Microsoft®
POWERPOINT®
2010

COMPREHENSIVE

**Sheffield
Career &
Technology
Center**

Microsoft®
POWERPOINT® 2010

COMPREHENSIVE

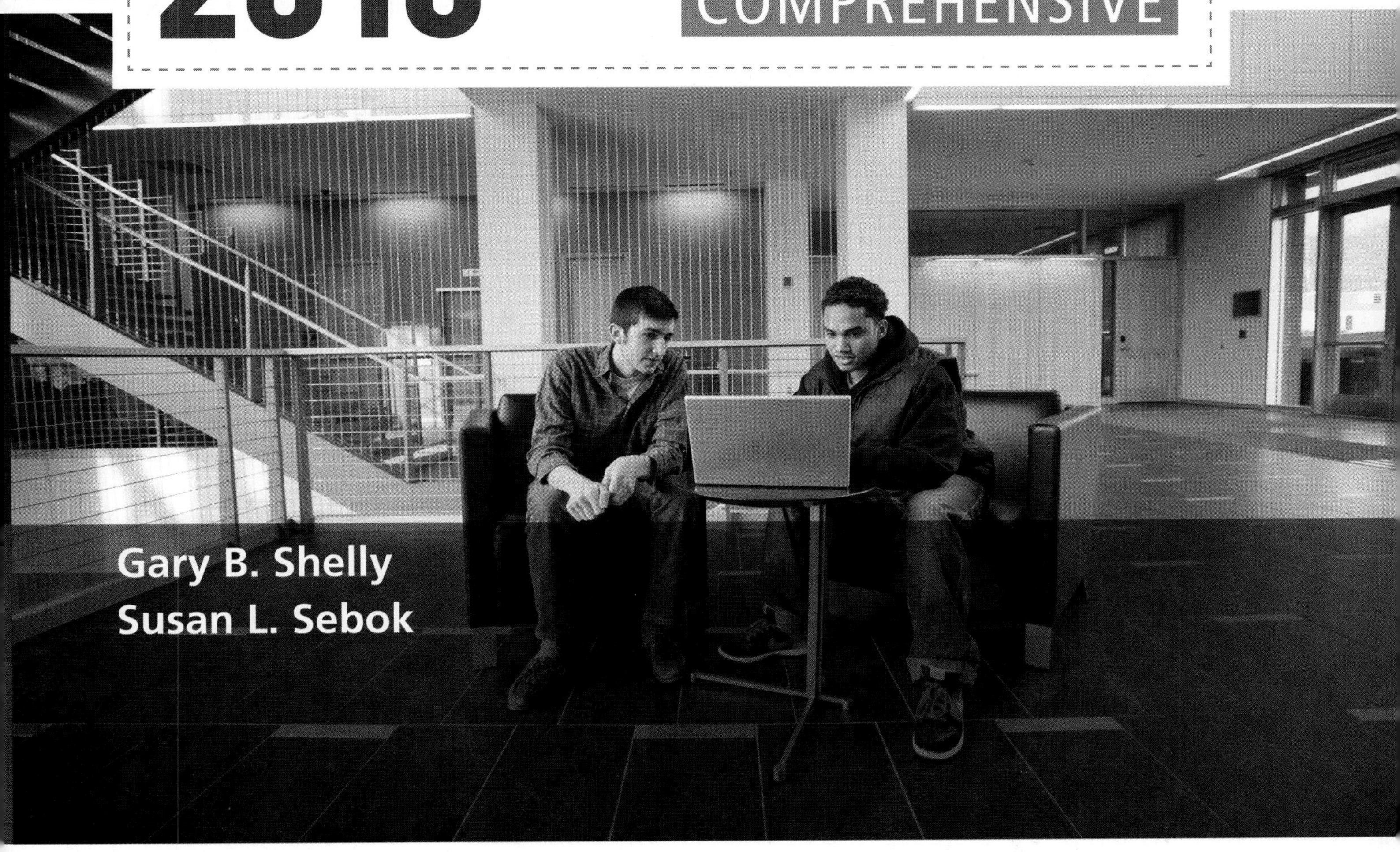

Gary B. Shelly
Susan L. Sebok

SHELLY
CASHMAN
SERIES®

Australia • Brazil • Japan • Korea • Mexico • Singapore • Spain • United Kingdom • United States

COURSE TECHNOLOGY
CENGAGE Learning

Microsoft® PowerPoint® 2010:
Comprehensive
Gary B. Shelly, Susan L. Sebok

Vice President, Publisher: Nicole Pinard

Executive Editor: Kathleen McMahon

Product Manager: Jon Farnham

Associate Product Manager: Aimee Poirier

Editorial Assistant: Angela Giannopoulos

Director of Marketing: Cheryl Costantini

Marketing Manager: Tristen Kendall

Marketing Coordinator: Adrienne Fung

Print Buyer: Julio Esperas

Director of Production: Patty Stephan

Senior Content Project Manager: Jill Braiewa

Development Editor: Deb Kaufmann

Copyeditor: Troy Lilly

Proofreader: Karen Annett

Indexer: Rich Carlson

QA Manuscript Reviewers: Chris Scriver, John
 Freitas, Serge Palladino, Susan Pedicini,
 Danielle Shaw

Art Director: Marissa Falco

Cover Designer: Lisa Kuhn, Curio Press, LLC

Cover Photo: Tom Kates Photography

Text Design: Joel Sadagursky

Compositor: PreMediaGlobal

For product information and technology assistance, contact us at
Cengage Learning Customer & Sales Support, 1-800-354-9706

For permission to use material from this text or product,
submit all requests online at **cengage.com/permissions**
Further permissions questions can be emailed to
permissionrequest@cengage.com

Library of Congress Control Number: 2010942460
ISBN-13: 978-1-4390-7903-4
ISBN-10: 1-4390-7903-X

Course Technology
20 Channel Center Street
Boston, MA 02210
USA

Microsoft and the Office logo are either registered trademarks or trademarks of Microsoft Corporation in the United States and/or other countries. Course Technology, a part of Cengage Learning, is an independent entity from the Microsoft Corporation, and not affiliated with Microsoft in any manner.

Cengage Learning is a leading provider of customized learning solutions with office locations around the globe, including Singapore, the United Kingdom, Australia, Mexico, Brazil, and Japan. Locate your local office at:
international.cengage.com/region

Cengage Learning products are represented in Canada by Nelson Education, Ltd.

Visit our Web site **www.cengage.com/ct/shellycashman** to share and gain ideas on our textbooks!

To learn more about Course Technology,
visit **www.cengage.com/coursetechnology**

Purchase any of our products at your local college bookstore or at our preferred online store **www.cengagebrain.com**

We dedicate this book to the memory of James S. Quasney (1940 – 2009), who for 18 years co-authored numerous books with Tom Cashman and Gary Shelly and provided extraordinary leadership to the Shelly Cashman Series editorial team. As series editor, Jim skillfully coordinated, organized, and managed the many aspects of our editorial development processes and provided unending direction, guidance, inspiration, support, and advice to the Shelly Cashman Series authors and support team members. He was a trusted, dependable, loyal, and well-respected leader, mentor, and friend. We are forever grateful to Jim for his faithful devotion to our team and eternal contributions to our series.

The Shelly Cashman Series Team

Printed in the United States of America
2 3 4 5 6 7 17 16 15 14 13 12 11

Microsoft
POWERPOINT® 2010
COMPREHENSIVE

Contents

Appendices

APPENDIX A
Project Planning Guidelines

What is the Microsoft® Office Specialist Program?

The Microsoft Office Specialist Program enables candidates to show that they have something exceptional to offer – proven expertise in certain Microsoft programs. Recognized by businesses and schools around the world, over 4 million certifications have been obtained in over 100 different countries. The Microsoft Office Specialist Program is the only Microsoft-approved certification program of its kind.

What is the Microsoft Office Specialist Certification?

 The Microsoft Office Specialist certification validates through the use of exams that you have obtained specific skill sets within the applicable Microsoft Office programs and other Microsoft programs included in the Microsoft Office Specialist Program. The candidate can choose which exam(s) they want to take according to which skills they want to validate.

The available Microsoft Office Specialist Program exams include*:

- Using Windows Vista®
- Using Microsoft® Office Word 2007
- Using Microsoft® Office Word 2007 – Expert
- Using Microsoft® Office Excel® 2007
- Using Microsoft® Office Excel® 2007 – Expert
- Using Microsoft® Office PowerPoint® 2007
- Using Microsoft® Office Access® 2007
- Using Microsoft® Office Outlook® 2007
- Using Microsoft SharePoint® 2007

The Microsoft Office Specialist Program 2010 exams will include*:

- Microsoft Word 2010
- Microsoft Word 2010 Expert
- Microsoft Excel® 2010
- Microsoft Excel® 2010 Expert
- Microsoft PowerPoint® 2010
- Microsoft Access® 2010
- Microsoft Outlook® 2010
- Microsoft SharePoint® 2010

What does the Microsoft Office Specialist Approved Courseware logo represent?

 The logo indicates that this courseware has been approved by Microsoft to cover the course objectives that will be included in the relevant exam. It also means that after utilizing this courseware, you may be better prepared to pass the exams required to become a certified Microsoft Office Specialist.

For more information:

To learn more about Microsoft Office Specialist exams, visit www.microsoft.com/learning/msbc

To learn about other Microsoft approved courseware from Cengage Learning, visit www.cengagebrain.com

Preface

The Shelly Cashman Series® offers the finest textbooks in computer education. We are proud that since Mircosoft Office 4.3, our series of Microsoft Office textbooks have been the most widely used books in education. With each new edition of our Office books, we make significant improvements based on the software and comments made by instructors and students. For this Microsoft PowerPoint 2010 text, the Shelly Cashman Series development team carefully reviewed our pedagogy and analyzed its effectiveness in teaching today's Office student. Students today read less, but need to retain more. They need not only to be able to perform skills, but to retain those skills and know how to apply them to different settings. Today's students need to be continually engaged and challenged to retain what they're learning.

With this Microsoft PowerPoint 2010 text, we continue our commitment to focusing on the user and how they learn best.

Objectives of This Textbook

Microsoft PowerPoint 2010: Comprehensive is intended for a ten- to fifteen-week period in a course that teaches PowerPoint 2010 as the primary component. No experience with a computer is assumed, and no mathematics beyond the high school freshman level is required. The objectives of this book are:

- To offer a comprehensive presentation of Microsoft PowerPoint 2010

- To expose students to practical examples of the computer as a useful tool

- To acquaint students with the proper procedures to create presentations suitable for coursework, professional purposes, and personal use

- To help students discover the underlying functionality of PowerPoint 2010 so they can become more productive

- To develop an exercise-oriented approach that allows learning by doing

New to this Edition

Microsoft PowerPoint 2010: Comprehensive offers a number of new features and approaches, which improve student understanding, retention, transference, and skill in using PowerPoint 2010. The following enhancements will enrich the learning experience:

- Office 2010 and Windows 7: Essential Concepts and Skills chapter presents basic Office 2010 and Windows 7 skills.
- Streamlined first chapter allows the ability to cover more advanced skills earlier.
- Chapter topic redistribution offers concise chapters that ensure complete skill coverage.
- New pedagogical elements enrich material, creating an accessible and user-friendly approach.
  - Break Points, a new boxed element, identify logical stopping points and give students instructions regarding what they should do before taking a break.
  - Within step instructions, Tab | Group Identifiers, such as (Home tab | Bold button), help students more easily locate elements in the groups and on the tabs on the Ribbon.
  - Modified step-by-step instructions tell the student what to do and provide the generic reason why they are completing a specific task, which helps students easily transfer given skills to different settings.

The Shelly Cashman Approach

A Proven Pedagogy with an Emphasis on Project Planning
Each chapter presents a practical problem to be solved, within a project planning framework. The project orientation is strengthened by the use of Plan Ahead boxes, which encourage critical thinking about how to proceed at various points in the project. Step-by-step instructions with supporting screens guide students through the steps. Instructional steps are supported by the Q&A, Experimental Step, and BTW features.

A Visually Engaging Book that Maintains Student Interest
The step-by-step tasks, with supporting figures, provide a rich visual experience for the student. Call-outs on the screens that present both explanatory and navigational information provide students with information they need when they need to know it.

Supporting Reference Materials (Appendices and Quick Reference)
The appendices provide additional information about the Application at hand and include such topics as project planning guidelines and certification. With the Quick Reference, students can quickly look up information about a single task, such as keyboard shortcuts, and find page references of where in the book the task is illustrated.

Integration of the World Wide Web
The World Wide Web is integrated into the PowerPoint 2010 learning experience by (1) BTW annotations; (2) BTW, Q&A, and Quick Reference Summary Web pages; and (3) the Learn It Online section for each chapter.

End-of-Chapter Student Activities

Extensive end-of-chapter activities provide a variety of reinforcement opportunities for students where they can apply and expand their skills.

Instructor Resources

The Instructor Resources include both teaching and testing aids and can be accessed via CD-ROM or at login.cengage.com.

Instructor's Manual Includes lecture notes summarizing the chapter sections, figures and boxed elements found in every chapter, teacher tips, classroom activities, lab activities, and quick quizzes in Microsoft Word files.

Syllabus Easily customizable sample syllabi that cover policies, assignments, exams, and other course information.

Figure Files Illustrations for every figure in the textbook in electronic form.

PowerPoint Presentations A multimedia lecture presentation system that provides slides for each chapter. Presentations are based on chapter objectives.

Solutions to Exercises Includes solutions for all end-of-chapter and chapter reinforcement exercises.

Test Bank & Test Engine Test Banks include 112 questions for every chapter, featuring objective-based and critical thinking question types, and including page number references and figure references, when appropriate. Also included is the test engine, ExamView, the ultimate tool for your objective-based testing needs.

Data Files for Students Includes all the files that are required by students to complete the exercises.

Additional Activities for Students Consists of Chapter Reinforcement Exercises, which are true/false, multiple-choice, and short answer questions that help students gain confidence in the material learned.

Book Resources

- 🔒 Additional Faculty Files
- 🔒 Blackboard Testbank
- 🔒 Data Files
- 🔒 Instructor's Manual
- 🔒 Lecture Success System
- 🔒 PowerPoint Presentations
- 🔒 Solutions to Exercises
- 🔒 Syllabus
- 🔒 Test Bank and Test Engine
- 🔒 WebCT Testbank

Chapter Reinforcement Exercises

Student Downloads

SAM: Skills Assessment Manager

SAM 2010 is designed to help bring students from the classroom to the real world. It allows students to train on and test important computer skills in an active, hands-on environment.

SAM's easy-to-use system includes powerful interactive exams, training, and projects on the most commonly used Microsoft Office applications. SAM simulates the Microsoft Office 2010 application environment, allowing students to demonstrate their knowledge and think through the skills by performing real-world tasks such as bolding word text or setting up slide transitions. Add in live-in-the-application projects, and students are on their way to truly learning and applying skills to business-centric documents.

Designed to be used with the Shelly Cashman Series, SAM includes handy page references so that students can print helpful study guides that match the Shelly Cashman textbooks used in class. For instructors, SAM also includes robust scheduling and reporting features.

Content for Online Learning

Course Technology has partnered with the leading distance learning solution providers and class-management platforms today. To access this material, instructors will visit our password-protected instructor resources available at login.cengage.com. Instructor resources include the following: additional case projects, sample syllabi, PowerPoint presentations per chapter, and more. For additional information or for an instructor user name and password, please contact your sales representative. For students to access this material, they must have purchased a WebTutor PIN-code specific to this title and your campus platform. The resources for students may include (based on instructor preferences), but are not limited to: topic review, review questions, and practice tests.

CourseNotes

Course Technology's CourseNotes are six-panel quick reference cards that reinforce the most important and widely used features of a software application in a visual and user-friendly format. CourseNotes serve as a great reference tool during and after the student completes the course. CourseNotes are available for software applications such as Microsoft Office 2010, Word 2010, Excel 2010, Access 2010, PowerPoint 2010, and Windows 7. Topic-based CourseNotes are available for Best Practices in Social Networking, Hot Topics in Technology, and Web 2.0. Visit www.cengagebrain.com to learn more!

A Guided Tour

Add excitement and interactivity to your classroom with "*A Guided Tour*" product line. Play one of the brief mini-movies to spice up your lecture and spark classroom discussion. Or, assign a movie for homework and ask students to complete the correlated assignment that accompanies each topic. "*A Guided Tour*" product line takes the prep work out of providing your students with information about new technologies and applications and helps keep students engaged with content relevant to their lives; all in under an hour!

About Our Covers

The Shelly Cashman Series is continually updating our approach and content to reflect the way today's students learn and experience new technology. This focus on student success is reflected on our covers, which feature real students from the University of Rhode Island using the Shelly Cashman Series in their courses, and reflect the varied ages and backgrounds of the students learning with our books. When you use the Shelly Cashman Series, you can be assured that you are learning computer skills using the most effective courseware available.

Textbook Walk-Through

The Shelly Cashman Series Pedagogy: Project-Based — Step-by-Step — Variety of Assessments

Plan Ahead boxes prepare students to create successful projects by encouraging them to think strategically about what they are trying to accomplish before they begin working.

Step-by-Step instructions now provide a context beyond the point-and-click. Each step provides information on why students are performing each task, or what will occur as a result.

Navigational callouts in red show students where to click.

Explanatory callouts summarize what is happening on screen.

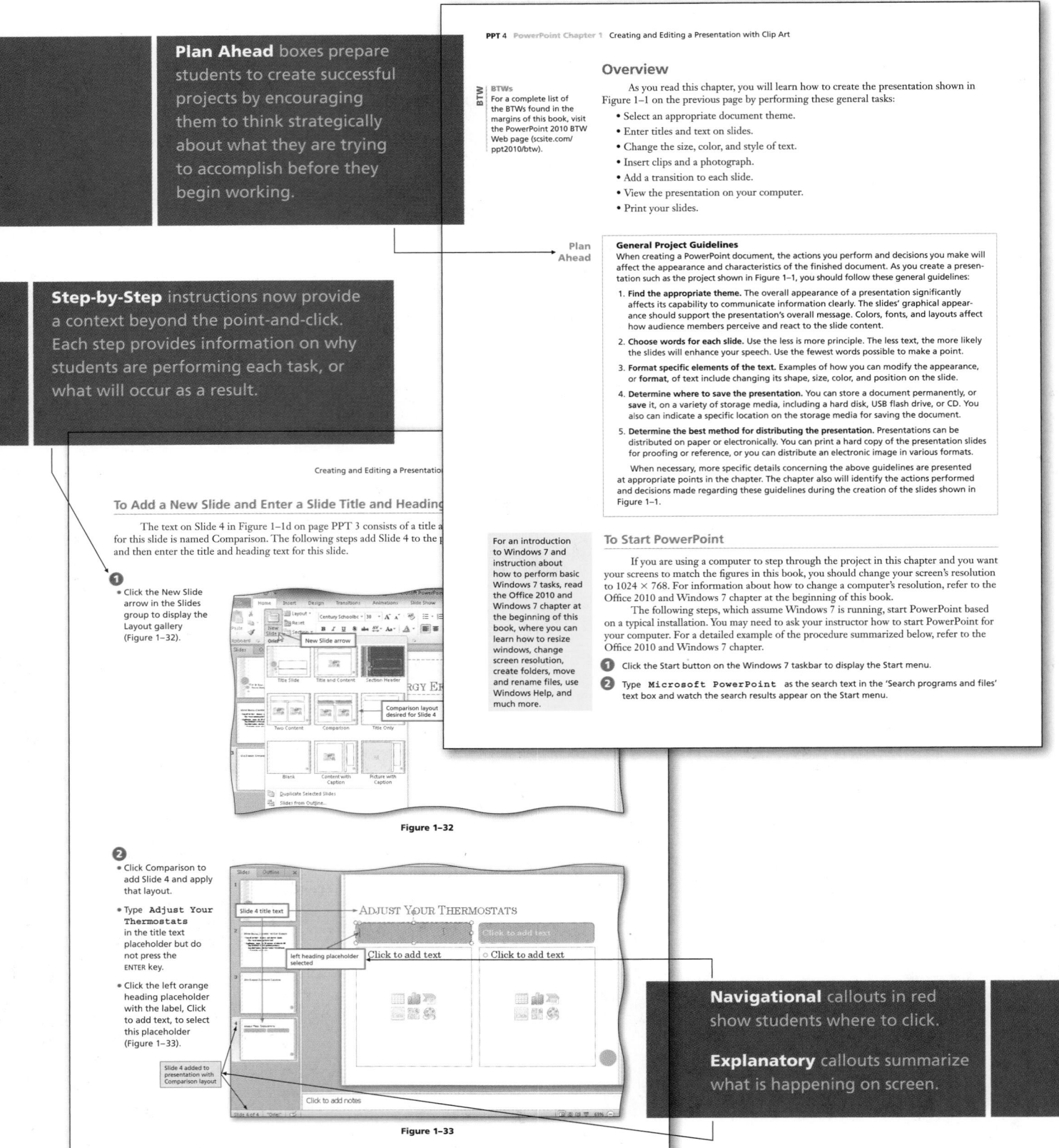

BTW
For a complete list of the BTWs found in the margins of this book, visit the PowerPoint 2010 BTW Web page (scsite.com/ppt2010/btw).

Overview

As you read this chapter, you will learn how to create the presentation shown in Figure 1–1 on the previous page by performing these general tasks:

- Select an appropriate document theme.
- Enter titles and text on slides.
- Change the size, color, and style of text.
- Insert clips and a photograph.
- Add a transition to each slide.
- View the presentation on your computer.
- Print your slides.

Plan Ahead

General Project Guidelines

When creating a PowerPoint document, the actions you perform and decisions you make will affect the appearance and characteristics of the finished document. As you create a presentation such as the project shown in Figure 1–1, you should follow these general guidelines:

1. **Find the appropriate theme.** The overall appearance of a presentation significantly affects its capability to communicate information clearly. The slides' graphical appearance should support the presentation's overall message. Colors, fonts, and layouts affect how audience members perceive and react to the slide content.

2. **Choose words for each slide.** Use the less is more principle. The less text, the more likely the slides will enhance your speech. Use the fewest words possible to make a point.

3. **Format specific elements of the text.** Examples of how you can modify the appearance, or **format**, of text include changing its shape, size, color, and position on the slide.

4. **Determine where to save the presentation.** You can store a document permanently, or **save** it, on a variety of storage media, including a hard disk, USB flash drive, or CD. You also can indicate a specific location on the storage media for saving the document.

5. **Determine the best method for distributing the presentation.** Presentations can be distributed on paper or electronically. You can print a hard copy of the presentation slides for proofing or reference, or you can distribute an electronic image in various formats.

When necessary, more specific details concerning the above guidelines are presented at appropriate points in the chapter. The chapter also will identify the actions performed and decisions made regarding these guidelines during the creation of the slides shown in Figure 1–1.

For an introduction to Windows 7 and instruction about how to perform basic Windows 7 tasks, read the Office 2010 and Windows 7 chapter at the beginning of this book, where you can learn how to resize windows, change screen resolution, create folders, move and rename files, use Windows Help, and much more.

To Start PowerPoint

If you are using a computer to step through the project in this chapter and you want your screens to match the figures in this book, you should change your screen's resolution to 1024 × 768. For information about how to change a computer's resolution, refer to the Office 2010 and Windows 7 chapter at the beginning of this book.

The following steps, which assume Windows 7 is running, start PowerPoint based on a typical installation. You may need to ask your instructor how to start PowerPoint for your computer. For a detailed example of the procedure summarized below, refer to the Office 2010 and Windows 7 chapter.

1. Click the Start button on the Windows 7 taskbar to display the Start menu.

2. Type `Microsoft PowerPoint` as the search text in the 'Search programs and files' text box and watch the search results appear on the Start menu.

Creating and Editing a Presentation

To Add a New Slide and Enter a Slide Title and Heading

The text on Slide 4 in Figure 1–1d on page PPT 3 consists of a title a [...] for this slide is named Comparison. The following steps add Slide 4 to the p [...] and then enter the title and heading text for this slide.

1
- Click the New Slide arrow in the Slides group to display the Layout gallery (Figure 1–32).

Figure 1–32

2
- Click Comparison to add Slide 4 and apply that layout.

- Type `Adjust Your Thermostats` in the title text placeholder but do not press the ENTER key.

- Click the left orange heading placeholder with the label, Click to add text, to select this placeholder (Figure 1–33).

Figure 1–33

Q&A boxes offer questions students may have when working through the steps and provide additional information about what they are doing right where they need it.

Experiment Steps within our step-by-step instructions, encourage students to explore, experiment, and take advantage of the features of the PowerPoint 2010 user interface. These steps are not necessary to complete the projects, but are designed to increase the confidence with the software and build problem-solving skills.

To Move Manually through Slides in a Slide Show

After you begin Slide Show view, you can move forward or backward through the slides. PowerPoint allows you to advance through the slides manually or automatically. During a slide show, each slide in the presentation shows on the screen, one slide at a time. Each time you click the mouse button, the next slide appears. The following steps move manually through the slides.

1
• Click each slide until Slide 5 (Be Green) is displayed (Figure 1–73).

Q&A
I see a small toolbar in the lower-left corner of my slide. What is this toolbar?

The Slide Show toolbar appears when you begin running a slide show and then move the mouse pointer. The buttons on this toolbar allow you to navigate to the next slide, the previous slide, to mark up the current slide, or to change the current display.

Figure 1–73

2
• Click the More button (Design tab | Themes group) to expand the gallery, which shows more Built-In theme gallery options (Figure 1–3).

Experiment
• Point to various document themes in the Themes gallery and watch the colors and fonts change on the title slide.

Q&A
Are the themes displayed in a specific order?

Yes. They are arranged in alphabetical order running from left to right. If you point to a theme, a ScreenTip with the theme's name appears on the screen.

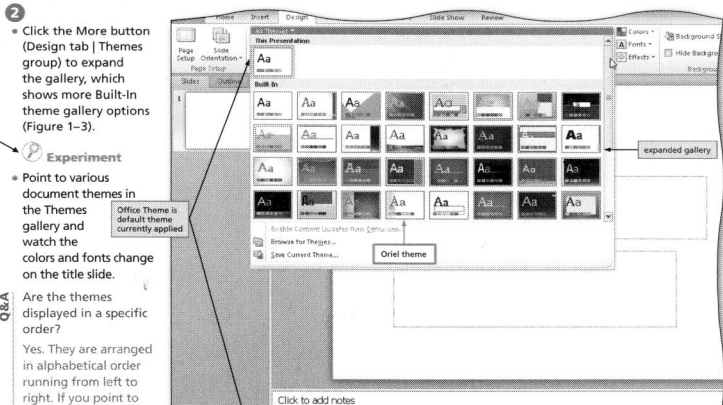

Figure 1–3

Q&A
What if I change my mind and do not want to select a new theme?
Click anywhere outside the All Themes gallery to close the gallery.

3
• Click the Oriel theme to apply this theme to Slide 1 (Figure 1–4).

Q&A
If I decide at some future time that this design does not fit the theme of my presentation, can I apply a different design?

Yes. You can repeat these steps at any time while creating your presentation.

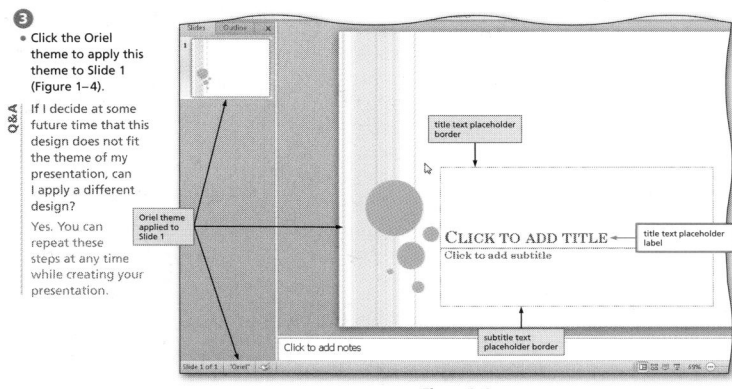

Figure 1–4

Textbook Walk-Through

Break Points identify logical breaks in the chapter if students need to stop before completing the project.

Break Point: If you wish to take a break, this is a good place to do so. You can quit PowerPoint now (refer to page PPT 50 for instructions). To resume at a later time, start PowerPoint (refer to pages PPT 4 and PPT 5 for instructions), open the file called Saving Energy (refer to pages PPT 50 and PPT 51 for instructions), and continue following the steps from this location forward.

Chapter Summary A concluding paragraph, followed by a listing of the tasks completed within a chapter together with the pages on which the step-by-step, screen-by-screen explanations appear.

To Quit PowerPoint

The project now is complete. The following steps quit PowerPoint. For a detailed example of the procedure summarized below, refer to the Office 2010 and Windows 7 chapter at the beginning of this book.

1. If you have one PowerPoint document open, click the Close button on the right side of the title bar to close the document and quit PowerPoint; or if you have multiple PowerPoint documents open, click File on the Ribbon to open the Backstage view and then click Exit in the Backstage view to close all open documents and quit PowerPoint.

2. If a Microsoft Office PowerPoint dialog box appears, click the Save button to save any changes made to the document since the last save.

Chapter Summary

In this chapter you have learned how to apply a document theme, create a title slide and text slides with a bulleted list, clip art, and a photograph, size and move clip art and a photograph, format and edit text, add a slide transition, and print slides as handouts. The items listed below include all the new [chapter].

Learn It Online

Test your knowledge of chapter content and key terms.

Instructions: To complete the Learn It Online exercises, start your browser, click the Address bar, and then enter the Web address **scsite.com/ppt2010/learn**. When the PowerPoint 2010 Learn It Online page is displayed, click the link for the exercise you want to complete and then read the instructions.

Chapter Reinforcement TF, MC, and SA
A series of true/false, multiple choice, and short answer questions that test your knowledge of the chapter content.

Flash Cards
An interactive learning environment where you identify chapter key terms associated with displayed definitions.

Practice Test
A series of multiple choice questions that test your knowledge of chapter content and key terms.

Who Wants To Be a Computer Genius?
An interactive game that challenges your knowledge of chapter content in the style of a television quiz show.

Wheel of Terms
An interactive game that challenges your knowledge of chapter key terms in the style of the television show *Wheel of Fortune*.

Crossword Puzzle Challenge
A crossword puzzle that challenges your knowledge of key terms presented in the chapter.

Apply Your Knowledge

Reinforce the skills and apply the concepts you learned in this chapter.

Modifying Character Formats and Paragraph Levels and Moving a Clip
Note: To complete this assignment, you will be required to use the Data Files for Students. See the inside back cover of this book for instructions on downloading the Data Files for Students, or contact your instructor for information about accessing the required files.

Instructions: Start PowerPoint. Open the presentation, Apply 1-1 Flu Season, from the Data Files for Students.
The two slides in the presentation discuss ways to avoid getting or spreading the flu. The document you open is an unformatted presentation. You are to modify the document theme, indent the paragraphs, resize and move the clip art, and format the text so the slides look like Figure 1–77 on the next page.

20. Insert a Clip from the Clip Organizer into the Title Slide (PPT 27)
21. Insert a Clip from the Clip Organizer into a Content Placeholder (PPT 30)
22. Insert a Photograph from the Clip Organizer into a Slide without a Content Placeholder (PPT 32)
23. Resize Clip Art (PPT 33)
24. Move Clips (PPT 36)
25. Duplicate a Slide (PPT 38)
26. Arrange a Slide (PPT 39)
27. Delete Text in a Placeholder (PPT 41)
28. Add a Transition between Slides (PPT 43)
29. Change Document Properties (PPT 46)
30. Save an Existing Presentation with the Same File Name (PPT 47)
31. Start Slide Show View (PPT 47)
32. Move Manually through Slides in a Slide Show (PPT 49)
33. Quit PowerPoint (PPT 50)
34. Open a Document from PowerPoint (PPT 50)
35. Print a Presentation (PPT 51)

Learn It Online Every chapter features a Learn It Online section that is comprised of six exercises. These exercises include True/False, Multiple Choice, Short Answer, Flash Cards, Practice Test, and Learning Games.

Apply Your Knowledge This exercise usually requires students to open and manipulate a file from the Data Files that parallels the activities learned in the chapter. To obtain a copy of the Data Files for Students, follow the instructions on the inside back cover of this text.

Continued >

Extend Your Knowledge

Extend the skills you learned in this chapter and experiment with new skills. You may need to use Help to complete the assignment.

Changing Slide Theme, Layout, and Text

Note: To complete this assignment, you will be required to use the Data Files for Students. See the inside back cover of this book for instructions on downloading the Data Files for Students, or contact your instructor for information about accessing the required files.

Instructions: Start PowerPoint. Open the presentation that you are going to prepare for your dental hygiene class, Extend 1–1 Winning Smile, from the Data Files for Students.
    You will choose a theme, format slides, and create a closing slide.

Perform the following tasks:
1. Apply an appropriate document theme.
2. On Slide 1, use your name in place of Student Name. Format the text on this slide using techniques you learned in this chapter, such as changing the font size and color and also bolding and italicizing words.
3. On Slide 2, change the slide layout and adjust the paragraph levels so that the lines of text are arranged under two headings: Discount Dental and Dental Insurance (Figure 1–78).
4. On Slide 3, create paragraphs and adjust the paragraph levels to create a bulleted list. Edit the text so that the slide meets the 7 × 7 rule, which states that each line should have a maximum of seven words, and each slide should have a maximum of seven lines.
5. Create an appropriate closing slide using the title slide as a guide.
6. The slides contain a variety of clips downloaded from the Microsoft Clip Organizer. Size and move them when necessary.
7. Apply an appropriate transition to all slides.
8. Change the document properties, as specified by your instructor. Save the presentation using the file name, Extend 1–1 Dental Plans.
9. Submit the revised document in the format specified by your instruc[tor.]

Extend Your Knowledge projects at the end of each chapter allow students to extend and expand on the skills learned within the chapter. Students use critical thinking to experiment with new skills to complete each project.

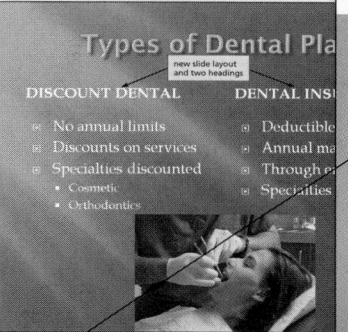

Types of Dental Pla[ns]

new slide layout and two headings

DISCOUNT DENTAL   DENTAL INS[URANCE]

- No annual limits   - Deductible
- Discounts on services   - Annual ma[ximum]
- Specialties discounted - Through e[mployer]
  - Cosmetic   - Specialties
  - Orthodontics

Figure 1–78

STUDENT ASSIGNMENTS

Make It Right

Analyze a presentation and correct all errors and/or improve the design.

Correcting Formatting and List Levels

Note: To complete this assignment, you will be required to use the Data Files for Students. See the inside back cover of this book for instructions on downloading the Data Files for Students, or contact your instructor for information about accessing the required files.

Instructions: Start PowerPoint. Open the presentation, Make It Right 1–1 Air Ducts, from the Data Files for Students.
    Members of your homeowners' association are having their semiannual meeting, and each member of the board is required to give a short presentation on the subject of energy savings. You have decided to discuss the energy-saving benefits of maintaining the air ducts in your home. Correct the formatting problems and errors in the presentation while keeping in mind the guidelines presented in this chapter.

Perform the following tasks:
1. Change the document theme from Origin, shown in Figure 1–79, to Module.
2. On Slide 1, replace the words, Student Name, with your name. Format your name so that it displays prominently on the slide.
3. Increase the size of the clip on Slide 1 and move it to the upper-right corner.
4. Move Slide 2 to the end of the presentation so that it becomes the new Slide 3.
5. On Slide 2, correct the spelling errors and then increase the font size of the Slide 2 title text, Check Hidden Air Ducts, to 54 point. Increase the size of the clip and move it up to fill the white space on the right of the bulleted list.
6. On Slide 3, correct the spelling errors and then change the font size of the title text, Energy Savings, to 54 point. Increase the indent levels for paragraphs 2 and 4. Increase the size of the clips. Center the furnace clip at the bottom of the slide.
7. Change the document properties, as specified by your instructor. Save the presentation using the file name, Make It Right 1–1 Ducts Presentation.
8. Apply the same transition and duration to all slides.
9. Submit the revised document in the format specified by your instructor.

Make It Right projects call on students to analyze a file, discover errors in it, and fix them using the skills they learned in the chapter.

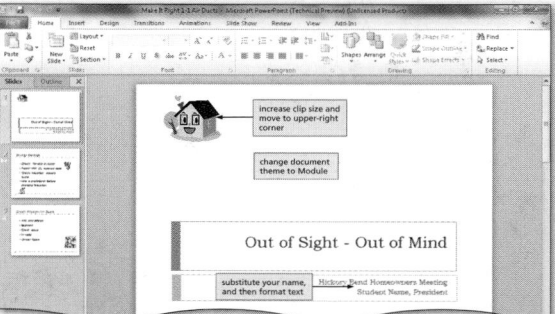

increase clip size and move to upper-right corner

change document theme to Module

Out of Sight - Out of Mind

substitute your name, and then format text

Figure 1–79

Textbook Walk-Through

In the Lab

Design and/or create a presentation using the guidelines, concepts, and skills presented in this chapter. Labs 1, 2, and 3 are listed in order of increasing difficulty.

Lab1: Creating a Presentation with Bulleted Lists, a Closing Slide, and Clips

Problem: You are working with upper-level students to host a freshmen orientation seminar. When you attended this seminar, you received some helpful tips on studying for exams. Your contribution to this year's seminar is to prepare a short presentation on study skills. You develop the outline shown in Figure 1–80 and then prepare the PowerPoint presentation shown in Figures 1–81a through 1–81d.

Studying for an Exam
Freshmen Orientation Seminar
Sarah Jones

Prepare in Advance
Location
    Quiet, well-lit
Timing
    15-minute breaks every hour
Material
    Quiz yourself

Exam Time
Day of Exam
    Rest properly
    Eat a good meal
    Wear comfy clothes
    Be early
    Be confident

Perform the following tasks:
1. Create a new presentation using the Aspect document theme.
2. Using the typed notes illustrated in Figure 1–80, create the title slide shown in Figure 1–81a, using your name in place of Sarah Jones. Italicize your name and increase the font size to 24 point. Increase the font size of the title text paragraph, Hit the Books, to 48 point. Increase the font size of the first paragraph of the subtitle text, Studying for an Exam, to 28 point.

In the Lab Three all new in-depth assignments per chapter require students to utilize the chapter concepts and techniques to solve problems on a computer.

Cases & Places exercises call on students to create open-ended projects that reflect academic, personal, and business settings.

Cases and Places

Apply your creative thinking and problem-solving skills to design and implement a solution.

Note: To complete these assignments, you may be required to use the Data Files for Students. See the inside back cover of this book for instructions on downloading the Data Files for Students, or contact your instructor for information about accessing the required files.

As you design the presentations, remember to use the 7 × 7 rule: a maximum of seven words on a line and a maximum of seven lines on one slide.

1: Design and Create a Presentation about Galileo

Academic
Italian-born Galileo is said to be the father of modern science. After the invention of the telescope by a Dutch eyeglass maker named Hans Lippershey, Galileo made his own telescope and made many discoveries. You decide to prepare a PowerPoint presentation to accompany a speech that is required in your Astronomy class. You create the outline shown in Figure 1–88 about Galileo. Use this outline, along with the concepts and techniques presented in this chapter, to develop and format a slide show with a title slide and three text slides with bulleted lists. Add photographs and clip art from the Microsoft Clip Organizer and apply a transition. Submit your assignment in the format specified by your instructor.

Galileo Galilei
    Father of Modern Science
    Astronomy 201
    Sandy Wendt

Major Role in Scientific Revolution
February 15, 1564 - January 8, 1642
    Physicist
    Mathematician
    Astronomer
    Philosopher

Galileo's Research Years
    1581 - Studied medicine
    1589-1592 - Studied math and physics
    1592-1607 - Padua University
        Developed Law of Inertia
    1609 - Built telescope
        Earth's moon
        Jupiter's moons

Galileo's Later Years
    Dialogue - Two Chief World Systems
        Controversy develops
    1633 - Rome
        Heresy trial
        Imprisoned
    1642 - Dies

Figure 1–88

Microsoft® POWERPOINT® 2010

COMPREHENSIVE

Office 2010 and Windows 7: Essential Concepts and Skills

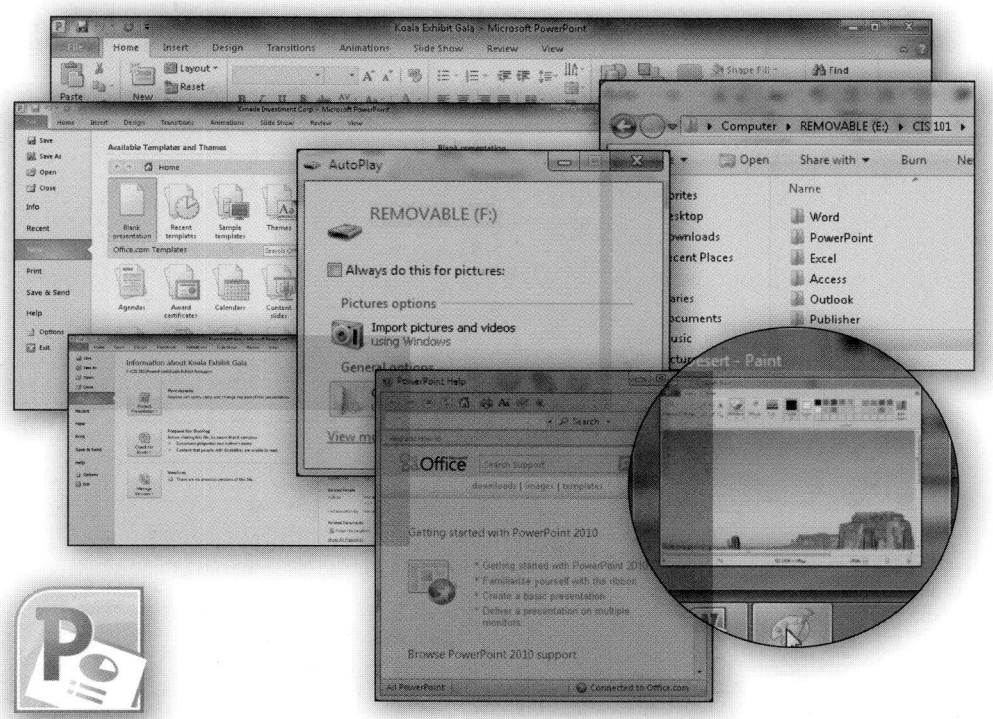

Objectives

You will have mastered the material in this chapter when you can:

- Perform basic mouse operations
- Start Windows and log on to the computer
- Identify the objects on the Windows 7 desktop
- Identify the programs in and versions of Microsoft Office
- Start a program
- Identify the components of the Microsoft Office Ribbon

- Create folders
- Save files
- Change screen resolution
- Perform basic tasks in Microsoft Office programs
- Manage files
- Use Microsoft Office Help and Windows Help

Office 2010 and Windows 7: Essential Concepts and Skills

Office 2010 and Windows 7

This introductory chapter uses PowerPoint 2010 to cover features and functions common to Office 2010 programs, as well as the basics of Windows 7.

Overview

As you read this chapter, you will learn how to perform basic tasks in Windows and PowerPoint by performing these general activities:

- Start programs using Windows.
- Use features in PowerPoint that are common across Office programs.
- Organize files and folders.
- Change screen resolution.
- Quit programs.

Introduction to the Windows 7 Operating System

Windows 7 is the newest version of Microsoft Windows, which is the most popular and widely used operating system. An **operating system** is a computer program (set of computer instructions) that coordinates all the activities of computer hardware such as memory, storage devices, and printers, and provides the capability for you to communicate with the computer.

The Windows 7 operating system simplifies the process of working with documents and programs by organizing the manner in which you interact with the computer. Windows 7 is used to run **application software**, which consists of programs designed to make users more productive and/or assist them with personal tasks, such as word processing.

Windows 7 has two interface variations, Windows 7 Basic and Windows 7 Aero. Computers with up to 1 GB of RAM display the Windows 7 Basic interface (Figure 1a). Computers with more than 1 GB of RAM also can display the Windows Aero interface (Figure 1b), which provides an enhanced visual appearance. The Windows 7 Professional, Windows 7 Enterprise, Windows 7 Home Premium, and Windows 7 Ultimate editions have the capability to use Windows Aero.

Using a Mouse

Windows users work with a mouse that has at least two buttons. For a right-handed user, the left button usually is the primary mouse button, and the right mouse button is the secondary mouse button. Left-handed people, however, can reverse the function of these buttons.

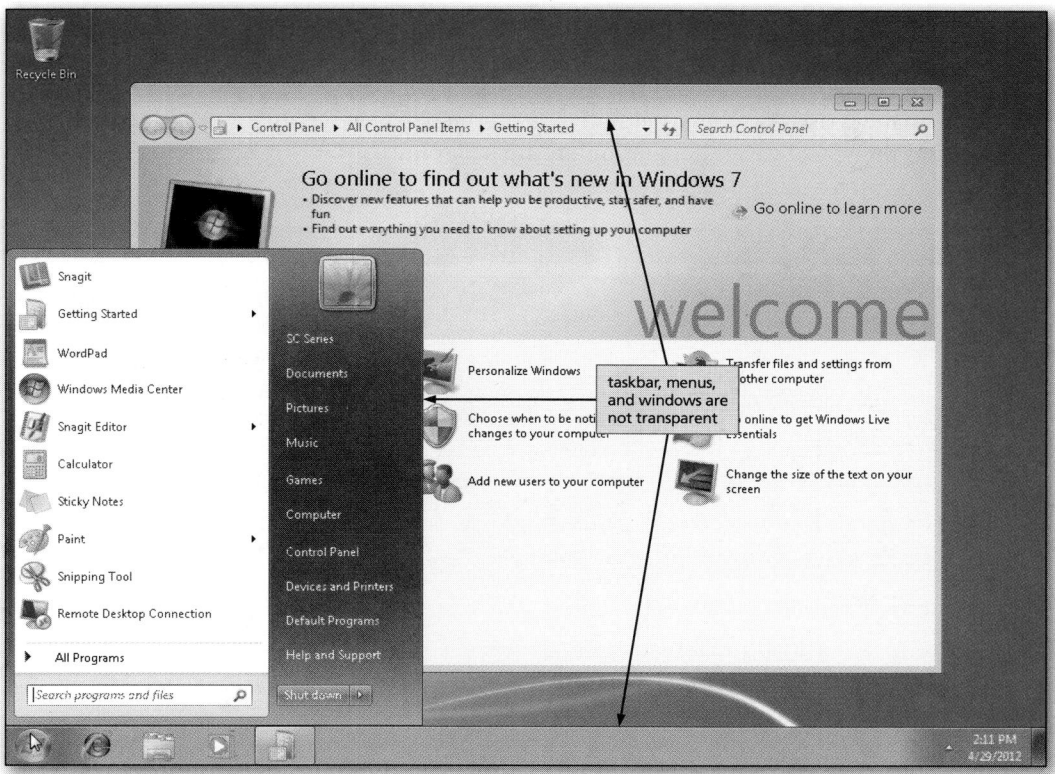

(a) Windows 7 Basic Interface

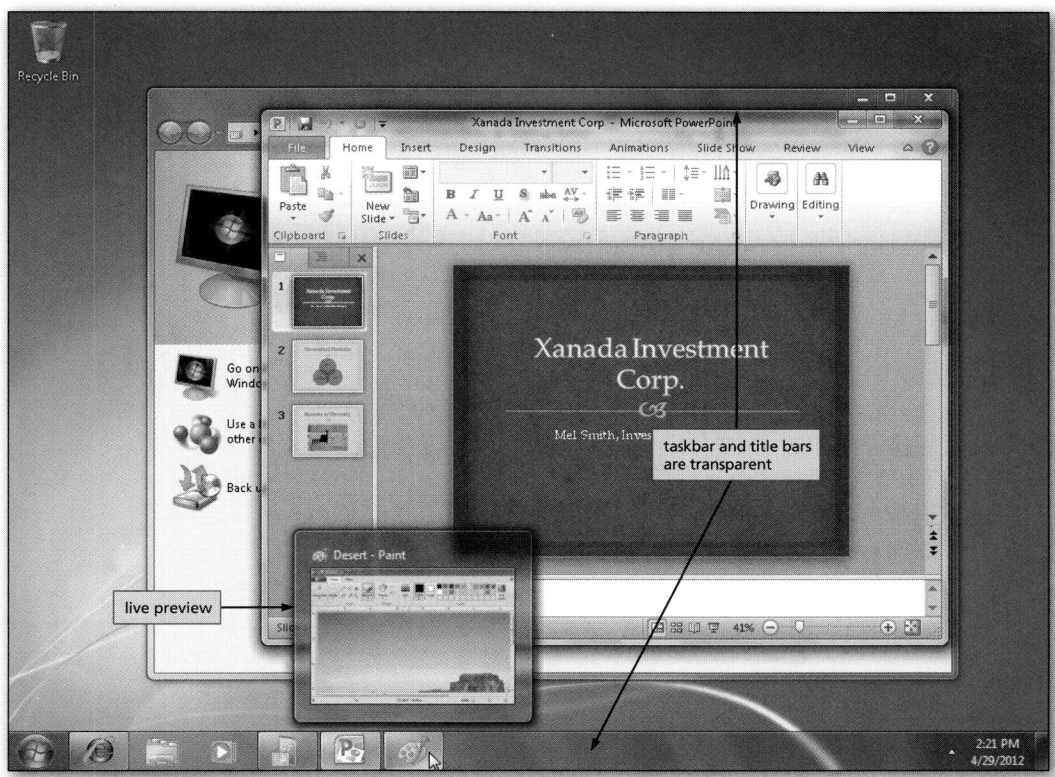

(b) Windows 7 Aero Interface

Figure 1

Table 1 explains how to perform a variety of mouse operations. Some programs also use keys in combination with the mouse to perform certain actions. For example, when you hold down the CTRL key while rolling the mouse wheel, text on the screen becomes larger or smaller based on the direction you roll the wheel. The function of the mouse buttons and the wheel varies depending on the program.

Table 1 Mouse Operations		
Operation	**Mouse Action**	**Example***
Point	Move the mouse until the pointer on the desktop is positioned on the item of choice.	Position the pointer on the screen.
Click	Press and release the primary mouse button, which usually is the left mouse button.	Select or deselect items on the screen or start a program or program feature.
Right-click	Press and release the secondary mouse button, which usually is the right mouse button.	Display a shortcut menu.
Double-click	Quickly press and release the left mouse button twice without moving the mouse.	Start a program or program feature.
Triple-click	Quickly press and release the left mouse button three times without moving the mouse.	Select a paragraph.
Drag	Point to an item, hold down the left mouse button, move the item to the desired location on the screen, and then release the left mouse button.	Move an object from one location to another or draw pictures.
Right-drag	Point to an item, hold down the right mouse button, move the item to the desired location on the screen, and then release the right mouse button.	Display a shortcut menu after moving an object from one location to another.
Rotate wheel	Roll the wheel forward or backward.	Scroll vertically (up and down).
Free-spin wheel	Whirl the wheel forward or backward so that it spins freely on its own.	Scroll through many pages in seconds.
Press wheel	Press the wheel button while moving the mouse.	Scroll continuously.
Tilt wheel	Press the wheel toward the right or left.	Scroll horizontally (left and right).
Press thumb button	Press the button on the side of the mouse with your thumb.	Move forward or backward through Web pages and/or control media, games, etc.

*Note: The examples presented in this column are discussed as they are demonstrated in this chapter.

Scrolling

A **scroll bar** is a horizontal or vertical bar that appears when the contents of an area may not be visible completely on the screen (Figure 2). A scroll bar contains **scroll arrows** and a **scroll box** that enable you to view areas that currently cannot be seen. Clicking the up and down scroll arrows moves the screen content up or down one line. You also can click above or below the scroll box to move up or down a section, or drag the scroll box up or down to move up or down to move to a specific location.

Shortcut Keys

In many cases, you can use the keyboard instead of the mouse to accomplish a task. To perform tasks using the keyboard, you press one or more keyboard keys, sometimes identified as

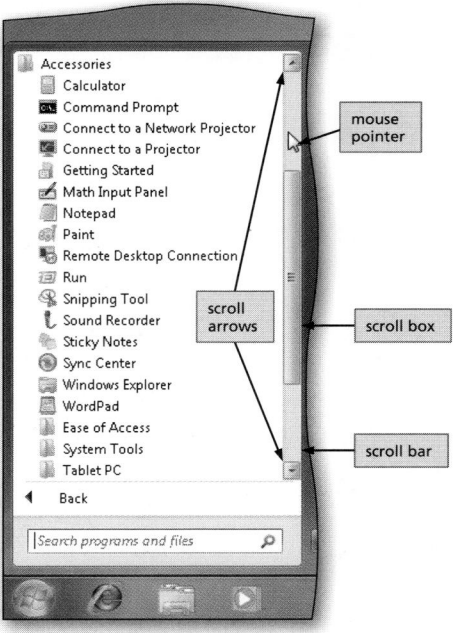

Figure 2

a **shortcut key** or **keyboard shortcut**. Some shortcut keys consist of a single key, such as the F1 key. For example, to obtain help about Windows 7, you can press the F1 key. Other shortcut keys consist of multiple keys, in which case a plus sign separates the key names, such as CTRL+ESC. This notation means to press and hold down the first key listed, press one or more additional keys, and then release all keys. For example, to display the Start menu, press CTRL+ESC, that is, hold down the CTRL key, press the ESC key, and then release both keys.

Starting Windows 7

It is not unusual for multiple people to use the same computer in a work, educational, recreational, or home setting. Windows 7 enables each user to establish a **user account**, which identifies to Windows 7 the resources, such as programs and storage locations, a user can access when working with a computer.

Each user account has a user name and may have a password and an icon, as well. A **user name** is a unique combination of letters or numbers that identifies a specific user to Windows 7. A **password** is a private combination of letters, numbers, and special characters associated with the user name that allows access to a user's account resources. A **user icon** is a picture associated with a user name.

When you turn on a computer, an introductory screen consisting of the Windows logo and copyright messages is displayed. The Windows logo is animated and glows as the Windows 7 operating system is loaded. After the Windows logo appears, depending on your computer's settings, you may or may not be required to log on to the computer. **Logging on** to a computer opens your user account and makes the computer available for use. If you are required to log on to the computer, the **Welcome screen** is displayed, which shows the user names of users on the computer (Figure 3). Clicking the user name or picture begins the process of logging on to the computer.

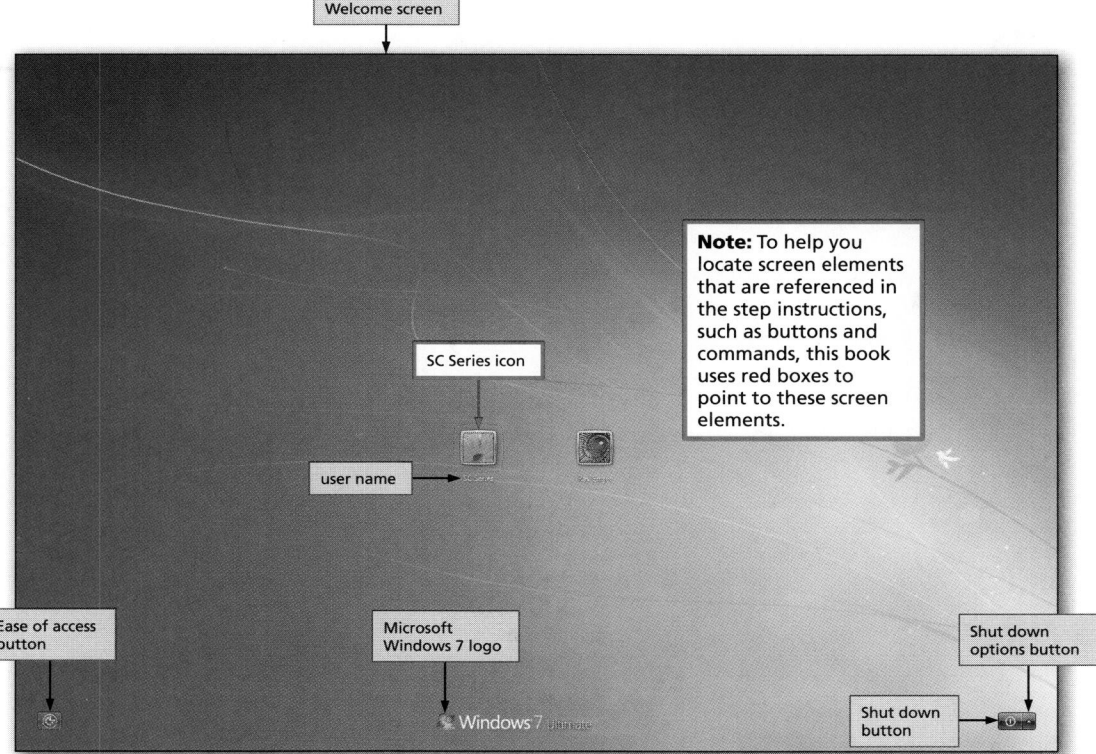

Figure 3

At the bottom of the Welcome screen is the 'Ease of access' button, the Windows 7 logo, a Shut down button, and a 'Shut down options' button. The following list identifies the functions of the buttons and commands that typically appear on the Welcome screen:

- Clicking the 'Ease of access' button displays the Ease of Access Center, which provides tools to optimize your computer to accommodate the needs of the mobility, hearing, and vision impaired users.
- Clicking the Shut down button shuts down Windows 7 and the computer.
- Clicking the 'Shut down options' button, located to the right of the Shut down button, provides access to a menu containing commands that perform actions such as restarting the computer, putting the computer in a low-powered state, and shutting down the computer. The commands available on your computer may differ.
  - The **Restart command** closes open programs, shuts down Windows 7, and then restarts Windows 7 and displays the Welcome screen.
  - The **Sleep command** waits for Windows 7 to save your work and then turns off the computer fans and hard disk. To wake the computer from the Sleep state, press the power button or lift a notebook computer's cover, and log on to the computer.
  - The **Shut down command** shuts down and turns off the computer.

To Log On to the Computer

After starting Windows 7, you might need to log on to the computer. The following steps log on to the computer based on a typical installation. You may need to ask your instructor how to log on to your computer. This set of steps uses SC Series as the user name. The list of user names on your computer will be different.

- Click the user icon (SC Series, in this case) on the Welcome screen (shown in Figure 3 on the previous page); depending on settings, this either will display a password text box (Figure 4) or will log on to the computer and display the Windows 7 desktop.

Q&A   Why do I not see a user icon?

Your computer may require you to type a user name instead of clicking an icon.

Q&A   What is a text box?

A text box is a rectangular box in which you type text.

Q&A   Why does my screen not show a password text box?

Your account does not require a password.

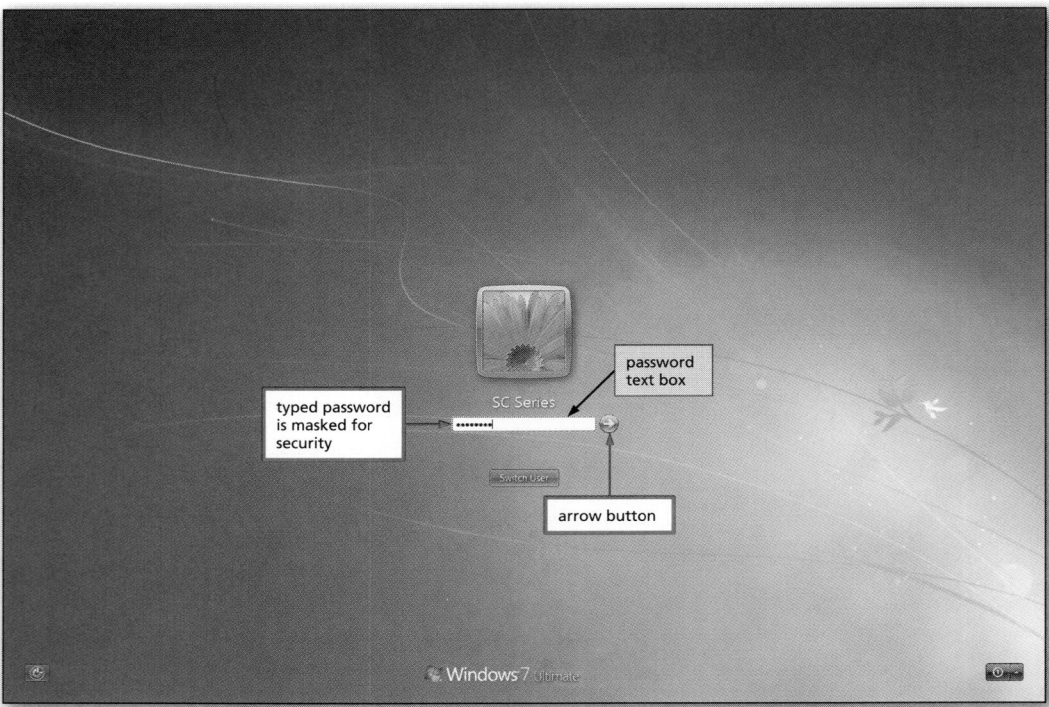

Figure 4

Office 2010 and Windows 7 Chapter

2

● If Windows 7 displays a password text box, type your password in the text box and then click the arrow button to log on to the computer and display the Windows 7 desktop (Figure 5).

Q&A

Why does my desktop look different from the one in Figure 5?

The Windows 7 desktop is customizable, and your school or employer may have modified the desktop to meet its needs. Also, your screen resolution, which affects the size of the elements on the screen, may differ from the screen resolution used in this book. Later in this chapter, you learn how to change screen resolution.

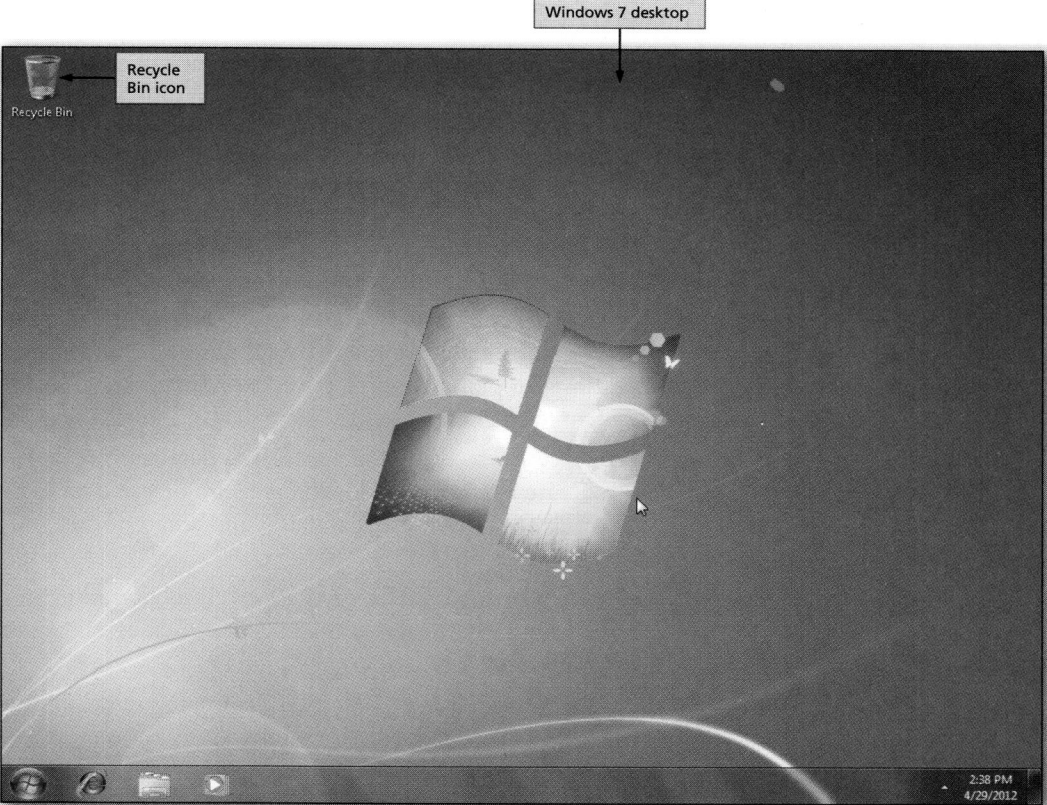

Figure 5

The Windows 7 Desktop

The Windows 7 desktop (Figure 5) and the objects on the desktop emulate a work area in an office. Think of the Windows desktop as an electronic version of the top of your desk. You can perform tasks such as placing objects on the desktop, moving the objects around the desktop, and removing items from the desktop.

When you start a program in Windows 7, it appears on the desktop. Some icons also may be displayed on the desktop. For instance, the icon for the **Recycle Bin**, the location of files that have been deleted, appears on the desktop by default. A **file** is a named unit of storage. Files can contain text, images, audio, and video. You can customize your desktop so that icons representing programs and files you use often appear on your desktop.

Introduction to Microsoft Office 2010

Microsoft Office 2010 is the newest version of Microsoft Office, offering features that provide users with better functionality and easier ways to work with the various files they create. These features include enhanced design tools, such as improved picture formatting tools and new themes, shared notebooks for working in groups, mobile versions of Office programs, broadcast presentation for the Web, and a digital notebook for managing and sharing multimedia information.

Microsoft Office 2010 Programs

Microsoft Office 2010 includes a wide variety of programs such as Word, PowerPoint, Excel, Access, Outlook, Publisher, OneNote, InfoPath, SharePoint Workspace, Communicator, and Web Apps:

- **Microsoft Word 2010**, or Word, is a full-featured word processing program that allows you to create professional-looking documents and revise them easily.
- **Microsoft PowerPoint 2010**, or PowerPoint, is a complete presentation program that allows you to produce professional-looking presentations.
- **Microsoft Excel 2010**, or Excel, is a powerful spreadsheet program that allows you to organize data, complete calculations, make decisions, graph data, develop professional-looking reports, publish organized data to the Web, and access real-time data from Web sites.
- **Microsoft Access 2010**, or Access, is a database management system that allows you to create a database; add, change, and delete data in the database; ask questions concerning the data in the database; and create forms and reports using the data in the database.
- **Microsoft Outlook 2010**, or Outlook, is a communications and scheduling program that allows you to manage e-mail accounts, calendars, contacts, and access to other Internet content.
- **Microsoft Publisher 2010**, or Publisher, is a desktop publishing program that helps you create professional-quality publications and marketing materials that can be shared easily.
- **Microsoft OneNote 2010**, or OneNote, is a note-taking program that allows you to store and share information in notebooks with other people.
- **Microsoft InfoPath 2010**, or InfoPath, is a form development program that helps you create forms for use on the Web and gather data from these forms.
- **Microsoft SharePoint Workspace 2010**, or SharePoint, is collaboration software that allows you to access and revise files stored on your computer from other locations.
- **Microsoft Communicator** is communications software that allows you to use different modes of communications such as instant messaging, videoconferencing, and sharing files and programs.
- **Microsoft Web Apps** is a Web application that allows you to edit and share files on the Web using the familiar Office interface.

Microsoft Office 2010 Suites

A **suite** is a collection of individual programs available together as a unit. Microsoft offers a variety of Office suites. Table 2 lists the Office 2010 suites and their components.

Programs in a suite, such as Microsoft Office, typically use a similar interface and share features. In addition, Microsoft Office programs use **common dialog boxes** for performing actions such as opening and saving files. Once you are comfortable working with these elements and this interface and performing tasks in one program, the similarity can help you apply the knowledge and skills you have learned to other Office programs. For example, the process for saving a file in PowerPoint is the same in Word, Excel, and the other Office programs. While briefly showing how to use PowerPoint, this chapter illustrates some of the common functions across the Office programs and also identifies the characteristics unique to PowerPoint.

Table 2 Microsoft Office 2010 Suites	Microsoft Office Professional Plus 2010	Microsoft Office Professional 2010	Microsoft Office Home and Business 2010	Microsoft Office Standard 2010	Microsoft Office Home and Student 2010
Microsoft Word 2010	✔	✔	✔	✔	✔
Microsoft PowerPoint 2010	✔	✔	✔	✔	✔
Microsoft Excel 2010	✔	✔	✔	✔	✔
Microsoft Access 2010	✔	✔	✗	✗	✗
Microsoft Outlook 2010	✔	✔	✔	✔	✗
Microsoft Publisher 2010	✔	✔	✗	✔	✗
Microsoft OneNote 2010	✔	✔	✔	✔	✔
Microsoft InfoPath 2010	✔	✗	✗	✗	✗
Microsoft SharePoint Workspace 2010	✔	✗	✗	✗	✗
Microsoft Communicator	✔	✗	✗	✗	✗

Starting and Using a Program

To use a program, such as PowerPoint, you must instruct the operating system to start the program. Windows 7 provides many different ways to start a program, one of which is presented in this section (other ways to start a program are presented throughout this chapter). After starting a program, you can use it to perform a variety of tasks. The following pages use PowerPoint to discuss some elements of the Office interface and to perform tasks that are common to other Office programs.

PowerPoint

PowerPoint is a complete presentation program that allows you to produce professional-looking presentations. A PowerPoint **presentation** also is called a **slide show**. To make presentations more impressive, you can add charts, diagrams, tables, pictures, video, sound, and animation effects. Additional PowerPoint features include the following:

- **Word processing** — Create bulleted lists, combine words and images, find and replace text, import text from an outline, and use multiple fonts and font sizes.
- **Inserting multimedia** — Insert artwork and multimedia files into a slide show.
- **Saving to the Web** — You can publish your slide show to the Internet or to an intranet.
- **Collaborating** — Share a presentation with friends and coworkers. Ask them to review the slides and then insert comments to enhance the presentation.

To Start a Program Using the Start Menu

Across the bottom of the Windows 7 desktop is the **taskbar**. The taskbar contains the **Start button**, which you use to access programs, files, folders, and settings on a computer. A **folder** is a named location on a storage medium that usually contains related documents. The taskbar also displays a button for each program currently running on a computer.

Clicking the Start button displays the Start menu. The **Start menu** allows you to access programs, folders, and files on the computer and contains commands that allow you to start programs, store and search for documents, customize the computer, and obtain help about thousands of topics. A **menu** is a list of related items, including folders, programs, and commands. Each **command** on a menu performs a specific action, such as saving a file or obtaining help.

The following steps, which assume Windows 7 is running, use the Start menu to start PowerPoint based on a typical installation. You may need to ask your instructor how to start PowerPoint for your computer. Although the steps illustrate starting the PowerPoint program, the steps to start any Office program are similar.

1
- Click the Start button on the Windows 7 taskbar to display the Start menu (Figure 6).

Q&A Why does my Start menu look different?

It may look different depending on your computer's configuration. The Start menu may be customized for several reasons, such as usage requirements or security restrictions.

2
- Click All Programs at the bottom of the left pane on the Start menu to display the All Programs list (Figure 7).

Q&A What is a pane?

A **pane** is an area of a window that displays related content. For example, the left pane on the Start menu contains a list of frequently used programs, as well as the All Programs command.

Q&A Why might my All Programs list look different?

Most likely, the programs installed on your computer will differ from those shown in Figure 7. Your All Programs list will show the programs that are installed on your computer.

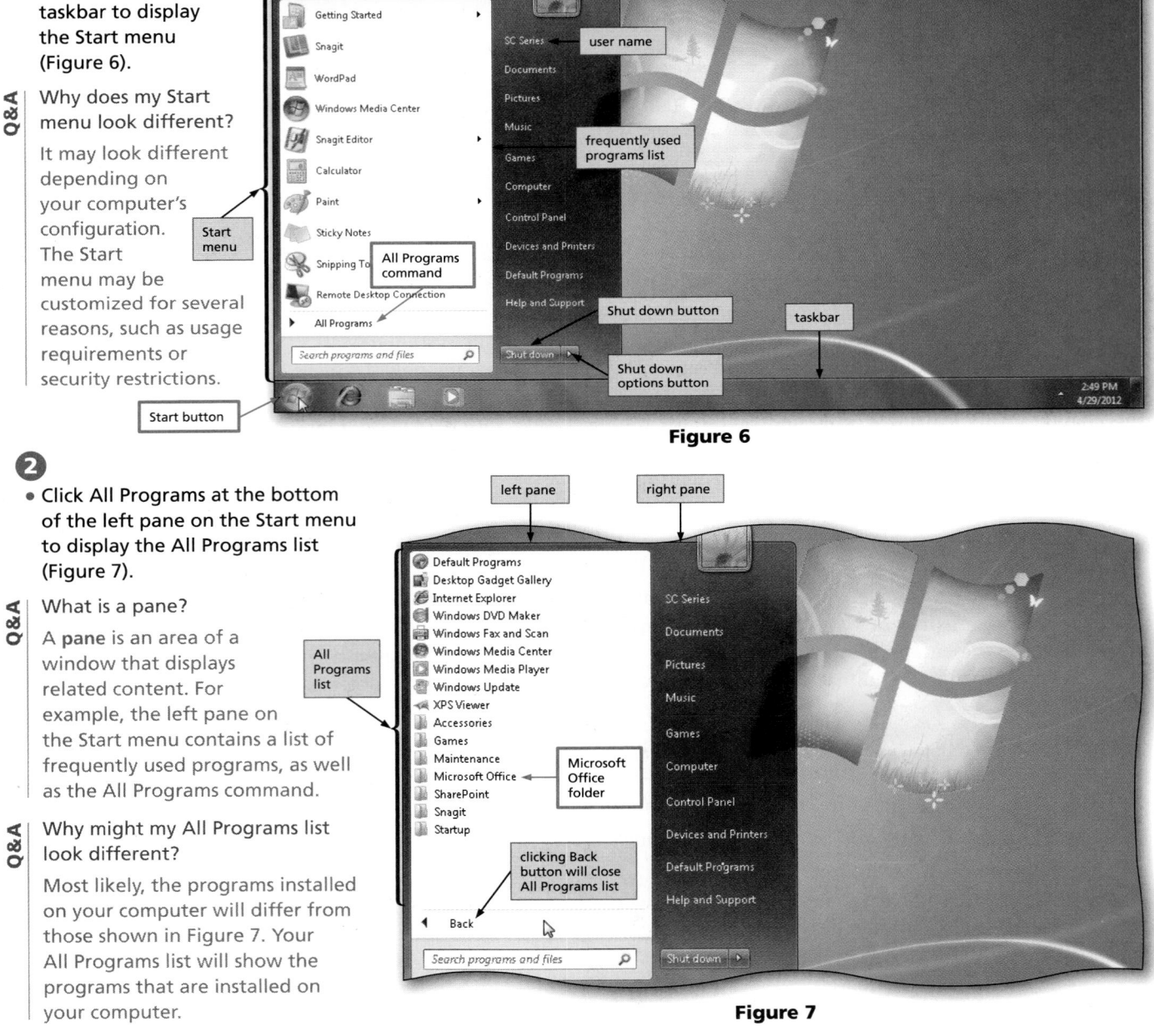

Figure 6

Figure 7

- If the program you wish to start is located in a folder, click or scroll to and then click the folder (Microsoft Office, in this case) in the All Programs list to display a list of the folder's contents (Figure 8).

Q&A | Why is the Microsoft Office folder on my computer?

During installation of Microsoft Office 2010, the Microsoft Office folder was added to the All Programs list.

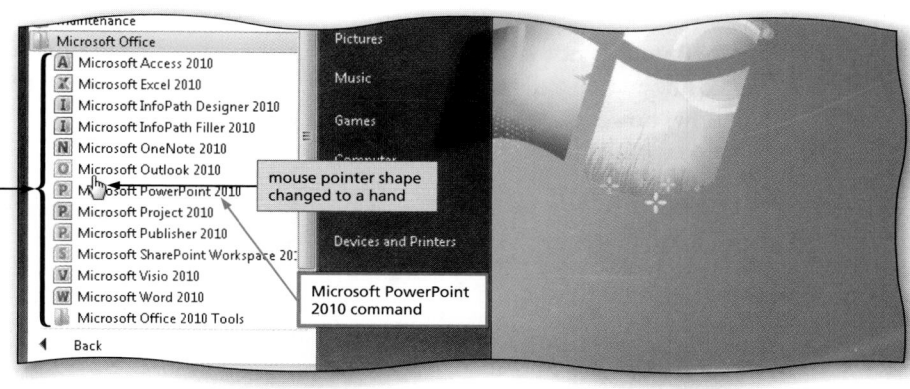

Figure 8

❹

- Click, or scroll to and then click, the program name (Microsoft PowerPoint 2010, in this case) in the list to start the selected program (Figure 9).

Q&A | What happens when you start a program?

Many programs initially display a blank document in a program window, as shown in the PowerPoint window in Figure 9; others provide a means for you to create a blank document. A **window** is a rectangular area that displays data and information. The top of a window has a **title bar**, which is a horizontal space that contains the window's name.

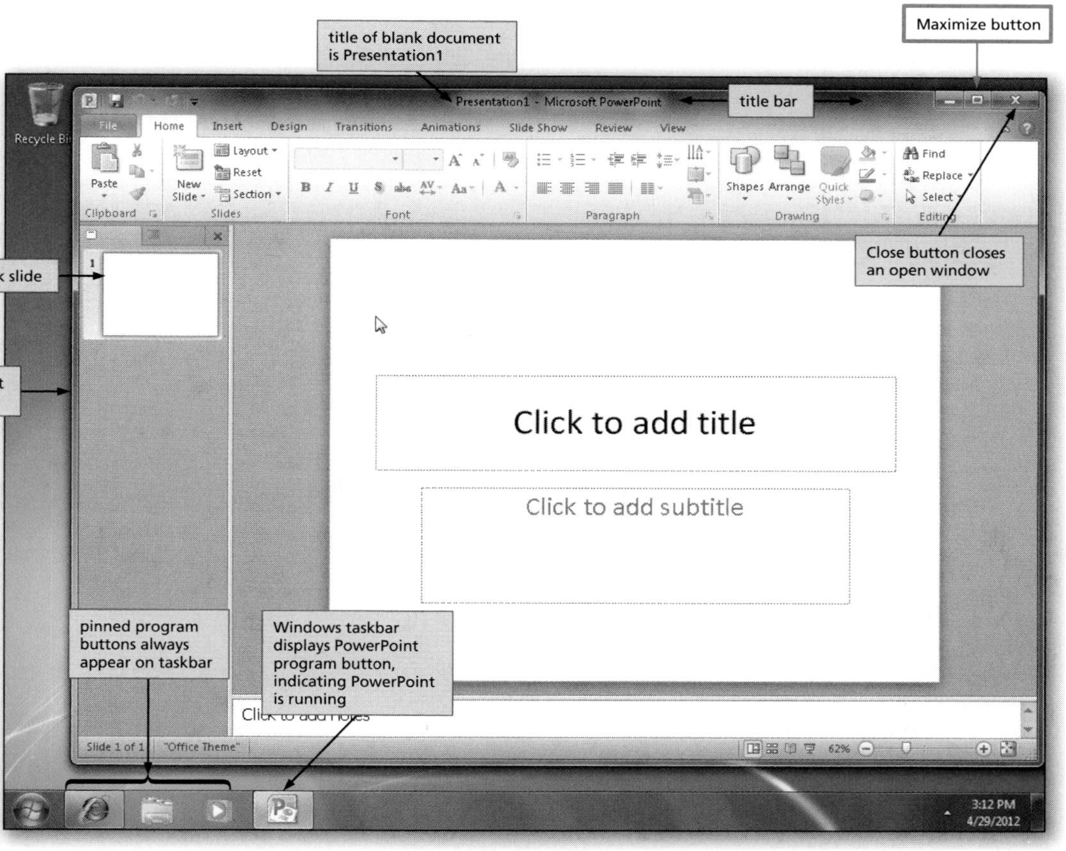

Figure 9

Q&A | Why is my program window a different size?

The PowerPoint window shown in Figure 9 is not maximized. Your PowerPoint window already may be maximized. The steps on the next page maximize a window.

Other Ways	
1. Double-click program icon on desktop, if one is present	3. Display Start menu, type program name in search box, click program name
2. Click program name in left pane of Start menu, if present	4. Double-click file created using program you want to start

To Maximize a Window

Sometimes content is not visible completely in a window. One method of displaying the entire contents of a window is to **maximize** it, or enlarge the window so that it fills the entire screen. The following step maximizes the PowerPoint window; however, any Office program's window can be maximized using this step.

- If the program window is not maximized already, click the Maximize button (shown in Figure 9 on the previous page) next to the Close button on the window's title bar (the PowerPoint window title bar, in this case) to maximize the window (Figure 10).

Q&A What happened to the Maximize button?

It changed to a Restore Down button, which you can use to return a window to its size and location before you maximized it.

Q&A How do I know whether a window is maximized?

A window is maximized if it fills the entire display area and the Restore Down button is displayed on the title bar.

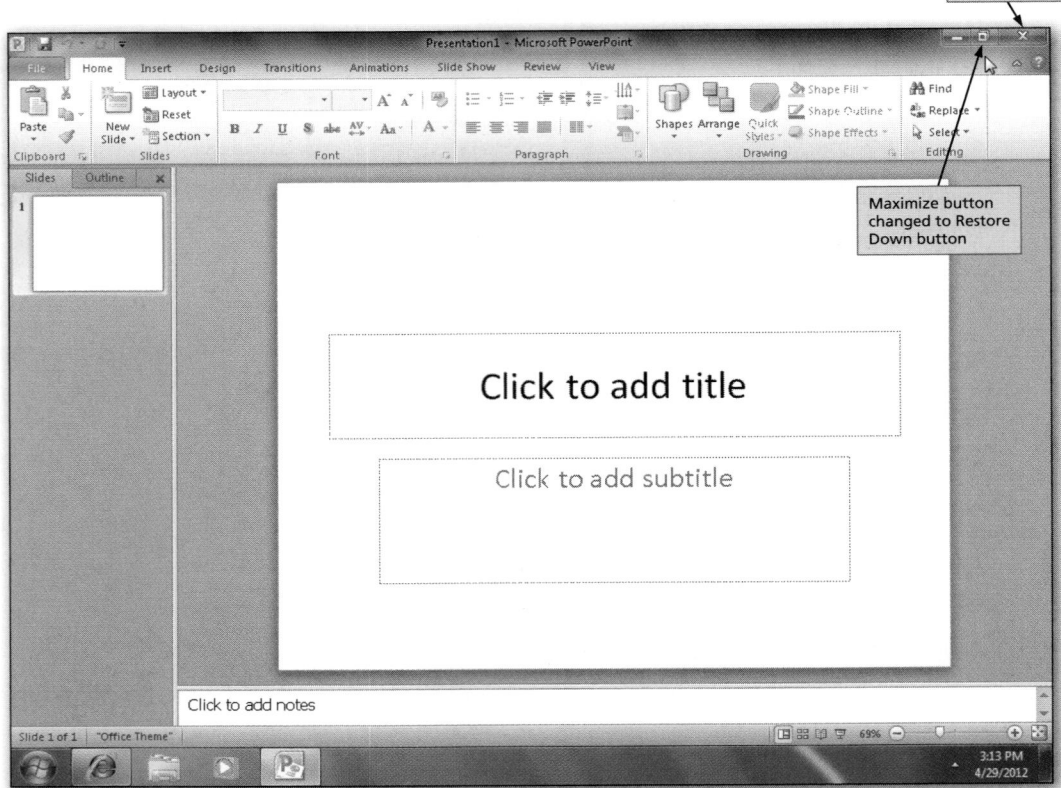

Figure 10

Other Ways

1. Double-click title bar
2. Drag title bar to top of screen

The PowerPoint Document Window, Ribbon, and Elements Common to Office Programs

The PowerPoint window consists of a variety of components to make your work more efficient and documents more professional: the window, Ribbon, Mini toolbar, shortcut menus, and Quick Access Toolbar. Many of these components are common to other Office programs and have been discussed earlier in this chapter. Other components, discussed in the following paragraphs and later in subsequent chapters, are unique to PowerPoint.

The basic unit of a PowerPoint presentation is a **slide**. A slide may contain text and objects, such as graphics, tables, charts, and drawings. **Layouts** are used to position this content on the slide. When you create a new presentation, the default **Title Slide** layout appears (Figure 11). The purpose of this layout is to introduce the presentation to the audience. PowerPoint includes eight other built-in standard layouts.

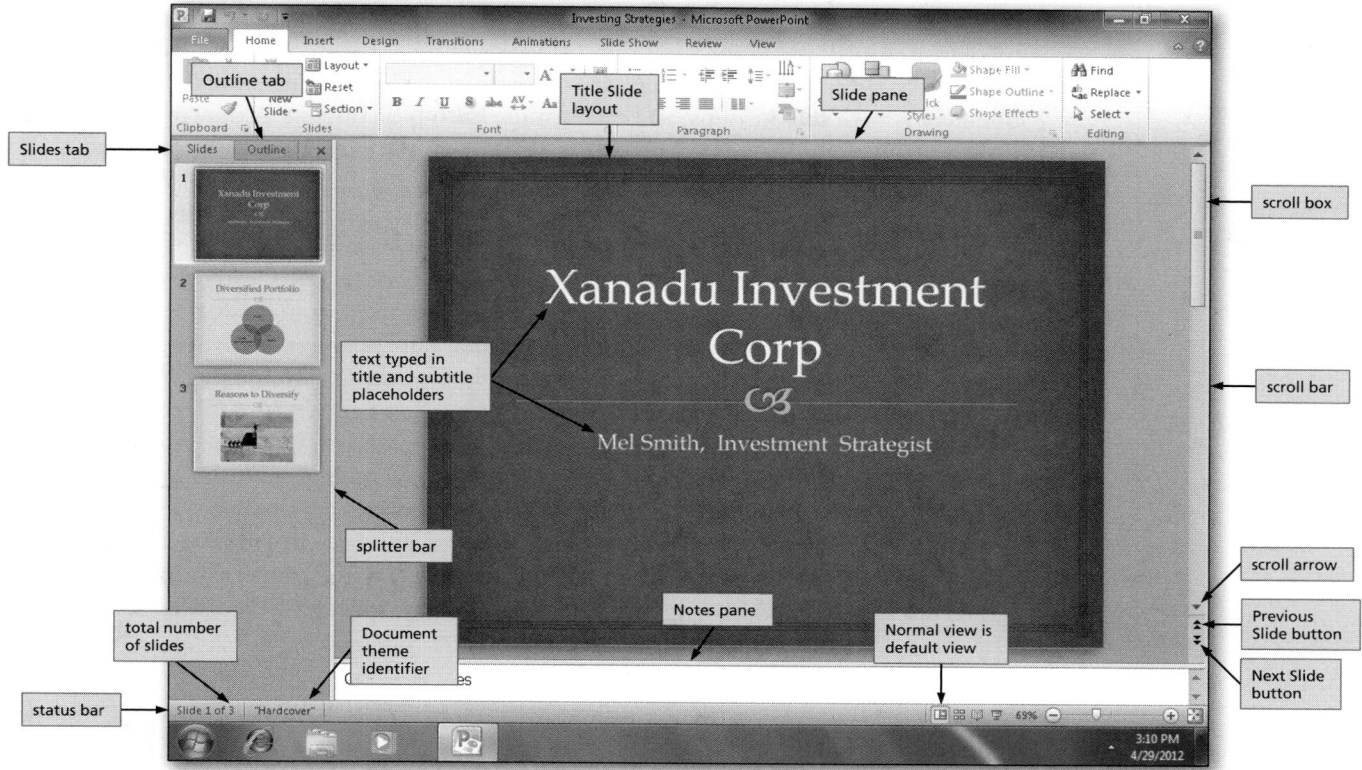

Figure 11

The default slide layouts are set up in **landscape orientation**, where the slide width is greater than its height. In landscape orientation, the slide size is preset to 10 inches wide and 7.5 inches high when printed on a standard sheet of paper measuring 11 inches wide and 8.5 inches high.

Placeholders   **Placeholders** are boxes with dotted or hatch-marked borders that are displayed when you create a new slide. All layouts except the Blank slide layout contain placeholders. Depending on the particular slide layout selected, placeholders are displayed for the slide title and subtitle; a content text placeholder is displayed for text, art, or a table, chart, picture, graphic, or movie. The title slide in Figure 11 has two text placeholders for the main heading, or title, of a new slide and the subtitle.

Scroll Bars   You use a scroll bar to display different portions of a document in the document window. At the right edge of the document window is a vertical scroll bar. If a document is too wide to fit in the document window, a horizontal scroll bar also appears at the bottom of the document window. On a scroll bar, the position of the scroll box reflects the location of the portion of the document that is displayed in the document window.

Status Bar   The **status bar**, located at the bottom of the document window above the Windows 7 taskbar, presents information about the document, the progress of current tasks, and the status of certain commands and keys; it also provides controls for viewing the document. As you type text or perform certain tasks, various indicators and buttons may appear on the status bar.

The left side of the status bar in Figure 11 shows the current slide followed by the total number of slides in the document and an icon to check spelling. The right side of the status bar includes buttons and controls you can use to change the view of a slide and adjust the size of the displayed document.

Ribbon   The Ribbon, located near the top of the window below the title bar, is the control center in PowerPoint and other Office programs (Figure 12). The Ribbon provides easy, central access to the tasks you perform while creating a document. The Ribbon consists of tabs, groups, and commands. Each **tab** contains a collection of groups, and each **group** contains related functions. When you start an Office program, such as PowerPoint, it initially displays several main tabs, also called default tabs. All Office programs have a **Home tab**, which contains the more frequently used commands.

In addition to the main tabs, Office programs display **tool tabs**, also called contextual tabs (Figure 13), when you perform certain tasks or work with objects such as pictures or tables. If you insert a picture in a PowerPoint document, for example, the Picture Tools tab and its related subordinate Format tab appear, collectively referred to as the Picture Tools Format tab. When you are finished working with the picture, the Picture Tools Format tab disappears from the Ribbon. PowerPoint and other Office programs determine when tool tabs should appear and disappear based on tasks you perform. Some tool tabs, such as the Table Tools tab, have more than one related subordinate tab.

Items on the Ribbon include buttons, boxes (text boxes, check boxes, etc.), and galleries (Figure 12). A **gallery** is a set of choices, often graphical, arranged in a grid or in a list. You can scroll through choices in an in-Ribbon gallery by clicking the gallery's scroll arrows. Or, you can click a gallery's More button to view more gallery options on the screen at a time.

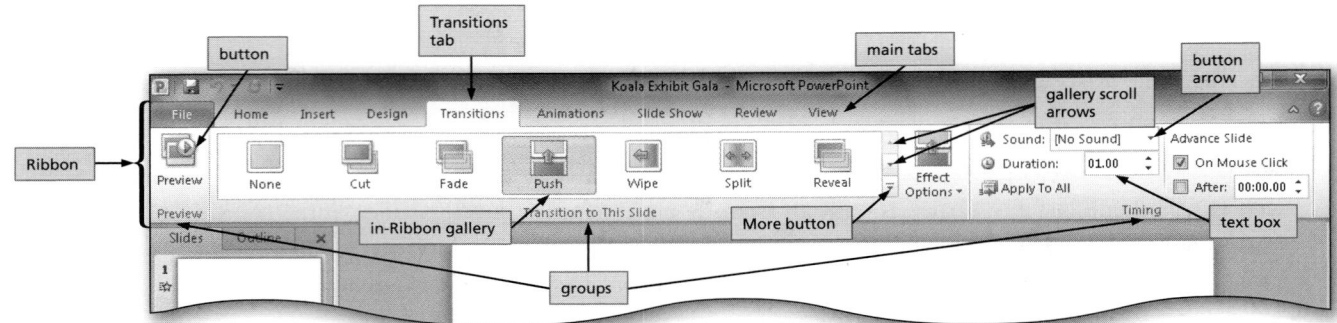

Figure 12

Some buttons and boxes have arrows that, when clicked, also display a gallery; others always cause a gallery to be displayed when clicked. Most galleries support **live preview**, which is a feature that allows you to point to a gallery choice and see its effect in the document — without actually selecting the choice (Figure 13).

Some commands on the Ribbon display an image to help you remember their function. When you point to a command on the Ribbon, all or part of the command glows in shades of yellow and orange, and an Enhanced ScreenTip appears on the screen. An **Enhanced ScreenTip** is an on-screen note that provides the name of the command, available keyboard shortcut(s), a description of the command, and sometimes instructions for how to obtain help about the command (Figure 14). Enhanced ScreenTips are more detailed than a typical ScreenTip, which usually displays only the name of the command.

Some groups on the Ribbon have a small arrow in the lower-right corner, called a **Dialog Box Launcher**, that when clicked, displays a dialog box or a task pane with additional options for the group (Figure 15). When presented with a dialog box, you make selections and must close the dialog box before returning to the document. A **task pane**, in contrast to a dialog box, is a window that can remain open and visible while you work in the document.

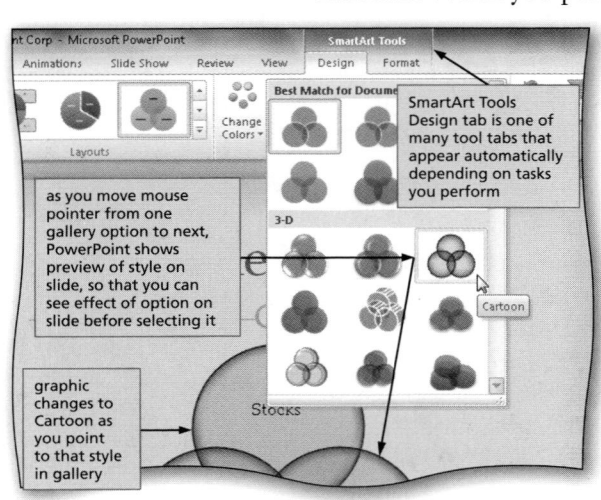

Figure 13

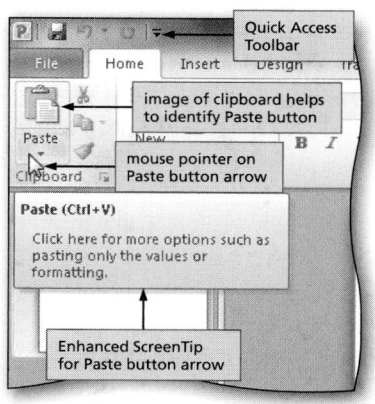

Figure 14

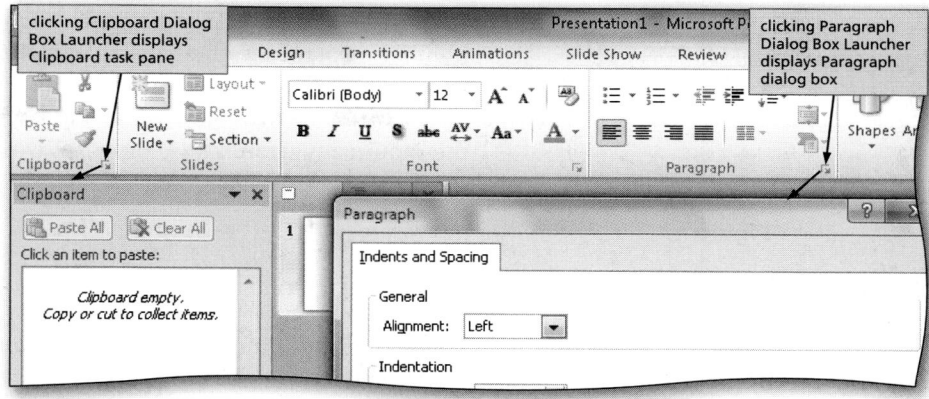

Figure 15

Mini Toolbar   The **Mini toolbar**, which appears automatically based on tasks you perform, contains commands related to changing the appearance of text in a document. All commands on the Mini toolbar also exist on the Ribbon. The purpose of the Mini toolbar is to minimize mouse movement.

When the Mini toolbar appears, it initially is transparent (Figure 16a). If you do not use the transparent Mini toolbar, it disappears from the screen. To use the Mini toolbar, move the mouse pointer into the toolbar, which causes the Mini toolbar to change from a transparent to bright appearance (Figure 16b). If you right-click an item in the document window, PowerPoint displays both the Mini toolbar and a shortcut menu, which is discussed in a later section in this chapter.

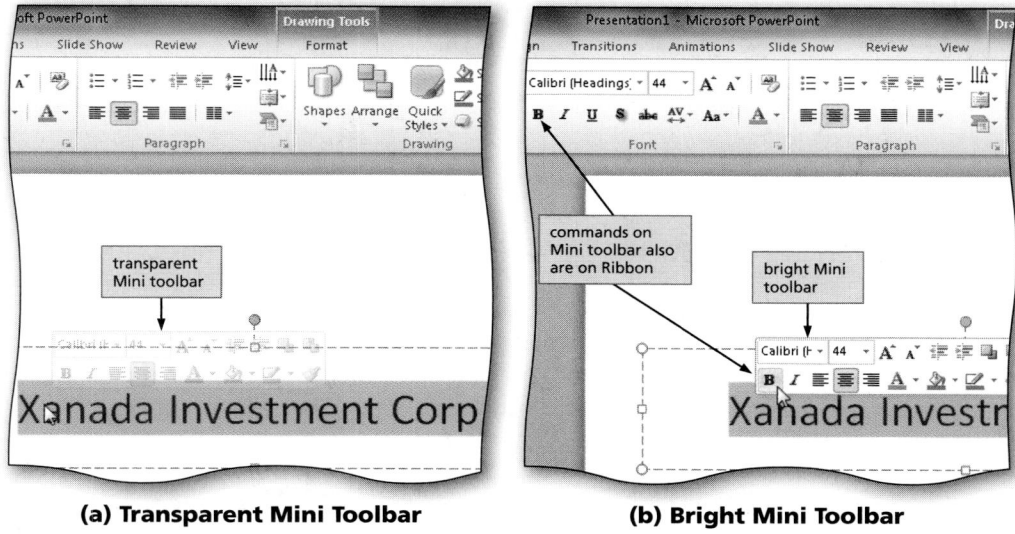

(a) Transparent Mini Toolbar   **(b) Bright Mini Toolbar**

Figure 16

BTW

Turning Off the Mini Toolbar
If you do not want the Mini toolbar to appear, click File on the Ribbon to open the Backstage view, click Options in the Backstage view, click General (Options dialog box), remove the check mark from the Show Mini Toolbar on selection check box, and then click the OK button.

Quick Access Toolbar   The **Quick Access Toolbar**, located initially (by default) above the Ribbon at the left edge of the title bar, provides convenient, one-click access to frequently used commands (Figure 14). The commands on the Quick Access Toolbar always are available, regardless of the task you are performing. The Quick Access Toolbar is discussed in more depth later in the chapter.

KeyTips   If you prefer using the keyboard instead of the mouse, you can press the ALT key on the keyboard to display **KeyTips**, or keyboard code icons, for certain commands

Figure 17

(Figure 17). To select a command using the keyboard, press the letter or number displayed in the KeyTip, which may cause additional KeyTips related to the selected command to appear. To remove KeyTips from the screen, press the ALT key or the ESC key until all KeyTips disappear, or click the mouse anywhere in the program window.

To Display a Different Tab on the Ribbon

When you start PowerPoint, the Ribbon displays nine main tabs: File, Home, Insert, Design, Transitions, Animations, Slide Show, Review, and View. The tab currently displayed is called the **active tab**.

The following step displays the Insert tab and makes it the active tab.

 1

- Click Insert on the Ribbon to display the Insert tab (Figure 18).

 **Experiment**

- Click the other tabs on the Ribbon to view their contents. When you are finished, click the Insert tab to redisplay the Insert tab.

Q&A If I am working in a different Office program, such as Word or Access, how do I display a different tab on the Ribbon?

Follow this same procedure; that is, click the desired tab on the Ribbon.

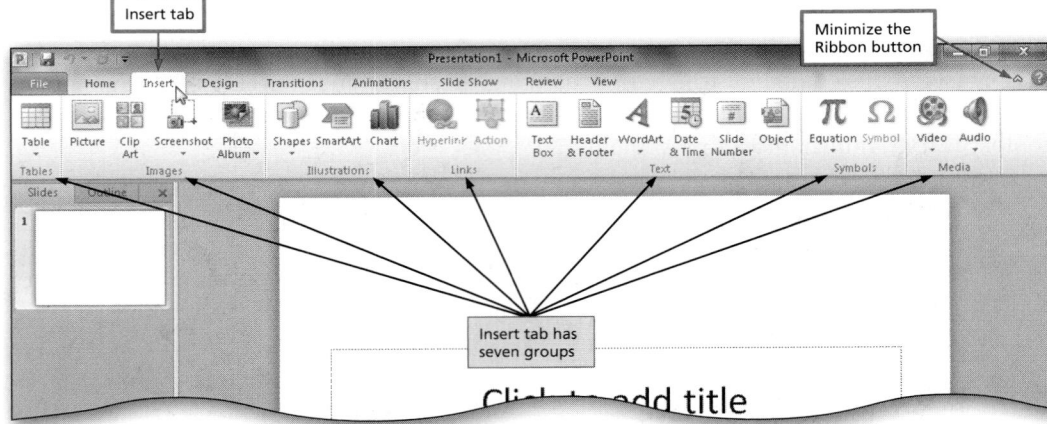

Figure 18

To Minimize, Display, and Restore the Ribbon

To display more of a document or other item in the window of an Office program, some users prefer to minimize the Ribbon, which hides the groups on the Ribbon and displays only the main tabs. Each time you start an Office program, such as PowerPoint, the Ribbon appears the same way it did the last time you used that Office program. The chapters in this book, however, begin with the Ribbon appearing as it did at the initial installation of the PowerPoint program.

The following steps minimize, display, and restore the Ribbon in an Office program.

 1

- Click the Minimize the Ribbon button on the Ribbon (shown in Figure 18) to minimize the Ribbon (Figure 19).

Q&A What happened to the groups on the Ribbon?

When you minimize the Ribbon, the groups disappear so that the Ribbon does not take up as much space on the screen.

Q&A What happened to the Minimize the Ribbon button?

The Expand the Ribbon button replaces the Minimize the Ribbon button when the Ribbon is minimized.

Figure 19

- Click Home on the Ribbon to display the Home tab (Figure 20).

Q&A

Why would I click the Home tab?

If you want to use a command on a minimized Ribbon, click the main tab to display the groups for that tab. After you select a command on the Ribbon, the groups will be hidden once again. If you decide not to use a command on the Ribbon, you can hide the groups by clicking the same main tab or clicking in the program window.

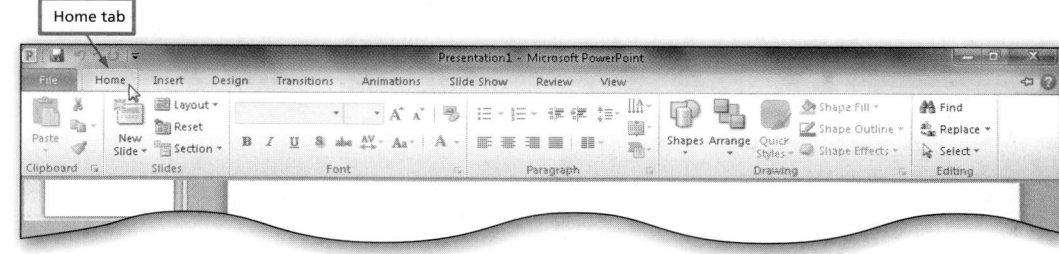

Figure 20

- Click Home on the Ribbon to hide the groups again (shown in Figure 19).

- Click the Expand the Ribbon button on the Ribbon (shown in Figure 19) to restore the Ribbon.

Other Ways
1. Double-click Home on the Ribbon
2. Press CTRL+F1

To Display and Use a Shortcut Menu

When you right-click certain areas of the PowerPoint and other program windows, a shortcut menu will appear. A **shortcut menu** is a list of frequently used commands that relate to the right-clicked object. When you right-click a scroll bar, for example, a shortcut menu appears with commands related to the scroll bar. When you right-click the Quick Access Toolbar, a shortcut menu appears with commands related to the Quick Access Toolbar. You can use shortcut menus to access common commands quickly. The following steps use a shortcut menu to move the Quick Access Toolbar, which by default is located on the title bar.

- Right-click the Quick Access Toolbar to display a shortcut menu that presents a list of commands related to the Quick Access Toolbar (Figure 21).

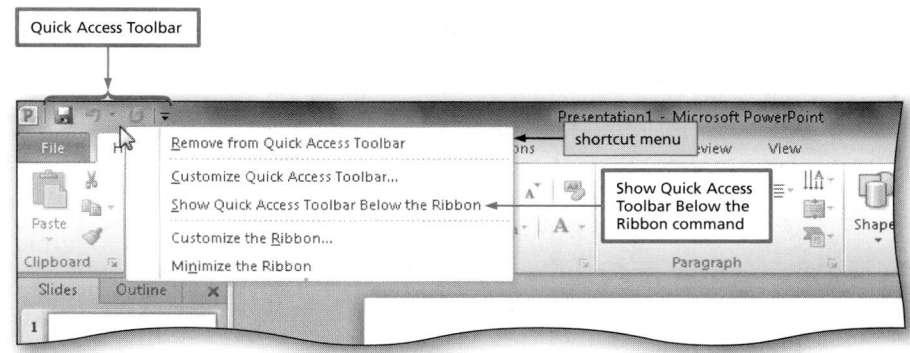

Figure 21

- Click Show Quick Access Toolbar Below the Ribbon on the shortcut menu to display the Quick Access Toolbar below the Ribbon (Figure 22).

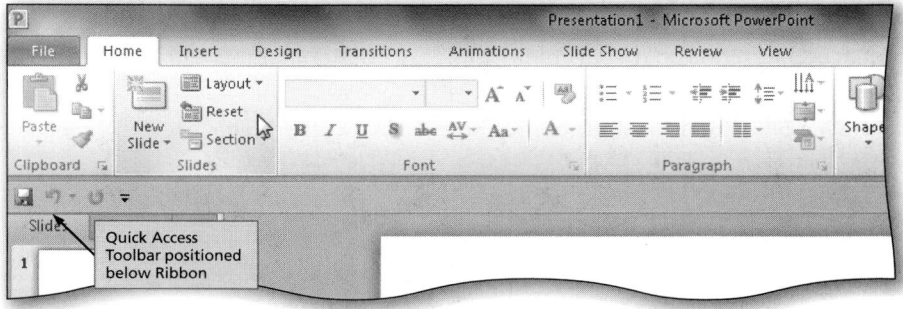

Figure 22

- Right-click the Quick Access Toolbar to display a shortcut menu (Figure 23).

- Click Show Quick Access Toolbar Above the Ribbon on the shortcut menu to return the Quick Access Toolbar to its original position (shown in Figure 21 on the previous page).

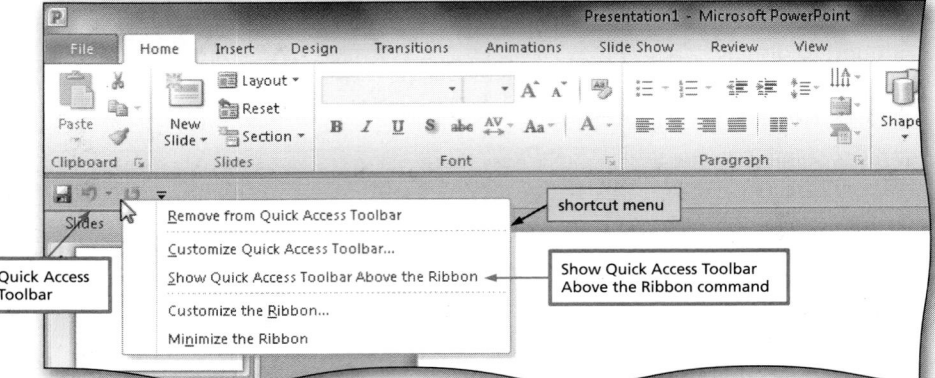

Figure 23

To Customize the Quick Access Toolbar

The Quick Access Toolbar provides easy access to some of the more frequently used commands in Office programs. By default, the Quick Access Toolbar contains buttons for the Save, Undo, and Redo commands. You can customize the Quick Access Toolbar by changing its location in the window, as shown in the previous steps, and by adding more buttons to reflect commands you would like to access easily. The following steps add the Quick Print button to the Quick Access Toolbar in the PowerPoint window.

- Click the Customize Quick Access Toolbar button to display the Customize Quick Access Toolbar menu (Figure 24).

Q&A Which commands are listed on the Customize Quick Access Toolbar menu?

It lists commands that commonly are added to the Quick Access Toolbar.

Q&A What do the check marks next to some commands signify?

Check marks appear next to commands that already are on the Quick Access Toolbar. When you add a button to the Quick Access Toolbar, a check mark will be displayed next to its command name.

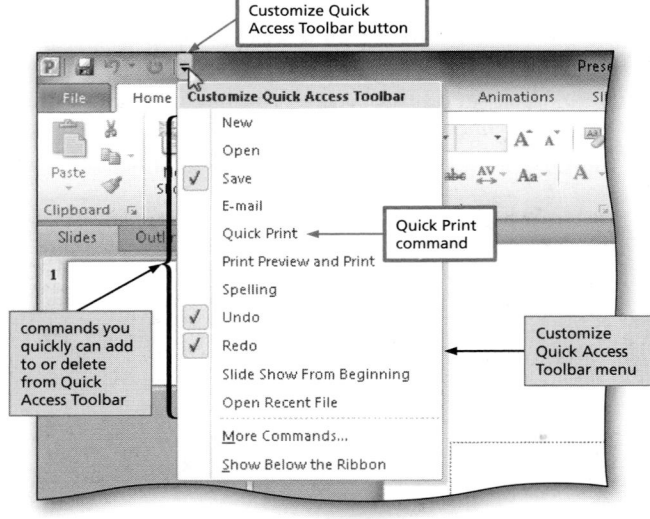

Figure 24

- Click Quick Print on the Customize Quick Access Toolbar menu to add the Quick Print button to the Quick Access Toolbar (Figure 25).

Q&A How would I remove a button from the Quick Access Toolbar?

You would right-click the button you wish to remove and then click Remove from Quick Access Toolbar on the shortcut menu. If you want your screens to match the screens in the remaining chapters in this book, you would remove the Quick Print button from the Quick Access Toolbar.

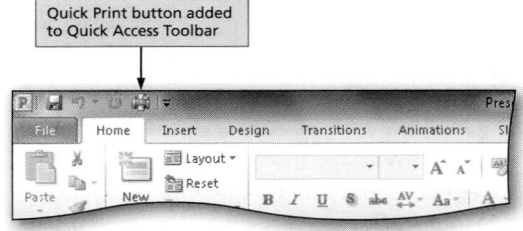

Figure 25

To Enter Content in a Title Slide

With the exception of a blank slide and a slide with a picture and caption, PowerPoint assumes every new slide has a title. Many of PowerPoint's layouts have both a title text placeholder and at least one content placeholder. To make creating a presentation easier, any text you type after a new slide appears becomes title text in the title text placeholder. As you begin typing text in the title text placeholder, the title text also is displayed in the Slide 1 thumbnail in the Slides tab. The presentation title for this presentation is Xanada Investment Corp. The following steps enter a presentation title on the title slide.

1

- Click the label 'Click to add title' located inside the title text placeholder to select the placeholder (Figure 26).

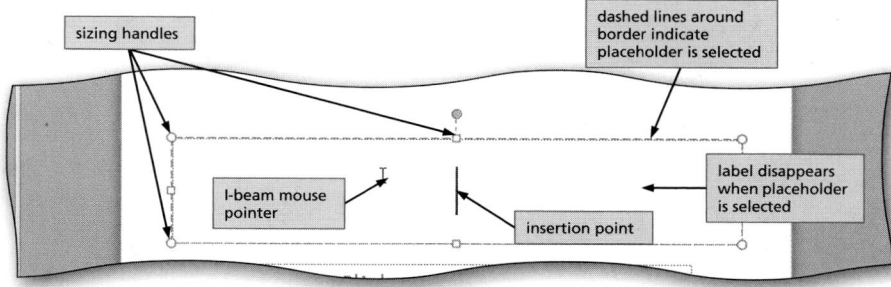

Figure 26

2

- Type **Xanada Investment Corp.** in the title text placeholder. Do not press the ENTER key because you do not want to create a new line of text (Figure 27).

Q&A

What are the white squares and circles that appear around the title text placeholder as I type the presentation title?

The white squares and circles are sizing handles, which you can drag to change the size of the title text placeholder. Sizing handles also can be found around other placeholders and objects within a presentation.

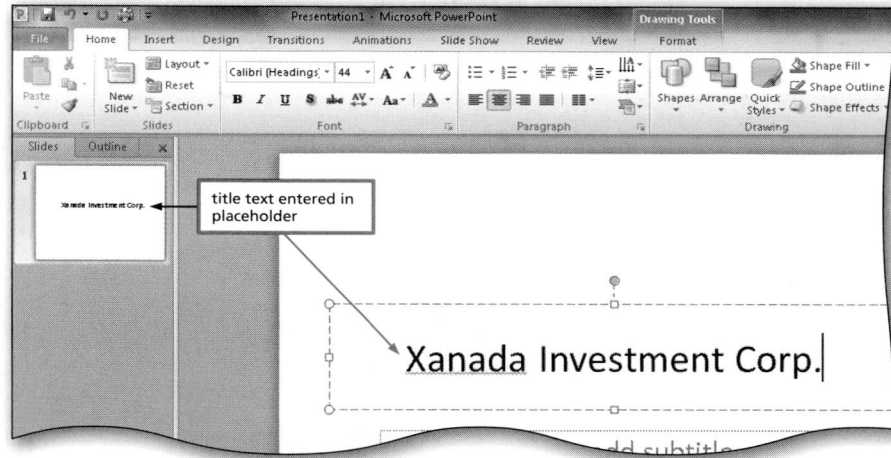

Figure 27

Saving and Organizing Files

While you are creating a document, the computer stores it in memory. When you save a document, the computer places it on a storage medium such as a hard disk, USB flash drive, or optical disc. A saved document is referred to as a file. A **file name** is the name assigned to a file when it is saved. It is important to save a document frequently for the following reasons:

- The document in memory might be lost if the computer is turned off or you lose electrical power while a program is running.
- If you run out of time before completing a project, you may finish it at a future time without starting over.

When saving files, you should organize them so that you easily can find them later. Windows 7 provides tools to help you organize files.

Organizing Files and Folders

A file contains data. This data can range from a research paper to an accounting spreadsheet to an electronic math quiz. You should organize and store these files in folders to avoid misplacing a file and to help you find a file quickly.

If you are a freshman taking an introductory computer class (CIS 101, for example), you may want to design a series of folders for the different subjects covered in the class. To accomplish this, you can arrange the folders in a hierarchy for the class, as shown in Figure 28.

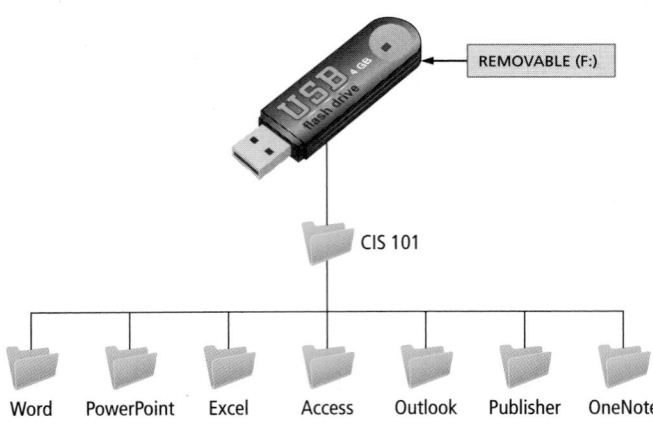

Figure 28

The hierarchy contains three levels. The first level contains the storage device, in this case a USB flash drive. Windows 7 identifies the storage device with a letter, and, in some cases, a name. In Figure 28, the USB flash drive is identified as REMOVABLE (F:). The second level contains the class folder (CIS 101, in this case), and the third level contains seven folders, one each for a different Office program that will be covered in the class (Word, PowerPoint, Excel, Access, Outlook, Publisher, and OneNote).

When the hierarchy in Figure 28 is created, the USB flash drive is said to contain the CIS 101 folder, and the CIS 101 folder is said to contain the separate Office folders (i.e., Word, PowerPoint, Excel, etc.). In addition, this hierarchy easily can be expanded to include folders from other classes taken during additional semesters.

The vertical and horizontal lines in Figure 28 form a pathway that allows you to navigate to a drive or folder on a computer or network. A **path** consists of a drive letter (preceded by a drive name when necessary) and colon, to identify the storage device, and one or more folder names. Each drive or folder in the hierarchy has a corresponding path.

Table 3 shows examples of paths and their corresponding drives and folders.

Table 3 Paths and Corresponding Drives and Folders	
Path	**Drive and Folder**
Computer ▶ REMOVABLE (F:)	Drive F (REMOVABLE (F:))
Computer ▶ REMOVABLE (F:) ▶ CIS 101	CIS 101 folder on drive F
Computer ▶ REMOVABLE (F:) ▶ CIS 101 ▶ PowerPoint	PowerPoint folder in CIS 101 folder on drive F

BTW

Saving Online
Instead of saving files on a USB flash drive, some people prefer to save them online so that they can access the files from any computer with an Internet connection. For more information, read Appendix C.

The following pages illustrate the steps to organize the folders for this class and save a file in one of those folders:

1. Create the folder identifying your class.
2. Create the PowerPoint folder in the folder identifying your class.
3. Save a file in the PowerPoint folder.
4. Verify the location of the saved file.

To Create a Folder

When you create a folder, such as the CIS 101 folder shown in Figure 28, you must name the folder. A folder name should describe the folder and its contents. A folder name can contain spaces and any uppercase or lowercase characters, except a backslash (\), slash (/), colon (:), asterisk (*), question mark (?), quotation marks ("), less than symbol (<), greater than symbol (>), or vertical bar (|). Folder names cannot be CON, AUX, COM1, COM2, COM3, COM4, LPT1, LPT2, LPT3, PRN, or NUL. The same rules for naming folders also apply to naming files.

To store files and folders on a USB flash drive, you must connect the USB flash drive to an available USB port on a computer. The following steps create your class folder (CIS 101, in this case) on a USB flash drive.

1

- Connect the USB flash drive to an available USB port on the computer to open the AutoPlay window (Figure 29).

Q&A Why does the AutoPlay window not open?

Some computers are not configured to open an AutoPlay window. Instead, they might display the contents of the USB flash drive automatically, or you might need to access contents of the USB flash drive using the Computer window. To use the Computer window to display the USB flash drive's contents, click the Start button, click Computer on the Start menu, click the icon representing the USB flash drive, and then proceed to Step 3 on the next page.

Q&A Why does the AutoPlay window look different from the one in Figure 29?

The AutoPlay window that opens on your computer might display different options. The type of USB flash drive, its contents, and the next available drive letter on your computer all will determine which options are displayed in the AutoPlay window.

2

- Click the 'Open folder to view files' link in the AutoPlay window to open the USB flash drive window (Figure 30).

Q&A Why does Figure 30 show REMOVABLE (F:) for the USB flash drive?

REMOVABLE is the name of the USB flash drive used to illustrate these steps. The (F:) refers to the drive letter assigned by Windows 7 to the USB flash drive. The name and drive letter of your USB flash drive probably will be different.

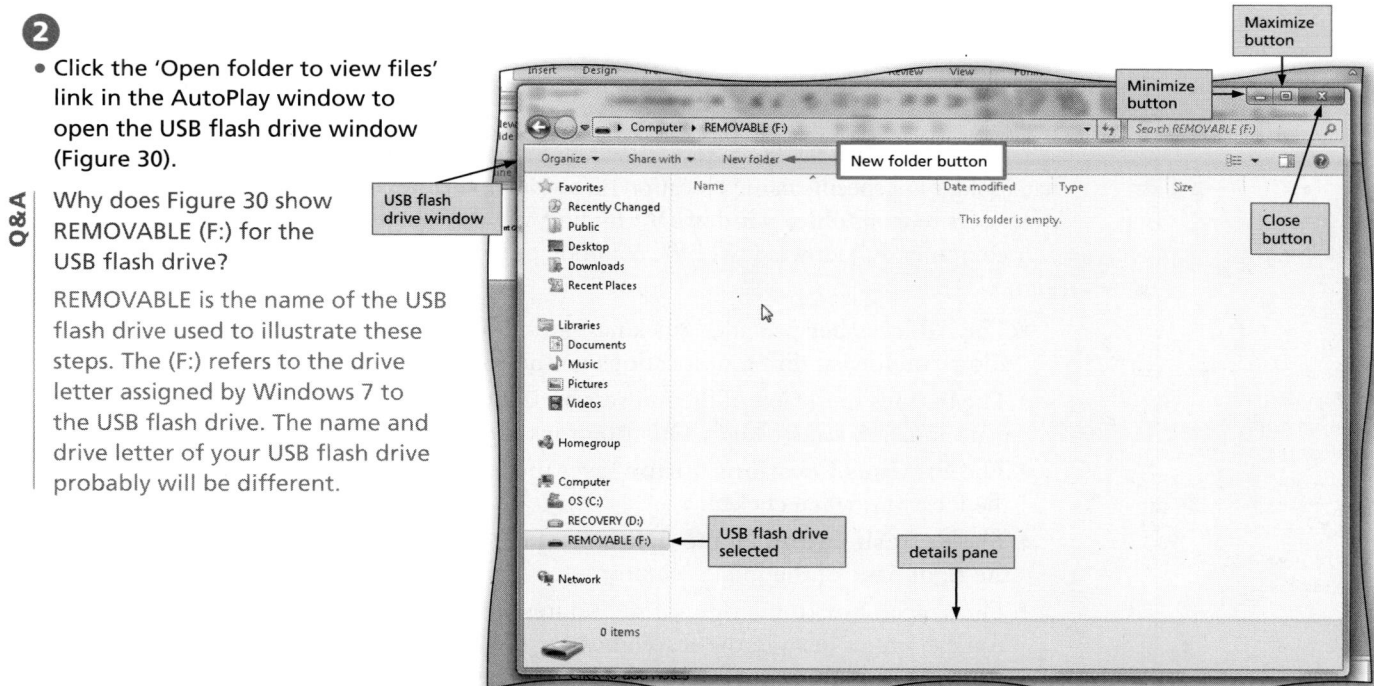

Figure 29

Figure 30

3

• Click the New folder button on the toolbar to display a new folder icon with the name, New folder, selected in a text box.

• Type **CIS 101** (or your class code) in the text box to name the folder.

• Press the ENTER key to create a folder identifying your class on the selected drive (Figure 31). If the CIS 101 folder does not appear in the Navigation pane, double-click REMOVABLE (F:) in the Navigation pane to display the folder just added. If the CIS 101 folder does not appear in the Navigation pane, double-click REMOVABLE (F:) in the Navigation pane to display the folder just added.

Q&A What happens when I press the ENTER key?

The class folder (CIS 101, in this case) is displayed in the File list, which contains the folder name, date modified, type, and size.

Q&A Why is the folder icon displayed differently on my computer?

Windows might be configured to display contents differently on your computer.

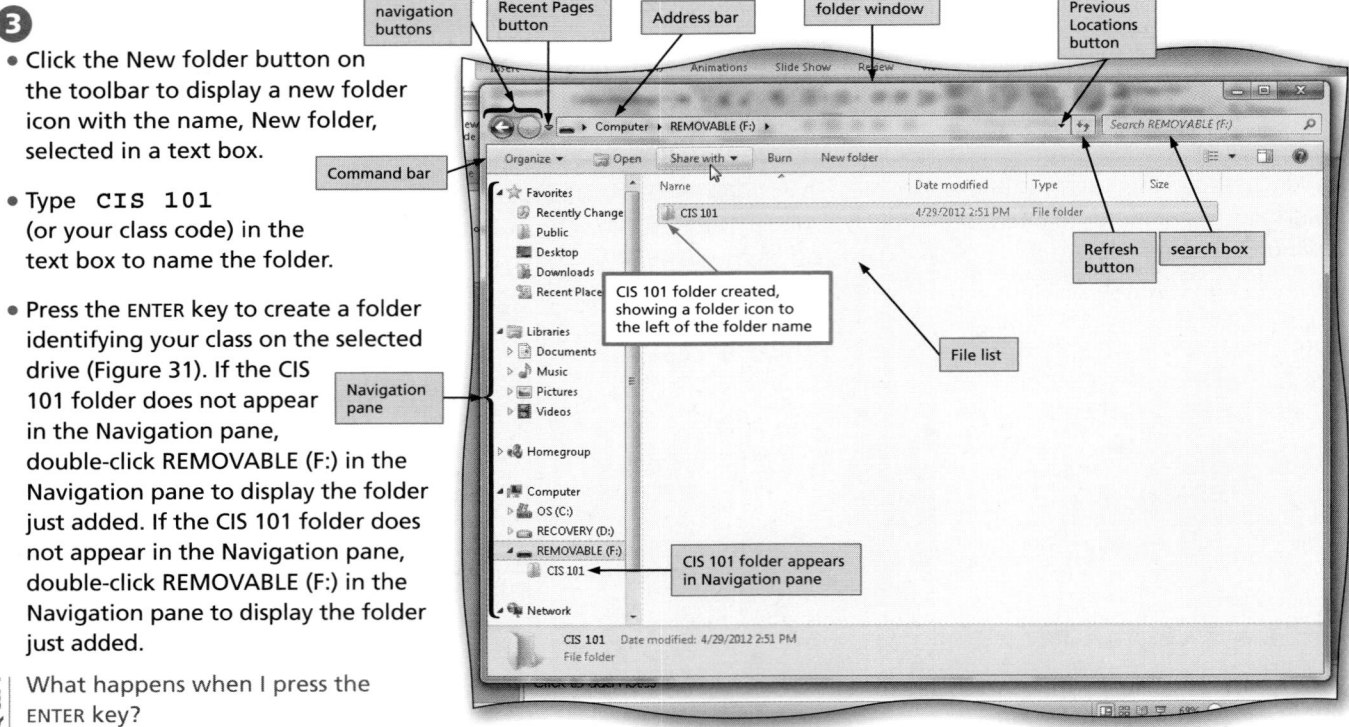

Figure 31

Folder Windows

The USB flash drive window (shown in Figure 31) is called a folder window. Recall that a folder is a specific named location on a storage medium that contains related files. Most users rely on **folder windows** for finding, viewing, and managing information on their computer. Folder windows have common design elements, including the following (Figure 31).

- The **Address bar** provides quick navigation options. The arrows on the Address bar allow you to visit different locations on the computer.
- The buttons to the left of the Address bar allow you to navigate the contents of the left pane and view recent pages. Other buttons allow you to specify the size of the window.
- The **Previous Locations button** saves the locations you have visited and displays the locations when clicked.
- The **Refresh button** on the right side of the Address bar refreshes the contents of the right pane of the folder window.
- The **search box** to the right of the Address bar contains the dimmed word, Search. You can type a term in the search box for a list of files, folders, shortcuts, and elements containing that term within the location you are searching. A **shortcut** is an icon on the desktop that provides a user with immediate access to a program or file.
- The **Command bar** contains five buttons used to accomplish various tasks on the computer related to organizing and managing the contents of the open window.
- The **Navigation pane** on the left contains the Favorites area, Libraries area, Computer area, and Network area.

- The **Favorites area** contains links to your favorite locations. By default, this list contains only links to your Desktop, Downloads, and Recent Places.
- The **Libraries area** shows links to files and folders that have been included in a library.

A **library** helps you manage multiple folders and files stored in various locations on a computer. It does not store the files and folders; rather, it displays links to them so that you can access them quickly. For example, you can save pictures from a digital camera in any folder on any storage location on a computer. Normally, this would make organizing the different folders difficult; however, if you add the folders to a library, you can access all the pictures from one location regardless of where they are stored.

To Create a Folder within a Folder

With the class folder created, you can create folders that will store the files you create using each Office program. The following steps create a PowerPoint folder in the CIS 101 folder (or the folder identifying your class).

- Double-click the icon or folder name for the CIS 101 folder (or the folder identifying your class) in the File list to open the folder (Figure 32).

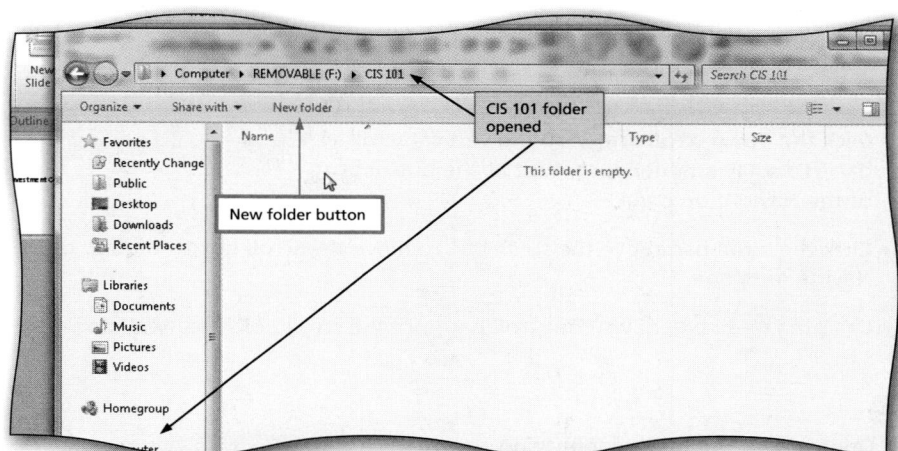

Figure 32

- Click the New folder button on the toolbar to display a new folder icon and text box for the folder.
- Type **PowerPoint** in the text box to name the folder.
- Press the ENTER key to create the folder (Figure 33).

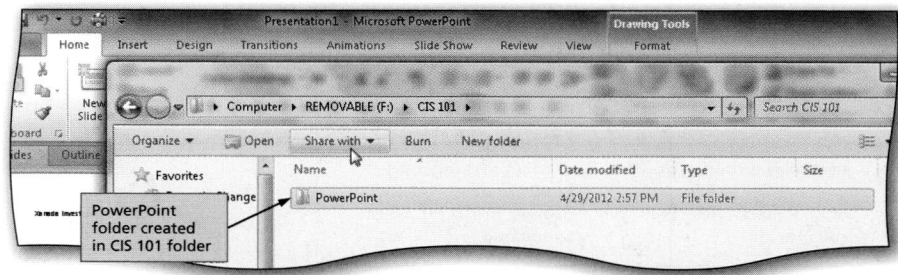

Figure 33

To Expand a Folder, Scroll through Folder Contents, and Collapse a Folder

Folder windows display the hierarchy of items and the contents of drives and folders in the right pane. You might want to expand a drive in the Navigation pane to view its contents, scroll through its contents, and collapse it when you are finished viewing its contents. When a folder is expanded, it lists all the folders it contains. By contrast, a collapsed folder does not list the folders it contains. These steps expand, scroll through, and then collapse the folder identifying your class (CIS 101, in this case).

• Double-click the folder identifying your class (CIS 101, in this case) in the Navigation pane, which expands the folder to display its contents and displays a black arrow to the left of the folder icon (Figure 34).

Q&A Why is the PowerPoint folder indented below the CIS 101 folder in the Navigation pane?

It shows that the folder is contained within the CIS 101 folder.

Q&A Why did a scroll bar appear in the Navigation pane?

When all contents cannot fit in a window or pane, a scroll bar appears. As described earlier, you can view areas currently not visible by (1) clicking the scroll arrows, (2) clicking above or below the scroll bar, and (3) dragging the scroll box.

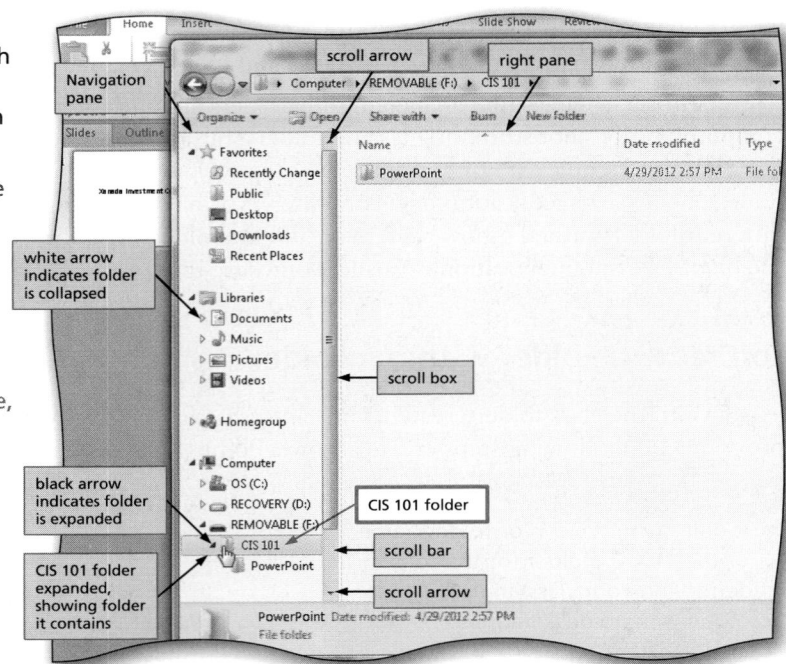

Figure 34

Experiment

• Click the down scroll arrow on the vertical scroll bar to display additional content at the bottom of the Navigation pane.

• Click the scroll bar above the scroll box to move the scroll box to the top of the Navigation pane.

• Drag the scroll box down the scroll bar until the scroll box is halfway down the scroll bar.

2

• Double-click the folder identifying your class (CIS 101, in this case) in the Navigation pane to collapse the folder (Figure 35).

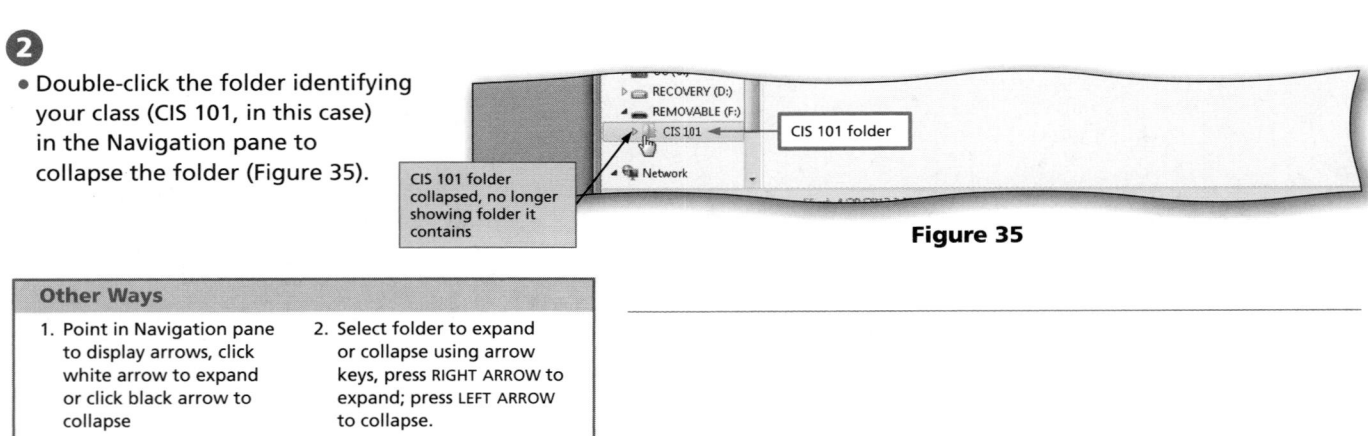

Figure 35

Other Ways
1. Point in Navigation pane to display arrows, click white arrow to expand or click black arrow to collapse	2. Select folder to expand or collapse using arrow keys, press RIGHT ARROW to expand; press LEFT ARROW to collapse.

To Switch from One Program to Another

The next step is to save the PowerPoint file containing the slide title you typed earlier. PowerPoint, however, currently is not the active window. You can use the program button on the taskbar and live preview to switch to PowerPoint and then save the document in the PowerPoint document window.

If Windows Aero is active on your computer, Windows displays a live preview window whenever you move your mouse on a button or click a button on the taskbar. If Aero is not supported or enabled on your computer, you will see a window title instead of a live preview. These steps use the PowerPoint program; however, the steps are the same for any active Office program currently displayed as a program button on the taskbar.

The next steps switch to the PowerPoint window.

- Point to the PowerPoint program button on the taskbar to see a live preview of the open document(s) or the window title(s) of the open document(s), depending on your computer's configuration (Figure 36).

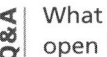

- Click the program button or the live preview to make the program associated with the program button the active window.

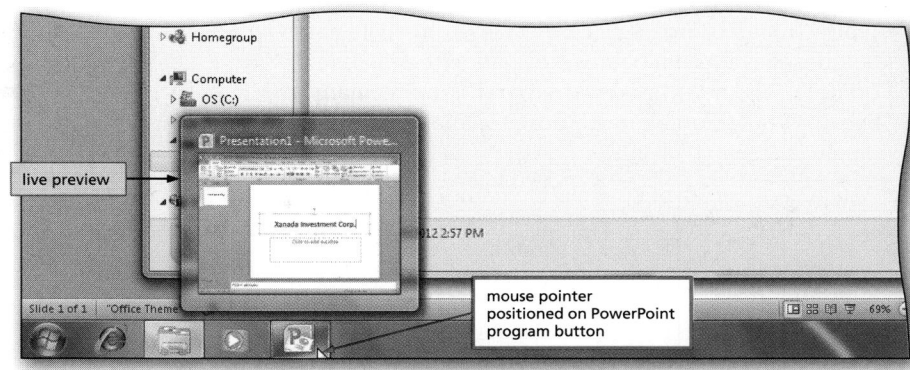

Figure 36

Q&A What if multiple documents are open in a program?

If Aero is enabled on your computer, click the desired live preview. If Aero is not supported or not enabled, click the window title.

To Save a File in a Folder

Now that you have created the folders for storing files, you can save the PowerPoint document. The following steps save a file on a USB flash drive in the PowerPoint folder contained in your class folder (CIS 101, in this case) using the file name, Investing Strategies.

- With a USB flash drive connected to one of the computer's USB ports, click the Save button on the Quick Access Toolbar to display the Save As dialog box (Figure 37).

Q&A Why does a file name already appear in the File name text box?

PowerPoint automatically suggests a file name the first time you save a document. The file name normally consists of the first few words contained in the document. Because the suggested file name is selected, you do not need to delete it; as soon as you begin typing, the new file name replaces the selected text.

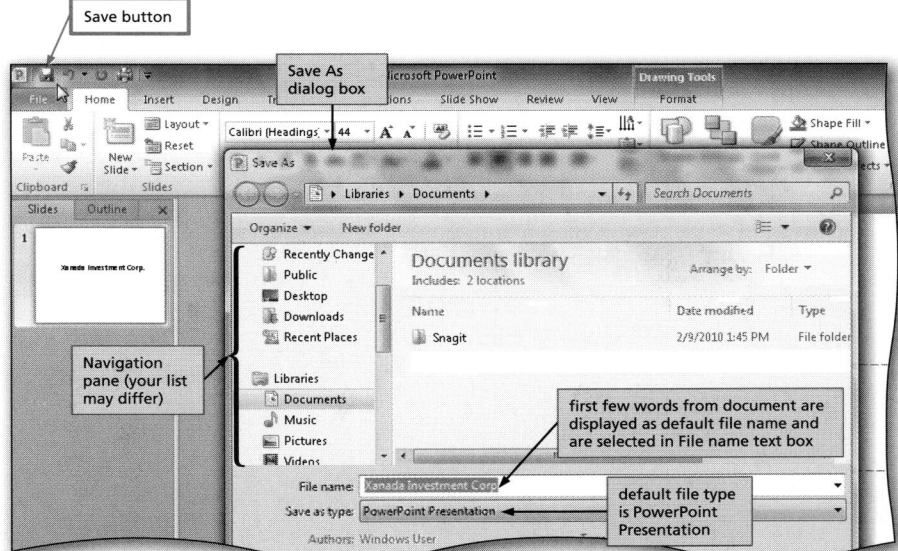

Figure 37

• Type **Investing Strategies** in the File name text box (Save As dialog box) to change the file name. Do not press the ENTER key after typing the file name because you do not want to close the dialog box at this time (Figure 38).

Q&A   What characters can I use in a file name?

The only invalid characters are the backslash (\), slash (/), colon (:), asterisk (*), question mark (?), quotation mark ("), less than symbol (<), greater than symbol (>), and vertical bar (|).

• Navigate to the desired save location (in this case, the PowerPoint folder in the CIS 101 folder [or your class folder] on the USB flash drive) by performing the tasks in Steps 3a, 3b, and 3c.

• If the Navigation pane is not displayed in the dialog box, click the Browse Folders button to expand the dialog box.

• If Computer is not displayed in the Navigation pane, drag the Navigation pane scroll bar until Computer appears.

• If Computer is not expanded in the Navigation pane, double-click Computer to display a list of available storage devices in the Navigation pane.

• If necessary, scroll through the dialog box until your USB flash drive appears in the list of available storage devices in the Navigation pane (Figure 39).

• If your USB flash drive is not expanded, double-click the USB flash drive in the list of available storage devices in the Navigation pane to select that drive as the new save location and display its contents in the right pane.

• If your class folder (CIS 101, in this case) is not expanded, double-click the CIS 101 folder to select the folder and display its contents in the right pane.

Q&A   What if I do not want to save in a folder?

Although storing files in folders is an effective technique for organizing files, some users prefer not to store files in folders. If you prefer not to save this file in a folder, skip all instructions in Step 3c and proceed to Step 4.

• Click the PowerPoint folder to select the folder and display its contents in the right pane (Figure 40).

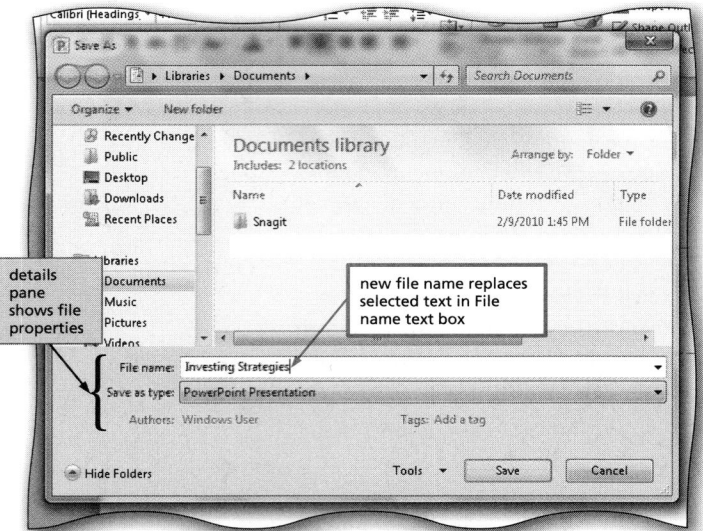

details pane shows file properties

new file name replaces selected text in File name text box

Figure 38

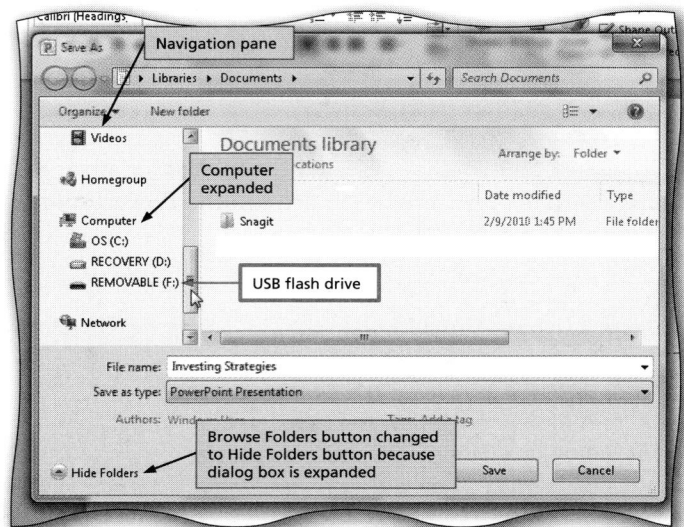

Navigation pane

Computer expanded

USB flash drive

Browse Folders button changed to Hide Folders button because dialog box is expanded

Figure 39

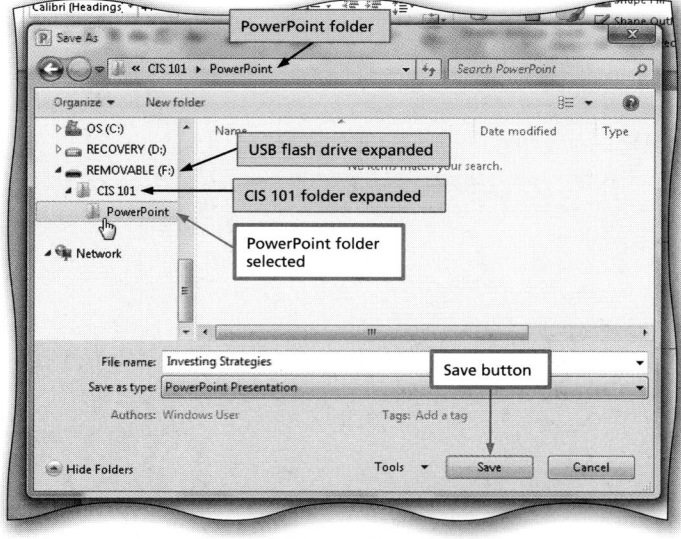

PowerPoint folder

USB flash drive expanded

CIS 101 folder expanded

PowerPoint folder selected

Save button

Figure 40

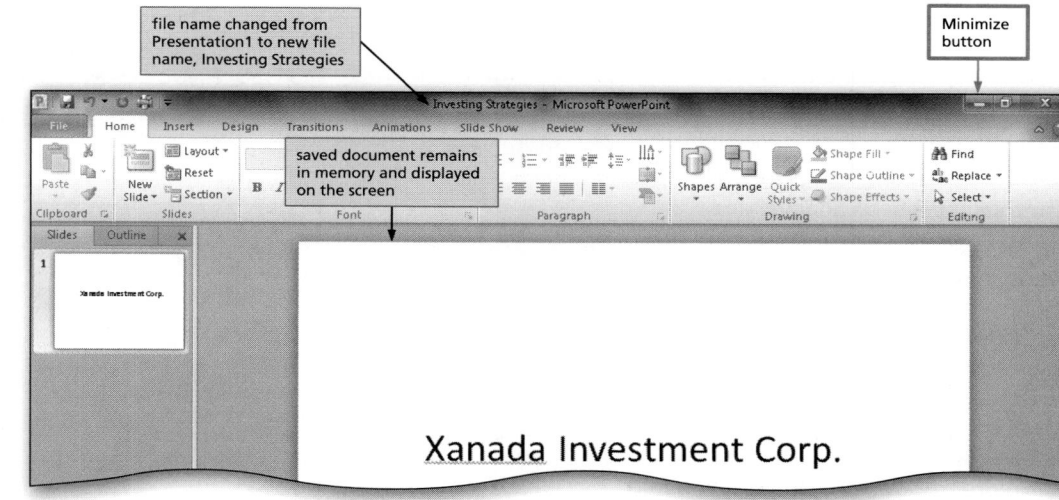

4

• Click the Save button (Save As dialog box) to save the document in the selected folder on the selected drive with the entered file name (Figure 41).

Q&A

How do I know that the file is saved?

While an Office program such as PowerPoint is saving a file, it briefly displays a message on the status bar indicating the amount of the file saved. In addition, the USB flash drive may have a light that flashes during the save process.

Figure 41

Other Ways

1. Click File on Ribbon, click Save, type file name, navigate to desired save location, click Save button
2. Press CTRL+S or press SHIFT+F12, type file name, navigate to desired save location, click Save button

Navigating in Dialog Boxes

Navigating is the process of finding a location on a storage device. While saving the Investing Strategies file, for example, you navigated to the PowerPoint folder located in the CIS 101 folder. When performing certain functions in Windows programs, such as saving a file, opening a file, or inserting a picture in an existing document, you most likely will have to navigate to the location where you want to save the file or to the folder containing the file you want to open or insert. Most dialog boxes in Windows programs requiring navigation follow a similar procedure; that is, the way you navigate to a folder in one dialog box, such as the Save As dialog box, is similar to how you might navigate in another dialog box, such as the Open dialog box. If you chose to navigate to a specific location in a dialog box, you would follow the instructions in Steps 3a – 3c on the previous page.

BTW

File Type
Depending on your Windows 7 settings, the file type .ppt may be displayed immediately to the right of the file name after you save the file. The file type .ppt is a PowerPoint 2010 document.

To Minimize and Restore a Window

Before continuing, you can verify that the PowerPoint file was saved properly. To do this, you will minimize the PowerPoint window and then open the USB flash drive window so that you can verify the file is stored on the USB flash drive. A **minimized window** is an open window hidden from view but that can be displayed quickly by clicking the window's program button on the taskbar.

In the following example, PowerPoint is used to illustrate minimizing and restoring windows; however, you would follow the same steps regardless of the Office program you are using.

The next steps minimize the PowerPoint window, verify that the file is saved, and then restore the minimized window.

1

- Click the Minimize button on the program's title bar (shown in Figure 41 on the previous page) to minimize the window (Figure 42).

Q&A Is the minimized window still available?

The minimized window, PowerPoint in this case, remains available but no longer is the active window. It is minimized as a program button on the taskbar.

- If necessary, click the Windows Explorer program button on the taskbar to open the USB flash drive window.

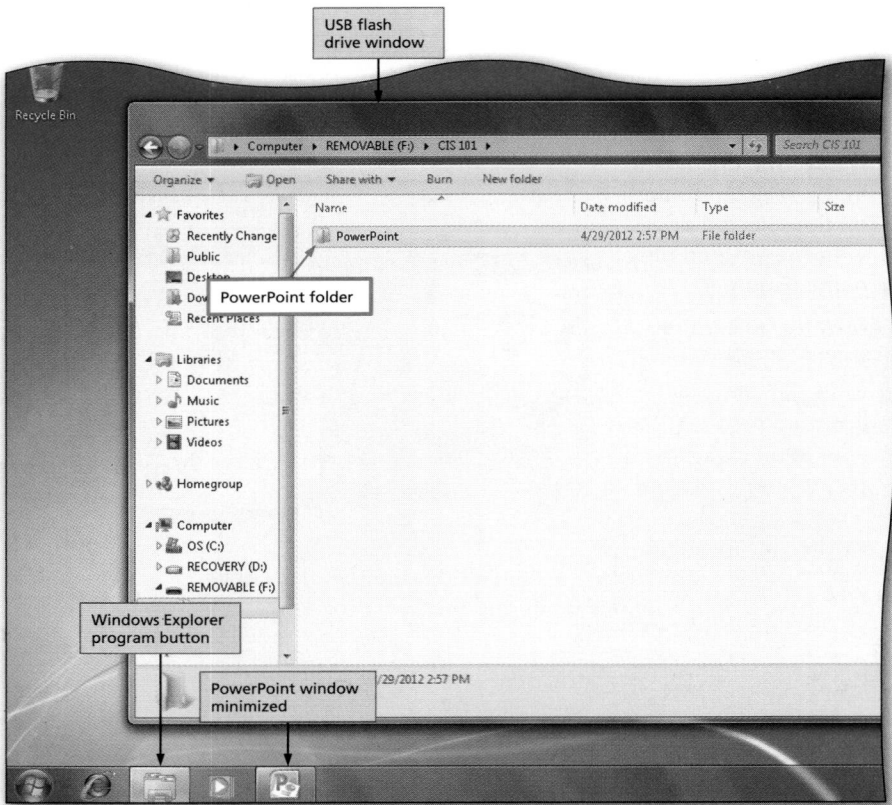

Figure 42

2

- Double-click the PowerPoint folder to select the folder and display its contents (Figure 43).

Q&A Why does the Windows Explorer button on the taskbar change?

The button changes to reflect the status of the folder window (in this case, the USB flash drive window). A selected button indicates that the folder window is active on the screen. When the button is not selected, the window is open but not active.

3

- After viewing the contents of the selected folder, click the PowerPoint program button on the taskbar to restore the minimized window (as shown in Figure 41 on the previous page).

Other Ways

1. Right-click title bar, click Minimize on shortcut menu, click taskbar button in taskbar button area
2. Press WINDOWS+M, press WINDOWS+SHIFT+M

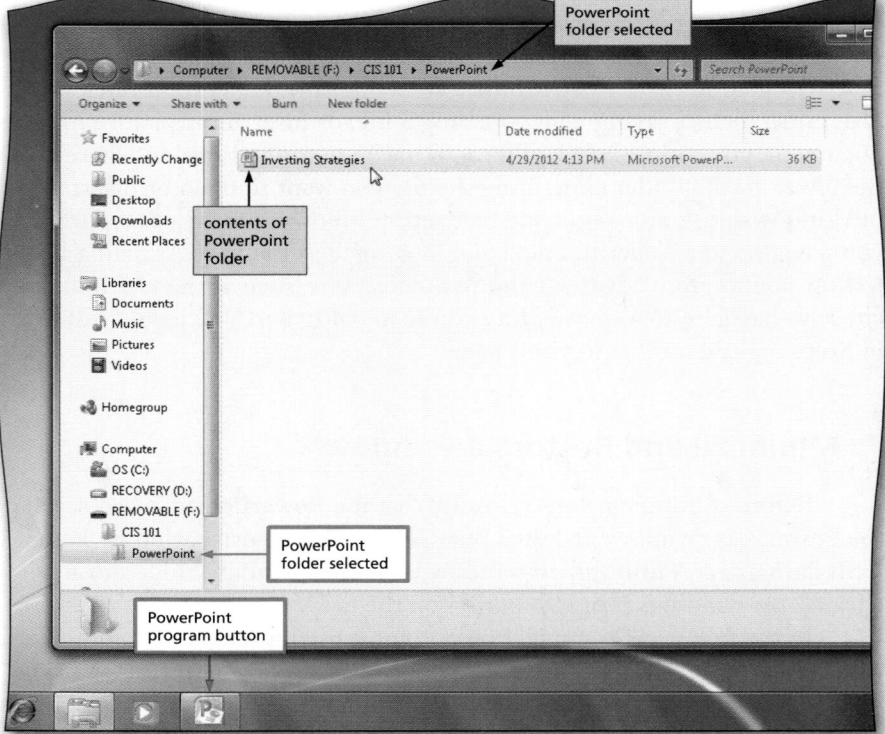

Figure 43

Screen Resolution

Screen resolution indicates the number of pixels (dots) that the computer uses to display the letters, numbers, graphics, and background you see on the screen. When you increase the screen resolution, Windows displays more information on the screen, but the information decreases in size. The reverse also is true: as you decrease the screen resolution, Windows displays less information on the screen, but the information increases in size.

Screen resolution usually is stated as the product of two numbers, such as 1024 × 768 (pronounced "ten twenty-four by seven sixty-eight"). A 1024 × 768 screen resolution results in a display of 1,024 distinct pixels on each of 768 lines, or about 786,432 pixels. Changing the screen resolution affects how the Ribbon appears in Office programs. Figure 44 shows the PowerPoint Ribbon at screen resolutions of 1024 × 768 and 1280 × 800. All of the same commands are available regardless of screen resolution. PowerPoint, however, makes changes to the groups and the buttons within the groups to accommodate the various screen resolutions. The result is that certain commands may need to be accessed differently depending on the resolution chosen. A command that is visible on the Ribbon and available by clicking a button at one resolution may not be visible and may need to be accessed using its Dialog Box Launcher at a different resolution.

Comparing the two Ribbons in Figure 44, notice the changes in content and layout of the groups and galleries. In some cases, the content of a group is the same in each resolution, but the layout of the group differs. For example, the same gallery and buttons appear in the Drawing group in the two resolutions, but the layouts differ. In other cases, the content and layout are the same across the resolution, but the level of detail differs with the resolution. In the Clipboard group, when the resolution increases to 1280 × 800, the names of all the buttons in the group appear in addition to the buttons themselves. At the lower resolution, only the buttons appear.

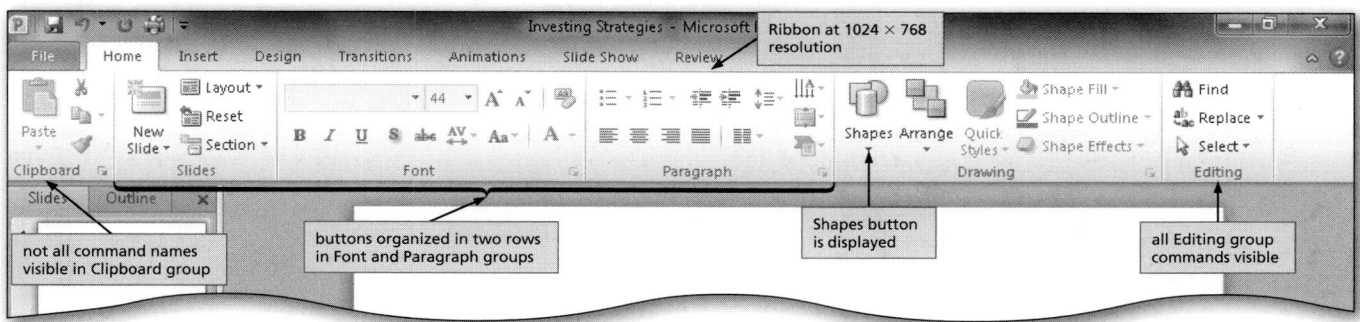

(a) Ribbon at Resolution of 1024 × 768

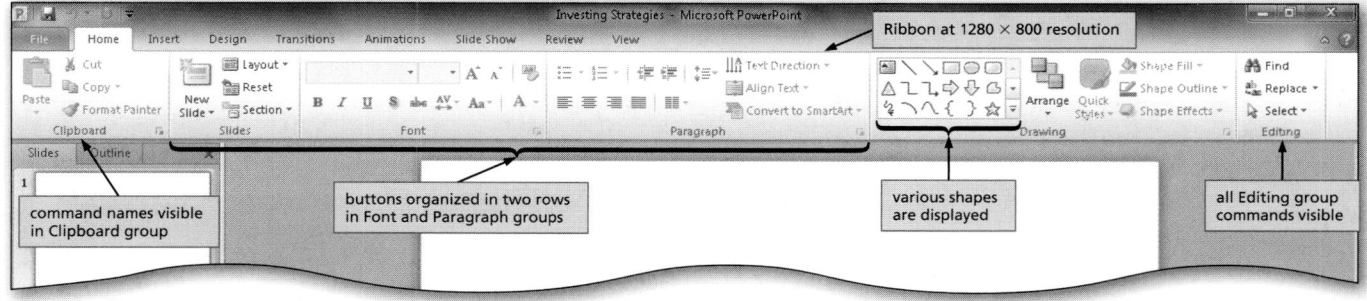

(b) Ribbon at Resolution of 1280 × 800

Figure 44

To Change the Screen Resolution

If you are using a computer to step through the chapters in this book and you want your screen to match the figures, you may need to change your screen's resolution. The figures in this book use a screen resolution of 1024 × 768. The following steps change the screen resolution to 1024 × 768. Your computer already may be set to 1024 × 768 or some other resolution. Keep in mind that many computer labs prevent users from changing the screen resolution; in that case, read the following steps for illustration purposes.

- Click the Show desktop button on the taskbar to display the Windows 7 desktop.

- Right-click an empty area on the Windows 7 desktop to display a shortcut menu that displays a list of commands related to the desktop (Figure 45).

Q&A

Why does my shortcut menu display different commands?

Depending on your computer's hardware and configuration, different commands might appear on the shortcut menu.

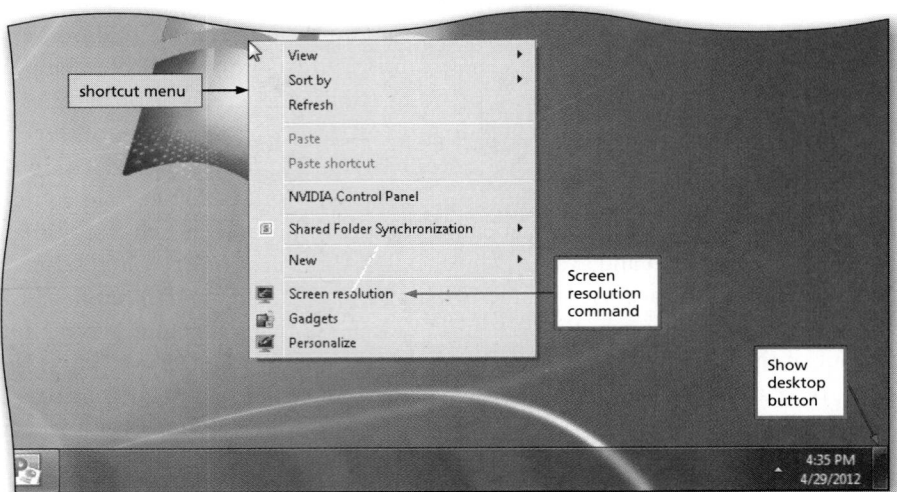

Figure 45

- Click Screen resolution on the shortcut menu to open the Screen Resolution window (Figure 46).

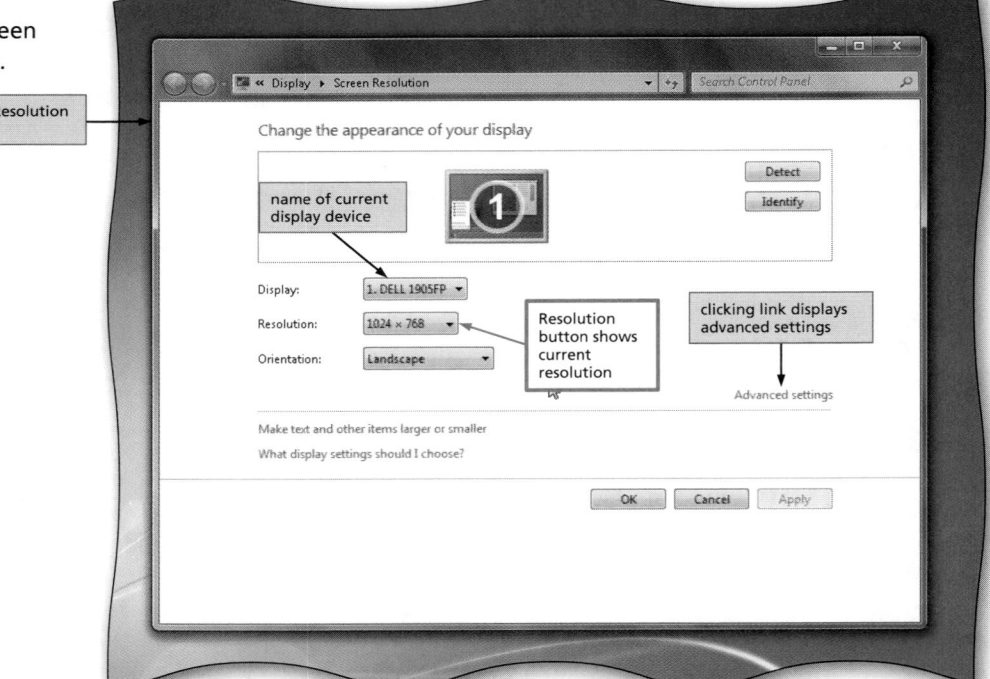

Figure 46

- Click the Resolution button in the Screen Resolution window to display the resolution slider.

Q&A What is a slider?

A **slider** is an object that allows users to choose from multiple predetermined options. In most cases, these options represent some type of numeric value. In most cases, one end of the slider (usually the left or bottom) represents the lowest of available values, and the opposite end (usually the right or top) represents the highest available value.

- If necessary, drag the resolution slider until the desired screen resolution (in this case, 1024 × 768) is selected (Figure 47).

Q&A What if my computer does not support the 1024 × 768 resolution?

Some computers do not support the 1024 × 768 resolution. In this case, select a resolution that is close to the 1024 × 768 resolution.

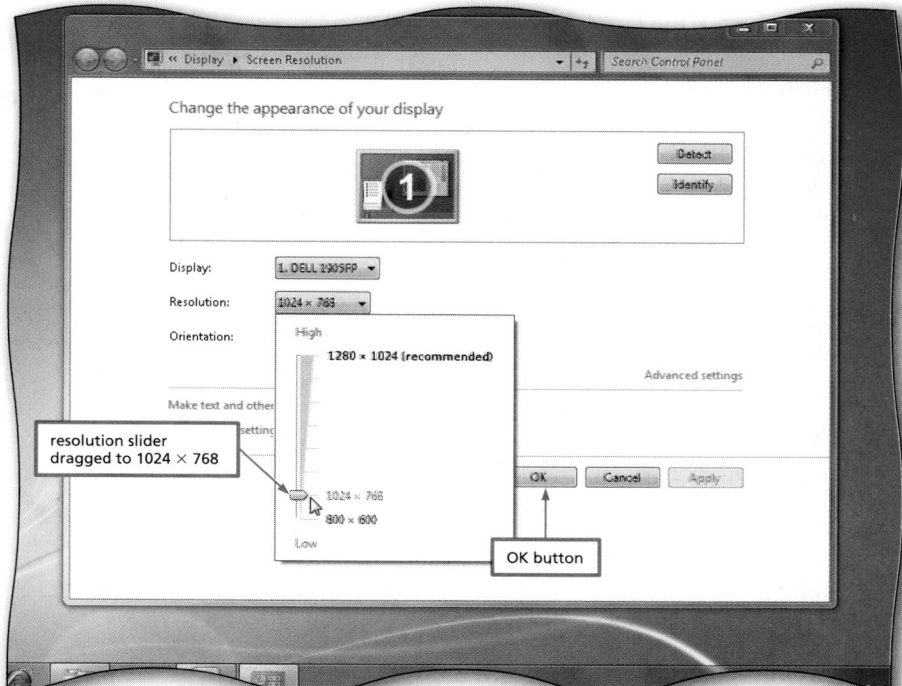

Figure 47

- Click an empty area of the Screen Resolution window to close the resolution slider.

- Click the OK button to change the screen resolution and display the Display Settings dialog box (Figure 48).

- Click the Keep changes button (Display Settings dialog box) to accept the new screen resolution.

Q&A Why does a message display stating that the image quality can be improved?

Some computer monitors are designed to display contents better at a certain screen resolution, sometimes referred to as an optimal resolution.

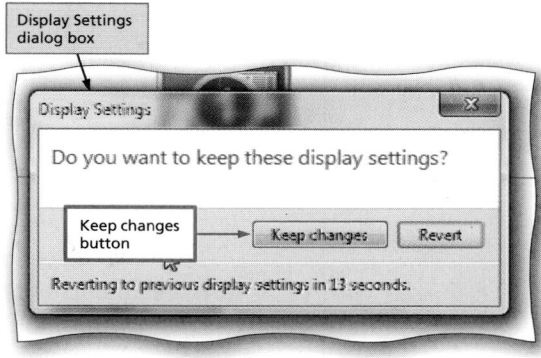

Figure 48

To Quit a Program with One Document Open

When you quit an Office program, such as PowerPoint, if you have made changes to a file since the last time the file was saved, the Office program displays a dialog box asking if you want to save the changes you made to the file before it closes the program window. The dialog box contains three buttons with these resulting actions: the Save button saves the changes and then quits the Office program, the Don't Save button quits the Office program without saving changes, and the Cancel button closes the dialog box and redisplays the file without saving the changes.

If no changes have been made to an open document since the last time the file was saved, the Office program will close the window without displaying a dialog box.

The following steps quit PowerPoint. You would follow similar steps in other Office programs.

- If necessary, click the PowerPoint program button on the taskbar to display the PowerPoint window on the desktop.
- Point to the Close button on the right side of the program's title bar, PowerPoint in this case (Figure 49).

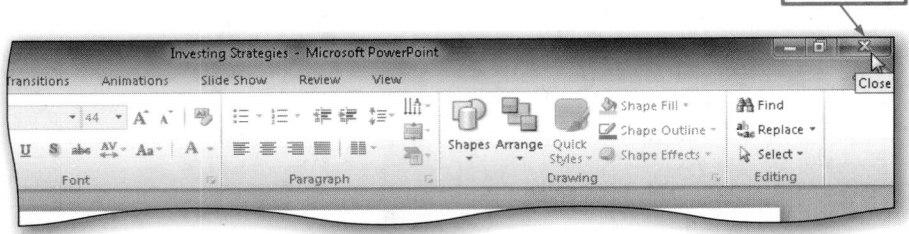

Figure 49

- Click the Close button to close the document and quit PowerPoint.

Q&A What if I have more than one document open in PowerPoint?

You would click the Close button for each open document. When you click the last open document's Close button, PowerPoint also quits. As an alternative, you could click File on the Ribbon to open the Backstage view and then click Exit in the Backstage view to close all open documents and quit PowerPoint.

Q&A What is the Backstage view?

The **Backstage view** contains a set of commands that enable you to manage documents and data about the documents. The Backstage view is discussed in more depth later in this chapter.

- If a Microsoft PowerPoint dialog box appears, click the Save button to save any changes made to the document since the last save.

Other Ways
1. Right-click the Office program button on Windows 7 taskbar, click Close window or 'Close all windows' on shortcut menu
2. Press ALT+F4

Break Point: If you wish to take a break, this is a good place to do so. To resume at a later time, continue to follow the steps from this location forward.

Additional Common Features of Office Programs

The previous section used PowerPoint to illustrate common features of Office and some basic elements unique to PowerPoint. The following sections continue to use PowerPoint to present additional common features of Office.

In the following pages, you will learn how to do the following:

1. Start an Office program (PowerPoint) using the search box.
2. Open a document in an Office program (PowerPoint).
3. Close the document.
4. Reopen the document just closed.
5. Create a blank Office document from Windows Explorer and then open the file.
6. Save the document with a new file name.

To Start a Program Using the Search Box

The next steps, which assume Windows 7 is running, use the search box to start PowerPoint based on a typical installation; however, you would follow similar steps to start any program. You may need to ask your instructor how to start programs for your computer.

- Click the Start button on the Windows 7 taskbar to display the Start menu.

- Type **Microsoft PowerPoint** as the search text in the 'Search programs and files' text box and watch the search results appear on the Start menu (Figure 50).

Q&A Do I need to type the complete program name or correct capitalization?

No, just enough of it for the program name to appear on the Start menu. For example, you may be able to type PowerPoint or powerpoint, instead of Microsoft PowerPoint.

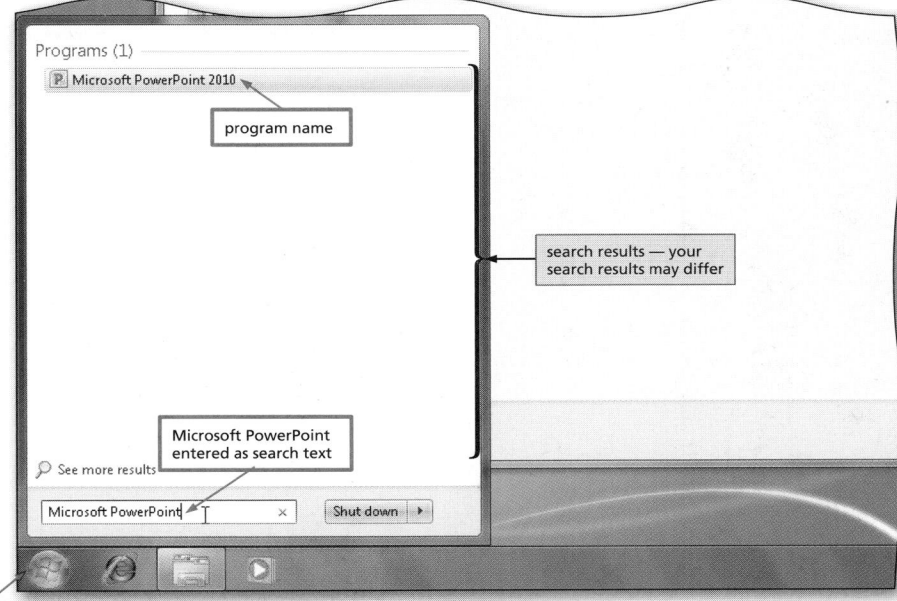

Figure 50

- Click the program name, Microsoft PowerPoint 2010 in this case, in the search results on the Start menu to start PowerPoint and display a new blank presentation in the PowerPoint window.

- If the program window is not maximized, click the Maximize button on its title bar to maximize the window (Figure 51).

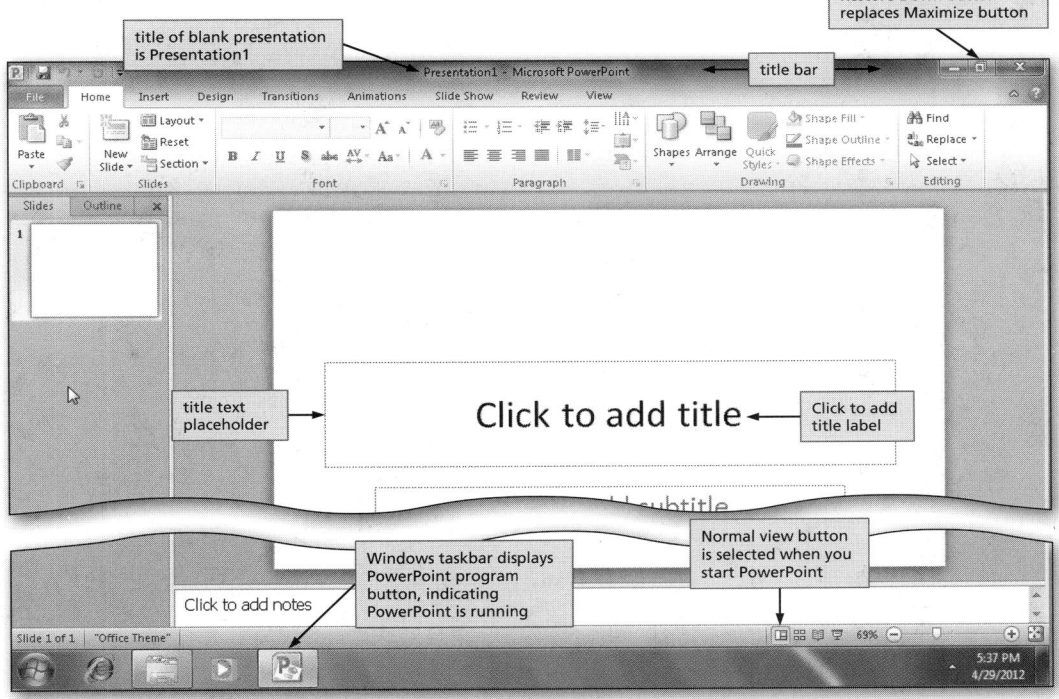

Figure 51

To Open an Existing Office File from the Backstage View

As discussed earlier, the Backstage view contains a set of commands that enable you to manage documents and data about the documents. From the Backstage view in PowerPoint, for example, you can create, open, print, and save presentations. You also can share presentations, manage versions, set permissions, and modify document properties. In other Office 2010 programs, the Backstage view may contain features specific to those programs.

Assume you wish to continue working on an existing file, that is, a file you previously saved. The following steps use the Backstage view to open a saved file, specifically the Investing Strategies file, from the USB flash drive.

- With your USB flash drive connected to one of the computer's USB ports, if necessary, click File on the Ribbon to open the Backstage view (Figure 52).

Q&A What is the purpose of the File tab?

The File tab is used to display the Backstage view for each Office program.

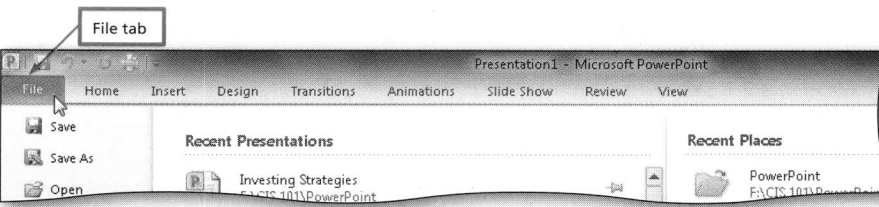

Figure 52

- Click Open in the Backstage view to display the Open dialog box (Figure 53).

- Navigate to the location of the file to be opened (in this case, the USB flash drive, then to the CIS 101 folder [or your class folder], and then to the PowerPoint folder). For detailed steps about navigating, see Steps 3a – 3c on OFF 26.

Q&A What if I did not save my file in a folder?

If you did not save your file in a folder, the file you wish to open should be displayed in the Open dialog box before navigating to any folders.

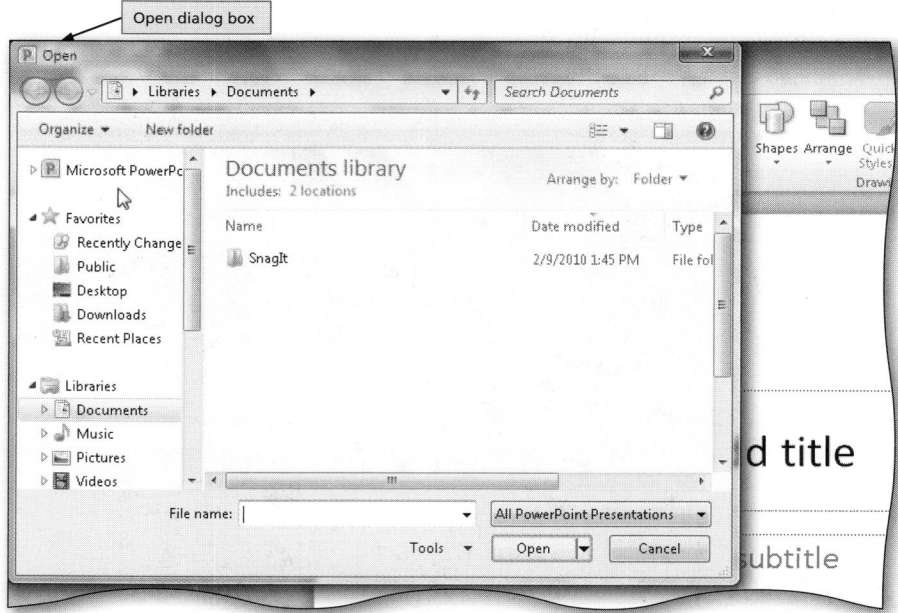

Figure 53

- Click the file to be opened, Investing Strategies in this case, to select the file (Figure 54).

- Click the Open button (Open dialog box) to open the selected file and display the opened file in the current program window.

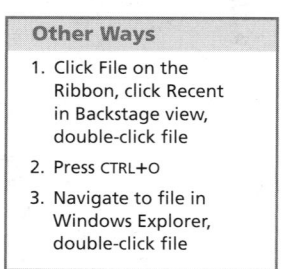

Other Ways

1. Click File on the Ribbon, click Recent in Backstage view, double-click file
2. Press CTRL+O
3. Navigate to file in Windows Explorer, double-click file

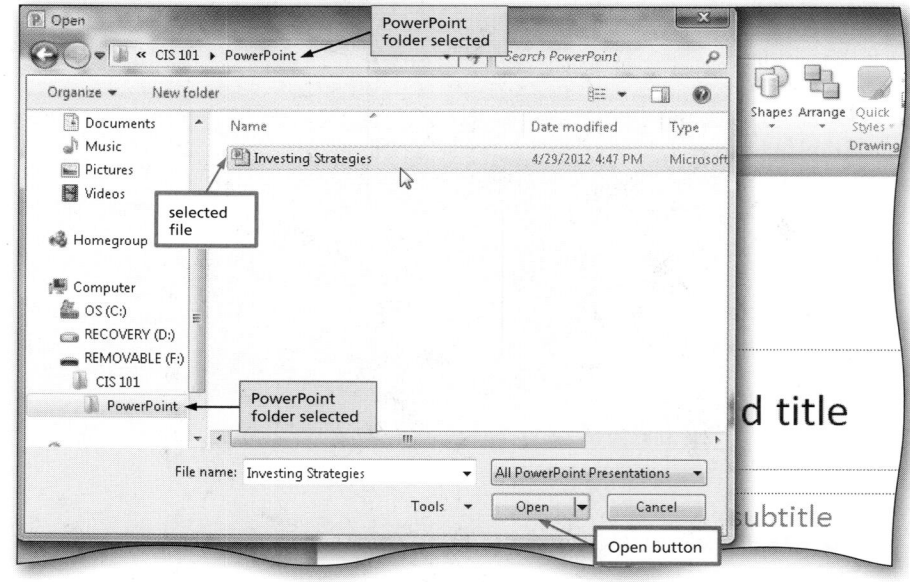

Figure 54

To Create a New Document from the Backstage View

You can create multiple documents at the same time in an Office program, such as PowerPoint. The following steps create a file, a blank presentation in this case, from the Backstage view.

1

- Click File on the Ribbon to open the Backstage view.
- Click the New tab in the Backstage view to display the New gallery (Figure 55).

Q&A

Can I create documents through the Backstage view in other Office programs?

Yes. If the Office program has a New tab in the Backstage view, the New gallery displays various options for creating a new file.

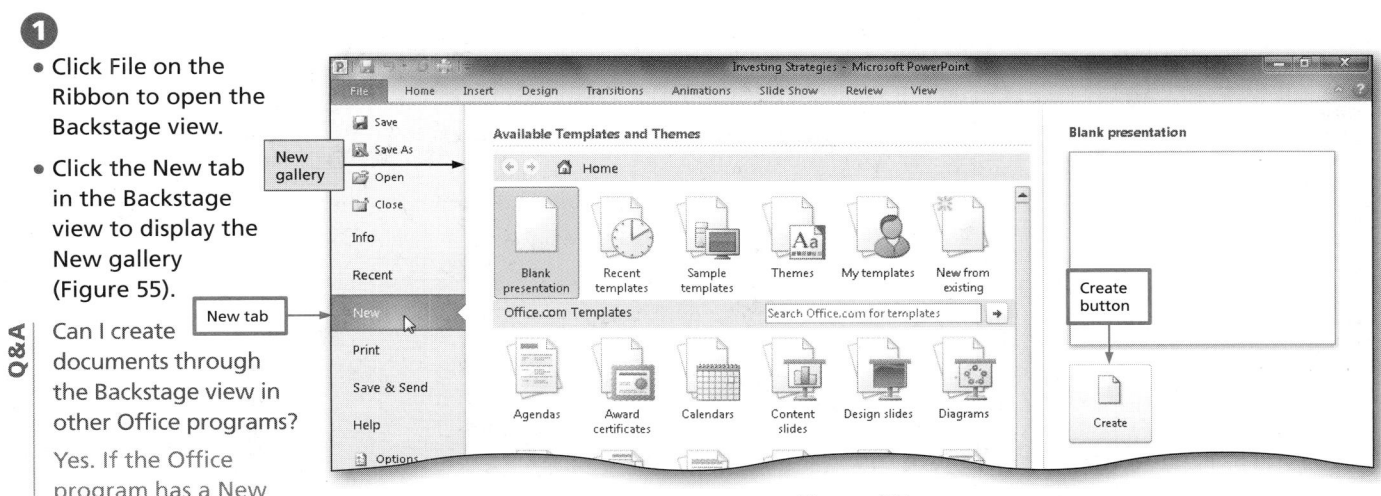

Figure 55

2

- Click the Create button in the New gallery to create a new presentation (Figure 56).

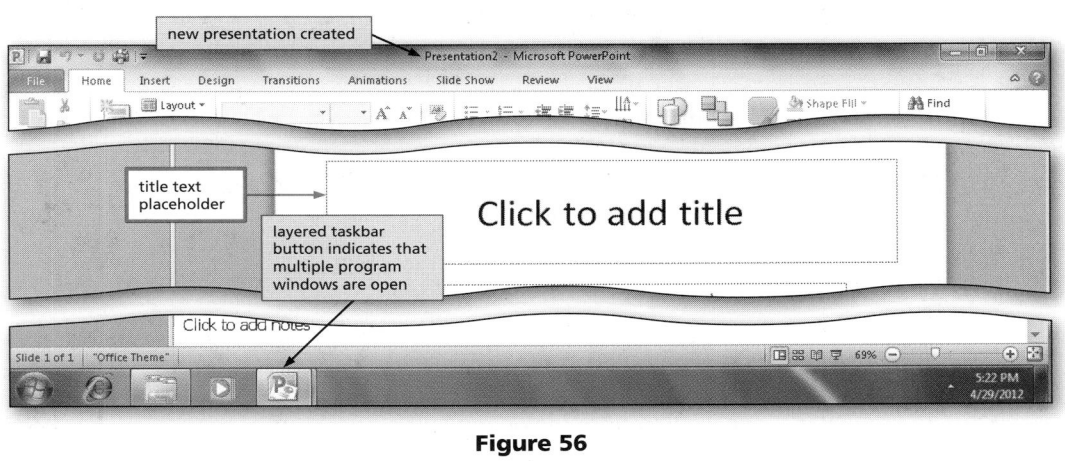

Figure 56

Other Ways

1. Press CTRL+N

To Enter Content in a Title Slide of a Second PowerPoint Presentation

The presentation title for this presentation is Koala Exhibit Gala. The following steps enter a presentation title on the title slide.

1 Click the title text placeholder (shown in Figure 56) to select it.

2 Type **Koala Exhibit Gala** in the title text placeholder. Do not press the ENTER key (Figure 57).

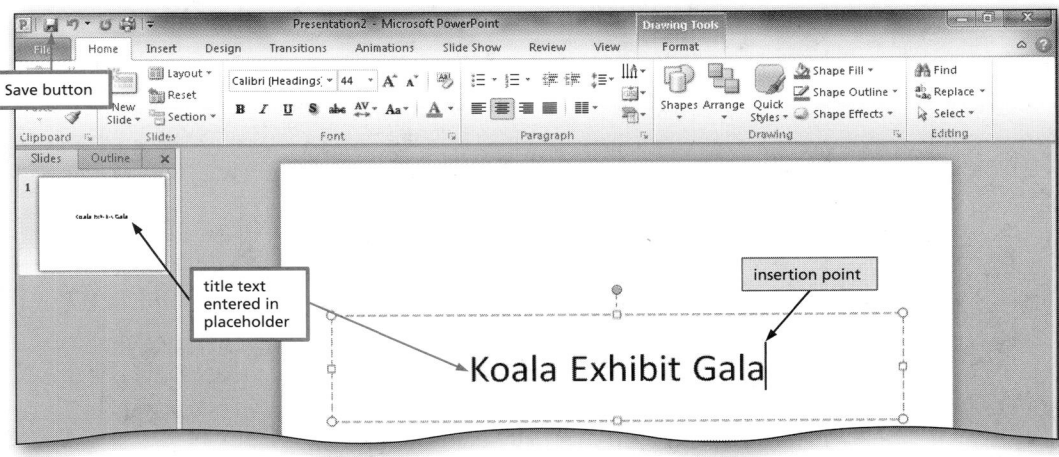

Figure 57

To Save a File in a Folder

The following steps save the second presentation in the PowerPoint folder in the class folder (CIS 101, in this case) on a USB flash drive using the file name, Koala Exhibit Gala.

1 With a USB flash drive connected to one of the computer's USB ports, click the Save button on the Quick Access Toolbar to display the Save As dialog box.

2 If necessary, type `Koala Exhibit Gala` in the File name text box to change the file name. Do not press the ENTER key after typing the file name because you do not want to close the dialog box at this time.

3 If necessary, navigate to the desired save location (in this case, the PowerPoint folder in the CIS 101 folder [or your class folder] on the USB flash drive).

4 Click the Save button (Save As dialog box) to save the presentation in the selected folder on the selected drive with the entered file name.

To Close a File Using the Backstage View

Sometimes, you may want to close an Office file, such as a PowerPoint presentation, entirely and start over with a new file. You also may want to close a file when you are finished working with it so that you can begin a new file. The following steps close the current active PowerPoint file (that is, the Koala Exhibit Gala presentation) without quitting the active program (PowerPoint in this case).

- Click File on the Ribbon to open the Backstage view (Figure 58).

- Click Close in the Backstage view to close the open file (Koala Exhibit Gala, in this case) without quitting the active program.

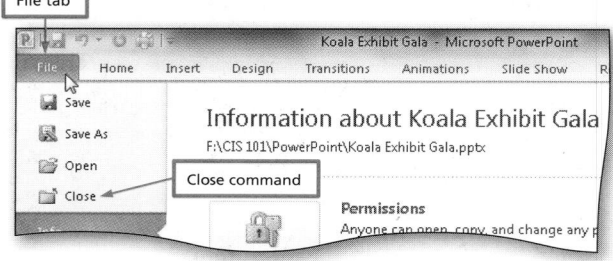

Figure 58

Q&A What if PowerPoint displays a dialog box about saving?

Click the Save button if you want to save the changes, click the Don't Save button if you want to ignore the changes since the last time you saved, and click the Cancel button if you do not want to close the document.

Q&A Can I use the Backstage view to close an open file in other Office programs, such as Word and Excel?

Yes.

To Open a Recent Office File Using the Backstage View

You sometimes need to open a file that you recently modified. You may have more changes to make such as adding more content or correcting errors. The Backstage view allows you to access recent files easily. The next steps reopen the Koala Exhibit Gala file just closed.

1

- Click File on the Ribbon to open the Backstage view.

- Click the Recent tab in the Backstage view to display the Recent gallery (Figure 59).

2

- Click the desired file name in the Recent gallery, Koala Exhibit Gala in this case, to open the file (shown in Figure 57 on OFF 35).

Q&A Can I use the Backstage view to open a recent file in other Office programs, such as Word and Excel?

Yes, as long as the file name appears in the list of recent files in the Recent gallery.

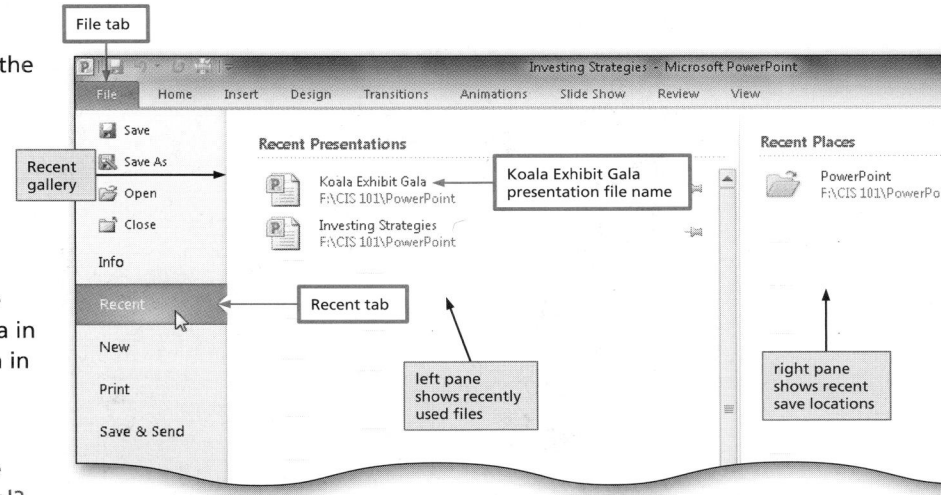

Figure 59

Other Ways
1. Click Start button, point to program name, click file name on submenu	2. Click File on Ribbon, click Open in Backstage view, navigate to file (Open | dialog box), click Open button

To Create a New Blank Office Document from Windows Explorer

Windows Explorer provides a means to create a blank Office document without ever starting an Office program. The following steps use Windows Explorer to create a blank PowerPoint document.

1

- Click the Windows Explorer program button on the taskbar to make the folder window the active window in Windows Explorer.

- If necessary, navigate to the desired location for the new file (in this case, the PowerPoint folder in the CIS 101 folder [or your class folder] on the USB flash drive).

- With the PowerPoint folder selected, right-click an open area in the right pane to display a shortcut menu.

- Point to New on the shortcut menu to display the New submenu (Figure 60).

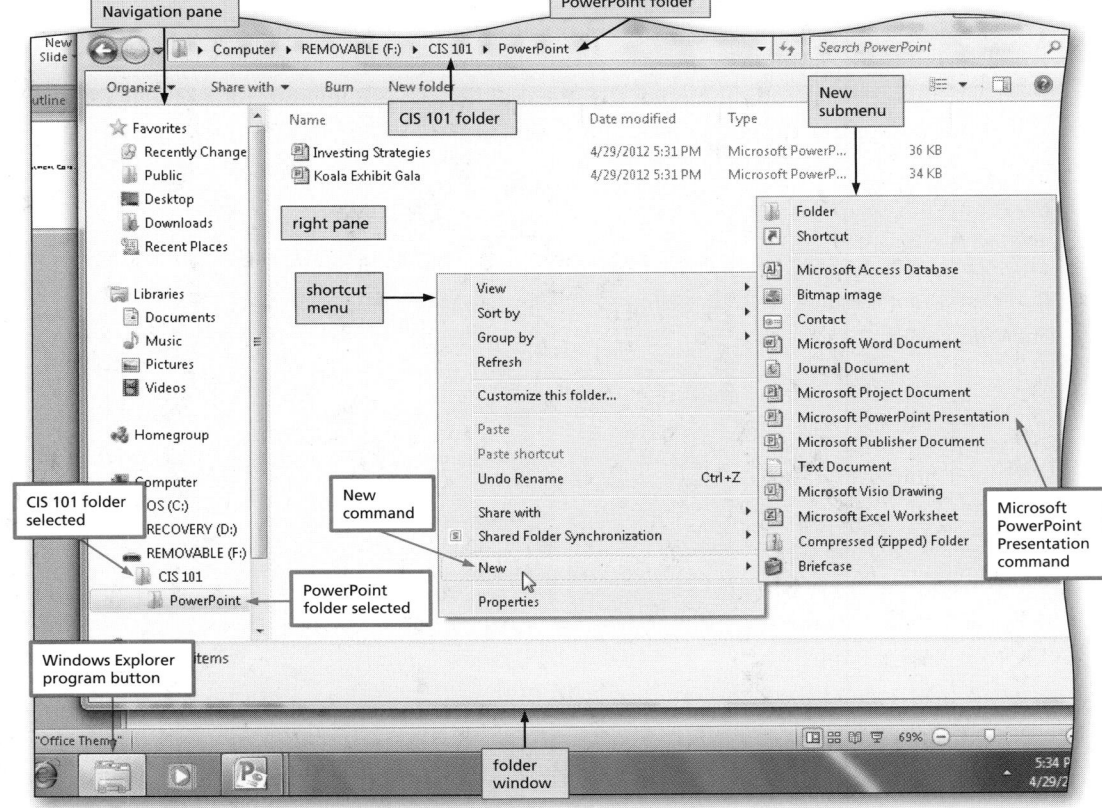

Figure 60

- Click Microsoft PowerPoint Presentation on the New submenu to display an icon and text box for a new file in the current folder window (Figure 61).

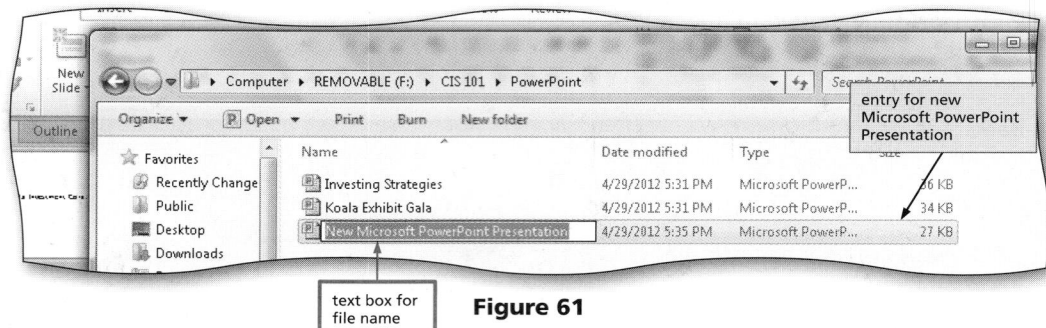

Figure 61

- Type **Koala Exhibit Gala Volunteers** in the text box and then press the ENTER key to assign a name to the new file in the current folder (Figure 62).

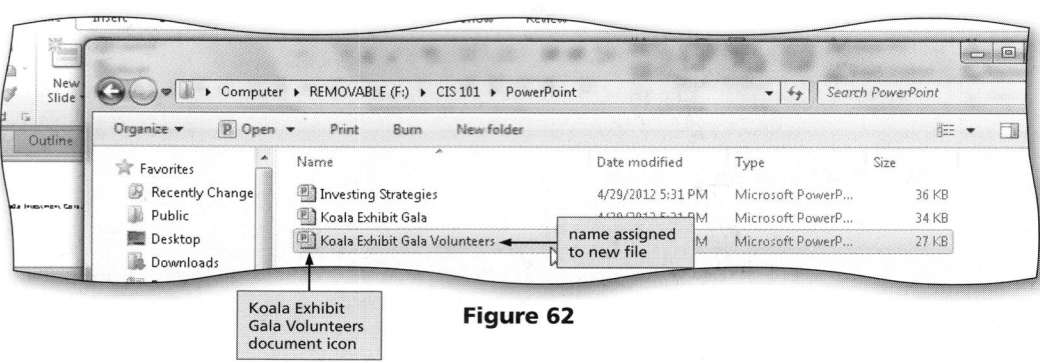

Figure 62

To Start a Program from Windows Explorer and Open a File

Previously, you learned how to start an Office program using the Start menu and the search box. Another way to start an Office program is to open an existing file from Windows Explorer, which causes the program in which the file was created to start and then open the selected file. The following steps, which assume Windows 7 is running, use Windows Explorer to start PowerPoint based on a typical installation. You may need to ask your instructor how to start PowerPoint for your computer.

- If necessary, display the file to open in the folder window in Windows Explorer (shown in Figure 62).

- Right-click the file icon or file name (Koala Exhibit Gala Volunteers, in this case) to display a shortcut menu (Figure 63).

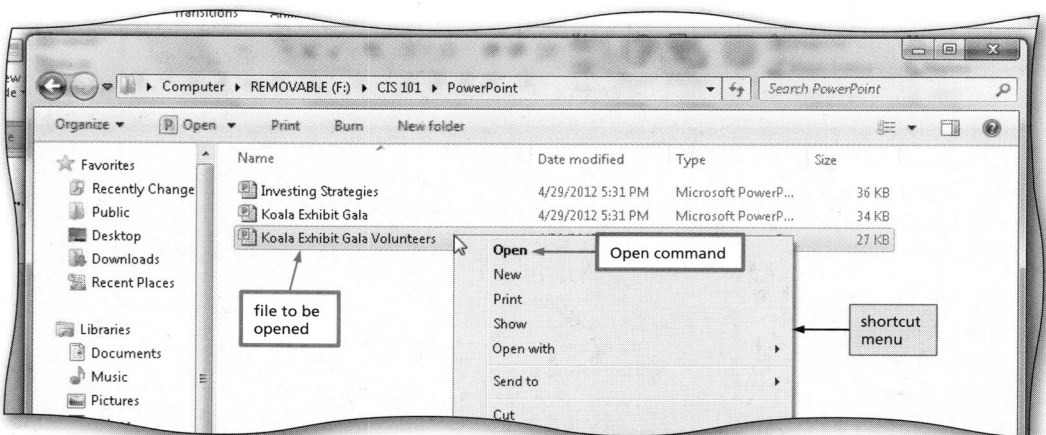

Figure 63

2

- Click Open on the shortcut menu to open the selected file in the program used to create the file, Microsoft PowerPoint in this case (Figure 64).

- If the program window is not maximized, click the Maximize button on the title bar to maximize the window.

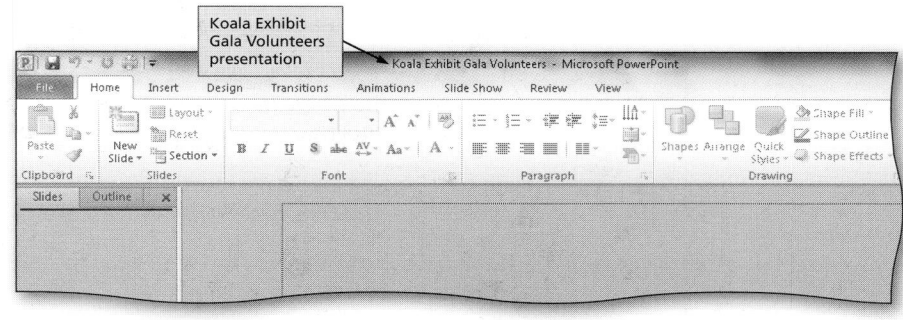

Koala Exhibit Gala Volunteers presentation

Figure 64

To Enter Text in a Slide

The next steps enter text in a blank slide.

1 Click the label, Click to add first slide, to display the title slide.

2 Click the label, Click to add title, located inside the title text placeholder.

3 Type **Koala Exhibit Staff and Volunteers** (shown in Figure 65).

To Save an Existing Document with the Same File Name

Saving frequently cannot be overemphasized. You have made modifications to the file (presentation) since you created it. Thus, you should save again. Similarly, you should continue saving files frequently so that you do not lose your changes since the time you last saved the file. You can use the same file name, such as Koala Exhibit Gala Volunteers, to save the changes made to the document. The following step saves a file again.

1

- Click the Save button on the Quick Access Toolbar to overwrite the previously saved file (Koala Exhibit Gala Volunteers, in this case) on the USB flash drive (Figure 65).

Q&A

Why did the Save As dialog box not appear?

Office programs, including PowerPoint, overwrite the document using the setting specified the first time you saved the document.

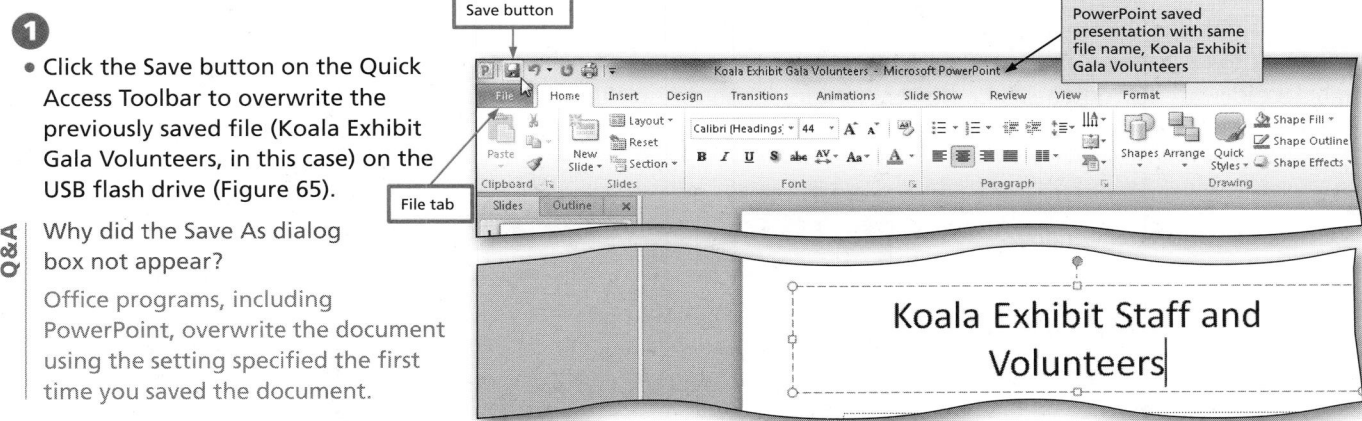

Save button

File tab

PowerPoint saved presentation with same file name, Koala Exhibit Gala Volunteers

Koala Exhibit Staff and Volunteers

Figure 65

Other Ways

1. Press CTRL+S or press SHIFT+F12

To Use Save As to Change the Name of a File

You might want to save a file with a different name and even to a different location. For example, you might start a homework assignment with a data file and then save it with a final file name for submitting to your instructor, saving it to a location designated by your instructor. The following steps save a file with a different file name.

1 With your USB flash drive connected to one of the computer's USB ports, click File on the Ribbon to open the Backstage view.

2 Click Save As in the Backstage view to display the Save As dialog box.

3 Type **Koala Exhibit Staff and Volunteers** in the File name text box (Save As dialog box) to change the file name. Do not press the ENTER key after typing the file name because you do not want to close the dialog box at this time.

4 Navigate to the desired save location (the PowerPoint folder in the CIS 101 folder [or your class folder] on the USB flash drive, in this case).

5 Click the Save button (Save As dialog box) to save the file in the selected folder on the selected drive with the new file name.

To Quit an Office Program

You are finished using PowerPoint. The following steps quit PowerPoint.

1 Because you have multiple PowerPoint documents open, click File on the Ribbon to open the Backstage view and then click Exit in the Backstage view to close all open documents and quit the PowerPoint program.

2 If a dialog box appears, click the Save button to save any changes made to the file since the last save.

Moving, Renaming, and Deleting Files

Earlier in this chapter, you learned how to organize files in folders, which is part of a process known as **file management**. The following sections cover additional file management topics including renaming, moving, and deleting files.

To Rename a File

In some circumstances, you may want to change the name of, or rename, a file or a folder. For example, you may want to distinguish a file in one folder or drive from a copy of a similar file, or you may decide to rename a file to better identify its contents. The PowerPoint folder shown in Figure 66 contains the PowerPoint document, Koala Exhibit Gala. The following steps change the name of the Koala Exhibit Gala file in the PowerPoint folder to Koala Exhibit Presentation.

- If necessary, click the Windows Explorer program button on the taskbar to display the folder window in Windows Explorer.

- If necessary, navigate to the location of the file to be renamed (in this case, the PowerPoint folder in the CIS 101 folder [or your class folder] on the USB flash drive) to display the file(s) it contains in the right pane.

- Right-click the Koala Exhibit Gala icon or file name in the right pane to select the Koala Exhibit Gala file and display a shortcut menu that presents a list of commands related to files (Figure 66).

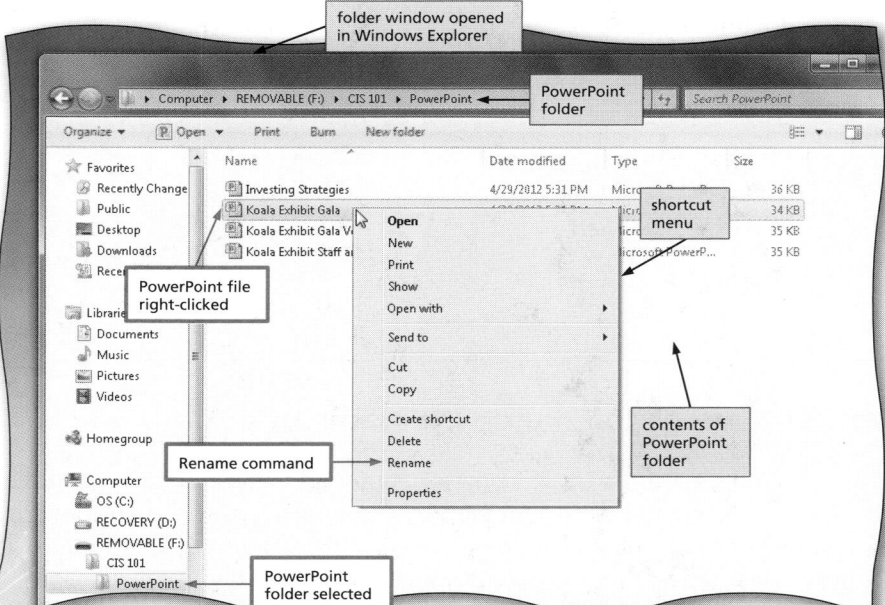

Figure 66

- Click Rename on the shortcut menu to place the current file name in a text box.

- Type **Koala Exhibit Presentation** in the text box and then press the ENTER key (Figure 67).

Q&A
Are any risks involved in renaming files that are located on a hard disk?

If you inadvertently rename a file that is associated with certain programs, the programs may not be able to find the file and, therefore, may not execute properly. Always use caution when renaming files.

Q&A
Can I rename a file when it is open?

No, a file must be closed to change the file name.

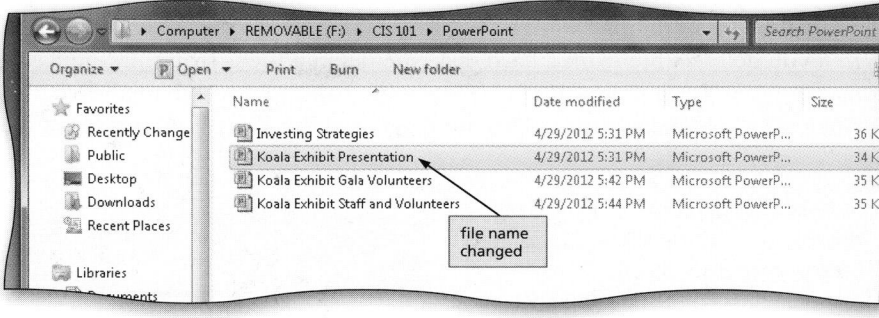

Figure 67

Other Ways

1. Select file, press F2, type new file name, press ENTER

To Move a File

At some time, you may want to move a file from one folder, called the source folder, to another, called the destination. When you move a file, it no longer appears in the original folder. If the destination and the source folders are on the same disk drive, you can move a file by dragging it. If the folders are on different disk drives, then you will need to right-drag the file. The following step moves the Koala Exhibit Gala Volunteers file from the PowerPoint folder to the CIS 101 folder.

1

- In Windows Explorer, if necessary, navigate to the location of the file to be moved (in this case, the PowerPoint folder in the CIS 101 folder [or your class folder] on the USB flash drive).

- Click the PowerPoint folder in the Navigation pane to display the files it contains in the right pane (Figure 68).

- Drag the Koala Exhibit Gala Volunteers file in the right pane to the CIS 101 folder in the Navigation pane.

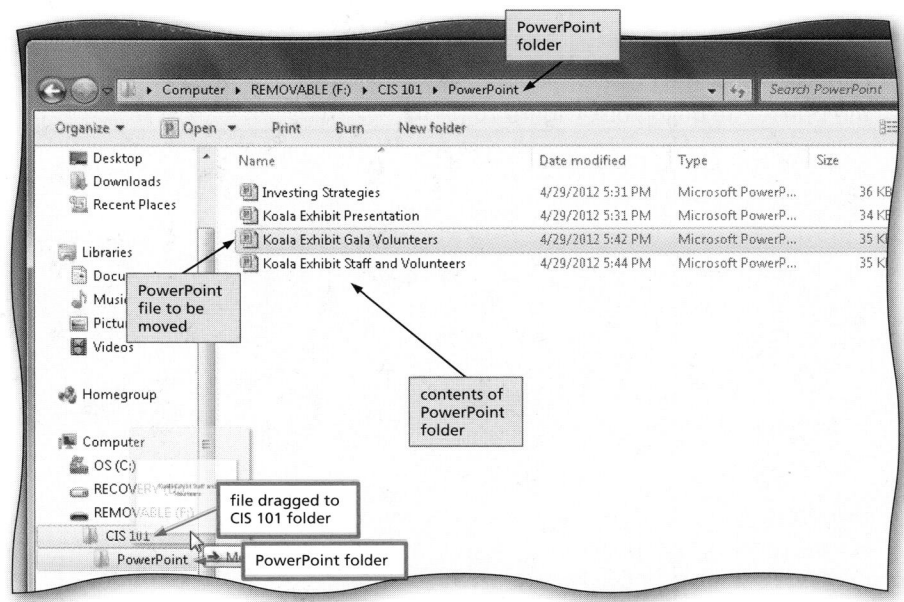

Figure 68

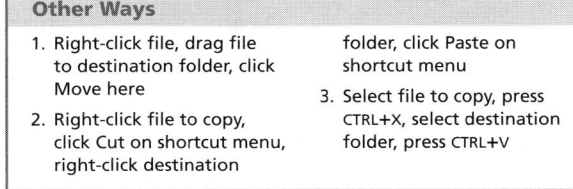

Other Ways

1. Right-click file, drag file to destination folder, click Move here

2. Right-click file to copy, click Cut on shortcut menu, right-click destination

folder, click Paste on shortcut menu

3. Select file to copy, press CTRL+X, select destination folder, press CTRL+V

To Delete a File

A final task you may want to perform is to delete a file. Exercise extreme caution when deleting a file or files. When you delete a file from a hard disk, the deleted file is stored in the Recycle Bin where you can recover it until you empty the Recycle Bin. If you delete a file from removable media, such as a USB flash drive, the file is deleted permanently. The next steps delete the Koala Exhibit Gala Volunteers file from the CIS 101 folder.

1

- In Windows Explorer, navigate to the location of the file to be deleted (in this case, the CIS 101 folder [or your class folder] on the USB flash drive).

- If necessary, click the CIS 101 folder in the Navigation pane to display the files it contains in the right pane.

- Right-click the Koala Exhibit Gala Volunteers icon or file name in the right pane to select the file and display a shortcut menu (Figure 69).

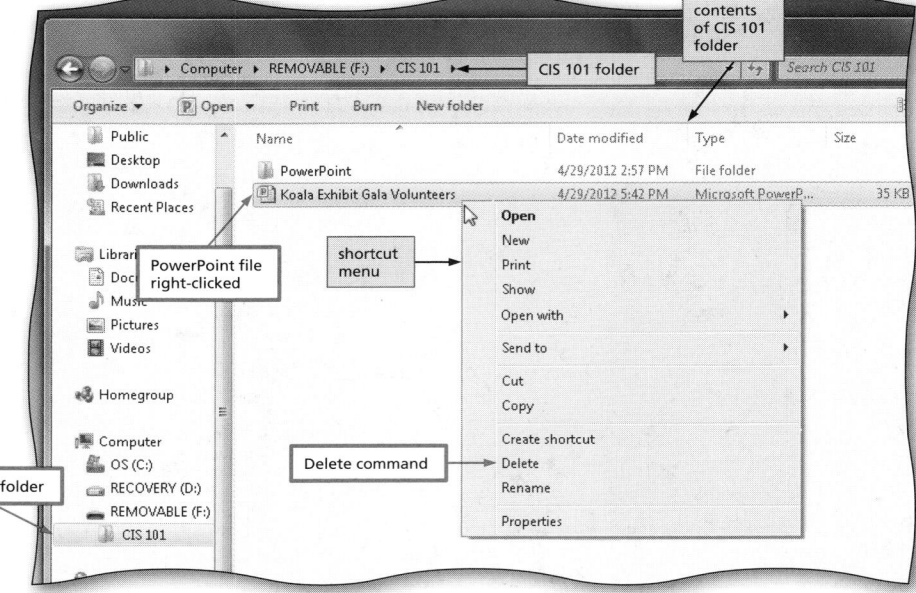

Figure 69

2

- Click Delete on the shortcut menu to display the Delete File dialog box (Figure 70).

- Click the Yes button (Delete File dialog box) to delete the selected file.

Q&A Can I use this same technique to delete a folder?

Yes. Right-click the folder and then click Delete on the shortcut menu. When you delete a folder, all of the files and folders contained in the folder you are deleting, together with any files and folders on lower hierarchical levels, are deleted as well.

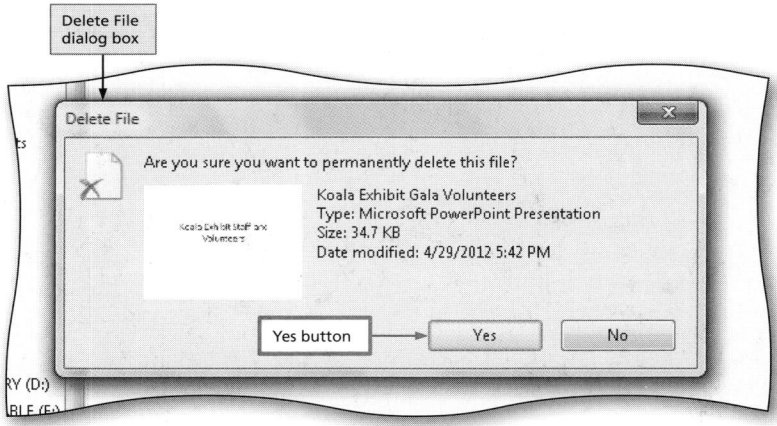

Figure 70

Other Ways

1. Select icon, press DELETE

Microsoft Office and Windows Help

At any time while you are using one of the Microsoft Office 2010 programs, such as PowerPoint, you can use Office Help to display information about all topics associated with the program. This section illustrates the use of PowerPoint Help. Help in other Office 2010 programs operates in a similar fashion.

In Office 2010, Help is presented in a window that has Web-browser-style navigation buttons. Each Office 2010 program has its own Help home page, which is the starting Help page that is displayed in the Help window. If your computer is connected to the Internet, the contents of the Help page reflect both the local help files installed on the computer and material from Microsoft's Web site.

To Open the Help Window in an Office Program

The following step opens the PowerPoint Help window. The step to open a Help window in other Office programs is similar.

- Start PowerPoint.

- Click the Microsoft PowerPoint Help button near the upper-right corner of the program window to open the PowerPoint Help window (Figure 71).

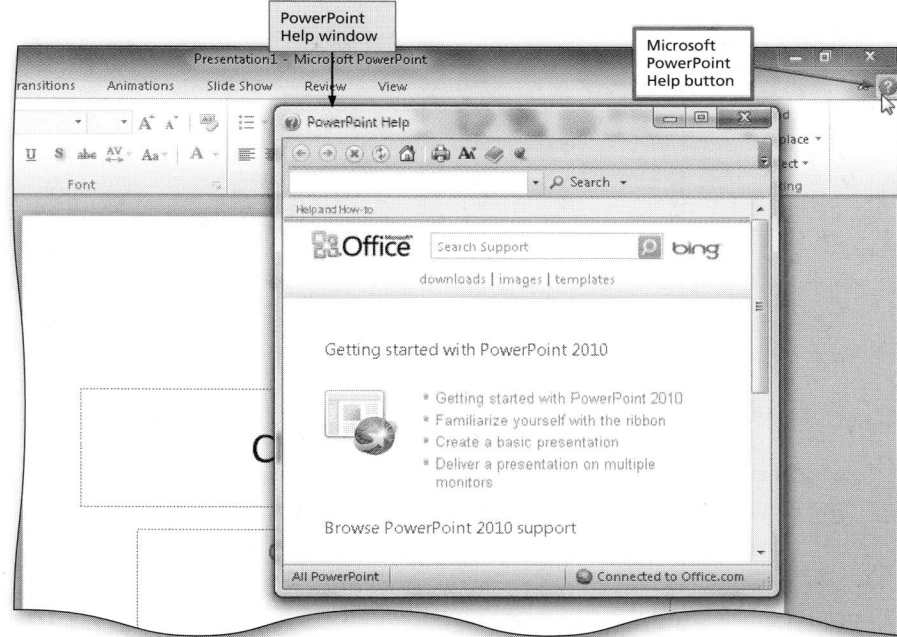

Figure 71

Other Ways
1. Press F1

Moving and Resizing Windows

Up to this point, this chapter has used minimized and maximized windows. At times, however, it is useful, or even necessary, to have more than one window open and visible on the screen at the same time. You can resize and move these open windows so that you can view different areas of and elements in the window. In the case of the Help window, for example, it could be covering slide elements in the PowerPoint window that you need to see.

To Move a Window by Dragging

You can move any open window that is not maximized to another location on the desktop by dragging the title bar of the window. The following step drags the PowerPoint Help window to the top left of the desktop.

1

- Drag the window title bar (the PowerPoint Help window title bar, in this case) so that the window moves to the top left of the desktop, as shown in Figure 72.

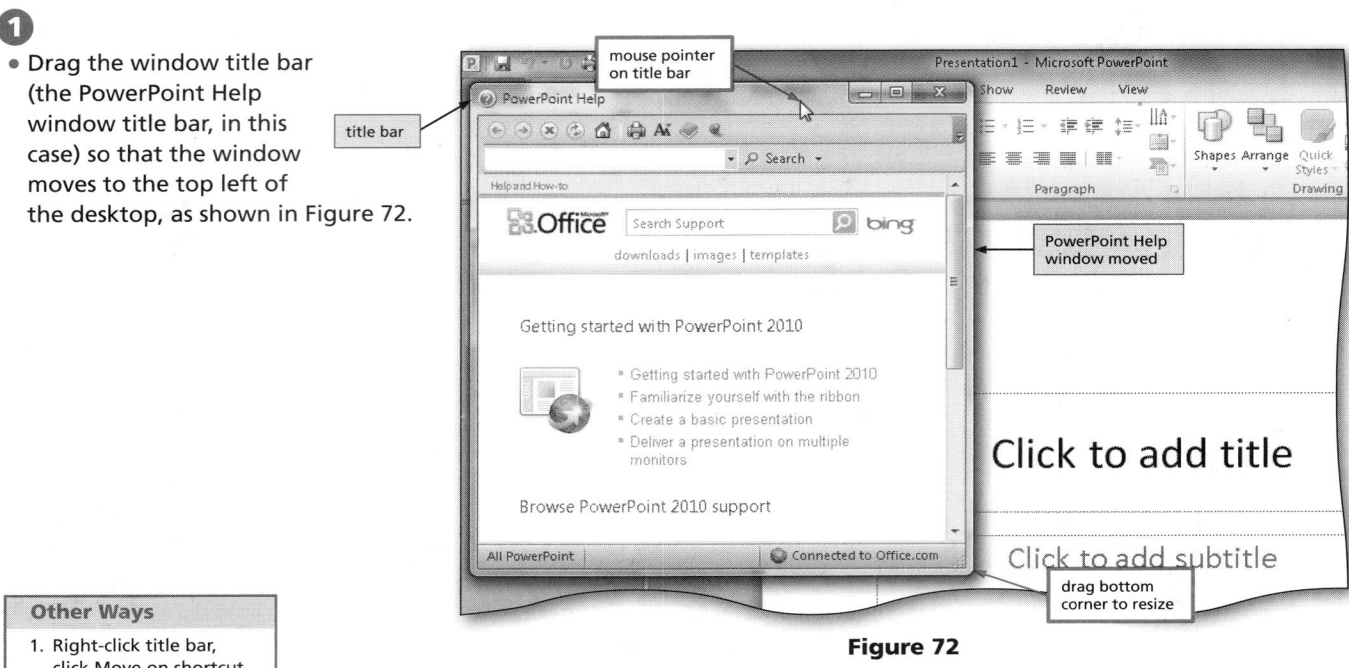

Figure 72

To Resize a Window by Dragging

Sometimes, information is not visible completely in a window. A method used to change the size of the window is to drag the window borders. The following step changes the size of the PowerPoint Help window by dragging its borders.

- Point to the lower-right corner of the window (the PowerPoint Help window, in this case) until the mouse pointer changes to a two-headed arrow.

- Drag the bottom border downward to display more of the active window (Figure 73).

Q&A Can I drag other borders on the window to enlarge or shrink the window?

Yes, you can drag the left, right, and top borders and any window corner to resize a window.

Q&A Will Windows 7 remember the new size of the window after I close it?

Yes. When you reopen the window, Windows 7 will display it at the same size it was when you closed it.

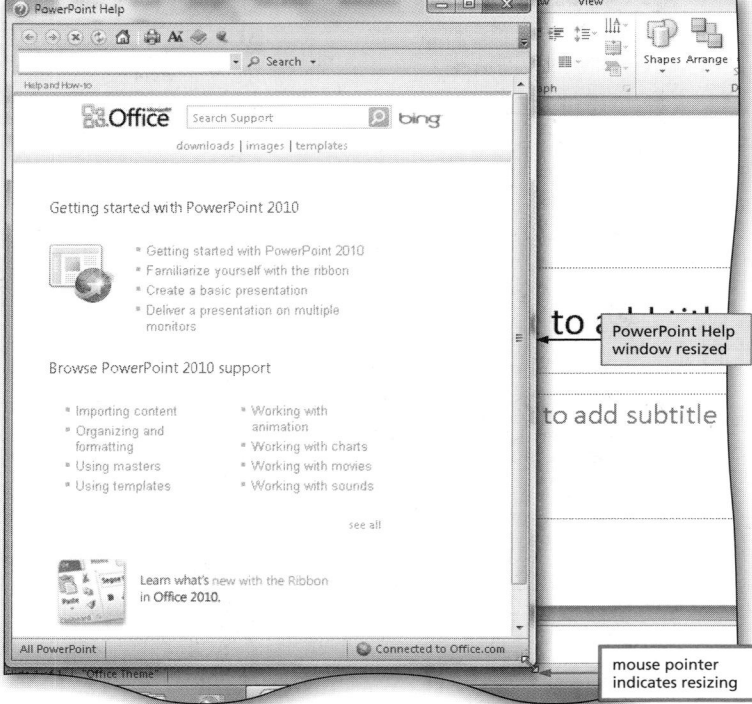

Figure 73

Using Office Help

Once an Office program's Help window is open, several methods exist for navigating Help. You can search for help by using any of the three following methods from the Help window:

1. Enter search text in the 'Type words to search for' text box.
2. Click the links in the Help window.
3. Use the Table of Contents.

To Obtain Help Using the 'Type words to search for' Text Box

Assume for the following example that you want to know more about the Backstage view. The following steps use the 'Type words to search for' text box to obtain useful information about the Backstage view by entering the word, Backstage, as search text.

1

- Type **Backstage** in the 'Type words to search for' text box at the top of the PowerPoint Help window to enter the search text.

- Click the Search button arrow to display the Search menu (Figure 74).

- If it is not selected already, click All PowerPoint on the Search menu, so that Help performs the most complete search of the current program (PowerPoint, in this case). If All PowerPoint already is selected, click the Search button arrow again to close the Search menu.

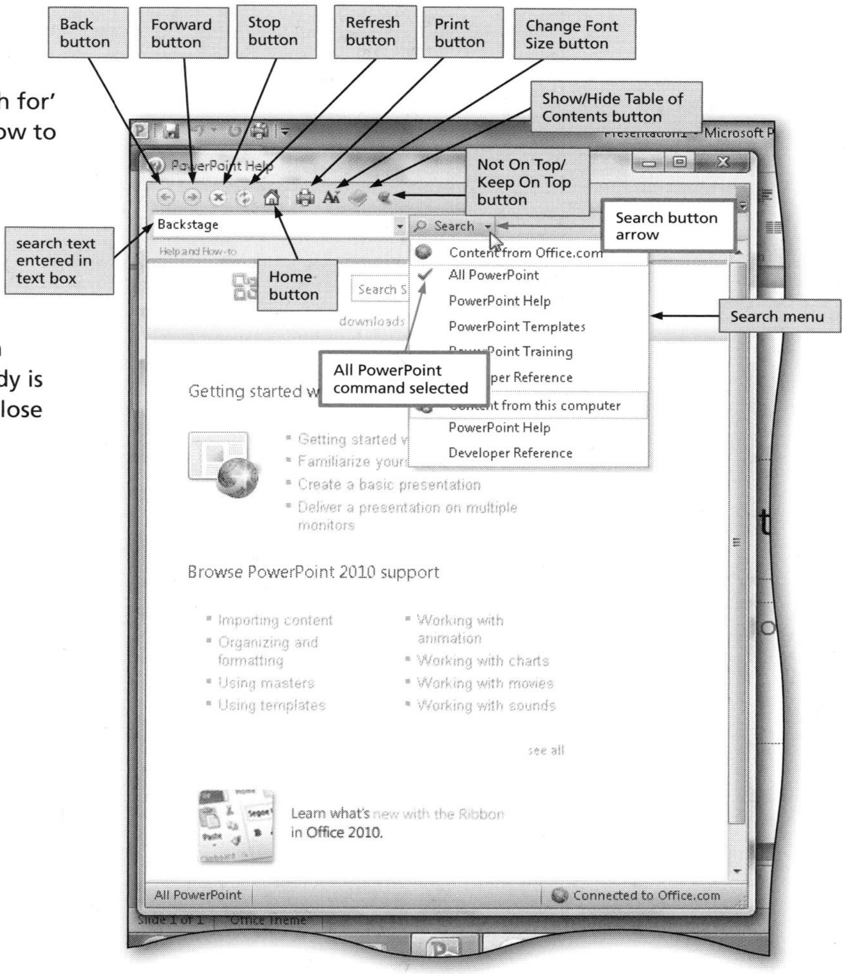

Figure 74

Q&A

Why select All PowerPoint on the Search menu?

Selecting All PowerPoint on the Search menu ensures that PowerPoint Help will search all possible sources for information about your search term. It will produce the most complete search results.

2

- Click the Search button to display the search results (Figure 75).

Q&A Why do my search results differ?

If you do not have an Internet connection, your results will reflect only the content of the Help files on your computer. When searching for help online, results also can change as material is added, deleted, and updated on the online Help Web pages maintained by Microsoft.

Q&A Why were my search results not very helpful?

When initiating a search, be sure to check the spelling of the search text; also, keep your search specific, with fewer than seven words, to return the most accurate results.

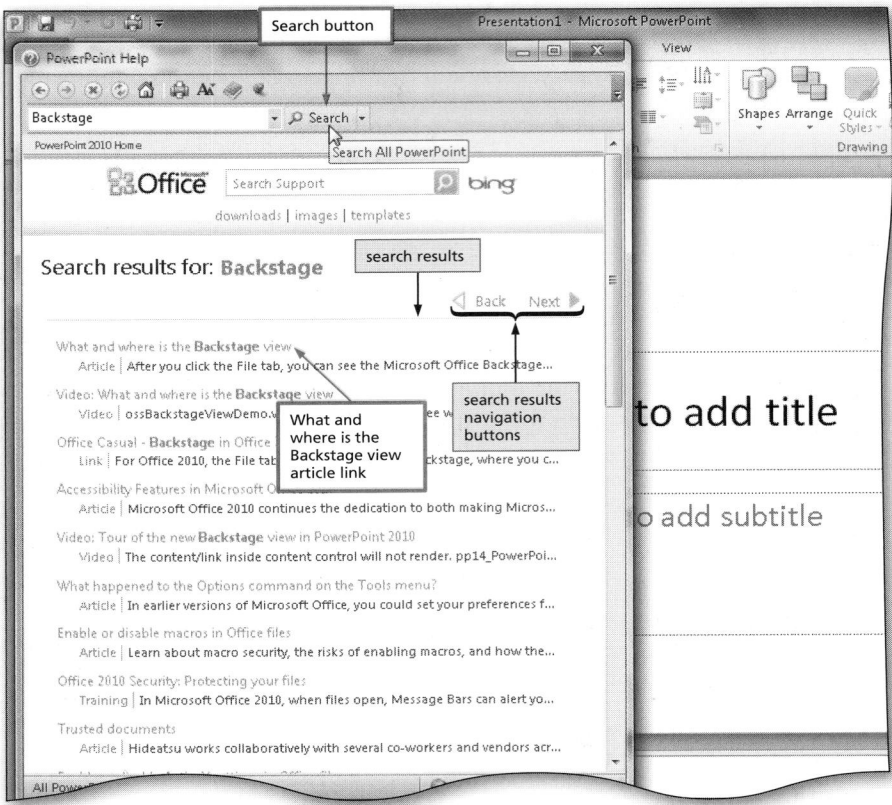

Figure 75

3

- Click the 'What and where is the Backstage view' link to open the Help document associated with the selected topic (Figure 76).

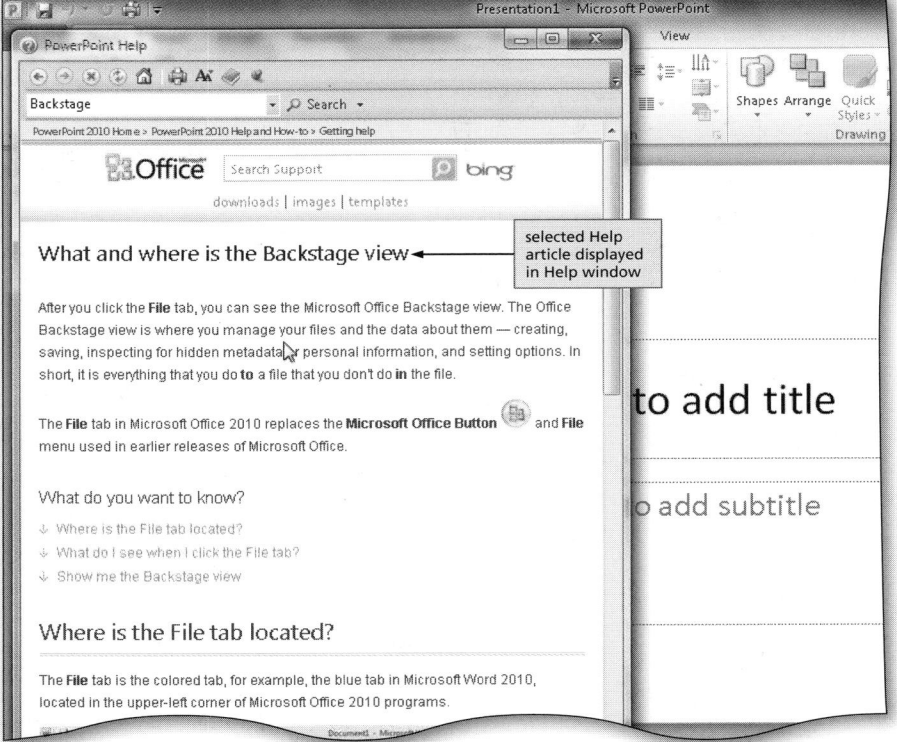

Figure 76

- Click the Home button on the toolbar to clear the search results and redisplay the Help home page (Figure 77).

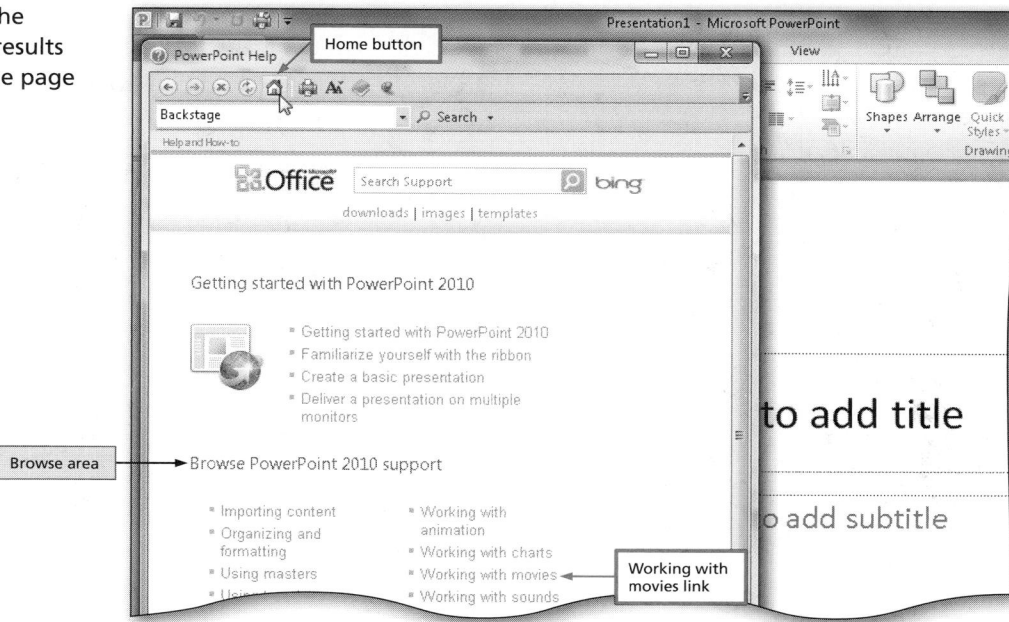

Figure 77

To Obtain Help Using the Help Links

If your topic of interest is listed in the Browse area of the Help window, you can click the link to begin browsing the Help categories instead of entering search text. You browse Help just as you would browse a Web site. If you know which category contains your Help information, you may wish to use these links. The following step finds the Working with movies Help information using the category links from the PowerPoint Help home page.

- Click the 'Working with movies' link on the Help home page (shown in Figure 77) to display the 'Working with movies' page (Figure 78).

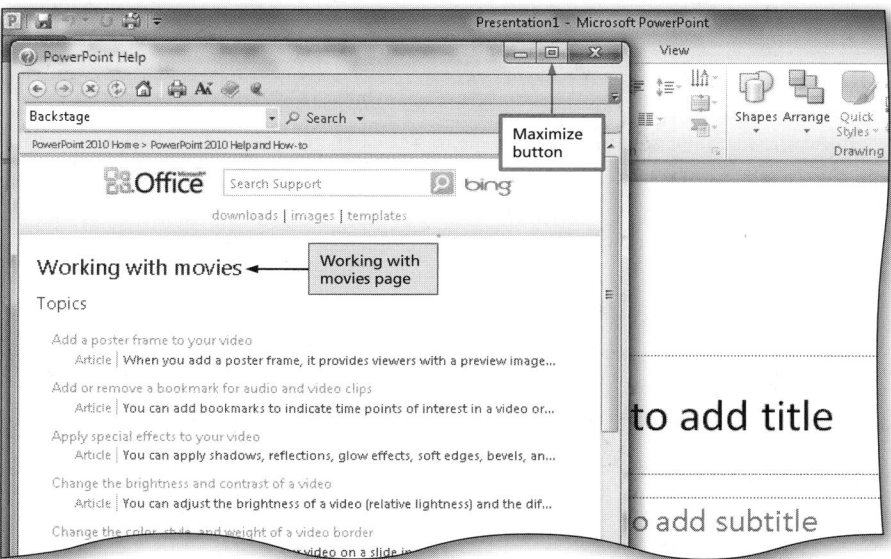

Figure 78

To Obtain Help Using the Help Table of Contents

A third way to find Help in Office programs is through the Help Table of Contents. You can browse through the Table of Contents to display information about a particular topic or to familiarize yourself with an Office program. The following steps access the Help information about slide layouts by browsing through the Table of Contents.

- Click the Home button on the toolbar to display the Help home page.

- Click the Show Table of Contents button on the toolbar to display the Table of Contents pane on the left side of the Help window. If necessary, click the Maximize button on the Help title bar to maximize the window (Figure 79).

Q&A

Why does the appearance of the Show Table of Contents button change?

When the Table of Contents is displayed in the Help window, the Hide Table of Contents button replaces the Show Table of Contents button.

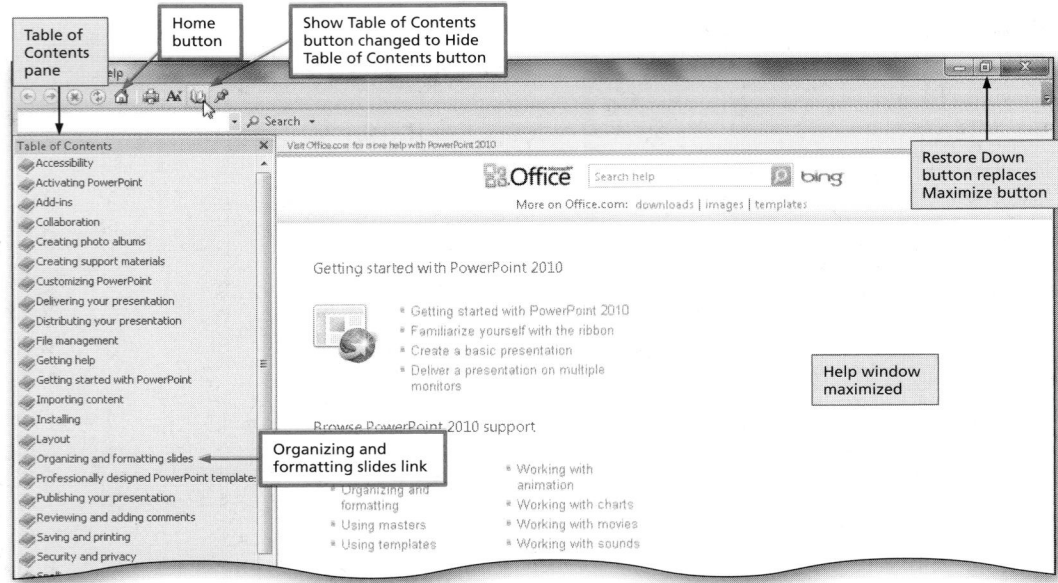

Figure 79

- Click the 'Organizing and formatting slides' link in the Table of Contents pane to view a list of Help subtopics.

- Click the 'Apply a layout to a slide' link in the Table of Contents pane to view the selected Help document in the right pane (Figure 80).

- After reviewing the page, click the Close button to quit Help.

- Click the PowerPoint Close button to quit the PowerPoint program.

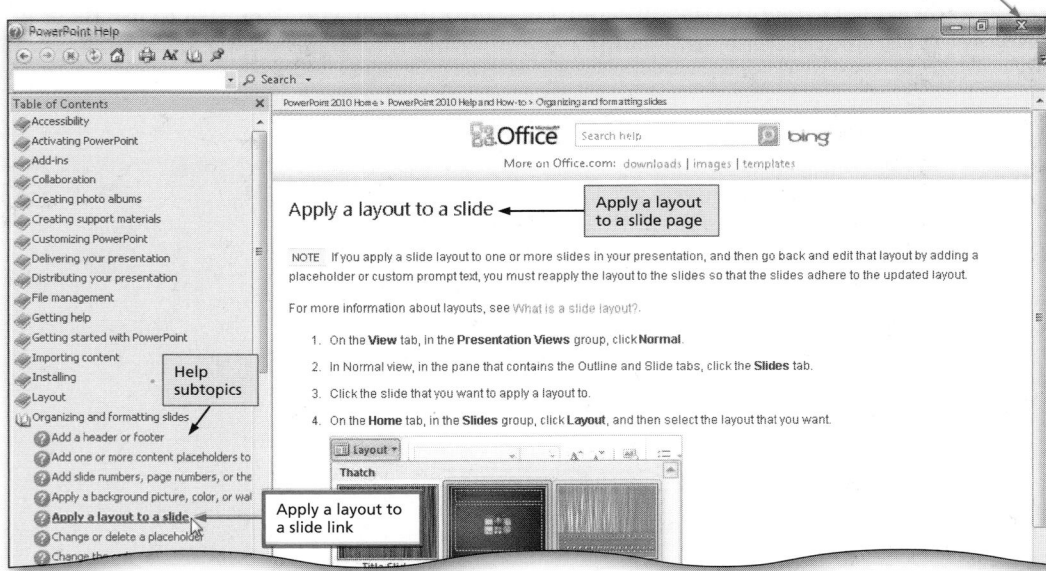

Figure 80

Q&A

How do I remove the Table of Contents pane when I am finished with it?

The Show Table of Contents button acts as a toggle. When the Table of Contents pane is visible, the button changes to Hide Table of Contents. Clicking it hides the Table of Contents pane and changes the button to Show Table of Contents.

Obtaining Help while Working in an Office Program

Help in Office programs, such as PowerPoint, provides you with the ability to obtain help directly, without the need to open the Help window and initiate a search. For example, you may be unsure about how a particular command works, or you may be presented with a dialog box that you are not sure how to use.

Figure 81 shows one option for obtaining help while working in PowerPoint. If you want to learn more about a command, point to the command button and wait for the Enhanced ScreenTip to appear. If the Help icon appears in the Enhanced ScreenTip, press the F1 key while pointing to the command to open the Help window associated with that command.

Figure 82 shows a dialog box that contains a Help button. Pressing the F1 key while the dialog box is displayed opens a Help window. The Help window contains help about that dialog box, if available. If no help file is available for that particular dialog box, then the main Help window opens.

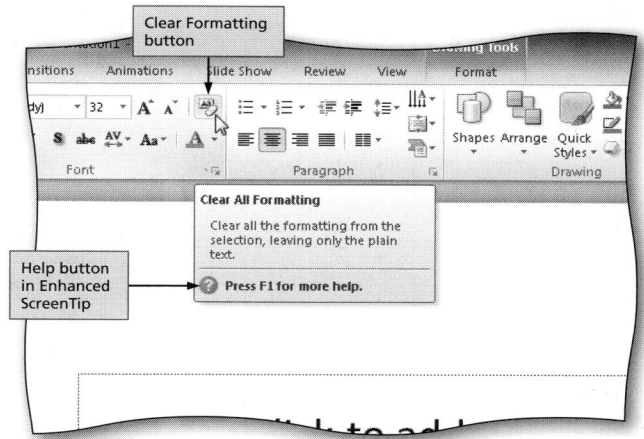

Figure 81

Using Windows Help and Support

One of the more powerful Windows 7 features is Windows Help and Support. **Windows Help and Support** is available when using Windows 7 or when using any Microsoft program running under Windows 7. This feature is designed to assist you in using Windows 7 or the various programs. Table 4 describes the content found in the Help and Support Center. The same methods used for searching Microsoft Office Help can be used in Windows Help and Support. The difference is that Windows Help and Support displays help for Windows 7, instead of for Microsoft Office.

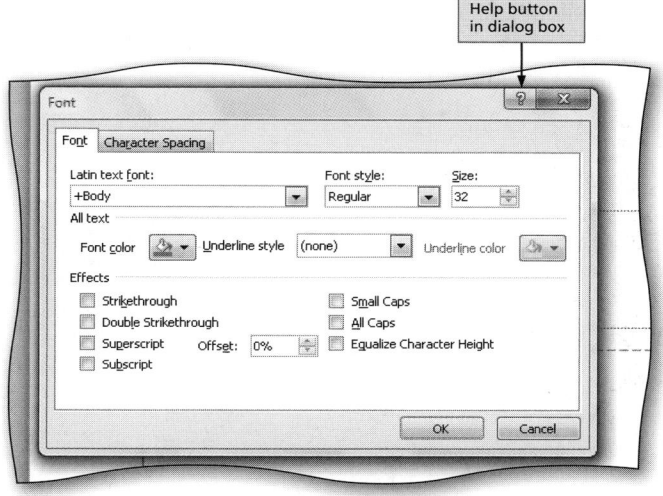

Figure 82

Table 4 Windows Help and Support Center Content Areas	
Area	**Function**
Find an answer quickly	This area contains instructions about how to do a quick search using the search box.
Not sure where to start?	This area displays three topics to help guide a user: How to get started with your computer, Learn about Windows Basics, and Browse Help topics. Clicking one of the options navigates to corresponding Help and Support pages.
More on the Windows website	This area contains links to online content from the Windows Web site. Clicking the links navigates to the corresponding Web pages on the Web site.

To Start Windows Help and Support

The following steps start Windows Help and Support and display the Windows Help and Support window, containing links to more information about Windows 7.

- Click the Start button on the taskbar to display the Start menu (Figure 83).

Q&A

Why are the programs that are displayed on the Start menu different?

Windows adds the programs you have used recently to the left pane on the Start menu. You have started PowerPoint while performing the steps in this chapter, so that program now is displayed on the Start menu.

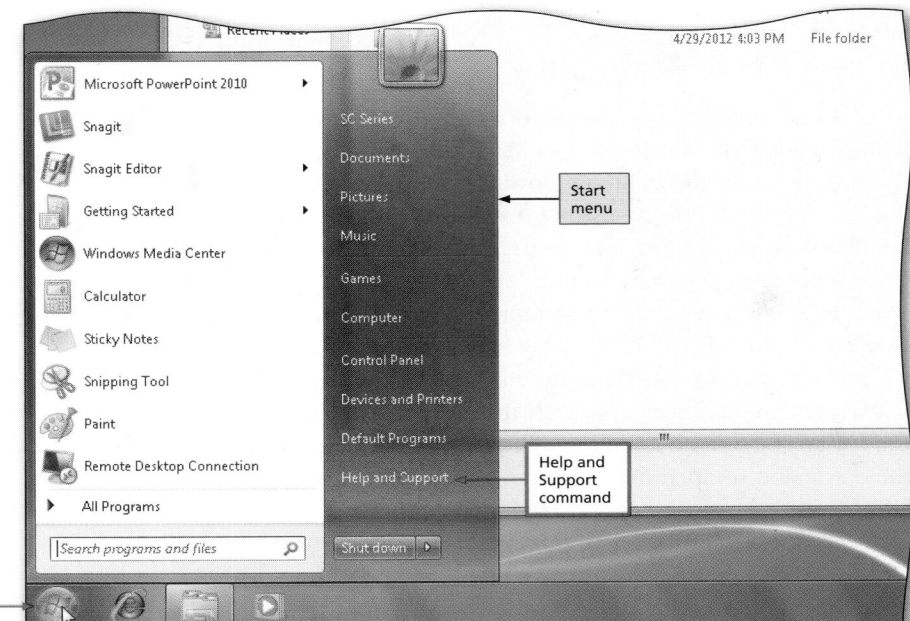

Figure 83

- Click Help and Support on the Start menu to open the Windows Help and Support window (Figure 84).

- After reviewing the Windows Help and Support window, click the Close button to quit Windows Help and Support.

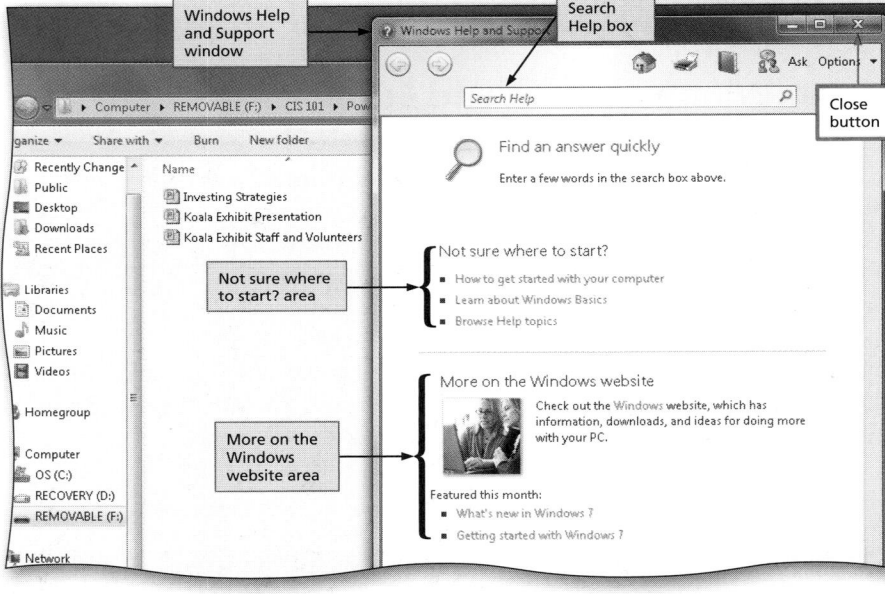

Figure 84

Other Ways

1. Press CTRL+ESC, press RIGHT ARROW, press UP ARROW, press ENTER
2. Press WINDOWS+F1

Chapter Summary

In this chapter, you learned about the Windows 7 interface. You started Windows 7, were introduced to the components of the desktop, and learned several mouse operations. You opened, closed, moved, resized, minimized, maximized, and scrolled a window. You used folder windows to expand and collapse drives and folders, display drive and folder contents, create folders, and rename and then delete a file.

You also learned some basic features of Microsoft PowerPoint 2010. As part of this learning process, you discovered the common elements that exist among Microsoft Office programs.

Microsoft Office Help was demonstrated, and you learned how to use the PowerPoint Help window. You were introduced to the Windows 7 Help and Support Center and learned how to use it to obtain more information about Windows 7.

The items listed below include all of the new Windows 7 and Office 2010 skills you have learned in this chapter.

1. Log On to the Computer (OFF 6)
2. Start a Program Using the Start Menu (OFF 10)
3. Maximize a Window (OFF 12)
4. Display a Different Tab on the Ribbon (OFF 16)
5. Minimize, Display, and Restore the Ribbon (OFF 16)
6. Display and Use a Shortcut Menu (OFF 17)
7. Customize the Quick Access Toolbar (OFF 18)
8. Enter Content in a Title Slide (OFF 19)
9. Create a Folder (OFF 20)
10. Create a Folder within a Folder (OFF 23)
11. Expand a Folder, Scroll through Folder Contents, and Collapse a Folder (OFF 23)
12. Switch from One Program to Another (OFF 24)
13. Save a File in a Folder (OFF 25)
14. Minimize and Restore a Window (OFF 27)
15. Change the Screen Resolution (OFF 30)
16. Quit a Program with One Document Open (OFF 31)
17. Start a Program Using the Search Box (OFF 32)
18. Open an Existing Office File from the Backstage View (OFF 33)
19. Create a New Document from the Backstage View (OFF 34)
20. Close a File Using the Backstage View (OFF 36)
21. Open a Recent Office File Using the Backstage View (OFF 36)
22. Create a New Blank Office Document from Windows Explorer (OFF 37)
23. Start a Program from Windows Explorer and Open a File (OFF 38)
24. Save an Existing Document with the Same File Name (OFF 39)
25. Rename a File (OFF 40)
26. Move a File (OFF 41)
27. Delete a File (OFF 42)
28. Open the Help Window in an Office Program (OFF 43)
29. Move a Window by Dragging (OFF 43)
30. Resize a Window by Dragging (OFF 44)
31. Obtain Help Using the 'Type words to search for' Text Box (OFF 45)
32. Obtain Help Using the Help Links (OFF 47)
33. Obtain Help Using the Help Table of Contents (OFF 48)
34. Start Windows Help and Support (OFF 49)

 If you have a SAM 2010 user profile, your instructor may have assigned an autogradable version of this assignment. If so, log into the SAM 2010 Web site at www.cengage.com/sam2010 to download the instruction and start files.

Learn It Online

Test your knowledge of chapter content and key terms.

Instructions: To complete the Learn It Online exercises, start your browser, click the Address bar, and then enter the Web address **scsite.com/office2010/learn**. When the Office 2010 Learn It Online page is displayed, click the link for the exercise you want to complete and then read the instructions.

Chapter Reinforcement TF, MC, and SA
A series of true/false, multiple choice, and short answer questions that test your knowledge of the chapter content.

Flash Cards
An interactive learning environment where you identify chapter key terms associated with displayed definitions.

Practice Test
A series of multiple choice questions that test your knowledge of chapter content and key terms.

Who Wants To Be a Computer Genius?
An interactive game that challenges your knowledge of chapter content in the style of a television quiz show.

Wheel of Terms
An interactive game that challenges your knowledge of chapter key terms in the style of the television show *Wheel of Fortune*.

Crossword Puzzle Challenge
A crossword puzzle that challenges your knowledge of key terms presented in the chapter.

Apply Your Knowledge

Reinforce the skills and apply the concepts you learned in this chapter.

Creating a Folder and a Document

Instructions: You will create a PowerPoint folder and then create a PowerPoint document and save it in the folder.

Perform the following tasks:

1. Connect a USB flash drive to an available USB port and then open the USB flash drive window.

2. Click the New folder button on the toolbar to display a new folder icon and text box for the folder name.

3. Type `PowerPoint` in the text box to name the folder. Press the ENTER key to create the folder on the USB flash drive.

4. Start PowerPoint.

5. Enter the text shown in Figure 85.

6. Click the Save button on the Quick Access Toolbar. Navigate to the PowerPoint folder on the USB flash drive and then save the document using the file name, Apply 1 Study Habits.

7. If your Quick Access Toolbar does not show the Quick Print button, add the Quick Print button to the Quick Access Toolbar. Print the document using the Quick Print button on the Quick Access Toolbar. When you are finished printing, remove the Quick Print button from the Quick Access Toolbar.

8. Submit the printout to your instructor.

9. Quit PowerPoint.

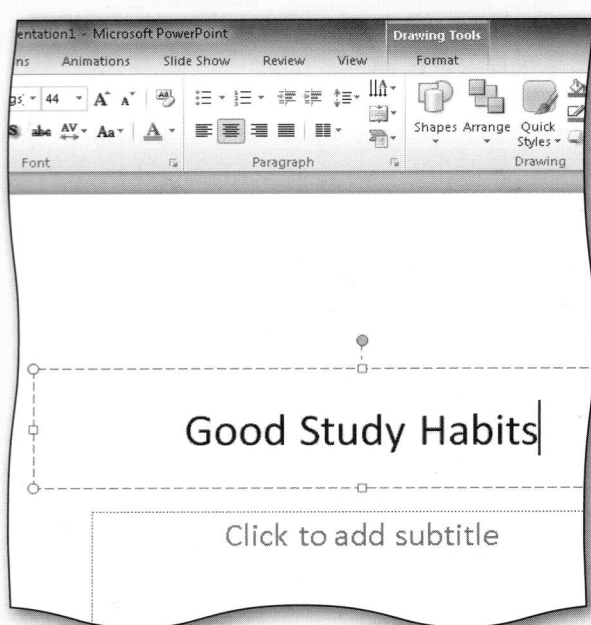

Figure 85

Extend Your Knowledge

Extend the skills you learned in this chapter and experiment with new skills. You will use Help to complete the assignment.

Using Help

Instructions: Use Office Help to perform the following tasks.

Perform the following tasks:

1. Start PowerPoint.

2. Click the Microsoft PowerPoint Help button to open the PowerPoint Help window (Figure 86).

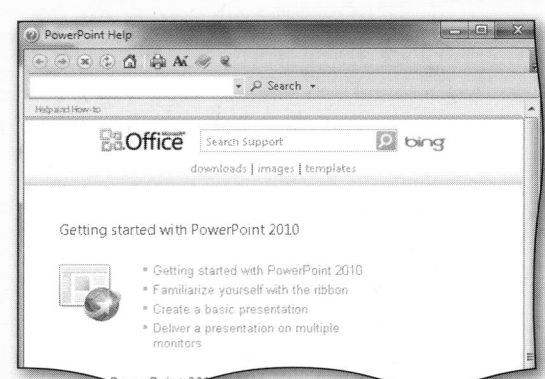

Figure 86

3. Search PowerPoint Help to answer the following questions.

   a. What are three features new to PowerPoint 2010?

   b. What type of training courses are available through Help?

   c. What steps add a new group to the Ribbon?

   d. What are Quick Parts?

   e. What are document properties?

   f. What is SmartArt?

   g. How do you print slides as a handout?

   h. What type of graphics can you insert?

   i. How do you add transitions between slides?

   j. What is the purpose of the Navigation pane?

4. Submit the answers from your searches in the format specified by your instructor.

5. Quit PowerPoint.

Make It Right

Analyze a file structure and correct all errors and/or improve the design.

Note: To complete this assignment, you will be required to use the Data Files for Students. See the inside back cover of this book for instructions on downloading the Data Files for Students, or contact your instructor for information about accessing the required files.

Organizing Vacation Photos

Instructions: Traditionally, you have stored photos from past vacations together in one folder. The photos are becoming difficult to manage, and you now want to store them in appropriate folders. You will create the folder structure shown in Figure 87. You then will move the photos to the folders so that they will be organized properly.

1. Connect a USB flash drive to an available USB port to open the USB flash drive window.

2. Create the hierarchical folder structure shown in Figure 87.

3. Move one photo to each folder in the folder structure you created in Step 2. The five photos are located on the Data Files for Students.

4. Submit your work in the format specified by your instructor.

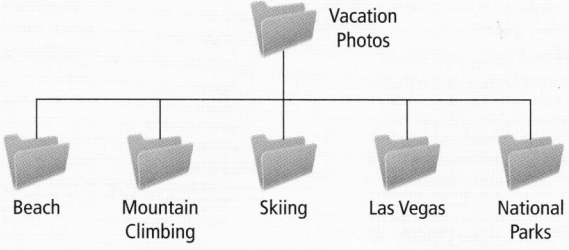

Figure 87

In the Lab

Use the guidelines, concepts, and skills presented in this chapter to increase your knowledge of Windows 7 and PowerPoint 2010. Labs are listed in order of increasing difficulty.

Lab 1: Using Windows Help and Support

Problem: You have a few questions about using Windows 7 and would like to answer these questions using Windows Help and Support.

Instructions: Use Windows Help and Support to perform the following tasks:

1. Display the Start menu and then click Help and Support to start Windows Help and Support.

2. Use the Help and Support Content page to answer the following questions.

   a. How do you reduce computer screen flicker?

   b. Which dialog box do you use to change the appearance of the mouse pointer?

   c. How do you minimize all windows?

   d. What is a VPN?

3. Use the Search Help text box in Windows Help and Support to answer the following questions.

   a. How can you minimize all open windows on the desktop?

   b. How do you start a program using the Run command?

   c. What are the steps to add a toolbar to the taskbar?

   d. What wizard do you use to remove unwanted desktop icons?

4. The tools to solve a problem while using Windows 7 are called **troubleshooters**. Use Windows Help and Support to find the list of troubleshooters (Figure 88), and answer the following questions.

   a. What problems does the HomeGroup troubleshooter allow you to resolve?

   b. List five Windows 7 troubleshooters that are not listed in Figure 88.

5. Use Windows Help and Support to obtain information about software licensing and product activation, and answer the following questions.

   a. What is genuine Windows?

   b. What is activation?

   c. What steps are required to activate Windows?

   d. What steps are required to read the Microsoft Software License Terms?

   e. Can you legally make a second copy of Windows 7 for use at home, work, or on a mobile computer or device?

   f. What is registration?

6. Close the Windows Help and Support window.

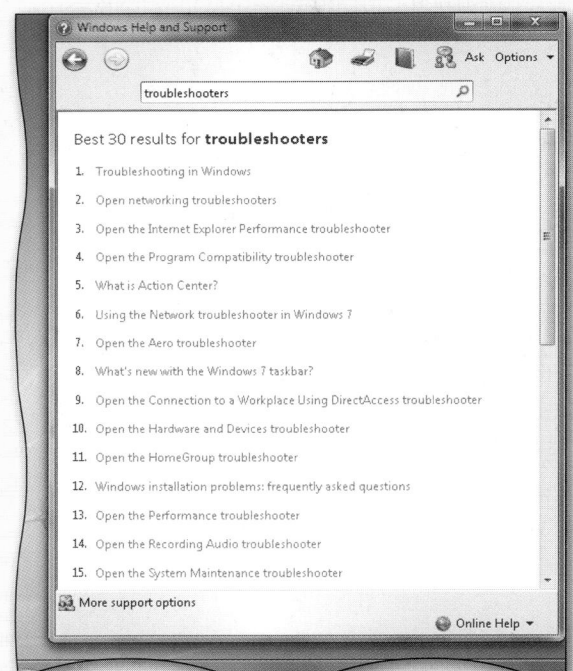

Figure 88

In the Lab

Lab 2: Creating Folders for a Pet Supply Store

Problem: Your friend works for Pete's Pet Supplies. He would like to organize his files in relation to the types of pets available in the store. He has five main categories: dogs, cats, fish, birds, and exotic. You are to create a folder structure similar to Figure 89.

Instructions: Perform the following tasks:

1. Connect a USB flash drive to an available USB port and then open the USB flash drive window.
2. Create the main folder for Pete's Pet Supplies.
3. Navigate to the Pete's Pet Supplies folder.
4. Within the Pete's Pet Supplies folder, create a folder for each of the following: Dogs, Cats, Fish, Birds, and Exotic.
5. Within the Exotic folder, create two additional folders, one for Primates and the second for Reptiles.
6. Submit the assignment in the format specified by your instructor.

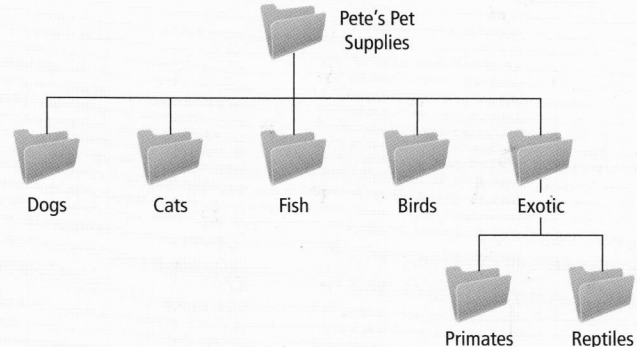

Figure 89

In the Lab

Lab 3: Creating PowerPoint Presentations and Saving Them in Appropriate Folders

Problem: You are taking a class that requires you to complete three PowerPoint chapters. You will save the work completed in each chapter in a different folder (Figure 90).

Instructions: Create the folders shown in Figure 90. Then, using PowerPoint, create a small file to save in each folder.

1. Connect a USB flash drive to an available USB port and then open the USB flash drive window.
2. Create the folder structure shown in Figure 90.
3. Navigate to the Chapter 1 folder.
4. Create a PowerPoint presentation containing the text, My Chapter 1 PowerPoint Document, and then save it in the Chapter 1 PowerPoint folder using the file name, PowerPoint Chapter 1 Document.
5. Navigate to the Chapter 2 folder.
6. Create another PowerPoint presentation containing the text, My Chapter 2 PowerPoint Document, and then save it in the Chapter 2 folder using the file name, PowerPoint Chapter 2 Document.
7. Navigate to the Chapter 3 folder.
8. Create another PowerPoint presentation containing the text, My Chapter 3 PowerPoint Document, and then save it in the Chapter 3 folder using the file name, PowerPoint Chapter 3 Document.
9. Quit PowerPoint.
10. Submit the assignment in the format specified by your instructor.

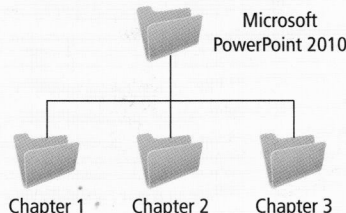

Figure 90

Cases and Places

Apply your creative thinking and problem solving skills to design and implement a solution.

Note: To complete these assignments, you may be required to use the Data Files for Students. See the inside back cover of this book for instructions on downloading the Data Files for Students, or contact your instructor for information about accessing the required files.

1: Creating Beginning Files for Classes

Academic

You are taking the following classes: Introduction to Engineering, Beginning Psychology, Introduction to Biology, and Accounting. Create folders for each of the classes. Use the following folder names: Engineering, Psychology, Biology, and Accounting, when creating the folder structure. In the Engineering folder, use PowerPoint to create a presentation with the name of the class and the class meeting location and time (MW 10:30 – 11:45, Room 317). In the Psychology folder, use PowerPoint to create your first lab presentation. It should begin with a title slide containing the text, Behavioral Observations. In the Biology folder, create another presentation with the title, Research. In the Accounting folder, create a PowerPoint presentation with the text, Tax Information. Use the concepts and techniques presented in this chapter to create the folders and files.

2: Using Help

Personal

Your parents enjoy working and playing games on their home computers. Your mother uses a notebook computer downstairs, and your father uses a desktop computer upstairs. They expressed interest in sharing files between their computers and sharing a single printer, so you offered to research various home networking options. Start Windows Help and Support, and search Help using the keywords, home networking. Use the link for installing a printer on a home network. Start PowerPoint and then create a presentation describing the main steps for installing a printer. Use the link for setting up a HomeGroup and then type the main steps for creating a HomeGroup in the PowerPoint presentation. Use the concepts and techniques presented in this chapter to use Help and create the PowerPoint presentation.

3: Creating Folders

Professional

Your boss at the bookstore where you work part-time has asked for help with organizing her files. After looking through the files, you decided upon a file structure for her to use, including the following folders: books, magazines, tapes, DVDs, and general merchandise. Within the books folder, create folders for hardback and paperback books. Within magazines, create folders for special issues and periodicals. In the tapes folder, create folders for celebrity and major release. In the DVDs folder, create a folder for book to DVD. In the general merchandise folder, create folders for novelties, posters, and games. Use the concepts and techniques presented in this chapter to create the folders.

1 Creating and Editing a Presentation with Clip Art

Objectives

You will have mastered the material in this chapter when you can:

- Select a document theme
- Create a title slide and a text slide with a multi-level bulleted list
- Add new slides and change slide layouts
- Insert clips and pictures into a slide with and without a content placeholder
- Move and size clip art

- Change font size and color
- Bold and italicize text
- Duplicate a slide
- Arrange slides
- Select slide transitions
- View a presentation in Slide Show view
- Print a presentation

1 | Creating and Editing a Presentation with Clip Art

Introduction

A PowerPoint **presentation,** also called a **slide show,** can help you deliver a dynamic, professional-looking message to an audience. PowerPoint allows you to produce slides to use in an academic, business, or other environment. One of the more common uses of these slides is to enhance an oral presentation. A speaker may desire to convey information, such as urging students to volunteer at a fund-raising event, explaining changes in employee compensation packages, or describing a new laboratory procedure. The PowerPoint slides should reinforce the speaker's message and help the audience retain the information presented. Custom slides can fit your specific needs and contain diagrams, charts, tables, pictures, shapes, video, sound, and animation effects to make your presentation more effective. An accompanying handout gives audience members reference notes and review material for your presentation.

Project Planning Guidelines

> The process of developing a presentation that communicates specific information requires careful analysis and planning. As a starting point, establish why the presentation is needed. Next, analyze the intended audience for the presentation and its unique needs. Then, gather information about the topic and decide what to include in the presentation. Finally, determine the presentation design and style that will be most successful at delivering the message. Details of these guidelines are provided in Appendix A. In addition, each project in this book provides practical applications of these planning considerations.

BTW

Energy-Saving Information
The U.S. Department of Energy's Web site has myriad information available on the topics of energy efficiency and renewable energy. These features can provide news and product research that you can share with audiences with the help of a PowerPoint presentation.

Project — Presentation with Bulleted Lists and Clip Art

In this chapter's project, you will follow proper design guidelines and learn to use PowerPoint to create, save, and print the slides shown in Figures 1–1a through 1–1e. The objective is to produce a presentation, called It Is Easy Being Green, to help consumers understand basic steps they can take to save energy in their homes. This slide show has a variety of clip art and visual elements to add interest and illustrate energy-cutting measures. Some of the text has formatting and color enhancements. Transitions help one slide flow gracefully into the next during a slide show. In addition, you will print a handout of your slides to distribute to audience members.

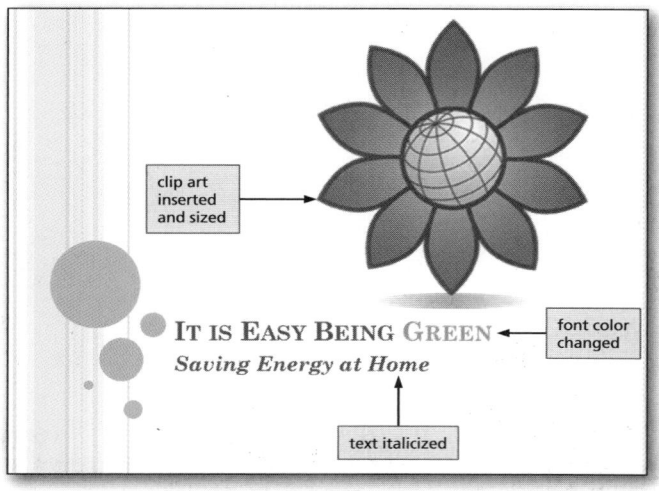

(a) Slide 1 (Title Slide with Clip Art)

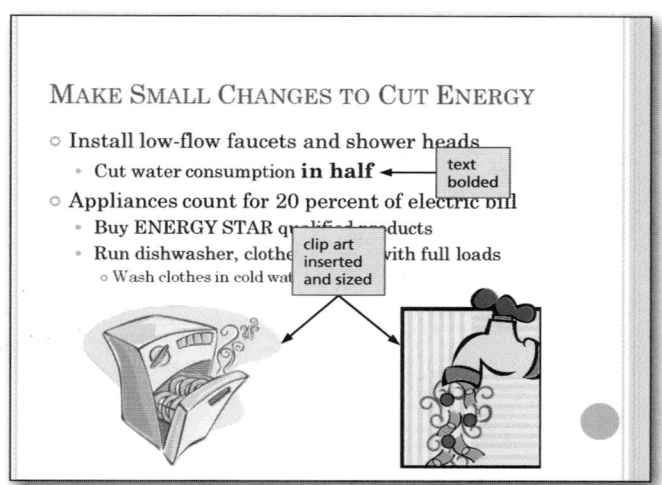

(b) Slide 2 (Multi-Level Bulleted List with Clip Art)

(c) Slide 3 (Title and Photograph)

(d) Slide 4 (Comparison Layout and Clip Art)

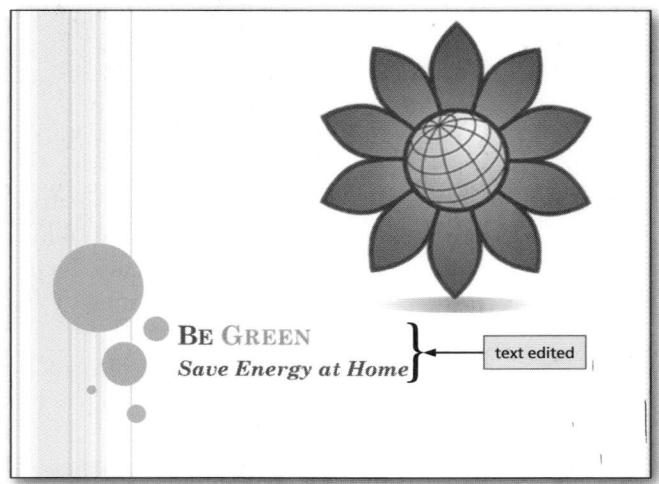

(e) Slide 5 (Closing Slide)

Figure 1–1

Overview

As you read this chapter, you will learn how to create the presentation shown in Figure 1–1 on the previous page by performing these general tasks:

- Select an appropriate document theme.
- Enter titles and text on slides.
- Change the size, color, and style of text.
- Insert clips and a photograph.
- Add a transition to each slide.
- View the presentation on your computer.
- Print your slides.

Plan
Ahead

> **General Project Guidelines**
> When creating a PowerPoint document, the actions you perform and decisions you make will affect the appearance and characteristics of the finished document. As you create a presentation such as the project shown in Figure 1–1, you should follow these general guidelines:
>
> 1. **Find the appropriate theme.** The overall appearance of a presentation significantly affects its capability to communicate information clearly. The slides' graphical appearance should support the presentation's overall message. Colors, fonts, and layouts affect how audience members perceive and react to the slide content.
>
> 2. **Choose words for each slide.** Use the less is more principle. The less text, the more likely the slides will enhance your speech. Use the fewest words possible to make a point.
>
> 3. **Format specific elements of the text.** Examples of how you can modify the appearance, or **format**, of text include changing its shape, size, color, and position on the slide.
>
> 4. **Determine where to save the presentation.** You can store a document permanently, or **save** it, on a variety of storage media, including a hard disk, USB flash drive, or CD. You also can indicate a specific location on the storage media for saving the document.
>
> 5. **Determine the best method for distributing the presentation.** Presentations can be distributed on paper or electronically. You can print a hard copy of the presentation slides for proofing or reference, or you can distribute an electronic image in various formats.
>
> When necessary, more specific details concerning the above guidelines are presented at appropriate points in the chapter. The chapter also will identify the actions performed and decisions made regarding these guidelines during the creation of the slides shown in Figure 1–1.

To Start PowerPoint

If you are using a computer to step through the project in this chapter and you want your screens to match the figures in this book, you should change your screen's resolution to 1024 × 768. For information about how to change a computer's resolution, refer to the Office 2010 and Windows 7 chapter at the beginning of this book.

The following steps, which assume Windows 7 is running, start PowerPoint based on a typical installation. You may need to ask your instructor how to start PowerPoint for your computer. For a detailed example of the procedure summarized below, refer to the Office 2010 and Windows 7 chapter.

1 Click the Start button on the Windows 7 taskbar to display the Start menu.

2 Type `Microsoft PowerPoint` as the search text in the 'Search programs and files' text box and watch the search results appear on the Start menu.

3 Click Microsoft PowerPoint 2010 in the search results on the Start menu to start PowerPoint and display a new blank document in the PowerPoint window.

4 If the PowerPoint window is not maximized, click the Maximize button next to the Close button on its title bar to maximize the window.

Choosing a Document Theme

You can give a presentation a professional and integrated appearance easily by using a document theme. A **document theme** provides consistency in design and color throughout the entire presentation by setting the color scheme, font set, and layout of a presentation. This collection of formatting choices includes a set of colors (the Theme Colors group), a set of heading and content text fonts (the Theme Fonts group), and a set of lines and fill effects (the Theme Effects group). These groups allow you to choose and change the appearance of all the slides or individual slides in your presentation. The left edge of the status bar in Figure 1–2 shows the current slide number followed by the total number of slides in the document and a document theme identifier.

Plan Ahead

Find the appropriate theme.
In the initial steps of this project, you will select a document theme by locating a particular built-in theme in the Themes group. You could, however, apply a theme at any time while creating the presentation. Some PowerPoint slide show designers create presentations using the default Office Theme. This blank design allows them to concentrate on the words being used to convey the message and does not distract them with colors and various text attributes. Once the text is entered, the designers then select an appropriate document theme.

To Choose a Document Theme

The document theme identifier shows the theme currently used in the slide show. PowerPoint initially uses the **Office Theme** until you select a different theme. The following steps change the theme for this presentation from the Office Theme to the Oriel document theme.

1

• Click Design on the Ribbon to display the Design tab (Figure 1–2).

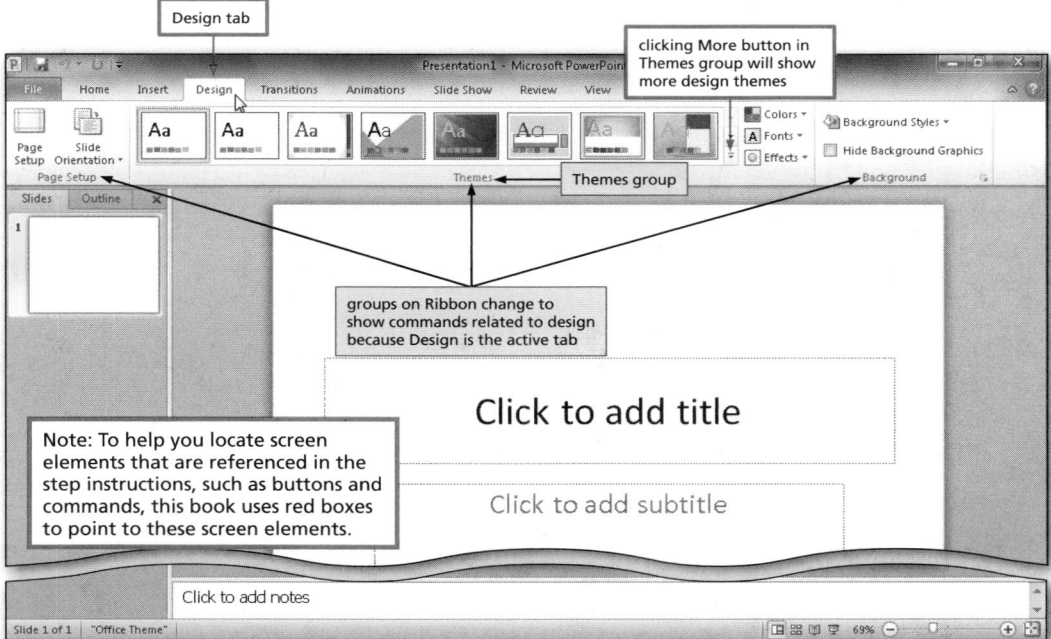

Figure 1–2

2

- Click the More button (Design tab | Themes group) to expand the gallery, which shows more Built-In theme gallery options (Figure 1–3).

Experiment

- Point to various document themes in the Themes gallery and watch the colors and fonts change on the title slide.

Q&A Are the themes displayed in a specific order?

Yes. They are arranged in alphabetical order running from left to right. If you point to a theme, a ScreenTip with the theme's name appears on the screen.

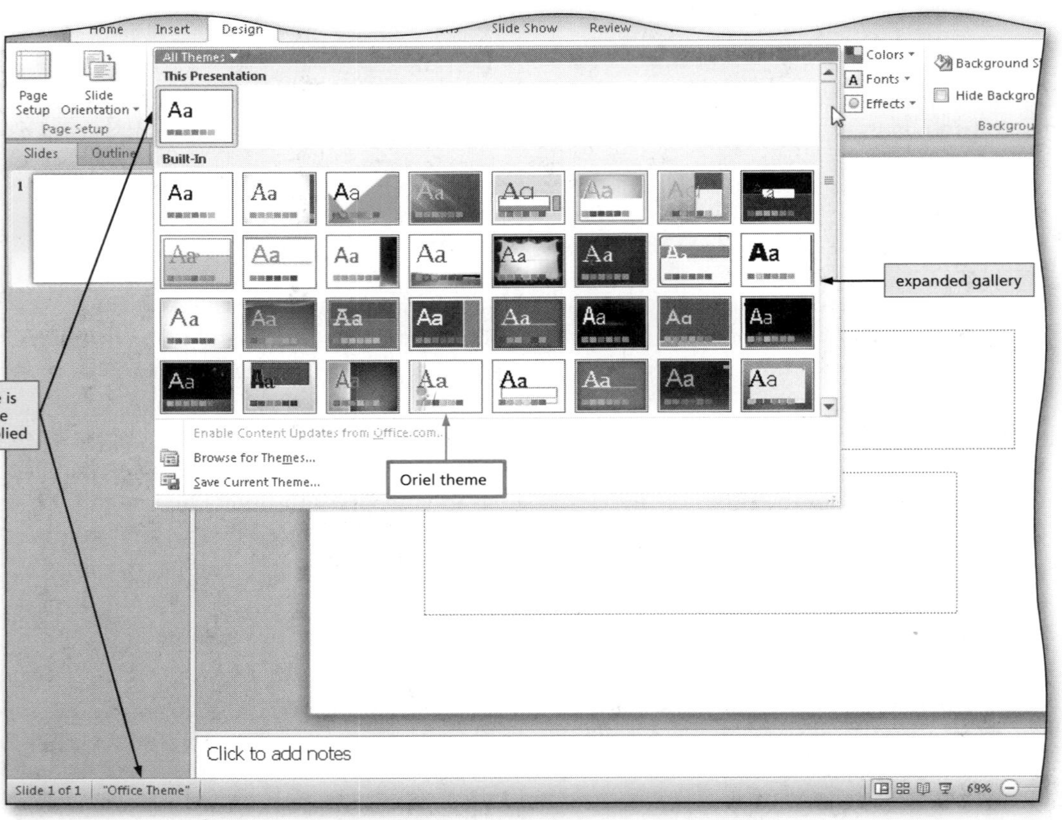

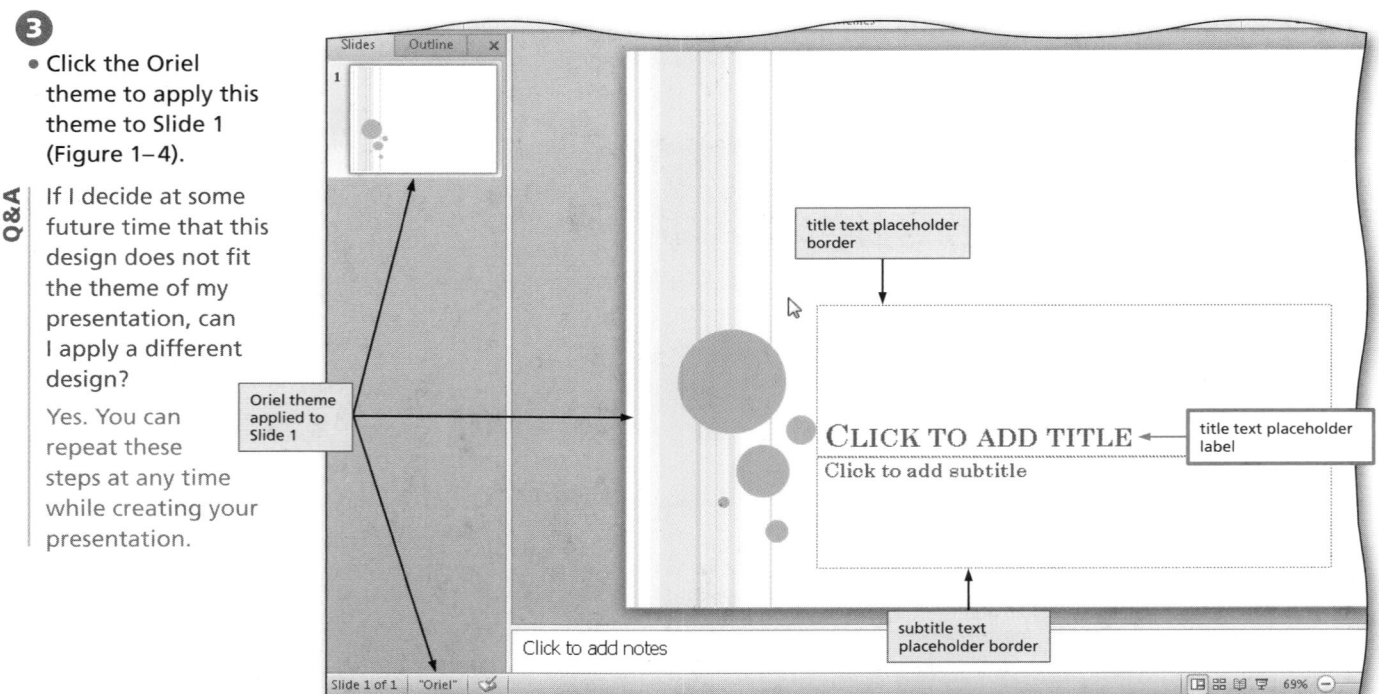

Figure 1–3

Q&A What if I change my mind and do not want to select a new theme?

Click anywhere outside the All Themes gallery to close the gallery.

3

- Click the Oriel theme to apply this theme to Slide 1 (Figure 1–4).

Q&A If I decide at some future time that this design does not fit the theme of my presentation, can I apply a different design?

Yes. You can repeat these steps at any time while creating your presentation.

Figure 1–4

Creating a Title Slide

When you open a new presentation, the default **Title Slide** layout appears. The purpose of this layout is to introduce the presentation to the audience. PowerPoint includes eight other built-in standard layouts. The default (preset) slide layouts are set up in **landscape orientation**, where the slide width is greater than its height. In landscape orientation, the slide size is preset to 10 inches wide and 7.5 inches high when printed on a standard sheet of paper measuring 11 inches wide and 8.5 inches high.

Placeholders are boxes with dotted or hatch-marked borders that are displayed when you create a new slide. Most layouts have both a title text placeholder and at least one content placeholder. Depending on the particular slide layout selected, title and sub-title placeholders are displayed for the slide title and subtitle; a content text placeholder is displayed for text, art, or a table, chart, picture, graphic, or movie. The title slide has two text placeholders where you can type the main heading, or title, of a new slide and the subtitle.

With the exception of a blank slide, PowerPoint assumes every new slide has a title. To make creating a presentation easier, any text you type after a new slide appears becomes title text in the title text placeholder. The following steps create the title slide for this presentation.

Plan Ahead

Choose the words for the slide.
No doubt you have heard the phrase, "You get only one chance to make a first impression." The same philosophy holds true for a PowerPoint presentation. The title slide gives your audience an initial sense of what they are about to see and hear. It is, therefore, extremely important to choose the text for this slide carefully. Avoid stating the obvious in the title. Instead, create interest and curiosity using key ideas from the presentation.

Some PowerPoint users create the title slide as their last step in the design process so that it reflects the tone of the presentation. They begin by planning the final slide in the presentation so that they know where and how they want to end the slide show. All the slides in the presentation should work toward meeting this final slide.

To Enter the Presentation Title

The presentation title for Project 1 is It Is Easy Being Green. This title creates interest by introducing the concept of simple energy conservation tasks. The following step creates the slide show's title.

- Click the label, Click to add title, located inside the title text placeholder to select the placeholder (Figure 1–5).

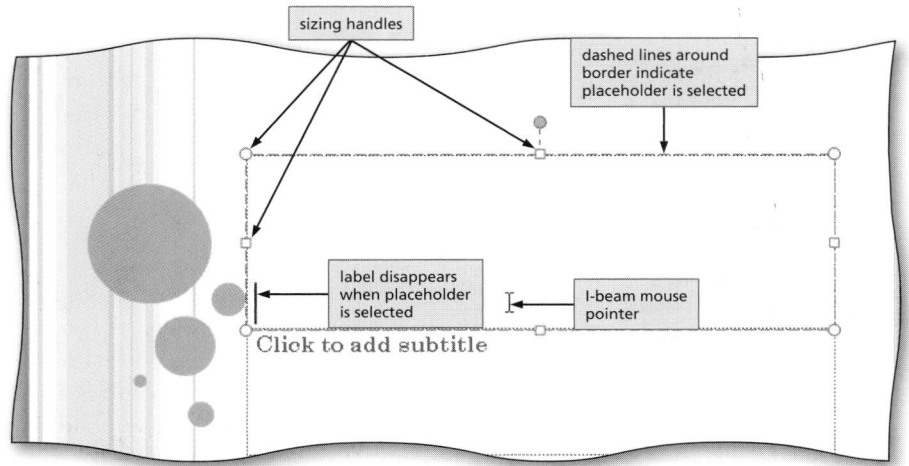

Figure 1–5

2

- Type **It Is Easy Being Green** in the title text placeholder. Do not press the ENTER key (Figure 1–6).

Q&A

Why does the text display with capital letters despite the fact I am typing uppercase and lowercase letters?

The Oriel theme uses the Small Caps effect for the title text. This effect converts lowercase letters to uppercase and reduces their size.

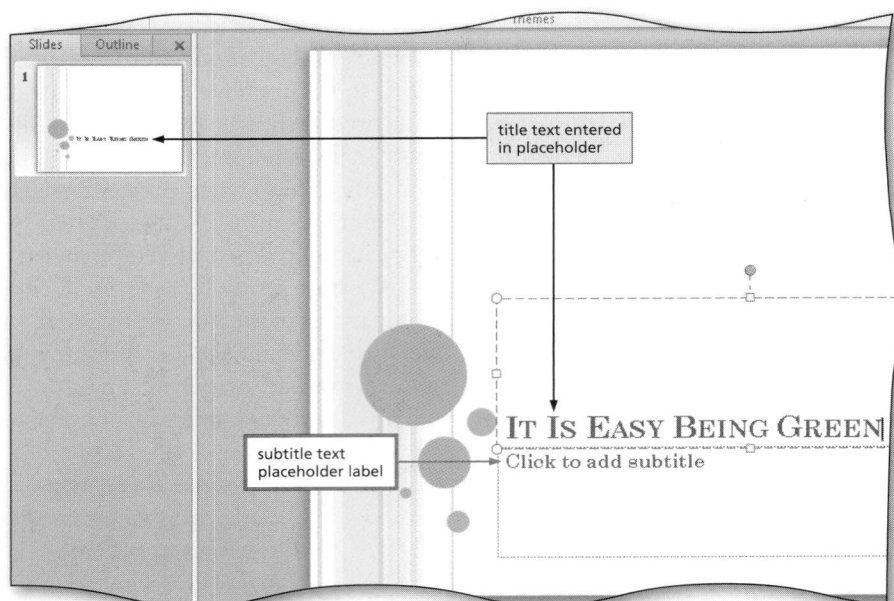

Figure 1–6

Correcting a Mistake When Typing

If you type the wrong letter, press the BACKSPACE key to erase all the characters back to and including the one that is incorrect. If you mistakenly press the ENTER key after typing the title and the insertion point is on the new line, simply press the BACKSPACE key to return the insertion point to the right of the letter n in the word, Green.

When you install PowerPoint, the default setting allows you to reverse up to the last 20 changes by clicking the Undo button on the Quick Access Toolbar. The ScreenTip that appears when you point to the Undo button changes to indicate the type of change just made. For example, if you type text in the title text placeholder and then point to the Undo button, the ScreenTip that appears is Undo Typing. For clarity, when referencing the Undo button in this project, the name displaying in the ScreenTip is referenced. You can reapply a change that you reversed with the Undo button by clicking the Redo button on the Quick Access Toolbar. Clicking the Redo button reverses the last undo action. The ScreenTip name reflects the type of reversal last performed.

Paragraphs

For an introduction to Office 2010 and instruction about how to perform basic tasks in Office 2010 programs, read the Office 2010 and Windows 7 chapter at the beginning of this book, where you can learn how to start a program, use the Ribbon, save a file, open a file, quit a program, use Help, and much more.

Text in the subtitle text placeholder supports the title text. It can appear on one or more lines in the placeholder. To create more than one subtitle line, you press the ENTER key after typing some words. PowerPoint creates a new line, which is the second paragraph in the placeholder. A **paragraph** is a segment of text with the same format that begins when you press the ENTER key and ends when you press the ENTER key again. This new paragraph is the same level as the previous paragraph. A **level** is a position within a structure, such as an outline, that indicates the magnitude of importance. PowerPoint allows for five paragraph levels.

To Enter the Presentation Subtitle Paragraph

The first subtitle paragraph links to the title by giving further detail that the presentation will focus on energy-saving measures at home. The following steps enter the presentation subtitle.

1

• Click the label, Click to add subtitle, located inside the subtitle text placeholder to select the placeholder (Figure 1–7).

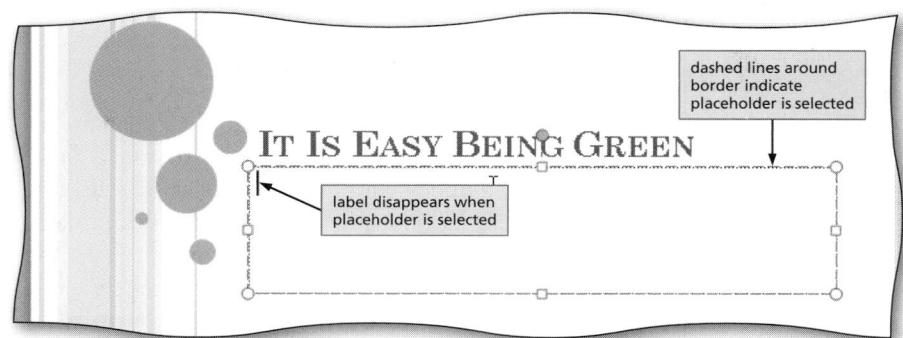

Figure 1–7

2

• Type `Saving Energy at Home` but do not press the ENTER key (Figure 1–8).

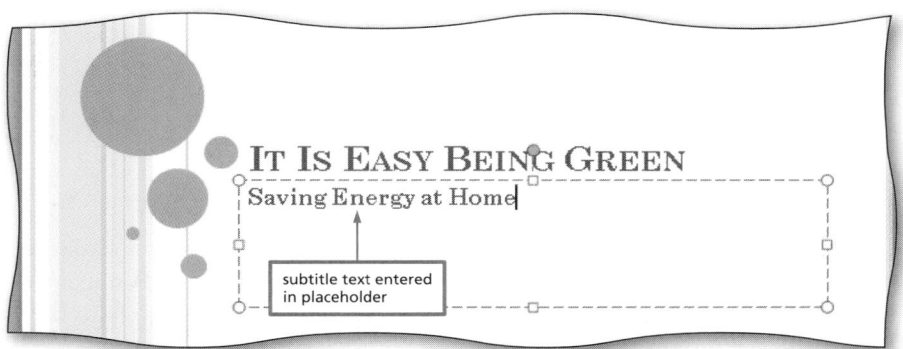

Figure 1–8

Identify how to format specific elements of the text.

Plan Ahead

Most of the time, you use the document theme's text attributes, color scheme, and layout. Occasionally, you may want to change the way a presentation looks, however, and still keep a particular document theme. PowerPoint gives you that flexibility.

Graphic designers use several rules when formatting text.

• Avoid all capital letters, if possible. Audiences have difficulty comprehending sentences typed in all capital letters, especially when the lines exceed seven words. All capital letters leaves no room for emphasis or inflection, so readers get confused about what material deserves particular attention. Some document themes, however, have a default title text style of all capital letters.

• Avoid text with a font size less than 30 point. Audience members generally will sit a maximum of 50 feet from a screen, and at this distance 30-point type is the smallest size text they can read comfortably without straining.

• Make careful color choices. Color evokes emotions, and a careless color choice may elicit the incorrect psychological response. PowerPoint provides a color gallery with hundreds of colors. The built-in document themes use complementary colors that work well together. If you stray from these themes and add your own color choices, without a good reason to make the changes, your presentation is apt to become ineffective.

Formatting Characters in a Presentation

Recall that each document theme determines the color scheme, font set, and layout of a presentation. You can use a specific document theme and then change the characters' formats any time before, during, or after you type the text.

BTW

Q&As
For a complete list of the Q&As found in many of the step-by-step sequences in this book, visit the PowerPoint 2010 Q&A Web page (scsite.com/ppt2010/qa).

Fonts and Font Styles

Characters that appear on the screen are a specific shape and size. Examples of how you can modify the appearance, or **format**, of these typed characters on the screen and in print include changing the font, style, size, and color. The **font**, or typeface, defines the appearance and shape of the letters, numbers, punctuation marks, and symbols. **Style** indicates how the characters are formatted. PowerPoint's text font styles include regular, italic, bold, and bold italic. **Size** specifies the height of the characters and is gauged by a measurement system that uses points. A **point** is 1/72 of an inch in height. Thus, a character with a font size of 36 is 36/72 (or 1/2) of an inch in height. **Color** defines the hue of the characters.

This presentation uses the Oriel document theme, which uses particular font styles and font sizes. The Oriel document theme default title text font is named Century Schoolbook. It has a bold style with no special effects, and its size is 30 point. The Oriel document theme default subtitle text font also is Century Schoolbook with a font size of 18 point.

To Select a Paragraph

You can use many techniques to format characters. When you want to apply the same formats to multiple words or paragraphs, it is efficient to select the desired text and then make the desired changes to all the characters simultaneously. The first formatting change you will make will apply to the title slide subtitle. The following step selects this paragraph.

• Triple-click the paragraph, Saving Energy at Home, in the subtitle text placeholder to select the paragraph (Figure 1–9).

Q&A
Can I select the paragraph using a technique other than triple-clicking?

Yes. You can move your mouse pointer to the left of the first paragraph and then drag to the end of the line.

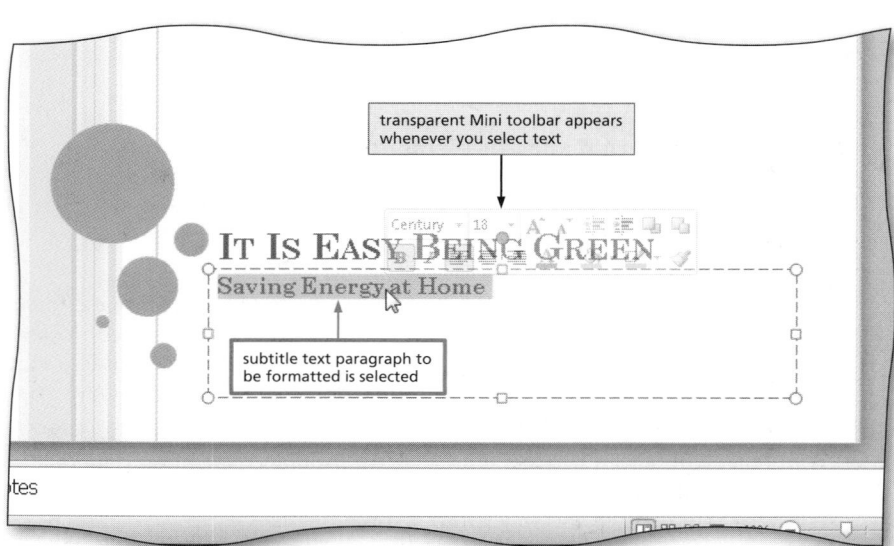

transparent Mini toolbar appears whenever you select text

IT IS EASY BEING GREEN

Saving Energy at Home

subtitle text paragraph to be formatted is selected

Figure 1–9

To Italicize Text

Different font styles often are used on slides to make them more appealing to the reader and to emphasize particular text. **Italicized** text has a slanted appearance. Used sparingly, it draws the readers' eyes to these characters. The following step adds emphasis to the second line of the subtitle text by changing regular text to italic text.

- With the subtitle text still selected, click the Italic button on the Mini toolbar to italicize that text on the slide (Figure 1–10).

Q&A If I change my mind and decide not to italicize the text, how can I remove this style?

Click the Italic button a second time or immediately click the Undo button on the Quick Access Toolbar or press CTRL+Z.

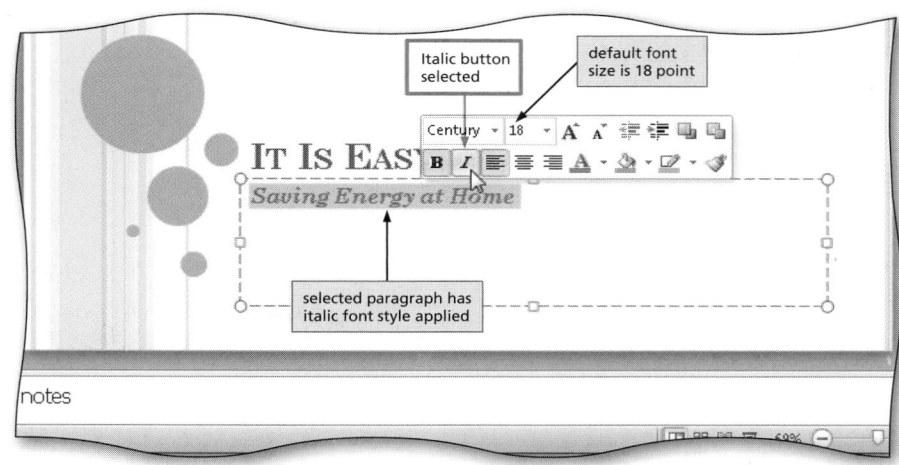

Figure 1–10

Other Ways
1. Right-click selected text, click Font on shortcut menu, click Font tab (Font dialog box), click Italic in Font style list, click OK button   2. Select text, click Italic button (Home tab | Font group)   3. Click Font Dialog Box Launcher (Home tab | Font group), click Font tab (Font dialog box), click Italic in Font style list, click OK button   4. Select text, press CTRL+I

To Increase Font Size

To add emphasis, you increase the font size for the subtitle text. The Increase Font Size button on the Mini toolbar increases the font size in preset increments. The following step uses this button to increase the font size.

1

- Click the Increase Font Size button on the Mini toolbar twice to increase the font size of the selected text from 18 to 24 point (Figure 1–11).

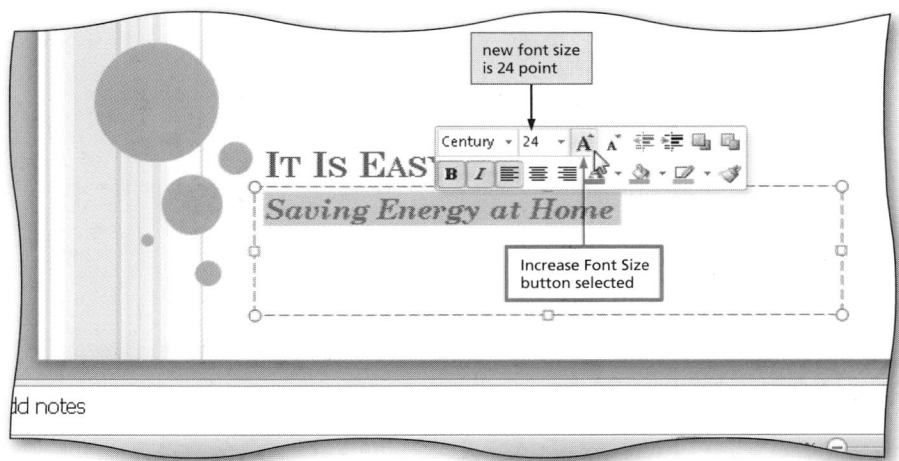

Figure 1–11

Other Ways
1. Click Font Size box arrow on Mini toolbar, click desired font size in Font Size gallery   2. Click Increase Font Size button (Home tab | Font group)   3. Click Font Size box arrow (Home tab | Font group), click desired font size in Font size gallery   4. Press CTRL+SHIFT+>

To Select a Word

PowerPoint designers use many techniques to emphasize words and characters on a slide. To add emphasis to the energy-saving concept of your slide show, you want to increase the font size and change the font color to green for the word, Green, in the title text. You could perform these actions separately, but it is more efficient to select the word and then change the font attributes. The following steps select a word.

- Position the mouse pointer somewhere in the word to be selected (in this case, in the word, Green) (Figure 1–12).

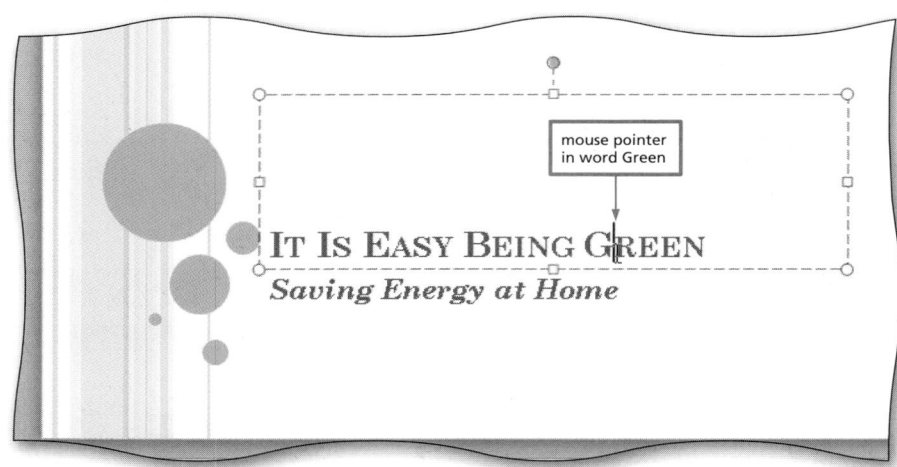

Figure 1–12

- Double-click the word to select it (Figure 1–13).

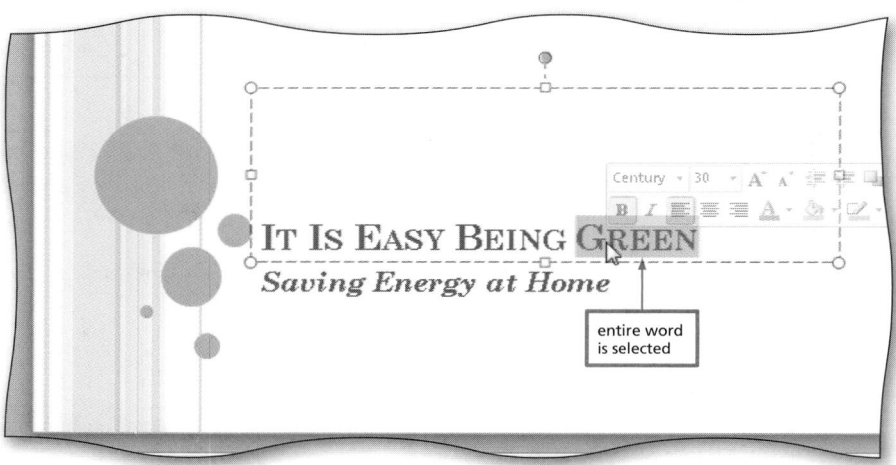

Figure 1–13

Other Ways

1. Position mouse pointer before first character, press CTRL+SHIFT+RIGHT ARROW

Plan Ahead

Format text colors.
When selecting text colors, try to limit using red. This color often is associated with dangerous or alarming situations. In addition, at least 15 percent of men have difficulty distinguishing varying shades of green or red. They also often see the color purple as blue and the color brown as green. This problem is more pronounced when the colors appear in small areas, such as slide paragraphs or line chart bars.

To Change the Text Color

PowerPoint allows you to use one or more text colors in a presentation. To add more emphasis to the word, Green, in the title slide text, you decide to change the color. The following steps add emphasis to this word by changing the font color from black to green.

- With the word, Green, selected, click the Font Color arrow on the Mini toolbar to display the gallery of Theme Colors and Standard Colors (Figure 1–14).

Q&A If the Mini toolbar disappears from the screen, how can I display it once again?

Right-click the text, and the Mini toolbar should appear.

Experiment

- Point to various colors in the gallery and watch the word's font color change.

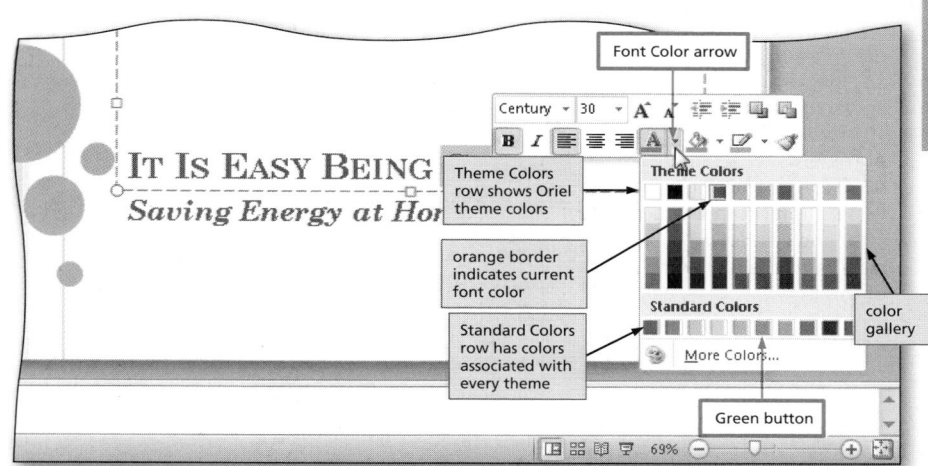

Figure 1–14

- Click the Green button in the Standard Colors row on the Mini toolbar (sixth color) to change the font color to green (Figure 1–15).

Q&A Why did I select the color Green?

Green is one of the 10 standard colors associated with every document theme, and it is a universal color to represent respecting natural resources. The color will emphasize the fact that the presentation focuses on green conservation measures.

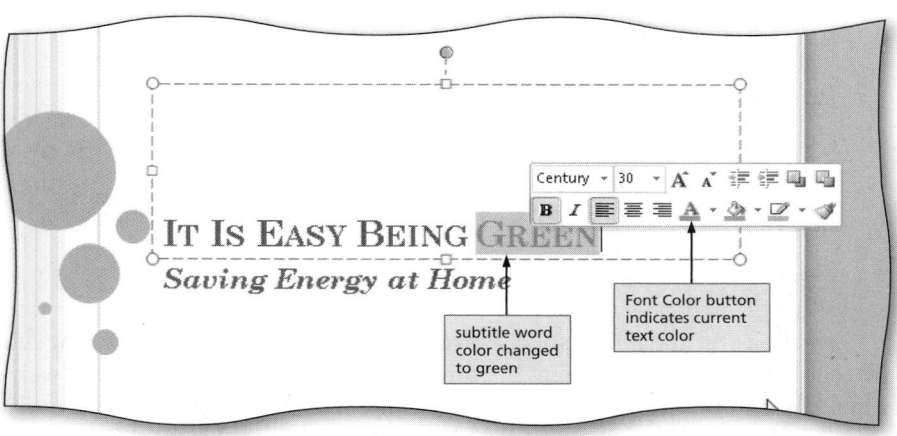

Figure 1–15

Q&A What is the difference between the colors shown in the Theme Colors area and the Standard Colors?

The 10 colors in the top row of the Theme Colors area are two text, two background, and six accent colors in the Oriel theme; the five colors in each column under the top row display different transparencies. These colors are available in every document theme.

- Click outside the selected area to deselect the word.

Other Ways

1. Right-click selected text, click Font on shortcut menu, click Font Color button, click Green in Standard Colors row
2. Click Font Color arrow (Home tab | Font group), click Green in Standard Colors row

BTW

Organizing Files and Folders
You should organize and store files in folders so that you easily can find the files later. For example, if you are taking an introductory computer class called CIS 101, a good practice would be to save all PowerPoint files in a PowerPoint folder in a CIS 101 folder. For a discussion of folders and detailed examples of creating folders, refer to the Office 2010 and Windows 7 chapter at the beginning of this book.

To Save a Presentation

You have performed many tasks while creating this slide and do not want to risk losing work completed thus far. Accordingly, you should save the document.

The following steps assume you already have created folders for storing your files, for example, a CIS 101 folder (for your class) that contains a PowerPoint folder (for your assignments). Thus, these steps save the document in the PowerPoint folder in the CIS 101 folder on a USB flash drive using the file name, Saving Energy. For a detailed example of the procedure summarized below, refer to the Office 2010 and Windows 7 chapter at the beginning of this book.

1 With a USB flash drive connected to one of the computer's USB ports, click the Save button on the Quick Access Toolbar to display the Save As dialog box.

2 Type **Saving Energy** in the File name text box to change the file name. Do not press the ENTER key after typing the file name because you do not want to close the dialog box at this time.

3 Navigate to the desired save location (in this case, the PowerPoint folder in the CIS 101 folder [or your class folder] on the USB flash drive).

4 Click the Save button (Save As dialog box) to save the document in the selected folder on the selected drive with the entered file name.

Adding a New Slide to a Presentation

With the text for the title slide for the presentation created, the next step is to add the first text slide immediately after the title slide. Usually, when you create a presentation, you add slides with text, clip art, graphics, or charts. Some placeholders allow you to double-click the placeholder and then access other objects, such as media clips, charts, diagrams, and organization charts. You can change the layout for a slide at any time during the creation of a presentation.

To Add a New Text Slide with a Bulleted List

When you add a new slide, PowerPoint uses the Title and Content slide layout. This layout provides a title placeholder and a content area for text, art, charts, and other graphics. A vertical scroll bar appears in the Slide pane when you add the second slide so that you can move from slide to slide easily. A thumbnail of this slide also appears in the Slides tab. The following steps add a new slide with the Title and Content slide layout.

1

- Click Home on the Ribbon to display the Home tab (Figure 1–16).

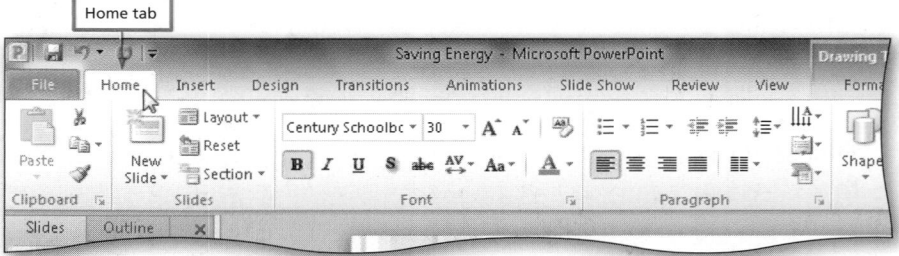

Figure 1–16

2

- Click the New Slide button (Home tab | Slides group) to insert a new slide with the Title and Content layout (Figure 1–17).

Q&A Why does the bullet character display an orange circle?

The Oriel document theme determines the bullet characters. Each paragraph level has an associated bullet character.

Q&A I clicked the New Slide arrow instead of the New Slide button. What should I do?

Click the Title and Content slide thumbnail in the layout gallery.

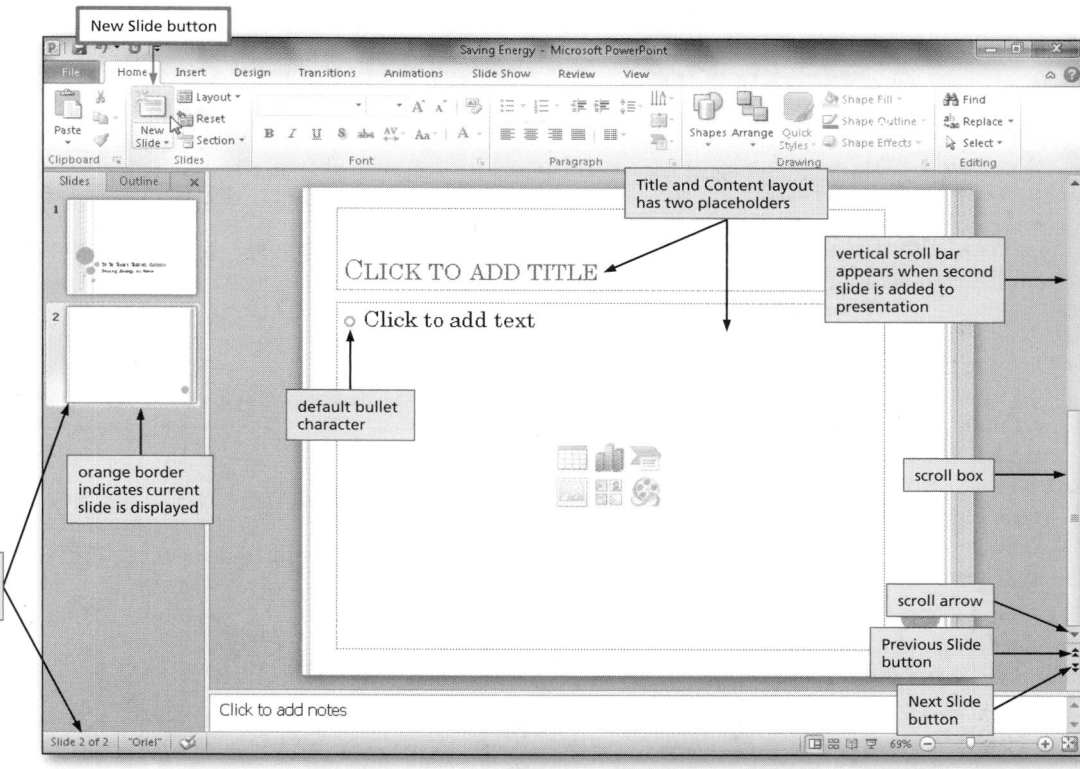

Figure 1–17

Other Ways

1. Press CTRL+M

Choose the words for the slide.
All presentations should follow the 7 × 7 rule, which states that each slide should have a maximum of seven lines, and each line should have a maximum of seven words. PowerPoint designers must choose their words carefully and, in turn, help viewers read the slides easily.

Avoid line wraps. Your audience's eyes want to stop at the end of a line. Thus, you must plan your words carefully or adjust the font size so that each point displays on only one line.

Plan Ahead

Creating a Text Slide with a Multi-Level Bulleted List

The information in the Slide 2 text placeholder is presented in a bulleted list with three levels. A **bulleted list** is a list of paragraphs, each of which is preceded by a bullet. A slide that consists of more than one level of bulleted text is called a **multi-level bulleted list slide**. In a multi-level bulleted list, a lower-level paragraph is a subset of a higher-level paragraph. It usually contains information that supports the topic in the paragraph immediately above it.

Two of the Slide 2 bullets appear at the same paragraph level, called the first level: Install low-flow faucets and shower heads, and Appliances count for 20 percent of electric bill. Beginning with the second level, each paragraph indents to the right of the preceding level and is pushed down to a lower level. For example, if you increase the indent of a first-level paragraph, it becomes a second-level paragraph. The second, fourth, and fifth paragraphs on Slide 2 are second-level paragraphs. The last paragraph, Wash clothes in cold water, is a third-level paragraph.

BTW

The Ribbon and Screen Resolution
PowerPoint may change how the groups and buttons within the groups appear on the Ribbon, depending on the computer's screen resolution. Thus, your Ribbon may look different from the ones in this book if you are using a screen resolution other than 1024 x 768.

Creating a text slide with a multi-level bulleted list requires several steps. Initially, you enter a slide title in the title text placeholder. Next, you select the content text placeholder. Then, you type the text for the multi-level bulleted list, increasing and decreasing the indents as needed. The next several sections add a slide with a multi-level bulleted list.

To Enter a Slide Title

PowerPoint assumes every new slide has a title. The title for Slide 2 is Make Small Changes to Cut Energy. The following step enters this title.

- Click the label, Click to add title, to select it and then type **Make Small Changes to Cut Energy** in the placeholder. Do not press the ENTER key (Figure 1–18).

Q&A

What are those six icons grouped in the middle of the slide?

You can click one of the icons to insert a specific type of content: table, chart, SmartArt graphic, picture, clip art, or media clip.

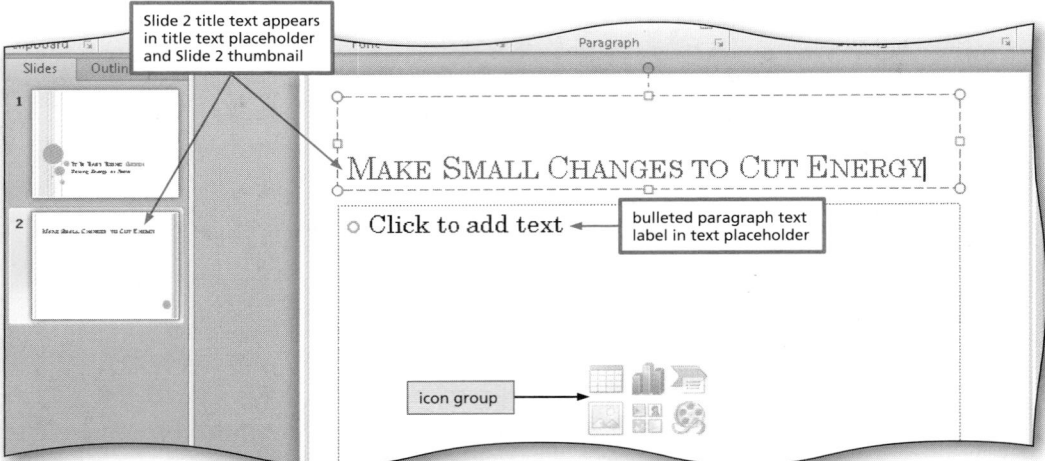

Figure 1–18

To Select a Text Placeholder

Before you can type text into the text placeholder, you first must select it. The following step selects the text placeholder on Slide 2.

- Click the label, Click to add text, to select the text placeholder (Figure 1–19).

Q&A

Why does my mouse pointer have a different shape?

If you move the mouse pointer away from the bullet, it will change shape.

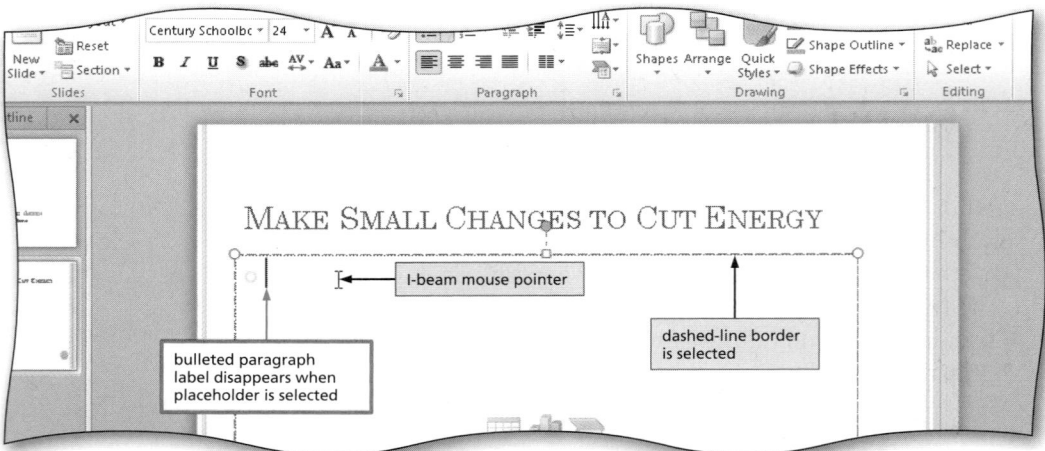

Figure 1–19

Other Ways

1. Press CTRL+ENTER

To Type a Multi-Level Bulleted List

The content placeholder provides an area for the text characters. When you click inside a placeholder, you then can type or paste text. As discussed previously, a bulleted list is a list of paragraphs, each of which is preceded by a bullet. A paragraph is a segment of text ended by pressing the ENTER key.

The content text placeholder is selected, so the next step is to type the multi-level bulleted list that consists of six paragraphs, as shown in Figure 1–1b on page PPT 3. Creating a lower-level paragraph is called **demoting** text; creating a higher-level paragraph is called **promoting** text. The following steps create a multi-level bulleted list consisting of three levels.

1
- Type `Install low-flow faucets and shower heads` and then press the ENTER key (Figure 1–20).

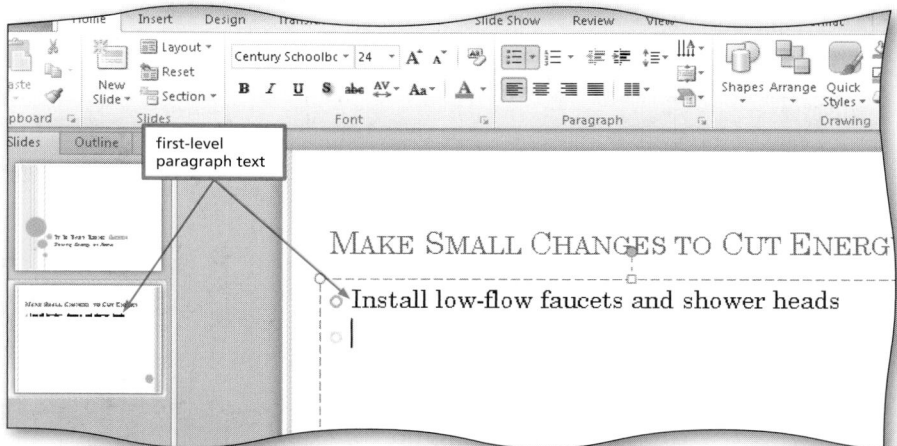

Figure 1–20

2
- Click the Increase List Level button (Home tab | Paragraph group) to indent the second paragraph below the first and create a second-level paragraph (Figure 1–21).

Q&A Why does the bullet for this paragraph have a different size and color?

A different bullet is assigned to each paragraph level.

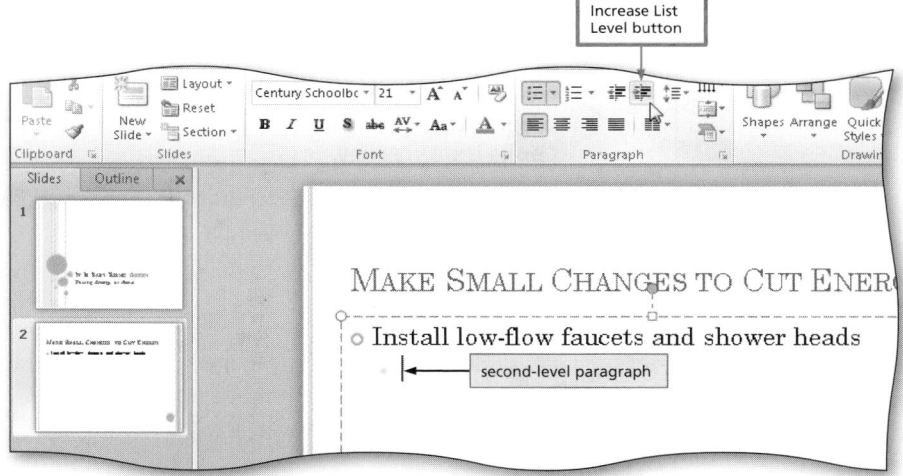

Figure 1–21

3
- Type `Cut water consumption in half` and then press the ENTER key (Figure 1–22).

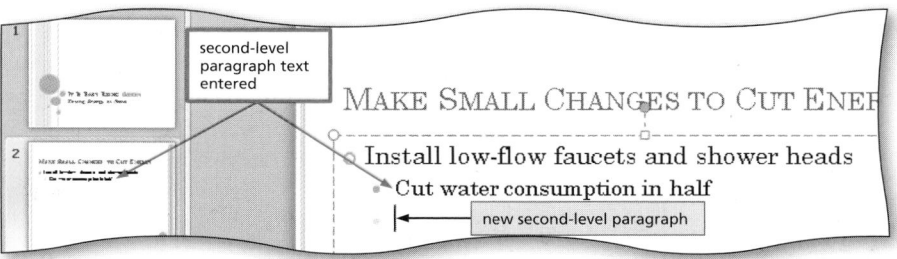

Figure 1–22

4

- Click the Decrease List Level button (Home tab | Paragraph group) so that the second-level paragraph becomes a first-level paragraph (Figure 1–23).

Q&A Can I delete bullets on a slide?

Yes. If you do not want bullets to display in a particular paragraph, click the Bullets button (Home tab | Paragraph group) or right-click the paragraph and then click the Bullets button on the shortcut menu.

Other Ways

1. Press TAB to promote paragraph; press SHIFT+TAB to demote paragraph

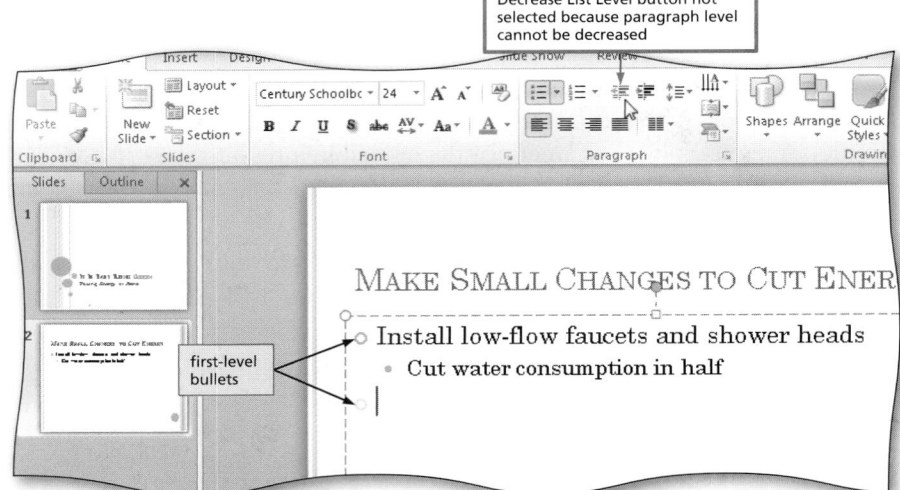

Decrease List Level button not selected because paragraph level cannot be decreased

first-level bullets

MAKE SMALL CHANGES TO CUT ENER

- Install low-flow faucets and shower heads
  - Cut water consumption in half

Figure 1–23

To Type the Remaining Text for Slide 2

The following steps complete the text for Slide 2.

1 Type `Appliances count for 20 percent of electric bill` and then press the ENTER key.

2 Click the Increase List Level button (Home tab | Paragraph group) to demote the paragraph to the second level.

3 Type `Buy ENERGY STAR qualified products` and then press the ENTER key to add a new paragraph at the same level as the previous paragraph.

4 Type `Run dishwasher, clothes washer with full loads` and then press the ENTER key.

5 Click the Increase List Level button (Home tab | Paragraph group) to demote the paragraph to the third level.

6 Type `Wash clothes in cold water` but do not press the ENTER key (Figure 1–24).

Q&A I pressed the ENTER key in error, and now a new bullet appears after the last entry on this slide. How can I remove this extra bullet?

Press the BACKSPACE key twice.

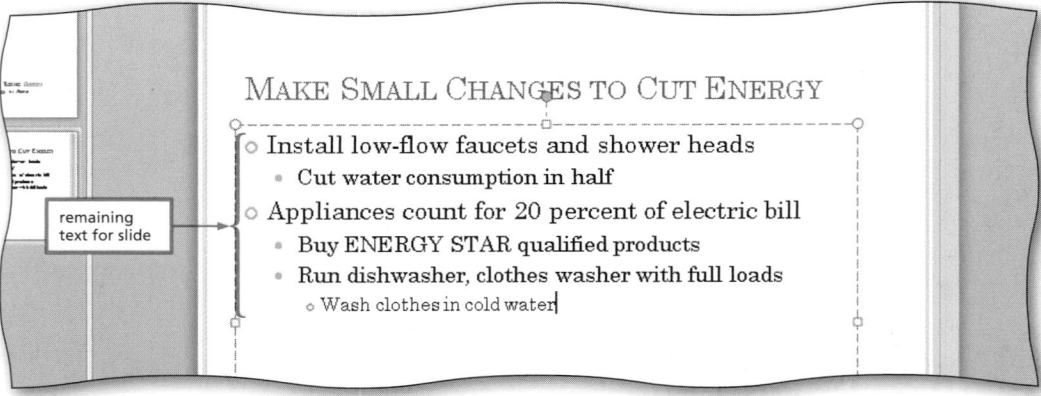

remaining text for slide

MAKE SMALL CHANGES TO CUT ENERGY

- Install low-flow faucets and shower heads
  - Cut water consumption in half
- Appliances count for 20 percent of electric bill
  - Buy ENERGY STAR qualified products
  - Run dishwasher, clothes washer with full loads
    - Wash clothes in cold water

Figure 1–24

To Select a Group of Words

PowerPoint designers use many techniques to emphasize words and characters on a slide. To add emphasis to your slide show's concept of saving natural resources, you want to bold and increase the font size of the words, in half, in the body text. You could perform these actions separately, but it is more efficient to select the words and then change the font attributes. The following steps select two words.

- Position the mouse pointer immediately to the left of the first character of the text to be selected (in this case, the i in the word, in) (Figure 1–25).

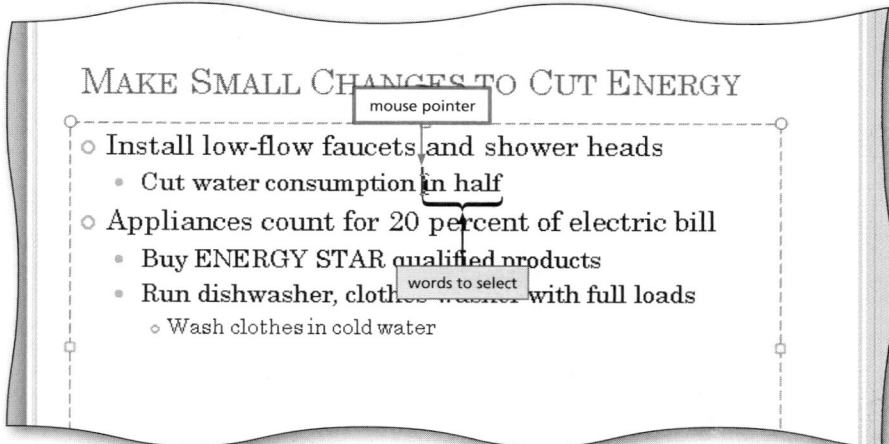

Figure 1–25

- Drag the mouse pointer through the last character of the text to be selected (in this case, the f in half) (Figure 1–26).

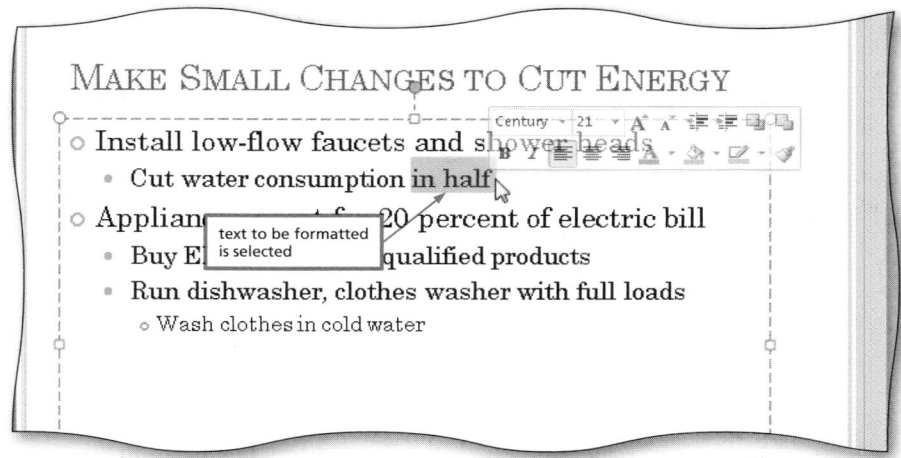

Figure 1–26

Other Ways
1. Press CTRL+SHIFT+RIGHT ARROW

To Bold Text

Bold characters display somewhat thicker and darker than those that display in a regular font style. Clicking the Bold button on the Mini toolbar is an efficient method of bolding text. To add more emphasis to the amount of water savings that can occur by installing low-flow faucets and shower heads, you want to bold the words, in half. The following step bolds this text.

1

• With the words, in half, selected, click the Bold button on the Mini toolbar to bold the two words (Figure 1–27).

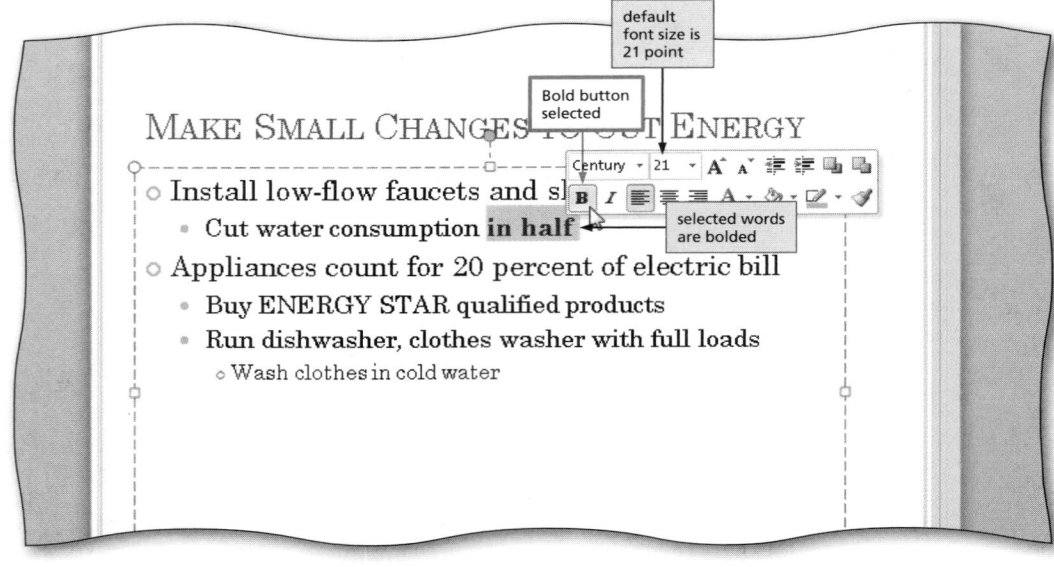

Figure 1–27

Other Ways
1. Click Bold button (Home tab | Font group)
2. Press CTRL+B

Formatting Words
To format one word, position the insertion point anywhere in the word. Then make the formatting changes you desire. The entire word does not need to be selected for the change to occur.

To Increase Font Size

To add emphasis, you increase the font size for the words, in half. The following step increases the font size from 21 to 24 point.

1 With the words, in half, still selected, click the Increase Font Size button on the Mini toolbar once (Figure 1–28).

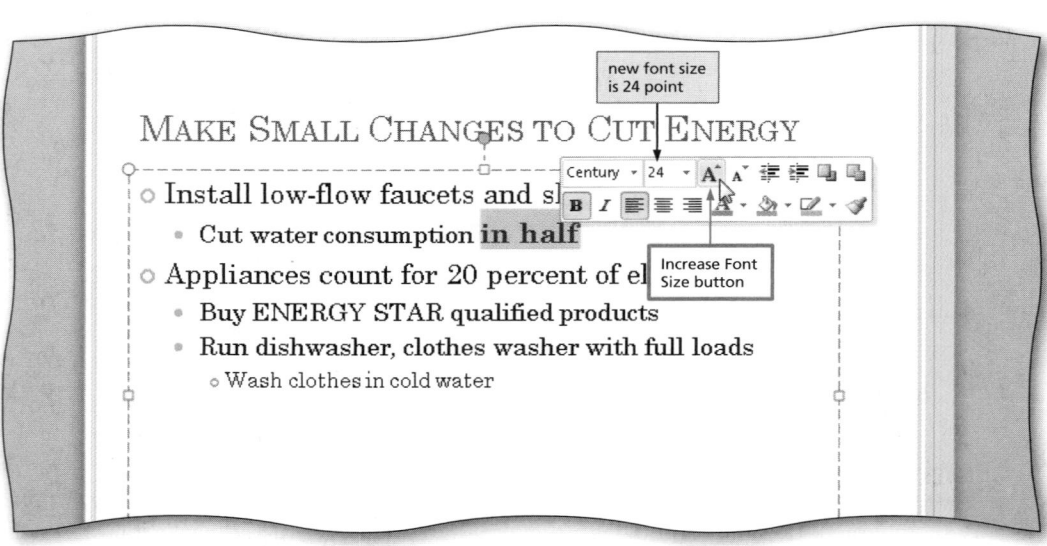

Figure 1–28

Adding New Slides and Changing the Slide Layouts

Slide 3 in Figure 1–1c on page PPT 3 contains a photograph and does not contain a bulleted list. When you add a new slide, PowerPoint applies the Title and Content layout. This layout along with the Title Slide layout for Slide 1 are the default styles. A **layout** specifies the arrangement of placeholders on a slide. These placeholders are arranged in various configurations and can contain text, such as the slide title or a bulleted list, or they can contain content, such as SmartArt graphics, pictures, charts, tables, shapes, and clip art. The placement of the text, in relationship to content, depends on the slide layout. You can specify a particular slide layout when you add a new slide to a presentation or after you have created the slide.

Using the **Layout gallery**, you can choose a slide layout. The nine layouts in this gallery have a variety of placeholders to define text and content positioning and formatting. Three layouts are for text: Title Slide, Section Header, and Title Only. Five are for text and content: Title and Content, Two Content, Comparison, Content with Caption, and Picture with Caption. The Blank layout has no placeholders. If none of these standard layouts meets your design needs, you can create a **custom layout**. A custom layout specifies the number, size, and location of placeholders, background content, and optional slide and placeholder-level properties.

When you change the layout of a slide, PowerPoint retains the text and objects and repositions them into the appropriate placeholders. Using slide layouts eliminates the need to resize objects and the font size because PowerPoint automatically sizes the objects and text to fit the placeholders.

To Add a Slide with the Title Only Layout

The following steps add Slide 3 to the presentation with the Title Only slide layout style.

1

- If necessary, click Home on the Ribbon to display the Home tab.

- Click the New Slide arrow (Home tab | Slides group) to display the Layout gallery (Figure 1–29).

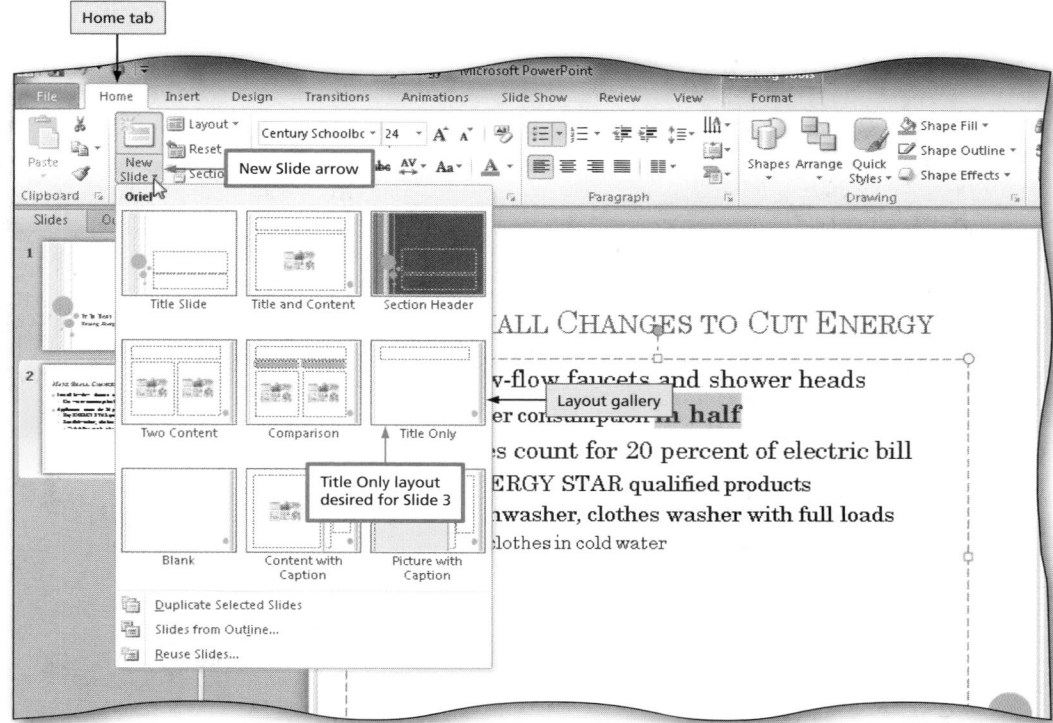

Figure 1–29

2

- Click Title Only to add a new slide and apply that layout to Slide 3 (Figure 1–30).

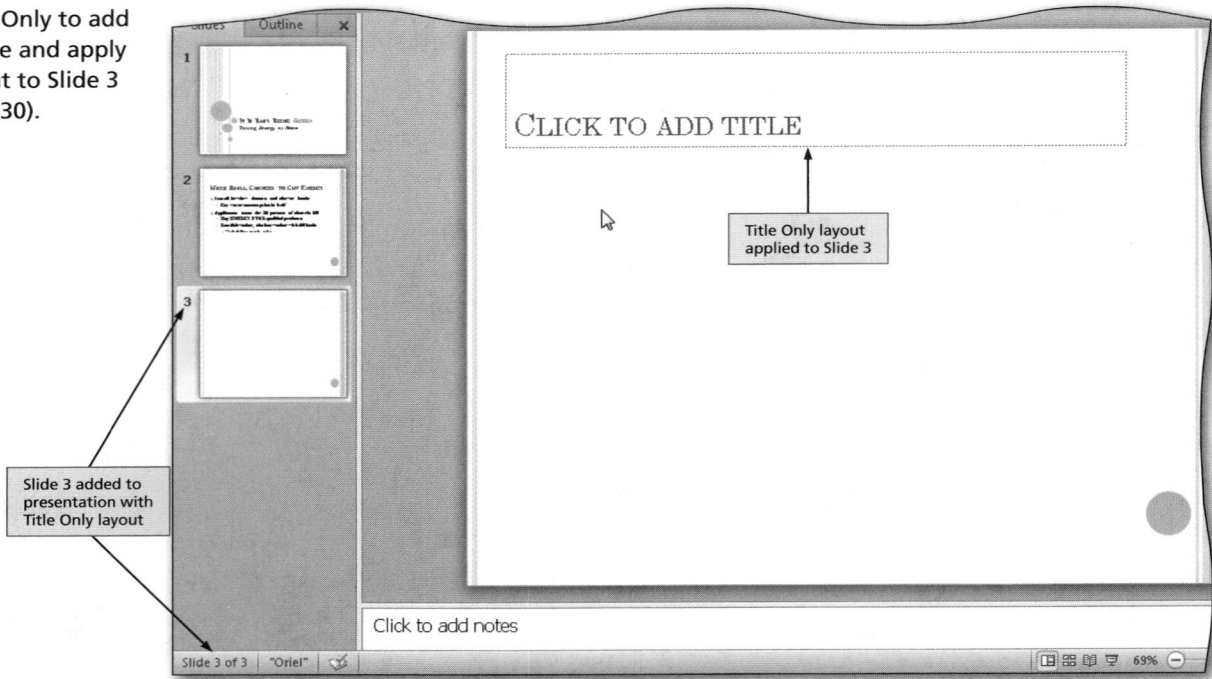

Figure 1–30

Other Ways

1. Press CTRL+M

To Enter a Slide Title

The only text on Slide 3 is the title. The following step enters the title text for this slide.

Portrait Page Orientation
If your slide content is dominantly vertical, such as a skyscraper or a person, consider changing the slide layout to a portrait page orientation. To change the orientation, click the Slide Orientation button (Design tab | Page Setup group) and then click the desired orientation.

1 Type **Use Energy Efficient Lighting** as the title text but do not press the ENTER key (Figure 1–31).

USE ENERGY EFFICIENT LIGHTING

Slide 3 title text

Figure 1–31

To Add a New Slide and Enter a Slide Title and Headings

The text on Slide 4 in Figure 1–1d on page PPT 3 consists of a title and two headings. The appropriate layout for this slide is named Comparison. The following steps add Slide 4 to the presentation with the Comparison layout and then enter the title and heading text for this slide.

1
- Click the New Slide arrow in the Slides group to display the Layout gallery (Figure 1–32).

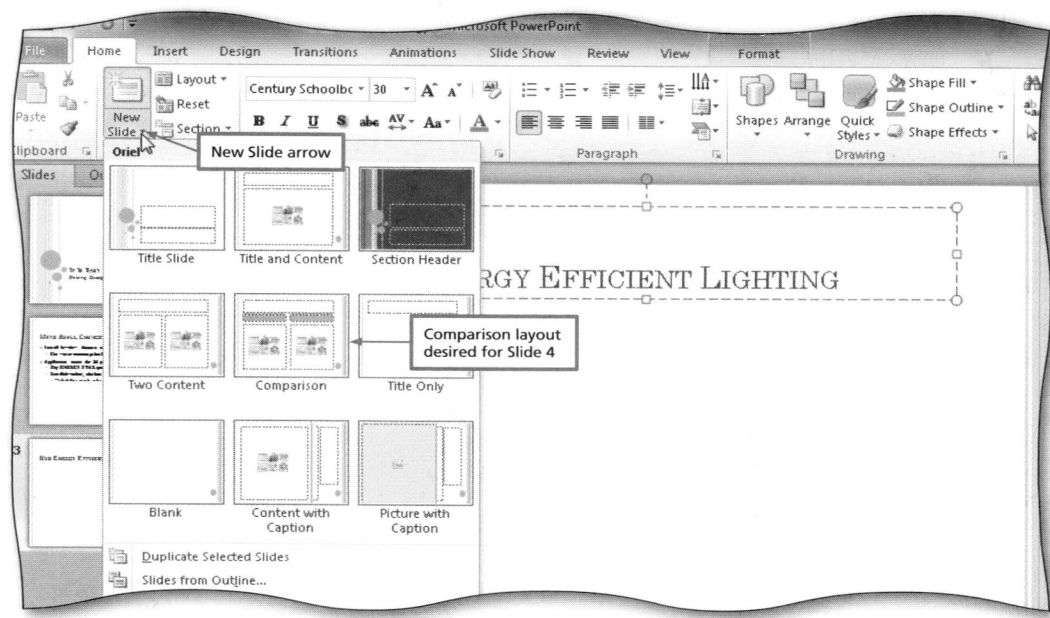

Figure 1–32

2
- Click Comparison to add Slide 4 and apply that layout.

- Type **Adjust Your Thermostats** in the title text placeholder but do not press the ENTER key.

- Click the left orange heading placeholder with the label, Click to add text, to select this placeholder (Figure 1–33).

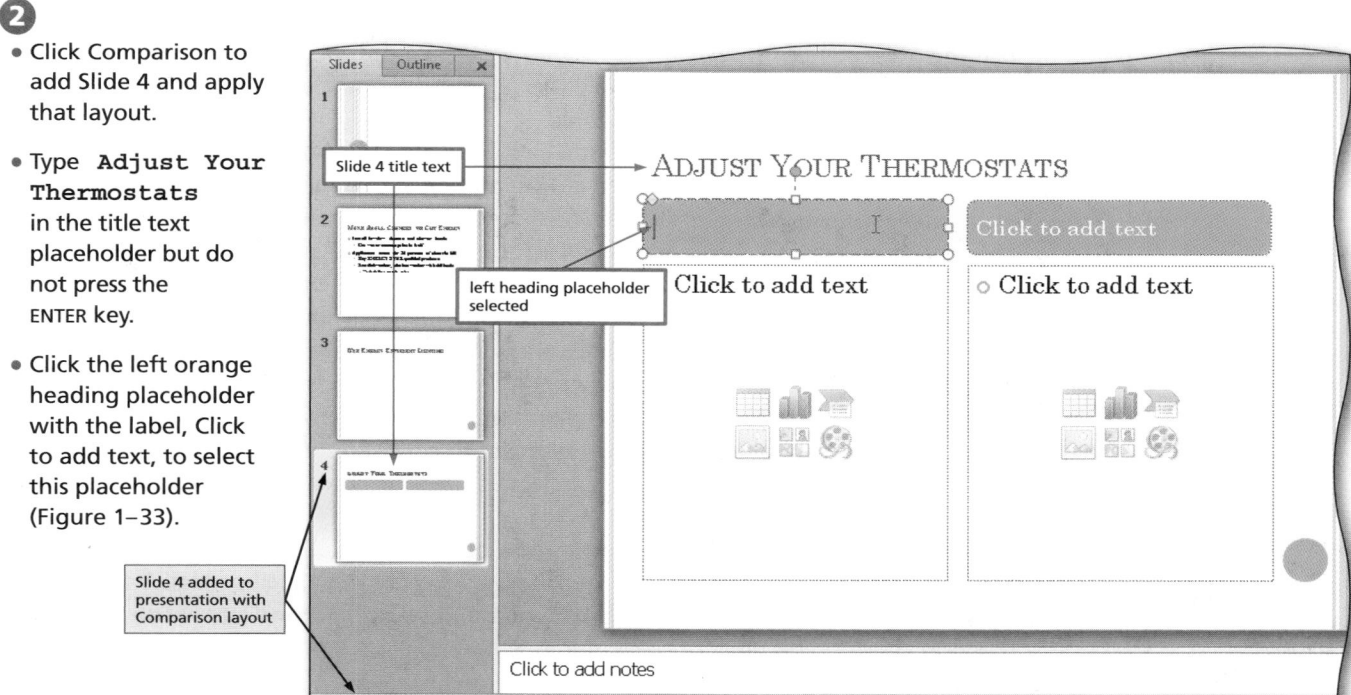

Figure 1–33

3

- Type **Furnace: 68 degrees** but do not press the ENTER key.

- Click the right orange heading placeholder and then type **Water heater: 120 degrees** but do not press the ENTER key (Figure 1–34).

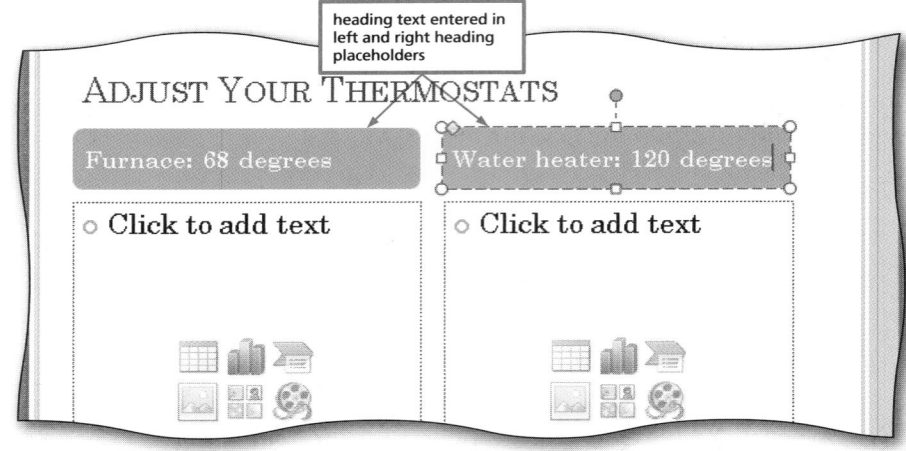

Figure 1–34

Break Point: If you wish to take a break, this is a good place to do so. You can quit PowerPoint now (refer to page PPT 50 for instructions). To resume at a later time, start PowerPoint (refer to pages PPT 4 and PPT 5 for instructions), open the file called Saving Energy (refer to pages PPT 50 and PPT 51 for instructions), and continue following the steps from this location forward.

PowerPoint Views

The PowerPoint window display varies depending on the view. A **view** is the mode in which the presentation appears on the screen. PowerPoint has four main views: Normal, Slide Sorter, Reading, and Slide Show. It also has another view, called Notes Page view, used for entering information about a slide.

The default view is **Normal view**, which is composed of three working areas that allow you to work on various aspects of a presentation simultaneously. The left side of the screen has a Tabs pane that consists of a **Slides tab** and an **Outline tab**. These tabs alternate between views of the presentation in a thumbnail, or miniature, view of the slides and an outline of the slide text. You can type the text of the presentation on the Outline tab and easily rearrange bulleted lists, paragraphs, and individual slides. As you type, you can view this text in the **Slide pane**, which shows a large view of the current slide on the right side of the window. You also can enter text, graphics, animations, and hyperlinks directly in the Slide pane. The **Notes pane** at the bottom of the window is an area where you can type notes and additional information. This text can consist of notes to yourself or remarks to share with your audience. If you want to work with your notes in full page format, you can display them in **Notes Page view**.

In Normal view, you can adjust the width of the Slide pane by dragging the **splitter bar** and the height of the Notes pane by dragging the pane borders. After you have created at least two slides, a scroll bar containing **scroll arrows** and **scroll boxes** will appear on the right edge of the window.

BTW

Using the Notes Pane
As you create your presentation, type comments to yourself in the Notes pane. This material can be used as part of the spoken information you will share with your audience as you give your presentation. You can print these notes for yourself or to distribute to your audience.

To Move to Another Slide in Normal View

When creating or editing a presentation in Normal view (the view you are currently using), you often want to display a slide other than the current one. Before continuing with developing this project, you want to display the title slide by dragging the scroll box on the vertical scroll bar. When you drag the scroll box, the **slide indicator** shows the number and title of the slide you are about to display. Releasing the mouse button shows the slide. The following steps move from Slide 4 to Slide 1 using the scroll box on the Slide pane.

- Position the mouse pointer on the scroll box.

- Press and hold down the mouse button so that Slide: 4 of 4 Adjust Your Thermostats appears in the slide indicator (Figure 1–35).

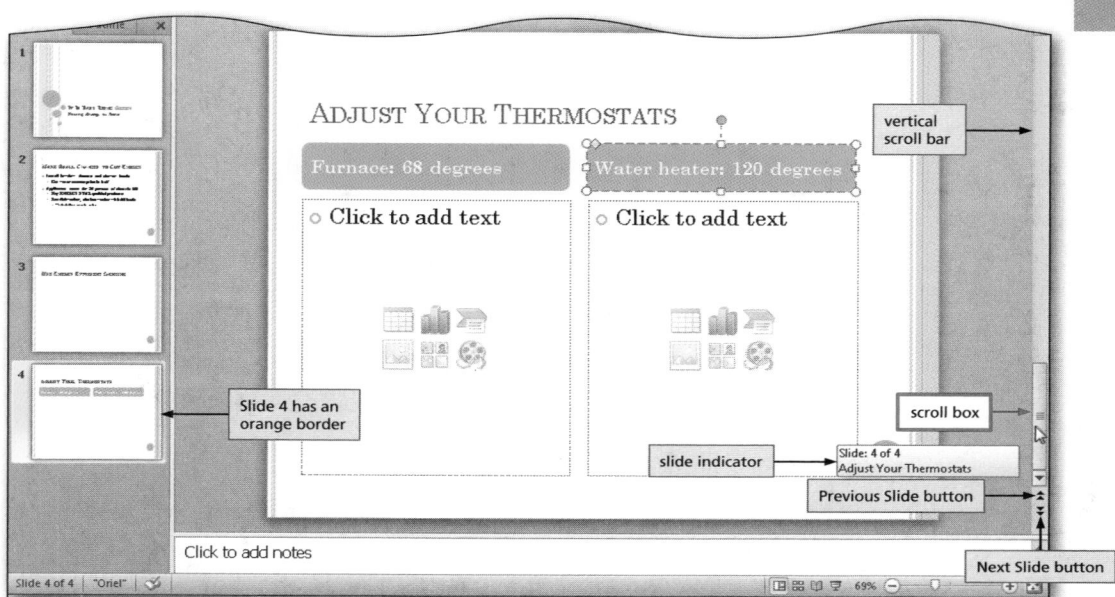

Figure 1–35

- Drag the scroll box up the vertical scroll bar until Slide: 1 of 4 It Is Easy Being Green appears in the slide indicator (Figure 1–36).

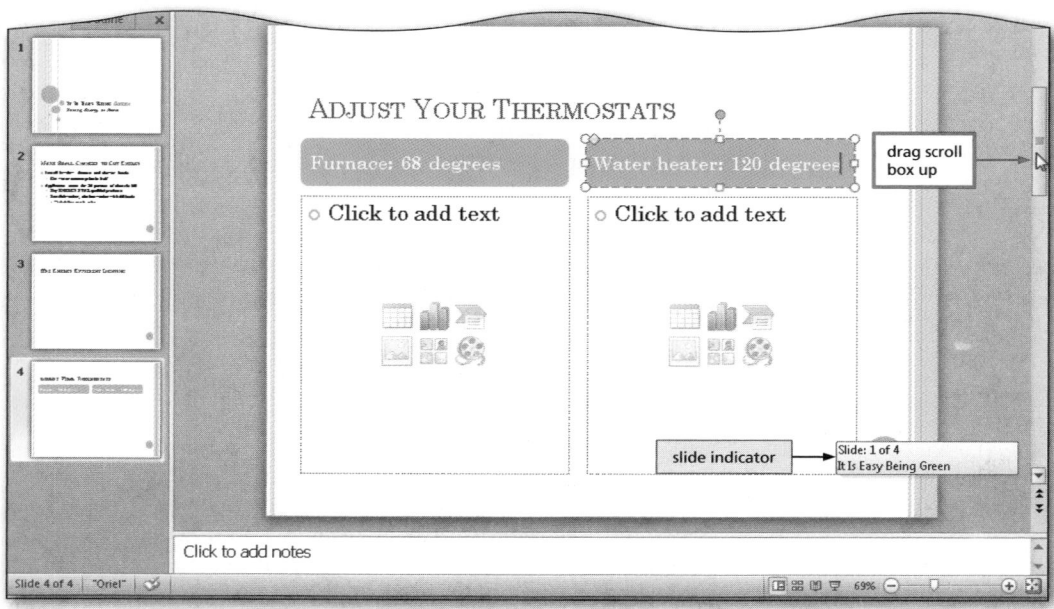

Figure 1–36

3

• Release the mouse button so that Slide 1 appears in the Slide pane and the Slide 1 thumbnail has an orange border in the Slides tab (Figure 1–37).

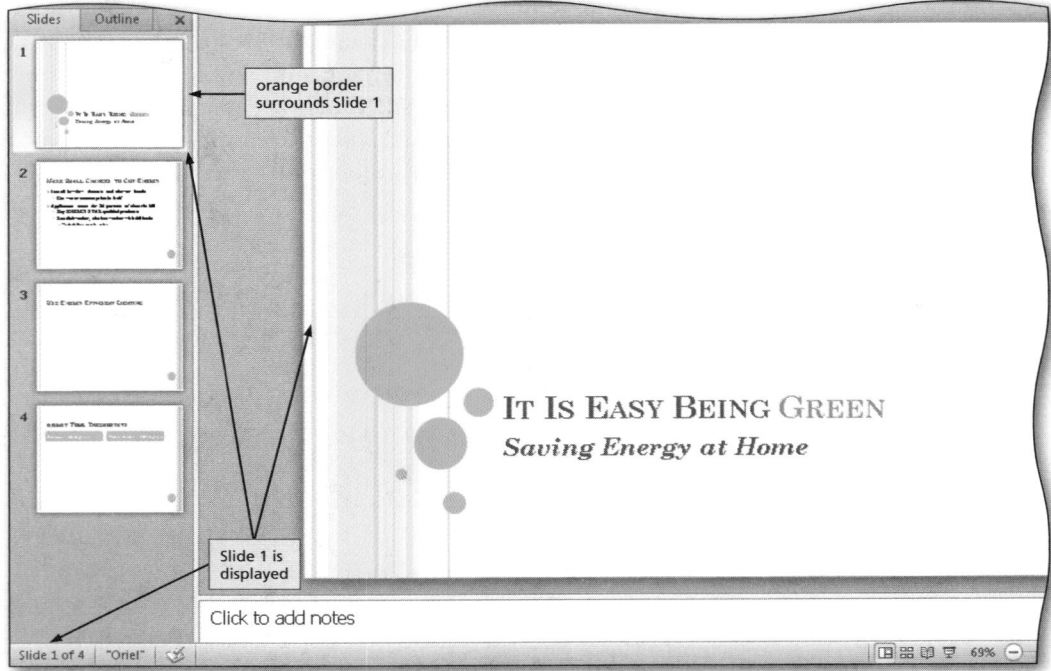

Figure 1–37

Other Ways

1. Click Next Slide button or Previous Slide button to move forward or back one slide
2. Click slide thumbnail on Slides tab
3. Press PAGE DOWN or PAGE UP to move forward or back one slide

Inserting Clip Art and Photographs into Slides

A **clip** is a single media file that can include art, sound, animation, or movies. Adding a clip can help increase the visual appeal of many slides and can offer a quick way to add professional-looking graphic images and sounds to a presentation without creating these files yourself. This art is contained in the **Microsoft Clip Organizer**, a collection of drawings, photographs, sounds, videos, and other media files shared among Microsoft Office applications. The **Office Collections** contains all these media files included with Microsoft Office.

You also can add your own clips to slides. You can insert these files directly from a storage medium, such as a USB flash drive. In addition, you can add them to the other files in the Clip Organizer so that you can search for and reuse these images, sounds, animations, and movies. When you create these media files, they are stored on your hard disk in **My Collections**. The Clip Organizer will find these files and create a new collection with these files. Two other locations for clips are Shared Collections and Web Collections. Files in the **Shared Collections** typically reside on a shared network file server and are accessible to multiple users. The **Web Collections** clips reside on the Microsoft Clip Art and Media Home page on the Microsoft Office Online Web site. They are available only if you have an active Internet connection.

The Clip Art Task Pane

You can add clips to your presentation in two ways. One way is by selecting one of the slide layouts that includes a content placeholder with a Clip Art button. A second method is by clicking the Clip Art button in the Images area on the Insert tab. Clicking the Clip Art button opens the Clip Art task pane. The **Clip Art task pane** allows you to search for clips by using descriptive keywords, file names, media file formats, and clip collections. Specific file formats could be for clip art, photographs, movies, and sounds.

Clips are organized in hierarchical **clip collections** that combine topic-related clips into categories, such as Academic, Business, and Technology.

Clips have one or more keywords associated with various entities, activities, labels, and emotions. In most instances, the keywords give the name of the clip and related categories. For example, an image of a cow in the Animals category has the keywords animals, cattle, cows, dairies, farms, and Holsteins. You can enter these keywords in the Search for text box to find clips when you know one of the words associated with the image. Otherwise, you might find it necessary to scroll through several categories to find an appropriate clip.

Depending on the installation of the Microsoft Clip Organizer on your computer, you might not have the clip art used in this chapter. Contact your instructor if you are missing clips used in the following steps. If you have an active connection to the Internet, clips from the Microsoft Office Online Web site will display automatically as the result of your search results.

Adhere to copyright regulations.

You have permission to use the clips from the Microsoft Clip Organizer. If you want to use a clip from another source, be certain you have the legal right to insert this file in your presentation. Read the copyright notices that may accompany the clip and may be posted on the Web site where you obtained the clip. The owners of these images and files often ask you to give them credit for using their work, which may be satisfied by stating where you obtained the images.

Plan Ahead

To Insert a Clip from the Clip Organizer into the Title Slide

Slide 1 uses the Title Slide layout, which has two placeholders for text but none for graphical content. You desire to place a graphic on Slide 1, so you will locate a clip art image of a green globe and flower and then insert it in this slide. Later in this chapter, you will size and position it in an appropriate location. The following steps add a clip to Slide 1.

- Click Insert on the Ribbon to display the Insert tab.

- Click the Clip Art button (Insert tab | Images group) to display the Clip Art task pane.

- Click the Search for text box in the Clip Art task pane, if necessary delete any letters that are present, and then type **green globe** in the Search for text box.

- If necessary, click the 'Include Office.com content' check box to select it (Figure 1–38).

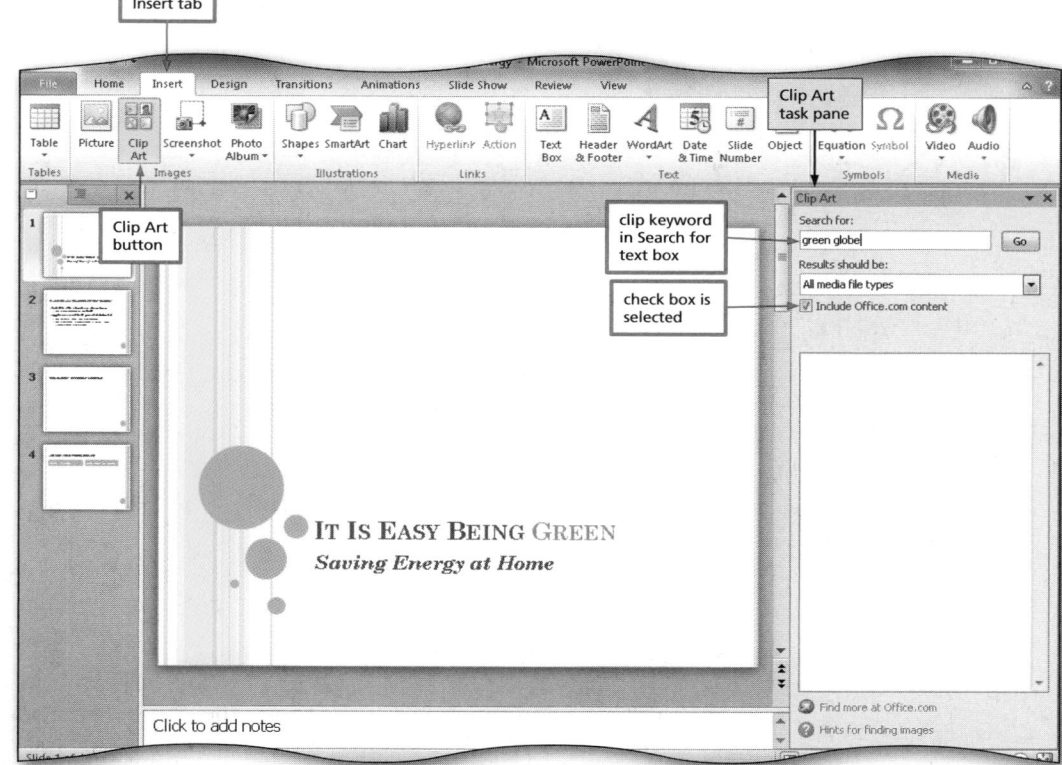

Figure 1–38

2

- Click the Go button so that the Microsoft Clip Organizer will search for and display all clips having the keywords, green globe.

- If necessary, click the Yes button if a Microsoft Clip Organizer dialog box appears asking if you want to include additional clip art images from Office.com.

- If necessary, scroll down the list to display the globe clip shown in Figure 1–39.

- Click the clip to insert it into the slide (Figure 1–39).

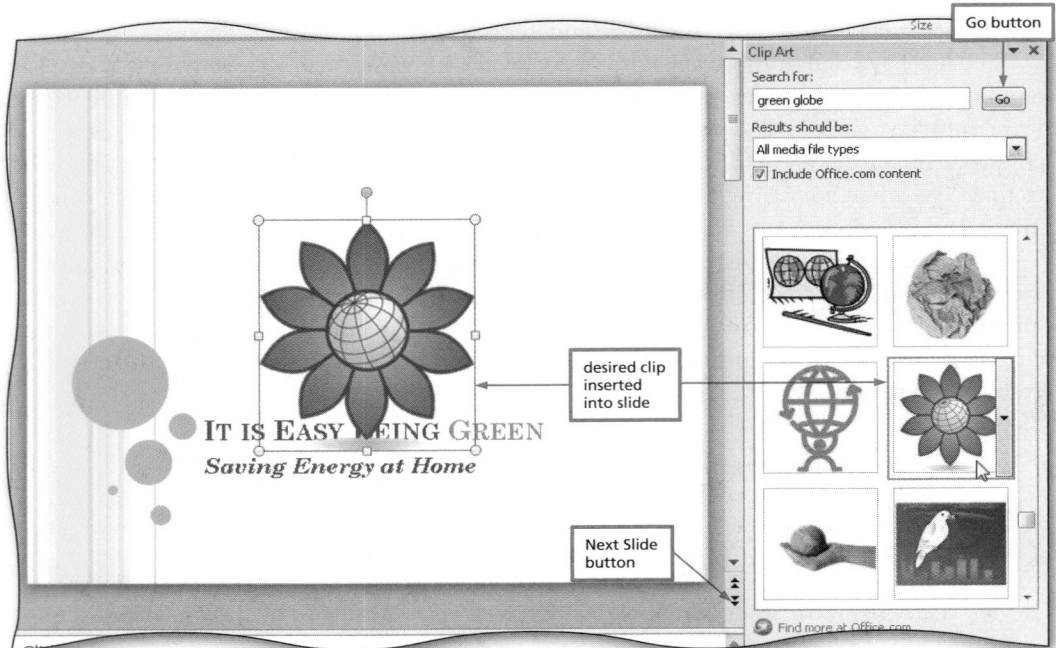

Figure 1–39

Q&A What if the globe image displayed in Figure 1–39 is not shown in my Clip Art task pane?

Select a similar clip. Your clips may be different depending on the clips installed on your computer and if you have an active connection to the Internet.

Q&A What is the yellow star image that displays in the lower-right corner of some clips in the Clip Art task pane?

The star indicates the image is animated and will move when the slide containing this clip is displayed during a slide show.

Q&A Why is this globe clip displayed in this location on the slide?

The slide layout does not have a content placeholder, so PowerPoint inserts the clip in the center of the slide.

To Insert a Clip from the Clip Organizer into a Slide without a Content Placeholder

The next step is to add two clips to Slide 2. Slide 2 has a bulleted list in the text placeholder, so the icon group does not display in the center of the placeholder. Later in this chapter, you will resize the inserted clips. The Clip Art task pane is displayed and will remain open until you close it. The following steps add one clip to Slide 2.

1 Click the Next Slide button to display Slide 2.

2 Click the Search for text box in the Clip Art task pane and then delete the letters in the Search for text box.

3 Type `faucets` and then click the Go button.

4 If necessary, scroll down the list to display the faucet clip shown in Figure 1–40 and then click the clip to insert it into Slide 2 (Figure 1–40).

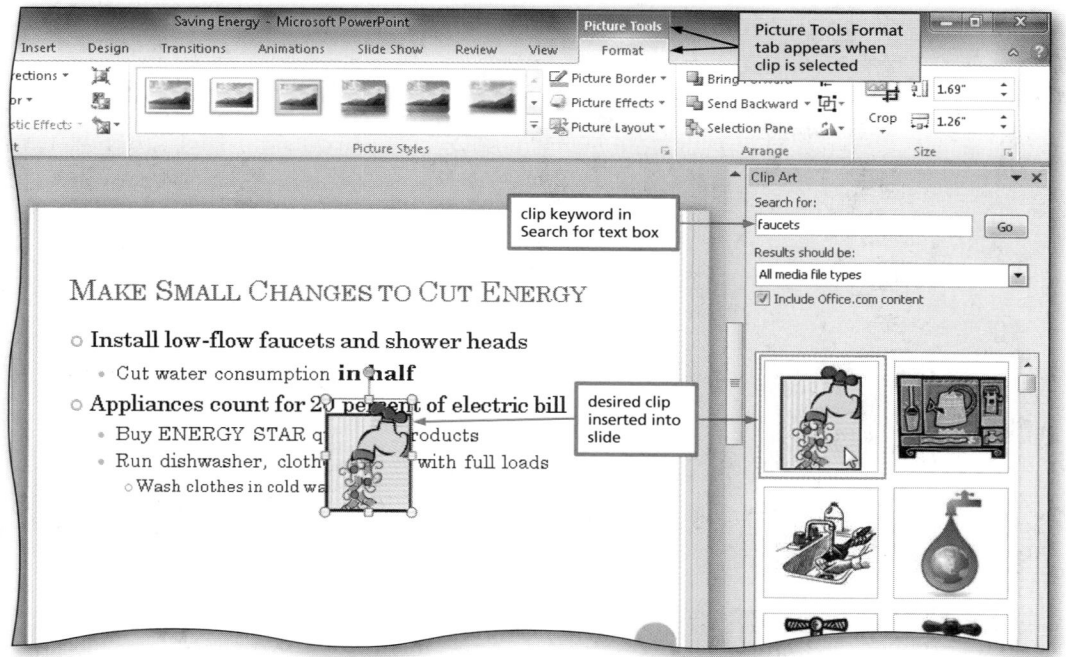

Figure 1–40

To Insert a Second Clip from the Clip Organizer into a Slide without a Content Placeholder

The following steps add a second clip to Slide 2. PowerPoint inserts this clip on top of the faucet clip in the center of the slide. Both clips will be moved and resized later in this project.

1 Click the Search for text box in the Clip Art task pane and then delete the letters in the text box.

2 Type **dishwasher**, click the Go button, locate the clip shown in Figure 1–41, and then click the clip to insert it into Slide 2 (Figure 1–41).

Clip Properties
Each clip has properties that identify its characteristics. When you right-click a clip in the Microsoft Clip Organizer, you will see details of the clip's name, file type, size, dimensions, keywords, and creation date. You also can preview the clip and edit its assigned keywords.

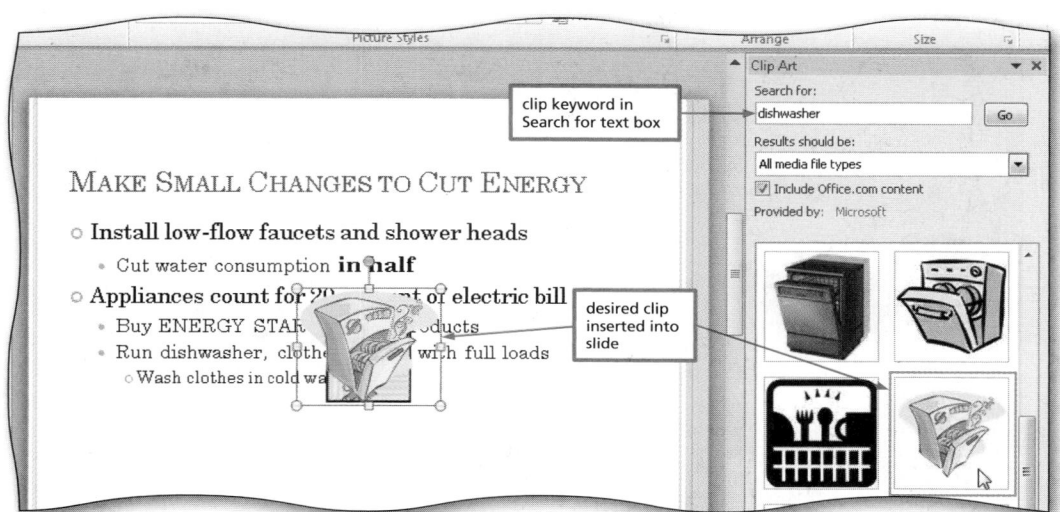

Figure 1–41

To Insert a Clip from the Clip Organizer into a Content Placeholder

Slide 4 uses the Comparison layout, which has a content placeholder below each of the two headings. You desire to insert clip art into both content placeholders to reinforce the concept that consumers should adjust the heating temperatures of their furnace and water heater. The following steps insert clip art of a furnace into the left content placeholder and a water heater into the right content placeholder on Slide 4.

- Click the Close button in the Clip Art task pane so that it no longer is displayed.

- Click the Next Slide button twice to display Slide 4.

- Click the Clip Art button in the left content placeholder to select that placeholder and to open the Clip Art task pane (Figure 1–42).

Q&A

Do I need to close the Clip Art task pane when I am finished inserting the two clips into Slide 2?

No. You can leave the Clip Art task pane open and then display Slide 4. It is often more convenient, however, to open this pane when you are working with a layout that has a content placeholder so that the clip is inserted in the desired location.

Figure 1–42

- Click the Search for text box in the Clip Art task pane, delete any letters that are present, type **furnace** in the Search for text box, and then click the Go button to search for and display all pictures having the keyword, furnace.

- If necessary, scroll down the list to display the furnace clip shown in Figure 1–43.

- Click the clip to insert it into the left content placeholder (Figure 1–43).

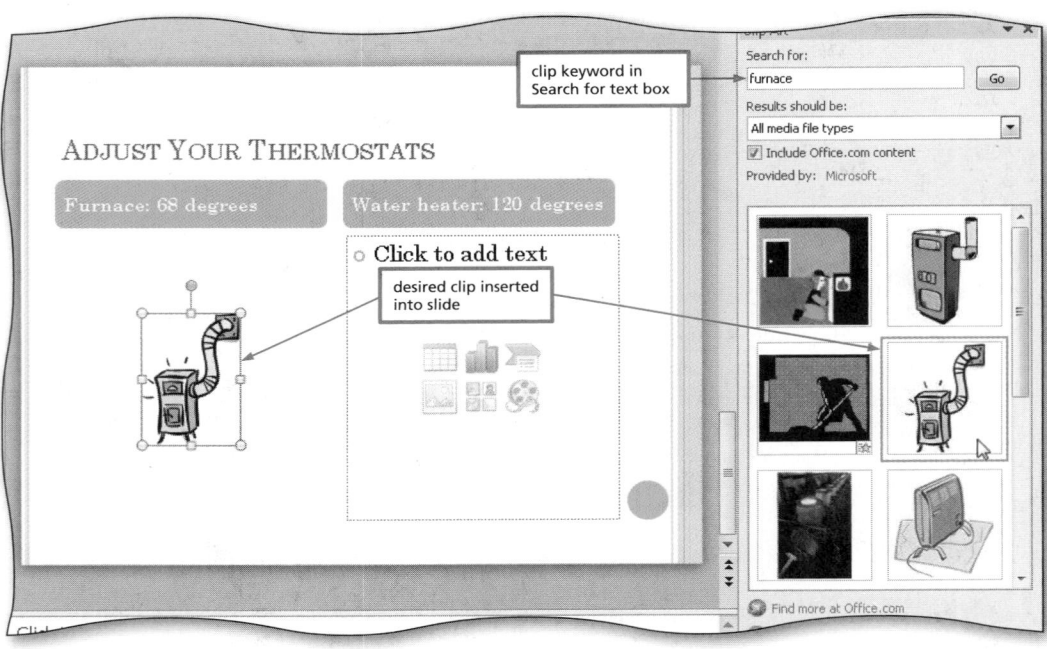

Figure 1–43

3

- Click anywhere in the right placeholder except one of the six icons to select the placeholder.

Q&A

I clicked the Clip Art icon by mistake, which closed the Clip Art task pane. How do I open it?

Click the Clip Art icon.

4

- Click the Search for text box in the Clip Art task pane, delete any letters that are present, type **water heater** in the Search for text box, and then click the Go button.

- If necessary, scroll down the list to display the water heater clip shown in Figure 1–44 and then click the clip to insert it into the right content placeholder (Figure 1–44).

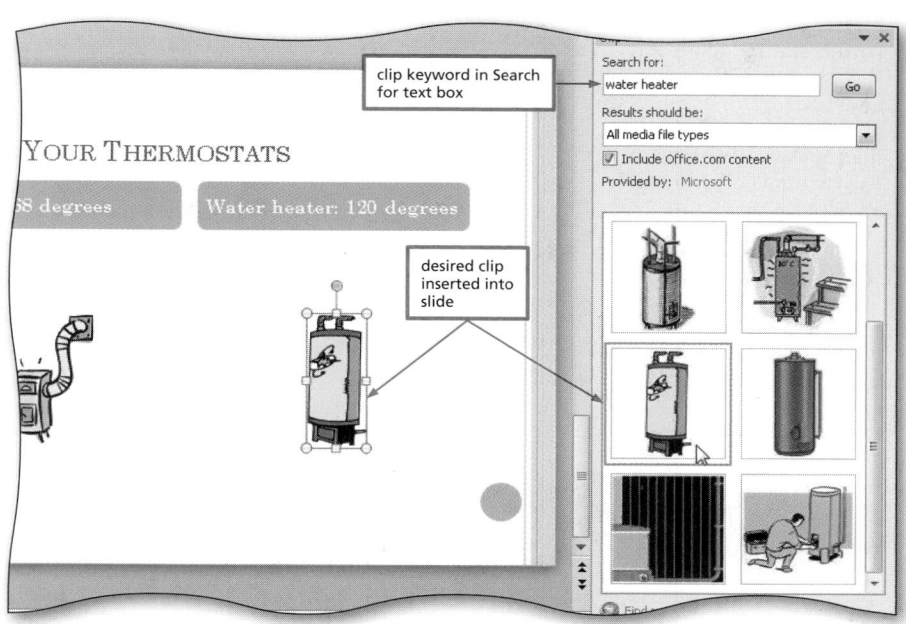

Figure 1–44

Photographs and the Clip Organizer

In addition to clip art, you can insert pictures into a presentation. These may include scanned photographs, line art, and artwork from storage media, such as USB flash drives, hard disks, optical discs, and memory cards. To insert a picture into a presentation, the picture must be saved in a format that PowerPoint can recognize. Table 1–1 identifies some of the formats PowerPoint recognizes.

Table 1–1 Primary File Formats PowerPoint Recognizes

Format	File Extension
Computer Graphics Metafile	.cgm
CorelDRAW	.cdr, .cdt, .cmx, and .pat
Encapsulated PostScript	.eps
Enhanced Metafile	.emf
FlashPix	.fpx
Graphics Interchange Format	.gif
Hanako	.jsh, .jah, and .jbh
Joint Photographic Experts Group (JPEG)	.jpg
Kodak PhotoCD	.pcd
Macintosh PICT	.pct
PC Paintbrush	.pcx
Portable Network Graphics	.png
Tagged Image File Format	.tif
Windows Bitmap	.bmp, .rle, .dib
Microsoft Windows Metafile	.wmf
WordPerfect Graphics	.wpg

BTW

Compressing File Size
When you add a picture to a presentation, PowerPoint automatically compresses this image. Even with this compression applied, a presentation that contains pictures usually has a large file size. To reduce this size, you can compress a picture further without affecting the quality of how it displays on the slide. To compress a picture, select the picture and then click the Compress Pictures button (Picture Tools Format tab | Adjust group). You can restore the picture's original settings by clicking the Reset Picture button (Picture Tools Format tab | Adjust group).

BTW

Wrapping Text around a Picture
PowerPoint 2010 does not allow you to wrap text around a picture or other graphics, such as tables, shapes, charts, or graphics. This feature, however, is available in Word 2010.

You can import files saved with the .emf, .gif, .jpg, .png, .bmp, .rle, .dib, and .wmf formats directly into PowerPoint presentations. All other file formats require separate filters that are shipped with the PowerPoint installation software and must be installed separately. You can download additional filters from the Microsoft Office Online Web site.

To Insert a Photograph from the Clip Organizer into a Slide without a Content Placeholder

Next, you will add a photograph to Slide 3. You will not insert this picture into a content placeholder, so it will display in the center of the slide. Later in this chapter, you will resize this picture. To start the process of locating this photograph, you do not need to click the Clip Art button in the content placeholder because the Clip Art task pane already is displayed. The following steps add a photograph to Slide 3.

1 Click the Previous Slide button to display Slide 3.

2 Click the Search for text box in the Clip Art task pane, delete the letters in the text box, type **CFL**, and then click the Go button.

3 If necessary, scroll down the list to display the picture of a light bulb shown in Figure 1–45, and then click the photograph to insert it into Slide 2 (Figure 1–45).

Q&A Why is my photograph a different size from the one shown in Figure 1–1c on page PPT 3?

The photograph was inserted into the slide and not into a content placeholder. You will resize the picture later in this chapter.

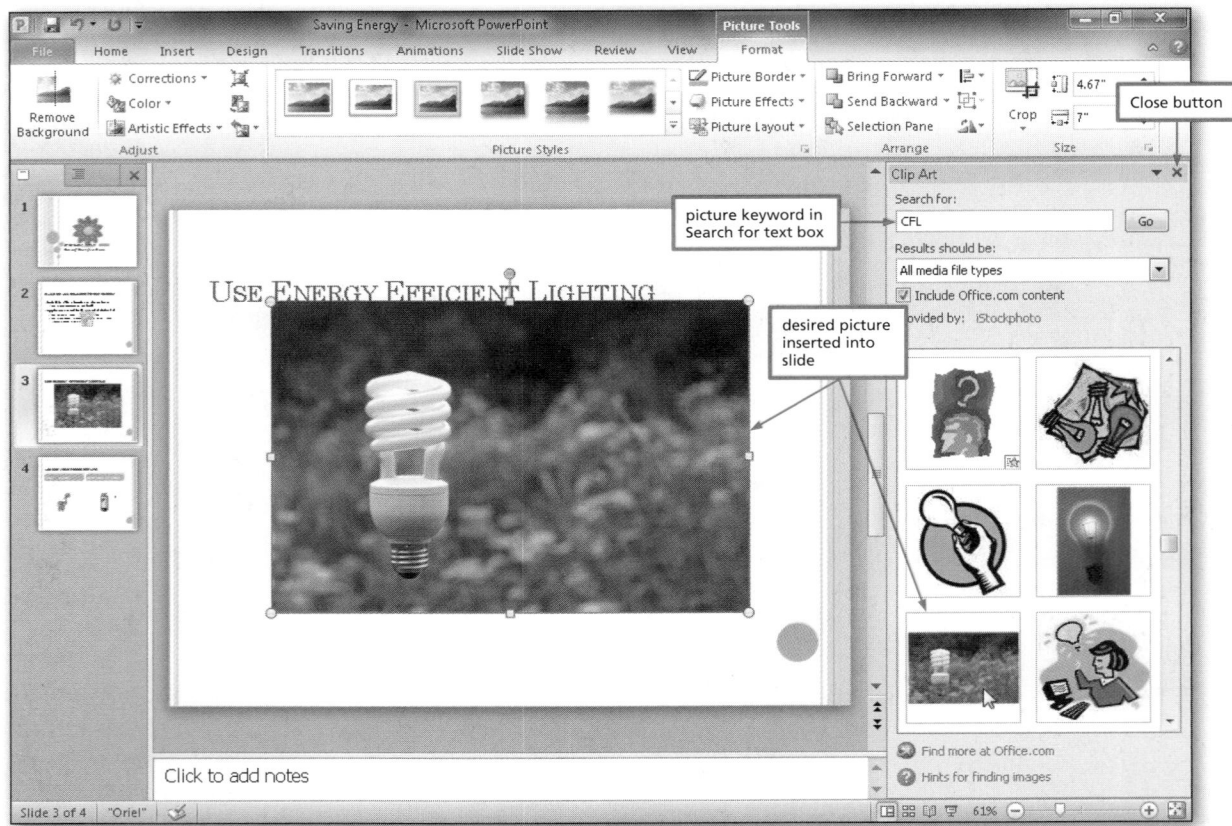

Figure 1–45

Break Point: If you wish to take a break, this is a good place to do so. You can quit PowerPoint now (refer to page PPT 50 for instructions). To resume at a later time, start PowerPoint (refer to pages PPT 4 and PPT 5 for instructions), open the file called Saving Energy (refer to pages PPT 50 and PPT 51 for instructions), and continue following the steps from this location forward.

Resizing Clip Art and Photographs

Sometimes it is necessary to change the size of clip art. **Resizing** includes enlarging or reducing the size of a clip art graphic. You can resize clip art using a variety of techniques. One method involves changing the size of a clip by specifying exact dimensions in a dialog box. Another method involves dragging one of the graphic's sizing handles to the desired location. A selected graphic appears surrounded by a **selection rectangle**, which has small squares and circles, called **sizing handles** or move handles, at each corner and middle location.

To Resize Clip Art

On Slides 1, 2, and 4, much space appears around the clips, so you can increase their sizes. Likewise, the photograph on Slide 3 can be enlarged to fill more of the space below the slide title. To change the size, drag the corner sizing handles to view how the clip will look on the slide. Using these corner handles maintains the graphic's original proportions. Dragging the square sizing handles alters the proportions so that the graphic's height and width become larger or smaller. The following steps increase the size of the Slide 1 clip using a corner sizing handle.

- Click the Close button in the Clip Art task pane so that it no longer is displayed.

- Click the Previous Slide button two times to display Slide 1.

- Click the globe clip to select it and display the selection rectangle.

- Point to the lower-left corner sizing handle on the clip so that the mouse pointer changes to a two-headed arrow (Figure 1–46).

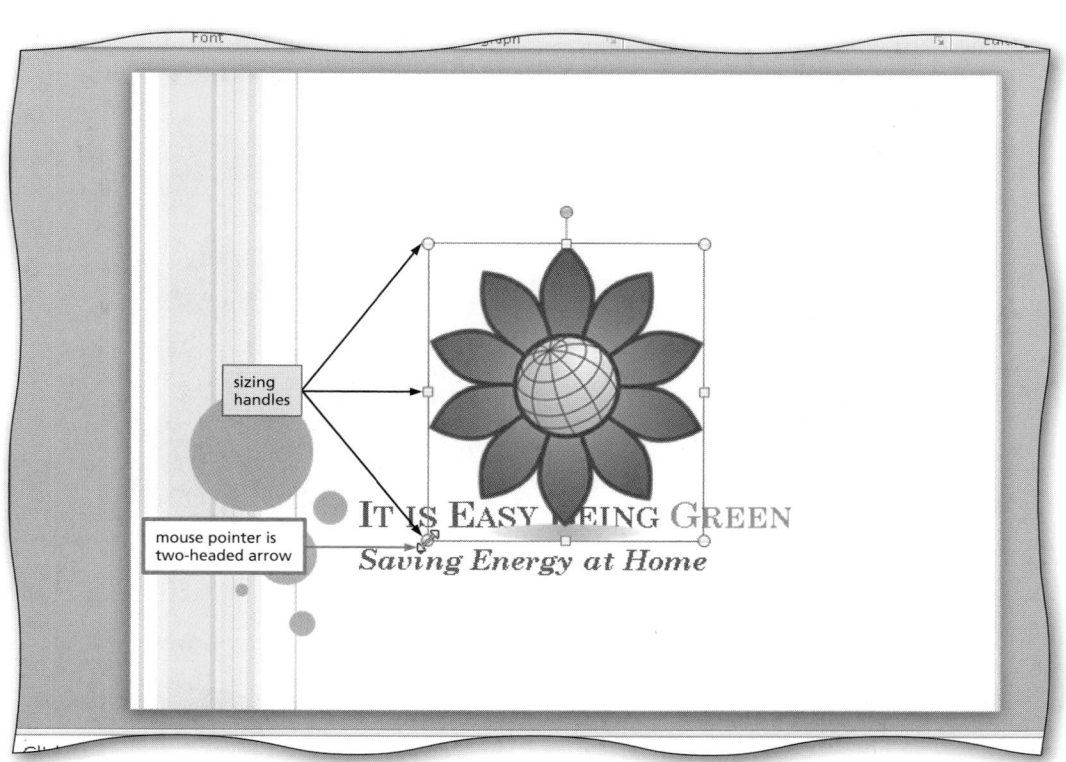

Figure 1–46

- Drag the sizing handle diagonally toward the lower-left corner of the slide until the mouse pointer is positioned approximately as shown in Figure 1–47.

Q&A What if the clip is not the same size as the one shown in Figure 1–47?

Repeat Steps 1 and 2.

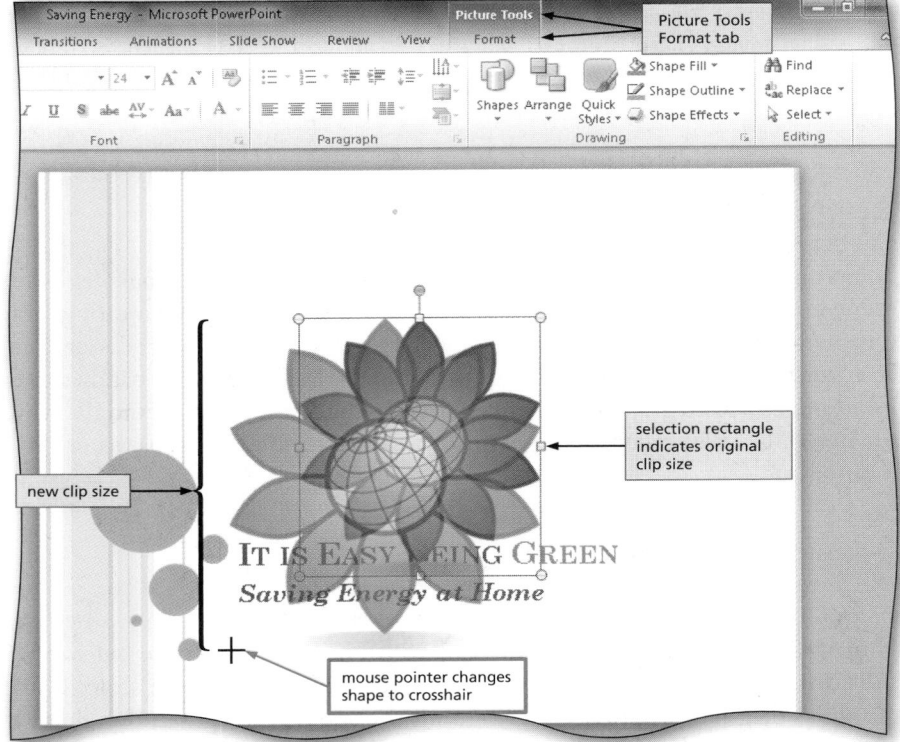

Figure 1–47

- Release the mouse button to resize the clip.
- Click outside the clip to deselect it (Figure 1–48).

Q&A What happened to the Picture Tools Format tab?

When you click outside the clip, PowerPoint deselects the clip and removes the Picture Tools Format tab from the screen.

Q&A What if I want to return the clip to its original size and start again?

With the graphic selected, click the Reset Picture button (Picture Tools Format tab | Adjust group).

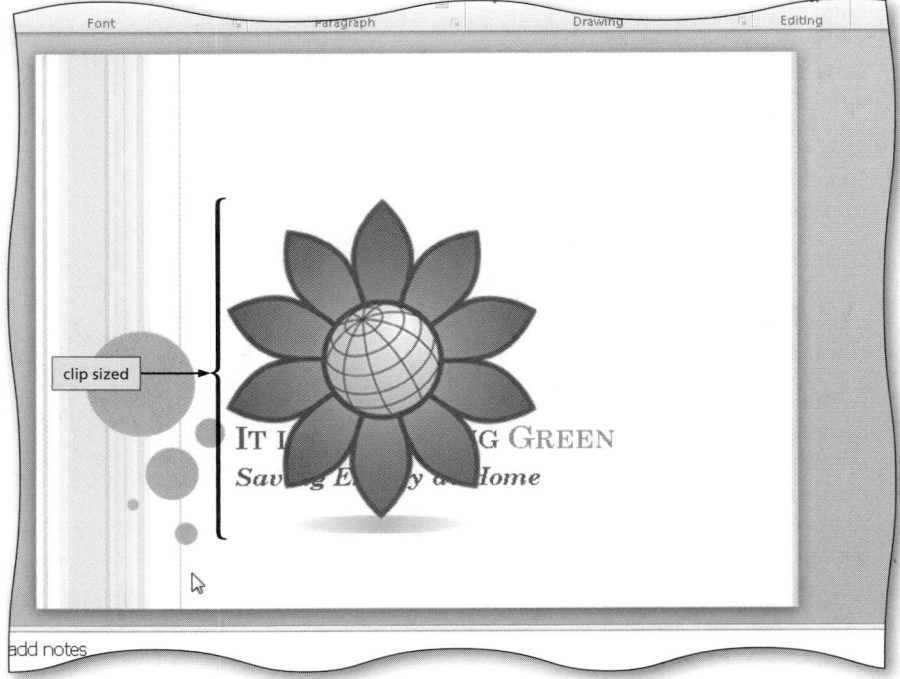

Figure 1–48

To Resize Clips on Slide 4

The two clip art images on Slide 4 also can be enlarged to fill much of the white space below the headings. You will reposition the clips in a later step. The following steps resize these clips using a sizing handle.

1 Click the Next Slide button three times to display Slide 4.

2 Click the furnace clip to select it.

3 Drag the lower-left corner sizing handle on the clip diagonally outward until the clip is resized approximately as shown in Figure 1–49.

4 Click the water heater clip to select it.

5 Drag the lower-right corner sizing handle on the clip diagonally outward until the clip is resized approximately as shown in Figure 1–49.

Figure 1–49

To Resize a Photograph

The light bulb picture in Slide 3 can be enlarged slightly to fill much of the space below the slide title. You resize a photograph in the same manner that you resize clip art. The following steps resize this photograph using a sizing handle.

1 Click the Previous Slide button to display Slide 3.

2 Click the light bulb photograph to select it.

BTW

Minimalist Design
Resist the urge to fill your slides with clips from the Microsoft Clip Organizer. Minimalist style reduces clutter and allows the slide content to display prominently. This simple, yet effective design helps audience members with short attention spans to focus on the message.

3 Drag the lower-left corner sizing handle on the photograph diagonally outward until the photograph is resized approximately as shown in Figure 1–50.

light bulb picture resized

Figure 1–50

To Move Clips

After you insert clip art or a photograph on a slide, you might want to reposition it. The light bulb photograph on Slide 3 could be centered in the space between the slide title and the left and right edges of the slide. The clip on Slide 1 could be positioned in the upper-right corner of the slide. On Slide 4, the furnace and water heater clips could be centered under each heading. The following steps move these graphics.

1

- If necessary, click the light bulb photograph on Slide 3 to select it.

- Press and hold down the mouse button and then drag the photograph diagonally downward below the title text (Figure 1–51).

- If necessary, select the photograph and then use the ARROW keys to position it precisely as shown in Figure 1–51.

 Q&A The photograph still is not located exactly where I want it to display. What can I do to align the photograph?

Press the CTRL key while you press the ARROW keys. This key combination moves the clip in smaller increments than when you press only an ARROW key.

light bulb picture moved to desired location on Slide 3

Figure 1–51

2

- Click the Next Slide button to display Slide 4.

- Click the furnace clip to select it, press and hold down the mouse button, and then drag the clip to center it under the furnace heading.

- Click the water heater clip and then drag the clip to center it under the water heater heading (Figure 1–52).

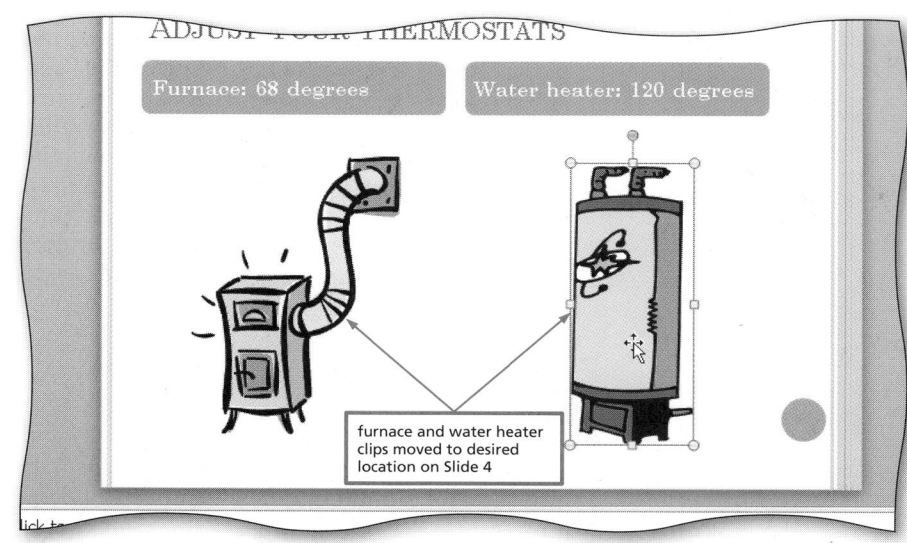

Figure 1–52

3

- Click the Previous Slide button twice to display Slide 2.

- Click the dishwasher clip, which is on top of the faucet clip, and then drag the clip to center it under the last bulleted paragraph, Wash clothes in cold water.

- Click the faucet clip and then drag the clip so that the faucet handle is centered under the words, full loads.

- Drag a corner sizing handle on the faucet clip diagonally outward until the clip is resized approximately as shown in Figure 1–53. You may need to drag the clip to position it in the desired location.

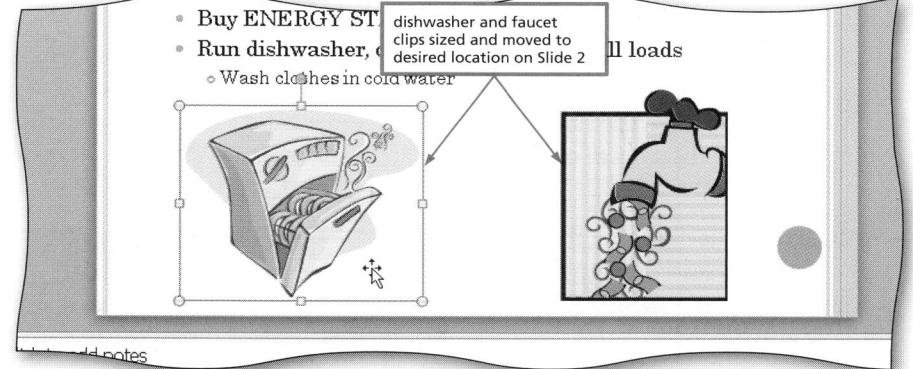

Figure 1–53

- Select the dishwasher clip and then resize and move it so that the clip displays approximately as shown in Figure 1–53.

4

- Click the Previous Slide button to display Slide 1.

- Click the globe clip and then drag it to the upper-right corner of the slide. You may want to adjust its size by selecting it and then dragging the corner sizing handles.

- Click outside the clip to deselect it (Figure 1–54).

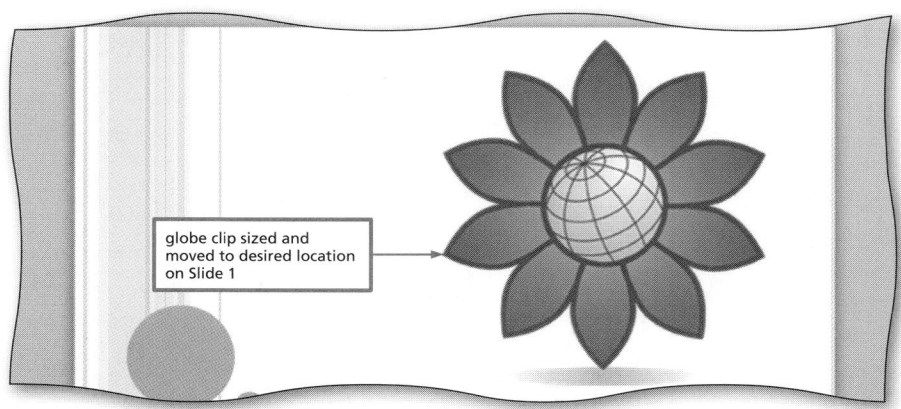

Figure 1–54

Plan Ahead

Choose a closing slide.
After the last slide appears during a slide show, the default PowerPoint setting is to end the presentation with a **black slide**. This black slide appears only when the slide show is running and concludes the slide show, so your audience never sees the PowerPoint window. It is a good idea, however, to end the presentation with a final closing slide to display at the end of the presentation. This slide ends the presentation gracefully and should be an exact copy, or a very similar copy, of your title slide. The audience will recognize that the presentation is drawing to a close when this slide appears. It can remain on the screen when the audience asks questions, approaches the speaker for further information, or exits the room.

Ending a Slide Show with a Closing Slide

All the text for the slides in the Saving Energy slide show has been entered. This presentation thus far consists of a title slide, one text slide with a multi-level bulleted list, a third slide for a photograph, and a fourth slide with a Comparison layout. A closing slide that resembles the title slide is the final slide to create.

To Duplicate a Slide

When two slides contain similar information and have the same format, duplicating one slide and then making minor modifications to the new slide saves time and increases consistency.

Slide 5 will have the same layout and design as Slide 1. The most expedient method of creating this slide is to copy Slide 1 and then make minor modifications to the new slide. The following steps duplicate the title slide.

1
• With Slide 1 selected, click the New Slide arrow (Home tab | Slides group) to display the Oriel layout gallery (Figure 1–55).

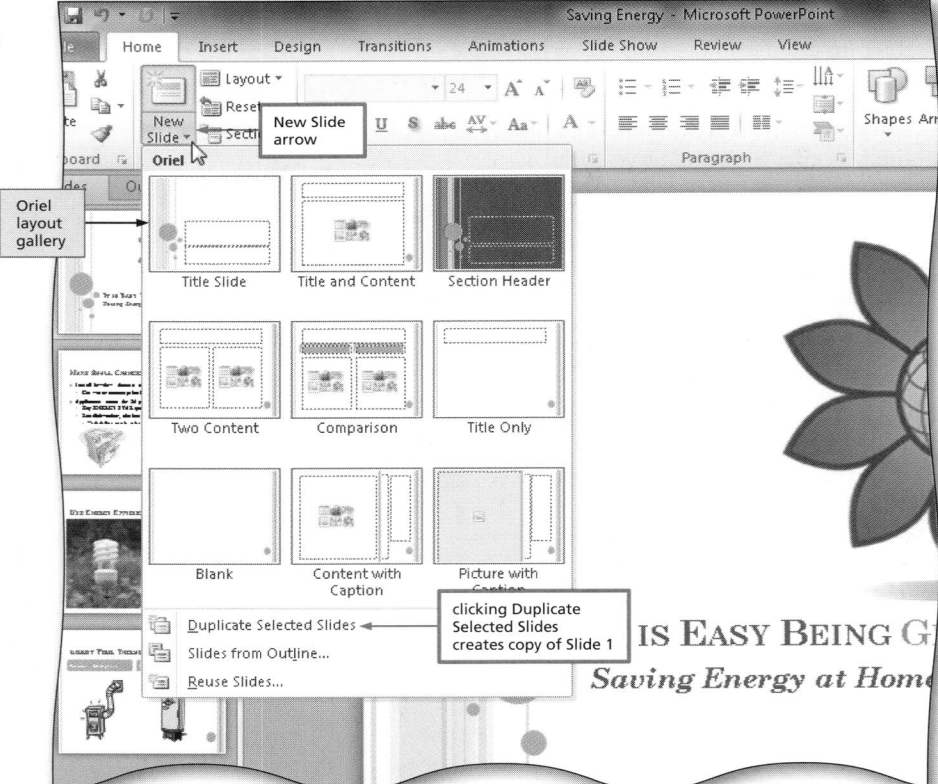

Figure 1–55

• Click Duplicate Selected Slides in the Oriel layout gallery to create a new Slide 2, which is a duplicate of Slide 1 (Figure 1–56).

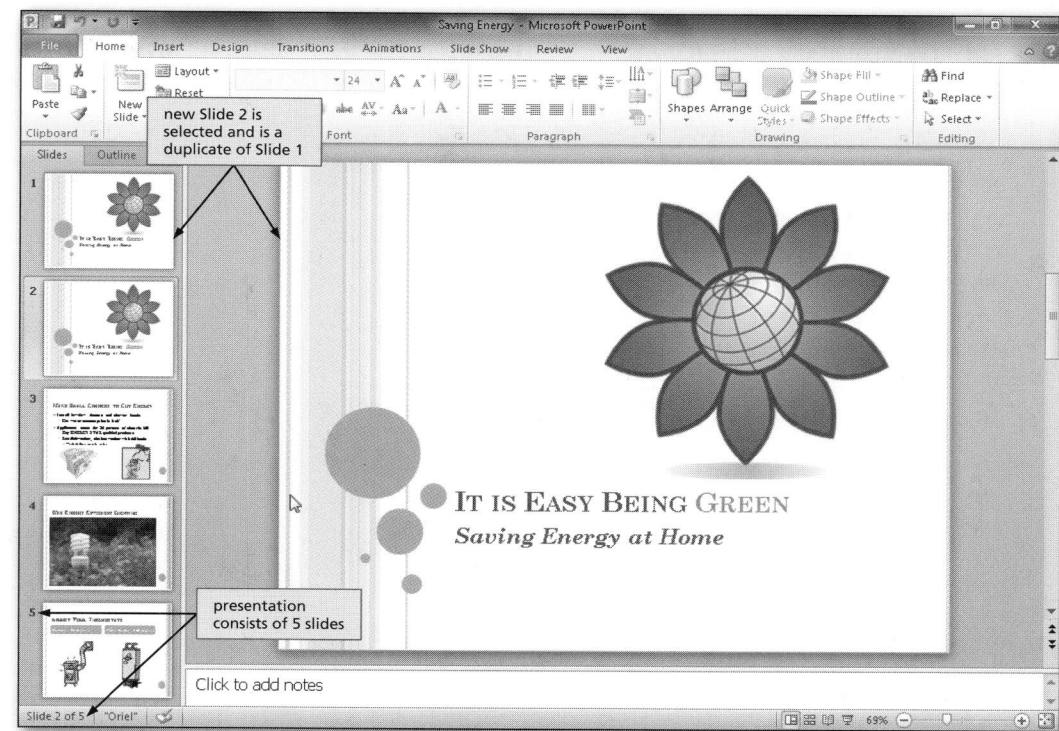

Figure 1–56

Break Point: If you wish to take a break, this is a good place to do so. You can quit PowerPoint now (refer to page PPT 50 for instructions). To resume at a later time, start PowerPoint (refer to pages PPT 4 and PPT 5 for instructions), open the file called Saving Energy (refer to pages PPT 50 and PPT 51 for instructions), and continue following the steps from this location forward.

To Arrange a Slide

The new Slide 2 was inserted directly below Slide 1 because Slide 1 was the selected slide. This duplicate slide needs to display at the end of the presentation directly after the final title and content slide.

Changing slide order is an easy process and is best performed in the Slides pane. When you click the slide thumbnail and begin to drag it to a new location, a line indicates the new location of the selected slide. When you release the mouse button, the slide drops into the desired location. Hence, this process of dragging and then dropping the thumbnail in a new location is called **drag and drop**. You can use the drag-and-drop method to move any selected item, including text and graphics. The following step moves the new Slide 2 to the end of the presentation so that it becomes a closing slide.

1

● With Slide 2 selected, drag the Slide 2 slide thumbnail in the Slides pane below the last slide thumbnail (Figure 1–57).

Q&A

The Slide 2 thumbnail is not visible in the Slides pane when I am dragging the thumbnail downward. How do I know it will be positioned in the desired location?

A blue horizontal bar indicates where the slide will move.

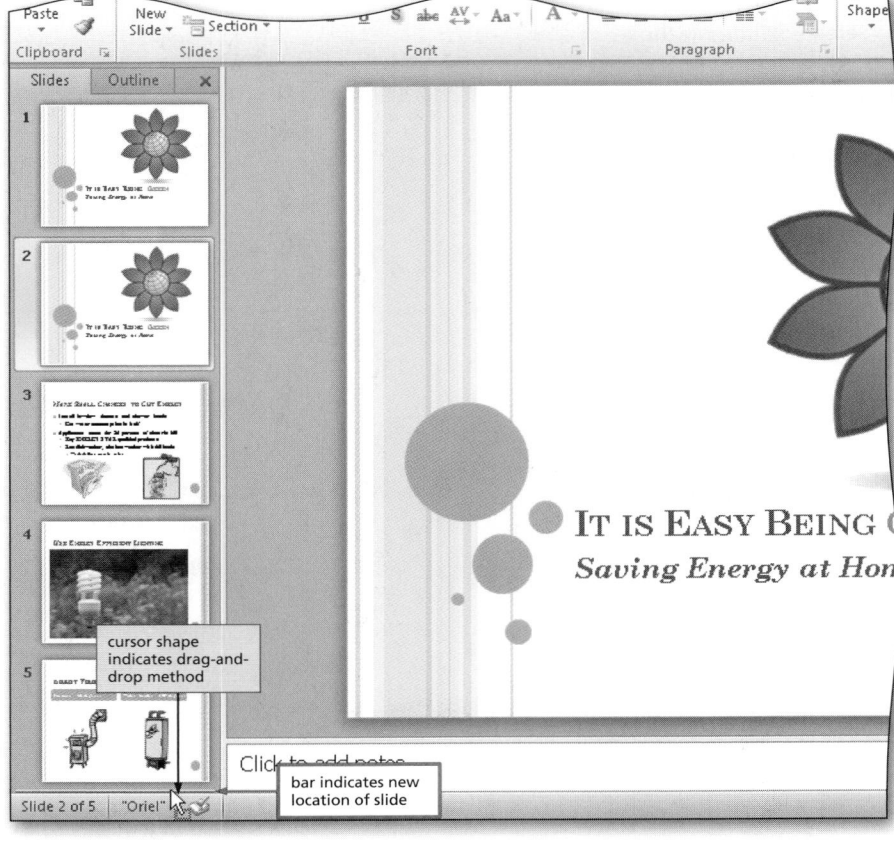

Figure 1–57

Other Ways

1. Click slide icon on Outline tab, drag icon to new location
2. Click Slide Sorter (View tab | Presentation Views group), click slide thumbnail, drag thumbnail to new location

Making Changes to Slide Text Content

After creating slides in a presentation, you may find that you want to make changes to the text. Changes may be required because a slide contains an error, the scope of the presentation shifts, or the style is inconsistent. This section explains the types of changes that commonly occur when creating a presentation.

You generally make three types of changes to text in a presentation: additions, replacements, and deletions.

- Additions are necessary when you omit text from a slide and need to add it later. You may need to insert text in the form of a sentence, word, or single character. For example, you may want to add the presenter's middle name on the title slide.

- Replacements are needed when you want to revise the text in a presentation. For example, you may want to substitute the word *their* for the word *there*.

- Deletions are required when text on a slide is incorrect or no longer is relevant to the presentation. For example, a slide may look cluttered. Therefore, you may want to remove one of the bulleted paragraphs to add more space.

Editing text in PowerPoint basically is the same as editing text in a word processing program. The following sections illustrate the most common changes made to text in a presentation.

Replacing Text in an Existing Slide

When you need to correct a word or phrase, you can replace the text by selecting the text to be replaced and then typing the new text. As soon as you press any key on the keyboard, the selected text is deleted and the new text is displayed.

PowerPoint inserts text to the left of the insertion point. The text to the right of the insertion point moves to the right (and shifts downward if necessary) to accommodate the added text.

Deleting Text

You can delete text using one of three methods. One is to use the BACKSPACE key to remove text just typed. The second is to position the insertion point to the left of the text you want to delete and then press the DELETE key. The third method is to drag through the text you want to delete and then press the DELETE or BACKSPACE key. Use the third method when deleting large sections of text.

To Delete Text in a Placeholder

To keep the ending slide clean and simple, you want to delete a few words in the slide show title and subtitle text. The following steps change It Is Easy Being Green to Be Green and then change Saving Energy at Home to Save Energy.

1

• With Slide 5 selected, position the mouse pointer immediately to the left of the first character of the text to be selected (in this case, the I in the word, It).

• Drag the mouse pointer through the last character of the text to be selected (in this case, the space after the y in Easy) (Figure 1–58).

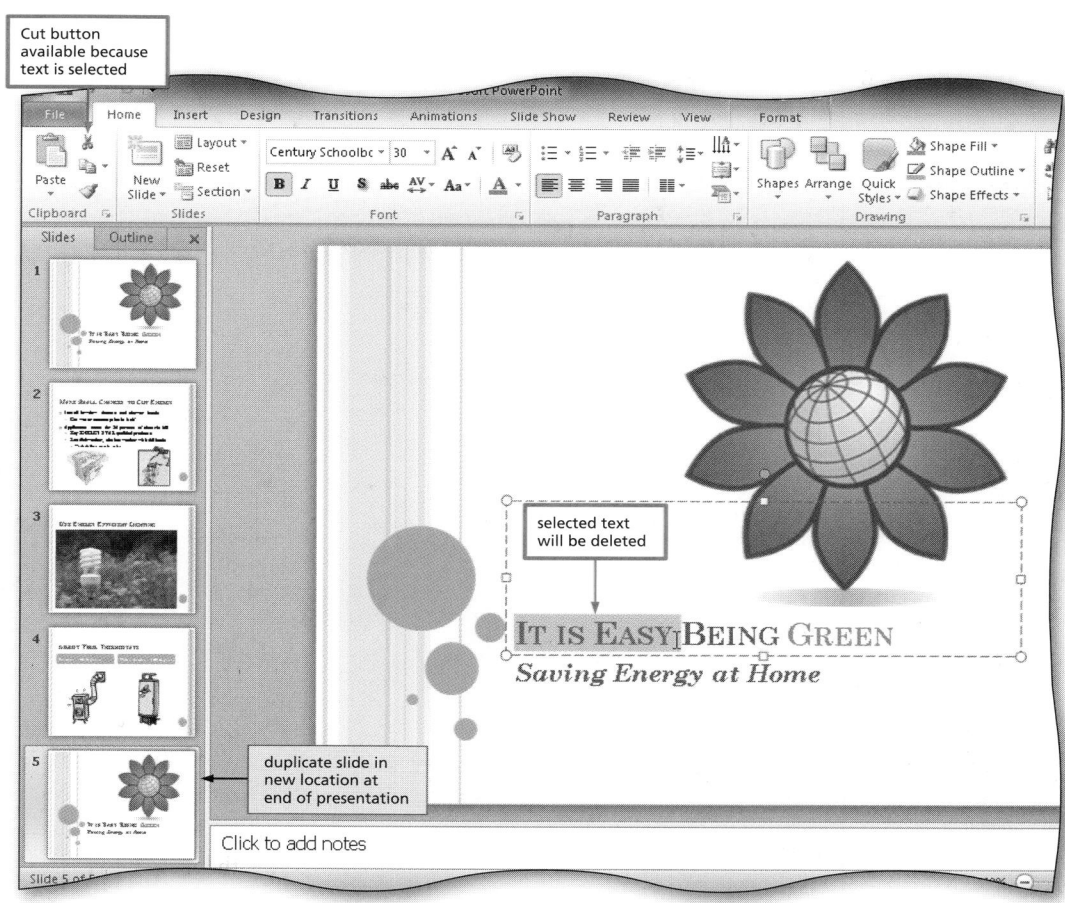

Cut button available because text is selected

selected text will be deleted

duplicate slide in new location at end of presentation

Figure 1–58

• Click the Cut button (Home tab | Clipboard group) to delete all the selected text (Figure 1–59).

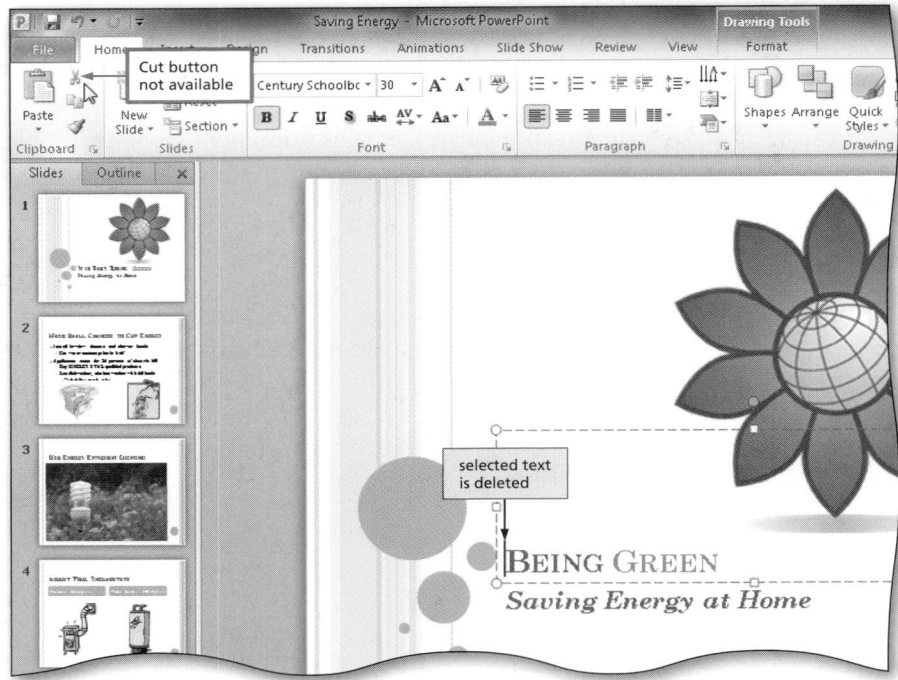

Figure 1–59

• Select the letters, ing, in the word, Being.

• Click the Cut button (Figure 1–60).

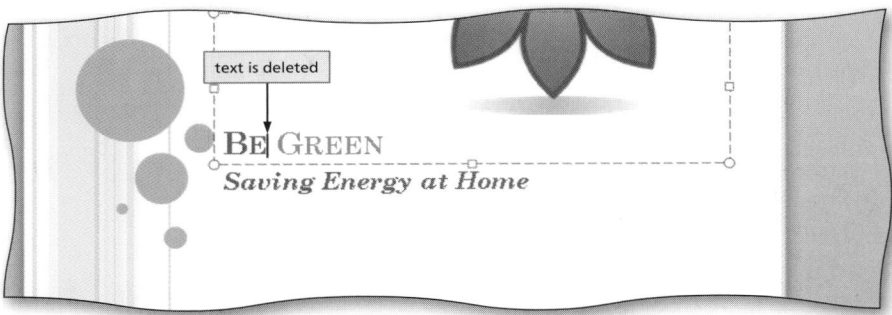

Figure 1–60

• Select the letters, ing, in the word, Saving, and then click the Cut button.

• Type e to change the word to Save (Figure 1–61).

Other Ways

1. Right-click selected text, click Cut on shortcut menu
2. Select text, press DELETE or BACKSPACE key
3. Select text, press CTRL+X

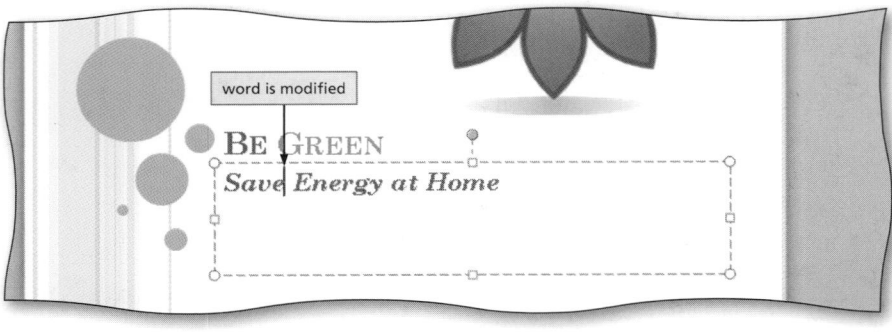

Figure 1–61

Adding a Transition

PowerPoint provides many animation effects to add interest and make a slide show presentation look professional. **Animation** includes special visual and sound effects applied to text or content. A **slide transition** is a special animation effect used to progress from one slide to the next in a slide show. You can control the speed of the transition effect and add a sound.

PowerPoint provides a variety of transitions arranged into three categories that describe the types of effects: Subtle, Exciting, and Dynamic Content.

To Add a Transition between Slides

In this presentation, you apply the Doors transition in the Exciting category to all slides and change the transition speed from 1.40 seconds to 2 seconds. The following steps apply this transition to the presentation.

1
- Click the Transitions tab on the Ribbon and then point to the More button (Transitions tab | Transition to This Slide group) (Figure 1–62).

Q&A Is a transition applied now?

No. The first slide icon in the Transitions group has an orange border, which indicates no transition has been applied.

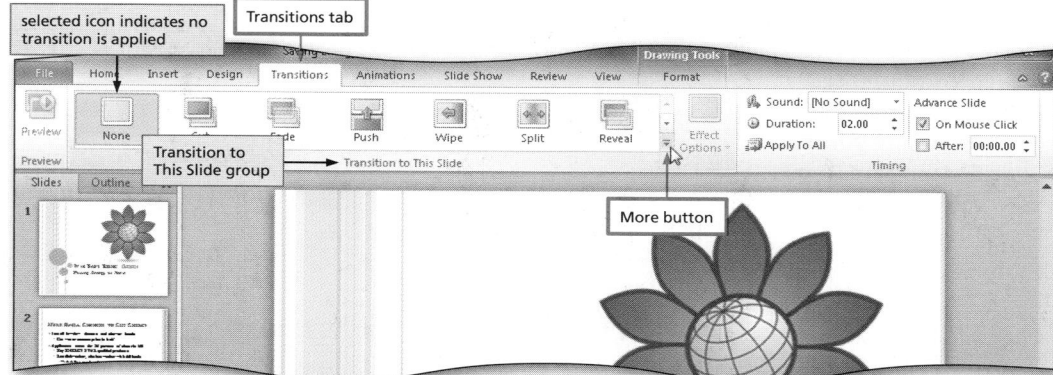

Figure 1–62

2
- Click the More button to expand the Transitions gallery.

- Point to the Doors transition in the Exciting category in the Transitions gallery (Figure 1–63).

Q&A Can I add a sound to play during this transition?

Yes. Click the Sound arrow (Transitions tab | Timing group) to display the Sound list and then select a sound from this list. You also can use your own sound if you select Other Sound in the list, select the desired sound (Add Audio dialog box), and then click the OK button.

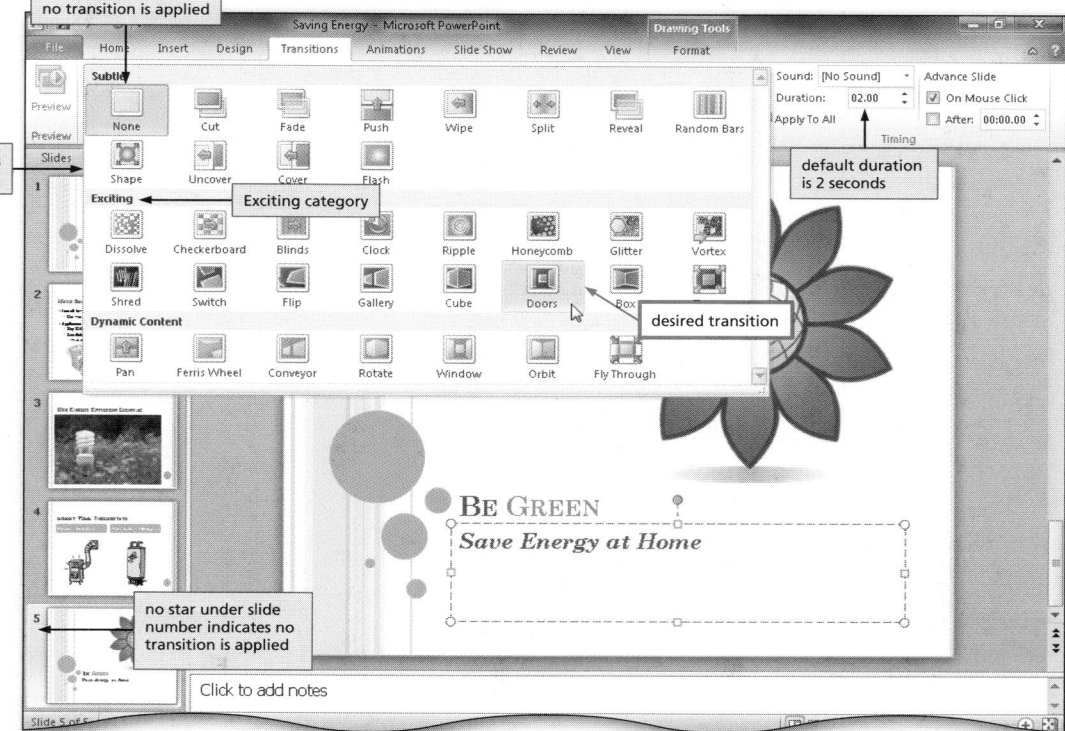

Figure 1–63

3

• Click Doors in the Exciting category in the Transitions gallery to apply this transition to the closing slide.

Q&A Why does a star appear next to Slide 5 in the Slides tab?

The star indicates that a transition animation effect is applied to that slide.

• Click the Duration up arrow (Transitions tab | Timing group) three times to change the transition speed from 01.40 seconds to 02.00 seconds (Figure 1–64).

Q&A Why did the time change?

Each transition has a default duration time. The Doors transition time is 1:40 seconds.

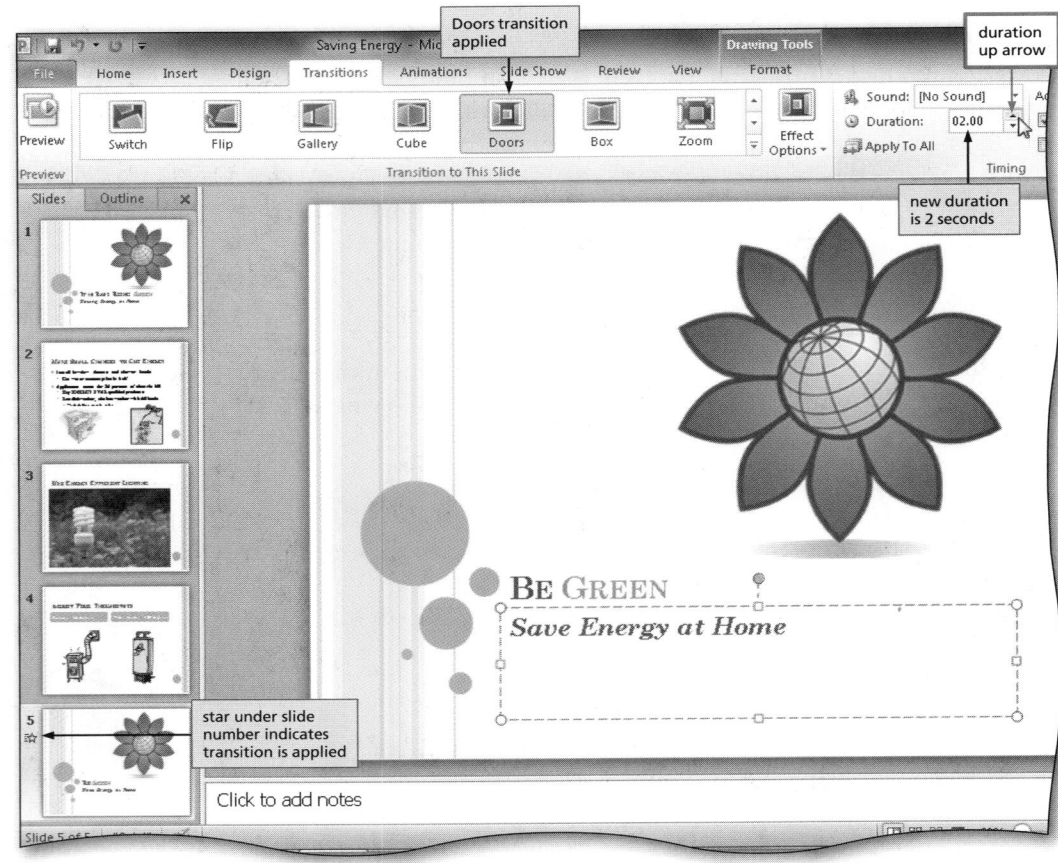

Figure 1–64

4

• Click the Preview Transitions button (Transitions tab | Preview area) to view the transition and the new transition time (Figure 1–65).

Q&A Can I adjust the duration time I just set?

Yes. Click the Duration up or down arrows or type a speed in the Duration text box and preview the transition until you find the time that best fits your presentation.

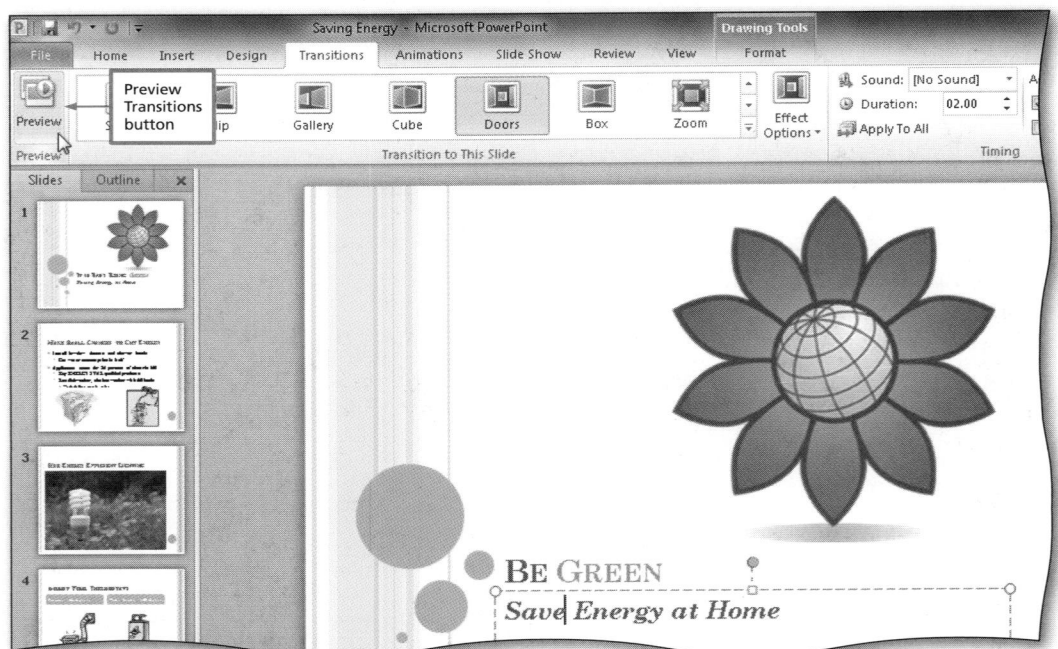

Figure 1–65

5

- Click the Apply To All button (Transitions tab | Timing group) to apply the Doors transition and the increased transition time to Slides 1 through 4 in the presentation (Figure 1–66).

Q&A

What if I want to apply a different transition and duration to each slide in the presentation?

Repeat Steps 2 and 3 for each slide individually.

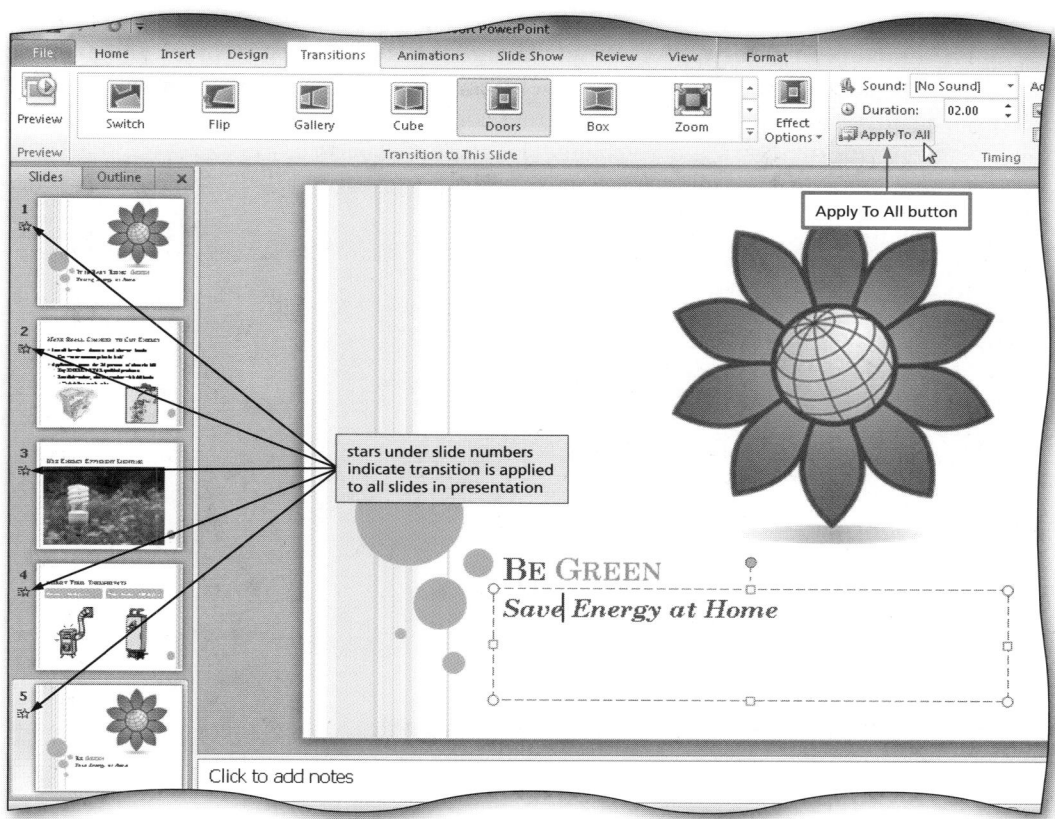

Figure 1–66

Changing Document Properties

PowerPoint helps you organize and identify your files by using **document properties**, which are the details about a file. Document properties, also known as **metadata**, can include information such as the project author, title, subject, and keywords. A **keyword** is a word or phrase that further describes the document. For example, a class name or document topic can describe the file's purpose or content.

Document properties are valuable for a variety of reasons:

- Users can save time locating a particular file because they can view a document's properties without opening the document.

- By creating consistent properties for files having similar content, users can better organize their documents.

- Some organizations require PowerPoint users to add document properties so that other employees can view details about these files.

Five different types of document properties exist, but the more common ones used in this book are standard and automatically updated properties. **Standard properties** are associated with all Microsoft Office documents and include author, title, and subject. **Automatically updated properties** include file system properties, such as the date you create or change a file, and statistics, such as the file size.

To Change Document Properties

The **Document Information Panel** contains areas where you can view and enter document properties. You can view and change information in this panel at any time while you are creating a document. Before saving the presentation again, you want to add your name and course information as document properties. The following steps use the Document Information Panel to change document properties.

- Click File on the Ribbon to open the Backstage view.

- If necessary, click the Info tab in the Backstage view to display the Info gallery (Figure 1–67).

Q&A How do I close the Backstage view?

Click File on the Ribbon or click the preview of the document in the Info gallery to return to the PowerPoint document window.

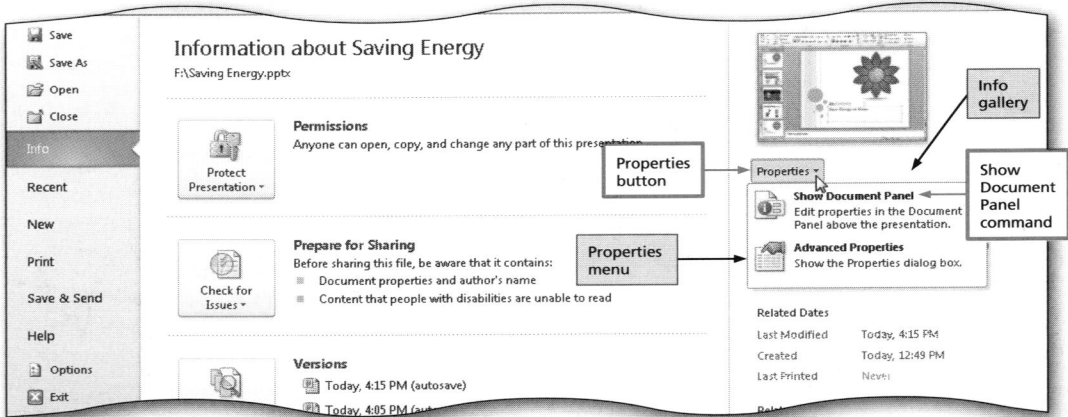

Figure 1–67

- Click the Properties button in the right pane of the Info gallery to display the Properties menu (Figure 1–68).

Figure 1–68

- Click Show Document Panel on the Properties menu to close the Backstage view and display the Document Information Panel in the PowerPoint document window (Figure 1–69).

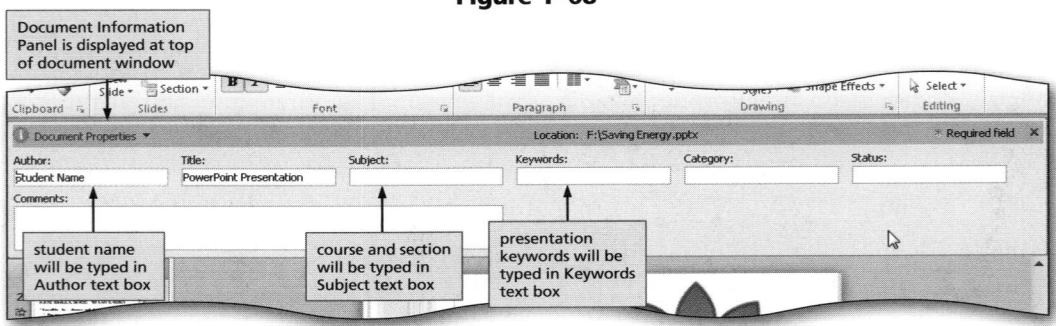

Figure 1–69

Q&A Why are some of the document properties in my Document Information Panel already filled in?

The person who installed Microsoft Office 2010 on your computer or network may have set or customized the properties.

- Click the Author text
  box, if necessary, and
  then type your name
  as the Author property.
  If a name already is
  displayed in the Author
  text box, delete it before
  typing your name.

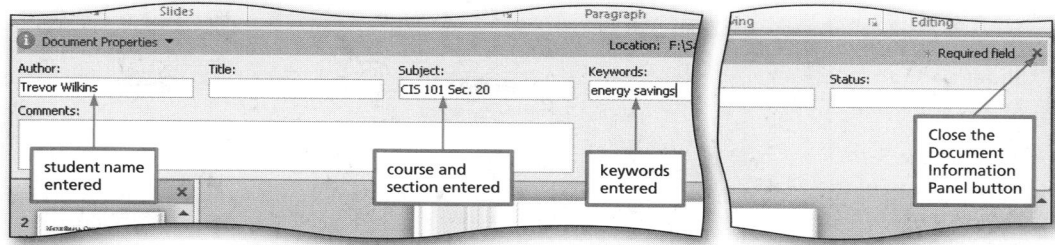

Figure 1–70

- Click the Subject text
  box, if necessary delete
  any existing text, and then type your course and section as the Subject property.

- If an AutoComplete dialog box appears, click its Yes button.

- Click the Keywords text box, if necessary delete any existing text, and then type **energy savings** as the Keywords property (Figure 1–70).

Q&A What types of document properties does PowerPoint collect automatically?

PowerPoint records details such as time spent editing a document, the number of times a document has been revised, and the fonts and themes used in a document.

5

- Click the Close the Document Information Panel button so that the Document Information Panel no longer is displayed.

Other Ways

1. Click File on Ribbon, click Info in Backstage view, if necessary click Show All Properties link in Info gallery, click property to change and type new information, close Backstage view

To Save an Existing Presentation with the Same File Name

You have made several modifications to the presentation since you last saved it. Thus, you should save it again. The following step saves the document again. For an example of the step listed below, refer to the Office 2010 and Windows 7 chapter at the beginning of this book.

1 Click the Save button on the Quick Access Toolbar to overwrite the previously saved file.

BTW

Saving in a Previous PowerPoint Format
To ensure that your presentation will open in PowerPoint 2003 or older versions of this software, you must save your file in PowerPoint 97-2003 format. These files will have the .ppt extension.

Viewing the Presentation in Slide Show View

The Slide Show button, located in the lower-right corner of the PowerPoint window above the status bar, allows you to show a presentation using a computer. The computer acts like a slide projector, displaying each slide on a full screen. The full-screen slide hides the toolbars, menus, and other PowerPoint window elements.

To Start Slide Show View

When making a presentation, you use **Slide Show view**. You can start Slide Show view from Normal view or Slide Sorter view. Slide Show view begins when you click the Slide Show button on the lower-right corner of the status bar. PowerPoint then shows the current slide on the full screen without any of the PowerPoint window objects, such as the menu bar or toolbars. The following steps start Slide Show view.

1

• Click the Slide 1 thumbnail in the Slides pane to select and display Slide 1.

• Point to the Slide Show button in the lower-right corner of the PowerPoint window on the status bar (Figure 1–71).

Q&A Why did I need to select Slide 1?

When you run a slide show, PowerPoint begins the show with the currently displayed slide. If you had not selected Slide 1, then only Slide 5 would have displayed in the slide show.

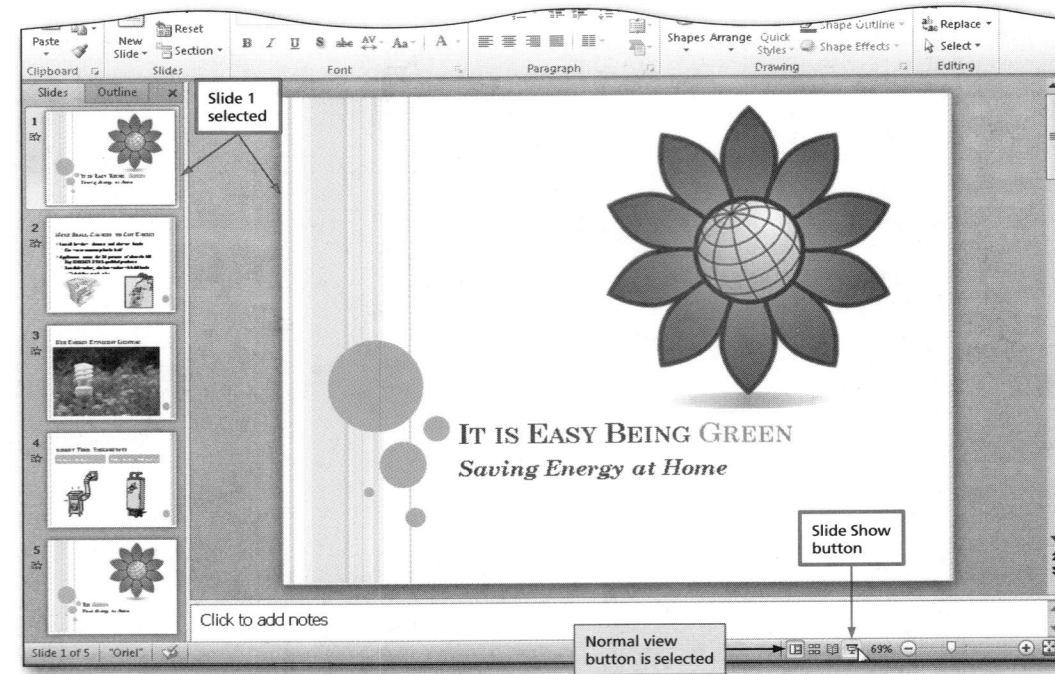

Figure 1–71

2

• Click the Slide Show button to display the title slide (Figure 1–72).

Q&A Where is the PowerPoint window?

When you run a slide show, the PowerPoint window is hidden. It will reappear once you end your slide show.

Other Ways

1. Click Slide Show From Beginning button (Slide Show tab | Start Slide Show group)
2. Press F5

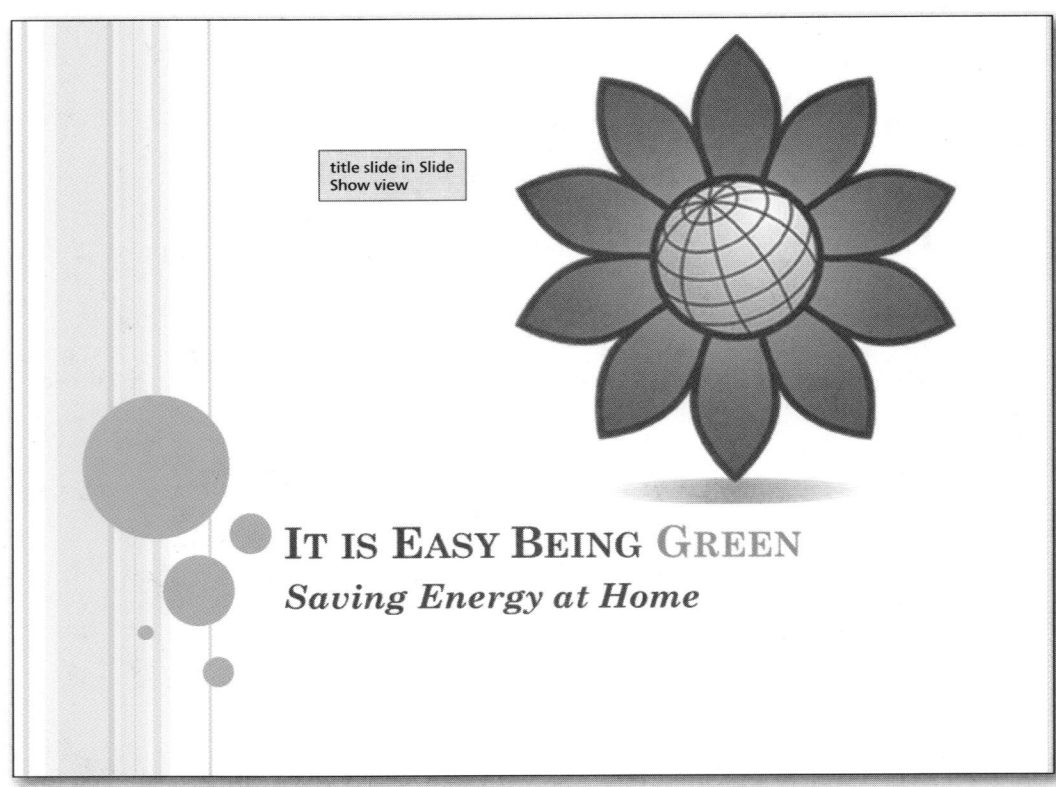

Figure 1–72

To Move Manually through Slides in a Slide Show

After you begin Slide Show view, you can move forward or backward through the slides. PowerPoint allows you to advance through the slides manually or automatically. During a slide show, each slide in the presentation shows on the screen, one slide at a time. Each time you click the mouse button, the next slide appears. The following steps move manually through the slides.

- Click each slide until Slide 5 (Be Green) is displayed (Figure 1–73).

Q&A I see a small toolbar in the lower-left corner of my slide. What is this toolbar?

The Slide Show toolbar appears when you begin running a slide show and then move the mouse pointer. The buttons on this toolbar allow you to navigate to the next slide, the previous slide, to mark up the current slide, or to change the current display.

Figure 1–73

- Click Slide 5 so that the black slide appears with a message announcing the end of the slide show (Figure 1–74).

Q&A How can I end the presentation at this point?

Click the black slide to return to Normal view in the PowerPoint window or press the ESC key.

Figure 1–74

Other Ways

1. Press PAGE DOWN to advance one slide at a time, or press PAGE UP to go back one slide at a time

2. Press RIGHT ARROW or DOWN ARROW to advance one slide at a time, or press LEFT ARROW or UP ARROW to go back one slide at a time

3. If Slide Show toolbar is displayed, click Next Slide or Previous Slide button on toolbar

BTW

Eliminating the Black Slide
By default, a black slide is displayed at the end of a slide show. If you do not want this slide to appear, click the File tab, click Options, and then click the Advanced link. In the Slide Show group, click 'End with black slide' to uncheck it.

To Quit PowerPoint

This project now is complete. The following steps quit PowerPoint. For a detailed example of the procedure summarized below, refer to the Office 2010 and Windows 7 chapter at the beginning of this book.

1 If you have one PowerPoint presentation open, click the Close button on the right side of the title bar to close the document and quit PowerPoint; or if you have multiple PowerPoint presentations open, click File on the Ribbon to open the Backstage view and then click Exit in the Backstage view to close all open documents and quit PowerPoint.

2 If a Microsoft PowerPoint dialog box appears, click the Save button to save any changes made to the document since the last save.

BTW

Certification
The Microsoft Office Specialist (MOS) program provides an opportunity for you to obtain a valuable industry credential — proof that you have the PowerPoint 2010 skills required by employers. For more information, visit the PowerPoint 2010 Certification Web page (scsite.com/ppt2010/cert).

To Start PowerPoint

Once you have created and saved a document, you may need to retrieve it from your storage medium. For example, you might want to revise the presentation or print it. The following steps, which assume Windows 7 is running, start PowerPoint so that you can open and modify the presentation. You may need to ask your instructor how to start PowerPoint for your computer. For a detailed example of the procedure summarized below, refer to the Office 2010 and Windows 7 chapter at the beginning of this book.

1 Click the Start button on the Windows 7 taskbar to display the Start menu.

2 Type **Microsoft PowerPoint** as the search text in the 'Search programs and files' text box and watch the search results appear on the Start menu.

3 Click Microsoft PowerPoint 2010 in the search results on the Start menu to start PowerPoint and display a new blank document in the PowerPoint window.

4 If the PowerPoint window is not maximized, click the Maximize button next to the Close button on its title bar to maximize the window.

To Open a Document from PowerPoint

Earlier in this chapter you saved your project on a USB flash drive using the file name, Saving Energy. The following steps open the Saving Energy file from the PowerPoint folder in the CIS 101 folder on the USB flash drive. For a detailed example of the procedure summarized below, refer to the Office 2010 and Windows 7 chapter at the beginning of this book.

1 With your USB flash drive connected to one of the computer's USB ports, click File on the Ribbon to open the Backstage view.

2 Click Open in the Backstage view to display the Open dialog box.

3 Navigate to the location of the file to be opened (in this case, the USB flash drive, then to the CIS 101 folder [or your class folder], and then to the PowerPoint folder).

④ Click Saving Energy to select the file to be opened.

⑤ Click the Open button (Open dialog box) to open the selected file and display the opened document in the PowerPoint window.

Printing a Presentation

After creating a presentation, you may want to print the slides. Printing a presentation enables you to distribute the document to others in a form that can be read or viewed but typically not edited. It is a good practice to save a presentation before printing it, in the event you experience difficulties printing.

Determine the best method for distributing the presentation.
The traditional method of distributing a presentation uses a printer to produce a hard copy. A **hardcopy** or **printout** is information that exists on a physical medium such as paper. For users who can receive fax documents, you can elect to print a hard copy on a remote fax machine. Hard copies can be useful for the following reasons:

- Many people prefer proofreading a hard copy of a document rather than viewing it on the screen to check for errors and readability.

- Hard copies can serve as reference material if your storage medium is lost or becomes corrupted and you need to recreate the document.

    Instead of distributing a hard copy of a presentation slides, users can choose to distribute the presentation as an electronic image that mirrors the original document's appearance. The electronic image of the document can be e-mailed, posted on a Web site, or copied to a portable storage medium such as a USB flash drive. Two popular electronic image formats, sometimes called fixed formats, are PDF by Adobe Systems and XPS by Microsoft. In PowerPoint, you can create electronic image files through the Print tab in the Backstage view, the Save & Send tab in the Backstage view, and the Save As dialog box. Electronic images of documents, such as PDF and XPS, can be useful for the following reasons.

- Users can view electronic images of documents without the software that created the original document (e.g., PowerPoint). Specifically, to view a PDF file, you use a program called Acrobat Reader, which can be downloaded free from Adobe's Web site. Similarly, to view an XPS file, you use a program called an XPS Viewer, which is included in the latest versions of Windows and Internet Explorer.

- Sending electronic documents saves paper and printer supplies. Society encourages users to contribute to **green computing**, which involves reducing the environmental waste generated when using a computer.

Plan Ahead

To Print a Presentation

With the completed presentation saved, you may want to print it. If copies of the presentation are being distributed to audience members, you will print a hard copy of each individual slide on a printer. The following steps print a hard copy of the contents of the saved Saving Energy presentation.

• Click File on the Ribbon to open the Backstage view.

• Click the Print tab in the Backstage view to display the Print gallery (Figure 1–75).

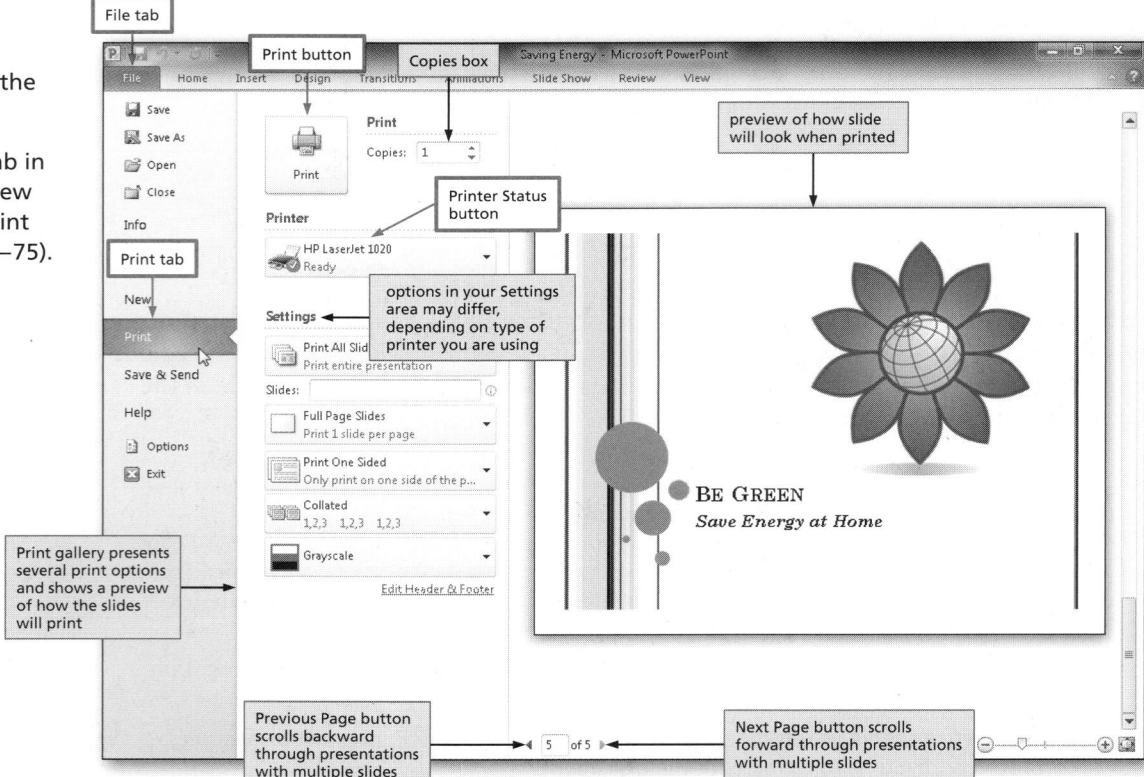

Figure 1–75

 How do I preview Slides 2 through 5?
Click the Next Page button in the Print gallery to scroll forward through pages in the document; similarly, click the Previous Page button to scroll backward through pages.

How can I print multiple copies of my slides?
Increase the number in the Copies box in the Print gallery.

What if I decide not to print the document at this time?
Click File on the Ribbon to close the Backstage view and return to the PowerPoint document window.

2

• Verify the printer name that appears on the Printer box Status button will print a hard copy of the document. If necessary, click the Printer Status button to display a list of available printer options and then click the desired printer to change the currently selected printer.

BTW

Quick Reference
For a table that lists how to complete the tasks covered in this book using the mouse, Ribbon, shortcut menu, and keyboard, see the Quick Reference Summary at the back of this book, or visit the PowerPoint 2010 Quick Reference Web page (scsite.com/ppt2010/qr).

- Click the Print button in the Print gallery to print the document on the currently selected printer.

- When the printer stops, retrieve the hard copy (Figure 1–76).

Q&A

Do I have to wait until my document is complete to print it?

No, you can follow these steps to print a document at any time while you are creating it.

Q&A

What if I want to print an electronic image of a document instead of a hard copy?

You would click the Printer Status button in the Print gallery and then select the desired electronic image option such as a Microsoft XPS Document Writer, which would create an XPS file.

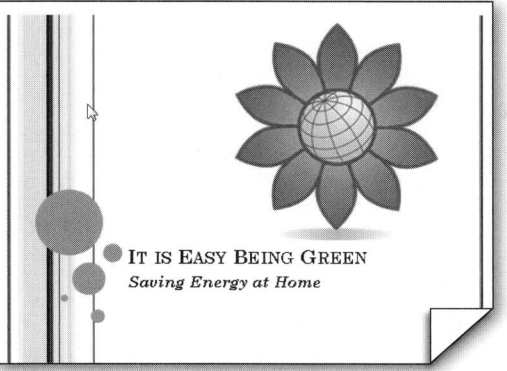

(a) Slide 1

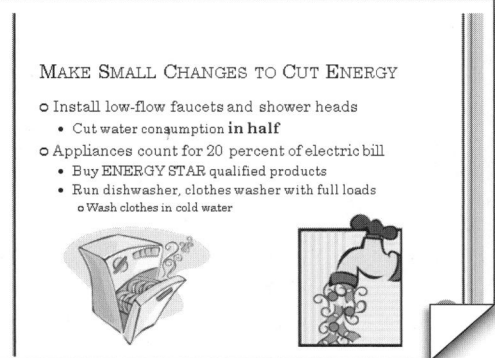

(b) Slide 2

(c) Slide 3

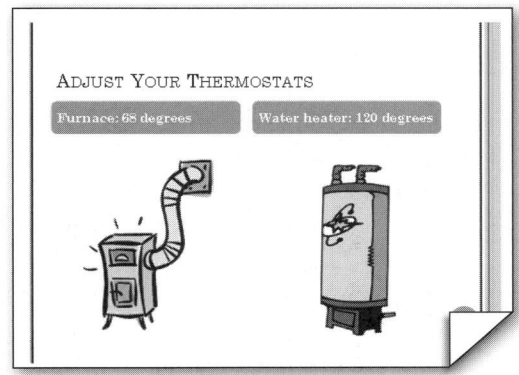

(d) Slide 4

(e) Slide 5

Figure 1–76

Other Ways
1. Press CTRL+P, press ENTER

To Quit PowerPoint

The project now is complete. The following steps quit PowerPoint. For a detailed example of the procedure summarized below, refer to the Office 2010 and Windows 7 chapter at the beginning of this book.

1 If you have one PowerPoint document open, click the Close button on the right side of the title bar to close the document and quit PowerPoint; or if you have multiple PowerPoint documents open, click File on the Ribbon to open the Backstage view and then click Exit in the Backstage view to close all open documents and quit PowerPoint.

2 If a Microsoft Office PowerPoint dialog box appears, click the Save button to save any changes made to the document since the last save.

Chapter Summary

In this chapter you have learned how to apply a document theme, create a title slide and text slides with a bulleted list, clip art, and a photograph, size and move clip art and a photograph, format and edit text, add a slide transition, view the presentation in Slide Show view, and print slides as handouts. The items listed below include all the new PowerPoint skills you have learned in this chapter.

1. Start PowerPoint (PPT 4)
2. Choose a Document Theme (PPT 5)
3. Enter the Presentation Title (PPT 7)
4. Enter the Presentation Subtitle Paragraph (PPT 9)
5. Select a Paragraph (PPT 10)
6. Italicize Text (PPT 11)
7. Increase Font Size (PPT 11)
8. Select a Word (PPT 12)
9. Change the Text Color (PPT 13)
10. Save a Presentation (PPT 14)
11. Add a New Text Slide with a Bulleted List (PPT 14)
12. Enter a Slide Title (PPT 16)
13. Select a Text Placeholder (PPT 16)
14. Type a Multi-Level Bulleted List (PPT 17)
15. Select a Group of Words (PPT 19)
16. Bold Text (PPT 19)
17. Add a Slide with the Title Only Layout (PPT 21)
18. Add a New Slide and Enter a Slide Title and Headings (PPT 23)
19. Move to Another Slide in Normal View (PPT 25)
20. Insert a Clip from the Clip Organizer into the Title Slide (PPT 27)
21. Insert a Clip from the Clip Organizer into a Content Placeholder (PPT 30)
22. Insert a Photograph from the Clip Organizer into a Slide without a Content Placeholder (PPT 32)
23. Resize Clip Art (PPT 33)
24. Move Clips (PPT 36)
25. Duplicate a Slide (PPT 38)
26. Arrange a Slide (PPT 39)
27. Delete Text in a Placeholder (PPT 41)
28. Add a Transition between Slides (PPT 43)
29. Change Document Properties (PPT 46)
30. Save an Existing Presentation with the Same File Name (PPT 47)
31. Start Slide Show View (PPT 47)
32. Move Manually through Slides in a Slide Show (PPT 49)
33. Quit PowerPoint (PPT 50)
34. Open a Document from PowerPoint (PPT 50)
35. Print a Presentation (PPT 51)

 If you have a SAM 2010 user profile, your instructor may have assigned an autogradable version of this assignment. If so, log into the SAM 2010 Web site at www.cengage.com/sam2010 to download the instruction and start files.

Learn It Online

Test your knowledge of chapter content and key terms.

Instructions: To complete the Learn It Online exercises, start your browser, click the Address bar, and then enter the Web address   **scsite.com/ppt2010/learn**.   When the PowerPoint 2010 Learn It Online page is displayed, click the link for the exercise you want to complete and then read the instructions.

Chapter Reinforcement TF, MC, and SA
A series of true/false, multiple choice, and short answer questions that test your knowledge of the chapter content.

Flash Cards
An interactive learning environment where you identify chapter key terms associated with displayed definitions.

Practice Test
A series of multiple choice questions that test your knowledge of chapter content and key terms.

Who Wants To Be a Computer Genius?
An interactive game that challenges your knowledge of chapter content in the style of a television quiz show.

Wheel of Terms
An interactive game that challenges your knowledge of chapter key terms in the style of the television show *Wheel of Fortune*.

Crossword Puzzle Challenge
A crossword puzzle that challenges your knowledge of key terms presented in the chapter.

Apply Your Knowledge

Reinforce the skills and apply the concepts you learned in this chapter.

Modifying Character Formats and Paragraph Levels and Moving a Clip
Note: To complete this assignment, you will be required to use the Data Files for Students. See the inside back cover of this book for instructions on downloading the Data Files for Students, or contact your instructor for information about accessing the required files.

Instructions: Start PowerPoint. Open the presentation, Apply 1-1 Flu Season, from the Data Files for Students.

The two slides in the presentation discuss ways to avoid getting or spreading the flu. The document you open is an unformatted presentation. You are to modify the document theme, indent the paragraphs, resize and move the clip art, and format the text so the slides look like Figure 1–77 on the next page.

Continued >

Apply Your Knowledge *continued*

Perform the following tasks:

1. Change the document theme to Urban. On the title slide, use your name in place of Student Name and bold and italicize your name. Increase the title text font size to 60 point. Resize and position the clip as shown in Figure 1–77a.

2. On Slide 2, increase the indent of the second, third, and fifth paragraphs (Cover mouth and nose with a tissue; No tissue? Use your elbow or sleeve; Use soap, warm water for 20 seconds) to second-level paragraphs. Then combine paragraphs six and seven (Drink fluids; Get plenty of rest) to read, Drink fluids and get plenty of rest, as shown in Figure 1–77b.

3. Change the document properties, as specified by your instructor. Save the presentation using the file name, Apply 1–1 Avoid the Flu. Submit the revised document in the format specified by your instructor.

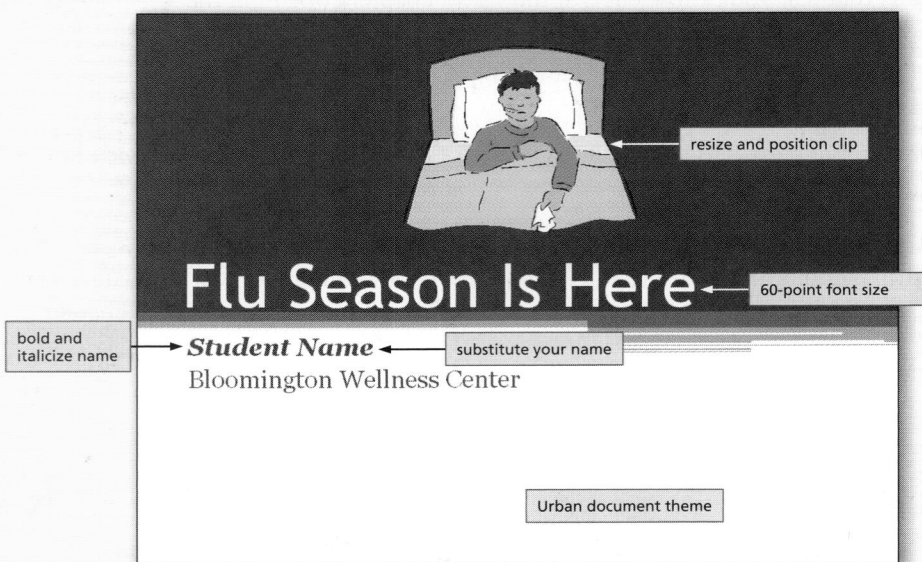

(a) Slide 1 (Title Slide with Clip Art)

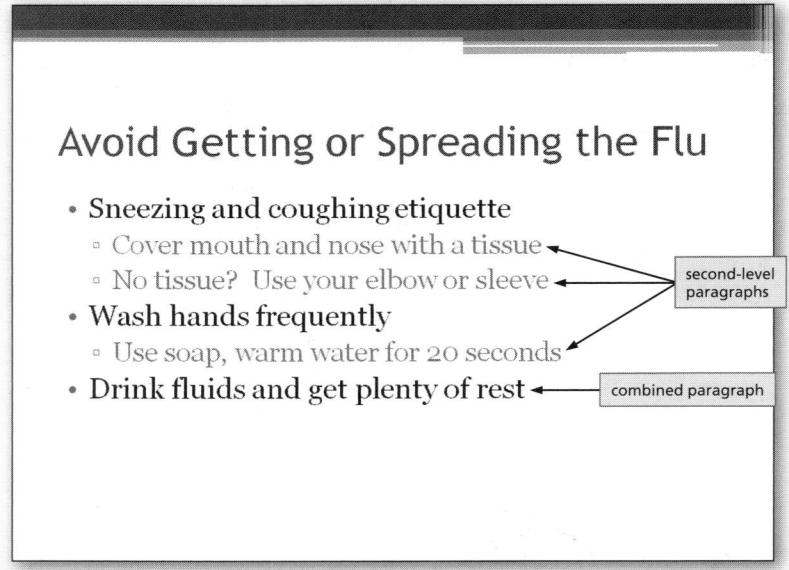

(b) Slide 2 (Multi-Level Bulleted List)

Figure 1–77

Extend Your Knowledge

Extend the skills you learned in this chapter and experiment with new skills. You may need to use Help to complete the assignment.

Changing Slide Theme, Layout, and Text

Note: To complete this assignment, you will be required to use the Data Files for Students. See the inside back cover of this book for instructions on downloading the Data Files for Students, or contact your instructor for information about accessing the required files.

Instructions: Start PowerPoint. Open the presentation that you are going to prepare for your dental hygiene class, Extend 1–1 Winning Smile, from the Data Files for Students.

You will choose a theme, format slides, and create a closing slide.

Perform the following tasks:

1. Apply an appropriate document theme.
2. On Slide 1, use your name in place of Student Name. Format the text on this slide using techniques you learned in this chapter, such as changing the font size and color and also bolding and italicizing words.
3. On Slide 2, change the slide layout and adjust the paragraph levels so that the lines of text are arranged under two headings: Discount Dental and Dental Insurance (Figure 1–78).
4. On Slide 3, create paragraphs and adjust the paragraph levels to create a bulleted list. Edit the text so that the slide meets the 7 × 7 rule, which states that each line should have a maximum of seven words, and each slide should have a maximum of seven lines.
5. Create an appropriate closing slide using the title slide as a guide.
6. The slides contain a variety of clips downloaded from the Microsoft Clip Organizer. Size and move them when necessary.
7. Apply an appropriate transition to all slides.
8. Change the document properties, as specified by your instructor. Save the presentation using the file name, Extend 1–1 Dental Plans.
9. Submit the revised document in the format specified by your instructor.

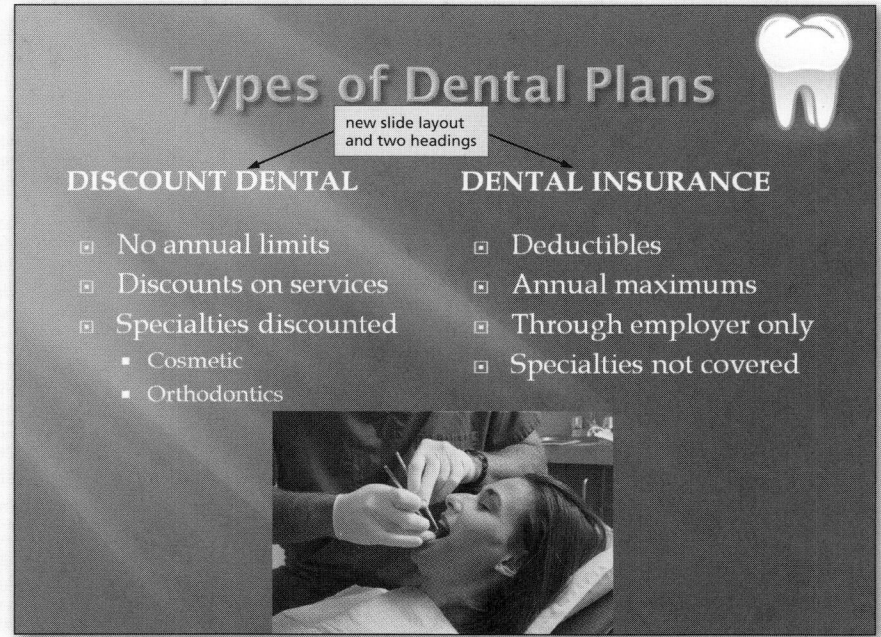

Figure 1–78

Make It Right

Analyze a presentation and correct all errors and/or improve the design.

Correcting Formatting and List Levels

Note: To complete this assignment, you will be required to use the Data Files for Students. See the inside back cover of this book for instructions on downloading the Data Files for Students, or contact your instructor for information about accessing the required files.

Instructions: Start PowerPoint. Open the presentation, Make It Right 1–1 Air Ducts, from the Data Files for Students.

Members of your homeowners' association are having their semiannual meeting, and each member of the board is required to give a short presentation on the subject of energy savings. You have decided to discuss the energy-saving benefits of maintaining the air ducts in your home. Correct the formatting problems and errors in the presentation while keeping in mind the guidelines presented in this chapter.

Perform the following tasks:

1. Change the document theme from Origin, shown in Figure 1–79, to Module.
2. On Slide 1, replace the words, Student Name, with your name. Format your name so that it displays prominently on the slide.
3. Increase the size of the clip on Slide 1 and move it to the upper-right corner.
4. Move Slide 2 to the end of the presentation so that it becomes the new Slide 3.
5. On Slide 2, correct the spelling errors and then increase the font size of the Slide 2 title text, Check Hidden Air Ducts, to 54 point. Increase the size of the clip and move it up to fill the white space on the right of the bulleted list.
6. On Slide 3, correct the spelling errors and then change the font size of the title text, Energy Savings, to 54 point. Increase the indent levels for paragraphs 2 and 4. Increase the size of the clips. Center the furnace clip at the bottom of the slide.
7. Change the document properties, as specified by your instructor. Save the presentation using the file name, Make It Right 1–1 Ducts Presentation.
8. Apply the same transition and duration to all slides.
9. Submit the revised document in the format specified by your instructor.

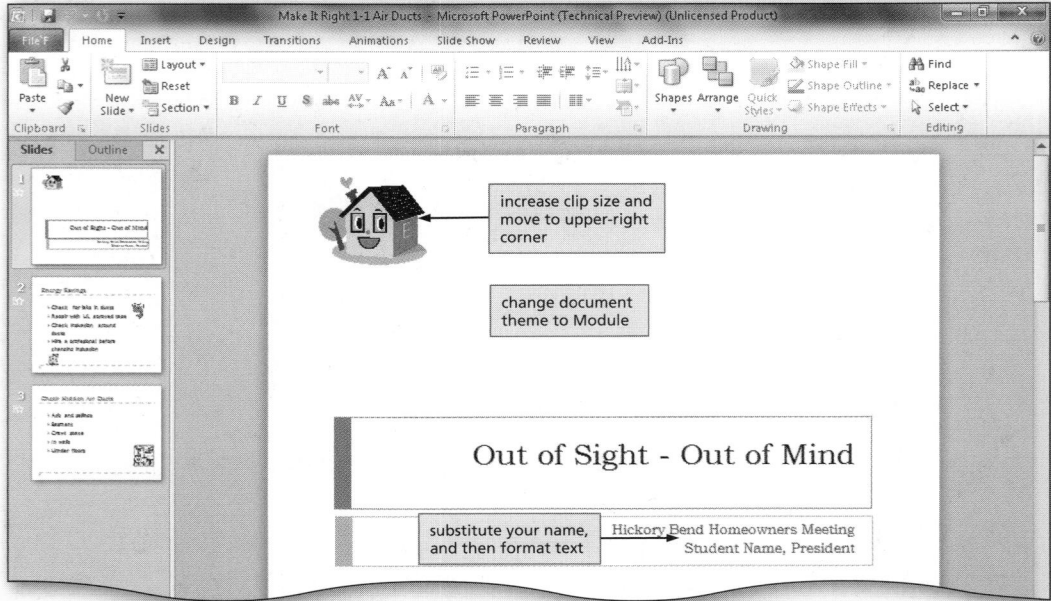

Figure 1–79

In the Lab

Design and/or create a presentation using the guidelines, concepts, and skills presented in this chapter. Labs 1, 2, and 3 are listed in order of increasing difficulty.

Lab1: Creating a Presentation with Bulleted Lists, a Closing Slide, and Clips

Problem: You are working with upper-level students to host a freshmen orientation seminar. When you attended this seminar, you received some helpful tips on studying for exams. Your contribution to this year's seminar is to prepare a short presentation on study skills. You develop the outline shown in Figure 1–80 and then prepare the PowerPoint presentation shown in Figures 1–81a through 1–81d.

Hit the Books
Studying for an Exam
Sarah Jones

Prepare in Advance
    Location
        Quiet, well-lit
    Timing
        15-minute breaks every hour
    Material
        Quiz yourself

Exam Time
    Day of Exam
        Rest properly
        Eat a good meal
        Wear comfy clothes
        Be early
        Be confident

Figure 1–80

Perform the following tasks:

1. Create a new presentation using the Aspect document theme.

2. Using the typed notes illustrated in Figure 1–80, create the title slide shown in Figure 1–81a, using your name in place of Sarah Jones. Italicize your name and increase the font size to 24 point. Increase the font size of the title text paragraph, Hit the Books, to 48 point. Increase the font size of the first paragraph of the subtitle text, Studying for an Exam, to 28 point.

(a) Slide 1 (Title Slide)
Figure 1–81

Continued >

In the Lab *continued*

3. Using the typed notes in Figure 1–80, create the two text slides with bulleted lists and find and insert clips from the Microsoft Clip Organizer, as shown in Figures 1–81b and 1–81c.

4. Create a closing slide by duplicating Slide 1, deleting your name, replacing the photograph with the photograph shown in Figure 1–81d, and moving the slide to the end of the presentation.

5. On Slide 3, change the font color of the words, Be confident, to Yellow (fourth color in the Standard Colors row) and then bold this text.

6. Apply the Uncover transition in the Subtle category to all slides. Change the duration to 1.25 seconds.

7. Drag the scroll box to display Slide 1. Click the Slide Show button to start Slide Show view. Then click to display each slide.

8. Change the document properties, as specified by your instructor. Save the presentation using the file name, Lab 1–1 Study Skills.

9. Submit the document in the format specified by your instructor.

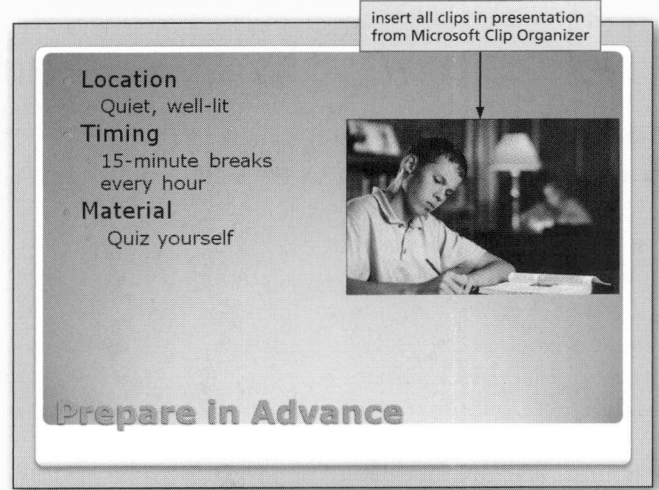

(b) Slide 2

(c) Slide 3

(d) Slide 4 (Closing Slide)
Figure 1–81 (continued)

In the Lab

Lab 2: Creating a Presentation with Bulleted Lists and Clips

Problem: Your health class instructor has assigned every student a different vitamin to research. She hands you the outline shown in Figure 1–82 and asks you to create the presentation about Vitamin D shown in Figures 1–83a through 1–83d on pages PPT 62 and PPT 63.

Vitamin D

The Sunshine Vitamin
Are You D-ficient?
Presented by Jim Warner

Why Is Vitamin D Important?
We need Vitamin D
Vital to our bodies
Promotes absorption of calcium and magnesium
For healthy teeth and bones
Maintains calcium and phosphorus in blood

Daily Requirements
How much do we need?
Child: 5 mcg (200 IU)
Adult: 10-20 mcg (400-600 IU)

Vitamin D Sources
Sunshine
Is our primary source
Vitamin manufactured by our body after exposure
Three times a week
For 10-15 minutes
Foods and Supplements
Contained in few foods
Some fish liver oils
Flesh of fatty fish
Fortified products
Milk and cereals
Available as supplement

Vitamin D History
Research began in 1924
Found to prevent rickets
United States and Canada
Instituted policy of fortifying foods with Vitamin D
Milk — food of choice
Other countries
Fortified cereal, bread, margarine

Figure 1–82

Continued >

In the Lab *continued*

Perform the following tasks:

1. Create a new presentation using the Solstice document theme.

2. Using the typed notes illustrated in Figure 1–82, create the title slide shown in Figure 1–83a, using your name in place of Jim Warner. Italicize the title, The Sunshine Vitamin, and increase the font size to 48 point. Change the font size of the first line of the subtitle text, Are You D-ficient?, to 36 point. Change the font color of the title text to Orange (third color in the Standard Colors row) and both lines of the subtitle text to Light Blue (seventh color in the Standard Colors row).

3. Using the typed notes in Figure 1–82, create the three text slides with bulleted lists shown in Figures 1–83b through 1–83d. Change the color of the title text on all slides and the text above the bulleted lists on Slides 2 and 3 to Orange.

4. Add the photographs and clip art shown in Figures 1–83a through 1–83d from the Microsoft Clip Organizer. Adjust the clip sizes when necessary.

5. Apply the Ripple transition in the Exciting category to all slides. Change the duration to 2.00 seconds.

6. Drag the scroll box to display Slide 1. Click the Slide Show button to start Slide Show view. Then click to display each slide.

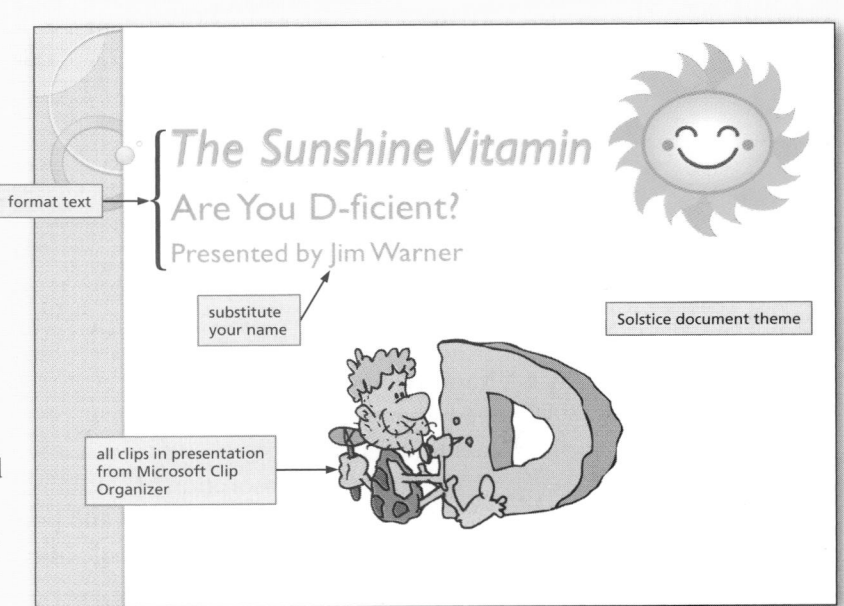

(a) Slide 1 (Title Slide)

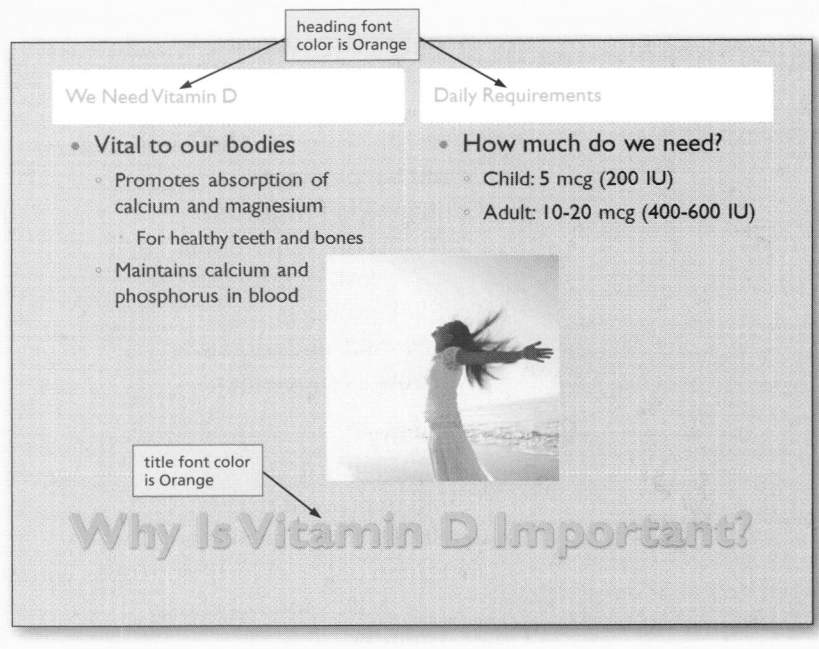

(b) Slide 2

Figure 1–83

7. Change the document properties, as specified by your instructor. Save the presentation using the file name, Lab 1–2 Vitamin D.

8. Submit the revised document in the format specified by your instructor.

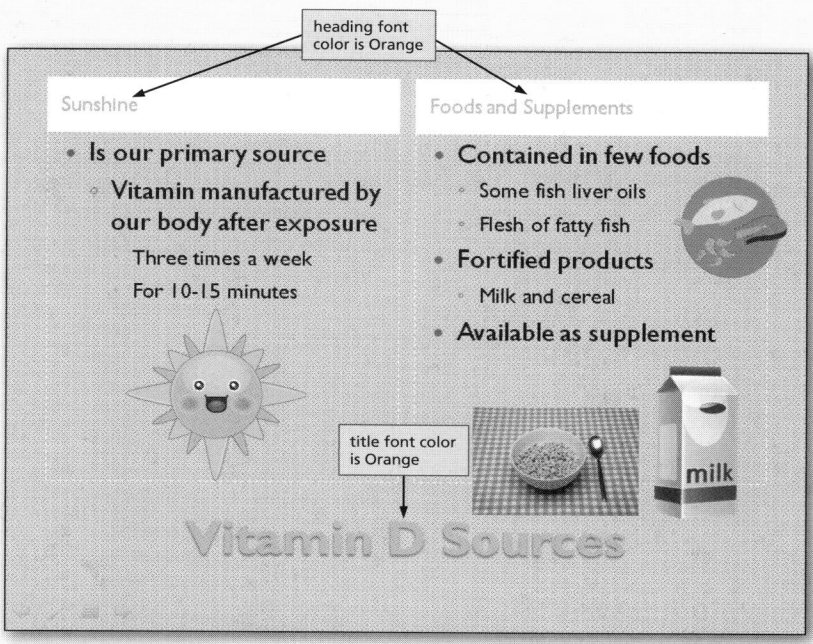

(c) Slide 3

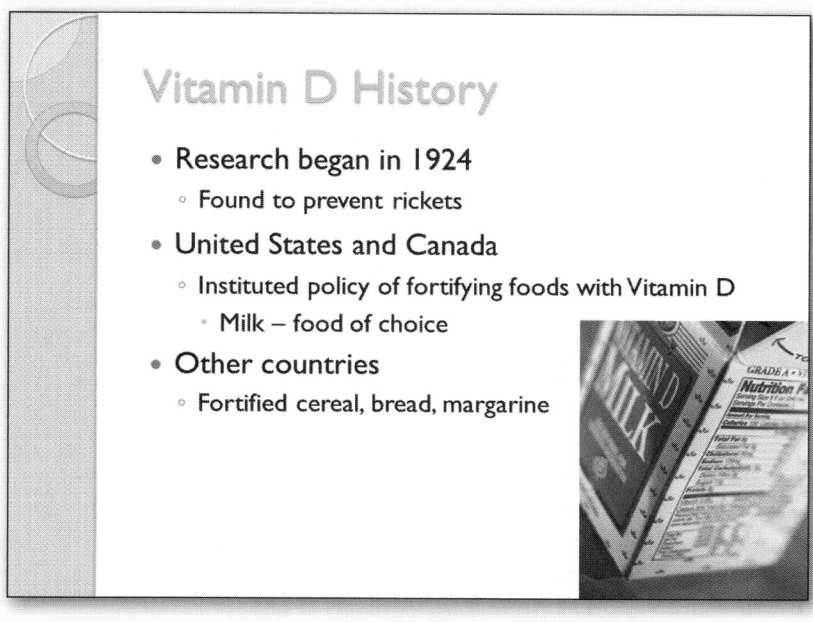

(d) Slide 4

Figure 1–83 (continued)

In the Lab

Lab 3: Creating and Updating Presentations with Clip Art

Problem: You are employed part time at your health club, and the Child Care Center director has asked you to put together a presentation for her to use at the next open house. The club has a large playroom that is perfect for children's parties.

Instructions Part 1: Using the outline in Figure 1–84, create the presentation shown in Figure 1–85. Use the Office Theme document theme. On the title slide shown in Figure 1–85a, increase the font size of the title paragraph, Make It a Party!, to 48, change the font color to Red, and change the text font style to italic. Decrease the font size of the entire subtitle paragraph to 28, and change the font color to Blue.

Make It a Party!
Host Your Child's
Next Birthday Party
at the Oaks Health Club

We Do the Work
You Enjoy the Moment
Two-hour party
Two chaperones
Lunch & cake provided
Game or craft activity available
Decorations

Two Party Packages
Package No. 1 - $8/child
Lunch
Hot Dogs
Pizza
Package No. 2 - $12/child
Lunch including beverage
Hot Dogs
Pizza
Game
Craft (age appropriate)

Reserve Your Party Date
Reserve 2 weeks in advance
Deposit required
Party room can hold 20 children
Sign up in the Child Care Center

Figure 1–84

Create the three text slides with multi-level bulleted lists, photographs, and clip art shown in Figures 1–85b through 1–85d on the next page. Adjust the clip sizes when necessary. Apply the Vortex transition in the Exciting category to all slides and decrease the duration to 3.00 seconds. Change the document properties, as specified by your instructor. Save the presentation using the file name, Lab 1–3 Part One Child Party.

(a) Slide 1 (Title Slide)

(b) Slide 2
Figure 1–85

Continued >

In the Lab continued

Two Party Packages

Package No. 1 - $8/child
- Lunch
  - Hot Dogs
  - Pizza

Package No. 2 - $12/child
- Lunch including beverage
  - Hot Dogs
  - Pizza
- Game
- Craft (age appropriate)

(c) Slide 3

Reserve Your Party Date

- Reserve 2 weeks in advance
- Deposit required
- Party room can hold 20 children
- Sign up in the Child Care Center

(d) Slide 4
Figure 1–85 (continued)

Instructions Part 2:   The children's parties have proved to be a great perk for members of the health club. A large group of older adults work out at the club and also meet socially once a month. These members have asked about renting the playroom to hold a retirement party for some of their friends. You decide to modify the children's party presentation to promote retirement parties. Use the outline in Figure 1–86 to modify the presentation created in Part 1 to create the presentation shown in Figure 1–87 on the next page. Required changes are indicated by a yellow highlight.

To begin, save the current presentation with the new file name, Lab 1–3 Part Two Retirement Party. Change the document theme to Flow. On Slide 3, change the pianist's name from Ms. Winn to your name. Apply the Fade transition in the Subtle category to all slides and change the duration speed to 2.25 seconds. View the slide show. Change the document properties, as specified by your instructor. Submit both Part One and Part Two documents in the format specified by your instructor.

Make It a Party!
   Host Your
   Retirement Party
   at the Oaks Health Club

We Do the Work
You Enjoy the Moment
   Two-hour party

   Lunch & cake provided

   Decorations
   Music

Two Party Packages
   Package No. 1 - $9/person
      Lunch
         Lasagna
         Salad & bread
   Package No. 2 - $20/person
      Lunch including beverage
         Lasagna
         Salad & bread
      Ms. Winn on piano
      Photo booth

Reserve Your Party Date
   Reserve 2 weeks in advance
   Deposit required
   Party room can hold 15 adults
   Sign up at the main desk

Figure 1–86

Continued >

In the Lab *continued*

(a) Slide 1 (Title Slide)

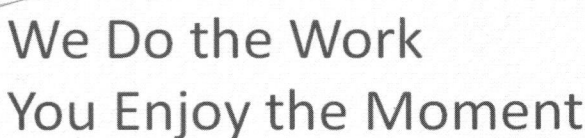

(b) Slide 2
Figure 1–87

(c) Slide 3

(d) Slide 4
Figure 1–87 (continued)

Cases and Places

Apply your creative thinking and problem-solving skills to design and implement a solution.

Note: To complete these assignments, you may be required to use the Data Files for Students. See the inside back cover of this book for instructions on downloading the Data Files for Students, or contact your instructor for information about accessing the required files.

As you design the presentations, remember to use the 7 × 7 rule: a maximum of seven words on a line and a maximum of seven lines on one slide.

1: Design and Create a Presentation about Galileo

Academic

Italian-born Galileo is said to be the father of modern science. After the invention of the telescope by a Dutch eyeglass maker named Hans Lippershey, Galileo made his own telescope and made many discoveries. You decide to prepare a PowerPoint presentation to accompany a speech that is required in your Astronomy class. You create the outline shown in Figure 1–88 about Galileo. Use this outline, along with the concepts and techniques presented in this chapter, to develop and format a slide show with a title slide and three text slides with bulleted lists. Add photographs and clip art from the Microsoft Clip Organizer and apply a transition. Submit your assignment in the format specified by your instructor.

Galileo Galilei
  Father of Modern Science
  Astronomy 201
  Sandy Wendt

Major Role in Scientific Revolution
February 15, 1564 –January 8, 1642
  Physicist
  Mathematician
  Astronomer
  Philosopher

Galileo's Research Years
  1581 - Studied medicine
  1589-1592 - Studied math and physics
  1592-1607 - Padua University
    Developed Law of Inertia
  1609 - Built telescope
    Earth's moon
    Jupiter's moons

Galileo's Later Years
  Dialogue - Two Chief World Systems
    Controversy develops
  1633 - Rome
    Heresy trial
    Imprisoned
  1642 - Dies

Figure 1–88

2: Design and Create a Presentation Promoting Hiking for Family Fitness

Personal

A great way for the entire family to get exercise is by participating in a hiking adventure. Employees at the local forest preserve district near your home have remodeled the nature center, and you have volunteered to give a presentation at the open house to help families plan their hikes. Use the outline shown in Figure 1–89 and then create an accompanying PowerPoint presentation. Use the concepts and techniques presented in this chapter to develop and format this slide show with a title slide, three text slides with bulleted lists, and clip art. Add photographs and clip art from the Microsoft Clip Organizer and apply a transition. Submit your assignment in the format specified by your instructor.

Take a Hike
    An Adventure with Kids
    Presented by Joshua Lind
    Pines Nature Center

Planning the Adventure
    Trail length — varies by child's age
        Ages 2 to 4: 1 to 2 miles
        Ages 5 to 7: 3 to 4 miles
        Ages 8 to 12: 5 to 7 miles
    Backpack — limit to 20 percent of child's weight

Packing Supplies
    Snacks and Drinks
        Child's favorite healthy foods
            Fruit and nuts
        Water
    Miscellaneous
        Sunscreen
        Insect repellent
        First-aid kit

Wearing the Right Clothes
    Dress in layers
        Children get cold quicker than adults
    Wear long pants and long-sleeved shirt
        Protect against insects and cuts
    Wear a hat and comfortable shoes
        Keep body warm

Figure 1–89

Continued >

Cases and Places *continued*

3: Design and Create a Landscaping Service Presentation

Professional

The home and garden center where you work is hosting weekend clinics for customers. The owner asks you to give a presentation about the center's new landscaping division and hands you the outline shown in Figure 1–90. Use the concepts and techniques presented in this chapter to develop and format a PowerPoint presentation with a title slide, three text slides with bulleted lists, and clip art. Add photographs and clip art from the Microsoft Clip Organizer and apply a transition. Submit your assignment in the format specified by your instructor.

Barry's Landscaping Service
Bensenville, Indiana

Full-Service Landscaping
    Initial design
    Installation
    Maintenance

Scope of Services
    Landscape design
    Irrigation
    Lighting
    Lawn-care programs
    Tree/shrub maintenance
    Masonry, carpentry
    Water features

Our Promise to You
    Deliver on-time service
    Provide highest level of workmanship
    Give maximum value for your dollar
    Install high-quality plants and materials
    Respond quickly to your needs

Figure 1–90

2 | Enhancing a Presentation with Pictures, Shapes, and WordArt

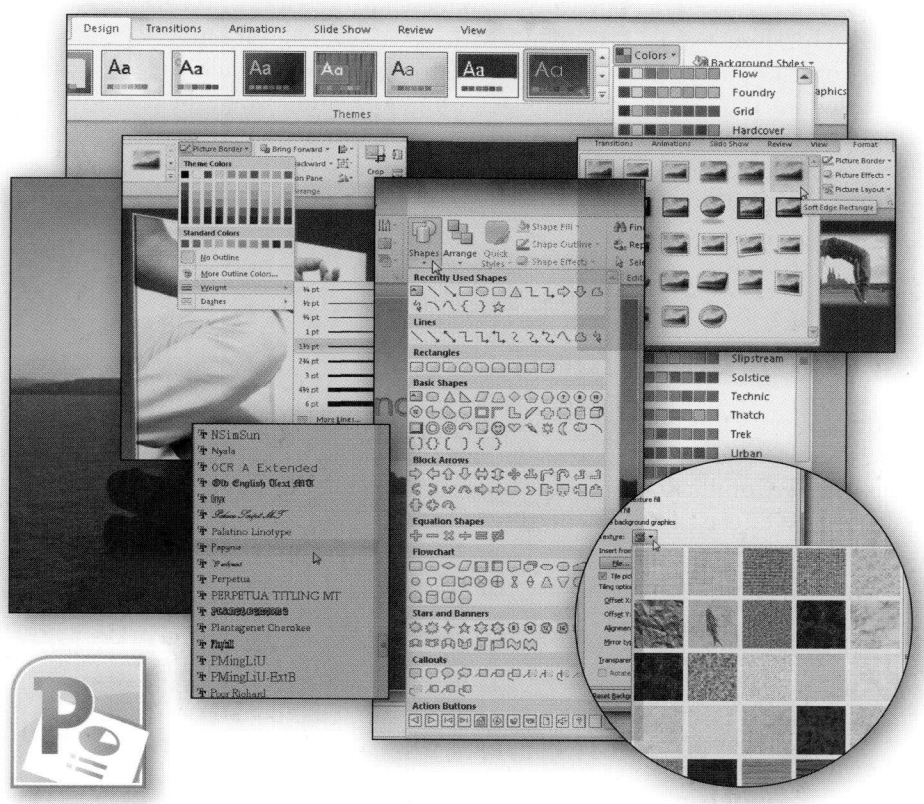

Objectives

You will have mastered the material in this chapter when you can:

- Change theme colors
- Insert a picture to create a background
- Format slide backgrounds
- Insert and size a shape
- Add text to a shape

- Apply effects to a shape
- Change the font and add a shadow
- Format pictures
- Apply a WordArt style
- Format WordArt
- Format text using the Format Painter

2 | Enhancing a Presentation with Pictures, Shapes, and WordArt

Introduction

In our visually oriented culture, audience members enjoy viewing effective graphics. Whether reading a document or viewing a PowerPoint presentation, people increasingly want to see photographs, artwork, graphics, and a variety of typefaces. Researchers have known for decades that documents with visual elements are more effective than those that consist of only text because the illustrations motivate audiences to study the material. People remember at least one-third more information when the document they are seeing or reading contains visual elements. These graphics help clarify and emphasize details, so they appeal to audience members with differing backgrounds, reading levels, attention spans, and motivations.

Project — Presentation with Pictures, Shapes, and WordArt

Yoga's Origins
The term, yoga, is derived from the Sanskrit word yuj, meaning to join or unite. Yogis have been practicing this system of exercises and philosophy of mental control for more than 26,000 years.

The project in this chapter follows graphical guidelines and uses PowerPoint to create the presentation shown in Figure 2–1. This slide show, which discusses yoga and meditation, has a variety of illustrations and visual elements. For example, pictures have particular shapes and effects. The enhanced type has a style that blends well with the background and illustrations. Pictures and type are formatted using Quick Styles and WordArt, which give your presentation a professional look.

Overview

As you read through this chapter, you will learn how to create the presentation shown in Figure 2–1 by performing these general tasks:

- Format slide backgrounds.
- Insert and format pictures by applying styles and effects.
- Insert and format shapes.
- Format text using WordArt.
- Print a handout of your slides.

(a) Slide 1 (Title Slide with Picture Background and Shapes)

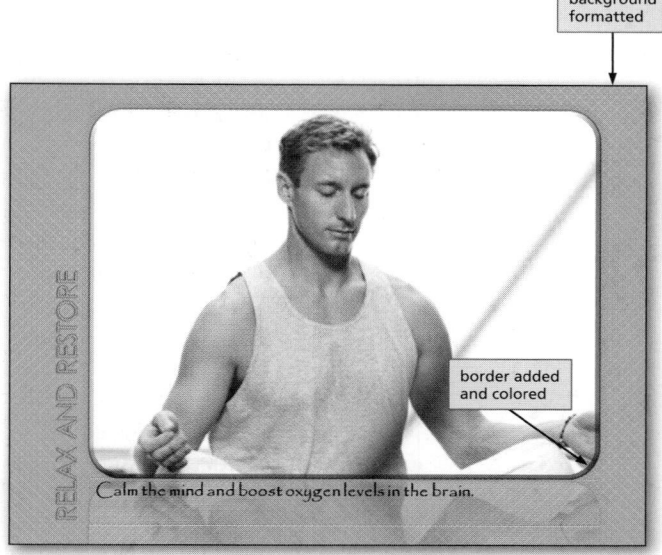

(b) Slide 2 (Formatted Picture)

(c) Slide 3 (Formatted Picture)

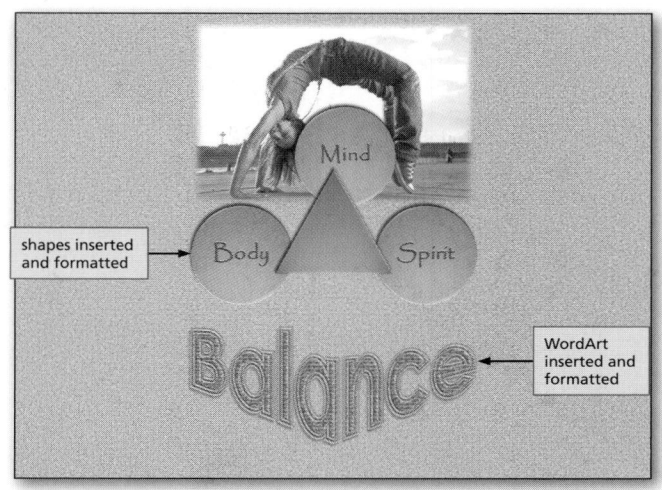

(d) Slide 4 (Inserted and Formatted Shapes)

Figure 2–1

Plan Ahead

General Project Guidelines

When creating a PowerPoint presentation, the actions you perform and decisions you make will affect the appearance and characteristics of the finished document. As you create a presentation with illustrations, such as the project shown in Figure 2–1, you should follow these general guidelines:

1. **Focus on slide text content.** Give some careful thought to the words you choose. Some graphic designers advise starting with a blank screen so that the document theme does not distract from or influence the words.

2. **Apply style guidelines.** Many organizations and publishers establish guidelines for writing styles. These rules apply to capitalization, punctuation, word usage, and document formats. Ask your instructor or manager for a copy of these guidelines or use popular writing guides, such as the *The Chicago Manual of Style*, *The Associated Press Stylebook*, and *The Elements of Style*.

3. **Use color effectively.** Your audience's eyes are drawn to color on a slide. Used appropriately, color can create interest by emphasizing material and promoting understanding. Be aware of symbolic meanings attached to colors, such as red generally representing danger, electricity, and heat.

4. **Adhere to copyright regulations.** Copyright laws apply to printed and electronic materials. You can copy an existing photograph or artwork if it is in the public domain, if your company owns the graphic, or if you have obtained permission to use it. Be certain you have the legal right to use a desired graphic in your presentation.

5. **Consider graphics for multicultural audiences.** In today's intercultural society, your presentation might be viewed by people whose first language is different from yours. Some graphics have meanings specific to a culture, so be certain to learn about your intended audience and their views.

6. **Use WordArt in moderation.** Used correctly, the graphical nature of WordArt can add interest and set a tone. Format text with a WordArt style only when needed for special emphasis.

When necessary, more specific details concerning the above guidelines are presented at appropriate points in the chapter. The chapter also will identify the actions you perform and decisions made regarding these guidelines during the creation of the presentation shown in Figure 2–1.

Starting PowerPoint

For an introduction to Windows 7 and instruction about how to perform basic Windows 7 tasks, read the Office 2010 and Windows 7 chapter at the beginning of this book, where you can learn how to resize windows, change screen resolution, create folders, move and rename files, use Windows Help, and much more.

Chapter 1 introduced you to starting PowerPoint, selecting a document theme, creating slides with clip art and a bulleted list, and printing a presentation. The following steps, which assume Windows 7 is running, start PowerPoint. You may need to ask your instructor how to start PowerPoint for your computer. For a detailed example of the procedure summarized on the next page, refer to pages OFF 33 through OFF 35 in the Office 2010 and Windows 7 chapter.

To Start PowerPoint and Apply a Document Theme

1 Click the Start button on the Windows 7 taskbar to display the Start menu.

2 Type `Microsoft PowerPoint` as the search text in the 'Search programs and files' text box.

3 Click Microsoft PowerPoint 2010 in the search results on the Start menu to start PowerPoint and display a new blank document.

4 If the PowerPoint window is not maximized, click the Maximize button.

5 Apply the Verve document theme.

Focus on slide text content.

Once you have researched your presentation topic, many methods exist to begin developing slide content.

• Select a document theme and then enter text, illustration, and tables.

• Open an existing presentation and modify the slides and theme.

• Import an outline created in Microsoft Word.

• Start with a blank presentation that uses the default Office Theme. Consider this practice similar to an artist who begins creating a painting with a blank, white canvas.

    Experiment using different methods of developing the initial content for slides. Experienced PowerPoint users sometimes find one technique works better than another to stimulate creativity or help them organize their ideas in a particular circumstance.

Plan Ahead

For an introduction to Office 2010 and instruction about how to perform basic tasks in Office 2010 programs, read the Office 2010 and Windows 7 chapter at the beginning of this book, where you can learn how to start a program, use the Ribbon, save a file, open a file, quit a program, use Help, and much more.

Creating Slides and Changing Font Colors and Background Style

In Chapter 1, you selected a document theme and then typed the content for the title and text slides. In this chapter, you will type the slide content for the title and text slides, select a background, insert and format pictures and shapes, and then insert and format WordArt. To begin creating the four slides in this presentation, you will enter text in four different layouts, change the theme colors, and then change the background style.

Apply style guidelines.

A good stylebook is useful to decide when to use numerals or words to represent numbers, as in the sentence, More than 25 students are waiting for the bus to arrive. Stylebooks also offer rules on forming possessives, capitalizing titles, and using commas. Once you decide on a style to use in your presentation, apply it consistently throughout your presentation.

Plan Ahead

To Create a Title Slide

    Recall from Chapter 1 that the title slide introduces the presentation to the audience. In addition to introducing the presentation, this project uses the title slide to capture the audience's attention by using title text and a background picture. The following steps create the slide show's title slide.

1 Type **Yoga and Meditation** in the title text placeholder.

2 Type **Unify Your Mind,** in the subtitle text placeholder.

3 Press the ENTER key and then type **Body,** as the second line in the subtitle text placeholder.

4 Press the ENTER key and then type **and Spirit** as the third line in the subtitle text placeholder. Change the capital letter 'A' in the word, And, at the beginning of this line to a lowercase 'a' (Figure 2–2).

Q&A Some stylebooks recommend using lowercase letters when using coordinating conjunctions (for, and, nor, but, or, yet, so) and also when using articles (a, an, the). Why is the case of the word, and, changed in the subtitle text?

By default, PowerPoint capitalizes the first word of each paragraph. For consistency, you can decide to lowercase this word to apply a particular style rule so that the word, and, is lowercase in both the title and subtitle text.

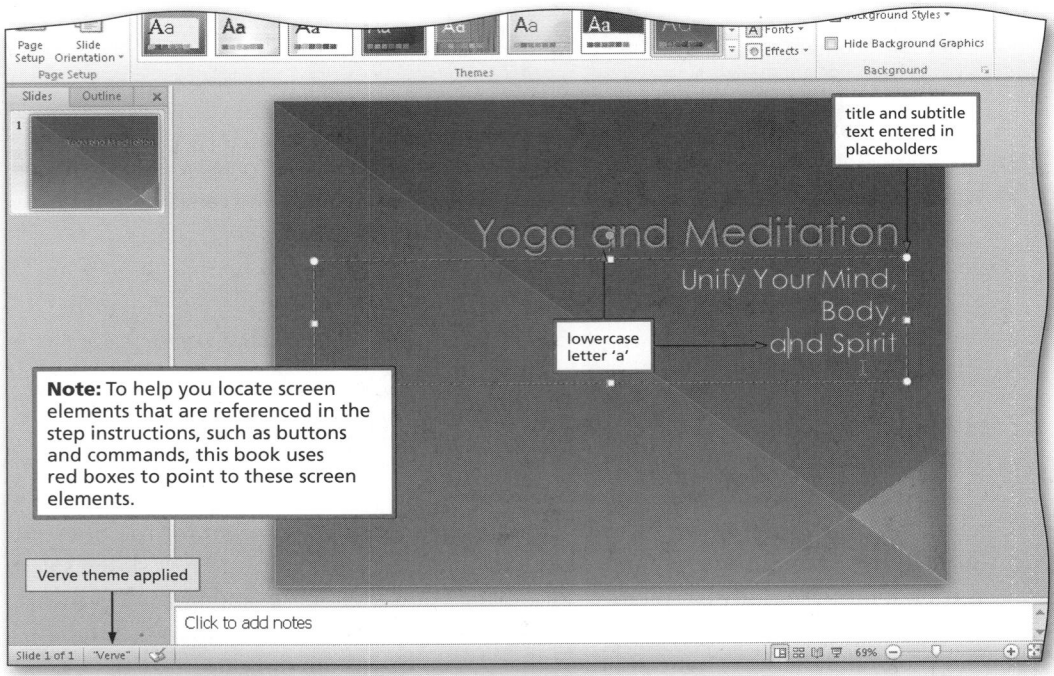

Figure 2–2

BTW

Q&As
For a complete list of the Q&As found in many of the step-by-step sequences in this book, visit the PowerPoint 2010 Q&A Web page (scsite.com/ppt2010/qa).

To Create the First Text Slide

The first text slide you create in Chapter 2 emphasizes the relaxation and restoration benefits derived from practicing yoga and meditation. The following steps add a new slide (Slide 2) and then create a text slide using the Picture with Caption layout.

1 Click Home on the Ribbon to display the Home tab, click the New Slide button arrow, and then click Picture with Caption in the Layout gallery to add a new slide with this layout.

2 Type **Relax and Restore** in the title text placeholder.

3 Press CTRL+ENTER to move to the caption placeholder and then type **Calm the mind and boost oxygen levels in the brain.** in this placeholder (Figure 2–3).

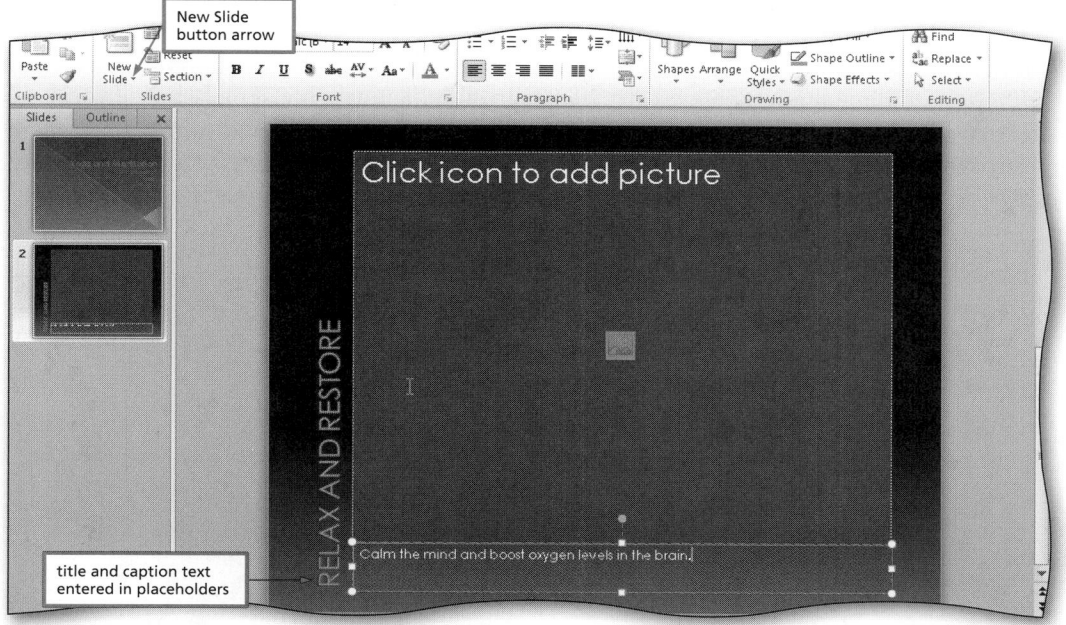

Figure 2–3

To Create the Second Text Slide

BTW

BTWs
For a complete list of the BTWs found in the margins of this book, visit the PowerPoint 2010 BTW Web page (scsite.com/ppt2010/btw).

The second text slide you create stresses the fact that yoga and meditation strengthen the body in multiple ways. The following steps add a new text slide (Slide 3) that uses the Content with Caption layout.

1 Click the New Slide button arrow and then click Content with Caption in the Layout gallery to add a new slide with this layout.

2 Type **Strengthen Body** in the title text placeholder.

3 Press CTRL+ENTER and then type **Increase flexibility and tone muscles.** in the caption placeholder (Figure 2–4).

Q&A   Why does the text display with capital letters despite the fact I am typing uppercase and lowercase letters?

The Verve theme uses the All Caps effect for the title text. This effect converts lowercase letters to uppercase.

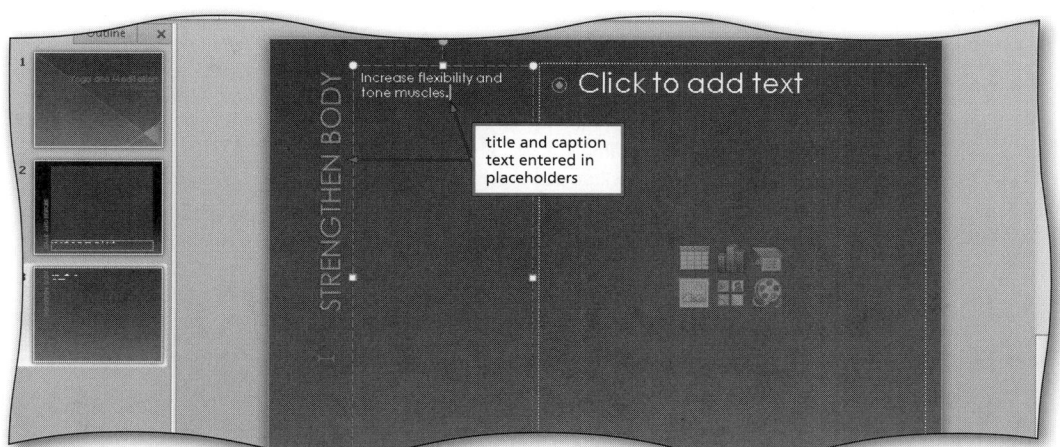

Figure 2–4

To Create the Third Text Slide

Yoga and meditation help create balance in an individual's life. The last slide you create uses graphics to depict the connection among the mind, body, and spirit. You will insert symbols later in this project to create this visual element. For now, you want to create the basic slide. The following step adds a new text slide (Slide 4) that uses the Blank layout.

1 Click the New Slide button arrow and then click Blank in the Layout gallery. (Figure 2–5).

Figure 2–5

Presentation Template Color Scheme

Each presentation template has 12 complementary colors, which collectively are called the **color scheme**. You can apply these colors to all slides, an individual slide, notes pages, or audience handouts. A color scheme consists of four colors for a background and text, six accent colors, and two hyperlink colors. The Theme Colors button on the Design tab contains a square with four colors; the top two colors indicate the primary text and background colors, and the bottom two colors indicate the accent colors. You also can customize the theme colors to create your own set and give them a unique name. Table 2–1 explains the components of a color scheme.

Table 2–1 Color Scheme Components	
Component	**Description**
Background color	The background color is the fundamental color of a PowerPoint slide. For example, if the background color is black, you can place any other color on top of it, but the fundamental color remains black. The black background shows everywhere you do not add color or other objects.
Text color	The text color contrasts with the background color of the slide. As a default, the text border color is the same as the text color. Together with the background color, the text and border colors set the tone for a presentation. For example, a gray background with black text and border sets a dramatic tone. In contrast, a red background with yellow text and border sets a vibrant tone.
Accent colors	Accent colors are designed as colors for secondary features on a slide. They often are used as fill colors on graphs and as shadows.
Hyperlink colors	The default hyperlink color is set when you type the text. When you click the hyperlink text during a presentation, the color changes to the Followed Hyperlink color.

To Change the Presentation Theme Colors

The first modification to make is to change the color scheme throughout the presentation. The following steps change the color scheme for the template from a gray title slide background with pink text and accents to a blue background with pink and orange accents.

- Click Design on the Ribbon and then click the Theme Colors button (Design tab | Themes group) to display the Theme Colors gallery.

- Scroll down and then point to the Oriel built-in theme to display a live preview of this color scheme (Figure 2–6).

 Experiment

- Point to various themes in the Theme Colors gallery and watch the colors change on Slide 4.

Q&A Why does a gold line surround the Verve color scheme in the Theme Colors gallery?

It shows the Verve document theme is applied, and those eight colors are associated with that theme.

Figure 2–6

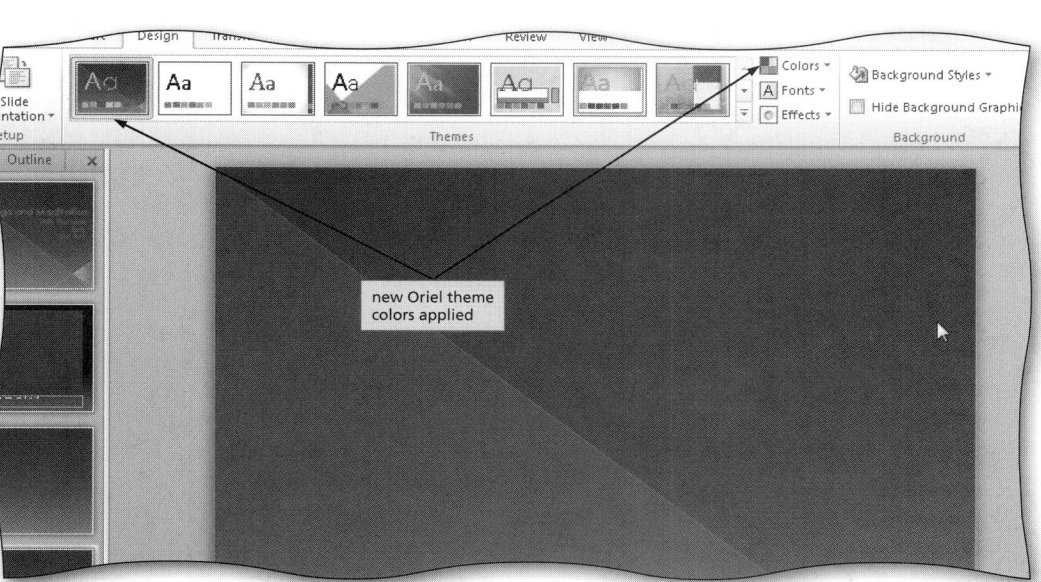

- Click Oriel in the Theme Colors gallery to change the presentation theme colors to Oriel (Figure 2–7).

Q&A What if I want to return to the original theme color?

You would click the Theme Colors button and then click Verve in the Theme Colors gallery.

Figure 2–7

Showing the Quick Access Toolbar below the Ribbon
By default, the Quick Access Toolbar is displayed in the upper-left corner of the PowerPoint window next to the PowerPoint icon. You can move this toolbar below the Ribbon in two ways: clicking the Customize Quick Access Toolbar button and then clicking Show Below the Ribbon in the list; or clicking the Show Quick Access Toolbar below the Ribbon check box in the Customize the Quick Access Toolbar pane (File tab | Options | Quick Access Toolbar | PowerPoint Options dialog box) to place a check mark in it. If you want to relocate the toolbar back to its original location, either click the Customize Quick Access toolbar button and then click Show Above the Ribbon or click the Show Quick Access Toolbar below the Ribbon check box to remove the check mark.

Inserting Watermarks
Checks, currency, business cards, and legal documents use watermarks to verify their authenticity. These semi-transparent images are visible when you hold this paper up to a light. You, likewise, can insert a clip art image or a picture as a watermark behind all or part of your slide to identify your unique PowerPoint presentation.

To Save a Presentation

You have performed many tasks while creating this slide and do not want to risk losing work completed thus far. Accordingly, you should save the document.

The following steps assume you already have created folders for storing your files, for example, a CIS 101 folder (for your class) that contains a PowerPoint folder (for your assignments). Thus, these steps save the document in the PowerPoint folder in the CIS 101 folder on a USB flash drive using the file name, Yoga. For a detailed example of the procedure summarized below, refer to pages OFF 27 through OFF 29 in the Office 2010 and Windows 7 chapter at the beginning of this book.

1 With a USB flash drive connected to one of the computer's USB ports, click the Save button on the Quick Access Toolbar to display the Save As dialog box.

2 Type **Yoga** in the File name text box to change the file name. Do not press the ENTER key after typing the file name because you do not want to close the dialog box at this time.

3 Navigate to the desired save location (in this case, the PowerPoint folder in the CIS 101 folder [or your class folder] on the USB flash drive).

4 Click the Save button (Save As dialog box) to save the document in the selected folder on the selected drive with the entered file name.

Inserting and Formatting Pictures in a Presentation

With the text entered and background formatted in the presentation, the next step is to insert digital pictures into the placeholders on Slides 2 and 3 and then format the pictures. These graphical images draw the viewers' eyes to the slides and help them retain the information presented.

In the following pages, you will perform these tasks:

1. Insert the first digital picture into Slide 3.
2. Insert the second digital picture into Slide 2.
3. Change the look of the first picture.
4. Change the look of the second picture.
5. Resize the second picture.
6. Insert a digital picture into the Slide 1 background.
7. Format slide backgrounds.

Adhere to copyright regulations.
You have permission to use the clips from the Microsoft Clip Organizer. If you want to use a clip from another source, be certain you have the legal right to insert this file in your presentation. Read the copyright notices that accompany the clip and are posted on the Web site. The owners of these images and files often ask you to give them credit for using their work, which may be satisfied by stating where you obtained the images.

Plan
Ahead

To Insert a Picture

The next step in creating the presentation is to insert one of the digital yoga pictures in the picture placeholder in Slide 3. The picture is available on the Data Files for Students. See the inside back cover of this book for instructions on downloading the Data Files for Students, or contact your instructor for information about accessing the required files.

The following steps insert a picture, which, in this example, is located in the PowerPoint Chapter 02 folder on the same USB flash drive that contains the saved presentation, into Slide 3.

- With your USB flash drive connected to one of the computer's USB ports, click the Previous Slide button to display Slide 3.

- Click the Insert Picture from File button in the content placeholder to display the Insert Picture dialog box.

- If Computer is not displayed in the navigation pane, drag the navigation pane scroll bar (Insert Picture dialog box) until Computer appears.

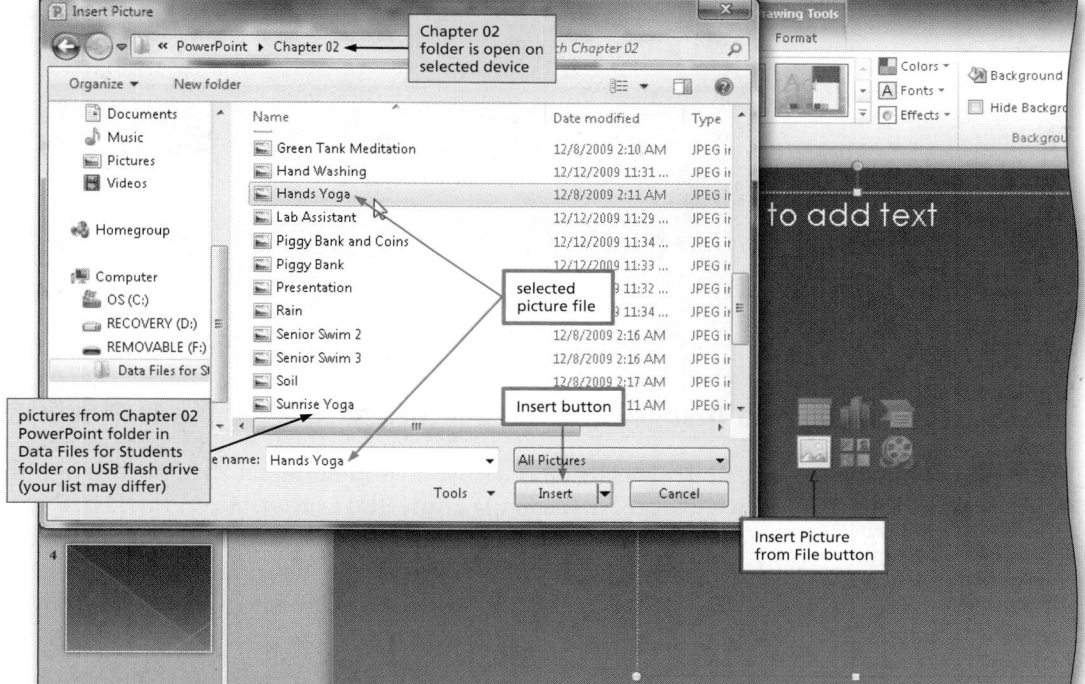

Figure 2–8

- Click Computer in the navigation pane to display a list of available storage devices in the Insert Picture dialog box. If necessary, scroll through the dialog box until your USB flash drive appears in the list of available storage devices.

- Double-click your USB flash drive in the list of available storage devices to display a list of files and folders on the selected USB flash drive. Double-click the Data Files for Students folder, double-click the PowerPoint folder, and then double-click the Chapter 02 folder to display a list of files in that folder.

- Scroll down and then click Hands Yoga to select the file name (Figure 2–8).

Q&A

What if the picture is not on a USB flash drive?

Use the same process, but select the drive containing the picture.

3

● Click the Insert button (Insert Picture dialog box) to insert the picture into the content placeholder in Slide 3 (Figure 2–9).

Q&A What are the symbols around the picture?

A selected graphic appears surrounded by a **selection rectangle**, which has small squares and circles, called **sizing handles**, at each corner and middle location.

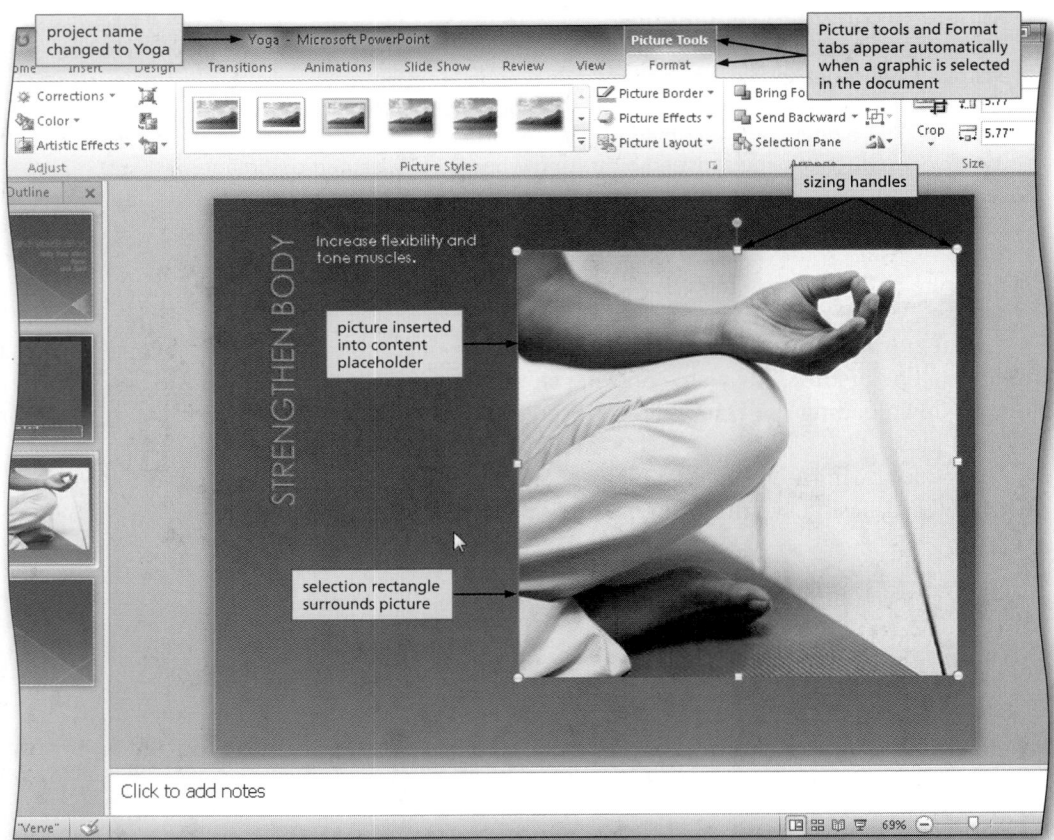

Figure 2–9

To Insert Another Picture into a Content Placeholder

The next step is to insert another digital yoga picture into the Slide 2 content placeholder. This second picture also is available on the Data Files for Students. See the inside back cover of this book for instructions on downloading the Data Files for Students, or contact your instructor for information about accessing the required files.

The following steps insert a picture into Slide 2.

1 Click the Previous Slide button to display Slide 2.

2 With your USB flash drive connected to one of the computer's USB ports, click the Insert Picture from File icon in the content placeholder to display the Insert Picture dialog box.

3 If the list of files and folders on the selected USB flash drive are not displayed in the Insert Picture dialog box, double-click your USB flash drive to display them and then navigate to the PowerPoint Chapter 02 folder.

4 Scroll down and then click Green Tank Meditation to select the file name.

5 Click the Insert button (Insert Picture dialog box) to insert the picture into the Slide 2 content placeholder (Figure 2–10).

picture inserted into content placeholder

RELAX AND RESTORE

Calm the mind and boost oxygen levels in the brain.

add notes

Figure 2–10

To Insert a Picture into a Slide without a Content Placeholder

In Chapter 1, you inserted a clip into a slide without a content placeholder. You also can insert a picture into a slide that does not have a content placeholder. The picture for Slide 4 is available on the Data Files for Students. See the inside back cover of this book for instructions on downloading the Data Files for Students, or contact your instructor for information about accessing the required files. The following steps insert a picture into Slide 4.

1

• Click the Next Slide button two times to display Slide 4.

• With your USB flash drive connected to one of the computer's USB ports, click Insert on the Ribbon (Figure 2–11).

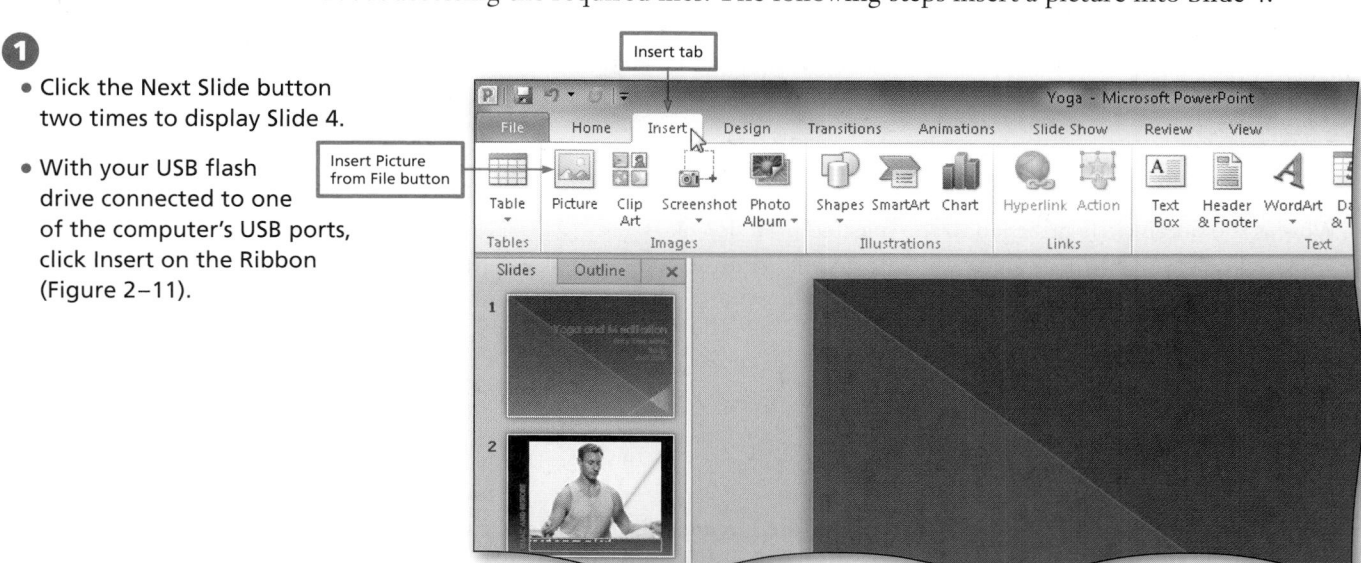

Figure 2–11

2
- Click Insert Picture from File (Insert tab | Images group) to display the Insert Picture dialog box. If the list of files and folders on the selected USB flash drive are not displayed in the Insert Picture dialog box, double-click your USB flash drive to display them and then navigate to the PowerPoint Chapter 02 folder.

- Click Arch Yoga to select the file name (Figure 2–12).

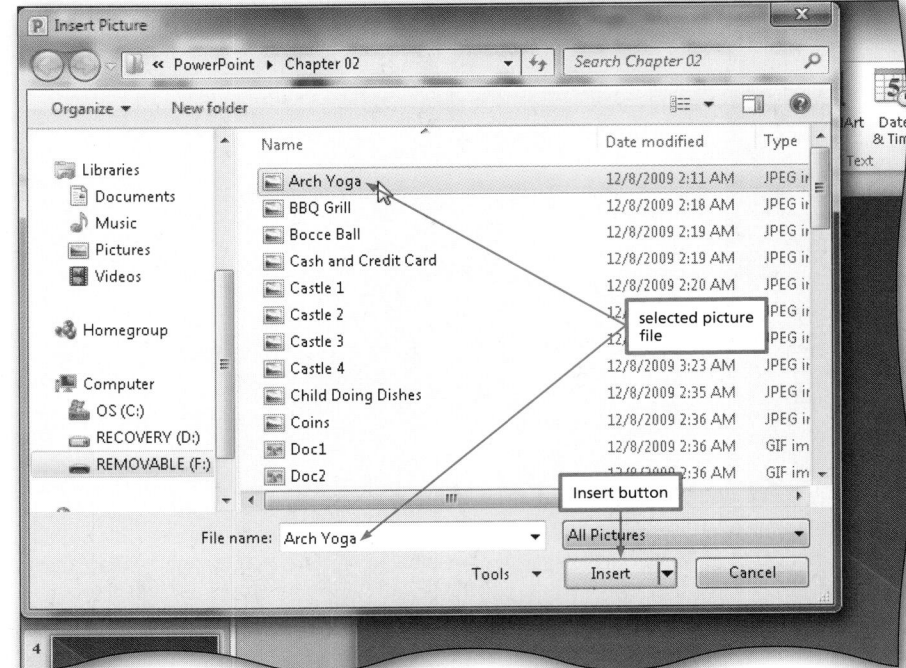

Figure 2–12

3
- Click the Insert button (Insert Picture dialog box) to insert the picture into the Slide 4 content placeholder.

- Move the picture so that it displays approximately as shown in Figure 2–13.

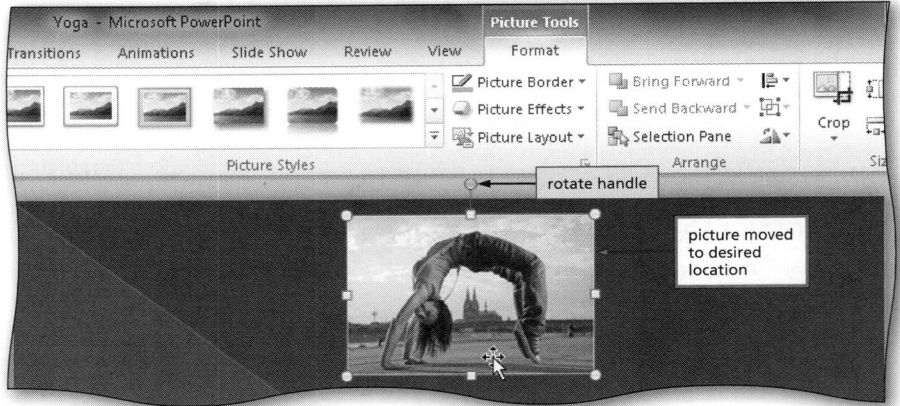

Figure 2–13

Q&A

What is the green circle attached to the selected graphic?
The green circle is a rotate handle. When you drag a graphic's rotate handle, the graphic moves in either a clockwise or counter clockwise direction.

To Correct a Picture

A photograph's color intensity can be modified by changing the brightness and contrast. **Brightness** determines the overall lightness or darkness of the entire image, whereas **contrast** is the difference between the darkest and lightest areas of the image. The brightness and contrast are changed in predefined percentage increments. The following step increases the brightness and decreases the contrast to intensify the picture colors.

1

- With the Arch Yoga picture on Slide 4 still selected, click the Corrections button (Picture Tools Format tab | Adjust group) to display the Corrections gallery.

- Point to Brightness: +20% Contrast: −40% (fourth picture in first row of Brightness and Contrast area) to display a live preview of these corrections on the picture (Figure 2–14).

Experiment

- Point to various pictures in the Brightness and Contrast area and watch the brightness and contrast change on the picture in Slide 4.

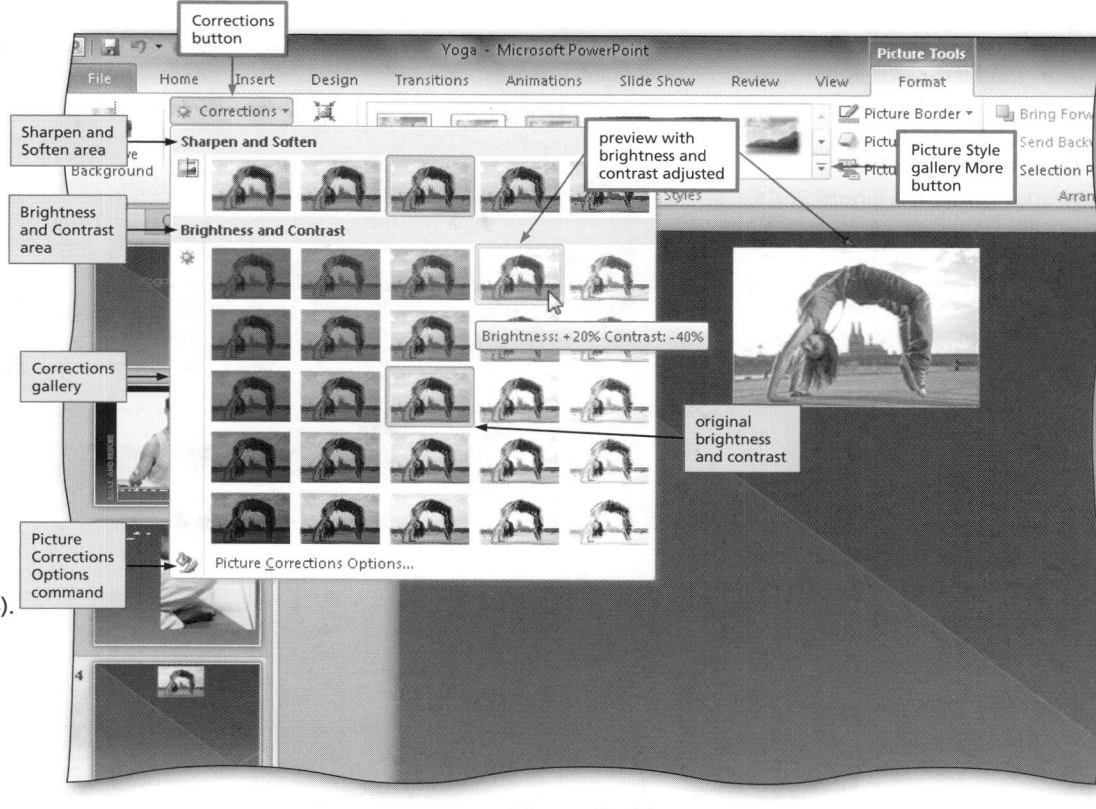

Figure 2–14

Q&A Why is a yellow border surrounding the picture in the center of the gallery?

The image on Slide 4 currently has normal brightness and contrast (0%), which is represented by this center image in the gallery.

- Click Brightness: +20% Contrast: −40% to apply this correction to the yoga picture.

Q&A How can I remove all effects from the picture?

Click the Reset Picture button (Picture Tools Format tab | Adjust group).

Other Ways

1. Click Picture Corrections Options, move Brightness or Contrast sliders or enter | number in box next to slider (Format Picture dialog box)

To Apply a Picture Style

The pictures on Slides 2, 3, and 4 grasp the audience's attention, but you can increase their visual appeal by applying a style. A **style** is a named group of formatting characteristics. PowerPoint provides more than 25 picture styles that enable you easily to change a picture's look to a more visually appealing style, including a variety of shapes, angles, borders, and reflections. The photos in Slides 2, 3, and 4 in this chapter use styles that apply soft edges, reflections, or angled perspectives to the pictures. The following steps apply a picture style to the Slide 4 picture.

BTW

Applying Sharpen and Soften Image Corrections
Applying sharpen and soften color corrections in the Corrections gallery can create spectacular pictures that enhance your slides. Sharpening an image enhances the details, and softening an image removes undesirable marks. You can display a live preview of a picture's blurriness by pointing to one of the pictures in the Sharpen and Soften area. To fine tune the degree of blurriness, click Picture Corrections Options in the Corrections gallery and then move the Sharpen and Soften slider or type a number in the text box next to the slider in the Sharpen and Soften area (Format Picture dialog box).

1

- With the Slide 4 picture selected, click the Picture Tools Format tab and then click the More button in the Picture Styles gallery (Picture Tools Format tab | Picture Styles group) (shown in Figure 2–14 on the previous page) to expand the gallery.

- Point to Soft Edge Rectangle in the Picture Styles gallery to display a live preview of that style applied to the picture in the document (Figure 2–15).

 Experiment

- Point to various picture styles in the Picture Styles gallery and watch the style of the picture change in the document window.

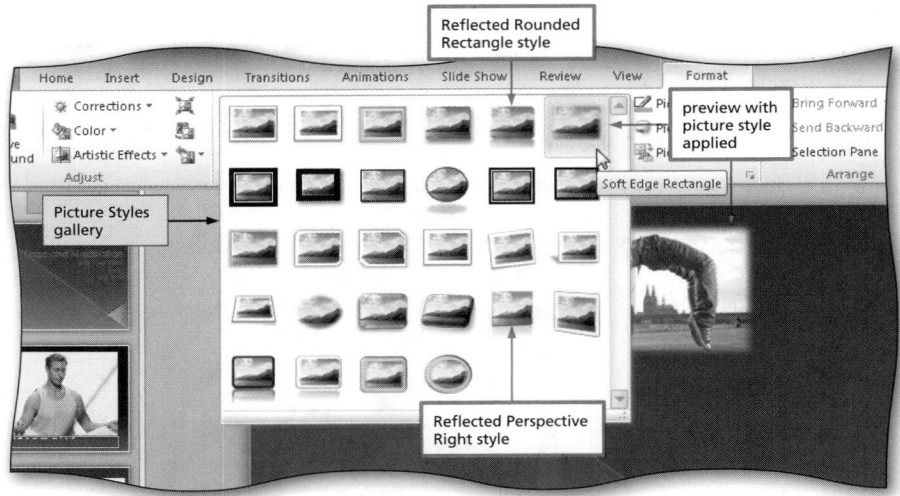

Figure 2–15

2

- Click Soft Edge Rectangle in the Picture Styles gallery to apply the style to the selected picture (Figure 2–16).

Figure 2–16

To Apply Other Picture Styles

The next step is to apply picture styles to the yoga pictures in Slides 3 and 2. To provide continuity, both of these styles will have a reflection. The following steps apply other picture styles to the Slide 3 and Slide 2 pictures.

1 Click the Previous Slide button to display Slide 3.

2 Click the Slide 3 picture to select it, click the Picture Tools Format tab, and then click the More button in the Picture Styles gallery to expand the gallery.

3 Click Reflected Perspective Right in the Picture Styles gallery to apply this style to the picture in Slide 3.

4 Click the Previous Slide button to display Slide 2.

5 Click the Slide 2 picture to select it, click the Picture Tools Format tab, and then click the More button in the Picture Styles gallery to expand the gallery.

6 Click Reflected Rounded Rectangle in the Picture Styles gallery to apply this style to the picture in Slide 2 (Figure 2–17).

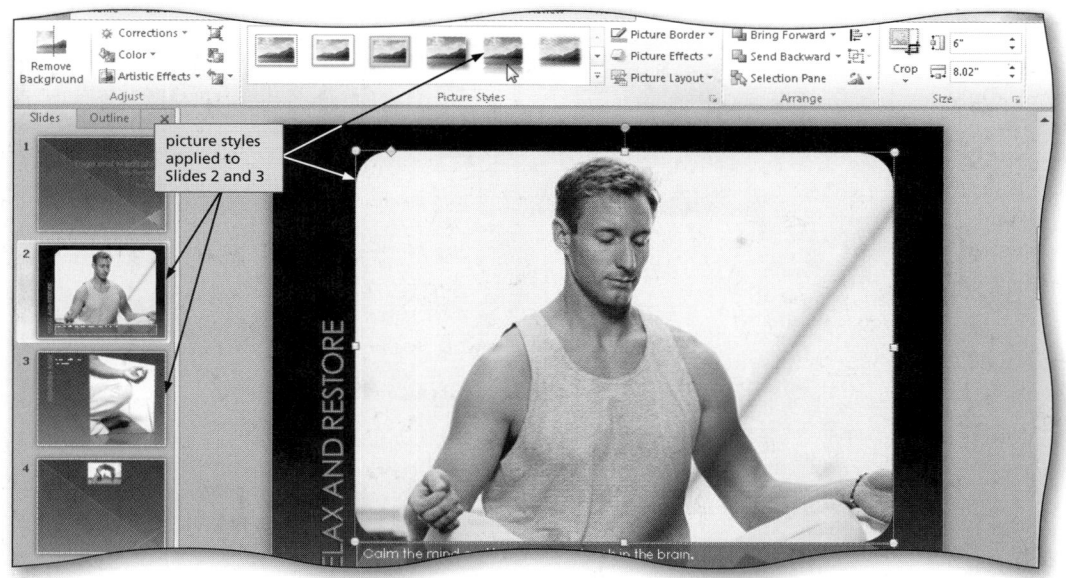

Figure 2–17

To Apply Picture Effects

PowerPoint provides a variety of picture effects so that you can further customize a picture. Effects include shadows, reflections, glow, soft edges, bevel, and 3-D rotation. The difference between the effects and the styles is that each effect has several options, providing you with more control over the exact look of the image.

In this presentation, the photos on Slides 2 and 3 have an orange glow effect and have a bevel applied to their edges. The following steps apply picture effects to the selected picture.

1

• With the Slide 2 picture selected, click the Picture Effects button (Picture Tools Format tab | Picture Styles group) to display the Picture Effects menu.

Q&A What if the Picture Tools Format tab no longer is displayed on my Ribbon?

Double-click the picture to display the Picture Tools and Format tabs.

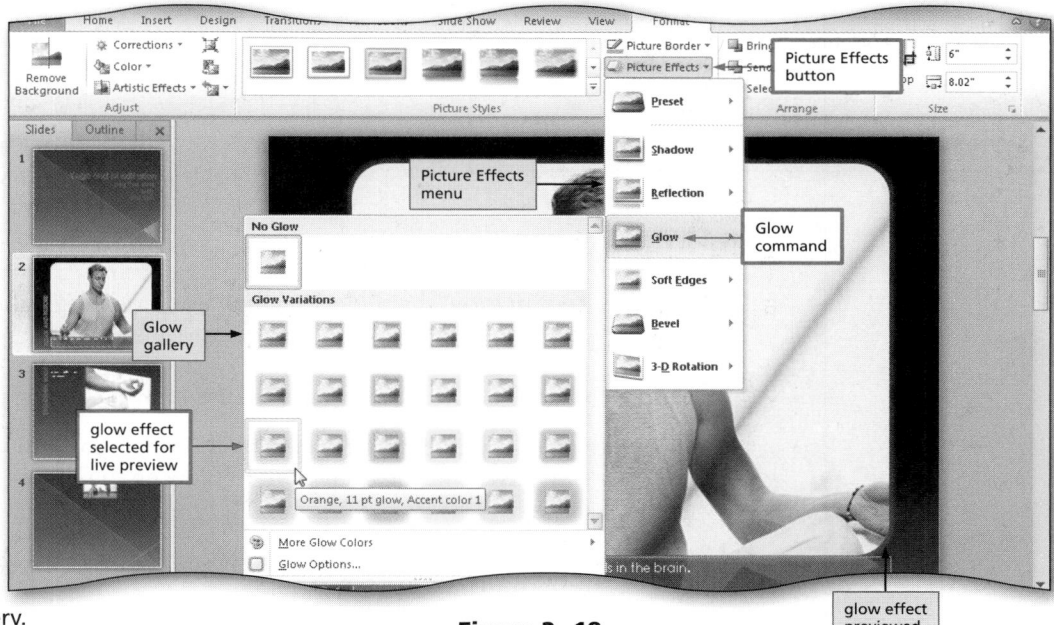

Figure 2–18

• Point to Glow on the Picture Effects menu to display the Glow gallery.

• Point to Orange, 11 pt glow, Accent color 1 in the Glow Variations area (leftmost glow in third row) to display a live preview of the selected glow effect applied to the picture in the document window (Figure 2–18).

Experiment

• Point to various glow effects in the Glow gallery and watch the picture change in the document window.

- Click Orange, 11 pt glow, Accent color 1 in the Glow gallery to apply the selected picture effect.

- Click the Picture Effects button (Picture Tools Format tab | Picture Styles group) to display the Picture Effects menu again.

- Point to Bevel on the Picture Effects menu to display the Bevel gallery.

- Point to Angle (leftmost bevel in second row) to display a live preview of the selected bevel effect applied to the Slide 2 picture (Figure 2–19).

 **Experiment**

- Point to various bevel effects in the Bevel gallery and watch the picture change in the slide.

4

- Click Angle in the Bevel gallery to apply the selected picture effect.

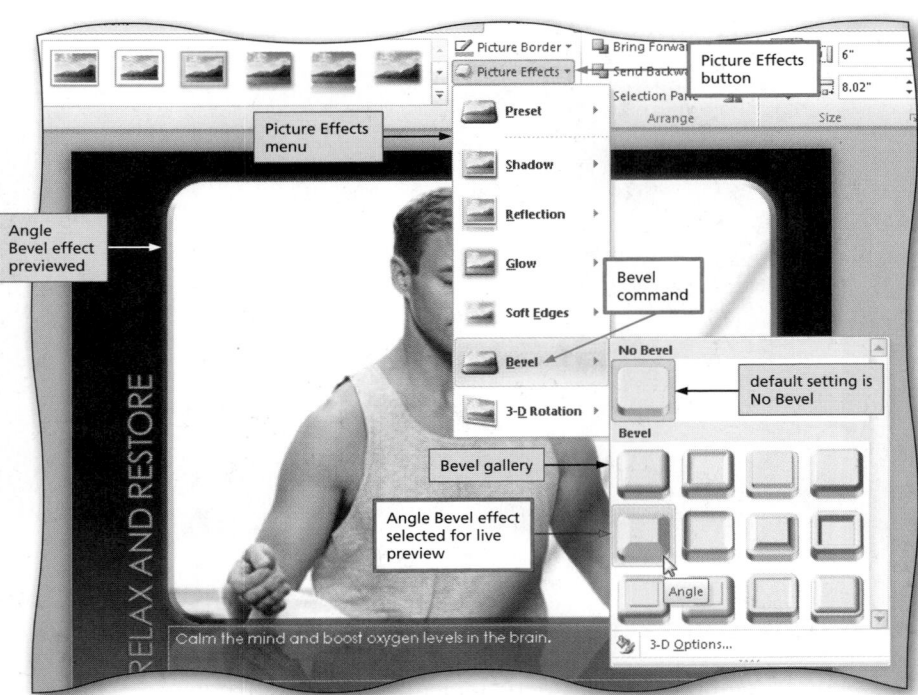

Figure 2–19

Other Ways
1. Right-click picture, click Format Picture on shortcut menu, select desired options (Format Picture dialog box), click Close button	Tools Format tab	Picture Styles group), select desired options (Format Picture dialog box), click Close button
2. Click Format Shape dialog box launcher (Picture	

To Apply a Picture Style and Effect to Another Picture

In this presentation, the Slide 3 picture also has orange glow and bevel effects. The following steps apply the picture style and picture effects to the picture.

1 Click the Next Slide button to display Slide 3 and then click the picture to select it.

2 Click the Picture Effects button (Picture Tools Format tab | Picture Styles group) to display the Picture Effects menu and then point to Glow on the Picture Effects menu to display the Glow gallery.

3 Click Orange, 11 pt glow, Accent color 1 (leftmost glow in third row) in the Glow gallery to apply the picture effect to the picture.

4 Click the Picture Effects button (Picture Tools Format tab | Picture Styles group) to display the Picture Effects menu again and then point to Bevel on the Picture Effects menu to display the Bevel gallery.

5 Click Convex (third bevel in second row) in the Bevel area to apply the picture effect to the selected picture (Figure 2–20).

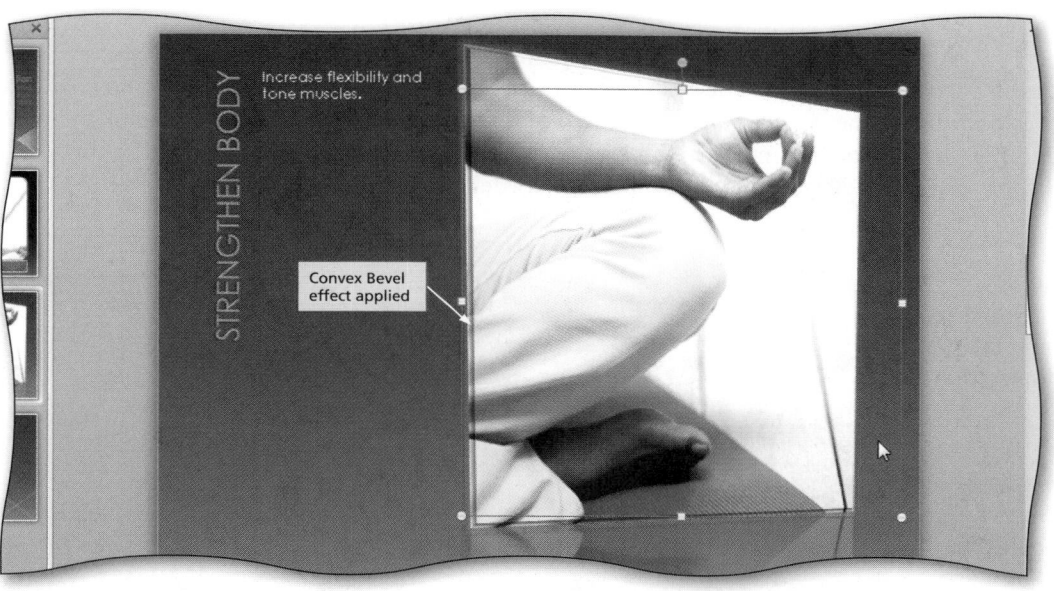

Figure 2–20

To Add a Picture Border

The next step is to add a small border to the Slide 3 picture. Some picture styles provide a border, but the Reflected Rounded Rectangle style you applied to this picture does not. The following steps add a border to the Slide 3 picture.

1

- With the Slide 3 picture still selected, click the Picture Border button (Picture Tools Format tab | Picture Styles group) to display the Picture Border gallery.

 What if the Picture Tools Format tab no longer is displayed on my Ribbon?

Double-click the picture to display the Picture Tools and Format tabs.

2

- Point to Weight on the Picture Border gallery to display the Weight list.

- Point to 1½ pt to display a live preview of this line weight on the picture (Figure 2–21).

 **Experiment**

- Point to various line weights in the Weight list and watch the line thickness change.

 Can I make the line width more than 6 pt?

Yes. Click More Lines and then increase the amount in the Width box.

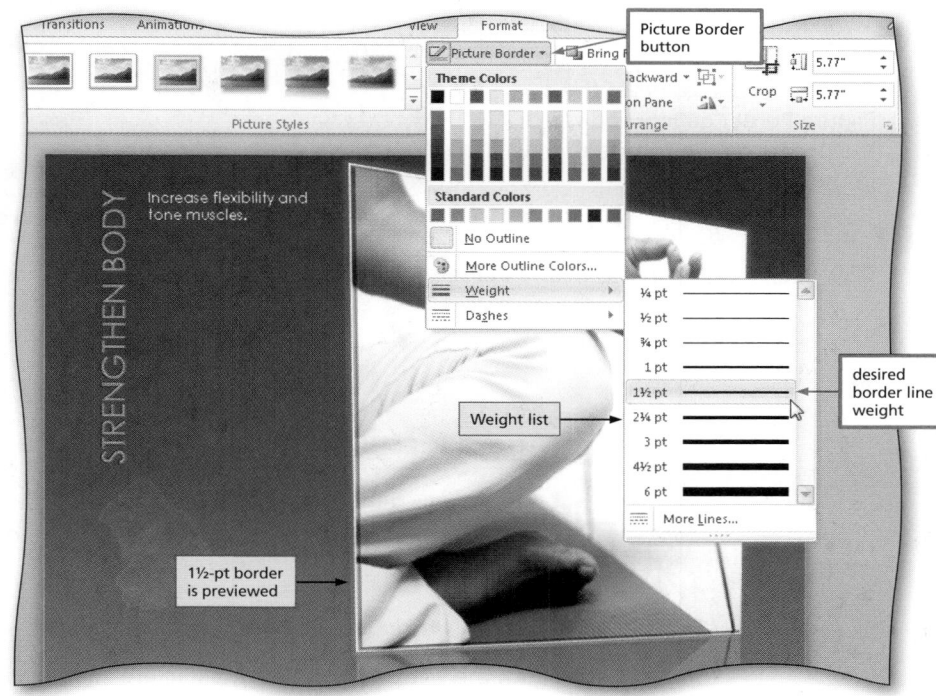

Figure 2–21

3

- Click 1½ pt to add this line weight to the picture.

To Change a Picture Border Color

The default color for the border you added to the Slide 3 picture is White. Earlier in this chapter, you changed the color scheme to Oriel. To coordinate the border color with the title text color and other elements of this theme, you will use a shade of red in the Oriel color scheme. Any color galleries you display show colors defined in this current color scheme. The following steps change the Slide 3 picture border color.

1

- With the Slide 3 photo still selected, click the Picture Border button (Picture Tools Format tab | Picture Styles group) to display the Picture Border gallery.

Q&A

What if the Picture Tools Format tab no longer is displayed on my Ribbon?

Double-click the picture to display the Picture Tools and Format tabs.

2

- Point to Red, Accent 3 (seventh theme color from left in first row) in the Picture Border gallery to display a live preview of that border color on the picture (Figure 2–22).

(magnifier icon) **Experiment**

- Point to various colors in the Picture Border gallery and watch the border on the picture change in the slide.

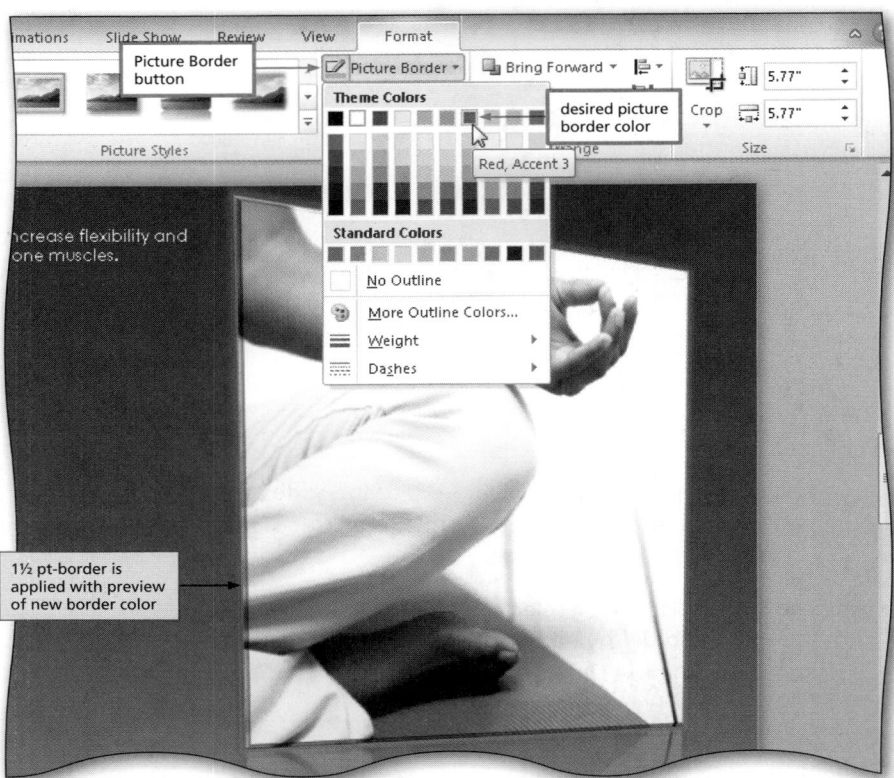

Figure 2–22

3

- Click Red, Accent 3 in the Picture Border gallery to change the picture border color.

To Add a Picture Border and Color to Another Picture

In this presentation, the Slide 2 picture does not have a border as part of the Reflected Perspective Right picture style. The following steps add a border to Slide 2 and change the color.

1 Click the Previous Slide button to display Slide 2 and then click the picture to select it.

2 Click the Picture Border button (Picture Tools Format tab | Picture Styles group) to display the Picture Border gallery.

3 Point to Weight on the Picture Border gallery to display the Weight list and then point to 1½ pt to display a live preview of this line weight on the picture.

4 Click 1½ pt to add this line weight to the picture.

5 Click the Picture Border button (Picture Tools Format tab | Picture Styles group) to display the Picture Border gallery again and then click Red, Accent 3 in the Picture Border gallery to change the picture border color (Figure 2–23).

Figure 2–23

To Resize a Graphic by Entering Exact Measurements

The next step is to resize the Slide 3 picture so that it fills much of the empty space in the slide. In Chapter 1, you resized clips by dragging the sizing handles. This technique also applies to changing the size of photos. You also can resize graphics by specifying exact height and width measurements. The yoga picture can be enlarged so that its height and width measurements are 6.0″. When a graphic is selected, its height and width measurements show in the Size group of the Picture Tools Format tab. The following steps resize the Slide 3 picture by entering its desired exact measurements.

1

- Click the Next Slide button to display Slide 3 and then select the picture. Click the Shape Height text box (Picture Tools Format tab | Size group) to select the contents in the text box and then type   6 as the height (Figure 2–24).

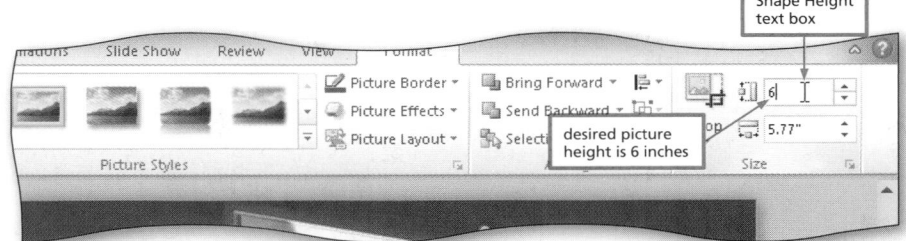

Figure 2–24

 | What if the contents of the Shape Height text box are not selected?

Triple-click the Shape Height text box.

 | Why did the width size also change?

PowerPoint kept the photo in proportion so that the width changed the same amount as the height changed.

2

- Click the Shape Width text box (Picture Tools Format tab | Size group) to select the contents in the text box and then type 6 as the width if this number does not display automatically.

- If necessary, move the photo to the location shown in Figure 2–25.

Q&A

What if I want to return a graphic to its original size and start again?

With the graphic selected, click the Size and Position dialog box launcher (Picture Tools Format tab | Size group), if necessary click the Size tab (Format Picture dialog box), click the Reset button, and then click the Close button.

Other Ways

1. Right-click picture, enter shape height and width values in text boxes on shortcut menu

   on shortcut menu, click Size (Format Picture dialog box), enter shape height and width values in text boxes, click Close button

2. Right-click picture, click Format Picture

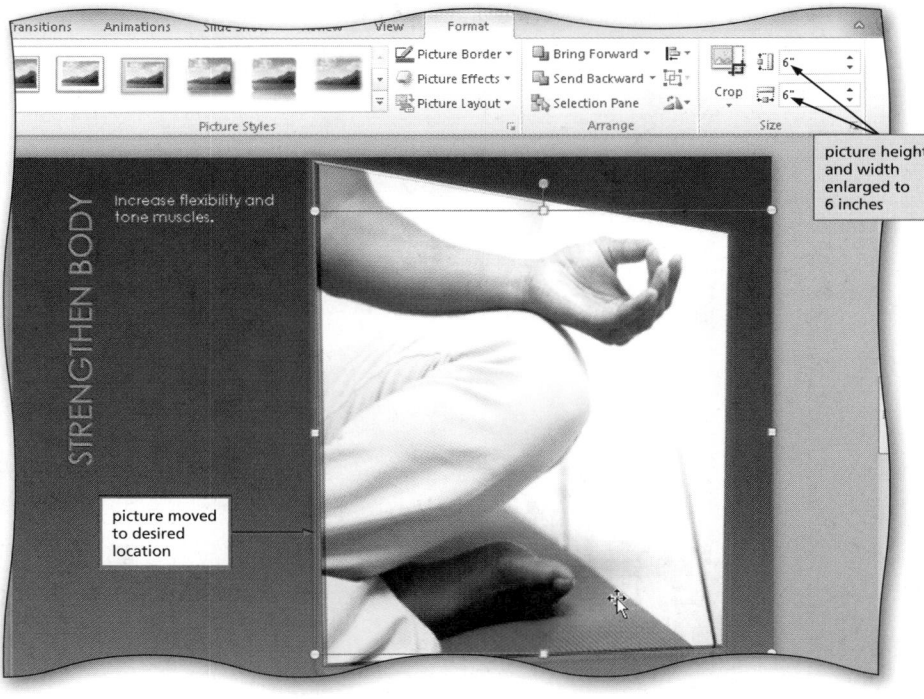

Figure 2–25

To Resize Another Graphic Using Exact Measurements

The Arch Yoga picture on Slide 4 also can be enlarged to fill space at the top of the slide. The yoga picture can be enlarged so that its height and width measurements are 3" and 4.48", respectively. The following steps resize the Slide 4 picture.

1 Click the Next Slide button to display Slide 4 and then select the picture. Click the Shape Height text box (Picture Tools Format tab | Size group) to select the contents in the text box and type 3 as the height.

2 Move the photo to the location shown in Figure 2–26.

Figure 2–26

To Save an Existing Document with the Same File Name

You have made several modifications to the document since you last saved it. Thus, you should save it again. The following step saves the document again. For an example of the step listed below, refer to page OFF 51 in the Office 2010 and Windows 7 chapter at the beginning of this book.

1 Click the Save button on the Quick Access Toolbar to overwrite the previously saved file.

Break Point: If you wish to take a break, this is a good place to do so. You can quit PowerPoint now. To resume at a later time, start PowerPoint, open the file called Yoga, and continue following the steps from this location forward.

Formatting Slide Backgrounds

A slide's background is an integral part of a presentation because it can generate audience interest. Every slide can have the same background, or different backgrounds can be used in a presentation. This background is considered **fill**, which is the content that makes up the interior of a shape, line, or character. Three fills are available: solid, gradient, and picture or texture. **Solid fill** is one color used throughout the entire slide. **Gradient fill** is one color shade gradually progressing to another shade of the same color or one color progressing to another color. **Picture or texture fill** uses a specific file or an image that simulates a material, such as cork, granite, marble, or canvas.

Once you add a fill, you can adjust its appearance. For example, you can adjust its **transparency**, which allows you to see through the background, so that any text on the slide is visible. You also can select a color that is part of the theme or a custom color. You can use **offsets**, another background feature, to move the background from the slide borders in varying distances by percentage. **Tiling options** repeat the background image many times vertically and horizontally on the slide; the smaller the tiling percentage, the greater the number of times the image is repeated.

BTW

Resetting Backgrounds
If you have made many changes to the background and want to start the process over, click the Reset Background button in the Format Background dialog box.

To Insert a Texture Fill

A wide variety of texture fills are available to give your presentation a unique look. The 24 pictures in the Textures gallery give the appearance of a physical object, such as water drops, sand, tissue paper, and a paper bag. You also can use your own texture pictures for custom backgrounds. When you insert a fill, PowerPoint assumes you want this custom background on only the current slide displayed. To make this background appear on all slides in the presentation, click the Apply to All button in the Format Background dialog box. The following steps insert the Sand fill on Slide 4 in the presentation.

• Right-click anywhere on the Slide 4 blue background to display the shortcut menu (Figure 2–27).

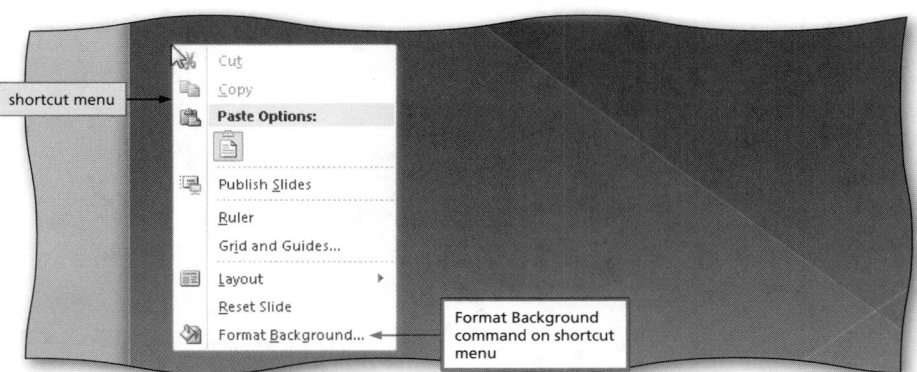

Figure 2–27

2

• Click Format Background on the shortcut menu to display the Format Background dialog box.

• With the Fill pane displaying, click 'Picture or texture fill' to expand the fill options (Figure 2–28).

Q&A | Why did the background change to a yellow texture?

This texture is the Papyrus background, which is the default texture fill.

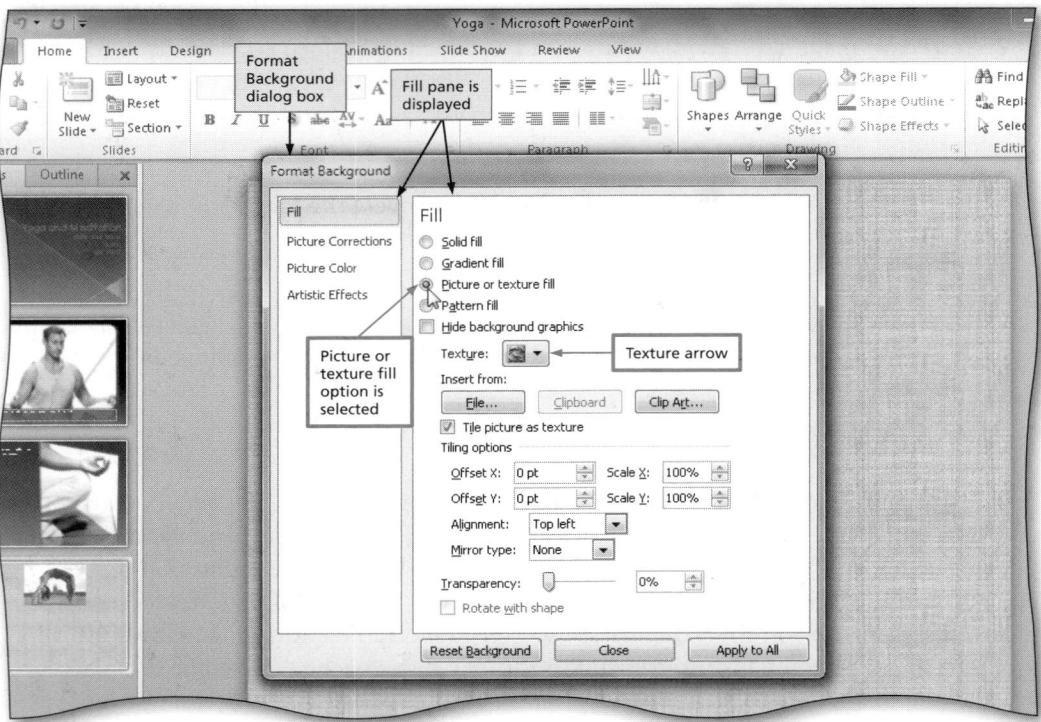

Figure 2–28

3

• Click the Texture arrow to display the Texture gallery (Figure 2–29).

Q&A | Is a live preview available to see the various textures on this slide?

No. Live preview is not an option with the background textures and fills.

Q&A | How does a texture fill differ from a gradient fill?

A texture fill can have the appearance of paper goods or a natural material, such as sand, water, or marble. A gradient fill blends two or more fill colors. PowerPoint includes several built-in gradient fills, and you also can create your own blend of desired colors. When you click the Gradient fill option, you can select a fill

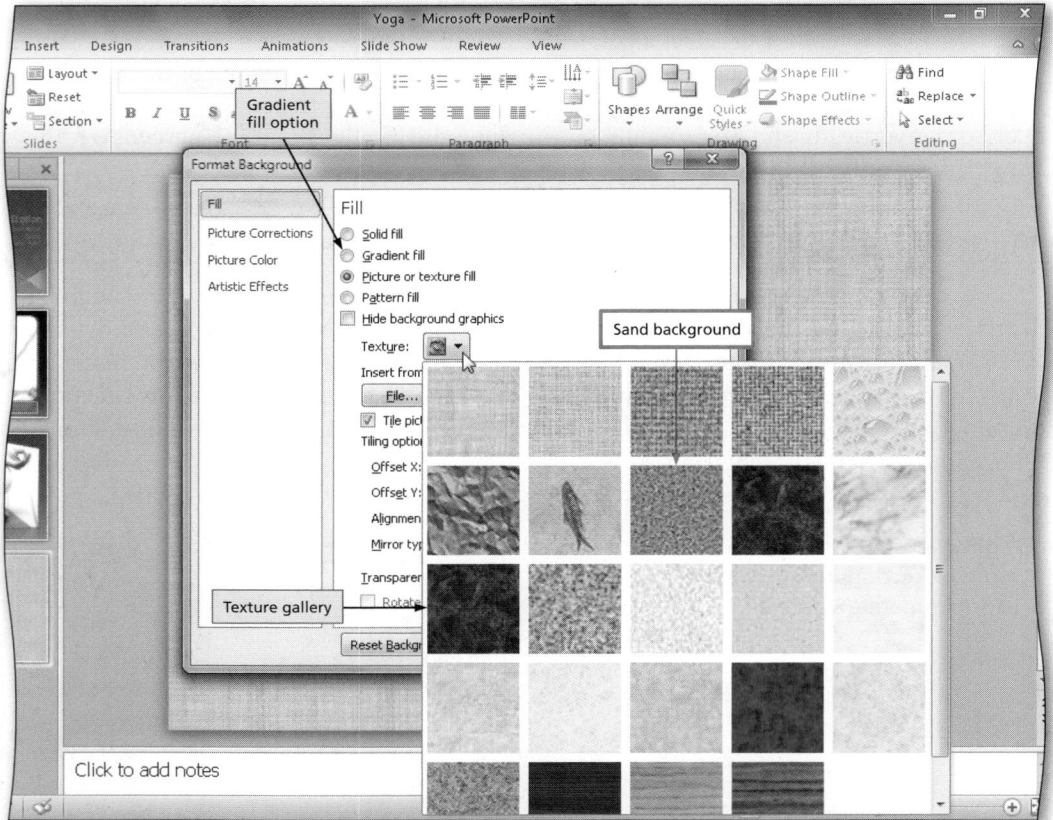

Figure 2–29

from the Light Variations and Dark Variations areas. If you click More Gradients, you can select the custom colors, the location, or stop, where the blending ends, the direction and angle of the blend, and the percentage of brightness and transparency.

4

- Click the Sand background (third texture in second row) to insert this background on Slide 4 (Figure 2–30).

Q&A The Format Background dialog box is covering part of the slide. Can I move this box?

Yes. Click the dialog box title and drag it to a different location so that you can view the slide.

Q&A Could I insert this background on all four slides simultaneously?

Yes. You would click the Apply to All button to insert the Sand background on all slides.

Other Ways

1. Click Design tab, Background Styles, click Format Background (Design tab | Background group)

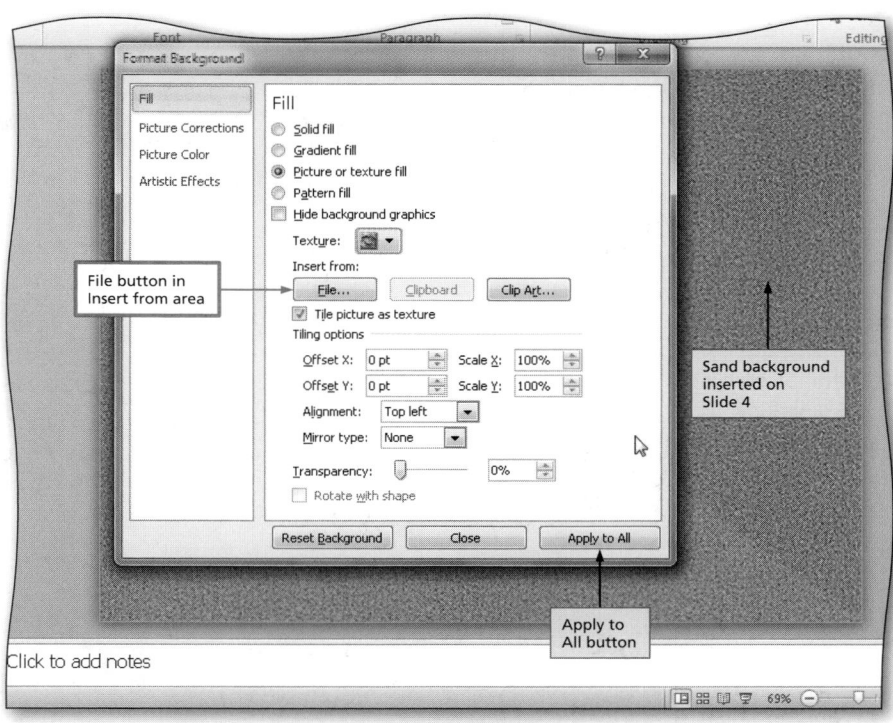

Figure 2–30

To Insert a Picture to Create a Background

For variety and interest, you want to use another yoga picture as the Slide 1 background. This picture is stored on the Data Files for Students. PowerPoint will stretch the height and width of this picture to fill the slide area. The following steps insert the picture, Sunrise Yoga, on only Slide 1.

1

- Click the Previous Slide button three times to display Slide 1.

- With the Fill pane displaying (Format Background dialog box), click 'Picture or texture fill'.

- Click the File button in the Insert from area (shown in Figure 2–30) to display the Insert Picture dialog box.

- If necessary, double-click your USB flash drive in the list of available storage devices to display a list of files and folders on the selected USB flash drive and then navigate to the PowerPoint Chapter 02 folder.

- Scroll down and then click Sunrise Yoga to select the file name (Figure 2–31).

Q&A What if the picture is not on a USB flash drive?

Use the same process, but select the drive containing the picture.

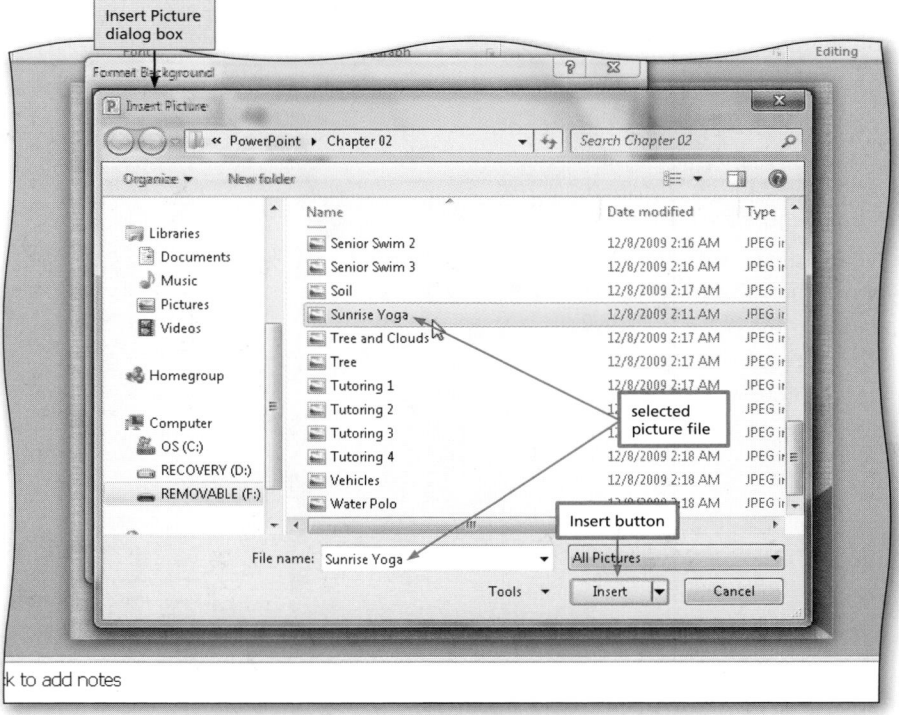

Figure 2–31

2

- Click the Insert button (Insert Picture dialog box) to insert the Sunrise Yoga picture as the Slide 1 background (Figure 2–32).

Q&A What if I do not want to use this picture?

Click the Undo button on the Quick Access Toolbar.

Q&A Why do the Left and Right offsets in the Stretch options area show a −6% value?

PowerPoint automatically reduced the photograph slightly so that it fills the entire slide.

Q&A Can I move the Format Background dialog box to the left so that I can see more of the subtitle text?

Yes. Click the dialog box title and then drag the box to the desired location on the slide.

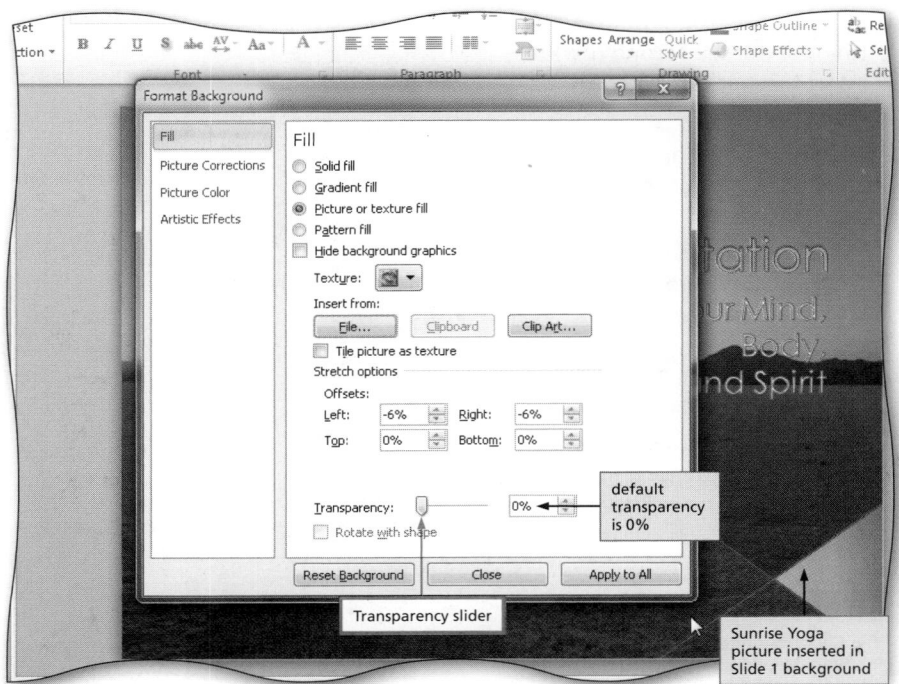

Figure 2–32

To Format a Background Picture Fill Transparency

The Sunrise Yoga picture on Slide 1 is a rich color and conflicts with the title and subtitle text. One method of reducing this richness is to change the transparency. The **Transparency slider** indicates the amount of opaqueness. The default setting is 0, which is fully opaque. The opposite extreme is 100%, which is fully transparent. To change the transparency, you can move the Transparency slider or enter a number in the text box next to the slider. The following step adjusts the transparency to 10%.

1

- Click the Transparency slider and drag it to the right until 10% is displayed in the Transparency text box (Figure 2–33).

Q&A Can I move the slider in small increments so that I can get a precise percentage easily?

Yes. Press the RIGHT ARROW or LEFT ARROW key to move the slider in one-percent increments.

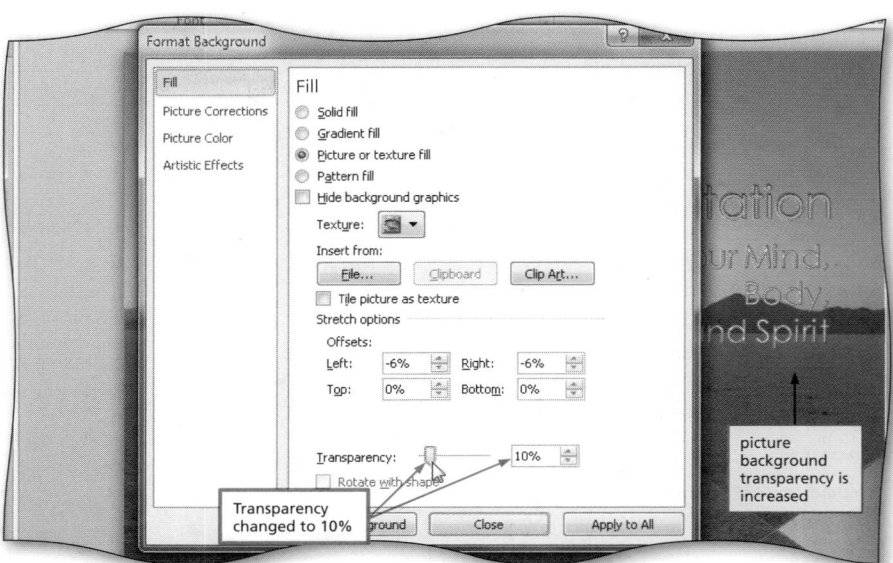

Figure 2–33

To Format a Background Texture Fill Transparency

The Sand texture on Slide 4 is dark and may not offer sufficient contrast with the symbols and text you are going to insert on this slide. You can adjust the transparency of slide texture in the same manner that you change a picture transparency. The following steps adjust the texture transparency to 50%.

1
- Click the Next Slide button three times to display Slide 4.
- Click the Transparency slider and drag it to the right until 50% is displayed in the Transparency text box (Figure 2–34).

2
- Click the Close button (Format Background dialog box).

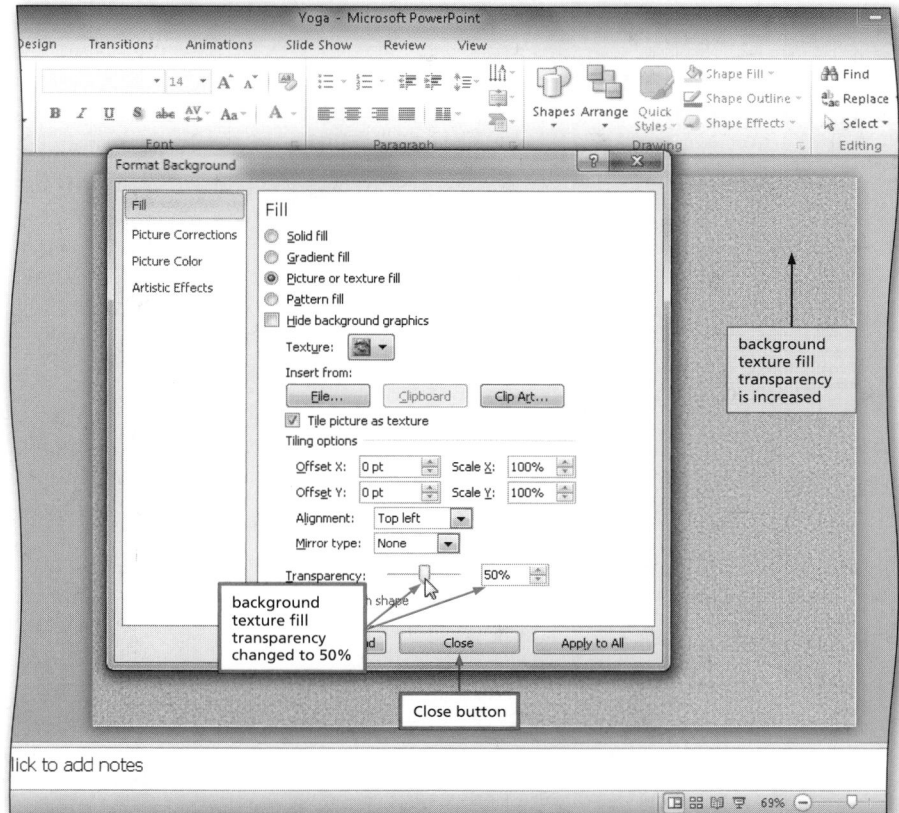

Figure 2–34

To Choose a Background Style

Now that the backgrounds for Slides 1 and 4 are set, and the title and text paragraphs for the presentation have been entered, you need to make design decisions for Slides 2 and 3. In this project, you will choose a background for these slides. For each theme, PowerPoint provides 12 **background styles** with designs that may include color, shading, patterns, and textures. **Fill effects** add pattern and texture to a background, which add depth to a slide. The following steps add a background style to Slides 2 and 3 in the presentation.

①

- Click the Previous Slide button once to display Slide 3 and then click the Design tab on the Ribbon.

- Click the Background Styles button (Design tab | Background group) to display the Background Styles gallery.

- Right-click Style 11 (third style in third row) to display the shortcut menu (Figure 2–35).

🔎 **Experiment**

- Point to various styles themes in the Background Styles gallery and watch the backgrounds change on the slide.

Q&A Are the backgrounds displayed in a specific order?

Yes. They are arranged in order from light to dark running from left to right. The first row has solid backgrounds; the middle row has darker fills at the top and bottom; the bottom row has fill patterns. If you point to a background, a ScreenTip with the background's name appears on the screen.

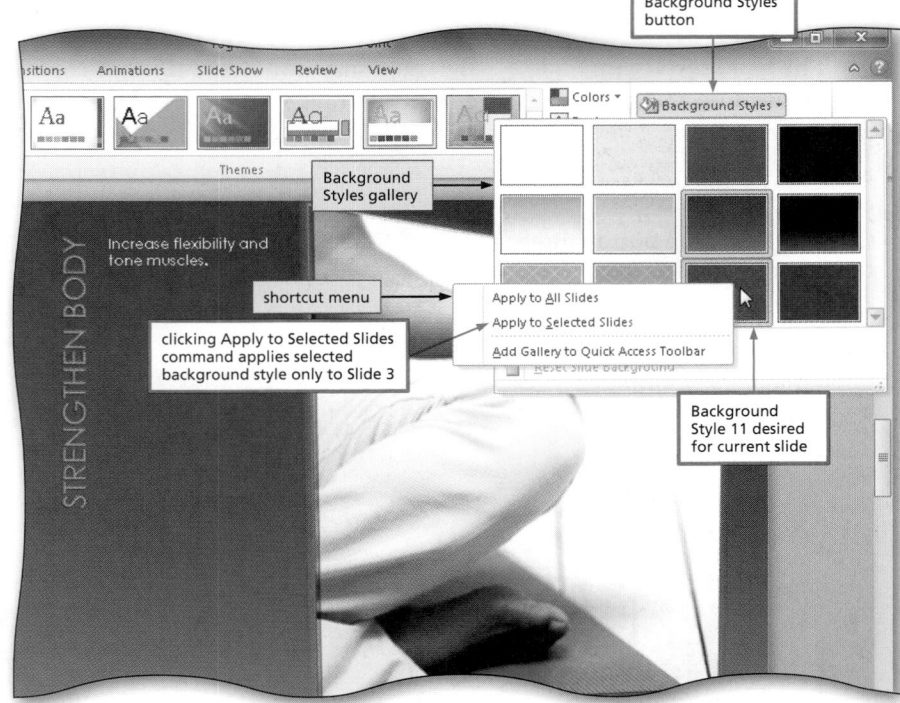

Figure 2–35

②

- Click Apply to Selected Slides to apply Style 11 to Slide 3 (Figure 2–36).

Q&A If I decide later that this background style does not fit the theme of my presentation, can I apply a different background?

Yes. You can repeat these steps at any time while creating your presentation.

Q&A What if I want to apply this background style to all slides in the presentation?

Click the desired style or click Apply to All Slides in the shortcut menu.

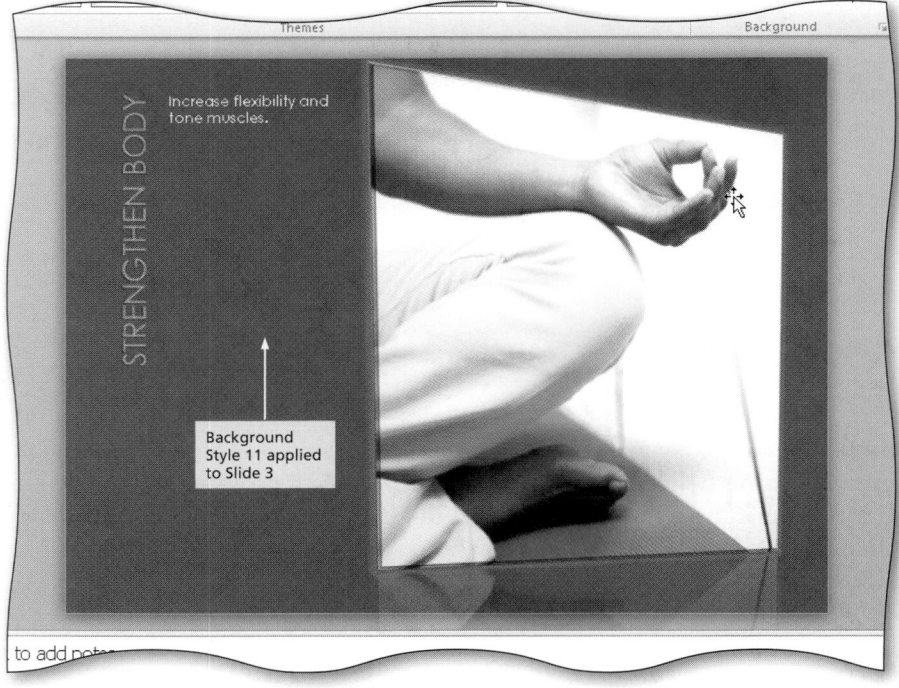

Figure 2–36

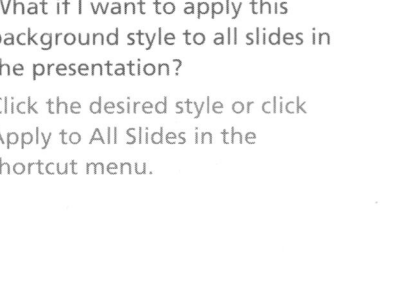

Other Ways

1. Click Background Styles, right-click desired background, press S

To Choose Another Background Style

In this presentation, the Slide 2 background can have a coordinating background to complement the yoga picture. The following steps add a background to Slide 2.

1 Click the Previous Slide button to display Slide 2. Click the Background Styles button (Design tab | Background group) and then right-click Style 10 (second style in third row) to display the shortcut menu.

2 Click Apply to Selected Slides to apply this background style to Slide 2 (Figure 2–37).

Figure 2–37

Formatting Title and Content Text

Choosing well-coordinated colors and styles for text and objects in a presentation is possible. Once you select a particular Quick Style and make any other font changes, you then can copy these changes to other text using the **Format Painter**. The Format Painter allows you to copy all formatting changes from one object to another.

To Change the Subtitle and Caption Font

The default Verve theme heading, subtitle, and caption text font is Century Gothic. To draw more attention to subtitle and caption text and to help differentiate these slide elements from the title text, you want to change the font from Century Gothic to Papyrus. To change the font, you must select the letters you want to format. In Chapter 1, you selected a paragraph and then formatted the characters. To format the text in multiple paragraphs quickly and simultaneously, you can select all the paragraphs to be formatted and then apply formatting changes. The following steps change the subtitle and caption font.

BTW

Introducing the Presentation
Before your audience enters the room, start the presentation and then display Slide 1. This slide should be visually appealing and provide general interest in the presentation. An effective title slide gives a good first impression.

- Click the Previous Slide button to display Slide 1. Move the mouse pointer to the left of the first subtitle paragraph, Unify Your Mind, until the mouse pointer changes to an I-beam (Figure 2–38).

Figure 2–38

- Drag downward to select all three subtitle lines that will be formatted (Figure 2–39).

Figure 2–39

- With the text selected, click Home on the Ribbon and then click the Font box arrow (Home tab | Font group) to display the Font gallery (Figure 2–40).

Q&A

Will the fonts in my Font gallery be the same as those shown in Figure 2–40?

Your list of available fonts may differ, depending on what fonts you have installed and the type of printer you are using.

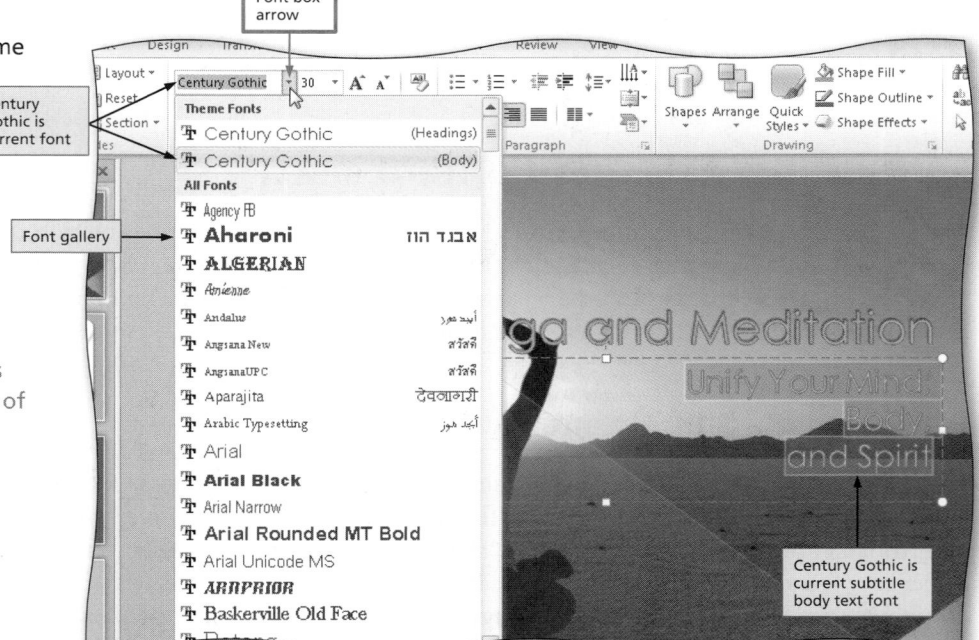

Figure 2–40

4

- Scroll through the Font gallery and then point to Papyrus (or a similar font) to display a live preview of the title text in the Papyrus font (Figure 2–41).

🔍 **Experiment**

- Point to various fonts in the Font gallery and watch the subtitle text font change on the slide.

- Click Papyrus (or a similar font) to change the font of the selected text to Papyrus.

Papyrus font is previewed for subtitle body text

Figure 2–41

Other Ways
1. Click Font box arrow on Mini toolbar, click desired font in Font gallery 2. Right-click selected text, click Font on shortcut menu (Font dialog box), click	Font tab, select desired font in Font list, click OK button 3. Click Font dialog box launcher (Home tab | Font group), click Font tab (Font dialog box), select	desired font in Font list, click OK button 4. Press CTRL+SHIFT+F, click Font tab (Font dialog box), select desired font in the Font list, click OK button

To Shadow Text

A **shadow** helps letters display prominently by adding a shadow behind the text. The following step adds a shadow to the selected subtitle text, Unify Your Mind, Body, and Spirit.

1

- With the subtitle text selected, click the Text Shadow button (Home tab | Font group) to add a shadow to the selected text (Figure 2–42).

Q&A

How would I remove a shadow?

You would click the Shadow button a second time, or you immediately could click the Undo button on the Quick Access Toolbar.

Text Shadow button

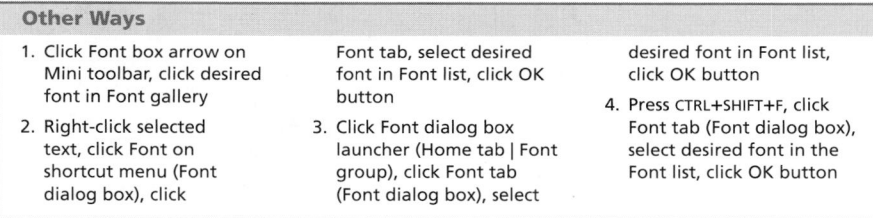

shadow applied to subtitle text

Figure 2–42

BTW

Formatting Text Effects
Text Shadow is one of a variety of effects PowerPoint provides in the Font group. If you click the Font dialog box launcher, you can select additional effects, such as Small Caps and Superscript, in the Font dialog box. In addition, you can format the letters by adding glow, reflection, 3-D, and other effects by selecting the text, clicking the Text Effects button (Drawing Tools Format tab | WordArt Styles group), pointing to an effect in the Text Effects menu, and then selecting an effect in the gallery.

To Format the Subtitle Text

To increase readability, you can format the Slide 1 subtitle text by bolding the characters and changing the font color to yellow. The following steps format the Slide 1 subtitle text.

1 With the subtitle text selected, click the Bold button (Home tab | Font group) to bold the text.

2 Click the Font Color arrow and change the color to Light Yellow, Text 2 (fourth color in first row) (Figure 2–43).

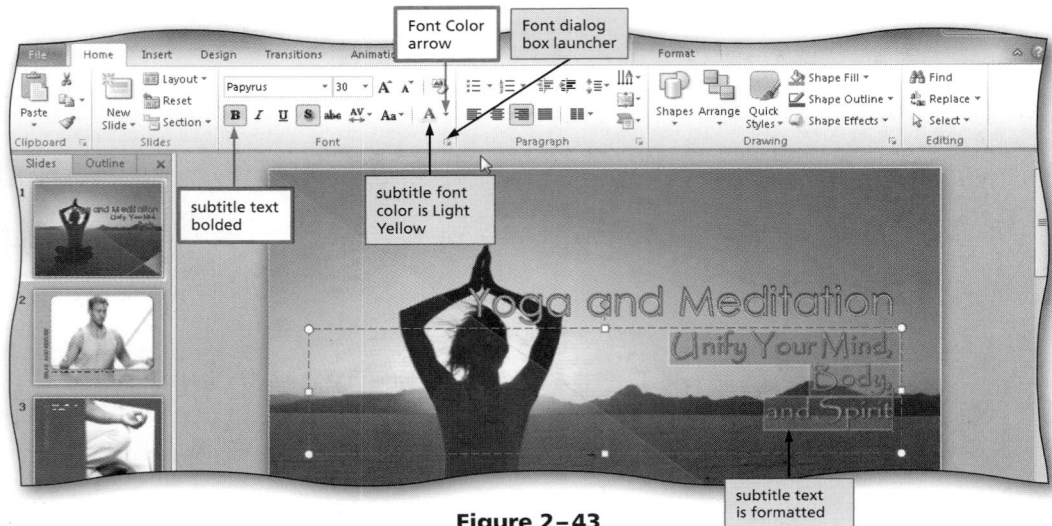

Figure 2–43

BTW

Decreasing Font Size
The Increase Font Size buttons on the Mini toolbar and in the Font group (Home tab) enlarge the selected characters in predetermined amounts. The Decrease Font Size buttons, which appear to the right of the Increase Font Size buttons, reduce the characters' size in the same predetermined point sizes.

To Format the Slide 2 Caption

The caption on a slide should be large enough for audience members to read easily and should coordinate with the font styles in other parts of the presentation. The caption on Slide 2 can be enhanced by changing the font, the font color, and the font size. The following steps format the Slide 2 caption text.

1 Click the Next Slide button to display Slide 2. Triple-click the caption text to select all the characters, click the Font box arrow on the Mini toolbar, and then scroll down and click Papyrus.

2 Click the Increase Font Size button on the Mini toolbar three times to increase the font size to 20 point.

3 Click the Bold button on the Mini toolbar to bold the text (Figure 2–44).

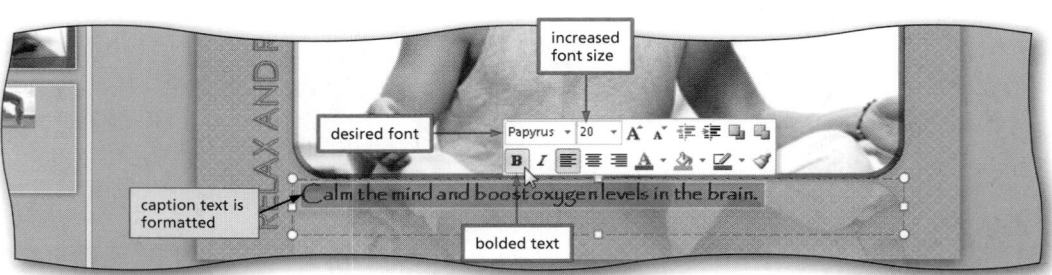

Figure 2–44

Format Painter

To save time and avoid formatting errors, you can use the Format Painter to apply custom formatting to other places in your presentation quickly and easily. You can use this feature in three ways:

- To copy only character attributes, such as font and font effects, select text that has these qualities.
- To copy both paragraph attributes, such as alignment and indentation and character attributes, select the entire paragraph.
- To apply the same formatting to multiple words, phrases, or paragraphs, double-click the Format Painter button and then select each item you want to format. You then can press the ESC key or click the Format Painter button to turn off this feature.

To Format Text Using the Format Painter

To save time and duplicated effort, you quickly can use the Format Painter to copy formatting attributes from the Slide 2 caption text and apply them to Slide 3. The following steps use the Format Painter to copy formatting features.

- With the Slide 2 caption text still selected, double-click the Format Painter button (Home tab | Clipboard group).

- Move the mouse pointer off the Ribbon (Figure 2–45).

Q&A Why did my mouse pointer change shape?

The mouse pointer changed shape by adding a paintbrush to indicate that the Format Painter function is active.

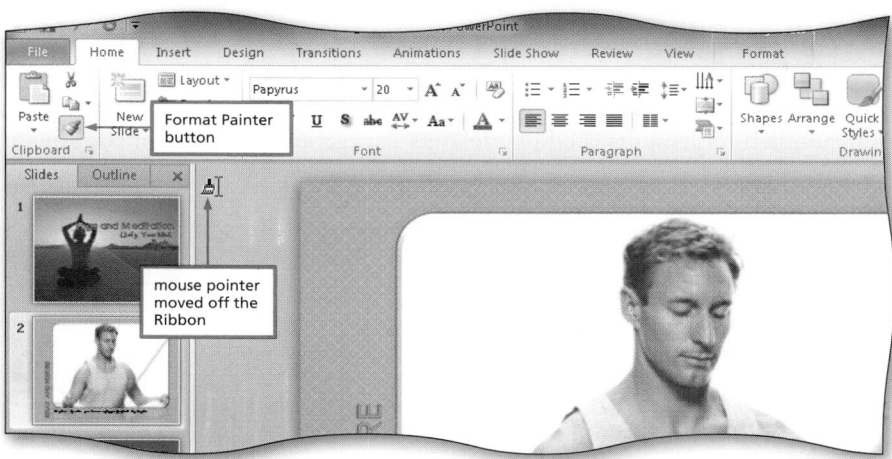

Figure 2–45

- Click the Next Slide button to display Slide 3. Triple-click the caption placeholder to apply the format to all the caption text (Figure 2–46).

- Press the ESC key to turn off the Format Painter feature.

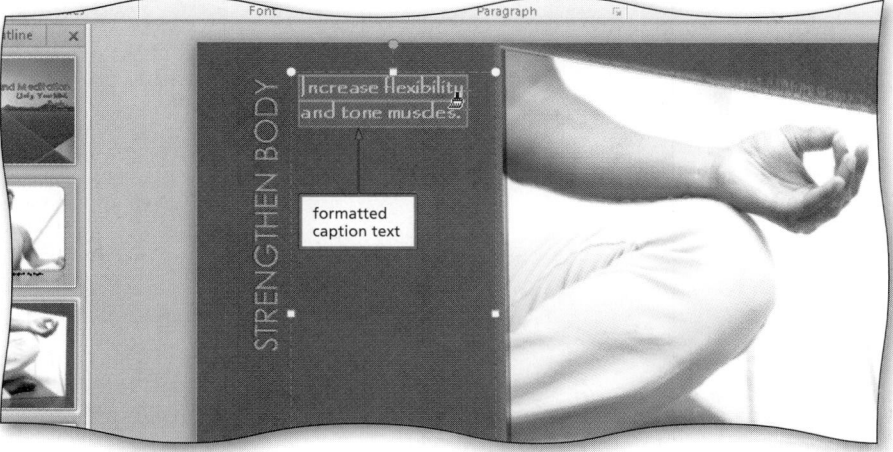

Figure 2–46

Other Ways

1. Click Format Painter button on Mini toolbar

Break Point: If you wish to take a break, this is a good place to do so. Be sure to save the Yoga file again and then you can quit PowerPoint. To resume at a later time, start PowerPoint, open the file called Yoga, and continue following the steps from this location forward.

Sizing Shapes
PowerPoint's Shapes gallery provides a wide variety of symbols that can help emphasize your major points on each slide. As you select the shapes and then size them, keep in mind that your audience will focus on the largest shapes first. The most important information, therefore, should be placed in or near the shapes with the most visual size.

Adding and Formatting a Shape

One method of getting the audience's attention and reinforcing the major concepts being presented is to have graphical elements on the title slide. PowerPoint provides a wide variety of predefined shapes that can add visual interest to a slide. Shape elements include lines, basic geometrical shapes, arrows, equation shapes, flowchart symbols, stars, banners, and callouts. After adding a shape to a slide, you can change its default characteristics by adding text, bullets, numbers, and styles. You also can combine multiple shapes to create a more complex graphic.

Slides 1 and 4 in this presentation are enhanced in a variety of ways. First, a sun shape is added to the Slide 1 title text in place of the letter o. Then a circle shape is inserted on Slide 4 and copied twice, and text is added to each circle and then formatted. Finally, a triangle is inserted on top of the three circle shapes on Slide 4.

To Add a Shape

Many of the shapes included in the Shapes gallery can direct the viewer to important aspects of the presentation. For example, the sun shape helps emphasize the presentation's theme of practicing yoga and meditation, and it complements the Sunrise Yoga background picture. The following steps add the Sun shape to Slide 1.

1
• Click the Previous Slide button two times to display Slide 1. Click the Shapes button (Home tab | Drawing group) to display the Shapes gallery (Figure 2–47).

Figure 2–47

Q&A
I do not see a Shapes button in the Drawing group. Instead, I have three rows of the shapes I have used recently in presentations. Why?

Monitor dimensions and resolution affect how buttons display on the Ribbon. Click the Shapes More button to display the entire Shapes gallery.

2

- Click the Sun shape in the Basic Shapes area of the Shapes gallery.

Q&A Why did my pointer change shape?

The pointer changed to a plus shape to indicate the Sun shape has been added to the Clipboard.

- Position the mouse pointer (a crosshair) above the person's hands in the picture, as shown in Figure 2–48.

Figure 2–48

3

- Click Slide 1 to insert the Sun shape (Figure 2–49).

Figure 2–49

Other Ways

1. Click More button (Drawing Tools Format tab | Insert Shapes group)

To Resize a Shape

The next step is to resize the Sun shape. The shape should be reduced so that it is approximately the same size as the letter o in the words Yoga and Meditation. The following steps resize the selected Sun shape.

1

- With the mouse pointer appearing as a two-headed arrow, drag a corner sizing handle on the picture diagonally inward until the Sun shape is resized approximately as shown in Figure 2–50.

Q&A What if my shape is not selected?

To select a shape, click it.

Q&A What if the shape has changed proportions?

To maintain a shape's proportions, hold down the SHIFT key when you drag a corner sizing handle.

Figure 2–50

2

- Release the mouse button to resize the shape.

- Drag the Sun shape on top of the letter o in the word, Yoga (Figure 2–51).

Q&A What if I want to move the shape to a precise location on the slide?

With the shape selected, press the ARROW keys or the CTRL+ARROW keys to move the shape to the desired location.

Figure 2–51

Other Ways

1. Enter shape height and width in Height and Width text boxes (Drawing Tools Format tab | Size group)

2. Click Size and Position dialog box launcher

(Drawing Tools Format tab | Size group), click Size tab, enter desired height and width values in text boxes, click Close button

To Copy and Paste a Shape

The next step is to copy the Sun shape. The duplicate shape will be placed over the letter 'o' in the word, Meditation. The following steps copy and move the identical second Sun shape.

1

- With the Sun shape still selected, click the Copy button (Home tab | Clipboard group) (Figure 2–52).

Q&A What if my shape is not selected?

To select a shape, click it.

Q&A How does the Copy button differ from the Cut button?

Clicking the Copy button leaves the shape in the slide while placing the same shape on the Office Clipboard. Clicking the Cut button removes the shape from the slide and then places it on the Office Clipboard.

Figure 2–52

2

- Click the Paste button on the Home tab to insert a duplicate Sun shape on Slide 1.

- Drag the Sun shape on top of the letter o in the word, Meditation, and release the mouse button when a dashed line connects this Sun shape to the Sun shape that is displaying in the word, Yoga (Figure 2–53).

Figure 2–53

Q&A What does the dashed line represent?

PowerPoint displays this Smart Guide when two shapes are aligned precisely. In this case, the two Sun shapes are centered horizontally.

Other Ways

1. Right-click selected shape, click Copy on shortcut menu, right-click, click Paste on shortcut menu
2. Select shape, press CTRL+C, press CTRL+V

BTW

Copying and Pasting Text

The process of copying text is similar to copying a shape. When you copy text, you place the word, phrase, sentence, or other letters on the Office Clipboard. When you paste this text, you copy the letters from the Office Clipboard into another location on a slide. To copy and paste text, select the text to be copied, click the Copy button (Home tab | Clipboard group), position the insertion point at the location where the text should be pasted, and then click the Paste button (Home tab | Clipboard group) to paste the copied text at the location of the insertion point.

To Add Other Shapes

Circles, squares, and triangles are among the geometric shapes included in the Shapes gallery. These shapes can be combined to show relationships among the elements, and they can help illustrate the basic concepts presented in your slide show. The following steps add the Oval and Isosceles Triangle shapes to Slide 4.

1

- Click the Next Slide button three times to display Slide 4 and then click the Shapes button (Home tab | Drawing group) to display the Shapes gallery (Figure 2–54).

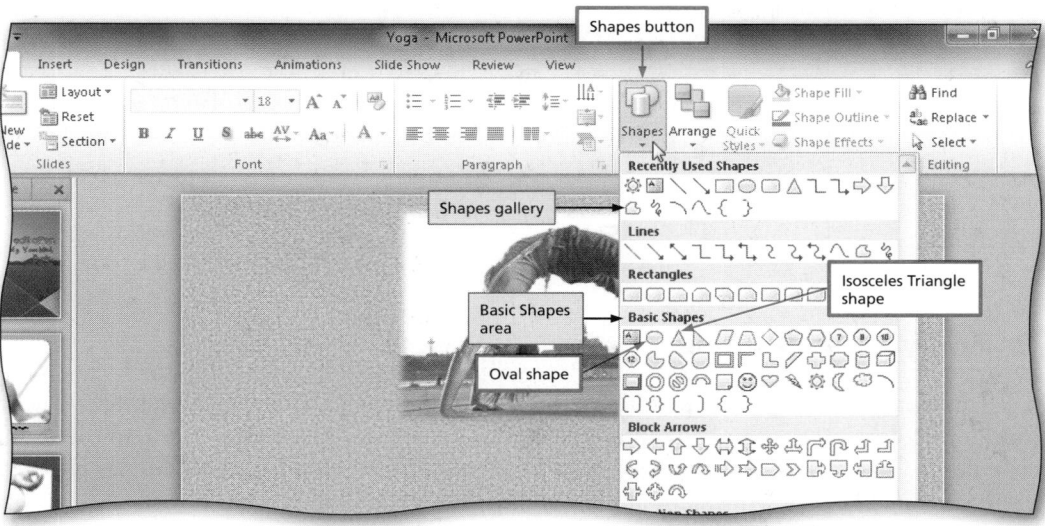

Figure 2–54

- Click the Oval shape in the Basic Shapes area of the Shapes gallery.

- Position the mouse pointer in the center of Slide 4 and then click to insert the Oval shape.

- Press and hold down the SHIFT key and then drag a corner sizing handle until the Oval shape forms a circle and is the size shown in Figure 2–55.

Q&A

Why did I need to press the SHIFT key while enlarging the shape?

Holding down the SHIFT key while dragging draws a perfect circle.

- Move the shape so it is positioned approximately as shown in the figure.

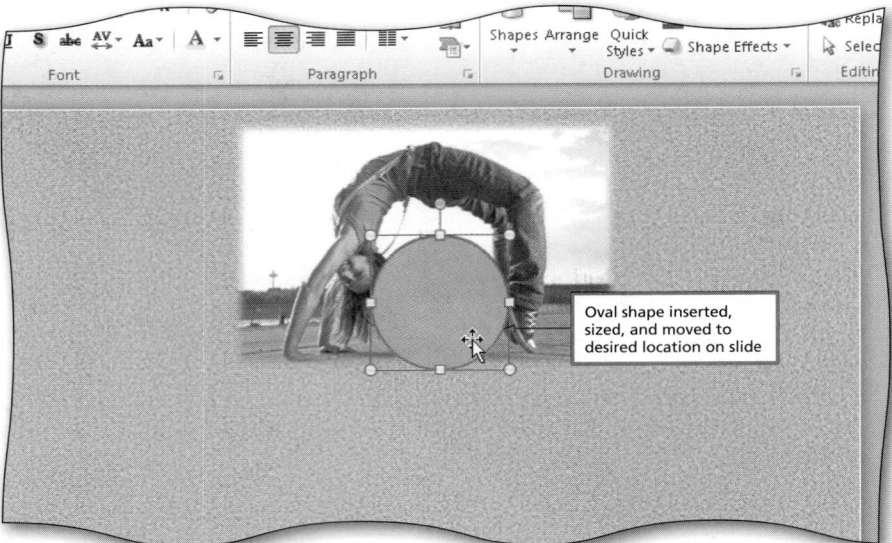

Figure 2–55

- Click the Shapes button (Home tab | Drawing group) and then click the Isosceles Triangle shape in the Basic Shapes area of the Shapes gallery.

- Position the mouse pointer in the right side of Slide 4 and then click to insert the Isosceles Triangle shape.

- Resize the shape so that it displays approximately as shown in Figure 2–56.

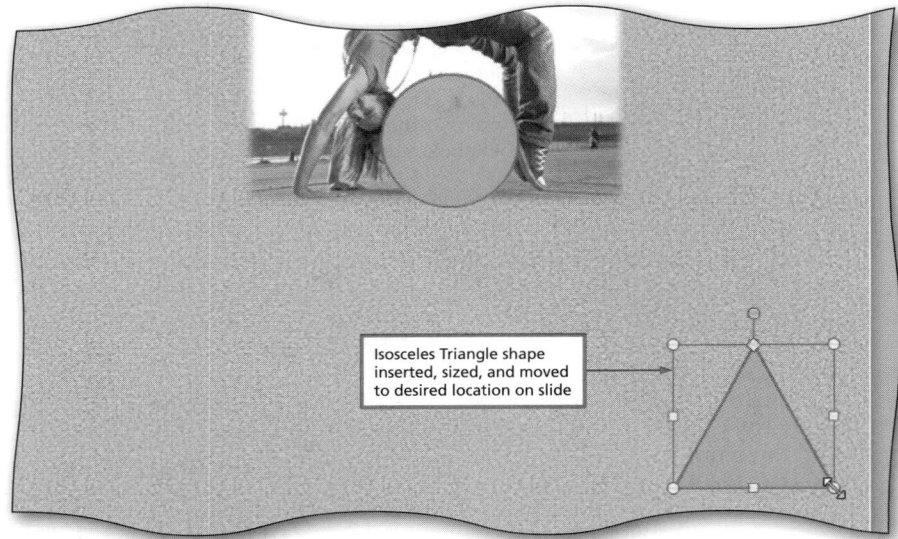

Figure 2–56

To Apply a Shape Style

Formatting text in a shape follows the same techniques as formatting text in a placeholder. You can change font, font color and size, and alignment. The next step is to apply a shape style to the oval so that it appears to have depth. The Shape Styles gallery has a variety of styles that change depending upon the theme applied to the presentation. The following steps apply a style to the Oval shape.

1

● Click the Oval shape to select it and then display the Drawing Tools Format tab (Figure 2–57).

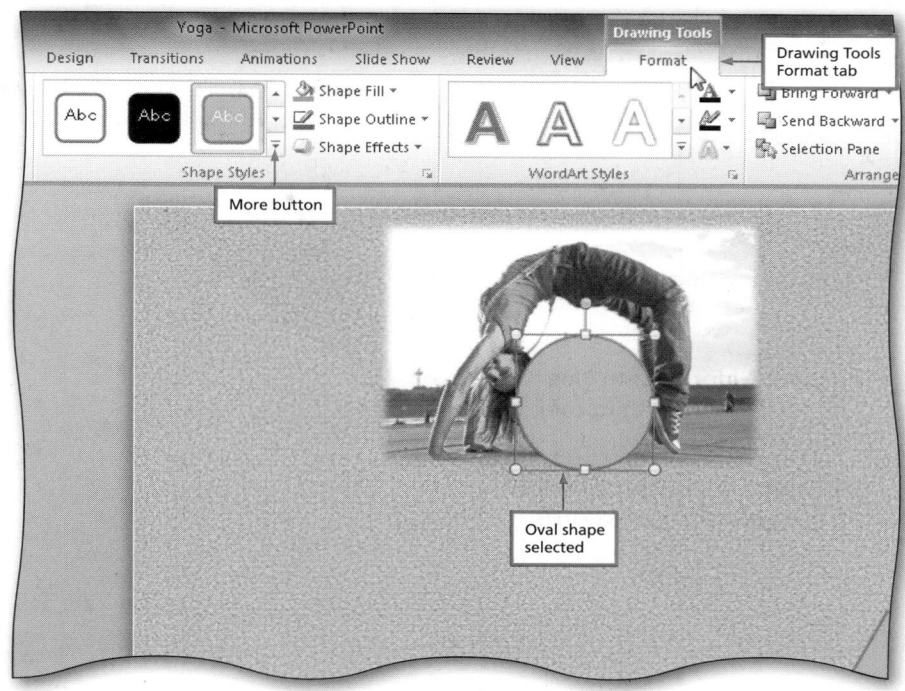

Figure 2–57

2

● Click the More button in the Shape Styles gallery (Drawing Tools Format tab | Shape Styles group) to expand the Shape Styles gallery.

● Point to Intense Effect – Orange, Accent 1 in the Shape Styles gallery (second shape in last row) to display a live preview of that style applied to the shape in the slide (Figure 2–58).

🔎 **Experiment**

● Point to various styles in the Shape Styles gallery and watch the style of the shape change.

3

● Click Intense Effect – Orange, Accent 1 in the Shape Styles gallery to apply the selected style to the Oval shape.

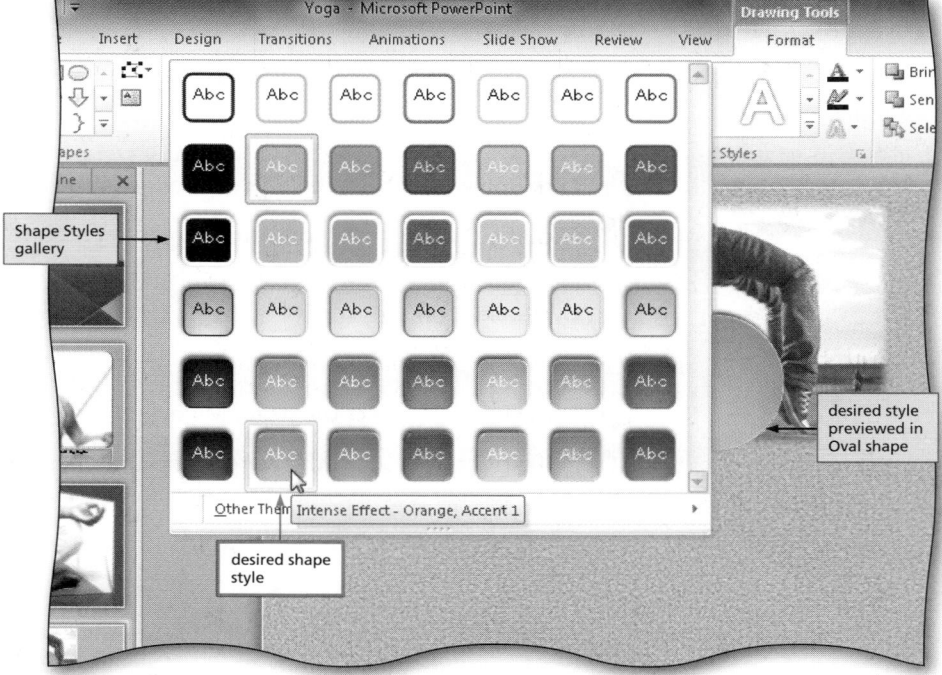

Figure 2–58

Other Ways
1. Click Format Shape dialog box launcher (Drawing Tools Format tab | Shape Styles group), select desired colors (Format Shape dialog box), click Close button   2. Right-click shape, click Format Shape on shortcut menu, select desired colors (Format Shape dialog box), click Close button

To Add Formatted Text to a Shape

Formatting text in a shape follows the same techniques as formatting text in a placeholder. You can change font, font color and size, and alignment. The next step is to add the word, Mind, to the shape, change the font to Papyrus and the font color to Blue-Gray, center and bold the text, and increase the font size to 24 point. The following step adds text to the Oval shape.

- With the Oval shape selected, type **Mind** in the shape.

- Change the font to Papyrus.

- Change the font color to Blue-Gray, Background 2 (third color in first Theme Colors row).

- Change the font size to 24 point and bold the text (Figure 2–59).

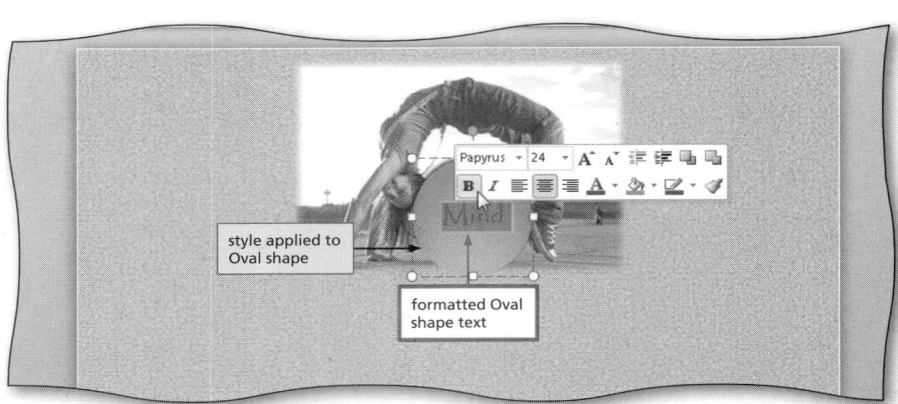

Figure 2–59

BTW

Drawing a Square
Holding down the SHIFT key while dragging a Rectangle shape draws a square.

To Copy a Shape

Your presentation emphasizes that mind, body, and spirit are equal components in finding balance in life. Each of these elements can be represented by an oval. The following steps copy the Oval shape.

1 Click Home on the Ribbon. Click the edge of the Oval shape so that it is a solid line.

2 Click the Copy button (Home tab | Clipboard group).

3 Click the Paste button (Home tab | Clipboard group) two times to insert two duplicate Oval shapes on Slide 4.

4 Move the Oval shapes so they appear approximately as shown in Figure 2–60.

5 In the left oval, select the word, Mind, and then type the word, **Body**, in the oval.

6 In the right oval, select the word, Mind, and then type the word, **Spirit**, in the oval (Figure 2–60). You may need to enlarge the size of the oval shapes slightly so that each word is displayed on one line.

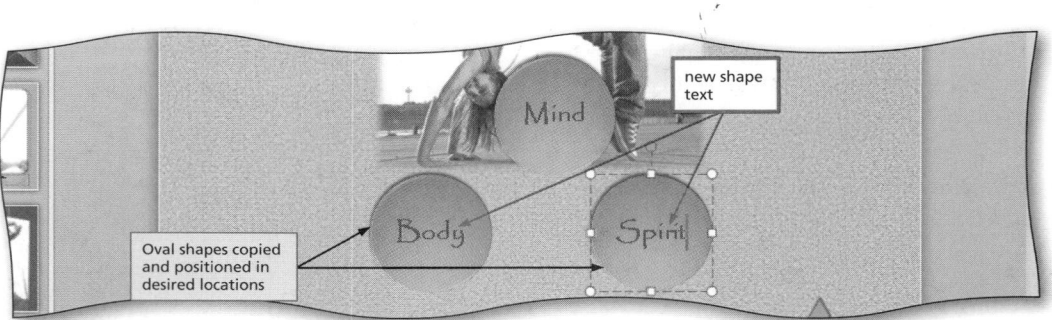

Figure 2–60

To Apply Another Style

The triangle shape helps show the unity among body, mind, and spirit. You can apply a coordinating shape style to the isosceles triangle and then place it on top of the three ovals. The following steps apply a style to the Isosceles Triangle shape.

1 Display the Drawing Tools Format tab. Click the Isosceles Triangle shape on Slide 4 to select it.

2 Click the More button in the Shape Styles gallery (Drawing Tools Format tab | Shape Styles group) to expand the Shape Styles gallery and then click Intense Effect – Blue, Accent 2 (third style in last row) to apply that style to the triangle.

3 Move the triangle shape to the center of the Ovals.

4 Click the Bring Forward button twice (Drawing Tools Format tab | Arrange group) to display the triangle on top of the ovals. Resize the triangle if necessary so that it displays as shown in Figure 2–61.

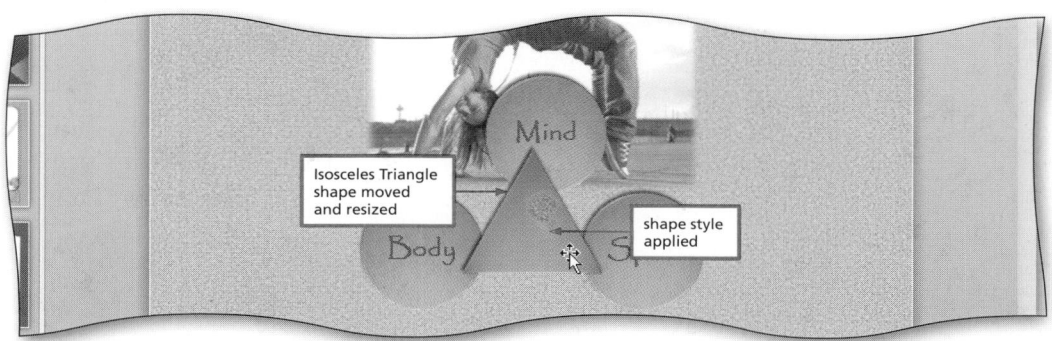

Figure 2–61

Break Point: If you wish to take a break, this is a good place to do so. Be sure to save the Yoga file again and then you can quit PowerPoint. To resume at a later time, start PowerPoint, open the file called Yoga, and continue following the steps from this location forward.

Using WordArt

One method of adding appealing visual elements to a presentation is by using **WordArt** styles. This feature is found in other Microsoft Office applications, including Word and Excel. This gallery of decorative effects allows you to type new text or convert existing text to WordArt. You then can add elements such as fills, outlines, and effects.

As with slide backgrounds, WordArt fill in the interior of a letter can consist of a solid color, texture, picture, or gradient. The WordArt **outline** is the exterior border surrounding each letter or symbol. PowerPoint allows you to change the outline color, weight, and style. You also can add an **effect**, which helps add emphasis or depth to the characters. Some effects are shadows, reflections, glows, bevels, and 3-D rotations.

BTW

Creating Logos
Many companies without graphic arts departments create their logos using WordArt. The bevels, glows, and shadows allow corporate designers to develop unique images with 3-D effects that give depth to their companies' emblems.

Plan Ahead

Use WordArt in moderation.
Some WordArt styles are bold and detailed, and they can detract from the message you are trying to present if not used carefully. Select a WordArt style when needed for special emphasis, such as a title slide that audience members will see when they enter the room. WordArt can have a powerful effect, so do not overuse it.

To Insert WordArt

Yoga and meditation can help individuals find balance among the mind, body, and spirit. The symbols on Slide 4 emphasize this relationship, and you want to call attention to the concept. You quickly can add a visual element to the slide by selecting a WordArt style from the WordArt Styles gallery and then applying it to a word. The following steps insert WordArt.

1
- With Slide 4 displaying, click Insert on the Ribbon.
- Click the WordArt button (Insert tab | Text group) to display the WordArt gallery (Figure 2–62).

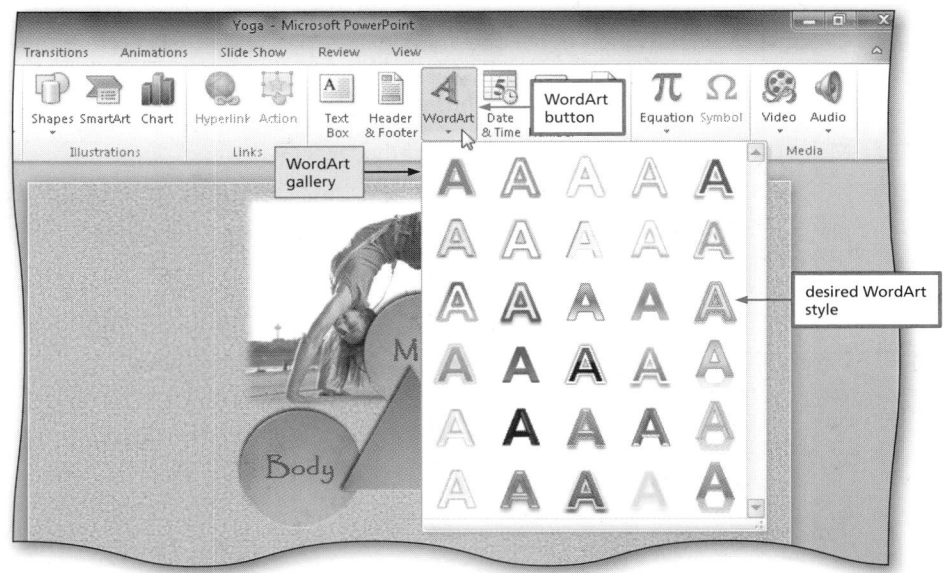

Figure 2–62

2
- Click Fill – Blue, Accent 2, Double Outline – Accent 2 (last letter A in third row) to display the WordArt text box (Figure 2–63).

Q&A What is a matte bevel style that is part of some of the styles in the gallery?

A matte finish gives a dull and rough effect. A bevel edge is angled or sloped and gives the effect of a three-dimensional object.

Figure 2–63

3
- Type **Balance** in the text box, as the WordArt text (Figure 2–64).

Q&A Why did the Format tab appear automatically in the Ribbon?

It appears when you select text to which you could add a WordArt style or other effect.

Figure 2–64

To Change a WordArt Shape

The WordArt text is useful to emphasize the harmony among the mind, body, and spirit. You can further emphasize this word by changing its shape. PowerPoint provides a variety of graphical shapes that add interest to text. The following steps change the WordArt to Triangle Down shape.

1

- With the Slide 4 text still selected, click the Text Effects button (Drawing Tools Format tab | WordArt Styles group) to display the Text Effects menu (Figure 2–65).

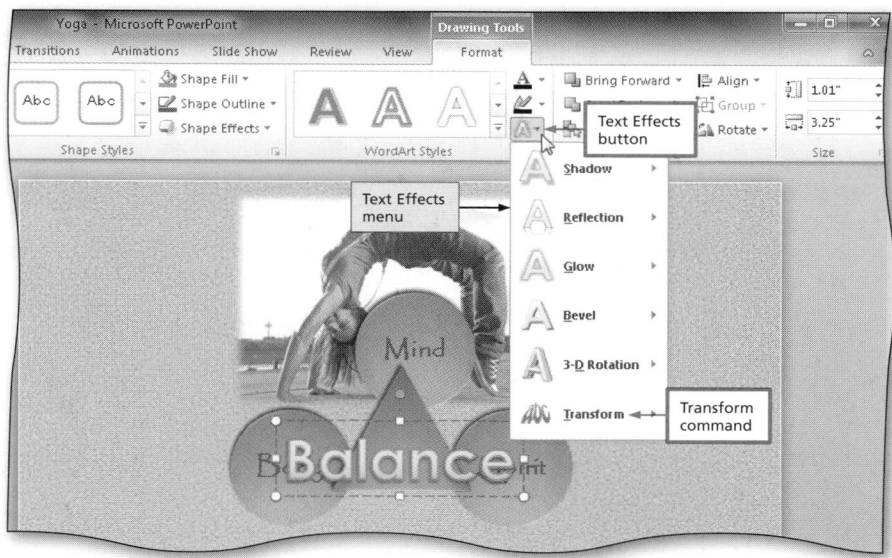

Figure 2–65

2

- Point to Transform in the Text Effects menu to display the WordArt Transform gallery (Figure 2–66).

 **Experiment**

- Point to various styles in the Transform gallery and watch the format of the text and borders change.

Q&A How can I see the preview of a Transform effect if the gallery is overlaying the WordArt letters?

Move the WordArt text box to the left or right side of the slide and then repeat Steps 1 and 2.

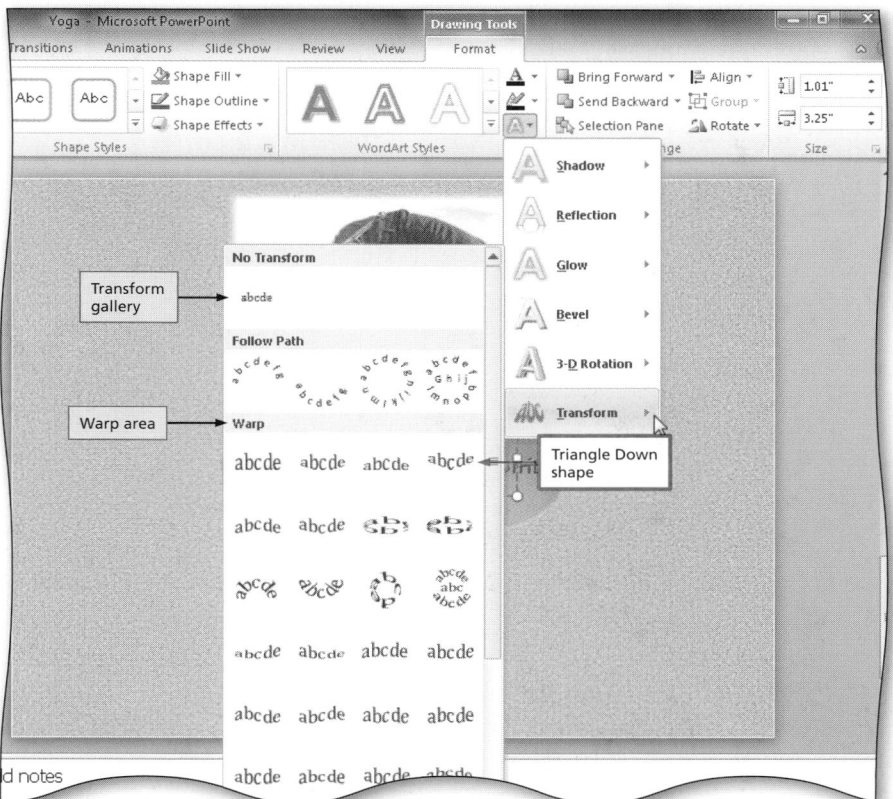

Figure 2–66

3

- Click the Triangle Down shape in the Warp area to apply the Triangle Down shape to the WordArt text (Figure 2–67).

Q&A Can I change the shape I applied to the WordArt?

Yes. Position the insertion point in the text box and then repeat Steps 1 and 2.

Figure 2–67

4

- Drag the WordArt downward until it is positioned approximately as shown in Figure 2–68.

- Drag a corner sizing handle diagonally outward until the WordArt is resized approximately as shown in the figure.

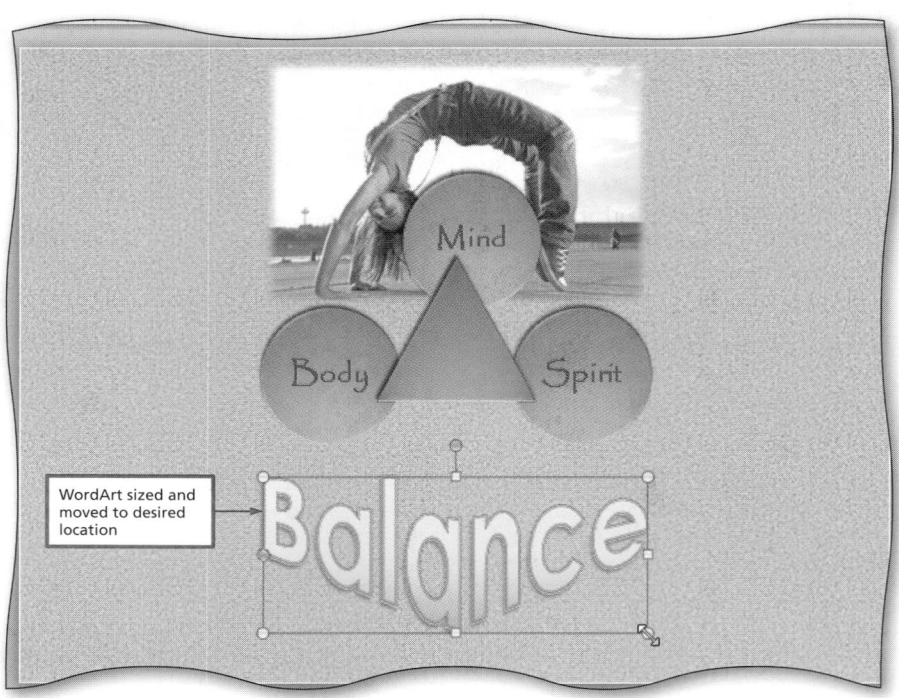

Figure 2–68

To Apply a WordArt Text Fill

The Slide 4 background has a Sand texture for the background, and you want to coordinate the WordArt fill with a similar texture. The following steps add the Denim texture as a fill for the WordArt characters.

1

● With the WordArt text selected, click the Text Fill button arrow (Drawing Tools Format tab | WordArt Styles group) to display the Text Fill gallery.

Q&A The Text Fill gallery did not display. Why not?

Be sure you click the Text Fill button arrow, which is to the right of the Text Fill button. If you mistakenly click the Text Fill button, PowerPoint places the default fill in the WordArt instead of displaying the Text Fill gallery.

● Point to Texture in the Text Fill gallery to display the Texture gallery (Figure 2–69).

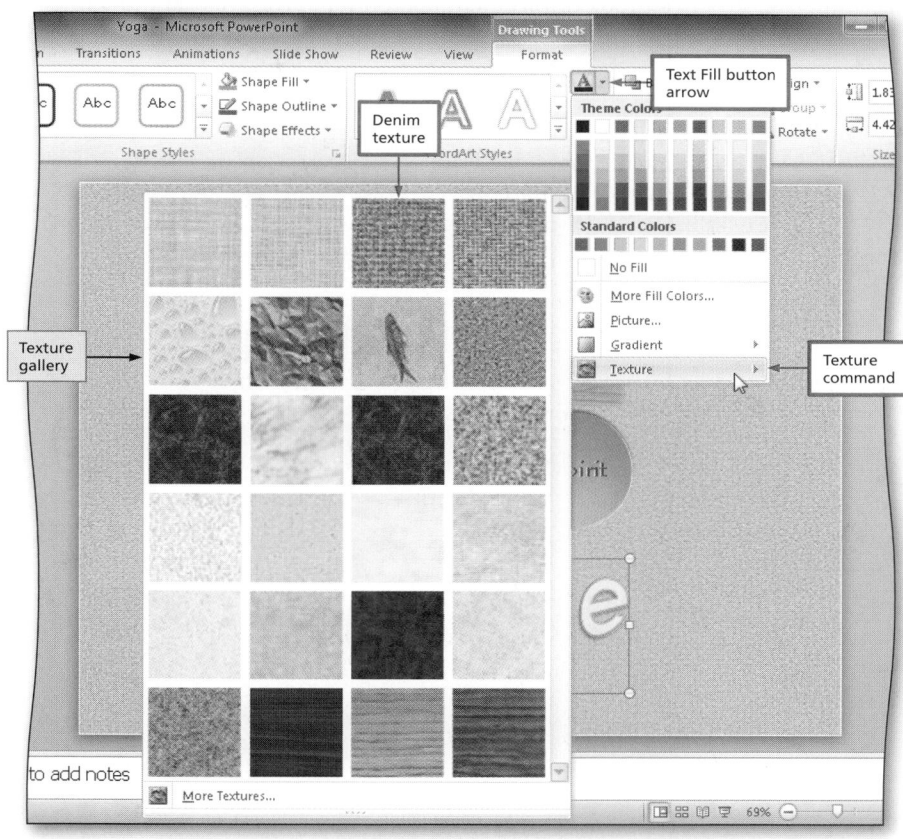

Figure 2–69

 Experiment

● Point to various styles in the Text Fill gallery and watch the fill change.

Q&A How can I see the preview of a fill if the gallery is overlaying the WordArt letters?

Move the WordArt text box to the left or right side of the slide and then repeat Step 1.

2

● Click the Denim texture (third texture in first row) to apply this texture as the fill for the WordArt.

Q&A Can I apply this texture simultaneously to text that appears in more than one place on my slide?

Yes. Select one area of text, press and then hold the CTRL key while you select the other text, and then apply the texture.

To Change the Weight of a WordArt Outline

The letters in the WordArt style applied have a double outline around the edges. To emphasize this characteristic, you can increase the width of the lines. As with font size, lines also are measured in point size, and PowerPoint gives you the option to change the line **weight**, or thickness, starting with ¼ point (pt) and increasing in one-fourth–point increments. Other outline options include modifying the color and the line style, such as changing to dots or dashes or a combination of dots and dashes. The following steps change the WordArt outline weight to 6 pt.

- With the WordArt still selected, click the Text Outline button arrow (Drawing Tools Format tab | WordArt Styles group) to display the Text Outline gallery.

- Point to Weight in the gallery to display the Weight list.

- Point to 6 pt to display a live preview of this line weight on the WordArt text outline (Figure 2–70).

Experiment

- Point to various line weights in the Weight list and watch the line thickness change.

Q&A Can I make the line width more than 6 pt?

Yes. Click More Lines and increase the amount in the Width box.

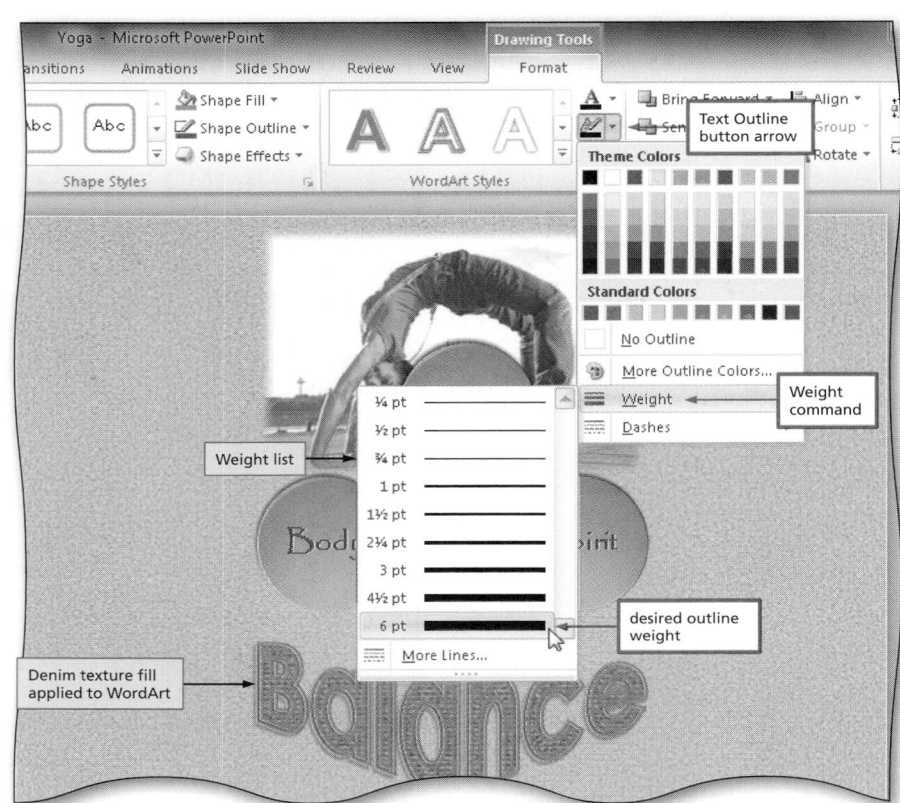

Figure 2–70

- Click 6 pt to apply this line weight to the title text outline.

Q&A Must my text have an outline?

No. To delete the outline, click No Outline in the Text Outline gallery.

To Change the Color of a WordArt Outline

The WordArt outline color is similar to the Denim fill color. To add variety, you can change the outline color. The following steps change the WordArt outline color.

1

- With the WordArt still selected, click the Text Outline button arrow (Drawing Tools Format tab | WordArt Styles group) to display the Text Outline gallery.

- Point to Orange, Accent 1 (fifth color in first row) to display a live preview of this outline color (Figure 2–71).

Experiment

- Point to various colors in the gallery and watch the outline colors change.

2

- Click Orange, Accent 1 to apply this color to the WordArt outline.

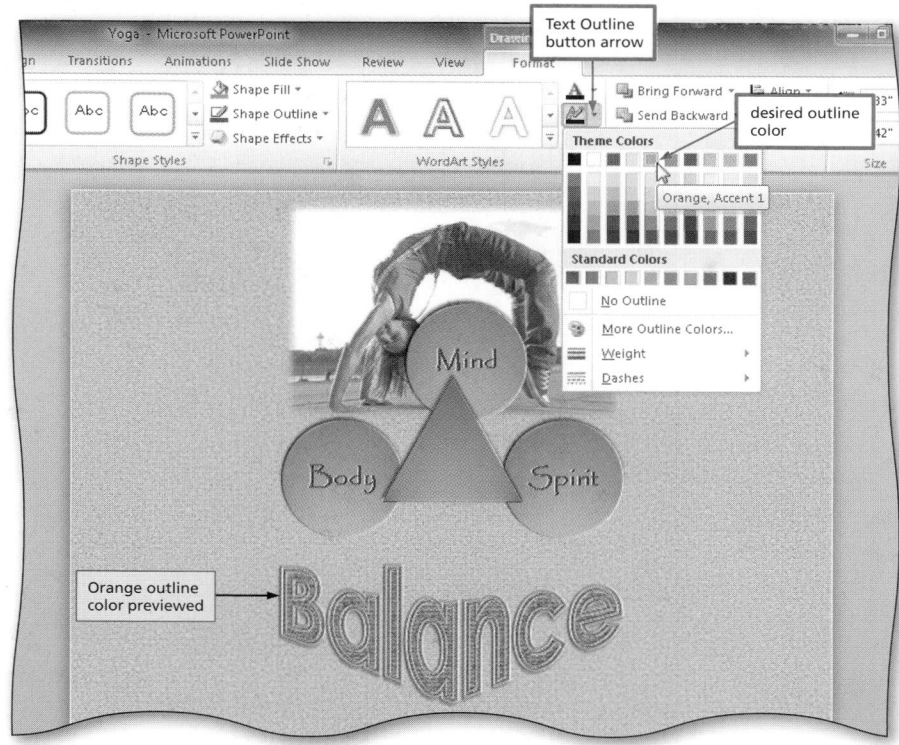

Figure 2–71

To Add a Transition between Slides

A final enhancement you will make in this presentation is to apply the Rotate transition in the Dynamic Content category to all slides and change the transition speed to Slow. The following steps apply this transition to the presentation.

1 Click Transitions on the Ribbon. Click the More button (Transitions tab | Transition to This Slide group) to expand the Transitions gallery.

2 Click the Rotate transition in the Dynamic Content category to apply this transition to Slide 4.

3 Click the Duration up arrow in the Timing group four times to change the transition speed from 02.00 to 03.00.

4 Click the Preview Transitions button (Transitions tab | Preview area) to view the new transition time.

5 Click the Apply To All button (Transitions tab | Timing group) to apply this transition and speed to all four slides in the presentation (Figure 2–72 on the next page).

BTW

Selecting Effect Options
Many PowerPoint transitions have options that you can customize to give your presentation a unique look. When you click the Effect Options button (Transitions tab | Transition to This Slide group), you can, for example, select the option to have a slide appear on the screen from the left or the right, or the screen can fade to black before the next slide is displayed.

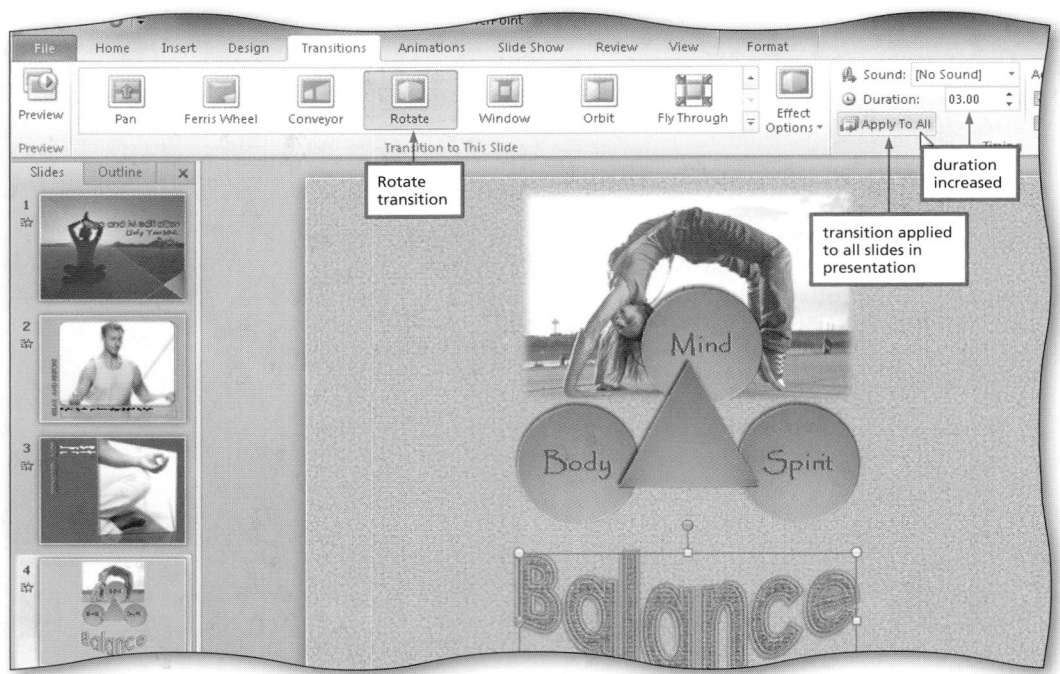

Figure 2–72

To Change Document Properties

Before saving the presentation again, you want to add your name, class name, and some keywords as document properties. The following steps use the Document Information Panel to change document properties.

1 Click File on the Ribbon to open the Backstage view. If necessary, click the Info tab.

2 Click the Properties button in the right pane of the Info gallery.

3 Click Show Document Panel on the Properties menu to close the Backstage view and display the Document Information Panel.

4 Click the Author box, if necessary, and then type your name as the Author property.

5 Click the Subject text box and then type your course and section as the Subject property.

6 Click the Keywords text box and then type `yoga, meditation` as the Keywords property.

7 Click the Close the Document Information Panel button so that the Document Information Panel no longer is displayed.

To Print a Presentation

With the completed presentation saved, you may want to print it. If copies of the presentation are being distributed to audience members, you will print a hard copy of each individual slide on a printer. The following steps print a hard copy of the contents of the saved Yoga presentation.

1 Click File on the Ribbon to open the Backstage view. Click the Print tab in the Backstage view to display the Print gallery.

2 Verify the printer name in the Printer box will print a hard copy of the document. If necessary, click the Printer box arrow to display a list of available Printer options and then click the desired printer to change the currently selected printer.

3 Click the Print button in the Print gallery to print the document on the currently selected printer. When the printer stops, retrieve the hard copy (Figure 2–73).

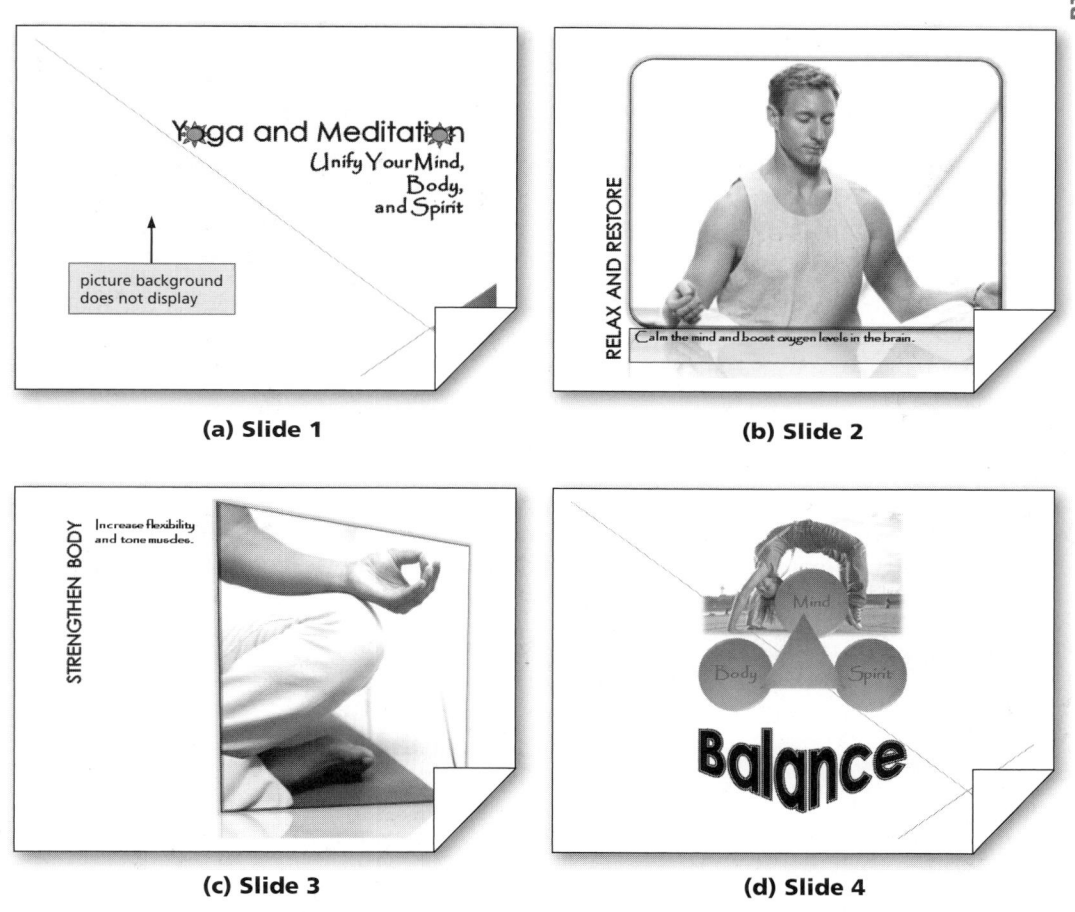

(a) Slide 1

(b) Slide 2

(c) Slide 3

(d) Slide 4

Figure 2–73   (Handouts printed using a black-and-white printer)

To Save an Existing Presentation with the Same File Name

You have made several changes to the presentation since you last saved it. Thus, you should save it again. The following step saves the document again.

1 Click the Save button on the Quick Access Toolbar to overwrite the previously saved file.

BTW

Saving and Recovering PowerPoint Files
A good computing practice is to save files regularly. If, however, PowerPoint closes abnormally due to a power outage or you mistakenly close a file without saving it, PowerPoint's AutoSave and AutoRecover features may help you restore some of your previous work. By default, PowerPoint saves your file every 10 minutes. To adjust this time, open the Backstage view, under Help click Options, click Save in the left pane (PowerPoint Options dialog box), and then modify the AutoRecover minutes in the Save presentations area. Also, be certain the 'Keep the last autosaved versions if I close without saving' check box is checked.

BTW

Quick Reference
For a table that lists how to complete the tasks covered in this book using the mouse, Ribbon, shortcut menu, and keyboard, see the Quick Reference Summary at the back of this book, or visit the PowerPoint 2010 Quick Reference Web page (scsite.com/ppt2010/qr).

To Run an Animated Slide Show

All changes are complete, and the presentation is saved. You now can view the Yoga presentation. The following steps start Slide Show view.

1 Click the Slide 1 thumbnail in the Slides tab to select and display Slide 1.

2 Click the Slide Show button to display the title slide and then click each slide to view the transition effect and slides.

To Quit PowerPoint

This project is complete. The following steps quit PowerPoint.

1 If you have one PowerPoint document open, click the Close Button on the right side of the title bar to close the document and then quit PowerPoint; or if you have multiple PowerPoint documents open, click File on the Ribbon to open the Backstage view and then click Exit in the Backstage view to close all open documents and quit PowerPoint.

2 If a Microsoft PowerPoint dialog box appears, click the Save button to save any changes made to the presentation since the last save.

Chapter Summary

In this chapter you have learned how to add a background style, insert and format pictures, add shapes, size graphic elements, apply styles, and insert WordArt. The items listed below include all the new PowerPoint skills you have learned in this chapter.

1. Change the Presentation Theme Colors (PPT 81)
2. Insert a Picture (PPT 83)
3. Insert a Picture into a Slide without a Content Placeholder (PPT 85)
4. Correct a Picture (PPT 86)
5. Apply a Picture Style (PPT 87)
6. Apply Picture Effects (PPT 89)
7. Add a Picture Border (PPT 91)
8. Change a Picture Border Color (PPT 92)
9. Resize a Graphic by Entering Exact Measurements (PPT 93)
10. Insert a Texture Fill (PPT 95)
11. Insert a Picture to Create a Background (PPT 97)
12. Format a Background Picture Fill Transparency (PPT 98)
13. Format a Background Texture Fill Transparency (PPT 99)
14. Choose a Background Style (PPT 99)
15. Change the Subtitle and Caption Font (PPT 101)
16. Shadow Text (PPT 103)
17. Format Caption Text Using the Format Painter (PPT 105)
18. Add a Shape (PPT 106)
19. Resize a Shape (PPT 107)
20. Copy and Paste a Shape (PPT 108)
21. Add Other Shapes (PPT 109)
22. Apply a Shape Style (PPT 110)
23. Add Formatted Text to a Shape (PPT 112)
24. Insert WordArt (PPT 114)
25. Change the WordArt Shape (PPT 115)
26. Apply a WordArt Text Fill (PPT 117)
27. Change the Weight of a WordArt Outline (PPT 118)
28. Change the Color of a WordArt Outline (PPT 118)

Learn It Online

Test your knowledge of chapter content and key terms.

Instructions: To complete the Learn It Online exercises, start your browser, click the Address bar, and then enter the Web address **scsite.com/ppt2010/learn**. When the PowerPoint 2010 Learn It Online page is displayed, click the link for the exercise you want to complete and then read the instructions.

Chapter Reinforcement TF, MC, and SA
A series of true/false, multiple choice, and short answer questions that test your knowledge of the chapter content.

Flash Cards
An interactive learning environment where you identify chapter key terms associated with displayed definitions.

Practice Test
A series of multiple choice questions that test your knowledge of chapter content and key terms.

Who Wants To Be a Computer Genius?
An interactive game that challenges your knowledge of chapter content in the style of a television quiz show.

Wheel of Terms
An interactive game that challenges your knowledge of chapter key terms in the style of the television show *Wheel of Fortune.*

Crossword Puzzle Challenge
A crossword puzzle that challenges your knowledge of key terms presented in the chapter.

Apply Your Knowledge

Reinforce the skills and apply the concepts you learned in this chapter.

Changing the Background and Adding Photographs, WordArt, and a Shape Quick Style
Note: To complete this assignment, you will be required to use the Data Files for Students. See the inside back cover of this book for instructions on downloading the Data Files for Students, or contact your instructor for information about accessing the required files.

Instructions: Start PowerPoint. Open the presentation, Apply 2-1 Lab Procedures, from the Data Files for Students.

The four slides in the presentation present laboratory safety procedures for your chemistry class. The document you open is an unformatted presentation. You are to add pictures, which are available on the Data Files for Students. You also will change the background style, change slide layouts, apply a transition, and use the Format Painter so the slides look like Figure 2–74.

Perform the following tasks:
1. Change the background style to Style 5 (row 2, column 1).
2. On the title slide (Figure 2–74a), create a background by inserting the picture called Lab Assistant. Change the transparency to 30%.
3. Apply the WordArt style, Fill – Red, Accent 2, Matte Bevel (row 6, column 3) to the title text and increase the font size to 54 point. Also, apply the WordArt Transform text effect, Chevron Up (row 2, column 1 in the Warp area) to this text.
4. In the Slide 1 subtitle area, replace the words, Student Name, with your name. Bold and italicize your name and the words, Presented by, and then apply the WordArt style, Fill – Red, Accent 2, Warm Matte Bevel (row 5, column 3). Position this subtitle text and the title text as shown in Figure 2–74a.

Continued >

STUDENT ASSIGNMENTS

Apply Your Knowledge *continued*

5. On Slide 2, change the layout to Two Content and insert the pictures shown in Figure 2–74b called Female in Lab Coat and Female with Goggles. In the left placeholder, apply the Rotated, White picture style to the inserted picture. In the right placeholder, apply the Reflected Bevel, Black picture style to the inserted picture and then change the picture border color to Purple.

6. On Slide 3, change the layout to Two Content and insert the Fire Extinguisher picture shown in Figure 2–74c. Apply the Soft Edge Oval picture style and change the picture brightness to +20% (row 3, column 4 in the Brightness and Contrast area).

7. On Slide 4, change the layout to Picture with Caption and then insert the picture, Hand Washing shown in Figure 2–74d. Increase the subtitle text font size to 18 point. Change the title text font size to 28 point, add a shadow, change font to Algerian, and change the font color to Purple.

(a) Slide 1

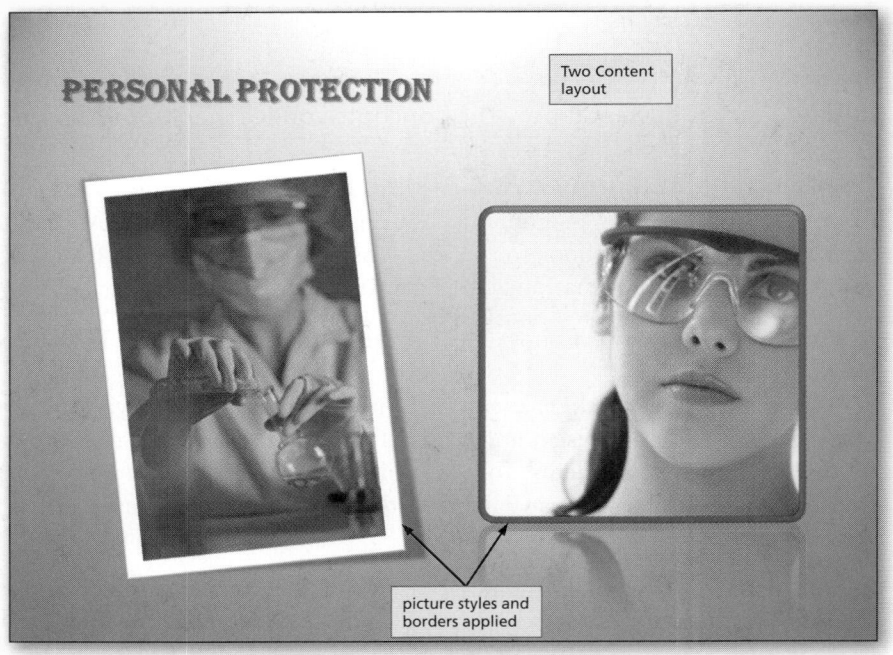

(b) Slide 2

Figure 2 – 74

8. Use the Format Painter to format the title text on Slides 2 and 3 with the same features as the title text on Slide 4.

9. Apply the Wipe transition in the Subtle category to all slides. Change the duration to 2.00 seconds.

10. Change the document properties, as specified by your instructor. Save the presentation using the file name, Apply 2-1 Chemistry Lab Safety. Submit the revised document in the format specified by your instructor.

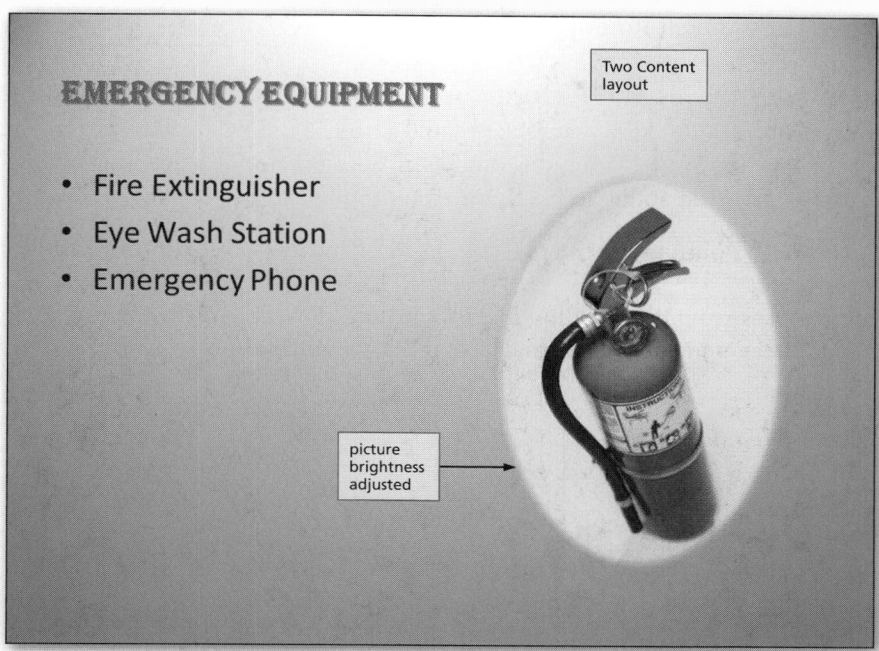

(c) Slide 3

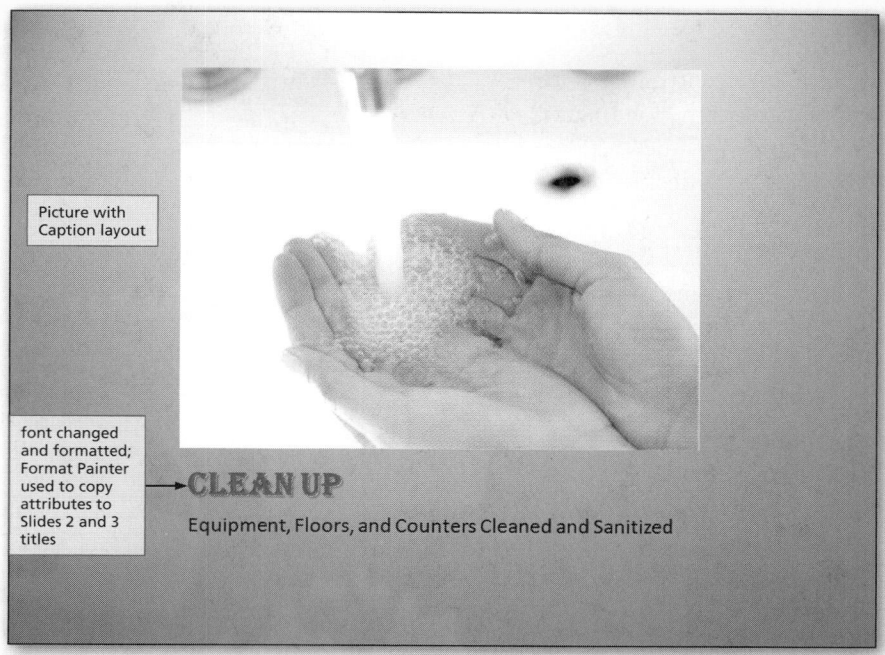

(d) Slide 4

Figure 2–74 (Continued)

STUDENT ASSIGNMENTS

Extend Your Knowledge

Extend the skills you learned in this chapter and experiment with new skills. You may need to use Help to complete the assignment.

Changing Slide Backgrounds and Picture Contrast, and Inserting Shapes and WordArt
Note: To complete this assignment, you will be required to use the Data Files for Students. See the inside back cover of this book for instructions on downloading the Data Files for Students, or contact your instructor for information about accessing the required files.

Instructions: Start PowerPoint. Open the presentation, Extend 2-1 Smith Family Reunion, from the Data Files for Students.
  You will create backgrounds including inserting a picture to create a background, apply a WordArt Style and Effect, and add shapes to create the presentation shown in Figure 2–75.

Perform the following tasks:

1. Change the background style to Denim (row 1, column 3) and change the transparency to 48%. On Slides 2 through 5, change the title text to bold.

2. On the title slide (Figure 2–75a), create a background by inserting the picture called Tree, which is available on the Data Files for Students. Change the transparency to 40%.

3. Apply the WordArt style, Gradient Fill – Blue, Accent 1, to the title text and increase the font size to 66 point. Also, apply the WordArt Transform text effect, Arch Up (row 1, column 1 in the Follow Path area), to this text.

4. In the Slide 1 subtitle area, insert the Wave shape in the Stars and Banners area. Also, apply the Shape Style, Subtle Effect – Orange, Accent 6 to the Wave shape. Type **Highlights From Our Last Reunion** and increase the font size to 40 point, change the text to bold italic and change the color to Green. Position the shape as shown in Figure 2–75a.

(a) Slide 1

(b) Slide 2

Figure 2–75

5. On Slide 2, change the layout to Two Content and insert the pictures shown in Figure 2–75b. The pictures to be inserted are called Bocce Ball and Frisbee Catcher and are available on the Data Files for Students. In the left placeholder, apply the Rotated White picture style to the inserted picture and change the picture border to Light Green. In the right placeholder, apply the Beveled Oval Black picture style to the inserted picture.

6. Insert the Plaque shape in the Basic Shapes area. Also, apply the Shape Style, Subtle Effect, Olive Green, Accent 3 and apply the Shape Effect, 3-D Rotation, Parallel, Off Axis 1 Right. Type **Cousin Tom & His Frisbee Moves** and increase the font size to 28 point. Move the shape as shown in Figure 2–75b.

(c) Slide 3

7. On Slide 3, change the layout to Picture with Caption and insert the picture shown in Figure 2–75c. The picture to be inserted is called BBQ Grill. Increase the title font size to 44 point. Also, increase the subtitle font size to 32 point, and then bold and italicize this text.

8. On Slide 4, change the layout to Two Content and insert the pictures shown in Figure 2–75d. The pictures to be inserted are called Reunion Boys and Reunion Toddler. In the left placeholder, apply the Rotated, White picture effect to the picture. In the right placeholder, apply the Bevel Perspective picture effect. Move the pictures as shown in Figure 2–75d.

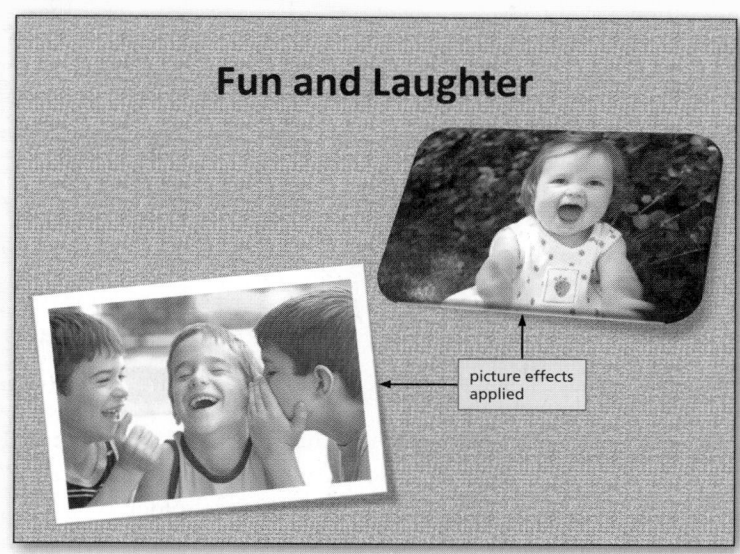

(d) Slide 4

Figure 2 – 75 (Continued)

Continued >

Extend Your Knowledge *continued*

9. On Slide 5, change the layout to Title and Content and insert the picture shown in Figure 2–75e. The picture to be inserted is called Reunion. Enlarge the picture as shown.

10. Insert the Oval Callout and Cloud Callout shapes in the Callouts area. In the Oval Callout shape, type **I hope Grandma makes cookies!** and change the font size to 24 point bold italic. Also add a Shape Style, Moderate Effect – Olive Green Accent 3 to this shape. In the Cloud Callout shape, type **I'm looking forward to our next reunion!** and change the font size to 24 point and the style to bold italic. Move the shapes as shown in Figure 2–75e. Use the adjustment handles (the yellow diamond below each shape) to move the callout arrows as shown in Figure 2–75e. You may need to use Help to learn how to move these arrows.

11. On Slide 6, change the layout to Picture with Caption and insert the picture shown in Figure 2–75f and change the picture contrast to +20. The picture to be inserted is called Reunion Tree.

12. Insert the Up Ribbon shape in the Stars and Banners area and type the words **Announcing Our Next Reunion**. Change the font color to Green, the font size to 32 point, and the style to bold italic. Also, apply the Shape Style, Subtle Effect – Orange Accent 6. In the title placeholder, type **Save the date – June 20, 2012** and change the font size to 28 point. Bold this text.

13. Add the Orbit transition under the Dynamic Content section to Slide 6 only. You may need to use Help to learn how to apply the transition to only one slide. Change the duration to 2.00 seconds.

14. Change the document properties, as specified by your instructor. Save the presentation using the file name, Extend 2-1 Smith Reunion.

15. Submit the revised document in the format specified by your instructor.

(e) Slide 5

(f) Slide 6

Figure 2–75 (Continued)

Make It Right

Analyze a presentation and correct all errors and/or improve the design.

Changing a Theme and Background Style

Note: To complete this assignment, you will be required to use the Data Files for Students. See the inside back cover of this book for instructions on downloading the Data Files for Students, or contact your instructor for information about accessing the required files.

Instructions: Start PowerPoint. Open the presentation, Make It Right 2-1 New Aerobics Classes, from the Data Files for Students.

Correct the formatting problems and errors in the presentation while keeping in mind the guidelines presented in this chapter.

Perform the following tasks:

1. Change the document theme from Flow, shown in Figure 2–76, to Waveform. Apply the Background Style 10 (row 3, column 2) to Slide 5 only.

2. On the title slide, change the title from New Aerobics Classes to New Pool Programs. Type your name in place of Northlake Fitness Center and change the font to bold italic.

3. Move Slide 2 to the end of the presentation so that it becomes the new Slide 5.

4. Adjust the picture sizes, font sizes, and shapes so they do not overlap text and are the appropriate dimensions for the slide content.

5. Apply the Ripple transition to all slides. Change the duration to 02.00.

6. Change the document properties, as specified by your instructor. Save the presentation using the file name, Make It Right 2-1 New Pool Programs.

7. Submit the revised document in the format specified by your instructor.

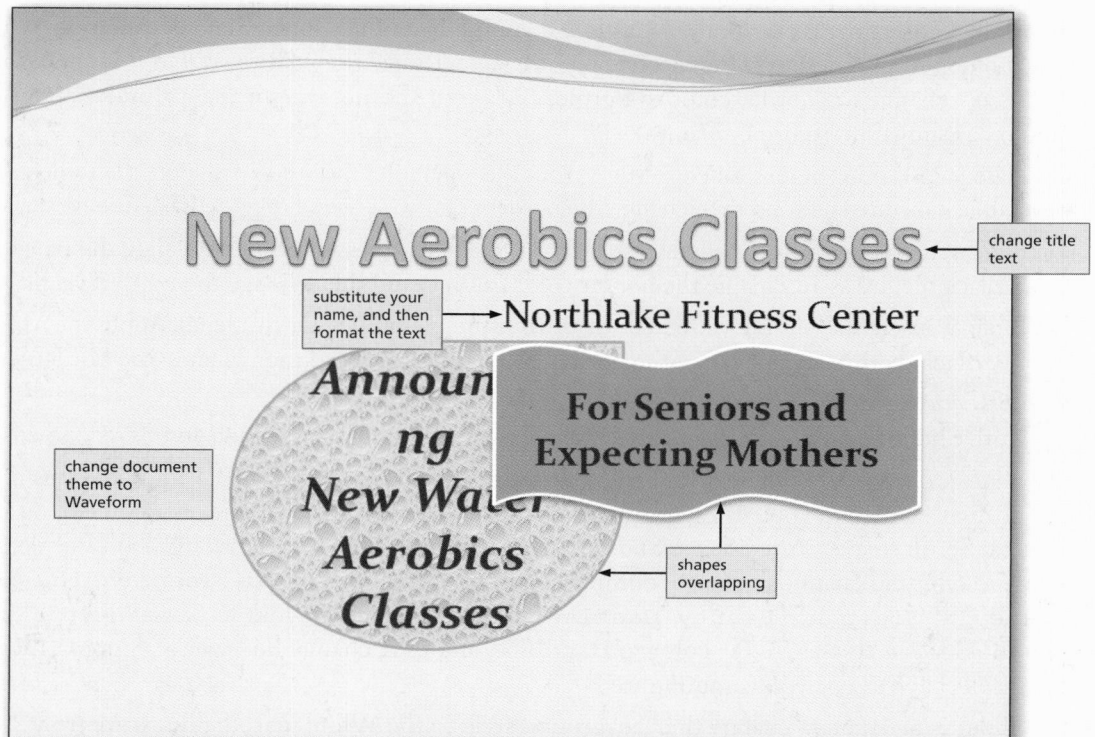

Figure 2–76

In the Lab

Design and/or create a presentation using the guidelines, concepts, and skills presented in this chapter. Labs 1, 2, and 3 are listed in order of increasing difficulty.

Lab 1: Creating a Presentation Inserting Pictures and Applying Picture Styles

Problem: You are studying German operas in your Music Appreciation class. Wilhelm Richard Wagner (pronounced 'va:gner') lived from 1813 to 1883 and was a composer, conductor, theatre director, and essayist known for his operas. Wagner wrote and composed many operas, and King Ludwig II of Bavaria was one of his biggest supporters. Because you recently visited southern Germany and toured King Ludwig's castles, you decide to create a PowerPoint presentation with some of your photos to accompany your class presentation. These pictures are available on the Data Files for Students. Create the slides shown in Figure 2–77 from a blank presentation using the Office Theme document theme.

Note: To complete this assignment, you will be required to use the Data Files for Students. See the inside back cover of this book for instructions on downloading the Data Files for Students, or contact your instructor for information about accessing the required files.

Instructions: Perform the following tasks:
1. On Slide 1, create a background by inserting the picture called Castle 1, which is available on the Data Files for Students.
2. Type **Fairy Tale Trip to Germany** as the Slide 1 title text. Apply the WordArt style, Fill – Tan, Text 2, Outline – Background 2, and increase the font size to 60 point. Change the text fill to the Papyrus texture, and then change the text outline weight to 1½ pt. Also, apply the Transform text effect, Arch Up (in the Follow Path area), to this text. Position this WordArt as shown in Figure 2–77a.
3. Type the title and content for the four text slides shown in Figure 2–77. Apply the Two Content layout to Slides 2 and 3 and the Picture with Caption layout to Slides 4 and 5.
4. On Slide 2, insert the picture called Castle 2 from the Data Files for Students in the right placeholder. Apply the Bevel Perspective picture style. Resize the picture so that it is approximately 4.5" × 6", change the border color to Purple, change the border weight to 6 pt, and then move the picture, as shown in Figure 2–77b.
5. On Slide 3, insert the picture called Castle 3 from the Data Files for Students. Apply the Reflected Bevel, Black picture style and then change the border color to Green. Do not change the border weight.
6. On Slide 4, insert the picture called Castle 4 from the Data Files for Students. Apply the Beveled Oval, Black picture style, change the border color to Blue, and then change the border weight to 6 pt.
7. On Slide 5, insert the picture called Castle 5 from the Data Files for Students. Apply the Moderate Frame, Black picture style, change the border color to Purple, and then change the border weight to 6 pt.
8. For both Slides 4 and 5, increase the title text size to 28 point and the caption text size to 24 point.
9. On Slide 2, change the title text font to Algerian, change the color to purple, and bold this text. Use the Format Painter to apply these formatting changes to the Slide 3 title text. In Slide 3, insert the Vertical Scroll shape located in the Stars and Banners area, apply the Subtle Effect – Purple, Accent 4 shape style, and change the shape outline weight to 3 pt. Type the text, **Inspiration for Disney's Sleeping Beauty Castle**, and then change the font to Curlz MT, or a similar font. Bold this text, change the color to Dark Blue, and then change the size to 28 point. Increase the scroll shape size, as shown in Figure 2–77c.
10. On Slides 2, 3, 4, and 5, change the background style to the White marble fill texture (row 2, column 5) and change the transparency to 35%. Apply the Glitter transition to all slides. Change the duration to 04.50.

11. Change the document properties, as specified by your instructor. Save the presentation using the file name, Lab 2-1 Trip to Germany.

12. Submit the revised document in the format specified by your instructor.

picture inserted as background

WordArt style, texture fill, and effect applied

(a) Slide 1

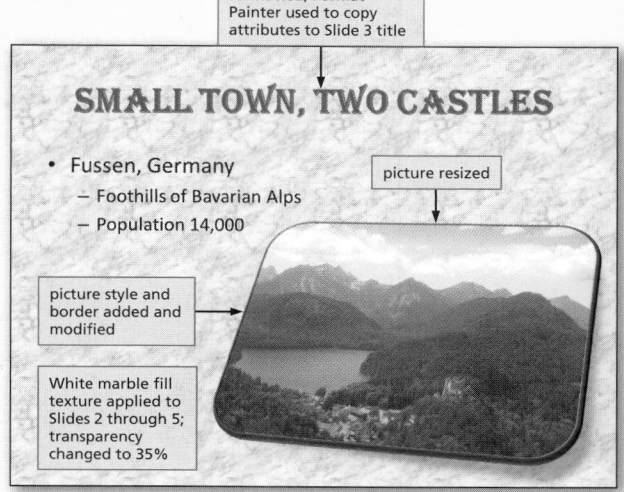

font changed and formatted; Format Painter used to copy attributes to Slide 3 title

picture resized

picture style and border added and modified

White marble fill texture applied to Slides 2 through 5; transparency changed to 35%

(b) Slide 2

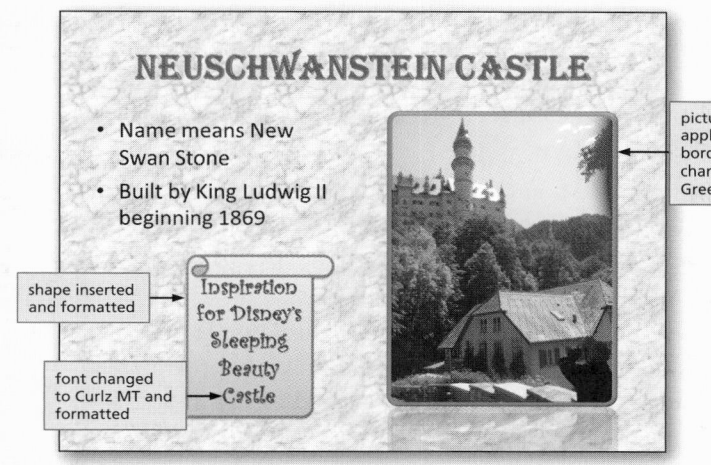

picture style applied and border color changed to Green

shape inserted and formatted

font changed to Curlz MT and formatted

(c) Slide 3

picture style applied and border color and weight changed

font size increased

(d) Slide 4

picture style applied and border color and weight changed

font size increased

(e) Slide 5

Figure 2 – 77

In the Lab

Lab 2: Creating a Presentation with a Shape and with WordArt

Problem: With the economy showing some improvement, many small businesses are approaching lending institutions for loans to expand their businesses. You work part-time for Loans Are Us, and your manager asked you to prepare a PowerPoint presentation for the upcoming Small Business Fair in your community. The pictures for this presentation are available on the Data Files for Students.

Note: To complete this assignment, you will be required to use the Data Files for Students. See the inside back cover of this book for instructions on downloading the Data Files for Students, or contact your instructor for information about accessing the required files.

Instructions: Perform the following tasks:

1. Create a new presentation using the Austin document theme.

2. Type the title and content for the title slide and the three text slides shown in Figure 2–78a–d. Apply the Title Only layout to Slide 2, the Two Content layout to Slide 3, and the Picture with Caption layout to Slide 4.

3. On both Slides 2 and 4, create a background by inserting the picture called Money. Change the transparency to 35%.

4. On Slide 1, insert the picture called Meeting. Apply the Reflected Bevel, White picture style. Resize the picture so that it is approximately 3.76" × 4.7", change the border color to Dark Blue, change the border weight to 3 pt, and then move the picture, as shown in Figure 2–78a. Increase the title text font size to 60 point, and then apply the WordArt style, Fill – Orange, Accent 6, Warm Matte Bevel.

5. Increase the subtitle text, Loans Are Us, font size to 28 point and then bold and italicize this text. Apply the WordArt style, Fill – Green, Accent 1, Metal Bevel, Reflection.

6. On Slide 2, bold the title text. Insert the pictures called Doc1, Doc2, and Doc3. Resize these pictures so they are approximately 3" × 2.7" and then move them to the locations shown in Figure 2–78b. Insert the Flowchart: Decision shape located in the Flowchart area, apply the Subtle Effect – Orange, Accent 6 shape style, and then resize the shape so that it is approximately 1.5" × 5.83". Change the shape outline weight to 6 pt. Type **Assets, Liabilities & Sales Reports** as the shape text, change the font to Aharoni, or a similar font, change the color to Dark Blue, and then change the size to 24 point.

7. On Slide 3, bold the title text. Insert the picture called Presentation into the right placeholder, apply the Beveled Oval, Black shape picture style, resize the picture so that it is approximately 3.5" × 5.25", and then sharpen the picture 50%.

8. On Slide 4, insert the picture called Cash and Credit Card. Change the title text font size to 36 point and bold this text. Change the subtitle text font size to 24 point and then bold and italicize these words.

9. Apply the Shape transition to all slides. Change the duration to 01.25.

10. Change the document properties, as specified by your instructor. Save the presentation using the file name, Lab 2-2 Small Business Loans.

11. Submit the document in the format specified by your instructor.

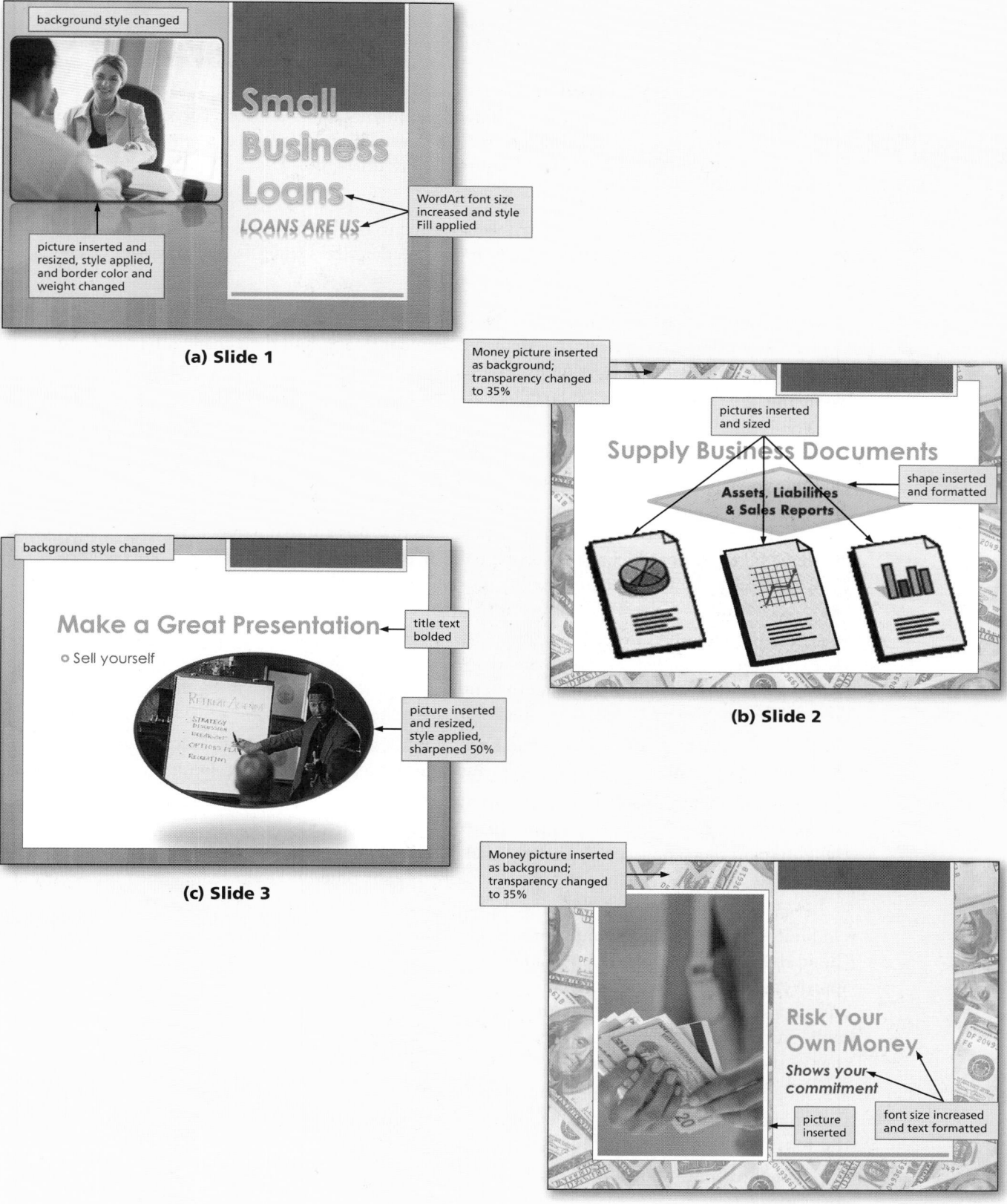

(a) Slide 1

(b) Slide 2

(c) Slide 3

(d) Slide 4

Figure 2–78

In the Lab

Lab 3: Creating a Presentation with Pictures and Shapes

Problem: One of your assignments in your child development class is to give a speech about teaching children the value of money, so you decide to create a PowerPoint presentation to add a little interest to your speech. Prepare the slides shown in Figures 2–79a through 2–79e. The pictures for this presentation are available on the Data Files for Students.

Note: To complete this assignment, you will be required to use the Data Files for Students. See the inside back cover of this book for instructions on downloading the Data Files for Students, or contact your instructor for information about accessing the required files.

Instructions: Perform the following tasks:

1. Create a new presentation using the Median document theme, and then change the presentation theme colors to Flow. This presentation should have five slides; apply the Title Slide layout to Slide 1, the Picture with Caption layout to Slides 2 and 5, the Comparison layout to Slide 3, and the Blank layout to Slide 4.

2. Type the title and content text for the title slide and the four text slides shown in Figure 2–79a–d.

3. On Slide 1, change the title text font size to 54 point. To make the letter 's' appear smaller than the other letters in the first word of the title slide title text placeholder, change the font size of this letter to 44 point. Insert the Oval shape, resize it so that it is approximately 0.5" × 0.5", and change the shape fill to white, which is the second color in the first row of the Theme Colors gallery. Type **$**, increase the font size to 48 point, change the color to green, and bold this dollar sign. Cover the letter 'o' in the word, Do, with this shape.

4. Insert the picture called Piggy Bank. Apply the Rounded Diagonal Corner, White picture style. Resize the picture so that it is approximately 4.4" × 5.03", change the border color to Light Blue, change the border weight to 3 pt, and then move the picture, as shown in Figure 2–79a. Change the subtitle font size to 32 point and then bold this text.

5. On Slide 2, insert the picture called Child Doing Dishes and then decrease the picture's contrast to −20%. Change the title text size to 36 point and bold this text. Change the caption text size to 32 point.

6. On Slide 3, change the background style to Style 6. Bold the title text. Change the heading title text size in both placeholders to 32 point. In the right placeholder, insert the picture called Father and Daughter and then apply the Reflected Bevel, White picture style. Resize the picture so that it is approximately 3" × 4", change the border color to Light Blue, and then change the border weight to 3 pt, as shown in Figure 2–79c.

7. On Slide 4, create a background by inserting the picture called Piggy Bank and Coins. Insert the Cloud shape located in the Basic Shapes area and then increase the cloud shape size so that it is approximately 3" × 5.6". Change the shape outline color to Yellow and then change the shape outline weight to 3 pt. Type **Teach your children to save for a big purchase.** as the shape text, and then change the font to Comic Sans MS. Bold and italicize this text and then change the font size to 32 point.

8. On Slide 5, create a background by inserting the picture called Coins. Insert the picture called Father and Child Shopping and then decrease the picture's brightness to −20%. Change the title text font size to 36 point and bold this text.

9. Apply the Box transition to all slides. Change the duration to 02.00. Check the spelling and correct any errors.

10. Change the document properties, as specified by your instructor. Save the presentation using the file name, Lab 2-3 ABCs of Money.

11. Submit the revised document in the format specified by your instructor.

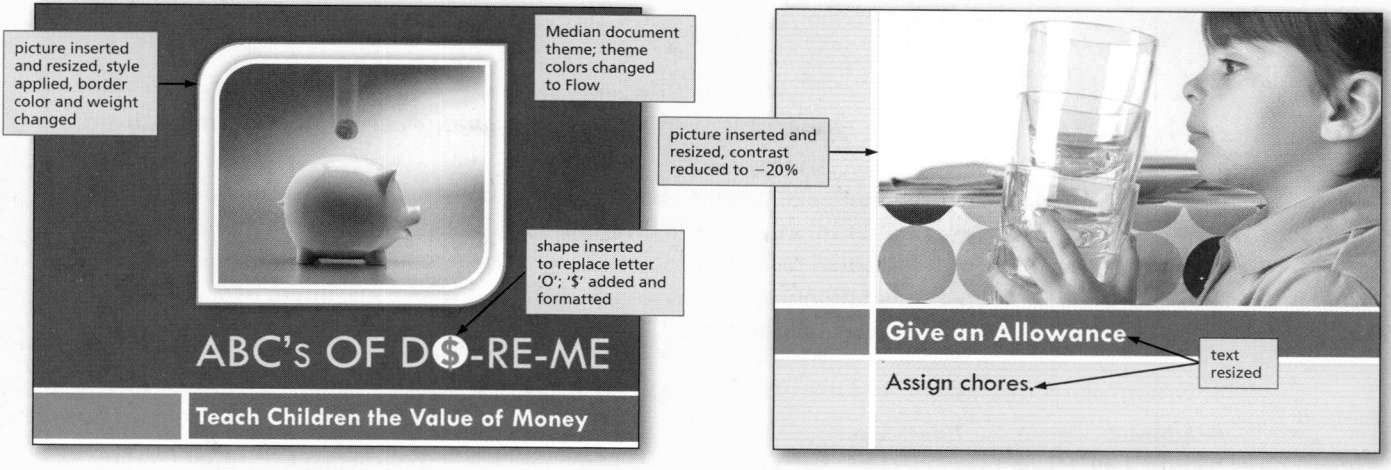

picture inserted and resized, style applied, border color and weight changed

Median document theme; theme colors changed to Flow

picture inserted and resized, contrast reduced to −20%

shape inserted to replace letter 'O'; '$' added and formatted

ABC's OF D$-RE-ME

Teach Children the Value of Money

Give an Allowance

Assign chores.

text resized

(a) Slide 1

(b) Slide 2

background style changed

Discuss Savings Rules

title text bolded

font size changed

How to Save

Make a Plan

☐ Determine amount to save.
☐ Open a bank account with your child.

picture inserted and resized, style applied, border color and weight changed

picture inserted as background

text added and formatted

Teach your children to save for a big purchase.

shape inserted and formatted

(c) Slide 3

(d) Slide 4

Coins picture inserted as background

picture inserted and brightness changed to −20%

Take Your Child Shopping

title text font size increased and bolded

(e) Slide 5

Figure 2–79

Cases and Places

Apply your creative thinking and problem-solving skills to design and implement a solution.

Note: To complete these assignments, you may be required to use the Data Files for Students. See the inside back cover of this book for instructions on downloading the Data Files for Students, or contact your instructor for information about accessing the required files.

As you design the presentations, remember to use the 7 × 7 rule: a maximum of seven words on a line and a maximum of seven lines on one slide.

1: Design and Create a Presentation about Acid Rain

Academic

Nature depends on the correct pH balance. Although some rain is naturally acidic with a pH level of around 5.0, human activities have increased the amount of acid in this water. Burning fossil fuels, including coal, oil, and natural gas, produces sulfur dioxide. Exhaust from vehicles releases nitrogen oxides. Both of these gases, when released into the atmosphere, mix with water droplets, forming acid rain. In your science class, you are studying about the causes and effects of acid rain. Create a presentation to show what causes acid rain and what effects it can have on humans, animals, plant life, lakes, and rivers. The presentation should contain at least three pictures appropriately resized. The Data Files for Students contains five pictures called Factory, Rain, Soil, Tree and Clouds, and Vehicles; you can use your own digital pictures or pictures from Office.com if they are appropriate for this topic. These pictures also should have appropriate styles and border colors. Use shapes such as arrows to show what gases are released into the atmosphere. Apply at least three objectives found at the beginning of this chapter to develop the presentation. Add a title slide with a shape and a closing slide. Be sure to check spelling.

2: Design and Create a Presentation about Tutoring

Personal

You have been helping some of your classmates with their schoolwork, and you have decided that you should start a small tutoring business. In the student center, there is a kiosk where students can find out about programs and activities on campus. The student center manager gave you permission to submit a short PowerPoint presentation promoting your tutoring business; this presentation will be added to the kiosk. The presentation should contain pictures appropriately resized. The Data Files for Students contains four pictures called Tutoring 1, Tutoring 2, Tutoring 3, and Tutoring 4, or you can use your own digital pictures or pictures from Office.com if they are appropriate for this topic. Change the contrast and brightness for at least one picture. Insert shapes and WordArt to enhance your presentation. Apply a transition in the Subtle area to all slides and increase the duration. Be sure to check spelling.

3: Design and Create a Presentation on Setting Up Children's Fish Tanks

Professional

Fish make great pets for young children, but there is a lot to learn before they can set up a fish tank properly. The owner of the pet store where you work has asked you to create a presentation for the store to give parents an idea of what they need to purchase and consider when setting up a fish tank. He would like you to cover the main points such as the appropriate size bowl or tank, setup procedures, filtration, water quality, types of fish, care, and feeding. The presentation should contain pictures appropriately resized. The Data Files for Students contains five pictures called Fish 1, Fish 2, Fish 3, Fish 4, and Fish 5, or you can use your own digital pictures or pictures from Office.com if they are appropriate for this topic. Add a title slide and closing slide to complete your presentation. Format the title slide with a shape and change the theme color scheme. Change the title text font on the title slide. Format the background with at least one picture and apply a background texture to at least one slide. This presentation is geared to parents of young children, so keep it colorful, simple, and fun.

3 | Reusing a Presentation and Adding Media

Objectives

You will have mastered the material in this chapter when you can:

- Color a picture
- Add an artistic effect to a picture
- Delete and move placeholders
- Align paragraph text
- Copy a slide element from one slide to another

- Ungroup, change the color, and regroup a clip
- Insert and edit a video clip
- Insert audio
- Control audio and video clips
- Check for spelling errors
- Print a presentation as a handout

3 | Reusing a Presentation and Adding Media

Introduction

At times, you will need to revise a PowerPoint presentation. Changes may include inserting and adding effects to pictures, altering the colors of clips and pictures, and updating visual elements displayed on a slide. Applying a different theme, changing fonts, and substituting graphical elements can give a slide show an entirely new look. Adding media, including sounds, video, and music, can enhance a presentation and help audience members retain the information being presented.

Project — Presentation with Video, Audio, and Pictures with Effects

BTW

PowerPoint 2010 Video Enhancements
New video tools in PowerPoint 2010 enable you to develop a presentation filled with professional-quality features. You now can embed and edit videos from within PowerPoint instead of needing to use a separate program to customize your media files. You can add fades and effects to captivate your audience, and you can trim specific pieces of the video file to show the exact scenes needed to make a point. Video and audio files now are embedded in your PowerPoint file, so they become part of the entire presentation. These enhanced features help make your media fit the message you are sending to your audience.

The project in this chapter follows graphical guidelines and uses PowerPoint to create the presentation shown in Figure 3–1. The slides in this revised presentation, which discusses Bird Migration, have a variety of audio and visual elements. For example, the pictures have artistic effects applied that soften the pictures and help the audience focus on other elements on the slides. The bird clip has colors that blend well with the background. The video has been edited to play only the portion with Bird Migration and has effects to add audience interest. Bird calls integrate with the visual elements. Overall, the slides have myriad media elements and effects that are exciting for your audience to watch and hear.

Overview

As you read through this chapter, you will learn how to create the presentation shown in Figure 3–1 by performing these general tasks:

- Format pictures by recoloring and adding artistic effects.
- Insert and format video and audio clips.
- Modify clip art.
- Vary paragraph alignment.
- Check a presentation for spelling errors.
- Print a handout of your slides.

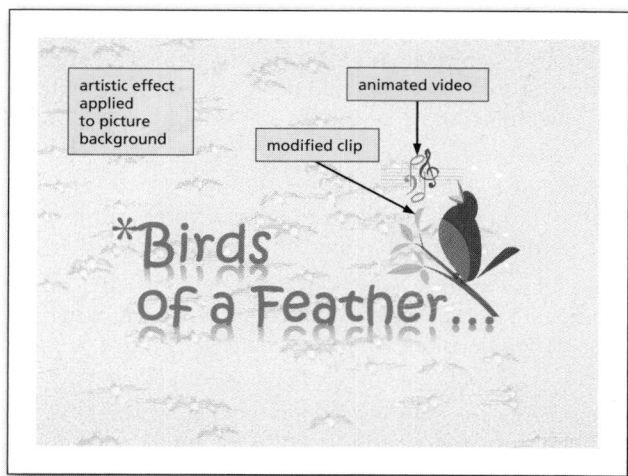

(a) Slide 1 (Title Slide with Picture Background, Modified Clip, and Animated Clip)

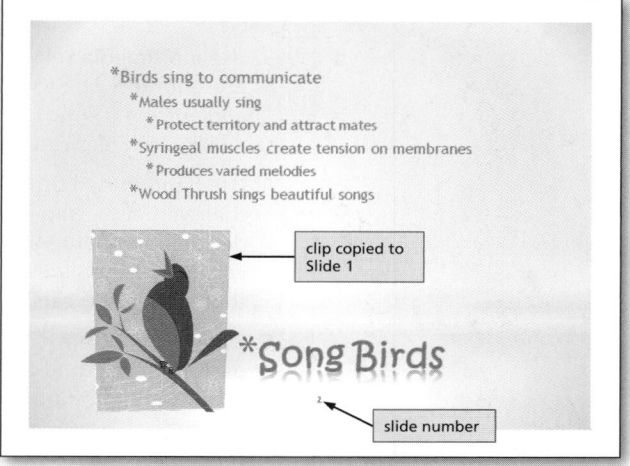

(b) Slide 2 (Bulleted List)

(c) Slide 3 (Picture Background and Video Clip)

(d) Slide 4 (Video Playing Full Screen)

Figure 3–1

Plan Ahead

General Project Guidelines

When creating a PowerPoint presentation, the actions you perform and the decisions you make will affect the appearance and characteristics of the finished document. As you create a presentation with illustrations, such as the project shown in Figure 3–1, you should follow these general guidelines:

1. **Use the color wheel to determine color choices.** Warm colors and cool colors evoke opposite effects on audience members. As you make decisions to color pictures, consider the emotions you want to generate and choose colors that match these sentiments.

2. **Vary paragraph alignment.** Different effects are achieved when text alignment shifts in a presentation. Themes dictate whether paragraph text is aligned left, center, or right in a placeholder, but you can modify these design decisions when necessary.

3. **Use multimedia selectively.** Video, music, and sound files can add interest to your presentation. Use these files only when necessary, however, because they draw the audience's attention away from the presenter and toward the slides. Using too many multimedia files can be overwhelming.

4. **Use handouts to organize your speech.** Effective speakers take much time to prepare their verbal message that will accompany each slide. They practice their speeches and decide how to integrate the material displayed. Viewing the thumbnails, or miniature versions of the slides, will help you associate the slide image with the script. These thumbnails also can be cut out and arranged when organizing the presentation.

5. **Evaluate your presentation.** As soon as you finish your presentation, critique your performance. You will improve your communication skills by eliminating the flaws and accentuating the positives.

When necessary, more specific details concerning the above guidelines are presented at appropriate points in the chapter. The chapter also will identify the actions performed and decisions made regarding these guidelines during the creation of the presentation shown in Figure 3–1.

For an introduction to Windows 7 and instruction about how to perform basic Windows 7 tasks, read the Office 2010 and Windows 7 chapter at the beginning of this book, where you can learn how to resize windows, change screen resolution, create folders, move and rename files, use Windows Help, and much more.

Starting PowerPoint

Chapter 1 introduced you to starting PowerPoint, selecting a document theme, creating slides with clip art and a bulleted list, and printing a presentation. Chapter 2 enhanced slides by adding pictures, shapes, and WordArt. The following steps, which assume Windows 7 is running, start PowerPoint and open the Birds presentation. For a detailed example of the procedure summarized below, refer to the Office 2010 and Windows 7 chapter at the beginning of this book.

BTW

The Ribbon and Screen Resolution
PowerPoint may change how the groups and buttons within the groups appear on the Ribbon, depending on the computer's screen resolution. Thus, your Ribbon may look different from the ones in this book if you are using a screen resolution other than 1024 × 768.

To Start PowerPoint and Open and Save a Presentation

1 Click the Start button on the Windows 7 taskbar to display the Start menu, type **Microsoft PowerPoint** as the search text in the 'Search programs and files' text box, and then click Microsoft PowerPoint 2010 in the search results on the Start menu to start PowerPoint and display a new blank document.

2 If the PowerPoint window is not maximized, click the Maximize button.

3 Open the presentation, Birds, from the Data Files for Students. See the inside back cover of this book for instructions on downloading the Data Files for Students, or contact your instructor for more information on accessing the required files.

4 Save the presentation using the file name, Bird Migration.

Inserting Pictures and Adding Effects

The Bird Migration presentation consists of four slides that have some text, a clip art image, a formatted background, and a transition applied to all slides. You will insert pictures into two slides and then modify them by adding artistic effects and recoloring. You also will copy the clip art from Slide 2 to Slide 1 and modify the objects in this clip. In Chapter 2, you inserted pictures, made corrections, and added styles and effects; the new effects you apply in this chapter will add to your repertoire of picture enhancements that increase interest in your presentation.

In the following pages, you will perform these tasks:

1. Insert the first digital picture into Slide 1.
2. Insert the second digital picture into Slide 3.
3. Recolor the Slide 3 picture.
4. Recolor and add an artistic effect to the Slide 1 picture.
5. Add an artistic effect to the Slide 3 picture.
6. Send the Slide 3 picture back behind all other slide objects.
7. Send the Slide 1 picture back behind all other slide objects.

> For an introduction to Office 2010 and instruction about how to perform basic tasks in Office 2010 programs, read the Office 2010 and Windows 7 chapter at the beginning of this book, where you can learn how to start a program, use the Ribbon, save a file, open a file, quit a program, use Help, and much more.

To Insert and Resize Pictures into Slides without Content Placeholders

The next step is to insert digital pictures into Slides 1 and 3. These pictures are available on the Data Files for Students. See the inside back cover of this book for instructions on downloading the Data Files for Students, or contact your instructor for information about accessing the required files.

The following steps insert pictures into Slides 1 and 3.

1 With Slide 1 displaying and your USB flash drive connected to one of the computer's USB ports, click Insert on the Ribbon to display the Insert tab and then click the Picture button (Insert tab | Images group) to display the Insert Picture dialog box.

2 If necessary, navigate to the picture location (in this case, the PowerPoint folder in the CIS 101 folder [or your class folder] on the USB flash drive). For a detailed example of this procedure, refer to Steps 3a–3c on pages OFF 28 and OFF 29 in the Office 2010 and Windows 7 chapter at the beginning of this book.

3 Click Birds in Sky to select the file.

4 Click the Insert button (Insert Picture dialog box) to insert the picture into Slide 1.

5 Resize the picture so that it covers the entire slide (approximately 7.5" × 10").

6 Display Slide 3, display the Insert tab, click the Picture button to display the Insert Picture dialog box, and then insert the Bird Reflect picture into Slide 3.

7 Resize the picture so that it covers the entire slide (approximately 7.5" × 10") (Figure 3–2).

Q&A How do I resize the picture so that it maintains its proportions?

Press and hold the SHIFT key while dragging a sizing handle away from or toward the center of the picture. To maintain the picture's proportions and keep its center in the same location, press and hold down both the CTRL and SHIFT keys while you drag a sizing handle.

BTW

Inserting Text Boxes
If you want to add text in an area of the slide where a content placeholder is not located, you can insert a text box. This object allows you to emphasize or set off text that you consider important for your audience to read. To create a text box, click the Text Box button (Insert tab | Text group), click the slide, and then drag this object to the desired location on the slide. Click inside the text box to add or paste text. You also can change the look and style of the text box characters by using formatting features (Home tab | Font group).

picture inserted and sized to cover entire slide

Note: To help you locate screen elements that are referenced in the step instructions, such as buttons and commands, this book uses red boxes to point to these screen elements.

Figure 3–2

Plan Ahead

Use the color wheel to determine color choices.
The color wheel is one of designers' basic tools. Twelve colors on the wheel are arranged in a specific order, with the three primary colors — red, yellow, and blue — forming a triangle. Between the primary colors are the secondary colors that are formed when the primary colors are mixed. For example, red and yellow mixed together form orange; red and blue form purple; and yellow and blue form green. The six other colors on the wheel are formed when the primary colors are mixed with the secondary colors.

Red, orange, and yellow are considered warm colors, and they display adjacent to each other on one side of the wheel. They are bold and lively, so you should use them when your message is intended to invigorate an audience and create a pleasing effect. Opposite the warm colors are the cool colors: green, blue, and purple. They generate a relaxing, calming atmosphere.

If you put a primary and secondary color together, such as red and purple, your slide will make a very bold and vivid statement. Be certain that effect is one you intend when planning your message.

Adjusting Picture Colors

BTW

Q&As
For a complete list of the Q&As found in many of the step-by-step sequences in this book, visit the PowerPoint 2010 Q&A Web page (scsite.com/ppt2010/qa).

PowerPoint allows you to adjust colors to match or add contrast to slide elements by coloring pictures. The Color Picture gallery has a wide variety of preset formatting combinations. The thumbnails in the gallery display the more common color saturation, color tone, and recolor adjustments. **Color saturation** changes the intensity of colors. High saturation produces vivid colors; low saturation produces gray tones. **Color tone** affects the coolness, called blue, or the warmness, called orange, of pictures. When a digital camera does not measure the tone correctly, a **color cast** occurs, and, as a result, one color dominates the picture. **Recolor** effects convert the picture into a wide variety of hues. The more common are **grayscale**, which changes the color picture into black, white, and shades of gray, and **sepia**, which changes the picture colors into brown, gold, and yellow, reminiscent of a faded photo. You also can fine-tune the color adjustments by clicking Picture Color Options and More Variations commands in the Color gallery.

To Color a Picture

The Slipstream theme and text on Slides 1 and 3 have many shades of blue. The inserted pictures, in addition, have blue backgrounds. The following steps recolor the Slide 3 picture to coordinate with the blue colors on the slide.

1

- With Slide 3 displaying and the Bird Reflect picture selected, click the Color button (Picture Tools Format tab | Adjust group) to display the Color gallery (Figure 3–3).

Q&A Why does the Adjust group look different on my screen?

Your monitor is set to a different resolution. See Chapter 1 for an explanation of screen resolution and the appearance of the Ribbon.

Q&A Why are yellow borders surrounding the thumbnails in the Color Saturation and Color Tone areas in the gallery?

The image on Slide 3 currently has normal color saturation and a normal color tone.

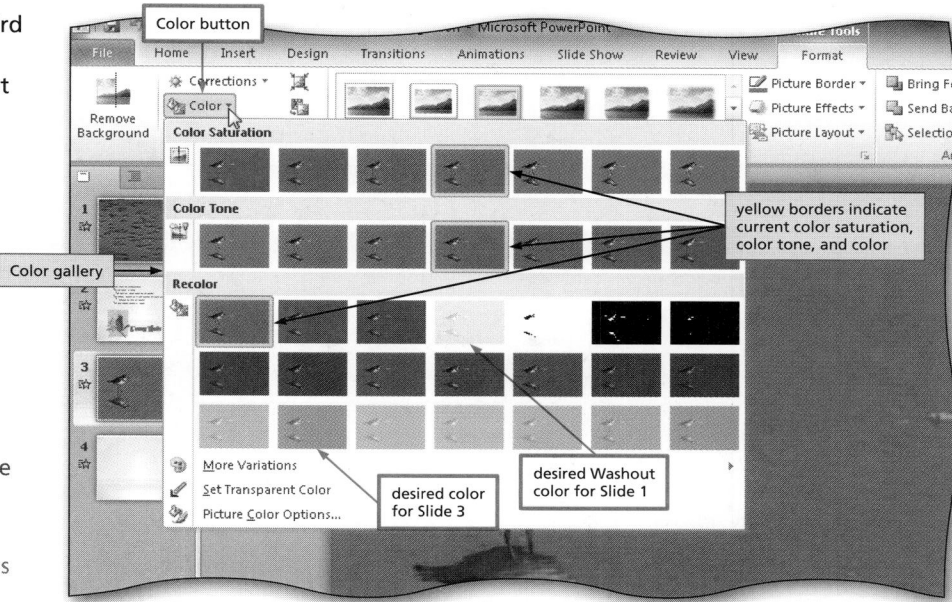

Figure 3–3

2

- Point to Blue, Accent color 1 Light (second picture in last row of Recolor area) to display a live preview of this adjustment on the picture.

 Experiment

- Point to various thumbnails in the Recolor area and watch the hues change on the picture in Slide 3.

- Click Blue, Accent color 1 Light to apply this correction to the Bird Reflect picture (Figure 3–4).

Q&A Could I have applied this correction to the picture if it had been a background instead of a file inserted into the slide?

No. Artistic effects cannot be applied to backgrounds.

Figure 3–4

To Color a Second Picture

The Slide 1 picture has rich hues and is very prominent on the slide. To soften its appearance and to provide continuity with the Slide 3 picture, you can color this picture. The following steps color the picture on the title slide.

1 Display Slide 1 and then click the picture to select it. Click the Color button (Picture Tools Format tab | Adjust group) to display the Color gallery.

2 Click Washout (fourth picture in first row of Recolor area) to apply this correction to the Bird Reflect picture (Figure 3–5).

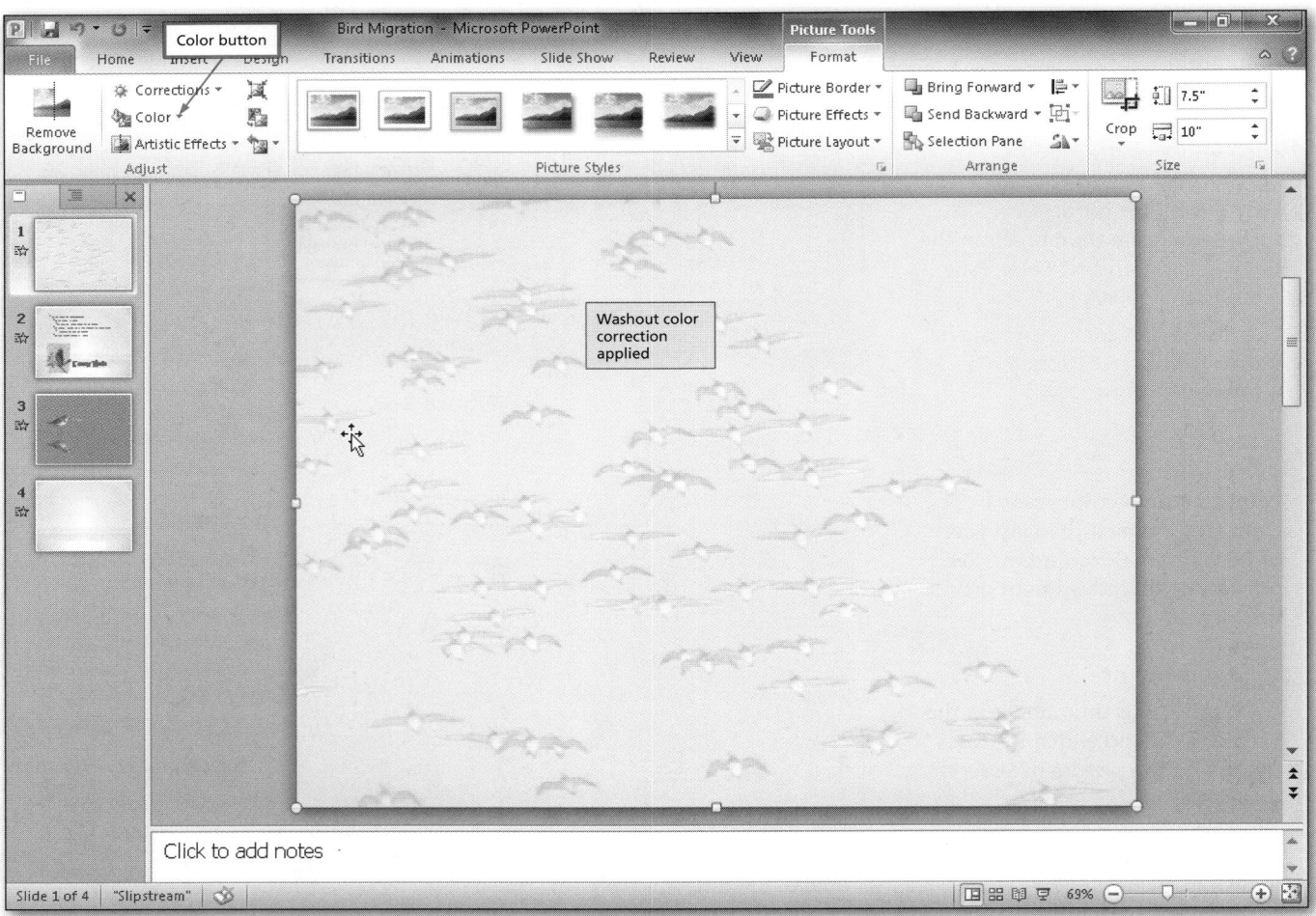

Figure 3–5

To Add an Artistic Effect to a Picture

Artists use a variety of techniques to create effects in their paintings. For example, they can vary the amount of paint on their brushstroke, use fine bristles to add details, mix colors to increase or decrease intensity, and smooth their paints together to blend the colors. You, likewise, can add similar effects to your pictures using PowerPoint's built-in artistic effects. The following steps add an artistic effect to the Slide 3 picture.

1

• With the Birds in Sky picture selected in Slide 1, click the Artistic Effects button (Picture Tools Format tab | Adjust group) to display the Artistic Effects gallery (Figure 3–6).

Q&A Why does the Adjust group look different on my screen?

Your monitor is set to a different resolution. See Chapter 1 for an explanation of screen resolution and the appearance of the Ribbon.

Q&A Why is a yellow border surrounding the first thumbnail in the gallery?

The first thumbnail shows a preview of the image on Slide 1 with no artistic effect applied.

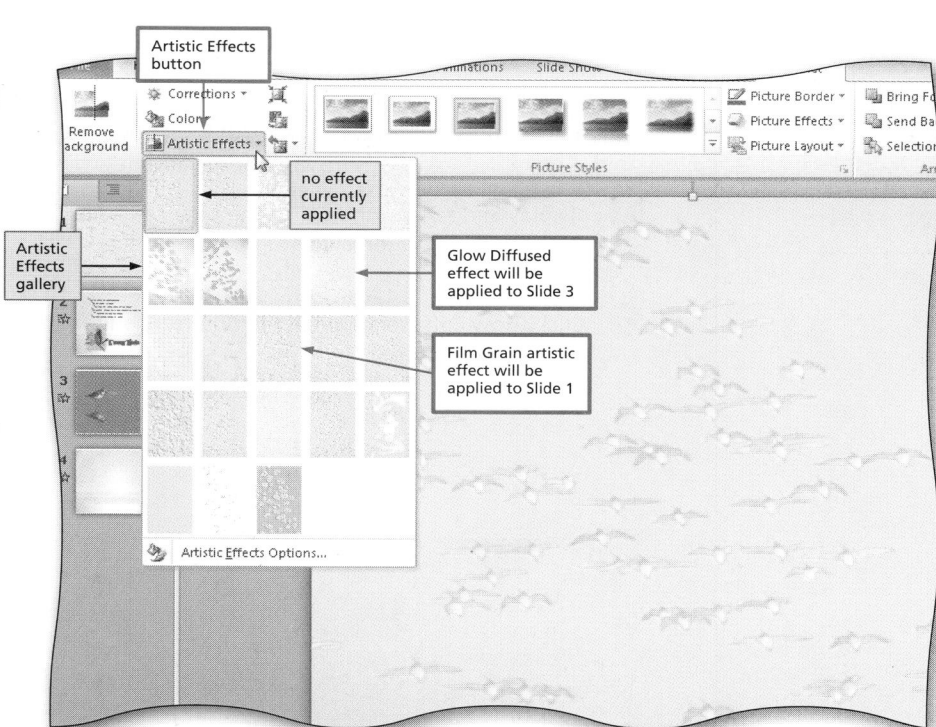

Figure 3–6

2

• Point to Film Grain (third picture in third row) to display a live preview of this adjustment on the picture.

 Experiment

• Point to various thumbnails and watch the hues change on the picture in Slide 1.

• Click Film Grain to apply this correction to the Birds in Sky picture (Figure 3–7).

Q&A Must I adjust a picture by recoloring and applying an artistic effect?

No. You can apply either a color or an effect. You may prefer at times to mix these adjustments to create a unique image.

Figure 3–7

To Add an Artistic Effect to a Second Picture

The Slide 3 picture was softened when you applied a blue accent color. You can further change the images and provide continuity with the Slide 1 picture by applying an artistic effect. The following steps add an artistic effect to the Slide 3 picture.

1 Display Slide 3 and then click the picture to select it. If necessary, click the Picture Tools Format tab and then click the Artistic Effects button (Picture Tools Format tab | Adjust group) to display the Artistic Effects gallery.

2 Click Glow Diffused (fourth picture in second row) to apply this effect to the Bird Reflect picture (Figure 3–8).

Figure 3–8

To Change the Stacking Order

The objects on a slide stack on top of each other, much like individual cards in a deck. On Slides 1 and 3, the pictures you inserted are on top of text placeholders. To change the order of these objects, you use the Bring Forward and Send Backward commands. **Bring Forward** moves an object toward the top of the stack, and **Send Backward** moves an object underneath another object. When you click the Bring Forward button arrow, PowerPoint displays a menu with an additional command, **Bring to Front**, which moves a selected object to the top of the stack. Likewise, when you click the Send Backward button arrow, the **Send to Back** button moves the selected object underneath all objects on the slide. The following steps arrange the Slide 3 and Slide 1 pictures by sending them to the bottom of the stack on each slide.

1

- With the Bird Reflect picture selected in Slide 3, click the Send Backward button arrow (Picture Tools Format tab | Arrange group) to display the Send Backward menu (Figure 3–9).

Q&A How can I see objects that are not on the top of the stack?

Press TAB or SHIFT+TAB to display each slide object.

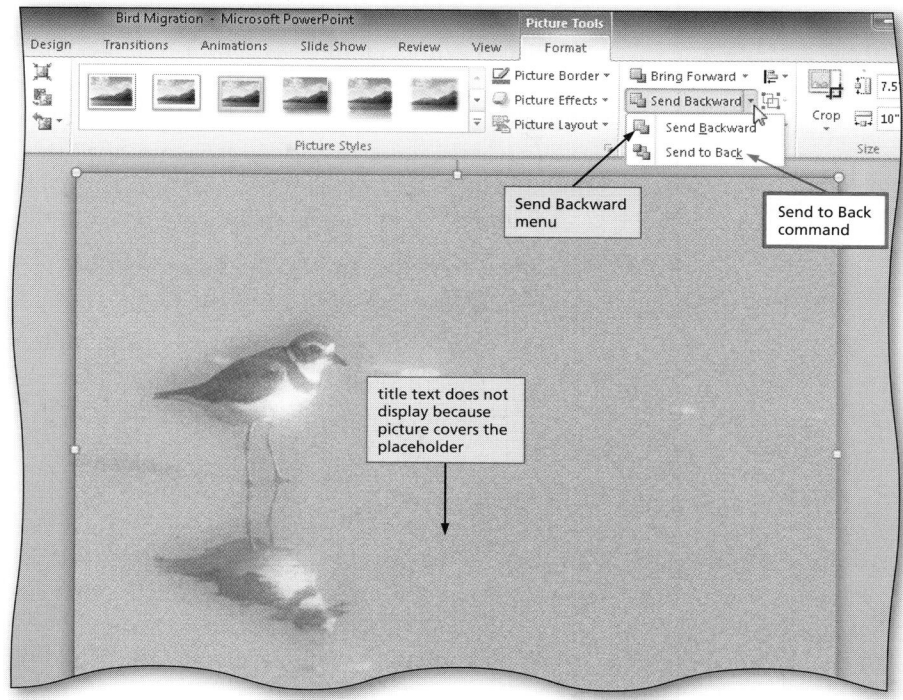

Figure 3–9

2

- Click Send to Back to move the picture underneath all slide objects (Figure 3–10).

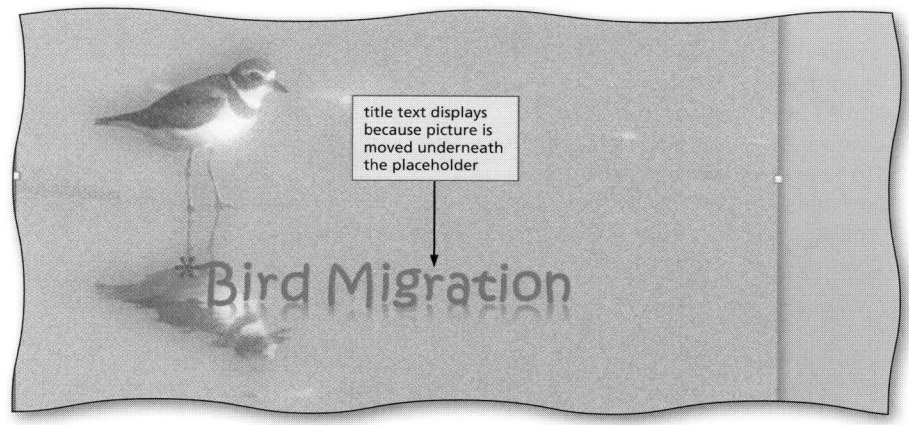

Figure 3–10

3

- Display Slide 1, select the Birds in Sky picture, and then click the Send Backward button arrow (Picture Tools Format tab | Arrange group).
- Click Send to Back to move the picture underneath all slide objects (Figure 3–11).

Figure 3–11

Other Ways	
1. Click Send to Back (Picture Tools Format tab | Arrange group), press K	2. Point to Send to Back on shortcut menu, click Send to Back

Modifying Placeholders and Deleting a Slide

BTW

BTWs
For a complete list of the BTWs found in the margins of this book, visit the PowerPoint 2010 BTW Web page (scsite.com/ppt2010/btw).

You have become familiar with inserting text and graphical content in the three types of placeholders: title, subtitle, and content. These placeholders can be moved, resized, and deleted to meet desired design requirements. In addition, placeholders can be added to a slide when needed. After you have modified the placeholder locations, you can view thumbnails of all your slides simultaneously by changing views.

In the following pages, you will perform these tasks:

1. Resize and move the Slide 1 title text placeholder.
2. Delete the Slide 1 subtitle text placeholder.
3. Align the Slide 1 and Slide 3 paragraph text.
4. Delete Slide 4.
5. Change views.

To Resize a Placeholder

The AutoFit button displays on the left side of the Slide 1 title text placeholder because the two lines of text exceed the placeholder's borders. PowerPoint attempts to reduce the font size when the text does not fit, and you can click this button to resize the existing text in the placeholder so the spillover text will fit within the borders. You also can resize the placeholder so that the letters fit within the rectangle. The following step increases the Slide 1 title text placeholder.

- With Slide 1 displaying, click somewhere in the title text paragraph to position the insertion point in the paragraph. Click the border of the title text placeholder to select it. Point to the bottom-middle sizing handle so that the mouse pointer changes to a two-headed arrow.

- Drag the bottom border downward to enlarge the text placeholder (Figure 3–12).

Q&A Can I drag other sizing handles to enlarge or shrink the placeholder?

Yes, you also can drag the left, right, top, and corner sizing handles to resize a placeholder.

Q&A How do the square sizing handles differ from circle sizing handles?

Dragging a square handle alters the shape of the text box so that it is wider or taller. Dragging a circle handle keeps the box in the same proportion and simply enlarges the overall shape.

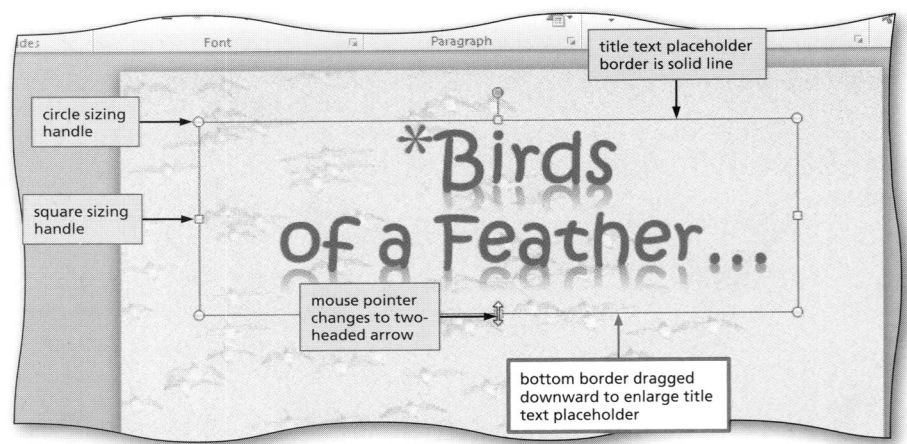

Figure 3–12

To Move a Placeholder

The theme layouts determine where the text and content placeholders display on the slide. If you desire to have a placeholder appear in a different area of the slide, you can move it to a new location. The Slide 1 title text placeholder currently displays in the upper third of the slide, but the text in this placeholder would be more aesthetically pleasing if it were moved toward the center of the slide. The following step moves the Slide 1 title text placeholder.

1

• With the Slide 1 title text placeholder border displaying as a solid line, point to an area of the bottom border between two sizing handles so that the mouse pointer changes to a four-headed arrow.

Q&A What if the placeholder border displays as a dotted line?

Click the border to change the line from dotted to solid.

Q&A Can I click any part of the border, or do I need to click the bottom edge?

You can click any of the four border lines.

• Drag the placeholder downward so that it overlaps part of the subtitle text placeholder (Figure 3–13).

• Click to set the placeholder in its new location.

Figure 3–13

To Delete a Placeholder

When you run a slide show, empty placeholders do not display. You may desire to delete unused placeholders from a slide so that they are not a distraction when you are designing slide content. The subtitle text placeholder on Slide 1 is not required for this presentation, so you can remove it. The following steps remove the Slide 1 subtitle text placeholder.

1 Click a border of the subtitle text placeholder so that it displays as a solid line or fine dots (Figure 3–14).

Q&A What if the placeholder border is displaying as a dotted line?

Click the border to change the line from dotted to solid or fine dots.

2 Press the DELETE key to remove the placeholder.

Q&A Can I click the Cut button (Home tab | Clipboard group) to delete the placeholder?

Yes. Clicking the Cut button deletes the placeholder if it does not contain any text.

BTW

Reusing Placeholders
If you need to show the same formatted placeholder on multiple slides, you may want to customize a slide master and insert a placeholder into a slide layout. Using a slide master saves you time because you do not need to type the same information in more than one slide. The slide master is useful when you have extremely long presentations. Every document theme has several slide masters that indicate the size and position of text and object placeholders. Any change you make to a slide master results in changing that component in every slide of the presentation.

Figure 3–14

Plan Ahead	**Vary paragraph alignment.** Designers use alignment within paragraphs to aid readability and to indicate relationships among slide elements. English language readers are accustomed to seeing paragraphs that are aligned left. When paragraphs are aligned right, the viewer's eyes are drawn to this unexpected text design. If your paragraph is short, consider centering or right-aligning the text for emphasis.

To Align Paragraph Text

The presentation theme determines the formatting characteristics of fonts and colors. It also establishes paragraph formatting, including the alignment of text. Some themes center the text paragraphs between the left and right placeholder borders, while others **left-align** the paragraph so that the first character of a text line is near the left border or **right-align** the paragraph so that the last character of a text line is near the right border. The paragraph also can be **justified** so that the text is aligned to both the left and right borders. When PowerPoint justifies text, it adds extras spaces between the words to fill the entire line.

The words, Birds of a Feather, are centered in the Slide 1 title text placeholder. Later, you will add clip art above the word, Feather, so you desire to left-align the paragraph to make room for this art. In addition, the words in the Slide 3 title text placeholder, Bird Migration, are covering the bird in the picture. You can right-align these words to uncover the bird in the lower-left corner. The following steps change the alignment of the Slide 1 and Slide 3 title placeholders.

- With the Home tab displayed, click somewhere in the title text paragraph of Slide 1 to position the insertion point in the paragraph to be formatted (Figure 3–15).

Figure 3–15

2

• Click the Align Text Left button (Home tab | Paragraph group) to left-align the paragraph (Figure 3–16).

Q&A What if I want to return the paragraph to center alignment?

Click the Center button (Home tab | Paragraph group).

3

• Display Slide 3. Click somewhere in the title text paragraph to position the insertion point in the paragraph to be formatted.

4

• Click the Align Text Right button (Home tab | Paragraph group) to right-align the paragraph.

5

• Move the Slide 3 title text placeholder downward so that it displays approximately as shown in Figure 3–17.

Q&A Can I align text vertically in a text box?

Yes. You can align paragraphs vertically in the top, middle, or bottom of a text box. Position the insertion point in a paragraph and then click the Align Text button (Home tab | Paragraph group) to display the Align Text gallery. You can experiment with the alignment by pointing to each of these three options and watching the paragraphs in the text box change position. If you click More Options at the bottom of the gallery, you can made additional alignment changes in the Format Text Effects dialog box.

Figure 3–16

Figure 3–17

Other Ways

1. Right-click paragraph, click Align Text Right button on Mini toolbar

2. Right-click paragraph, click Paragraph on shortcut menu, click Indents and Spacing tab (Paragraph dialog box), click Alignment box arrow, click Right, click OK button

3. Click Paragraph Dialog Box Launcher (Home tab | Paragraph group), click Indents and Spacing tab (Paragraph dialog box), click Alignment box arrow, click Right, click OK button

4. Press CTRL+R

To Delete a Slide

The Bird Migration presentation has a blank slide at the end. You decide that you will not use this slide, so you need to remove it from the file. The following steps delete Slide 4 from the presentation.

1

• Right-click the Slide 4 thumbnail in the Slides tab to display the shortcut menu (Figure 3–18).

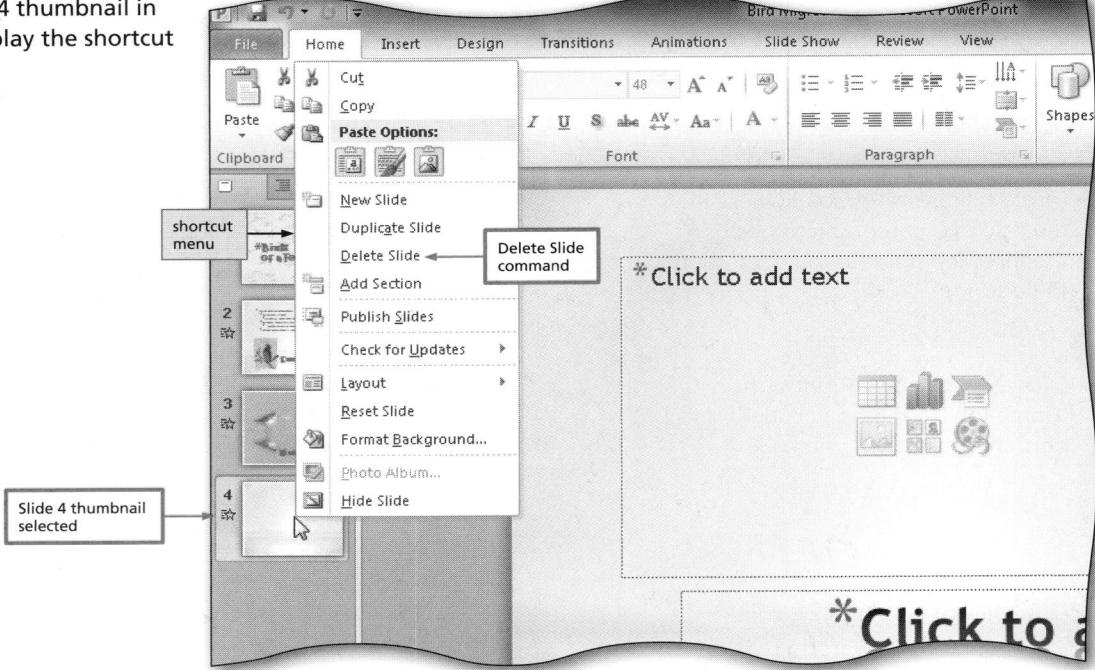

Figure 3–18

2

• Click Delete Slide to delete Slide 4 from the presentation (Figure 3–19).

Figure 3–19

Q&A

Can I delete multiple slides simultaneously?

Yes. If the slides are sequential, click the first slide you want to delete, press and hold the SHIFT key, click the last slide that you want to delete, right-click any selected slide, and then click Delete Slide on the shortcut menu. If the slides are not sequential, press and hold the CTRL key while you click each slide that you want to delete, right-click any selected slide, and then click Delete Slide on the shortcut menu.

Changing Views

You have been using Normal view to create and edit your slides. Once you completed your slides, you reviewed the final products by displaying each slide in Slide Show view, which occupies the full computer screen. You were able to view how the transitions, graphics, and effects will display in an actual presentation before an audience.

PowerPoint has other views to help review a presentation for content, organization, and overall appearance. Slide Sorter view allows you to look at several slides at one time. Reading view is similar to Slide Show view because each slide displays individually, but the slides do not fill the entire screen. Using this view, you easily can control the progression through the slides forward or backward with simple controls at the bottom of the window. Switching between Slide Sorter view, Reading view, and Normal view helps you review your presentation, assess whether the slides have an attractive design and adequate content, and make sure they are organized for the most impact. After reviewing the slides, you can change the view to Normal so that you may continue working on the presentation.

BTW

Using the Ribbon to Adjust Views
While it is convenient to change views by clicking the controls on the bar at the bottom of the PowerPoint Window, you also can change views by using the Ribbon. The Presentation Views group on the View tab has four buttons that allow you to change to Normal, Slide Sorter, Reading, and Slide Show views.

To Change Views

You have made several modifications to the slides, so you should check for balance and consistency. The following steps change the view from Normal view to Slide Sorter view, then Reading view, and back to Normal view.

1
- Click the Slide Sorter view button in the lower right of the PowerPoint window to display the presentation in Slide Sorter view (Figure 3–20).

Q&A Can I view only the slide title text in Slide Sorter View?

Yes. Press and hold the ALT key while you press and hold the mouse button. Each slide title will display against a white background.

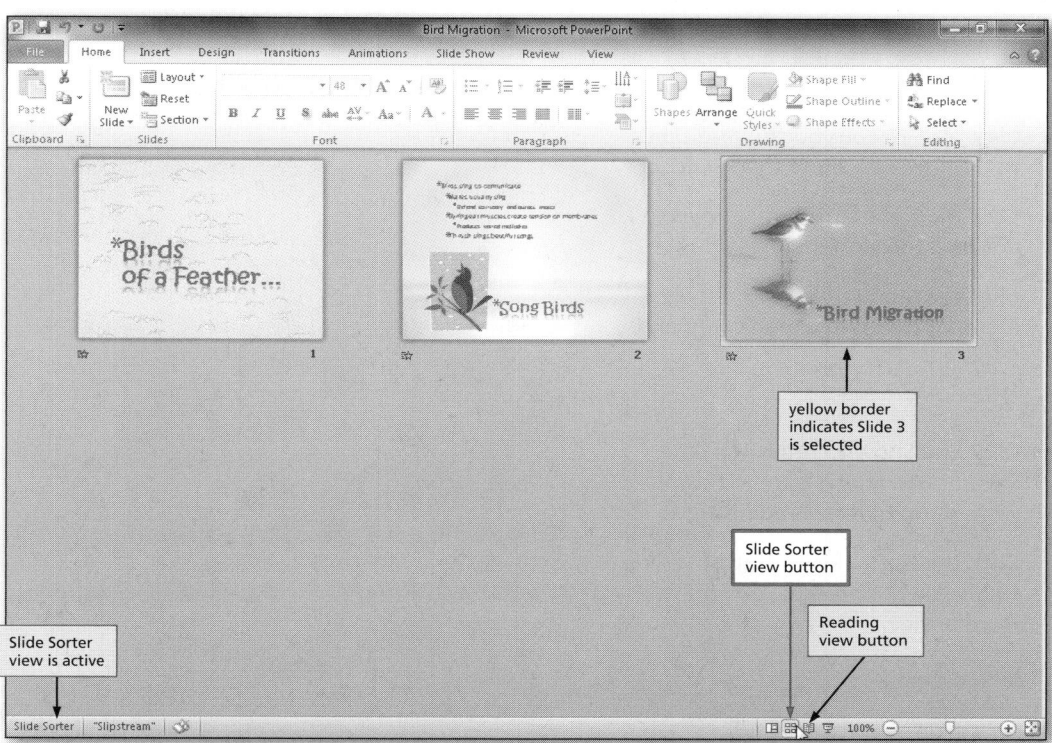

Figure 3–20

Q&A Why is Slide 3 selected?

It is the current slide in the Slide pane.

2

● Click the Reading view button in the lower right of the PowerPoint window to display Slide 3 of the presentation in Reading view (Figure 3–21).

Figure 3–21

3

● Click the Previous button two times to display Slide 2 and then Slide 1.

● Click the Next button two times to advance through the presentation.

● Click the Menu button to display a menu of commonly used commands (Figure 3–22).

4

● Click End Show to return to Slide Sorter view, which is the view you were using before Reading view.

● Click the Normal view button to display the presentation in Normal view.

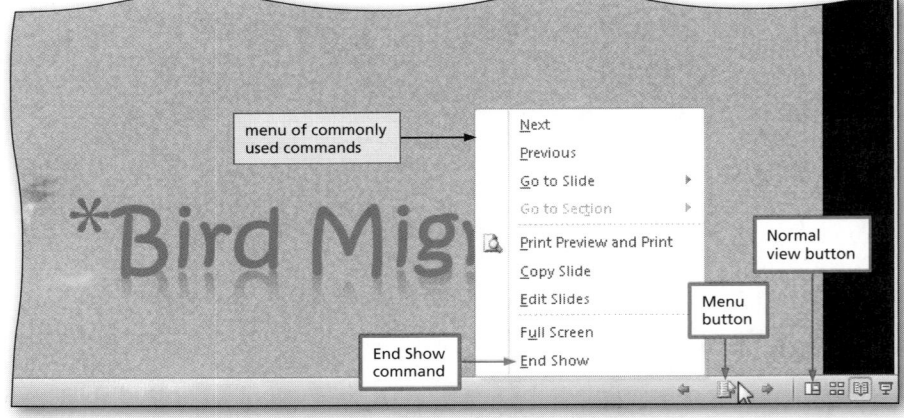

Figure 3–22

Other Ways

1. Click desired view button (View tab | Presentation Views group)

Copying and Modifying a Clip

Slide 1 (shown in Figure 3–1a on PPT 139) contains a modified version of a songbird. You may want to modify a clip art picture for various reasons. Many times, you cannot find a clip art picture that precisely illustrates your topic. For example, you want a picture of a red sports car, but the only available clip art picture is painted black.

Occasionally, you may want to remove or change a portion of a clip art picture or you might want to combine two or more clip art pictures. For example, you can use one clip art picture for the background and another picture as the foreground. Other times, you may want to combine a clip art picture with another type of object. In this presentation, the bird picture has a yellow background that is not required to display on the slide, so you will ungroup the clip art picture and remove the background.

Modifying the clip on Slide 1 requires several steps. You first must copy it using the Office Clipboard and then paste it in the desired location. The **Office Clipboard** is a temporary storage location that can hold a maximum of 24 text or graphics items copied from any Office program. The same procedure of copying and pasting objects works for copying and pasting text from one placeholder to another. In the following pages, you will perform these tasks:

1. Copy the clip from Slide 2 to Slide 1.
2. Zoom Slide 1 to examine the clip.
3. Ungroup the clip.
4. Edit and change the clip colors.
5. Delete a clip object.
6. Regroup the clip.

To Copy a Clip from One Slide to Another

The bird clip on Slide 2 also can display in a modified form on the title slide. The following steps copy this slide element from Slide 2 to Slide 1.

1
- Display Slide 2. With the Home tab displayed, click the bird clip to select it and then click the Copy button (Home tab | Clipboard group) (Figure 3–23).

Q&A Why are some words on Slide 2 underlined with red wavy lines?

Those words are not in PowerPoint's main or custom dictionaries, so PowerPoint indicates that they may be misspelled. For example, the word, Syringeal, is spelled correctly, but is not in PowerPoint's dictionaries.

2
- Display Slide 1 and then click the Paste button (Home tab | Clipboard group) to insert the bird clip into the title slide.

Q&A Is the clip deleted from the Office Clipboard when I paste it into the slide?

No.

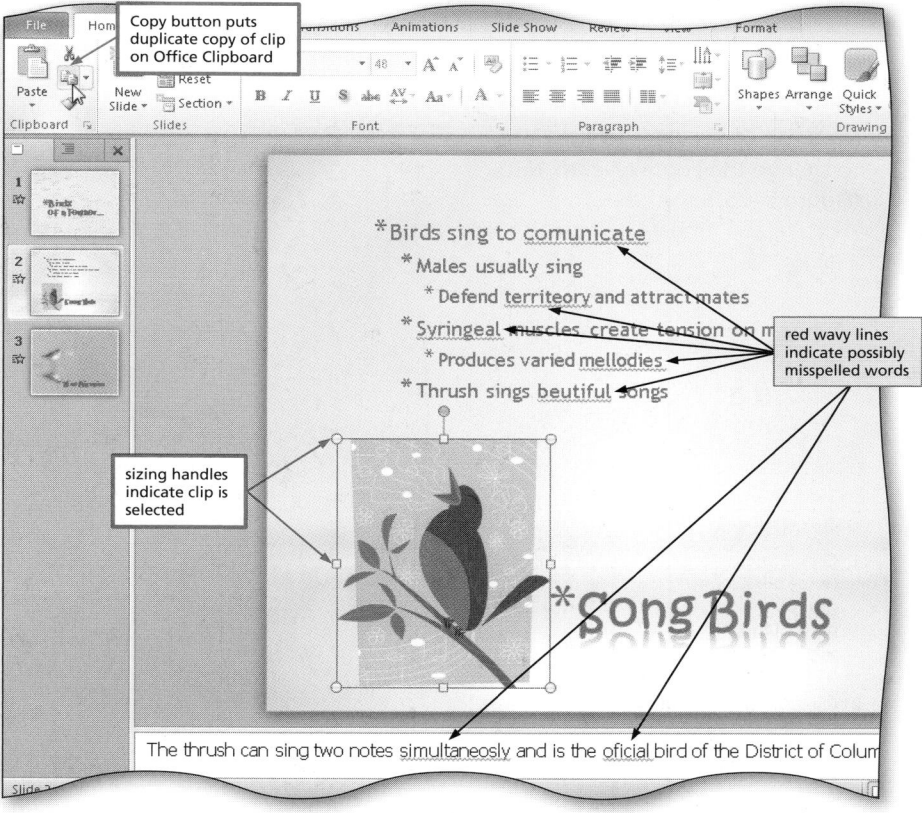

Figure 3–23

- Decrease the clip size by dragging one of the corner sizing handles inward until the clip is the size shown in Figure 3–24. Drag the clip to the location shown in this figure.

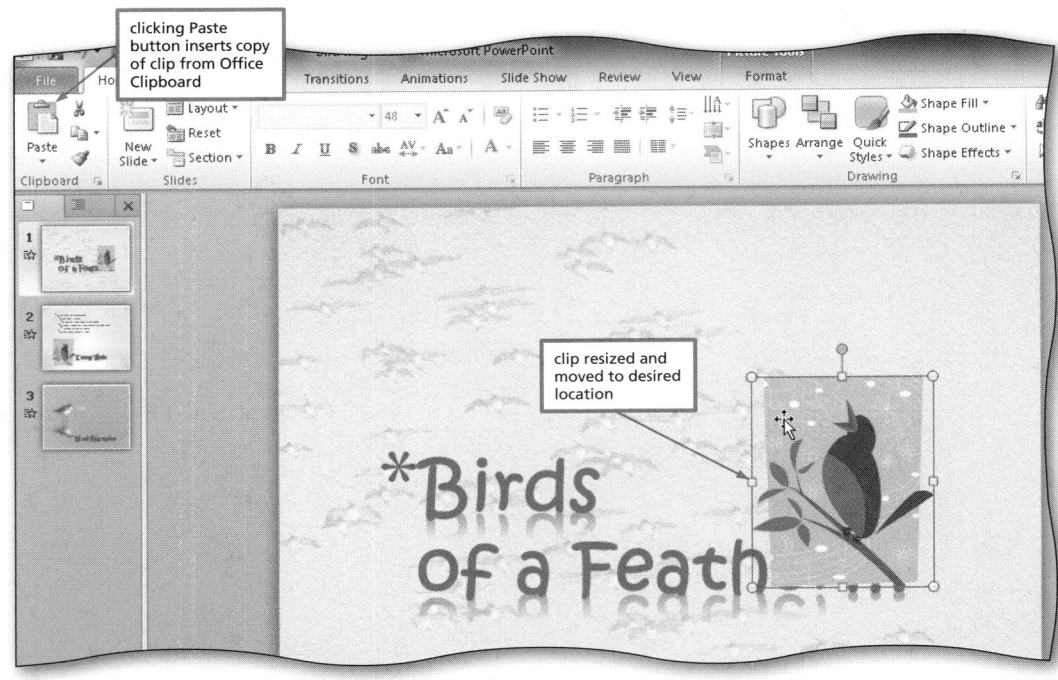

Figure 3–24

To Zoom a Slide

You will be modifying small areas of the clip, so it will help you select the relevant pieces if the graphic is enlarged. The following step changes the zoom to 150 percent.

- Drag the Zoom slider to the right to change the zoom level to 150% (Figure 3–25).

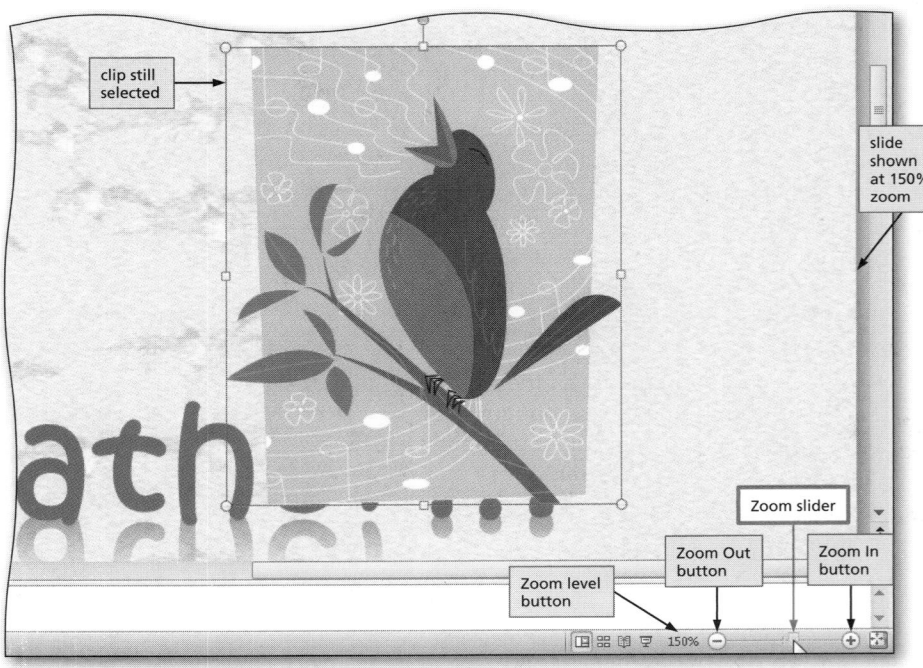

Figure 3–25

Other Ways

1. Click Zoom button (View tab | Zoom group), change percentage in Percent text box (Zoom dialog box), click OK button
2. Click Zoom In button at end of slider
3. Click Zoom level on left side of slider, change percentage in Percent text box (Zoom dialog box), click OK button

To Ungroup a Clip

The next step is to ungroup the bird clip on Slide 1. When you **ungroup** a clip art picture, PowerPoint breaks it into its component objects. A clip may be composed of a few individual objects or several complex groups of objects. These groups can be ungrouped repeatedly until they decompose into individual objects. Because a clip art picture is a collection of complex groups of objects, you may need to ungroup a complex object into less complex objects before being able to modify a specific object. When you ungroup a clip and click the Yes button in the Microsoft PowerPoint dialog box, PowerPoint converts the clip to a PowerPoint object. The following steps ungroup a clip.

1

- With the bird clip selected, click Format on the Ribbon to display the Picture Tools Format tab.

- Click the Group button (Picture Tools Format tab | Arrange group) to display the Group menu (Figure 3–26).

 Why does the Group button look different on my screen?

Your monitor is set to a different resolution. See Chapter 1 for an explanation of screen resolution and the appearance of the Ribbon.

Figure 3–26

2

- Click Ungroup on the Group menu to display the Microsoft PowerPoint dialog box (Figure 3–27).

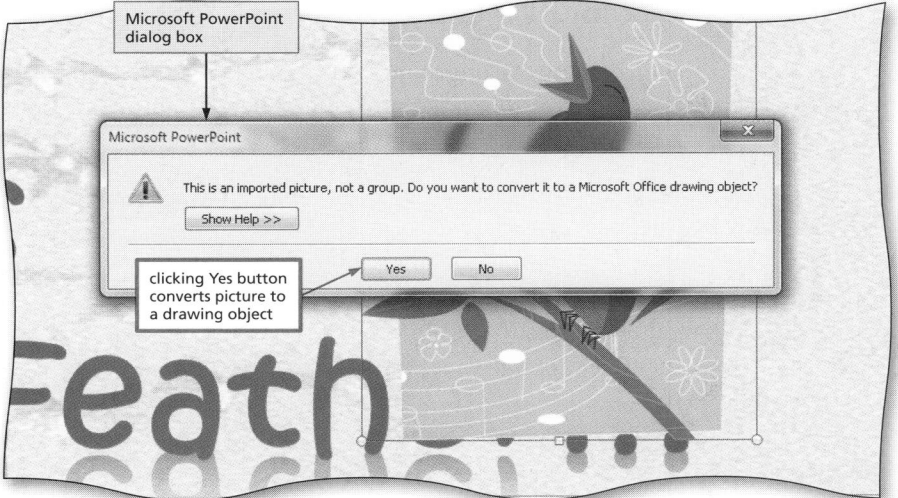

Figure 3–27

- Click the Yes button (Microsoft PowerPoint dialog box) to convert the clip to a Microsoft Office drawing.

Q&A What happens if I click the No button?

The clip will remain displayed on the slide as a clip art picture and will not ungroup.

- Click Format on the Ribbon to display the Drawing Tools Format tab. Click the Group button (Drawing Tools Format tab | Arrange group) and then click Ungroup again.

Q&A Why does the Drawing Tools Format tab show different options this time?

The clip has become a drawing object, so tools related to drawing now display.

- With the Drawing Tools Format tab displayed, click the Group button (Drawing Tools Format tab | Arrange group), and then click Ungroup a third time to display the objects that constitute the bird clip (Figure 3–28).

Q&A Why do all those circles and squares display in the clip?

The circles and squares are sizing handles for each of the clip's objects, which resemble pieces of a jigsaw puzzle.

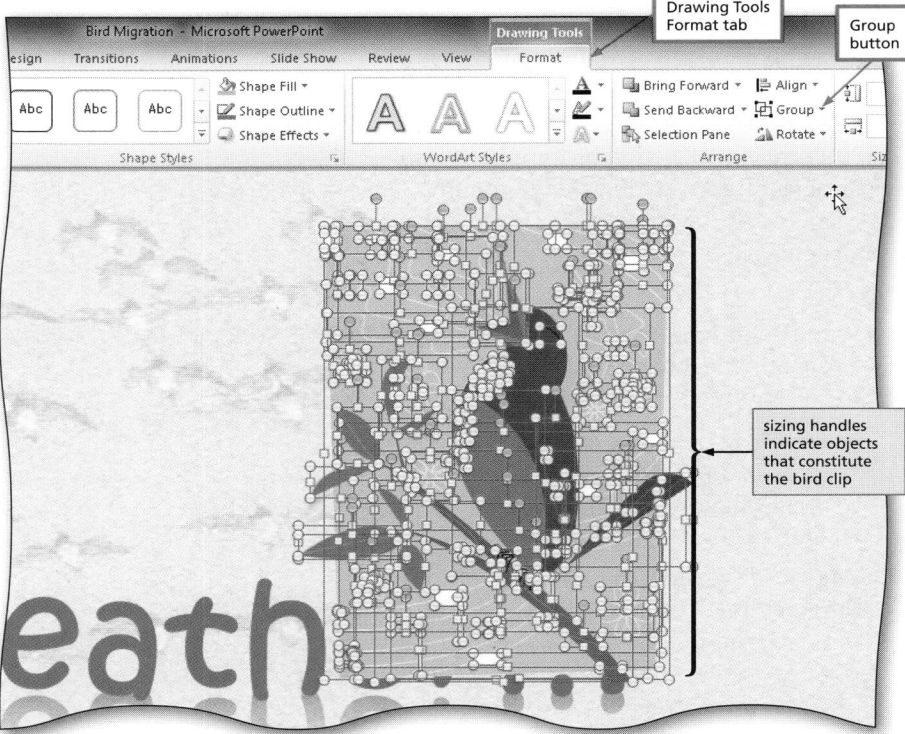

Figure 3–28

Other Ways

1. Right-click clip, point to Group on shortcut menu, click Ungroup
2. Press SHIFT+CTRL+G

To Change the Color of a Clip Object

Now that the bird picture is ungrouped, you can change the color of the objects. The clip is composed of hundreds of objects, so you must exercise care when selecting the correct object to modify. The following steps change the color of the bird's mouth and the leaves.

- Click outside the clip area to display the clip without the sizing handles around the objects.

- Click the bird's mouth to display sizing handles around the colored area (Figure 3–29).

Q&A What if I selected a different area by mistake?

Click outside the clip and retry.

Figure 3–29

2

- Click the Shape Fill button arrow (Drawing Tools Format tab | Shape Styles group) to display the Shape Fill gallery.

- Point to Yellow in the Standard Colors area (fourth color) to display a live preview of the mouth color (Figure 3–30).

🔍 **Experiment**

- Point to various colors and watch the bird's mouth color change.

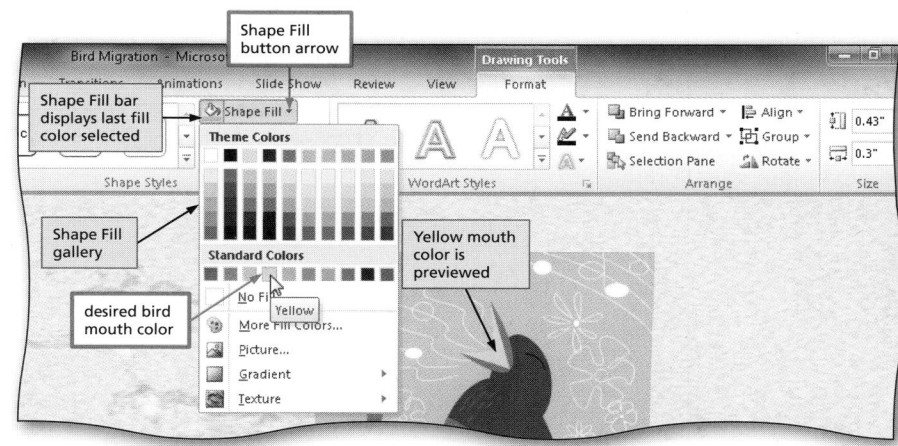

Figure 3–30

3

- Click the color Yellow to change the bird's mouth color.

Q&A Why is the bar under the Shape Fill button now yellow?

The button displays the last fill color selected.

- Click a leaf on the branch to display the sizing handles around the colored area (Figure 3–31).

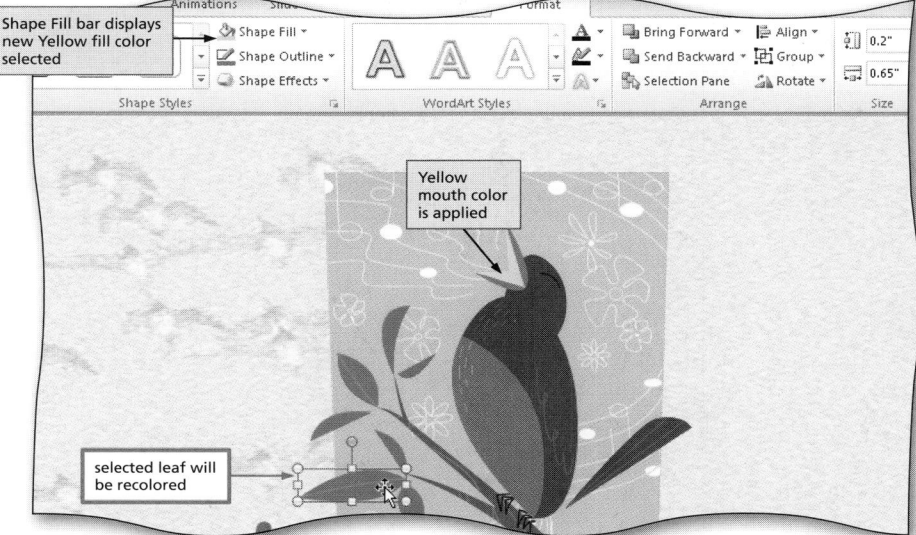

Figure 3–31

4

- Click the Shape Fill button arrow (Drawing Tools Format tab | Shape Styles group) and then point to Green, Accent 3 in the Theme Colors area (seventh color in first row) to display a live preview of the color of the selected leaf in the graphic (Figure 3–32).

🔍 **Experiment**

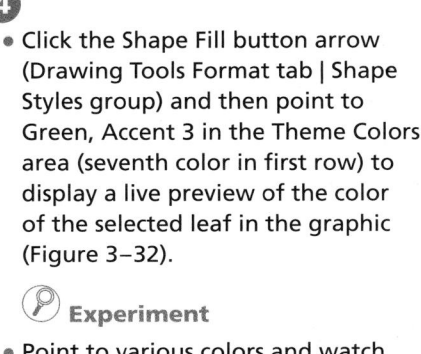

- Point to various colors and watch the leaf color change.

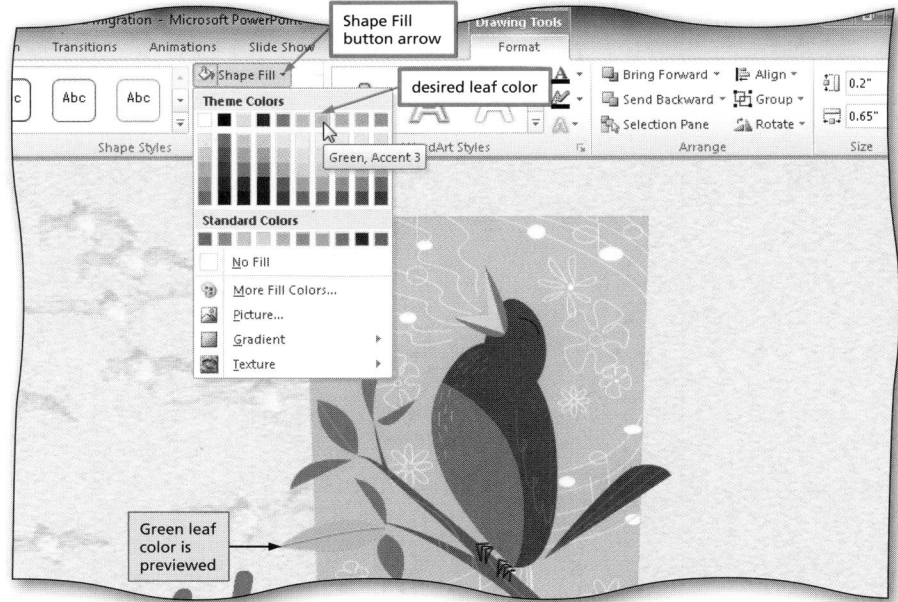

Figure 3–32

5

- Click the Green, Accent 3 color to change the leaf color.

6

- Click another leaf on the branch to select it.

- Click the Shape Fill button to change the leaf color to Green, Accent 3 (Figure 3–33).

Q&A Why did I not need to click the Shape Fill button arrow to select this color?

PowerPoint uses the last fill color selected. This color displays in the bar under the bucket icon on the button.

Figure 3–33

7

- Repeat Step 6 until all the leaves have been recolored (Figure 3–34).

Q&A Can I open the Microsoft Clip Organizer when I am not using PowerPoint?

Yes. On the Start menu, point to All Programs, point to Microsoft Office, point to Microsoft Office 2010 Tools, and then click Microsoft Clip Organizer.

Other Ways

1. Right-click object, click Format Shape on shortcut menu, click Color button

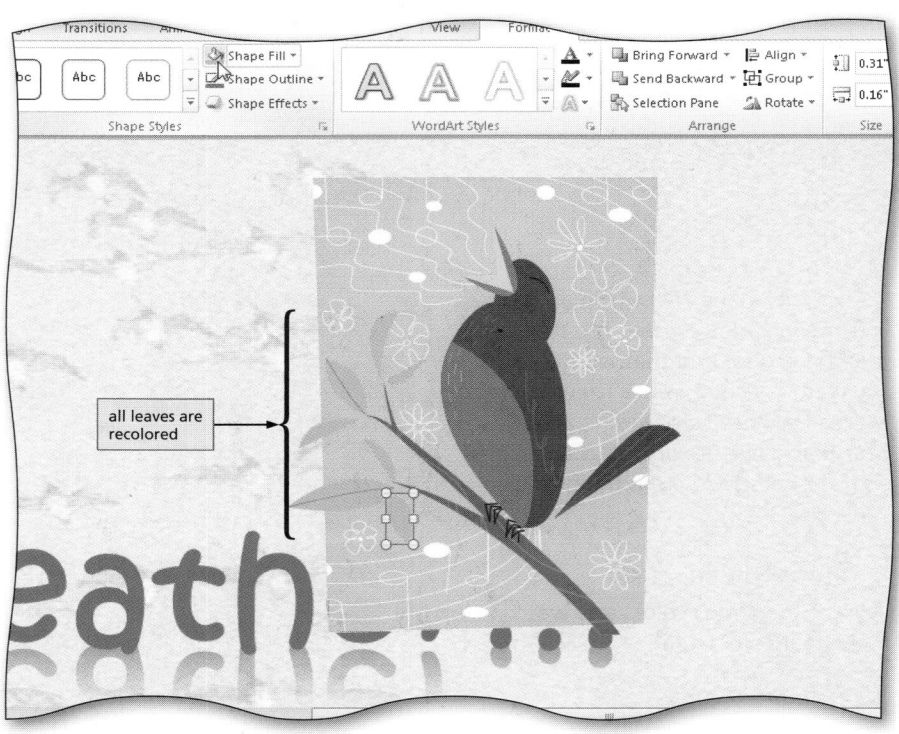

Figure 3–34

To Delete a Clip Object

With the bird mouth and leaf colors changed, you want to delete the gold background object. The following steps delete this object.

- Click the background in any area where the gold color displays to select this object (Figure 3–35).

Q&A Can I select multiple objects so I can delete them simultaneously?

Yes. While pressing the SHIFT key, click the unwanted elements to select them.

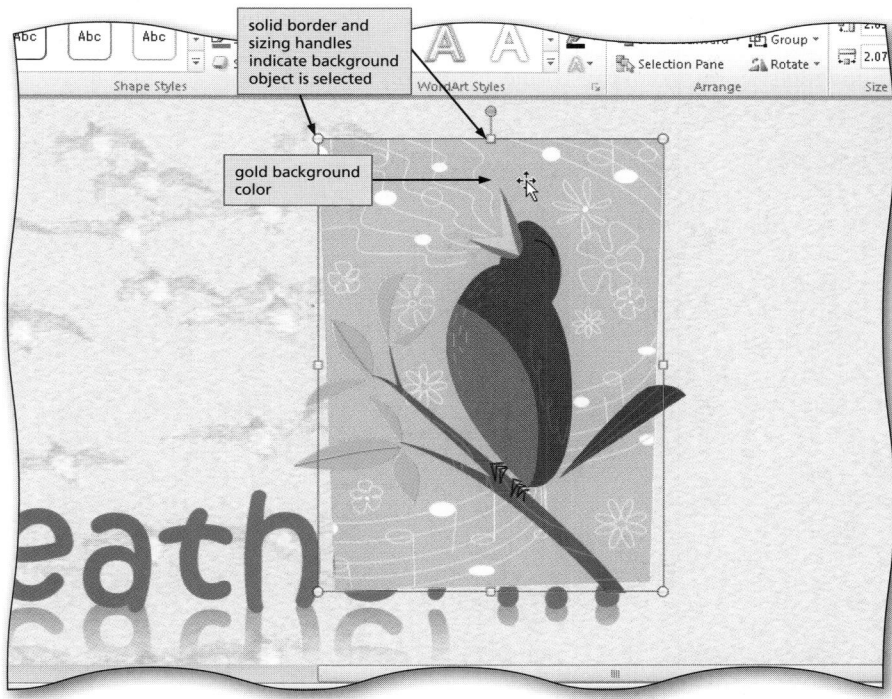

Figure 3–35

- Press the DELETE key to delete this object (Figure 3–36).

Q&A Should the white musical staff display on the slide?

Yes. It is part of the bird clip.

Figure 3–36

To Regroup Objects

When you ungrouped the bird clip, you eliminated the embedding data or linking information that tied all the individual pieces together. If you attempt to move or size this clip now, you might encounter difficulties because it consists of hundreds of objects and is no longer one unified piece. Dragging or sizing affects only a selected object, not the entire collection of objects, so you must use caution when objects are not completely regrouped. All of the ungrouped objects in the bird clip must be regrouped so they are not accidentally moved or manipulated. The following steps regroup these objects into one object.

- With the clip selected, click the Drawing Tools Format tab and then click the Group button (Drawing Tools Format tab | Arrange group) to display the Group menu (Figure 3–37).

- Click Regroup to combine all the objects.

- Use the Zoom slider to change the zoom level to 69%.

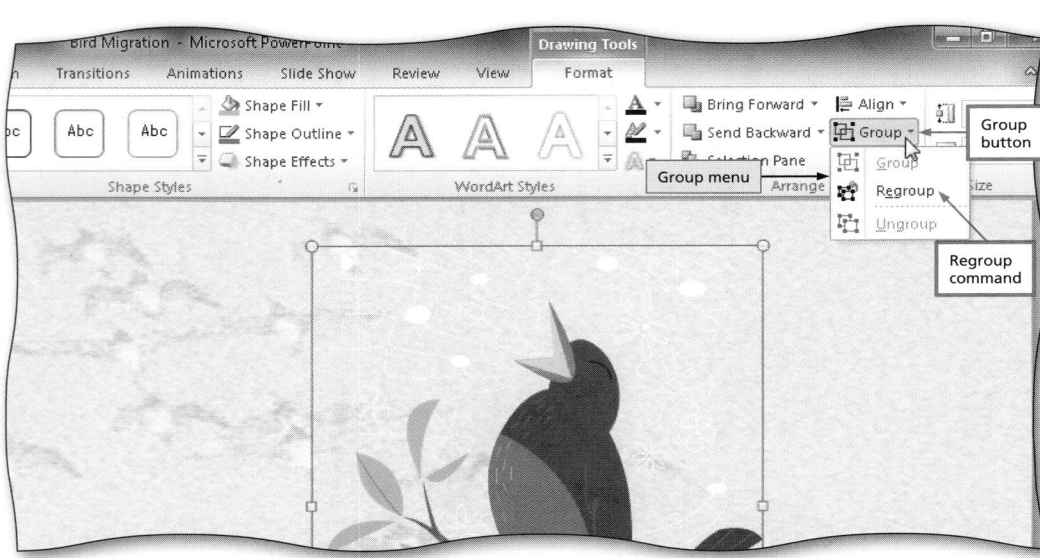

Figure 3–37

Other Ways

1. Right-click clip, point to Group on shortcut menu, click Regroup
2. Press CTRL+G

Plan Ahead

Use multimedia selectively.
PowerPoint makes it easy to insert multimedia into a presentation. Well-produced video clips add value when they help explain a procedure or show movement that cannot be captured in a photograph. Music can help calm or energize an audience, when appropriate. A sound, such as applause when a correct answer is given, can emphasize an action. Before you insert these files on a slide, however, consider whether they really add any value to your overall slide show. If you are inserting them just because you can, you might want to reconsider your decision. Audiences quickly tire of extraneous sounds and movement on slides, and they will find these media clips annoying. Keep in mind that the audience's attention should focus primarily on the presenter; extraneous or inappropriate media files may divert their attention and, in turn, decrease the quality of the presentation.

Break Point: If you wish to take a break, this is a good place to do so. Be sure to save the Bird Migration file again and then you can quit PowerPoint. To resume at a later time, start PowerPoint, open the file called Bird Migration, and continue following the steps from this location forward.

Adding Media to Slides

Media files can enrich a presentation if they are used correctly. Movies files can have two formats: digital video produced with a camera and editing software or animated GIF (Graphics Interchange Format) files composed of multiple images combined into a single file. Sound files can be from the Microsoft Clip Organizer, files stored on your computer, or an audio track on a CD. To hear the sounds, you need a sound card and speakers on your system.

In the following pages, you will perform these tasks:

1. Insert a video file into Slide 3.
2. Trim the video file so only the final few seconds play.
3. Add video options that determine the clip's appearance and playback.
4. Insert audio files.
5. Add audio options that determine the clips' appearance and playback.
6. Add a video style to the Slide 3 clip.
7. Resize the video.
8. Insert a movie clip into Slide 1.

To Insert a Video File

Slide 3 has the title, Bird Migration, and you have a video clip that is composed of many scenes featuring various animals and birds. A short segment of this clip shows a flock of birds on a beach, and you want to use only this part of the clip in your presentation. PowerPoint allows you to insert this clip into your slide and then trim the file so that just a portion will play when you preview the clip or run the slide show. This clip is available on the Data Files for Students. See the inside back cover of this book for instructions on downloading the Data Files for Students, or contact your instructor for more information about accessing the required file. The following steps insert this video clip into Slide 3.

1

• Display Slide 3 and then display the Insert tab. With your USB flash drive connected to one of the computer's USB ports, click the Insert Video button (Insert tab | Media group) to display the Insert Video dialog box.

• If the list of files and folders on the selected USB flash drive are not displayed in the Insert Video dialog box, double-click your USB flash drive to display them.

• Click Wildlife to select the file (Figure 3–38).

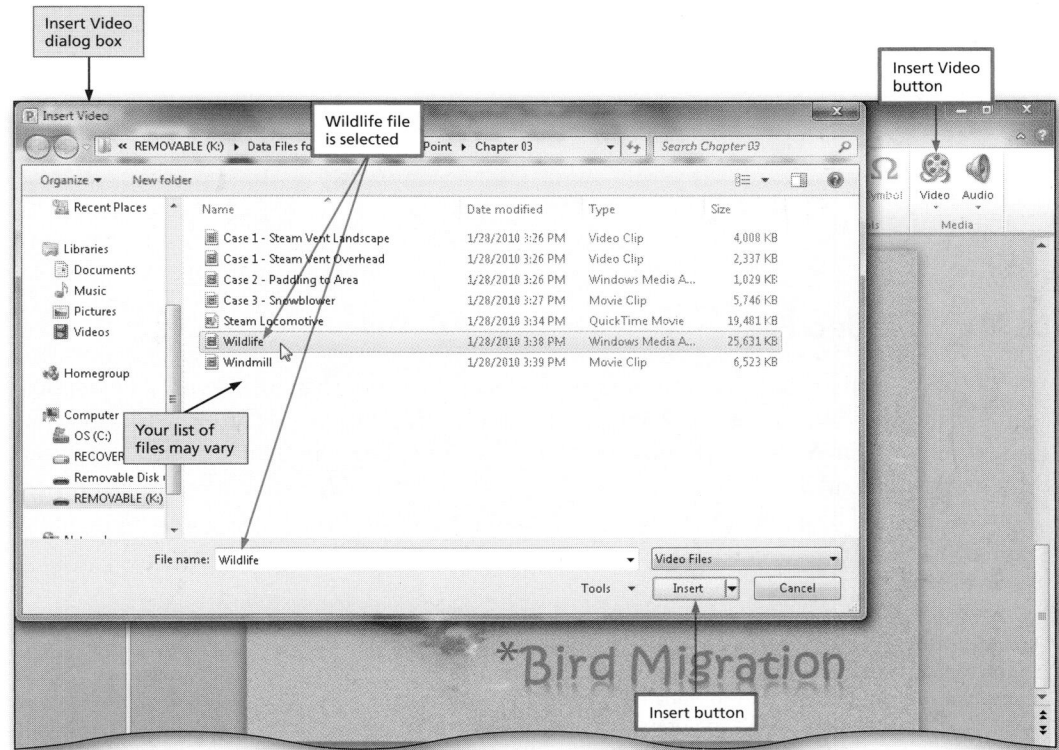

Figure 3–38

2

- Click the Insert button (Insert Video dialog box) to insert the movie clip into Slide 3 (Figure 3–39).

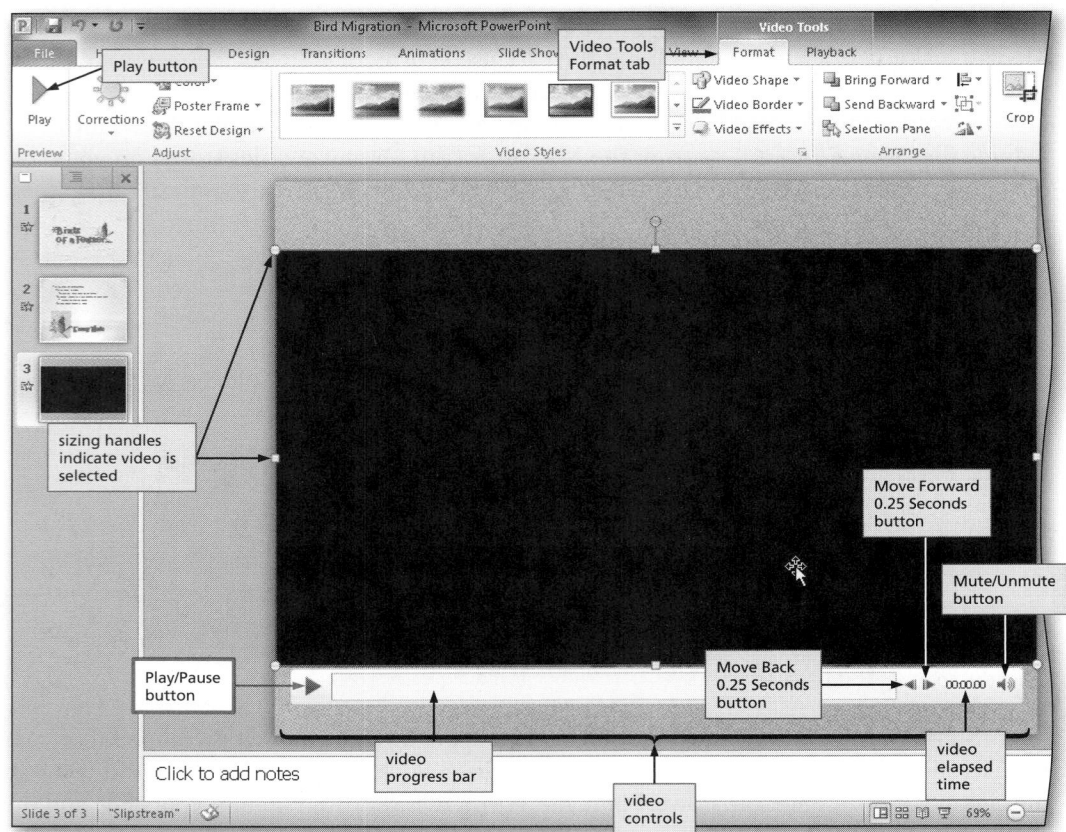

Figure 3–39

Q&A

Can I adjust the color of a video clip?

Yes. You correct the brightness and contrast, and you also recolor a video clip using the same methods you learned in this chapter to color a picture.

To Trim a Video File

The Wildlife video has a running time of slightly more than 30 seconds. The approximately six-second segment that you want to use in your presentation begins 24 seconds into the file and finishes at the end of the clip. PowerPoint's **Trim Video** feature allows you to trim the beginning and end of your clip by designating your desired Start Time and End Time. These precise time measurements are accurate to one-thousandth of a second. The start point is indicated by a green marker, and the end point is indicated by a red marker. The following steps trim the Wildlife video clip.

BTW

Using Codecs

Digital media file sizes often are quite large, so video and audio content developers use a codec (**co**mpressor/**dec**ompressor) to reduce the required storage space and to transfer the files across the Internet quickly and smoothly. Your computer can play any compressed file if the specific codec used to compress the file is available on your computer. If the codec is not installed or is not recognized, your computer attempts to download this file from the Internet. Microsoft Windows Media Encoder is a free program that makes some media files compatible with PowerPoint.

1

- With the video clip selected on Slide 3, click the Play/Pause button to play the entire video.

Q&A Can I play the video by clicking the Play button in the Preview group?

Yes. This Play button plays the entire clip. You may prefer to click the Play/Pause button displayed in the Video Controls to stop the video and examine one of the frames.

- Click Playback on the Ribbon to display the Video Tools Playback tab. Click the Trim Video button (Editing group) to display the Trim Video dialog box (Figure 3–40).

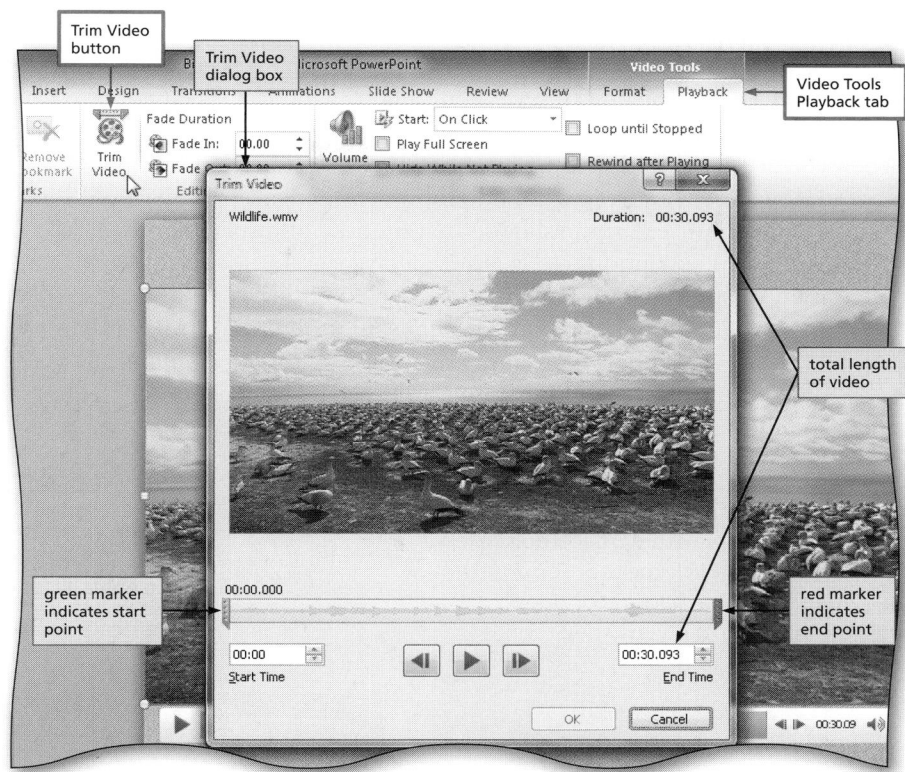

Figure 3–40

2

- Point to the start point, which is indicated by the green marker on the left side, so that the mouse pointer changes to a two-headed arrow.

- Drag the green marker to the right until the Start Time is 00:24:634 (Figure 3–41).

Q&A Can I specify the start or end times without dragging the markers?

Yes. You can enter the time in the Start Time or End Time boxes, or you can click the Start Time or End Time box arrows. You also can click the Next Frame and Previous Frame buttons (Trim Video dialog box).

Q&A How would I indicate an end point if I want the clip to end at a time other than at the end of the clip?

You would drag the red marker to the left until the desired end time displays.

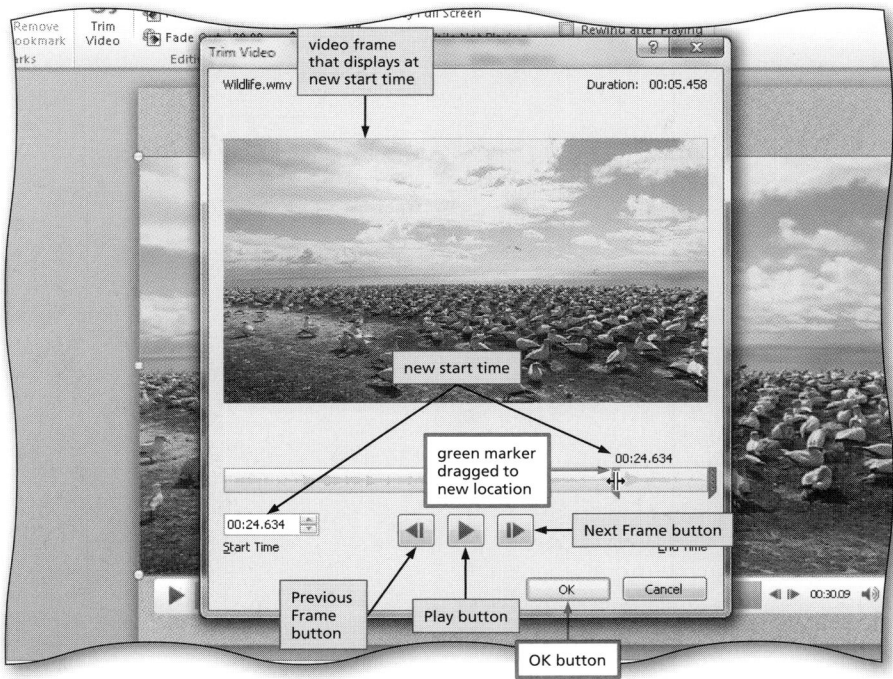

Figure 3–41

3

- Click the Play button (Trim Video dialog box) to review the shortened video clip.

- Click the OK button to set the Start Time and End Time and to close the Trim Video dialog box.

Other Ways

1. Right-click clip, click Trim Video on shortcut menu

To Add Video Options

Once the video clip is inserted into Slide 3, you can specify options that affect how the file is displayed and played. For example, you can have the video play automatically when the slide is displayed, or you can click the slide when you are ready to start the playback. You also can have the video fill the entire slide, which is referred to as **full screen**. If you decide to play the slide show automatically and have it display full screen, you can drag the video frame to the gray area off the slide so that it does not display briefly before going to full screen. You can select the Loop until Stopped option to have the video repeat until you click the next slide, or you can choose to not have the video frame display on the slide until you click the slide.

If your video clip has recorded sounds, the volume controls give you the option to set how loudly this audio will play. They also allow you to mute the sound so that your audience will hear no background noise or music.

The following steps add the options of playing the video full screen automatically when Slide 3 is displayed and also mutes the background music recorded on the video clip.

- If necessary, click Playback on the Ribbon to display the Video Tools Playback tab. Click the Start box (Video Tools Playback tab | Video Options group) to view the Start menu (Figure 3–42).

Q&A What does the On Click option do?

The video clip would begin playing when a presenter clicks the slide during the slide show.

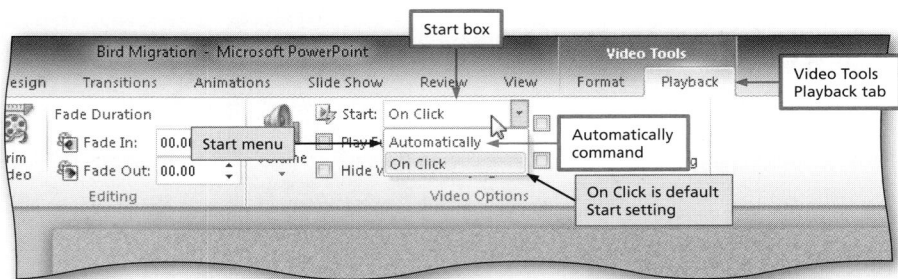

Figure 3–42

- Click Automatically in the Start menu (Figure 3–43).

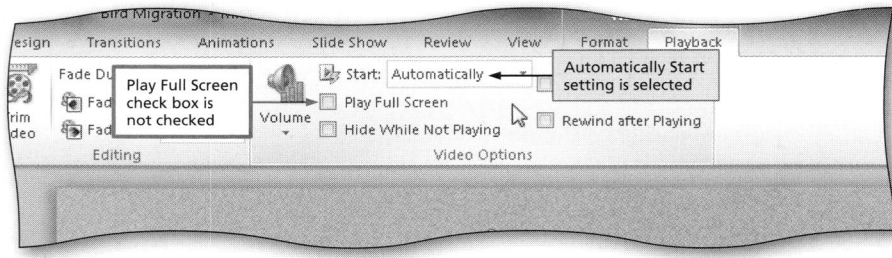

Figure 3–43

- Click the Play Full Screen check box (Video Tools Playback tab | Video Options group) to place a check mark in it.

- Click the Volume button (Video Tools Playback tab | Video Options group) to display the Volume menu (Figure 3–44).

4
- Click Mute in the Volume menu.

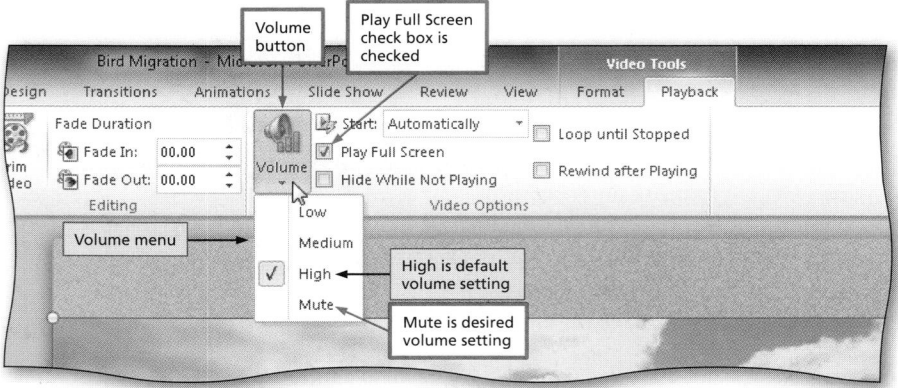

Figure 3–44

To Insert an Audio File

Avid bird watchers listen to the songs and calls birds make to each other. The Microsoft Clip Organizer and Office.com have several of these sounds in audio files that you can download and insert into your presentation. Once these audio files are inserted into a slide, you can add options that specify how long and how loudly the clip will play; these options are similar to the video options you just selected for the Wildlife video clip. The following steps insert an audio clip into Slide 3.

1

- With Slide 3 displaying, click Insert on the Ribbon to display the Insert tab and then click the Insert Audio button arrow (Insert tab | Media group) to display the Insert Audio menu (Figure 3–45).

Figure 3–45

2

- Click Clip Art Audio in the Insert Audio menu to open the Clip Art task pane.

- If necessary, click the 'Results should be' box arrow, click the 'All media types' check box to remove the check mark from each of the four types of media files, and then click the Audio check box to place a check mark in it (Figure 3–46).

 Can I use this technique to search solely for videos, photographs, or illustrations?

Yes. You also can search for a combination of these file types, such as both video and audio files.

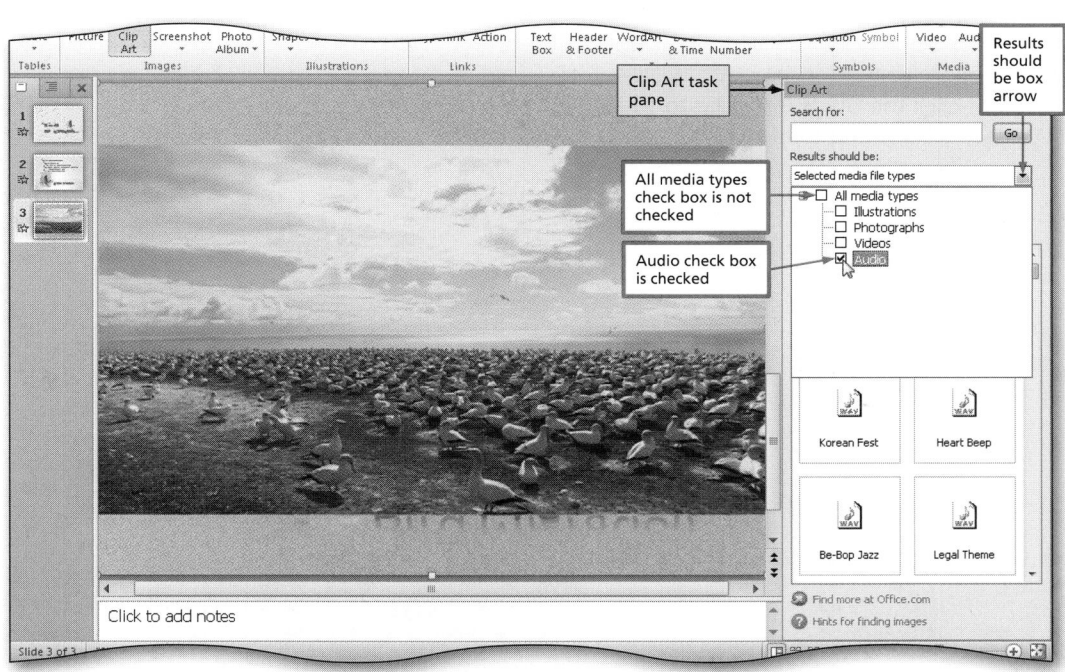

Figure 3–46

- If necessary, delete any letters that are present in the Search for text box and then type `Glade Birds` in the Search for text box. If necessary, click the 'Include Office.com content' check box to select it.

- Click the Go button so that the Microsoft Clip Organizer will search for and display all clips having the keyword or title, Glade Birds.

4

- Point to the Glade Birds clip to display the properties of this file (Figure 3–47).

Q&A What if the Glade Birds audio clip is not shown in my Clip Art task pane?

Select a similar clip. Your clips may be different depending on the clips installed on your computer and if you have an active Internet connection.

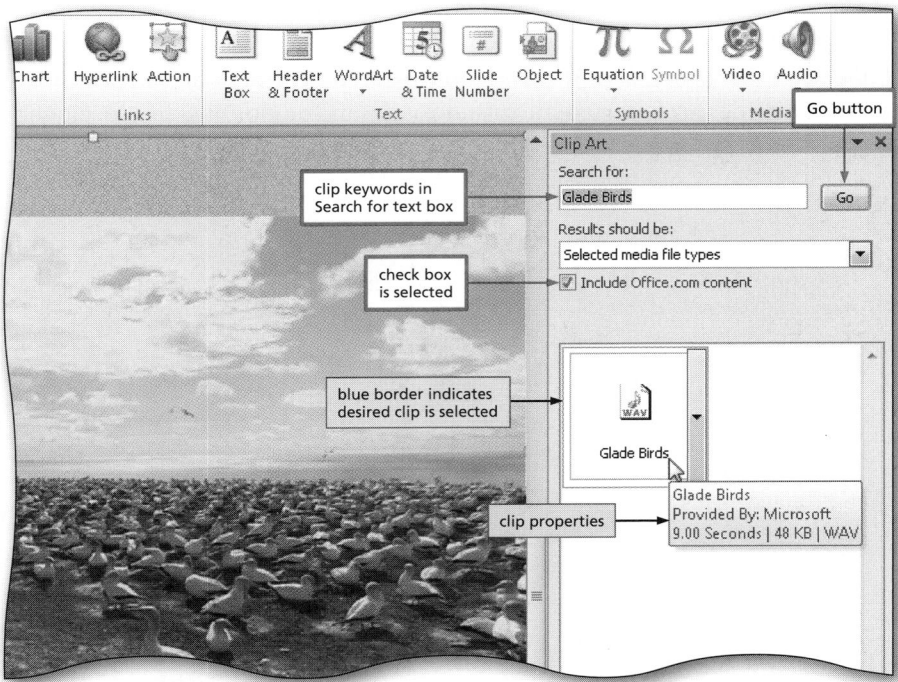

Figure 3–47

Q&A What are the properties associated with this clip?

The properties include the number of seconds of playing time, the file size, and the type of audio file. This file is a **Windows waveform (.wav)** file, which uses a standard format to encode and communicate music and sound between computers, music synthesizers, and instruments.

5

- Right-click the Glade Birds clip to select the clip and to display the Edit menu (Figure 3–48).

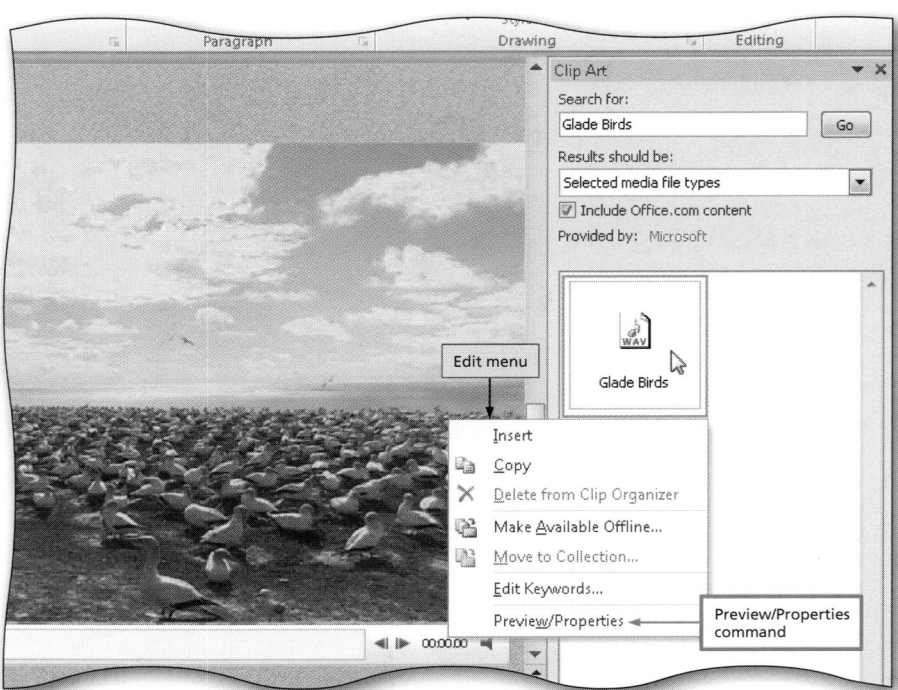

Figure 3–48

6

- Click Preview/Properties to display the Preview/Properties dialog box and to hear the clip (Figure 3–49).

Q&A What are the words listed in the Keywords box?

Those words are the search terms associated with the file. If you enter any of those words in the Search for text box, this audio file would display in the results list.

Q&A Can I preview the clip again?

Yes. Click the Play button in the Preview/Properties dialog box.

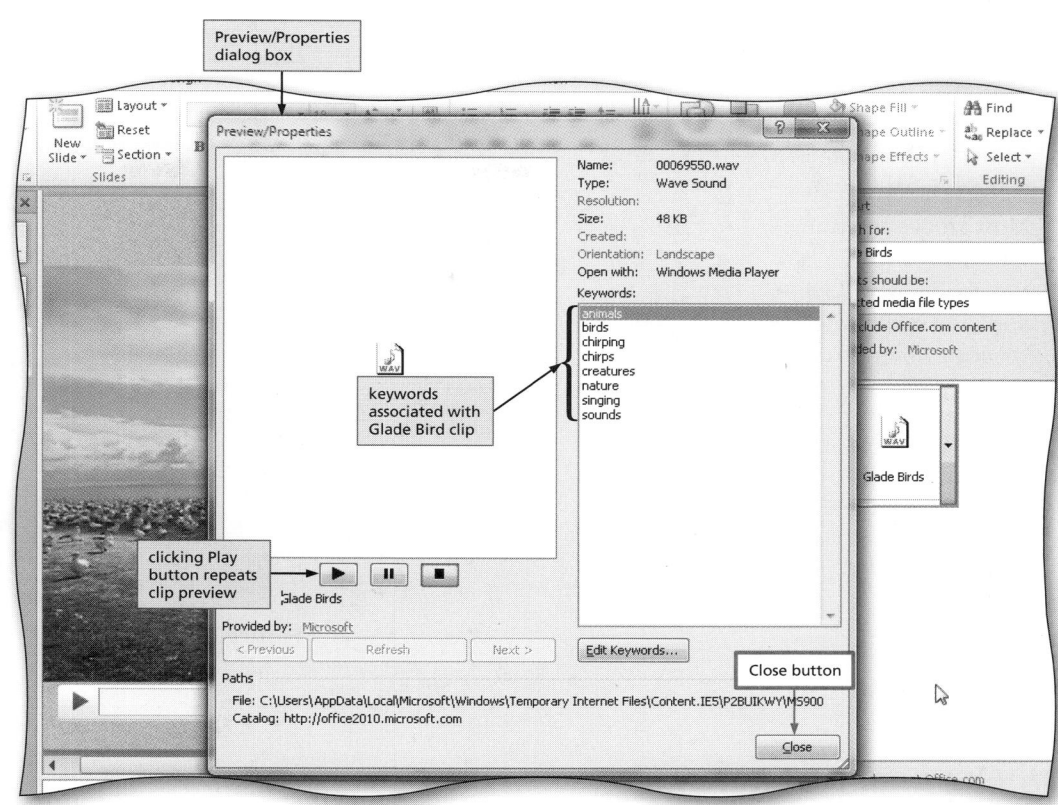

Figure 3–49

7

- Click the Close button (Preview/Properties dialog box) to close the dialog box.

- Click Glade Birds in the results list (Clip Art task pane) to insert that file into Slide 3 (Figure 3–50).

Q&A Why does a sound icon display in the video?

The icon indicates an audio file is inserted.

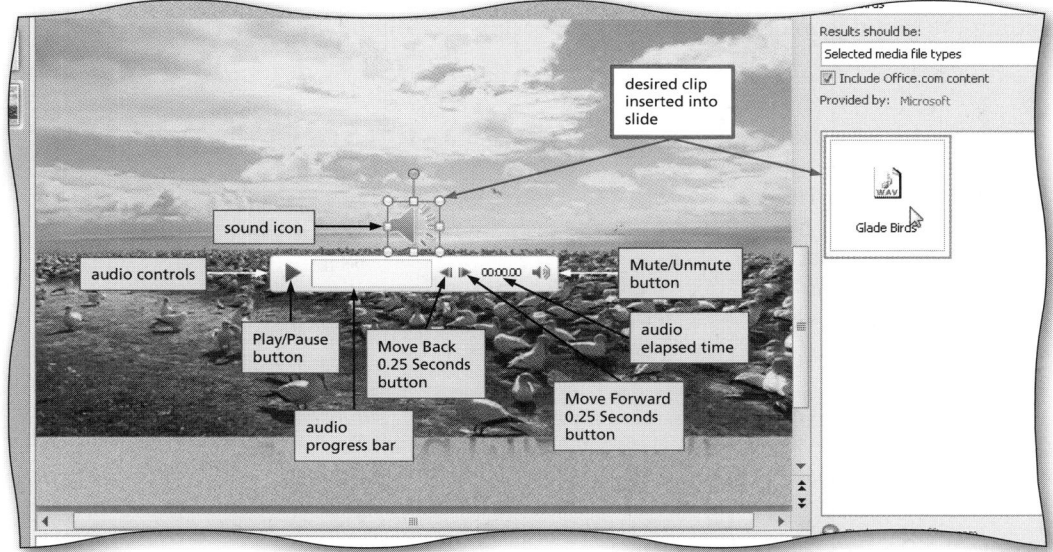

Figure 3–50

Q&A Do the Audio Controls buttons have the same functions as the Video Controls buttons that displayed when I inserted the Wildlife clip?

Yes. The controls include playing and pausing the sound, moving back or forward 0.25 seconds, audio progress, elapsed time, and muting or unmuting the sound.

● Drag the sound icon to the upper-left corner of the slide (Figure 3–51).

Q&A

Must I move the icon on the slide?

No. Although your audience will not see the icon when you run the slide show, it is easier for you to see the media elements when they are separated on the slide rather than stacked on top of each other.

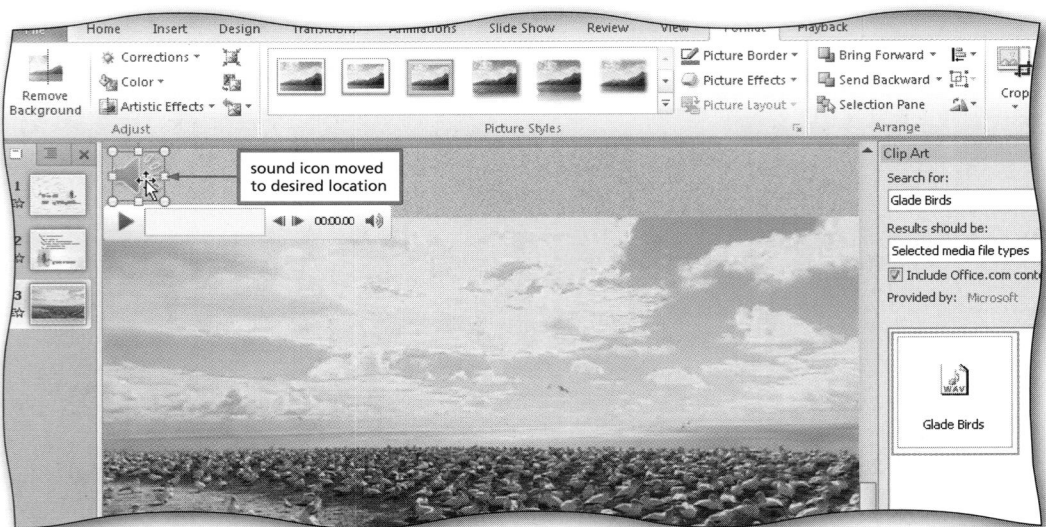

Figure 3–51

To Add Audio Options

Once an audio clip is inserted into a slide, you can specify options that control playback and appearance. As with the video options you applied to the Wildlife clip, the audio clip can play either automatically or when clicked, it can repeat the clip while a particular slide is displayed, and you can drag the sound icon off the slide and set the volume.

The following steps add the options of starting automatically and playing until the slide no longer is displayed, hiding the sound icon on the slide, and increasing the volume.

● Click Playback on the Ribbon to display the Audio Tools Playback tab. Click the Start box (Audio Tools Playback tab | Audio Options group) to display the Start box menu (Figure 3–52).

● Click Automatically in the Start menu.

Q&A

Does the On Click option function the same way for an audio clip as On Click does for a video clip?

Yes. If you were to select On Click, the sound would begin playing only after the presenter clicks Slide 1 during a presentation.

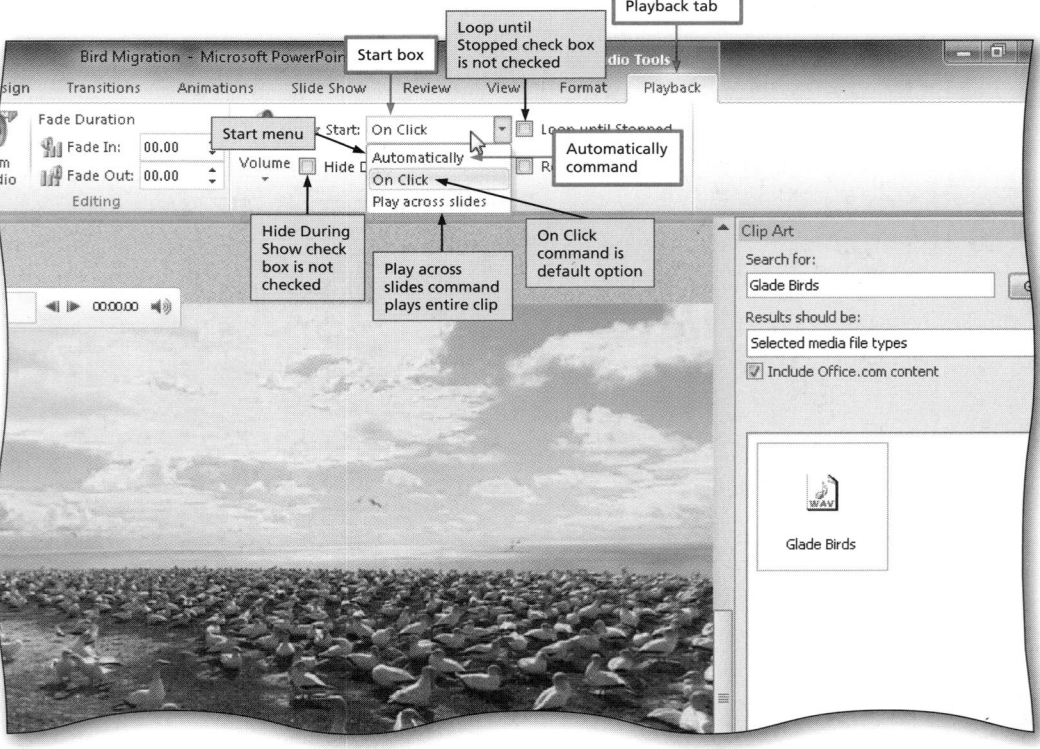

Figure 3–52

3

- Click the Loop until Stopped check box (Audio Tools Playback tab | Audio Options group) to place a check mark in it.

Q&A What is the difference between the Loop until Stopped option and the Play across slides option?

The audio clip in the Loop until Stopped option repeats for as long as one slide is displayed. In contrast, the Play across slides option clip would play only once, but it would continue to play while other slides in the presentation are displayed. Once the end of the clip is reached, the sound would end and not repeat.

4

- Click the Hide During Show check box (Video Tools Playback tab | Audio Options group) to place a check mark in it (Figure 3–53).

Q&A Why would I want the icon to display during the show?

If you had selected the On Click start option, you would need to find this icon on the slide and click it to start playing the clip.

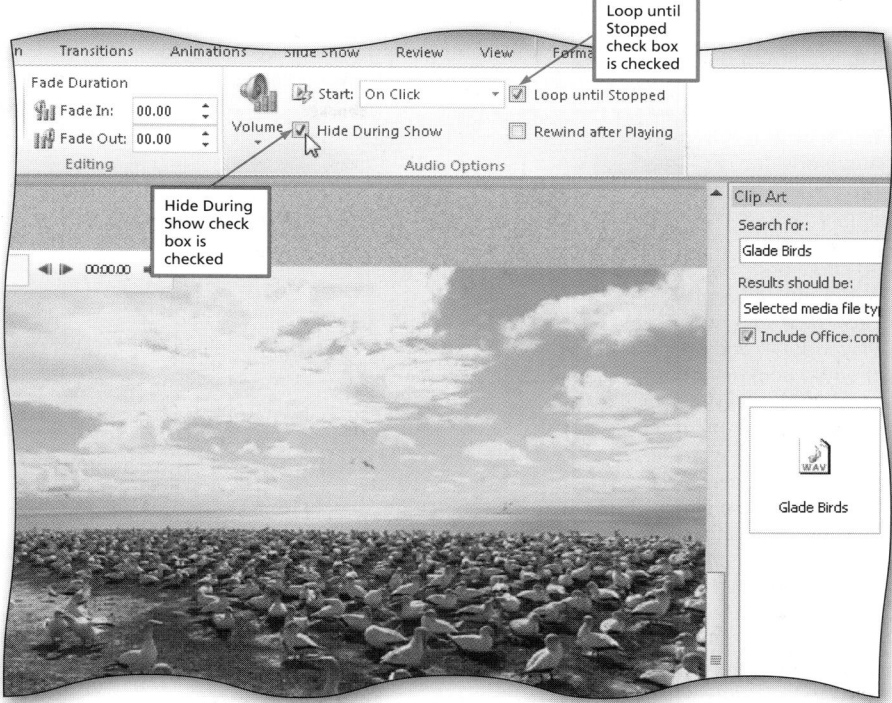

Figure 3–53

To Insert an Additional Audio File and Set Options

Having an audio clip play when Slide 1 is displayed would add interest and help set the tone of the presentation. Only one bird appears on that slide, and it appears to be singing heartily. A single bird singing would coordinate nicely with this clip art image. The following steps insert a songbird audio clip into Slide 1 and set playback options.

1 Display Slide 1, delete any letters that are present in the Search for text box, and then type **Birds at dawn** in the Search for text box (Clip Art task pane), and search for this audio clip.

2 Insert the Birds at dawn clip into Slide 1 and then drag the sound icon to the lower-left corner of the slide.

3 Close the Clip Art task pane.

4 Display the Audio Tools Playback tab. Click the Start box (Audio Tools Playback tab | Audio Options group) and then click Automatically in the Start menu.

5 Click the Loop until Stopped check box (Audio Tools Playback tab | Audio Options group) to place a check mark in it.

BTW

Playing Audio Continuously
You can play one audio file throughout an entire presentation instead of only when one individual slide is displayed. When you select the 'Play across slides' option in the Start box (Audio Tools Playback tab | Audio Options group), the audio clip will play continuously as you advance through the slides in your presentation. If you select this option, be certain the length of the clip exceeds the total time you will display all slides in your slide show.

BTW

Using Bookmarks in Audio and Video Clips
While delivering a presentation, bookmarks are useful in helping you find specific locations in an audio or video clip. They can start an animation or jump to a specific location in the audio or video file. To add a bookmark to an audio clip as it is playing, click the Audio Tools Playback tab and then click the Add Bookmark button (Audio Tools Playback tab | Bookmarks group) at the time when you want to add the bookmark. To add a bookmark to a video clip as it is playing, click the Video Tools Playback tab and then click the Add Bookmark button (Video Tools Playback tab | Bookmarks group) when you see the frame where you want to add the bookmark.

BTW

Trimming an Audio Clip
You can shorten an audio clip to play only a specific part of the file. The steps for trimming an audio file are similar to those used for trimming a video file. Select the clip, click the Play/Pause button, and

⑥ Click the Hide During Show check box (Audio Tools Playback tab | Audio Options group).

⑦ Click the Volume button (Audio Tools Playback tab | Audio Options group) and then change the volume to Medium (Figure 3–54).

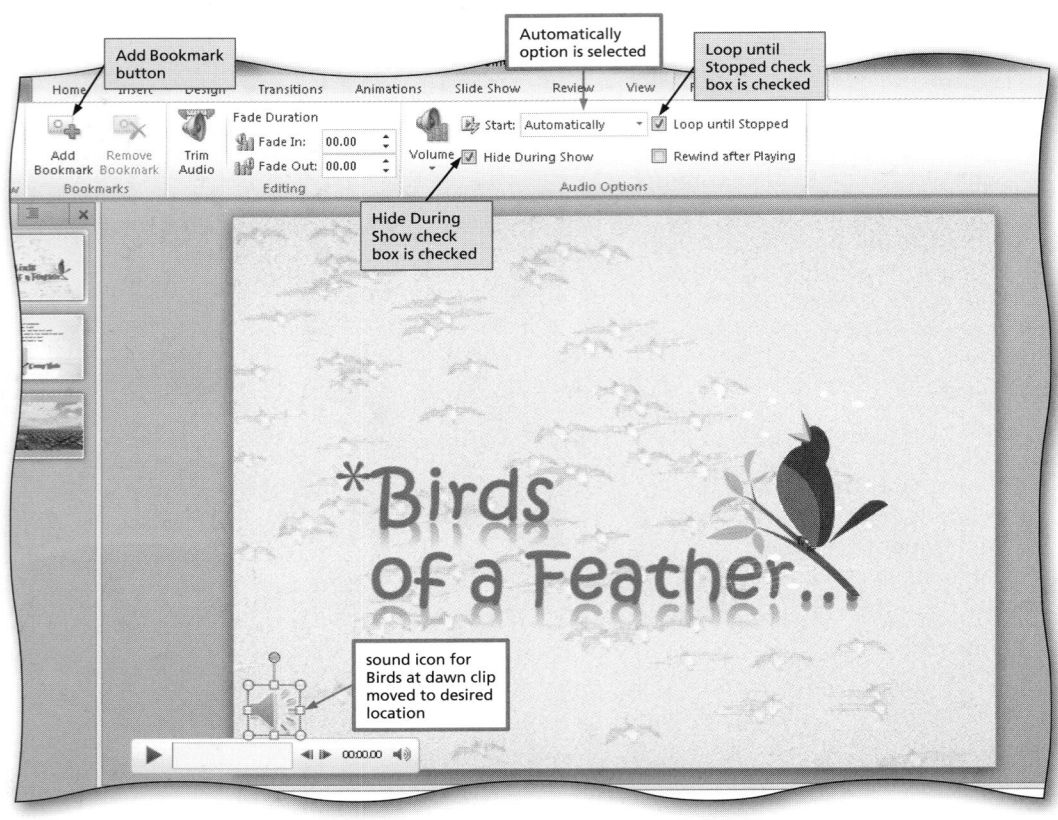

Figure 3–54

then click the Trim Audio button (Audio Tools Playback tab | Editing group). When the Trim Audio dialog box is displayed, you then can drag the green start point marker to the desired starting position and the red end point marker to the desired ending position.

To Add a Video Style

The Wildlife video clip on Slide 3 displays full screen when it is playing, but you can increase the visual appeal of the clip when it is not playing by applying a video style. The video styles are similar to the picture styles you applied in Chapter 2 and include various shapes, angles, borders, and reflections. The following steps apply a video style to the Wildlife clip on Slide 3.

①
• Display Slide 3 and select the video. Click Format on the Ribbon to display the Video Tools Format tab (Figure 3–55).

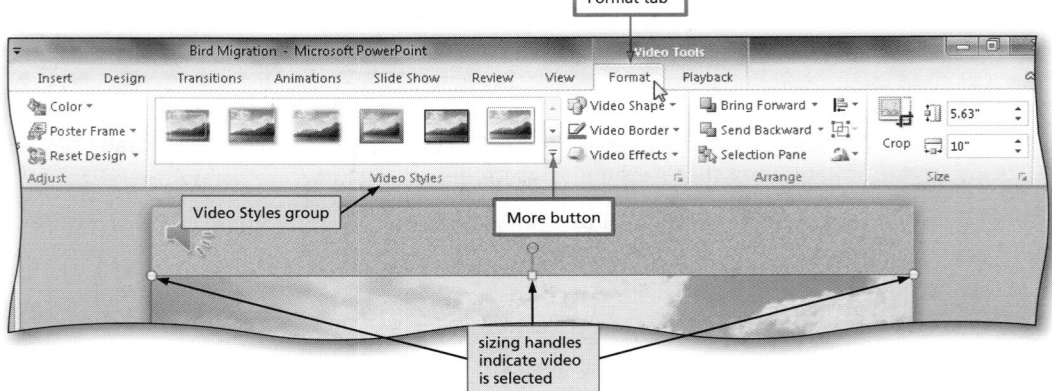

Figure 3–55

2

- With the video selected, click the More button in the Video Styles gallery (Video Tools Format tab | Video Styles group) (shown in Figure 3–55) to expand the gallery.

- Point to Bevel Perspective in the Intense area of the Video Styles gallery to display a live preview of that style applied to the video on the slide (Figure 3–56).

 Experiment

- Point to various picture styles in the Video Styles gallery and watch the style of the video frame change in the document window.

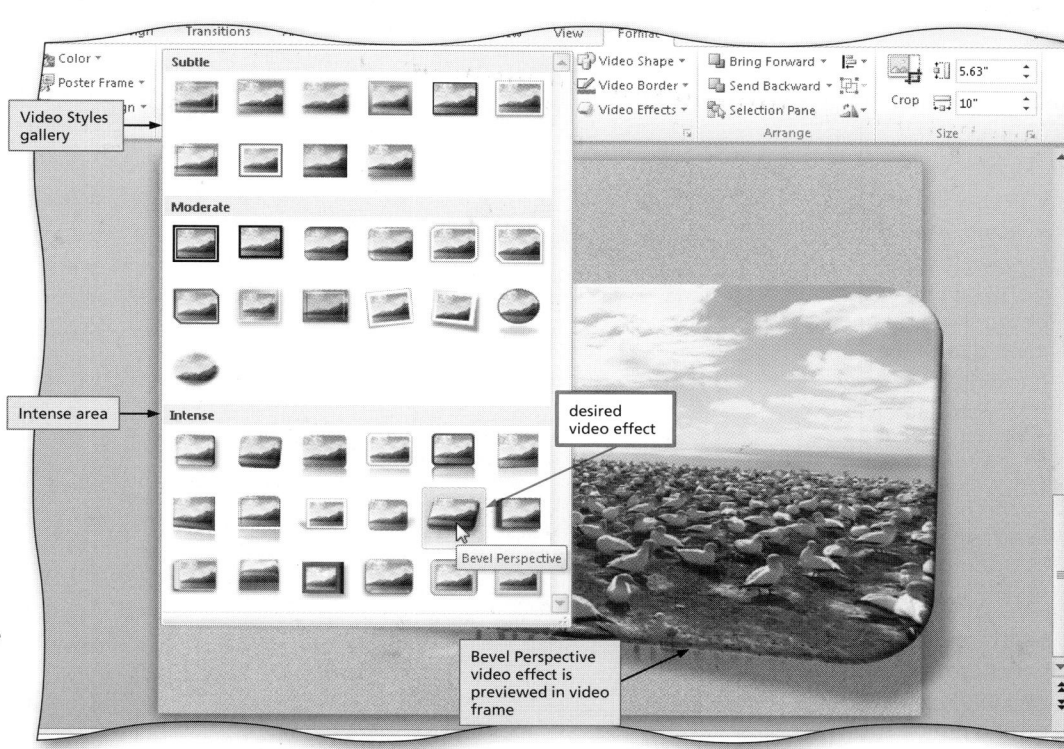

Figure 3–56

3

- Click Bevel Perspective in the Video Styles gallery to apply the style to the selected video (Figure 3–57).

Q&A Can I preview the movie clip?

Yes. Point to the clip and then click the Play/Pause button on the Video Controls below the video.

Q&A Can I add a border to a video style?

Yes. You add a border using the same method you learned in Chapter 2 to add a border to a picture. Click the Video Border button (Video Tools Format tab | Video Styles gallery) and then select a border line weight and color.

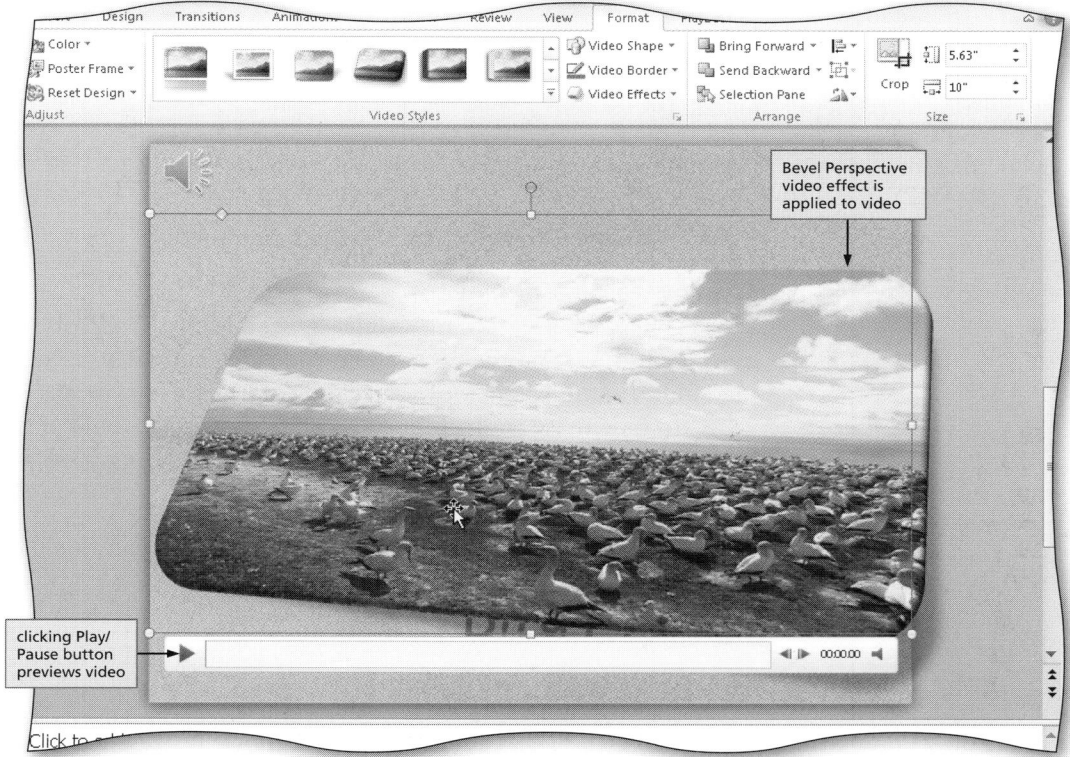

Figure 3–57

To Resize a Video

The Wildlife video size can be decreased to fill the space on the right side of the slide. You resize a video clip in the same manner that you resize clip art and pictures. The following steps resize this video using a sizing handle.

- With the video clip selected, drag the lower-left corner sizing handle on the photograph diagonally inward until the photograph is resized to approximately 3.9″ × 6.93″.

- Drag the clip to the location shown in Figure 3–58.

Q&A

Can I rearrange the order in which video and audio clips play during a slide show?

Yes. You can change the sequence by clicking the Animation Pane button (Animations tab | Advanced Animation group) to open

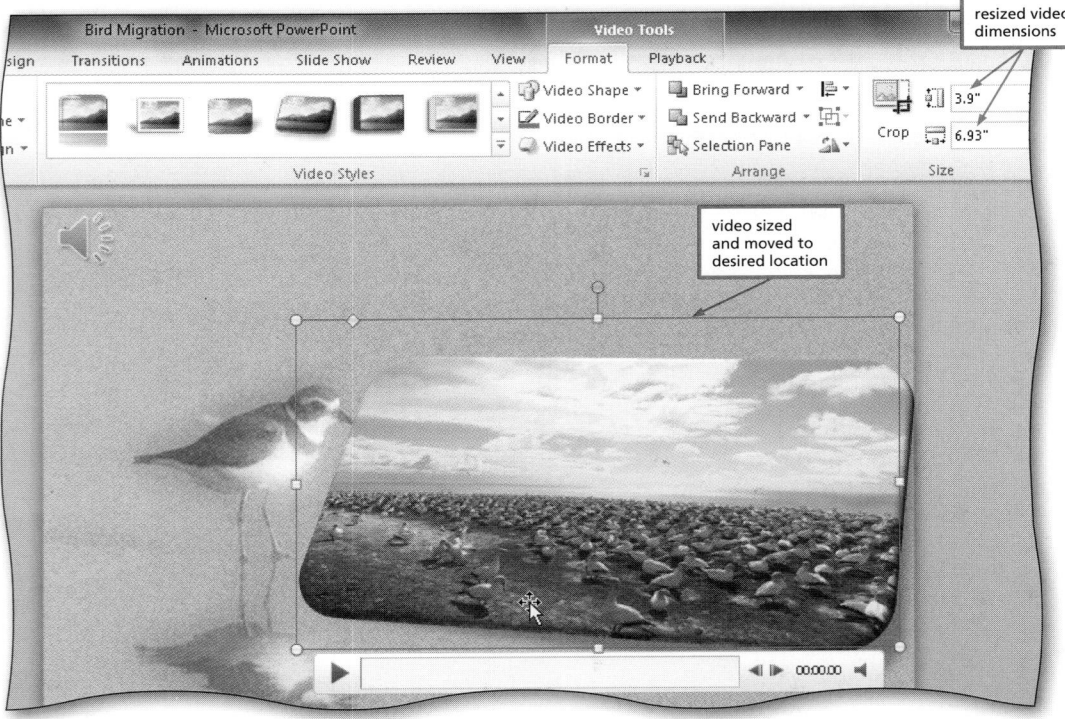

Figure 3–58

the Animation Pane, selecting one of the clips in the list, and then clicking the up or down Re-Order arrows at the bottom of the task pane. You also can select one of the clips and then click the Move Earlier or Move Later buttons (Animations tab | Timing group).

TO SHOW MEDIA CONTROLS

When you are running a slide show, slide show controls display by default when you move your mouse pointer over audio and video clips. These controls allow you to pause, play, mute, unmute, and move the clip forward and backward.

To hide these controls during a slide show, you would perform the following step.

1. Click the Show Media Controls check box (Slide Show tab | Set Up group) to remove the check mark.

If you want to show the hidden media controls, you would perform the following step.

1. Click the Show Media Controls check box (Slide Show tab | Set Up group) to place a check mark in it.

To Insert a Movie Clip

PowerPoint classifies animated GIF files as a type of video or movie because the clips have movement or action. These files are commonplace on Web sites. They also are found in PowerPoint presentations when you want to call attention to material on a particular slide. You can insert them into a PowerPoint presentation in the same manner that you insert video and audio files. They play automatically when the slide is displayed. The following steps insert a music notes video clip into Slide 1.

1

- Display Slide 1 and then display the Insert tab.

- Click the Picture button (Insert tab | Images group) to display the Insert Picture dialog box.

- If necessary, navigate to the Chapter 3 files on your USB drive.

- Click Music Notes to select the file (Figure 3–59).

Q&A Why does my list of files look different?

The list of picture files can vary depending upon the contents of your USB drive and the organization of those files into folders for each chapter.

Q&A Can I search for animated GIF files in the Microsoft Clip Organizer?

Yes. Click the Video button arrow (Insert tab | Media group), click Clip Art Video, click the Videos check box (Clip Art task pane), type the search text, and then click the Go button.

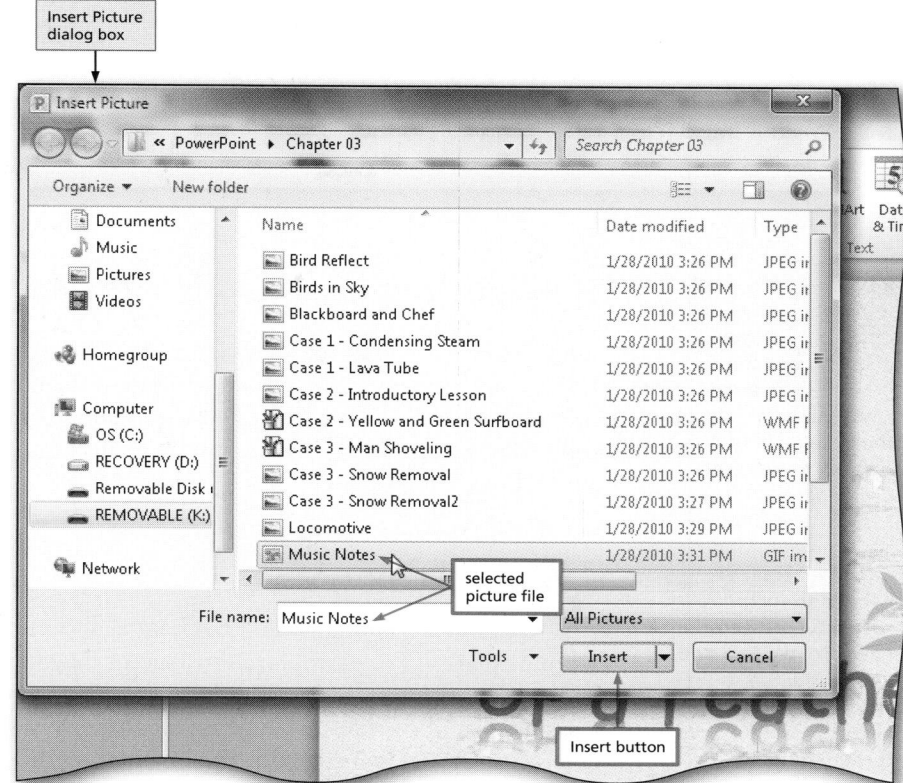

Figure 3–59

2

- Click the Insert button (Insert Picture dialog box) to insert the Music Notes animated GIF clip into Slide 1.

- Resize the clip so that it is approximately 1" × 1.47".

- Drag the clip to the location shown in Figure 3–60.

Q&A Why is the animation not showing?

Animated GIF files move only in Slide Show view and Reading view.

Figure 3–60

Break Point: If you wish to take a break, this is a good place to do so. Be sure to save the Bird Migration file again and then you can quit PowerPoint. To resume at a later time, start PowerPoint, open the file called Bird Migration, and continue following the steps from this location forward.

BTW

Revising Your Text
Generating ideas, revising slides, editing graphics and text, and then proofreading all slide text are required as part of the development process. A good PowerPoint developer has the ability to write and then revise slide content. Multiple drafts generally are needed to complete a successful presentation. PowerPoint's Find and Replace feature is useful if you need to change all instances of a word throughout a large presentation when you are revising slides.

Reviewing and Revising Individual Slides

The text and graphics for all slides in the Bird Migration presentation have been entered. Once you complete a slide show, you might decide to change elements. PowerPoint provides several tools to assist you with making changes. They include finding and replacing text, inserting a synonym, and checking spelling. The following pages discuss these tools.

Replace Dialog Box

At times, you might want to change all occurrences of a word or phrase to another word or phrase. For example, an instructor may have one slide show to accompany a lecture for several introductory classes, and he wants to update slides with the particular class name and section that appear on several slides. He manually could change the characters, but PowerPoint includes an efficient method of replacing one word with another. The Find and Replace feature automatically locates specific text and then replaces it with desired text.

In some cases, you may want to replace only certain occurrences of a word or phrase, not all of them. To instruct PowerPoint to confirm each change, click the Find Next button in the Replace dialog box instead of the Replace All button. When PowerPoint locates an occurrence of the text, it pauses and waits for you to click either the Replace button or the Find Next button. Clicking the Replace button changes the text; clicking the Find Next button instructs PowerPoint to disregard that particular instance and look for the next occurrence of the Find what text.

To Find and Replace Text

While reviewing your slides, you realize that you could give more specific information regarding the type of thrush discussed in Slide 2. The Wood Thrush's songs especially are melodic and beautiful, so you decide to add the word, Wood, to the bird's name. In addition, you want to capitalize the word, Thrush, because it is a specific type of thrush. To perform this action, you can use PowerPoint's Find and Replace feature, which automatically locates each occurrence of a word or phrase and then replaces it with specified text. The word, thrush, displays twice on Slide 2. The following steps use Find and Replace to replace all occurrences of the word, thrush, with the words, Wood Thrush.

BTW

Matching Case and Finding Whole Words
Two options in the Replace dialog box are useful when revising slides. Match case maintains the upper- or lowercase letters within a word, such as a capitalized word at the beginning of a sentence. In addition, the 'Find whole words only' option specifies that PowerPoint makes replacements only when the word typed in the Find what box is a complete word and is not embedded within another word. For example, if you want to change the word 'diction' to 'pronunciation,' clicking the 'Find whole words only' option prevents PowerPoint from changing the word, dictionary, to 'pronunciationary.'

1

- Display the Home tab and then display Slide 2. Click the Replace button (Home tab | Editing group) to display the Replace dialog box.

- Type **thrush** in the Find what text box (Replace dialog box).

- Press the TAB key. Type **Wood Thrush** in the Replace with text box (Figure 3–61).

Q&A Do I need to display the slide that contains the words for which I want to search?

No. But to allow you to see the results of this search and replace action, you can display the slide where the changes will occur.

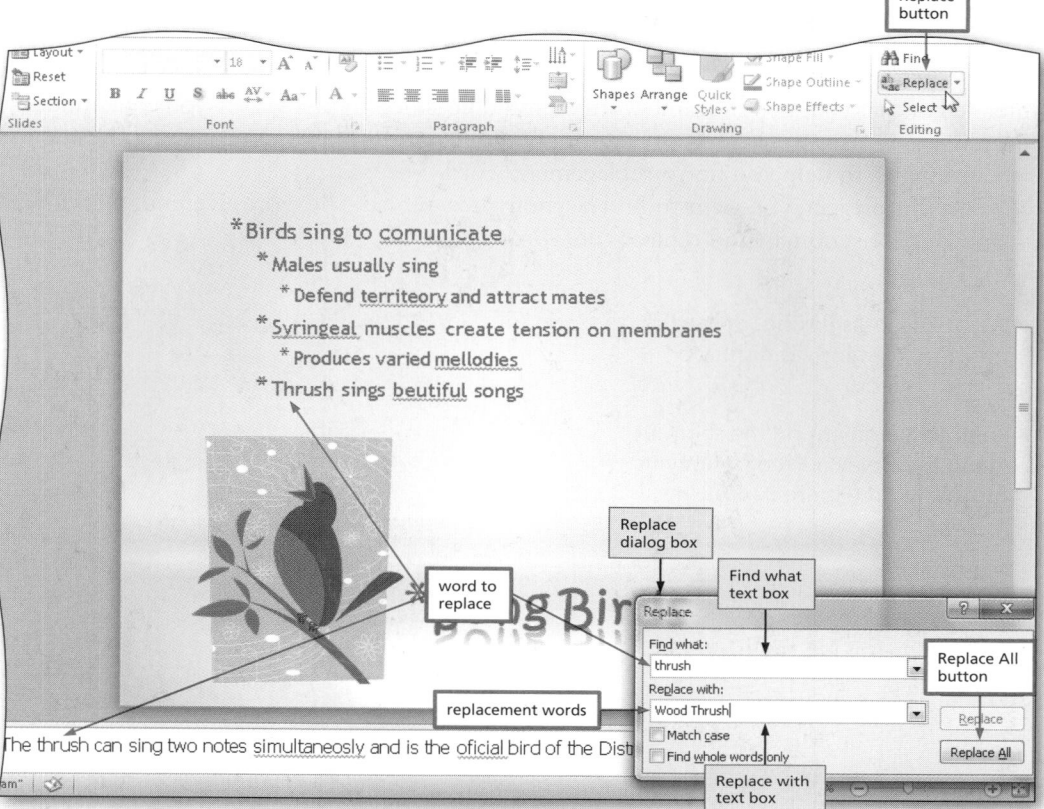

Figure 3–61

2

- Click the Replace All button (Replace dialog box) to instruct PowerPoint to replace all occurrences of the Find what word, thrush, with the Replace with words, Wood Thrush (Figure 3–62).

Q&A If I accidentally replaced the wrong text, can I undo this replacement?

Yes. Click the Undo button on the Quick Access Toolbar to undo all replacements. If you had clicked the Replace button instead of the Replace All button, PowerPoint would undo only the most recent replacement.

Figure 3–62

3

- Click the OK button (Microsoft PowerPoint dialog box).

- Click the Close button (Replace dialog box).

Other Ways
1. Press CTRL+H

To Find and Insert a Synonym

When reviewing your slide show, you may decide that a particular word does not express the exact usage you intended or that you used the same word on multiple slides. In these cases, you could find a **synonym**, or word similar in meaning, to replace the inappropriate or duplicate word. PowerPoint provides a **thesaurus**, which is a list of synonyms and antonyms, to help you find a replacement word.

In this project, you want to find a synonym to replace the word, Defend, on Slide 2. The following steps locate an appropriate synonym and replace the word.

1
- With Slide 2 displaying, right-click the word, Defend, to display a shortcut menu.

- Point to Synonyms on the shortcut menu to display a list of synonyms for this word (Figure 3–63).

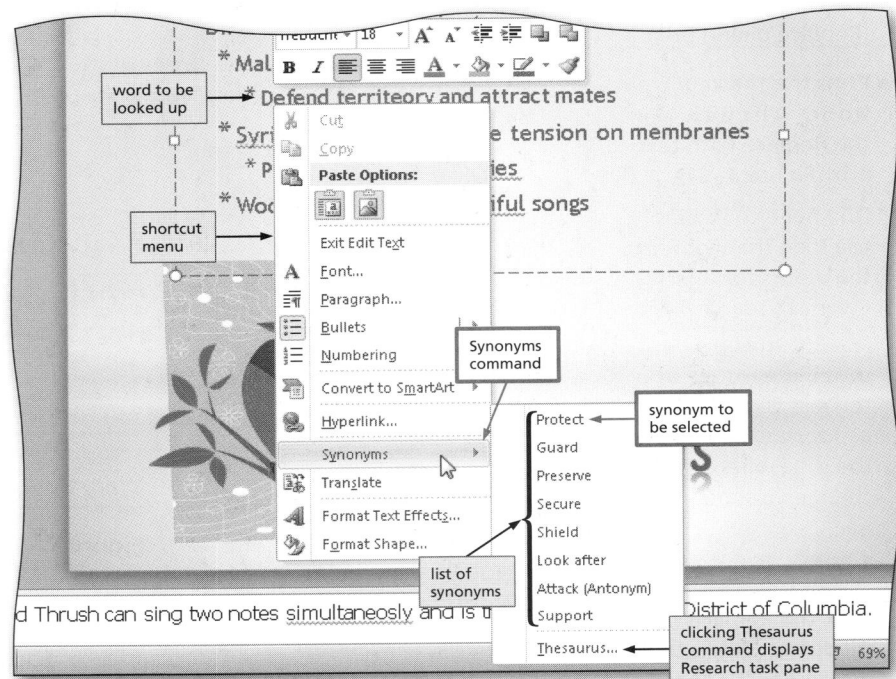

Figure 3–63

2
- Click the synonym you want (Protect) on the Synonyms submenu to replace the word, Defend, in the presentation with the word, Protect (Figure 3–64).

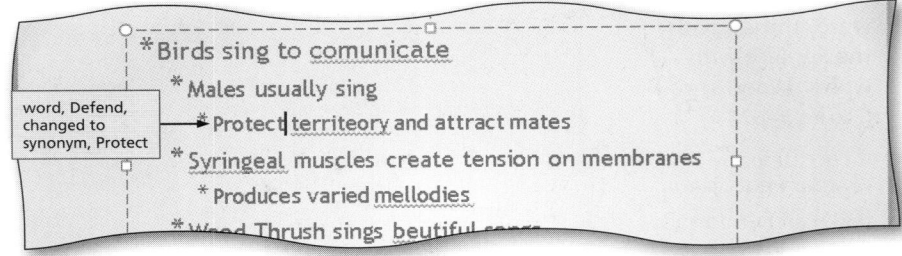

Figure 3–64

Q&A What if a suitable word does not display in the Synonyms submenu?

You can display the thesaurus in the Research task pane by clicking Thesaurus on the Synonyms submenu. A complete thesaurus with synonyms displays in the Research task pane along with an **antonym**, which is a word with an opposite meaning.

BTW
Foreign Language Synonyms
The thesaurus contains synonyms for languages other than English. To look up words in the thesaurus of another language, click the Thesaurus button (Review tab | Proofing group), click Research options (Research task pane), select the desired languages in the Reference Books area, and then click the OK button.

Other Ways
1. Click Thesaurus (Review tab | Proofing group)
2. Press SHIFT+F7

To Add Notes

As you create slides, you may find material you want to state verbally and do not want to include on the slide. You can type and format notes in the **Notes pane** as you work in Normal view and then print this information as **notes pages**. After adding comments, you can print a set of speaker notes. These notes will print below a small image of the slide. Charts, tables, and pictures added to the Notes pane also print on these pages. In this project, comments were included on Slide 2 when you opened that file. The following steps add text to the Notes pane on Slides 1 and 3.

1

- Display Slide 1, click the Notes pane, and then type **More than 10,000 species of birds exist in the world. The largest bird is the ostrich, and the smallest is the hummingbird. They generally live in small groups, but some form huge flocks with**

Figure 3–65

thousands of members and a variety of species. Flocks help keep the birds safe while they search for food. (Figure 3–65).

Q&A

What if I cannot see all the lines I typed?

You can drag the splitter bar up to enlarge the Notes pane. Clicking the Notes pane scroll arrows allows you to view the entire text.

2

- Display Slide 3, click the Notes pane, and then type **Birds migrate to benefit from warm weather. Some can fly more than 6,000 miles without stopping. We can help bird migration by providing food, shelters, nest sites, and water.** (Figure 3–66).

Figure 3–66

BTW

Using AutoCorrect Features
Microsoft Office programs use the AutoCorrect feature to correct typing mistakes and commonly misspelled words. When you install Microsoft Office, a default list of typical misspellings is created. To view this list, click File on the Ribbon to open the Backstage view, under Help click Options, click Proofing in left pane (PowerPoint Options dialog box), and then click the AutoCorrect Options button. If necessary, click the AutoCorrect tab (AutoCorrect dialog box). The first column of this list contains the word that you often mistype, and the second column contains the replacement text. You can modify the AutoCorrect list with words you are apt to misspell. The AutoCorrect feature also inserts symbols, such as replacing (c) with the copyright symbol, ©.

Checking Spelling

After you create a presentation, you should check it visually for spelling errors and style consistency. In addition, you use PowerPoint's Spelling tool to identify possible misspellings on the slides and in the notes. Do not rely on the spelling checker to catch all your mistakes. Although PowerPoint's spelling checker is a valuable tool, it is not infallible. You should proofread your presentation carefully by pointing to each word and saying it aloud as you point to it. Be mindful of commonly misused words such as its and it's, through and though, and to and too.

PowerPoint checks the entire presentation for spelling mistakes using a standard dictionary contained in the Microsoft Office group. This dictionary is shared with the other Microsoft Office applications such as Word and Excel. A **custom dictionary** is available if you want to add special words such as proper names, cities, and acronyms. When checking a presentation for spelling errors, PowerPoint opens the standard dictionary and the custom dictionary file, if one exists. When a word appears in the Spelling dialog box, you can perform one of several actions, as described in Table 3–1.

Table 3–1 Spelling Dialog Box Buttons and Actions

Button Name	When To Use	Action
Ignore	Word is spelled correctly but not found in dictionaries	PowerPoint continues checking rest of the presentation but will flag that word again if it appears later in document.
Ignore All	Word is spelled correctly but not found in dictionaries	PowerPoint ignores all occurrences of the word and continues checking rest of presentation.
Change	Word is misspelled	Click proper spelling of the word in Suggestions list. PowerPoint corrects word, continues checking rest of presentation, but will flag that word again if it appears later in document.
Change All	Word is misspelled	Click proper spelling of word in Suggestions list. PowerPoint changes all occurrences of misspelled word and continues checking rest of presentation.
Add	Add word to custom dictionary	PowerPoint opens custom dictionary, adds word, and continues checking rest of presentation.
Suggest	Correct spelling is uncertain	Lists alternative spellings. Click the correct word from the Suggestions box or type the proper spelling. Corrects the word and continues checking the rest of the presentation.
AutoCorrect	Add spelling error to AutoCorrect list	PowerPoint adds spelling error and its correction to AutoCorrect list. Any future misspelling of word is corrected automatically as you type.
Close	Stop spelling checker	PowerPoint closes spelling checker and returns to PowerPoint window.

The standard dictionary contains commonly used English words. It does not, however, contain many proper names, abbreviations, technical terms, poetic contractions, or antiquated terms. PowerPoint treats words not found in the dictionaries as misspellings.

To Check Spelling

The following steps check the spelling on all slides in the Bird Migration presentation.

1

• Click Review on the Ribbon to display the Review tab.

• Click the Spelling button (Review Tab | Proofing group) to start the spelling checker and display the Spelling dialog box (Figure 3–67).

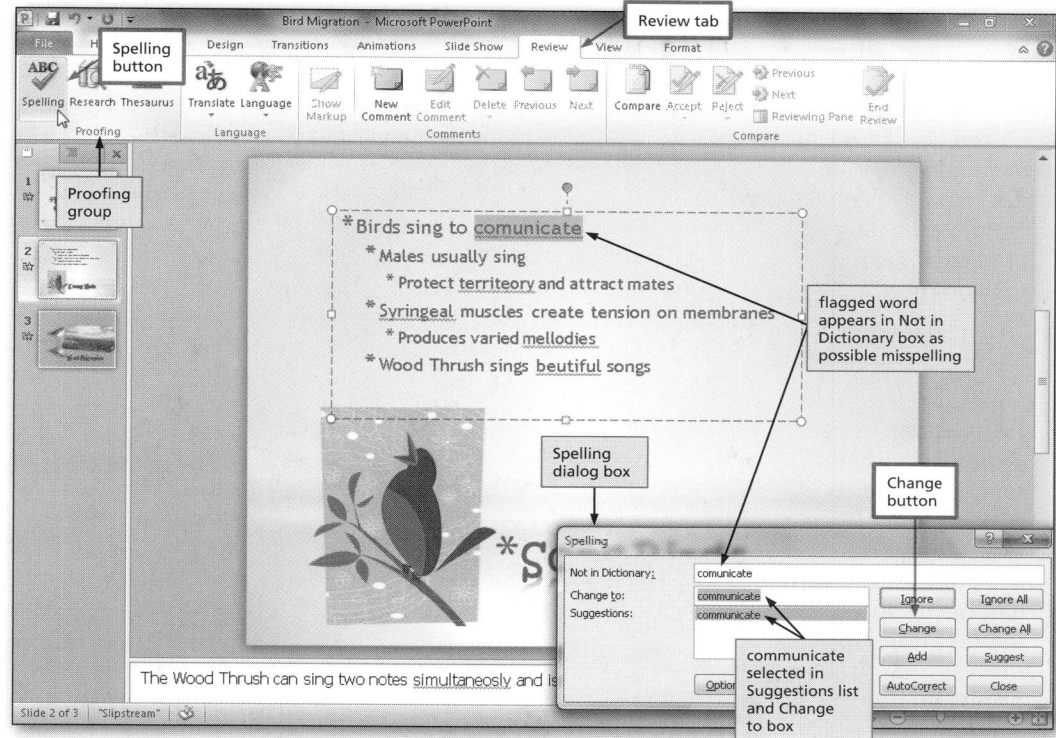

Figure 3–67

2

• With the word, communicate, selected in the Suggestions list, click the Change button (Spelling dialog box) to replace the misspelled flagged word, comunicate, with the selected correctly spelled word, communicate, and then continue the spelling check (Figure 3–68).

Q&A Could I have clicked the Change All button instead of the Change button?

Yes. When you click the Change All button, you change the current and future occurrences of the misspelled word.

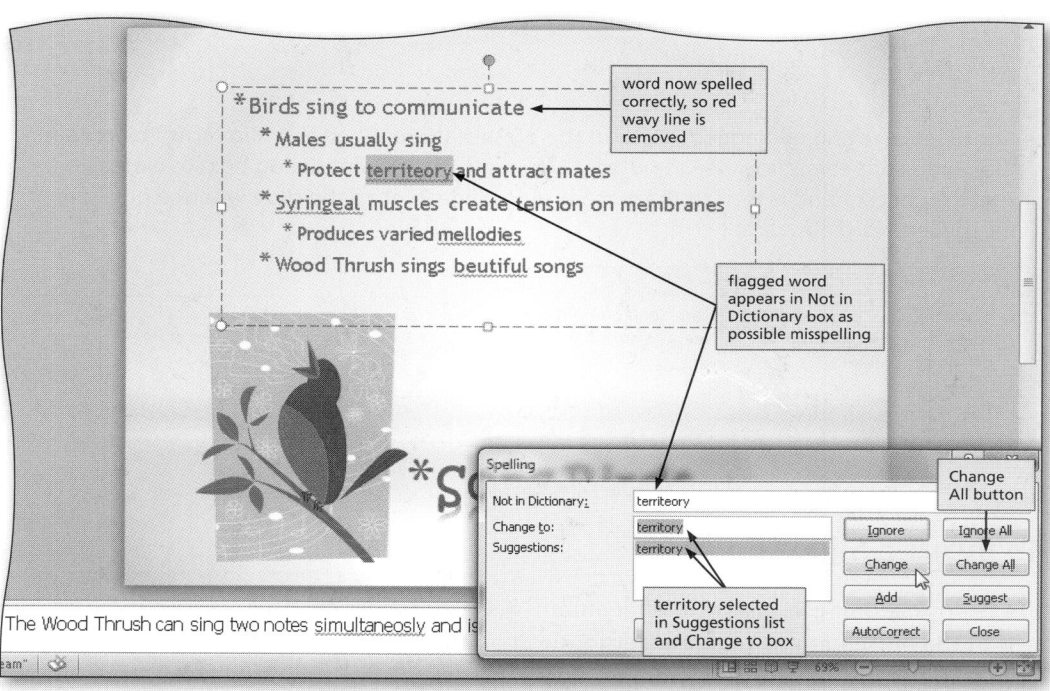

Figure 3–68

The misspelled word, comunicate, appears only once in the presentation, so clicking the Change or the Change All button in this instance produces identical results.

3

- Replace the misspelled word, territeory, with the word, territory (Figure 3–69).

- When the word, Syringeal, is flagged, click the Ignore button (Spelling dialog box) to skip the correctly spelled word, Syringeal, and then continue the spelling check.

Q&A Syringeal is flagged as a possible misspelled word. Why?

Your custom dictionary does not contain the word, so it is recognized as spelled incorrectly. You can add this word to a custom dictionary to prevent the spelling checker from flagging it as a mistake.

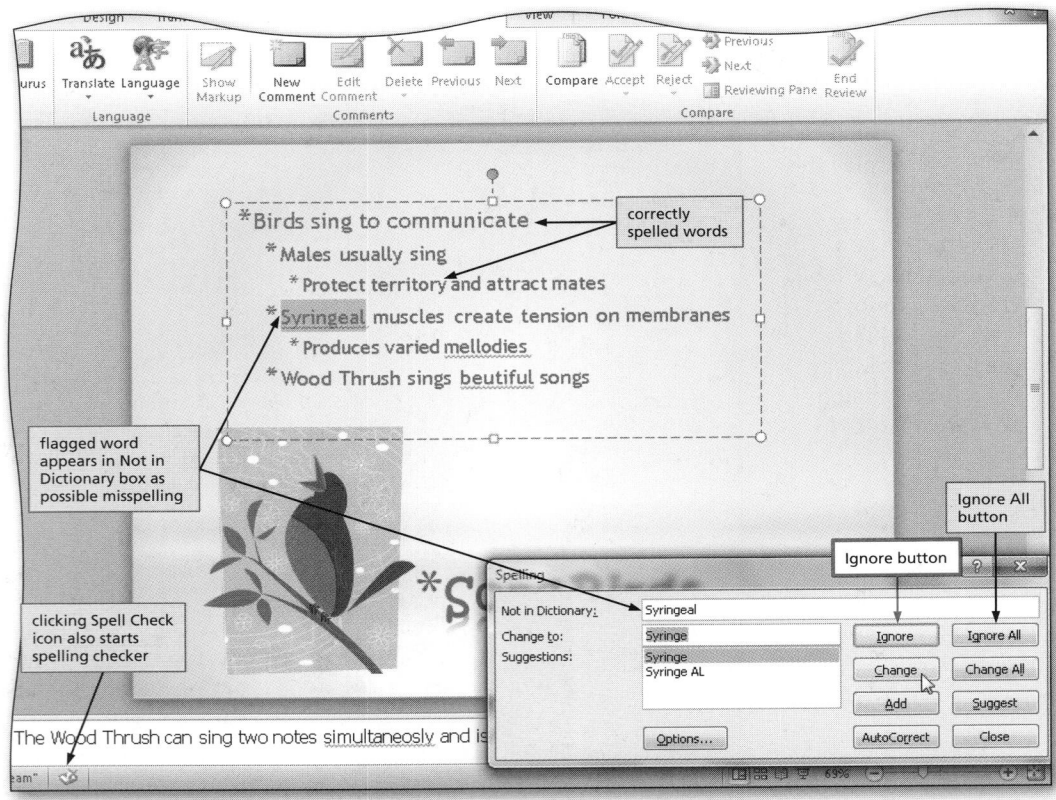

Figure 3–69

Q&A Could I have clicked the Ignore All button instead of the Ignore button?

Yes. When you click the Ignore All button, you ignore the current and future occurrences of the word.

4

- Continue checking all flagged words in the presentation. When the Microsoft PowerPoint dialog box appears, click the OK button (Microsoft PowerPoint dialog box) to close the spelling checker and return to the current slide, Slide 2, or to the slide where a possible misspelled word appeared.

Other Ways	
1. Click Spell Check icon on status bar, click Spelling on shortcut menu	click Spelling on shortcut menu
2. Right-click flagged word, click correct word or	3. Press F7

To Insert a Slide Number

PowerPoint can insert the slide number on your slides automatically to indicate where the slide is positioned within the presentation. The number location on the slide is determined by the presentation theme. You have the option to not display this slide number on the title slide. The following steps insert the slide number on all slides except the title slide.

1

- If a word in the Notes pane is selected, click the Slide 2 Slide pane. Display the Insert tab and then click the Insert Slide Number button (Insert tab | Text group) to display the Header and Footer dialog box (Figure 3–70).

Q&A Why did I need to click the Slide pane?

The page number would have been inserted in the Notes pane instead of on the slide.

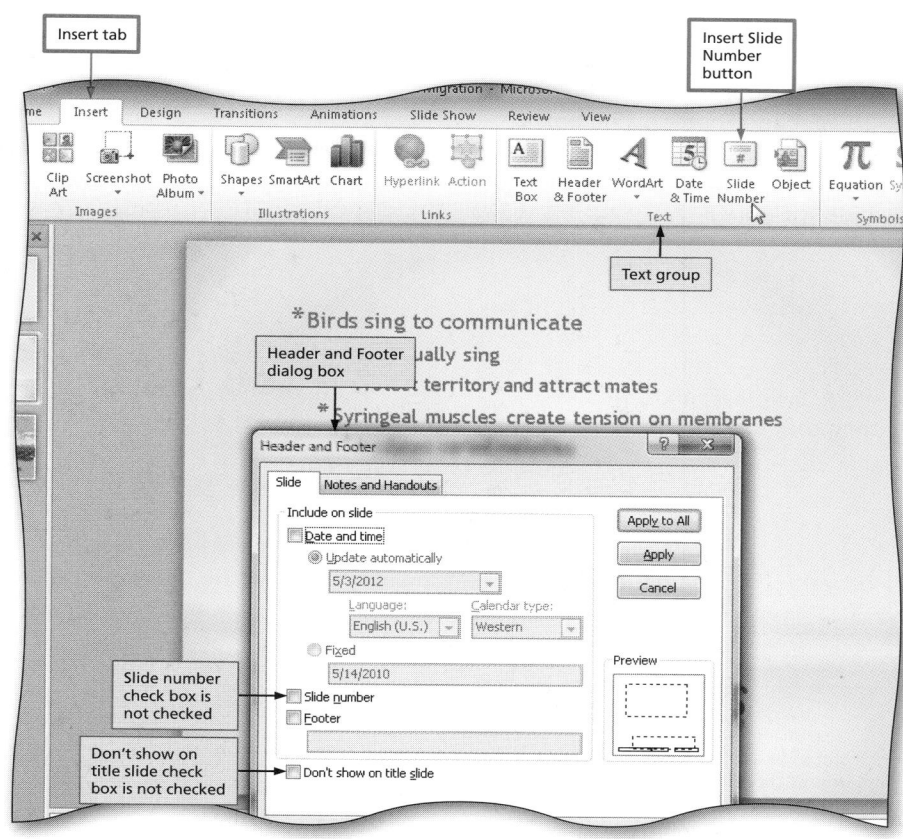

Figure 3–70

2

- Click the Slide number check box (Header and Footer dialog box) to place a check mark in it.

- Click the 'Don't show on title slide' check box (Header and Footer dialog box) to place a check mark in it (Figure 3–71).

Q&A Where does the slide number display on the slide?

Each theme determines where the slide number is displayed in the footer. In the Slipstream theme, the slide number location is the center of the footer, as indicated by the black box at the bottom of the Preview area.

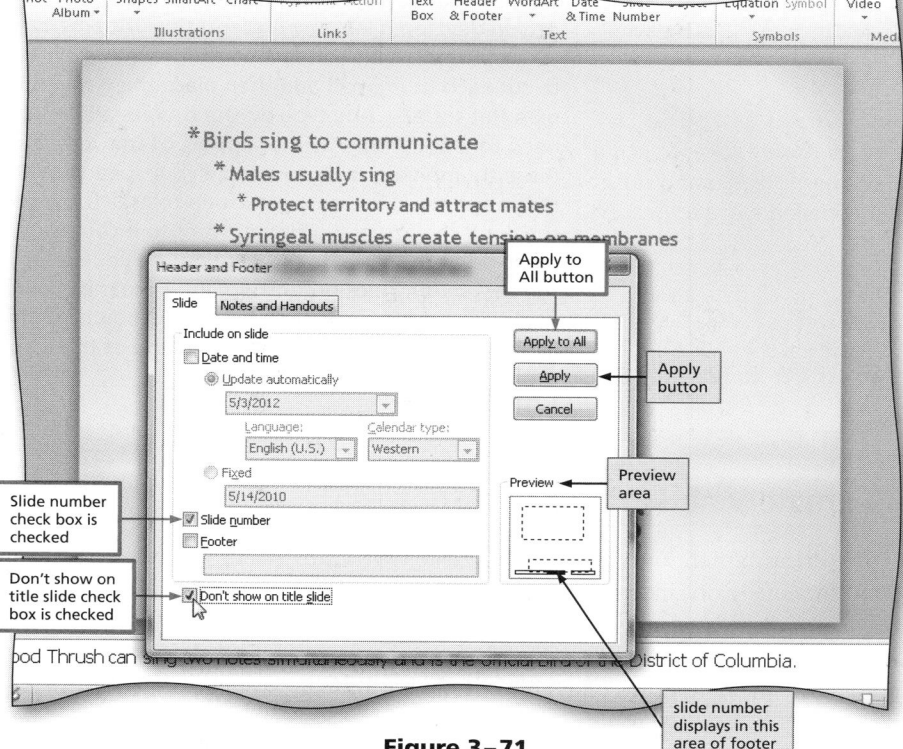

Figure 3–71

• Click the Apply to All button (Header and Footer dialog box) to close the dialog box and insert the slide number on all slides except Slide 1 (Figure 3–72).

Figure 3–72

Q&A

How does clicking the Apply to All button differ from clicking the Apply button?

The Apply button inserts the slide number only on the currently displayed slide whereas the Apply to All button inserts the slide number on every slide.

Other Ways

1. Click Header & Footer button (Insert tab | Text group), click Slide Number box (Header and Footer dialog box), click 'Slide number' and 'Don't show on title slide' boxes, click Apply to All button

Plan Ahead

Use handouts to organize your speech.

As you develop a lengthy presentation with many visuals, handouts may help you organize your material. Print handouts with the maximum number of slides per page. Use scissors to cut each thumbnail and then place these miniature slide images adjacent to each other on a flat surface. Any type on the thumbnails will be too small to read, so the images will need to work with only the support of the verbal message you provide. You can rearrange these thumbnails as you organize your speech. When you return to your computer, you can rearrange the slides on your screen to match the order of your thumbnail printouts. Begin speaking the actual words you want to incorporate in the body of the talk. This process of glancing at the thumbnails and hearing yourself say the key ideas of the speech is one of the best methods of organizing and preparing for the actual presentation. Ultimately, when you deliver your speech in front of an audience, the images on the slides or on your note cards should be sufficient to remind you of the accompanying verbal message.

To Preview and Print a Handout

Printing handouts is useful for reviewing a presentation because you can analyze several slides displayed simultaneously on one page. Additionally, many businesses distribute handouts of the slide show before or after a presentation so attendees can refer to a copy. Each page of the handout can contain reduced images of one, two, three, four, six, or nine slides. The three-slides-per-page handout includes lines beside each slide so that your audience can write notes conveniently. The following steps preview and print a presentation handout.

1

- Click File on the Ribbon to open the Backstage view and then click the Print tab to display Slide 2 in the Print gallery.

- Click Full Page Slides in the Settings area to display the Full Page Slides gallery (Figure 3–73).

Q&A Why does the preview of my slide appear in color?

Your printer determines how the preview appears. If your printer is not capable of printing color images, the preview will not appear in color.

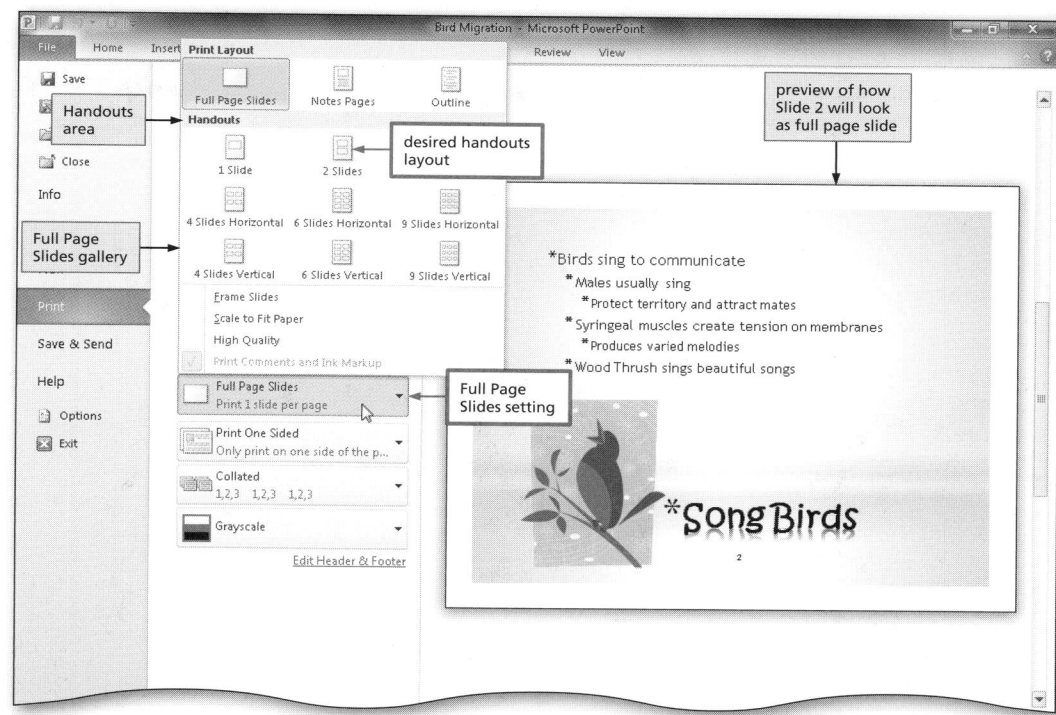

Figure 3–73

2

- Click 2 Slides in the Handouts area to select this option and display a preview of the handout (Figure 3–74).

Q&A The current date displays in the upper-right corner of the handout, and the page number displays in the lower-right corner of the footer. Can I change their location or add other information to the header and footer?

Yes. Click the Edit Header & Footer link at the bottom of the Print gallery, click the Notes and Handouts tab (Header and Footer dialog box), and then decide what content to include on the handout page.

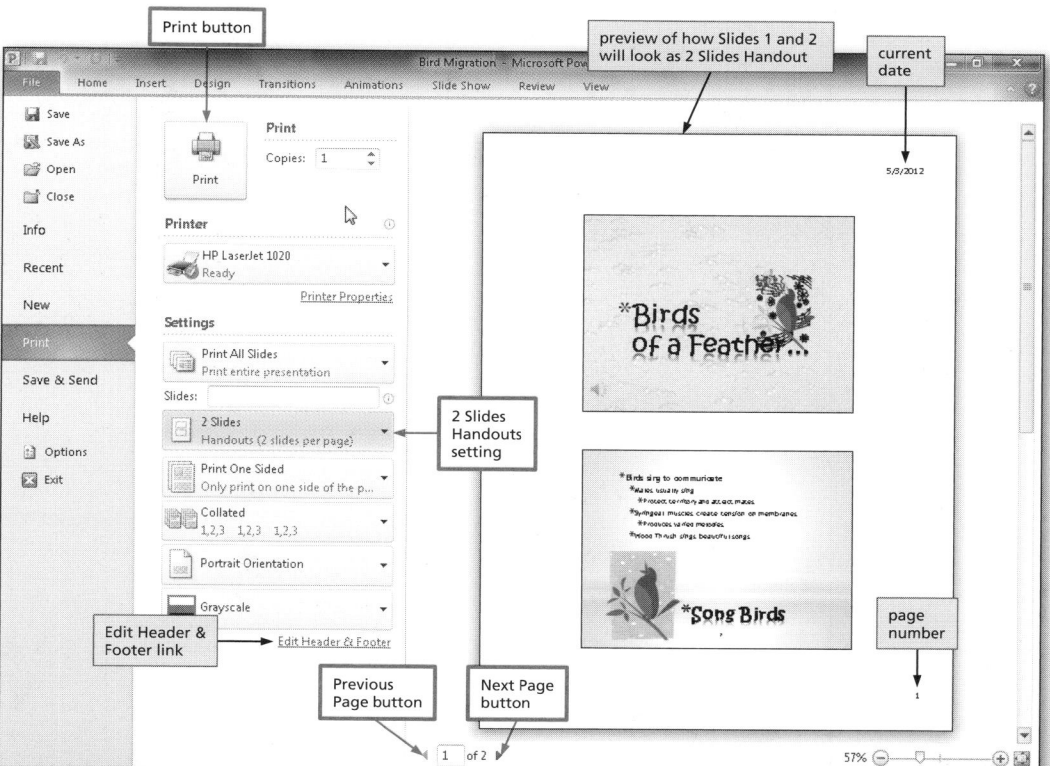

Figure 3–74

● Click the Next Page and Previous Page buttons to display previews of the two pages in the presentation.

● Click the Print button in the Print gallery to print the handout.

● When the printer stops, retrieve the printed handout (Figure 3–75).

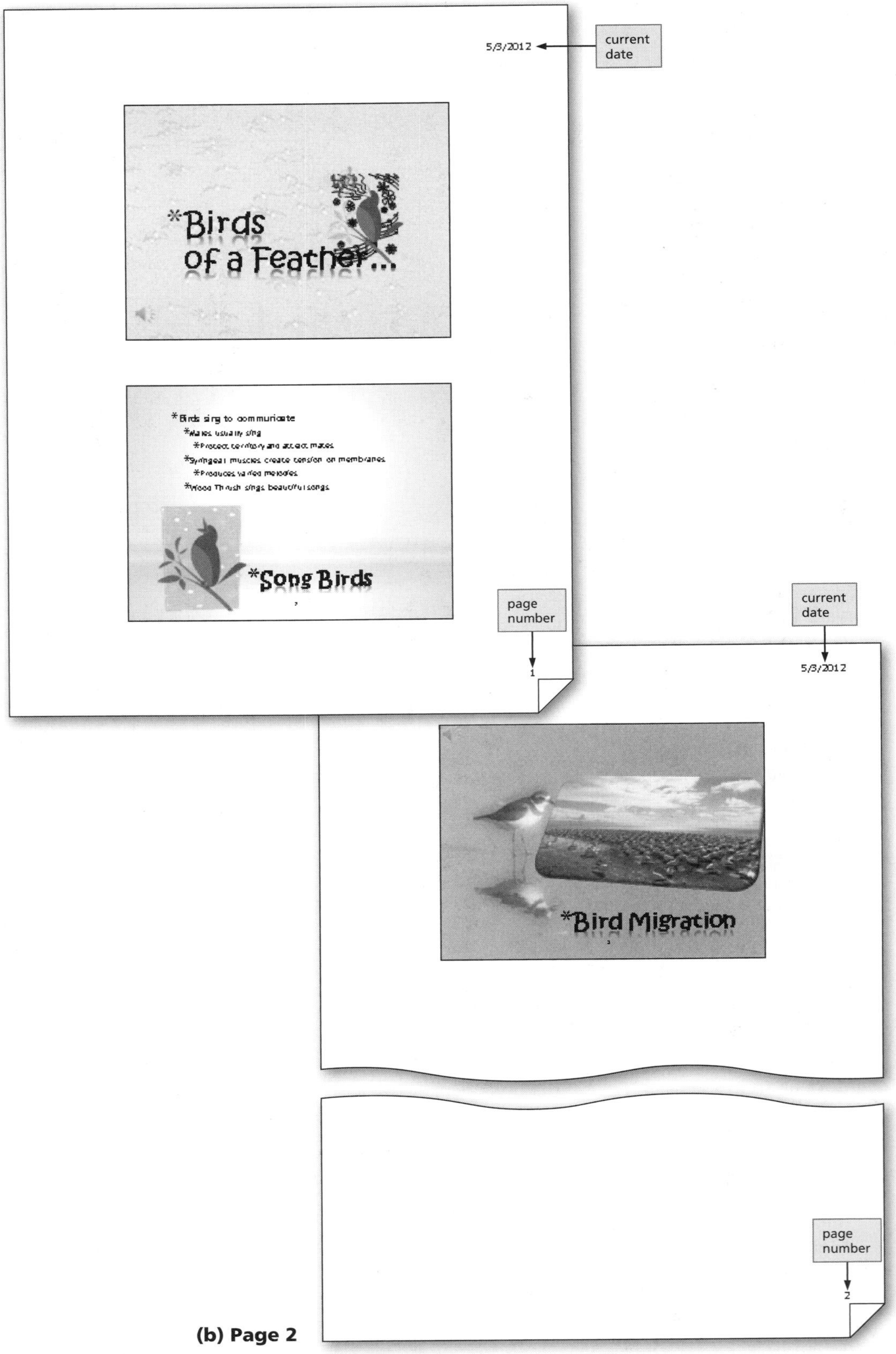

5/3/2012 ◄———— current date

*Birds of a Feather...

*Birds sing to communicate
  *Males usually sing
    *Protect territory and attract mates
  *Syringeal muscles create tension on membranes
    *Produces varied melodies
  *Wood Thrush sings beautiful songs

*Song Birds

page number

1

(a) Page 1

current date

5/3/2012

*Bird Migration

page number

2

(b) Page 2

Figure 3–75

To Print Speaker Notes

Comments added to slides in the Notes pane give the speaker information that supplements the text on the slide. They will print with a small image at the top and the comments below the slide. The following steps print the speaker notes.

1

• Click the Print tab in the Backstage view and then click 2 Slides in the Settings area to display the gallery (Figure 3–76).

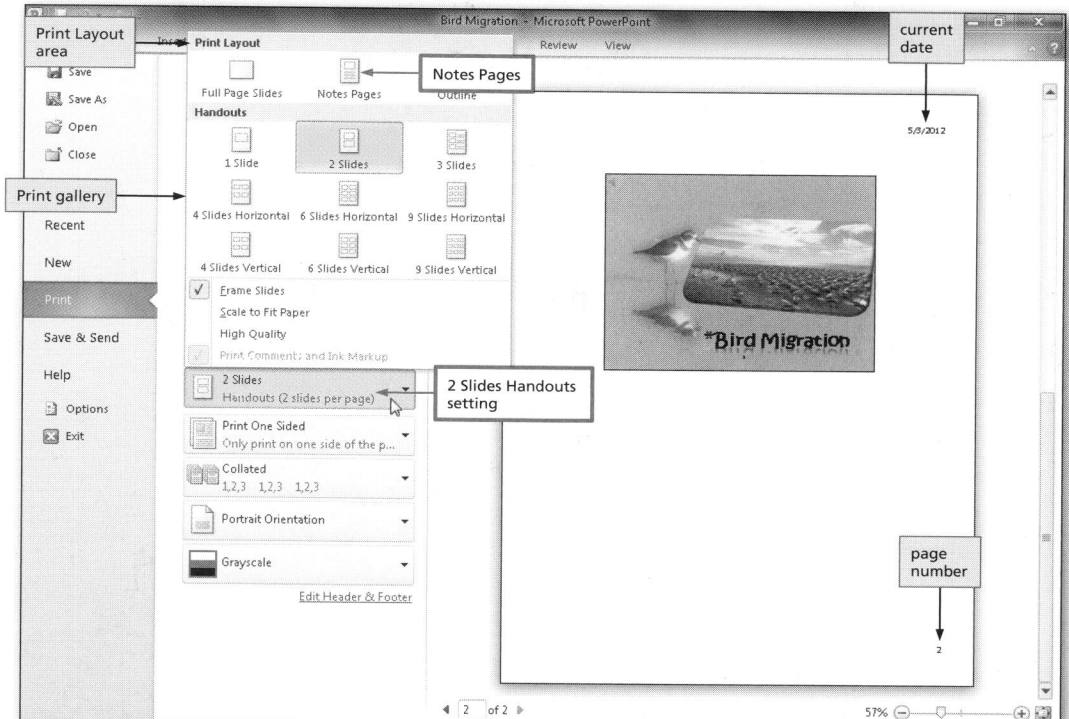

Figure 3–76

2

• Click Notes Pages in the Print Layout area to select this option and display a preview of the current page (Figure 3–77).

• Click the Previous Page and Next Page buttons to display previews of other pages in the presentation.

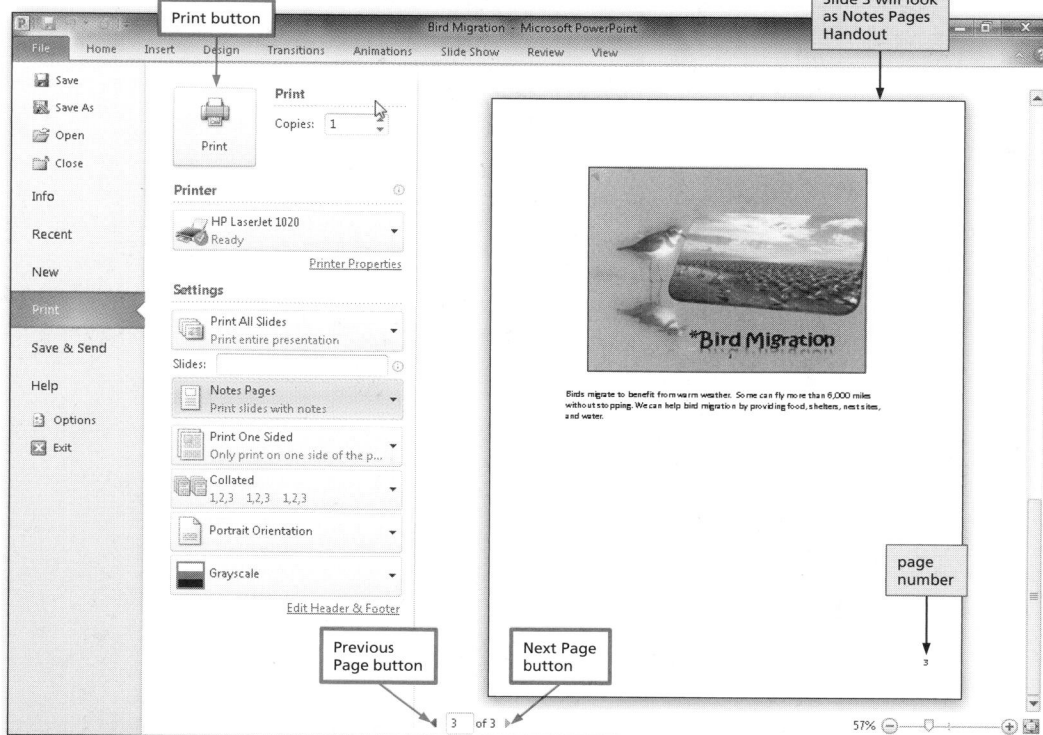

Figure 3–77

3

- Click the Print button in the Print gallery to print the notes.

- When the printer stops, retrieve the printed pages (Figure 3–78).

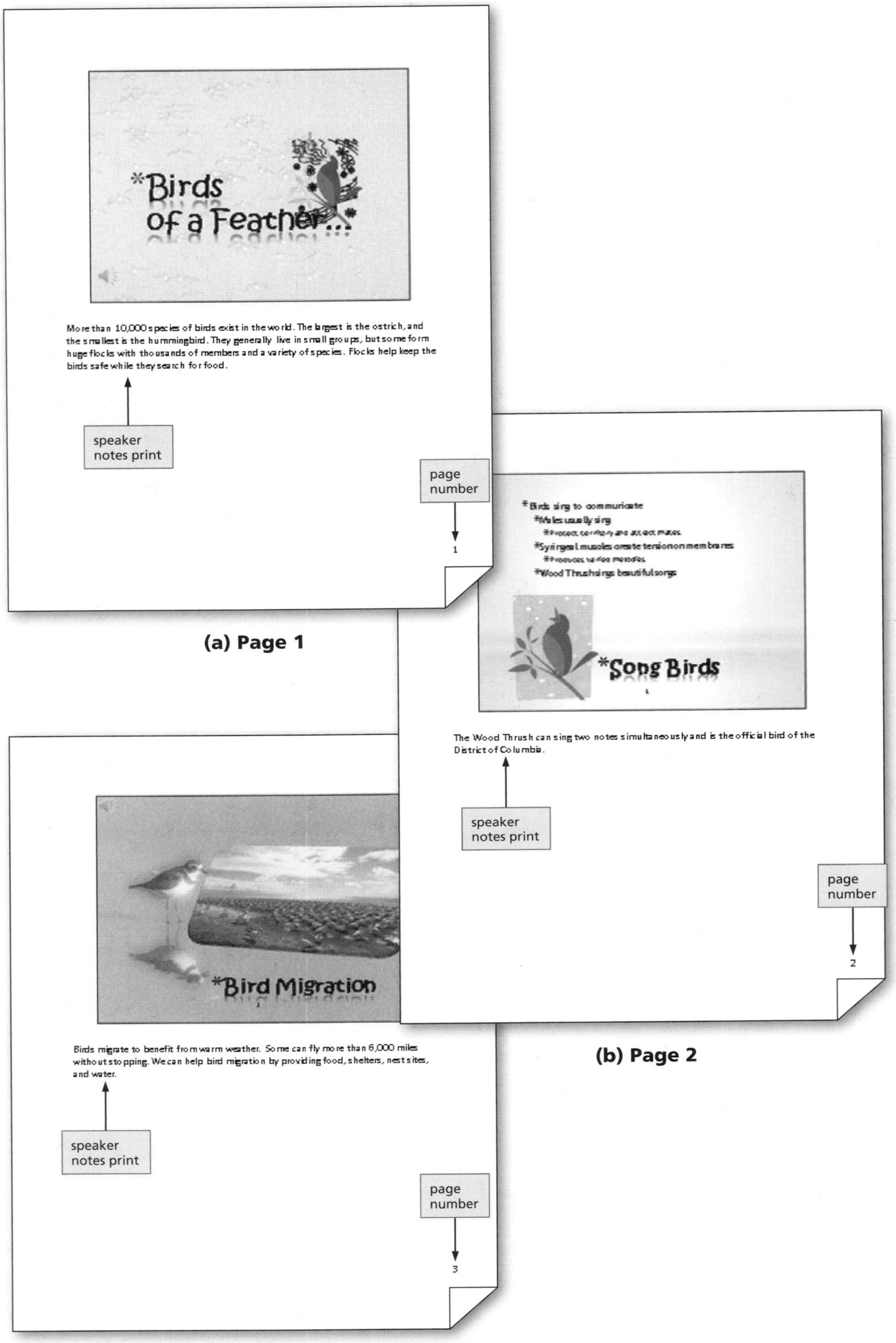

*Birds of a Feather...

More than 10,000 species of birds exist in the world. The largest is the ostrich, and the smallest is the hummingbird. They generally live in small groups, but some form huge flocks with thousands of members and a variety of species. Flocks help keep the birds safe while they search for food.

speaker notes print

page number

1

(a) Page 1

*Birds sing to communicate
  *Males usually sing
    *Protect territory and attract mates
  *Syringeal muscles create tension on membranes
    *Produces varied melodies
  *Wood Thrush sings beautiful songs

*Song Birds

The Wood Thrush can sing two notes simultaneously and is the official bird of the District of Columbia.

speaker notes print

page number

2

(b) Page 2

*Bird Migration

Birds migrate to benefit from warm weather. Some can fly more than 6,000 miles without stopping. We can help bird migration by providing food, shelters, nest sites, and water.

speaker notes print

page number

3

(c) Page 3

Figure 3–78

Plan
Ahead

Evaluate your presentation.
One of the best methods of improving your communication skills is to focus on what you learned from the experience. Respond to these questions:

- How successfully do you feel you fulfilled your assignment?
- What strategies did you use to develop your slides and the accompanying oral presentation?
- What revisions did you make?
- If you could go back to the speaking engagement and change one thing, what would it be?
- What feedback did you receive from your instructor or audience?

To Change Document Properties

Before saving the presentation again, you want to add your name, class name, and some keywords as document properties. The following steps use the Document Information Panel to change document properties.

1 In the Backstage view, click the Properties button in the right pane of the Info gallery, and then click Show Document Panel on the Properties menu to close the Backstage view and display the Document Information Panel.

2 Enter your name in the Author text box. Enter your course and section in the Subject text box. Enter the text, **bird, migration, singing** in the Keywords text box.

3 Close the Document Information Panel.

4 Click the Save button on the Quick Access Toolbar to overwrite the previous Bird Migration file on the USB flash drive.

BTW Quick Reference
For a table that lists how to complete the tasks covered in this book using the mouse, Ribbon, shortcut menu, and keyboard, see the Quick Reference Summary at the back of this book, or visit the PowerPoint 2010 Quick Reference Web page (scsite.com/ppt2010/qr).

To Run a Slide Show with Media

All changes are complete, and the presentation is saved. You now can view the Bird Migration presentation. The following steps start Slide Show view.

1 Click the Slide 1 thumbnail in the Slide pane to select and display Slide 1.

2 Click the Slide Show button to display the title slide, watch the animations, and listen to the bird calls. Allow the audio clip to repeat several times.

3 Press the SPACEBAR to display Slide 2.

4 Press the SPACEBAR to display Slide 3. Listen to the audio clip, watch the video clip, and then allow the audio clip to repeat several times.

5 Press the SPACEBAR to end the slide show and click to exit the slide show.

BTW Certification
The Microsoft Office Specialist (MOS) program provides an opportunity for you to obtain a valuable industry credential — proof that you have the PowerPoint 2010 skills required by employers. For more information, visit the PowerPoint 2010 Certification Web page (scsite.com/ppt2010/cert).

To Quit PowerPoint

This project is complete. The following steps quit PowerPoint.

1 Click the Close button on the right side of the title bar to close the document and then quit PowerPoint.

2 If a Microsoft PowerPoint dialog box appears, click the Save button to save any changes made to the presentation since the last save.

Chapter Summary

In this chapter you have learned how to enhance an existing presentation by adding video, audio, and pictures with effects. You also learned to modify placeholders, align text, and review a presentation by checking spelling and creating handouts. The items listed below include all the new PowerPoint skills you have learned in this chapter.

1. Color a Picture (PPT 143)
2. Add an Artistic Effect to a Picture (144)
3. Change the Stacking Order (PPT 146)
4. Resize a Placeholder (PPT 148)
5. Move a Placeholder (PPT 148)
6. Delete a Placeholder (PPT 149)
7. Align Paragraph Text (PPT 150)
8. Delete a Slide (PPT 152)
9. Change Views (PPT 153)
10. Copy a Clip from One Slide to Another (PPT 155)
11. Zoom a Slide (PPT 156)
12. Ungroup a Clip (PPT 157)
13. Change the Color of a Clip Object (PPT 158)
14. Delete a Clip Object (PPT 161)
15. Regroup Objects (PPT 162)
16. Insert a Video File (PPT 163)
17. Trim a Video File (PPT 164)
18. Add Video Options (PPT 166)
19. Insert an Audio File (PPT 167)
20. Add Audio Options (PPT 170)
21. Add a Video Style (PPT 172)
22. Resize a Video (PPT 174)
23. Insert a Movie Clip (PPT 174)
24. Find and Replace Text (PPT 176)
25. Find and Insert a Synonym (PPT 178)
26. Add Notes (PPT 179)
27. Check Spelling (PPT 181)
28. Insert a Slide Number (PPT 182)
29. Preview and Print a Handout (PPT 184)
30. Print Speaker Notes (PPT 187)

If you have a SAM 2010 user profile, your instructor may have assigned an autogradable version of this assignment. If so, log into the SAM 2010 Web site at www.cengage.com/sam2010 to download the instruction and start files.

Learn It Online

Test your knowledge of chapter content and key terms.

Instructions: To complete the Learn It Online exercises, start your browser, click the Address bar, and then enter the Web address **scsite.com/ppt2010/learn**. When the PowerPoint 2010 Learn It Online page is displayed, click the link for the exercise you want to complete and then read the instructions.

Chapter Reinforcement TF, MC, and SA
A series of true/false, multiple choice, and short answer questions that test your knowledge of the chapter content.

Flash Cards
An interactive learning environment where you identify chapter key terms associated with displayed definitions.

Practice Test
A series of multiple choice questions that test your knowledge of chapter content and key terms.

Who Wants To Be a Computer Genius?
An interactive game that challenges your knowledge of chapter content in the style of a television quiz show.

Wheel of Terms
An interactive game that challenges your knowledge of chapter key terms in the style of the television show *Wheel of Fortune*.

Crossword Puzzle Challenge
A crossword puzzle that challenges your knowledge of key terms presented in the chapter.

Apply Your Knowledge

Reinforce the skills and apply the concepts you learned in this chapter.

Adding Artistic Effects to Pictures, Moving a Placeholder, and Inserting and Controlling Audio Clips

Note: To complete this assignment, you will be required to use the Data Files for Students. See the inside back cover of this book for instructions on downloading the Data Files for Students, or contact your instructor for information about accessing the required files.

Instructions: Start PowerPoint. Open the presentation, Apply 3-1 SAD, from the Data Files for Students.
The five slides in the presentation, shown in Figure 3–79, present information about Seasonal Affective Disorder, also known as SAD, which is a mood disorder that occurs generally during the winter months. The document you open is composed of slides containing pictures and clip art, and you will apply artistic effects or modify some of these graphic elements. You also will insert audio clips from Office.com. In addition, you will move the placeholder on the final slide.

Perform the following tasks:

1. Insert the audio clip, Sad Piano Music, into Slide 1 (Figure 3–79a). Change the volume to Medium, start the clip automatically, and hide the sound icon during the slide show. Then copy this audio clip to Slides 2, 3, and 4 with the same options. Insert the audio clip, Variety Hour, into Slide 5, change the volume to Medium, start the clip automatically, and hide the sound icon during the slide show.

2. On Slide 2, color the picture by selecting Yellow, Accent color 2 Dark from the Recolor area, as shown in Figure 3–79b.

3. On Slide 3, apply the Watercolor Sponge artistic effect to the picture, as shown in Figure 3–79c.

4. On Slide 4, select the lamp clip and then change the Zoom level to 120%. Ungroup the lamp clip and then recolor the arms to Dark Teal, Text 2, Lighter 10% (last color in fourth Theme Colors column), as shown in Figure 3–79d. Regroup the clip. Change the Zoom level to 69%.

5. On Slide 5, move the WordArt placeholder above the bird in the picture, as shown in Figure 3–79e.

6. On Slide 1, type **Up to 9 percent of U.S. adults may suffer from SAD.** in the Notes pane.

7. Check the slides for spelling errors and then run the revised presentation.

8. Change the document properties, as specified by your instructor. Save the presentation using the file name, Apply 3-1 Seasonal Affective Disorder.

9. Submit the revised document in the format specified by your instructor.

(a) Slide 1

(b) Slide 2

Figure 3–79

Continued >

STUDENT ASSIGNMENTS

Apply Your Knowledge *continued*

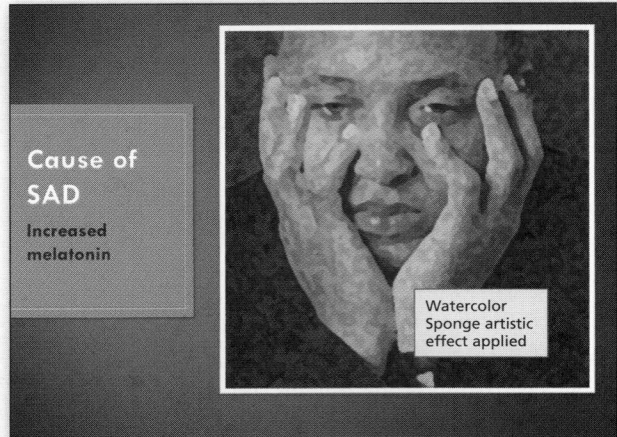

(c) Slide 3

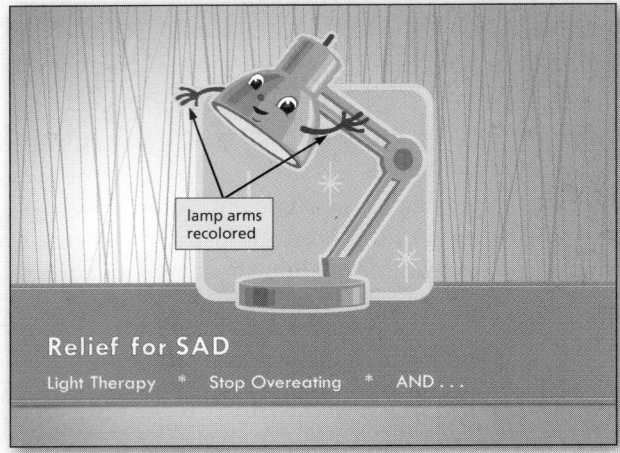

(d) Slide 4

(e) Slide 5

Figure 3–79 (Continued)

Extend Your Knowledge

Extend the skills you learned in this chapter and experiment with new skills. You may need to use Help to complete the assignment.

Formatting a Video Border, Deleting Audio, Adding a Font Effect, and Pausing and Resuming Video Playback

Note: To complete this assignment, you will be required to use the Data Files for Students. See the inside back cover of this book for instructions on downloading the Data Files for Students, or contact your instructor for information about accessing the required files.

Instructions: Start PowerPoint. Open the presentation, Extend 3-1 Nature, from the Data Files for Students. You will add the Small Caps font effect to the title text on the title slide, delete an audio clip, and format a video border, as shown in Figure 3–80a. While the slide show is running, you will adjust the video playback to pause and then resume playing the clip.

Perform the following tasks:

1. On Slide 1, move the title text placeholder up so that it is positioned in the upper-right corner of the slide, as shown in Figure 3–80a. Right-align the title text and then add the Small Caps font effect to these letters. *Hint:* Font effects are located in the Font dialog box (Home tab | Font group).

2. On the title slide, delete the audio clip positioned in the upper-left corner of the slide. The three audio clips on the right side of the slide will remain.

3. Change the video style from Soft Edge Oval to Beveled Oval, Black (in the Moderate area). Then change the video border color to Gold, Accent 2 and change the border weight to 10 pt. *Hint:* Click More Lines in the Video Border Weight gallery and then change the Border Style Width.

4. On Slide 2, add a border to each of the six pictures that surround the center deer video frame, and then change the border colors and the border weights. Use Figure 3–80b as a guide. Add the Compound Frame, Black video style (in the Moderate area) to the bird feeder clip.

5. Change the document properties, as specified by your instructor. Save the presentation using the file name, Extend 3-1 Observing Nature.

6. Start the slide show. When a few seconds of the video have elapsed, pause the video and then move your mouse pointer to an area other than the video and listen to the bird audio clips. Then move the mouse pointer over the video clip to display the Video Controls. Resume the video playback.

7. Submit the revised document in the format specified by your instructor.

(a) Slide 1

(b) Slide 2

Figure 3–80

Make It Right

Analyze a presentation and correct all errors and/or improve the design.

Editing Clips, Finding and Replacing Text, and Correcting Spelling

Note: To complete this assignment, you will be required to use the Data Files for Students. See the inside back cover of this book for instructions on downloading the Data Files for Students, or contact your instructor for information about accessing the required files.

Instructions: Start PowerPoint. Open the presentation, Make It Right 3-1 Flamingos, from the Data Files for Students.

Correct the formatting problems and errors in the presentation while keeping in mind the guidelines presented in this chapter.

Perform the following tasks:

1. On Slide 1 (Figure 3–81), change the audio clip volume to High and hide the sound icon during the show. Loop this clip for the duration of the slide show.

2. On Slide 2, add the Reflection video effect located in the Reflection Variations area, Tight Reflection 4 pt offset (first reflection in second row) to the video.

3. Trim the Slide 2 video so that the Start Time is 00:21.087 and the End Time is 01:44.273. The duration should be 01:23.186 minutes.

4. Copy the flamingo clip from Slide 4 to Slide 3 and then delete Slide 4. Place this clip on the left side of the picture frame and then adjust the picture frame size so it is the appropriate dimension for the slide content. Ungroup the flamingo clip and then recolor the flamingo to match the color of its legs, the palm tree leaves to a shade of green, and the bird to a shade of blue. Regroup the clip.

5. Find the word, Antarctica, in the Slide 1 Notes pane, and then replace it with the words, South America. Then find the number, 14, and replace it with the number, 4.

6. Check the slides for spelling errors and then run the revised presentation.

7. Change the document properties, as specified by your instructor. Save the presentation using the file name, Make It Right 3-1 Chilean Flamingos.

8. Submit the revised document in the format specified by your instructor.

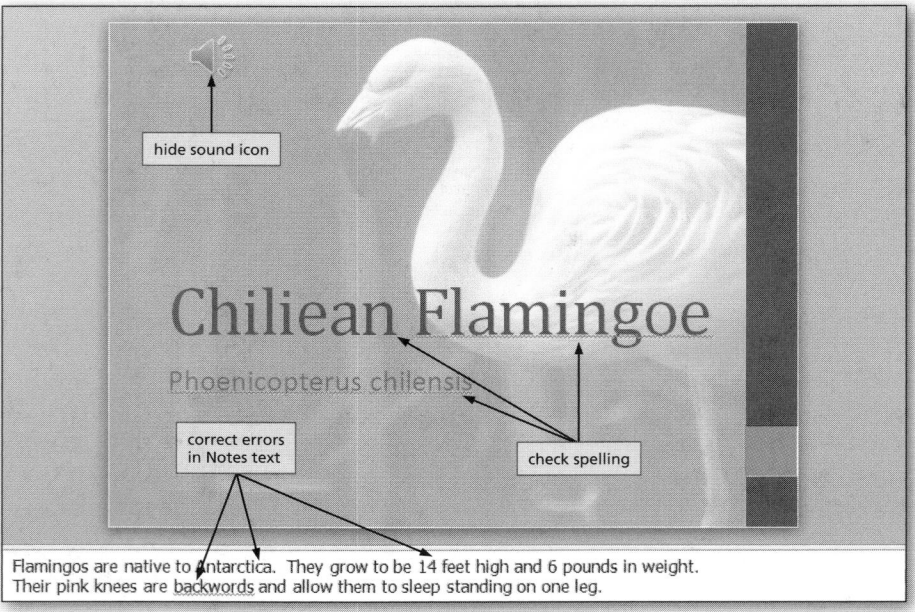

Figure 3–81

In the Lab

Design and/or create a presentation using the guidelines, concepts, and skills presented in this chapter. Labs 1, 2, and 3 are listed in order of increasing difficulty.

Lab 1: Inserting Audio Clips, Coloring a Picture, and Applying Artistic Effects to Pictures

Note: To complete this assignment, you will be required to use the Data Files for Students. See the inside back cover of this book for instructions on downloading the Data Files for Students, or contact your instructor for information about accessing the required files.

Problem: Start PowerPoint. Open the presentation, Lab 3-1 Cooking, from the Data Files for Students.
Your college has an outstanding culinary program, and you are preparing a PowerPoint presentation to promote an upcoming seafood cooking class. The slides will feature audio clips and graphics with applied effects. Create the slides shown in Figure 3–82.

Instructions: Perform the following tasks.

1. On Slide 1, insert the Mr. Light music audio clip from Office.com. Change the volume to Low, play across slides, and hide the sound icon during the show. Move the subtitle text placeholder downward to the location shown in Figure 3–82a and center both paragraphs.

2. On Slide 2, insert the picture called Blackboard and Chef, which is available on the Data Files for Students. Change the color of the picture to Gold, Accent color 3 Dark (Recolor area). Add a border to this picture using Dark Red, Accent 5, and then change the border weight to 6 pt., as shown in Figure 3–82b.

(a) Slide 1

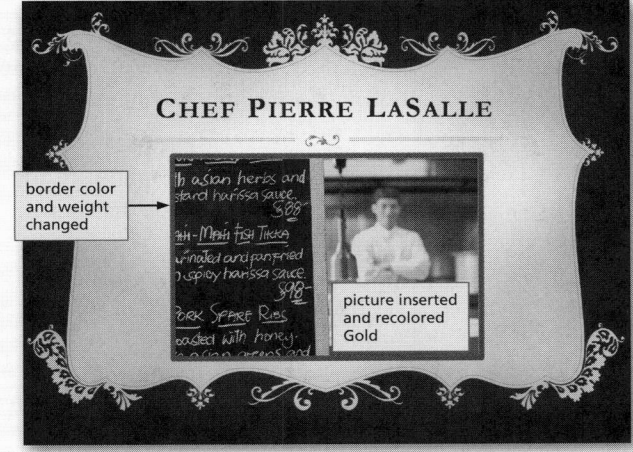

(b) Slide 2

Figure 3–82

Continued >

In the Lab *continued*

3. On Slide 3, right-align all the text. Insert the Chef video clip from Office.com and resize this clip so that it is approximately 4.08" × 3.99", as shown in Figure 3–82c. Insert the Pepper Grinder video clip from Office.com and resize this clip so that it is approximately 3.81" × 2.25". Move the Pepper Grinder video clip to the lower-left corner of the slide. Insert the audio clips, Pepper Grinder and Cartoon Crash, from Office.com. Start these clips automatically, hide the sound icons during the show, and loop until stopped.

4. On Slide 4, apply the Watercolor Sponge artistic effect to the lobster picture in the left content placeholder and the Plastic Wrap artistic effect to the paella picture in the right content placeholder, as shown in Figure 3–82d.

5. On Slide 5, insert the Bottle Open audio clip from Office.com. Move the sound icon to the lower-right corner of the slide. Start this clip on click. Center the text in the caption placeholder and then move this placeholder downward to the location shown in Figure 3–82e.

6. Review the slides in Slide Sorter view to check for consistency, and then change the view to Normal.

7. Drag the scroll box to display Slide 1. Start Slide Show view and display each slide.

8. Change the document properties, as specified by your instructor. Save the presentation using the file name, Lab 3-1 Cooking Classes.

9. Submit the revised document in the format specified by your instructor.

(c) Slide 3

(d) Slide 4

(e) Slide 5

Figure 3–82 (Continued)

In the Lab

Lab 2: Adding Slide Numbers, Applying Artistic Effects to Pictures, and Recoloring a Video

Note: To complete this assignment, you will be required to use the Data Files for Students. See the inside back cover of this book for instructions on downloading the Data Files for Students, or contact your instructor for information about accessing the required files.

Problem: The Dutch tradition is continuing with Klompen dancers, who take their name from their traditional wooden clog shoes. You attended an annual festival this past spring and captured some video clips of teenagers dancing a traditional dance. In addition, you have some video of a hand-built windmill. In your speech class, you desire to inform your classmates of a few aspects of Dutch life, so you prepare the presentation shown in Figure 3–83.

Instructions: Perform the following tasks.

1. Start PowerPoint. Open the presentation, Lab 3-2 Dancers, from the Data Files for Students. On Slide 1, apply the Mosaic Bubbles artistic effect to the tulips picture, as shown in Figure 3–83a. Insert the audio clip, Spring Music, from Office.com. Start this clip automatically, hide the sound icon during the show, and change the volume to Medium.

2. On Slide 2, apply the Marker artistic effect to the wooden shoe picture, as shown in Figure 3–83b. Change the Start option for the video clip from On Click to Automatically. Apply the Rotated, Gradient video style (Moderate area) to the video clip, change the video border color to Tan, Accent 6, and then change the border width to 18 pt.

3. On Slide 2, type **Many dancers wear traditional, hand-sewn Dutch costumes. Dancers wear thick socks to make the wooden shoes comfortable during this annual event.** in the Notes pane.

(a) Slide 1

(b) Slide 2

Figure 3–83

Continued >

STUDENT ASSIGNMENTS

In the Lab *continued*

4. On Slide 3, insert the video clip called Windmill from the Data Files for Students. Apply the Reflected Bevel, White video style (Intense area). Change the color of the video to Dark Blue, Accent color 3 Dark (Recolor area). Start this clip automatically and loop until stopped. Center the text in the title placeholder, as shown in Figure 3–83c.

5. Use the thesaurus to change the word, Custom, to Tradition. Check the slides for spelling errors.

6. Add the slide number to all slides except the title slide.

7. Review the slides in Slide Sorter view to check for consistency. Then click the Reading view button to display the current slide and click the Next and Previous buttons to display each slide. Change the view to Normal.

8. Change the document properties, as specified by your instructor. Save the presentation using the file name, Lab 3-2 Klompen Dancers.

9. Submit the revised document in the format specified by your instructor.

video style applied

video clip recolored to Dark Blue

title text centered

thesaurus used to find synonym

A Long-Time Dutch Tradition

(c) Slide 3

Figure 3–83 (Continued)

In the Lab

Lab 3: Applying Artistic Effects to and Recoloring Pictures, Inserting Audio, and Trimming Video

Note: To complete this assignment, you will be required to use the Data Files for Students. See the inside back cover of this book for instructions on downloading the Data Files for Students, or contact your instructor for information about accessing the required files.

Problem: Your Uncle Barney is an avid railroad buff, and he especially is interested in viewing steam locomotives. He has a collection of video clips and photographs of historic steam engines, and he asks you to create a presentation for the next Hessville Train Club meeting he is planning to attend. Start PowerPoint and then open the presentation, Lab 3-3 Locomotives, from the Data Files for Students. Prepare the slides shown in Figures 3–84a through 3–84c.

Instructions: Perform the following tasks.

1. Delete the subtitle text placeholder on Slide 1. Then insert the picture, Steamer 624, from the Data Files for Students and apply the Glow Diffused artistic effect. Position the picture as shown in Figure 3–84a. Center the title text. Insert the audio clip, Train Whistle By, from Office.com. Start this clip automatically, hide the sound icon during the show, and loop until stopped.

2. On Slide 2, insert the picture, Locomotive, from the Data Files for Students and resize it so that it fills the entire slide height and width (approximately 7.5" × 10"). Change the color of the picture to Tan, Accent color 1 Light (Recolor area), as shown in Figure 3–84b.

3. Insert the video clip, Steam Locomotive, from the Data Files for Students. Resize this clip to approximately 4.54" × 8.07" and move the clip to the location shown in Figure 3–84b. Apply the Metal Rounded Rectangle video style (Intense area). Change the color of the border to Olive Green, Accent 2. Trim the Slide 2 video so that the Start Time is 00:06.186 and the End Time is 00:23.432. The duration should be 00:17.246 seconds. Start this clip automatically and loop until stopped.

4. On Slide 3, insert the picture, Railroad Track Border, and the video clip, Red Locomotive, from the Data Files for Students. Resize the Red Locomotive clip to approximately 2.78" × 5.36" and move it to the location shown in Figure 3–84c. Also, insert the audio clip, Steam Train Pass, from Office. com, and move this sound icon to the lower-left corner of the slide. Copy the audio clip, Train Whistle By, from Slide 1 and then move the sound icon to the upper-right corner of the slide. Start both audio clips automatically, hide the sound icons during the show, and loop until stopped.

5. Review the slides in Slide Sorter view. Then click the Reading view button to display the current slide and click the Next and Previous buttons to display each slide. Change the view to Normal.

6. Change the document properties, as specified by your instructor. Save the presentation using the file name, Lab 3-3 Steam Locomotives.

7. Submit the revised document in the format specified by your instructor.

(a) Slide 1

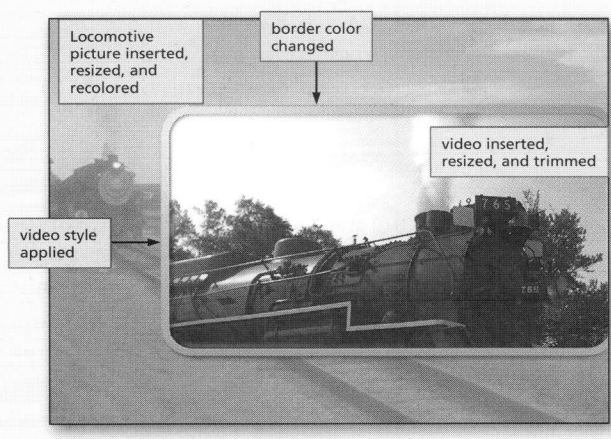

(b) Slide 2

(c) Slide 3

Figure 3–84

Cases and Places

Apply your creative thinking and problem-solving skills to design and implement a solution.

Note: To complete these assignments, you will be required to use the Data Files for Students. See the inside back cover of this book for instructions on downloading the Data Files for Students, or contact your instructor for information about accessing the required files.

As you design the presentations, remember to use the 7 × 7 rule: a maximum of seven words on a line and a maximum of seven lines on one slide.

1: Design and Create a Presentation about Kilauea Volcano

Academic

Most of the volcanic eruptions in Hawaii have occurred within Hawaii Volcanoes National Park. One of these volcanoes, Kilauea, has been erupting since 1983, and visitors to the National Park can drive on two roads to see lava tubes, steam vents, and plants returning to the barren landscape. Rainwater drains through cracks in the ground, is heated, and then is released through fissures and condenses in the cool air. Lava flows in underground tubes, and vents release volcanic gases that consist mainly of carbon dioxide, steam, and sulfur dioxide. During your recent trip to Hawaii Volcanoes National Park, you drove on these roads and captured these geological wonders with your video and digital cameras. You want to share your experience with your Geology 101 classmates. Create a presentation to show the pictures and video clips, which are located in the Data Files for Students and begin with the file name, Case 1. You also can use pictures from Office.com if they are appropriate for this topic. Apply appropriate styles and effects, and use at least three objectives found at the beginning of this chapter to develop the presentation. Be sure to check spelling.

2: Design and Create a Presentation about Surfing

Personal

During your summer vacation, you took surfing lessons and enjoyed the experience immensely. You now want to share your adventure with friends, so you decide to create a short PowerPoint presentation with video clips of the surf and of your paddling on your surfboard to the instruction area in the ocean. You also have pictures of your introductory lesson on shore and of your first successful run catching a wave. The Data Files for Students contains these media files that begin with the file name, Case 2. You also can use your own digital pictures or pictures from Office.com if they are appropriate for this topic. Use the clip, Case 2 - Yellow and Green Surfboard, on one slide, but ungroup this clip and then change the surfboard's colors to your school's team colors. Trim the video clips and apply appropriate styles and effects. Use at least three objectives found at the beginning of this chapter to develop the presentation. Be sure to check spelling.

3: Design and Create a Presentation to Promote Your Snow Removal Business

Professional

Record snowfalls have wreaked havoc in your neighborhood, so you have decided to earn tuition money by starting a snow removal business. You are willing to clear sidewalks and driveways when snowfall exceeds three inches. To promote your business, you desire to create a PowerPoint presentation to run behind the counter at the local hardware store. The Data Files for Students contains pictures and a video clip that begin with the file name, Case 3. You also can use your own digital pictures or pictures from Office.com if they are appropriate for this topic. Use the clip, Case 3 - Man Shoveling, on one slide, but ungroup this clip and then zoom in and delete the white area of the clip depicting the man's breath. Also, recolor at least one picture and apply an artistic effect. Be sure to check spelling.

4 Working with Information Graphics

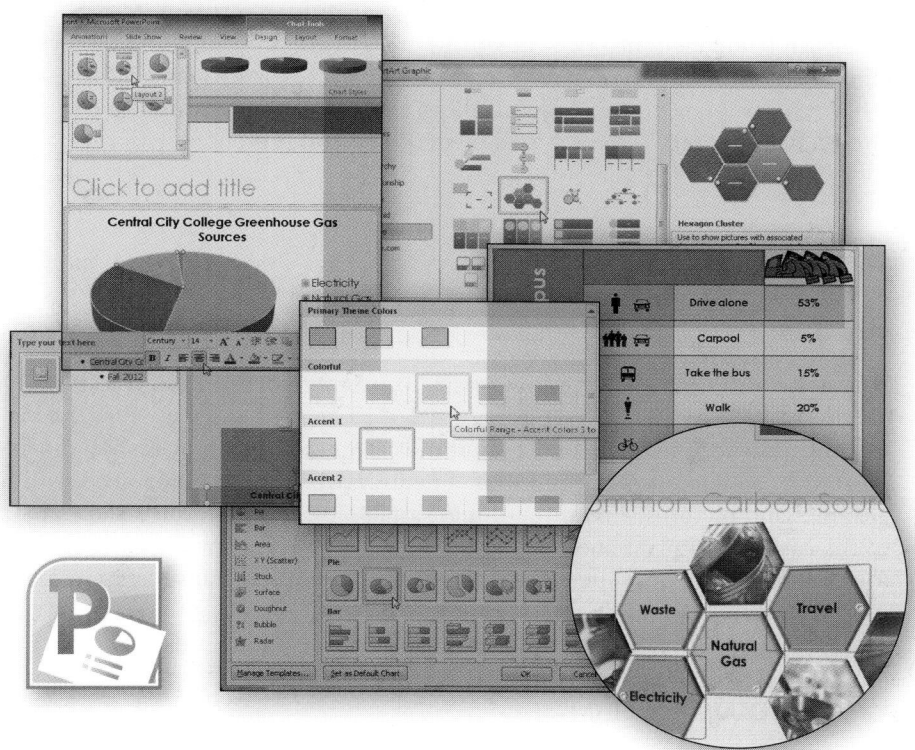

Objectives

You will have mastered the material in this chapter when you can:

- Insert a SmartArt graphic
- Insert images from a file into a SmartArt graphic
- Convert text to a SmartArt graphic
- Format a SmartArt graphic
- Create and format a chart
- Change the chart slice outline weight and color

- Rotate a chart
- Change the chart title and legend
- Create and format a table
- Change table text alignment and orientation
- Add an image to a table
- Insert a symbol

4 | Working with Information Graphics

Introduction

Audiences generally focus first on the visual elements displayed on a slide. Graphical elements increase **visual literacy**, which is the ability to examine and assess these images. They can be divided into two categories: images and information graphics. Images are the clips and photographs you have used in Chapters 1, 2, and 3, and information graphics are tables, charts, graphs, and diagrams. Both sets of visuals help audience members interpret and retain material, so they should be designed and presented with care.

BTW

Scheduling Preparation Time
Developing a presentation incorporating charts and tables generally requires extra preparation time. You need to gather data from reputable and current sources to incorporate into these visual elements. Be certain to start well in advance of assignment deadlines and create a schedule so that you have adequate time to prepare clear information graphics.

Project — Presentation with SmartArt, a Chart, and a Table

The project in this chapter follows visual content guidelines and uses PowerPoint to create the presentation shown in Figure 4–1. The slide show uses several visual elements to help audience members understand the carbon footprint, or carbon dioxide emissions, created by college students and staff. The first two slides are enhanced with SmartArt graphics and pictures. The three-dimensional pie chart on Slide 3 shows four contributors to the carbon footprint and emphasizes that the largest contributor is electricity. The four-column table on Slide 4 lists the five most common transportation methods students use to arrive on campus.

BTW

Increasing Presenter Confidence
When you rehearse your presentation that includes tables and charts, keep in mind that your audience will be studying these visual elements during your actual presentation and will not be focusing on you. The graphics, therefore, should give you confidence as a presenter because they are supporting your verbal message and helping to reinforce the message you are trying to convey.

Overview

As you read through this chapter, you will learn how to create the presentation shown in Figure 4–1 by performing these general tasks:

- Insert and modify a SmartArt graphic.
- Add styles and effects to SmartArt.
- Create a table and a chart.
- Add borders to tables and charts.
- Change table text alignment and orientation.
- Change chart and table styles and colors.

(a) Slide 1 (Title Slide with SmartArt Enhanced with a Picture)

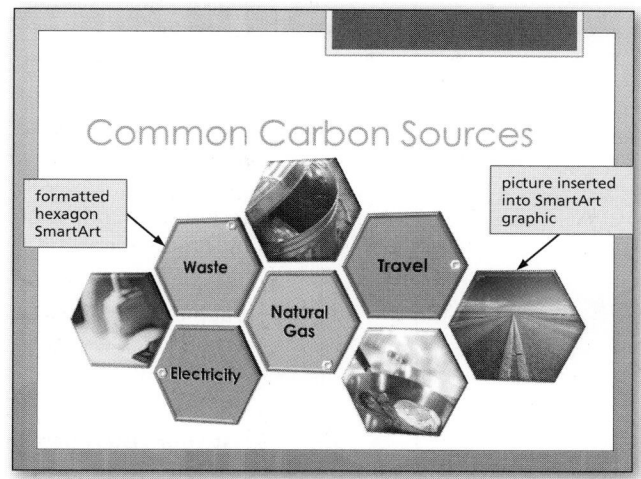

(b) Slide 2 (SmartArt Enhanced with Pictures)

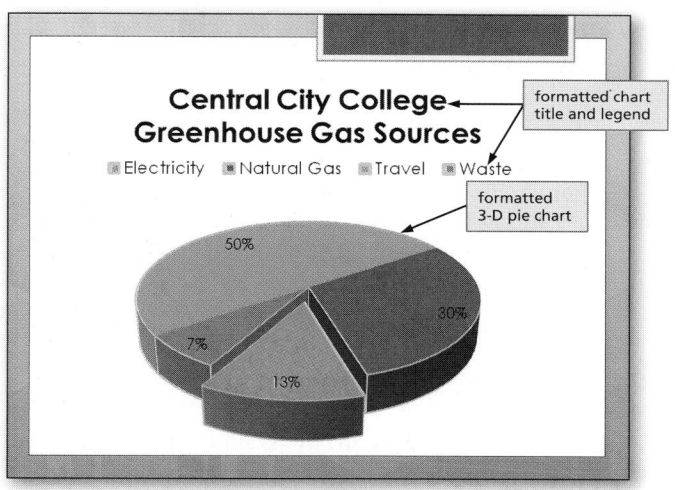

(c) Slide 3 (3-D Chart)

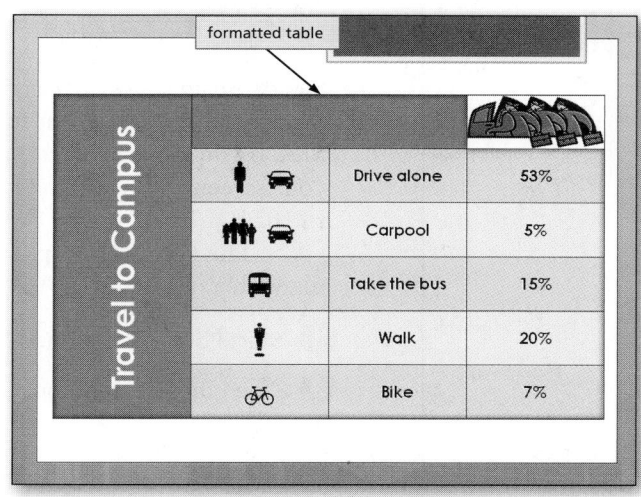

(d) Slide 4 (Four-Column Table)

Figure 4–1

General Project Guidelines

When creating a PowerPoint presentation, the actions you perform and the decisions you make will affect the appearance and characteristics of the finished document. As you create a presentation with illustrations, such as the project shown in Figure 4–1 on the previous page, you should follow these general guidelines:

1. **Consider the graphic's function.** Decide precisely what message you want the chart, table, or illustration to convey to the audience. Determine the graphic's purpose.

2. **Choose an appropriate SmartArt layout.** SmartArt illustrations represent ideas and concepts graphically. Audiences can grasp these visual concepts and recall them more quickly and accurately than when viewing text alone. Many SmartArt layouts are available (see Table 4–1), so select the one that best represents the concept you are attempting to present.

3. **Choose an appropriate chart style.** Most audience members like charts to help them understand the relationships between groups of data. Charts express numbers visually, but you must decide which chart type best conveys the points you are attempting to make in your presentation. PowerPoint presents a variety of chart layouts, and you must decide which one is effective in presenting the relationships between numbers and indicating important trends.

4. **Obtain information for the graphic from credible sources.** The text or numbers in the graphics should be current and correct. Verify the sources of the information and be certain you have typed the data correctly. On the slide or during your presentation, acknowledge the source of the information. If necessary, give credit to the person or organization that supplied the information for your graphics.

5. **Test your visual elements.** Show your slides to several friends or colleagues and ask them to interpret what they see. Time the duration they studied each slide. Have them verbally summarize the information they perceived.

When necessary, more specific details concerning the above guidelines are presented at appropriate points in the chapter. The chapter also will identify the actions performed and decisions made regarding these guidelines during the creation of the presentation shown in Figure 4–1.

BTW

BTWs
For a complete list of the BTWs found in the margins of this book, visit the PowerPoint 2010 BTW Web page (scsite.com/ppt2010/btw).

To Start PowerPoint and Open and Save a Presentation

To begin this presentation, you will open a file located on the Data Files for Students. See the inside back cover of this book for instructions on downloading the Data Files for Students, or contact your instructor for more information about accessing the required files. If you are using a computer to step through the project in this chapter and you want your screens to match the figures in this book, you should change your screen's resolution to 1024 × 768.

The following steps start PowerPoint, open the Carbon presentation, and save the file with a new name.

1 Start PowerPoint. If necessary, maximize the PowerPoint window.

2 Open the presentation, Carbon, located on the Data Files for Students.

3 Save the presentation using the file name, Carbon Footprint.

**Plan
Ahead**

Consider the graphic's function.
Determine why you are considering using an information graphic. The SmartArt, chart, or table should introduce meaningful information, support information in your speech, and help you convey details. If you are inserting the graphic simply for the sake of enlivening the presentation, do not use it. Graphics should help your audience understand and retain information and should not merely repeat details they have seen or heard up to this point in the slide show.

Take care in placing a manageable amount of information in your chart or table. Avoid overwhelming your audience with numerous lines in your table or slices or bars in your chart. If your audience is confused or struggling with comprehending the graphic, chances are they simply will abandon the task and wait for you to display the next slide.

Creating and Formatting a SmartArt Graphic

An illustration often can help convey relationships between key points in your presentation. Numerous studies have shown that audience members recall information more readily and accurately when it is presented graphically rather than textually. Microsoft Office 2010 includes **SmartArt graphics**, which are visual representations of your ideas. The SmartArt layouts have a variety of shapes, arrows, and lines to correspond to the major points you want your audience to remember.

You can create a SmartArt graphic in two ways: Select a type and then add text and pictures or convert text or pictures already present on a slide to a graphic. Once the SmartArt graphic is present, you can customize its look by changing colors, adding and deleting shapes, adding fill and effects, adding pictures, and including animation. Table 4–1 lists the SmartArt types and their uses.

BTW

Improving Audience Retention
Audience members need to use both senses of sight and hearing when they view graphics and listen to a speaker. When they become engaged in the presentation, they tune out distractions, which ultimately increases their retention of the material being presented. Although the exact amount of measured retention varies, one study found that an audience recalled five times more material when it was presented both verbally and visually.

Table 4–1 SmartArt Graphic Layout Types and Purposes	
Type	**Purpose**
List	Show non-sequential information
Process	Show steps in a process or timeline
Cycle	Show a continual process
Hierarchy	Create an organizational chart
Relationship	Illustrate connections
Matrix	Show how parts relate to a whole
Pyramid	Show proportional relationships with the largest component at the top or bottom
Picture	Include a placeholder for pictures within the graphic
Office.com	Use SmartArt available on the Office.com Web site

In the following pages, you will follow these general steps to create two SmartArt graphics:

1. Insert a SmartArt graphic.
2. Add text and then format these characters.
3. Insert a picture from a file into the SmartArt graphic.
4. Add a SmartArt Style to the graphics.
5. Change the SmartArt color.
6. Convert text to a SmartArt graphic.
7. Adjust the SmartArt size and location on the slide.

Choose an appropriate SmartArt layout.
If a slide contains key points that show a process or relationship, consider using a SmartArt graphic to add visual appeal and enhance audience comprehension. As you select a layout, determine the number of ideas you need to present and then select a graphic that contains the same number of shapes. For example, the Counterbalance Arrows layout in the Relationship area resembles a teeter-totter; it represents the notion that one concept conversely affects another concept, such as the economic principle that supply has an inverse relationship to demand.

To Insert a SmartArt Graphic

A picture of Central City students and staff would complement the theme of showing the results of the campus's carbon footprint survey. Several SmartArt graphics have placeholders for one or more pictures, and they are grouped in the Picture category. The Snapshot Picture List graphic has one area for a picture and another for text. The following steps insert the Snapshot Picture List SmartArt graphic on Slide 1.

1

- Display the Insert tab and then click the SmartArt button (Insert tab | Illustrations group) to display the Choose a SmartArt Graphic dialog box.

- Click Picture in the left pane to display the Picture gallery.

- Click the Snapshot Picture List graphic (last graphic in first row) to display a preview of this graphic in the right pane (Figure 4–2).

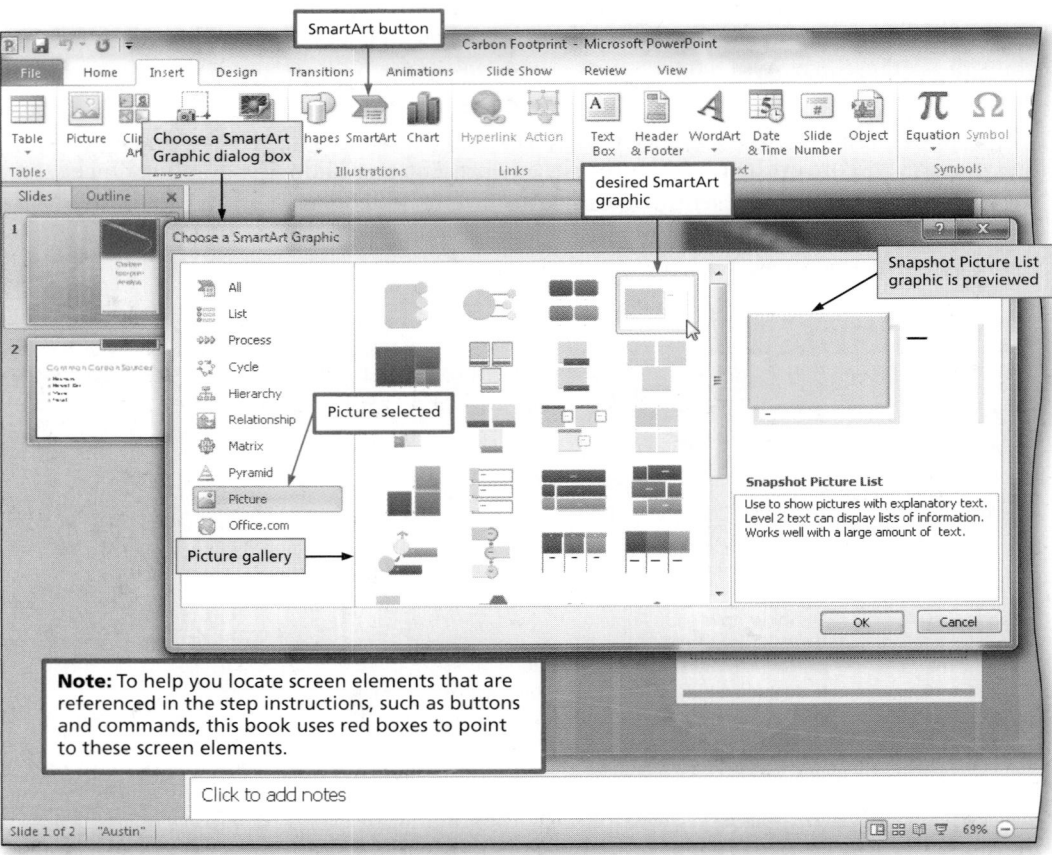

Figure 4–2

2

- Click the OK button to insert this SmartArt graphic on Slide 1 (Figure 4–3).

- If necessary, click the Text Pane button (SmartArt Tools Design tab | Create Graphic group) to open the Text pane if it does not display automatically.

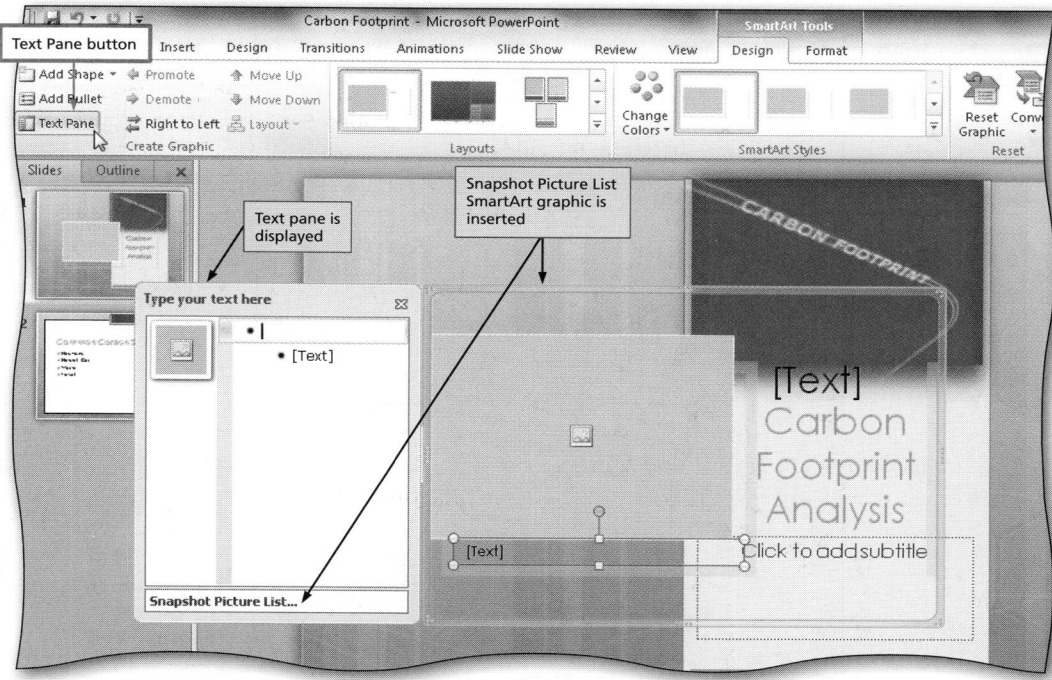

Figure 4–3

Text Pane

The **Text pane** assists you in creating a graphic because you can direct your attention to developing and editing the message without being concerned with the actual graphic. This Text pane consists of two areas: The top portion has the text that will appear in the SmartArt graphic and the bottom portion gives the name of the graphic and suggestions of what type of information is best suited for this type of visual. Each SmartArt graphic has an associated Text pane with bullets that function as an outline and map directly to the image. You can create new lines of bulleted text and then indent and demote these lines. You also can check spelling. Table 4–2 shows the character shortcuts you can use to enter Text pane characters.

BTW

The Ribbon and Screen Resolution
PowerPoint may change how the groups and buttons within the groups appear on the Ribbon, depending on the computer's screen resolution. Thus, your Ribbon may look different from the ones in this book if you are using a screen resolution other than 1024 × 768.

Table 4–2 Text Pane Keyboard Shortcuts	
Activity	**Shortcut**
Indent text	TAB or ALT+SHIFT+RIGHT ARROW
Demote text	SHIFT+TAB or ALT+SHIFT+LEFT ARROW
Add a tab character	CTRL+TAB
Create a new line of text	ENTER
Check spelling	F7
Merge two lines of text	DELETE at the end of the first text line
Display the shortcut menu	SHIFT+F10
Switch between the SmartArt drawing canvas and the Text pane	CTRL+SHIFT+F2
Close the Text pane	ALT+F4
Switch the focus from the Text pane to the SmartArt graphic border	ESC

To Enter Text in a SmartArt Graphic

The following steps insert two lines of text in the Text pane and in the corresponding SmartArt shapes on Slide 1.

1
- Type **Central City College** in the first bullet line and then press the DOWN ARROW key to move the insertion point to the second bullet line (Figure 4–4).

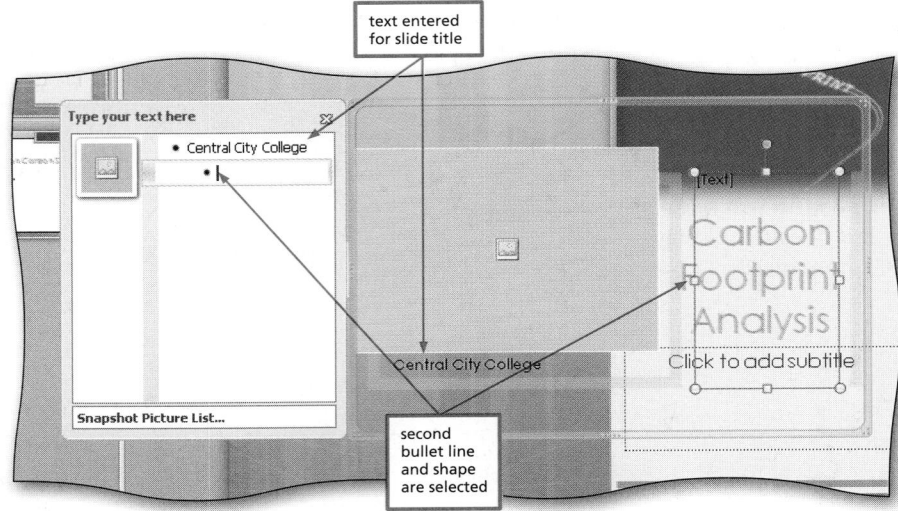

Figure 4–4

2
- Type **Fall 2012** in the second bullet line. Do not press the ENTER or DOWN ARROW keys (Figure 4–5).

 Q&A I mistakenly pressed the ENTER key. How can I delete the bullet line I just added?

Press the BACKSPACE key twice to delete the line.

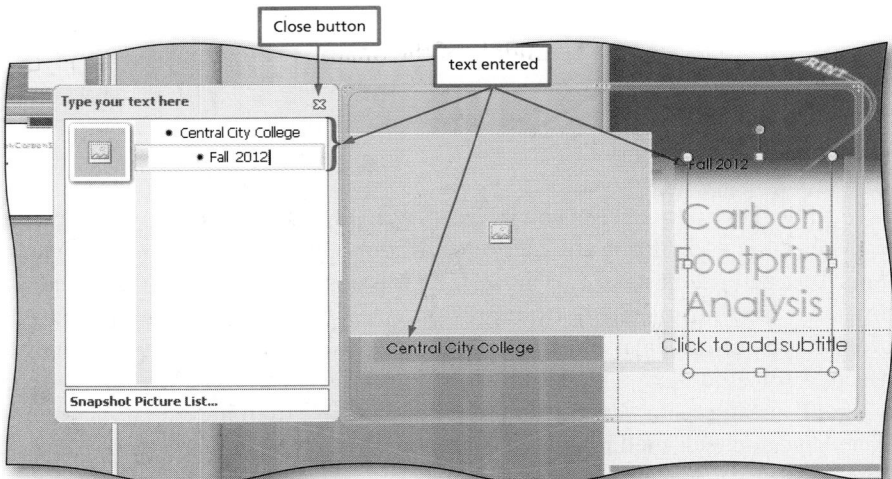

Figure 4–5

To Format Text Pane Characters

Once the desired characters are entered in the Text pane, you can change the font size and apply formatting features, such as bold, italic, and underlined text. The following steps format the text by changing the shape text font color and bolding the letters.

1
- With the Text pane open, drag through both bulleted lines to select the text and display the Mini toolbar.

Q&A If my Text pane no longer is displayed, how can I get it to appear?

Click the control, which is the tab with two arrows pointing to the right and left, on the left side of the SmartArt graphic.

- Display the Font Color gallery and change the font color to Dark Blue.

- Bold the text.

- Center the text (Figure 4–6).

Q&A These formatting changes did not appear in the Text pane. Why?

Not all the formatting changes are evident in the Text pane, but they appear in the corresponding shape.

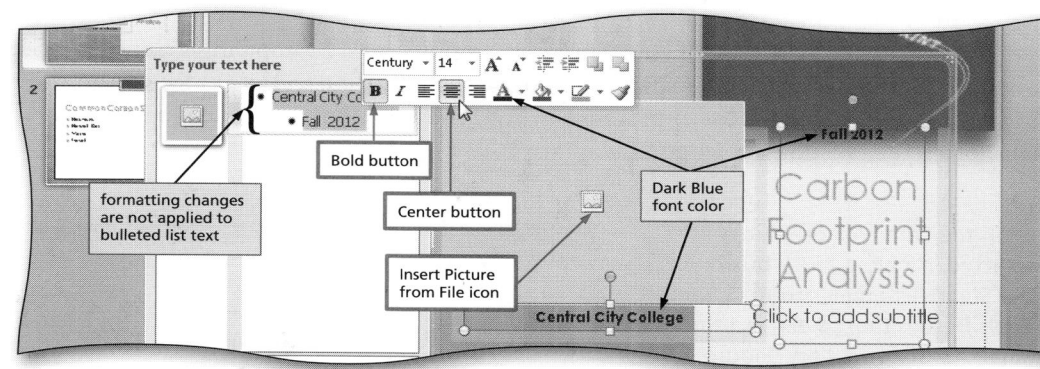

Figure 4–6

3

- Click the Close button in the SmartArt Text pane so that it no longer is displayed.

To Insert a Picture from a File into a SmartArt Graphic

The picture icon in the middle of the Snapshot Picture List SmartArt graphic indicates that the rectangular shape is designed to hold an image. You can select files from the Clip Organizer or from images you have obtained from other sources, such as a photograph taken with your digital camera. The following steps insert an image located on the Data Files for Students into the SmartArt graphic.

1

- With your USB flash drive connected to one of the computer's USB ports, click the Insert Picture from File icon in the rectangle picture placeholder to display the Insert Picture dialog box.

- If the list of files and folders on the selected USB flash drive are not displayed in the Insert Picture dialog box, double-click your USB flash drive to display them.

- Click Students and Staff to select the file name (Figure 4–7).

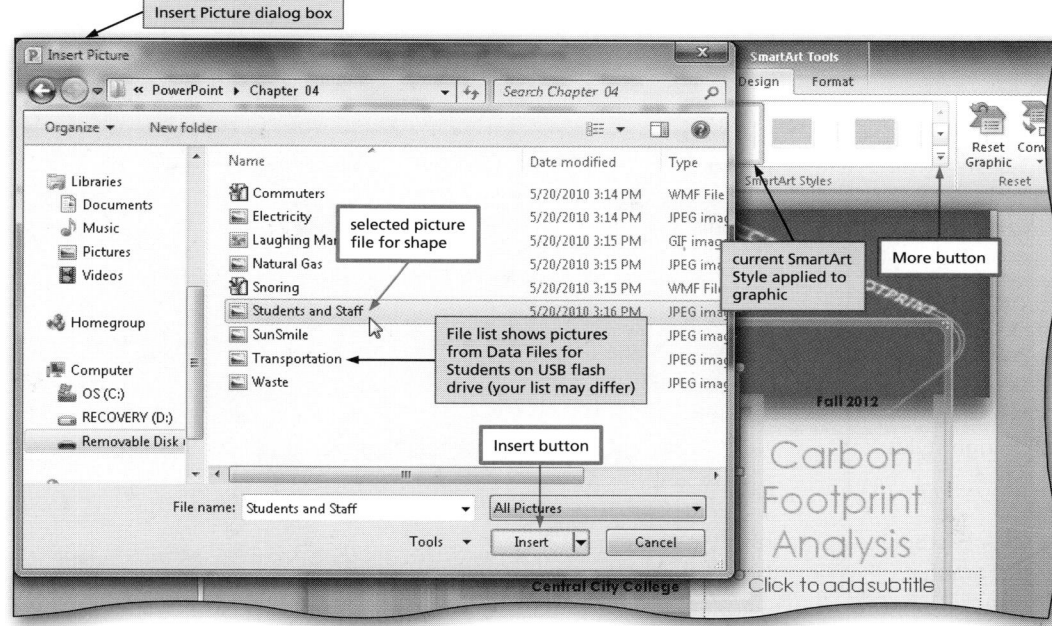

Figure 4–7

Q&A What if the picture is not on a USB flash drive?

Use the same process, but be certain to select the location containing the picture in the File list.

- Click the Insert button (Insert Picture dialog box) to insert the picture into the SmartArt picture placeholder.

To Apply a SmartArt Style

You can change the look of your SmartArt graphic easily by applying a **SmartArt Style**. These professionally designed effects have a variety of shape fills, edges, shadows, line styles, gradients, and three-dimensional styles that allow you to customize the appearance of your presentation. The following steps add the Cartoon Style to the Snapshot Picture List SmartArt graphic.

- With the SmartArt graphic still selected, click the More button in the SmartArt Styles group (SmartArt Tools Design tab) to expand the SmartArt Styles gallery (Figure 4–8).

Q&A

How do I select the graphic if it no longer is selected?

Click the graphic anywhere except the picture you just added.

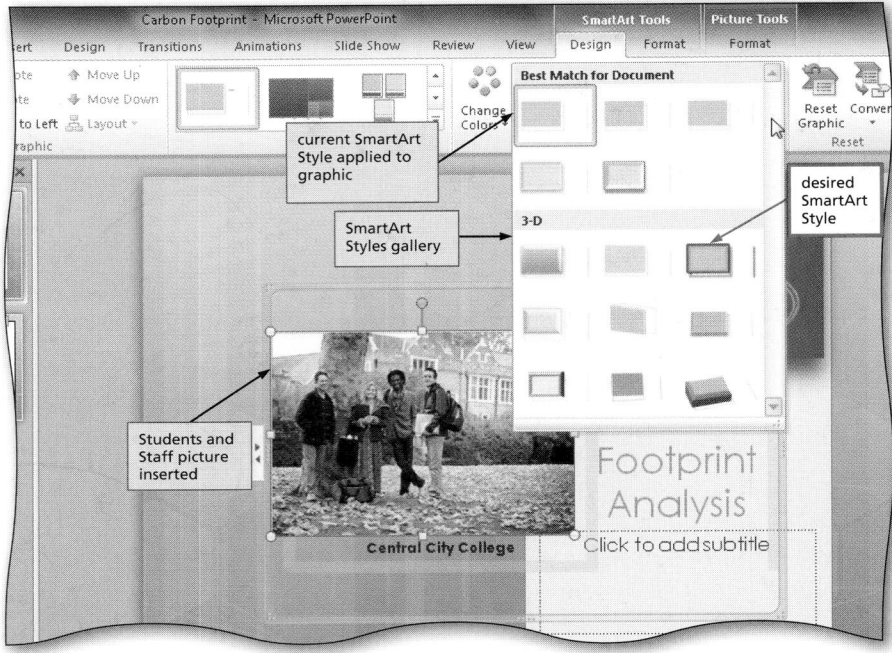

Figure 4–8

- Point to the Cartoon Style in the 3-D area (third style in first row) in the SmartArt Styles gallery to display a live preview of this style (Figure 4–9).

 **Experiment**

- Point to various styles in the SmartArt Styles gallery and watch the Snapshot Picture List graphic change styles.

- Click Cartoon to apply this style to the graphic.

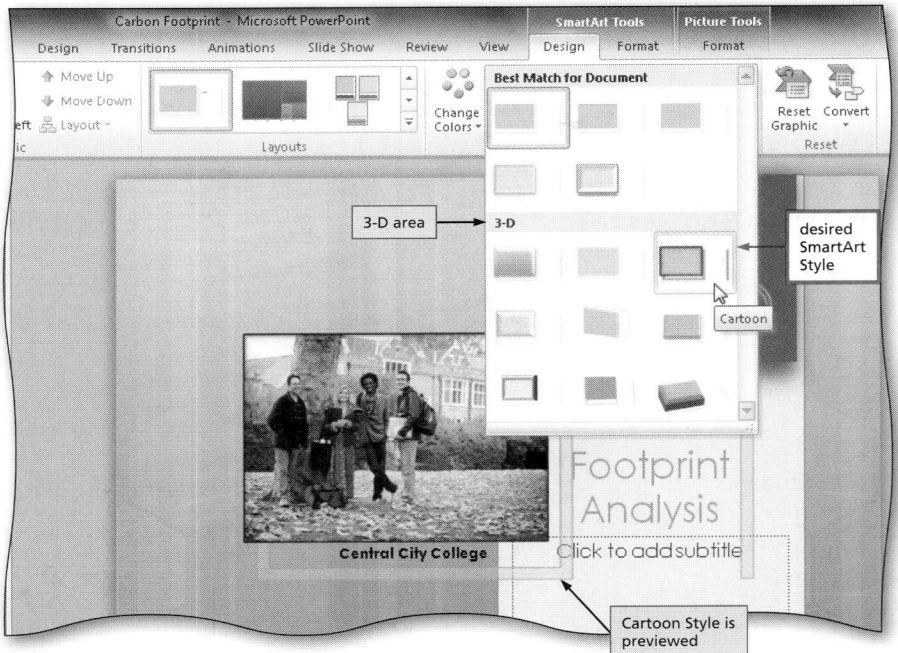

Figure 4–9

To Change SmartArt Color

Another modification you can make to your SmartArt graphic is to change its color. As with the WordArt Style gallery, PowerPoint provides a gallery of color options you can preview and evaluate. The following steps change the SmartArt graphic color to a Colorful range.

1

- With the SmartArt graphic still selected, click the Change Colors button (SmartArt Tools Design tab | SmartArt Styles group) to display the Change Colors gallery (Figure 4–10).

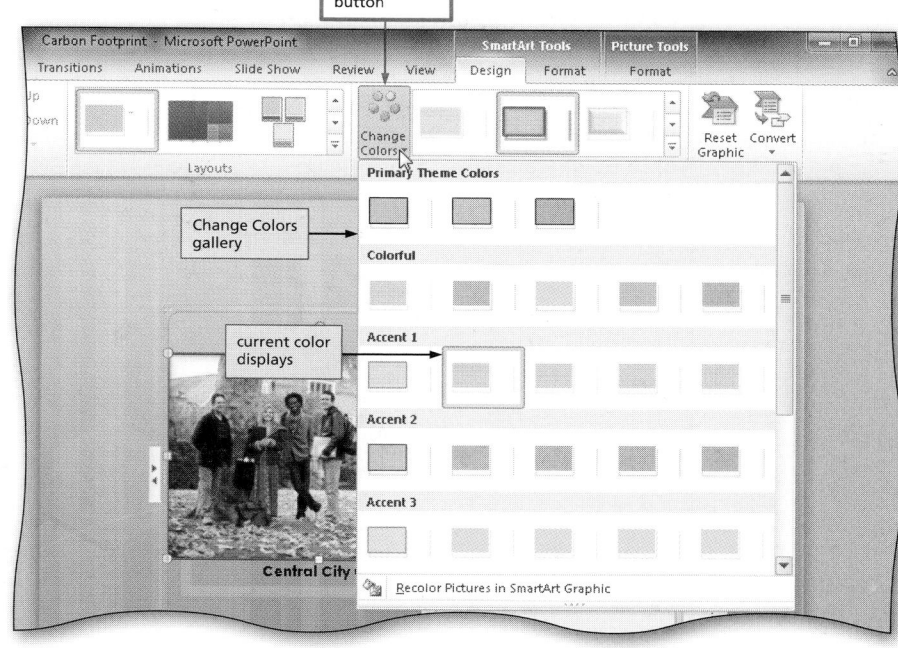

Figure 4–10

2

- Point to Colorful Range – Accent Colors 3 to 4 in the Colorful area (third color) to display a live preview of these colors (Figure 4–11).

🔍 **Experiment**

- Point to various colors in the Change Colors gallery and watch the shapes change colors.

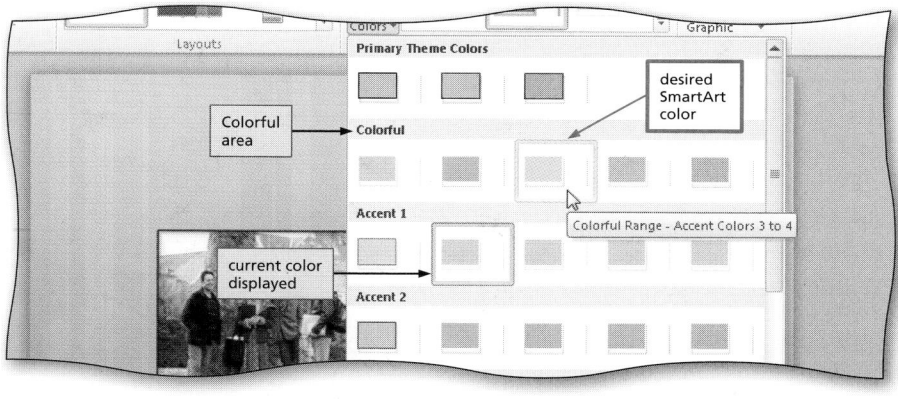

Figure 4–11

3

- Click Colorful Range – Accent Colors 3 to 4 to apply this color variation to the graphic (Figure 4–12).

Figure 4–12

To Resize a SmartArt Graphic

When you view the completed graphic, you may decide that individual shapes or the entire piece of art needs to be enlarged or reduced. If you change the size of one shape, the other shapes also may change size to maintain proportions. Likewise, the font size may change in all the shapes if you increase or decrease the font size of one shape. On Slide 1, the SmartArt graphic size can be increased to fill the space and add readability. All the shapes will enlarge proportionally when you adjust the graphic's height and width. The following steps resize the SmartArt graphic.

1

- With the SmartArt graphic still selected, point to the lower-left sizing handle and drag downward and to the left, as shown in Figure 4–13.

Figure 4–13

2

- Release the mouse button to resize the graphic.

- Press the UP and RIGHT ARROW keys to position the graphic, as shown in Figure 4–14.

Figure 4–14

To Convert Text to a SmartArt Graphic

You quickly can convert small amounts of slide text and pictures into a SmartArt graphic. Once you determine the type of graphic, such as process or cycle, you then have a wide variety of styles from which to choose in the SmartArt Graphic gallery. As with other galleries, you can point to the samples and view a live preview if you desire. The following steps convert the four bulleted text paragraphs on Slide 2 to the Hexagon Cluster graphic, which is part of the Picture category.

1
- Click the Next Slide button to display Slide 2.

- With the Home tab displayed, select the four bulleted list items and then click the Convert to SmartArt Graphic button (Home tab | Paragraph group) to display the SmartArt Graphics gallery (Figure 4–15).

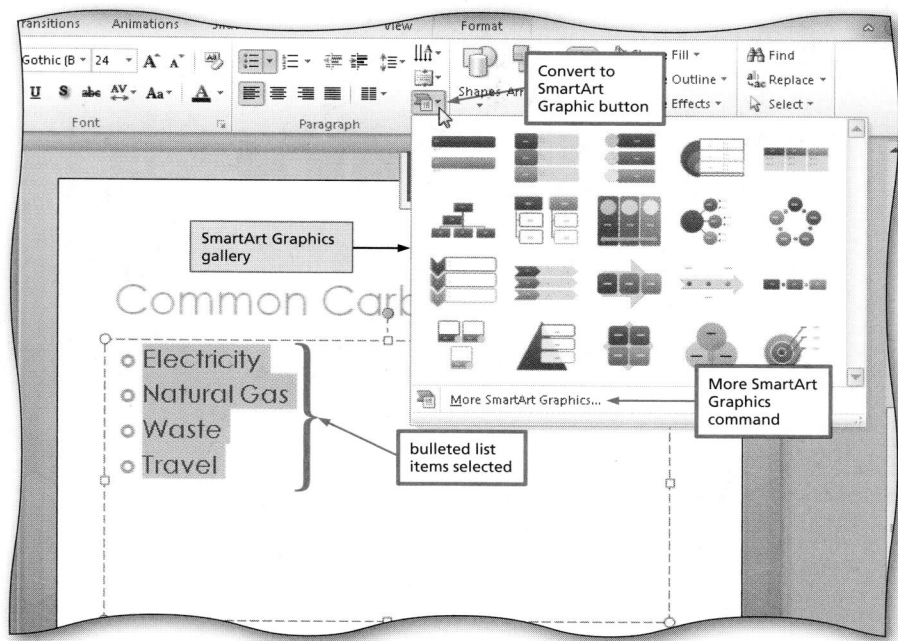

Figure 4–15

2
- Click More SmartArt Graphics in the SmartArt Graphics gallery to display the Choose a SmartArt Graphic dialog box.

- Click Picture in the left pane to display the Picture gallery.

- Scroll down and then click the Hexagon Cluster graphic (second graphic in sixth row) to display a preview of this graphic in the right pane (Figure 4–16).

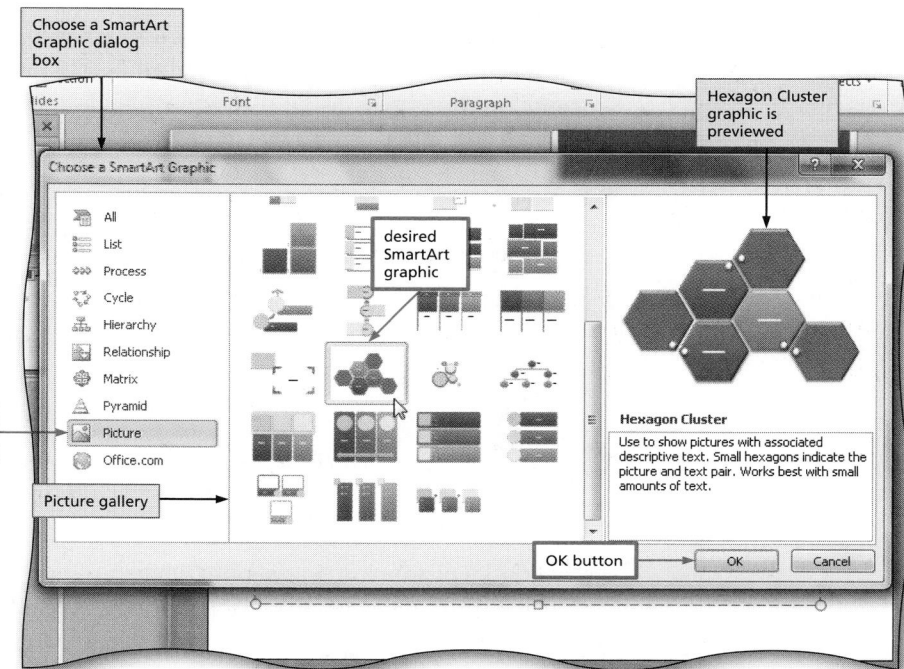

Figure 4–16

3

- Click the OK button (Choose a SmartArt Graphic dialog box) to apply this shape and convert the text (Figure 4–17).

Q&A

How can I edit the text that displays in the four shapes?

You can click the text and then make the desired changes. Also, if you display the Text pane on the left side of the graphic, you can click the text you want to change and make your edits.

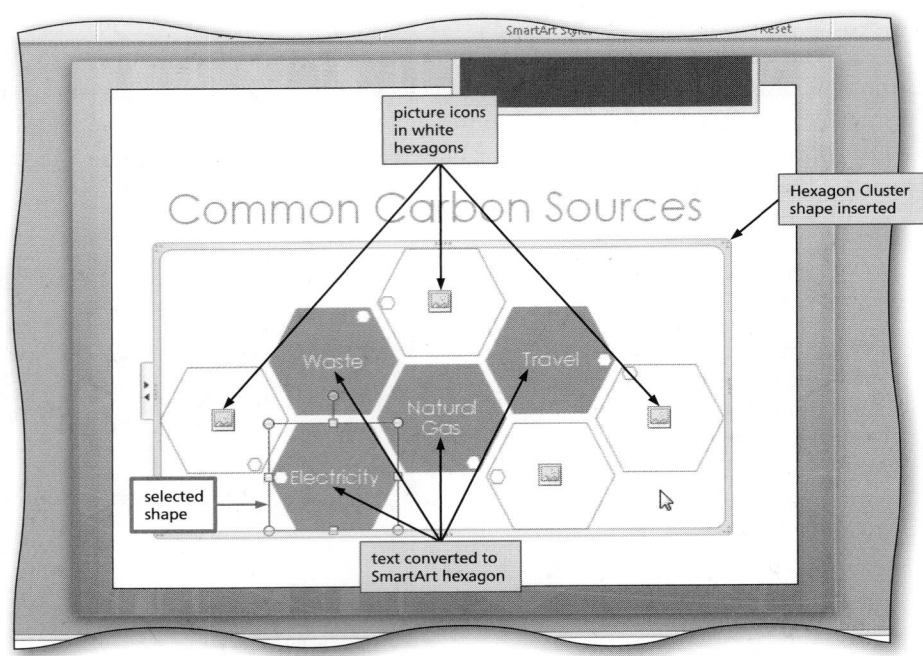

Figure 4–17

Other Ways

1. Click Convert to SmartArt on shortcut menu

BTW

Q&As
For a complete list of the Q&As found in many of the step-by-step sequences in this book, visit the PowerPoint 2010 Q&A Web page (scsite.com/ppt2010/qa).

To Insert Pictures from a File into a SmartArt Graphic

The picture icon in each of the four white hexagons in the SmartArt graphic indicates the shape is designed to hold an image. In this presentation, you will add images located on the Data Files for Students. The following steps insert pictures into the SmartArt graphic.

1 With Slide 2 displaying and your USB flash drive connected to one of the computer's USB ports, click the Insert picture from file icon in the top white hexagon under the word, Carbon, to display the Insert Picture dialog box.

2 Click Waste in the list of picture files and then click the Insert button (Insert Picture dialog box) to insert the picture into the top SmartArt picture placeholder.

3 Click the Insert picture from file icon in the left white hexagon to display the Insert Picture dialog box and then insert the picture with the file name, Electricity, into the placeholder.

4 Click the picture icon in the white hexagon to the right of the word, Natural Gas (below the word, Travel), and insert the picture with the file name, Natural Gas, into the placeholder.

5 Click the picture icon in the right white hexagon and then insert the picture with the file name, Transportation, into the placeholder (Figure 4–18).

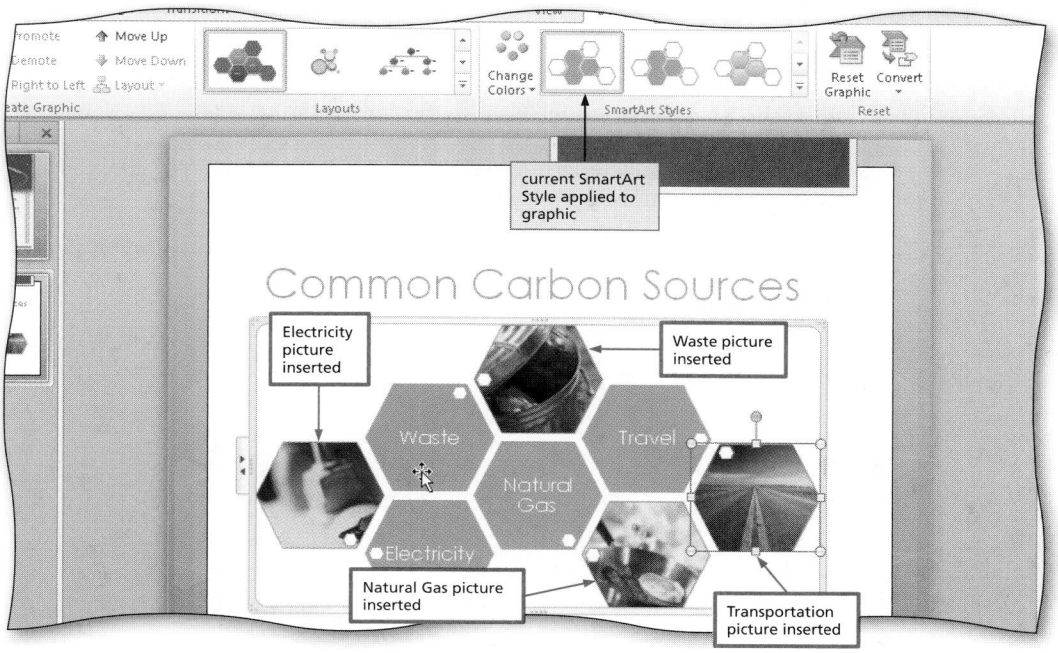

Figure 4–18

To Add a SmartArt Style to the Graphic

To enhance the appearance of the group of hexagons, you can add a three-dimensional style. The following steps add the Metallic Scene Style to the Hexagon Cluster graphic.

1 With the SmartArt graphic still selected, click the More button in the SmartArt Styles group (SmartArt Tools Design tab) to expand the SmartArt Styles gallery.

2 Click Metallic Scene in the 3-D area (first graphic in third row) to apply this style to the graphic (Figure 4–19).

BTW

Addressing Your Audiences

As you show your information graphics, resist the urge to turn to the screen and talk to the graphics instead of talking to your audience. If you turn toward the screen, your audience will get the impression that you are not prepared and must read information displayed on the graphics. Point with your hand nearest the screen and keep eye contact with your audience.

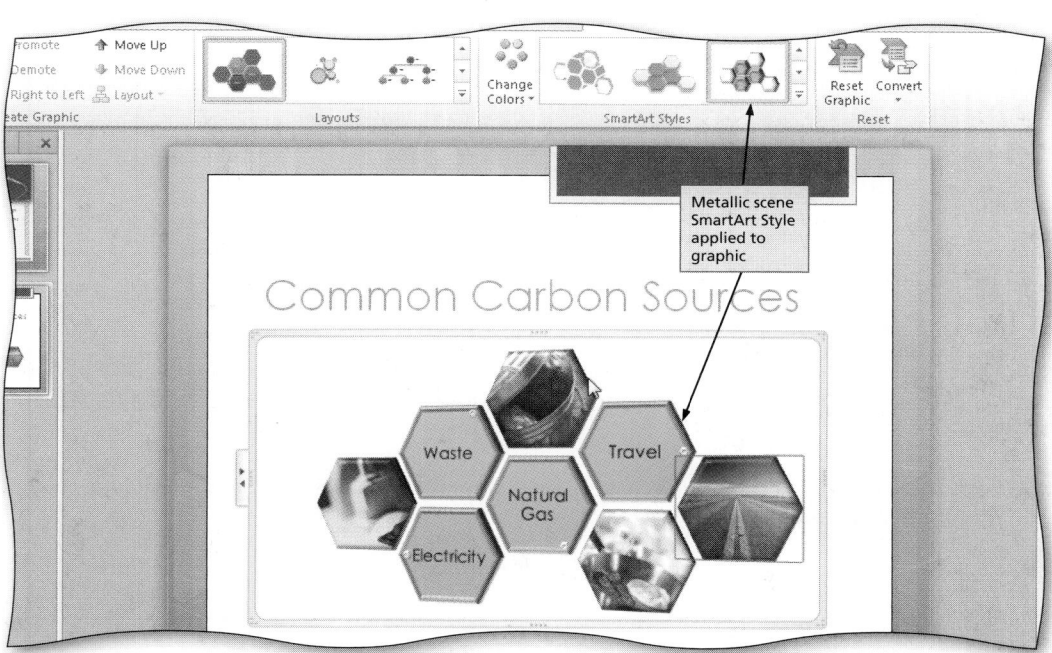

Figure 4–19

BTW

Choosing Contrasting Colors
Black or dark blue type on a white screen is an extremely effective color combination because the contrast increases readability. If you add a background color, be certain it has sufficient contrast with the font color. This contrast is especially important if your presentation will be delivered in a room with bright lighting that washes out the screen.

To Change the SmartArt Color

Adding more colors to the SmartArt graphic would enhance its visual appeal. The following steps change the SmartArt graphic color to a Colorful range.

1 With the SmartArt graphic still selected, click the Change Colors button (SmartArt Tools Design tab | SmartArt Styles group) to display the Change Colors gallery.

2 Click Colorful Range – Accent Colors 3 to 4 to apply this color variation to the graphic (Figure 4–20).

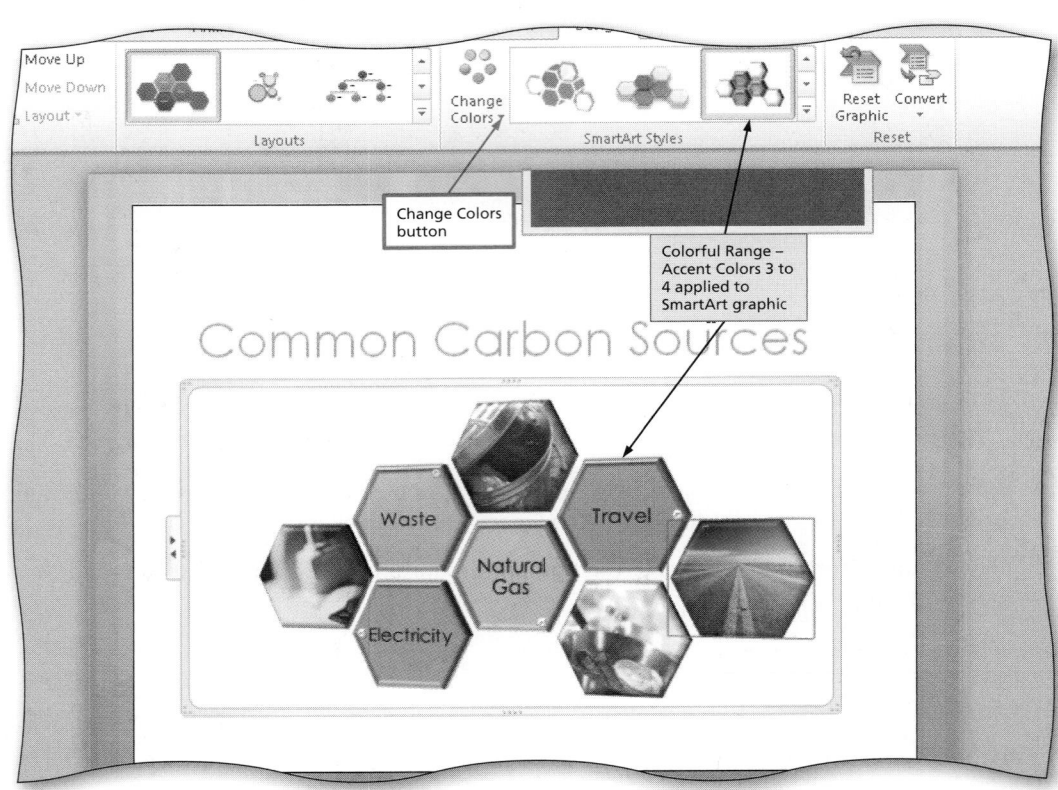

Figure 4–20

BTW

Avoid Distorting Graphics
Take care in preparing your visual elements so that you do not distort their physical appearance and mislead the audience. Edward R. Tufte's classic book, *The Visual Display of Quantitative Information,* presents guidelines for presenting information graphics and gives examples of accurate and inaccurate representations of data.

To Resize a SmartArt Graphic

Although white space on a slide generally is good to have, Slide 2 has sufficient space to allow the SmartArt graphic size to increase slightly. When you adjust the graphic's height and width, all the hexagons will enlarge proportionally. The following steps resize the SmartArt graphic.

1 With the SmartArt graphic still selected, drag one of the corner sizing handles diagonally outward, as shown in Figure 4–21.

2 Position the graphic so it is centered in the lower area of the slide (shown in Figure 4–22).

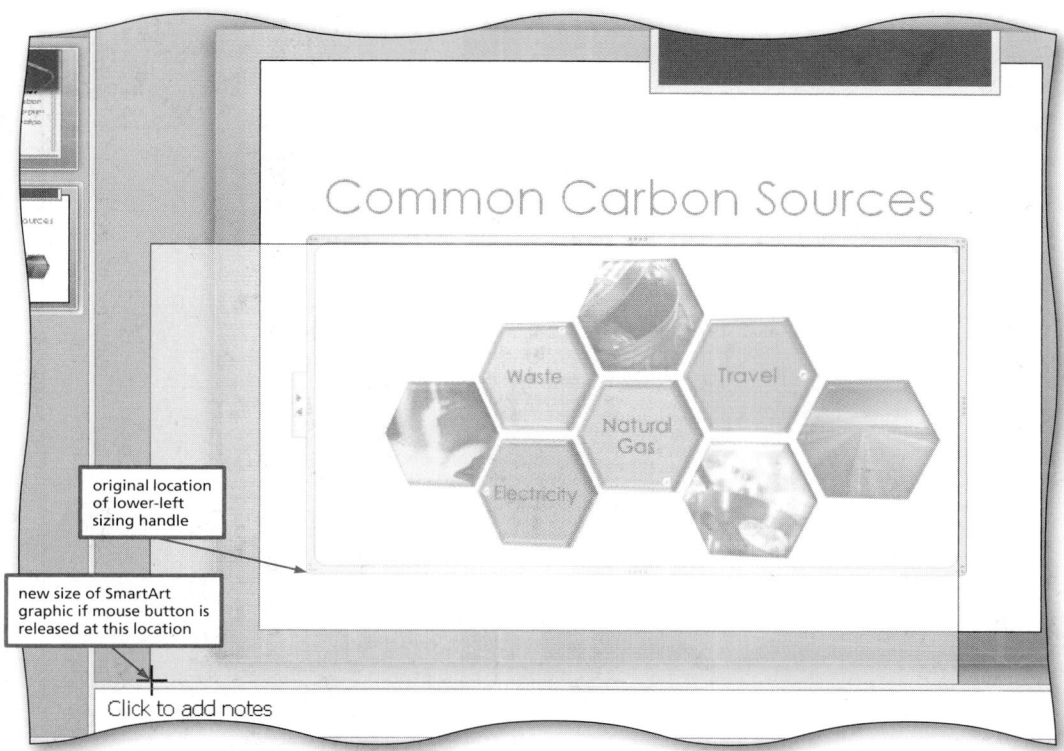

Figure 4–21

To Bold SmartArt Graphic Text

The text in the four hexagons can be bolded for readability. For consistency and efficiency, you can select all four hexagons and then change the text simultaneously. These hexagons are separate items in the SmartArt graphic, so you select these objects by selecting one hexagon, pressing and holding down the CTRL key, and then selecting the second, third, and fourth hexagons. The following steps simultaneously bold the hexagon text.

1

• Click the hexagon labeled Waste to select it. Press and hold down the CTRL key and then click the Electricity, Natural Gas, and Travel hexagons (Figure 4–22).

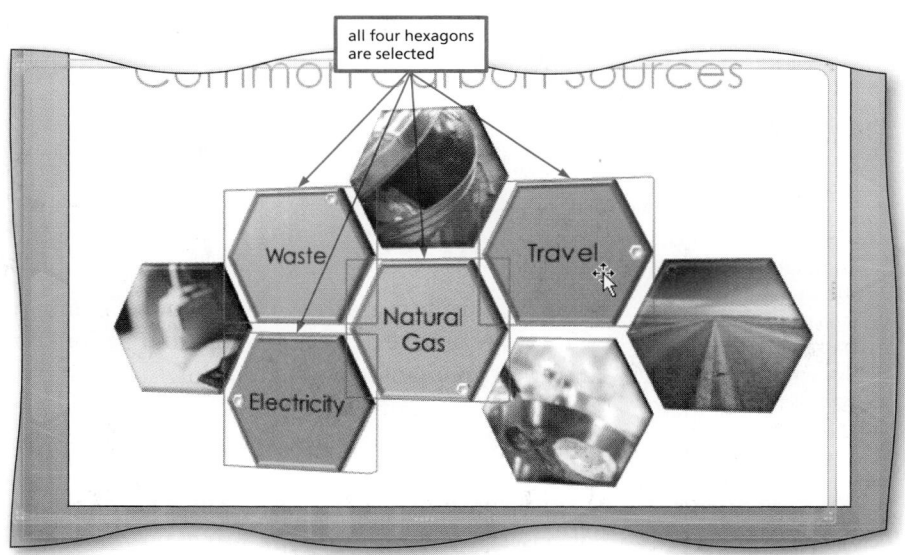

Figure 4–22

2

- Display the Home tab and then click the Bold button (Home tab | Font group) (Figure 4–23).

Q&A

Can I make other formatting changes to the graphics' text?

Yes. You can format the text by making such modifications as increasing the font size, changing the text color, and adding an underline and shadow.

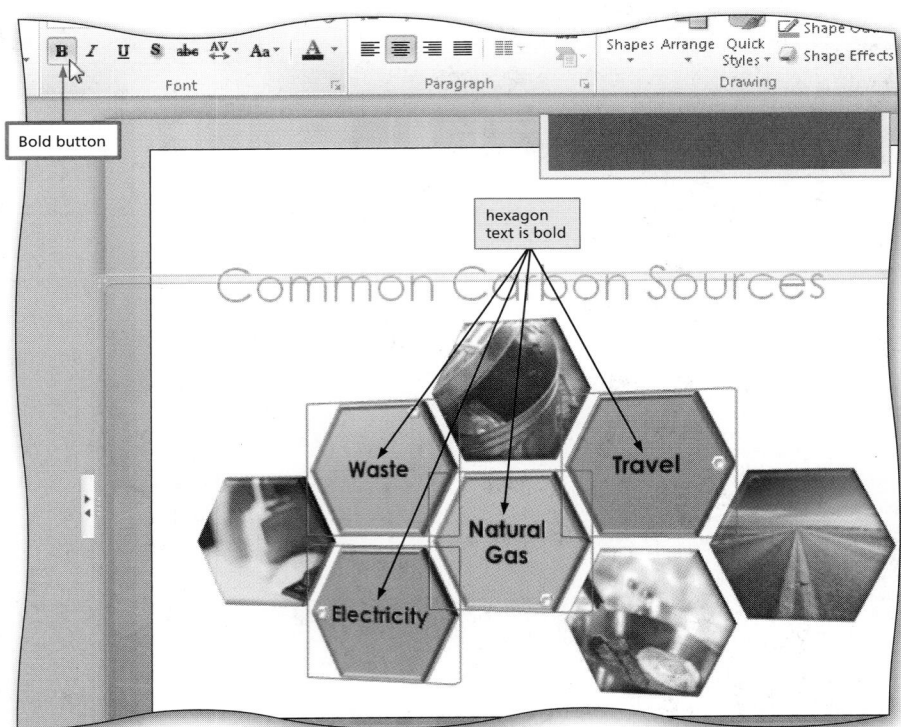

Figure 4–23

To Save an Existing Presentation with the Same File Name

You have made several modifications to the presentation since you last saved it. Thus, you should save it again. The following step saves the presentation again.

1 Click the Save button on the Quick Access Toolbar to overwrite the previously saved file.

Break Point: If you wish to take a break, this is a good place to do so. You can quit PowerPoint now. To resume at a later time, start PowerPoint, open the file called Carbon Footprint, and continue following the steps from this location forward.

BTW

Conducting Research
Use reputable sources to obtain data for your charts. Do not assume that something published on the Internet is accurate and reliable. Instead, focus your research on relevant, unbiased sources. The reference librarian at your school can recommend specific databases and Web sites that will provide you with current, accurate data.

Adding a Chart to a Slide and Formatting

Carbon dioxide is a natural by-product of combustion, and administrators at Central City College have determined that four major elements contribute to the campus's carbon ("greenhouse gas") footprint. One-half of the greenhouse gas comes from using electricity, most of which is produced from hydropower dams, coal-burning generators, and nuclear reactors. Another large contributor is natural gas, which is used on campus to heat buildings. Transportation to and from campus adds to carbon dioxide production because most of Central City College's students and staff commute to campus using cars or buses. A fourth carbon footprint contributor is waste; microscopic bacteria eat trash in landfills and convert this garbage into carbon dioxide and methane. The chart on Slide 3, shown in Figure 4–1c on page PPT 203, shows the proportion of these four greenhouse gas sources on campus.

Microsoft Excel and Microsoft Graph

PowerPoint uses one of two programs to develop a chart. It opens Microsoft Excel if that software is installed on your system. If Excel is not installed, PowerPoint opens Microsoft Graph and displays a chart with its associated data in a table called a datasheet. Microsoft Graph does not have the advanced features found in Excel. In this chapter, the assumption is made that Excel has been installed. When you start to create a chart, Excel opens and displays a chart in the PowerPoint slide. The default chart type is a **Clustered Column chart**. The Clustered Column chart is appropriate when comparing two or more items in specified intervals, such as comparing how inflation has risen during the past 10 years. Other popular chart types are line, bar, and pie, the latter of which you will use in Slide 3.

The figures for the chart are entered in a corresponding **Microsoft Excel worksheet**, which is a rectangular grid containing vertical columns and horizontal rows. Column letters display above the grid to identify particular **columns**, and row numbers display on the left side of the grid to identify particular **rows**. **Cells** are the intersections of rows and columns, and they are the locations for the chart data and text labels. For example, cell A1 is the intersection of column A and row 1. Numeric and text data are entered in the **active cell**, which is the one cell surrounded by a heavy border. You will replace the sample data in the worksheet by typing entries in the cells, but you also can import data from a text file, import an Excel worksheet or chart, or paste data obtained from another program. Once you have entered the data, you can modify the appearance of the chart using menus and commands.

In the following pages, you will perform these tasks:

1. Insert a chart and then replace the sample data.
2. Apply a chart style.
3. Change the line and shape outline weights.
4. Change the chart layout.
5. Resize the chart and then change the title and legend font size.
6. Separate a pie slice.
7. Rotate the chart.

BTW

Giving Credit to Your Sources
If you insert a chart that was created by someone else, you must give credit to this person and might need to ask permission to reproduce this graphic. This attribution informs your audience that you did not conduct your own research to construct this chart and that you are relying upon the expertise of another person.

Choose an appropriate chart style.
General adult audiences are familiar with bar and pie charts, so those chart types are good choices. Specialized audiences, such as engineers and architects, are comfortable reading scatter and bubble charts.

Common chart types and their purposes are as follows:

- Column — Vertical bars compare values over a period of time.

- Bar — Horizontal bars compare two or more values to show how the proportions relate to each other.

- Line — A line or lines show trends, increases and decreases, levels, and costs during a continuous period of time.

- Pie — A pie chart divides a single total into parts to illustrate how the segments differ from each other and the whole.

- Scatter — A scattterplot displays the effect on one variable when another variable changes.

In general, three-dimensional charts are more difficult to comprehend than two-dimensional charts. The added design elements in a three-dimensional chart add clutter and take up space. Also, legends help keep the chart clean, so use them prominently on the slide.

Plan Ahead

To Insert a Chart

The next step in developing the presentation is to insert a chart. The following steps insert a chart with sample data into Slide 3.

- Click the New Slide button to add Slide 3 to the presentation (Figure 4–24).

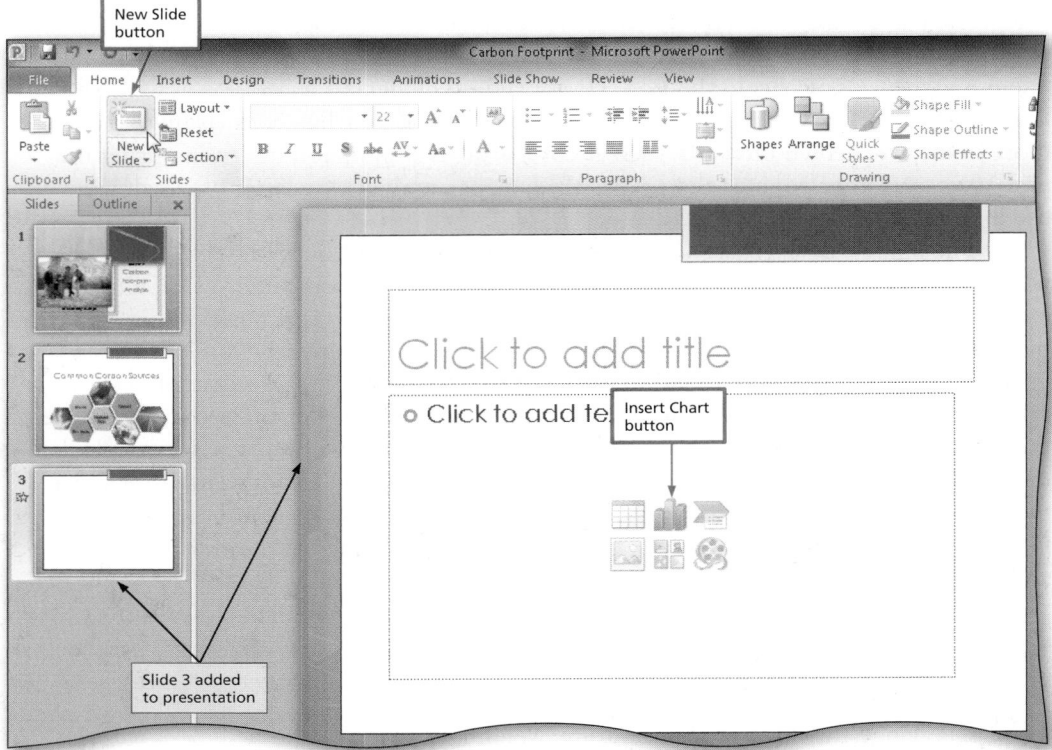

Figure 4–24

- Click the Insert Chart button in the content placeholder to display the Insert Chart dialog box.

- Scroll down and then click the Pie in 3-D chart button in the Pie area to select that chart style (Figure 4–25).

Q&A

Can I change the chart style after I have inserted a chart?

Yes. Click the Change Chart Type button in the Type group on the SmartArt Tools Design tab to display the Change Chart Type dialog box and then make another selection.

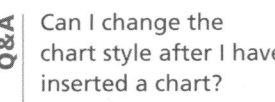
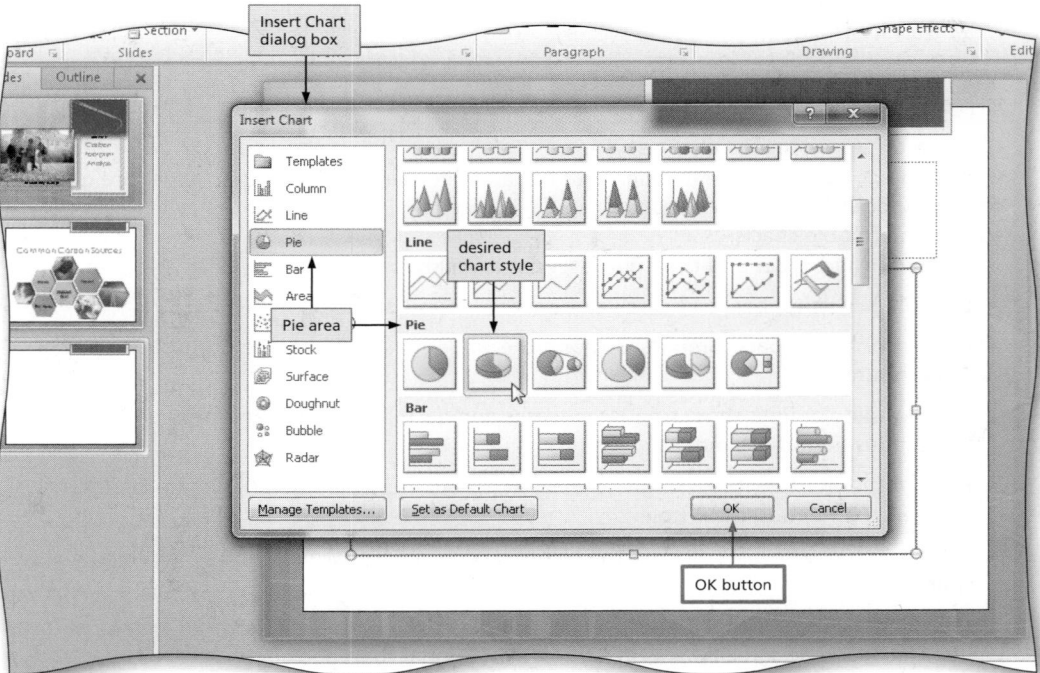

Figure 4–25

3

- Click the OK button (Insert Chart dialog box) to start the Microsoft Excel program and open a worksheet tiled on the right side of your Carbon Footprint presentation (Figure 4–26).

Q&A

What do the numbers in the worksheet and the chart represent?

Excel places sample data in the worksheet and charts the sample data in the default chart type.

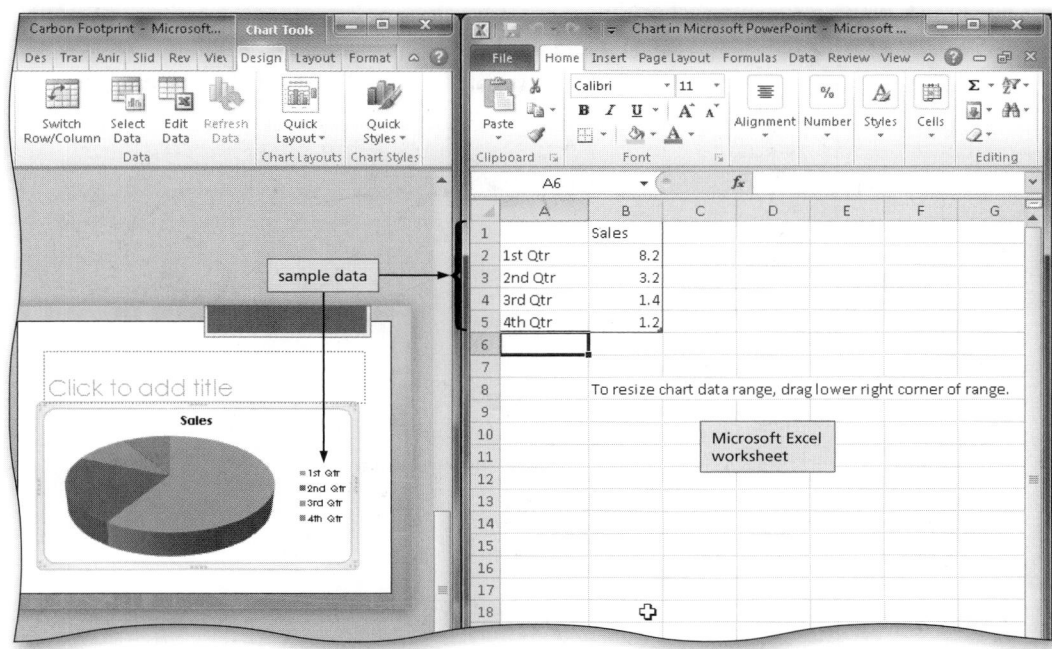

Figure 4–26

Other Ways

1. Click Pie button (Insert tab | Chart group)

Obtain information for the graphic from credible sources.
At times, you are familiar with the data for your chart or table because you have conducted in-the-field, or primary, research by interviewing experts or taking measurements. Other times, however, you have gathered the data from secondary sources, such as magazine articles, newspaper articles, or Web sites. General circulation magazines and newspapers, such as *Newsweek* and the *Wall Street Journal*, use experienced journalists and editors to verify their information. Also, online databases, such as EBSCOhost, OCLC FirstSearch, LexisNexis Academic, and NewsBank Info Web contain articles from credible sources.

On the other hand, some sources have particular biases and present information that supports their causes. Political, religious, and social publications and Web sites often are designed for specific audiences who share a common point of view. You should, therefore, recognize that data from these sources can be skewed.

If you did not conduct the research yourself, you should give credit to the source of your information. You are acknowledging that someone else provided the data and giving your audience the opportunity to obtain the same materials you used. Type the source at the bottom of your chart or table, especially if you are distributing handouts of your slides. At the very least, state the source during the body of your speech.

Plan Ahead

To Replace Sample Data

The next step in creating the chart is to replace the sample data, which will redraw the chart. The sample data is displayed in two columns and five rows. The first row and left column contain text labels and will be used to create the chart title and legend. A **legend** is a box that identifies each slice of the pie chart and coordinates with the colors assigned to the slice categories. The other cells contain numbers that are used to determine the size of the pie slices. The following steps replace the sample data in the worksheet.

1

- Click cell B1, which is the intersection of column B and row 1, to select it.

Q&A Why did my mouse pointer change shape?

The mouse pointer changes to a block plus sign to indicate a cell is selected.

- Type **Central City College Greenhouse Gas Sources** in cell B1 to replace the sample chart title (Figure 4–27).

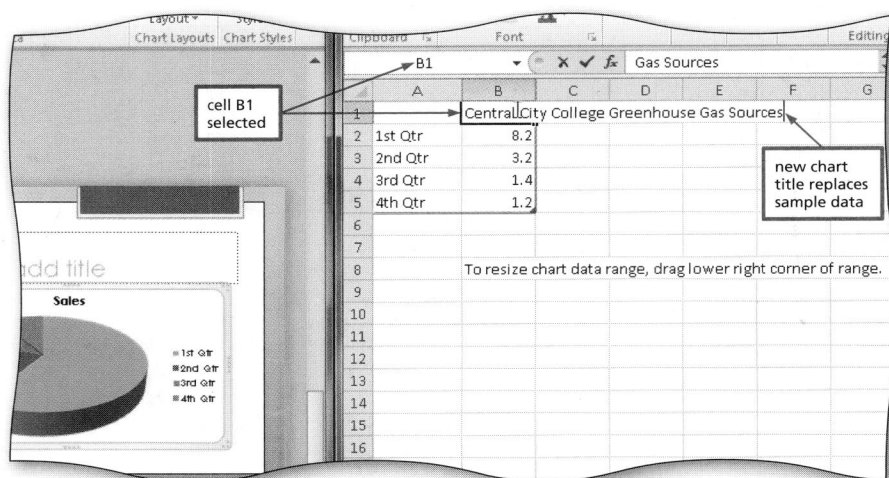

Figure 4–27

2

- Click cell A2 to select that cell.

- Type **Electricity** in cell A2 (Figure 4–28).

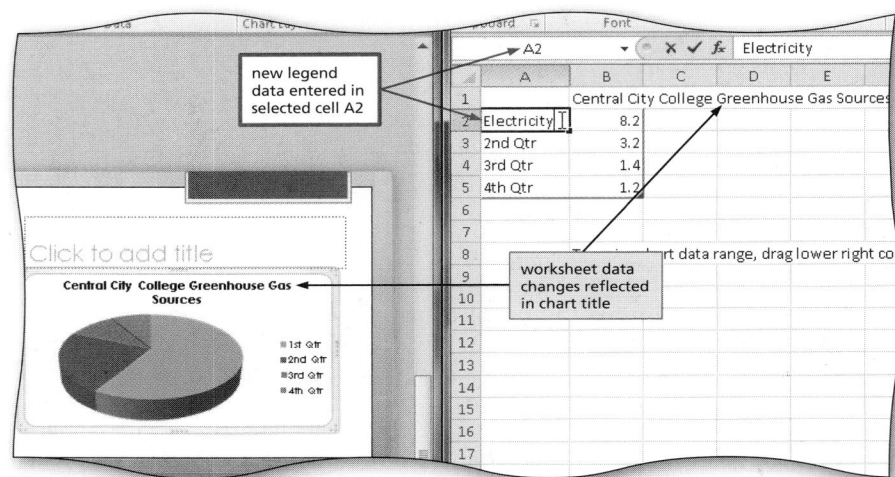

Figure 4–28

3

- Press the DOWN ARROW key to move the mouse pointer to cell A3.

- Type **Natural Gas** in cell A3 and then press the DOWN ARROW key to move the mouse pointer to cell A4.

4

- Type **Travel** in cell A4 and then press the DOWN ARROW key.

- Type **Waste** in cell A5 (Figure 4–29).

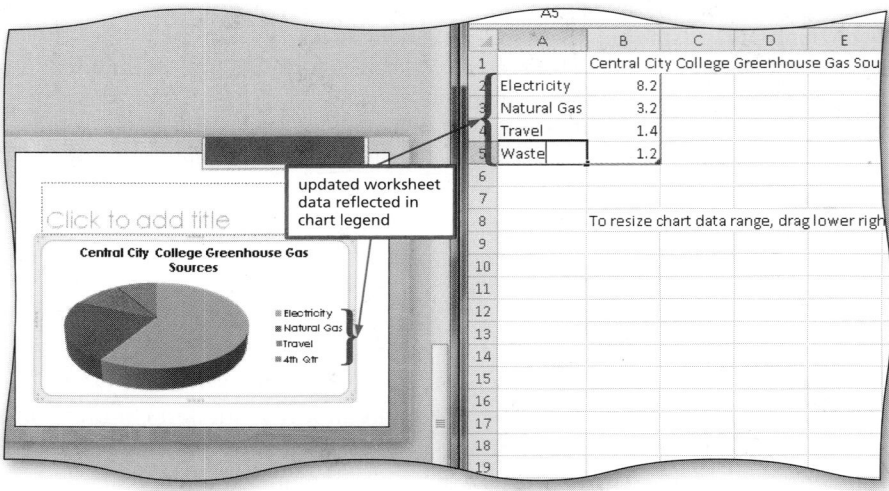

Figure 4–29

⑤

• Click cell B2, type 50 in that cell, and then press the DOWN ARROW key to move the mouse pointer to cell B3.

• Type 30 in cell B3 and then press the DOWN ARROW key.

• Type 13 in cell B4 and then press the DOWN ARROW key.

• Type 7 in cell B5. Press the ENTER key (Figure 4–30).

Q&A Why do the slices in the PowerPoint pie chart change locations?

As you enter data in the Excel worksheet, the chart slices rotate to reflect these new figures.

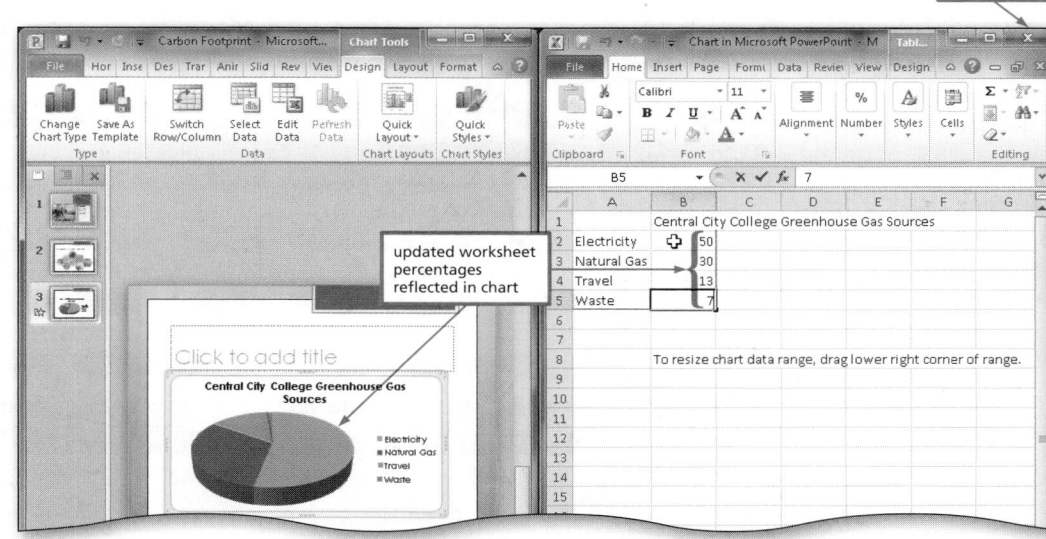

Figure 4–30

⑥

• Close Excel by clicking its Close button.

Q&A Can I open the Excel spreadsheet once it has been closed?

Yes. Click the chart to select it and then click the Edit Data button (Chart Tools Design tab | Data group).

To Apply a Chart Style

Each chart type has a variety of styles that can change the look of the chart. If desired, you can change the chart from two dimensions to three dimensions, add borders, and vary the colors of the slices, lines, and bars. When you inserted the Pie in 3-D chart, a style was applied automatically. Thumbnails of this style and others are displayed in the Chart Styles gallery. The following steps apply a chart style to the Slide 3 pie chart.

①

• If the entire pie chart area is not selected, click a white space near the pie chart and then click the Chart Tools Design tab to display the Chart Tools Design Ribbon (Figure 4–31).

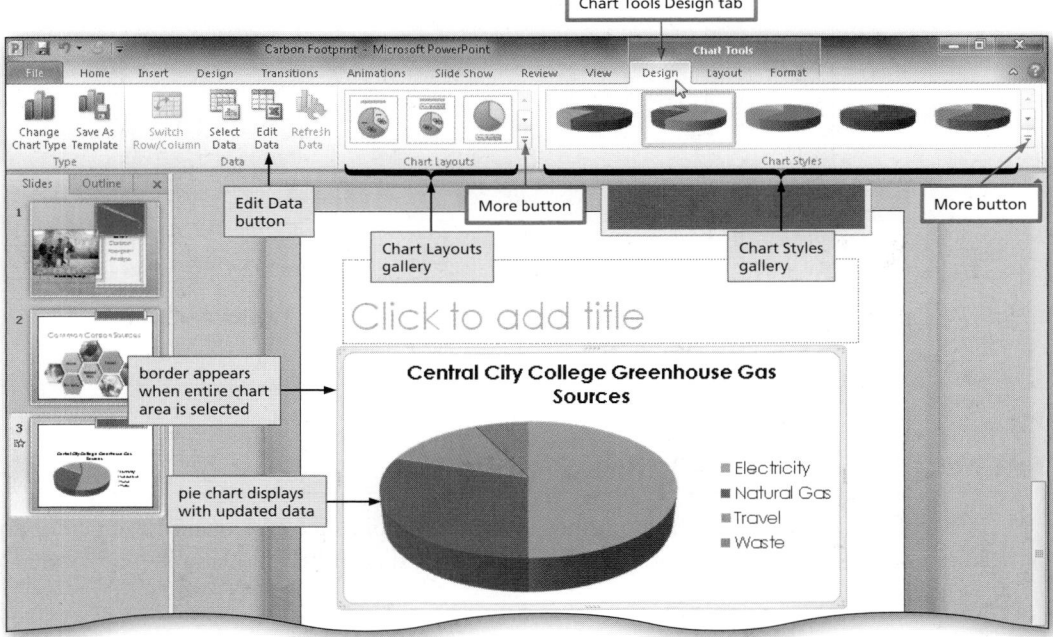

Figure 4–31

2

• Click the More button in the Chart Styles gallery to expand the gallery.

• Point to Style 10 (second chart in second row) (Figure 4–32).

Q&A Does the Chart Styles gallery have a live preview feature?

This feature is not available.

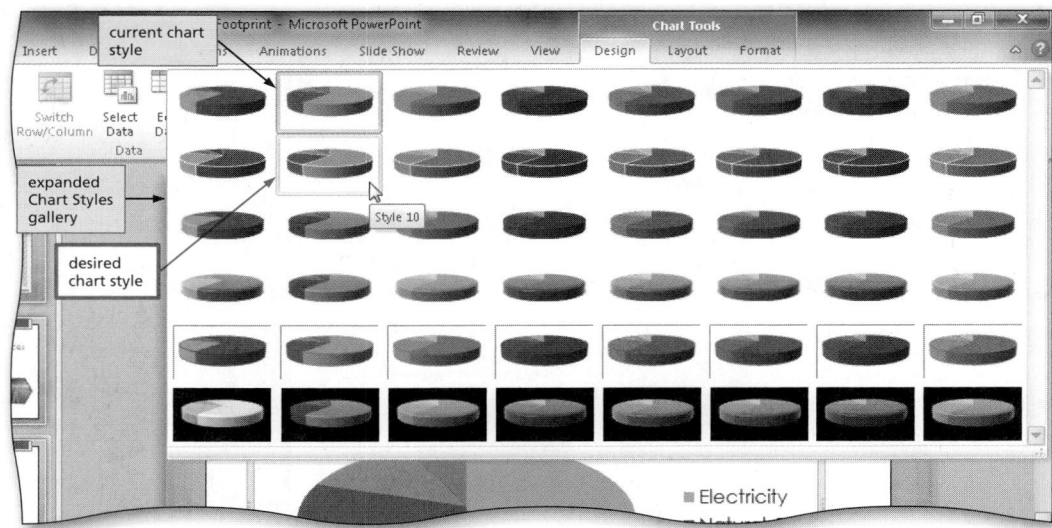

Figure 4–32

3

• Click Style 10 in the Chart Styles gallery to apply the selected style to the chart (Figure 4–33).

Q&A Can I change the chart type?

Yes. Click the Change Chart Type button (Chart Tools Design tab | Type group) and then select a different type.

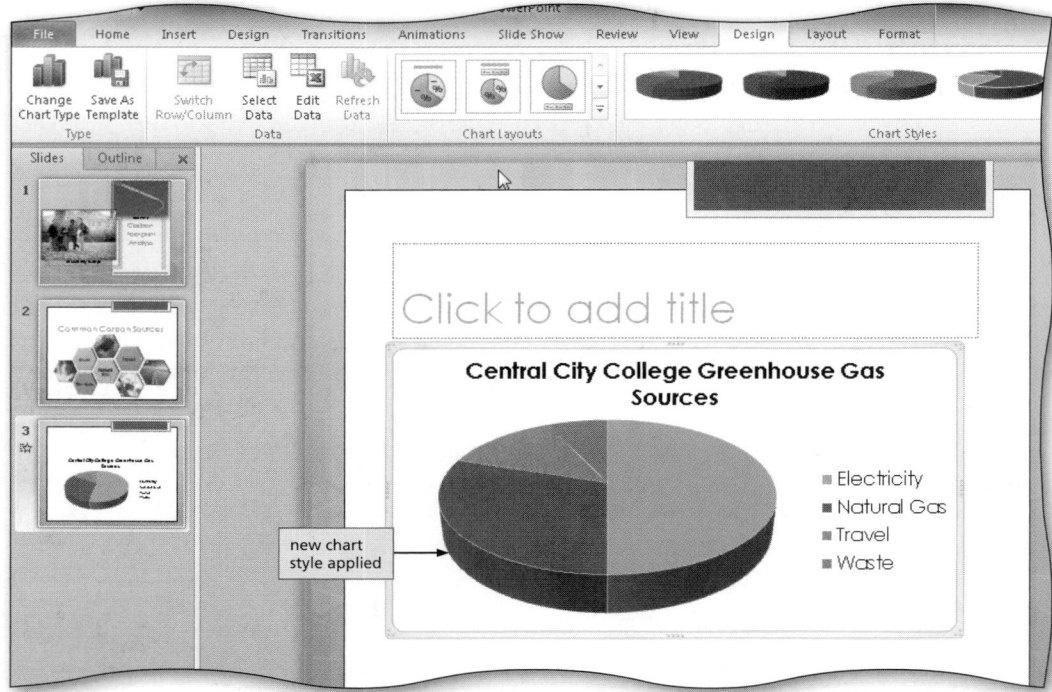

Figure 4–33

To Change the Shape Outline Weight

Chart Style 10 has thin white outlines around each pie slice and around each color square in the legend. You can change the weight of these lines to accentuate each slice. The following steps change the outline weight.

1

- Click the Chart Tools Format tab to display the Chart Tools Format Ribbon.

- Click the center of the pie chart to select it and display the sizing handles around each slice.

- Click the Shape Outline button arrow (Chart Tools Format tab | Shape Styles group) to display the Shape Outline gallery.

- Point to Weight in the Shape Outline gallery to display the Weight list (Figure 4–34).

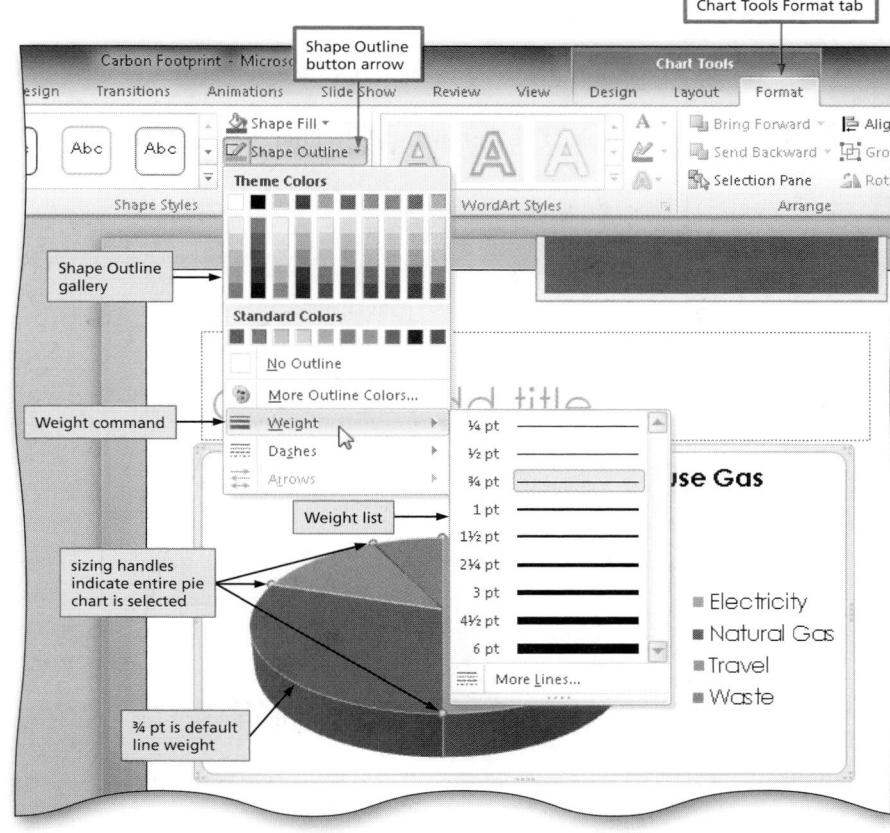

Figure 4–34

2

- Point to 4½ pt to display a live preview of this outline line weight (Figure 4–35).

Experiment

- Point to various weights on the submenu and watch the border weights on the pie slices change.

3

- Click 4½ pt to increase the border around each slice to that width.

Q&A Can I add a border to other chart elements?

Yes. Select the chart, click the Chart Tools Format tab, and then click the Chart Elements button arrow (Chart Tools Format tab | Current Selection area) to display a list of chart elements that you can format. Click the desired element, click the Format Selection button (Chart Tools Format Tab | Current Selection area), click Border Styles in the dialog box, and then select the formatting changes you desire. You also can change the border color and add effects.

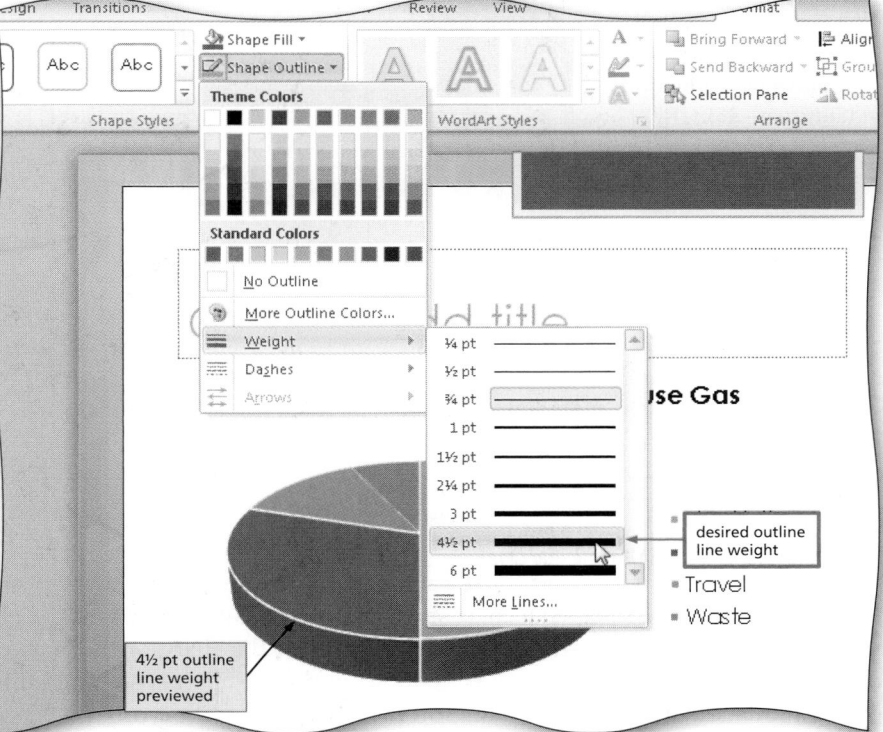

Figure 4–35

To Change the Shape Outline Color

Style 10 has white outlines around each pie slice and around each color square in the legend. At this point, you can't see the border around the legend squares because it is white. You can change this color to add contrast to each slice and legend color square. The following steps change the border color.

• Click the Shape Outline button arrow (Chart Tools Format tab | Shape Styles group) and then point to Orange in the Standard Colors area to display a live preview of that border color on the pie slice shapes and legend squares.

Experiment

• Point to various colors in the Shape Outline gallery and watch the border colors on the pie slices change.

• Click Orange to add orange borders around each slice and also around the color squares in the legend (Figure 4–36).

Q&A Can I add effects to the borders and other chart elements?

Yes. Each chart element has predetermined types of effects that you can apply, so preset, reflection, and bevel effects may not be available for the element you want to manipulate. Select the desired element, click the Shape Effects button (Chart Tools Format tab | Shape Styles group), click an available effect on the menu, and then click the desired effect in the gallery.

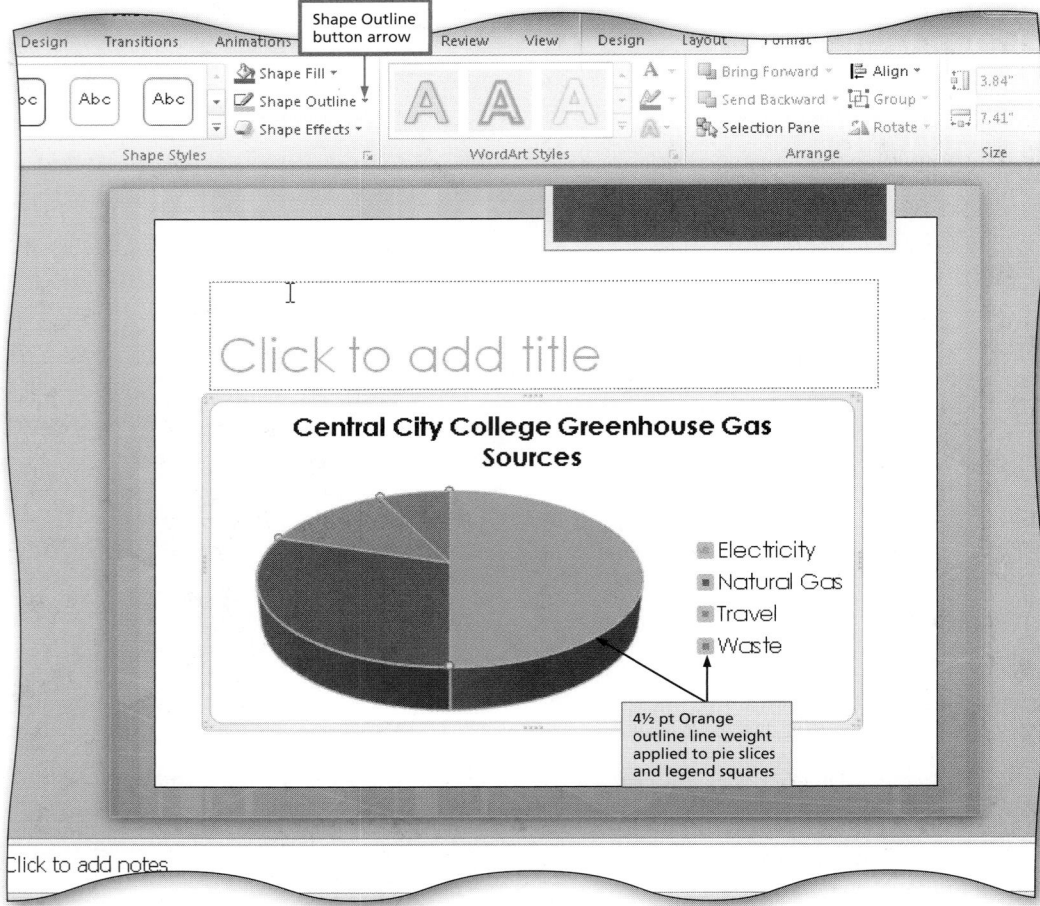

Figure 4–36

To Change a Chart Layout

Once you have selected a chart style, you can modify the look of the chart elements by changing its layout. The various layouts move the legend above or below the chart, or they move some or all of the legend data directly onto the individual chart pieces. For example, in the pie chart type, seven different layouts display only percentages on the pie slices, only the identifying information, such as the word, Electricity, or combinations of this data. If the chart layout displays a title that provides sufficient information to describe the chart's purpose, you may want to delete the slide title text placeholder. The following steps apply a chart layout with a title, legend, and percentages to the Slide 3 pie chart and then delete the title text placeholder.

1

• With the chart still selected, click the Chart Tools Design tab to display the Chart Tools Design Ribbon and then click the More button in the Chart Layouts gallery to expand the gallery.

• Point to Layout 2 (second chart in first row) (Figure 4–37).

Q&A

Does the Chart Layouts gallery have a live preview feature?

This feature is not available.

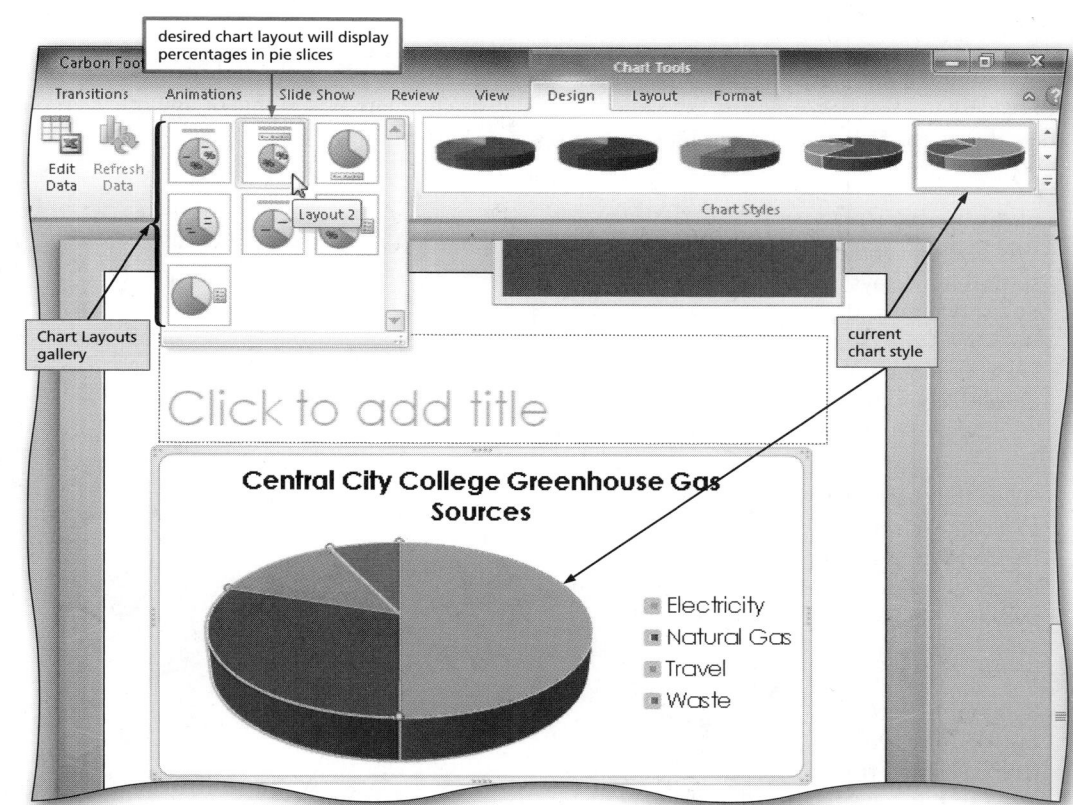

Figure 4–37

2

• Click Layout 2 in the Chart Layouts gallery to apply the selected layout to the chart (Figure 4–38).

Q&A

Can I change the chart layout?

Because a live preview is not available, you may want to sample the various layouts to evaluate their effectiveness. To change these layouts, repeat Steps 1 and 2 with different layouts.

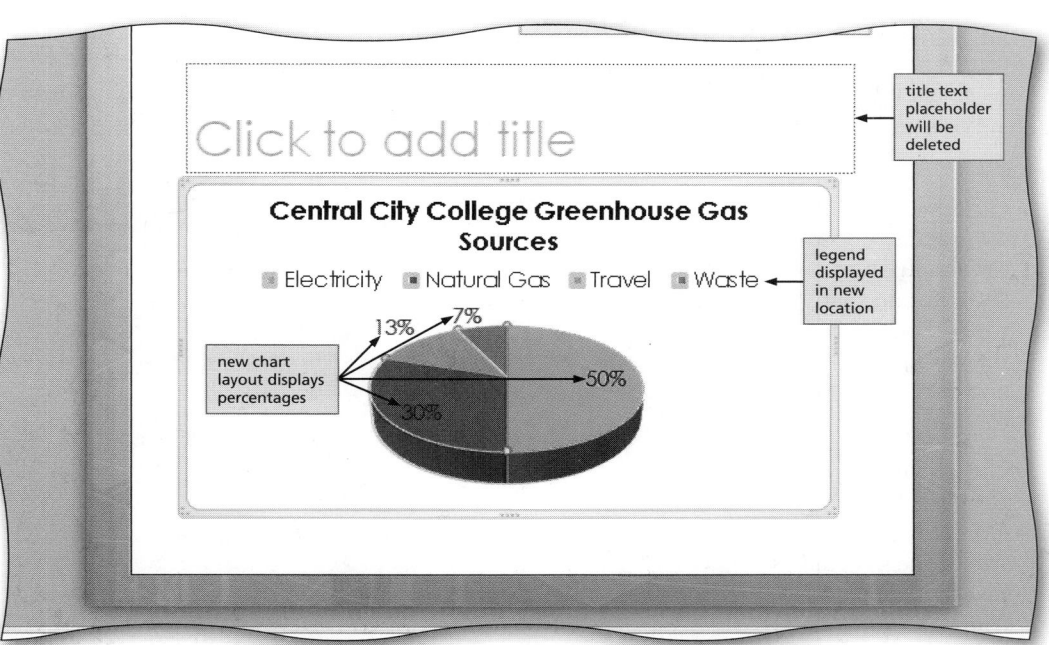

Figure 4–38

To Resize a Chart

Removing the title text placeholder increases the white space on the slide, so you are able to enlarge the chart and aid readability. You resize a chart the same way you resize a SmartArt graphic or any other graphical object. The following steps delete the title text placeholder and resize the chart to fill Slide 3.

- Click a border of the title text placeholder so that it displays as a solid line and then press the DELETE key to remove the placeholder.

- Select the chart, point to a corner sizing handle, and then drag diagonally outward, as shown in Figure 4–39.

- Release the mouse button to resize the chart. Position the chart so it is centered in the slide.

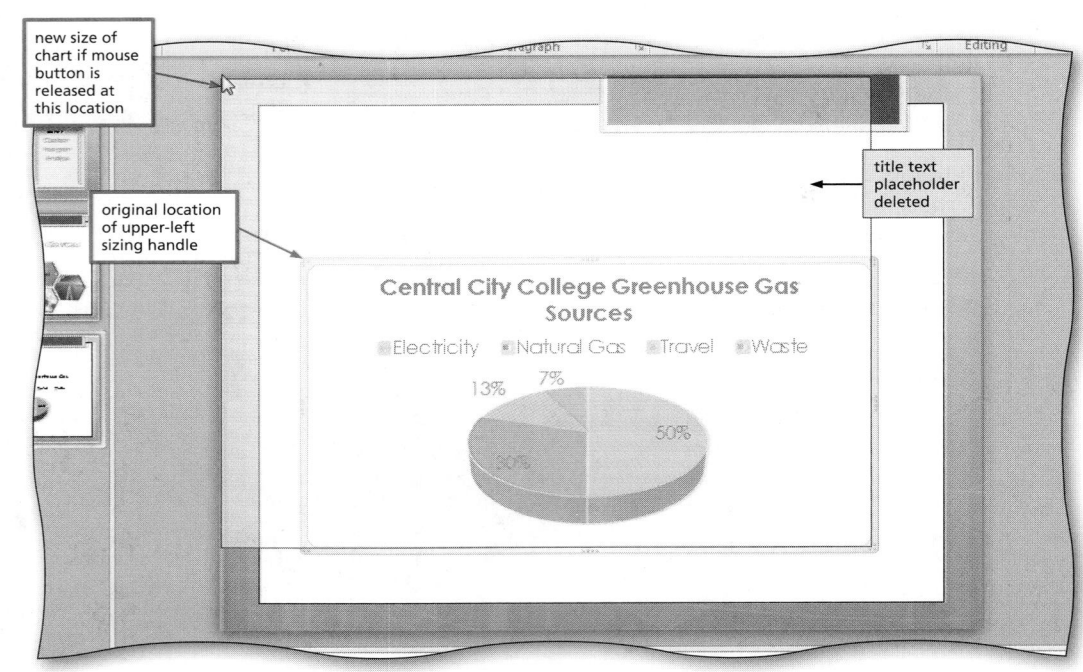

Figure 4–39

To Change the Title and Legend Font Size

Depending upon the complexity of the chart and the overall slide, you may want to increase the font size of the chart title and legend to increase readability. The following steps change the font size of both of these chart elements.

- Click the chart title, Central City College Greenhouse Gas Sources, and then triple-click to select the paragraph of text and display the Mini toolbar.

- Click the Increase Font Size button to increase the font size of the selected text to 32 point (Figure 4–40).

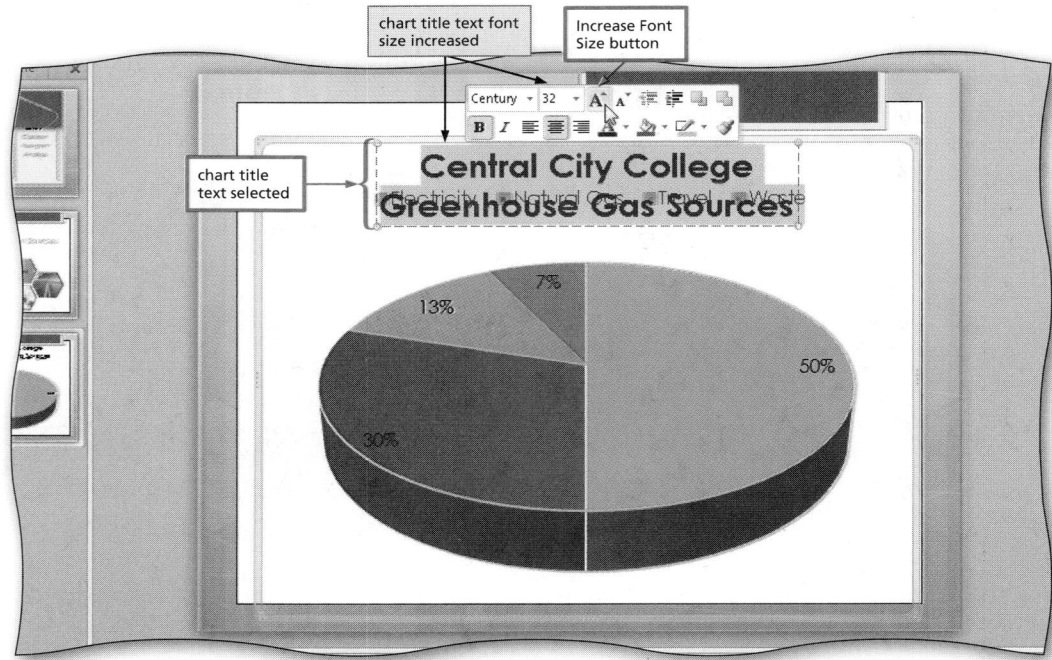

Figure 4–40

2

- Click an area of the chart other than the title to position the new title text.

- Right-click the legend in the chart to display the Mini toolbar and a legends shortcut menu.

- Click the Increase Font Size button on the Mini toolbar to increase the font size of the legend text to 20 point (Figure 4–41).

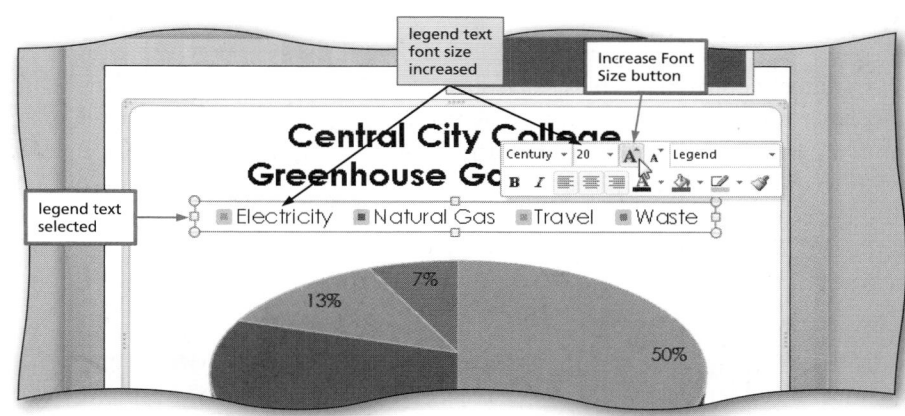

Figure 4–41

To Separate a Pie Slice

At times, you may desire to draw the viewers' attention to a particular area of the pie chart. To add this emphasis, you can separate, or explode, one or more slices. For example, you can separate the orange Travel slice of the chart to stress that Central City College students and staff contribute significantly to greenhouse gas production when traveling to and from campus. The following steps separate a chart slice.

1

- Click the orange Travel slice of the pie chart to select it.

- Click and hold down the mouse button and then drag the Travel slice diagonally toward the word, Electricity (Figure 4–42).

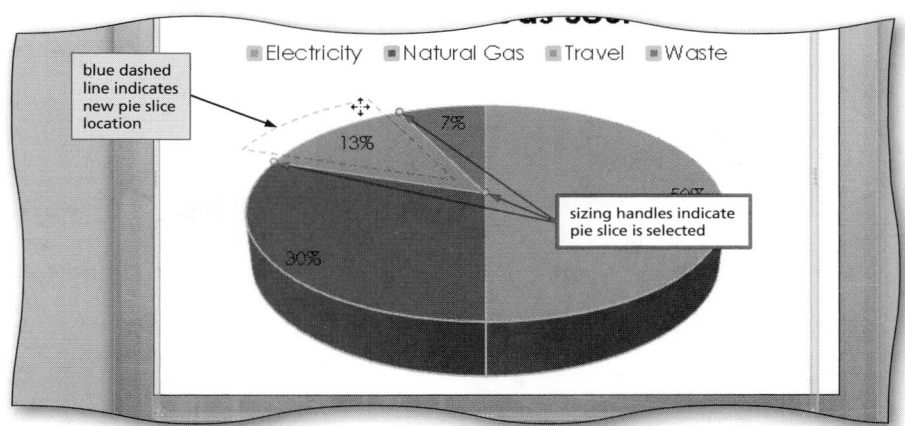

Figure 4–42

2

- Release the mouse button to position the slice in a new location on the slide (Figure 4–43).

Q&A

Can I change the size of chart objects?

Charts are composed of several elements, including the horizontal and vertical axes, plot area, chart area, and legend. When you select one of these objects, you then can point to a sizing handle and drag outward or inward to adjust the object's size.

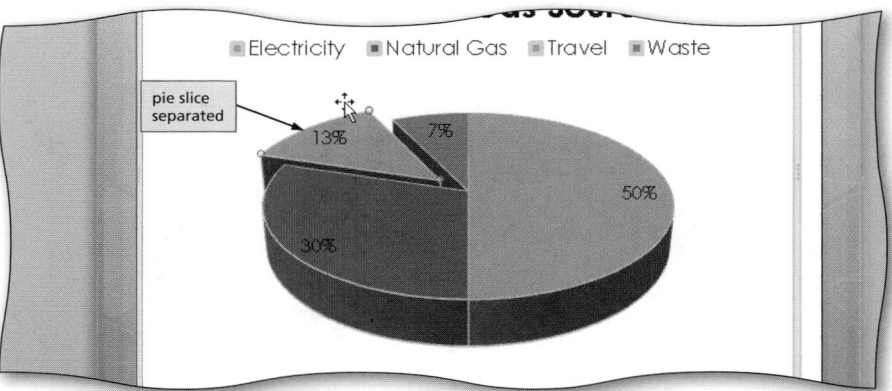

Figure 4–43

To Rotate a Chart

Excel determines where each slice of pie is positioned in the chart. You may desire to have a specific slice display in a different location, such as at the top or bottom of the circle. You can rotate the entire chart clockwise until a particular part of the chart displays where you desire. A circle's circumference is 360 degrees, so if you want to move a slice from the top of the chart to the bottom, you would rotate it halfway around the circle, or 180 degrees. Similarly, if you a want a slice to move one-quarter of the way around the slide, you would rotate it either 90 degrees or 270 degrees. The following steps rotate the chart so that the orange Travel slice displays at the bottom of the chart.

- With the orange Travel slice of the pie chart still selected, click the Chart Tools Format tab to display the Chart Tools Format Ribbon.

- Click the Format Selection button (Chart Tools Format tab | Current Selection group) to display the Format Data Point dialog box (Figure 4–44).

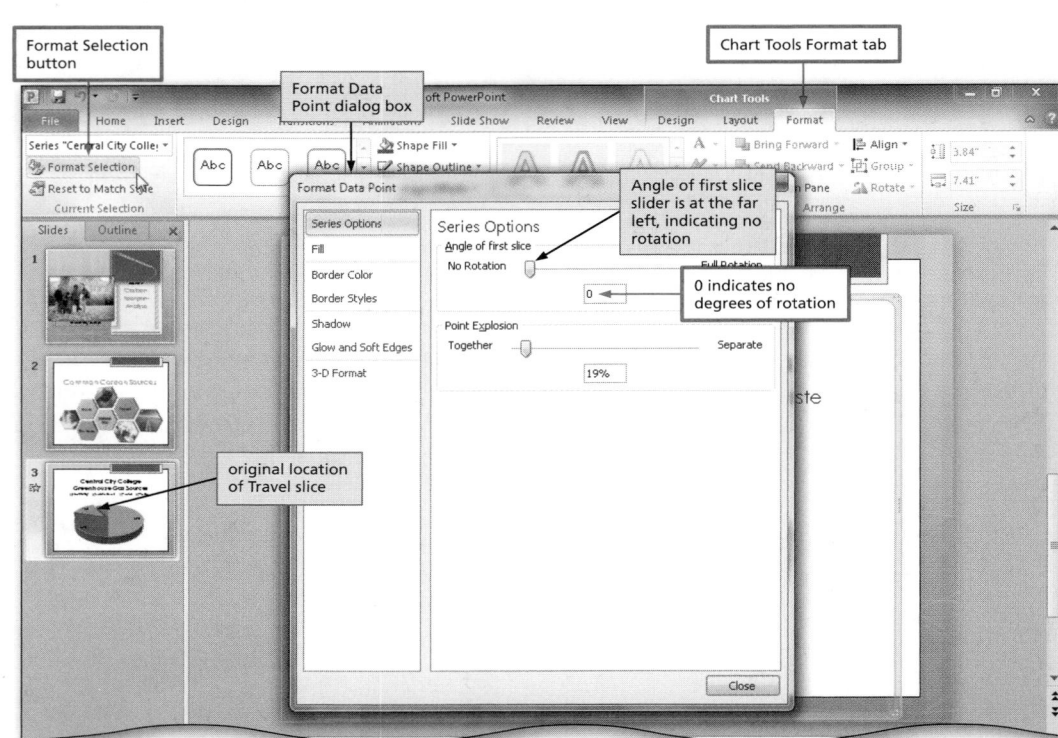

Figure 4–44

- Click the 'Angle of first slice' text box, delete the text, and then type 235 in the box to specify that the Travel slice rotates 235 degrees to the right (Figure 4–45).

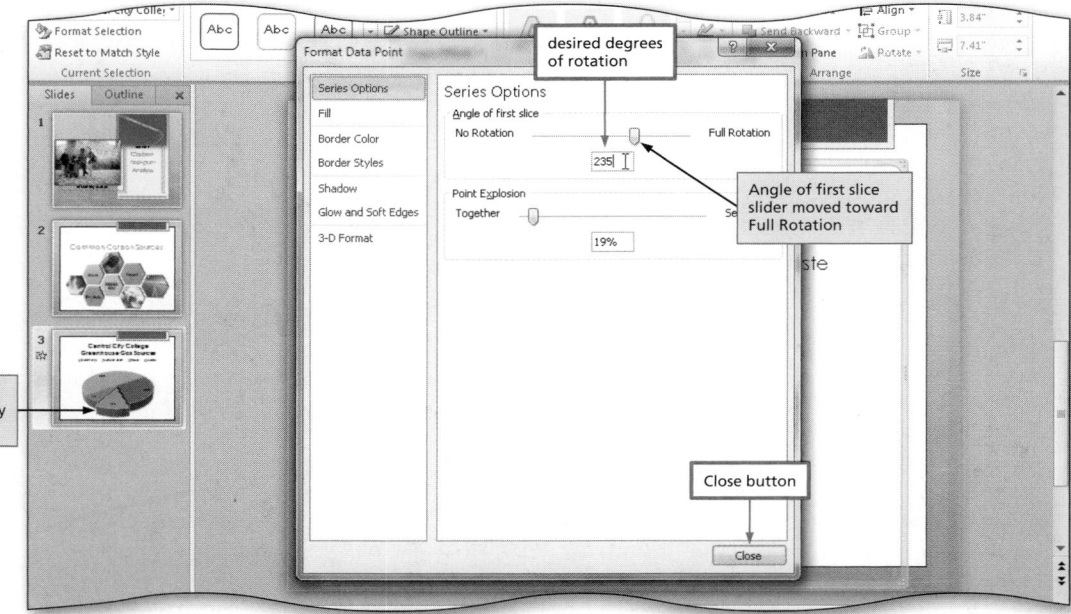

Figure 4–45

3

• Click the Close button to close the dialog box and rotate the chart (Figure 4–46).

Q&A

Can I specify a precise position where the chart will display on the slide?

Yes. Right-click the edge of the chart, click Format Chart Area on the shortcut menu, click Position in the left pane (Format Chart Area dialog box), and then enter measurements in the Horizontal and Vertical text boxes and specify whether these distances are from the Top Left Corner or the Center of the slide.

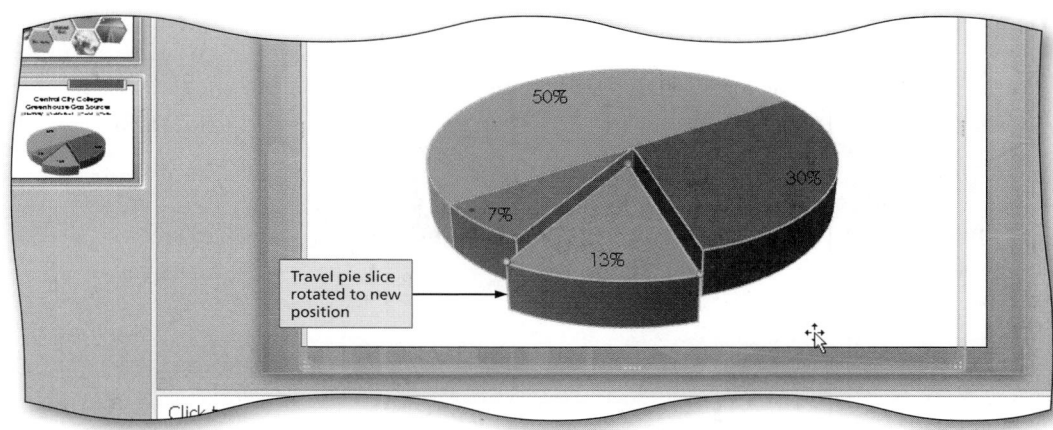

Travel pie slice rotated to new position

Figure 4–46

Break Point: If you wish to take a break, this is a good place to do so. Be sure to save the Carbon Footprint file again and then you can quit PowerPoint. To resume at a later time, start PowerPoint, open the file called Carbon Footprint, and continue following the steps from this location forward.

Adding a Table to a Slide and Formatting

One effective method of organizing information on a slide is to use a **table**, which is a grid consisting of rows and columns. You can enhance a table with formatting, including adding colors, lines, and backgrounds, and changing fonts.

In the following pages, you will perform these tasks:

1. Insert a table and then enter data and symbols.
2. Apply a table style.
3. Add borders and an effect.
4. Resize the table.
5. Add an image.
6. Merge cells and then display text in the cell vertically.
7. Align text in cells.
8. Format table data.

Tables

The table on Slide 4 (shown in Figure 4–1d on page PPT 203) contains information about the five major methods students and staff use to travel to campus. This data is listed in four columns and six rows. The intersections of these rows and columns are **cells**.

To begin developing this table, you first must create an empty table and insert it into the slide. You must specify the table's **dimension**, which is the total number of rows and columns. This table will have a 4 × 6 dimension; the first number indicates the number of columns, and the second specifies the number of rows. You will fill the cells with data pertaining to transportation to campus. Then you will format the table using a table style.

BTW

Entering Table Data
The table you create on Slide 4 has four columns and six rows. Many times, however, you may need to create much larger tables and then enter data into many cells. In these cases, experienced PowerPoint designers recommend clearing all formatting from the table so that you can concentrate on the numbers and letters and not be distracted by the colors and borders. To clear formatting, click the Clear Table command at the bottom of the Table Styles gallery (Table Tools Design tab | Table Styles group). Then, add a table style once you have verified that all table data is correct.

To Insert an Empty Table

The next step in developing the presentation is to insert an empty table. The following steps insert a table with four columns and six rows into Slide 4.

- Add a new slide to the presentation (Figure 4–47).

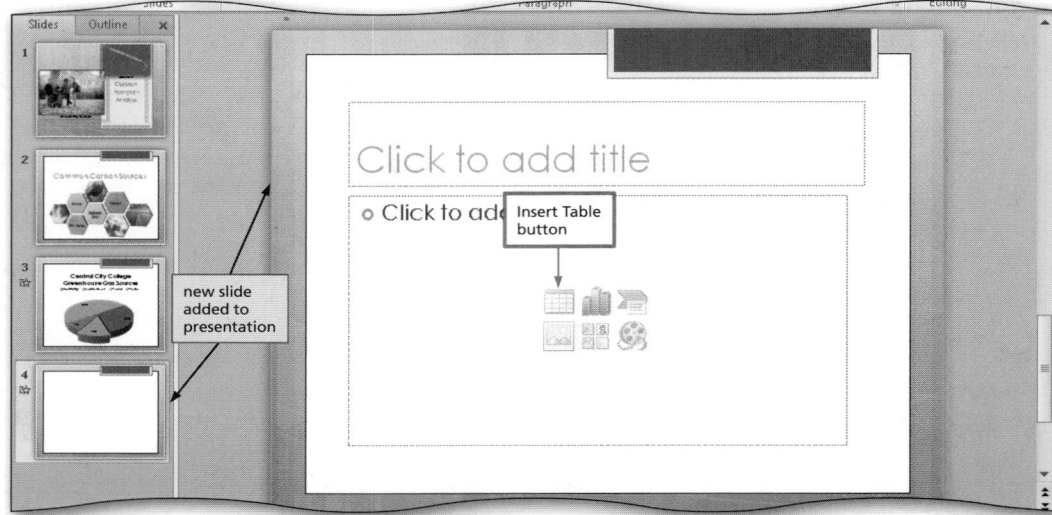

Figure 4–47

- Click the Insert Table button in the content placeholder to display the Insert Table dialog box.

- Click the down arrow to the right of the 'Number of columns' text box one time so that the number 4 appears in the box.

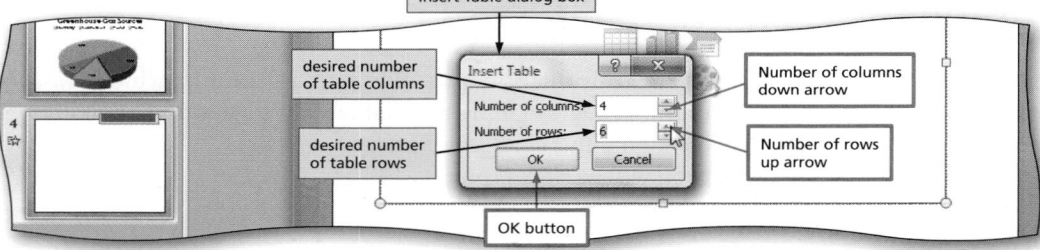

Figure 4–48

- Click the up arrow to the right of the 'Number of rows' text box four times so that the number 6 appears in the box (Figure 4–48).

- Click the OK button (Insert Table dialog box) to insert the table into Slide 4 (Figure 4–49).

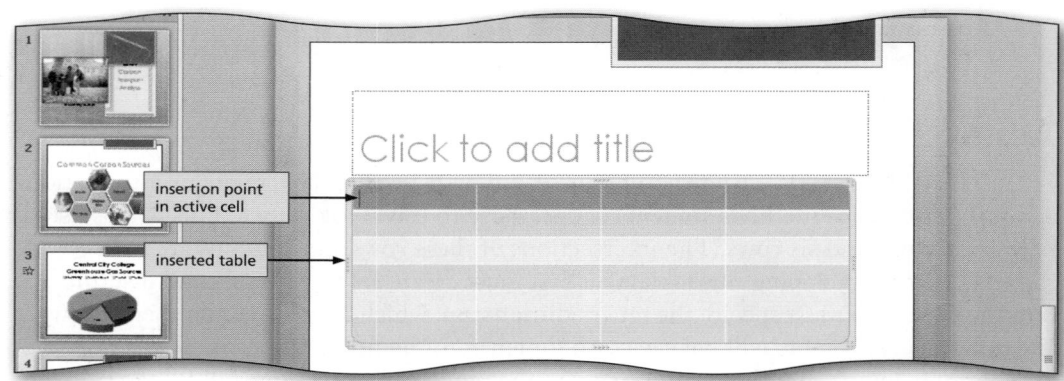

Figure 4–49

Other Ways

1. Click Table on Insert tab, drag to select columns and rows, press ENTER

To Enter Data in a Table

The Slide 4 table title will display vertically in the first column. The three columns to the right of this title will contain data with symbols representing the type of travel, words describing this travel, and the percent of students and staff using these modes of travel. The next step is to enter data in the cells of the empty table. To place data in a cell, you click the cell and then type text. The following steps enter the data in the table.

1

- Click the second cell in the third column to place the insertion point in this cell. Type **Drive alone** and then press the TAB key to advance the insertion point to the adjacent right column cell.

- Type **53%** and then press the TAB key three times to advance to the cell below the words, Drive Alone.

- Type **Carpool** and then press the TAB key.

- Type **5%** and then press the TAB key three times (Figure 4–50).

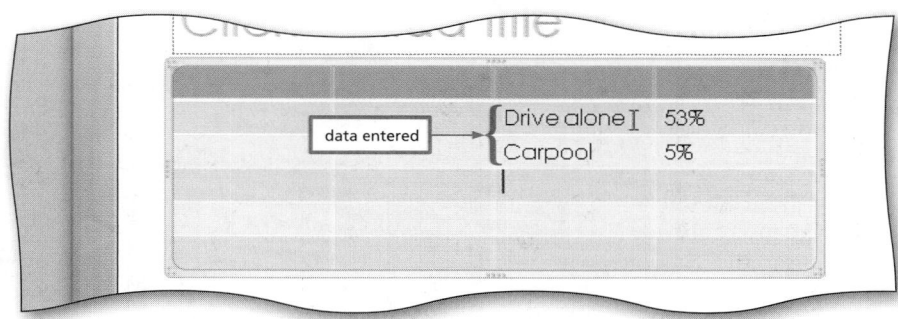

Figure 4–50

How do I correct cell contents if I make a mistake?

Click the cell and then correct the text.

Can I use the arrow keys to move the insertion point in the table cells?

Yes.

2

- Enter the data for the remaining table cells in the third and fourth columns, using Figure 4–51 as a guide.

What if I pressed the TAB key after filling in the last cell and added another row?

Right-click the unnecessary row and then click Delete Rows on the shortcut menu.

How would I add more rows to the table?

When the insertion point is positioned in the bottom-right cell, press the TAB key.

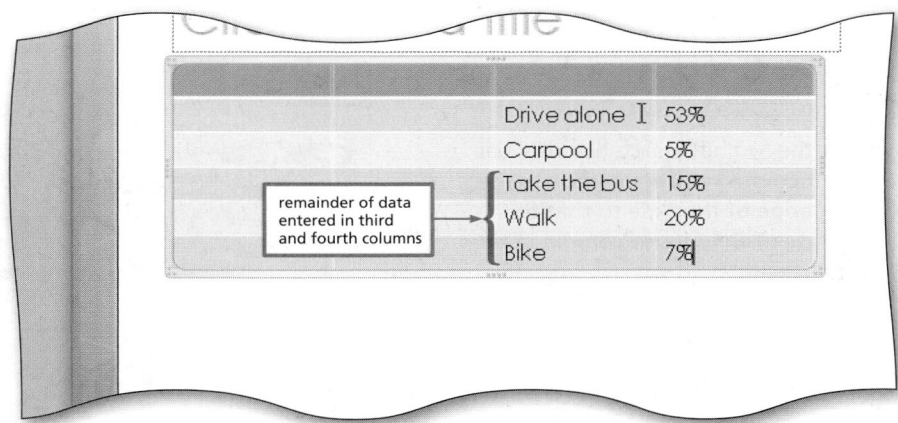

Figure 4–51

To Insert a Symbol

The Slide 4 table title will display vertically in the first column. The three columns to the right of this title will contain symbols and words describing the type of travel and the percent of students and staff using these modes of travel. The second column of the table contains symbols depicting the various modes of transportation. Although you could add clip art or pictures to these table cells, you also can insert special symbols. You insert symbols, such as mathematical characters and dots, using the Symbol dialog box.

The following steps insert symbols in the second table column.

1

● Click the second cell in the second column to place the insertion point in this cell.

● Display the Insert tab.

● Click the Symbol button (Insert tab | Symbols group) to display the Symbol dialog box (Figure 4–52).

Q&A
What if the symbol I want to insert already appears in the Symbol dialog box?

You can click any symbol shown in the dialog box to insert it in the slide.

Q&A
Why does my 'Recently used symbols' list display different symbols from those shown in Figure 4–52?

As you insert symbols, PowerPoint places them in the 'Recently used symbols' list.

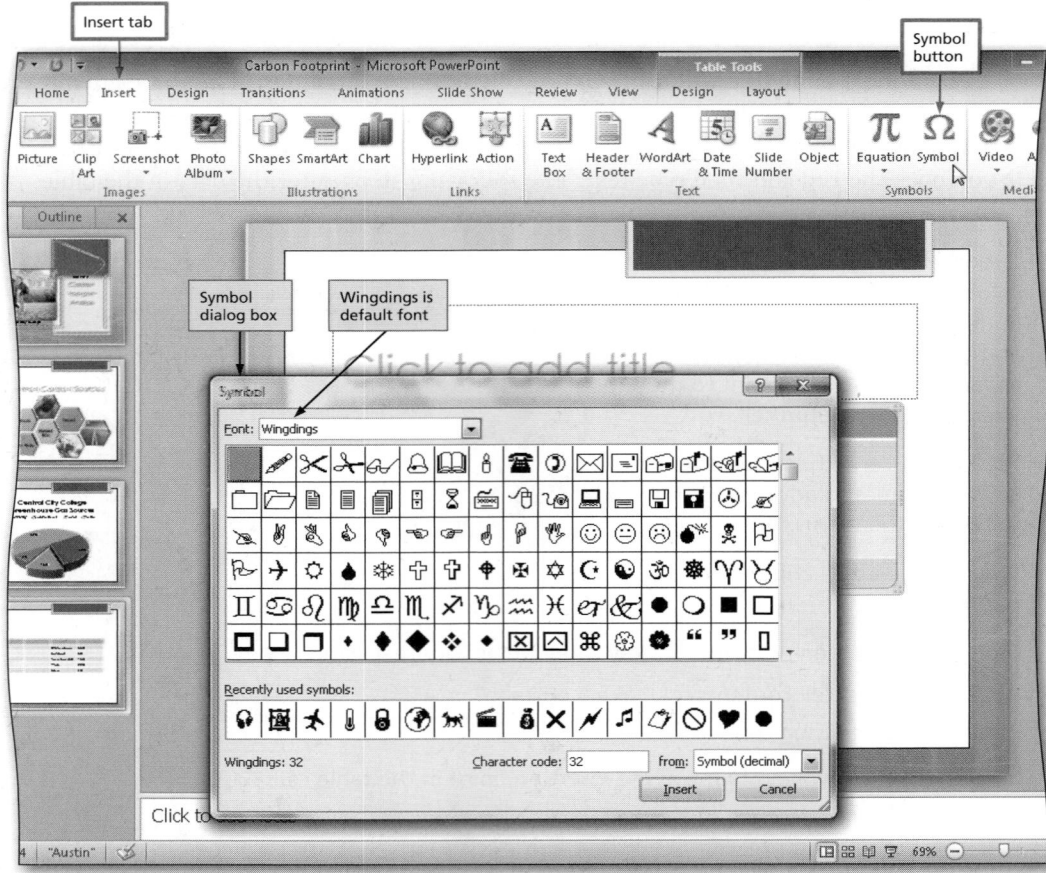

Figure 4–52

2

● Click the Symbol dialog box title bar and then drag the dialog box to the right edge of the slide so that the left side of the second column in the table is visible.

3

● If Webdings is not the font displayed in the Font box, click the Font box arrow (Symbol dialog box) and then scroll to Webdings and click it.

● In the list of symbols, if necessary, scroll to and then click the man symbol shown in Figure 4–53.

● Click the Insert button (Symbol dialog box) to place the man symbol in the selected table cell (Figure 4–53).

Q&A
Why is the Symbol dialog box still open?

The Symbol dialog box remains open, allowing you to insert additional symbols.

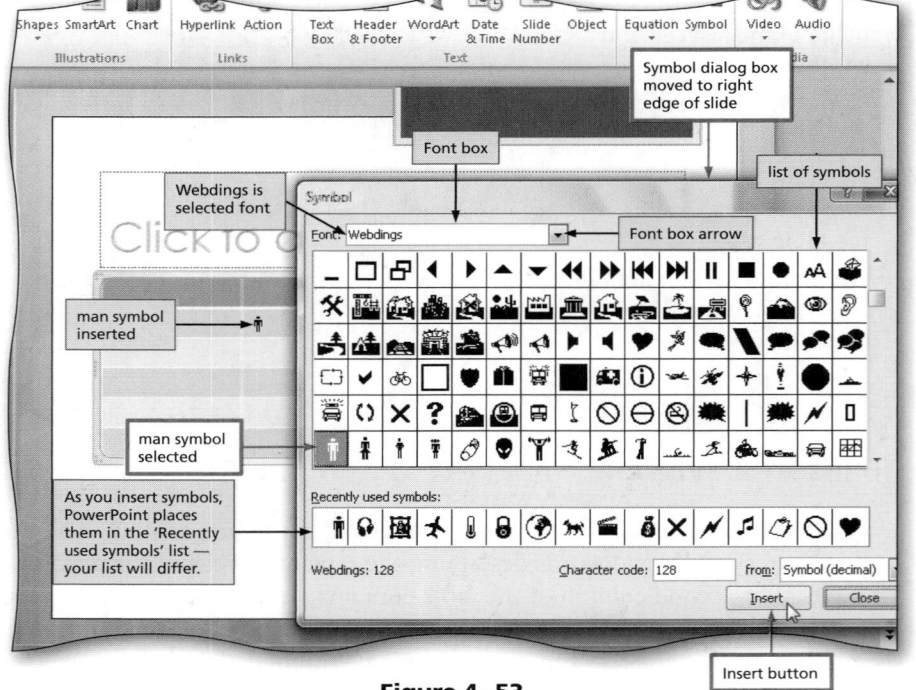

Figure 4–53

4

- In the list of symbols, click the car symbol shown in Figure 4–54.

- Click the Insert button (Symbol dialog box) to place the car symbol beside the man symbol in the selected table cell (Figure 4–54).

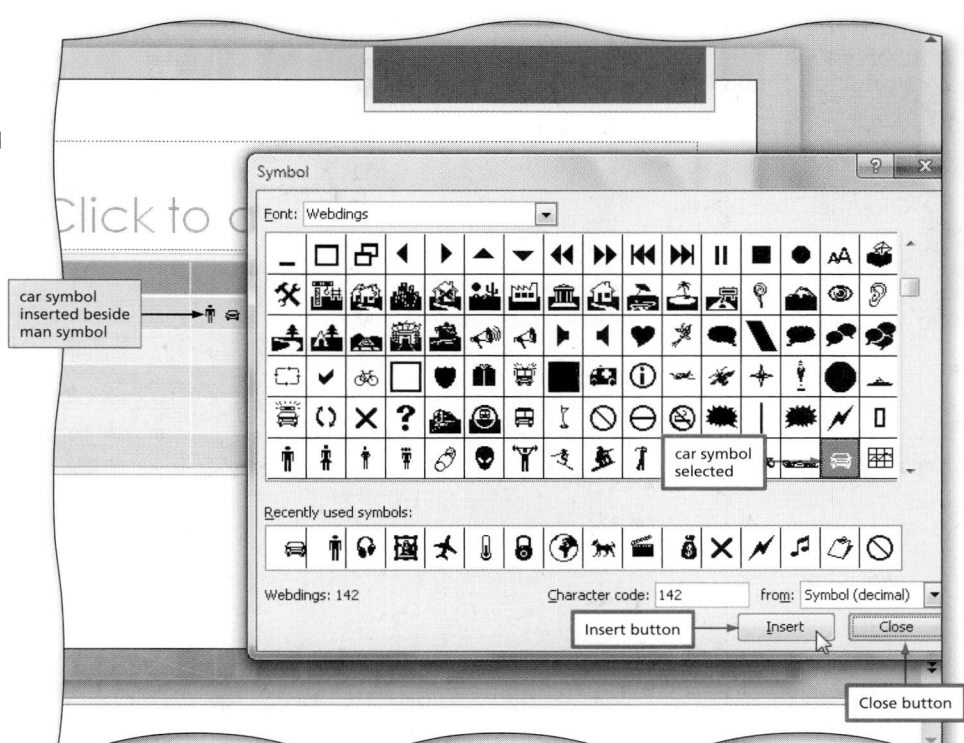

Figure 4–54

 5

- Click the Close button (Symbol dialog box).

 6

- Press the DOWN ARROW key to move the insertion point to the third cell in the second table column.

- Display the Symbol dialog box and then insert the people and car symbols shown in Figure 4–55.

Q&A

Can I insert the car symbol from the 'Recently used symbols' list?

Yes. PowerPoint designers generally reuse a set of symbols, which conveniently are displayed in this list for this purpose.

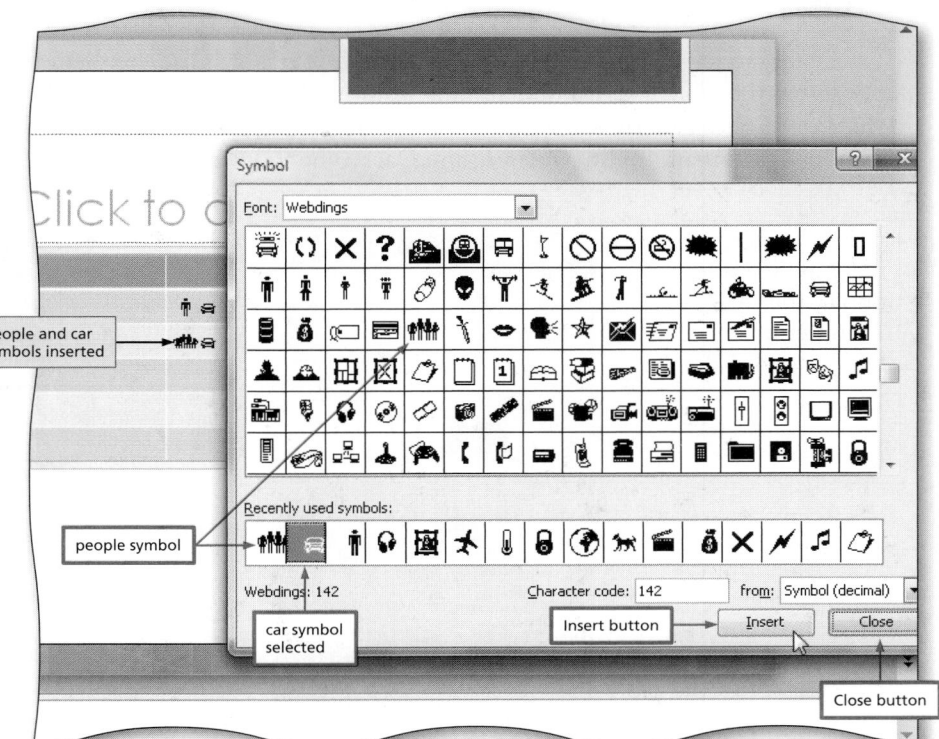

Figure 4–55

- Using Figure 4–56 as a guide, continue inserting symbols in the second column.

- Click the Close button (Symbol dialog box).

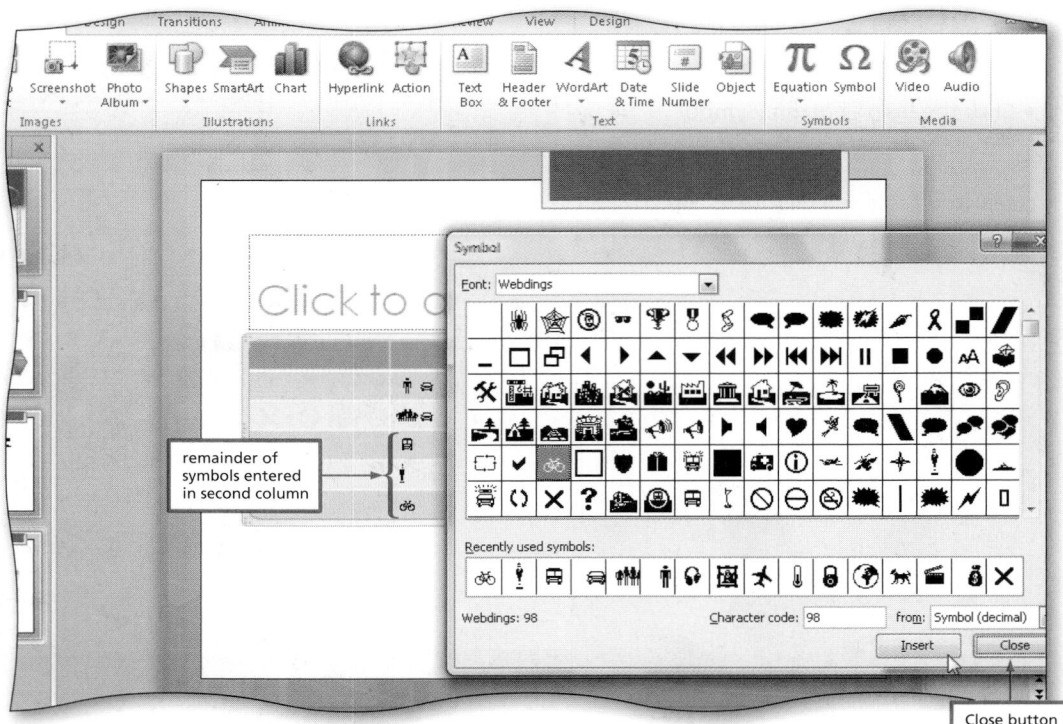

Figure 4–56

To Apply a Table Style

A table style is a combination of formatting options that use the theme colors applied to the presentation. When you inserted the table, PowerPoint automatically applied a style. Thumbnails of this style and others are displayed in the Table Styles gallery. These styles use a variety of colors and shading and are grouped in the categories of Best Match for Document, Light, Medium, and Dark. The following steps apply a table style to the Slide 4 table.

- With the insertion point in the table, display the Table Tools Design tab (Figure 4–57).

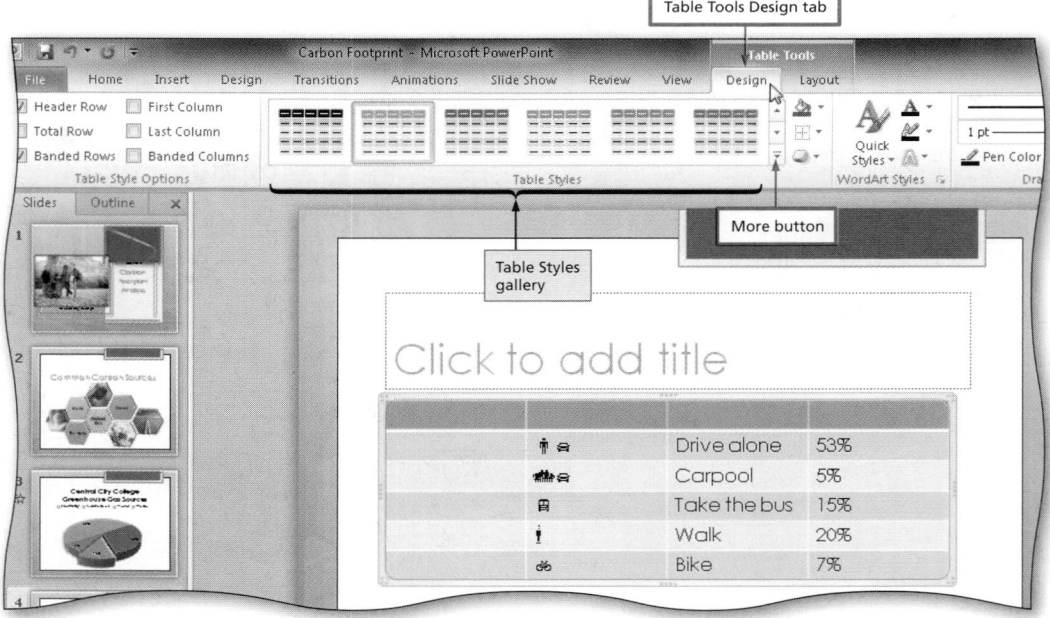

Figure 4–57

2
• Click the More button in the Table Styles gallery to expand the Table Styles gallery.

• Scroll down and then point to Dark Style 2 - Accent 3/Accent 4 in the Dark area (third table in last row) (Figure 4–58).

Q&A Does the Table Styles gallery have a live preview feature?

Yes, but the gallery is covering most of the table, greatly limiting your ability to preview table styles.

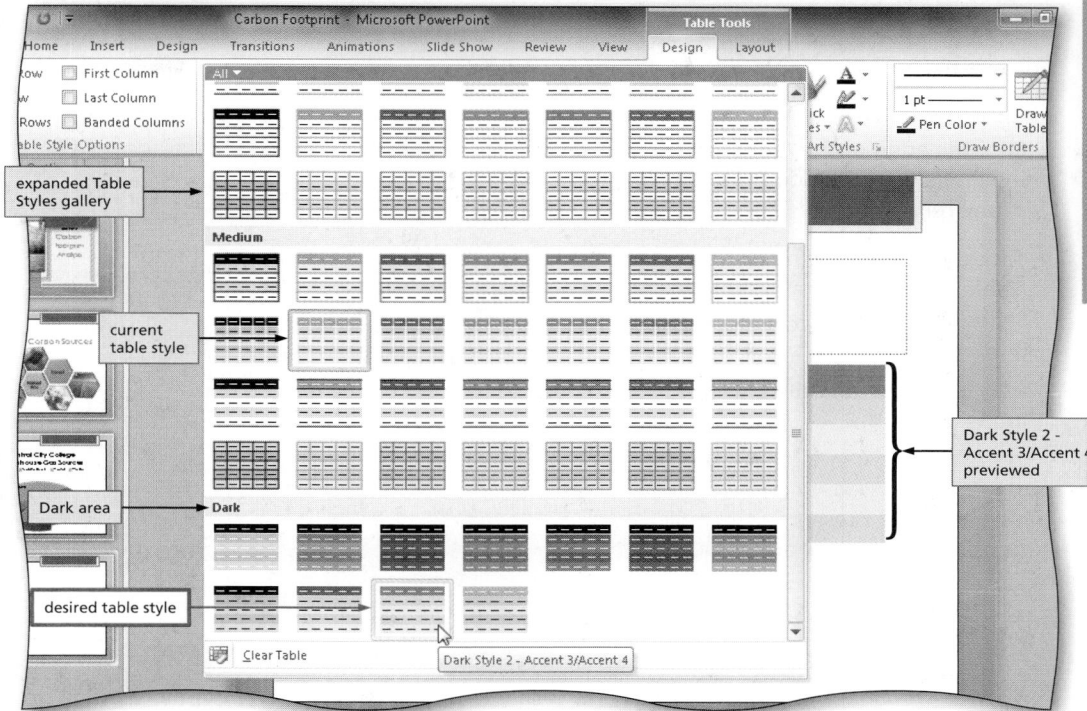

Figure 4–58

3
• Click Dark Style 2 - Accent 3/Accent 4 in the Table Styles gallery to apply the selected style to the table (Figure 4–59).

Q&A Can I resize the columns and rows or the entire table?

Yes. To resize columns or rows, drag a **column boundary** (the border to the right of a column) or the **row boundary** (the border at the bottom of a row) until the column or row is the desired width or height. To resize the entire table, drag a **table resize handle**.

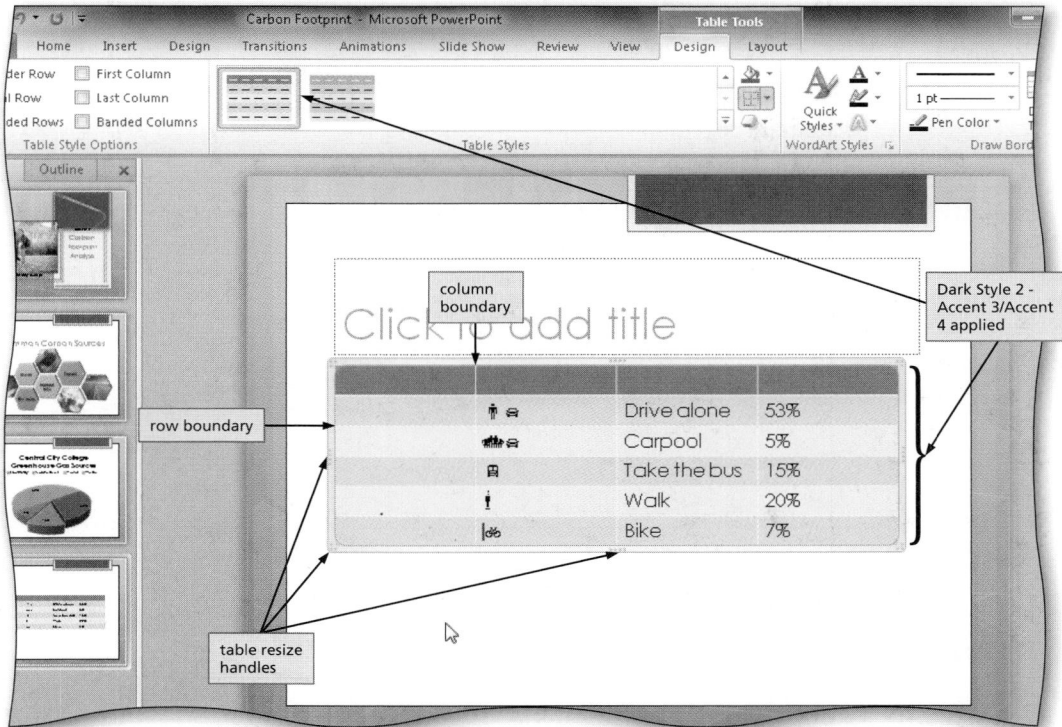

Figure 4–59

To Add Borders to a Table

The Slide 4 table does not have borders around the entire table or between the cells. The following steps add borders to the entire table.

- Click the edge of the table so that the insertion point does not appear in any cell.

- Click the Border button arrow (Table Tools Design tab | Table Styles group) to display the Border gallery (Figure 4–60).

Q&A Why is the button called No Border in the ScreenTip?

The ScreenTip name for the button will change based on the type of border, if any, present in the table. Currently no borders are applied.

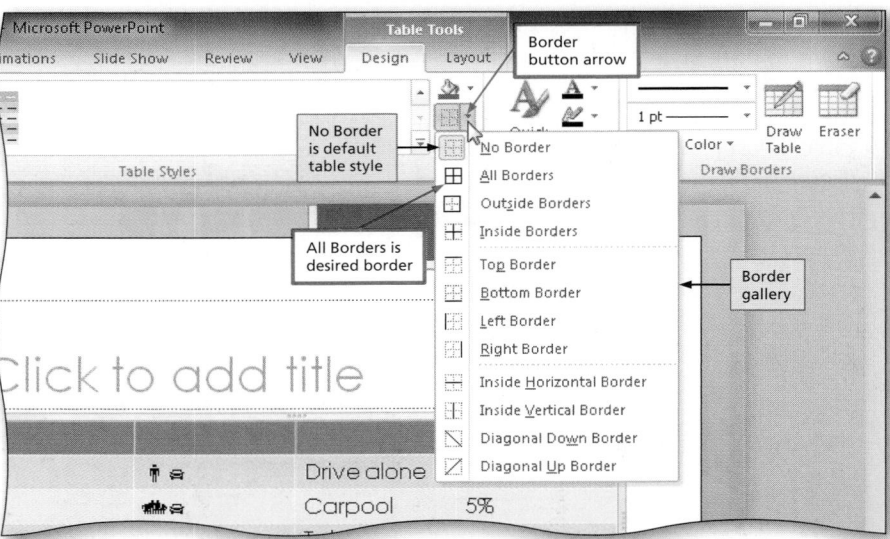

Figure 4–60

- Click All Borders in the Border gallery to add borders around the entire table and to each table cell (Figure 4–61).

Q&A Why is the border color black?

PowerPoint's default border color is black. This color is displayed on the Pen Color button (Table Tools Design tab | Draw Borders group).

Q&A Can I apply any of the border options in the Border gallery?

Yes. You can vary the look of your table by applying borders only to the cells, around the table, to the top, bottom, left or right edges, or a combination of these areas.

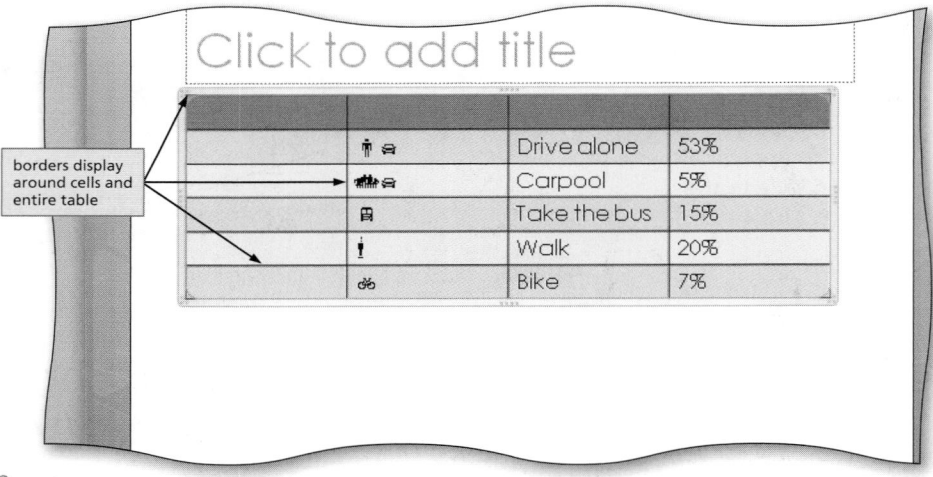

Figure 4–61

To Add an Effect to a Table

To enhance the visual appeal of the table, you can add an effect. PowerPoint gives you the option of applying a bevel to specified cells so they have a three-dimensional appearance. You also can add a shadow or reflection to the entire table. The following steps add a shadow and give a three-dimensional appearance to the entire table.

1

• With the table selected, click the Effects button (Table Tools Design tab | Table Styles group) to display the Effects menu.

Q&A What is the difference between a shadow and a reflection?

A shadow gives the appearance that a light is displayed on the table, which causes a shadow behind the graphic. A reflection gives the appearance that the table is shiny, so a mirror image appears below the actual graphic.

2

• Point to Shadow to display the Shadow gallery (Figure 4–62).

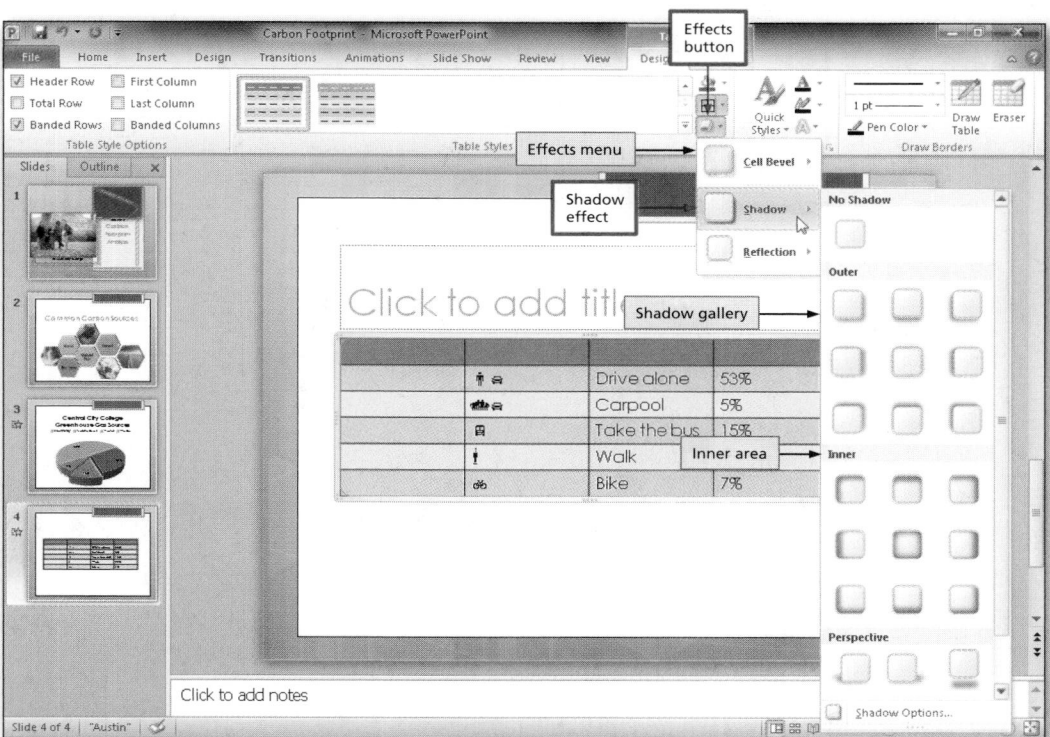

Figure 4–62

Q&A How do the shadows differ in the Outer, Inner, and Perspective categories?

The Outer shadows are displayed on the outside of the table, whereas the Inner shadows are displayed in the interior cells. The Perspective shadows give the illusion that a light is shining from the right or left side of the table or from above, and the table is casting a shadow.

3

• Point to Inside Center in the Inner category (second shadow in second row) to display a live preview of this shadow (Figure 4–63).

Experiment

• Point to the various shadows in the Shadow gallery and watch the shadows change in the table.

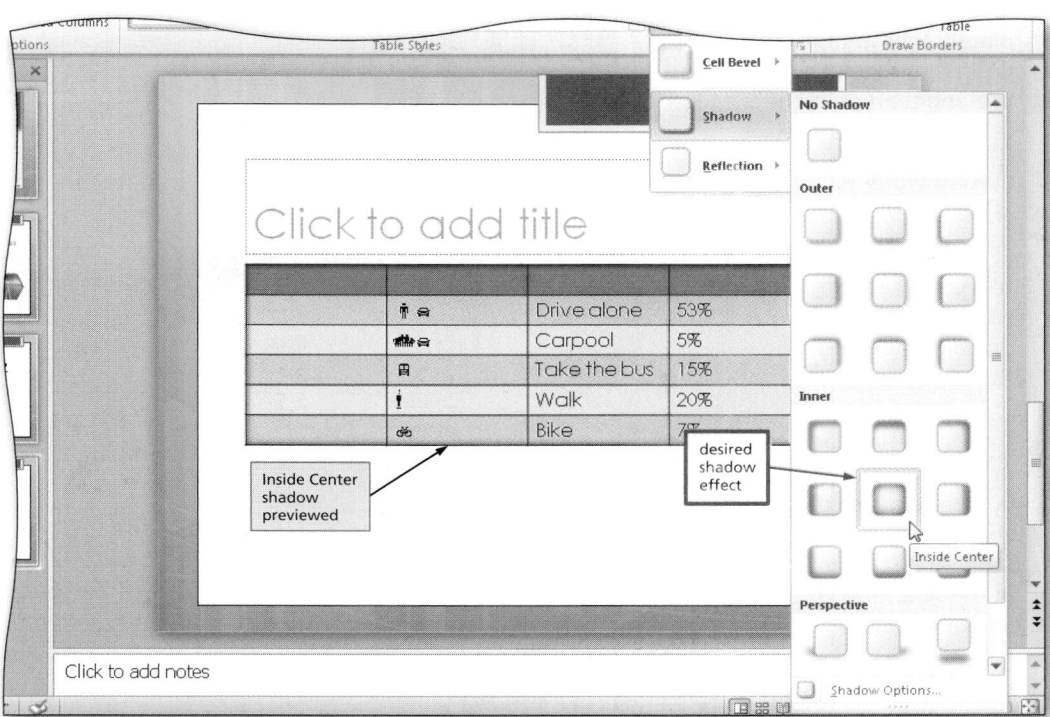

Figure 4–63

- Click Inside Center to apply this shadow to the table (Figure 4–64).

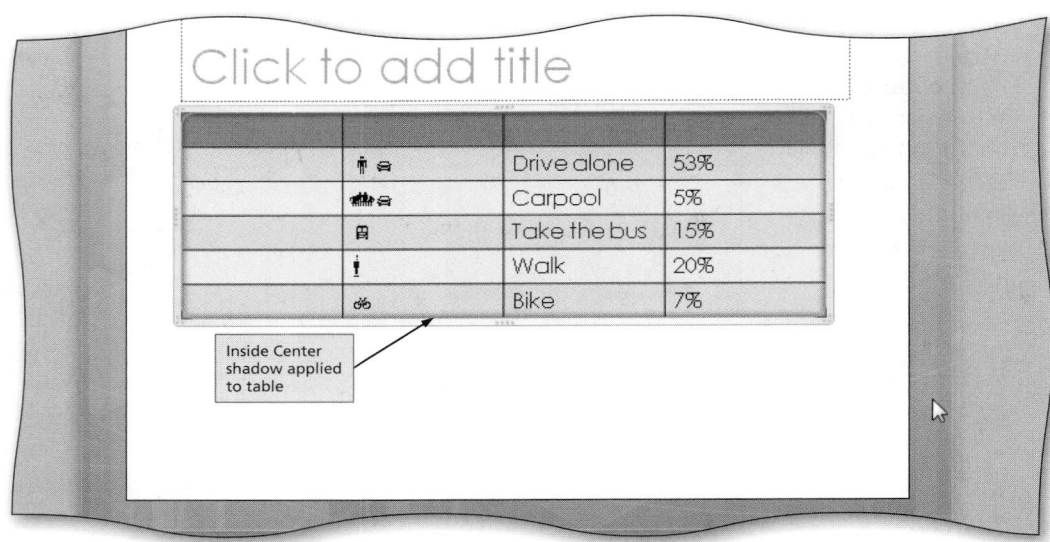

Figure 4–64

To Resize a Table

You resize a table the same way you resize a chart, a SmartArt graphic, or any other graphical object. On Slide 4, you can remove the title text placeholder because the table will have the title, Travel to Campus, in the first column. The following steps resize the table to fill Slide 4.

- Click a border of the title text placeholder so that it displays as a solid line and then press the DELETE key to remove the placeholder.

- Select the table, point to a corner sizing handle, and then drag diagonally outward, as shown in Figure 4–65.

❸
- Release the mouse button to resize the chart. Position the table so it is centered in the slide (shown in Figure 4–66).

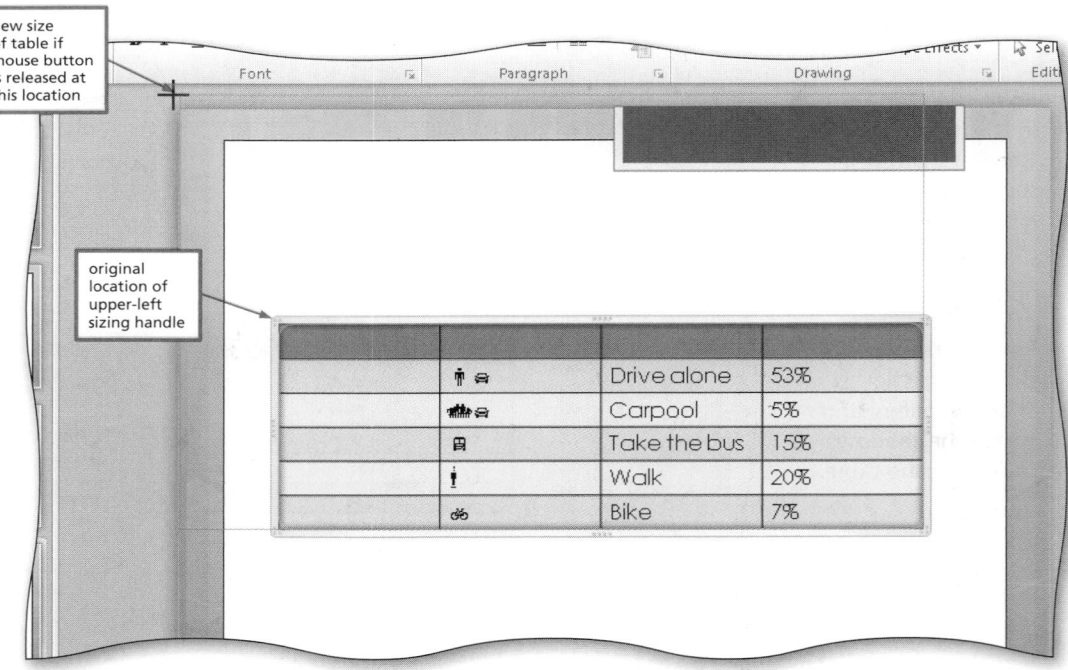

Figure 4–65

To Add an Image to a Table

Another table enhancement you can make is to add a picture or clip to a table cell. The following steps add a commuter picture to the upper-right table cell.

1

• Right-click the upper-right table cell to display the shortcut menu and Mini toolbar (Figure 4–66).

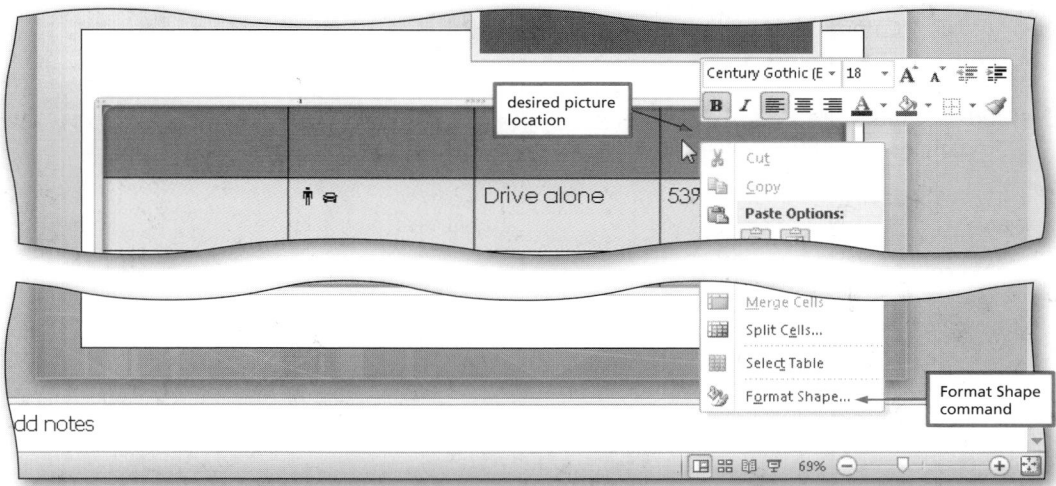

Figure 4–66

2

• Click Format Shape to display the Format Shape dialog box and then click 'Picture or texture fill' (Figure 4–67).

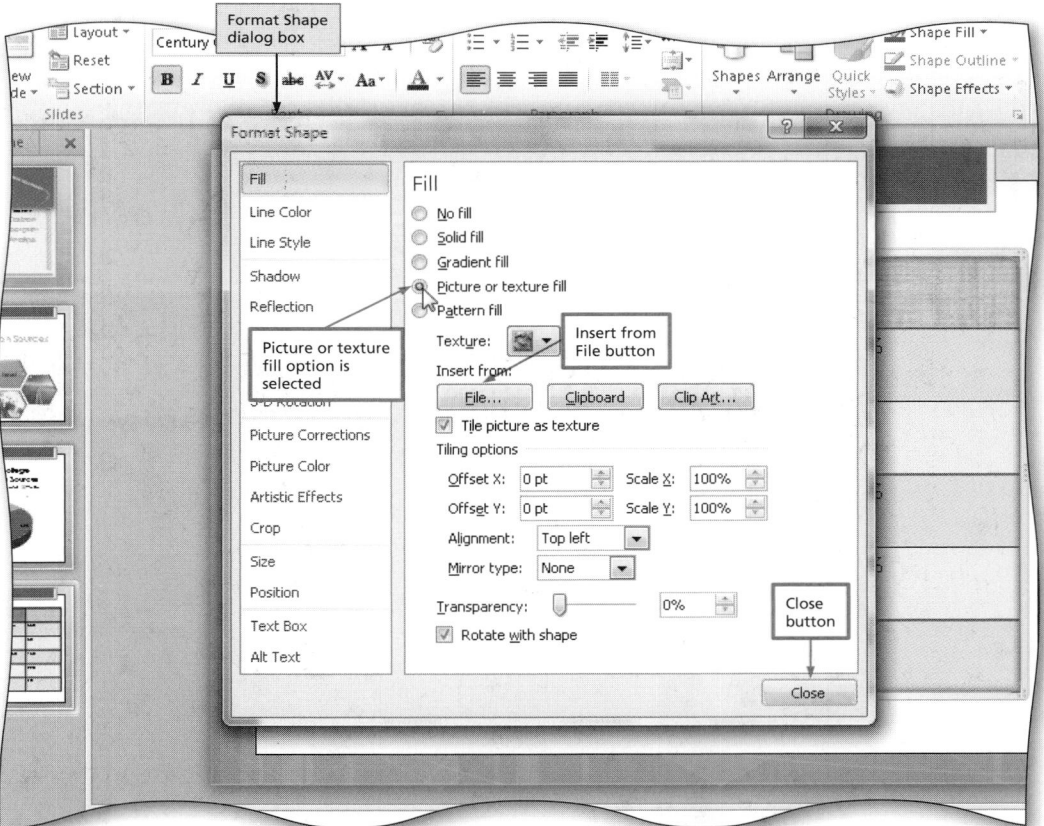

Figure 4–67

- Click the Insert from File button to display the Insert Picture dialog box.

- Select the Commuters picture located on the Data Files for Students and then click the Insert button in the Insert Picture dialog box to insert the picture into the table cell.

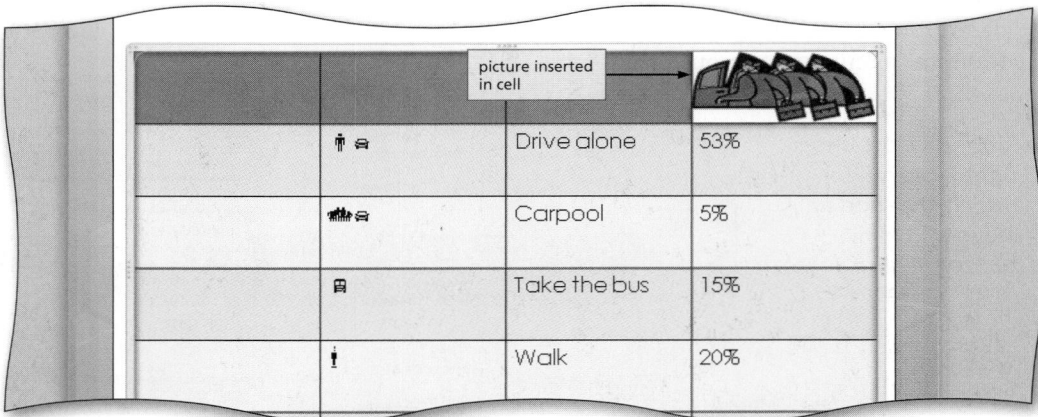

Figure 4–68

- Click the Close button (Format Shape dialog box) (Figure 4–68).

To Merge Cells

To provide space for the table title to stretch across the entire table height, you can merge all the cells in the first column. In addition, the top row of the table will contain only the picture you added to the upper-right cell, so you can merge cells in the top row so it looks like a single cell. The following steps merge the six cells in the first column into a single cell and merge two cells in the first table row.

- Drag through all six cells in the first table column to select these cells (Figure 4–69).

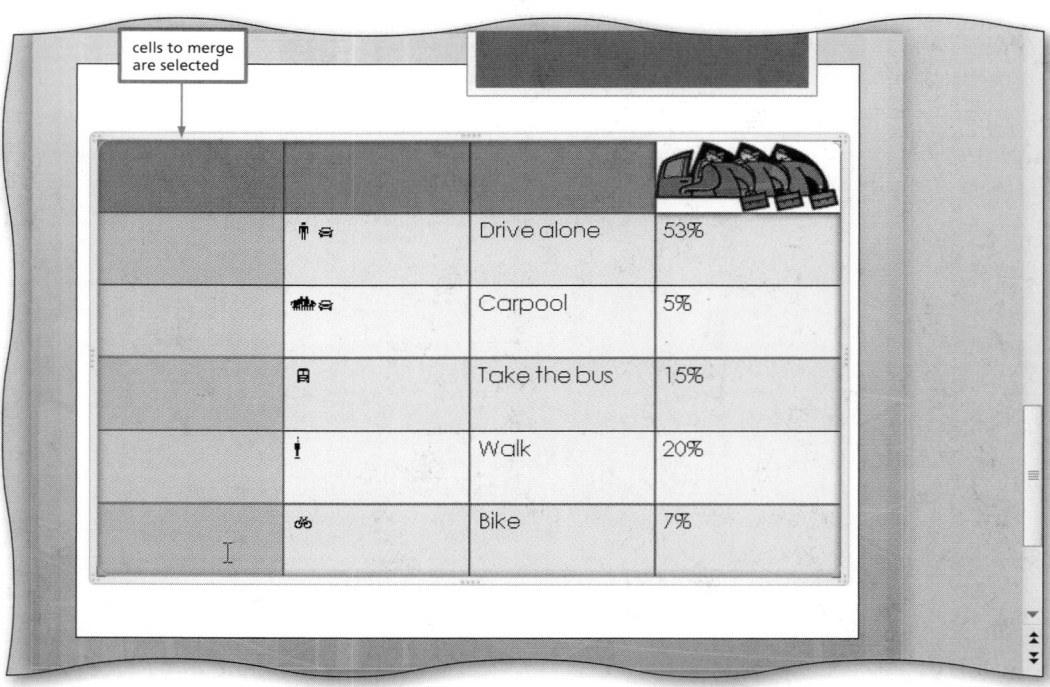

Figure 4–69

2

- Click the Table Tools Layout tab to display the Table Tools Layout Ribbon.

- Click the Merge Cells button (Table Tools Layout tab | Merge group) to merge the six column cells into one cell (Figure 4–70).

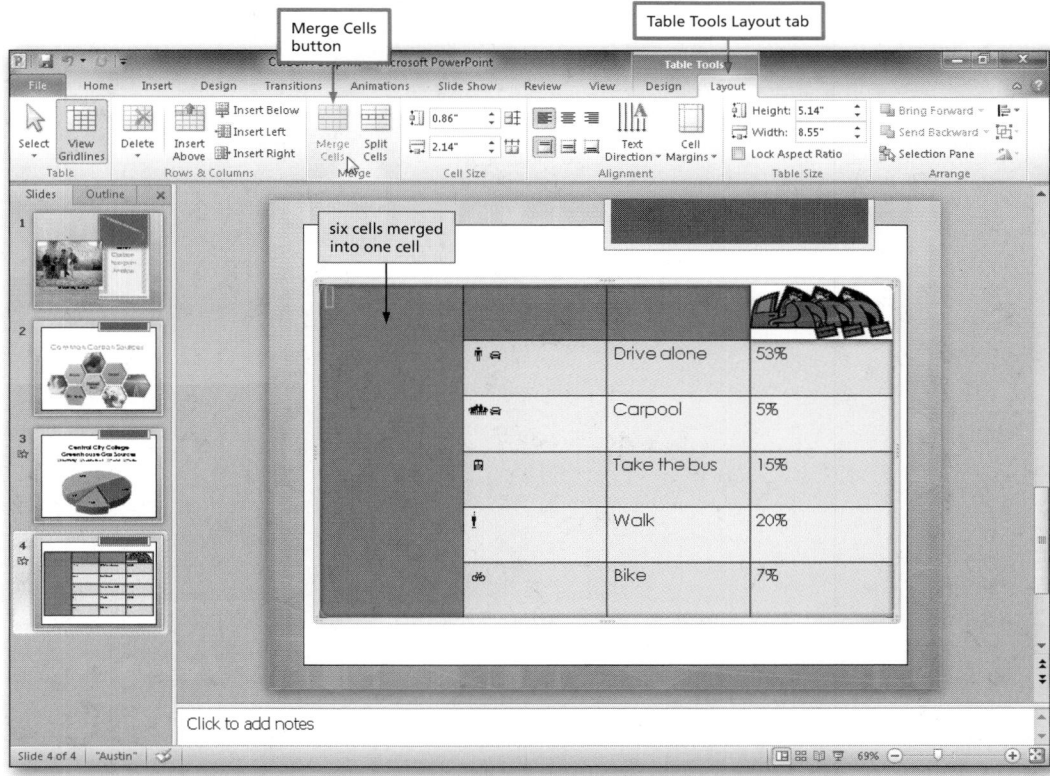

Figure 4–70

3

- Drag through the second and third column cells in the first table row to select these two cells (Figure 4–71).

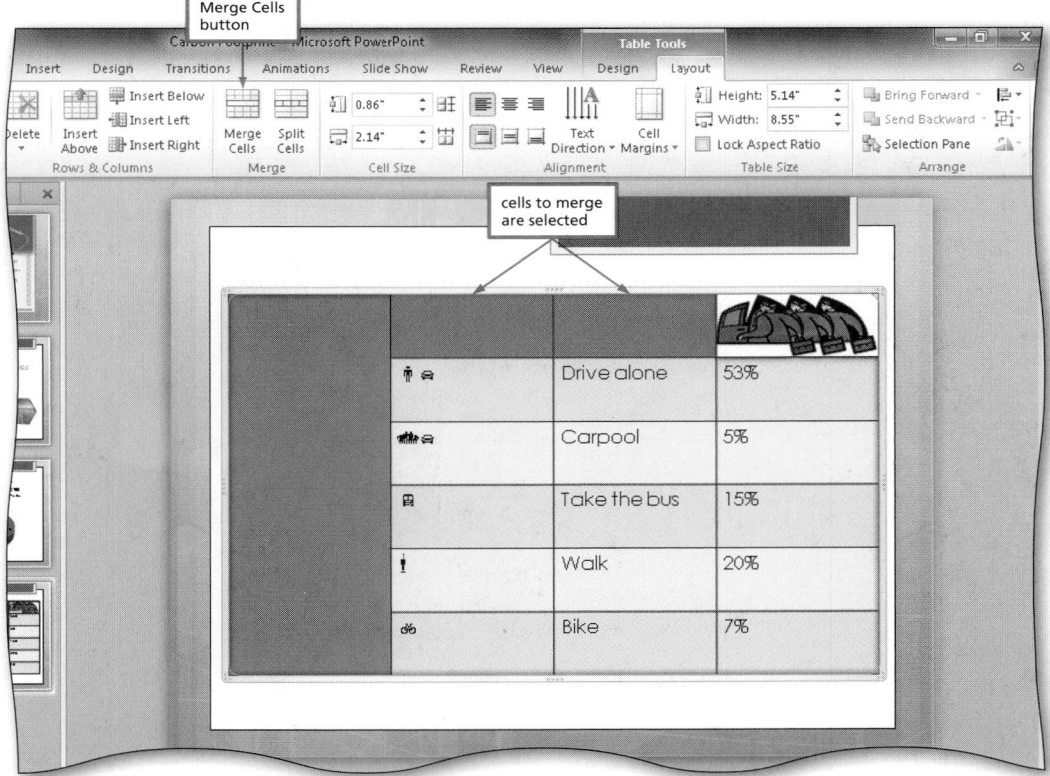

Figure 4–71

- Click the Merge Cells button to merge these cells (Figure 4–72).

Q&A

Could I have merged the cells in the first row before merging the first column cells?

Yes, but you would have achieved different results. If you merge the row one cells, then you would need to merge all first column cells except the first cell.

Other Ways

1. Right-click selected cells, click Merge Cells on shortcut menu

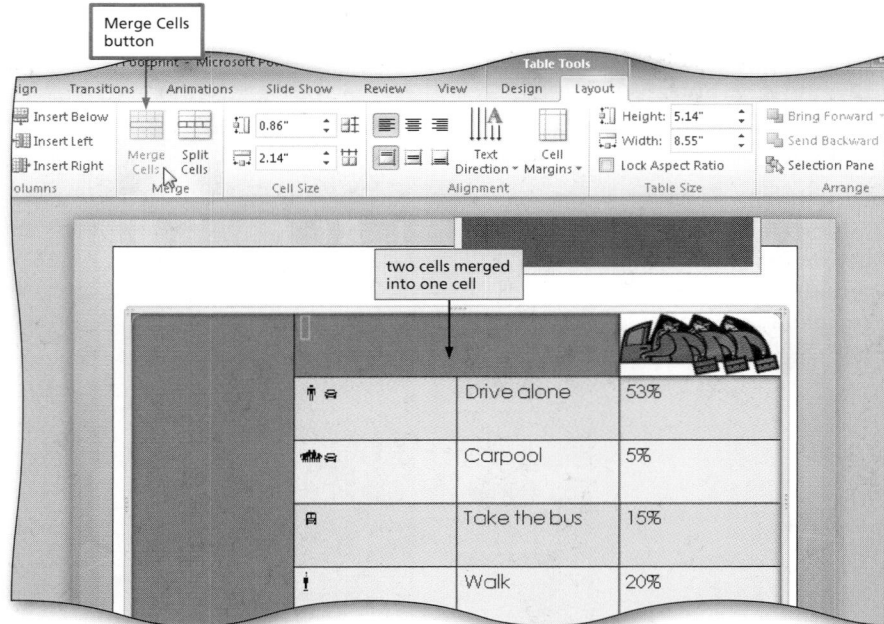

Figure 4–72

To Display Text in a Cell Vertically

The default orientation of table cell text is horizontal. You can change this direction to stack the letters so they display above and below each other, or you can rotate the direction in 90-degree increments. The following steps rotate the text in the first column cell.

- With the Table Tools Layout tab displayed, click the column 1 cell.

- Type **Travel to Campus** in the table cell.

- Click the Text Direction button (Table Tools Layout tab | Alignment group) to display the Text Direction gallery (Figure 4–73).

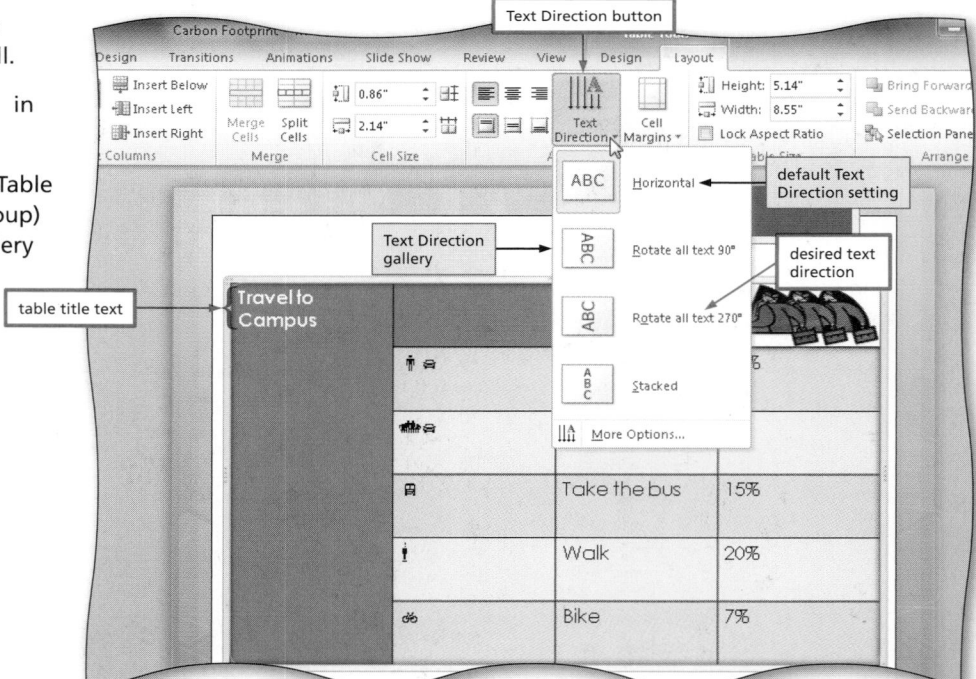

Figure 4–73

2

- Click 'Rotate all text 270°' to rotate the text in the cell (Figure 4–74).

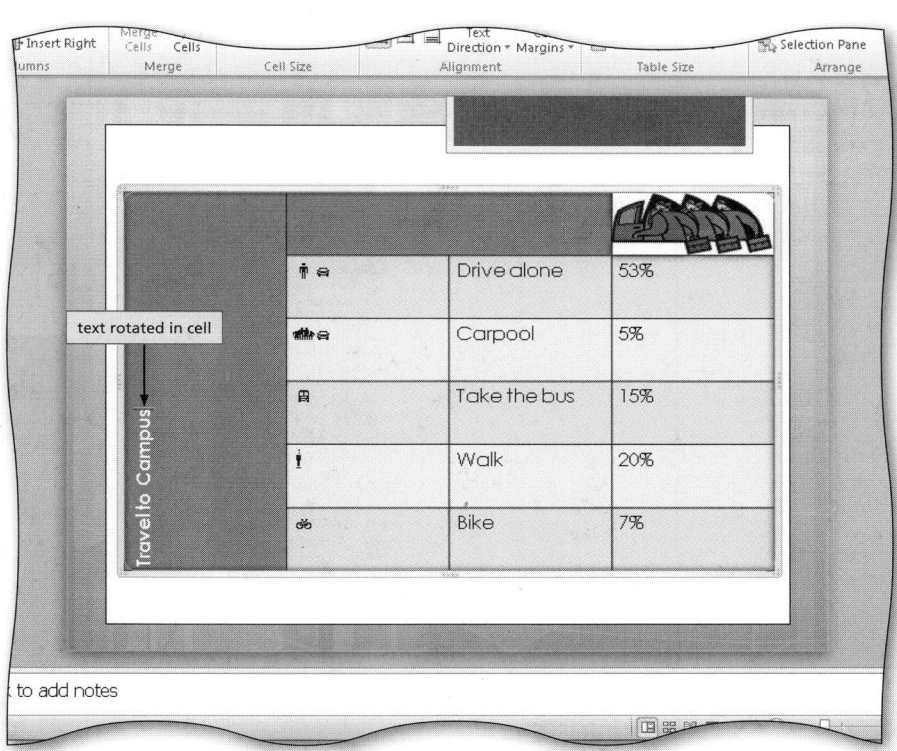

Figure 4–74

<table>
<tr><td>**Other Ways**</td></tr>
<tr><td>1. Right-click selected cells, click Format Shape on shortcut menu, click Text Box, click Text direction arrow</td></tr>
</table>

To Align Text in Cells

The data in each cell can be aligned horizontally and vertically. You change the horizontal alignment of each cell in a similar manner as you center, left-align, or right-align text in a placeholder. You also can change the vertical alignment so that the data displays at the top, middle, or bottom of each cell. The following steps center the text both horizontally and vertically in each table cell.

- With the Table Tools Layout tab displayed, click the Select button (Table group) to display the Select menu (Figure 4–75).

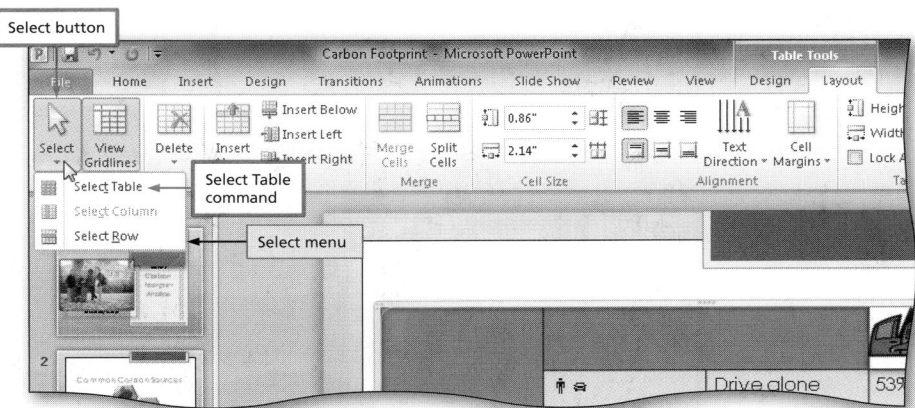

Figure 4–75

2

- Click Select Table in the Select menu to select the entire table.

- Click the Center button (Table Tools Layout tab | Alignment group) to center the text between the left and right borders of each cell in the table (Figure 4–76).

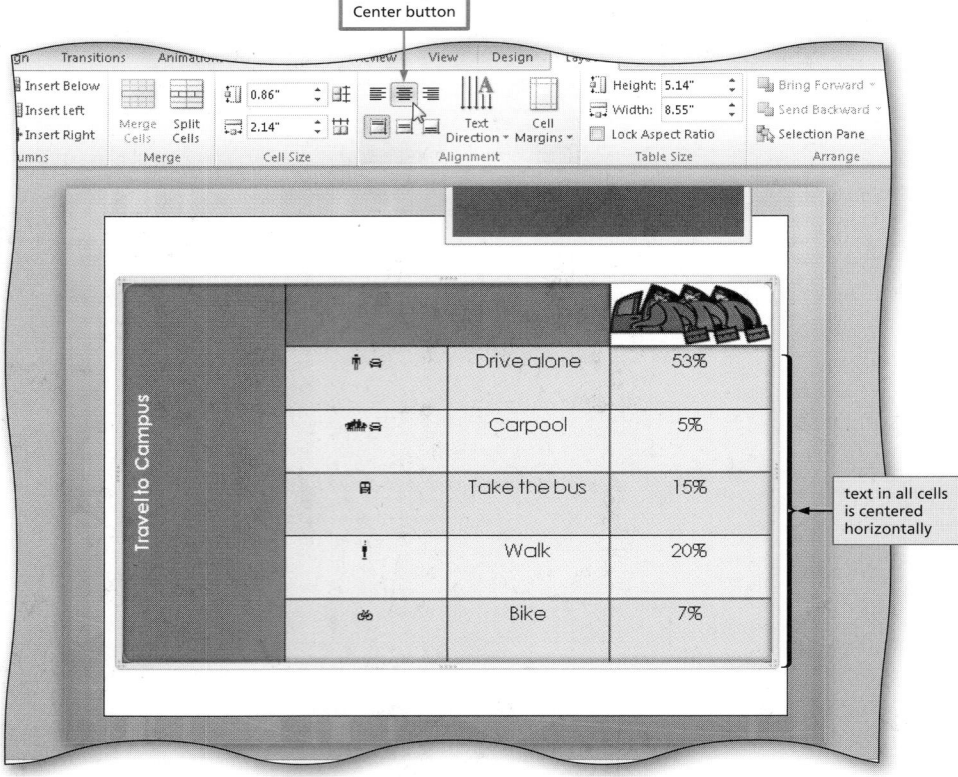

Figure 4–76

3

- Click the Center Vertically button (Table Tools Layout tab | Alignment group) to center the text between the top and bottom borders of each cell in the table (Figure 4–77).

Q&A Must I center all the table cells, or can I center only specific cells?

You can center as many cells as you desire at one time by selecting one or more cells.

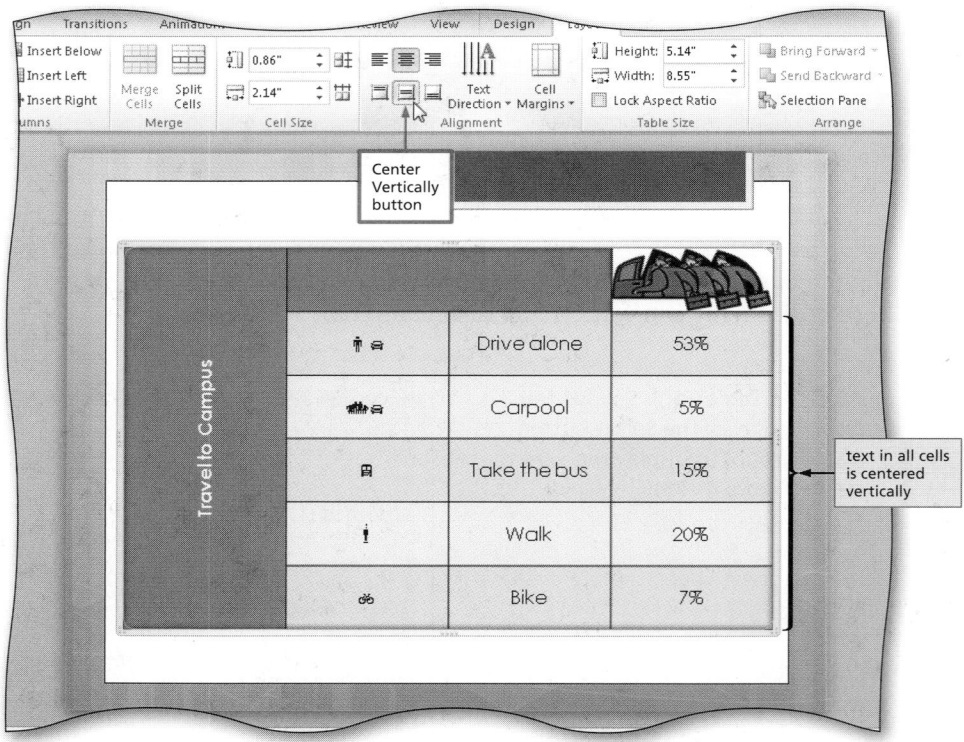

Figure 4–77

Other Ways

1. Right-click selected cells, click Format Shape on shortcut menu, click Text Box, click Vertical alignment arrow

To Format Table Data

The final table enhancement is to bold the text in all cells and increase the font size of the title and the symbols. The entire table is selected, so you can bold all text simultaneously. The title and symbols will have different font sizes. The following steps format the data.

1 Display the Home tab and then click the Bold button (Font group) to bold all text in the table.

2 Select the table title text in the first column and then increase the font size to 36 point.

3 Select the symbols in the second column and then increase the font size to 44 point (Figure 4–78).

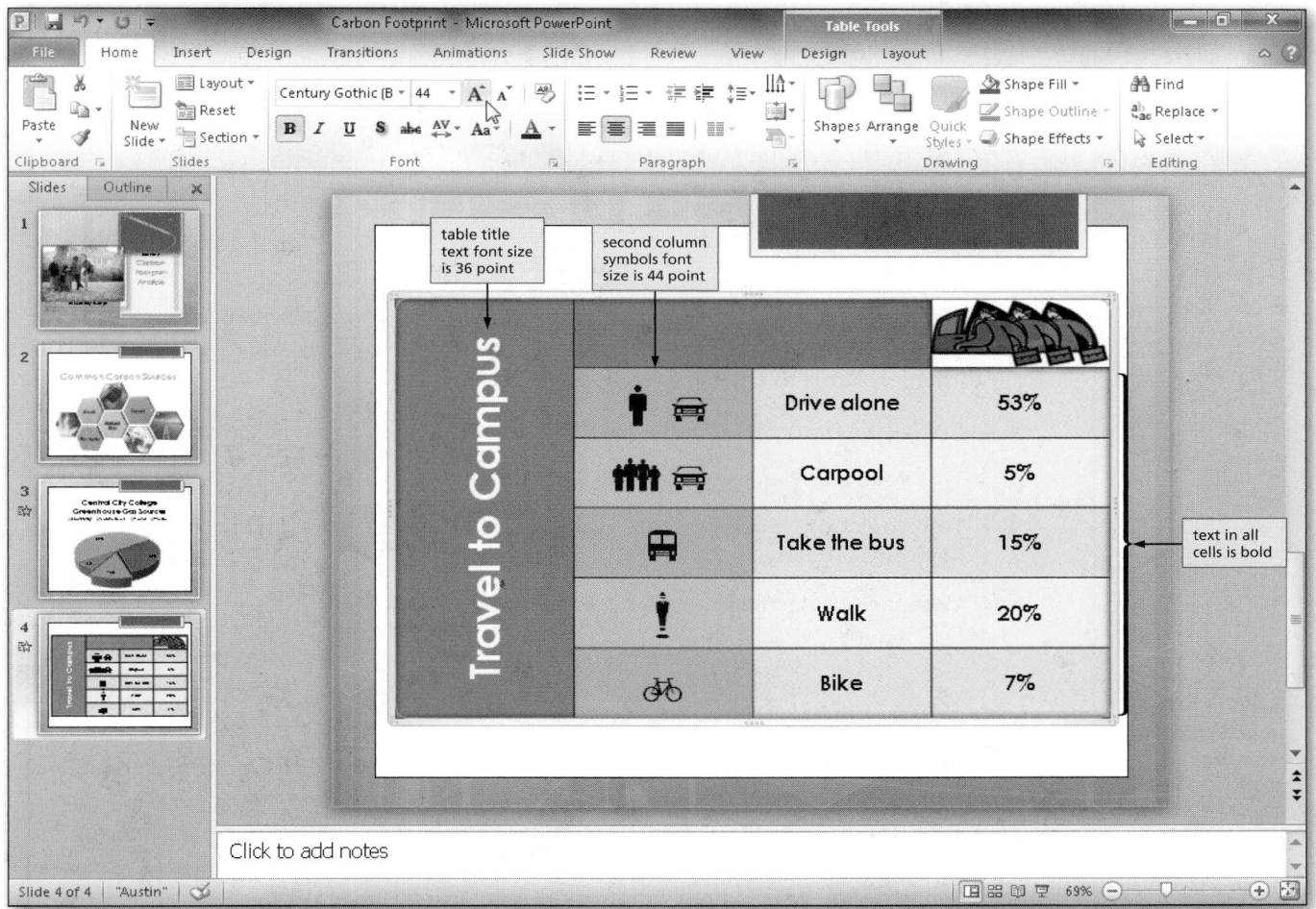

Figure 4–78

Plan Ahead

Test your visual elements.

Proofread your charts and tables carefully using these guidelines:

- Verify that your charts and tables contain the correct data. It is easy to make mistakes when inputting large quantities of numbers or entering many lines of text. Check that numbers are not transposed and that pie chart percentages total 100.

- Be certain that graphics are clearly labeled. The slide title text or the chart title should state the graphic's purpose. Table column headings must indicate the data below them. Chart legends must accompany the graphic if the data is not displayed on the chart itself. Units of measurement, such as degrees, dollars, or inches, should appear for clarity.

- Show your graphic to people unfamiliar with your topic. Ask them to explain verbally what they gather from viewing the material. Determine how long it takes them to state their interpretations. If they pause or look confused, your graphic either has too much or too little information and needs revision.

BTW

Quick Reference
For a table that lists how to complete the tasks covered in this book using the mouse, Ribbon, shortcut menu, and keyboard, see the Quick Reference Summary at the back of this book, or visit the PowerPoint 2010 Quick Reference Web page (scsite.com/ppt2010/qr).

To Add a Transition between Slides

A final enhancement you will make in this presentation is to apply the Orbit transition in the Dynamic Content category to all slides and change the transition speed to 3.00. The following steps apply this transition to the presentation.

1 Apply the Orbit transition in the Dynamic Content category to all four slides in the presentation.

2 Change the transition speed from 01.60 to 03.00.

To Change Document Properties

Before saving the presentation again, you want to add your name, class name, and some keywords as document properties. The following steps use the Document Information Panel to change document properties.

1 Display the Document Information Panel and then type your name as the Author property.

2 Type your course and section in the Subject property.

3 Type `carbon footprint, greenhouse gas, transportation` as the Keywords property.

4 Close the Document Information Panel.

BTW

Certification
The Microsoft Office Specialist (MOS) program provides an opportunity for you to obtain a valuable industry credential — proof that you have the PowerPoint 2010 skills required by employers. For more information, visit the PowerPoint 2010 Certification Web page (scsite.com/ppt2010/cert).

To Save, Print, and Quit PowerPoint

The presentation now is complete. You should save the slides, print a handout, and then quit PowerPoint.

1 Save the presentation again with the same file name.

2 Print the slide as a handout with two slides per page (Figure 4–79).

3 Quit PowerPoint, closing all open documents.

(a) Page 1

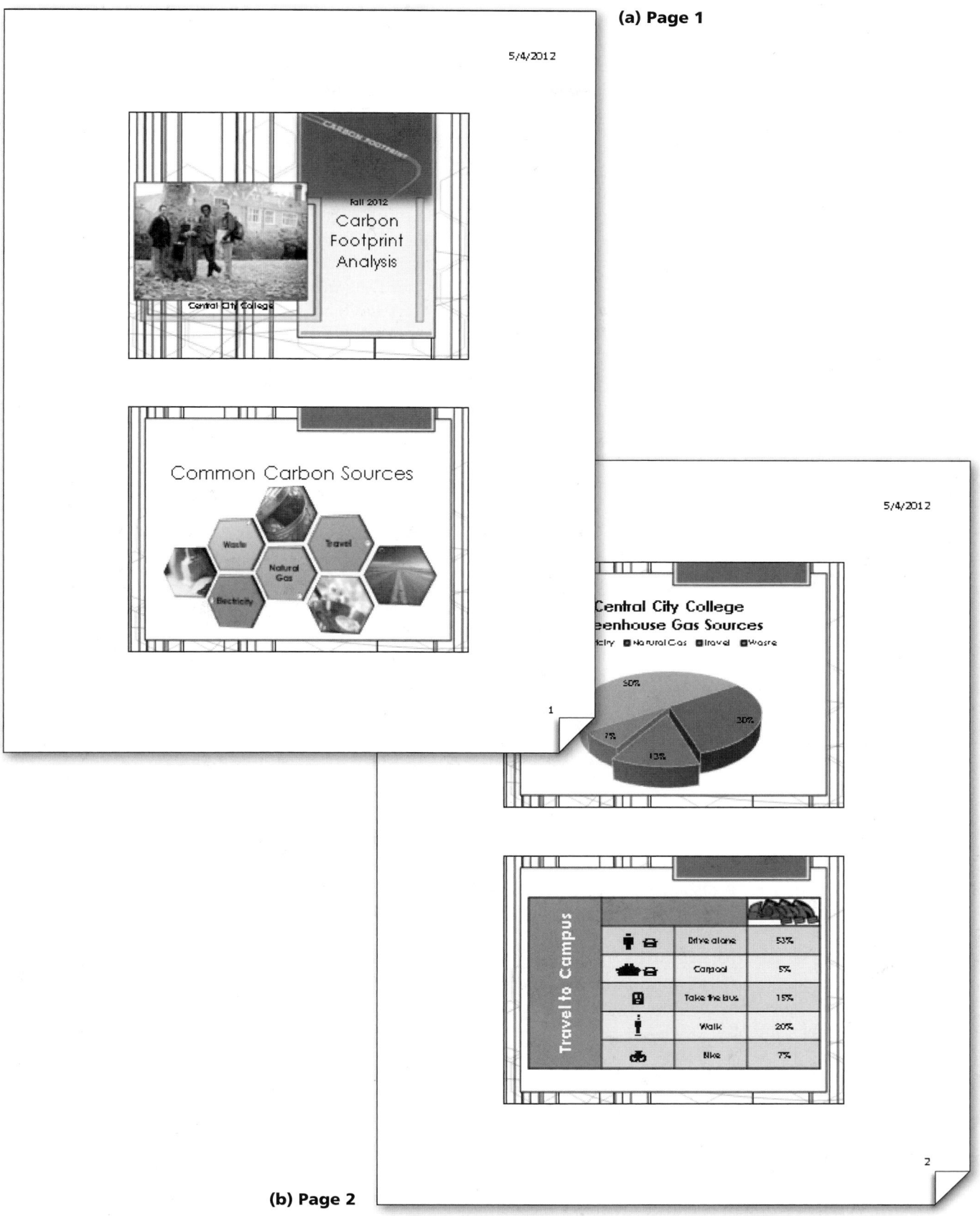

(b) Page 2

Figure 4–79

PowerPoint Chapter 4

Chapter Summary

In this chapter you have learned how to insert a SmartArt graphic and then add a picture and text, convert pictures to a SmartArt graphic, create and format a chart and a table, change table text alignment and orientation, and insert symbols. The items listed below include all the new PowerPoint skills you have learned in this chapter.

1. Insert a SmartArt Graphic (PPT 206)
2. Enter Text in a SmartArt Graphic (PPT 208)
3. Format Text Pane Characters (PPT 208)
4. Insert a Picture from a File into a SmartArt Graphic (PPT 209)
5. Apply a SmartArt Style (PPT 210)
6. Change SmartArt Color (PPT 211)
7. Resize a SmartArt Graphic (PPT 212)
8. Convert Text to a SmartArt Graphic (PPT 213)
9. Bold SmartArt Graphic Text (PPT 217)
10. Insert a Chart (PPT 220)
11. Replace Sample Data (PPT 221)
12. Apply a Chart Style (PPT 223)
13. Change the Shape Outline Weight (PPT 224)
14. Change the Shape Outline Color (PPT 226)
15. Change a Chart Layout (PPT 226)
16. Resize a Chart (PPT 228)
17. Change the Title and Legend Font Size (PPT 228)
18. Separate a Pie Slice (PPT 229)
19. Rotate a Chart (PPT 230)
20. Insert an Empty Table (PPT 232)
21. Enter Data in a Table (PPT 233)
22. Insert a Symbol (PPT 233)
23. Apply a Table Style (PPT 236)
24. Add Borders to a Table (PPT 238)
25. Add an Effect to a Table (PPT 238)
26. Resize a Table (PPT 240)
27. Add an Image to a Table (PPT 241)
28. Merge Cells (PPT 242)
29. Display Text in a Cell Vertically (PPT 244)
30. Align Text in Cells (PPT 245)

If you have a SAM 2010 user profile, your instructor may have assigned an autogradable version of this assignment. If so, log into the SAM 2010 Web site at www.cengage.com/sam2010 to download the instruction and start files.

Learn It Online

Test your knowledge of chapter content and key terms.

Instructions: To complete the Learn It Online exercises, start your browser, click the Address bar, and then enter the Web address **scsite.com/ppt2010/learn**. When the PowerPoint 2010 Learn It Online page is displayed, click the link for the exercise you want to complete and then read the instructions.

Chapter Reinforcement TF, MC, and SA
A series of true/false, multiple choice, and short answer questions that test your knowledge of the chapter content.

Flash Cards
An interactive learning environment where you identify chapter key terms associated with displayed definitions.

Practice Test
A series of multiple choice questions that test your knowledge of chapter content and key terms.

Who Wants To Be a Computer Genius?
An interactive game that challenges your knowledge of chapter content in the style of a television quiz show.

Wheel of Terms
An interactive game that challenges your knowledge of chapter key terms in the style of the television show *Wheel of Fortune*.

Crossword Puzzle Challenge
A crossword puzzle that challenges your knowledge of key terms presented in the chapter.

Apply Your Knowledge

Reinforce the skills and apply the concepts you learned in this chapter.

Converting Text to a SmartArt Graphic

Note: To complete this assignment, you will be required to use the Data Files for Students. See the inside back cover of this book for instructions on downloading the Data Files for Students, or contact your instructor for information about accessing the required files.

Instructions: Start PowerPoint. Open the presentation, Apply 4-1 Medical, located on the Data Files for Students.

   The slide in the presentation presents information about when injured people should seek medical care at a hospital emergency room or an urgent care facility. The document you open is an unformatted presentation. You are to convert the two separate lists to SmartArt and format these graphics so the slide looks like Figure 4–80.

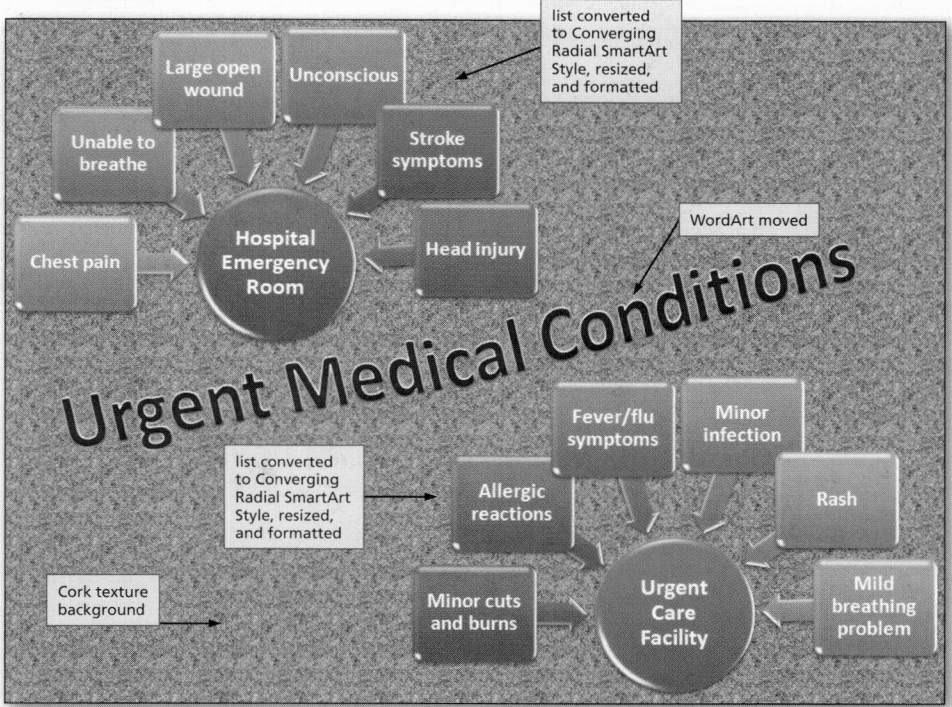

Figure 4–80

Perform the following tasks:

1. Convert the upper-left Hospital Emergency Room list to SmartArt by applying the Converging Radial Style (Relationship area). Change the colors to Colorful Range – Accent Colors 3 to 4.

2. Resize this SmartArt graphic to approximately 4.5" × 5.25". With the Text pane open, select the six Level 2 bulleted lines and then increase the font size to 16 point and bold this text. Select all six SmartArt graphic squares and then click the Larger button (SmartArt Tools Format tab | Shapes group) three times to increase the size of the selected shapes.

3. Select the center Hospital Emergency Room circle, increase the font size to 18 point, and bold this text. Click the Larger button two times to increase the size of the selected shape.

4. Apply the Polished (3-D area) Style and then move this SmartArt graphic to the area shown in Figure 4–80.

5. Convert the lower-right Urgent Care Facility list to SmartArt by applying the Converging Radial Style (Relationship area). Change the colors to Colorful Range – Accent Colors 2 to 3.

Continued >

6. Resize this SmartArt graphic to approximately 4.5" × 5.25". With the Text pane open, select the six Level 2 bulleted lines and then increase the font size to 16 point and bold this text. Select all six SmartArt graphic squares and then click the Larger button (SmartArt Tools Format tab | Shapes group) three times to increase the size of the selected shapes.

7. Select the center Urgent Care Facility circle, decrease the font size to 18 point, and bold this text. Click the Larger button two times to increase the size of the selected shape.

8. Apply the Polished (3-D area) Style to this SmartArt graphic.

9. Move the center WordArt title, Urgent Medical Conditions, to the location shown in Figure 4–80 on the previous page.

10. Insert the Cork texture to format the background.

11. Apply the Clock transition (Exciting area) and then change the duration to 2.00 seconds.

12. Check the spelling and then change the document properties as specified by your instructor. Save the presentation using the file name, Apply 4-1 Urgent Medical. Submit the revised document in the format specified by your instructor.

Extend Your Knowledge

Extend the skills you learned in this chapter and experiment with new skills. You may need to use Help to complete the assignment.

Changing Chart Type and Style and Creating a SmartArt Graphic from Text

Note: To complete this assignment, you will be required to use the Data Files for Students. See the inside back cover of this book for instructions on downloading the Data Files for Students, or contact your instructor for information about accessing the required files.

Instructions: Start PowerPoint. Open the presentation, Extend 4-1 College, located on the Data Files for Students.

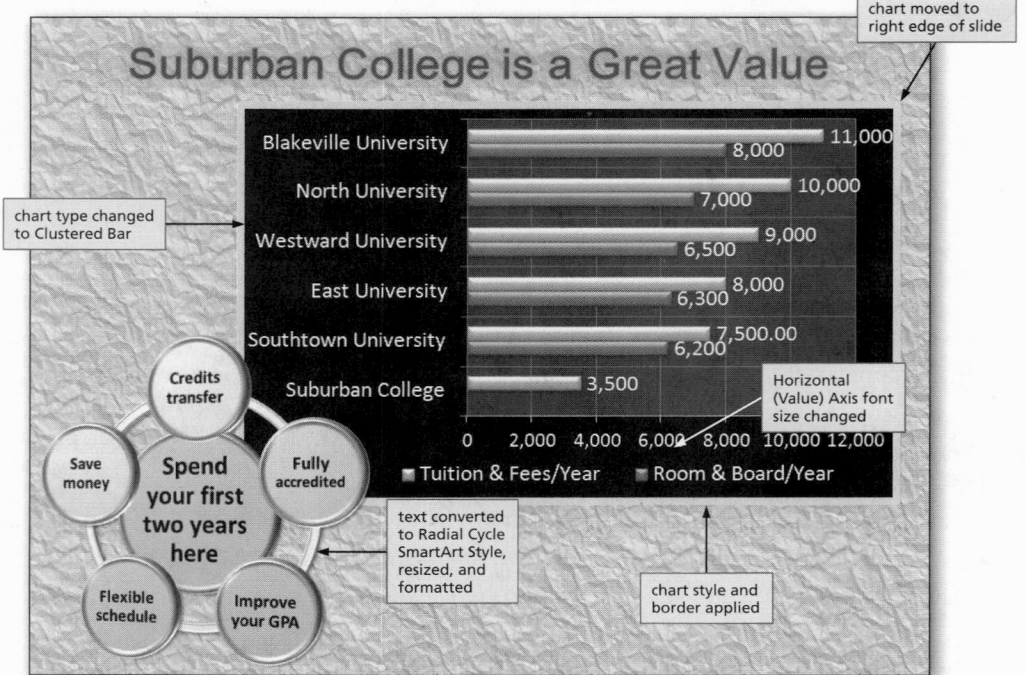

Figure 4–81

You will format a chart by applying a type and style, and then you will create a graphic by converting text to SmartArt.

Perform the following tasks:

1. Change the chart type from Clustered Column to Clustered Bar. *Hint:* Click the chart to select it and then click the Change Chart Type button (Chart Tools Design tab | Type group).

2. Apply chart Style 43 (last style in blue column) and then add a 6 pt. Yellow border to the chart. Move the chart to the right edge of the slide, as shown in Figure 4–81 on the previous page. Right-click the Horizontal (Value) Axis to display the Mini toolbar and then decrease the font size to 16 point.

3. Convert the text in the lower-left corner of the slide to the Radial Cycle layout (first layout in third row in Cycle area) SmartArt graphic. Change the color to Colored Fill – Accent 3 (second color in Accent 3 area). Apply the Metallic Scene design in the 3-D area.

4. Resize this SmartArt graphic to approximately 3.8" × 6.5" and then move the graphic to the location shown in Figure 4–81.

5. Select all six SmartArt graphic circles and then click the Larger button (SmartArt Tools Format tab | Shapes group) three times to increase the size of the selected shapes. Select the center shape and then click the Larger button once to increase the size of this circle. Increase the font size of the center circle text to 24 point and the outer circle text to 16 point. Change the font size of the word, Accredited, to 14 point so it displays on one line. Bold the text in the six circles.

6. Change the document properties, as specified by your instructor. Save the presentation using the file name, Extend 4-1 Suburban College.

7. Submit the revised document in the format specified by your instructor.

Make It Right

Analyze a presentation and correct all errors and/or improve the design.

Modifying a Table

Note: To complete this assignment, you will be required to use the Data Files for Students. See the inside back cover of this book for instructions on downloading the Data Files for Students, or contact your instructor for information about accessing the required files.

Instructions: Start PowerPoint. Open the presentation, Make It Right 4-1 Media World, located on the Data Files for Students.

In your sociology class, you have learned that women tend to have more friends than men do in their personal and online relationships. Table 4–3 lists the more popular social networking Web sites and the percentages of women and men who participate in these groups. This table is displayed partially on the slide in the Media World presentation (Figure 4–82 on the next page). Correct the formatting problems and errors in the presentation while keeping in mind the guidelines presented in this chapter.

Table 4–3 Social Media World		
Males		**Females**
43%	Facebook	57%
45%	Flickr	55%
36%	MySpace	64%
43%	Twitter	57%

Continued >

STUDENT ASSIGNMENTS

Make It Right *continued*

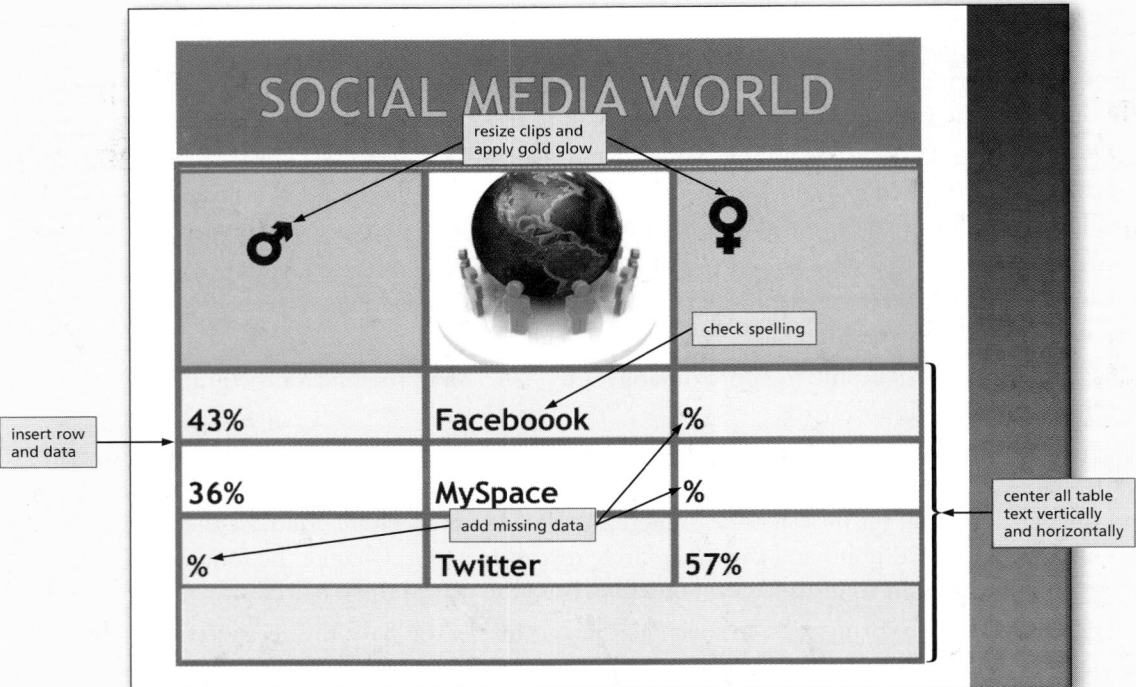

Figure 4-82

Perform the following tasks:

1. Resize the male symbol clip in the cell at the upper-left corner of the table to approximately 1.25" × 1.25". Apply the Gold, 18 pt glow, Accent color 4 (Glow Variations area) picture effect to this clip. Resize the female symbol clip in the cell at the upper-right corner of the table to approximately 1.35" × 0.88". Apply the Pink, 18 pt glow, Accent color 5 (Glow Variations area) picture effect to this clip. Center the male and female clips in the cells.

2. Use Table 4-3 on the previous page to add the missing data in three table cells. Insert a row for the Flickr data by right-clicking any cell in the Facebook row, pointing to Insert on the shortcut menu, and then clicking Insert Rows Below. Using Table 4-3, type the percentages and the word, Flickr, in this new row.

3. Select the table and then apply the Circle effect (Cell Bevel, Bevel area) to the table.

4. Select the four social media rows, center the text horizontally in the cells, and then middle-align this text vertically.

5. Change the slide transition from Shred to Orbit (Dynamic Content area) and then change the duration to 3.00 seconds.

6. Check the slide for spelling errors and then change the document properties, as specified by your instructor. Save the presentation using the file name, Make It Right 4-1 Social Media World.

7. Submit the revised document in the format specified by your instructor.

In the Lab

Design and/or create a presentation using the guidelines, concepts, and skills presented in this chapter. Labs 1, 2, and 3 are listed in order of increasing difficulty.

Lab 1: Inserting and Formatting SmartArt

Note: To complete this assignment, you will be required to use the Data Files for Students. See the inside back cover of this book for instructions on downloading the Data Files for Students, or contact your instructor for information about accessing the required files.

Problem: A pineapple is a type of fruit enjoyed throughout the world. People living in the Caribbean first called this fruit *anana*, meaning excellent fruit. European explorers to the Caribbean then changed the name to pineapple because they thought the outside looked like a pinecone and the inside texture resembled an apple. You visited Hawaii recently and toured a pineapple plantation. Several of the pictures you took are on the slides shown in Figure 4–83 and are on the Data Files for Students. You will convert the four pictures on Slide 1 to SmartArt and add descriptive text. Then you will convert the bulleted list on Slide 2 to a SmartArt graphic, change colors, apply a style, and add a shape fill.

(a) Slide 1

(b) Slide 2

Figure 4–83

Continued >

In the Lab *continued*

Perform the following tasks:

1. Open the presentation, Lab 4-1 Pineapples, located on the Data Files for Students.

2. On Slide 1, change the order of the pictures to match the order shown in Figure 4-83a on the previous page by selecting the picture you want to move and then clicking the Move Up or Move Down buttons (SmartArt Tools Design tab | Create Graphic group).

3. In the SmartArt Text pane, type `Pineapple` as the top Level 1 text that will appear over the central pineapple picture. Type `28,000 plants per acre` as the second Level 1 text that will appear to the right of the first circle, `Needs iron-rich soil` as the text for the middle circle, and `Fruit ready to pick` for the third circle.

4. Change the font for the word, Pineapple, to Forte. Bold this word and then change the font color to Orange. Decrease the size of the placeholder for the word, Pineapple, by dragging the bottom square sizing handle upward being careful not to decrease the size of the word, Pineapple. Move the placeholder toward the top of the slide, as shown in Figure 4–83a on the previous page.

5. Apply the Orange, 18 pt glow, Accent color 6 (Glow Variations area) picture effect to the large pineapple picture.

6. On Slide 2, convert the bulleted list to the Circle Accent Timeline (Process area) SmartArt Graphic. Change the color to Colored Fill – Accent 3 (Accent 3 area). Apply the Subtle Effect (Best Match for Document area) SmartArt Style to the entire graphic.

7. Select all text in the Text pane and then add a shape fill by clicking the Shape Fill button arrow (SmartArt Tools Format tab | Shape Styles group) and then clicking the color, Orange, Accent 6, Lighter 40% (Theme Colors area), as shown in Figure 4–83b on the previous page.

8. For all slides, apply the Reveal transition (Subtle area) and change the duration to 5.00 seconds.

9. Change the document properties, as specified by your instructor. Save the presentation using the file name, Lab 4-1 Growing Pineapples.

10. Submit the revised document in the format specified by your instructor.

In the Lab

Lab 2: Creating a Presentation by Inserting SmartArt and a Chart

Note: To complete this assignment, you will be required to use the Data Files for Students. See the inside back cover of this book for instructions on downloading the Data Files for Students, or contact your instructor for information about accessing the required files.

Problem: Adults generally have four or five sleep cycles every night. Each cycle lasts approximately 90 minutes and is composed of four steps, which are light sleep, intermediate sleep, deep sleep, and rapid eye movement (REM) sleep. Nearly one-fifth of people sleep fewer than six hours each night, and the average hours slept are indicated in Table 4–4. Your speech teacher has assigned an informative speech, and you desire to explain the sleep cycle and the hours slept as part of your talk. You create two slides of a PowerPoint presentation shown in Figure 4–84a and Figure 4–84b. These slides contain clips that are on the Data Files for Students.

Table 4–4 Hours Slept			
Fewer than 6	6 – 6.9	7 – 7.9	More than 8
19%	27%	30%	24%

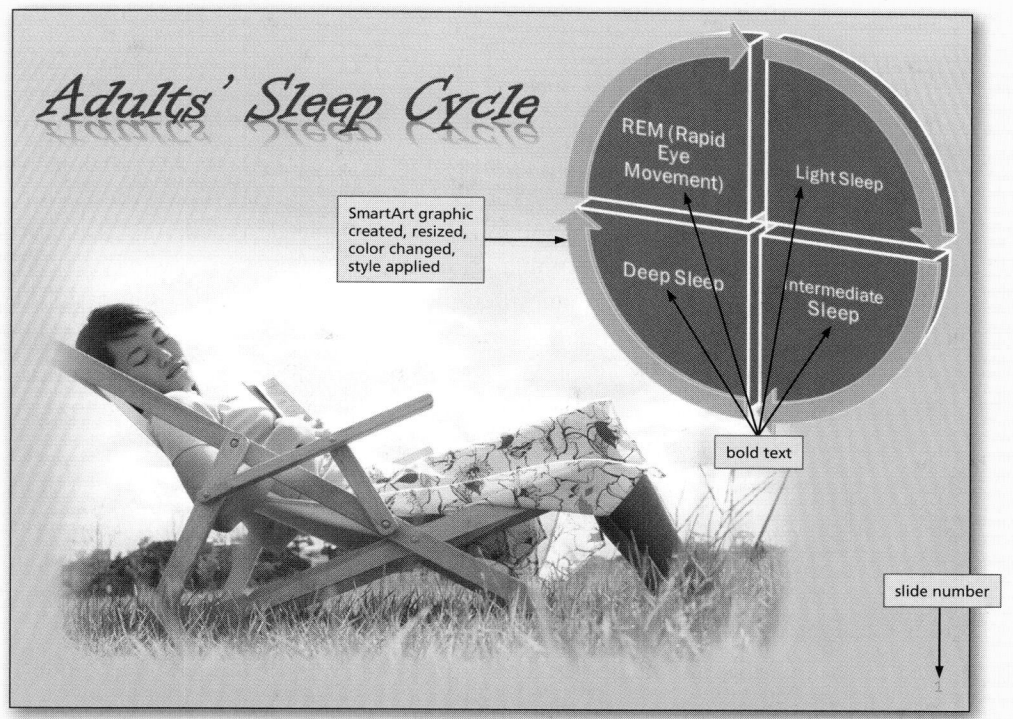

(a) Slide 1

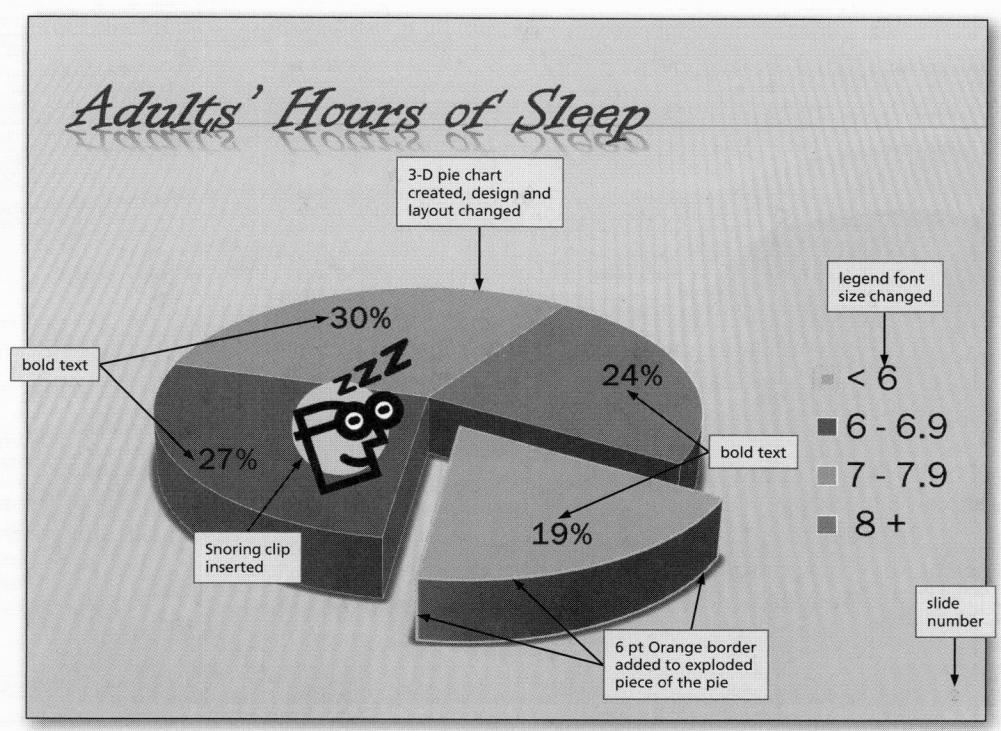

(b) Slide 2

Figure 4–84

Continued >

In the Lab *continued*

Perform the following tasks:

1. Open the presentation, Lab 4-2 Sleep, located on the Data Files for Students.

2. On Slide 1, create the SmartArt graphic shown in Figure 4–84a on the previous page. Replace the sample data with the data in Table 4–4 on the previous page starting with the words, Light Sleep, and moving clockwise. Apply the Segmented Cycle (Cycle area). Change the colors to Colored Fill – Accent 5 (Accent 5 group). Apply the Brick Scene (3-D area) Style. Resize the SmartArt graphic to approximately 5" × 7" and then move this graphic to the upper-right corner of the slide. Bold all words in the graphic.

3. On Slide 2, create the Pie in 3-D chart (second chart in Pie area) shown in Figure 4–84b on the previous page. Apply chart design Style 10 and then change the chart layout to Layout 6. Select the chart title text, Sales, and then press the DELETE key to delete this text.

4. Increase the legend font size to 28 point and the percentages on each pie slice to 24 point bold.

5. Select the chart and rotate it approximately 120 degrees so that the green slice is at the bottom of the pie. Explode the green slice, which represents the percentage of people sleeping fewer than 6 hours, as shown in Figure 4–84. Add a 6 pt border to this slice and then change the border color to Orange.

6. Insert the Man Snore audio clip located on the Data Files for Students into Slide 1, play the clip across slides, hide the sound icon during the show, and loop until stopped.

7. Insert the Snoring clip located on the Data Files for Students into Slide 2 and move it to the location shown in Figure 4–84.

8. Insert the slide number on both slides. Apply the Ripple transition (Exciting area) to all slides. Change the duration to 3.00 seconds. Check the spelling and correct any errors.

9. Change the document properties, as specified by your instructor. Save the presentation using the file name, Lab 4-2 Sleep Cycle.

10. Submit the revised document in the format specified by your instructor.

In the Lab

Lab 3: Creating a Presentation with SmartArt and a Table

Note: To complete this assignment, you will be required to use the Data Files for Students. See the inside back cover of this book for instructions on downloading the Data Files for Students, or contact your instructor for information about accessing the required files.

Problem: Laughter is the best medicine, according to the adage. Sharing a humorous situation with others can have many health benefits, as outlined in Table 4–5. You have read about the positive effects of laughter, and you want to share your knowledge with students enrolled in your health class. You create the presentation in Figure 4–85 that consists of three slides. Pictures and a clip for the presentation are on the Data Files for Students.

Table 4–5 Benefits of Laughter

Benefits of Laughter			
Physical	Lowers blood pressure	Boosts immunity	Decreases pain
Mental	Relieves stress	Eases anxiety	Improves mood
Social	Strengthens relationships	Promotes teamwork	Minimizes conflict

Perform the following tasks:

1. Open the presentation, Lab 4-3 Laughter, located on the Data Files for Students. Change the presentation theme colors to Austin.

2. On Slide 1, insert the Funnel graphic (Process area) SmartArt graphic shown in Figure 4–85a. Type the keywords, Smile, Laugh, Love, in the first three Level 1 bulleted lines in the Text pane, and type the word, HEALTH, in the fourth line. Bold the word, HEALTH.

3. Resize the SmartArt graphic to approximately 5.4" × 7.58". Change the graphic's colors to Colorful Range – Accent Colors 3 to 4. Add the Sunset Scene (3-D area) Style. Move this graphic to the left side of the slide.

(a) Slide 1

Figure 4–85

Continued >

In the Lab *continued*

4. On Slide 2, create a background by inserting the SunSmile picture located on the Data Files for Students and then change the transparency to 80%. Create the SmartArt graphic shown in Figure 4–85b using the Vertical Box List graphic (List area) and the text shown in Figure 4–85b. Change the graphic's colors to Colorful Range – Accent Colors 5 to 6. Apply the Cartoon (3-D area) Style and the Tight Reflection 4 pt offset (Reflection Variations area) shape effect reflection to the graphic.

5. Apply the Shape Outline Green, Accent 1 color to the four blank rectangle shapes in the SmartArt graphic and then change the weight to 4½ pt.

6. Insert the clip of the person laughing, shown in Figure 4–85b, from Office.com. Resize the clip to approximately 2.33" × 1.96" and then move this clip to the lower-left corner of the slide.

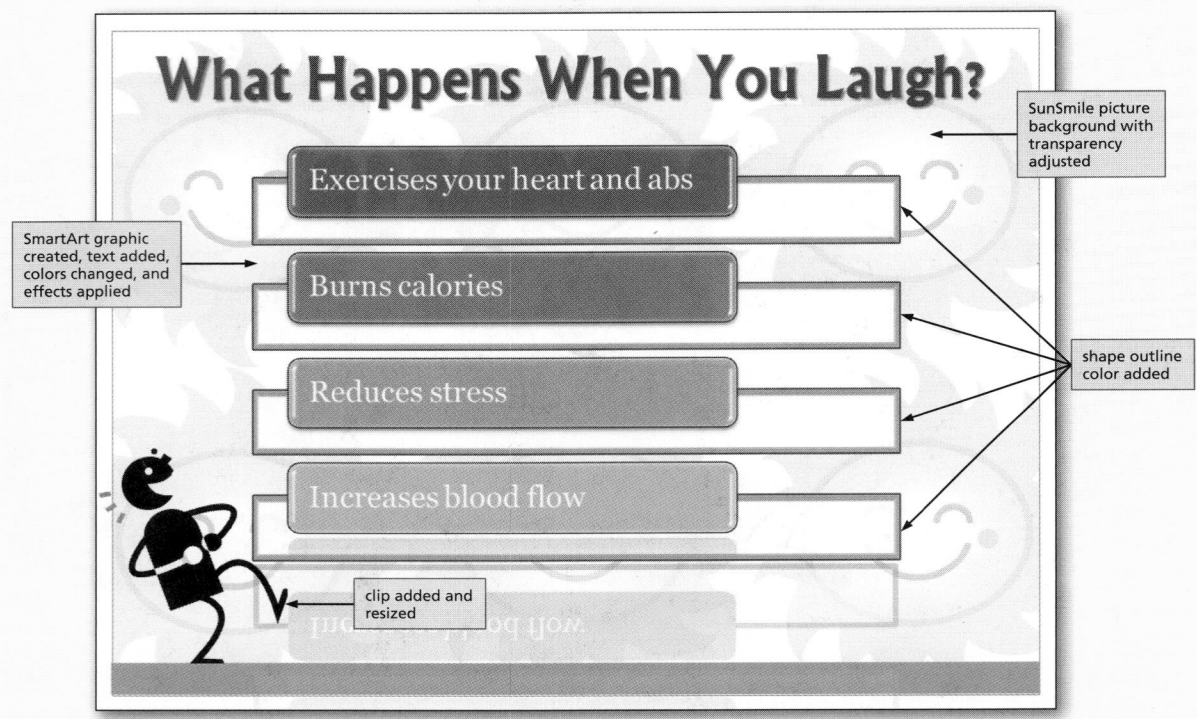

(b) Slide 2

Figure 4–85 (Continued)

7. On Slide 3, insert a table with four columns and four rows, as shown in Figure 4–85c. Merge the second, third, and fourth cells in the Header Row and then change the font size to 48 point.

8. Type the table header and text using the data in Table 4–5 on page PPT 258. Change the font for all cells to Narkisim and then middle-align this text vertically and center this text horizontally.

9. For all cells other than the Header Row, change the font size to 24 point. Bold the text in the first column and rotate the text direction to 270 degrees.

10. Move the table to the location shown in Figure 4–85c and increase the table size. Change the shading of the second, third, and fourth cells in the first column to Green, Accent 1. If the upper-left table cell has a green fill, apply a No Fill format to this cell so that only the cells below it have a green fill.

11. In the first table cell, insert the picture called Laughing Man located on the Data Files for Students. If necessary, increase the size of this clip in the cell, as shown in Figure 4-85c. Then insert the audio clip, Long Laugh, located on the Data Files for Students. Start the audio clip automatically, hide the sound icon during the show, and loop until stopped.

12. Apply the Riblet (Bevel area) Cell Bevel effect to the table.

13. Apply the Doors transition and change the duration to 03.00. Check the spelling and correct any errors.

14. Change the document properties, as specified by your instructor. Save the presentation using the file name, Lab 4-3 Laughter Benefits.

15. Submit the revised document in the format specified by your instructor.

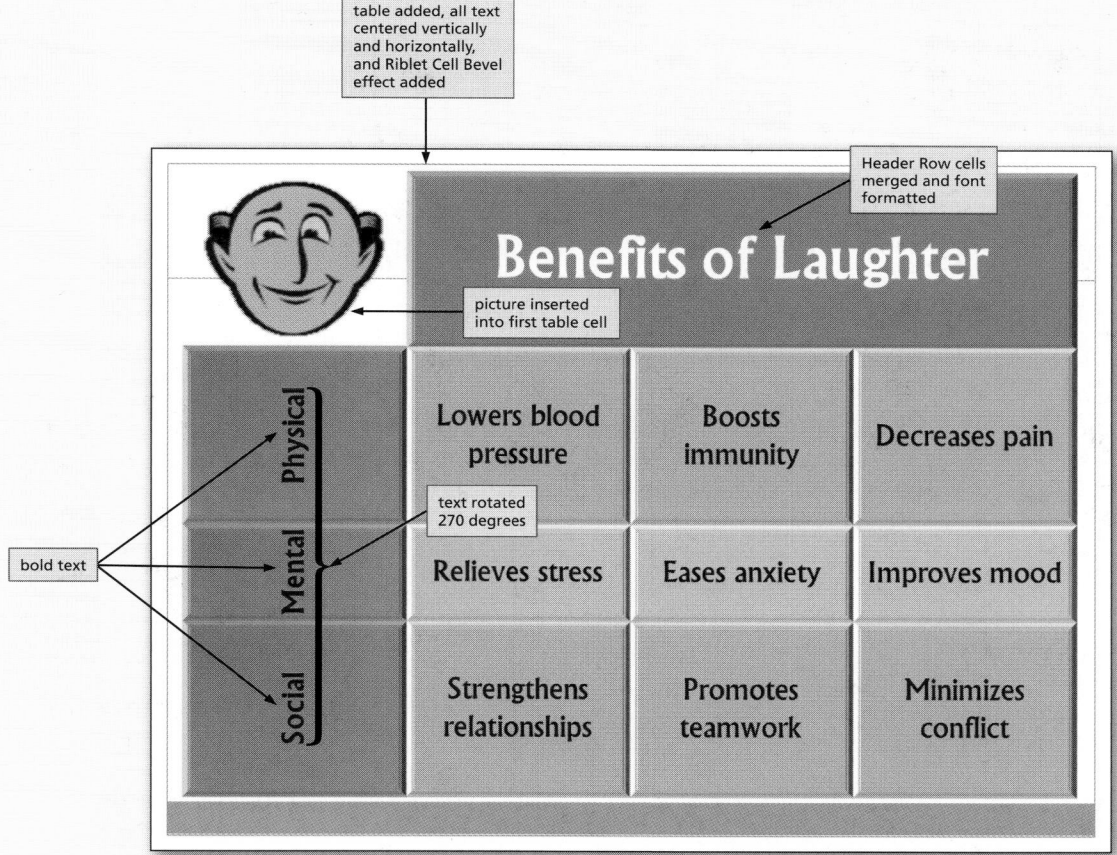

(c) Slide 3

Figure 4–85 (Continued)

Cases and Places

Apply your creative thinking and problem-solving skills to design and implement a solution.

Note: To complete these assignments, you may be required to use the Data Files for Students. See the inside back cover of this book for instructions on downloading the Data Files for Students, or contact your instructor for information about accessing the required files.

As you design the presentations, remember to use the 7 × 7 rule: a maximum of seven words on a line and a maximum of seven lines on one slide.

1: Designing and Creating a Presentation about Temperature Conversions

Academic

Students in your chemistry class are struggling to convert temperatures from Fahrenheit to Celsius to Kelvin, so you have decided to help them understand the formulas. In addition, you provide some facts to help them see the relationship among the numbers, such as ice melting at 32 degrees Fahrenheit, 0 degrees Celsius, and 273 degrees Kelvin, and water boiling at 212 degrees Fahrenheit, 100 degrees Celsius, and 373 degrees Kelvin. Create a presentation to show the formulas and temperature conversions in two tables. Use the data in Tables 4-6 and 4-7 to create your tables. Apply table styles and add borders and effects, and use at least three objectives found at the beginning of this chapter to develop the presentation. Use pictures from Office.com if they are appropriate for this topic. Be sure to check spelling.

Table 4–6 Temperature Conversion Formulas

Temperature		
From	**To**	**Formula**
Fahrenheit (degrees F)	Celsius (degrees C)	$5 \div 9 \,(F - 32)$
Celsius (degrees C)	Fahrenheit (degrees F)	$9 \div 5 \,C + 32$
Fahrenheit (degrees F)	Kelvin (degrees K)	$(F + 459.67) \times (5/9)$

Table 4–7 Temperature Conversions

Quick Temperature Conversions		
Fahrenheit	**Celsius**	**Kelvin**
212	100	373
86	30	303
68	20	293
50	10	283
32	0	273
14	−10	263
−4	−20	253

2: Designing and Creating a Presentation about Dogs and Cats

Personal

On weekends, you volunteer at an animal shelter, and you notice that fewer dogs and cats are adopted by people living alone than by households having multiple people. You decide to survey the adopting families to see how likely a household is to adopt a dog or a cat if the household has one, two, three, or four members. The data you collect is summarized in Tables 4–8 and 4–9. Share your findings by creating a PowerPoint presentation that contains two pie charts representing survey results. Use at least three objectives found at the beginning of this chapter to develop the presentation. Be sure to check spelling.

Table 4–8 Dogs by Family Size

Dogs by Family Size	
Household Size	Percent
4 or more people	33
3 people	21
2 people	32
1 person	14

Table 4–9 Cats by Family Size

Cats by Family Size	
Household Size	Percent
4 or more people	29
3 people	20
2 people	33
1 person	18

Continued >

Cases and Places *continued*

3: Designing and Creating a Presentation about Light Bulbs

Professional
You are employed at a local hardware store, and many customers desire to change their light bulbs from incandescent to compact fluorescent (CFL). Your manager has asked you to develop a presentation that provides information about equivalent light output, which is measured in lumens. In addition, she wants you to include an explanation that describes the color temperatures recommended for indoor general and task lighting. For example, warm colors (2700–3600 K) are preferred for living spaces because they complement clothing and skin tones; cool colors (3600–5500 K) are best for reading and household tasks because they provide contrast. These temperatures are not related to the heat generated from bulb usage. You decide to create a table using the data in Table 4–10 and a SmartArt graphic using the data in Table 4–11. Insert images in the table and SmartArt graphics from Office.com or your own digital pictures if they are appropriate for this topic. Apply at least one style, border, and effect. Be certain to check spelling.

Table 4–10 Light Bulbs

Incandescent Bulbs vs. CFL Bulbs		
Incandescent	**Minimum Light Output**	**CFL**
40 watts	450 lumens	9–13 watts
60 watts	800 lumens	13–15 watts
75 watts	1,100 lumens	18–25 watts
100 watts	1,600 lumens	23–30 watts
150 watts	2,600 lumens	30–52 watts

Table 4–11 Color Temperatures

Light Sources Warmth and Coolness	
Kelvin (K) Temperature	**Bulb Type**
2600	Incandescent
3000	Warm white
3100	Halogen
4200	Cool white
5000	Daylight

5 | Collaborating on and Delivering a Presentation

Objectives

You will have mastered the material in this chapter when you can:

- Combine slide shows
- Accept and reject a reviewer's proposed changes
- Insert, modify, and delete comments
- Reuse slides from an existing presentation
- Capture part of a slide using screen clipping
- Insert slide footer content

- Set slide and presentation resolution
- Save a file as a PowerPoint show
- Package a presentation for storage on a compact disc
- Save a presentation in a previous PowerPoint format
- Inspect and protect files
- Annotate slide shows with a pen and highlighter

5 | Collaborating on and Delivering a Presentation

BTW

Integrating Differing Perspectives
Audience members often have diverse educational levels, technical skills, and cultural backgrounds. It is important for you to understand how they may interpret material on your slides. Terms and graphics that seem clear to you may raise questions among people viewing your slides. The issues raised and the comments made during the review cycle play an important role in the development of a successful PowerPoint presentation.

Introduction

Often presentations are enhanced when individuals collaborate to fine-tune text, visuals, and design elements on the slides. A **review cycle** occurs when a slide show designer shares a file with reviewers so they can make comments and changes to their copies of the slides and then return the file to the designer. A **comment** is a description that normally does not display as part of the slide show. It can be used to clarify information that may be difficult to understand, to pose questions, or to communicate suggestions. The designer then can display the comments, modify their content, and ask the reviewers to again review the presentation, and continue this process until the slides are satisfactory. Once the presentation is complete, the designer can protect the file so no one can open it without a password or alter comments and other information. The designer also can save the presentation to an optical disc or as a PowerPoint show that will run without opening the PowerPoint application. In addition, a presenter can use PowerPoint's variety of tools to run the show effectively and to emphasize various elements on the screen.

Project — Presentation with Comments, Inserted Slides, and Protection

BTW

Documenting Your Thoughts
Your PowerPoint slides are formal documentation of the thoughts you are attempting to present to an audience, so you should seek comments to help ensure that your words and graphic elements are as clear as possible. The words you use on your slides and the handouts you provide are important documents that audience members may reference in the future. Your efforts, consequently, may be visible long after the verbal presentation has concluded.

The six slides in the Windstorms presentation (Figure 5–1) give information on and provide images of two particular types of windstorms: tornadoes and hurricanes. The initial presentation began with three slides, which were sent to a reviewer, Mary Halen. She suggested changes and created a new slide.

When you are developing a presentation, it often is advantageous to ask a variety of people to review your work in progress. These individuals can evaluate the wording, art, and design, and experts in the subject can check the slides for accuracy. They can add comments to the slides in specific areas, such as a paragraph, a graphic, or a table. You then can review their comments and use them to modify and enhance your work. You also can insert slides from other presentations into your file. The Windstorms presentation includes two slides from the file, Hurricanes.pptx.

Once you develop the final set of slides, you can complete the file by removing any comments and personal information, by adding a password so that unauthorized people cannot see or change the file contents without your permission, by saving the file as a PowerPoint show that runs automatically when you open a file, and by saving the file to an optical disc.

When running your presentation, you may decide to show the slides nonsequentially. For example, you may need to review a slide you discussed already, or you may want to skip slides and jump forward. You also may want to emphasize, or **annotate**, material on the slides by highlighting text or writing on the slides. You can save your annotations to review during or after the presentation.

(a) Slide 1 (Title Slide Enhanced from Reviewer)

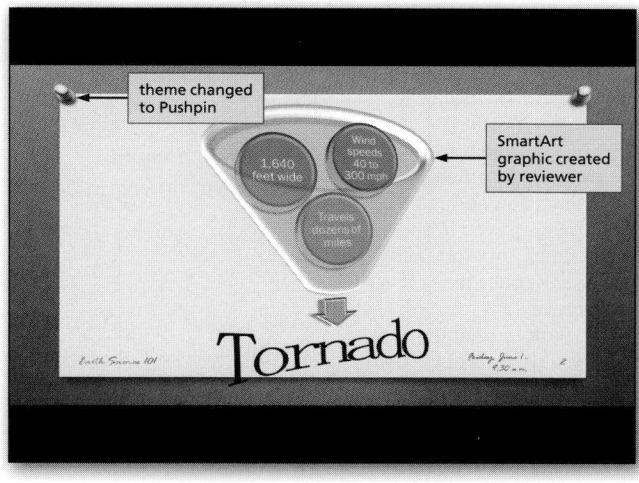

(b) Slide 2 (SmartArt from Reviewer)

(c) Slide 3 (Inserted from Reviewer's Presentation)

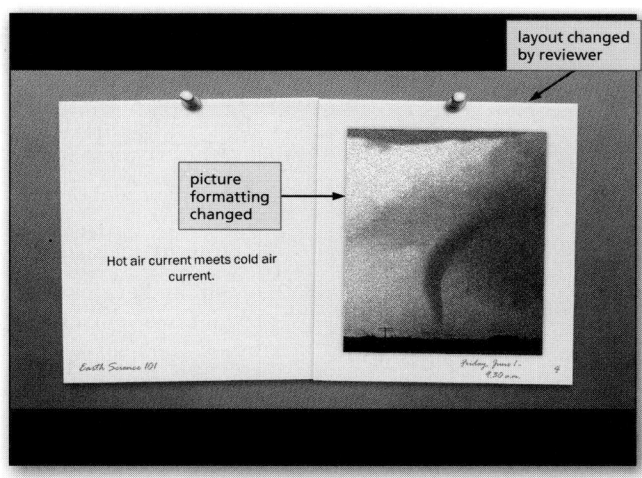

(d) Slide 4 (Enhanced from Reviewer)

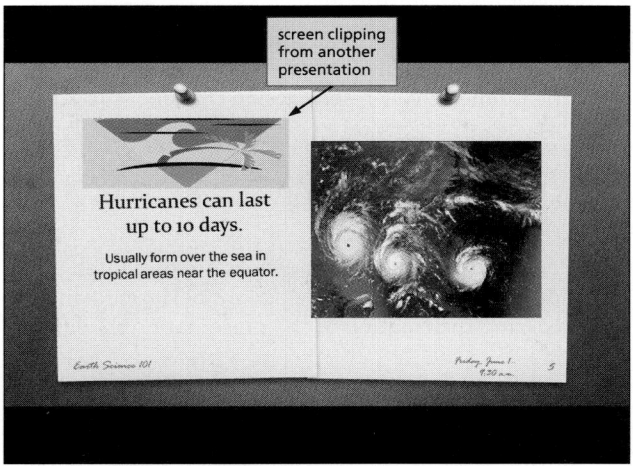

(e) Slide 5 (Inserted from Reviewer's Presentation)

(f) Slide 6 (Inserted from Reviewer's Presentation)

Figure 5–1

BTW

Considering Reviewers' Technology
People who receive copies of your presentation to review may not be able to open a PowerPoint 2010 file saved in the default .pptx format because they may have a previous version of this software or may not have Internet access available readily. For these reasons, you need to know their software and hardware limitations and distribute your file or handouts accordingly.

Overview

As you read through this chapter, you will learn how to create the presentation shown in Figure 5–1 on the previous page by performing these general tasks:

- Review a merged presentation.
- Insert slides and content clipped from slides.
- Secure and share a presentation.
- Use presentation tools.
- Package a presentation for a CD or DVD.
- Save a presentation in a variety of formats.
- Annotate a presentation.

Plan Ahead

General Project Guidelines
When creating a PowerPoint presentation, the actions you perform and the decisions you make will affect the appearance and characteristics of the finished document. As you create a presentation with illustrations, such as the project shown in Figure 5–1, you should follow these general guidelines:

1. **Develop a collaboration plan.** Planning tasks for group members to follow helps ensure success. Collaborators must understand the overall group goal, set short-term and long-term goals, identify subtasks that must be completed, and set a schedule.

2. **Accept and evaluate criticism.** Feedback, both positive and negative, that enables you to improve yourself and your work, is called **criticism**. Written and oral comments from others can help reinforce the positive aspects and also identify flaws. Seek comments from a variety of people who genuinely want to help you develop an effective slide show.

3. **Give constructive criticism.** If you are asked to critique a presentation, begin and end with positive comments. Give specific details about a few key areas that can be improved. Be honest, but be tactful.

4. **Use slide numbers to guide your speech.** A speaker can view the slide numbers to organize the speech, jump to particular slides, and control timing.

5. **Determine the screen show ratio.** Consider where the presentation will be shown and the type of hardware that will be available. Wide-screen displays are prevalent in the home office and corporate world, but their dimensions present design challenges for the PowerPoint developer.

6. **Select an appropriate password.** A **password** is a private combination of characters that allows users to open a file. To prevent unauthorized people from viewing your slides, choose a good password and keep it confidential.

When necessary, more specific details concerning the above guidelines are presented at appropriate points in the chapter. The chapter also will identify the actions performed and decisions made regarding these guidelines during the creation of the presentation shown in Figure 5–1.

To Start PowerPoint and Open and Save a Presentation

To begin this presentation, you will open a file located on the Data Files for Students. See the inside back cover of this book for instructions on downloading the Data Files for Students, or contact your instructor for more information about accessing the required files. If you are using a computer to step through the project in this chapter and you want your screens to match the figures in this book, you should change your screen's resolution to 1024 × 768.

The following steps start PowerPoint, open a file, and then save it with a new file name.

1 Start PowerPoint. If necessary, maximize the PowerPoint window.

2 Open the presentation, Windstorms, located on the Data Files for Students.

3 Save the presentation using the file name, Windstorms Final.

Plan Ahead

Develop a collaboration plan.
Working with your classmates can yield numerous benefits. Your peers can assist in brainstorming, developing key ideas, revising your project, and keeping you on track so that your presentation meets the assignment goals.

The first step when collaborating with peers is to define success. What, ultimately, is the goal? For example, are you developing a persuasive presentation to school administrators in an effort to fund a new club? Next, you can set short-term and long-term goals that help lead you to completing the project successfully. These goals can be weekly tasks to accomplish, such as interviewing content experts, conducting online research, or compiling an annotated bibliography. After that, you can develop a plan to finish the project by stating subtasks that each member must accomplish. Each collaborator should inform the group members when the task is complete or if problems are delaying progress. When collaborators meet, whether in person or online, they should establish an agenda and have one member keep notes of topics discussed.

Collaborating on a Presentation

PowerPoint provides several methods to collaborate with friends or coworkers who can view your slide show and then provide feedback. When you **collaborate**, you work together on a document with other PowerPoint users who are cooperating jointly and assisting willingly with the endeavor. You can distribute your slide show physically to others by exchanging a compact disc or a flash drive. You also can share your presentation through the Internet by sending the file as an e-mail attachment or saving the file to a storage location, such as Windows Live SkyDrive.

In the following pages, you will follow these general steps to collaborate with Mary Halen, who has reviewed your Windstorms presentation:

1. Combine a presentation.
2. Print slides and comments.
3. Review and accept or reject changes.
4. Delete a comment.
5. Modify a comment.
6. Insert a comment.

BTW

Slide Library
In a business environment, PowerPoint presentations may be stored on a centrally located Slide Library that resides on a server. These slide shows may be shared, reused, and accessed by many individuals who then can copy materials into their individual presentations. The Slide Library time stamps when an individual has borrowed a particular slide or presentation and then time stamps the slide or presentation when it is returned. If a particular slide in the Slide Library has been updated, anyone who has borrowed that slide is notified that the content has changed. People creating PowerPoint presentations can track the changes to presentations, locate the latest versions of slides, and check for slide updates.

To Merge a Presentation

Mary Halen reviewed the Windstorms presentation and made several comments about the design. She converted the Slide 1 title text to WordArt and the Slide 2 bulleted list to a SmartArt graphic. She also added a transition to all slides, changed the theme, edited some paragraphs, and added two slides. The following steps merge this reviewer's file with the original Windstorms presentation.

1

- With the Windstorms Final presentation active, display the Review tab (Figure 5–2).

 Can I track my changes in PowerPoint as I can in other Office 2010 products, such as Word 2010?

No. To detect differences between your presentation and another presentation, you must merge the files.

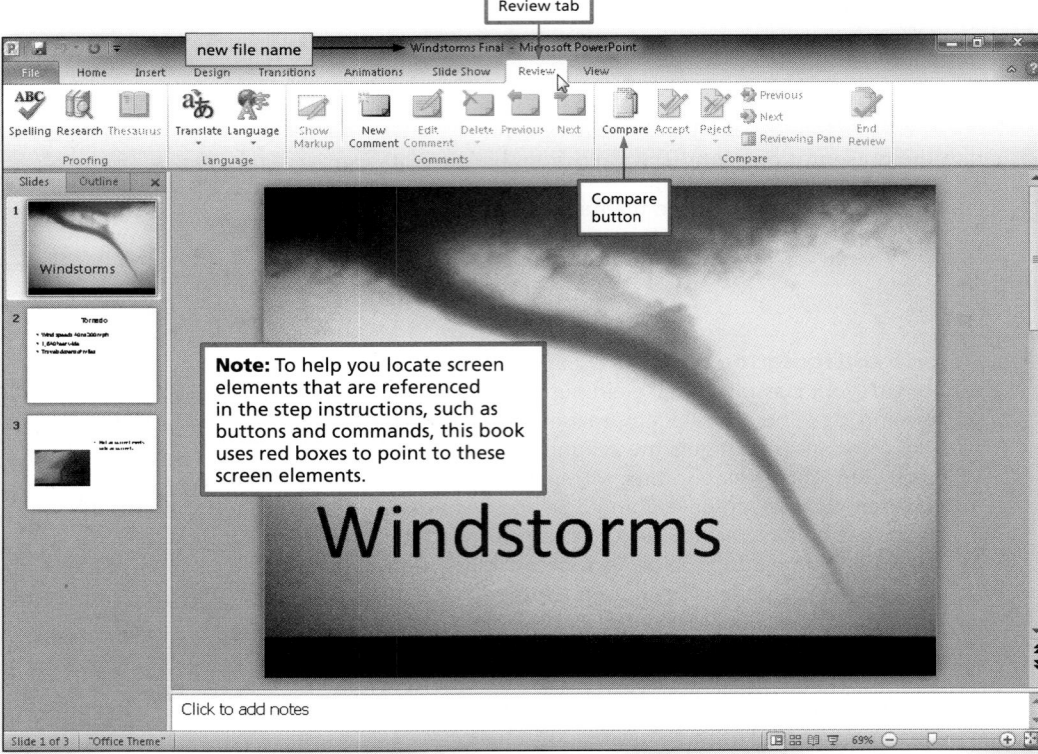

Figure 5–2

2

- Click the Compare button (Review tab | Compare group) to display the Choose File to Merge with Current Presentation dialog box.

- With the list of files and folders on your USB flash drive displaying, click Windstorms – Mary Halen to select the file name (Figure 5–3).

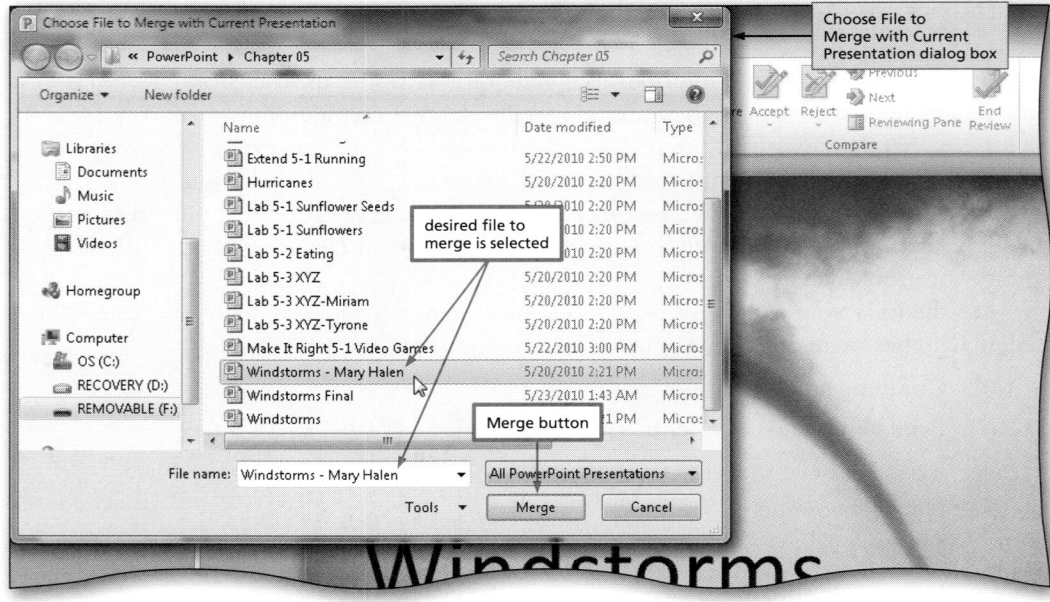

Figure 5–3

3

- Click the Merge button (Choose File to Merge with Current Presentation dialog box) to merge Mary Halen's presentation with the Windstorms presentation and to display the Revisons task pane (Figure 5–4).

Q&A

If several reviewers have made comments and suggestions, can I merge their files, too?

Yes. Repeat Steps 1 and 2. Each reviewer's initials display in a color-coded comment box.

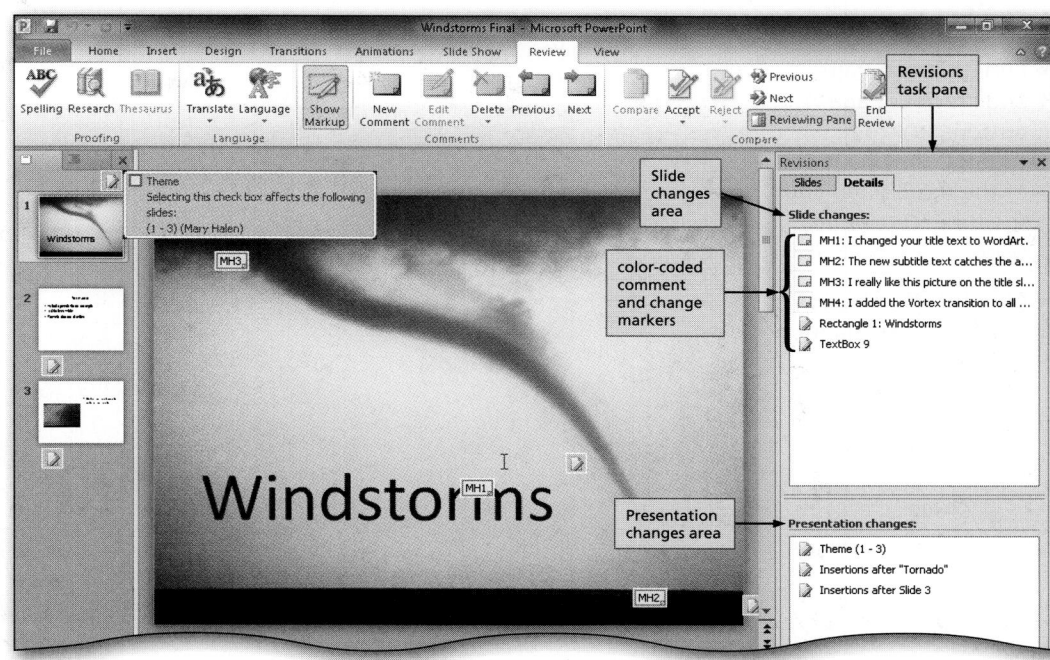

Figure 5–4

To Print Comments

As owner of the original presentation, you want to review the comments and modifications and then make decisions about whether to accept these suggestions. You can print each slide and the comments a reviewer has made before you begin to accept and reject each suggestion. PowerPoint can print these slides and comments on individual pages. The following steps use this slide show to illustrate printing these suggestions.

1

- Open the Backstage view and then click the Print tab to display the Print gallery.

- Click Full Page Slides to display the Print Layout gallery.

- If necessary, click Print Comments and Ink Markup to select this option (Figure 5–5).

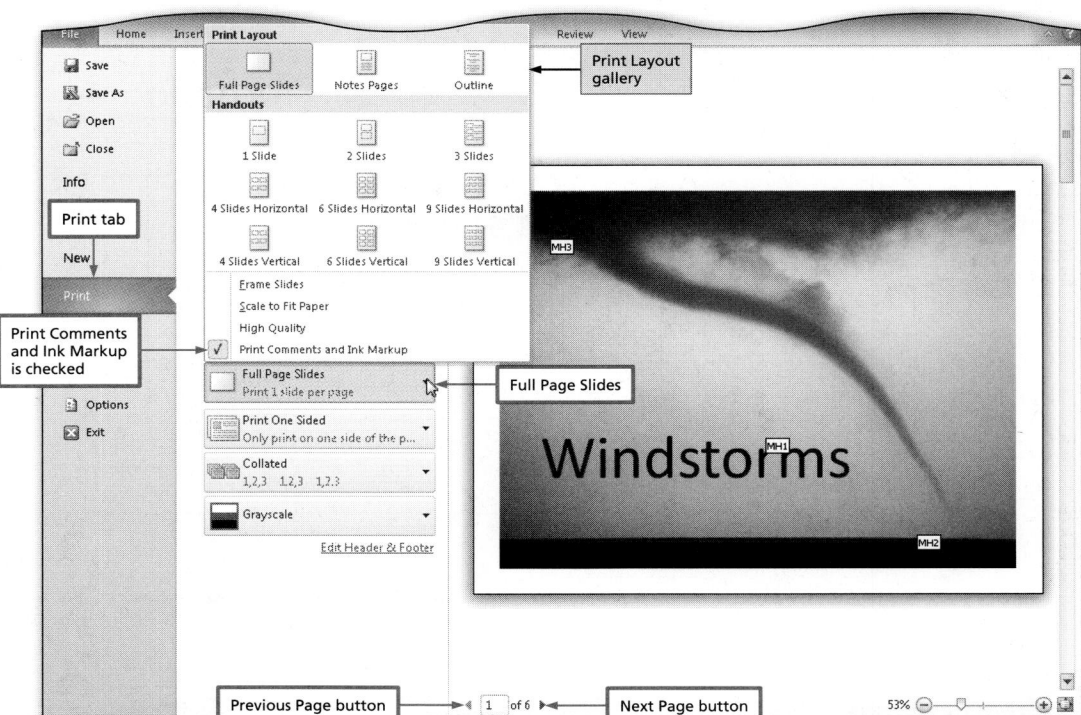

Figure 5–5

2
- Click the Next Page and Previous Page buttons to scroll through the previews of the three slides and the three comment pages.
- Click the Print button to print the six pages (Figure 5–6).

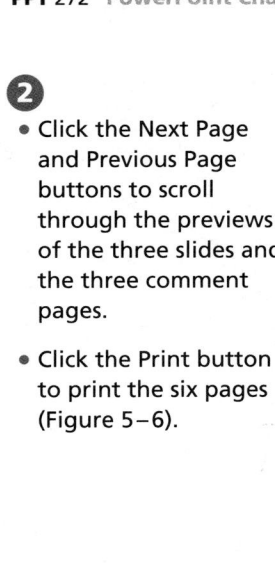

(a) Page 1 (Title Slide)

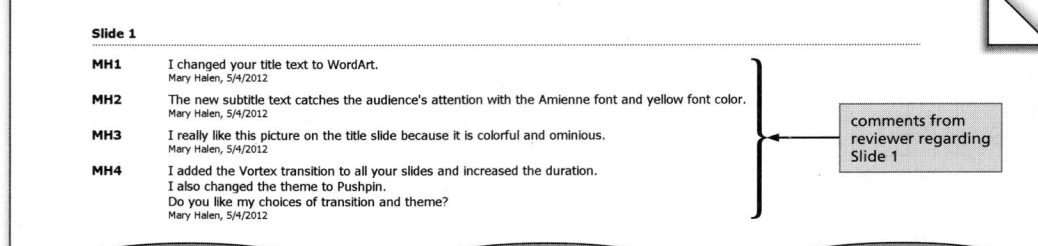

Slide 1

MH1	I changed your title text to WordArt. Mary Halen, 5/4/2012
MH2	The new subtitle text catches the audience's attention with the Amienne font and yellow font color. Mary Halen, 5/4/2012
MH3	I really like this picture on the title slide because it is colorful and ominous. Mary Halen, 5/4/2012
MH4	I added the Vortex transition to all your slides and increased the duration. I also changed the theme to Pushpin. Do you like my choices of transition and theme? Mary Halen, 5/4/2012

comments from reviewer regarding Slide 1

(b) Page 2 (Comments from Reviewer)

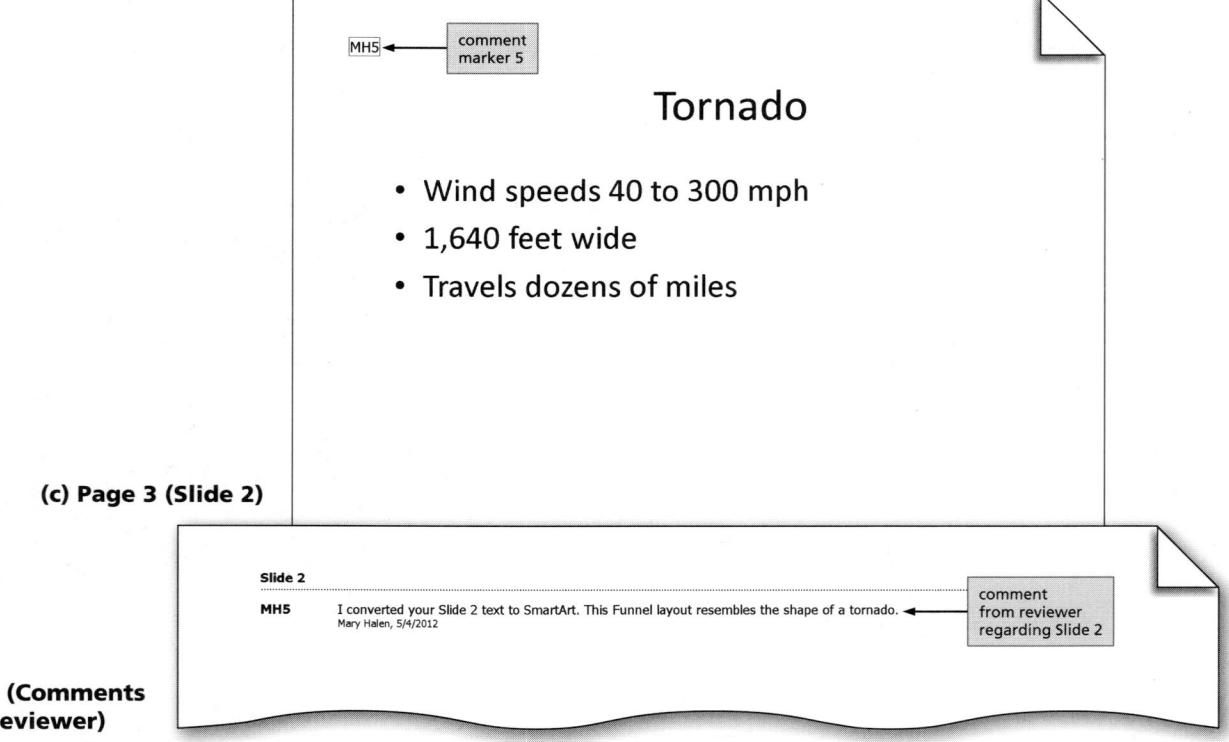

(c) Page 3 (Slide 2)

Slide 2

MH5	I converted your Slide 2 text to SmartArt. This Funnel layout resembles the shape of a tornado. Mary Halen, 5/4/2012

comment from reviewer regarding Slide 2

(d) Page 4 (Comments from Reviewer)

Figure 5–6

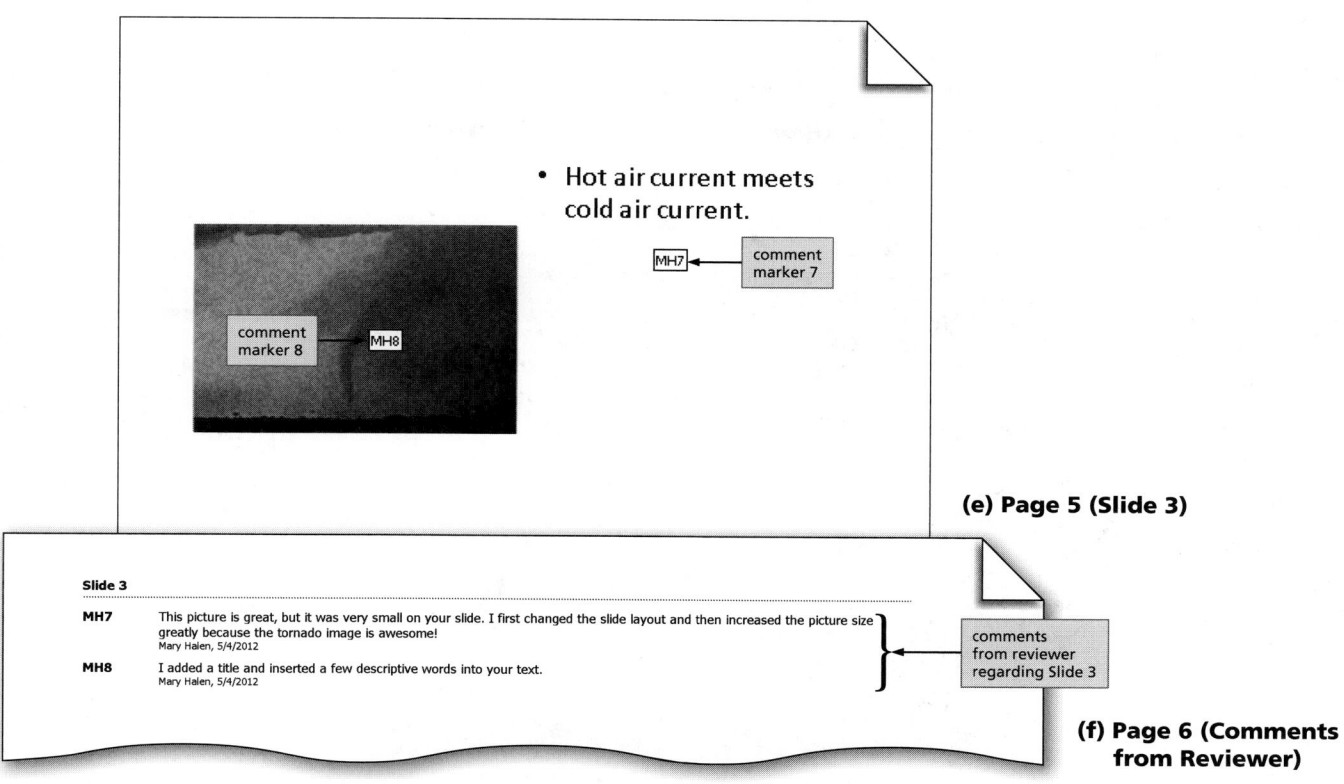

(e) Page 5 (Slide 3)

Slide 3

MH7   This picture is great, but it was very small on your slide. I first changed the slide layout and then increased the picture size greatly because the tornado image is awesome!
Mary Halen, 5/4/2012

MH8   I added a title and inserted a few descriptive words into your text.
Mary Halen, 5/4/2012

comments from reviewer regarding Slide 3

(f) Page 6 (Comments from Reviewer)

Figure 5–6 (Continued)

To Preview Presentation Changes

The reviewer made several changes to the overall presentation and then edited your three slides. You can preview her modifications to obtain an overview of her suggestions. Seeing her edits now can help you decide later whether to accept or reject each change as you step through each revision. The following steps preview the merged presentation.

- If necessary, display the Review tab and then click the Reviewing Pane button (Review tab | Compare group) to display the Revisions task pane. With Slide 1 displaying, click the Slides tab in the Revisions task pane to display a thumbnail of merged Slide 1 (Figure 5–7).

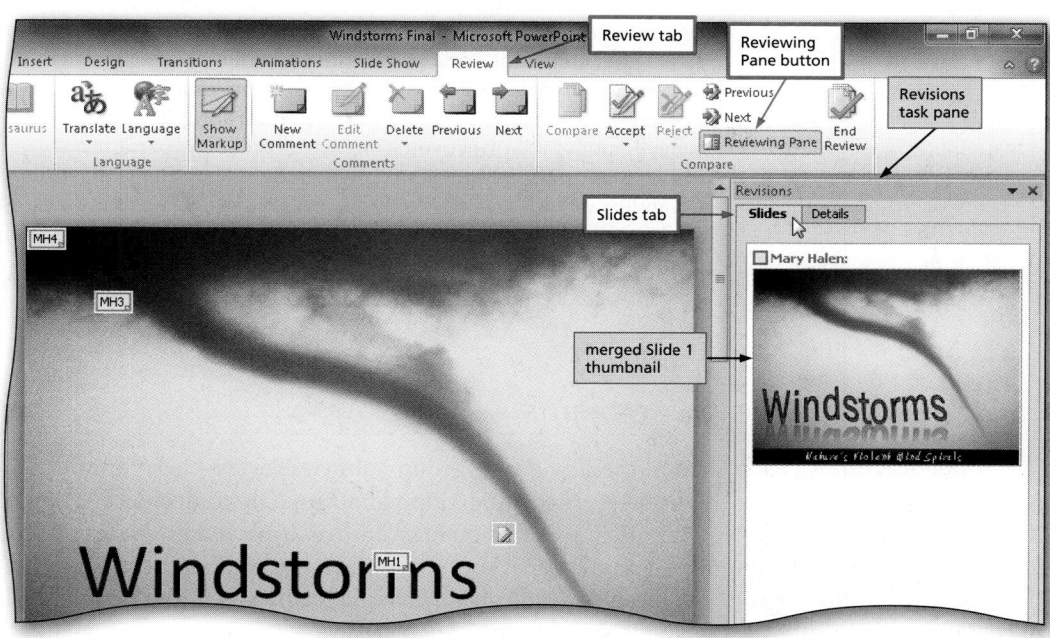

Figure 5–7

- Click the Mary Halen check box above the Slide 1 thumbnail to view the proposed changes in the Slide pane (Figure 5–8).

- Click the Mary Halen check box again to reject the changes.

Q&A

Can I make some, but not all, of the reviewer's changes on Slide 1?

Yes. PowerPoint allows you to view each proposed change individually and then either accept or reject the modification.

Figure 5–8

Plan Ahead

Accept and evaluate criticism.
Receiving feedback from others ultimately should enhance your presentation. If several of your reviewers make similar comments, such as too much text appears on one slide or that a chart would help present your concept, then you should heed their criticism and modify your slides. Criticism from a variety of people, particularly if they are from different cultures or vary in age, gives a wide range of viewpoints. Some reviewers might focus on the font size, others on color and design choices, while others might single out the overall message. These individuals should make judgments on your work, such as saying that the overall presentation is good or that a particular paragraph is confusing, and then offer reasons why elements are effective or how you can edit a paragraph.

When you receive these comments, do not get defensive. Ask yourself why your reviewers would have made these comments. Perhaps they lack a background in the subject matter, or, on the other hand, they may have a particular interest in this topic and can add their expertise.

To Review and Delete Comments

The Revisions task pane and the Reviewing group help you review each comment. These notes from the reviewer may guide you through the revisions and help you ultimately to decide whether to accept changes or delete the suggestions. Color-coded comment and change markers are displayed in the Revisions task pane. The reviewer's initials display in the rectangular comment marker on the slide and next to the comment marker in the task pane; the initials are followed by a numeral that indicates the sequence by which the reviewer added comments to the presentation. The following steps view and then delete the reviewer's comments for Slide 1.

1

- Click the Details tab in the Revisions task pane to display the comment markers and the change markers in the Slide changes and Presentation changes areas.

Q&A How do I distinguish between the comment markers and the change markers?

The comment markers are horizontal rectangles followed by the reviewer's initials and a number; the change markers are vertical rectangles with a pencil overlay.

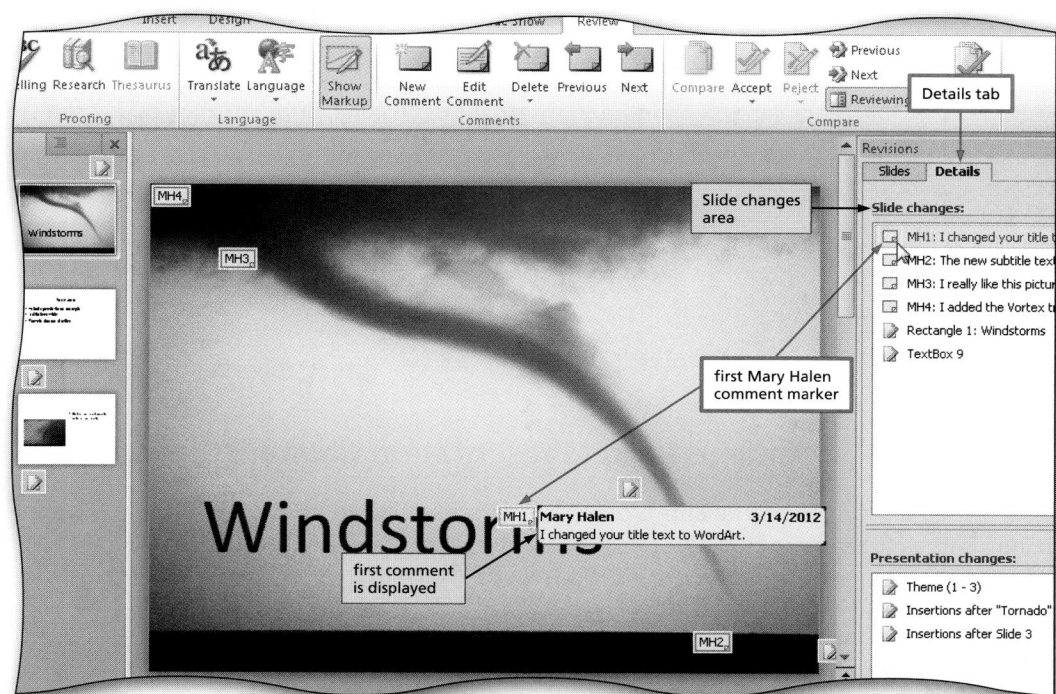

Figure 5–9

- Click the first Mary Halen comment marker, MH1, in the Slides changes area to display the comment (Figure 5–9).

Q&A Why does the number 1 display after the commenter's initials?

The number indicates it is the first comment the reviewer inserted.

Q&A Can I read the comment without clicking the comment marker on the Details tab?

Yes. You can mouse over or click the comment marker on the slide.

2

- Read the comment and then click the Delete Comment button (Review tab | Comments group) to delete Mary Halen's first comment.

- Click the Next Comment button (Review tab | Comments group) to view the second comment (Figure 5–10).

Q&A Can I click the comment marker on the Details tab to display the comment instead of clicking the Next button?

Yes. Either method displays the comment.

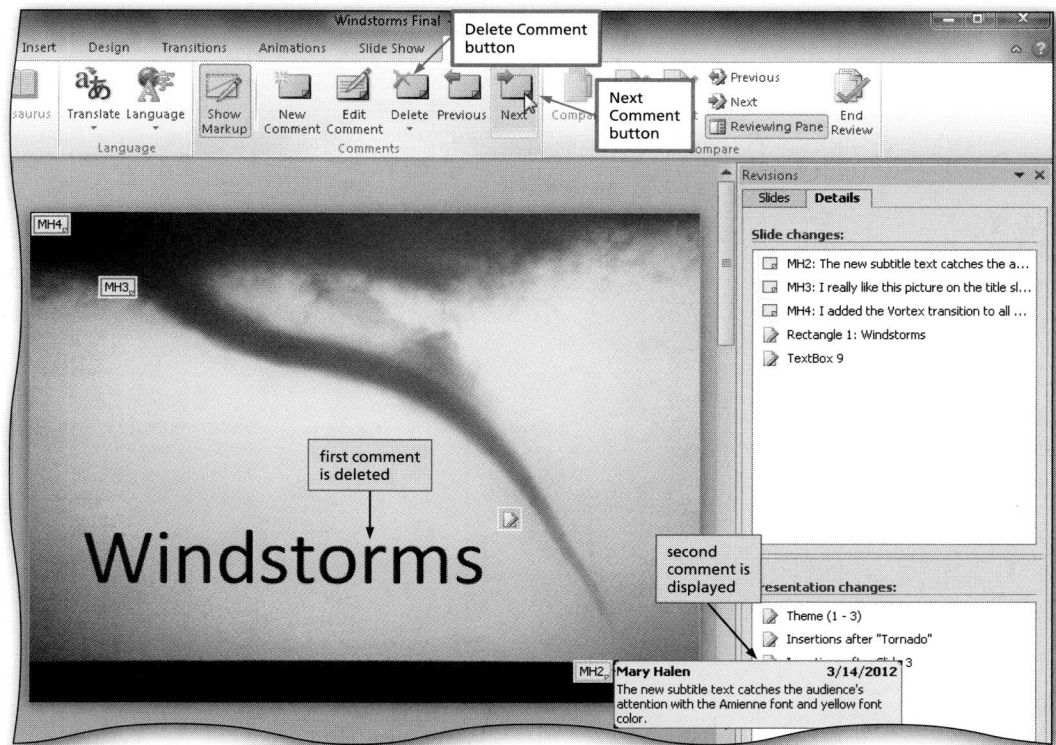

Figure 5–10

- Delete the second comment.

- Review the third comment for Slide 1 and then delete this comment marker.

- Review the fourth comment for Slide 1 but do not delete this comment marker.

Q&A Why should I not delete Mary Halen's fourth comment?

Mary indicates that she added a transition and changed the presentation theme. You have not accepted her changes yet, so you do not know if you agree with her modifications. You will respond to her question after you have made the changes.

To Review, Accept, and Reject Presentation Changes

Changes that affect the entire presentation are indicated in the Presentation changes area of the Revisions task pane. These changes can include transitions, color schemes, fonts, backgrounds, and slide insertions. The following steps display and accept the reviewer's three revisions in the presentation.

- Click the first presentation change marker, Theme (1 – 3), in the Presentation changes area to display the Theme box with an explanation of the proposed change for all slides in the presentation (Figure 5–11).

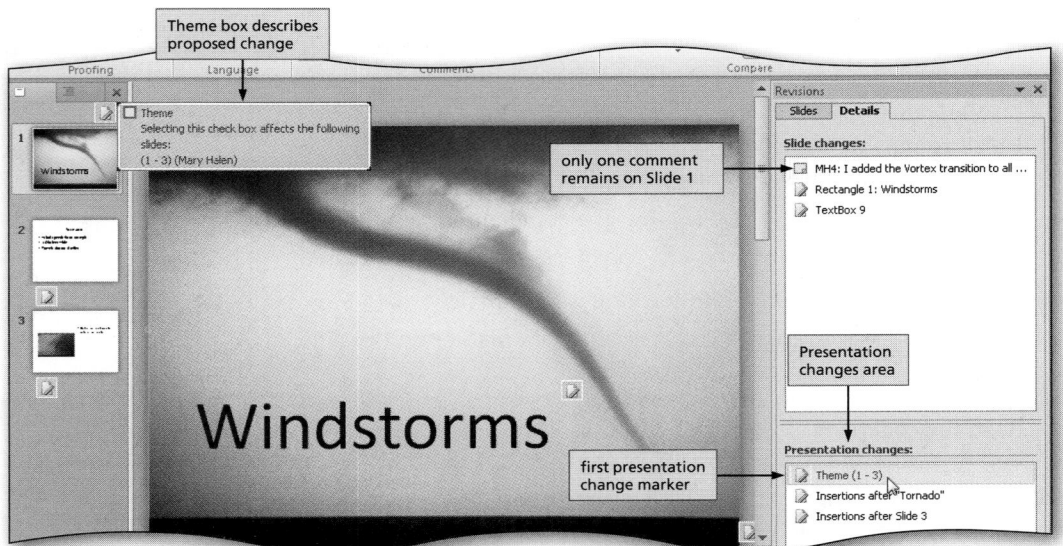

Figure 5–11

- Click the Accept Change button (Review tab | Compare group) to view the new Pushpin theme on all slides (Figure 5–12).

Q&A Can I also apply the change by clicking the Theme check box?

Yes. Either method applies the Pushpin theme.

Q&A If I decide to not apply the new theme, can I reverse this change?

Yes. Click the Reject Change button (Review tab | Compare group) or click the check box to remove the check mark and reject the reviewer's theme modification.

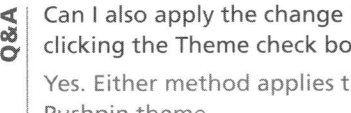
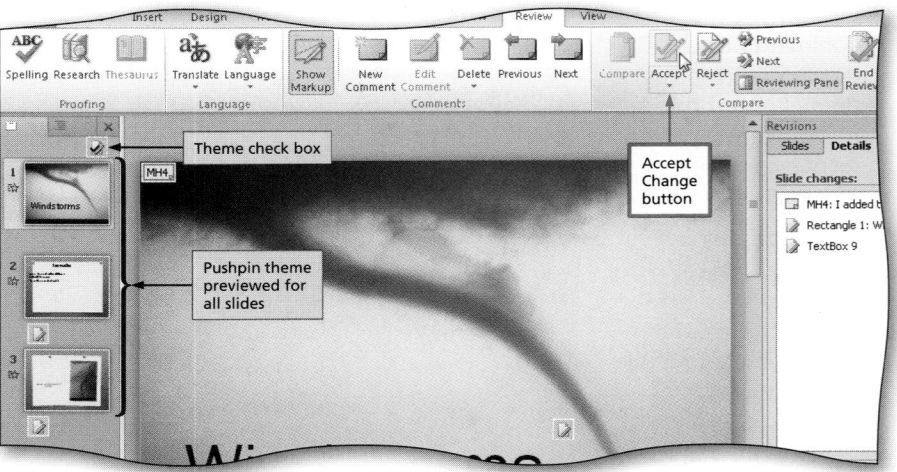

Figure 5–12

Click the second presentation change marker, Insertions after "Tornado", in the Presentation changes area to display the review content thumbnail with an explanation of the proposed new slide (Figure 5–13).

Q&A

Why does a check mark appear in the Theme (1 – 3) change marker?

The check mark indicates you have applied the proposed change.

Click the Accept Change button to insert the new slide.

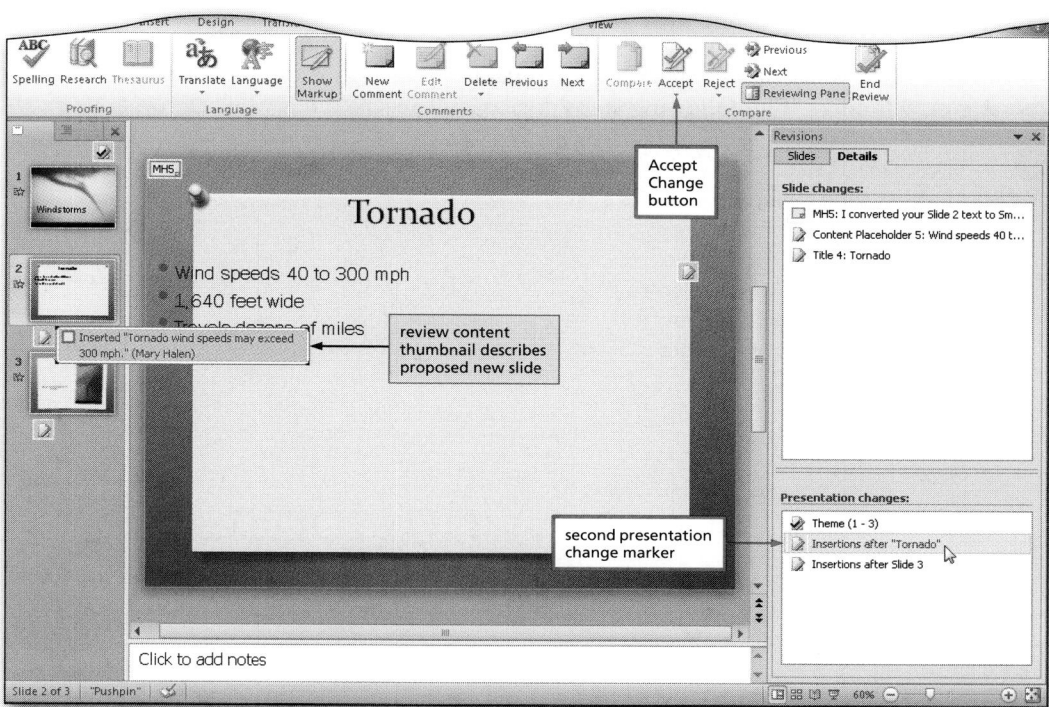

Figure 5–13

Click the third presentation change marker, Insertions after Slide 4, to display the review content thumbnail with a proposed slide to insert in the presentation (Figure 5–14).

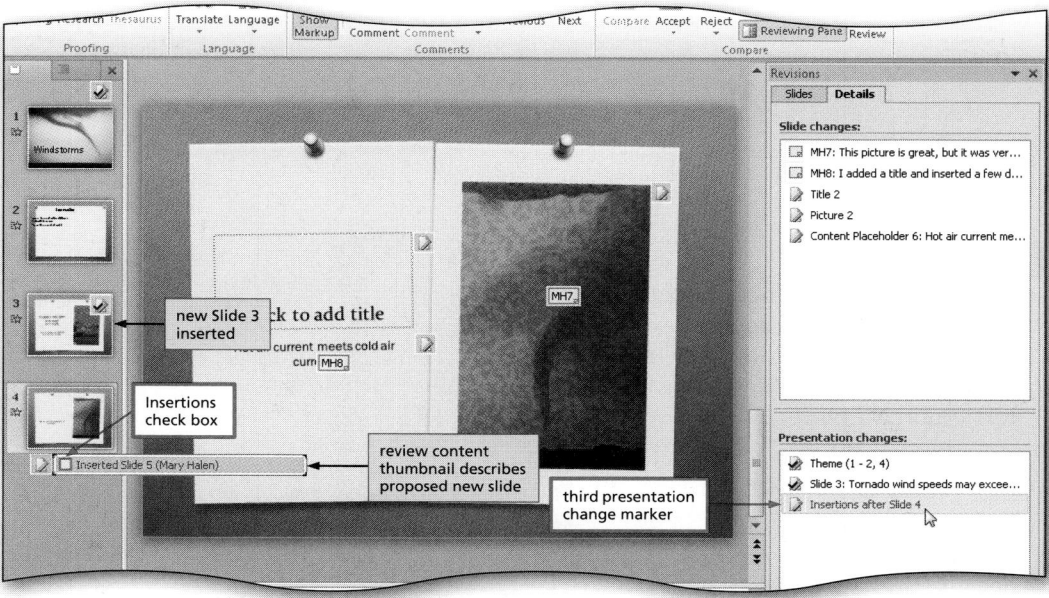

Click the Insertions check box to insert the new Slide 5.

Figure 5–14

To Review, Accept, and Reject Slide Changes

Changes that affect only the displayed slide are indicated in the Slide changes area of the Revisions task pane. A reviewer can modify many aspects of the slide, such as adding and deleting pictures and clips, editing text, and moving placeholders. The following steps display and accept the reviewer's revisions to Slide 1.

1
• Click the first slide change, Rectangle 1: Windstorms, in the Slide changes area to display the Rectangle 1 box with Mary Halen's three proposed changes for the Windstorms text in the rectangle (Figure 5–15).

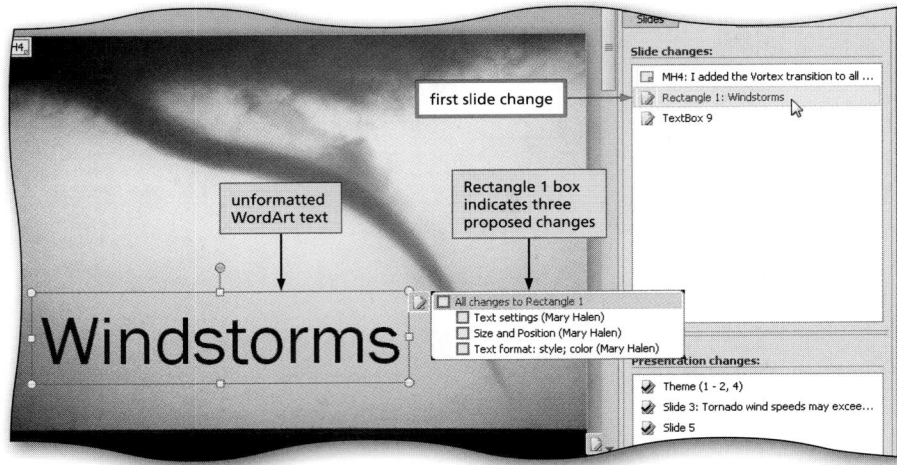

Figure 5–15

2
• Click the All changes to Rectangle 1 check box to preview the three proposed changes to the Windstorms text (Figure 5–16).

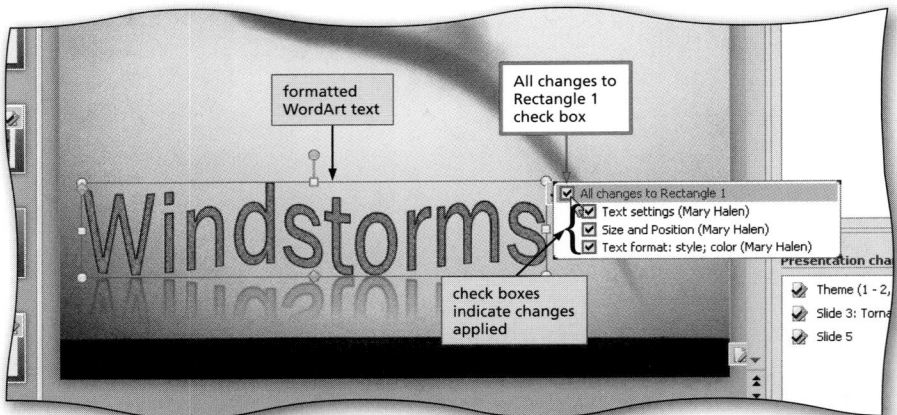

Figure 5–16

3
• Click the Size and Position check box to preview only the proposed Text settings and the Text format: style, color changes to the Windstorms text (Figure 5–17).

 Q&A

Can I select any combination of the check boxes to modify the text in the rectangle?

Yes. Click the individual check boxes to preview the reviewer's modifications.

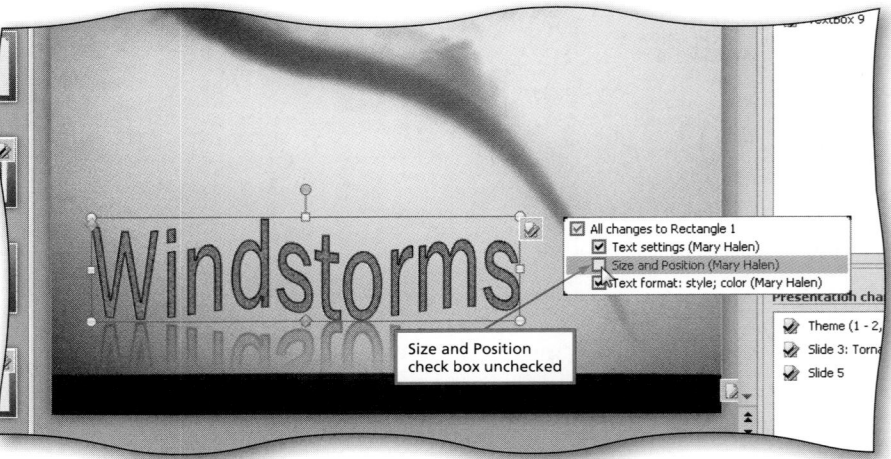

Figure 5–17

4
- Click the second slide change, TextBox, in the Slide changes area to display the Inserted TextBox box.

- Click the Inserted TextBox check box to view the proposed text box (Figure 5–18).

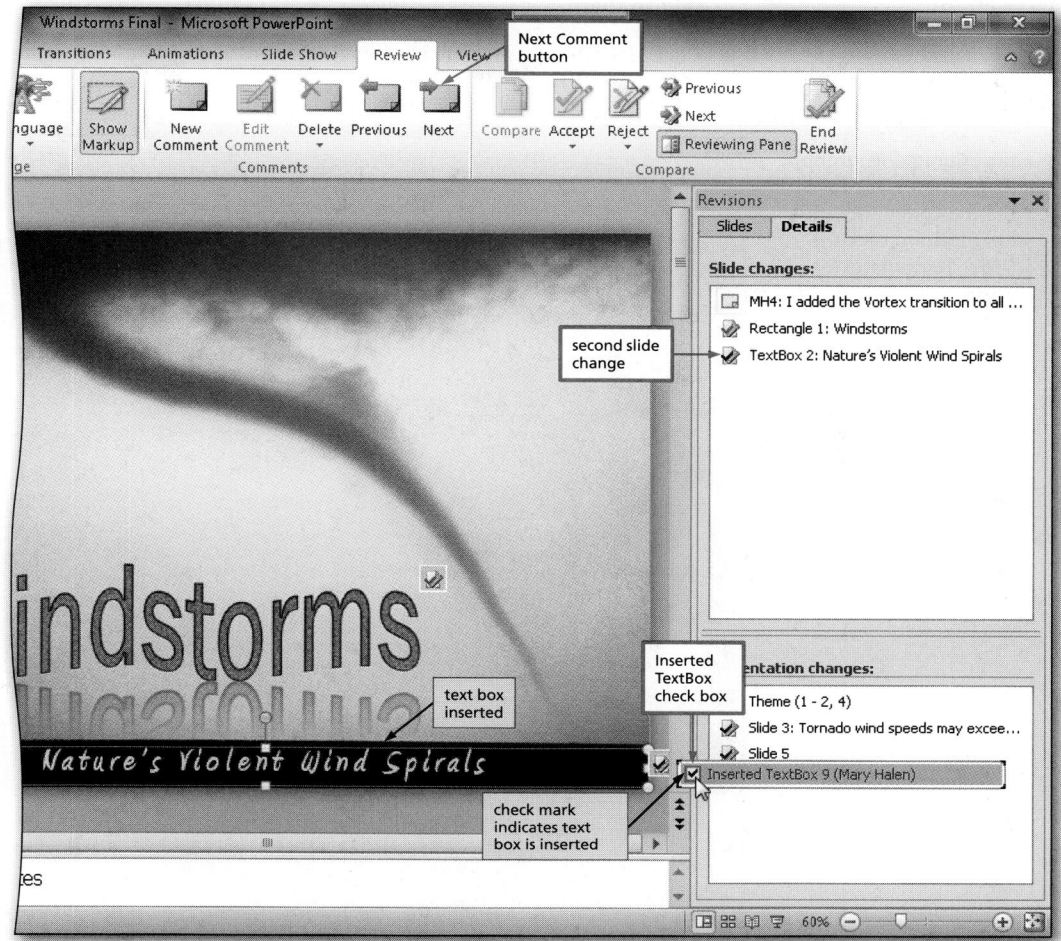

Figure 5–18

To Review and Accept Slide Changes on the Remaining Slides

You have accepted all of Mary Halen's presentation changes and most of her Slide 1 changes. She also inserted comments in and made changes to other slides. The following steps review her comments and accept her modifications.

1 Click the Next Comment button (Review tab | Comments group) to display Slide 2.

2 Read comment 5 and then delete the comment.

3 Click the Content Placeholder 5 slide change and then apply the Canvas contents change.

4 Click the Title 4: Tornado slide change and then accept the change to delete the title text placeholder.

5 Click the Next Comment button to display Slide 3. Read comment 6, but do not delete it.

BTW

Showing or Hiding Markup
You can view the slides without the comments and other annotations by clicking the Show Markup button (Review tab | Comments group). If you then want to see the comments and annotations, click the Show Markup button again.

6 Click the Next Comment button to display Slide 4. Read comments 7 and 8 and then delete them.

7 Click the Next Comment button to display Slide 5. Read comment 9, but do not delete it (Figure 5–19).

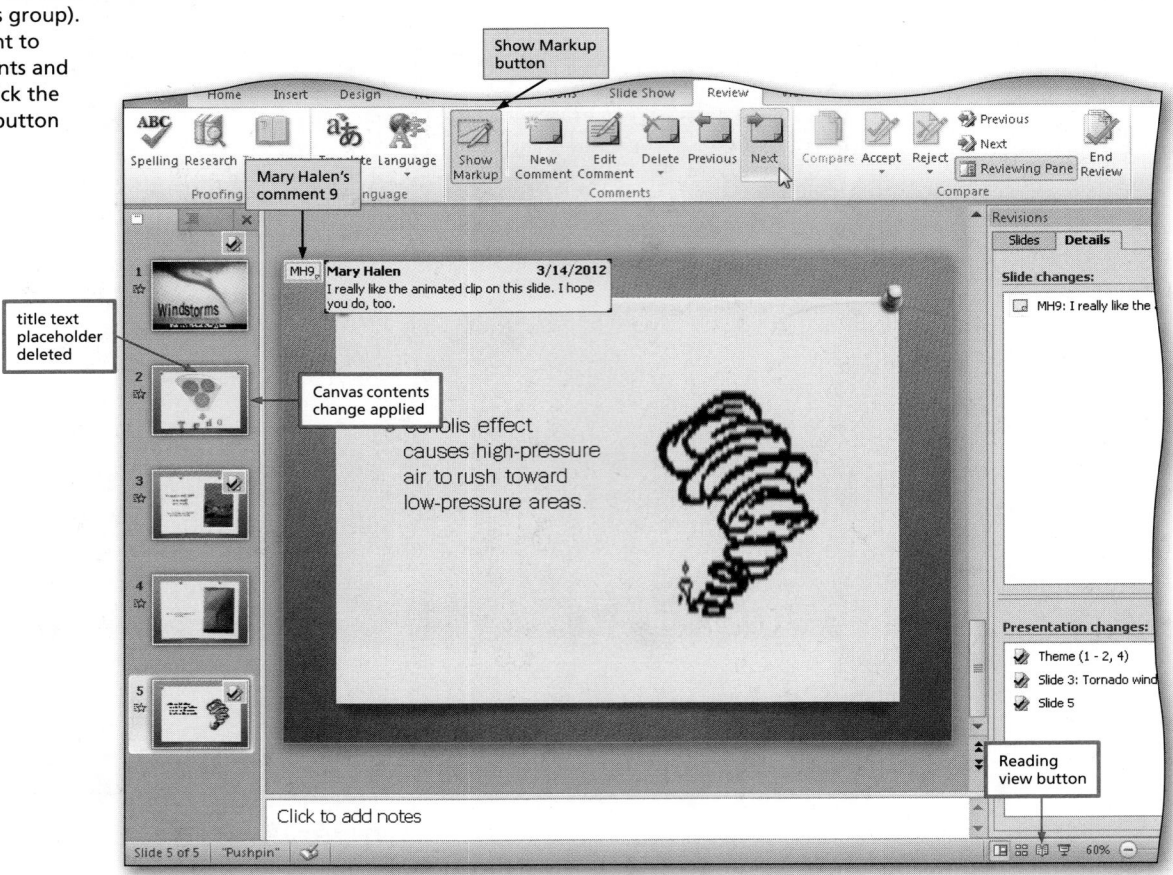

Figure 5–19

BTW

Q&As
For a complete list of the Q&As found in many of the step-by-step sequences in this book, visit the PowerPoint 2010 Q&A Web page (scsite.com/ppt2010/qa).

To Run the Revised Presentation in Reading View

Mary's changes modified the original presentation substantially, so it is a good idea to review the new presentation. The following steps review the revised slides.

1 Display Slide 1 and then click the Reading view button.

2 Click the Next and Previous buttons to review the changes on each slide.

3 After viewing the animated tornado on Slide 5, click the Normal view button.

To Reject a Slide Revision

After running the presentation, you decide that the animation on Slide 5 is distracting and that the text is not part of the material you desire to display in the slide show. Although you initially accepted Mary's change to insert the slide, you decide to reject this modification. The following steps display and reject the reviewer's revision to insert Slide 5.

1

• Click the change marker on the Slide 5 thumbnail in the Slides tab to display the Inserted Slide 5 box (Figure 5–20).

2

• Click the Reject Change button (Review tab | Compare group) to delete Slide 5 from the presentation.

Q&A Could I have deleted the slide by clicking the Inserted Slide 5 check box to remove the check mark?

Yes.

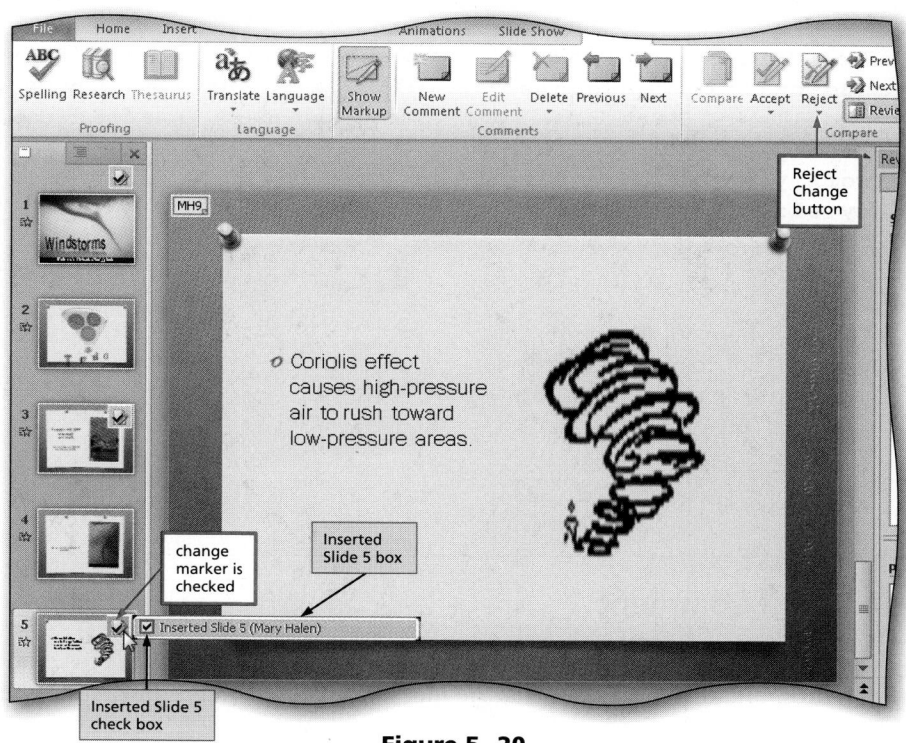

Figure 5–20

Give constructive criticism.
If you are asked to critique a presentation, begin and end with positive comments. Give specific details about a few key areas that can be improved. Be honest, but be tactful. Avoid using the word, you. For example, instead of writing, "You need to give some statistics to support your viewpoint," write "I had difficulty understanding which departments' sales have declined in the past five months. Perhaps a chart with specific losses would help depict how dramatically revenues have fallen."

Plan Ahead

To Insert a Comment

Mary Halen's comments and changes greatly enhanced your slide show, and you would like to send her a copy of the presentation so that she can see what modifications you accepted. You want to insert a comment to her on Slide 1 to thank her for taking the time to review your original slides. The following steps insert a comment on Slide 1.

1

• With Slide 1 displaying, click the Slide pane. Click the Insert Comment button, which displays as New Comment, (Review tab | Comments group) to open a comment box at the top of the slide (Figure 5–21).

Q&A Why do my initials and name differ from those shown in the figure?

The initials and name reflect the information that was entered when Microsoft Office 2010 was installed on your computer.

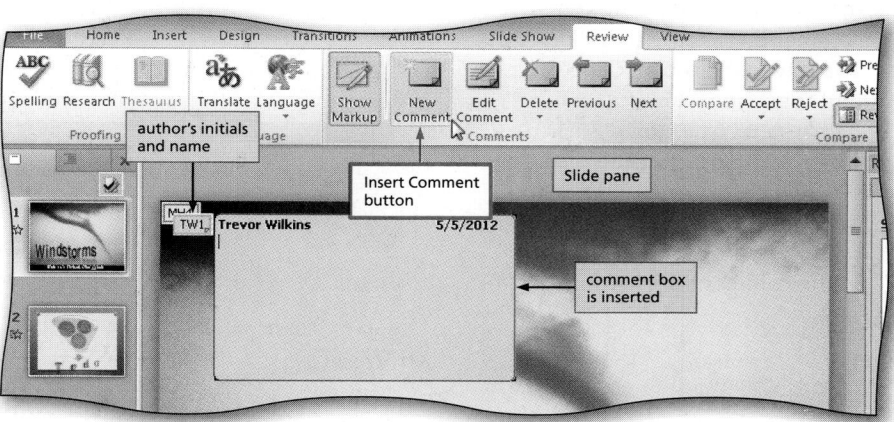

Figure 5–21

2
- Type **Your suggestions and modifications are excellent, Mary. I really appreciate the work you did to enhance my slides.** in the comment box (Figure 5–22).

3
- Click anywhere outside the comment box to hide the text and lock in the comment.

Q&A
Can I move the comment on the slide?
Yes. Select the comment and then drag it to another location on the slide.

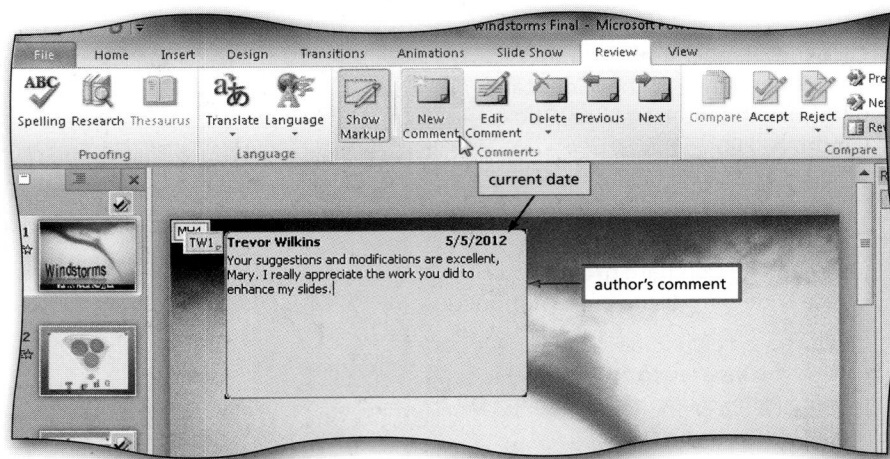

Figure 5–22

To Edit a Comment

Mary asked some questions in the comments she made in her presentation. You want to provide feedback to her by responding to her queries. One method of responding is by editing the comments she made. The following steps edit the comments on Slides 1 and 3.

1
- With Slide 1 displaying, click the MH4 comment marker on the slide to display Mary's fourth comment.

Q&A
Can I click the MH4 comment marker in the Revisions task pane to display Mary's comment?
Yes.

- Click the Edit Comment button (Review tab | Comments group) to change the marker comment color and display your initials and name (Figure 5–23).

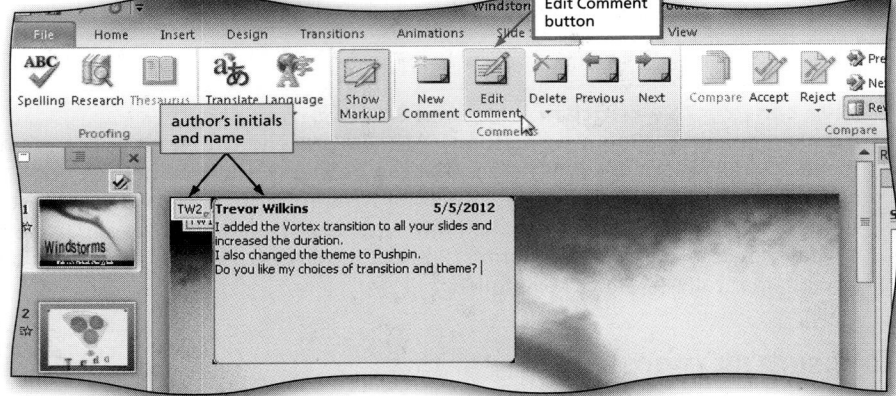

Figure 5–23

2
- Press the ENTER key to move the insertion point below Mary's comment. Press the ENTER key again to insert a blank line and then type **The Vortex transition complements the windstorm topic well. The Pushpin theme is excellent for displaying the photos.** in the comment box (Figure 5–24).

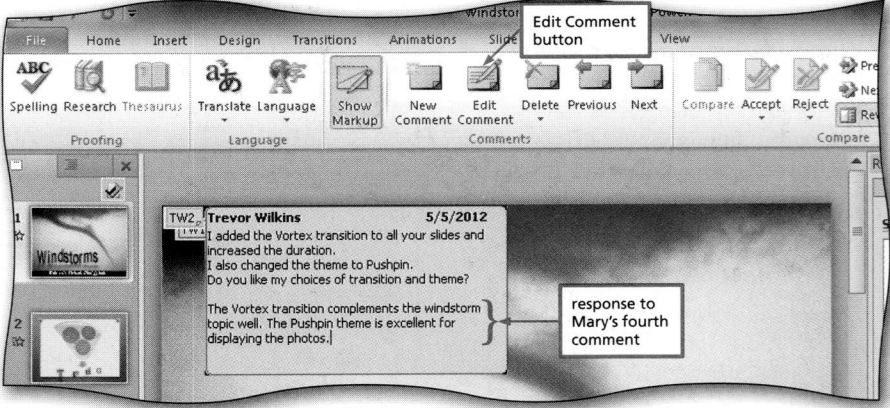

Figure 5–24

- Display Slide 3 and then click the MH6 comment marker on the slide to display Mary's comment.

- Click the Edit Comment button (Review tab | Comments group), press the ENTER key twice, and then type **The devastation from that tornado is amazing! Your slide is outstanding.** in the comment box immediately after Mary's comment (Figure 5–25).

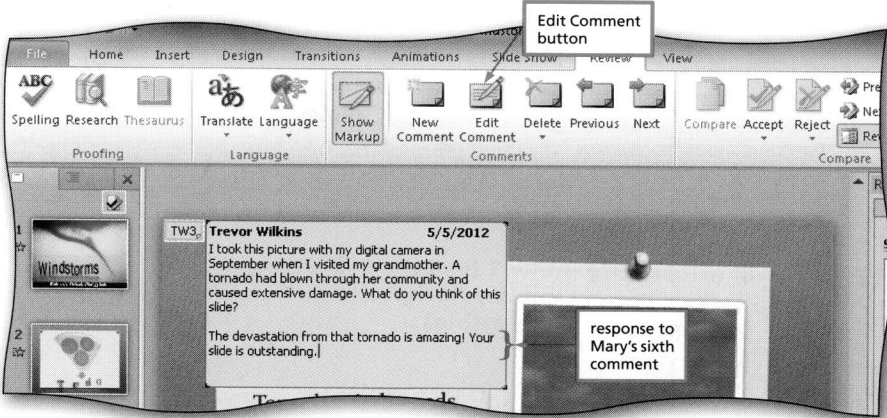

Figure 5–25

To End the Review

You have analyzed all of the reviewer's proposed changes and replied to some of her questions. Your review of the merged presentation is complete, so you can apply all the changes and close the Revisions task pane. Be mindful that you cannot undo these changes after the review has ended. The following steps end the review of the merged slides.

- Click the End Review button (Review tab | Compare group) to display the Microsoft PowerPoint dialog box (Figure 5–26).

2

- Click the Yes button (Microsoft PowerPoint dialog box) to apply the changes you accepted and discard the changes you rejected.

Q&A

Which changes are discarded?

You did not apply the size and position change to the Windstorms rectangle on Slide 1, and you did not insert Mary's proposed Slide 5.

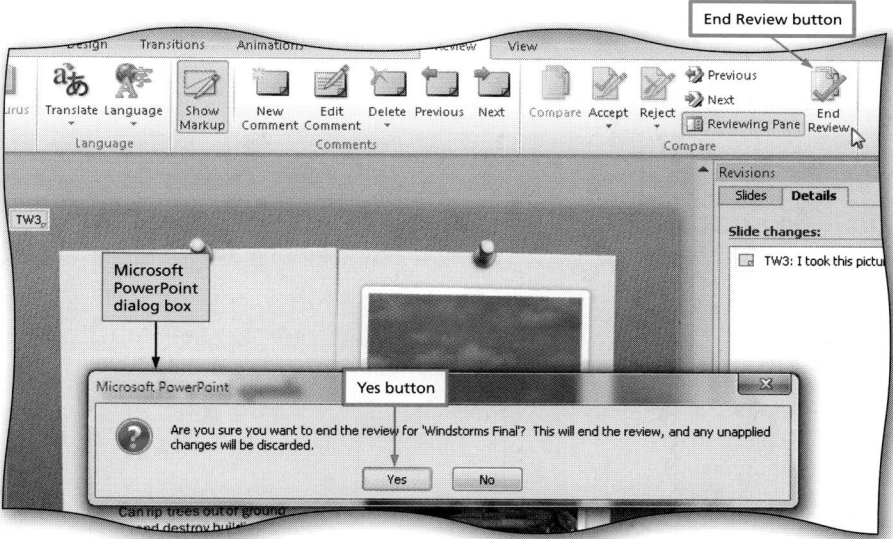

Figure 5–26

Reusing Slides from an Existing Presentation

Occasionally you may want to insert a slide from another presentation into your presentation. PowerPoint offers two methods of obtaining these slides. One way is to open the second presentation and then copy and paste the desired slides. The second method is to use the Reuse Slides task pane to view and then select the desired slides. The presentation can be stored on a storage medium or in a Slide Library, which is a folder where individual slides are saved.

BTW

BTWs
For a complete list of the BTWs found in the margins of this book, visit the PowerPoint 2010 BTW Web page (scsite.com/ppt2010/btw).

BTW

Copying Content from Other Applications
Collaboration can involve combining PowerPoint slides from two or more files, and it also can involve sharing content or objects created using other software. These programs can be other Microsoft Office programs, such as Word and Excel, as well as other programs that support object linking and embedding. A linked object maintains a connection to the program that created it and is updated if the source file is changed. An embedded object, on the other hand, loses its connection to the original software and becomes part of the presentation file. To link or embed content copied from another program, you select and copy the information in that program, position the insertion point at the location on the slide where you want that content to appear, click the Paste button arrow (Home tab | Clipboard group), and then click Paste Special in the Paste Options menu to display the Paste Special dialog box. Click Paste link if you want to link the object to the original software. Or, if you want to embed the object, click Paste (Paste Special dialog box) and then click the entry in the As box that has the word "object" in its name. For example, if you copied part of an Excel worksheet, you would click Microsoft Excel Worksheet Object.

The PowerPoint presentation with the file name, Hurricanes, has colorful pictures and useful text. It contains three slides, and you would like to insert two of these slides, shown in Figure 5–27, into your Windstorms Final presentation. You will capture part of the diamond graphic on Slide 3 and copy this snip to one Windstorms Final slide. The Hurricanes presentation is located on your Data Files for Students. See the inside back cover of this book for instructions on downloading the Data Files for Students, or contact your instructor for more information about accessing the required files.

(a) Slide 1 (Insert and Use Pushpin Formatting)

(b) Slide 2 (Insert and Keep Original Formatting)

(c) Slide 3 (Snip Part of Graphic)

Figure 5–27

The inserted slides will be placed in the presentation directly after Slide 4. PowerPoint converts inserted slides to the theme and styles of the current presentation, so the first slide will inherit the styles of the current Pushpin theme and Windstorms Final presentation. You will, in contrast, specify that the second slide keep the source formatting of the Hurricanes presentation, which uses the Apothecary theme. You will need to add the Vortex transition to the second slide because you are not applying the Windstorms Final formatting.

To Reuse Slides from an Existing Presentation

The following steps add two slides from the Hurricanes presentation to your presentation.

1

- With your USB flash drive connected to one of the computer's USB ports, display Slide 4 and then display the Home tab.

- Click the New Slide button arrow to display the Pushpin layout gallery (Figure 5–28).

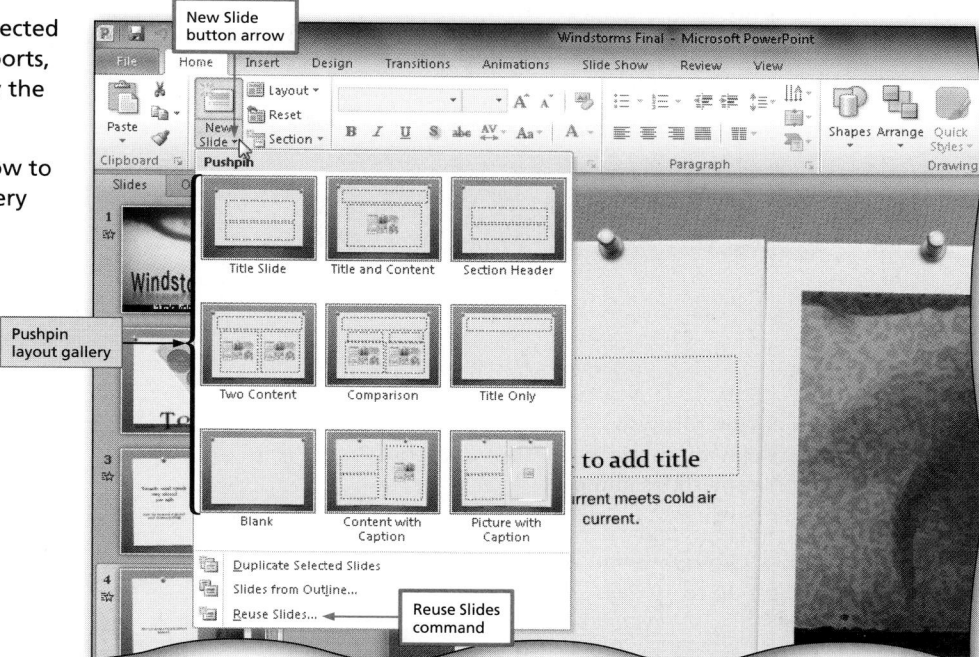

Figure 5–28

2

- Click Reuse Slides in the Pushpin layout gallery to display the Reuse Slides task pane.

- Click the Browse button (Figure 5–29).

Q&A

What are the two Browse options shown?

If the desired slides are in a Slide Library, you would click Browse Slide Library to select individual slides that you want to use. The slides you need, however, are on your Data Files for Students, so you need to click Browse File.

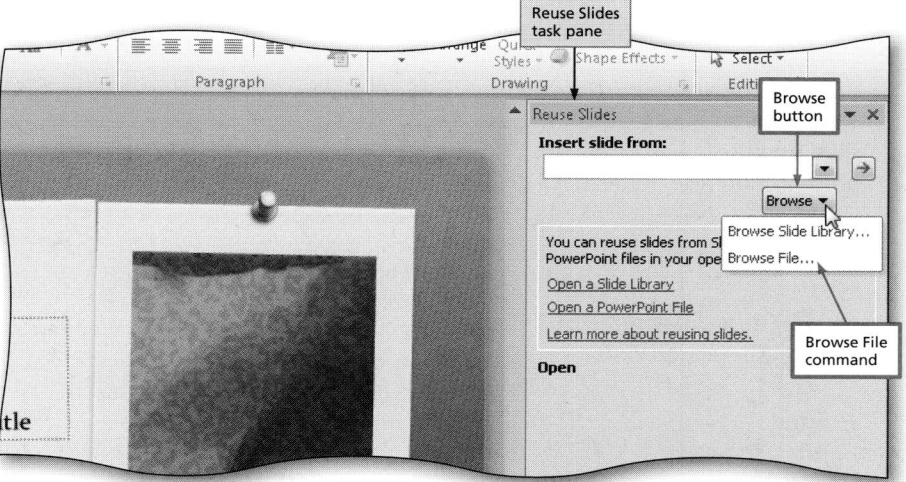

Figure 5–29

- Click Browse File to display the Browse dialog box.

- If necessary, double-click your USB flash drive in the list of available storage devices to display a list of files and folders on the selected USB flash drive.

- Click Hurricanes to select the file (Figure 5–30).

Q&A What if the file is not on a USB flash drive?

Use the same process, but select the drive containing the file.

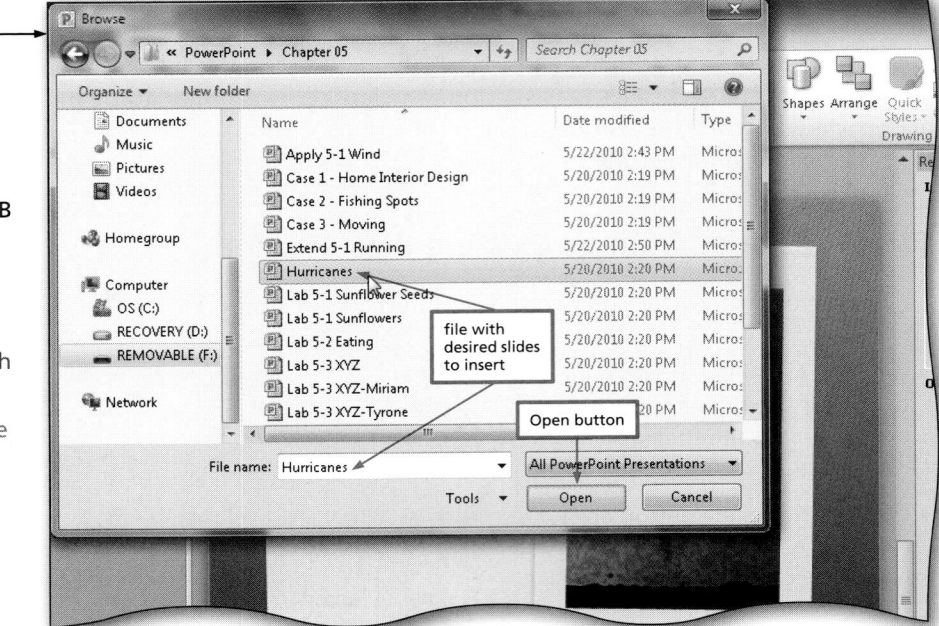

Figure 5–30

- Click the Open button (Browse dialog box) to display thumbnails of the three Hurricane slides in the Reuse Slides task pane.

- Point to the first slide thumbnail, Hurricanes can last up to 10 days (Figure 5–31).

Experiment

- Point to each of the thumbnails in the Reuse Slides task pane to see a larger preview of that slide.

5

- Click the Hurricanes can last up to 10 days thumbnail to insert this slide into the Windstorms Final presentation after Slide 4.

Q&A Can I insert all the slides in the presentation in one step instead of selecting each one individually?

Yes. Right-click any thumbnail and then click Insert All Slides.

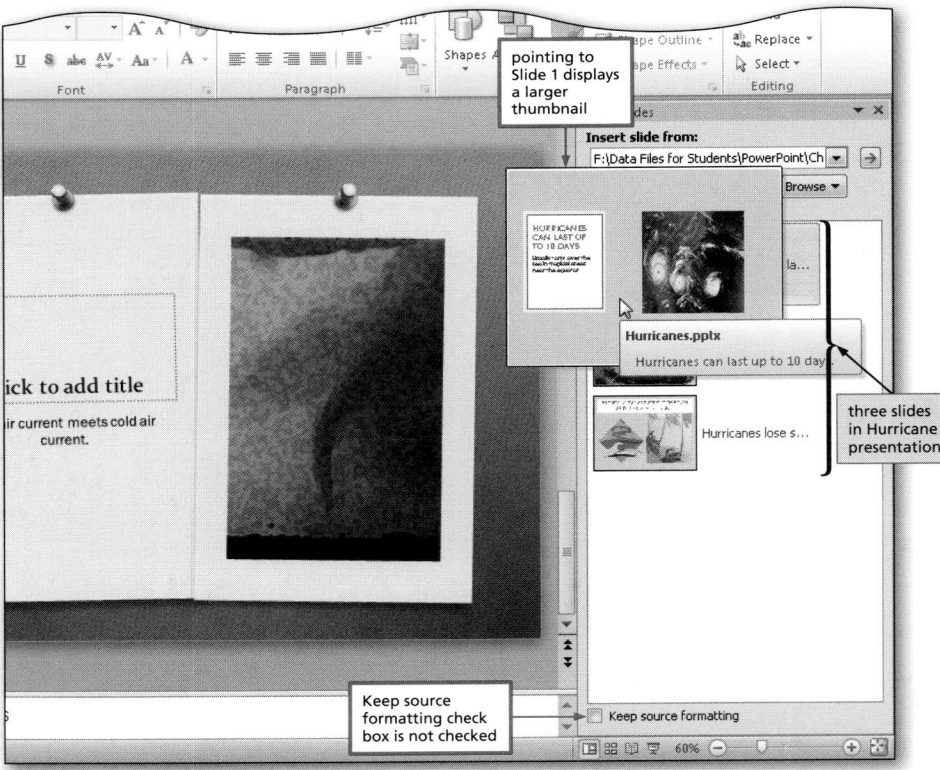

Figure 5–31

6

- Click the 'Keep source formatting' check box at the bottom of the Reuse Slides task pane to preserve the Hurricanes presentation formatting.

Q&A What would happen if I did not check this box?

PowerPoint would change the formatting to the characteristics found in the Pushpin theme.

- Point to the second slide, which has an aerial picture of a hurricane (Figure 5–32).

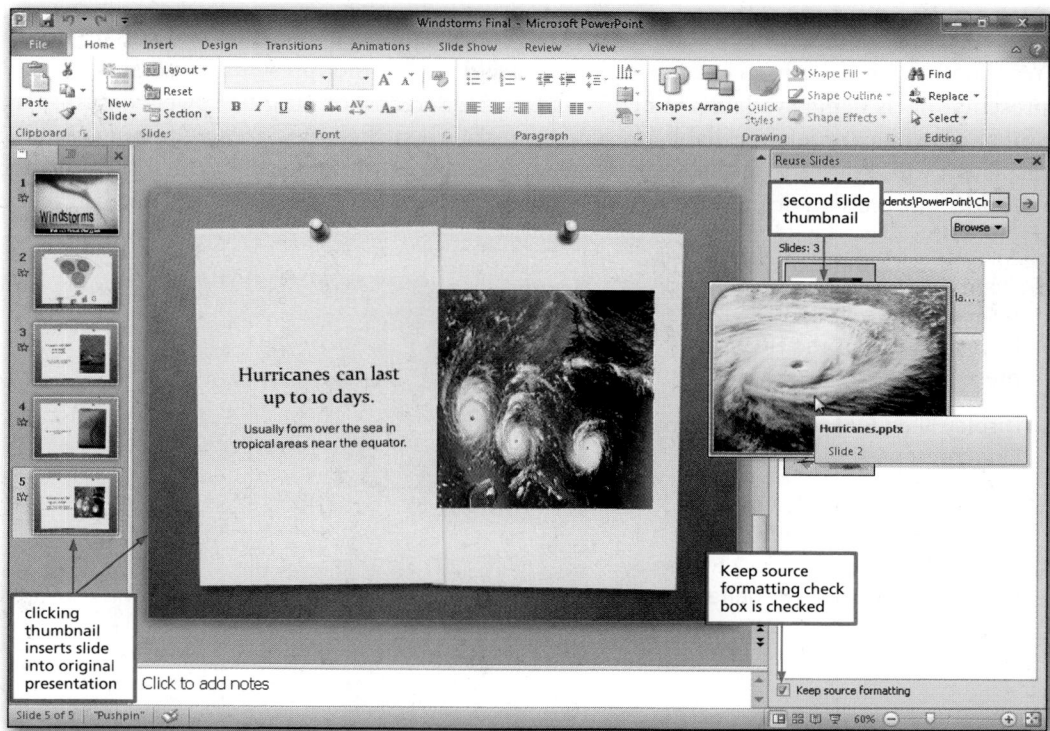

Figure 5–32

7

- Click the second slide thumbnail to insert this slide into the presentation as the last slide in the Windstorms Final presentation (Figure 5–33).

8

- Click the Close button in the Reuse Slides task pane so that it no longer is displayed.

- Apply the Vortex transition to Slide 6.

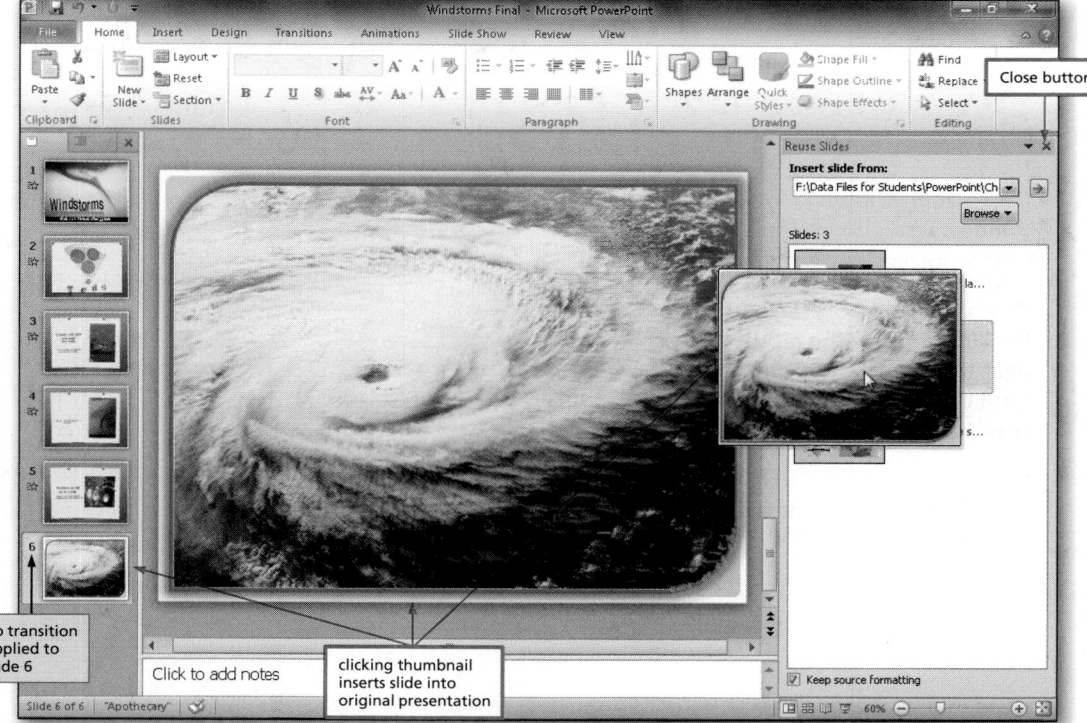

Figure 5–33

To Capture Part of a Screen Using Screen Clipping

At times you may be developing a presentation and need a portion of a clip or picture in another presentation. You can capture, or **snip**, part of an object on a slide in another presentation that is open. PowerPoint refers to this presentation as being available. When you click the Screenshot button, PowerPoint displays a dialog box and asks you to select a particular available presentation. You then click the Screen Clipping command, and PowerPoint displays a white overlay on the available slide until you capture the snip. The following steps snip part of an image on Slide 3 of the Hurricanes presentation and paste it on Slide 5 in the Windstorms Final presentation.

1

- Open the Hurricanes presentation from your USB flash drive. Display Slide 3 of the Hurricanes presentation.

- Display Slide 5 of the Windstorms Final presentation.

- Display the Insert tab and then click the Screenshot button (Insert tab | Images group) to display the Available Windows gallery (Figure 5–34).

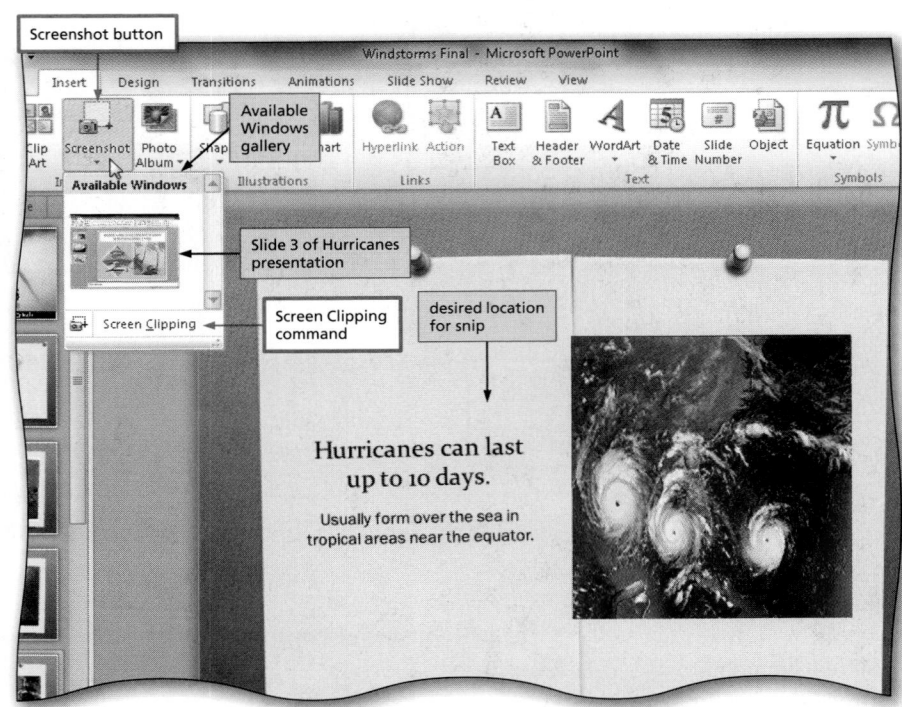

Figure 5–34

2

- Click Screen Clipping (Available Windows gallery) to display Slide 3 of the Hurricanes presentation.

- When the white overlay displays on Slide 3, move the mouse pointer near the left point of the diamond until the pointer changes to a cross hair.

- Drag downward and to the right to select the lower half of the diamond (Figure 5–35).

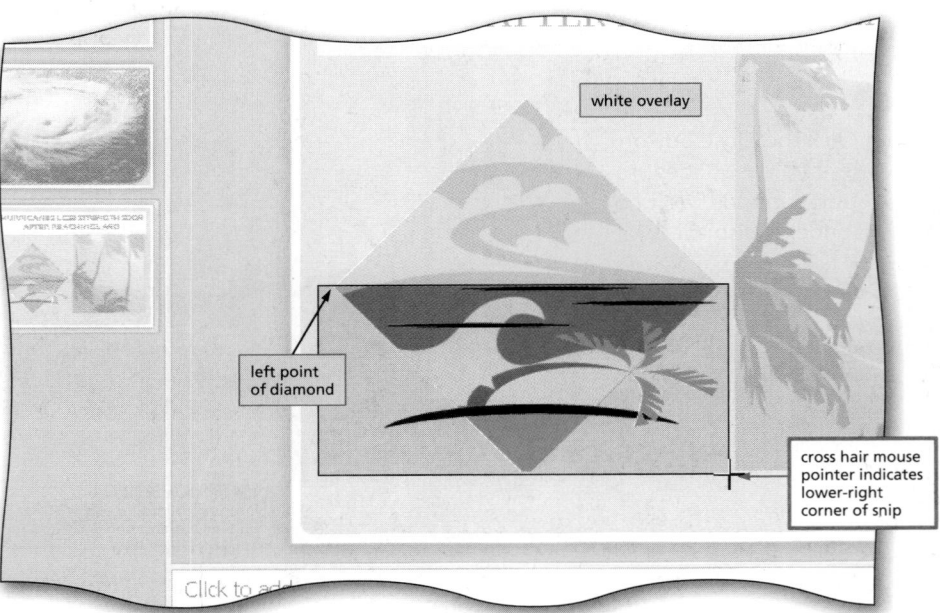

Figure 5–35

3
- Release the mouse button. When the snip displays on Slide 5 of the Windstorms Final presentation, drag the snip above the title text (Figure 5–36).

Figure 5–36

Use slide numbers to guide your speech.
Slide numbers help a presenter organize a talk. While few audience members are cognizant of this aspect of a slide, the presenter can glance at the number and know which slide contains particular information. If an audience member asks a question pertaining to information contained on a slide that had been displayed previously or is on a slide that has not been viewed yet, the presenter can jump to that slide in an effort to answer the question. In addition, the slide number helps pace the slide show. For example, a speaker could have the presentation timed so that Slide 4 is displaying three minutes into the talk.

Plan Ahead

To Add a Footer with Fixed Information

Slides can contain information at the top or bottom. The area at the top of a slide is called a **header**, and the area at the bottom is called a **footer**. As a default, no information is displayed in the header or footer. You can choose to apply only a header, only a footer, or both a header and footer. In addition, you can elect to have the header or footer display on single slides, all slides, or all slides except the title slide.

PowerPoint gives the option of displaying the current date and time obtained from the system or a fixed date and time that you specify. In addition, you can add relevant information, such as your name, your school or business name, or the purpose of your presentation in the footer. The following steps add a slide number, a fixed date, and footer text to all slides in the presentation except the title slide.

1

- Display the Insert tab.

- Click the Header & Footer button (Insert tab | Text group) to display the Header and Footer dialog box.

- If necessary, click the Slide tab to display the Slide sheet (Figure 5–37).

Q&A Can I change the starting slide number?

Yes. The first slide number is 1 by default. To change this number, click the Page Setup button (Design tab | Page Setup group) and then click the 'Number slides from' up button (Page Setup dialog box).

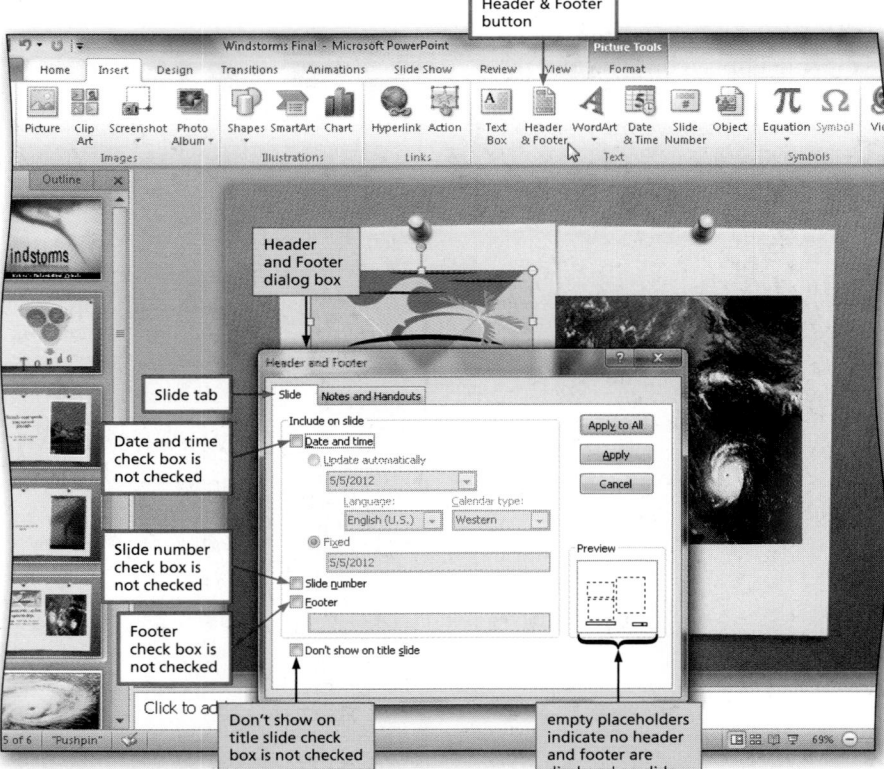

Figure 5–37

2

- Click 'Date and time' to select this check box.

- If necessary, click Fixed to select this option. Type **Friday, June 1 - 9:30 a.m.** in the Fixed box.

- Click Slide number to select this check box.

- Click Footer to select this check box.

- Type **Earth Science 101** in the Footer box (Figure 5–38).

Q&A What are the black boxes in the Preview area?

The black box in the left footer placeholder indicates where the footer information will appear on the slide; the black box in the right footer placeholder indicates where the date and time information and the page number will appear.

Q&A What if I want the current date and time to appear?

Click the Update automatically option in the 'Date and time' area.

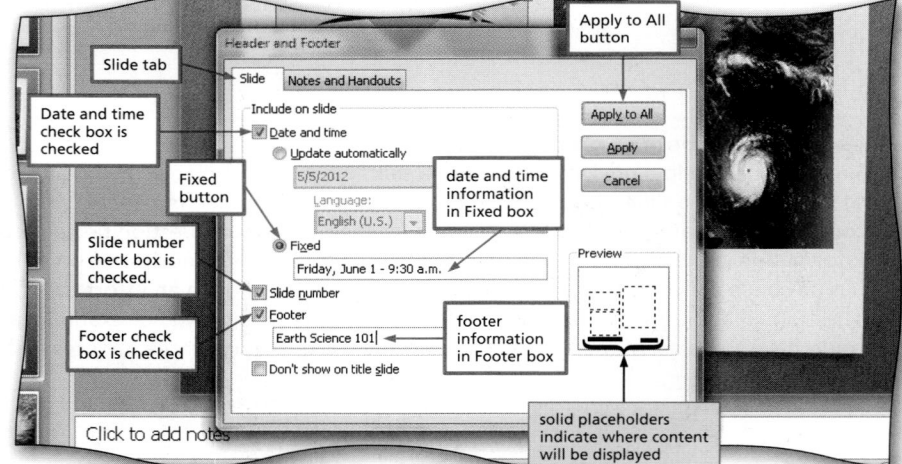

Figure 5–38

3

- Click the Apply to All button to display the date, time, footer text, and slide number on all slides.

Q&A When would I click the Apply button instead of the Apply to All button?

Click the Apply button when you want the slide number to appear only on the slide currently selected.

To Clear Formatting and Apply an Artistic Effect

PowerPoint provides myriad options to enhance pictures. You can, for example, format the images by recoloring, changing the color saturation and tone, adding artistic effects, and altering the picture style. After adding various effects, you may desire to reset the picture to its original state. The tornado picture on Slide 4 has several formatting adjustments, and now you want to see the original unformatted picture. The following steps remove all formatting applied to the tornado picture on Slide 4 and then apply the Film Grain artistic effect.

1

• Display Slide 4, select the tornado picture, and then display the Picture Tools Format tab (Figure 5–39).

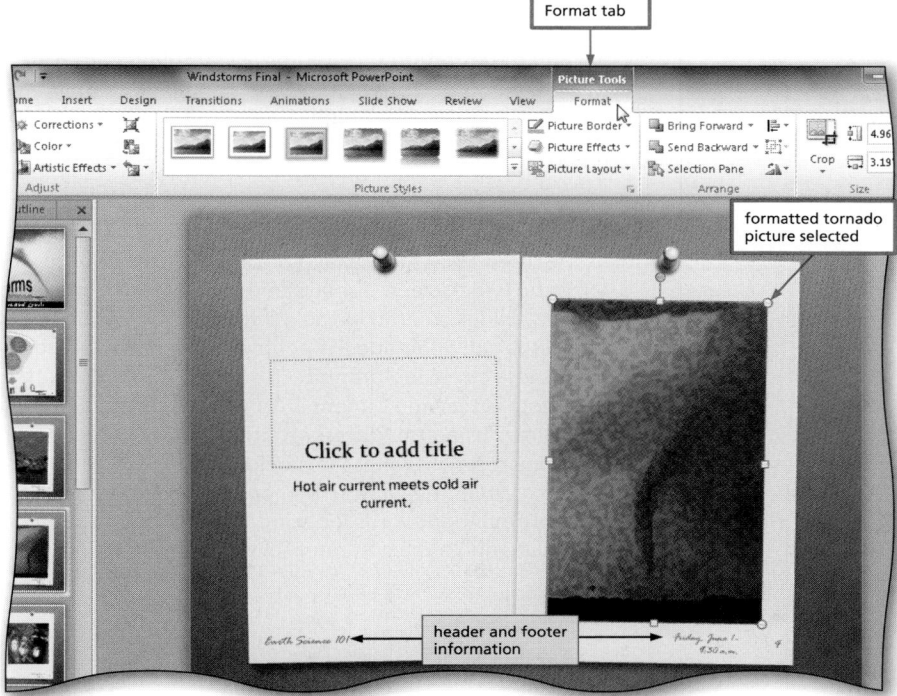

Figure 5–39

2

• Click the Reset Picture button (Picture Tools Format tab | Adjust group) to remove all formatting from the picture.

• Click the Artistic Effects button (Picture Tools Format tab | Adjust group) to display the Artistic Effects gallery (Figure 5–40).

3

• Apply the Film Grain effect (third effect in the third row) to the tornado picture.

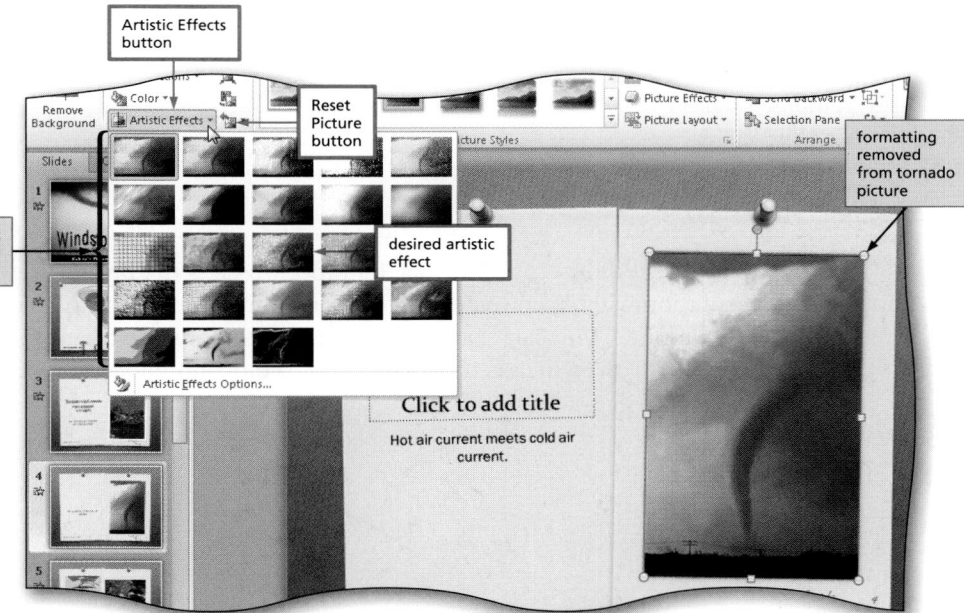

Figure 5–40

Break Point: If you wish to take a break, this is a good place to do so. Be sure to save the Windstorms Final file again and then you can quit PowerPoint. To resume at a later time, start PowerPoint, open the file called Windstorms Final, and continue following the steps from this location forward.

Plan Ahead

Determine the screen show ratio.

Your presentation can be viewed on one of three different screen sizes. A standard monitor has a ratio of 4:3. Many new wide-screen notebook computers have a 16:10 ratio, and high-definition televisions have displays with a 16:9 ratio. These numbers describe the dimensions of the screen. For example, a display with a 4:3 ratio would be four feet wide if it were three feet high. Similarly, a notebook computer screen would be 16 inches wide if it were 10 inches high. While these exact measurements do not fit all displays and screens, the hardware height and width dimensions remain in the same proportion using these ratios.

Changing the default ratio offers many advantages. Audience members perceive a presentation in the wide-screen format as being trendy and new. In addition, the wider screen allows more layout area to display photographs and clips. In rooms with low ceilings, the wide-screen displays mirror the room dimensions and blend with the environment.

Slides created in the 4:3 format and then converted to 16:9 or 16:10 may look distorted, especially if images of people or animals are inserted. You consequently may need to adjust these stretched graphics if they look unnatural. If you present your slide show frequently on computers and screens with varying formats, you may want to save the slide show several times using the different ratios and then open the presentation that best fits the environment where it is being shown.

While the wide screen presents the opportunity to place more text on a slide, resist the urge to add words. Continue to use the 7 × 7 guideline (a maximum of seven lines on a slide and a maximum of seven words on a line).

BTW

Pixels
Screen resolution specifies the amount of pixels displayed on your screen. The word, pixel, combines the words pix ("pictures") and el ("element").

Setting Slide Size and Slide Show Resolution

Today's technology presents several options you should consider when developing your presentation. The on-screen show ratio determines the height and width proportions. The screen resolution affects the slides' clarity.

To Set Slide Size

By default, PowerPoint sets a slide in a 4:3 ratio, which is the proportion found on a standard monitor. If you know your presentation will be viewed on a wide-screen high-definition television (HDTV) or you are using a wide-screen notebook computer, you can change the slide size to optimize the proportions. The following steps change the default size ratio to 16:9, which is the proportion of most notebook computers.

1
- Display the Design tab and then click the Page Setup button (Design tab | Page Setup group) to display the Page Setup dialog box.

- Click the 'Slides sized for' box arrow to display the size list (Figure 5–41).

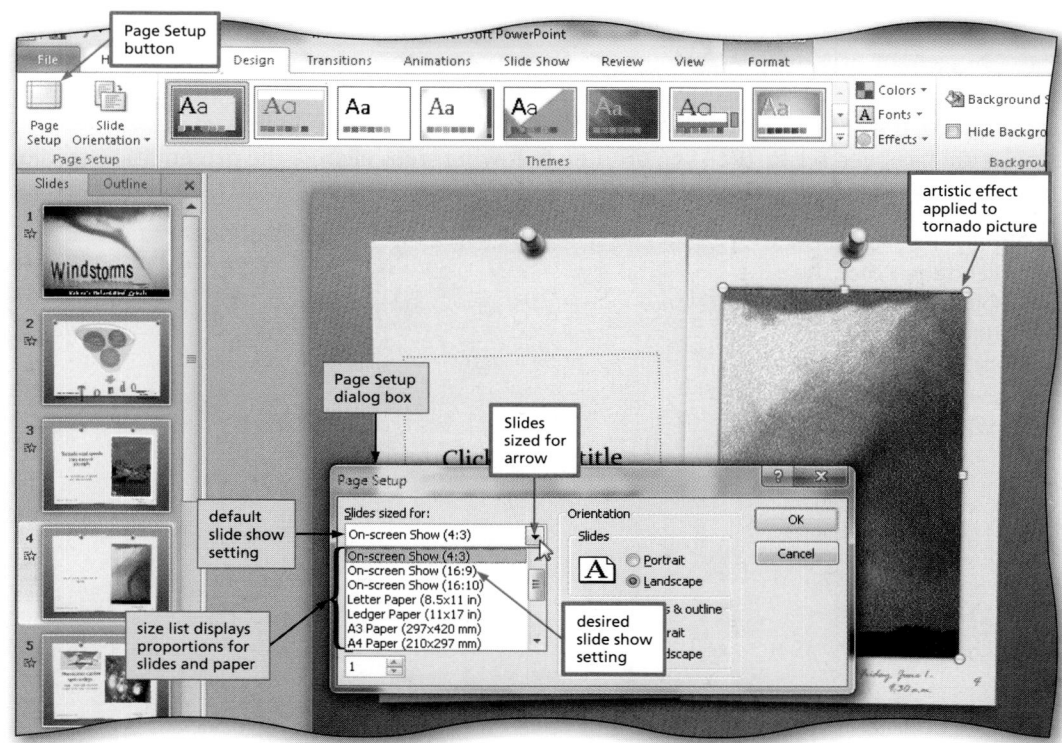

Figure 5–41

2
- Click On-screen Show (16:9) to change the slide size setting (Figure 5–42).

Q&A

Can I also change the default slide orientation from Landscape to Portrait?

Yes, but all slides in the presentation will change to this orientation. You cannot mix Portrait and Landscape orientations in one presentation. If you need to use both orientations during a speech, you can use a hyperlink to seamlessly jump from one slide show in Landscape orientation to another in Portrait orientation. Hyperlinks are discussed in Chapter 6.

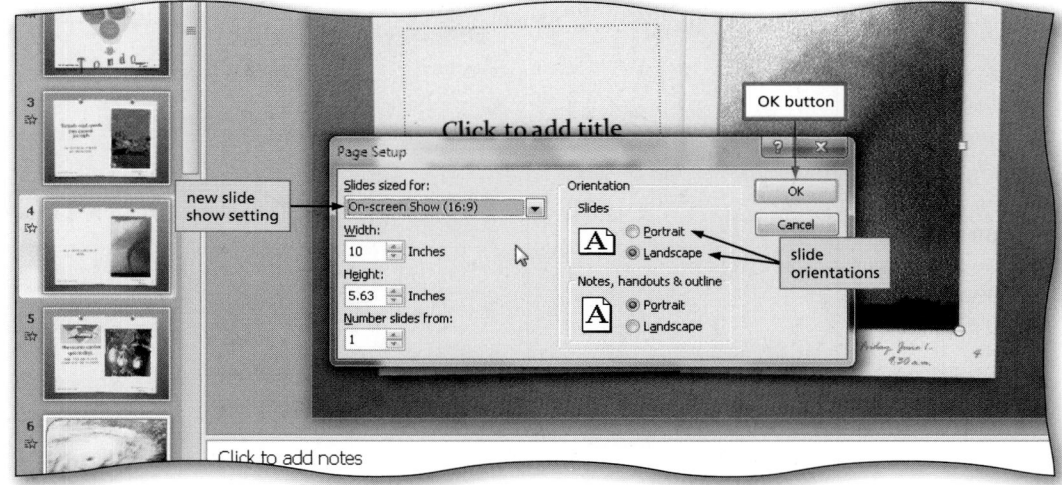

Figure 5–42

3
- Click the OK button to change the slide size in the presentation.

4
- Save the Windstorms Final presentation.

To Select Slide Show Resolution

Screen, or presentation, resolution affects the number of pixels that are displayed on your screen. When screen resolution is increased, more information is displayed, but it is decreased in size. Conversely, when screen resolution is decreased, less information is displayed, but that information is increased in size. Throughout this book, the screen resolution has been set to 1024×768. The following steps change the presentation resolution to 800×600.

1

- Display the Slide Show tab and then click the Resolution box arrow (Slide Show tab | Monitors group) to display the Resolution list (Figure 5–43).

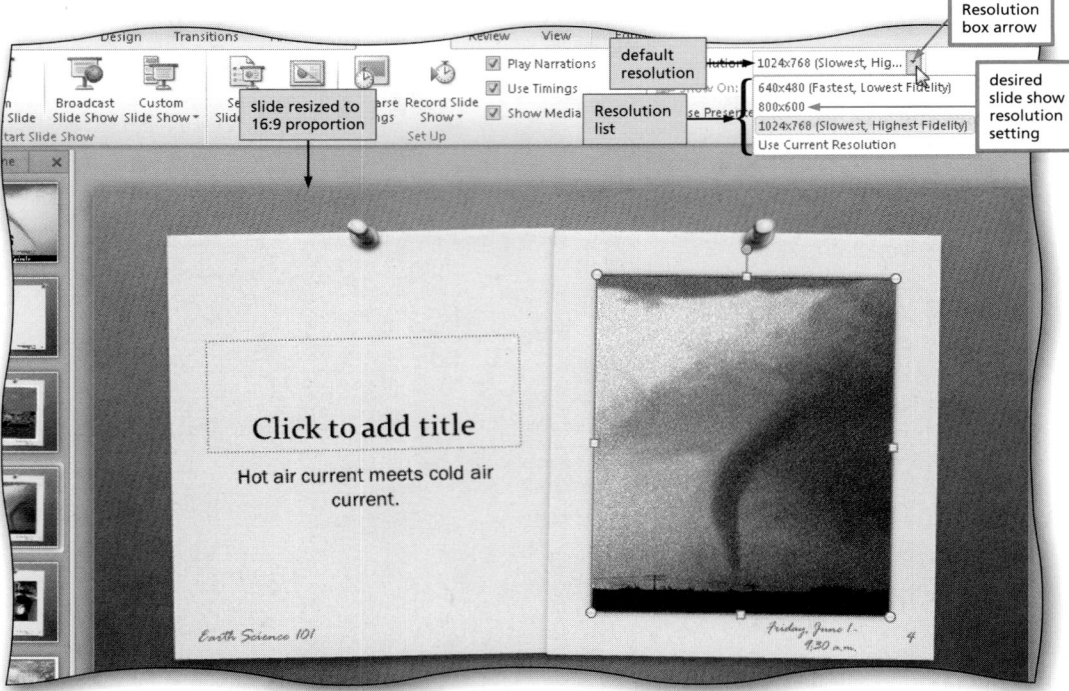

Figure 5–43

2

- Click 800 × 600 to change the slide show resolution setting (Figure 5–44).

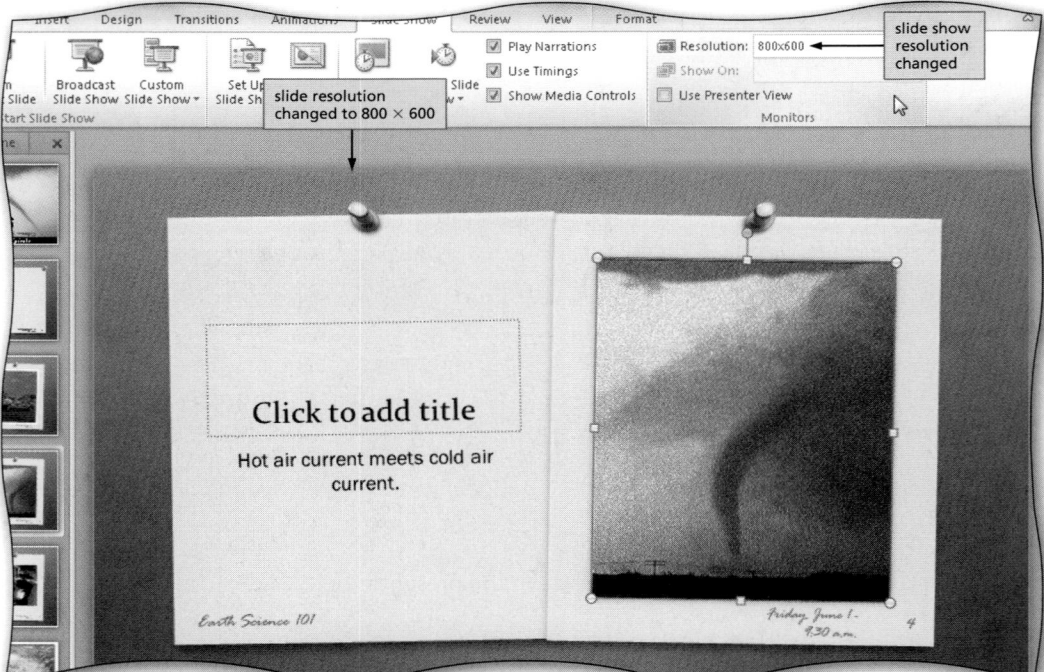

Figure 5–44

Saving and Packaging a Presentation

Both PowerPoint 2010 and PowerPoint 2007 save files, by default, as a PowerPoint Presentation with a .pptx file extension. You can, however, select other file types that allow other computer users to view your slides if they do not have one of the newer PowerPoint versions installed. You also can save the file as a PowerPoint show so that it runs automatically when opened. Another option is to save one slide as an image that can be inserted into another program, such as Microsoft Word, or can be e-mailed.

In the following pages, you will follow these general steps to save the slides in four file types:

1. Save the presentation as a PowerPoint show.
2. Save one slide as an image.
3. Package the presentation for a CD.
4. Save the presentation in the PowerPoint 97–2003 format.

BTW

Saving a Presentation as a PDF or an XPS Document
Electronic images of your slides are identical to the original slides and can be viewed using free viewers, including Acrobat Reader for PDF files and XPS Viewer for XPS files. To save your presentation in one of these formats, open the Backstage view, display the Save & Send tab, click Create PDF/XPS Document in the File Types area, and then click the Create PDF/XPS button in the Create a PDF/XPS Document area. When the Publish as PDF or XPS dialog box is displayed, click the 'Save as type' arrow and then select PDF or XPS in the list. Click 'Standard (publishing online and printing)' if you are going to print high-quality documents or 'Minimum size (publishing online)' if you desire to keep the file size small.

To Save a File as a PowerPoint Show

To simplify giving a presentation in front of an audience, you may want your slide show to start running without having to start PowerPoint, open a file, and then click the Slide Show button. When you save a presentation as a **PowerPoint show** (**.ppsx**), it automatically begins running when opened. The following steps save the Windstorms Final file as a PowerPoint show.

1

- Open the Backstage view, display the Save & Send tab, and then click Change File Type in the File Types area.

- Click PowerPoint Show in the Presentation File Types area (Figure 5–45).

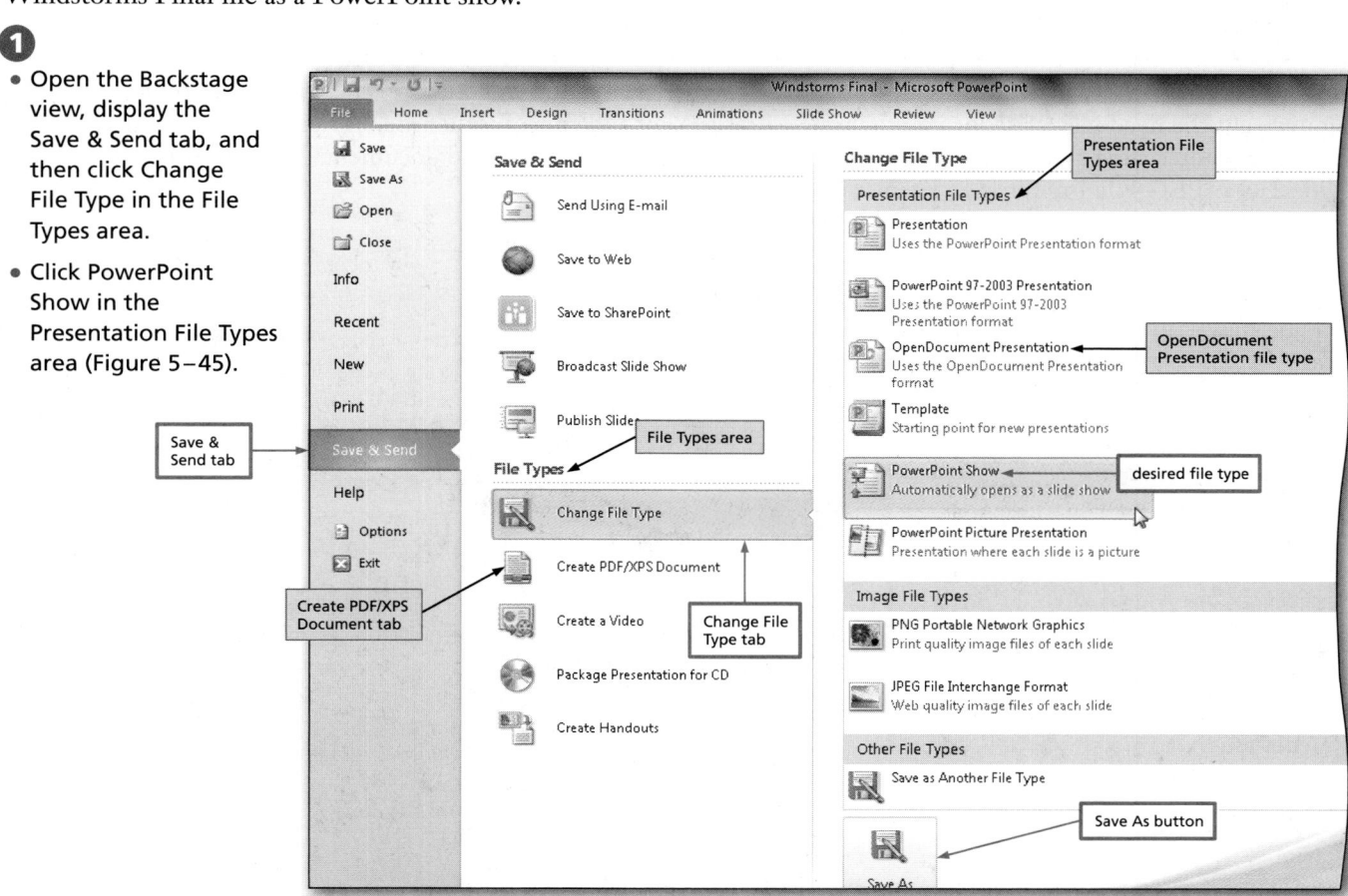

Figure 5–45

2
• Click the Save As button below the Other File Types area to display the Save As dialog box.

• Type **Windstorms Final Show** in the File name text box (Figure 5–46).

3
• Click the Save button (Save As dialog box) to save the Windstorms Final presentation as a PowerPoint show.

4
• Close both the current PowerPoint file and the Hurricanes presentation.

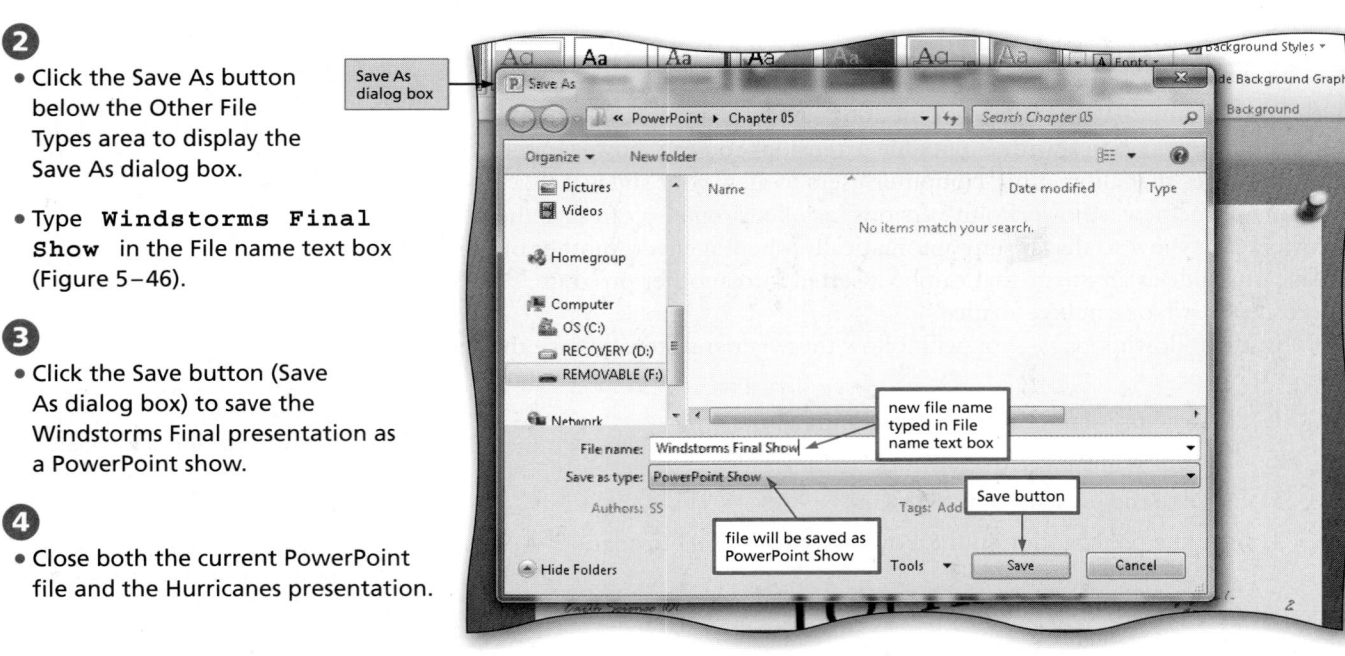

Figure 5–46

Other Ways

1. Click File on Ribbon, click Save As in Backstage view, click 'Save as type' arrow, select PowerPoint Show, click Save button

2. Double-click PowerPoint Show in Presentation File Types area

To Save a Slide as an Image

To create visually interesting slides, you insert pictures, clips, and video files into your presentation. Conversely, the need may arise for you to insert a PowerPoint slide into another file. For example, you can save the information on a slide as an image and insert the image into a Microsoft Word document. The following steps save Slide 2 as a JPEG File Interchange Format image.

1
• Open the Windstorms Final presentation from your USB flash drive.

Q&A
Why do I want to open this presentation?

It is best to use the final .pptx version of the presentation to complete the remaining tasks in this chapter.

• Display Slide 2.

• Open the Backstage view, display the Save & Send tab, and then click Change File Type in the File Types area.

• Click JPEG File Interchange Format in the Image File Types area (Figure 5–47).

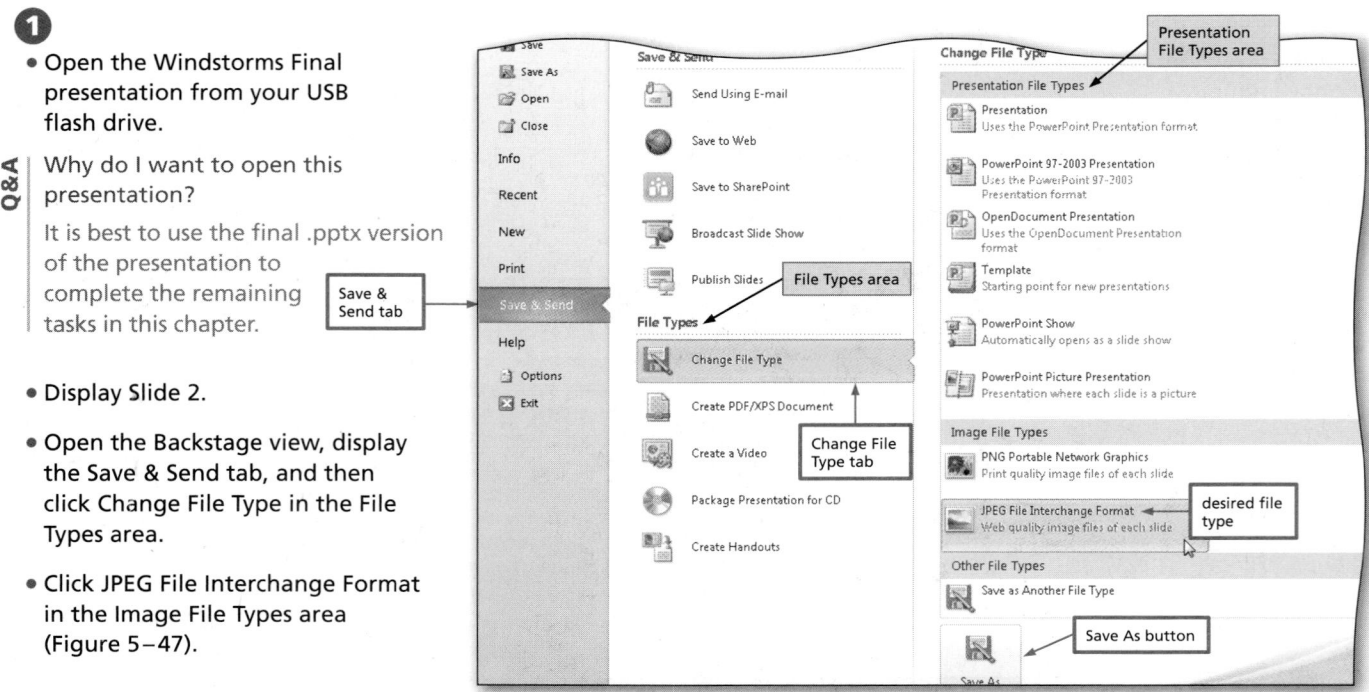

Figure 5–47

2

- Click the Save As button to display the Save As dialog box.

- Type **Tornadoes SmartArt** in the File name text box (Figure 5–48).

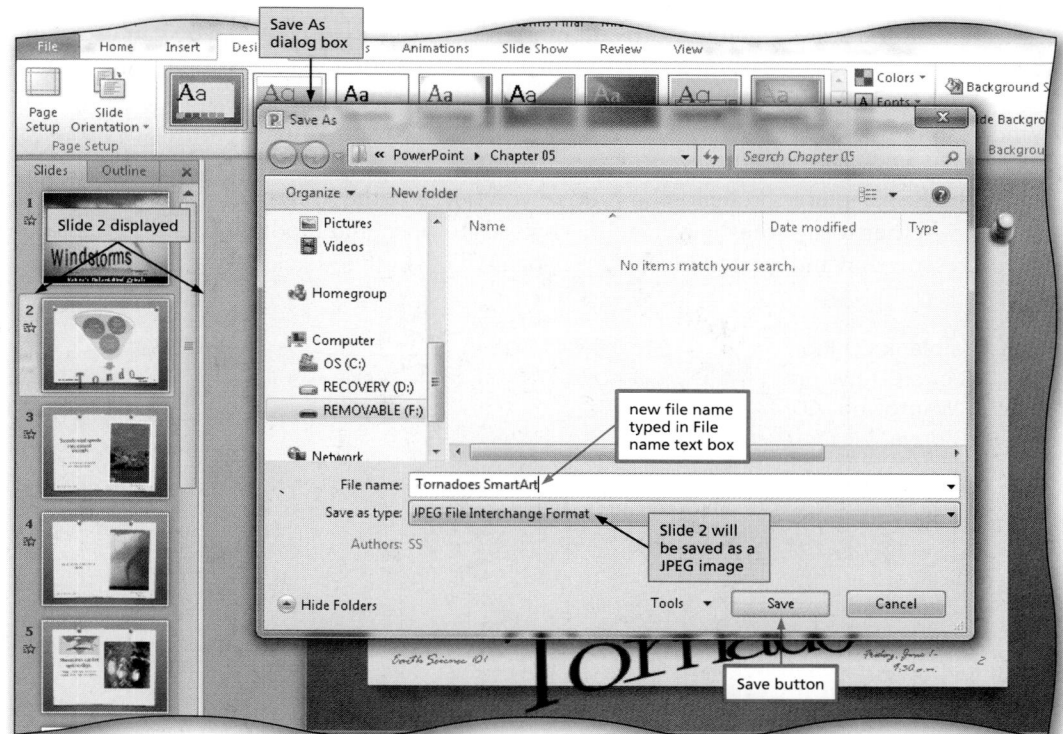

Figure 5–48

3

- Click the Save button (Save As dialog box) to display the Microsoft PowerPoint dialog box (Figure 5–49).

4
- Click the Current Slide Only button (Microsoft PowerPoint dialog box) to save only Slide 2 as a file in JPEG (.jpg) format.

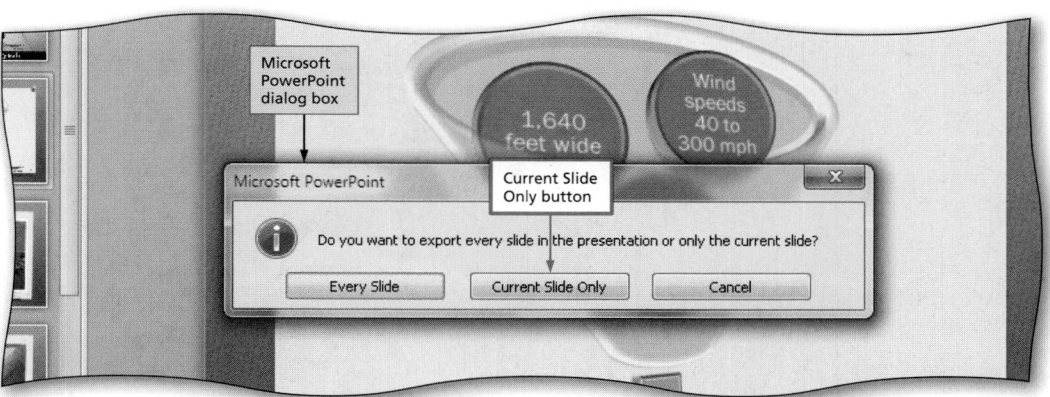

Figure 5–49

Other Ways

1. Click File on Ribbon, click Save As in Backstage view, click 'Save as type' arrow, select JPEG File Interchange Format, click Save button

2. Double-click JPEG File Interchange Format in Image File Types area

To Package a Presentation for Storage on a CD or DVD

If your computer has compact disc (CD) or digital video disc (DVD) burning hardware, the Package for CD option will copy a PowerPoint presentation and linked files onto a CD or DVD. Two types of CDs or DVDs can be used: recordable (CD-R or DVD-R) and rewritable (CD-RW or DVD-RW). You must copy all the desired files in a single operation if you use PowerPoint for this task because you cannot add any more files after the first set is copied. If, however, you want to add more files to the CD or DVD, you can use Windows Explorer to copy additional files. If you are using a CD-RW or DVD-RW with existing content, these files will be overwritten.

The PowerPoint Viewer is included so you can show the presentation on another computer that has Microsoft Windows but does not have PowerPoint installed. The **PowerPoint Viewer** also allows users to view presentations created with PowerPoint 2003, 2000, and 97.

The Package for CD dialog box allows you to select the presentation files to copy, linking and embedding options, whether to add the Viewer, and passwords to open and modify the files. The following steps show how to save a presentation and related files to a CD or DVD using the Package for CD feature.

- Insert a blank CD-R or DVD-R or a CD-RW or DVD-RW into your CD or DVD drive.

- Open the Backstage view, display the Save & Send tab, and then click Package Presentation for CD in the File Types area (Figure 5–50).

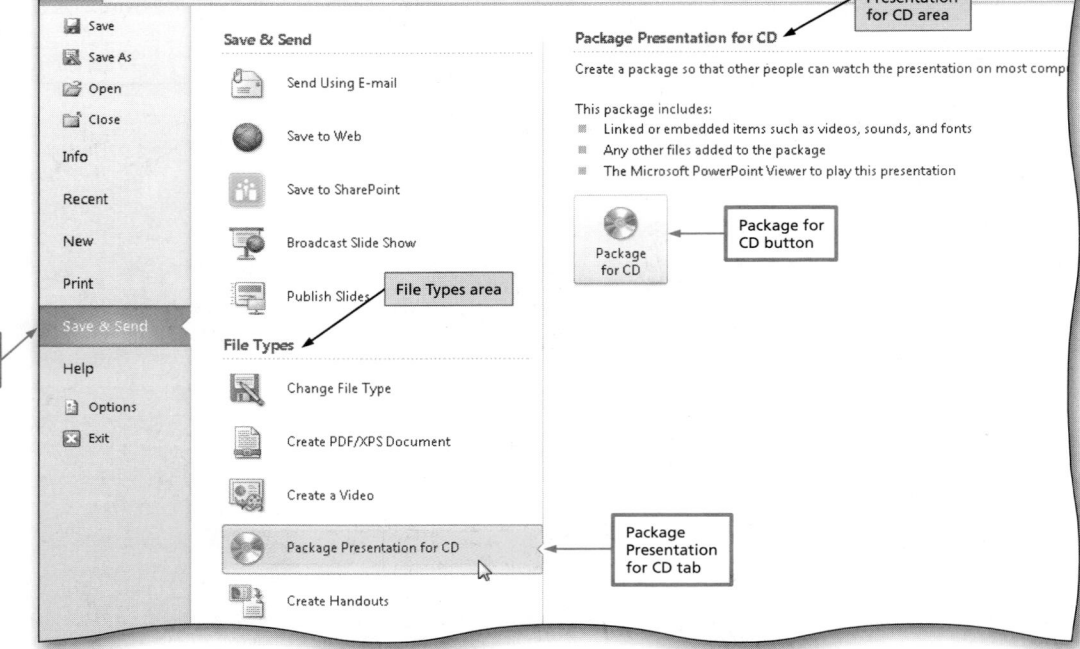

Figure 5–50

❷
- Click the Package for CD button in the Package Presentation for CD area to display the Package for CD dialog box.

- Type **Windstorms** in the Name the CD text box (Package for CD dialog box) (Figure 5–51).

Q&A

What if I want to add more files to the CD?

Click the Add button and then locate the files you want to write on the CD.

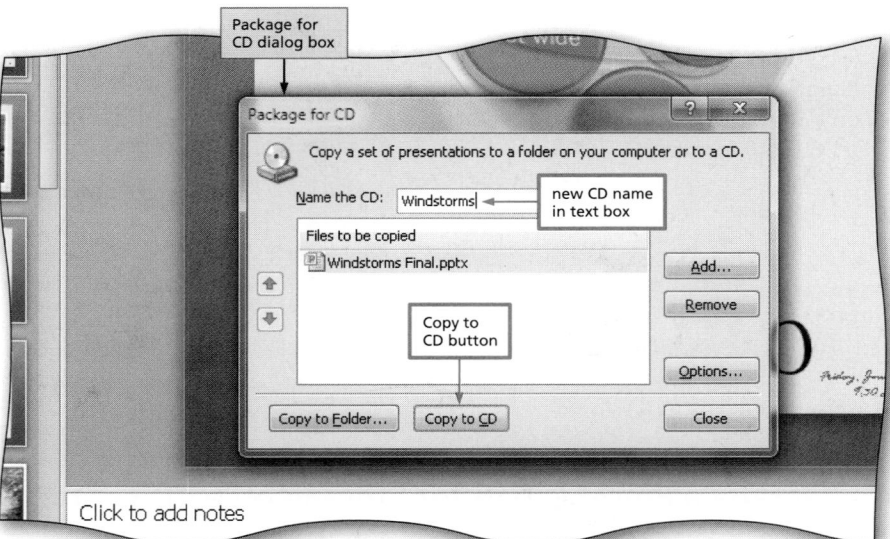

Figure 5–51

- Click the Copy to CD button to begin packaging the presentation files and to display the Microsoft PowerPoint dialog box (Figure 5–52).

Q&A What is the purpose of the Copy to Folder button?

If you are copying your presentation to a folder on a network or on your storage device instead of on a CD, you would click this button.

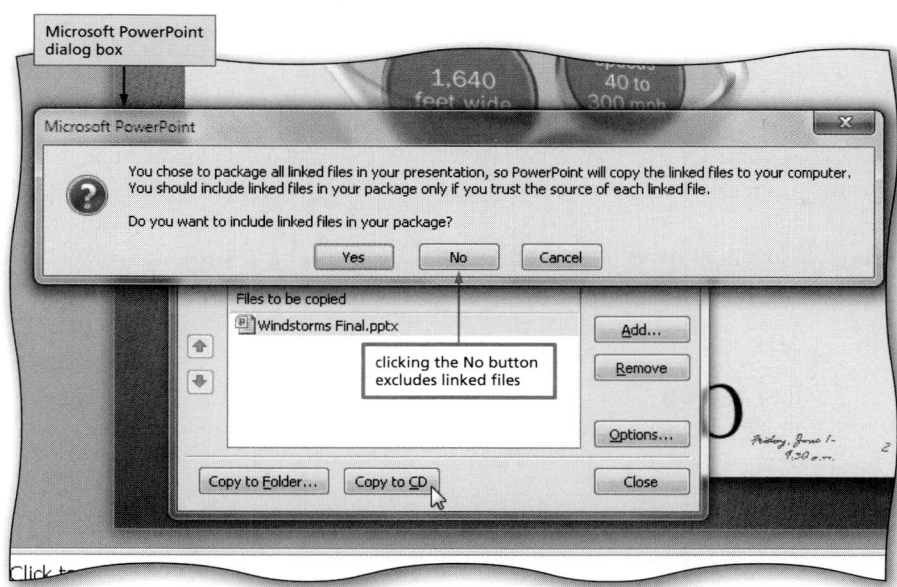

Figure 5–52

- Click the No button (Microsoft PowerPoint dialog box) to not include linked files and to display another Microsoft PowerPoint dialog box (Figure 5–53).

- Click the Continue button (Microsoft PowerPoint dialog box) to continue copying the presentation to a CD without the comments added to the slides.

6

- When the files have been written, click the No button (Microsoft PowerPoint dialog box) to not copy the files to another CD.

7

- Click the Close button (Package for CD dialog box) to finish saving the presentation to a CD.

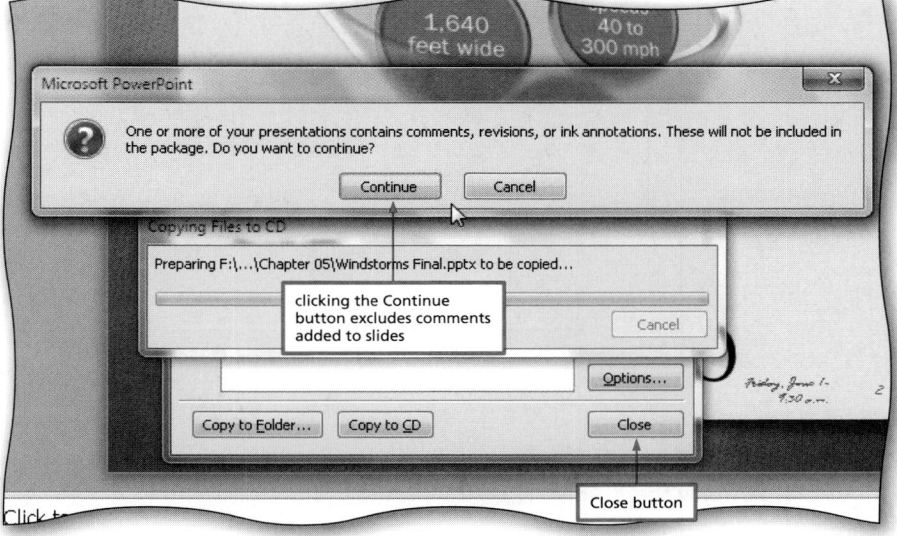

Figure 5–53

TO VIEW A POWERPOINT SHOW USING THE POWERPOINT VIEWER

When you arrive at a remote location, you will run the packaged presentation. The following steps explain how you would run the presentation using the PowerPoint Viewer.

1. Insert your CD or DVD into the CD or DVD drive.

2. Accept the licensing agreement for the PowerPoint Viewer to open and run the slide show.

To Save a File in a Previous PowerPoint Format

Prior to Microsoft Office 2007, PowerPoint saved files, by default, as a .ppt type. The earlier versions of PowerPoint cannot open the .pptx type that PowerPoint 2010 and 2007 create by default. The Microsoft Office Downloads and Updates Web site has converters for users who are using these earlier versions of the program and also for other Microsoft Office software. The Microsoft Compatibility Pack for Word, Excel, and PowerPoint will open, edit, and save Office 2010 and 2007 documents. You cannot assume that people who obtain a .pptx file from you have installed the Compatibility Pack, so to diminish frustration and confusion, you can save a presentation as a .ppt type. The following steps save the Windstorms Final file as a PowerPoint 97–2003 Presentation.

1

- Open the Backstage view, display the Save & Send tab, and then click Change File Type in the File Types area.

- Click PowerPoint 97–2003 Presentation in the Presentation File Types area (Figure 5–54).

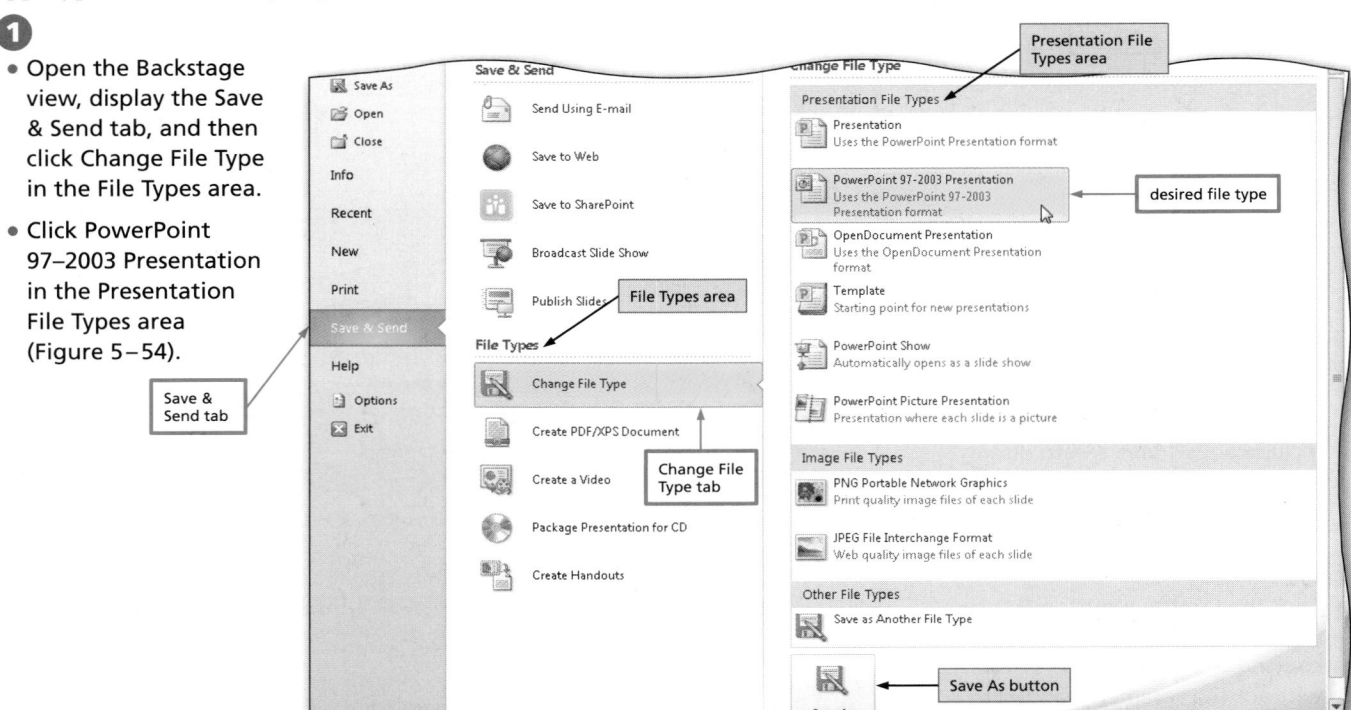

Figure 5–54

2

- Click the Save As button to display the Save As dialog box.

- Type **Windstorms Final Previous Version** in the File name text box (Figure 5–55).

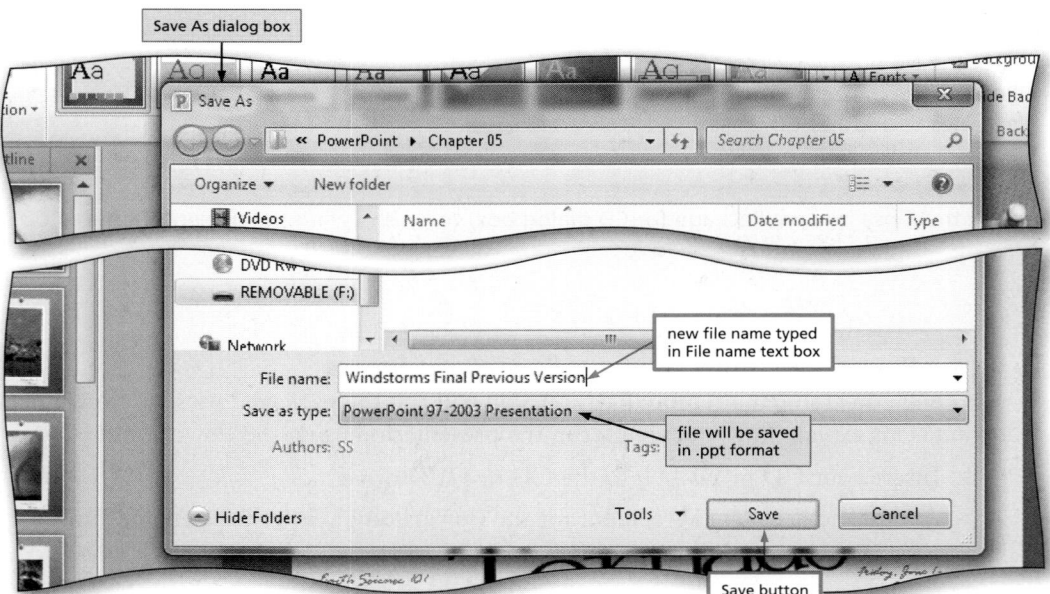

Figure 5–55

3

- Click the Save button (Save As dialog box) to save the Windstorms Final Previous Version presentation as a .ppt type and display the Microsoft PowerPoint Compatibility Checker.

Q&A Why does this Compatibility Checker dialog box display?

PowerPoint is alerting you that the older file version will not keep some of the features used in the presentation. You will learn more about the Compatibility Checker in the next section of this chapter.

4

- Click the Continue button (Microsoft PowerPoint Compatibility Checker) to continue to save the presentation.

5

- Close the current PowerPoint file and then open the Windstorms Final presentation from your USB flash drive.

Q&A Why do I want to open this presentation instead of using the current file?

The current file is saved in a previous version of PowerPoint, so some features are not available when you run the final version of the slide show. It is best to use the more current version of the presentation to complete the remaining tasks in this chapter.

Other Ways
1. Click File on Ribbon, click Save As in Backstage view, click 'Save as type' arrow, select PowerPoint 97–2003 Presentation, click Save button
2. Double-click PowerPoint 97–2003 Presentation in Presentation File Types area

---

Protecting and Securing a Presentation

When your slides are complete, you can perform additional functions to finalize the file and prepare it for distributing to other users or for running on a computer other than the one used to develop the file. For example, the Compatibility Checker reviews the file for any feature that will not work properly or display on computers running a previous PowerPoint version. In addition, the Document Inspector locates inappropriate information, such as comments, in a file and allows you to delete these slide elements. With passwords and digital signatures, you add security levels to prevent people from distributing, viewing, or modifying your slides. When the review process is complete, you can indicate this file is the final version.

In the following pages, you will follow these general steps to ensure your presentation contains appropriate information and that the contents will not be changed without authorization:

1. Identify features not supported by versions prior to PowerPoint 2007.
2. Remove personal information.
3. Select a password to open the file.
4. Identify the presentation as the final version.
5. Create a digital certificate to state the file contents have not been altered.

BTW

Digital Signatures
A digital signature verifies that the contents of a file have not been altered and that an imposter is not trying to commit forgery by taking ownership of the document. This signature encrypts, or converts, readable data into unreadable characters. To read the file, a user must decrypt, or decipher, the data into a readable form.

To Identify Presentation Features Not Supported by Previous Versions

PowerPoint 2010 has many new features not found in some previous versions of PowerPoint, especially versions older than PowerPoint 2007. For example, WordArt formatted with Quick Styles is an enhancement found only in PowerPoint 2010 and PowerPoint 2007. If you give your file to people who have an earlier PowerPoint version installed on their computers, they will be able to open the file but may not be able to see or edit some special features and effects. You can use the **Compatibility Checker** to see which presentation elements will not function in earlier versions of PowerPoint. The following steps run the Compatibility Checker and display a summary of the elements in your Windstorms Final presentation that will be lost if your file is opened in some earlier PowerPoint versions.

1

- Open the Backstage view and then click the Check for Issues button (Info tab | Prepare for Sharing area) to display the Prepare for Sharing menu (Figure 5–56).

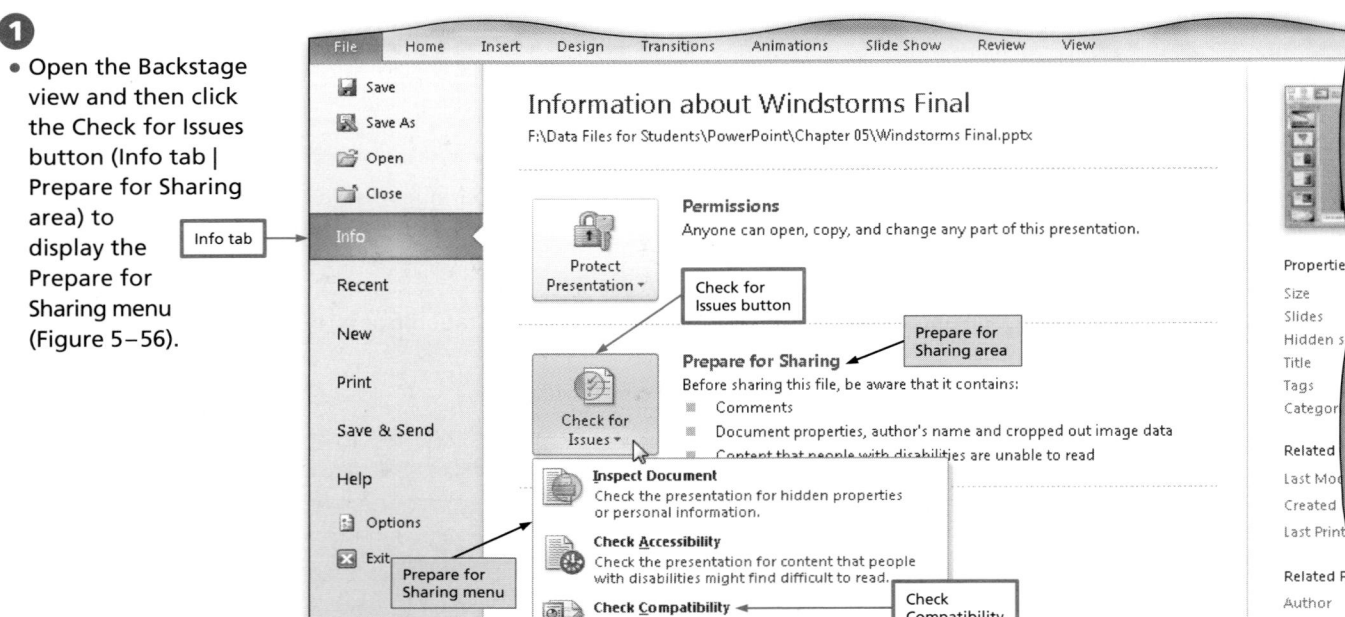

Figure 5–56

2

- Click Check Compatibility to have PowerPoint examine the file and then, after a short period, display the Microsoft PowerPoint Compatibility Checker dialog box.

- In the Summary area, view the comments regarding the three features that are not supported by earlier versions of PowerPoint (Figure 5–57).

Q&A Why do the numbers 1, 1, and 6 display in the Occurrences column in the right side of the Summary area?

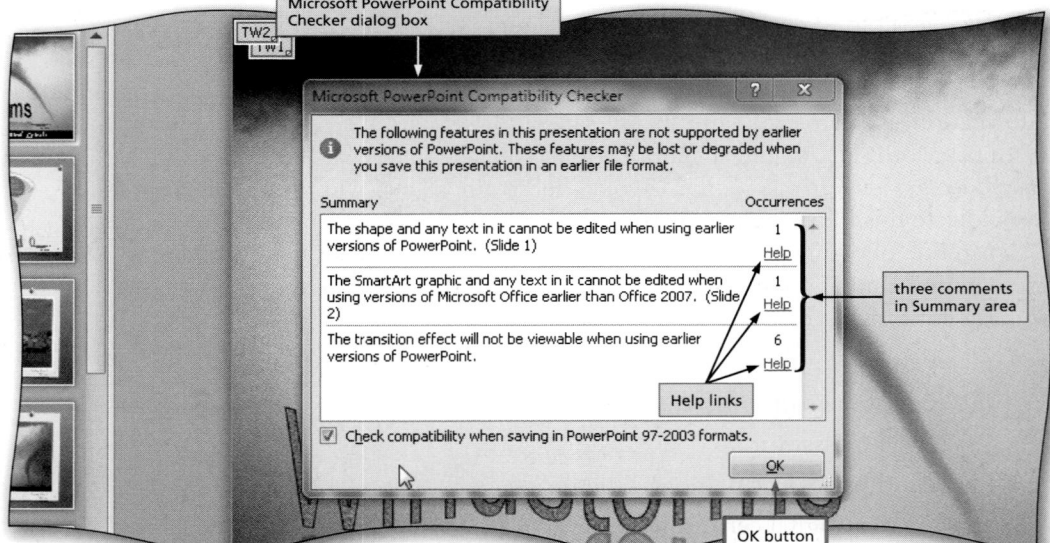

Figure 5–57

The Compatibility Checker found one shape and one SmartArt graphic in your presentation that cannot be edited in previous versions. These graphics will be converted to bitmap images in older versions, so they cannot be ungrouped and modified. In addition, the Vortex transition applied to all six slides will not display if the presentation is opened with any previous version of PowerPoint.

Q&A What happens if I click the Help links in the Summary area?

PowerPoint will provide additional information about the particular incompatible slide element.

3

- Click the OK button (Microsoft PowerPoint Compatibility Checker dialog box) to close the dialog box and return to the presentation.

To Remove Inappropriate Information

As you work on your presentation, you might add information meant only for you to see. For example, you might write comments to yourself or put confidential information in the Document Information Panel. You would not want other people to access this information if you give a copy of the presentation file to them. You also added a comment and replied to Mary Halen's questions, and you may not want anyone other than Mary to view this information. The Document Inspector provides a quick and efficient method of searching for and deleting inappropriate or confidential information.

If you tell the Document Inspector to delete content, such as personal information, comments, invisible slide content, or notes, and then decide you need to see those slide elements, quite possibly you will be unable to retrieve the information by using the Undo command. For that reason, it is a good idea to make a duplicate copy of your file and then inspect this new second copy. The following steps save a duplicate copy of your Windstorms Final presentation, run the Document Inspector on this new file, and then delete comments.

1

- Open the Backstage view, click Save As to open the Save As dialog box, and then type **Windstorms Final Duplicate** in the File name text box.

- Click the Save button to change the file name and save another copy of this presentation.

2

- Open the Backstage view and then click the Check for Issues button (Info tab | Prepare for Sharing area) to display the Prepare for Sharing menu (Figure 5–58).

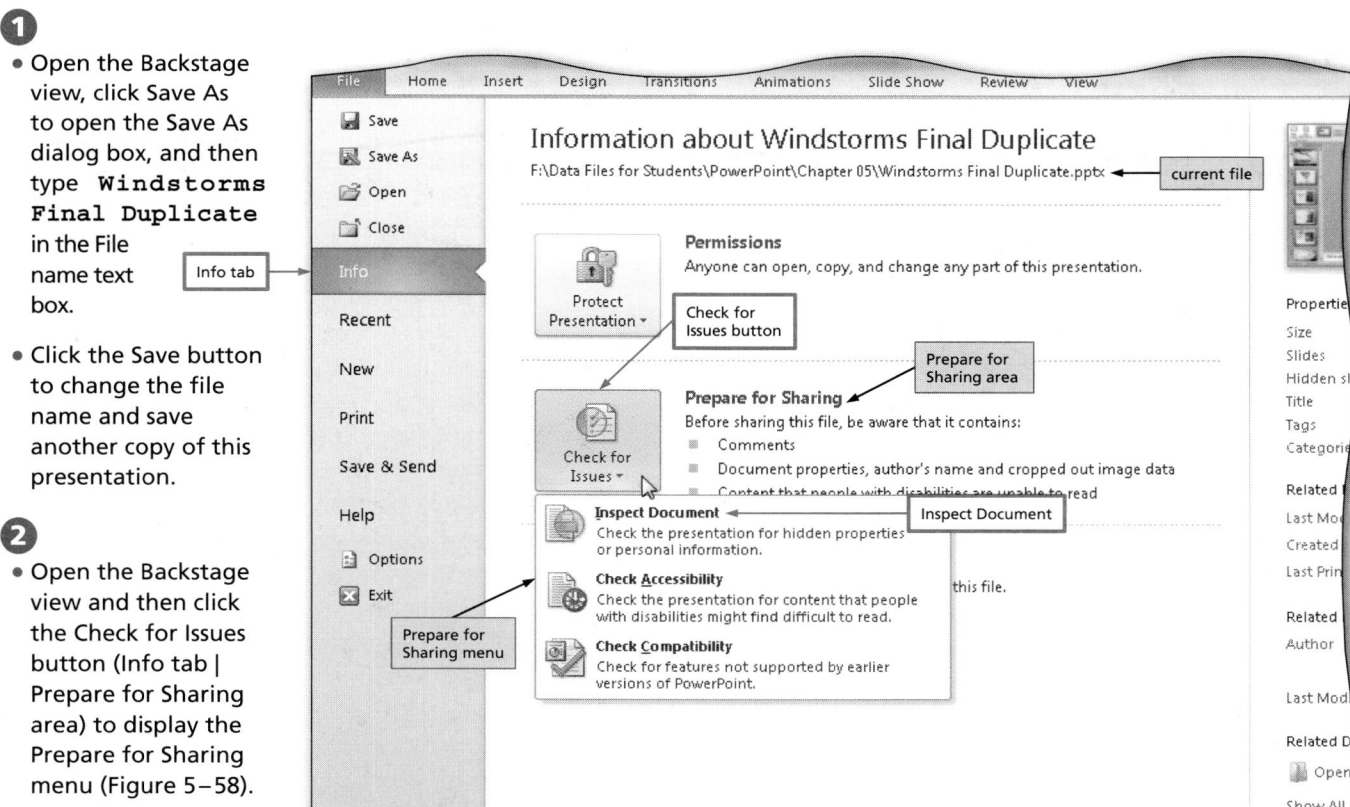

Figure 5–58

3

- Click Inspect Document to display the Document Inspector dialog box (Figure 5–59).

Q&A

What information does the Document Inspector check?

This information includes text in the Document Information Panel, such as your name and company. Other information includes details of when the file was last saved, objects formatted as invisible, graphics and text you dragged off a slide, presentation notes, and e-mail headers.

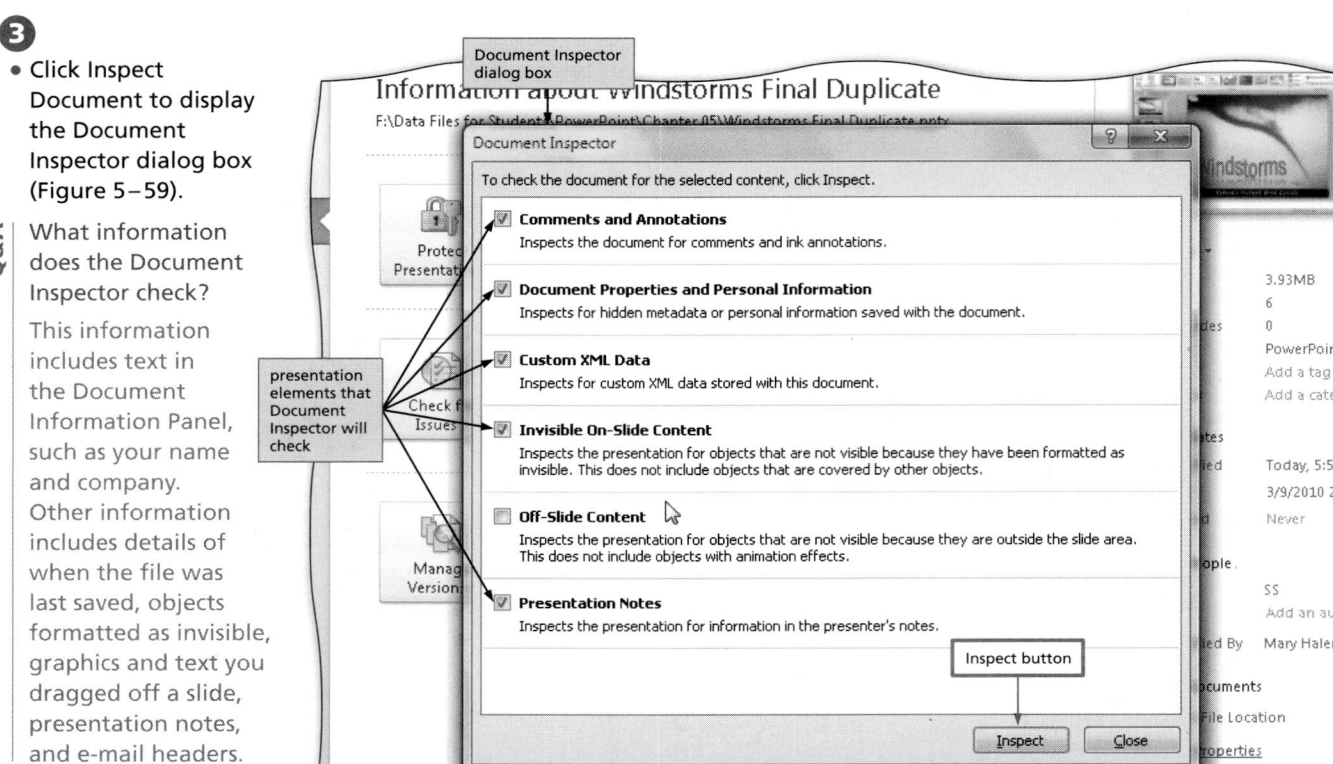

Figure 5–59

4

- Click the Inspect button to check the document and display the inspection results (Figure 5–60).

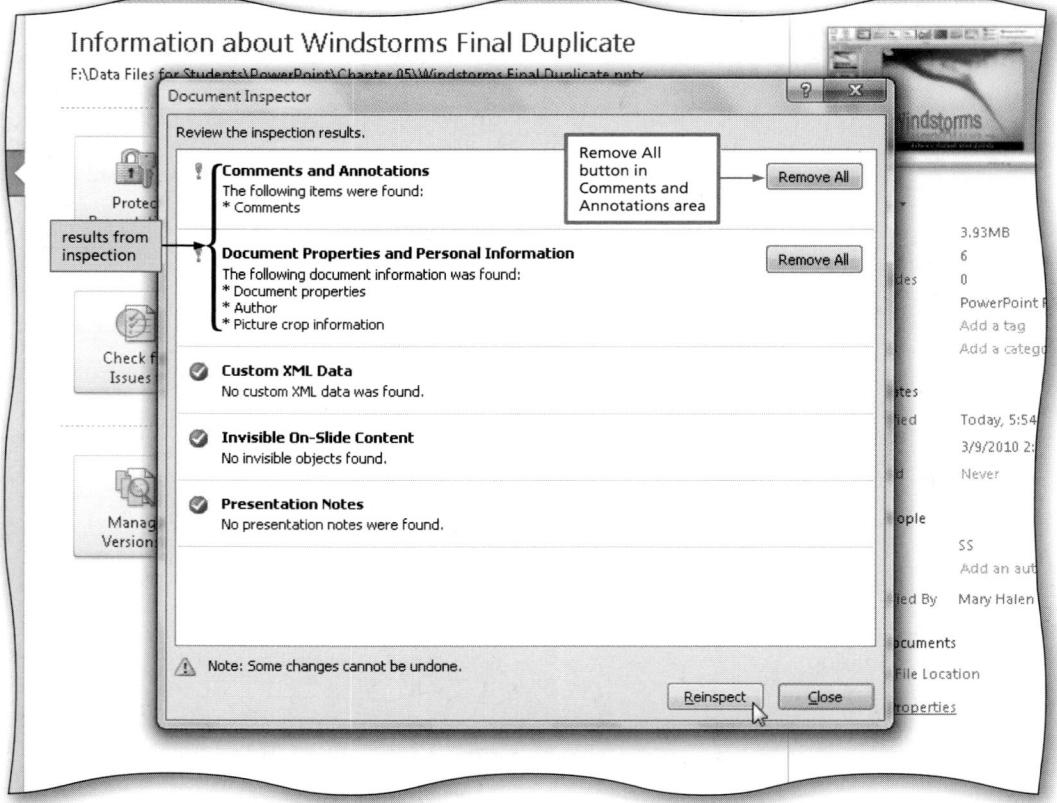

Figure 5–60

5

- Click the Remove
  All button in the
  Comments and
  Annotations area
  of the inspection
  results to remove
  the comments from
  the presentation
  (Figure 5–61).

Q&A

Should I also remove
the document
properties and
personal information?

You might want to
delete this information
so that no identifying
information is saved.
This information
includes text that
displays in the
Document Information
Panel, such as your
name, course number,
and keywords.

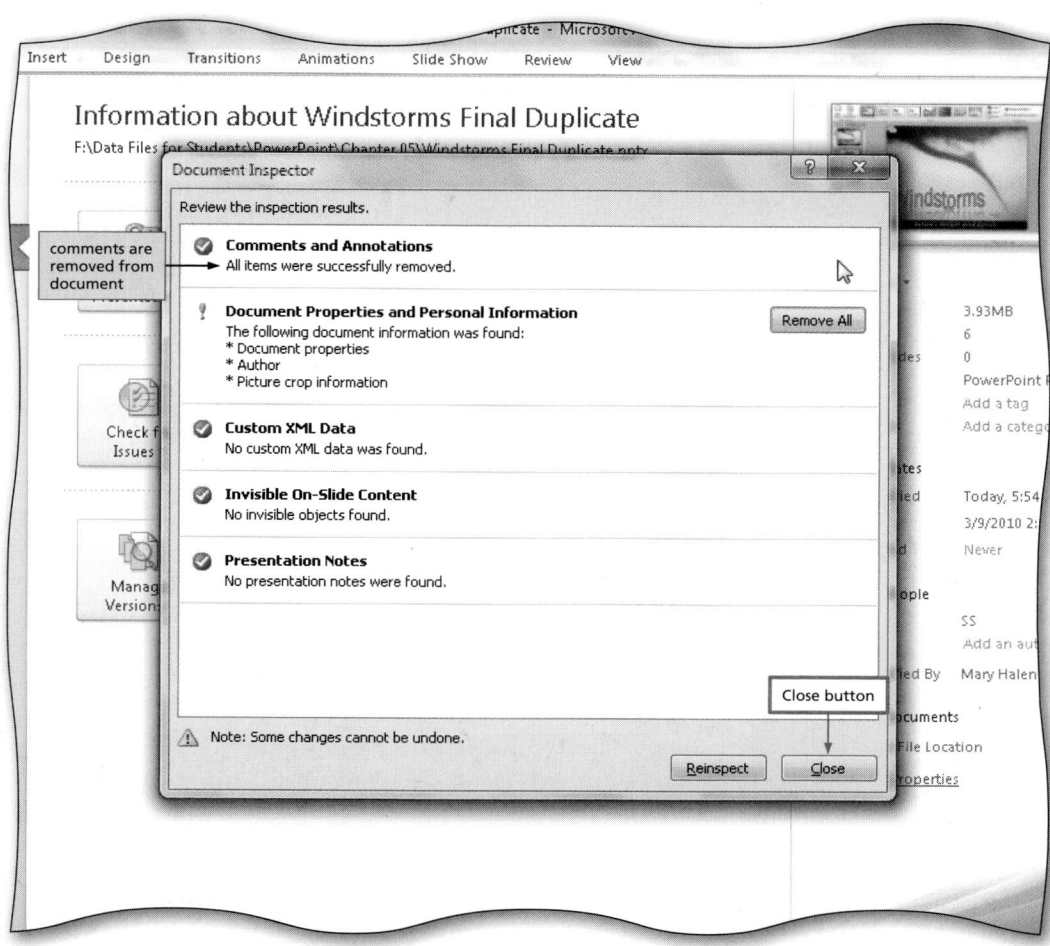

Figure 5–61

 6

- Click the Close button (Document Inspector dialog box) to close the dialog box.

Select an appropriate password.
A password should be at least eight characters and contain a combination of letters and
numbers. Using both uppercase and lowercase letters is advised. Do not use a password that
someone could guess, such as your first or last name, spouse's or child's name, telephone
number, birth date, street address, license plate number, or Social Security number.

Once you develop this password, write it down in a secure place. Underneath your
keyboard is not a secure place, nor is your middle desk drawer.

**Plan
Ahead**

To Set a Password

You can protect your slide content by using passwords. The passwords specify whether a user can look at or
modify a file. The following steps set a password for the Windstorms Final Duplicate file.

- With the Backstage view open and the Info tab displaying, click the Protect Presentation button (Info tab | Permissions area) menu to display the Permissions menu (Figure 5–62).

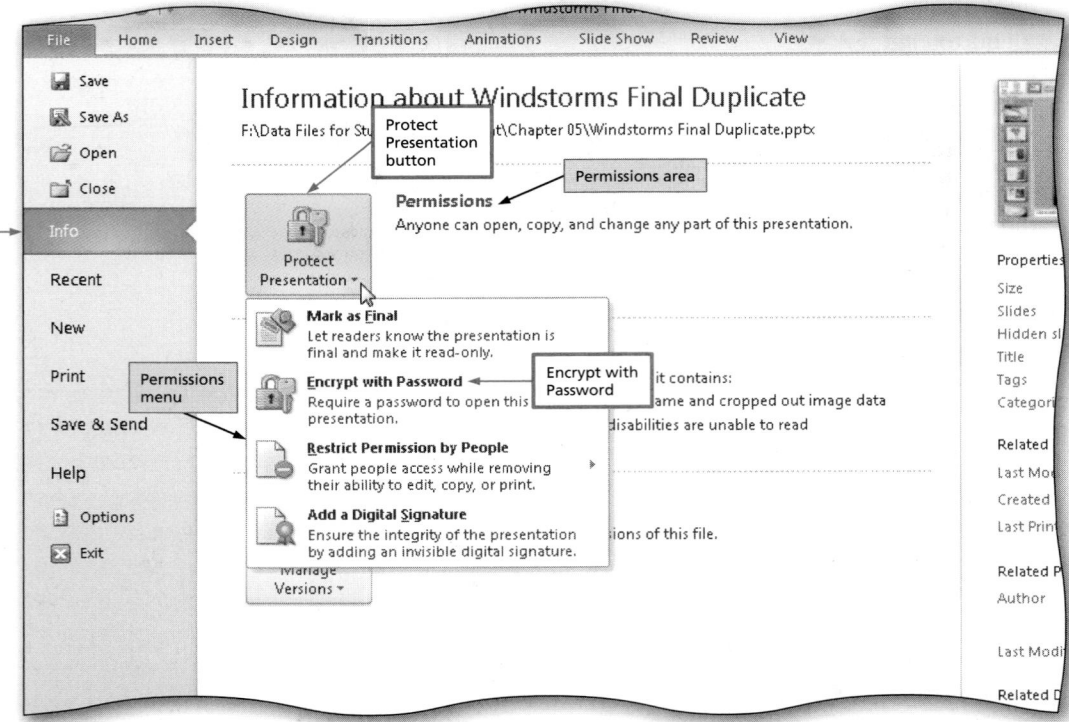

Figure 5–62

- Click Encrypt with Password to display the Encrypt Document dialog box.

- Type **Tornado2Windy** in the Password text box (Figure 5–63).

Q&A

Why do dots appear instead of the characters I typed?

PowerPoint does not display the actual letters and numbers for security reasons. In the next step, you are prompted to reenter the characters to ensure you pressed the desired keys.

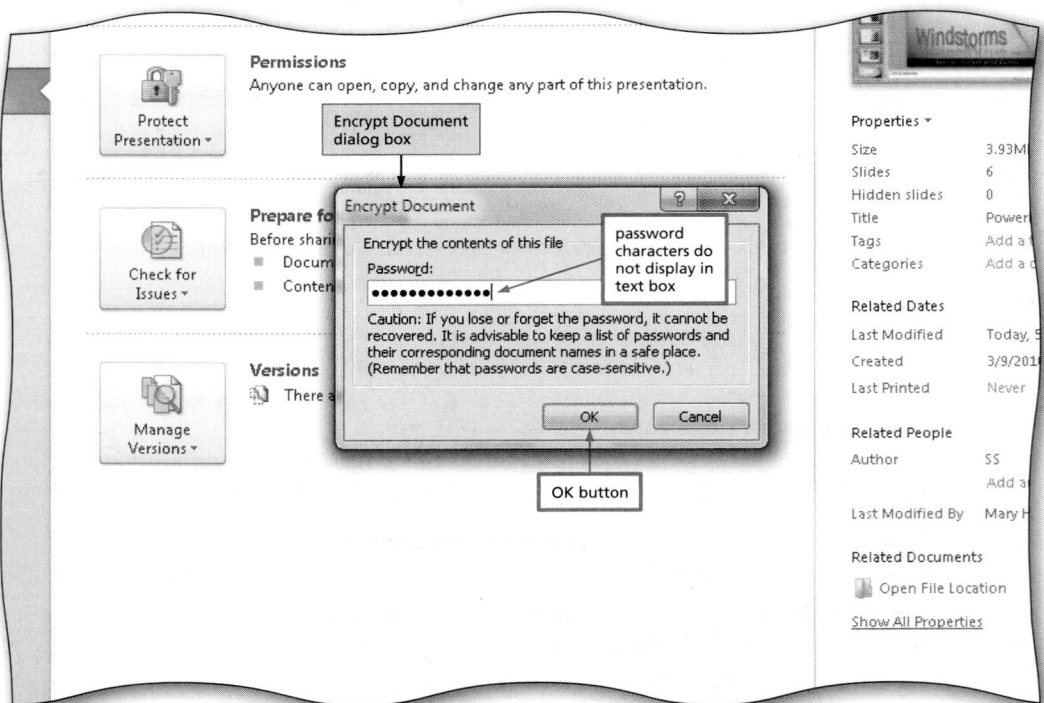

Figure 5–63

- Click the OK button to display the Confirm Password dialog box.

- Type **Tornado2Windy** in the Reenter password text box (Figure 5–64).

Q&A

What if I forget my password?

You will not be able to open your file. For security reasons, Microsoft or other companies cannot retrieve a lost password.

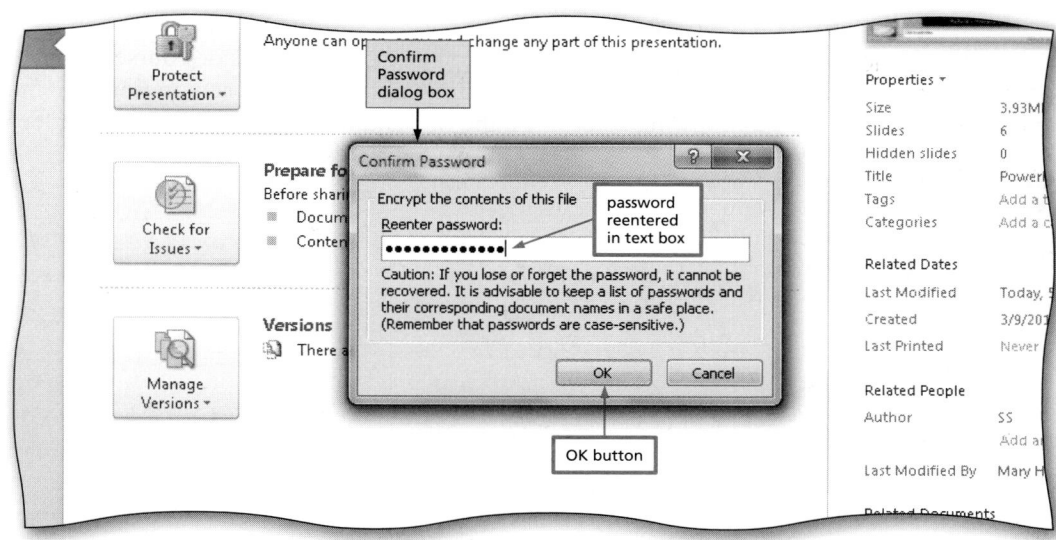

Figure 5–64

4

- Click the OK button in the Confirm Password dialog box.

Q&A

When does the password take effect?

You will need to enter your password the next time you open your presentation.

TO OPEN A PRESENTATION WITH A PASSWORD

To open a file that has been protected with a password, you would perform the following steps.

1. Display the Open dialog box, locate the desired file, and then click the Open button to display the Password dialog box.

2. When the Password dialog box appears, type the password in the Password text box and then click the OK button to display the presentation.

TO CHANGE THE PASSWORD OR REMOVE PASSWORD PROTECTION

To change a password that you added to a file or to remove all password protection from the file, you would perform the following steps.

1. Display the Open dialog box, locate the desired file, and then click the Open button to display the Password dialog box.

2. When the Password dialog box appears, type the password in the Password text box and then click the OK button to display the presentation.

3. Open the Backstage view and then click Save As to display the Save As dialog box. Click the Tools button and then click General Options in the Tools list.

4. Select the contents of the 'Password to open' text box or the 'Password to modify' text box. To remove the password, delete the password text. To change the password, type the new password and then click the OK button. When prompted, retype your password to reconfirm it, and then click the OK button.

5. Click the OK button, click the Save button, and then click the Yes button to resave the presentation.

BTW

Selecting Passwords
Common passwords are 123456, 12345, 123456789, password, and iloveyou. Security experts recommend using passwords or passphrases that have at least eight characters and are a combination of numbers, letters, and capital letters.

To Mark a Presentation as Final

When your slides are completed, you may want to prevent others or yourself from accidentally changing the slide content or features. If you use the **Mark as Final** command, the presentation becomes a read-only document and cannot be edited. The following steps mark the presentation as a final (read-only) document.

1
• With the Backstage view open and the Info tab displaying, click Protect Presentation to display the Permissions menu (Figure 5–65).

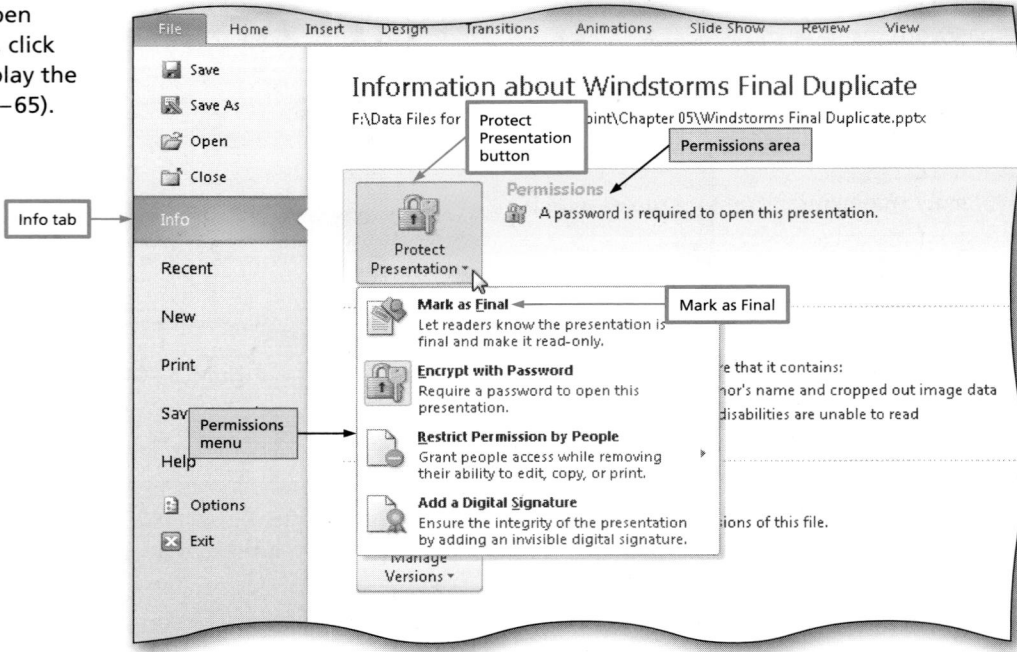

Figure 5–65

2
• Click Mark as Final to display the Microsoft PowerPoint dialog box indicating that the presentation will be saved as a final document (Figure 5–66).

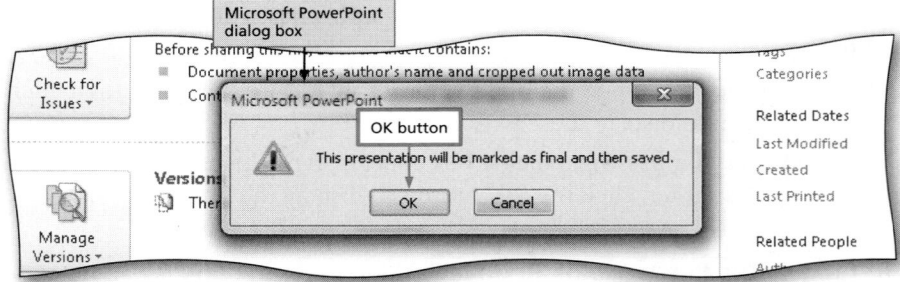

Figure 5–66

3
• Click the OK button (Microsoft PowerPoint dialog box) to save the file and to display another Microsoft PowerPoint dialog box with information about a final version of a document and indicating that the presentation is final (Figure 5–67).

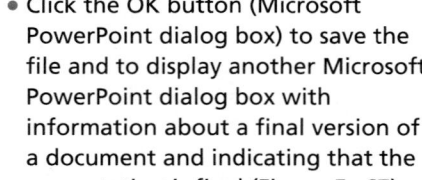

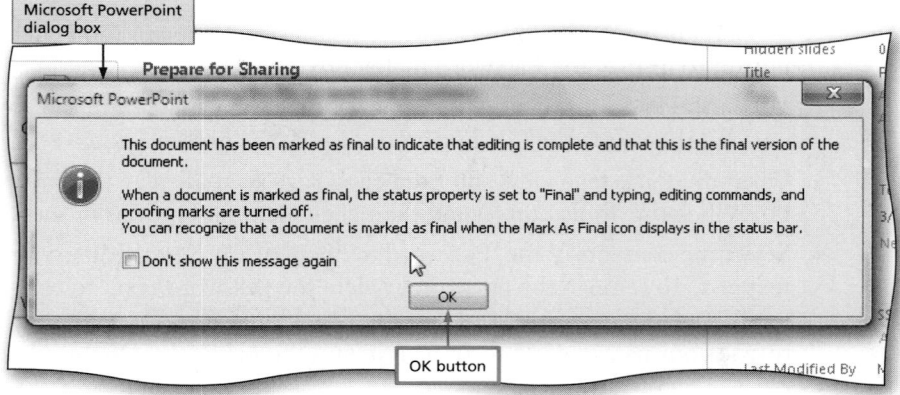

Figure 5–67

Collaborating on and Delivering a Presentation **PowerPoint Chapter 5** **PPT** 309

 Q&A Can I turn off this read-only status so that I can edit the file?

Yes. Click Mark as Final in the Permissions menu to toggle off the read-only status.

4

• Click the OK button (Microsoft PowerPoint dialog box) to return to the Backstage view.

To Create a Digital Signature and Add It to a Document

A digital signature or ID is more commonly known as a **digital certificate**. It verifies that file contents are authentic and valid. Files protected with this certificate cannot be viewed in the PowerPoint Viewer or sent as an e-mail attachment. You can add a digital signature to files that require security, such as a presentation about a company's prototype or a patent application that will be submitted shortly. Only users with Office PowerPoint 2003 or later can view presentations protected by the digital signature. You can obtain an authentic digital certificate from a Microsoft partner, or you can create one yourself. The following steps create a digital signature and add it to the Windstorms Final Duplicate file.

1

• With the Backstage view open and the Info tab displaying, click the Protect Presentation button (Info tab | Permissions area) to display the Permissions menu (Figure 5–68).

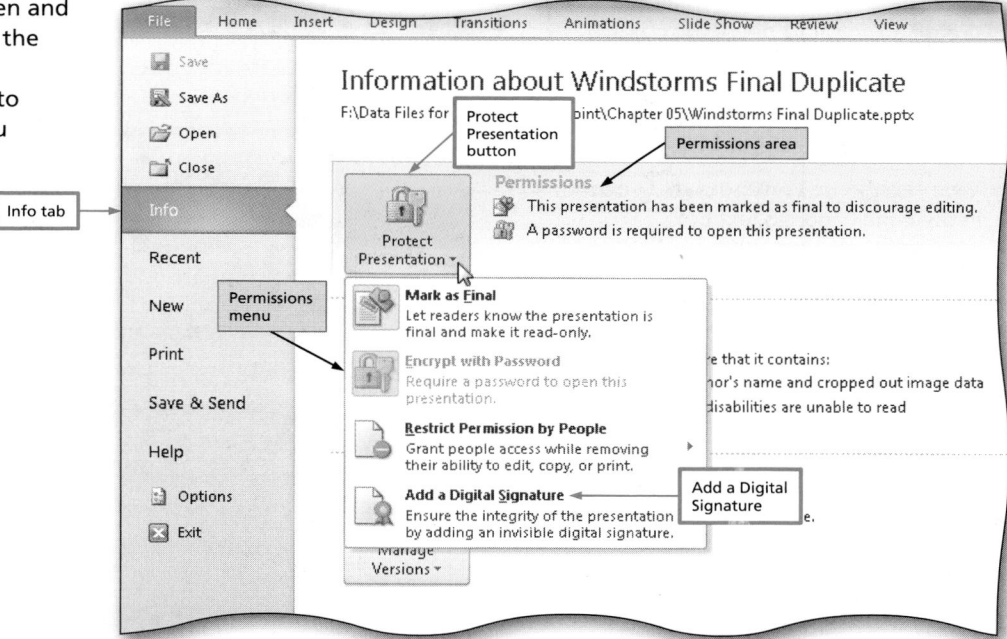

Figure 5–68

2

• Click Add a Digital Signature to display the Microsoft PowerPoint dialog box (Figure 5–69).

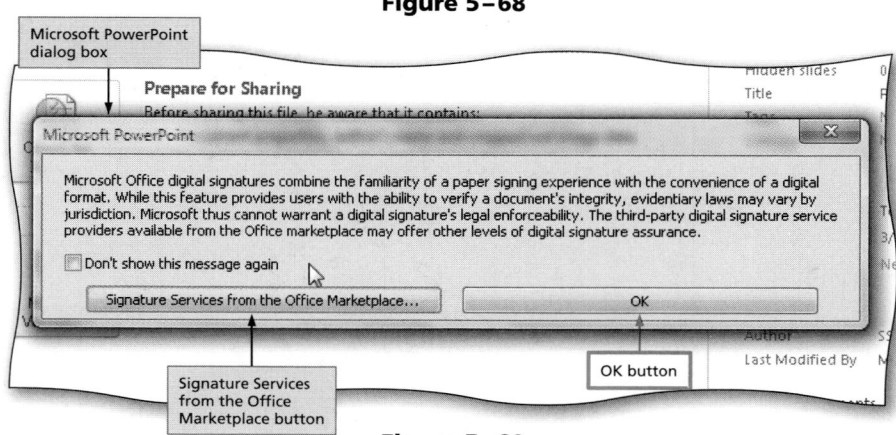

Figure 5–69

3

- Click the OK button to display the Get a Digital ID dialog box.

- Click 'Create your own digital ID' (Get a Digital ID dialog box) (Figure 5–70).

Q&A

What would have happened if I had clicked the Signature Services from the Office Marketplace button instead of the OK button?

You would have been connected to the Microsoft Office Marketplace, which is the same process that will occur if you click the 'Get a digital ID from a Microsoft partner' option button.

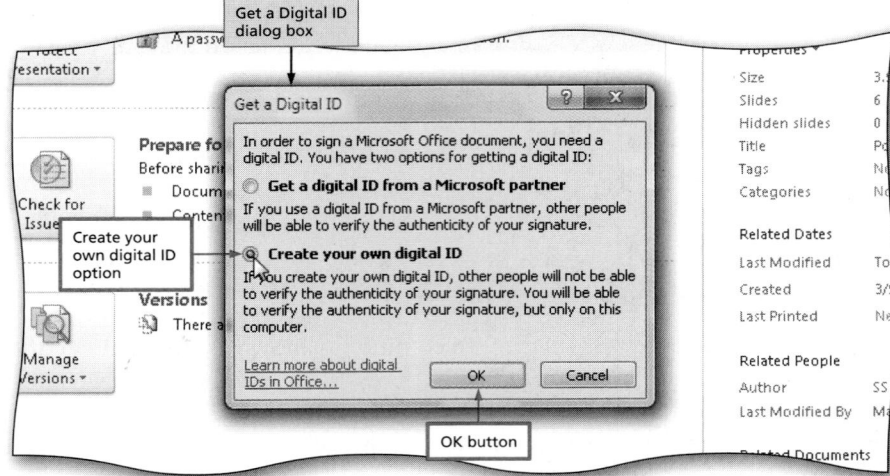

Figure 5–70

4

- Click the OK button to display the Create a Digital ID dialog box.

- If necessary, select the text in the Name text box, and then type **Mary Halen** in this text box.

- Type **mary_halen@hotmail.com** in the E-mail address text box.

- Type **Mary's Weather** in the Organization text box.

- Type **Chicago, IL** in the Location text box (Figure 5–71).

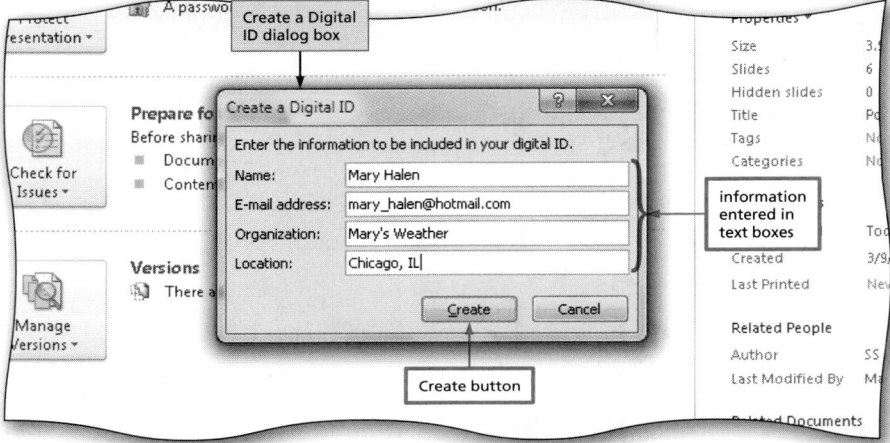

Figure 5–71

5

- Click the Create button to display the Sign dialog box (Figure 5–72).

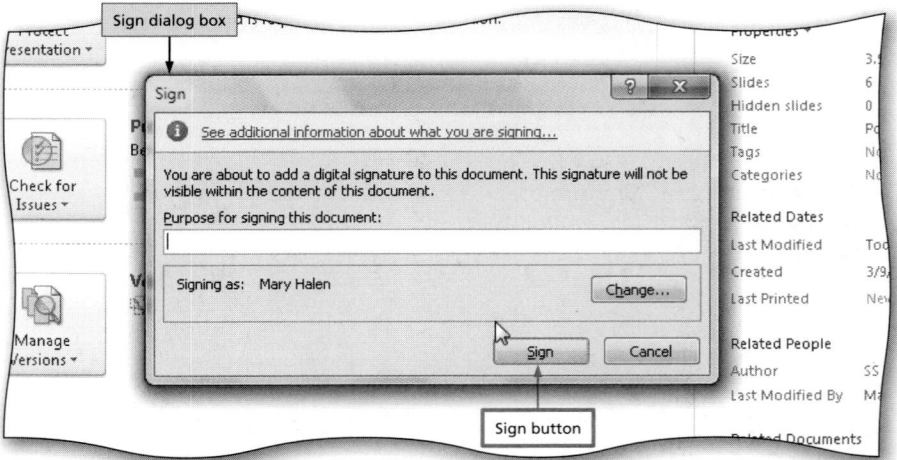

Figure 5–72

6

- Click the Sign button to display the Signature Confirmation dialog box (Figure 5–73).

Q&A Why would a company want to add a digital signature to a document?

The publisher, who is the signing person or organization, is trusted to ensure the source and integrity of the digital information. A signature confirms that the file contents have not been altered since it was signed.

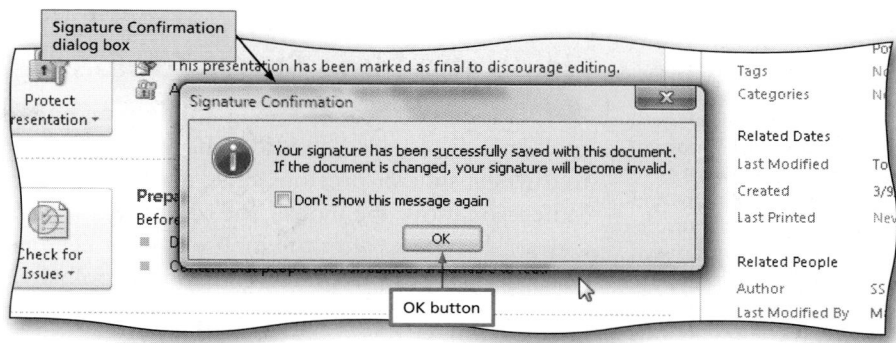

Figure 5–73

Q&A Can I remove a digital signature that has been applied?

Yes. Point to a signature in the Signatures task pane, click the list arrow, click Remove Signature, click the Yes button, and then, if necessary, click the OK button.

7

- Click the OK button to close the Signature Confirmation dialog box and return to the Backstage view.

Using Presentation Tools to Navigate

When you display a particular slide and view the information, you may want to return to one of the other slides in the presentation. Jumping to particular slides in a presentation is called **navigating**. A set of keyboard shortcuts can help you navigate to various slides during the slide show. When running a slide show, you can press the F1 key to see a list of these keyboard controls. These navigational features are listed in Table 5–1.

BTW

Displaying a Black or White Screen
If an audience member interrupts your planned presentation and asks a question not pertaining to the current slide, you should consider displaying a black or white screen temporarily while you are answering the query.

Table 5–1 Slide Show Navigation Shortcut Keys	
Keyboard Shortcut	**Purpose**
N Click SPACEBAR RIGHT ARROW DOWN ARROW ENTER PAGE DOWN	Advance to the next slide
P BACKSPACE LEFT ARROW UP ARROW PAGE UP	Return to the previous slide
Number followed by ENTER	Go to a specific slide
B PERIOD	Display a black screen Return to slide show from a black screen
W COMMA	Display a white screen Return to slide show from a white screen
ESC CTRL + BREAK HYPHEN	End a slide show

Saving Annotations
Many presenters highlight and write on individual slides during the slide show to emphasize important points. They, in turn, save these markups and then print handouts with these annotations so that audience members can have a set of notes reflecting the key discussion points.

Delivering and Navigating a Presentation Using the Slide Show Toolbar

When you begin running a slide show and move the mouse pointer, the Slide Show toolbar is displayed. The **Slide Show toolbar** contains buttons that allow you to navigate to the next slide or previous slide, mark up the current slide, or change the current display. When you move the mouse, the toolbar displays faintly in the lower-left corner of the slide; it disappears after the mouse has not been moved for three seconds. Table 5–2 describes the buttons on the Slide Show toolbar.

Table 5–2 Slide Show Toolbar Buttons

Description	Image	Function
Previous		Previous slide or previous animated element on the slide
Pointer		Shortcut menu for arrows, pens, and highlighters
Navigation		Shortcut menu for slide navigation and screen displays
Next		Next slide or next animated element on the slide

To Highlight Items on a Slide

You click the arrow buttons on either end of the toolbar to navigate backward or forward through the slide show. The Pointer button has a variety of functions, most often to emphasize, or **highlight**, words or to add **ink** notes or drawings to your presentation in order to emphasize aspects of slides or make handwritten notes. When the presentation ends, PowerPoint will prompt you to keep or discard the ink annotations. The following steps highlight items on a slide in Slide Show view.

- Display the Home tab and then click the Edit Anyway button in the yellow Marked as Final Message Bar near the top of the screen to enable editing the presentation.

- Click the Slide 1 thumbnail in the Slides tab and then run the slide show.

- If the Slide Show toolbar is not visible, move the mouse pointer on the slide.

- Click the Pointer button on the Slide Show toolbar to display the shortcut menu (Figure 5–74).

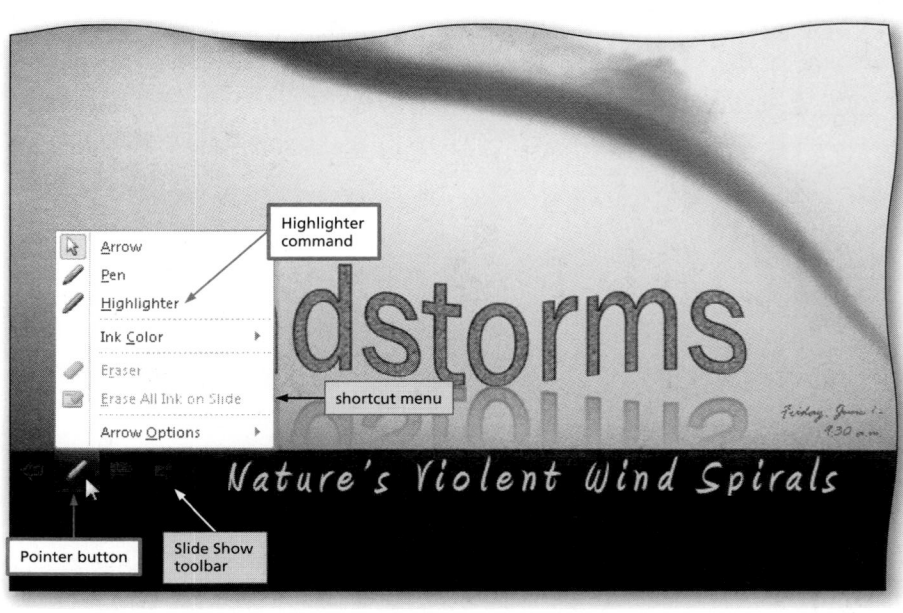

Figure 5–74

● Click Highlighter and then drag the
mouse over the word, Windstorms.
Repeat this action until all the letters
are highlighted (Figure 5–75).

Figure 5–75

To Change Ink Color

Instead of the Highlighter, you also can click Pen to draw or write notes on the slides. The following steps
change the pointer to a pen and change the color of ink during the presentation.

● Display Slide 2. Click the Pointer
button on the Slide Show toolbar
and then click Pen on the
shortcut menu.

● Click the Pointer button on
the Slide Show toolbar and
then point to Ink Color
(Figure 5–76).

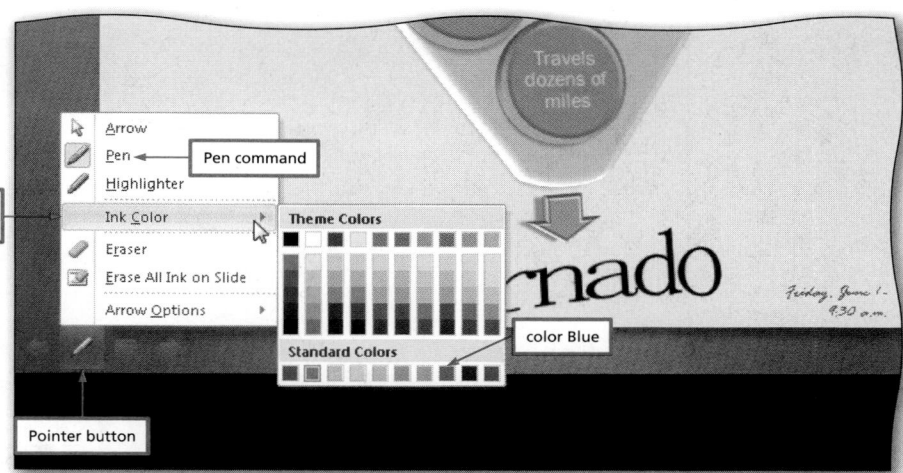

Figure 5–76

● Click the color Blue in the Standard
Colors row.

● Drag the mouse around the SmartArt
graphic to draw a circle around this
object (Figure 5–77).

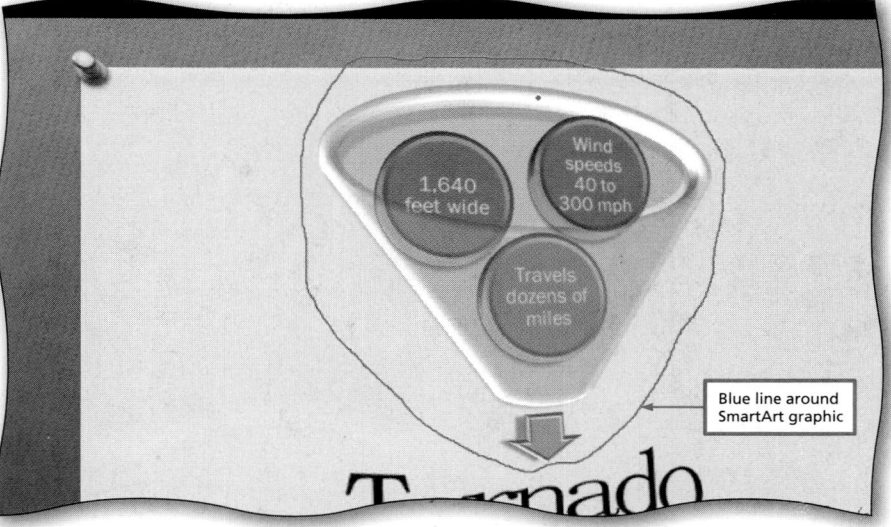

Figure 5–77

- Right-click the slide to display the shortcut menu (Figure 5–78).

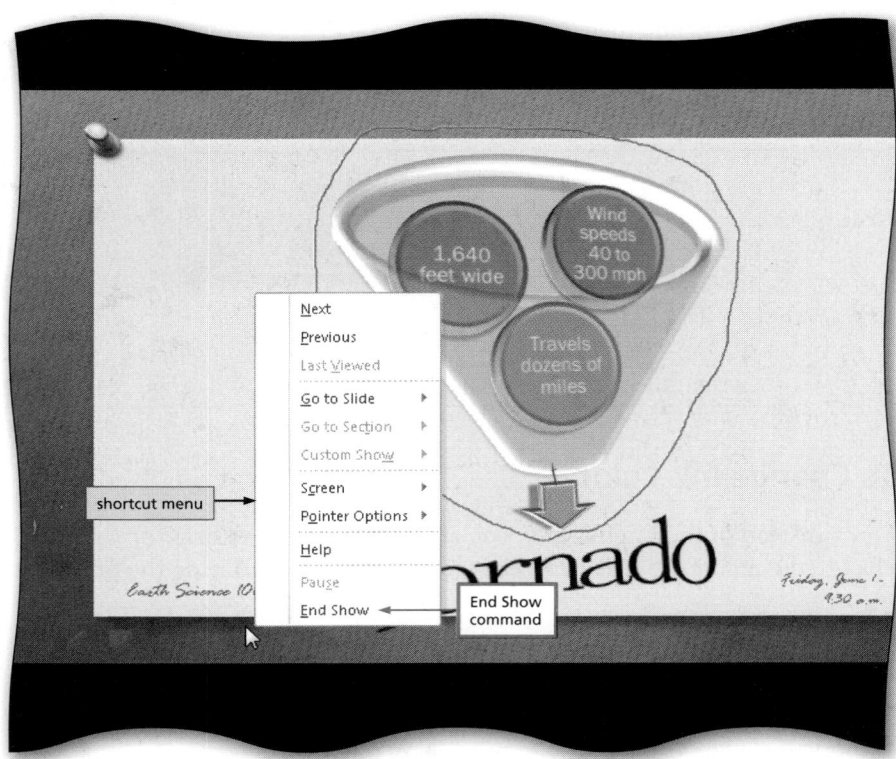

Figure 5–78

- Click End Show to display the Microsoft PowerPoint dialog box (Figure 5–79).

- Click the Discard button (Microsoft PowerPoint dialog box) to end the presentation without saving the annotations.

If I clicked the Keep button in error, can I later discard the annotations?

Yes. Display the slide, click the annotation line to select it, and then press the DELETE key.

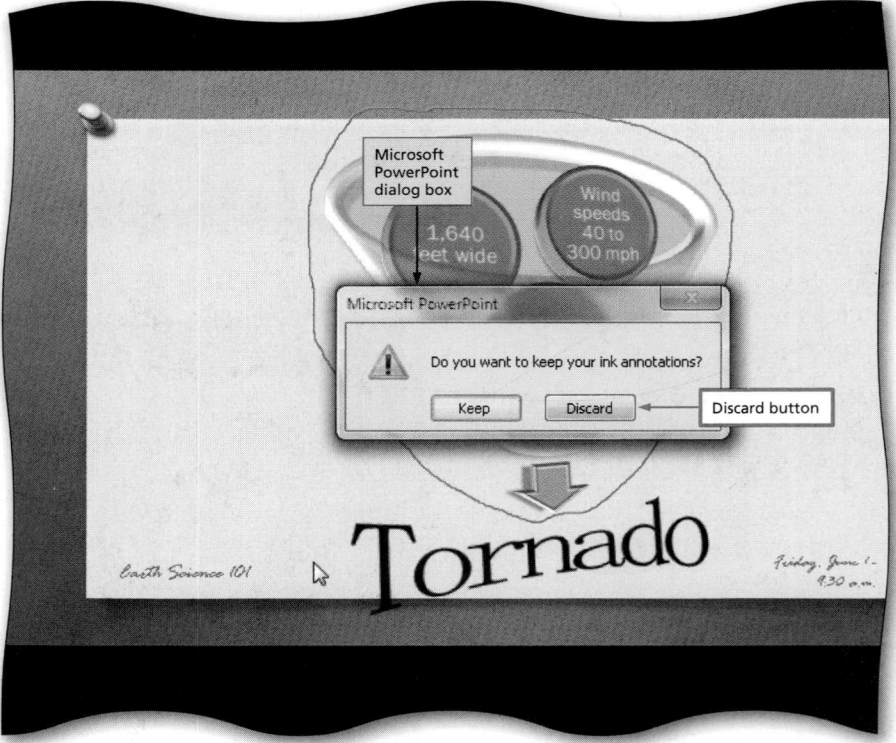

Figure 5–79

TO HIDE THE MOUSE POINTER AND SLIDE SHOW TOOLBAR
To hide the mouse pointer and Slide Show toolbar during the slide show, you would perform the following step.

1. Click the Pointer button on the Slide Show toolbar, point to Arrow Options, and then click Hidden.

TO CONSTANTLY DISPLAY THE MOUSE POINTER AND SLIDE SHOW TOOLBAR
By default, the mouse pointer and toolbar are set at Automatic, which means they are hidden after three seconds of no movement. After you hide the mouse pointer and toolbar, they remain hidden until you choose one of the other commands on the Pointer Options submenu. They are displayed again when you move the mouse.

To keep the mouse pointer and toolbar displayed at all times during a slide show, you would perform the following step.

1. Click the Pointer button on the Slide Show toolbar, point to Arrow Options, and then click Visible.

To Change Document Properties

Before saving the presentation again, you want to add your name, class name, and some keywords as document properties. The following steps use the Document Information Panel to change document properties.

1 Display the Document Information Panel and then type your name as the Author property.

2 Type your course and section in the Subject property.

3 Type `windstorm, hurricane, tornado` as the Keywords property.

4 Close the Document Information Panel.

To Save, Print, and Quit PowerPoint

The presentation now is complete. You should save the slides, print a handout, and then quit PowerPoint.

1 Save the Windstorms Final presentation again with the same file name.

2 Print the presentation as a handout with two slides per page. Do not print the comment pages (Figure 5–80 on the following page).

3 Click the Page Setup button (Design tab | Page Setup group) and then change the slide size to On-screen Show (4:3).

4 Click the Resolution box arrow (Slide Show tab | Monitors group) and then change the slide show resolution to 1024 × 768.

5 Quit PowerPoint, closing all open documents.

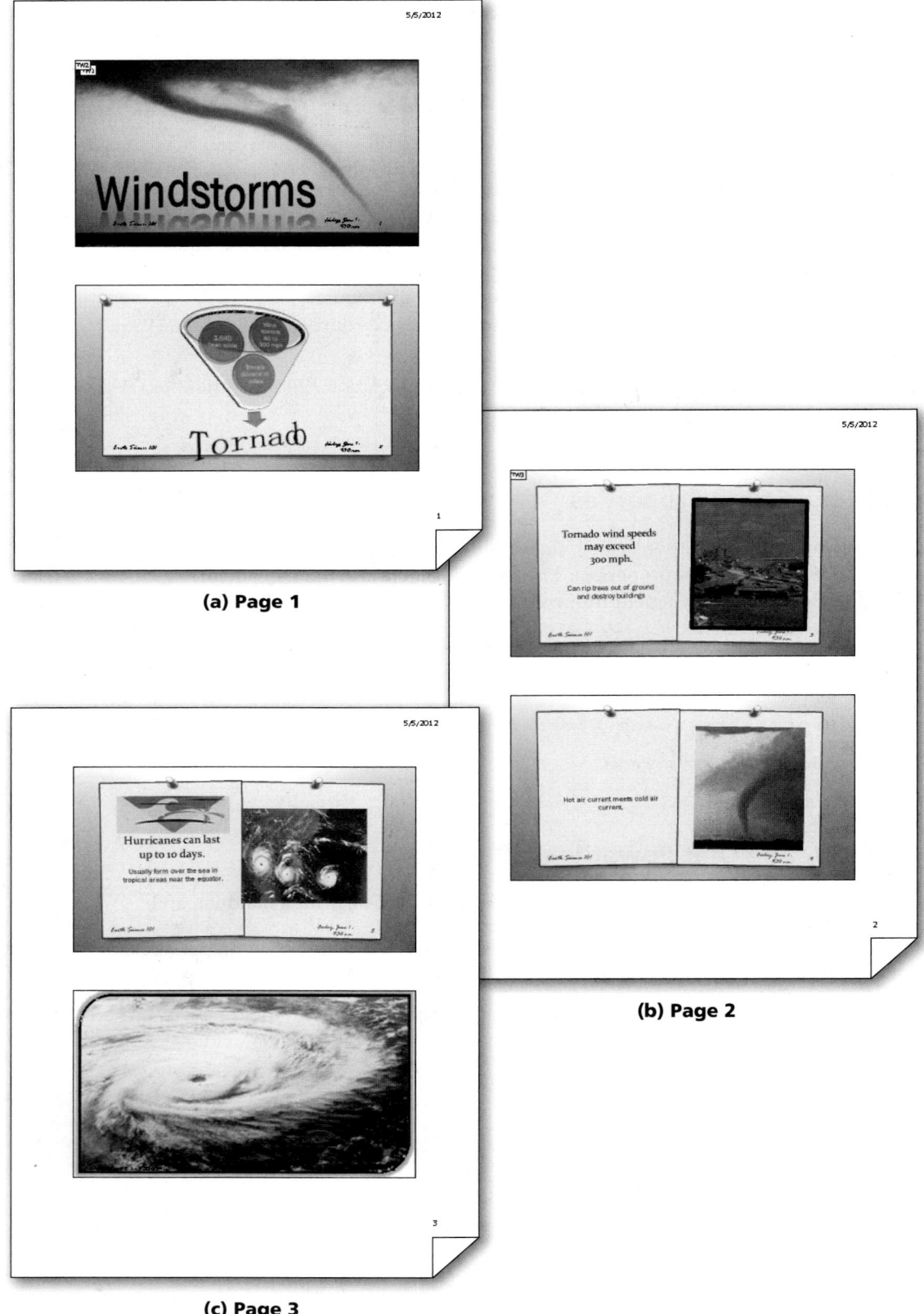

(a) Page 1

(b) Page 2

(c) Page 3

Figure 5–80

Chapter Summary

In this chapter you have learned how to merge presentations, review a reviewer's comments, and then accept or reject proposed changes. You changed the slide size and presentation resolution, protected and secured the file with a password and digital signature, checked compatibility, removed inappropriate information, and then saved the presentation in a variety of formats. Finally, you ran the presentation and annotated the slides with a highlighter and pen. The items listed below include all the new PowerPoint skills you have learned in this chapter.

1. Merge a Presentation (PPT 270)
2. Print Comments (PPT 271)
3. Preview Presentation Changes (PPT 273)
4. Review and Delete Comments (PPT 274)
5. Review, Accept, and Reject Presentation Changes (PPT 276)
6. Review, Accept, and Reject Slide Changes (PPT 278)
7. Reject a Slide Revision (PPT 280)
8. Insert a Comment (PPT 281)
9. Edit a Comment (PPT 282)
10. End the Review (PPT 283)
11. Reuse Slides from an Existing Presentation (PPT 285)
12. Capture Part of a Screen Using Screen Clipping (PPT 288)
13. Add a Footer with Fixed Information (PPT 289)
14. Clear Formatting and Apply an Artistic Effect (PPT 291)
15. Set Slide Size (PPT 292)
16. Select Slide Show Resolution (PPT 294)
17. Save a File as a PowerPoint Show (PPT 295)
18. Save a Slide as an Image (PPT 296)
19. Package a Presentation for Storage on a CD or DVD (PPT 297)
20. Save a File in a Previous PowerPoint Format (PPT 300)
21. Identify Presentation Features Not Supported by Previous Versions (PPT 301)
22. Remove Inappropriate Information (PPT 303)
23. Set a Password (PPT 305)
24. Mark a Presentation as Final (PPT 308)
25. Create a Digital Signature and Add It to a Document (PPT 309)
26. Highlight Items on a Slide (PPT 312)
27. Change Ink Color (PPT 313)

 If you have a SAM 2010 user profile, your instructor may have assigned an autogradable version of this assignment. If so, log into the SAM 2010 Web site at www.cengage.com/sam2010 to download the instruction and start files.

Learn It Online

Test your knowledge of chapter content and key terms.

Instructions: To complete the Learn It Online exercises, start your browser, click the Address bar, and then enter the Web address **scsite.com/ppt2010/learn**. When the PowerPoint 2010 Learn It Online page is displayed, click the link for the exercise you want to complete and then read the instructions.

Chapter Reinforcement TF, MC, and SA
A series of true/false, multiple choice, and short answer questions that test your knowledge of the chapter content.

Flash Cards
An interactive learning environment where you identify chapter key terms associated with displayed definitions.

Practice Test
A series of multiple choice questions that test your knowledge of chapter content and key terms.

Who Wants To Be a Computer Genius?
An interactive game that challenges your knowledge of chapter content in the style of a television quiz show.

Wheel of Terms
An interactive game that challenges your knowledge of chapter key terms in the style of the television show *Wheel of Fortune*.

Crossword Puzzle Challenge
A crossword puzzle that challenges your knowledge of key terms presented in the chapter.

Apply Your Knowledge

Reinforce the skills and apply the concepts you learned in this chapter.

Inserting Comments, Adding a Header and a Footer, Marking as Final, and Saving As a Previous Version

Note: To complete this assignment, you will be required to use the Data Files for Students. See the inside back cover of this book for instructions on downloading the Data Files for Students, or contact your instructor for information about accessing the required files.

Instructions: Start PowerPoint. Open the presentation, Apply 5-1 Wind, located on the Data Files for Students.

The slides in the presentation present information about wind energy. You will insert a comment, add a footer, and then save the file as PowerPoint 2010 (.pptx) document. The slides should look like Figure 5–81a and 5–81b. You then will remove inappropriate information, mark the presentation as final, and save the files as a PowerPoint 97–2003 (.ppt) document. Figure 5–81c shows the new Slide 1.

Perform the following tasks:

1. On Slide 1, add a comment on the picture with the following text: **To be consistent with kilowatts, I suggest you show wind speeds in kilometers per hour instead of miles per hour. I converted them for you: 12 mph = 19.31 Km/H and 14 mph = 22.53 Km/H.**

2. Display the Header and Footer dialog box and add the slide number and the automatic date and time. Type your name as the footer text. Do not show on title slide.

3. Check the spelling and then change the document properties, as specified by your instructor. Save the presentation using the file name, Apply 5-1 Wind Energy.

4. Remove all inappropriate information.

5. Mark the presentation as final.

6. Save the presentation as a PowerPoint 97-2003 (.ppt) document using the file name, Apply 5-1 Wind Energy PPT. Submit the revised documents in the format specified by your instructor.

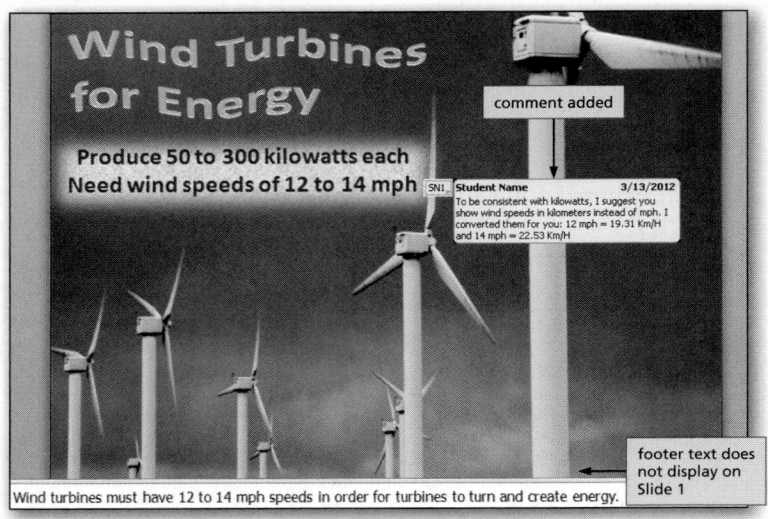

(a) Slide 1

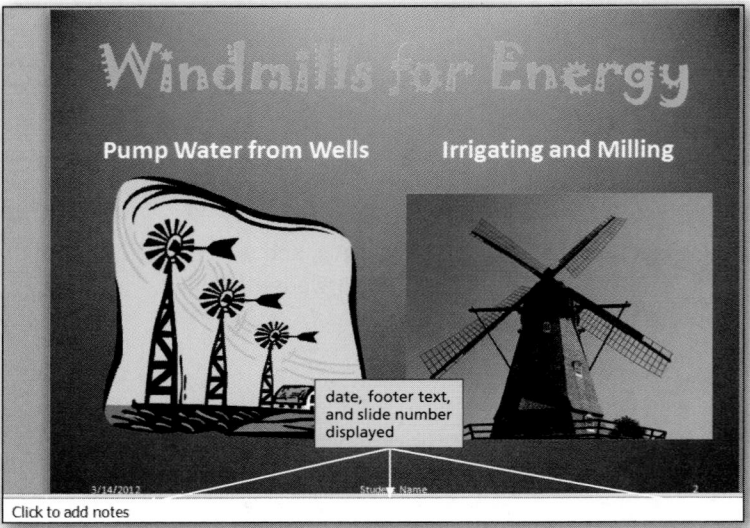

(b) Slide 2

Figure 5–81

(c) Revised Slide 1

Figure 5–81 (Continued)

Extend Your Knowledge

Extend the skills you learned in this chapter and experiment with new skills. You may need to use Help to complete the assignment.

Changing Headers and Footers on Slides and Handouts and Inserting a Screenshot

Note: To complete this assignment, you will be required to use the Data Files for Students. See the inside back cover of this book for instructions on downloading the Data Files for Students, or contact your instructor for information about accessing the required files.

Instructions: Start PowerPoint. Open the presentation, Extend 5-1 Running, located on the Data Files for Students.

You will add a footer and a fixed date to all slides in the presentation (Figure 5–82) and format this text on the title slide. You also will insert a screenshot of marathon information on one slide.

Perform the following tasks:

1. Display the Header and Footer dialog box and then add your next birthday as the fixed date footer text on all slides. Type your school's name as the footer text, followed by the words, Running Club.

2. Display the Notes and Handouts tab (Header and Footer dialog box) and then add the same date and footer text to the notes and handouts.

3. Increase the font size of the Slide 1 footer date to 16 point and change the font color to Red. Italicize this text (Figure 5–82a).

(a) Slide 1

Figure 5–82

Continued >

Extend Your Knowledge *continued*

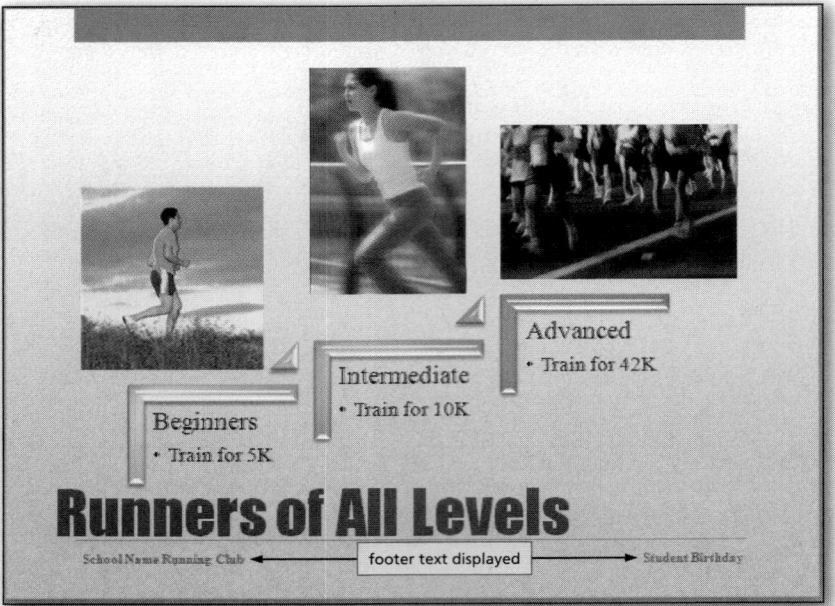

(b) Slide 2

(c) Slide 3

Figure 5–82 (Continued)

4. Insert a comment on Slide 1 as a reminder to yourself to verify the training dates and times with your school's running club president.

5. Locate information about marathons on the Internet. This information could list previous winners, record times, or routes. Insert a screenshot of one Web page on Slide 3 (Figure 5–82c). You may need to make the screenshot smaller or reduce the size of the two photos at the top of Slide 3.

6. Change the document properties, as specified by your instructor. Save the presentation using the file name, Extend 5–1 Running Club.

7. Submit the revised document in the format specified by your instructor.

Make It Right

Analyze a presentation and correct all errors and/or improve the design.

Clearing Formatting and Correcting Headers and Footers

Note: To complete this assignment, you will be required to use the Data Files for Students. See the inside back cover of this book for instructions on downloading the Data Files for Students, or contact your instructor for information about accessing the required files.

Instructions: Start PowerPoint. Open the presentation, Make It Right 5-1 Video Games, located on the Data Files for Students.

In your psychology class, you are studying the habits of teenagers and if playing video games can have negative effects on their behavior. You contact a local high school and get permission to conduct a survey among the students to find out how they spend their leisure time. Correct the formatting problems and errors in the presentation, shown in Figure 5–83, while keeping in mind the guidelines presented in this chapter.

Perform the following tasks:

1. Change the design from Trek to Slipstream.

2. Set the slide size to On-screen Show (16:9). Change the slide show resolution to 800 × 600.

3. On Slide 1, adjust the chart size so that all text on the chart is visible. Decrease the slide title text font size to 44 point.

4. Adjust the size of the picture and move it to the upper-right corner of the slide so that it is not covering the title text.

5. On Slide 2, decrease the font size of the bulleted text to 20 point and decrease the title text font size to 54 point.

6. Clear the formatting from the picture and adjust the size so that it fits below the bulleted text in the right text placeholder.

7. Display the Header and Footer dialog box, remove the student name from the footer on Slide 2, and do not show the slide number on the title slide.

8. Change the Transition from Fly Through to Cube on all slides.

9. Change the document properties, as specified by your instructor. Save the presentation using the file name, Make It Right 5-1 Teens and Video Games.

10. Submit the revised document in the format specified by your instructor.

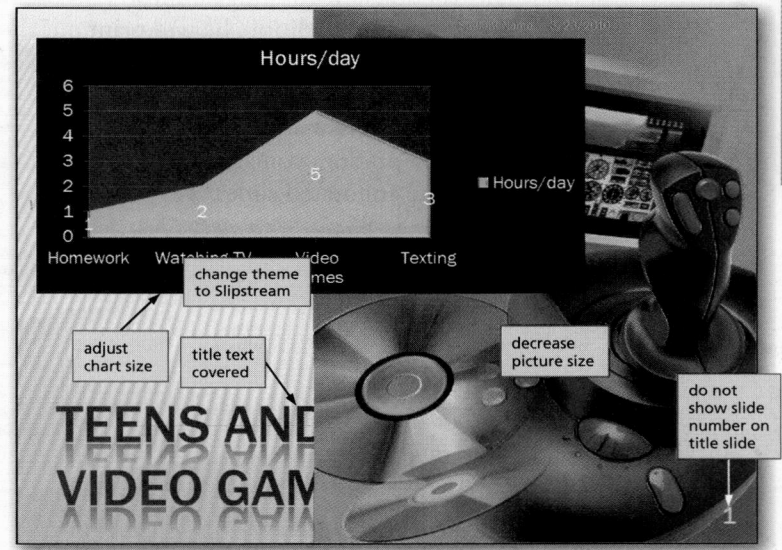

(a) Slide 1

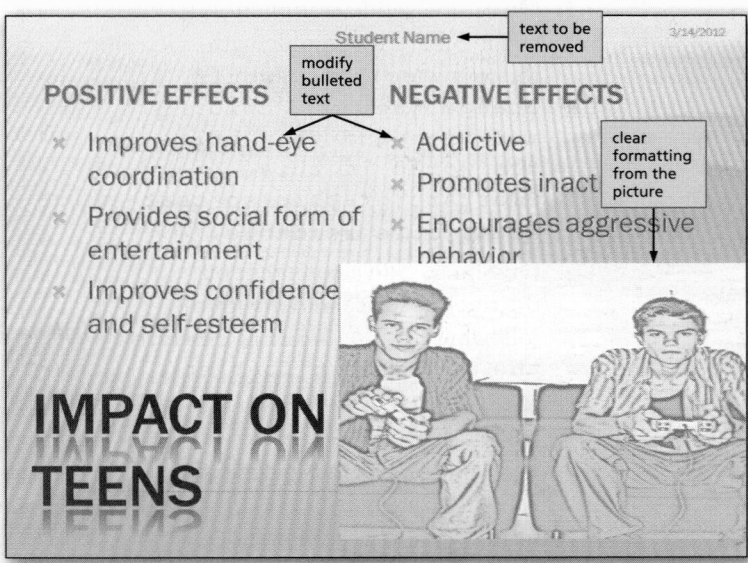

(b) Slide 2

Figure 5–83

In the Lab

Design and/or create a presentation using the guidelines, concepts, and skills presented in this chapter. Labs 1, 2, and 3 are listed in order of increasing difficulty.

Lab 1: Adding Comments to and Protecting a Presentation and Inserting a Slide

Note: To complete this assignment, you will be required to use the Data Files for Students. See the inside back cover of this book for instructions on downloading the Data Files for Students, or contact your instructor for information about accessing the required files.

Problem: The garden center where you work is putting together small gift baskets to hand out to local senior citizens at an upcoming fair. One of the items in the gift basket is a packet of sunflower seeds. Last spring your manager, John Wind, created a PowerPoint presentation about sunflower seeds. He sent you two sets of slides and requested comments. One PowerPoint presentation that he sent to you includes instructions for roasting sunflower seeds, and he would like those instructions to be added to the presentation. In addition, he will print out the instructions to include with the sunflower seeds. You add several comments, insert a slide, check the slides for compatibility with previous PowerPoint versions, and then protect the presentation with a password. When you run the presentation, you add annotations. The annotated slides are shown in Figure 5–84.

Perform the following tasks:

1. Open the presentation, Lab 5-1 Sunflowers, located on the Data Files for Students.

2. On Slide 1, replace Calista Lindy's name with your name. Add a comment on the picture with the following text: **I suggest you enlarge this picture and add a 6 pt Gold border.**

3. On Slide 2, add a comment in the SmartArt graphic with the following text: **I would change the text color and size and then bold the words in this SmartArt graphic so that it is more readable.**

4. On Slide 3, add a comment on the title text placeholder with the following text: **I would change the title text font so it matches the title text font on Slide 2.**

5. After Slide 2, insert Slide 2 (which becomes the new Slide 3, and former Slide 3 becomes Slide 4) from the Lab 5-1 Sunflower Seeds file located on the Data Files for Students. Keep the source formatting.

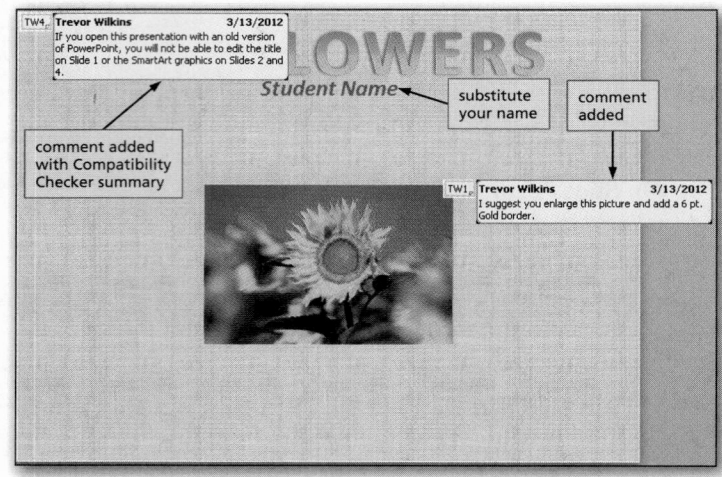

(a) Slide 1

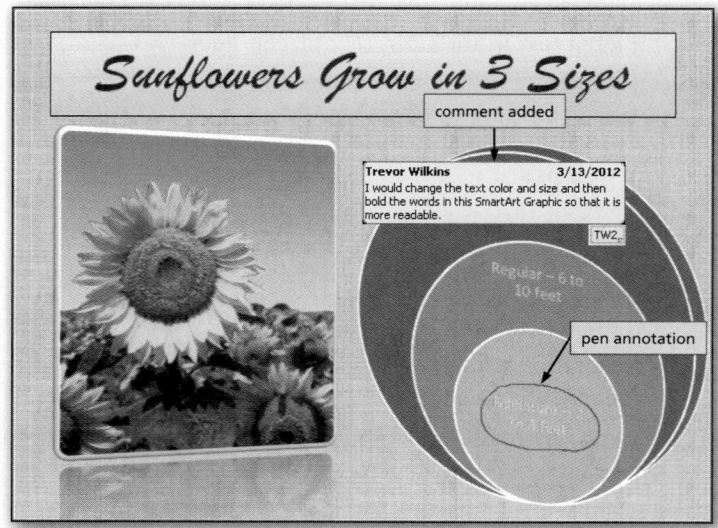

(b) Slide 2

Figure 5–84

6. On the new Slide 3, clear the formatting from the picture.

7. Run the Compatibility Checker to identify the presentation features not supported in previous PowerPoint versions. Summarize these features in a comment placed on Slide 1.

8. Protect the presentation with the password, Sunflowers2Grow.

9. Change the document properties, as specified by your instructor. Save the presentation using the file name, Lab 5-1 Growing Sunflowers.

10. Print the slides. In addition, print Slide 3 again.

11. Run the presentation. On Slide 2, click the Pointer button, point to Ink Color on the shortcut menu, and then click Blue in the Standard Colors row. Click the Pen, draw a circle around the text, Miniature – 2 to 4 feet, in the SmartArt graphic. Click the Next button on the toolbar, click Highlighter, point to Ink Color, and then click Light Green in the Standard Colors row. Highlight the text, Soak seeds overnight in salted water. Save the annotations.

12. Print the slides with annotations.

13. Submit the revised document in the format specified by your instructor.

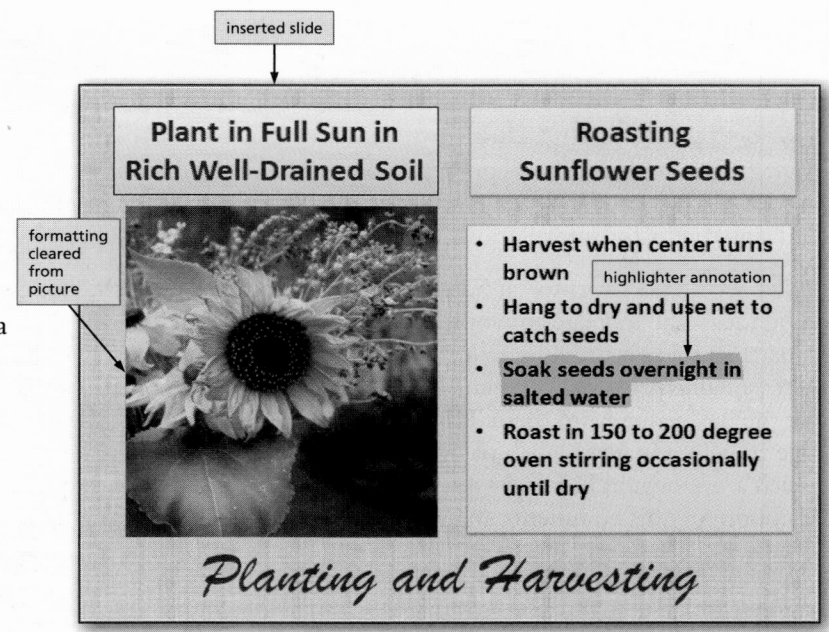

(c) Slide 3 (Inserted Slide)

(d) Slide 4

Figure 5–84 (Continued)

In the Lab

Lab 2: Modifying and Deleting Comments in a Protected Presentation

Note: To complete this assignment, you will be required to use the Data Files for Students. See the inside back cover of this book for instructions on downloading the Data Files for Students, or contact your instructor for information about accessing the required files.

Problem: In an effort to eat healthy and shop economically, stocking up on vegetables and fruits is a good idea. The manager of your local grocery store contacts you about doing a display for the produce department. He is listening to his customers and trying to provide more healthy choices of fresh produce at reasonable prices. Several customers have expressed a concern about handling the fresh produce to get the best value from them. He knows you are studying biology in school and thought you might be able to help. He gives you a password-protected file that he created and asks you to review the slides, which are shown in Figure 5–85. He has inserted comments with questions. You offer some suggestions by modifying his comments and removing inappropriate information.

Perform the following tasks:

1. Open the presentation, Lab 5-2 Eating, located on the Data Files for Students. The password is Produce4Us.

2. Insert the date, time, and your name in the footer on all slides except the title slide. On Slide 1, modify the comment on the title by adding the following text: `Yes, I think the title is a great attention-getter. You really want your customers to eat healthy and make better food choices.`

3. On Slide 2, modify the comment by adding the following text: `You could change the word microbial to bacterial. The statement is good because a lot of people might not know they should not wash produce before storing.`

4. On Slide 3, modify comment 3 by adding the following text: `The presentation will be printed in color and displayed throughout the produce department. These slides will be enlarged, so shoppers should see the pictures easily.` Delete comment 4 on the title text placeholder.

(a) Slide 1

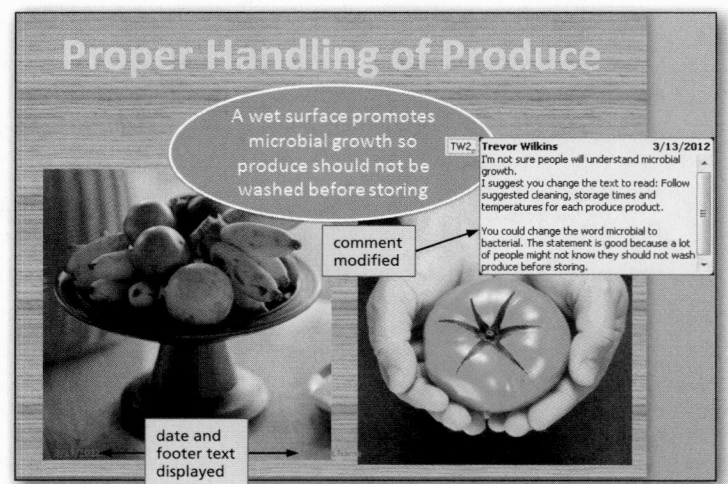

(b) Slide 2

Figure 5–85

5. Mark the presentation as final.

6. Add a digital signature by creating your own digital ID. Enter your name in the Name text box, `mary_halen@hotmail.com` in the E-mail address text box, `John's Supermarket` in the Organization text box, and `Chicago, IL` in the Location text box.

7. Inspect the document and then remove all document properties and personal information.

8. Save the presentation using the file name, Lab 5-2 Healthy Eating. Then save the slides as a PowerPoint 97-2003 Presentation (.ppt) type using the same file name.

9. Print the slides and comments.

10. Submit the revised document in the format specified by your instructor.

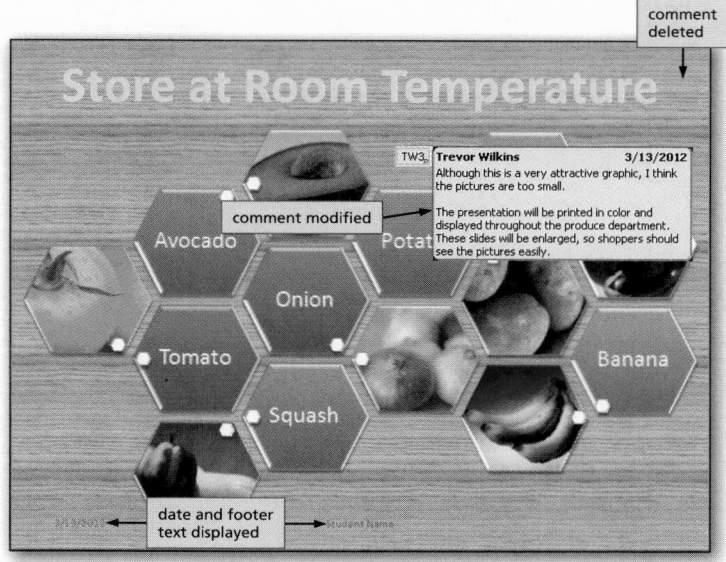

(c) Slide 3

Figure 5–85 (Continued)

In the Lab

Lab 3: Reviewing and Accepting Comments, Using Screen Clipping, and Packaging the Presentation for Storage on a Compact Disc

Note: To complete this assignment, you will be required to use the Data Files for Students. See the inside back cover of this book for instructions on downloading the Data Files for Students, or contact your instructor for information about accessing the required files.

Problem: The XYZ Corporation is promoting its software products. You work in the Marketing department and have developed a PowerPoint presentation, which is shown in Figures 5–86a and 5–86b on the next page, as part of the marketing strategy. You ask your coworker, Miriam Lind, to review the presentation by inserting comments and making revisions on the slides. You use her input to create the final presentation shown in Figures 5–86c through 5–86e on page PPT 327. You also obtain a picture of your department's new director, Sanjai Rukah, from another PowerPoint presentation. In addition, you use the Package for CD feature to distribute the presentation to local businesses.

Perform the following tasks:

1. Open the presentation, Lab 5-3 XYZ, located on the Data Files for Students.

2. Merge Miriam's revised file, Lab 5-3 XYZ-Miriam, located on the Data Files for Students. Accept both presentation changes so that the transition is added and Slide 3 is inserted. Review all of Miriam's comments on Slide 1 and Slide 2. Preview the slides, and then print the slides and the comments.

Continued >

STUDENT ASSIGNMENTS

In the Lab *continued*

3. On Slide 1, accept all changes except Miriam's computer clip (Picture 6) at the bottom of the slide.

4. On Slide 2, accept the SmartArt change.

5. On Slide 3, review all of Miriam's comments. Change the layout to Picture with Caption. Type **Meet Our New IT Director** as the title text. Type **Sanjai Rukah** as the caption text below the title text placeholder, as shown in Figure 5–86e. Increase the title text and the caption text font size. Bold and italicize the caption text.

6. Open the presentation, Lab 5-3 XYZ-Tyrone, located on the Data Files for Students. Then display Lab 5-3 XYZ. With Slide 3 still displayed, use screen clipping to capture Sanjai's head shot in Lab 5-3 XYZ-Tyrone. Resize the screen clipping and move it to the location shown in Figure 5–86e.

7. Delete all markup in the presentation.

8. On Slide 1, enhance the building picture by applying the Reflected Bevel, White picture style. Change the color to Tan, Accent color 1 Dark. Resize the picture.

9. Change the document properties, as specified by your instructor. Save the presentation using the file name, Lab 5-3 XYZ Corporation.

10. Save Slide 3 as a .jpg image with the file name, Lab 5-3 XYZ-Sanjai Rukah.

11. Save the presentation using the Package for CD feature. Name the CD XYZ Corporation.

12. Submit the revised PowerPoint file, the Slide 3 .jpg file, and the CD in the format specified by your instructor.

(a) Slide 1

(b) Slide 2

Figure 5–86

(c) Slide 3 (Revised Slide 1)

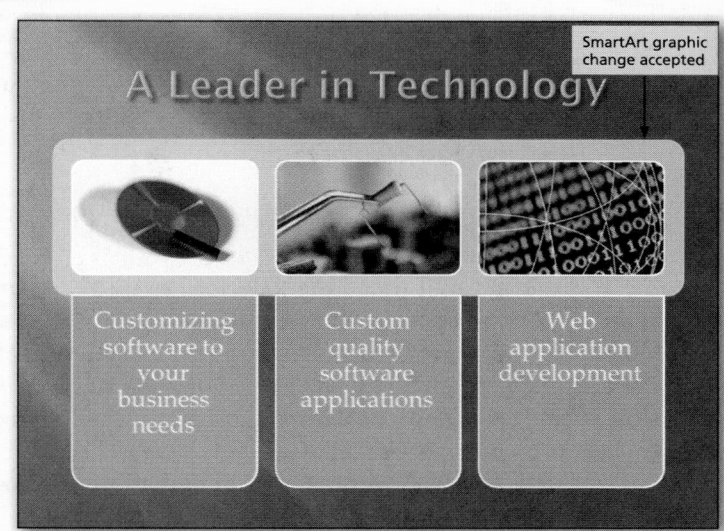

(d) Slide 4 (Revised Slide 2)

(e) Slide 5 (Inserted Slide 3)

Figure 5–86 (Continued)

Cases and Places

Apply your creative thinking and problem-solving skills to design and implement a solution.

Note: To complete these assignments, you will be required to use the Data Files for Students. See the inside back cover of this book for instructions on downloading the Data Files for Students, or contact your instructor for information about accessing the required files.

As you design the presentations, remember to use the 7 × 7 rule: a maximum of seven words on a line and a maximum of seven lines on one slide.

1: Designing and Creating a Presentation about Interior Design

Academic

For an assignment in your Interior Design class, you must put together a slide presentation showing a variety of home interior designs. Create a presentation to show at least two examples of living rooms, bedrooms, kitchens, and dining rooms. Apply at least three objectives found at the beginning of this chapter to develop the presentation. Use the file, Home Interior Design, located on the Data Files for Students and insert at least two pictures from each slide. Use pictures from Office.com if they are appropriate for this topic. Insert and modify comments, set slide size, and select a presentation resolution. Add a header and footer with your name included. Be sure to check spelling. Save the presentation in a previous PowerPoint format.

2: Designing and Creating a Presentation about Fishing

Personal

You and your friends have decided to take a summer fishing trip. You volunteered to find the best fishing spots. You have found several destinations, and you want to relay the information to your friends. Use at least three objectives found at the beginning of this chapter to develop the presentation. Using the file, Fishing Spots, located on the Data Files for Students, insert slides into your presentation and capture part of a screen using screen clipping. Add comments to the presentation. Encrypt the presentation with a password and create a digital signature. Be sure to check spelling. Save an individual slide and save the presentation in the PowerPoint 97-2003 format.

3: Designing and Creating a Presentation about Moving

Professional

You are employed at a moving company. Your manager has asked you to develop a presentation to promote the business and show the many services your company provides. He wants you to give customers some hints for making their moving experience a little easier. You create a presentation using at least three of the pictures in the file, Moving, located on the Data Files for Students. Insert comments so you can share your thoughts with your boss. Create two similar presentations and compare and combine the presentations. Be certain to check spelling. Save the file as a slide show so that when your manager opens the file, it displays automatically as a slide show. Package the presentation for storage on a compact disc.

6 | Navigating Presentations Using Hyperlinks and Action Buttons

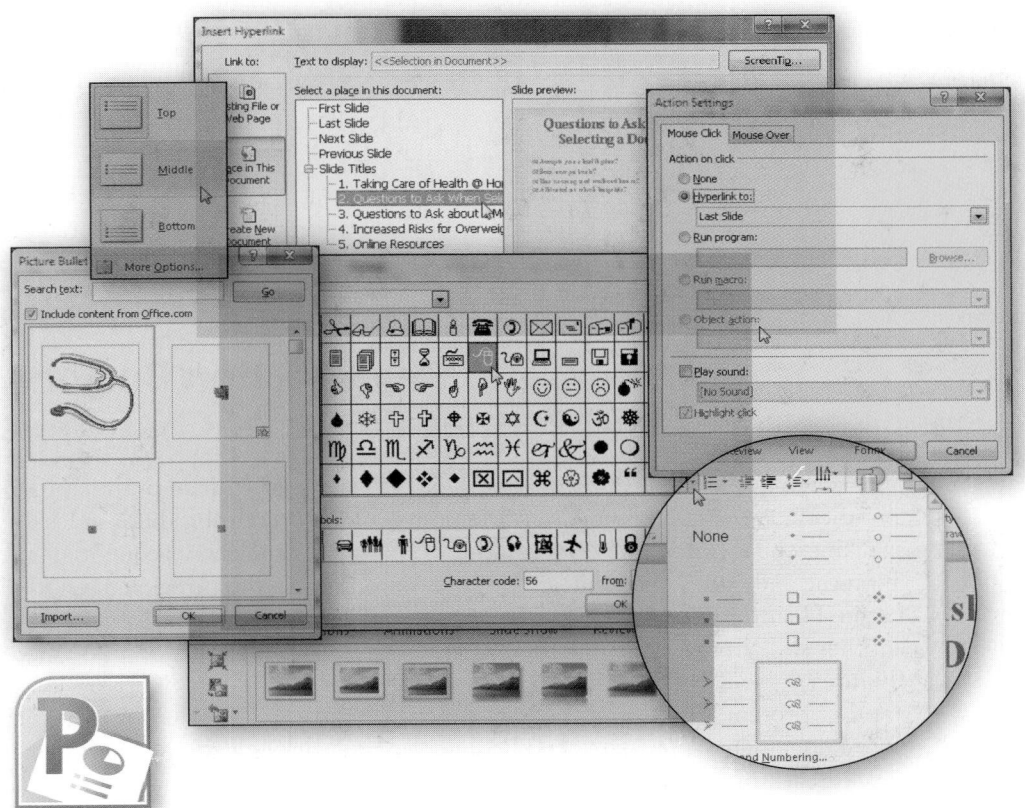

Objectives

You will have mastered the material in this chapter when you can:

- Create a presentation from a Microsoft Word outline
- Add hyperlinks to slides and objects
- Hyperlink to other Microsoft Office documents
- Add action buttons and action settings
- Display guides to position slide elements

- Set placeholder margins
- Create columns in a placeholder
- Change paragraph line spacing
- Format bullet size and color
- Change bullet characters to pictures and numbers
- Hide slides

6 | Navigating Presentations Using Hyperlinks and Action Buttons

BTW

Using Outlines to Organize Thoughts
Two types of outlines can help you get and stay organized. As you plan a speech, a scratch outline is a type of rough sketch of possible major points you would like to make and the order in which they might appear. Once you determine your material and the sequence of topics, you can develop a formal outline to arrange your thoughts in multiple levels of major and supporting details.

Introduction

Many writers begin composing reports and documents by creating an outline. Others review their papers for consistency by saving the document with a new file name, removing all text except the topic headings, and then saving the file again. An outline created in Microsoft Word or another word-processing program works well as a shell for a PowerPoint presentation. Instead of typing text in PowerPoint, as you did in previous projects, you can import this outline, add visual elements such as clip art, photos, and graphical bullets, and ultimately create an impressive slide show. When delivering the presentation, you can navigate forward and backward through the slides using hyperlinks and action buttons to emphasize particular points, to review material, or to address audience concerns.

BTW

Organizing with Sections
One of PowerPoint 2010's new features can help you organize presentations composed of dozens of slides. You can create logical sections, which are groups of related slides, and then customize and give them unique names to help identify their content or purpose. While giving a presentation, you can jump to a particular section. You also can print the slides in a specific section.

Project — Presentation with Action Buttons, Hyperlinks, and Formatted Bullet Characters

Speakers may elect to begin creating their presentations with an outline (Figure 6–1a) and then add formatted bullets and columns. When presenting these slides during a speaking engagement, they can run their PowerPoint slides nonsequentially depending upon the audience's needs and comprehension. Each of the three pictures on the Home Health title slide (Figure 6–1b on page PPT 332) branches, or hyperlinks, to another slide in the presentation. Action buttons and hyperlinks on Slides 2, 3, and 4 (Figures 6–1c – 6–1e) allow the presenter to jump to Slide 5 (Figure 6–1f), slides in another presentation (Figures 6–1g and 6–1h on page PPT 333), or to a Microsoft Word document (Figure 6–1i). The five resources on Slide 5 are hyperlinks that display specific health-related Web sites when clicked during a presentation. The slides in the presentation have a variety of embellishments, including a two-column list on Slide 4 that provides details of the factors associated with obesity, formatted graphical bullets on Slides 2 and 5 in the shape of stethoscopes and computer mice, and a numbered list on Slide 3.

Overview

As you read through this chapter, you will learn how to create the presentation shown in Figure 6–1 by performing these general tasks:

- Open a Microsoft Word outline as a presentation.
- Insert, use, and remove hyperlinks.
- Insert and format action buttons.
- Indent and align text in placeholders.
- Create columns and adjust column spacing.
- Change and format bullet characters.
- Run a slide show with hyperlinks and action buttons.

BTW

Defining Outline Levels

Imported outlines can contain up to nine outline levels, whereas PowerPoint outlines are limited to six levels (one for the title text and five for body paragraph text). When you import an outline, all text in outline levels six through nine is treated as a fifth-level paragraph.

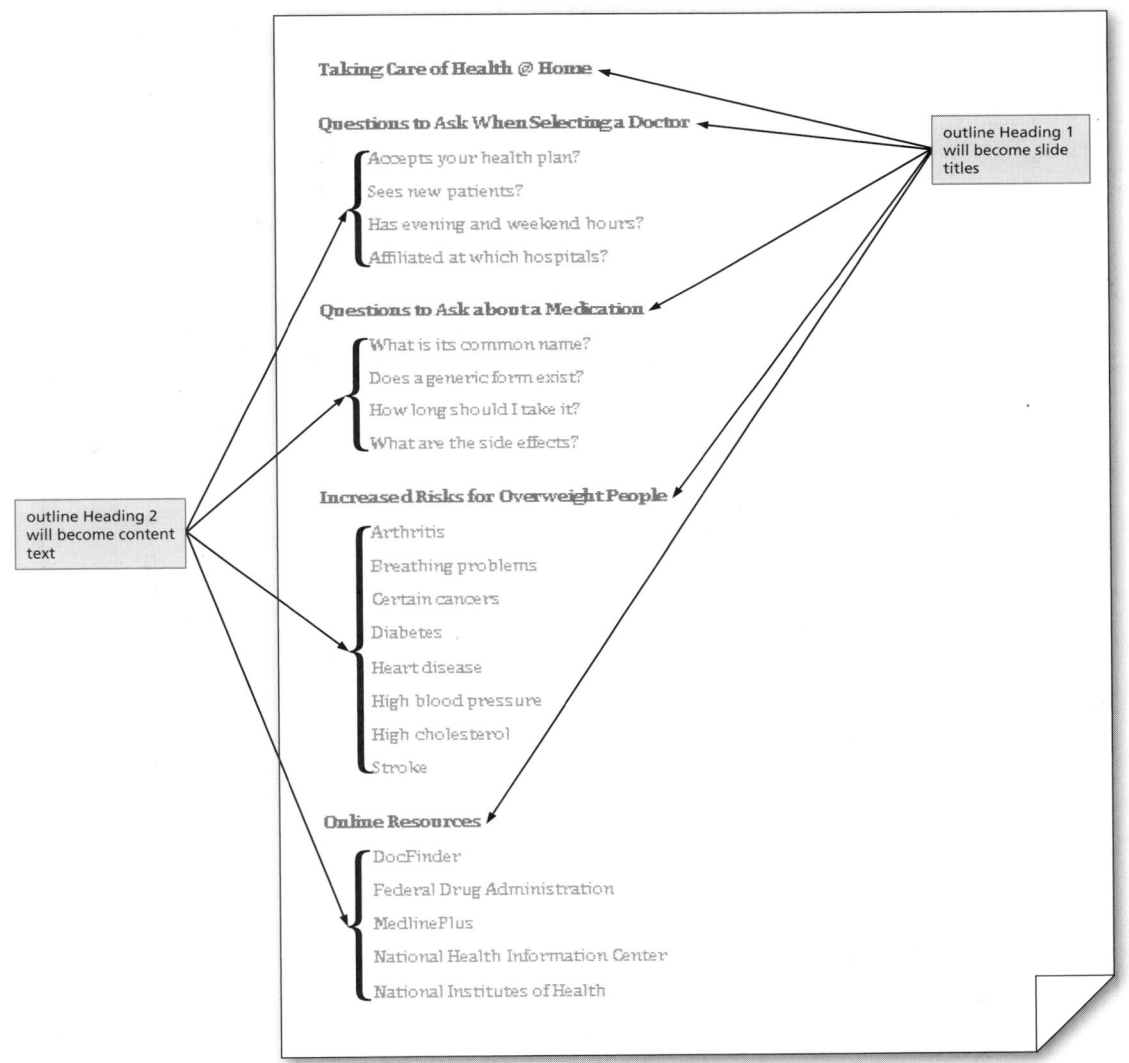

(a) Health Outline (Microsoft Word Document)

Figure 6–1

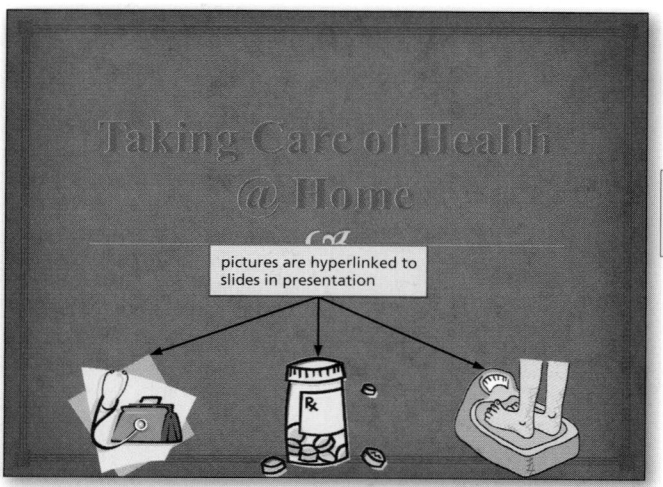

(b) Slide 1 (Title Slide with Picture Hyperlinks)

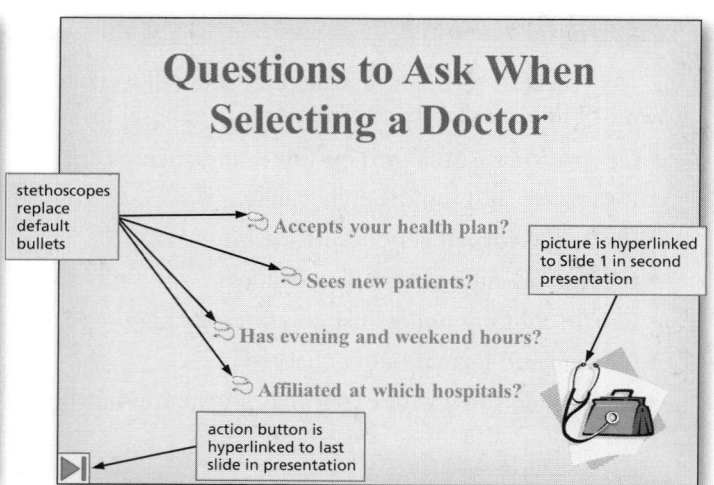

(c) Slide 2 (Centered List with Graphical Bullets)

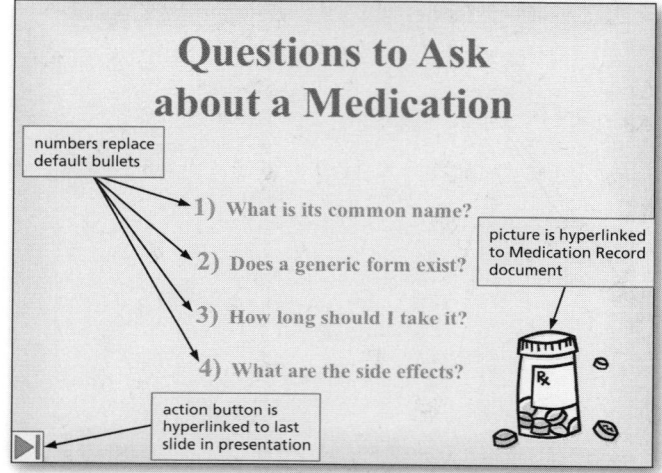

(d) Slide 3 (Numbered List)

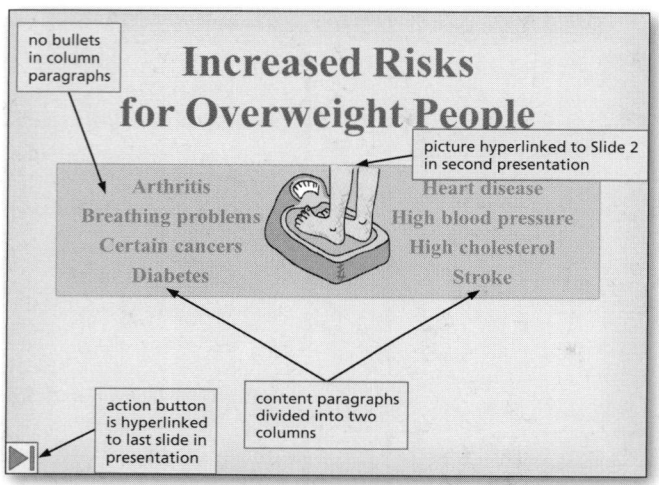

(e) Slide 4 (Two-Column List)

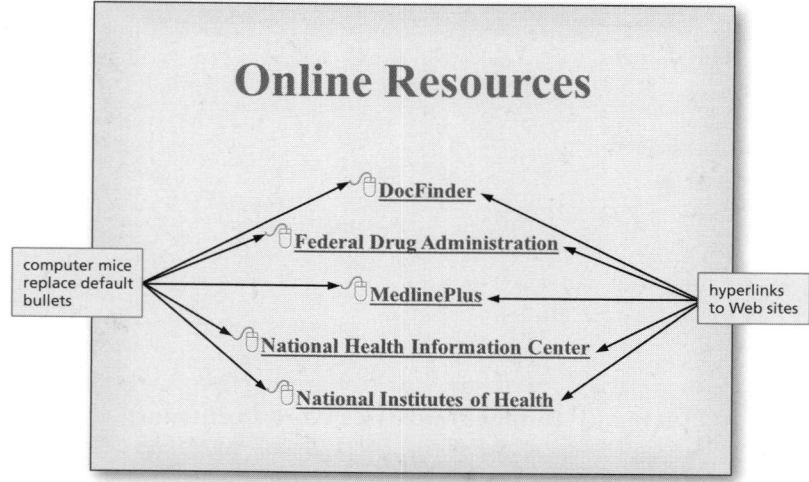

(f) Slide 5 (Hyperlinks to Web Sites)

Figure 6–1 (Continued)

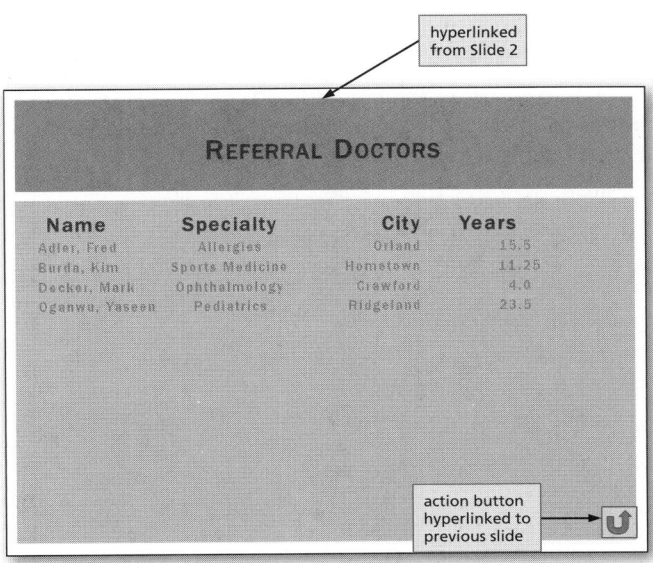

(g) Slide 1 (Hyperlinked from First Presentation)

(h) Slide 2 (Hyperlinked from First Presentation)

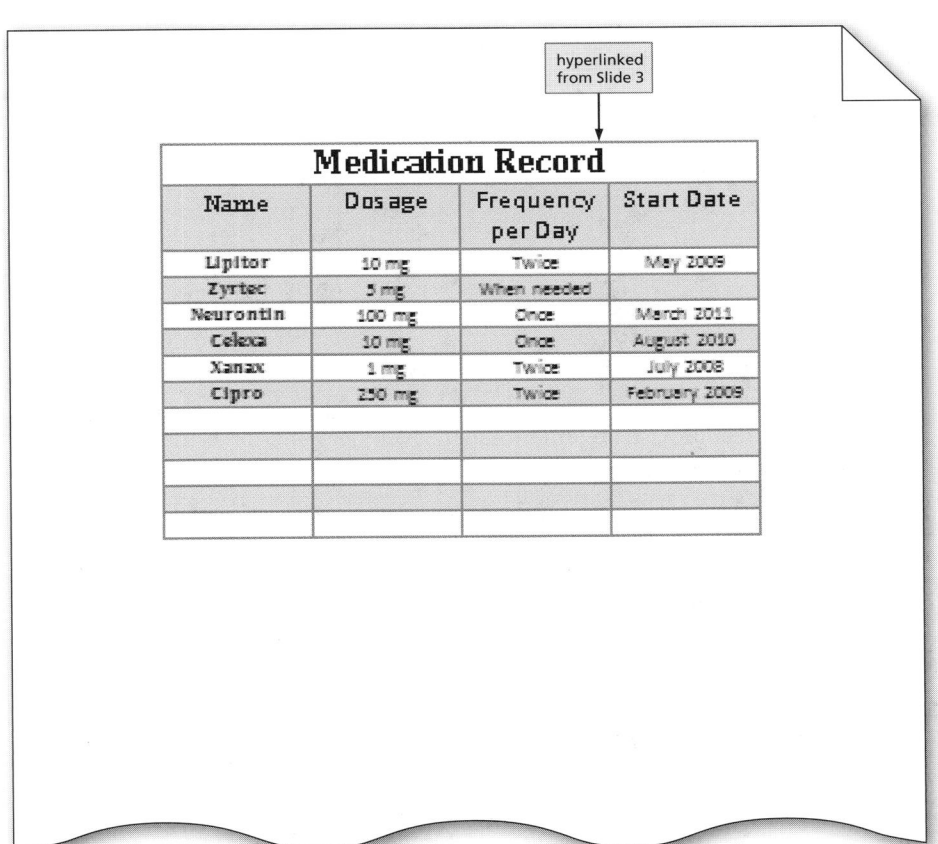

(i) Medication Record (Microsoft Word Document)

Figure 6–1 (Continued)

Plan Ahead

> **General Project Guidelines**
>
> When creating a PowerPoint presentation, the actions you perform and the decisions you make will affect the appearance and characteristics of the finished document. As you create a presentation with illustrations, such as the project shown in Figure 6–1 on pages PPT 331 through PPT 333, you should follow these general guidelines:
>
> 1. **Think threes.** Many aspects of our lives are grouped in threes: sun, moon, stars; reduce, reuse, recycle; breakfast, lunch, dinner. Your presentation and accompanying presentation likewise can be grouped in threes: introduction, body, and conclusion.
>
> 2. **Choose outstanding hyperlink images or text.** Make the hypertext graphics or letters large so a speaker is prompted to click them easily during a speaking engagement.
>
> 3. **Customize action buttons for a unique look.** The icons on the action buttons indicate their functions, but you also can add clip art, pictures, and other graphic elements to add interest or make the button less obvious to your viewers.
>
> 4. **Be mindful of prepositional phrases.** A preposition at the end of a title or a bulleted line is disconcerting to audience members. For example, if you say, "This is something I am thinking about," or "Retiring soon is something I dream of," your audience could be waiting for you to continue your thought.
>
> 5. **Consider the audience's interests.** Audience members desire to hear speeches and view presentations that benefit them in some way based on their personal needs. A presenter, in turn, must determine the audience's physical and psychological needs and then tailor the presentation to fit each speaking engagement.
>
> When necessary, more specific details concerning the above guidelines are presented at appropriate points in the chapter. The chapter also will identify the actions performed and decisions made regarding these guidelines during the creation of the presentation shown in Figure 6–1.

BTW

Widening the Tabs Pane
The Outline and Slides tabs display an icon when the pane becomes narrow. If the Outline tab is hidden, widen the pane by dragging the right border. Work in Outline view when you want to make global edits, get an overview of the presentation, change the sequence of bullets or slides, or apply formatting changes.

Creating a Presentation from a Microsoft Word 2010 Outline

An outline created in Microsoft Word or another word-processing program works well as a shell for a PowerPoint presentation. Instead of typing text in PowerPoint, you can import this outline, add visual elements such as clip art, pictures, and graphical bullets, and ultimately create an impressive slide show.

To Start PowerPoint

To begin this presentation, you will open a file located on the Data Files for Students. See the inside back cover of this book for instructions on downloading the Data Files for Students, or contact your instructor for more information about accessing the required files. If you are using a computer to step through the project in this chapter and you want your screens to match the figures in this book, you should change your screen's resolution to 1024 × 768.

The following step starts PowerPoint.

 Start PowerPoint. If necessary, maximize the PowerPoint window.

Converting Documents for Use in PowerPoint

PowerPoint can produce slides based on an outline created in Microsoft Word, another word-processing program, or a Web page if the text was saved in a format that PowerPoint can recognize. Microsoft Word 2010 and 2007 files use the **.docx** file extension in their file names. Text originating in other word-processing programs for later use with PowerPoint should be saved in Rich Text Format (.rtf) or plain text (.txt). Web page documents that use an HTML extension (.htm or .html) also can be imported.

PowerPoint automatically opens Microsoft Office files, and many other types of files, in the PowerPoint format. The **Rich Text Format (.rtf)** file type is used to transfer formatted documents between applications, even if the programs are running on different platforms, such as Windows and Macintosh. When you insert a Word or Rich Text Format document into a presentation, PowerPoint creates an outline structure based on heading styles in the document. A Heading 1 in a source document becomes a slide title in PowerPoint, a Heading 2 becomes the first level of content text on the slide, a Heading 3 becomes the second level of text on the slide, and so on.

If the original document contains no heading styles, PowerPoint creates an outline based on paragraphs. For example, in a .docx or .rtf file, for several lines of text styled as Normal and broken into paragraphs, PowerPoint turns each paragraph into a slide title.

To Open a Microsoft Word Outline as a Presentation

The text for the Home Health presentation is contained in a Microsoft Word 2010 file. The following steps open this Microsoft Word outline as a presentation located on the Data Files for Students.

1
- With your USB flash drive connected to one of the computer's USB ports, open the Backstage view and then click the Open command in the Backstage view to display the Open dialog box.
- If necessary, navigate to the PowerPoint folder on your USB flash drive (Open dialog box) so that you can open the Health Outline file in that location.
- Click the File Type arrow to display the File Type list (Figure 6–2).

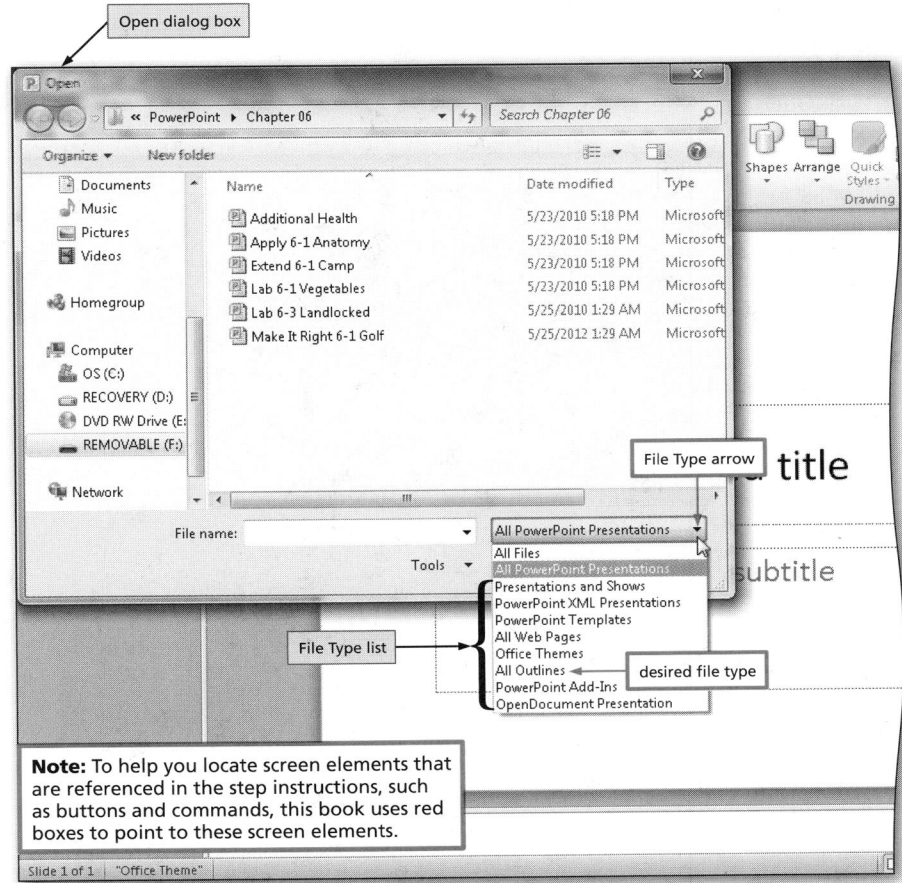

Figure 6–2

- Click All Outlines to select this file type.

- Click Health Outline to select the file (Figure 6–3).

Q&A

What if the file is not on a USB flash drive?

Use the same process, but select the drive containing the file.

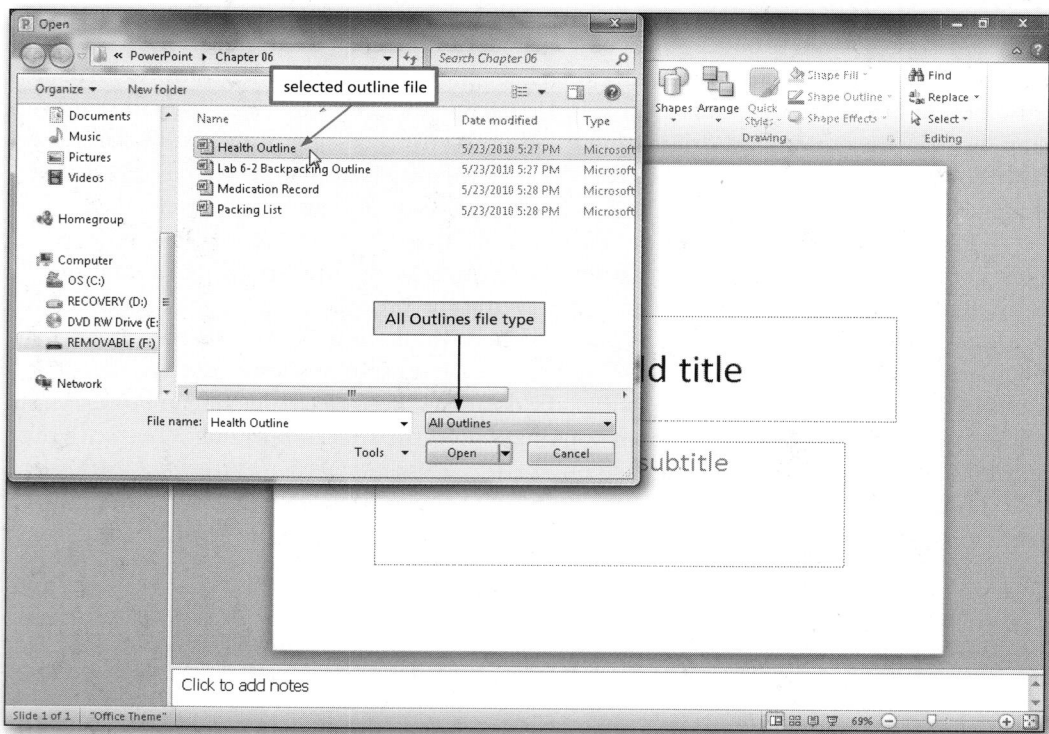

Figure 6–3

- Click Open to create the five slides in your presentation (Figure 6–4).

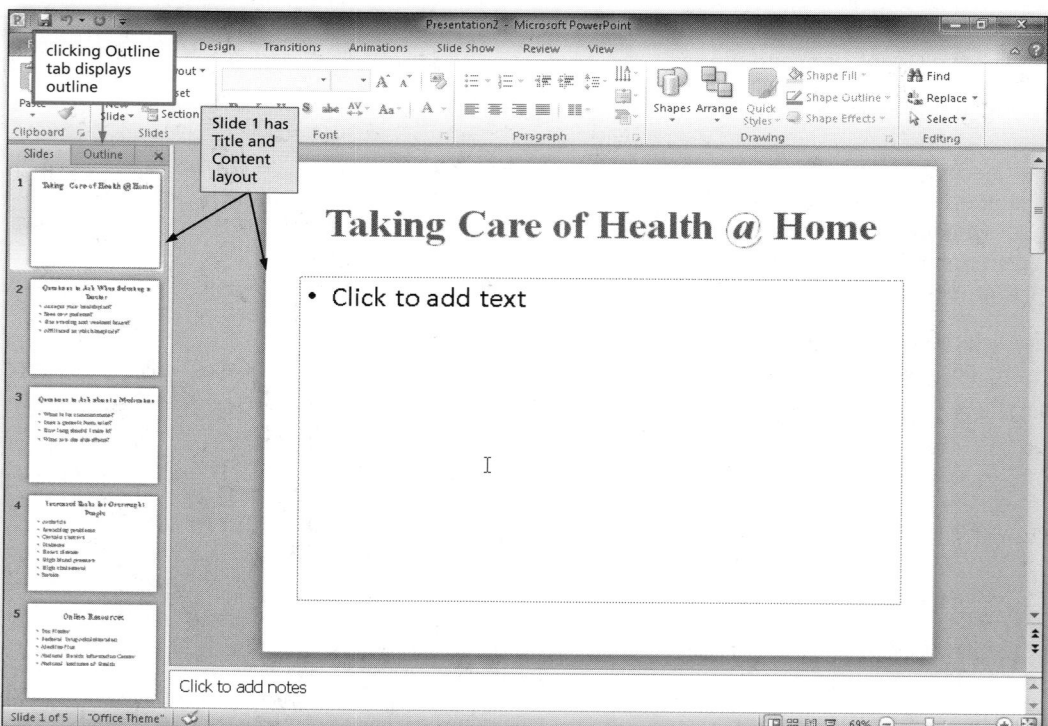

Figure 6–4

4

- Click the Outline tab in the Tabs pane to view the outline (Figure 6–5).

Q&A Do I need to see the text as an outline in the Outline tab now?

No, but sometimes it is helpful to view the content of your presentation in this view before looking at individual slides.

Q&A Do I need to change to the Slides tab to navigate between slides?

No, you can click the slide number in Outline view to navigate to slides.

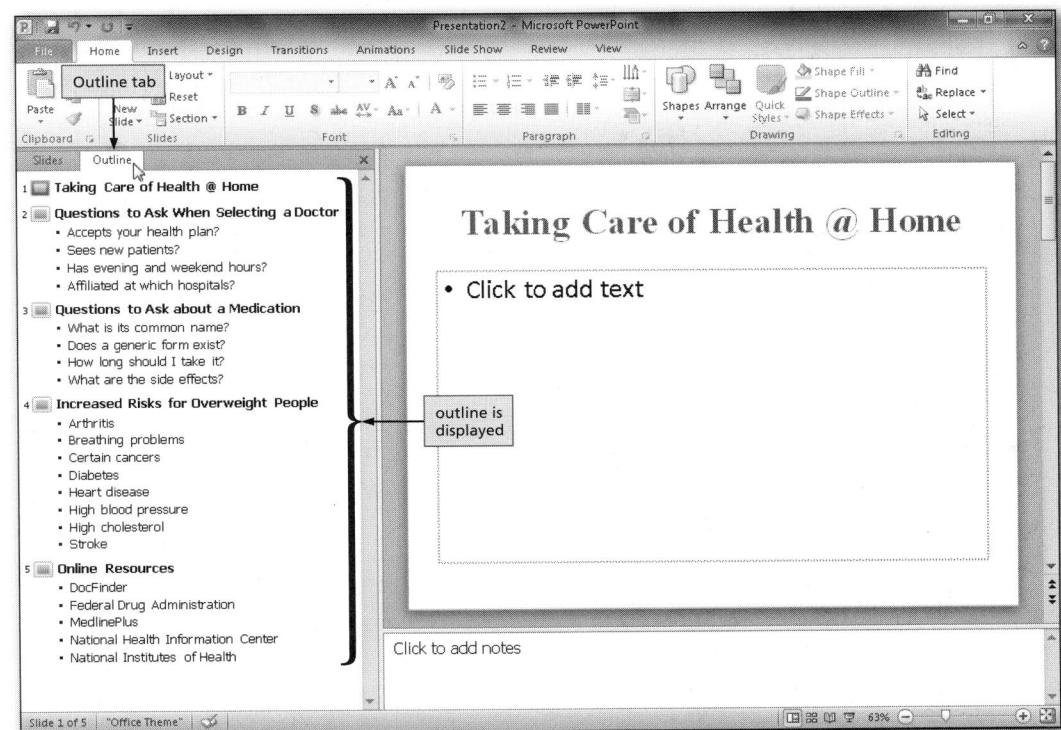

Figure 6–5

Other Ways

1. Click New Slide button arrow (Home tab | Slides group), click Slides from Outline, click File Type arrow, click All Outlines, click Health Outline, click Open button

To Change the Slide 1 Layout, Apply a Document Theme, and Change the Theme Colors

When you created the new slides from the Word outline, PowerPoint applied the Title and Text slide layout to all slides. You want to apply the Title Slide layout to Slide 1 to introduce the presentation. The following steps change the Slide 1 slide layout.

1 With Slide 1 displaying, click the Layout button (Home tab | Slides group) and then click Title Slide to apply that layout to Slide 1.

2 Apply the Hardcover document theme.

3 Change the presentation theme colors to Clarity.

Plan Ahead

Think threes.
Speechwriters often think of threes as they plan their talks and PowerPoint presentations. The number three is considered a symbol of balance, as in an equilateral triangle that has three 60-degree angles, the three meals we eat daily, or the three parts of our day — morning, noon, and night. A speech generally has an introduction, a body, and a conclusion. Audience members find balance and harmony seeing three objects on a slide, so whenever possible, plan visual components on your slides in groups of three.

BTW

The Ribbon and Screen Resolution
PowerPoint may change how the groups and buttons within the groups appear on the Ribbon, depending on the computer's screen resolution. Thus, your Ribbon may look different from the ones in this book if you are using a screen resolution other than 1024 × 768.

To Insert and Size Pictures

Health-related pictures will serve two purposes in this presentation. First, they will add visual interest and cue the viewers to the three topics of doctor visits, medications, and weight-control measures. The three pictures are located on the Data Files for Students. Later in this chapter, you will position the pictures in precise locations. The following steps insert and then size the three pictures on Slides 1, 2, 3, and 4.

1 On the title slide, insert the pictures called Stethoscope, Prescription, and Scale, which are located on the Data Files for Students, in the area below the title text.

2 Display the Picture Tools Format tab and then resize the three pictures so that they are approximately 2″ × 2″ (Figure 6–6).

3 Copy the stethoscope picture to the lower-right corner of Slide 2, the prescription picture to the lower-right corner of Slide 3, and the scale picture to the lower-right corner of Slide 4.

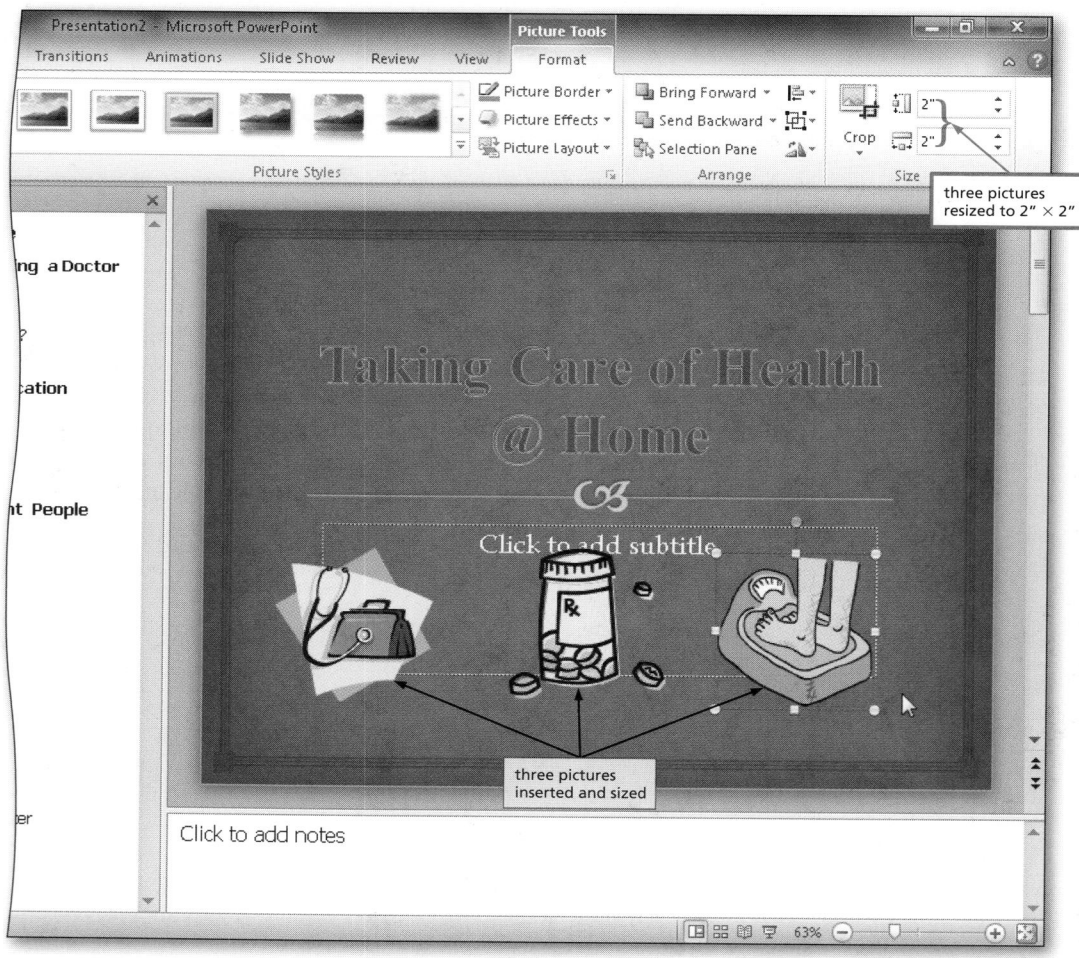

Figure 6–6

To Save the Presentation

With all five slides created, you should save the presentation. The following steps save the slides.

1 Click the Save button on the Quick Access Toolbar to display the Save As dialog box.

2 Save the file on your USB flash drive using **Home Health** as the file name.

> **Choose outstanding hyperlink images or text.**
> Good speakers are aware of their audiences and know their speech material well. They have rehearsed their presentations and know where the hypertext is displayed on the slides. During a presentation, however, they sometimes need to divert from their planned material. Audience members may interrupt with questions, the room may not have optimal acoustics or lighting, or the timing may be short or long. It is helpful, therefore, to make the slide hyperlinks as large and noticeable to speakers as possible. The presenters can glance at the slide and receive a visual cue that it contains a hyperlink. They then can decide whether to click the hyperlink to display a Web page.

Plan Ahead

Adding Hyperlinks and Action Buttons

Speakers sometimes skip from one slide to another in a presentation in response to audience needs or timing issues. In addition, if Internet access is available, they may desire to display a Web page during a slide show to add depth to the presented material and to enhance the overall message. When presenting the Home Health slide show and discussing medical information on Slides 1, 2, 3, or 4, a speaker might want to skip to the last slide in the presentation and then access a Web site for further specific health information. Or the presenter may be discussing information on Slide 5 and want to display Slide 1 to begin discussing a new topic.

One method of jumping nonsequentially to slides is by clicking a hyperlink or an action button on a slide. A **hyperlink**, also called a **link**, connects one slide to a Web page, another slide, a custom show consisting of specific slides in a presentation, an e-mail address, or a file. A hyperlink can be any element of a slide. This includes a single letter, a word, a paragraph, or any graphical image such as a clip, picture, shape, or graph.

BTW

BTWs
For a complete list of the BTWs found in the margins of this book, visit the PowerPoint 2010 BTW Web page (scsite.com/ppt2010/btw).

To Add a Hyperlink to a Picture

In the Home Health presentation, each piece of clip art on Slide 1 will hyperlink to another slide in the same presentation. When you point to a hyperlink, the mouse pointer becomes the shape of a hand to indicate the text or object contains a hyperlink. The following steps create the first hyperlink for the stethoscope picture on Slide 1.

- Display Slide 1, select the stethoscope picture, and then display the Insert tab.

- Click the Insert Hyperlink button (Insert tab | Links group) to display the Insert Hyperlink dialog box.

- If necessary, click the Place in This Document button in the Link to area.

- Click 2. Questions to Ask When Selecting a Doctor in the 'Select a place in this document' area (Insert Hyperlink dialog box) to select and display a preview of this slide (Figure 6–7).

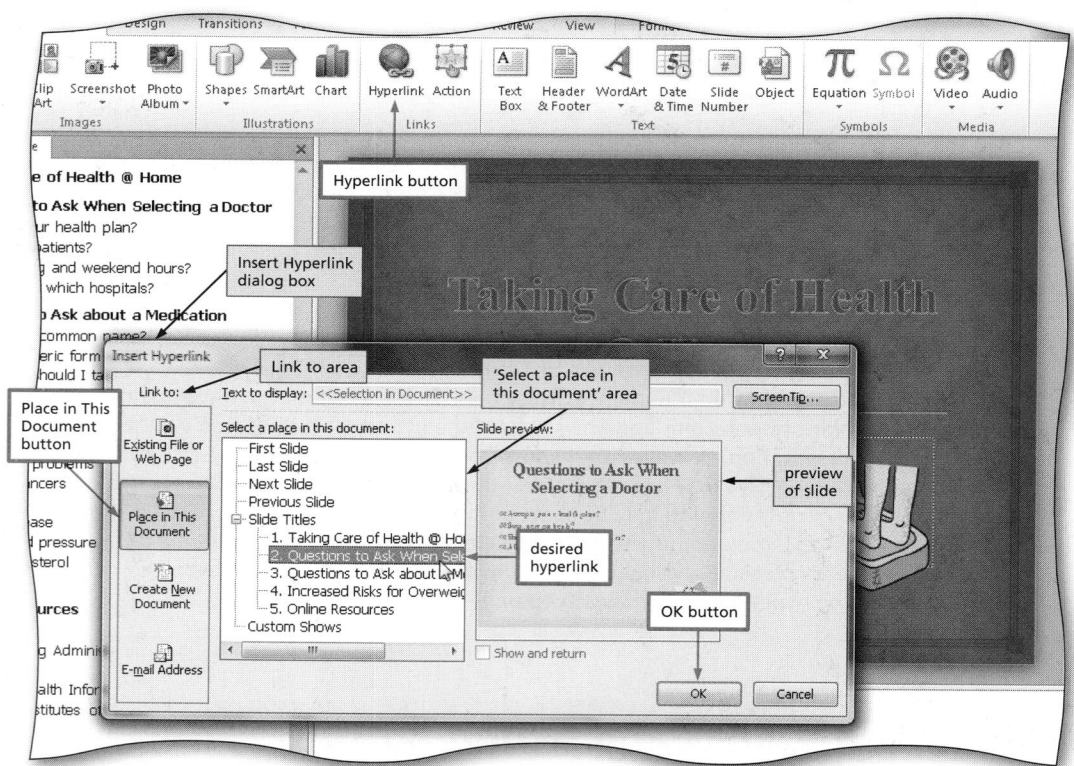

Figure 6–7

Q&A Could I also have selected the Next Slide link in the 'Select a place in this document' area?

Yes. Either action would create the hyperlink to Slide 2.

- Click the OK button to insert the hyperlink.

Q&A I clicked the stethoscope picture, but Slide 2 did not display. Why?

Hyperlinks are active only when you run the presentation, not when you are creating it in Normal, Reading, or Slide Sorter view.

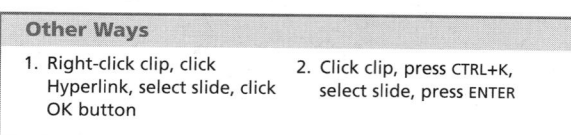

Other Ways	
1. Right-click clip, click Hyperlink, select slide, click OK button	2. Click clip, press CTRL+K, select slide, press ENTER

To Add a Hyperlink to the Remaining Slide 1 Pictures

The hyperlink for the stethoscope clip is complete. The next task is to create the hyperlinks for the other two pictures on Slide 1.

1 On Slide 1, click the prescription picture.

2 Click the Insert Hyperlink button and then click 3. Questions to Ask about a Medication to select this slide as the hyperlink. Click the OK button.

3 Click the scale picture, click the Insert Hyperlink button, and then click 4. Increased Risks for Overweight People. Click the OK button.

To Add a Hyperlink to a Paragraph

On Slide 5, each second-level paragraph will be a hyperlink to a health organization's Web page. If you are connected to the Internet when you run the presentation, you can click each of these paragraphs, and your Web browser will open a new window and display the corresponding Web page for each hyperlink. By default, hyperlinked text is displayed with an underline and in a color that is part of the color scheme. The following steps create a hyperlink for the first paragraph.

1
- Display Slide 5 and then double-click the second-level paragraph that appears first, DocFinder, to select the text.

- Display the Insert Hyperlink dialog box and then click the Existing File or Web Page button in the Link to area (Figure 6–8).

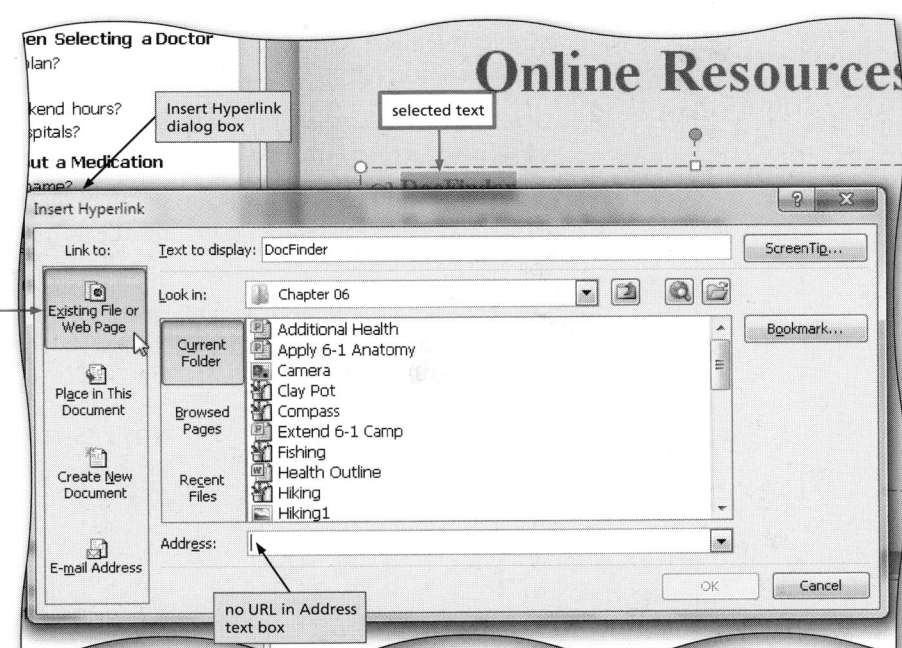

Figure 6–8

2
- Type **www.docboard.org** in the Address text box (Figure 6–9).

3
- Click the OK button to insert the hyperlink.

Q&A Why is this paragraph now underlined and displaying a new font color?

The default style for hyperlinks is underlined text. The Clarity built-in theme hyperlink color is Blue, so PowerPoint formatted the paragraph to that color automatically.

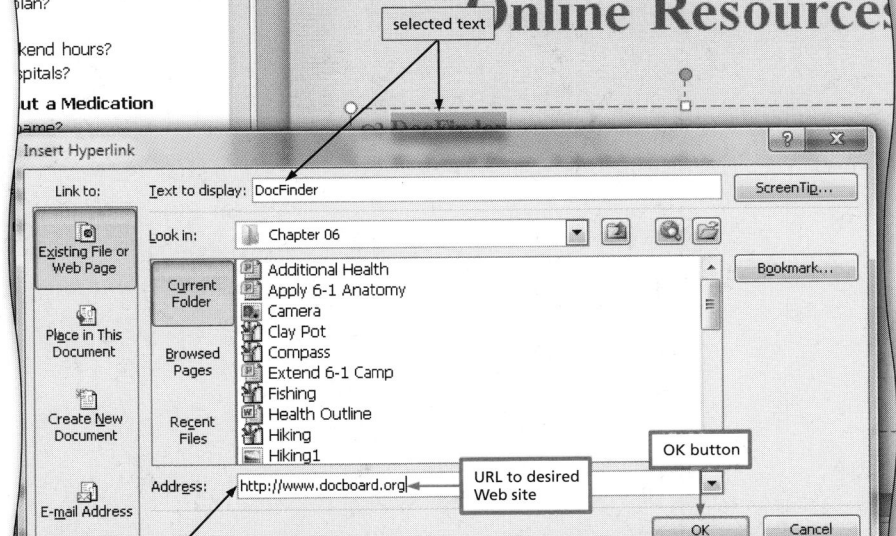

Figure 6–9

Other Ways
1. Right-click selected text, click Hyperlink, type address, click OK button   2. Select text, press CTRL+K, type address, press ENTER

To Add a Hyperlink to the Remaining Slide 5 Paragraphs

The hyperlink for the second-level paragraph that appears first is complete. The next task is to create the hyperlinks for the other second-level paragraphs on Slide 5.

1 Triple-click the second-level paragraph that appears second, Federal Drug Administration, to select this text.

2 Display the Insert Hyperlink dialog box and then type `www.fda.gov` in the Address text box. Click the OK button.

3 Select the third paragraph, MedlinePlus, display the Insert Hyperlink dialog box, type `www.medlineplus.gov` in the Address text box, and then click the OK button.

4 Select the fourth paragraph, National Health Information Center, display the Insert Hyperlink dialog box, type `www.health.gov/nhic` in the Address text box, and then click the OK button.

5 Select the fifth paragraph, National Institutes of Health, display the Insert Hyperlink dialog box, type `www.nih.gov` in the Address text box, and then click the OK button (Figure 6–10).

Q&A

I clicked the hyperlink, but the Web page did not display. Why?

Hyperlinks are active only when you run the presentation, not when you are creating it in Normal, Reading, or Slide Sorter view.

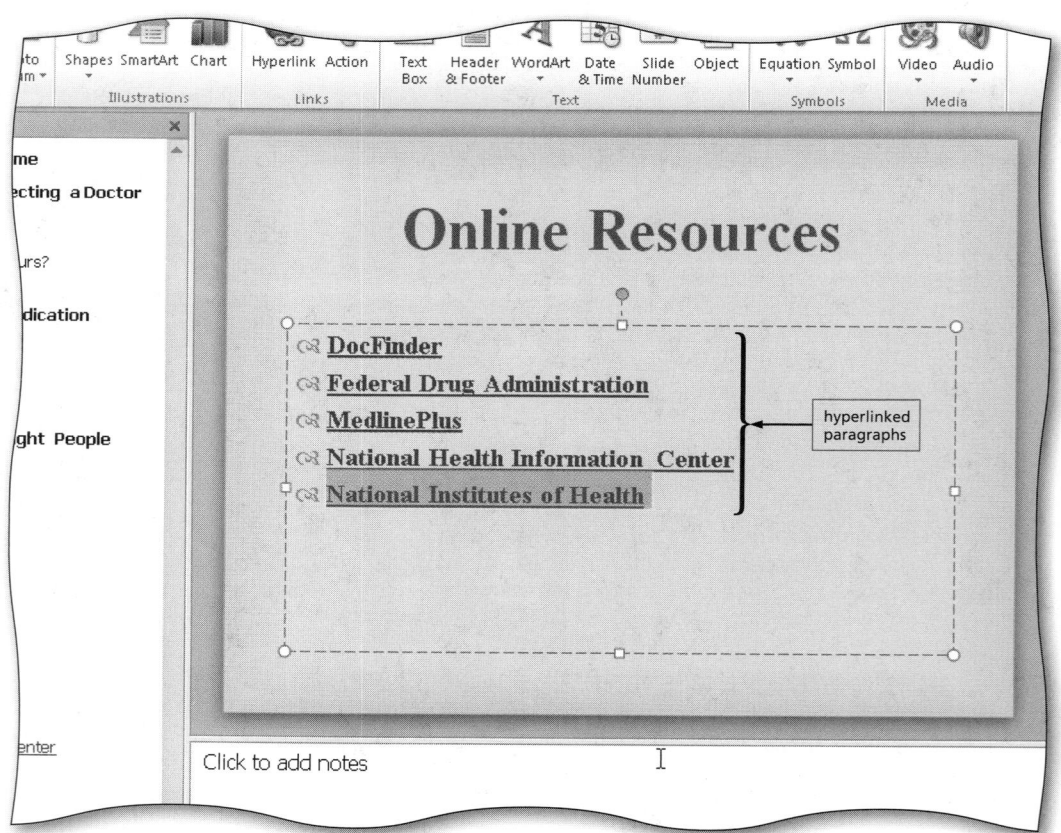

Figure 6–10

Customize action buttons for a unique look.
PowerPoint's built-in action buttons have icons that give the presenter an indication of their function. Designers frequently customize these buttons with images related to the presentation. For example, in a grocery store presentation, the action buttons may have images of a coupon, dollar sign, and question mark to indicate links to in-store coupons, sale items, and the customer service counter. Be creative when you develop your own presentations and attempt to develop buttons that have specific meanings for your intended audience.

**Plan
Ahead**

Action Buttons

PowerPoint provides 12 built-in action buttons. An **action button** is a particular type of hyperlink that has a built-in function. Each action button performs a specific task, such as displaying the next slide, providing help, giving information, or playing a sound. In addition, the action button can activate a hyperlink that allows users to jump to a specific slide in the presentation. The picture on the action button indicates the type of function it performs. For example, the button with the house icon represents the home slide, or Slide 1. To achieve a personalized look, you can customize an action button with a photograph, piece of clip art, logo, text, or any graphic you desire. Table 6–1 describes each of the built-in action buttons.

BTW
Q&As
For a complete list of the Q&As found in many of the step-by-step sequences in this book, visit the PowerPoint 2010 Q&A Web page (scsite.com/ppt2010/qa).

Table 6–1 Built-In Action Buttons

Button Name	Image	Description
Back or Previous		Returns to the previous slide displayed in the same presentation.
Forward or Next		Jumps to the next slide in the presentation.
Beginning		Jumps to Slide 1. This button performs the same function as the Home button.
End		Jumps to the last slide in the presentation.
Home		Jumps to Slide 1. This button performs the same function as the Beginning button.
Information		Does not have any predefined function. Use it to direct a user to a slide with details or facts.
Return		Returns to the previous slide displayed in any presentation. For example, you can place it on a hidden slide or on a slide in a custom slide show and then return to the previous slide.
Movie		Does not have any predefined function. You generally would use this button to jump to a slide with an inserted video clip.
Document		Opens a program other than PowerPoint. For example, you can open Microsoft Word or Microsoft Excel and display a page or worksheet.
Sound		Does not have any predefined function. You generally would use this button to jump to a slide with an inserted audio clip.
Help		Does not have any predefined function. Use it to direct a user to a slide with instructions or contact information.
Custom		Does not have any predefined function. You can add a clip, picture, graphic, or text and then specify a unique purpose.

To Insert an Action Button

In the Home Health slide show, the action buttons on Slides 2, 3, and 4 hyperlink to the last slide, Slide 5. You will insert and format the action button shape on Slide 2 and copy it to Slides 3 and 4, and then create a link to Slide 5 so that you will be able to display Slide 5 at any point in the presentation by clicking the action button. When you click the action button, a sound will play. This sound will vary depending upon which slide is displayed. The following steps insert an action button on Slide 2 and link it to Slide 5.

1

- Display Slide 2 and then click the Shapes button (Insert tab | Illustrations group) to display the Shapes gallery.

- Point to the Action Button: End shape in the Action Buttons area (fourth image) (Figure 6–11).

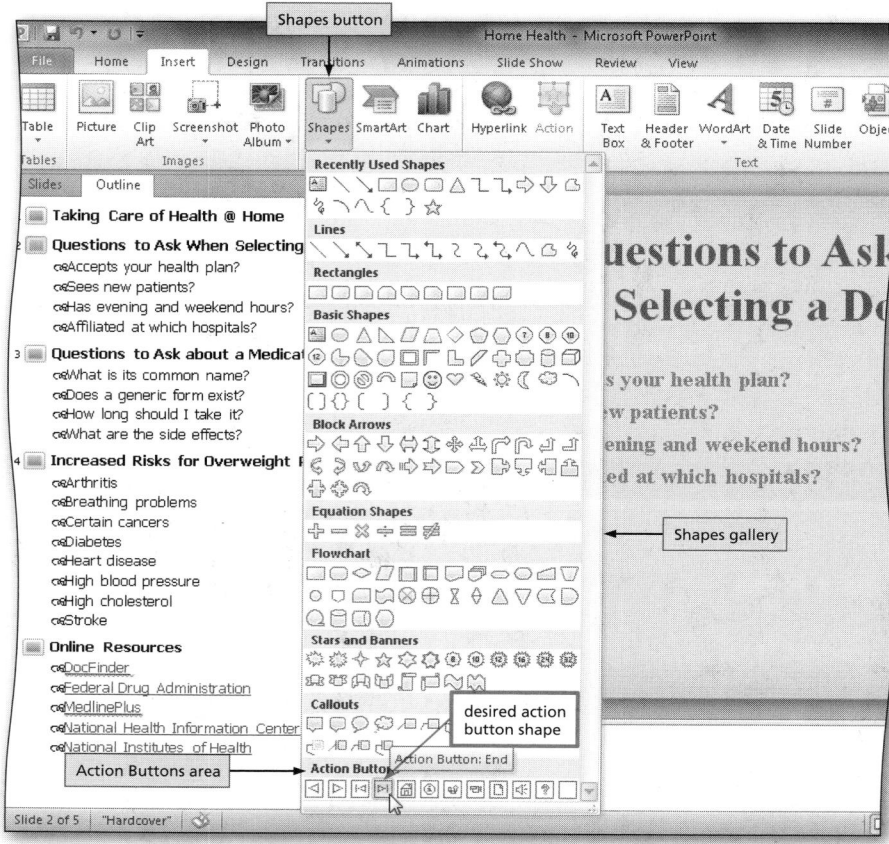

Figure 6–11

2

- Click the Action Button: End shape.

- Click the lower-left corner of the slide to insert the action button and to display the Action Settings dialog box.

- If necessary, click the Mouse Click tab (Action Settings dialog box) (Figure 6–12).

Q&A — Why is the default setting the action to hyperlink to the last slide?

The End shape establishes a hyperlink to the last slide in a presentation.

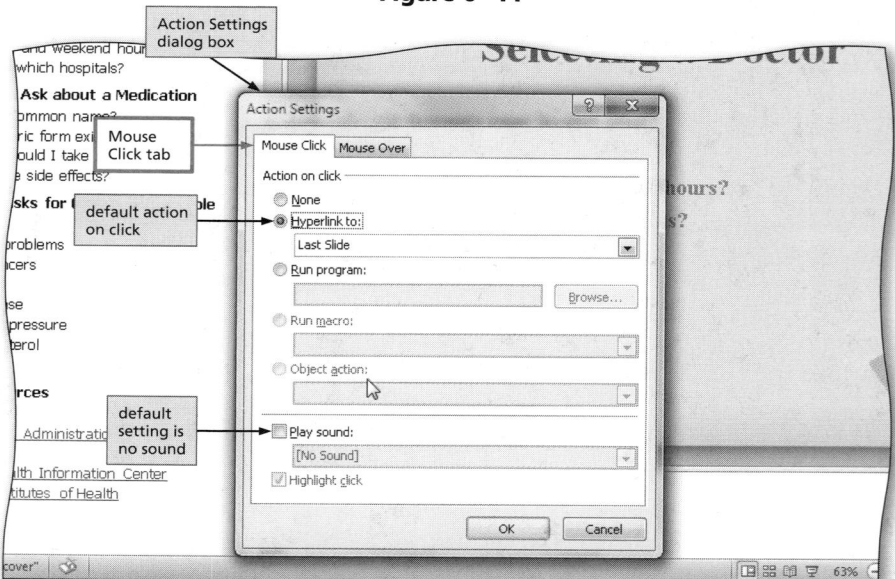

Figure 6–12

3

• Click the Play sound check box and then click the Play sound arrow to display the Play Sound list (Figure 6–13).

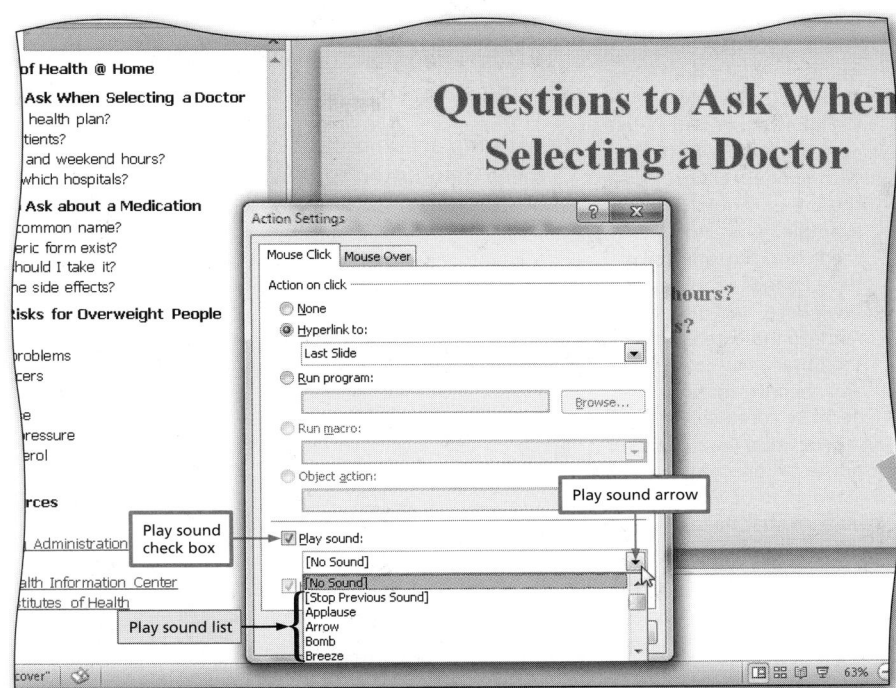

Figure 6–13

4

• Scroll down and then click Push to select that sound (Figure 6–14).

Q&A | I did not hear the sound when I selected it. Why not?

The Push sound will play when you run the slide show and click the action button.

5

• Click the OK button to apply the hyperlink setting and sound to the action button and to close the Action Settings dialog box.

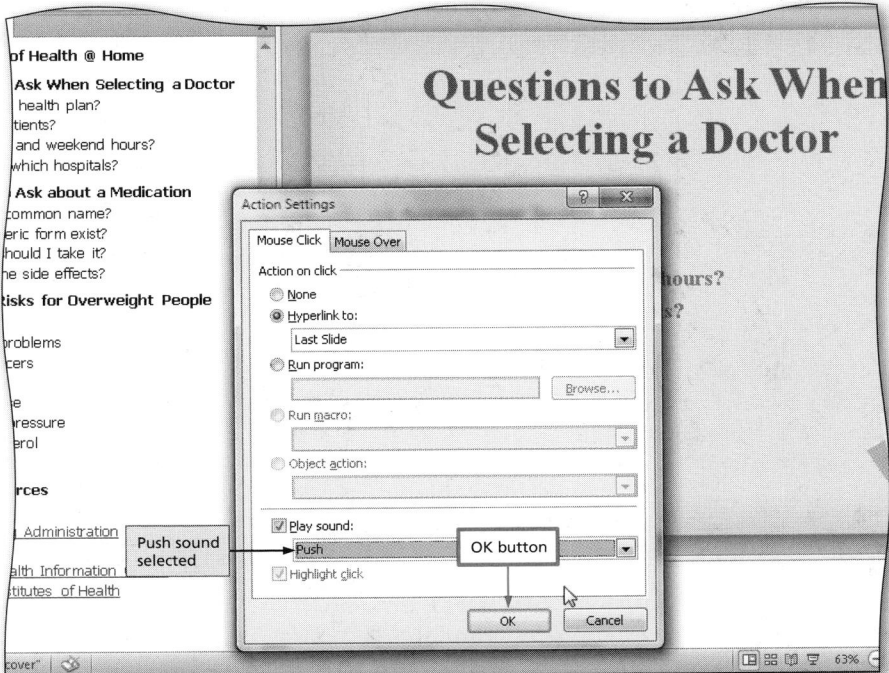

Figure 6–14

Customizing Action Buttons

This project uses one of PowerPoint's built-in action buttons. Designers frequently customize these buttons with images related to the presentation. For example, in a school the action buttons may have images of a book, silverware, and question mark to indicate links to the library, the cafeteria, and the information desk. Be creative when you develop your own presentations and attempt to develop buttons that have a specific meaning for your intended audience.

To Size an Action Button

The action button size can be decreased to make it less obvious on the slide. The following step resizes the selected action button.

1 With the action button still selected, display the Drawing Tools Format tab and then size the action button so that it is approximately 0.5" × 0.5". If necessary, move the action button to the location shown in Figure 6–15.

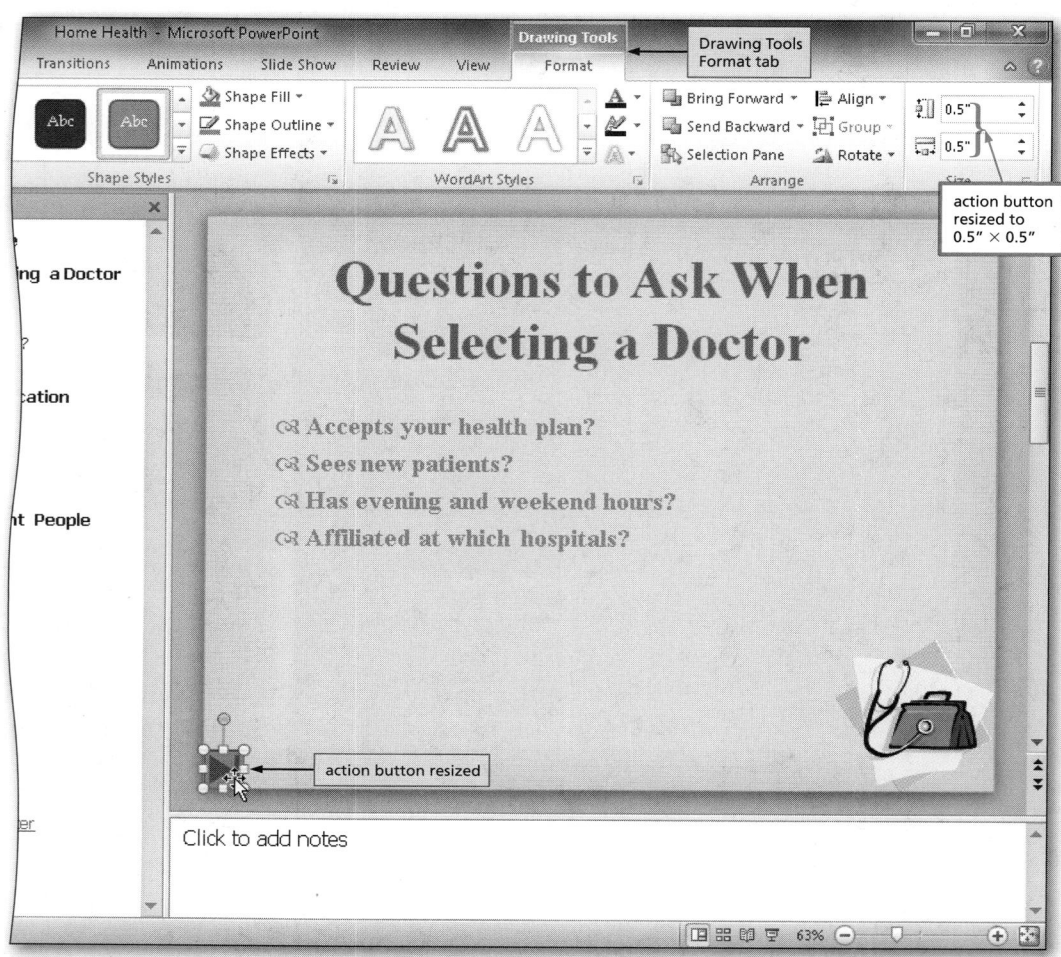

Figure 6–15

To Change an Action Button Fill Color

The action button's Gray interior color does not blend well with the light yellow border on the slide. You can select a new fill color to coordinate with the slide edges. The following steps change the fill color from Gray to Light Yellow.

1

- With the action button still selected, click the Shape Fill button arrow (Drawing Tools Format tab | Shape Styles gallery) to display the Shape Fill gallery (Figure 6–16).

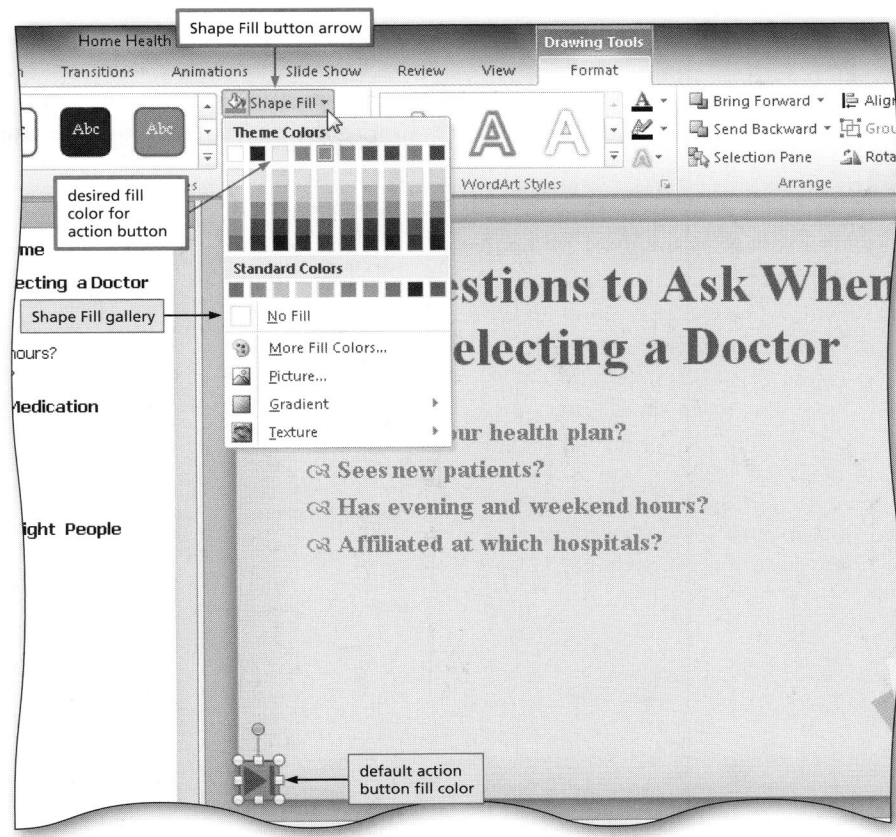

Figure 6–16

2

- Point to Light Yellow, Background 2 (third color from left in first row) to display a live preview of that fill color on the action button (Figure 6–17).

Experiment

- Point to various colors in the Shape Fill gallery and watch the fill color change in the action button.

3

- Click Light Yellow, Background 2 to apply this color to the action button.

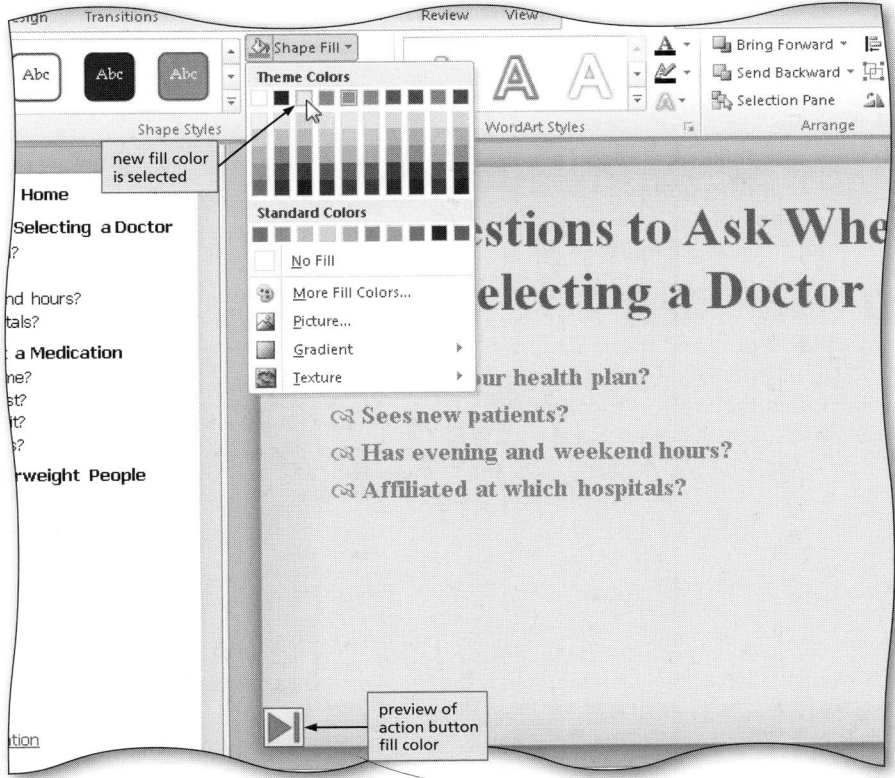

Figure 6–17

To Copy an Action Button

The Slide 2 action button is formatted and positioned correctly. You can copy this shape to Slides 3 and 4. The following steps copy the Slide 2 action button to the next two slides in the presentation.

1

- Right-click the action button on Slide 2 to display the shortcut menu (Figure 6–18).

Q&A

Why does my shortcut menu have different commands?

Depending upon where you right-clicked, you might see a different shortcut menu. As long as this menu displays the Copy command, you can use it. If the Copy command is not visible, click the slide again to display another shortcut menu.

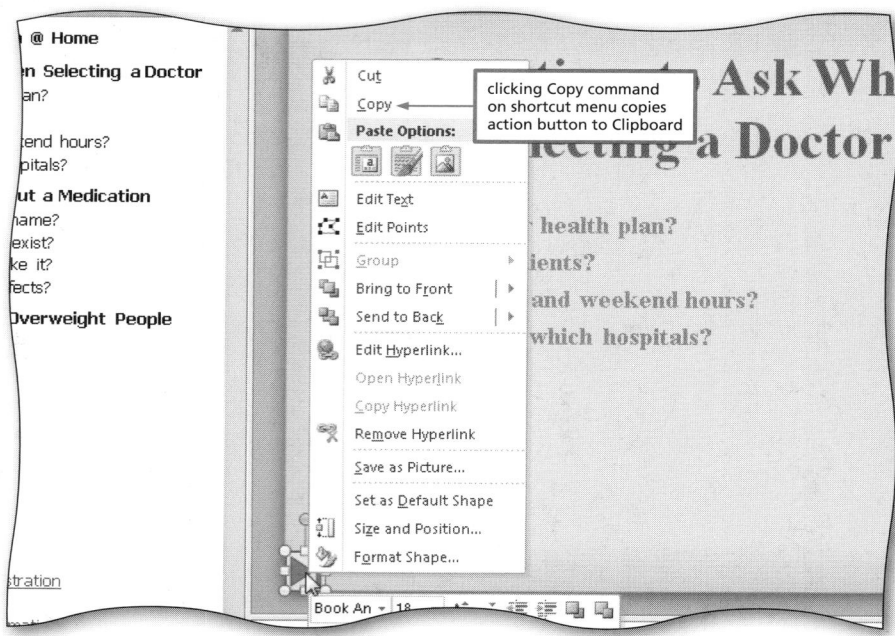

Figure 6–18

2

- Click Copy on the shortcut menu to copy the action button to the Clipboard.

- Display Slide 3 and then click the Paste button (Home tab | Clipboard group) to paste the action button in the lower-left corner of Slide 3 (Figure 6–19).

3

- Display Slide 4 and then click the Paste button to paste the action button in the lower-left corner of Slide 4.

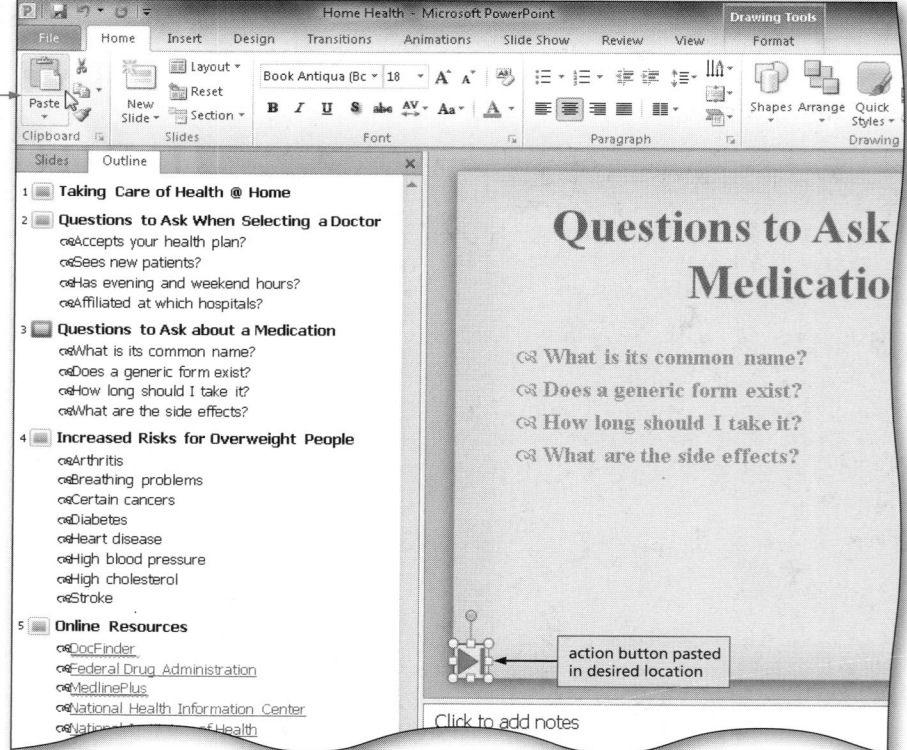

Figure 6–19

To Edit an Action Button Action Setting

When you copied the action button, PowerPoint retained the settings to hyperlink to the last slide and to play the Push sound. For variety, you want to change the sounds that play for the Slide 3 and Slide 4 action buttons. The following steps edit the Slide 3 and Slide 4 hyperlink sound settings.

- With the action button still selected on Slide 4, display the Insert tab and then click the Action button (Insert tab | Links group) to display the Action Settings dialog box.

- Click the Play sound arrow to display the Play sound menu (Figure 6–20).

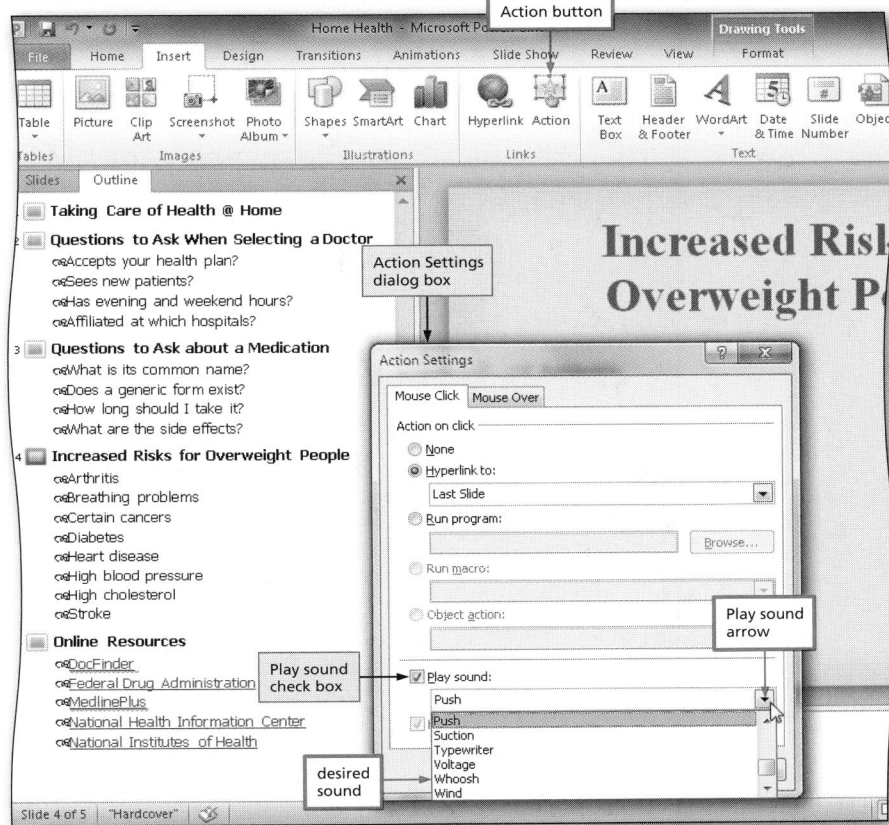

Figure 6–20

- Click Whoosh in the Play sound list to select the Whoosh sound to play when the action button is clicked (Figure 6–21).

- Click the OK button (Action Settings dialog box) to apply the new sound setting to the Slide 4 action button.

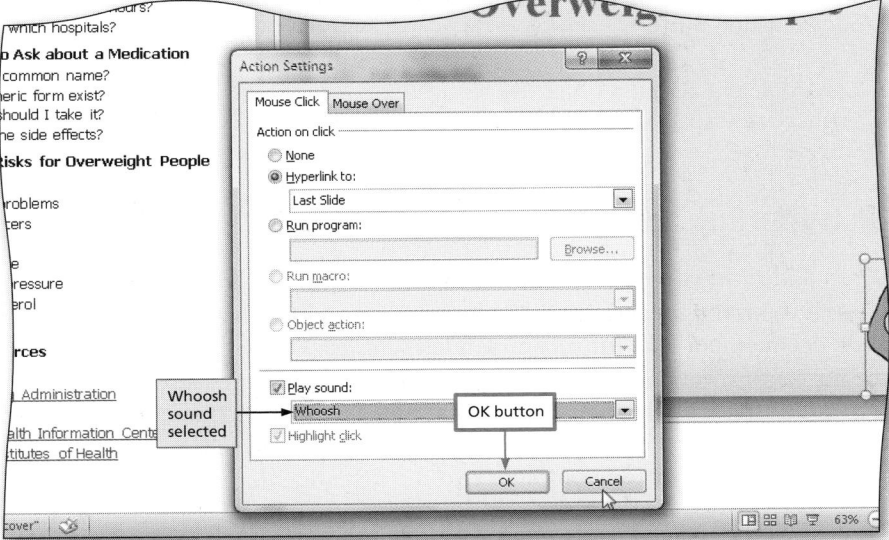

Figure 6–21

- Display Slide 3, select the action button, and then click the Action button (Insert tab | Links group) to display the Action Settings dialog box.

- Click the Play sound arrow to display the Play sound menu.

- Scroll up and then click Breeze in the Play sound list (Figure 6–22).

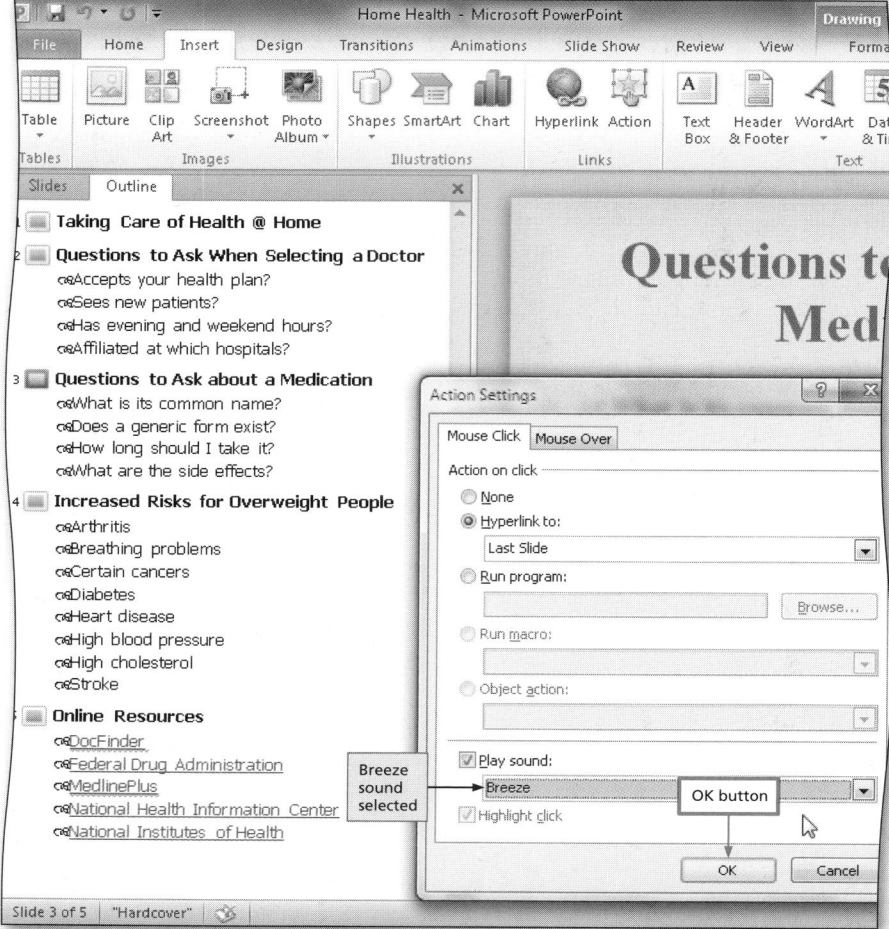

Figure 6–22

- Click the OK button (Action Settings dialog box) to apply the new sound setting to the Slide 3 action button.

To Hyperlink to Another PowerPoint File

Slide 2 in your presentation provides information for patients to ask a potential doctor. When running a presentation, the speaker may decide some useful information might be a list of referral doctors, especially if an audience member asks for recommended physicians. While hyperlinks are convenient tools to navigate through the current PowerPoint presentation or to Web pages, they also allow you to open a second PowerPoint presentation and display a particular slide in that file. The first slide in another presentation, Additional Home Health, lists details about several doctors, including their names, specialties, and number of years of practice. The following steps hyperlink the stethoscope on Slide 2 to the first slide in the second presentation.

1

- Display Slide 2 and then select the stethoscope picture.

- If necessary, display the Insert tab and then click the Action button (Insert tab | Links group) to display the Action Settings dialog box.

- Click Hyperlink to in the 'Action on click' area and then click the Hyperlink to arrow to display the Hyperlink to menu (Figure 6–23).

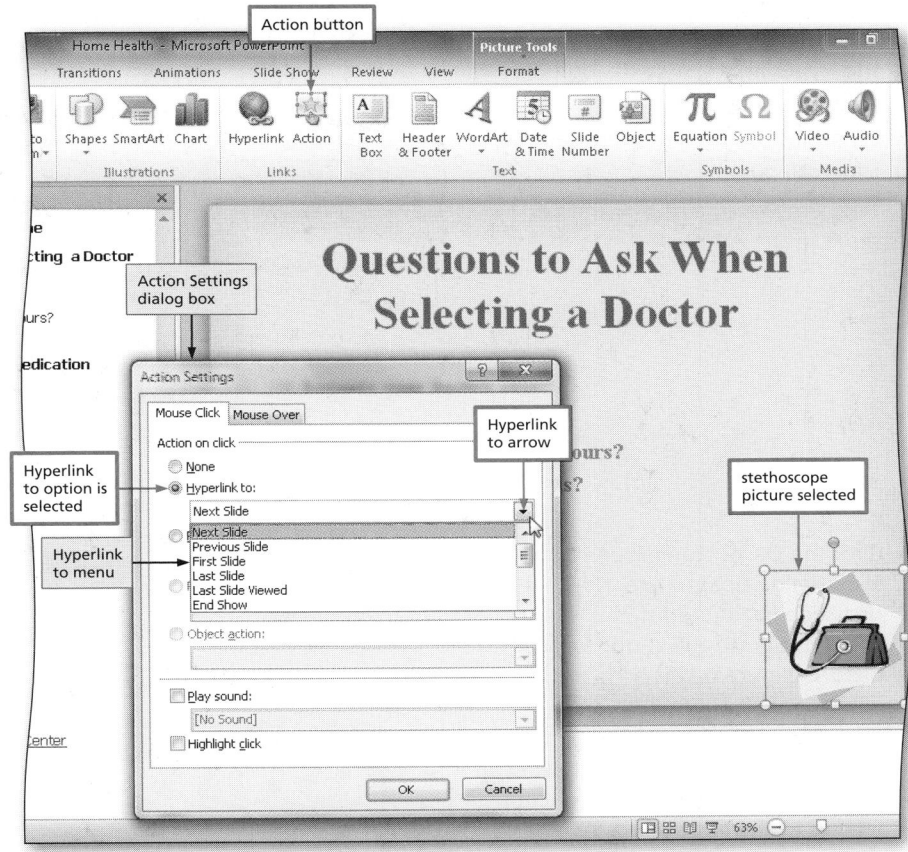

Figure 6–23

2

- Scroll down and then click Other PowerPoint Presentation to display the Hyperlink to Other PowerPoint Presentation dialog box.

- Click Additional Health to select this file as the hyperlinked presentation (Figure 6–24).

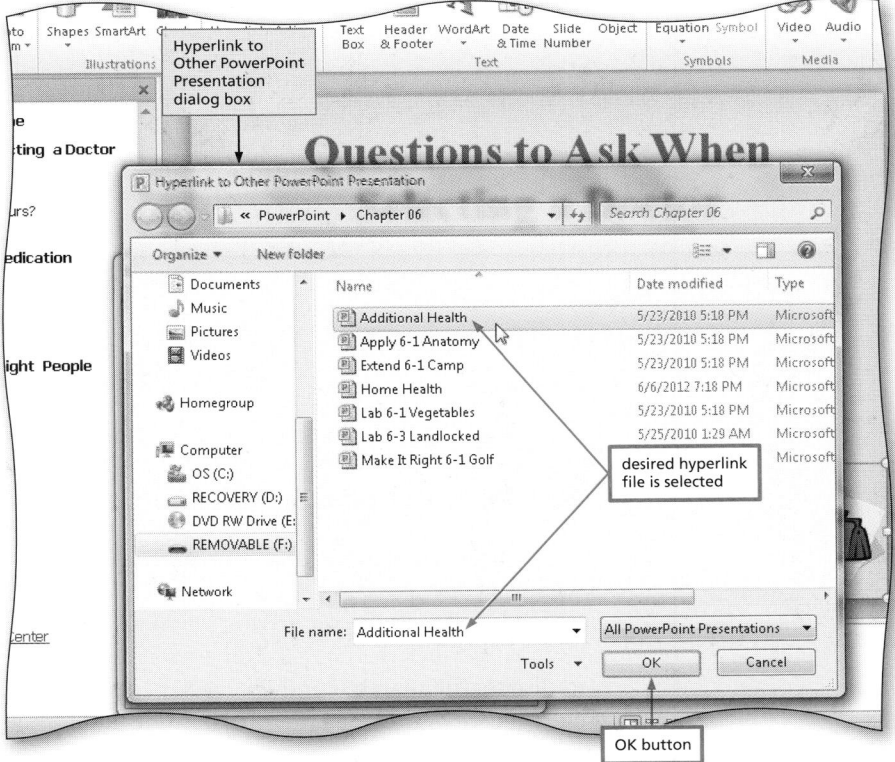

Figure 6–24

3

● Click the OK button to display the Hyperlink to Slide dialog box (Figure 6–25).

Q&A

What are the two items listed in the Slide title area?

They are the title text of the two slides in the Additional Health file.

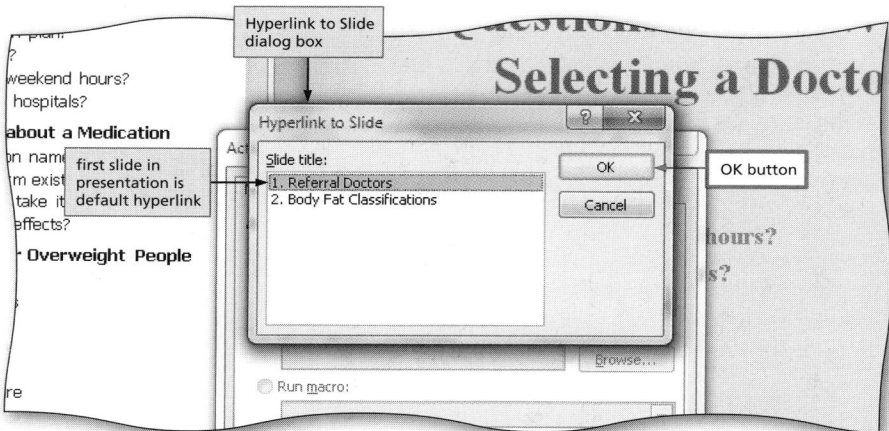

Figure 6–25

4

● Click the OK button (Hyperlink to Slide dialog box) to hyperlink the first slide in the Additional Health presentation to the stethoscope picture (Figure 6–26).

5

● Click the OK button (Action Settings dialog box) to apply the new action setting to the Slide 2 picture.

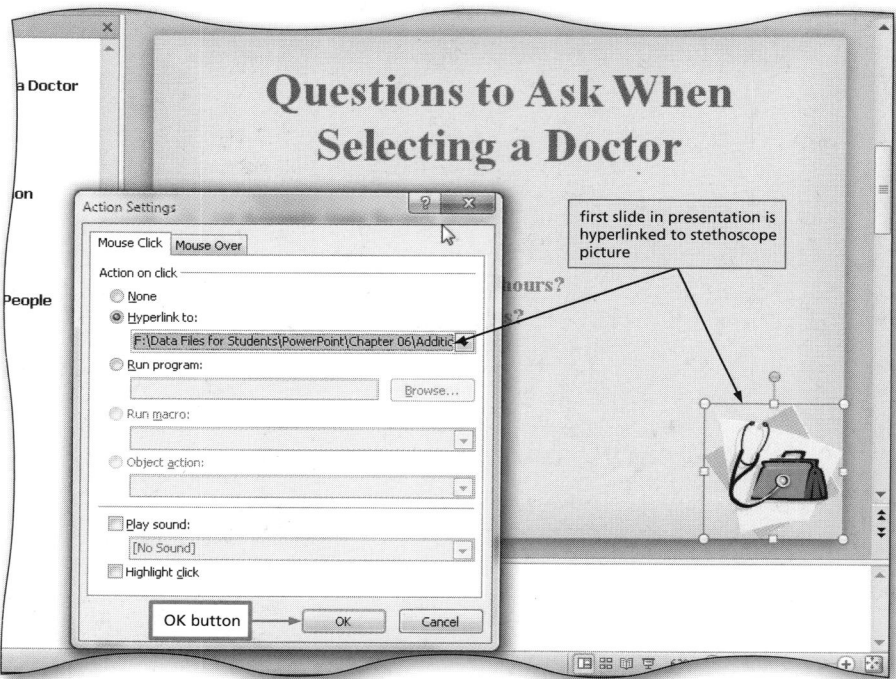

Figure 6–26

To Hyperlink to a Second Slide in Another PowerPoint File

A table on the second slide in the Additional Health presentation has information regarding the five classifications of male and female body fat. This slide might be useful to display during a presentation when a speaker is discussing the information on Slide 4, which describes the health risks associated with being overweight. If the speaker has time to discuss the material and the audience needs to know these specific body fat percentages, he could click the scale picture on Slide 4 and then hyperlink to Slide 2 in the second presentation. The following steps hyperlink Slide 4 to the second slide in the Additional Health presentation.

1 Display Slide 4, select the scale picture, and then click the Action button (Insert tab | Links group) to display the Action Settings dialog box.

2 Click Hyperlink to in the 'Action on click' area, click the Hyperlink to arrow, and then scroll down and click Other PowerPoint Presentation in the Hyperlink to menu.

3 Click Additional Health in the Hyperlink to Other PowerPoint Presentation dialog box to select this file as the hyperlinked presentation and then click the OK button.

4 Click 2. Body Fat Classifications (Hyperlink to Slide dialog box) (Figure 6–27).

5 Click the OK button (Hyperlink to Slide dialog box) to hyperlink the second slide in the Additional Health presentation to the scale picture.

6 Click the OK button (Action Settings dialog box) to apply the new action setting to the Slide 4 picture.

BTW

Verifying Hyperlinks
Always test your hyperlinks prior to giving a presentation. Web addresses change frequently, so if your hyperlinks are to Web sites, be certain your Internet connection is working, the Web sites are active, and that the content on these pages is appropriate for your viewers. If your hyperlinks direct PowerPoint to display specific slides and to open files, click the hyperlinks to verify your desired actions are followed and that the files exist.

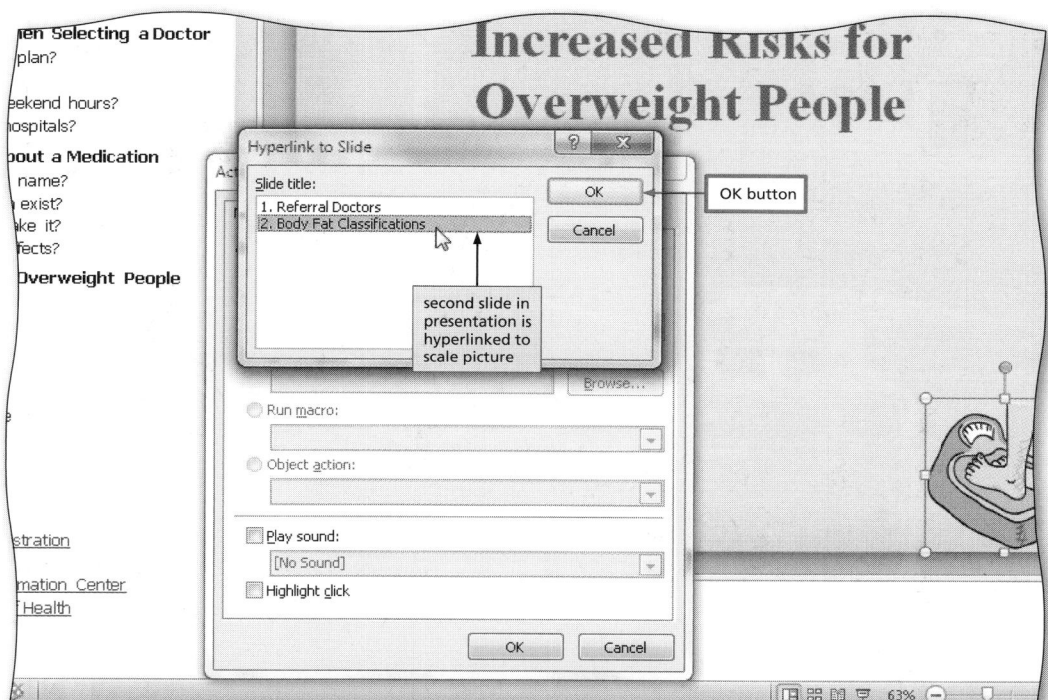

Figure 6–27

To Hyperlink to a Microsoft Word File

Doctors recommend their patients keep a current record of all prescribed and over-the-counter medications. This list should include the name of the drug, the amount taken per day, and the date when the patient started taking this medication. A convenient form for recording these details is located on the Data Files for Students. The file, Medication Record, was created using Microsoft Word, and it would be useful to display this document when discussing the information on Slide 3 of your presentation. PowerPoint allows a speaker to hyperlink to other Microsoft Office documents in a similar manner as linking to another PowerPoint file. The following steps hyperlink the prescription picture on Slide 3 to the Microsoft Word document with the file name, Medication Record.

1

- Display Slide 3, select the prescription picture, and then click the Action button (Insert tab | Links group) to display the Action Settings dialog box.

- Click Hyperlink to, click the Hyperlink to arrow to display the Hyperlink to menu, and then scroll down to the end of the Hyperlink to list (Figure 6–28).

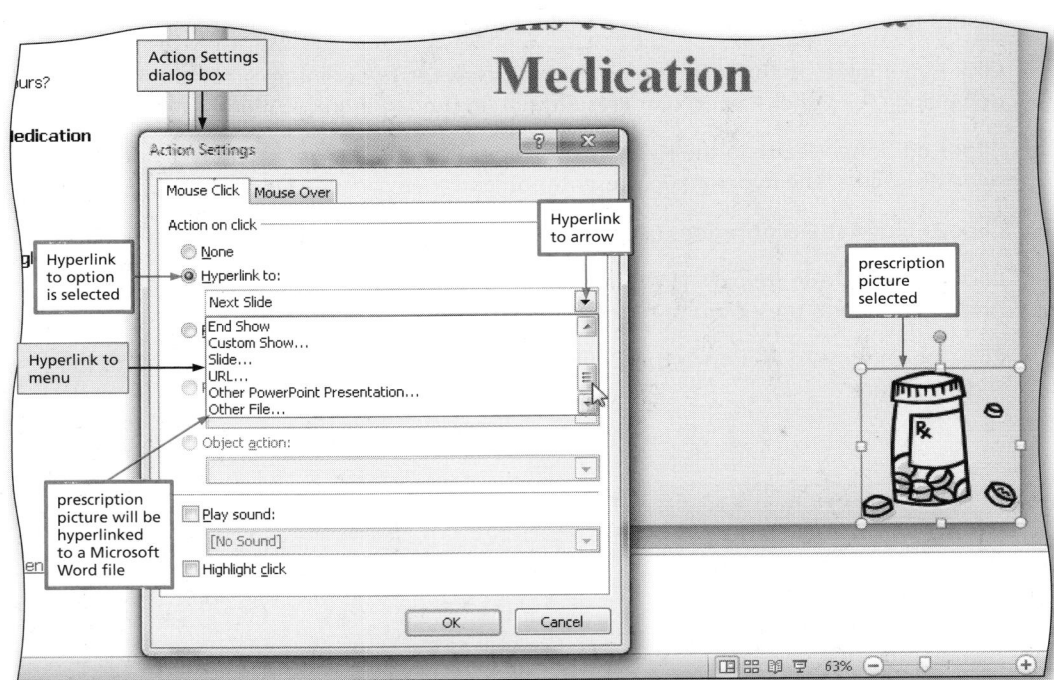

Figure 6–28

2

- Click Other File to display the Hyperlink to Other File dialog box, scroll down, and then click Medication Record to select this file as the hyperlinked document (Figure 6–29).

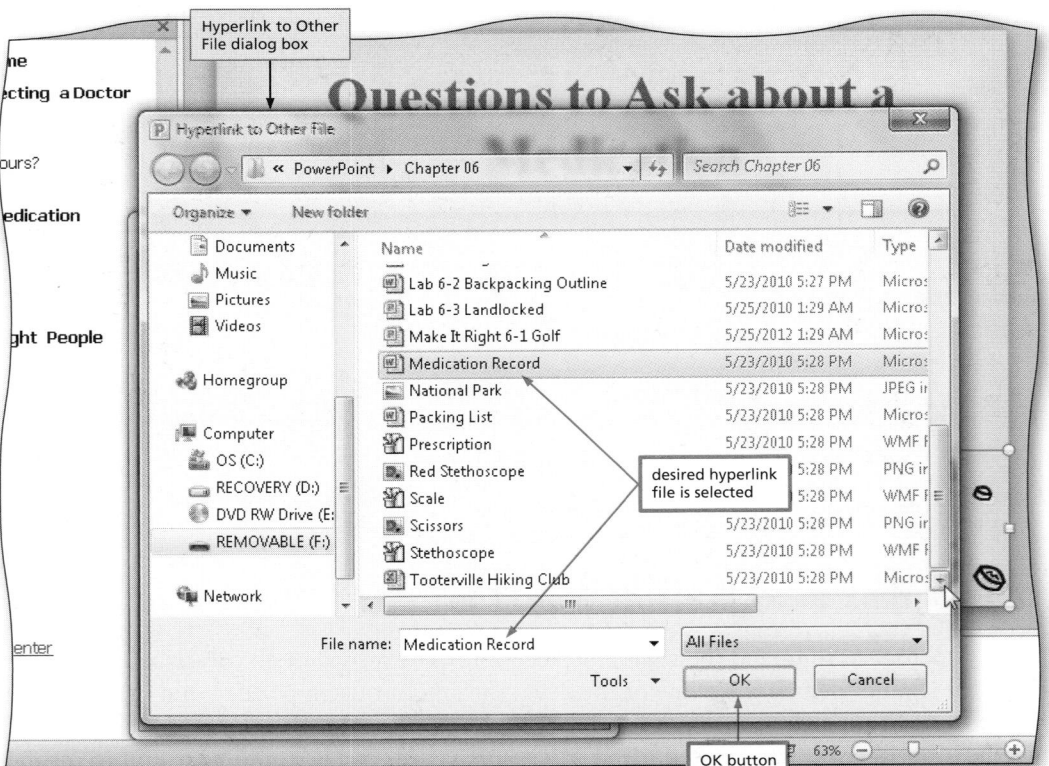

Figure 6–29

- Click the OK button (Hyperlink to Other File dialog box) to hyperlink this file to the prescription picture action button (Figure 6–30).

4

- Click the OK button (Action Settings dialog box) to apply the new action setting to the Slide 3 picture.

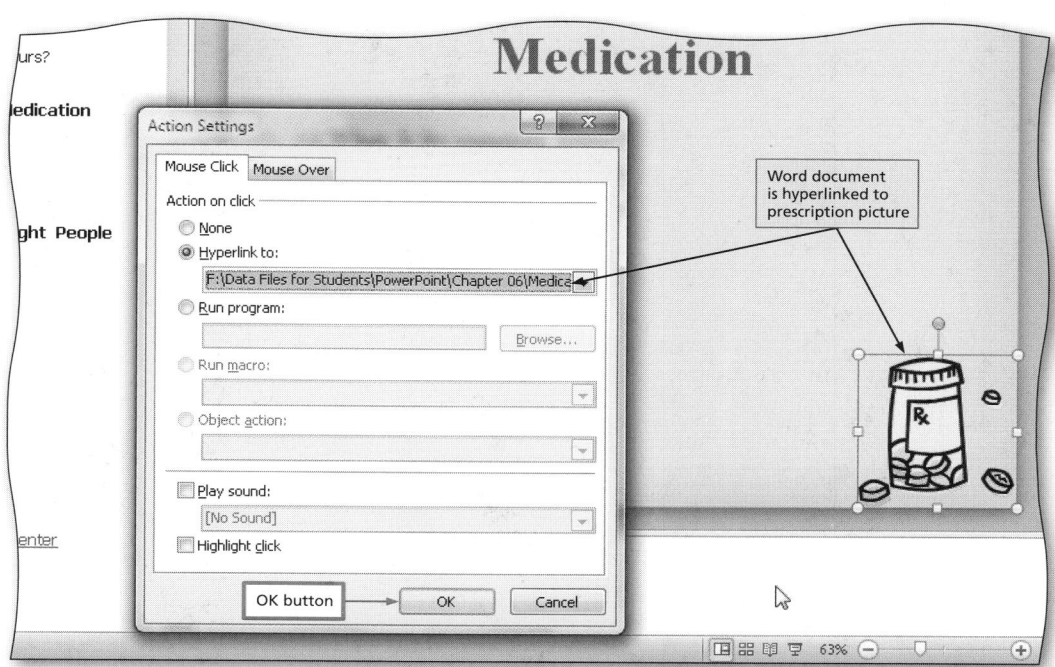

Figure 6–30

To Insert and Format Action Buttons on the Hyperlinked File

The action buttons on Slide 2 and Slide 3 hyperlink to slides in the Additional Health file. While running the presentation, if you click an action button that opens and then displays either Slide 1 or Slide 2, you may need to review this slide and then return to the previous slide displayed in the first presentation. The Return action button performs this function. The following steps open the Additional Health file and then insert and format the Return action button on both slides.

1 In the Backstage view, click the Open command to display the Open dialog box, click the File Type arrow to display the File Type list, and then click All PowerPoint Presentations to select this file type.

2 Open the Additional Health file located on the Data Files for Students.

3 With Slide 1 displaying, click the Shapes button (Insert tab | Illustrations group), and then click the Action Button: Return shape (seventh image).

4 Insert the action button in the lower-right corner of the slide.

5 Display the Action Settings dialog box and then hyperlink the action button to Slide 2 (Questions to Ask When Selecting a Doctor) in the Home Health presentation.

6 Size the action button so that it is approximately 0.5" × 0.5".

7 Change the action button fill color to Tan, Background 2, Lighter 40% (fourth color in third column).

8 Copy the action button to the same location on Slide 2 (Figure 6–31 on the next page). Display the Action Settings dialog box and then hyperlink this action button to Slide 4 (Increased Risks for Overweight People) in the Home Health presentation.

BTW

Showing a Range of Slides
If your presentation consists of many slides, you may want to show only a portion of them in your slide show. For example, if your 30-slide presentation is designed to accompany a 30-minute speech and you are given only 10 minutes to present, you may elect to display only the first 10 slides. Rather than have the show end abruptly after Slide 10, you can elect to show a range of slides. To specify this range, display the Slide Show tab, click the Set Up Slide Show button, and then specify the starting and ending slide numbers in the From and To boxes in the Show slides area (Set Up Show dialog box).

9 Save the file using the same file name.

10 Close the Additional Health file.

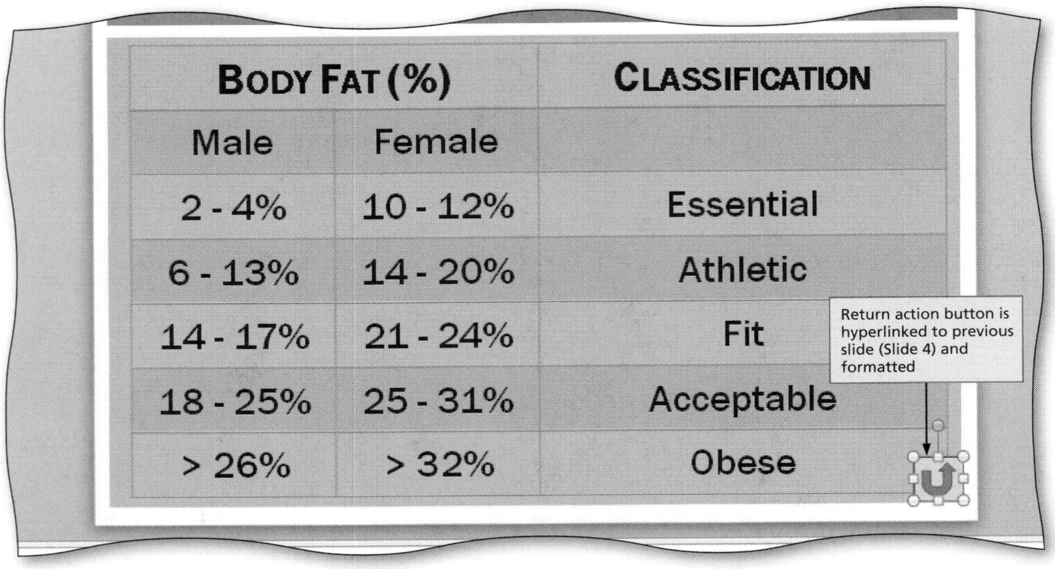

Body Fat (%)		Classification
Male	Female	
2 - 4%	10 - 12%	Essential
6 - 13%	14 - 20%	Athletic
14 - 17%	21 - 24%	Fit
18 - 25%	25 - 31%	Acceptable
> 26%	> 32%	Obese

Return action button is hyperlinked to previous slide (Slide 4) and formatted

Figure 6–31

Break Point: If you wish to take a break, this is a good place to do so. Be sure to save the Home Health file again and then you can quit PowerPoint. To resume at a later time, start PowerPoint, open the file called Home Health, and continue following the steps from this location forward.

BTW

Measurement System
The vertical and horizontal rulers display the units of measurement in inches by default. This measurement system is determined by the settings in Microsoft Windows. You can change the measurement system to centimeters by customizing the numbers format in the Clock, Language, and Region area of Control Panel.

Positioning Slide Elements

At times you may desire to arrange slide elements in precise locations. PowerPoint provides useful tools to help you position shapes and objects on slides. **Drawing guides** are two straight dotted lines, one horizontal and one vertical. When an object is close to a guide, its corner or its center (whichever is closer) **snaps**, or aligns precisely on top of the guide. You can drag a guide to a new location to meet your alignment requirements. Another tool is the vertical or horizontal **ruler**, which can help you drag an object to a precise location on the slide. The center of a slide is 0.00 on both the vertical and the horizontal rulers.

Aligning and Distributing Objects

If you display multiple objects, PowerPoint can **align** them above and below each other (vertically) or side by side (horizontally). The objects, such as SmartArt graphics, clip art, shapes, text boxes, and WordArt, can be aligned relative to the slide so that they display along the top, left, right, or bottom borders or in the center or middle of the slide. They also can be aligned relative to each other, meaning that you position either the first or last object in the desired location and then command PowerPoint to move the remaining objects in the series above, below, or beside it. Depending on the alignment option that you click, objects will move straight up, down, left, or right, and might cover an object already located on the slide. Table 6–2 describes alignment options.

Table 6–2 Alignment Options	
Alignment	**Action**
Left	Aligns the edges of the objects to the left
Center	Aligns the objects vertically through the centers of the objects
Right	Aligns the edges of the objects to the right
Top	Aligns the top edges of the objects
Middle	Aligns the objects horizontally through the middles of the objects
Bottom	Aligns the bottom edges of the objects
to Slide	Aligns one object to the slide

One object remains stationary when you align objects relative to each other by their edges. For example, Align Left aligns the left edges of all selected objects with the left edge of the leftmost object. The leftmost object remains stationary, and the other objects are aligned relative to it. Objects aligned to a SmartArt graphic are aligned to the leftmost edge of the SmartArt graphic, not to the leftmost shape in the SmartArt graphic. Objects aligned relative to each other by their middles or centers are aligned along a horizontal or vertical line that represents the average of their original positions. All of the objects might move.

Smart Guides appear automatically when two or more shapes are in spatial alignment with each other, even if the shapes vary in size. To evenly space multiple objects horizontally or vertically, you **distribute** them. PowerPoint determines the total length between either the outermost edges of the first and last selected object or the edges of the entire slide. It then inserts equal spacing among the items in the series. You also can distribute spacing by using the Size and Position dialog box, but the Distribute command automates this task.

To Display the Drawing Guides

Guides help you align objects on slides. When you point to a guide and then press and hold the mouse button, PowerPoint displays a box containing the exact position of the guide on the slide in inches. An arrow is displayed below the guide position to indicate the vertical guide either left or right of center. An arrow also is displayed to the right of the guide position to indicate the horizontal guide either above or below center. The following step displays the guides.

• With the Home Health presentation displayed, click the View tab, and then click the Guides check box (View tab | Show group) to display the horizontal and vertical guides (Figure 6–32).

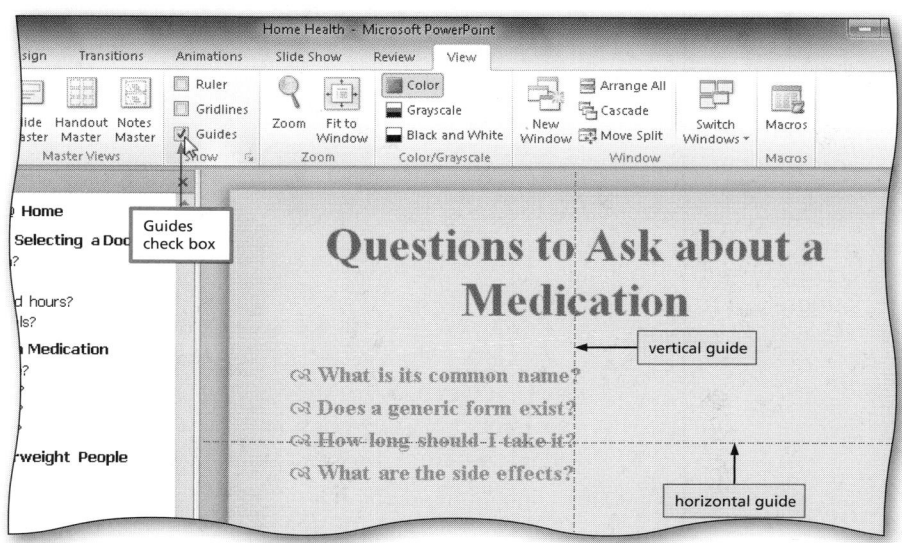

Figure 6–32

Other Ways

1. Right-click area of slide other than a placeholder or object, click Grid and Guides on shortcut menu, click 'Display drawing guides on screen' check box

2. Press ALT+F9

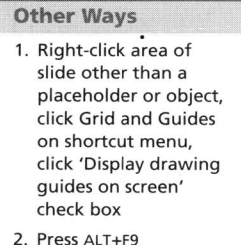

To Position a Picture Using Guides

The three pictures on Slides 2, 3, and 4 should be displayed in precisely the same location so they appear static as you transition from one slide to the next during the slide show. In addition, the top border of the three pictures on Slide 1 should align evenly. The following steps position the picture on Slide 3.

1

- Point to the horizontal guide anywhere except the text.

Q&A Why does 0.00 display when I hold down the mouse button?

The ScreenTip displays the horizontal guide's position. A 0.00 setting means that the guide is precisely in the middle of the slide and is not above or below the center.

- Click and then drag the horizontal guide to 1.50 inches below the center. Do not release the mouse button (Figure 6–33).

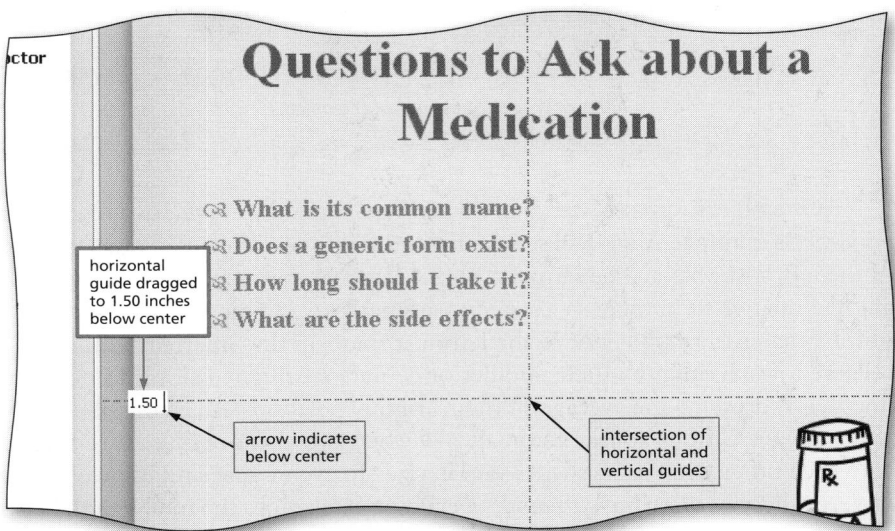

Figure 6–33

2

- Release the mouse button to position the horizontal guide at 1.50, which is the intended location of the picture's top border.

- Point to the vertical guide anywhere except the text in the content placeholder.

- Click and then drag the vertical guide to 2.50 inches right of the center and then release the mouse button to position the vertical guide.

- Drag the upper-left corner of the picture to the intersection of the vertical and horizontal guides to position the picture in the desired location (Figure 6–34).

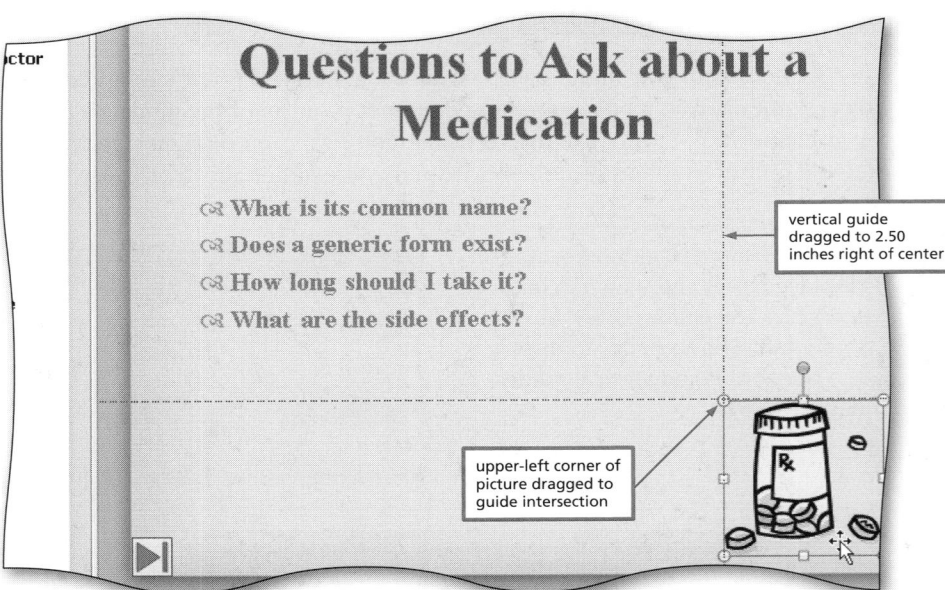

Figure 6–34

Q&A Can I add guides to help me align multiple objects?

Yes. Position the mouse pointer over one guide and then press the CTRL key. When you drag your mouse pointer, a second guide appears.

To Position the Slide 4 and Slide 2 Pictures

The pictures on Slide 4 and Slide 2 should be positioned in the same location as the Slide 3 picture. The guides will display in the same location as you display each slide, so you easily can align similar objects on multiple slides. The following steps position the pictures on Slide 4 and Slide 2.

1 Display Slide 4 and then drag the upper-left corner of the scale picture to the intersection of the guides.

2 Repeat Step 1 to position the stethoscope picture on Slide 2 (Figure 6–35).

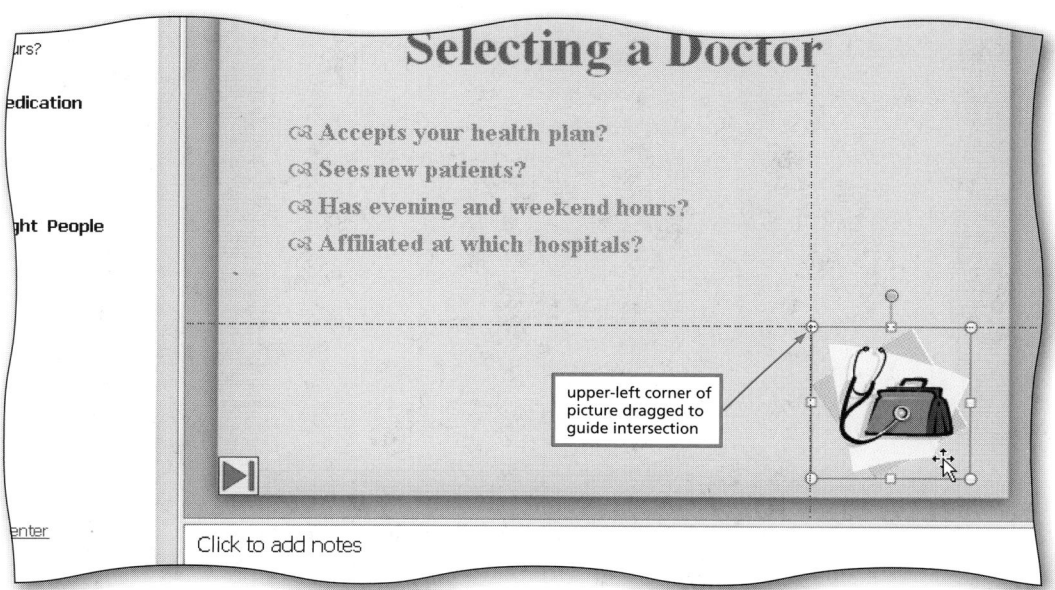

Figure 6–35

To Hide Guides

The three pictures on Slides 2, 3, and 4 are positioned in the desired locations, so the guides no longer are needed. The following step hides the guides.

1 If necessary, display the View tab and then click the Guides check box to remove the check mark.

Other Ways
1. Right-click area of slide other than a placeholder or object, click Grid and Guides on shortcut menu,   click 'Display drawing guides on screen' check box   2. Press ALT+F9

To Display the Rulers

To begin aligning the three Slide 1 objects, you need to position either the left or the right object. The vertical or horizontal **ruler** can help you drag an object to a precise location on the slide. The center of a slide is 0.00 on both the vertical and the horizontal rulers. The following step displays the rulers.

1

- If necessary, display the View tab and then click the Ruler check box (View tab | Show group) to display the vertical and horizontal rulers (Figure 6–36).

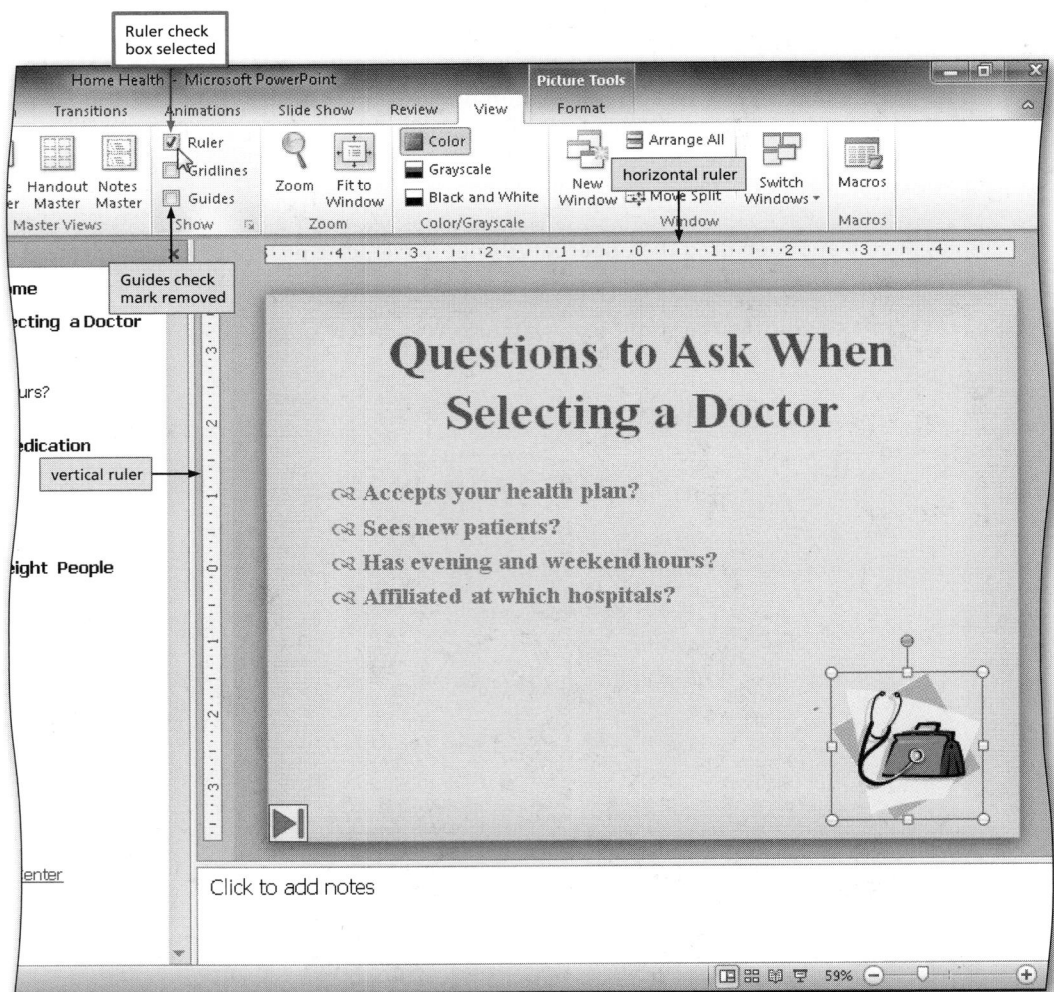

Figure 6–36

To Align Pictures

The three pictures on Slide 1 will look balanced if the bottom edges are aligned. One method of creating this orderly appearance is by dragging the borders to a guide. Another method that is useful when you have multiple objects is to use one of PowerPoint's align commands. On Slide 1, you will position the far left picture of the stethoscope and then align its bottom edge with those of the prescription and scale pictures. The following steps align the Slide 1 pictures.

1

- Display Slide 1 and then position the mouse pointer over the handle of the doctor's bag in the stethoscope picture.

- Drag the picture so that the bag handle is positioned 3 inches left of the center and 2½ inches below the center (Figure 6–37).

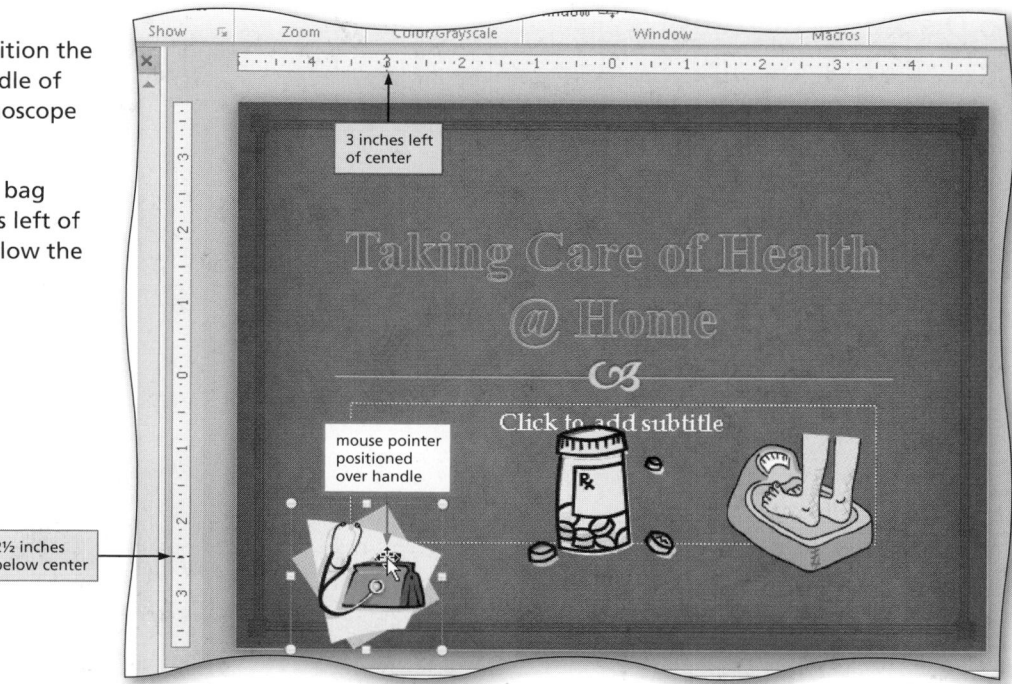

Figure 6–37

2

- Drag the prescription picture toward the bottom of the slide until the Smart Guide appears in the center of the stethoscope and prescription pictures (Figure 6–38).

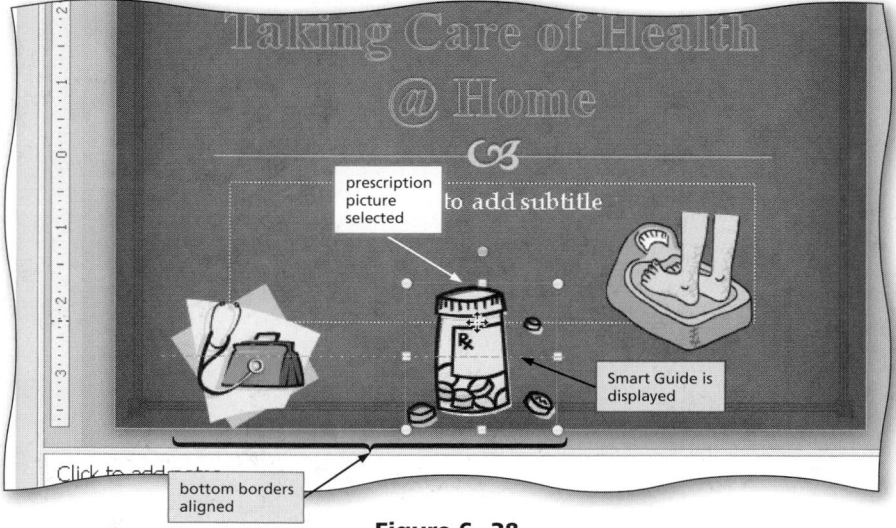

Figure 6–38

3

- Drag the scale picture toward the bottom of the slide until the Smart Guide appears in the center of all three pictures on the slide (Figure 6–39).

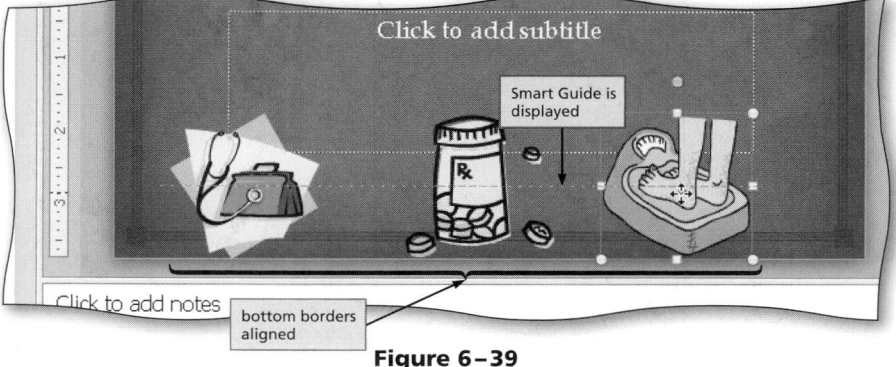

Figure 6–39

To Distribute Pictures

Now that the three Slide 1 pictures are aligned along their bottom edges, you can have PowerPoint place the same amount of space between the first and second pictures and the second and third pictures. You have two distribution options: Align to Slide spaces all the selected objects evenly across the entire width of the slide; Align Selected Objects spaces only the middle objects between the fixed right and left objects. The following steps use the Align to Slide option to horizontally distribute the Slide 1 pictures.

1
- Select the three Slide 1 pictures, display the Picture Tools Format tab, and then click the Align button (Picture Tools Format tab | Arrange group) to display the Align menu.

2
- If necessary, click Align to Slide so that PowerPoint will adjust the spacing of the pictures evenly between the slide edges and then click the Align button to display the Align menu again (Figure 6–40).

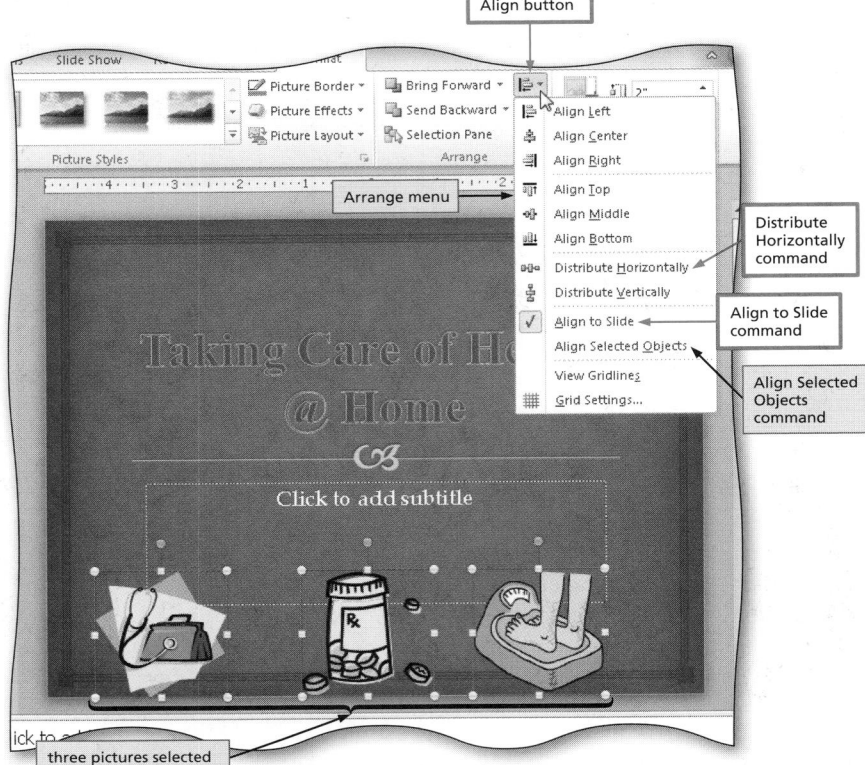

Figure 6–40

3
- Click Distribute Horizontally to adjust the spacing (Figure 6–41).

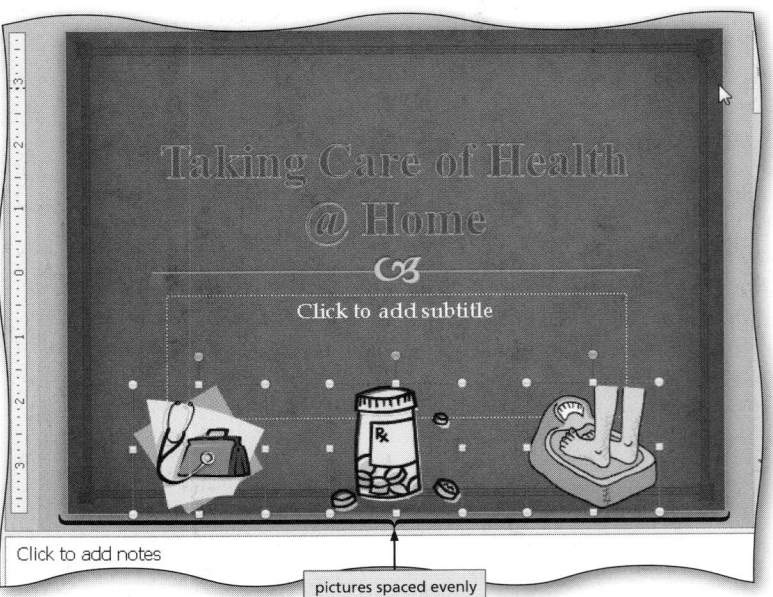

Figure 6–41

To Hide Rulers

The three pictures on Slide 1 are positioned in the desired locations, so the rulers no longer need to display. The following step hides the rulers.

1 Display the View tab and then click the Ruler check box to remove the check mark.

Hiding a Slide

Slides 2, 3, and 4 present a variety of health information with hyperlinks. Depending on the audience's needs and the time constraints, you may decide not to display one or more of these slides. If need be, you can use the **Hide Slide** command to hide a slide from the audience during the normal running of a slide show. When you want to display the hidden slide, press the H key. No visible indicator displays to show that a hidden slide exists. You must be aware of the content of the presentation to know where the supporting slide is located.

When you run your presentation, the hidden slide does not display unless you press the H key when the slide preceding the hidden slide is displaying. For example, Slide 4 does not display unless you press the H key when Slide 3 displays in Slide Show view. You continue your presentation by clicking the mouse or pressing any of the keys associated with running a slide show. You skip the hidden slide by clicking the mouse and advancing to the next slide.

To Hide a Slide

Slide 4 discusses health problems that overweight people face. If time permits, or if the audience requires information on this subject, you can display Slide 4. As the presenter, you decide whether to show Slide 4. You hide a slide in Slide Sorter view so you can see the slashed square surrounding the slide number, which indicates a slide is hidden. The following steps hide Slide 4.

1

- Click the Slide Sorter view button to display the slide thumbnails.

- Click Slide Show on the Ribbon to display the Slide Show tab and then click the Slide 4 thumbnail to select it (Figure 6–42).

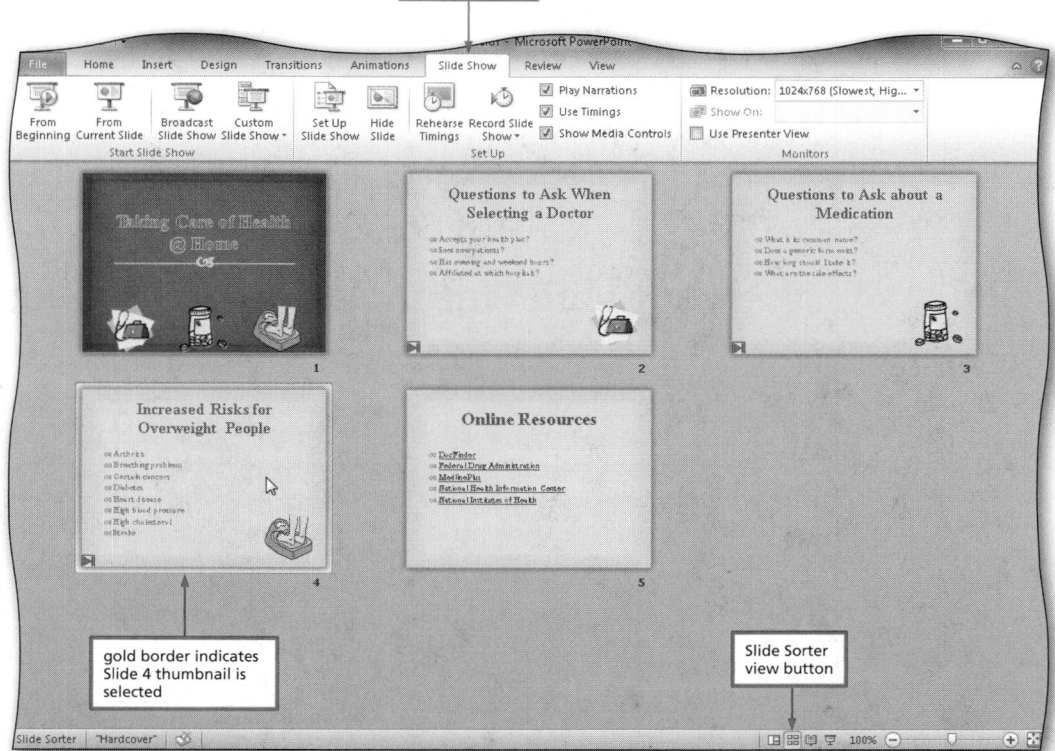

Figure 6–42

- Click the Hide Slide button (Slide Show tab | Set Up group) to hide Slide 4 (Figure 6–43).

Q&A How do I know that Slide 4 is hidden?

The rectangle with a slash surrounds the slide number to indicate Slide 4 is a hidden slide.

Q&A What if I decide I no longer want to hide a slide?

Repeat Steps 1 and 2. The Hide Slide button is a toggle; it either hides or displays a slide.

- Click the Normal view button to display Slide 4.

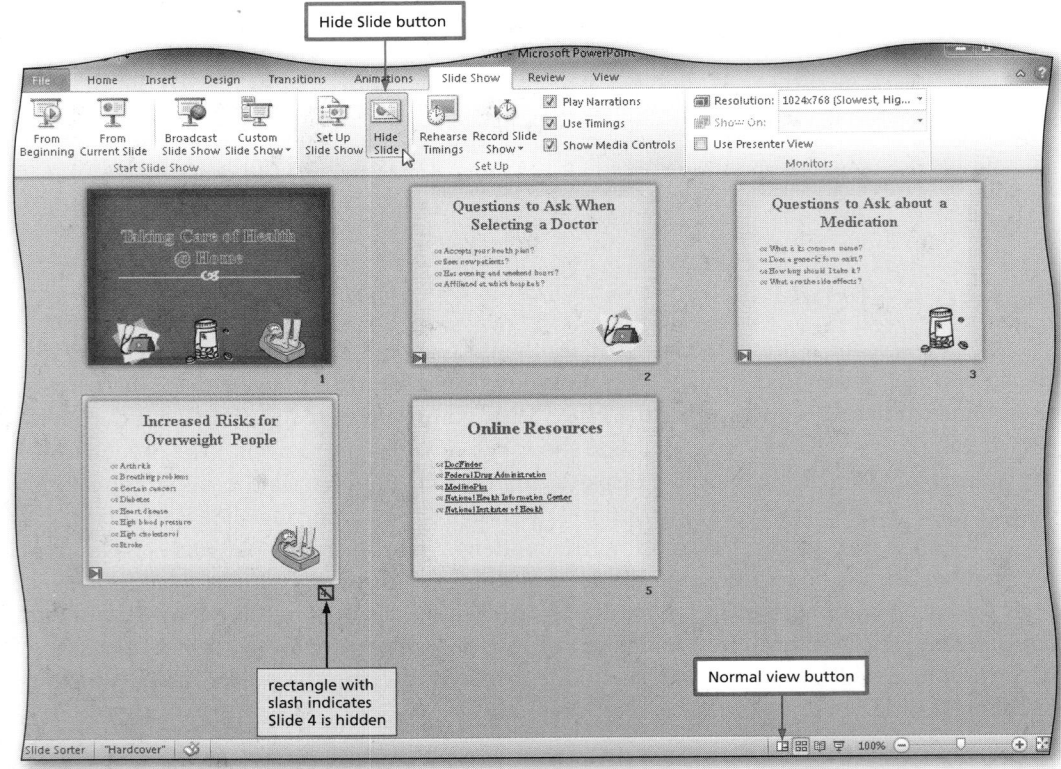

Figure 6–43

Other Ways

1. Change view to Slide Sorter, right-click desired slide, click Hide Slide on shortcut menu

2. Right-click slide thumbnail in Slides tab, click Hide Slide on shortcut menu

Break Point: If you wish to take a break, this is a good place to do so. Be sure to save the Home Health file again and then you can quit PowerPoint. To resume at a later time, start PowerPoint, open the file called Home Health, and continue following the steps from this location forward.

Modifying Placeholder Text Settings

The PowerPoint design themes specify default alignment of and spacing for text within a placeholder. For example, the text in most paragraphs is **left-aligned**, so the first character of each line is even with the first character above or below it. Text alignment also can be horizontally **centered** to position each line evenly between the left and right placeholder edges; **right-aligned**, so that the last character of each line is even with the last character of each line above or below it; and **justified**, where the first and last characters of each line are aligned and extra space is inserted between words to spread the characters evenly across the line.

When you begin typing text in most placeholders, the first paragraph is aligned at the top of the placeholder with any extra space at the bottom. You can change this default **paragraph alignment** location to position the paragraph lines centered vertically between the top and bottom placeholder edges, or you can place the last line at the bottom of the placeholder so that any extra space is at the top.

The design theme also determines the amount of spacing around the sides of the placeholder and between the lines of text. An internal **margin** provides a cushion of space between text and the top, bottom, left, and right sides of the placeholder. **Line spacing** is the amount of vertical space between the lines of text in a paragraph, and **paragraph spacing** is the amount of space above and below a paragraph. PowerPoint adjusts the line spacing and paragraph spacing automatically to accommodate various font sizes within the placeholder.

Long lists of items can be divided into several **columns** to fill the placeholder width and maximize the slide space. Once you have created columns, you can adjust the amount of space between the columns to enhance readability.

To Center Placeholder Text

By default, all placeholder text in the Hardcover document theme is left-aligned. For variety, you want the text to be centered, or placed with equal space horizontally between the left and right placeholder edges. The following steps center the text in the content placeholders on Slides 2, 3, 4, and 5.

1
• Display Slide 2 and then select the four paragraphs in the content placeholder (Figure 6–44).

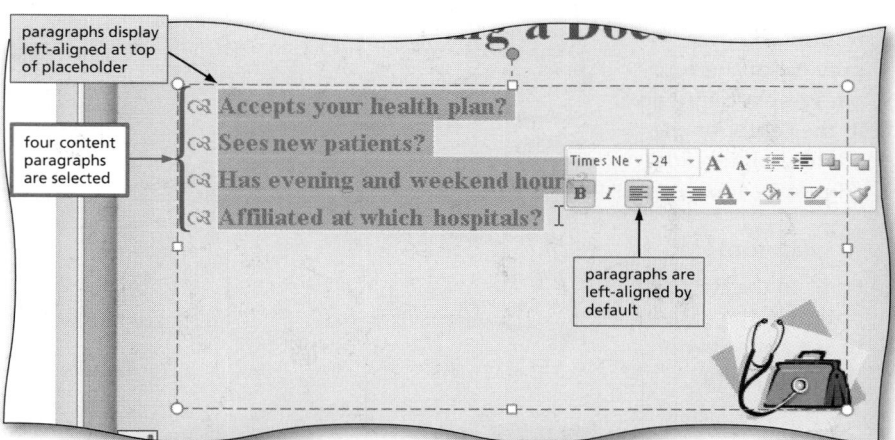

Figure 6–44

2
• Click the Center button on the Mini toolbar to center these paragraphs (Figure 6–45).

3
• Repeat Steps 1 and 2 to center the paragraph text in the content placeholders on Slides 3, 4, and 5.

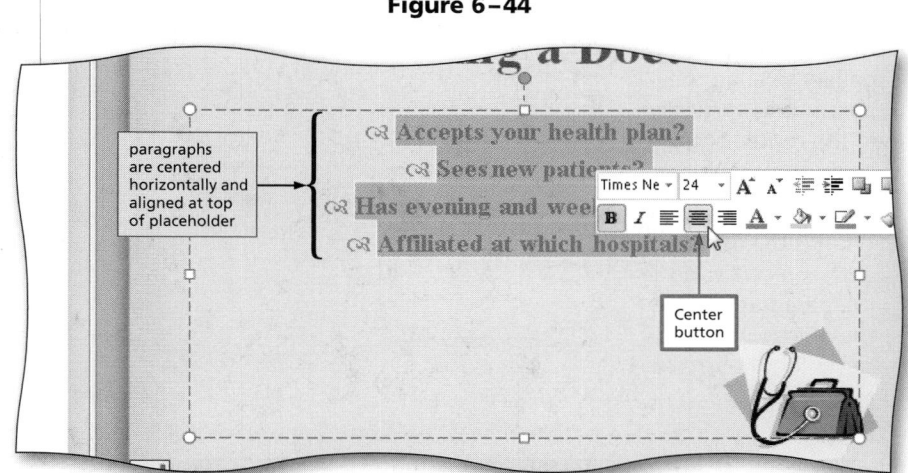

Figure 6–45

Other Ways
1. Click Center button (Home tab | Font group)
2. Right-click selected text, click Paragraph on shortcut menu, click Alignment box arrow (Paragraph dialog box), click Centered, click OK button
3. Click Paragraph Dialog Box Launcher (Home tab | Paragraph group), click Alignment box arrow (Paragraph dialog box), click Centered, click OK button
4. Press CTRL+E

To Align Placeholder Text

The Hardcover document theme aligns the text paragraphs at the top of the content placeholders. This default setting can be changed easily so that the paragraphs either are centered or aligned at the bottom of the placeholder. The following steps align the paragraphs vertically in the center of the content placeholders on Slides 2, 3, 4, and 5.

1

- With the Slide 5 paragraphs still selected, display the Home tab and then click the Align Text button (Home tab | Paragraph group) to display the Align Text gallery.

- Point to Middle in the Align Text gallery to display a live preview of the four paragraphs aligned in the center of the content placeholder (Figure 6–46).

 **Experiment**

- Point to the Bottom option in the gallery to see a preview of that alignment.

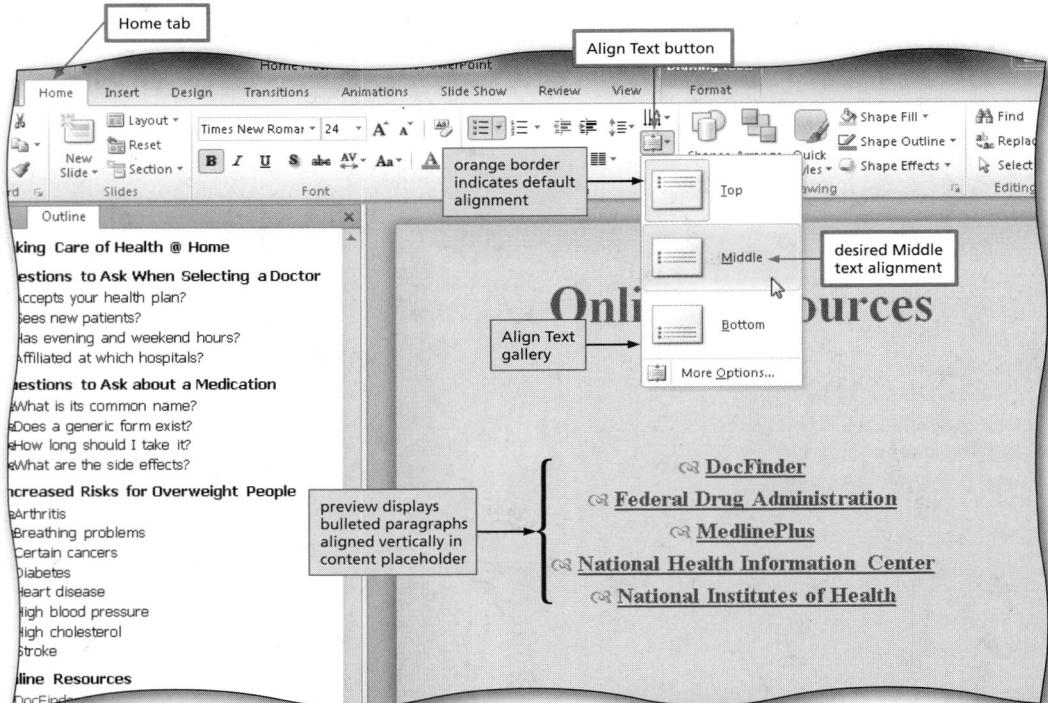

Figure 6–46

2

- Click Middle in the Align Text gallery to align the paragraphs vertically in the center of the content placeholder (Figure 6–47).

Q&A What is the difference between centering the paragraphs in the placeholder and centering the text?

Clicking the Align Text button and then clicking Middle moves the paragraphs up or down so that the first and last paragraphs are equal distances from the top and bottom placeholder borders. The Center button, on the other hand, moves the paragraphs left or right so that the first and last words in each line are equal distances from the left and right text box borders.

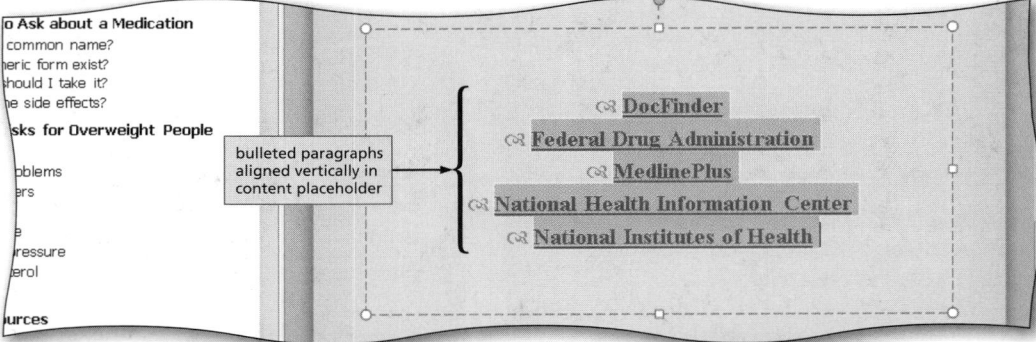

Figure 6–47

3

- Repeat Steps 1 and 2 to center the paragraph text in the middle of the content placeholders on Slides 2, 3, and 4.

To Change Paragraph Line Spacing

The vertical space between paragraphs is called **line spacing**. PowerPoint adjusts the amount of space based on font size. Default line spacing is 1.0, which is considered single spacing. Other preset options are 1.5, 2.0 (double spacing), 2.5, and 3.0 (triple spacing). You can specify precise line spacing intervals between, before, and after paragraphs in the Indents and Spacing tab of the Paragraph dialog box. The following steps increase the line spacing of the content paragraphs from single (1.0) to double (2.0) on Slides 2, 3, and 5.

1

- With the Home tab displayed, display Slide 2 and select the four content paragraphs.

- Click the Line Spacing button (Home tab | Paragraph group) to display the Line Spacing gallery.

- Point to 2.0 in the Line Spacing gallery to display a live preview of this line spacing (Figure 6–48).

Experiment

- Point to each of the line spacing options in the gallery to see a preview of that paragraph spacing.

2

- Click 2.0 in the Line Spacing gallery to change the paragraph line spacing to double.

3

- Repeat Steps 1 and 2 to change the line spacing for the paragraph text in the content placeholders on Slides 3 and 5. Do not change the line spacing on Slide 4.

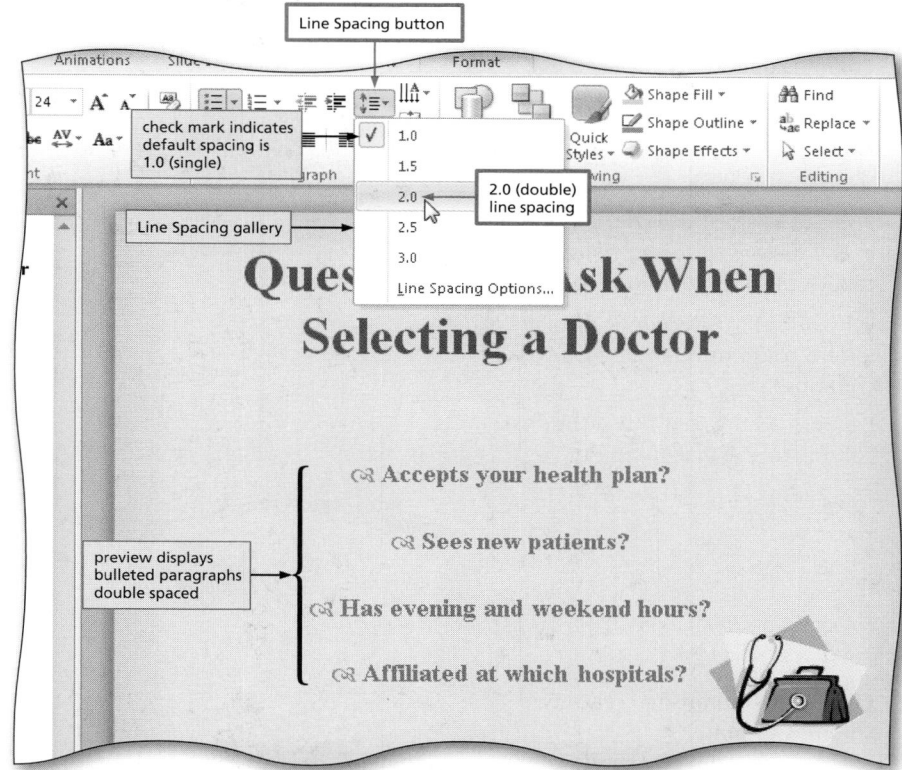

Figure 6–48

Q&A Why is the line spacing not changing on Slide 4?

The content placeholder paragraphs will be changed into columns, so spacing is not a design concern at this time.

Other Ways
1. Right-click selected text, click Paragraph on shortcut menu, click Line Spacing box arrow (Paragraph dialog box), click Double, click OK button   2. Click Paragraph Dialog Box Launcher (Home tab | Paragraph group), click Line Spacing box arrow (Paragraph dialog box), click Double, click OK button

To Create Columns in a Placeholder

The list of health risks in the Slide 4 placeholder is lengthy and lacks visual appeal. You can change these items into two, three, or more columns and then adjust the column widths. The following steps change the placeholder elements into columns.

1

- Display Slide 4 and then click the content placeholder to select it.

- With the Home tab displayed, click the Columns button (Home tab | Paragraph group) to display the Columns gallery.

- Point to Two Columns in the Columns gallery to display a live preview of the text in the first column (Figure 6–49).

🔍 **Experiment**

- Point to each of the column options in the gallery to see a preview of the text displaying in various columns.

Q&A Why doesn't the content display in two columns if I selected two columns?

Because all the text fits in the first column in the placeholder.

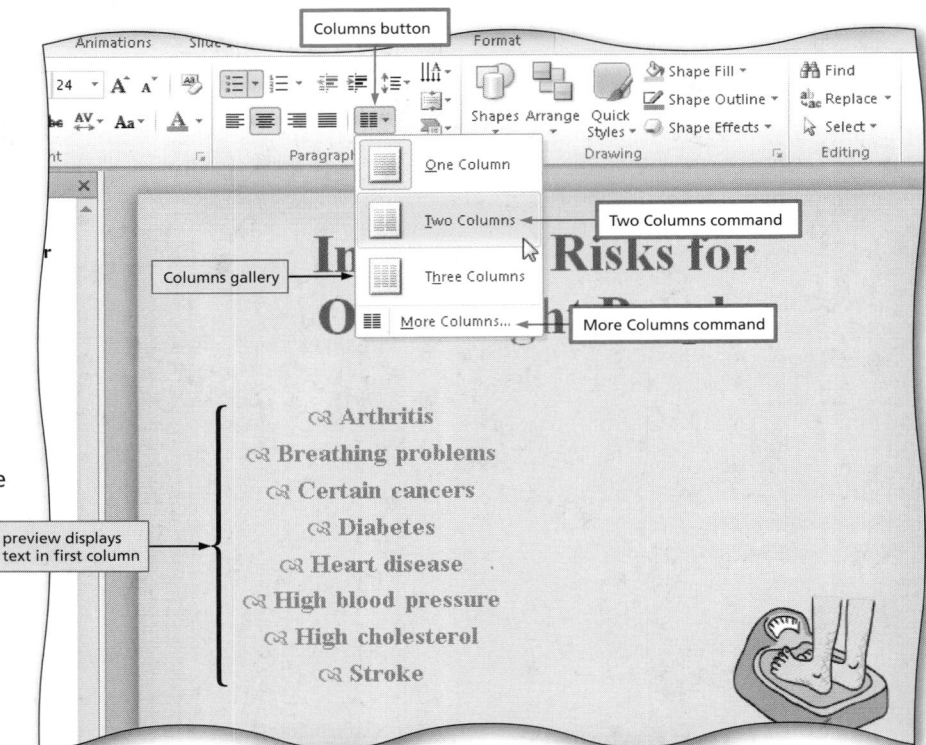

Figure 6–49

2

- Click Two Columns to create two columns of text.

- Drag the bottom sizing handle up to the location shown in Figure 6–50.

Q&A Why is the bottom sizing handle between the Diabetes and Heart Disease paragraphs?

Eight risks are listed in the content placeholder, so dividing the paragraphs in two groups of four will balance the layout.

3

- Release the mouse button to resize the content placeholder and create the two columns of text.

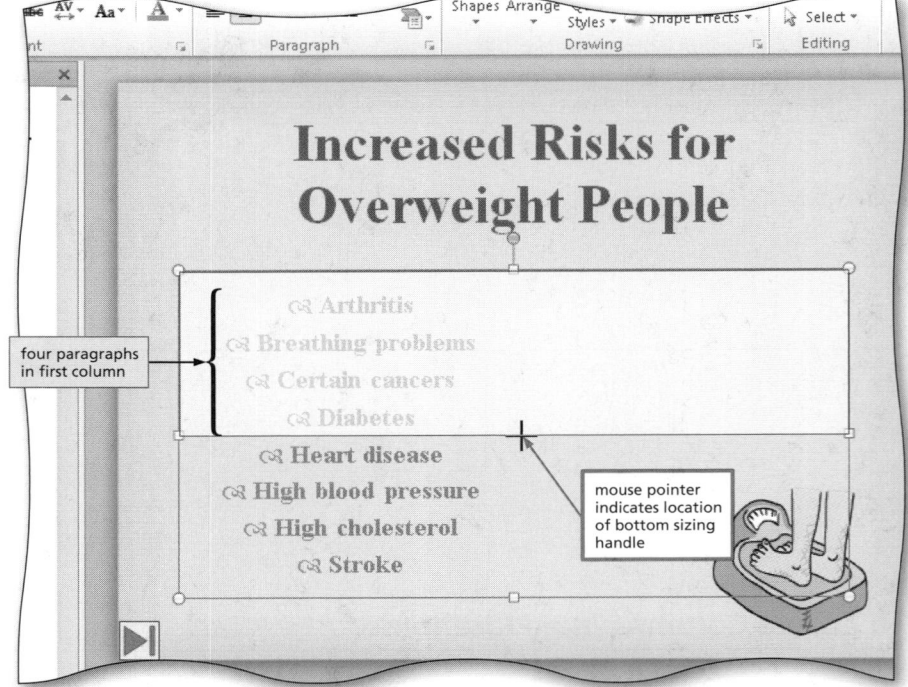

Figure 6–50

To Adjust Column Spacing

The space between the columns in the placeholder can be increased to make room for the scale picture in the lower-right corner. The following steps increase the spacing between the columns.

1

- With the placeholder selected, click the Columns button and then click More Columns.

- Click the Spacing box up arrow (Columns dialog box) until 1.5″ is displayed (Figure 6–51).

Q&A Can I type a number in the text box instead of clicking the up arrow?

Yes. Double-click the text box and then type the desired measurement expressed in inches.

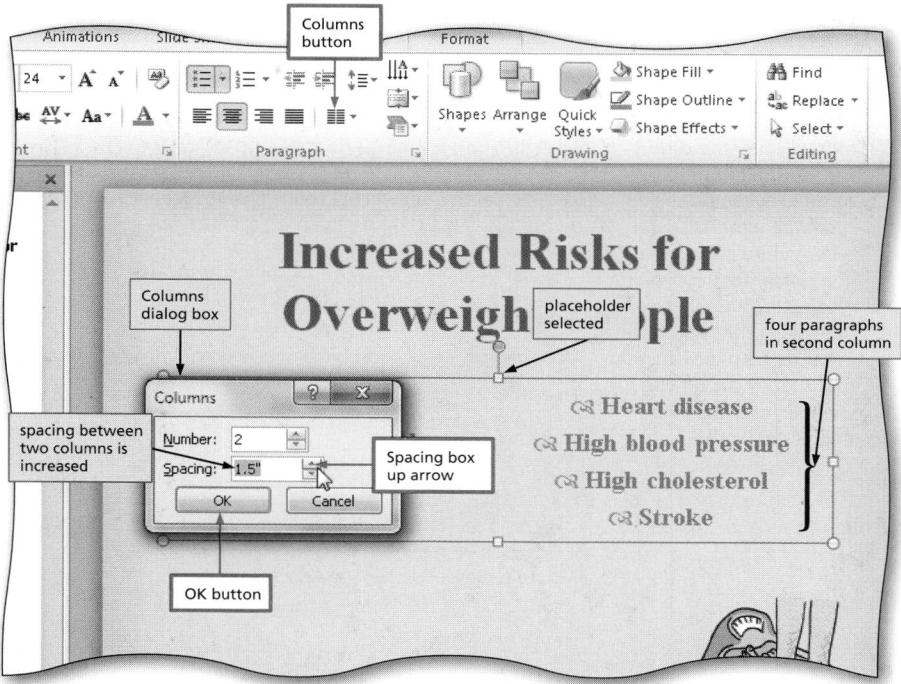

Figure 6–51

2

- Click the OK button to increase the spacing between the columns (Figure 6–52).

Q&A Can I change the paragraphs back to one column easily?

Yes. Click the Columns button and then click One Column.

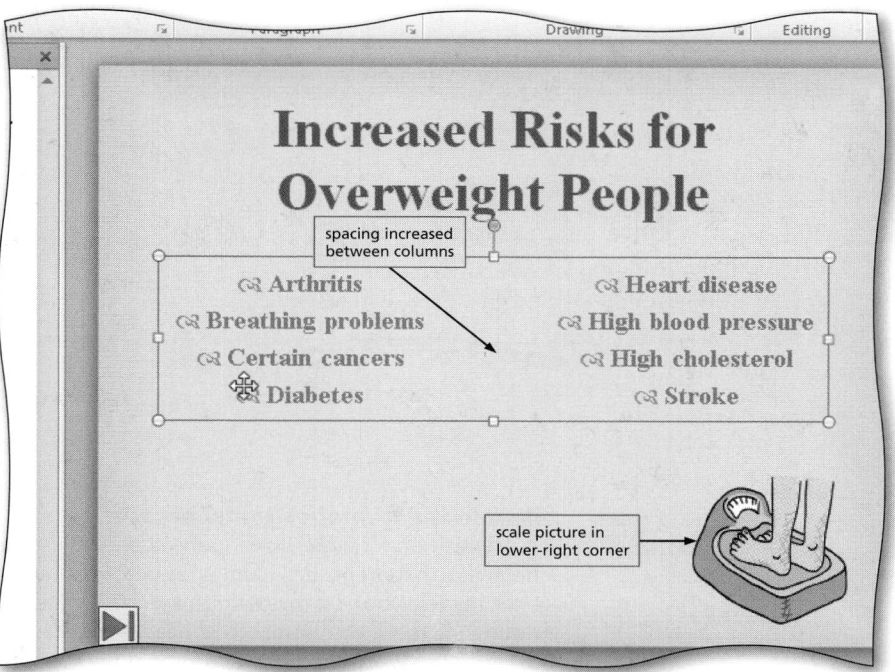

Figure 6–52

BTW

Displaying Slides
Slide 4 in this presentation has important information about potential health problems related to obesity. Your audience needs time to read and contemplate the risks listed in the content placeholder, so you must display the slide for a sufficient amount of time. Some public speaking experts recommend each slide in a presentation should display for at least one minute so that audience members can look at the material, focus on the speaker, and then refer to the slide again.

To Format the Content Placeholder

To add interest to the Slide 4 content placeholder, apply a Quick Style and then move the scale picture from the lower-right corner to the space between the columns. The following steps apply a green Subtle Effect style to the placeholder and then change the picture location.

1 With the placeholder selected, click the Quick Styles button (Home tab | Drawing group) to display the Quick Styles gallery.

2 Click Subtle Effect – Gray-50%, Accent 1 (second style in fourth row).

3 Move the scale clip from the lower-right corner to the area between the two columns (Figure 6–53).

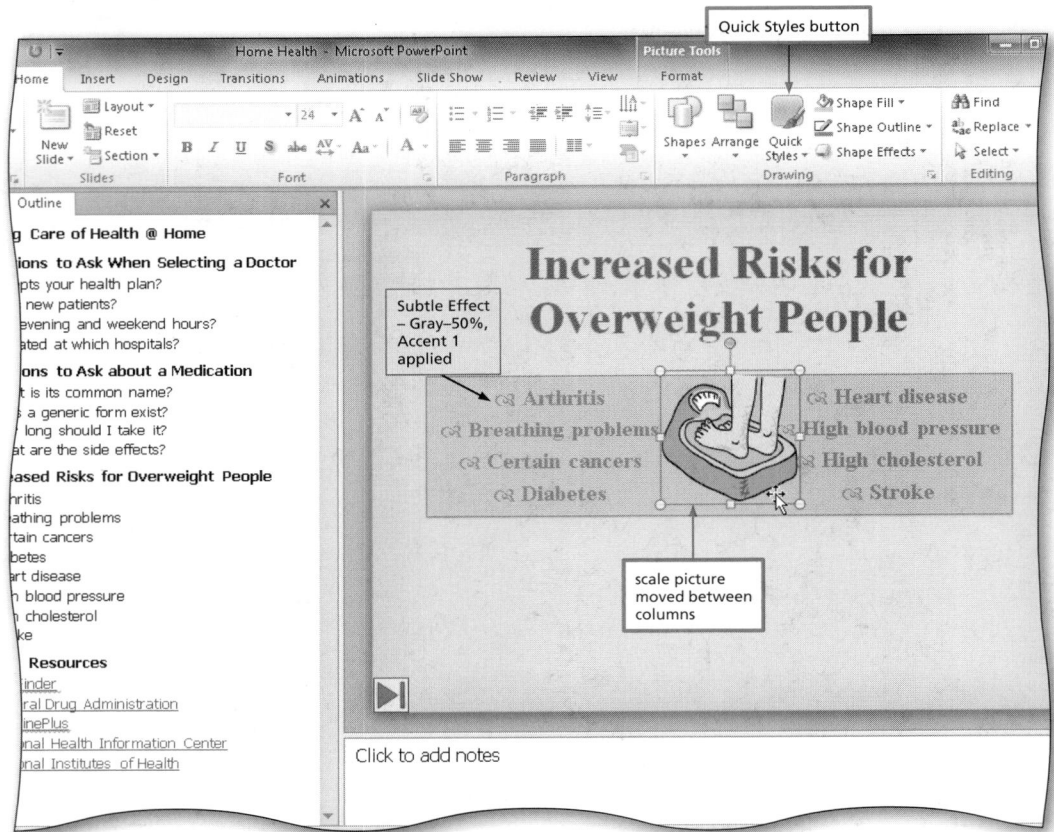

Figure 6–53

Plan Ahead

Be mindful of prepositional phrases.
A prepositional phrase links nouns and pronouns to the rest of a sentence. The phrase begins with a preposition and ends with a noun or pronoun. For example, in the sentence, I left my textbook on my desk, the word "on" is a preposition and the word "desk" is a noun. The more commonly used prepositions are at, by, for, from, in, of, on, to, and with. Because the words in the prepositional phrase work together as a unit, PowerPoint audience members often find it awkward when the entire prepositional phrase does not appear together in one line on the slide. It therefore is best to reword slide text or split multiple paragraph lines so that the prepositional phrase stays intact.

To Enter a Line Break

Slides 3 and 4 in your presentation have prepositional phrases in the title text placeholders. On Slide 3, the words, about a Medication, and on Slide 4 the words, for Overweight People, start on the first line and then continue to the second line. This break in the middle of the phrase can be disconcerting to your viewers who interpret each line as a separate thought. It is advisable to display all words in a prepositional phrase together on one line. If you press the ENTER key at the end of a line, PowerPoint automatically applies paragraph formatting, which could include indents and bullets. To prevent this formatting from occurring, you can press SHIFT+ENTER to place a **line break** at the end of the line, which moves the insertion point to the beginning of the next line. The following steps place a line break at the beginning of the prepositional phrases on Slide 3 and Slide 4.

- Display Slide 3 and then place the insertion point before the word, about (Figure 6–54).

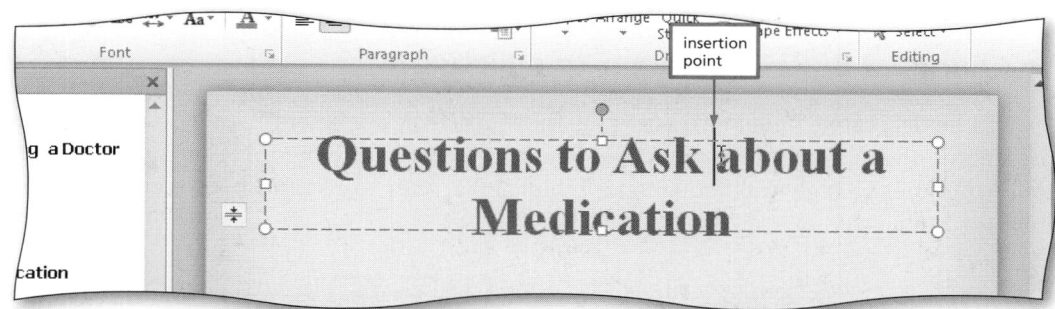

Figure 6–54

- Press SHIFT+ENTER to insert a line break character and move the word, about, to the second line in the placeholder.

- Display Slide 4, place the insertion point before the word, for, and then press SHIFT+ENTER to insert a line break character and move the word, for, to the second line (Figure 6–55).

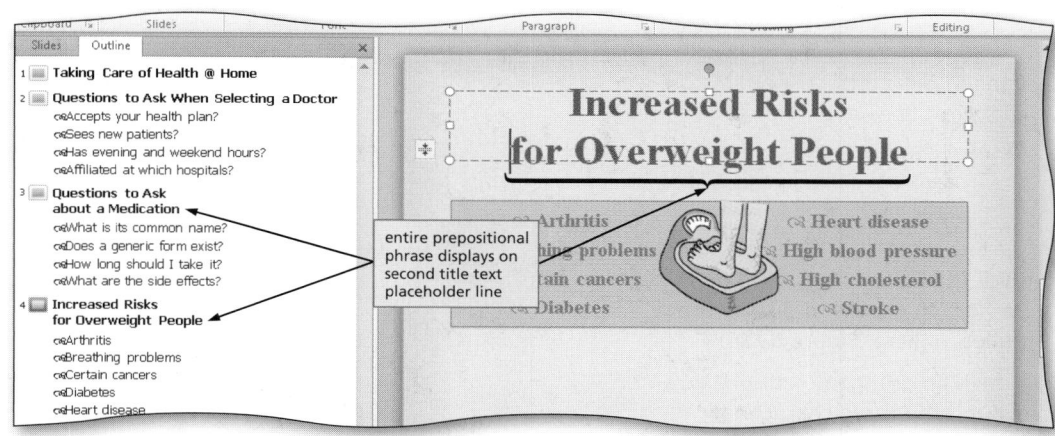

Figure 6–55

Modifying Bullets

PowerPoint allows you to change the default appearance of bullets in a slide show. The document themes determine the bullet character. A **bullet character** is a symbol, traditionally a closed circle, that sets off items in a list. It can be a predefined style, a variety of fonts and characters displayed in the Symbol gallery, or a picture from a file or the Clip Organizer. You may want to change a character to add visual interest and variety. Once you change the bullet character, you also can change its size and color.

If desired, you can change every bullet in a presentation to a unique character. If your presentation has many bulleted slides, however, you would want to have a consistent look on all slides by making the bullets a similar color and size.

To customize your presentation, you can change the default slide layout bullets to numbers by changing the bulleted list to a numbered list. PowerPoint provides a variety of numbering options, including Arabic and Roman numerals. These numbers can be sized and recolored, and the starting number can be something other than 1 or I. In addition, PowerPoint's numbering options include upper- and lowercase letters.

To Change a Bullet Character to a Picture

The decorative bullet characters for the Hardcover document theme do not fit the serious nature of a presentation with the topic of medicine. One method of modifying these bullets is to use a relevant picture. The following steps change the first paragraph bullet character to a stethoscope picture, which is located on the Data Files for Students.

- With the Home tab still displaying and your USB flash drive connected to one of the computer's USB ports, display Slide 2 and then select all four content placeholder paragraphs.

Q&A Can I insert a different bullet character in each paragraph?

Yes. Select only a paragraph and then perform the steps below for each paragraph.

- Click the Bullets arrow (Home tab | Paragraph group) to display the Bullets gallery (Figure 6–56).

Q&A Why is an orange box displayed around the three characters?

They are the default first-level bullet characters for the Hardcover document theme.

Experiment

- Point to each of the bullets displayed in the gallery to see a preview of the characters.

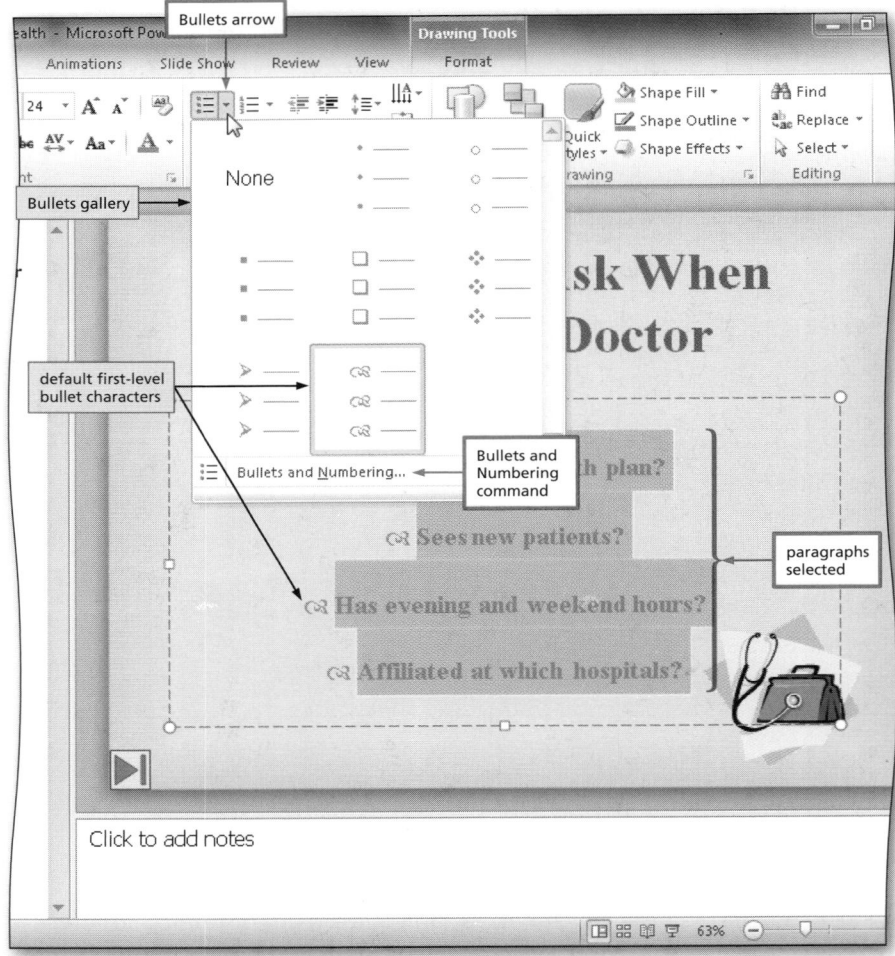

Figure 6–56

2

- Click Bullets and Numbering to display the Bullets and Numbering dialog box (Figure 6–57).

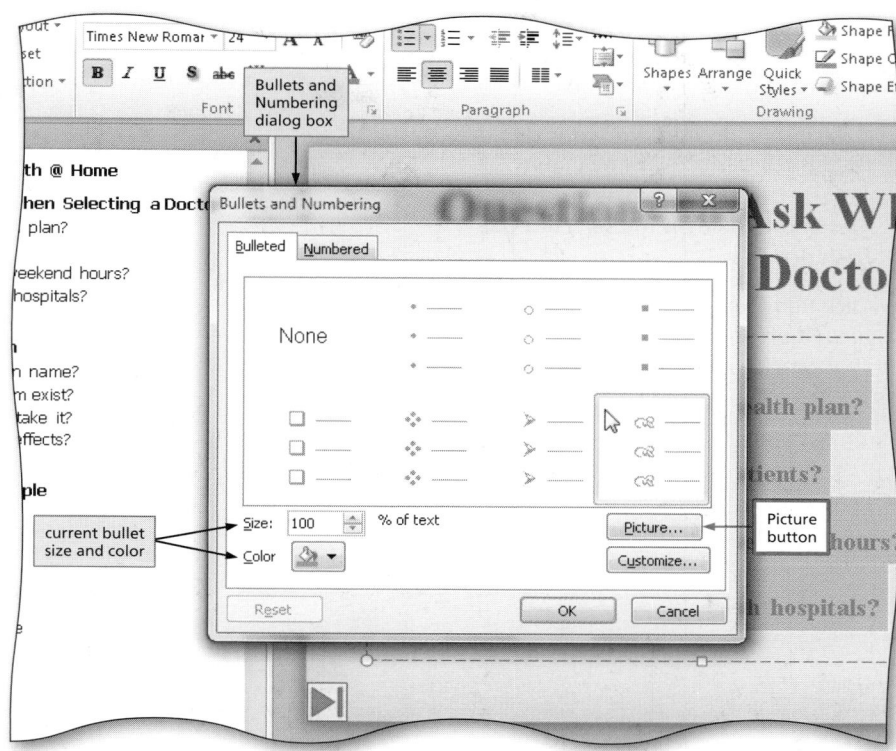

Figure 6–57

3

- Click the Picture button (Bullets and Numbering dialog box) to display the Picture Bullet dialog box (Figure 6–58).

Why are my bullets different from those displayed in Figure 6–58?

The bullets most recently inserted are displayed as the first items in the dialog box.

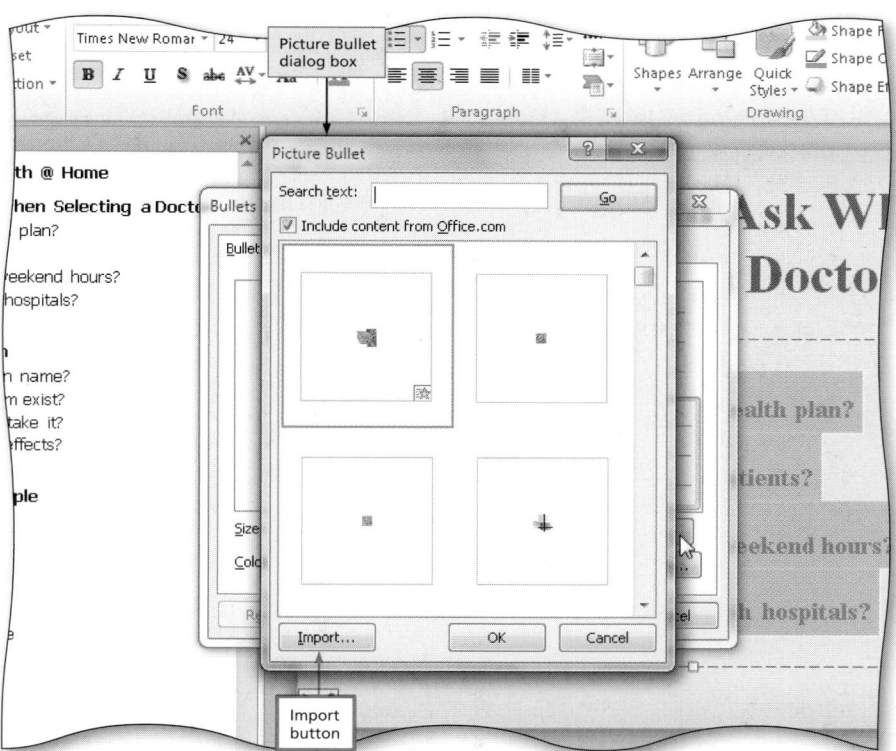

Figure 6–58

4

- Click the Import button (Picture Bullet dialog box) to display the Add Clips to Organizer dialog box.

- If necessary, double-click your USB flash drive in the list of available storage devices to display a list of files and folders on the selected USB flash drive.

- Click Red Stethoscope to select the file (Figure 6–59).

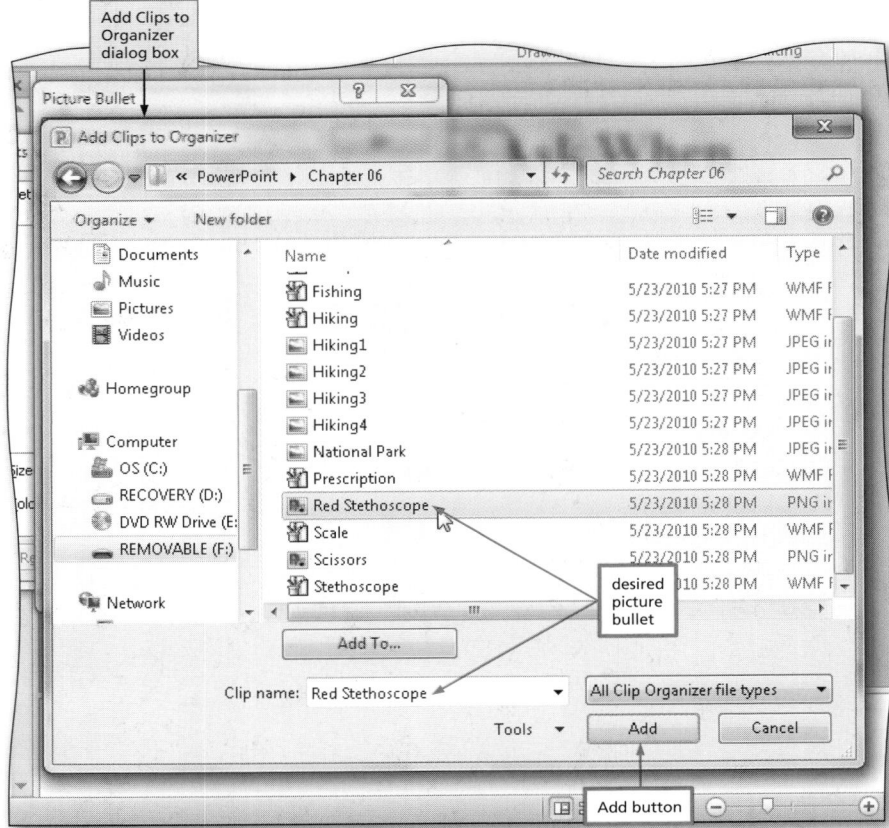

Figure 6–59

5

- Click the Add button (Add Clips to Organizer dialog box) to import the clip to the Microsoft Clip Organizer (Figure 6–60).

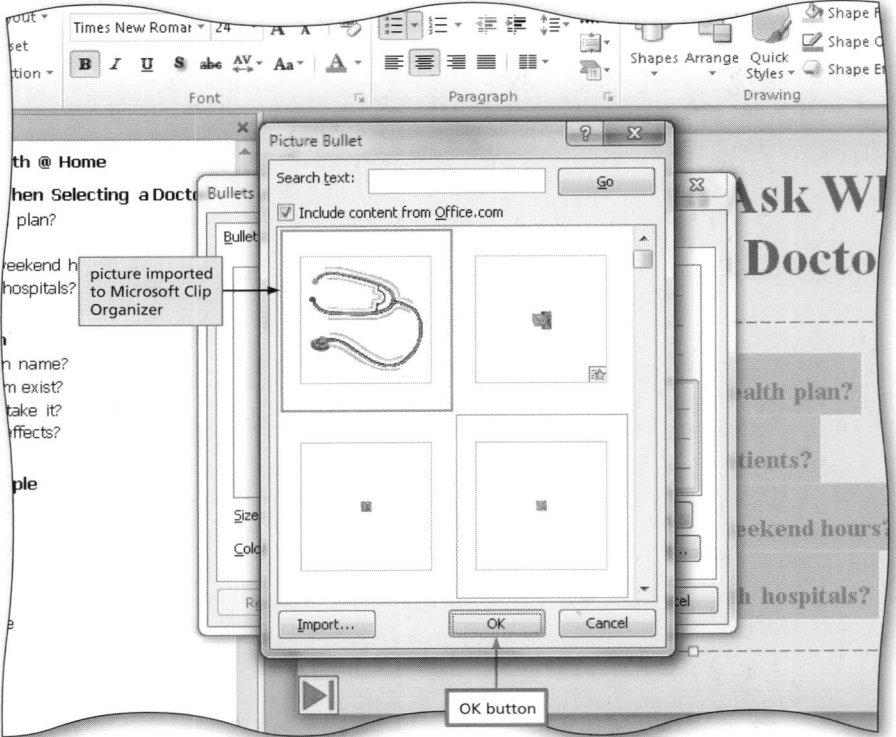

Figure 6–60

- Click the OK button (Picture Bullet dialog box) to insert the Red Stethoscope picture as the paragraph bullet character (Figure 6–61).

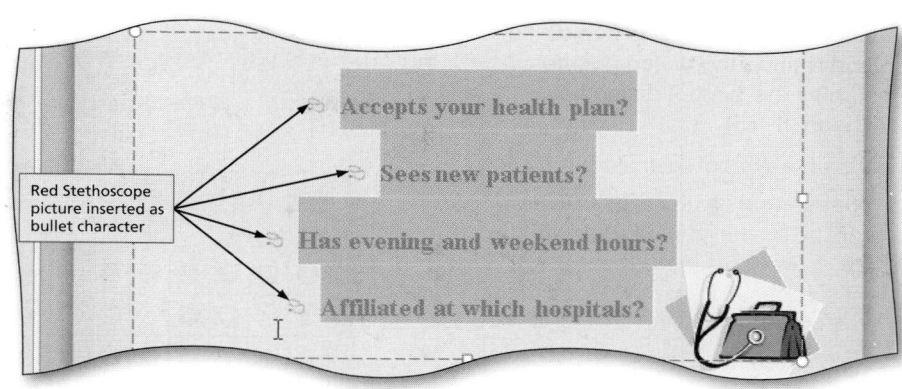

Figure 6–61

To Change a Bullet Character to a Symbol

Picture bullets add a unique quality to your presentations. Another bullet change you can make is to insert a symbol as the character. Symbols are found in several fonts, including Webdings, Wingdings, Wingdings 2, and Wingdings 3. The following steps change the bullet character on Slide 5 to a computer mouse symbol in the Wingdings font.

- Display Slide 5, select all five hyperlinked paragraphs, click the Bullets arrow, and then click Bullets and Numbering to display the Bullets and Numbering dialog box (Figure 6–62).

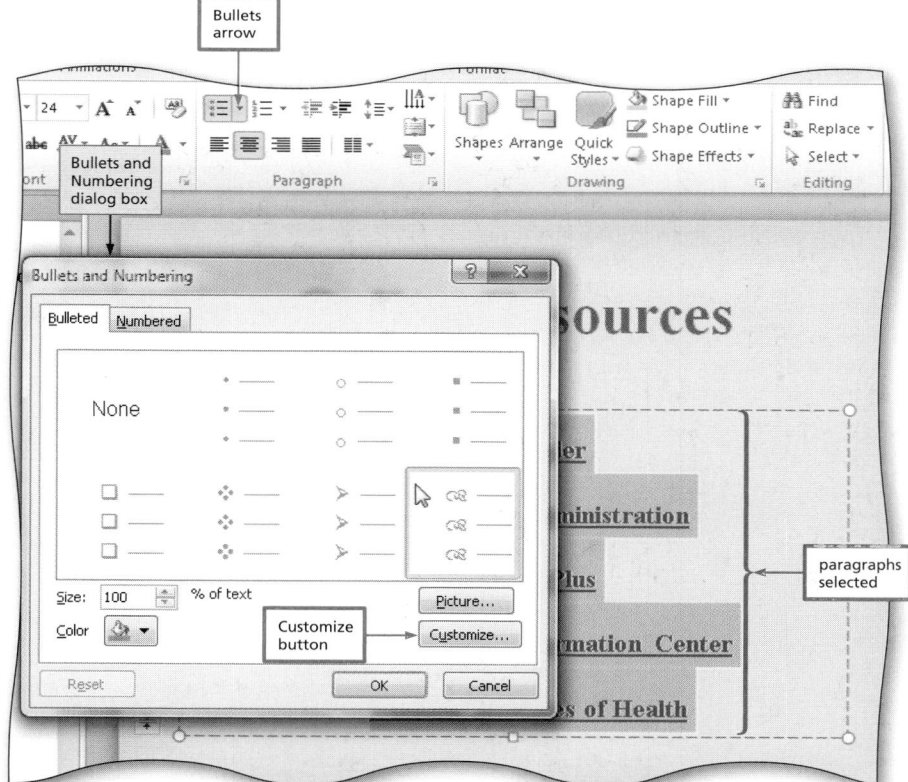

Figure 6–62

2

- Click the Customize button (Bullets and Numbering dialog box) to display the Symbol dialog box (Figure 6–63).

Q&A Why is a symbol selected?

That symbol is the default bullet for the first-level paragraphs in the Hardcover document theme.

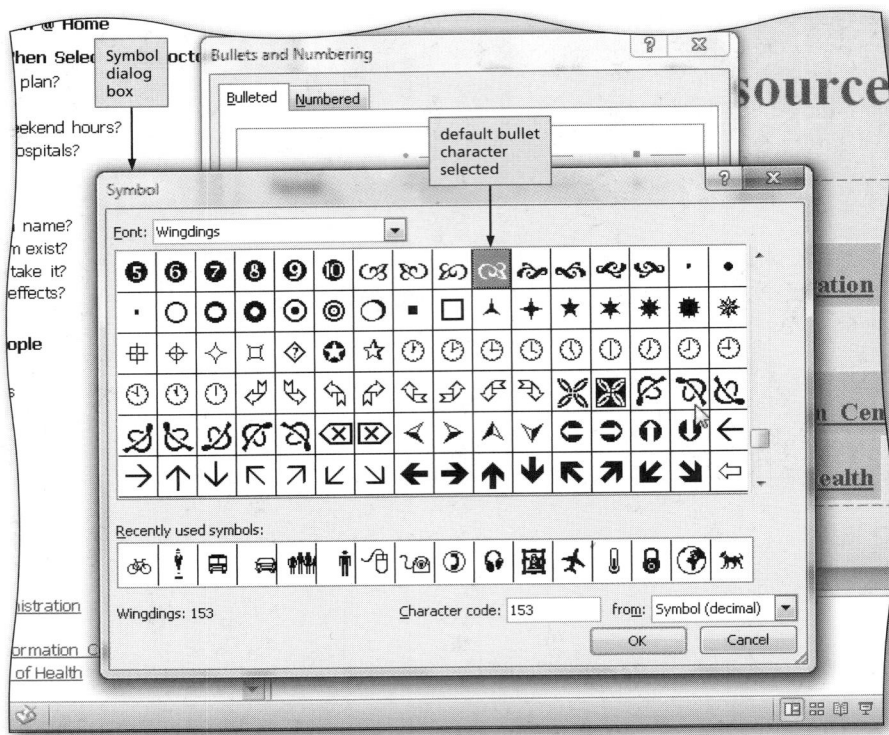

Figure 6–63

3

- Scroll up to locate the computer mouse symbol.

- Click the computer mouse symbol to select it (Figure 6–64).

Q&A Why does my dialog box have more rows of symbols and different fonts from which to choose?

The rows and fonts displayed depend upon how PowerPoint was installed on your system.

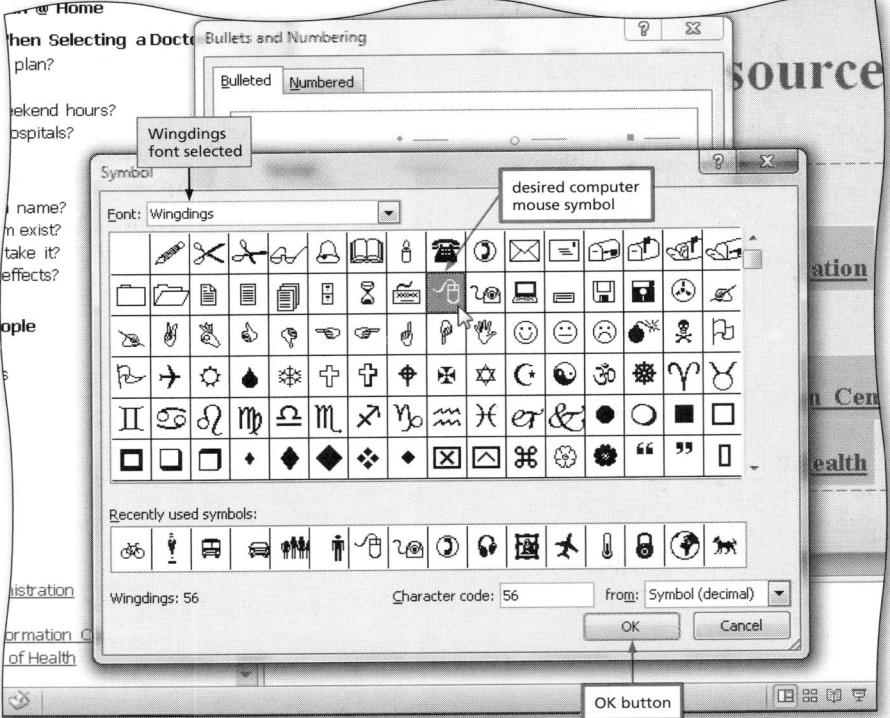

Figure 6–64

4

- Click the OK button (Symbol dialog box) to display the computer mouse bullet in the Bullets and Numbering dialog box (Figure 6–65).

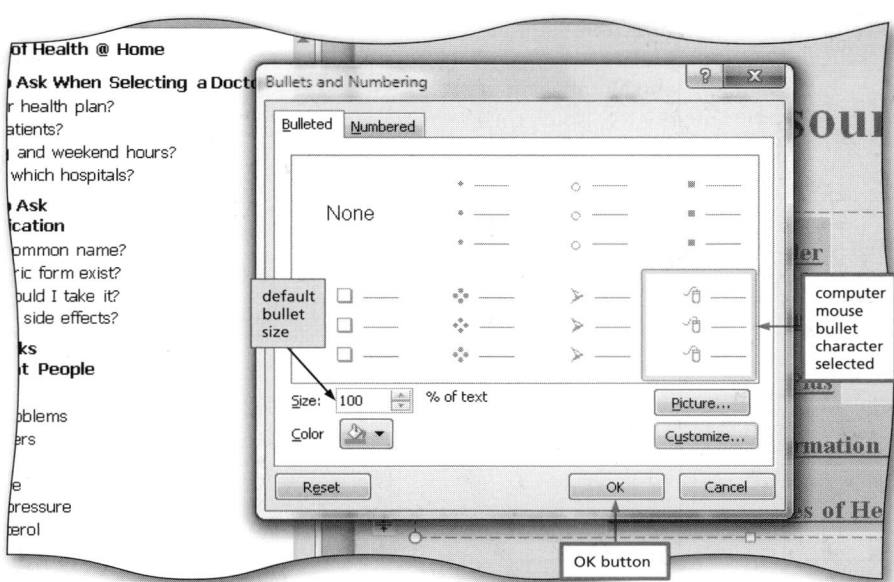

Figure 6–65

5

- Click the OK button (Bullets and Numbering dialog box) to insert the computer mouse symbol as the paragraph bullet (Figure 6–66).

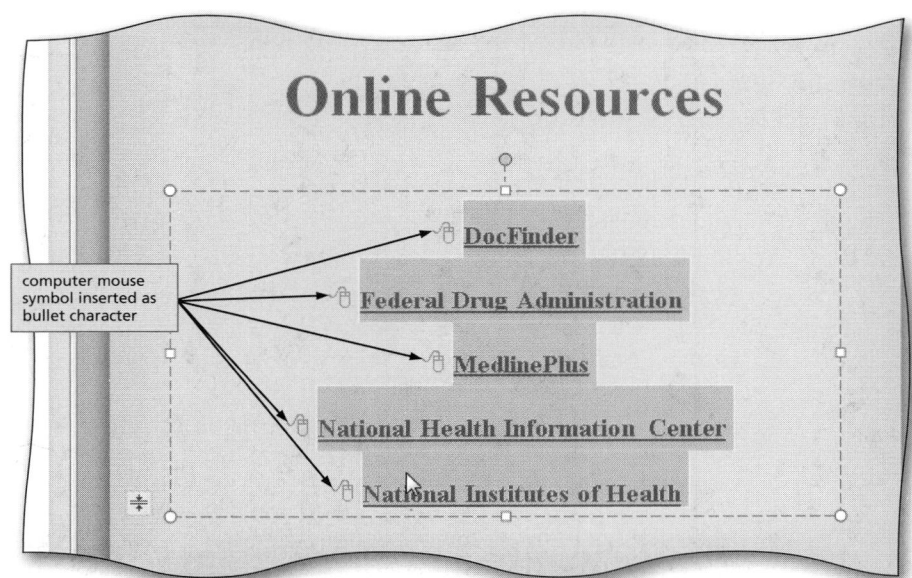

Figure 6–66

To Format a Bullet Size

Bullets have a default size determined by the document theme. **Bullet size** is measured as a percentage of the text size and can range from 25 to 400 percent. The following steps change the computer mouse character size.

1

- With the Slide 5 paragraphs still selected, click the Bullets arrow and then click Bullets and Numbering in the Bullets gallery to display the Bullets and Numbering dialog box.

- Click and hold down the mouse button on the Size box up arrow until 150 is displayed (Figure 6–67).

 Q&A Can I type a number in the text box instead of clicking the up arrow?

Yes. Double-click the text box and then type the desired percentage.

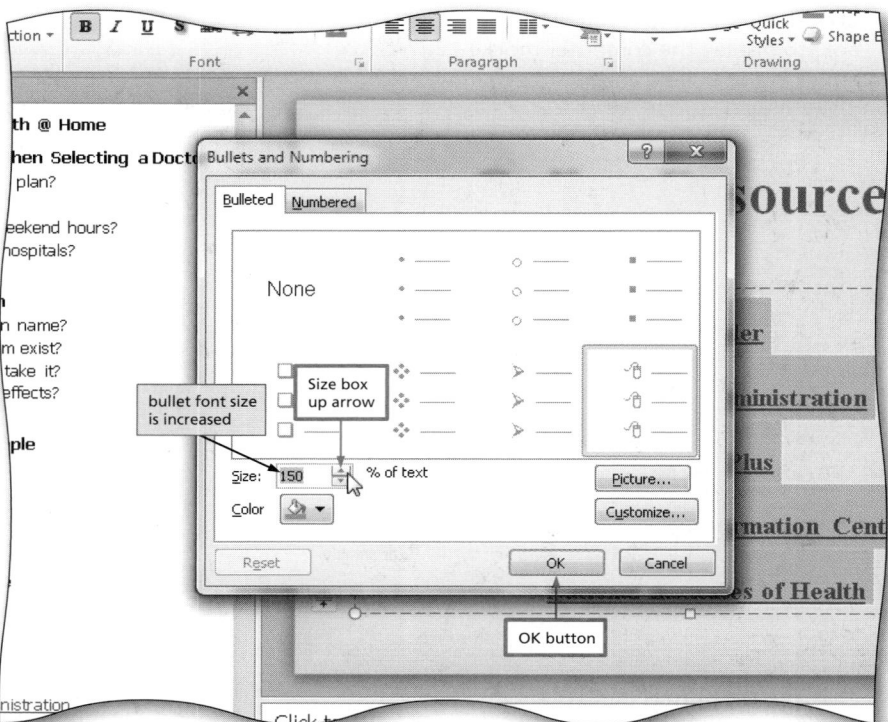

Figure 6–67

2

- Click the OK button to increase the computer mouse bullet size to 150 percent of its original size (Figure 6–68).

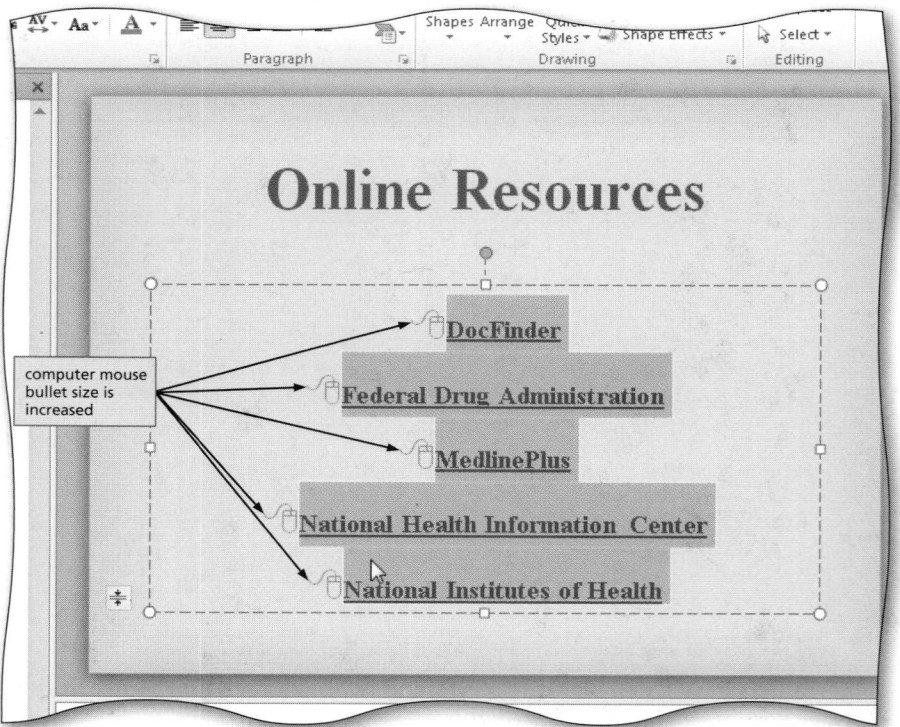

Figure 6–68

To Change the Size of Other Bullet Characters

For consistency, the bullet character on Slide 2 should have a similar size as that on Slide 5. The following steps change the size of the Red Stethoscope bullets.

1 Display Slide 2 and then select the four paragraphs in the content placeholder.

2 Display the Bullets and Numbering dialog box, increase the bullet size to 160% of text, and then click the OK button (Figure 6–69).

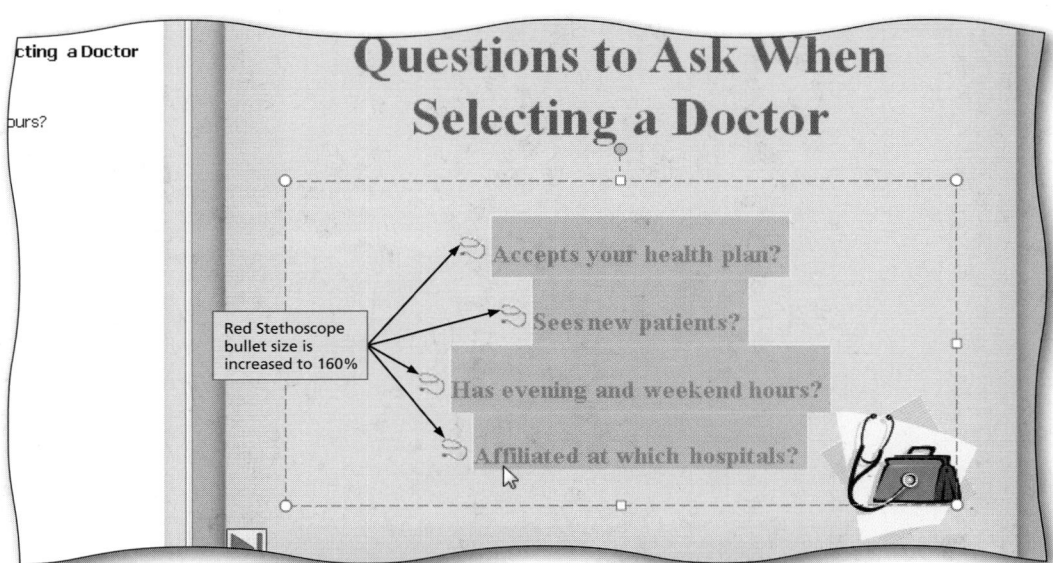

Figure 6–69

To Format a Bullet Color

A default **bullet color** is based on the eight colors in the design theme. Additional standard and custom colors also are available. The following steps change the computer mouse bullet color to Red.

1

• Display Slide 5, select the five hyperlinked paragraphs, display the Bullets and Numbering dialog box, and then click the Color button to display the Color gallery (Figure 6–70).

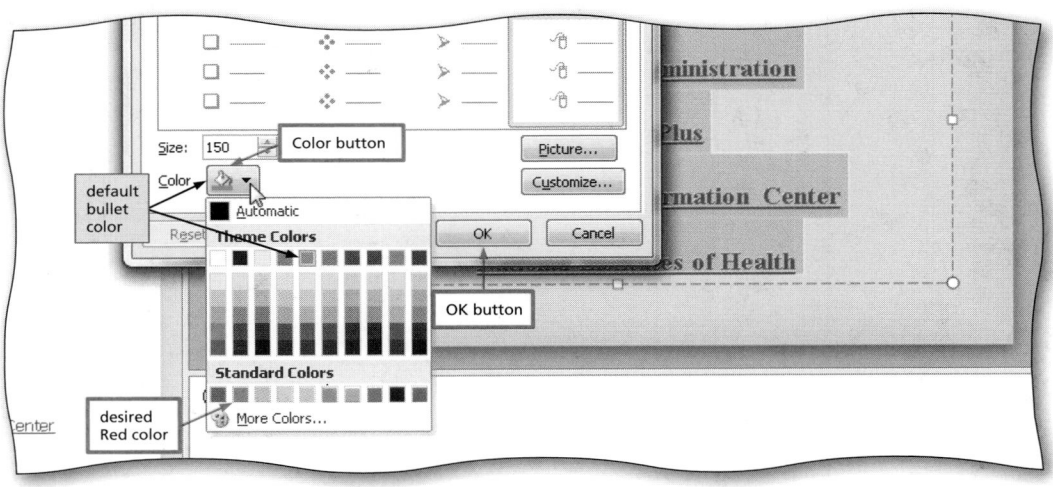

Figure 6–70

• Click the color Red in the Standard
Colors area to change the bullet
color to Red (second color in the
Standard Colors area) (Figure 6–71).

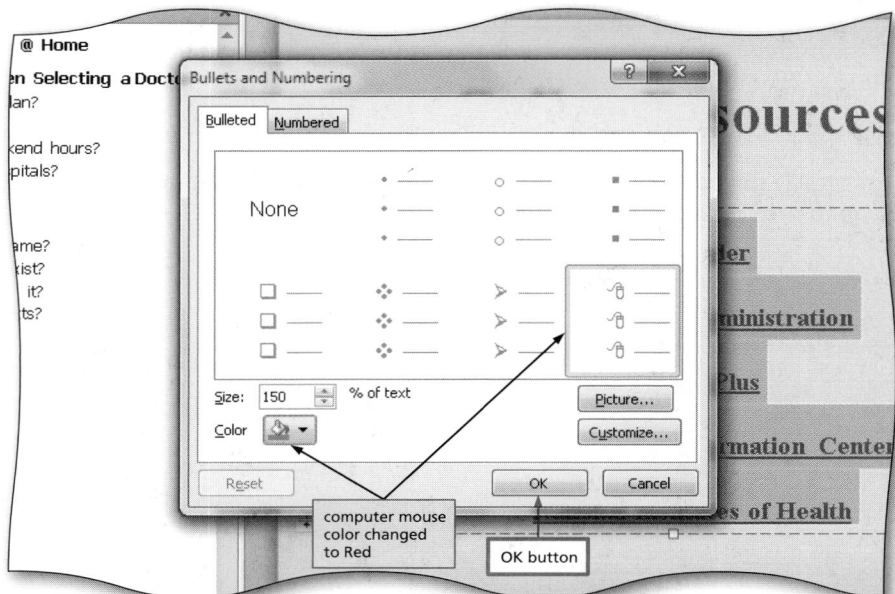

Figure 6–71

• Click the OK button to apply the
color Red to the computer mouse
bullet (Figure 6–72).

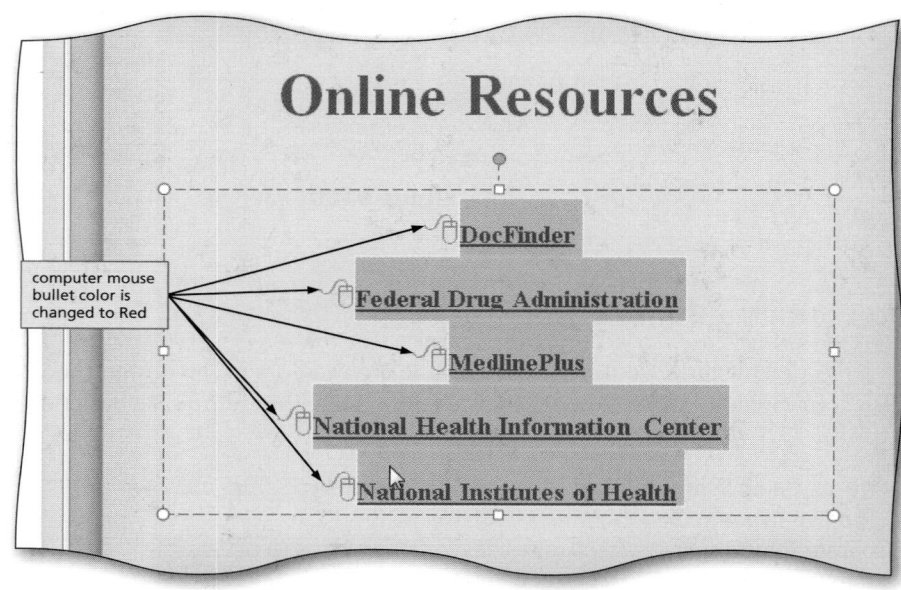

Figure 6–72

Other Ways

1. Right-click paragraph,
   point to Bullets
   on shortcut menu,
   click Bullets and
   Numbering, select
   color

To Change a Bullet Character to a Number

PowerPoint allows you to change the default bullets to numbers. The process of changing the bullet characters
is similar to the process of changing bullets to symbols. The following steps change the first-level paragraph bullet
characters on Slide 3 to numbers.

1

- Display Slide 3 and then select all four content paragraphs.

- With the Home tab still displaying, click the Numbering button arrow (Home tab | Paragraph group) to display the Numbering gallery.

- Point to the 1) 2) 3) numbering option in the Numbering gallery to display a live preview of these numbers (Figure 6–73).

Experiment

- Point to each of the numbers in the Numbering gallery to watch the numbers change on Slide 3.

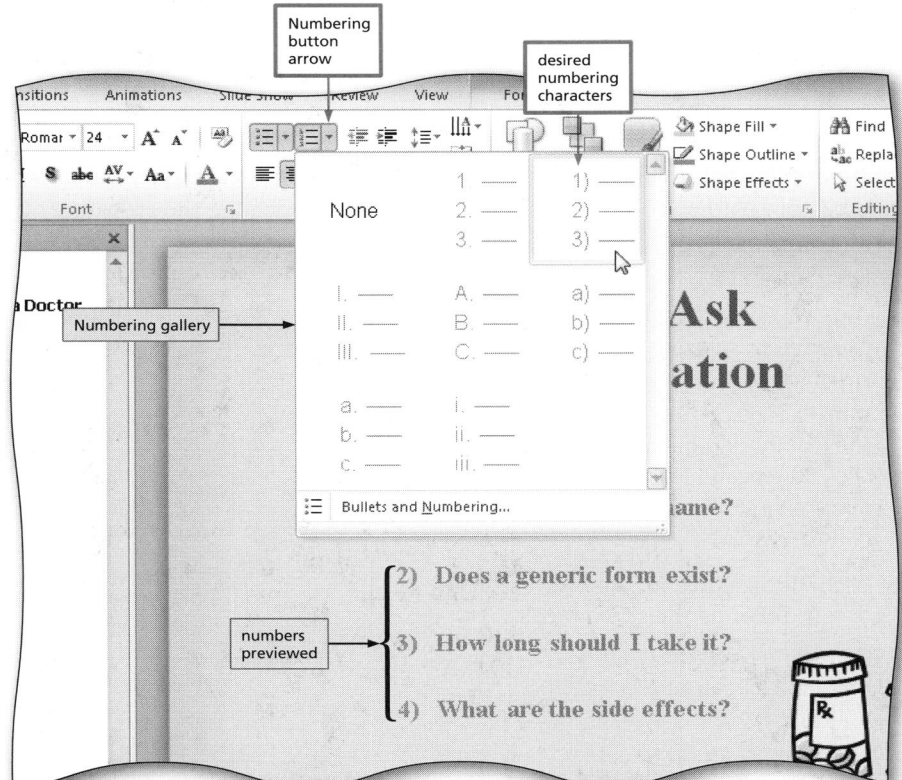

Figure 6–73

2

- Click the 1) 2) 3) numbering option to insert these numbers as the first-level paragraph characters (Figure 6–74).

Q&A

How do I change the first number in the list?

Click Bullets and Numbering at the bottom of the Numbering gallery and then click the up or down arrow in the Start at text box to change the number.

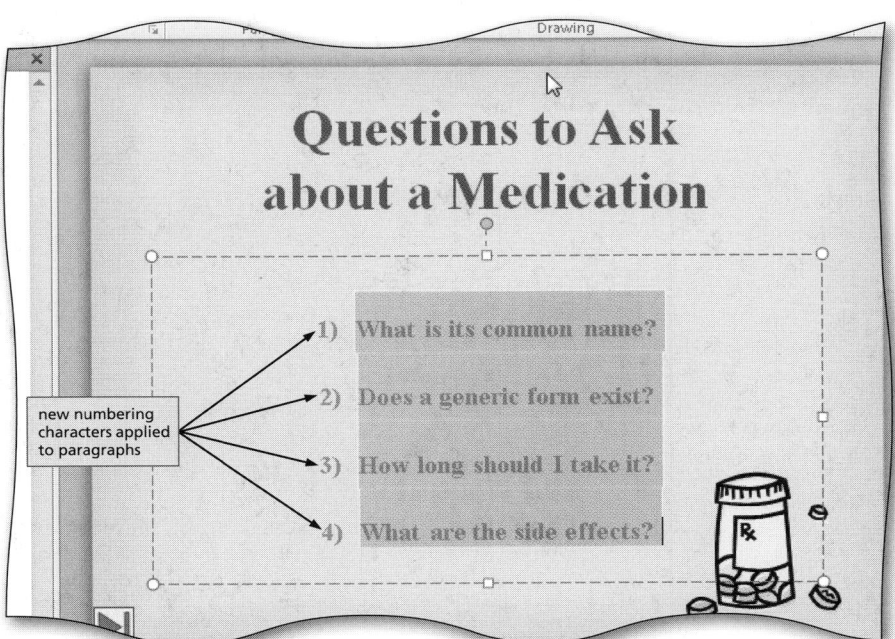

Figure 6–74

Other Ways

1. Right-click paragraph, point to Numbering on shortcut menu, select numbering characters

To Format a Numbered List

To add emphasis, you can increase the size of the new numbers inserted in Slide 3. As with bullets, these characters are measured as a percentage of the text size and can range from 25 to 400 percent. The color of these numbers also can change. The original color is based on the eight colors in the design theme. Additional standard and custom colors are available. The following steps change the size and colors of the numbers to 125 percent and Red, respectively.

 1

- With the Slide 3 content paragraphs still selected, click the Numbering button arrow (Home tab | Paragraph group) to display the Numbering gallery and then click Bullets and Numbering to display the Bullets and Numbering dialog box.

- Click the Size box up arrow several times to change the size to 125%.

 Can I type a number in the text box instead of clicking the up arrow?

Yes. Double-click the text box and then type the desired percentage.

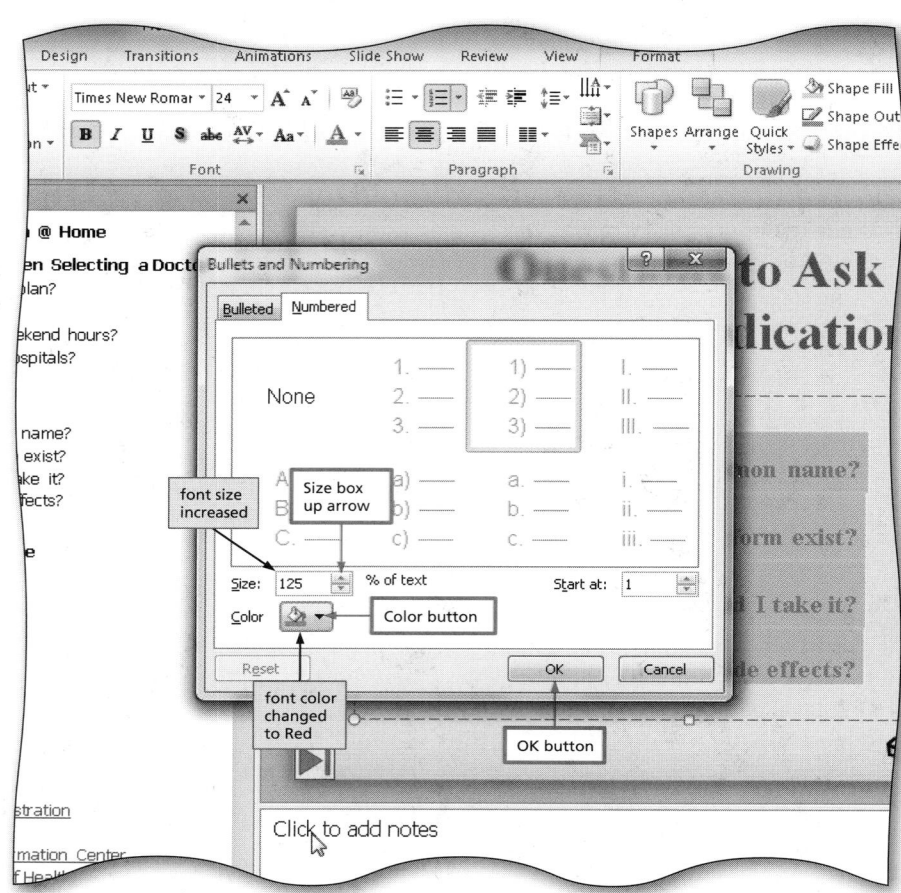

2

- Click the Color button to display the Color gallery and then click Red (second color in the Standard Colors area) to change the numbers' font color (Figure 6–75).

3

- Click the OK button to apply the new numbers' font size and color.

Figure 6–75

Other Ways
1. Right-click paragraph, point to Numbering on shortcut menu, click Bullets and Numbering, click up or down Size arrow until desired size is displayed, click Color button, select color, click OK button

To Remove Bullet Characters

The health risks listed in the two Slide 4 columns are preceded by an ornate bullet character. The slide may appear less cluttered if you remove the bullets. The following steps remove the bullet characters from the items in the two columns on Slide 4.

1

- Display Slide 4, select all the text in the two columns, and then click the Bullets button arrow.

- Point to the None option in the Bullets gallery to display a live preview of how the slide will appear without bullets (Figure 6–76).

2

- Click the None option to remove the bullet characters on Slide 4.

- If necessary, move the scale picture to center it between the two columns.

Q&A Would I use the same technique to remove numbers from a list?

Yes. The None option also is available in the Numbering gallery.

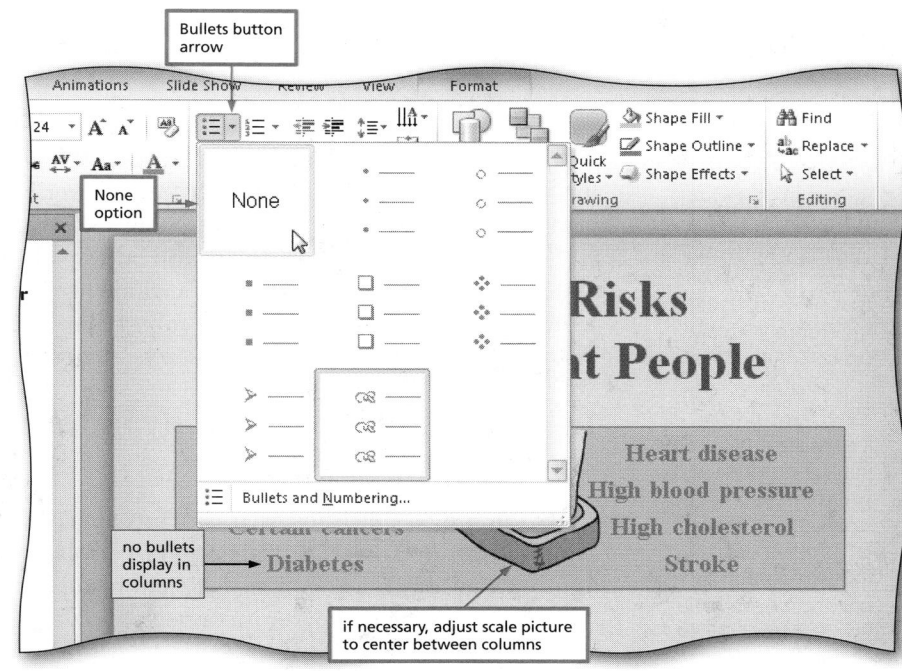

Figure 6–76

To Change Document Properties

Before saving the presentation again, you want to add your name, class name, and some keywords as document properties. The following steps use the Document Information Panel to change document properties.

1 Display the Document Information Panel and then type your name as the Author property.

2 Type your course and section in the Subject property.

3 Type `home health, medication record, doctor selection, overweight risks` as the Keywords property.

4 Close the Document Information Panel.

Consider the audience's interests.
As audience members start to view your presentation, they often think about their personal needs and wonder, "How will this presentation benefit me?" As you may have learned in your psychology classes, Maslow's hierarchy of needs drives much of your behavior, starting with basic sustenance and moving on to safety, belonging, ego-status, and self-actualization. Audience members cannot move to the next higher level of needs until their current level is satisfied. For example, an individual must first satisfy his needs of hunger and thirst before he can consider partaking in leisure time activities. Your presentations must meet the requirements of your audience members; otherwise, these people will not consider your talk as benefiting their needs. Having hyperlinks and action buttons can help you tailor a presentation to fulfill the audience's satisfaction level.

Plan Ahead

BTW

Quick Reference
For a table that lists how to complete the tasks covered in this book using the mouse, Ribbon, shortcut menu, and keyboard, see the Quick Reference Summary at the back of this book, or visit the PowerPoint 2010 Quick Reference Web page (scsite.com/ppt2010/qr).

BTW

Certification
The Microsoft Office Specialist (MOS) program provides an opportunity for you to obtain a valuable industry credential — proof that you have the PowerPoint 2010 skills required by employers. For more information, visit the PowerPoint 2010 Certification Web page (scsite.com/ppt2010/cert).

BTW

Saving the Presentation as an Outline
You began this project by opening a Microsoft Word outline, and you can save the presentation as an outline to use in a word processor or another PowerPoint project. An outline is saved in Rich Text Format (.rtf) and contains only text. To save the presentation as an outline, open the Backstage view, click Save As, type a file name in the File name text box (Save As dialog box), click the 'Save as type' arrow and select Outline/RTF in the Save as type list, and then click the Save button.

Running a Slide Show with Hyperlinks and Action Buttons

The Home Health presentation contains a variety of useful features that provide value to an audience. The graphics should help viewers understand and recall the information being presented. The hyperlinks on Slide 5 show useful Web sites that give current medical information. In addition, the action button allows a presenter to jump to Slide 5 while Slides 2 or 3 are being displayed. If an audience member asks a question or if the presenter needs to answer specific questions regarding weight when Slide 3 is displaying, the information on the hidden Slide 4 can be accessed immediately by pressing the H key.

To Run a Slide Show with Hyperlinks, Action Buttons, and a Hidden Slide

Running a slide show that contains hyperlinks and action buttons is an interactive experience. A presenter has the option to display slides in a predetermined sequence or to improvise based on the audience's reaction and questions. When a presentation contains hyperlinks and the computer is connected to the Internet, the speaker can click the links to command the default browser to display the Web sites. The following steps run the Home Health presentation.

1. Click Slide 1 on the Outline tab. Click the Slide Show button to run the slide show and display Slide 1.

2. Click the stethoscope picture to display Slide 2.

3. On Slide 2, click the stethoscope picture to link to the first slide in the Additional Health presentation.

4. Click the Return action button on the first slide to return to Slide 2 in the Home Health presentation.

5. Press the ENTER key to display Slide 3. Click the prescription picture to start Microsoft Word and open the Medication Record file. View the information and then click the Close button on the title bar to quit Word and return to Slide 3.

6. Press the H key to display Slide 4. Click the scale picture to link to the second slide in the Additional Health presentation. Click the Return action button on the second slide to return to Slide 4 in the Home Health presentation.

7. Press the ENTER key to display Slide 5. Click the first hyperlink to start your browser and access the DocFinder online physician directory Web page. If necessary, maximize the Web page window when the page is displayed. Click the Close button on the Web page title bar to close the browser.

8. Continue using the hyperlinks and action buttons and then end the presentation.

To Save, Print, and Quit PowerPoint

The presentation now is complete. You should save the slides, print a handout, and then quit PowerPoint.

1. Save the Home Health presentation again with the same file name.

2. Print the presentation as a handout with two slides per page (Figure 6–77).

3. Quit PowerPoint, closing all open documents.

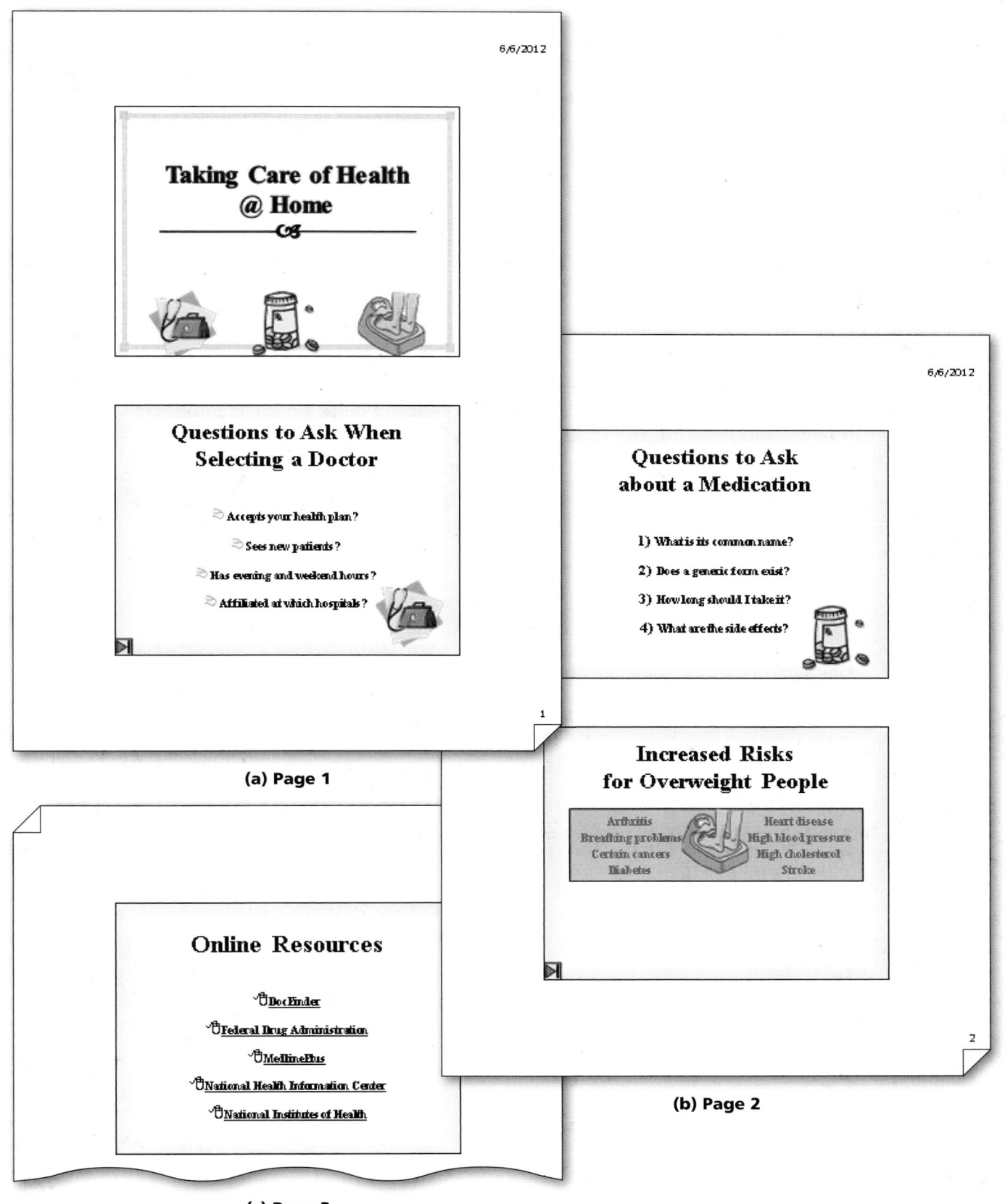

(a) Page 1

(b) Page 2

(c) Page 3

Figure 6–77

Chapter Summary

In this chapter you have learned how to open a Microsoft Word outline as a PowerPoint presentation, develop slides with hyperlinks and action buttons, position slide elements using the drawing guides and rulers, align and distribute pictures, center and align placeholder text, and create columns and then adjust the width. You then learned to change a bullet character to a picture or a symbol and then change its size and color. Finally, you ran the presentation using the action buttons and hyperlinks. The items listed below include all the new PowerPoint skills you have learned in this chapter.

1. Open a Microsoft Word Outline as a Presentation (PPT 335)
2. Add a Hyperlink to a Picture (PPT 339)
3. Add a Hyperlink to a Paragraph (PPT 341)
4. Insert an Action Button (PPT 344)
5. Change an Action Button Fill Color (PPT 346)
6. Copy an Action Button (PPT 348)
7. Edit an Action Button Action Setting (PPT 349)
8. Hyperlink to Another PowerPoint File (PPT 350)
9. Hyperlink to a Microsoft Word File (PPT 353)
10. Display the Drawing Guides (PPT 357)
11. Position a Picture Using Guides (PPT 358)
12. Display the Rulers (PPT 359)
13. Align Pictures (PPT 360)
14. Distribute Pictures (PPT 362)
15. Hide a Slide (PPT 363)
16. Center Placeholder Text (PPT 365)
17. Align Placeholder Text (PPT 366)
18. Change Paragraph Line Spacing (PPT 367)
19. Create Columns in a Placeholder (PPT 367)
20. Adjust Column Spacing (PPT 369)
21. Enter a Line Break (PPT 371)
22. Change a Bullet Character to a Picture (PPT 372)
23. Change a Bullet Character to a Symbol (PPT 375)
24. Format a Bullet Size (PPT 377)
25. Format a Bullet Color (PPT 379)
26. Change a Bullet Character to a Number (PPT 380)
27. Format a Numbered List (PPT 382)
28. Remove Bullet Characters (PPT 382)

If you have a SAM 2010 user profile, your instructor may have assigned an autogradable version of this assignment. If so, log into the SAM 2010 Web site at www.cengage.com/sam2010 to download the instruction and start files.

Learn It Online

Test your knowledge of chapter content and key terms.

Instructions: To complete the Learn It Online exercises, start your browser, click the Address bar, and then enter the Web address **scsite.com/ppt2010/learn**. When the Office 2010 Learn It Online page is displayed, click the link for the exercise you want to complete and then read the instructions.

Chapter Reinforcement TF, MC, and SA
A series of true/false, multiple choice, and short answer questions that test your knowledge of the chapter content.

Flash Cards
An interactive learning environment where you identify chapter key terms associated with displayed definitions.

Practice Test
A series of multiple choice questions that test your knowledge of chapter content and key terms.

Who Wants To Be a Computer Genius?
An interactive game that challenges your knowledge of chapter content in the style of a television quiz show.

Wheel of Terms
An interactive game that challenges your knowledge of chapter key terms in the style of the television show *Wheel of Fortune*.

Crossword Puzzle Challenge
A crossword puzzle that challenges your knowledge of key terms presented in the chapter.

Apply Your Knowledge

Reinforce the skills and apply the concepts you learned in this chapter.

Revising a Presentation with Action Buttons, Bullet Styles, and Hidden Slides

Note: To complete this assignment, you will be required to use the Data Files for Students. See the inside back cover of this book for instructions on downloading the Data Files for Students, or contact your instructor for information about accessing the required files.

Instructions: Start PowerPoint. Open the presentation, Apply 6-1 Anatomy, located on the Data Files for Students.

   The six slides in the presentation identify names seldom used for parts of the body. You plan to use the presentation as a study guide for your anatomy class. The document you open is an unformatted presentation. You are to add a style to the pictures; insert action buttons on Slide 1; hide Slides 2, 3, 4, and 5; and format the bullets on Slides 2 through 6 so the slides look like Figure 6–78 on the next page.

Perform the following tasks:

1. Change the document theme to Grid. Apply the WordArt style, Fill – Tan, Accent 2, Warm Matte Bevel, to the title text and add the Chevron Up text effect.

2. On Slide 1, apply the Rotated, White picture style to the upper-left picture, apply the Metal Frame picture style to the upper-right picture, apply the Metal Rounded Rectangle picture style to the lower-left picture, and apply the Bevel Perspective Left, White picture style to the lower-right picture, as shown in Figure 6–78a.

3. Hyperlink each picture to the corresponding slide. For example, the upper-left picture should hyperlink to Slide 2. The other three pictures should hyperlink to Slides 3, 4, and 5, respectively.

4. Center the subtitle text and then bold this text.

5. On Slide 2, insert a Home action button and hyperlink it to the first slide. Change the action button fill color to Yellow, and then change the transparency to 60%. Do not play a sound. Size the button so that it is approximately 0.75" × 0.75" and then move it to the location shown in Figure 6–78b. Copy this action button to Slides 3, 4, and 5.

6. On Slides 2 through 6, add Arrow Bullets to the content text paragraphs and then increase the size of the bullets to 135% of text. Change the color of the body part terms at the beginning of each paragraph to Tan, Accent 1 on all slides.

7. Hide Slides 2, 3, 4, and 5.

8. Change the Transition from Zoom to Split. Change the duration to 02.50.

9. Display the revised presentation in Slide Sorter view to check for consistency.

10. Change the document properties, as specified by your instructor. Save the presentation using the file name, Apply 6-1 Parts of the Body. Submit the revised document in the format specified by your instructor.

Continued >

Apply Your Knowledge *continued*

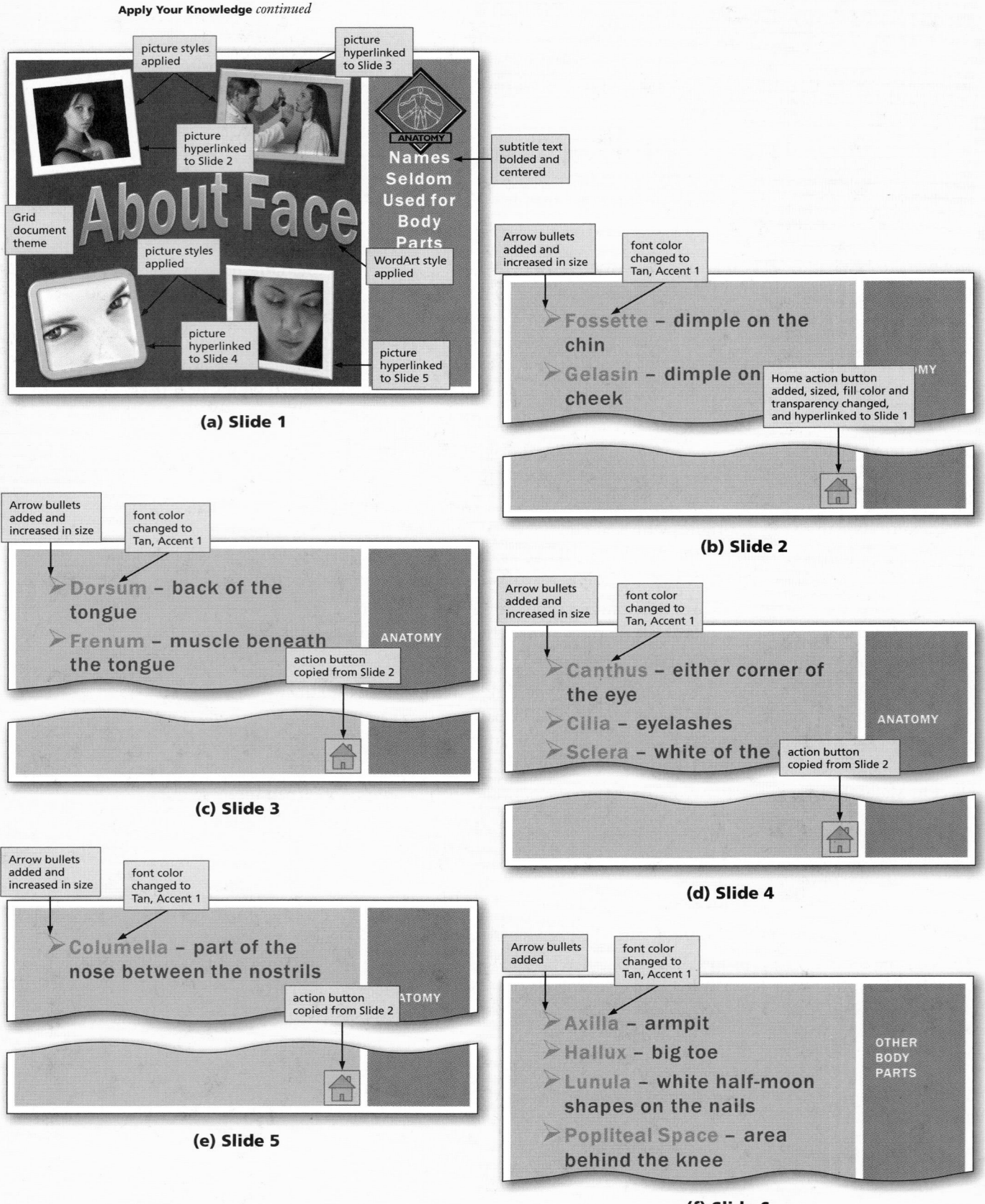

Figure 6–78

Extend Your Knowledge

Extend the skills you learned in this chapter and experiment with new skills. You may need to use Help to complete the assignment.

Inserting a Picture into an Action Button and Changing a Bullet Character to a Picture

Note: To complete this assignment, you will be required to use the Data Files for Students. See the inside back cover of this book for instructions on downloading the Data Files for Students, or contact your instructor for information about accessing the required files.

Instructions: Start PowerPoint. Open the presentation, Extend 6-1 Camp, located on the Data Files for Students.

You will insert hyperlinks on the title slide; enter the data from Table 6–3 on Slide 2; insert action buttons on Slides 2, 3, and 4; and change the bullet characters to pictures on Slides 5 and 6, as shown in Figure 6–79 on the next page.

Table 6–3 Adams Family Camp Trails

Trail	Length	Trail Head
Mountainview	10.2 miles	Behind clubhouse
Lakeside	11.5 miles	Main dock
Upper Bend	12.8 miles	Behind clubhouse

Perform the following tasks:

1. On Slide 1, hyperlink each picture to the corresponding slide. For example, the top picture should hyperlink to Slide 2. The other two pictures should hyperlink to Slides 3 and 4, respectively. Use the Smart Guides to align the three pictures to the slide and then distribute these images vertically. Once the pictures are distributed vertically, use the Arrange list to align their centers as well.

2. On Slide 2, insert a Custom action button in the lower-left area of the slide and hyperlink it to the first slide. Format this shape by inserting the picture, Hiking, located on the Data Files for Students, as shown in Figure 6–79b.

3. Enter the data from Table 6–3 in the text box on Slide 2. Change the paragraph line spacing to 1.5 and center all text.

4. On Slide 3, insert a Custom action button in the lower-left corner of the slide and hyperlink it to the first slide. Format this shape by inserting the picture, Fishing, located on your Data Files for Students, as shown in Figure 6–79c.

5. On Slide 4, insert a Forward or Next action button in the lower-right corner of the slide.

6. On Slide 5, change the bullet character to the Scissors picture located on the Data Files for Students. Increase the size of the bullets to 150% of text.

7. On Slide 6, insert a picture bullet by importing the Camera picture located on the Data Files for Students, and then increase the size of the bullets to 150% of text.

8. Change the title text paragraph alignment on Slides 5 and 6 to Distributed by selecting the title text, displaying the Home tab, clicking the Paragraph Dialog Box Launcher button (Home tab | Paragraph group), clicking the Alignment box arrow, and then clicking Distributed.

9. Apply a transition to all slides.

10. Change the document properties, as specified by your instructor. Save the presentation using the file name, Extend 6-1 Family Summer Camp.

11. Submit the revised document in the format specified by your instructor.

Continued >

Extend Your Knowledge *continued*

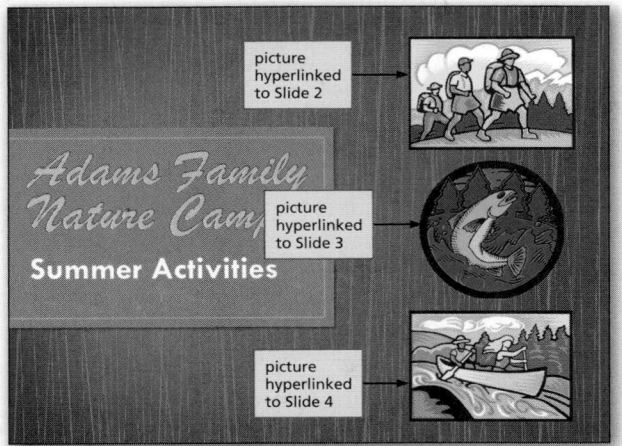

(a) Slide 1

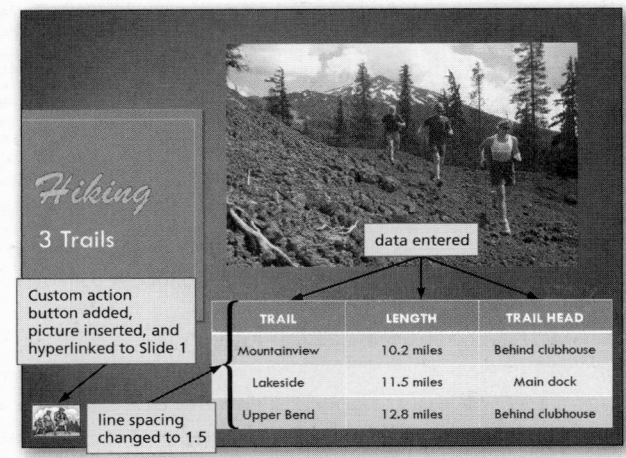

(b) Slide 2

(c) Slide 3

(d) Slide 4

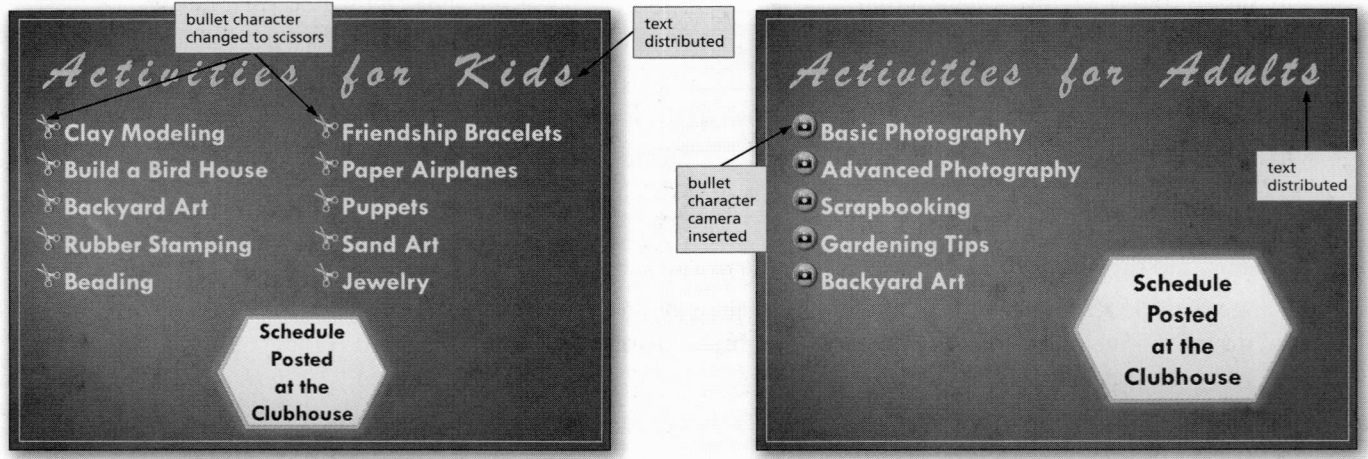

(e) Slide 5

(f) Slide 6

Figure 6–79

Make It Right

Analyze a presentation and correct all errors and/or improve the design.

Modifying Text and Line Spacing in a Placeholder

Note: To complete this assignment, you will be required to use the Data Files for Students. See the inside back cover of this book for instructions on downloading the Data Files for Students, or contact your instructor for information about accessing the required files.

Instructions: Start PowerPoint. Open the presentation, Make It Right 6-1 Golf, located on the Data Files for Students. Correct the formatting problems and errors in the presentation while keeping in mind the guidelines presented in this chapter.

Perform the following tasks:

1. On Slide 1, shown in Figure 6–80, select the four words, What's in Your Bag?, at the top of the slide and then decrease the font size to 28 point. Make sure that these four words show in the box. Change the title text font size to 40 point and then right-align this text. Center the text in both subtitle placeholders.

2. Remove the artistic effect from the picture and change the style to Rotated, White.

3. Increase the font size of the text in the right placeholder to 22 point.

4. Align the text in both placeholders vertically in the center.

5. Increase the size of the bullets to 200% of the text size.

6. Check the spelling and correct the misspellings.

7. Change the document properties, as specified by your instructor. Save the presentation using the file name, Make It Right 6-1 Golf Clubs.

8. Submit the revised document in the format specified by your instructor.

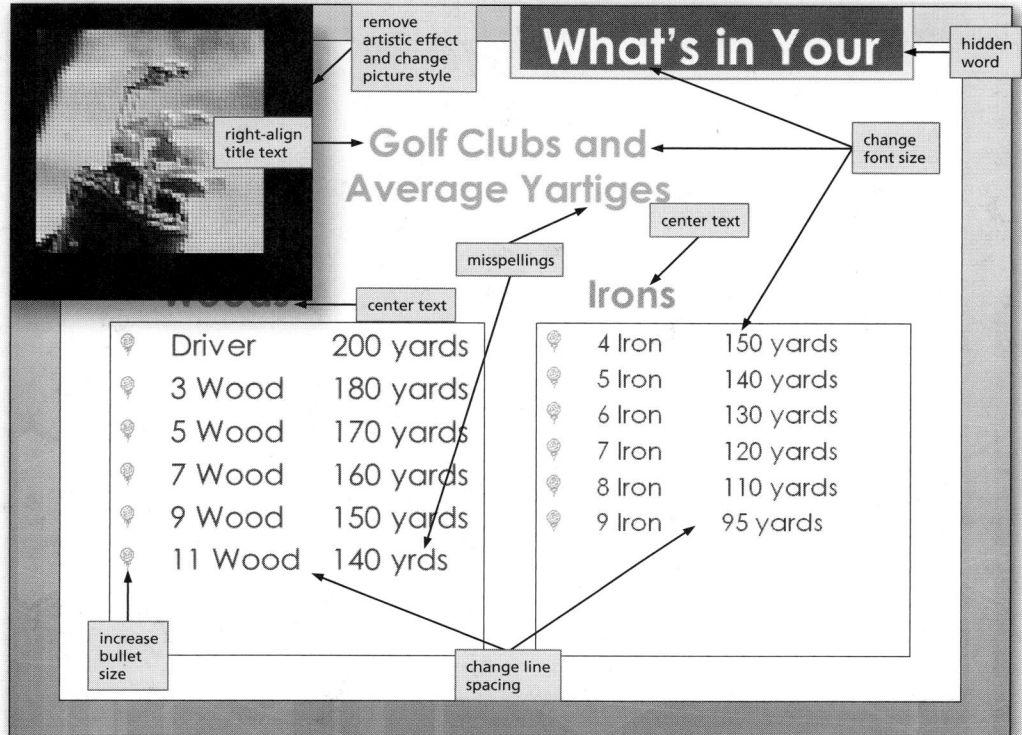

Figure 6–80

In the Lab

Design and/or create a presentation using the guidelines, concepts, and skills presented in this chapter. Labs 1, 2, and 3 are listed in order of increasing difficulty.

Lab 1: Aligning Text and Creating Columns in a Text Box, Moving a Placeholder, and Changing a Bullet Character to a Picture

Note: To complete this assignment, you will be required to use the Data Files for Students. See the inside back cover of this book for instructions on downloading the Data Files for Students, or contact your instructor for information about accessing the required files.

Problem: You belong to a garden club in the city and find that many members have limited yard space for planting a garden. The president of the club asked if you would modify an existing presentation that describes the basics of container gardening. You create the slides shown in Figure 6–81 using files located on the Data Files for Students.

Perform the following tasks:

1. Open the presentation, Lab 6-1 Vegetables, located on the Data Files for Students.

2. Change the presentation theme colors to Hardcover.

3. On Slide 1, change the title text placeholder vertical alignment to Top. Insert a line break after the dash in the first line and then delete the space before the word, No, in the second line. Change the font size to 54 point, and the font color to Light Green, and then bold this text. Change the subtitle text font to Vani and the font size to 36 point. Increase the size of the three clips, as shown in Figure 6–81a, and then use the Smart Guides to align the two flowerpots.

4. On Slide 2, add bullets and then change the bullet character to the Clay Pot picture located on the Data Files for Students. Increase the size of these bullets to 250% of text.

5. On Slide 3, change the four bullet characters to the 1) 2) 3) numbering format. Change the numbering color to Orange, Accent 2 and the size to 100% of text.

6. On Slide 4, create three columns in the text box, adjust the column spacing to 1", and then change the line spacing to 1.5. Move the two clips to the locations shown in Figure 6–81d.

7. Apply the Window transition and change the duration to 2.25 for all slides.

8. Change the document properties, as specified by your instructor. Save the presentation using the file name, Lab 6-1 Container Vegetable Garden.

9. Submit the revised document in the format specified by your instructor.

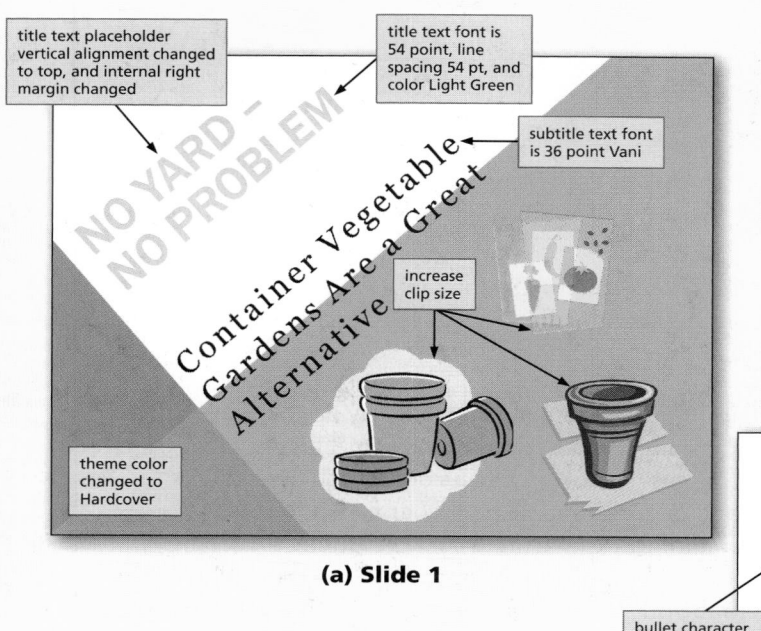

title text placeholder vertical alignment changed to top, and internal right margin changed

title text font is 54 point, line spacing 54 pt, and color Light Green

subtitle text font is 36 point Vani

increase clip size

theme color changed to Hardcover

(a) Slide 1

LOCATION

- Need sun
- Keep containers small enough to move
- Ensure proper drainage

bullet character changed to clay pot

(b) Slide 2

bullet characters changed and formatted

WATERING AND FEEDING

1) Must be well watered
2) Use mulch around top of container
3) May need additional fertilizer due to extra watering
4) Use a diluted water-soluble fertilizer

(c) Slide 3

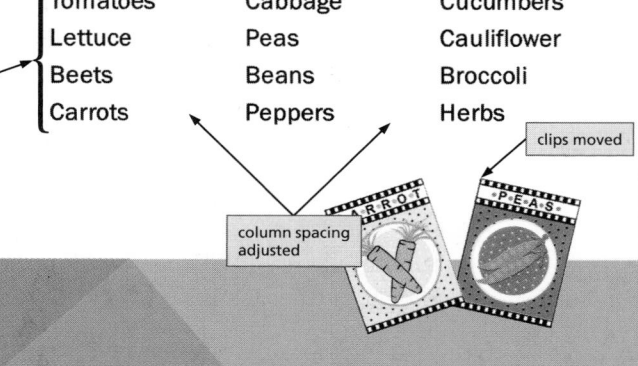

VEGETABLES TO CONSIDER

Tomatoes	Cabbage	Cucumbers
Lettuce	Peas	Cauliflower
Beets	Beans	Broccoli
Carrots	Peppers	Herbs

three-column textbox

clips moved

column spacing adjusted

(d) Slide 4

Figure 6–81

In the Lab

Lab 2: Creating a Presentation from a Microsoft Word Outline, Inserting Hyperlinks to Other Office Documents, Hiding Slides, and Copying and Editing Action Buttons

Note: To complete this assignment, you will be required to use the Data Files for Students. See the inside back cover of this book for instructions on downloading the Data Files for Students, or contact your instructor for information about accessing the required files.

Problem: The members of your school's hiking club are planning an eight-day backpacking trip in a national park. As program chairman, you are working on the details of the trip. The president asks you to give a presentation at your next meeting to discuss some of the trip's details and gives you a Microsoft Word outline with points to cover during your speech. To supplement your talk, the treasurer gives you an Excel file that has the club's membership information, and you have created a Microsoft Word document that lists items everyone should pack and bring on the trip. You will use the outline as the basis for your presentation and create hyperlinks to the other documents to display during your presentation. You borrowed photos from your cousin, who took a trip to this park, and you will use those pictures in your presentation. The trip will include visits to Baer Woods, Ruff Summit, Pine Cone Valley, and Stoop Falls. You create the slides shown in Figure 6–82 using files located on the Data Files for Students.

Perform the following tasks:

1. Create a new presentation using the Office Theme. Import the outline, Lab 6-2 Backpacking Outline, shown in Figure 6–82a, located on the Data Files for Students. Change the new Slide 1 layout to Title Slide.

2. On Slide 1, create a background by inserting the picture called National Park located on the Data Files for Students. Change the transparency to 62%.

3. Increase the title text font size to 54 point. Create a hyperlink for all the title text to the Excel document, Tooterville Hiking Club (Figure 6–82i), located on the Data Files for Students. Bold the subtitle text.

4. On Slide 2, convert the bulleted list to SmartArt by applying the Continuous Picture List (List area). Change the colors to Colorful Range – Accent Colors 2 to 3 and then apply the Polished 3D style to the graphic. Insert the pictures, Hiking1, Hiking2, Hiking3, and Hiking4, from the Data Files for Students, as shown in Figure 6–82b.

5. On all slides except the title slide, change the background to Style 10.

6. On Slide 3 (Figure 6–82c), change the bullet character to the Compass picture located on the Data Files for Students. Increase the size of the bullets to 110% of the text. Insert the Return action button in the lower-right corner of this slide and then hyperlink the button to the Last Slide Viewed, which will be Slide 2 when you run the presentation.

7. Duplicate Slide 3 three times to add the new three slides to create new Slides 4, 5, and 6. The current Slide 4 becomes Slide 7.

8. On Slide 2, insert a hyperlink on each picture. Link the Baer Woods picture to Slide 3, the Ruff Summit picture to Slide 4, the Pine Cone Valley picture to Slide 5, and the Stoop Falls picture to Slide 6. Play the sound, Camera, for each hyperlink.

9. On Slides 3, 4, 5, and 6, change the font color of the bulleted paragraphs to match the corresponding SmartArt graphic color, as shown in Figures 6–82d through 6–82g. The Baer Woods color is Red, Accent 2; the Ruff Summit color is Orange, Accent 6; the Pine Cone Valley color is Orange; and the Stoop Falls color is Olive Green, Accent 3, Darker 50%. Bold each of the colored paragraphs.

10. Hide Slides 3, 4, 5, and 6.

11. On Slide 7 (Figure 6–82h), insert a hyperlink in the title text to the Word document, Packing List (Figure 6–82j), located on the Data Files for Students. Change the six bullet characters to the 1.2.3. numbering format, the color to Blue, and the size to 125% of the text. Bold all the numbered paragraphs on the slide.

12. Apply the Honeycomb transition and then change the duration to 3.25 for all slides.

13. Check the spelling and correct any errors.

14. Change the document properties, as specified by your instructor. Save the presentation using the file name, Lab 6-2 Backpacking Trip.

15. Submit the revised document in the format specified by your instructor.

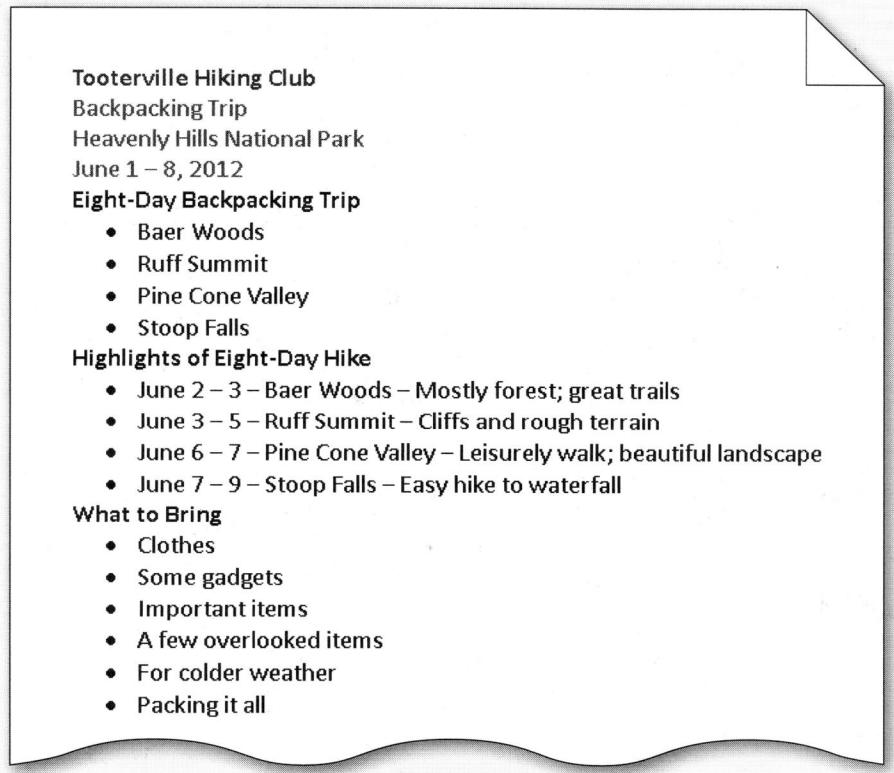

(a) Backpacking Outline — Microsoft Word Document

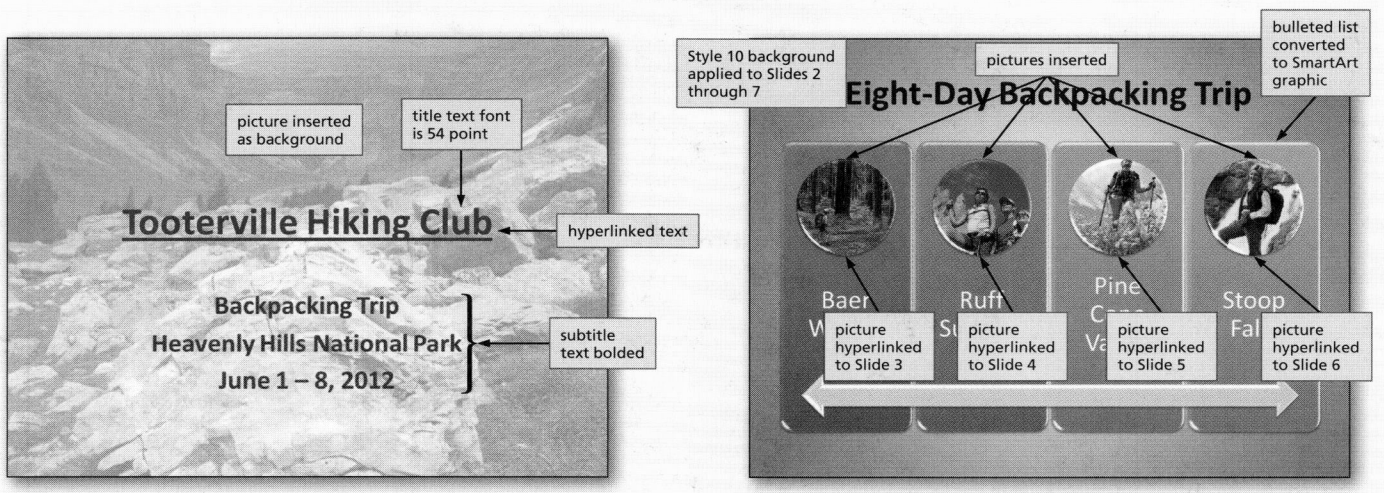

(b) Slide 1

(c) Slide 2

Figure 6–82

Continued >

In the Lab *continued*

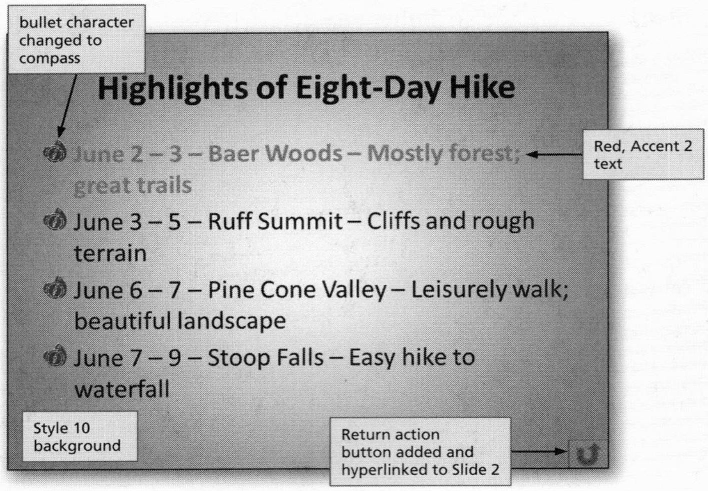

bullet character changed to compass

Highlights of Eight-Day Hike

Red, Accent 2 text

- June 2 – 3 – Baer Woods – Mostly forest; great trails
- June 3 – 5 – Ruff Summit – Cliffs and rough terrain
- June 6 – 7 – Pine Cone Valley – Leisurely walk; beautiful landscape
- June 7 – 9 – Stoop Falls – Easy hike to waterfall

Style 10 background

Return action button added and hyperlinked to Slide 2

(d) Slide 3

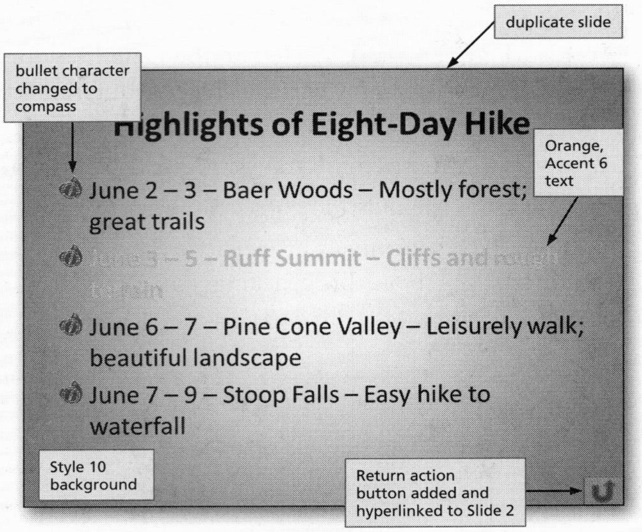

duplicate slide

bullet character changed to compass

Highlights of Eight-Day Hike

Orange, Accent 6 text

- June 2 – 3 – Baer Woods – Mostly forest; great trails
- June 3 – 5 – Ruff Summit – Cliffs and rough terrain
- June 6 – 7 – Pine Cone Valley – Leisurely walk; beautiful landscape
- June 7 – 9 – Stoop Falls – Easy hike to waterfall

Style 10 background

Return action button added and hyperlinked to Slide 2

(e) Slide 4

duplicate slide

bullet character changed to compass

Highlights of Eight-Day Hike

- June 2 – 3 – Baer Woods – Mostly forest; great trails
- June 3 – 5 – Ruff Summit – Cliffs and rough terrain
- June 6 – 7 – Pine Cone Valley – Leisurely walk; beautiful landscape

Orange text

- June 7 – 9 – Stoop Falls – Easy hike to waterfall

Style 10 background

Return action button added and hyperlinked to Slide 2

(f) Slide 5

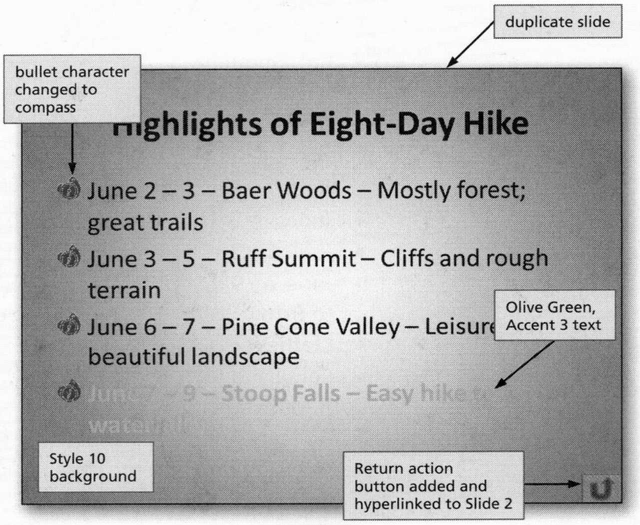

duplicate slide

bullet character changed to compass

Highlights of Eight-Day Hike

- June 2 – 3 – Baer Woods – Mostly forest; great trails
- June 3 – 5 – Ruff Summit – Cliffs and rough terrain
- June 6 – 7 – Pine Cone Valley – Leisure beautiful landscape

Olive Green, Accent 3 text

- June 7 – 9 – Stoop Falls – Easy hike waterfall

Style 10 background

Return action button added and hyperlinked to Slide 2

(g) Slide 6

bullet characters changed to numbers formatted

What to Bring

hyperlinked text

1. Clothes
2. Some gadgets
3. Important items
4. A few overlooked items
5. For colder weather
6. Packing it all

text bolded

Style 10 background

(h) Slide 7

Figure 6–82 (Continued)

	A	B	C	D	E	F	G	H	I	J	K	L	M
1	**Tooterville Hiking Club - Membership Roster**												
2	**Name**		**Joined**	**Dues Paid**	June 2012 Trip								
3	Abbot	Carol	2006	Yes	No								
4	Anders	Robert	2009	Yes	Yes								
5	Bolt	Abigail	2009	Yes	Yes								
6	Conners	Jimmie	2008	Yes	No								
7	Cranz	Nancy	2009	Yes	Yes								
8	Cravin	Joe	2008	Yes	Yes								
9	Davis	Sandy	2009	Yes	Yes								
10	Dorm	Janie	2006	No	No								
11	Evins	Erick	2006	Yes	Yes								
12	Flap	Susan	2007	No	Yes								
13	Foster	Chris	2006	Yes	No								
14	Hope	Candy	2006	No	Yes								
15	Jones	Felix	2006	Yes	No								
16	Kwik	Joshua	2008	Yes	No								
17	Morgan	Nicholas	2009	Yes	Yes								
18	Mullin	Benjamin	2009	Yes	No								
19	Nallon	Miriam	2007	No	No								
20	Olson	Jack	2008	Yes	Yes								
21	Platt	Calista	2009	Yes	Yes								
22	Wyatt	Brian	2008	No	No								
23	Yore	Suzie	2007	Yes	No								
24	Yulepp	Kendra	2009	Yes	Yes								
25	Zanders	Amy	2008	Yes	Yes								
26													
27													

Sheet1 / Sheet2 / Sheet3

Sunday, April 04, 2010

(i) Membership Roster — Microsoft Excel File

Clothes
- Shirts (long- and short-sleeved)
- Thin fleece jacket
- Socks and underwear
- Two pair of jeans
- Baseball hat, sun hat
- Swimming gear
- Hiking boots/shoes and sandals

Some gadgets
- Camera and spare battery
- Chargers and plug adaptor if needed
- Mini LED flashlight or head light
- Cell phone
- Calculator

Important Items
- ATM, credit card, and cash
- Sun glasses
- Glasses and contacts lenses and solutions
- First aid/medicine kit
- Shower kit
- Mosquito net and tape
- Documents: emergency numbers, insurance cards, flight details, etc.
- Guidebook

A few overlooked items
- Pen and notepad
- Packets of tissues
- Towel
- Sleeping sac
- Entertainment: book(s), magazine(s), cards, MP3 player, handheld games
- Umbrella or waterproof shell
- Earplugs, eye mask
- Snacks

For colder weather
- Heavy fleece jacket
- Thermal vest
- Gloves, knit hat, thick socks, an outer windproof shell, thermal leggings

Packing it all
- Money belt
- Mini padlock and cable lock
- Shoulder bag or fanny pack for day use
- Small plastic bags and containers for storage
- A bag/backpack to store everything

(j) Packing List — Microsoft Word File

Figure 6–82 (Continued)

In the Lab

Lab 3: Inserting Hyperlinks and Action Buttons, Hiding Slides, Using Guides, and Formatting Bullets

Note: To complete this assignment, you will be required to use the Data Files for Students. See the inside back cover of this book for instructions on downloading the Data Files for Students, or contact your instructor for information about accessing the required files.

Problem: Your public speaking instructor has assigned an informative speech, and you have decided to discuss landlocked countries. You create the presentation in Figure 6–83 that consists of six slides with hyperlinks, and you decide to hide four slides. Required files are located on the Data Files for Students.

Perform the following tasks:

1. Open the presentation, Lab 6-3 Landlocked, from the Data Files for Students. Change the document theme to Civic and then change the presentation theme colors to Adjacency.

2. On Slide 1, change the title text font to Algerian. Increase the font size of the first line of the title text to 48 point, and then decrease the second line's font size to 36 point. Convert the bulleted list to SmartArt by applying the Vertical Circle List (List area). Decrease the font size of the first line to 30 point and the countries' names to 24 point. Apply the Bevel Perspective picture style to the picture.

3. On Slides 2, 3, and 4, resize the globe and map pictures so that they are approximately 3.39" × 5.4" and then move them to the locations shown in Figure 6–83. Display the rulers, click to the left and below the center of the globe, and then move the graphic so that the mouse pointer is positioned at the center of both the vertical and horizontal rulers. Hide the rulers.

4. On Slides 2, 3, and 4, resize the country symbols in the lower-right corners so that they are approximately 0.75" × 1.67". Display the drawing guides. Set the horizontal guide to 2.33 below center and the vertical guide to 3.17 right of center. Move the country symbols so that their upper-left sizing handles align with the intersection of the guides. Hide the guides.

5. On Slide 5, change the color of the map to Tan, Accent color 5 Dark.

6. On Slide 6, center all six content text paragraphs and then align these paragraphs in the middle of the placeholder.

7. On Slide 1, insert a hyperlink for each country. Kazakhstan should be hyperlinked to Slide 2, Mongolia should be hyperlinked to Slide 3, and Hungary should be hyperlinked to Slide 4.

8. On Slides 2, 3, and 4, insert a hyperlink for each country symbol to Slide 1. Then insert a hyperlink for each country's name to the country's Web site shown in Slide 6.

9. On Slide 5, change the bullets to the Star Bullets, change the color to Orange, and then increase the size of the two first-level paragraph bullets to 130% of text and the four countries to 120% of text. Right-align all six bulleted paragraphs.

10. Hide Slides 2, 3, 4, and 6.

11. Apply the Flip transition to all slides and then change the duration to 2.50.

12. Click the Slide Sorter view button, view the slides for consistency, and then click the Normal view button.

13. Change the document properties, as specified by your instructor. Save the presentation using the file name, Lab 6-3 Landlocked Countries.

14. Submit the revised document in the format specified by your instructor.

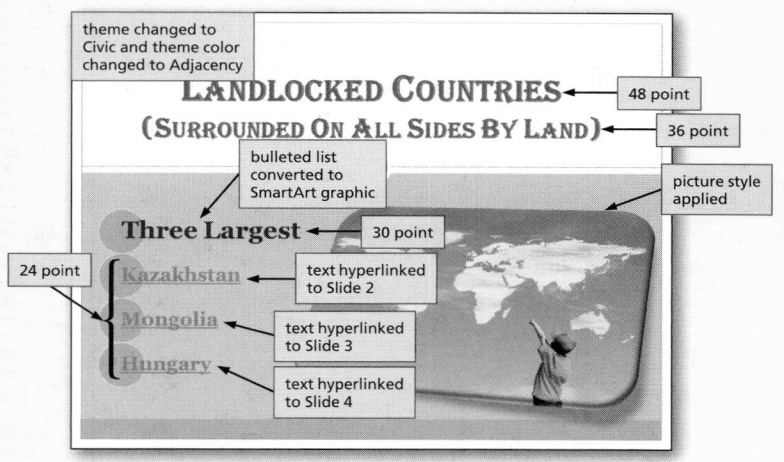

(a) Slide 1

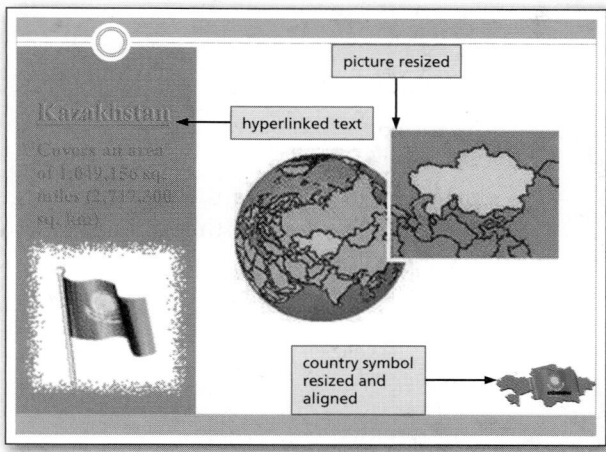

(b) Slide 2

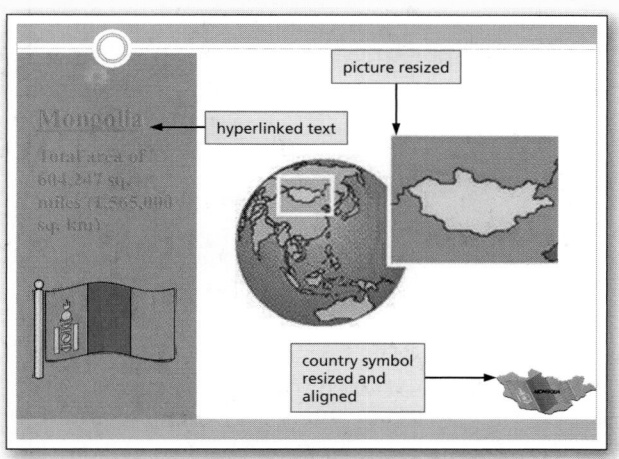

(c) Slide 3

(d) Slide 4

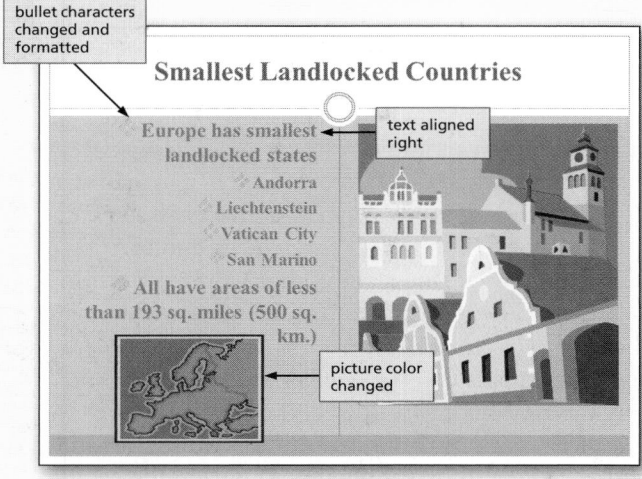

(e) Slide 5

(f) Slide 6 (Hidden Slide)

Figure 6–83

Cases and Places

Apply your creative thinking and problem-solving skills to design and implement a solution.

Note: To complete these assignments, you may be required to use the Data Files for Students. See the inside back cover of this book for instructions on downloading the Data Files for Students, or contact your instructor for information about accessing the required files.

As you design the presentations, remember to use the 7×7 rule: a maximum of seven words on a line and a maximum of seven lines on one slide.

1: Designing and Creating a Presentation about Hurricane Names

Academic

You are studying tropical cyclones in your Earth Science class and learning about the names given to hurricanes worldwide. The World Meteorological Organization (WMO) manages the 10 lists of agreed-upon names for the storms throughout the world. The National Hurricane Center developed the original lists of names in 1953. Create a presentation for your class with columns of hurricane names for the Atlantic and North Pacific oceans. Also include the history of naming hurricanes, including when men's names were added to the rotation, when names are retired, and how often the lists are rotated. Apply at least three objectives found at the beginning of this chapter to develop the presentation. Hide at least one slide. Be sure to check spelling.

2: Designing and Creating a Presentation about First Aid Kits

Personal

To be prepared for emergencies, it is a good idea to have a first aid kit in your home and vehicle. You can purchase a kit at a local store or you can assemble one yourself. The Red Cross (www.redcross.org) and the Ready America (www.ready.gov) Web sites provide lists of recommended items to include in a first aid kit. Visit these Web sites and use the information regarding basic first aid kit supplies to create a presentation to share with your family, urging them to buy their own kits or check their current kits. Create a title slide introducing the topic, and create text slides containing columns of supplies that should be included in a first aid kit. Create another slide reminding your family to check the kit contents' expiration dates and flashlight batteries. Also include a hyperlink to your local Red Cross chapter for details on taking a class, donating blood, and volunteering. Use at least three objectives found at the beginning of this chapter to develop the presentation. Use bullets related to medical or emergency themes. Be sure to check spelling.

3: Designing and Creating a Presentation about Sound Levels

Professional

You work in a noisy factory and are concerned about the sound levels and how they are affecting your hearing. More than nine million workers are subjected to loud noises on the job that can lead to hearing loss. Sound levels are measured in decibels (dB). According to the American Speech-Language-Hearing Association (ASHA), noises louder than 80 dB can damage the inner ear and the auditory nerve. Visit the ASHA (www.asha.org) and National Institute on Deafness and Other Communication Disorders (NIDCD) (www.nidcd/nih.org) Web sites and read the information regarding noise levels in the workplace and the relationship to noise-induced hearing loss (NIHL).

Develop a Microsoft Word outline regarding specific sounds and the decibel levels, prolonged exposure to loud noises, and hearing protection. Insert this outline into a PowerPoint presentation that you can share with your boss and your coworkers about working around hazardous noise. Include a table showing the decibel levels of various sounds. Also include information about how employees can benefit physiologically and psychologically from reduced noise levels in the workplace and how they can protect their hearing. Include hyperlinks to the ASHA, NIDCD, and the National Institute for Occupational Safety and Health (www.cdc.gov/niosh) Web sites. Include action buttons and bullet characters that have been changed to pictures or symbols. Be certain to check spelling.

7 | Creating a Self-Running Presentation Containing Animation

Objectives

You will have mastered the material in this chapter when you can:

- Remove a picture background
- Crop and compress a picture
- Insert entrance, emphasis, and exit effects
- Add and adjust motion paths
- Reorder animation sequences
- Associate sounds with animations

- Control animation timing
- Animate SmartArt graphics and charts
- Insert and animate a text box
- Animate bulleted lists
- Rehearse timings
- Set slide show timings manually

7 | Creating a Self-Running Presentation Containing Animation

BTW

Animation Enhancements
Microsoft made many changes and enhancements to animation features in PowerPoint 2010. The Animation tab is reorganized and contains the Animation group to add effects to slide objects. The Timing group allows designers to change the order of elements and set the precise time when they appear on each slide. In addition, the transitions that appeared on the PowerPoint 2007 Animation tab are moved to their own tab.

Introduction

One method used for disseminating information is a **kiosk**. This freestanding, self-service structure is equipped with computer hardware and software and is used to provide information or reference materials to the public. Some have a touch screen or keyboard that serves as an input device and allows users to select various options so they can browse or find specific information. Advanced kiosks allow customers to place orders, make payments, and access the Internet. Many kiosks have multimedia devices for playing sound and video clips.

Various elements on PowerPoint slides can have movement to direct the audience's attention to the point being made. For example, each paragraph in a bulleted list can fade or disappear after being displayed for a set period of time. Each SmartArt graphic component can appear in sequence. A picture can grow, shrink, bounce, or spin, depending upon its relationship to other slide content. PowerPoint's myriad animation effects allow you to use your creativity to design imaginative and distinctive presentations.

Project — Presentation with Adjusted Pictures, Animated Content, and Slide Timings

BTW

Animation Effect Icon Colors
Animation effects allow you to control how objects enter, move on, and exit slides. Using a traffic signal analogy may help you remember the sequence of events. Green icons indicate when the animation effect starts on the slide. Yellow icons represent the object's motion; use them with caution so they do not distract from the message you are conveying to your audience. Red icons indicate when the object stops appearing on a slide.

Interest in the sport of snowboarding, which also is called boarding, has grown since its commercial start in the 1970s and its entry into the Olympics in 1998. Today, almost every North American ski resort allows snowboarders to perform their jumps and aerial feats. Downhill enthusiasts of all ages have experienced the sport, with the average age ranging between 18 and 24 years. Approximately 25 percent of the boarding population is women. The snowboarding project in this chapter (Figure 7–1) explores the sport and uses animation to give a feeling of the twists and turns the boarders experience while on the slopes. The title slide (Figure 7–1a) has animated title text and a snowboarder who performs a flip as she cruises down the mountain. The second slide (Figure 7–1b) shows a snowboarder clip that carves graceful turns during a gentle snowfall. The third slide (Figure 7–1c) uses animated SmartArt to explain how to find the correct snowboard length based on the boarder's height. The growth of the snowboarding industry is depicted in the animated chart on Slide 4 (Figure 7–1d). The last slide (Figure 7–1e) has two lists that describe the essential gear a snowboarder needs to have an enjoyable day on the slopes and an upward-rolling credit line to end the presentation.

(a) Slide 1 (Title Slide with Animated WordArt and Picture)

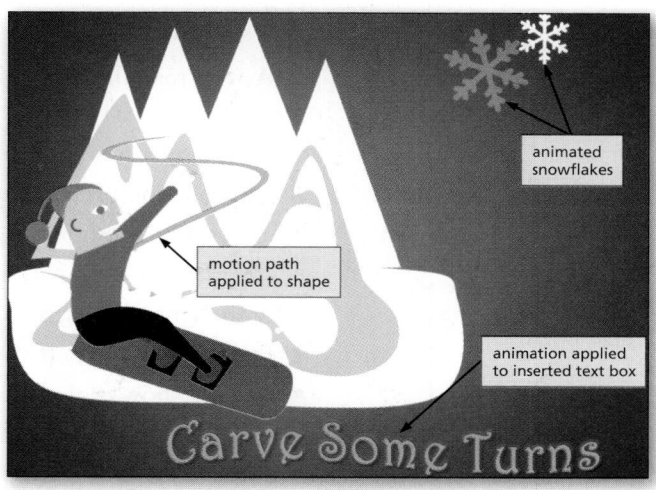

(b) Slide 2 (Animated Clip with Motion Path and Sound)

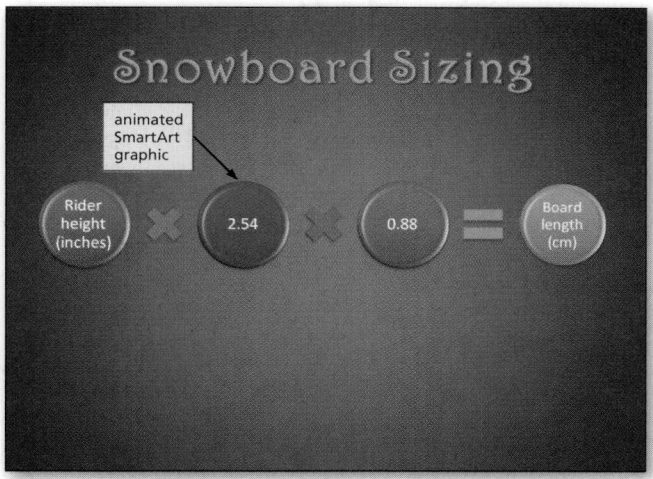

(c) Slide 3 (Animated SmartArt)

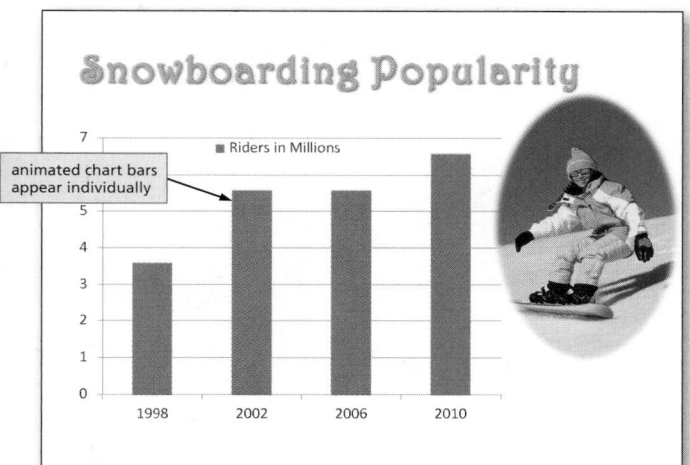

(d) Slide 4 (Animated Chart)

(e) Slide 5 (Animated Bulleted List and Credits)

Figure 7 – 1

BTW

The Ribbon and Screen Resolution
PowerPoint may change how the groups and buttons within the groups appear on the Ribbon, depending on the computer's screen resolution. Thus, your Ribbon may look different from the ones in this book if you are using a screen resolution other than 1024 × 768.

Overview

As you read through this chapter, you will learn how to create the presentation shown in Figure 7–1 by performing these general tasks:

- Remove picture backgrounds.
- Crop and compress pictures.
- Add entrance, emphasis, and exit animations.
- Create custom animations.
- Animate text boxes, SmartArt, and charts.
- Change transition effect options.
- Set slide show timings.

Plan Ahead

General Project Guidelines

When creating a PowerPoint presentation, the actions you perform and the decisions you make will affect the appearance and characteristics of the finished document. As you create a presentation with illustrations, such as the project shown in Figure 7–1 on the previous page, you should follow these general guidelines:

1. **Use animation sparingly.** Prior to using an animation effect, think about why you need it and how it will affect your presentation. Do not use animation merely for the sake of using animation.

2. **Select colors for dimming text.** Paragraphs of text can change color after they display on the slide. This effect, called dimming, can be used effectively to emphasize important points and draw the audience's attention to another area of the slide. Select dimming colors that suit the purpose of the presentation.

3. **Use quotations judiciously.** At times, the words of noted world leaders, writers, and prominent entertainers can create interest in your presentation and inspire audiences. If you choose to integrate their quotations into your slide show, give credit to the source and keep the original wording.

4. **Give your audience sufficient time to view your slides.** On average, an audience member will spend only eight seconds viewing a basic slide with a simple graphic or a few words. They need much more time to view charts, graphs, and SmartArt graphics. When you are setting slide timings, keep this length of time in mind, particularly when the presentation is viewed at a kiosk without a speaker's physical presence.

When necessary, more specific details concerning the above guidelines are presented at appropriate points in the chapter. The chapter also will identify the actions performed and decisions made regarding these guidelines during the creation of the presentation shown in Figure 7–1.

To Start PowerPoint, Open a Presentation, and Rename the Presentation

To begin this presentation, you will open a file located on the Data Files for Students. See the inside back cover of this book for instructions on downloading the Data Files for Students, or contact your instructor for more information about accessing the required files. If you are using a computer to step through the project in this chapter and you want your screens to match the figures in this book, you should change your screen's resolution to 1024 × 768.

The following steps start PowerPoint, open a file, and then save it with a new file name.

1 Start PowerPoint. If necessary, maximize the PowerPoint window.

2 Open the presentation, Snowboarding, located on the Data Files for Students.

3 Save the presentation using the file name, Animated Snowboarding.

Adjusting and Cropping a Picture

At times you may desire to emphasize one section of a picture and eliminate distracting background content. PowerPoint includes picture formatting tools that allow you to edit pictures. The **Remove Background** command isolates the foreground from the background, and the **Crop** command removes content along the top, bottom, left, or right edges. Once you format the picture to include only the desired content, you can **compress** the image to reduce the file size.

To Remove a Background

The title slide in the Animated Snowboarding presentation has a picture of a snowboarder wearing tan and white clothes in the foreground. Snow is present in the background of this picture, and you want to eliminate it to direct the viewers' attention to the snowboarder. PowerPoint 2010's Background Removal feature makes it easy to eliminate extraneous aspects. When you click the Remove Background button, PowerPoint attempts to select the foreground of the picture and overlay a magenta marquee selection on this area. You then can adjust the marquee shape and size to contain all foreground picture components you want to keep. The following steps remove the background from the snowboarder picture.

1

- With the title slide displaying, double-click the snowboarder picture in the foreground to display the Picture Tools Format tab.

- Click the Remove Background button (Picture Tools Format tab | Adjust group) to display the Background Removal tab and a marquee selection area (Figure 7–2).

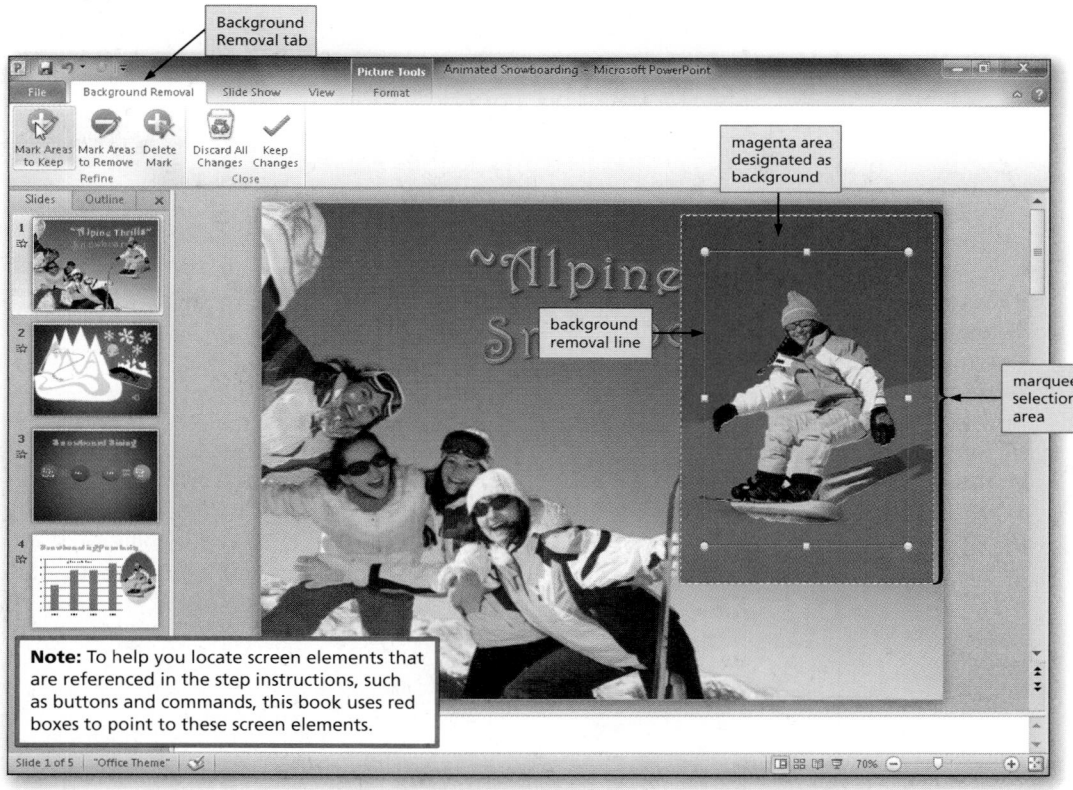

Figure 7–2

Q&A How does PowerPoint determine the area to display within the marquee?

Microsoft Research software engineers developed the algorithms that determine the portions of the picture in the foreground.

2
- Click and drag the handles on the background removal lines so that the snowboarder and her snowboard are contained within the marquee (Figure 7–3).

Q&A

Why do some parts of the background, such as the area under her right arm and below her knees, still display?

The removal tool was not able to determine that those areas are part of the background. You will remove them in the next set of steps.

Figure 7–3

3
- Click the Keep Changes button (Background Removal tab | Close group) to discard the unwanted picture background (Figure 7–4).

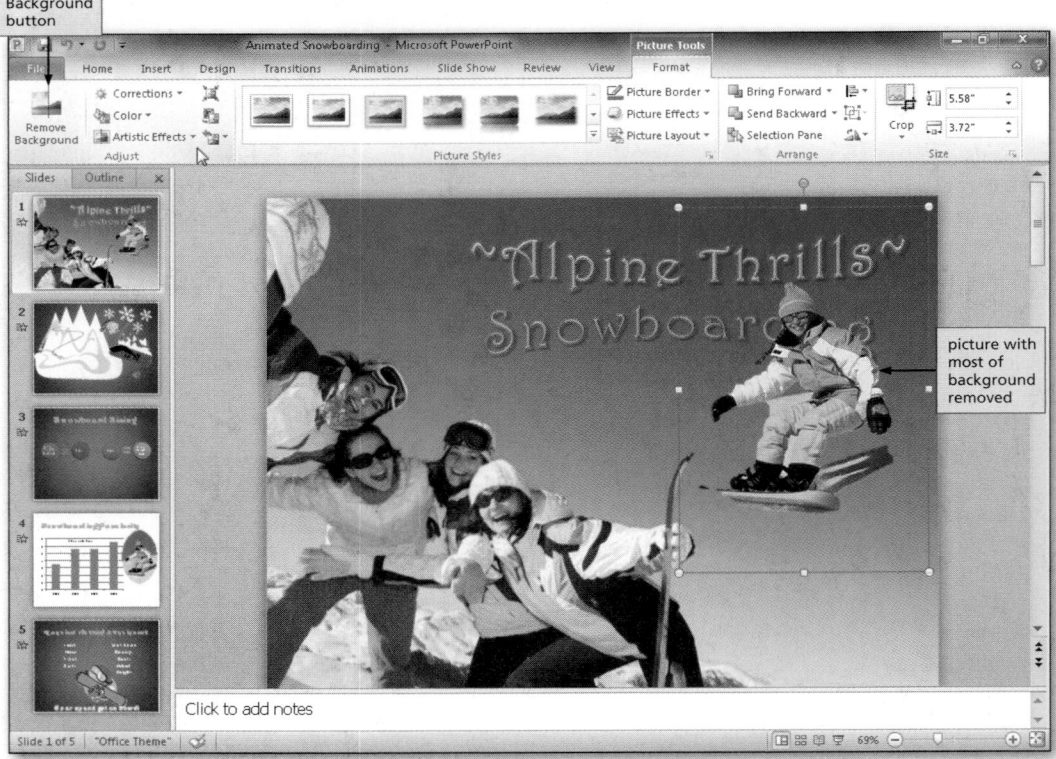

Figure 7–4

To Refine Background Removal

In many cases, the Remove Background command discards all the undesired picture components. Occasionally, however, some pieces remain when the background is integrated closely with the foreground picture. In the title slide snowboarding picture, for example, the algorithms could not distinguish the snow and sky between the boarder's right arm and torso, below her knees, and directly behind her. Tools on the Background Removal tab allow you to mark specific areas to remove. The following steps remove the unwanted background areas from around the snowboarder.

1

• Click the Remove Background button again to display the Background Removal tab and the marquee selection area.

• Click the Mark Areas to Remove button (Background Removal tab | Refine group) and then position the mouse pointer in the white area above the snowboarder's right knee (Figure 7–5).

Q&A | Why did my mouse pointer change shape?

The mouse pointer changed to a pencil to indicate you are about to draw on a precise area of the picture.

Figure 7–5

2

• Click and then drag the mouse pointer to the snowboarder's jacket to indicate the portion of the background to delete (Figure 7–6).

Q&A | Why does a circle with a minus sign display on the dotted line?

That symbol indicates that you manually specified the deletion of a portion of the background.

Q&A | Why does some of the background remain on my picture?

The location where you drew your line determines the area that PowerPoint deletes. You may need to make several passes to remove all of the unwanted background.

Figure 7–6

- Repeat Step 2 to delete the white area below her knees and the area to the right of her left boot (Figure 7–7).

Q&A I mistakenly removed the snowboard when I tried to remove some of the background. How can I keep the snowboard in the picture?

You can mark the snowboard as an area to keep and then delete the background.

Figure 7–7

Q&A If I marked an area with a line and now want to keep it, can I reverse my action?

Yes. Click the Delete Mark button (Background Removal tab | Refine area) and then click the line to remove it. You also can press CTRL+Z immediately after you draw the line.

- Click the Keep Changes button to review the results of your background refinements.

Q&A The tail no longer is connected to the rest of the board, or my entire board is removed. Can I add this missing piece?

Yes. In the next step, you will instruct PowerPoint to keep any necessary area that was discarded.

- Click the Remove Background button again, click the Mark Areas to Keep button (Background Removal tab | Refine group), and then position the mouse pointer on the snow on the tail of the snowboard.

- Click and then drag the mouse pointer to the front of the snowboard (Figure 7–8).

- Click the Keep Changes button to review the results of your background refinement.

Figure 7–8

Q&A If I want to see the original picture at a later time, can I display the components I deleted?

Yes. If you click the Discard All Changes button (Background Removal tab | Close area), all the deleted pieces will reappear.

To Crop a Picture

The Remove Background command deleted the snow and sky components of the picture from your view, but they still remain in the picture. Because you will not need to display the background in this presentation, you can remove the unnecessary edges of the picture. When you crop a picture, you trim the vertical or horizontal sides so that the most important area of the picture is displayed. Any picture file type except animated GIF can be cropped. The following steps crop the title slide snowboarder picture.

- With the snowboarder picture still selected, click the Crop button (Picture Tools Format tab | Size group) to display the cropping handles on the picture.

- Position the mouse pointer over the center cropping handle on the right side of the picture (Figure 7–9).

Q&A Why did my mouse pointer change shape?

The mouse pointer changed to indicate you are about to crop a picture.

Figure 7–9

- Drag the center cropping handle inward so that the right edge of the marquee is beside the snowboarder's glove on her left hand.

- Drag the center cropping handles on the left, upper, and lower edges of the background removal lines inward to frame the picture (Figure 7–10).

Q&A Does cropping actually cut the picture's edges?

No. Although you cannot see the cropped edges, they exist until you save the file.

Figure 7–10

- Click an area of the slide other than the picture to crop the edges.

Q&A Can I change the crop lines?

If you have not saved the file, you can undo your crops by clicking the Undo button on the Quick Access Toolbar, clicking the Reset Picture button (Picture Tools Format tab | Adjust group), or pressing CTRL+Z.

Other Ways

1. Enter dimensions in Left, Right, Top, and Bottom boxes in Crop position   area (Format Picture dialog box | Crop tab)

To Compress a Picture

Pictures inserted into slides greatly increase the total PowerPoint file size. PowerPoint automatically compresses picture files inserted into slides by eliminating details, generally with no visible loss of quality. You can increase the compression and, in turn, decrease the file size if you instruct PowerPoint to compress a picture you have cropped so you can save space on a storage medium such as a hard disk, USB flash drive, or optical disk. Although these storage devices generally have a large storage capacity, you might want to reduce the file size for e-mailing the file or reducing the download time from an FTP or Web site.

The snowboard picture on the title slide picture is cropped and displays only the female snowboarder. You will not need any of the invisible portions of the picture, so you can delete them permanently and reduce the picture file size. The following steps compress the title slide snowboarder picture.

1
- Double-click the snowboarder picture to display the Picture Tools Format tab. Click the Compress Pictures button (Picture Tools Format tab | Adjust group) to display the Compress Pictures dialog box (Figure 7–11).

Q&A Should I apply an artistic effect prior to or after compressing a picture?

Compress a picture and then apply the artistic effect.

2
- Click the OK button (Compress Pictures dialog box) to delete the cropped portions of this picture and compress the image.

Q&A Can I undo the compression?

Yes, as long as you have not closed the file.

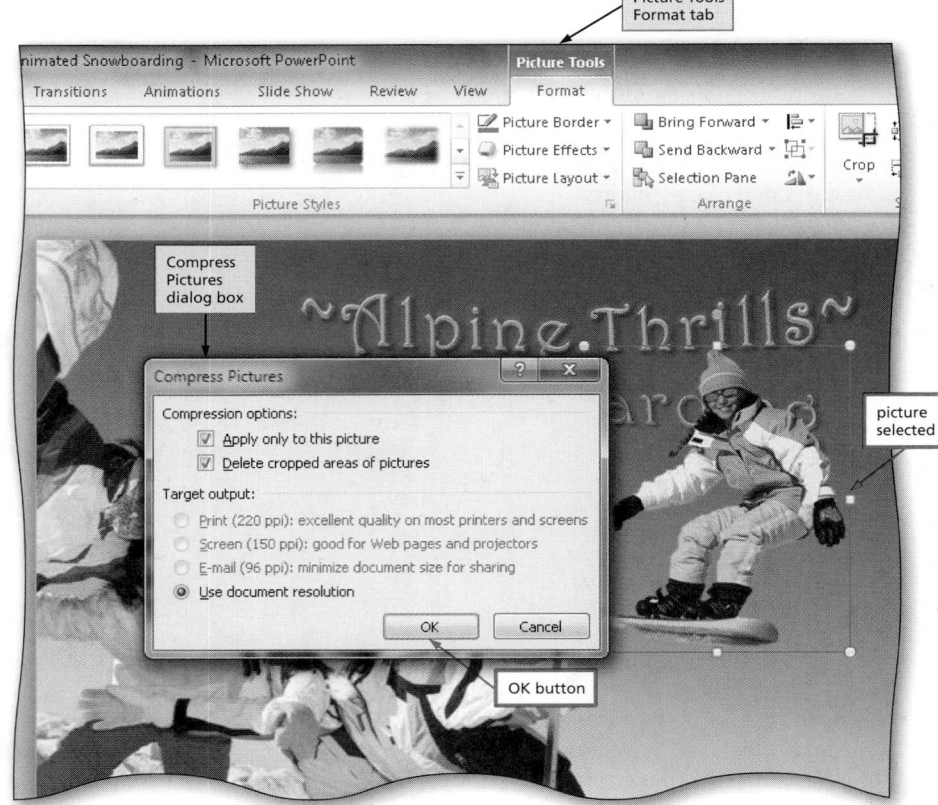

Figure 7–11

Animating Slide Content

Animation includes special visual and sound effects applied to text or other content. You already are familiar with one form of animation: transitions between slides. To add visual interest and clarity to a presentation, you can animate various parts of an individual slide, including clips, shapes, text, and other slide elements. For example, each paragraph on the slide can spin as it is displayed. Individual letters and shapes also can spin or move in a wide variety of motions. PowerPoint has a variety of built-in animations that will fade, wipe, or fly-in text and graphics.

Custom Animations

You can create your own **custom animations** to meet your unique needs. Custom animation effects are grouped in categories: entrance, exit, emphasis, and motion paths. **Entrance** effects, as the name implies, determine how slide elements first appear on a slide. **Exit** animations work in the opposite manner as entrance effects: They remove slide elements. **Emphasis** effects modify text and objects displayed on the screen. For example, letters may darken or increase in font size. The entrance, exit, and emphasis animations are grouped into categories: Basic, Subtle, Moderate, and Exciting. You can set the animation speed to Very Fast, Fast, Medium, Slow, or Very Slow.

The Slide 1 background picture shows skiing enthusiasts posing on a ski slope. When the presentation begins, the audience will view these skiers and then see a snowboarder enter from the upper-left corner, slide down the slope, perform an aerial trick as she reaches the center of the slide, and then continue down the slope toward the lower-right corner. To create this animation on the slide, you will use entrance, emphasis, and exit effects.

If you need to move objects on a slide once they are displayed, you can define a **motion path**. This predefined movement determines where an object will be displayed and then travel. Motion paths are grouped into the Basic, Lines & Curves, and Special categories. You can draw a **custom path** if none of the predefined paths meets your needs.

Plan Ahead

Use animation sparingly.
PowerPoint audience members usually take notice the first time an animation is displayed on the screen. When the same animation effect is applied throughout a presentation, the viewers generally become desensitized to the effect unless it is highly unusual or annoying. Resist the urge to use animation effects simply because PowerPoint provides the tools to do so. You have options to decide how text or a slide element enters and exits a slide and how it is displayed once it is present on the slide; your goal, however, is to use these options wisely. Audiences soon tire of a presentation riddled with animations, causing them to quickly lose their impact.

To Animate a Picture Using an Entrance Effect

The snowboarder you modified will not appear on Slide 1 when you begin the presentation. Instead, she will enter the slide from the uphill part of the slope, which is in the upper-left corner of the slide, to give the appearance she is snowboarding down the mountain. She will then continue downhill until she reaches the center of the slide. Entrance effects are colored green in the Animation gallery. The following steps apply an entrance effect to the snowboarder picture.

- With Slide 1 displaying, move the snowboarder picture to the center of the slide, as shown in Figure 7–12.

Q&A

Why am I moving the picture to this location?

This area of the slide is where you want the picture to stop moving after she enters the slide in the upper-left corner.

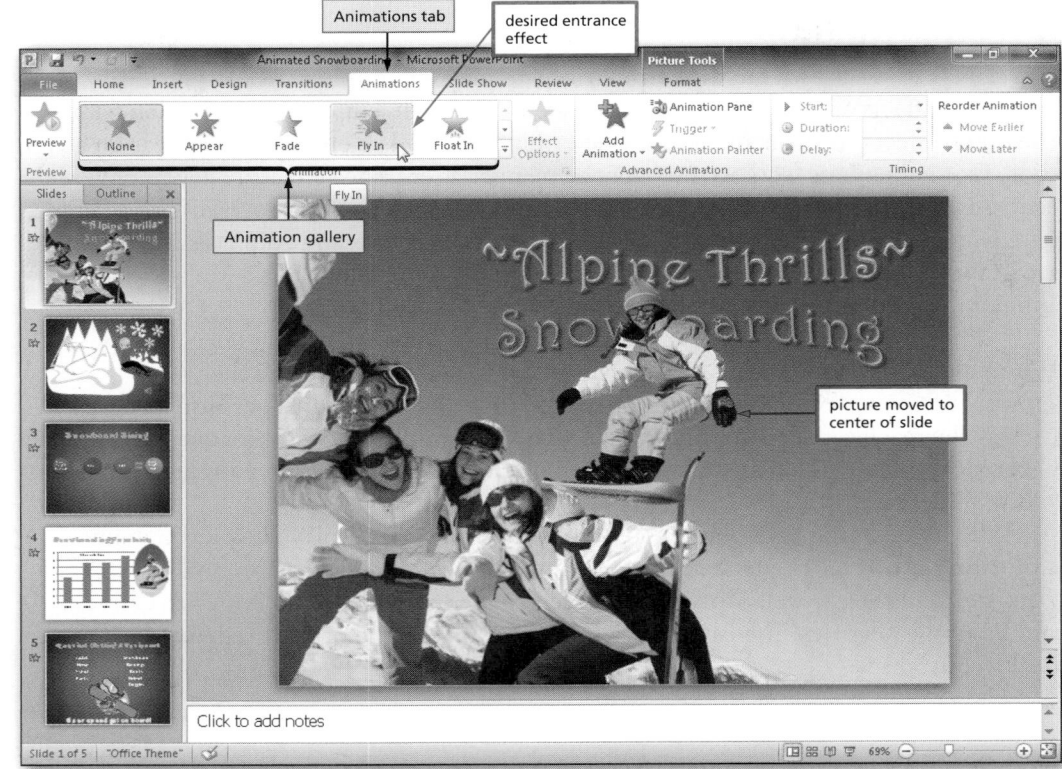

Figure 7–12

- Click the Animations tab on the Ribbon and then point to the Fly In animation in the Animation gallery (Animation group) to display a live preview of this animation (Figure 7–12).

 **Experiment**

- Point to three other animations shown in the Animation gallery and watch the snowboarder enter the slide.

Q&A

Are more entrance animations available?

Yes. Click the More button in the Animation gallery to see additional animations. You can select one of the 13 entrance animations that are displayed, or you can click the More Entrance Effects command to expand the selection.

- Click Fly In to apply this entrance animation to the snowboarder picture.

Q&A

Why does the number 1 appear in a box on the left side of the picture?

The 1 is a sequence number and indicates Fly In is the first animation that will appear on the slide when you click the mouse.

To Change Animation Direction

By default, the picture appears on the slide by entering from the bottom edge. You can modify this direction and specify that it enters from another side or from a corner. The following steps change the snowboard picture entrance animation direction to the upper-left corner.

1

- Click the Effect Options button (Animations tab | Animation group) to display the Direction gallery (Figure 7–13).

Q&A Why does a gold box appear around the From Bottom arrow?

From Bottom is the default entrance direction applied to the animation.

- Point to From Top-Left in the Direction gallery to display a live preview of this animation effect.

🔎 **Experiment**

- Point to various arrows in the Direction gallery and watch the snowboarder enter the slide from different sides and corners.

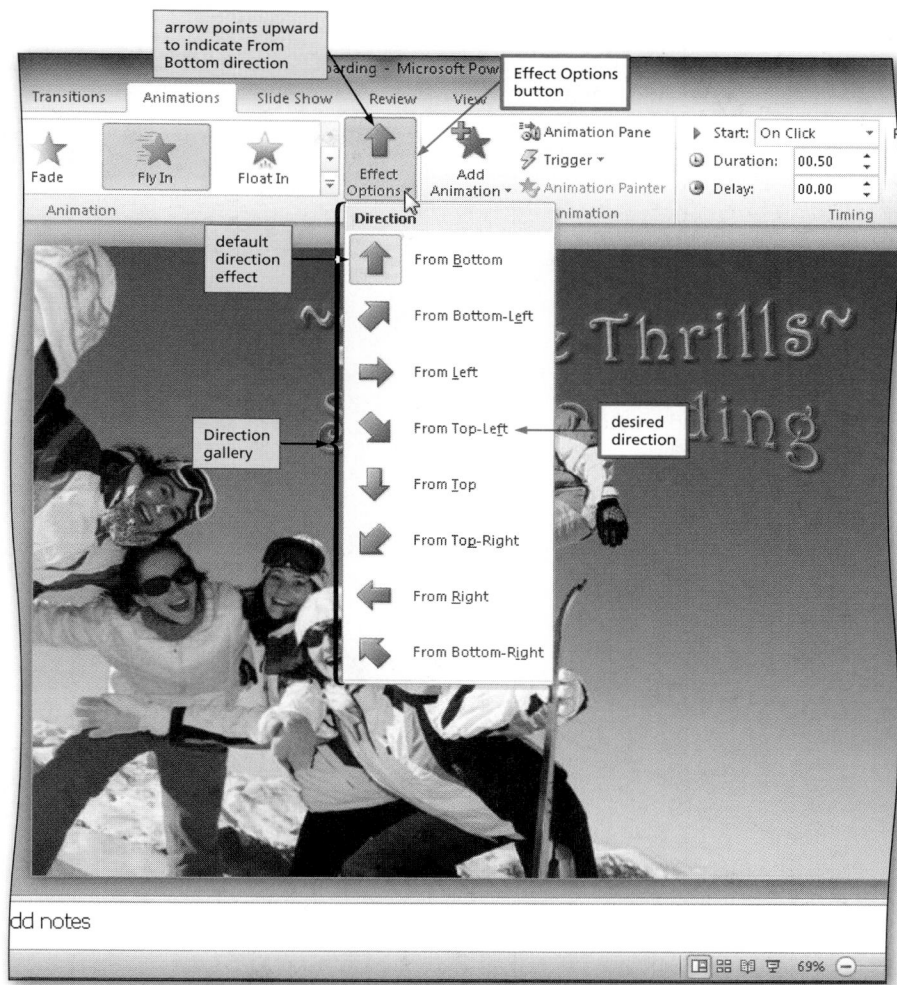

Figure 7–13

2

- Click the From Top-Left arrow to apply this direction to the entrance animation.

Q&A Can I change this entrance effect?

Yes. Repeat Step 1 to select another direction.

To Animate a Picture Using an Emphasis Effect

The snowboarder will enter the slide from the upper-left corner and stop in the center of the slide. You then want her to perform an acrobatic trick. PowerPoint provides several effects that you can apply to a picture once it appears on a slide. These movements are categorized as emphasis effects, and they are colored yellow in the Animation gallery. You already have applied an entrance effect to the snowboarder picture, so you want to add another animation to this picture. The following steps apply an emphasis effect to the snowboarder picture after the entrance effect.

- With the snowboarder picture still selected, click the Add Animation button (Animations tab | Advanced Animation group) to expand the Animation gallery.

- Point to Spin in the Emphasis area to display a live preview of this effect (Figure 7–14).

Experiment

- Point to various effects in the Emphasis area and watch the snowboarder.

Are more emphasis effects available in addition to those shown in the Animation gallery?

Yes. To see additional emphasis effects, click More Emphasis Effects in the lower portion of the Animation gallery. The effects are arranged in the Basic, Subtle, Moderate, and Exciting categories.

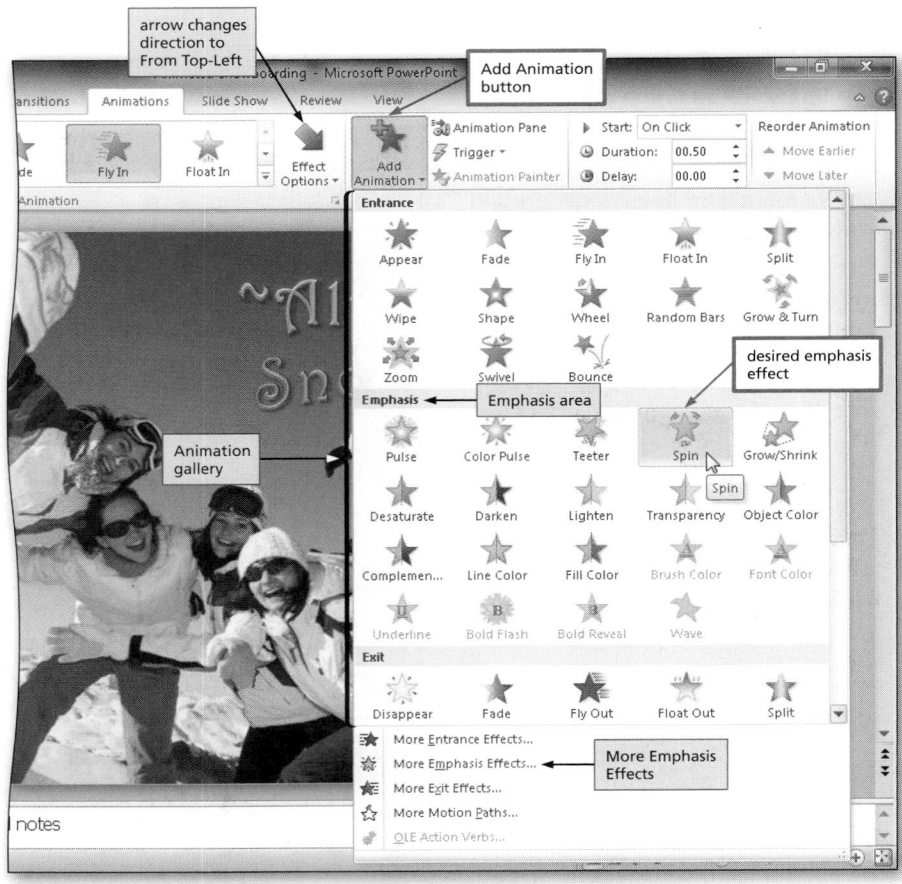

Figure 7–14

- Click Spin to apply this emphasis effect to the snowboarder picture.

Do I need to use both an entrance and an emphasis effect, or can I use only an emphasis effect?

You can use one or the other effect, or both effects.

Why does the number 2 appear in a box below the number 1 on the left side of the picture?

The 2 in the numbered tag indicates a second animation is applied in the animation sequence.

To Animate a Picture Using an Exit Effect

The animated snowboarder picture will enter the slide from the upper-left corner, stop in the center of the slide, and then perform a spin trick. She then will continue down the slope and snowboard off the slide in the lower-right corner. To continue this animation sequence, you first need to apply an exit effect. As with the entrance and emphasis effects, PowerPoint provides a wide variety of effects that you can apply to remove a picture from a slide. These exit effects are colored red in the Animation gallery. You already have applied the Fly In entrance effect, so the Fly Out exit effect would give continuity to the animation sequence. The following steps add this exit effect to the snowboarder picture after the emphasis effect.

1

• With the snowboarder picture still selected, click the Add Animation button again to expand the Animation gallery.

• Point to Fly Out in the Exit area to display a live preview of this effect (Figure 7–15).

Experiment

• Point to various effects in the Exit area and watch the snowboarder. You will not be able to view all the effects because they are hidden by the Animation gallery, but you can move the snowboarder clip to the left side of the slide to view the effects and then move her back to the middle of the slide.

Q&A Are more exit effects available in addition to those shown in the Animation gallery?

Yes. To see additional exit effects, click More Exit Effects in the lower portion of the Animation gallery. The effects are arranged in the Basic, Subtle, Moderate, and Exciting categories.

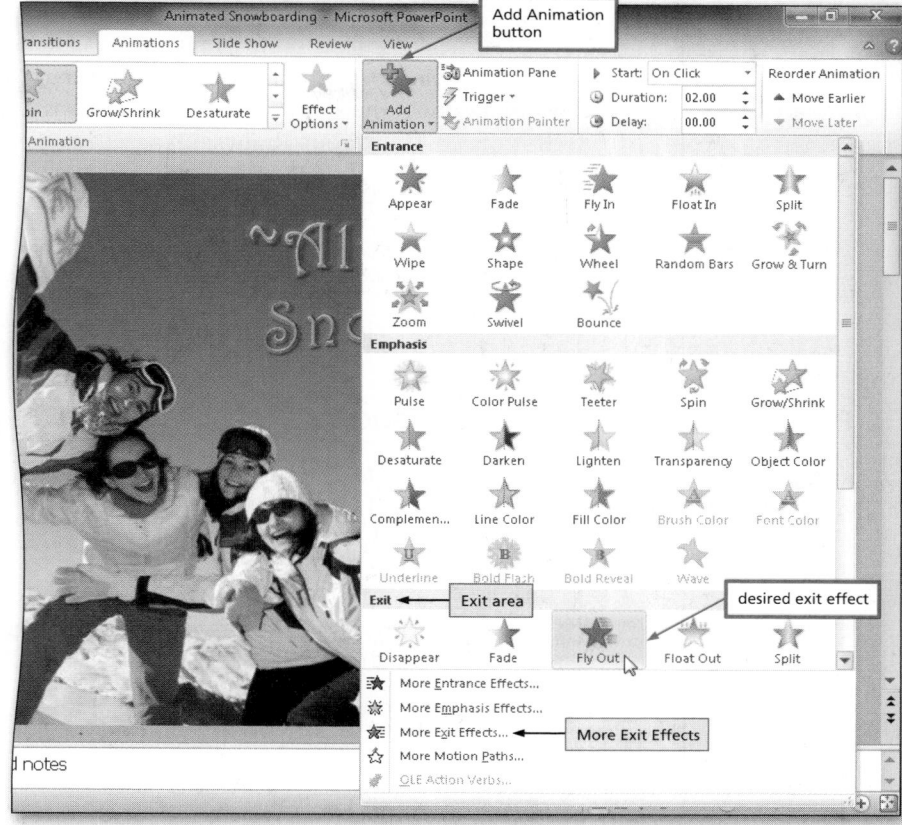

Figure 7–15

2

• Click Fly Out to add this exit effect to the sequence of snowboarder picture animations (Figure 7–16).

Q&A How can I tell that this exit effect has been applied?

The Fly Out effect is displayed in the Animation gallery (Animations tab | Animation group), and the number 3 is displayed to the left of the snowboarder picture.

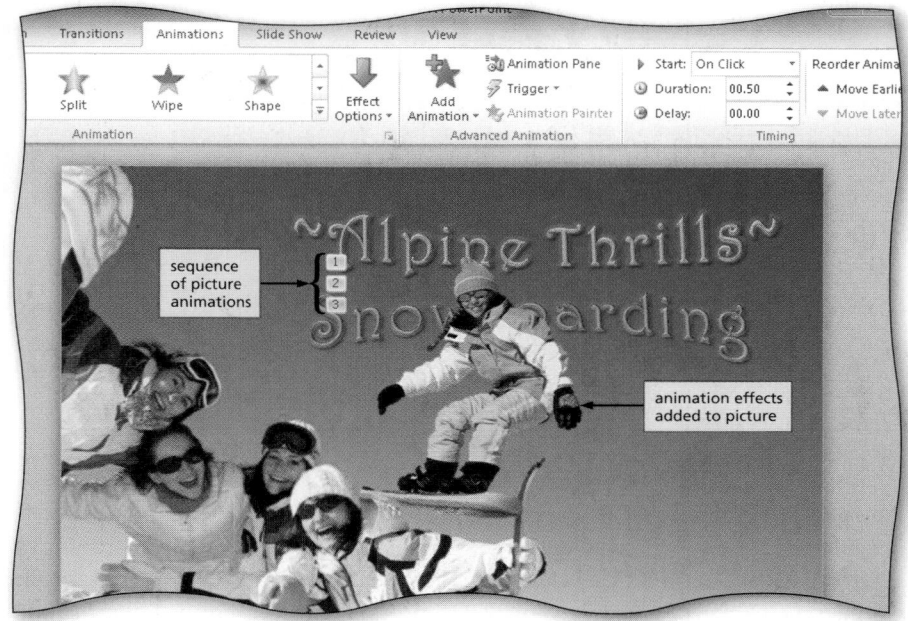

Figure 7–16

To Change Exit Animation Direction

The default direction for a picture to exit a slide is To Bottom. In this presentation, you want the snowboarder to exit in the lower-right corner to give the impression she is continuing down the slope. The following steps change the exit animation direction from To Bottom to To Bottom-Right.

1 Click the Effect Options button (Animations tab | Animation group) to display the Direction gallery.

2 Click the To Bottom-Right arrow to apply this direction to the exit animation effect.

To Preview an Animation Sequence

Although you have not completed developing the presentation, you should view the animation you have added. By default, the entrance, emphasis, and exit animations will be displayed when you run the presentation and click the mouse. The following step runs the presentation and displays the three animations.

1

• Click the Preview button (Animations tab | Preview group) to view all the Slide 1 animations (Figure 7–17).

Why does a red square appear in the middle of the circle on the Preview button when I click that button?

The red square indicates the animation sequence is in progress. Ordinarily, a green arrow is displayed in the circle.

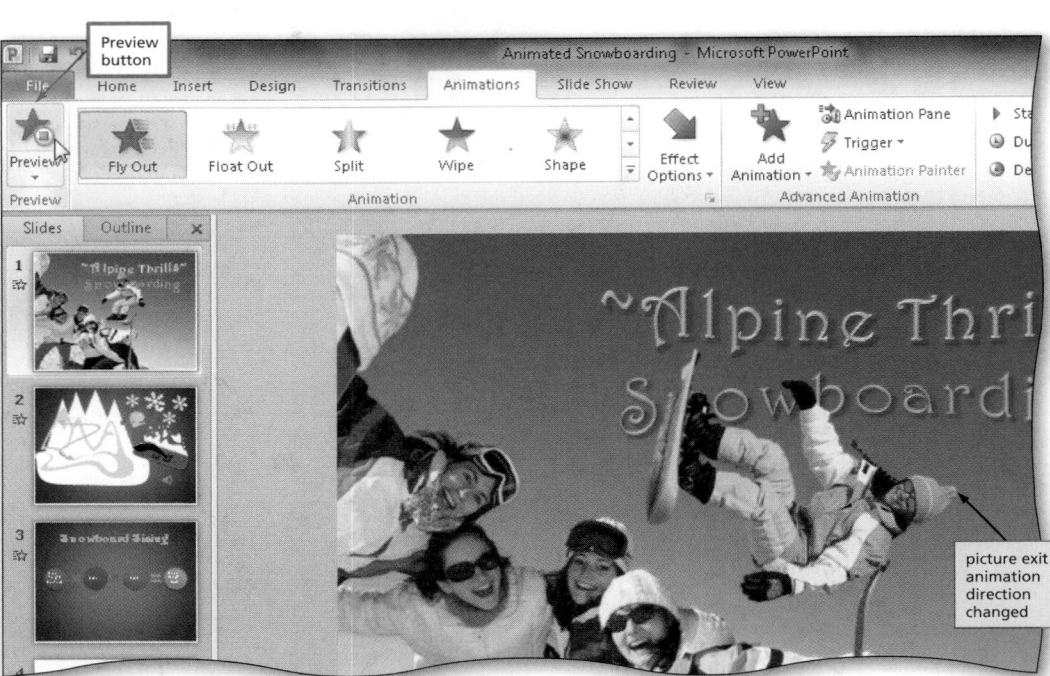

Figure 7–17

To Modify Entrance Animation Timing

The three animation effects are displayed quickly. To create a dramatic effect, you can change the timing so that the background picture displays and then, a few seconds later, the snowboarder starts to glide down the mountain slowly. The default setting is to start each animation with a mouse click, but you can change this setting so that the entrance effect is delayed until a specified number of seconds has passed. The following steps modify the start, delay, and duration settings for the entrance animation.

● Click the 1 numbered tag on the left side of the snowboarder picture and then click the Start Animation Timing button arrow (Animations tab | Timing group) to display the Start menu (Figure 7–18).

● Click After Previous to change the start timing setting.

Q&A Why did the numbered tags change from 1, 2, 3 to 0, 1, 2?

The first animation now occurs automatically without a mouse click. The first and second mouse clicks now will apply the emphasis and exit animations.

Q&A What is the difference between the With Previous and After Previous settings?

The With Previous setting starts the effect simultaneously with any prior animation; the After Previous setting starts the animation after a prior animation has ended. If the prior animation is fast or a short duration, it may be difficult for a viewer to discern the difference between these two settings.

Figure 7–18

● Click the Animation Duration up arrow (Animations tab | Timing group) several times to increase the time from 00.50 second to 05.00 seconds (Figure 7–19).

● Click the Preview button to view the animations.

Q&A What is the difference between the duration time and the delay time?

The duration time is the length of time in which the animation occurs; the delay time is the length of time that passes before the animation begins.

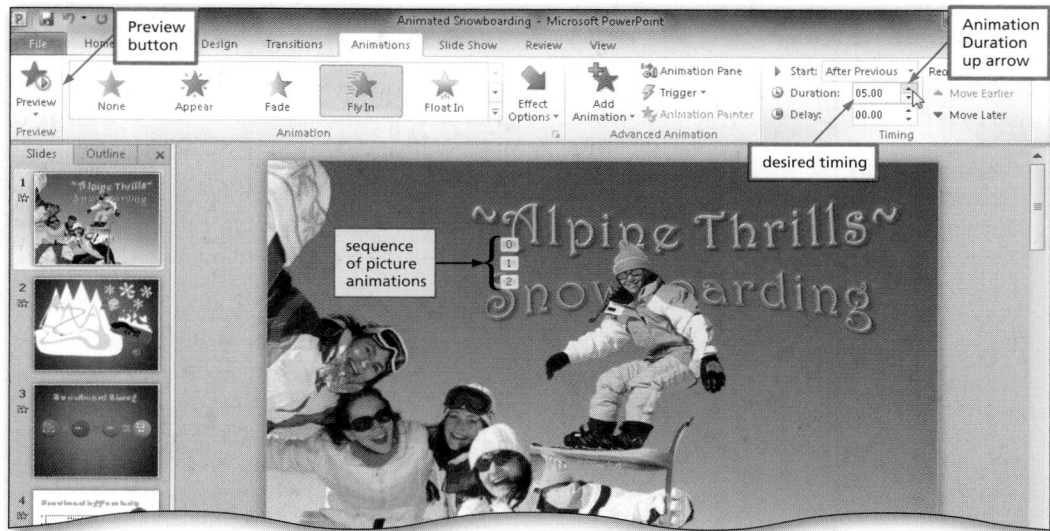

Figure 7–19

Q&A Can I type the speed in the Duration text box instead of clicking the arrow to adjust the speed?

Yes. Typing the numbers allows you to set a precise timing.

4

- Click the Animation Delay up arrow (Animations tab | Timing group) several times to increase the time from 00.00 seconds to 04.00 seconds (Figure 7–20).

- Click the Preview button to view the animations.

Q&A Can I adjust the delay time I just set?

Yes. Click the Animation Delay up or down arrows and run the slide show to display Slide 1 until you find the time that best fits your presentation.

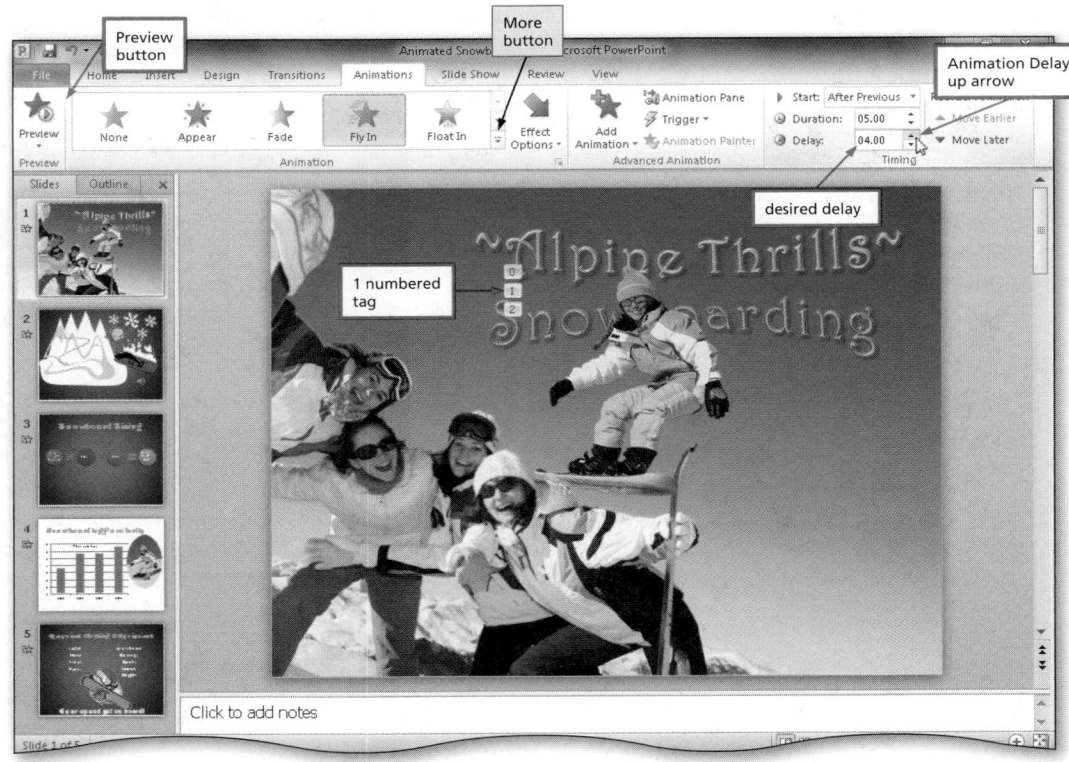

Figure 7–20

To Modify Emphasis and Exit Timings

Now that the entrance animation settings have been modified, you then can change the emphasis and exit effects for the snowboarder picture. The emphasis effect can occur once the entrance effect has concluded, and then the exit effect can commence. With gravity's effect, the snowboarder should be able to glide more quickly down the lower part of the mountain, so you will shorten the duration of her exit effect compared with the duration of the entrance effect. The animation sequence should flow without stopping, so you will not change the default delay timing of 00.00 seconds. The following steps modify the start and duration settings for the emphasis and exit animations.

1 Click the 1 sequence number, which represents the emphasis effect, on the left side of the snowboarder picture, click the Start Animation Timing button arrow (Animations tab | Timing group) to display the Start menu and then click After Previous to change the start timing option setting.

2 Click the Animation Duration up arrow (Animations tab | Timing group) several times to increase the time to 03.00 seconds.

3 Click the 1 sequence number, which now represents the exit effect, click the Start Animation Timing button arrow, and then click After Previous.

4 Click the Animation Duration up arrow several times to increase the time to 04.00 seconds.

5 Preview the Slide 1 animation.

To Animate Title Text Placeholder Paragraphs

The snowboarder picture on Slide 1 has one entrance, one emphasis, and one exit animation, and you can add similar animations to the two paragraphs in the Slide 1 title text placeholder. For a special effect, you can add several emphasis animations to one slide element. The following steps add one entrance and two emphasis animations to the title text paragraphs.

- Double-click the Slide 1 title text placeholder border so that it displays as a solid line.

- Click the More button (shown in Figure 7–20) in the Animation gallery (Animations tab | Animation group) to expand the Animation gallery (Figure 7–21).

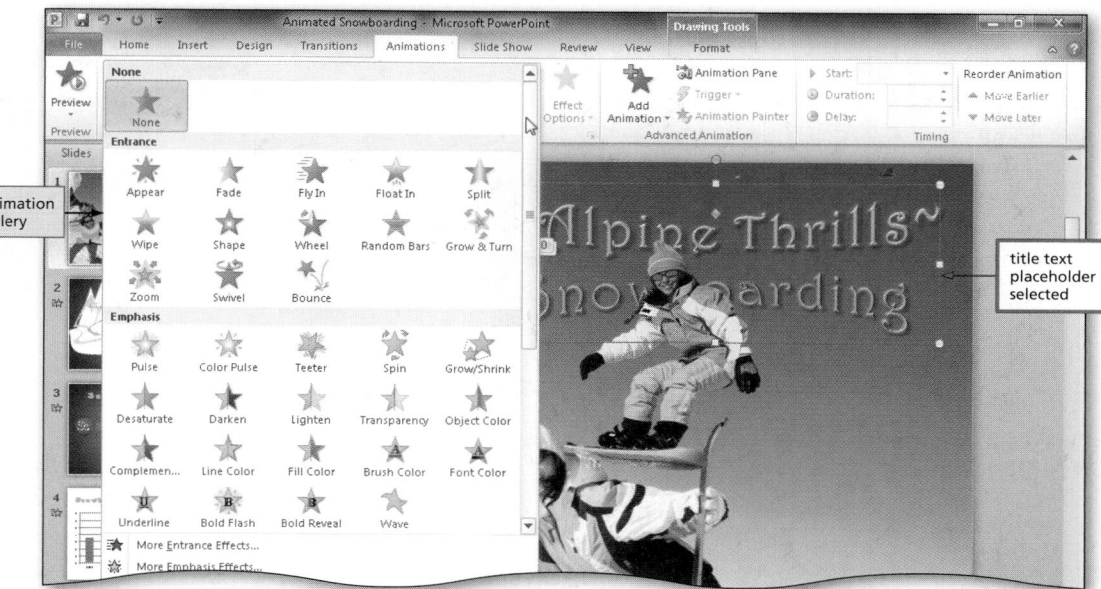

Figure 7–21

- Point to the Zoom entrance effect in the Animation gallery to display a live preview of this effect.

Experiment

- Point to various effects in the Entrance area and watch the title text. You will not be able to view all the effects because they are hidden by the Animation gallery, but you can move the title text placeholder to the left side of the slide to view the effects and then move the placeholder back to its original position.

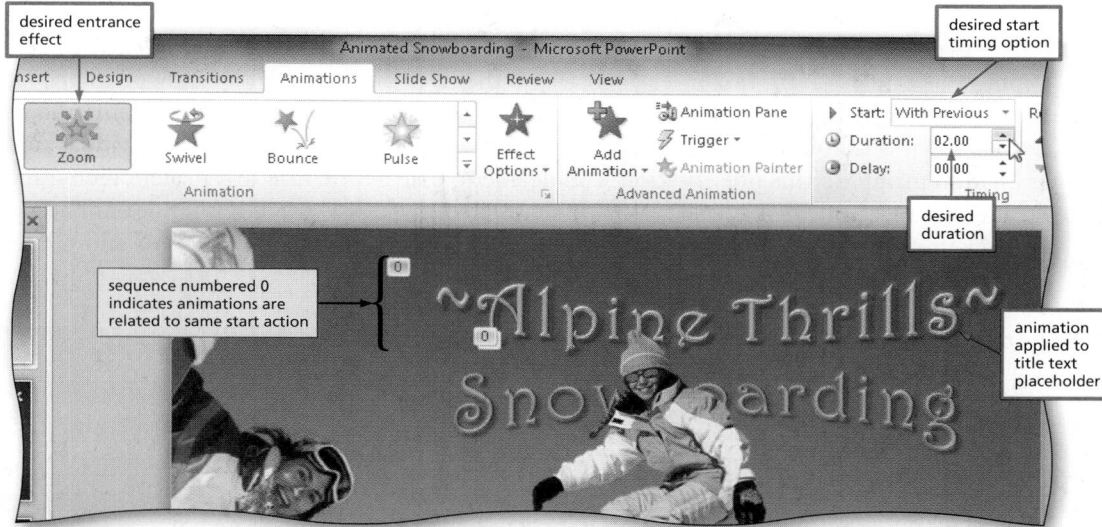

Figure 7–22

- Click the Zoom entrance effect in the Animation gallery to add this animation.

- Change the start timing option to With Previous.

- Change the duration time to 02.00 seconds (Figure 7–22).

Q&A
Do I need to change the delay time?

No. The title text placeholder can start appearing on the slide when the snowboarder exit effect is beginning.

3

- Click the Add Animation button and then click the Font Color emphasis animation effect.

- Change the start timing option to After Previous.

- Click the Add Animation button and then click the Underline emphasis animation effect.

- Change the start timing option to With Previous (Figure 7–23).

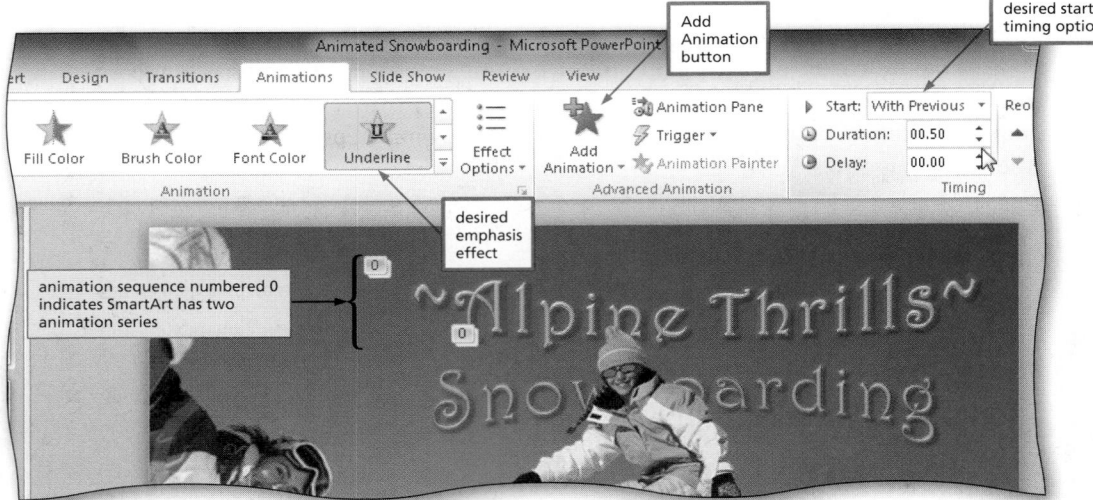

Figure 7–23

Q&A Why is a second set of animation numbered tags starting with 0 displaying on the left side of the title text placeholder?

They represent the three animations associated with the paragraphs in that placeholder.

To Change Animation Order

Two title slide elements have animations: the snowboarder picture and the title text placeholder. PowerPoint applies the animations in the order you created them, so on this slide the snowboarder picture animations will appear first and then the title text placeholder animation will follow. You can reorder animation elements if you decide one set of animation should appear before another set, and you also can reorder individual animation elements within an animation group. In this presentation, you decide to display the title text placeholder animation first, and then you decide that the Underline emphasis effect should appear before the Font Color emphasis effect. The following steps reorder the two animation groups on the slide and then reorder the Font Color and Underline emphasis effects.

1

- Double-click the Slide 1 title text placeholder border so that it displays as a solid line. Click the far-left orange sequence order tag to display the Animation Pane task pane (Figure 7–24).

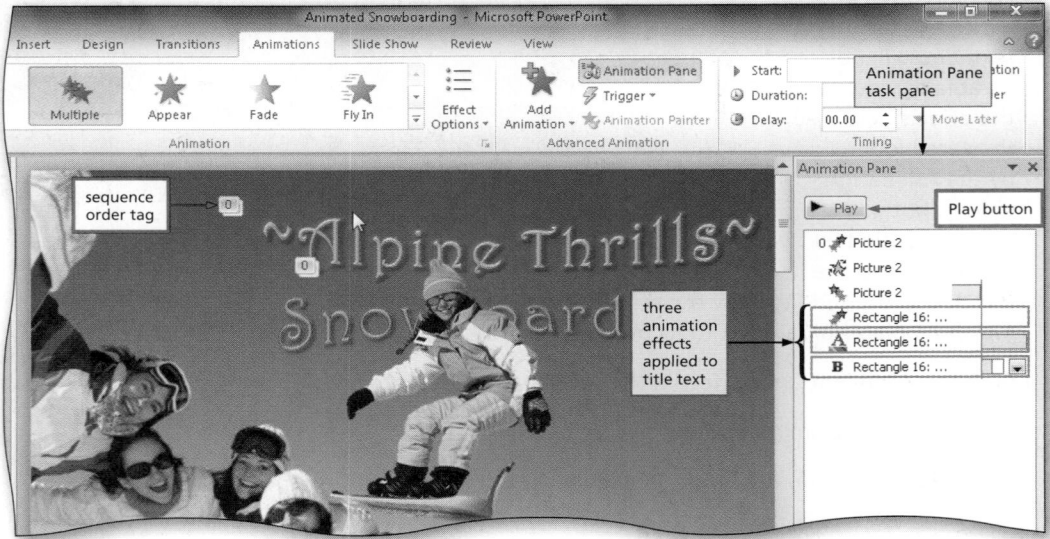

Figure 7–24

Q&A Why do blue lines appear around the three Rectangle effects?

The lines correspond to the three animation effects that you applied to the title text placeholder. The green star indicates the entrance effect, the A with the multicolor underline indicates the Font Color emphasis effect, and the black B indicates the Underline emphasis effect.

Q&A Why do I see a different number after the Rectangle label?

PowerPoint numbers slide elements consecutively, so you may see a different number if you have added and deleted pictures, text, and other graphics. You will rename these labels in a later set of steps.

2

- Click the Move Earlier button (Animations tab | Timing group) three times to move the three Rectangle animations above the Picture animations (Figure 7–25).

- Click the Play button (Animation Pane task pane) to see the reordered animation.

Q&A Can I click the Re-Order up button at the bottom of the Animation Pane task pane instead of the Move Earlier button on the Ribbon?

Yes. Either button will change the animation order.

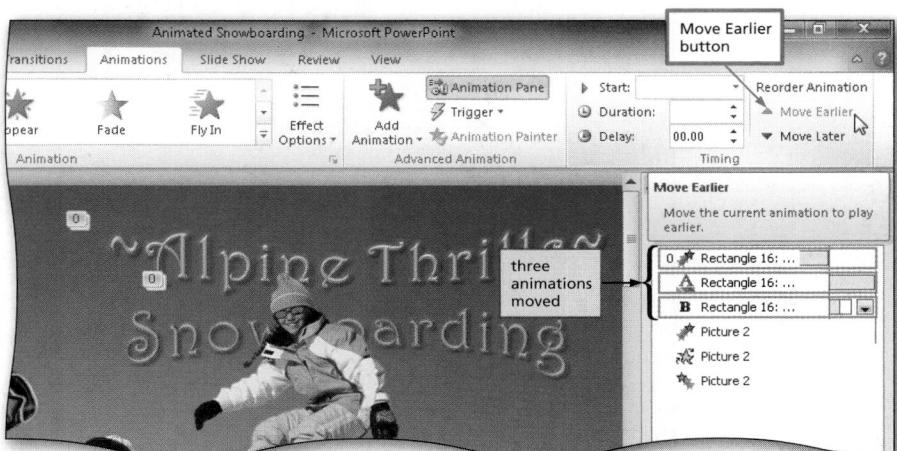

Figure 7–25

3

- In the Animation Pane task pane, click the second Rectangle label representing the Font Color animation to select it and then click the Move Later button (Animations tab | Timing group) to move this animation below the Rectangle label representing the Underline animation (Figure 7–26).

- Click the Play button (Animation Pane task pane) to see the reordered text placeholder animation.

Figure 7–26

Q&A Can I view the Animation Pane task pane at any time when I am adding and adjusting animation effects?

Yes. Click the Animation Pane button (Animations tab | Advanced Animation group) to display the Animation Pane task pane.

To Rename Slide Objects

The two animated title slide elements are listed in the Animation Pane task pane as Rectangle and Picture. You can give these objects meaningful names so that you can identify them in the animation sequence. The following steps rename the animated Slide 1 objects.

- Display the Home tab and then click Select (Home tab | Editing group) to display the Select menu (Figure 7–27).

Figure 7–27

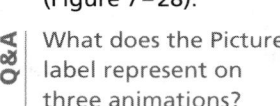

- Click Selection Pane in the Select menu to display the Selection and Visibility task pane.

- Click the Picture label in the Shapes on this Slide area and then click the label again to place the insertion point in the text box (Figure 7–28).

What does the Picture label represent on three animations?

The green entry, yellow emphasis, and red exit animations are applied to the snowboarder picture.

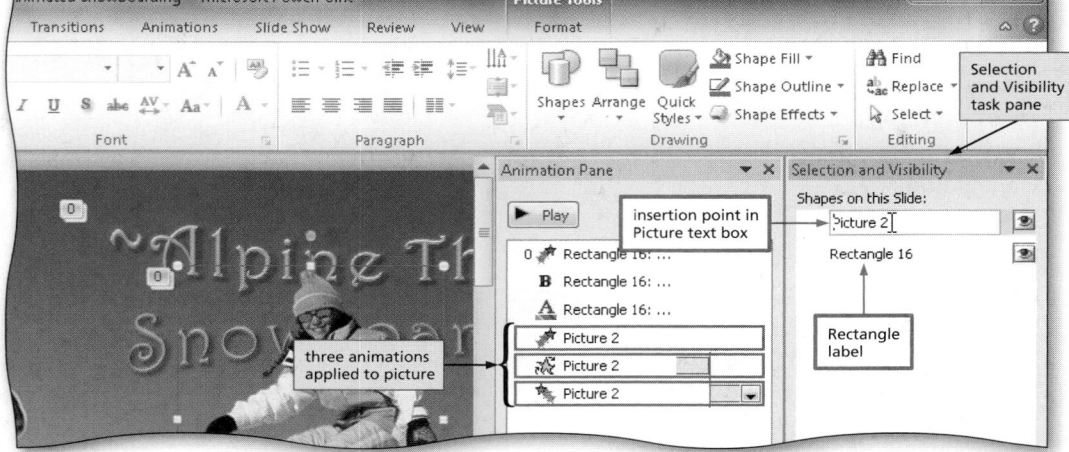

Figure 7–28

3

- Delete the text and then type **Snowboarder** in the Picture text box.

- Click the Rectangle label in the Shapes on this Slide area, click the label again, delete the text, and then type **Title Text** in the Rectangle text box (Figure 7–29).

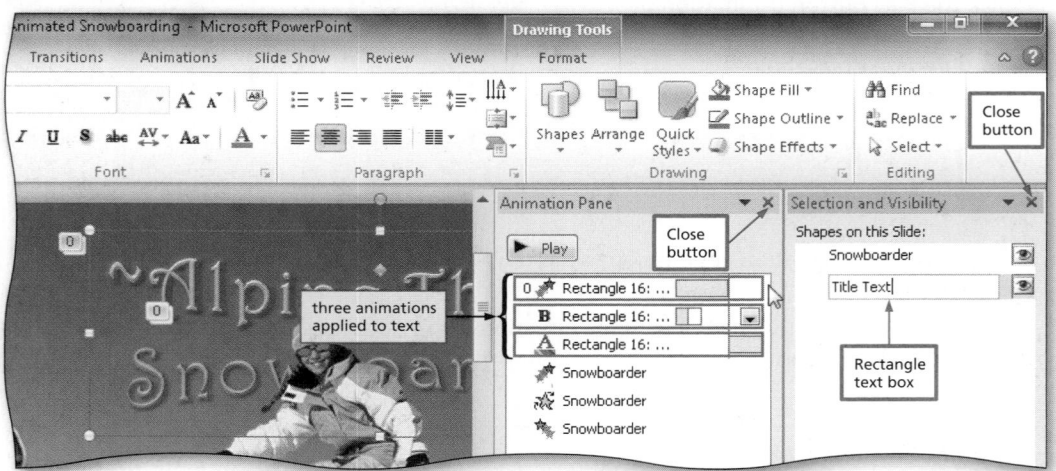

Figure 7–29

What does the Rectangle label represent on three animations?

The green entry and two emphasis animations are applied to the title text placeholder.

4

• Click the Close button on the Selection and Visibility task pane.

• Click the Close button on the Animation Pane task pane.

BTW

Selecting Text Animation Options
Multi-level bulleted list paragraphs can have animation effects that help direct the audience's attention. For example, you can animate the second-level paragraphs so they are displayed individually along with any associated third-level paragraphs. To specify a text animation option, display the Animation Pane, click an animation you want to manipulate in the list, click this animation's list arrow to display a menu, click Effect Options in the list, and then click the Text Animation tab. If desired, you can click the Group Text arrow and select a paragraph level, such as 2nd level, in the list. Click the Automatically after check box and enter a time if you want the next bulleted paragraph to appear after a specific number of seconds. In addition, click the 'In reverse order' check box to build the paragraphs from the bottom to the top of the slide.

Break Point: If you wish to take a break, this is a good place to do so. Be sure to save the Animated Snowboarding file again and then you can quit PowerPoint. To resume at a later time, start PowerPoint, open the file called Animated Snowboarding, and continue following the steps from this location forward.

To Insert a Text Box and Format Text

Slide 2 contains three elements that you will animate. First, you will add a text box, format and animate the text, and add a motion path and sound. Next, you will add an entrance effect and custom motion path to the snowboarder clip. Finally, you will animate one snowflake and copy the animation to the other snowflakes using the Animation Painter.

You can add the parts of the animation in any order and then change the sequence. You can save time, however, if you develop the animation using the sequence in which the elements will display on the slide. The first sequence will be a text box in the lower-left corner of the slide. The following steps add a text box to Slide 2.

1

• Display Slide 2 and then display the Insert tab.

• Click the Text Box button (Insert tab | Text group) and then position the mouse pointer in the blue area in the lower-left corner of the slide (Figure 7–30).

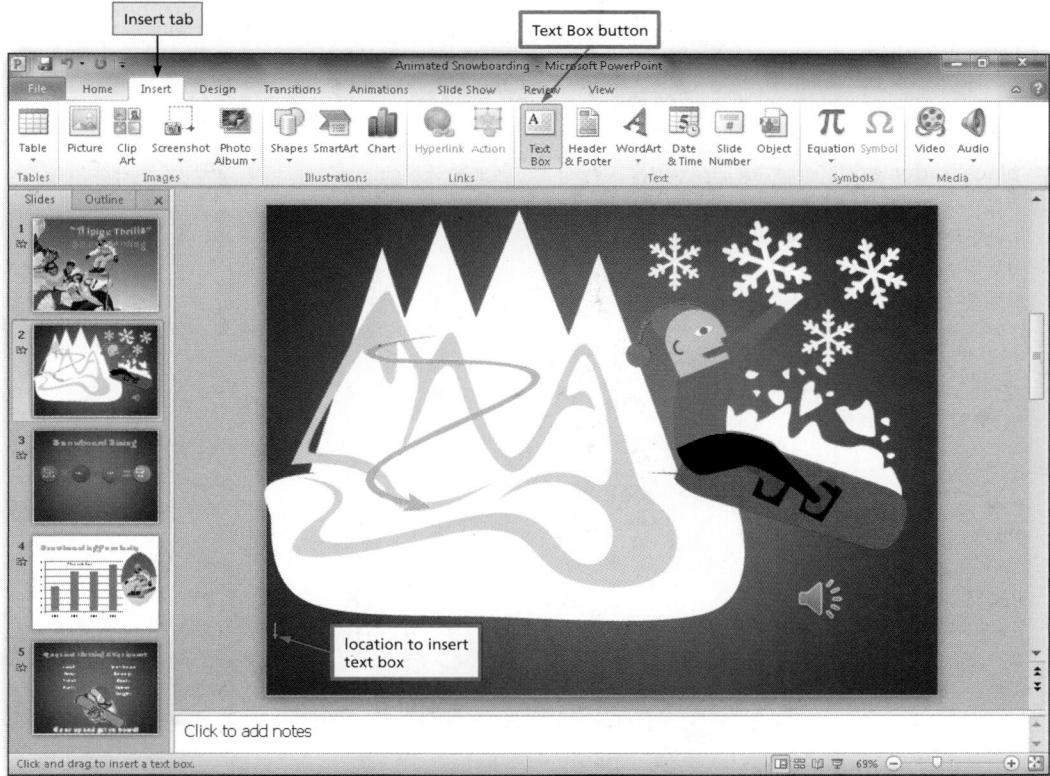

Figure 7–30

● Click the slide and
then type **Carve
Some Turns**
in the text box
(Figure 7–31).

Figure 7–31

● Display Slide 1,
position the mouse
pointer in the second
line of the title text
placeholder, and
then double-click the
Format Painter button
(Home tab | Clipboard
group) (Figure 7–32).

Figure 7–32

4

- Display Slide 2 and then triple-click the inserted text box to apply the Slide 1 title text format to the text in the text box.

- Press the ESC key to turn off the Format Painter feature.

- Display the Drawing Tools Format tab, click the Text Effects button (Drawing Tools Format tab | WordArt Styles group), and then apply the Wave 1 WordArt text effect (first effect in fifth row of the Warp area of the Transform gallery) to the words in the text box (Figure 7–33). If

Figure 7–33

necessary, move the text box so that all the letters display on the slide.

To Animate a Text Box Using an Entrance Effect

Text boxes can have the same animation effects applied to pictures and placeholders. Entrance, emphasis, and exit animations can add interest to slides, and the default timings can be changed to synchronize with the slide content. The 13 effects shown in the Entrance area of the Animation gallery are some of the more popular choices; PowerPoint provides many more effects that are divided into the Basic, Subtle, Moderate, and Exciting categories. The following steps add an entrance effect to the text box.

1

- If necessary, click the text box to select it and then display the Animations tab.

- Click the More button in the Animation gallery (Animations tab | Animation group) to expand the Animation gallery (Figure 7–34).

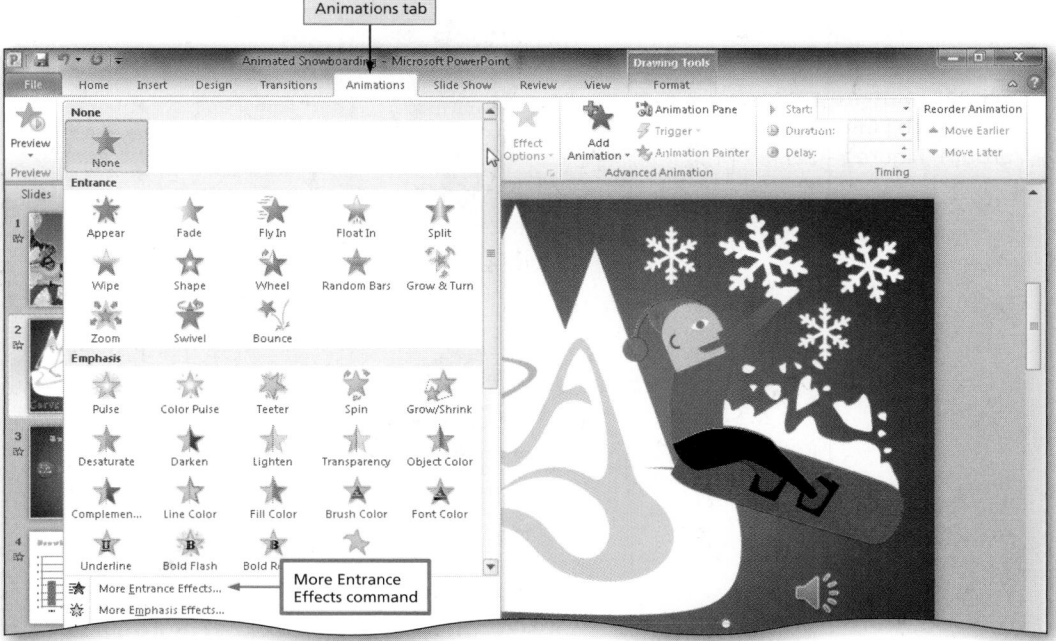

Figure 7–34

• Click More Entrance Effects in the Animation gallery to display the Change Entrance Effect dialog box (Figure 7–35).

🔎 **Experiment**

• Click some of the entrance effects in the various areas and watch the effect preview in the text box on Slide 2.

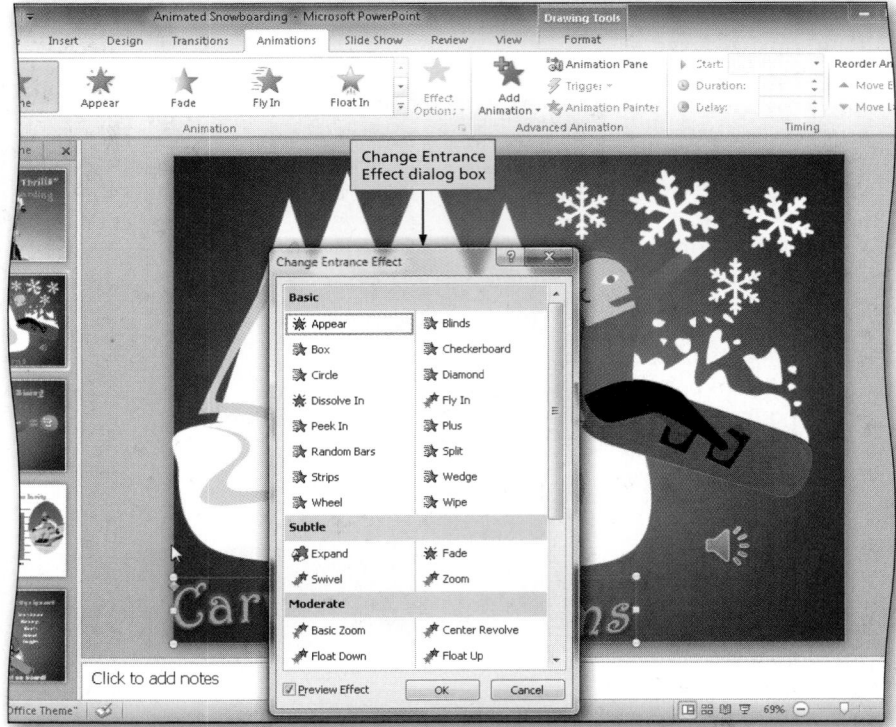

Figure 7–35

Q&A Can I move the dialog box so that I can see the effect preview?

Yes. Drag the dialog box title bar so that the dialog box does not cover the text box.

• Scroll down and then click Flip in the Exciting area (Figure 7–36).

Q&A Why do I see a preview of the effects when I click their names?

The Preview Effect box is selected. If you do not want to see previews, click the box to deselect it.

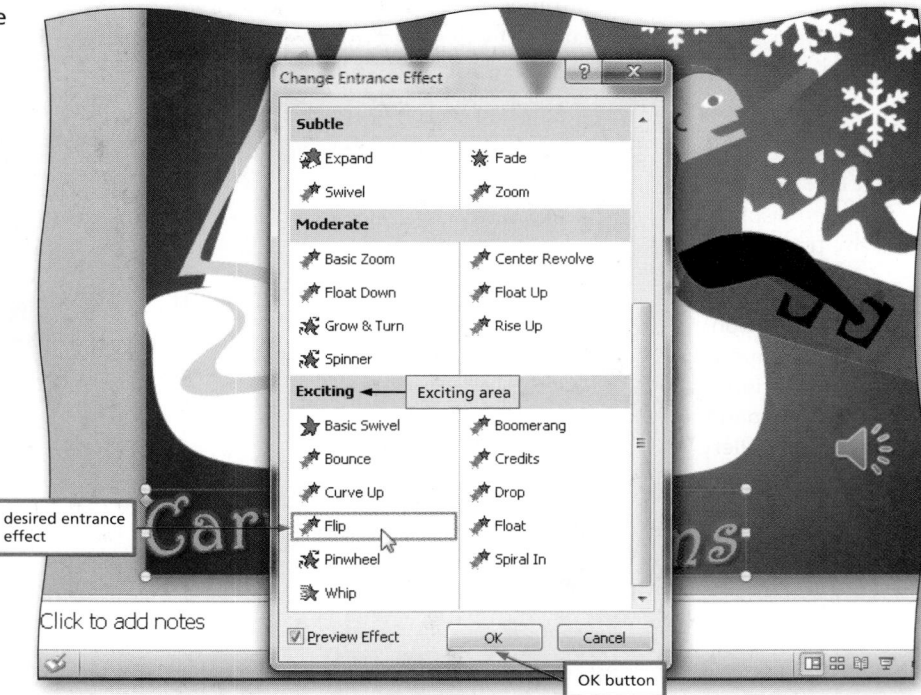

Figure 7–36

4

- Click the OK button to apply the Flip entrance effect to the text.

- Change the start timing option to With Previous.

- Change the duration to 02.00 seconds (Figure 7–37).

Q&A
Can I remove an animation?

Yes. Click None (Animations tab | Animation group). You may need to click the More button to see None.

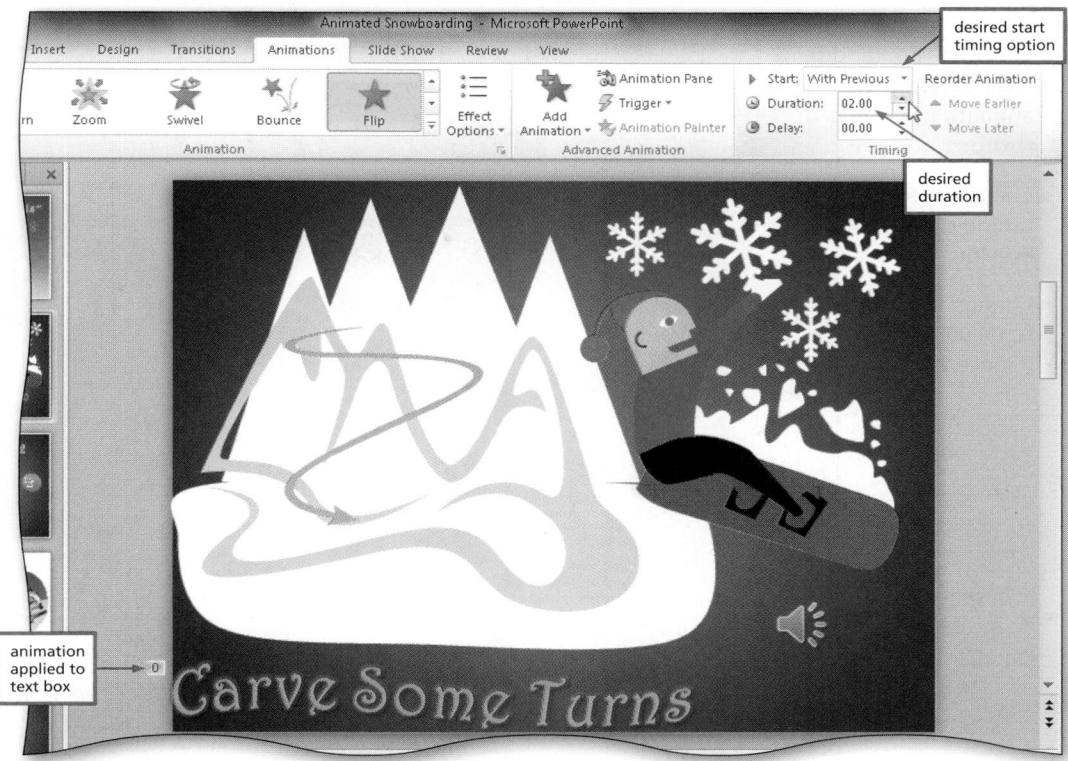

Figure 7–37

To Animate a Text Box by Applying a Motion Path

One of the more effective methods of animating slide objects is to use a motion path to predetermine the route the object will follow. In your presentation, the text box will move from the left side of the slide to the right side in a curving motion that simulates a snowboarder's sideslip ride across the slope. The following steps apply a motion path to the Slide 2 text box.

1

- Click the Add Animation button (Animations tab | Advanced Animation group) to expand the Animation gallery.

- Scroll down until the Motion Paths area is visible (Figure 7–38).

 Experiment

- Point to some of the motion paths and watch the animation preview in the text box.

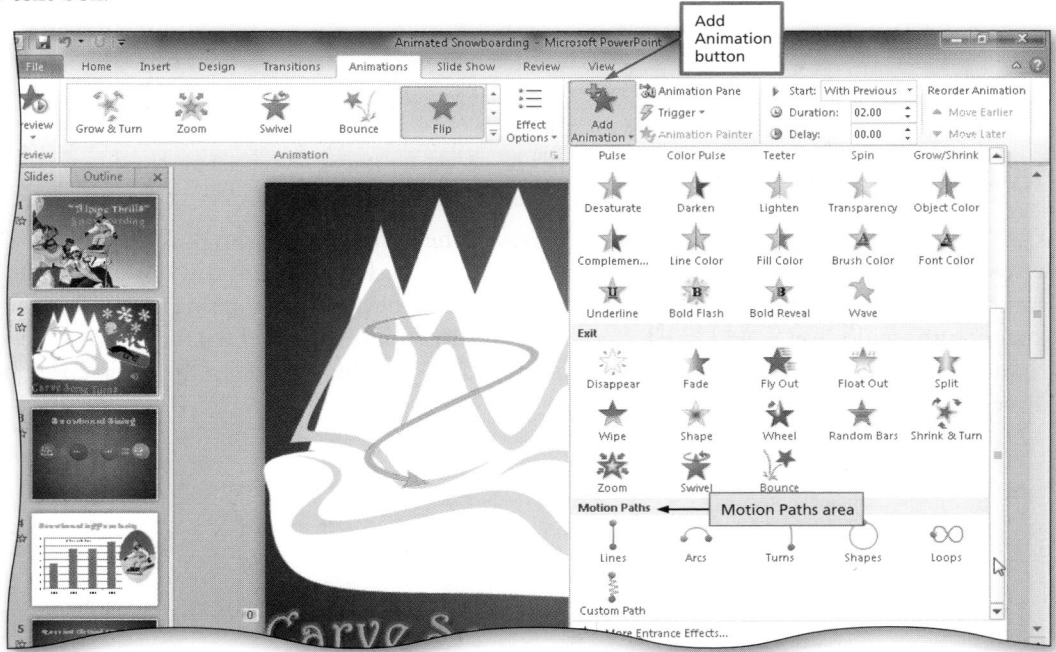

Figure 7–38

- Click the Arcs motion path to apply the animation to the text box.

- Change the start timing option to After Previous.

- Change the duration to 04.00 seconds (Figure 7–39).

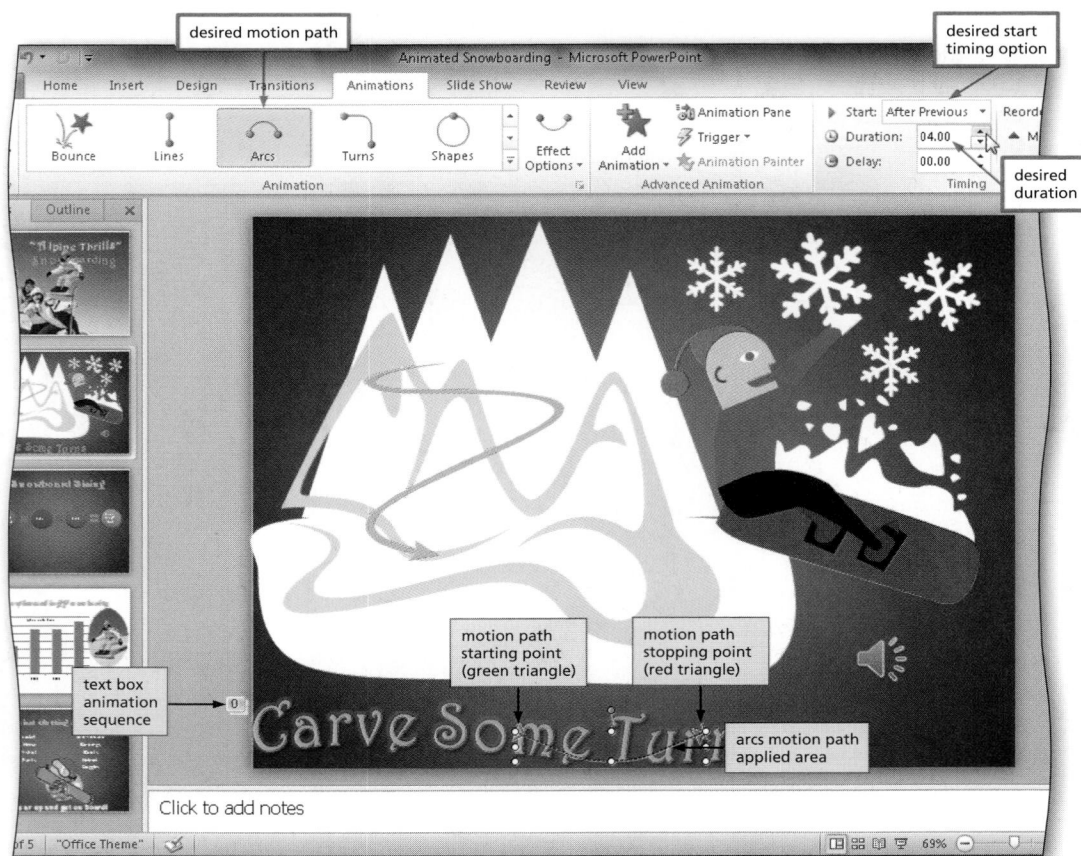

Figure 7–39

Q&A

Are more motion paths available in addition to those shown in the Animation gallery?

Yes. To see additional motion paths, click More Motion Paths in the lower portion of the Animation gallery. The motion paths are arranged in the Basic, Lines & Curves, and Special categories.

To Adjust a Motion Path

The Arcs motion path moves the text box in the correct directions, but the path can be extended to move across the entire width of the slide. The green triangle in the middle of the word, Some, indicates the starting point, and the red triangle in the middle of the word, Turns, indicates the stopping point. For the maximum animation effect on the slide, you would like to move the starting point toward the left edge and the stopping point toward the right edge. The following steps move the starting and stopping points on the Slide 2 text box and then reverse the direction of the arc.

1

- With the motion path selected in the text box, click the red stopping point and position the cursor over the upper-right sizing handle so that your cursor is displayed as a two-headed arrow.

- Drag the red stopping point to the location shown in Figure 7–40.

Q&A
My entire motion path moved. How can I move only the red stopping point arrow?

Be certain your cursor is a two-headed arrow and not a four-headed arrow.

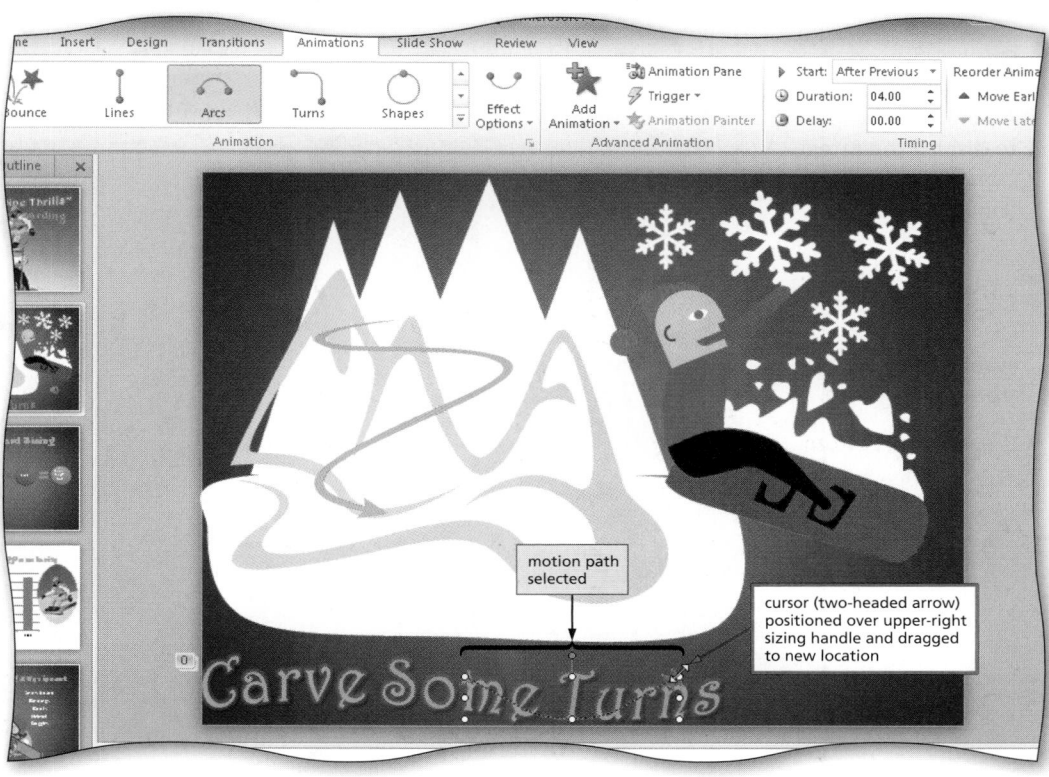

Figure 7–40

2

- Drag the green starting point to the location shown in Figure 7–41.

- Drag the upper-center sizing handle to the location shown in Figure 7–41.

- Preview the custom animation (Figure 7–41).

Q&A
My animation is not exactly like the path shown in Figure 7–41. Can I change the path?

Yes. Continue adjusting the starting and stopping points and playing the animation until you are satisfied with the effect.

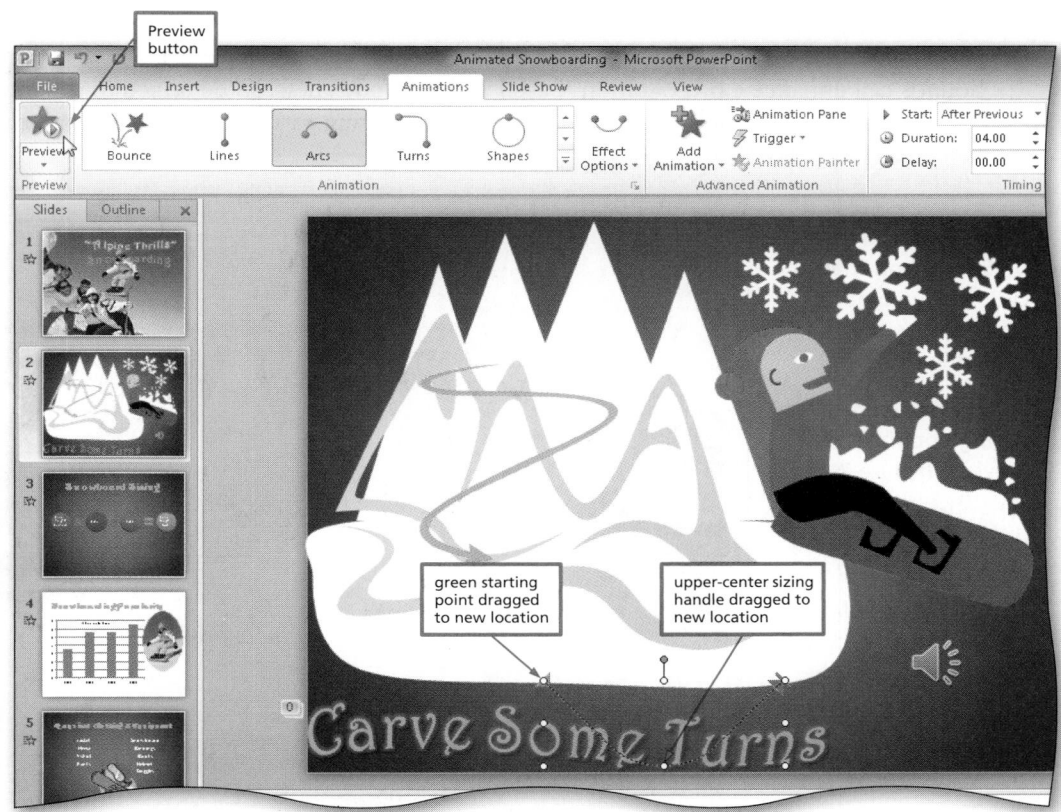

Figure 7–41

3
- Click the Effect Options button (Animations tab | Animation group) to display the Effect Options gallery (Figure 7–42).

4
- Click Up in the Direction area to reverse the direction from Down to Up.

- Preview the custom animation.

Figure 7–42

To Associate a Sound with an Animation

Sounds can enhance a presentation if used properly, and they can be linked to other animations on the slide. Slide 2 already has the inserted sound of a snowboarder carving turns. The following step associates a sound with the text box on Slide 2.

1
- Click the sound icon on Slide 2 and then click Play animation (Animations tab | Animation group).

- Change the start timing option to With Previous (Figure 7–43).

Q&A

What does the duration Auto setting control?

The sound will play automatically and will repeat as long as the text box is animated.

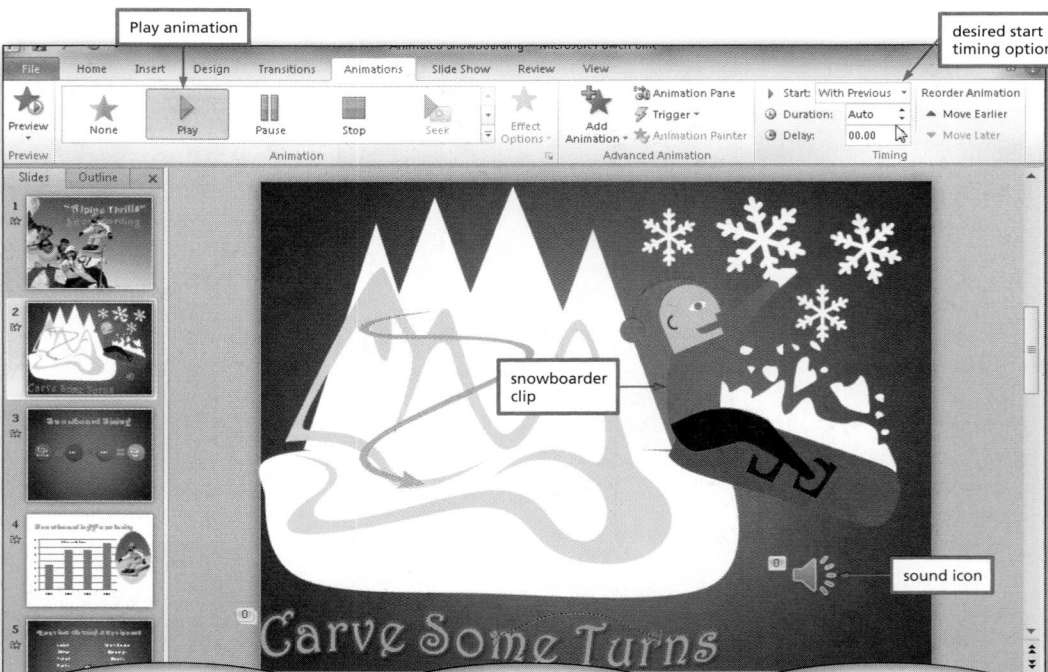

Figure 7–43

To Draw a Custom Motion Path

Although PowerPoint supplies a wide variety of motion paths, at times they may not fit the precise animations your presentation requires. In that situation, you can draw a custom path that specifies the unique movement your slide element should make. Slide 2 has a clip of a mountain and another clip of a snowboarder. The mountain has an orange curvy line running down the face of the slope, and you can animate the snowboarder to follow this line. No preset motion path presents the exact motion you want to display, so you will draw your own custom path.

Drawing a custom path requires some practice and patience. You click the mouse to begin drawing the line. If you want the line to change direction, such as to curve, you click again. When you have completed drawing the path, you double-click to end the line. The following steps draw a custom motion path.

1

- Select the snowboarder clip, apply the Fade entrance effect, and then change the start timing option to After Previous.

- Click the Add Animation button and then scroll down until the entire Motion Paths area is visible (Figure 7–44).

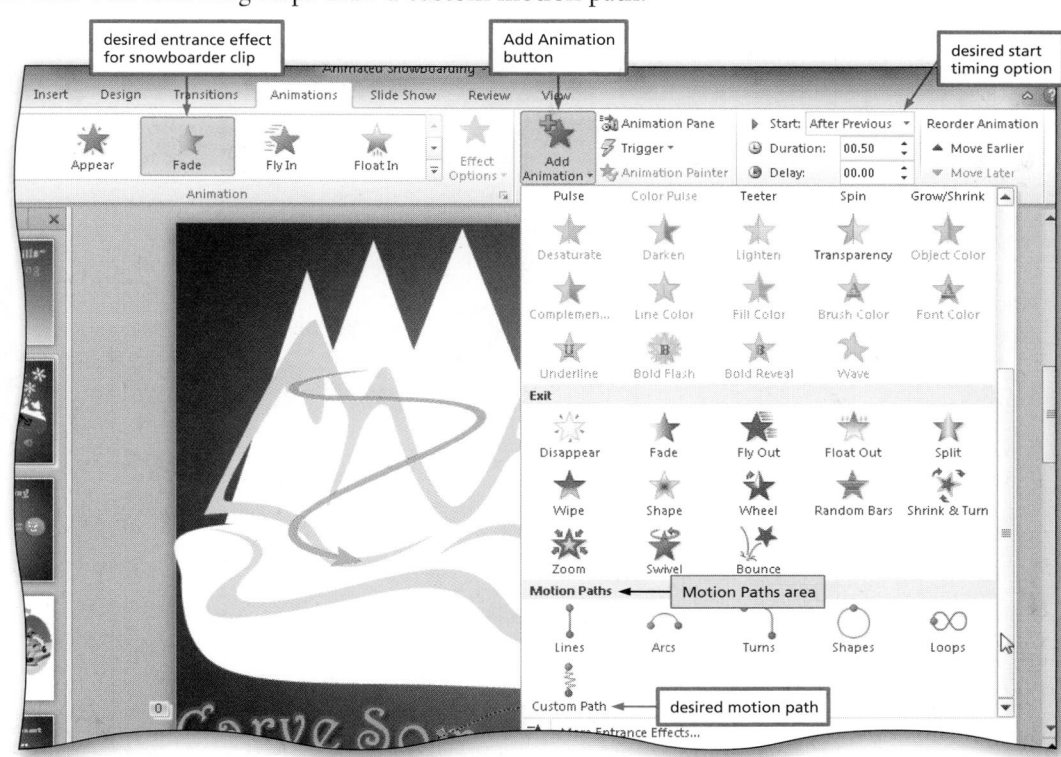

Figure 7–44

2

- Click Custom Path in the Motion Paths gallery to add this animation.

- Click the Effect Options button (Animations tab | Animation group) to display the Type gallery (Figure 7–45).

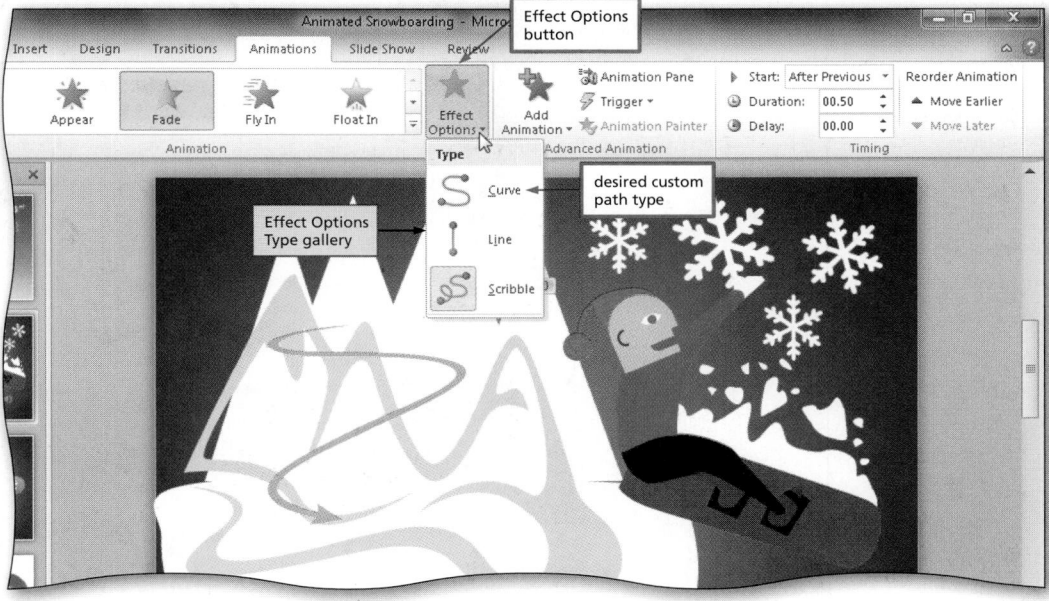

Figure 7–45

- Click Curve in the Type gallery and then position the mouse pointer at the beginning of the orange line at the top of the mountain.

Q&A

Why did I need to change the option from Scribble to Curve?

Your custom motion path will follow the orange curves on the mountain clip, and the Curve type will create rounded edges to connect the lines you draw. The Scribble option would draw only straight lines, so the snowboarder would not carve smooth turns as he comes downhill.

- Click the mouse to indicate where the curve will start and then move the mouse pointer to the location shown in Figure 7–46, which is where the curve will change direction.

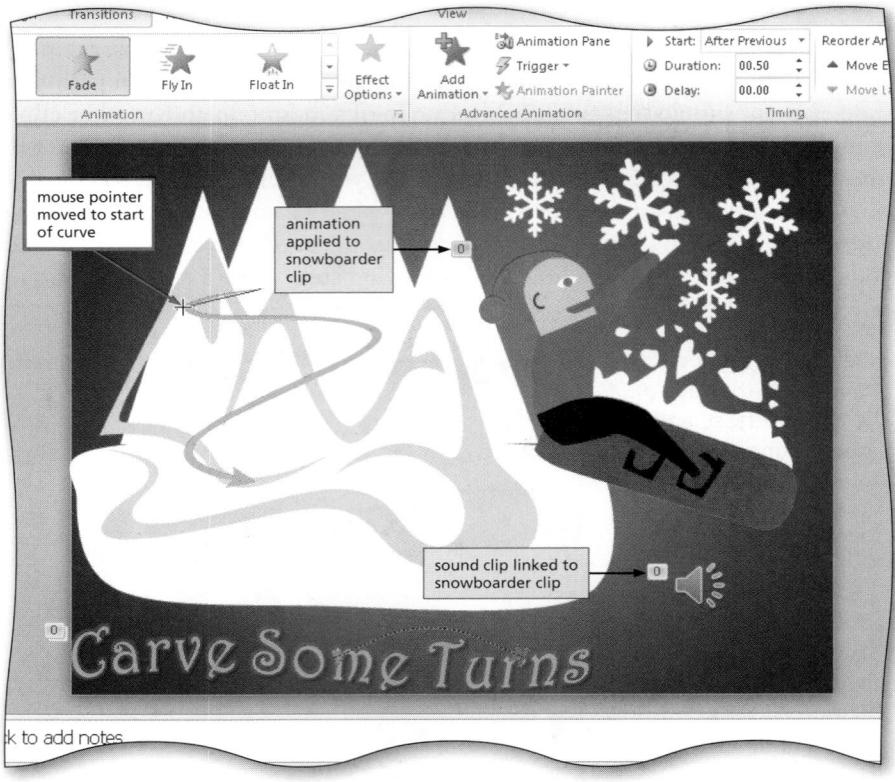

Figure 7–46

- Click the mouse, position the mouse pointer at the top of the far-right orange curve, and then click to indicate the end of this direction of travel.
- Position the mouse pointer at the top of the lower-left curve and then click to indicate the end of this curve (Figure 7–47).

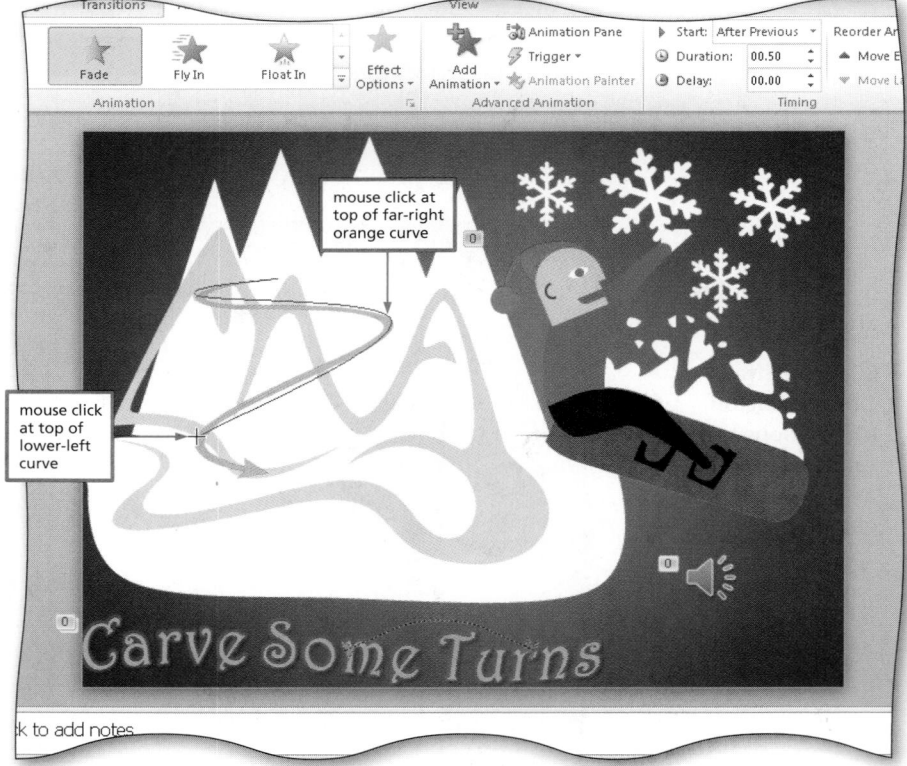

Figure 7–47

5

- Position the mouse pointer at the tip of the orange arrowhead and then double-click to indicate the end of the motion path and preview the animation (Figure 7–48).

- Change the start timing option to With Previous and the duration setting to 05.00 seconds.

Q&A

If my curve is not correct, can I delete it?

Yes. Select the motion path, press the DELETE key, and then repeat the previous steps.

Figure 7–48

To Use the Animation Painter to Animate a Clip

At times, you may desire to apply the same animation effects to several objects on a slide. On Slide 2, for example, you want to animate the four snowflakes with identical entrance, emphasis, and exit effects. As with the Format Painter that is used to duplicate font and paragraph attributes, the Animation Painter copies animation effects. Using the Animation Painter can save time by duplicating numerous animations quickly and consistently. The following steps animate one snowflake and then use the Animation Painter to copy these effects to three other snowflakes.

1

- Select the snowflake in the upper-right corner of the slide and then apply the Fly In entrance effect.

- Click the Effect Options button and then change the direction to From Top.

- Change the start timing option to With Previous and the duration to 06.00 seconds (Figure 7–49).

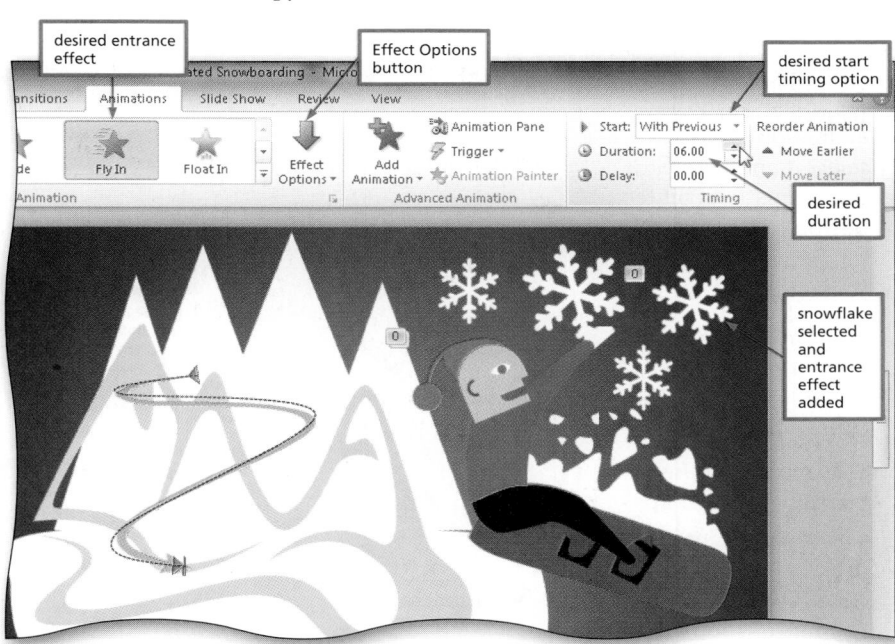

Figure 7–49

● With the snowflake still selected, add the Teeter emphasis effect, change the start timing option to After Previous, and then change the duration to 01.50 seconds (Figure 7–50).

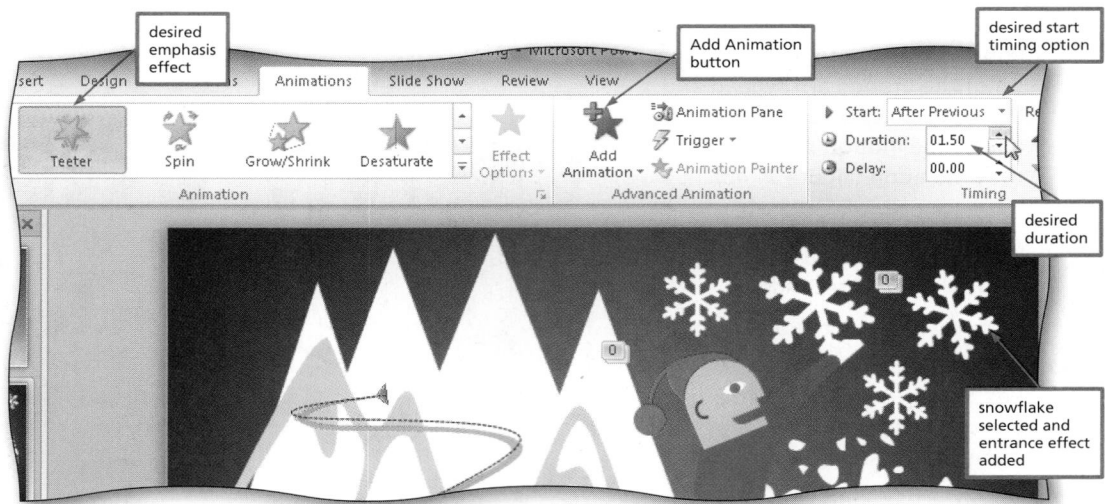

Figure 7–50

● Add the Fade exit effect, change the start timing option to After Previous, and then change the duration to 03.00 seconds (Figure 7–51).

Q&A

Can I copy the animation to an object on another slide?

Yes. Once you establish the desired animation effects, you can copy them to any object that can be animated on any slide.

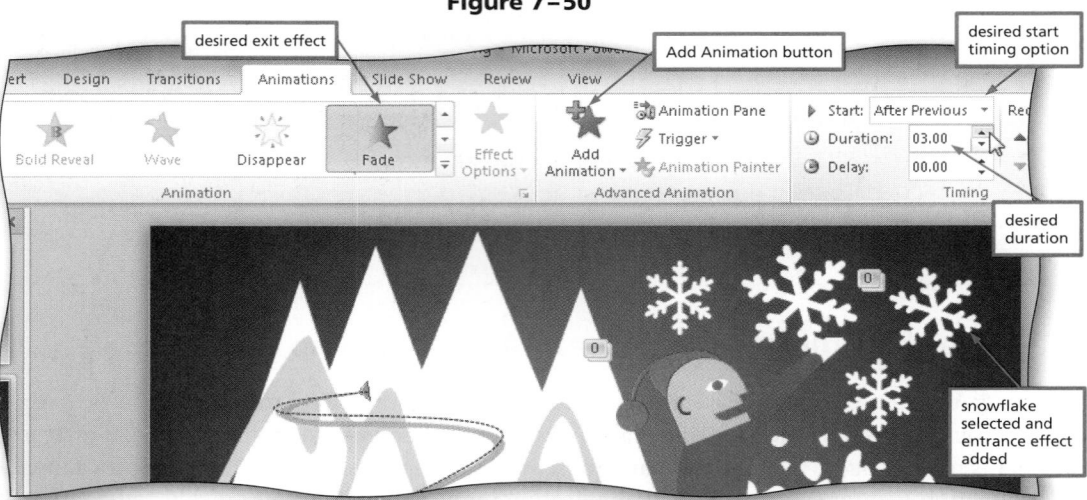

Figure 7–51

● Click the upper-right snowflake with the animation effects to select it and then click the Animation Painter button (Animations tab | Advanced Animation group).

● Position the mouse pointer over the upper-left snowflake (Figure 7–52).

Q&A

Why did my mouse pointer change shape?

The mouse pointer changed shape by displaying a paintbrush to indicate that the Animation Painter function is active.

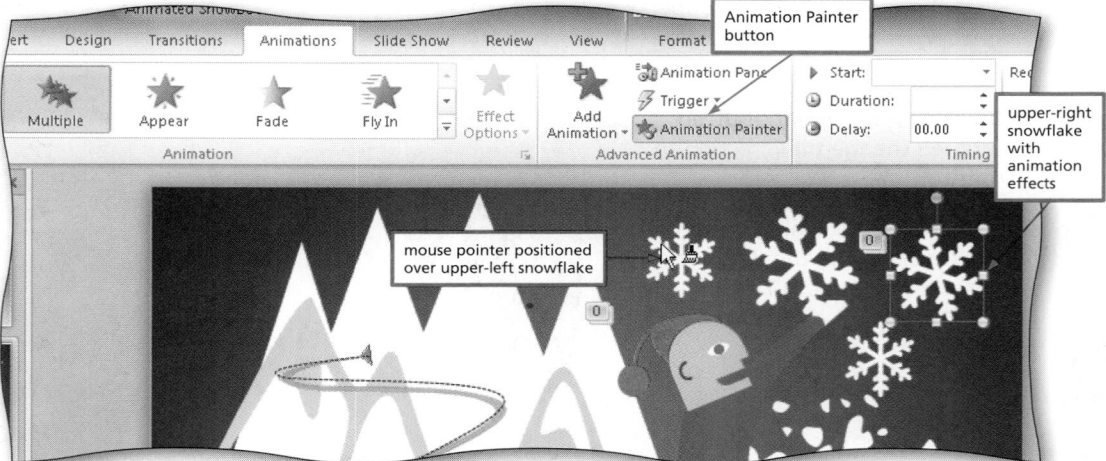

Figure 7–52

5

- Click the upper-left snowflake to apply the same entrance, emphasis, and exit animation effects as those added to the upper-right snowflake.

- Click the Animation Painter button and then click the center snowflake.

- Click the Animation Painter button again and then click the lower-right snowflake (Figure 7–53).

- Preview the animation effects.

Q&A Can I copy the animation to more than one object simultaneously?

No. Unlike using the Format Painter, you must click the Animation Painter button each time you want to copy the animation to an object on the slide.

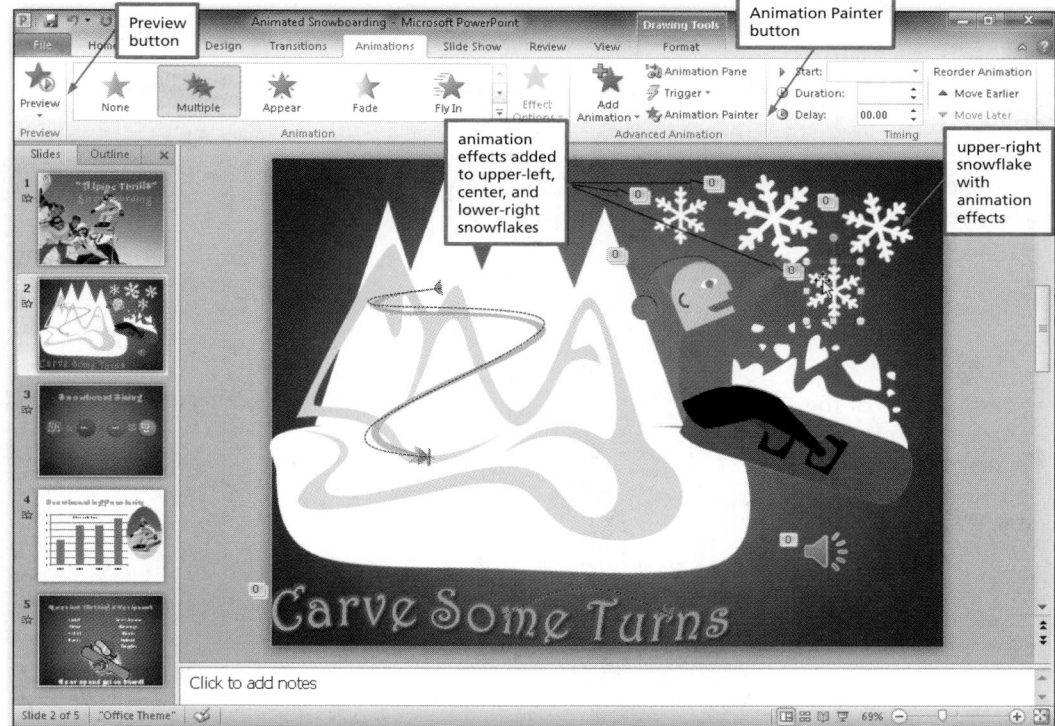

Figure 7–53

Break Point: If you wish to take a break, this is a good place to do so. Be sure to save the Animated Snowboarding file again and then you can quit PowerPoint. To resume at a later time, start PowerPoint, open the file called Animated Snowboarding, and continue following the steps from this location forward.

To Animate a SmartArt Graphic

The bulleted lists on the text slides are animated, and you can build on this effect by adding animation to the Slide 3 SmartArt graphic. You can add a custom animation to each shape in the cycle, but you also can use one of PowerPoint's built-in animations to simplify the animation procedure. The following steps apply an entrance animation effect to the Equation diagram.

1

- Display Slide 3 and then select the SmartArt graphic.

- Display the Animation gallery and then point to the Zoom entrance effect to display a live preview of this effect (Figure 7–54).

🔍 **Experiment**

- Point to some of the entrance effects and watch the animation preview in the SmartArt objects.

2

- Select the Zoom entrance effect.

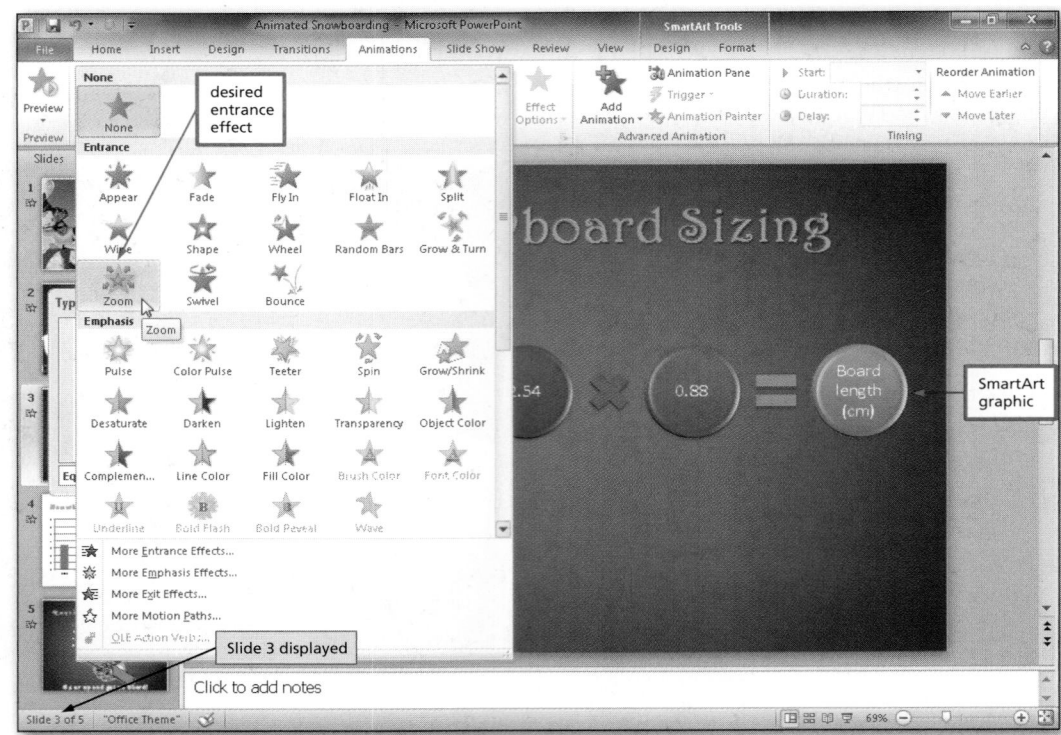

Figure 7–54

To Change a SmartArt Graphic Animation Sequence

By default, all SmartArt graphic components enter the slide simultaneously. You can modify this setting and change the entrance sequence so that each element enters one at a time and builds the mathematical sequence from left to right. The following steps change the sequence for the SmartArt animation to One by One.

1

- Click the Effect Options button to display the Effect Options gallery (Figure 7–55).

Q&A Can I reverse the order of individual shapes in the SmartArt sequence?

No. You can reverse the order of the entire SmartArt graphic but not individual shapes within the sequence.

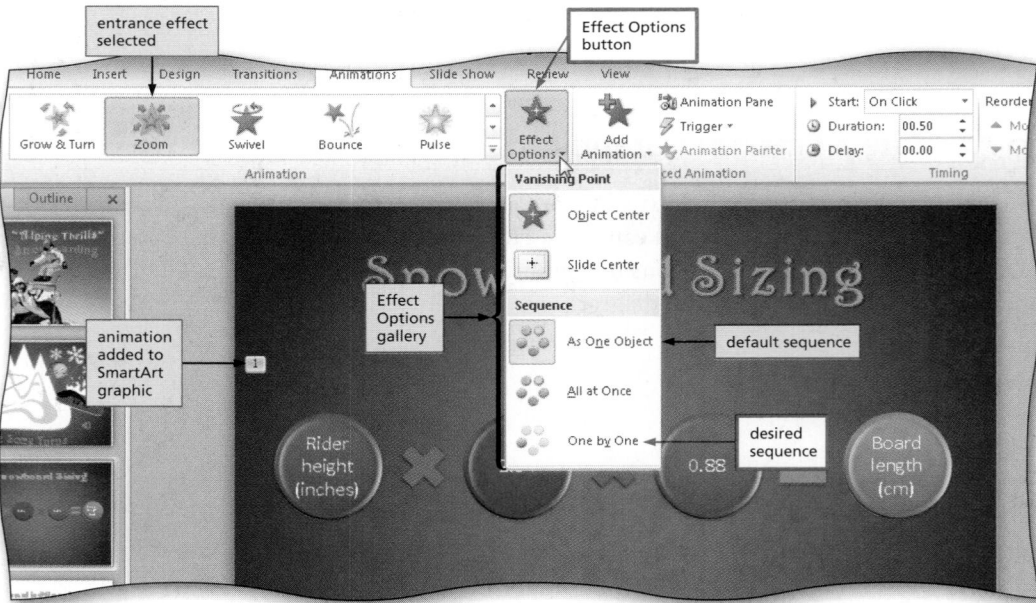

Figure 7–55

2

- Click One by One in the Sequence area to change the animation order.

- Change the start timing option to After Previous, the duration to 5.00 seconds, and the delay to 01.00 second (Figure 7–56).

Figure 7–56

TO TRIGGER AN ANIMATION EFFECT

If you select the On Click start timing option and run the slide show, PowerPoint starts the animation when you click any part of the slide or press the SPACEBAR. You may, however, want the option to play an animation in a particular circumstance. For example, you may have an animated sequence ready to show if time permits or if you believe your audience needs time to understand a process and would understand the concept more readily if you revealed one part of a SmartArt graphic at a time. A **trigger** specifies when an animation or other action should occur. It is linked to a particular component of a slide so that the action occurs only when you click this slide element. If you click any other part of the slide, PowerPoint will display the next slide in the presentation. If you need to set a slide object as the trigger to start an animation, you would follow these steps.

1. Click the Trigger button (Animations tab | Advanced Animation group) to display the Trigger menu and then point to On Click Of to display the list of slide elements.

2. Click the desired slide element to set the trigger on the click of that object.

BTW

Displaying Equations
One of PowerPoint 2010's enhancements is the Equation Tools Design tab. This feature allows you to type mathematical symbols and insert structures, including functions, integrals, operators, and radicals.

To Animate a Chart

The chart on Slide 4 depicts the growth of the sport of snowboarding. In 10 years, the number of snowboarders practically has doubled. To emphasize this increase in popularity, you can animate the bars of the chart so that each one enters the slide individually. As with the SmartArt animation, PowerPoint gives you many options to animate the chart data. The following steps animate the Slide 4 chart bars.

1
- Display Slide 4 and then click an edge of the chart so that the frame is displayed. Display the Animation gallery (Figure 7–57).

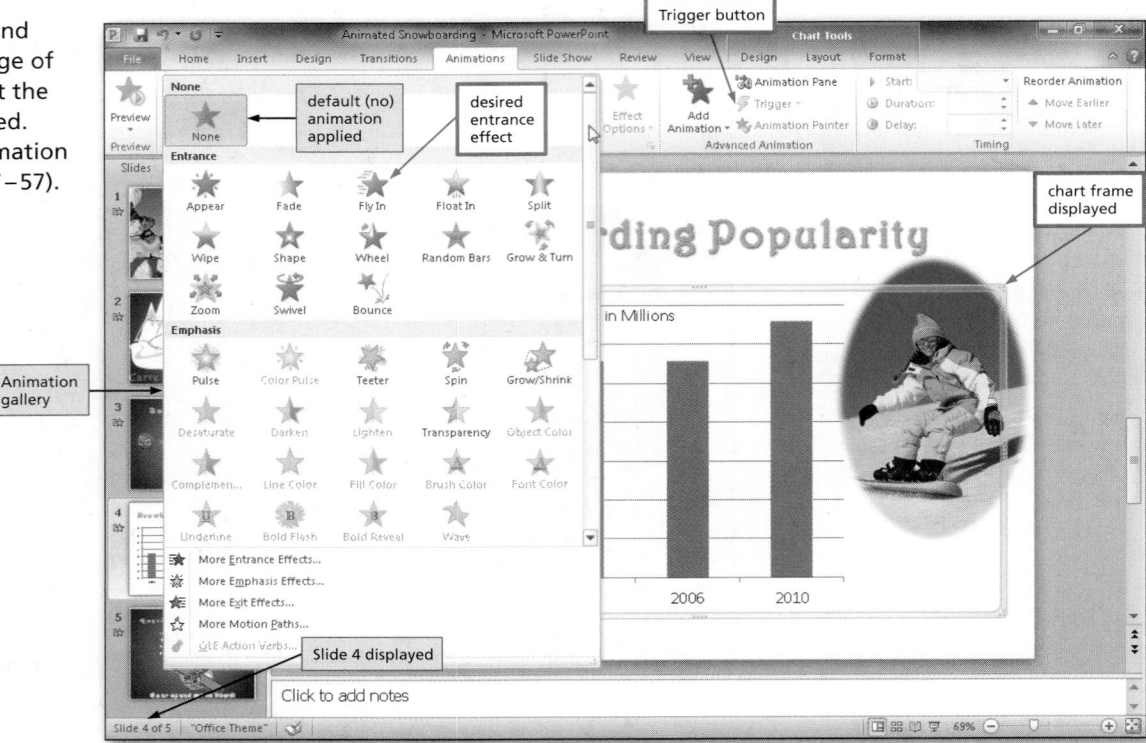

Figure 7–57

2
- Click the Fly In entrance effect, change the start timing option to After Previous, change the duration to 02.00 seconds, and change the delay to 02.50 seconds.

3
- Click the Effect Options button to display the Effect Options gallery (Figure 7–58).

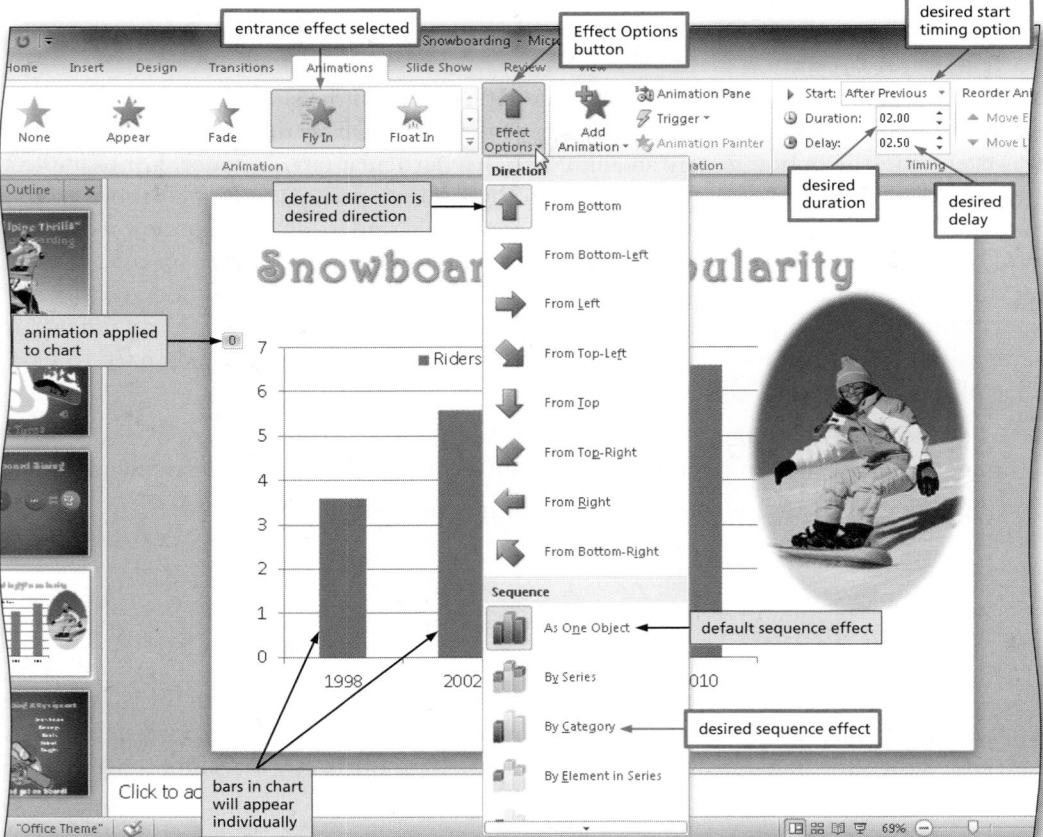

Figure 7–58

4

- Point to By Category to preview the chart animation so that each bar for the first category, Number of Snowboarders in Millions, appears individually for each year.

⌕ Experiment

- Point to some of the animations in the various categories and watch the animations preview on Slide 4.

- Click By Category to change the chart animation for the first category.

- Change the start timing option to After Previous, change the duration to 03.00 seconds, and change the delay to 03.50 seconds.

To Animate a List

The two lists on Slide 5 give the minimum clothing and equipment required to snowboard warmly and safely. Each item in the placeholder is a separate paragraph. To add interest during a presentation, you can have each paragraph in the left list enter the slide individually. When the entire list has displayed, the list can disappear and then each paragraph in the right list can appear. The following steps animate the Slide 5 paragraph lists.

1

- Display Slide 5 and then select the four items in the left text placeholder.

- Apply the Shape entrance animation effect, change the start timing option to After Previous, change the duration to 03.00 seconds, and change the delay to 01.50 seconds (Figure 7–59).

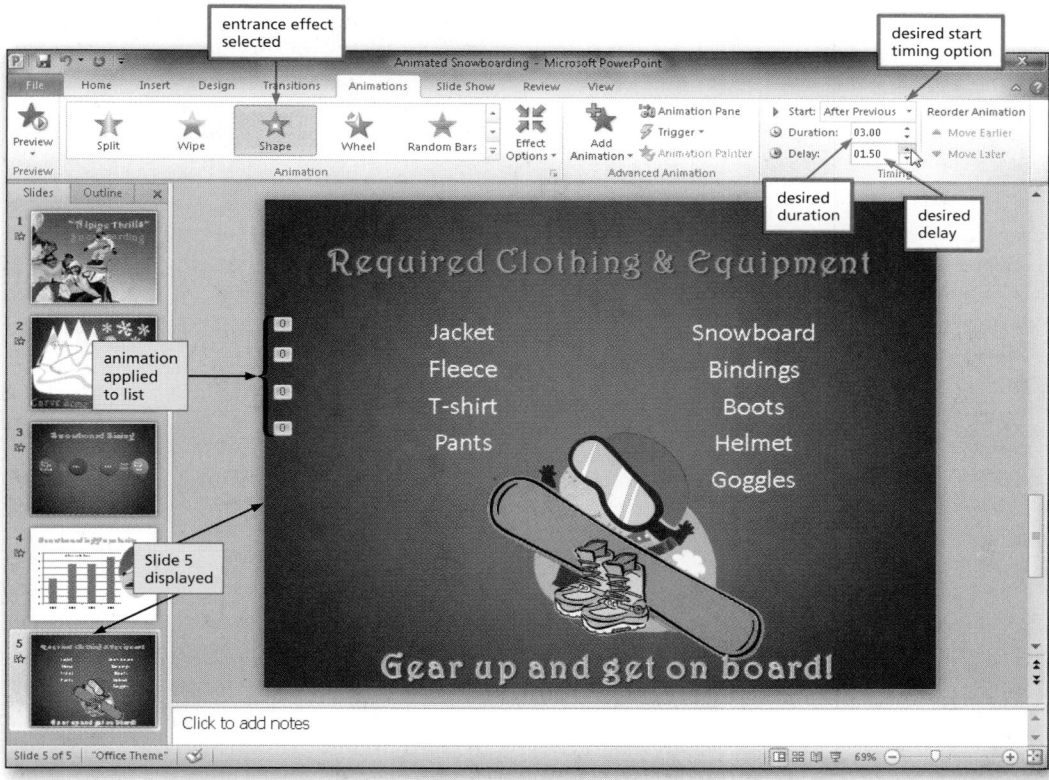

Figure 7–59

- Click the Effect Options button to display the Effect Options gallery (Figure 7–60).

Experiment

- Point to the Out direction and the Box, Diamond, and Plus Shapes and watch the animations preview on the Slide 5 left list paragraphs.

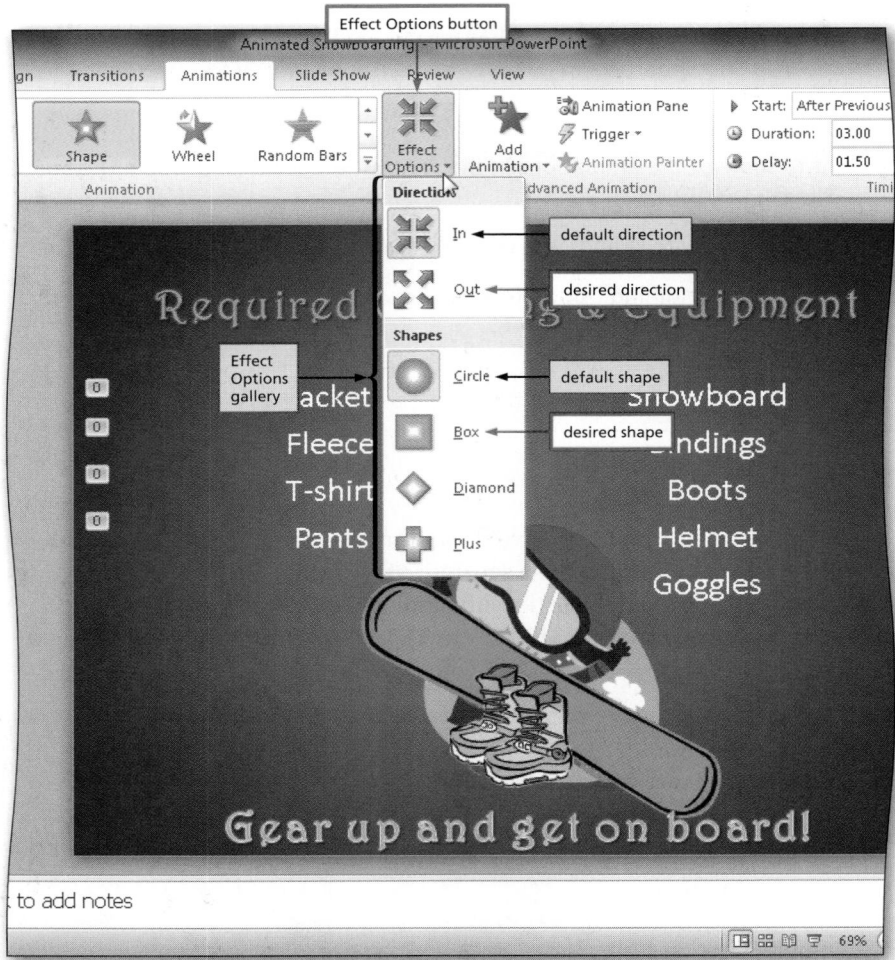

Figure 7–60

- Change the Shapes from Circle to Box.

- Click the Effect Options button again and then change the Direction to Out.

Plan Ahead

Select colors for dimming text.
After paragraphs of text are displayed, you can change the color, or dim the text, to direct the audience's attention to another area of the slide. Choose the dimming colors carefully. For example, use cool colors, such as blue, purple, and turquoise, as backgrounds so that the audience focuses on the next brighter, contrasting color on the slide. Avoid using light blue because it often is difficult to see, especially against a dark background. In addition, use a maximum of three colors unless you have a compelling need to present more variety.

To Dim Text after Animation

As each item in the list is displayed, you may desire to have the previous item removed from the screen or to have the font color change, or **dim**. PowerPoint provides several options for you to alter this text by specifying an After Animation effect. The following steps dim each item in the left placeholder list by changing the font color to Purple.

- Select the four paragraphs in the left placeholder and then click the Animation Pane button (Animations tab | Advanced Animation group) to display the Animation Pane task pane.

- Click the Pants Animation Order list arrow to display the Animation Order menu (Figure 7–61).

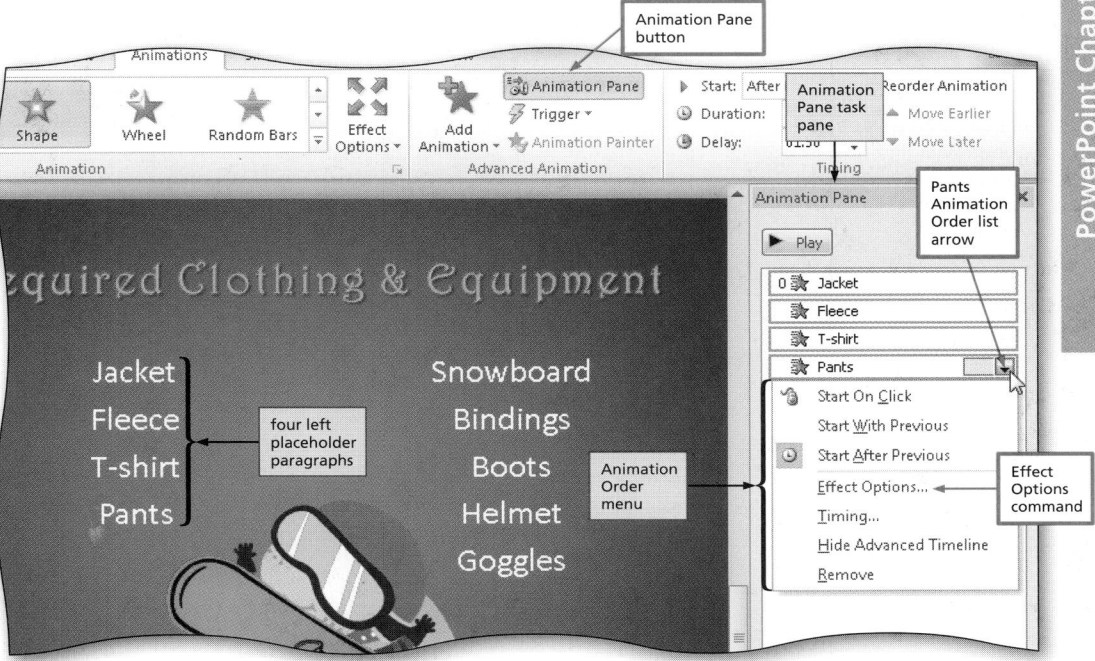

Figure 7–61

- Click Effect Options on the Animation Order list to display the Box dialog box.

- Click the After animation list arrow to display the After animation menu (Figure 7–62).

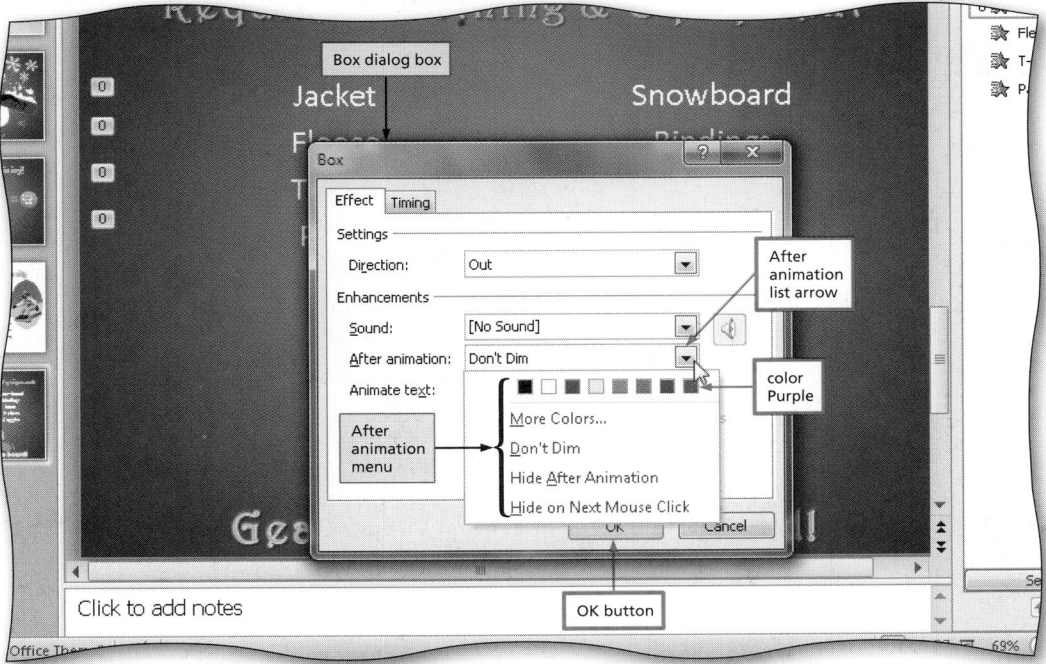

Figure 7–62

3

- Click the color Purple (last color in the row of colors) to select this color for the dim effect.

- Click the OK button (Box dialog box) to apply the dim effect to the four items in the left placeholder on Slide 5.

- Close the Animation Pane task pane.

BTW

Animation Painter
Using the Animation Painter helps to save time and ensure consistency if you desire to apply the same animations to multiple objects. This tool is a new PowerPoint 2010 element.

To Use the Animation Painter to Copy Animations

All animations have been applied to the left placeholder paragraphs. You now can copy these animations to the five items in the right text placeholder. The following steps use the Animation Painter to copy the animation.

1 Click one item in the list in the left text placeholder and then click the Animation Painter button.

2 Click the word, Snowboard, in the right list to copy the animations in the left list to the five words in the right list.

3 Select the five words in the list in the right placeholder and then change the start timing option to After Previous, the duration to 03.00 seconds, and the delay to 01.50 seconds (Figure 7–63).

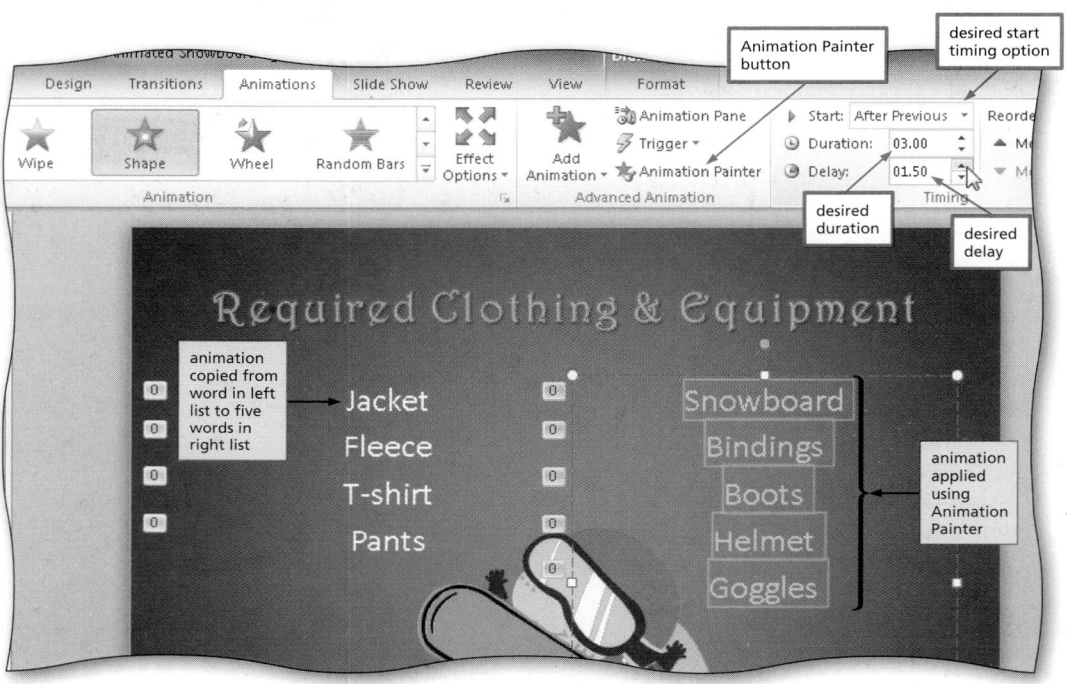

Figure 7–63

Plan Ahead

Use quotations judiciously.
Quotations and sayings are available from a variety of print sources, such as *Quotable Quotes, The Merriam-Webster Dictionary of Quotations,* and *Bartlett's Familiar Quotations.* Web sites, including bartleby.com and quotations.com, also provide direct quotes organized into specific categories. These words often add insight to the beginning or the end of a slide show. If you use a quotation, give credit to the person who said or wrote the words. Also, do not change the wording unless it is offensive or biased.

To Create Credits

Many motion pictures use rolling credits at the end of the movie to acknowledge the people who were involved in the filmmaking process or to provide additional information about the actors or setting. You, too, can use a credit or closing statement at the end of your presentation to thank individuals or companies who helped you develop your slide show or to leave your audience with a final thought. The following steps display text as an ascending credit line on Slide 5.

1

- With Slide 5 displaying, click the text box with the words, Gear up and get on board!, at the bottom of the slide to select it.

- Display the Animation gallery and then click More Entrance Effects (Figure 7–64).

Figure 7–64

2

- Click the Credits entrance animation effect in the Exciting area and then click the OK button (Change Entrance Effect dialog box) to apply the effect.

3

- Change the start timing option to After Previous, the duration to 18.00 seconds, and the delay to 01.00 second (Figure 7–65).

- Preview the animation.

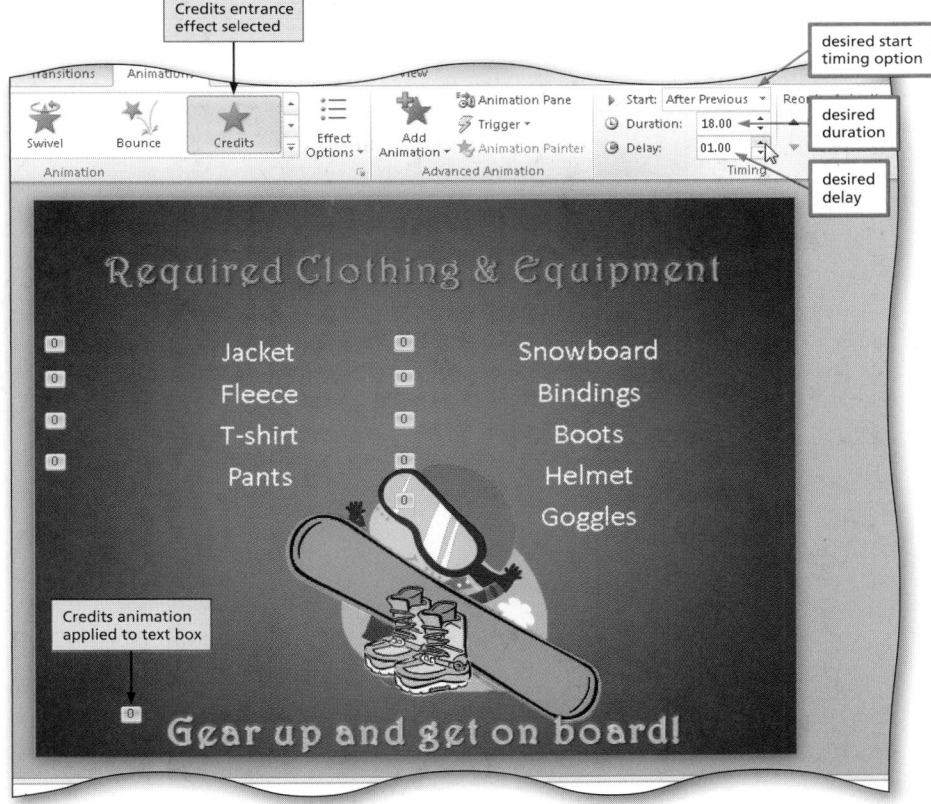

Figure 7–65

BTW

Quick Reference
For a table that lists how to complete the tasks covered in this book using the mouse, Ribbon, shortcut menu, and keyboard, see the Quick Reference Summary at the back of this book, or visit the PowerPoint 2010 Quick Reference Web page (scsite.com/ppt2010/qr).

Preparing for a Self-Running Presentation

In previous slide shows, you clicked to advance from one slide to the next. Because all animations have been added to the slides in the presentation, you now can set the time each slide is displayed on the screen. You can set these times in one of two ways. The first method is to specify each slide's display time manually. The second method is to use PowerPoint's **rehearsal feature**, which allows you to advance through the slides at your own pace, and the amount of time you view each slide is recorded. You will use the second technique in this chapter and then adjust the last slide's timing manually.

When you begin rehearsing a presentation, the Rehearsal toolbar is displayed. The **Rehearsal toolbar** contains buttons that allow you to start, pause, and repeat viewing the slides in the slide show and to view the times for each slide as well as the elapsed time. Table 7–1 describes the buttons on the Rehearsal toolbar.

Table 7–1 Rehearsal Toolbar Buttons

Button Name	Image	Description
Next	⮕	Displays the next slide or next animated element on the slide.
Pause Recording	⏸	Stops the timer. Click the Next or Pause Recording button to resume timing.
Slide Time	0:00:00	Indicates the length of time a slide has been displayed. You can enter a slide time directly in the Slide Time box.
Repeat	↩	Clears the Slide Time box and resets the timer to 0:00:00.
Elapsed Time	0:00:00	Indicates slide show total time.

Plan Ahead

Give your audience sufficient time to view a slide.
The presentation in this chapter is designed to run continuously at a kiosk without a speaker's physical presence. Your audience, therefore, must read or view each slide and absorb the information without your help as a narrator. Be certain to give them time to read the slide and grasp the concept you are presenting. They will become frustrated if the slide changes before they have finished viewing and assimilating the material. As you set the slide timings, read each slide aloud and note the amount of time that elapses. Add a few seconds to this time and use this amount for the total time the slide is displayed.

To Rehearse Timings

You need to determine the length of time each slide should be displayed. Audience members need sufficient time to read the text and watch the animations. Table 7–2 indicates the desired timings for the five slides in the snowboarding presentation. Slide 1 is displayed and then the title text and animated snowboarder picture appear for 25 seconds. The Slide 2 title text, sound, and clip are displayed for 50 seconds. Slide 3 has the animated SmartArt, and it takes one minute for the elements to display. The bars on the Slide 4 chart can display in 40 seconds, and the two lists and rolling credits on Slide 5 display for one minute, five seconds.

Table 7–2 Slide Rehearsal Timings		
Slide Number	**Display Time**	**Elapsed Time**
1	0:00	0:25
2	0:50	1:15
3	1:00	2:15
4	0:40	2:55
5	1:05	4:00

The following steps add slide timings to the slide show.

1

- Display Slide 1 and then click Slide Show on the Ribbon to display the Slide Show tab (Figure 7–66).

Figure 7–66

2

- Click the Rehearse Timings button (Slide Show tab | Set Up group) to start the slide show and the counter (Figure 7–67).

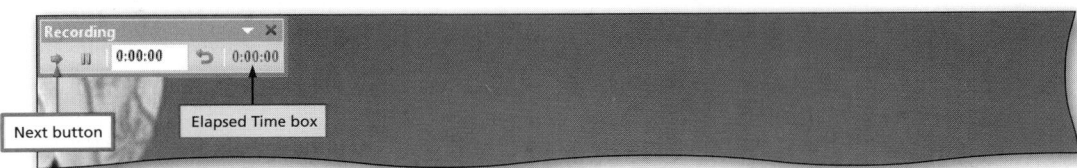

Figure 7–67

3

- When the Elapsed Time displays 0:25, click the Next button to display Slide 2.

- When the Elapsed Time displays 1:15, click the Next button to display Slide 3.

- When the Elapsed Time displays 2:15, click the Next button to display Slide 4.

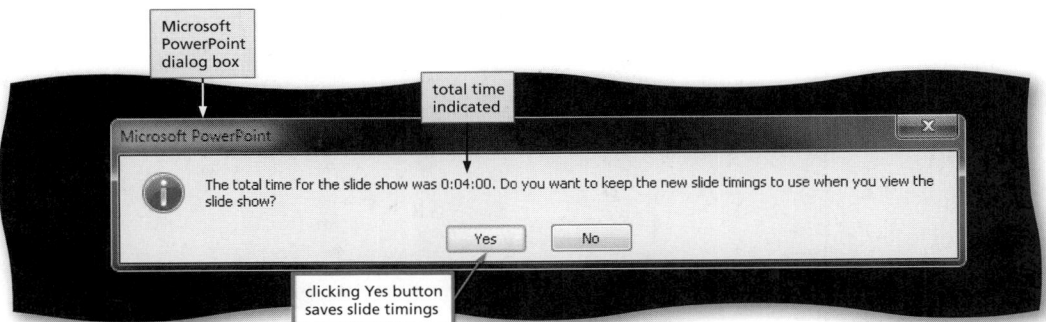

Figure 7–68

- When the Elapsed Time displays 2:55, click the Next button to display Slide 5.

- When the Elapsed Time displays 4:00, click the Next button to display the black slide (Figure 7–68).

4
- Click the Yes button in the Microsoft Office PowerPoint dialog box to keep the new slide timings with an elapsed time of 4:00.

- Review each slide's timing displayed in the lower-left corner in Slide Sorter view (Figure 7–69).

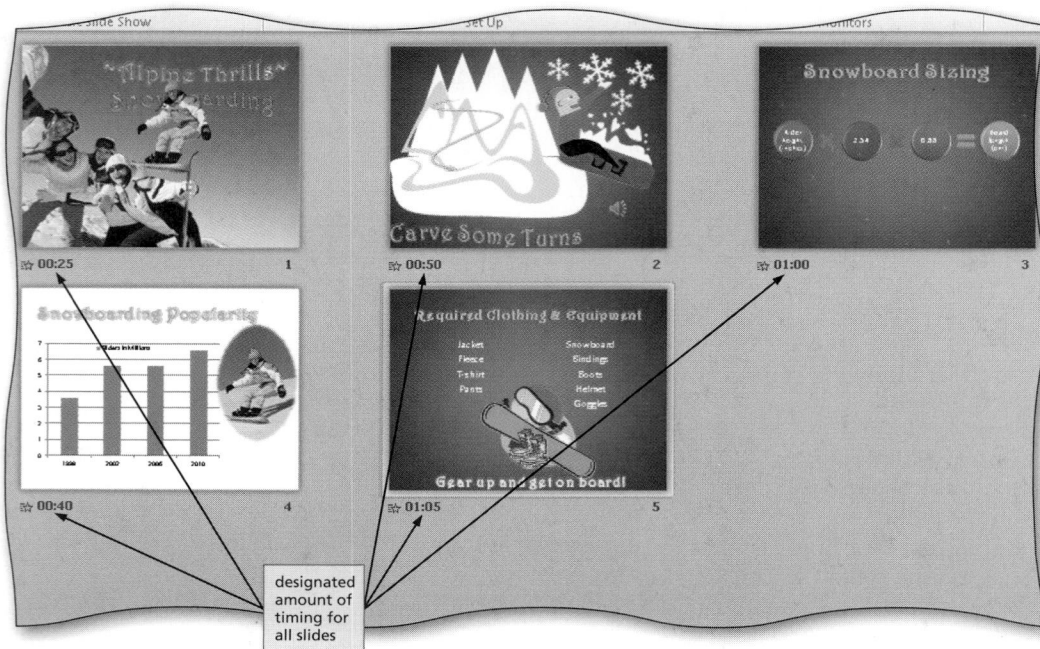

designated amount of timing for all slides

Figure 7–69

To Adjust Timings Manually

If the slide timings need adjustment, you manually can change the length of time each slide is displayed. In this presentation, you decide to display Slide 4 for 30 seconds instead of 40 seconds. The following step decreases the Slide 4 timing.

1
- In Slide Sorter view, display the Transitions tab and then select Slide 4.

- Click and hold down the Advance Slide After down arrow (Transitions tab | Timing group) until 00:30.00 is displayed (Figure 7–70).

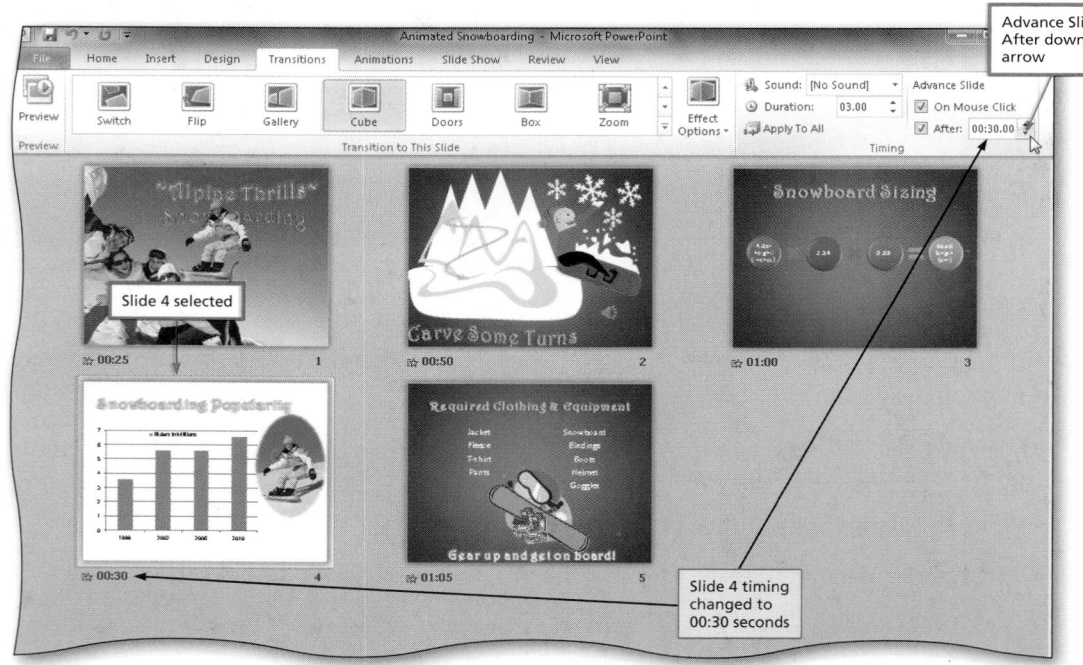

Advance Slide After down arrow

Slide 4 selected

Slide 4 timing changed to 00:30 seconds

Figure 7–70

To Modify a Transition Effect

The Cube transition is applied to the five slides in this presentation. The default rotation is From Right, so the current slide turns to the left while the new slide appears from the right side of the screen. To keep the downhill theme of the presentation in mind, you can change the Cube rotation so that the current slide moves to the bottom of the screen and the new slide appears from the top. The following steps modify the Transition Effect for all slides in the presentation.

1

- With the Transitions tab still selected, click the Effect Options button (Transitions tab | Transition to This Slide group) to display the Effect Options gallery (Figure 7–71).

Q&A

Are the same four effects available for all transitions?

No. The transition effects vary depending upon the particular transition selected.

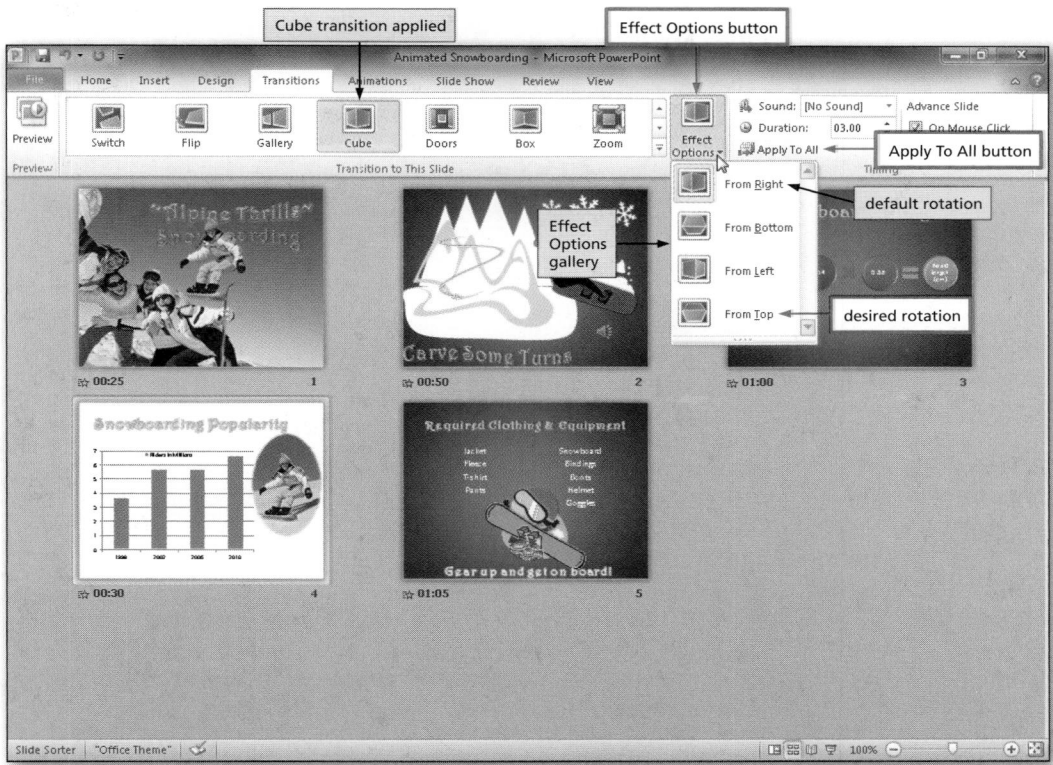

Figure 7–71

2

- Click the From Top effect to change the rotation.

- Click the Apply To All button (Transitions tab | Timing group) to set the From Top transition effect for all slides in the presentation.

To Create a Self-Running Presentation

The snowboarding presentation can accompany a speech, but it also can run unattended at sporting goods stores and ski resorts. When the last slide in the presentation is displayed, the slide show **loops**, or restarts, at Slide 1. PowerPoint has the option of running continuously until the user presses the ESC key. The following steps set the slide show to run in this manner.

1

- Display the Slide Show tab and then click the Set Up Slide Show button (Slide Show tab | Set Up group) to display the Set Up Show dialog box (Figure 7–72).

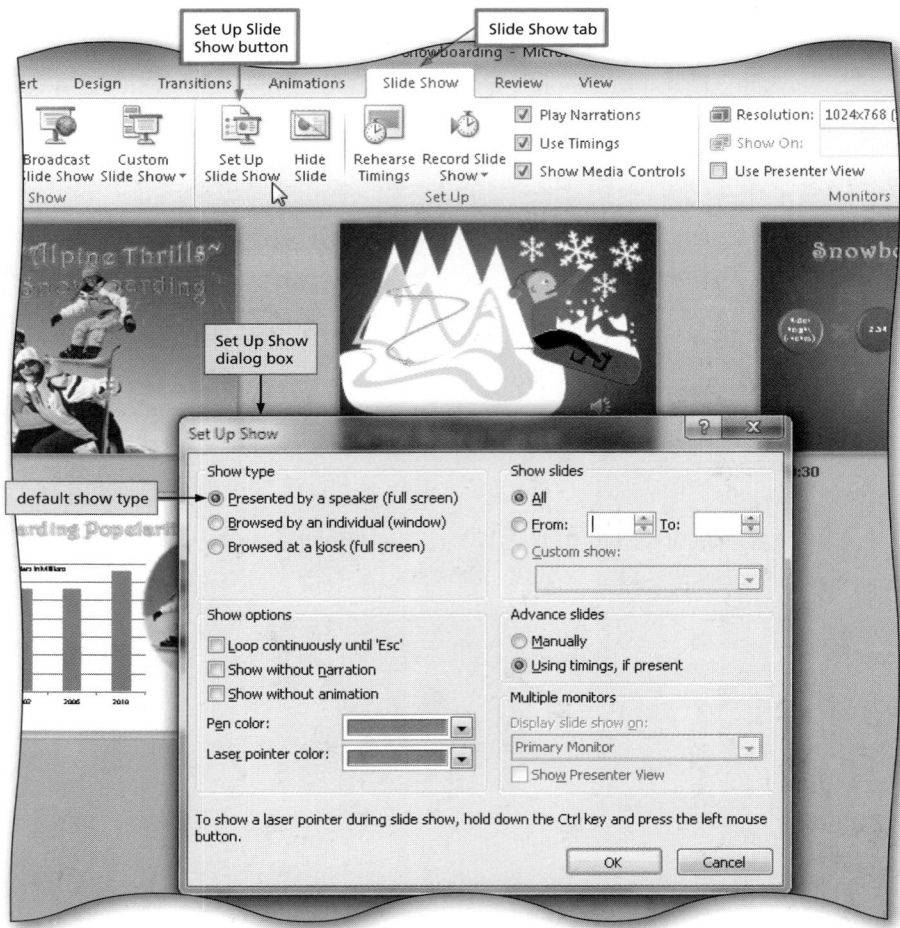

Figure 7–72

2

- Click 'Browsed at a kiosk (full screen)' in the Show type area (Figure 7–73).

3

- Click the OK button to apply this show type.

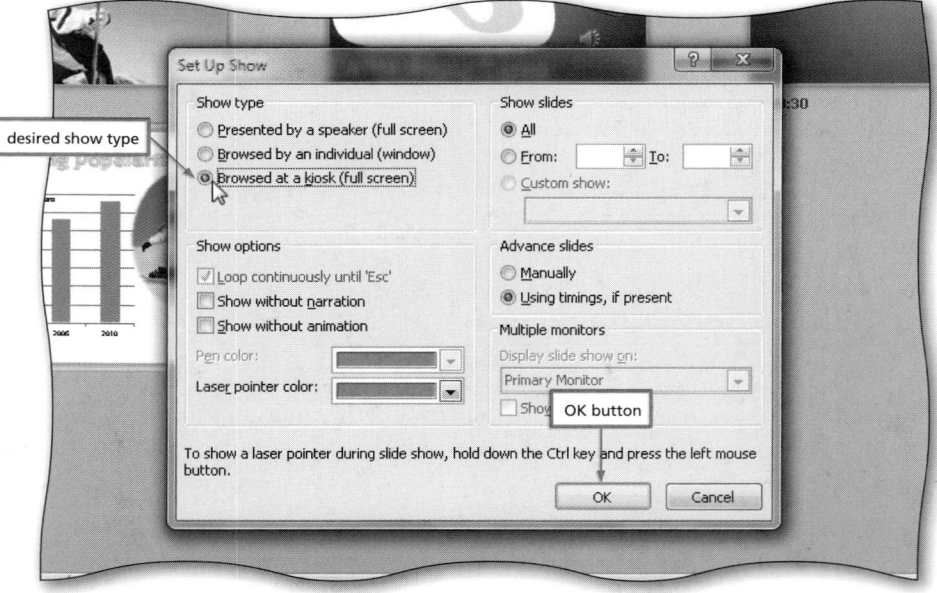

Figure 7–73

To Run an Animated Slide Show

All changes are complete. You now can view the Animated Snowboarding presentation. The following steps run the slide show.

1 Click the Normal View button, display the title slide, and then click the Slide Show button to start the presentation.

2 As each slide automatically is displayed, review the information.

3 When Slide 1 is displayed again, press the ESC key to stop the presentation.

To Change Document Properties

Before saving the presentation again, you want to add your name, class name, and some keywords as document properties. The following steps use the Document Information Panel to change document properties.

1 Display the Document Information Panel and then type your name as the Author property.

2 Type your course and section in the Subject property.

3 Type `snowboarding, snowboard size, popularity, clothing, equipment` as the Keywords property.

4 Close the Document Information Panel.

To Save, Print, and Quit PowerPoint

The presentation now is complete. You should save the slides, print a handout, and then quit PowerPoint.

1 Save the Animated Snowboarding presentation again with the same file name.

2 Print the presentation as a handout with two slides per page (Figure 7–74 on the next page).

3 Quit PowerPoint, closing all open documents.

BTW

Certification
The Microsoft Office Specialist (MOS) program provides an opportunity for you to obtain a valuable industry credential — proof that you have the PowerPoint 2010 skills required by employers. For more information, visit the PowerPoint 2010 Certification Web page (scsite.com/ppt2010/cert).

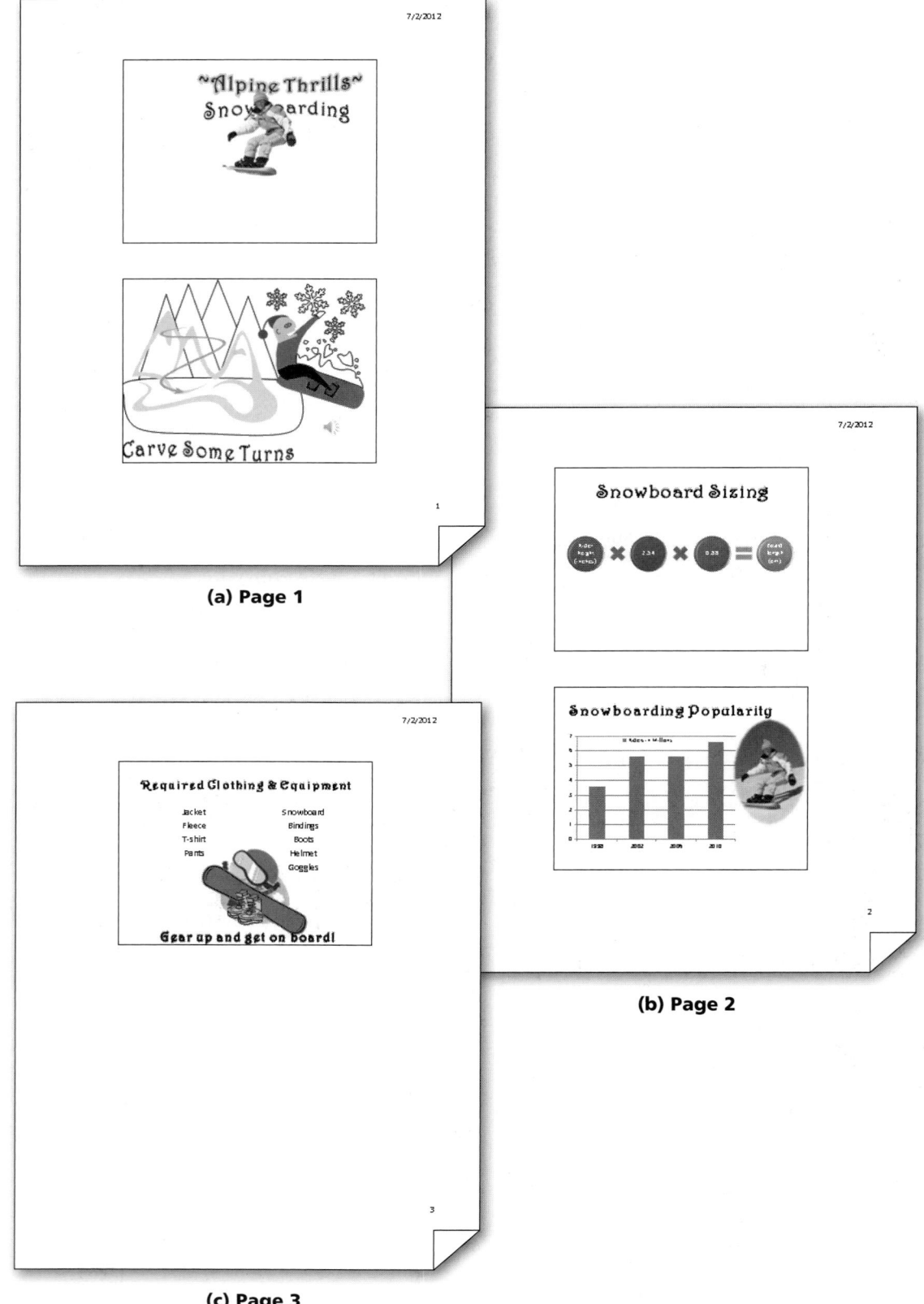

(a) Page 1

(b) Page 2

(c) Page 3

Figure 7–74

Chapter Summary

In this chapter you have learned how to remove a background from a picture and then crop and compress the image. You then applied entrance, emphasis, and exit effects to slide content and created a custom animation using a motion path. Also, you inserted and animated a text box and associated a sound with this text. You animated a SmartArt graphic, a chart, and two lists. Then, you set timing so that the slide show runs automatically. The items listed below include all the new PowerPoint skills you have learned in this chapter.

1. Remove a Background (PPT 405)
2. Refine Background Removal (PPT 407)
3. Crop a Picture (PPT 409)
4. Compress a Picture (PPT 410)
5. Animate a Picture Using an Entrance Effect (PPT 411)
6. Change Animation Direction (PPT 412)
7. Animate a Picture Using an Emphasis Effect (PPT 413)
8. Animate a Picture Using an Exit Effect (PPT 414)
9. Preview an Animation Sequence (PPT 416)
10. Modify Entrance Animation Timing (PPT 416)
11. Animate Title Text Placeholder Paragraphs (PPT 419)
12. Change Animation Order (PPT 420)
13. Rename Slide Objects (PPT 422)
14. Insert a Text Box and Format Text (PPT 423)
15. Animate a Text Box Using an Entrance Effect (PPT 425)
16. Animate a Text Box by Applying a Motion Path (PPT 427)
17. Adjust a Motion Path (PPT 428)
18. Associate a Sound with an Animation (PPT 430)
19. Draw a Custom Motion Path (PPT 431)
20. Use the Animation Painter to Animate a Clip (PPT 433)
21. Animate a SmartArt Graphic (PPT 435)
22. Change a SmartArt Graphic Animation Sequence (PPT 436)
23. Animate a Chart (PPT 437)
24. Animate a List (PPT 439)
25. Dim Text after Animation (PPT 440)
26. Create Credits (PPT 442)
27. Rehearse Timings (PPT 444)
28. Adjust Timings Manually (PPT 446)
29. Modify a Transition Effect (PPT 447)
30. Create a Self-Running Presentation (PPT 447)

 If you have a SAM 2010 user profile, your instructor may have assigned an autogradable version of this assignment. If so, log into the SAM 2010 Web site at www.cengage.com/sam2010 to download the instruction and start files.

Learn It Online

Test your knowledge of chapter content and key terms.

Instructions: To complete the Learn It Online exercises, start your browser, click the Address bar, and then enter the Web address **scsite.com/ppt2010/learn**. When the Office 2010 Learn It Online page is displayed, click the link for the exercise you want to complete and then read the instructions.

Chapter Reinforcement TF, MC, and SA
A series of true/false, multiple choice, and short answer questions that test your knowledge of the chapter content.

Flash Cards
An interactive learning environment where you identify chapter key terms associated with displayed definitions.

Practice Test
A series of multiple choice questions that test your knowledge of chapter content and key terms.

Who Wants To Be a Computer Genius?
An interactive game that challenges your knowledge of chapter content in the style of a television quiz show.

Wheel of Terms
An interactive game that challenges your knowledge of chapter key terms in the style of the television show *Wheel of Fortune*.

Crossword Puzzle Challenge
A crossword puzzle that challenges your knowledge of key terms presented in the chapter.

Apply Your Knowledge

Reinforce the skills and apply the concepts you learned in this chapter.

Applying Entrance Effects
Note: To complete this assignment, you will be required to use the Data Files for Students. See the inside back cover of this book for instructions on downloading the Data Files for Students or contact your instructor for information about accessing the required files.

Instructions: Start PowerPoint. Open the presentation, Apply 7-1 Losing Weight, located on the Data Files for Students.

The slide in this presentation gives a few suggestions on losing weight. The document you open is an unformatted presentation. You are to add an entrance effect to the title, convert the text to a SmartArt graphic, and then add an entrance effect to the SmartArt graphic so the slide looks like Figure 7–75.

Perform the following tasks:
1. Change the document theme to Angles and change the presentation theme colors to Clarity.
2. Apply the Brown, Accent 2 WordArt text fill and the Dark Red, Accent 6 WordArt text outline to the title text. Then change the text outline weight to 2¼ pt. Also apply the WordArt Transform text effect, Fade Right, in the Warp area, to this text. Increase the size of the WordArt to 1.27" × 8.23".
3. Click More Entrance Effects in the Animation gallery and then apply the Grow & Turn entrance effect in the Moderate category to the title text. Change the start timing setting to After Previous and the duration to 02.00 seconds.

4. Reduce the picture size to 3.62" × 2.42" and apply the Soft Edges, 10 Point effect. Move the picture to the lower-right corner of the slide, as shown in Figure 7–75. Then apply the Appear entrance effect and change the duration from Auto to 01.00 second. Change the start timing setting to After Previous.

5. Convert the bulleted text to the Basic Target layout (Relationship area) SmartArt graphic. Change the color to the Colorful Range - Accent Colors 5 to 6 in the Colorful area. Apply the Polished 3-D SmartArt Style and then resize this graphic to approximately 5.5" × 10".

6. Increase the font size of the SmartArt graphic to 22 point. Change the width of the first three text boxes in the SmartArt graphic to 3.5". Use the Ruler and Guides to align the first three text boxes with the fourth and fifth text boxes.

7. Apply the Zoom entrance effect to the SmartArt graphic. Add the One by One effect option. Change the duration to 02.50 seconds. Move the SmartArt graphic to the location shown in Figure 7–75.

8. Change the transition from Reveal to Shape and then change the duration to 03.50 seconds.

9. Change the document properties, as specified by your instructor. Save the presentation using the file name, Apply 7-1 Aim for Losing Weight. Submit the revised document in the format specified by your instructor.

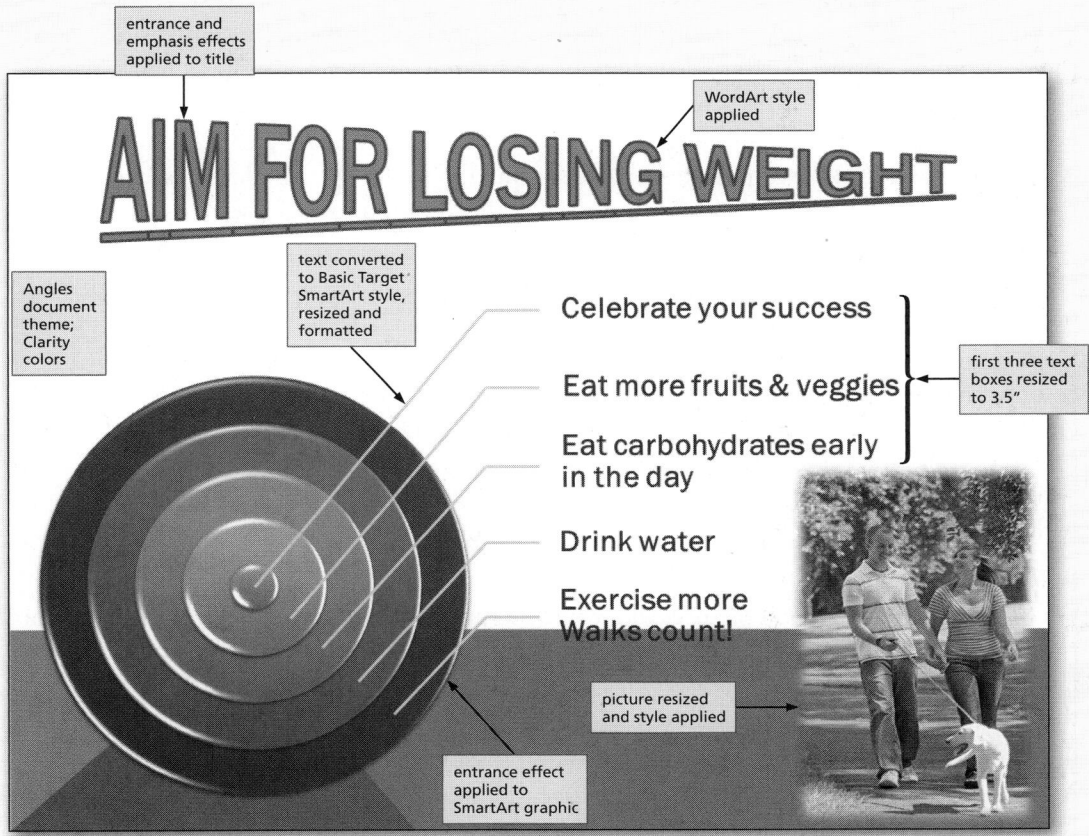

Figure 7–75

Extend Your Knowledge

Extend the skills you learned in this chapter and experiment with new skills. You may need to use Help to complete the assignment.

Changing and Reordering Animations, Adding Sound to Animations, Inserting a Text Box, and Cropping a Picture to a Shape

Note: To complete this assignment, you will be required to use the Data Files for Students. See the inside back cover of this book for instructions on downloading the Data Files for Students or contact your instructor for information about accessing the required files.

Instructions: Start PowerPoint. Open the presentation, Extend 7-1 Blue Moon, located on the Data Files for Students. You will change the title text animations, animate a bulleted list, dim text after animation, add sound to animations, and insert a text box, as shown in Figure 7–76. You will need to show more entrance, emphasis, and exit effects to locate the required animations.

Perform the following tasks:

1. On the Slide 1 title, change the Bounce entrance effect to the Float In entrance effect. Change the start timing option from On Click to After Previous, the duration to 02.00 seconds, and the direction to Float Down. Add the Wave emphasis effect in the Advanced Animation area, change the start timing option to After Previous, and change the duration to 05.50 seconds. Have the Brass Wind Chime sound, which is next to the title text on the slide, play with the Wave emphasis effect, and hide the sound icon during the show.

2. Apply the Fly In from Bottom Left Entrance animation to the three bulleted paragraphs so that they enter one at a time on click and then change the duration to 03.75 seconds.

3. Apply the Fly In from Left entrance animation to the moon clip. Change the duration to 03.00 seconds. Change the start timing option to After Previous. Have the Drum Roll Loud sound, which is next to the moon clip, play with this clip, change the volume to High, and hide the sound icon during the show.

4. Change the font of the vertically rotated text, Next Blue Moon 2015, to Eras Bold ITC, the color of the text to Dark Blue, and the font size to 40 point. Center this text. Add the Dissolve In entrance effect to this text. Change the start timing option to After Previous and the duration to 02.50 seconds. Add the Grow With Color emphasis to the text. Click the Effect Options button and select the teal color (ninth color in Theme Colors row). Change the start timing option to After Previous and change the duration to 03.00 seconds.

5. Apply the Flash transition to Slide 1 and change the duration to 04.50 seconds.

6. On Slide 2, select the moon picture, and, while holding down the CTRL key, move the picture to the right to duplicate it. Remove the background from the duplicate picture, click the handles on the marquee, and then drag the lines so that the moon is centered in the picture. Change the color of this picture to Blue, Accent Color 1 Dark and then move this picture on top of the original picture until the blue moon is lined up directly on top of the white moon.

7. Apply the Shrink & Turn exit effect to the blue moon picture, change the start timing option to After Previous, and change the duration to 05.00 seconds. Change the name of the blue moon picture in the Animation pane from Picture 4 to Blue Moon.

8. On Slide 2, select the Wave shape and add the Float In entrance effect. Change the direction to Float Down. Change the start timing option to After Previous and the duration to 2.00. Resize the oval shape so that it is approximately 2.19" × 2.25", and also reduce the font size to fit into the shape. Add the Fly In entrance effect, change the direction to From Right, and then change the start timing option to After Previous and the duration to 02.50 seconds.

9. Insert the Moon picture located on the Data Files for Students. Crop the picture so that the moon is centered within the black background. Increase the size of the picture to 3.28" × 3.66" and then

crop the picture to fill the Moon shape. You may need to use Help to learn how to crop to a shape. Move the Moon picture to the location shown in the figure.

10. Apply the Orbit transition to Slide 2 and change the duration to 04.50 seconds.

11. Change the document properties, as specified by your instructor. Save the presentation using the file name, Extend 7-1 Once in a Blue Moon.

12. Submit the revised document in the format specified by your instructor.

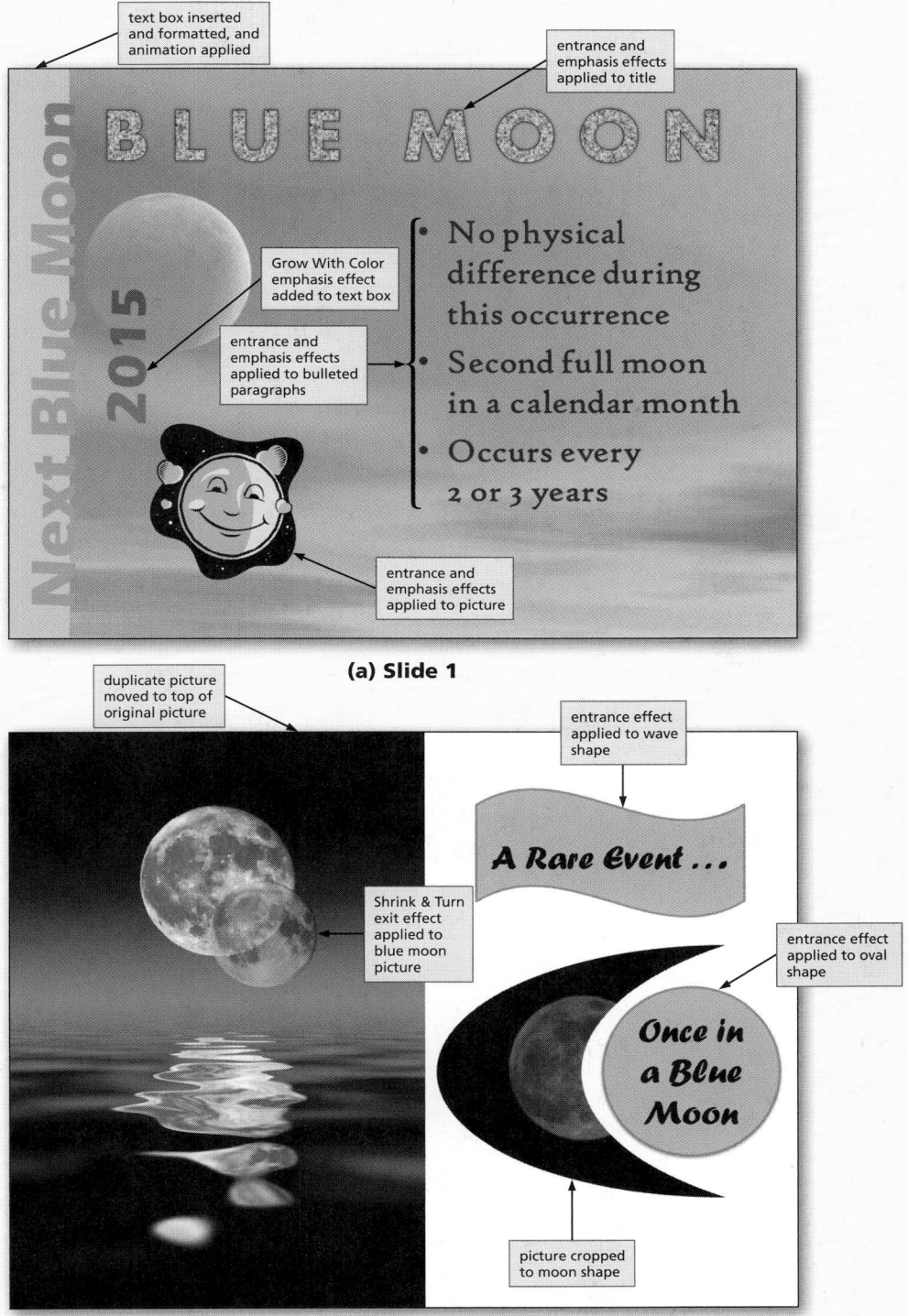

(a) Slide 1

(b) Slide 2

Figure 7–76

Make It Right

Analyze a presentation and correct all errors and/or improve the design.

Removing and Changing Animation, and Copying Animation Using the Animation Painter

Note: To complete this assignment, you will be required to use the Data Files for Students. See the inside back cover of this book for instructions on downloading the Data Files for Students or contact your instructor for information about accessing the required files.

Instructions: Start PowerPoint. Open the presentation, Make It Right 7-1 Footprints, located on the Data Files for Students.

Correct the formatting problems and errors in the presentation while keeping in mind the guidelines presented in this chapter. This presentation was created as part of an interactive exhibit for children at the local nature center. The instructions for the matching game are as follows: First, select the green number 1; then, click on the animal's picture. The correct picture will display with a Grow & Turn animation and an orange border. Then click on green number 2. Continue selecting the green numbers to match all the animals with their tracks.

The footprints and pictures shown in Figure 7–77 are not in the correct order. You volunteer to modify the presentation so that the animals match their tracks.

Perform the following tasks:

1. Display the Animation tab, and remove the animation from all the footprints except number 1. Remove the animation from all the pictures except the skunk picture. Use the Animation Painter to copy the animation from the first footprint picture to the five remaining footprint pictures. Then copy the animation from the skunk picture to the five remaining animal pictures.

2. Reorder the animations so that the animal picture follows the footprint. Footprint number 1 is the skunk, footprint number 2 is the deer, footprint number 3 is the squirrel, footprint number 4 is the mink, footprint number 5 is the wolf, and footprint number 6 is the fox.

3. Change the Fade transition to Rotate, change the Camera sound to the Wolves sound, and then change the duration to 04.50 seconds.

4. Change the document properties, as specified by your instructor. Save the presentation using the file name, Make It Right 7-1 Animal Footprints.

5. Submit the revised document in the format specified by your instructor.

Figure 7–77

In the Lab

Design and/or create a presentation using the guidelines, concepts, and skills presented in this chapter. Labs 1, 2, and 3 are listed in order of increasing difficulty.

Lab 1: Creating a Presentation with an Animated Chart

Note: To complete this assignment, you will be required to use the Data Files for Students. See the inside back cover of this book for instructions on downloading the Data Files for Students or contact your instructor for information about accessing the required files.

Problem: In many countries around the world, people do not have clean drinking water. You belong to a science club, and your group has decided to develop a water project that can change salt water to fresh water. You decide to create a PowerPoint presentation to introduce the basic facts about water on Earth. You create the slides shown in Figure 7–78 on pages PPT 458 and PPT 459 using files located on the Data Files for Students. You will need to show more entrance and emphasis effects to locate the required animations.

Perform the following tasks:
1. Open the presentation, Lab 7-1 Water, located on the Data Files for Students.
2. On Slide 1, apply the Wedge entrance effect to the title text. Change the start timing option to With Previous and the duration to 03.50 seconds. Then add a Wave emphasis effect to the title text, change the start timing option to With Previous, and change the duration to 04.00 seconds.

Continued >

In the Lab *continued*

3. On Slide 2, apply the Wheel entrance effect to the title text. Change the start timing option to After Previous and change the duration to 03.50 seconds.

4. Apply the Random Bars entrance effect to the clip. Change the start timing option to After Previous and change the duration to 04.50 seconds.

5. Apply the Wipe entrance effect to the chart. Change the duration to 05.25 seconds.

6. Apply the Fly In From Left entrance effect to all paragraphs in the content placeholder. Change the duration to 02.50 seconds.

7. Dim the second bulleted paragraph (Ocean and seas), the third bulleted paragraph, and the three second-level paragraphs (Fresh water; Lakes, Rivers; Glaciers; Ground) after animation using a blue and a green color displayed in the pie chart. To select these colors, click the After animation arrow in the Enhancements area (Fly In dialog box), click More Colors in the After animation menu, and then click the colors that best match the chart colors.

8. Add the Style 5 background style to Slide 2. *Hint:* Right-click Style 5 and then click Apply to Selected Slides in the shortcut menu.

9. Apply the Ripple transition and change the duration to 03.00 seconds for all slides.

10. Change the document properties, as specified by your instructor. Save the presentation using the file name, Lab 7-1 Water on Earth.

11. Submit the revised document in the format specified by your instructor.

entrance and emphasis effects applied to title text

(a) Slide 1
Figure 7–78

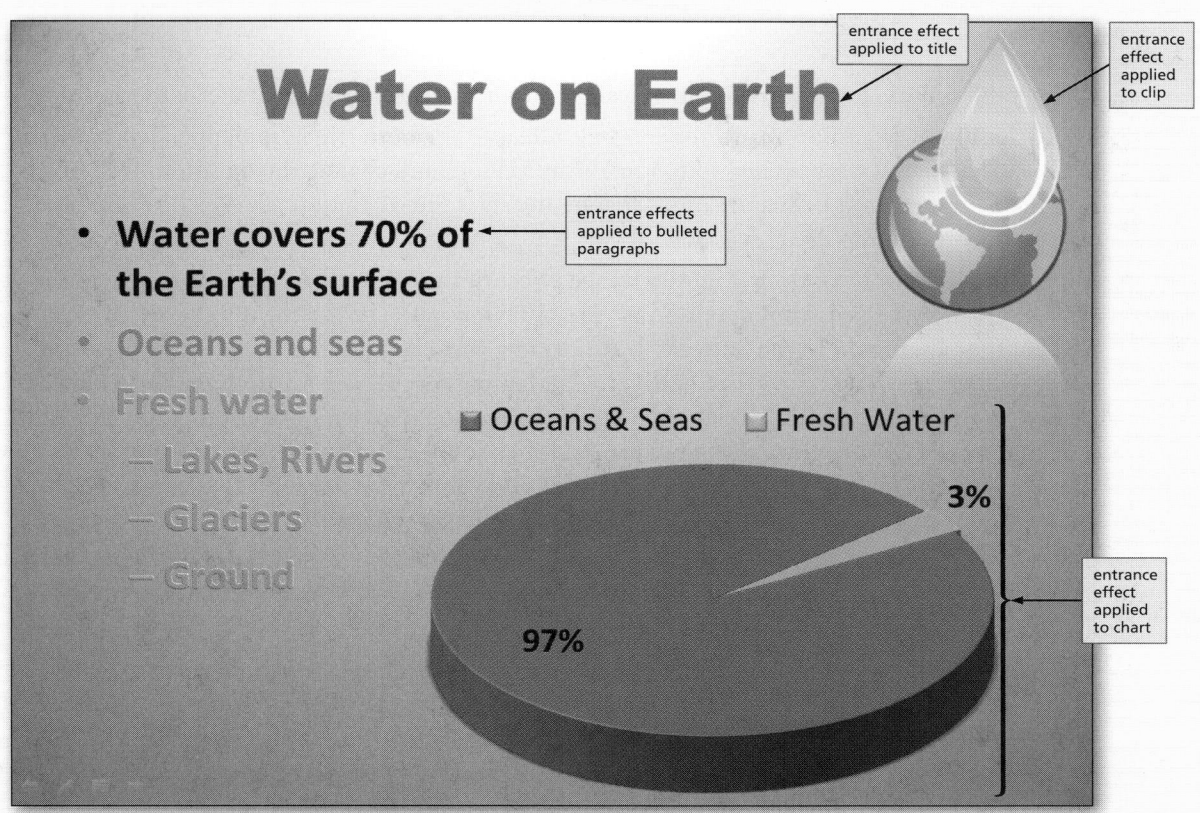

(b) Slide 2

Figure 7–78

In the Lab

Lab 2: Creating a Self-Running Presentation and Animating a Clip Using a Motion Path

Note: To complete this assignment, you will be required to use the Data Files for Students. See the inside back cover of this book for instructions on downloading the Data Files for Students or contact your instructor for information about accessing the required files.

Problem: You are studying botany and work part time at a local botanic garden. The garden's directors announced recently that a butterfly conservatory will be opening next year. In the interim, they are setting up a temporary exhibit. The master gardener, who is overseeing the planting of flowers and bushes that attract butterflies, has asked you to assist with the design of the conservatory. One of your assignments is to create a self-running PowerPoint presentation that will be viewed on a kiosk at the temporary exhibit. He asked you to gear your presentation to children because the botanic gardens are visited frequently by groups of children on field trips, and the butterfly conservatory will be designed with children in mind. You create the slides shown in Figure 7–79 on pages PPT 460 and PPT 461 using files located on the Data Files for Students.

Perform the following tasks:

1. Open the presentation, Lab 7-2 Butterfly, located on the Data Files for Students, and then add the Slipstream document theme.

2. On Slide 1, increase the size of the picture and add the Reflected Bevel, White picture style. Change the border to Turquoise, Accent 2.

3. Increase the title text font size to 54 point so that it is on two lines, as shown in Figure 7–79a.

Continued >

In the Lab *continued*

4. Change the subtitle font to Eurostyle or a similar font and then bold and italicize the author's name.

5. Apply the Fly In from Bottom-Right entrance effect to the butterfly in the upper-left corner of Slide 1. Change the start timing option to With Previous and change the duration to 02.50 seconds. Add the Loops motion path animation, change the start timing option to After Previous, and change the duration to 03.00 seconds.

6. Apply the Fly In from Bottom-Right entrance effect to the butterfly in the lower-right corner of Slide 1. Change the start timing option to After Previous and change the duration to 01.75 seconds. Add another animation to the butterfly by drawing a custom motion path. To draw the path, select the butterfly, click the More button in Animation group, click Custom Path, click the Effect Options button, and then click Scribble. Draw the motion path so it starts at the left side of the slide and moves upward toward the picture, and then loops down to the right corner of the slide. Change the start timing option to After Previous and change the duration to 02.75 seconds.

7. On Slide 2, insert the Butterfly picture located on the Data Files for Students. Crop the picture to show more of the butterfly and then resize the picture so that it is close to the size of the caterpillar picture (4.25" × 2.81"). Add the Beveled Oval Black picture style to both pictures and then move the pictures to the locations shown in Figure 7–79b.

8. Convert the bulleted text to the Block Cycle SmartArt graphic, change the color to Accent Colors 4 to 5, and apply the Sunset Scene style. Increase the size of the graphic to approximately 5.25" × 7.25" and move it to the location shown in Figure 7–79b. Apply the Fly In, One by One (in Sequence area), entrance effect to the SmartArt graphic. Change the start timing option to After Previous and change the duration to 02.75 seconds.

9. Apply the Honeycomb transition and then change the duration to 04.00 seconds for all slides.

10. Rehearse the presentation and then set the slide timings to 22 seconds for Slide 1 and 28 seconds for Slide 2.

11. Change the document properties, as specified by your instructor. Save the presentation using the file name, Lab 7-2 Butterfly Mystique.

12. Submit the revised document in the format specified by your instructor.

(a) Slide 1

Figure 7–79

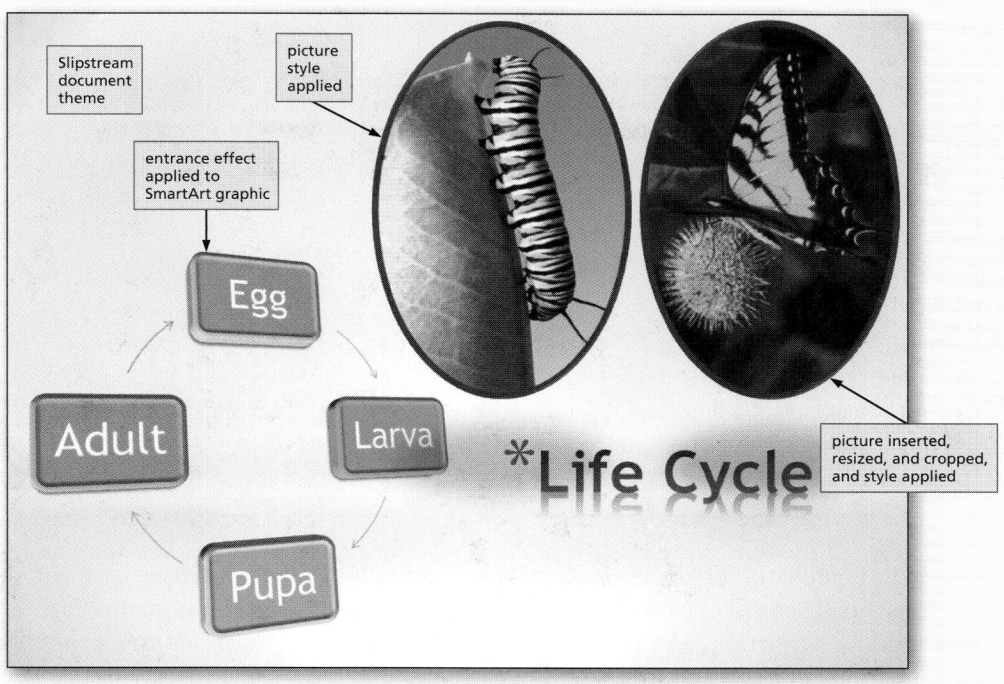

(b) Slide 2

Figure 7–79

In the Lab

Lab 3: Animating a Chart, Adding Credits, and Removing a Background from a Picture

Note: To complete this assignment, you will be required to use the Data Files for Students. See the inside back cover of this book for instructions on downloading the Data Files for Students or contact your instructor for information about accessing the required files.

Problem: You volunteer a few days each week at the local animal shelter, and the manager of the shelter asks if you would create a PowerPoint presentation to show to prospective dog owners. You create the presentation in Figure 7–80 on page PPT 463 consisting of three slides and a closing slide.

Perform the following tasks:
1. Open the presentation, Lab 7-3 Dog, located on the Data Files for Students, and change the document theme to Trek.
2. On Slide 1, add the Bounce entrance effect to the WordArt. Change the start timing option to After Previous and change the duration to 02.75 seconds.
3. Change the subtitle so that the text is on three lines, increase font size to 40 point, and then move the subtitle to the location shown in Figure 7–80a. Add the Fade entrance effect to the subtitle. Change the start timing option to After Previous and change the duration to 01.50 seconds. Add the Wipe From Top exit effect to this text, change the start timing option to After Previous, change the duration to 03.00 seconds, and change the delay to 02.25 seconds.
4. On Slide 2, remove the background from the German Shepherd picture and then increase the size of the picture to approximately 5.19" x 4.14", as shown in Figure 7–80b.
5. Apply the animation effects to the seven bulleted paragraphs and pictures using Table 7–3 as a guide.

Continued >

In the Lab *continued*

Table 7–3 Slide 2 Animation Effects

Text or Picture	Entrance Effect	Start	Duration	Delay
First bulleted paragraph	Appear	After Previous	3.00	2.00
Second bulleted paragraph	Fly In From Left	On Click	2.50	—
White dog picture	Float Down	With Previous	2.50	—
Third bulleted paragraph	Fly In From Left	On Click	2.50	—
Brown puppy picture	Float Down	With Previous	2.50	—
Fourth bulleted paragraph	Fly In From Left	On Click	2.50	—
German Shepherd picture	Fly In From Right	With Previous	2.50	—
Fifth, sixth, and seventh bulleted paragraphs	Fly In From Left	On Click	2.50	—

6. On Slide 3, apply the Fly In From Left – By Element in Category (Sequence group in Effect Options) entrance effect to the chart, as shown in Figure 7–80c. Change the start timing option for only the first animation, which is the chart background, to After Previous. Change the duration for all animations to 03.25 seconds.

7. Apply Background Style 6 to Slides 2 and 3.

8. Create a fourth slide for a closing slide and use the Title and Content layout. In the title text placeholder, type **Thank You for Your Support**. Change the font color to Orange, Accent 1 and then center and italicize this text, as shown in Figure 7–80d. Apply the Dissolve In entrance animation effect (Basic group) and then change the duration to 07.00 seconds.

9. Insert the Bulldog picture located in the Data Files for Students on Slide 4. Remove the background from the picture and then refine the background removal by keeping and removing areas around the bulldog. Crop the picture, resize it so that it is approximately 5" × 6.76", and then move it to the location shown in the figure. Compress this picture.

10. Insert a text box at the bottom of the slide and type **Clifford Mason, Manager** as the first paragraph and **Southtown Animal Shelter** as the second paragraph. Change the font color to Light Yellow, Text 2 and the font size to 32 point. Center this text. Bring this text box forward so that the text will be in front of the bulldog. Apply the Credits entrance animation, change the start timing option to With Previous, and change the duration to 13.00 seconds. Add the Applause sound to this text and change the volume to the highest level.

11. Apply Background Style 3 to Slide 4.

12. Add a trigger to display the Thank You for Your Support text box when the bulldog picture is clicked. Rename the trigger animation Bulldog Picture.

13. Change the document properties, as specified by your instructor. Save the presentation using the file name, Lab 7-3 Adopting a Dog.

14. Submit the revised document in the format specified by your instructor.

(a) Slide 1

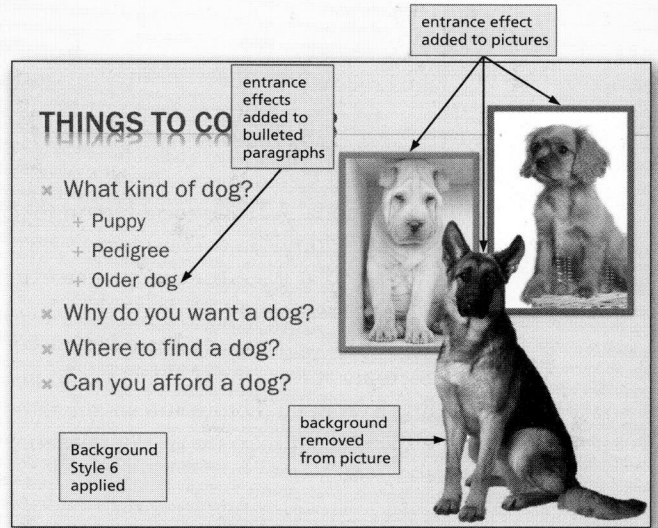

(b) Slide 2

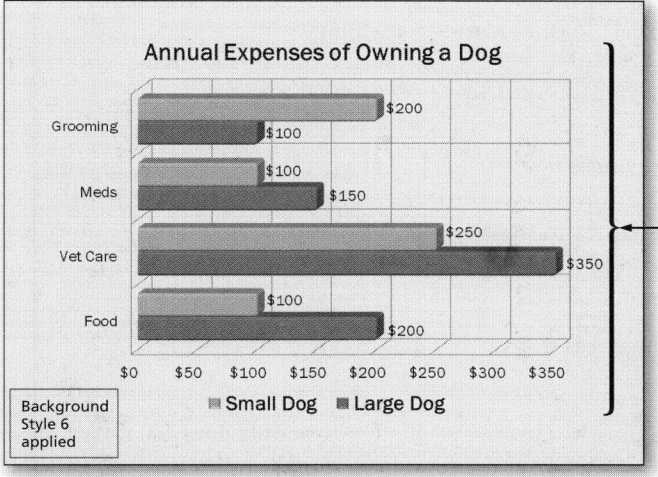

(c) Slide 3

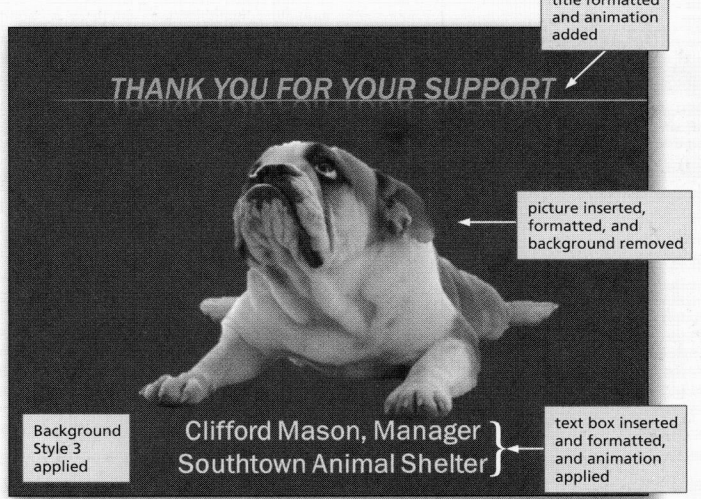

(d) Slide 4

Figure 7–80

Cases and Places

Apply your creative thinking and problem-solving skills to design and implement a solution.

Note: To complete these assignments, you may be required to use the Data Files for Students. See the inside back cover of this book for instructions on downloading the Data Files for Students, or contact your instructor for information about accessing the required files.

As you design the presentations, remember to use the 7 × 7 rule: a maximum of seven words on a line and a maximum of seven lines on one slide.

1: Designing and Creating a Presentation about the Dwarf Planet Pluto

Academic

The International Astronomical Union (IAU) determined, after changing the definition of what constitutes a planet, that Pluto is now considered a dwarf planet. Even though Pluto was once considered the ninth planet in our solar system, other planets have been discovered since that are larger than Pluto. In your Astronomy class, you are studying the planets in our solar system. You decide to create a PowerPoint presentation to explain why Pluto is now considered a dwarf planet. Include information about other dwarf planets. Apply at least three objectives found at the beginning of this chapter to develop the presentation, including a cropped picture and an animated picture or a SmartArt graphic. Use pictures and diagrams from Office.com if they are appropriate for this topic. Be sure to check spelling.

2: Designing and Creating a Presentation about Sailing

Personal

You always have wanted to learn how to sail. You and a few friends have registered for sailing lessons and want to learn some things in advance to better prepare you for the sailing lessons. Use at least three objectives found at the beginning of this chapter to develop the presentation, including a motion path and dimmed text. Use pictures from Office.com if they are appropriate for this topic or use your personal digital pictures. Be sure to check spelling.

3: Designing and Creating a Presentation about Planning a Retirement Community

Professional

You work for an architectural firm that is developing a retirement village for people ages 55 and older. The 30-acre village will have condominiums, townhomes, and a few single-family homes. It will offer a community clubhouse with an indoor-outdoor swimming pool, a fitness center, party rooms, a large banquet room, a small movie theater, and a game room. Your firm has assigned you the job of putting together a presentation listing all the amenities this retirement village will offer. There will also be a community garden for residents to plant vegetables and flowers; tennis courts; shuffleboard courts; and a small landscaped park that will feature a fountain, a pond, benches, and picnic tables. You will be showing your slide show at a town hall meeting for community residents and also plan to run the self-running presentation at a kiosk. Use pictures from Office.com if they are appropriate for this topic or use your personal digital pictures. Add credits on the last slide. Be certain to check spelling.

8 | Customizing a Template and Handouts Using Masters

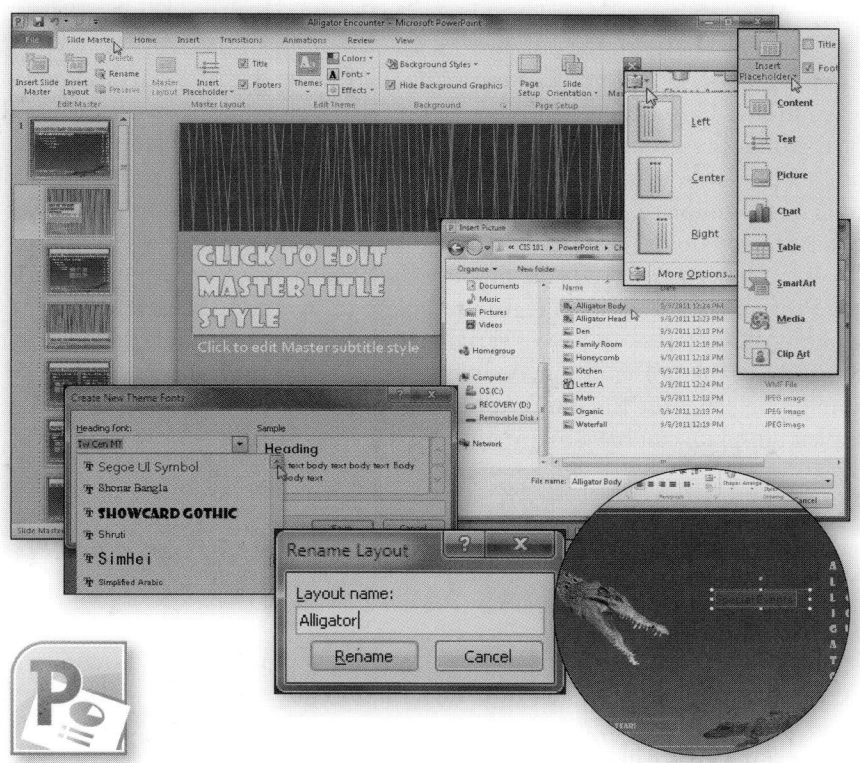

Objectives

You will have mastered the material in this chapter when you can:

- Apply slide and font themes to a slide master

- Change a slide master background

- Add a background style and graphic to a slide master

- Insert a placeholder into a slide layout

- Apply a Quick Style to a placeholder

- Change text direction and character spacing

- Hide background graphics on individual slides

- Apply a fill to a text box and change transparency

- Rename a slide master

- Save a slide master as a template

- Create handouts using the handout master

- Create speaker notes using the notes master

8 | Customizing a Template and Handouts Using Masters

Introduction

PowerPoint provides a variety of designs and layouts to meet most presenters' needs. At times, however, you may need a different set of colors, fonts, placeholders, or graphics to display throughout a presentation. PowerPoint allows you to customize the master layouts for slides, handouts, and speaker notes. These masters specify the precise locations and styles of placeholders, pictures, text boxes, and other slide and handout elements.

Once you determine your custom specifications in these masters, you can save the file as a template so that you can reuse these key elements as a starting point for multiple presentations. This unique **template** is a set of special slides you create and then use to create similar presentations. A template consists of a general master slide layout that has elements common to all the slide layouts. One efficient way to create similar presentations is to create a template, save the template, open the template, and then save the slides as a different PowerPoint presentation each time a new presentation is required.

Templates help speed and simplify the process of creating a presentation, so many PowerPoint designers create a template for common presentations they develop frequently. Templates can have a variable number of slide layouts depending upon the complexity of the presentation. A simple presentation can have a few slide layouts; for example, the Alligator Encounter presentation will have three slide layouts. A more complex template can have many slide masters and layouts.

Project — Presentation with Customized Slide, Handout, and Notes Masters

Alligators have existed on Earth for more than 200 million years. Found in the southeastern United States and in China, these reptiles can weigh more than 1,000 pounds and grow to a length of more than 19 feet. Having approximately 80 teeth, their bone-crushing jaws can catch unsuspecting prey, such as fish, mammals, and other reptiles. Many nature parks, including the Alligator Encounter you will feature in this project, offer excursions into freshwater swamps and allow visitors to view the alligators in a natural habitat. The project in this chapter (Figure 8–1) promotes these safaris. All three slides are created by starting with a template file that contains two basic slide elements: the nature center's name on a formatted placeholder and an alligator picture. The overall template, called the **slide master** (Figure 8–1a), is formatted with a theme, customized title and text fonts, and customized footer placeholders for the slide layouts. The Title Slide Layout (Figure 8–1b) is used to create Slide 1 (Figure 8–1c), which introduces audiences to the nature center. Similarly, the Blank Layout (Figure 8–1d) is used for Slide 2 (Figure 8–1e), which promotes the nighttime tours in June. The Title and Content Layout (Figure 8–1f) is used to create the text and graphic on Slide 3 (Figure 8–1g). In addition, the custom handout master (Figure 8–1h) is used to create a handout with an alligator picture and header and footer text (Figure 8–1i). Likewise, the custom notes master (Figure 8–1j) is used to create speaker notes pages (Figures 8–1k, 8–1l, and 8–1m).

BTW

The Power of Using Masters
Use masters to give your presentation a unique and uniform look. They are convenient when you have presentations with many slides because they allow you to make universal style changes to every slide in your presentation, including ones added later. You can customize the presentation theme and slide layouts, including the background, color, fonts, effects, and placeholder sizes and location. Using slide masters saves time because you don't have to format every slide or type the same information repeatedly.

BTW

Multiple Slide Masters
PowerPoint allows you to insert additional slide masters in one file so that one presentation can have two or more different styles. Each slide master has a related set of layout masters. In contrast, however, one presentation can have only one handout master and one notes master.

Overview

As you read through this chapter, you will learn how to create the presentation and handouts shown in Figure 8–1 on this page through page PPT 469 by performing these general tasks:

- Customize slide masters.
- Format and arrange slide master footers.
- Insert pictures and a placeholder into slide layouts.
- Insert and format text boxes.
- Rename and delete slide layouts.
- Customize handout and notes masters.
- Create a new presentation using a custom template.

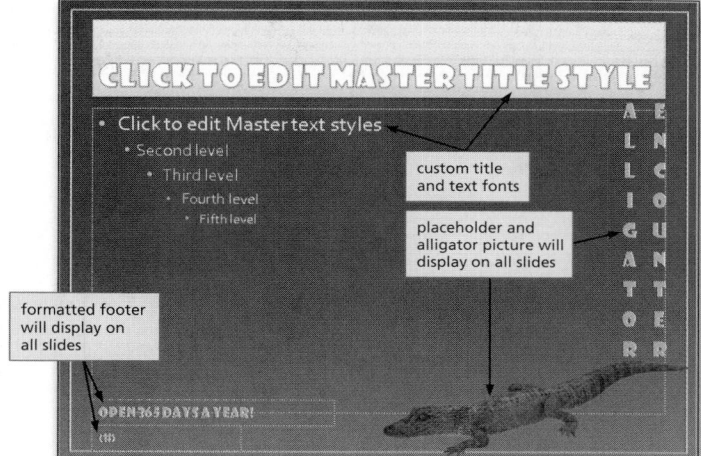

(a) Slide Master

(b) Title Slide Layout

(c) Slide 1

Figure 8–1

BTW

Inserting Objects into the Slide Master
In this project you will add a placeholder, text box, and pictures to the layout. You can, however, insert other objects, including clip art and video and audio files. Corporations often insert their company logos into a slide master.

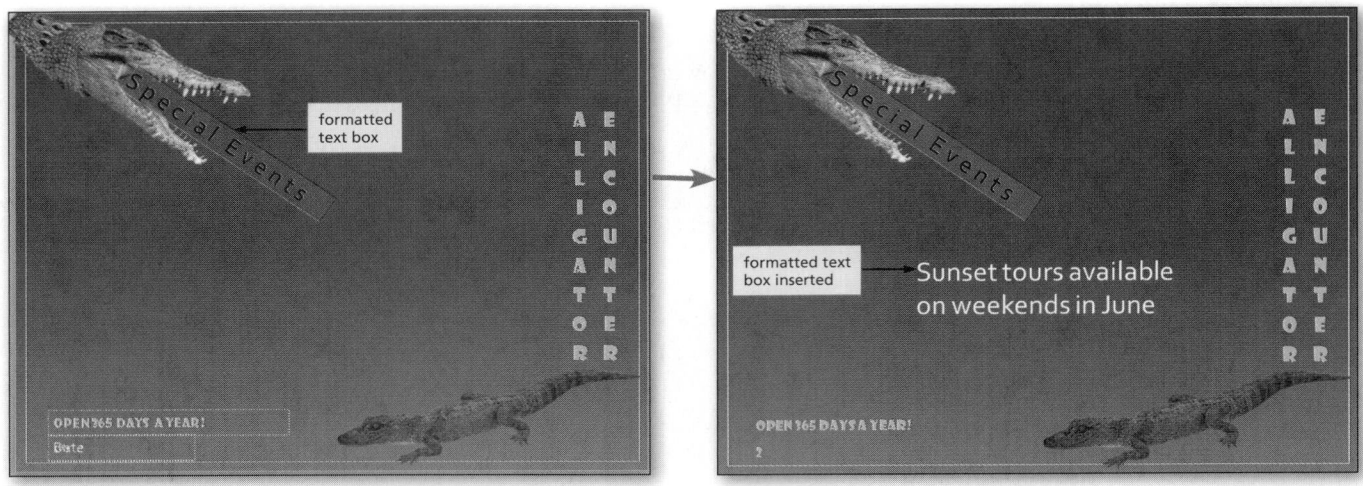

(d) Blank Layout

(e) Slide 2

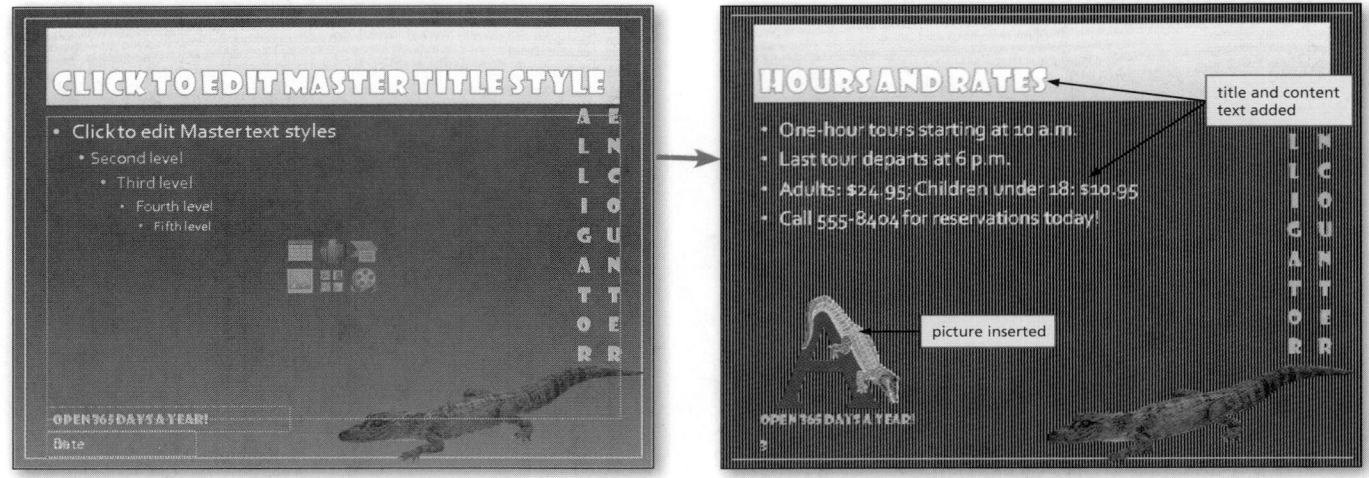

(f) Title and Content Layout

(g) Slide 3

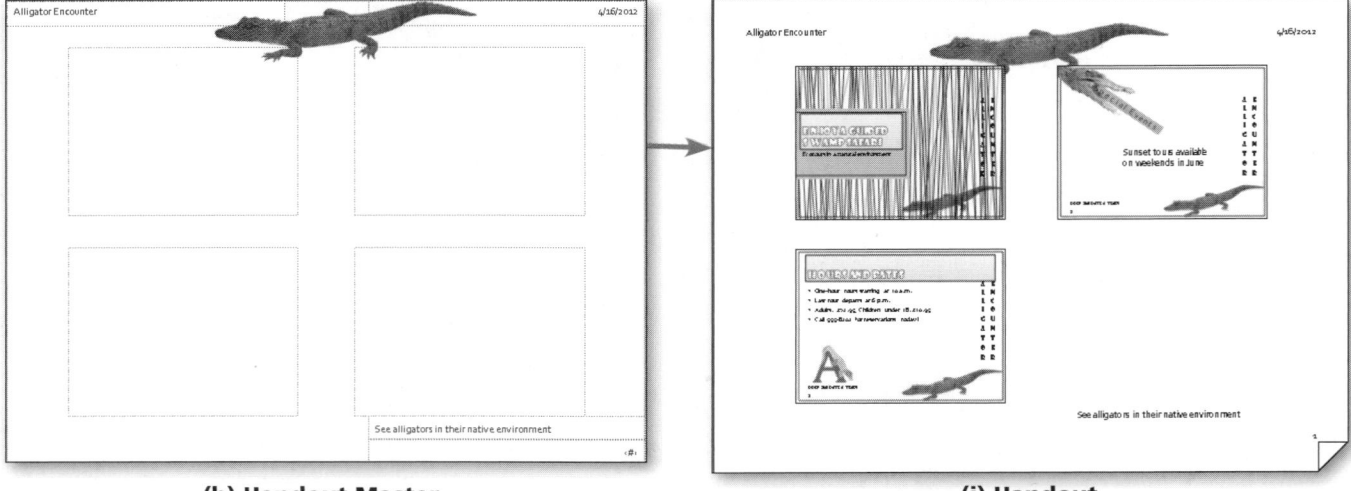

(h) Handout Master

(i) Handout

Figure 8–1 (Continued)

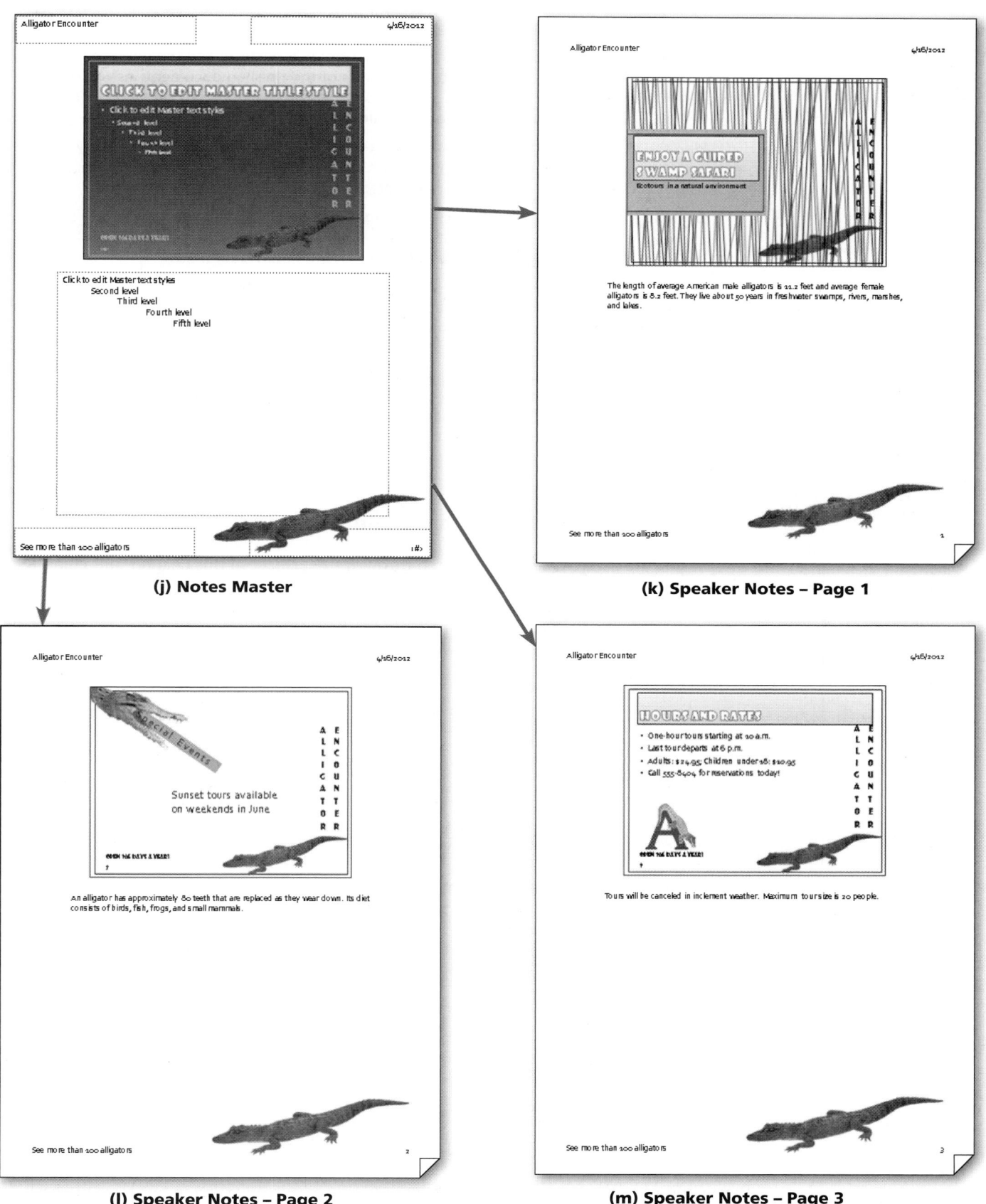

(j) Notes Master

(k) Speaker Notes – Page 1

(l) Speaker Notes – Page 2

(m) Speaker Notes – Page 3

Figure 8–1 (Continued)

Plan
Ahead

General Project Guidelines

When creating a PowerPoint presentation, the actions you perform and the decisions you make will affect the appearance and characteristics of the finished document. As you create a presentation with illustrations, such as the project shown in Figure 8–1 on pages PPT 467 to PPT 469, you should follow these general guidelines:

1. **Plan the slide master.** Using a new slide master gives you the freedom to plan every aspect of your slide. Take care to think about the overall message you are trying to convey before you start PowerPoint and select definite elements for this master.

2. **Develop the slide master prior to creating presentation slides.** You can save time and create consistency when you design and build your master at the start of your PowerPoint session rather than after you have created individual slides.

3. **Decide how to distribute copies of slides.** Some audience members will desire printed copies of your slides. To conserve paper and ink, you may decide to limit the number of copies you print or to post the presentation electronically in a shared location for users to print the presentation if they so choose.

When necessary, more specific details concerning the above guidelines are presented at appropriate points in the chapter. The chapter also will identify the actions performed and decisions made regarding these guidelines during the creation of the presentation shown in Figure 8–1.

BTW

The Ribbon and Screen Resolution
PowerPoint may change how the groups and buttons within the groups appear on the Ribbon, depending on the computer's screen resolution. Thus, your Ribbon may look different from the ones in this book if you are using a screen resolution other than 1024 × 768.

To Start PowerPoint and Save a File

If you are using a computer to step through the project in this chapter and you want your screens to match the figures in this book, you should change your computer's resolution to 1024 × 768. The following steps start PowerPoint and then save a file.

1 Start PowerPoint. If necessary, maximize the PowerPoint window.

2 Save the presentation using the file name, Alligator Encounter.

Plan
Ahead

Plan the slide master.

Using a new slide master gives you the freedom to specify every slide element. Like an artist with a new canvas or a musician with blank sheet music, only your imagination prevents you from creating an appealing master that conveys the overall look of your presentation.

Before you start developing the master, give your overall plan some careful thought. The decisions you make at this point should be reflected on every slide. A presentation can have several master layouts, but you should change these layouts only if you have a compelling need to change them. Use the Plan Ahead concepts you have read throughout the chapters in this book to guide your decisions about fonts, colors, backgrounds, art, and other essential slide elements.

Customizing Presentation Slide Master Backgrounds and Fonts

PowerPoint has many template files with the file extension .potx. Each template file has three masters: slide, handout, and notes. A slide master has at least one layout; you have used many of these layouts, such as Title and Content, Two Content, and Picture with

Caption, to create presentations. A **handout master** designates the placement of text, such as page numbers, on a sheet of paper intended to distribute to audience members. A **notes master** defines the formatting for speaker's notes.

Slide Master

If you select a document theme and want to change one of its components on every slide, you can override that component by changing the slide master. In addition, if you want your presentation to have a unique design, you might want to create a slide master rather than attempt to modify a current document theme. A slide master indicates the size and position of text and object placeholders, font styles, slide backgrounds, transitions, and effects. Any change to the slide master results in changing that component on every slide in the presentation. For example, if you change the second-level bullet on the slide master, each slide with a second-level bullet will display this new bullet format.

One presentation can have more than one slide master. You may find two or more slide masters are necessary when your presentation reuses special slide layouts. In this Alligator Encounter presentation, for example, one slide will have the title slide to introduce the overall concept, another will have a blank slide to showcase a special event for the month, and a third slide will have a title and a bulleted list to give specific information about the nature park's hours, admission prices, and telephone number. All slides will have an alligator picture and the name of the safari company, Alligator Encounter, on the slide master.

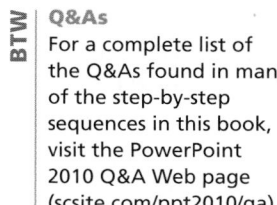

BTW

Q&As
For a complete list of the Q&As found in many of the step-by-step sequences in this book, visit the PowerPoint 2010 Q&A Web page (scsite.com/ppt2010/qa).

To Display a Slide Master

To begin developing a unique design for the Alligator Encounter slides, you need to display the slide master so that you can customize the slide components. The following steps display the slide master.

- Click View on the Ribbon to display the View tab (Figure 8–2).

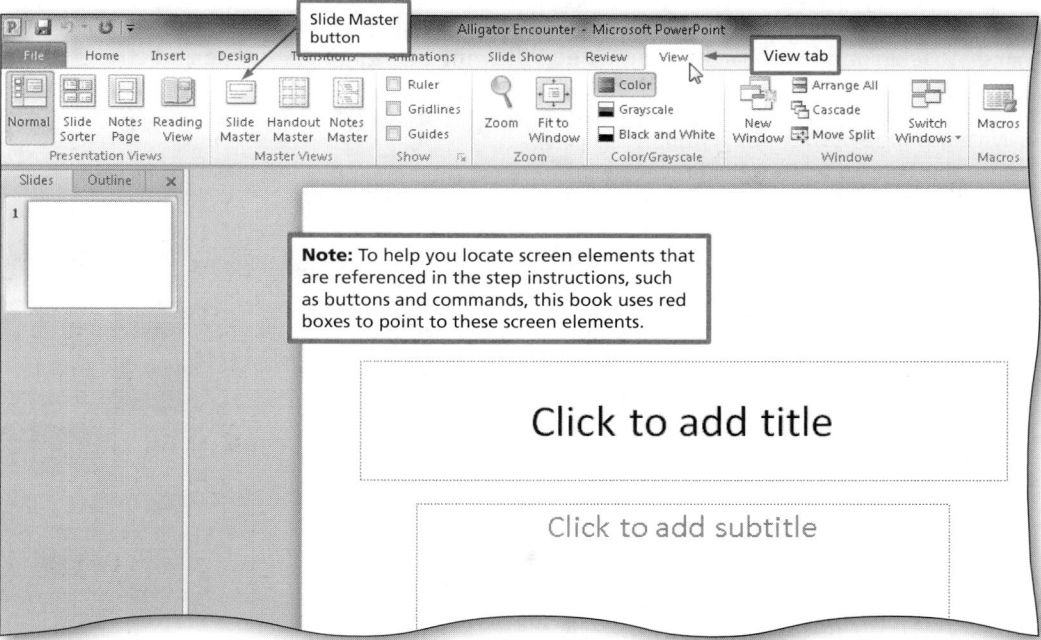

Figure 8–2

- Click the Slide Master button (View tab | Master Views group) to display the Slide Master tab and the slide thumbnails in the Overview pane.

- Click the Office Theme Slide Master layout (Figure 8–3).

Q&A What are all the other thumbnails in the left pane below the slide master?

They are all the slide layouts associated with this slide master. You have used many of these layouts in the presentations you have developed in the exercises in this book.

Q&A Why is the layout given this name?

The slide layout names begin with the theme applied to the slides. In this case, the default Office Theme is applied. The first slide layout in the list is called the master because it controls the colors, fonts, and objects that are displayed on all the other slides in the presentation.

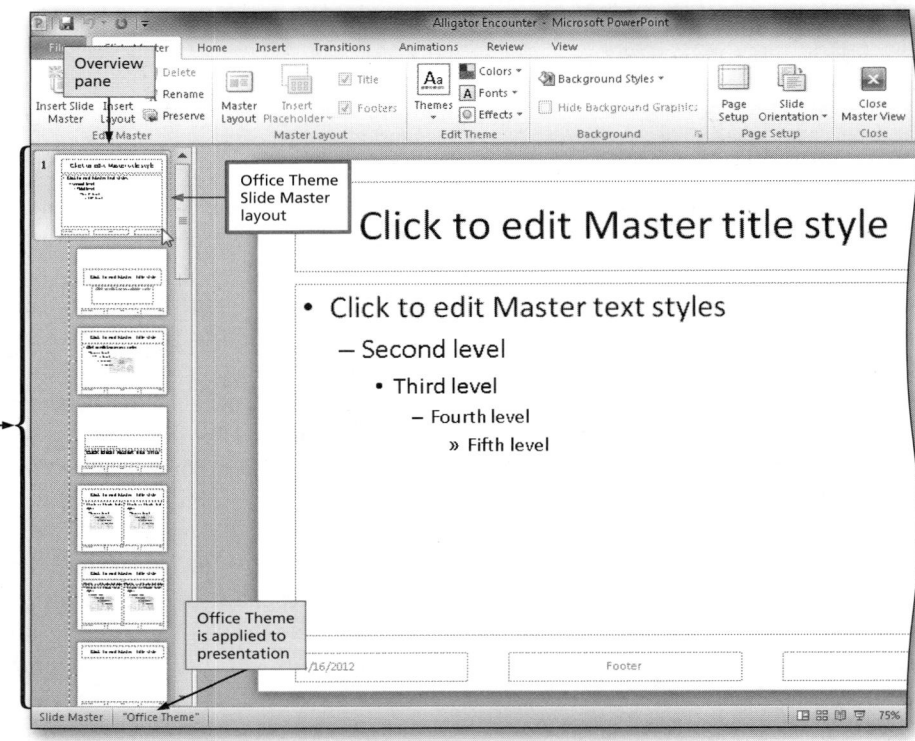

Figure 8–3

To Apply Slide and Font Themes to a Slide Master

You can change the look of an entire presentation by applying formats to the slide master in the same manner that you apply these formats to individual slides. Alligators live in swampy areas, so you want your slides to reflect a marshy background and earthy tones. The following steps apply a theme and change the font theme colors.

- With the slide master displaying, click the Themes button (Slide Master tab | Edit Theme group) to display the Themes gallery.

- Scroll down to display the Thatch theme in the gallery (Figure 8–4).

Experiment

- Point to various themes in the Themes gallery and watch the colors and fonts change on the slide master.

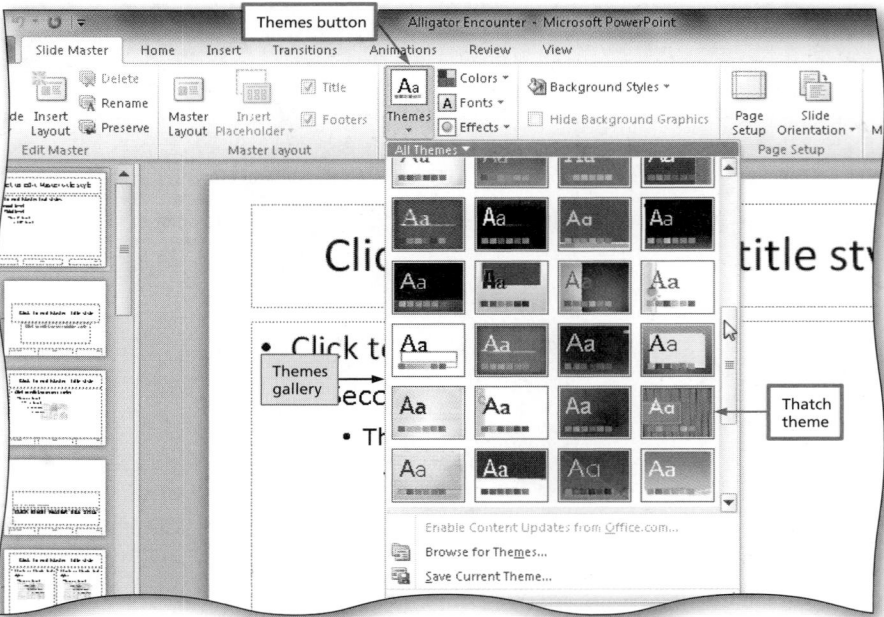

Figure 8–4

- Click the Thatch theme to apply this theme to the slide master.

- Click the Theme Colors button (Slide Master tab | Edit Theme group) to display the Theme Colors gallery.

- Scroll down to display the Paper theme color scheme in the gallery (Figure 8–5).

Experiment

- Point to various themes in the Theme Colors gallery and watch the colors and fonts change on the slide master.

- Click Paper in the Theme Colors gallery to change the slide master colors to Paper.

Q&A Can I insert another set of slide masters to give other slides in the presentation a unique look?

Yes. PowerPoint allows you to insert multiple masters into an existing presentation.

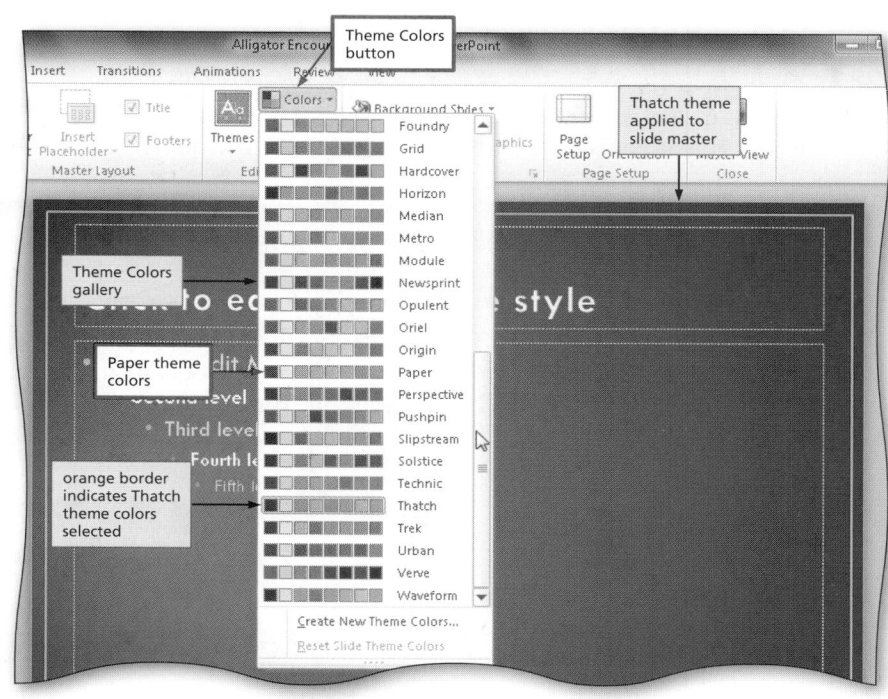

Figure 8–5

To Customize Theme Fonts

Each theme has a heading font and a body font applied to it. At times both fonts are the same. For example, the Thatch theme you applied to the slide master uses the Twentieth Century MT font for both the heading and body. Other times, the heading font differs from the body font, but both fonts coordinate with each other. You can customize theme fonts by selecting your own combination of heading and body font and then giving the new theme font set a unique name. The following steps apply a new heading and body font to the Thatch theme.

❶
- Click the Theme Fonts button (Slide Master tab | Edit Theme group) to display the Theme Fonts gallery (Figure 8–6).

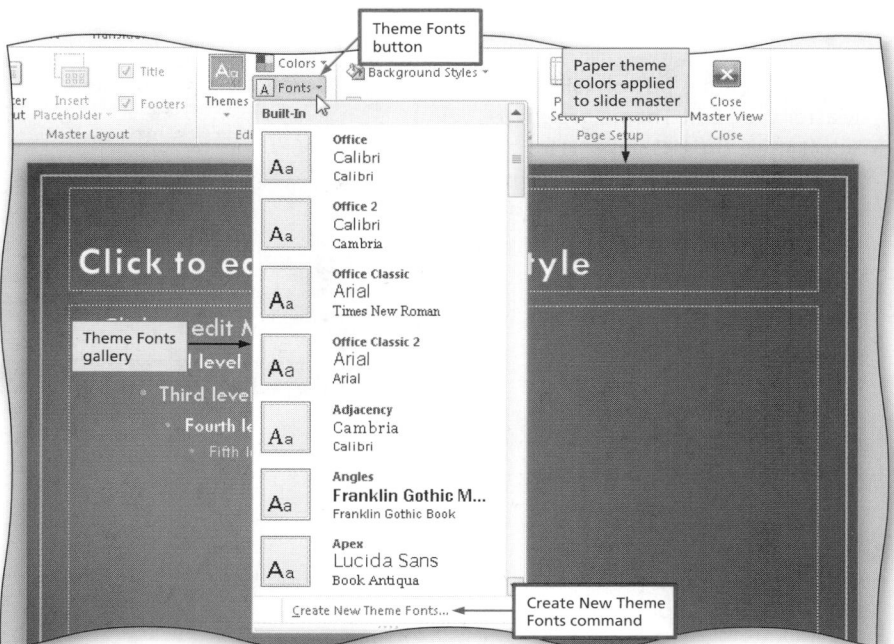

Figure 8–6

- Click Create New Theme Fonts in the Theme Fonts gallery to display the Create New Theme Fonts dialog box.

- Click the Heading font arrow and then scroll up to display Showcard Gothic in the list (Figure 8–7).

Q&A

Can I preview the fonts to see how they are displayed on the slide master?

No preview is available when using the Create New Theme Fonts dialog box. Once you select the font, however, PowerPoint will display text in the Sample box.

Figure 8–7

- Click Showcard Gothic to apply that font as the new heading text font.

- Click the Body font arrow and then scroll up to display Corbel in the list (Figure 8–8).

Q&A

What if the Showcard Gothic or Corbel fonts are not in my list of fonts?

Select fonts that resemble the fonts shown in Figure 8–8.

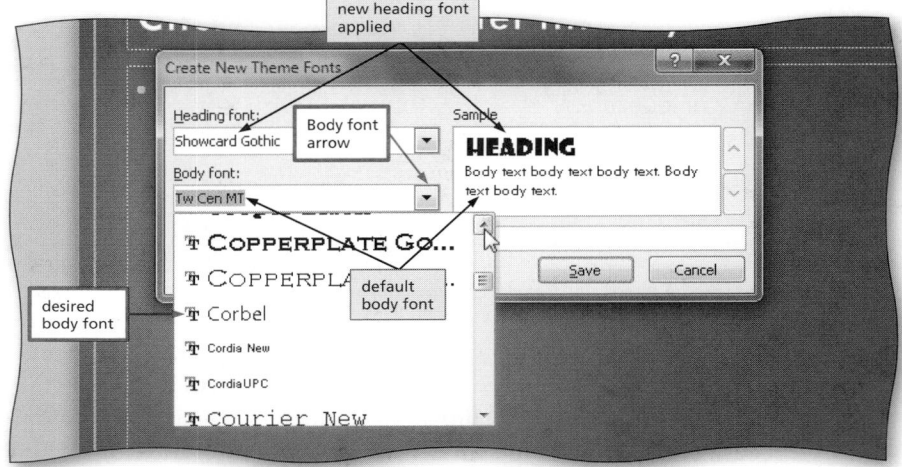

Figure 8–8

- Click Corbel to apply that font as the new body text font.

- Select the words, Custom 1, in the Name text box and then type **Alligator** to name the new font set (Figure 8–9).

Q&A

Must I name this font set I just created?

No. If you name the set, however, you easily will recognize this combination in your font set if you want to use it in new presentations. It will display in the Custom area of the Fonts gallery fonts.

Figure 8–9

- Click the Save button (Create New Theme Fonts dialog box) to save this new font set with the name, Alligator.

To Format a Slide Master Background and Apply a Quick Style

Once you have applied a theme to the slide master and determined the fonts for the presentation, you can further customize the presentation. The following steps format the slide master background and then apply a Quick Style.

1

- Click the Background Styles button (Slide Master tab | Background group) to display the Background Styles gallery (Figure 8–10).

Experiment

- Point to various styles themes in the Background Styles gallery and watch the backgrounds change on the slide master title text placeholder.

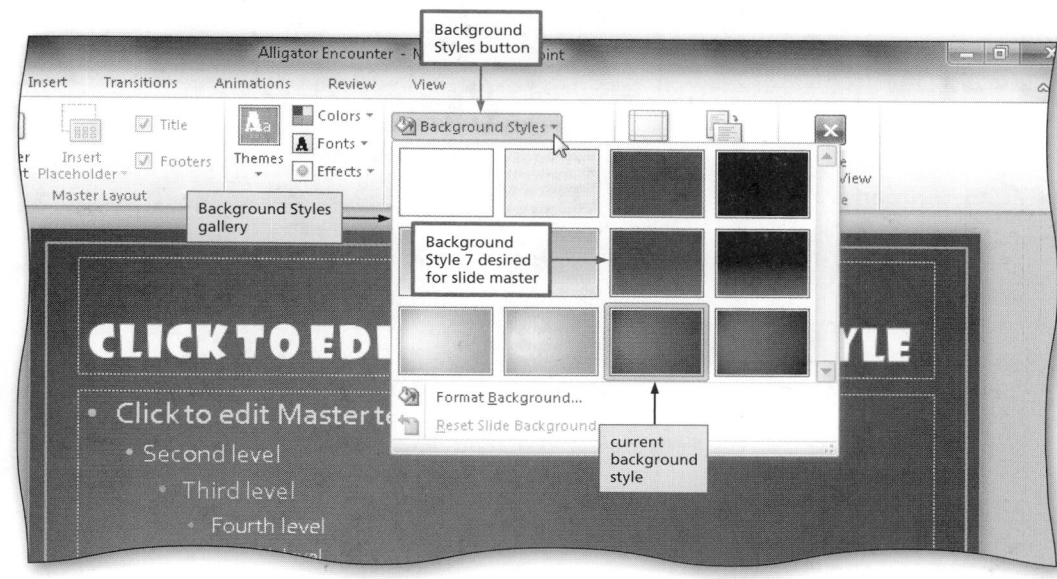

Figure 8–10

2

- Click Background Style 7 (third style in second row) to apply this background to the slide master (Figure 8–11).

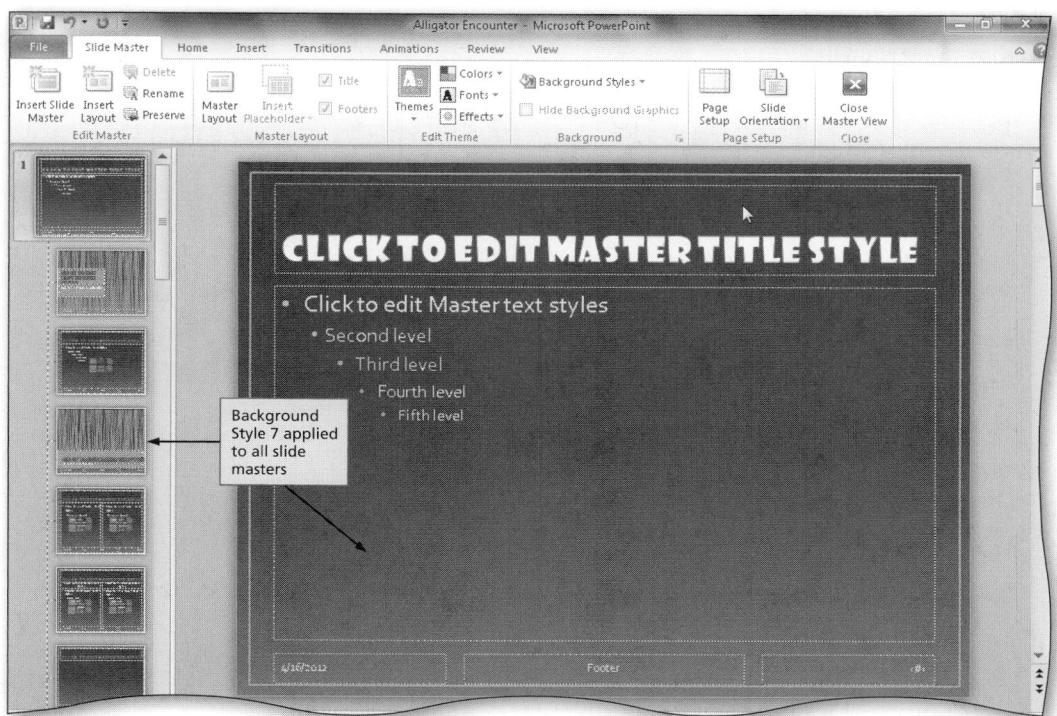

Figure 8–11

- Click the border of the slide master title text placeholder to select it.

- Display the Home tab and then click the Quick Styles button (Home tab | Drawing group) to display the Quick Styles gallery (Figure 8–12).

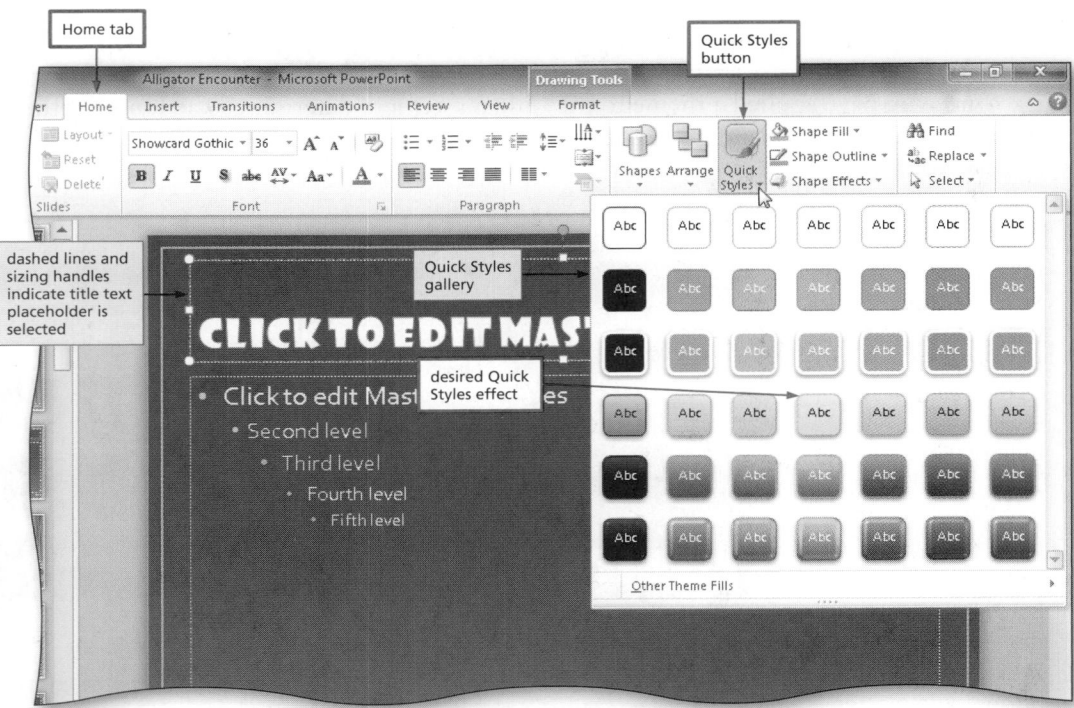

Experiment

- Point to various styles in the Quick Styles gallery and watch the background and borders change on the slide master title text placeholder.

Figure 8–12

- Click the Subtle Effect – Gold, Accent 3 Quick Style (fourth style in fourth row) to apply this style to the title text placeholder (Figure 8–13).

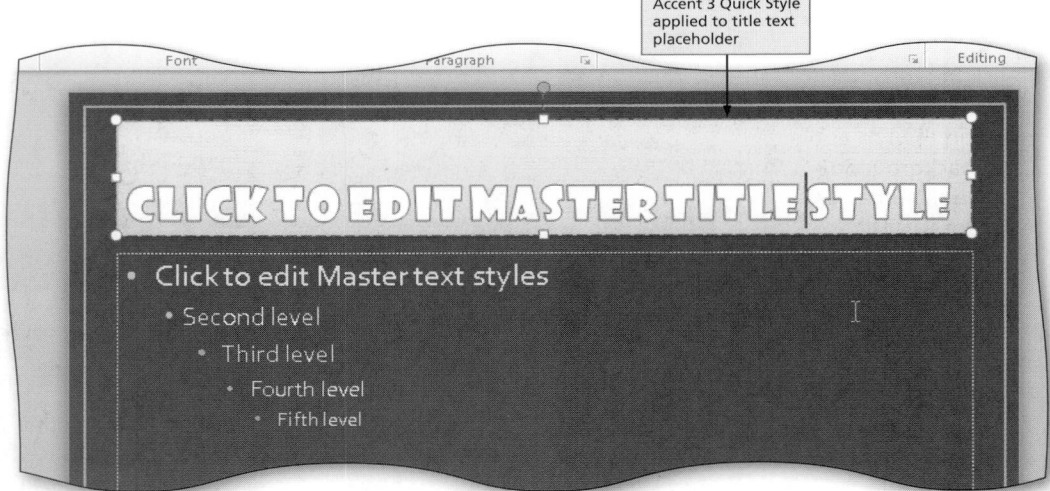

Figure 8–13

To Delete, Move, and Add Text to a Slide Master Footer

Slide numbers, the date and time, and footer text can be displayed anywhere on a slide, not just in the default footer placeholder locations. The following steps delete one footer placeholder, move the footer placeholders, and then add footer text.

1

- With the slide master displaying, click the border of the date footer placeholder to select it (Figure 8–14).

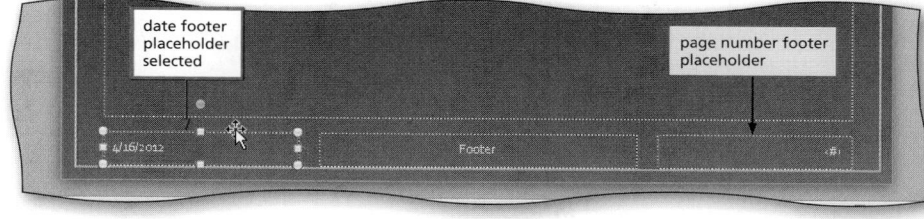

Figure 8–14

2

- Press the DELETE key to delete the date placeholder.

Q&A What should I do if the placeholder still is showing on the slide?

Be certain you clicked the placeholder border and not just the text. The border must display as a solid line before you can delete it.

- Click the page number footer placeholder to select it and then drag it to the location where the date placeholder originally appeared.

3

- Click the content footer placeholder and then drag it above the page number placeholder (Figure 8–15).

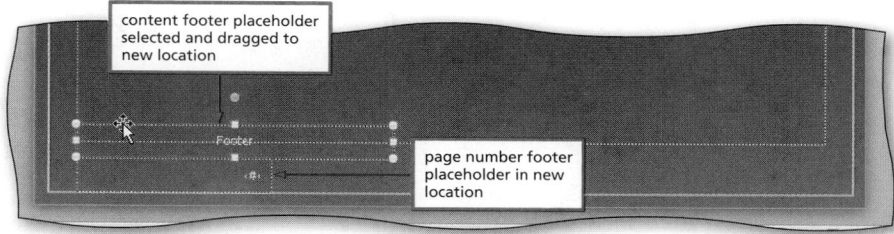

Figure 8–15

4

- Display the Insert tab, click the Header & Footer button (Insert tab | Text group), and then place a check mark in the Slide number check box.

- Place a check mark in the Footer check box and then type `Open 365 days a year!` in the Footer text box.

- Place a check mark in the 'Don't show on title slide' check box (Figure 8–16).

Q&A Can I verify where the footer placeholders will display on the slide layout?

Yes. The black boxes in the bottom of the Preview area indicate the footer placeholders' locations.

5

- Click the Apply to All button (Header and Footer dialog box) to add the slide number and footer text to the slide master.

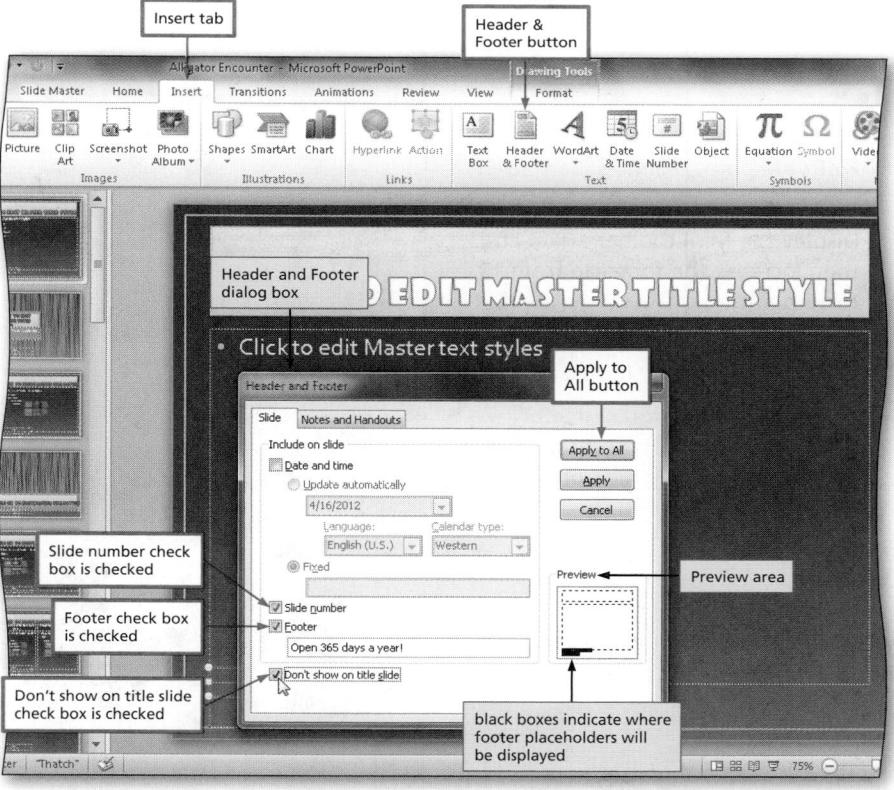

Figure 8–16

To Format Slide Master Footer Text

You can format footer text using the same font styles and text attributes available to title and subtitle text. The following steps format the footer text.

1

• Select the content footer placeholder text and then click the Font box arrow on the Mini toolbar to display the Font gallery (Figure 8–17).

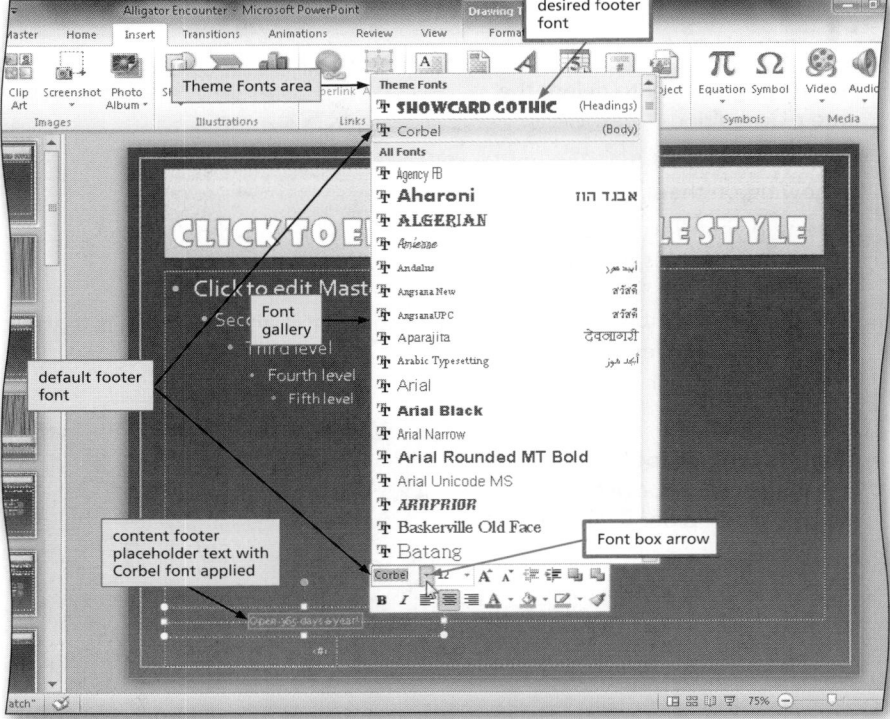

Figure 8–17

2

• Click Showcard Gothic in the Theme Fonts area of the Font gallery to change the footer font.

• Display the Mini toolbar again and then increase the font size from 12 to 16 point.

• Change the font color to Orange, Accent 2 (sixth color in first row).

• Use the Format Painter to apply the content footer placeholder formatting to the page number placeholder.

• Click the Align Text Left button to move both the content and page number footer text toward the left border of the placeholder (Figure 8–18).

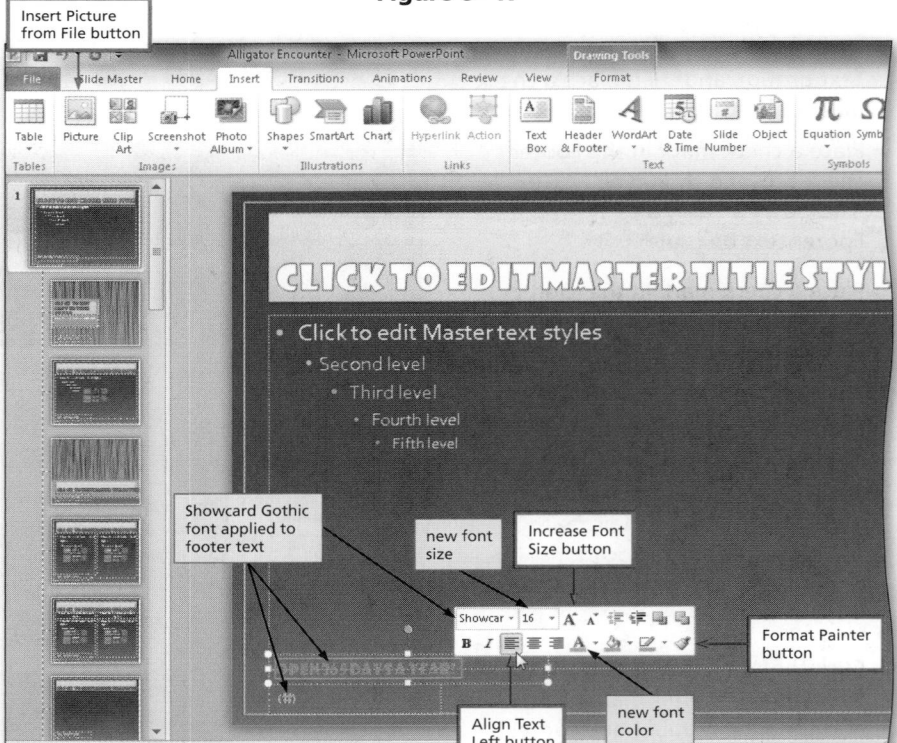

Figure 8–18

To Insert a Background Graphic into a Slide Master

The theme, fonts, footer, and background colors are set. The next step is to draw the viewers' attention to the presentation by placing Alligator Body picture, located on the Data Files for Students, in the same location on every slide. See the inside back cover of this book for instructions on downloading the Data Files for Students, or contact your instructor for more information on accessing the required files. The repetition of this picture creates consistency and helps reinforce the message. The following steps insert an alligator picture into the slide master.

1
- With the slide master and Insert tab displaying, click the Insert Picture from File button (Insert tab | Images group) to display the Insert Picture dialog box.

- With your USB flash drive connected to one of the computer's USB ports and the list of files and folders on your flash drive displaying, click Alligator Body to select the file name (Figure 8–19).

Q&A

What if the picture is not on a USB flash drive?

Use the same process, but select the device containing the picture. Another option is to locate this picture or a similar one in the Microsoft Clip Organizer. You may need to remove the picture background to call attention to the alligator.

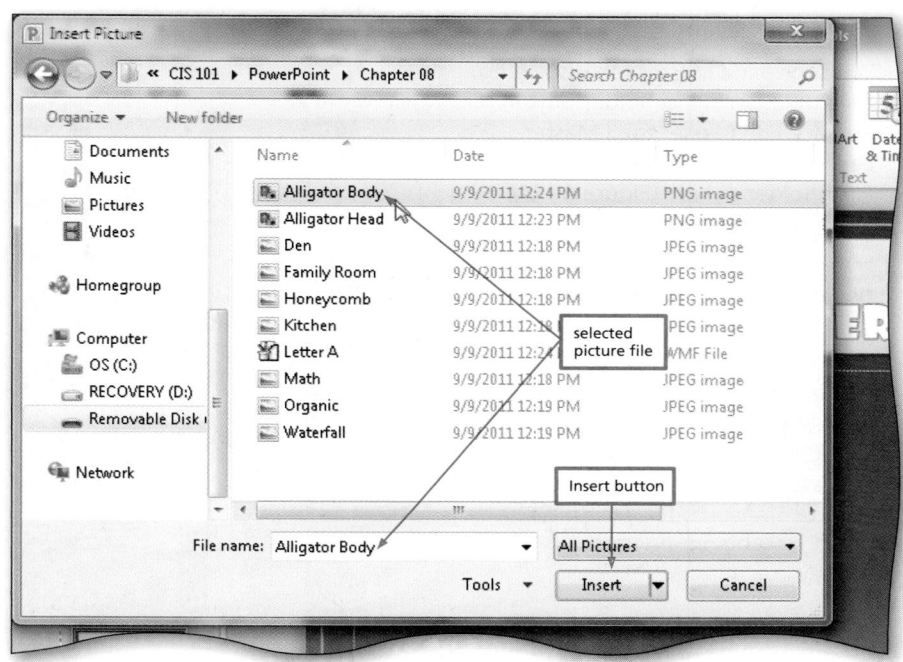

Figure 8–19

2
- Click the Insert button (Insert Picture dialog box) to insert the picture into the slide master.

- Drag the picture to the location shown in Figure 8–20.

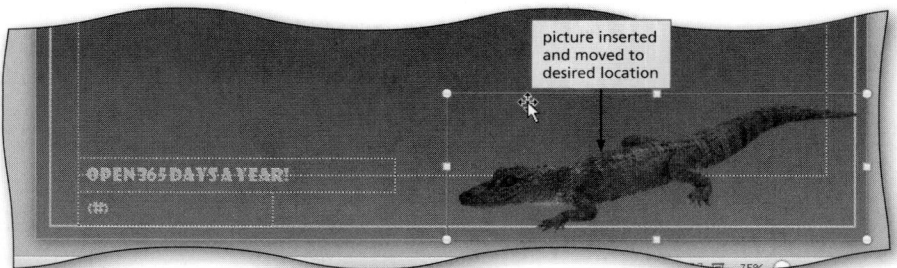

Figure 8–20

Break Point: If you wish to take a break, this is a good place to do so. Be sure to save the Alligator Encounter file again and then you can quit PowerPoint. To resume at a later time, start PowerPoint, open the file called Alligator Encounter, and continue following the steps from this location forward.

Adding and Formatting Placeholders

Each design theme determines where placeholders appear on individual layouts. The slide master has placeholders for bulleted lists, title text, pictures, and other graphical elements. At times, you may find that you need a specific placeholder for a design element not found on any of the slide master layouts. You can add a placeholder in Slide Master view for text, SmartArt, charts, tables, and other graphical elements.

To Insert a Placeholder into a Blank Layout

The words, Alligator Encounter, will appear on the title slide. To emphasize the name, you can add these words to every text slide. One efficient method of adding this text is to insert a placeholder, type the words, and, if necessary, format the characters. The following steps insert a placeholder into the Blank Layout.

• In the Overview pane, scroll down and then click the Blank Layout to display this layout.

• With the Slide Master tab displaying, click the Insert Placeholder button arrow (Slide Master tab | Master Layout group) to display the Insert Placeholder gallery (Figure 8–21).

Q&A Why does the Insert Placeholder button on my screen differ from the button shown in Figure 8–21?

The image on the button changes based on the type of placeholder content that was last inserted. A placeholder can hold any content, including text, pictures, and tables. If the last type of placeholder inserted was for SmartArt, for example, the Insert Placeholder button would display the SmartArt icon.

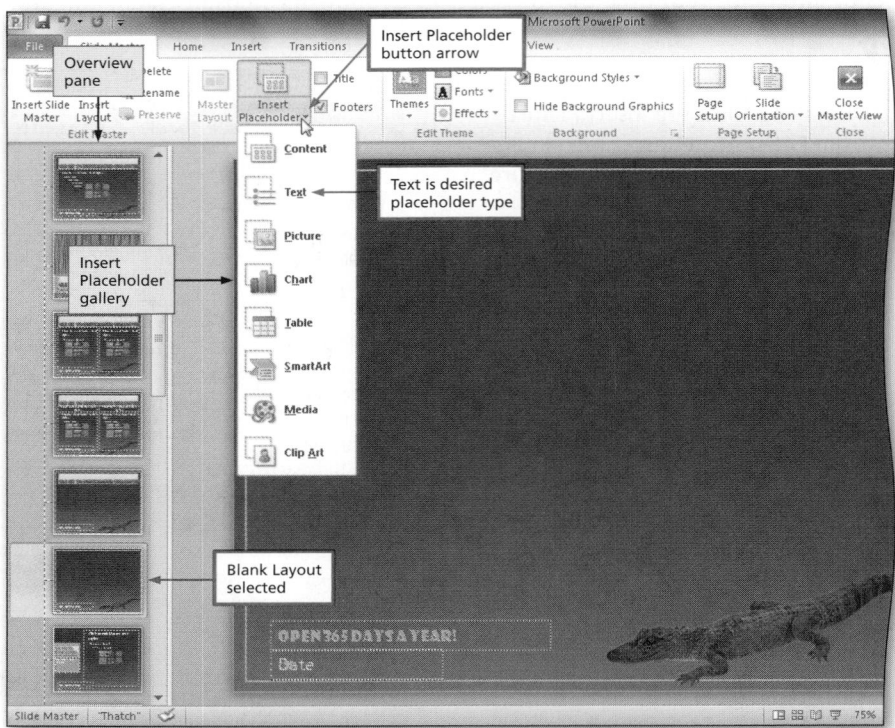

Figure 8–21

• Click Text in the gallery to change the mouse pointer to a crosshair.

Q&A Could I have inserted a Content placeholder rather than a Text placeholder?

Yes. The Content placeholder is used for any of the seven types of slide content: text, table, chart, SmartArt, picture, clip art, or media. In this project, you will insert text in the placeholder. If you know the specific kind of content you want to place in the placeholder, it is best to select that placeholder type.

• Position the mouse pointer at the upper-right area of the layout (Figure 8–22).

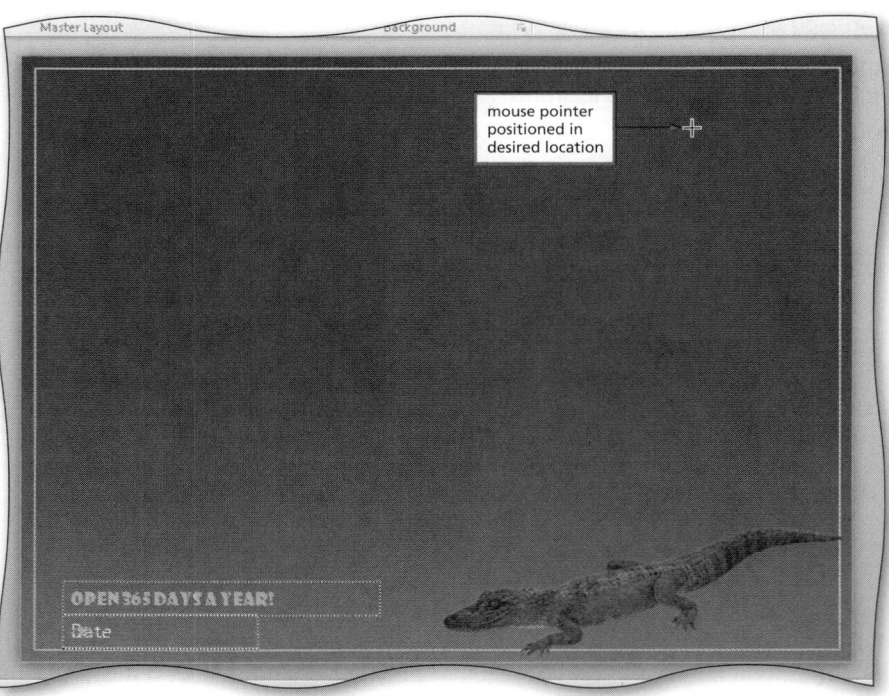

Figure 8–22

3

• Click to insert the new placeholder into the Blank Layout (Figure 8–23).

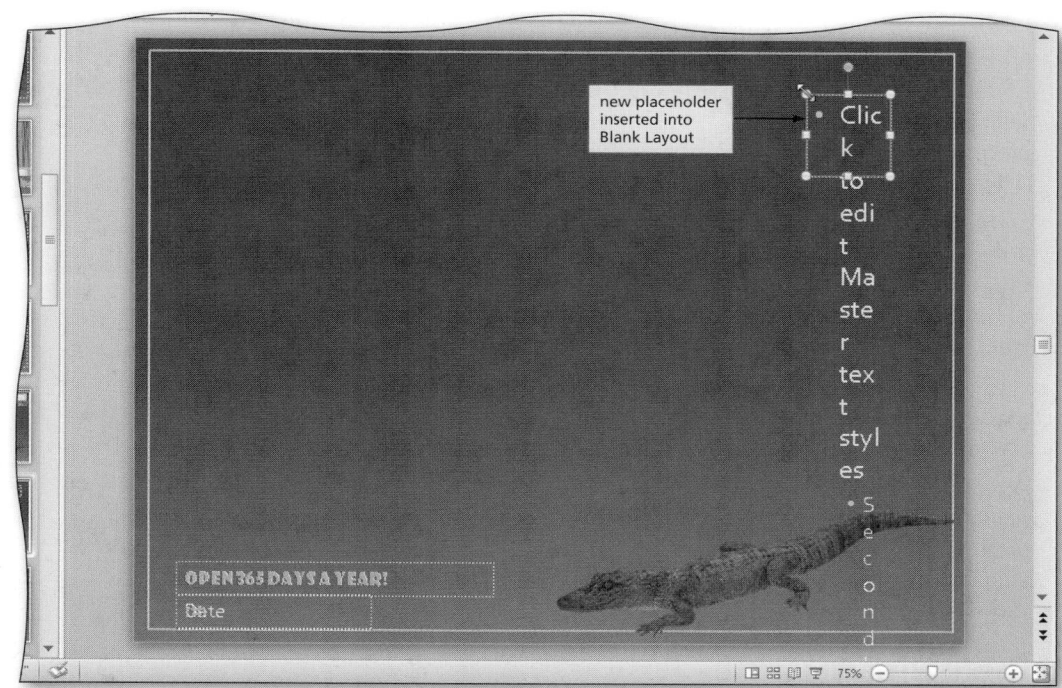

Figure 8–23

To Add and Format Placeholder Text

Now that the text placeholder is positioned, you can add the desired text and then format the characters. You will need to delete the second-, third-, fourth-, and fifth-level bullets in this placeholder because they are not being used. The following steps add and format the words in the new Blank Layout placeholder.

1

• Click inside the new placeholder, press and hold down the CTRL key, and then press the A key to select all the text in the placeholder (Figure 8–24).

Figure 8–24

2

- Press the DELETE key to delete all the selected text in the placeholder.

- Display the Home tab and then click the Bullets button (Home tab | Paragraph group) to remove the bullet from the placeholder.

- Type **Alligator Encounter** in the placeholder.

- Drag the bottom sizing handle down until it is above the alligator picture, as shown in Figure 8–25.

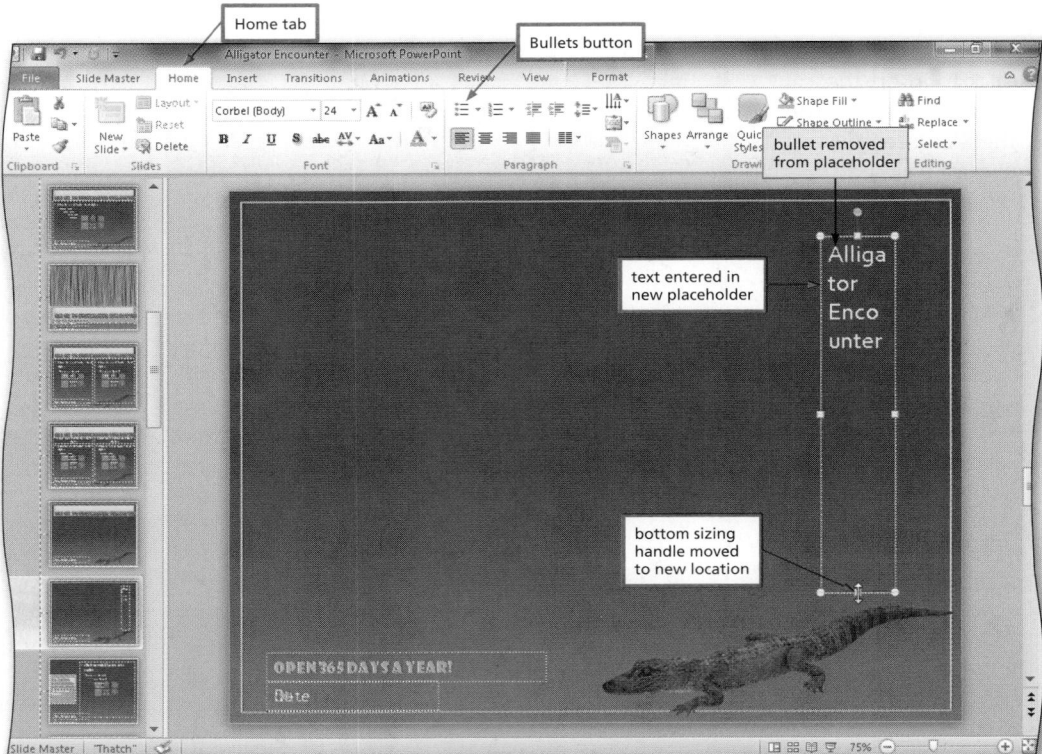

Figure 8–25

3

- Click the Text Direction button (Home tab | Paragraph group) to open the Text Direction gallery (Figure 8–26).

Experiment

- Point to various directions in the Text Direction gallery and watch the two words in the placeholder change direction on the layout.

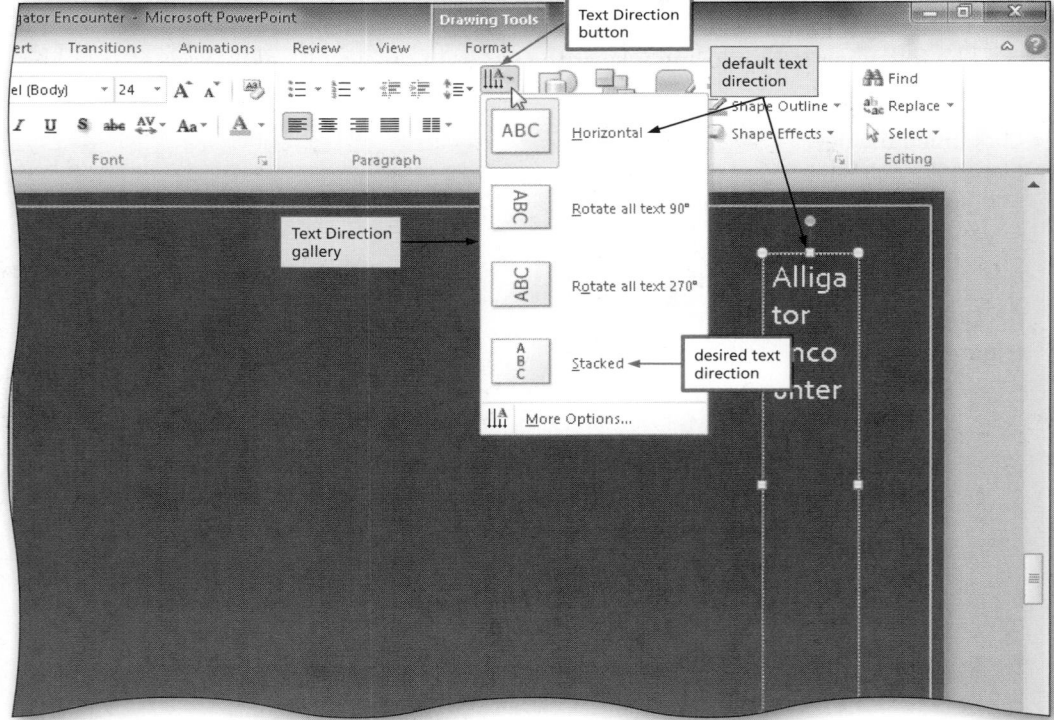

Figure 8–26

4

- Click Stacked to display the text vertically.

- Click the Align Text button (Home tab | Paragraph group) to display the Align Text gallery (Figure 8–27).

🔎 **Experiment**

- Point to the Center and Right icons in the Align Text gallery and watch the two words in the placeholder change alignment on the layout.

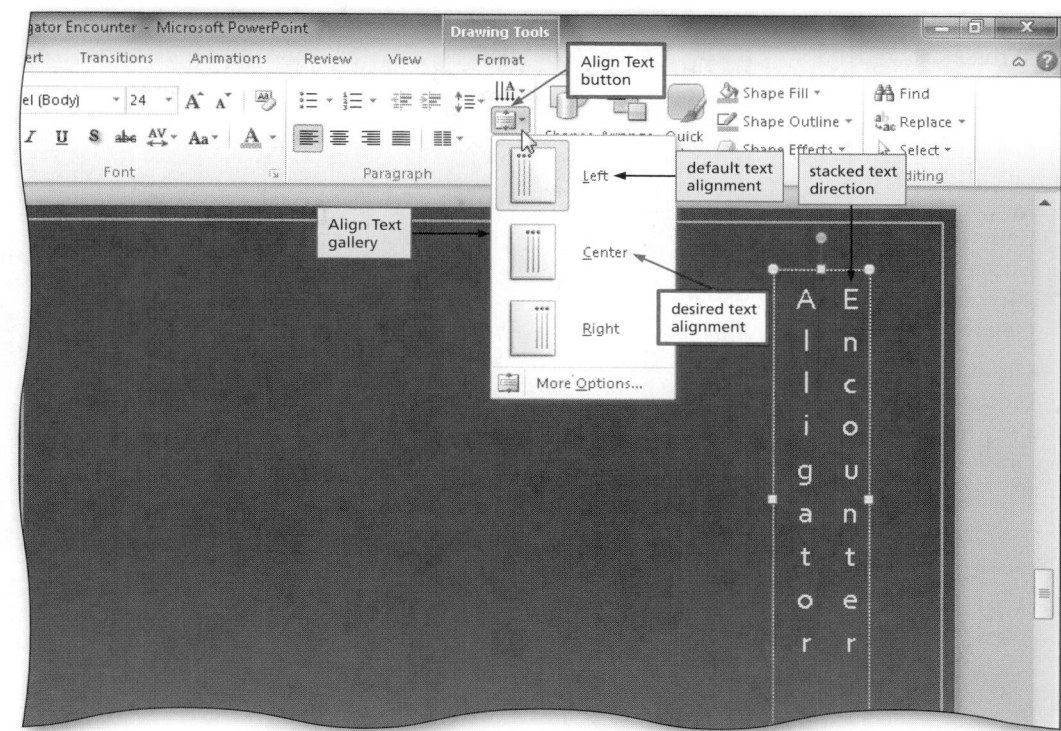

Figure 8–27

5

- Click Center to display the text in the middle of the placeholder (Figure 8–28).

 Q&A

What is the difference between the Center button in the Paragraph group and the Center button in the Align gallery?

The Center button in the Paragraph group positions the text between the top and bottom borders of the placeholder. The Center button in the Align gallery centers the text between the left and right borders.

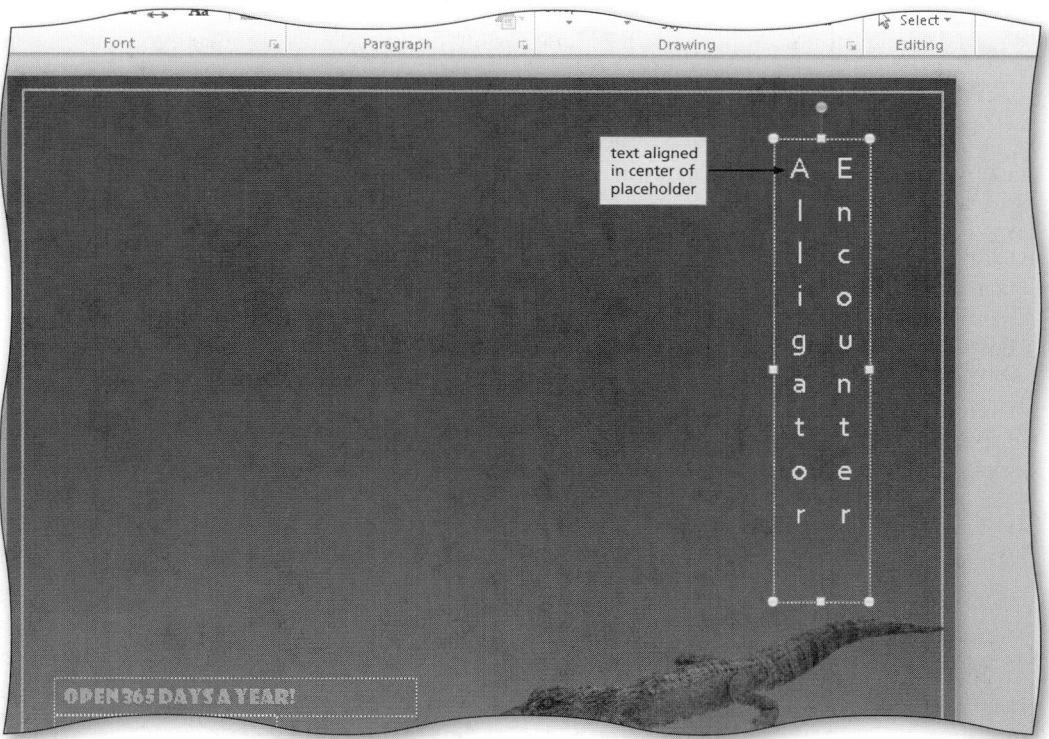

Figure 8–28

6
- Right-click the text in the placeholder to display the Mini toolbar and shortcut menu, click the Font box arrow on the Mini toolbar, and then select Showcard Gothic in the Theme Fonts area of the Font gallery.

- Click the Font Color button to change the font color to Orange, Accent 2 (Figure 8–29).

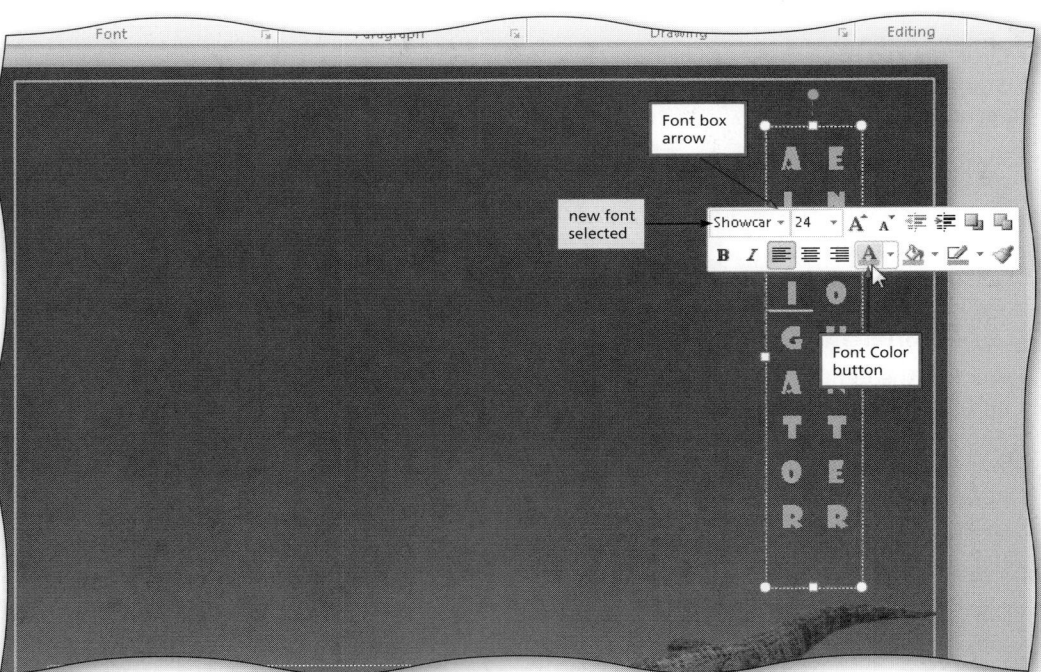

Figure 8–29

To Cut a Placeholder and Paste It into a Slide Master

The new formatted placeholder appears only on the Blank Layout. If you selected any other layout in your presentation, such as Two Content or Title Only, this placeholder would not display. For consistency, this placeholder should appear on all text slides. You are not given the opportunity to insert a placeholder into the slide master, but you can paste a placeholder that you copied or cut from another slide. The following steps cut the new placeholder from the Blank Layout and paste it into the slide master.

- With the Home tab displaying, click the new placeholder border and then click the Cut button (Home tab | Clipboard group) to delete the placeholder from the layout and copy it to the Clipboard (Figure 8–30).

Q&A

Why did I click the Cut button instead of the Copy button?

Clicking the Cut button deletes the placeholder. Clicking the Copy button keeps the original placeholder on the slide, so if you paste the placeholder on the slide master, a second, identical placeholder would display on the Blank Layout.

Figure 8–30

2

- Scroll up and then click the Thatch Slide Master thumbnail in the Overview pane to display the slide master.

- Click the Paste button (Home tab | Clipboard group) to copy the placeholder from the Clipboard to the slide master.

- Drag the placeholder to the location shown in Figure 8–31.

Figure 8–31

Break Point: If you wish to take a break, this is a good place to do so. Be sure to save the Alligator Encounter file again and then you can quit PowerPoint. To resume at a later time, start PowerPoint, open the file called Alligator Encounter, and continue following the steps from this location forward.

To Insert a Picture and a Text Box into a Blank Layout

One slide in the completed presentation will feature the Alligator Encounter's new events. The content on this slide can vary depending upon the occasion; it might be photographs of newborn alligators, video from nighttime tours, or airboat rides. To ensure continuity when publicizing special events and promotions, you can insert another picture into the Blank Layout and then add and format a text box. This layout includes the Alligator Encounter placeholder you inserted into the slide master. The following steps insert a picture and a text box into the Blank Layout and then add text in the text box.

1 Scroll down and then click the Blank Layout thumbnail in the Overview pane.

2 Display the Insert tab, insert the Alligator Head picture from your USB flash drive into the Blank Layout, and then move the picture to the location shown in Figure 8–32 (on the next page).

3 Display the Insert tab, click the Text Box button (Insert tab | Text group) and then insert a new text box in a blank area in the center of the layout.

4 Type `Special Events` as the text box text, change the font color to Black, Background 1 (first color in first row), and then increase the font size to 28 point (Figure 8–32).

BTW

Adjusting Text Using AutoFit
When text is too large to fit in a placeholder, PowerPoint displays the AutoFit Options box on the side of the placeholder. If you continue typing, PowerPoint will adjust the text by reducing the line spacing and font size. If you click the AutoFit Options button, you can decide whether to AutoFit or stop fitting the text in this placeholder. You can specify that PowerPoint not use AutoFit by clicking the AutoFit Options button and then clicking Control AutoCorrect Options in the menu to display the AutoCorrect dialog box. Click the 'AutoFit title text to placeholder' and 'AutoFit body text to placeholder' (AutoFormat As You Type tab | AutoCorrect dialog box) to stop PowerPoint from sizing any text as you type. You also can display the AutoCorrect dialog box by opening the Backstage view, clicking Options, clicking Proofing, and then clicking the AutoCorrect Options button.

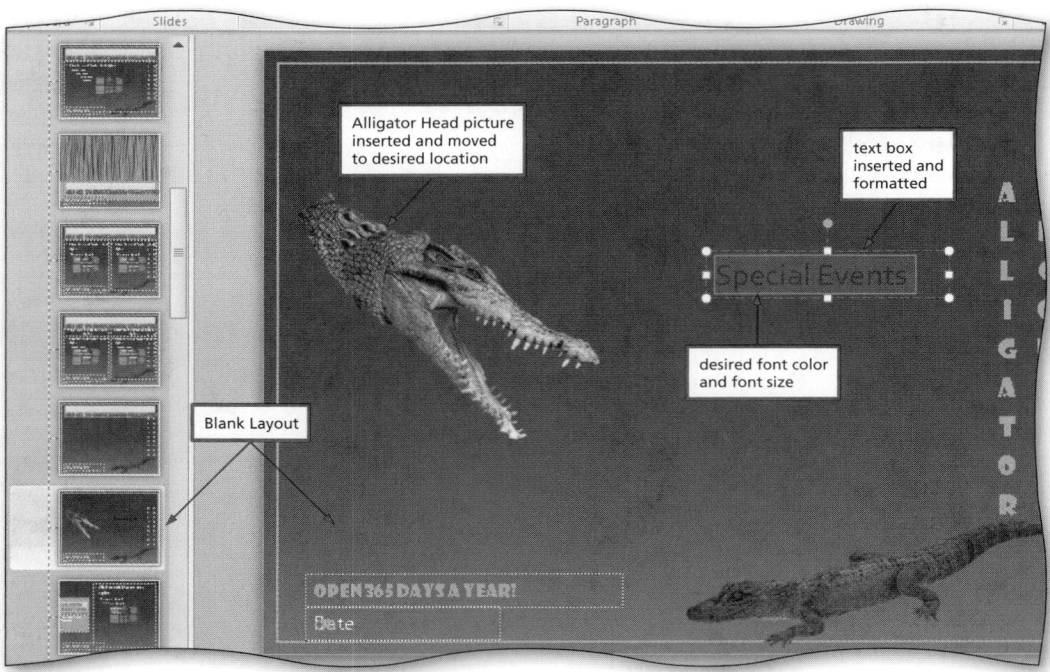

Figure 8–32

To Change Character Spacing

Now that the text is added, you can change the spacing between the letters in the placeholder. The amount of space, called **character spacing**, can be increased or decreased from the Normal default in one of four preset amounts: Very Tight, Tight, Loose, or Very Loose. In addition, you can specify a precise amount of space in the Character Spacing tab of the Font dialog box. In this presentation, you will move the text box inside of the alligator's mouth, which is very long, so the letters in the text box can be stretched to fit the length of the mouth. The following steps increase the character spacing in the text box.

1

- With the text in the new text box selected, click the Character Spacing button (Home tab | Font group) to display the Character Spacing gallery (Figure 8–33).

Experiment

- Point to the spacing options in the gallery and watch the characters in the placeholder change.

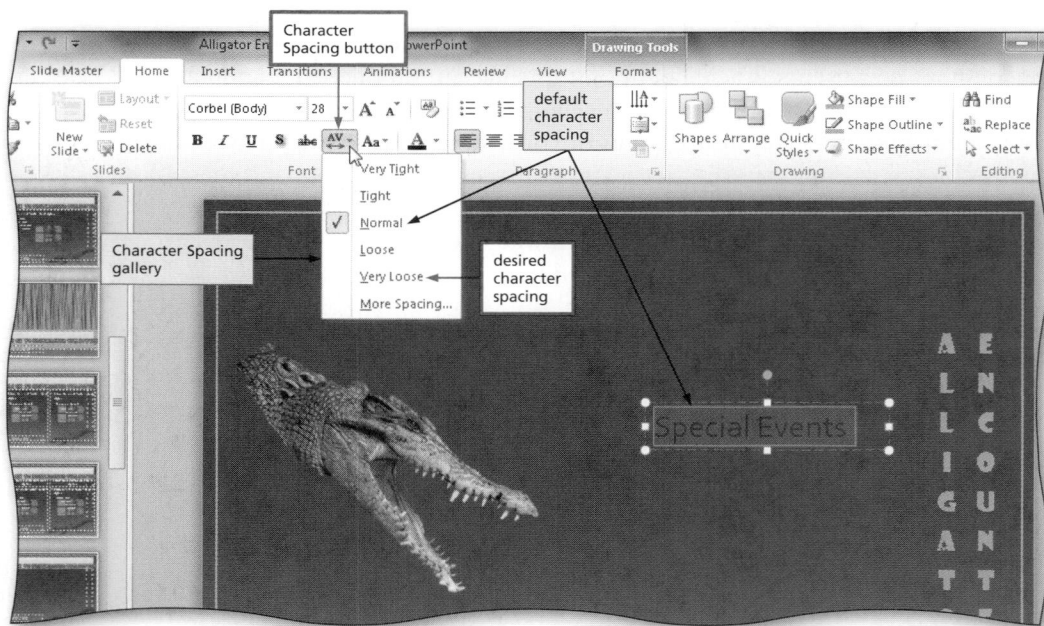

Figure 8–33

- Click Very Loose in the gallery to change the character spacing in the text box (Figure 8–34).

Figure 8–34

Other Ways

1. Click Character Spacing tab (Font dialog box), select Expanded or Condensed in Spacing box and point size in By text box

To Apply a Fill to a Text Box and Increase Transparency

Now that the text is added, you can format the text box. A **fill** refers to the formatting of the interior of a shape. The fill can be a color, picture, texture, pattern, or the presentation background. If a color fill is desired, you can increase the transparency so that some of the background color or pattern mixes with the fill color. **Transparency** determines how much you can see through a picture or other slide element. A fully opaque object is solid, and it is represented by the default transparency percentage of 0. In contrast, the transparency percentage of 100 is fully transparent and allows all of the background to display. The following steps apply a fill to the text box on the Blank Layout and increase the transparency.

- Click the text inside the Special Events text box to remove the selection from the letters.

- Click the Shape Fill button arrow (Home tab | Drawing group) to display the Shape Fill gallery.

🔍 **Experiment**

- Point to various colors in the Shape Fill gallery and watch the placeholder background change.

- Click Red (second color in Standard Colors row) to fill the text box.

- Click the Drawing Dialog Box Launcher (Home tab | Drawing group) to display the Format Shape dialog box (Figure 8–35).

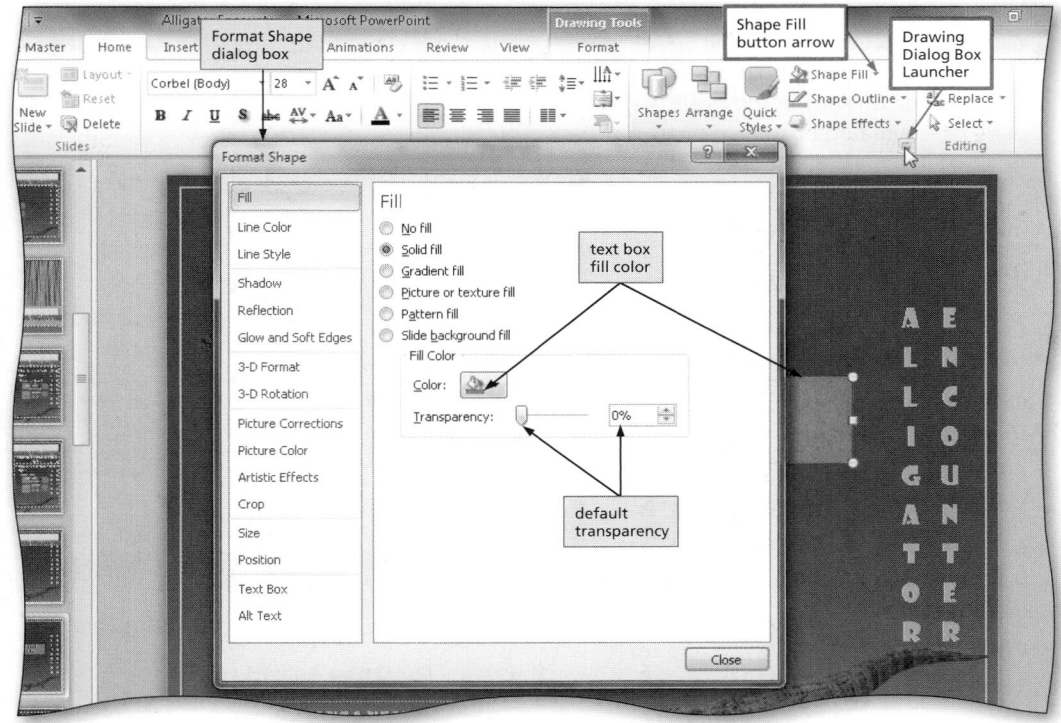

Figure 8–35

- If necessary, drag the Format Shape dialog box to the left side of the layout so that it does not cover the Special Events text box.

- Click the Transparency slider in the Fill pane and drag it to the right until 50% is displayed in the Transparency text box (Figure 8–36).

🔍 **Experiment**

- Drag the Transparency slider to the left and right, and watch the text box background change.

Other Ways
1. Enter percentage in Transparency text box
2. Click Transparency up or down arrow

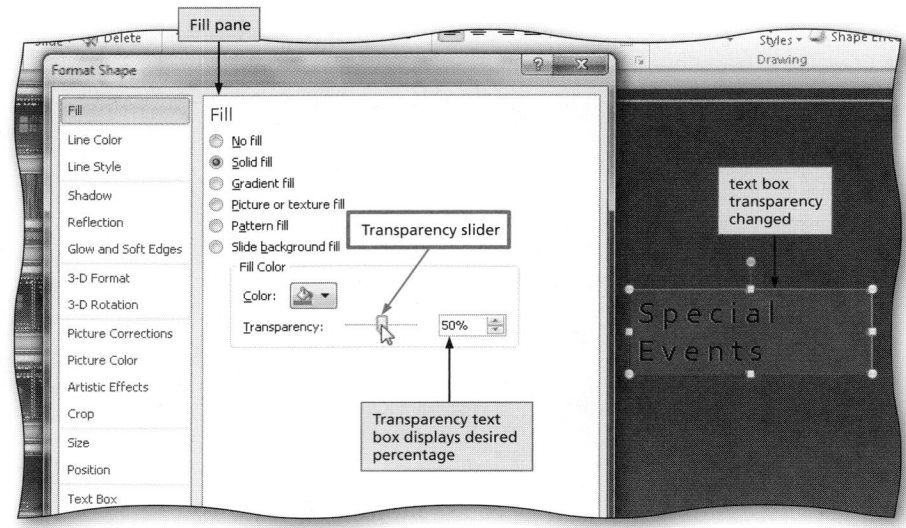

Figure 8–36

To Change a Text Box Internal Margin

Each placeholder and text box has preset internal margins, which are the spaces between the border and the contents of the box. The default left and right margins are 0.1", and the default top and bottom margins are 0.05". You can change one, two, three, or all four internal margins depending upon the placeholder shape and the amount of text entered. In this project, you will drag the text box into the alligator's mouth, so you want the text to align as closely as possible against the left, top, and bottom borders of the box and the right margin to extend out of the alligator's mouth. The following steps change all four text box margins.

- Click Text Box in the left pane (Format Shape dialog box) to display the Text Box options in the right pane of the dialog box.

- Click the Left down arrow in the Internal margin area one time to decrease the margin to 0".

- Click the Right up arrow two times to increase the margin to 0.3".

- Click the Top down arrow one time to decrease the margin to 0".

- Click the Bottom down arrow one time to decrease the margin to 0".

- Click the 'Wrap text in shape' check box to remove the check mark in it (Figure 8–37).

Q&A What is the purpose of wrapping text?

You wrap text when you want the letters to appear on multiple lines instead of one line inside the text box.

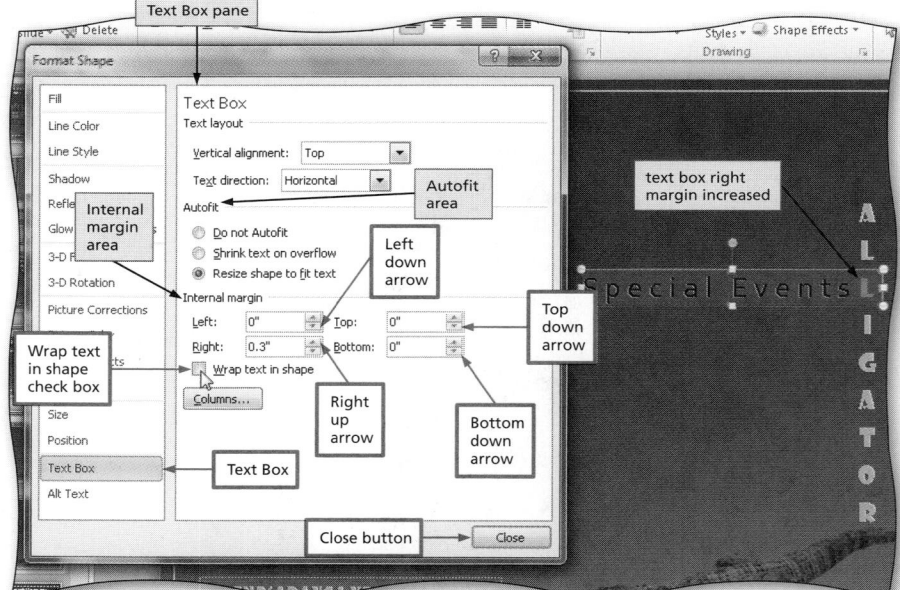

Figure 8–37

- Click the Close button (Format Shape dialog box).

BTW **Using Autofit Options**

The Autofit area of the Format Shape dialog box has several options that allow you to adjust text in a text box. The 'Resize shape to fit text' option automatically increases the vertical text box size so that all the letters fit inside the box. If you do not want this action to occur automatically, click the 'Do not Autofit' option. In addition, the 'Shrink text on overflow' option reduces the size of the text so that it fits in the specified text box size.

To Rotate a Picture and a Text Box

To balance the pictures on the slide, you can move the Alligator Head picture farther into the upper-left corner and then move the Special Events text box inside of the alligator's open mouth. For a dramatic effect, you can change the orientation of the picture and the placeholder on the slide by rotating them. Dragging the green **rotation handle** above a selected object allows you to rotate an object in any direction. The following steps move and rotate the Alligator Head picture and the Special Events text box.

1
- Click the Alligator Head picture to select it and then position the mouse pointer over the rotation handle so that it changes to a Free Rotate pointer (Figure 8–38).

 I selected the picture, but I cannot see the rotation handle. Why?

The rotation handle may not be visible at the top of the slide layout. Drag the picture downward, and the rotation hand will appear.

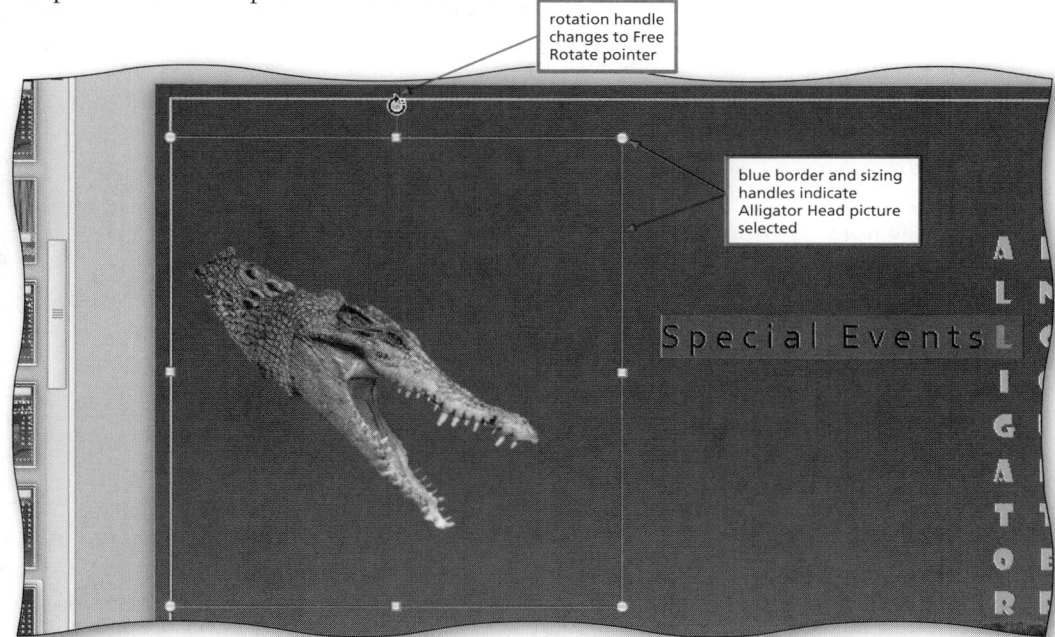

Figure 8–38

2
- Drag the mouse pointer counterclockwise so that it is displayed as shown in Figure 8–39.

3
- Drag the picture to position it in the upper-left corner of the slide layout.

 How do I move the picture in small increments?

To move or nudge the picture in very small increments, hold down the CTRL key with the picture selected while pressing the UP ARROW, DOWN ARROW, RIGHT ARROW, or LEFT ARROW keys.

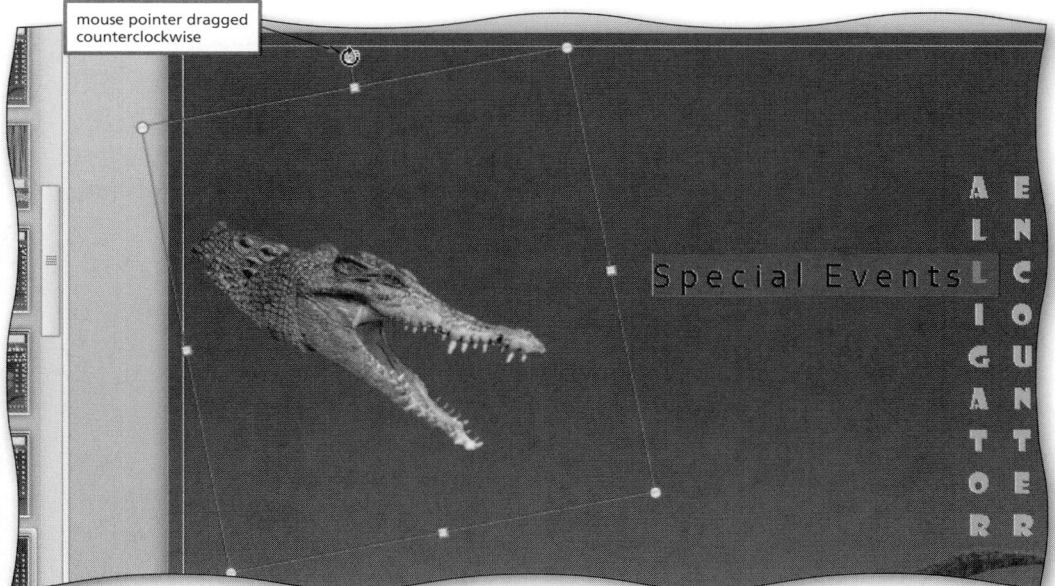

Figure 8–39

4

- Click the Special Events text box to select it, position the mouse pointer over the rotation handle so that it changes to a Free Rotate pointer, and then drag the text box clockwise so that it is at the same angle as the alligator's mouth.

- Drag the text box into the alligator's mouth as shown in Figure 8–40.

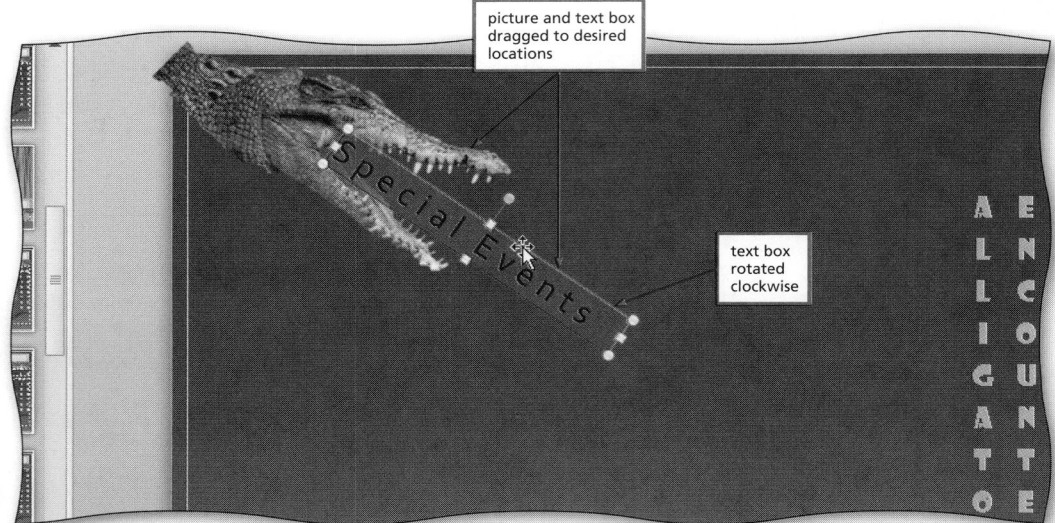

Figure 8–40

To Hide and Unhide Background Graphics

The placeholder, text box, pictures, and other graphical elements are displayed on some slide master layouts and are hidden on others. You have the ability to change the default setting by choosing to hide or unhide the background graphics. The Title Slide Layout, by default, hides the background elements. Because alligators often hide in the marshy swamps, you want to convey this setting by displaying the Alligator Encounter placeholder and the alligator picture you inserted. The following steps unhide the background graphics on the Title Slide Layout, which is the first layout below the Thatch Slide Master in the Overview pane.

1

- Scroll up to display the Title Slide Layout and then display the Slide Master tab (Figure 8–41).

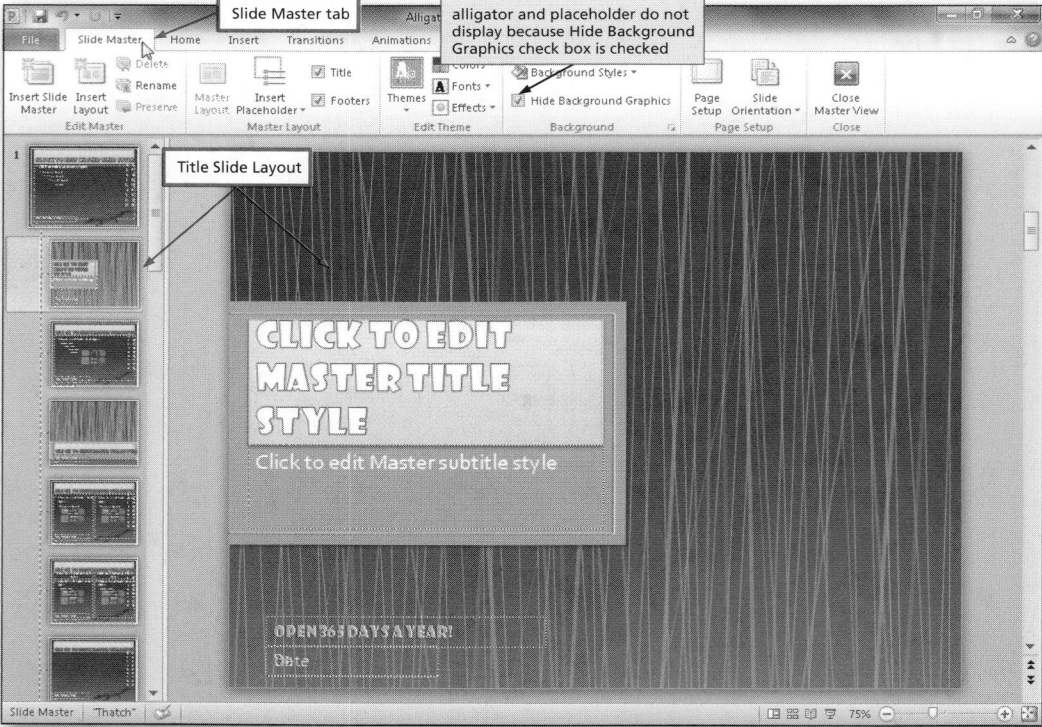

Figure 8–41

2

- Click the Hide Background Graphics check box (Slide Master tab | Background group) to remove the check mark in it (Figure 8–42).

Q&A

If I decide to hide the graphics, do I click the same check box to make them disappear?

Yes. The Hide Background Graphics check box is a toggle that displays and conceals the graphics.

Figure 8–42

To Rename a Slide Master and a Slide Layout

Once all the changes are made to a slide master and a slide layout, you may want to rename them with meaningful names that describe their functions or features. The new slide master name will be displayed on the status bar; the new layout name will be displayed in the Slide Layout gallery. The following steps rename the Thatch Slide Master, the Title Slide Layout, the Blank Layout, and the Title and Content Layout.

1

- Display the Thatch Slide Master and then click the Rename button (Slide Master tab | Edit Master group) to display the Rename Layout dialog box.

- Delete the text in the Layout name text box (Rename Layout dialog box) and then type **Alligator** in the text box (Figure 8–43).

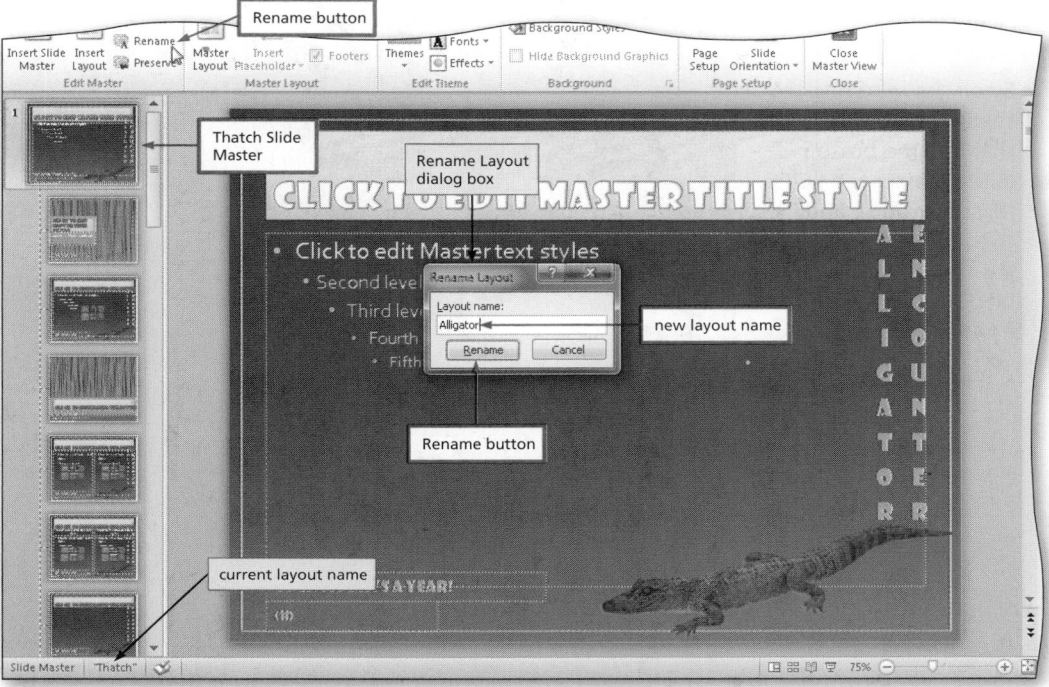

Figure 8–43

- Click the Rename button (Rename Layout dialog box) to give the layout the new name, Alligator Slide Master.

- Display the Title Slide Layout, click the Rename button (Slide Master tab | Edit Master group), and then type **Alligator Hiding** as the new layout name (Figure 8–44).

Figure 8–44

4

- Click the Rename button (Rename Layout dialog box) to rename the Title Slide layout.

- Scroll down to display the Blank Layout, click the Rename button (Slide Master tab | Edit Master group), and then type **Special Events** as the new layout name (Figure 8–45).

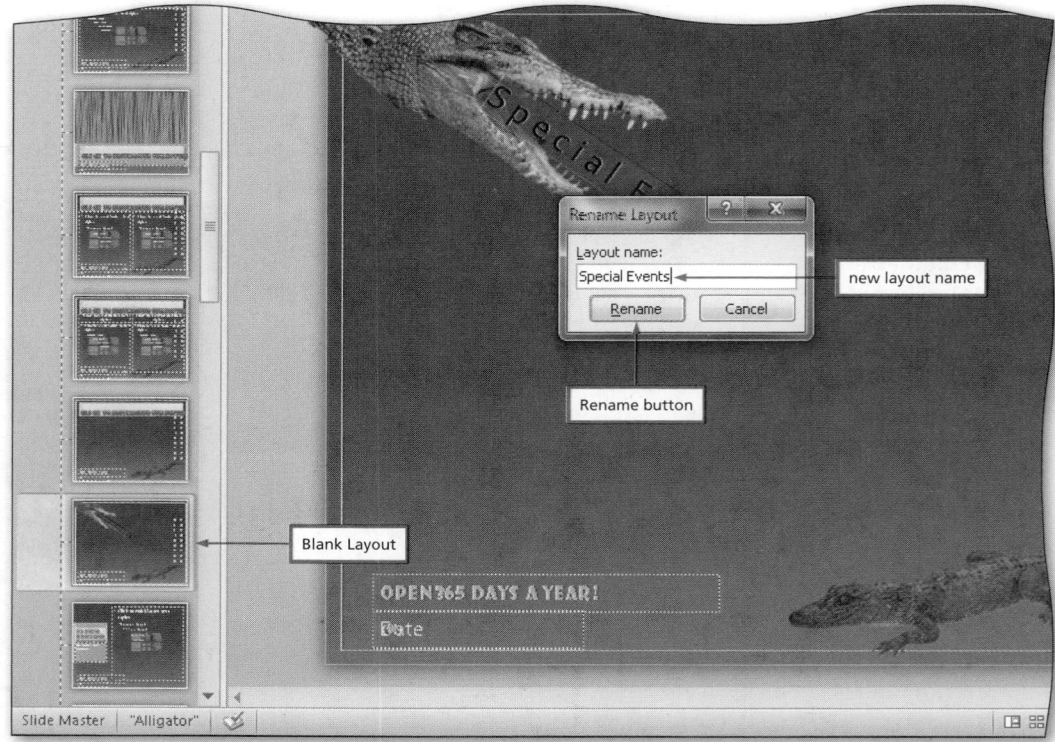

Figure 8–45

- Click the Rename button (Rename Layout dialog box).
- Scroll up to display the Title and Content Layout, click the Rename button (Slide Master tab | Edit Master group), and then type **Miscellaneous** as the new layout name (Figure 8–46).

- Click the Rename button (Rename Layout dialog box).

Figure 8–46

To Delete a Slide Layout

You have made many changes to the slide master and two slide layouts. You will use these layouts and the Title and Content Layout, which is now called the Miscellaneous layout, when you close Master view and then add text, graphics, or other content to the presentation in Normal view. You can delete the other layouts in the Overview pane because you will not use them. The following steps delete slide layouts that will not be used to create the presentation.

- Click the Section Header Layout in the Overview pane to select it (Figure 8–47).

Figure 8–47

- Press and hold down the SHIFT key and then click the Title Only Layout to select four consecutive layouts (Figure 8–48).

Q&A Why did I select only these four layouts?

The layout below the Title Only Layout is the Special Events Layout, and you will use that layout when you create Slide 2 in your presentation.

Figure 8–48

- Press the DELETE key to delete the four layouts.

- Click the Content with Caption Layout, press and hold down the SHIFT key, and then click the last layout, which is the Vertical Title and Text Layout, in the Overview pane (Figure 8–49).

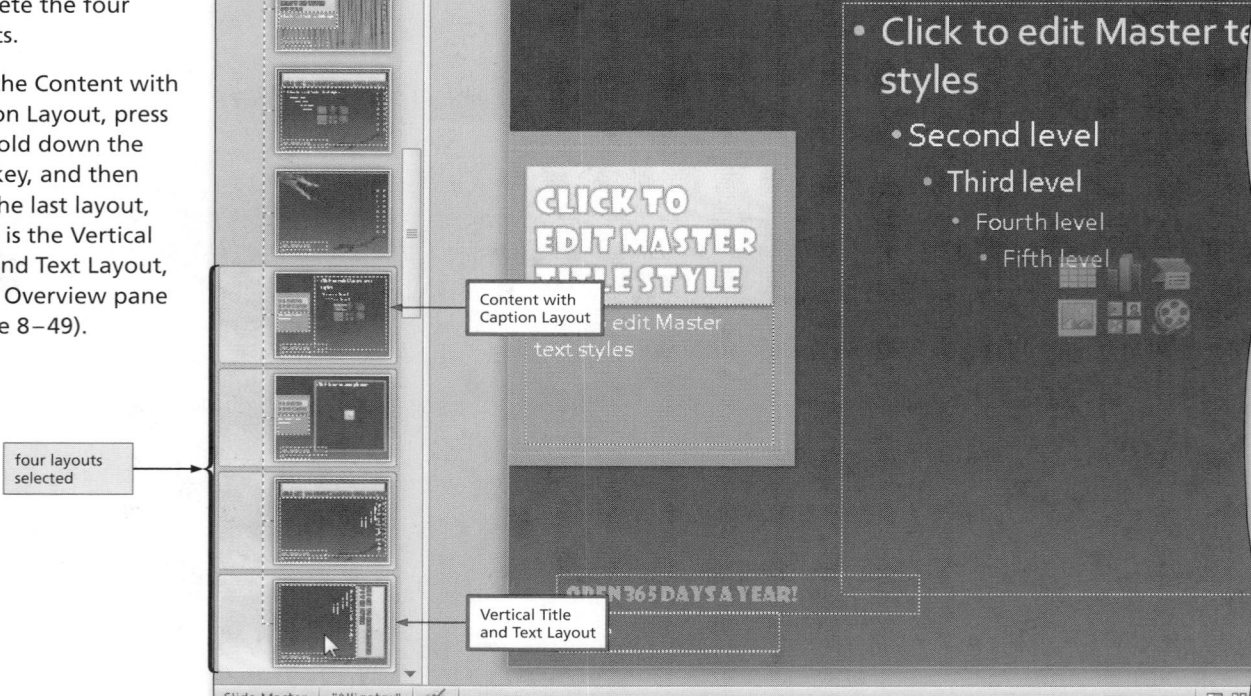

Figure 8–49

4

• Press the DELETE key to delete the four layouts (Figure 8–50).

Q&A
Now that I have created this slide master, can I ensure that it will not be changed when I create future presentations?

Yes. Normally a slide master is deleted when a new design template is selected. To keep the original master as part of your presentation, you can preserve it by selecting the thumbnail and then clicking the Preserve button in the Edit Master group. An icon in the shape of a pushpin

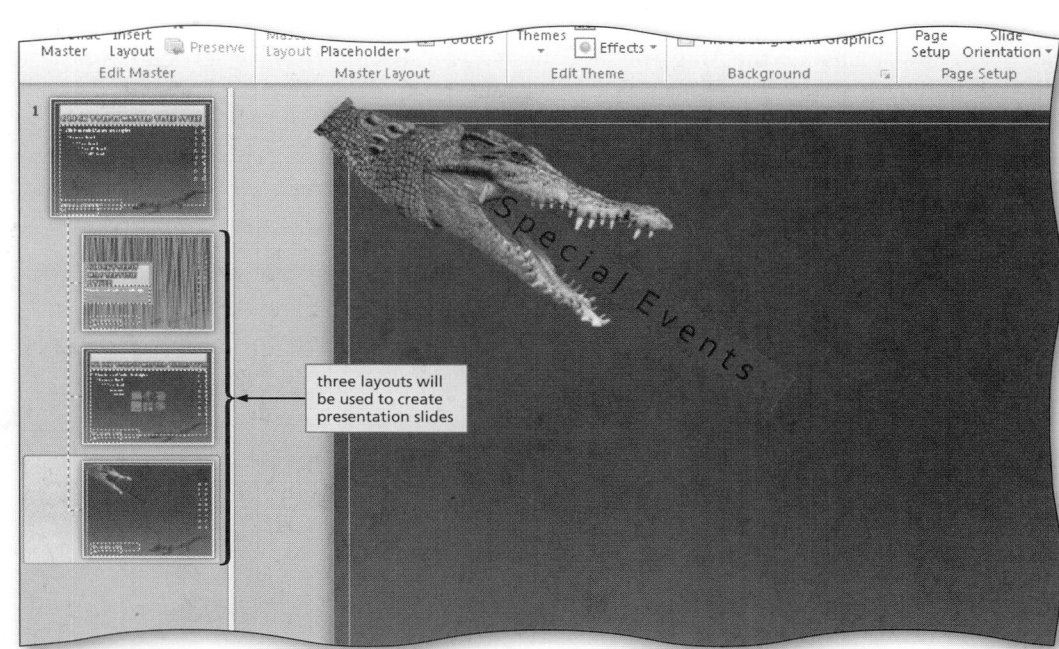

three layouts will be used to create presentation slides

Figure 8–50

is displayed below the slide number to indicate the master is preserved. If you decide to unpreserve a slide master, select this thumbnail and then click the Preserve button.

Other Ways
1. Click Delete button (Home tab | Slides group)
2. Right-click selected slide, click Delete Layout on shortcut menu

Break Point: If you wish to take a break, this is a good place to do so. You can quit PowerPoint now. To resume at a later time, start PowerPoint and continue following the steps from this location forward.

Decide how to distribute copies of slides.
Printed copies of your slides or handouts can give your audience the ability to follow the main points of your presentation and to write notes. Depending upon the venue and the audience, you might decide to limit the number of copies of the printed version of your presentation. As an alternative, you can put the file in a shared location, such as a Web site or a company's intranet. You can tell your audience members before the presentation where to locate the slides, and they can decide whether they want to download and print the copies. This option conserves ink and paper.

Plan Ahead

Customizing Handout and Notes Masters

You have used PowerPoint's slide master template file to create unique slide layouts for the Alligator Encounter presentation. PowerPoint also has master template files to create handouts and notes. If you are going to distribute handouts to your audience, you can customize the handout master so that it coordinates visually with the presentation slides and reinforces your message. In addition, if you are going to use speaker notes to guide you through a presentation, you can tailor the notes master to fit your needs.

BTW
Formatting the Date and Time Placeholder
The 'Date and time' footer can have a variety of formats. When you click the Update automatically arrow, you can choose among formats that display the day, date, and time in a variety of combinations.

To Customize a Handout Using a Handout Master

When you created the Alligator slide master, you specified the background, fonts, theme, and pictures for all slides. You likewise can create a specific handout master to determine the layout and graphics that will display on the printed page. Possible customization includes moving, restoring, and formatting the header and footer placeholders; setting the page number orientation; adding graphics; and specifying the number of slides to print on each page. The following steps use the handout master to create a custom handout.

1

- Display the View tab (Figure 8–51).

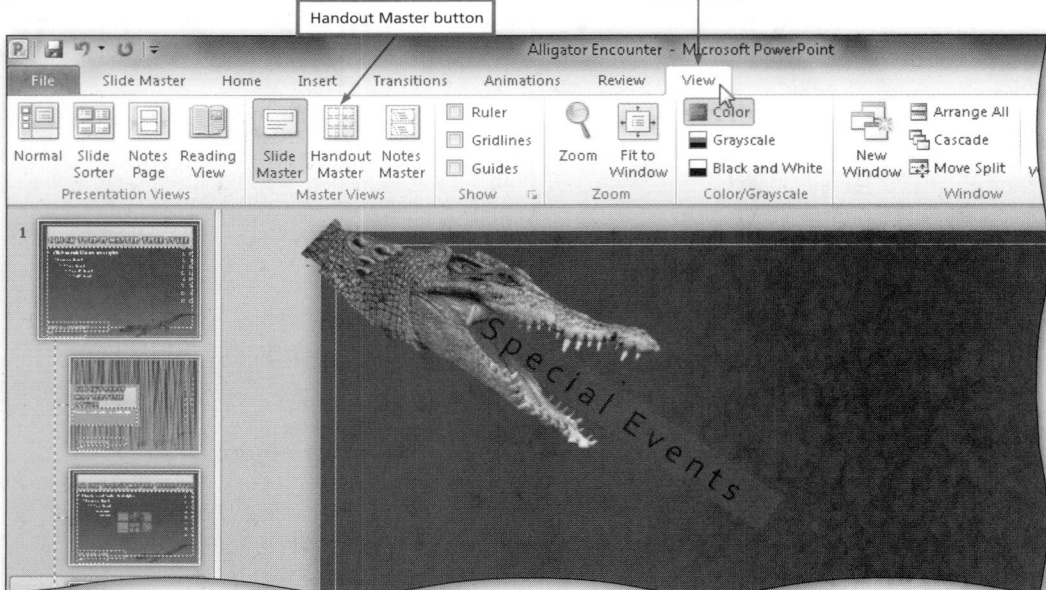

Figure 8–51

2

- Click the Handout Master button (View tab | Master Views group) to display the Handout Master tab and then click the Slides Per Page button (Handout Master tab | Page Setup group) to display the Slides Per Page gallery (Figure 8–52).

Q&A

Is 6 Slides the default layout for all themes?

Yes. If you have fewer than six slides in your presentation or want to display slide details, then choose a handout layout with 1, 2, 3, or 4 slides per sheet of paper.

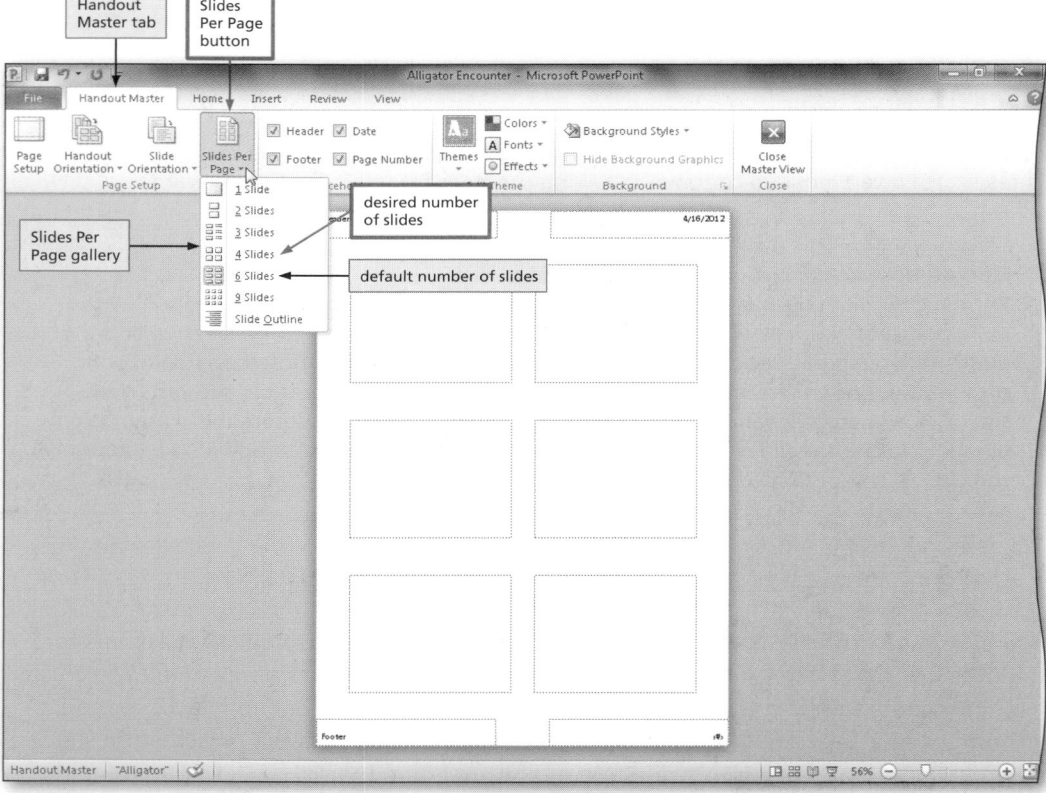

Figure 8–52

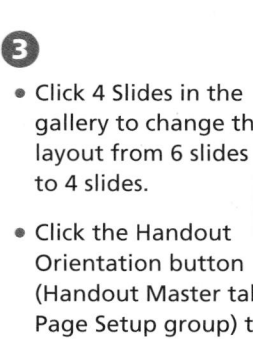

- Click 4 Slides in the gallery to change the layout from 6 slides to 4 slides.

- Click the Handout Orientation button (Handout Master tab | Page Setup group) to display the Handout Orientation gallery (Figure 8–53).

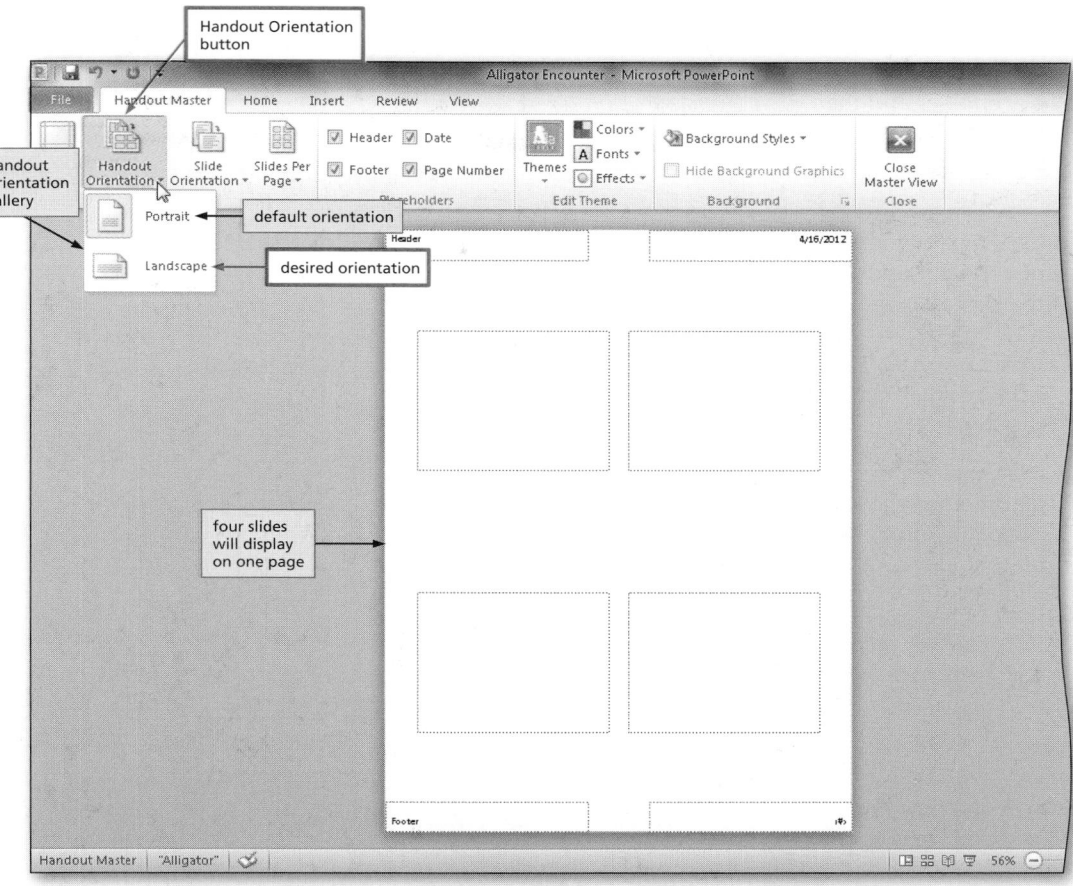

Figure 8–53

- Click Landscape in the gallery to display the page layout in landscape orientation (Figure 8–54).

Q&A

When should I change the orientation from portrait to landscape?

If your slide content is dominantly vertical, such as an athlete running or a skyscraper in a major city, consider using the default portrait orientation. If, however, your slide content has long lines of text or pictures of four-legged animals, landscape orientation may be a more appropriate layout.

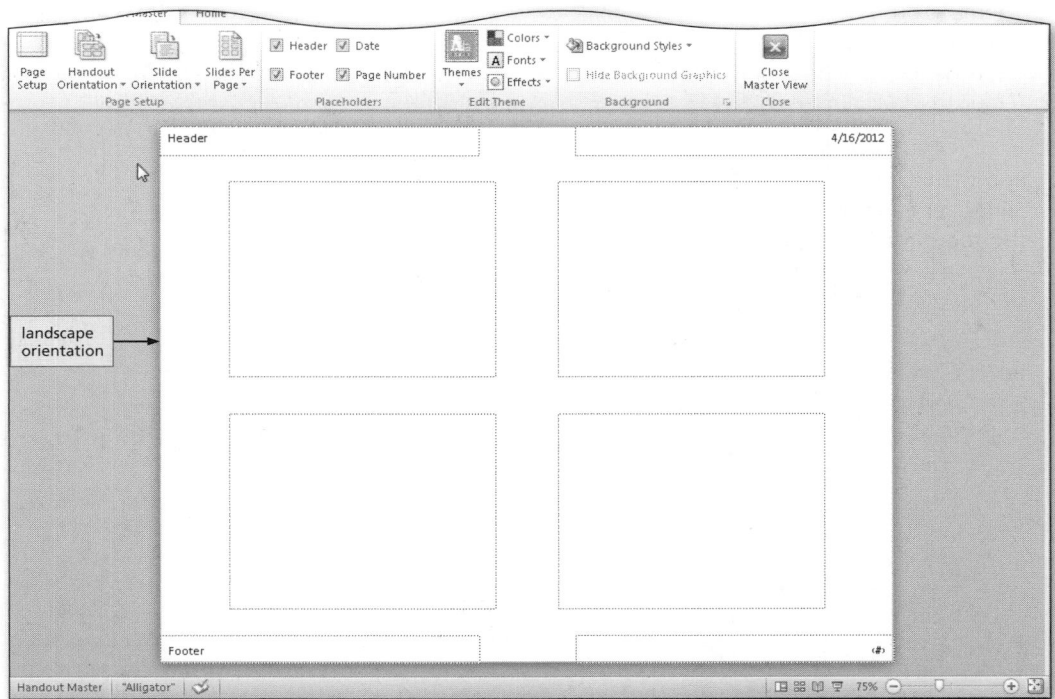

Figure 8–54

5

- Click the Header placeholder and then type **Alligator Encounter** as the header text.

- Click the Footer placeholder and then type **See alligators in their native environment** as the footer text.

- Drag the Footer placeholder above the page number placeholder (Figure 8–55).

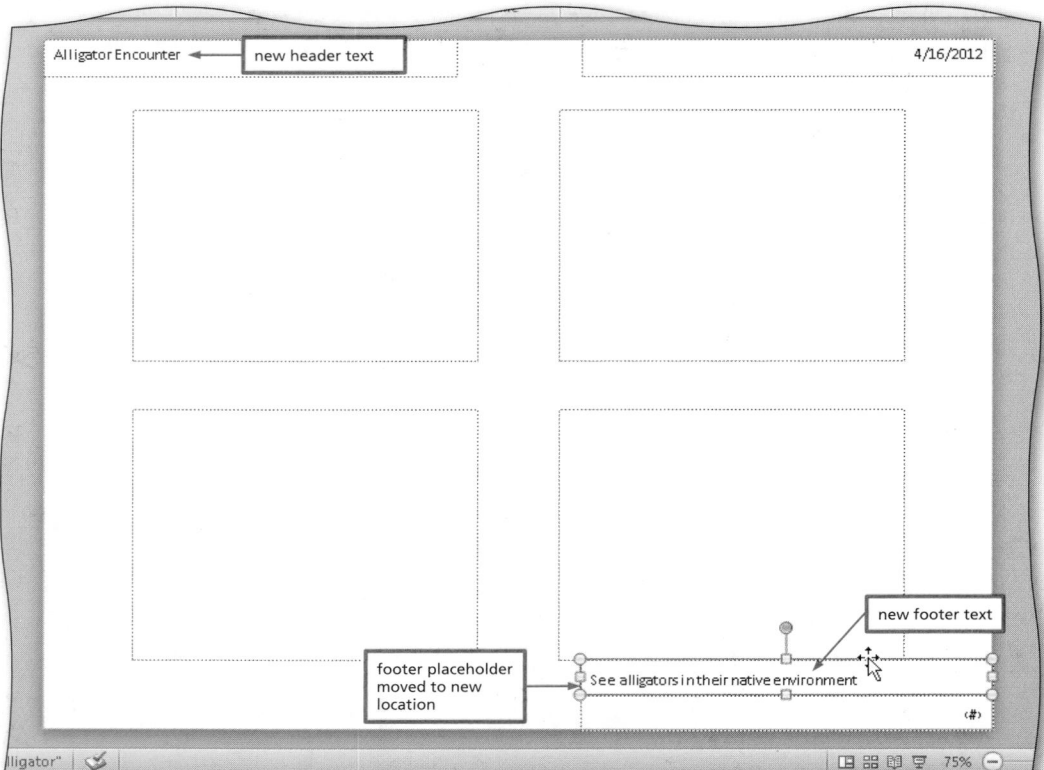

Figure 8–55

6

- Click the Theme Fonts button (Handout Master tab | Edit Theme group) to display the Theme Fonts gallery (Figure 8–56).

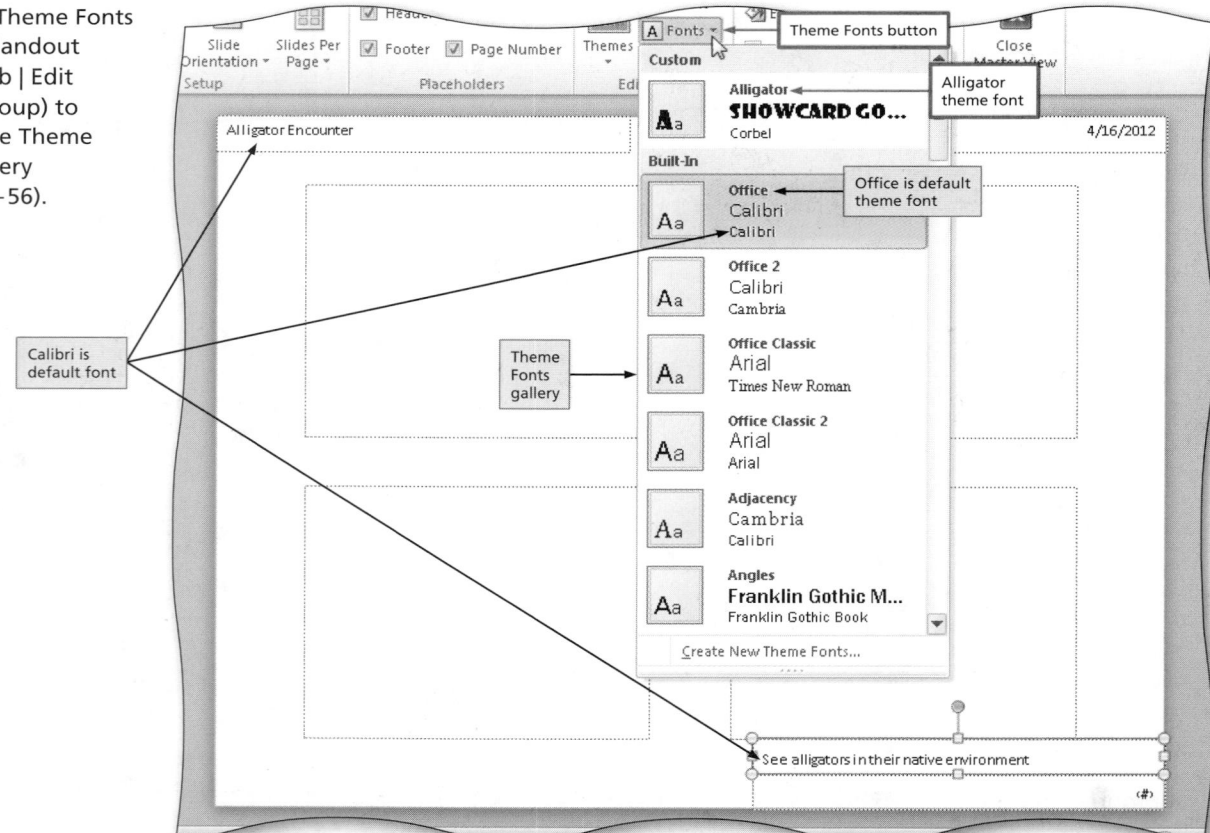

Figure 8–56

7

- Click Alligator in the Custom area of the gallery to apply the Corbel font to the text in the placeholders.

8

- Display the Insert tab, click the Insert Picture from File button (Insert tab | Images group), and then insert the Alligator Body picture located on the Data Files for Students.

- Rotate the Alligator Body picture clockwise, resize the picture so it is approximately 1.5" × 4.24", and then center it along the upper edge of the handout layout, as shown in Figure 8–57.

9

- Display the Insert tab, click the Header & Footer button (Insert tab | Text group), and then place a check mark in the 'Date and time' check box.

- Place a check mark in the Header check box.

- Place a check mark in the Footer check box (Figure 8–58).

10

- Click the Apply to All button (Header and Footer dialog box) to add the header and footer text and date to the handout master.

Q&A

Where will the header and footer display on the handout?

The black boxes in the Preview area show where these placeholders are located.

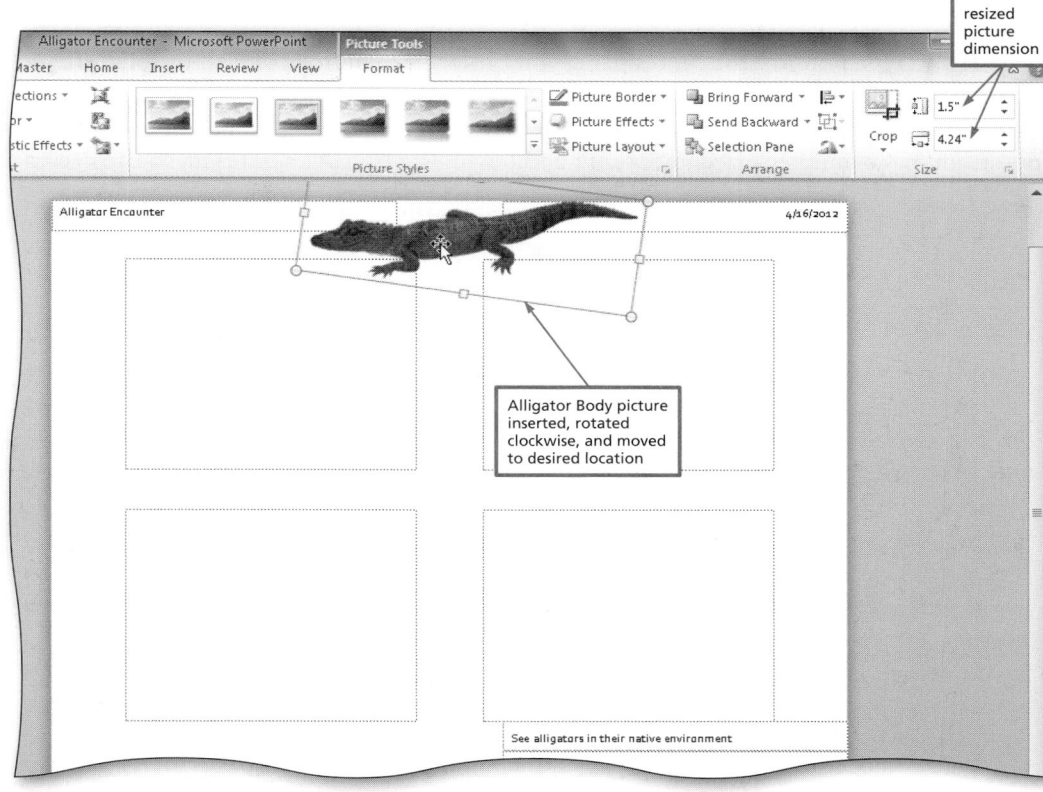

Figure 8–57

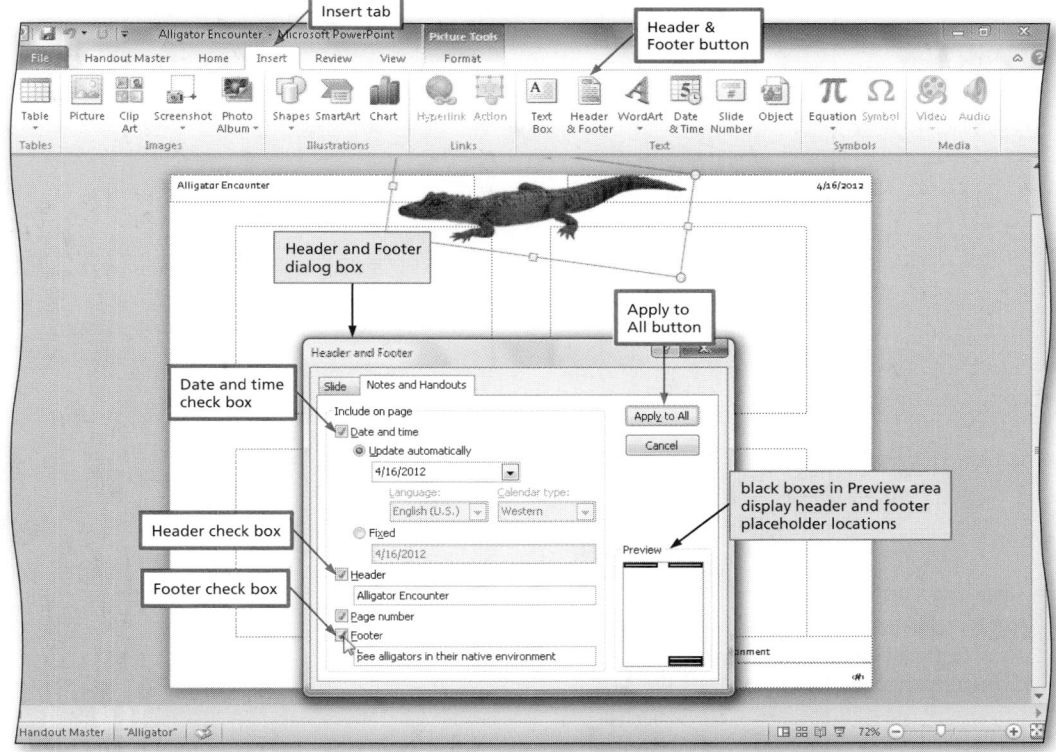

Figure 8–58

To Customize a Notes Page Using a Notes Master

If you type notes in the Notes pane, you can print them for yourself or for your audience. The basic format found in the Backstage view generally suffices for handouts, but you may desire to alter the layout using the notes master. As with the slide master and handout master, you can add graphics and rearrange and format the header, footer, and page number placeholders. The following steps use the notes master to create a custom handout.

- Display the View tab (Figure 8–59).

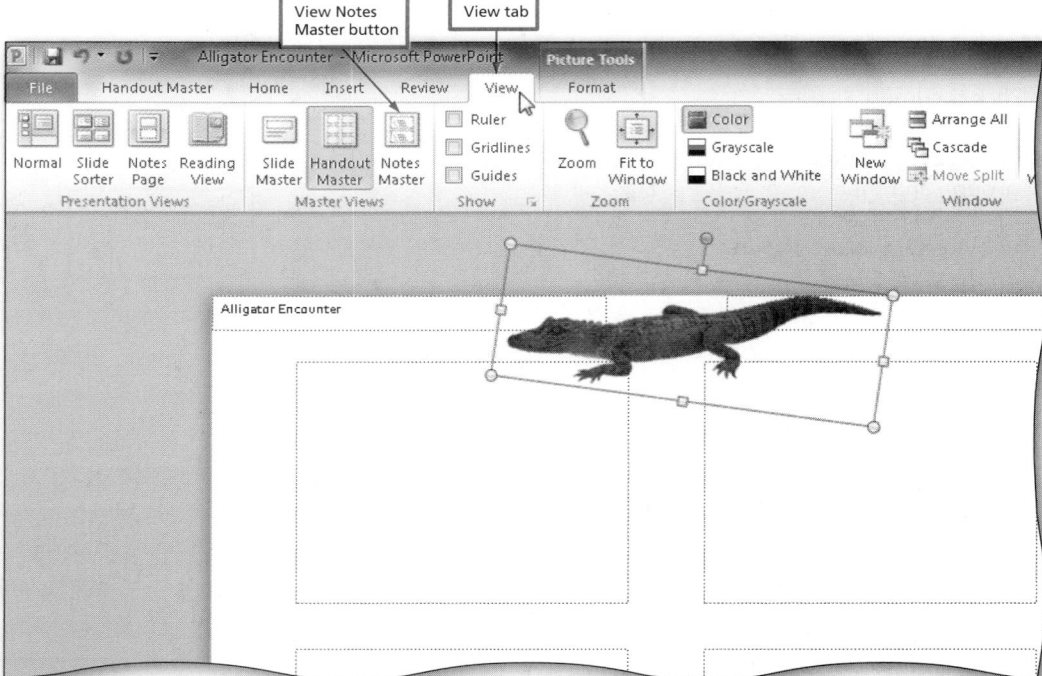

Figure 8–59

- Click the View Notes Master button (View tab | Master Views group) to display the Notes Master tab.

- Click the Footer placeholder, delete the text, and then type See more than 100 alligators as the new footer text.

- Click the Theme Fonts button (Notes Master tab | Edit Theme group) to display the Theme Fonts gallery (Figure 8–60).

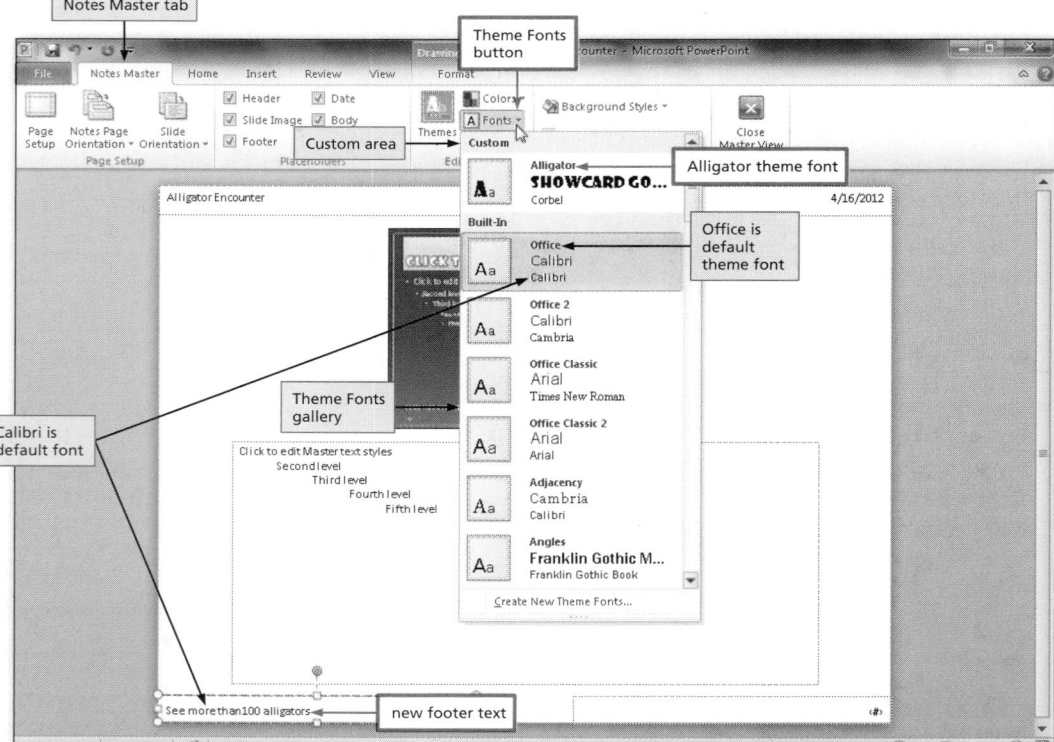

Figure 8–60

4

- Click Alligator in the Custom area of the Theme Fonts gallery to apply the Corbel font to the text in the header, footer, date, and page number placeholders.

- Click the Notes Page Orientation button (Notes Master tab | Page Setup group) to display the Notes Page Orientation gallery (Figure 8–61).

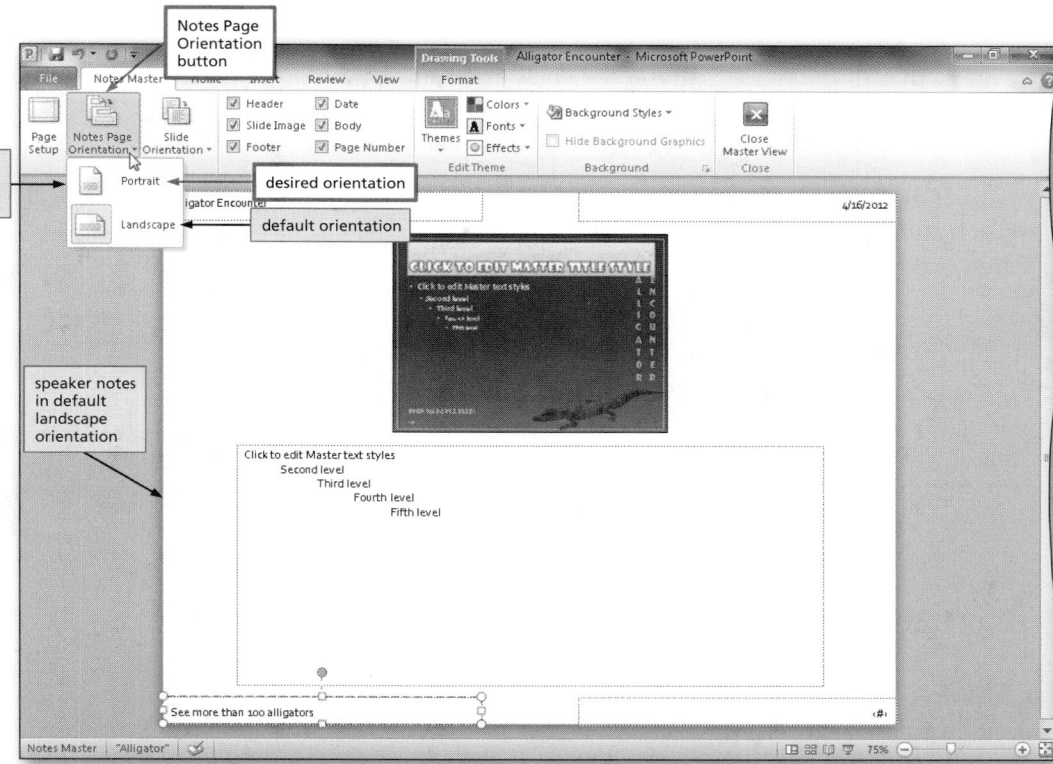

Figure 8–61

5

- Click Portrait in the gallery to display the page layout in portrait orientation.

- Display the Insert tab, click the Insert Picture from File button (Insert tab | Images group), and then insert the Alligator Body picture located on the Data Files for Students.

- Resize the picture so that it is approximately 1.25" × 4".

- Move the picture to the lower-right corner of the layout, as shown in Figure 8–62.

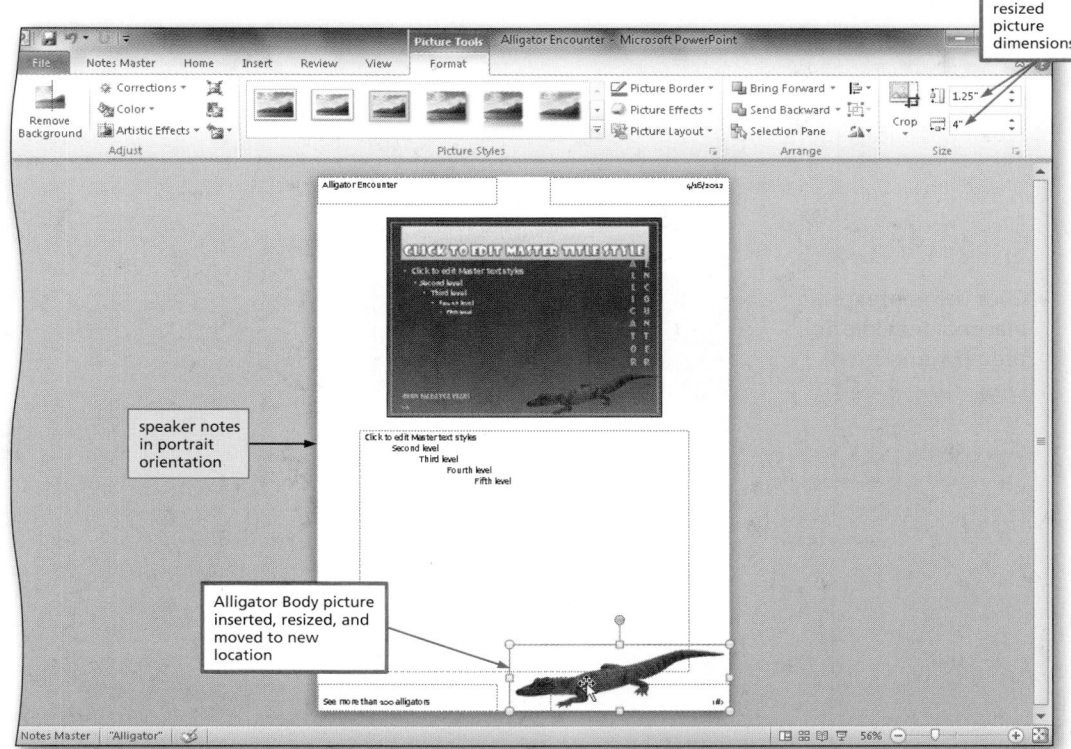

Figure 8–62

To Close Master View

Now that all the changes to the slide master, handout master, and notes master are complete, you can exit Master view and return to Normal view. The following steps close Master view.

- Display the Notes Master tab (Figure 8–63).

- Click the Close Master View button (Notes Master tab | Close group) to exit Master view and return to Normal view.

Figure 8–63

To Save a Master as a Template

The changes and enhancements you have made to the Alligator Encounter slide master, handout master, and notes master are excellent starting points for future presentations. The background text and graphics allow users to add text boxes, pictures, SmartArt, tables, and other elements depending upon the specific message that needs to be communicated to an audience. You can save your slide layouts as a template to use for a new presentation and use the revised handout and notes masters to print unique pages. The following steps save the Alligator masters as a template on your USB drive.

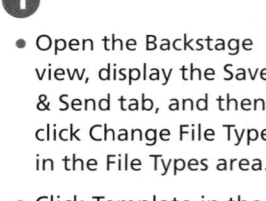

- Open the Backstage view, display the Save & Send tab, and then click Change File Type in the File Types area.

- Click Template in the Presentation File Types area (Figure 8–64).

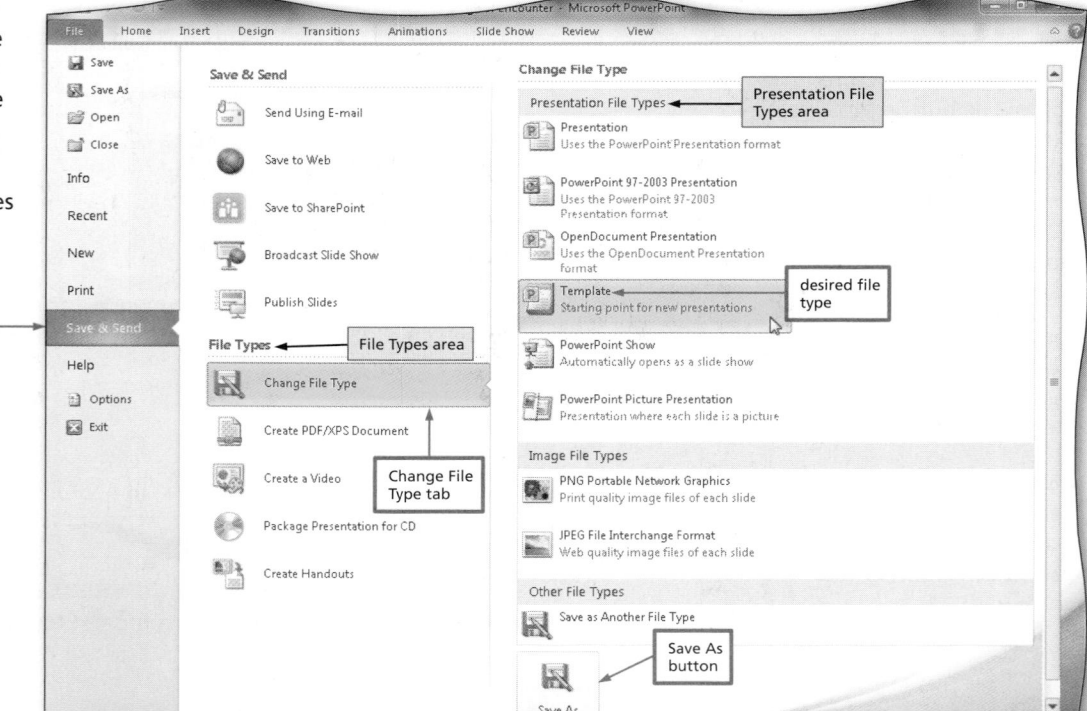

Figure 8–64

- Click the Save As button below the Other File Types area to display the Save As dialog box.

- Type **Alligator Template** in the File name text box (Figure 8–65).

- If necessary, navigate to the desired location to save the file and then click the Save button (Save As dialog box) to save the Alligator Encounter presentation as a template.

❹

- Close the Alligator Template file.

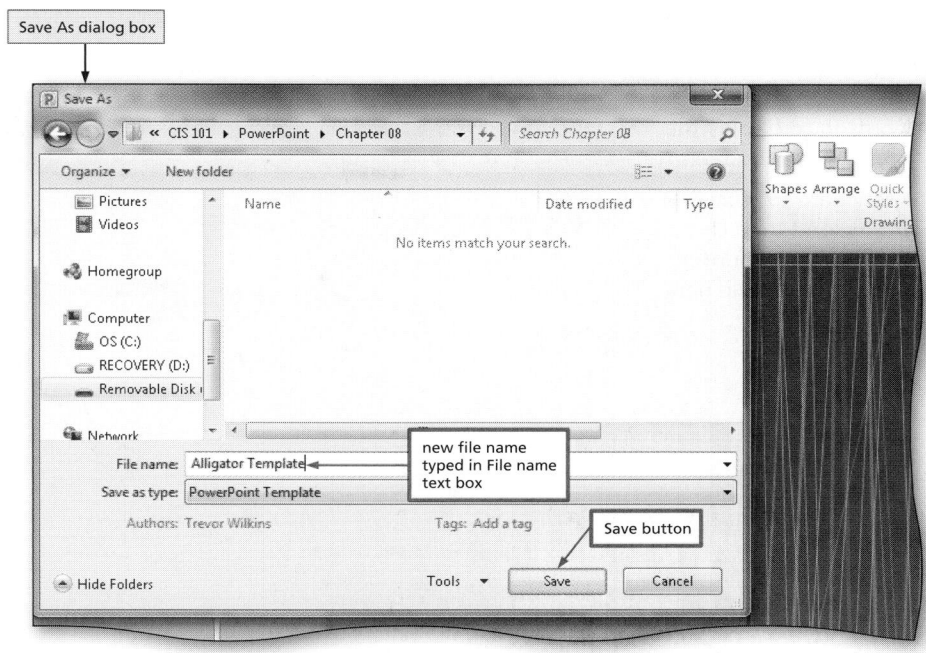

Figure 8–65

Break Point: If you wish to take a break, this is a good place to do so. You can quit PowerPoint now. To resume at a later time, start PowerPoint and continue following the steps from this location forward.

To Open a Template and Save a Presentation

The Alligator Template file you created is a convenient start to a new presentation. The graphical elements and essential slide content are in place; you then can customize the layouts for a specific need, such as a new event or special program. The following steps open the Alligator Template file and save the presentation with the Alligator Encounter name.

❶

- Open the file, Alligator Template, from your USB flash drive.

- Open the Backstage view, display the Save & Send tab, and then click Change File Type in the File Types area.

- Click Presentation in the Presentation File Types area (Figure 8–66).

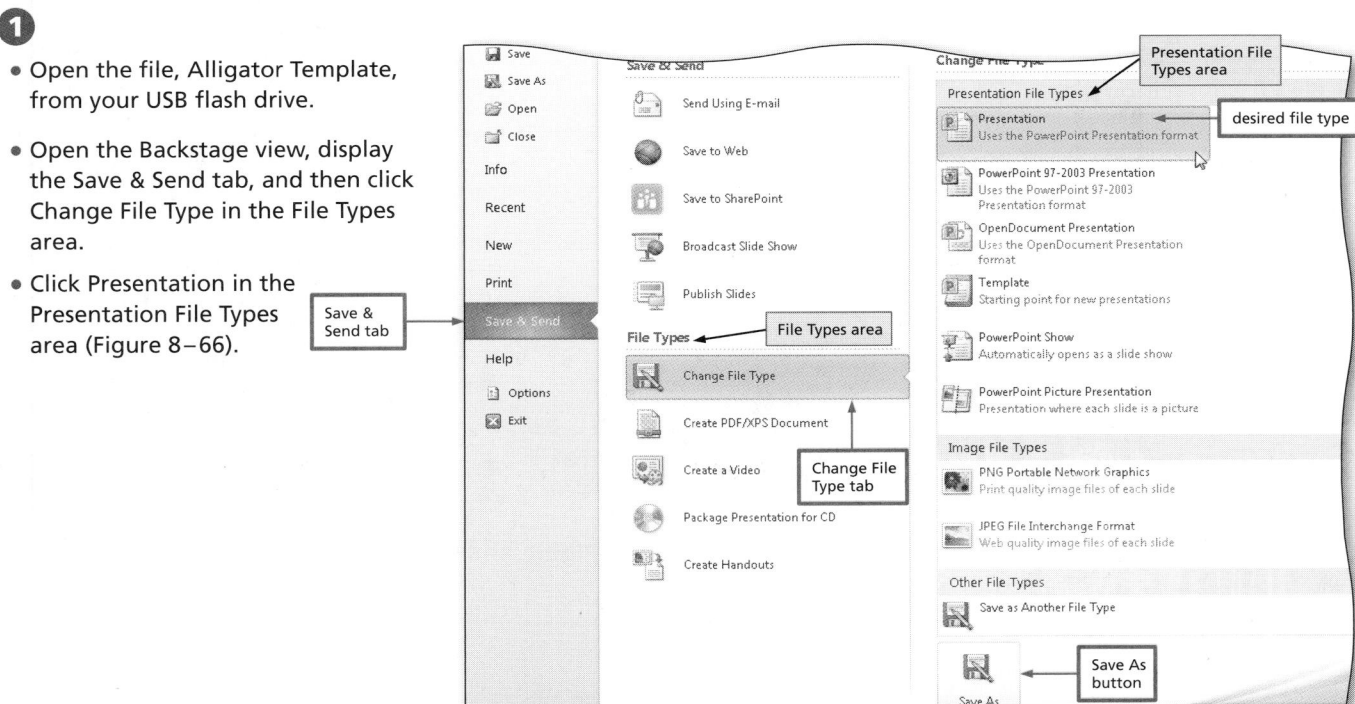

Figure 8–66

- Click the Save As button to display the Save As dialog box.
- Navigate to your USB drive and then click Alligator Encounter to select the file name (Figure 8–67).

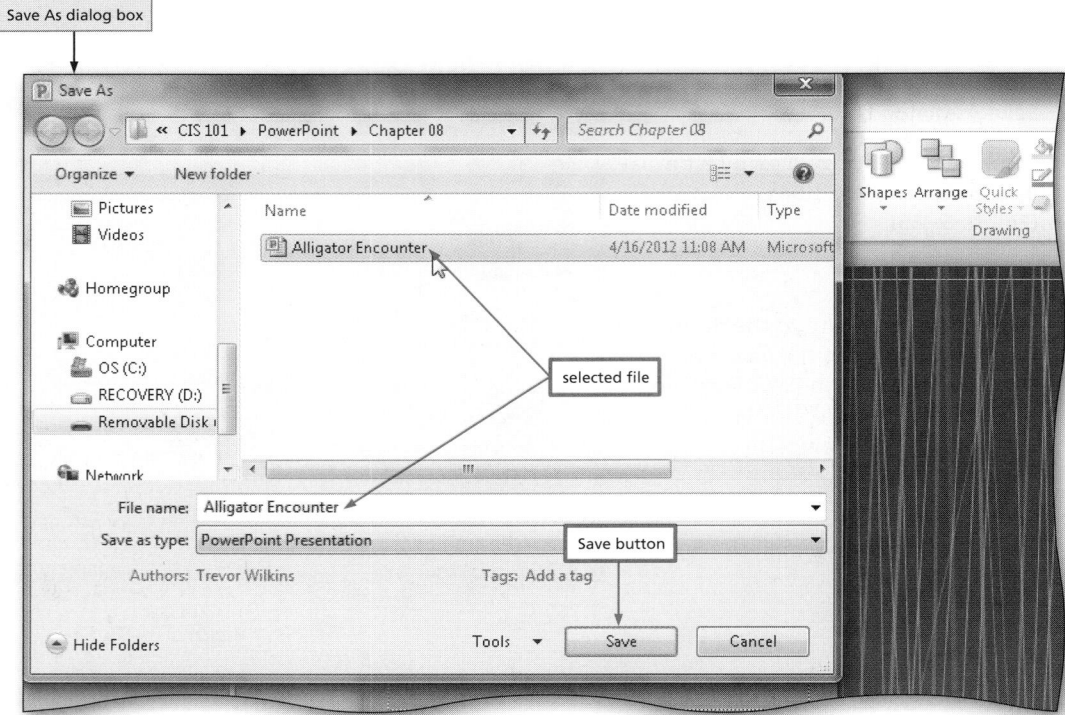

Figure 8–67

- Click the Save button (Save As dialog box) to display the Confirm Save As dialog box (Figure 8–68).

- Click the Yes button to replace the file.

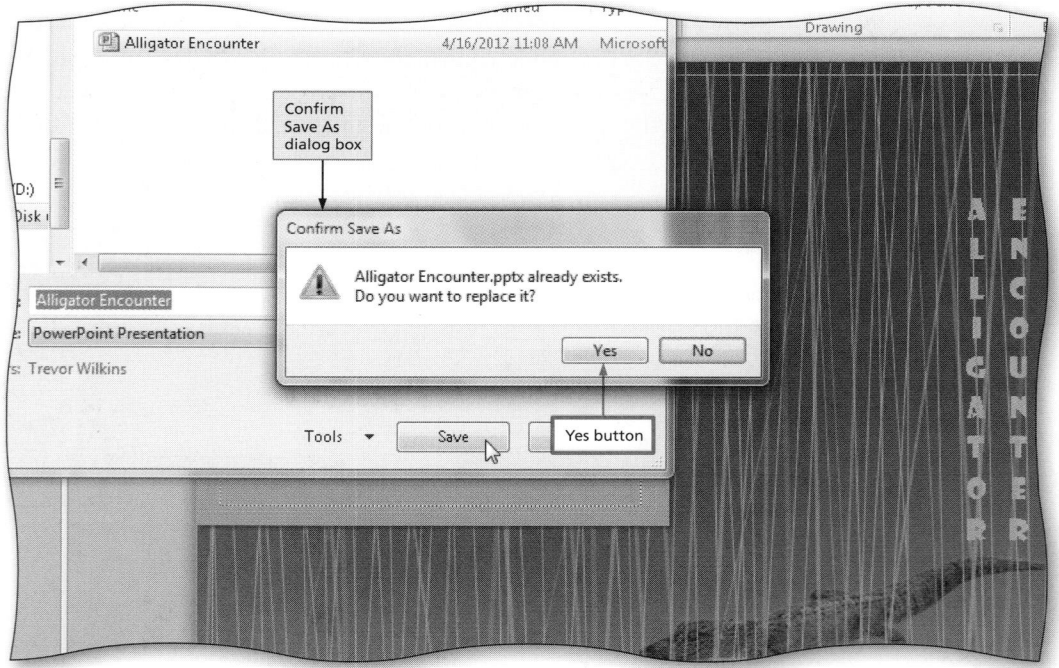

Figure 8–68

To Add Text and Notes to the Title Slide

By default, the Title Slide Layout, which was renamed Alligator Hiding, is applied to the first slide. The following steps add text and speaker notes to Slide 1.

1 With the title slide displaying, type `Enjoy a Guided Swamp Safari` as the title text and `Ecotours in a natural environment` as the subtitle text.

2 Click the Notes pane and type `The length of average American male alligators is 11.2 feet and average female alligators is 8.2 feet. They live about 50 years in freshwater swamps, rivers, marshes, and lakes.` (Figure 8–69).

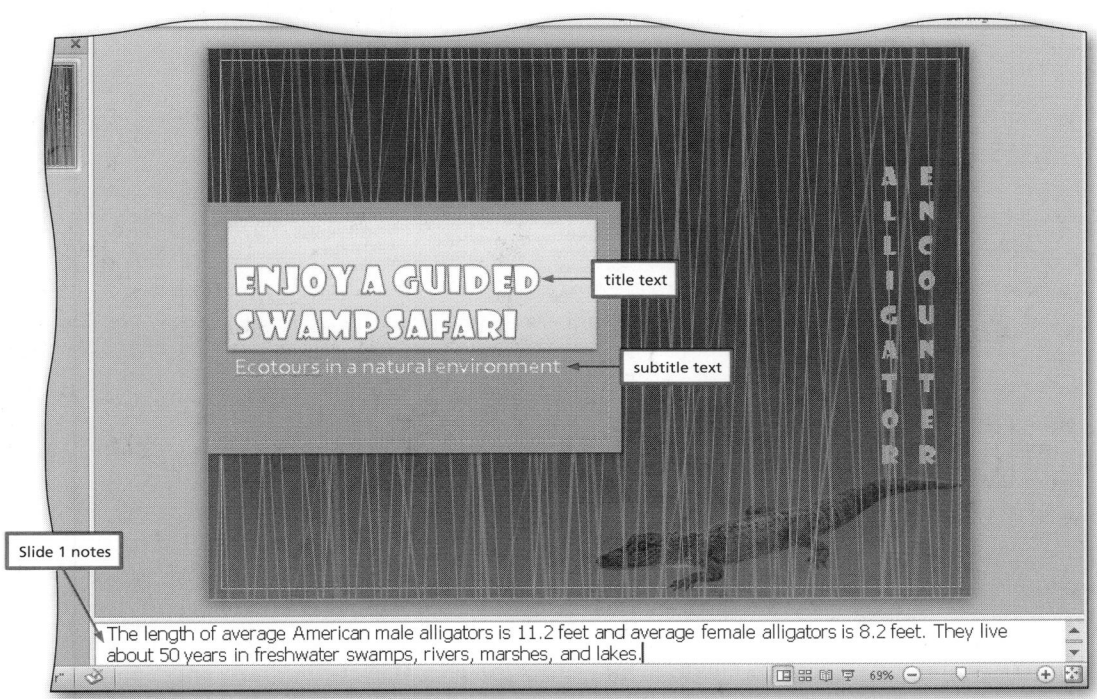

Figure 8–69

To Add Text and Notes to the Blank Layout

The second slide in your presentation will feature the June special event, which is a night excursion into the swamp. The Special Events slide layout, which is the new name for the Blank Layout, is designed so that you can add variable slide content below the alligator picture in the upper-left corner. The following steps add a text box and speaker notes to Slide 2.

1 Insert a slide with the Special Events layout and then insert a text box between the two alligator pictures. Type `Sunset tours available on weekends in June` as the text box text.

2 Increase the text box font size to 32 point and then, if necessary, adjust the text box borders so the text is displayed on two lines.

3 In the Notes pane, type `An alligator has approximately 80 teeth that are replaced as they wear down. Its diet consists of birds, fish, frogs, and small mammals.` (Figure 8–70).

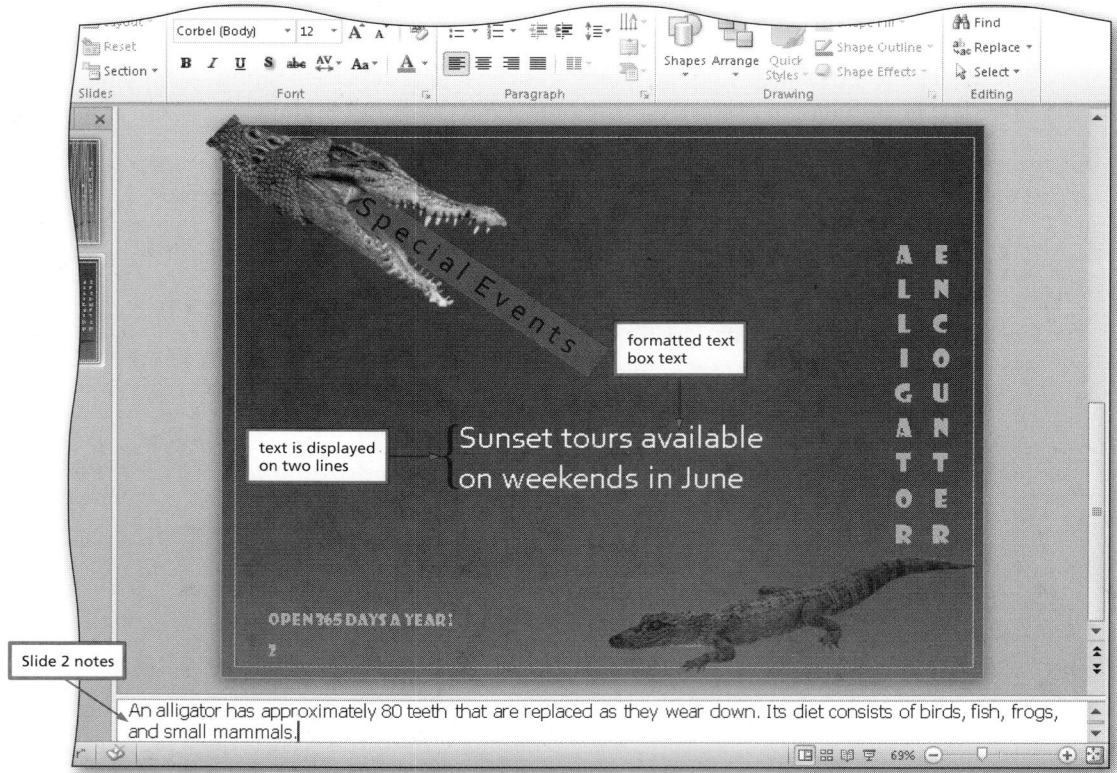

Figure 8–70

BTW

Customer Experience Improvement Program
You can contribute to the design and development of Microsoft products by participating in the company's Customer Experience Improvement Program (CEIP). If you choose to sign up for the program, your computer will send information to Microsoft automatically about how you use Microsoft products and other third-party applications. CEIP reports include your computer's configuration, the programs' performance and reliability, and how you use the programs' features. Microsoft uses the data to improve frequently used elements and to solve common problems.

To Add Text, Notes, and a Picture to the Title and Content Layout

The third slide in your presentation will list details about the nature park's admission and tour prices, swamp tour hours, and telephone number. The Miscellaneous layout, which is the new name for the Title and Content slide layout, will allow you to insert text into the content placeholder. The following steps insert a slide and add text and a picture to the title and content placeholder.

1 Insert a slide with the Miscellaneous layout and then type `Hours and Rates` as the title text.

2 Type `One-hour tours starting at 10 a.m.` as the first content placeholder paragraph.

3 Type `Last tour departs at 6 p.m.` as the second paragraph.

4 Type `Adults: $24.95; Children under 18: $10.95` as the third paragraph.

5 Type `Call 555-8404 for reservations today!` as the fourth paragraph.

6 In the Notes pane, type `Tours will be canceled in inclement weather. Maximum tour size is 20 people.`

7 Insert the picture with the file name, Letter A, located on the Data Files for Students, and then move the picture above the content footer placeholder (Figure 8–71).

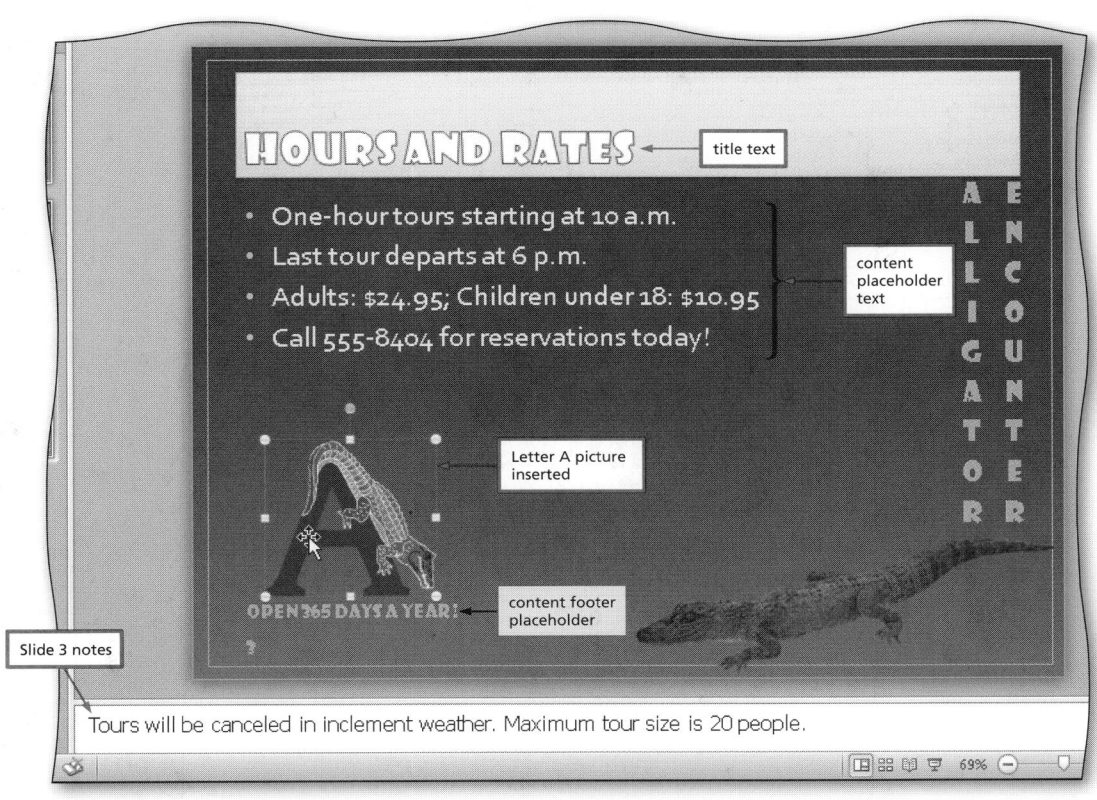

Figure 8–71

To Apply a Fill Color to a Slide

Earlier in this project, you formatted the interior of the Special Event text box by applying a fill. In a similar manner, you can apply a fill to an entire slide by selecting a color from the Shape Fill gallery. If desired, you can increase the transparency to soften the color. Because the Special Events text box on Slide 2 is red, you can coordinate the Slide 3 fill color by changing the Slide 3 background to red. The following steps apply a fill to Slide 3 and increase the transparency.

1

- With Slide 3 displaying, right-click anywhere on the green background to display the shortcut menu.

- Click Format Background on the shortcut menu to display the Format Background dialog box (Figure 8–72).

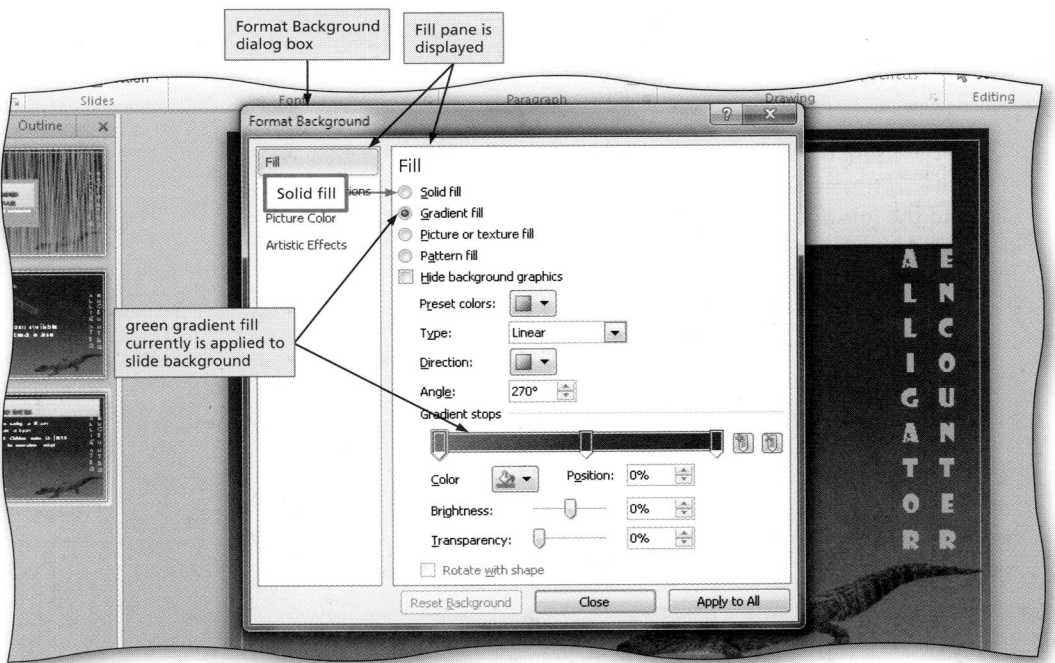

Figure 8–72

2

• With the Fill pane displaying, click Solid fill to reduce the fill options and to display the Fill Color area.

• Click the Color button in the Fill Color area to display the Fill Color gallery (Figure 8–73).

Q&A Can I experiment with previewing the background colors?

No live preview feature is available.

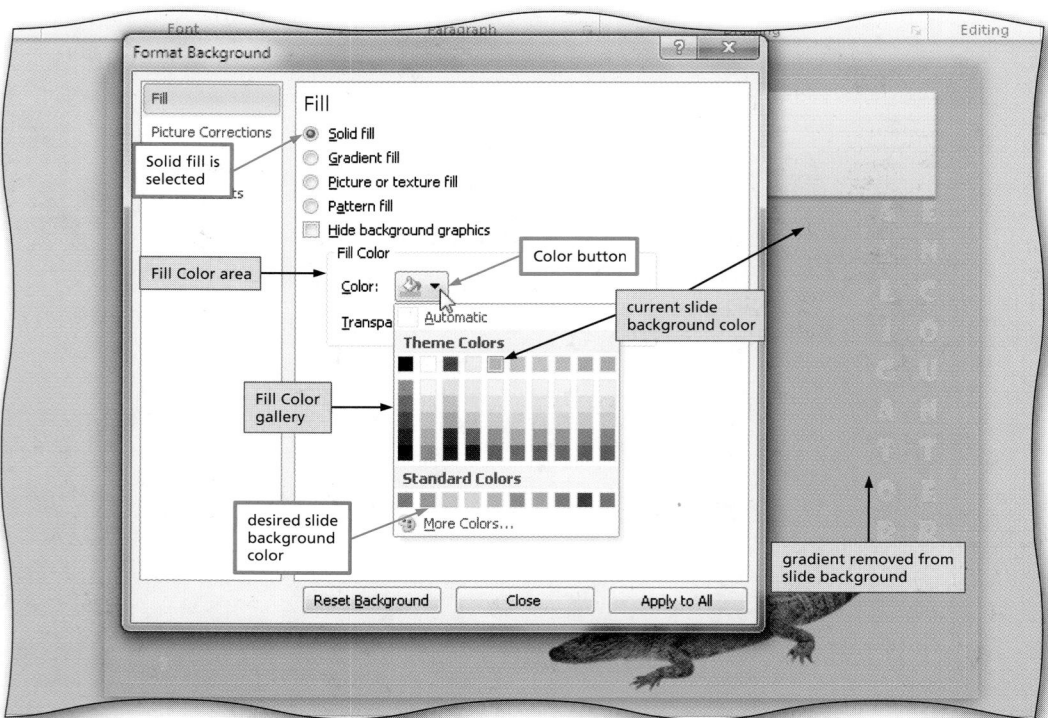

Figure 8–73

3

• Click Red (second color in Standard Colors row) to change the slide background color.

• Click the Transparency slider in the Fill Color area and drag it to the right until 20% is displayed in the Transparency text box (Figure 8–74).

 **Experiment**

• Drag the Transparency slider to the left and right, and watch the text box background change.

Q&A How can I delete a fill color if I decide not to apply one to my slide?

Any fill effect in the Format Background dialog box is applied immediately. If this dialog box is displayed, click the Reset Background button. If you already have applied the fill color, you must click the Undo button on the Quick Access Toolbar.

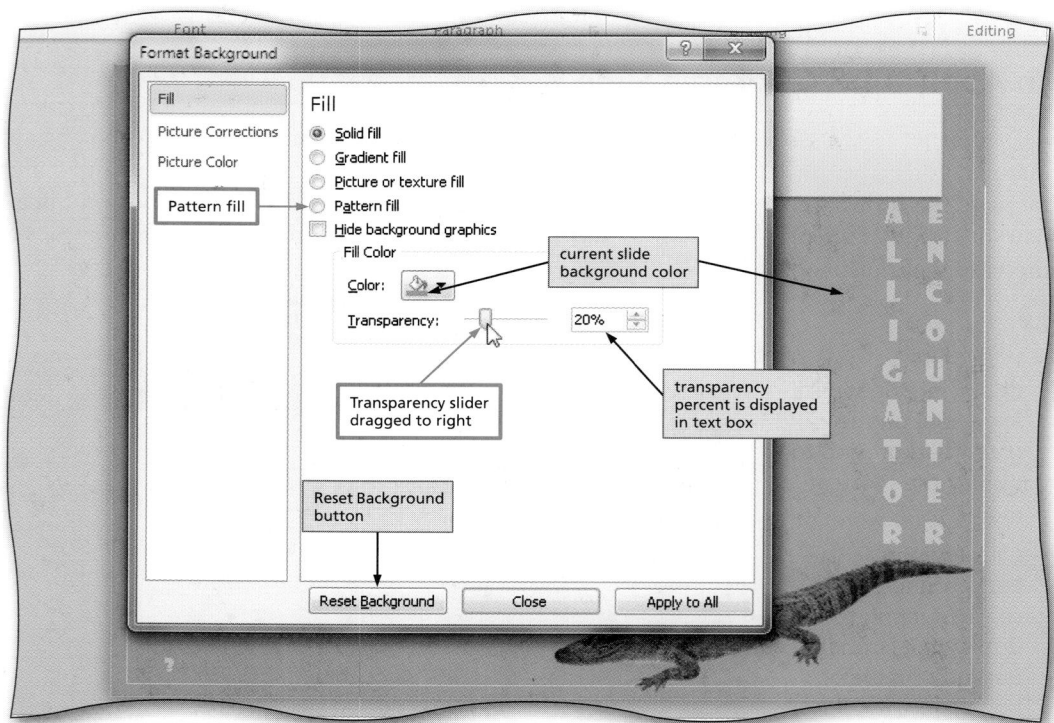

Figure 8–74

Other Ways

1. Enter percentage in Transparency text box	2. Click Transparency up or down arrow

To Apply a Pattern to a Slide

You add variety to a slide by adding a **pattern fill**. This design of repeating horizontal or vertical lines, dots, dashes, or stripes can enhance the visual appeal of one or more slides in the presentation. If you desire to change the colors in the pattern, PowerPoint allows you to select the fill foreground and background colors by clicking the Color button and then choosing the desired colors. The following steps apply a pattern to Slide 3.

1

- With the Format Background dialog box displaying, click Pattern fill to display the Pattern gallery and the 5% pattern on Slide 3 (Figure 8–75).

Experiment

- Click various patterns in the Pattern gallery and watch the patterns change on the slide.

Q&A How can I delete a pattern if I decide not to apply one to my slide?

If the Format Background dialog box is displayed, click the Reset Background button. If you already have applied the pattern, you must click the Undo button on the Quick Access Toolbar.

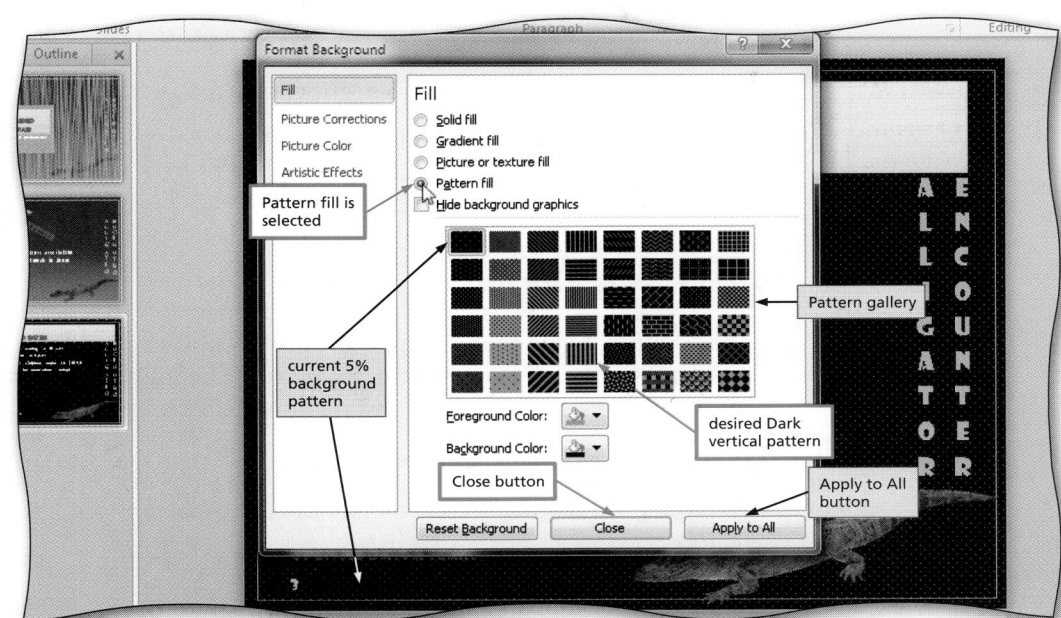

Figure 8–75

2

- Click the Dark vertical pattern (fourth color in fifth row) to apply this pattern to the Slide 3 background (Figure 8–76).

Q&A Can I apply this pattern to all the slides in the presentation?

Yes. You would click the Apply to All button in the Format Background dialog box.

3

- Click the Close button to close the Format Background dialog box.

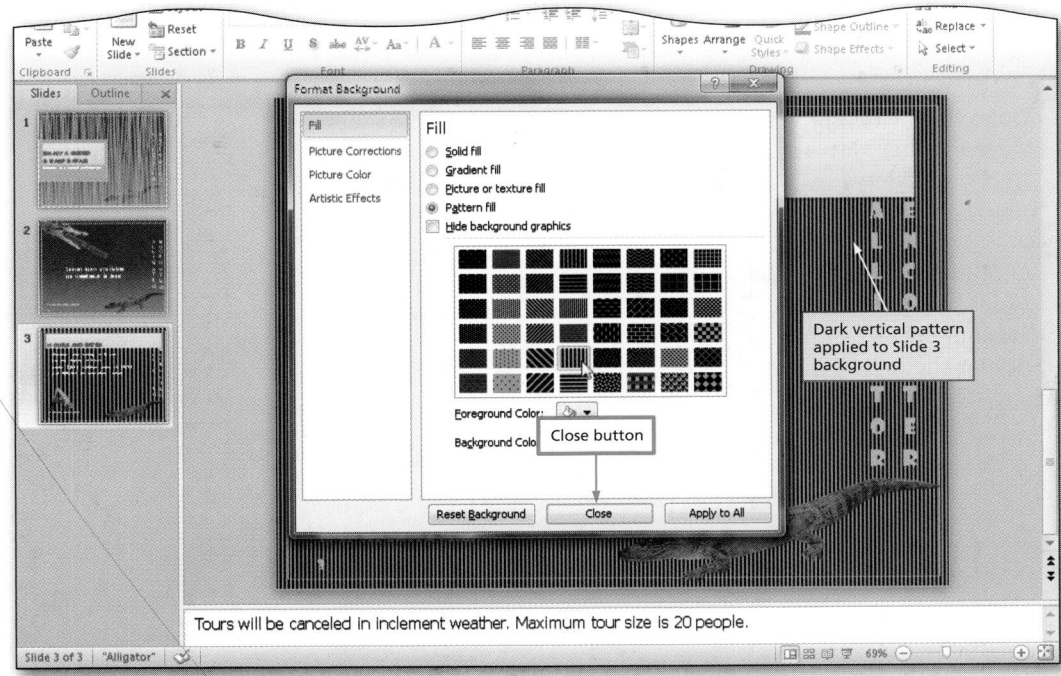

Figure 8–76

BTW

Quick Reference
For a table that lists how to complete the tasks covered in this book using the mouse, Ribbon, shortcut menu, and keyboard, see the Quick Reference Summary at the back of this book, or visit the PowerPoint 2010 Quick Reference Web page (scsite.com/ppt2010/qr).

To Add a Slide Transition

A final enhancement you will make in this presentation is to apply the Shred transition to all slides and then change the transition speed to 6.00 and the effect option to Particles Out. The following steps apply this transition and effect to the presentation.

1 Apply the Shred transition in the Exciting category.

2 Change the transition speed from 03.00 to 06.00.

3 Change the Effect Option from Strips In to Particles Out.

4 Apply these transitions to all slides in the presentation.

To Change Document Properties

Before saving the presentation again, you want to add your name, class name, and some keywords as document properties. The following steps use the Document Information Panel to change document properties.

1 Display the Document Information Panel and then type your name as the Author property.

2 Type your course and section in the Subject property.

3 Type `alligator, special events, safari` as the Keywords property.

4 Close the Document Information Panel.

To Print a Handout Using the Handout Master

The handout master you created has header and footer text using the Corbel font, a revised location for the footer placeholder, and the Alligator Body picture in the lower-right corner. The following steps print a handout using the handout master.

1
- Open the Backstage view and then display the Print gallery.

2
- Click the Full Page Slides button in the Settings area to display the gallery (Figure 8–77).

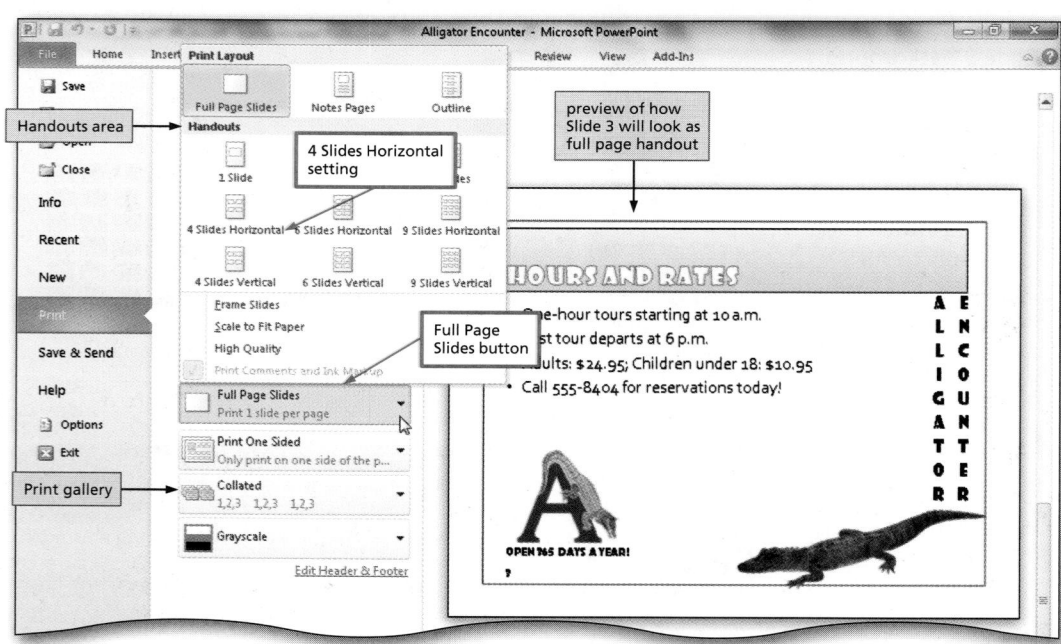

Figure 8–77

- Click 4 Slides Horizontal in the Handouts area.
- Click the Portrait Orientation button in the Settings area to display the Orientation gallery (Figure 8–78).

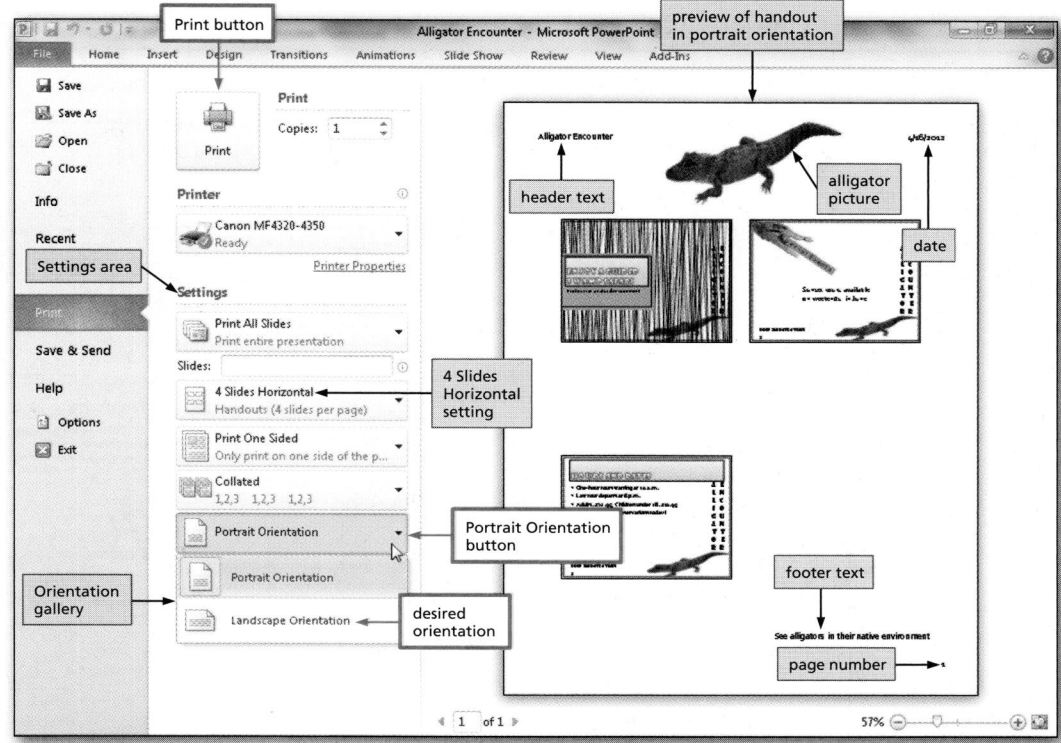

Figure 8–78

4

- Click Landscape Orientation to change the setting.
- Verify that 4 Slides Horizontal is selected as the option in the Settings area and that the preview of Page 1 shows the header text, date, footer text, page number, alligator picture, and three slides in landscape orientation.
- Click the Print button in the Print gallery to print the handout (Figure 8–79).

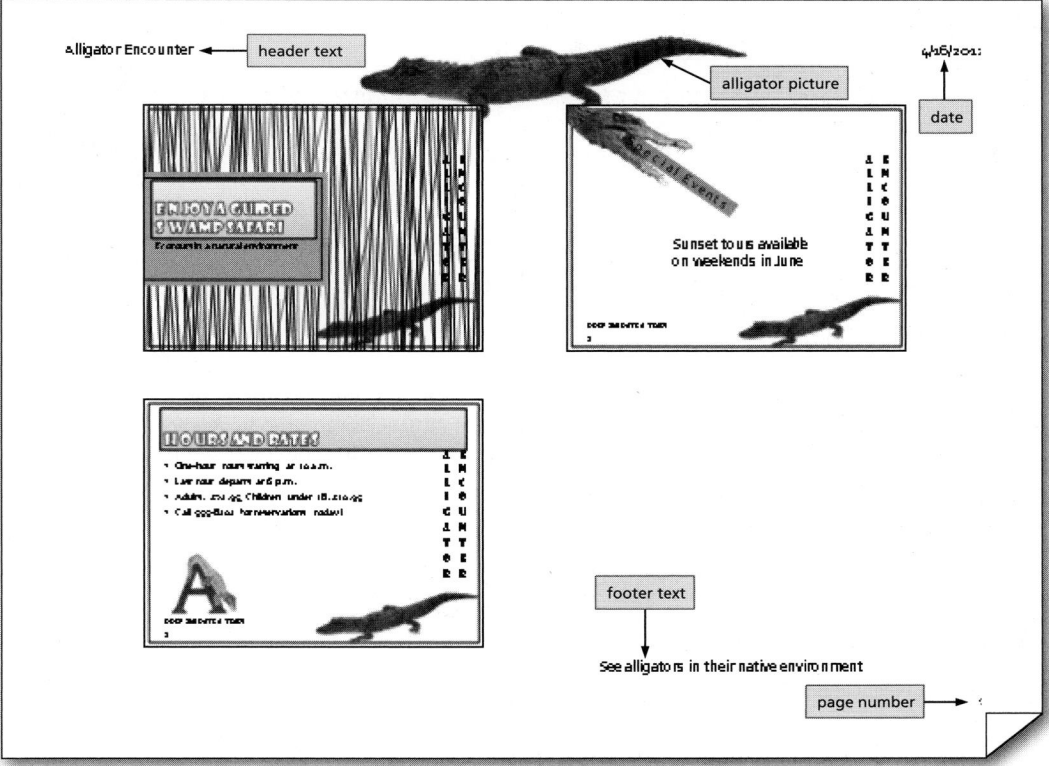

Figure 8–79

To Print Speaker Notes Using the Notes Master

You also can print speaker notes while the Backstage view is displayed. The custom notes master you created has the same footer as the handout master, revised footer text using the Corbel font, the current date, and the resized Alligator Body picture in the lower-right corner. The following steps print notes pages using the notes master.

1
- With the Backstage view open, click the 4 Slides Horizontal button to display the gallery and then click Notes Pages in the Print Layout area.

- Click Landscape Orientation in the Settings area and then click Portrait Orientation in the gallery to change the setting.

- Verify that the page preview shows the header text, date, speaker notes, revised footer text, alligator picture, and page number in portrait orientation (Figure 8–80).

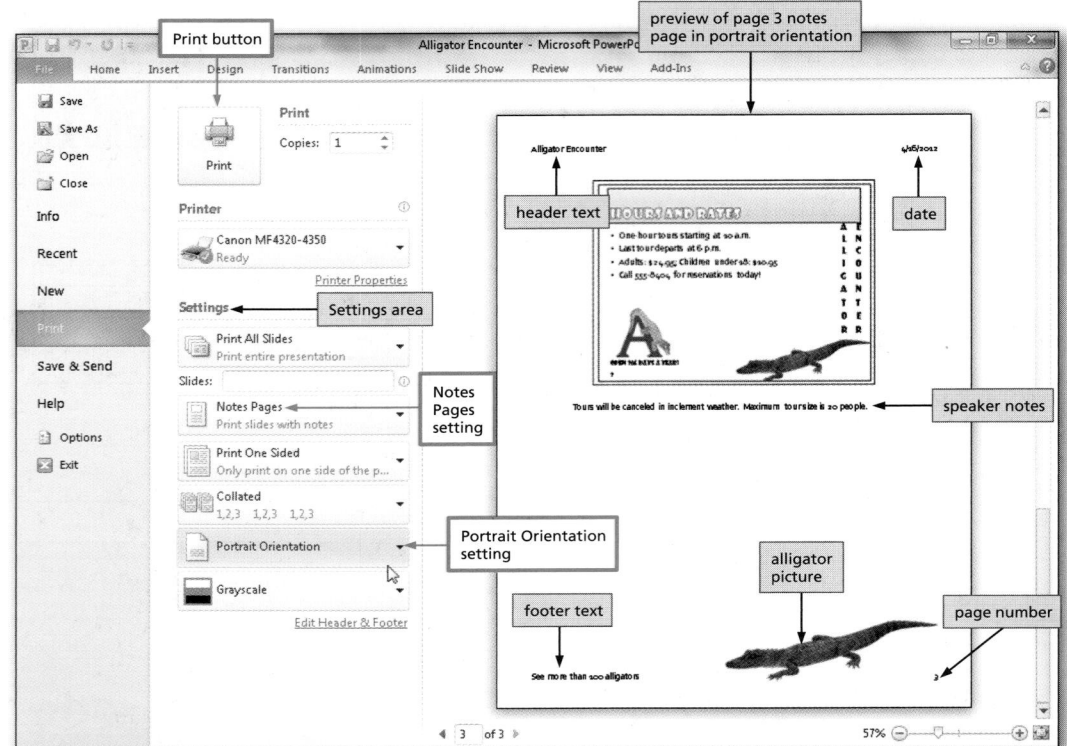

Figure 8–80

2
- Click the Previous Page and Next Page buttons to display previews of the other pages.
- Click the Print button in the Print gallery to print the notes (Figure 8–81).

BTW

Certification
The Microsoft Office Specialist (MOS) program provides an opportunity for you to obtain a valuable industry credential – proof that you have the PowerPoint 2010 skills required by employers. For more information, visit the PowerPoint 2010 Certification Web page (scsite.com/ppt2010/cert).

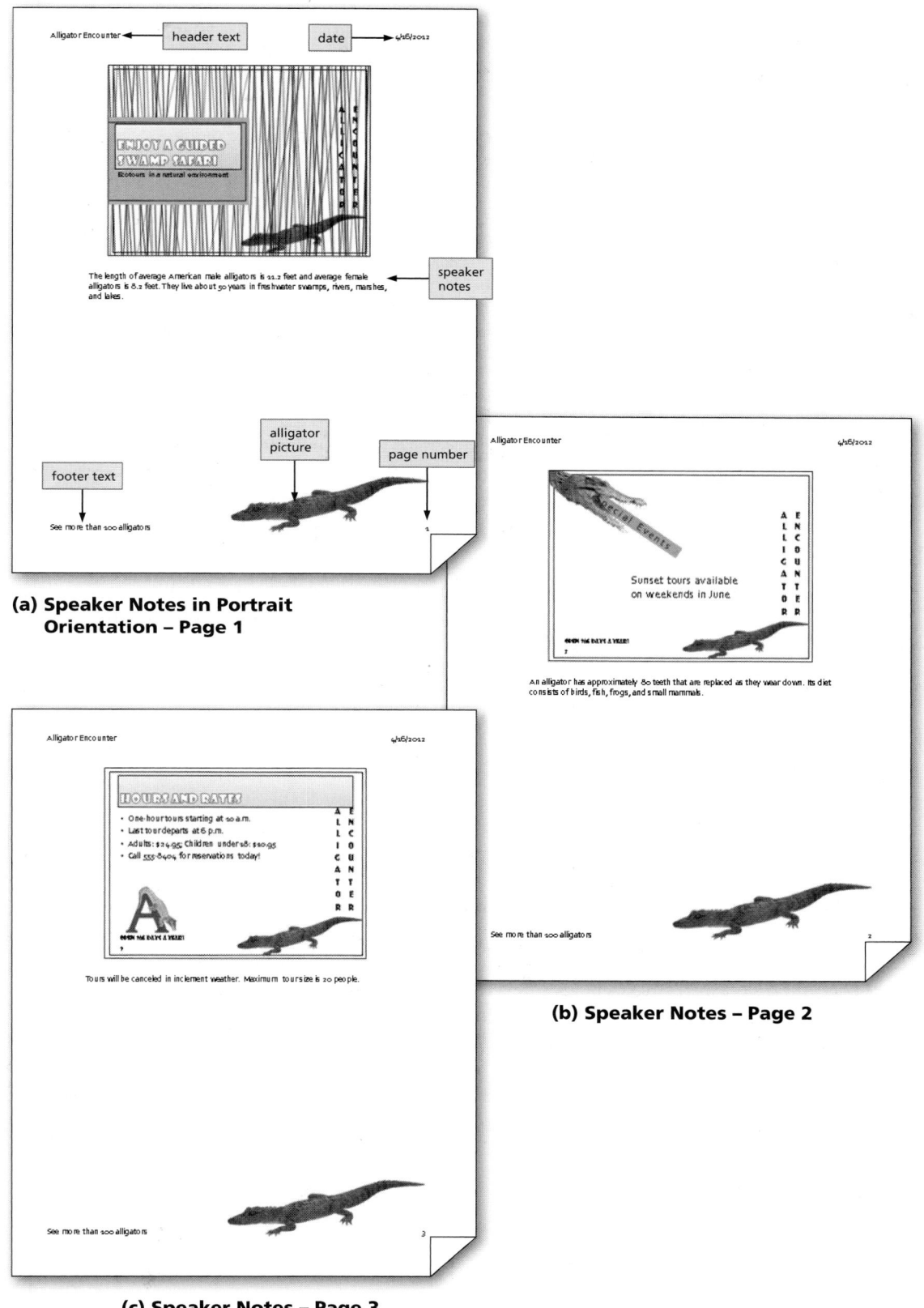

(a) Speaker Notes in Portrait Orientation – Page 1

(b) Speaker Notes – Page 2

(c) Speaker Notes – Page 3

Figure 8–81

To Save and Quit PowerPoint

The presentation now is complete. You should save the slides and then quit PowerPoint.

1 Save the Alligator Encounter presentation again with the same file name.

2 Quit PowerPoint, closing all open documents.

Chapter Summary

In this chapter you have learned how to customize master slide layouts by changing the slide and font themes, formatting the background and footers, and adding background graphics. You then inserted a placeholder, added and formatted text, applied a fill, and changed the internal margins. Also, you rotated a picture and a placeholder, displayed the background graphics, and renamed and deleted slide layouts. Then you customized the handouts and notes masters by adding a picture and changing the layout orientation. You then saved the slide master as a template, opened this template, added slide content, and printed a handout and speaker notes pages. The items listed below include all the new PowerPoint skills you have learned in this chapter.

1. Display a Slide Master (PPT 471)
2. Apply Slide and Font Themes to a Slide Master (PPT 472)
3. Customize a Theme Font (PPT 473)
4. Format a Slide Master Background and Apply a Quick Style (PPT 475)
5. Delete, Move, and Add Text to a Slide Master Footer (PPT 476)
6. Format Slide Master Footer Text (PPT 478)
7. Insert a Background Graphic into a Slide Master (PPT 479)
8. Insert a Placeholder into a Blank Layout (PPT 480)
9. Add and Format Placeholder Text (PPT 481)
10. Cut a Placeholder and Paste It into a Slide Master (PPT 484)
11. Change Character Spacing (PPT 486)
12. Apply a Fill to a Text Box and Increase Transparency (PPT 487)
13. Change a Text Box Internal Margin (PPT 488)
14. Rotate a Picture and a Text Box (PPT 489)
15. Hide and Unhide Background Graphics (PPT 490)
16. Rename a Slide Master and a Slide Layout (PPT 491)
17. Delete a Slide Layout (PPT 493)
18. Customize a Handout Using a Handout Master (PPT 496)
19. Customize a Notes Page Using a Notes Master (PPT 500)
20. Close Master View (PPT 502)
21. Save a Master as a Template (PPT 502)
22. Open a Template and Save a Presentation (PPT 503)
23. Apply a Fill Color to a Slide (PPT 507)
24. Apply a Pattern to a Slide (PPT 509)
25. Print a Handout Using the Handout Master (PPT 510)
26. Print Speaker Notes Using the Notes Master (PPT 512)

 If you have a SAM 2010 user profile, your instructor may have assigned an autogradable version of this assignment. If so, log into the SAM 2010 Web site at www.cengage.com/sam2010 to download the instruction and start files.

Learn It Online

Test your knowledge of chapter content and key terms.

Instructions: To complete the Learn It Online exercises, start your browser, click the Address bar, and then enter the Web address `scsite.com/ppt2010/learn`. When the Office 2010 Learn It Online page is displayed, click the link for the exercise you want to complete and then read the instructions.

Chapter Reinforcement TF, MC, and SA
A series of true/false, multiple choice, and short answer questions that test your knowledge of the chapter content.

Flash Cards
An interactive learning environment where you identify chapter key terms associated with displayed definitions.

Practice Test
A series of multiple choice questions that test your knowledge of chapter content and key terms.

Who Wants To Be a Computer Genius?
An interactive game that challenges your knowledge of chapter content in the style of a television quiz show.

Wheel of Terms
An interactive game that challenges your knowledge of chapter key terms in the style of the television show *Wheel of Fortune*.

Crossword Puzzle Challenge
A crossword puzzle that challenges your knowledge of key terms presented in the chapter.

Apply Your Knowledge

Reinforce the skills and apply the concepts you learned in this chapter.

Applying a Slide Theme to a Slide Master, Creating a New Theme Font, and Changing a Slide Master Background

Note: To complete this assignment, you will be required to use the Data Files for Students. See the inside back cover of this book for instructions on downloading the Data Files for Students, or contact your instructor for information about accessing the required files.

Instructions: Start PowerPoint. Open the presentation, Apply 8–1 Mathematics, located on the Data Files for Students.

The four slides in this presentation discuss the careers available to mathematics majors. The document you open is an unformatted presentation. You will apply a slide theme to a slide master, create a new theme font, and change the slide master background so the slides look like Figure 8–82.

Perform the following tasks:
1. Display the Slide Master view. Change the document theme to Angles, the colors to Civic, and then create a new Theme Font named Math using Bernard MT Condensed for the heading font and Microsoft Sans Serif for the body font, as shown in Figure 8–82a. Close Slide Master view.

2. On Slide 1, center the title text, change the size to 80 point, and then change the color to Red, Accent 1. Center the subtitle text, change the size to 48 point, and change the color to Blue-Gray, Text 2. Adjust the line break so that the word, CAREERS, is on the first line by itself. Resize the pictures and move them to the positions shown in Figure 8–82b. Adjust the color to Washout (Recolor area) on the bottom (abacus) picture.

Continued >

Apply Your Knowledge *continued*

3. On Slide 2, change the title text to 40 point and the color to Teal, Accent 3. Increase the size of the body text to 36 point and change the color to Dark Blue. Use the Format Painter to apply the same formatting changes to the title and body text on Slide 3. Increase the size of the clips on Slides 2 and 3 and move them to the locations shown in Figures 8–82c and 8–82d.

4. On Slide 4, change the layout to Picture with Caption. Insert the Math picture located on the Data Files for Students. Change the title text to 44 point and the color to Teal, Accent 3, and then move the text placeholder as shown in Figure 8–82e. Change the subtitle text to 28 point and the color to Dark Blue, and move the subtitle text placeholder to the location shown.

5. Change the arrow shape, as shown in Figure 8–82e, increase the font size to 36 point, change the text color to Yellow, and then bold this text. Apply the Intense Effect – Teal, Accent 3 Quick Style to the arrow, and then move the arrow to the location shown.

6. For all slides, change the transition to Cube and the duration to 03.00 seconds.

7. Change the document properties, as specified by your instructor. Save the presentation using the file name, Apply 8–1 Mathematics Careers. Submit the revised document in the format specified by your instructor.

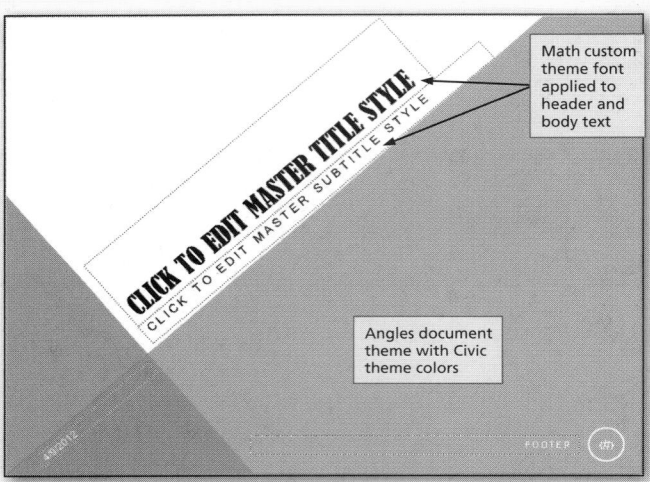

(a) Slide Master Title Slide Layout

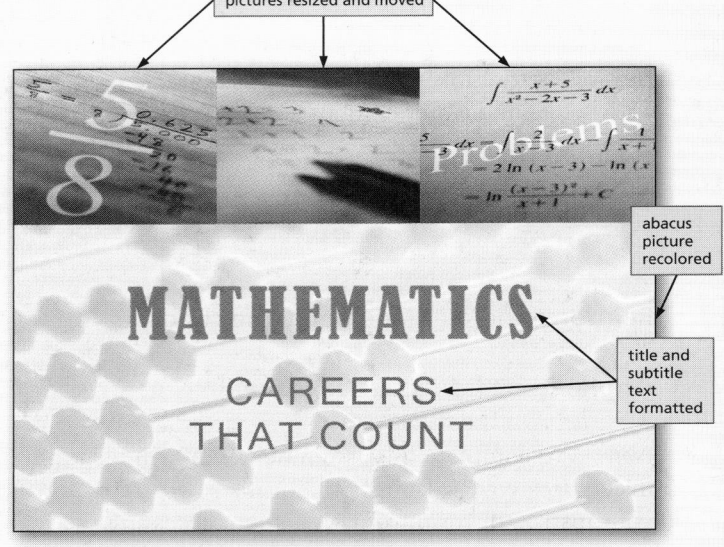

(b) Slide 1

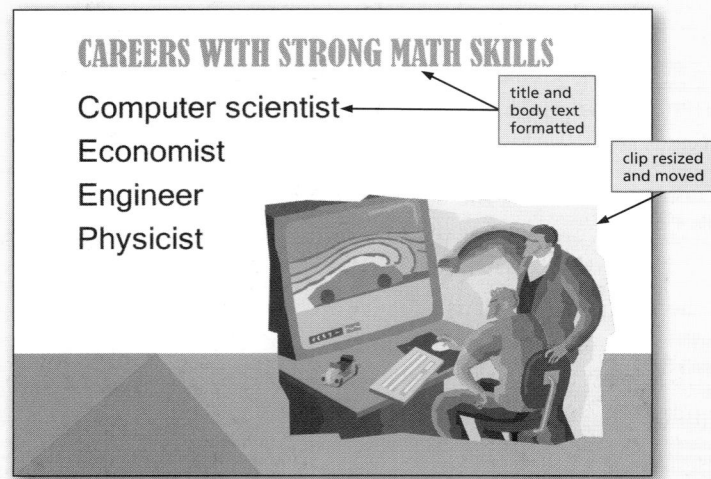

(c) Slide 2

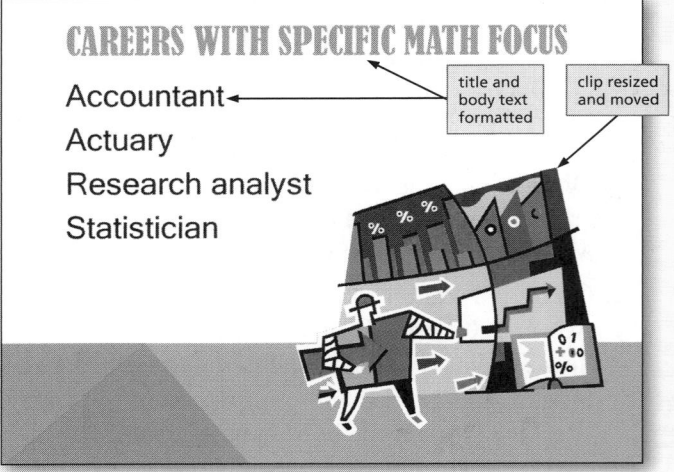

(d) Slide 3

Figure 8–82

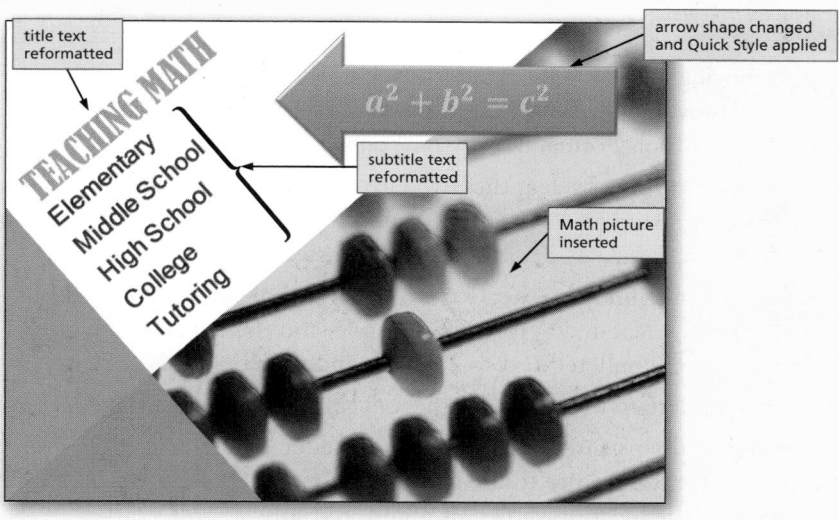

(e) Slide 4

Figure 8–82 (Continued)

Extend Your Knowledge

Extend the skills you learned in this chapter and experiment with new skills. You may need to use Help to complete the assignment.

Adding a Background Graphic to a Slide Master and Adjusting Footer Content and Placeholders

Note: To complete this assignment, you will be required to use the Data Files for Students. See the inside back cover of this book for instructions on downloading the Data Files for Students, or contact your instructor for information about accessing the required files.

Instructions: Start PowerPoint. Open the presentation, Extend 8–1 Bees, located on the Data Files for Students. You will add a background graphic to a slide master; add footer slide numbers, date, and time; delete a footer placeholder; and move a footer placeholder, as shown in Figure 8–83.

Perform the following tasks:
1. Open Slide Master view and then select the Slide Master thumbnail. Add the slide number, date, and time to the footer placeholders. *Hint:* You may need to use Help to learn how to insert the time into the footer. Delete the center text placeholder in the footer area. Move the 'Date and time' footer placeholder to the upper-right area of the slide master. Right-align the 'Date and time' placeholder text, change the color to Black, and then bold this text, as shown in Figure 8–83a.
2. Add a background style by selecting Brass from the Preset colors in the Gradient fill area. Insert the Bees audio clip, located on the Data Files for Students, on the slide master, have it start automatically, and hide the sound icon during the show. You may need to use Help to learn how to insert the sound icon into the slide master. Close Slide Master view.
3. On the title slide, select the title text and change the font to Aharoni. Apply the Fill – White, Drop Shadow WordArt style to the title text, change the text fill color to Orange, the outline color to Black, and the outline line weight to 4.5 pt. Apply the Can Down text effect to the title, decrease the width of the title text to 7.5", and then move it to the location shown in Figure 8–83b.
4. Change the color of the subtitle text to Black and the font size to 44 point. Bold this text and then move the subtitle placeholder to the lower part of the slide.
5. On Slide 1, move the Beekeeper avatar picture to Slide 2. Increase the size of the bee clip and move it to the location shown in Figure 8–83b. Duplicate the bee clip by selecting it, holding the CTRL

Continued >

STUDENT ASSIGNMENTS

Extend Your Knowledge *continued*

key, and then moving the duplicate clip to the upper-right corner of the slide. Flip the second clip horizontally and move to the location shown. *Hint:* Select the bee clip and then select Rotate: Flip Horizontal (Picture Tools Format tab | Arrange group).

6. Open Slide Master view and select the Two Content Layout. Add the Honeycomb picture, located on the Data Files for Students, as a background graphic to this layout, and change the transparency to 65%, as shown in Figure 8–83c. Close Slide Master view.

7. Change the layout for Slide 2 to the Two Content Layout. Increase the size of the picture in the left placeholder, apply the Rotated White picture style, and then change the border color to Orange. Increase the size of the bulleted text to 28 point and then bold this text.

8. Change the title text font to Broadway and the font size to 54 point. Change the color of the text to Black.

9. Increase the size of the picture in the right placeholder, apply the Simple Frame, Black picture style, and then move the picture to the location shown. Increase the size of the Beekeeper avatar clip and move it to the location shown in Figure 8–83d.

10. Apply the Honeycomb transition to all slides and change the duration to 05.00 seconds.

11. Change the document properties, as specified by your instructor. Save the presentation using the file name, Extend 8–1 Beekeepers.

12. Submit the revised document in the format specified by your instructor.

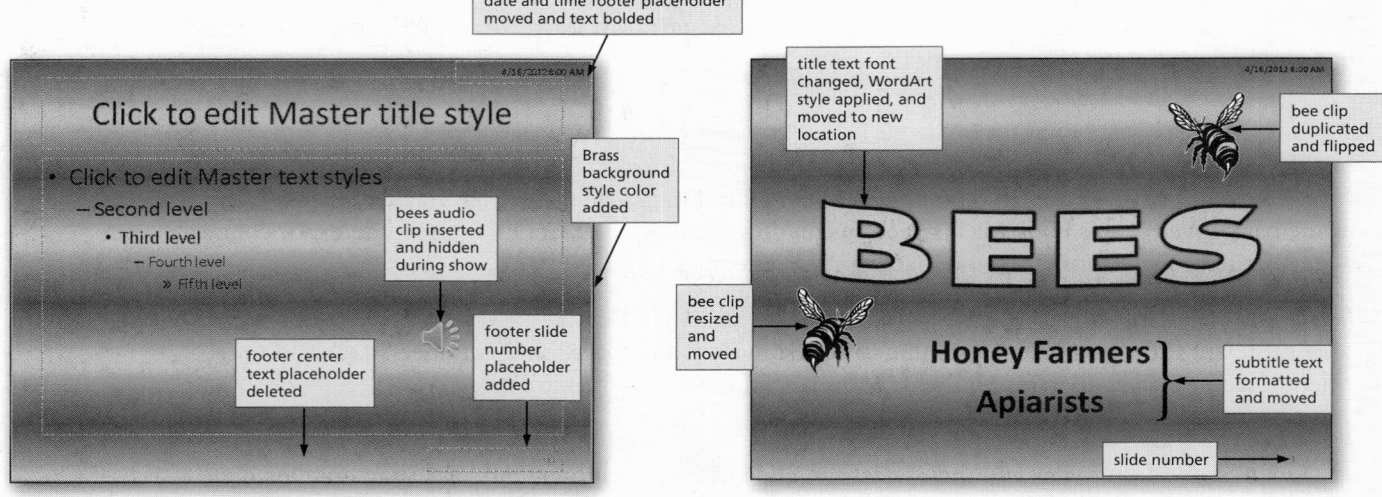

(a) Slide Master

(b) Slide 1

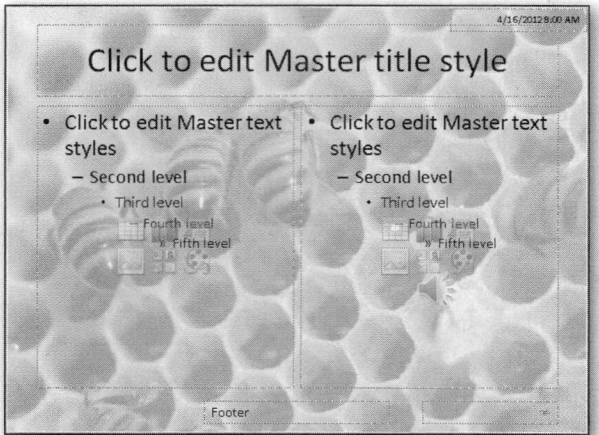

(c) Slide Master Two Content Layout

(d) Slide 2

Figure 8–83

Make It Right

Analyze a presentation and correct all errors and/or improve the design.

Changing a Font Theme and Background Style, Deleting a Placeholder and a Graphic, and Rotating a Placeholder on a Slide Master

Note: To complete this assignment, you will be required to use the Data Files for Students. See the inside back cover of this book for instructions on downloading the Data Files for Students, or contact your instructor for information about accessing the required files.

Instructions: Start PowerPoint. Open the presentation, Make It Right 8-1 Hang Gliding, located on the Data Files for Students.

Correct the formatting problems and errors in the presentation while keeping in mind the guidelines presented in this chapter.

Perform the following tasks:

1. Open Slide Master view, select the Office Theme Slide Master (Figure 8–84a), and delete the clip from the lower-right area of the slide. Change the font theme to Elemental. Also, delete the Date and time, Slide number, and Footer placeholders.

2. Select the Title Slide Layout (Figure 8–84b) and change the background style to the style of your choice. Increase the font size of the title text and then right-align this text. Rotate the subtitle text placeholder right 90 degrees and then move the placeholder under the title text placeholder. Delete the text placeholder in the upper-right corner of the Title Slide Layout, and also delete the three footer placeholders.

3. Select the Title and Content Layout, change the content placeholder left and right internal margins to 0.1", and change the top margin to 1.7". Close Slide Master view.

4. On Slide 1, change the layout to Title Slide. Delete the text and the text placeholder in the upper-right area of the slide. Change the title text font size to an appropriate size and insert a line break so it fits on two lines, bold this text, and then center it. Change the subtitle text font size and add line breaks so it fits on three lines, change the color, bold this text, and then center it. Increase the size of the picture and move the picture, the title text, and the subtitle text to the locations shown in Figure 8–84c.

5. On Slide 2 (Figure 8–84d), delete the first bulleted paragraph, bold the remainder of the text in the placeholder, and then move the placeholder downward. Insert a cloud shape, cut and paste the last bulleted paragraph into the cloud shape, increase the font size, and then move the shape to the upper-right area of the slide. Resize and move the title text placeholder so the title fits on one line above the cloud, increase the size of the font, bold the text, and then change the color.

6. Change the transition to Fly Through and the Effect Options to Out, and then change the duration to 3.00 for all slides.

7. Change the document properties, as specified by your instructor. Save the presentation using the file name, Make It Right 8-1 Hang Gliding School.

8. Submit the revised document in the format specified by your instructor.

Continued >

Make It Right *continued*

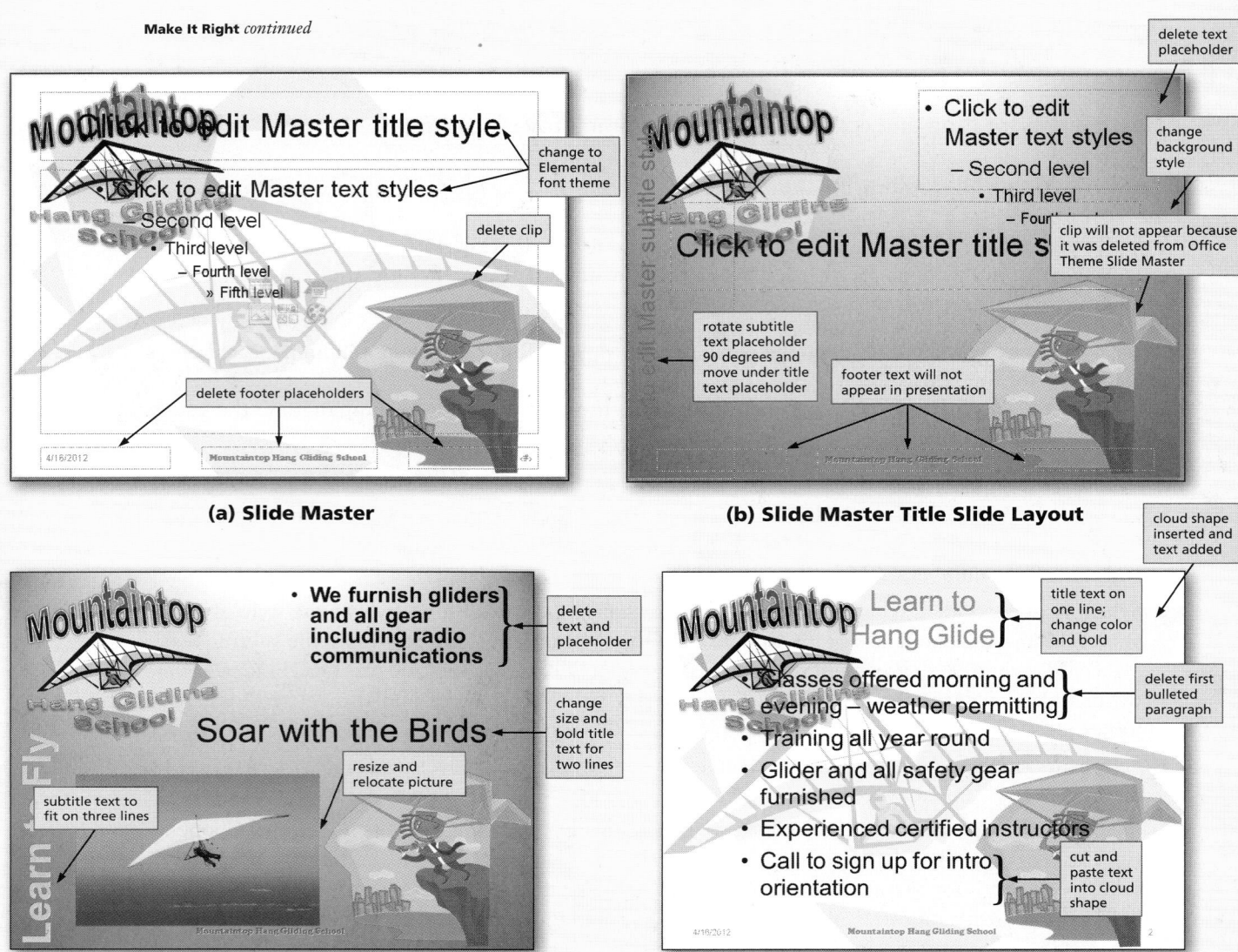

(a) Slide Master

(b) Slide Master Title Slide Layout

(c) Slide 1

(d) Slide 2

Figure 8–84

In the Lab

Design and/or create a presentation using the guidelines, concepts, and skills presented in this chapter. Labs 1, 2, and 3 are listed in order of increasing difficulty.

Lab 1: Formatting a Slide Master by Inserting a Placeholder, Applying a Fill, and Changing the Internal Margin

Note: To complete this assignment, you will be required to use the Data Files for Students. See the inside back cover of this book for instructions on downloading the Data Files for Students or contact your instructor for information about accessing the required files.

Problem: In your biology class, you learned that half of the world's animal species live in all four layers of rain forests. You decide to create a PowerPoint presentation to identify a few of these animal species and to give an example of which animals live in each rain forest layer. You create the slides shown in Figure 8–85 using files located on the Data Files for Students.

Perform the following tasks:

1. Open the presentation, Lab 8-1 Rain Forest, located on the Data Files for Students.

2. Open Slide Master view and select the Slide Master thumbnail. Apply the Austin document theme. On the Austin Slide Master, delete the slide number and date placeholders from the upper-right area of the slide, as shown in Figure 8–85a.

3. Insert a Picture placeholder in the left side of the Title Slide Layout. Adjust the size of the Picture placeholder so that it is approximately 6" × 4", as shown in Figure 8–85b. Close Slide Master view.

4. On Slide 1, select the layout, 1_Title Slide. Change the title text to **Rain Forest Animals** and then change the text font to 44-point bold, center the text, and then align the text in the middle of the placeholder. Increase the subtitle text font to 25 point, change the color to Black, Text 1, center the text, bold and italicize this text, and then align the text in the middle of the placeholder.

5. On Slide 1, insert the Waterfall picture located on the Data Files for Students in the Picture placeholder. Increase the size of the Frog picture and move it to the location shown in Figure 8–85c and then apply the Soft Edge Rectangle picture style to the picture.

6. Open Slide Master view. Select the Two Content Layout and then apply the Linear Down Gradient Fill to both content placeholders. Also, change the left internal margin to .5" in both content placeholders, as shown in Figure 8–85d. Close Slide Master view.

7. Apply the Two Content slide layout to Slides 2 and 3.

8. On Slides 2 and 3, bold and center the title text. Bold the text in both placeholders. Adjust the size of the pictures and move them to the locations shown in Figure 8–85e and Figure 8–85f. Apply the Rotated, White picture style to the snake picture and the Bevel Perspective style to the frog picture in Slide 2. Apply the Reflected Bevel, Black picture style to the gorilla picture and the Center Shadow Rectangle style to the toucan picture in Slide 3.

9. On Slide 4, change the title font to 40 point, bold this text, and then insert a line break after the word, Forests', to display the title text on two lines. Move the title text placeholder down slightly, as shown in Figure 8–85g.

10. Increase the size of the rain forest picture to 4.5" × 3.17" and move the picture to the left side of the slide. Add a 6 pt Orange border to the picture.

11. Increase the size of the SmartArt graphic to 4.5" × 5.5" and move the graphic to the right side of the slide. Apply the Colorful – Accent Colors and the Intense Effect SmartArt style to the graphic.

12. Apply the Ripple transition and change the duration to 04.00 seconds for all slides.

13. Change the document properties, as specified by your instructor. Save the presentation using the file name, Lab 8-1 Rain Forest Animals.

14. Submit the revised document in the format specified by your instructor.

Continued >

In the Lab continued

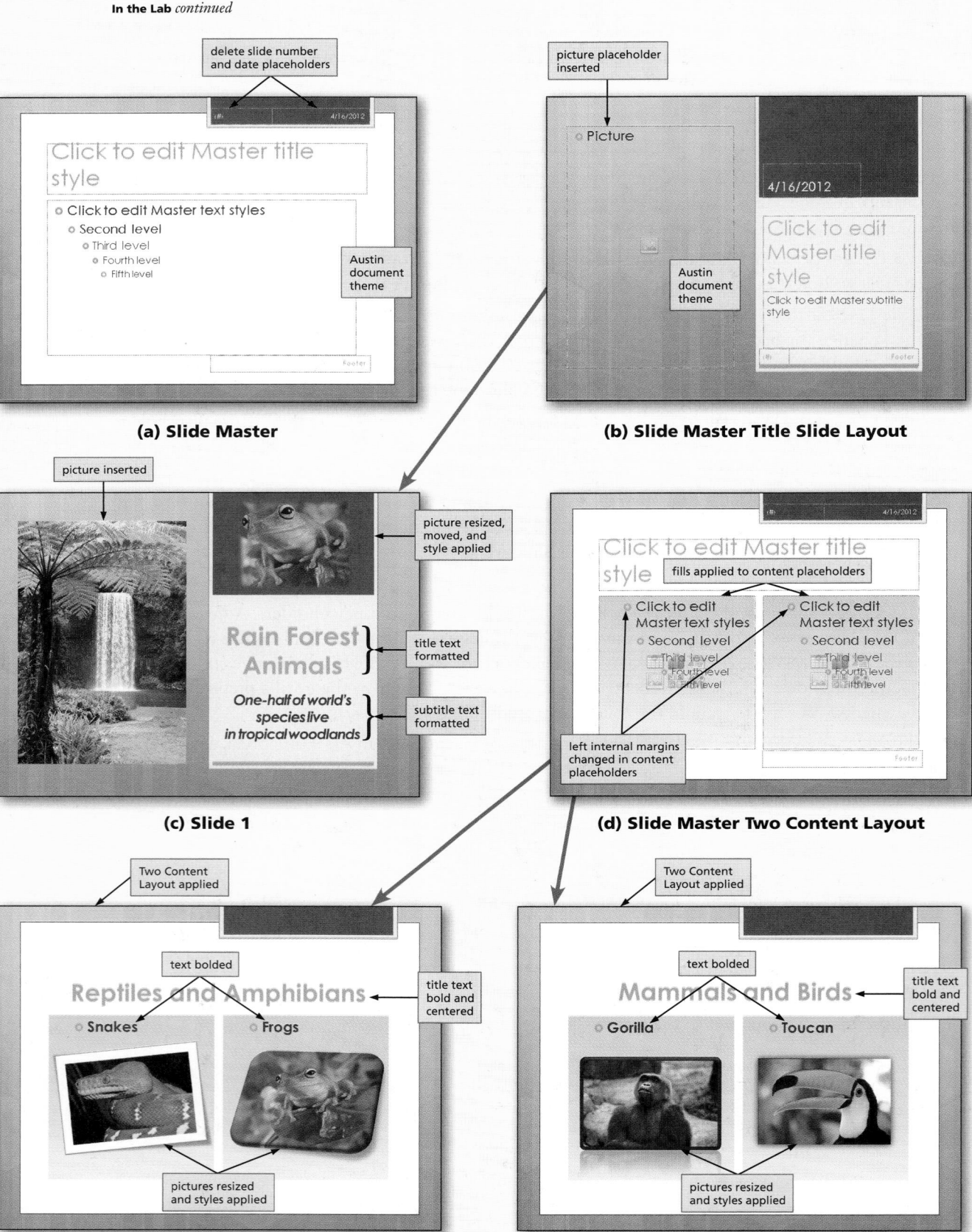

(a) Slide Master

(b) Slide Master Title Slide Layout

(c) Slide 1

(d) Slide Master Two Content Layout

(e) Slide 2

(f) Slide 3

Figure 8–85

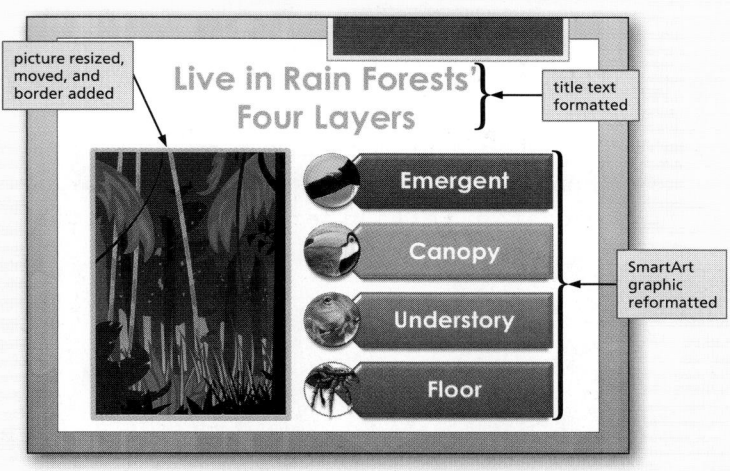

(g) Slide 4

Figure 8–85 (Continued)

In the Lab

Lab 2: Formatting and Renaming Slide Masters and Creating Handouts Using the Handout and Notes Masters

Note: To complete this assignment, you will be required to use the Data Files for Students. See the inside back cover of this book for instructions on downloading the Data Files for Students or contact your instructor for information about accessing the required files.

Problem: Many consumers grow and eat organic foods. Your garden club members have asked you to prepare a presentation about organic gardening for your next meeting. You create the slides shown in Figure 8–86 using files located on the Data Files for Students.

Perform the following tasks:

1. Open the presentation, Lab 8-2 Organic, located on the Data Files for Students.

2. Open Slide Master view. Select the Title and Content Layout, duplicate the title text placeholder, rotate it left 90 degrees, reduce the size to 1.25 × 7.5, and then move it to the left edge of the slide. Apply the Intense Effect – Olive Green, Accent 3 Quick Style.

3. Type `ORGANIC` in the rotated placeholder. Bold this text and then change the font to Cooper Black, the font size to 54 point, the character spacing to Very Loose, and the text direction to Stacked.

4. Apply Background Style 10 to the Title Slide, Title and Content, and Blank layouts. On the Title and Content Layout master, decrease the size of the title and the content placeholders by dragging the left sizing handles to the right until they are 7.67" wide, as shown in Figure 8–86a.

5. Change the Title and Content Layout name to Organic Title. Copy the rotated placeholder from the Organic Title layout to the Blank layout, as shown in Figure 8–86b.

6. Delete the Vertical Title and Text and the Title and Vertical Text layouts. Rename this slide master Organic. Close Slide Master view.

7. On Slide 1, change the title font to Cooper Black and the text color to Green. Increase the font size to 54 point and then bold this text. Increase the subtitle font size to 36 point, change the color to Purple, and then bold this text. Adjust the size of the subtitle text placeholder so that the text is displayed on two lines and then left-align this text. Insert a line break after the word, Plan, to display the subtitle text on two lines. Move the title and subtitle text placeholders to the locations shown in Figure 8–86c.

8. Resize and move the vegetable picture and then apply the Relaxed Perspective, White style to the picture, as shown in Figure 8–86c.

Continued >

In the Lab *continued*

9. On Slide 2, change the layout to Blank. Increase the size of the wheat picture so that it measures 7.5" × 8.74". Change the color to Orange, Accent color 6 Light, move the wheat picture so that it fills the slide, and then send this picture to the back. Increase the size of the second organic picture and move it to the location shown in Figure 8–86d. Insert a text box and type `In organic gardening, no synthetic fertilizers or pesticides are used.` Open

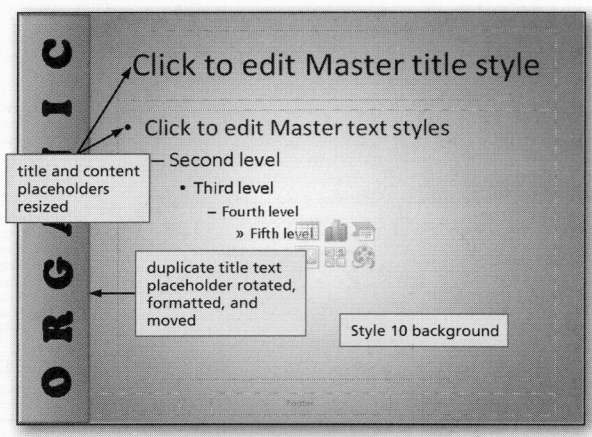

(a) Slide Master Title and Content Layout

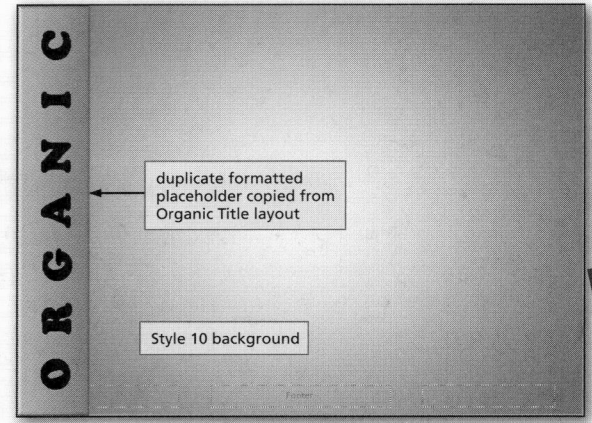

(b) Slide Master Blank Layout

(c) Slide 1

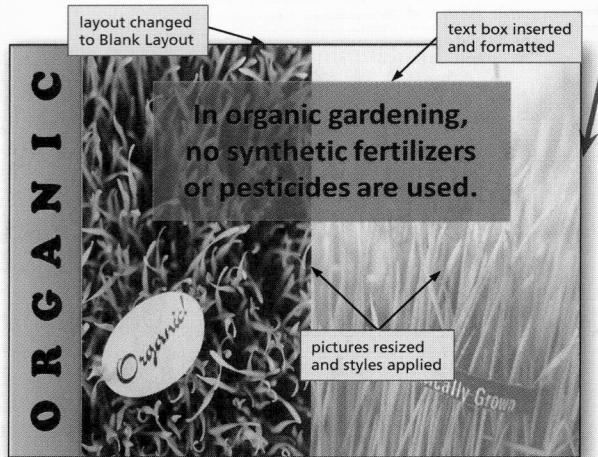

(d) Slide 2

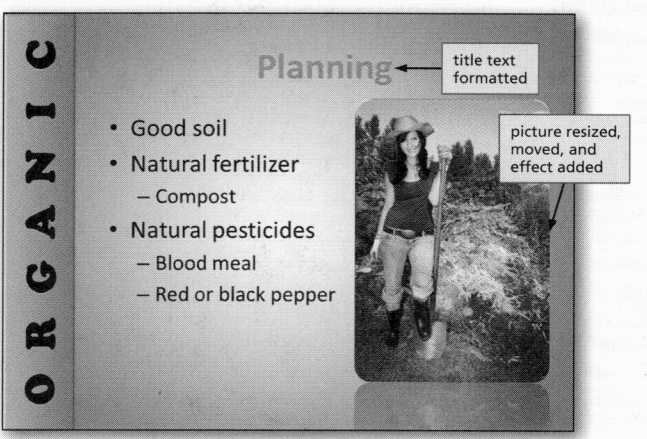

(e) Slide 3

(f) Slide 4

Figure 8–86

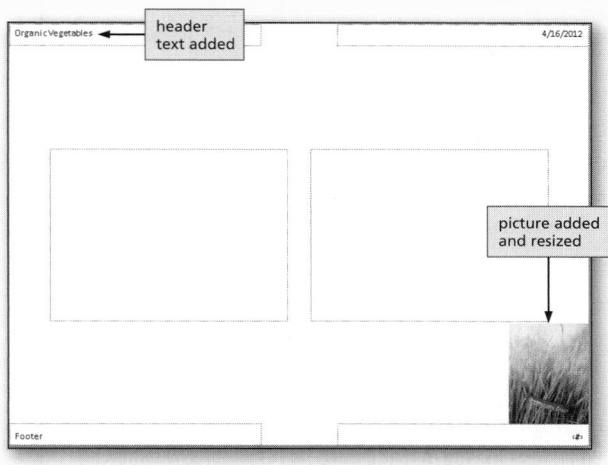

(g) Handout Master

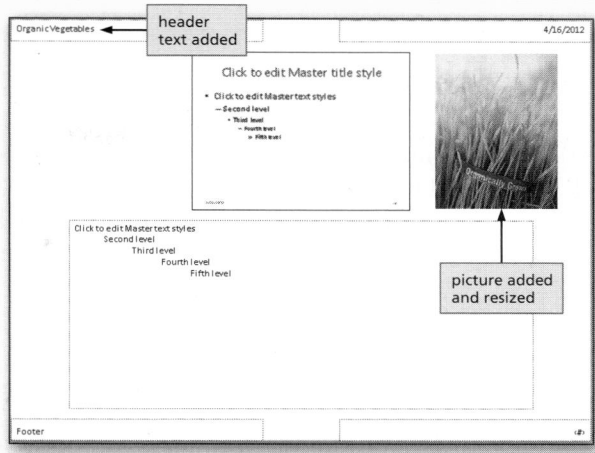

(h) Notes Master

Figure 8–86 (Continued)

the Format Shape dialog box and make sure the Wrap text in shape check box is checked. Change the left and right internal margins to 0.5" and the top and bottom internal margins to 0.25". Increase the size of the text to 40 point and then bold and center the text. Apply an Orange, Accent 6, Darker 25% solid fill color to the text box and change the transparency to 40%. If necessary, change the size of the text box so that the text is on three lines and then move it to the location shown in Figure 8–86d.

10. On Slide 3, change the title text font color to Orange, Accent 6, Darker 25%, change the font size to 48 point, and then bold this text. Increase the size of the picture, add the Reflected Rounded Rectangle picture style, and then move the picture to the location shown in Figure 8–86e.

11. On Slide 4, change the title text font color to Orange, Accent 6, Darker 25%, change the font size to 48 point, and then bold this text. Apply the Light downward diagonal pattern to this slide and change the foreground color to Orange, Accent 6. Increase the size of the picture, add the Beveled Oval, Black picture style, and then move the picture to the location shown in Figure 8–86f.

12. Apply the Cover transition and then change the duration to 03.00 seconds for all slides.

13. Open the handout master, change the orientation to landscape, and then change the Slides per page to 2 Slides. Type **Organic Vegetables** as the header text. Insert the Organic picture, change the size to 1.8" × 1.38", and then move it to the lower-right area of the handout master, as shown in Figure 8–86g.

14. Open the notes master and then type **Organic Vegetables** as the header text. Insert the Organic picture, change the size to 2.75" × 2.11", and then move it to the right side of the notes master, as shown in Figure 8–86h. Close the Slide Master view.

15. Change the document properties, as specified by your instructor. Save the presentation using the file name, Lab 8-2 Organic Vegetables.

16. Submit the revised document in the format specified by your instructor.

In the Lab

Lab 3: Adding and Formatting Placeholders, Adding a Graphic, Hiding Background Graphics on Individual Slides, and Saving a Slide Master as a Template

Note: To complete this assignment, you will be required to use the Data Files for Students. See the inside back cover of this book for instructions on downloading the Data Files for Students or contact your instructor for information about accessing the required files.

Continued >

In the Lab *continued*

Problem: You work for a home remodeling company. Your manager has decided to run monthly ads for his company in two local newspapers. Each newspaper will run a 10" × 8" ad that can be revised each month. Your manager plans to insert pictures of the remodeling jobs he has completed. He has asked you to set up a template so that he can insert a picture and change the text each month. He also has asked you to prepare the first month's ads. You create the slide master template shown in Figure 8–87a and then create the ads for the month, as shown in Figure 8–87.

Perform the following tasks:

1. Open the presentation, Lab 8-3 Handy Man, located on the Data Files for Students.

2. Select everything on the slide by using the Select All button (Home tab | Editing group), click the Copy button in the Clipboard group, and then open Slide Master view and paste it onto the Office Theme Slide Master. Decrease the width of the title text placeholder to 5.83". Add the Style 5 background style and change the theme font to Essential. Add the text, `Ad for month of:`, in the center footer placeholder and change the font color to Black, as shown in Figure 8–87a.

3. Hide the logo and text box background graphics on the Title Slide Layout only.

4. Select the Title and Content Layout, delete the content placeholder, and then insert a Picture placeholder. Resize the placeholder to 4.92" × 5.83" and then move it to the location shown in Figure 8–87b. Insert a text placeholder, resize it to 3.08" × 3", change the font size of the first level text to 24 point, delete the second-, third-, fourth-, and fifth-level text, and then position it on the right side of the slide below the logo and text box. Delete the footer placeholder. Rename this layout, Ad1.

5. Select the Two Content layout, delete the two content placeholders, and then insert a picture placeholder. Resize the placeholder to 3.17" × 4.33" and then move it to the location shown on the left side of Figure 8–87c. Duplicate this picture placeholder and move it to the right side of the slide below the logo and text box. Insert a text placeholder below the left picture placeholder, change the font size of the first level text to 24 point, and then delete the second-, third-, fourth,- and fifth-level text. Resize the placeholder to 1.5" × 4.33". Delete the footer placeholder. Rename this layout, Ad2.

6. Delete all the layouts in the slide master except for the Title Slide, Ad1, and Ad2 layouts. Close the Slide Master view and change the Slide 1 layout to Title Slide.

7. Save this slide master as a template and name it Lab 8-3 Handy Max.

8. Create a new presentation using the Lab 8-3 Handy Max template (Figure 8–87b). Save the presentation using the file name, Lab 8-3 Handy Max Ad1.

9. On Slide 1, type `Kitchens` in the title text placeholder, type `Southside Chronicle` in the subtitle text placeholder, and then type `April` after the text in the footer placeholder. Delete the logo and text box (Figure 8–87d).

10. Insert a new slide and select the Ad1 layout. On Slide 2 (Figure 8–87e), type `Kitchen Remodeling` in the title text placeholder and change the font color to Purple. Insert the picture, Kitchen, located on the Data Files for Students, in the picture placeholder. Insert the Flowchart: Punched Tape shape in the lower part of the picture, type `Does Your Kitchen Need an Update?`, and then apply the Intense Effect – Aqua, Accent 5 to the shape. Increase the size of the font to 24 point, change the font color to Yellow, and then bold this text.

11. In the text placeholder, type the text shown in Figure 8–87e. Bold this text. Add the White marble Shape Fill texture to the text placeholder.

12. Change the document properties, as specified by your instructor. Save the presentation again.

13. Create a new presentation by using the Lab 8-3 Handy Max template (Figure 8–87c). Save the presentation using the file name, Lab 8-3 Handy Max Ad2.

14. On Slide 1, type `Living/Family Rooms` in the title text placeholder, type `Northside Chronicle` in the subtitle text placeholder, and then type `April` after the text in the footer placeholder. Delete the logo and text box (Figure 8–87f).

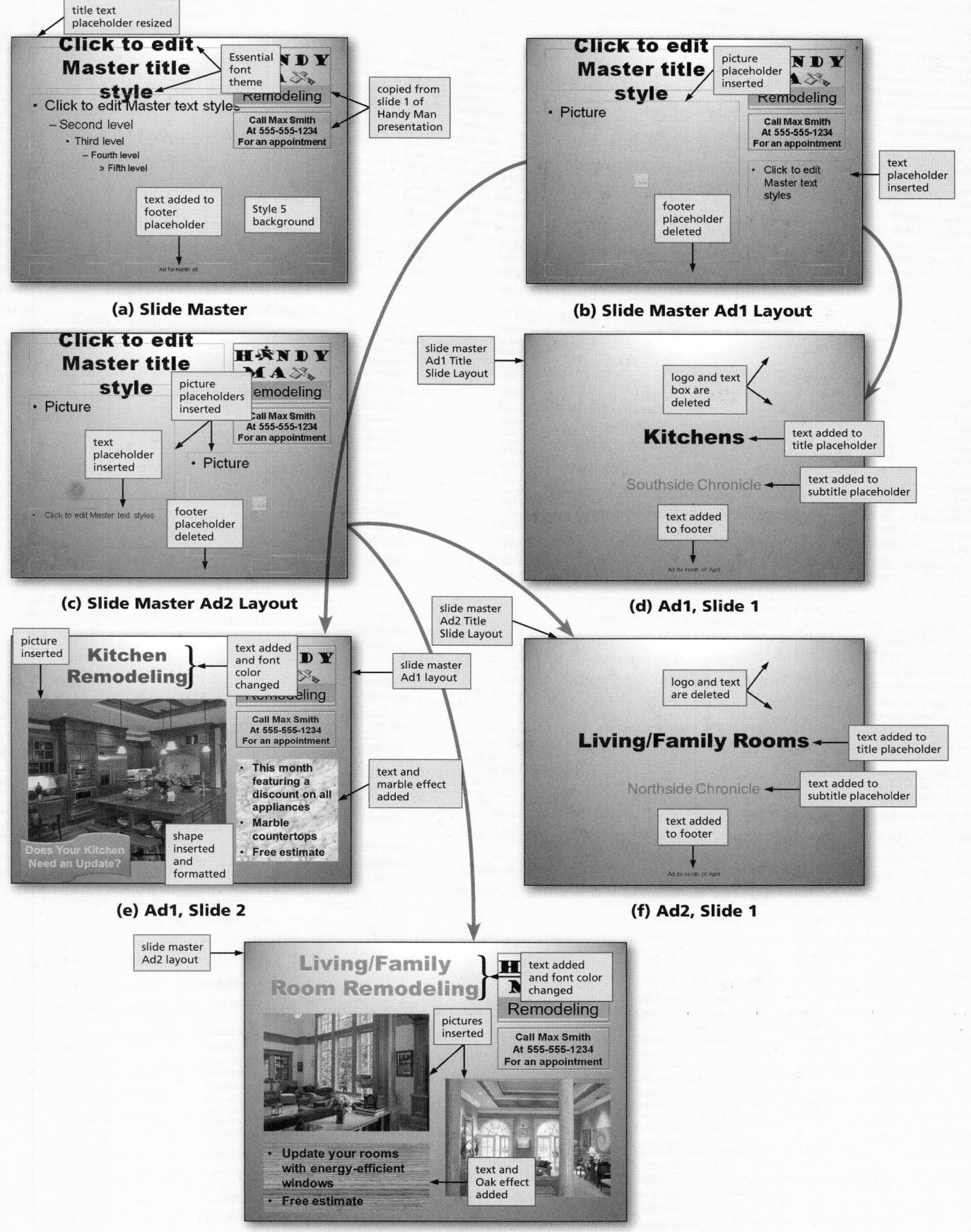

Figure 8–87

Continued >

In the Lab *continued*

15. Insert a new slide and select Ad2 layout. On Slide 2 (Figure 8–87g), type `Living/Family Room Remodeling` in the title text placeholder and change the font color to Green. Insert the pictures Den and Family Room, located on the Data Files for Students, in the picture placeholders.

16. In the text placeholder, type the text shown in Figure 8–87g. Bold this text. Add the Oak Shape Fill texture to the text placeholder. *Note:* You may need to increase the size of the text placeholder.

17. Change the document properties, as specified by your instructor. Save the presentation again.

18. Submit the revised documents in the format specified by your instructor.

Cases and Places

Apply your creative thinking and problem-solving skills to design and implement a solution.

Note: To complete these assignments, you may be required to use the Data Files for Students. See the inside back cover of this book for instructions on downloading the Data Files for Students, or contact your instructor for information about accessing the required files.

As you design the presentations, remember to use the 7 × 7 rule: a maximum of seven words on a line and a maximum of seven lines on one slide.

1: Designing and Creating a Presentation about Smart Phones

Academic

In your technical writing class, you have been assigned the topic of how to purchase a smart phone. You decide to focus on selecting a wireless carrier and plan, deciding on a style, comparing battery life, determining memory and storage space, and checking out accessories. Your instructor gives you permission to make a PowerPoint presentation instead of writing a paper to explain this topic to the class. Apply at least three objectives found at the beginning of this chapter to develop the presentation, including creating a new font theme, rotating a placeholder, and changing text direction. Use pictures and diagrams from Office.com if they are appropriate for this topic. Be sure to check spelling.

2: Designing and Creating a Presentation about Neighborhood Trees

Personal

Your community of 100 homes and townhomes is about three years old, and many residents have expressed a desire to add some trees to the public areas and parkways in front of their homes. Your homeowners' association has extra money in the budget, and the board members have asked you, as president of your association, to develop a presentation for the next meeting. You research the topic and decide on at least three or four kinds of trees. Use at least three objectives found at the beginning of this chapter to develop the presentation, including adding a picture or graphic of a tree as a slide master background. Use pictures from Office.com if they are appropriate for this topic or use your personal digital pictures. Be sure to check spelling.

3: Designing and Creating a Presentation about Your Computer Repair Business

Professional

To help with expenses during your last year of school, you decide to put your skills to use and start a small computer repair business. Your slide show will be running on a kiosk in the school library. Apply at least three objectives found at the beginning of this chapter to develop the presentation, including changing the slide master background and adding a footer, date, and time. Use pictures and clips from Office.com if they are appropriate for this topic or use your personal digital pictures. Add a picture to the handout master and create handouts that will be copied and made available next to the kiosk. Be certain to check spelling.

9 | Modifying a Presentation Using Graphical Elements

Objectives

You will have mastered the material in this chapter when you can:

- Change a text box outline color, weight, and style
- Set text box formatting as the default for new text boxes
- Apply a gradient, texture, pattern, and effects to a text box
- Convert WordArt to SmartArt
- Reorder SmartArt shapes
- Promote and demote SmartArt text
- Add and remove SmartArt shapes
- Convert a SmartArt graphic to text
- Customize the Ribbon
- Combine and subtract shapes
- Save the presentation as a picture presentation
- Create a handout by exporting files to Microsoft Word

9 | Modifying a Presentation Using Graphical Elements

Introduction

PowerPoint's themes determine the default characteristics of slide objects. Colors, border weights and styles, fills, effects, and other formatting options give the slides a unique character. You can create your own designs for text boxes, shapes, lines, and other slide content, and then reuse these graphical objects throughout the presentation. Once you learn to format one type of object, such as a text box, you can use similar techniques to format other slide objects, such as SmartArt and shapes. One efficient way to create consistent graphical elements is to save your settings as the default. Then, when you insert the same objects later during the presentation design process, they will have the same characteristics as the initial element.

SmartArt graphics have individual layouts, styles, and color schemes. If one of these designs does not meet the specific needs of your slide content, you can modify the graphic by adding shapes, reordering the current shapes, and changing each element's size and location. You also can convert the SmartArt to text or to a shape if SmartArt is not the best method of conveying your ideas to an audience. PowerPoint's myriad formatting options allow you to tailor graphical elements to best fit your unique design needs.

Project — Presentation with Customized Text Boxes, SmartArt, and Shapes

Hot air ballooning has fascinated flight enthusiasts for more than two centuries. The freedom of flying silently through scenic landscapes is a thrill that pilots and their passengers experience throughout the world.

Hot air balloon rides often are scheduled during the summer months. Morning and evening are preferred times to fly because the winds are light and the balloon altitude is easy to control. First-time passengers often are given a ground school lesson that includes a discussion of the balloon parts and flight dynamics. The presentation you create in this chapter (Figure 9–1) would be useful to show during the ground school lesson. All four slides are created by modifying a starting file that has a variety of content. The title slide (Figure 9–1a) contains a text box that is formatted with an outline style, a weight, and a color. These modifications are saved as the default settings for all other text boxes inserted into other slides. The second slide (Figure 9–1b) features a new colorful picture and a formatted text box. The text on Slide 3 (Figure 9–1c) is converted from WordArt to a SmartArt graphic. The layout, style, color, and shapes are changed and enhanced. The final slide (Figure 9–1d) has bulleted text converted from a SmartArt graphic; it also has a hot air balloon composed of formatted shapes. After the slides are created, you save the presentation as a picture presentation and export the file to Microsoft Word to create a handout (Figures 9–1e and 9–1f).

BTW

Identifying Shapes
Most objects in our world are composed of shapes: a circle, square, and triangle. Artists see objects as combinations of these shapes and begin their drawings by sketching these basic forms in proportion to each other. For example, a tree has the form of a circle for the branches and a rectangle for the trunk. A car has the form of a rectangle for the body, a smaller rectangle for the passenger compartment, and four circles for the wheels. Become observant of the relationships between objects in your world as you learn to use PowerPoint's drawing tools.

BTW

Hot Air Balloon Festivals
The largest hot air balloon festival occurs each October in Albuquerque, New Mexico. More than 700 balloonists launch their brilliantly colored and imaginative balloons during the nine-day event. The city also is home to the Anderson-Abruzzo International Balloon Museum, which features exhibits of historical balloons and a flight simulator.

Overview

As you read through this chapter, you will learn how to create the presentation and handout shown in Figure 9–1 below and on the following page by performing these general tasks:

- Format text boxes.
- Set formatting as default.
- Draw and insert shapes, lines, and arrows.
- Convert WordArt to SmartArt.
- Add and remove SmartArt shapes.
- Promote and demote bullet levels in SmartArt.
- Convert SmartArt to text.
- Customize the Ribbon.

BTW

Vector Graphics
Geometric shapes, lines, arrows, and action buttons are vector graphics, which are drawn using mathematical formulas. The size, color, line width, starting and ending points, and other formatting attributes are stored as numeric values and are recalculated when you resize or reformat each shape. Most clip art and video games also use vector graphics.

(a) Slide 1

(b) Slide 2

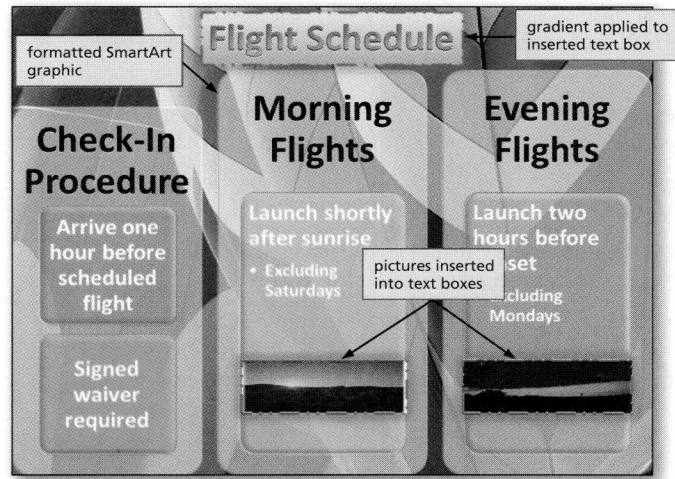

(c) Slide 3

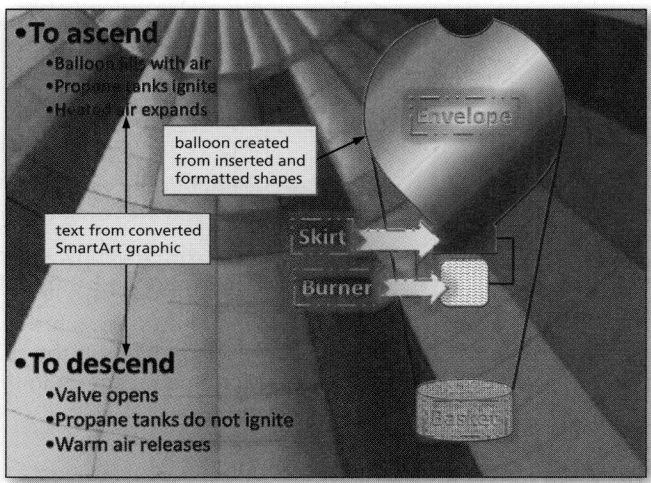

(d) Slide 4

Figure 9–1

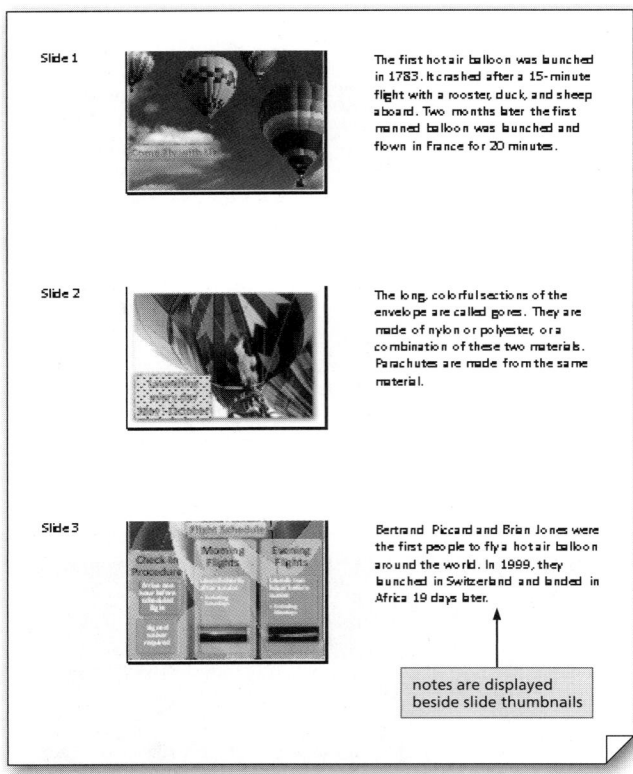

notes are displayed
beside slide thumbnails

(e) Microsoft Word Handout – Page 1

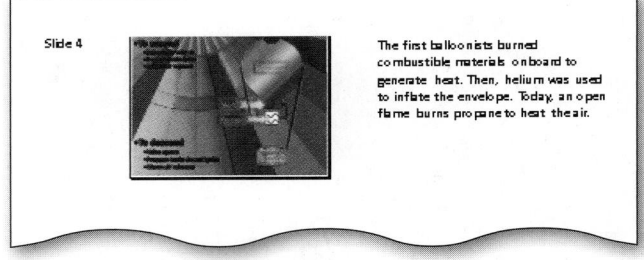

(f) Microsoft Word Handout – Page 2

Figure 9–1 (Continued)

Plan Ahead

General Project Guidelines

When creating a PowerPoint presentation, the actions you perform and the decisions you make will affect the appearance and characteristics of the finished document. As you create a presentation with illustrations, such as the project shown in Figure 9–1 on the previous page and this page, you should follow these general guidelines:

1. **Choose colors wisely.** The appropriate use of color can add interest and help audience members retain information. Used inappropriately, however, mismatched colors will generate confusion and create an impression of unprofessionalism.

2. **Use keywords in SmartArt graphics.** The words you type into your SmartArt graphic can serve as a prompt of the key points you want to make in the presentation.

3. **Use politically correct language.** When you type words into text boxes, be mindful of the terms you are using to identify the images.

4. **Work with a buddy.** As you develop your slide content and then rehearse the presentation, ask a friend or work associate to assist you with various tasks.

When necessary, more specific details concerning the above guidelines are presented at appropriate points in the chapter. The chapter also will identify the actions performed and decisions made regarding these guidelines during the creation of the presentation shown in Figure 9–1.

To Start PowerPoint and Save a File

If you are using a computer to step through the project in this chapter and you want your screens to match the figures in this book, you should change your computer's resolution to 1024 × 768. The following steps start PowerPoint and then save a file.

1 Start PowerPoint. If necessary, maximize the PowerPoint window.

2 Open the presentation, Balloons, located on the Data Files for Students.

3 Save the presentation using the file name, Hot Air Balloons.

Choose colors wisely.
Color can create interest in the material on your slides, so you need to think about which colors best support the message you want to share with your audience. The color you add to text boxes signals that the viewer should pay attention to the contents. Orange, red, and yellow are considered warm colors and will be among the first colors your viewers perceive on your slide. Blue and green are considered cool colors, and they often blend into a background and are less obvious than the warm colors.

**Plan
Ahead**

Formatting Text Boxes

Text boxes can be formatted in a variety of ways to draw attention to slide content. You can apply formatting, such as fill color, gradient, texture, and pattern. You can add a picture; change the outline color, weight, and style; and then set margins and alignment. Once you determine the desired effects for a text box, you can save these settings as a default to achieve consistency and save time. Then, each time you insert another text box, the same settings will be applied.

> In the following pages, you will perform these tasks on Slide 1:
>
> 1. Insert a text box into Slide 1.
> 2. Type text into the text box.
> 3. Change the text box outline color.
> 4. Change the text box outline weight.
> 5. Change the text box outline style.
> 6. Apply a glow effect to the text box.
> 7. Change the text box text to WordArt.
> 8. Increase the WordArt font size and center the paragraph in the text box.
> 9. Set the text box formatting as the default for new text boxes.
>
> Once the text box formatting is complete on Slide 1, you then will perform these tasks on Slide 2:
>
> 1. Insert a text box and enter text.
> 2. Apply a pattern to the text box.
> 3. Change the text box pattern foreground and background colors.
> 4. Change the Slide 2 picture.
>
> You also will perform these tasks on Slide 3:
>
> 1. Insert a text box and enter text.
> 2. Apply a gradient to the text box.
> 3. Align the text box in the center of the slide.

BTW

The Ribbon and Screen Resolution
PowerPoint may change how the groups and buttons within the groups appear on the Ribbon, depending on the computer's screen resolution. Thus, your Ribbon may look different from the ones in this book if you are using a screen resolution other than 1024 × 768.

To Insert a Text Box and Text

The default text box is displayed with the Calibri font and has no border, fill, or effects. To begin customizing the Hot Air Balloons presentation, you will insert a text box and then type the text that serves as the title to your presentation. The following steps insert a text box and enter text into the text box.

Can I change the
shape of the text
box?

Yes. By default, a
rectangular text
box is inserted. If
you want to use
a different shape,
select the text box,
display the Drawing
Tools Format tab,
click the Edit Shape
button (Drawing
Tools Format tab |
Shapes group), point
to Change Shape in
the list, and then
click the desired
new shape.

1 Display the Insert tab, click the Text Box button (Insert tab | Text group), position the
mouse pointer over the large cloud on Slide 1, and then click to insert the new text box.

2 Type **Come Fly with Us** as the text box text (Figure 9–2).

Figure 9–2

To Change a Text Box Outline Weight

The first graphical change you will make to the text box is to increase the thickness of its border, which
is called the outline. The weight, or thickness, of the text box border is measured in points. The following steps
increase the outline weight.

- Click Format on the
Ribbon to display the
Drawing Tools Format
tab.

- Click the Shape
Outline button arrow
(Drawing Tools Format
tab | Shape Styles
group) to display the
Shape Outline gallery.

- Point to Weight in the
Shape Outline gallery
to display the Weight
list (Figure 9–3).

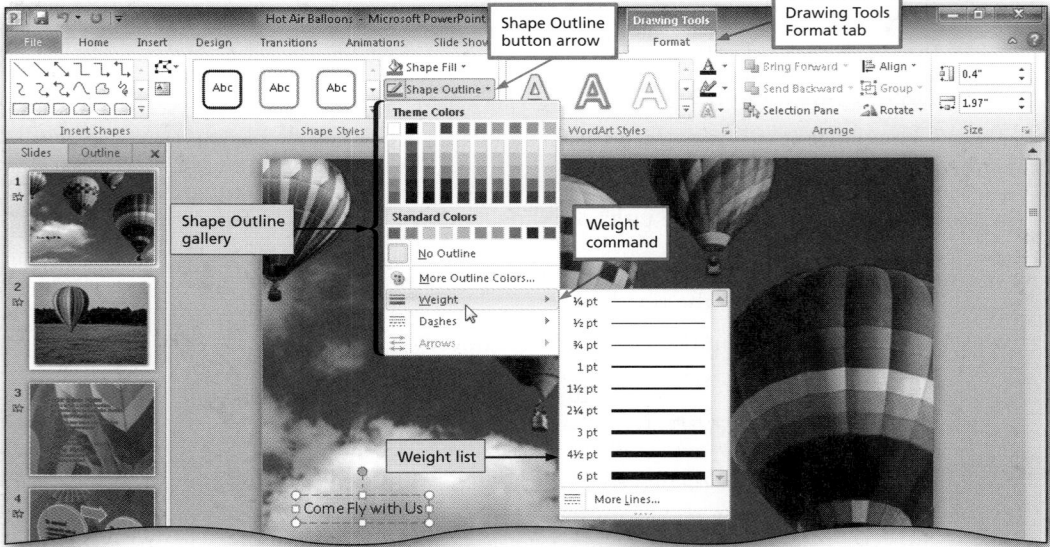

Figure 9–3

- Point to 3 pt to display a live preview of this outline line weight (Figure 9–4).

Experiment

- Point to various line weights on the Weight list and watch the border weights on the text box change.

- Click 3 pt to add an outline around the text box.

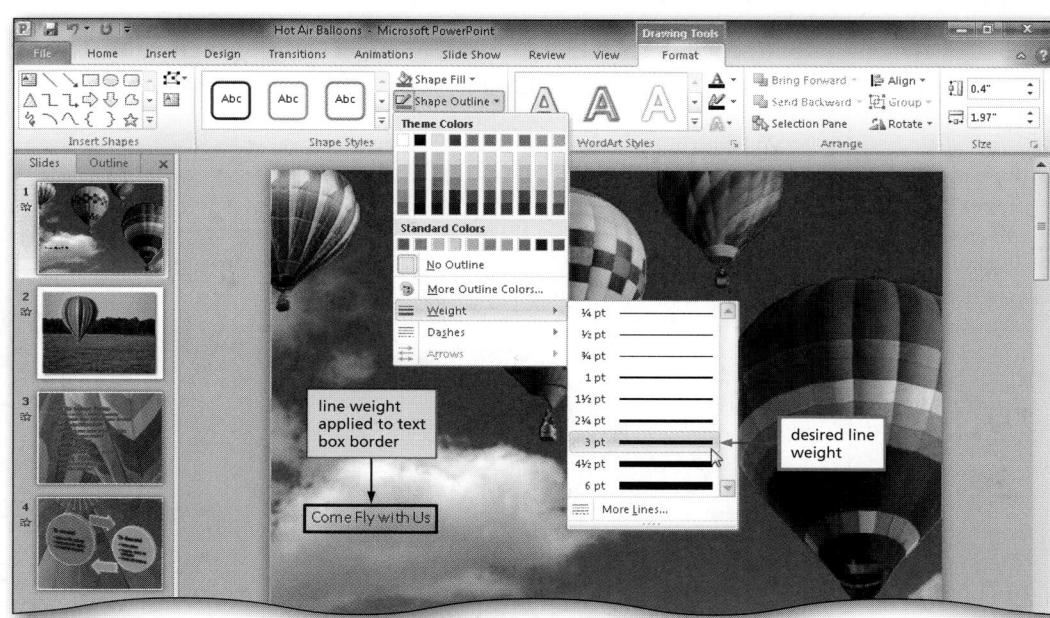

Figure 9–4

To Change a Text Box Outline Color

The default outline color in the Office Theme is black. To coordinate with the colorful balloon picture and blue sky, you can change the outline color to a bright color. The following steps change the text box outline color.

- Click the Shape Outline button arrow (Drawing Tools Format tab | Shape Styles group) to display the Shape Outline gallery and then point to Blue in the Standard Colors area to display a live preview of that outline color on the text box (Figure 9–5).

Experiment

- Point to various colors in the Shape Outline gallery and watch the border colors on the text box change.

- Click Blue to change the text box border color.

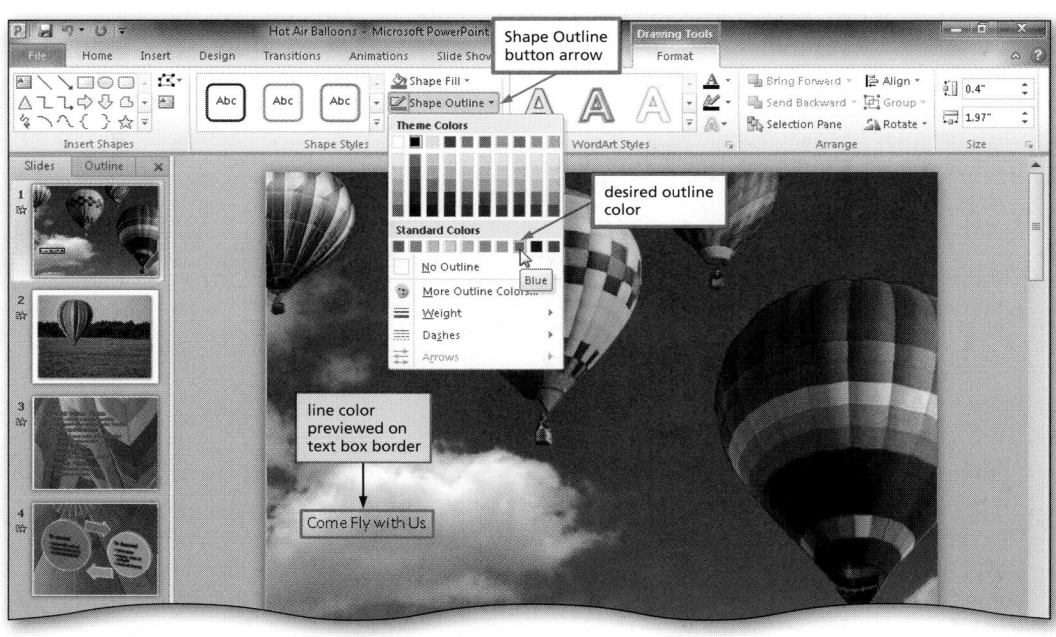

Figure 9–5

To Change a Text Box Outline Style

The default outline style is a solid line. You can add interest by changing the style to dashes, dots, or a combination of dashes and dots. The following steps change the text box outline style.

- Click the Shape Outline button arrow (Drawing Tools Format tab | Shape Styles group) to display the Shape Outline gallery and then point to Dashes to display the Dashes list.

- Point to Long Dash Dot Dot to display a live preview of this outline style (Figure 9–6).

 Experiment

- Point to various styles in the Shape Outline gallery and watch the borders on the text box change.

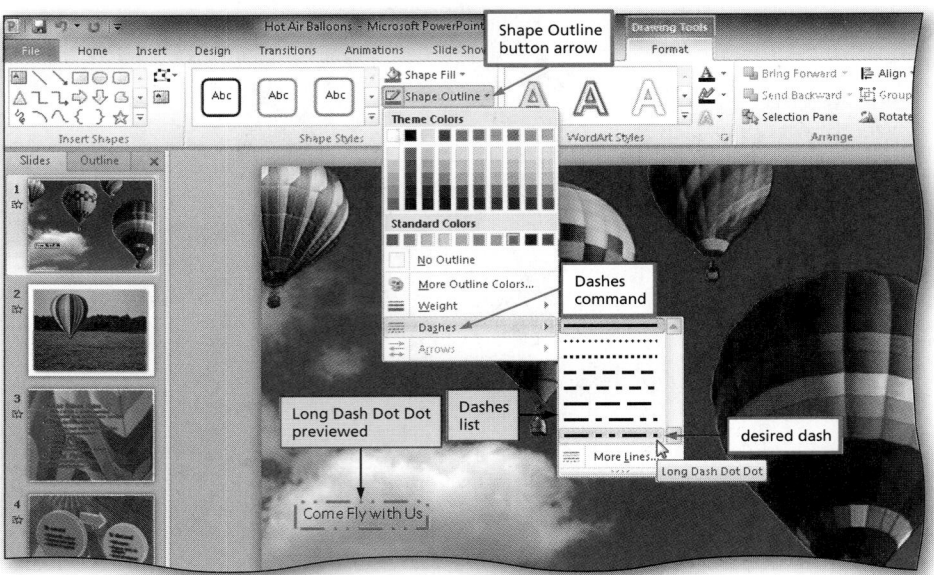

2

- Click Long Dash Dot Dot to change the text box border style.

Figure 9–6

To Apply an Effect to a Text Box

PowerPoint provides a variety of visual effects to add to the text box. They include shadow, glow, reflection, and 3-D rotation. The clouds in the Slide 1 background have uneven and transparent edges, so you can coordinate with this soft effect by adding a glow effect to the text box. The following steps apply an effect to the text box.

- Click the Shape Effects button (Drawing Tools Format tab | Shape Styles group) to display the Shape Effects gallery.

- Point to Glow to display the Glow gallery (Figure 9–7).

 **Experiment**

- Point to various effects in the Glow gallery and watch the glow edges change on the text box.

- Click the Blue, 18 pt glow, Accent color 1 (first color in fourth row) variation in the Glow Variations area to apply the glow effect.

Figure 9–7

To Format Text Box Text

The text box outline color, width, line style, and effect are set, so you now can choose a font and font size that complement the formatting changes. A WordArt style can add visual interest to the text box. The following steps change the text box text to WordArt, change the font size, and center the text in the text box.

1 Select all the text box text, click the WordArt Styles More button (Drawing Tools Format tab | WordArt Styles group) to expand the gallery, and then click Gradient Fill – Orange, Accent 6, Inner Shadow (second letter A in fourth row) to apply this style.

2 Increase the font size to 44 point.

3 Center the text in the text box. If necessary, drag the text box to the location shown in Figure 9–8.

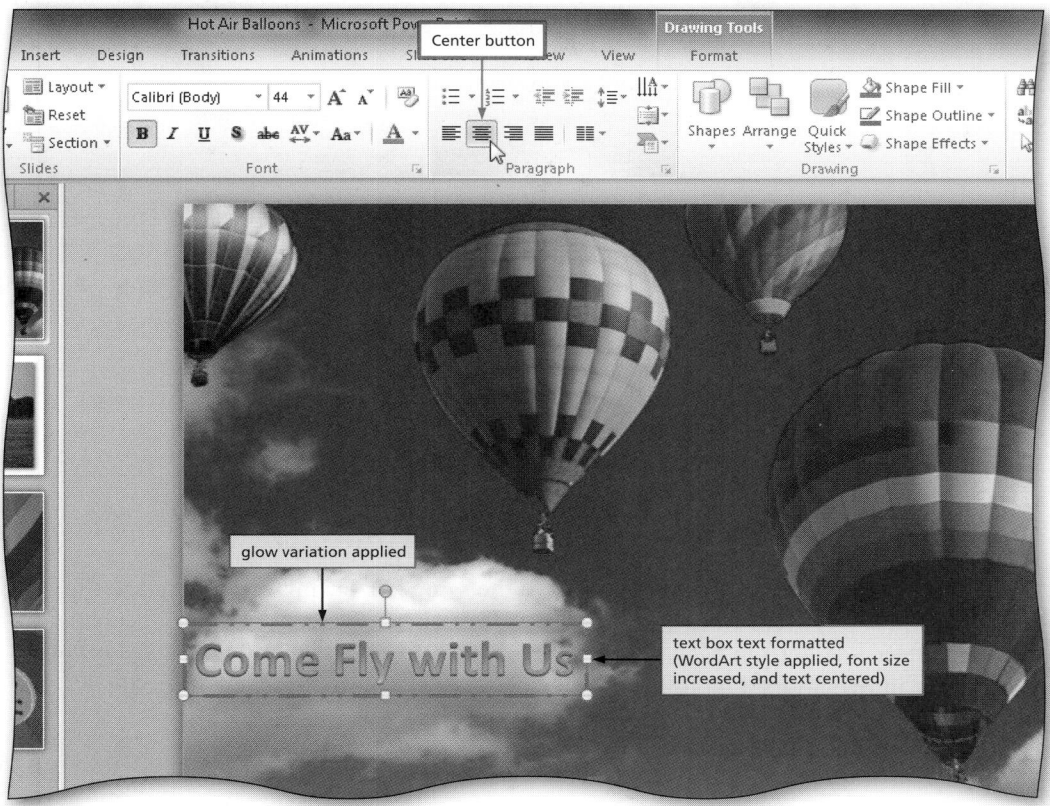

Figure 9–8

To Set Text Box Formatting as the Default

The text box you inserted and formatted has a variety of visual elements that work well with the Hot Air Balloons picture and overall theme. For consistency, you can insert text boxes with the same formatting into other slides in the presentation. To save time and ensure all the formatting changes are applied, you can set the formatting of one text box as the default for all other text boxes you insert into the presentation. The following steps set the text box on Slide 1 as the default.

- Right-click the text box outline to display the shortcut menu (Figure 9–9).

2

- Click Set as Default Text Box on the shortcut menu to set the text box formatting as the default for any new text boxes.

Q&A
What should I do if the Set as Default Text Box command is not displayed on the shortcut menu?

Repeat Step 1 and be certain to click the text box border, not the interior of the box.

Q&A
Does setting the default text box affect all presentations or just the current one?

Only the current presentation is affected.

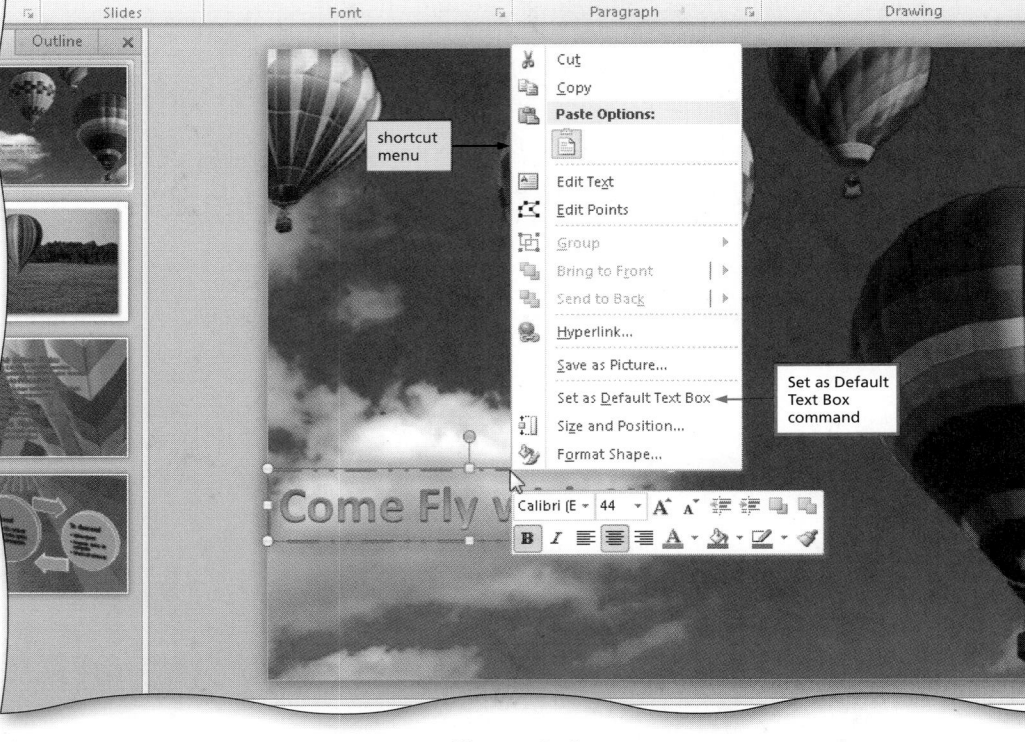

Figure 9–9

BTW

Q&As
For a complete list of the Q&As found in many of the step-by-step sequences in this book, visit the PowerPoint 2010 Q&A Web page (scsite.com/ppt2010/qa).

To Insert a Formatted Text Box and Enter Text

Any new text boxes you insert will have the same formatting you applied to the Slide 1 text box. You want to emphasize to your presentation viewers that hot air balloon rides are offered daily from May through October, so a text box on Slide 2 is a good place to state this information. The following steps insert a formatted text box into Slide 2 and enter text.

1 Display Slide 2, display the Insert tab, and then click the Text Box button.

2 Insert the text box into the lower-left corner of the slide and then type `Launching` as the first line of the text box text.

3 Press SHIFT+ENTER to insert a line break and then type `every day` as the second text box line.

4 Press SHIFT+ENTER to insert a line break and then type `May - October` as the third text box line.

5 If necessary, drag the text box to the location shown in Figure 9–10.

Figure 9–10

To Apply a Pattern to a Text Box

A pattern fill can call attention to a text box. PowerPoint provides a Pattern gallery, allowing you to change the appearance of the text box with a variety of horizontal and vertical lines, dots, dashes, and stripes. If desired, you can change the default fill foreground and background colors. The following steps apply a pattern to the Slide 2 text box and change the foreground and background colors.

1

- Right-click anywhere on the Slide 2 text box to display the shortcut menu.

- Click Format Shape on the shortcut menu to display the Format Shape dialog box. Drag the dialog box to the right so that you can view the text box (Figure 9–11).

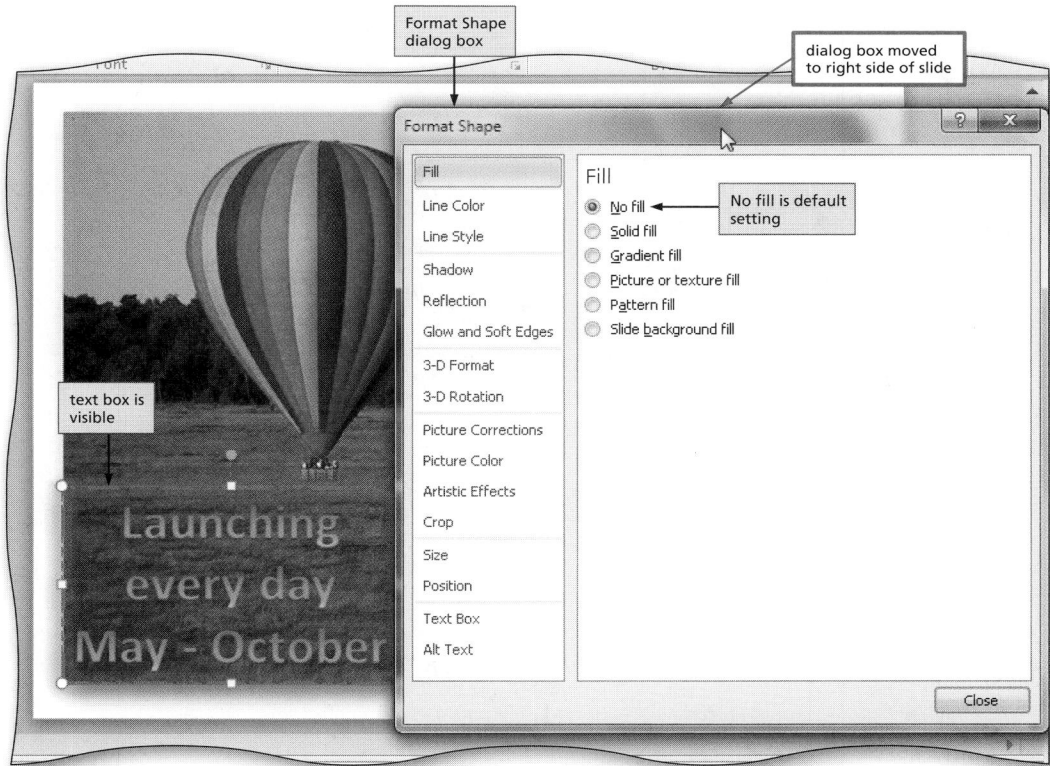

Figure 9–11

2

- Click Pattern fill (Format Shape dialog box) to display the Pattern gallery and the 5% pattern on the text box (Figure 9–12).

Q&A Can I experiment with previewing the patterns on the text box?

No, the live preview function is not available.

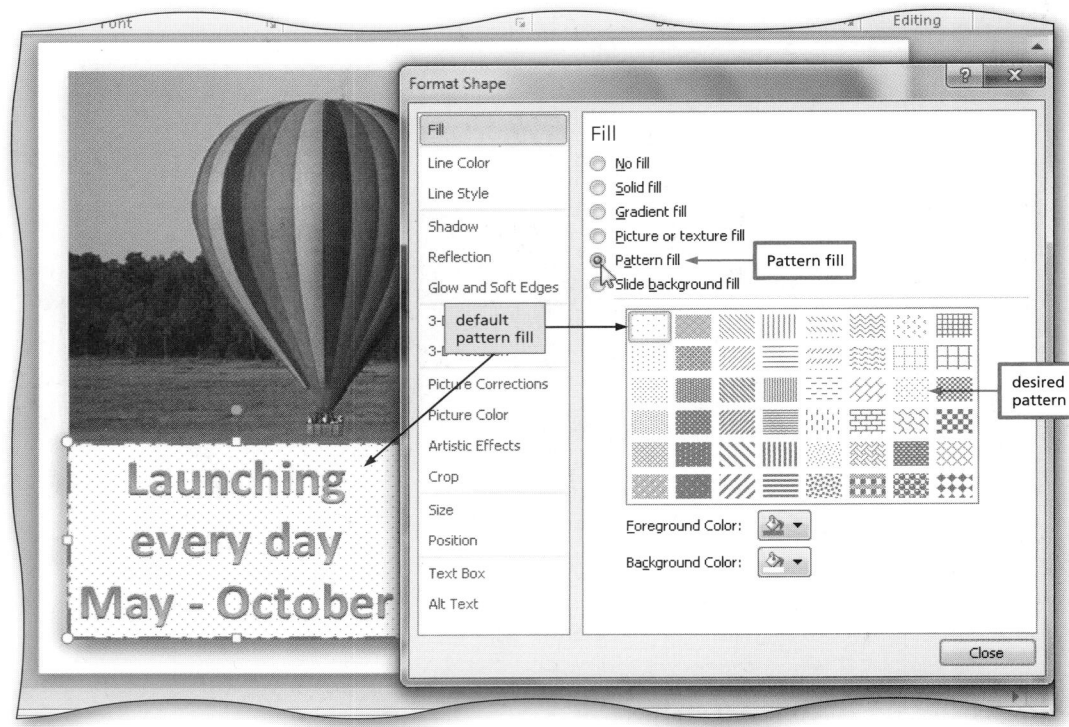

Figure 9–12

3

- Click the Dotted diamond pattern (seventh color in third row) to apply this pattern to the Slide 2 text box.

Q&A How can I delete a pattern if I decide not to apply one to my slide?

If you already have applied the pattern, click the Undo button on the Quick Access Toolbar.

- Click the Foreground Color button (Format Shape dialog box) to display a color gallery (Figure 9–13).

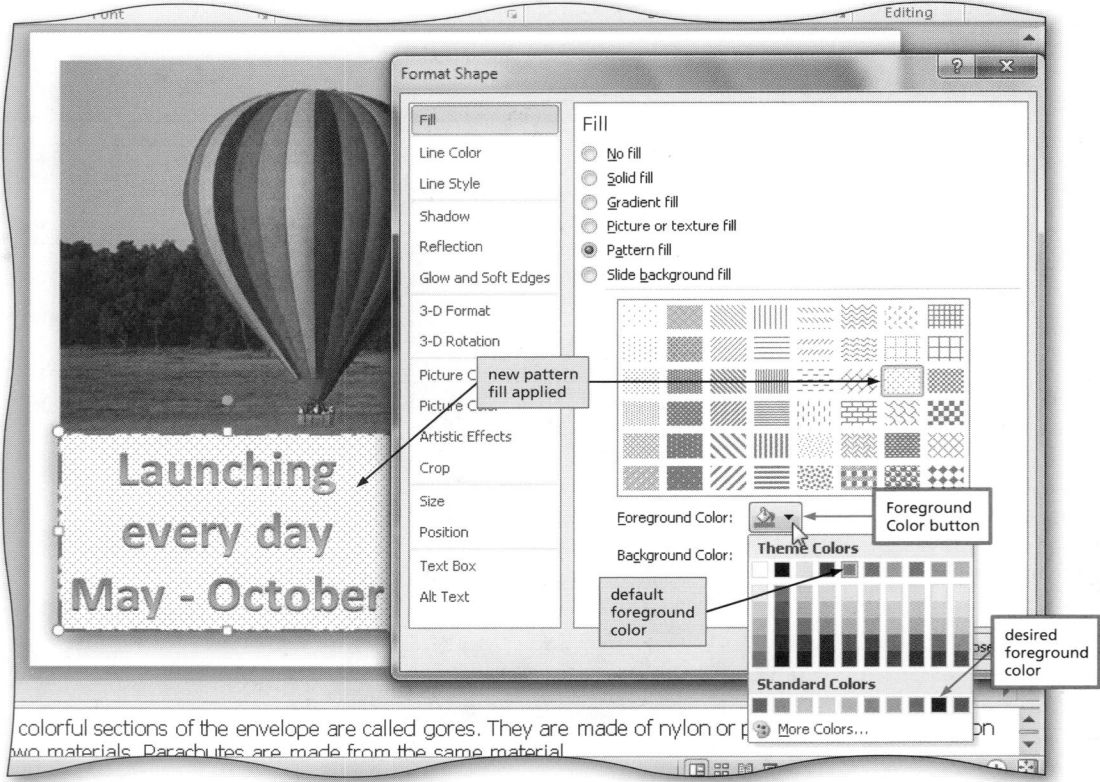

Figure 9–13

• Click Dark Blue (ninth color in Standard Colors row) to apply this color to the text box pattern and to display the Pattern gallery with the new foreground color.

• Click the Background Color button (Format Shape dialog box) to display a color gallery (Figure 9–14).

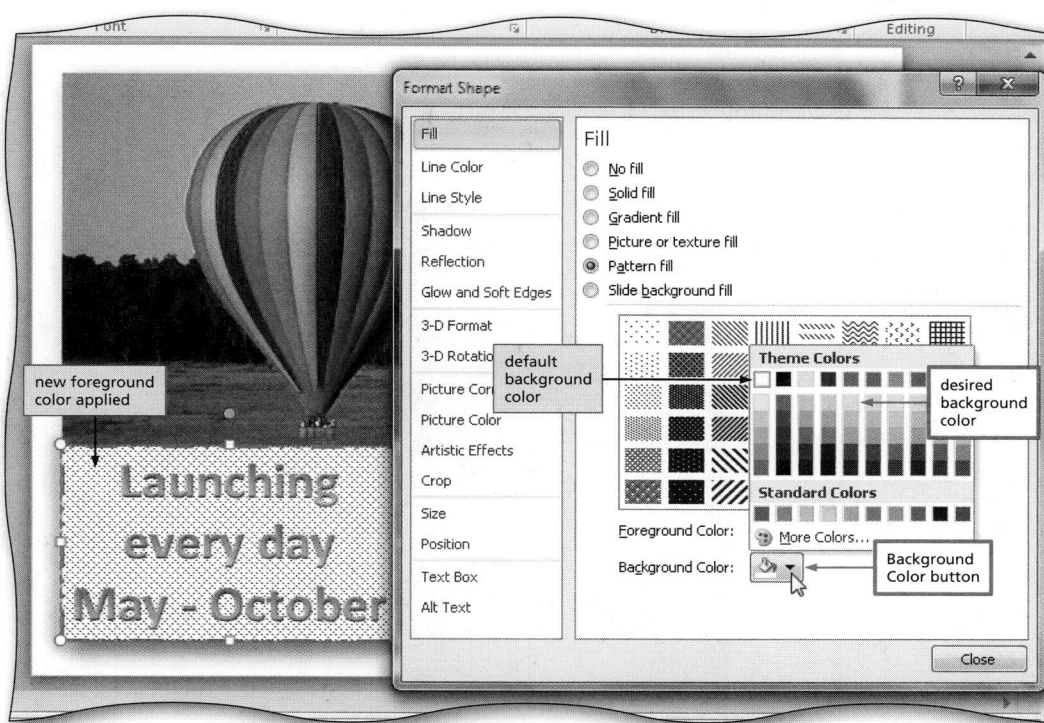

Figure 9–14

• Click Blue, Accent 1, Lighter 80% (fifth color in second Theme Colors row) to apply this color to the text box background and to display the Pattern gallery with the new background color (Figure 9–15).

• Click the Close button to close the Format Shape dialog box.

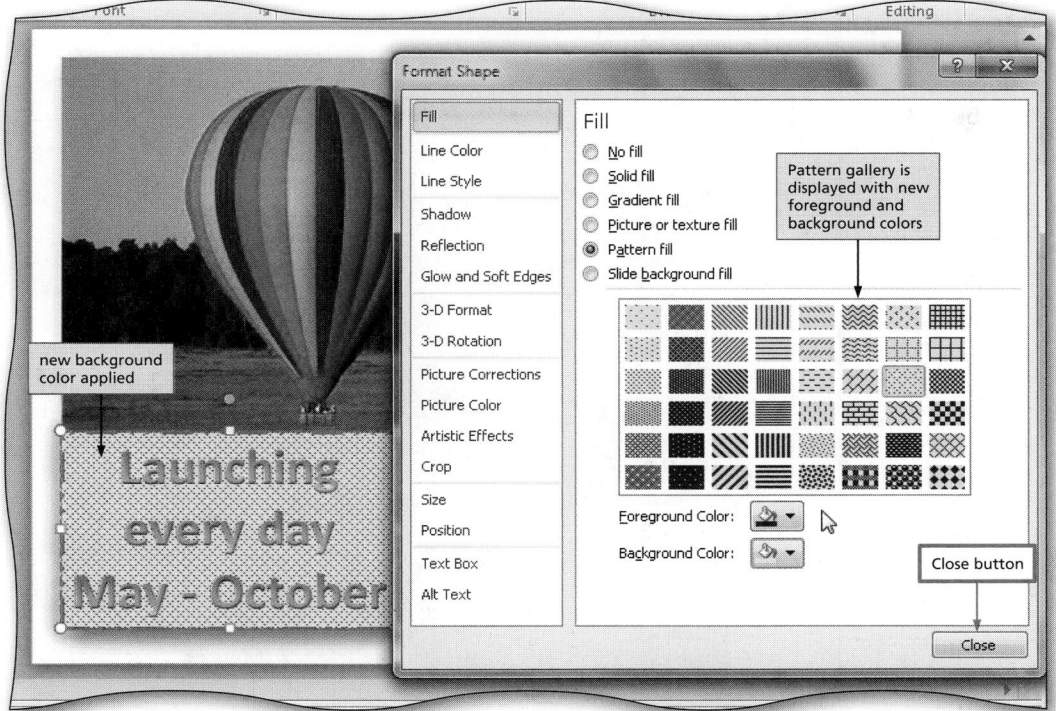

Figure 9–15

To Apply a Gradient Fill to a Text Box

A gradient fill is another type of format you can apply to create interest in a slide element. It blends one color into another shade of the same color or another color. PowerPoint provides several preset gradients, or you can create your own custom color mix. The following steps insert a text box into Slide 3 and then apply a gradient fill.

1

- Display Slide 3, display the Insert tab, and then insert a text box near the top of the slide.

- Type **Flight Schedule** as the text box text, and if necessary, drag the text box to the location shown in Figure 9–16.

Figure 9–16

2

- Click the Drawing Tools Format tab and then click the Shape Fill button arrow (Drawing Tools Format tab | Shape Styles group) to display the Shape Fill gallery.

- Point to Gradient to display the Gradient gallery (Figure 9–17).

Experiment

- Point to various fills in the Gradient gallery and watch the interior of the text box change.

3

- Click the Linear Up (second variation in third row) variation in the Light Variations area to apply the gradient fill.

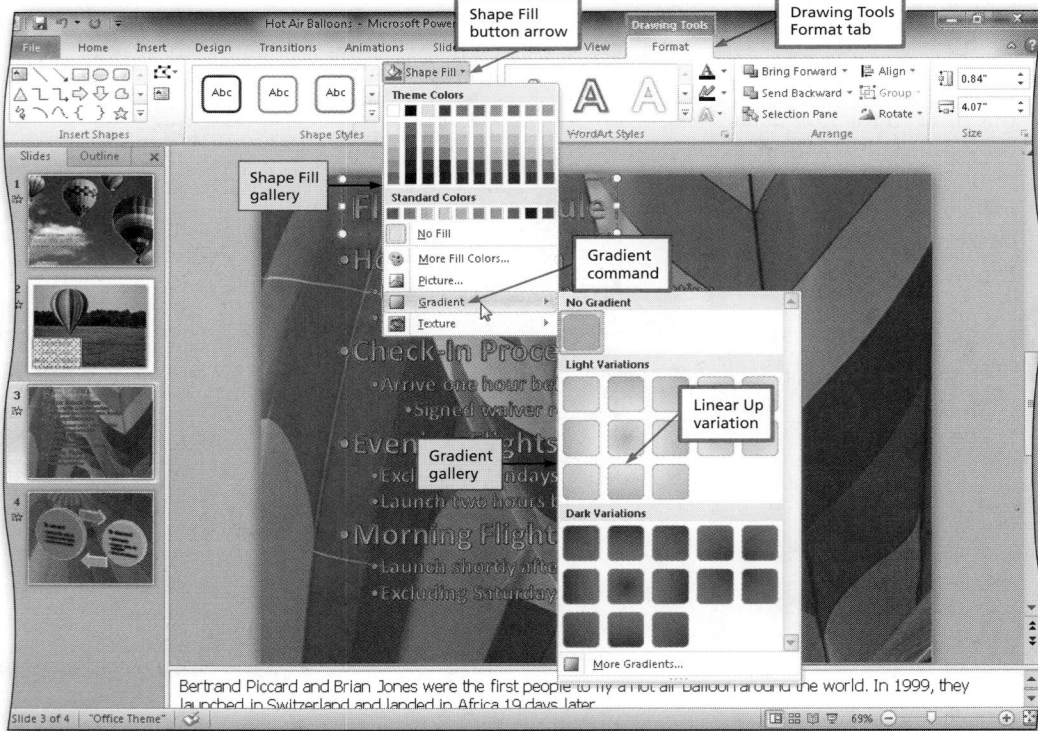

Figure 9–17

To Center a Text Box

The text box on Slide 3 will serve as the title. You could attempt to center it horizontally on the slide and use the rulers to aid you in this process. A more efficient method of centering the text box between the left and right edges of the slide, however, is to use PowerPoint's align feature. You can align a slide element horizontally along the left or right sides or in the center of the slide, and you also can align an element vertically along the top, bottom, or middle of the slide. The following steps align the Slide 3 text box horizontally.

1

- With the Slide 3 text box selected, click the Align button (Drawing Tools Format tab | Arrange group) to display the Align menu (Figure 9–18).

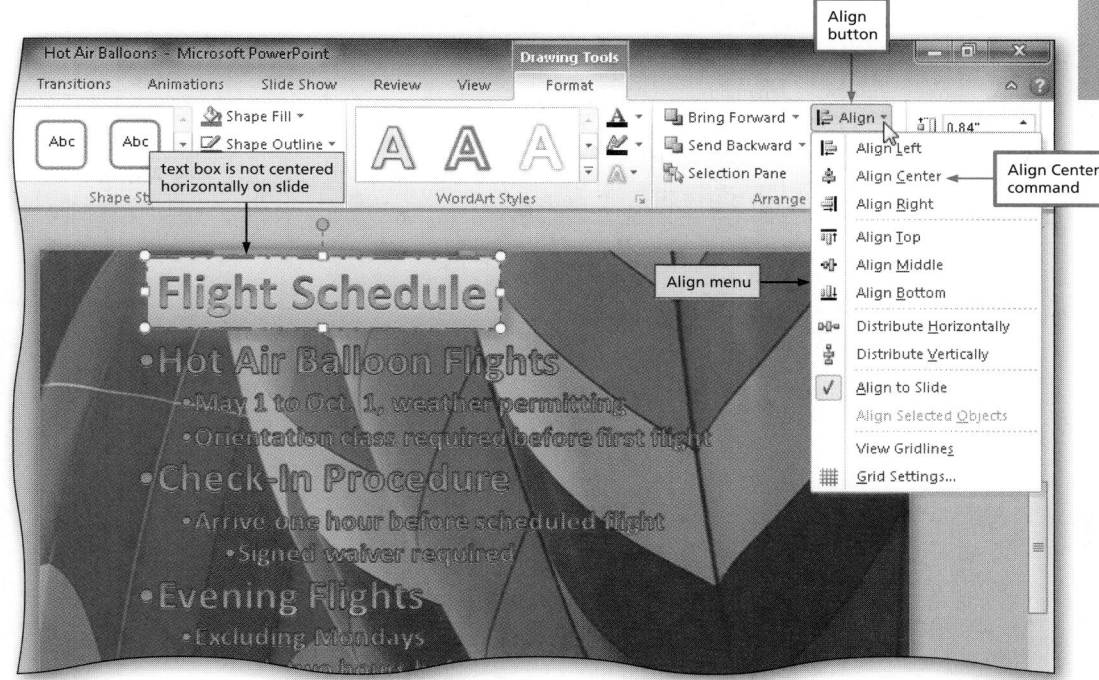

Figure 9–18

2

- Click Align Center to center the text box horizontally on the slide (Figure 9–19).

Q&A Can I position a text box in a precise location on a slide?

Yes. With the text box selected, right-click a border of the box to display the shortcut menu and then click Format Shape on the shortcut menu to display the Format Shape dialog box. Click Position (Format Shape dialog box) to display the Position pane and then enter Horizontal and Vertical measurements in the 'Position on slide' area. Specify if these measurements should be from the Top Left Corner or the Center of the text box and then click the Close button.

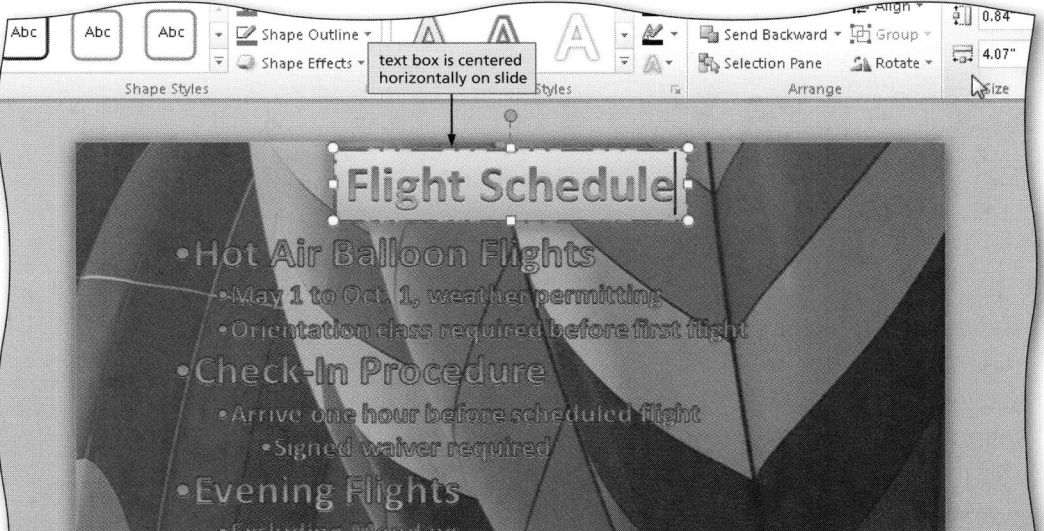

Figure 9–19

To Change a Slide Picture

The picture on Slide 2 features a colorful balloon, but the brown grass that dominates the slide does not complement the formatted text box. A dramatic picture of a colorful balloon is located on the Data Files for Students. PowerPoint allows you to change a picture on a slide easily. The following steps change the Slide 2 picture.

1

- Display Slide 2, click anywhere on the picture except the text box to select the picture, and then click the Picture Tools Format tab (Figure 9–20).

Figure 9–20

2

- Click the Change Picture button (Picture Tools Format tab | Adjust group) to display the Insert Picture dialog box.

- If necessary, select your USB flash drive in the list of available storage devices to display a list of files and folders on the selected USB flash drive and then navigate to the PowerPoint Chapter 09 folder.

- Click Balloon Burner to select the file name (Figure 9–21).

Q&A
What if the picture is not on a USB flash drive?

Use the same process, but select the drive containing the picture.

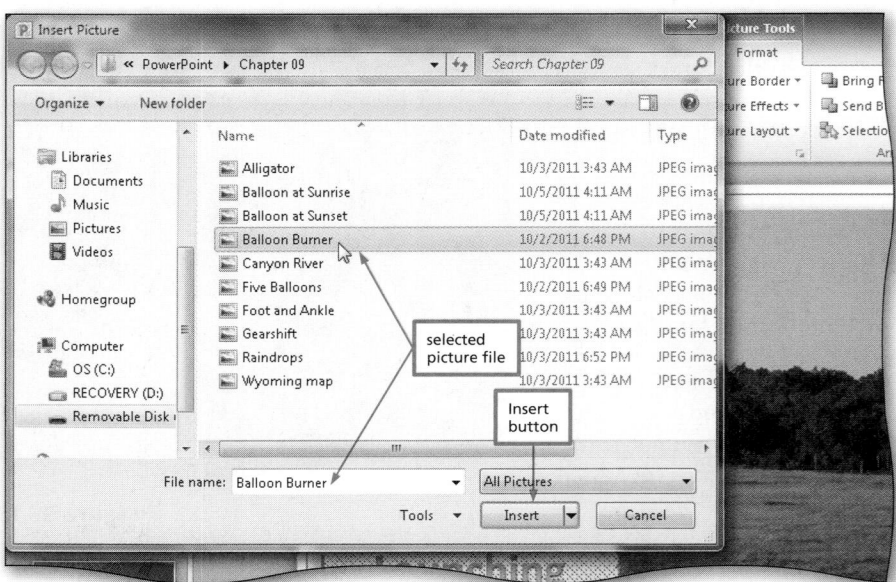

Figure 9–21

3

- Click the Insert button (Insert Picture dialog box) to change the Slide 2 picture (Figure 9–22).

Q&A What if I do not want to use this picture?

Click the Undo button on the Quick Access Toolbar.

Figure 9–22

Break Point: If you wish to take a break, this is a good place to do so. Be sure to save the Hot Air Balloons file again and then you can quit PowerPoint. To resume at a later time, start PowerPoint, open the file called Hot Air Balloons, and continue following the steps from this location forward.

Manipulating SmartArt

Every SmartArt layout has a unique design and graphical elements. The shapes maximize vertical and horizontal space for text and pictures. When your presentation calls for special design needs or additional shapes, you can change the defaults that specify where each SmartArt element is displayed. You can add, subtract, and reorder shapes; promote and demote text; make a single shape smaller or larger; and change the SmartArt fill, outline, and colors.

In the following pages, you will perform these tasks on Slide 3:

1. Convert WordArt paragraphs to a SmartArt Target List.
2. Reorder two shapes in the SmartArt layout.
3. Reorder two bulleted paragraphs in one shape.
4. Promote and demote bulleted paragraphs.
5. Change the SmartArt layout and style.
6. Resize the entire SmartArt layout and one shape within the layout.
7. Apply two pictures to SmartArt shapes.
8. Convert the SmartArt graphic to text.

BTW

SmartArt in Handouts
SmartArt diagrams are composed of individual vector graphics. Some presenters decide to include these diagrams in a handout but not as part of a presentation so that audience members can study the relationships among the shapes after the presentation has concluded.

Plan Ahead	**Use keywords in SmartArt graphics.**
	Most SmartArt shapes have very limited space for text. You must, therefore, carefully choose each word you are going to display in the graphic. The text you select can serve as keywords, or a speaking outline. If you glance at the SmartArt when you are presenting the slide show in front of an audience, each word should prompt you for the main point you are going to make. These keywords should jog your memory if you lose your train of thought or are interrupted.

To Convert WordArt to SmartArt

The bulleted paragraphs on Slide 3 are formatted as WordArt. Although WordArt can add visual interest, using a graphical element such as SmartArt can be even more effective in helping the audience to grasp essential concepts. SmartArt diagrams are creative means to show processes, lists, cycles, and other relationships. PowerPoint suggests layouts that might fit the concept you are trying to present and then easily converts WordArt to SmartArt. The following steps convert WordArt to SmartArt.

- Display Slide 3, right-click anywhere in the WordArt bulleted list paragraphs to display the shortcut menu, and then point to Convert to SmartArt to display the SmartArt gallery.

Q&A
Does it matter where I place the cursor to right-click the WordArt?

No. As long as the cursor is placed in the WordArt text, you will be able to convert the paragraphs to SmartArt.

- Point to Target List in the gallery to display a live preview of that layout applied to the WordArt paragraphs (Figure 9–23).

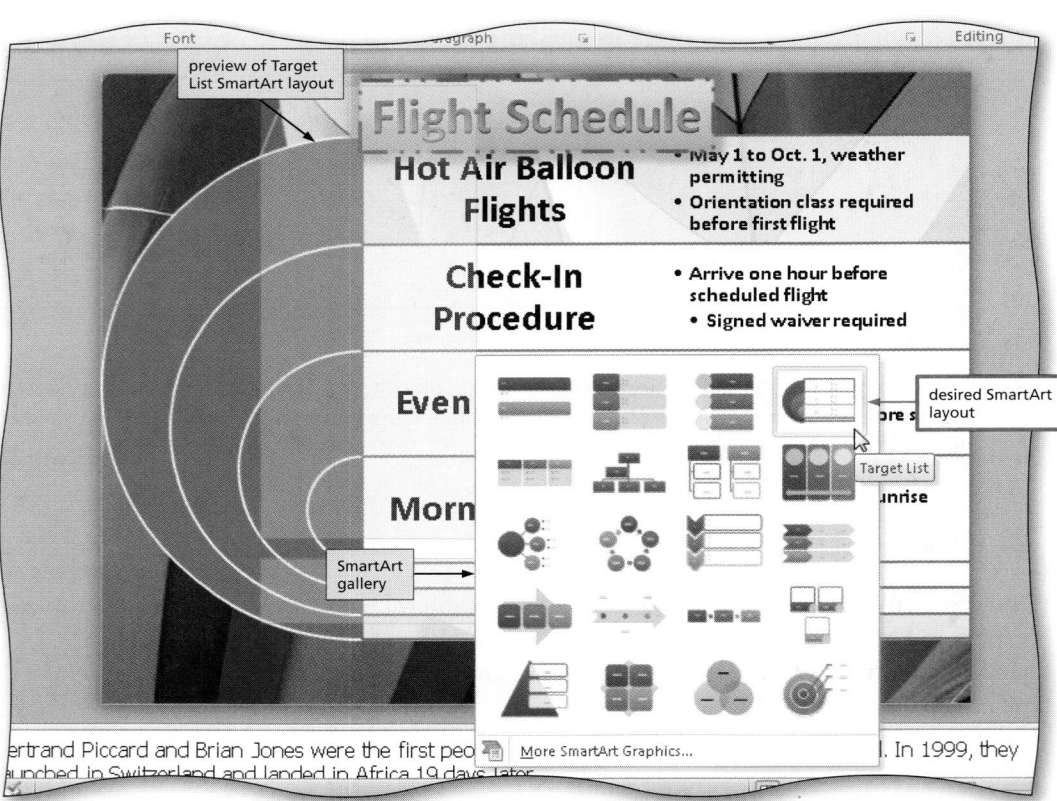

Figure 9–23

 **Experiment**
- Point to various graphics in the SmartArt gallery and watch the layouts change.

- Click Target List in the SmartArt gallery to convert the WordArt to that layout.

How is the text arranged in the Target List layout?

The four first-level paragraphs are in the middle column of the graphic and have a larger font size than the eight bulleted second-level paragraphs.

To Reorder SmartArt Shapes

Now that the SmartArt layout is created, you can modify the graphic. One change you can make is to change the order of the shapes. You decide that two items in the graphic should be displayed in a different order. First, the information regarding the morning flights should precede the details for the evening flights. Also, for consistency, you decide that the second bulleted paragraph in the morning and evening flight shapes should refer to the day of the week excluded from the schedule. Currently, the Excluding Mondays bulleted paragraph in the Evening Flights shape is the second item, and the Excluding Saturdays bulleted paragraph in the Morning Flights shape is the first item. PowerPoint provides tools to move shapes and paragraphs in a vertical layout up or down and the shapes and paragraphs in a horizontal layout right or left. The following steps reorder the Morning and Evening Flights shapes and the two bulleted paragraphs in the Evening Flights shape.

- Position the mouse pointer in the Morning Flights shape and then click to select it and the two bulleted paragraphs (Figure 9–24).

Q&A Why are both shapes selected?

The Morning Flights shape is a first-level paragraph, and the two bulleted second-level paragraphs are associated with it. When a first-level paragraph is selected, any related paragraphs also are selected with it.

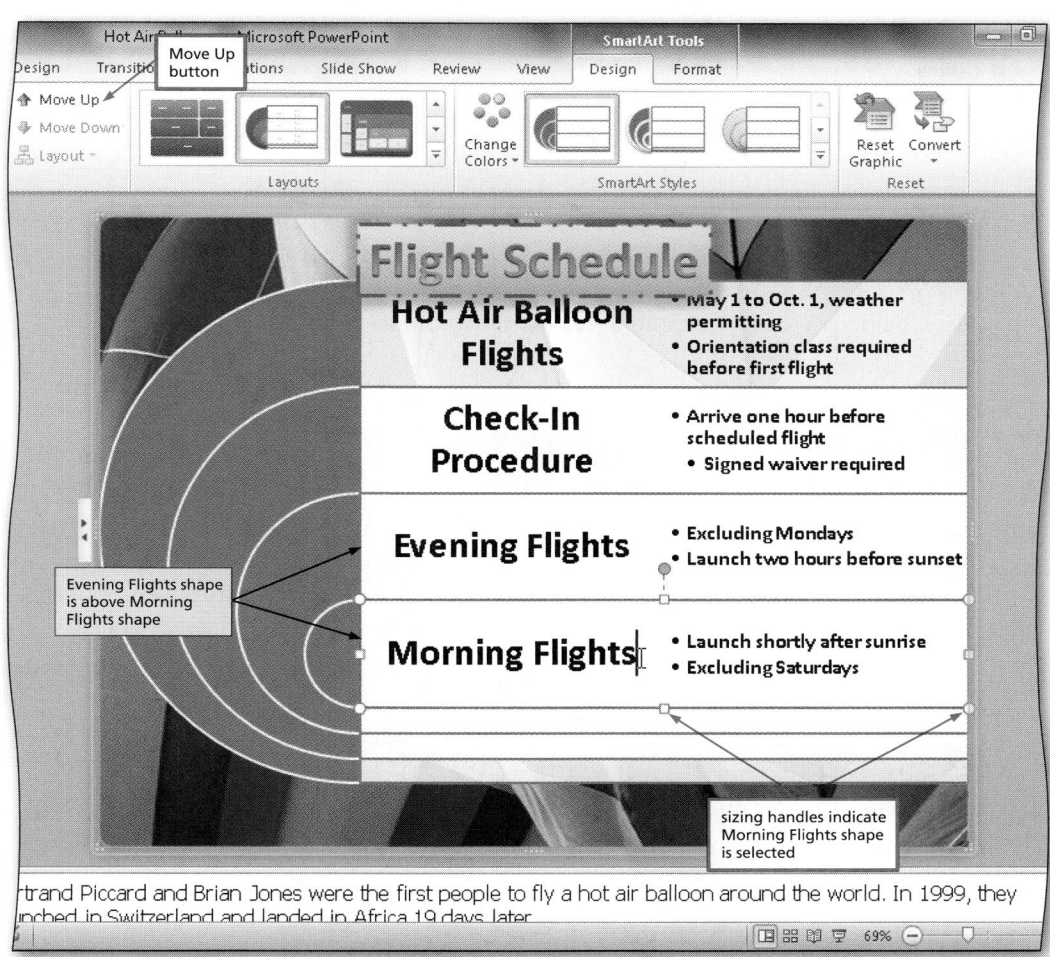

Figure 9–24

Q&A Why is the signed waiver bullet indented in the Check-In Procedure shape?

The original PowerPoint slide designer categorized this waiver as a subset of the one-hour preflight time paragraph. You now want to emphasize that this document is an important part of the check-in procedure and decide that it deserves equal prominence on the slide. You will, therefore, change this bulleted paragraph to the same level as the bullet above it in the next set of steps.

- With the SmartArt
Tools Design tab
displayed, click the
Move Up button
(SmartArt Tools Design
tab | Create Graphic
group) to reorder the
Morning Flights shape
above the Evening
Flights shape.

- Position the mouse
pointer in the
bulleted paragraph,
Excluding Mondays
(Figure 9–25).

- Click the Move Down
button (SmartArt
Tools Design tab | Create
Graphic group) to reorder the bulleted paragraph, Excluding
Mondays, below the bulleted paragraph, Launch two hours before sunset.

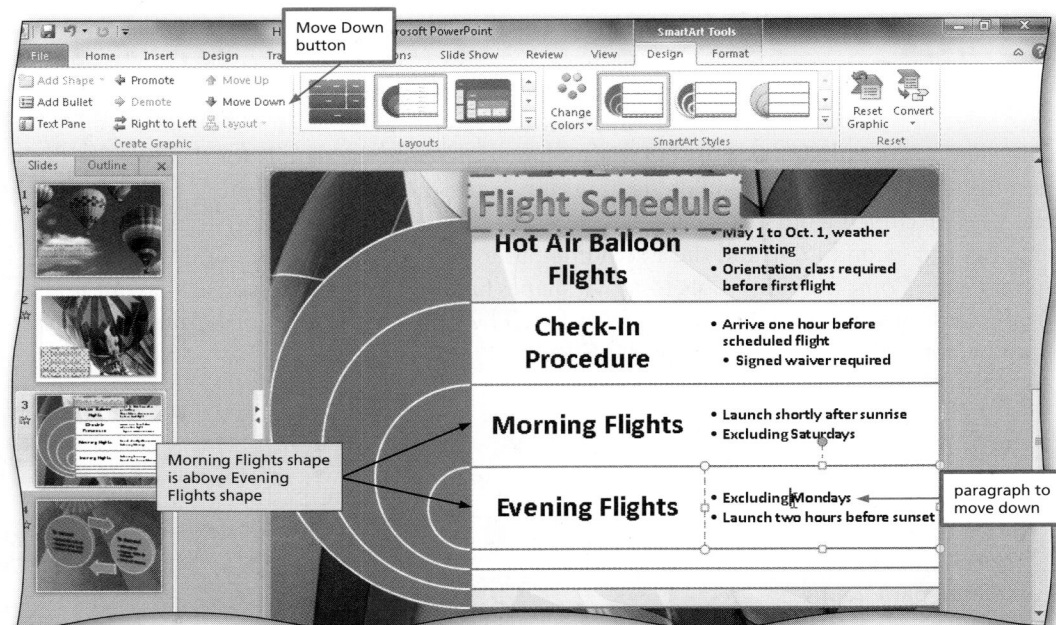

Figure 9–25

To Promote a SmartArt Bullet Level

PowerPoint provides tools that allow you to promote and demote bulleted text. These tools function in the same manner as the Increase List Level and Decrease List Level buttons that change the indents for bulleted text.

Another change you want to make on Slide 3 is to promote the bulleted paragraph, Signed waiver required, to the same level as the bullet above it, because this document is an important part of the check-in procedure. The following steps promote the second bullet in the Check-In Procedure shape.

- Position the mouse
pointer in the bulleted
paragraph, Signed
waiver required
(Figure 9–26).

- With the SmartArt
Tools Design tab
displayed, click the
Promote button
(SmartArt Tools Design
tab | Create Graphic
group) to decrease the
indent of the bulleted
paragraph.

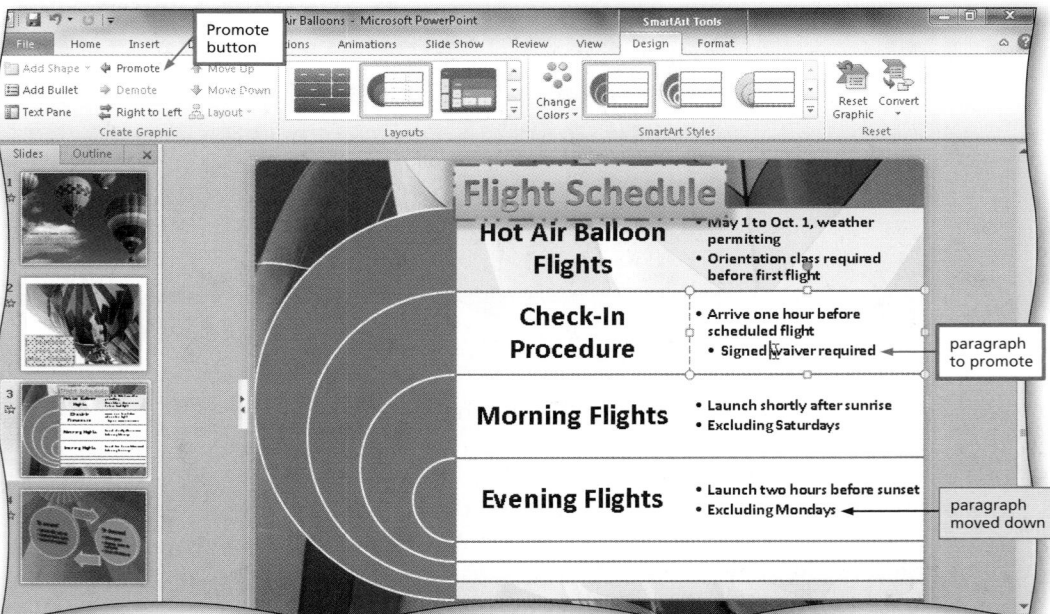

Figure 9–26

To Demote a SmartArt Bullet Level

The two bulleted items in the Morning Flights and Evening Flights shapes both are second-level paragraphs. You decide that the two days that are excluded from the weekly schedule are not as important to emphasize as the launch times, so you want to demote those paragraphs. The following steps demote the second-level bulleted paragraphs.

1

- Position the mouse pointer in the bulleted paragraph, Excluding Saturdays (Figure 9–27).

Figure 9–27

2

- With the SmartArt Tools Design tab displayed, click the Demote button (SmartArt Tools Design tab | Create Graphic group) to increase the indent of the bulleted paragraph.

- Position the mouse pointer in the bulleted paragraph, Excluding Mondays, and then click the Demote button to increase the indent of this paragraph (Figure 9–28).

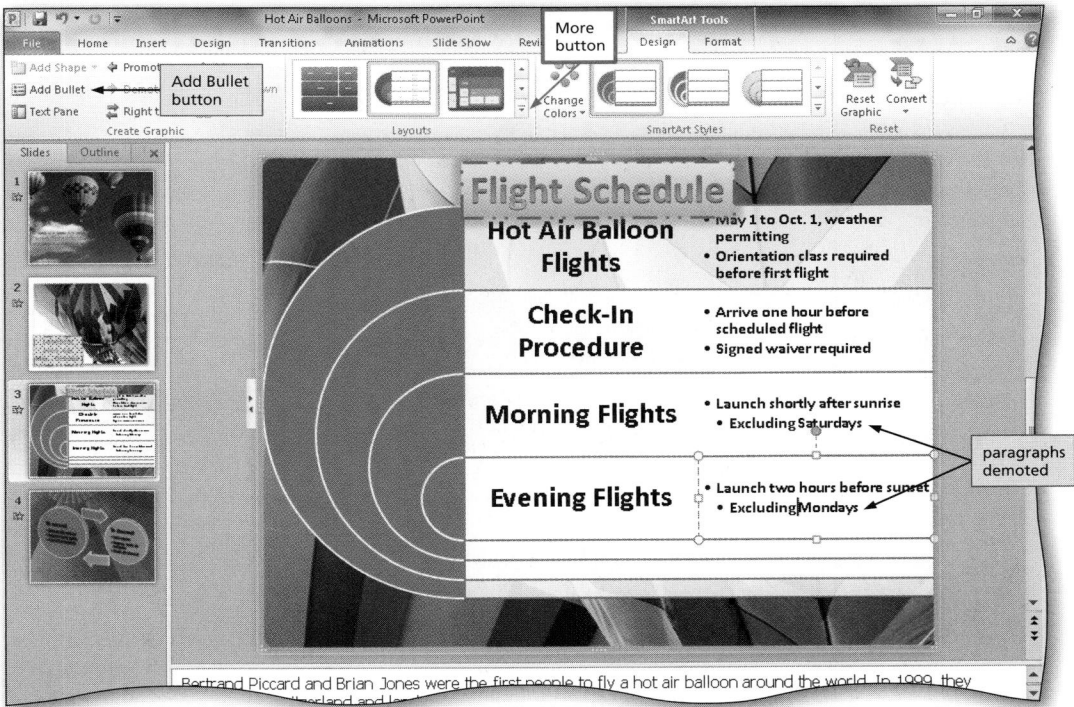

Figure 9–28

To Add a SmartArt Bullet

If you need to add information to a SmartArt shape, you can create a new bulleted paragraph. This text would display below the last bulleted paragraph in the shape. If you wanted to add a SmartArt bullet, you would perform the following steps.

1. Select the SmartArt graphic shape where you want to insert the bulleted paragraph.
2. Click the Add Bullet button (SmartArt Tools Design tab | Create Graphic group) to insert a new bulleted paragraph below any bulleted text.

To Change the SmartArt Layout

Once you begin formatting a SmartArt shape, you may decide that another layout better conveys the message you are communicating to an audience. PowerPoint allows you to change the layout easily. Any graphical changes that were made to the original SmartArt, such as moving shapes or promoting and demoting paragraphs, are applied to the new SmartArt layout. The following steps change the SmartArt layout.

- With the SmartArt Tools Design tab displaying, click the More button in the Layouts group to expand the Layouts gallery (Figure 9–29).

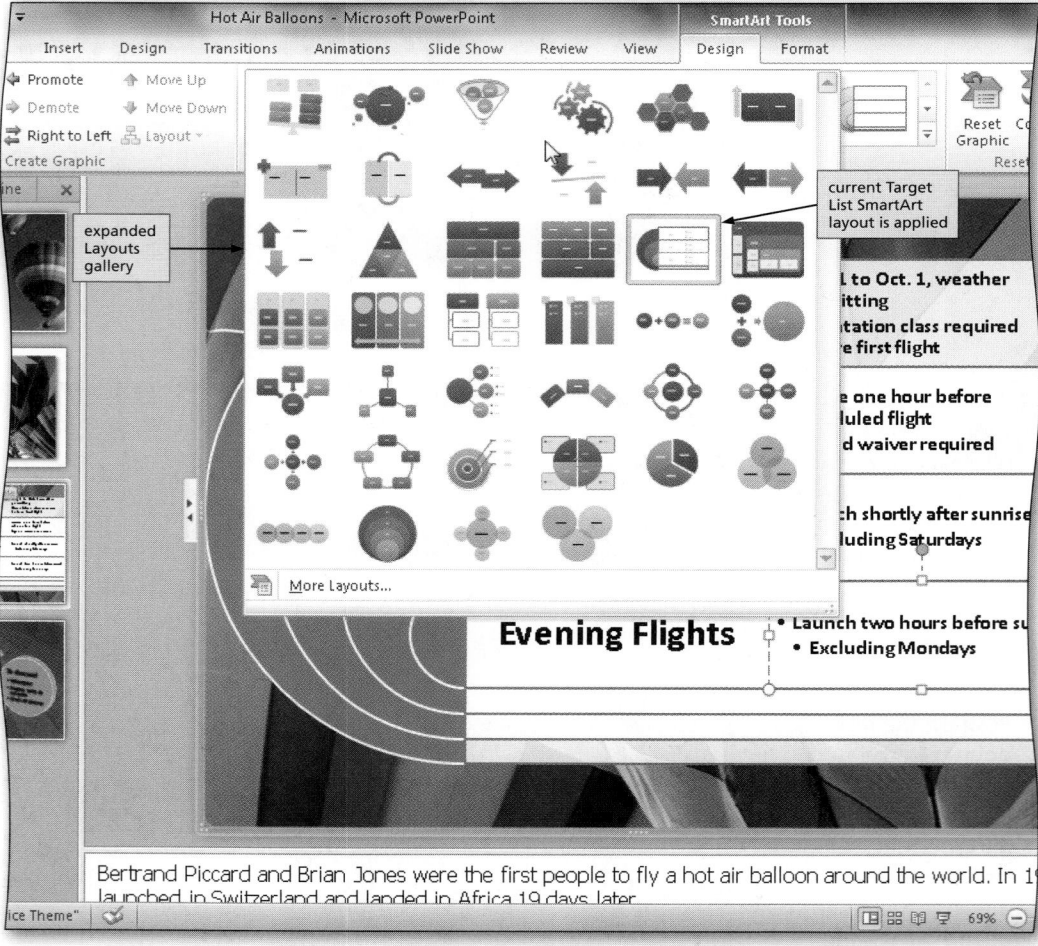

Figure 9–29

2

- Point to the Grouped List layout (first layout in fourth row) to display a live preview of this SmartArt layout (Figure 9–30).

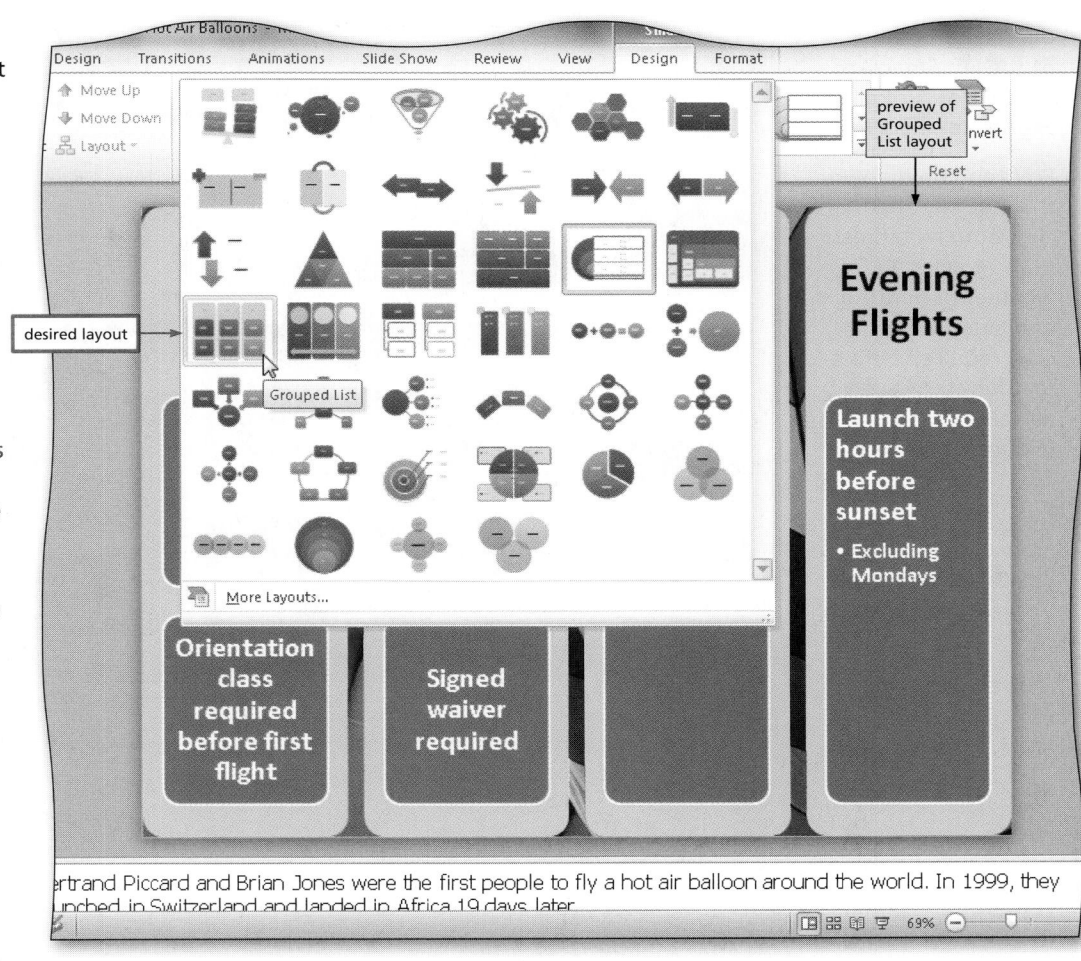

Experiment

- Point to various layouts in the gallery and watch the SmartArt layouts change.

Q&A Are additional layouts available other than those displayed in the gallery?

Yes. Click More Layouts to display the Choose a SmartArt Graphic dialog box and then select another layout.

3

- Click Grouped List to change the layout.

Figure 9–30

To Remove a SmartArt Shape

Now that the new SmartArt layout is created, you can modify the graphic. One change you can make is to delete unnecessary elements. Slide 2 has similar information found in the first shape regarding the months when the flights are scheduled. In addition, the next slide you will create will have information about material covered in the orientation class. You can, therefore, delete the first shape to eliminate redundancy. The following steps remove a SmartArt shape.

BTW

Line Spacing Measurements
The lower part of each letter rests on an imaginary line called the baseline. The space between the baseline of one row of type and the baseline of the row beneath it is called line spacing. Typically, the line spacing is 120 percent of the font size. For example, if the font size is 10 point, the line spacing is 12 point so that two points of space are displayed between the lines.

- Click a light blue area of the left SmartArt shape, Hot Air Balloon Flights, to select it.

- Press and hold down the CTRL key and then click both rectangles, May 1 to Oct. 1, weather permitting and Orientation class required before first flight, to select all three shapes (Figure 9–31).

- Press the DELETE key to delete the entire left SmartArt shape.

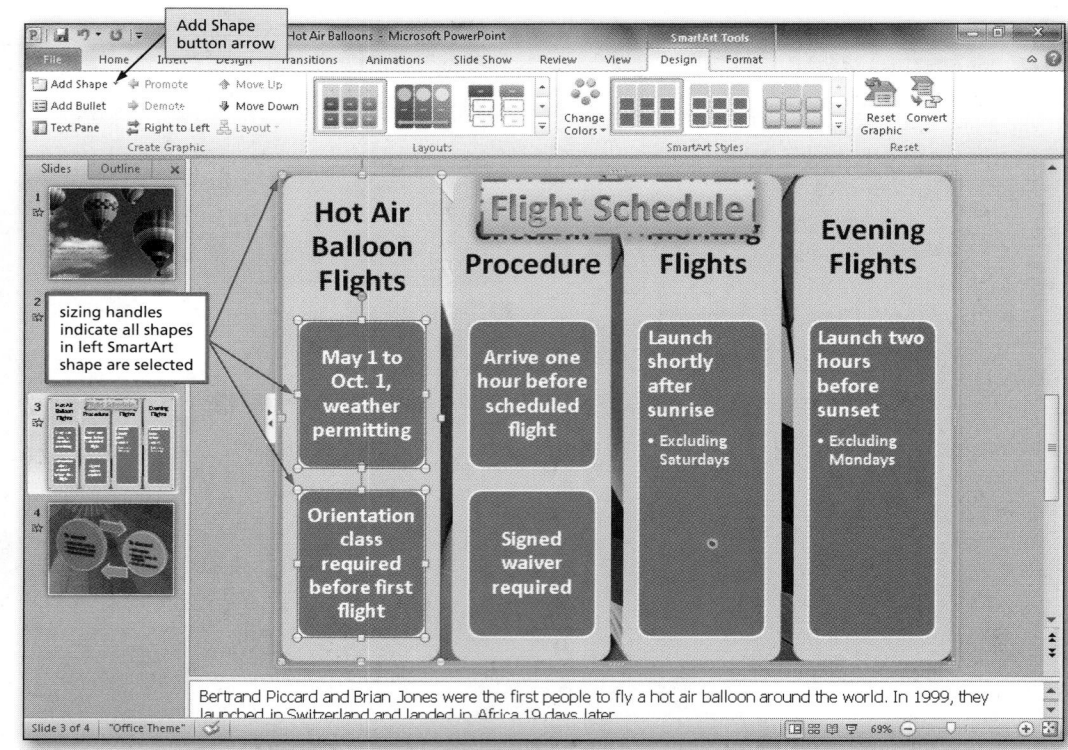

Figure 9–31

TO ADD A SMARTART SHAPE

You may add a new SmartArt shape to the layout if you need to display additional information. PowerPoint gives you the option of adding this shape above or below a selected shape or to the left or the right side of the shape. If you wanted to add a SmartArt shape, you would perform the following steps.

1. Select a SmartArt graphic shape near where you want to insert another shape.
2. Click the Add Shape button arrow (SmartArt Tools Design tab | Create Graphic group) to display the Add Shape menu.
3. Click the desired location for the new shape, which would be after, before, above, or below the selected shape.

To Resize a SmartArt Graphic by Entering an Exact Measurement

The SmartArt shape overlaps the Flight Schedule text box, so you can reduce the size of the shape. You can resize this slide element by dragging the sizing handles or by specifying exact measurements for the height and width. The following steps resize the SmartArt graphic by entering an exact measurement.

1

- Select the entire SmartArt graphic by clicking an outer edge of the graphic near the edge of the slide (Figure 9–32).

Q&A

How will I know the entire graphic is selected?

You will see the Text pane control and sizing handles around the outer edge of the SmartArt.

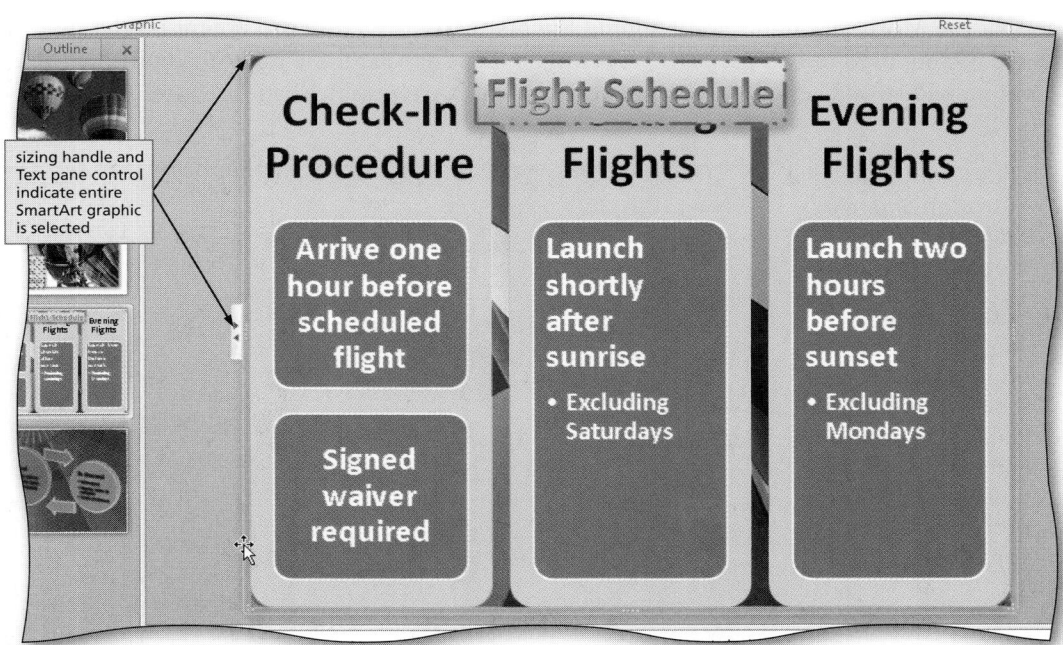

Figure 9–32

2

- Display the SmartArt Tools Format tab and then click the SmartArt Size button.

- Click the Shape Height down arrow repeatedly until 6.5" is displayed in the Height box (Figure 9–33).

3

- Drag the SmartArt graphic downward so its lower edge is aligned with the lower edge of the slide.

Other Ways

1. Right-click graphic, click Size and Position on shortcut menu, click Size tab (Layout dialog box), enter graphic height and width values in boxes, click OK button

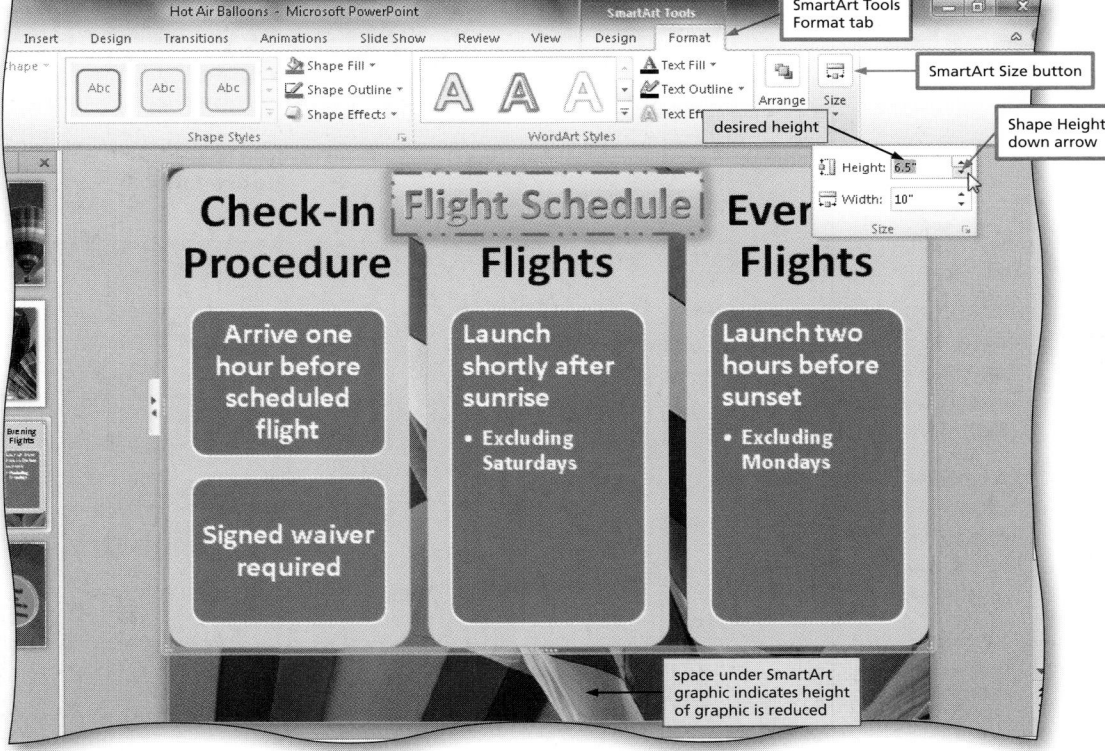

Figure 9–33

To Resize a SmartArt Graphic Shape

The entire SmartArt shape and the text box now are the proper proportions to display together on the slide. In addition to changing the height and width of the SmartArt graphic, you also can change the height and width of one individual SmartArt shape in the graphic. You decide that you want to deemphasize the Check-In Procedure shape so that the Morning Flights and Evening Flights shapes are more prominent on the slide. The Check-In Procedure shape is composed of two parts: the outer light-blue shape and the inner medium-blue shape. Each shape must be sized individually. The following steps resize a SmartArt graphic shape.

1

- Click a light blue area of the left SmartArt shape, Check-In Procedure, to select it.

- With the SmartArt Tools Format tab displaying, click the Smaller button (SmartArt Tools Format tab | Shapes group) once to decrease the shape size (Figure 9–34).

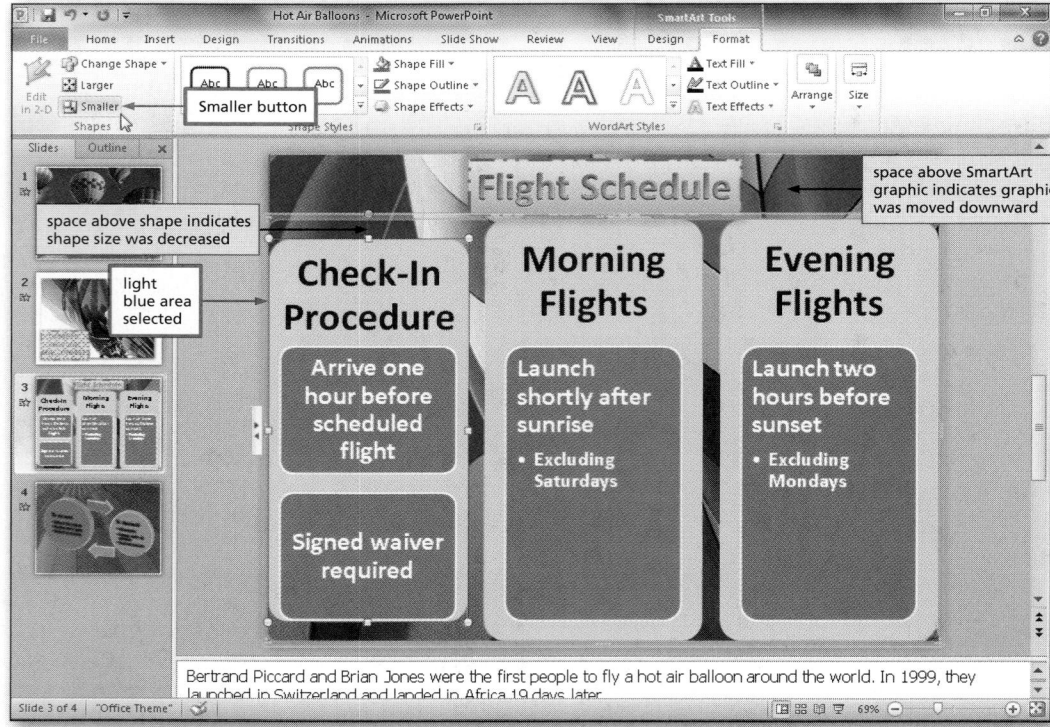

Figure 9–34

2

- Click the left shape, Arrive one hour before scheduled flight, to select it and then click the Smaller button two times (Figure 9–35).

Q&A

Can I select both shapes in the Check-In Procedure shape and size them simultaneously?

No. Each shape must be sized independently.

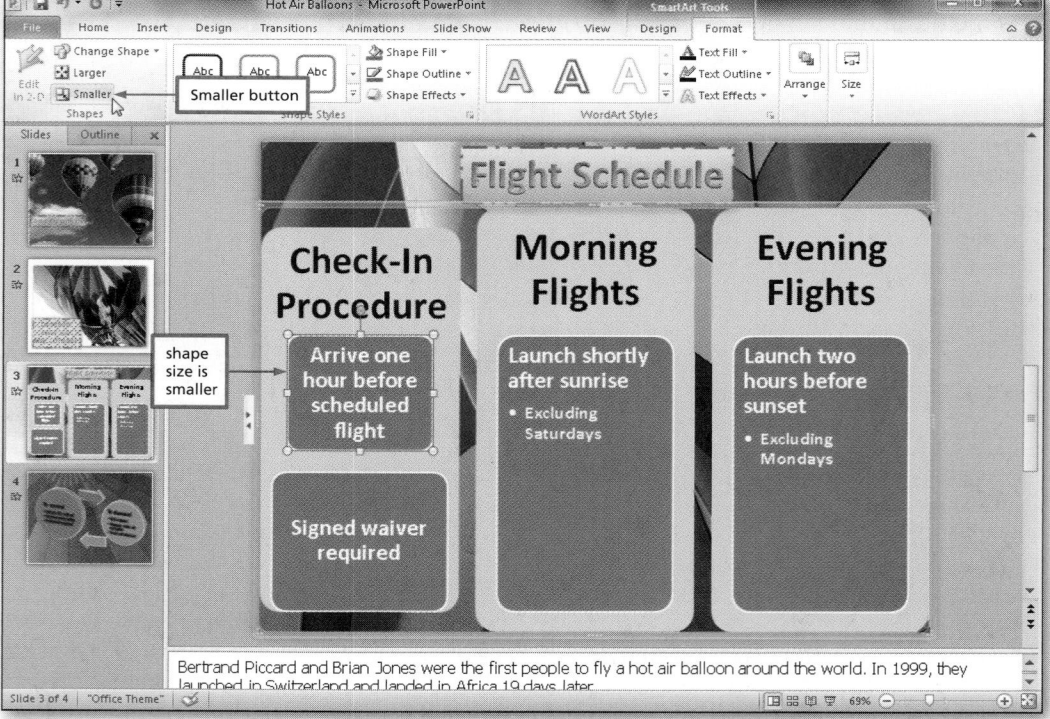

Figure 9–35

3

- Click the left shape, Signed waiver required, to select it and then click the Smaller button twice.

- Click a light blue area of the shape and then drag the shape downward so its lower edge is aligned with the lower edge of the slide.

- Drag the Arrive one hour before scheduled flight shape downward so that it displays as shown in Figure 9–36.

Other Ways

1. Right-click graphic, click Size and Position on shortcut menu, click Size tab (Layout dialog box), enter graphic height and width values in boxes, click OK button

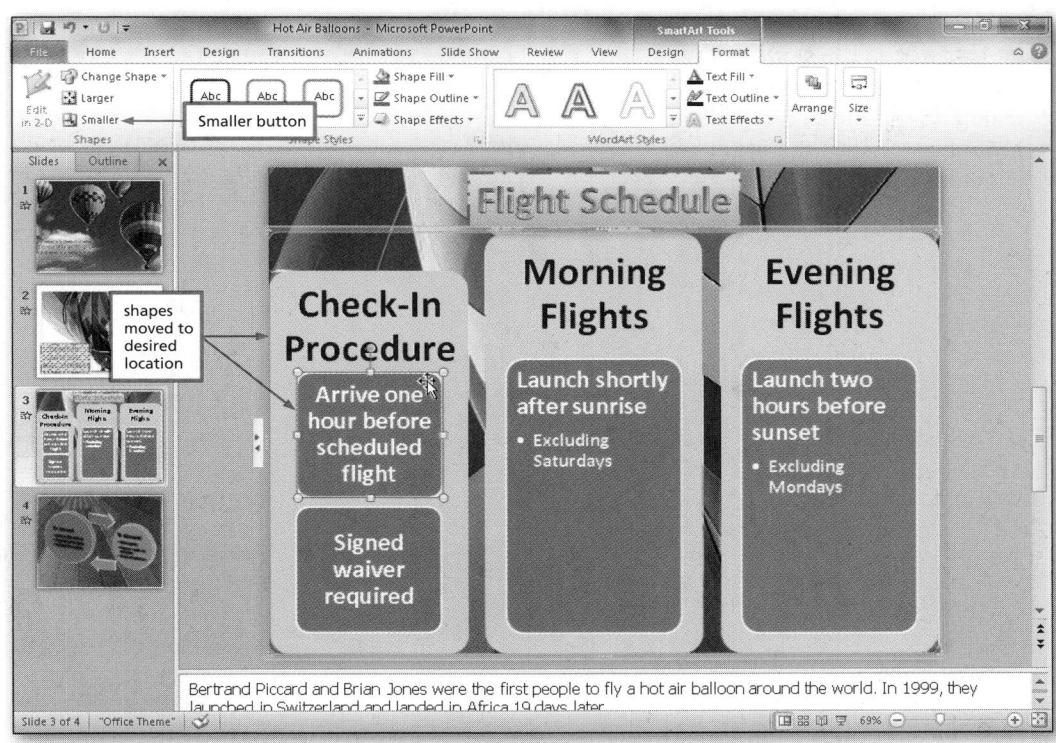

Figure 9–36

To Apply a Picture to a Text Box

Sufficient space exists in the lower halves of the Morning Flights and Evening Flights shapes to insert a picture. For consistency with the slide title, you can insert a text box that has the default formatting and then add a picture. The following steps add a text box and then apply a picture into two SmartArt graphic shapes.

1

- Insert a text box below the bulleted paragraph, Excluding Saturdays, in the middle SmartArt shape.

- Click the Shape Fill button (Drawing Tools Format tab | Drawing group) to display the Shape Fill gallery (Figure 9–37).

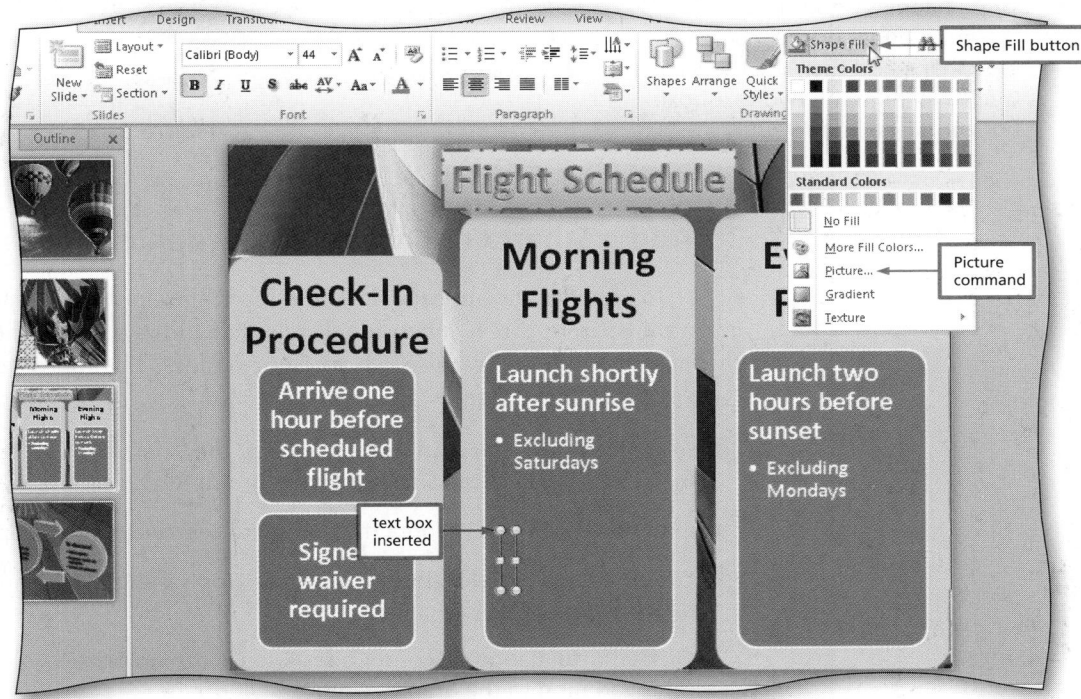

Figure 9–37

2

- Click Picture in the Shape Fill gallery to display the Insert Picture dialog box and then click Balloon at Sunrise to select the file name (Figure 9–38).

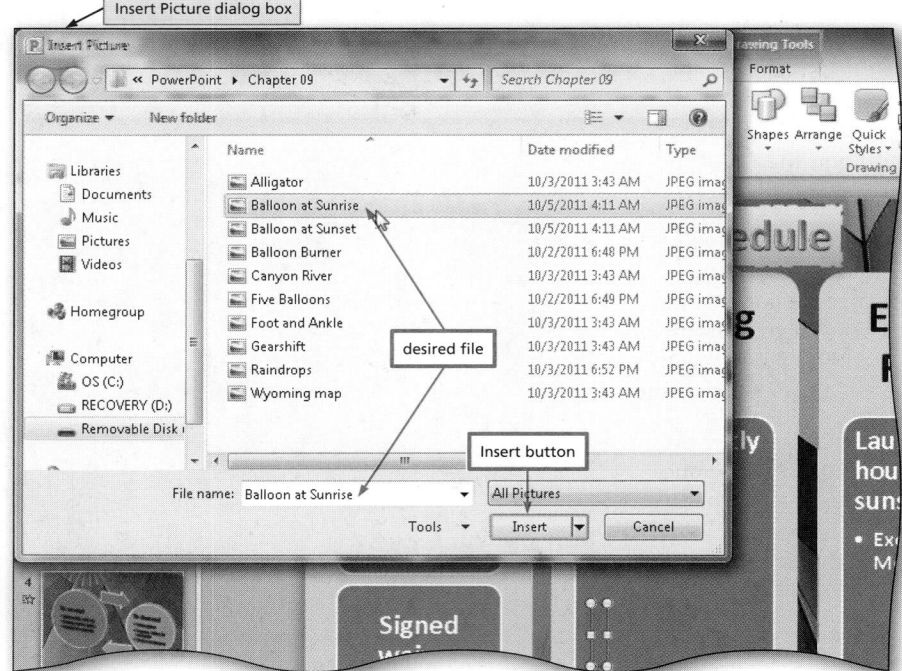

Insert Picture dialog box

desired file

Insert button

Figure 9–38

3

- Click the Insert button (Insert Picture dialog box) to insert the picture into the text box.

- Insert a text box below the bulleted paragraph, Excluding Mondays, in the right SmartArt shape, display the Shape Fill gallery, and then insert the picture, Balloon at Sunset.

- If necessary, drag the left and right sizing handles of both boxes to the outer edges of the medium-blue shape and then use the Smart Guides to align the two text boxes horizontally (Figure 9–39).

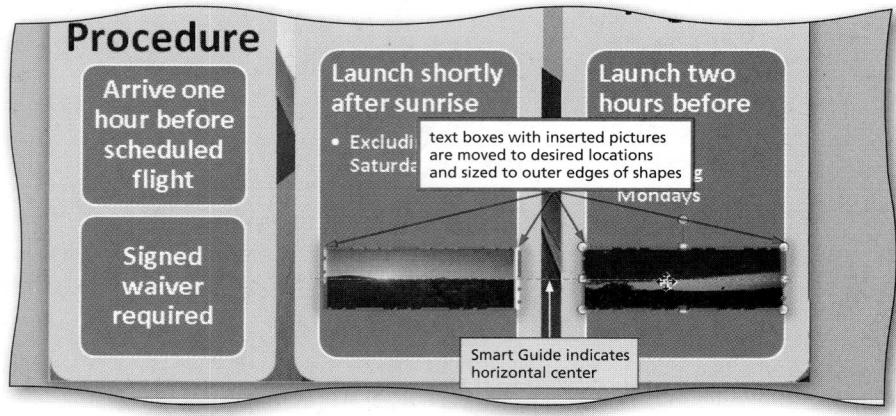

text boxes with inserted pictures are moved to desired locations and sized to outer edges of shapes

Smart Guide indicates horizontal center

Figure 9–39

To Add a SmartArt Style to the Graphic and Change the Color

To enhance the appearance of the rectangles in the Grouped List layout, you can add a transparent three-dimensional style that allows some of the background to show through the graphic. You also can add more colors. The following steps add the Powder style and a Colorful range.

1 Select the entire SmartArt graphic, display the SmartArt Tools Design tab, and then click the More button in the SmartArt Styles group to expand the SmartArt Styles gallery.

2 Click Powder in the 3-D area (first graphic in second row) to apply this style to the graphic.

3 Click the Change Colors button (SmartArt Tools Design tab | SmartArt Styles group) to display the Change Colors gallery.

4 Click Colorful Range – Accent Colors 5 to 6 (fifth graphic in Colorful row) to apply this color variation to the graphic (Figure 9–40).

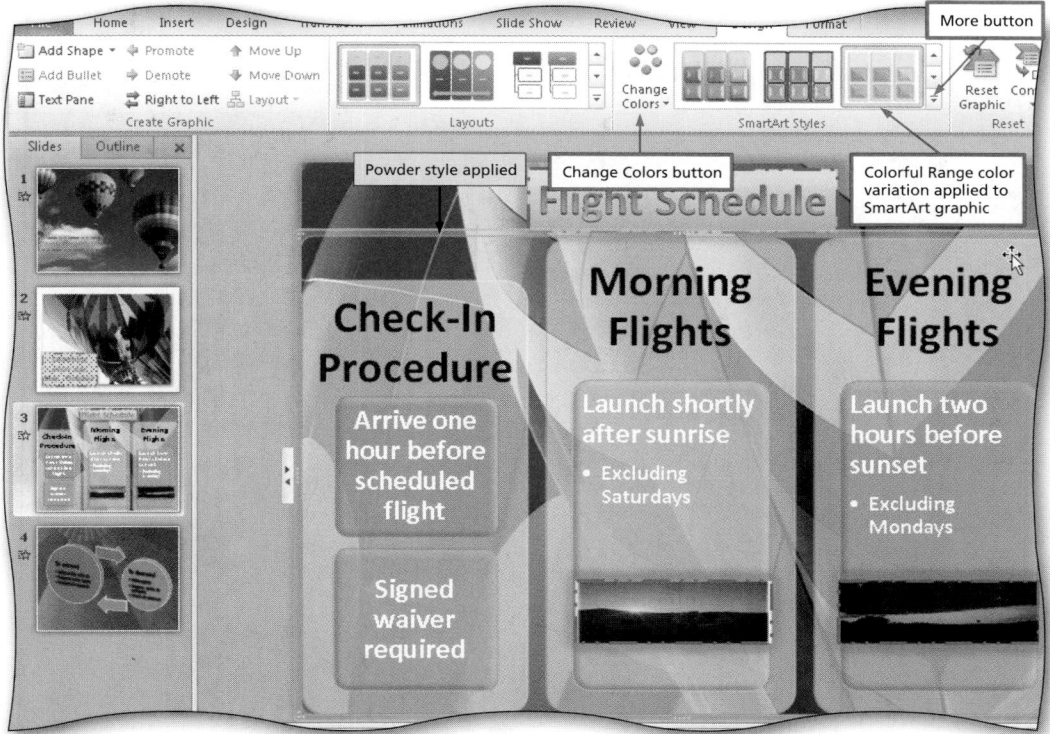

Figure 9–40

To Convert a SmartArt Graphic to Text

Hot air balloon pilots must learn the techniques of ascending and descending, and the SmartArt shape on Slide 4 states the basic principles of how the pilot controls altitude. At times, you may decide that SmartArt is not the optimal method of presenting information to an audience and instead want to depict the same concept using text. PowerPoint allows you to remove the shapes and change the text in the graphic to a bulleted list. The following steps convert the SmartArt graphic to text.

1

- Display Slide 4 and then select the entire SmartArt graphic.

If one of the SmartArt shapes is selected, how do I select the entire graphic?

Be certain to click the edge of the slide. You will see sizing handles and the Text pane control when the SmartArt graphic is selected.

- With the SmartArt Tools Design tab displaying, click the Convert button (SmartArt Tools Design tab | Reset group) to display the Convert menu (Figure 9–41).

Figure 9–41

2

- Click Convert to Text to display the SmartArt text as eight bulleted list paragraphs.

Q&A

Why would I want to convert the SmartArt graphic?

The bulleted list might be useful for instructional purposes. At times, audiences may prefer seeing instructions as paragraphs and not be distracted by the graphical SmartArt elements.

- Position the mouse pointer between the bullet character and the word, To, in the paragraph, To descend (Figure 9–42).

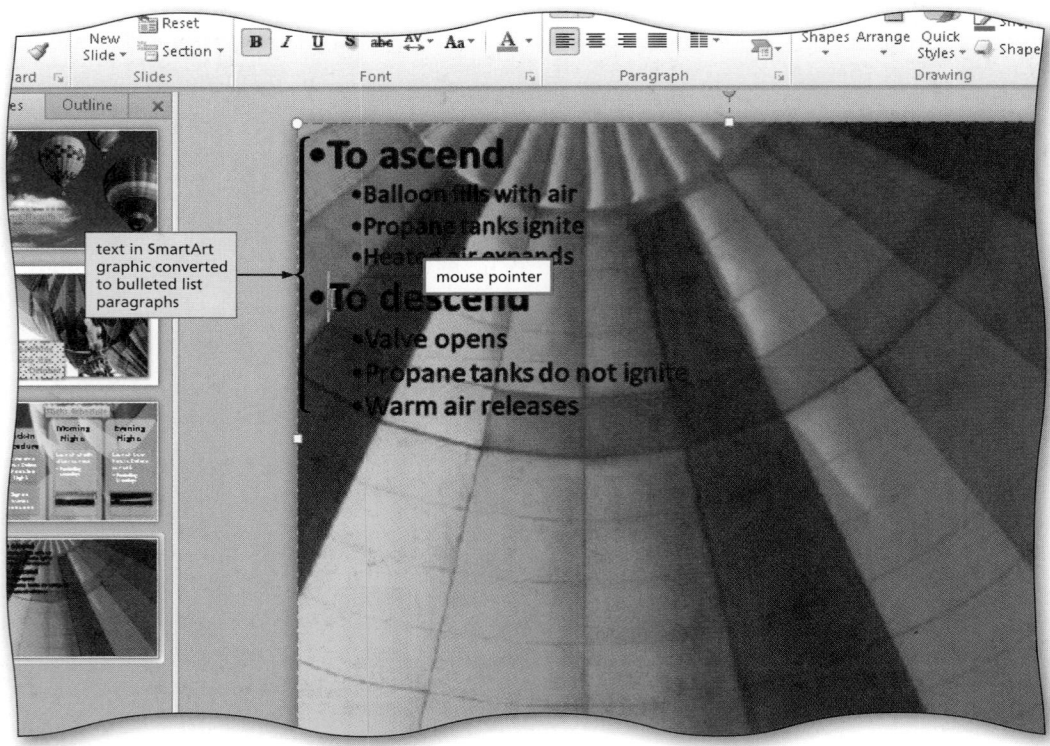

Figure 9–42

3

- Press the ENTER key six times to move the four paragraphs downward (Figure 9–43).

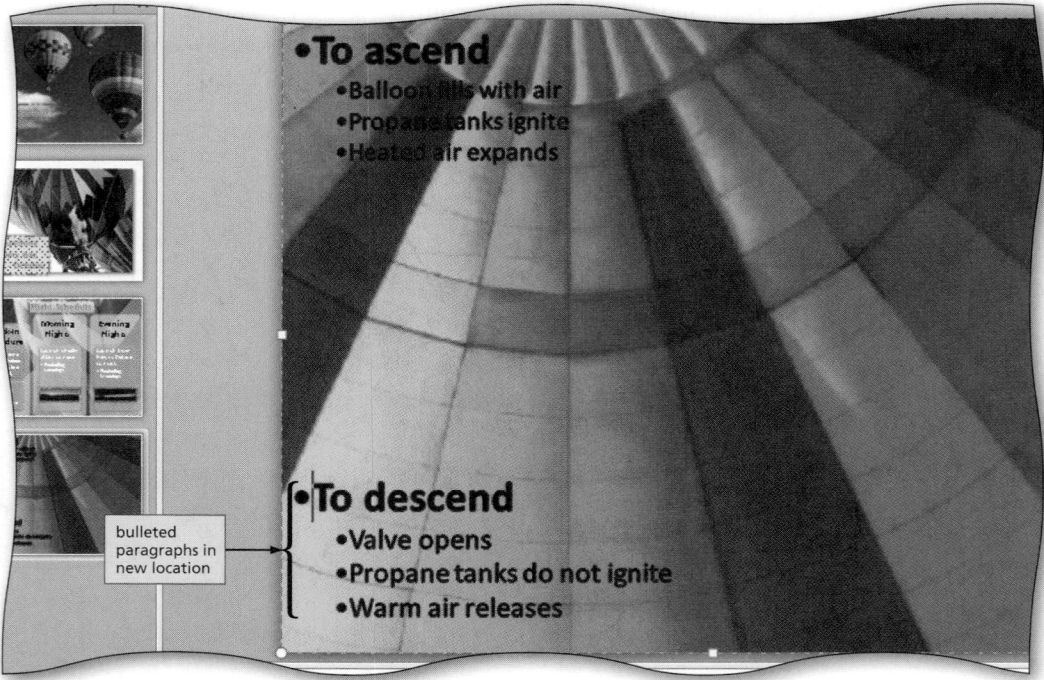

Figure 9–43

To Convert a SmartArt Graphic to Shapes

An alternative to changing a graphic to text is changing a graphic to shapes. In this manner, a shape can be moved, resized, or deleted independently of any other shape in the SmartArt. If you wanted to convert a SmartArt graphic to shapes, you would perform the following steps.

1. Select the entire SmartArt graphic.
2. Click the Convert button (SmartArt Tools Design tab | Reset group) to display the Convert menu.
3. Click Convert to Shapes.

> **Break Point:** If you wish to take a break, this is a good place to do so. Be sure to save the Hot Air Balloons file again and then you can quit PowerPoint. To resume at a later time, start PowerPoint, open the file called Hot Air Balloons, and continue following the steps from this location forward.

Inserting and Modifying Shapes

Diagrams with labels often help audiences identify the parts of an object. Text boxes with clear, large type and an arrow pointing to a precise area of the object work well in showing relationships between components. The items in the Shapes gallery provide a variety of useful shapes you can insert into slides.

A hot air balloon has several components: They include the envelope, which is the colorful balloon that inflates; the skirt; the burner unit that releases heat into the envelope; and a basket to hold the pilot and the passengers. These parts can be depicted with a variety of items found in the Shapes gallery. At times, you may be unable to find a shape in the gallery that fits your specific needs. In those instances, you might find a similar shape and then alter it to your specifications.

To Insert Shapes and an Arrow

You can draw four parts of the hot air balloon with shapes located in the Shapes gallery: Teardrop for the envelope, two rectangles for the skirt and the burner unit, and Flowchart: Magnetic Disk for the basket. In addition, the Notched Right Arrow shape can be inserted to serve as a leader line for labeling a hot air balloon part. The following steps insert four shapes and an arrow into Slide 4.

1 With Slide 4 displaying, click the Shapes button (Home tab | Drawing group) to display the Shapes gallery and then click the Teardrop shape in the Basic Shapes area (fourth shape in second row).

2 Position the mouse pointer near the top of the slide and then click to insert the Teardrop shape.

3 Display the Shapes gallery and then click the Snip Same Side Corner Rectangle shape (fourth shape in Rectangles area).

4 Position the mouse pointer below the Teardrop and then click to insert the Snip Same Side Corner Rectangle shape.

5 Display the Shapes gallery, click the Rounded Rectangle shape (second shape in Rectangles area), and then insert this shape below the Snip Same Side Corner Rectangle shape.

6 Display the Shapes gallery, click the Flowchart: Magnetic Disk shape in the Flowchart area (second shape in third row), and then insert this shape below the Rounded Rectangle shape.

7 Use the Smart Guides to align the four shapes vertically.

BTW

Using Metaphorical Shapes
Use your imagination to use simple shapes and objects as metaphors. For example, a broken pencil can represent a stressful situation whereas a slice of cake can serve as imagery for a simple task. Make the shape large and bold, and use as few words as possible. Your audience should be able to understand and relate to the images without much explanation on the slides or from the speaker.

8 Display the Shapes gallery, click the Notched Right Arrow shape in the Block Arrows **area** (sixth shape in second row), and then insert this shape in the middle of the slide (Figure 9–44).

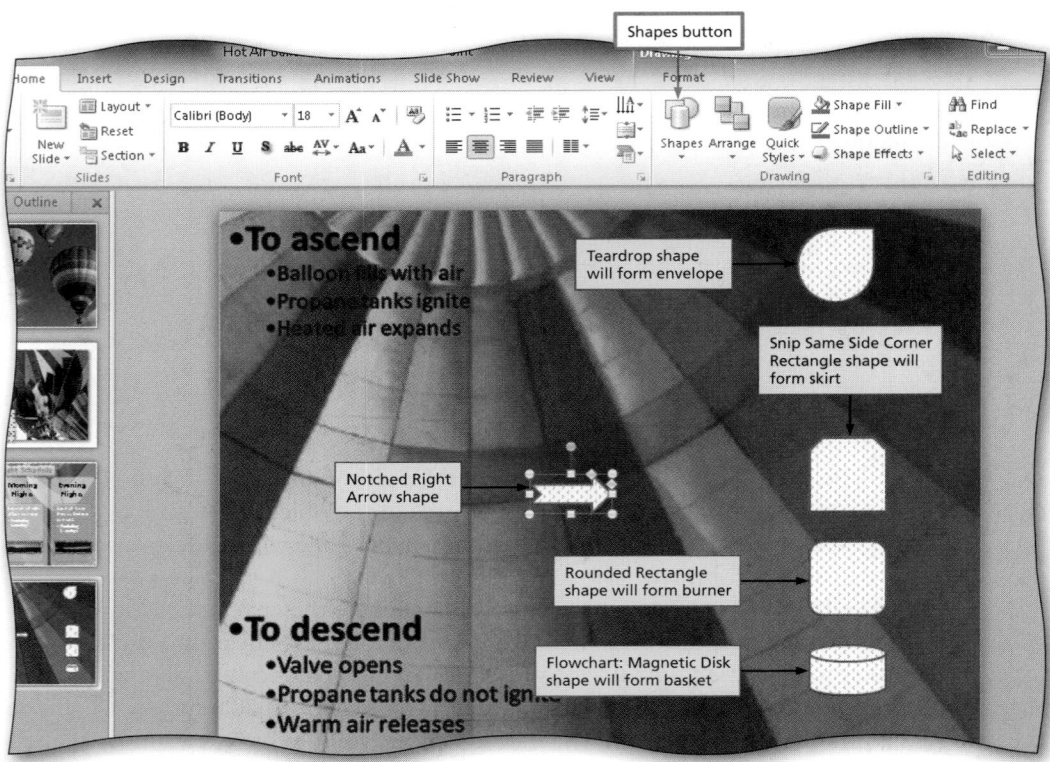

Figure 9–44

To Resize and Move a Shape

The five shapes on Slide 5 are the default sizes, and they need to be proportioned to reflect accurate hot air balloon dimensions. When you want to keep the resized shape proportions identical to the original shape, press the SHIFT key when clicking a sizing handle and then drag the mouse pointer inward or outward to decrease or increase the size. If you do not hold down the SHIFT key, you can elongate the height or the width to draw an object that is not identical to the shape shown in the Shapes gallery. If you want to alter the shape's proportions, drag one of the sizing handles inward or outward. The following steps resize the shapes and arrow.

1 Select the Teardrop, press and hold down the SHIFT key, and then drag the lower-left corner sizing handle downward to the middle of the slide.

2 Position the mouse pointer over the Teardrop rotation handle so that it changes to a Free Rotate pointer and then drag the mouse pointer clockwise so that the tip of the shape points to the lower edge of the slide.

3 Select the Snip Same Side Corner Rectangle and then drag the middle sizing handle on the lower edge upward to the middle of the shape.

4 Select the Rounded Rectangle, press and hold down the SHIFT key, and then drag a corner sizing handle inward.

5 Select the Flowchart: Magnetic Disk, press and hold down the SHIFT key, and then drag a corner sizing handle outward.

6 Select the Notched Right Arrow, press and hold down the SHIFT key, and then drag a corner sizing handle outward.

7 Drag the shapes to the locations shown in Figure 9–45 using the Smart Guide to help you align the shapes vertically.

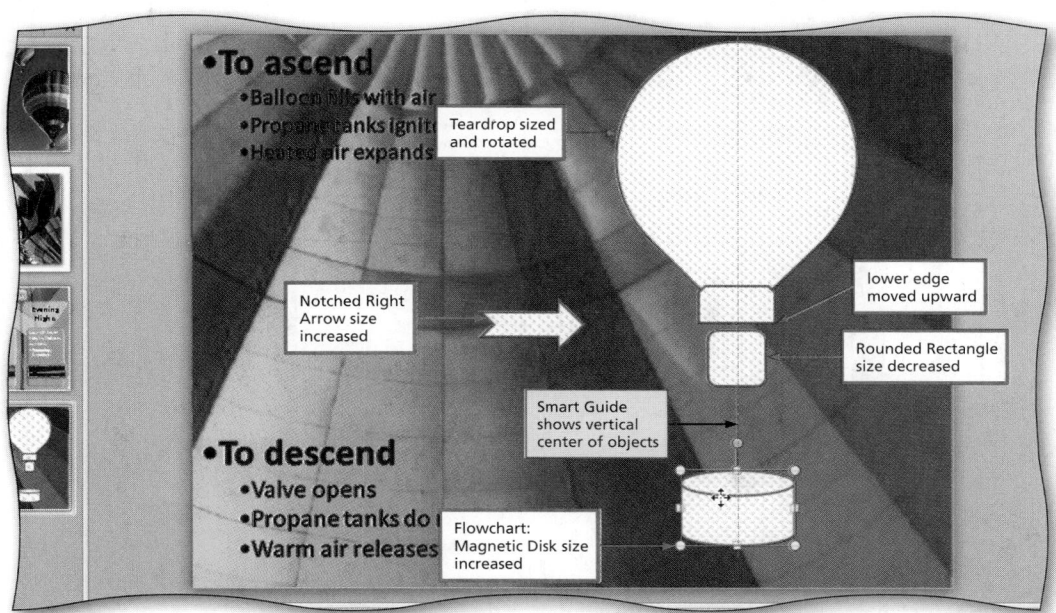

Figure 9–45

To Apply a Fill to a Shape

The shapes on Slide 4 have a Light Green Divot fill. You can change the shape fill using the same types of fills you used for the text boxes in this presentation. For example, you can apply a gradient, pattern, texture, or picture. The method of applying these fill effects is similar to the steps you used to format text boxes. The following steps apply fills to the shapes.

1

- Select the Teardrop, click the Shape Fill button arrow (Drawing Tools Format tab | Drawing group) to display the Shape Fill gallery, and then point to Gradient to display the Gradient gallery (Figure 9–46).

🔍 **Experiment**

- Point to various gradients in the Gradient gallery and watch the interior of the Teardrop shape change.

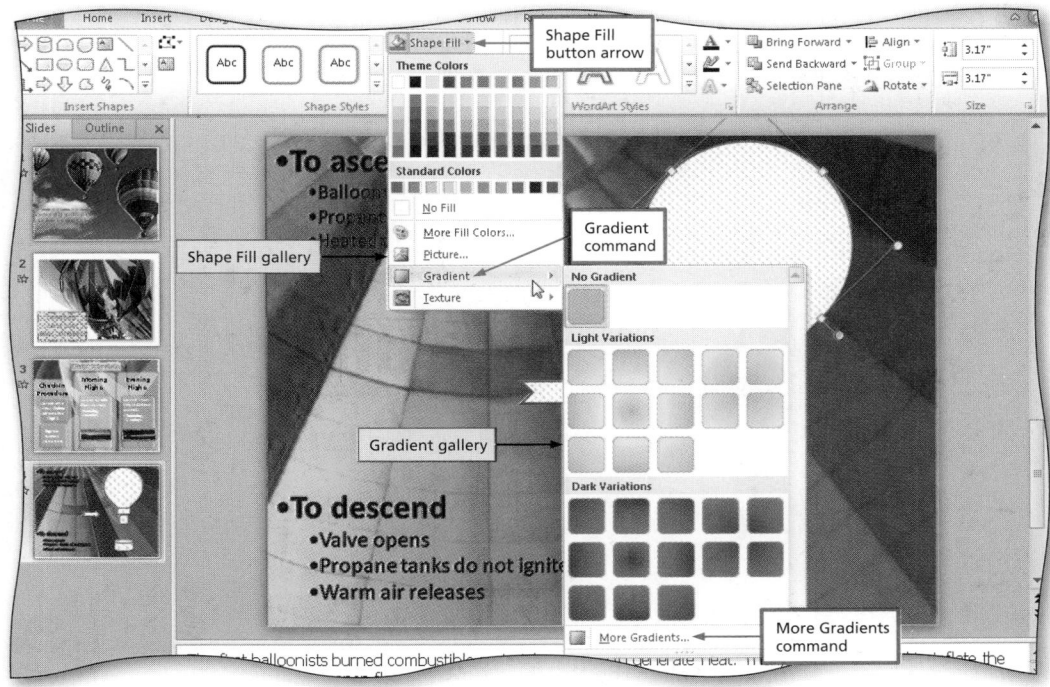

Figure 9–46

• Click More Gradients in the Gradient gallery to display the Format Shape dialog box. Drag the dialog box to the left so that you can view the balloon shapes.

• With the Fill pane displaying, click Gradient fill to expand the gradient options and then click the Preset colors button to display the Preset colors gallery (Figure 9–47).

Q&A

Can I experiment with previewing the gradient colors?

No, the live preview feature is not available.

• Click Rainbow in the Preset colors gallery to apply the gradient fill to the Teardrop.

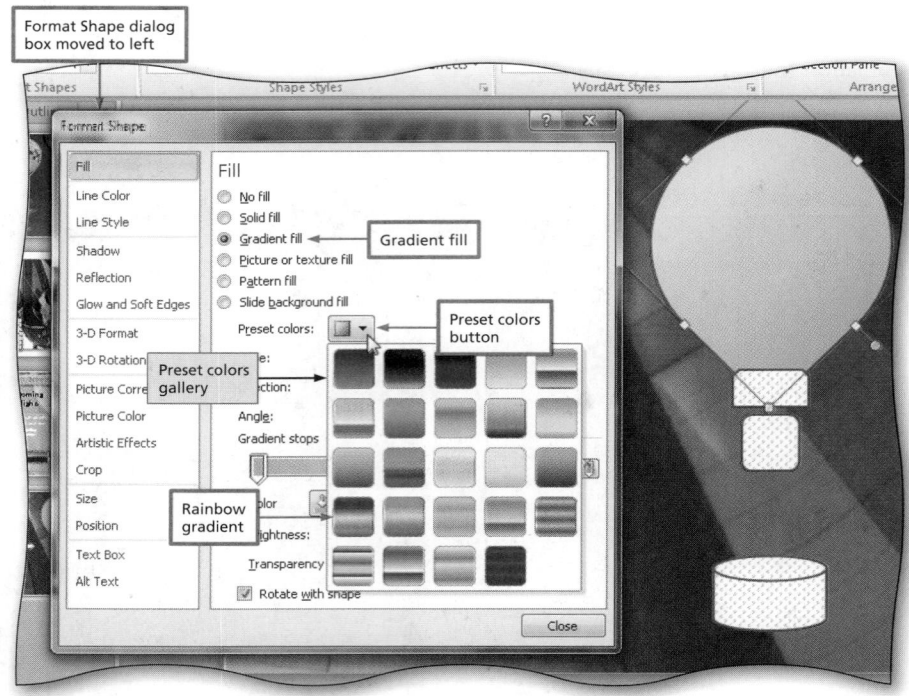

Figure 9–47

Q&A

How can I delete a gradient fill if I decide not to apply one to the shape?

If you already have applied the pattern, you must click the Undo button on the Quick Access Toolbar.

• Select the Snip Same Side Corner Rectangle shape and then click Solid fill to display the Fill Color area.

• Click the Color button in the Fill Color area to display the Color palette (Figure 9–48).

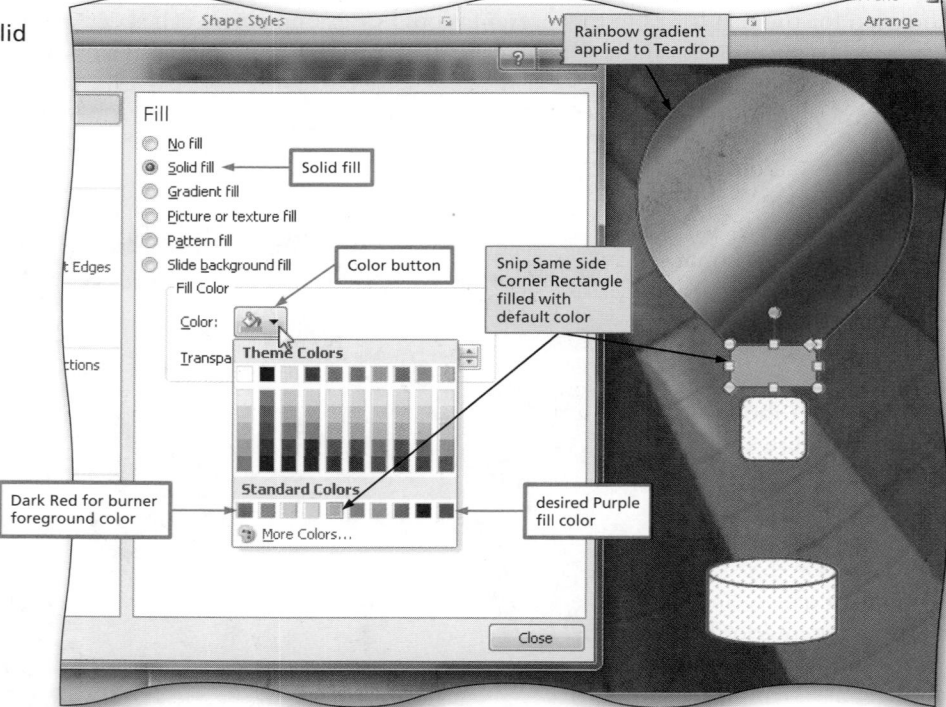

Figure 9–48

5

- Click Purple (last color in Standard Colors row) to apply the color to the shape.

- Select the Rounded Rectangle shape, click the Wave pattern (sixth color in second row) in the Pattern gallery, and then change the foreground color to Dark Red (first color in Standard Colors row) (Figure 9–49).

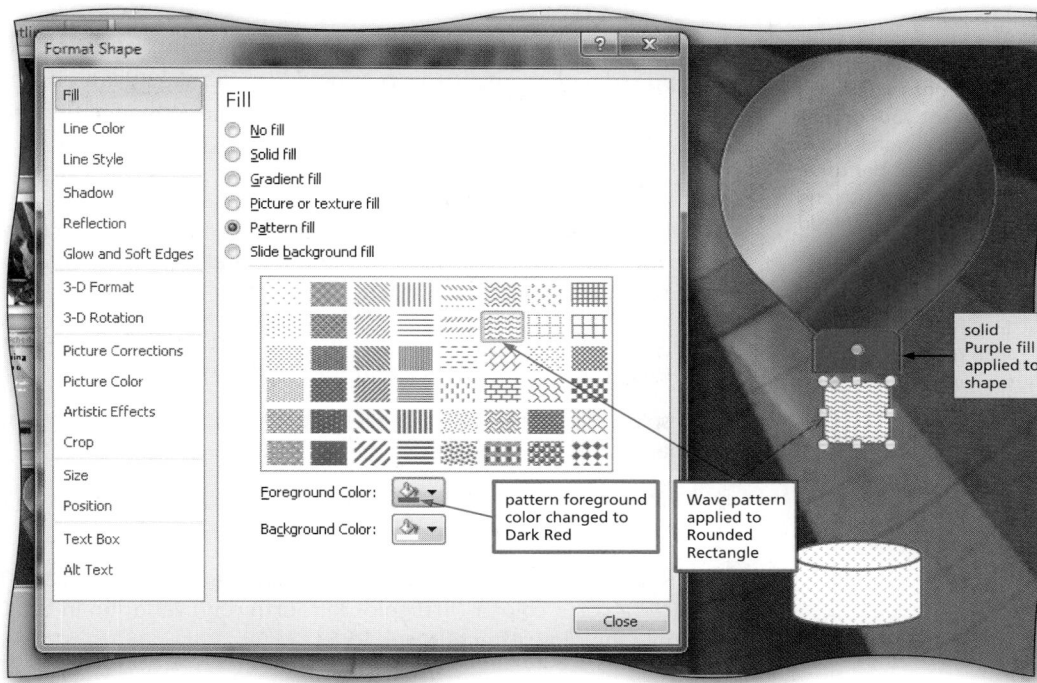

Figure 9–49

6

- Select the Flowchart: Magnetic Disk shape, click Picture or texture fill, and then click the Texture button to display the Texture gallery (Figure 9–50).

7

- Click Woven Mat (fourth texture in first row) to apply this texture to the shape.

- Click the Close button to close the Format Picture dialog box.

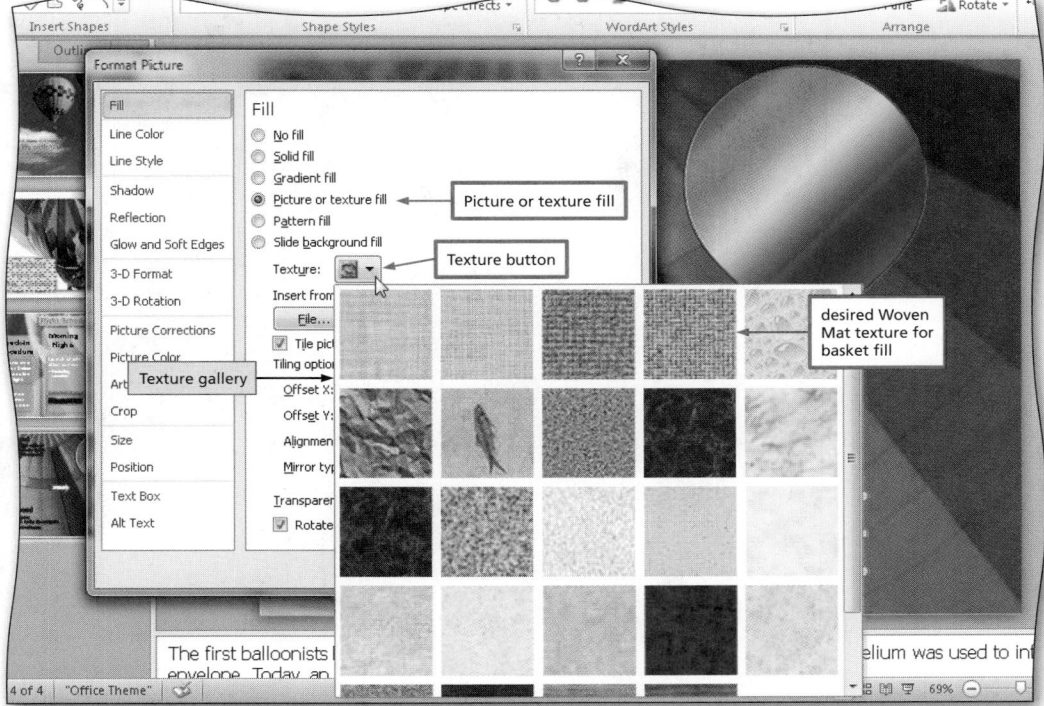

Figure 9–50

Adding Contrast for Energy
The samples in the Color palette columns range from light to dark. If you want your graphic to have a high level of energy, consider using colors at opposite ends of the columns to add a dramatic effect. The greater the contrast, the higher the energy. In contrast, if your goal is to give your graphic a peaceful feeling, use colors in the same row that have the same levels of intensity.

To Change a Shape Fill and Outline and Apply Effects

Earlier in this project, you changed a text box outline color, weight, and style. You also applied a glow effect to a text box. You, similarly, can change the outline formatting and effects for a shape. For consistency, you can enhance the arrow by using the same formatting changes that you applied to the text box. The following steps change the arrow shape outline and apply an effect.

1 Select the Notched Right Arrow, click the Shape Fill button (Drawing Tools Format tab | Shape Styles group), display the Gradient gallery, and then click Linear Right (first gradient in second row) in the Light Variations area.

2 Click the Shape Outline button arrow (Drawing Tools Format tab | Shape Styles group), display the Weight gallery, and then click 3 pt.

3 Display the Shape Outline gallery again and then click Blue in the Standard Colors area to change the shape border color.

4 Display the Shape Outline gallery again, display the Dashes gallery, and then click Long Dash Dot Dot to change the border style.

5 Display the Shape Effects gallery, display the Glow gallery, and then click the Blue, 18 pt glow, Accent color 1 (first color in fourth row) variation in the Glow Variations area to apply the glow effect (Figure 9–51).

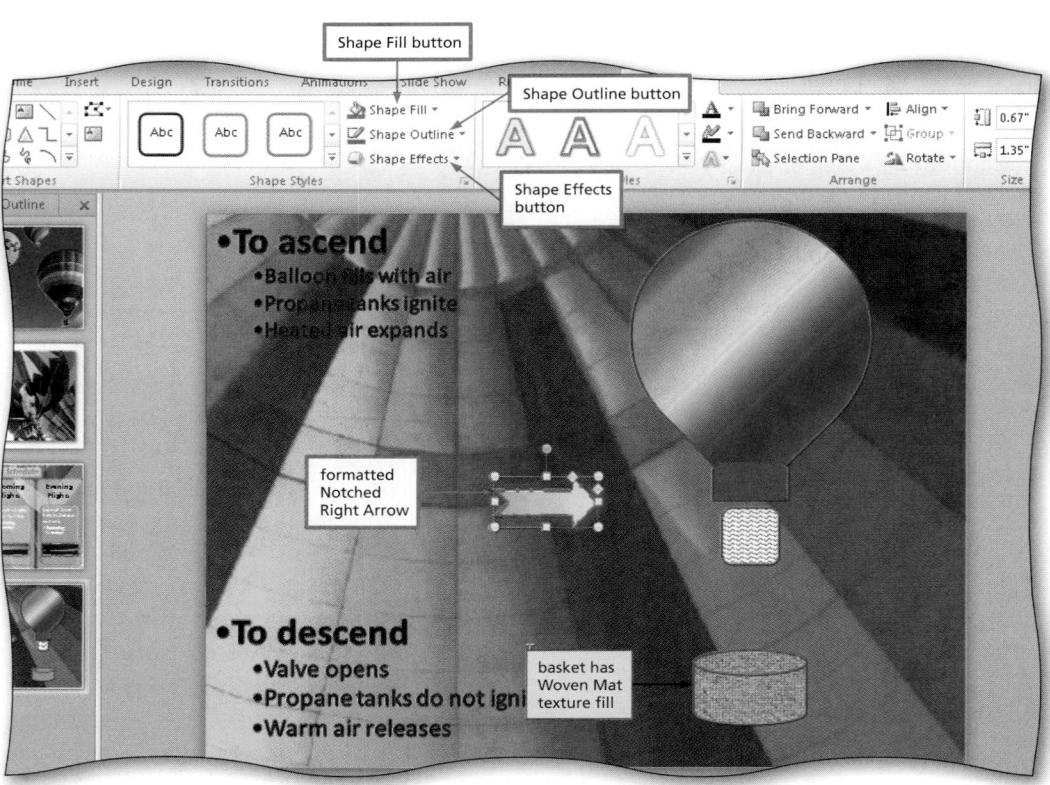

Figure 9–51

To Set Shape Formatting as the Default

The Notched Right Arrow shape you inserted and formatted complements the default text box you inserted on the slides in the presentation. You will use this shape on several parts of Slide 4 to help identify parts of the hot air balloon. To save time and ensure all the formatting changes are applied, you can set the formatting of one shape as the default for all other shapes you insert into the presentation. The following steps set the arrow shape formatting on Slide 4 as the default.

1

- Right-click the Notched Right Arrow shape to display the shortcut menu (Figure 9–52).

2

- Click Set as Default Shape on the shortcut menu to set the shape formatting as the default for any new shapes.

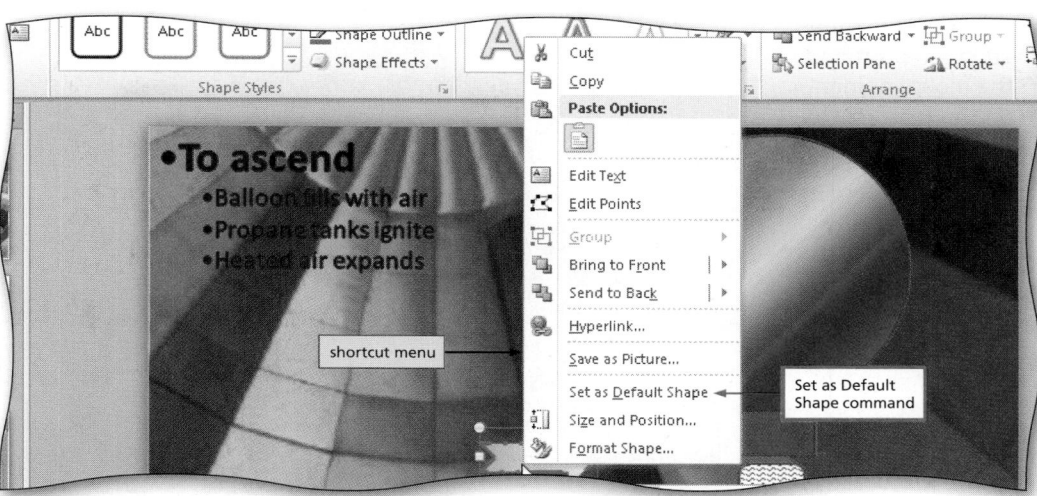

Figure 9–52

To Draw a Line

The shapes on Slide 4 help identify the parts of a hot air balloon. To complete the drawing, you need to connect the Teardrop, which represents the balloon's envelope, to the Flowchart: Magnetic Disk, which represents the basket. Line shapes are included in the Shapes gallery, and they include three straight lines, three straight elbow connectors, a Curve, a Freeform, and a Scribble line. The lines and connectors have zero, one, or two arrowheads. The following steps draw two straight lines without arrowheads and position these shapes on Slide 4.

1

- Display the Shapes gallery and then point to the Line shape (first shape in the Lines area) (Figure 9–53).

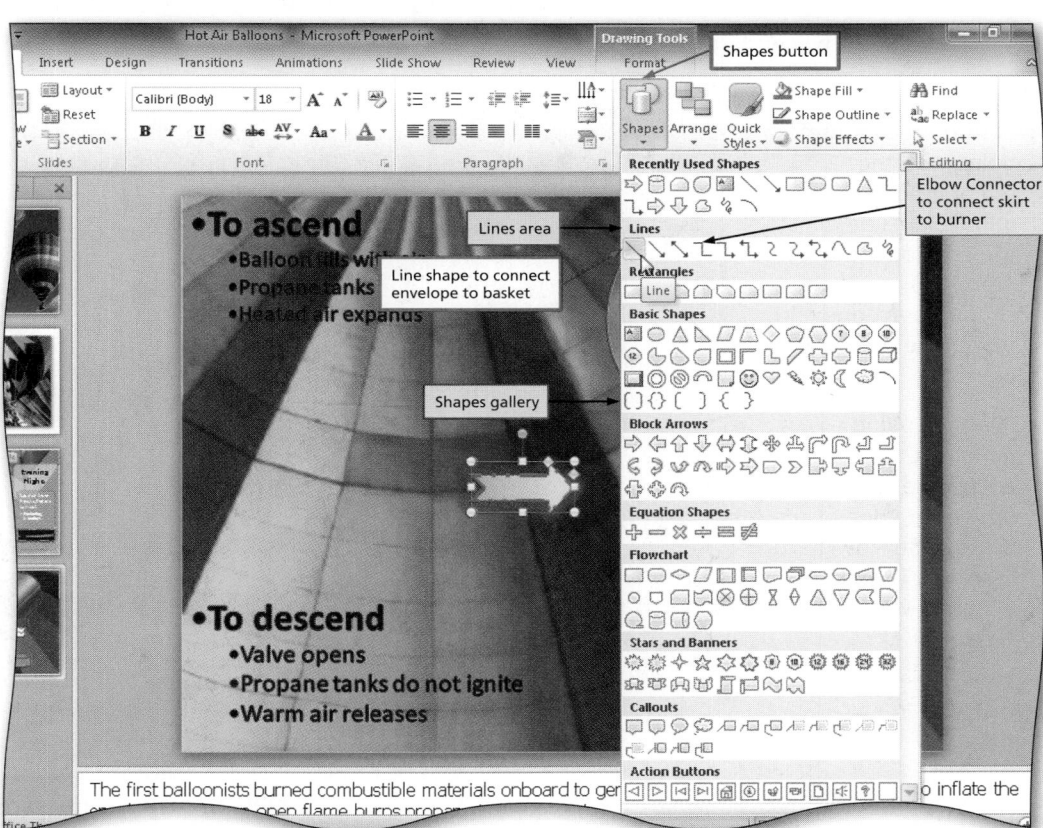

Figure 9–53

• Click the Line shape and then position the mouse pointer on the Teardrop to display the points (Figure 9–54).

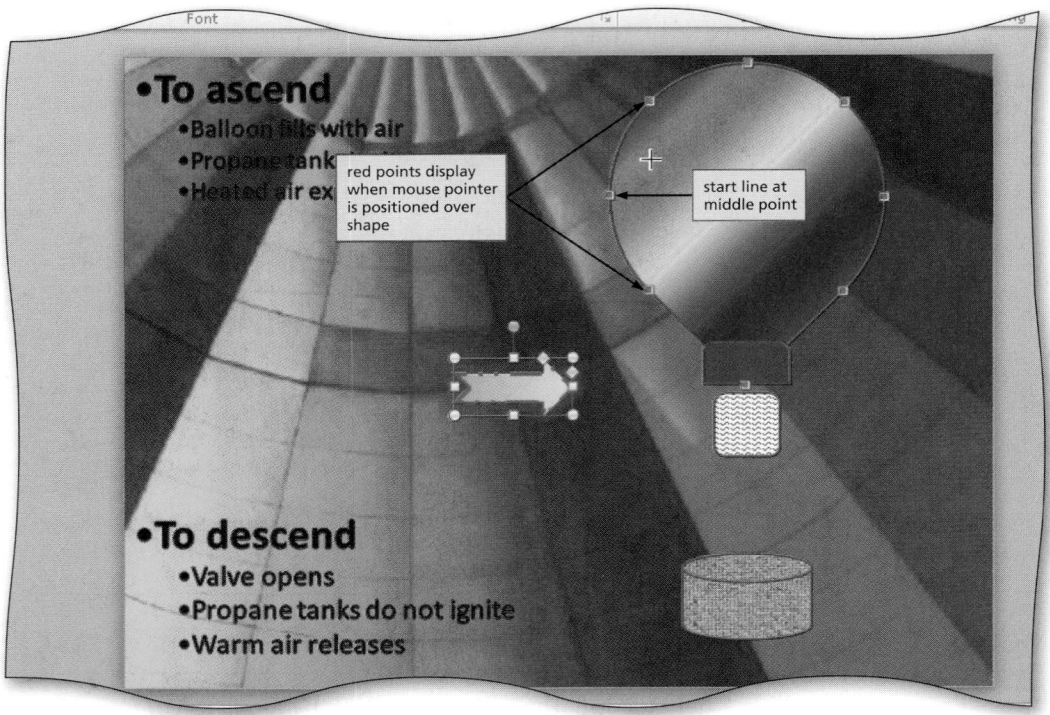

Figure 9–54

Q&A

What are the red squares on the perimeter of the Teardrop?

The squares are called points. Every shape is formed by a series of points connected with lines that are straight or curved. If desired, you can drag a point to alter the shape's form.

❸

• Position the mouse pointer on the red point on the middle left side of the envelope (the Teardrop) and then click to insert one end of the line on this point.

• Drag the sizing handle at the other end of the line to the upper-left edge of the basket (the Flowchart: Magnetic Disk shape) (Figure 9–55).

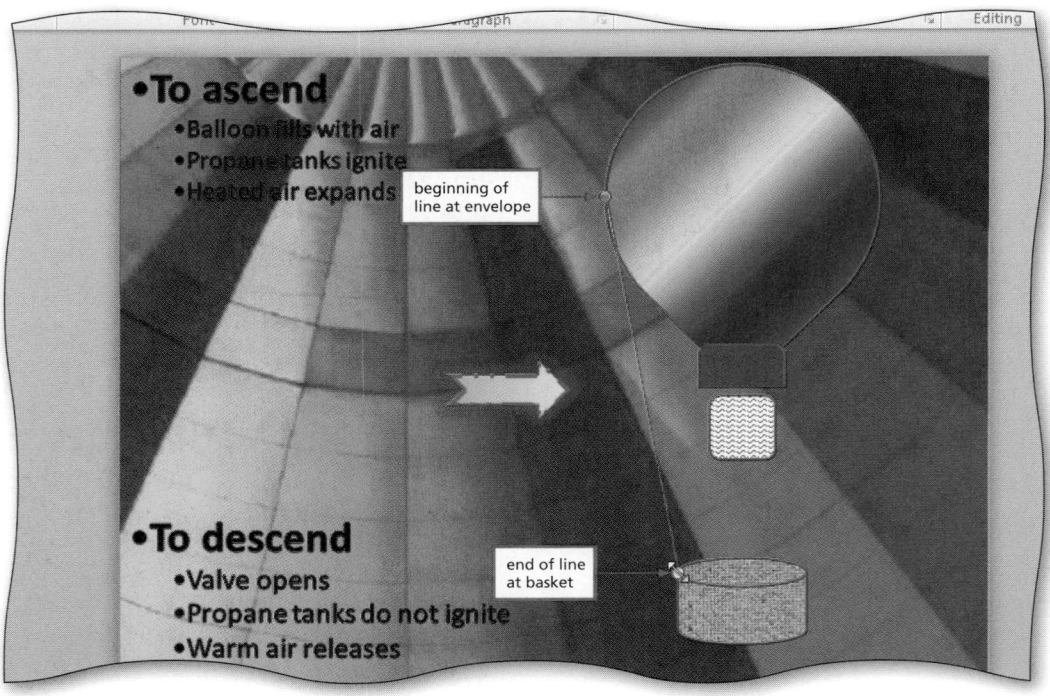

Figure 9–55

To Change a Line Weight and Color

In this project, you changed a text box and shape outline color and weight. In a similar fashion, you can change line outline formatting. The line you drew on Slide 4 is thin, and the color does not display well against the colorful background. You can increase the line thickness and change its color to enhance the shape. The following steps change the line thickness and color.

1

- With the line selected, click the Shape Outline button (Drawing Tools Format tab | Drawing group) and then point to Weight to display the Weight gallery.

- Point to 2¼ pt to see a preview of that weight applied to the line (Figure 9–56).

Experiment

- Point to various weights in the Weight gallery and watch the line thickness change.

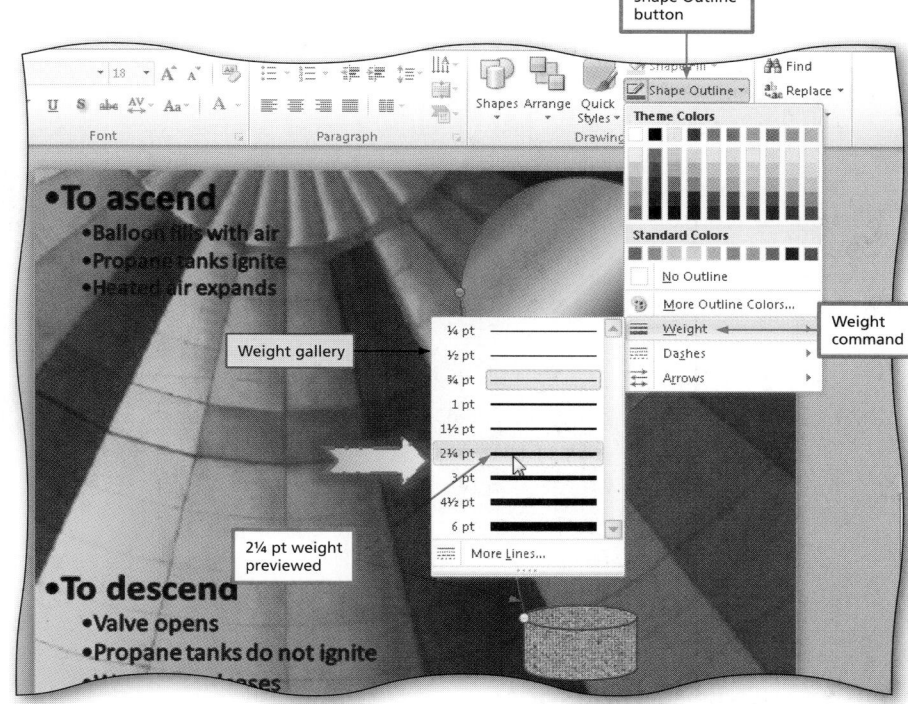

Figure 9–56

2

- Click 2¼ pt in the Weight gallery to apply that weight to the line.

- Click the Shape Outline button again and then point to Dark Blue (ninth color in Standard Colors area) to see a preview of that color applied to the line (Figure 9–57).

Experiment

- Point to various colors in the Theme Colors gallery and watch the line color change.

3

- Click Dark Blue to apply that color to the line.

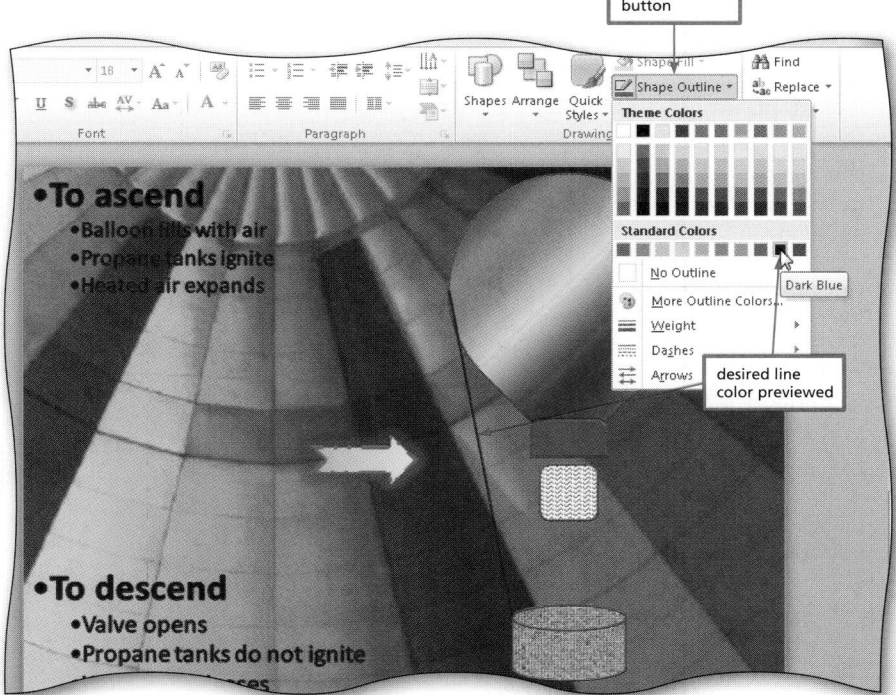

Figure 9–57

To Set Line Formatting as the Default

The line you inserted and formatted will be used to complete the hot air balloon diagram. You can set these line attributes as the default for all other lines you will draw in the presentation. The following steps set the line shape on Slide 4 as the default.

1
- Right-click the line to display the shortcut menu (Figure 9–58).

2
- Click Set as Default Line on the shortcut menu to set the line formatting as the default for any new lines.

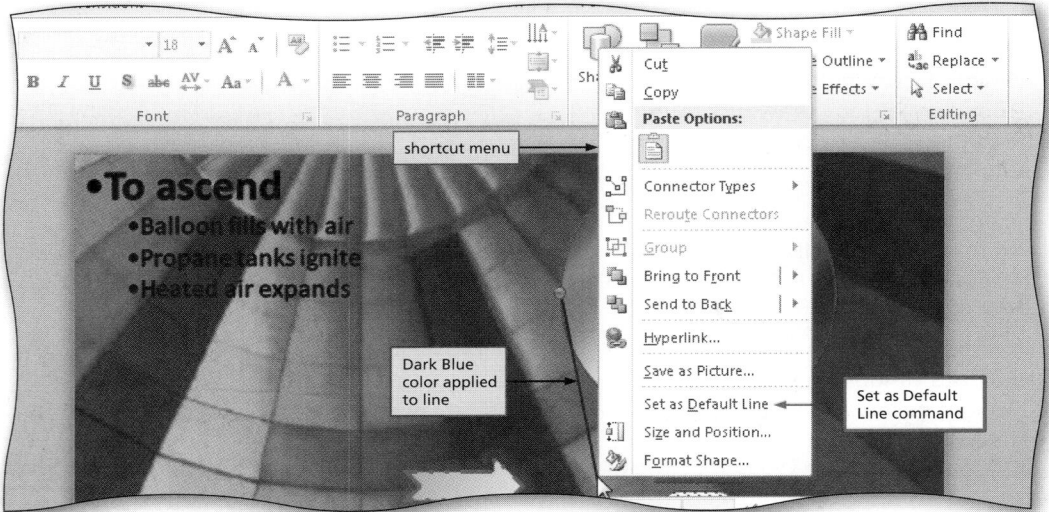

Figure 9–58

To Draw Additional Lines

One more line is needed to connect the right side of the hot air balloon envelope to the right side of the basket. In addition, two lines are needed to connect the burner to the skirt. The following steps draw these lines.

1
- Display the Shapes gallery, select the Line shape, position the mouse pointer on the envelope, and then click the red point on the right side of the envelope to insert the line at this point.

- Drag the sizing handle at the other end of the line to the upper-right edge of the basket (Figure 9–59).

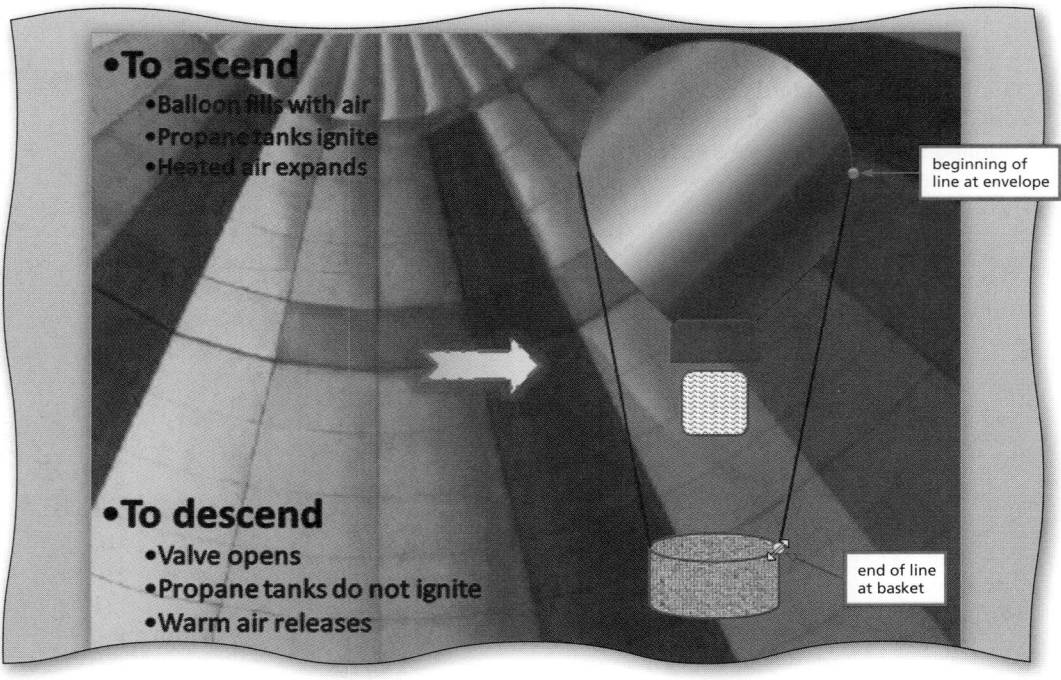

Figure 9–59

- Display the Shapes gallery and then point to the Elbow Connector (fourth line in the Lines area) (Figure 9–60).

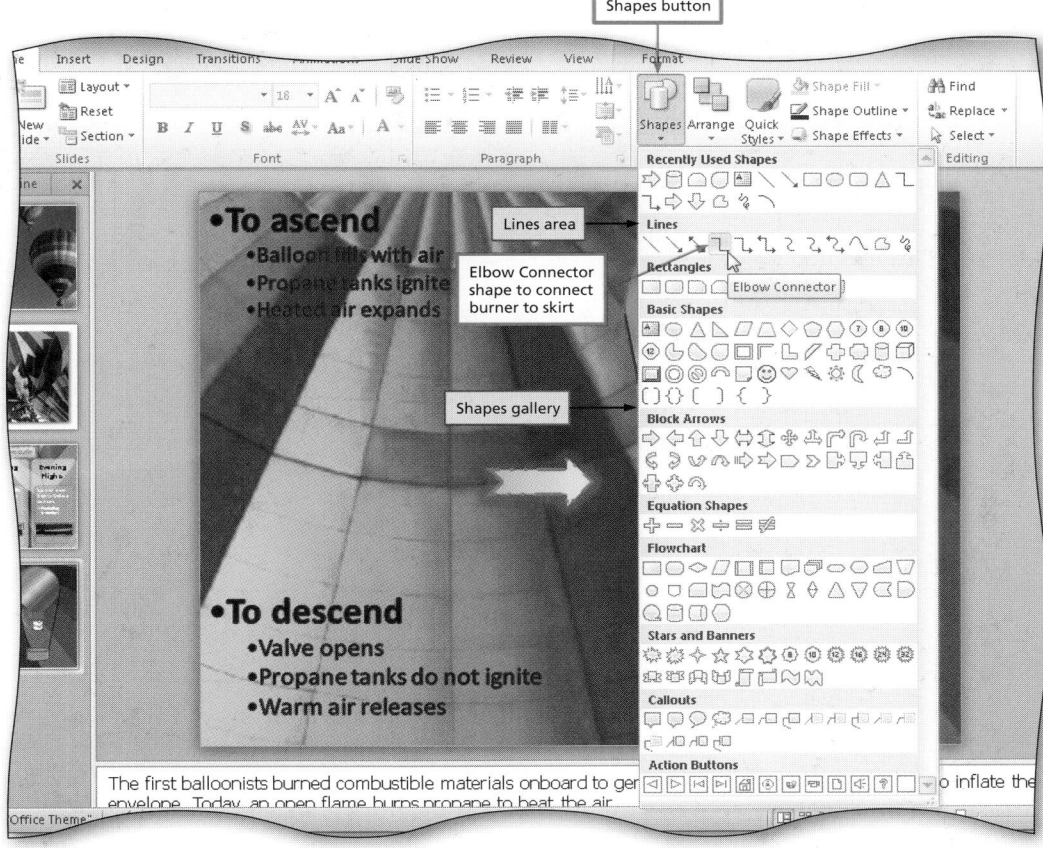

Figure 9–60

- Click the Elbow Connector, position the mouse pointer on the red point on the left side of the skirt (the Snip Same Side Corner Rectangle), and then click to insert one end of the line at this location.

- Drag the sizing handle at the other end of the line to the middle-left edge of the burner (the Rounded Rectangle) (Figure 9–61).

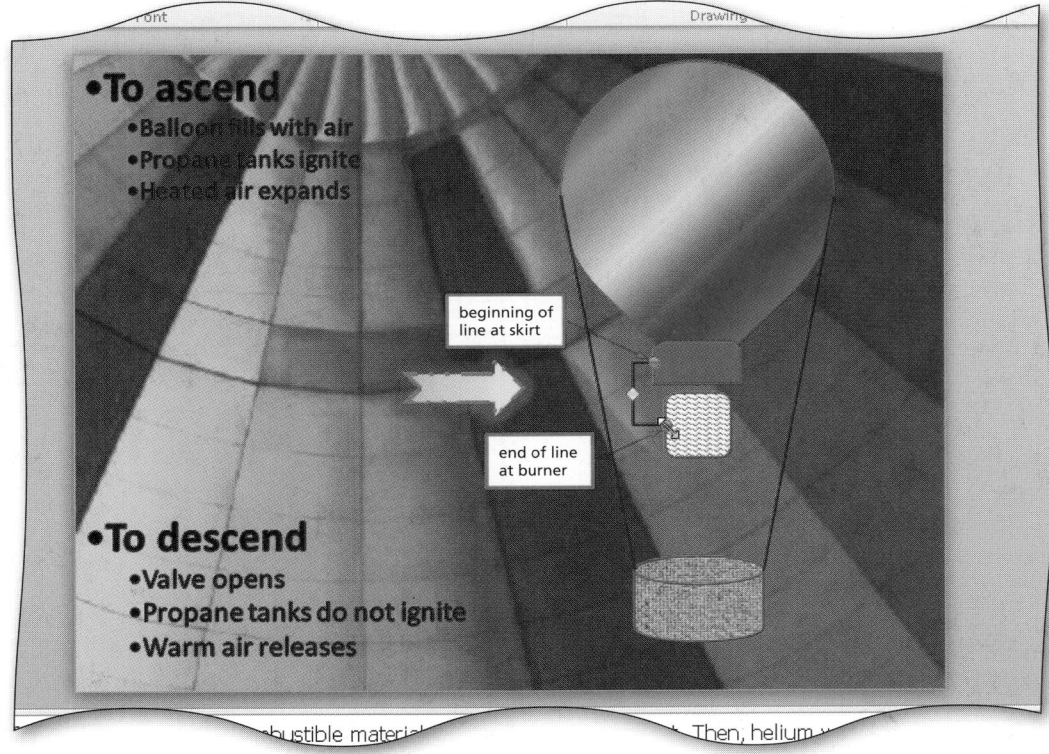

Figure 9–61

• Display the Shapes gallery, select the Elbow Connector, insert one end of the line on the red point on the right side of the skirt, and then drag the other end of the line to the middle-right edge of the burner (Figure 9–62).

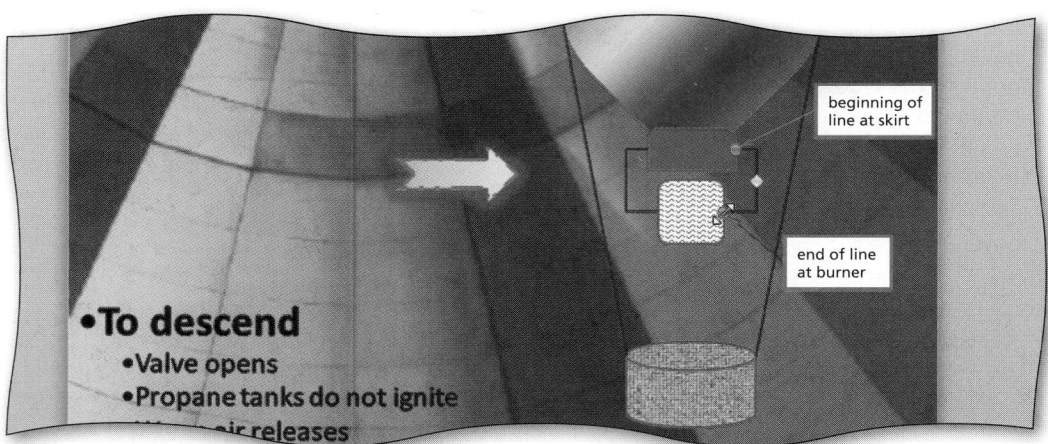

Figure 9–62

To Customize the Ribbon

Many commands available in PowerPoint are not included on any of the tabs on the Ribbon. You can, however, add such commands to the Ribbon or to the Quick Access Toolbar. One command combines shapes, and you could use it in this project to join all the shapes that form the hot air balloon. A second command subtracts shapes, so it would be useful to create a vent hole at the top of the balloon's envelope. The following steps customize the Ribbon by adding the Shape Combine and Shape Subtract commands to the Ribbon and then arranging their order in the group.

• With the Home tab displaying, open the Backstage view and then click Options to display the PowerPoint Options dialog box.

• Click Customize Ribbon in the left pane to display the Customize the Ribbon pane (Figure 9–63).

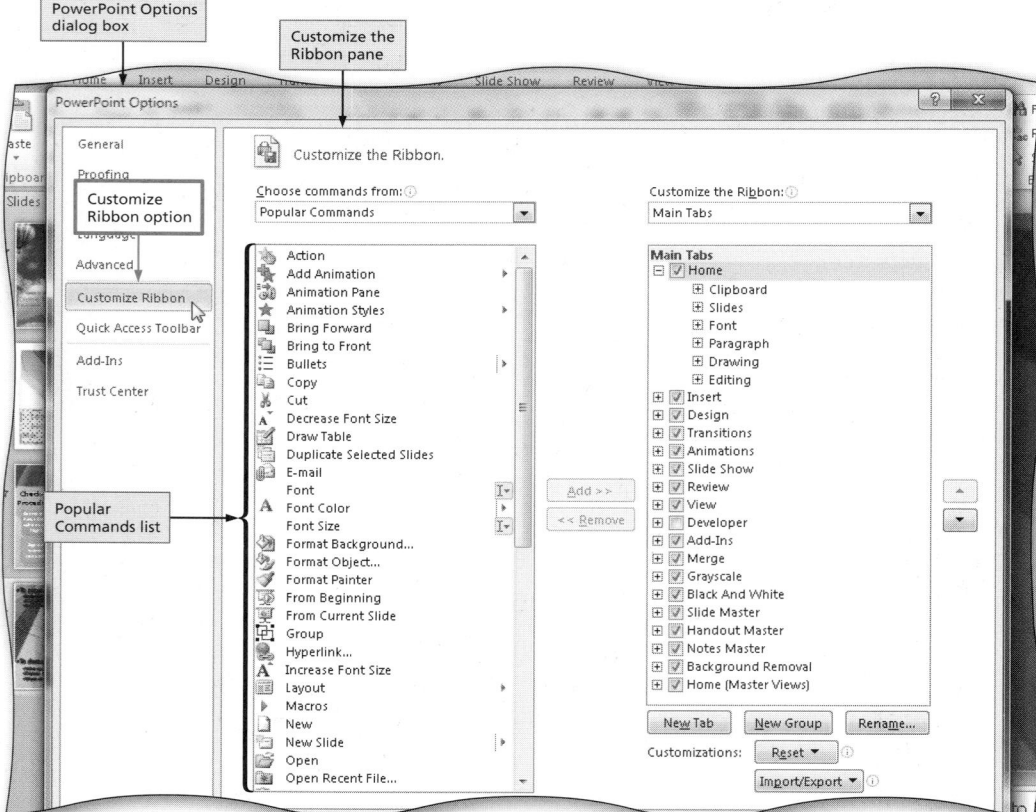

Figure 9–63

2

• Click the 'Choose commands from' box arrow to display the 'Choose commands from' list (Figure 9–64).

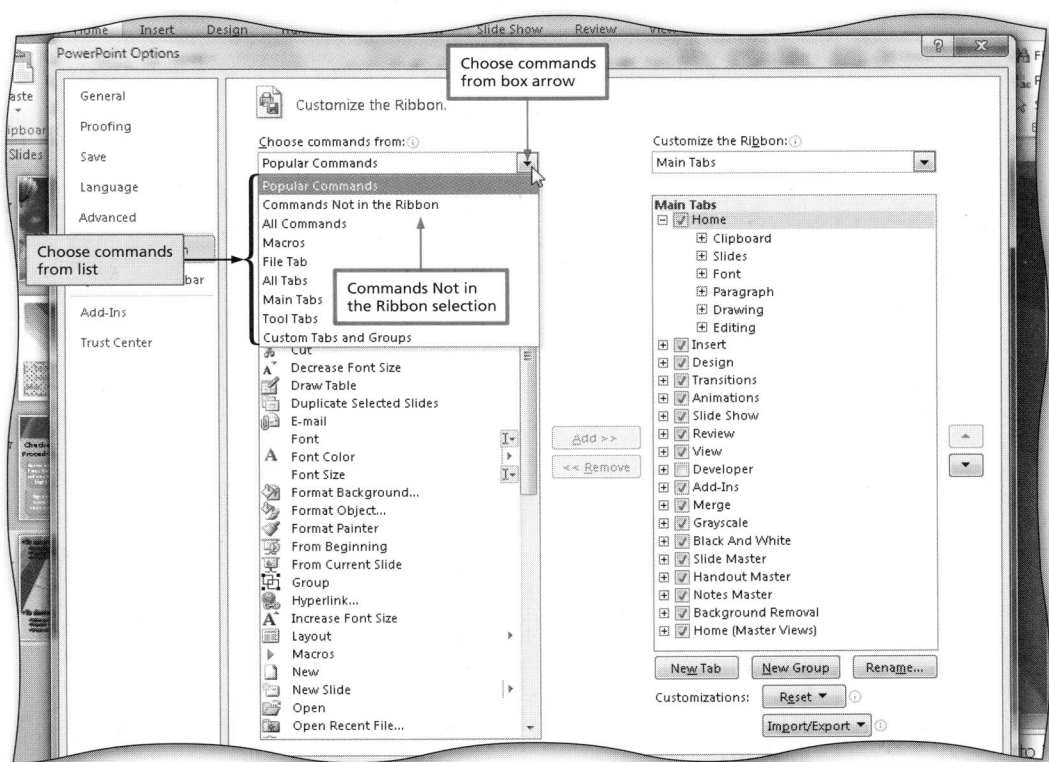

Figure 9–64

3

• Click Commands Not in the Ribbon in the 'Choose commands from' list to display a list of commands that do not display on the Ribbon (Figure 9–65).

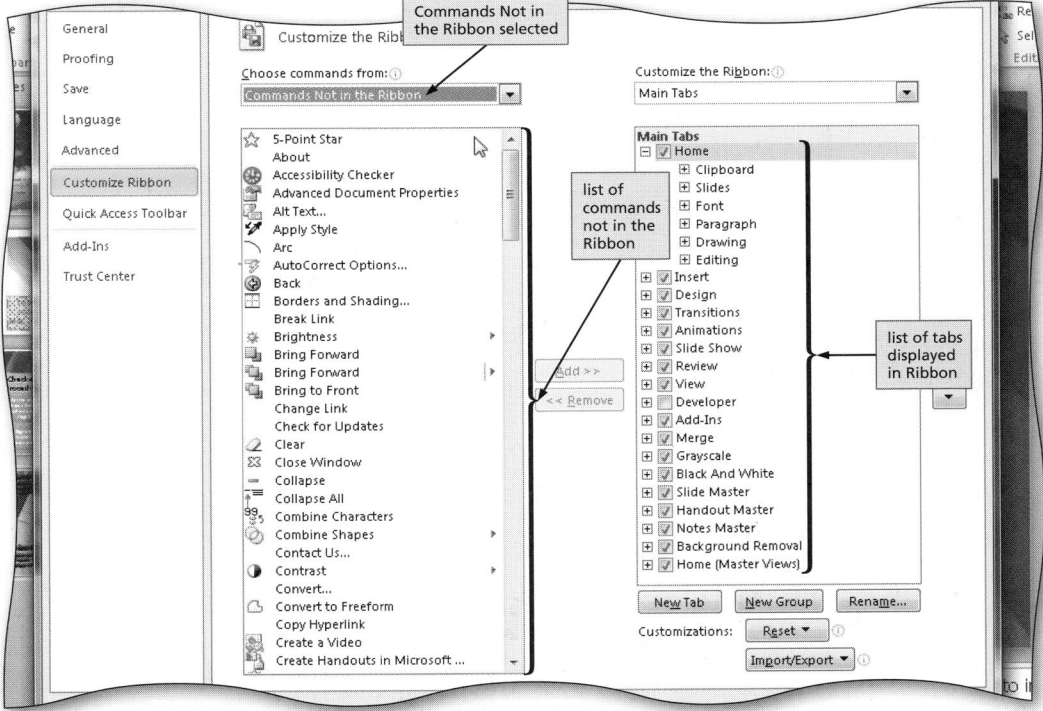

Figure 9–65

- Scroll to the bottom of the list and then click Shape Union to select this button.

- Click Drawing in the Main Tabs area to specify that the Shape Union button will be added in a new group between the Drawing and Editing groups on the Home tab (Figure 9–66).

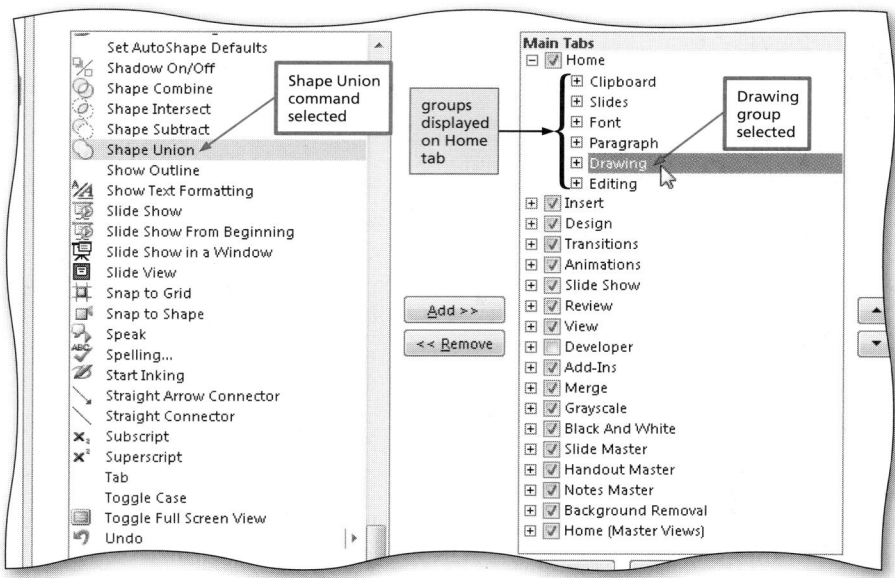

Figure 9–66

- Click the New Group button to create a new group.

- Click the Rename button and then type **Change Shape** as the new group name in the Display name text box (Rename dialog box) (Figure 9–67).

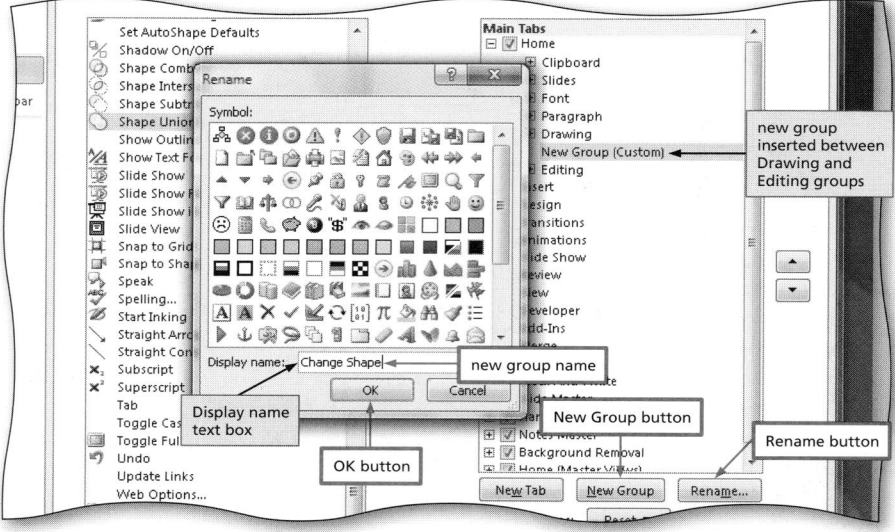

Figure 9–67

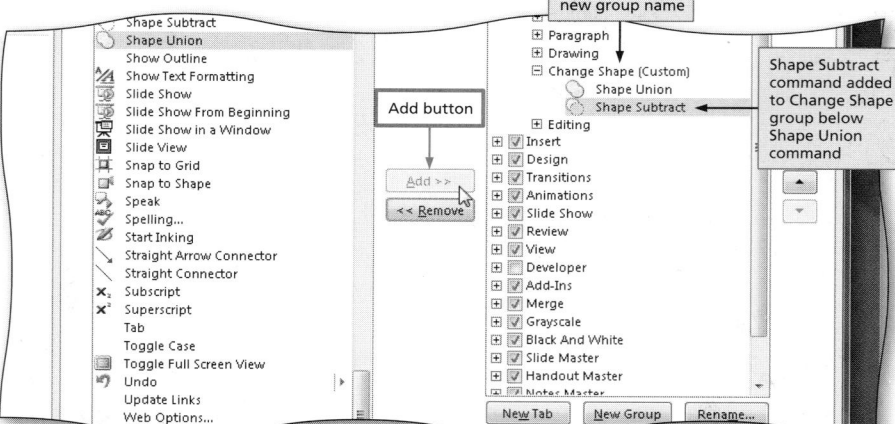

- Click the OK button (Rename dialog box) to rename the new group.

- Click the Add button to add the Shape Union button to the Change Shape group.

- Click Shape Subtract in the list of Commands Not in the Ribbon and then click the Add button to add the button to the Change Shape group (Figure 9–68).

Figure 9–68

7

- Click the Move Up button (PowerPoint Options dialog box) to move the Shape Subtract button above the Shape Union button (Figure 9–69).

8

- Click the OK button to close the PowerPoint Options dialog box and display the two buttons in the new Change Shape group on the Home tab in the Ribbon.

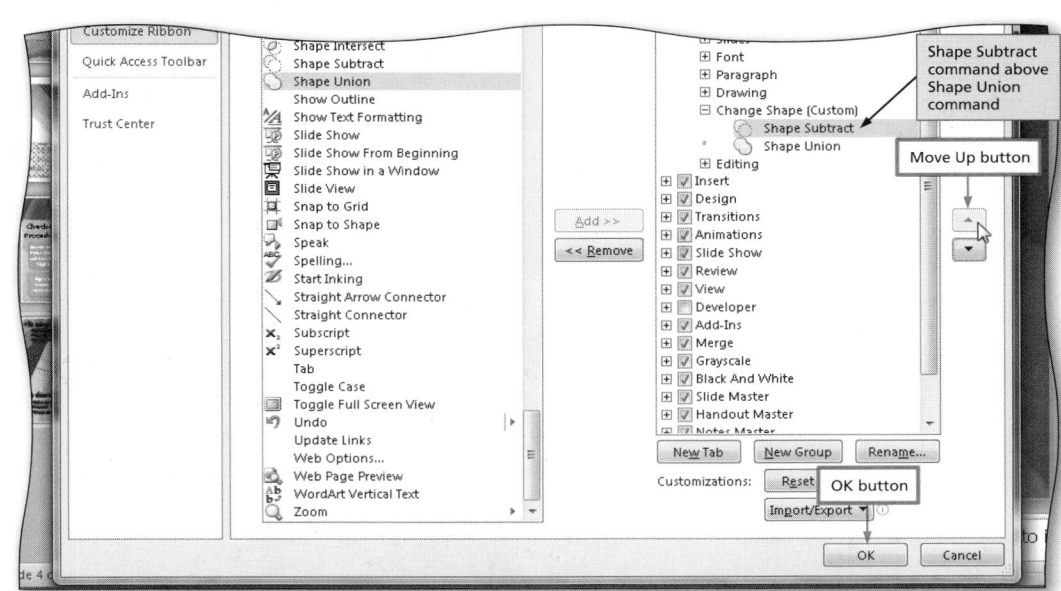

Figure 9–69

To Subtract a Shape and Combine Shapes

The hot air balloon's envelope has a vent at the top to release air. You will add this vent to the Teardrop shape on Slide 4. One method of creating this vent is to overlap an Oval shape and the Teardrop shape and then use the Shape Subtract command you just added to the Ribbon to delete the overlapped portion. The following steps insert an Oval shape and then subtract this object.

1

- Display the Shapes gallery, select the Oval shape in the Basic Shapes area (second shape in first row), and then insert the shape on the top of the envelope (Teardrop).

- Use the Smart Guides to align the Oval shape vertically, as shown in Figure 9–70.

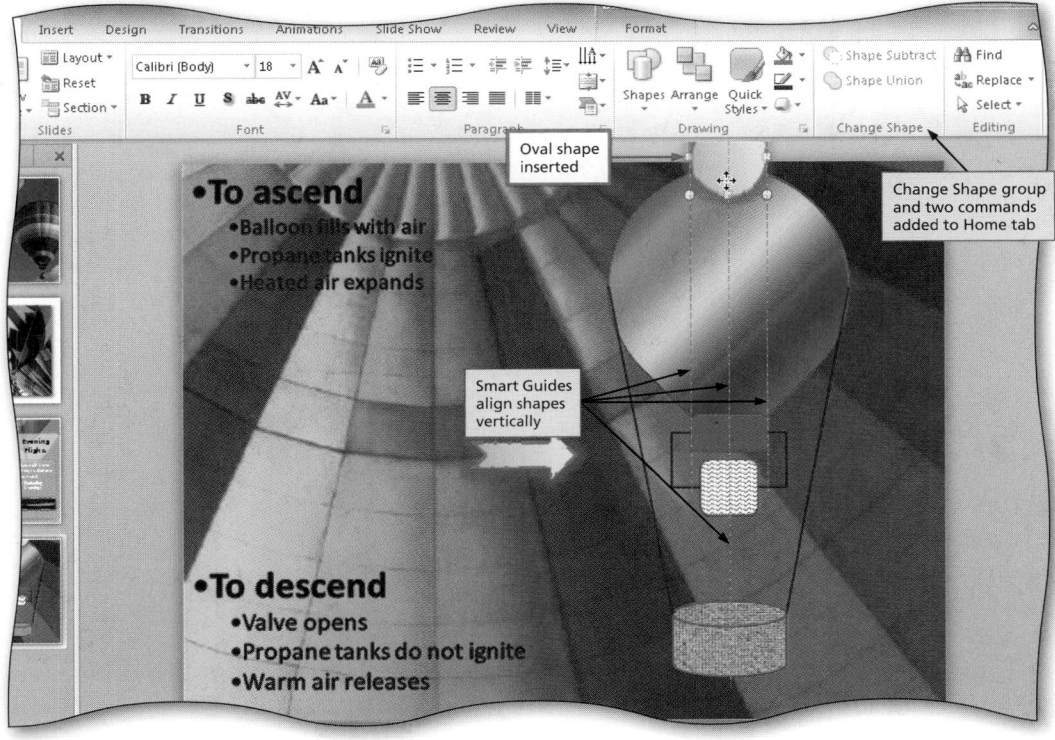

Figure 9–70

- Click the envelope to select it, press and hold down the CTRL key, and then click the oval to select both shapes (Figure 9–71).

Q&A

Do I need to select the shapes in this order?

Yes. When using the Shape Subtract command, you first select the shape that you want to keep and then click the shape that you want to delete.

- Click the Shape Subtract button (Home tab | Change Shape group) to delete the overlapped portion of the envelope.

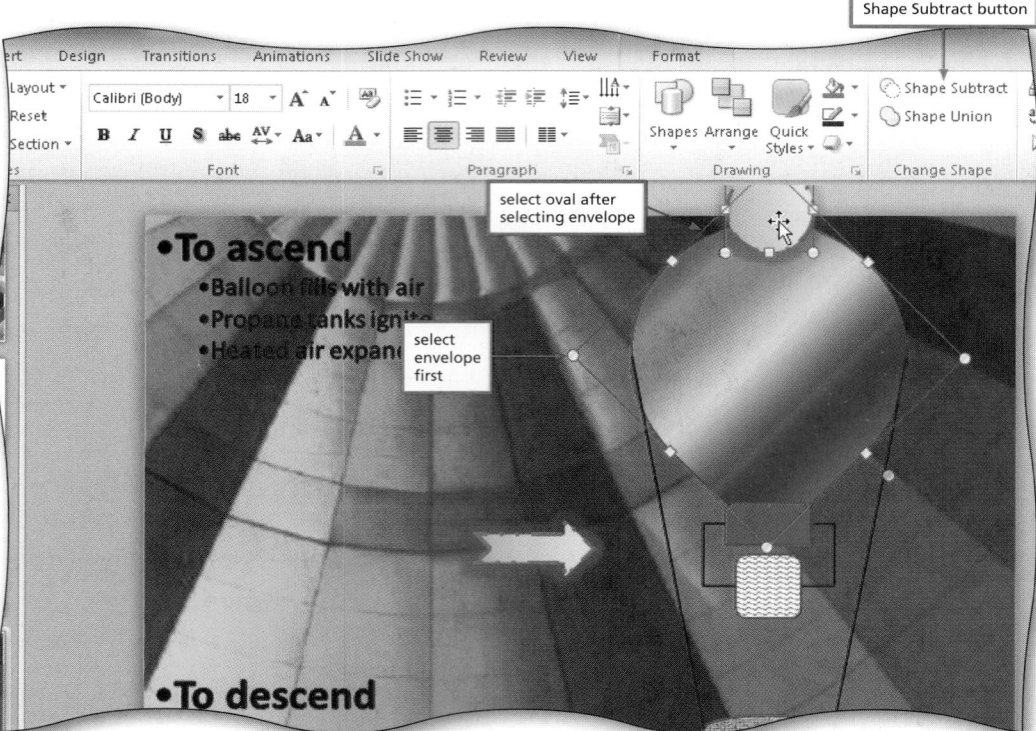

Figure 9–71

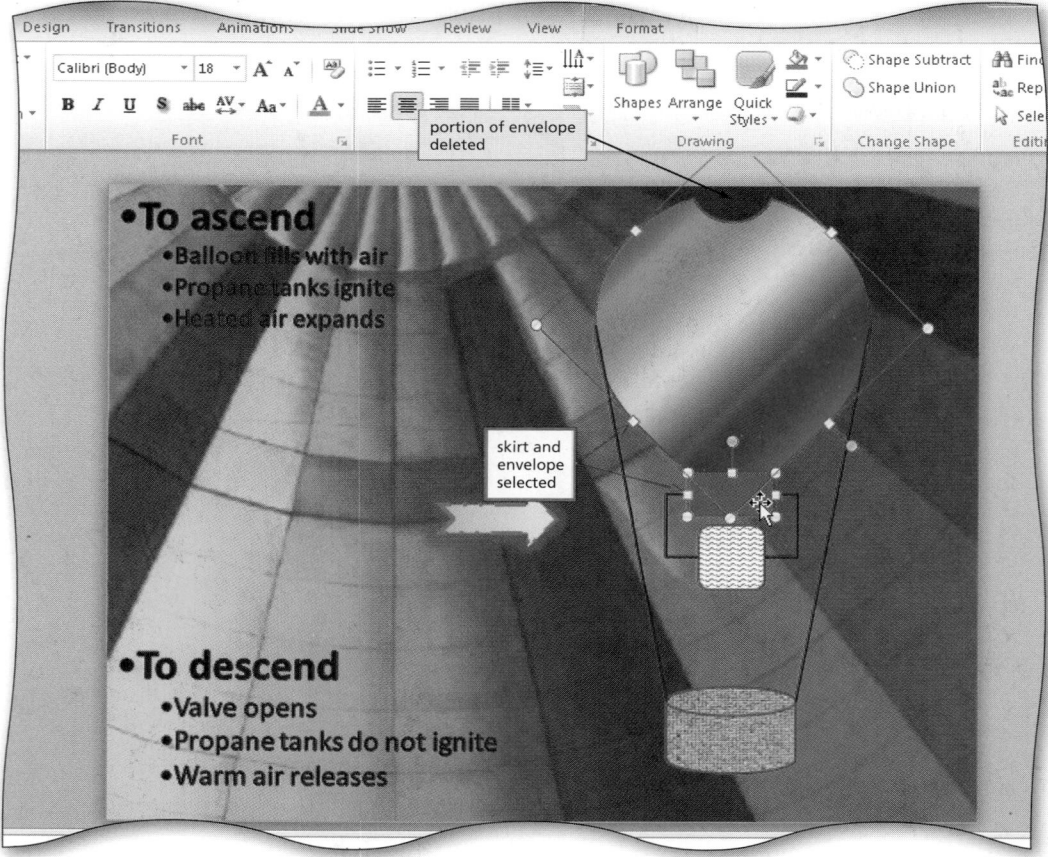

- Press and hold down the CTRL key and then click the skirt (Snip Same Side Corner Rectangle) to select it and the envelope (Figure 9–72).

Figure 9–72

5

• Click the Shape Union button (Home tab | Change Shape group) to combine the hot air balloon envelope and skirt shapes (Figure 9–73).

• Press and hold down the CTRL key, click all the hot air balloon shapes to select the objects, and then click the Shape Union button to combine all the shapes.

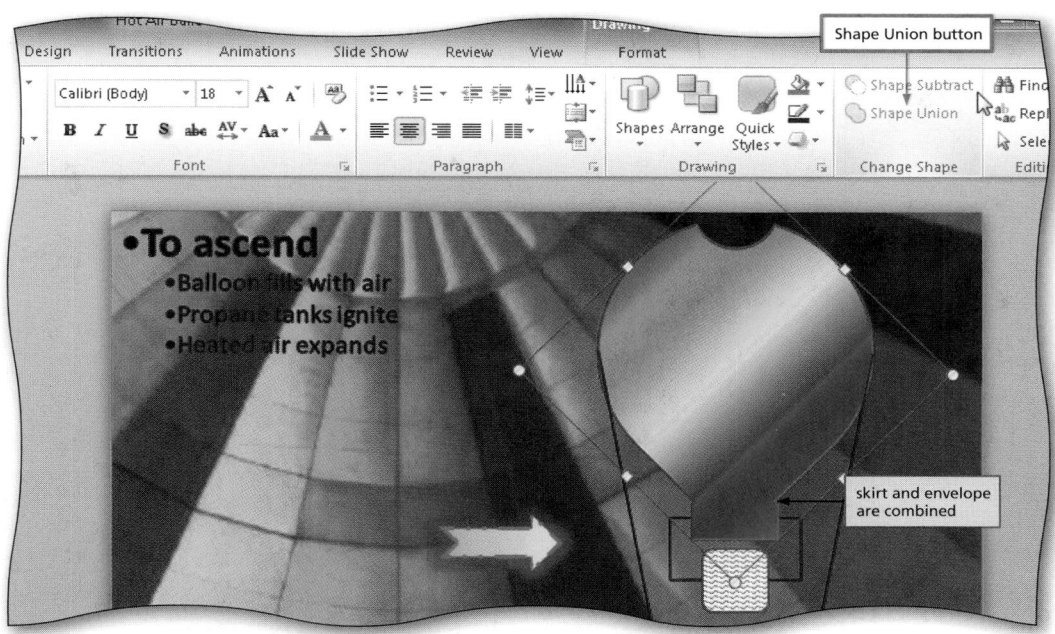

Figure 9–73

Use politically correct language.	Plan
Many companies have strict policies in order to prevent harassment in the workplace. These guidelines are developed to protect employees from adverse treatment based on race, religion, national origin, gender, or other personal traits. Keep these policies in mind as you label components on your slides. For example, some females may be offended if you refer to an adult woman as a "girl," or an older athlete may resent being labeled as an "aging" rather than as a "veteran" player.	Ahead

To Label the Shapes

The final step in creating Slide 4 is to label the parts of the hot air balloon. The Notched Right Arrow shape and the text box are formatted as defaults, so the labeling process is easy to accomplish. The following steps insert text boxes and arrows into Slide 4 and then enter text in the text boxes.

1 With Slide 4 displaying, insert a text box into the lower-right corner of the slide, type `Basket` in the text box, decrease the font size to 28 point, and move the text box to the middle of the basket.

2 Insert a text box into the center of the slide, type `Envelope` in the text box, decrease the font size to 28 point, and move the text box to the middle of the envelope.

3 Insert a text box into the center of the slide, type `Skirt` in the text box, decrease the font size to 28 point, and move the text box to the left side of the skirt and the left line.

4 Insert a text box into the center of the slide, type `Burner` in the text box, decrease the font size to 28 point, and move the text box to the left side of the burner and the left line.

5 Drag the Notched Right arrow between the Skirt text box and the hot air balloon skirt.

BTW

Quick Reference
For a table that lists how to complete the tasks covered in this book using the mouse, Ribbon, shortcut menu, and keyboard, see the Quick Reference Summary at the back of this book, or visit the PowerPoint 2010 Quick Reference Web page (scsite.com/ppt2010/qr).

6️⃣ Insert a Notched Right arrow and drag it between the Burner text box and the hot air balloon burner.

7️⃣ Press and hold down the SHIFT key, right-click the left elbow connector and the left line connecting the envelope to the basket, point to Send to Back, and then click Send to Back (Figure 9–74).

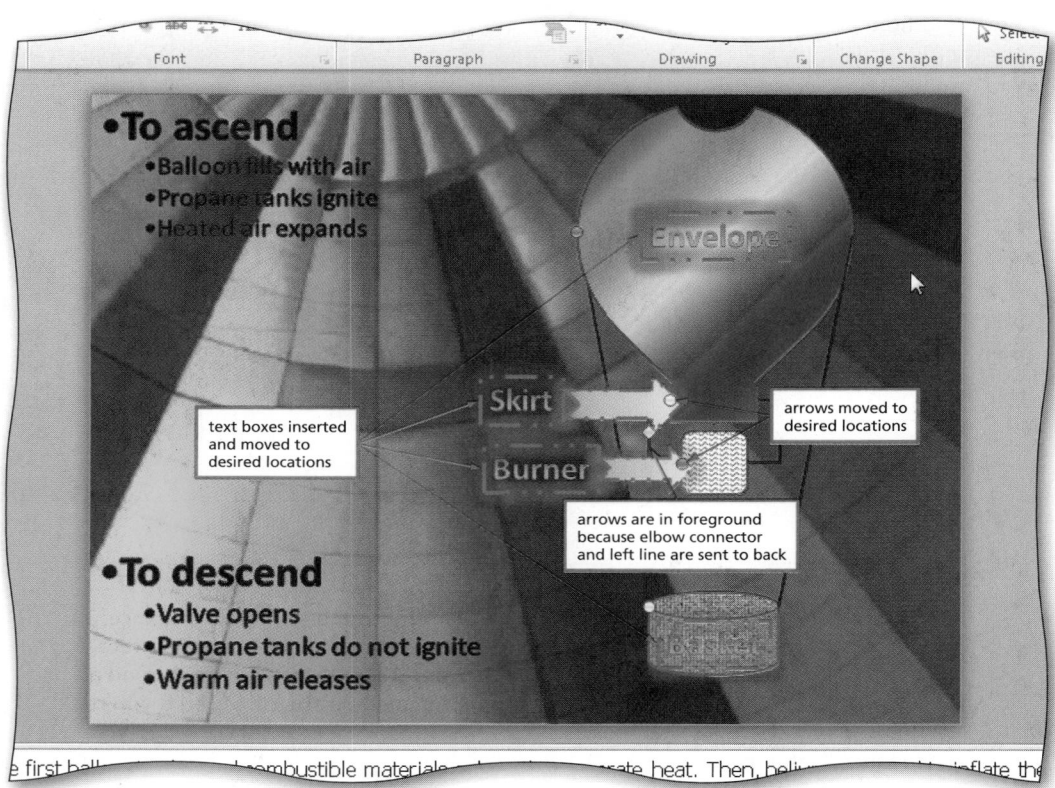

Figure 9–74

Plan Ahead	**Work with a buddy.** Although you may believe you create your best work when you work alone, research shows that the work product generally improves when two or more people work together on a creative task. A classmate or team member at work can assist you in many ways. For example, this person can help you gather research for your graphics and bulleted text or provide feedback on the slides' clarity and readability. As you rehearse, a buddy can time your talk and identify the times when the presentation lacks interest. If a buddy attends your actual presentation, he can give objective feedback on the components that worked and those that can use revision for the next time you present the material.

To Save the Presentation as a Picture Presentation

If you are going to share your slides with other presenters and do not want them to alter the slide content, you can save each slide as a picture. When they run the slide show, each slide is one complete picture, so the text and shapes cannot be edited. You also can use an individual slide picture as a graphic on another slide or in another presentation. The following steps save a copy of the presentation as a picture presentation.

1

- Open the Backstage view, display the Save & Send tab, and then click Change File Type in the File Types area.

- Click PowerPoint Picture Presentation in the Presentation File Types area (Figure 9–75).

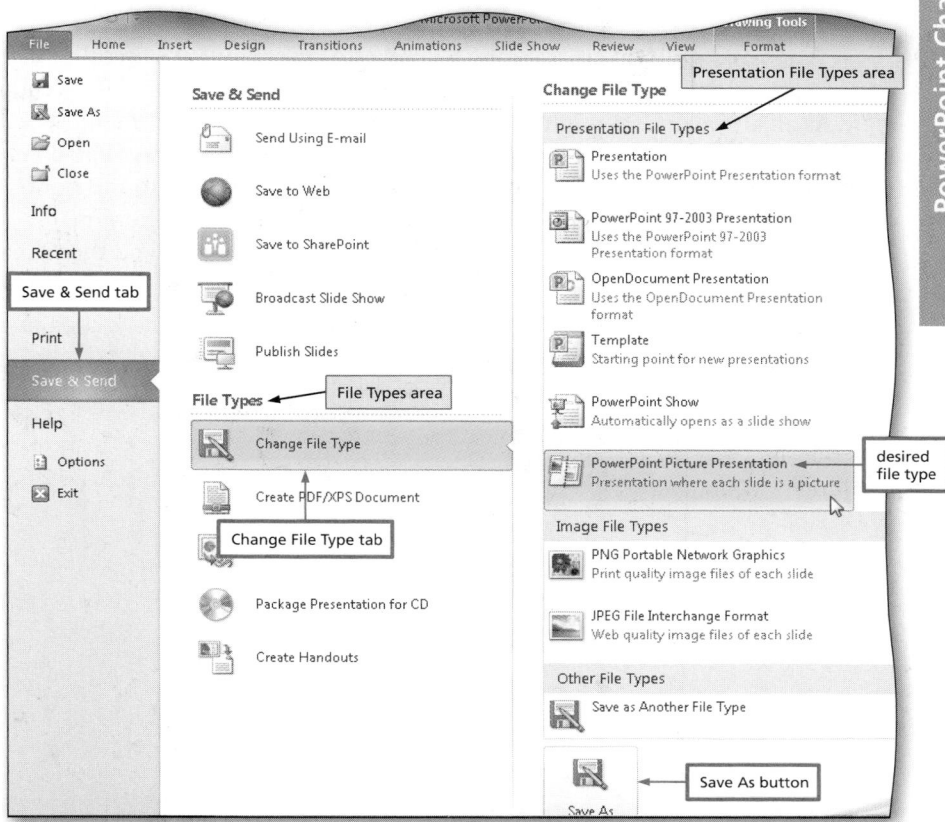

Figure 9–75

2

- Click the Save As button to display the Save As dialog box.

- Type **Balloon Picture Presentation** in the File name text box (Figure 9–76).

3

- Click the Save button (Save As dialog box) to save the presentation as a picture presentation.

- Click the OK button (Microsoft PowerPoint dialog box).

Q&A Will the PowerPoint presentation and the PowerPoint Picture Presentation have the same file names?

Yes. PowerPoint creates a new picture presentation and also retains the slide show presentation with identical file names.

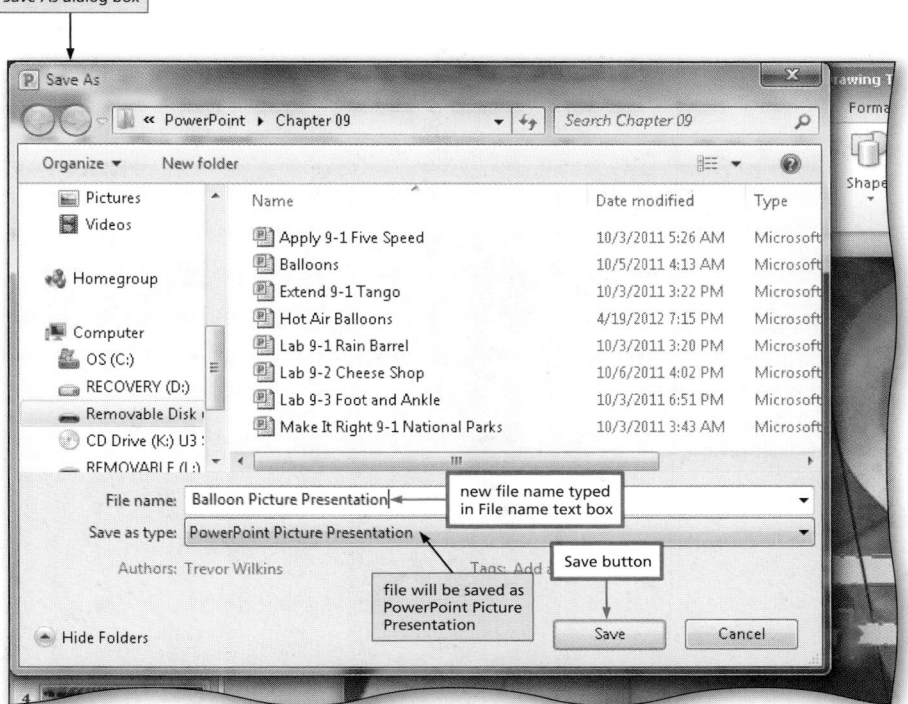

Figure 9–76

To Create a Handout by Exporting a File to Microsoft Word

The handouts you create using Microsoft PowerPoint are useful to distribute to audiences. Each time you need to create these handouts, however, you need to open the file in PowerPoint and then print from the Backstage view. As an alternative, it might be convenient to save, or export, the file as a Microsoft Word document if you are going to be using Microsoft Word to type a script or lecture notes. The handout can have a variety of layouts; for example, the notes you type in the Notes pane can be displayed to the right of or beneath the slide thumbnails, blank lines can be displayed to the right of or beneath the slide thumbnails, or just an outline can be displayed. The following steps export the presentation to Microsoft Word and then create a handout.

- Open the Backstage view, display the Save & Send tab, and then click Create Handouts in the File Types area (Figure 9–77).

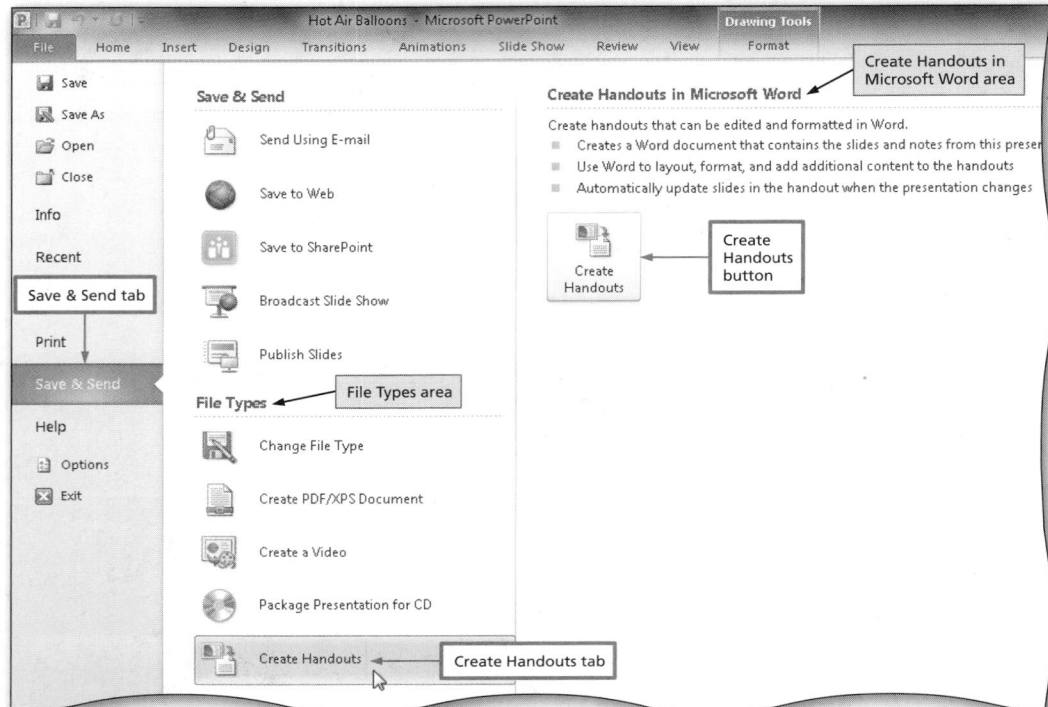

Figure 9–77

- Click Create Handouts in the Create Handouts in Microsoft Word area to display the Send to Microsoft Word dialog box (Figure 9–78).

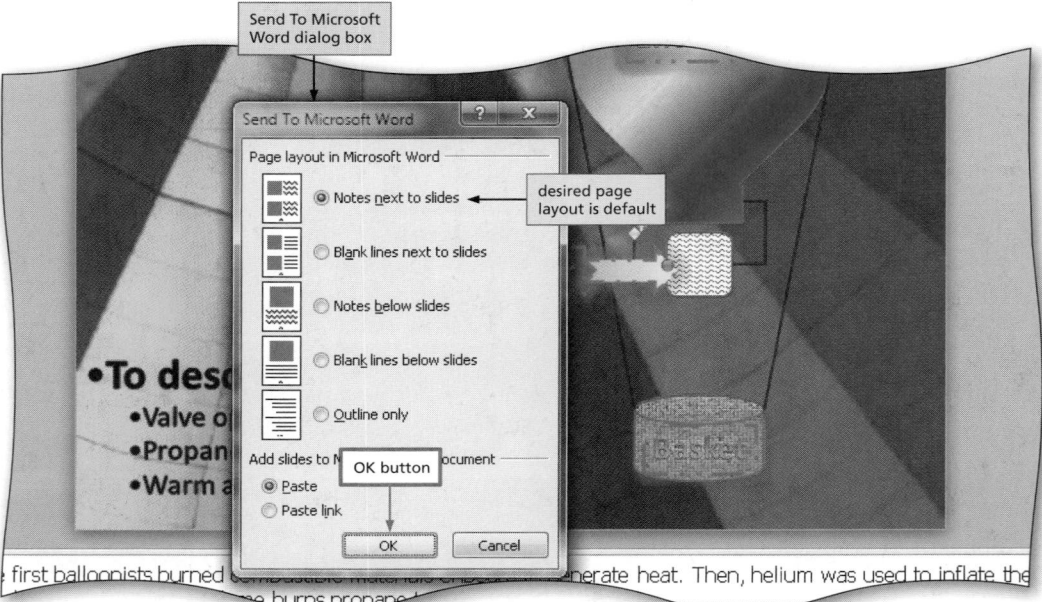

Figure 9–78

3

- Click the OK button to save the file with the default 'Notes next to slides' layout.

- If the handout does not display in a new Microsoft Word window, point to the Microsoft Word program button on the Windows taskbar to see a live preview of the handout (Figure 9–79).

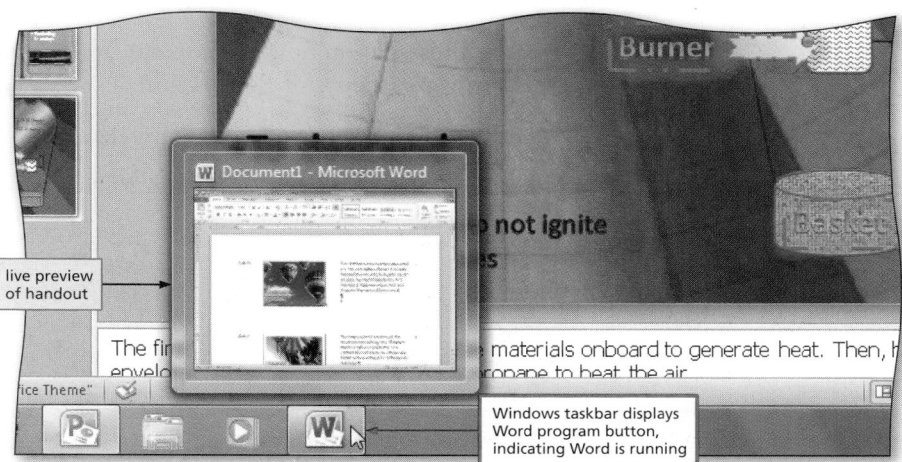

Figure 9–79

To Reset the Ribbon

Your work with the PowerPoint presentation is complete. The following steps remove the Change Shape group and the Shape Combine and Shape Subtract commands from the Home tab.

1 Display the Backstage view, click Options to display the PowerPoint Options dialog box, and then click Customize Ribbon in the left pane to display the Customize the Ribbon pane.

2 Click the Reset button (PowerPoint Options dialog box) to display the Reset menu and then click Reset all customizations.

3 Click the Yes button (Microsoft Office dialog box) to delete all customizations.

4 Click the OK button (PowerPoint Options dialog box) to close it.

Q&A

Do I need to remove the group and commands from the Ribbon?

No. For consistency, the Ribbon is reset after the added group and commands are no longer needed. If you share a computer with others, you should reset the Ribbon.

To Change Document Properties

Before saving the presentation again, you want to add your name, class name, and some keywords as document properties. The following steps use the Document Information Panel to change document properties.

1 Display the Document Information Panel and then type your name as the Author property.

2 Type your course and section in the Subject property.

3 Type `hot air balloon, orientation, schedule` as the Keywords property.

4 Close the Document Information Panel.

BTW

Certification
The Microsoft Office Specialist (MOS) program provides an opportunity for you to obtain a valuable industry credential – proof that you have the PowerPoint 2010 skills required by employers. For more information, visit the PowerPoint 2010 Certification Web page (scsite.com/ppt2010/cert).

To Print, Save, and Quit PowerPoint

The presentation now is complete. You should print the slides, save the presentation, and then quit PowerPoint.

1 Print the Hot Air Balloons presentation as a handout with two slides per page.

2 Save the Hot Air Balloons presentation again with the same file name.

3 Quit PowerPoint, closing all open documents.

Chapter Summary

In this chapter you have learned how to modify a presentation using text boxes, SmartArt, and shapes. You customized a text box, set it as the default, and then inserted new text boxes and applied formatting, including a texture, gradient, and pattern. You also converted WordArt to SmartArt and then formatted the shapes and bulleted paragraphs. Then you created a diagram from shapes, which had gradients and patterns applied. Finally, you saved the presentation as a picture presentation and exported the file to Microsoft Word to create a handout. The items listed below include all the new PowerPoint skills you have learned in this chapter.

1. Change a Text Box Outline Weight (PPT 534)
2. Change a Text Box Outline Color (PPT 535)
3. Change a Text Box Outline Style (PPT 536)
4. Apply an Effect to a Text Box (PPT 536)
5. Set Text Box Formatting as the Default (PPT 537)
6. Apply a Pattern to a Text Box (PPT 539)
7. Apply a Gradient Fill to a Text Box (PPT 542)
8. Center a Text Box (PPT 543)
9. Change a Slide Picture (PPT 544)
10. Convert WordArt to SmartArt (PPT 546)
11. Reorder SmartArt Shapes (PPT 547)
12. Promote a SmartArt Bullet Level (PPT 548)
13. Demote a SmartArt Bullet Level (PPT 549)
14. Change the SmartArt Layout (PPT 550)
15. Remove a SmartArt Shape (PPT 551)
16. Resize a SmartArt Graphic by Entering an Exact Measurement (PPT 552)
17. Resize a SmartArt Graphic Shape (PPT 553)
18. Apply a Picture to a Text Box (PPT 555)
19. Convert a SmartArt Graphic to Text (PPT 557)
20. Apply a Fill to a Shape (PPT 561)
21. Set Shape Formatting as the Default (PPT 564)
22. Draw a Line (PPT 565)
23. Change a Line Weight and Color (PPT 567)
24. Set Line Formatting as the Default (PPT 568)
25. Draw Additional Lines (PPT 568)
26. Customize the Ribbon (PPT 570)
27. Subtract a Shape and Combine Shapes (PPT 573)
28. Save the Presentation as a Picture Presentation (PPT 576)
29. Create a Handout by Exporting a File to Microsoft Word (PPT 578)

If you have a SAM 2010 user profile, your instructor may have assigned an autogradable version of this assignment. If so, log into the SAM 2010 Web site at www.cengage.com/sam2010 to download the instruction and start files.

Learn It Online

Test your knowledge of chapter content and key terms.

Instructions: To complete the Learn It Online exercises, start your browser, click the Address bar, and then enter the Web address `scsite.com/ppt2010/learn`. When the Office 2010 Learn It Online page is displayed, click the link for the exercise you want to complete and then read the instructions.

Chapter Reinforcement TF, MC, and SA
A series of true/false, multiple choice, and short answer questions that test your knowledge of the chapter content.

Flash Cards
An interactive learning environment where you identify chapter key terms associated with displayed definitions.

Practice Test
A series of multiple choice questions that test your knowledge of chapter content and key terms.

Who Wants To Be a Computer Genius?
An interactive game that challenges your knowledge of chapter content in the style of a television quiz show.

Wheel of Terms
An interactive game that challenges your knowledge of chapter key terms in the style of the television show *Wheel of Fortune*.

Crossword Puzzle Challenge
A crossword puzzle that challenges your knowledge of key terms presented in the chapter.

Apply Your Knowledge

Reinforce the skills and apply the concepts you learned in this chapter.

Formatting Text Boxes, Manipulating SmartArt, Adding and Reordering SmartArt Shapes, and Changing a Picture

Note: To complete this assignment, you will be required to use the Data Files for Students. See the inside back cover of this book for instructions on downloading the Data Files for Students, or contact your instructor for information about accessing the required files.

Instructions: Start PowerPoint. Open the presentation, Apply 9-1 Five Speed, located on the Data Files for Students.

The slides in this presentation give instructions for learning to drive a five-speed vehicle. The document you open is a partially formatted presentation. You will apply a gradient and a pattern to a text box and a shape, change the outline style of a text box, add and reorder SmartArt shapes, and change a picture so the slides look like Figure 9–80.

Perform the following tasks:
1. On Slide 1, change the gradient fill in the text box to From Center. Change the outline color of the text box to Dark Red, change the outline weight to 3 pt, and then change the outline style to Long Dash.

2. Change the picture in the lower-left corner of the slide to Gearshift, located on the Data Files for Students. Increase the picture size to 3.37" × 2.25" and move the picture to the lower-right corner of the slide, as shown in Figure 9–80a on the next page.

3. Start the audio clip on Slide 1 automatically and hide the icon during the show.

4. On Slide 2, insert a text box, type `Clutch` in the text box, increase the font size to 32 point, change the font color to White, center the text, and then bold this text. Apply a Black fill and then apply the Preset 5 effect to the text box. Set the current text box formatting as the default for new text boxes.

Continued >

Apply Your Knowledge *continued*

5. Insert three additional text boxes into Slide 2. Type **Brake** in one text box, type **Gas** in the second text box, and then type **5-Speed Setup** in the third text box. Decrease the font size of the third text box text to 20 point. Move the text boxes to the locations shown in Figure 9–80b.

6. Insert the Rectangle shape, apply the Dark vertical pattern, and then change the foreground color to Black. Set the shape outline to No Outline. Apply the Preset 5 effect to the shape and then set the shape as the default for future shapes. Change the size of this shape to 0.75" × 0.75" and move it below the Clutch text box.

7. Insert the Rectangle shape, change the size to 0.58" × 1.25", and then move this shape below the Brake text box. Insert another Rectangle shape, change the size to 0.92" × 0.5", and then move this shape below the Gas text box.

8. Use the Smart Guides to align the text boxes and shapes, as shown in Figure 9–80b. Copy the four text boxes and three shapes from Slide 2 to Slide 3 and Slide 4 and reposition if necessary, as shown in Figures 9–80c and 9–80d.

9. On Slide 2, add a shape before the first shape in the SmartArt graphic. Type **Check your pedals.** in the shape, change the font size to 20 point, and then bold this text.

10. On Slide 4, move the fifth shape in the SmartArt graphic (second shape in second row) so that it is the last shape, as shown in Figure 9–80d.

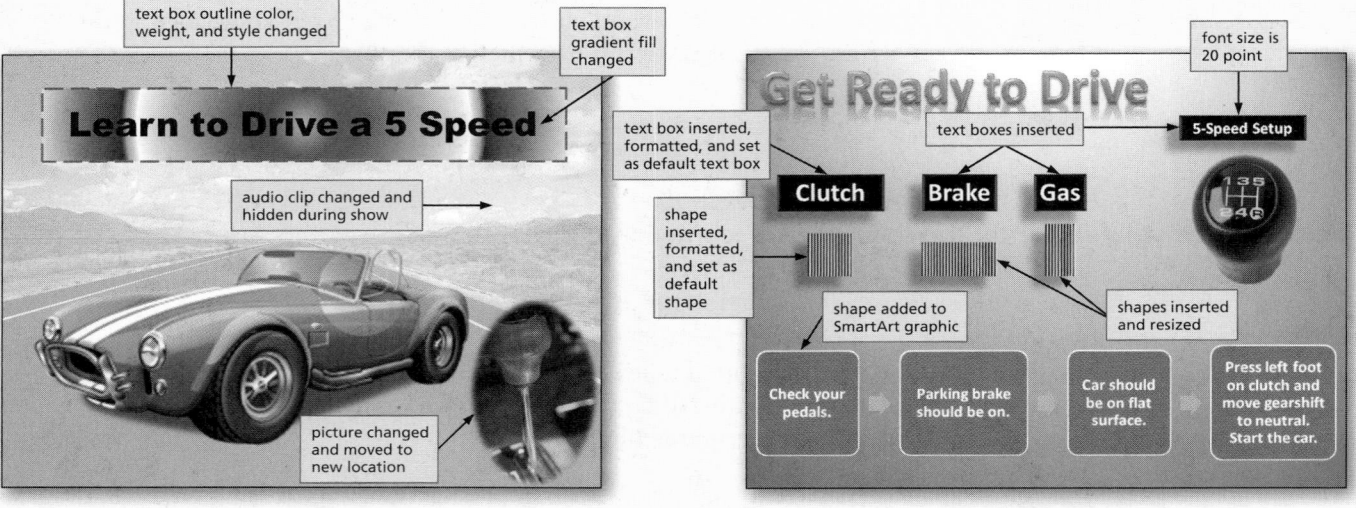

(a) Slide 1

(b) Slide 2

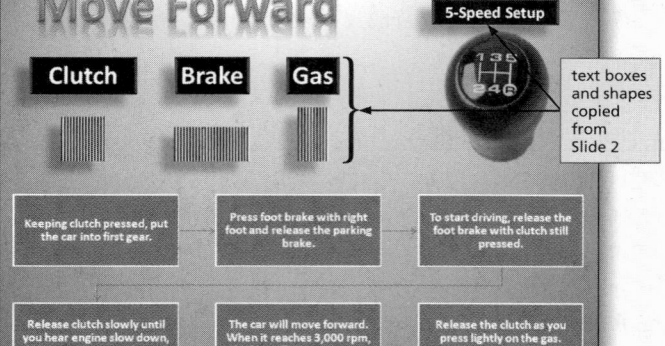

(c) Slide 3

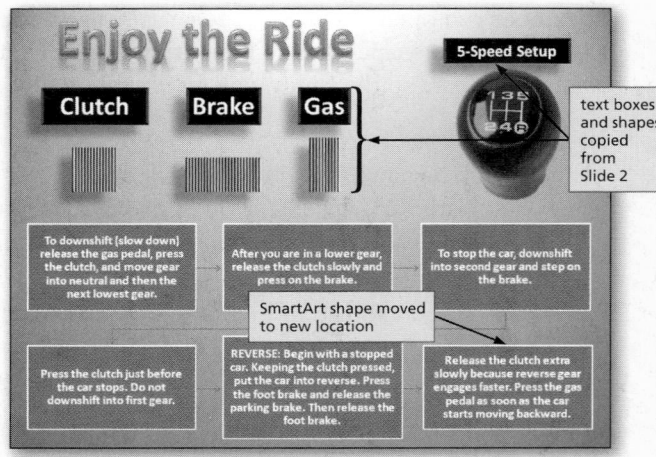

(d) Slide 4

Figure 9–80

11. Change the transition for all slides from Window to Zoom and then change the duration to 03.00 seconds.

12. Change the document properties, as specified by your instructor. Save the presentation using the file name, Apply 9-1 Drive a 5 Speed. Submit the revised document in the format specified by your instructor.

Extend Your Knowledge

Extend the skills you learned in this chapter and experiment with new skills. You may need to use Help to complete the assignment.

Applying a Texture and Changing the Outline Color of a Text Box, Demoting SmartArt Bullet Levels, and Inserting Arrows

Note: To complete this assignment, you will be required to use the Data Files for Students. See the inside back cover of this book for instructions on downloading the Data Files for Students, or contact your instructor for information about accessing the required files.

Instructions: Start PowerPoint. Open the presentation, Extend 9-1 Tango, located on the Data Files for Students. You will apply a texture and change the outline color of a text box, demote a SmartArt bullet level, and insert arrows, as shown in Figure 9–81 on the next page.

Perform the following tasks:
1. On Slide 1, insert a text box, type **Step by Step**, change the font to Arial, change the font size to 36 point, change the font color to White, and then bold this text. Apply a Purple mesh texture to the text box, add a 1½ pt outline, and then change the outline color to Orange. Set the current text box formatting as the default for new text boxes. Move the text box to the location shown in Figure 9–81a.

2. On Slide 2, insert a text box and type **Tango Styles** in the box. Center the text box on the slide, as shown in Figure 9–81b.

3. Remove the three white square shapes in the SmartArt graphic on Slide 2.

4. On Slide 3, insert a text box and type **Tango Attire** in the box. Center the text box on the slide horizontally, as shown in Figure 9–81c.

5. In the SmartArt graphic on Slide 3, demote the text **Gauchos, boots, and spurs** so that it is indented under the word, Men. With the SmartArt graphic still selected, click the Change Colors button (SmartArt Tools Design Tab | SmartArt Styles group) and then click Recolor Pictures in SmartArt Graphic to change the color of the pictures.

6. On Slide 4, insert a text box and type **Basic Steps** in the box. Center the text box on the slide horizontally, as shown in Figure 9–81d.

7. Change the pattern fill in the three right footprints on Slide 4 to Outlined diamond.

8. Insert an Arrow line shape (second shape in the Lines area) behind the number 1 circle, change the line weight to 2¼ pt, and then change the color to Red, as shown in Figure 9–81d. Set the current line formatting as the default. Click the end of the arrow and then rotate the shape upward.

9. Insert four more Arrow line shapes and move the shapes to the locations shown in Figure 9–81d. Send the arrows to the back so they are underneath the numbers.

10. Apply the Flip transition to all slides and change the duration to 02:50 seconds.

11. Change the document properties, as specified by your instructor. Save the presentation using the file name, Extend 9-1 Learn to Tango.

12. Submit the revised document in the format specified by your instructor.

Continued >

Extend Your Knowledge *continued*

(a) Slide 1

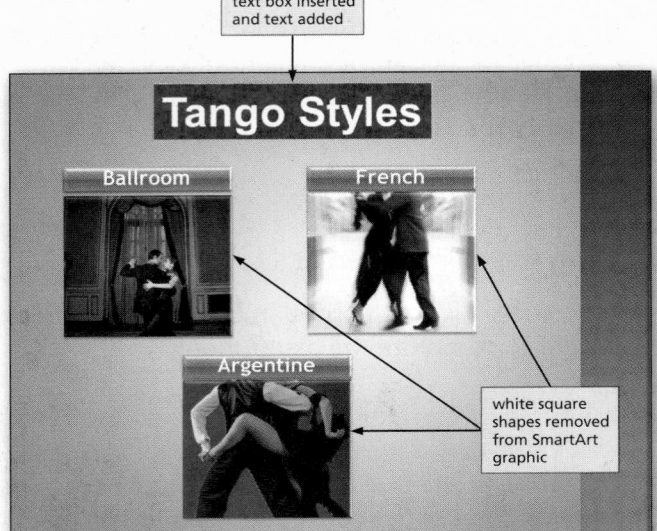

(b) Slide 2

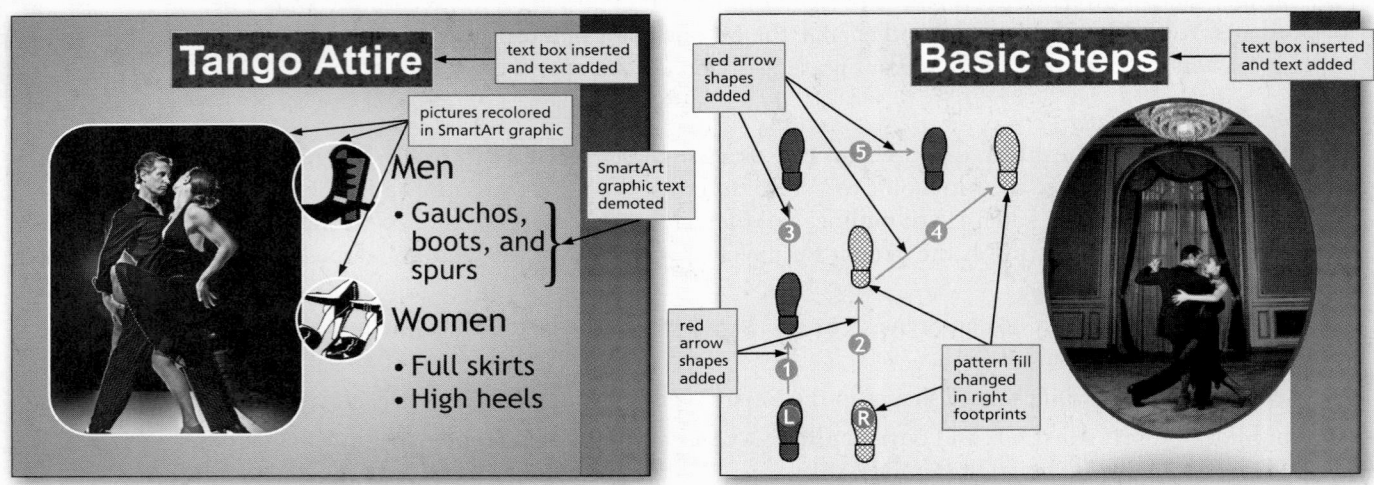

(c) Slide 3

(d) Slide 4

Figure 9–81

Make It Right

Analyze a presentation and correct all errors and/or improve the design.

Changing a Text Box Fill, Reordering SmartArt Shapes, and Changing a Picture

Note: To complete this assignment, you will be required to use the Data Files for Students. See the inside back cover of this book for instructions on downloading the Data Files for Students, or contact your instructor for information about accessing the required files.

Instructions: Start PowerPoint. Open the presentation, Make It Right 9-1 National Parks, located on the Data Files for Students.

Correct the formatting problems and errors in the presentation while keeping in mind the guidelines presented in this chapter.

Perform the following tasks:

1. On Slide 1 (Figure 9–82a), change the Ranked by Total Acreage text box fill to Linear Down Gradient and remove the outline. Increase the font size to 36 point, change the font color to Brown, Accent 2, and then adjust the size of the text box. Move the text box to the lower-right corner of the slide.

2. On Slide 2 (Figure 9–82b), change the acreage for the Grand Canyon from 2.4 to 1.2 and reorder the SmartArt shapes so that the Grand Canyon is listed in the tenth position below Everglades, Florida. Also, switch the layout of the graphic so that the acreage figures are on the right side of the SmartArt graphic. *Hint:* With the SmartArt graphic selected, select the Right to Left button (SmartArt Tools Design tab | Create Graphic group).

3. On Slide 3 (Figure 9–82c on the next page), correct the information to state that Wrangell-St. Elias is the largest National Park. Also, change the weight and color of the arrow shape to match the weight and color of the outline shape on the text box.

4. On Slide 4 (Figure 9–82d), change the Montana map picture to the Wyoming map picture, located on the Data Files for Students. Change the Wyoming picture style to Reflected Bevel, White.

5. On Slide 5 (Figure 9–82e), change the Iguana picture to the Alligator picture, located on the Data Files for Students. Remove the artistic effect from the Florida map picture.

6. On Slide 6 (Figure 9–82f), change the top river picture to the Canyon River picture, located on the Data Files for Students, and increase the size of the picture to 3.24" × 4.08". If necessary, bring the title text to the front of this picture.

7. For all slides, apply the Fly Through transition, change the Effect Option to Out, and change the duration to 02:50 seconds.

8. Change the document properties, as specified by your instructor. Save the presentation using the file name, Make It Right 9-1 Largest US National Parks.

9. Submit the revised document in the format specified by your instructor.

(a) Slide 1

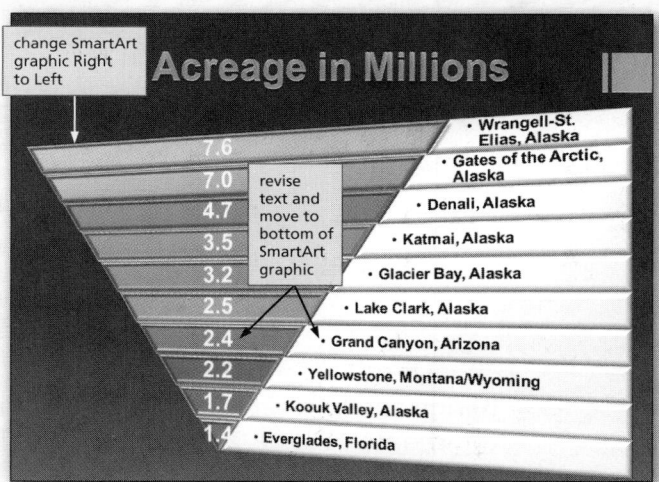

(b) Slide 2

Figure 9–82

Continued >

STUDENT ASSIGNMENTS

Make It Right *continued*

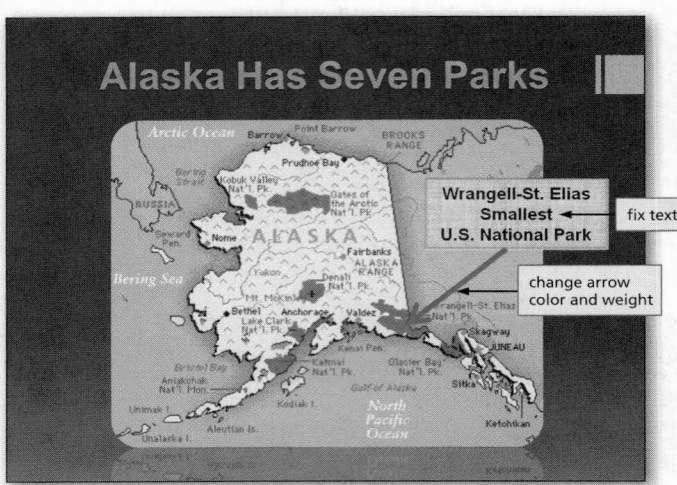

(c) Slide 3

(d) Slide 4

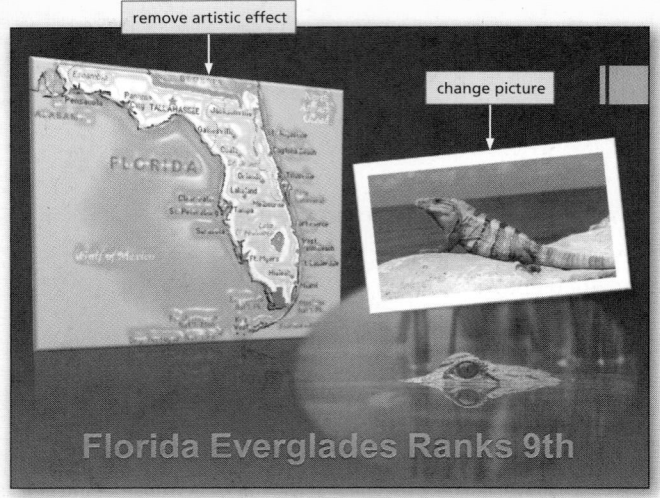

(e) Slide 5

(f) Slide 6

Figure 9–82 (Continued)

In the Lab

Design and/or create a presentation using the guidelines, concepts, and skills presented in this chapter. Labs 1, 2, and 3 are listed in order of increasing difficulty.

Lab 1: Applying a Picture to a Text Box, Converting SmartArt to Shapes, and Converting SmartArt to Text

Note: To complete this assignment, you will be required to use the Data Files for Students. See the inside back cover of this book for instructions on downloading the Data Files for Students or contact your instructor for information about accessing the required files.

Problem: Saving and using rain water can be a great way to conserve water. Whether you are watering your garden or washing your car, rain water is a great way to use one of our most valuable natural resources.

A rain barrel is an excellent way to catch rain and store it. Members of your garden club have been discussing building a rain barrel, and you decide to create a PowerPoint presentation to give some basic instructions. You create the slides shown in Figure 9–83 using files located on the Data Files for Students.

Perform the following tasks:

1. Open the presentation, Lab 9-1 Rain Barrel, located on the Data Files for Students.

2. On Slide 1, remove the background from the umbrella picture, increase the size, and move it to the lower-left corner of the slide, as shown in Figure 9–83a.

3. Insert a text box, type **CATCH THE RAIN** in the text box, change the font to Broadway, change the font color to White, and then center the text in the text box. Change the font size to 60 point for the words, Catch the, and 88 point for the word, Rain. Change the outline color to White, the outline weight to 3 pt, and then increase the size of the text box to 3.74" × 5". Apply the Raindrops picture to the text box and then move it to the position shown in Figure 9–83a.

4. Change the font size of the text in the text box located at the bottom of the slide to 36 point, change the font color to Dark Red, and then bold this text. Adjust the size of the text box so that the text fits on four lines, as shown in Figure 9–83a. Change the outline weight of the text box to 3 pt and then change the outline style to Round Dot.

5. On Slide 2, convert the SmartArt graphic at the top of the slide to shapes. Apply a Subtle Effect – Red, Accent 2 Quick Style effect to the three text shapes and change the font to Broadway, as shown in Figure 9–83b.

6. Apply the Water droplets texture to the Teardrop shape on the left side of Slide 2.

7. Convert the SmartArt graphic on the right side of Slide 2 to text. Increase the font size of the text to 34 point, change the font color to black, and then change the bullets to Checkmark Bullets. Change the size of the text box, apply the Water droplets texture, change the outline color of the text box to Red, and then change the outline weight to 3 pt. Move the text box to the location shown in Figure 9–83b.

8. Add the Style 7 background style to Slide 2.

9. Apply the Ripple transition and change the duration to 03.75 seconds for all slides.

10. Change the document properties, as specified by your instructor. Save the presentation using the file name, Lab 9-1 Catch the Rain.

11. Submit the revised document in the format specified by your instructor.

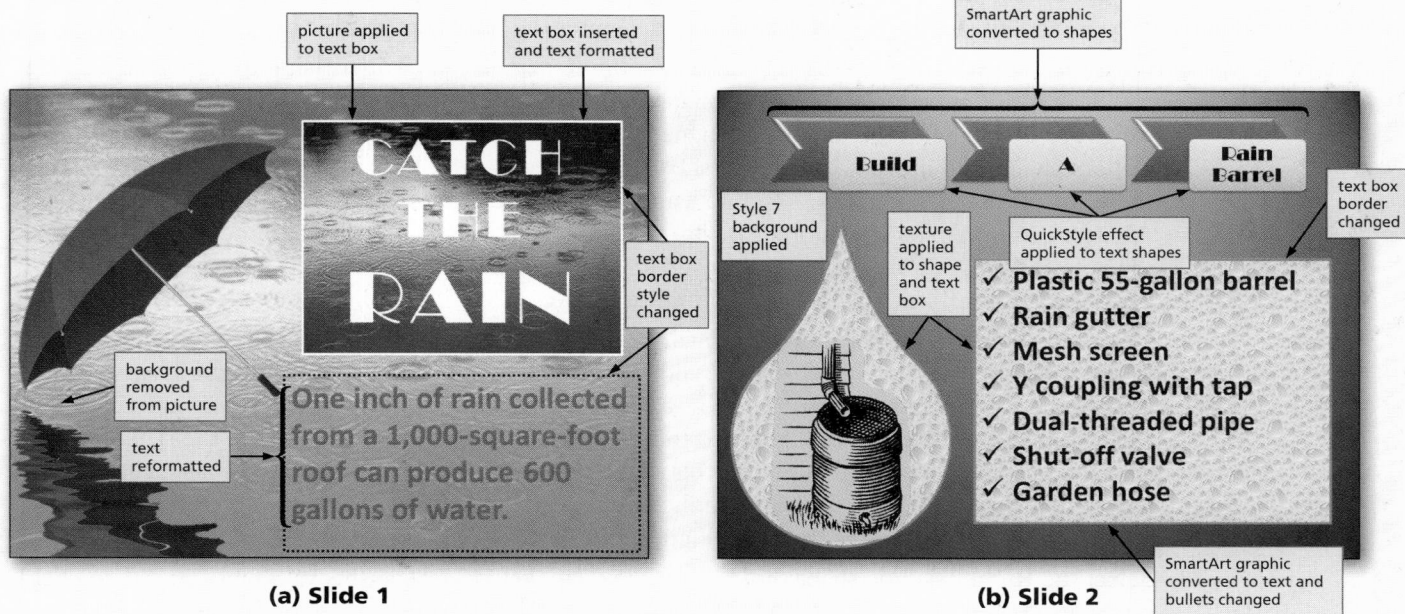

(a) Slide 1   **(b) Slide 2**

Figure 9–83

In the Lab

Lab 2: Inserting and Drawing Shapes, Creating a Handout by Exporting a File to Microsoft Word, and Saving a Presentation as a Picture Presentation

Note: To complete this assignment, you will be required to use the Data Files for Students. See the inside back cover of this book for instructions on downloading the Data Files for Students or contact your instructor for information about accessing the required files.

Problem: Your family is opening a cheese store in northern Wisconsin. The store will offer cheese from local farmers, imported cheese, and sausage. The store will also feature gift baskets and some small specialty items, such as homemade jams. You volunteered to put together a small advertising campaign for the new store, and you decide to create a PowerPoint presentation to share your ideas with the family. You will create an ad for the local newspaper and a sign to hang in the library and the village hall. You create the slides shown in Figure 9–84.

Perform the following tasks:

1. Open the presentation, Lab 9-2 Cheese Shop, located on the Data Files for Students.

2. On Slide 1, apply the Oak texture to the text box in the lower-left corner of the slide, and then remove the yellow outline on the text box. Move the text box to the left side of the yellow rectangle above the canopy in the cheese shop picture, as shown in Figure 9–84a.

3. Insert the Explosion 1 shape into the upper-left corner of the slide, type **Coming Soon**, and then increase the size of the shape to 2.5" × 3.12". Increase the font size to 28 point, change the font color to Black, and then bold this text. Change the shape fill color to Yellow, change the shape outline color to Olive Green, Accent 3, and then change the line weight to 3 pt.

4. On Slide 2, insert a text box and type **The Grate Cheese Store Products** in the box. Change the font to Bernard MT Condensed and increase the font size to 36 point. Apply the Small grid pattern fill to the text box and change the foreground color to Yellow. Move the text box to the area shown in Figure 9–84b and center the text box horizontally on the slide.

5. Convert the WordArt text on Slide 2 to the Vertical Bracket List SmartArt graphic. Change the size of the SmartArt graphic to 6.53" × 7.83", change the color to Transparent Gradient Range – Accent 6, and then apply the Sunset Scene SmartArt style. Move the Sausage shape up so that it is above the Gift Baskets shape. Demote the two paragraphs, Swiss and Cheddar, in the first shape so they are indented below the word, Imported. Center the SmartArt graphic horizontally on the slide.

6. On Slide 3, create the baseboard by inserting the Rectangle shape, increasing the size of the shape to 1.17" × 10", applying a White fill, changing the outline color to Black, and changing the outline weight to 2¼ pt. Send the baseboard shape backward until it is behind the mouse and Cloud Callout shape, and move it to the area shown in Figure 9–84c. Also, insert the Flowchart: Delay shape, increase the size to 1.42" × 1.15", and then Rotate Left 90° (Drawing Tools Format tab | Arrange group). Apply the Subtle Effect – Black, Dark 1 Shape QuickStyle to the shape. Move the shape to the position shown in Figure 9–84c. Duplicate this shape, move it slightly to the right, and then apply a Black fill, as shown in Figure 9–84c.

7. Create the cheese for Slide 3 by customizing the Ribbon and adding the Shape Subtract command in a new group named Cheese. Insert a slide with the Blank layout. Insert the Right Triangle shape, change the size of the shape to 2.5" × 3.5", apply a Yellow fill, and then change the outline weight to No Line. Apply the Preset 9 effect to the shape. Insert the Oval shape, change the size of the shape to .5" × .5", and then duplicate this shape two times. Insert another Oval shape, change the size of the shape to .75" × .75", and duplicate this shape two times. Move the six oval shapes on the Right Triangle shape, as shown in Figure 9–84d.

8. Select the Right Triangle shape, hold down the CTRL key, select the six oval shapes, and then click the Shape Subtract button on the Ribbon. Copy the cheese shape to the cloud shape on Slide 3. Delete Slide 4.

9. Reset the Ribbon. Change the document properties, as specified by your instructor. Save the presentation using the file name, Lab 9-2 The Grate Cheese Shop.

10. Save the presentation as a picture presentation using the file name, Lab 9-2 Cheese Shop Picture Presentation. Open the picture presentation, display Slide 3, change the size of the picture to 1.7" × 2.35", and then copy the picture to the Clipboard. Close the Lab 9-2 Cheese Shop Picture Presentation file without saving. Paste the picture on Slide 1 in the file, Lab 9-2 The Grate Cheese Shop. Move the picture to the right side of the yellow rectangle in the cheese store clip, as shown in Figure 9–84a.

11. Type **Ad for The Chronicle.** in the Slide 1 Notes pane. Type **Sign for the library.** in the Slide 2 Notes pane. Type **Sign for Small Business News bulletin board at the library.** in the Slide 3 Notes pane.

12. Create a handout in Microsoft Word using the 'Notes next to slides' page layout, as shown in Figure 9–84e on the next page.

13. Submit the revised document in the format specified by your instructor.

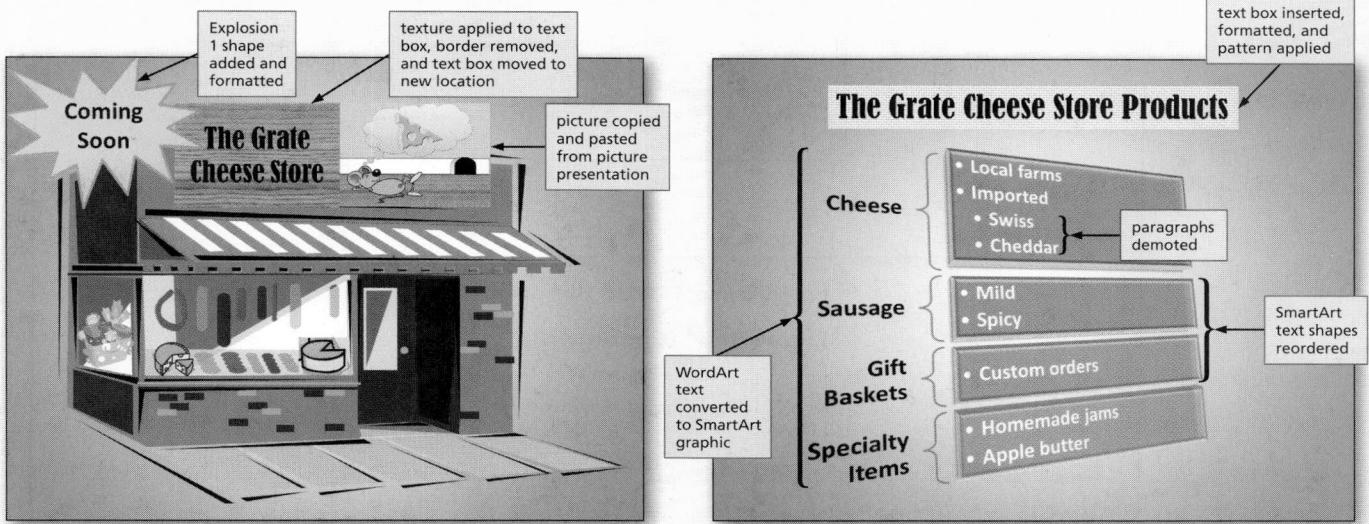

(a) Slide 1

(b) Slide 2

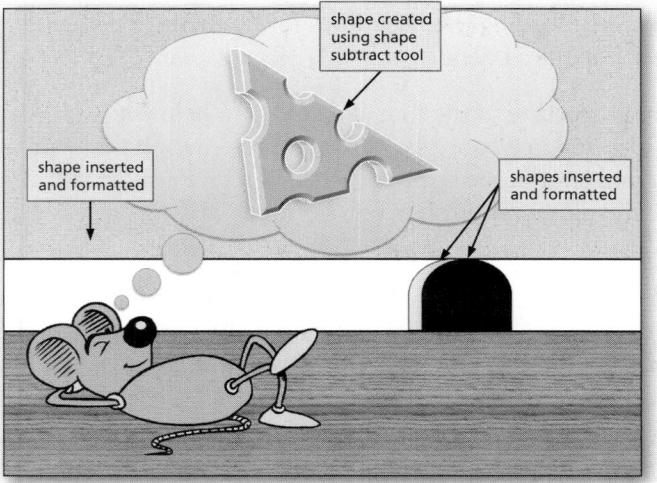

(c) Slide 3

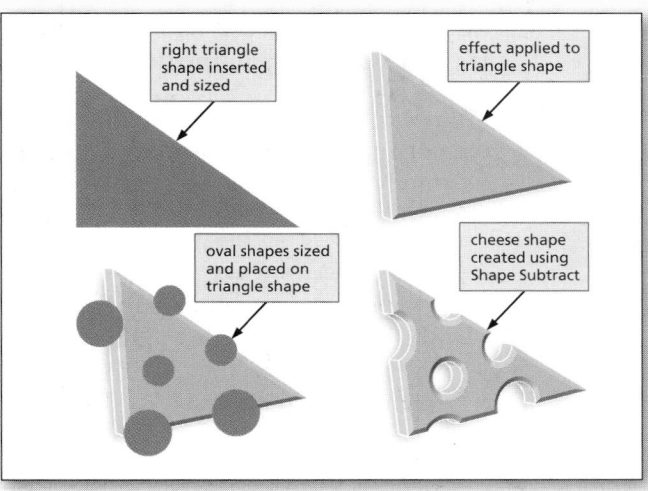

(d) Cheese Diagram

Figure 9–84

Continued >

In the Lab *continued*

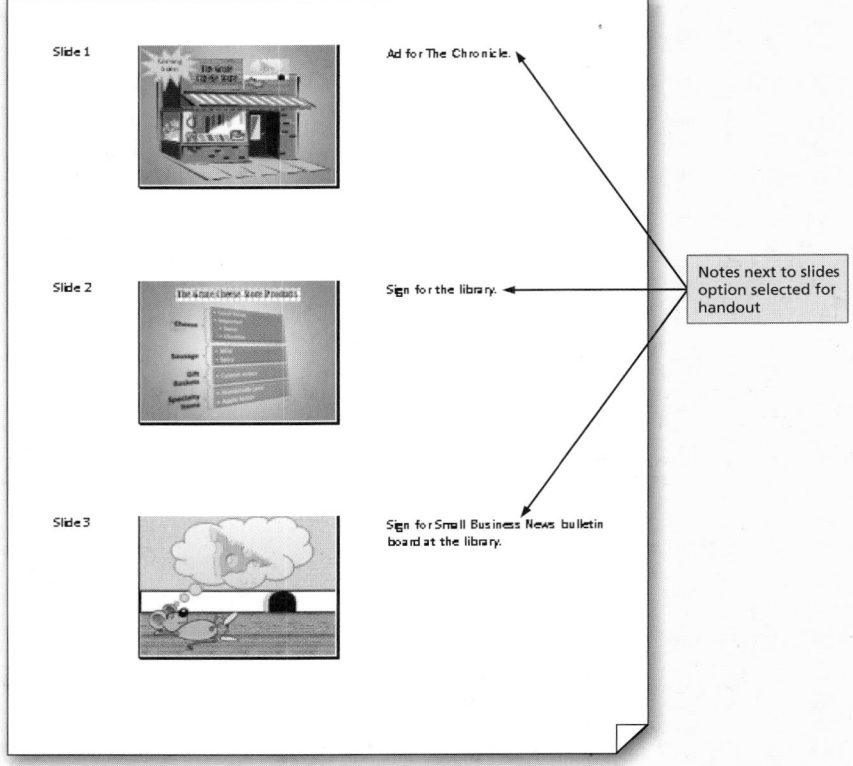

(e) Microsoft Word Handout

Figure 9–84 (Continued)

In the Lab

Lab 3: Changing a SmartArt Layout, Sizing SmartArt Shapes, Formatting Text Boxes, and Inserting Arrow Shapes

Note: To complete this assignment, you will be required to use the Data Files for Students. See the inside back cover of this book for instructions on downloading the Data Files for Students or contact your instructor for information about accessing the required files.

Problem: Your anatomy class is studying the bone structure of the foot and ankle. To help you memorize and learn the names of the bones, you decide to create a PowerPoint presentation that will be a study guide now and also will be a valuable tool later in the semester when you give a short talk about this subject to your classmates. You create the presentation shown in Figure 9–85.

Perform the following tasks:

1. Open the presentation, Lab 9-3 Foot and Ankle, located on the Data Files for Students. Change the built-in font style to Office Classic 2. On Slide 1, insert the Rectangle shape, change the size to 7.5" × 3.75", apply a Black fill, and then move the shape to the left side of the slide, as shown in Figure 9–85a.

2. Change the SmartArt layout on Slide 1 to Vertical Process. Change the size of the SmartArt graphic to 7" × 3.98" and move it on top of the black rectangle shape. Bring the graphic to the front. Change the font size to 28 point and then bold this text. Change the size of each SmartArt shape to 0.84" × 3.08". Change the colors to Colorful Range – Accent Colors 5 to 6 and the style to Inset, and then change the font color to Black.

3. On Slide 1, insert a text box and type **Anatomy of the Foot and Ankle** in the text box. Change the font size to 44 point, center the text in the text box, and then bold this text. Use line

breaks to display the text in the text box in five lines, as shown in Figure 9–85a. Apply the Dotted grid pattern fill to the text box, change the foreground color to Light Green, and then change the background color to Yellow. Apply the Preset 4 effect to the text box, change the outline color of the text box to Green, and then change the outline weight to 4½ pt. Move the text box to the location shown in Figure 9–85a. Apply the Style 9 background to the slide.

4. Display Slide 2 and then change the picture to Foot and Ankle, located on the Data Files for Students.

5. Customize the Ribbon by adding a group called Foot to the Home tab and then adding the Shape Union command to this new group.

6. To create arrow callouts, insert the Rectangle shape, change the size to 0.53" × 2.09", and then remove the outline. Insert the Chevron shape (from the Block Arrows area), remove the outline, and then duplicate the shape. Overlap the chevrons at each end of the rectangle, select the rectangle, select the two chevron shapes so that the three shapes are selected, and then click Shape Union on the Home tab to create the arrow callout shown in Figure 9–85b. Change the shape fill color to Aqua, Accent 5, apply a Preset 4 effect to the arrow shape, and then change the transparency to 30%. Type **Fibula** in the arrow shape, change the font size to 24 point, and then bold this text. Set the arrow as a default shape.

7. Duplicate the Fibula arrow callout three times. Type **Tibia** in the second arrow callout and change the color to Green. Type **Talus** in the third arrow callout and change the color to Olive Green, Accent 3. Type **Malleolus** in the fourth arrow callout and change the color to Light Green. Move these four arrows to the locations shown in Figure 9–85b.

8. On Slide 2, insert the Down Arrow Callout from the Block Arrows area and type **Metatarsals** in the shape, change the color of the shape to Yellow, increase the size of the shape, and then move it to the location shown in Figure 9–85b. Insert the Down Arrow Callout, type **Phalanges** in the shape, change the color to Orange, Accent 6, increase the size of the shape, and then move it to the location shown in Figure 9–85b.

9. Insert the Oval shape into Slide 2 and change the size to 1.38" × 2.42". Change the color of the shape fill to Yellow, change the transparency to 70%, add an outline and change the color to Black, and then change the outline weight to 2¼ pt. Move this shape to the location shown. Duplicate this oval shape and change the size to 1.08" × 2.25". Change the color of the shape fill to Orange, Accent 6 and move this shape to the location shown in Figure 9–85b.

10. Apply Background Style 9 to Slide 2.

11. Apply the Cube transition and change the duration to 03.00 seconds for all slides.

12. Reset the Ribbon. Change the document properties, as specified by your instructor. Save the presentation using the file name, Lab 9-3 Anatomy of Foot and Ankle.

13. Submit the revised document in the format specified by your instructor.

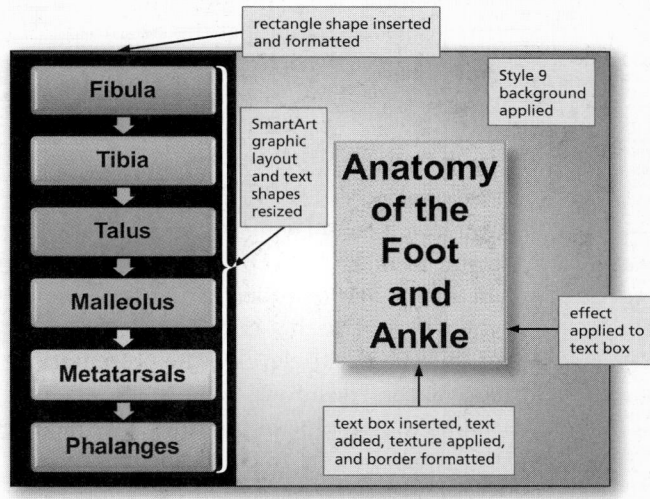

(a) Slide 1

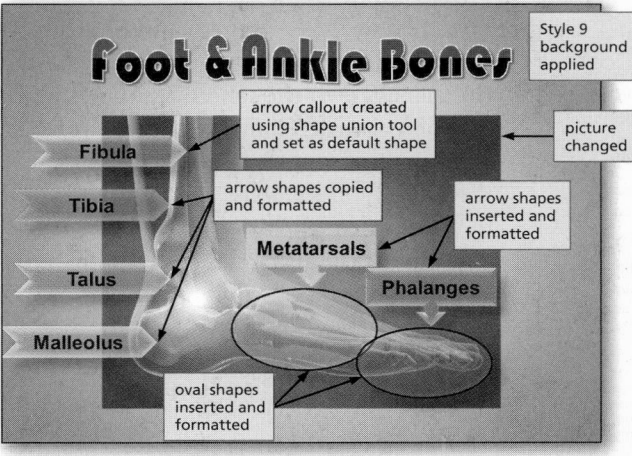

(b) Slide 2

Figure 9–85

Cases and Places

Apply your creative thinking and problem-solving skills to design and implement a solution.

Note: To complete these assignments, you may be required to use the Data Files for Students. See the inside back cover of this book for instructions on downloading the Data Files for Students, or contact your instructor for information about accessing the required files.

As you design the presentations, remember to use the 7 × 7 rule: a maximum of seven words on a line and a maximum of seven lines on one slide.

1: Designing and Creating a Presentation about Communication Devices for People with Special Needs

Academic

As an education major, you are researching communication devices that assist people with special needs. One of your relatives is visually impaired and has shown you some of the gadgets he uses, such as a voice-command television, computer, and printer. He uses a scanner to copy and then play back the contents of his mail and other documents in a computer program. He also has a modified mouse and a braille keyboard for his computer. You decide to do a PowerPoint presentation to explain the devices your family member uses and to list other devices you find in your research. Apply at least three objectives found at the beginning of this chapter to develop the presentation, including applying borders and effects to text boxes and adding or removing SmartArt shapes. Use pictures and diagrams from Office.com if they are appropriate for this topic. Be sure to check spelling.

2: Designing and Creating a Presentation about Soccer

Personal

You have been playing soccer for many years and, in addition to playing, are coaching an adult soccer team. You decide to create a PowerPoint presentation to explain some of the soccer rules to new team members. Some of the current team members have difficulty understanding what off sides means, so you will explain that in the presentation as well. Apply at least three objectives found at the beginning of this chapter to develop the presentation, including using shapes to show a diagram of the soccer field and players' positions. You can also include a SmartArt graphic and change the layout and size of the shapes to list some of the rules. Use pictures and diagrams from Office.com if they are appropriate for this topic. Be sure to check spelling.

3: Designing and Creating a Presentation about School Funding

Professional

You are a member of the board of directors of the ABC Charter School. After several years of financial crisis at the school, a very large sum of money was donated to the school. Members of the board and the managers of the school are meeting to decide how this money will be used. The director of the school has received many ideas from faculty, staff members, students, and parents. He has shared these ideas with you and asks you to prepare a PowerPoint presentation for the upcoming meeting. Some of the ideas submitted are: updating the computer lab, expanding the library, building a greenhouse next to the science lab, hiring an additional art teacher, expanding the music program to include a band or an orchestra, and starting a competitive basketball program for boys and girls. You may have a few ideas of your own to share. The presentation should include applying pictures, textures, or patterns to text boxes and a Microsoft Word handout to be distributed at the meeting. Use pictures from Office.com if they are appropriate for this topic or use your personal digital pictures. Be sure to check spelling.

10 | Developing a Presentation with Content from Outside Sources

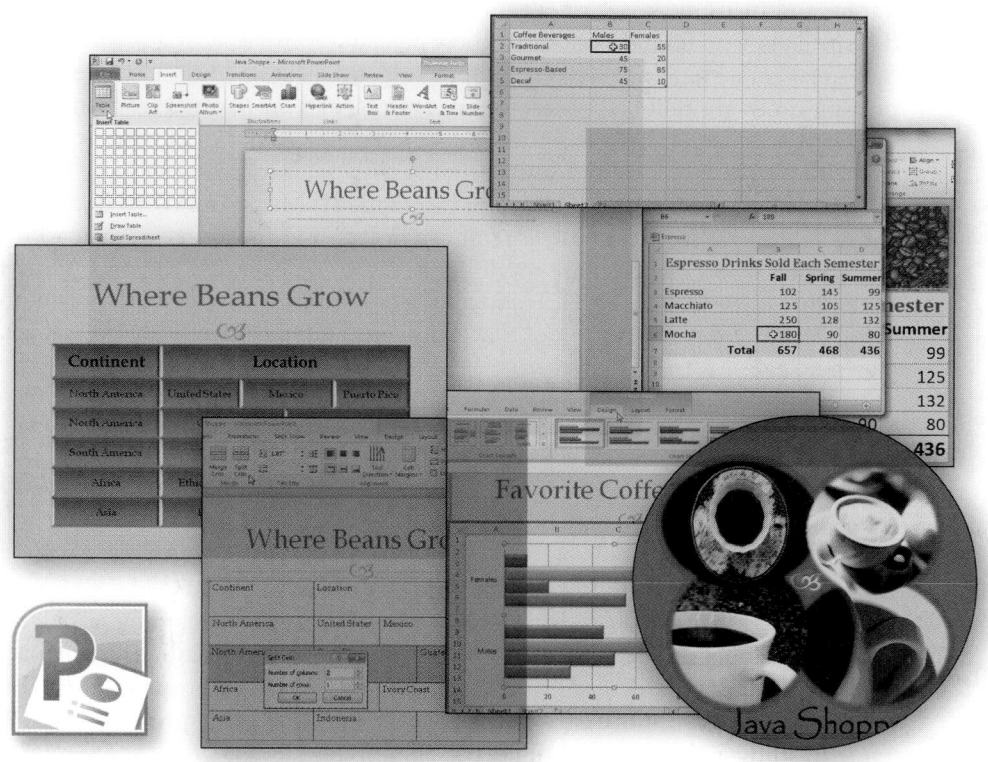

Objectives

You will have mastered the material in this chapter when you can:

- Insert an object from a file
- Draw and format a table
- Resize, split, distribute, and arrange table columns and rows
- Embed and edit a file
- Apply effects and borders to chart elements
- Add a hyperlink to a chart element

- Change a chart type
- Switch chart rows and columns
- Edit chart data
- Use chart labels, axes, gridlines, and backgrounds
- Apply a Quick Style to a chart
- Arrange chart elements
- Create a hyperlink to a PDF

10 Developing a Presentation with Content from Outside Sources

Introduction

BTW

Using Charts and Tables
Charts and tables can be outstanding tools to give meaning to the figures and facts you want to emphasize in your presentation and to help audiences understand abstract concepts and the relationships between sets of data. Overloading your slides with data may confuse your audience and defeat the purpose of these graphical elements. Present only one main idea in a chart or table.

Adding visuals to a presentation could help audience members remember the important facts you want to share. Researchers have found that adding such graphics as tables, charts, graphs, and maps increases retention by more than 50 percent. The audience also believes that speakers who include visuals in their presentations are more qualified and believable than speakers who do not have accompanying visuals. In addition, studies have shown that meeting times are reduced and decisions are reached more quickly when group members have seen visuals that help them reach a consensus.

PowerPoint has many features that allow you to insert visuals and then modify them directly on the slide. For example, you can embed a Microsoft Word document and then edit its text or replace its graphics. You can link an Excel worksheet with a PowerPoint slide so that when numbers are modified in the worksheet, the corresponding numbers on the PowerPoint slide also are updated. These tools help you work productively and generate slides with graphics that help your audience comprehend and remember your message.

Project — Presentation with Embedded Files and Formatted Charts and Table

BTW

Coffee Preferences
More than one-half of adults consume at least one cup of coffee each day, according to the National Coffee Association. One-third of this group prefers an elaborate drink made with milk, and another one-third favors black coffee or espresso. A 16-ounce cup of name-brand coffee has approximately 330 mg of caffeine, which is the same amount of caffeine found in seven 12-ounce cans of diet cola.

More than one-half of adults drink at least one coffee beverage daily. Gourmet coffee drinks, such as espresso-based and milk-based beverages, are gaining popularity and now account for approximately 40 percent of the coffee consumed. Consumers patronize chain and independent coffeehouses to relax, chat with friends, or browse the Internet. The locally owned coffee shops on or near college campuses often provide an outstanding venue to study and complete homework assignments.

The presentation you create in this chapter (Figure 10–1) would be useful to show to the Java Shoppe owners who are deciding what types of drinks to offer at their new campus location. You begin Slide 1 (Figure 10–1a) by inserting a flyer with graphics and text (Figure 10–1b). You then learn that the name of the shop will change from Java Stop to Java Shoppe, so you edit the name directly on the slide. The second slide (Figure 10–1c) includes a chart that you draw and enhance using PowerPoint's tools and graphical features. You insert the table on Slide 3 (Figure 10–1d on page 596) from a Microsoft Excel worksheet (Figure 10–1e) that contains the results of a year long student survey. Students who drink espresso-based beverages were asked to indicate which beverage they preferred. When you learn that some of the surveys were not included in the table, you edit several of the numbers, and then Microsoft Excel updates the totals automatically. The last slide (Figure 10–1f) features a Microsoft Excel chart (Figure 10–1g) that you insert and then enhance. If you click the chart when running the presentation, a hyperlinked Adobe Acrobat file (Figure 10–1h) displays.

Overview

As you read through this chapter, you will learn how to create the presentation shown in Figure 10–1 on this page and the next by performing these general tasks:

- Insert a graphic from a file.
- Insert a Microsoft Excel worksheet.
- Link and embed a file.
- Edit a linked object and an embedded file.
- Format chart elements.
- Arrange chart elements.
- Draw and modify a table.
- Create a hyperlink to a PDF document.

BTW

First Impressions
The first slide in your presentation sets the tone of your entire presentation. Before you say one word, your audience sees what you have projected on the screen and forms a first impression of whether the speech is going to be interesting, professional, and relevant. Take care in designing an opening slide that meets the audience's expectations and generates interest in the remainder of the presentation.

(a) Slide 1 (Title Slide)

(b) Microsoft Word Document

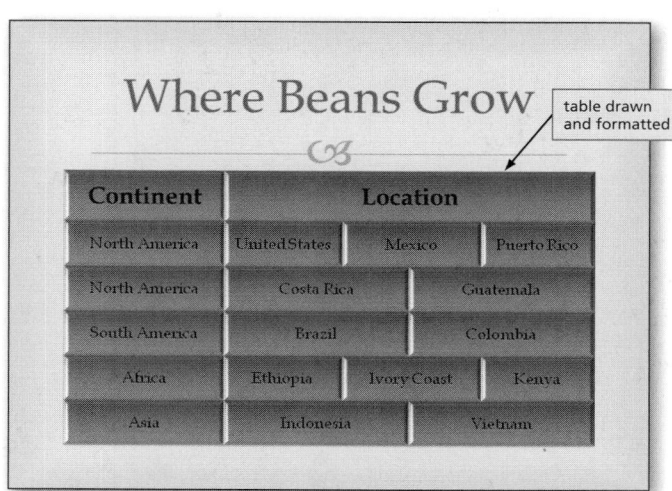

(c) Slide 2

Figure 10–1

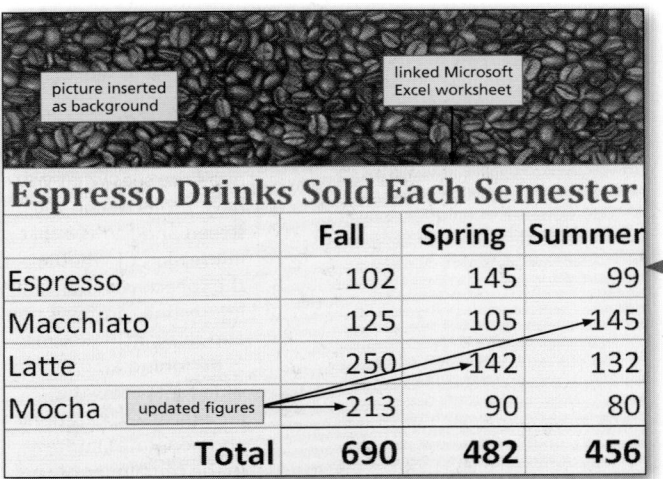

picture inserted as background
linked Microsoft Excel worksheet
Espresso Drinks Sold Each Semester
Fall | Spring | Summer
Espresso 102 145 99
Macchiato 125 105 145
Latte 250 142 132
Mocha 213 90 80
Total 690 482 456
updated figures

(d) Slide 3

A B C D
1 Espresso Drinks Sold Each Semester
2 Fall Spring Summer
3 Espresso 102 145 99
4 Macchiato 125 105 125
5 Latte 250 128 132
6 Mocha 180 90 80
7 Total 657 468 436
figures will be updated

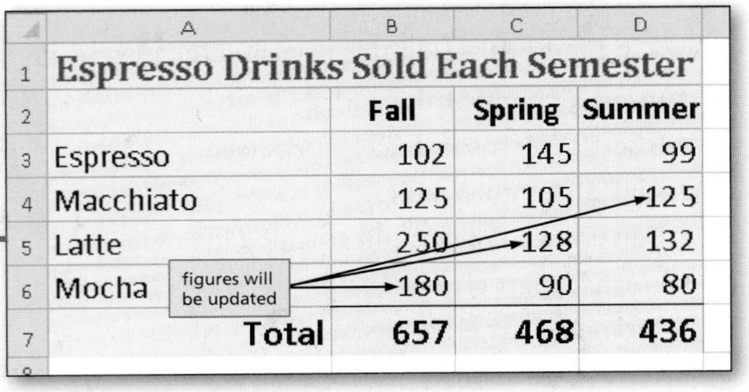

(e) Original Microsoft Excel Worksheet

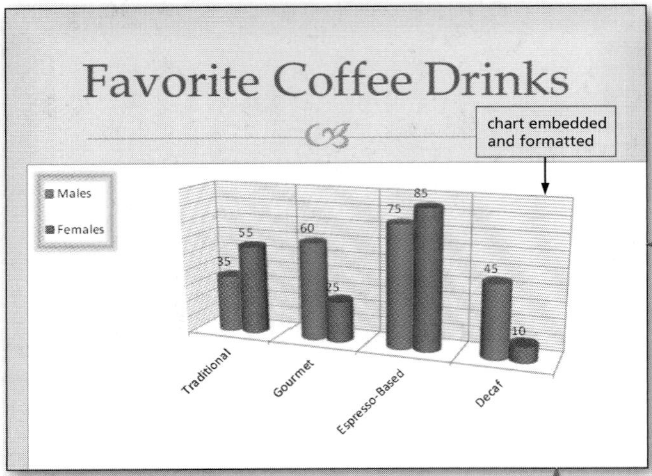

Favorite Coffee Drinks
chart embedded and formatted
Males
Females
35
55
60
25
75
85
45
10
Traditional
Gourmet
Espresso-Based
Decaf

(f) Slide 4

Females
Males
0
20
40
60
80
100
Decaf
Espresso-Based
Gourmet
Traditional

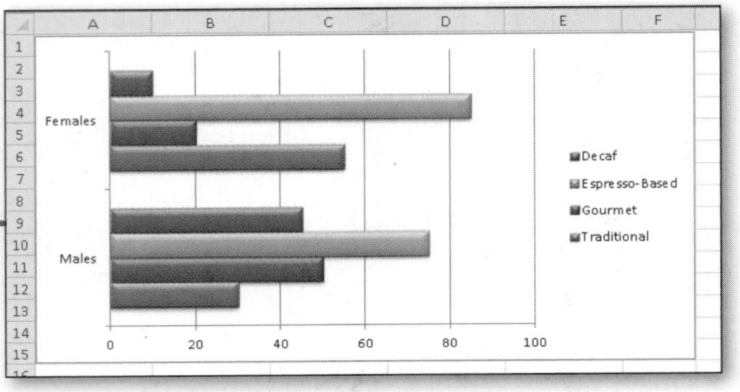

(g) Original Microsoft Excel Chart

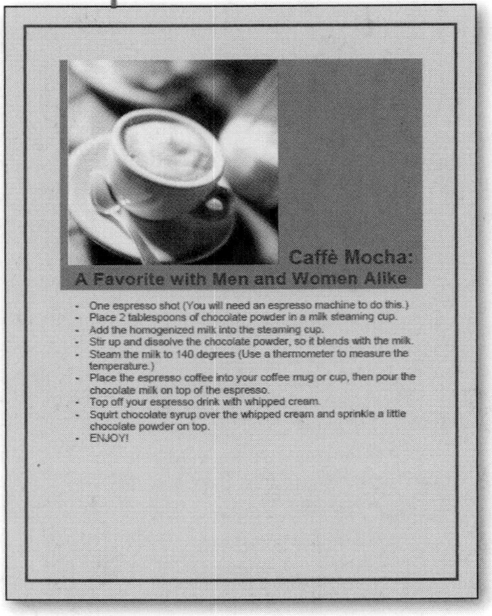

Caffè Mocha:
A Favorite with Men and Women Alike
- One espresso shot (You will need an espresso machine to do this.)
- Place 2 tablespoons of chocolate powder in a milk steaming cup.
- Add the homogenized milk into the steaming cup.
- Stir up and dissolve the chocolate powder, so it blends with the milk.
- Steam the milk to 140 degrees (Use a thermometer to measure the temperature.)
- Place the espresso coffee into your coffee mug or cup, then pour the chocolate milk on top of the espresso.
- Top off your espresso drink with whipped cream.
- Squirt chocolate syrup over the whipped cream and sprinkle a little chocolate powder on top.
- ENJOY!

(h) Hyperlinked Adobe Acrobat Document

Figure 10–1 (Continued)

General Project Guidelines

When creating a PowerPoint presentation, the actions you perform and the decisions you make will affect the appearance and characteristics of the finished document. As you create a presentation with illustrations, such as the project shown in Figure 10–1 on pages PPT 595 to PPT 596, you should follow these general guidelines:

1. **Use powerful words to accompany the text on your slides.** The slides are meant to enhance your talk by clarifying main points and calling attention to key ideas. Your speech should use words that explain and substantiate your visuals.

2. **Develop tables that are clear and meaningful.** Tables are extremely useful vehicles for presenting complex relationships. Their design plays an important part of successfully conveying the information to the audience.

3. **Use appropriate colors when formatting graphics you want people to remember.** Numerous studies have shown that appropriate graphics help audiences comprehend and remember the information presented during a speech. Color has been shown to increase retention by as much as 80 percent. When choosing colors for your graphics, use hues that fit the tone and objective of your message.

When necessary, more specific details concerning the above guidelines are presented at appropriate points in the chapter. The chapter also will identify the actions performed and decisions made regarding these guidelines during the creation of the presentation shown in Figure 10–1.

To Start PowerPoint and Save a File

If you are using a computer to step through the project in this chapter and you want your screens to match the figures in this book, you should change your computer's resolution to 1024 × 768. The following steps start PowerPoint and then save a file.

1 Start PowerPoint. If necessary, maximize the PowerPoint window.

2 Apply the Hardcover document theme.

3 Save the presentation using the file name, Java Shoppe.

Use powerful words to accompany the text on your slides.

Carefully plan the speech that coordinates with the slides in your presentation. Use examples that substantiate the objects on the slides, and use familiar, precise words and terms that enlighten the audience. Do not include obvious material as filler because audience members will reach the conclusion that you are wasting their time with meaningless information that they do not need to know.

Inserting Graphics or Other Objects from a File

PowerPoint allows you to insert many types of objects into a presentation. You can insert clips, pictures, video and audio files, and symbols, and you also can copy and paste or drag and drop objects from one slide to another. At times you may want to insert content created with other Microsoft Office programs, such as a Word flyer, an Excel table or graph, a Paint graphic, or a document created with another Microsoft Windows-based application. The original document is called the **source**, and the new document that contains this object is called the **destination**. When you want to copy a source document object, such as a Word flyer, to a destination document, such as your PowerPoint slide, you can use one of three techniques.

- **Embedding** — An **embedded object** becomes part of the destination slide, but you edit and modify the contents using the source program's commands and features. In this project, for example, you will embed a Word document and then edit the text using Microsoft Word without leaving PowerPoint. In addition, you will embed an Excel chart and then modify the object using Microsoft Excel while Slide 4 is displayed. The embedded file is static, meaning that any changes you make to the object in PowerPoint will be reflected only on the destination PowerPoint slide and not in the original source file.

- **Linking** — Similar to an embedded object, a **linked object** also is created in another application and is stored in the **source file**, the original file in which the object was created. The linked object maintains a connection to its source and does not become part of the destination slide. Instead, a connection, or link, made between the source and destination objects gives the appearance that the objects are independent. In reality, the two objects work together so that when one is edited, the other is updated. If the original object is changed, the linked object on the slide also changes. In this project, for example, you will link a Microsoft Excel table and then edit the data using Excel. As the numbers in the table change, the numbers in the linked table on the PowerPoint slide also are updated to reflect those changes. Likewise, if you change data to the linked table in your PowerPoint slide, that data will change in the Excel source document.

- **Copying and pasting** — An object that you copy from a source document and then paste in a destination document becomes part of the destination program. Any edits that you make are done using the destination software. For example, if you copy a picture from a Word document, paste it into your slide, and then recolor or remove the background, those changes are made using PowerPoint's commands and do not affect the source object.

The first two techniques described above are termed **object linking and embedding** (**OLE**, pronounced o-lay). This means of sharing material developed in various sources and then updating the files within a destination program is useful when you deliver presentations frequently that display current data that changes constantly. For example, your PowerPoint presentation may contain a chart reflecting current student registration statistics for the upcoming semester, or you may include a table with election tallies for Student Government Association candidates.

To Insert a File with Graphics and Text

The first object you will add to your presentation is a graphical flyer created in Microsoft Word. This flyer contains artwork and text developed as part of an advertising campaign for the new coffee shop on campus, and you desire to use this document in your slide show to promote this business. The following steps insert a Microsoft Word file with a graphic and text.

①

- Click Insert on the Ribbon and then click the Insert Object button (Insert tab | Text group) to display the Insert Object dialog box (Figure 10–2).

What is the difference between the Create new and the 'Create from file' options?

The Create new option opens an application and allows you to develop an original object. In contrast, the 'Create from file' option prompts you to locate a file that already is created and saved so you can modify the object using the program that was used to create it.

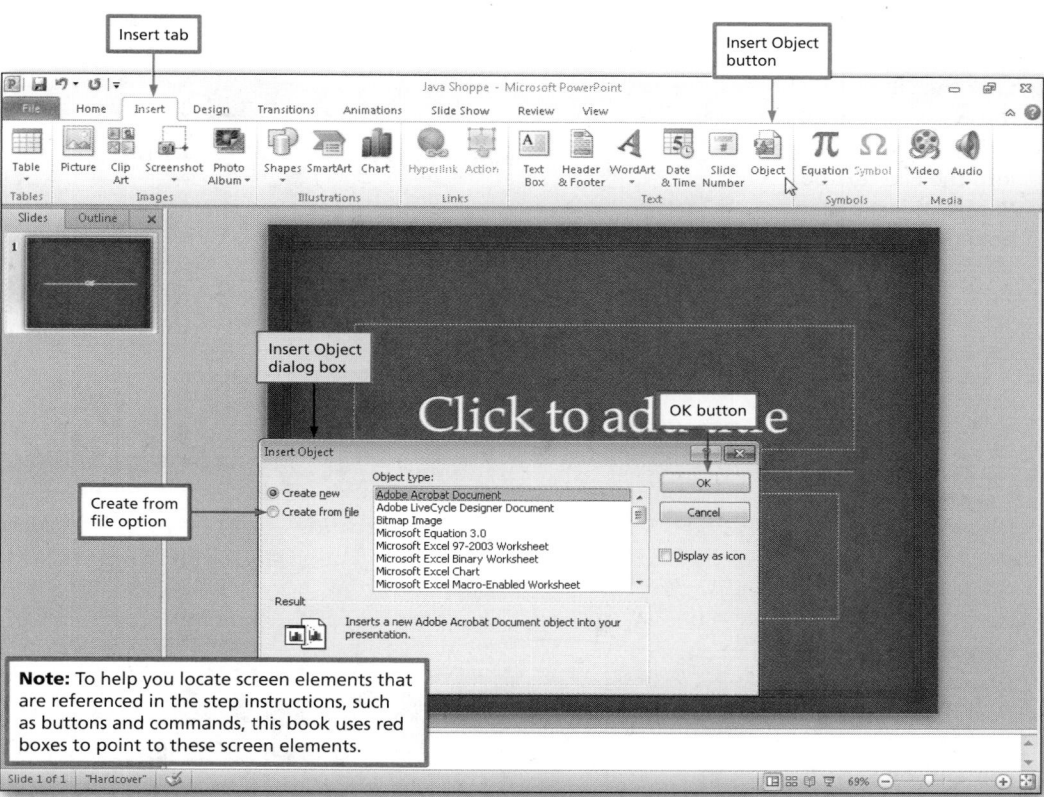

Figure 10–2

②

- Click 'Create from file' (Insert Object dialog box) to display the File text box.

- Click the Browse button and then navigate to the PowerPoint Chapter 10 folder.

- Click Java Stop Flyer to select the Microsoft Word file (Figure 10–3).

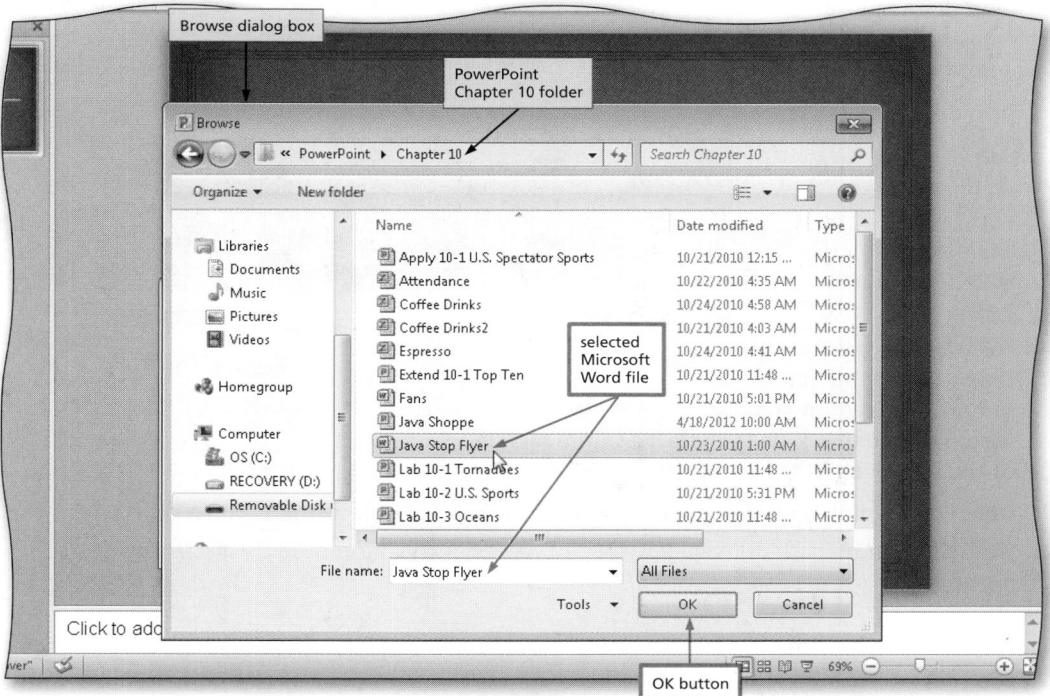

Figure 10–3

- Click the OK button (Browse dialog box) to insert the file name into the File text box (Insert Object dialog box) (Figure 10–4).

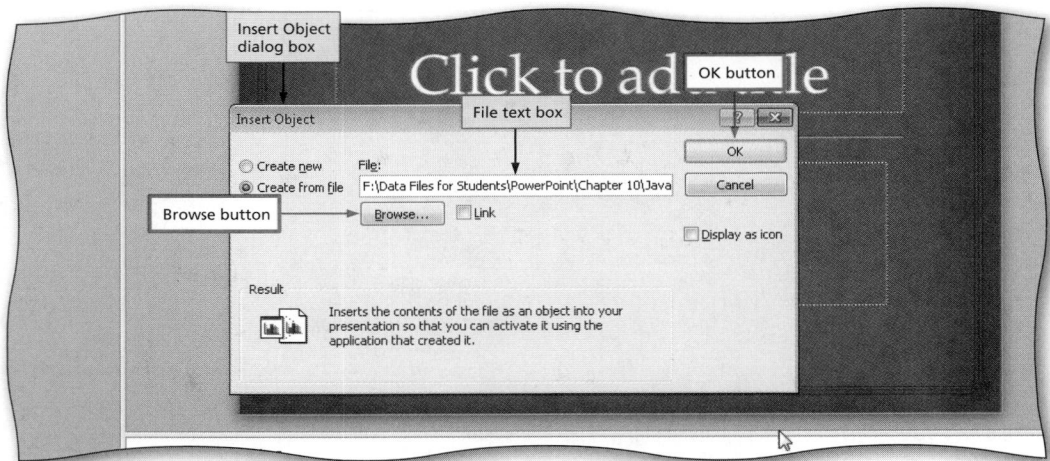

Figure 10–4

- Click the OK button (Insert Object dialog box) to display the Java Stop Flyer contents on Slide 1.

Q&A Why did several seconds pass before this flyer was displayed on the slide?

PowerPoint takes more time to insert embedded and linked inserted objects than it takes to perform an ordinary cut-and-paste or copy-and-paste action. You must be patient while PowerPoint is inserting the object.

Figure 10–5

- Position the object in the center of the slide so that the decorative design on the title slide is displayed in the middle of the four ovals in the object (Figure 10–5).

Q&A Does PowerPoint take more time to position embedded objects than copied objects?

Yes, you must be patient while PowerPoint responds to your mouse or ARROW key movements.

Q&A How can I center the object precisely over the decorative object?

Drag the object so that it is near the decoration and then use the ARROW keys to move the object in small increments.

To Edit an Embedded File

The flyer provides an excellent graphic and text to use on Slide 1, but the business has changed its name since the document was created. You want to change the word, Stop, to the word, Shoppe. PowerPoint allows you to edit an embedded file easily by opening the source program, which in this case is Microsoft Word. The following steps edit the Microsoft Word text.

1

- Double-click the embedded coffee object to start the Microsoft Word program and open the document on Slide 1 (Figure 10–6).

Q&A

Why are the horizontal and vertical rulers displayed in my Word document but not in the Word document shown in Figure 10–6?

Your Microsoft Word setting to show the rulers is checked.

Figure 10–6

2

- Double-click the word, Stop, to select it and then type **Shoppe** as the replacement text (Figure 10–7).

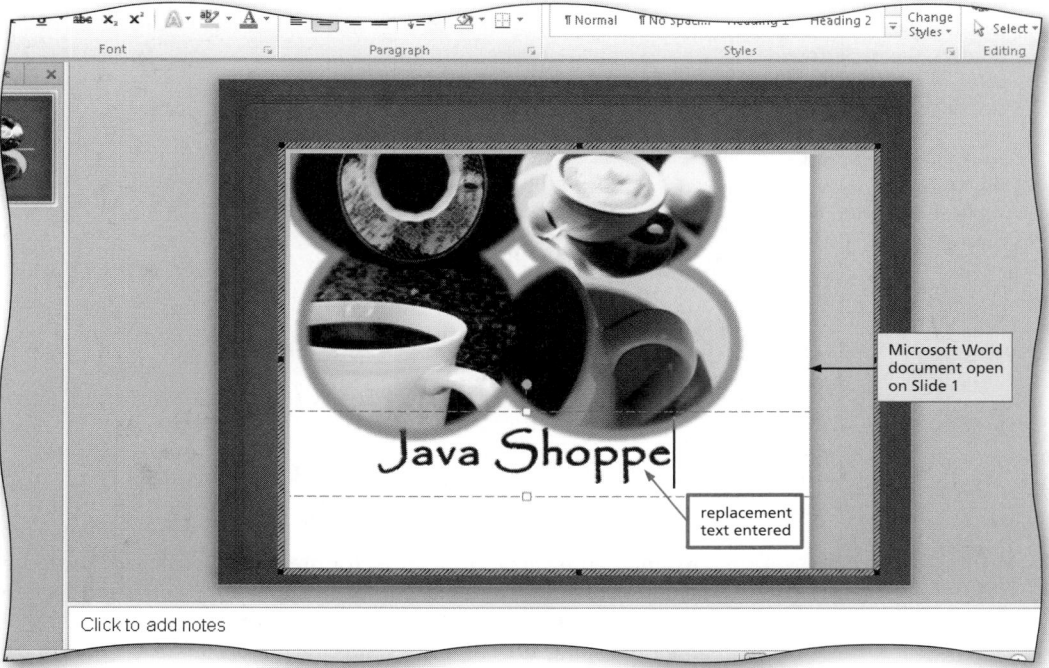

Figure 10–7

3

- Click outside the Word document to close Microsoft Word and display the edited flyer object on Slide 1.

- If necessary, position the object as shown in Figure 10–8.

edited flyer object on Slide 1

Figure 10–8

Other Ways

1. Right-click Word object, point to Document Object on shortcut menu, click Edit

Drawing and Adjusting a Table

Tables are useful graphical elements to present data organized in descriptive rows and columns. Each cell created from the intersection of a row and column has a unique location name and contains numeric or textual data that you can edit.

In the following pages, you will perform these tasks on Slide 2:

1. Draw a table.
2. Draw table rows.
3. Draw table columns.
4. Erase a table line.
5. Split a table column and row.
6. Add shading to a table.
7. Add a gradient fill to a table.
8. Add a cell bevel.
9. Distribute table rows.
10. Resize table columns and rows.
11. Center the table.

Plan Ahead

Develop tables that are clear and meaningful.
Use a table to present complex material, but be certain the information makes useful comparisons. Tables generally are used to show relationships between sets of data. For example, they may show prices for grades of gasoline in three states, the number of in-state and out-of-state students who have applied for admission to various college programs, or the rushing and passing records among quarterbacks in a particular league. The units of measurement, such as dollars, specific majors, or yards, should be expressed clearly on the slides. The data in the rows and columns should be aligned uniformly. Also, the table labels should be meaningful and easily read.

To Draw a Table

PowerPoint allows you to insert a table in several ways. You can click the Table button on the Insert tab and either click the Insert Table command or drag your mouse pointer to specify the number of rows and columns you need. You also can click the Insert Table button in a content placeholder. Another method that allows flexibility is to use the mouse pointer as a pencil to draw the outer edges and then add the columns and rows. The following steps draw a table on Slide 2.

1

- Insert a new slide with the Title Only layout. Type **Where Beans Grow** as the title text.

- Display the View tab and then click the Ruler check box (View tab | Show group) to display the horizontal and vertical rulers.

- Display the Insert tab and then click the Table button (Insert tab | Tables group) to display the Table gallery (Figure 10–9).

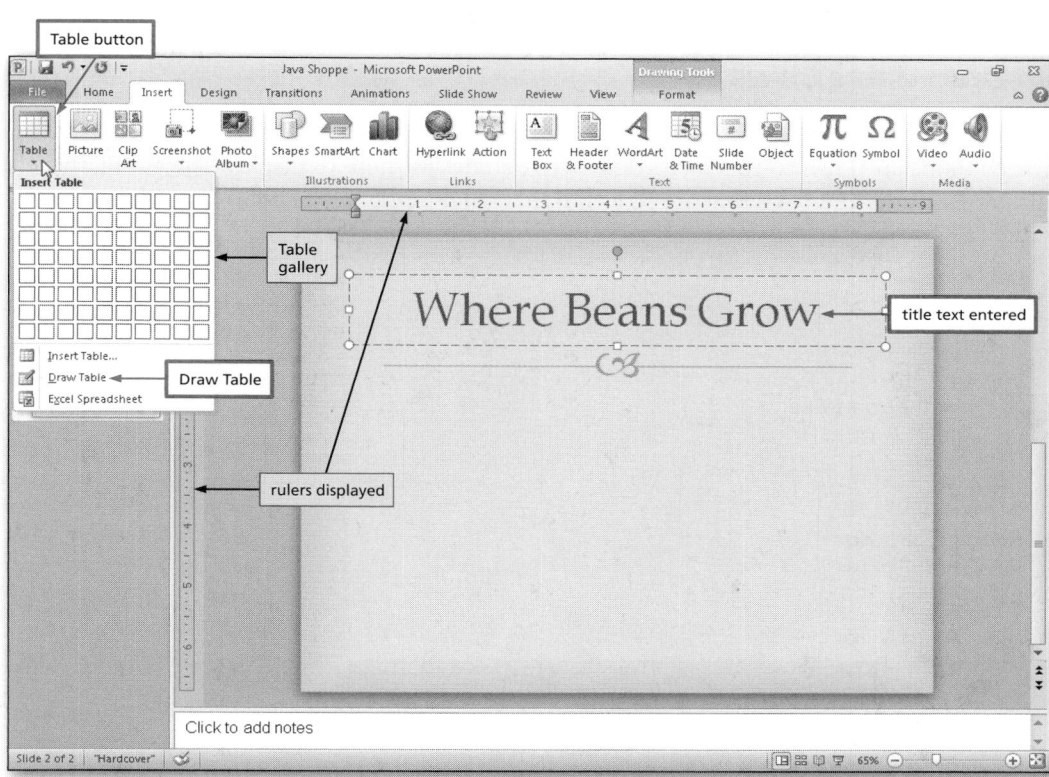

Figure 10–9

2

- Click Draw Table and then position the mouse pointer, which has the shape of a pencil, in the upper-left area below the slide title.

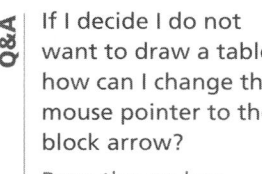 If I decide I do not want to draw a table, how can I change the mouse pointer to the block arrow?

Press the ESC key.

- Drag the pencil pointer to the lower-right corner of the slide to draw the outer edges of the table (Figure 10–10).

Figure 10–10

• Release the mouse button to create the table frame.

Q&A Must my table be the same size or be positioned in the same location shown in the figure?

No. You will resize and reposition the table later in this project.

To Draw Table Rows

Once you draw the four sides of the table, you then can use the mouse pointer as a pencil to draw lines for the columns and rows in the positions where you desire them to display. You could, therefore, draw columns having different widths and rows that are spaced in irregular heights. The following steps draw four lines to create five table rows.

• Position the pencil pointer inside the table approximately 1" from the top table edge (Figure 10–11).

Q&A How can I get my pencil pointer to reappear if it no longer is displaying?

Click the Draw Table button (Table Tools Design tab | Draw Borders group).

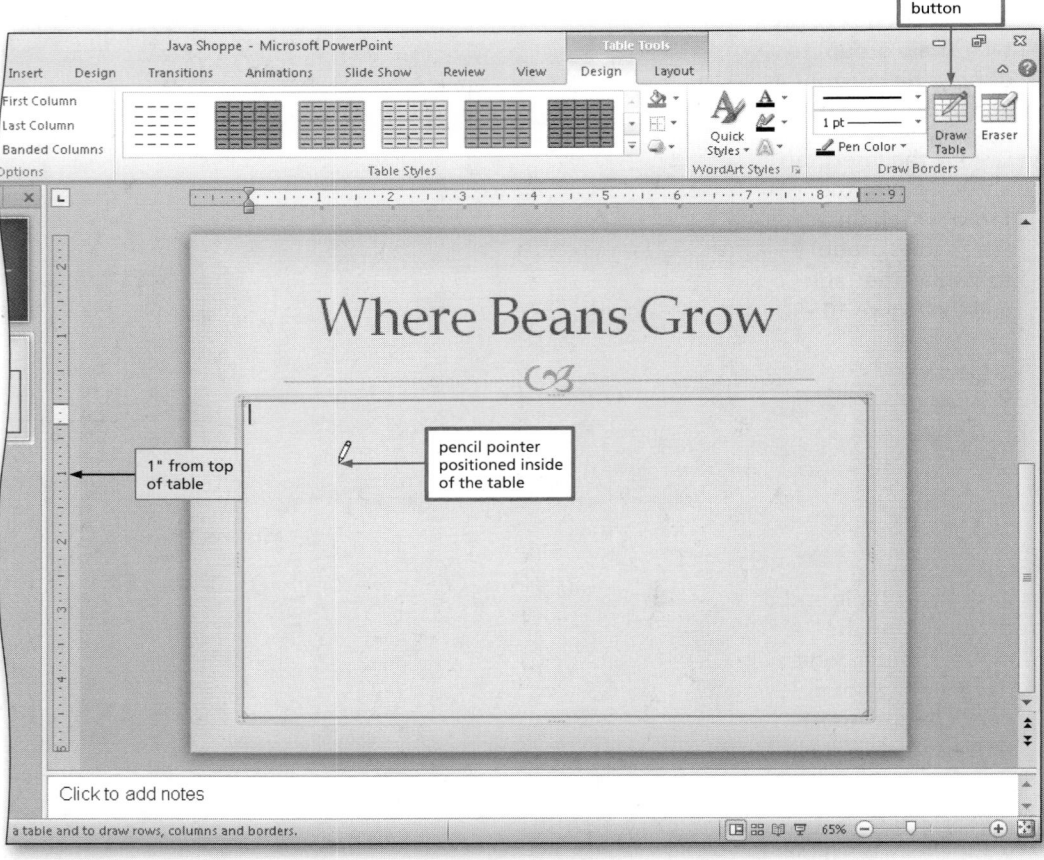

Figure 10–11

2

• Drag the pencil pointer to the right to draw a horizontal line across the entire table and divide the table into two cells (Figure 10–12), then release the mouse button.

Q&A Should I drag the pencil pointer to the right edge of the table?

No. PowerPoint will draw a complete line when you begin to move the pencil pointer in one direction.

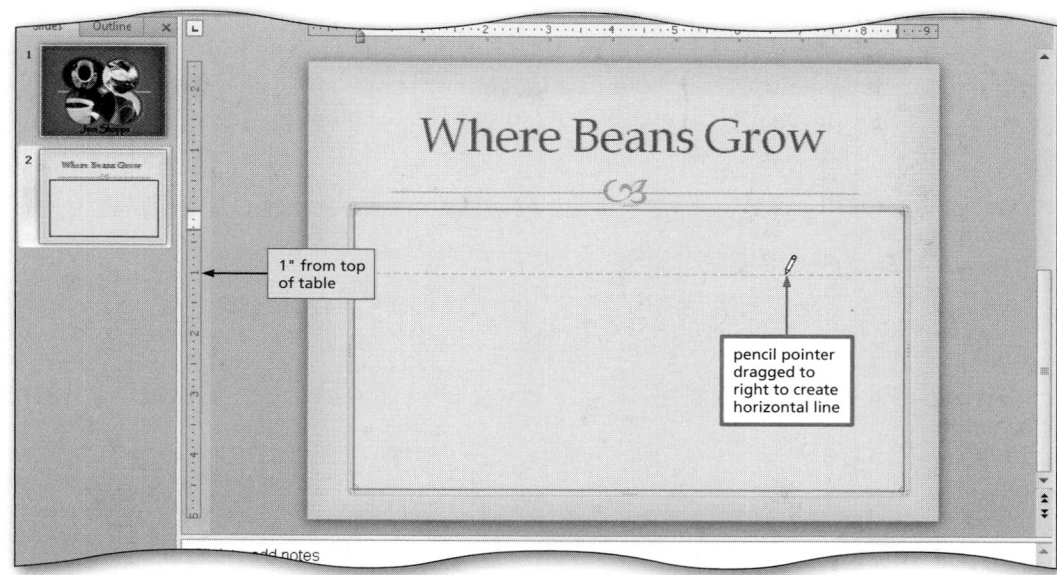

Figure 10–12

Q&A If I drew the line in the incorrect location, how can I erase it?

Press the ESC key or click the Eraser button (Table Tools Design tab | Draw Borders group) and then click the line.

3

• Draw three additional horizontal lines, as shown in Figure 10–13, and then release the mouse pointer.

Q&A Do I need to align the lines in the precise positions shown?

No. You will create evenly spaced rows later in this project.

Figure 10–13

To Draw Table Columns

The pencil pointer is useful to draw table columns with varying widths. The two major categories in the table are continents and countries. The countries column will be subdivided to show the countries where coffee beans are grown. The following steps draw six vertical lines to create columns.

1

• Position the pencil pointer inside the table approximately 2.5" from the left table edge (Figure 10–14).

Q&A Can I change the line color?

Yes. Click the Pen Color button (Table Tools Design tab | Draw Borders group) and then select a different color.

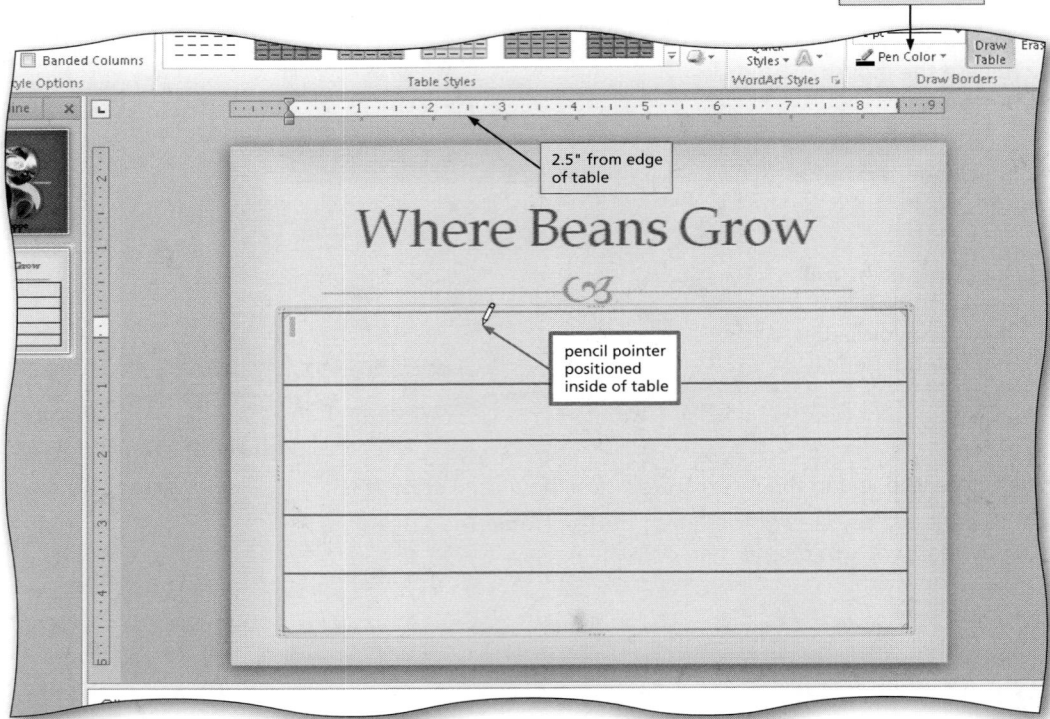

Figure 10–14

2

• Drag the pencil pointer down through all the horizontal lines to draw a vertical line that divides the table into 10 cells.

• Position the pencil pointer inside the second cell in the second row approximately 4.5" from the left table edge, as shown in Figure 10–15.

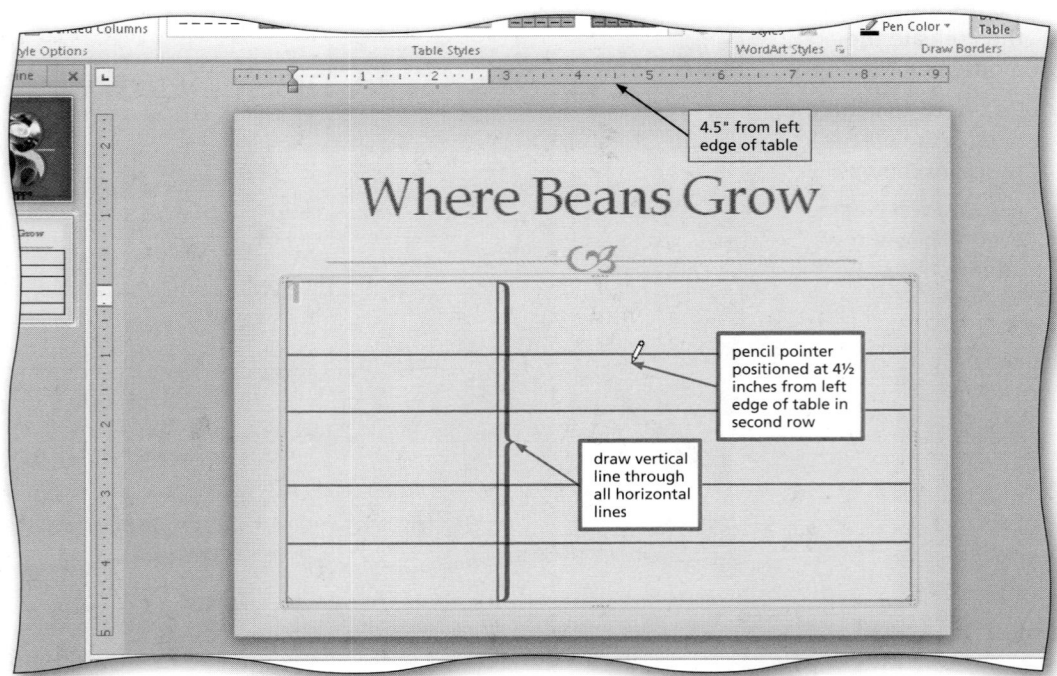

Figure 10–15

3

- Drag the pencil pointer down slightly to draw a vertical line in only that cell (Figure 10–16) and then release the mouse button.

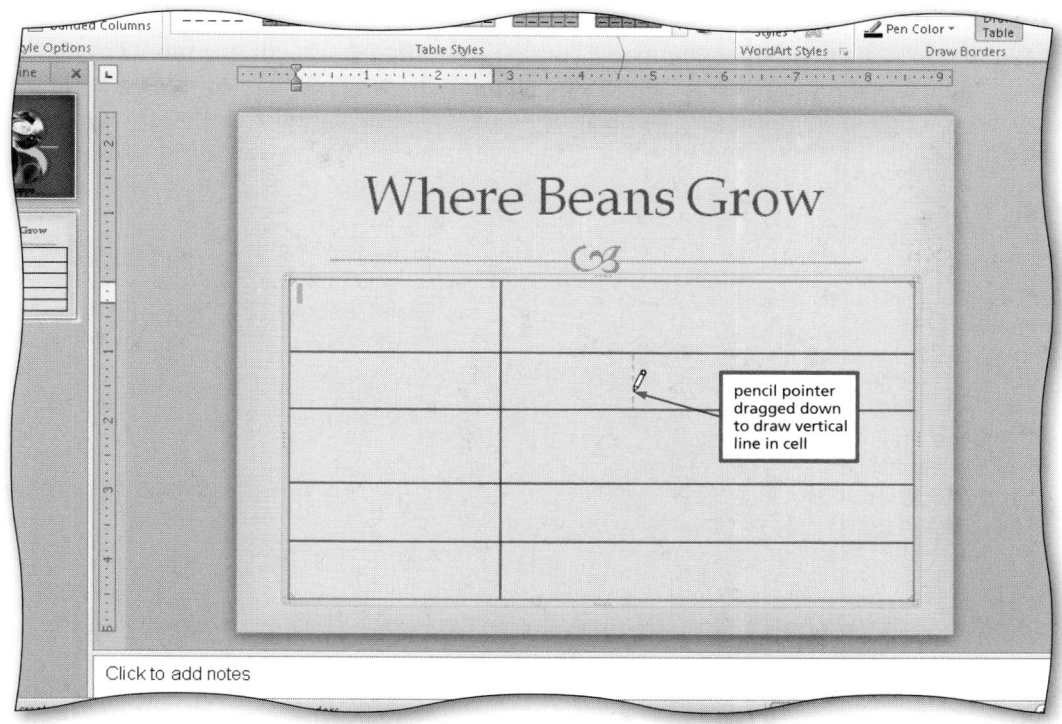

Figure 10–16

4

- Draw four additional vertical lines, as shown in Figure 10–17, and then release the mouse button.

Q&A

Are vertical and horizontal lines the only types of lines I can draw?

No. You also can draw a diagonal line from one corner of a cell to another corner.

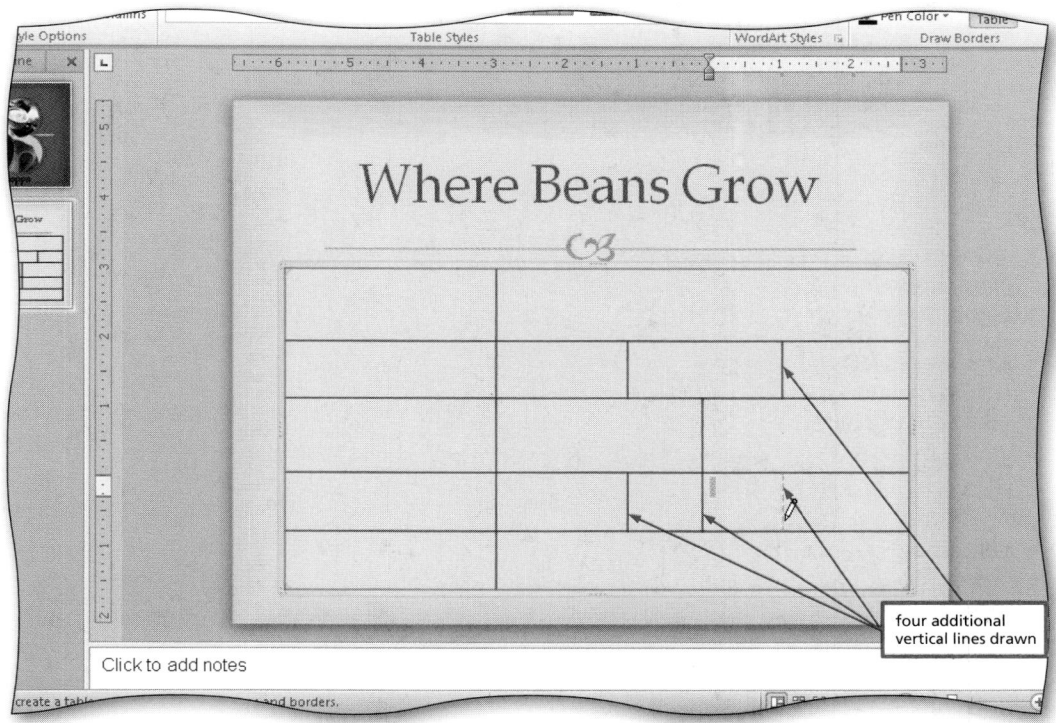

Figure 10–17

To Erase a Table Line

Because the number of countries is different for each continent, the number of cells in each row varies. The eraser pointer is useful to delete unnecessary column lines. The fourth row in the table should be identical to the second row and have four cells. PowerPoint supplies an eraser tool that allows you to delete vertical and horizontal lines in a table. The following steps use the eraser to delete one vertical line in a row.

- Click the Table Eraser button (Table Tools Design tab | Draw Borders group).

- Position the mouse pointer, which has the shape of an eraser, over the third line in the fourth row (Figure 10–18).

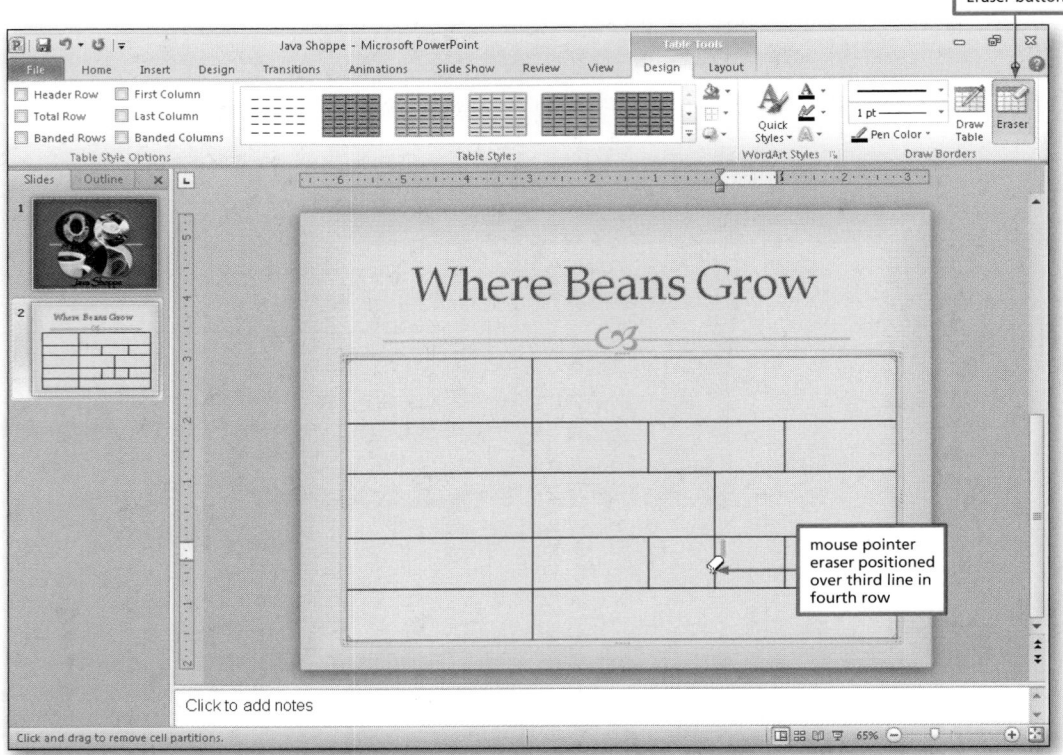

Figure 10–18

- Click the vertical line to erase it (Figure 10–19).

- Press the ESC key to change the mouse pointer to the block arrow.

- If necessary, drag the edges of the cells so the cell widths are similar to those in the figure.

- Display the View tab and then click the Ruler check box (View tab | Show group) to hide the horizontal and vertical rulers.

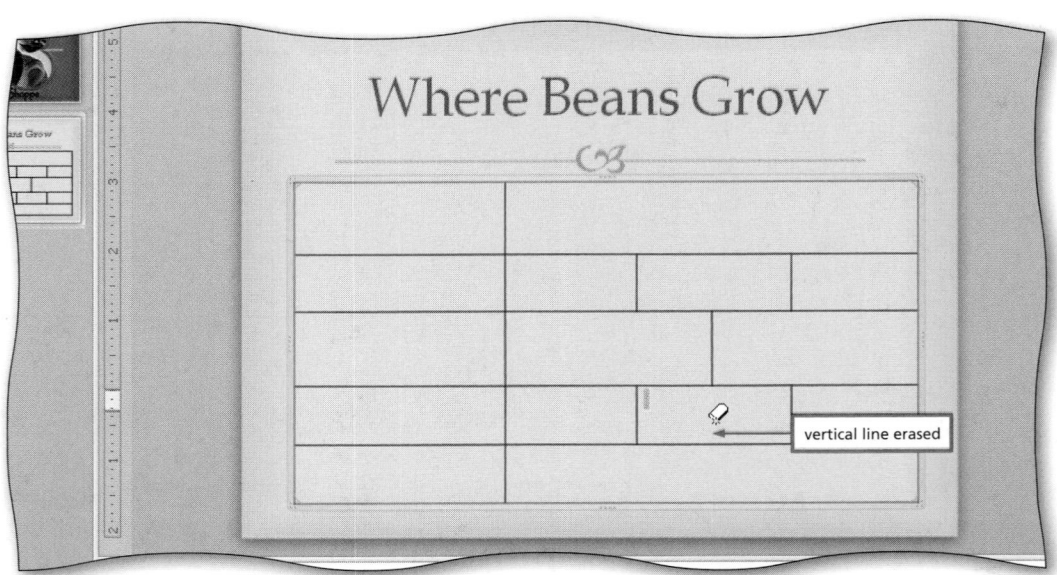

Figure 10–19

To Enter Data in a Table

Coffee beans are grown in several countries throughout the world. The table you created will list the continent names on the left side of each row and the location names on the right side. The first row will label the two parts of the table. To place data in a cell, you click the cell and then type text. The following steps enter data in the cells of the empty table.

1 Position the mouse pointer in the upper-left cell of the table, type `Continent` in the cell, and then press the TAB key to advance the insertion point to the next cell.

2 Type `Location` in the upper-right cell and then press the TAB key to advance the insertion point to the first cell in the second row.

3 Type `North America` and then press the TAB key to advance the insertion point to the next cell. Type `United States` and then press the TAB key to advance the insertion point to the next cell. Type `Mexico` and then press the TAB key to advance the insertion point to the next cell. Type `Puerto Rico` and then press the TAB key to advance the insertion point to the first column of the third row.

4 In the third row, type `North America` in the first column, `Costa Rica` in the second column, and `Guatemala` in the third column. Press the TAB key to advance the insertion point to the first column of the fourth row.

5 In the fourth row, type `Africa` in the first column, `Ethiopia` in the second column, `Ivory Coast` in the third column, and `Kenya` in the fourth column. Press the TAB key to advance the insertion point to the first column of the fifth row.

6 In the fifth row, type `Asia` in the first column and `Indonesia` in the second column (Figure 10–20).

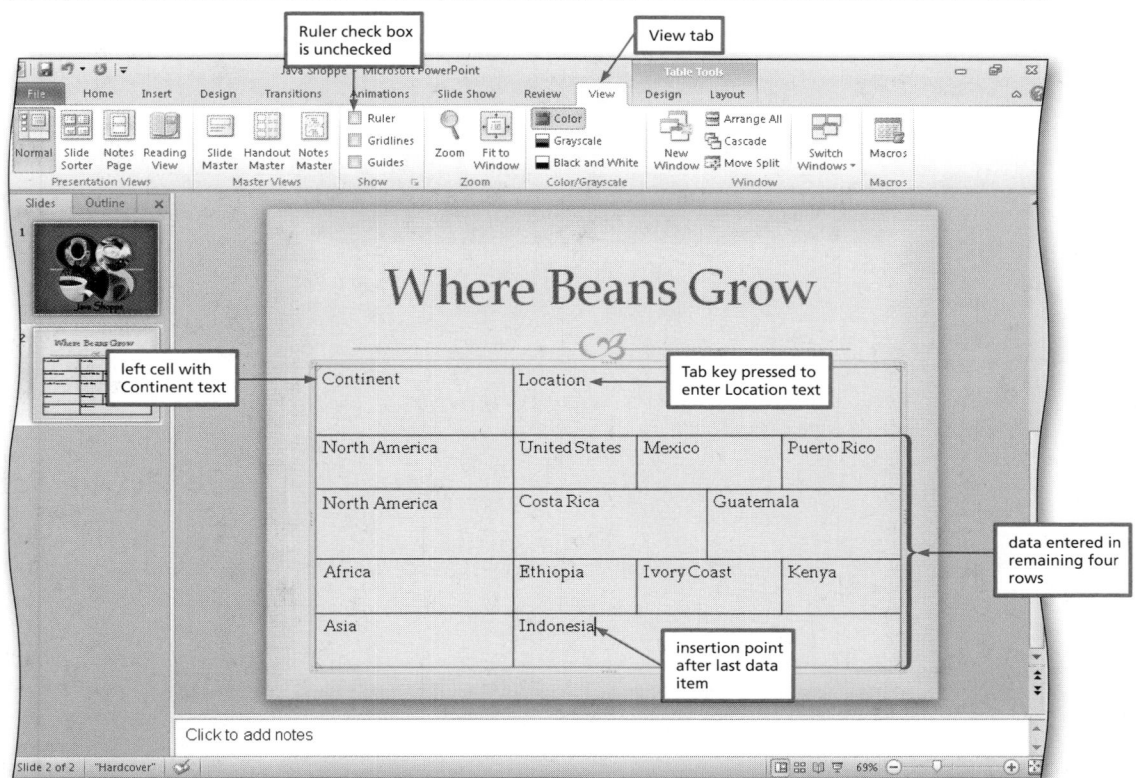

Figure 10–20

To Split a Table Column and Row

The Asia row in the table identifies Indonesia as the only location growing coffee beans. Your research indicates that the Vietnamese also grow coffee plants, so you need to add that location to the right side of the last row. The layout of this row should be identical to the second North America row. In addition, you learn that coffee also is grown in Brazil and Colombia, which are located in South America. You easily can create additional table columns and rows by dividing current cells and rows. The following steps split a column and a row.

1

- With the mouse pointer positioned in the Indonesia cell, click the Table Tools Layout tab to display the Table Tools Layout Ribbon and then click the Split Cells button (Table Tools Layout tab | Merge group) to display the Split Cells dialog box (Figure 10–21).

Q&A

Are the default numbers in the dialog box always 2 columns and 1 row?

Yes, but you can increase the numbers if you need to divide the cell into more than two halves or need to create two or more rows within one cell.

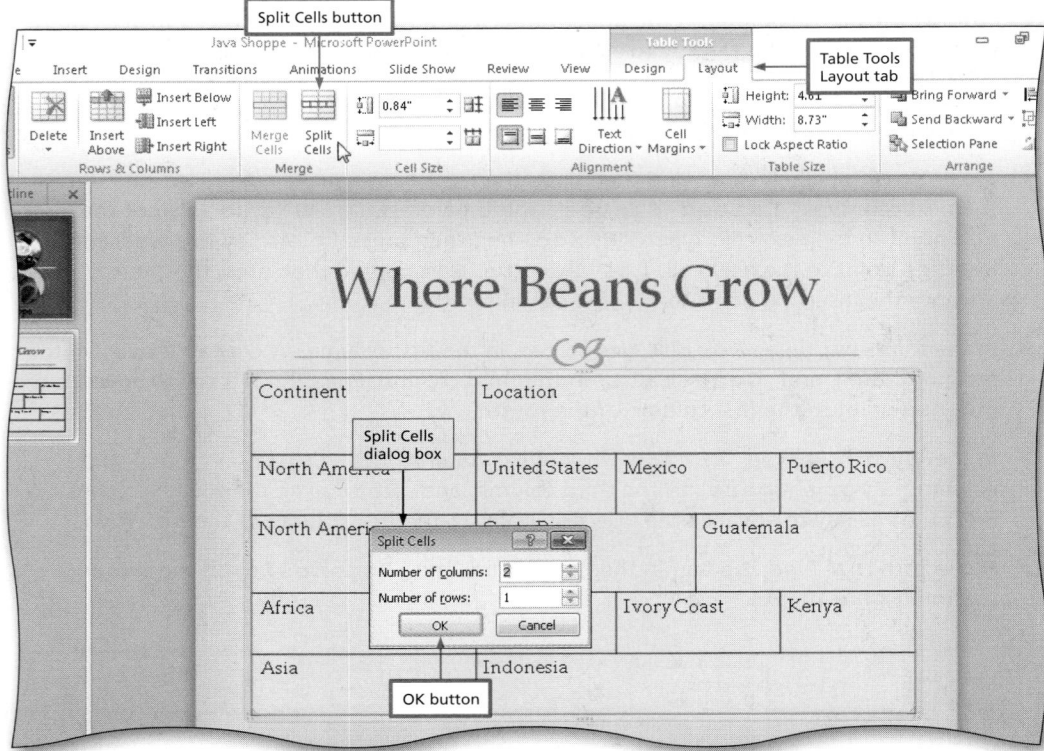

Figure 10–21

2

- Click the OK button (Split Cells dialog box) to create a third cell in the Asia row.

- Position the mouse pointer in the second North America cell.

- Click the Select button (Table Tools Layout tab | Table group) to display the Select menu (Figure 10–22).

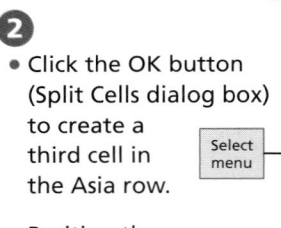

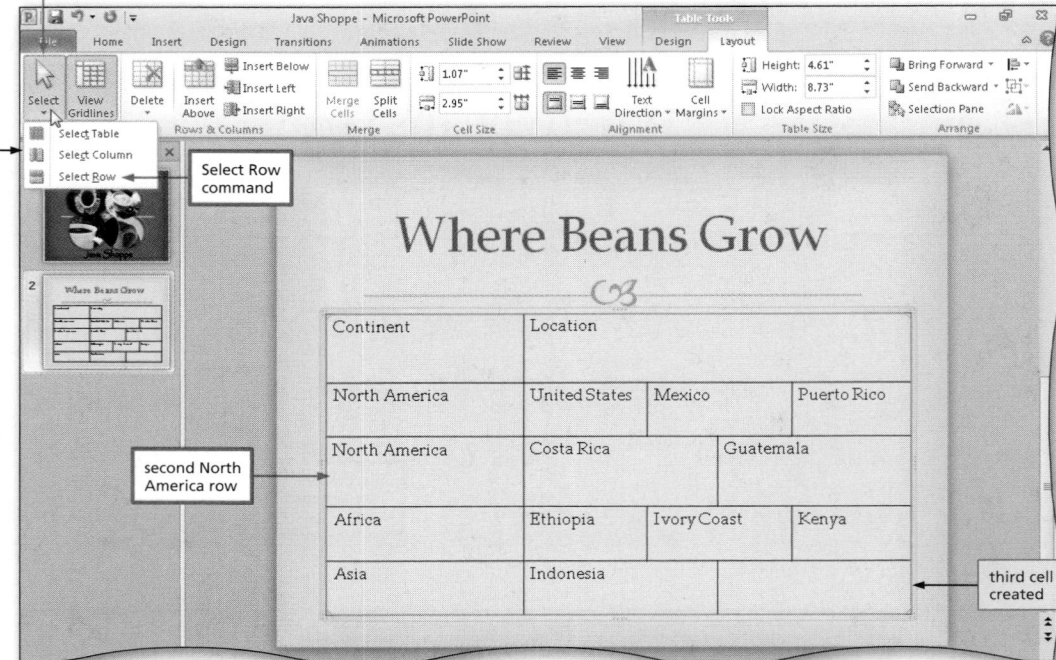

Figure 10–22

3

- Click Select Row in the Select menu to select the second North America row.

- With the Table Tools Layout tab displaying, click the Split Cells button (Table Tools Layout tab | Merge group) to display the Split Cells dialog box (Figure 10–23).

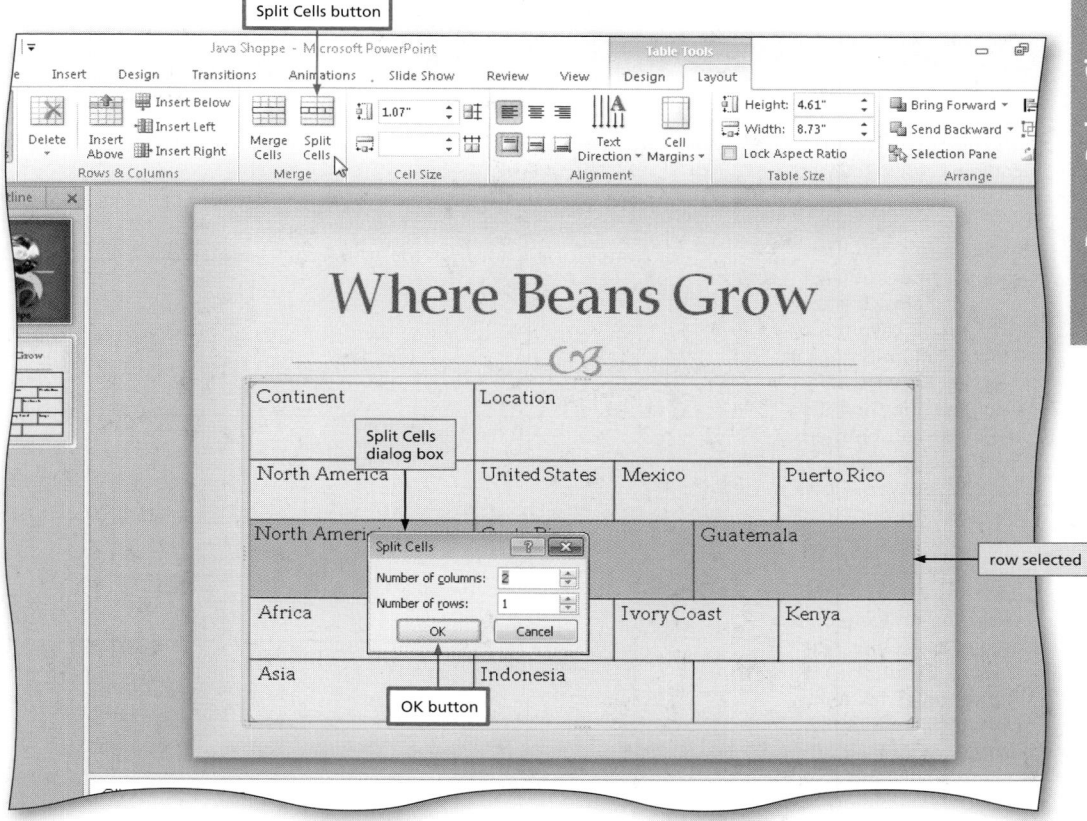

Figure 10–23

4

- Click the 'Number of columns' box down arrow one time to decrease the number of columns to 1.

- Click the 'Number of rows' box up arrow one time to increase the number of rows to 2 (Figure 10–24).

Q&A

How many rows and columns can I create by splitting the cells?

The maximum number varies depending upon the width and height of the selected cell.

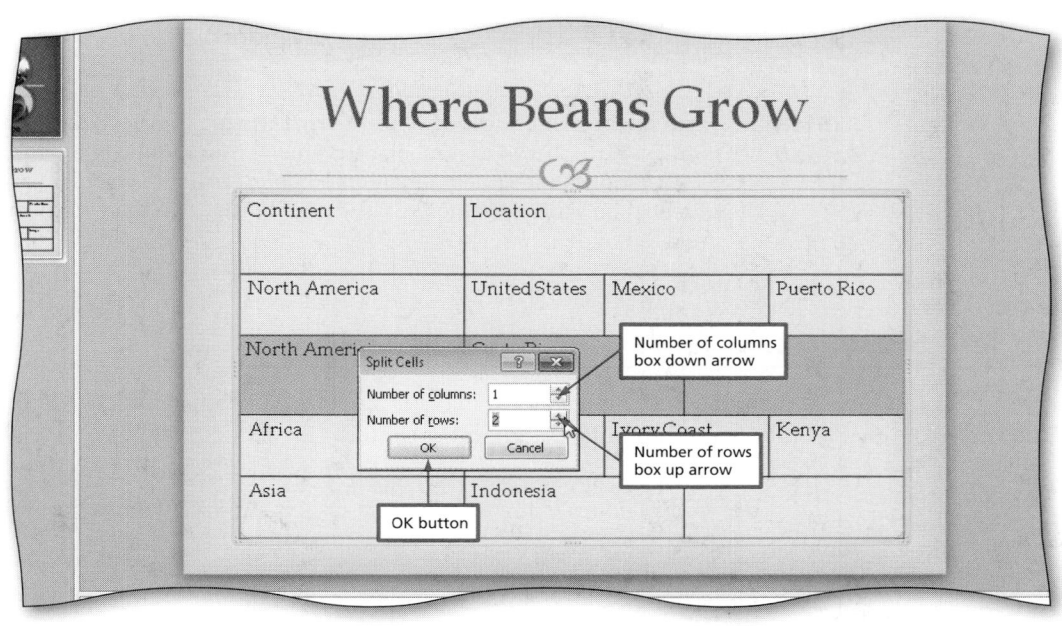

Figure 10–24

5

- Click the OK button (Split Cells dialog box) to create a row below the second North America row.

Other Ways

1. Right-click table, click Split Cells on shortcut menu, enter number of columns and rows, click OK button

Inserting and Deleting Rows and Columns

Once you have drawn a table, you can insert and delete rows and columns easily. To insert an entire row, select a row where you want to add a row and then click the Insert Above or Insert Below buttons (Table Tools Layout tab | Rows & Columns group). You can, likewise, select a column and then click the Insert Left or Insert Right buttons (Table Tools Layout tab | Rows & Columns group) to insert a column. If you desire to delete an entire row or a column, select this unwanted area of the table, click the Delete button (Table Tools Layout tab | Rows & Columns group) to display the Delete menu, and then click Delete Columns or Delete Rows in the Delete menu.

To Enter Additional Data in a Table

With the additional row and column added to the table, you now can add the South America data in the inserted row and also add the location, Vietnam, to the new cell in the Asia row. The following steps enter data in the new cells.

1 If necessary, position the mouse pointer in the first cell of the fourth row and then type `South America` in the cell. Press the TAB key to advance the insertion point to the adjacent right column cell and then type `Brazil` and `Colombia` in the cells in this row.

2 Press the DOWN ARROW key two times to position the mouse pointer in the new cell in the Asia row and then type `Vietnam` in the cell (Figure 10–25).

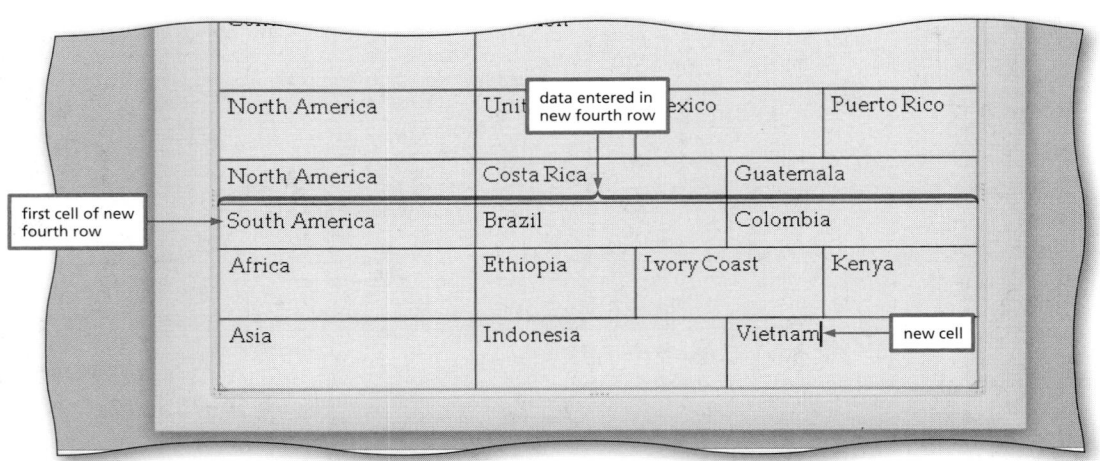

Figure 10–25

<table>
<tr><td>**Plan Ahead**</td><td>**Use appropriate colors when formatting graphics you want people to remember.** Studies have shown that men and women differ slightly in their recall of graphics formatted with various colors. Men remembered objects colored with shades of violet, dark blue, olive green, and yellow. Women recalled objects they had seen with dark blue, olive green, yellow, and red hues.</td></tr>
</table>

To Add Shading to a Table

You can format the table in several ways to make it more visually appealing. By adding shading, you can color the background. The following steps add shading to the table.

1
- Click the Select button (Table Tools Layout tab | Table group) to display the Select menu (Figure 10–26).

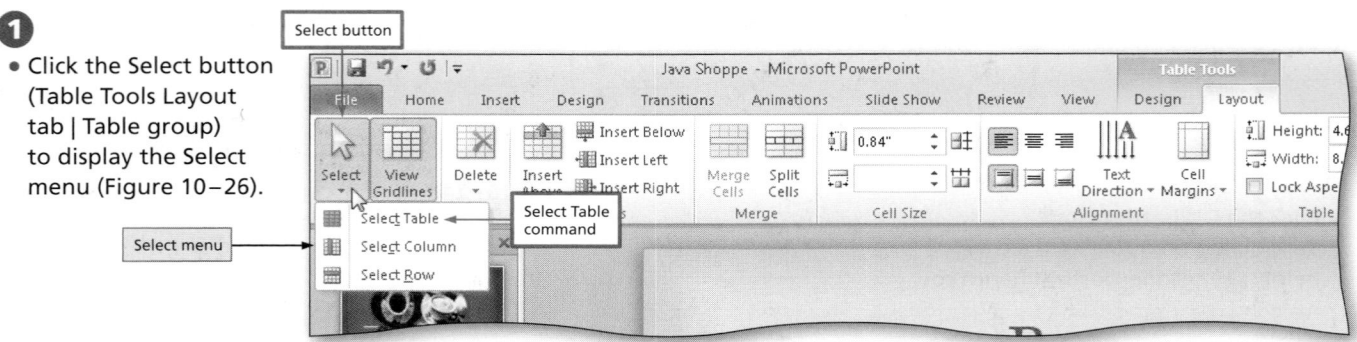

Figure 10–26

2

- Click Select Table in the Select menu to select the entire table.

- Click the Table Tools Design tab and then click the Shading button arrow (Table Tools Design tab | Table Styles group) to display the Shading gallery.

- Point to Olive Green, Accent 6 (rightmost color in first Theme Colors row) in the Shading gallery to display a live preview of that color applied to the table in the slide (Figure 10–27).

🔎 **Experiment**

- Point to various colors in the Shading gallery and watch the background of the table change.

3

- Click Olive Green, Accent 6 in the Shading gallery to apply the selected color to the table.

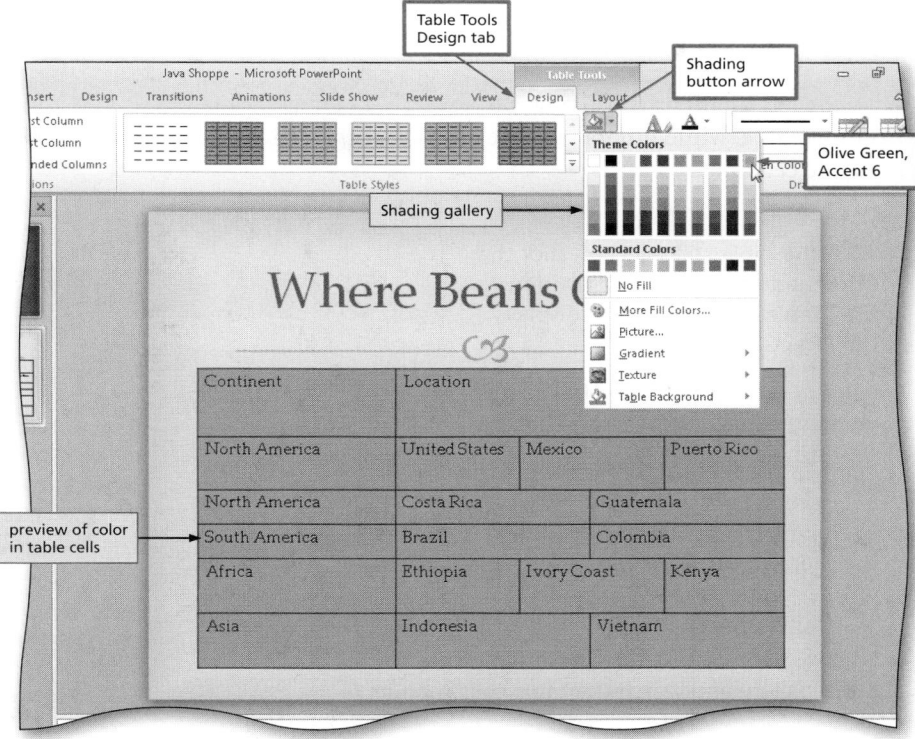

Figure 10–27

To Add a Gradient Fill to a Table

Another enhancement you can make to the table is to add a gradient fill so that one shade of the olive green color gradually progresses to another shade of the same color. The following steps add a gradient fill to the table.

1

- With the table still selected, click the Shading button arrow (Table Tools Design tab | Table Styles group) again to display the Shading menu.

- Point to Gradient to display the Gradient gallery and then point to Linear Down in the Dark Variations area (second gradient in first row) to display a live preview of that gradient applied to the table in the slide (Figure 10–28).

🔎 **Experiment**

- Point to various gradients in the Gradient gallery and watch the background of the table change.

2

- Click Linear Down in the Shading gallery to apply the selected gradient to the table.

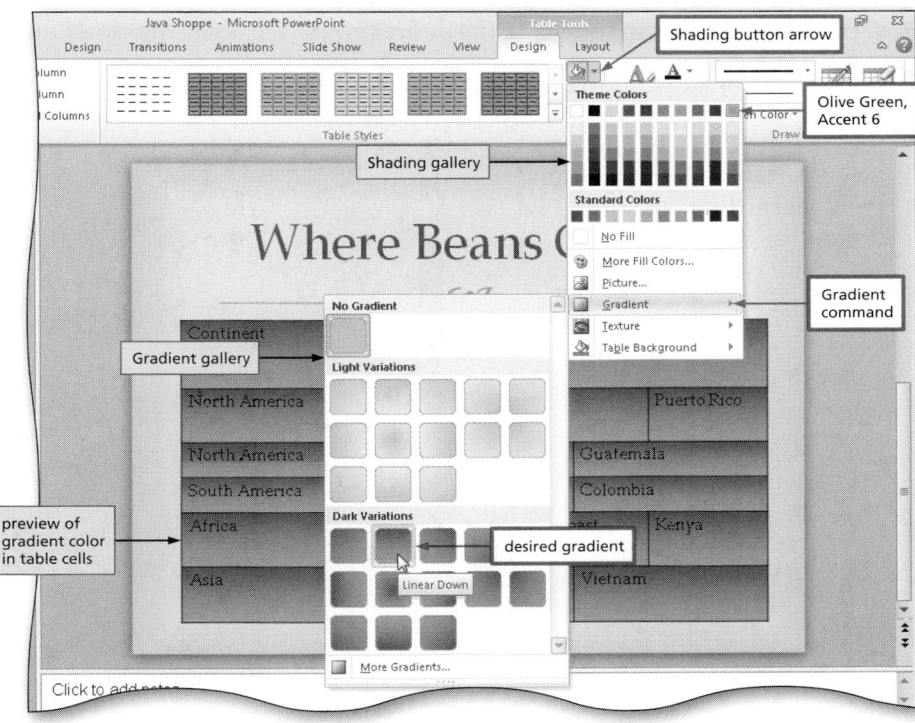

Figure 10–28

To Add a Cell Bevel

Bevels modify the cell edges to give a 3-D effect. Some bevels give the appearance that the cell is protruding from the table, while others give the effect that the cell is depressed into the table. The following steps add a bevel to the table cells.

- With the table still selected, click the Effects button (Table Tools Design tab | Table Styles group) to display the Effects menu.

- Point to Cell Bevel on the Effects menu to display the Cell Bevel gallery.

- Point to Art Deco (rightmost bevel in last row) to display a live preview of that bevel applied to the table in the slide (Figure 10–29).

- Point to various bevel effects in the Bevel gallery and watch the table cells change.

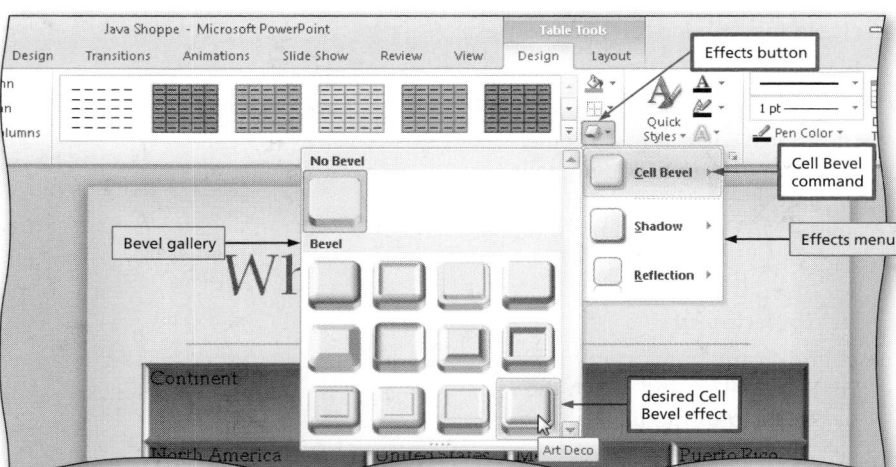

Figure 10–29

- Click Art Deco in the Bevel gallery to apply the selected bevel effect to the table.

To Distribute Table Rows

The horizontal lines you drew are not spaced equidistant from each other. At times you may desire the row heights to vary. In the Slide 2 table, however, you desire the heights of the rows to be uniform. To make each selected row the same height, you distribute the desired rows. The following steps distribute table rows.

- With the table still selected, display the Table Tools Layout tab and then select the cells in the second, third, fourth, fifth, and sixth rows (Figure 10–30).

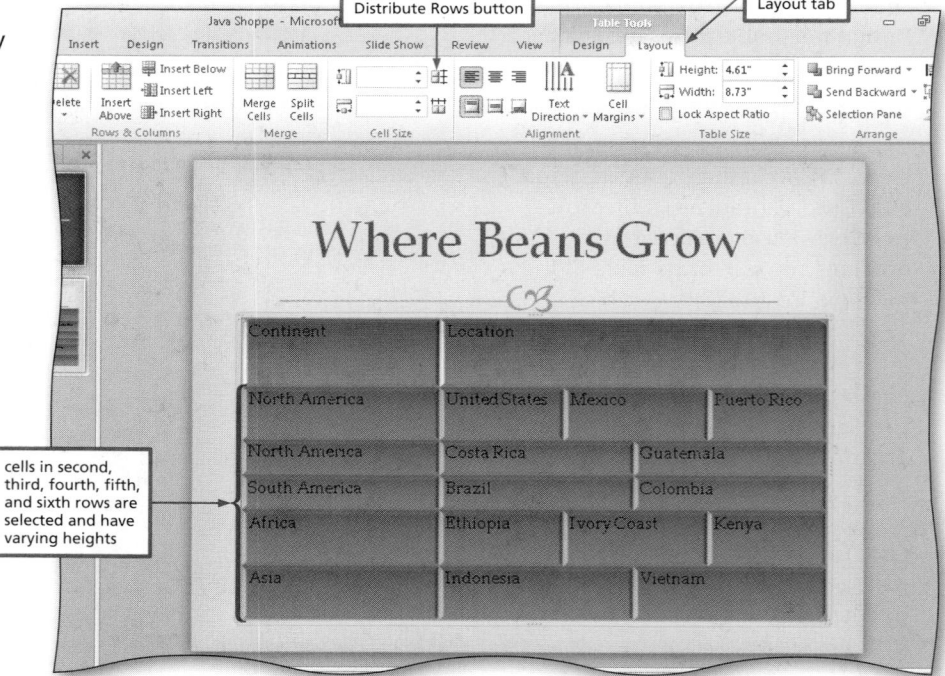

Figure 10–30

2

- Click the Distribute Rows button (Table Tools Layout tab | Cell Size group) to equally space the five continent rows vertically (Figure 10–31).

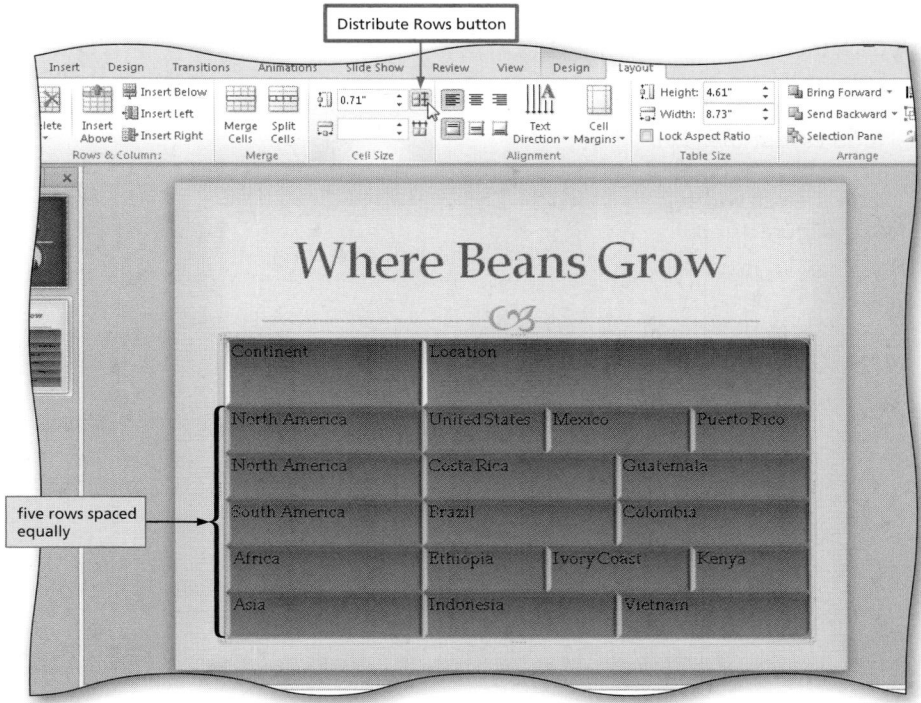

Figure 10–31

To Resize Table Columns and Rows

The first table row should have a taller height than the rows beneath it because it signifies the two table categories. In addition, the continents portion of the table should be narrower than the countries portion because it has fewer words and only one cell per row. The following steps resize the table columns and rows.

1

- With the Table Tools Layout tab displaying, position the insertion point in the Continent cell in the first row.

- Click the Table Row Height box down arrow (Table Tools Layout tab | Cell Size group) as needed to reduce the height to 0.8" (Figure 10–32).

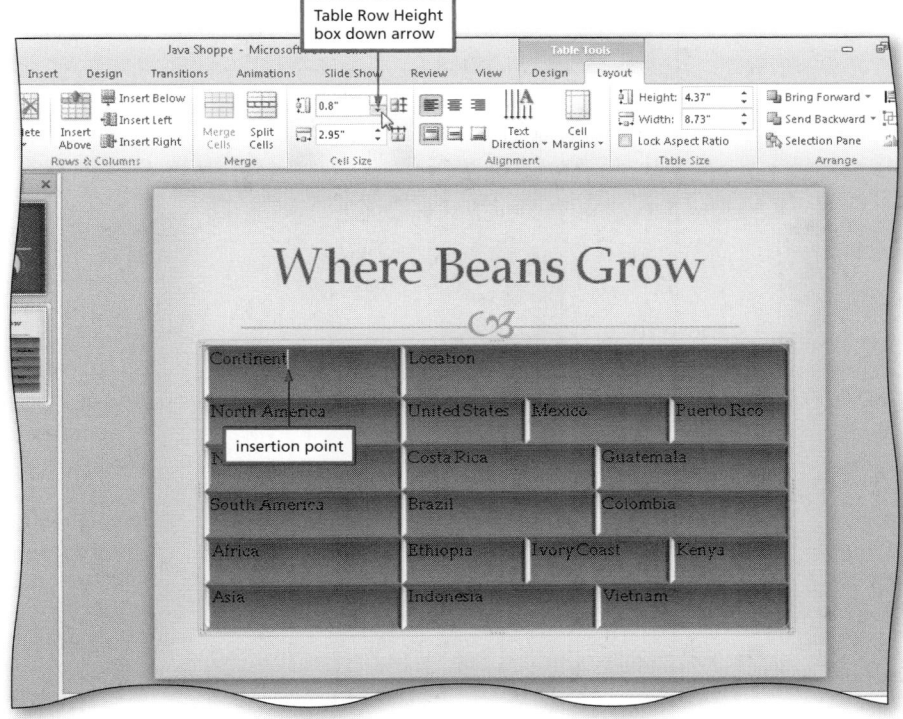

Figure 10–32

2
- Click the Table Column Width box down arrow (Table Tools Layout tab | Cell Size group) as needed until the cell width is 2.5" (Figure 10–33).

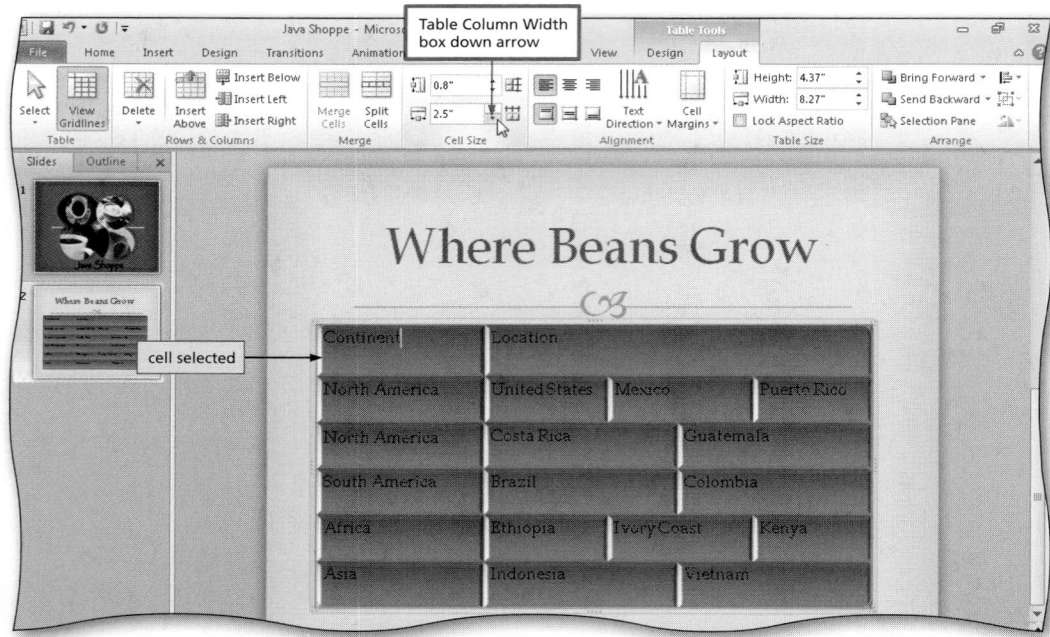

Figure 10–33

To Align Data in Cells

The next step is to change the alignment of the data in all the table cells. In addition to aligning text horizontally in a cell (left, center, or right), you can align it vertically within a cell (top, middle, or bottom). The following steps center data in the table both horizontally and vertically.

1 Select all the table cells and then click the Center button (Table Tools Layout tab | Alignment group) to center the text horizontally in the cells.

2 Click the Center Vertically button (Table Tools Layout tab | Alignment group) to center the contents of the cells vertically (Figure 10–34).

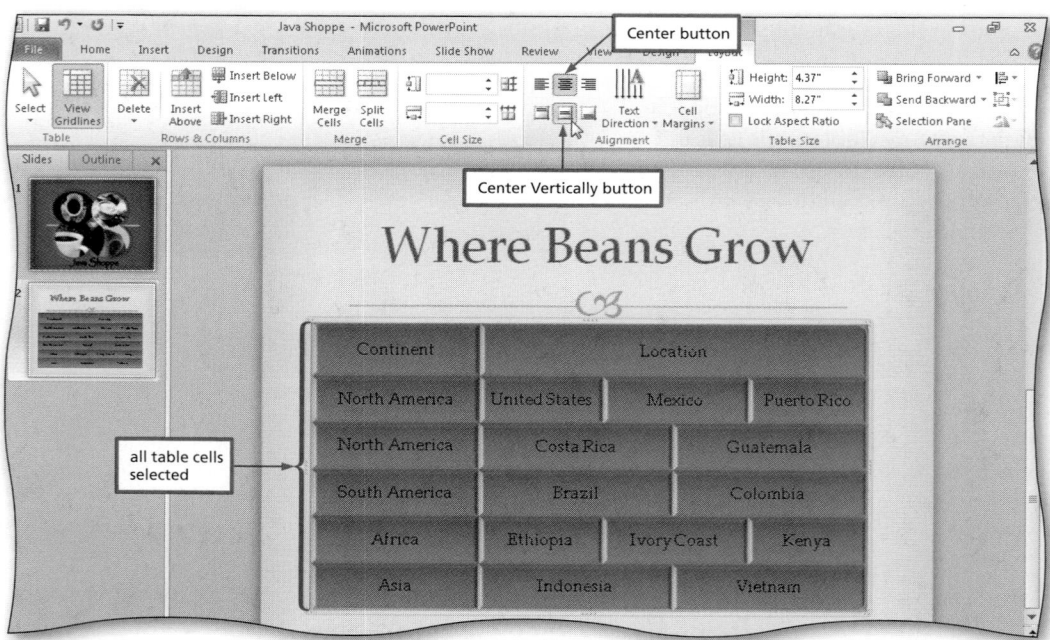

Figure 10–34

To Center the Table

The table should be positioned an equal distance between the left and right slide edges. To center the table, you align it in the middle of the slide. The following steps center the table horizontally.

1

- With the insertion point in the table, click the Align button (Table Tools Layout tab | Arrange group) to display the Align menu (Figure 10–35).

2

- Click Align Center on the Align menu, so PowerPoint adjusts the position of the table evenly between the left and right sides of the slide. If necessary, adjust the table vertically on the slide, so that it is displayed below the decorative slide background element.

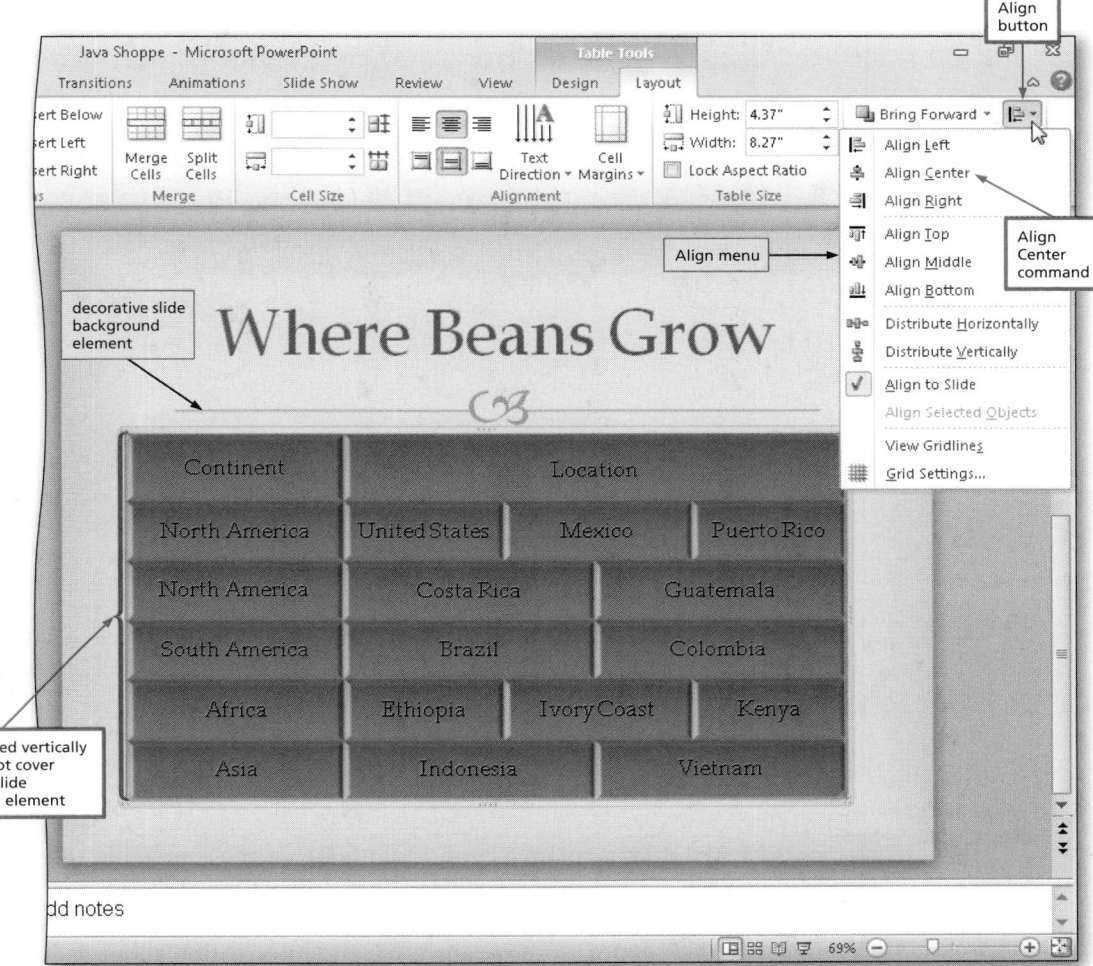

Figure 10–35

To Format Table Data

The final table enhancement is to bold and increase the font size of the text in the first row. The following steps bold the text in the first row and then increase the font size.

1 Select the first row, display the Home tab, and then click the Bold button to bold the text.

2 Increase the font size to 28 point (Figure 10–36).

BTW

Positioning a Table
At times you might desire to place a table, text box, shape, or other element in a precise location on the slide. To specify a position, right-click the object, click Format Object or Format Shape on the shortcut menu, click Position in the left pane of the Format Object or Format Shape dialog box, and then enter the precise measurements of the horizontal and vertical distances from either the top-left corner or the center of the slide.

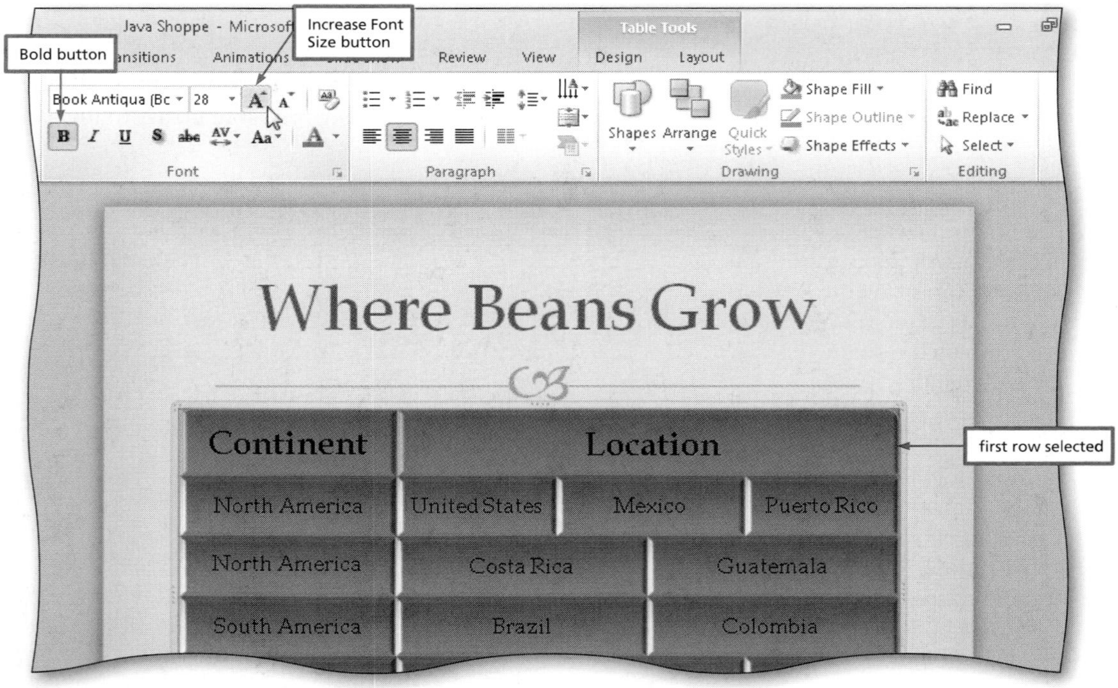

Figure 10–36

Break Point: If you wish to take a break, this is a good place to do so. Be sure to save the Java Shoppe file again and then you can quit PowerPoint. To resume at a later time, start PowerPoint, open the file called Java Shoppe, and continue following the steps from this location forward.

BTW

File Sizes
Files with embedded objects typically have larger file sizes than those with linked objects because the source data is stored in the presentation. In order to keep file sizes manageable, Microsoft recommends inserting a linked object rather than an embedded object when the source file is large or complex.

Inserting a Linked Spreadsheet

Linked files maintain a connection between the source file and the destination file. When you select the **Link check box** in the Insert Object dialog box, the object is inserted as a linked object instead of an embedded object. Your PowerPoint presentation stores a representation of the original file and information about its location. If you later move or delete the source file, the link is broken, and the object will not be available. Consequently, if you make a presentation on a computer other than the one on which the presentation was created, and the presentation contains linked objects, be certain to include a copy of the source files. The source files must be stored in the exact location as originally specified when you linked them to your presentation.

PowerPoint associates a linked file with a specific application, which PowerPoint bases on the file extension. For example, if you select a source file with the file extension **.docx**, PowerPoint recognizes the file as a Microsoft Word file. Additionally, if you select a source file with the file extension **.xlsx**, PowerPoint recognizes the file as a Microsoft Excel file.

In the following pages, you will insert a linked Excel worksheet, align it on the slide, and then edit three cells.

To Insert a Linked Excel Worksheet

An Excel worksheet contains a table with tallies of the number of students expressing a preference for a particular espresso drink. You can insert this object and specify that it is linked from the PowerPoint slide to the Excel worksheet so that any edits made to specific cells are reflected in both the source and destination files. The following steps insert and link the Microsoft Excel worksheet.

1

- Insert a new slide with the Blank layout.

- Insert the Coffee Beans picture from your USB flash drive as a background for the new slide (Figure 10–37).

Figure 10–37

2

- Click Insert on the Ribbon and then click the Insert Object button (Insert tab | Text group) to display the Insert Object dialog box.

- Click 'Create from file' (Insert Object dialog box) to display the File text box (Figure 10–38).

Figure 10–38

- Click the Browse button, navigate to the PowerPoint Chapter 10 folder, and then click Espresso to select the file name (Figure 10–39).

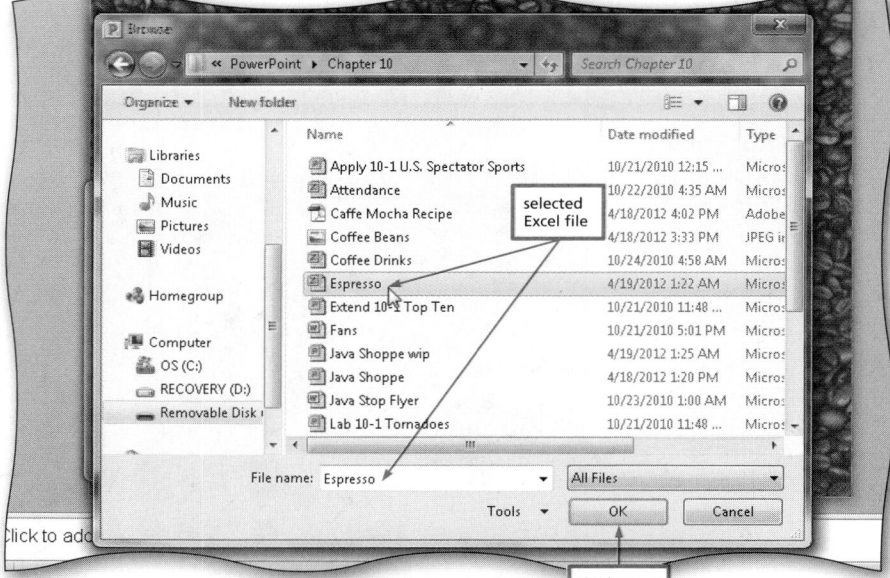

Figure 10–39

- Click the OK button (Browse dialog box) to insert the file name into the File text box (Insert Object dialog box).

- Click the Link check box (Insert Object dialog box) to place a check mark in it (Figure 10–40).

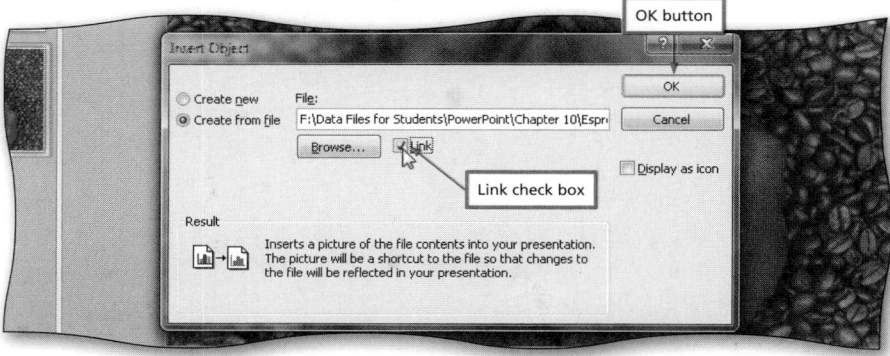

Figure 10–40

- Click the OK button (Insert Object dialog box) to insert the Espresso Excel worksheet into Slide 3.

- Display the Drawing Tools Format tab and then click the Shape Height box up arrow repeatedly to change the worksheet height to 5" (Figure 10–41).

Q&A

Why did the worksheet width change when I changed the height measurement?

The worksheet's width and height stay in proportion to each other, so when you change one dimension, the other dimension changes accordingly.

Figure 10–41

To Align a Worksheet

PowerPoint inserts the table on Slide 3 in a location that is not visually appealing. You can drag the table to a location, but you also can have PowerPoint precisely align the object horizontally in the left, center, or right areas of the slide, and vertically in the top, middle, or bottom of the slide. The following steps align the table horizontally and vertically on Slide 3.

1

- With the Drawing Tools Format tab displaying, click the Align button (Drawing Tools Format tab | Arrange group) to display the Align menu (Figure 10–42).

Figure 10–42

2

- Click Align Center on the Align menu to position the worksheet evenly between the left and right edges of the slide.

- Click the Align button again to display the Align menu and then click Align Bottom to position the worksheet at the lower edge of the slide (Figure 10–43).

Figure 10–43

To Edit a Linked Worksheet

Each table or worksheet cell is identified by a unique address, or **cell reference**, representing the intersection of a column and row. The column letter is first and is followed by the row number. For example, cell B6 is located at the intersection of the second column, B, and the sixth row. Three cells need updating in the worksheet to reflect additional survey results. When the numbers in the cell change, the totals at the bottom of each column change to reflect the updated sum of each column. The following steps edit cells in the linked table.

1
- Double-click the table to open Microsoft Excel and display the worksheet.
- Click the Mocha cell for the Fall semester to make cell B6 the active cell (Figure 10–44).

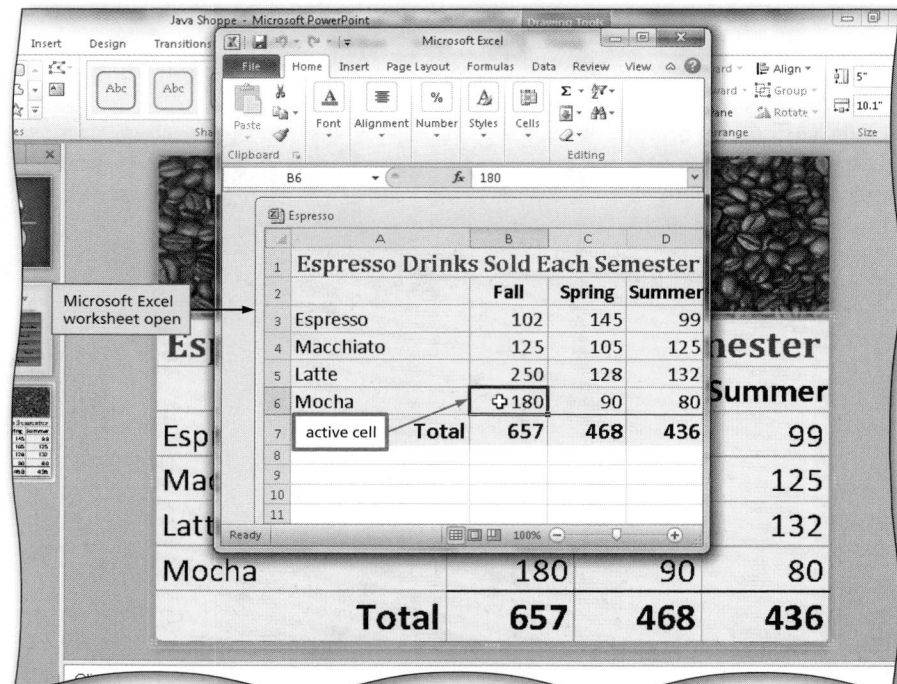

Figure 10–44

2
- Type **213** as the replacement number and then press the ENTER key to recalculate the Fall total.
- Click the Latte cell for the Spring semester, type **142** as the replacement number, and then press the ENTER key to recalculate the Spring total.
- Click the Macchiato cell for the Summer semester, type **145** as the replacement number, and then press the ENTER key to recalculate the Summer total (Figure 10–45).

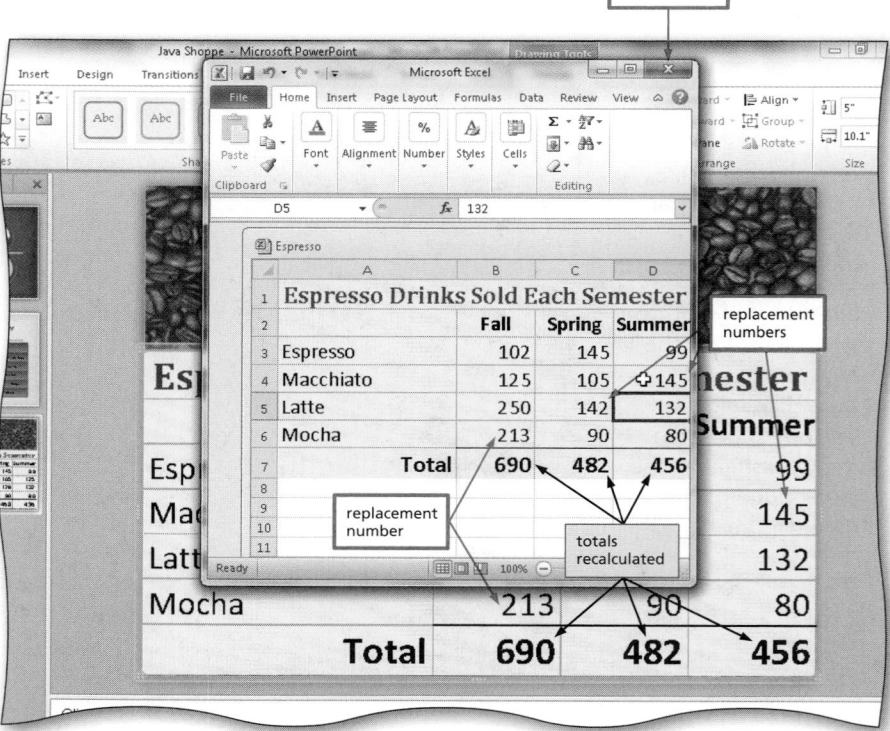

Figure 10–45

3

- Click the Close button in the upper-right corner of the Microsoft Excel window to quit Excel (Figure 10–46).

- Click the Save button (Microsoft Excel dialog box) to save your edited numbers in the worksheet and to display the updated table in Slide 3.

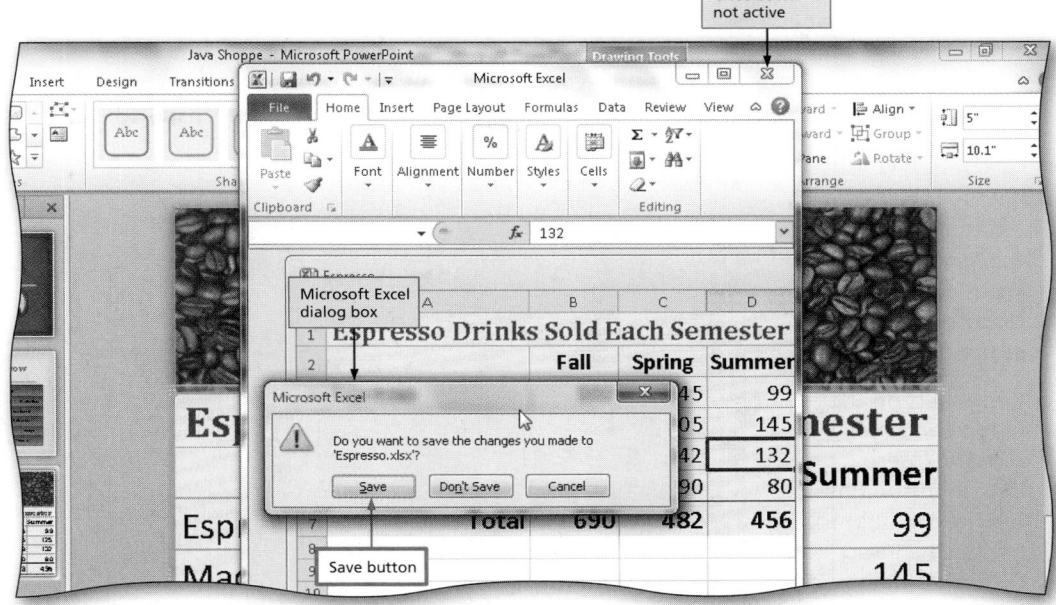

Figure 10–46

Break Point: If you wish to take a break, this is a good place to do so. Be sure to save the Java Shoppe file again and then you can quit PowerPoint. To resume at a later time, start PowerPoint, open the file called Java Shoppe, and continue following the steps from this location forward. Note: PowerPoint will prompt you to update the Excel file that you modified.

Inserting and Modifying an Embedded Excel Chart

The Microsoft Word file you inserted into Slide 1 is an embedded object. You edited the business name using the Microsoft Word source program, but the change is stored only on the PowerPoint slide, not the original Word document. You, likewise, will insert and then modify a Microsoft Excel chart on Slide 4. This object will be embedded, so any changes you make to the layout, legend, or background will be reflected in the destination object on the slide.

In the following pages, you will perform these tasks on Slide 4:

1. Insert a chart from a file.
2. Align the chart.
3. Switch rows and columns.
4. Change a chart type.
5. Apply a Quick Style.
6. Format a legend.
7. Display chart labels.
8. Hide an axis.
9. Display gridlines.
10. Format the background.
11. Edit data.
12. Add a hyperlink.

BTW

Using Excel within PowerPoint
The Microsoft Excel chart you insert in this project is located on the Data Files for Students. When you want to create your own chart, you can open Excel from within PowerPoint, enter data, and then create a chart. The chart becomes an embedded Excel object, so you later can modify the worksheet or use Excel's formatting tools to enhance the chart. To open Excel within PowerPoint, display the Insert tab, click the Table button (Insert tab | Tables group), and then click Excel Spreadsheet.

To Insert a Chart from a File

The chart you want to insert into your slide show was created in Microsoft Excel. The file consists of two sheets: one for the chart and another for the numbers used to create the chart. The chart is on Sheet 1. The following steps insert a chart from Sheet 1 of the Microsoft Excel file.

- Insert a new slide with the Title Only layout. Type **Favorite Coffee Drinks** as the title text.

- Click Insert on the Ribbon and then click the Insert Object button (Insert tab | Text group) to display the Insert Object dialog box (Figure 10–47).

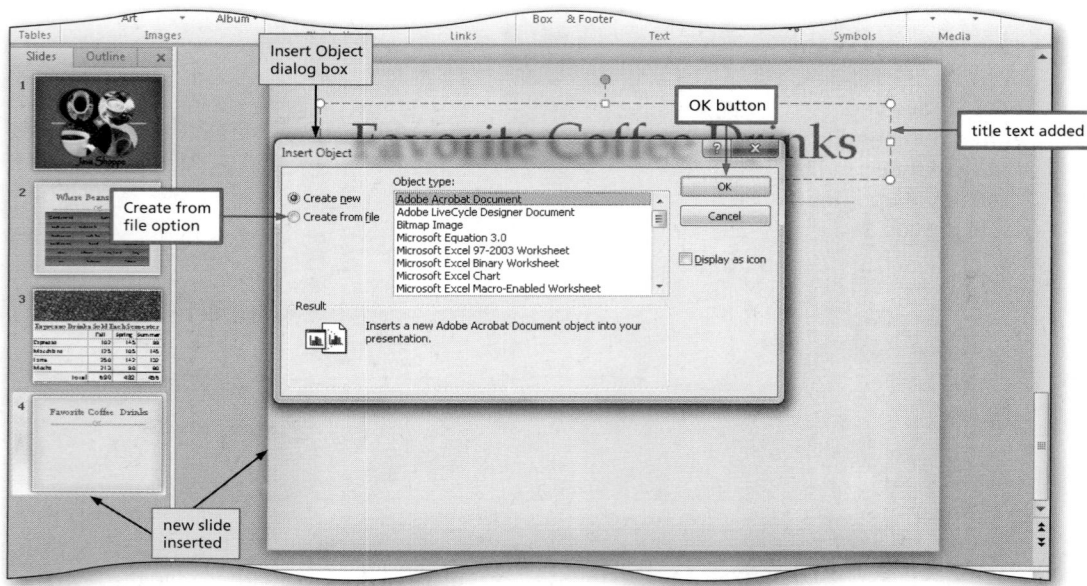

Figure 10–47

- Click 'Create from file' (Insert Object dialog box) to display the File text box.

- Click the Browse button, navigate to the PowerPoint Chapter 10 folder, and then click Coffee Drinks to select the Excel file name (Figure 10–48).

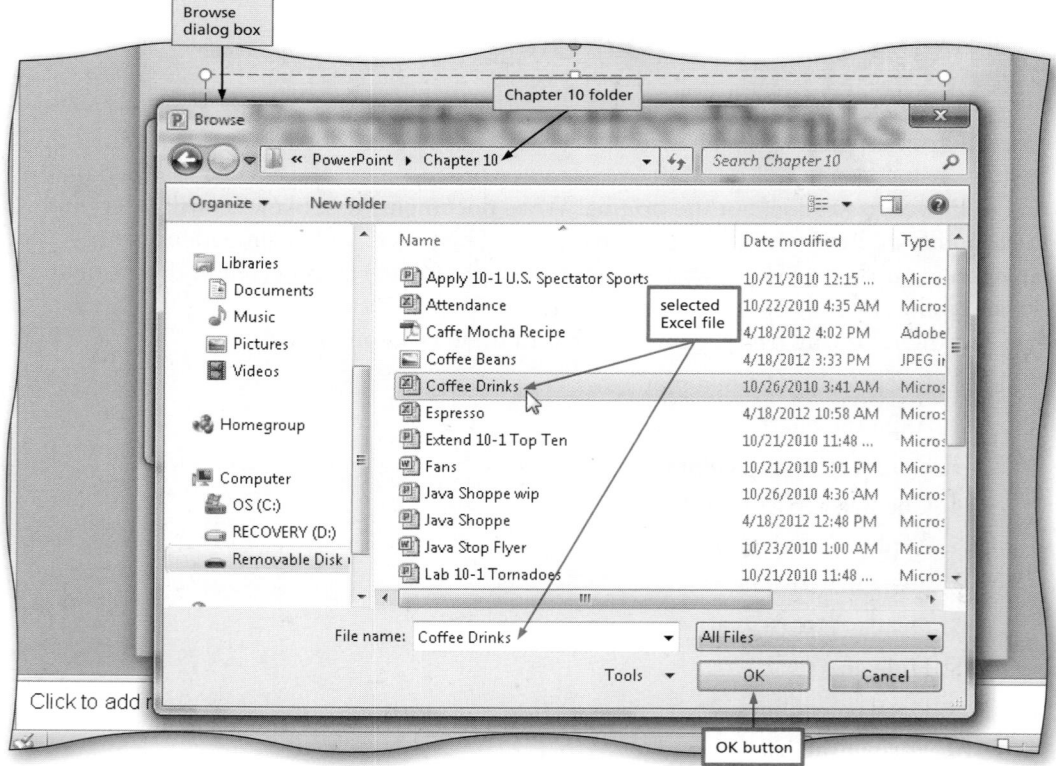

Figure 10–48

3

- Click the OK button (Browse dialog box) to display the File text box and then click the OK button (Insert Object dialog box) to insert an Excel chart into Slide 4.

- Display the Drawing Tools Format tab and then click the Shape Height box up arrow repeatedly to change the worksheet height to 5" (Figure 10–49).

Q&A

Why did the chart width change when I changed the height measurement?

The chart's width and height stay in proportion to each other, so when you change one dimension, the other dimension changes accordingly.

Other Ways

1. Right-click Excel chart, click Copy, exit Microsoft Excel, click Paste button arrow (Home tab | Clipboard group), click Use Destination Theme & Embed Excel Workbook

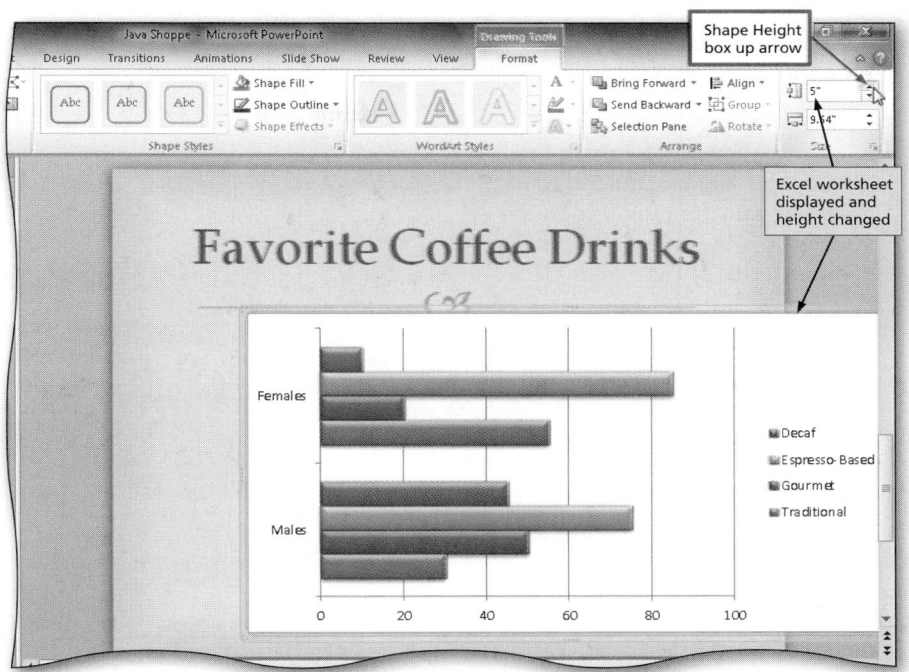

Figure 10–49

To Align a Chart

You aligned the table on Slide 3 horizontally and vertically. You, likewise, want to align the chart on Slide 3 so that it is displayed in an appropriate location on the slide. Although you can drag the chart on the slide, you also can use PowerPoint commands to align the object horizontally in the left, center, or right areas of the slide, and vertically in the top, middle, or bottom of the slide. The following steps align the chart horizontally and vertically on Slide 4.

1

- With the Drawing Tools Format tab displaying, click the Align button (Drawing Tools Format tab | Arrange group) to display the Align menu (Figure 10–50).

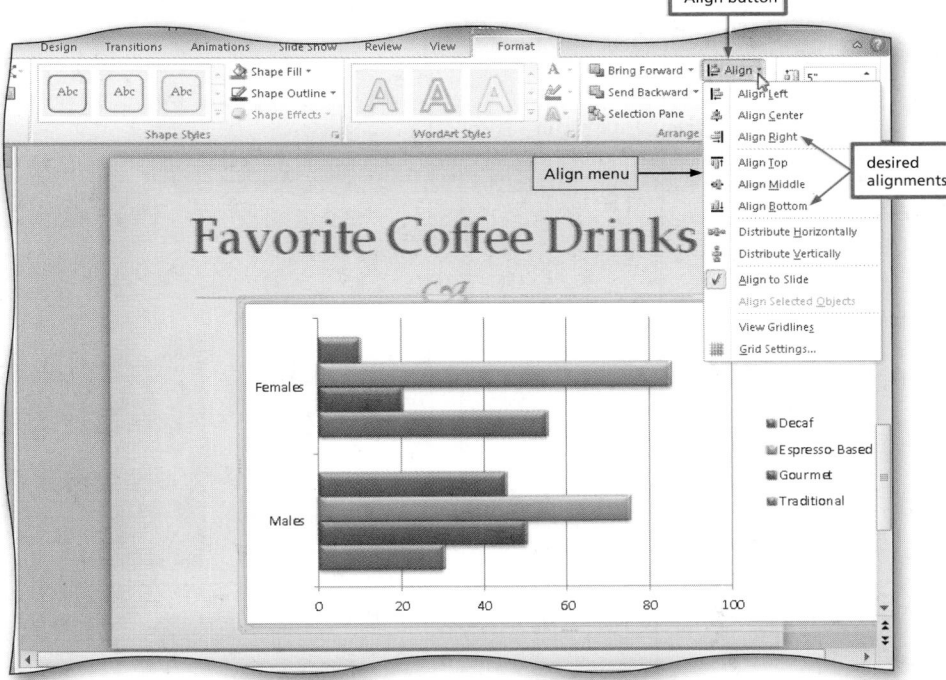

Figure 10–50

2

- Click Align Right on the Align menu to position the chart along the right edge of the slide.

- Click the Align button again to display the Align menu and then click Align Bottom to position the chart at the lower edge of the slide (Figure 10–51).

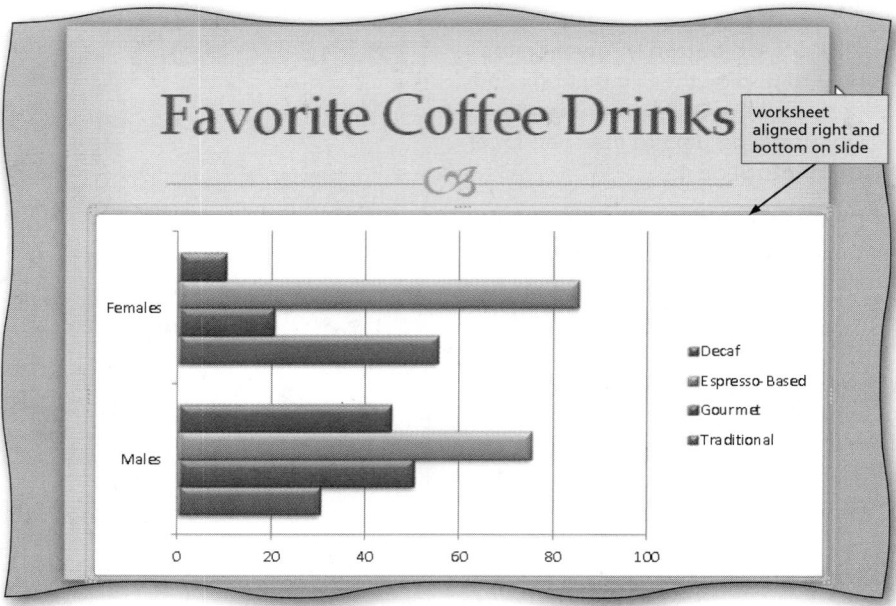

Figure 10–51

To Switch Rows and Columns in a Chart

Excel created the chart on Slide 4 (Sheet 1 in the Excel file) based on the values in the worksheet on Sheet 2 of the Excel file. The scale is based on the values in the **y-axis**, which also is called the **vertical axis** or **value axis**. The titles along the **x-axis**, also referred to as the **horizontal axis** or **category axis**, are derived from the top row of the Slide 2 worksheet and are displayed above the bottom edge of the chart. Each bar in the chart has a specific color to represent one of the four coffee drinks preferred by males and females. You can switch the data in the chart so that a male and female bar is displayed for each of the four coffee drinks. The following steps switch the rows and columns in the chart.

1

- Double-click the Slide 4 chart to start the Microsoft Excel program and open the document.

- Click the plot area to select it and then display the Chart Tools Design tab on the Ribbon (Figure 10–52).

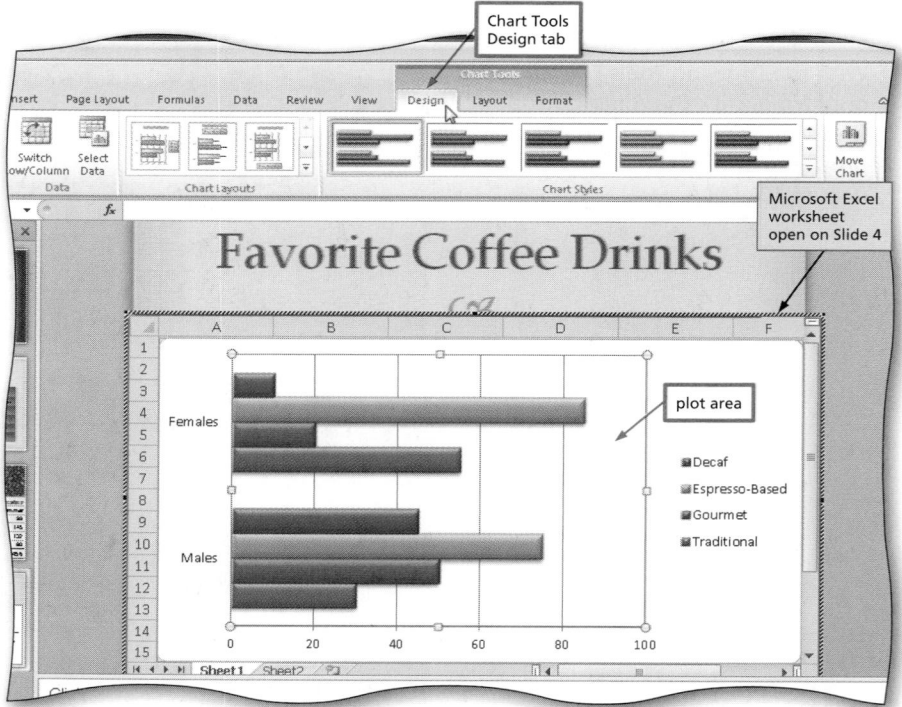

Figure 10–52

- Click the Switch Row/Column button (Chart Tools Design tab | Data group) to swap the data charted on the x-axis with the data on the y-axis (Figure 10–53).

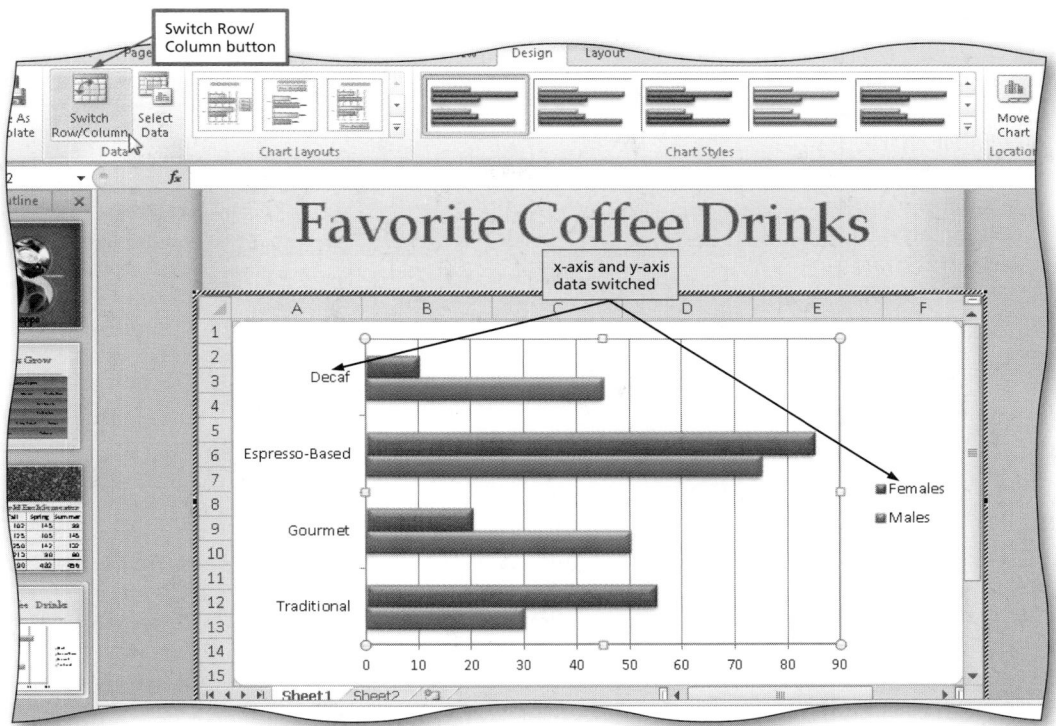

Figure 10–53

To Change a Chart Type

The bar chart represents data horizontally for each of the four coffee drinks. You can change the chart appearance by selecting another type in the Insert Chart dialog box. The sample charts are divided into a variety of categories, including bar, column, and pie. The cylinder type that you want to use in the presentation is located in the Column area. The following steps change the chart to a Clustered Cylinder chart type.

- Click the Change Chart Type button (Chart Tools Design tab | Type group) to display the Change Chart Type dialog box (Figure 10–54).

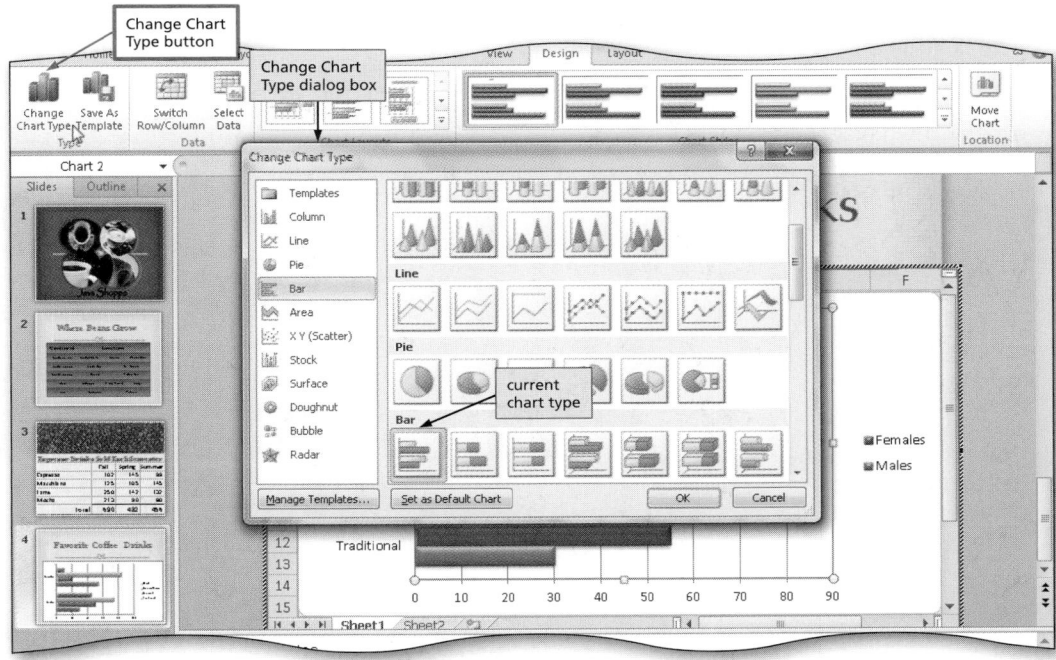

Figure 10–54

- Scroll up and then click the Clustered Cylinder chart type (first chart in second row) in the Column area to select this chart type (Figure 10–55).

Q&A Is a preview available?

No live preview is available when using the Change Chart Type dialog box.

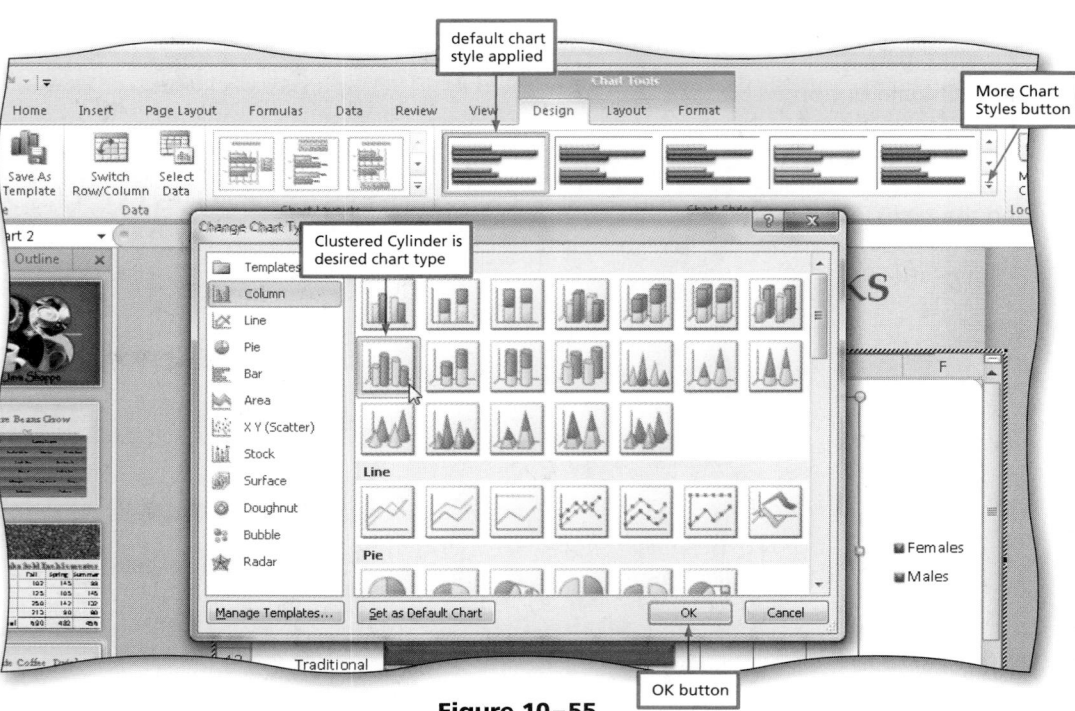

Figure 10–55

- Click the OK button (Change Chart Type dialog box) to change the chart in the selection rectangle to Clustered Cylinder.

To Apply a Quick Style to a Chart

You can modify the chart's appearance easily by selecting one of the 36 styles available in the Chart Styles gallery. These styles have a variety of colors and backgrounds and display in both 2-D and 3-D. The following steps apply a Quick Style to the chart.

- Click the More button in the Chart Styles gallery (Chart Tools Design tab | Chart Styles group) to expand the gallery (Figure 10–56).

- Click Style 34 in the Chart Styles gallery (second style in fifth row) to apply the chart style to the chart.

Q&A Does the Chart Styles gallery have a live preview feature?

No. This feature is not available.

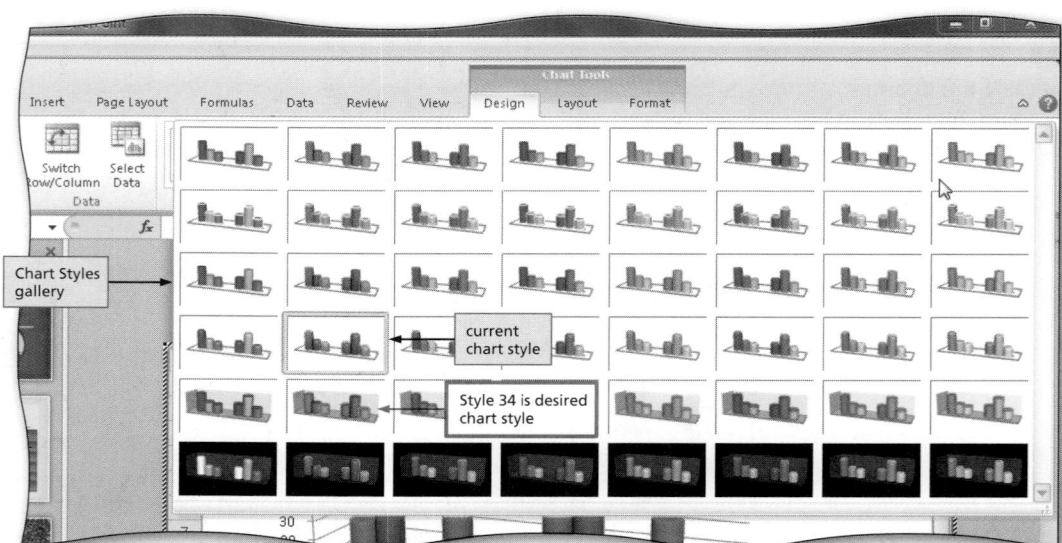

Figure 10–56

To Format a Chart Legend

The legend on the right side of the chart identifies the colors assigned to each of the cylinders. You can modify the default legend in a variety of ways, including moving its location, changing the fill and outline, adding an effect, and changing the font. The following steps format the legend.

1

- Display the Chart Tools Layout tab and then click the Legend button (Chart Tools Layout tab | Labels group) to display the Legend menu (Figure 10–57).

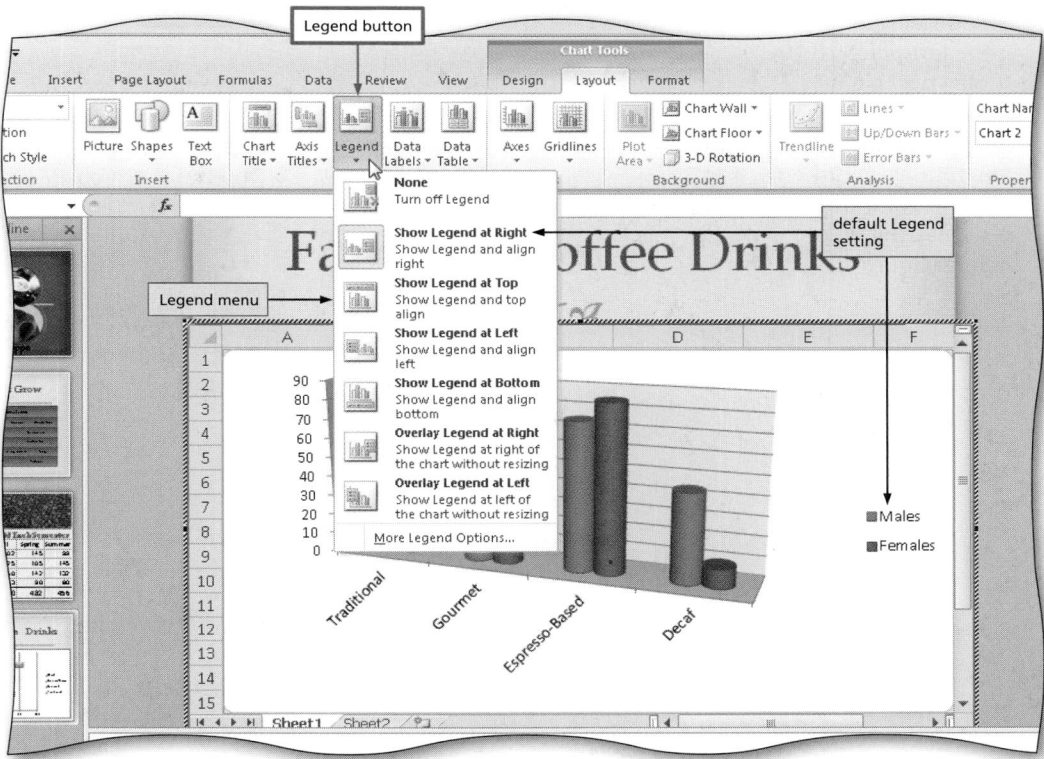

Figure 10–57

2

- Click Show Legend at Left to display the legend on the left side of the selection rectangle.

Q&A Is a live preview available?

No, this feature is not offered.

- Click the Legend button again to display the Legend menu (Figure 10–58).

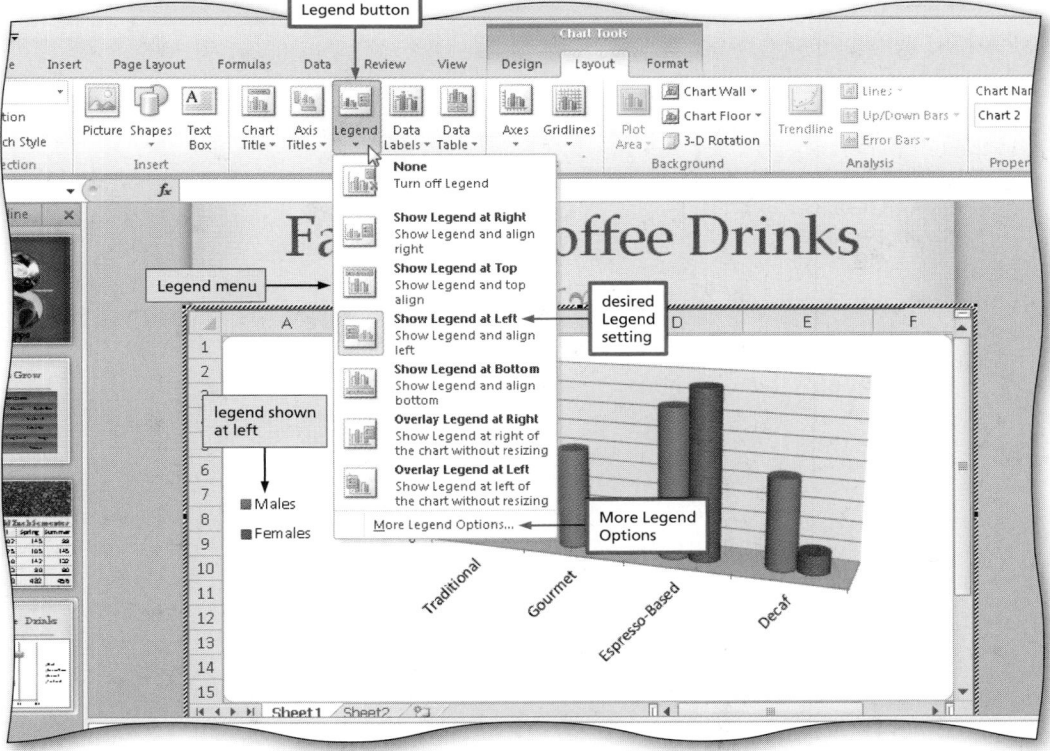

Figure 10–58

- Click More Legend Options to display the Format Legend dialog box.

- Click Border Color in the left panel to display the Border Color pane, click Solid line to expand the line options, and then click the Color button to display the Color gallery (Figure 10–59).

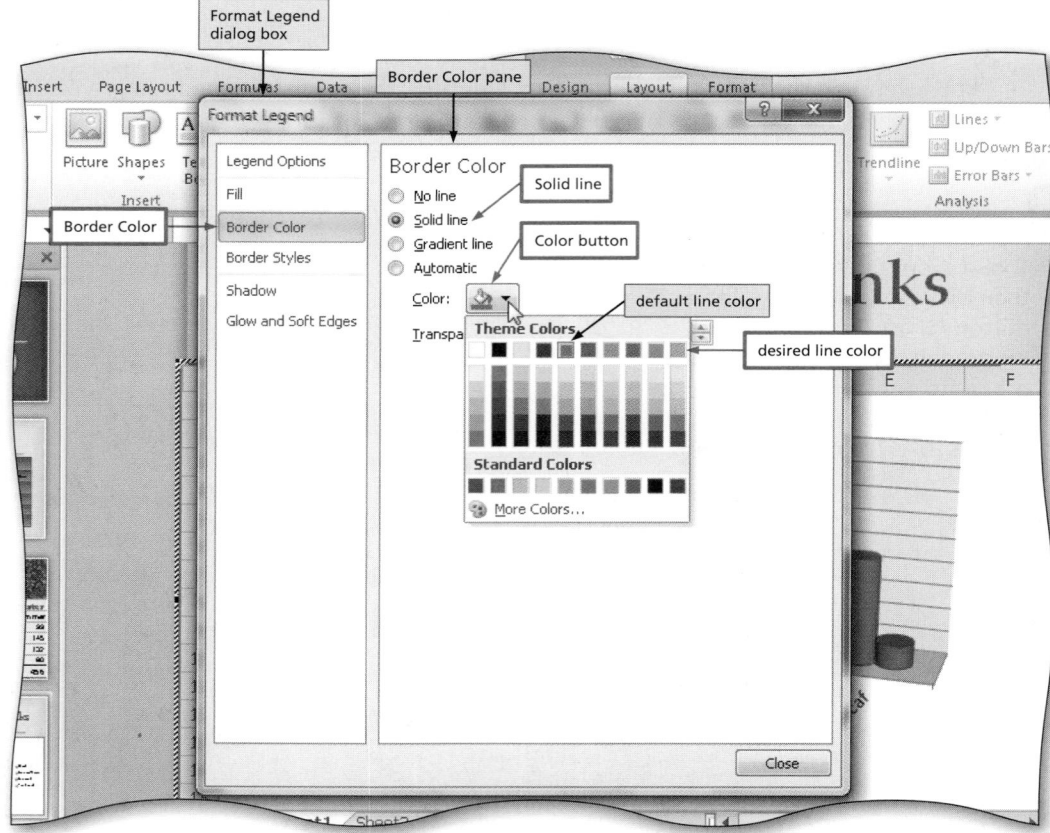

Figure 10–59

- Click Orange, Accent 6 (rightmost color in first Theme Colors row) to change the line color.

- Click Border Styles in the left panel to display the Border Styles pane and then click the Width box up arrow repeatedly until 2 pt is displayed in the Width box (Figure 10–60).

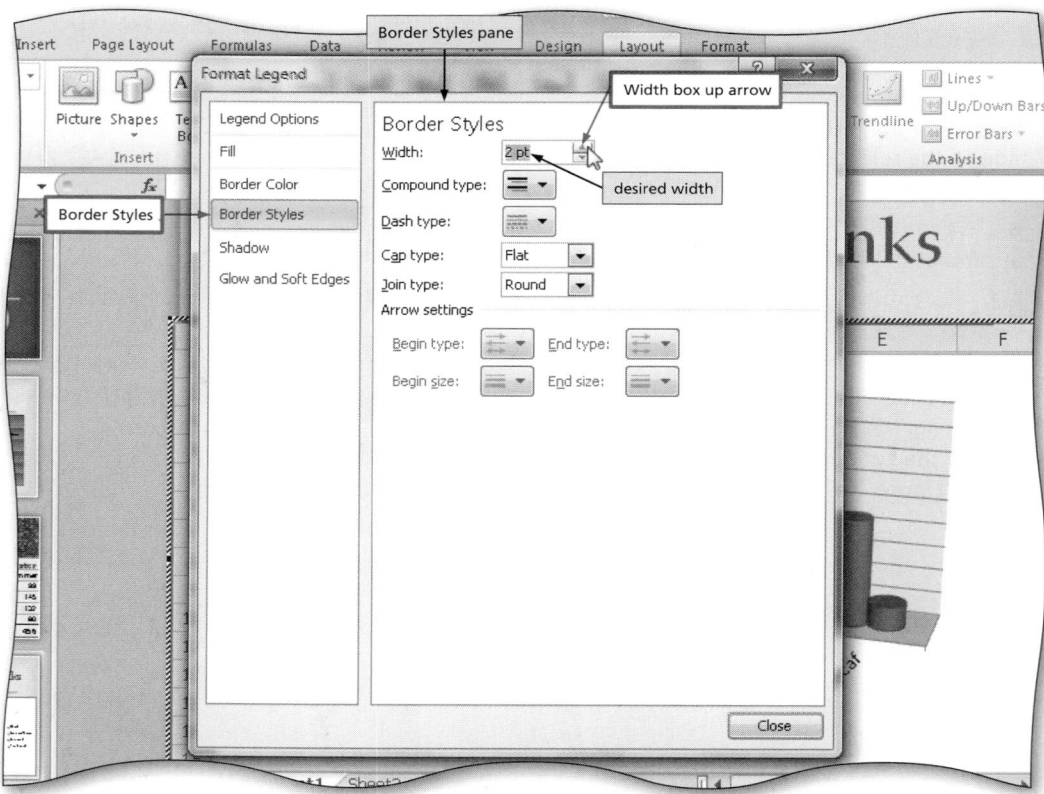

Figure 10–60

- Click Glow and Soft Edges in the left pane to display the Glow and Soft Edges pane and then click the Presets button in the Glow area to display the Glow gallery (Figure 10–61).

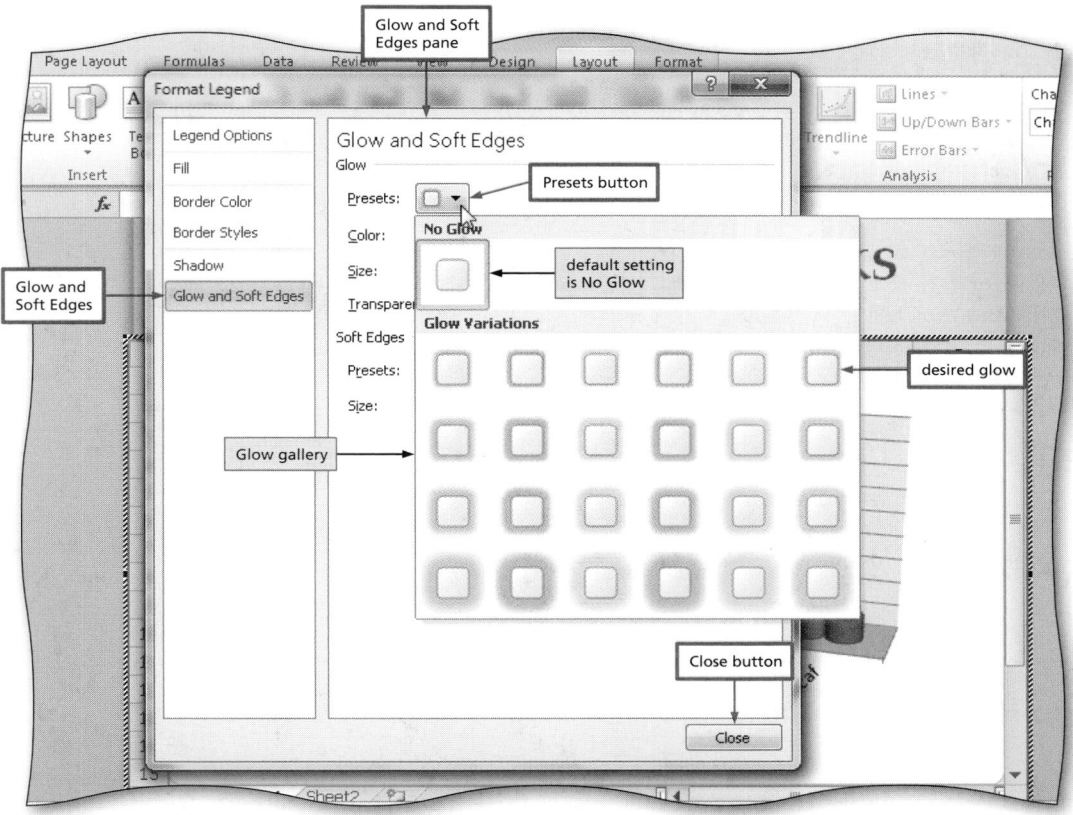

Figure 10–61

- Click Orange, 5 pt glow, Accent color 6 (last variation in first row) to select this Glow preset.

- Click the Close button (Format Legend dialog box) to apply the formatting changes to the legend.

- Drag the legend to the upper-left corner of the selection rectangle and then drag the lower sizing handle downward to increase the size of the legend, as shown in Figure 10–62.

Other Ways

1. Right-click legend, click Format Legend on shortcut menu

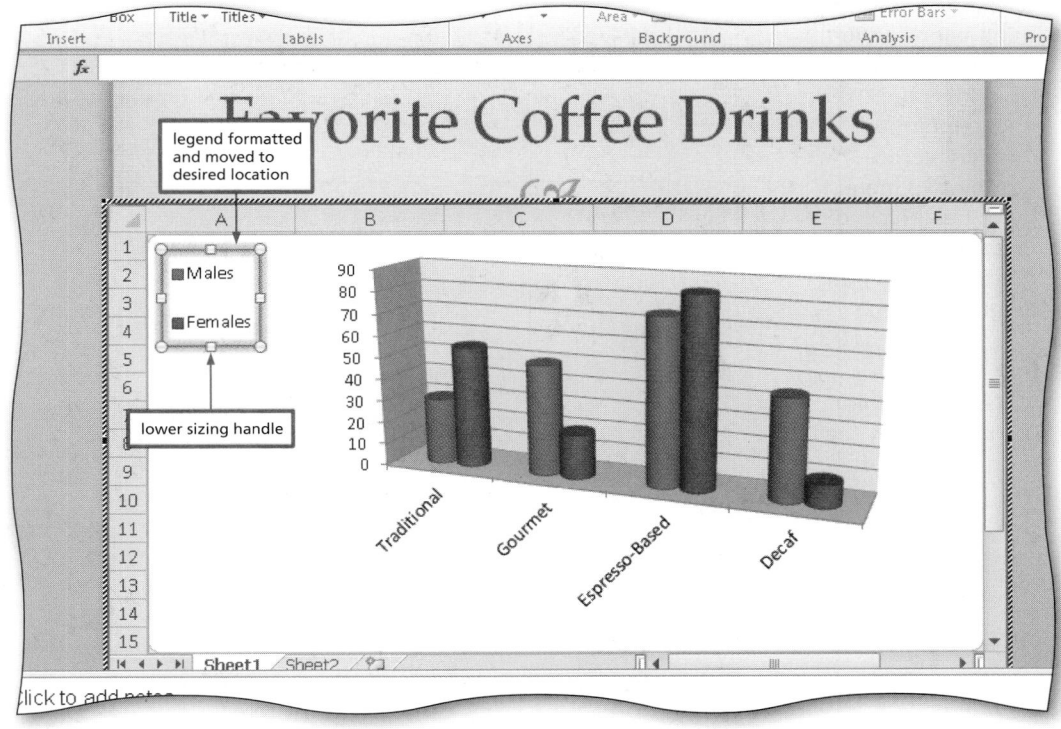

Figure 10–62

To Display Chart Labels

To increase readability, you can display the exact value of each cylinder in the chart. These values are linked to the values in the worksheet that was used to create the original chart. They update automatically when you change the data in the worksheet cells. If desired, you can change the labels' appearance and style. The following steps display the chart labels.

- Click the Data Labels button (Chart Tools Layout tab | Labels group) to display the Data Labels menu (Figure 10–63).

- Click Show to turn on the data labels above each chart cylinder.

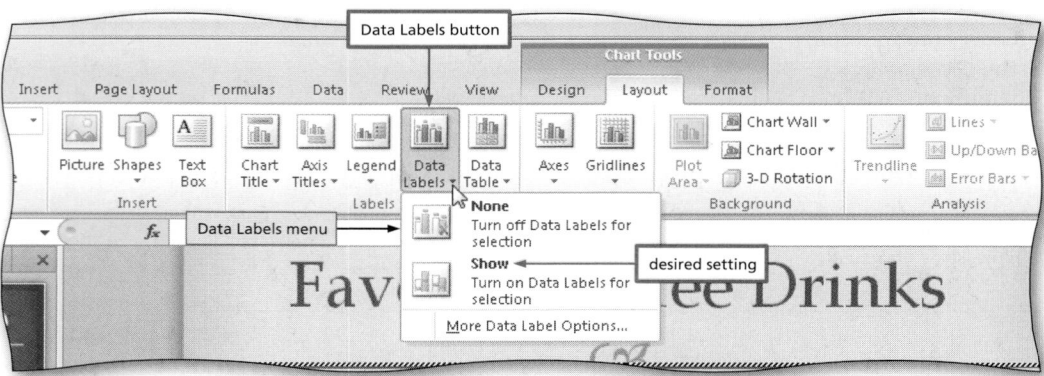

Figure 10–63

To Hide a Chart Axis

The chart labels you just added display the totals for male and female coffee drinkers' preferences. The same information is displayed in the vertical axis on the left side of the chart. To eliminate this duplication, you can choose not to display the y-axis. The following steps hide a chart axis.

- Click the Axes button (Chart Tools Layout tab | Axes group) to display the Axes menu, point to Primary Vertical Axis on the Axis menu, and then point to None on the Primary Vertical Axis menu (Figure 10–64).

- Click None to hide the vertical axis on the left side of the chart.

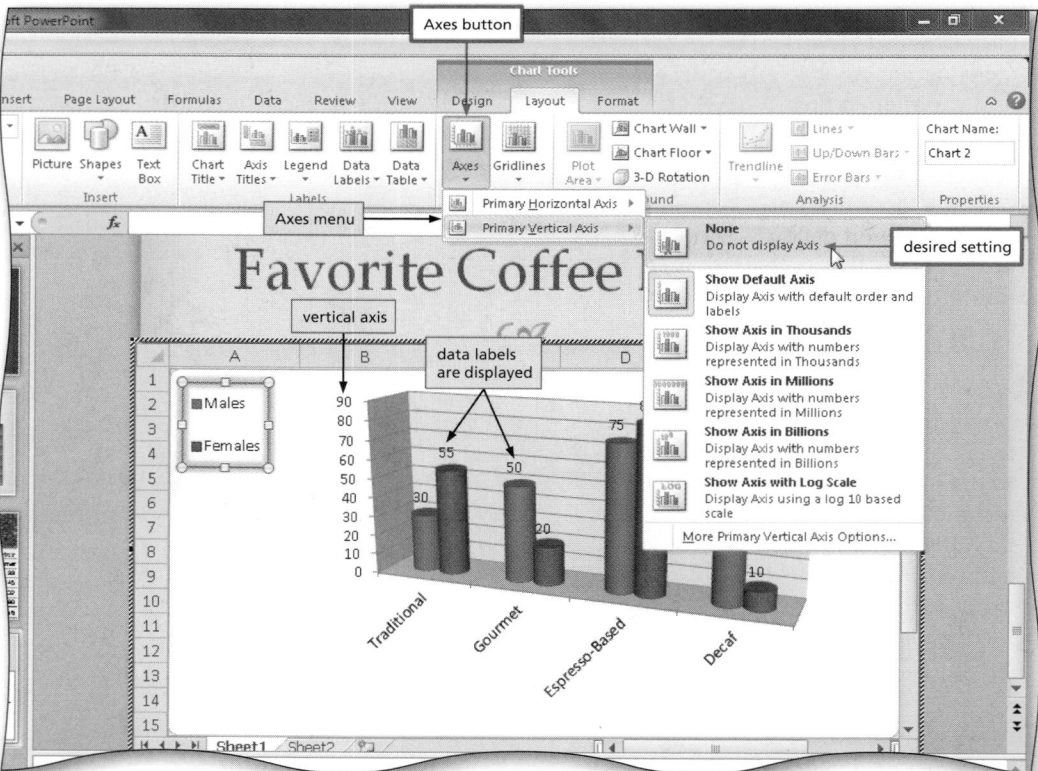

Figure 10–64

To Display Chart Gridlines

Horizontal and vertical gridlines can display on a chart to help viewers identify the values represented by each bar. The gridlines align with the horizontal and vertical axes and extend across the plot area from left to right or top to bottom. The following steps display both horizontal and vertical gridlines.

1

- Click the Gridlines button (Chart Tools Layout tab | Axes group) to display the Gridlines menu, point to Primary Horizontal Gridlines on the Gridlines menu, and then point to Major & Minor Gridlines on the Primary Horizontal Gridlines menu (Figure 10–65).

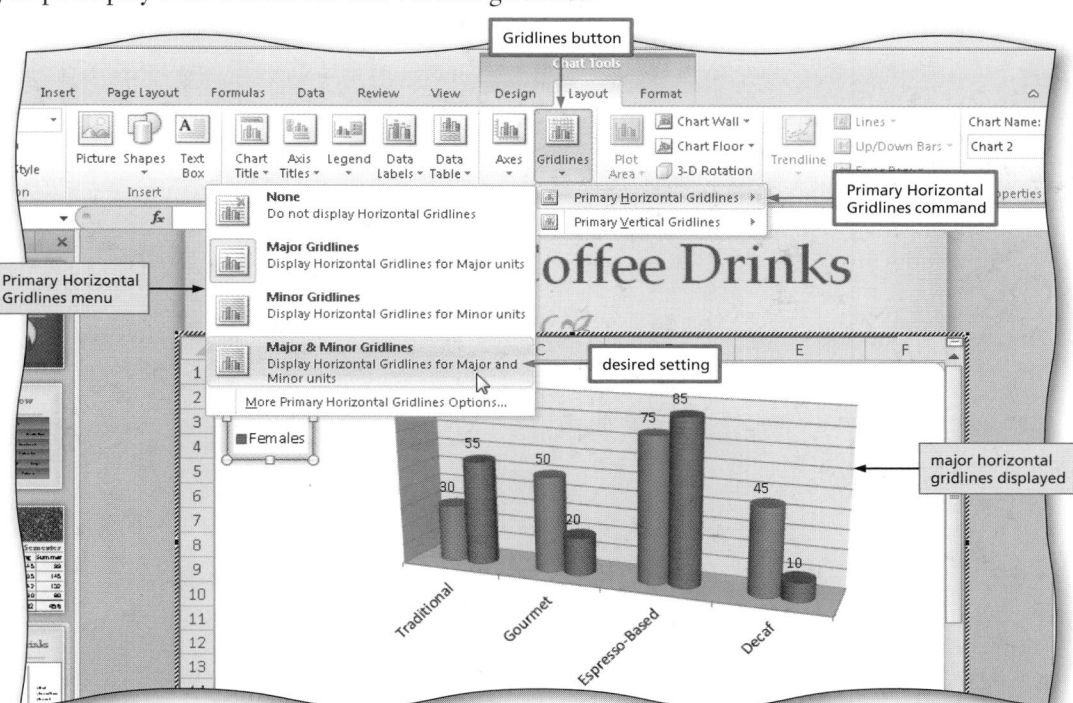

Figure 10–65

2

- Click Major & Minor Gridlines to display both types of gridline units on the left and rear sides of the chart.

- Click the Gridlines button again to display the Gridlines menu, point to Primary Vertical Gridlines on the Gridlines menu, and then point to Major Gridlines on the Primary Vertical Gridlines menu (Figure 10–66).

3

- Click Major Gridlines to display vertical gridline units on the rear side of the chart.

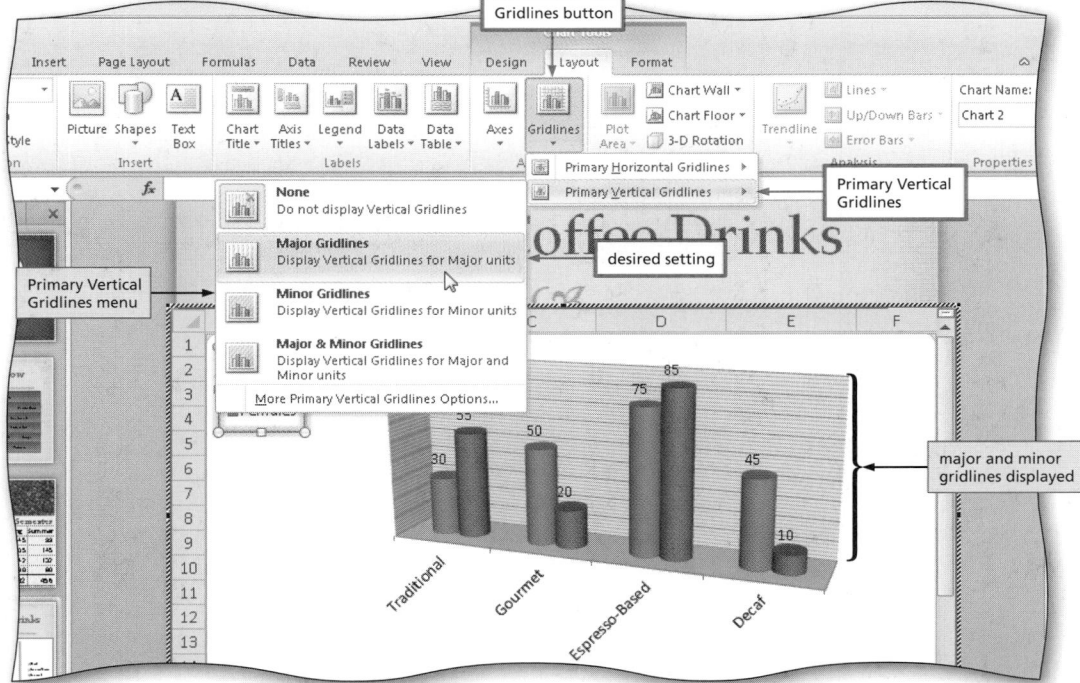

Figure 10–66

Q&A How would I hide gridlines if I did not want them to display?

Click the Gridlines button, point to either Primary Horizontal Gridlines or Primary Vertical Gridlines, and then click None.

To Format a Chart Background

The area behind the chart cylinders is called the **chart wall**, and the area below the cylinders is called the **chart floor**. Both of these chart elements are considered part of the chart background. You can modify the wall and floor in a variety of ways, including clearing all background elements. The following steps clear the chart wall and chart floor fill.

1
- Click the Chart Wall button (Chart Tools Layout tab | Background group) to display the Chart Wall menu (Figure 10–67).

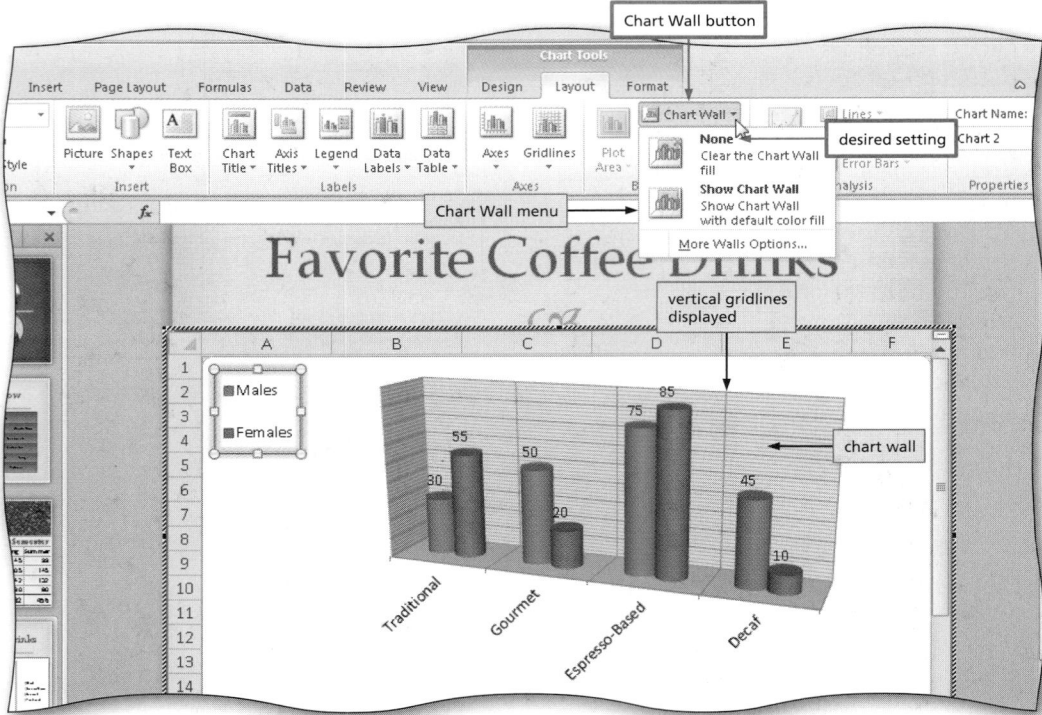

Figure 10–67

2
- Click None on the Chart Wall menu to clear the chart wall fill.

- Click the Chart Floor button (Chart Tools Layout tab | Background group) to display the Chart Floor menu (Figure 10–68).

3
- Click None on the Chart Floor menu to clear the chart floor fill.

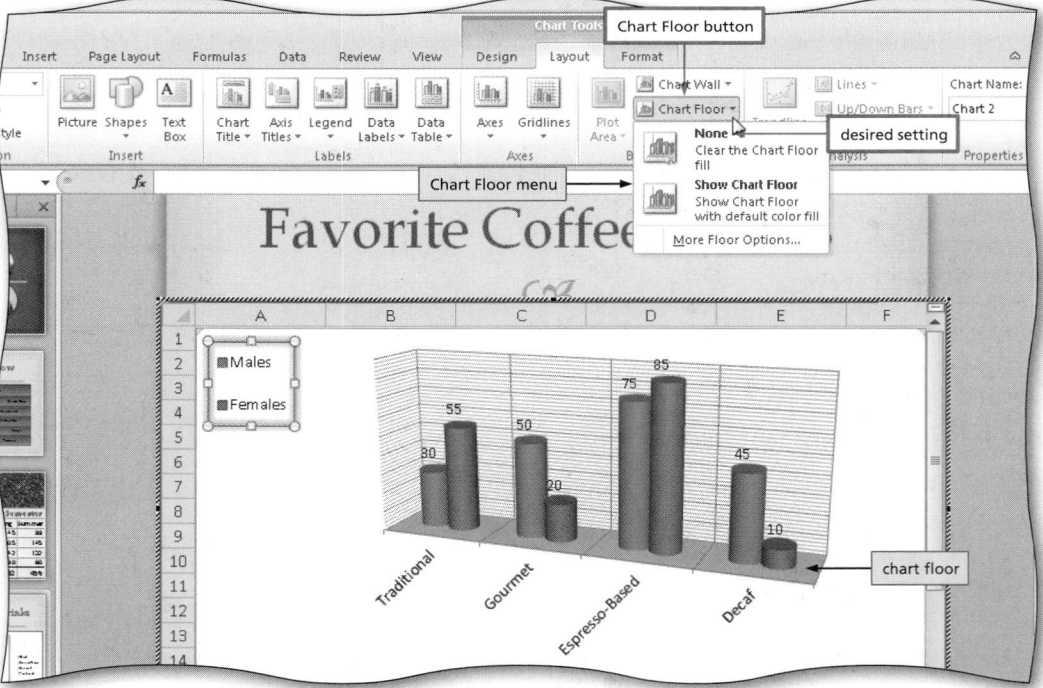

Figure 10–68

To Edit Data in a Chart

The data in Sheet 2 of the worksheet is used to create the chart on Slide 1. If you edit this data, the corresponding cylinders in the chart change height to reflect new numbers. The chart is an embedded object, so when you double-click this object to open it, Microsoft Excel opens within PowerPoint. When you modify the data and close the worksheet, the chart will reflect the changes. The original file stored on your Data Disk for Students, however, will not change. The following steps edit three cells in the worksheet.

1

- Click the Sheet 2 tab to display the worksheet.

- Click the Traditional cell for Males to make cell B2 the active cell (Figure 10–69).

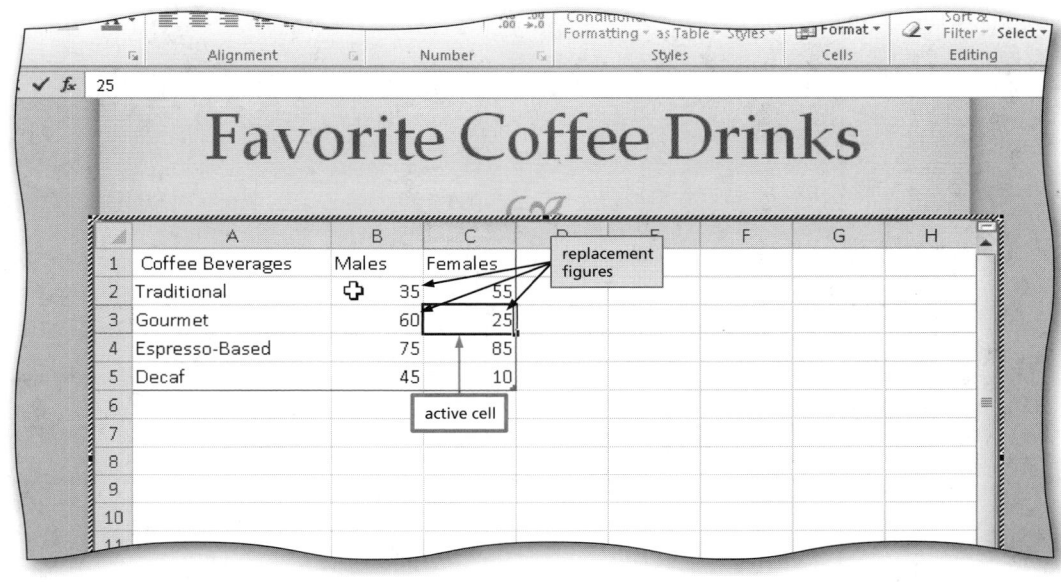

Figure 10–69

2

- Type **35** as the replacement number and then press the DOWN ARROW key to make cell B3 (Males Gourmet) the active cell.

- Type **60** as the replacement number and then press the RIGHT ARROW key to make cell C3 (Females Gourmet) the active cell.

- Type **25** as the replacement number (Figure 10–70).

Figure 10–70

- Click the Sheet 1 tab to display the updated chart (Figure 10–71).

- Click outside the selection rectangle to close Microsoft Excel and display the formatted and edited chart on Slide 4.

Q&A Can I change the range of data displayed in chart?

Yes. Click the Select Data button (Chart Tools Design tab | Data group) to display the Select Data Source dialog box. You can modify the 'Chart data range' value that is used to display the chart. You also can edit values in the Series and Category areas.

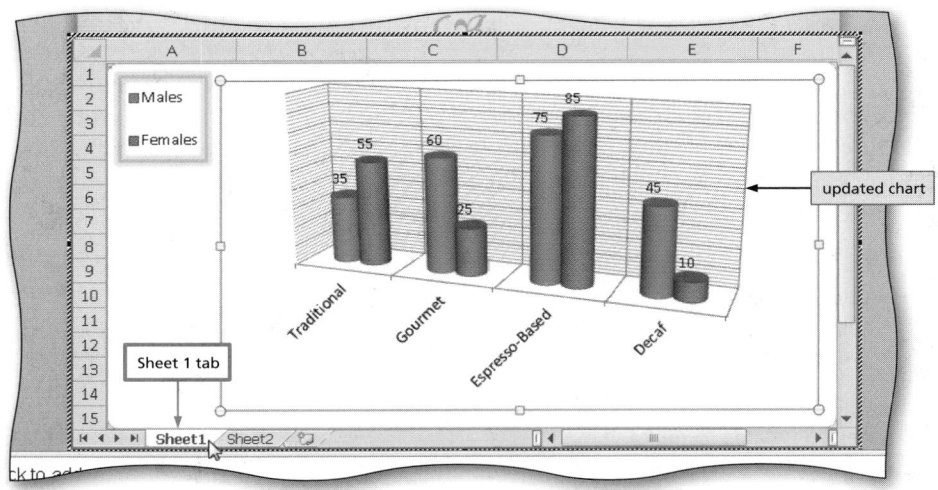

Figure 10–71

To Add a Hyperlink to a Chart

A hyperlink connects one element on a slide to another slide, presentation, picture, file, Web page, or e-mail address. Presenters use hyperlinks to display these elements to an audience. In this Java Shoppe presentation, you will create a hyperlink from the chart on Slide 4 to an Adobe Acrobat PDF document giving the recipe for a specific coffee drink. When you click the chart during a slide show, Adobe Acrobat starts and then opens this PDF. The following steps hyperlink the chart to an Adobe Acrobat document.

- With the table selected, display the Insert tab and then click the Hyperlink button (Insert tab | Links group) to display the Insert Hyperlink dialog box.

- If necessary, click the Existing File or Web Page button in the Link to area.

- If necessary, click the Current Folder button in the Look in area and then navigate to the PowerPoint Chapter 10 folder.

- Click Caffe Mocha Recipe to select this file as the hyperlink (Figure 10–72).

2

- Click the OK button (Insert Hyperlink dialog box) to insert the hyperlink.

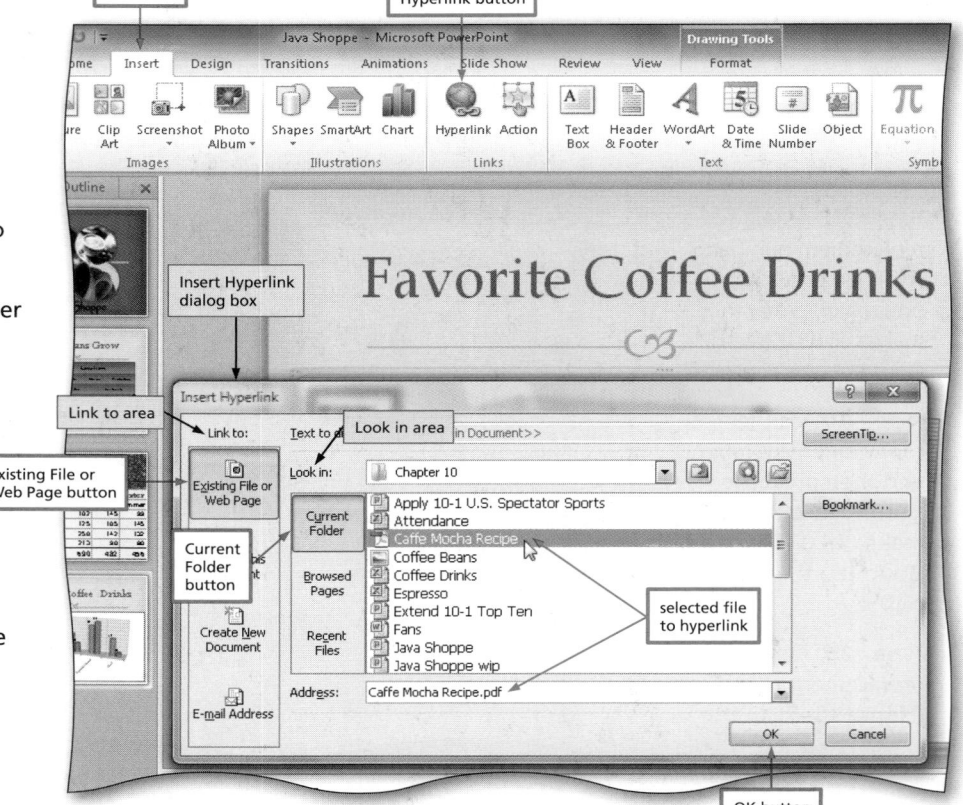

Figure 10–72

To Add a Transition between Slides

A final enhancement you will make in this presentation is to apply a transition, change the effect option, and change the transition speed. The following steps apply this transition to the presentation.

1 Apply the Flip transition in the Exciting category to all slides.

2 Change the effect option to Left.

3 Change the transition speed from 1.20 to 3.00 seconds.

To Change Document Properties

Before saving the presentation again, you want to add your name, class name, and some keywords as document properties. The following steps use the Document Information Panel to change document properties.

1 Display the Document Information Panel and then type your name as the Author property.

2 Type your course and section in the Subject property.

3 Type `coffee drinks, java shoppe, coffee beans` as the Keywords property.

4 Close the Document Information Panel.

BTW

Quick Reference
For a table that lists how to complete the tasks covered in this book using the mouse, Ribbon, shortcut menu, and keyboard, see the Quick Reference Summary at the back of this book, or visit the PowerPoint 2010 Quick Reference Web page (scsite.com/ppt2010/qr).

To Run, Print, Save, and Quit PowerPoint

The presentation now is complete. You should run the presentation, view the hyperlinked file, print the slides, save the presentation, and then quit PowerPoint.

1 Run the Java Shoppe presentation. When Slide 4 is displayed, click the chart to display the Caffe Mocha Recipe document as the hyperlinked file.

2 Click the Close button in the upper-right corner of the Adobe Acrobat window to quit the program and return to Slide 4. End the slide show.

3 Print the Java Shoppe presentation as a handout with two slides per page (Figure 10–73 on the next page).

4 Save the Java Shoppe presentation again with the same file name.

5 Quit PowerPoint, closing all open documents.

BTW

Certification
The Microsoft Office Specialist (MOS) program provides an opportunity for you to obtain a valuable industry credential — proof that you have the PowerPoint 2010 skills required by employers. For more information, visit the PowerPoint 2010 Certification Web page (scsite.com/ppt2010/cert).

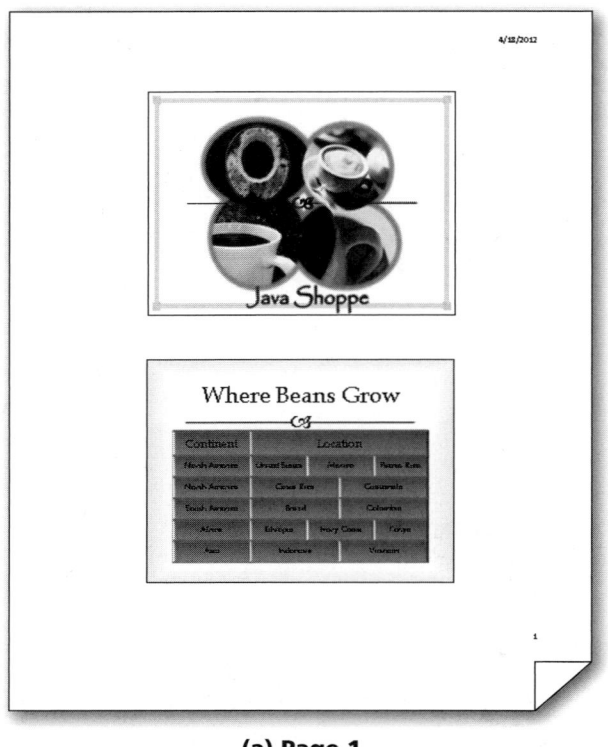

(a) Page 1

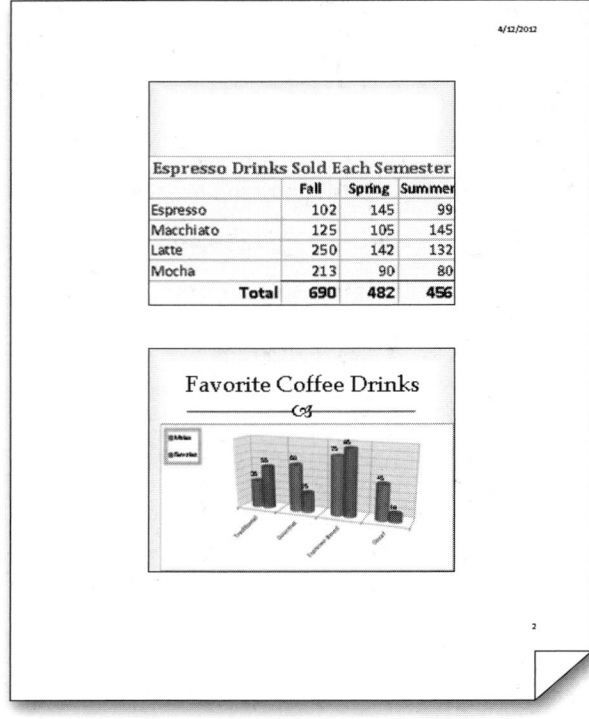

(b) Page 2

Figure 10–73

Chapter Summary

In this chapter you have learned how to develop a presentation using information you inserted from a Microsoft Word flyer and Microsoft Excel table and chart. These documents were either embedded or linked, and you edited each of them to update words or numbers. You also drew a table and enhanced this object by changing the chart type, background, gridlines, and legend. Finally, you hyperlinked an Adobe Acrobat file to the chart. The items listed below include all the new PowerPoint skills you have learned in this chapter.

1. Insert a File with Graphics and Text (PPT 598)
2. Edit an Embedded File (PPT 601)
3. Draw a Table (PPT 603)
4. Draw Table Rows (PPT 604)
5. Draw Table Columns (PPT 606)
6. Erase a Table Line (PPT 608)
7. Split a Table Column and Row (PPT 610)
8. Add Shading to a Table (PPT 612)
9. Add a Gradient Fill to a Table (PPT 613)
10. Add a Cell Bevel (PPT 614)
11. Distribute Table Rows (PPT 614)
12. Resize Table Columns and Rows (PPT 615)
13. Center the Table (PPT 617)
14. Insert a Linked Excel Worksheet (PPT 618)
15. Align a Worksheet (PPT 621)
16. Edit a Linked Worksheet (PPT 622)
17. Insert a Chart from a File (PPT 624)
18. Align a Chart (PPT 625)
19. Switch Rows and Columns in a Chart (PPT 626)
20. Change a Chart Type (PPT 627)
21. Apply a Quick Style to a Chart (PPT 628)
22. Format a Chart Legend (PPT 629)
23. Display Chart Labels (PPT 632)
24. Hide a Chart Axis (PPT 632)
25. Display Chart Gridlines (PPT 633)
26. Format a Chart Background (PPT 634)
27. Edit Data in a Chart (PPT 635)
28. Add a Hyperlink to a Chart (PPT 636)

If you have a SAM 2010 user profile, your instructor may have assigned an autogradable version of this assignment. If so, log into the SAM 2010 Web site at www.cengage.com/sam2010 to download the instruction and start files.

Learn It Online

Test your knowledge of chapter content and key terms.

Instructions: To complete the Learn It Online exercises, start your browser, click the Address bar, and then enter the Web address `scsite.com/ppt2010/learn`. When the Office 2010 Learn It Online page is displayed, click the link for the exercise you want to complete and then read the instructions.

Chapter Reinforcement TF, MC, and SA
A series of true/false, multiple choice, and short answer questions that test your knowledge of the chapter content.

Flash Cards
An interactive learning environment where you identify chapter key terms associated with displayed definitions.

Practice Test
A series of multiple choice questions that test your knowledge of chapter content and key terms.

Who Wants To Be a Computer Genius?
An interactive game that challenges your knowledge of chapter content in the style of a television quiz show.

Wheel of Terms
An interactive game that challenges your knowledge of chapter key terms in the style of the television show *Wheel of Fortune*.

Crossword Puzzle Challenge
A crossword puzzle that challenges your knowledge of key terms presented in the chapter.

Apply Your Knowledge

Reinforce the skills and apply the concepts you learned in this chapter.

Embedding and Editing an Excel Chart, and Inserting Graphics from a Word Document

Note: To complete this assignment, you will be required to use the Data Files for Students. See the inside back cover of this book for instructions on downloading the Data Files for Students, or contact your instructor for information about accessing the required files.

Instructions: Start PowerPoint. Open the presentation, Apply 10-1 U.S. Spectator Sports, located on the Data Files for Students.

The slides in this presentation provide data about the total attendance for popular U.S. spectator sports. The document you open is a partially formatted presentation. You will insert an Excel chart, edit the chart, and insert a graphic from a Word document so the slides look like the ones shown in Figure 10–74 on the next page.

Perform the following tasks:
1. You will not make any changes to Slide 1 (Figure 10–74b). Open the Attendance Excel workbook (Figure 10–74a), located on the Data Files for Students. Copy the Total Attendance bar chart to the Clipboard.
2. On Slide 2, delete the title placeholder and then paste the bar chart into the content placeholder using the Use Destination Theme & Embed Workbook pasting option. Close the Excel workbook.
3. Using the Chart Tools Design tab, apply Chart Style 26 to the chart. Using the Chart Tools Format tab, apply the Gradient fill – Olive Green, Accent 4, Reflection WordArt Style to the chart title. Resize the chart and center it on the slide, as shown in Figure 10–74c.

Continued >

STUDENT ASSIGNMENTS

Apply Your Knowledge *continued*

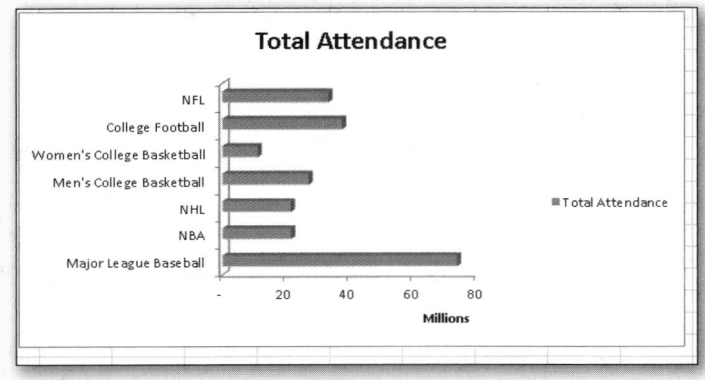

(a) Excel Workbook

(b) Slide 1

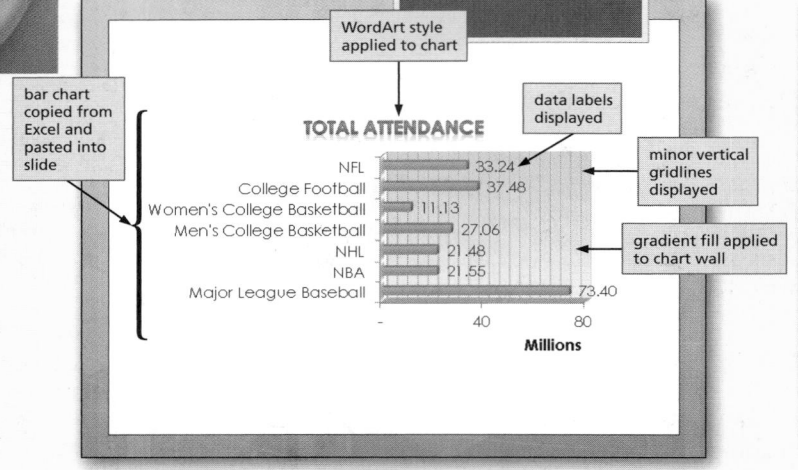

(c) Slide 2

(d) Fans Word Document

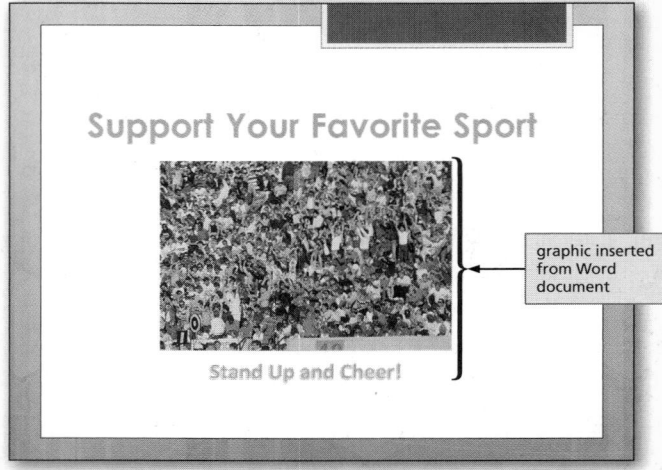

(e) Slide 3

Figure 10–74

4. Using the Chart Tools Layout tab, change the Legend label option to None for the chart. For the Primary Vertical Gridlines, display the minor gridlines. Display the data labels for the chart. Apply the Linear Gradient fill to the chart wall.

5. On Slide 3, use the Create from file option of the Insert Object dialog box to insert a graphic from the Fans Word document (Figure 10–74d). Resize the graphic and move it to the location shown in Figure 10–74e.

6. Apply the Cube transition in the Exciting group to all slides and then change the duration to 02.50 seconds.

7. Change the document properties, as specified by your instructor. Save the presentation using the file name, Apply 10-1 U.S. Spectator Sports Attendance. Submit the revised document in the format specified by your instructor.

Extend Your Knowledge

Extend the skills you learned in this chapter and experiment with new skills. You may need to use Help to complete the assignment.

Drawing and Formatting a Table

Note: To complete this assignment, you will be required to use the Data Files for Students. See the inside back cover of this book for instructions on downloading the Data Files for Students, or contact your instructor for information about accessing the required files.

Instructions: Start PowerPoint. Open the presentation, Extend 10-1 Top Ten, located on the Data Files for Students. You will draw and format a table, copy the table to another slide, and complete the tables, as shown in Figure 10–75.

Perform the following tasks:
1. You will not make any changes to Slide 1 (Figure 10–75a).

(a) Slide 1

Figure 10–75

Continued >

Extend Your Knowledge *continued*

2. Display Slide 2 and then click the Table button. Click the Draw Table button and then draw the shape of the table shown in Figure 10–75b. Change the line weight to 3 pt and the pen color to Orange, Accent 2 (Table Tools Design tab | Draw Borders group). Click the Draw Table button and then click the four main borders of the table to apply the new border settings. (*Hint:* Click each border on its inside edge.) Add four columns and six rows, similar to those shown in Figure 10–75b. If necessary, adjust the size of column 1 to look like Figure 10–75b. Select columns 2, 3, and 4, and then click Distribute Columns (Table Tools Layout tab | Cell Size group). Select all the rows and then click Distribute Rows.

3. Apply an Ice Blue, Background 2 Shading to all the cells, as shown in Figure 10–75b.

4. On Slide 2, use Table 10–1 to enter the headings and data for the top five cities. Align the text of all cells to center vertically. Center the first row and then change the font size to 20 and the font color to White. Center the first column and then change the font size to 20 and the font color to White. Center the last column. Change the font for all cells to Calibri. For all cells except the first row and first column, center the text, and bold the text in the cells.

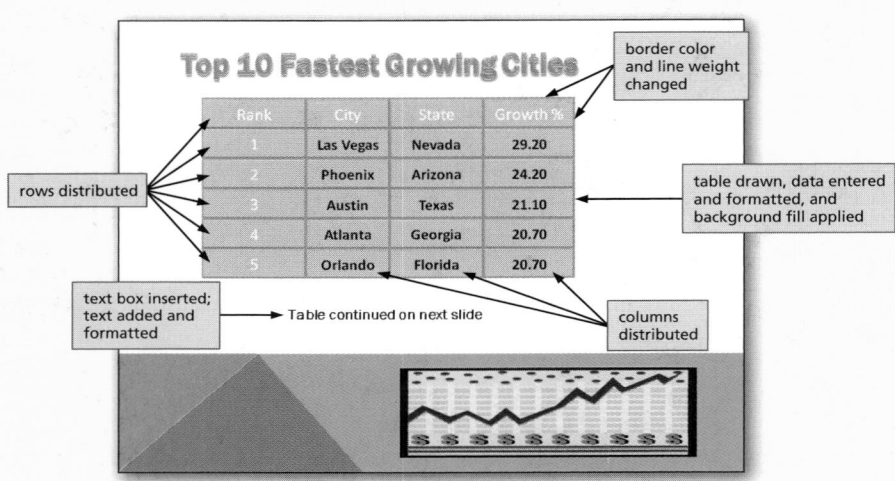

(b) Slide 2

Figure 10–75 (Continued)

Table 10–1 Top 10 Fastest Growing Cities			
Rank	City	State	Growth %
1	Las Vegas	Nevada	29.20
2	Phoenix	Arizona	24.20
3	Austin	Texas	21.10
4	Atlanta	Georgia	20.70
5	Orlando	Florida	20.70
6	Charlotte	North Carolina	19.00
7	Houston	Texas	17.50
8	Dallas	Texas	16.30
9	Sacramento	California	15.00
10	Jacksonville	Florida	13.80

5. Insert a text box below the table and type **Table continued on next slide** in the box. Center the text, bold it, and then move the text box to the location shown in Figure 10–75b. Copy the table and the text box from Slide 2 to Slide 3.

6. On Slide 3, replace the data in the table with the bottom five cities' data shown in Table 10–1. If necessary, adjust size of columns so the table appears as shown. Replace the text in the text box with **Table continued from previous slide** and move the text box above the table, as shown in Figure 10–75c.

7. Change the transition from Push to Clock in the Exciting area and change the duration to 03:00 seconds.

8. Change the document properties, as specified by your instructor. Save the presentation using the file name, Extend 10-1 Top Ten U.S. Cities.

9. Submit the revised document in the format specified by your instructor.

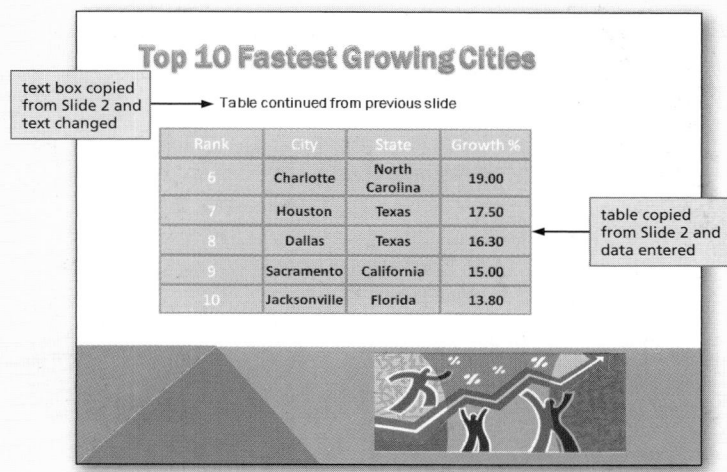

(c) Slide 3

Figure 10–75 (Continued)

Make It Right

Analyze a presentation and correct all errors and/or improve the design.

Changing a Chart and Editing a Table

Note: To complete this assignment, you will be required to use the Data Files for Students. See the inside back cover of this book for instructions on downloading the Data Files for Students, or contact your instructor for information about accessing the required files.

Instructions: Start PowerPoint. Open the presentation, Make It Right 10-1 U.S. Longest Rivers, located on the Data Files for Students.

Correct the formatting problems and errors in the presentation while keeping in mind the guidelines presented in this chapter.

Continued >

Make It Right *continued*

STUDENT ASSIGNMENTS

Perform the following tasks:

1. You will not make any changes to Slide 1 (Figure 10–76a). On Slide 2 (Figure 10–76b), select the second column. Split the column into two columns using the Split Cells button. Select rows 2–10 in column 2. Using the Format Painter, copy the formatting to rows 2–10 in column 3. Enter the data from Table 10–2 in the second column. If necessary, adjust the size of the table. Distribute the columns so that each column has the same width. Add an Offset Diagonal Top Left shadow effect to the table. *Hint:* Click the Effects button (Table Tools Design tab | Table Styles group). Change the size of the Blur shadow to 7 pt.

(a) Slide 1

Figure 10–76

Table 10–2 Longest Rivers Data
Runs Along
10 states
5 states
1 state
3 states
2 states
3 states
2 states
2 states
3 states
5 states

2. On Slide 3 (Figure 10–76c), change the chart type of the line chart to the Clustered Horizontal Cylinder bar chart. Switch the row and column data for the chart. Apply the Style 34 chart style to the chart. Select the chart legend, click the Shape Outline button arrow, and then apply a light blue (seventh in Standard Colors row) border around the legend.

3. For all slides, apply the Ripple transition, change the Effect Option to From Bottom-Left, and then change the duration to 02:50 seconds.

4. Change the document properties, as specified by your instructor. Save the presentation using the file name, Make It Right 10-1 U.S. Longest Rivers in Miles.

5. Submit the revised document in the format specified by your instructor.

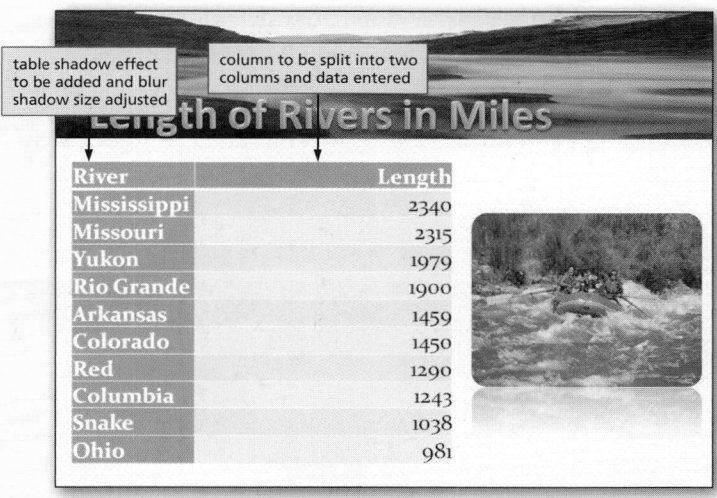

(b) Slide 2

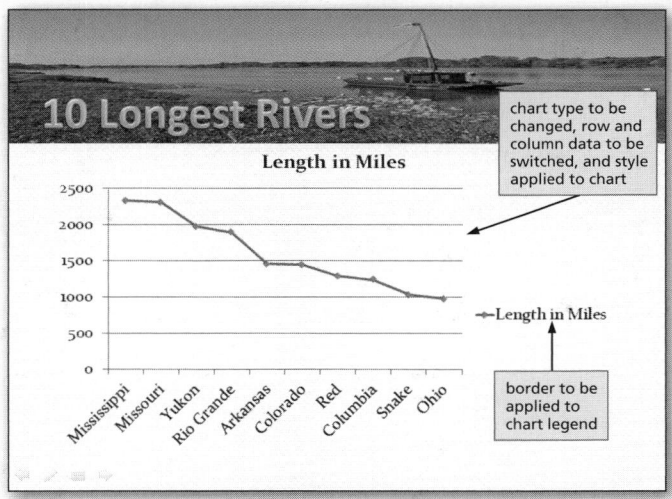

(c) Slide 3

Figure 10–76 (Continued)

In the Lab

Design and/or create a presentation using the guidelines, concepts, and skills presented in this chapter. Labs 1, 2, and 3 are listed in order of increasing difficulty.

Lab 1: Linking a Chart from a File, Embedding a File, and Editing an Embedded File
Note: To complete this assignment, you will be required to use the Data Files for Students. See the inside back cover of this book for instructions on downloading the Data Files for Students or contact your instructor for information about accessing the required files.

Problem: You are doing a report on tornadoes for a class project. You have acquired data on the top five states with the most tornadoes as well as the top five states with the most severe tornadoes. Using this data, you create the slides shown in Figure 10–77.

Perform the following tasks:
1. Open the presentation, Lab 10-1 Tornadoes, located on the Data Files for Students. You will not make any changes to Slide 1 (Figure 10–77a).

(a) Slide 1

Figure 10–77

2. Open the Severe Tornadoes Excel workbook located on the Data Files for Students (Figure 10–77b). Copy the chart to the Clipboard. On Slide 2 (Figure 10–77c), select the content placeholder and then paste the chart, keeping the source formatting and linking it. In the Severe Tornadoes Excel workbook, change the average number of storms for Oklahoma to `17`. Save and close the Excel workbook. If necessary, adjust the size of the chart and move it to the location shown in Figure 10–77c.

3. Select the chart title on Slide 2. Click the Hyperlink button (Insert tab | Links group), enter the following URL as the address, and then click the OK button: `http://www.nssl.noaa` `.gov/edu/safety/tornadoguide.html`

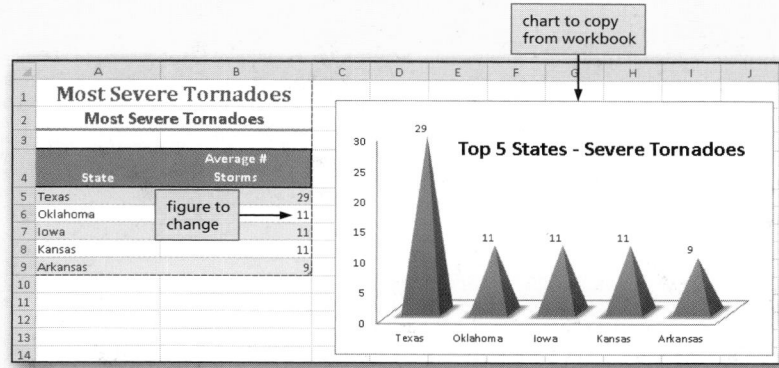

(b) Severe Tornadoes Excel Workbook

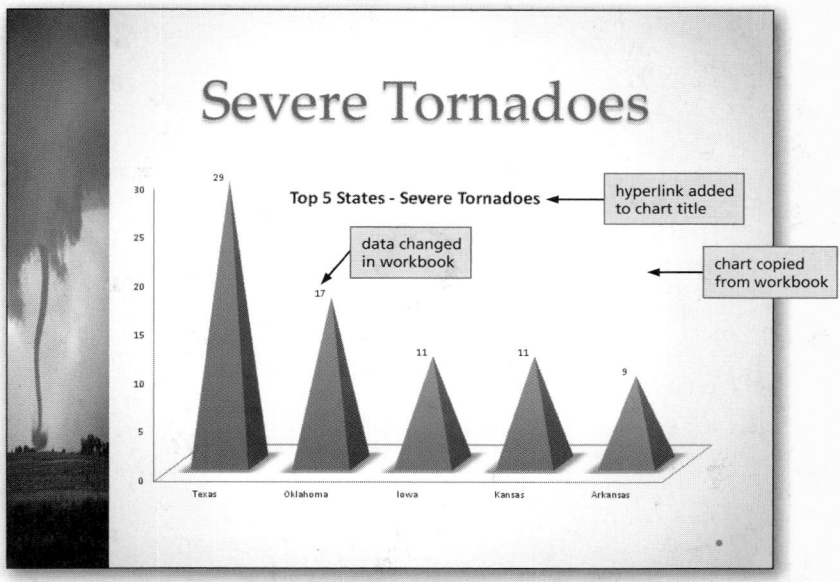

(c) Slide 2

Figure 10–77 (Continued)

Continued >

In the Lab continued

4. On Slide 3, select the content placeholder and then embed the Tornadoes Excel workbook (Figure 10–77d), located on the Data Files for Students. Edit the Violent Storms column in the embedded file by entering **29** for Texas, **7** for Oklahoma, **17** for Florida, **11** for Kansas, and **7** for Nebraska, then click outside the worksheet (Figure 10–77e).

5. Apply the Vortex transition and change the duration to 03:00 seconds for all slides.

6. Change the document properties, as specified by your instructor. Save the presentation using the file name, Lab 10-1 Tornadoes – Forces of Nature.

7. Submit the revised document in the format specified by your instructor.

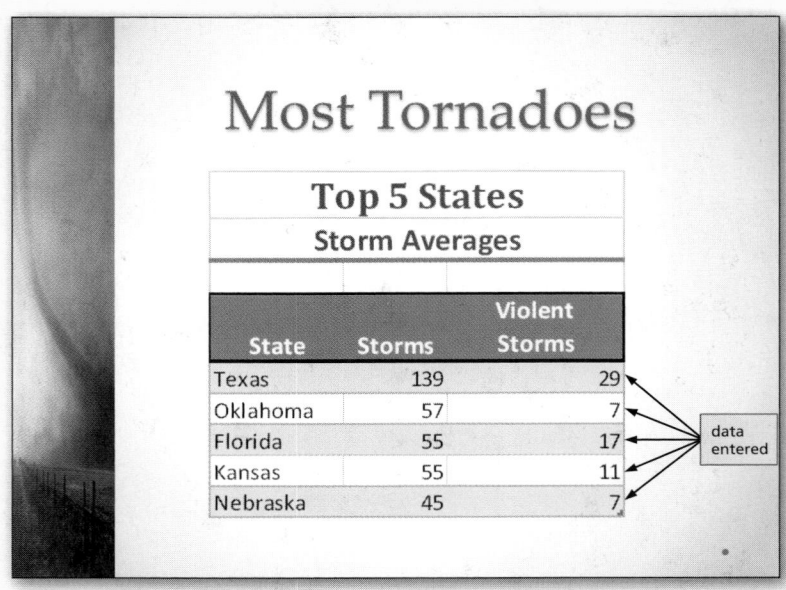

	A	B	C
1	**Top 5 States**		
2	**Storm Averages**		
3			
4	**State**	**Storms**	**Violent Storms**
5	Texas	139	
6	Oklahoma	57	
7	Florida	55	
8	Kansas	55	
9	Nebraska	45	
10			

data to be entered

(d) Tornadoes Excel Workbook

Most Tornadoes

Top 5 States		
Storm Averages		
State	**Storms**	**Violent Storms**
Texas	139	29
Oklahoma	57	7
Florida	55	17
Kansas	55	11
Nebraska	45	7

data entered

(e) Slide 3

Figure 10–77 (Continued)

In the Lab

Lab 2: Linking and Editing a File, Changing a Chart Type, and Inserting a Graphic from a File

Note: To complete this assignment, you will be required to use the Data Files for Students. See the inside back cover of this book for instructions on downloading the Data Files for Students or contact your instructor for information about accessing the required files.

Problem: Sports have been a part of society since at least 4000 BC and are played throughout the world. You have gathered data about 10 popular sports in the United States for males and females who are seven years of age and older. You decide to create a presentation to display the results you have found. You create the slides shown in Figure 10–78 using files located on the Data Files for Students.

Perform the following tasks:
1. Open the presentation, Lab 10-2 U.S. Sports, located on the Data Files for Students. You will not make any changes to Slide 1 (Figure 10–78a).
2. On Slide 2, select the content placeholder and then insert the Excel workbook (Figure 10–78b on the next page) by linking to the Popular Sports workbook, located on the Data Files for Students.

(a) Slide 1

Figure 10–78

Continued >

STUDENT ASSIGNMENTS

In the Lab continued

3. Edit the Popular Sports workbook. Change the walking female percentage to **38%**. Change the bicycling male percentage to **25%**. Change the golfing male percentage to **18%**. Save and close the workbook. The percentages in the table should now match those shown in Figure 10–78c. If they do not match, right-click the table and then click Update Link on the shortcut menu. If necessary, adjust the size of the table and move it to the location shown in Figure 10–78c.

workbook to insert into Slide 2

	A	B	C
1	Sport	Male	Female
2	Walking	23%	38%
3	Swimming	26%	26%
4	Bicycling	25%	19%
5	Weight Training	19%	19%
6	Camping	20%	17%
7	Fishing	24%	11%
8	Bowling	17%	15%
9	Basketball	18%	6%
10	Hiking	12%	8%
11	Golfing	18%	5%
12			

data changed in workbook

(b) Popular Sports Excel Workbook

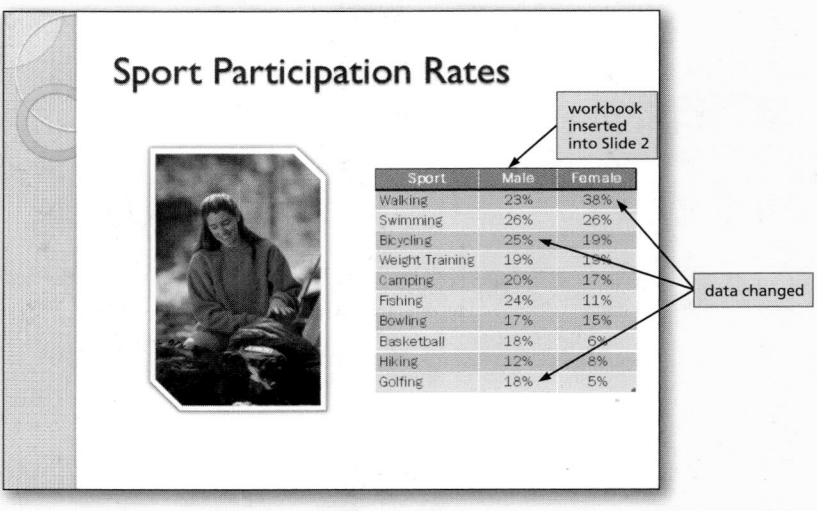

(c) Slide 2

Figure 10–78 (Continued)

4. On Slide 3, change the chart type of the column chart to Clustered Bar in 3-D. Change the chart layout to Layout 7. Show Major horizontal and, if necessary, Major & Minor vertical gridlines. Change the vertical axis title to `Sport Activity` and the horizontal axis title to `Participation Rate`. Put a black border around the legend. The chart should appear as shown in Figure 10–78d.

5. On Slide 4, select the content placeholder and insert the graphic from the Reasons Word document. If necessary, adjust the size of the graphic and move it to the location shown in Figure 10–78e.

6. Apply the Shape transition and change the duration to 02.25 seconds for all slides.

7. Change the document properties, as specified by your instructor. Save the presentation using the file name, Lab 10-2 Most Popular U.S. Sports Activities.

8. Submit the revised document in the format specified by your instructor.

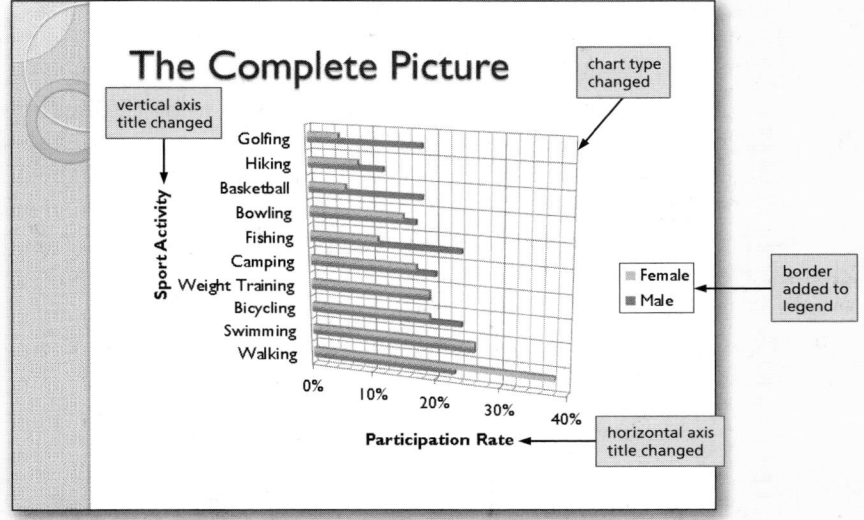

(d) Slide 3

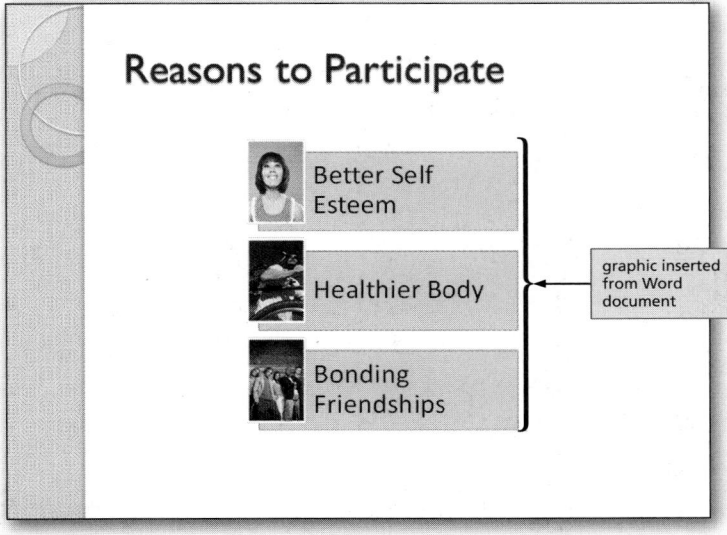

(e) Slide 4

Figure 10–78 (Continued)

In the Lab

Lab 3: Drawing and Formatting a Table, Inserting and Formatting a Bar Chart, and Inserting an Excel Spreadsheet

Note: To complete this assignment, you will be required to use the Data Files for Students. See the inside back cover of this book for instructions on downloading the Data Files for Students or contact your instructor for information about accessing the required files.

Problem: As part of your work-study program for an aquatic park, you are tasked with creating a presentation about the world's oceans and seas. You have collected data on the relative sizes of the oceans and seas and will use them in your presentation. You create the presentation shown in Figure 10–79.

Perform the following tasks:
1. Open the presentation, Lab 10-3 Oceans, located on the Data Files for Students. You will not make any changes to Slide 1 (Figure 10–79a).
2. On Slide 2 (Figure 10–79b), delete the content placeholder using the Cut button and then draw a table that has two columns and 10 rows. Select all the rows and then distribute the rows (Table Tools Layout tab | Cell Size group). Enter the data for rows 2–10, using the data from the first nine rows of Table 10–3. Right-align the text in the second column. Erase the divider between the cells in the first row. Enter **Area in Square Miles** in the first row, center this text, bold it, and then designate it as the header row. Apply the Light Style 2 - Accent 1 table style to the table. If necessary, adjust the size of the table, as shown in Figure 10–79b.
3. Insert a text box below the table and then type **Continued on next slide** in the box. Center the text and then move the text box to the location shown.

(a) Slide 1

Figure 10–79

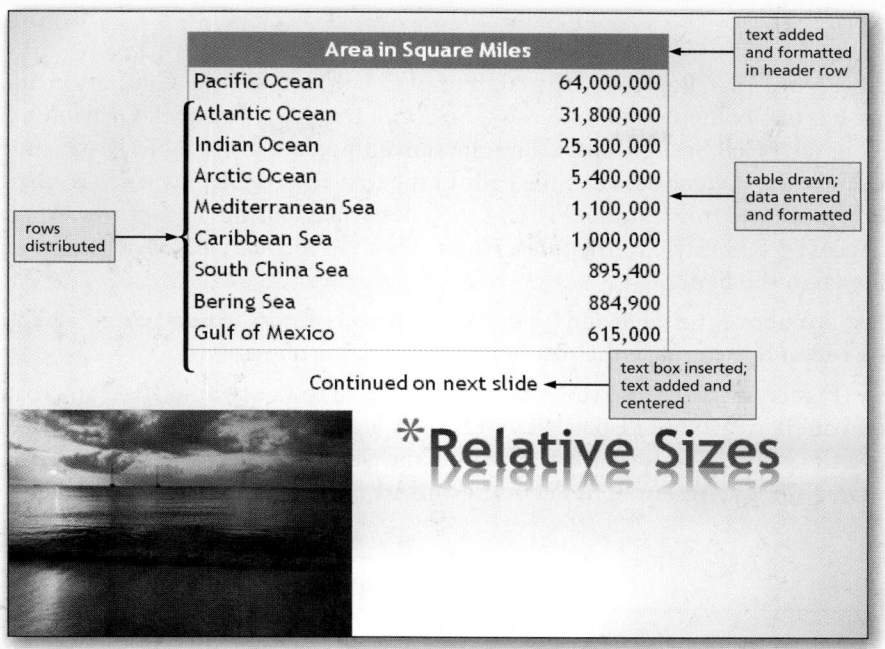

(b) Slide 2

Figure 10–79 (Continued)

Table 10–3 Table Data for Slides 2 and 3	
Pacific Ocean	64,000,000
Atlantic Ocean	31,800,000
Indian Ocean	25,300,000
Arctic Ocean	5,400,000
Mediterranean Sea	1,100,000
Caribbean Sea	1,000,000
South China Sea	895,400
Bering Sea	884,900
Gulf of Mexico	615,000
Okhotsk Sea	613,800
East China Sea	482,300
Hudson Bay	475,800
Japan Sea	389,100
Andaman Sea	308,100
North Sea	222,100
Red Sea	169,100
Baltic Sea	163,000

Continued >

In the Lab *continued*

4. On Slide 3 (Figure 10–79c), delete the content placeholder using the Cut button and then draw a table that has two columns and nine rows. Select all the rows, and click Distribute Rows (Table Tools Layout tab | Cell Size group). Using the remaining data from Table 10–3, enter the data for rows 2–9. Erase the divider between the cells in the first row. Enter `Area in Square Miles` in the first row, center this text, bold it, and then designate it as the header row. Apply the Light Style 2 – Accent 1 table style to the table. Right-align the second column. Position and size the table as shown in the figure.

5. Insert a text box above the table and type `Continued from previous slide` in the box. Center the text and then move the text box to the location shown.

6. On Slide 4 (Figure 10–79d), use the data in the first five rows of Table 10–3 to create a Clustered Bar in 3-D bar chart. Do not display a chart title or legend. Display the major horizontal gridlines and remove the primary vertical axis title. Apply the Style 27 chart style to the chart. Apply the Gradient Fill – Green, Accent 4, Reflection WordArt Style to the vertical axis labels.

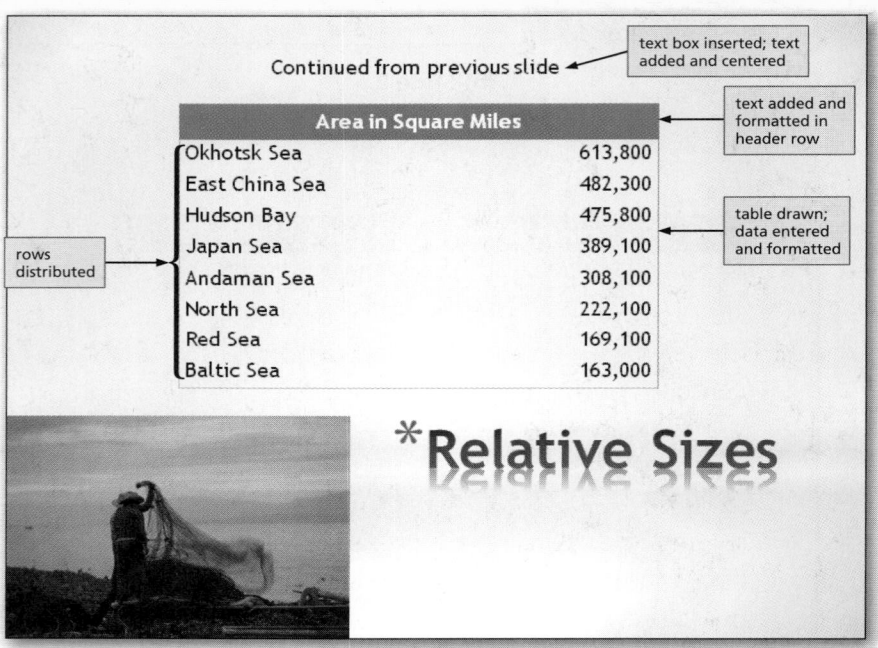

(c) Slide 3

Figure 10–79 (Continued)

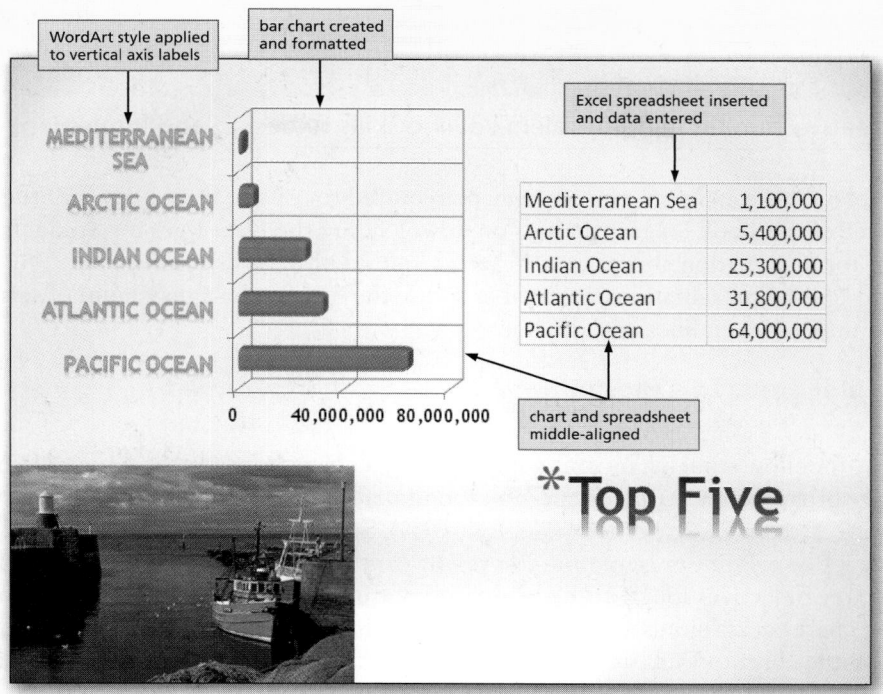

(d) Slide 4

Figure 10–79 (Continued)

7. Insert an Excel spreadsheet on Slide 4 and enter the five largest ocean names and square mileage data, as shown in the figure. Select the bar chart and spreadsheet and middle-align them on the slide as shown in the figure.

8. Apply the Doors transition and change the duration to 02.75 seconds for all slides.

9. Change the document properties, as specified by your instructor. Save the presentation using the file name, Lab 10-3 Oceans and Seas.

10. Submit the revised document in the format specified by your instructor.

Cases and Places

Apply your creative thinking and problem-solving skills to design and implement a solution.

Note: To complete these assignments, you may be required to use the Data Files for Students. See the inside back cover of this book for instructions on downloading the Data Files for Students, or contact your instructor for information about accessing the required files.

As you design the presentations, remember to use the 7 × 7 rule: a maximum of seven words on a line and a maximum of seven lines on one slide.

1: Designing and Creating a Presentation about Studying Abroad

Academic

While talking with fellow students in your study group, you have learned that some of them have chosen to study abroad. Researching online, you found that the most popular countries where U.S. students study are Mexico (7%), France (8%), Italy (9%), Spain (9%), and Great Britain (24%). You decide to create a PowerPoint presentation to present your findings at your next study group meeting. Apply at least three objectives found at the beginning of this chapter to develop the presentation, including using chart backgrounds and adding hyperlinks to chart elements. You can hyperlink the country labels in the chart to Web sites about each country. Use pictures and diagrams from Office.com if they are appropriate for this topic. Be sure to check spelling.

2: Designing and Creating a Presentation about Why People Travel

Personal

You enjoy traveling, and you have been curious about the purpose people have for traveling in general. You have researched and found that, according to surveys done by the U.S. Travel Data Center and Nation Travel Survey, the reasons reported for trips have been ranked in terms of millions of trips per year. Pleasure is responsible for 434 million trips, business or conventions for 220 million trips, and other reasons for 34 million trips. You decide to create a PowerPoint presentation to explain the reasons to your family members, who have been asking about why people travel. Apply at least three objectives found at the beginning of this chapter to develop the presentation, including drawing a table and arranging table columns and rows. You can also include a chart displaying the number of times you have traveled over the past five years (3, 7, 5, 9, and 6 trips, respectively). Use pictures and diagrams from Office.com if they are appropriate for this topic or use your personal digital pictures. Be sure to check spelling.

3: Designing and Creating a Presentation about Recycled Tires

Professional

You are employed as a customer service representative at a local tire store. Customers often ask you about recycling their old tires. You explain that instead of being taken to a landfill, more than 50 million worn tires each year are processed into tire crumb, which is a granulated product used to manufacture footwear, playground equipment, trash cans, and asphalt. To better explain the benefits of tire recycling, you will prepare a presentation that explains the uses of recycled rubber. Apply at least three objectives found at the beginning of this chapter to develop the presentation, and include a chart showing recycled tire components and a table with the countries that produce natural rubber. Use pictures from Office.com if they are appropriate for this topic or use your personal digital pictures. Be sure to check spelling.

11 | Organizing Slides and Creating a Photo Album

Objectives

You will have mastered the material in this chapter when you can:

- Create a section break
- Rename a section
- Reorder a section
- Create a custom slide show
- Set up a custom size
- Create a photo album
- Reorder pictures in a photo album
- Adjust the quality of pictures in a photo album

- Add captions to pictures in a photo album
- Use the Research task pane to look up information
- Change slide orientation
- Copy and compress a video file
- E-mail a presentation
- Create a video from a presentation

11 | Organizing Slides and Creating a Photo Album

Introduction

Using Photographs
The adage, "A picture is worth a thousand words," is relevant when PowerPoint slides are displayed to an audience. One picture can evoke emotions and create a connection between the speaker and the listeners. A carefully selected image with an engaging message conveys a message that your audience will remember long after the presentation has ended.

Sharing photographs and videos has become a part of our everyday lives. We often use digital cameras and visit online social media Web sites to share our adventures, special occasions, and business activities. The presentations can be organized into sections so that particular slides are shown to specific audiences. For example, one large presentation created for freshmen orientation can be divided into one section for registration, another for financial aid, and a third for campus activities, and each section would be shown to different audiences.

In addition, PowerPoint's ability to create a photo album allows you to organize and distribute your pictures by adding interesting layouts, vibrant backgrounds, and meaningful captions. These photo albums can be e-mailed, published to a Web site, or turned into a video to distribute to friends and business associates, who do not need PowerPoint installed on their computers to view your file.

Project — Presentation with Sections and a Photo Album

Gardening Benefits Health
Gardening as a hobby improves physical and mental health. Planting, weeding, and digging in the garden give a cardiovascular workout that can burn up to 600 calories per hour. These activities also increase endurance, strength, and flexibility. In addition, working in a garden can reduce stress, especially if plants with soothing scents and colors are grown.

Gardening is a hobby that provides relaxation, satisfaction, and beautification to millions of people in a wide variety of climates. Many communities have organized gardening clubs where members share advice and show photographs of their beautiful yards and flower beds. The Granville Garden Club officers are planning their annual spring meeting where they will announce the winners of the photo contest and display pictures of members' gardening accomplishments.

The presentation you create in this chapter (Figure 11–1) will be shown at the spring meeting. You divide the slide show into sections for the photo contest winners (Figure 11–1a), the members' favorite perennials, favorite annuals, and favorite spring bulbs. You then create a photo album, add members' pictures and make adjustments to brightness and contrast, and add captions (Figures 11–1b and 11–1c). You also create a second photo album with black-and-white images (Figure 11–1d). In addition, you create two slides with a custom size to use as a marketing tool to promote the annual meeting and insert a video file on one of the slides (Figure 11–1e). You then e-mail the meeting announcement file to a member and also convert another file to a video so that members who do not have PowerPoint installed on their computers can view the photo contest winners' pictures in the presentation.

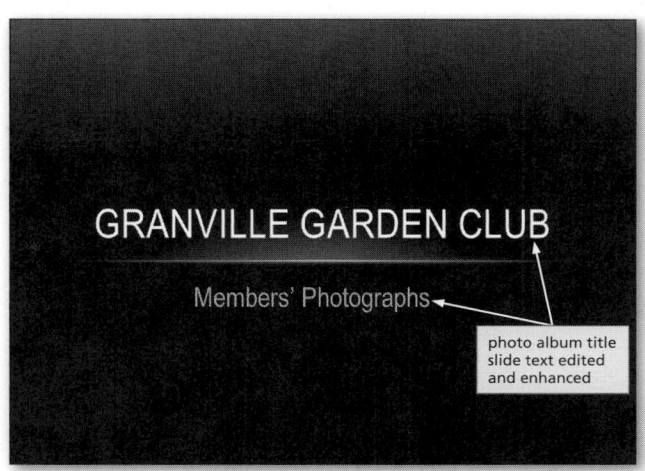

Hardcover document theme

text inserted into placeholder for Section Header layout

(a) Photo Contest Section Slide

photo album title slide text edited and enhanced

(b) Photo Album Title Slide

photo enhanced

caption edited

(c) Photo Album Slide

black-and-white picture in photo album

(d) Black-and-White Photo Album Slide

custom size slide has portrait orientation

video copied and compressed

(e) Custom Size Slide

Figure 11–1

BTW

Designing Postcards
Marketing personnel have found that a postcard is an effective means of sending information to a specific audience. The customary 6″ × 4″ size is large enough to support eye-catching images yet small enough to get the message into the readers' hands. Designers recommend using two-thirds of the postcard for a graphic and one-third for text.

Overview

As you read through this chapter, you will learn how to create the presentation shown in Figure 11–1 on page PPT 659 by performing these general tasks:

- Create and organize sections.
- Create a custom slide show.
- Start a photo album and add color and black-and-white photos.
- Enhance photo album elements.
- Perform research.
- Specify a custom slide size.
- Copy and compress a video file.
- Create a video from a presentation.

Plan Ahead

> **General Project Guidelines**
>
> When creating a PowerPoint presentation, the actions you perform and the decisions you make will affect the appearance and characteristics of the finished document. As you create a presentation with illustrations, such as the project shown in Figure 11–1 on page PPT 659, you should follow these general guidelines:
>
> 1. **Use photographs with sharp focus and contrast.** The adage, "A picture is worth a thousand words," is relevant in a PowerPoint presentation. When your audience can see a visual representation of the concept you are describing during your talk, they are apt to understand and comprehend your message. Be certain your pictures are sharp and clear.
>
> 2. **Use hyperlinks to show slides with landscape and portrait orientations.** All slides in one presentation must be displayed in either landscape or portrait orientation. If you want to have variety in your slide show or have pictures or graphics that display best in one orientation, consider using hyperlinks to mix the two orientations during your presentation.
>
> 3. **Rehearse, rehearse, rehearse.** Outstanding slides lose their value when the presenter is unprepared to speak. Always keep in mind that the visual aspects are meant to supplement a speaker's verbal message. Practice your presentation before different types of audiences to solicit feedback, and use their comments to improve your speaking style.
>
> When necessary, more specific details concerning the above guidelines are presented at appropriate points in the chapter. The chapter also will identify the actions performed and decisions made regarding these guidelines during the creation of the presentation shown in Figure 11–1.

To Start PowerPoint and Save a File

If you are using a computer to step through the project in this chapter and you want your screens to match the figures in this book, you should change your computer's resolution to 1024 × 768. The following steps start PowerPoint and then save a file.

1 Start PowerPoint. If necessary, maximize the PowerPoint window.

2 Open the presentation, Garden Club, located on the Data Files for Students.

3 Save the presentation using the file name, Granville Garden Club.

Creating Sections and a Custom Slide Show

Quality PowerPoint presentations are tailored toward specific audiences, and experienced presenters adapt the slides to meet the listeners' needs and expectations. Speakers can develop one slide show and then modify the content each time they deliver the presentation. In the Granville Garden Club slide show, for example, a speaker may decide to place the slides that announce the photo contest winners at the end of the presentation to build suspense. Or, these slides can appear at the beginning of the presentation to generate discussion.

You can divide the slides into **sections** to help organize the slides. These sections serve the same function as dividers in a notebook or tabs in a manual: They help the user find required information and move material in a new sequence. In PowerPoint, you can create sections, give them unique names, and then move slides into each section. You then can move one entire section to another part of the slide show or delete the section if it no longer is needed. Each section can be displayed or printed individually.

A **custom show** is an independent set of slides to show to a specific audience. These slides can be in a different order than in the original presentation. For example, you may desire to show a title slide, the last nine slides, and then Slides 2, 5, and 8, in that order. One PowerPoint file can have several custom shows to adapt to specific audiences.

To Insert Slides with a Section Layout

You can help your audience understand the organization of your slide show if you have one slide announcing the content of each section. One of PowerPoint's layouts is named Section Header, and it is similar to the Title Slide layout because it has a title and a subtitle placeholder. Your presentation will have four sections: photo contest winners, favorite annuals, favorite perennials, and favorite spring bulbs. To ensure consistency and save time, you can create one slide with a Section Header layout and then duplicate and modify it for each section. The following steps insert the four section slides.

1

- With Slide 1 selected and the Home tab displaying, click the New Slide button arrow (Home tab | Slides group) to display the Office Theme gallery (Figure 11–2).

Figure 11–2

2

- Click Duplicate Selected Slides in the Office Theme gallery to create a new Slide 2 that is a duplicate of Slide 1.

- Click the Slide Layout button (Home tab | Slides group) to display the Office Theme layout gallery (Figure 11–3).

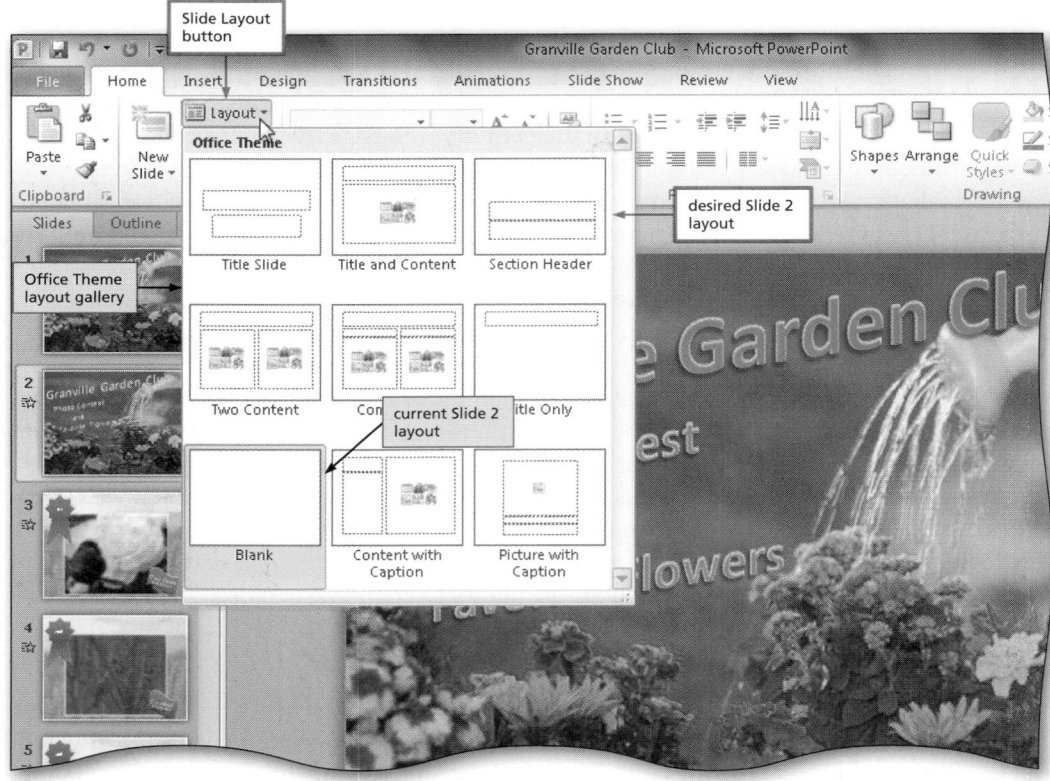

Figure 11–3

3

- Click the Section Header layout to apply that layout to the new Slide 2 (Figure 11–4).

Figure 11–4

Other Ways

1. Right-click Slide 1, click Duplicate Slide on shortcut menu

To Apply an Artistic Effect and Add a Title

The slide with the Section Header layout should have characteristics similar to the title slide to give the presentation continuity. One method of slightly altering the title slide is to apply an artistic effect that shows some of the slide's distinctive traits. The following steps apply an artistic effect to the new slide.

1 With Slide 2 displaying, select the picture, and then display the Picture Tools Format tab.

2 Click the Artistic Effects button (Picture Tools Format tab | Adjust group) to display the Artistic Effects gallery.

3 Click Blur (last effect in second row) to apply this effect to the Slide 2 picture.

4 Click in the title text placeholder and then type `Photo Contest Winners` as the title text.

5 Change the title text font color to Yellow (fourth color in Standard Colors row) and then click the Character Spacing button (Home tab | Font group) and change the character spacing to Very Loose (Figure 11–5).

Figure 11–5

BTW

The Ribbon and Screen Resolution
PowerPoint may change how the groups and buttons within the groups appear on the Ribbon, depending on the computer's screen resolution. Thus, your Ribbon may look different from the ones in this book if you are using a screen resolution other than 1024 × 768.

BTW

Q&As
For a complete list of the Q&As found in many of the step-by-step sequences in this book, visit the PowerPoint 2010 Q&A Web page (scsite. com/ppt2010/qa).

To Duplicate and Edit the Section Slides

Slide 2 is formatted appropriately to display at the beginning of the photo contest section of the slide show. A similar slide should display at the beginning of the favorite annuals, favorite perennials, and favorite spring bulbs sections. The following steps duplicate Slide 2 and edit the title text.

1 With Slide 2 selected and the Home tab displaying, click the New Slide button arrow and then click Duplicate Selected Slides.

2 Repeat Step 1 twice to insert two additional duplicate slides.

3 Display Slide 3, select the title text, and then type `Favorite Annuals` in the title text placeholder.

4 Display Slide 4, select the title text, and then type `Favorite Perennials` in the title text placeholder.

5 Display Slide 5, select the title text, and then type `Favorite Spring Bulbs` in the title text placeholder (Figure 11–6).

Figure 11–6

To Arrange Slides in Slide Sorter View

The four slides with a Section Header layout currently are displayed after the title slide. They are followed by 12 slides grouped into four categories, each of which has a distinct background. The photo contest winners' slides have a pastel sky and field, the annuals have a tan field background, the perennials have a green background, and the spring bulbs have a pink background. One of the four section slides you formatted should be positioned at the beginning of each category. When the presentation has only a few slides, you easily can drag and drop the slide thumbnails in the Slides pane. Your Granville Garden Club presentation, however, has 13 slides. To easily arrange the slides, you can change to Slide Sorter view and drag and drop the thumbnails into their desired locations. The following steps arrange the slides in Slide Sorter view.

1

- Click the Slide Sorter view button to display the slides in Slide Sorter view and then click the Slide 3 thumbnail (Favorite Annuals) to select it.

- Drag the Zoom slider to the left to change the zoom percentage to 60% so that all the slides are displayed (Figure 11–7).

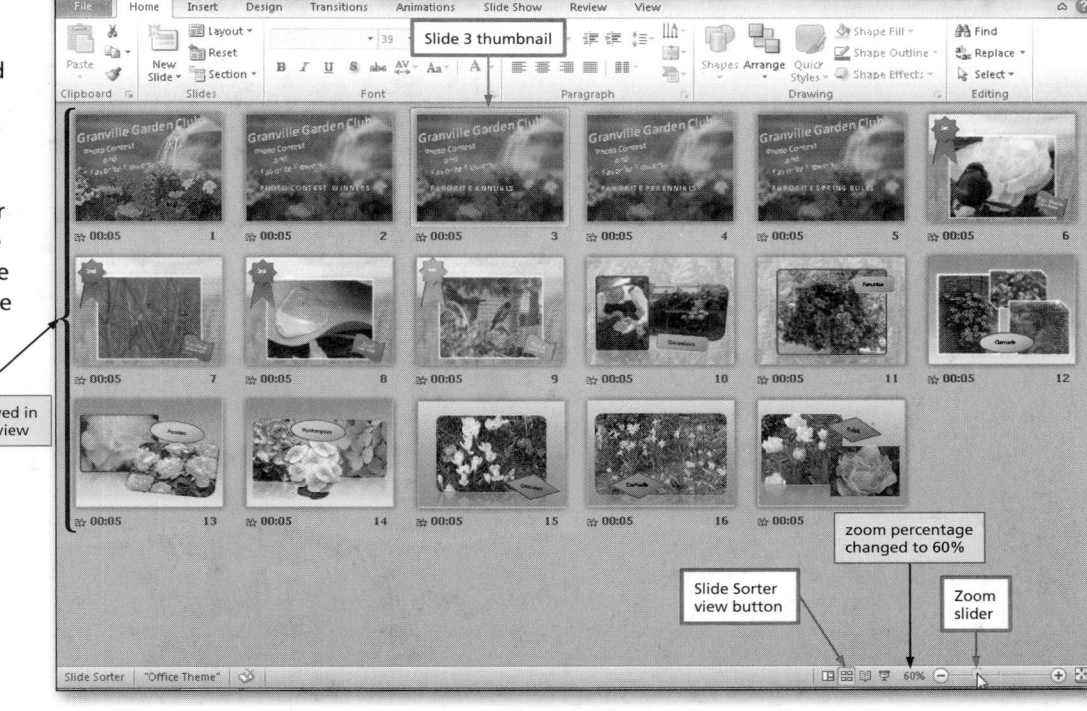

Figure 11–7

2

- Drag the Slide 3 thumbnail between the Slide 9 and Slide 10 thumbnails so that a vertical bar is displayed in the desired location for Slide 3 (Figure 11–8).

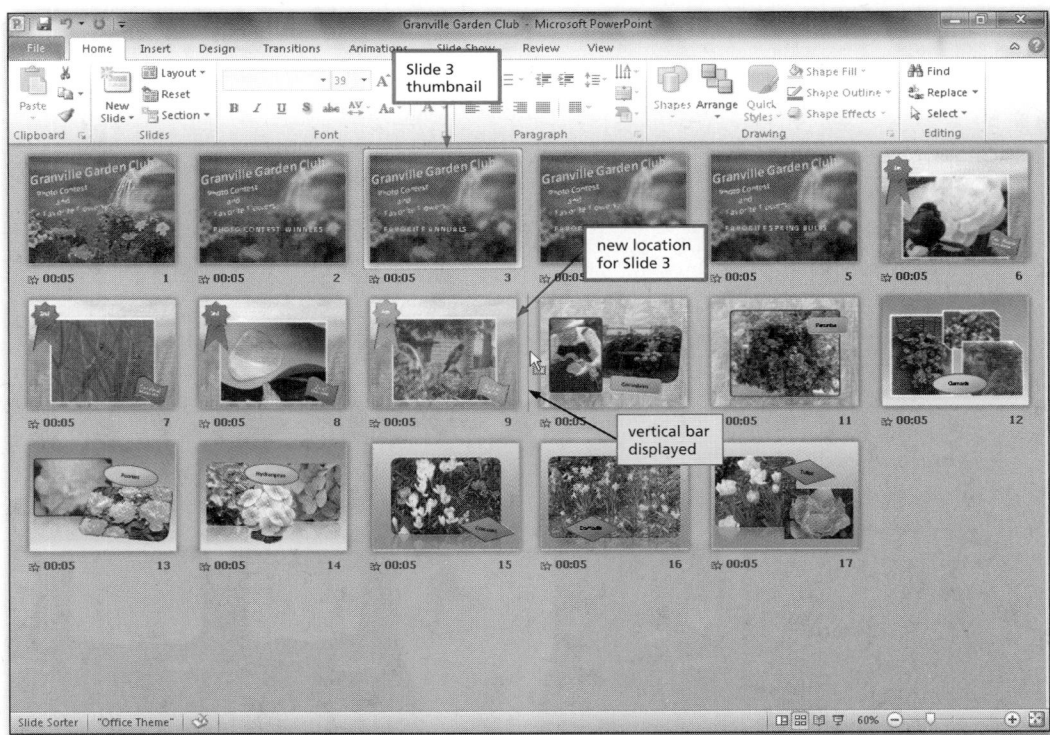

Figure 11–8

● Release the mouse button to display the Slide 3 thumbnail in a new location as Slide 9.

● Select the new Slide 3 (Favorite Perennials) and drag it between Slide 11 and Slide 12.

● Select the new Slide 3 (Favorite Spring Bulbs) and drag it between Slide 14 and Slide 15 (Figure 11–9).

Figure 11–9

To Create a Section Break

The slides in the presentation are divided into four categories: photo contest winners, annuals, perennials, and spring bulbs. At times, you may want to display slides from one particular category or move this particular group to another part of the presentation. You can create a section break to organize slides into a particular group. The following steps create five sections in the presentation.

1

● In Slide Sorter view, position the mouse pointer between Slide 1 and Slide 2 and then click once to display the vertical bar (Figure 11–10).

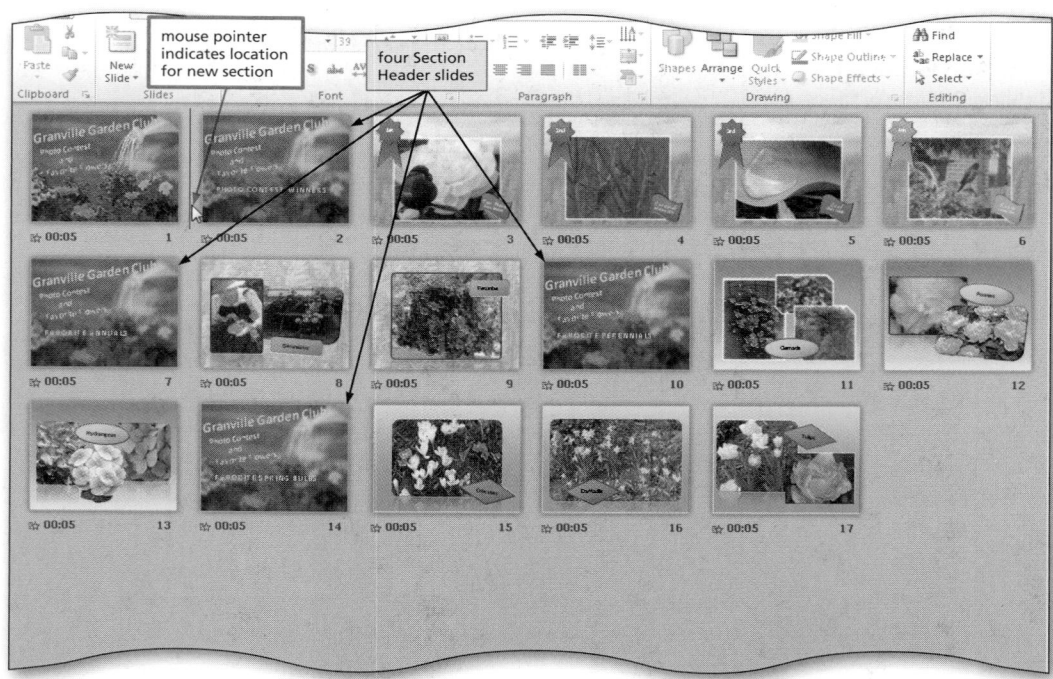

Figure 11–10

2

- With the Home tab displaying, click the Section button (Home tab | Slides group) to display the Section menu (Figure 11–11).

Figure 11–11

3

- Click Add Section in the menu to create a section.

- Scroll up to verify that the new section is named Default Section and consists of Slide 1.

Q&A

Why is a section name shown as Untitled Section instead of Default Section?

If you place the mouse pointer before Slide 1, the section is named Untitled Section; if you place the mouse pointer between Slides 1 and 2, then it is named Default Section.

- Position the mouse pointer between Slide 6 and Slide 7, which is the start of the slides with annuals, and then click once to display the vertical bar (Figure 11–12).

Figure 11–12

4

- Click the Section button (Home tab | Slides group) to display the Section menu and then click Add Section in the menu to create a section with the name, Untitled Section.

- Position the mouse pointer between Slide 9 and Slide 10, which is the start of the slides with perennials (Figure 11–13).

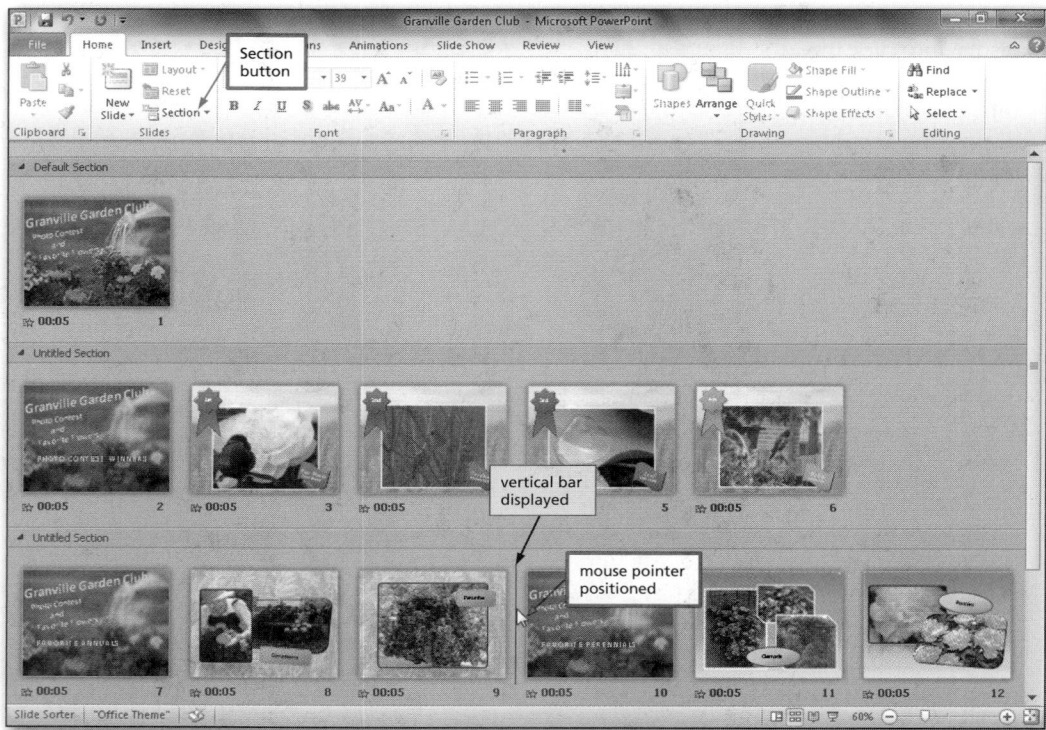

Figure 11–13

- Click the Section button and then click Add Section in the menu to create a section with the name, Untitled Section.

- Scroll down to display the final slides in the presentation, position the mouse pointer between Slide 13 and Slide 14, and then create a section (Figure 11–14).

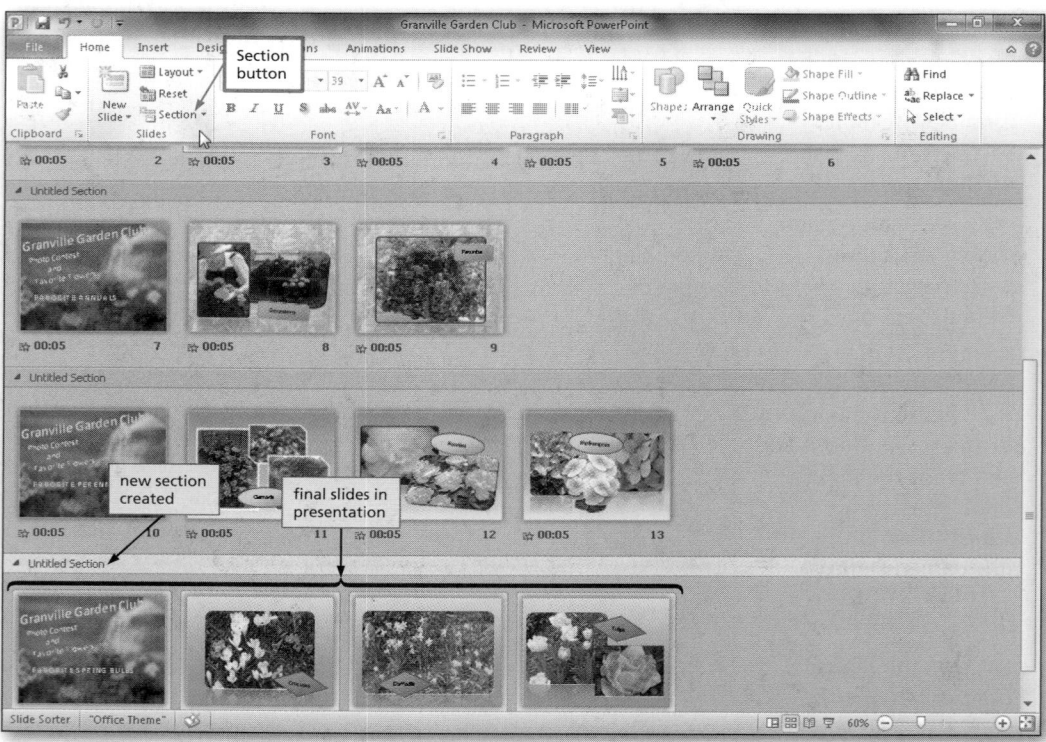

Figure 11–14

To Rename a Section

The default section names, Untitled and Default, do not identify the content of the slides in the group. You can give each section a unique name to easily categorize the slides. The following steps rename each of the five sections in the presentation.

1

• With the last section featuring the spring bulbs selected and the Home tab displaying, click the Section button (Home tab | Slides group) to display the Section menu (Figure 11–15).

Q&A

If the spring bulbs section is not highlighted, how can I select it?

Click the divider between the sections. You will know the section is selected when the divider is gold.

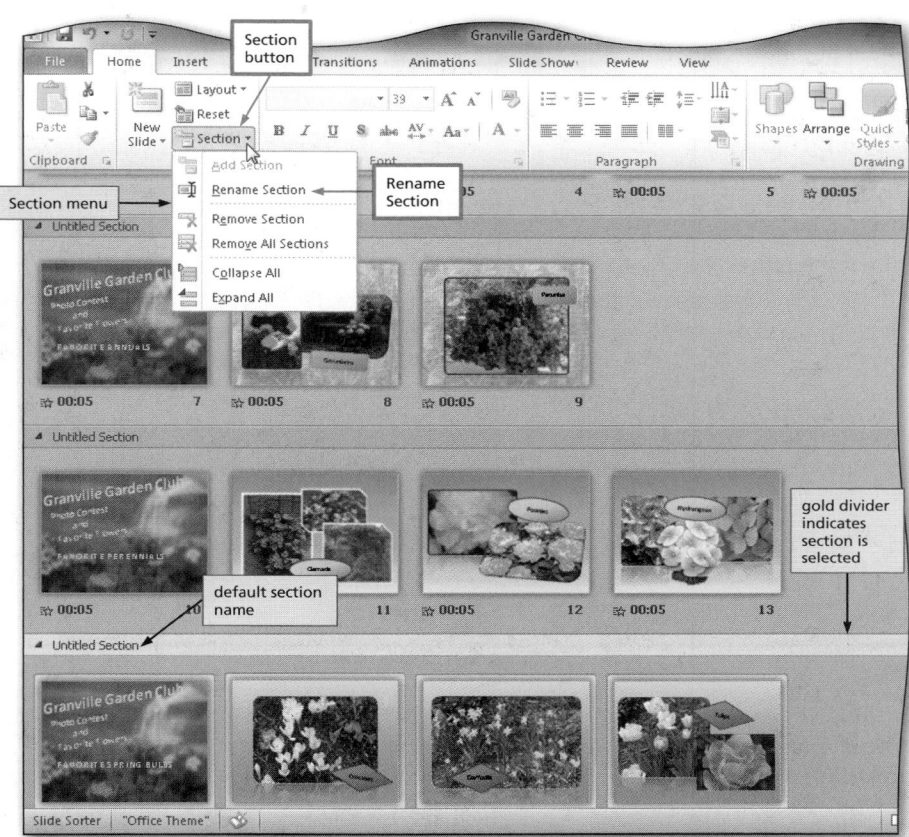

Figure 11–15

2

• Click Rename Section in the menu to display the Rename Section dialog box.

• Type **Spring Bulbs** in the Section name text box (Figure 11–16).

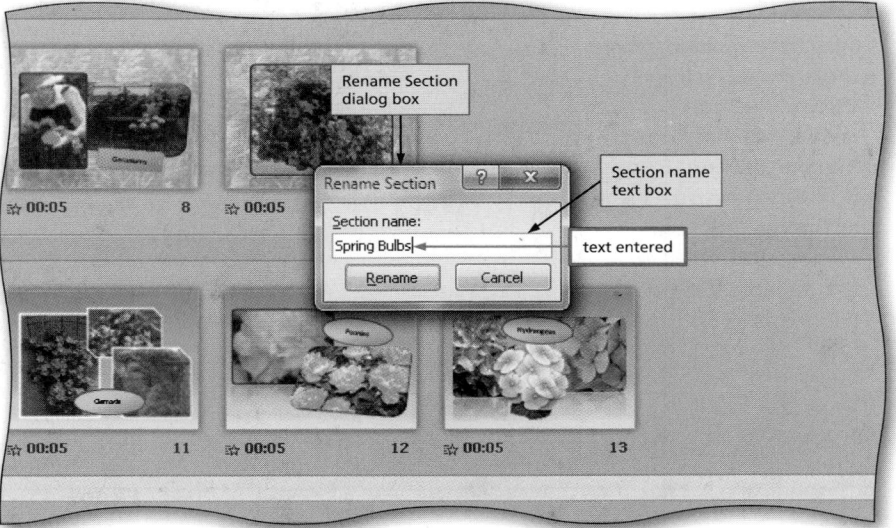

Figure 11–16

3

• Click the Rename button (Rename Section dialog box) to change the section name.

• Click the divider for the perennials section (Slide 10 through Slide 13) to select it and then click the Section button (Home tab | Slides group) to display the Section menu (Figure 11–17).

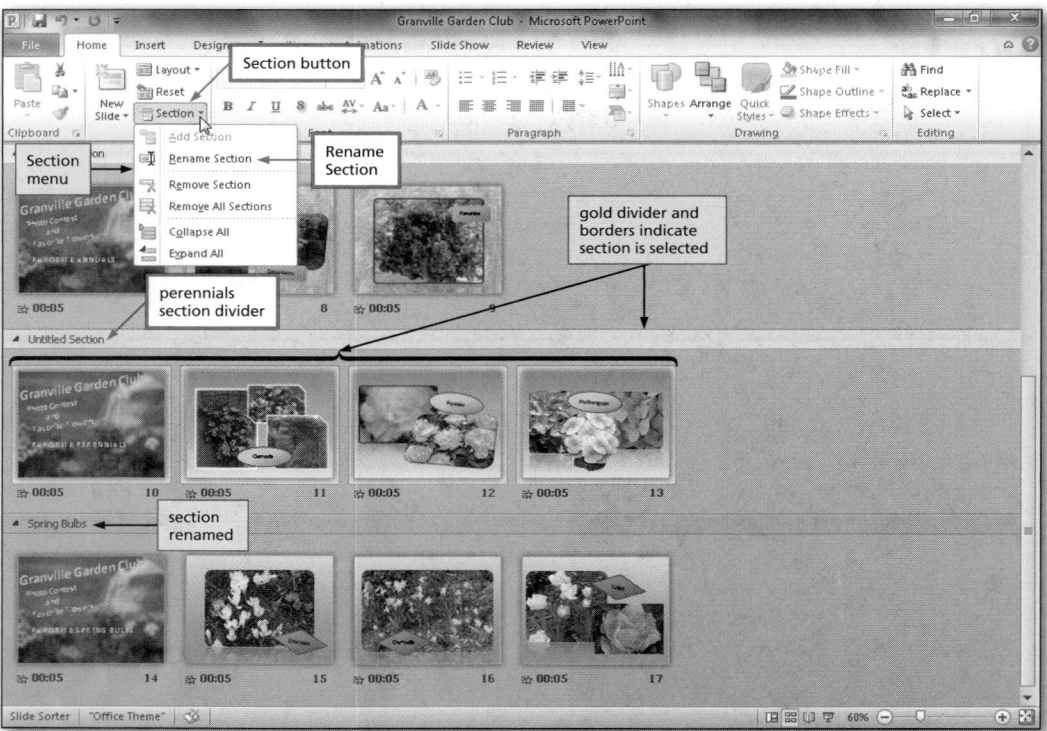

Figure 11–17

4

• Click Rename Section to display the Rename Section dialog box, type **Perennials** in the Section name text box, and then click the Rename button to change the section name.

• Select the divider for the annuals section (Slide 7 through Slide 9), display the Rename Section dialog box, type **Annuals** as the new section name, and then click the Rename button (Figure 11–18).

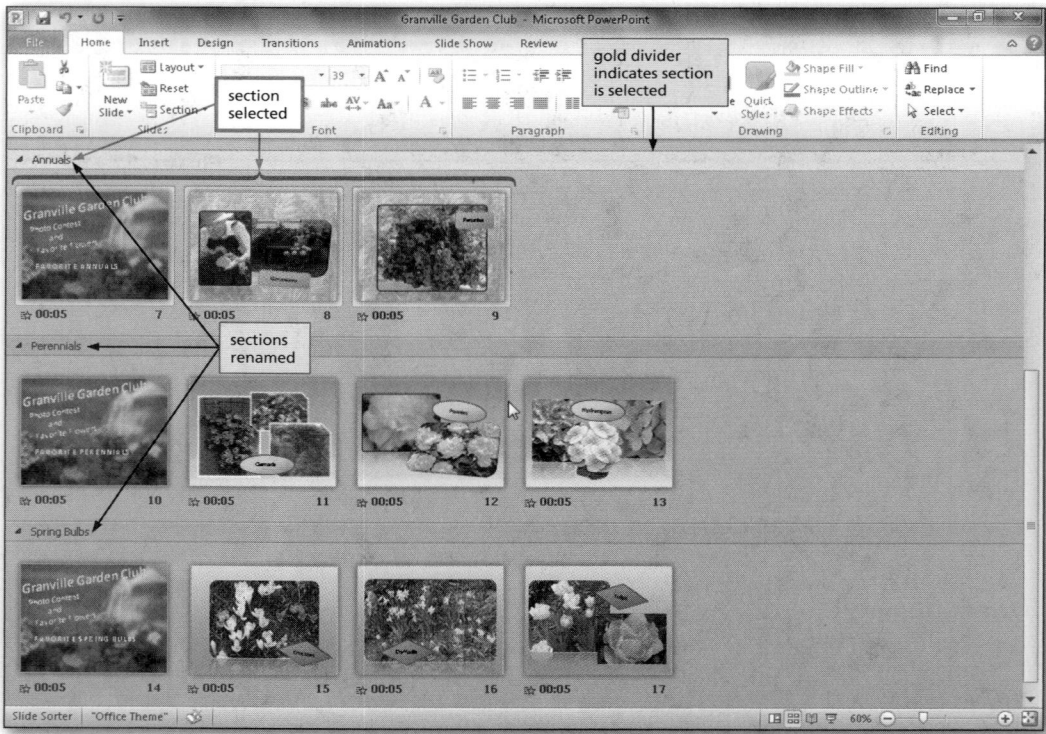

Figure 11–18

5

- Scroll up to display the first two sections, select the divider for the photo contest winners slides (Slide 2 through Slide 6), display the Rename Section dialog box, type **Photo Contest Winners** as the new section name, and then click the Rename button.

- Select the divider for Slide 1, display the Rename Section dialog box, type **Garden Club Title** as the new section name, and then click the Rename button (Figure 11–19).

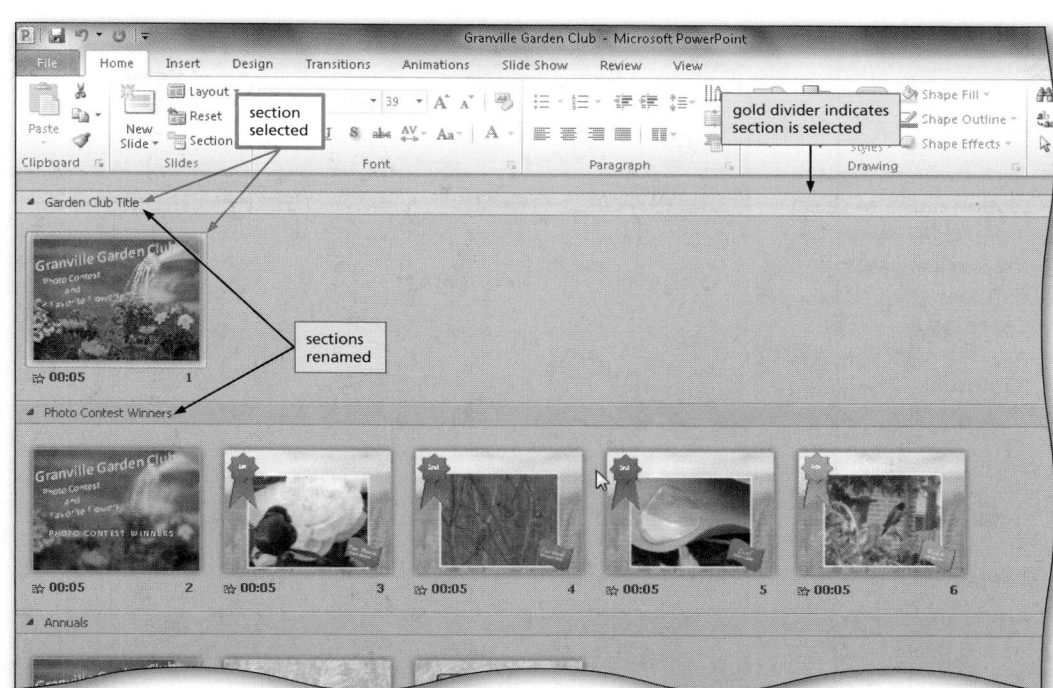

Figure 11–19

Other Ways

1. Right-click section divider, click Rename Section on shortcut menu

To Collapse and Reorder Sections

When slides are organized into sections, it is easy to change the order in which the sections display. Garden Club members have expressed much more interest this year in perennials than annuals, so you want to change the order of these two sets of slides in your presentation. Because your presentation consists of multiple sections, you can collapse the sections so that only the section titles are displayed. You then can reorder the sections and expand the sections. The following steps collapse the sections, reorder the annual and perennial sections, and expand the sections.

1

- With the first section featuring the Garden Club Title selected and the Home tab displaying, click the Section button (Home tab | Slides group) to display the Section menu (Figure 11–20).

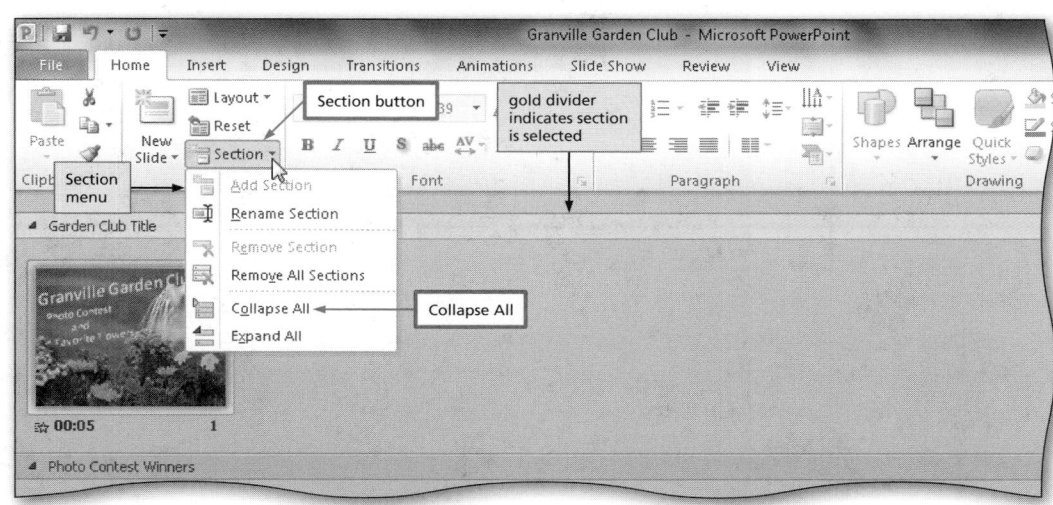

Figure 11–20

2

- Click Collapse All in the Section menu to display only the section names.

- Click the Perennials section name to select it and then drag the section upward between the Photo Contest Winners and Annuals sections (Figure 11–21).

Q&A

How do I know when I am dragging the section name if the slides will be positioned in the desired location?

A vertical bar indicates where the slides in the section will move.

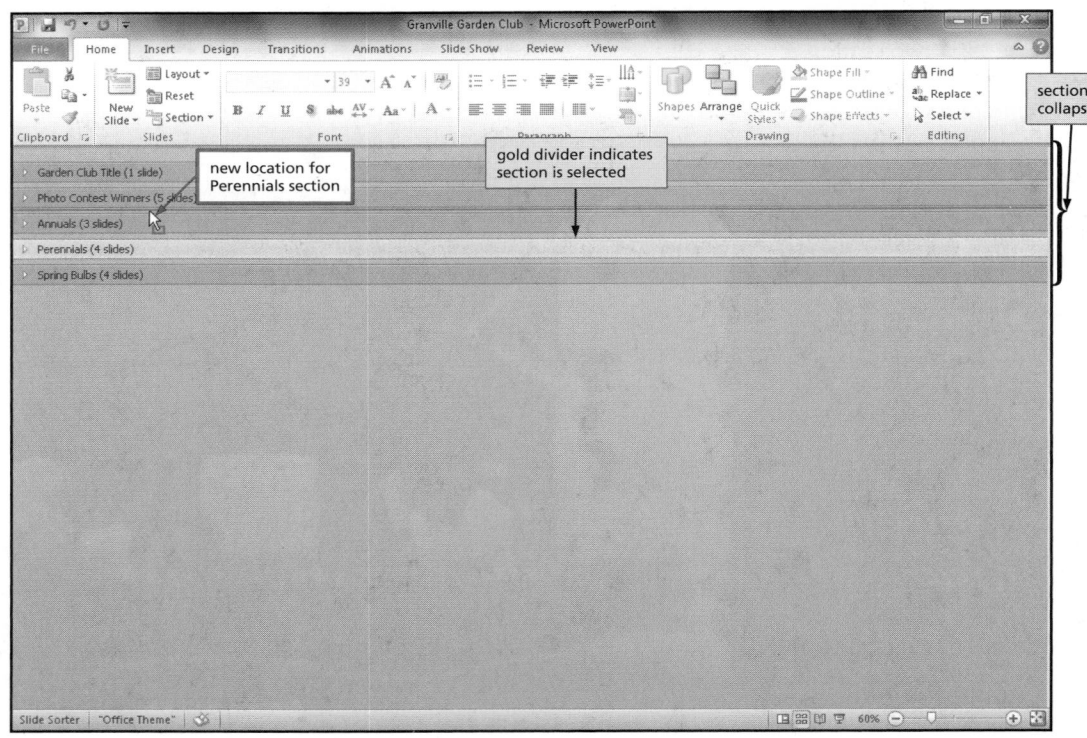

Figure 11–21

3

- Release the mouse button to move the Perennials section between the Photo Contest Winners and Annuals sections.

- Click the Section button (Home tab | Slides group) to display the Section menu (Figure 11–22).

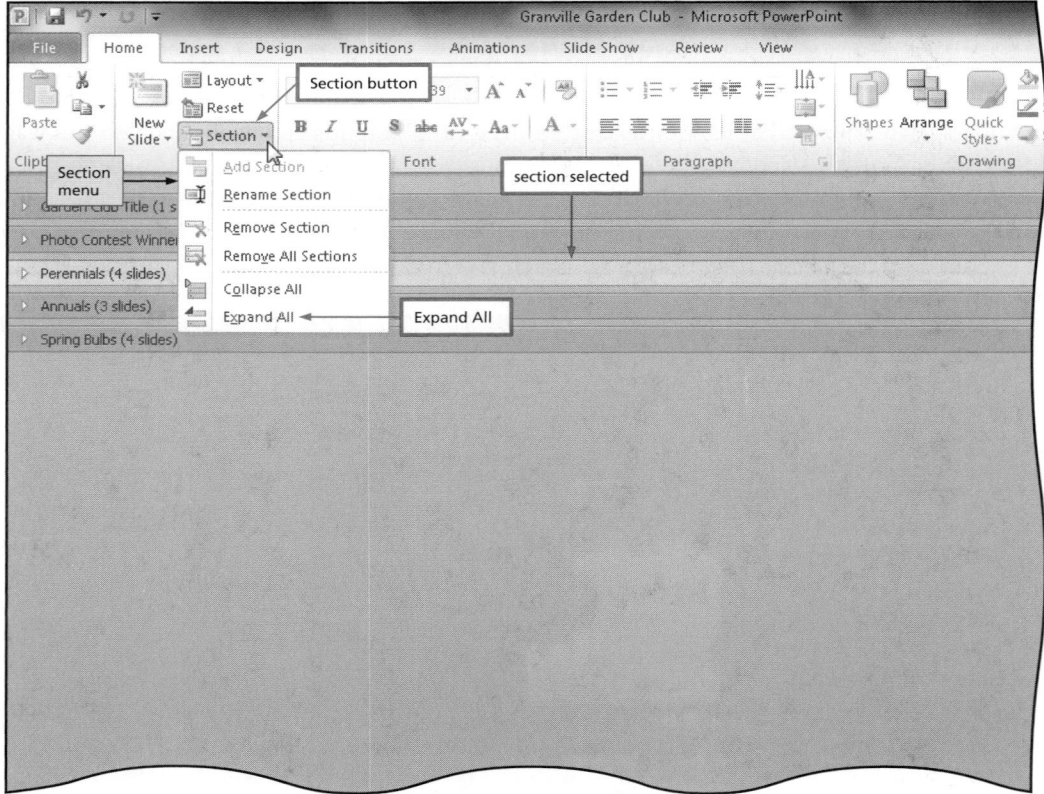

Figure 11–22

4
- Click Expand All in the Section menu to display all the slides in their corresponding sections (Figure 11–23).

5
- Run the presentation to display all the slides in the desired order.

Figure 11–23

TO SHOW A PRESENTATION WITH MANUAL TIMING

The Granville Garden Club slides are set to display for specified times. If you desire to override the automatic timings and advance the slides manually, you would perform the following steps.

1. Display the Slide Show tab and then click the Set Up Slide Show button (Slide Show tab | Set Up group) to display the Set Up Show dialog box.

2. Click Manually in the Advance slides area (Set Up Show dialog box) and then click the OK button.

Break Point: If you wish to take a break, this is a good place to do so. Be sure to save the Granville Garden Club file again and then you can quit PowerPoint. To resume at a later time, start PowerPoint, open the file called Granville Garden Club, and continue following the steps from this location forward.

To Create a Custom Slide Show

Many presenters deliver their speeches in front of targeted audiences. For example, the director of human resources may present one set of slides for new employees, another set for potential retirees, and a third for managers concerned with new regulations and legislation. Slides for all these files may be contained in one file, and the presenter can elect to show particular slides to accompany specific speeches. PowerPoint allows you to create a **custom show** that displays only selected slides. The following steps create a custom show.

1

• Click the Normal view button to display the slides in Normal view and then display the Slide Show tab.

• Click the Custom Slide Show button (Slide Show tab | Start Slide Show group) to display the Custom Slide Show list (Figure 11–24).

Figure 11–24

2

• Click Custom Shows to open the Custom Shows dialog box (Figure 11–25).

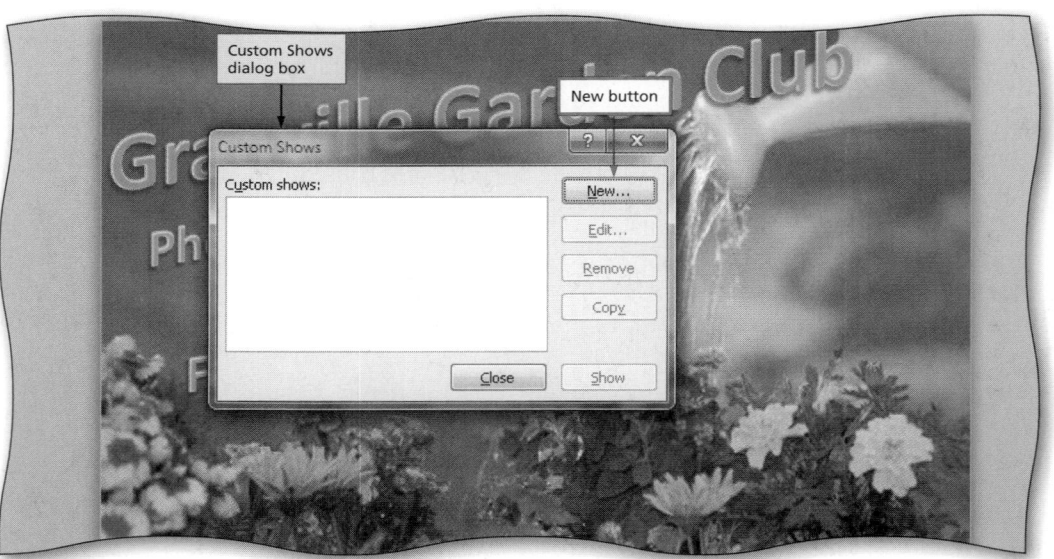

Figure 11–25

3

• Click the New button (Custom Shows dialog box) to display the Define Custom Show dialog box.

• Click Slide 1 in the 'Slides in presentation' area to select this slide (Figure 11–26).

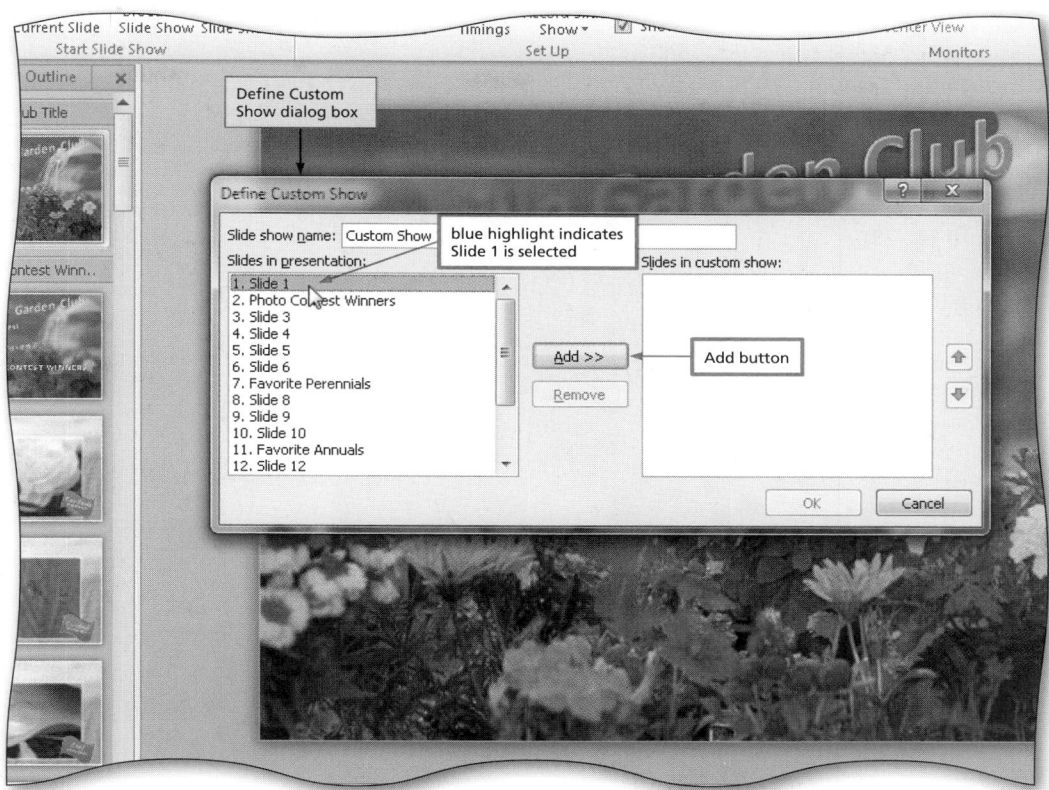

Figure 11–26

4

• Click the Add button (Define Custom Show dialog box) to add this slide to the 'Slides in custom show' area.

• Scroll down, press and hold down the CTRL key, and then click Slide 8, Slide 9, Slide 10, Slide 12, Slide 13, Slide 15, Slide 16, and Slide 17 in the 'Slides in presentation' area.

• Click the Add button (Define Custom Show dialog box) to add these slides to the 'Slides in custom show' area (Figure 11–27).

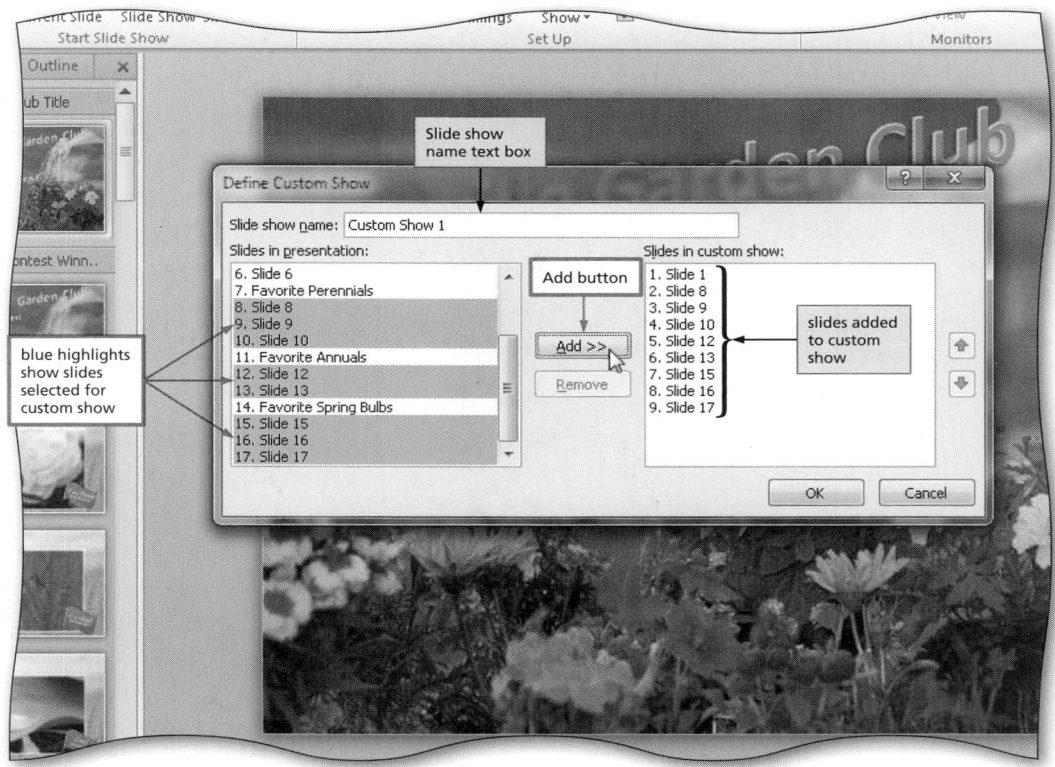

Figure 11–27

5

- Select the text in the 'Slide show name' text box (Define Custom Show dialog box) and then type **Garden Club Favorites** as the new name (Figure 11–28).

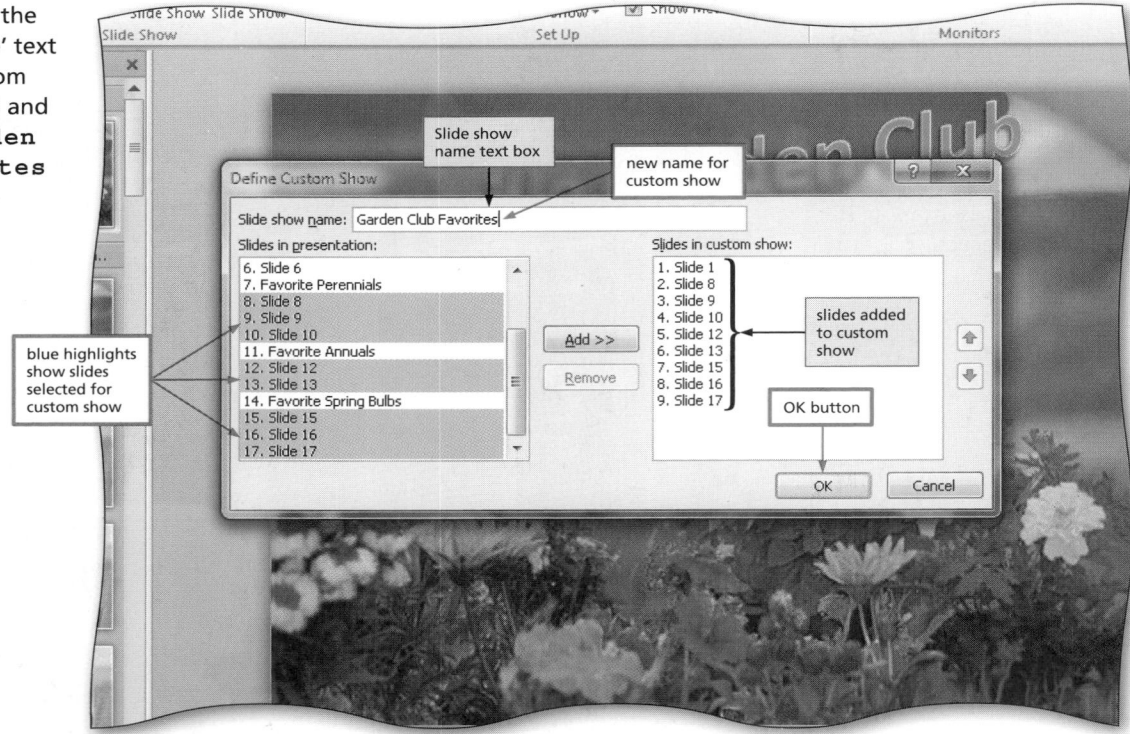

Figure 11–28

6

- Click the OK button (Define Custom Show dialog box) to create the new Garden Club Favorites custom show and display the Custom Shows dialog box (Figure 11–29).

7

- Click the Close button (Custom Shows dialog box) to close the dialog box.

Figure 11–29

To Open and Edit a Custom Slide Show

A PowerPoint file may have several custom slide shows. You can elect to display one of them at any time depending upon the particular needs of your audience. If you need to reorder the slides, you can change the sequence easily. The following steps open a custom show and edit the slide sequence.

1

- With the Slide Show tab displaying, click the Custom Slide Show button (Slide Show tab | Start Slide Show group) to display the Custom Slide Show list (Figure 11–30).

Q&A

Why does Garden Club Favorites display in the Custom Slide Show list?

The names of any custom shows will be displayed in the list. If desired, you could click this custom show name to run the slide show and display the selected slides.

Figure 11–30

2

- Click Custom Shows to display the Custom Shows dialog box (Figure 11–31).

Figure 11–31

3

• With the Garden Club Favorites custom show selected in the Custom shows area, click the Edit button (Custom Shows dialog box) to display the Define Custom Show dialog box.

• Click Slide 15 in the 'Slides in custom show' area to select it (Figure 11–32).

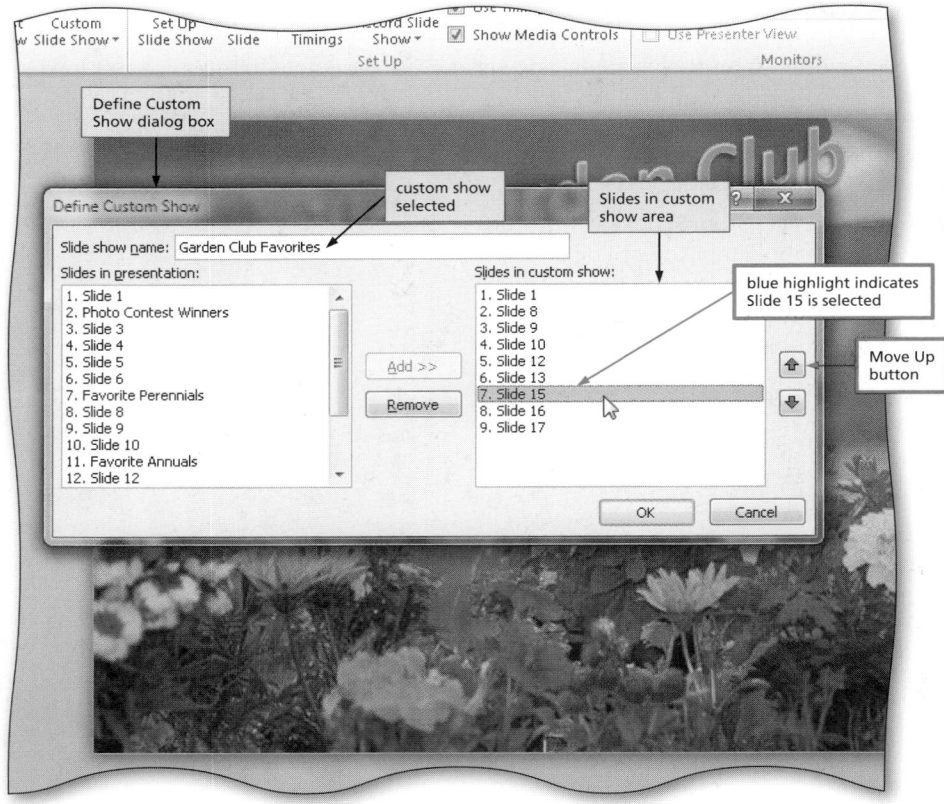

Figure 11–32

4

• Click the Move Up button five times to move Slide 15 below Slide 1 as the second slide in the custom show (Figure 11–33).

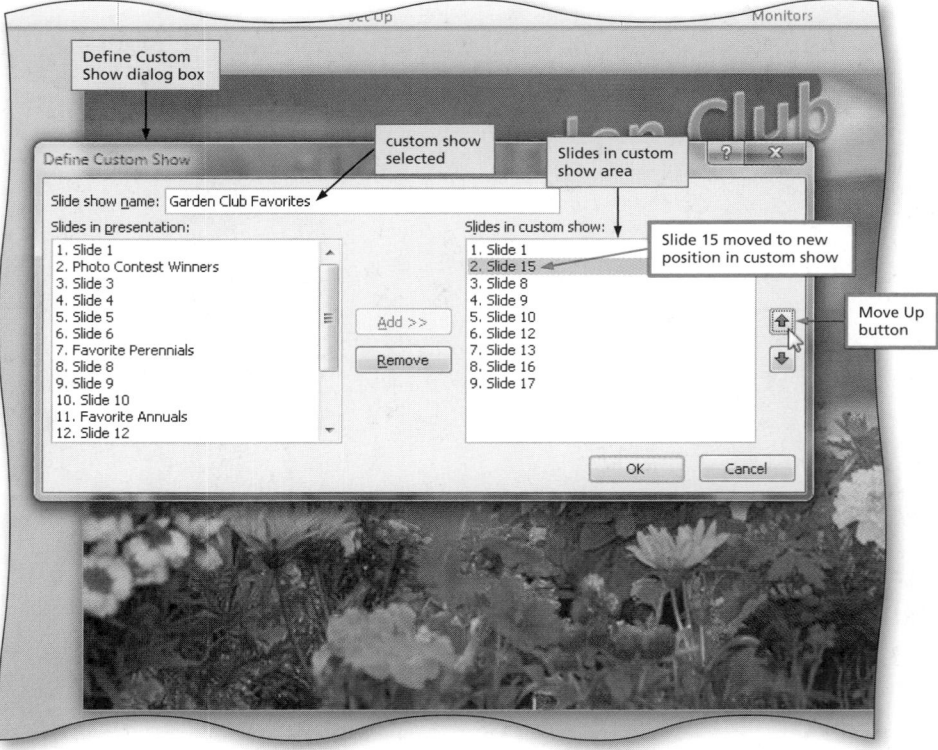

Figure 11–33

5

- Click Slide 16 in the 'Slides in custom show' area to select it and then click the Move Up button five times to move Slide 16 below Slide 15 as the third slide in the custom show.

- Click Slide 17 in the 'Slides in custom show' area to select it and then click the Move Up button seven times to move Slide 17 below Slide 1 as the second slide in the custom show (Figure 11–34).

Q&A Can I move the slides so they display later in the custom show?

Yes. Select the slide you want to reorder and then click the Move Down button.

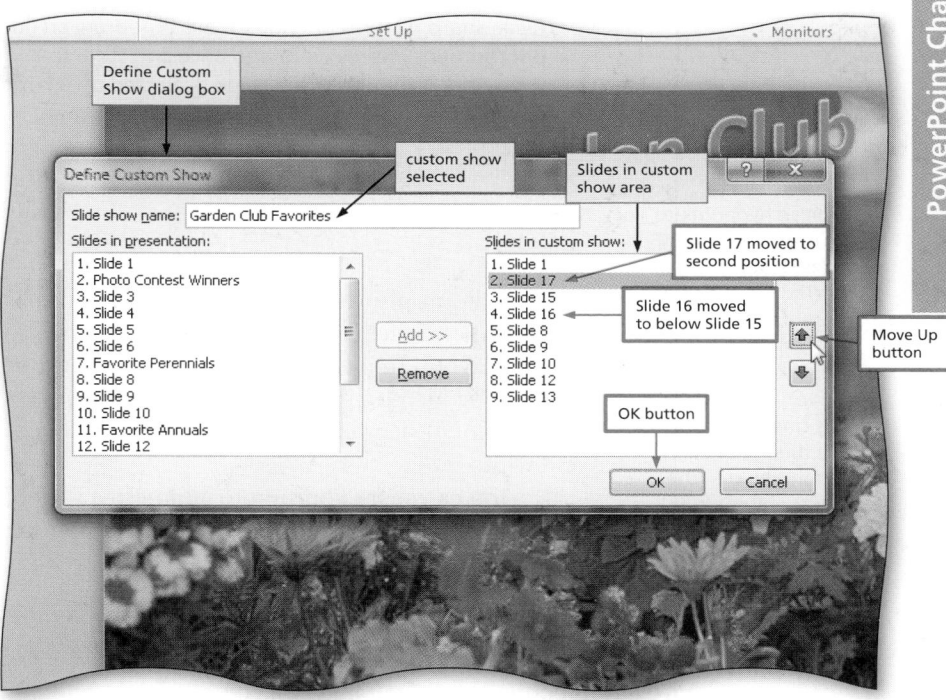

Figure 11–34

6

- Click the OK button (Define Custom Show dialog box) to create the revised Garden Club Favorites custom show and display the Custom Shows dialog box (Figure 11–35).

7

- Click the Show button (Custom Shows dialog box) to run the Garden Club Favorites custom show.

- When all the slides have displayed, press the ESC button to end the custom show.

- Save the Granville Garden Club file. Do not close this file.

Figure 11–35

Break Point: If you wish to take a break, this is a good place to do so. You can quit PowerPoint now. To resume at a later time, start PowerPoint, open the file called Granville Garden Club, and continue following the steps from this location forward.

Plan
Ahead

> **Use photographs with sharp focus and contrast.**
> Clear, sharp pictures provide details that draw an audience into your presentation. High-quality photographs impress your audience and state that you have an eye for detail and take pride in your work. When your slides are projected on a large screen, any imperfection is magnified, so you must take care to select photographs that are in focus and have high contrast.

BTW

Hyperlinking Custom Shows
You can hyperlink to a custom show with slides relating to a specific topic in your presentation. Click the Hyperlink button (Insert tab | Links group), click the Place in This Document button, and then select the custom show in the 'Select a place in this document' list.

Creating a Photo Album

A PowerPoint **photo album** is a presentation that contains pictures to share with friends and business colleagues. It can contain a theme, a vibrant background, custom captions, a specific layout, frames around pictures, and text boxes. You can enhance the quality of the pictures by increasing or decreasing brightness and contrast, and you also can rotate the pictures in 90-degree increments. You also can change color pictures to display in black and white.

You can share your photo album in a variety of ways. You can, for example, e-mail the file, publish it to the Web, or print the pictures as handouts.

To Start a Photo Album and Add Pictures

Once you have gathered files of digital pictures, you can begin building a photo album. You initially create the album and then later enhance its appearance. The following steps start a photo album and add pictures.

1

- Display the Insert tab and then click the New Photo Album button, which is displayed on the Ribbon as the Photo Album button (Insert tab | Images group), to display the Photo Album dialog box (Figure 11–36).

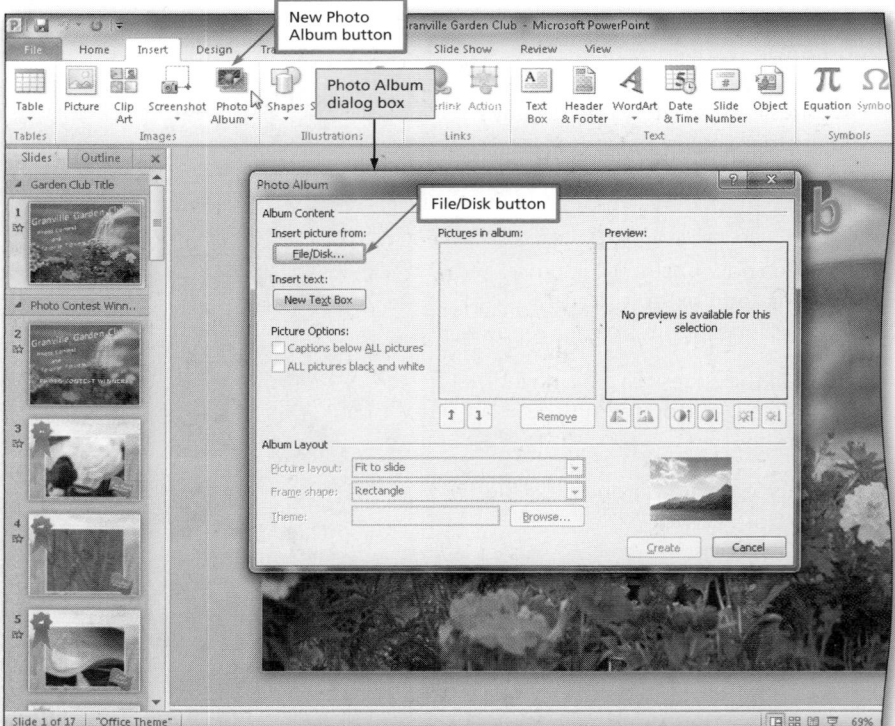

Figure 11–36

- Click the File/Disk button to display the Insert New Pictures dialog box.

- If necessary, double-click your USB flash drive in the list of available storage devices to display a list of files and folders on the selected USB flash drive and then navigate to the PowerPoint Chapter 11 folder (Figure 11–37).

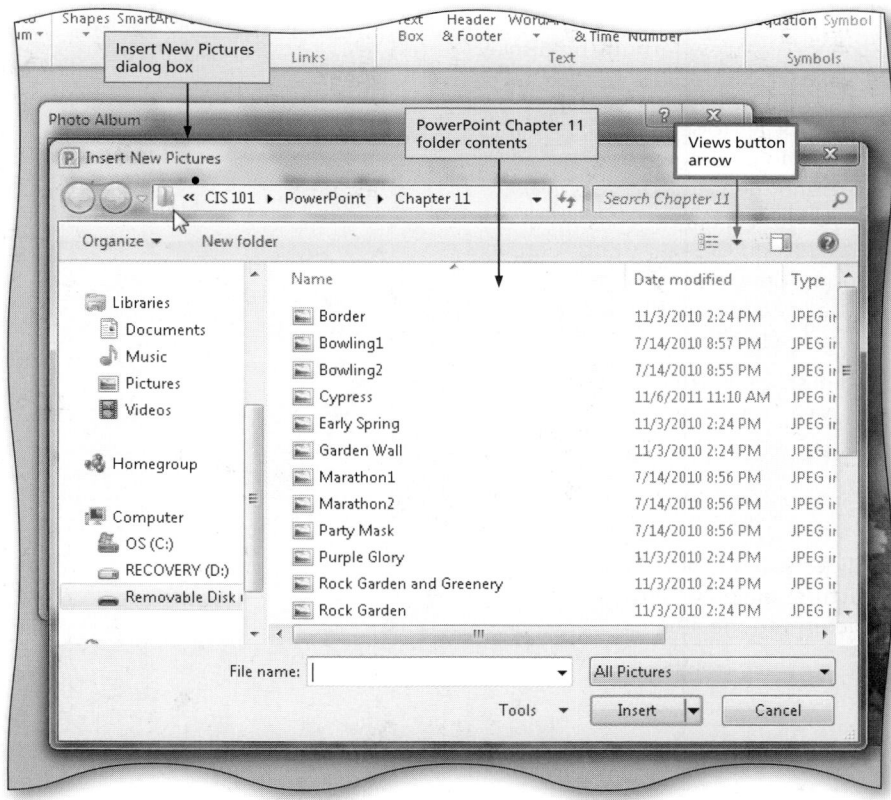

Figure 11–37

3

- Click the Views button arrow on the toolbar (Insert New Pictures dialog box) to display the view settings (Figure 11–38).

Figure 11–38

4

- Click List in the view settings to change the view setting and display only the picture file names.

- Click Border to select the file name, press and hold down the CTRL key, and then click Early Spring, Garden Wall, Purple Glory, Rock Garden and Greenery, Rock Garden, Spring Time, and Summer Time to select additional files to insert (Figure 11–39).

Q&A

If I mistakenly select a file name, how can I remove the selection?

Click the file name again.

5

- Click the Insert button (Insert New Pictures dialog box) to add the pictures to the album.

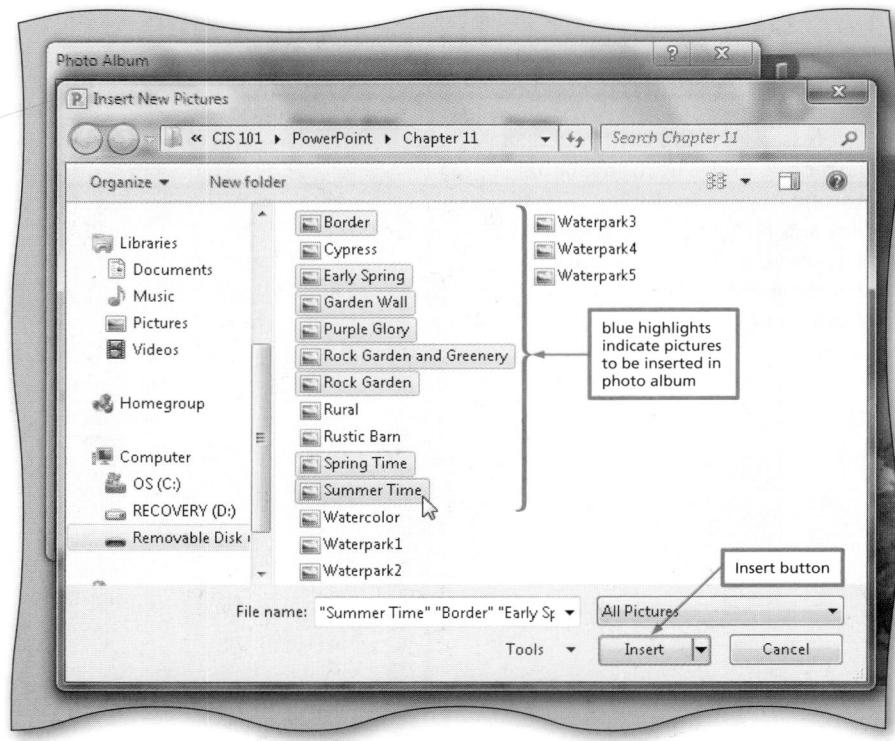

Figure 11–39

To Reorder Pictures in a Photo Album

PowerPoint inserted the pictures in alphabetical order, which may not be the desired sequence for your album. You easily can change the order of the pictures in the same manner that you change the slide order in a custom show. The following steps reorder the photo album pictures.

1

- Click the second picture, Early Spring, to select it (Figure 11–40).

2

- Click the Move Down button four times to move the Early Spring photo downward between the Rock Garden and Spring Time photos so that it now is picture 6 in the album.

- Select the third picture, Purple Glory, and then click the Move Up button one time to move this picture upward between the Border and Garden Wall photos so that it now is the second picture.

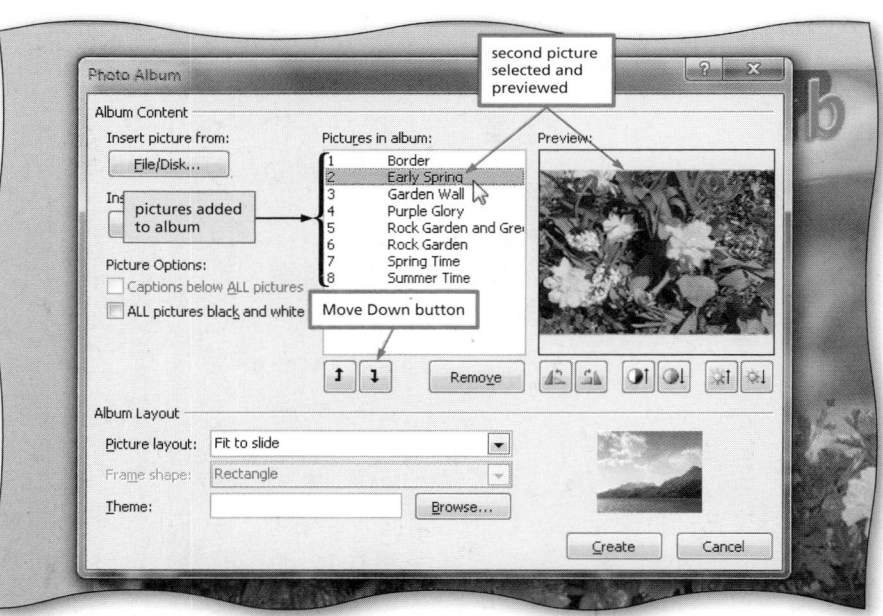

Figure 11–40

To Adjust the Rotation of a Photo Album Image

Digital images have either a portrait (vertical) or landscape (horizontal) orientation. If a picture is displayed in your album with the wrong orientation, you can rotate the image in 90-degree increments to the left or the right. The following steps rotate a photo album picture.

1

• Click the third picture, Garden Wall, to select it and display a preview (Figure 11–41).

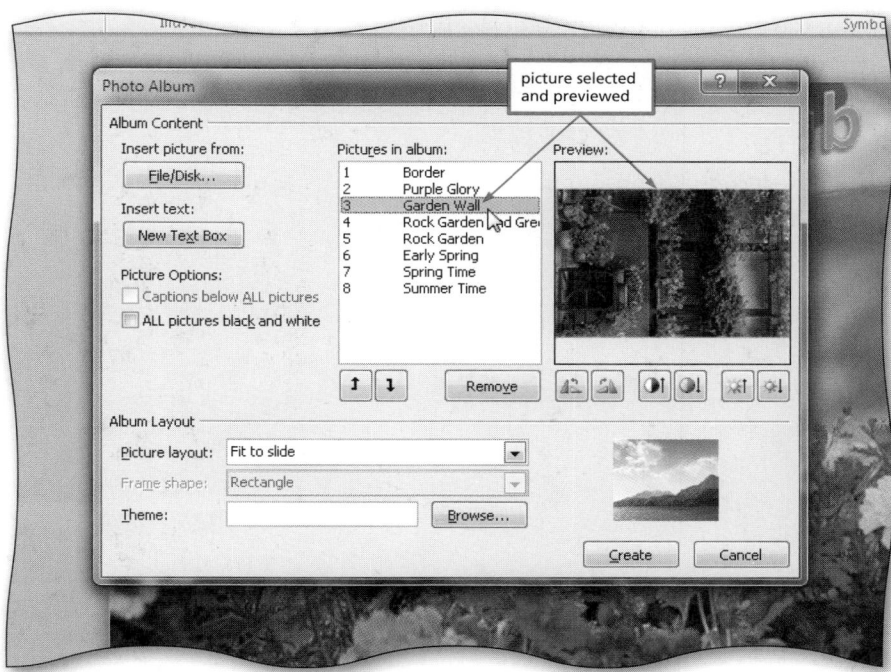

Figure 11–41

2

• Click the Rotate Left 90° button (Photo Album dialog box) to turn the picture to the left (Figure 11–42).

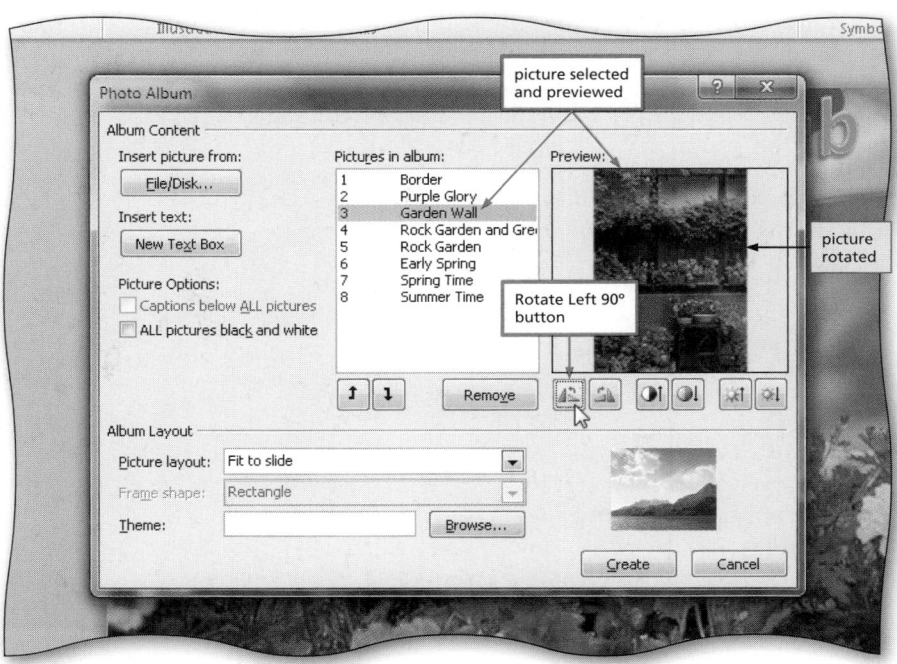

Figure 11–42

To Adjust the Contrast of a Photo Album Image

A picture you insert may need correcting to enhance its visual appeal. You can adjust the difference between the darkest and lightest areas of the picture by increasing or decreasing the contrast. The following steps adjust the contrast of a photo album picture.

1
- Click the fifth picture, Rock Garden, to select it and display a preview (Figure 11–43).

2
- Click the Increase Contrast button (Photo Album dialog box) six times to change the contrast of this picture.

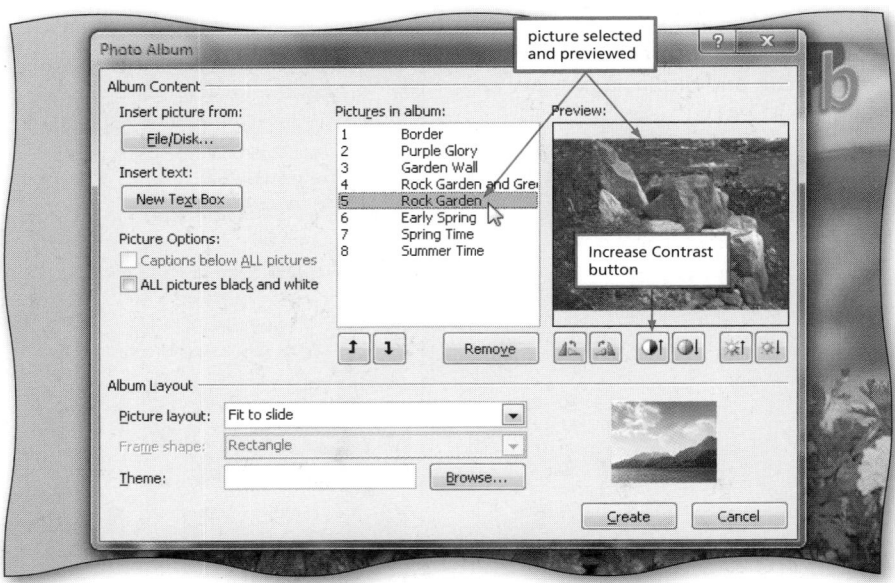

Figure 11–43

To Adjust the Brightness of a Photo Album Image

If a picture in the photo album is too light or too dark, you can adjust its brightness to enhance its appearance. The following step adjusts the contrast of a photo album picture.

1
- With the Rock Garden picture selected, click the Decrease Brightness button (Photo Album dialog box) four times to darken the picture (Figure 11–44).

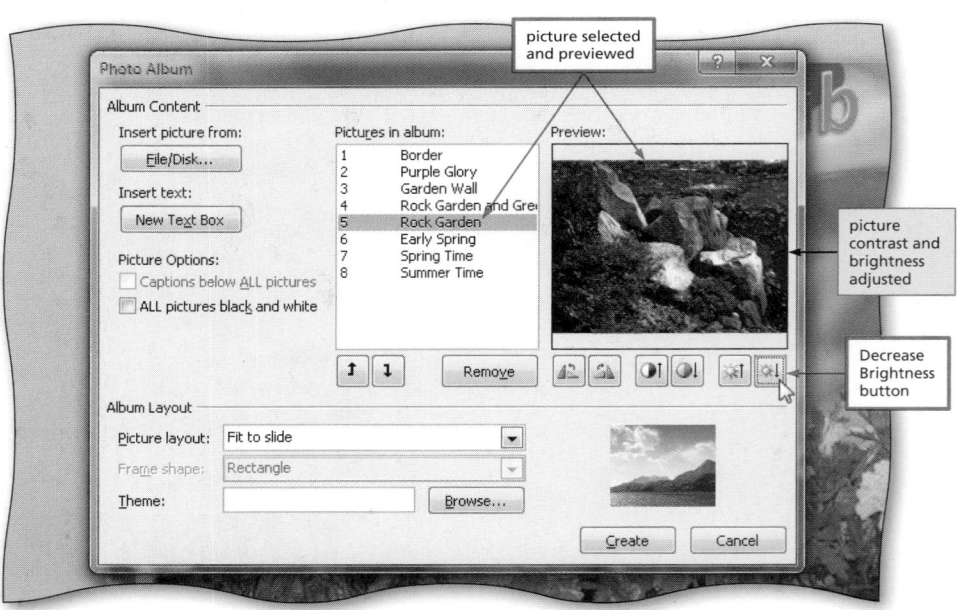

Figure 11–44

To Change a Photo Album Layout

PowerPoint inserts each photo album picture so that it fills, or fits, one entire slide. You can modify this layout to display two or four pictures on a slide, display a title, or add white space between the image and the slide edges. You also can add a white or black border around the perimeter of each picture. The following steps change an album layout.

1

- With the Photo Album dialog box displayed, click the Picture layout box arrow in the Album Layout area (Photo Album dialog box) to display the Picture layout list (Figure 11–45).

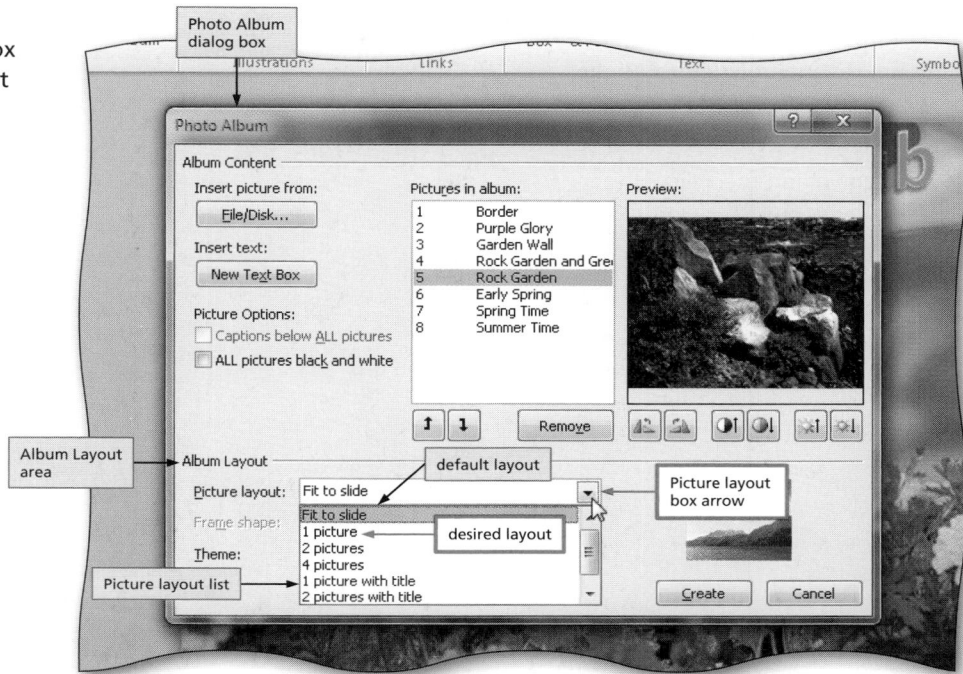

Figure 11–45

2

- Click 1 picture in the Picture layout list to change the layout so that one picture is displayed on each slide and a rectangular border is displayed around each picture.

- Click the Frame shape box arrow in the Album Layout area (Photo Album dialog box) to display the Frame shape list (Figure 11–46).

3

- Click Simple Frame, Black in the Frame shape list to add a black border around the picture.

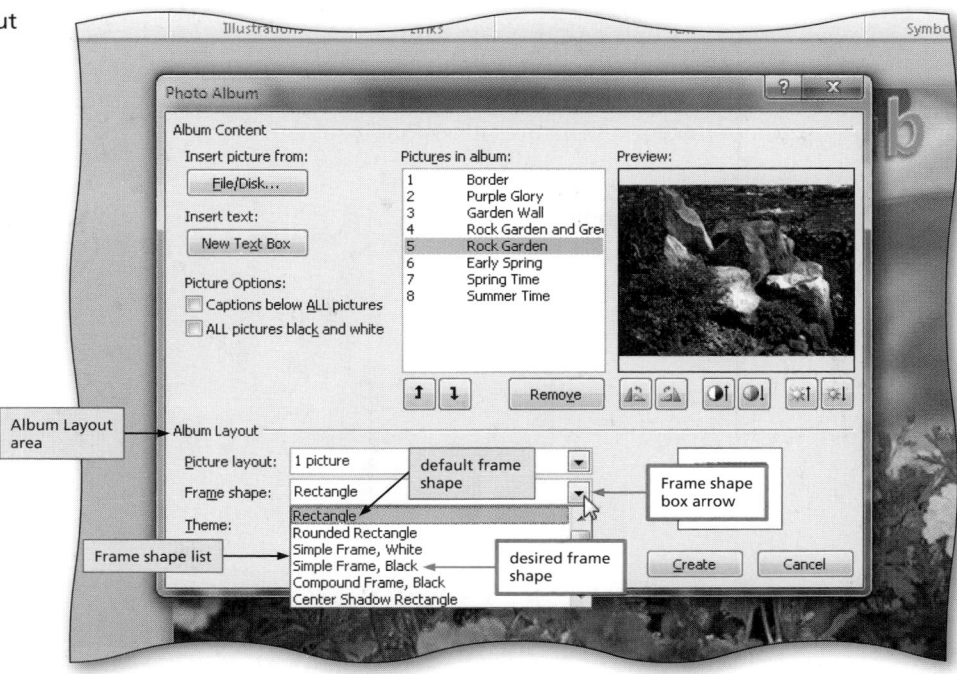

Figure 11–46

To Add a Photo Album Theme

The themes that are used to design a presentation also are available to add to a photo album. These themes determine the colors and fonts that complement each other and increase the visual appeal of the slides. The following steps add a theme to the photo album.

- Click the Browse button in the Album Layout area (Photo Album dialog box) to display the Choose Theme dialog box.

- Scroll down and then click Horizon in the theme list to select this theme (Figure 11–47).

- Click the Select button (Choose Theme dialog box) to apply this theme to the presentation.

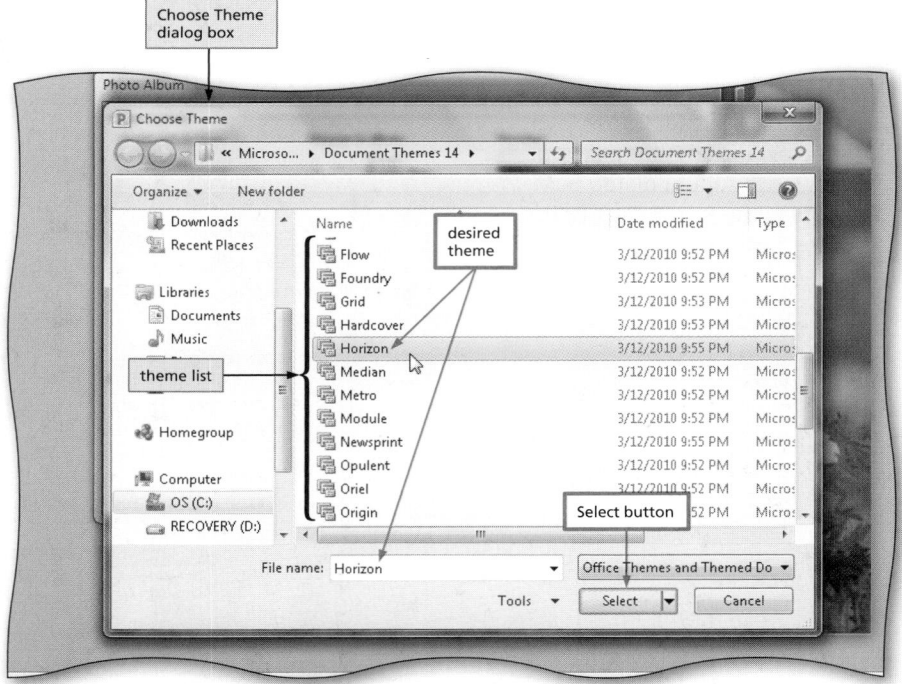

Figure 11–47

To Add Captions below All Pictures

If you desire a caption below each picture, you can request PowerPoint add this feature to the slides. The file name is displayed as the caption text, but you can edit and add effects to this text. The following step selects the picture option to add a caption below all pictures in the photo album.

- In the Picture Options area (Photo Album dialog box), click the 'Captions below ALL pictures' check box to add a check mark (Figure 11–48).

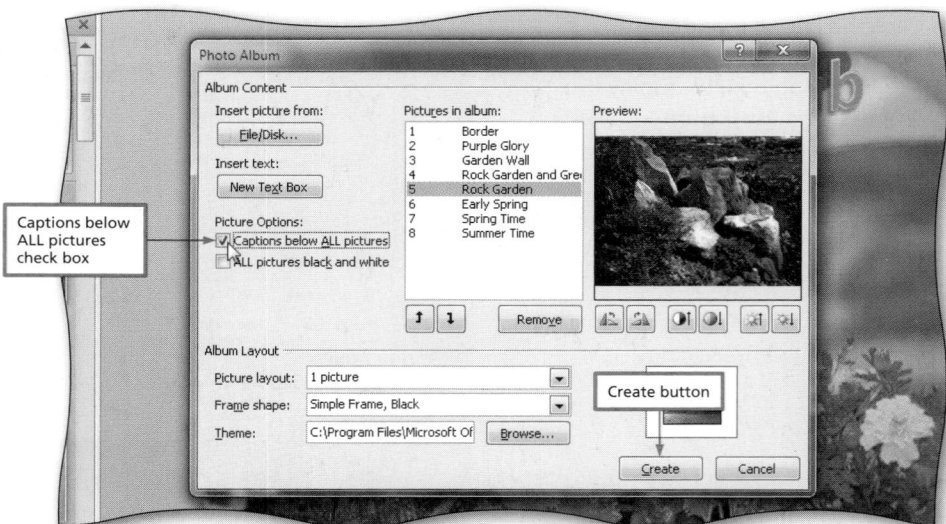

Figure 11–48

To Create a Photo Album

Once you have determined the picture sequence, layout, and frame shape, you are ready to make the photo album. The following step creates the photo album.

1

- Click the Create button (Photo Album dialog box) to close the dialog box and create a photo album with a title page and eight pictures (Figure 11–49).

 Why does a particular name display below the Photo Album title?

PowerPoint displays the user name that was entered when the program was installed. To see this name, display the Backstage view, click Options to display the PowerPoint Options dialog box, and then view or change the name entered in the User name text box in the Personalize your copy of Microsoft Office area.

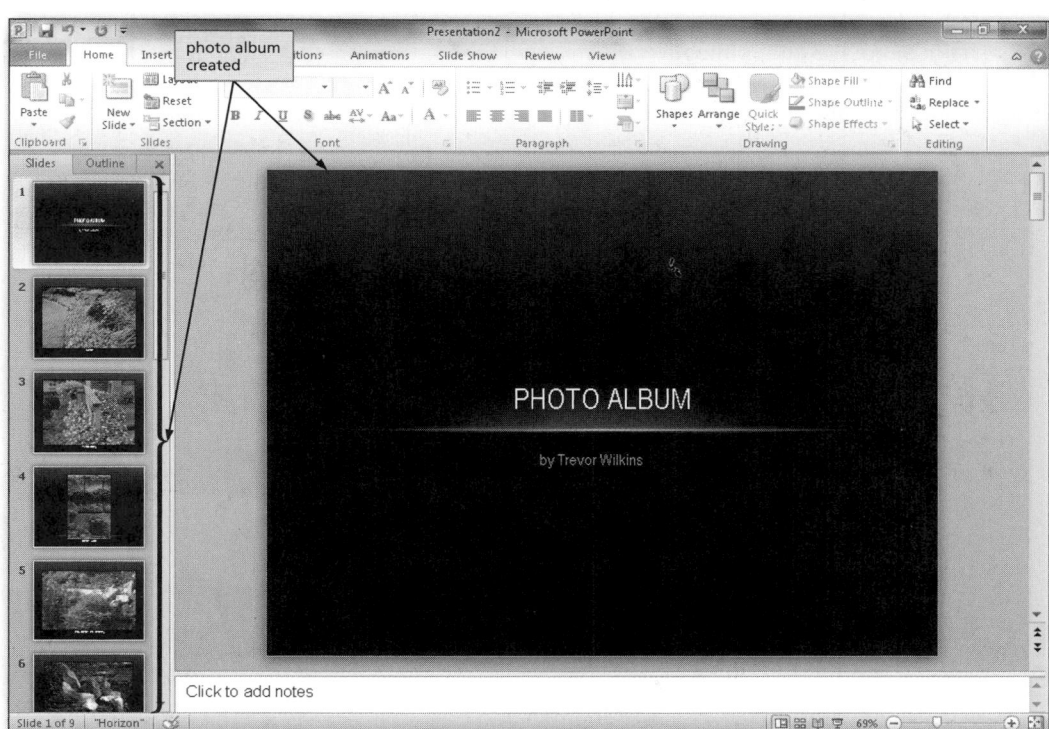

Figure 11–49

To Edit a Photo Album

Once you review the photo album PowerPoint creates, you can modify the contents by adding and deleting pictures, changing the layout and borders, and adding transitions. The following steps edit the photo album by changing the border color and adding a text box on a new slide.

1

- Display the Insert tab and then click the New Photo Album button arrow (Insert tab | Images group) to display the Photo Album menu (Figure 11–50).

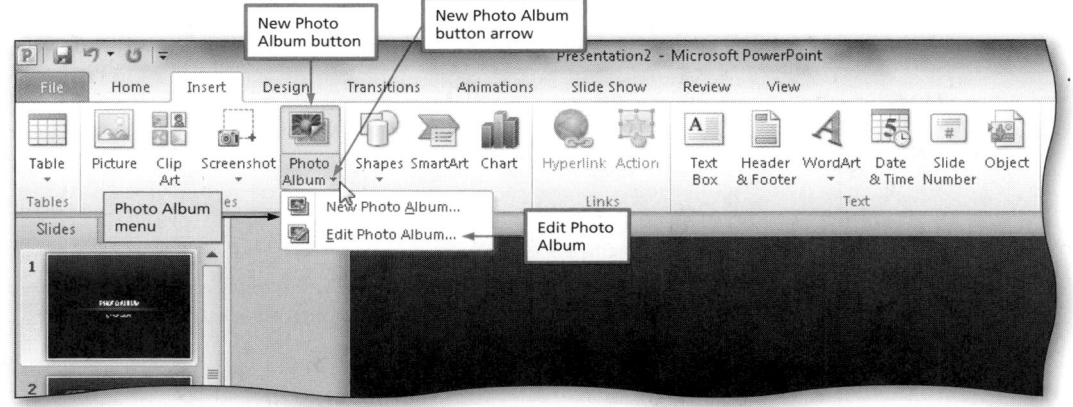

Figure 11–50

2

- Click Edit Photo Album in the menu to display the Edit Photo Album dialog box.

- Click the Frame shape box arrow to display the Frame shape list and then click Simple Frame, White in the list to change the border color from black to white.

- Click the New Text Box button (Edit Photo Album dialog box) to insert a new slide as Slide 9 in the album with the name, Text Box.

- Click the Move Up button eight times to move this picture upward as the first picture in the slide show (Figure 11–51).

Q&A Can I insert a text box on one slide that already has a picture?

Yes. Click the Text Box button (Insert tab | Text group) and then click the slide where you want to insert the text box. You then can arrange the text box and picture on the slide.

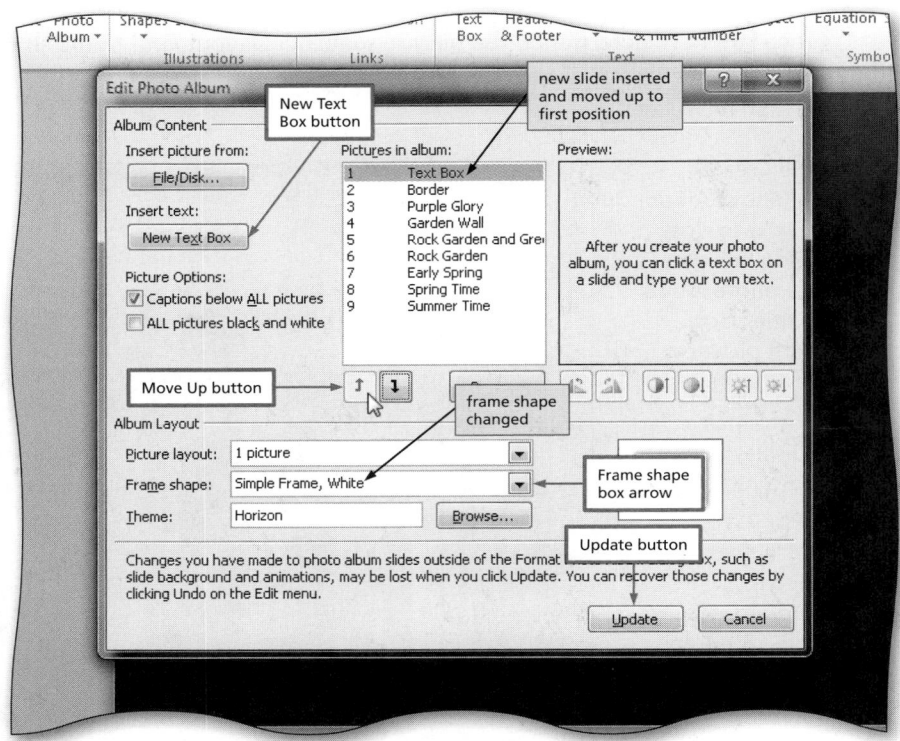

Figure 11–51

3

- Click the Update button (Edit Photo Album dialog box) to make the changes to the photo album.

- Apply the Glitter transition and then change the duration to 5 seconds for all slides.

BTW

Linking Files
If you link one file in landscape orientation to another in portrait orientation, you can give the impression that you have mixed the orientations. It is suggested you save both presentations in one folder so that the links will remain connected if you move or copy the folder.

To Insert and Format Text in a Photo Album

PowerPoint inserts text into the slides, such as the file name for captions and the user name associated with the Microsoft Office installation as the subtitle text on the title slide. You can revise and format this text by changing the font, font size, color, and any other font styles and effects. The following steps edit text in the photo album.

1 With Slide 1 displaying, select the title text, Photo Album, and then type `Granville Garden Club` as the replacement text.

2 Select the subtitle text and then type `Members' Photographs` as the replacement text.

3 Increase the font size of the title text to 48 point and the subtitle text to 32 point.

4 Display Slide 2, select the words, Text Box, and then type `The Granville Garden Club is celebrating its 10`th` year of community beautification.` as the replacement text.

5 Press the ENTER key two times and then type, `These photographs reflect our members' tremendous gardening talents.` as the second paragraph.

6 Display Slide 3, select the caption text, and then type `Colorful flowers make attractive borders.` as the new caption.

7 Display Slide 7, select the caption text, and then type `Boulders create an interesting garden focal point.` as the new caption.

8 Display Slide 1 and then run the slide show.

To Change Document Properties and Save the Photo Album Presentation

Before saving the photo album presentation, you want to add your name, class name, and some keywords as document properties. The following steps use the Document Information Panel to change document properties and then save the document.

1 Display the Document Information Panel and then type your name as the Author property.

2 Type your course and section in the Subject property.

3 Type `garden club, photo contest, annuals, perennials, bulbs` as the Keywords property.

4 Close the Document Information Panel.

5 Save the presentation with the file name, Granville Photo Album (Figure 11–52).

BTW

Resetting Placeholders
You can reset all customization changes to the preset options. Click the Reset button (Home tab | Slides group) or right-click the slide or thumbnail and then click Reset Slide on the shortcut menu. To retain custom formatting changes and move the placeholders to their original locations, right-click the slide or thumbnail and then click the Layout button (Home tab | Slides group) and reapply the active layout from the Layout gallery.

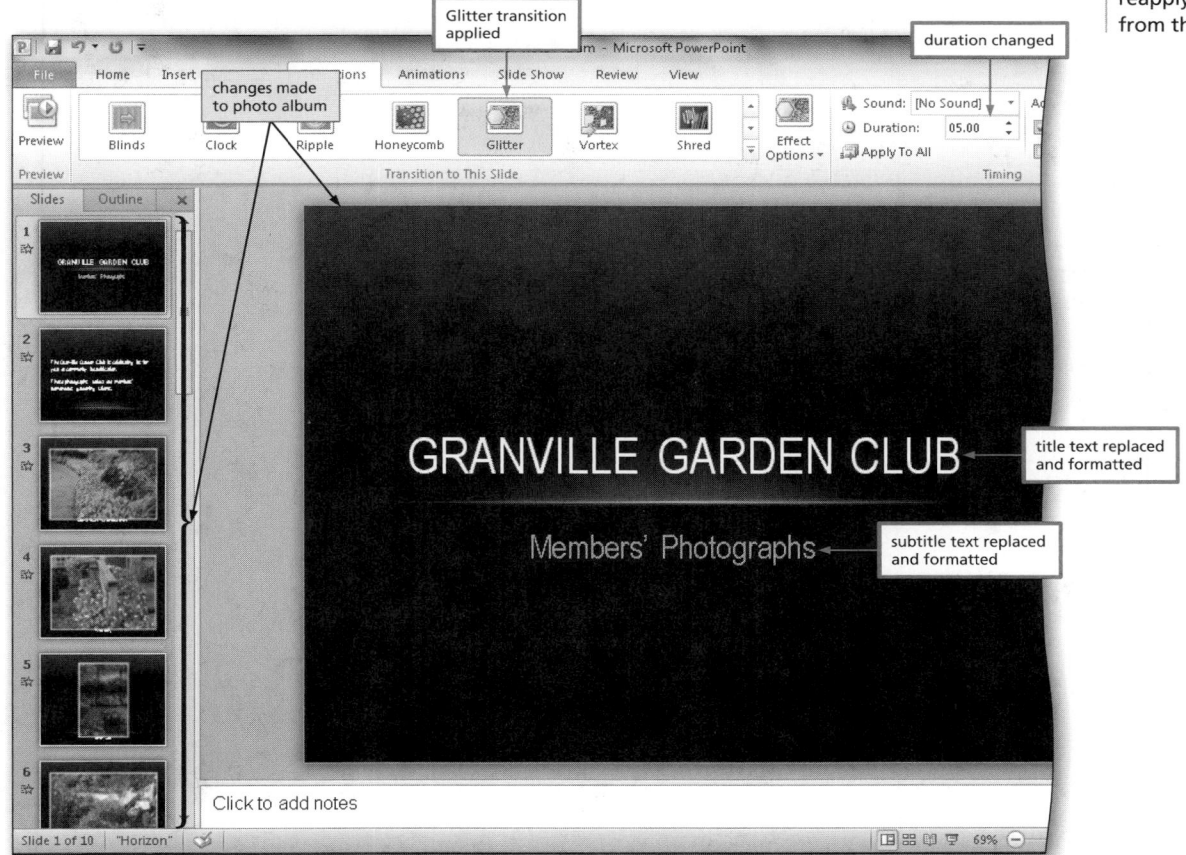

Figure 11–52

To Create Black-and-White Images in a Photo Album

Black-and-white pictures often generate interest and give a unique version of the color photographs. The series of shades ranging from black to white, or grayscale, provide a different perspective on our world. The following steps edit a photo album to use black-and-white images.

1

- Display the Insert tab, click the New Photo Album button arrow and then click Edit Photo Album.

- Click the 'ALL pictures black and white' check box to add a check mark (Figure 11–53).

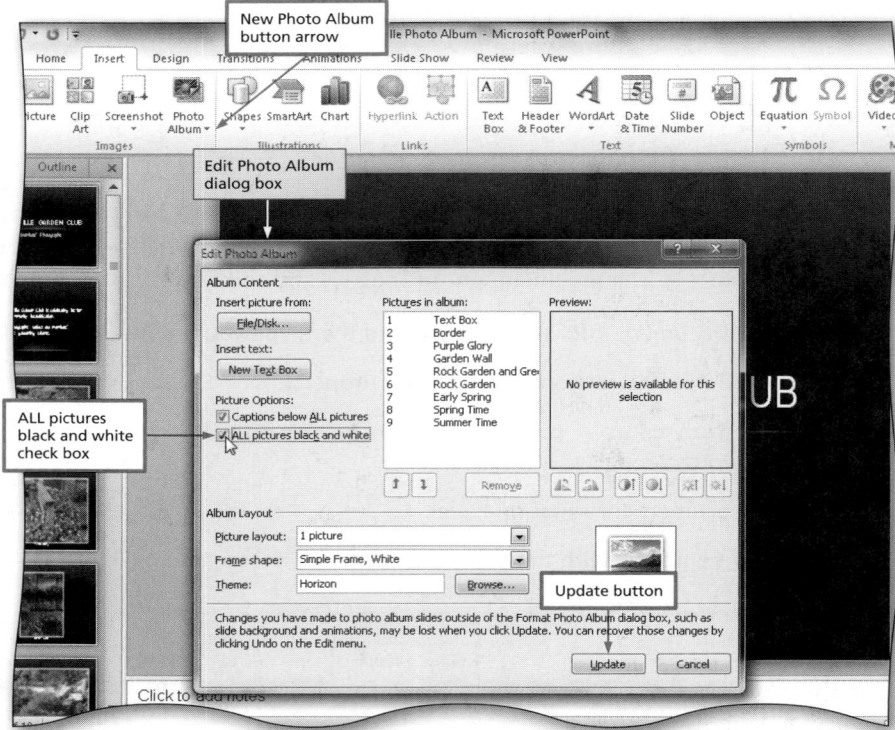

Figure 11–53

2

- Click the Update button (Edit Photo Album dialog box) to change the photographs from color to black-and-white images on the slides.

- Run the slide show.

- Save the presentation with the file name, Granville Photo Album Black and White.

- Print the presentation as a handout with two slides per page (Figure 11–54).

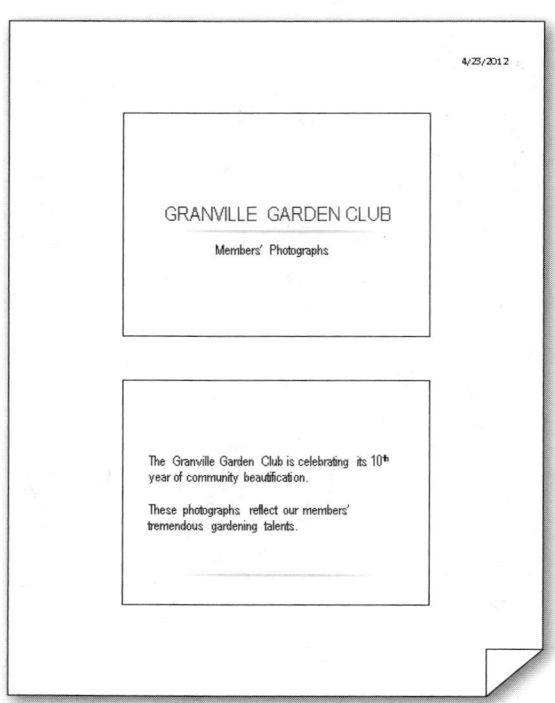

(a) Handout Page 1

Figure 11–54

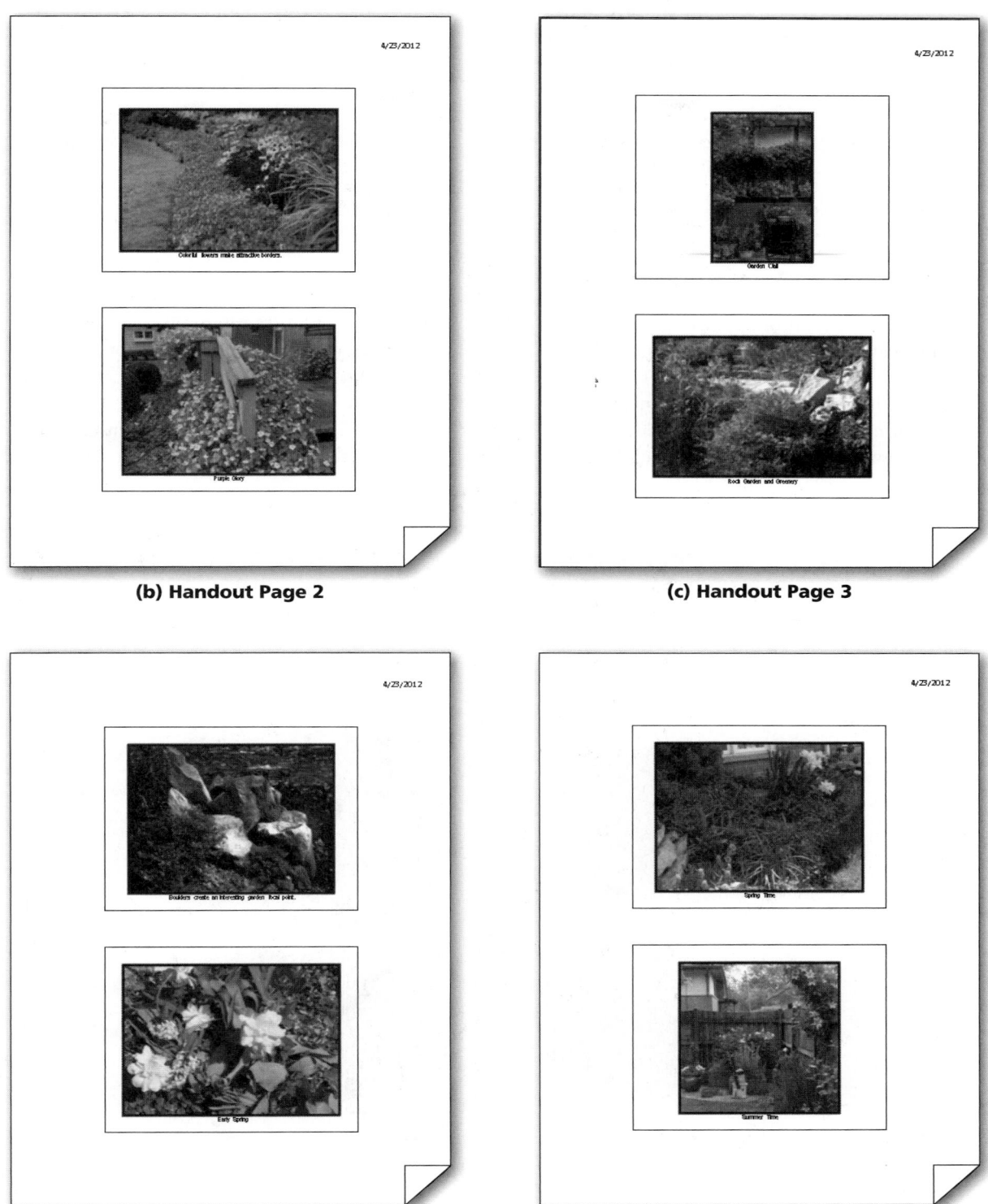

(b) Handout Page 2

(c) Handout Page 3

(d) Handout Page 4

(e) Handout Page 5

Figure 11–54 (Continued)

To Close a Presentation

The second photo album with the black-and-white pictures is complete. The following step closes the Granville Photo Album Black and White file.

1 With the Backstage view open, click Close to close the open Granville Photo Album Black and White file without quitting PowerPoint.

To Use the Research Pane to Find Information

You can search for information regarding a wide variety of topics using PowerPoint's reference materials. A commonly used research tool is the thesaurus to find synonyms for words on your slides or in the Notes pane. The Research task pane also includes a dictionary, encyclopedia, and translation services. In addition, if you are connected to the Web, it provides a search engine and other useful Web sites.

Assume you desire to learn about geraniums, which are featured on Slide 12 in the Granville Garden Club presentation. The following steps use the Research task pane to locate Web sites that provide information about this particular flower.

1

- If necessary, open the Granville Garden Club presentation.

- Display the Review tab and then click the Research button (Review tab | Proofing group) to display the Research task pane (Figure 11–55).

Q&A

Why does my Research task pane look different?

Your computer's settings and Microsoft's Web site search settings determine the way your Research task pane is displayed.

Figure 11–55

2

- Type **geranium** in the Search for text box and then click the Start searching button to perform an Internet search for Web sites with information about this search term (Figure 11–56).

Q&A What is Bing?

It is the name of Microsoft's search engine, which is a program that locates Web sites, Web pages, images, videos, news, maps, and other information related to a specific topic.

Q&A What should I do if I see the message, No results were found, instead of a list of search results?

If a 'Get updates to your services' icon is displayed at the bottom of the Research pane, click it, follow instructions to update your services, and then repeat your search.

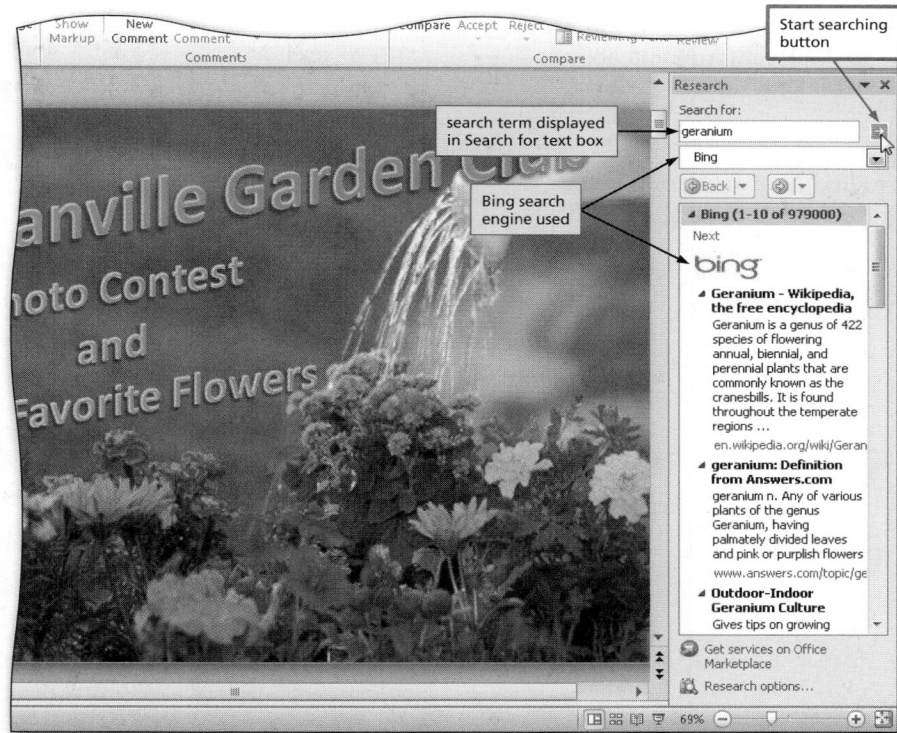

Figure 11–56

3

- Click the Search for box arrow in the Research task pane to display a list of search locations (Figure 11–57).

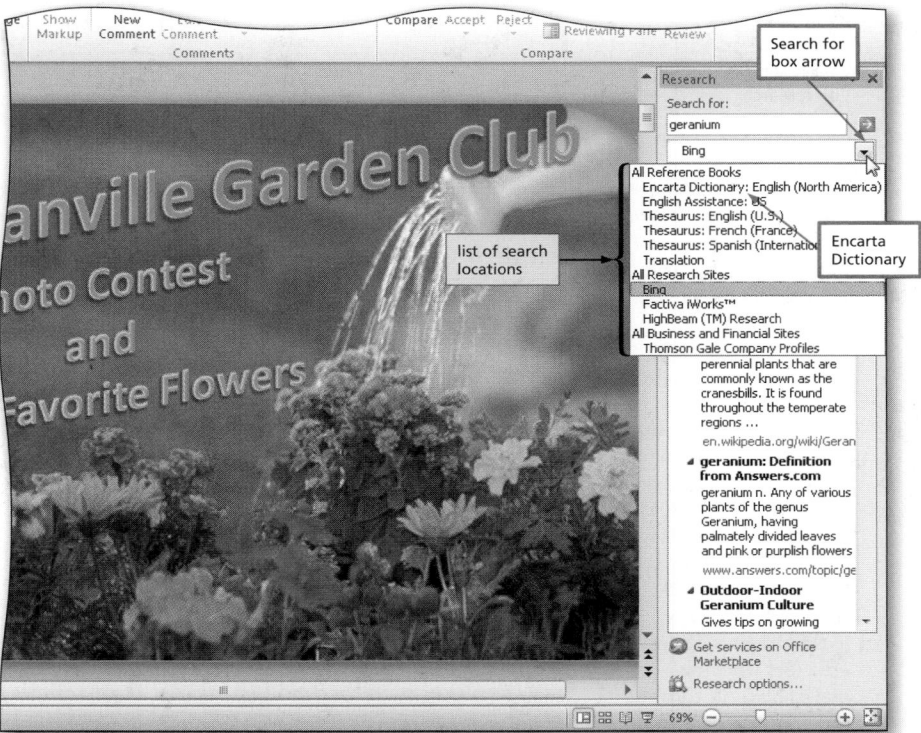

Figure 11–57

4
- Click Encarta Dictionary in the list to display information about a geranium (Figure 11–58).

5
- Click the Close button in the Research task pane.

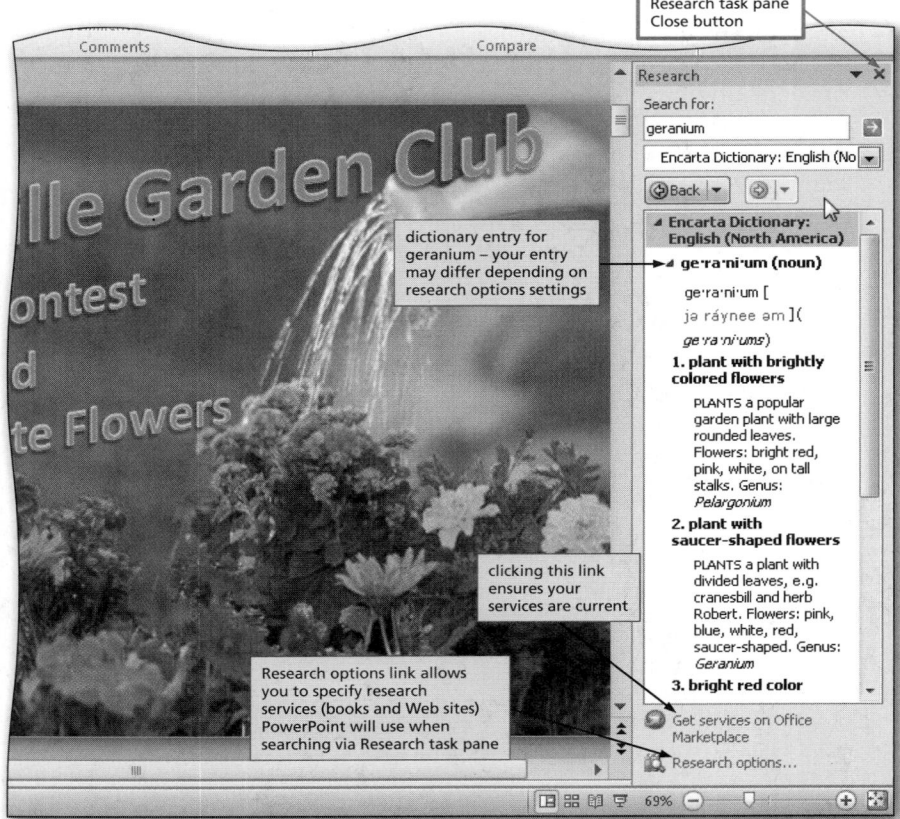

Figure 11–58

BTW

Turn Off Slide Timings
If you recorded narration with slide timings, you might decide to play the comments for your audience but want to advance the slides manually. PowerPoint gives you the option to turn slide timings off and then turn them back on without having to recreate them. Click the Set Up Slide Show button (Slide Show tab | Set Up group) and then click Manually in the Advance slides area (Set Up Show dialog box). To turn the slide timings back on, click 'Using timings, if present' in the Advance slides area (Set Up Show dialog box).

TO RECORD NARRATION

In some situations, you may want your viewers to hear recorded narration that accompanies slides. If your topic is flowers grown by local gardeners, you may want to hear their voices describe the plants that are displayed on slides. You can record narration separately and then add this file to the slide. You also can record narration while the slide show is running. To record this narration, you would perform the following steps.

1. Display the Slide Show tab and then click the Record Slide Show button arrow (Slide Show tab | Set Up group).

2. Click Start Recording from Beginning if you want to begin with the first slide or click Start Recording from Current Slide if you want to begin with the slide that is displaying on your screen.

3. Click the Narrations and laser pointer check box (Record Slide Show dialog box) and, if appropriate, click the Slide and animation timings check box (Record Slide Show dialog box) to select or remove the check mark.

4. Click the Start Recording button (Record Slide Show dialog box).

5. When you have finished speaking, right-click the slide and then click End Show on the shortcut menu.

To Preview Narration

Once you have recorded narration, you can play the audio to review the sound. To preview this narration, you would perform the following steps.

1. In Normal view, click the sound icon on the slide.

2. Display the Audio Tools Playback tab and then click the Play button (Audio Tools Playback tab | Preview group).

To Show a Presentation with or without Narration

If you have recorded narration to accompany your slides, you can choose whether to include this narration when you run your slide show. You would perform the following steps to run the slide show either with or without narration.

1. Display the Slide Show tab and then click the Set Up Slide Show button (Slide Show tab | Set Up group) to display the Set Up Show dialog box.

2. If you do not want the narration to play, click the 'Show without narration' check box in the Show options area (Set Up Show dialog box) and then click the OK button.

3. If you have chosen to show the presentation without narration and then desire to allow audience members to hear this recording, click the 'Show without narration' check box in the Show options area (Set Up Show dialog box) to uncheck this option and then click the OK button.

BTW

Golden Rectangle Proportion
Research has determined that people prefer reading a sheet of paper that is approximately the size of their head. This ideal size has the proportion, called the golden rectangle, which is one-and-one-half times longer than its width.

Break Point: If you wish to take a break, this is a good place to do so. You can quit PowerPoint now. To resume at a later time, start PowerPoint, open the file called Granville Garden Club, and continue following the steps from this location forward.

Sharing and Distributing a Presentation

Many people design PowerPoint presentations to accompany a speech given in front of an audience, and they also develop the slide shows to share with family, work associates, and friends in a variety of ways. For example, they can print a slide on thick paper and send the document through the mail. They also can e-mail the file or create a video to upload to a Web site or view on a computer. Video files can become quite large in file size, so PowerPoint allows you to reduce the size by compressing the file.

Use hyperlinks to show slides with landscape and portrait orientations.
When you are creating your presentation, you have the option to display all your slides in either the default landscape orientation or in portrait orientation. You may, however, desire to have slides with both orientations during a single presentation. Using hyperlinks is one solution to mixing the orientations. Apply a hyperlink to an object on the last slide in one orientation and then hyperlink to another presentation with slides in the other orientation. If you desire to hyperlink to one particular slide in a second presentation, click the Bookmark button in the Insert Hyperlink dialog box and then select the title of the slide you want to use as your link. Once you have displayed the desired slides in the second presentation, create another hyperlink from that presentation back to a slide in your original presentation.

Plan Ahead

To Change the Slide Orientation

By default, PowerPoint displays slides in landscape orientation, where the width dimension is greater than the height dimension. You can change this setting to specify that the slides display in portrait orientation, so the height dimension is greater than the width dimension. The portrait orientation is useful to display tall objects, people who are standing, or faces. The following steps change the slide orientation.

1
- Open the presentation, Spring Meeting, located on the Data Files for Students.

- Display the Design tab and then click the Slide Orientation button (Design tab | Page Setup group) to display the Slide Orientation gallery (Figure 11–59).

2
- Click Portrait to change the slide orientation from landscape to portrait.

Figure 11–59

To Set Up a Custom Size

To announce the Granville Garden Club's spring meeting and encourage members to attend, you want to mail postcards to the members' homes. To simplify the process, you can create a PowerPoint slide that is the precise measurement of a postcard, print the card on heavy paper stock, and mail the card to club members. You can specify that your PowerPoint slides are a precise dimension. The following steps change the slide size to a custom size.

1
- With the Design tab displaying, click the Page Setup button (Design tab | Page Setup group) to display the Page Setup dialog box.

- Click the 'Slides sized for' box arrow to display the size list (Figure 11–60).

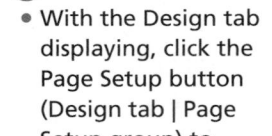
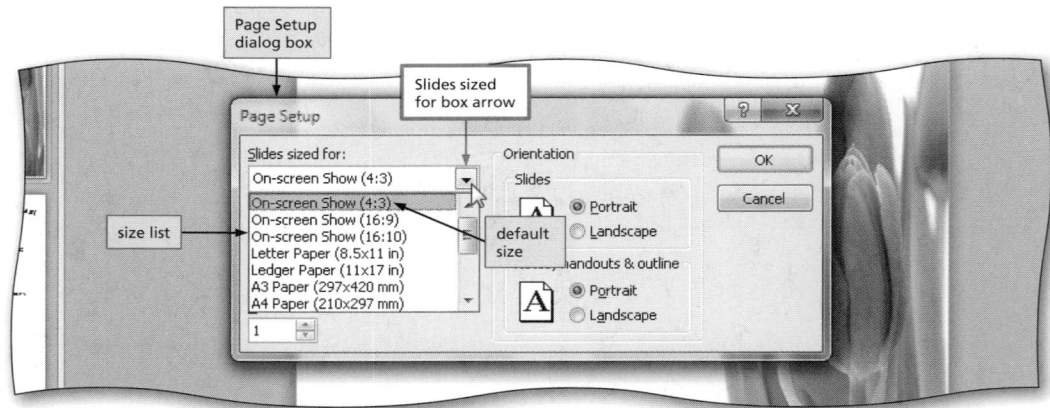

Figure 11–60

2

- Scroll down and then click Custom in the size list.

- Click the Width down arrow repeatedly until 5 is displayed in the Width text box.

- Click the Height down arrow repeatedly until 7 is displayed in the Height text box (Figure 11–61).

Q&A

Can I type the width and height measurements in the text boxes instead of clicking the down arrows repeatedly?

Yes. You also can click and hold down the mouse button instead of repeatedly clicking the arrows until the desired dimensions are displayed.

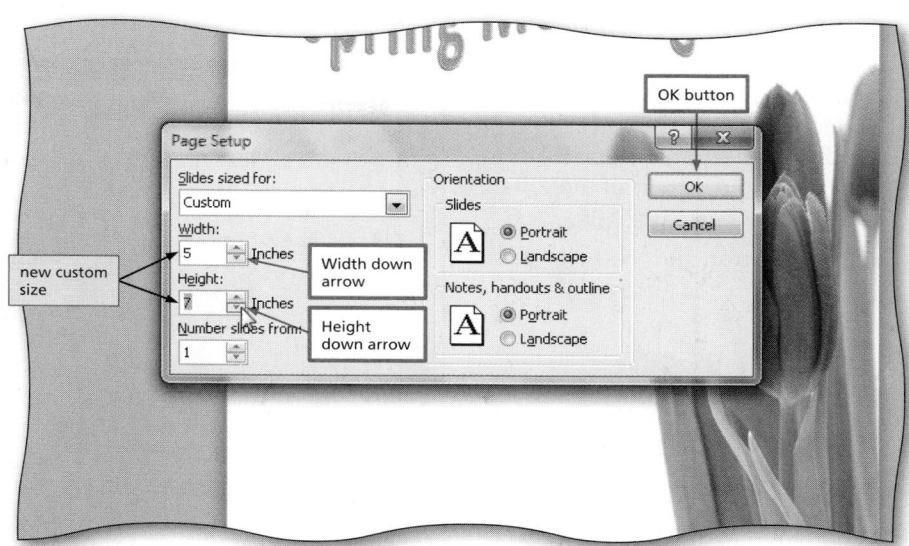

Figure 11–61

3

- Click the OK button (Page Setup dialog box) to apply the custom sizes and close the dialog box.

To Display Multiple Presentation Windows Simultaneously

When you are reviewing elements of several presentations, it often is efficient and convenient to open both presentations and display them simultaneously on the screen. The following steps display three open presentations simultaneously.

1

- Open the presentation, Alpine Beauty, located on the Data Files for Students and then display the View tab (Figure 11–62).

Figure 11–62

2

- Click the Cascade button (View tab | Window group) to display the three open presentations – Alpine Beauty, Spring Meeting, and Granville Garden Club – from the upper-left to the lower-right corners of the screen.

Q&A

What is the difference between the Cascade button and the Arrange All button?

When you click the Cascade button, the open windows display overlapped, or stacked, on each other. Clicking the Arrange All button tiles all the open windows side by side on the screen. Each window may display narrower than in normal view so that all the open windows are visible simultaneously.

- If necessary, click the Alpine Beauty presentation title bar to display that presentation in the front of the screen (Figure 11–63).

Q&A

The Alpine Beauty title bar is not visible on my screen. Can I move the presentation windows so that it is visible?

Yes. You can drag the presentation title bars to arrange the windows.

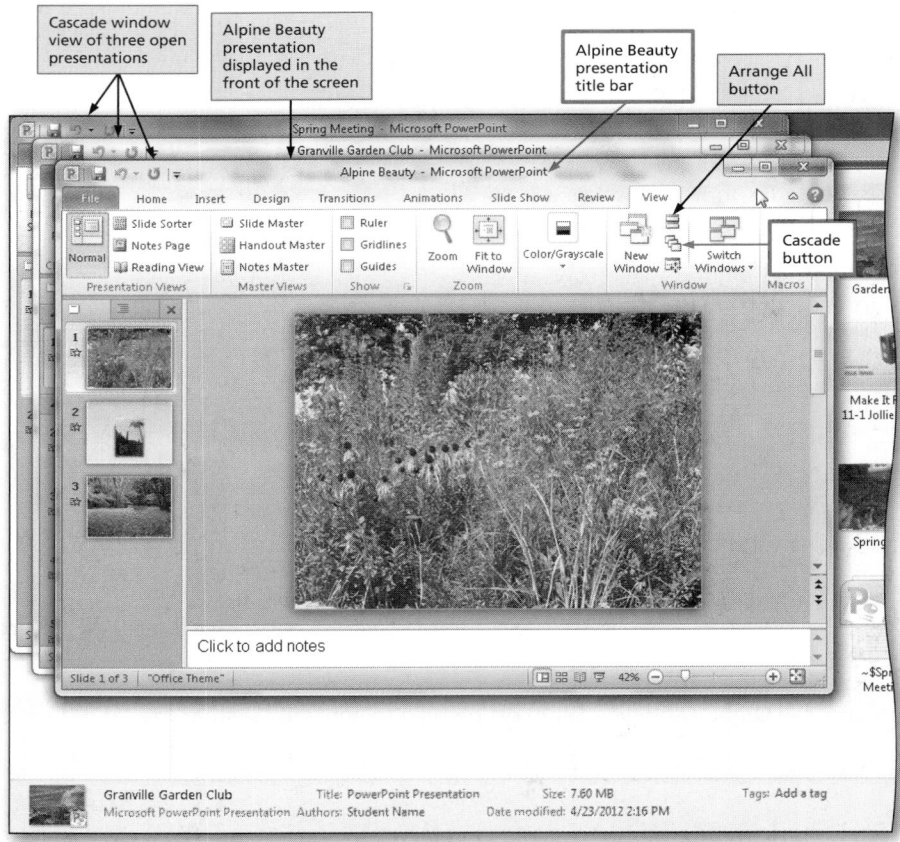

Figure 11–63

To Copy a Video File

Slide 2 in the Alpine Beauty presentation contains a video clip of a stream that you want to insert at the bottom of Slide 2 in the Spring Meeting file. With multiple presentations open simultaneously on your screen, you can view all the slides quickly and decide which elements of one presentation you desire to copy to another. The following steps copy the video file from Slide 2 of the Alpine Beauty presentation to Slide 2 of the Spring Meeting presentation.

BTW

Use the buttons in the View tab's Windows group to help you manipulate PowerPoint windows. As the button names imply, the New Window button opens a new window with an identical view of the open window; the Switch Windows button changes the view from one open window to another. The Arrange All button tiles all the open windows side-by-side on the screen, and the Cascade Windows button overlaps these windows diagonally. The Move Split button allows you to move the splitter bars that separate the parts of the window; use the ARROW keys to increase or decrease the size of the Notes pane, the Slide pane, or the pane that contains the Outline and Slides tabs and then press the ENTER key to return to your open document.

1

• Click the Slide 2 thumbnail of the Alpine Beauty presentation to display that slide.

• Right-click the video image in the center of the slide to select it and to display the shortcut menu (Figure 11–64).

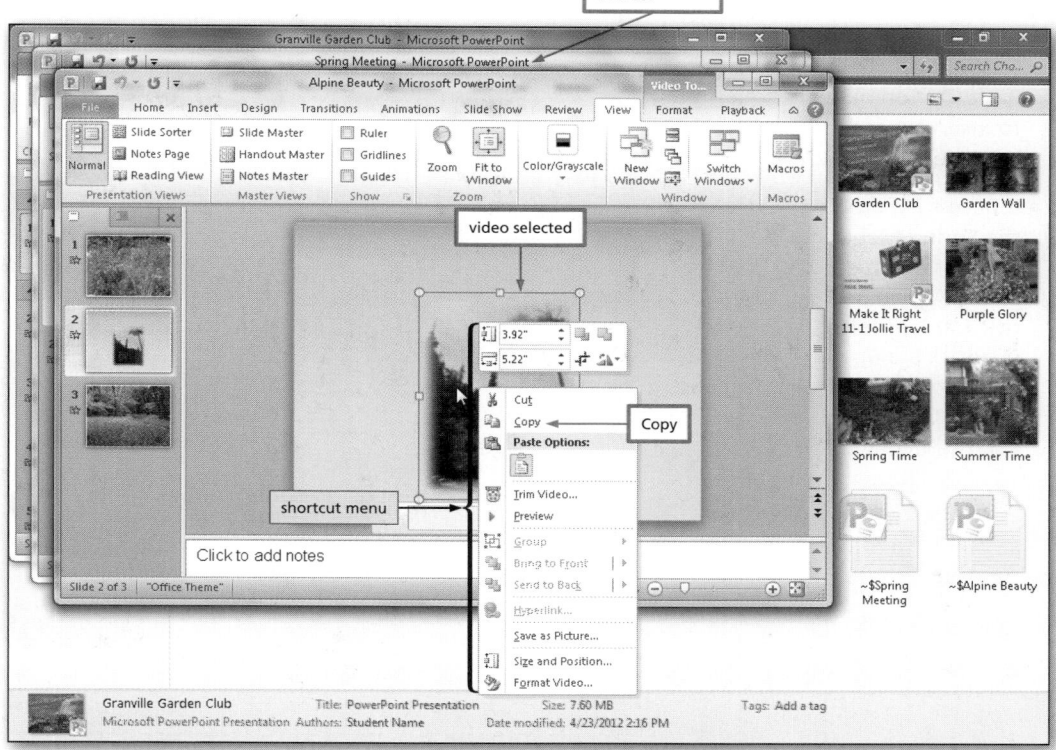

Figure 11–64

2

• Click Copy on the shortcut menu.

• Click the Spring Meeting presentation title bar to display that presentation in the front of the screen.

• If necessary, click the Slide 2 thumbnail of the Spring Meeting presentation to display that slide.

• Right-click the slide to display the shortcut menu and then point to the Use Destination Theme Paste Option button to display a preview of the video clip on that slide (Figure 11–65).

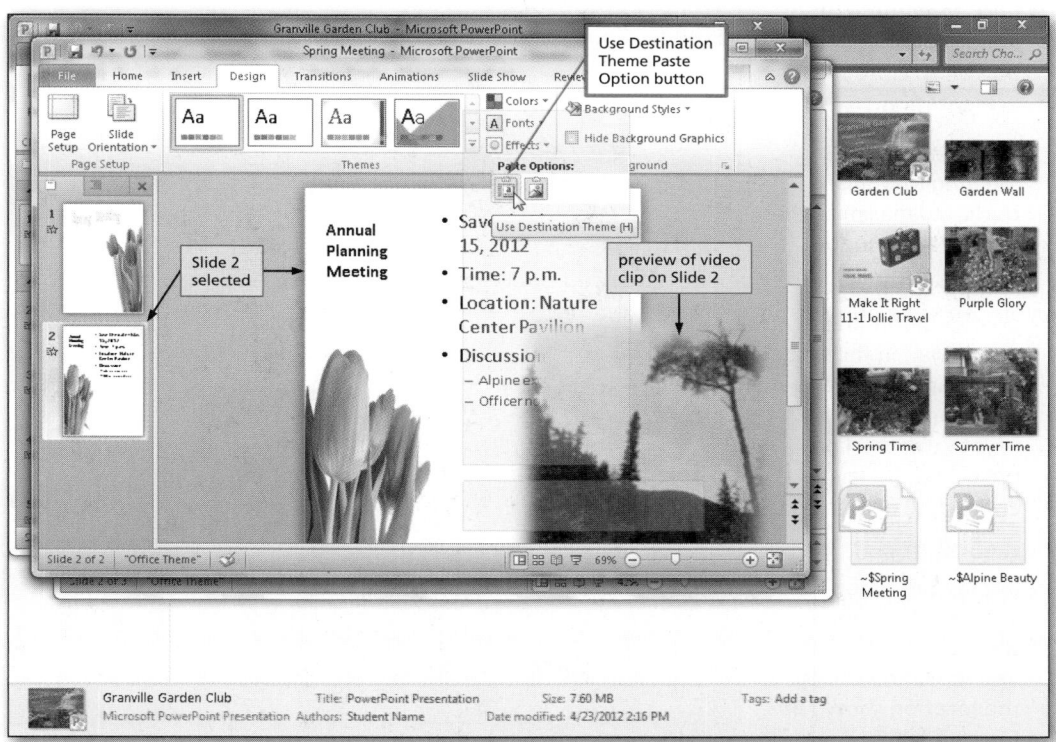

Figure 11–65

3

- Click the Use Destination Theme Paste Option button to insert the video into the slide.

- If necessary, drag the Spring Meeting title bar downward so the Alpine Beauty title bar is visible (Figure 11–66).

Figure 11–66

4

- Click the Alpine Beauty Close button to close that presentation.

- Click the Spring Meeting Maximize button to maximize the PowerPoint window.

- Position the mouse pointer before the word, May, in the first paragraph and then press the SHIFT+ENTER keys to create a line break and display the entire date on one line.

- Select the video, display the Video Tools Format tab, size the video to 3" × 4", and move the clip to the location shown in Figure 11–67.

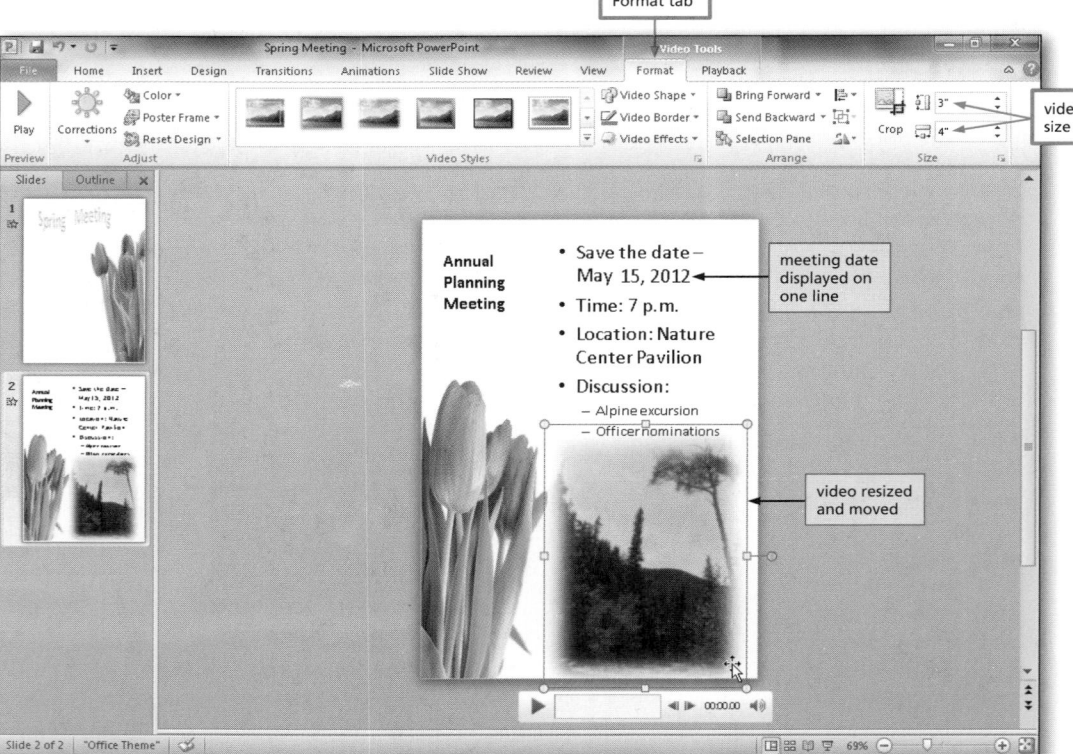

Figure 11–67

To Compress a Video File

The file size of videos can be quite large. This size can pose a problem if you desire to e-mail a presentation or if the space on a storage device is small. PowerPoint includes a feature that will compress your file to reduce its size. You can specify one of three compression qualities: Presentation, Internet, or Low. In this project, you are going to e-mail the Spring Meeting file, so you desire to keep the file size as small as possible without sacrificing too much resolution quality. The following steps compress the video file.

1
- With the video clip selected on Slide 2, display the Backstage view and then click the Compress Media button (Info tab | Media Size and Performance area) to display the Media Size and Performance menu (Figure 11–68).

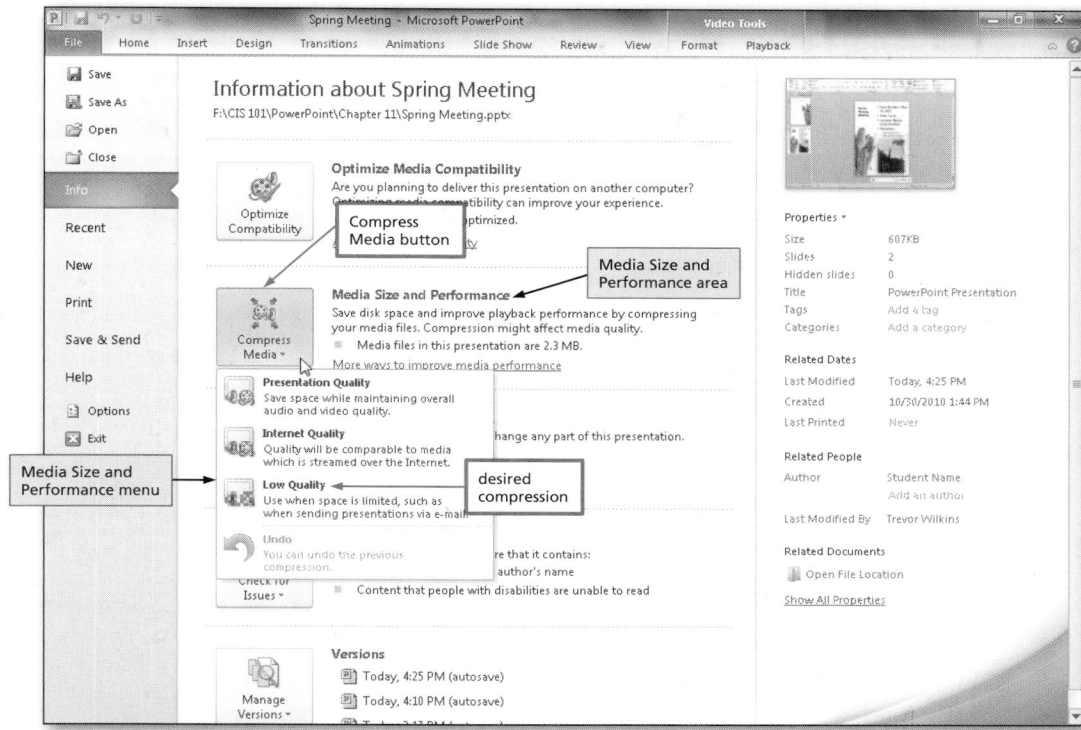

Figure 11–68

2
- Click Low Quality to display the Compress Media dialog box and compress the file (Figure 11–69).

3
- Click the Close button (Compress Media dialog box) to return to the Backstage view.

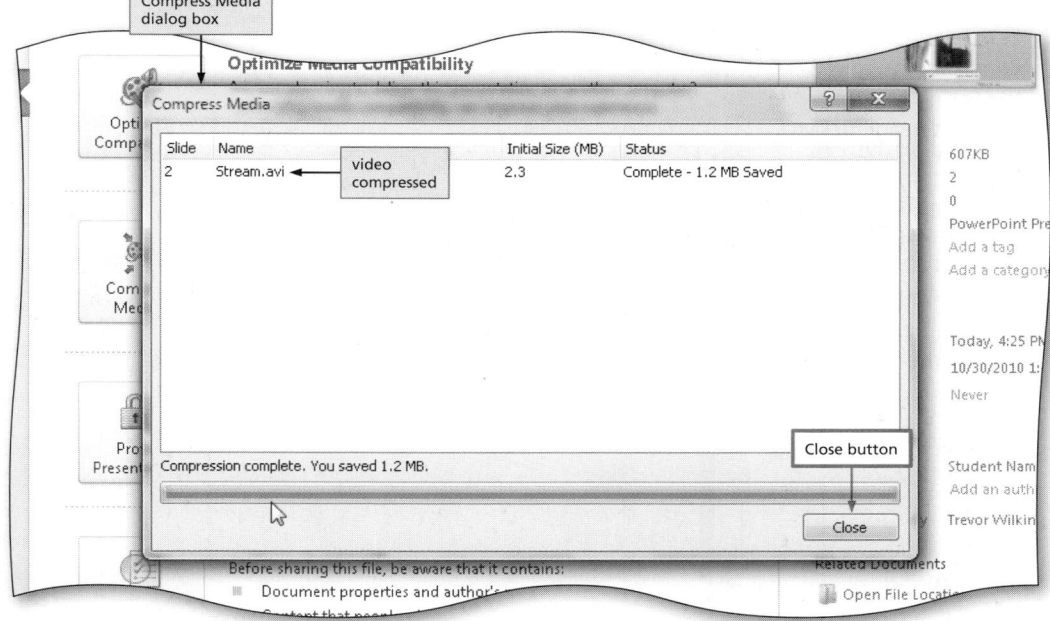

Figure 11–69

To E-Mail a Slide Show from within PowerPoint

Presenters often e-mail their presentations to friends and colleagues to solicit feedback and share their work. PowerPoint offers a convenient method of e-mailing a presentation directly within PowerPoint. The following steps e-mail the slide show.

1

• With the Backstage view displaying, display the Save & Send tab (Figure 11–70).

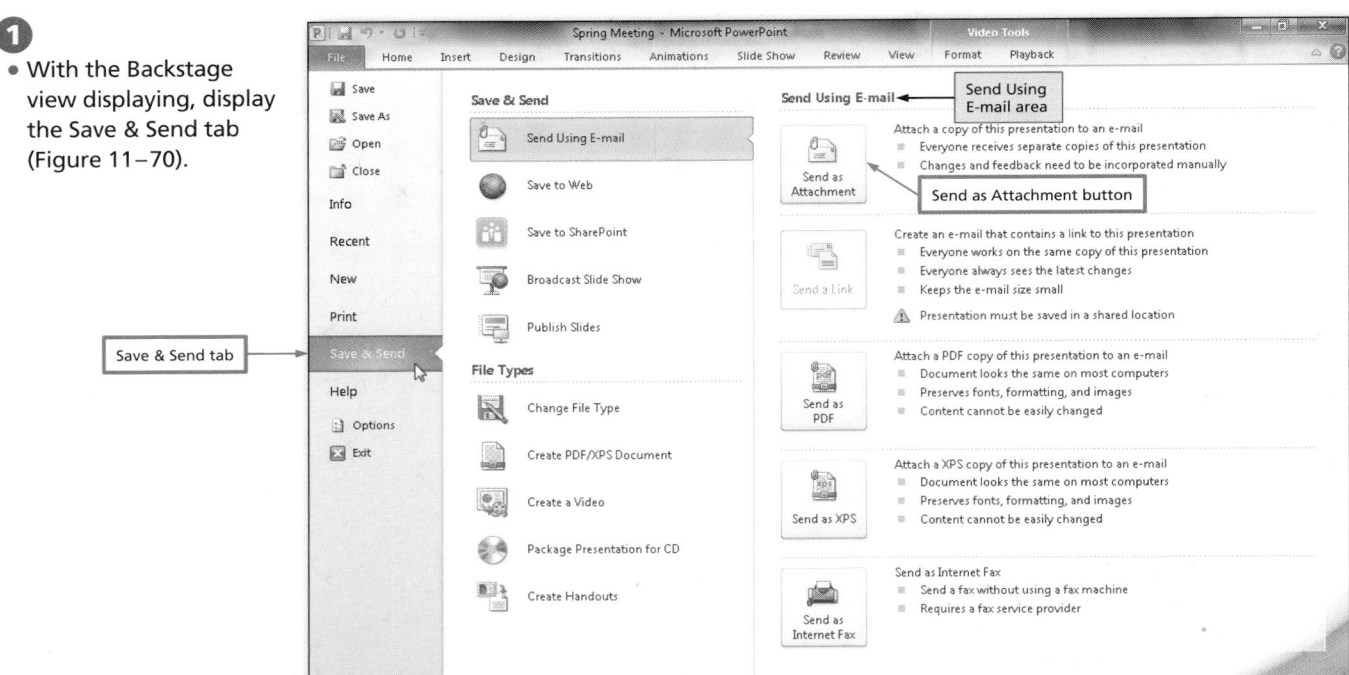

Figure 11–70

2

• Click the Send as Attachment button in the Send Using E-mail area to open the Spring Meeting. pptx – Message (HTML) window in Microsoft Outlook (Figure 11–71).

Q&A

Must I use Microsoft Outlook to send this e-mail message?

No, you do not have to have Outlook installed; however, you should have an e-mail program installed in Windows to send the e-mail. If you don't use Outlook, you could install Windows Live Mail or another e-mail program. An e-mail program must be installed for the step to work.

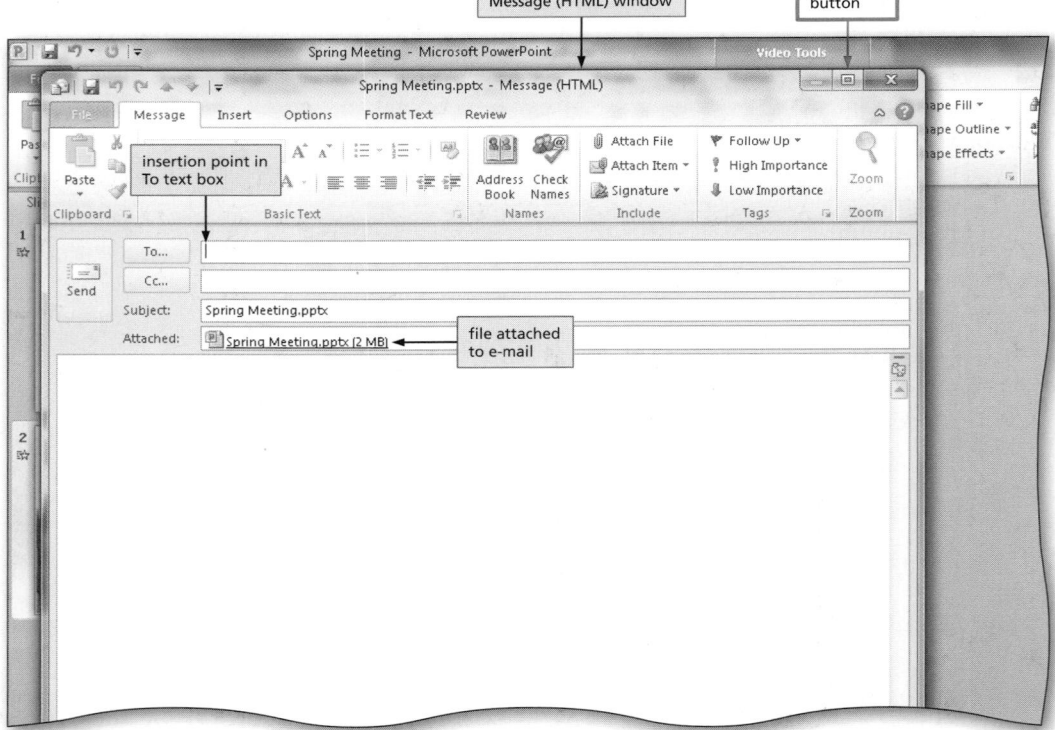

Figure 11–71

3

- If necessary, click the Maximize button in the Spring Meeting. pptx – Message (HTML) window to maximize the window.

- With the insertion point in the To text box, type `rose. stewart@ hotmail.com` (with no spaces) to enter the e-mail address of the recipient.

- Click to position the insertion point in the Subject text box, select the file name that is displaying, and then type `Upcoming Meeting` as the subject.

- Press the TAB key two times to move the insertion point into the message area (Figure 11–72).

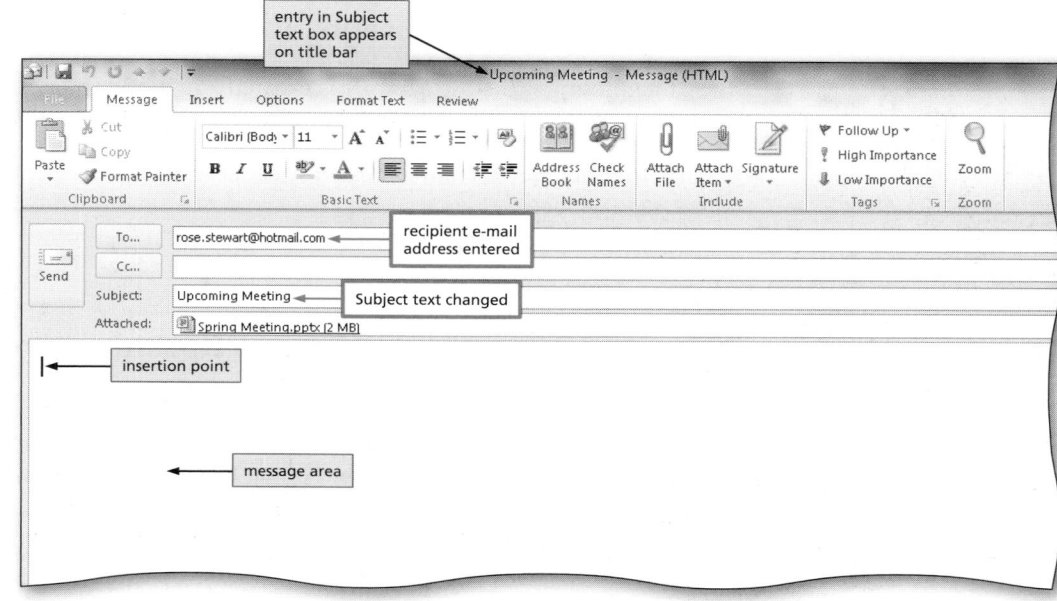

Figure 11–72

4

- Type `Ms. Stewart,` as the greeting line.

- Press the ENTER key to move the insertion point to the beginning of the next line.

- Type `The announcement for our upcoming Spring Meeting is attached. I hope you will be able to join us.` to enter the message text.

- Press the ENTER key twice to insert a blank line and move the insertion point to the beginning of the next line. Type `Trevor Wilkins` as the signature line (Figure 11–73).

Figure 11–73

Q&A

May I type my own name instead of Trevor's name?

Yes. You may desire to have your name on the title slide, or your instructor may request that you substitute your name or provide other identifying information.

To Send an E-Mail Message

The message to Rose Stewart is created and ready to be sent. The following step sends the completed e-mail message and attached presentation to Rose Stewart.

1 Click the Send button in the message header to send the e-mail message and to close the message window.

To Run the Presentation, Change Document Properties, and Save the Presentation

When you run the Spring Meeting presentation, the video will play automatically because the file had that setting in the Alpine Beauty presentation. Before saving the presentation, you want to add your name, class name, and some keywords as document properties. The following steps run the slide show, use the Document Information Panel to change document properties, and then save the document.

1 Display Slide 1 and then run the presentation.

2 Display the Document Information Panel and then type your name as the Author property.

3 Type your course and section in the Subject property.

4 Type `annual spring meeting, alpine excursion, officers nominations` as the Keywords property.

5 Close the Document Information Panel.

6 Save the presentation with the file name, Spring Meeting Mailer.

7 Display the Backstage view and then click Close to close the Spring Meeting Mailer file without quitting PowerPoint.

Plan Ahead

Rehearse, rehearse, rehearse.
Speakers should spend as much time practicing their presentations as they do preparing their PowerPoint slides. Frequently, however, they use the majority of their preparation time designing and tweaking the slides. Audience members expect to see a presenter who is prepared, confident, and enthusiastic. Practicing the presentation helps convey this image. As you rehearse, focus on a strong introduction that grasps the audience's attention and previews the main points of your talk. You have only one chance to make a good first impression, so begin the speech by establishing eye contact with audience members in various parts of the room. Resist the urge to stare at the slides projected on the screen. Your audience came to your presentation to hear you speak, and rehearsing will help you deliver a high-quality talk that exceeds their expectations.

TO BROADCAST A SLIDE SHOW

PowerPoint's broadcast slide show feature allows you to share your presentation remotely with anyone having an Internet connection. As you display your slides, they see a synchronized view of your slide show in their Web browser, even if they do not have PowerPoint installed on their computers. To broadcast your presentation, you would perform the following steps.

1. Click the Broadcast Slide Show button (Slide Show tab | Start Slide Show group).

2. Ensure that PowerPoint Broadcast Service is selected in the Broadcast Service area and then click the Start Broadcast button (Broadcast Slide Show dialog box).

3. Enter your Windows Live ID e-mail address and password (Connecting to pptbroadcast.officeapps.live.com dialog box) and then click the OK button.

PowerPoint connects to the PowerPoint broadcast service, prepares the broadcast, and then provides a link that you can share with a maximum of 50 remote users. When these people visit the Web site and you start the slide show, they view your presentation with any annotations you make. When you have displayed the last slide, click the End Broadcast button below the Ribbon.

To Create a Video

Watching video files is a common activity with the advent of easy-to-use recording devices and Web sites that host these files. You can convert your PowerPoint presentation to a video file and upload it to a Web site or share the file with people who do not have PowerPoint installed on their computers. The following steps create a video of the Granville Garden Club presentation.

1

- Display the Granville Garden Club file and, if necessary, click the Maximize button in the title bar to maximize the window.

- Display the Backstage view and then display the Save & Send tab.

- Click the Create a Video tab in the File Types area to display the Create a Video area (Figure 11–74).

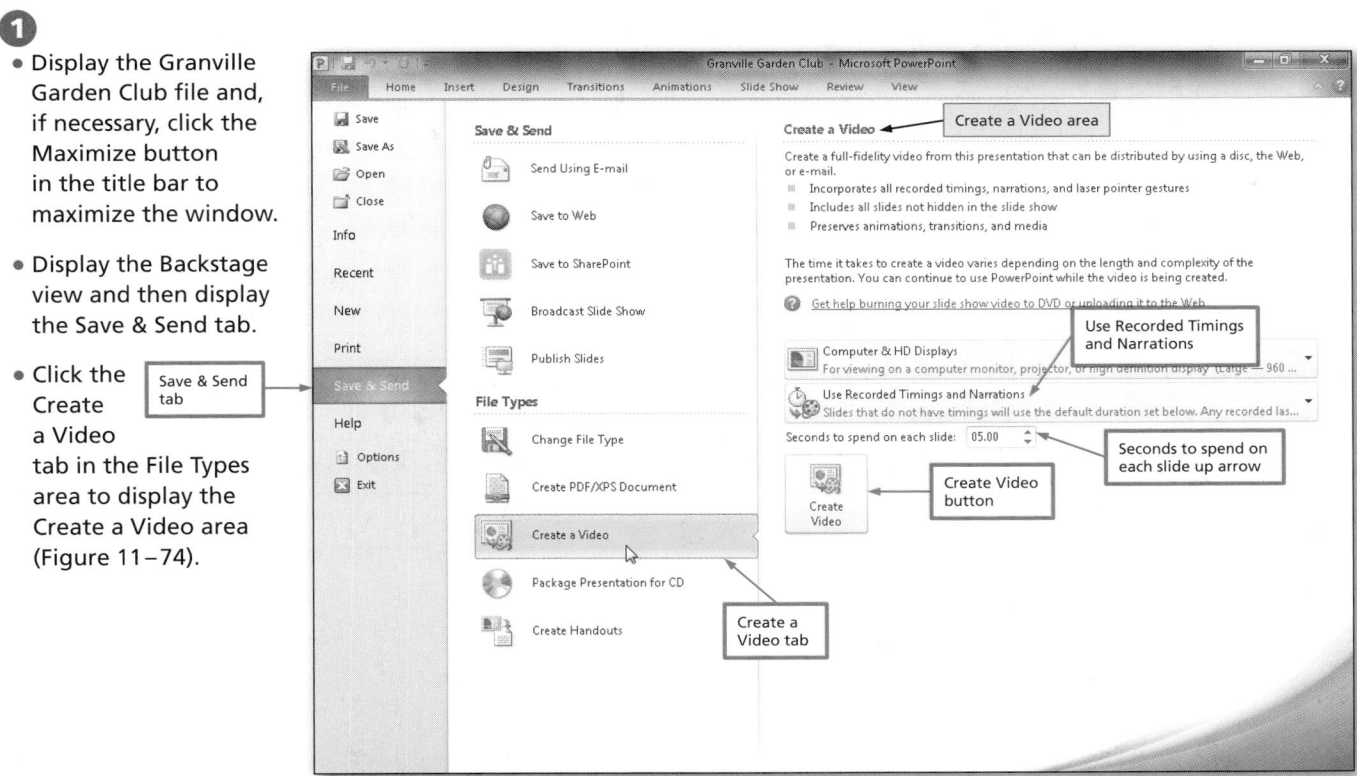

Figure 11–74

- Click Use Recorded
  Timings and
  Narrations in the
  Create a Video area
  to display the Use
  Recorded Timings
  and Narrations menu
  (Figure 11–75).

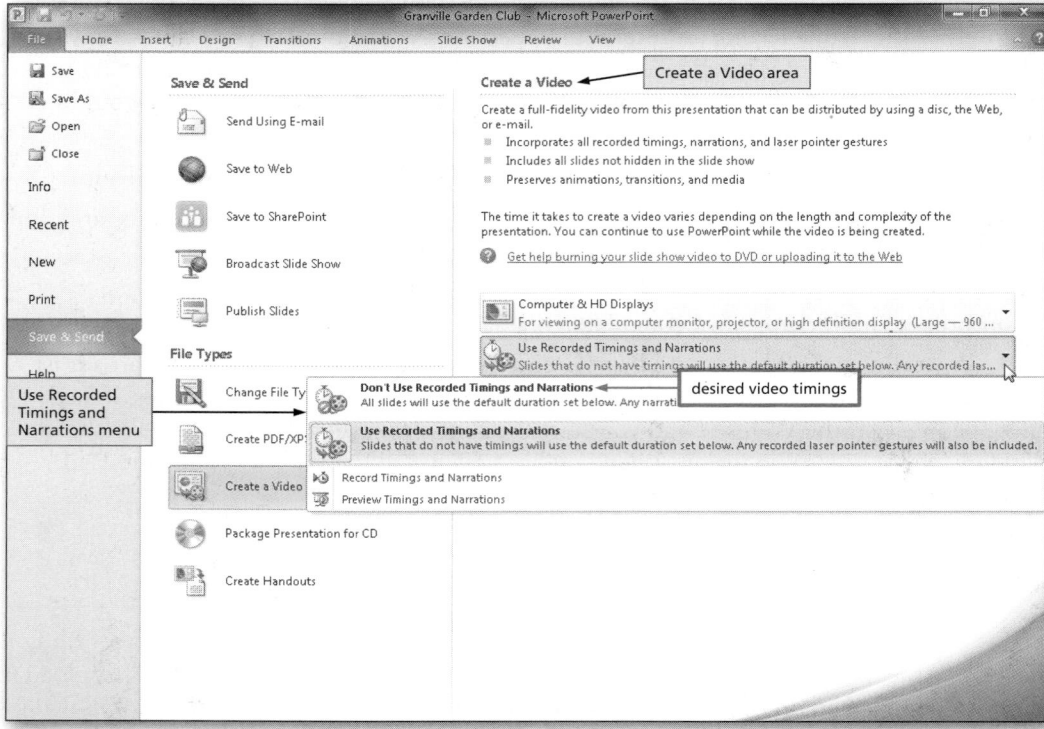

Figure 11–75

- Click Don't Use
  Recorded Timings and
  Narrations to select
  that option.

- Click the 'Seconds
  to spend on each
  slide' up arrow five
  times to increase the
  time to 10 seconds
  (Figure 11–76).

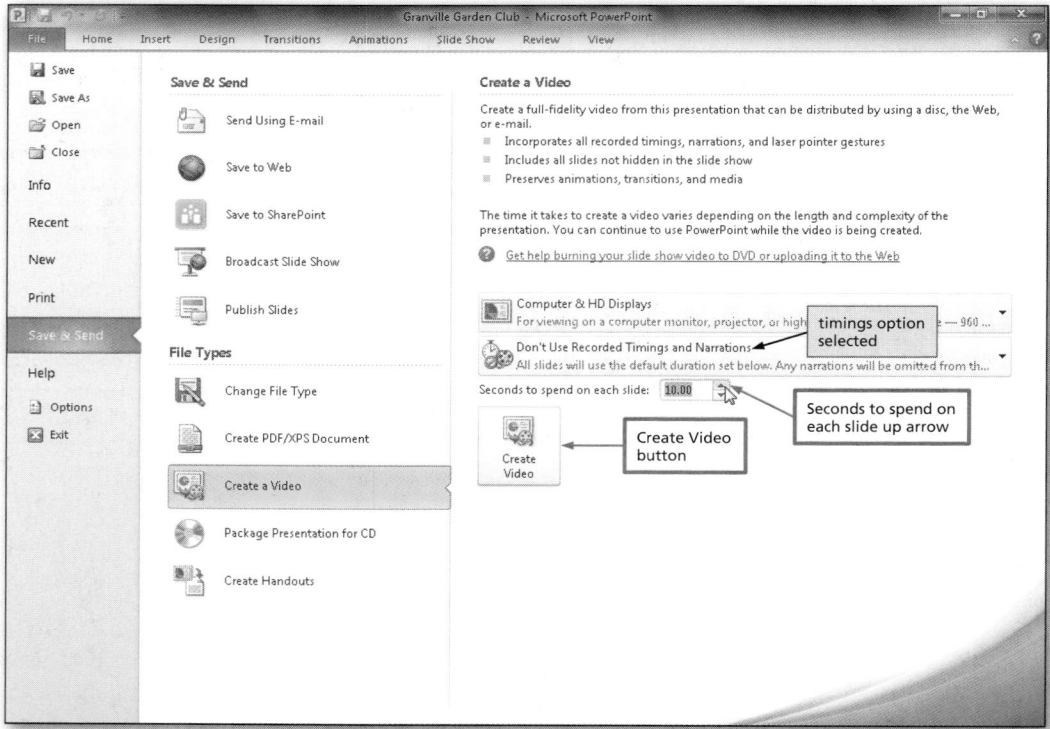

Figure 11–76

4

- Click the Create Video button to open the Save As dialog box.

- Change the video file name to Granville Garden Club Video (Figure 11–77).

5

- Click the Save button (Save As dialog box) to begin creating the Granville Garden Club Video file.

Q&A

Does PowerPoint use a long period of time to create the video?

Yes. It may take several minutes to export the presentation to a video. Windows Media Player will display an error message stating that the file is in use if you attempt to open the video file while it is being created.

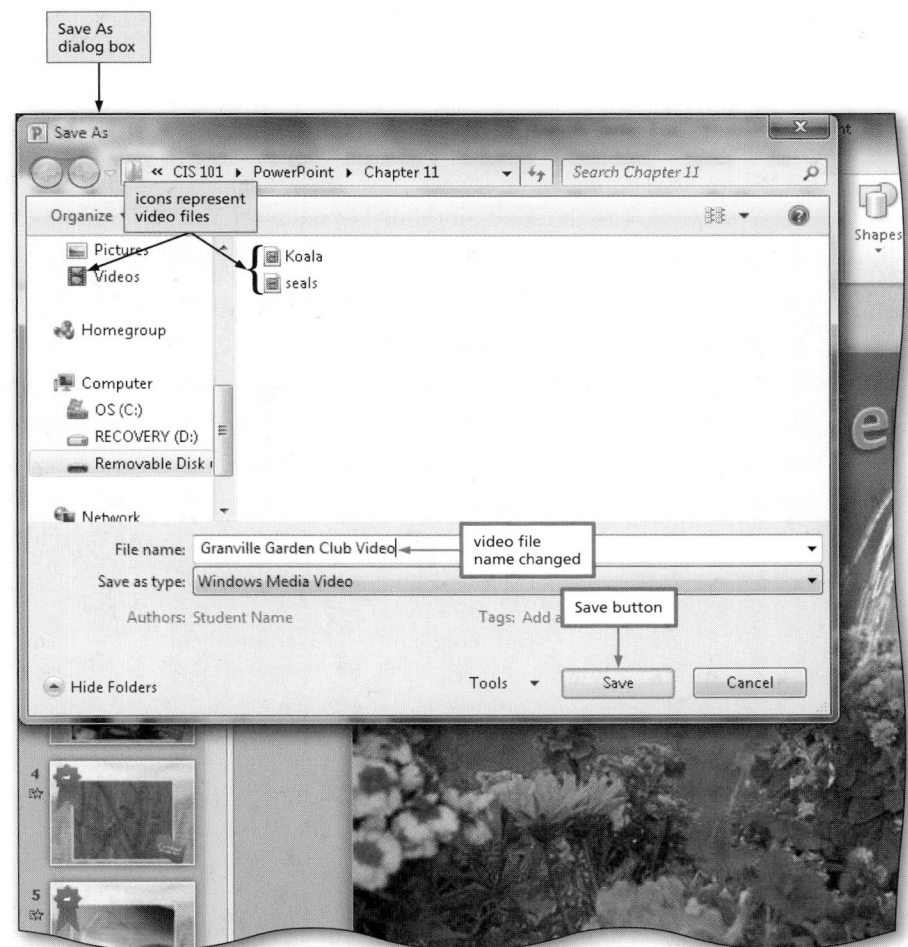

Figure 11–77

To Change Document Properties and Save the Presentation

Before saving the presentation, you want to add your name, class name, and some keywords as document properties. The following steps use the Document Information Panel to change document properties and then save the document.

1 Display the Document Information Panel and then type your name as the Author property.

2 Type your course and section in the Subject property.

3 Type `photo contest, perennials, annuals, bulbs` as the Keywords property.

4 Close the Document Information Panel.

5 Save the presentation again.

BTW

Quick Reference
For a table that lists how to complete the tasks covered in this book using the mouse, Ribbon, shortcut menu, and keyboard, see the Quick Reference Summary at the back of this book, or visit the PowerPoint 2010 Quick Reference Web page (scsite.com/ppt2010/qr).

BTW

Certification
The Microsoft Office Specialist (MOS) program provides an opportunity for you to obtain a valuable industry credential – proof that you have the PowerPoint 2010 skills required by employers. For more information, visit the PowerPoint 2010 Certification Web page (scsite.com/ppt2010/cert).

TO USE PRESENTER VIEW

Experienced speakers often deliver a presentation using two monitors: one to display their speaker notes privately, and a second to display the slides and project them on a large screen for the audience to view. PowerPoint's **Presenter view** supports the use of two monitors connected to one computer so they can view the slide currently being projected while viewing the slide thumbnails, reading their speaker notes, viewing the elapsed time, lightening or darkening the audience's screen, or customizing the presentation by skipping the next slide or reviewing a slide previously displayed. A computer must support the use of multiple monitors and must be configured to use this feature. To use Presenter view, you would perform the following steps.

1. Display the Slide Show tab and then click the Use Presenter View check box (Slide Show tab | Monitors group) to select it to display the Display Settings dialog box.

2. On the Monitor tab, click the icon that represents the monitor you desire to use for your private use and then click the 'This is my main monitor' check box to select it.

3. Click the icon that represents the second monitor that your audience will view, click the 'Extend my Windows Desktop onto this monitor' check box to select it, and then click the OK button.

4. Ensure that the audience's monitor icon is displayed in the Show On list (Slide Show tab | Monitors group).

5. Click the Set Up Slide Show button (Slide Show tab | Set Up group) to display the Set Up Show dialog box.

6. Select the desired options and then click the OK button (Set Up Show dialog box).

7. Run the slide show.

To Run and Print the Presentation

The presentation now is complete. You should run the slide show, print handouts, and then quit PowerPoint.

1 Run the slide show.

2 Print the presentation as a handout with six horizontal slides per page (Figure 11–78).

3 Quit PowerPoint, closing all open documents.

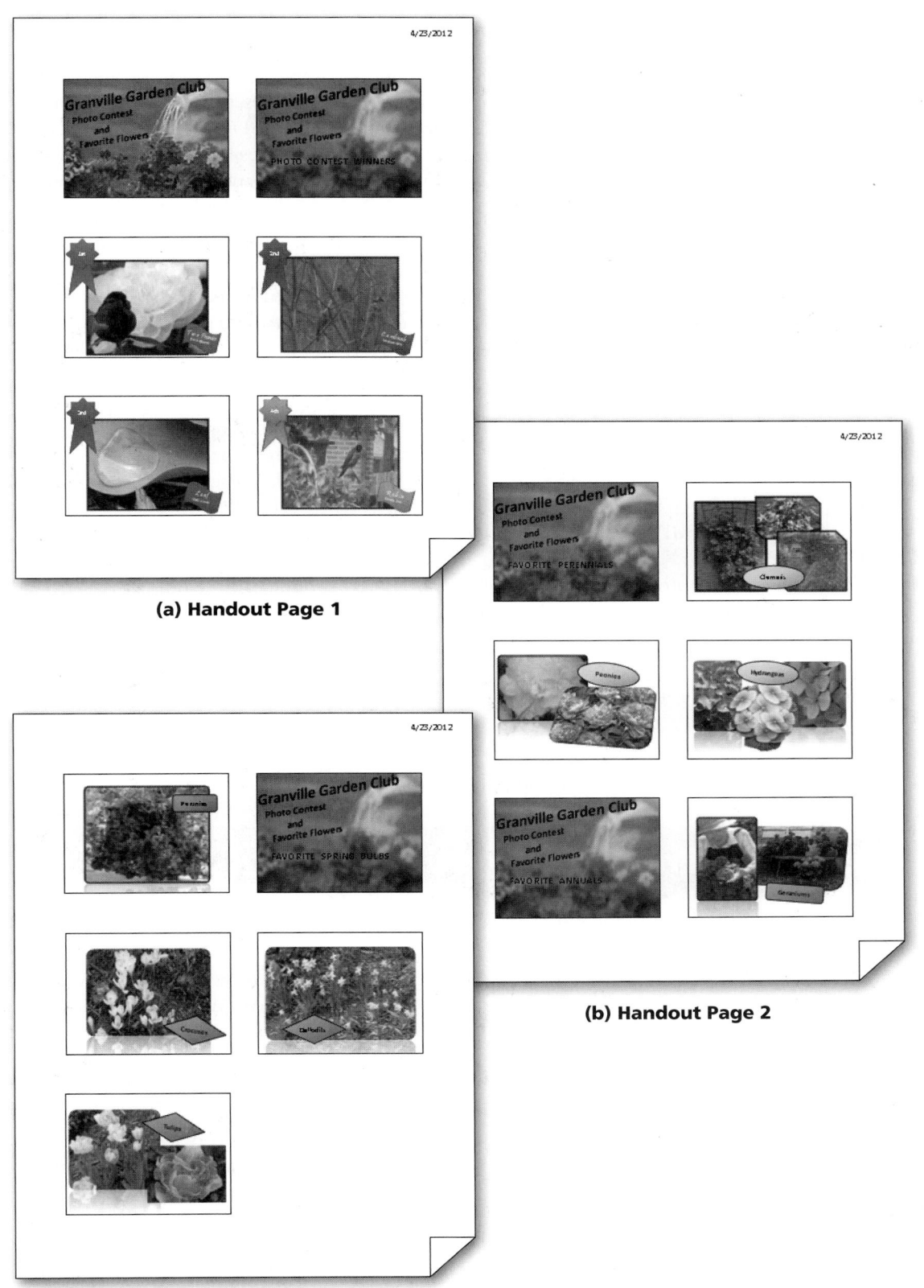

(a) Handout Page 1

(b) Handout Page 2

(c) Handout Page 3

Figure 11–78

Chapter Summary

In this chapter you have learned how to organize a presentation into sections and then rename and move entire sections in the file. You then created a photo album, added and organized pictures, selected a theme and layout, adjusted a picture's contrast and brightness, and edited captions. You also changed the images to black and white in a separate photo album. Then, you specified a custom size and modified two slides by changing the slide orientation to portrait and inserting and compressing a video file. You then e-mailed the file and converted another file to video. The items listed below include all the new PowerPoint skills you have learned in this chapter.

1. Insert Slides with a Section Layout (PPT 661)
2. Arrange Slides in Slide Sorter View (PPT 664)
3. Create a Section Break (PPT 666)
4. Rename a Section (PPT 669)
5. Collapse and Reorder Sections (PPT 671)
6. Create a Custom Slide Show (PPT 674)
7. Open and Edit a Custom Slide Show (PPT 677)
8. Start a Photo Album and Add Pictures (PPT 680)
9. Reorder Pictures in a Photo Album (PPT 682)
10. Adjust the Rotation of a Photo Album Image (PPT 683)
11. Adjust the Contrast of a Photo Album Image (PPT 684)
12. Adjust the Brightness of a Photo Album Image (PPT 684)
13. Change a Photo Album Layout (PPT 685)
14. Add a Photo Album Theme (PPT 686)
15. Add Captions below All Pictures (PPT 686)
16. Create a Photo Album (PPT 687)
17. Edit a Photo Album (PPT 687)
18. Create Black-and-White Images in a Photo Album (PPT 690)
19. Use the Research Pane to Find Information (PPT 692)
20. Change the Slide Orientation (PPT 696)
21. Set Up a Custom Size (PPT 696)
22. Display Multiple Presentation Windows Simultaneously (PPT 697)
23. Copy a Video File (PPT 698)
24. Compress a Video File (PPT 701)
25. E-Mail a Slide Show from within PowerPoint (PPT 702)
26. Create a Video (PPT 705)

If you have a SAM 2010 user profile, your instructor may have assigned an autogradable version of this assignment. If so, log into the SAM 2010 Web site at www.cengage.com/sam2010 to download the instruction and start files.

Learn It Online

Test your knowledge of chapter content and key terms.

Instructions: To complete the Learn It Online exercises, start your browser, click the Address bar, and then enter the Web address `scsite.com/ppt2010/learn`. When the Office 2010 Learn It Online page is displayed, click the link for the exercise you want to complete and then read the instructions.

Chapter Reinforcement TF, MC, and SA
A series of true/false, multiple choice, and short answer questions that test your knowledge of the chapter content.

Flash Cards
An interactive learning environment where you identify chapter key terms associated with displayed definitions.

Practice Test
A series of multiple choice questions that test your knowledge of chapter content and key terms.

Who Wants To Be a Computer Genius?
An interactive game that challenges your knowledge of chapter content in the style of a television quiz show.

Wheel of Terms
An interactive game that challenges your knowledge of chapter key terms in the style of the television show *Wheel of Fortune*.

Crossword Puzzle Challenge
A crossword puzzle that challenges your knowledge of key terms presented in the chapter.

Apply Your Knowledge

Reinforce the skills and apply the concepts you learned in this chapter.

Creating and Reordering Sections and Creating Custom Slide Shows

Note: To complete this assignment, you will be required to use the Data Files for Students. See the inside back cover of this book for instructions on downloading the Data Files for Students, or contact your instructor for information about accessing the required files.

Instructions: Start PowerPoint. Open the presentation, Apply 11-1 Hantel Lodge, located on the Data Files for Students.

The slides in this presentation provide data about the activities available at the Hantel Lodge. The document you open is a partially formatted presentation. You will insert section breaks, reorder and rename sections, change the slide orientation, and create two custom slide shows so that the presentation matches the one shown in Figure 11–79.

Perform the following tasks:

1. You will not make any changes to Slide 1 (Figure 11–79a). Select Slide 2 and add a section break. Select the section divider and rename the section `Ski`.

2. Select Slide 4 and add a section break. Select the section divider and rename the section **`Snowboard`.**

3. Select the Default Section divider (before Slide 1) and rename the section **`Hantel Lodge`.**

4. Reorder the sections by moving the Snowboard section before the Ski section. The slides should now appear in the order shown in Figures 11–79b through 11–79e on the next page.

5. Change the slide orientation of the presentation to Portrait.

6. Create a custom slide show called Skiing. Include only Slides 1, 4, and 5 in the custom slide show.

7. Create a second custom slide show called Snowboarding. Include only Slides 1, 2, and 3 in this custom slide show.

8. Change the document properties, as specified by your instructor. Save the presentation using the file name, Apply 11-1 Hantel Lodge Activities. Submit the revised document in the format specified by your instructor.

slide orientation changed to Portrait

(a) Slide 1

Figure 11–79

Continued >

Apply Your Knowledge *continued*

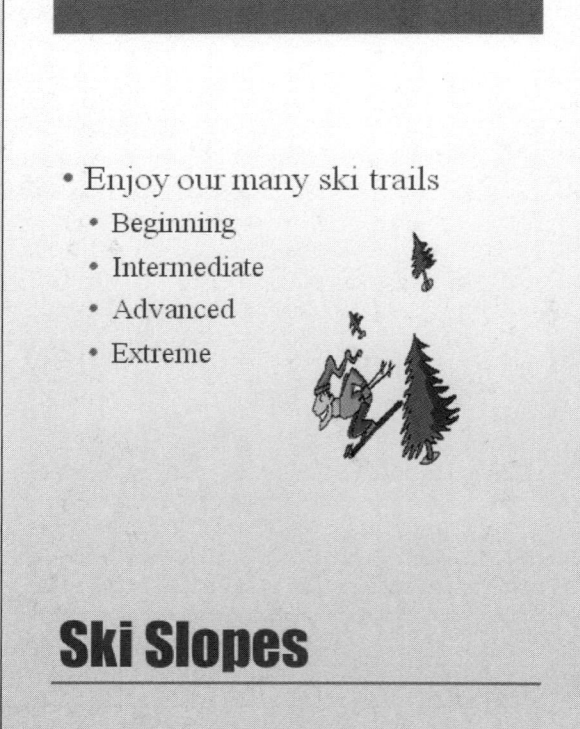

(b) Slide 2

slide orientation
changed to
Portrait

(c) Slide 3

(d) Slide 4

slide orientation
changed to
Portrait

(e) Slide 5

Figure 11–79 (Continued)

Extend Your Knowledge

Extend the skills you learned in this chapter and experiment with new skills. You may need to use Help to complete the assignment.

Formatting Sections and Broadcasting a Presentation

Note: To complete this assignment, you will be required to use the Data Files for Students. See the inside back cover of this book for instructions on downloading the Data Files for Students, or contact your instructor for information about accessing the required files.

Instructions: Start PowerPoint. Open the presentation, Extend 11-1 Fun Festival, located on the Data Files for Students. You will add and format sections to create the presentation shown in Figure 11–80. You will then broadcast your presentation.

Perform the following tasks:

1. You will not make any changes to Slide 1 (Figure 11–80a).
2. Select Slide 2. Add a section break and rename it `Seasonal`. Select Slide 4. Add a section break and rename it `Special Occasion`.
3. Select the Seasonal section and then change the transition from Checkerboard to Reveal to this section only, and change the duration to 02.00 seconds. Select the Special Occasion section and then change the transition from Checkerboard to Random Bars to this section only, and change the duration to 02.50 seconds. Change the document properties, as specified by your instructor. Save the presentation as Extend 11-1 Fun Festival Party Supplies. The slides should appear as shown in Figures 11–80a through 11–80e on this page and pages PPT 714 to PPT 715.
4. Broadcast the slide show to your instructor and to two classmates.
5. Submit the document in the format specified by your instructor.

(a) Slide 1

Figure 11–80

Continued >

Extend Your Knowledge *continued*

(b) Slide 2

(c) Slide 3

Figure 11–80 (Continued)

(d) Slide 4

(e) Slide 5

Figure 11–80 (Continued)

Make It Right

Analyze a presentation and correct all errors and/or improve the design.

Selecting a Custom Size, Modifying Sections, and Proofing a Presentation

Note: To complete this assignment, you will be required to use the Data Files for Students. See the inside back cover of this book for instructions on downloading the Data Files for Students, or contact your instructor for information about accessing the required files.

Instructions: Start PowerPoint. Open the presentation, Make It Right 11-1 Jollie Travel, located on the Data Files for Students.

Correct the formatting problems and errors in the presentation while keeping in mind the guidelines presented in this chapter.

Perform the following tasks:

1. Change the size of the slides to a custom width of 11" and a height of 8".
2. Display the slides in Slide Sorter view (Figure 11–81a). Select the Travel section and rename the section `Jollie Travel`. Select the Untitled Section and rename the section `Hawaii`. Select the Alaska section and move it before the Hawaii section. The Alaskan Getaway slide should now appear before the two Hawaiian Getaway slides.
3. On Slide 4 (Figure 11–81b), use the Research proofing tool to look up the word, Hello, in Hawaiian. (*Hint:* Type `Hello in Hawaiian` in the research search box.) Enter the Hawaiian word in row 2, column 2 of the table. Look up the phrase, Thank You, in Hawaiian. Enter the Hawaiian word in row 3, column 2 of the table. Finally, look up the word, Family, in Hawaiian. Enter the Hawaiian word in row 4, column 2.
4. Change the document properties, as specified by your instructor. Save the presentation using the file name, Make It Right 11-1 Jollie Travel Packages.
5. Submit the revised document in the format specified by your instructor.

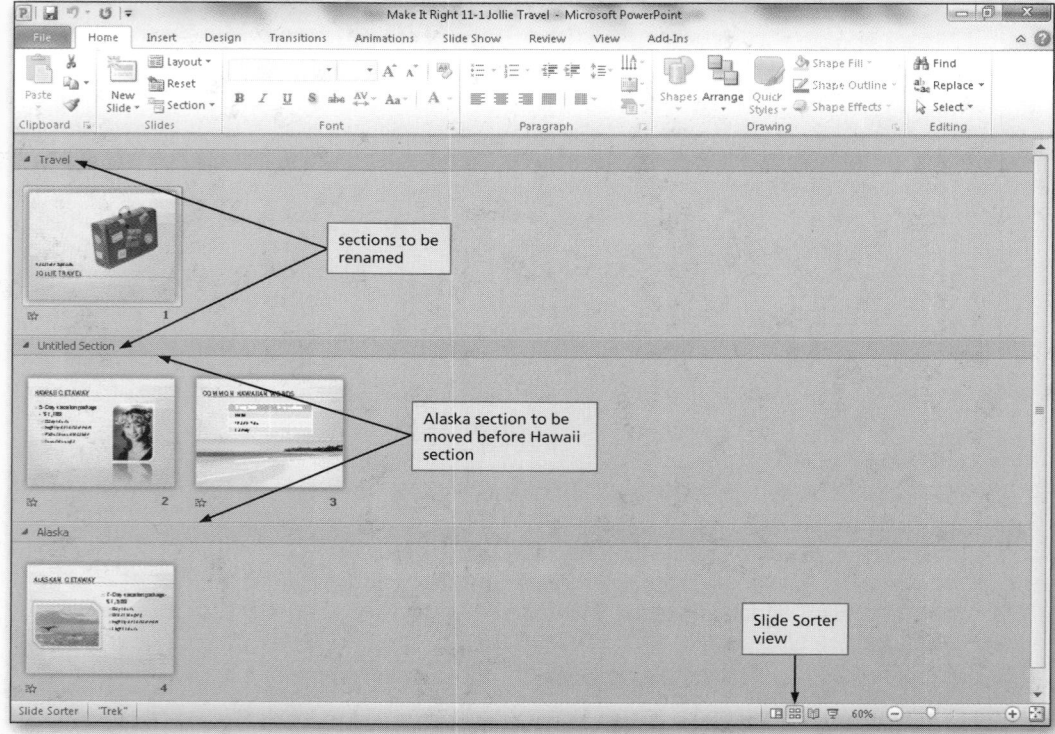

(a) Presentation in Slide Sorter View

Figure 11–81

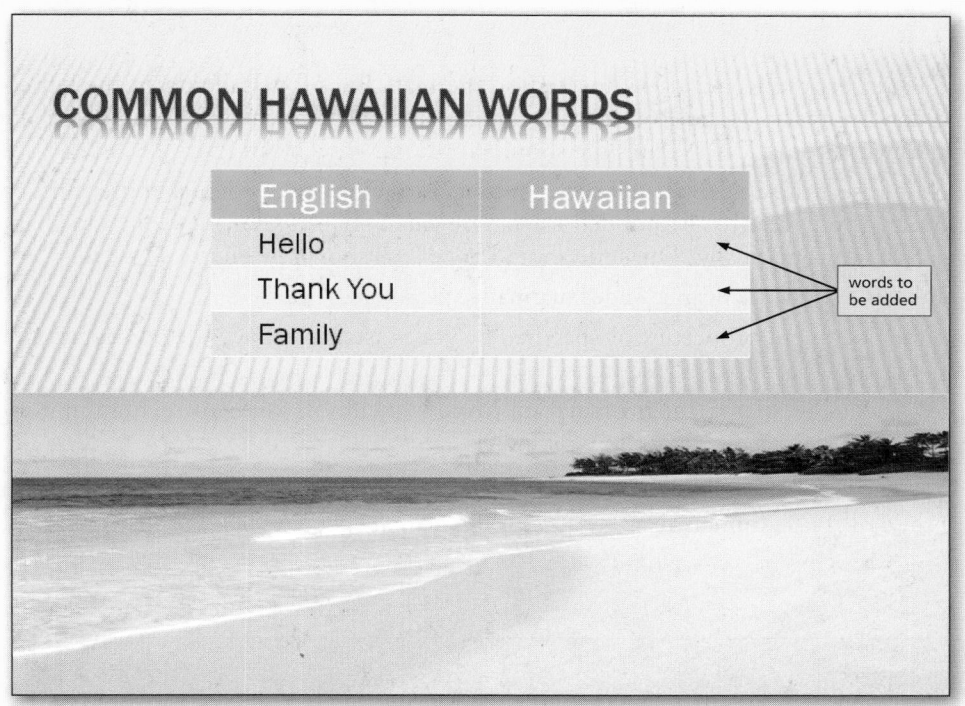

(b) Slide 4
Figure 11–81 (Continued)

In the Lab

SAM

Design and/or create a presentation using the guidelines, concepts, and skills presented in this chapter. Labs 1, 2, and 3 are listed in order of increasing difficulty.

Lab 1: Working with Multiple Presentation Windows Simultaneously, Setting Manual Timing, Compressing Media Files, and E-Mailing a Presentation

Note: To complete this assignment, you will be required to use the Data Files for Students. See the inside back cover of this book for instructions on downloading the Data Files for Students or contact your instructor for information about accessing the required files.

Problem: You are volunteering for a local zoo and decide to enhance a presentation for a grade school class by adding videos of horses, koalas, and seals in the wild. One of the videos is in a separate presentation. You create the slides shown in Figure 11–82 on pages PPT 718 through PPT 720.

Perform the following tasks:
1. Open the presentation, Lab 11-1 Animals, located on the Data Files for Students. You will not make any changes to Slide 1 (Figure 11–82a).
2. Open the Horses presentation located on the Data Files for Students and then cascade the two open document windows on the screen. Select Slide 2 (Figure 11–82b) of the Horses presentation. Copy the video clip from Slide 2 and paste it into the right content placeholder of Slide 2 of the Lab 11-1 Animals presentation (Figure 11–82c). In the Lab 11-1 Animals presentation, change the video to Start Automatically. Close the Horses presentation. Maximize the Lab 11-1 Animals presentation.

Continued >

In the Lab *continued*

3. On Slide 3, insert the Koala video, located on the Data Files for Students, in the left content placeholder. Apply the Metal Rounded Rectangle video style to the video clip and change the video to Start Automatically. The slide should appear as shown in Figure 11–82d.

4. On Slide 4, insert the Seals video, located on the Data Files for Students, in the right content placeholder. Apply the Metal Rounded Rectangle video style to the video clip and change the video to Start Automatically. The slide should appear as shown in Figure 11–82e.

5. Set up the slide show to advance slides manually.

6. Change the document properties, as specified by your instructor. Save the presentation using the file name, Lab 11-1 Animals Presentation.

7. Compress the media files in the presentation to Low Quality. Save the presentation using the file name, Lab 11-1 Animals Presentation – E-mail.

8. E-mail the Lab 11-1 Animals Presentation – E-mail to your instructor.

9. Submit the Lab 11-1 Animals Presentation in the format specified by your instructor.

(a) Slide 1

Figure 11–82

(b) Slide 2 Horses Presentation

(c) Slide 2 Animals Presentation

Figure 11–82 (Continued)

Continued >

In the Lab *continued*

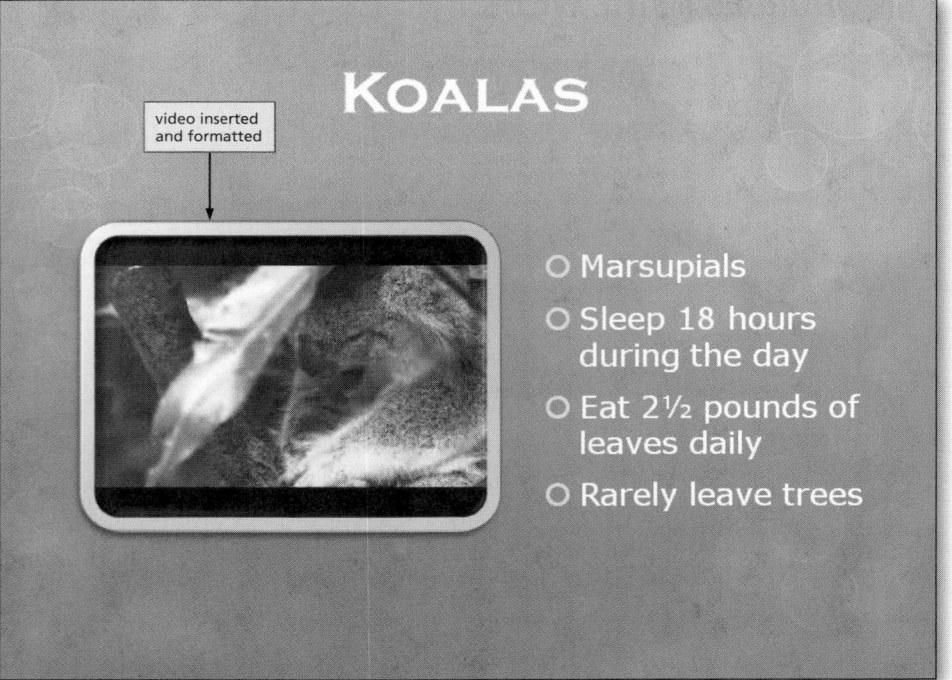

(d) Slide 3

(e) Slide 4

Figure 11–82 (Continued)

In the Lab

Lab 2: Creating a Photo Album, Adding Captions, Reordering Pictures, Adjusting Rotation of Images, and Recording from the Current Slide

Note: To complete this assignment, you will be required to use the Data Files for Students. See the inside back cover of this book for instructions on downloading the Data Files for Students or contact your instructor for information about accessing the required files.

Problem: You work part time at a water park and have been asked to create a presentation for an upcoming advertising campaign. You decide to put together a photo album using photos from the park and create the slides shown in Figure 11–83 on pages PPT 722 to PPT 724 using files located on the Data Files for Students.

Instructions Part 1: Start PowerPoint.
Perform the following tasks:

1. Insert a new photo album.

2. Insert the Waterpark1, Waterpark2, Waterpark3, Waterpark4, and Waterpark5 pictures located on the Data Files for Students. Do not create the album until you are asked to do so.

3. Select the Waterpark2 picture in the album and move it above the Waterpark1 picture. Rotate the picture counterclockwise.

4. Select the Waterpark5 picture in the album and rotate the picture clockwise.

5. Change the Picture layout to '1 picture with title.' Select the 'Captions below All pictures' picture option.

6. Select the Executive theme for the photo album. Create the photo album.

7. On Slide 1, change the title to `SlideNPlay Waterpark`. The slide should appear as shown in Figure 11–83a.

8. On Slide 2, change the caption to `Mega Slides`. The slide should appear as shown in Figure 11–83b.

9. On Slide 3, change the caption to `Speed Races`. The slide should appear as shown in Figure 11–83c.

10. On Slide 4, change the caption to `Pick Your Path`. The slide should appear as shown in Figure 11–83d.

11. On Slide 5, change the caption to `Survey the Ruins`. The slide should appear as shown in Figure 11–83e.

12. On Slide 6, change the caption to `See You Later`. The slide should appear as shown in Figure 11–83f.

13. Apply the Gallery transition and change the duration to 02.50 seconds for all slides

14. Change the document properties, as specified by your instructor. Save the presentation using the file name, Lab 11-2 SlideNPlay Waterpark.

15. Submit the document in the format specified by your instructor.

Instructions Part 2: If necessary, open the file called Lab 11-2 SlideNPlay Waterpark.
Perform the following tasks:

1. Select Slide 4. Record the slide show from the current slide. *Note:* The following steps contain narration that you will read while progressing through the slides. For Slide 4, read the following narration: `"We offer great rides for you and your family to enjoy all day long, ranging from this downhill water slide"`

2. Advance to Slide 5, read the following narration: `"to this slide through ancient ruins, where you will slide past images of previous civilizations until you exit into our wading pool."`

3. Advance to Slide 6, and read the following narration: `"Above all else, we want you to have fun in our park and come back to visit us again all season long."`

4. Stop the presentation so that the recording session ends.

Continued >

In the Lab *continued*

5. Display Slide 1 and then run the slide show to view the presentation and to hear the narration you just recorded.

6. Save the presentation using the file name, Lab 11-2 SlideNPlay Waterpark – Narration.

7. Submit the revised document in the format specified by your instructor.

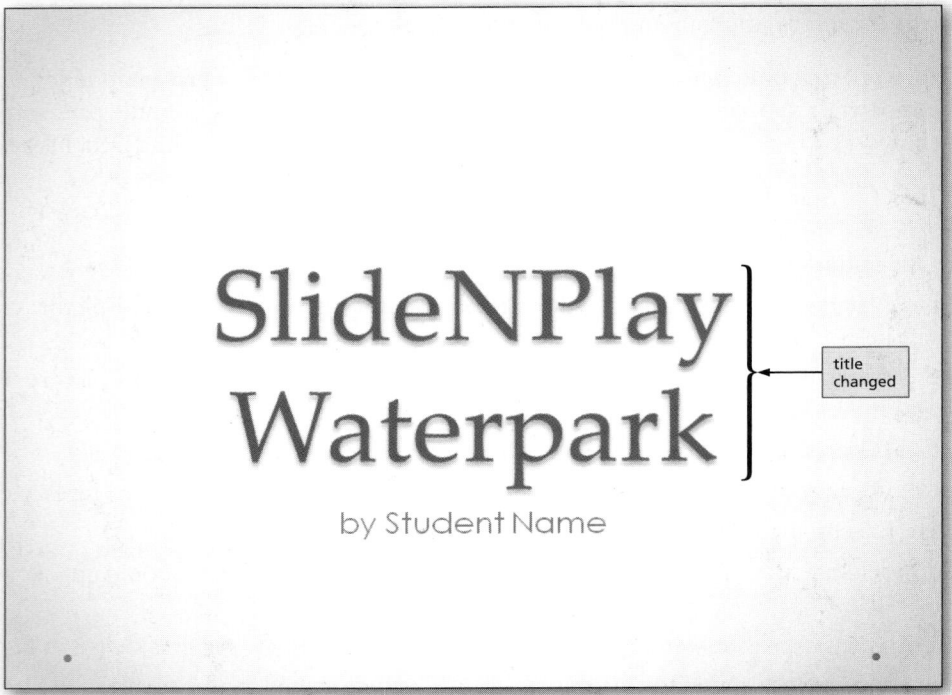

(a) Slide 1

(b) Slide 2

Figure 11–83

(c) Slide 3

(d) Slide 4
Figure 11–83 (Continued)

Continued >

In the Lab *continued*

Survey the Ruins ← caption changed

(e) Slide 5

See You Later ← caption changed

(f) Slide 6

Figure 11–83 (Continued)

In the Lab

Lab 3: Creating a Black-and-White Photo Album, Adjusting Images, Inserting Text, Using Presenter View, and Recording from the Beginning of a Slide Show

Note: To complete this assignment, you will be required to use the Data Files for Students. See the inside back cover of this book for instructions on downloading the Data Files for Students or contact your instructor for information about accessing the required files.

Problem: As part of your volunteer work at a local museum, you are tasked with creating a presentation featuring some of the local artists whose works are on display. You have collected the necessary pictures and will include them in your presentation. As an added artistic effect, you decide to present them all in black and white. You create the presentation shown in Figure 11–84 on pages PPT 726 to PPT 727.

Instructions Part 1: Start PowerPoint.
Perform the following tasks:

1. Insert a new photo album.

2. Insert the Rural, Cypress, Watercolor, and Rustic Barn pictures located on the Data Files for Students, in that order. Do not create the album until you are asked to do so.

3. Select the 'All pictures black and white' picture option, the 1 picture layout, and the Simple Frame, White Frame shape.

4. Select the Cypress picture in the album and increase the brightness of the picture four times.

5. Select the Rustic Barn picture in the album and decrease the contrast of the picture two times.

6. Select the Paper theme for the photo album. Create the photo album.

7. On Slide 1, change the title to **W. L. Surr Gallery**. Use your name in place of Student Name.

8. On Slide 5 (Figure 11–84e), insert a text box below the picture. Center the text box. Enter the text, **Come See Our Exhibit!** in the text box. Change the font size to 28 pt. Apply the Fill – Olive Green, Text 1, Inner Shadow WordArt style (third style in second row) to this text.

9. Apply the Shape transition and change the duration to 02.00 seconds for all slides.

10. Set up the presentation to run in Presenter view. The slides should appear as shown in Figures 11–84a through 11–84e.

11. Change the document properties, as specified by your instructor. Save the presentation using the file name, Lab 11-3 Surr Gallery.

12. Submit the document in the format specified by your instructor.

Instructions Part 2: If necessary, open the file called Lab 11-3 Surr Gallery.
Perform the following tasks:

1. Select Slide 1. Record the slide show from the beginning. *Note:* The following steps contain narration that you will read while progressing through the slides. For this slide, read the following narration: **"Welcome to the W.L. Surr Gallery's exhibit of local artwork."**

2. Advance to Slide 2 and read the following narration: **"This submission is from an artist who was visiting a rural area up north and was inspired to create this painting."**

3. Advance to Slide 3 and read the following narration: **"From the ocean side, the next artist found a lone cypress tree and decided to share its beauty with us."**

4. Advance to Slide 4 and read the following narration: **"This next landscape captures an old West scene using water colors to bring out the landscape."**

Continued >

In the Lab *continued*

5. Advance to Slide 5 and read the following narration: **"Finally, this rustic barn exudes that old-time comfort feeling. Please come visit our exhibit to see these and even more works by local artists."**

6. Stop the presentation so that the recording session ends.

7. Run the slide show from beginning to see the slide show and play the narration you just recorded.

8. Save the presentation using the file name, Lab 11-3 Surr Gallery – Narration.

9. Save the presentation as a video using the file name, Lab 11-3 Surr Gallery – Video.

10. Submit the revised document and the video in the format specified by your instructor.

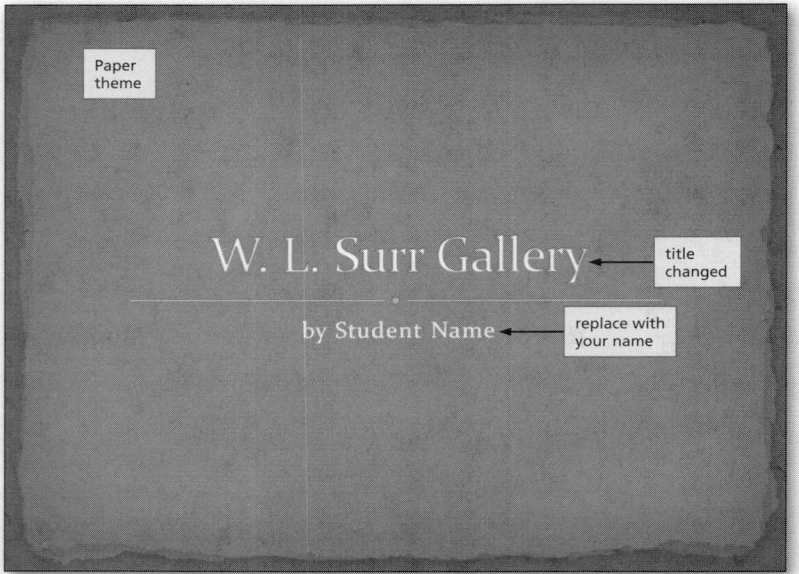

(a) Slide 1

(b) Slide 2

Figure 11–84

(c) Slide 3

(d) Slide 4

(e) Slide 5

Figure 11–84 (Continued)

Cases and Places

Apply your creative thinking and problem-solving skills to design and implement a solution.

Note: To complete these assignments, you may be required to use the Data Files for Students. See the inside back cover of this book for instructions on downloading the Data Files for Students, or contact your instructor for information about accessing the required files.

As you design the presentations, remember to use the 7 × 7 rule: a maximum of seven words on a line and a maximum of seven lines on one slide.

1: Designing and Creating a Presentation about Club Activities

Academic

While working with fellow students in your student club, you have been given photos of different activities your club has sponsored. You have pictures from the last bowling night (Bowling1.jpg and Bowling2.jpg), marathon (Marathon1.jpg and Marathon2.jpg), and Mardi Gras mask building party (Party Mask.jpg). You decide to create a PowerPoint photo album presentation using the photos to display at a future club meeting. Apply at least three objectives found at the beginning of this chapter to develop the presentation, including adding captions to pictures and inserting text in a photo album. Use the pictures located on the Data Files for Students or other pictures and diagrams from Office.com if they are appropriate for this topic. Be sure to check spelling.

2: Designing and Creating a Presentation about Youth Summer Camp

Personal

You are volunteering for a local youth club summer camp this upcoming summer. You have been asked to create a PowerPoint presentation to illustrate various camp activities using pictures from last year's camp. Apply at least three objectives found at the beginning of this chapter to develop the presentation, including creating one section for each activity and adding a caption to each picture. You also can include narration describing how much fun each activity can provide. Use your personal digital pictures or pictures and diagrams from Office.com if they are appropriate for this topic. Be sure to check spelling.

3: Designing and Creating a Presentation about Conference Meeting Rooms

Professional

Your company is researching meeting rooms for an upcoming conference. You decide to create a photo album of the available meeting rooms so the committee can select the appropriate rooms. The conference will have lab sessions, guest speakers, and hands-on demonstrations. Apply at least three objectives found at the beginning of this chapter to develop the presentation, and include captions and text in the photo album to describe the functionality of each room. Use pictures from Office.com if they are appropriate for this topic or use your personal digital pictures. Be sure to check spelling.

NOTES

NOTES

NOTES

NOTES

Appendix A
Project Planning Guidelines

Using Project Planning Guidelines

The process of communicating specific information to others is a learned, rational skill. Computers and software, especially Microsoft Office 2010, can help you develop ideas and present detailed information to a particular audience.

Using Microsoft Office 2010, you can create projects such as Word documents, PowerPoint presentations, Excel spreadsheets, and Access databases. Productivity software such as Microsoft Office 2010 minimizes much of the laborious work of drafting and revising projects. Some communicators handwrite ideas in notebooks, others compose directly on the computer, and others have developed unique strategies that work for their own particular thinking and writing styles.

No matter what method you use to plan a project, follow specific guidelines to arrive at a final product that presents information correctly and effectively (Figure A–1). Use some aspects of these guidelines every time you undertake a project, and others as needed in specific instances. For example, in determining content for a project, you may decide that a chart communicates trends more effectively than a paragraph of text. If so, you would create this graphical element and insert it in an Excel spreadsheet, a Word document, or a PowerPoint slide.

Determine the Project's Purpose

Begin by clearly defining why you are undertaking this assignment. For example, you may want to track monetary donations collected for your club's fund-raising drive. Alternatively, you may be urging students to vote for a particular candidate in the next election. Once you clearly understand the purpose of your task, begin to draft ideas of how best to communicate this information.

Analyze Your Audience

Learn about the people who will read, analyze, or view your work. Where are they employed? What are their educational backgrounds? What are their expectations? What questions do they have?

PROJECT PLANNING GUIDELINES

1. DETERMINE THE PROJECT'S PURPOSE
Why are you undertaking the project?

2. ANALYZE YOUR AUDIENCE
Who are the people who will use your work?

3. GATHER POSSIBLE CONTENT
What information exists, and in what forms?

4. DETERMINE WHAT CONTENT TO PRESENT TO YOUR AUDIENCE
What information will best communicate the project's purpose to your audience?

Figure A–1

Design experts suggest drawing a mental picture of these people or finding photos of people who fit this profile so that you can develop a project with the audience in mind.

By knowing your audience members, you can tailor a project to meet their interests and needs. You will not present them with information they already possess, and you will not omit the information they need to know.

Example: Your assignment is to raise the profile of your college's nursing program in the community. How much do they know about your college and the nursing curriculum? What are the admission requirements? How many of the applicants admitted complete the program? What percent pass the state board exams?

Gather Possible Content

Rarely are you in a position to develop all the material for a project. Typically, you would begin by gathering existing information that may reside in spreadsheets or databases. Web sites, pamphlets, magazine and newspaper articles, and books could provide insights of how others have approached your topic. Personal interviews often provide perspectives not available by any other means. Consider video and audio clips as potential sources for material that might complement or support the factual data you uncover.

Determine What Content to Present to Your Audience

Experienced designers recommend writing three or four major ideas you want an audience member to remember after reading or viewing your project. It also is helpful to envision your project's endpoint, the key fact you wish to emphasize. All project elements should lead to this ending point.

As you make content decisions, you also need to think about other factors. Presentation of the project content is an important consideration. For example, will your brochure be printed on thick, colored paper or posted on the Web? Will your PowerPoint presentation be viewed in a classroom with excellent lighting and a bright projector, or will it be viewed on a notebook computer monitor? Determine relevant time factors, such as the length of time to develop the project, how long readers will spend reviewing your project, or the amount of time allocated for your speaking engagement. Your project will need to accommodate all of these constraints.

Decide whether a graph, photo, or artistic element can express or emphasize a particular concept. The right hemisphere of the brain processes images by attaching an emotion to them, so audience members are more apt to recall these graphics long term rather than just reading text.

As you select content, be mindful of the order in which you plan to present information. Readers and audience members generally remember the first and last pieces of information they see and hear, so you should place the most important information at the top or bottom of the page.

Summary

When creating a project, it is beneficial to follow some basic guidelines from the outset. By taking some time at the beginning of the process to determine the project's purpose, analyze the audience, gather possible content, and determine what content to present to the audience, you can produce a project that is informative, relevant, and effective.

Appendix B

Publishing Office 2010 Web Pages Online

With Office 2010 programs, you use the Save As command in the Backstage view to save a Web page to a Web site, network location, or FTP site. **File Transfer Protocol (FTP)** is an Internet standard that allows computers to exchange files with other computers on the Internet.

You should contact your network system administrator or technical support staff at your Internet access provider to determine if their Web server supports Web folders, FTP, or both, and to obtain necessary permissions to access the Web server.

Using an Office Program to Publish Office 2010 Web Pages

When publishing online, someone first must assign the necessary permissions for you to publish the Web page. If you are granted access to publish online, you must obtain the Web address of the Web server, a user name, and possibly a password that allows you to connect to the Web server. The steps in this appendix assume that you have access to an online location to which you can publish a Web page.

TO CONNECT TO AN ONLINE LOCATION

To publish a Web page online, you first must connect to the online location. To connect to an online location using Windows 7, you would perform the following steps.

1. Click the Start button on the Windows 7 taskbar to display the Start menu.

2. Click Computer in the right pane of the Start menu to open the Computer window.

3. Click the 'Map network drive' button on the toolbar to display the Map Network Drive dialog box. (If the 'Map network drive' button is not visible on the toolbar, click the 'Display additional commands' button on the toolbar and then click 'Map network drive' in the list to display the Map Network Drive dialog box.)

4. Click the 'Connect to a Web site that you can use to store your documents and pictures' link (Map Network Drive dialog box) to start the Add Network Location wizard.

5. Click the Next button (Add Network Location dialog box).

6. Click 'Choose a custom network location' and then click the Next button.

7. Type the Internet or network address specified by your network or system administrator in the text box and then click the Next button.

8. Click 'Log on anonymously' to deselect the check box, type your user name in the User name text box, and then click the Next button.

9. If necessary, enter the name you want to assign to this online location and then click the Next button.

10. Click to deselect the Open this network location when I click Finish check box, and then click the Finish button.

11. Click the Cancel button to close the Map Network Drive dialog box.

12. Close the Computer window.

TO SAVE A WEB PAGE TO AN ONLINE LOCATION

The online location now can be accessed easily from Windows programs, including Microsoft Office programs. After creating a Microsoft Office file you wish to save as a Web page, you must save the file to the online location to which you connected in the previous steps. To save a Microsoft Word document as a Web page, for example, and publish it to the online location, you would perform the following steps.

1. Click File on the Ribbon to display the Backstage view and then click Save As in the Backstage view to display the Save As dialog box.

2. Type the Web page file name in the File name text box (Save As dialog box). Do not press the ENTER key because you do not want to close the dialog box at this time.

3. Click the 'Save as type' box arrow and then click Web Page to select the Web Page format.

4. If necessary, scroll to display the name of the online location in the navigation pane.

5. Double-click the online location name in the navigation pane to select that location as the new save location and display its contents in the right pane.

6. If a dialog box appears prompting you for a user name and password, type the user name and password in the respective text boxes and then click the Log On button.

7. Click the Save button (Save As dialog box).

The Web page now has been published online. To view the Web page using a Web browser, contact your network or system administrator for the Web address you should use to connect to the Web page.

Appendix C

Saving to the Web Using Windows Live SkyDrive

Introduction

Windows Live SkyDrive, also referred to as **SkyDrive**, is a free service that allows users to save files to the Web, such as documents, spreadsheets, databases, presentations, videos, and photos. Using SkyDrive, you also can save files in folders, providing for greater organization. You then can retrieve those files from any computer connected to the Internet. Some Office 2010 programs including Word, PowerPoint, and Excel can save files directly to an Internet location such as SkyDrive. SkyDrive also facilitates collaboration by allowing users to share files with other SkyDrive users (Figure C–1).

Figure C–1

Note: An Internet connection is required to perform the steps in this appendix.

To Save a File to Windows Live SkyDrive

You can save files directly to SkyDrive from within Word, PowerPoint, and Excel using the Backstage view. The following steps save an open PowerPoint presentation (Xanada Investment Corp, in this case) to SkyDrive. These steps require you to have a Windows Live account. Contact your instructor if you do not have a Windows Live account.

1

- Start PowerPoint and then open a document you want to save to the Web (in this case, the Xanada Investment Corp presentation).
- Click File on the Ribbon to display the Backstage view (Figure C–2).

Figure C–2

2

- Click the Save & Send tab to display the Save & Send gallery (Figure C–3).

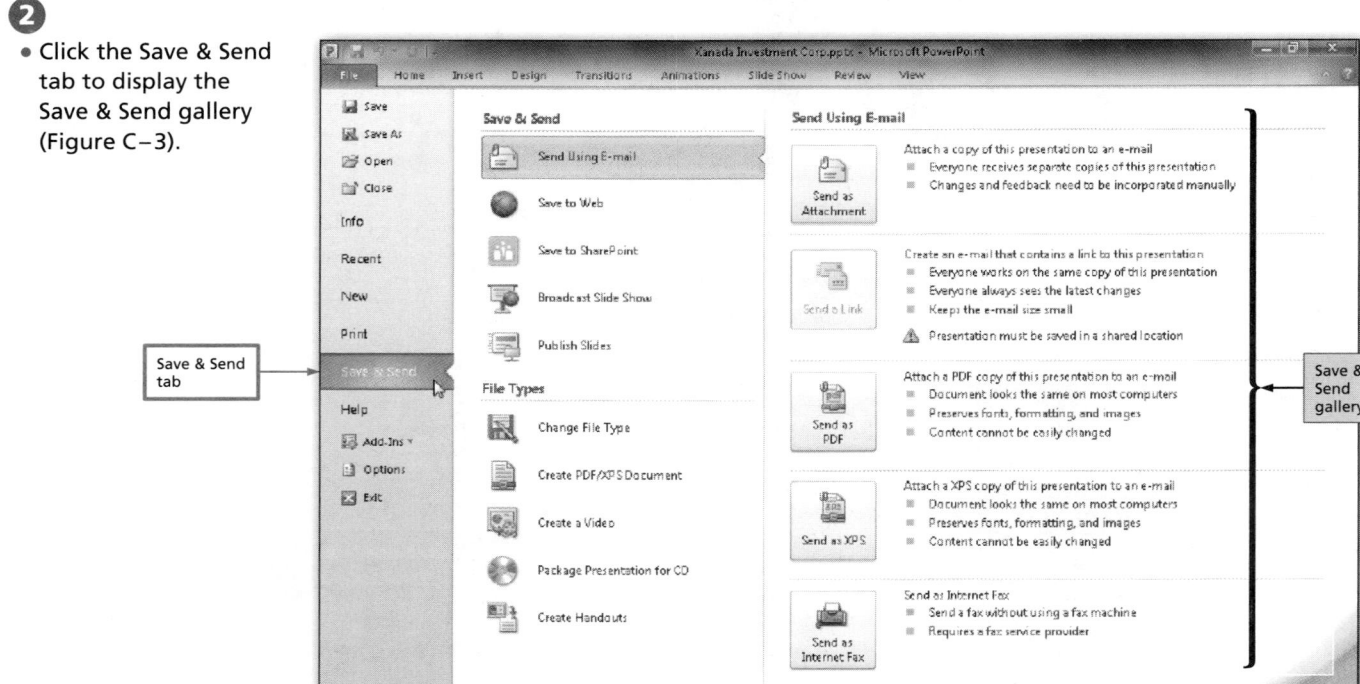

Figure C–3

3

- Click Save to Web in the Save & Send gallery to display information about saving a file to the Web (Figure C–4).

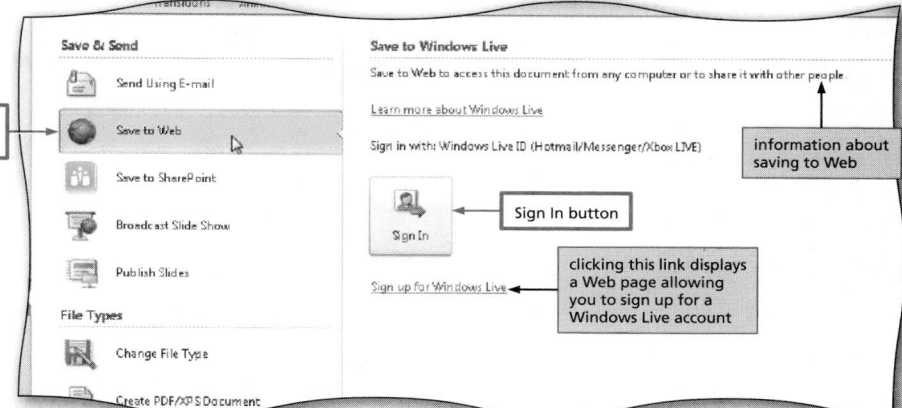

Figure C–4

4

- Click the Sign In button to display a Windows Live login dialog box that requests your e-mail address and password (Figure C–5).

Q&A

What if the Sign In button does not appear?

If you already are signed into Windows Live, the Sign In button will not be displayed. Instead, the contents of your Windows Live SkyDrive will be displayed. If you already are signed into Windows Live, proceed to Step 6.

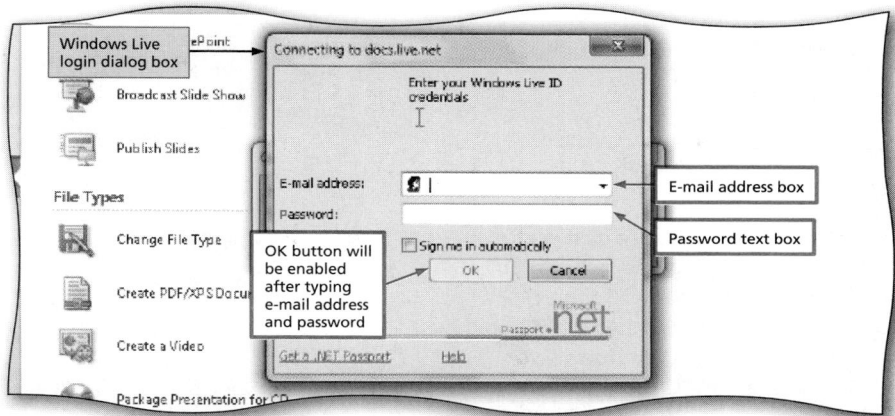

Figure C–5

5

- Enter your Windows Live e-mail address in the E-mail address box (Windows Live login dialog box).

- Enter your Windows Live password in the Password text box.

- Click the OK button to sign into Windows Live and display the contents of your Windows Live SkyDrive in right pane of the Save & Send gallery.

- If necessary, click the My Documents folder to set the save location for the document (Figure C–6).

Q&A

What if the My Documents folder does not exist?

Click another folder to select it as the save location. Record the name of this folder so that you can locate and retrieve the file later in this appendix.

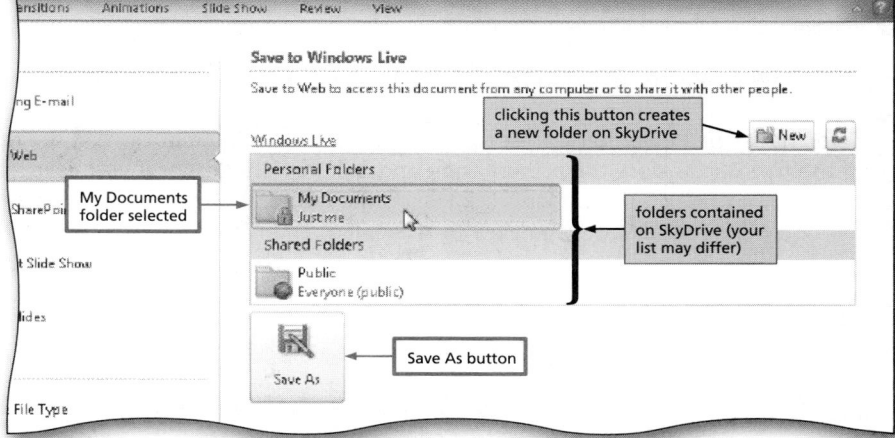

Figure C–6

Q&A

What is the difference between the personal folders and the shared folders?

Personal folders are private and are not shared with anyone. Shared folders can be viewed by SkyDrive users to whom you have assigned the necessary permissions.

• Click the Save As button in the right pane of the Save & Send gallery to contact the SkyDrive server (which may take some time, depending on the speed of your Internet connection) and then display the Save As dialog box (Figure C–7).

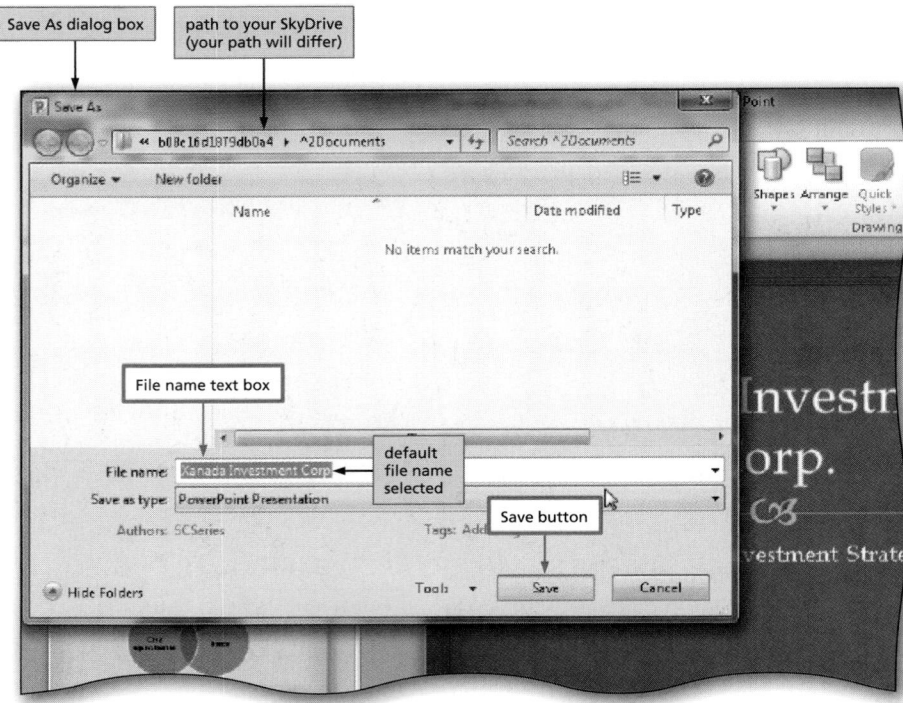

Figure C–7

• Type **Xanada Investment Web** in the File name text box to enter the file name and then click the Save button (Save As dialog box) to save the file to Windows Live SkyDrive (Figure C–8).

Q&A

Is it necessary to rename the file?

It is good practice to rename the file. If you download the file from SkyDrive to your computer, having a different file name will preserve the original file.

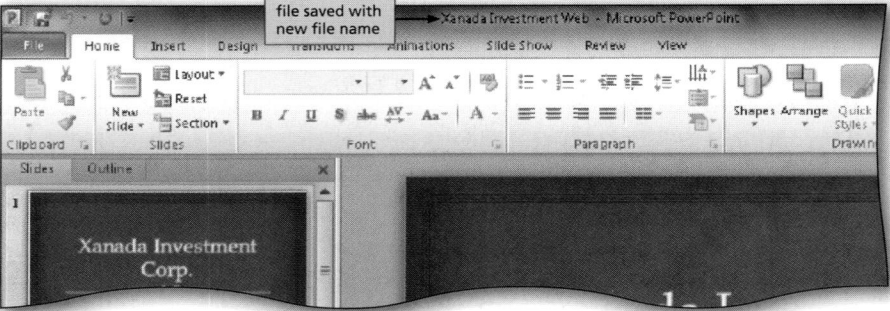

Figure C–8

• If you have one PowerPoint presentation open, click the Close button on the right side of the title bar to close the presentation and quit PowerPoint; or if you have multiple PowerPoint presentations open, click File on the Ribbon to open the Backstage view and then click Exit in the Backstage view to close all open presentations and quit PowerPoint.

Web Apps

Microsoft has created a scaled-down, Web-based version of its Microsoft Office suite, called **Microsoft Office Web Apps,** or **Web Apps.** Web Apps contains Web-based versions of Word, PowerPoint, Excel, and OneNote that can be used to view and edit files that are saved to SkyDrive. Web Apps allows users to continue working with their files even while they are not using a computer with Microsoft Office installed. In addition to working with files located on SkyDrive, Web Apps also enables users to create new Word documents, PowerPoint presentations, Excel spreadsheets, and OneNote notebooks. After returning to a computer with the Microsoft Office suite, some users choose to download files from SkyDrive and edit them using the associated Microsoft Office program.

To Open a File from Windows Live SkyDrive

Files saved to SkyDrive can be opened from a Web browser using any computer with an Internet connection. The following steps open the Xanada Investment Web file using a Web browser.

1

- Click the Internet Explorer program button pinned on the Windows 7 taskbar to start Internet Explorer.

- Type **skydrive.live.com** in the Address bar and then press the ENTER key to display a SkyDrive Web page requesting you sign in to your Windows Live account (Figure C–9).

Q&A Why does the Web address change after I enter it in the Address bar?

The Web address changes because you are being redirected to sign into Windows Live before you can access SkyDrive.

Q&A Can I open the file from Microsoft PowerPoint instead of using the Web browser?

If you are opening the file on the same computer from which you saved it to the SkyDrive, click File on the Ribbon to open the Backstage view. Click the Recent tab and then click the desired file name (Xanada Investment Web, in this case) in the Recent Presentations list, or click Open and then navigate to the location of the saved file (for a detailed example of this procedure, refer to the Office 2010 and Windows 7 chapter at the beginning of this book).

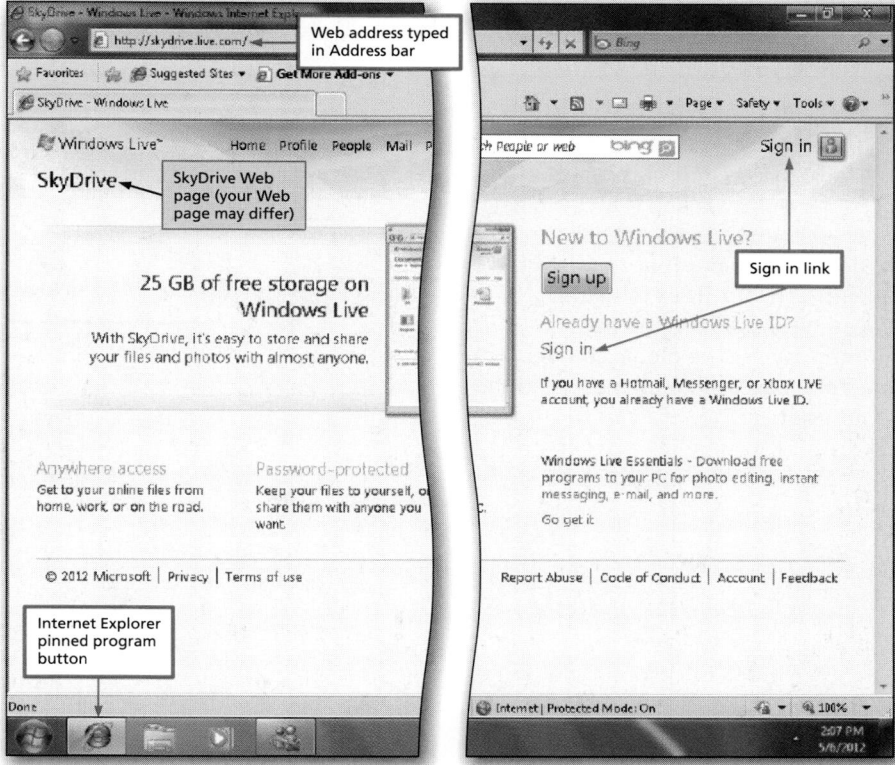

Figure C–9

2

- Click the Sign in link to display the Windows Live ID and Password text boxes (Figure C–10).

Q&A Why can I not locate the Sign in link?

If your computer remembers your Windows Live sign in credentials from a previous session, your e-mail address already may be displayed on the SkyDrive Web page. In this case, point to your e-mail address to display the Sign in button, click the Sign in button, and then proceed to Step 3. If you cannot locate your e-mail address or Sign in link, click the Sign in with a different Windows Live ID link and then proceed to Step 3.

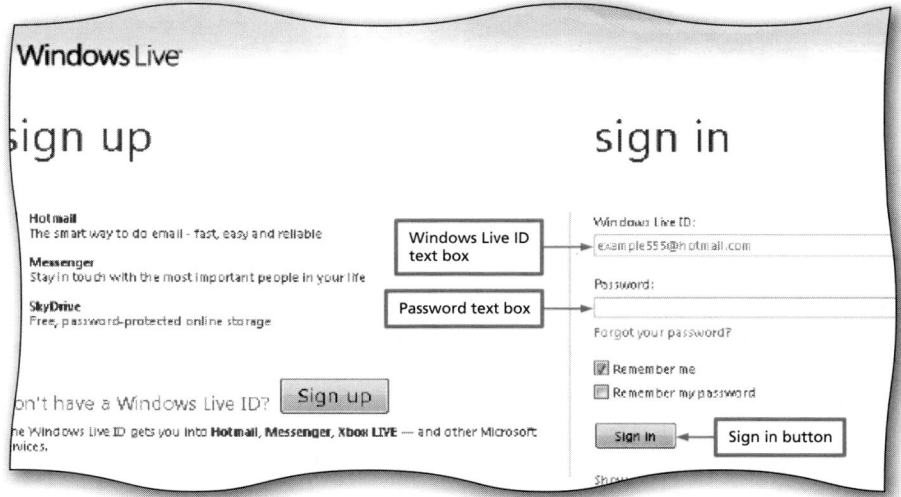

Figure C–10

- If necessary, enter your Windows Live ID and password in the appropriate text boxes and then click the Sign in button to sign into Windows Live and display the contents of your SkyDrive (Figure C–11).

Q&A

What do the icons beside the folders mean?

The lock icon indicates that the folder is private and is accessible only to you. The people icon signifies a folder that can be shared with SkyDrive users to whom you have assigned the necessary permissions. The globe icon denotes a folder accessible to anyone on the Internet.

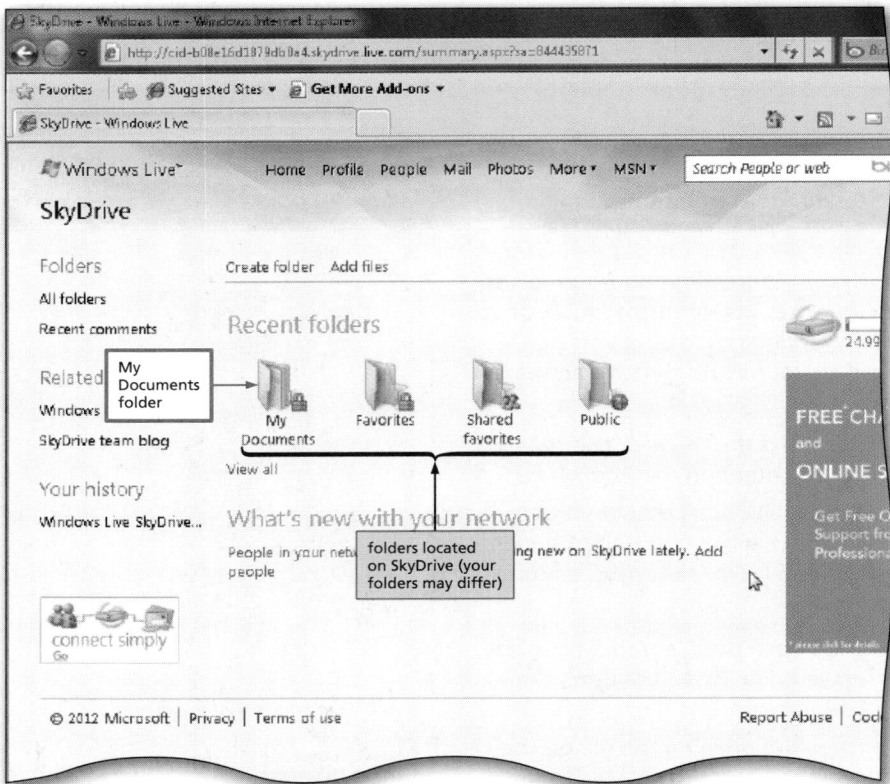

Figure C–11

- Click the My Documents folder, or the folder containing the file you wish to open, to select the folder and display its contents (Figure C–12).

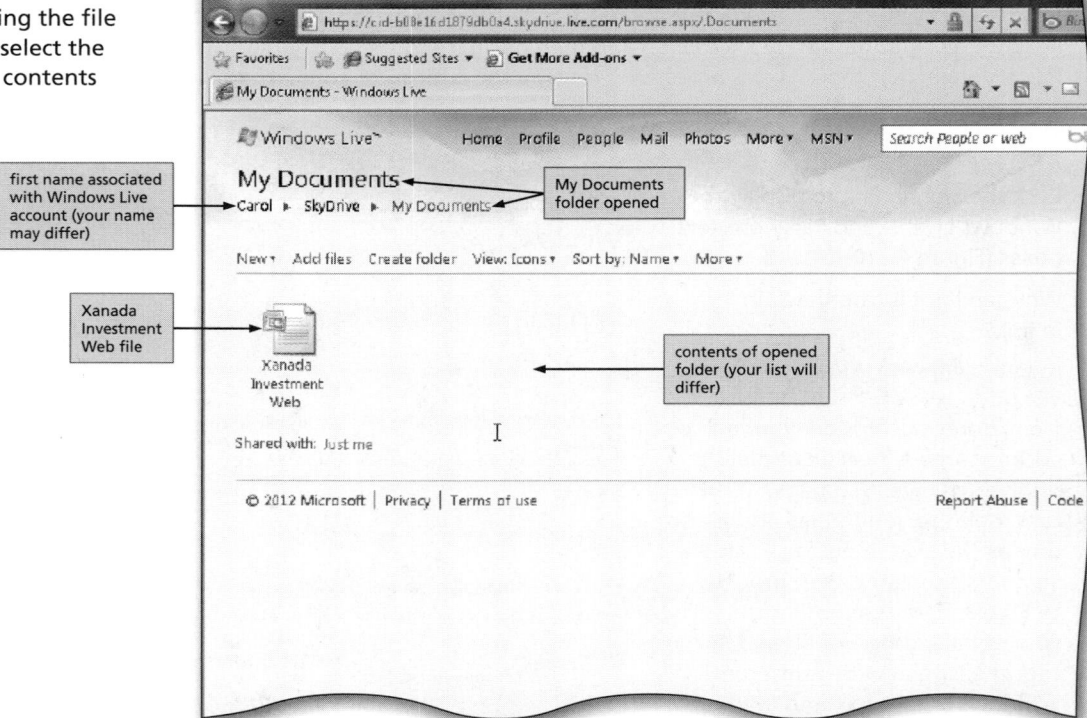

Figure C–12

5

• Click the Xanada
Investment Web file
to select the file and
display information
about it (Figure C–13).

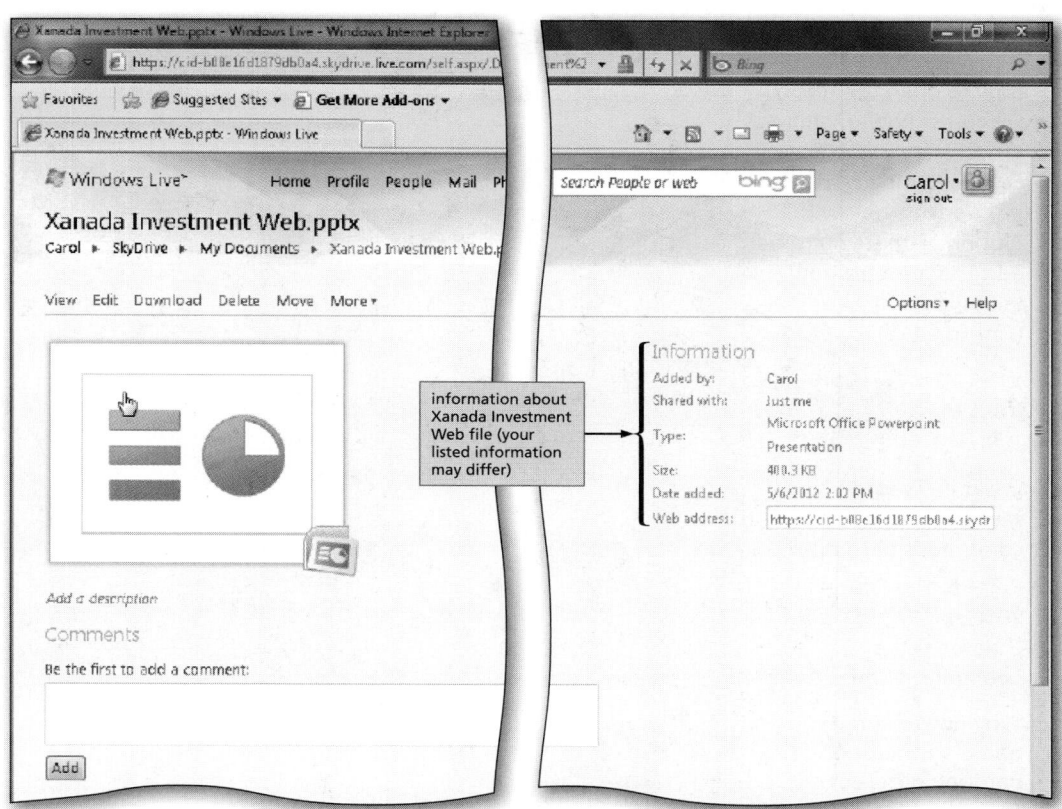

Figure C–13

6

• Click the Download
link to display the File
Download dialog box
(Figure C–14).

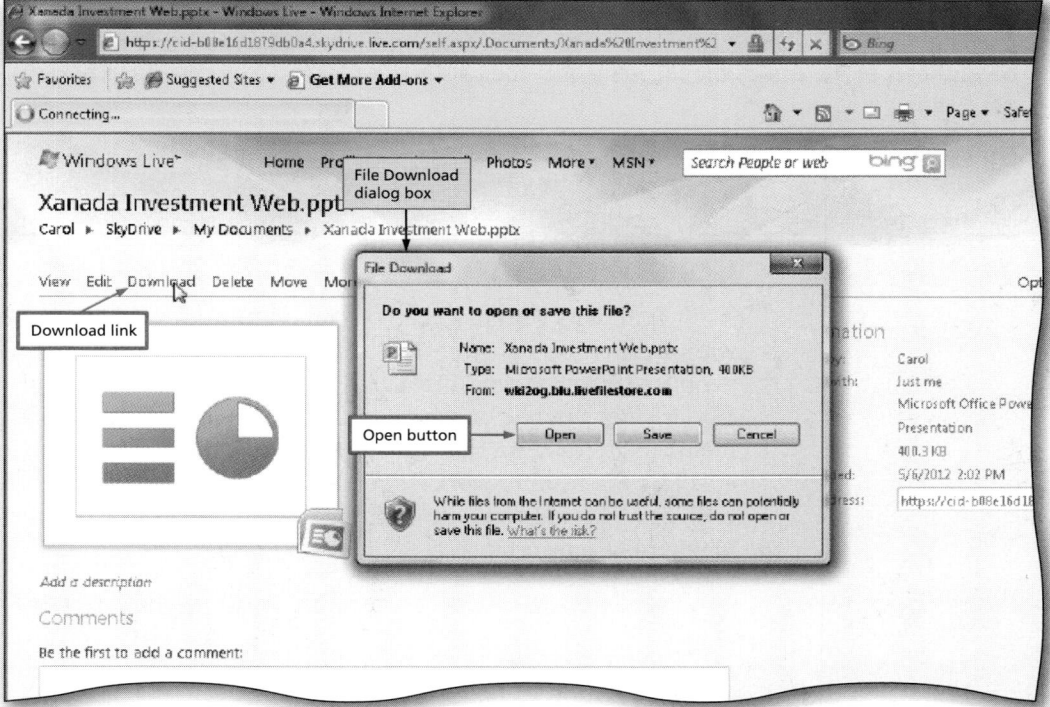

Figure C–14

- Click the Open button (File Download dialog box) to open the file in Microsoft PowerPoint. If necessary, click the Enable Editing button if it appears below the Ribbon so that you can edit the presentation in PowerPoint (Figure C–15).

Q&A

What if I want to save the file on my computer's hard disk?

Refer to the Office 2010 and Windows 7 chapter at the beginning of this book.

Q&A

Why does the file name on the title bar look different from the file name I typed when saving the document?

Because you are opening the file directly from SkyDrive without first saving it to your computer, the file name may differ slightly. For example, spaces may be replaced with "%20" and a number in parentheses at the end of the file name may indicate you are opening a copy of the original file that is stored online.

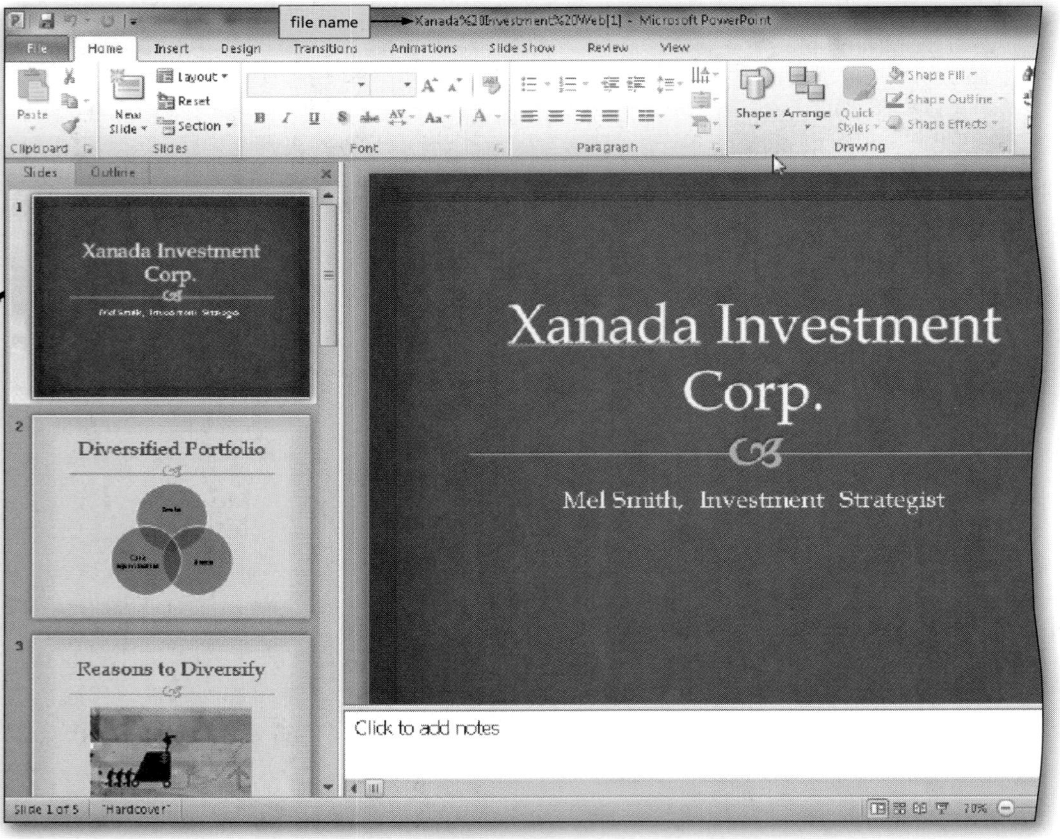

Figure C–15

Collaboration

In today's workplace, it is common to work with others on projects. Collaborating with the members of your team often requires sharing files. It also can involve multiple people editing and working with a certain set of files simultaneously. Placing files on SkyDrive in a public or shared folder enables others to view or modify the files. The members of the team then can view and edit the files simultaneously using Web Apps, enabling the team to work from one set of files. Collaboration using Web Apps not only enables multiple people to work together, it also can reduce the amount of time required to complete a project.

Appendix D

Microsoft Office 2010 Specialist and Expert Certifications

What Are Microsoft Office Specialist and Expert Certifications?

Microsoft Corporation has developed a set of standardized, performance-based examinations that you can take to demonstrate your overall expertise with Microsoft Office 2010 programs, including Microsoft Word 2010, Microsoft PowerPoint 2010, Microsoft Excel 2010, Microsoft Access 2010, and Microsoft Outlook 2010. When you successfully complete an examination for one of these Office programs, you will have earned the designation as a specialist or as an expert in that particular Office program.

These examinations collectively are called the Microsoft Office 2010 Specialist and Microsoft Office 2010 Expert certification exams. The information in Table D–1 identifies each of these examinations.

Table D–1 Microsoft Office Specialist and Expert Certifications			
Certification Exam	**Description**	**Requirement**	**Credential Earned**
Microsoft Word 2010 Specialist	Indicates you have proficiency in using at least 80 percent of the features and capabilities of Word 2010	Successfully complete Exam 77-881	Microsoft Office Specialist: Microsoft Word 2010
Microsoft Word 2010 Expert	Indicates you have proficiency in using Word 2010 at the feature and functionality levels, together with advanced features of Word 2010	Successfully complete Exam 77-887	Microsoft Office Specialist: Microsoft Word 2010 Expert
Microsoft PowerPoint 2010 Specialist	Indicates you have proficiency in using PowerPoint 2010 by creating complex slide shows using sophisticated data presented in visual formats	Successfully complete Exam 77-883	Microsoft Office Specialist: Microsoft PowerPoint 2010

Table D–1 Microsoft Office Specialist and Expert Certifications *(continued)*

Certification Exam	Description	Requirement	Credential Earned
Microsoft Excel 2010 Specialist	Indicates you have proficiency in using at least 80 percent of the features and capabilities of Excel 2010	Successfully complete Exam 77-882	Microsoft Office Specialist: Microsoft Excel 2010
Microsoft Excel 2010 Expert	Indicates you have proficiency in using Excel 2010 at the feature and functionality levels, together with advanced features of Excel 2010	Successfully complete Exam 77-888	Microsoft Office Specialist: Microsoft Excel 2010 Expert
Microsoft Access 2010	Indicates you have proficiency in using Access 2010 by creating, modifying, and extending functionality of basic database objects	Successfully complete Exam 77-885	Microsoft Office Specialist: Microsoft Access 2010
Microsoft Outlook 2010	Indicates you have proficiency in using Outlook 2010 by formatting message content, creating contact records and appointments, scheduling meetings, and sharing schedules	Successfully complete Exam 77-884	Microsoft Office Specialist: Microsoft Outlook 2010

You will notice in Table D–1 that Word and Excel have an Expert certification. The other programs do not.

Microsoft provides one other level of Office certification: 2010 Microsoft Office Master certification. To be certified as a 2010 Microsoft Office Master, you must successfully complete the following exams:

- 77-887: Word 2010 Expert
- 77-888: Excel 2010 Expert
- 77-883: PowerPoint 2010

and either

- 77-885: Access 2010

or

- 77-884: Outlook 2010

Why Should You Be Certified?

Microsoft Office 2010 certification provides a number of benefits for both you and your potential employer. The benefits for you include the following:

- You can differentiate yourself in the employment marketplace from those who are not Microsoft Office Specialist or Expert certified.
- You have proved your skills and expertise when using Microsoft Office 2010.
- You will be able to perform at a higher skill level in your job.
- You will be working at a higher professional level than those who are not certified.
- You will broaden your employment opportunities and advance your career more rapidly.

For employers, Microsoft Office 2010 certification offers the following advantages:

- When hiring or promoting employees, employers have immediate verification of employees' skills.
- Companies can maximize their productivity and efficiency by employing Microsoft Office 2010 certified individuals.

Taking the Microsoft Office 2010 Certification Exams

The Certiport Company administers the Microsoft Office 2010 Specialist and Expert certification exams. You can contact Certiport at 888-999-9830 x138 or at the Web site, http://www.certiport.com. On the Web site, click the Microsoft Office 2010 Specialist link. Be sure to explore the links on these Certiport pages to obtain a thorough understanding of the Microsoft Office 2010 certification exams.

To take an exam, you must register and pay a fee. The fee varies depending on the test and the testing center. Each exam requires that you complete specified tasks using the program on which you are being tested, that is, tasks you would perform while at work. Remember—these are performance-based exams, so you will be using the software, not answering questions about the software.

You can find testing centers by following the links on the Certiport Web site and then clicking Find a Testing Center.

How Do I Prepare for the Microsoft Office 2010 Specialist Exam?

The Shelly Cashman Series offers Microsoft-approved textbooks for the certification exams listed in Table D–1 on pages APP 13 and APP 14. These textbooks can be found by visiting the Web site, www.cengagebrain.com, and then entering the search topic, Shelly. Using any of the approved textbooks will prepare you to take and pass the indicated Microsoft Office 2010 Specialist or Expert exam. For a list of skill sets specific to this book, see Table D–2 on pages APP 16 through APP 20. The use of all appropriate Shelly Cashman Series Office 2010 textbooks will prepare you for the 2010 Microsoft Office Master certification.

For further information from Microsoft regarding Microsoft Office 2010 certification, please visit http://www.microsoft.com/learning/en/us/certification/mos.aspx and http://office.microsoft.com/en-us/word-help/should-you-become-a-microsoft-office-specialist-HA001211101.aspx.

Table D–2 Specialist-Level Skill Sets and Locations in Book for Microsoft PowerPoint 2010

Skill Set	Page Number
Managing the PowerPoint Environment	
Adjust views.	
Adjust views by using ribbon	PPT 153
Adjust views by status bar commands	PPT 47, PPT 153, PPT 154, PPT 664
Manipulate the PowerPoint window.	
Work with multiple presentation windows simultaneously	PPT 697, PPT 698
Configure the Quick Access Toolbar.	
Show the Quick Access Toolbar (QAT) below the ribbon	PPT 82
Configure PowerPoint file options.	
Use PowerPoint Proofing	PPT 180, PPT 692
Use PowerPoint Save options	PPT 295
Creating a Slide Presentation	
Construct and edit photo albums.	
Add captions to picture	PPT 686
Insert text	PPT 688
Insert images in black and white	PPT 690
Reorder pictures in an album	PPT 682
Adjust image	
Rotation	PPT 683
Brightness	PPT 684
Contrast	PPT 684
Apply slide size and orientation settings.	
Set up a custom size	PPT 696
Change the orientation	PPT 696
Add and remove slides.	
Insert an outline	PPT 335
Reuse slides from a saved presentation	PPT 285
Reuse slides from a slide library	PPT 269, PPT 285
Duplicate selected slides	PPT 38, PPT 662
Delete multiple slides simultaneously	PPT 152
Include non-contiguous slides in a presentation	PPT 285, PPT 674
Format slides.	
Format sections	PPT 666, PPT 669, PPT 671
Modify themes	PPT 81, PPT 101
Switch to a different slide layout	PPT 21
Apply a formatting to a slide	
Fill color	PPT 507
Gradient	PPT 95, PPT 96
Picture	PPT 97
Texture	PPT 95
Pattern	PPT 509
Set up slide footers	PPT 289, PPT 476
Enter and format text.	
Use text effects	PPT 103, PPT 104, PPT 115
Change text format	
Indentation	PPT 488
Alignment	PPT 150, PPT 151, PPT 365, PPT 366

Table D–2 Specialist-Level Skill Sets and Locations in Book for Microsoft PowerPoint 2010 *(continued)*

Skill Set	Page Number
Line Spacing	PPT 367
Direction	PPT 482
Change the formatting of bulleted and numbered lists	PPT 377, PPT 379, PPT 382
Enter text in a placeholder text box	PPT 7, PPT 9
Convert text to SmartArt	PPT 213
Copy and paste text	PPT 109
Use Paste Special	PPT 284
Use Format Painter	PPT 105
Format text boxes.	
Apply formatting to a text box	
Fill color	PPT 487
Gradient	PPT 542
Picture	PPT 539
Texture	PPT 487
Pattern	PPT 539
Change the outline of a text box	
Color	PPT 535
Weight	PPT 534
Style	PPT 536
Change the shape of the text box	PPT 534
Apply effects	PPT 536
Set the alignment	PPT 543
Create columns in a text box	PPT 367
Set internal margins	PPT 488
Set the current text box formatting as the default for new text boxes	PPT 537
Adjust text in a text box	
Wrap	PPT 488
Size	PPT 488
Position	PPT 489, PPT 543, PPT 617
Use AutoFit	PPT 485, PPT 488
Working with Graphical and Multimedia Elements	
Manipulate graphical elements.	
Arrange graphical elements	PPT 146, PPT 157, PPT 162
Position graphical elements	PPT 36
Resize graphical elements	PPT 33, PPT 93
Apply effects to graphical elements	PPT 89
Apply styles to graphical elements	PPT 87, PPT 110
Apply borders to graphical elements	PPT 91
Add hyperlinks to graphical elements	PPT 339
Manipulate images.	
Apply color adjustments	PPT 143
Apply image corrections	
Sharpen	PPT 87
Soften	PPT 87
Brightness	PPT 87
Contrast	PPT 87

Table D–2 Specialist-Level Skill Sets and Locations in Book for Microsoft PowerPoint 2010 *(continued)*

Skill Set	Page Number
Add artistic effects to an image	PPT 144
Remove a background	PPT 405, PPT 407
Crop a picture	PPT 409, PPT 317
Compress selected pictures or all pictures	PPT 410
Change a picture	PPT 544
Reset a picture	PPT 291
Modify WordArt and shapes.	
Set the formatting of the current shape as the default for future shapes	PPT 564
Change the fill color or texture	PPT 117
Change the WordArt	PPT 115
Convert WordArt to SmartArt	PPT 546
Manipulate SmartArt.	
Add and remove shapes	PPT 550, PPT 551
Change SmartArt styles	PPT 210, PPT 556
Change the SmartArt layout	PPT 550
Reorder shapes	PPT 547
Convert a SmartArt graphic to text	PPT 557
Convert SmartArt to shapes	PPT 559
Make shapes larger or smaller	PPT 553
Promote bullet levels	PPT 548
Demote bullet levels	PPT 549
Edit video and audio content.	
Apply a style to video or audio content	PPT 172
Adjust video or audio content	PPT 164, PPT 172
Arrange video or audio content	PPT 174
Size video or audio content	PPT 174
Adjust playback options	PPT 166, PPT 170
Creating Charts and Tables	
Construct and modify tables.	
Draw a table	PPT 603, PPT 604, PPT 606
Insert a Microsoft Excel spreadsheet	PPT 618
Set table style options	PPT 236
Add shading	PPT 612
Add borders	PPT 238
Add effects	PPT 238
Columns and Rows	
Change the alignment	PPT 617
Resize	PPT 240, PPT 615
Merge	PPT 242
Split	PPT 610
Distribute	PPT 614
Arrange	PPT 604, PPT 606, PPT 608, PPT 612
Insert and modify charts.	
Select a chart type	PPT 220
Enter chart data	PPT 221
Change the chart type	PPT 627
Change the chart layout	PPT 226

Table D–2 Specialist-Level Skill Sets and Locations in Book for Microsoft PowerPoint 2010 *(continued)*

Skill Set	Page Number
Switch row and column	PPT 626
Select data	PPT 635
Edit data	PPT 635
Apply chart elements.	
Use chart labels	PPT 632
Use axes	PPT 632
Use gridlines	PPT 633
Use backgrounds	PPT 634
Manipulate chart layouts.	
Select chart elements	PPT 224, PPT 226
Format selections	PPT 224, PPT 226
Manipulate chart elements.	
Arrange chart elements	PPT 229, PPT 230
Specify a precise position	PPT 230, PPT 231, PPT 625, PPT 629
Apply effects	PPT 226, PPT 629
Resize chart elements	PPT 228, PPT 229
Apply Quick Styles	PPT 628
Apply a border	PPT 225, PPT 629
Add hyperlinks	PPT 636
Applying Transitions and Animations	
Apply built-in and custom animations.	
Use More Entrance	PPT 411
Use More Emphasis	PPT 413
Use More Exit effects	PPT 414
Use More Motion paths	PPT 427, PPT 428, PPT 431
Apply effect and path options.	
Set timing	PPT 446
Set start options	PPT 416
Manipulate animations.	
Change the direction of an animation	PPT 412
Attach a sound to an animation	PPT 430
Use Animation Painter	PPT 433
Reorder animation	PPT 420
Select text options	PPT 423
Apply and modify transitions between slides.	
Modify a transition effect	PPT 447
Add a sound to a transition	PPT 43
Modify transition duration	PPT 43
Set up manual or automatically timed advance options	PPT 446, PPT 673
Collaborating on Presentations	
Manage comments in presentations.	
Insert and edit comments	PPT 281, PPT 282
Show or hide markup	PPT 280
Move to the previous or next comment	PPT 276
Delete comments	PPT 274

Table D–2 Specialist-Level Skill Sets and Locations in Book for Microsoft PowerPoint 2010 *(continued)*

Skill Set	Page Number
Apply proofing tools.	
Use Spelling and Thesaurus features	PPT 181, PPT 187
Compare and combine presentations	PPT 270
Preparing Presentations for Delivery	
Save presentations.	
Save the presentation as a picture presentation	PPT 576
Save the presentation as a PDF	PPT 51, PPT 295
Save the presentation as an XPS	PPT 51, PPT 295
Save the presentation as an outline	PPT 384
Save the presentation as an OpenDocument	PPT 295
Save the presentation as a show (.ppsx)	PPT 295
Save a slide or object as a picture file	PPT 296
Share presentations.	
Package a presentation for CD delivery	PPT 297
Create video	PPT 705
Create handouts (send to Microsoft Word)	PPT 578
Compress media	PPT 701
Print presentations.	
Adjust print settings	PPT 184, PPT 187, PPT 271, PPT 510, PPT 512
Protect presentations.	
Set a password	PPT 305
Change a password	PPT 307
Mark a presentation as final	PPT 308
Delivering Presentations	
Apply presentation tools.	
Add pen and highlighter annotations	PPT 312
Change the ink color	PPT 313
Erase an annotation	PPT 314
Discard annotations upon closing	PPT 314
Retain annotations upon closing	PPT 314
Set up slide shows.	
Set up a Slide Show	PPT 292, PPT 294, PPT 447, PPT 673, PPT 694, PPT 695, PPT 708
Play narrations	PPT 695
Set up Presenter view	PPT 708
Use timings	PPT 673
Show media controls	PPT 174
Broadcast presentations	PPT 705
Create a Custom Slide Show	PPT 674, PPT 677
Set presentation timing.	
Rehearse timings	PPT 444
Keep timings	PPT 446
Adjust a slide's timing	PPT 446
Record presentations.	
Start recording from the beginning of a slide show	PPT 725
Start recording from the current slide of the slide show	PPT 694, PPT 721

Index

Quick Reference Summary

Microsoft PowerPoint 2010 Quick Reference Summary

Task	Page Number	Mouse	Ribbon	Shortcut Menu	Keyboard Shortcut
Action Button, Copy	PPT 348		Copy button (Home tab | Clipboard group)	Copy	CTRL+C
Action Button, Edit Setting	PPT 349		Action button (Insert tab | Links group)		
Action Button, Insert	PPT 344		Shapes button (Insert tab | Illustrations group), Action Buttons area		
Animated GIF (Movie), Insert	PPT 174		Picture button (Insert tab | Images group)		
Animation, Add after Existing Effect	PPT 413, 414		Add Animation button (Animations tab | Advanced Animation group)		
Animation, Associate Sound with	PPT 430		Add sound to slide, click sound icon, Play button (Animations tab | Animation group), With Previous		
Animation, Change Direction	PPT 412		Effect Options button (Animations tab | Animation group)		
Animation, Change Order	PPT 420		Animation Pane button (Animations tab | Advanced Animation group)		
Animation, Dim Text After	PPT 440		Animation Pane button (Animations tab | Advanced Animation group), Animation Order list arrow, Effect Options, After animation list arrow		
Animation, Modify Timing	PPT 416		Start Animation Timing button arrow (Animations tab | Timing group)		
Animation, Preview Sequence	PPT 416		Preview button (Animations tab | Preview group)		
Animation Painter, Use to Copy Animations	PPT 433		Animation Painter button (Animations tab | Advanced Animation group)		
Audio File, Insert	PPT 167		Insert Audio button (Insert tab | Media group)		

Microsoft PowerPoint 2010 Quick Reference Summary *(continued)*

Task	Page Number	Mouse	Ribbon	Shortcut Menu	Keyboard Shortcut
Audio Options, Add	PPT 170		Audio options check boxes (Audio Tools Playback tab | Audio Options group)		
Broadcast Presentation	PPT 705		Broadcast Slide Show button (Slide Show tab | Start Slide Show group), Start Broadcast button (Broadcast Slide Show dialog box)		
Bullet, Format Color	PPT 379		Bullets button arrow (Home tab | Paragraph group), Bullets and Numbering, Color button	Bullets, Bullets and Numbering	
Bullet, Format Size	PPT 377		Bullets button arrow (Home tab | Paragraph group), Bullets and Numbering, Size box	Bullets, Bullets and Numbering	
Bullet Character, Change to Number	PPT 380		Numbering button arrow (Home tab | Paragraph group)	Bullets, Bullets and Numbering	
Bullet Character, Change to Picture	PPT 372		Bullets button arrow (Home tab | Paragraph group), Bullets and Numbering, Picture button (Bullets and Numbering dialog box)		
Bullet Character, Change to Symbol	PPT 375		Bullets button arrow (Home tab | Paragraph group), Bullets and Numbering, Customize button (Bullets and Numbering dialog box)		
Bullet Characters, Remove	PPT 382		Bullets button arrow (Home tab | Paragraph group), None	Bullets, None	
Character Spacing, Change	PPT 486		Character Spacing button (Home tab | Font group); Font Dialog Box Launcher (Home tab | Font Group), Character Spacing tab		
Chart, Align	PPT 625		Align button (Drawing Tools Format tab | Arrange group) or (Chart Tools Format tab | Arrange group)		
Chart, Animate	PPT 437		More button (Animations tab | Animation group)		
Chart, Apply Quick Style	PPT 628		More button (Chart Tools Design tab | Chart Styles group)		
Chart, Apply Style	PPT 223		More button (Chart Tools Design tab | Chart Styles group)		
Chart, Change Layout	PPT 226		More button (Chart Tools Design tab | Chart Layouts group)		
Chart, Change Type	PPT 627		Change Chart Type button (Chart Tools Design tab | Type group)		
Chart, Display Gridlines	PPT 633		Gridlines button (Chart Tools Layout tab | Axes group)		
Chart, Display Labels	PPT 632		Data Labels button (Chart Tools Layout tab | Labels group)		

Microsoft PowerPoint 2010 Quick Reference Summary *(continued)*

Task	Page Number	Mouse	Ribbon	Shortcut Menu	Keyboard Shortcut
Chart, Format Background	PPT 634		Chart Wall button (Chart Tools Layout tab | Background group)		
Chart, Format Legend	PPT 629		Legend button (Chart Tools Layout tab | Labels group)	Format Legend	
Chart, Hide Axis	PPT 632		Axes button (Chart Tools Layout tab | Axes group), Primary Vertical Axis or Primary Horizontal Axis, None		
Chart, Insert	PPT 220	Insert Chart button in content placeholder	Chart button (Insert tab | Illustrations group)		
Chart, Insert from Excel	PPT 624		Insert Object button (Insert tab | Text group), Create from file, browse to file with chart	Copy chart in Microsoft Excel, exit Microsoft Excel, Paste button arrow (Home tab | Clipboard group), Use Destination Theme & Embed Workbook	
Chart, Resize	PPT 228	Drag sizing handle to desired location			
Chart, Rotate	PPT 230		Format Selection button (Chart Tools Format tab | Current Selection group)		
Chart, Separate a Pie Slice	PPT 229	Select slice and drag			
Chart, Switch Rows and Columns	PPT 626		Switch Row/Column button (Chart Tools Design tab | Data group)		
Chart Shape, Change Outline Color	PPT 226		Shape Outline button arrow (Chart Tools Format tab | Shape Styles group)		
Chart Shape, Change Outline Weight	PPT 224		Shape Outline button arrow (Chart Tools Format tab | Shape Styles group), Weight		
Clip Art, Insert	PPT 27	Clip Art button in content placeholder	Clip Art button (Insert tab | Images group)		
Clip Art, Photo, or Shape, Move	PPT 36	Drag			ARROW KEYS move selected image in small increments
Clip Art, Regroup	PPT 162		Group button (Drawing Tools Format tab | Arrange group), Regroup	Group, Regroup	
Clip Art, Ungroup	PPT 157		Group button (Picture Tools Format tab | Arrange group), Ungroup	Group, Ungroup	
Clip Object, Recolor	PPT 158		Shape Fill button (Drawing Tools Format tab | Shape Styles group)	Format Shape, Solid fill option button, Color button (Format Shape dialog box)	
Columns, Adjust Spacing	PPT 369		Columns button (Home tab | Paragraph group), More Columns, Spacing box		

Microsoft PowerPoint 2010 Quick Reference Summary *(continued)*

Task	Page Number	Mouse	Ribbon	Shortcut Menu	Keyboard Shortcut
Columns, Create in a Placeholder	PPT 367		Columns button (Home tab | Paragraph group)		
Comment, Delete	PPT 274		Delete Comment button (Review tab | Comments group)		
Comment, Edit	PPT 282		Edit Comment button (Review tab | Comments group)		
Comment, Insert	PPT 281		New Comment button (Review tab | Comments group)		
Comments, Print	PPT 271		Page Layout button (File tab | Print tab), check 'Print Comments and Ink Markup' box		CTRL+P
Copy	PPT 108, 155, 348		Copy button (Home tab | Clipboard group)	Copy	CTRL+C
Credits, Create	PPT 442		More button (Animations tab | Animation group), More Entrance Effects, Credits		
Custom Slide Show, Create	PPT 674		In Normal view, Custom Slide Show button (Slide Show tab | Start Slide Show group), Custom Shows, New		
Custom Slide Show, Edit	PPT 677		In Normal view, Custom Slide Show button (Slide Show tab | Start Slide Show group), Custom Shows, select show, Edit		
Digital Signature, Create and Add	PPT 309		Protect Presentation button (File tab | Info tab), Add a Digital Signature		
Document Inspector, Start	PPT 303		Check for Issues button (File tab | Info tab), Inspect Document		
Document Properties, Change	PPT 46		Properties button (File tab | Info tab)		
Document Theme, Change Color	PPT 81		Colors button (Design tab | Themes group)		
Document Theme, Choose	PPT 5		More button (Design tab | Themes group)		
Embedded File, Edit	PPT 601	Double-click embedded object to open source program		Document Object, Edit	
File with Graphics and Text, Insert	PPT 598		Insert Object button (Insert tab | Text group), Create from file		
Fill Color, Apply to Slide	PPT 507		Background Styles button (Design tab | Background group), Format Background, Fill pane	Format Background, Fill pane	
Fill Color, Set Transparency	PPT 507		Background Styles button (Design tab | Background group), Format Background, Fill pane, Transparency slider	Format Background, Fill pane, Transparency slider	
Font, Change	PPT 102	Font box arrow on Mini toolbar	Font box arrow (Home tab | Font group)	Font, Font tab (Font dialog box)	CTRL+SHIFT+F

Microsoft PowerPoint 2010 Quick Reference Summary *(continued)*

Task	Page Number	Mouse	Ribbon	Shortcut Menu	Keyboard Shortcut
Font, Change Color	PPT 13	Font Color button or Font Color button arrow on Mini toolbar	Font Color button or Font Color button arrow (Home tab | Font group)	Font, Font tab (Font dialog box)	CTRL+SHIFT+F
Font Size, Decrease	PPT 104	Decrease Font Size button or Font Size box arrow on Mini toolbar	Decrease Font Size button or Font Size box arrow (Home tab | Font group)		CTRL+SHIFT+<
Font Size, Increase	PPT 11	Increase Font Size button or Font Size box arrow on Mini toolbar	Increase Font Size button or Font Size box arrow (Home tab | Font group)		CTRL+SHIFT+>
Footer, Add	PPT 289, 476		Header & Footer button (Insert tab | Text group)		
Format Painter	PPT 105	Format Painter button on Mini toolbar	Format Painter button (Home tab | Clipboard group)		
Guides, Display	PPT 357		Guides check box (View tab | Show group)	Grid and Guides, 'Display drawing guides on screen' check box	ALT+F9
Handout, Create by Exporting File to Microsoft Word	PPT 578		Create Handouts button (File tab | Save & Send tab)		
Handout, Print	PPT 184, 510		Print button (File tab | Print tab)		
Handout Master, Use	PPT 496, 510		Handout Master button (View tab | Master Views group)		
Header, Add	PPT 289		Header & Footer button (Insert tab | Text group)		
Hyperlink, Add	PPT 339, 341, 636		Hyperlink button (Insert tab | Links group)	Hyperlink	CTRL+K
Hyperlink to Another PowerPoint File	PPT 350		Action button (Insert tab | Links group), Hyperlink to list arrow, Other PowerPoint Presentation		
Hyperlink to a Word File	PPT 353		Action button (Insert tab | Links group), Hyperlink to list arrow, Other File		
Line, Change Weight or Color	PPT 567		Shape Outline button (Drawing Tools Format tab | Shape Styles group), Weight or choose color		
Line, Draw	PPT 565		More button (Drawing Tools Format tab | Insert Shapes group), click desired Line shape		
Line, Set Formatting as Default	PPT 568			Set as Default Line	
Line Break, Enter	PPT 371				SHIFT+ENTER
Line Spacing, Change	PPT 367		Line Spacing button (Home tab | Paragraph group)	Paragraph	
Linked File, Insert	PPT 618		Insert Object button (Insert tab | Text group), Create from file, Link check box		
Linked Worksheet, Edit	PPT 622	Double-click linked object to open source program			
List, Animate	PPT 439		More button (Animations tab | Animation group)		

Microsoft PowerPoint 2010 Quick Reference Summary *(continued)*

Task	Page Number	Mouse	Ribbon	Shortcut Menu	Keyboard Shortcut
List Level, Decrease	PPT 18	Decrease List Level button on Mini toolbar	Decrease List Level button (Home tab | Paragraph group)		SHIFT+TAB or ALT+SHIFT+LEFT ARROW
List Level, Increase	PPT 17	Increase List Level button on Mini toolbar	Increase List Level button (Home tab | Paragraph group)		TAB or ALT+SHIFT+RIGHT ARROW
Manual Timing, Show Presentation with	PPT 673		Set Up Slide Show button (Slide Show tab | Set Up group), Manually (Set Up Show dialog box)		
Master View	PPT 471		Slide Master button (View tab | Master Views group)		
Merge a Presentation	PPT 270		Compare button (Review tab | Compare group)		
Narration, Record	PPT 694		Record Slide Show button arrow (Slide Show tab | Set Up group), Start Recording from Beginning or Start Recording from Current Slide, Narrations and laser pointer check box (Record Slide Show dialog box), Start Recording button (Record Slide Show dialog box), End Show		
Next Slide	PPT 25	Next Slide button on vertical scroll bar or next slide thumbnail on Slides tab			PAGE DOWN
Normal View	PPT 153	Normal view button at lower-right PowerPoint window	Normal View button (View tab | Presentation Views group)		
Notes Master, Use	PPT 500, 512		View Notes Master button (View tab | Master Views group)		
Numbered List, Format	PPT 382		Numbering button arrow (Home tab | Paragraph group), Bullets and Numbering	Numbering, Bullets and Numbering	
Open Presentation	PPT 50		Open (File tab)		CTRL+O
Outline, Open as Presentation	PPT 335		Open (File tab), File Type arrow, All Outlines, select Word file, Open button		
Password, Set	PPT 305		Protect Presentation button (File tab | Info tab), Encrypt with Password		
Paste	PPT 109		Paste button (Home tab | Clipboard group)	Paste	CTRL+V
Pattern Fill, Apply to Slide	PPT 509		Background Styles button (Design tab | Background group), Format Background, Fill pane, Pattern fill	Format Background, Fill pane, Pattern fill	
Photo, Insert	PPT 32, 83	Insert Picture from File button in content placeholder or Insert Clip Art button in content placeholder	Picture button or Clip Art button (Insert tab | Images group)		

Microsoft PowerPoint 2010 Quick Reference Summary *(continued)*

Task	Page Number	Mouse	Ribbon	Shortcut Menu	Keyboard Shortcut
Photo Album, Add Captions Below All Pictures	PPT 686		New Photo Album button arrow (Insert tab | Images group), Captions below ALL pictures check box (Photo Album dialog box)		
Photo Album, Add Theme	PPT 686		New Photo Album button arrow (Insert tab | Images group), Browse button in Album Layout area (Photo Album dialog box)		
Photo Album, Change Layout	PPT 685		New Photo Album button arrow (Insert tab | Images group), Picture layout box arrow (Photo Album dialog box)		
Photo Album, Create	PPT 687		New Photo Album button arrow (Insert tab | Images group), Create button (Photo Album dialog box)		
Photo Album, Create Black-and-White Images	PPT 690		New Photo Album button arrow (Insert tab | Images group), ALL pictures black and white check box (Photo Album dialog box), Update		
Photo Album, Edit	PPT 687		New Photo Album button arrow (Insert tab | Images group), Edit Photo Album		
Photo Album, Reorder Pictures	PPT 682		New Photo Album button arrow (Insert tab | Images group), Move Up or Move Down button (Photo Album dialog box)		
Photo Album, Start and Add Pictures	PPT 680		New Photo Album button (Insert tab | Images group)		
Photo Album Image, Adjust Brightness	PPT 684		New Photo Album button arrow (Insert tab | Images group), Increase Brightness or Decrease Brightness button (Photo Album dialog box)		
Photo Album Image, Adjust Contrast	PPT 684		New Photo Album button arrow (Insert tab | Images group), Increase Contrast or Decrease Contrast button (Photo Album dialog box)		
Photo Album Image, Adjust Rotation	PPT 683		New Photo Album button arrow (Insert tab | Images group), Rotate Left 90° or Rotate Right 90° button (Photo Album dialog box)		
Picture, Add an Artistic Effect	PPT 145		Artistic Effects button (Picture Tools Format tab | Adjust group)	Format Picture, Artistic Effects (Format Picture dialog box)	

Microsoft PowerPoint 2010 Quick Reference Summary (continued)

Task	Page Number	Mouse	Ribbon	Shortcut Menu	Keyboard Shortcut
Picture, Add Border	PPT 91		Picture border button (Picture Tools Format tab | Picture Styles group)		
Picture, Animate	PPT 411, 414, 415, 425		Select picture, choose animation in Animation gallery (Animations tab | Animation group)		
Picture, Change	PPT 544		Change Picture button (Picture Tools Format tab | Adjust group), select new picture file		
Picture, Clear Formatting	PPT 291		Reset Picture button (Picture Tools Format tab | Adjust group)		
Picture, Compress	PPT 410		Compress Pictures button (Picture Tools Format tab | Adjust group)		
Picture, Correct	PPT 87		Corrections button (Picture Tools Format tab | Adjust group)	Format Picture, Picture Corrections (Format Picture dialog box)	
Picture, Crop	PPT 409		Crop button (Picture Tools Format tab | Size group), drag cropping handles		
Picture, Recolor	PPT 143		Color button (Picture Tools Format tab | Adjust group)	Format Picture, Picture Color (Format Picture dialog box)	
Picture, Remove Background	PPT 405, 407		Remove Background button (Picture Tools Format tab | Adjust group)		
Picture, Rotate	PPT 489	Drag rotation handle			
Picture Border, Change Color	PPT 92		Picture Border button (Picture Tools Format tab | Picture Styles group)		
Picture Effects, Apply	PPT 89		Picture Effects button (Picture Tools Format tab | Picture Styles group)	Format Picture	
Picture Presentation, Save as	PPT 576		Change File Type (File tab | Save & Send tab), PowerPoint Picture Presentation		
Picture Style, Apply	PPT 87		More button (Picture Tools Format tab | Picture Styles group)		
Pictures, Align	PPT 360, 362		Align button (Picture Tools Format tab | Arrange group)		
Placeholder, Delete	PPT 149				Select placeholder, DELETE
Placeholder, Move	PPT 148	Drag			
Placeholder, Resize	PPT 148	Drag sizing handles			
Presentation, Check for Compatibility	PPT 301		Check for Issues button, (File tab | Info tab), Check Compatibility		

Microsoft PowerPoint 2010 Quick Reference Summary *(continued)*

Task	Page Number	Mouse	Ribbon	Shortcut Menu	Keyboard Shortcut
Presentation, Create Self-Running	PPT 447		Set Up Slide Show button (Slide Show tab | Set Up group), 'Browsed at a kiosk (full screen)' option		
Presentation, Display Multiple Windows Simultaneously	PPT 697		With multiple presentations open, Cascade button or Arrange All button (View tab | Window group)		
Presentation, Mark as Final	PPT 308		Protect Presentation button, (File tab | Info tab), Mark as Final		
Presentation, Package for CD or DVD	PPT 297		Package Presentation for CD (File tab | Send & Save tab), Package Presentation for CD button		
Presentation, Print	PPT 51, 184, 271		Print button (File tab | Print tab)		CTRL+P
Presentation Change, Accept	PPT 276		Accept Change button (Review tab | Compare group)		
Presentation Change, Reject	PPT 278, 280		Reject Change button (Review tab | Compare group)		
Presentation Changes, End Review	PPT 283		End Review button (Review tab | Compare group)		
Presentation Changes, Review	PPT 273		Reviewing Pane button (Review tab | Compare group)		
Presenter View, Use	PPT 708		Use Presenter View check box (Slide Show tab | Monitors group), icon on Monitor tab, 'This is my main monitor' check box, icon that represents second monitor, 'Extend my Windows Desktop onto this monitor' check box, Set Up Slide Show button (Slide Show tab | Set Up group)		
Previous Slide	PPT 26	Previous Slide button on vertical scroll bar or click previous slide thumbnail on Slides tab			PAGE UP
Quit PowerPoint	PPT 50	Close button on title bar	Exit (File tab)	Right-click Microsoft PowerPoint button on taskbar, click Close window	ALT+F4
Reading View	PPT 154	Reading view button at lower-right PowerPoint window	Reading View button (View tab | Presentation Views group)		
Research Pane, Use to Find Information	PPT 692		Research button (Review tab | Proofing group)		Press ALT and click word to research

Microsoft PowerPoint 2010 Quick Reference Summary *(continued)*

Task	Page Number	Mouse	Ribbon	Shortcut Menu	Keyboard Shortcut
Resize	PPT 33, 93, 148	Drag sizing handles	Enter height and width values (Picture Tools Format tab | Size group or Drawing Tools Format tab | Size group)	Format Picture or Format Shape, Size tab, or enter height and width in Shape Height and Shape Width boxes	
Ribbon, Customize	PPT 570		Options (File tab), Customize Ribbon (PowerPoint Options dialog box)		
Ribbon, Reset	PPT 579		Options (File tab), Customize Ribbon, Reset button (PowerPoint Options dialog box)		
Rulers, Display	PPT 359		Ruler check box (View tab | Show group)	Ruler	
Save a Presentation	PPT 14, 295, 297, 300	Save button on Quick Access Toolbar	Save or Save As (File tab)		CTRL+S or F12
Save a Slide as an Image	PPT 296		Change File Type (File tab, Save & Send tab), JPEG File Interchange Format, Save As button		
Save as a PowerPoint Show	PPT 295		Change File Type (File tab | Save & Send tab), PowerPoint Show, Save As button		
Save in a Previous Format	PPT 300		Change File Type (File tab | Save & Send tab), PowerPoint 97-2003 Presentation, Save As button		
Screen Clipping, Use	PPT 288		Screenshot button (Insert tab | Images group), Screen Clipping command		
Section, Create Break	PPT 666	Click mouse where section break desired, then follow Ribbon steps	In Slide Sorter view, Section button (Home tab | Slides group), Add Section		
Section, Rename	PPT 669		Section button (Home tab | Slides group), Rename Section	Rename Section	
Sections, Collapse or Expand	PPT 671		Section button (Home tab | Slides group), Collapse All or Expand All	Collapse All or Expand All	
Sections, Reorder	PPT 682	Drag section name		Move Section Up or Move Section Down	
Shape, Apply Fill	PPT 561		Shape Fill button (Drawing Tools Format tab | Shape Styles group) or Shape Fill button (Home tab | Drawing group)	Format Shape, Fill pane	
Shape, Apply Style	PPT 110		More button or Format Shape Dialog Box Launcher in Shapes Style gallery (Drawing Tools Format tab | Shape Styles group)	Format Shape	

Microsoft PowerPoint 2010 Quick Reference Summary (continued)

Task	Page Number	Mouse	Ribbon	Shortcut Menu	Keyboard Shortcut
Shape, Change Fill Color	PPT 347		Shape Fill button arrow (Drawing Tools Format tab | Shape Styles group)		
Shape, Insert	PPT 106		Shapes button (Home tab | Drawing group), More button (Drawing Tools Format tab | Insert Shapes group)		
Shape Fill, Increase Transparency	PPT 487		Drawing Dialog Box Launcher (Home tab | Drawing group), Fill Pane, Transparency slider (Format Shape dialog box)		
Shape Formatting, Set as Default	PPT 564			Set as Default Shape	
Slide, Add	PPT 14		New Slide button (Home tab | Slides group)		CTRL+M
Slide, Arrange	PPT 39	Drag slide in Slides tab or Outline tab to new position, or in Slide Sorter view drag to new position			
Slide, Delete	PPT 152			Delete Slide	DELETE
Slide, Duplicate	PPT 38		New Slide button arrow (Home tab | Slides group), Duplicate Selected Slides	Duplicate Slide	
Slide, Format Background	PPT 95		Background Styles button (Design tab | Background group)	Format Background	
Slide, Hide	PPT 363		Hide Slide button (Slide Show tab | Set Up group)	Hide Slide (Slide Sorter view or thumbnail on Slides tab)	
Slide, Insert Picture as Background	PPT 97		Background Styles button (Design tab | Background group)	Format Background, Picture or texture fill, Insert from File (Format Background dialog box)	
Slide, Reuse from an Existing Presentation	PPT 285		New Slide button arrow (Home tab | Slides group), Reuse Slides command		
Slide, Select Layout	PPT 21		Layout button or New Slide button arrow (Home tab | Slides group)		
Slide, Set Size	PPT 292		Page Setup button (Design tab | Page Setup group), 'Slides sized for' box arrow		
Slide, Set Up Custom Size	PPT 696		Page Setup button (Design tab | Page Setup group), 'Slides sized for' box arrow, Custom		
Slide Layout, Delete	PPT 493		Delete button (Home tab | Slides group) (must be in Slide Master view)	Delete Layout	DELETE
Slide Master, Apply Slide and Font Themes	PPT 472		Themes button (Slide Master tab | Edit Theme group)		

Microsoft PowerPoint 2010 Quick Reference Summary (continued)

Task	Page Number	Mouse	Ribbon	Shortcut Menu	Keyboard Shortcut
Slide Master, Display	PPT 471		Slide Master button (View tab | Master Views group)		
Slide Master, Format Background and Apply a Quick Style	PPT 475		Background Styles button (Slide Master tab | Background group)		
Slide Master, Hide and Unhide Background Graphics	PPT 490		Hide/Unhide Background Graphics check box (Slide Master tab | Background group)		
Slide Master, Insert a Background Graphic	PPT 479		Insert Picture button (Insert tab | Images group)		
Slide Master, Insert Placeholder	PPT 480, 484		Insert Placeholder button (Slide Master tab | Master Layout group)		
Slide Master and Slide Layout, Rename	PPT 491		Rename button (Slide Master tab | Edit Master group)		
Slide Number, Insert	PPT 182		Insert Slide Number button (Insert tab | Text group) or Header & Footer button (Insert tab | Text group), Slide number check box		
Slide Objects, Rename	PPT 422		Select button (Home tab | Editing group), Selection Pane		
Slide Orientation, Change	PPT 696		Slide Orientation button (Design tab | Page Setup group)		
Slide Show, Adjust Timings Manually	PPT 446		Select slide and set timing (Transitions tab | Timing group)		
Slide Show, Draw on Slides During Show	PPT 313		Pointer button, Pen (Slide Show toolbar), drag mouse to draw		
Slide Show, E-mail from within PowerPoint	PPT 702		Send Using E-mail (File tab | Save & Send tab), Send as Attachment button		
Slide Show, End	PPT 49	Click black ending slide		End Show	ESC or HYPHEN
Slide Show, Highlight Items During Show	PPT 312		Pointer button, Highlighter (Slide Show toolbar), drag mouse to highlight		
Slide Show, Rehearse Timings	PPT 444		Rehearse Timings button (Slide Show tab | Set Up group)		
Slide Show, Set Resolution	PPT 294		Resolution box arrow (Slide Show tab | Monitors group)		
Slide Show View	PPT 47	Slide Show view button at lower-right PowerPoint window	From Beginning button (Slide Show tab | Start Slide Show group)		F5
Slide Sorter View	PPT 153, 664	Slide Sorter view button at lower-right PowerPoint window	Slide Sorter button (View tab | Presentation Views group)		
Slides, Insert with a Section Layout	PPT 661		Slide Layout button (Home tab | Slides group), Section Header layout		
SmartArt, Change Layout	PPT 550		More button (SmartArt Tools Design tab | Layouts group)		

Microsoft PowerPoint 2010 Quick Reference Summary *(continued)*

Task	Page Number	Mouse	Ribbon	Shortcut Menu	Keyboard Shortcut
SmartArt, Convert to Text or Shapes	PPT 557, 559		Convert button (SmartArt Tools Design tab | Reset group)		
SmartArt, Remove Shape	PPT 551				Select shape, DELETE
SmartArt, Resize Graphic Shape	PPT 554		Smaller or Larger button (SmartArt Tools Format tab | Shapes group)	Size and Position, Size tab	
SmartArt Bullet Level, Promote or Demote	PPT 548, 549		Promote button or Demote button (SmartArt Tools Design tab | Create Graphic group)		
SmartArt Graphic, Add Text	PPT 208		Text Pane button (SmartArt Tools Design tab | Create Graphic group)		See Table 4–2, PPT 207
SmartArt Graphic, Animate	PPT 435, 436		More button (Animations tab | Animation group)		
SmartArt Graphic, Apply Style	PPT 210		More button (SmartArt Tools Design tab | SmartArt Styles group)		
SmartArt Graphic, Change Color	PPT 211		Change Colors button (SmartArt Tools Design tab | SmartArt Styles group)		
SmartArt Graphic, Insert	PPT 206		SmartArt button (Insert tab | Illustrations group)		
SmartArt Graphic, Insert Picture	PPT 209	Insert Picture from File button in picture placeholder			
SmartArt Graphic, Resize	PPT 212, 553	Drag sizing handle to desired location	Shape width and Shape height boxes (SmartArt Tools Format tab | Size group)	Size and Position, Size tab	
SmartArt Shapes, Reorder	PPT 547		Move Up or Move Down button (SmartArt Tools Design tab | Create Graphic group)		
Speaker Notes, Add	PPT 179	In Normal view, click Notes pane and type notes			
Speaker Notes, Print	PPT 187, 512		Page Layout button (File tab | Print tab), Notes Pages		
Spelling, Check	PPT 181		Spelling button (Review tab | Proofing group)	Spelling (or click correct word on shortcut menu)	F7
Stacking Order, Change	PPT 146		Bring Forward or Send Backward button (Picture Tools Format tab | Arrange group)	Send to Back or Bring to Front	
Symbol, Insert	PPT 233		Symbol button (Insert tab | Symbols group)		
Synonym, Find and Insert	PPT 178		Thesaurus button (Review tab | Proofing group)	Synonyms	SHIFT+F7
Table, Add Borders	PPT 238		Border button arrow (Table Tools Design tab | Table Styles group)		
Table, Add Cell Effects	PPT 614		Effects button (Table Tools Design tab | Table Styles group)		
Table, Add Effect	PPT 238		Effects button (Table Tools Design tab | Table Styles group)		

Microsoft PowerPoint 2010 Quick Reference Summary *(continued)*

Task	Page Number	Mouse	Ribbon	Shortcut Menu	Keyboard Shortcut
Table, Add Gradient Fill	PPT 613		Shading button arrow (Table Tools Design tab | Table Styles group), Gradient		
Table, Add Shading	PPT 612		Shading button arrow (Table Tools Design tab | Table Styles group)		
Table, Align	PPT 617		Align button (Table Tools Layout tab | Arrange group)		
Table, Apply Style	PPT 236		More button (Table Tools Design tab | Table Styles group)		
Table, Distribute Rows	PPT 614		Distribute Rows button (Table Tools Layout tab | Cell Size group)		
Table, Draw	PPT 603		Table button (Insert tab | Tables group), Draw Table, drag pencil pointer		
Table, Insert	PPT 232	Insert Table button in content placeholder	Table button (Insert tab | Tables group)		
Table, Merge Cells	PPT 242		Merge Cells button (Table Tools Layout tab | Merge group)	Merge Cells	
Table, Resize	PPT 240	Drag sizing handle to desired location	Height and Width boxes (Table Tools Layout tab | Table Size group)		
Table, Resize Columns and Rows	PPT 615	Drag column or row borders	Table Row Height or Table Column Width arrows (Table Tools Layout tab | Cell Size group)		
Table, Split Columns or Rows	PPT 610		Split Cells button (Table Tools Layout tab | Merge group)	Split Cells	
Table Cell, Add Image	PPT 241			Format Shape, Picture or texture fill	
Table Cell, Center Text Vertically	PPT 245		Center Vertically button (Table Tools Layout tab | Alignment group)	Format Shape, Text Box, Vertical alignment arrow	
Table Cell, Change Text Direction	PPT 244		Text Direction button (Table Tools Layout tab | Alignment group)	Format Shape, Text Box, Text direction arrow	
Table Line, Erase	PPT 608		Table Eraser button (Table Tools Design tab | Draw Borders group), click line to erase		
Table Rows and Columns, Draw	PPT 604, 606		Draw Table button (Table Tools Design tab | Draw Borders group), drag pencil pointer		
Template, Save a Master As	PPT 502		Change File type (File tab | Save & Send tab), Template, Save As button		
Text, Add Shadow	PPT 103		Text Shadow button (Home tab | Font group)		
Text, Align Horizontally	PPT 150	Align Text buttons on Mini toolbar	Align Text buttons (Home tab | Paragraph group)	Paragraph, Alignment box (Paragraph dialog box)	CTRL+R (right), CTRL+L (left), CTRL+E (center)

Microsoft PowerPoint 2010 Quick Reference Summary *(continued)*

Task	Page Number	Mouse	Ribbon	Shortcut Menu	Keyboard Shortcut
Text, Align Vertically	PPT 366		Align Text button (Home tab | Paragraph group), Top, Middle, or Bottom		
Text, Animate	PPT 425, 427		More button in Animation gallery (Animations tab | Animation group)		
Text, Bold	PPT 20	Bold button on Mini toolbar	Bold button (Home tab | Font group)	Font, Font tab (Font dialog box)	CTRL+B
Text, Change Color	PPT 13	Font Color button or Font Color button arrow on Mini toolbar	Font Color button or Font Color button arrow (Home tab | Font group)	Font, Font tab (Font dialog box)	
Text, Change Direction	PPT 482		Text Direction button (Home tab | Paragraph group)		
Text, Convert to SmartArt Graphic	PPT 213		Convert to SmartArt Graphic button (Home tab | Paragraph group)	Convert to SmartArt	
Text, Delete	PPT 41		Cut button (Home tab | Clipboard group)	Cut	DELETE or CTRL+X or BACKSPACE
Text, Find and Replace	PPT 176		Replace button (Home tab | Editing group)		CTRL+H
Text, Italicize	PPT 11	Italic button on Mini toolbar	Italic button (Home tab | Font group)	Font, Font tab (Font dialog box)	CTRL+I
Text, Select Paragraph	PPT 10	Triple-click paragraph			SHIFT+DOWN ARROW or SHIFT+UP ARROW
Text, Select Word	PPT 12	Double-click word			CTRL+SHIFT+RIGHT ARROW or CTRL+SHIFT+LEFT ARROW
Text Box, Align	PPT 543		Align button (Drawing Tools Format tab | Arrange group)		
Text Box, Animate	PPT 425, 427		More button (Animations tab | Animation group)		
Text Box, Apply Effect	PPT 536		Shape Effects button (Drawing Tools Format tab | Shape Styles group)		
Text Box, Apply Fill	PPT 487		Shape Fill button (Home tab | Drawing group)		
Text Box, Apply Gradient Fill	PPT 542		Shape Fill button arrow (Drawing Tools Format tab | Shape Styles group), Gradient	Format Shape, Fill pane, Gradient fill	
Text Box, Apply Pattern Fill	PPT 539		Shape Fill button arrow (Drawing Tools Format tab | Shape group), Gradient, More Gradients, Pattern fill (Format Shape dialog box)	Format Shape, Fill pane, Pattern fill	
Text Box, Apply Picture Fill	PPT 555		Shape Fill button arrow (Drawing Tools Format tab | Drawing group), Picture		
Text Box, Change Internal Margin	PPT 488		Drawing Dialog Box Launcher (Home tab | Drawing group), Text box (Format Shape dialog box)		

Microsoft PowerPoint 2010 Quick Reference Summary *(continued)*

Task	Page Number	Mouse	Ribbon	Shortcut Menu	Keyboard Shortcut
Text Box, Change Outline Weight, Color, or Style	PPT 534, 535, 536		Shape Outline button arrow (Drawing Tools Format tab | Shape Styles group), choose Weight, color, or Dashes		
Text Box, Insert	PPT 423		Text Box button (Insert tab | Text group)		
Text Box, Rotate	PPT 489	Drag rotation handle			
Text Box, Set Formatting as Default	PPT 537			Set as Default Text Box	
Theme Font, Customize	PPT 473		Theme Fonts button (Slide Master tab | Edit Theme group)		
Transition, Add	PPT 43		Click transition in Transitions gallery (Transitions tab | Transition to This Slide group)		ALT+K
Transition Effect, Modify	PPT 447		Effect Options button (Transitions tab | Transition to This Slide group)		
Transparency, Change	PPT 98		Background Styles button (Design tab | Background group), Format Background, move Transparency slider	Format Background, Transparency slider	
Video, Create from Presentation	PPT 705		Create a Video (File tab | Save & Send tab), Create Video button		
Video File, Compress	PPT 701		Compress Media button (File tab	Info tab		
Video File, Insert	PPT 163		Insert Video button (Insert tab | Media group)		
Video File, Trim	PPT 165		Trim Video button (Video Tools Playback tab | Editing group), drag video start/end points or edit Start Time and End Time boxes		
Video Options	PPT 166		Video options check boxes (Video Tools Playback tab | Video Options group)		
Video Style, Add	PPT 172		More button (Video Tools Format tab | Video Styles group)		
WordArt, Add Text Effects	PPT 115		Text Effects button (Drawing Tools Format tab | WordArt Styles group)		
WordArt, Convert to SmartArt	PPT 546			Convert to SmartArt	
WordArt, Insert	PPT 114		WordArt button (Insert tab | Text group)		
Worksheet, Align	PPT 621		Align button (Drawing Tools Format tab | Arrange group)		
Zoom for Viewing Slides	PPT 156	Drag Zoom slider on status bar; click Zoom In or Zoom Out button on Zoom slider; change percentage in Zoom level box on left side of slider	Zoom button (View tab | Zoom group)		

YOUR EXAM PREP JOURNEY
STARTS NOW

 P9-CRV-600

Welcome to the Becker CPA Exam Review course and congratulations on taking the first steps to becoming a CPA! With more than 60 years of experience and a time-tested learning approach, we're here to help you gain the confidence you need to pass the CPA Exam.

GET STARTED ON YOUR PATH TO CPA EXAM SUCCESS WITH THESE STEPS:

1. ACCESS BECKER'S CPA EXAM REVIEW COURSE

▸ Log in to Becker's CPA Exam Review at **online.becker.com**

▸ Watch the orientation video

▸ Download the mobile app to access your course and study on the go; Available for Apple® and Android™ tablets and smartphones

Pick up right where you left off. Your progress will automatically synchronize among all your devices.

2. DEVELOP YOUR STUDY PLAN

▸ Create your customized study plan using Becker's interactive **Study Planner**

3. START STUDYING

▸ Follow your study plan and reach out for academic support

4. CONNECT WITH US

▸ Visit our blog at **beckerpinnacle.com** to stay up-to-date on our latest tips, stories, and advice

▸ You can also find us on Facebook, Twitter, LinkedIn, YouTube, and Google+

▸ For more information on getting started, visit **becker.com/cpagettingstarted**

THE PINNACLE from BECKER

BECKER
PROFESSIONAL EDUCATION®

For Exams Scheduled After December 31, 2018

CPA EXAM REVIEW
BUSINESS

ACADEMIC HELP

Click on Customer and Academic Support under CPA Resources at
http://www.becker.com/cpa-review.html

CUSTOMER SERVICE AND TECHNICAL SUPPORT

Call 1-877-CPA-EXAM (outside the U.S. +1-630-472-2213)
or click Customer and Academic Support under CPA Resources at
http://www.becker.com/cpa-review.html

This textbook contains information that was current at the time of printing.
Your course software will be updated on a regular basis as the content
that is tested on the CPA Exam evolves and as we improve our materials.
Note the version reference below and click on Replacement Textbooks under
CPA Resources at http://www.becker.com/cpa-review.html to learn if a newer
version of this book is available to be ordered.

BECKER
PROFESSIONAL EDUCATION®

V 3.2

COURSE DEVELOPMENT TEAM

Timothy F. Gearty, CPA, MBA, JD, CGMA . . . . Editor in Chief, Financial/Regulation (Tax) National Editor

Angeline S. Brown, CPA, CGMA. . . . . .Sr. Director, Product Management

Mike Brown, CPA, CMA, CGMA . . . . .Director, Product Management

Valerie Funk Anderson, CPA . . . . Sr. Manager, Curriculum

Stephen Bergens, CPA . . . . Manager, Accounting Curriculum

Patrice W. Johnson, CPA . . . . Sr. Manager, Curriculum

Tom Cox, CPA, CMA . . . . Financial (GASB & NFP) National Editor

Steven J. Levin, JD . . . . .Regulation (Law) National Editor

Pete Console . . . . .Sr. Director, Educational Technologies

Brian Cave . . . . Sr. Manager, Software Development

Dan Corrales . . . . Sr. Manager, Curriculum Quality Assurance

Danita De Jane . . . . Director, Course Development

Anson Miyashiro. . . . . Manager, Course Development

John Ott . . . . Manager, Visual Design

Tim Munson . . . . .Project Manager, Course Development

Linda Finestone. . . . . Sr. Course Editor

Naomi Oseida . . . . Course Development

Eric Vasquez . . . . Course Development

Andrea Horton . . . . Course Development

CONTRIBUTING EDITORS

Teresa C. Anderson, CPA, CMA, MPA	Michelle Moshe, CPA, DipIFR
Katie Barnette, CPA	Peter Olinto, JD, CPA
Jim DeSimpelare, CPA, MBA	Sandra Owen, CPA, MBA, JD
Tara Z. Fisher, CPA	Michelle M. Pace, CPA
Melisa F. Galasso, CPA	Jennifer J. Rivers, CPA
R. Thomas Godwin, CPA, CGMA	Josh Rosenberg, MBA, CPA, CFA, CFP
Holly Hawk, CPA, CGMA	Jonathan R. Rubin, CPA, MBA
Julie D. McGinty, CPA	Michael Rybak, CPA, CFA
Sandra McGuire, CPA, MBA	Denise M. Stefano, CPA, CGMA, MBA
Stephanie Morris, CPA, MAcc	Elizabeth Lester Walsh, CPA, CITP

LICENSE AGREEMENT—TERMS & CONDITIONS

DO NOT DOWNLOAD, ACCESS, AND/OR USE ANY OF THESE MATERIALS (AS THAT TERM IS <u>DEFINED</u> <u>BELOW</u>) UNTIL YOU HAVE READ THIS LICENSE AGREEMENT CAREFULLY. IF YOU DOWNLOAD, ACCESS, AND/OR USE ANY OF THESE MATERIALS, YOU ARE AGREEING AND CONSENTING TO BE BOUND BY AND ARE BECOMING A PARTY TO THIS LICENSE AGREEMENT ("AGREEMENT").

The printed Materials provided to you and/or the Materials provided for download to your computer and/or provided via a web application to which you are granted access are NOT for sale and are not being sold to you. You may NOT transfer these Materials to any other person or permit any other person to use these Materials. You may <u>only</u> acquire a license to use these Materials and <u>only</u> upon the terms and conditions set forth in this Agreement. Read this Agreement carefully <u>before</u> downloading, and/or accessing, and/or using these Materials. <u>Do not</u> download and/or access, and/or use these Materials <u>unless</u> you agree with <u>all</u> terms of this Agreement.

NOTE: You may already be a party to this Agreement if you registered for a Becker Professional Education CPA program (the "Program") or placed an order for these Materials online or using a printed form that included this License Agreement. Please review the termination section regarding your rights to terminate this License Agreement and receive a refund of your payment.

Grant: Upon your acceptance of the terms of this Agreement, in a manner set forth above, Becker Professional Development Corporation ("Becker") hereby grants to you a non-exclusive, revocable, non-transferable, non-sublicensable, limited license to use (as defined below) the Materials by downloading them onto a computer and/or by accessing them via a web application using a user ID and password (as defined below), and any Materials to which you are granted access as a result of your license to use these Materials and/or in connection with the Program on the following terms:

During the Term (as defined below) of this Agreement, you may:

- use the Materials for preparation for one or more parts of the CPA Exam (the "Exam"), and/or for your studies relating to the subject matter covered by the Program and/or the Exam), and/or for your studies relating to the subject matter covered by the Materials and/or the Exam, including taking electronic and/or handwritten notes during the Program, provided that all notes taken that relate to the subject matter of the Materials are and shall remain Materials subject to the terms of this Agreement;
- download the Materials onto any single device;
- download the Materials onto a second device so long as the first device and the second device are not used simultaneously;
- download the Materials onto a third device so long as the first, second, and third device are not used simultaneously; and
- download the Materials onto a fourth device so long as the first, second, third, and fourth device are not used simultaneously.

The number of installations may vary outside of the U.S. Please review your local office policies and procedures to confirm the number of installations granted—your local office's policies and procedures regarding the number of allowable activations of downloads supersedes the limitations contained herein and is controlling.

You may not:

- use the Materials for any purpose other than as expressly permitted above;
- use the downloaded Materials on more than one device, computer terminal, or workstation at the same time;
- make copies of the Materials;
- rent, lease, license, lend, or otherwise transfer or provide (by gift, sale, or otherwise) all or any part of the Materials to anyone;
- permit the use of all or any part of the Materials by anyone other than you; or
- reverse engineer, decompile, disassemble, or create derivate works of the Materials.

Materials: As used in this Agreement, the term "Materials" means and includes any printed materials provided to you by Becker, and/or to which you are granted access by Becker (directly or indirectly) in connection with your license of the Materials and/or the Program, and shall include notes you take (by hand, electronically, digitally, or otherwise) while using the Materials relating to the subject matter of the Materials; any and all electronically-stored/accessed/delivered, and/or digitally-stored/ accessed/delivered materials included under this License via download to a computer or via access to a web application, and/or otherwise provided to you and/or to which you are otherwise granted access by Becker (directly or indirectly), including, but not limited to, applications downloadable from a third party, for example Google® or Amazon®, in connection with your license of the Materials.

Title: Becker is and will remain the owner of all title, ownership rights, intellectual property, and all other rights and interests in and to the Materials that are subject to the terms of this Agreement. The Materials are protected by the copyright laws of the United States and international copyright laws and treaties.

Use of Navigator 2.0: If your employer or college/university has instructed Becker to use its Navigator 2.0 to track your studies, the following will occur: a) once you have activated your software (course log-in), you will be asked to set up your study planner. In order to do this, you may be required to provide information about yourself as part of the Program registration process, or as part of your continued use of the Materials. You agree that any registration information you give to Becker will be shared by Becker with your employer or college/university ; and b) once that is done, Navigator 2.0 will automatically track if you are behind in your studies based on your study planner, your office location, your service line within the firm, your college/university course, which course parts were purchased (Audit and Attestation, Financial Accounting and Reporting, Business Environment and Concepts, and Regulation), what format are you using (online, live, self-study), your course progress, study time details (hours/min in course, # of log-ins, last log in), exam progress details including: whether you applied to take the exam, and if so, the state to which you applied; whether you received your NTS (notice to schedule), and if so, its expiration date; whether you scheduled your exam, and if so, the date; whether you received any scores and what they were; and the number of attempts to pass each of the four parts.

Navigator 2.0 Liability Provisions: You hereby waive any claims, causes of action, and damages, and agree to hold harmless and indemnify Becker and its affiliates, officers, agents, and employees from any claim, suit or action arising from or related to your use of the Materials, the sharing of any of your information by Becker with your employer or violation of these terms, including any liability or expense arising from claims, losses, damages, suits, judgments, litigation costs and attorneys' fees.

SUBJECT TO THE OVERALL PROVISION ABOVE, YOU EXPRESSLY UNDERSTAND AND AGREE THAT BECKER, ITS PARENT CORPORATION, SUBSIDIARIES AND AFFILIATES, AND THE OFFICERS, AGENTS AND EMPLOYEES OF THOSE ENTITIES, SHALL NOT BE LIABLE TO YOU FOR ANY LOSS OR DAMAGE THAT MAY BE INCURRED BY YOU, INCLUDING BUT NOT LIMITED TO LOSS OR DAMAGE AS A RESULT BECKER SHARING YOUR INFORMATION WITH YOUR EMPLOYER OR COLLEGE/UNIVERSITY.

THE LIMITATIONS ON BECKER'S LIABILITY TO YOU IN THE PARAGRAPHS ABOVE SHALL APPLY WHETHER OR NOT BECKER HAS BEEN ADVISED OF OR SHOULD HAVE BEEN AWARE OF THE POSSIBILITY OF ANY SUCH LOSSES ARISING.

Termination: The license granted under this Agreement commences upon your receipt of these Materials. This license shall terminate the earlier of: (i) ten (10) business days after notice to you of non-payment of or default on any payment due Becker which has not been cured within such 10-day period; or (ii) immediately if you fail to comply with any of the limitations described above; or (iii) upon expiration of the period ending eighteen (18) months after you log-in to access the Materials, that is, the first time you visit the Becker Program homepage and log-in using your user identification and password; or upon expiration of the twenty-four (24) month period beginning upon your purchase of the Material, whichever of these periods first transpires (the "Term"). In addition, upon termination of this license for any reason, you must delete or otherwise remove from your computer and other device any Materials you downloaded, including, but not limited to, any archival copies you may have made. The Title, Exclusion of Warranties, Exclusion of Damages, Indemnification and Remedies, Severability of Terms and Governing Law provisions, and any amounts due, shall survive termination of the license.

Your Limited Right to Terminate this License and Receive a Refund: You may terminate this license for the in-class, online, and self-study Programs in accordance with Becker's refund policy as provided below.

Cancellations and Refunds: To cancel your enrollment and receive a refund, contact Becker Professional Education at 800-868-3900.

Textbooks should be returned within 10 days of notification of withdrawal. Students should contact Becker for a "Return Materials Authorization" number prior to shipping returns. Students should ship materials by certified mail or an alternative traceable method. Flashcards and the material license fees for the Becker Promise are non-refundable. The cost to return materials is the responsibility of the student. Refunds will be made within 30 days from the date of cancellation. Non-receipt of shipment disputes must be made with 90 days of original purchase date.

All returns must be sent to: Becker Professional Education.
Attn: Becker Returns, 200 Finn Ct., Farmingdale NY 11735

For **Online CPA Exam Review Course and CPA Final Review course students***, a full tuition refund (less any applicable savings and fees) will be issued within 10 days of initial purchase or first login, whichever comes first.

For **Live Format and Cohort Program CPA Review students***, a full tuition refund (minus all applicable savings) will be issued to students who withdraw on or before the 5th business day or if students do not attend any part of the course (no-shows) after the start date of the scheduled section and provided that electronic course materials are not accessed. Thereafter, no refund will be issued as full access to course content has been granted.

Under certain circumstances, a live class may be cancelled up to 5 days in advance of the scheduled start date. Students will be provided with rescheduling options which could include access to self-study materials when live courses are not available. If rescheduling efforts are not successful, a refund for the cancelled course section may be issued and access suspended provided that the section content has not been accessed.

No Shows are students who never attend a live/live online class and do not access any portion of the course software/electronic materials.

For **Atlanta Intensive and Final Review students***, a full tuition refund (minus all applicable savings) will be issued to students who withdraw on or before the 2nd class of the first scheduled part. Thereafter, no refund will be issued as full access to course content has been granted.

For **SkillMaster Workshops:** A full refund will be issued to students who withdraw at least 10 business days before the scheduled workshop. Thereafter, no refund will be issued.

(*Applicable in all states except those noted below.)

The following cancellation policy is applicable for students in Alabama, Arkansas, District of Columbia, Kansas, Kentucky, Louisiana, Nebraska, Nevada, New Hampshire, New Mexico, Oklahoma, West Virginia:

If cancellation occurs within 3 business days of registration, all monies paid by the student will be refunded even if classes have already started.

A full tuition refund (minus all applicable savings and fees) will be issued to students who withdraw on or before the 5th business day after the start date of the first scheduled section; thereafter, students are entitled to a prorated refund (minus all applicable savings and fees) for the unused portion through 60% of the part taken (75% in Arkansas and DC).

For example, the refund for a candidate who withdraws after completing 12 hours (3 sessions) of Audit classes will be calculated as follows:

- Amount Paid $1131.00
- Amount to be Prorated $1131.00
- 8 Hours Cancelled / 20 Hours Scheduled × $1131.00 = $452.00 (Amount Refunded)

Residents are not required to submit written notification of withdrawal.

New Hampshire Students: Any buyer may cancel this transaction any time prior to midnight of the third business day after the date of this transaction.

Oklahoma Students: Becker Professional Education is licensed by Oklahoma Board of Private Vocational Schools, 700 N. Classen Blvd. #250, Oklahoma City, OK 73118.

Classroom Locations: University of Oklahoma, 307 West Brooks, Room 200, Norman, OK 73019, Oklahoma Christian University, 2501 E Memorial Rd., Edmond, OK 73136, and Oklahoma State University, 108 Gunderson Hall, Stillwater, OK 74078.

Holder in Due Course Rule: Any holder of this consumer credit contract is subject to all claims and defenses which the debtor could assert against the seller of goods and services obtained pursuant hereto or with the proceeds hereof. Recovery hereunder by the debtor shall not exceed that paid by the debtor. (This Federal TradeCom Regulation became in effect 5/14/75.)

Becker Professional Education is licensed by Oklahoma Board of Private Vocational Schools, 700 N. Classen Blvd. #250, Oklahoma City, OK 73118.

Tennessee Students: At a minimum, refunds are calculated as follows:

Date of Withdrawal During:	Percent Refund of Tuition (Less Administrative Fee)
First day of scheduled classes	100%
Balance of week 1	90%
Week 2	75%
Weeks 3 and 4	25%
Weeks 5–8	0%

Refunds are to be prorated as of last day of actual attendance, notification is not required. All monies paid by an applicant will be refunded if requested within three days after signing an enrollment agreement and making an initial payment.

NON-REFUNDABLE ITEMS: Charges for Flashcards, Supplemental Multiple-Choice Questions, 0% APR* Financing Processing Fee and the Becker Promise material license fee are non-refundable.

*Annual Percentage Rating

Attendance:

CPA Exam Review Courses—Live Classroom Non-F1 Students

Attendance is defined as a student physically attending a live classroom on the enrolled/registered dates and times. BPE tracks attendance through rosters at live classes for students who selected and enrolled in this format. Classroom coordinators or student assistants are responsible for collecting attendance information. The faculty member supervises the attendance process at each class.

The purpose of BPE's CPA Exam review course is to prepare students for the CPA Exam. BPE does not issue grades, degrees, licenses or diplomas at course completion. A student may request a live course completion certificate by calling Becker's customer service at 800-868-3900. CPA live course completion certificates are offered for each section of the course (Audit, Business, Financial and Regulation). A student must attend a minimum of 50% of the live lectures for each section to receive the course completion certificate for that section. The student must complete any classes not attended live by viewing the corresponding lecture content (which is similar in length and content as the Live Course) using Becker's e-learning platform. The student must demonstrate completion of the relevant e-learning lectures by providing the Performance Summary report. Upon confirmation that the student has completed 100% of the lectures with at least 50% of the lectures in the live classroom, the student will receive the course completion certificate.

Students who are tardy or depart early must notify the instructor who will note on the attendance sheet with "T" for tardy (arriving 20 or more minutes late) and/or "ED" at early departure (leaving 20 or more minutes before the end of class). All students are required to sign in upon arrival at the class. Note that receiving a "T" or "ED" means that student may not count that class toward the live attendance requirement to receive a completion certificate.

No Shows are students who never attend a live/live online class and do not access any portion of the course software/electronic materials.

CPA Exam Review Courses—LiveOnline (LiveOnline courses are not I-20 eligible)

Attendance is defined as a student logging in to a LiveOnline webcast on the enrolled/registered dates and times. BPE tracks attendance using the webinar platform's built-in tracking of when registered students log in and log off. LiveOnline webcast registration and attendance tracking are the responsibility of the U.S. Accounting Operations team.

The purpose of BPE's CPA Exam review course is to prepare students for the CPA Exam. BPE does not issue grades, degrees, licenses or diplomas at course completion. A student may request a LiveOnline course completion certificate by calling Becker's customer service at 800-868-3900. CPA LiveOnline course completion certificates are offered for each section of the course (Audit, Business, Financial and Regulation). A student must attend a minimum of 50% of the LiveOnline lectures for each section to receive the course completion certificate for that section. The student must complete any classes not attended via webcast by viewing the corresponding lecture content using Becker's e-learning platform. The student must demonstrate completion of the relevant e-learning lectures by providing the Performance Summary report. Upon confirmation that the student has completed 100% of the lectures with at least 50% of the lectures via LiveOnline webcast, the student will receive the course completion certificate. Students who arrive more than 20 minutes late or leave more than 20 minutes early may not count that class toward the LiveOnline attendance requirement.

No Shows are students who never attend a live/live online class and do not access any portion of the course software/electronic materials.

Course Overview: To review Becker's full live course overview, catalog and policies applicable to live course enrollment, please visit https://www.becker.com/content/dam/bpe/cpa/live/pdf/cpa_exam_review_course_catalog_4-6-18.pdf

Auditing: This course includes 18 hours of live instruction* and prepares students to pass the Auditing and Attestation section of the CPA Exam.

Business: This course includes 18 hours of live instruction* and prepares students to pass the Business Environment and Concepts section of the CPA Exam.

Financial: This course includes 30 hours of live instruction* and prepares students to pass the Financial Accounting and Reporting section of the CPA Exam.

Regulation: This course includes 24 hours of live instruction* and prepares students to pass the Regulation section of the CPA Exam.

*Hours of instruction represent allotted schedule time for live classes. Actual pre-recorded lecture hours may vary.

Exclusion of Warranties: YOU EXPRESSLY ASSUME ALL RISK FOR USE OF THE MATERIALS. YOU AGREE THAT THE MATERIALS ARE PROVIDED TO YOU "AS IS" AND "AS AVAILABLE" AND THAT BECKER MAKES NO WARRANTIES, EXPRESS OR IMPLIED, WITH RESPECT TO THE MATERIALS, THEIR MERCHANTABILITY OR FITNESS FOR A PARTICULAR PURPOSE AND NO WARRANTY OF NONINFRINGEMENT OF THIRD PARTIES' RIGHTS. NO DEALER, AGENT OR EMPLOYEE OF BECKER IS AUTHORIZED TO PROVIDE ANY SUCH WARRANTY TO YOU. BECAUSE SOME JURISDICTIONS DO NOT ALLOW THE EXCLUSION OF IMPLIED WARRANTIES, THE ABOVE EXCLUSION OF IMPLIED WARRANTIES MAY NOT APPLY TO YOU. BECKER DOES NOT WARRANT OR GUARANTEE THAT YOU WILL PASS ANY EXAMINATION.

Exclusion of Damages: UNDER NO CIRCUMSTANCES AND UNDER NO LEGAL THEORY, TORT, CONTRACT, OR OTHERWISE, SHALL BECKER OR ITS DIRECTORS, OFFICERS, EMPLOYEES, OR AGENTS BE LIABLE TO YOU OR ANY OTHER PERSON FOR ANY CONSEQUENTIAL, INCIDENTAL, INDIRECT, PUNITIVE, EXEMPLARY OR SPECIAL DAMAGES OF ANY CHARACTER, INCLUDING, WITHOUT LIMITATION, DAMAGES FOR LOSS OF GOODWILL, WORK STOPPAGE, COMPUTER FAILURE OR MALFUNCTION OR ANY AND ALL OTHER DAMAGES OR LOSSES, OR FOR ANY DAMAGES IN EXCESS OF BECKER'S LIST PRICE FOR A LICENSE TO THE MATERIALS, EVEN IF BECKER SHALL HAVE BEEN INFORMED OF THE POSSIBILITY OF SUCH DAMAGES, OR FOR ANY CLAIM BY ANY OTHER PARTY. Some jurisdictions do not allow the limitation or exclusion of liability for incidental or consequential damages, so the above limitation or exclusion may not apply to you.

Indemnification and Remedies: You agree to indemnify and hold Becker and its employees, representatives, agents, attorneys, affiliates, directors, officers, members, managers, and shareholders harmless from and against any and all claims, demands, losses, damages, penalties, costs or expenses (including reasonable attorneys' and expert witnesses' fees and costs) of any kind or nature, arising from or relating to any violation, breach, or nonfulfillment by you of any provision of this license. If you are obligated to provide indemnification pursuant to this provision, Becker may, in its sole and absolute discretion, control the disposition of any indemnified action at your sole cost and expense. Without limiting the foregoing, you may not settle, compromise, or in any other manner dispose of any indemnified action without the consent of Becker. If you breach any material term of this license, Becker shall be entitled to equitable relief by way of temporary and permanent injunction without the need for a bond and such other and further relief as any court with jurisdiction may deem just and proper.

Confidentiality: The Materials are considered confidential and proprietary to Becker. You shall keep the Materials confidential and you shall not publish or disclose the Materials to any third party without the prior written consent of Becker.

Use of Your Data: You understand that you will be providing personal information if you register for the Program and that the following will occur: (a) once you have registered, logged in, and activated your account, you will be asked to provide information about yourself as part of the registration process, or as part of your continued use of the Materials. You agree that any registration information you give to Becker will be used and stored by Becker. By using the Materials, you hereby consent to Becker retaining your personal information for purposes of the Program and for future purposes in marketing to you regarding other Becker Products.

Waiver of Liability: You hereby waive any claims, causes of action, and damages, and agree to hold harmless and indemnify Becker and its affiliates, officers, agents, and employees from any claim, suit, or action arising from or related to your use of the Materials, the use and storing of any of your information by Becker, or violation of these terms, including any liability or expense arising from claims, losses, damages, suits, judgments, litigation costs, and attorneys' fees.

SUBJECT TO THE OVERALL PROVISION ABOVE, YOU EXPRESSLY UNDERSTAND AND AGREE THAT BECKER, ITS PARENT CORPORATION, SUBSIDIARIES AND AFFILIATES, AND THE OFFICERS, AGENTS, AND EMPLOYEES OF THOSE ENTITIES, SHALL NOT BE LIABLE TO YOU FOR ANY LOSS OR DAMAGE THAT MAY BE INCURRED BY YOU, INCLUDING BUT NOT LIMITED TO LOSS OR DAMAGE AS A RESULT OF BECKER USING OR STORING YOUR INFORMATION WITH YOUR PROFESSOR OR COLLEGE/UNIVERSITY.

THE LIMITATIONS ON BECKER'S LIABILITY TO YOU IN THE PARAGRAPHS ABOVE SHALL APPLY WHETHER OR NOT BECKER HAS BEEN ADVISED OF, OR SHOULD HAVE BEEN AWARE OF, THE POSSIBILITY OF ANY SUCH LOSSES ARISING.

Severability of Terms: If any term or provision of this license is held invalid or unenforceable by a court of competent jurisdiction, such invalidity shall not affect the validity or operation of any other term or provision and such invalid term or provision shall be deemed to be severed from the license. This Agreement may only be modified by written agreement signed by both parties.

Governing Law: This Agreement shall be governed and construed according to the laws of the State of Illinois, United States of America, excepting that State's conflicts of laws rules. The parties agree that the jurisdiction and venue of any dispute subject to litigation is proper in any state or federal court in Chicago, Illinois, USA. The parties hereby agree to waive application of the UN Convention on the Sale of Goods. If the State of Illinois adopts the current proposed Uniform Computer Information Transactions Act (UCITA, formerly proposed Article 2B to the Uniform Commercial Code), or a version of the proposed UCITA, that part of the laws shall not apply to any transaction under this Agreement.

NOTICE TO STUDENTS: ACCET COMPLAINT PROCEDURE

This institution is recognized by the Accrediting Council for Continuing Education & Training (ACCET) as meeting and maintaining certain standards of quality. It is the mutual goal of ACCET and the institution to ensure that educational training programs of quality are provided. When problems arise, students should make every attempt to find a fair and reasonable solution through the institution's internal complaint procedure, which is required of ACCET accredited institutions and frequently requires the submission of a written complaint. Refer to the institution's written complaint procedure which is published in the institution's catalog or otherwise available from the institution, upon request. Note that ACCET will process complaints which involve ACCET standards and policies and, therefore, are within the scope of the accrediting agency.

In the event that a student has exercised the institution's formal student complaint procedure, and the problem(s) have not been resolved, the student has the right and is encouraged to take the following steps:

1. Complaints should be submitted in writing and mailed, or emailed to the ACCET office. Complaints received by phone will be documented, but the complainant will be requested to submit the complaint in writing.

2. The letter of complaint must contain the following:

    a. Name and location of the ACCET institution;

    b. A detailed description of the alleged problem(s);

    c. The approximate date(s) that the problem(s) occurred;

    d. The names and titles/positions of all individual(s) involved in the problem(s), including faculty, staff, and/or other students;

    e. What was previously done to resolve the complaint, along with evidence demonstrating that the institution's complaint procedure was followed prior to contacting ACCET;

    f. The name, email address, telephone number, and mailing address of the complainant. If the complainant specifically requests that anonymity be maintained, ACCET will not reveal his or her name to the institution involved; and

    g. The status of the complainant with the institution (e.g., current student, former student, etc.).

3. In addition to the letter of complaint, copies of any relevant supporting documentation should be forwarded to ACCET (e.g., student's enrollment agreement, syllabus or course outline, correspondence between the student and the institution).

4. **SEND TO:**
    ACCET
    CHAIR, COMPLAINT REVIEW COMMITTEE
    1722 N Street, NW
    Washington, DC 20036
    Telephone: (202) 955-1113
    Fax: (202) 955-1118 or (202) 955-5306
    Email: complaints@accet.org
    Website: accet.org

Note: Complainants will receive an acknowledgement of receipt within 15 days.

NOTES

BUSINESS

Program Attendance Record

Student: _____   Location: _____

BUSINESS 1	BUSINESS 2
Attendance Stamp	Attendance Stamp
BUSINESS 3	**BUSINESS 4**
Attendance Stamp	Attendance Stamp
BUSINESS 5	**BUSINESS 6**
Attendance Stamp	Attendance Stamp

IMPORTANT NOTES TO STUDENTS REGARDING "THE BECKER PROMISE"

- The attendance sheet must be stamped at the end of each class attended. This is the only acceptable record of your classroom attendance.
- An overall percentage correct of 90% or higher is required on MCQs and simulations to qualify for The Becker Promise.
- Please e-mail documentation to beckerpromise@becker.com or fax to 866-398-7375 no later than 45 days following the completion of each section.
- For Becker Promise redemption policies and procedures, visit becker.com/promise.

NOTES

BUSINESS
Table of Contents

Introduction
BEC

NOTES

Business Environment and Concepts (BEC) Overview

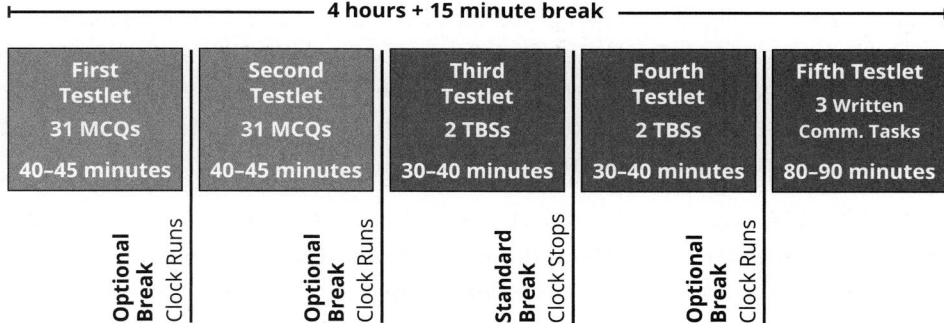

BEC Exam—Summary Blueprint

Content Area Allocation	Weight
Corporate Governance	17–27%
Economic Concepts and Analysis	17–27%
Financial Management	11–21%
Information Technology	15–25%
Operations Management	15–25%
Skill Allocation	Weight
Evaluation	—
Analysis	20–30%
Application	50–60%
Remembering and Understanding	15–25%

The complete BEC exam blueprint appears in the back of the book.

Written Communication—Lecture

For the Business section of the CPA Exam, candidates will be required to complete three written communication tasks. The written communication tasks will appear in the fifth and final testlet of the exam.

- Each written communication will give you a situation, a request for a response, and a series of instructions. Your answer will be typed in the designated response area using a simple word processor.

- For additional guidance on the written communication task, view the written communications lecture in your CPA Exam Review course.

Becker's CPA Exam Review—Course Introduction

Becker Professional Education's CPA Exam Review products were developed with you, the candidate, in mind. To that end we have developed a series of tools designed to tap all of your learning and retention capabilities. The Becker lectures, comprehensive texts, and course software are designed to be fully integrated to give you the best chance of passing the CPA Exam.

Passing the CPA Exam is difficult, but the professional rewards a CPA enjoys make this a worthwhile challenge. We created our CPA Exam Review after evaluating the needs of CPA candidates and analyzing the CPA Exam over the years. Our course materials comprehensively present topics you must know to pass the examination, teaching you the most effective tactics for learning the material.

Becker Customer and Academic Support

You can access Becker's Customer and Academic Support under CPA Resources at:

http://www.becker.com/cpa-review.html

You can also access Academic Support by clicking on the Academic Support button in the Becker software. You can access customer service and technical support from Customer and Academic Support or by calling 1-877-CPA-EXAM (outside the U.S. + 1-630-472-2213).

The Uniform CPA Exam—Overview

Exam Sections

The CPA Examination consists of four sections:

Financial Accounting and Reporting

The *Financial* section consists of a four-hour exam covering financial accounting and reporting for commercial entities under U.S. GAAP, governmental accounting, not-for-profit accounting, and the differences between IFRS and U.S. GAAP.

Auditing and Attestation

The *Auditing* section consists of a four-hour exam. This section covers all topics related to auditing, including audit reports and procedures, generally accepted auditing standards, attestation and other engagements, and government auditing.

Regulation

The *Regulation* section consists of a four-hour exam, combining topics from business law and federal taxation, including the taxation of property transactions, individuals, and entities.

Business Environment and Concepts

The *Business* section consists of a four-hour exam covering general business topics, such as corporate governance, economics, financial management, information technology, and operations management, including managerial accounting.

Question Formats

The chart below illustrates the question format breakdown by exam section.

Section	Multiple-Choice Questions		Task-Based Simulations or Written Communication Tasks	
	Percentage	*Number*	*Percentage*	*Number*
Financial	50%	66	50%	8 TBSs
Auditing	50%	72	50%	8 TBSs
Regulation	50%	76	50%	8 TBSs
Business	50%	62	50%	4 TBSs/3 WC

Each exam will contain testlets. A testlet is either a series of multiple-choice questions, a set of task-based simulations, or a set of written communications. For example, the Business examination will contain five testlets. The first two testlets will be multiple-choice questions, the third and fourth testlets will contain task-based simulations, and the last testlet will contain three written communication tasks. Each testlet must be finished and submitted before continuing to the next testlet. Candidates cannot go back to view a previously completed testlet or go forward to view a subsequent testlet before closing and submitting the earlier testlet. Our mock exams contain these types of restrictions so that you can familiarize yourself with the functionality of the CPA Exam.

Exam Schedule

The computer-based CPA Exam is offered during the first two months and 10 days of each calendar quarter. Candidates can schedule an exam date directly with Prometric (www.prometric.com/cpa) after receiving a notice to schedule.

Eligibility and Application Requirements

Each state sets its own rules of eligibility for the examination. Please visit www.becker.com/state as soon as possible to determine your eligibility to sit for the exam.

Application Deadlines

With the computer-based exam format, set application deadlines generally do not exist. You should apply as early as possible to ensure that you are able to schedule your desired exam dates. Each state has different application requirements and procedures, so be sure to gain a thorough understanding of the application process for your state.

Grading System

You must pass all four parts of the examination to earn certification as a CPA. You must score 75 or better on a part to receive a passing grade and you must pass all four exams in 18 months or you will lose credit for the earliest exam that you passed.

Corporate Governance and Financial Risk Management

Module

1 Introduction to COSO

The Committee of Sponsoring Organizations (COSO), an independent private sector initiative, was initially established in the mid-1980s to study the factors that lead to fraudulent financial reporting. The private "sponsoring organizations" include the five major financial professional associations in the United States: the American Accounting Association (AAA), the American Institute of Certified Public Accountants (AICPA), the Financial Executives Institute (FEI), the Institute of Internal Auditors (IIA), and the Institute of Management Accountants (IMA).

In 1992, COSO issued *Internal Control—Integrated Framework* ("the framework") to assist organizations in developing comprehensive assessments of internal control effectiveness.

In 2013, the framework received an update to deal with changes in technology, business models, globalization, outsourcing, and regulatory environment. One significant enhancement to the 2013 update was the formalization of fundamental concepts that were part of the original 1992 framework. Specifically, these fundamental concepts have evolved into 17 principles that have been categorized within the five major internal control components. COSO's framework is widely regarded as an appropriate and comprehensive basis to document the assessment of internal controls over financial reporting.

2 COSO Internal Control Framework

The framework is used by company *management* and its board of directors to obtain an initial understanding of what constitutes an effective system of internal control and to provide insight as to when internal controls are being properly applied within the organization. The framework also provides confidence to external stakeholders that an organization has a system of internal control in place that is conducive to achieving its objectives.

Pass Key

An effective system of internal control requires more than adherence to policies and procedures by management, the board of directors, and the internal auditors. It requires the use of judgment in determining the sufficiency of controls, in applying the proper controls, and in assessing the effectiveness of the system of internal controls. The principles-based approach of the framework supports the emphasis on the importance of management judgment.

Material from *Internal Control—Integrated Framework,* © 2013 Committee of Sponsoring Organizations of the Treadway Commission (COSO). Used with permission.

2.1   Definition of Internal Control

Internal control is a process that is designed and implemented by an organization's management, board of directors, and other employees to provide reasonable assurance that the organization will achieve its operating, reporting, and compliance objectives.

2.2   Application to Management and Board

The framework assists an entity's management and board of directors in the following areas:

- Effectively applying internal control within the overall organization, on a divisional (operating) unit level or at a functional level.

- Determining the requirements of an effective system of internal control by ascertaining whether the components and principles exist and are functioning properly.

- Allowing judgment and flexibility in the design and implementation of the system of internal control within all operational and functional areas of the organization.

- Identifying and analyzing risks and then developing acceptable actions to mitigate or minimize these risks to an acceptable level.

- Eliminating redundant, ineffective, or inefficient controls.

- Extending internal control application beyond an organization's financial reporting.

2.3   Application to Stakeholders

The framework also provides value to external stakeholders and other parties that interact with the organization by providing:

- Greater understanding of what constitutes an effective system of internal controls.

- Greater confidence that management will be able to eliminate ineffective, redundant, or inefficient controls.

- Greater confidence that the board has effective oversight of the organization's internal controls.

- Improved confidence that the organization will achieve its stated objectives and will be capable of identifying, analyzing, and responding to risks affecting the organization.

2.4   COSO Cube

The 2013 framework continues to use a cube to depict the relationship between an entity's objectives, integrated internal control components, and organizational structure. The three categories of *objectives* (operations, xreporting, and compliance) are shown as columns on the cube, and the five *internal control components* (control environment, risk assessment, control activities, information and communication, and monitoring activities) are depicted as rows. Additionally, the entity's *organizational structure* (entity level, division, operating unit, and function) is shown on the cube as a third dimension.

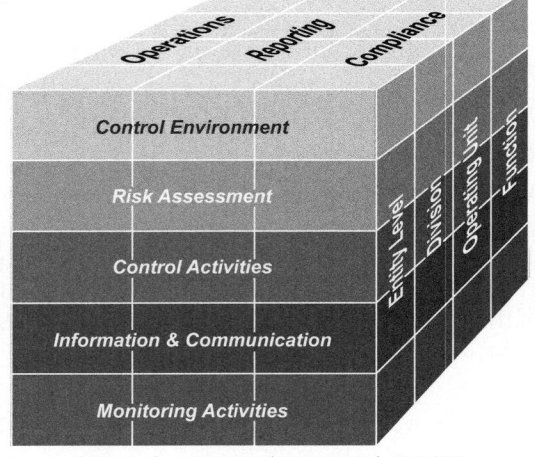

Internal Control—Integrated Framework, © 2013 Committee of Sponsoring Organizations of the Treadway Commission (COSO). Used with permission.

2.5   Framework Objectives

There are three *categories of objectives* within the framework.

1.   Operations Objectives

Operations objectives relate to the effectiveness and efficiency of an entity's operations. This category includes financial and operational performance goals as well as ensuring that the assets of the organization are adequately safeguarded against potential losses.

2.   Reporting Objectives

Reporting objectives pertain to the reliability, timeliness, and transparency of an entity's external and internal financial and nonfinancial reporting as established by regulators, accounting standard setters, or the firm's internal policies.

3.   Compliance Objectives

Compliance objectives are established to ensure the entity is adhering to all applicable laws and regulations.

2.6   Components of Internal Control (**CRIME**)

The updated framework retained the original five integrated *components* of internal control, including the control environment, risk assessment, information and communication, monitoring activities, and (existing) control activities. These components and the 17 related fundamental principles are needed to achieve the three *objectives* of internal control.

Each of the 17 principles is intended to be suitable to all entities and is presumed to be relevant. However, management may determine that a principle is not relevant to a component.

In addition, the framework introduces 81 points of focus. Some points of focus may not be suitable or relevant, and others may be identified. They are intended to facilitate designing, implementing, and conducting internal control by providing examples. They are not intended to be used as a checklist, and there is no requirement to separately assess whether points of focus are in place.

Pass Key

The COSO framework does not prescribe which controls an entity should implement for effective internal control. Instead, an organization's selection of controls requires management's judgment based on factors unique to the entity.

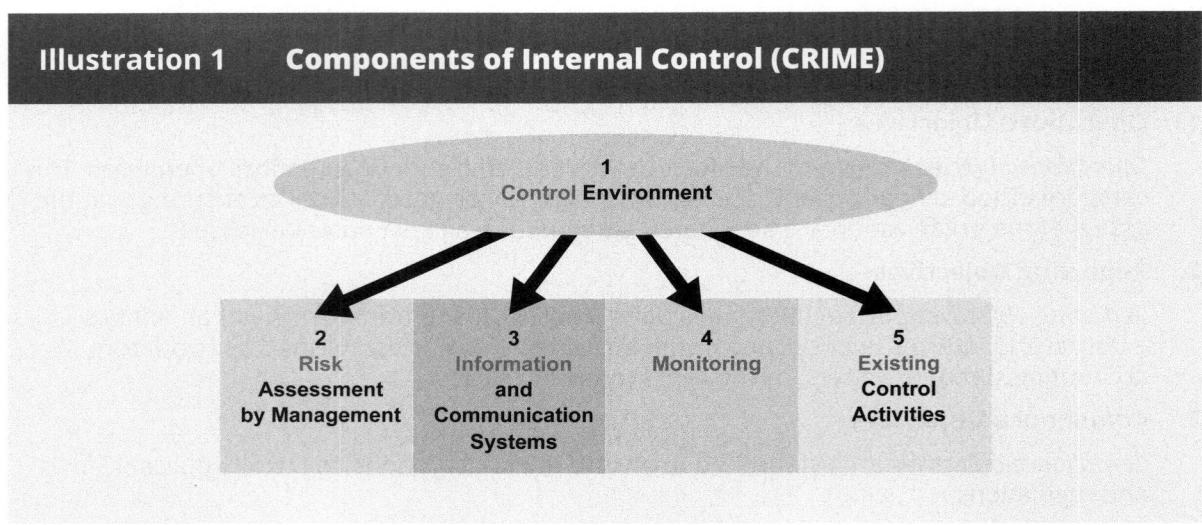

Illustration 1   Components of Internal Control (CRIME)

Pass Key

Remember that it would be a **CRIME** if you forgot the five components of internal control:

- **Control** Environment
- **Risk** Assessment
- **Information** and Communication
- **Monitoring**
- **(Existing)** Control Activities

2.6.1   Control Environment

The control environment includes the processes, structures, and standards that provide the foundation for an entity to establish a system of internal control. The importance of internal control and expected standards of conduct is established through a "tone at the top" approach taken by the senior management and board of directors of an entity. The five principles related to the control environment are:

1. **Commitment to Ethics and Integrity:** There is a commitment to ethical values and overall integrity throughout the organization. Points of focus include setting the tone at the top, establishing standards of conduct, evaluating adherence to standards of conduct, and addressing deviations in a timely manner.

2. **Board Independence and Oversight:** The board is independent from management and oversees the development and performance of internal control. Points of focus include establishing oversight responsibilities and providing oversight for the system of internal control.

3. **Organizational Structure:** Management establishes an organizational structure. Points of focus include establishing reporting lines, as well as defining, assigning, and limiting authorities and responsibilities that are appropriate to the organization's objectives.

4. **Commitment to Competence:** There is a commitment to hire, develop, and retain competent employees. Other points of focus include evaluating competence and addressing shortcomings in addition to succession planning.

5. **Accountability:** Individuals are held accountable for their internal control responsibilities. Points of focus include establishing performance measures, incentives, and rewards, and evaluating those for ongoing relevance while considering excessive pressures.

2.6.2 Risk Assessment

Risk assessment is an entity's identification and analysis of risks to the achievement of its objectives. The four principles related to risk assessment are:

1. **Specify Objectives:** The organization creates objectives that allow for identification and assessment of the risks related to those objectives. Points of focus include identifying objectives that reflect management's choices while complying with applicable accounting standards, laws, and regulations.

2. **Identify and Analyze Risks:** The organization identifies risks across the entity and analyzes risks in order to determine how the risks should be managed. Points of focus include analyzing internal and external factors, involving appropriate levels of management and determining how to respond to risks.

3. **Consider Potential for Fraud:** The organization considers the potential for fraud in assessing risks. Points of focus include assessing incentives and pressures, opportunities and attitudes, and rationalizations.

4. **Identify and Assess Changes:** The organization identifies and assesses changes that could significantly affect the system of internal control. Points of focus include assessing changes in the external environment, business model, and leadership.

2.6.3 Information and Communication

Information and communication systems support the identification, capture, and exchange of information in a timely and useful manner. The three principles related to information and communications are:

1. **Obtain and Use Information:** The organization obtains or generates and uses relevant, high-quality information to support the functioning of internal control. Points of focus include management identifying and defining information requirements within the internal control component level.

2. **Internally Communicate Information:** The organization internally communicates information necessary to support the functioning of internal controls, including relevant objectives and responsibilities. Points of focus include the flow of information up, down, and across the organization using a variety of methods and channels.

3. **Communicate With External Parties:** The organization communicates with external parties regarding matters that affect the functioning of internal control. Points of focus include management having open, two-way external communication channels using a variety of methods and channels.

2.6.4 Monitoring Activities

Monitoring is the process of assessing the quality of internal control performance over time by assessing the design and operation of controls on a timely basis and taking the necessary corrective actions. The two principles related to monitoring activities are:

1. **Ongoing and/or Separate Evaluations:** The organization selects, develops, and performs ongoing and/or separate evaluations to ascertain whether the components of internal control are present and functioning. One point of focus is to consider establishing baseline understandings.

2. **Communication of Deficiencies:** The organization evaluates and communicates internal control deficiencies in a timely manner to parties responsible for taking corrective action. One point of focus is monitoring corrective actions.

2.6.5 (Existing) Control Activities

Control activities are set forth by an entity's policies and procedures to ensure that the directives initiated by management to mitigate risks are performed.

Control activities may be detective or preventive in nature and may include automated and manual activities (e.g., approvals, reconciliations, verifications). Segregation of duties is usually part of the control activities developed by an organization, and when not practical, management should develop alternative controls. The three principles related to control activities are:

1. **Select and Develop Control Activities:** The organization selects and develops control activities that contribute to the mitigation of risks to acceptable levels. Points of focus include integrating with risk assessment when selecting activities and considering entity-specific factors.

2. **Select and Develop Technology Controls:** The organization selects and develops general control activities over technology to support the achievement of objectives. Points of focus include determining dependencies between the use of technology in business processes and establishing relevant technology infrastructure control activities.

3. **Deployment of Policies and Procedures:** The organization deploys control activities through policies that establish what is expected and procedures that put policies into action. Points of focus include establishing responsibility and accountability for executing policies and procedures and taking corrective action.

Pass Key

The candidate should be familiar with the five components of internal control (in bold) and each of the 17 principles within the components.

Control Environment

- Commitment to ethical values and integrity
- Board independence and oversight
- Organizational structure
- Commitment to competence
- Accountability

Risk Assessment

- Specify objectives
- Identify and analyze risks
- Consider the potential for fraud
- Identify and assess changes

(continued)

(continued)

Information and Communication

- Obtain and use information
- Internally communicate information
- Communicate with external parties

Monitoring Activities

- Ongoing and/or separate evaluations
- Communication of deficiencies

(Existing) Control Activities

- Select and develop control activities
- Select and develop technology controls
- Deploy through policies and procedures

Illustration 2   COSO Application

- **Risk:** Management is unaware of risks that could affect the company.

  —**Component:** Risk assessment.

  —**Principle:** The company identifies risks to achieving its objectives and analyzes risks to determine how the risks should be managed.

  —**Control Activity:** Periodic risk assessments are reviewed by management, including internal audit assessments.

- **Risk:** Employees act in an unethical or unlawful manner.

  —**Component:** Control environment.

  —**Principle:** The company demonstrates a commitment to integrity and ethical values.

  —**Control Activity:** A code of conduct or ethics policy exists and includes provisions about conflicts of interest, related party transactions, illegal acts, and the monitoring of the code by management, the audit committee, and board of directors.

2.7   Effective Internal Control

2.7.1   General Requirements

The framework indicates that an effective system of internal control provides reasonable assurance that the entity's objectives will be achieved. Under the framework, an effective system of internal control requires:

- All five components and 17 principles that are relevant to be both *present* and *functioning*.

    - **Present (Design):** The term "present" means that the components and relevant principles are included in the design and implementation of the internal control system.

    - **Functioning (Operating Effectively):** The term "functioning" demonstrates that the components and relevant principles are currently operating as designed in the internal control system.

- That all five components operate together as an *integrated* system in order to reduce, to an acceptable level, the risk that the entity will not achieve its objectives.

2.7.2   Specific Requirements

To be considered an effective system of internal control, senior management and the board must have reasonable assurance that the entity:

- Achieves effective and efficient operations when:

    - external threats are considered unlikely to have a significant impact on the achievement of objectives; or

    - the organization can reasonably predict and mitigate the impact of external events to an acceptable level.

- Understands the extent to which operations are managed effectively and efficiently when:

    - external events may have a significant impact on the achievement of objectives; or

    - the organization can reasonably predict and mitigate the impact of external events to an acceptable level.

- Complies with all applicable rules, regulations, external standards, and laws.

- Prepares reports that are in conformity with the entity's reporting objectives and all applicable standards, rules, and regulations.

Pass Key

The framework requires judgment in designing, implementing, and conducting internal control and in assessing the effectiveness of internal control.

2.7.3   Ineffective Internal Control: COSO

Internal control deficiencies are shortcomings in a component or components and relevant principles that reduce the likelihood of an entity achieving its objectives.

Although U.S. GAAS uses the terms "significant deficiency" and "material weakness," the COSO framework uses the term "major deficiency."

A major deficiency represents a material internal control deficiency, or combination of deficiencies, that significantly reduces the likelihood that an organization can achieve its objectives.

When a major deficiency is identified pertaining to the presence and functioning of a component or relevant principle, or with respect to the components operating together in an integrated manner, the entity may not conclude that it has met the requirements for an effective internal control system under the COSO framework.

2.8   Internal Control (Framework) Limitations

Although internal control provides reasonable assurance that a firm will achieve its stated objectives, it does not prevent bad decisions or eliminate all external events that may prevent the achievement of the entity's operational goals. The following are inherent limitations that may exist even in an effective internal control system:

- Breakdowns in internal control due to errors or human failure
- Faulty or biased judgment used in decision making
- Issues relating to the suitability of the entity's objectives
- External events beyond the control of the entity
- Circumvention of controls through collusion
- Management override of internal controls

Question 1	CPA-06748

The external auditors for the Horace Company assess the achievement of internal control objectives each year and communicate the assessment to management and the board. Communication by the external auditor illustrates which principle of the information and communication component of the Committee of Sponsoring Organizations' Integrated Framework?

    a.   Financial Reporting Information

    b.   Internal Control Information

    c.   Internal Communication

    d.   External Communication

Question 2	CPA-06483

A company that retains a CPA with the appropriate knowledge, skills, and abilities to prepare timely and effective financial reporting is applying the ideas from which principle of effective internal control over financial reporting?

    a.   Integrity and ethical values

    b.   Management philosophy and operating style

    c.   Accountability

    d.   Financial reporting competencies

3 Applying the Internal Control Framework

The COSO framework may be used to manage the application of internal controls, evaluate their effectiveness, and serve as a basis for management's assertions regarding the existence or absence of internal control deficiencies. Inherent in both the concept and application of the framework is the existence of risk to achievement of objectives and the implementation of controls to mitigate risk. Applying the COSO internal control framework is intended to reduce assessed risk to acceptable levels.

3.1 Using the COSO Framework Document

Management will logically compile and document the internal control assessment using the following steps as supported by the COSO framework guidance:

- **Overall Assessment:** Overall assessments are supported by component evaluations.

- **Component Evaluation:** Component evaluations are supported by principal evaluations.

- **Principal Evaluation:** Principal evaluations serve as the source for isolating and defining internal control deficiencies.

- **Summary of Internal Control Deficiencies (if any):** Internal control deficiencies are summarized and impact the overall assessment.

This overall assessment may trigger a reevalution of the components.

3.2 Common Risks Identified Using the COSO Framework

3.2.1 Material Omission or Misstatement

Management identifies risks that could individually or in combination result in material omissions or misstatements of the financial statements. The process for evaluating risk is dynamic and ongoing. Risks vary as entities operate in:

- Multiple industries, markets, and geographic areas

- Multiple regulatory environments with different standards

- Transactional environments with numerous contracts

- An active merger, acquisition, and divestiture environment

- A dynamic technological environment

- A high executive turnover environment

3.2.2 Fraud

The risk of fraud is typically characterized by either fraudulent financial reporting (intentional misstatements of financial reports designed to deceive users) and misappropriation of assets (theft).

Specific risks encountered include:

- Management bias in exercising judgment

- The degree of estimates and judgments underlying accounting and reporting

- Incentives for fraud (e.g., bonuses)

- Attitudes and rationalizations by individuals
- Unusual transactions
- Vulnerability to management override

A system of internal control over external financial reporting is designed and implemented to prevent or detect in a timely manner any material omissions within or misstatements of the financial statements due to error or fraud.

3.2.3 Management Override

Management override refers to actions taken by management in an attempt to override controls for personal gain. Management override of controls can lead to fraud.

Pass Key

Management intervention is not the same as management override. It represents the fully appropriate involvement of management in unusual transactions.

3.2.4 Illegal Acts

Illegal acts represent violations of government regulations that could have a material impact on the financial statements. Assessments of potential illegal acts include:

- Existence of investigations
- Reports of regulatory examiners
- Payments for unspecified services
- Delinquent tax returns

3.3   Controls

Management considers how the risk of material omissions and misstatements should be managed across the entity. Management selects, develops, and deploys controls to effectively apply principles within each component to respond to assessed risk. As part of its response, management considers:

- Laws, rules, regulations, and standards that apply to the entity
- The nature of the entity's business and the markets in which it operates
- Scope and nature of the operating model
- Competence of personnel
- Use and dependence on technology

3.3.1   Selection and Development of Controls

The selection and development of controls can include any of the following approaches:

- Use workshops or control activity inventories to map risks to controls.
- Implement control activities over outsourced functions.
- Consider the types of control activities.

- Consider alternative control to segregation of duties.

- Identify incompatible functions.

3.3.2 Selection and Development of General Controls Over Technology

The selection and development of general controls over technology can include any of the following approaches:

- Use risk-control matrices to document technology dependencies.

- Evaluate end-user computing.

- Implement or monitor control activities when outsourcing IT functions.

- Configure the IT infrastructure to support restricted access and segregation of duties.

- Configure the IT system to support the complete, accurate, and valid processing of transactions and data.

- Administer security and access.

- Apply a system development life cycle over packaged and internally developed software.

3.3.3 Deploying Controls Through Policies and Procedures

Deploying controls through policies and procedures may include any of the following approaches:

- Develop and document policies and procedures.

- Deploy control activities through the business unit of functional leaders.

- Conduct regular and ad hoc assessments of control activities.

1 Introduction to Enterprise Risk Management

In 2004, COSO issued *Enterprise Risk Management (ERM)—Integrated Framework* ("the framework") to assist organizations in developing a comprehensive response to risk management. In recognition of the changing complexity of risk, the emergence of new risks, and the enhanced awareness of risk management by both boards and executive oversight bodies, COSO published *Enterprise Risk Management—Integrating With Strategy and Performance* in 2017.

According to COSO, "Risk is the possibility that events will occur and affect the achievement of strategy and business objectives."

1.1 Value

The underlying premise of ERM is that every entity exists to provide value for stakeholders and that all entities face risk in the pursuit of value for their stakeholders. Management decisions will affect the development of value, including its *creation, preservation, erosion, and realization*.

Pass Key

Value is defined by the type of entity.

For-profit commercial entities: Value is usually shaped by strategies that balance market opportunities against the risks of pursuing those opportunities.

Not-for-profit and governmental entities: Value may be shaped by delivering goods and services that balance the opportunity to serve the broader community against any associated risk.

1.1.1 Value Creation

Value is created when benefits of value exceed the cost of resources used. Resources may include people, financial capital, technology, process, and brand (market presence).

Illustration 1   Value Creation

Silky & Shiny & Smooth Skin Products has a full line of skin care products. The company decides to develop shampoos and conditioners using a companion product line. The successful and profitable launch of the new product line represents value creation.

Material from *Enterprise Risk Management—Integrating With Strategy and Performance,* © 2017 Committee of Sponsoring Organizations of the Treadway Commission (COSO). Used with permission.

1.1.2   Value Preservation

Value is preserved when ongoing operations efficiently and effectively sustain created benefits. High customer satisfaction with profitable product lines is evidence of value preservation.

1.1.3   Value Erosion

Value is eroded when faulty strategy and inefficient/ineffective operations cause value to decline.

Illustration 2	Value Erosion

Silky & Shiny & Smooth Skin Products has a full line of skin care products. The company decides to develop shampoos and conditioners using a companion product line. The unsuccessful launch of the new product line represents value erosion. Not only are financial resources lost, but the brand name suffers as well.

1.1.4   Value Realization

Value is realized when benefits created by the organization are received by stakeholders in either monetary or nonmonetary form.

Illustration 3	Value Realization

Value realization is illustrated by increased profitability and stock prices for company owners, increased customer satisfaction, consistent product and brand usage, market leadership, and consistent innovation that not only enhances the company but improves the economy.

1.2   Mission, Vision, and Core Values

Mission, vision, and core values define what an entity strives to be and how it wants to conduct business.

1.2.1   Mission

Mission represents the core purpose of the entity. The mission represents why the company exists and what it hopes to accomplish.

1.2.2   Vision

Vision represents the aspirations of the entity and what it hopes to achieve over time.

1.2.3   Core Values

Core values represent an organization's beliefs and ideals about what is good or bad, acceptable and unacceptable, and they influence the behavior of the organization.

Each enterprise is unique. The ERM framework helps identify the individual features that make an enterprise stand out.

2 Definition of Enterprise Risk Management

As defined by COSO:

> Enterprise risk management is the *culture, capabilities, and practices, integrated with strategy-setting and performance*, that organizations rely on to *manage risk* in creating, preserving, and realizing *value*.

2.1 Culture

Culture represents the collective thinking of the people within an organization. Individuals have unique points of reference that influence how they identify, assess, and respond to risk. Culture plays an important role in shaping decisions regarding risk.

Pass Key

Core values correlate with culture.

2.2 Capabilities (Competitive Advantage)

Competitive advantage produces value for an entity. Exploitation of competitive advantage and adaptation to change are skill sets embedded within ERM.

2.3 Practices

ERM is an organizational practice continually applied to the entire scope of activities of the business. It is part of management decisions at all levels of the entity. It is neither static nor is it an adjunct or add-on to the business.

2.4 Integration With Strategy-Setting and Performance

Strategy is set in a manner that aligns with mission and vision. Business objectives flow from strategy. Business objectives drive the activities of all business units and functions.

ERM integrates with strategy-setting and operating activities to promote an understanding of how risk potentially affects the entity overall.

Pass Key

Mission and vision correlate with strategy and business objectives.

2.5   Managing Risk Linked to Value

ERM practices are intended to provide the management and the board with a reasonable expectation that the organization's overall strategy and business objectives can be achieved. Reasonable expectation means the amount of risk of achieving strategy and business objectives is appropriate for that entity.

An organization must continually review and manage the types and amounts of risk it is willing to accept in its pursuit of value.

2.5.1   Risk Appetite

Risk appetite represents the types and amounts of risk, on a broad level, that an organization is willing to accept in pursuit of value. Risk appetite is a range rather than a specific limit and provides guidance on the practices an organization is encouraged to pursue or not pursue.

- Risk appetite is expressed first in mission and vision.

- Risk appetite varies between products, business units, or over time in line with changing capabilities for managing risk and must be flexible enough to adapt to changing business conditions without approvals.

2.5.2   Relationship of Value and Risk Appetite

Managing risk within risk appetite enhances an organization's ability to create, preserve, and realize value. ERM seeks to align anticipated value creation with risk appetite and capabilities for managing risk over time.

3   Enterprise Risk Management Themes and Terms

Enterprise Risk Management encompasses numerous themes and uses very specific terminology.

An entity's culture, driven by core values, defines a mission to create value and recognizes that an inventory of risks exist that threaten the achievement of the mission and the creation of value. The application of ERM is intended to provide management with a reasonable expectation of success.

- **Risk Inventory:** All risk that could impact an entity.

- **Reasonable Expectation:** The amount of risk of having strategy and business objectives that is appropriate for an entity, recognizing that no one can predict risk with precision.

Core values affect the amount of risk an organization is willing to accept within the context of the business. The organization makes overall decisions regarding risk appetite and, based on that determination, assesses its risk capacity and develops a risk profile.

- **Business Context:** The trends, events, relationships, and other factors that may influence, clarify, or change an entity's current and future strategy and business objectives.

- **Risk Capacity:** The maximum amount of risk that an entity is able to absorb in the pursuit of strategy and business objectives.

- **Risk Profile:** A composite view of the risk assumed at a particular level of the entity or aspect of the business that positions management to consider the types, severity, and interdependencies of risk and how they may affect performance relative to the strategy and business objectives.

Although risk is evaluated at a departmental and divisional level, entity-wide risks use a portfolio view. Related ideas include the ability of the entity to absorb risk and its ongoing management efforts.

- **Portfolio View:** A composite view of risk the entity faces which positions management and the board to consider the types, severity, and interdependencies of risk and how they may affect the entity's performance relative to its strategy and business objectives.

- **Organizational Sustainability:** The ability of an entity to withstand the impact of large-scale events.

- **Performance Management:** The measurement of efforts to achieve or exceed the strategy and business objectives.

4 Enterprise Risk Management Interrelationships

Enterprise Risk Management is depicted as a series of sequential yet intertwined components that drive an organization toward enhanced value.

The tone at the top and communication are linked, and weave into the similarly linked efforts to develop overall strategy, specific business objectives, and manage performance to the achievement of value.

Mission, vision, and values drive the process but are also affected by performance, as management constantly reviews its risks and its ability to create value.

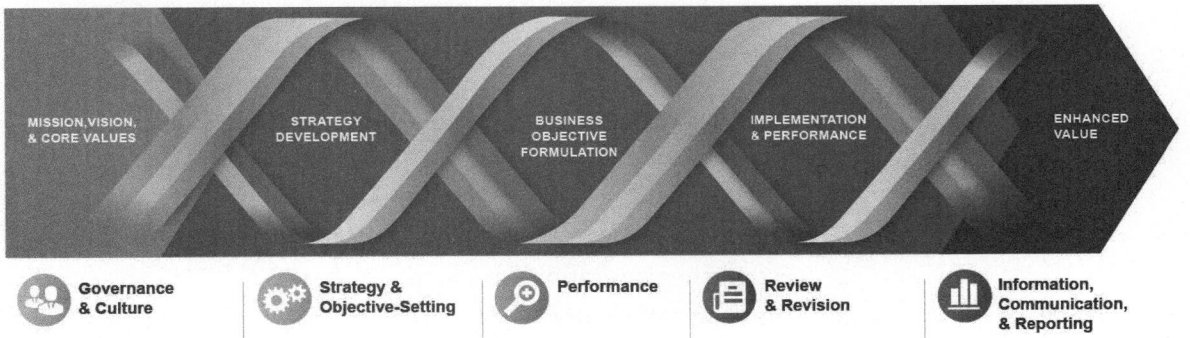

Enterprise Risk Management—Integrating With Strategy and Performance, © 2017 Committee of Sponsoring Organizations of the Treadway Commission (COSO). Used with permission.

5 Components of Enterprise Risk Management

Enterprise risk management is defined by five interrelated components and is supported by 20 risk management principles. The components somewhat resemble the COSO cube for internal control but address the broader issues of risk as it impacts an entity.

1. Governance and Culture

2. Strategy and Objective-Setting

3. Performance

4. Review and Revision

5. Information, Communication, and Reporting (Ongoing)

Pass Key

Knowing the logical order of the enterprise management framework has been a topic of released questions. Memorize the five components as you **GO PRO** with ERM.

Governance and Culture

Strategy and **O**bjective-Setting

Performance

Review and Revision

Information, Communication, and Reporting (**O**ngoing information-gathering and feedback)

Pass Key

The five components of ERM are supported by 20 principles. Recollecting which principles support which components is a potential source of multiple-choice points, summarized below:

Governance and Culture	Strategy and Objective-Setting	Performance	Review and Revision	Information, Communication, and Reporting (Ongoing)
DOVES	SOAR	VAPIR	SIR	TIP

Governance and Culture	**D**	Defines **d**esired culture
	O	Exercises board **o**versight
	V	Demonstrates commitment to core **v**alues
	E	Attracts, develops, and retains capable individuals (**e**mployees)
	S	Establishes operating **s**tructure
Strategy and Objective-Setting	**S**	Evaluates alternative **s**trategies
	O	Formulates business **o**bjectives
	A	**A**nalyzes business context
	R	Defines **r**isk appetite
Performance	**V**	Develops portfolio **v**iew
	A	**A**ssesses severity of risk
	P	**P**rioritizes risk
	I	**I**dentifies risks (events)
	R	Implements risk **r**esponses
Review and Revision	**S**	Assesses **s**ubstantial change
	I	Pursues **i**mprovement in Enterprise Risk Management
	R	**R**eviews risk and performance
Information, Communication, and Reporting (Ongoing)	**T**	Leverages information and **t**echnology
	I	Communicates risk **i**nformation
	P	Reports on risk, culture, and **p**erformance

5.1   Governance and Culture (**DOVES**)

Governance and culture together form a base for all other components of enterprise risk management.

- Governance sets the entity's tone at the top, serves to endorse the importance of enterprise risk management, and establishes oversight responsibilities for ERM.

- Culture is reflected in decision making.

5.1.1   Exercises Board **O**versight

The board of directors provides oversight for an entity's strategy and carries out governance responsibilities to support management in achieving strategy and business objectives. The board is expected to have the skills, experience, and business knowledge to understand the entity's strategy; stay informed on relevant issues; and maintain an active and accountable role that is independent and conscious of potential bias.

Illustration 4   Board Oversight
Active and accountable board oversight is often characterized by frequent conversations with management to determine the suitability of ERM design and effectiveness in enhancing value.

5.1.2   Establishes Operating **S**tructure

Operating structures are established to pursue strategy and business objectives. Operating structures describe how an entity organizes and carries out its day-to-day operations and contributes to the alignment of risk management practices with core values.

5.1.3   Defines **D**esired Culture

The organization defines the desired behaviors that characterize the entity's desired culture. An entity's culture influences how the organization identifies risk, what types of risk it accepts, and how it manages risk. Culture is a spectrum that progresses from Risk Averse to Risk Neutral and extends to Risk Aggressive.

Pass Key
The ability of an organization to successfully achieve its strategy and business objectives is impeded when the behaviors and decisions of the organization (culture) do not align with its core values.

5.1.4   Demonstrates Commitment to Core **V**alues

The organization demonstrates a commitment to the entity's core values. Without support from the top of the organization, risk awareness can be undermined and risk-inspired decisions may be inconsistent with those values.

5.1.5   Attracts, Develops, and Retains Capable Individuals (Employees)

Commitment to building human capital in alignment with the strategy and business objectives is a principle of the governance and culture component. The ultimate accountability for development and retention of capable individuals starts with the board and its selection of executive leadership. The selection of team members is typically delegated to appropriate levels of management. Human resources professionals assist management in assembling competent team members through consideration of the following factors:

- Knowledge, skills, and experience

- Nature and degree of judgment and limitations of authority to be applied to a specific position

- The costs and benefit of different skill levels and experience

The ongoing process of attracting, developing, and retaining individuals includes attracting or seeking out competent individuals and training them, then mentoring, evaluating, and ultimately retaining them with appropriate incentives and rewards.

No less important than maintenance of the current talent pool is preparation for succession, a process that may involve identifying more than one person who could fill a crucial role.

5.2   Strategy and Objective-Setting (SOAR)

Enterprise risk management is integrated into the entity's strategic plan through the process of setting strategy and business objectives that considers both internal and external factors and their effect on risk framed by business context.

- An organization sets its risk appetite in conjunction with strategy-setting.

- The business objectives allow strategy to be put into practice and shape the entity's day-to-day operations and priorities.

5.2.1   Analyzes Business Context

Consideration of the potential effects of business context on risk profile is a principle supporting the strategy and objective-setting component. Business context may be dynamic, complex, and even unpredictable. Business context usually considers both external and internal environments.

5.2.2   Defines Risk Appetite

The organization defines risk appetite in the context of creating, preserving, and realizing value.

- Entities consider risk appetite in qualitative terms, while others may be quantitative. The best approach for an entity is one that aligns with the analyses used to assess risk in general, whether that is qualitative or quantitative.

- General terms such as "low appetite" or "high appetite" are sufficient expressions of risk appetite. Referencing "targets," "ranges," "ceilings," or "floors" may also be used.

Ultimately, risk appetite is expressed in the context of objectives.

5.2.3   Evaluates Alternative Strategies

Evaluation of alternative strategies and the potential effect on risk profile is a principle supporting the strategy and objective-setting component. Strategy is evaluated from two perspectives:

- The possibility that the strategy does not align with the mission, vision, and core values of the entity

- The implications from the chosen strategy

Misaligned strategies may impede achievement of the mission and fulfillment of the entity's mission.

The implications of each strategy include risks and opportunities of each strategy. Identified risks collectively form a risk profile and serve as the basis for developing and evaluating alternative strategies.

■ The development of alternative strategies considers the supporting assumptions relating to the business context, resources, and capabilities. The level of confidence associated with each supporting assumption will affect the risk profile of each of the strategies.

■ Development of a risk profile for a strategy enables consideration of the types and amount of risk faced by the organization.

Successful strategy is carried out within the organization's risk appetite. Strategy may change as the evaluation of risk or the ability to perform changes.

5.2.4 Formulates Business Objectives

Business objectives are the measurable steps that an organization makes to achieve its strategy. The alignment of business objectives to strategy supports the entity in achieving its mission and vision.

■ Business objectives are developed that are specific, measurable or observable, attainable, and relevant (to the achievement of strategy).

■ Business objectives may relate to financial performance, customer aspirations, operational efficiency, compliance obligations, or innovation.

The organization sets targets to monitor the performance of the entity and support the achievement of its business objectives.

Monitoring performance includes the concept of tolerance. Tolerance is the range of acceptable outcomes related to achieving a business objective within the risk appetite. Tolerance is also referred to as the acceptable variance in performance.

5.3 Performance (VAPIR)

Identification and assessment of risks that may affect an entity's ability to achieve its strategy and business objectives represent the performance component.

■ Organizations identify and assess risks that may affect the achievement of strategy and business objectives.

■ Risk is prioritized according to severity and in consideration of the entity's risk appetite.

■ The organization then selects risk responses and monitors performance for change.

■ The resulting portfolio view describes the amount of risk the entity has assumed in the pursuit of its strategy and entity-level business objectives.

5.3.1 Identifies Risks

Organizations identify risks that affect their performance in achieving strategy and business objectives. New and emerging risks are identified, and currently assessed risks are reevaluated using various techniques.

5.3.2 Assesses Severity of Risk

The severity of risk is evaluated after it has been identified. Resources and capabilities are deployed to keep the risk within the entity's risk appetite based on the assessment.

The severity of a risk is assessed at multiple levels (across divisions, functions, and operating units) in line with the business objectives it may affect. Risks deemed severe at the operating level may be less of a concern at the division or entity level.

Severity measures relate to impact (result or effect of the risk) and likelihood (possibility of the risk occurring). Likelihood may be expressed qualitatively or quantitatively.

Risk assessment includes the concepts of inherent risk, target residual risk, and actual residual risk.

- Inherent risk is the risk to an entity in the absence of any direct or focused actions by management to alter its severity.

- Target residual risk is the amount of risk that an entity prefers to assume in the pursuit of its strategy and business objectives knowing that management will implement or has implemented direct or focused actions to alter the severity of the risk.

- Actual residual risk is the risk remaining after management has taken action.

The organization strives to identify triggers that will prompt a reassessment of severity when required.

5.3.3 Prioritizes Risk

Prioritization of risk as a basis for determining risk response is a principle underlying the performance component. Risks that result in the entity approaching the risk appetite for specific business objectives are typically given higher priority.

5.3.4 Implements Risk Responses

Risk responses are generally classified as:

- **Accept:** No action is taken to change the severity of the risk. Acceptance is most appropriate as a risk response when risk to strategy and business objectives is within the entity's risk appetite.

- **Avoid:** Action is taken to remove the risk (leaving a line of business, etc.). Avoidance is appropriate when an entity cannot devise a risk response that will mitigate the risk to objectives.

- **Pursue:** Action is taken that accepts increased risk to achieve improved performance. Pursuit of risk is appropriate when management understands the nature and extent of any changes required to achieve desired performance while not exceeding the boundaries of acceptable tolerance.

- **Reduce:** Action is taken to reduce the severity of the risk. Management designs risk mitigation techniques to reduce risk to an amount of severity aligned with the target risk profile and risk appetite.

- **Share:** Action is taken to reduce the severity of the risk. Sharing risk with such techniques as outsourcing and insurance lower residual risk in alignment with risk appetite.

Risk responses may trigger a review of strategic and business objectives.

5.3.5 Develops Portfolio View

The organization develops and evaluates a portfolio (entity-wide) view of risk. A portfolio view allows management and the board to consider the type, severity, and interdependencies of risks and how they may affect performance and align with the overall risk appetite.

5.4   Review and Revision (SIR)

By reviewing enterprise risk management capabilities and practices, and the entity's performance relative to its targets, an organization can consider how well the enterprise risk management capabilities and practices have increased value over time and will continue to drive value in light of substantial changes.

5.4.1 Assesses Substantial Change

The entity identifies and assesses changes that may substantially affect strategy and business objectives; it is a principle supporting the review and revision component. Assessments may include identifying internal and external environmental changes related to the business context as well as changes in culture.

5.4.2 Reviews Risk and Performance

The organization reviews entity performance and considers risk, including the capabilities and practices of the organization. Evaluations may relate to potentially incorrect assumptions, poorly implemented practices, entity capability, or cultural factors.

5.4.3 Pursues Improvement in Enterprise Risk Management

The organization pursues improvement of enterprise risk management. Opportunities to revisit and improve efficiency and usefulness may occur in any area.

5.5   Information, Communication, and Reporting (Ongoing) (TIP)

Communication is the continual, iterative process of obtaining information and sharing it throughout the entity.

- Management uses relevant information from both internal and external sources to support enterprise risk management.

- The organization leverages information systems to capture, process, and manage data and information. By using information that applies to all components, the organization reports on risk, culture, and performance.

5.5.1 Leverages Information and Technology

The organization leverages the entity's information and technology systems to support the organization with relevant information. Relevant information helps the organization be more agile in its decision making and provides a competitive advantage.

Illustration 5	How Information Supports Decisions

Different types of information support different levels of the decision making:

Governance and culture-related practices. The organization may need information on the standards of conduct and individual performance in relation to those standards.

Strategy and objective-setting practices. The organization may need information on stakeholder expectations about risk appetite.

Performance-related practices. Organizations may need information on their competitors to assess changes in the amount of risk.

Review and revision-related practices. Organizations may need information on emerging trends in enterprise risk management.

Information is generally characterized as structured (e.g., database files, etc.) and unstructured (e.g., volumes of e-mail, photos, etc.). The ability to accumulate and analyze data effectively is constantly evolving. Classifying information using common risk categories helps with risk assessment (e.g., information from internal audit, information management, etc.)

Data management is integral to risk-aware decisions. Effective data management considers three key elements:

- Data and information governance promote standardization of high-quality data.

- Processes and controls promote data reliability.

- Data management architecture refers to the fundamental design of the technology. Design is driven by value defined by management's needs.

5.5.2 Communicates Risk Information

The organization uses communication channels to support enterprise risk management. Communications are made to internal and external stakeholders and with the board of directors. Communication techniques vary widely. Communication methods must be evaluated for effectiveness.

5.5.3 Reports on Risk, Culture, and Performance

The organization reports on risk, culture, and performance at multiple levels and across the entity. Reporting may be either quantitative or qualitative and be made to a wide range of users, including management, risk owners, assurance providers, external stakeholders, and others.

Types of reports include:

- Portfolio view of risk (outlining the severity of risk at the entity level)

- Profile view of risk (outlining the severity of risk at different levels within the entity, e.g., a division, etc.)

Reporting on culture seeks to measure and provide feedback on behavior and attitudes. Reporting can be complex and may be embodied by:

- Analytics of cultural trends
- Benchmarking to other entities or standards
- Compensation schemes and the potential influence on decision making
- "Lessons learned" analysis
- Reviews of behavioral trends
- Surveys of risk attitudes and risk awareness

The frequency of reporting should be commensurate with the severity and priority of risk.

Question 1   **CPA-06480**

According to the Committee of Sponsoring Organizations (COSO) of the Treadway Commission, which of the following components of enterprise risk management addresses an entity's commitment to core values?

   a. Governance and Culture

   b. Strategy and Objective-Setting

   c. Performance

   d. Review and Revision

Question 2   **CPA-06754**

Able Corporation owns numerous businesses along the coast of Florida. The company's management has identified business interruption events as a potential risk resulting from storm damage caused by hurricanes. The company elects to not only insure its properties but to "buy down" standard deductibles with additional premium. Able's response to potential risks is known as:

   a. Avoidance

   b. Reduction

   c. Sharing

   d. Acceptance

NOTES

1 Introduction to the Sarbanes-Oxley Act of 2002

The Sarbanes-Oxley Act of 2002 has had a profound effect on the financial reporting requirements of public companies. In particular, there are numerous provisions for expanded disclosures by corporations and specific representations required by officers of public companies that must accompany published financial statements. Key provisions of the act related to those disclosures are described in Title III and Title IV of the act. Title VIII and Title IX describe penalties for violating the act. Title XI covers guidelines for rules and punishments concerned with fraudulent corporate activities.

2 Title III (Corporate Responsibility)

The corporate responsibility section of the act relates to the establishment of an audit committee and the representations made by key corporate officers, typically the chief executive officer (CEO) and the chief financial officer (CFO).

2.1 Public Company Audit Committees

- Public companies are responsible for establishing an audit committee that is directly responsible for the appointment, compensation, and oversight of the work of the public accounting firm employed by that public company (also referred to as an issuer).
  - The auditor reports directly to the audit committee.
  - The audit committee is responsible for resolving disputes between the auditor and management.
- Audit committee members are to be members of the issuer's board of directors but are to be otherwise independent. Independence criteria are as follows:
  - Audit committee members may not accept compensation from the issuer for consulting or advisory services.
  - Audit committee members may not be an affiliated person of the issuer. (Affiliation means a person having the ability to influence financial decisions).
- Audit committees must establish procedures to accept reports of complaints regarding audit, accounting, or internal control issues (whistle-blower hotlines).
  - Procedures must accommodate confidential, anonymous reports by employees of the issuer.
  - Procedures must accommodate receipt and retention of complaints as well as a method to address those complaints.

2.2   Corporate Responsibility for Financial Reports

Corporate officials, typically the CEO and CFO, must sign certain representations regarding annual and quarterly reports, including their assertion that:

■   They have reviewed the report.

■   The report does not contain untrue statements or omit material information.

■   The financial statements fairly present in all material respects the financial condition and results of operations of the issuer.

■   The CEO and CFO signing the report have assumed responsibility for internal controls, including assertions that:

   •   Internal controls have been designed to ensure that material information has been made available.

   •   Internal controls have been evaluated for effectiveness as of a date within 90 days prior to the report.

   •   Their report includes their conclusions as to the effectiveness of internal controls based on their evaluation.

■   The CEO and CFO signing the report assert that they have made the following disclosures to the issuer's auditors and the audit committee:

   •   All significant deficiencies and material weaknesses in the design or operation of internal controls which might adversely affect the financial statements.

   •   Any fraud (regardless of materiality) that involves management or any other employee with a significant role in internal controls.

■   The CEO and CFO signing the report must also represent whether there have been any significant changes to internal controls.

2.3   Improper Influence on the Conduct of Audits

No officer or director, or any person acting under the direction thereof, may take any action that would fraudulently influence, coerce, mislead, or manipulate the auditor in a manner that would make the financial statements materially misleading.

2.4   Forfeiture of Certain Bonuses and Profits

If an issuer is required to prepare an accounting restatement due to material noncompliance with any financial reporting requirement under the securities laws, the CEO and CFO may be required to reimburse the issuer for:

■   bonuses or incentive-based or equity-based compensation.

■   gains on sale of securities during that 12-month period.

3   Title IV (Enhanced Financial Disclosures)

The enhanced financial disclosures associated with issuer reports include additional details regarding the financial statements, internal controls, and the operations of the audit committee.

3.1   Disclosures in Periodic Reports (Generally Quarterly or Annually)

Financial statement disclosures are intended to ensure that the application of GAAP reflects the economics of the transactions included in the report and that those transactions are transparent to the reader. Enhanced disclosure requirements include the following:

- All material correcting adjustments identified by the auditor should be reflected in the financial statements.
- The financial statements should disclose all material off-balance sheet transactions:
  - Operating leases
  - Contingent obligations
  - Relationships with unconsolidated subsidiaries
- Conformance of pro forma financial statements to the following requirements:
  - No untrue statements
  - No omitted material information
  - Reconciled with GAAP basis financial statements
- Use of special purpose entities (SPEs).

3.2   Conflict of Interest Provisions

Issuers are generally prohibited from making personal loans to directors or executive officers.

- Exceptions apply if the consumer credit loans are made in the ordinary course of business by the issuer.
- Exceptions apply if the terms offered to the officer are generally made available to the public under similar terms and conditions with no preferential treatment.

3.3   Disclosure of Transactions Involving Management and Principal Stockholders

- Disclosures are required for persons who generally have direct or indirect ownership of more than 10 percent of any class of most any equity security. Disclosures are made by filing a statement.
- Statements are filed at the following times:
  - At the time of registration
  - When the person achieves 10 percent ownership
  - If there has been a change in ownership

3.4   Management Assessment of Internal Controls

The assessment of internal controls is commonly referred to as Section 404. Each annual report is required to contain a report that includes the following:

- A statement that management is responsible for establishing and maintaining an adequate internal control structure and procedures for financial reporting.

- An assessment, as of the end of the most recent fiscal year of the issuer, of the effectiveness of the internal control structure and procedures for financial reporting.

The auditor must attest to management's assessment of internal control.

3.5   Certain Exemptions

Investment companies are exempt from this act.

3.6   Code of Ethics for Senior Officers

- Issuers must disclose whether the issuer has adopted a code of conduct for senior officers (e.g., CEO, CFO, controller, and chief accountant). If no code of conduct has been adopted, the issuer must disclose the reasons.

- The code of ethics contemplates standards that promote:

  - Honest and ethical conduct (including handling of conflicts of interest).

  - Full, fair, accurate, and timely disclosures in periodic financial reports.

  - Compliance with laws, rules, and regulations.

- Changes to or waivers from the code must be reported on a Form 8-K.

3.7   Disclosure of Audit Committee Financial Expert

At least one member of the audit committee should be a financial expert. Financial reports of the issuer must disclose the existence of a financial expert on the committee or the reasons why the committee does not have a member who is a financial expert.

- A financial expert qualifies through education, past experience as a public accountant, or past experience as a principal financial officer, controller, or principal accounting officer for an issuer.

- Knowledge of the financial expert should include:

  - Understanding of GAAP.

  - Experience in the preparation or auditing of financial statements for comparable issuers.

  - Application of GAAP.

  - Experience with internal controls.

  - Understanding of audit committee functions.

3.8   Enhanced Review of Periodic Disclosures by Issuers

The Securities and Exchange Commission (SEC) is required to review disclosures made by issuers, including those in Form 10-K, on a regular and systematic basis for the protection of investors. When scheduling reviews, the SEC should consider the following:

- Issuers that have issued material restatements of financial results.

- Issuers that experience significant volatility in their stock prices when compared to other issuers.

- Issuers with the largest market capitalization.

- Emerging companies with disparities in price-to-earning ratios.

- Issuers whose operations significantly affect any material sector of the economy.

4   Title VIII (Corporate and Criminal Fraud Accountability)

4.1   Criminal Penalties for Altering Documents

- Individuals who alter, destroy, mutilate, conceal, cover up, falsify, or make false entry in any record, document, or tangible object with the intent to impede, obstruct, or influence an investigation will be fined, imprisoned for not more than 20 years, or both.

- Auditors of issuers should retain all audit and review workpapers for a period of seven years from the end of the fiscal period in which the audit or review was conducted. Failure to do so will result in a fine, imprisonment for not more than 10 years, or both.

4.2   Statute of Limitations for Securities Fraud

The statute of limitations for securities fraud is no later than the earlier of two years after the discovery of the facts constituting the violation, or five years after the violation.

4.3   Whistle-Blower Protection

An employee who lawfully provides evidence of fraud may not be discharged, demoted, suspended, threatened, harassed, or in any other matter discriminated against for providing such information. An employee who alleges discharge or other discrimination for providing evidence of fraud may file a complaint with the Secretary of Labor and may be provided with compensatory damages, including:

- reinstatement with the same seniority status that the employee would have had;

- back pay with interest; and

- compensation for any special damages as a result of the discrimination including litigation costs, expert witness fees, and reasonable attorney fees.

4.4   Criminal Penalties for Securities Fraud

An individual who knowingly executes, or attempts to execute, securities fraud will be fined, imprisoned not more than 25 years, or both.

5   Title IX (White-Collar Crime Penalty Enhancements)

5.1   Attempt and Conspiracy

An individual who attempts (conspires) to commit any white-collar offense will be subject to the same penalties as those who commit the offense, as predetermined by the United States Sentencing Commission. The penalties for mail and wire fraud were increased from 5 years to 20 years. The penalties for violating ERISA were increased from not more than $5,000 to not more than $100,000 and from not more than 1 year to not more than 10 years for individuals. (Either or both of the fine and the sentence may be imposed.) Fines imposed upon persons who are not individuals cannot exceed $500,000.

Module 3   B1–33

5.2   Amendment to Sentencing Guidelines Related to Certain White-Collar Offenses

■ The United States Sentencing Commission ("Sentencing Commission") will review and amend, as needed, the Federal Sentencing Guidelines and policy statements to carry out the provisions of the Attempt and Conspiracy Act. This includes ensuring that the sentencing guidelines and policy statements take into account the nature of any offense and that the corresponding penalties are commensurate with the provisions of the act. In the event the Sentencing Commission determines a growing trend of a particular offense, it will review to determine whether any modifications to the Sentencing Guidelines or policy statements are necessary.

■ The Sentencing Commission will review any additional aggravating or mitigating circumstances for a particular offense that could justify an exception to the existing sentencing ranges.

5.3   Failure of Corporate Officers to Certify Financial Reports

■ Any issuer periodic report which contains financial statements that is filed with the SEC must be accompanied by the following:

- A written statement that the periodic report fully complies with the Securities Exchange Act of 1934.

- A written statement that the information contained in the report fairly presents, in all material respects, the financial condition and operating results of the issuer.

- The written statements above must be signed by the chief executive officer and chief financial officer (or equivalent) of the issuer (who bear responsibility for these statements).

■ Any party that certifies the periodic financial report and/or its content knowing that it does not satisfy all the requirements shall be fined and/or imprisoned. Specifically, a party who:

- *certifies* any statement knowing that it does not comply with all requirements will be fined not more than $1,000,000 and/or imprisoned not more than 10 years; or

- *willfully* certifies any statement knowing that it does not comply with all requirements will be fined not more than $5,000,0000 and/or imprisoned not more than 20 years.

6   Title XI (Corporate Fraud Accountability)

6.1   Tampering With Record or Impeding an Official Proceeding

Any individual who alters, destroys, or conceals a document (record) with the intent to modify the document and its integrity or the availability of the document in an official proceeding shall be fined and/or subject to not more than a 20-year prison term.

6.2   Temporary Freeze Authority for the SEC

If during an investigation pertaining to potential violations of federal securities laws by an issuer of publicly traded securities (or a director, officer, or employee acting on its behalf) the SEC determines it is likely that the issuer will be required to make penalty payments, the SEC may petition a federal district court to require the issuer to escrow the payments in an interest-bearing account for 45 days.

6.3 Authority of the SEC to Prohibit Persons From Serving as Officers or Directors

For any cease-and-desist proceedings, the SEC may issue an order to conditionally or unconditionally prohibit an individual from serving as an officer or director of the issuer for a stipulated period (or permanently) if that individual has violated securities rules and regulations and the SEC determines that this individual is unfit to serve as an officer or director of an issuer.

6.4 Retaliation Against Informants

Any individual who knowingly takes any harmful action against another person with the intent to retaliate for that person providing truthful information to the SEC regarding a possible federal offense shall be fined and/or imprisoned for not more than 10 years.

Question 1	CPA-07014

Which of the following is necessary to be an audit committee financial expert, according to the criteria specified in the Sarbanes-Oxley Act of 2002?

    a. A limited understanding of generally accepted auditing standards.

    b. Education and experience as a certified financial planner.

    c. Experience with internal accounting controls.

    d. Experience in the preparation of tax returns.

Question 2	CPA-06491

Conflict-of-interest provisions of the Sarbanes-Oxley Act of 2002 generally prohibit the directors or executive officers of an issuer from:

    a. Owning more than 10 percent of common stock.

    b. Owning more than 10 percent of any form of equity.

    c. Receiving a personal loan from the issuer not in the ordinary course of business.

    d. Receiving perquisite compensation.

NOTES

Financial Risk Management: Part 1

1 Trade-offs Between Risk and Return

1.1 Definitions

Risk and return are a function of both market conditions and the risk preferences of the parties involved.

- **Risk:** May be defined as the chance of financial loss. More formally, the term "risk" may be used interchangeably with the term "uncertainty" to refer to the variability of returns associated with a given asset.

- **Return:** May be defined as the total gain or loss experienced on behalf of the owner of an asset over a given period. Typically, greater risk yields greater returns. The seller of financial securities compensates the buyer of financial securities with increased opportunity for profit by offering a higher rate of return.

1.2 Risk Preferences

Different managers have varying attitudes toward risk. Three basic risk preference behaviors exist:

- **Risk-Indifferent Behavior:** reflects an attitude toward risk in which an increase in the level of risk does not result in an increase in management's required rate of return.

- **Risk-Averse Behavior:** reflects an attitude toward risk in which an increase in the level of risk results in an increase in management's required rate of return. Risk-averse managers require higher expected returns to compensate for greater risk. Most managers are risk-averse.

- **Risk-Seeking Behavior:** reflects an attitude toward risk in which an increase in the level of risk results in a decrease in management's required rate of return. Risk-seeking managers are willing to settle for lower expected returns as the level of risk increases.

2 Types of Risk

Measurements of risk attempt to capture the multiple dimensions of risk. Risk exposures include interest rate, market, default, credit, liquidity, and price risk.

2.1 Interest Rate Risk (or Yield Risk)

Interest rate risk (or yield risk) is often used in the context of financial instruments and represents the exposure of the owner of the instrument to fluctuations in the value of the instrument in response to changes in interest rates.

Illustration 1   Interest Rate Risk

Thayer Thermodynamics Inc. owns a five-year, $10,000 Duffy International coupon bond purchased at a discount. Recently, the market rate of interest increased 1 percent, causing the market value of the bond to decline to $9,610. Assuming the bond's carrying value on the financial statements was $9,840 at the time the market rate of interest abruptly increased, Thayer Thermodynamics suffered a $230 market loss in bond value as a result of its exposure to interest rate risk.

2.2   Market/Systematic/Nondiversifiable Risk

The exposure of a security or firm to fluctuations in value as a result of operating within an economy is referred to as *market risk*. Market risk is sometimes referred to as *nondiversifiable risk* because it is a risk inherent in operating within the economy. Nondiversifiable risk is attributable to factors such as war, inflation, international incidents, and political events.

Illustration 2   Market Risk

The prices on publicly traded stocks generally increase and decrease together with overall market activity. Although the prices may not increase or decrease identically, they often move in the same direction. A technology company's stock, for example, might increase in value on a given day from $37.00 per share to $37.75 per share. This increase in the stock price is consistent with the overall 2 percent increase in the NASDAQ on that trading day.

2.3   Unsystematic/Firm-Specific/Diversifiable Risk

Diversifiable risk (which is also referred to as *nonmarket, unsystematic,* or *firm-specific risk*) represents the portion of a firm's or industry's risk that is associated with random causes and can be eliminated through diversification. Diversifiable risk is attributable to firm-specific or industry-specific events (e.g., strikes, lawsuits, regulatory actions, or the loss of a key account).

Pass Key

It is important to be able to classify risk into two broad categories:

D   Diversifiable risk

U   Unsystematic risk (nonmarket/firm-specific)

N   Nondiversifiable risk

S   Systematic risk (market)

Remember the mnemonic **DUNS** to keep these risk types and their alternative names clear.

2.4   Credit Risk

Credit risk affects borrowers. Exposure to credit risk includes a company's inability to secure financing or secure favorable credit terms as a result of poor credit ratings. As credit ratings decline, the interest rate demanded by lenders increases, collateral may be required, and other terms are generally less favorable to the borrower.

Illustration 3	Credit Risk

Duffy International seeks to borrow $10,000 for five years, but the company has a history of late payments and displays a high debt-to-income ratio and high debt-to-equity ratio (measurements discussed later). Although market rates of interest are 7 percent, lenders may only loan money to Duffy International at an 8 percent rate, require a lien on the company's inventory as collateral, and insist on shortening the term of the loan to three years. Duffy International's inability to borrow the funds it needs at the market rate of interest and under favorable terms illustrates the company's exposure to credit risk and demonstrates the creditors' attempt to mitigate default risk (see below).

2.5   Default Risk

Default risk affects lenders. Creditors are exposed to default risk to the extent that it is possible that its debtors may not repay the principal or interest due on their indebtedness on a timely basis.

Illustration 4	Default Risk

Thayer Thermodynamics Inc. (TTI) holds $100,000 worth of $1,000 face value bonds recently issued by Duffy International. During the third quarter of the year, Duffy fails to make its quarterly interest payment on its outstanding bond issue. The loss incurred by TTI results from the company's exposure to default risk or the possibility that the debtor will not make its debt service payments as outlined in the bond agreement (indenture).

2.6   Liquidity Risk

Liquidity risk affects lenders (investors). Lenders or investors are exposed to liquidity risk when they desire to sell their security, but cannot do so in a timely manner or when material price concessions have to be made to do so.

Illustration 5	Liquidity Risk

Smithfield Company holds several fixed-income securities of Johnson Manufacturing Company. Due to its current operational needs, Smithfield attempts to sell $250,000 of Johnson's 10-year bonds but is unsuccessful in attracting willing buyers at current market prices. As the company's working capital requirements increase, Smithfield significantly discounts the bonds to obtain the proceeds from the Johnson bond investments. Smithfield is exposed to liquidity risk, as evidenced by its inability to sell the bonds on a timely basis and the need to make concessions to attract willing investors.

2.7   Price Risk

Price Risk represents the exposure that investors have to a decline in the value of their individual securities or portfolios. Factors unique to individual investments and/or portfolios contribute to price risk, which becomes an even greater concern with increased market volatility. Price risk is related to diversifiable (unsystematic) risk.

3   Computation of Return

Return compensates investors and creditors for assumed risk. Return is often stated or measured by interest rates. Interest can be expressed as either a cost (interest expense) to debtors or income (interest income) to investors.

3.1   Stated Interest Rate

- **Definition:** The *stated interest rate* (sometimes referred to as nominal interest rate) represents the rate of interest charged before any adjustment for compounding or market factors.

- **Computation:** The *stated interest rate* is the rate shown in the agreement of indebtedness (e.g., a bond indenture or promissory note).

Example 1 ▸   Stated Interest Rate

Facts: A $10,000 promissory note states that payments will be made quarterly at a 10 percent interest rate per annum.

Required: Calculate the stated interest rate. *Hint:* You do not need a calculator.

Solution: Stated rate = 10 percent

3.2   Effective Interest Rate

- **Definition:** The *effective interest rate* represents the actual finance charge associated with a borrowing after reducing loan proceeds for charges and fees related to a loan origination.

- **Computation:** Effective interest rates are computed by dividing the amount of interest paid based on the loan agreement by the net proceeds received.

Example 2 ▸   Effective Interest Rate

Facts: A $10,000 promissory note has a stated rate of 10 percent per annum and is due in one year. The bank charges a loan origination fee of $75 and the state in which the loan is made levies a $50 documentary stamp charge. Taxes and fees are taken from loan proceeds.

Required: Compute the effective interest rate.

Solution:

Interest paid (10,000 × 10%)	$ 1,000
Divided by net proceeds (10,000 − 75 − 50)	÷ 9,875
Effective interest rate	10.13%

3.3   Annual Percentage Rate

- **Definition:** The *annual percentage rate* of interest represents a noncompounded version of the effective annual percentage rate described and computed below. The annual percentage rate is the rate required for disclosure by federal regulations.

- **Computation:** Annual percentage rates are computed as the effective periodic interest rate times the number of periods in a year. Annual percentage rate emphasizes the amount paid relative to funds available.

Example 3   Annual Percentage Rate

Facts: A $10,000 promissory note displays a stated rate of 8 percent with interest to be paid semiannually. The bank charges a $75 loan origination fee and a documentary tax of $50 is assessed by the state.

Required: Calculate the annual percentage rate.

Solution:

Step 1: Compute the effective periodic interest rate (as per above)

Interest paid (10,000 × 8% × 6/12)	$ 400
Divided by available funds (10,000 − 75 − 50)	÷ 9,875
Effective periodic interest rate	4.05%

Step 2: Multiply the effective periodic interest rate by the number of periods in a year

Effective periodic interest rate	4.05%
Periods in a year	× 2
Annual percentage rate	8.10%

3.4   Effective Annual Percentage Rate

- **Definition:** The *effective annual percentage rate* represents the stated interest rate adjusted for the number of compounding periods per year. The effective annual percentage rate is abbreviated APR.

- **Computation:** The effective APR is computed as follows:

$$\text{Effective annual interest rate} = [1 + (i/p)]^p - 1$$

i = Stated interest rate

p = Compounding periods per year

Example 4	Effective Annual Percentage Rate

Facts: A note has an 8 percent stated rate of interest compounded semiannually (two times per year).

Required: Compute the effective annual percentage rate or APR.

Solution:

Effective annual interest rate = $[1 + (i/p)]^p - 1$

Effective annual interest rate = $[1 + (0.08/2)]^2 - 1$

Effective annual interest rate = $[1 + (0.04)]^2 - 1$

Effective annual interest rate = $1.0816 - 1$

Effective annual interest rate = 8.16%

3.5 Simple Interest (Amount)

■   **Definition:** Simple interest is the amount represented by interest paid only on the original amount of principal without regard to compounding.

■   **Computation:** Simple interest is formulated as follows:

$$SI = P_0(i)(n)$$

$$P_0 = \text{Original principal}$$

$$i = \text{Interest rate per time period}$$

$$n = \text{Number of time periods}$$

Example 5	Simple Interest

Facts: A $10,000 promissory note bears simple interest at 8 percent for two years.

Required: What is the simple interest on this obligation?

Solution:

$SI = P_0(i)(n)$

$SI = \$10,000(8\%)(2)$

$SI = \$1,600$

3.6   Compound Interest (Amount)

- **Definition:** Compound interest is the amount represented by interest earnings or expense that is based on the original principal plus any unpaid interest earnings or expense. Interest earnings or expense, therefore, compounds and yields an amount higher than simple interest.

- **Computation:** Compound interest is computed as a future value as follows:

$$FV_n = P_0(1 + i)^n$$

P_0 = Original principal

i = Interest rate

n = Number of periods

Example 6   Compound Interest

Facts: A promissory note for $10,000 carries an interest rate of 8 percent for two years, compounded annually.

Required: Compute the maturity value of the promissory note.

Solution:

$FV_n = P_0(1 + i)^n$

$FV_n = \$10,000(1 + 0.08)^2$

$FV_n = \$10,000(1.1664)$

$FV_n = \$11,664$

3.7   Required Rate of Return

The required rate of return is calculated adding the following risk premiums to the risk-free rate:

- **Maturity Risk Premium (MRP):** Is the compensation that investors demand for exposure to interest rate risk over time. This risk increases with the term to maturity.

- **Purchasing Power Risk or Inflation Premium (IP):** Is the compensation investors require to bear the risk that price levels will change and affect asset values or the purchasing power of invested dollars (e.g., real estate).

- **Liquidity Risk Premium (LP):** Is the additional compensation demanded by lenders (investors) for the risk that an investment security (e.g., junk bonds) cannot be sold on a short notice without making significant price concessions. Liquidity is defined as the ability to quickly convert an asset to cash at fair market value.

- **Default Risk Premium (DRP):** Is the additional compensation demanded by lenders (investors) for bearing the risk that the issuer of the security will fail to pay interest and/or principal due on a timely basis.

Module 4   B1–43

Illustration 6	**Default Risk Premium**

A bank desires to purchase a corporate bond for its investment portfolio. Given the characteristics of the bond issue/issuer and current financial market conditions, a required rate of return of 8 percent is deemed appropriate for the bond issue, as follows:

	Real rate of return	3%
+	Inflation premium (IP)	2%
	Nominal rate of return	5%
+	Risk premium:	
	Interest rate risk (MRP)	
	Liquidity risk (LP)	
	Default risk (DRP)	3%
	Required rate of return	8%

4 Mitigating and Controlling Financial Risk

Business entities must be able to not only identify and assess various financial risks, but also implement strategies to mitigate and control the impact these risks can have on their operations and finances.

4.1 Diversification

Diversifiable risk represents the portion of a single asset's risk that is associated with random causes and can be eliminated through diversification. Diversification is the process of building a portfolio of investments of different and offsetting risks. Although diversification can reduce certain risks, business are exposed to risks that cannot be managed through diversification (i.e., nondiversifiable risks). A diversified investor should be concerned only with nondiversifiable (systematic) risk because, in theory, an investor can create a portfolio of assets that eliminates all (or virtually all) diversifiable risk.

4.2 Strategies to Mitigate and Control Specific Financial Risks

Companies use many different strategies to reduce their exposure and vulnerability to the various financial risks.

4.2.1 Mitigating Interest Rate Risk

An investor can mitigate interest rate risk by investing in floating rate debt securities, which do not change in value when interest rates change and also generate higher coupon payments when interest rates rise. Derivatives such as forward rate agreements (FRAs) or interest rate swaps, in which the investor pays a fixed interest rate and receives a floating interest rate, can also be used to mitigate interest rate risk.

Illustration 7   Interest Rate Swap

East Company has invested in $1,000,000 of 8 percent fixed rate bonds. East expects interest rates to increase during the next 12 months. On January 1, East Company enters into an interest rate swap with West Company in which East Company agrees to make to West Company a series of future payments equal to the fixed interest rate of 8 percent on the principal amount of $1,000,000. In exchange, West Company agrees to make to East Company a series of future payments equal to a floating interest rate of LIBOR* + 1 percent on the principal amount of $1,000,000.

Underlying:	East Company—8%, and West Company—LIBOR + 1%
Notional amount:	$1,000,000
Initial net investment:	$0 (no cost to enter into the swap contract)
Settlement amount:	East Company—8% × $1,000,000 = $80,000, and West Company—(LIBOR + 1%) × $1,000,000

On the first settlement date, LIBOR was 8.5 percent and the following amounts were exchanged:

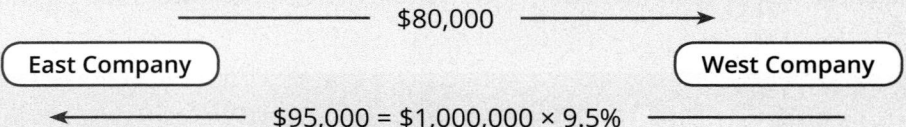

Derivatives generally have multiple settlement options. This derivative could be settled in the following ways:

1. East Company could pay $80,000 to West Company, and West Company could pay $95,000 to East Company.

2. West Company could pay $15,000 ($95,000 − $80,000) to East Company. This is a net settlement and is the most likely form of settlement in this example.

*LIBOR (London Interbank Offered Rate) is a benchmark rate that some of the world's leading banks charge each other for short-term loans.

4.2.2 Mitigating Market Risk

Market risk, because it is inherent in the marketplace and overall economy, is not as easy to mitigate. Market risk cannot be mitigated through diversification. One way to control market risk is to invest in derivatives that provide gains to the investor when the market declines. Short selling (selling an investment in the hopes of buying it back at a lower price later) is another strategy that provides returns when the market declines.

Illustration 8   Short Sale

The CFO of Dillon Bank is concerned that falling oil prices may lead to an overall stock market decline in the coming months. In order to protect the bank's investment portfolios against a market decline, the CFO opens several short positions in index funds designed to track the S&P 500. She will earn a profit if the market does decline, as she can buy back the funds at lower prices. However, if the market rises, she will eventually have to buy back the funds at higher prices than the original sale price.

4.2.3 Mitigating Unsystematic Risk

Unsystematic risk can be minimized through diversification. If an investor has a broad portfolio of investments, then an event that has a negative effect on one firm, industry, or investment type would have less of an effect on the value of the portfolio as a whole.

4.2.4 Mitigating Credit Risk

Credit risk is managed through improvements in credit ratings, which are assigned at entity and individual debt levels. When credit ratings are higher, borrowing can occur at more favorable terms (such as lower interest rates). Factors evaluated in determining credit ratings include overall economic outlook, industry conditions, cash flow measures, leverage, capital structure, management strength, historical performance, and financial ratios measuring solvency, liquidity, profitability, etc. Management has various degrees of control over these factors, but awareness of them and understanding of how changes can affect credit ratings are crucial to controlling this risk.

4.2.5 Mitigating Default Risk

Default risk can be mitigated in several ways. As a lender, an entity may choose to lend only to borrowers with low risk of default. Another option is to adjust the interest rates charged to better reflect the risk of each borrower, such that higher-risk borrowers will pay higher interest rates.

> **Illustration 9 Default Risk**
>
> Miller Inc. wants to reduce its default risk and is considering two plans. Miller can either reduce the population of potential customers by extending credit to customers with credit ratings only above a certain threshold, or it can continue extending credit to all customers but charge higher interest rates to borrowers that pose greater risks of not paying back money owed.

4.2.6 Mitigating Liquidity Risk

Liquidity risk is higher for investments that don't have active markets (e.g., forward contracts, limited partnerships). Liquidity risk is mitigated by allocating a greater percentage of capital to investments that trade on active markets, such as equities, corporate bonds, futures contracts, and options.

4.2.7 Mitigating Price Risk

Price risk can be minimized through diversification. Price risk also can be mitigated through short selling or derivatives, such as put options.

Illustration 10   Put Option

Roberts Company owns 10,000 shares of Buy Big Inc. stock. Roberts plans to sell the stock during January and is concerned that the price of the stock will fall below the current price of $75/share. On January 1, Roberts purchased a put option on the stock of Buy Big. The option gives Roberts the right to sell the 10,000 shares of Buy Big stock at $75/share during the next 30 days. Roberts paid a premium of $2/share to enter into the option. Roberts exercises the option when Buy Big stock was selling for $69/share.

Underlying:	$75/share
Notional amount:	10,000 shares of Buy Big stock
Initial net investment:	$2/share × 10,000 shares = $20,000
Settlement amount:	$75/share × 10,000 shares = $750,000

Derivatives generally have multiple settlement options. This derivative could be settled in the following ways:

1. Roberts could deliver 10,000 shares of Buy Big stock to the option writer in exchange for $750,000. Roberts would realize a gain of $60,000 [($75/share exercise price − $69/share market price) × 10,000 shares. The option writer would realize a loss of $60,000 because the option writer must pay $75/share for stock with a market value of $69/share.

2. The option writer could pay Roberts $60,000 to settle the contract. This is a net settlement.

Because $20,000 was paid to purchase the put option, Roberts will report a net gain of $40,000 ($60,000 gain − $20,000 premium). If the stock price had remained above $75/share during the 30-day period, Roberts would not have exercised the option and would have sold the stock for the market price.

Question 1   CPA-05788

A company has an outstanding one-year bank loan of $500,000 at a stated interest rate of 8 percent. The company is required to maintain a 20 percent compensating balance in its checking account. The company would maintain a zero balance in this account if the requirement did not exist. What is the effective interest rate of the loan?

a. 8 percent

b. 10 percent

c. 20 percent

d. 28 percent

NOTES

1 Currency Exchange Rate Risk

Within domestic environments, a single currency defines the value of assets, liabilities, and operating transactions. In international settings, the values of assets, liabilities, and operating transactions are established not only in terms of the single currency, but also in relation to other currencies. Exchange rate (FX) risk exists because the relationship between domestic and foreign currencies may be subject to volatility.

1.1 Factors Influencing Exchange Rates

Circumstances that give rise to changes in exchange rates are generally divided between trade-related factors (including differences in inflation, income, and government regulation) and financial factors (including differences in interest rates and restrictions on capital movements between companies).

1.1.1 Trade Factor (Relative Inflation Rates)

When domestic inflation exceeds foreign inflation, holders of domestic currency are motivated to purchase foreign currency to maintain the purchasing power of their money. The increase in demand for foreign currency forces the value of the foreign currency to rise in relation to the domestic currency, thereby changing the rate of exchange between the domestic and foreign currency.

Illustration 1	Relative Inflation Rates

Assume that the U.S. dollar is relatively stable while the Mexican peso is suffering from sudden inflationary pressures. As the Mexican peso buys less in the domestic Mexican economy, Mexicans and their banking institutions seek the safe haven of the U.S. dollar to maintain the purchasing power of their liquid resources. The demand for U.S. dollars created by Mexicans buying them with Mexican pesos makes the U.S. dollar more valuable in terms of the peso and drives up the exchange rate. The U.S. dollar commands more pesos in an exchange of currency.

1.1.2 Trade Factor (Relative Income Levels)

As income increases in one country relative to another, exchange rates change as a result of increased demand for foreign currencies in the country in which income is increasing.

Illustration 2   Relative Income Levels

The income level in the United States increases significantly in the second quarter. Americans flock to Mexico City on vacation to buy piñatas. The increased supply of American dollars seeking to buy pesos to purchase Mexican goods causes the value of the American dollar to fall in relation to a stated number of pesos. The exchange rate is thus affected by relative income levels and the associated demand for foreign currency created by higher domestic income.

1.1.3 Trade Factor (Government Controls)

Various trade and exchange barriers that artificially suppress the natural forces of supply and demand affect exchange rates.

Illustration 3   Government Controls

A tariff on imported piñatas would have the effect of discouraging the purchase of imports, thereby reducing demand for the peso and maintaining the exchange rate.

1.1.4 Financial Factors (Relative Interest Rates and Capital Flows)

Interest rates create demand for currencies by motivating either domestic or foreign investments. The forces of supply and demand create changes in the exchange rate as investors seek fixed returns. The effect of interest rates is directly affected by the volume of capital that is allowed to flow between countries.

Illustration 4   Relative Interest Rates and Capital Flows

Assume that returns on institutional investments in Mexico skyrocket in the third quarter while returns on comparable institutional investments remain significantly lower in the United States. U.S. investors find the opportunity to earn high returns with similar risks in Mexican financial institutions irresistible. The demand for pesos increases as American investment increases. The exchange rate changes as the peso commands more U.S dollars.

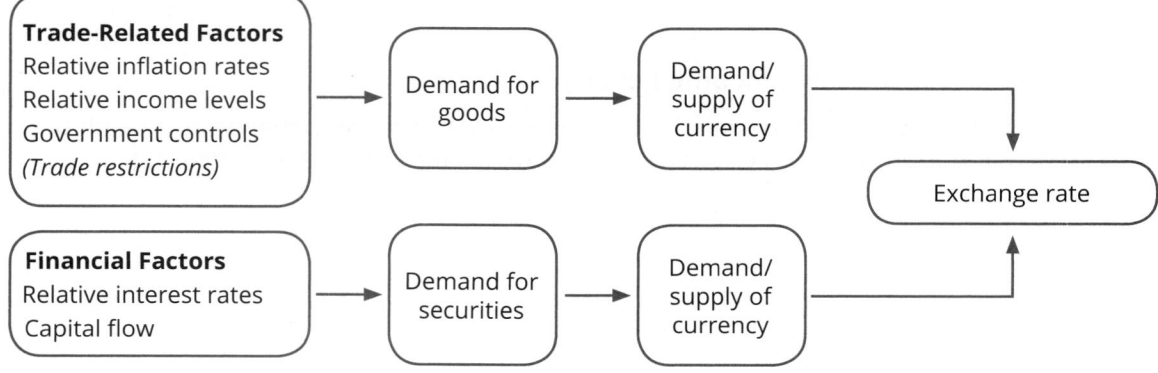

Summary Chart: Circumstances That Impact Exchange Rates

Trade-Related Factors
Relative inflation rates
Relative income levels
Government controls
(Trade restrictions)

Demand for goods

Demand/ supply of currency

Exchange rate

Financial Factors
Relative interest rates
Capital flow

Demand for securities

Demand/ supply of currency

1.2   Risk Exposure Categories

1.2.1   Transaction Exposure

Exchange rate risk is defined, in part, by *transaction exposure*. Transaction exposure is defined as the potential that an organization could suffer economic loss or experience economic gain upon settlement of individual transactions as a result of changes in the exchange rates. Transaction exposure is generally measured in relation to currency variability or currency correlation. Measurement of transaction exposure is generally done in two steps:

1.   Project foreign currency inflows and foreign currency outflows.

2.   Estimate the variability (risk) associated with the foreign currency.

Illustration 5   Transaction Exposure

Seattle Import/Export, a U.S. import/export company, imports commodities from Canada that it pays for in Canadian dollars and exports commodities to Canada for which it receives Canadian dollars. If Seattle Import/Export anticipated that it would export C\$10,000,000 to Canada over the next year while importing C\$8,000,000 over the same period, the net exposure in Canadian dollars is a C\$2,000,000 inflow (receivable).

If the current exchange rate is \$0.75/C\$1, the net exposure in U. S. dollars is \$1,500,000 (C\$2,000,000 × 0.75). If the rate is anticipated to fluctuate five cents, between \$0.70 and \$0.80, the total U.S. dollar fluctuation exposure would be expected to be between \$1,400,000 and \$1,600,000.

1.2.2   Economic Exposure

In addition to transaction exposure, exchange rate risk is defined, in part, by *economic exposure*. Economic exposure is defined as the potential that the present value of an organization's cash flows could increase or decrease as a result of changes in the exchange rates. Economic exposure is generally defined through local currency appreciation or depreciation and is measured in relation to organization earnings and cash flows.

▪ **Currency Appreciation and Depreciation**

Currency appreciation (depreciation) refers to the strengthening (weakening) of a currency in relation to other currencies.

• **Effect of Currency Appreciation**

As a domestic currency appreciates in value or becomes stronger, it becomes more expensive in terms of a foreign currency. As a currency appreciates, the volume of outflows tends to decline as domestic exports become more expensive. However, the volume of inflows tends to increase as foreign imports become less expensive.

• **Effect of Currency Depreciation**

As a domestic currency depreciates in value or becomes weaker, it becomes less expensive in terms of a foreign currency. As a currency depreciates, the volume of outflows tends to rise as domestic exports become less expensive. However, the volume of inflows tends to decline as foreign imports become more expensive.

The economic exposure created by domestic currency appreciation or depreciation with respect to a foreign currency depends on the net inflow or outflow of foreign currency.

1.2.3 Translation Exposure

In addition to the transaction and economic exposures, exchange rate risk is defined in part by *translation exposure*. Translation exposure is the risk that assets, liabilities, equity, or income of a consolidated organization that includes foreign subsidiaries will change as a result of changes in exchange rates. Translation exposure is generally defined by the degree of foreign involvement, the location of foreign subsidiaries, and the accounting methods used and measured in relation to the effect on the organization's earnings or comprehensive income.

■ **Degree of Foreign Involvement**: Translation exposure increases as the proportion of foreign involvement by subsidiaries increases.

Illustration 6   Translation Risk

Domestic International Inc. has no foreign subsidiaries but is deeply involved in exporting to neighboring countries. Global International Inc. has 12 foreign subsidiaries which, combined, make up 65 percent of consolidated revenues. Domestic International has less translation exposure than Global International because it has no foreign subsidiaries. Domestic's international business does expose the company to exchange rate risks, however, in terms of both transaction and economic exposure.

Because of Global International's extensive foreign operations, the parent company has significant exposure to foreign currency translation exposure, and depending on the entity's export/import activity, Global International may also be exposed to foreign exchange transaction and economic risks.

■ **Locations of Foreign Investments:** Measurements of financial results of foreign investments frequently occur in the foreign currency in which the investee company operates. The exposure of the parent company to translation risk is affected by the stability of the foreign currency in comparison to the parent's domestic currency. The more stable the exchange rate, the lower the translation risk. The more volatile the exchange rate, the higher the translation risk.

2 Mitigating and Controlling Transaction Exposure

Businesses have various methods of managing the transaction exposure associated with exchange rate risks. The use of financial instruments and hedging attempts to mitigate the effect of exchange rate fluctuations on individual transactions. The following discussion analyzes hedging as it relates to foreign currency transactions.

2.1 Measuring Specific Net Transaction Exposure

Net transaction exposure is the amount of gain or loss that might result from either a favorable or an unfavorable settlement of a transaction.

2.1.1 Selective Hedging

Hedging is a financial risk management technique in which an organization, seeking to mitigate the risk of fluctuations in value, acquires a financial instrument that behaves in the opposite manner from the hedged item. In effect, hedging is a process of reducing the uncertainty of the future value of a transaction or position (e.g., asset, liability, income) by actively engaging in various derivative investments.

Illustration 7   Hedging

Worldwide Sweet Peaches buys shipping crates for its product from Mexico. The company incurs liabilities denominated in pesos that it satisfies in pesos bought with U.S. dollars at the time of transaction settlement. The company incurs a significant liability in pesos at a spot rate of $0.10. Worldwide management expects that the peso will strengthen to $0.20 by the time the bill is due and thereby double its cost. To mitigate this perceived transaction risk, the company decides to hedge its position by locking in the current peso spot rate of $0.10.

2.1.2 Identifying Net Transaction Exposure

Consolidated entities consider their net transaction exposure prior to considering hedge strategies. Net transaction exposure considers the effect of transaction exposure on the entity taken as a whole rather than on individual subsidiaries. Although exchange rate issues might adversely affect one subsidiary, they might favorably affect another. The net transaction exposure is the aggregate exposure associated with a particular foreign currency for a particular time and is computed as follows:

1. Accumulate the inflows and outflows of foreign currencies by subsidiary.

2. Consolidate the effects on the subsidiary by currency type.

3. Compute the net effect in total.

2.1.3 Adjusting Invoice Policies

International companies may hedge transactions without complex instruments by timing the payment for imports with the collection from exports.

2.2 Mitigating Transaction Exposure: Futures Hedge

A *futures hedge* entitles its holder to either purchase or sell a particular number of currency units of an identified currency for a negotiated price on a stated date. Futures hedges are denominated in standard amounts and tend to be used for smaller transactions.

2.2.1 Accounts Payable Application

■ Accounts payable denominated in a foreign currency represents a potential transaction exposure to exchange rate risk in the event that the *domestic currency weakens* in relation to the foreign currency. Should the domestic currency weaken relative to the foreign currency, more domestic currency will be required to purchase the foreign currency, thereby increasing the company's cost of settling the liability. If management does not hedge this liability exposure, the company will incur a foreign exchange transaction loss.

- A *futures hedge contract* to buy the foreign currency at a specific price at the time the account payable is due will mitigate the risk of a weakening domestic currency.

Illustration 8   Futures Contract

Worldwide Sweet Peaches buys crates from Mexico. On the date that Worldwide Sweet Peaches buys crates and incurs a significant liability in pesos, the spot rate is $0.10. Because the company fears that the peso will strengthen to $0.20 by the time the bill is due in 30 days, the company enters into a futures contract that will allow it to purchase the pesos needed to pay the liability for $0.10 per peso in 30 days.

2.2.2   Accounts Receivable Application

- Accounts receivable denominated in a foreign currency represent a potential transaction exposure to exchange rate risk in the event that the *domestic currency strengthens* in relation to the foreign currency. Should the domestic currency strengthen, less domestic currency (than originally anticipated from the sale that created the receivable) can be purchased with the foreign currency received. An exchange loss will result.

- A *futures hedge contract to sell* the foreign currency received in satisfaction of the receivable at a specific price at the time the accounts receivable is due will mitigate the risk of a strengthening domestic currency.

Illustration 9   Futures Hedge Contract

Running Apparel International, a U.S.-based retailer, has international retail operations in several countries, including significant business in Japan. Company management expects that the Japanese retail operations will generate and liquidate a significant amount of its accounts receivables in 30 days. Although the current $/¥ spot rate is $1/¥98.02, company management expects the $/¥ spot rate to be $1/¥102.09 in 30 days. To mitigate this expected foreign exchange loss caused by the appreciation of the U.S. dollar (relative to the Japanese yen), the company enters into a futures contract to sell yen at the current spot rate ($1/¥98.02) in 30 days, thereby locking in the current value of these foreign receivables.

2.3   Mitigating Transaction Exposure: Forward Hedge

A *forward hedge* is similar to a futures hedge in that it entitles its holder to either purchase or sell currency units of an identified currency for a negotiated price at a future point. Although futures hedges tend to be used for smaller transactions, forward hedges are contracts between businesses and commercial banks and normally are larger transactions. Although a futures hedge might hedge a particular transaction, a forward hedge would anticipate a company's needs to either buy or sell a foreign currency at a particular point.

2.3.1   Accounts Payable Application

- Accounts payable denominated in a foreign currency represent a potential transaction exposure to exchange rate risk in the event that the *foreign currency strengthens*.

- A *forward hedge contract to buy* the foreign currency at a specific price at the time accounts payable are due for an entire subsidiary will mitigate the risk of a weakening domestic currency.

2.3.2   Accounts Receivable Application

▪ Accounts receivable denominated in a foreign currency represent a potential transaction exposure to exchange rate risk in the event that the *domestic currency strengthens*.

▪ A *forward hedge contract to sell* the foreign currency received in satisfaction of the receivables at a specific price at the time the accounts receivable are due or on the monthly cycle of a particular subsidiary will mitigate the risk of a strengthening domestic currency.

2.4   Mitigating Transaction Exposure: Money Market Hedge

A *money market hedge* uses international money markets to plan to meet future currency requirements. A money market hedge uses domestic currency to purchase a foreign currency at current spot rates and invest them in securities timed to mature at the same time as related payables.

2.4.1   Money Market Hedge: Payables (Excess Cash)

Firms with excess cash use money market hedges to lock in the exchange rate associated with the foreign currency needed to satisfy payables when they come due. Money market hedges for payables satisfaction include the following steps:

1. Determine the amount of the payable.

2. Determine the amount of interest that can be earned prior to settling the payable.

3. Discount the amount of the payable to the net investment required.

4. Purchase the amount of foreign currency equal to the net investment required and deposit the proceeds in the appropriate money market vehicle.

Illustration 10   Money Market Hedge: Payables (Excess Cash)

Duffy's Discount Piñatas has a payable due to its Mexican suppliers in the amount of 1,000,000 pesos in 90 days. The current exchange rate is $0.08 per peso and Mexican interest rates are 16 percent. Duffy has $100,000 in excess cash and elects to use a money market hedge to mitigate transaction exposure to exchange rate risk. Duffy performs the following steps:

1. Determine the required investment in pesos at Mexican interest rates: 1,000,000 / 1.04 = 961,538.

   (**Note:** A 16 percent annual interest rate for 90 days is equal to approximately 4 percent).

2. Purchase 961,538 pesos with $76,923 (961,538 pesos × 0.08).

3. Invest pesos at Mexican interest rates and satisfy payables upon maturity of the investment.

Duffy has secured the satisfaction of its current $80,000 payable for $76,923.

2.4.2   Money Market Hedge: Payables (Borrowed Funds)

Firms that do not have excess cash follow the same basic procedure for a money market hedge on payables, except that they first borrow funds domestically and invest them internationally to satisfy the payable denominated in a foreign currency.

Illustration 11 — Money Market Hedge: Payables (Borrowed Funds)

Duffy's Discount Piñatas has a payable due to its Mexican suppliers in the amount of 1,000,000 pesos in 90 days. The current exchange rate is $0.08 per peso, Mexican interest rates are 16 percent, and U.S. interest rates are 6 percent. Duffy computes that it must borrow $76,923 to use a money market hedge to mitigate transaction exposure to exchange rate risk consistent with the first money market hedge example, but has no excess cash. Duffy borrows the needed amount for 90 days in the United States.

Duffy has secured the satisfaction of its current $80,000 payable for $78,077 (76,923 × 1.015 or 6% for 90 days).

2.4.3 Money Market Hedge: Receivables

A money market hedge used for receivables denominated in foreign currencies effectively involves factoring receivables with foreign bank loans. Foreign currency amounts are borrowed in discounted amounts that are repaid in the ultimate maturity value of the receivable denominated in the foreign currency. Borrowed foreign currency amounts are converted into the domestic currency.

Illustration 12 — Money Market Hedge: Receivables

Duffy's Discount Piñatas has a receivable from a Mexican customer in the amount of 1,000,000 pesos due in 90 days. The current exchange rate is $0.08 per peso and Mexican interest rates are 16 percent. Duffy needs available cash and cannot wait to receive $80,000 in 90 days. Because Duffy needs the money now, the company elects to use a money market hedge technique to expedite collection and mitigate any transaction exposure to exchange rate risk.

Duffy computes that it can borrow 961,538 pesos and convert them to $76,923 consistent with the first money market hedge example. Duffy borrows the pesos from Mexican financial institutions.

Duffy will be able to meet whatever its current cash requirements are in the United States with the $76,923, and when the 90-day discounted note for 961,538 pesos matures for 1,000,000 pesos, Duffy will satisfy it with the collections from the foreign accounts receivable.

2.5 Mitigating Transaction Exposure: Currency Option Hedges

Currency option hedges use the same principles as forward hedge contracts and money market hedge transactions. However, instead of requiring a commitment to a transaction, the currency option hedge gives the business the option of executing the option contract or purely settling its originally negotiated transaction without the benefit of the hedge, depending on which result is most favorable.

2.5.1 Currency Option Hedges: Payables

A call option (an option to buy) is the currency option hedge used to mitigate the transaction exposure associated with exchange rate risk for payables.

- Similar to a futures contract or forward contract, the business plans to buy a foreign currency at a low rate in anticipation of the foreign currency strengthening in comparison to the domestic currency in order to ensure that it can settle its liability at the predicted value.

■ The business has the option (not the obligation) to purchase the security at the option (strike or exercise) price. The business evaluates the relationship between the option price and the exchange rate at the settlement date. Generally, if the option price is less than the exchange rate at the time of settlement, the business will exercise its option. If the option price is more than the exchange rate at the time of settlement, the business will allow the option to expire. Although option premiums are used to compute any net savings associated with option transactions, they are a sunk cost and are irrelevant to the decision to exercise the options.

Example 1	Currency Option Hedge: Payables

Facts: Gearty International owes its Mexican supplier 1,000,000 pesos due in 30 days. Although the peso is currently exchanged for the U.S. dollar at $0.08, the company is fearful that the Mexican peso will strengthen in comparison to the dollar before the settlement to as much as $0.10. Gearty International pays a $0.005 option premium to secure a call option to buy 1,000,000 pesos in 30 days for $0.08/peso.

Required: Compute Gearty's net savings, assuming that Gearty is correct in its assessment of international exchange rates and the exchange rate at the time of the settlement (the spot rate) increases as predicted.

Solution:

Spot Rate at Settlement	Option Price	Premium	Total Option	Settlement Cost for 1,000,000 Pesos
$0.10	–	–	–	$100,000
–	$0.08	$0.005	$0.085	(85,000)
Net savings				$ 15,000

Gearty's consideration for the option, the $0.005 option premium, is $5,000 and is paid regardless of whether the option is exercised. The gross savings of $20,000 [(0.10 − 0.08) × 1,000,000 pesos] is reduced by the $5,000 option premium to reflect a $15,000 net savings. Because the option premium is a sunk cost, it does not affect the company's decision to exercise the call option.

Facts: Same as above

Required: Calculate Gearty's loss, assuming that Gearty is incorrect in its assessment of international exchange rates, the exchange rates stay constant at $0.08, and the company allows its option to expire.

Solution:

Spot Rate at Settlement	Option Price	Premium	Total Option	Settlement Cost for 1,000,000 Pesos
$0.08	–	–	–	$80,000
–	$0.08	$0.005	$0.085	(85,000)
Loss				$ (5,000)

Exercising the option is actually equal to simply settling the transaction at the spot rate. Gearty will likely buy pesos at the spot rate regardless of the loss associated with the premium.

2.5.2 Currency Option Hedges: Receivables

A put option (an option to sell) is the currency option hedge used to mitigate the transaction exposure associated with exchange rate risk for receivables.

- Similar to a futures contract or forward contract, the business plans to sell a foreign currency at a higher rate, in anticipation of the foreign currency weakening in comparison to the domestic currency, to ensure that it can capitalize on receivable collections at a stable or predicted value.

- The business has the option (not the obligation) to sell the collected amount of the foreign currency from the receivable at the option (strike or exercise) price. The business evaluates the relationship between the option price and the exchange rate at the settlement date. Generally, if the option price is more than the exchange rate at the time of settlement, the business will exercise its put option. If the put option price is less than the exchange rate at the time of settlement, the business will allow the put option to expire. Although premiums are used to compute any net preserved value associated with option transactions, they are a sunk cost and irrelevant to the decision to exercise the options.

Example 2 — Currency Options Hedge: Receivables

Facts: Gearty International is owed 1,000,000 pesos due in 30 days from its Mexican customer. Although the peso is currently exchanged for the U.S. dollar at $0.08, the company is fearful that the Mexican peso will weaken in comparison to the dollar before the settlement to as little as $0.06. Gearty International pays a $0.005 put premium to secure a put option to sell 1,000,000 pesos in 30 days for $0.08.

Required: Compute the net preserved value assuming that Gearty is correct in its assessment of international exchange rates and the exchange rate at the time of the settlement (the spot rate) decreases.

Solution:

Spot Rate at Settlement	Option Price	Premium	Total Option	Settlement Cost for 1,000,000 Pesos
$0.06	–	–	–	$(60,000)
–	$0.08	$0.005	$0.075	75,000
Net preserved value				$ 15,000

Gearty's consideration for the put option, the $0.005 put premium, is $5,000 and is paid regardless of whether the put option is exercised. The gross value "preserved" of $20,000 [(0.08 − 0.06) × 1,000,000 pesos] is reduced by the $5,000 put premium paid to reflect a net $15,000 preserved receivable value. Because the put premium is a sunk cost, it is not included in the decision to exercise the option.

(continued)

(continued)

Facts: Same as above

Required: Calculate Gearty's loss, assuming that Gearty is incorrect in its assessment of international exchange rates, the exchange rates stay constant at $0.08, and Gearty allows the put option to expire.

Solution:

Spot Rate at Settlement	Option Price	Premium	Total Option	Settlement Cost for 1,000,000 Pesos
$0.08	–	–	–	$(80,000)
–	$0.08	$0.005	$0.075	75,000
Loss				$ (5,000)

Exercising the put option would actually be equal to simply settling the transaction at the spot rate when the receivables are received. Gearty will likely sell pesos at the spot rate regardless of the loss associated with the premium.

2.6 Mitigating Transaction Exposure: Long-Term Transactions

The following hedge transactions are used to mitigate exchange rate risk presented by transaction exposure.

2.6.1 Long-Term Forward Contracts

Mechanically, *long-term forward contracts* deal with the same issues as any other forward contracts. Long-term forward contracts are set up to stabilize transaction exposure over long periods. Long-term purchase contracts may be hedged with long-term forward contracts.

2.6.2 Currency Swaps

Transaction exposure associated with exchange rate risk for longer-term transactions can be mitigated with *currency swaps*.

- **Two Firms**

    Two firms with coincidental needs for international currencies may agree to swap currencies collected in a future period at a specified exchange rate. The two entities essentially swap their currencies in an exchange negotiation completed years in advance of their receipt of the currencies.

- **Financial Intermediaries**

    Typically, financial intermediaries are contacted to broker or to match firms with currency needs.

- **Parallel Loan**

    Two firms may mitigate their transaction exposure to long-term exchange rate loss by exchanging or swapping their domestic currencies for a foreign currency and simultaneously agreeing to re-exchange or repurchase their domestic currency at a later date.

Example 3	Currency Swap

Facts: In order to hedge its future raw material purchases for its operations, in Poland, a U.S. manufacturing firm (U.S. counterparty) agrees to enter into a currency swap with a Polish multinational firm (foreign counterparty) whereby the U.S. counterparty agrees to provide the following quarterly notional amounts in U.S. dollars to the foreign counterparty in exchange for the following quarterly notional amounts in Polish zlotys.

Quarter End	U.S. Counterparty Receives	Foreign Counterparty Receives
1	1,500,000 zloty	500,000 USD
2	900,000 zloty	300,000 USD
3	750,000 zloty	250,000 USD
4	1,800,000 zloty	600,000 USD

Assume that the exchange rates are 3.25 zloty/1.0 USD and 2.85 zloty/1.0 USD at the end of quarter 1 and quarter 2, respectively.

Required: Calculate the U.S. manufacturing firm's foreign currency gain or loss recorded at the end of the first and second quarters on the currency swap.

Solution: The U.S. manufacturing firm (U.S. counterparty) entered into a fixed notional amount currency swap with a foreign counterparty when the exchange rates were 3.0 zloty/1.0 USD. Because the contractual quarterly payments made in U.S. dollars to the Polish firm are fixed at that exchange rate throughout the swap, any movement up or down of these two exchange rates will result in a foreign currency gain or loss.

In the first quarter, the U.S. dollar appreciates versus the Polish zloty, so the U.S. counterparty incurs a foreign currency loss. Under the terms of the currency swap, the U.S. counterparty pays 500,000 U.S. dollars and receives 1,500,000 zloty (based on an exchange rate of 3.0 zloty/1.0 USD). The 1,500,000 zloty received are worth only 461,538 U.S. dollars based on the end of quarter exchange rate of 3.25 zloty/1.0 USD:

> 1,500,000 / 3.25 = 461,538 USD

Paying 500,000 U.S. dollars and receiving zloty worth only 463,538 U.S. dollars represents a loss of 38,462 U.S. dollars:

> 500,000 − 461,538 = 38,462 USD

In the second quarter, the U.S. dollar depreciates versus the Polish zloty. As a result of the swap, the U.S. counterparty incurs a foreign currency gain. The U.S. counterparty pays 300,000 U.S. dollars and receives 900,000 zloty. The value in U.S. dollars of 900,000 zloty based on the end of quarter exchange rate of 2.85 zloty/1.0 USD is 315,789 U.S. dollars.

> 900,000 / 2.85 = 315,789

Paying 300,000 U.S. dollars and receiving zloty worth 315,789 U.S. dollars represents a gain of 15,789 in U.S. dollars:

> 315,789 − 300,000 = 15,789 USD

2.7   Mitigating Transaction Exposure: Alternative Hedging Techniques

The following hedge transactions are used to mitigate exchange rate risk presented by transaction exposure.

2.7.1   Leading and Lagging

Leading and lagging represent transactions between subsidiaries or a subsidiary and a parent. The entity that is owed may bill in advance if the exchange rate warrants (leading) or possibly wait until the exchange rate is favorable before settling (lagging).

2.7.2 Cross-Hedging

The technique known as *cross-hedging* involves hedging one instrument's risk with a different instrument by taking a position in a related derivatives contract. This is often done when there is no derivatives contract for the instrument being hedged, or when a suitable derivatives contract exists but the market is highly illiquid.

2.7.3 Currency Diversification

The simplest hedge for long-term transactions is to diversify foreign currency holdings over time. A substantial decline in the value of one currency would not affect the overall dollar value of the firm if the currency represented only one of many foreign currencies.

3 Mitigating and Controlling Economic and Translation Exposure

Businesses have various methods of managing the economic and translation exposure associated with exchange rate risks. Generally, the use of organization-wide solutions related to the entity itself and related reporting requirements are included in the approach.

3.1 Assessing Economic Exposure

Economic exposure is defined by the degree to which cash flows of the business can be affected by fluctuations in exchange rates. The extent to which revenues and expenses are denominated in different currencies could seriously affect the profitability of an organization and represents economic exposure.

Illustration 13   Economic Exposure

Pete's Primo Piñatas manufactures piñatas in Mexico. The company's expenses paid to local suppliers are denominated in the peso. The company exports nearly 80 percent of its product to the United States and receives revenues denominated in U.S. dollars from upscale Mexican theme-party planners. If the peso were to strengthen in relation to the dollar, then import revenues could be significantly less than domestic expenses. Pete's Primo Piñatas would suffer economic losses as a result of its economic exposure to exchange rate risk.

3.2 Techniques for Economic Exposure Mitigation

Economic exposures typically relate to organization-wide issues and can usually only be mitigated with organization-wide approaches that involve restructuring and adjustments to the business plan.

3.2.1 Restructuring

Economic exposure to currency fluctuations can be mitigated by restructuring the sources of income and expense to the consolidated entity.

- **Decreases in Sales**

  A company fearful of a depreciating foreign currency used by a foreign subsidiary may elect to reduce foreign sales to preserve cash flows.

■ **Increases in Expenses**

A company anticipating a depreciating foreign currency may elect to increase reliance on those suppliers to take advantage of paying for raw materials or supplies with cheaper currency.

3.2.2 Characteristics of Restructuring and Economic Exposure

Restructuring tends to be more difficult than ordinary hedges. Economic exposures to exchange rate fluctuations are viewed as more difficult to manage than transaction exposures.

Question 1	CPA-05860

If the dollar price of the euro rises, which of the following will occur?

 a. The dollar depreciates against the euro.

 b. The euro depreciates against the dollar.

 c. The euro will buy fewer European goods.

 d. The euro will buy fewer U.S. goods.

Question 2	CPA-05590

What is the effect when a foreign competitor's currency becomes weaker compared with the U.S. dollar?

 a. The foreign company will have an advantage in the U.S. market.

 b. The foreign company will be disadvantaged in the U.S. market.

 c. The fluctuation in the foreign currency's exchange rate has *no* effect on the U.S. company's sales or cost of goods sold.

 d. It is better for the U.S. company when the value of the U.S. dollar strengthens.

Question 3	CPA-05767

Platinum Co. has a receivable due in 30 days for 30,000 euros. The treasurer is concerned that the value of the euro relative to the dollar will drop before the payment is received. What should Platinum do to reduce this risk?

 a. Buy 30,000 euros now.

 b. Enter into an interest rate swap contract for 30 days.

 c. Enter into a forward contract to sell 30,000 euros in 30 days.

 d. Platinum cannot effectively reduce this risk.

BEC

2

Financial Management

Module

1 Capital Structure Components

An entity's capital structure is the mix of debt (long-term and short-term) and equity (common and preferred) used to finance operations and growth.

1.1 Debt Financing

Entities use various forms of short-term and long-term debt in their capital structures. Common forms of short-term debt include short-term notes payable, commercial paper, and line-of-credit arrangements. Long-term debt may include long-term notes payable, debentures, bonds, and finance leases.

1.1.1 Commercial Paper

Commercial paper is an unsecured, short-term debt instrument issued by a corporation. Commercial paper matures in 270 days or less (the threshold above which commercial paper must be registered with the SEC) and typically matures in 30 days. The proceeds from commercial paper must be used to finance current assets such as account receivable or inventory, or to meet short-term obligations.

1.1.2 Debentures

A debenture represents an unsecured obligation of the issuing company. In the event of default, the holder of a debenture has the status of a general creditor. Risks associated with debentures may be mitigated by a negative-pledge clause that stops a company from pledging assets to additional debt.

1.1.3 Subordinated Debentures

A subordinated debenture is a bond issue that is unsecured and ranks behind senior creditors in the event of an issuer liquidation. Subordinated debentures command higher interest rates than debentures to allow for additional risk.

1.1.4 Income Bonds

Income bonds represent securities that pay interest only upon achievement of target income levels. Income bonds represent a risky bond that typically only is used in reorganizations.

1.1.5 Junk Bonds

Junk bonds are characterized by high default risk and high return. Junk bonds are classified as "noninvestment grade" bonds by the major credit rating agencies given their more likely default on principal and/or interest payments by the issuer. Junk bonds are frequently used to raise capital for acquisitions and leveraged buyouts.

Illustration 1   Junk Bonds

Rust Belt Industries is looking to close its machinery plant in the small town of Oxidation, Ohio. The company is the only major employer in Oxidation. To preserve their way of life, employees have decided to buy the company from its current owners. The group of employees completed a leveraged buyout of the owners by issuing noninvestment grade (junk) bonds.

1.1.6   Mortgage Bonds

A mortgage is a loan that is secured by residential or commercial real property. Mortgages are usually pooled together and issued as mortgage bonds, with bondholders protected from default by a lien on the pooled real property assets. A distinguishing feature of mortgage bonds is that trustees act on behalf of bondholders to foreclose on mortgage assets in the event of default.

1.1.7   Leasing

A lease represents a contractual agreement in which the owner of an asset, the lessor, allows another party, the lessee, to use the property (asset) in exchange for periodic lease payments.

A lessee will classify a lease on its books as either an operating lease or a finance lease. Both types of leases will result in the lessee recording a right-of-use (ROU) asset and a lease liability on the balance sheet. The ROU asset will be amortized and the lease liability will be paid down over the life of the lease.

For an operating lease, "lease expense" representing interest expense and the amortization of the ROU asset will be recorded on the income statement for every payment made. For a finance lease, interest expense and amortization expense are accounted for separately on the income statement.

Assuming that certain parameters are met, a lessee can make an accounting policy election to not recognize ROU assets and lease liabilities for leases with terms of 12 months or less.

In order to classify a lease as a finance lease, a lessee must meet one of the following five criteria:

- **Ownership** transfer at the end of the lease.

- **Written** purchase option that the lessee is reasonably certain to exercise.

- **Net** present value of all lease payments and guaranteed residual value is equal to or substantially exceeds the underlying asset's fair value.

- **Economic** life of the underlying asset is primarily encompassed within the term of the lease.

- **Specialized** asset such that it will not have an expected alternative use to the lessor when the lease ends.

If none of the above criteria are met, or if the lease is short term (12 months or less), it will be classified as an operating lease.

Illustration 2	Leasing

Phillips Manufacturing Company is working on its strategic plan for the upcoming year. Due to increased product demand, the company must expand its manufacturing by either constructing a new building or leasing an existing manufacturing facility for the next five years.

Management carefully weighs both options and recommends leasing the facility using a lease based on the following factors:

1. There are tax advantages offered by leasing, given Phillips' existing marginal tax rates;

2. The company has low financial leverage, which means that the lease liability recorded on the balance sheet will not have as harmful an impact as it would if the company had high financial leverage; and

3. Local real estate prices have been highly volatile. Leasing provides additional flexibility, allowing management to reassess the lease-versus-buy decision and the level of product demand in five years.

1.2   Equity Financing

Equity financing involves the issuance of equity (stock) securities that represent different forms of ownership of the company. A distinguishing feature of equity securities is the rights of shareholders to a firm's assets in a bankruptcy (liquidation) are less than that of both secured and unsecured bondholders.

1.2.1   Preferred Stock

Preferred stock is a hybrid equity security that has features similar to both debt and equity. Preferred shares offer or require a fixed dividend payment to their holders, which is similar to coupon payments made on debt instruments. They are like equity because the timing of the dividend payment is at the discretion of the board of directors (not mandatory) and the dividend payments are not tax deductible. Preferred shares may have the following features and uses:

- **Cumulative Dividends**

   A cumulative provision on preferred stock may require that (unpaid) *dividends in arrears* on preferred stock from a prior period be paid prior to the distribution of common stock dividends.

- **Participating Feature**

   Preferred shares may participate in declared dividends along with common shareholders to the extent that undistributed dividends exist after satisfying both preferred dividend requirements and common shareholder requirements at the preferred dividend rate.

- **Voting Rights**

   In rare circumstances, preferred shares are given voting rights. Usually these situations are associated with dividends in arrears for significant periods.

1.2.2 Common Stock

Common stock represents the basic equity ownership security of a corporation. Common stock includes voting rights with optional dividend payments by the issuer. Most common stock is issued with a stated par value. When the common stock is issued at a given market price, the proceeds received by the issuer are separated between the common stock account (i.e., par value times the number of shares issued) and the additional paid-in capital account. A negative feature of common equity is that common shareholders have the lowest claim to a firm's assets in a liquidation.

Pass Key

The following table summarizes some of the general characteristics of debt and equity financing:

	Debt	Equity
Flexibility	No	Yes
Tax deductibility	Yes	No
EPS dilution	No	Yes
Increased financial risk	Yes	No
Security issuance costs	Low	High
Investor return	Fixed	Variable

2 Weighted Average Cost of Capital

The *weighted average cost of capital* (WACC) serves as a major link between the long-term investment decisions associated with a corporation's capital structure and the wealth of a corporation's owners. The weighted average cost of capital is the average cost of all forms of financing used by a company. WACC is often used internally as a hurdle rate for capital investment decisions. The theoretical optimal capital structure is the mix of financing instruments that produces the lowest WACC.

Pass Key

The value of a firm can be computed as the present value of the cash flow it produces, discounted by the costs of capital used to finance it. The mixture of debt and equity financing that produces the lowest WACC maximizes the value of the firm.

2.1 Computing the Weighted Average Cost of Capital (WACC)

The *weighted average cost of capital* (WACC) is the average cost of debt and equity financing associated with a firm's existing assets and operations.

2.1.1 Formula

The weighted average cost of capital is determined by weighting the cost of each specific type of capital by its proportion to the firm's total capital structure.

$$\text{WACC} = \left(\frac{E}{V}\right)(R_e) + \left(\frac{P}{V}\right)(R_p) + \left(\frac{D}{V}\right)\left[R_d(1-T)\right]$$

Where:

V = The summed market values of the individual components of the firm's capital structure: common stock equity (E), preferred stock equity (P), and debt (D)

R = The required rate of return (also known as the "cost") of the various components

T = The corporate tax rate

- The percentage equity and percentage debt in the capital structure is calculated using the market values of the outstanding debt and equity, if market values are available.

Example 1	Calculating WACC

Facts: Assume that the cost of common stock equity for XYZ Company is 8.4 percent, the cost of preferred stock equity is 6.8 percent, and the weighted average interest rate on the company's debt is 6.0 percent. Also, assume that the market value percentages of each component of the capital structure are 55 percent common stock, 20 percent preferred stock, and 25 percent debt. The corporate tax rate is 30 percent.

Required: Compute XYZ's WACC.

Solution:

1. Cost of debt (after tax):

   = Interest rate × (1 − Tax rate)

   = 6.0% × (1 − 30%)

   = 4.2%

2. WACC = (8.4% × 55%) + (6.8% × 20%) + (4.2% × 25%) = 7.03%

If XYZ is using its WACC as the hurdle rate, then it should invest in any project that will yield a return higher than 7.03%.

2.1.2 Individual Capital Components

Individual capital components include both long-term and short-term elements of a firm's permanent financing mix.

- **Long-Term Elements:** *Long-term elements* include long-term debt, preferred stock, common stock, and retained earnings.

- **Short-Term Elements:** *Short-term elements* may include short-term interest-bearing debt (e.g., notes payable). Other forms of current liabilities (e.g., accounts payables and accruals) are rarely, if ever, included in the cost-of-capital estimate, because they generally represent interest-free capital.

- **After-Tax Cash Flows:** In evaluating the cost of the components of capital structure, *after-tax cash flows* are the most relevant. The cost of debt is computed on an after-tax basis because interest expense is tax deductible.

2.2   Weighted Average Cost of Debt

The relevant cost of *long-term debt* is the after-tax cost of raising long-term funds through borrowing. Sources of long-term debt generally include issuance of bonds or long-term loans. Debt costs are generally stated as the interest rate of the various debt instruments. In some cases, debt costs are stated according to basis points above U.S. Treasury bond rates (where 1 basis point is equal to one-hundredth of 1 percent, or 0.01 percent). The weighted average interest rate is calculated by dividing a company's total interest obligations on an annual basis by the debt outstanding:

$$\text{Weighted average interest rate} = \frac{\text{Effective annual interest payments}}{\text{Debt outstanding}}$$

2.2.1   Pretax Cost of Debt

The *pretax cost of debt* represents the cost of debt before considering the tax shielding effects of the debt.

2.2.2   After-Tax Cost of Debt

Because interest on debt is tax deductible, the tax savings reduces the actual cost of debt. The formula for computing the after-tax cost of debt is:

$$\text{After-tax cost of debt} = \text{Pretax cost of debt} \times (1 - \text{Tax rate})$$

Example 2   After-Tax Cost of Long-Term Debt

Facts: Assume that the long-term debt component of the weighted average cost of capital for a firm includes a pretax cost of debt of 12.5 percent and a 30 percent tax rate.

Required: Compute the after-tax cost of long-term debt.

Solution:

$$
\begin{aligned}
\text{After-tax cost of long-term debt} &= \text{Pretax cost of debt} \times (1 - \text{Tax rate}) \\
&= 0.125 \times (1 - 0.30) \\
&= 0.125 \times 0.7 \\
&= 0.0875 = 8.75\%
\end{aligned}
$$

Although the pretax interest rate is 12.5 percent, the after-tax interest rate, after considering the deductibility of the interest expense, is 8.75 percent. Note that if the tax rate increased to 40 percent, the cost of debt would decrease to 7.5 percent [12.5% × (1 − 0.40)].

Pass Key

- Debt carries the lowest cost of capital and the interest is tax deductible.
- The higher the tax rate, the more incentive exists to use debt financing.

2.3 Cost of Preferred Stock

The cost of preferred stock is the dividends paid to preferred stockholders. After-tax considerations are irrelevant with equity securities because dividends are not tax deductible.

2.3.1 Formula

$$\text{Cost of preferred stock} = \frac{\text{Preferred stock dividends}}{\text{Net proceeds of preferred stock}}$$

2.3.2 Preferred Stock Dividends

Preferred stock dividends can be stated as a dollar amount or a percentage. For example, 5 percent preferred stock pays an annual dividend of 5 percent of par value, if dividends are declared by the corporation.

2.3.3 Net Proceeds of Preferred Stocks

The net proceeds from a preferred stock issuance can be calculated as the proceeds net of flotation costs (i.e., issuance costs).

Example 3	Cost of Preferred Stock

Facts: Assume that the preferred stock component of the weighted average cost of capital for a firm is 10 percent, $100 par value preferred stock that was issued at par value with a flotation cost of $5 per share.

Required: Compute the cost of preferred stock.

Solution:

Preferred stock dividend = Dividend percentage times par value = 10% × $100 = $10

Cost of preferred stock = Dividends / Net proceeds

= $10 / ($100 − $5)

= $10 / $95

= 0.1053 = 10.53%

2.4   Cost of Retained Earnings

The cost of equity capital obtained through retained earnings is equal to the rate of return required by the firm's common stockholders. A firm should earn at least as much on any earnings retained and reinvested in the business as stockholders could have earned on alternative investments of equivalent risk. As mentioned above, after-tax considerations are irrelevant to equity securities because dividends are not tax deductible. Arriving at the components of the formula for the cost of retained earnings can be difficult and potentially subjective.

2.4.1   Three Common Methods of Computing the Cost of Retained Earnings

1.   Capital asset pricing model (CAPM)

2.   Discounted cash flow (DCF)

3.   Bond yield plus risk premium (BYRP)

2.4.2   The Capital Asset Pricing Model (CAPM)

■   **Key Assumptions**

- The cost of retained earnings is equal to the risk-free rate plus a risk premium.

- The market risk premium is equal to the systematic (nondiversifiable) risks associated with the overall stock market.

- The beta coefficient is a numerical representation of the volatility (risk) of the stock relative to the volatility of the overall market. A beta equal to 1 means the stock is as volatile as the market, and a beta greater (less) than 1 means the stock is more (less) volatile than the market.

- The risk premium is the stock's beta coefficient multiplied by the market risk premium.

- The market risk premium is the market rate of return minus the risk-free rate.

■   **Cost of Retained Earnings Formula (CAPM)**

Cost of retained earnings = Risk-free rate + Risk premium
= Risk-free rate + (Beta × Market risk premium)
= Risk-free rate + [Beta × (Market return − Risk-free rate)]

Example 4	Capital Asset Pricing Model

Facts: Assume that a firm's beta is 1.25, the risk-free rate is 8.75 percent, and the market rate of return is 14.25 percent.

Required: Compute the cost of retained earnings using the capital asset pricing model (CAPM).

Solution: Cost of retained earnings using the capital asset pricing model (CAPM):

Cost of retained earnings = Risk-free rate + [Beta × (Market return − Risk-free rate)]
= 0.0875 + [1.25 × (0.1425 − 0.0875)]
= 0.0875 + [1.25 × 0.0550]
= 0.0875 + 0.0688
= 0.1563 = 15.63%

2.4.3   Discounted Cash Flow (DCF)

■ **Key Assumptions**

- Stocks are normally in equilibrium relative to risk and return.
- The estimated expected rate of return will yield an estimated required rate of return.
- The expected growth rate may be based on projections of past growth rates, a retention growth model, or analysts' forecasts.

■ **Formula**

$$\text{Cost of retained earnings} = \frac{D_1}{P_0} + g$$

Where:

P_0 = Current market value or price of the outstanding common stock

D_1 = The dividend per share expected at the end of one year

g = The constant rate of growth in dividends

Example 5	Discounted Cash Flow

Facts: Assume that a firm is a constant growth firm that just paid an annual common stock dividend of $2.00, has a dividend growth rate of 7.5 percent, and a current market price for common stock of $25.25 per share.

Required: Compute the cost of retained earnings using the discounted cash flow (DCF) method.

Solution: Compute the dividend per share expected at the end of the year as follows:

$D_1 = D_0 \times (1 + g)$

$D_1 = \$2.00 \times (1 + 0.075)$

$D_1 = \$2.00 \times 1.075$

$D_1 = \$2.15$

Cost of retained earnings using the discounted cash flow (DCF) method:

$$\begin{aligned}
\text{Cost of retained earnings} &= (D_1 / P_0) + g \\
&= (\$2.15 / \$25.25) + 0.075 \\
&= 0.0851 + 0.075 \\
&= 0.1601 = 16.01\%
\end{aligned}$$

2.4.4   The Bond Yield Plus Risk Premium (BYRP)

■ **Key Assumptions**

- Equity and debt security values are comparable before taxes.
- Risks are associated with both the individual firm and the state of the economy. Risk premiums depend on nondiversifiable risk.
- Risk estimation can be derived by using a market analysts' survey approach or by subtracting the yield on an average (A-rated) corporate long-term bond from an estimate of the return on the equity market.

▪ Formula

> Cost of retained earnings = Pretax cost of long-term debt + Market risk premium

---

Example 6   Bond Yield Plus Risk Premium

Facts: Assume that a firm has estimated its market risk premium at 4.5 percent and has determined that the yield to maturity on its own bonds is 11.34 percent.

Required: Compute the cost of retained earnings using the bond yield plus risk premium (BYRP) method.

Solution: Cost of retained earnings using the bond yield plus risk premium method:

Cost of retained earnings = Firm's own bond yield + Market risk premium
$$= 0.1134 + 0.045$$
$$= 0.1584 = 15.84\%$$

2.4.5 Comparison of the CAPM, DCF, and BYRP Methods

Each method is a valid method of calculating the cost of retained earnings.

The average of the three cost amounts could be used as the estimate of the cost of retained earnings if there is sufficient consistency in the results of the three methods.

Example 7   Cost of Retained Earnings

Facts: The cost of retained earnings under:

CAPM method = 15.63%
DCF method = 16.01%
BYRP method = 15.84%

Required: Compute the average cost of retained earnings.

Solution: Average cost of retained earnings:

$$\text{Average} = \frac{(\text{CAPM} + \text{DCF} + \text{BYRP})}{3}$$

$$= \frac{(15.63\% + 16.01\% + 15.84\%)}{3}$$

$$= 15.83\%$$

Question 1	**CPA-03385**

DQZ Telecom is considering a project for the coming year, which will cost $50 million. DQZ plans to use the following combination of debt and equity to finance the investment.

- Issue $15 million of 20-year bonds at a price of 101, with a coupon rate of 8 percent, and flotation costs of 2 percent of par.

- Use $35 million of funds generated from (retained) earnings.

The equity market is expected to earn 12 percent. U.S. Treasury bonds are currently yielding 5 percent. The beta coefficient for DQZ is estimated to be 0.60. DQZ is subject to an effective corporate income tax rate of 40 percent. Assume that the after-tax cost of debt is 7 percent and the cost of equity is 12 percent. Determine the weighted average cost of capital.

  a. 10.50 percent

  b. 8.50 percent

  c. 9.50 percent

  d. 6.30 percent

Question 2	**CPA-03420**

Using the capital asset pricing model (CAPM), the required rate of return for a firm with a beta of 1.25 when the market return is 14 percent and the risk-free rate of 6 percent is:

  a. 14 percent.

  b. 7.5 percent.

  c. 17.5 percent.

  d. 16 percent.

NOTES

1 Optimal Capital Structure

The *optimal cost of capital* is the ratio of debt to equity that produces the lowest WACC. Required rates of return demanded by debt and equity holders fluctuate as the ratio of debt to equity changes. At some point as debt to equity increases, leverage becomes more pronounced and debtors will demand a greater return for the high level of default risk. In addition, equity holders also will require a greater return due to the negative effect of high leverage on their potential future cash flows.

1.1 Determination of Lowest WACC

The following graph displays an example of the cost of using equity financing, the cost of using debt financing, and the resulting WACC as debt and equity conditions change. In this example, the firm achieves its lowest WACC when its debt-to-equity ratio is at 4.0.

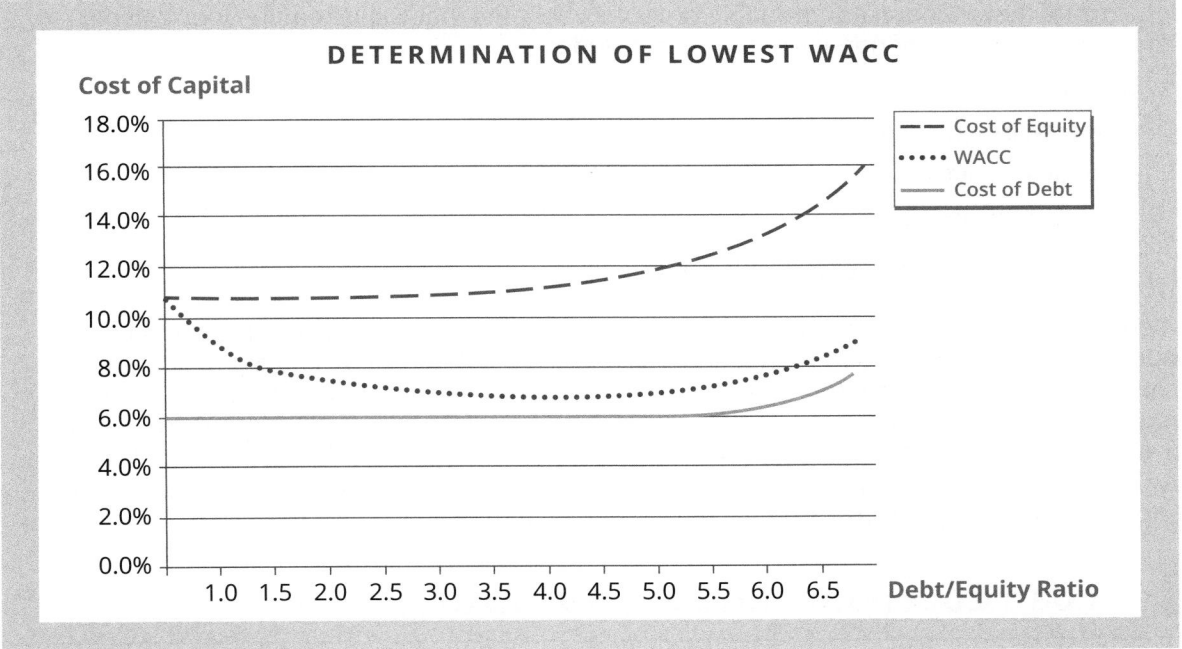

1.2 Application to Capital Budgeting

Generally, new projects are funded by sources of capital that maintain the optimum capital structure (ratio of debt to equity) and meet or exceed the hurdle rate implied by its cost. The historic weighted average cost of capital may not be appropriate for use as a discount rate for a new capital project unless the project carries the same risk as the corporation and results in identical leveraging characteristics. Appropriate application of the weighted average cost of capital as a hurdle rate for capital projects involves use of the weighted average cost of each additional new dollar of capital raised at the margin as that capital need arises.

2   Asset Structure

While a firm's capital structure relates to the debt and equity components of its balance sheet, the asset structure relates to the composition of assets on its balance sheet. Specifically, asset structure describes the dollar amounts in each line on the balance sheet and the proportions of the assets that are classified as current and long-term.

2.1   Current Assets

Current assets are expected to provide economic benefits to the company within the 12-month period following the balance sheet date. Examples of current assets include:

- Cash and cash equivalents
- Inventory
- Accounts receivable
- Notes receivable
- Prepaid expenses
- Marketable security investments classified as trading

2.2   Non-current Assets

Non-current assets represent probable economic benefits that will extend beyond the next 12 months. Examples of non-current assets include:

- Long-term investments
- Property, plant, and equipment
- Intangible assets
- Deferred tax assets

2.3   Influence of Capital Structure

An entity's asset structure is influenced by and influences its capital structure. Debt and equity issuances may be used to fund long-term assets such as building construction and the acquisition of other companies. When a company issues new debt or equity, it receives an immediate cash infusion that boosts current assets. With debt in the capital structure, cash (or other current assets that can easily be converted to cash) are needed to fund interest and principal payments when they come due. With equity, the company may choose to pay dividends, which require cash payments (typically each quarter).

3   Loan Covenants and Capital Structure

Lenders use debt covenants to protect their interests by limiting or prohibiting the actions of borrowers that might negatively affect the position of the lenders. An entity's capital structure influences the extent to which it is subjected to loan covenants. If a borrower's capital structure is heavily weighted toward equity, its financial leverage will be low and its fixed obligations associated with debt will be relatively minimal. In these situations, loan covenants may not be particularly stringent or difficult to maintain because there is less risk that the borrower will be unable to make its interest and principal payments. However, when a borrower has a significant amount of outstanding debt relative to equity, loan covenants will typically increase and become more stringent because there is more risk for the lender.

4   Growth and Profitability

Investors, creditors/lenders, and individuals who do business with a company want to see sustainable growth and profitability over time; this provides assurance that the company will meet its obligations and provide a positive return on investment for its stakeholders. Both growth and profitability are affected by an entity's capital structure.

4.1   Growth Rate

The growth rate associated with a company's earnings is a key component of financial valuation. A company's annual earnings are allocated between dividend payments to shareholders and retained earnings.

$$\text{Growth rate (g)} = \frac{\text{Return on assets} \times \text{Retention}}{1 - (\text{Return on assets} \times \text{Retention})}$$

Where: Retention (the retention ratio) is equal to the addition to retained earnings divided by net income. This also can be thought of as the portion of net income not paid out in the form of dividends to stockholders.

Example 1   Growth Rate

Facts: A company calculates return on assets of 7.5 percent in the current year and follows a policy of paying out 40 percent of all earnings as dividends.

Required: Calculate the company's expected growth rate.

Solution: If 40 percent of all earnings are paid out as dividends, then 60 percent are retained by the company.

$$\text{Growth rate (g)} = \frac{0.075 \times 0.60}{1 - (0.075 \times 0.60)} = 4.7\%$$

4.1.1   Influence of Capital Structure

An entity's capital structure influences its growth rate. The retention ratio is influenced by the level of equity. Dividends paid to shareholders increase the dividend payout ratio and decrease the retention ratio and the overall growth rate. Return on equity is affected by an entity's net income (which is reduced by interest expense associated with a company's debt) and the amount of equity (relative to debt) in a firm's capital structure. Lower net income and/or higher equity decrease the growth rate.

4.2   Profitability

A key financial measure of success for a company is profitability. Measures of profitability include return on sales (ROS), return on investment (ROI), return on assets (ROA), and return on equity (ROE). All else being equal, a higher profitability ratio (over time for a single company or relative to its peers when comparing companies) is desirable.

$$\text{Return on sales (ROS)} = \frac{\text{Income before interest income, interest expense, and taxes}}{\text{Sales (net)}}$$

$$\text{Return on investment (ROI)} = \frac{\text{Net income}}{\text{Average invested capital}}$$

$$\text{Return on assets (ROA)} = \frac{\text{Net income}}{\text{Average total assets}}$$

$$\text{Return on equity (ROE)} = \frac{\text{Net income}}{\text{Average total equity}}$$

4.2.1 Influence of Capital Structure

ROS, ROI, ROA, and ROE measure profitability after accounting for capital structure decisions. Net income is the bottom line of the income statement after both interest expense and taxes are taken into account. The higher an entity's debt, the greater the impact of interest expense on net income. Dividend payments affect these ratios in the sense that dividend payments reduce assets and retained earnings (equity).

5 Leverage and Risk

Leverage affects the variability of company profits and, therefore, affects the risk assumed (and return required) by creditors and owners. Leverage is a significant consideration as a factor in designing capital structure. Financial managers must consider both operating leverage and financial leverage.

5.1 Operating Leverage

5.1.1 Definition

Operating leverage is the degree to which a company uses fixed operating costs rather than variable operating costs. Capital-intensive industries often have high operating leverage. Labor-intensive industries generally have low operating leverage.

5.1.2 Implications

A company with high operating leverage must produce sufficient sales revenue to cover its high fixed-operating costs. High operating leverage is beneficial when sales revenue is high. High contribution margin indicates high operating leverage.

A company with high operating leverage will have greater risk but greater possible returns. There is risk because the variability of profits is greater with higher operating leverage.

When sales decline, a company with high operating leverage may struggle to cover its fixed costs. However, beyond the breakeven point, a company with higher fixed costs will retain a higher percentage of additional revenues as operating income (earnings before interest and taxes or EBIT).

Illustration 1   Operating Leverage

When Pat Jones compared his company's operating leverage with a competitor's operating leverage, Jones found that his company experienced a 21 percent increase in EBIT as a result of a 5 percent increase in sales, while the competitor experienced a 10 percent increase in EBIT as a result of a 5 percent increase in sales. Jones' company has higher operating leverage than the competitor, which implies that fixed costs constitute a higher proportion of his company's total costs compared with the competitor. As a result, Jones' company will need to generate more revenue to cover its fixed costs, but will be highly profitable once those fixed costs are met.

Illustration 2   High Operating Leverage

Nursing homes and hospitals are required to meet minimum staffing levels to maintain bed capacity. Salaries represent a fixed cost of maintaining capacity and result in higher operating leverage.

Illustration 3   Low Operating Leverage

Big box retailers have high variable operating costs in their cost of goods sold and part-time labor pool, resulting in low operating leverage.

5.2   Financial Leverage

5.2.1   Definition

When making financing decisions, a firm can choose to issue debt or equity. When debt is issued, the firm generally must pay fixed interest costs. Equity issuances do not result in an increase in fixed costs because dividend payments are not required. Financial leverage is the degree to which a company uses debt rather than equity to finance the company.

5.2.2   Implications

A company that issues debt must produce sufficient operating income (EBIT) to cover its fixed interest costs. However, once fixed interest costs are covered, additional EBIT will go straight to net income and earnings per share. A higher degree of financial leverage implies that a relatively small change in earnings before interest and taxes (increase or decrease) will have a greater effect on profits and shareholder value. Another benefit of financial leverage is that interest costs are tax deductible, whereas dividends are not.

Companies that are highly leveraged may be at risk of bankruptcy if they are unable to make payments on their debt. They also may be unable to find new lenders in the future.

Illustration 4   Financial Leverage

If a firm with significant debt experiences a 42 percent increase in EPS as a result of a 21 percent increase in EBIT, the firm has more than enough operating income to cover its fixed interest costs. As a result, EPS has been magnified. If the firm had issued equity rather than debt, EPS most likely would have decreased because the number of shares outstanding would have increased. The higher a firm's financial leverage, the greater its potential profitability (but also the greater its risk).

Illustration 5   Financial Leverage

Jax Company issues new common equity to obtain cash for the purchase of new equipment for $1,000,000. Jax is not using financial leverage, and has no fixed financing costs associated with this transaction. Jax may or may not pay dividends to the new stockholders.

Max Company borrows $900,000 and uses its own cash of $100,000 to buy equipment. Max is using financial leverage, and now must pay fixed interest costs annually.

In the next year, the economy enters recession, and profits do not materialize for Jax or Max as each had expected. Max must pay the fixed interest cost on the loan, which further erodes its already tight cash flow. Jax has no interest expense and protects its cash by not declaring a dividend.

In future years, as sales improve, Max Company will benefit from financial leverage because interest is a fixed charge and is tax deductible. Additional earnings in excess of the interest charges will go straight to EPS. Jax, however, has no such guarantee because dividends are not fixed and shareholders may require larger returns. In addition, Jax has more shares of stock outstanding, which dilutes EPS.

5.3   Value of a Levered Firm

5.3.1   Definition

A "levered firm" is a company that has debt in its capital structure, whereas an unlevered firm has only equity (and no debt) in its structure. The formula for calculating the value of a levered firm, assuming that the debt is permanent, is shown below:

$$\text{Value of a levered firm} = \text{Value of an unlevered firm} + \text{Present value of the interest tax savings}$$

Where:

$$\text{Present value of interest tax savings} = \frac{T \times (r_{debt} \times D)}{r_{debt}}$$

T = Corporate tax rate

r = Interest rate on debt

D = Amount of debt

5.3.2 Implications

A firm that uses debt benefits from the tax deductibility of the interest payments. These cumulative tax savings, discounted to today's dollars, represent the difference between the value of a firm with no debt and a firm with debt in its capital structure.

Example 2   **Value of a Levered Firm**

Facts: The value of a company with no debt in its capital structure is $130 million. The company has recently issued $25 million in debt at an interest rate of 5.75 percent.

Required: Assuming that the corporate tax rate is 30 percent, calculate the value of the levered firm.

Solution:

$$\text{Value of the levered firm} = \$130 \text{ million} + \frac{0.30 \times (0.0575 \times \$25 \text{ million})}{0.0575} = \$137.5 \text{ million}$$

---

6 Impact of Capital Structure on Financial Ratios

An entity's solvency, or ability to meet its long-term obligations, is affected by the amount of debt in its capital structure. Solvency can be measured using ratios such as the total debt ratio, debt to equity, and debt to assets. The times interest earned ratio measures the company's ability to meet its interest obligations on long-term debt.

6.1 Total Debt Ratio

$$\text{Total debt ratio} = \frac{\text{Total liabilities}}{\text{Total assets}}$$

■ **Interpretation:** The total debt ratio provides indications related to an organization's long-term debt-paying ability. The lower the ratio, the greater the level of solvency and the greater the presumed ability to pay debts.

■ **Variations:** Some analysts adjust the total debt ratio to exclude certain items from the denominator (such as reserves, deferred taxes, minority shareholder interests, and redeemable preferred stock) as a basis for refining the amount truly available to liquidate debt.

6.2 Debt-to-Equity Ratio

Although comprehensive ratios provide insights into the overall solvency, relationships between the elements of capital structure provide more refined views of solvency.

$$\text{Debt-to-equity ratio} = \frac{\text{Total liabilities}}{\text{Total equity}}$$

- **Interpretation:** The debt-to-equity ratio relates the two major categories of capital structure to each other and indicates the degree of leverage used. The lower the ratio, the lower the risk involved.

- **Variations:** Some analysts use the reciprocal of this ratio (total shareholders' equity to total debt) to measure the amount of equity backing up every dollar of debt. Another alternative version of this ratio uses only long-term debt in the numerator to purely compare only the long-term elements of capital structure.

6.3   Equity Multiplier

The equity multiplier represents the value of assets on the firm's balance sheet relative to the value of its equity. This ratio is also used to convert return on assets (ROA) to return on equity (ROE).

$$\text{Equity multiplier} = \frac{\text{Total assets}}{\text{Total equity}}$$

Interpretation: On a firm's balance sheet, total assets are equal to total liabilities plus total equity. A greater percentage of debt utilized by the firm results in more assets allocated to debt relative to equity and a higher equity multiplier.

6.4   Times Interest Earned Ratio

The times interest earned ratio shows the number of times the interest charges are covered by net operating income.

$$\text{Times interest earned ratio} = \frac{\text{Earnings before interest expense and taxes (EBIT)}}{\text{Interest expense}}$$

- **Interpretation:** The times interest earned ratio measures the ability of the company to pay its interest charges as they come due. It is a measure of long-term solvency.

Question 1	**CPA-03431**

Sylvan Corporation has the following capital structure:

Debenture bonds	$10,000,000
Preferred equity	1,000,000
Common equity	39,000,000

The financial leverage of Sylvan Corp. would increase as a result of:

   a.   Issuing common stock and using the proceeds to retire preferred stock.

   b.   Issuing common stock and using the proceeds to retire debenture bonds.

   c.   Financing its future investments with a higher percentage of bonds.

   d.   Financing its future investments with a higher percentage of equity funds.

---

1 Working Capital

Working capital policy and working capital management involve managing cash so that a company can meet its short-term obligations, and include all aspects of the administration of current assets (CA) and current liabilities (CL). The goal of working capital management is shareholder wealth maximization. The optimal mix of current assets and current liabilities depends on the nature of the business and the industry and requires offsetting the benefit of CA and CL against the probability of technical insolvency.

1.1 Definition of Net Working Capital

Net working capital is defined as the difference between current assets (CA) and current liabilities (CL).

1.2 Balancing Profitability and Risk

Working capital must be financed either with long-term or short-term debt or with stockholders' equity. Adequate working capital reserves mitigate risk, and thereby increase profitability. Less working capital increases risk by exposing a company to the likelihood of a possible failure to meet current obligations and potentially reducing a firm's ability to obtain additional short-term financing.

1.3 Analysis of Working Capital

Working capital metrics should be evaluated regularly. A ratio on its own will have some value, but significant value lies in examining ratio trends and making comparisons for both a single entity across time and comparisons to industry/peers at a point in time. Ratios provide quantitative support for understanding and explaining trends and changes in financial and business operations.

2 Working Capital Ratios

2.1 Current Ratio

2.1.1 Formula

$$\text{Current ratio} = \frac{\text{Current assets}}{\text{Current liabilities}}$$

2.1.2 Interpretation

The net amount of working capital (CA minus CL) measures the amount by which current assets exceed current liabilities, and the current ratio (CA divided by CL) measures the number of times current assets exceed current liabilities and is a way of measuring short-term solvency. This ratio demonstrates a firm's ability to generate cash to meet its short-term obligations.

2.1.3   Analysis

In general, a higher current ratio is better. The current ratio is generally considered to be the best single indicator of a company's ability to meet short-term obligations. The current ratio measures liquidity at a point in time, but it is not indicative of future cash flows.

■ **Deteriorating Current Ratio**

A decline in the current ratio, which implies a reduced ability to generate cash, can be attributable to increases in short-term debt, decreases in current assets, or a combination of both.

■ **Improving Current Ratio**

An increase or improvement in the current ratio implies an increased ability to pay off current liabilities and may be attributable to using long-term borrowing to repay short-term debt (in cases in which a firm lacks cash to reduce current debts).

2.1.4   Limitations of the Current Ratio (and Other Liquidity Ratios)

Unless short-term liquidity is a relevant issue, the current ratio is not necessarily the best measure of the health of a business.

Illustration 1   Current Ratio

A restaurant might have low CA (e.g., accounts receivable and inventory) relative to CL (e.g., accounts payable and payroll obligations), but might otherwise be healthy in terms of increasing cash flows, growing reputation, good location, and limited long-term debt obligations.

A bookstore might have a high CA (e.g., inventory) relative to CL (e.g., accounts payable), but might otherwise be unhealthy in terms of diminishing cash flows, poor location, increased competition from Internet vendors, and low inventory turnover.

2.2   Quick Ratio

2.2.1   Formula

$$\text{Quick ratio} = \frac{\text{Cash and cash equivalents} + \text{Short-term marketable securities} + \text{Receivables (net)}}{\text{Current liabilities}}$$

Some analysts elect to include prepaid assets in the numerator of the quick ratio, but it is more conservative to exclude such items.

2.2.2   Interpretation

The quick ratio is a more rigorous test of liquidity than the current ratio because inventory and prepaids are excluded from current assets. Inventory is the least liquid of current assets. The ability to meet current obligations without liquidating inventory is important.

2.2.3   Analysis

The higher the quick ratio (or acid-test ratio), the better.

2.3   Cash Conversion Cycle

2.3.1   Formula

Pass Key

Turnover ratios generally use average balances [i.e., (beginning balance + ending balance) / 2] for balance sheet components. However, on some recent CPA Exam questions, candidates have been instructed to use year-end balances instead. Please be sure to read the question carefully to determine the appropriate method to use.

$$\text{Cash conversion cycle} = \text{Days in inventory} + \text{Days sales in accounts receivable} - \text{Days of payables outstanding}$$

2.3.2   Interpretation

The cash conversion cycle (sometimes called net operating cycle) is the length of time from the date of the initial expenditure for production to the date cash is collected from the customers offset by the length of time it takes to pay vendors for the initial expenditures.

2.3.3   Elements of the Cash Conversion Cycle Formula

The elements of the cash conversion cycle can most easily be calculated using the related turnover ratios.

■ **Days in Inventory**

The inventory turnover ratio (the number of times a year inventory is sold) and the days in inventory (the average number of days inventory is held before it is sold) are measures of the effectiveness of an entity's inventory management. The days in inventory measures the degree to which resources have been devoted to inventory to support sales.

$$\text{Inventory turnover} = \frac{\text{Cost of goods sold}}{\text{Average inventory}}$$

$$\text{Days in inventory} = \frac{\text{Ending inventory}}{\text{Cost of goods sold} / 365}$$

■ **Days Sales in Accounts Receivable**

The accounts receivable turnover ratio and the days sales in accounts receivable are measures of the effectiveness of a company's credit policy. The accounts receivable turnover ratio measures the number of times receivables are collected over an accounting period (typically one year). The days sales in accounts receivable measures the number of days after a typical credit sale is made until the firm receives payment:

$$\text{Accounts receivable turnover} = \frac{\text{Sales (net)}}{\text{Average accounts receivable (net)}}$$

$$\text{Days sales in accounts receivable} = \frac{\text{Ending accounts receivable (net)}}{\text{Sales (net) / 365}}$$

■ **Days of Payables Outstanding**

The accounts payable turnover ratio (the number of times a year a company pays its suppliers) and the days of payables outstanding (the average number of days it takes for a company to pay its suppliers) are measures of the effectiveness of a company's attempt to delay payment to creditors.

$$\text{Accounts payable turnover} = \frac{\text{Cost of goods sold}}{\text{Average accounts payable}}$$

$$\text{Days of payables outstanding} = \frac{\text{Ending accounts payable}}{\text{Cost of goods sold / 365}}$$

Example 1	Cash Conversion Cycle

Facts: ABC Computers has annual sales of $36 million. On average, the company carries $5 million in inventory, $3 million in accounts receivable, and $3 million in accounts payable.

Required: If the annual cost of goods sold for ABC is $27 million, what is the length of the cash conversion cycle for the firm?

Solution:

$$\text{Days in inventory} = \frac{\$5,000,000}{\$27,000,000 \, / \, 365} = 67.6 \text{ days}$$

$$\text{Days sales in accounts receivable} = \frac{\$3,000,000}{\$36,000,000 \, / \, 365} = 30.4 \text{ days}$$

$$\text{Days of payables outstanding} = \frac{\$3,000,000}{\$27,000,000 \, / \, 365} = 40.6 \text{ days}$$

$$\text{Cash conversion cycle} = 67.6 \text{ days} + 30.4 \text{ days} - 40.6 \text{ days} = 57.4 \text{ days}$$

2.3.4 Analysis

A company should minimize the amount of time it takes to convert inventory to cash while maximizing the amount of time it takes to pay vendors. Therefore, the lower the cash conversion cycle, the better. Each component of the cash conversion cycle should be analyzed individually.

- **Days in inventory**

  A company is doing well when it quickly converts inventory into sales. More days in inventory could mean that inventory becomes obsolete and ultimately a sunk cost to the entity. If the days in inventory is too short, the company may not have enough inventory on hand to support potential sales.

- **Days Sales in Accounts Receivable**

  Fewer days sales in accounts receivable is ideal, although a company may lose sales if its credit or collection policies are too strict. Too many days sales in accounts receivable indicates that the company is struggling to collect from its customers.

- **Days of Payables Outstanding**

  A company conserves cash by delaying payment to vendors for purchases on credit. Too short of a period presents the risk of not fully utilizing cash to the advantage of the company. Too long of a period may cause the company's relationship with its vendors to deteriorate.

2.4 Working Capital Turnover

2.4.1 Formula

$$\text{Working capital turnover} = \frac{\text{Sales}}{\text{Average working capital}}$$

Average working capital is the beginning-of-period plus end-of-period working capital divided by 2.

2.4.2 Interpretation

Working capital turnover is a measure of how effective a company is at generating sales based on funds used in operations.

2.4.3 Analysis

A higher working capital turnover ratio implies that a company is doing a relatively good job converting its working capital into sales. Too low of a ratio implies too much money is invested in current assets such as receivables and inventory relative to the amount of sales a company is generating from that capital. Too high of a ratio implies that there may not be enough capital in place to continue to support operations and sales.

Question 1	CPA-03528

Which one of the following would increase the working capital of a firm?

- **a.** Cash collection of accounts receivable.
- **b.** Refinancing of accounts payable with a two-year note payable.
- **c.** Cash payment of accounts payable.
- **d.** Payment of a 30-year mortgage payable with cash.

Question 2	CPA-03456

Which of the following transactions would increase the current ratio and decrease net profit?

- **a.** A federal income tax payment due from the previous year is paid.
- **b.** A long-term bond is retired before maturity at a discount.
- **c.** A dividend is paid.
- **d.** Vacant land is sold for less than the net book value.

1 Inventory Management

Inventory may represent the most significant current noncash resource of an organization. Inventory typically is most significant in businesses that involve the sale or manufacture of goods.

1.1 Types of Inventory

Inventory may be classified as raw materials, work-in-process, and finished goods.

- **Raw Materials:** Inventory held for use in the production process.

- **Work-in-Process:** Inventory in production but incomplete.

- **Finished Goods:** Production inventory that is complete and ready for sale.

1.2 Inventory Valuation

1.2.1 Lower of Cost, Market, or Net Realizable Value

Inventory is generally accounted for at cost, which is the price paid to acquire an asset. When the value of the inventory falls below original cost, the inventory must be restated to the lower of market value or net realizable value. Inventory costed using LIFO or the retail inventory method is measured at the lower of cost or market value. Inventory costed using other methods is measured at the lower of cost or net realizable value.

1.2.2 Market Value

Market value represents the median value of the item's replacement cost, the market ceiling, and the market floor.

- **Replacement Cost:** Replacement cost is equal to the cost to purchase the inventory on the valuation date.

- **Market Ceiling:** The market ceiling is the net selling price less the costs to complete and dispose of the inventory.

- **Market Floor:** The market floor is equal to the market ceiling less a normal profit margin.

1.2.3 Net Realizable Value

Net realizable value is equal to the net selling price less costs to complete and dispose. This is also known as the market ceiling.

Example 1	Lower of Cost or Market

Facts: Six months ago, Duffy Inc. purchased inventory for $55 per unit. The current replacement cost is $48 per unit, while the net selling price less costs to complete (net realizable value) is $51 and the normal profit margin is $5.

Required: Determine the value of the inventory on the balance sheet if the inventory is costed using LIFO and FIFO.

Solution: Under LIFO, the inventory is valued at the lower of cost or market:

$$\text{Cost} = \$55$$
$$\text{Market} = \$48$$

Market is the median value of the replacement cost ($48), market ceiling ($51), and market floor ($46 = $51 − $5).

The value of the inventory per unit on the balance sheet will be $48.

Under FIFO, the inventory is valued at the lower of cost and net realizable value:

$$\text{Cost} = \$55$$
$$\text{Net realizable value} = \$51$$

The value of the inventory per unit on the balance sheet will be $51.

1.3 Periodic vs. Perpetual Inventory Systems

1.3.1 Periodic Inventory System

In a periodic inventory system, inventory quantities are determined by physical counts performed at least annually. Inventory units are valued at the end of the accounting period and actual cost of goods sold for the period is determined after each physical inventory by calculating the difference between beginning inventory plus purchases less ending inventory.

1.3.2 Perpetual Inventory System

With a perpetual inventory system, the inventory balance is updated for each purchase and each sale, and is always current. Cost of goods sold is determined and recorded with each sale.

1.4 Cost Flow Assumptions

Inventory valuation depends on the inventory system employed and the cost flow assumption chosen by an entity.

1.4.1 Specific Identification Method

Under specific identification, the cost of each item in inventory is uniquely identified to that item. The cost follows the physical flow of the item in and out of inventory to cost of goods sold.

1.4.2 First In, First Out (FIFO) Method

Under FIFO, the first costs inventoried are the first costs transferred to cost of goods sold. Ending inventory on the balance sheet includes the most recently incurred costs and therefore approximates replacement cost. The periodic and perpetual inventory systems can be used with FIFO.

1.4.3   Last In, First Out (LIFO) Method

Under LIFO, the last costs inventoried are the first costs transferred to cost of goods sold. The ending inventory balance typically does not approximate replacement cost because ending inventory includes the oldest inventory. The periodic and perpetual inventory systems can be used with LIFO.

1.4.4   Weighted Average Method

The weighted average method calculates an average cost per item at the end of the period by dividing the total costs of inventory available by the total number of units of inventory available. This average cost is used for both the ending inventory balance and cost of goods sold. The weighted average method works with a periodic inventory system.

1.4.5   Moving Average Method

The moving average method computes the weighted average cost of the inventory after each purchase by dividing the total cost of inventory available after each purchase (inventory plus current purchase) by the total units available after each purchase. The moving average method requires the perpetual inventory system.

Illustration 1   Cost Flow Assumptions

If a company chooses to use FIFO, the oldest costs inventoried are included in the cost of goods sold, leaving more recent purchases in the ending inventory balance on the balance sheet. When prices are falling, the older costs are the more expensive costs. Therefore, the cost of goods sold will be higher under FIFO and net income will be lower. In terms of working capital, current assets will be lower because inventory on the balance sheet will include the more recently purchased lower price inventory. As a result, working capital will be lower.

---

2   Inventory Management Strategies

2.1   Factors Influencing Inventory Levels

Inventory depends on the accuracy of sales forecasts. Lack of inventory can result in lost sales, and excessive inventory can result in burdensome carrying costs, including:

- Storage costs
- Insurance costs
- Opportunity costs of inventory investment
- Lost inventory due to obsolescence or spoilage

Pass Key

The lower the carrying costs of inventory, the more inventory companies are willing to carry.

2.2 Optimal Levels of Inventory

Numerous factors affect the optimal level of inventory, including the usage rate of inventory per period of time, cost per unit of inventory, cost of placing orders for inventory, and the time required to receive inventory. Concepts related to the determination of the optimal level of inventory include:

- Inventory turnover
- Safety stock
- Reorder point
- Economic order quantity
- Materials requirements planning

2.3 Safety Stock

Many companies maintain safety stock to ensure that manufacturing or customer supply requirements are met. The determination of safety stock depends on the following factors:

- Reliability of sales forecasts
- Possibility of customer dissatisfaction resulting from back orders
- Stockout costs (the cost of running out of inventory), including loss of income, the cost of restoring goodwill with customers, and the cost of expedited shipping to meet customer demand
- Lead time (the time that elapses from the placement to the receipt of an order)
- Seasonal demands on inventory

2.4 Reorder Point

The reorder point is the inventory level at which a company should order or manufacture additional inventory to meet demand and to avert incurring stockout costs. The reorder point can be calculated using the following formula:

Reorder point = Safety stock + (Lead time × Sales during lead time)

Example 2 | Reorder Point

Facts: Worldwide Widgets sells 8,000 widgets per year, manufactures widgets in groups of 1,500, and requires five weeks of lead time for widget production. Worldwide also maintains an absolute minimum safety stock of 1,200 widgets.

Required: Assuming a 50-week year and constant demand, compute Worldwide's reorder point for widgets.

Solution:

Worldwide sells an average of 160 widgets per week (8,000 widgets per year / 50 weeks).

Reorder point = Safety stock + (Lead time × Sales during lead time)

Reorder point = 1,200 widgets + (5 weeks × 160 widgets per week) = 2,000 widgets

Worldwide will manufacture additional widgets when its inventory of widgets falls to 2,000 units.

2.5 Economic Order Quantity

When managing inventory, there is a trade-off between carrying costs (the costs of holding inventory) and ordering costs (the costs of ordering additional inventory). For example, if the order quantity is small then carrying costs are low, but inventory must be ordered more frequently to meet demand, which increases ordering costs.

Ordering costs typically represent the costs of labor associated with order placement. The costs are driven by order frequency (rather than quantity per order) and they include the costs of entering the purchase order, processing the receipt of the inventory, inspecting the inventory to ensure that the goods received (typically a sample) are acceptable, and processing of the vendor invoice and consequent payment.

The *economic order quantity* (EOQ) inventory model attempts to minimize total ordering and carrying costs. The model can be applied to the management of any exchangeable good.

2.5.1 Assumptions

EOQ assumes that demand is known and is constant throughout the year, so EOQ does not consider stockout costs, nor does it account for costs of safety stock. EOQ also assumes that carrying costs per unit and ordering costs per unit are fixed.

2.5.2 The EOQ Equation and Equation Components

$$E = \sqrt{\frac{2SO}{C}}$$

- Order size (**EOQ**)
- Annual **Sales** (in units)
- Cost per Purchase **Order**
- Annual **Carrying** cost per unit

Example 3   EOQ

Facts: Maximus Company incurs carrying costs of $50 a month and each order costs the firm $5,625.

Required: Calculate Maximus' economic order quantity if Maximus goes through 100 units of inventory monthly.

Solution:

$$E = \sqrt{\frac{2SO}{C}}$$

$$E = \sqrt{\frac{2 \times 100 \times \$5,625}{\$50}}$$

$$E = 150 \text{ units}$$

When Maximus orders inventory, it should order 150 units to minimize total ordering costs and carrying costs.

Note: Although the formula calls for annual sales and carrying costs, using monthly sales in the numerator and monthly carrying costs in the denominator will produce the same result.

2.6   Other Inventory Management Issues

2.6.1   Just-in-Time Inventory Models

The *just-in-time (JIT) inventory model* was developed to reduce the lag time between inventory arrival and inventory use. JIT ties delivery of components to the speed of the assembly line. JIT reduces the need of manufacturers to carry large inventories, but requires a considerable degree of coordination between manufacturer and supplier. The benefits of JIT implementation include tying production scheduling with demand, more efficient flow of goods between warehouses and production, reduced setup time, and greater employee efficiencies.

2.6.2   Kanban Inventory Control

Kanban inventory control techniques give visual signals that a component required in production must be replenished. This technique prevents oversupply or interruption of the entire manufacturing process as the result of lacking a component.

2.6.3   Computerized Inventory Control

Computerized inventory control operates by establishing real-time communication links between the cashier and the stock room. Every purchase is recognized instantaneously by the inventory database, as is every product return. Computers are programmed to alert inventory managers as to reorder requirements. In some cases, company databases interface directly with supplier software to allow for instantaneous reorders, thereby removing the human element.

3   Supply Chain Management/Integrated Supply Chain Management (ISCM)

Integrated supply chain management (ISCM) exists when a firm and the entire supply chain (suppliers, producers, distributors, retailers, customers, and service providers) are able to reasonably predict the expected demand of consumers for a product and then plan accordingly to meet that demand. Integrated supply chain management is a collaborative effort between buyers and sellers.

3.1   Goal Is to Understand Needs and Preferences of Customers

The goal of ISCM is to better understand the needs and preferences of customers and cultivate the relationship with them. If the actual demand of the customer is met and excess supply does not exist in the market, the firm will be able to minimize costs all along the supply chain (e.g., raw materials, production, packaging, shipping, etc.).

3.2   Supply Chain Operations Reference (SCOR) Model

The SCOR model was developed by the Supply Chain Council, which attempted to create a generic model for supply chain analysis. The SCOR model assists a firm in mapping out its true supply chain and then configuring it to best fit the needs of the firm. There are four key management processes or core activities pertaining to SCOR: plan, source, make, and deliver.

3.2.1   Plan

The process of planning consists of developing a way to properly balance demand and supply within the goals and objectives of the firm and prepare for the necessary infrastructure. According to the Supply Chain Council, examples of activities associated with "plan" are:

- Determining the demand requirements
- Assessing the ability of the suppliers to supply resources
- Planning the inventory levels

- Planning the distribution of inventory
- Planning for the purchase of raw materials
- Assessing capacity concerns and capabilities
- Identifying viable distribution channels
- Configuring the supply chain
- Managing the product's life cycle
- Making make/buy decisions

3.2.2 Source

Once demand has been planned, it is necessary to procure the resources required to meet it and to manage the infrastructure that exists for the sources. According to the Supply Chain Council, this process deals with the following types of activities:

- Selecting vendors
- Obtaining vendor feedback and certification
- Overseeing and obtaining proper vendor contracts
- Collecting and processing vendor payments
- Ordering, inspecting, and storing inputs to the production process
- Overseeing the quality assurance process
- Assessing vendor performance

3.2.3 Make

The "make" process encompasses all the activities that turn the raw materials into finished products that are produced to meet a planned demand. According to the Supply Chain Council, the process includes the following types of activities:

- Managing the production process
- Implementing changes in engineering
- Requesting products for use in the production process
- Manufacturing the product
- Testing the product
- Packaging the product
- Releasing inventory for shipment
- Maintaining the production equipment and the facilities
- Performing quality assurance measures
- Scheduling production runs
- Analyzing capacity availability

3.2.4 Deliver

The "deliver" process encompasses all the activities of getting the finished product into the hands of the ultimate consumers to meet their planned demand. According to the Supply Chain Council, this process includes the following types of activities:

- Managing of orders (e.g., provide quotes, grant credit, enter orders, etc.)
- Forecasting
- Pricing

- Managing transportation (e.g., freight, import/export issues, truck coordination, etc.)
- Managing accounts receivable and collections
- Shipping of products
- Labeling of products
- Scheduling installation of products
- Delivering the inventory according to channel distribution rules

---

Illustration 2   Supply Chain Operations Reference (SCOR) Model

Steel Products Inc. (SPI) manufactures custom steel rolls and standardized cut steel sheets. Despite its relatively small size, the company uses the SCOR model to assist in its supply chain management. Key features of SPI's SCOR model are as follows:

Plan: Prior to each new operating year, the plant manager estimates specific demand for SPI's steel products. The manager then estimates year-end inventory levels for each of SPI's standardized products. Once this is determined, the manager develops a plan to purchase the generic steel inputs.

Source: The next step is for the plant manager to select the vendors for purchasing the steel inputs used for the upcoming year's production. The steel is ordered from the vendors and then stored in the receiving section of the main plant. As part of the receiving supervisor's responsibilities, he is required to inspect the quality of each of the steel shipments and assess the dependability of each vendor.

Make: The plant manager, along with an outside consultant, assesses the current year's production process to determine whether any production changes should be made for the current year. At the start of the new operating year, the company manufactures its steel products from customer orders received. As new orders are obtained from the sales department, the plant manager schedules the weekly production runs.

Deliver: Once the steel orders are completed, they are priced using a combination of market intelligence and production cost inputs. The products are then shipped using the company's semitrailer trucks for regional orders and a national trucking company for longer-distance deliveries.

3.3 Benefits of Implementing Supply Chain Management

Examples of benefits derived from implementing supply chain management include:

- Reduced costs in inventory management
- Reduced costs in warehousing
- Optimization of the distribution network and facility locations
- Enhanced revenues
- Improved service times
- Strategic shipment consolidation
- Reduced cost in packaging
- Improved delivery times

- Cross-docking (the minimization of handling and storage costs while receiving and processing of goods in the shortest time possible)
- Identification of inefficiencies in supply chain activities
- Integration of suppliers
- Management of suppliers

4   Accounts Payable Management

4.1   Trade Credit

Trade credit (or accounts payable) generally provides the largest source of short-term credit for small firms. Trade credit represents the purchases of goods and services as part of usual and customary business transactions for which payment is made 30 to 45 days after acquisition.

4.2   Accruals

Accruals represent routine transactions that remain unpaid at the end of an accounting period (e.g., wages payable and taxes payable) purely as a result of transaction timing. Accruals are another common form of short-term credit.

4.3   Discounts

Although extension of payments under trade credit arrangements can be very effective in preserving cash balances and financing current operations, the effective annual interest cost can be extremely high if discounts are offered and foregone as part of this working capital management strategy.

4.3.1   Calculating Payment Discounts

The formula for calculating the annual cost (APR) of a quick payment discount (assuming a 360-day year) follows:

$$\text{APR of quick payment discount} = \frac{360}{\text{Pay period} - \text{Discount period}} \times \frac{\text{Discount}}{100 - \text{Discount \%}}$$

Example 4	Payment Discounts (APR)

Facts: Terranova Company's main vendor offers a quick payment discount of 1/10, net 30 to its customers.

Required: Assuming a 360-day year, calculate the annual cost to Terranova of not taking advantage of the discount.

Solution:

$$\frac{360}{30 - 10} \times \frac{1\%}{100\% - 1\%} = \frac{360}{20} \times \frac{1\%}{99\%} = 18.2\%$$

4.3.2 Factors Affecting Discount Policy

As shown in the previous example, there can be a high cost associated with a customer not taking advantage of a discount offered by the vendor. The decision whether or not to pay early and take the discount depends on several factors, including whether:

- The company has the cash on hand to pay that particular vendor early.

- The company wants to preserve its cash position for other purposes (investments, projects, maintaining a reserve, etc.).

- There is potential to negotiate even more favorable terms with vendors, including greater discounts or longer discount periods.

4.4 Use of Electronic Funds Transfer

The electronic movement of funds from one institution to another is called electronic funds transfer, or EFT. Electronic funds transfer can be used to ensure timely payment.

4.5 Optimal Vendor Payment Schedule

Companies need to find an optimal balance between conserving cash and ensuring that vendors are paid in a timely manner. If a company is a regular buyer and/or a large volume buyer from a particular vendor, it may be able to negotiate more favorable terms in order to either take advantage of discounts or extend payment periods. If, for example, the discount period is 10 days, a company will want to pay on the 10th day. If the overall payment is due in 30 days and the discount is not taken, the company should pay on the 30th day. Setting up automatic payments to pay vendors at the end of the payment period is ideal, as it allows the company to conserve cash as long as it can and still pay in a timely manner.

Illustration 3   Optimal Vendor Payment Schedule

Riggs Corp. pays for gas and electricity costs from Lancor, with monthly payments due on the 12th of each month. Rather than issuing paper checks from its Accounts Payable department, Riggs sets up the payments in its automated bill-pay system such that the amount due is automatically wired from Riggs' bank to Lancor on the morning of the 12th. Setting up the payments in this manner allows Riggs to conserve cash and meet the payment deadline without worrying about remembering to issue checks.

4.6 Methods to Delay Disbursements

4.6.1 Defer Payments

Postponing payment of accounts payable provides a spontaneous source of credit to which management can resort if the company is confronted with a short-term cash shortage. Communications to creditors that payments will arrive later than usual serve to mitigate possible damage to credit ratings.

4.6.2 Line of Credit

Establishing a line of credit with a bank serves to slow down payments. A line of credit extends the company's trade credit by paying off the company's trade accounts with borrowed funds and allowing the company a longer period to pay back that loan to the bank.

Question 1	**CPA-03458**

Garo Company, a retail store, is considering foregoing sales discounts in order to delay using its cash. Supplier credit terms are 2/10, net 30. Assuming a 360-day year, what is the annual cost of credit if the cash discount is *not* taken and Garo pays net 30?

- **a.** 24.0 percent
- **b.** 24.5 percent
- **c.** 36.0 percent
- **d.** 36.7 percent

Question 2	**CPA-06627**

An increase in which of the following should cause management to reduce the average inventory?

- **a.** The cost of placing an order.
- **b.** The cost of carrying inventory.
- **c.** The annual demand for the product.
- **d.** The lead time needed to acquire inventory.

NOTES

1   Cash and Credit Management

1.1   Management of Cash and Cash Equivalents

Factors influencing the levels of cash include the volume of collections and their timing, the volume of disbursements and their timing, and the degree to which idle cash is invested in marketable securities.

Businesses use various techniques to maximize cash balances, including managing float, synchronizing cash inflows and outflows, speeding collections and deposits, and mitigating risks with overdraft systems or compensating balances.

1.1.1   Motives for Holding Cash

Companies hold cash to make routine payments for business transactions, to repay loans and other financing costs, to maintain compensating balances for banks, to prepare for future uncertainties, and to prepare for future opportunities. Motives for holding cash include:

- **Transaction Motive:** A company may hold cash to meet payments arising from the ordinary course of business.

- **Speculative Motive:** Cash may be needed to take advantage of temporary opportunities.

- **Precautionary Motive:** It is important to have enough cash on hand to maintain a safety cushion to meet unexpected needs.

1.1.2   Disadvantages of High Cash Levels

Maintaining high levels of cash can be a disadvantage because of:

- The "negative arbitrage" effect (i.e., interest obligations exceed interest income from cash reserves).

- Increased attractiveness as a takeover target.

- Investor dissatisfaction with allocation of assets (i.e., failure to pay dividends).

1.1.3   Primary Methods of Increasing Cash Levels (Reducing the Operating Cycle)

Either speeding up cash inflows or slowing down cash outflows increases cash balances. Improved rates of cash collection are generally achieved through faster accounts receivable collections. Reduced cash outflows are often achieved through delayed (or deferred) disbursements. The combination of current cash inflows and current cash outflows related to a business is called the operating cycle. The objective of financial managers is to shorten the operating cycle.

1.2   Management of Accounts Receivable

1.2.1   Credit Policy

Credit policy is one of the major determinants of demand for a firm's products or services, along with price, product quality, and advertising. The credit policy of a company is typically established by a committee of senior company executives. Credit policy variables include:

1. **Credit Period:** Credit period is the length of time buyers are given to pay for their purchases. A commonly used credit period is 30 days. If the credit period is too long, the company may experience cash shortages. A credit period that is too short may damage relationships with customers and negatively affect future sales.

2. **Credit Standards:** Credit standards refer to the required financial strength of credit customers. Extending credit to only financially strong customers minimizes uncollectible receivables, but also limits potential sales. Extending credit to a broader base of customers increases sales, but adds risk in that a greater percentage of receivables are likely to be written off.

3. **Collection Policy:** Collection policy is measured by its stringency or laxity in collecting delinquent accounts. This is also a balancing act between wanting to collect cash owed quickly versus maintaining positive relationships with customers.

4. **Discounts:** Discounts include the discount percentage and period. Offering discounts to customers who pay early may result in faster receivables collection, depending on the terms of the discount and the customer's own cash needs and capacity to pay early.

1.2.2   Accounts Receivable Ratios

Financial ratios can be used to evaluate the effectiveness of an entity's credit policy. The list below represents common metrics used to evaluate AR collections.

■ **Accounts Receivable Turnover (ART):** The number of times (per year, typically) a company is converting its receivables into cash.

$$\text{Accounts receivable turnover} = \frac{\text{Sales (net)}}{\text{Average accounts receivable (net)}}$$

■ **Days Sales in Accounts Receivable:** A key component of the cash conversion cycle, this represents how many days on average it takes a company to convert its credit sales into cash.

$$\text{Days sales in accounts receivable} = \left(\frac{\text{Ending accounts receivable (net)}}{\text{Sales (net)}} \right) \times \frac{\text{Number of days}}{\text{in the period}}$$

1.2.3   Methods to Speed Collections

■ **Customer Screening and Credit Policy:** A company can choose to extend credit to more responsible customers, who are more likely to pay bills promptly.

■ **Prompt Billing:** Timely billing of charges to credit customers ultimately serves to speed collections.

■ **Payment Discounts:** Offering payment discounts may influence customers to pay faster and can result in improved cash collections. Discounts foregone represent a higher cost to the customer than a bank loan for similar financing.

- **Expedite Deposits:** Financial managers not only must collect credit sales in a timely manner, but also must ensure that funds are deposited and credited to their account quickly. The following techniques reduce the time during which payments received by a firm remain uncollected (not yet credited as cash in the bank).

  - **Electronic Funds Transfer:** The electronic movement of funds from one institution to another is called electronic funds transfer, or EFT. Electronic funds transfer and credit cards ensure timely payment. Having funds sent electronically to a company's bank account facilitates immediate collection rather than waiting for checks to be deposited.

  - **Lockbox Systems:** Lockbox systems expedite cash inflows by having a bank receive payments from a company's customers directly via mailboxes to which the bank has access. Payments that arrive in these mailboxes are deposited into the company's account immediately.

- **Concentration Banking:** Concentration banking is characterized by the designation of a single bank as a central depository. Advantages of concentration banking include:

  - Improved controls over inflows and outflows of cash

  - Reduced idle balances

  - Improved effectiveness for investments

1.2.4 Factoring

Factoring accounts receivable entails turning over the collection of accounts receivable to a third-party factor in exchange for a discounted short-term loan. Cash is collected from the factor immediately rather than from the customer according to the credit terms.

Example 1	Factoring

Facts: Radon Technologies enters into an agreement with a firm that will factor the company's accounts receivable. The factor agrees to buy the company's receivables, which average $50,000 a month, and have an average collection period of 30 days. The factor will advance up to 80 percent of the face value of receivables at an annual rate of 12 percent and charge a fee of 2 percent on all receivables purchased. The controller of the company estimates that the company would save $10,000 in collection expenses over the year. Fees and interest are not deducted in advance. Assuming a 360-day year, what is the annual cost of financing?

Required: Assuming a 360-day year, compute the annual cost of financing.

Solution:

	AR	× Fee	× (Days in year / Days in period)	Subtotals
AR submitted	$ 50,000	2%	360 / 30	$ 12,000
Amount withheld (20%)	(10,000)			
Amount subject to interest	$ 40,000	12% / 12	360 / 30	4,800
Cost to company				16,800
Less expense saved (due to outsourced collections)				(10,000)
Net cost				$ 6,800

Net cost/average amount advanced = $6,800 / $40,000 = 17% (APR)

2 Corporate Banking Arrangements

Debt involves risk, but it also provides management with the funds needed for operations and growth. One source of debt is borrowing from banks and other lending institutions that offer various forms of credit to companies.

2.1 Letter of Credit

A letter of credit represents a third-party guarantee, generally by a bank, of financial obligations incurred by the company. Letters of credit represent an external credit enhancement used by a company issuing otherwise unsecured debt to enhance its credit or can be required by a creditor to ensure payment.

Illustration 1 Letter of Credit

WUTFUN Toy Company is stocking up for its year-end inventory requirements and seeks to issue commercial paper to its suppliers upon delivery of stock. Toy wholesalers expect weak sales and are reluctant to accept unsecured debt. WUTFUN arranges for a letter of credit to guarantee payment of its indebtedness in order to ensure delivery of inventory.

2.2 Line of Credit

A line of credit represents a revolving loan with a bank, or group of banks, that is up to a specific dollar maximum amount for a defined term and is renewable upon the maturity date. Any outstanding balances under the line of credit reduce the future availability of funds that may be drawn by the company under that line. Lines of credit that are drawn represent a loan from the bank(s).

A company may also have a seasonal revolving credit facility that allows additional capital availability for a limited time period. Seasonal revolving credit facilities are used by companies during periods of high working capital needs.

Illustration 2 Line of Credit

Lacey's Stores Inc. is a soft goods general retailer. Through the first six months of the current operating year, the company has been able to cover its operating costs and working capital needs through its internal cash flow generation and the issuance of commercial paper. As the summer season begins to wind down, the retailer is planning a significant buildup of retail inventory for the upcoming holiday season. In order to obtain the necessary capital for this working capital expansion, the retailer draws down 80 percent of the availability under its master revolving line of credit facility. Several months later, Lacey's uses its seasonal revolving line of credit to cover its additional retail inventory needs. As the holiday season ends, the retailer pays down all outstanding balances under the master revolving credit facility and seasonal revolving line of credit (which is subsequently terminated at operating year-end).

2.3   Borrowing Capacity

A company's borrowing capacity, or borrowing limit, represents the amount of money in the form of credit or loans that a given lender, such as a bank, is willing to extend/lend to the company. Financial strength and stability (often summarized in the form of a credit rating) are key factors in this determination, as is the collateral a borrower has available to pledge toward the borrowed amount. In the event the borrower defaults on its obligation, the collateral is in place to protect the lender. Another key factor is the income level (and stability) of the borrower, as this will ultimately be the source of repayments to the lender.

Both lenders and borrowers have to manage their risk, and the borrowing capacity is protection for both sides such that the borrower does not take on more debt than it can reasonably manage and ultimately pay back. If a lender thinks that the borrower has no capacity to take on debt, the borrowing capacity is zero and no money will be lent.

2.4   Debt Covenants

Creditors use debt covenants in lending agreements to protect their interests by limiting or prohibiting the actions of debtors that might negatively affect the positions of the creditors. Covenants contained in a lending agreement may be positive or negative. A positive covenant may include the requirement that the issuer provides quarterly financial reporting (information) to the investors; a negative covenant may involve a restriction on asset sales for a stipulated time frame. When issuing debt instruments, company management should consider the potential effect of debt covenants on a firm's solvency, as highly restrictive covenants could hinder the company's basic operating decisions.

2.4.1   Common Debt Covenants

Debt covenants vary widely. Debt covenants may be positive (specifying something the borrower will do) or negative (specifying something the borrower will not do). Common debt covenants include:

- Limitations on issuing additional debt
- Restrictions on the payment of dividends
- Limitations on the disposal of certain assets
- Limitations on how the borrowed money can be used
- Minimum working capital requirements
- Maintenance of specific financial ratios, including:
    - Maximum debt-to-total-capital ratio (debt ratio)
    - Maximum debt-to-EBITDA ratio (cash flow coverage)
    - Minimum interest coverage ratio (times interest earned)
- Providing monthly, quarterly, or annual financial statements to bondholders (lenders)

2.4.2   Violation of Debt Covenants

When debt covenants are violated, the debtor is in technical default and the creditor can demand repayment of the entire principal. Most of the time, concessions are negotiated and real default, as opposed to technical default, is avoided. Concessions can result in the violated covenant(s) being waived temporarily or permanently. Concessions also can result in a change in the interest rate or other terms of the debt.

3 Financing Decisions and Working Capital

Companies use a mix of short-term and long-term financing to meet their capital requirements. Short-term and long-term financing have different advantages and disadvantages, and different effects on working capital.

3.1 Short-Term Financing

3.1.1 Characteristics

Short-term financing is generally classified as current and will mature within one year.

- **Rates:** Rates associated with short-term financing tend to be lower than long-term rates and presume greater liquidity on the part of the organization using short-term financing.

- **Effect on Working Capital:** Short-term financing is classified as a current liability and decreases working capital. The extent to which an organization uses short-term financing is dependent on both the amount of current assets it maintains and the risk tolerance of management. Shorter-term financing strategies require current asset levels to be sufficient to meet short-term obligations.

3.1.2 Advantages

- **Increased Profitability:** Rapid conversion of operating cycle components (e.g., inventory, receivables) into cash in order to meet short-term obligations carries the potential of increased profitability (and improved liquidity).

- **Decreased Financing Cost:** Short-term interest rates are generally lower than long-term interest rates given the shorter duration of the financing instruments.

3.1.3 Disadvantages

- **Increased Interest Rate Risk:** Interest rates may abruptly change, and given shorter maturities, may require greater financing charges than anticipated on future refinancing.

- **Decreased Capital Availability:** Lender evaluation of creditworthiness may change and thereby make financing impossible or less favorable by virtue of increased rates and/or less favorable terms.

3.2 Long-Term Financing

3.2.1 Characteristics

Long-term financing is generally classified as non-current and will mature after one year.

- **Rates:** Rates associated with long-term financing tend to be higher than short-term rates and presume less liquidity on the part of the organization using long-term financing.

- **Effect on Working Capital:** Long-term financing is classified as non-current and is not included in the calculation of working capital. However, dividend, interest, and principal repayments all require cash, which can reduce working capital over time. The extent to which an organization uses long-term financing is dependent on both the amount of current assets it maintains and the risk tolerance of management. Long-term financing increases financial leverage.

3.2.2 Advantages

- **Decreased Interest Rate Risk:** For the borrower, long-term financing locks in an interest rate over a long period, thereby reducing the exposure to fluctuations in rates.

- **Increased Capital Availability:** Securing long-term debt guarantees financing over a long period and reduces the company's exposure to any risk that refinancing might be denied or modified with less favorable terms.

3.2.3 Disadvantages

- **Decreased Profitability:** Higher financing costs reduce profitability.

- **Increased Financing Costs:** Long-term debt generally carries a higher interest rate given the longer duration of the financing instruments.

  - **Interest Rate Risk: Lender's Perspective**

    For the lenders, a higher interest rate is charged for longer-term debt because the likelihood that interest rates will change over the period of the loan increases as the term of the loan increases. Higher financing charges compensate the lender for increased interest rate risk. Therefore, the lenders recognize their exposure to interest rate risk with long-term financing and charge a premium to the borrower in the form of higher rates.

  - **Interest Rate Risk: Borrower's Perspective**

    The borrowers, on the other hand, lock themselves into a long-term interest rate to reduce their exposure to interest rate risk, and pay a premium to do so.

Question 1	CPA-05315

What would be the primary reason for a company to agree to a debt covenant limiting the percentage of its long-term debt?

    a. To cause the price of the company's stock to rise.

    b. To lower the company's bond rating.

    c. To reduce the risk for existing bondholders.

    d. To reduce the coupon rate on the bonds being sold.

NOTES

1 Security Valuation

1.1 Absolute Value Models

Absolute value models assign an intrinsic value to an asset based on the present value of its future cash flows. Estimates of cash flows are derived and discounted based on interest rates applicable to the level of risk and required return associated with the asset and its projected cash flows.

1.1.1 Annuities

An annuity is a series of equal cash flows to be received over a number of periods. The traditional approach to asset valuation is the annuity present value formula, which divides future cash flows by a rate of return in order to determine the value of the annuity in today's dollars.

- **Calculating the Present Value of an Annuity**

$$\text{Annuity present value} = C \times (1 - \text{Present value factor})/r$$

$$= C \times \frac{1 - \dfrac{1}{(1+r)^t}}{r}$$

Terms are defined as follows:

C = Amount of annuity (equal future cash flows)

r = Rate of return

t = Number of years

- **Assumptions:** Key assumptions implied by the variables of the formula include:

  - **Recurring Amount of the Annuity:** The amount of the periodic annuity must be specified (e.g., $10,000 per year).

  - **Appropriate Discount Rate:** Assumptions must specify the discount rate (e.g., the company requires a 15 percent return per year).

  - **Duration of the Annuity:** Assumptions must specify how long the annuity will continue (e.g., 2 years, 10 years, or even perpetuity, etc.).

  - **Timing of the Annuity:** An annuity may be received or paid in any number of ways. Assumptions must specify if the annuity payment occurs monthly, quarterly, annually, etc. The assumptions also must specify whether the annuity occurs at the beginning or the end of the period. The formula above assumes that annuity payments are made at the end of each period.

1.1.2 Perpetuities (Zero Growth Stock)

When the periodic cash flows paid by an annuity last forever, the annuity is called a perpetuity or perpetual annuity. The traditional annuity formula for perpetual cash flow streams is simplified, because no duration is known. When a company is expected to pay the same dividend each period, the perpetuity formula can be used to determine the value of the company's stock. This is the method used to value preferred stock.

- **Per-Share Valuation**

> **Present value of a perpetuity = Stock value per share = P = D/R**
>
> Terms are defined as follows:
>
> P = Stock price
>
> D = Dividend
>
> R = Required return

- **Assumptions**

  - The assumptions must specify the dividend (and assume that it will never change).

  - The assumptions must specify the required return.

Example 1   Perpetuities

Facts: Baker Corporation pays a constant annual dividend per share of $5 per year. Able wants to invest in Baker and earn a 20 percent return.

Required: Calculate the value of Baker's stock.

Solution:

P = D/R

P = $5/20%

P = $25

Able should pay $25 for a share of Baker.

1.1.3 Constant (Gordon) Growth Dividend Discount Model (DDM)

The dividend discount model (DDM) assumes that dividend payments are the cash flows of an equity security and that the intrinsic value of the company's stock is the present value of the expected future dividends. If dividends are assumed to grow at a constant rate, the constant (Gordon) growth DDM can be used to determine the value of the company's stock.

■   **Per-Share Valuation With Assumed Growth**

  •   **Value (Price) of Equity Formula (Dividend Growth Model)**

$$P_t = \frac{D_{(t)}(1 + G)}{(R - G)}$$

Terms are defined as follows:

P_t =   Current price (price at period "t")

$D_{(t+1)}$ =   Dividend one year after period "t"

R =   Required return

G =   (Sustainable) Growth rate

The candidate may be given the dividend at time = 0 or D_0. To determine D_1, the numerator of the formula becomes: $D_0(1 + G)$

  •   **Determining the Required Rate of Return (R)**

The capital asset pricing model (CAPM) is often used to determine the required return for the DDM model as follows:

$$R_{ce} = R_f + \beta_i[(E(R_m) - R_f]$$

Where:

R_{ce} =   Required rate of return on the (common) equity security

R_f =   Risk-free rate of return

β_i =   Beta on the security

$E(R_m)$ =   Expected return on market (portfolio)

Under the CAPM formula, the $[E(R_m) - R_f]$ term is also known as the equity risk premium.

■   **Assumptions**

  •   The assumptions must specify (or allow for the calculation of) dividends one year beyond the year in which you are determining the price.

  •   The assumptions must include a required return.

  •   The assumptions must include a constant growth rate of dividends.

  •   The formula implies that the stock price will grow at the same rate as the dividend, in perpetuity.

  •   The formula assumes that the required rate of return is greater than the dividend growth rate. If this relationship does not hold true, the formula will not work.

Example 2	Dividend Growth Model

Facts: Baker Corporation pays a current dividend per share of $5 per year and is projected to grow at 4 percent per year. Able wants to invest in Baker and earn a 20 percent return.

Required: Calculate the value of Baker's stock today.

Solution:

$$P_t = D_{(t+1)}/(R - G)$$
$$D_{(t+1)} = \$5 \times 1.04$$
$$D_{(t+1)} = \$5.20$$
$$P_t = \$5.20/(0.20 - 0.04)$$
$$P_t = \$5.20/(0.16)$$
$$P_t = \$32.50$$

The intrinsic value of Baker's stock today is $32.50.

Example 3	Dividend Discount Model

Facts: Baker Corporation pays a current dividend per share of $5 per year and is projected to grow at 4 percent per year. Able wants to invest in Baker and earn a 20 percent return.

Required: Calculate the amount that Able will pay for Baker's stock three years from today.

Solution:

$$P_t = D_{(t+1)}/(R - G)$$
$$D_{(t+1)} = \$5 \times 1.04 \times 1.04 \times 1.04 \times 1.04, \text{ or}$$
$$D_{(t+1)} = \$5 \times (1.04)^4$$
$$D_{(t+1)} = \$5 \times 1.1698586$$
$$D_{(t+1)} = \$5.85$$
$$P_t = D_{(t+1)}/(R - G)$$
$$P_t = (\$5.85)/(0.20 - 0.04)$$
$$P_t = \$5.85/(0.16)$$
$$P_t = \$36.56$$

In order to value Baker in three years, the dividend to be paid in the fourth year is required. Able should pay $36.56 for Baker in three years.

1.1.4   Introduction to Discounted Cash Flow Analysis

Discounted cash flow (DCF) analysis attempts to determine the intrinsic (true) value of an equity security by determining the present value of its expected future cash flows. To apply DCF analysis, an analyst takes the following steps:

- Choose an appropriate model.

  - Dividend discount models (DDM) use the stock's expected dividends as the relevant cash flows. The Gordon constant growth model is an example of a simple dividend discount model.

  - Free cash flow models including free cash flow to the firm (FCFF) and free cash flow to equity (FCFE). The free cash flow models discount the cash flow left over by the firm after satisfying certain required obligations including working capital needs and fixed capital investment.

  - Residual income models represent the income left over after the firm satisfies the investor's required return.

- Forecast the security's cash flows using one of the model approaches above.

- Select a discount rate methodology. The CAPM is a popular method used to estimate the required return for an equity security.

- Estimate the discount rate and apply to the appropriate DCF model.

- Calculate the equity security's intrinsic value and compare to its current market value.

1.2   Relative Valuation Models

Relative valuation models use the value of comparable stocks to determine the value of similar stocks. Price multiples are useful metrics in relative valuation.

Price multiples represent ratios of a stock's market price to another measure of fundamental value per share. Investors use price multiples to determine if a stock is undervalued, fairly valued, or overvalued.

1.2.1   Price-Earnings (P/E) Ratio

The P/E ratio is the most widely used multiple when valuing equity securities. The rationale for using this measure is that earnings are a key driver of investment value (stock price). This multiple is widely used by the investment community and empirical research has shown that changes in a company's P/E are tied to the long-run stock performance of that company.

- **Calculating the P/E Ratio**

$$\text{P/E ratio} = P_0 / E_1$$

Terms are defined as follows:

P_0 = Stock price or value today

E_1 = EPS expected in one year (next four quarters)

Note: The above formula is termed the "forward P/E" as the denominator is based on expected earnings over the next year or four quarters.

■ Valuing Equity With the P/E Ratio

The P/E ratio, once calculated, can be multiplied by anticipated future earnings in order to determine the current stock price. It requires that earnings be greater than zero.

Example 4	P/E Ratio

Facts: Assume that Baker Corporation has current-year earnings per share of $1.50 and anticipates earnings per share in the coming year of $2.

Required: If the P/E ratio is 7.5x, calculate the expected value of Baker's shares.

Solution:

$$(P_0) = (P_0/E_1) \times E_1$$
$$(P_0) = 7.5 \times \$2$$
$$(P_0) = \$15$$

The P/E ratio of 7.5x implies that the current stock price should be 7.5x the anticipated earnings per share of $2. An investor would expect the current stock price to therefore be $15.

■ Trailing vs. Forward P/E

The numerator in the P/E ratio is unambiguous, as the stock price for publicly traded companies is readily available. This is not the case for the denominator of the ratio, as the earnings used in the P/E ratio can either be past earnings or expected future earnings.

When past earnings are used in the P/E ratio, such as earnings for the past four quarters or trailing 12-month EPS, the ratio calculated is the *trailing P/E*. When expected earnings of the company next year is used in the denominator, the ratio is the *forward P/E*.

The trailing P/E is the preferred calculation method when a company's forecasted earnings are unavailable, while the forward P/E is the preferred method when the company's historical earnings is not representative of its future earnings. The formula for the trailing P/E ratio is as follows:

$$\text{Trailing P/E ratio} = P_0/E_0$$

Terms are defined as follows:

P_0 = Stock price or value today

E_0 = EPS for the past year (past four quarters)

1.2.2 PEG Ratio

The PEG ratio is a measure that shows the effect of earnings growth on a company's P/E, assuming a linear relationship between P/E and growth. Generally, stocks that have lower PEG ratios are more attractive to investors than stocks that have higher PEG ratios.

Calculating the PEG Ratio

$$PEG = (P_0/E_1)/G$$

Terms are defined as follows:

P_0 = Stock price or value today

E_1 = Expected EPS

G = Growth rate = 100 × Expected growth rate

Valuing Equity With the PEG Ratio

The PEG ratio calculates the P/E ratio per unit of growth. The PEG ratio can be multiplied by both forecasted future earnings and the growth rate to determine the current price of the stock.

$$(P_0) = PEG \times E_1 \times G$$

Terms are defined as follows:

P_0 = Stock price or value today

E_1 = Expected EPS

G = Growth rate = 100 × Expected growth rate

Example 5 | PEG Ratio

Facts: Baker wants to use the PEG ratio to estimate the price of its stock. The company's PEG ratio is 2.5x and its current earnings per share is $5. The growth rate for earnings is anticipated to be 4 percent.

Required: Calculate the current price of Baker's stock.

Solution:

E_1 = 5.00 × 1.04 = $5.20

(P_0) = PEG × E_1 × G

(P_0) = 2.5 × $5.20 × 4

(P_0) = $52.00

1.2.3 Price-to-Sales Ratio

Similar to the P/E ratio, this price multiple ratio can be used to estimate the current stock price. The rationale for using the price-to-sales ratio is that sales are less subject to manipulation than earnings or book values; sales are always positive so this multiple can be used even when EPS is negative; and this ratio is not as volatile as the P/E ratio, which includes the effect of financial and operating leverage. Empirical studies have shown that P/S is an appropriate measure to value stocks that are associated with mature or cyclical companies.

■ **Calculating the Price-to-Sales Ratio**

$$\text{Price-to-sales ratio} = P_0/S_1$$

Terms are defined as follows:

P_0 = Stock price or value today

S_1 = Expected sales in one year

■ **Valuing Equity With the Price-to-Sales Ratio**

The value of equity can then be calculated as follows:

$$(P_0) = (P_0/S_1) \times S_1$$

1.2.4 Price-to-Cash-Flow Ratio

The price-to-cash-flow ratio may also be used to calculate the current stock price. The rationale for using this price multiple is that cash flow is harder for companies to manipulate than earnings; P/CF is a more stable measure than P/E; and empirical research has shown that changes in a company's P/CF ratios over time are positively related to changes in a company's long-term stock returns.

■ **Calculating the Price-to-Cash-Flow Ratio**

$$\text{Price-to-cash-flow ratio} = P_0/CF_1$$

Terms are defined as follows:

P_0 = Stock price or value today

CF_1 = Expected cash flow in one year

■ **Valuing Equity With the Price-to-Cash-Flow Ratio**

The value of equity can then be calculated as follows:

$$(P_0) = (P_0/CF_1) \times CF_1$$

1.2.5   Price-to-Book Ratio

The price-to-book (P/B) ratio is another price multiple used by analysts that focuses on the balance sheet rather than the income statement or statement of cash flows. The rationale for using this multiple is that a firm's book value of common equity (assets minus liabilities and preferred stock) is more stable than earnings per share, especially when a firm's EPS is extremely high or low for a given period. Because P/B is usually positive, this multiple can be used even when a firm's EPS is negative or zero. Research indicates that the P/B ratio can explain a firm's average stock returns over the long run.

■   **Calculating the P/B Ratio**

$$\text{P/B ratio} = P_0 / B_0$$

Terms are defined as follows:

P_0 = **Stock price or value today**

B_0 = **Book value of common equity**

■   **Valuing Equity With the P/B Ratio**

The value of equity can then be calculated as follows:

$$(P_0) = (P_0 / B_0) \times B_0$$

Example 6	Price-to-Book Ratio

Facts: An analyst assembles the following financial and market data for Bolden Corporation's most recent year-end. The analyst projects that the firm's operating cash flow will increase 20 percent in the upcoming year.

Market Data

Common stock price	$18
Common shares outstanding	10,000,000

Financial Data

Total assets	$250,000,000
Total liabilities	110,000,000
Preferred stock	20,000,000
Common stock	25,000,000
Additional paid-in capital	45,000,000
Retained earnings	50,000,000
Total stockholders' equity	140,000,000
Cash flow from operations	25,000,000

Required: Using the previous data, calculate the P/B and P/CF multiples.

(continued)

(continued)

Solution:

The P/B multiple for Bolden Corporation's current year is derived as follows:

1. Determine book value of common equity

    $25,000,000 (CS) + $45,000,000 (APIC) + $50,000,000 (RE) = $120,000,000

2. Determine book of common equity per share

    $120,000,000 / 10,000,000 shares = $12

3. Calculate P/B multiple

    $$P_0/B_0 = \$18/\$12$$
    $$= 1.5$$

Based on the previous data and the analyst's operating cash flow forecast, the P/CF multiple is derived as follows:

1. Determine the firm's expected cash flow per share

    $$CF_1 = \$25,000,000 \times 1.20 = \$30,000,0000$$
    $$CF_1/Sh. = \$30,000,000/10,000,000 \text{ shares} = \$3$$

2. Calculate P/CF multiple

    $$P_0/CF_1 = \$18/\$3$$
    $$= 6.0$$

1.2.6 Assumptions

The price multiple ratios have similar assumption requirements, each of which can be influenced by management behaviors, including:

- Future earnings
- Future cash flows
- Future sales
- Future growth rate
- The duration of sales, earnings, or cash flow trends

1.2.7 Relative Valuation

Once an analyst calculates a set of price multiple ratios for a given company (stock), these ratios are used as a method of comparison to the same corresponding ratios calculated for similar companies (stocks) within that industry sector to determine a ranking for each price multiple ratio and ultimately provide important input into a particular company's stock valuation.

| Example 7 | Relative Valuation Models |

Facts: An investor is comparing market ratios for the XLX Company to those of its industry. The following ratios were calculated at the end of the current fiscal year:

Ratio	XLX Company	Industry
P/E	16.2	14.9
PEG	4.8	5.3
P/S	18.1	19.4
P/CF	13.6	13.7
P/B	19.2	17.8

Required: Discuss what each ratio indicates regarding XLX stock valuation and how the numbers can be interpreted.

Solution:

- **P/E Ratio:** XLX has a higher P/E ratio than its industry peer group. This measure, on its own, would indicate that the stock price for XLX is overvalued relative to that of its peers. Investors would expect the price of XLX stock to decline in order to align the P/E ratio with that of its peers.

- **PEG Ratio:** XLX has a lower PEG ratio than its industry. For XLX, the growth rate is equal to 3.38 percent (PE of 16.2 divided by PEG of 4.8). For the industry, the growth rate is equal to 2.81 percent (PE of 14.9 divided by PEG of 5.3). Given the higher level of growth for XLX versus its industry, the PEG ratio indicates that XLX stock may actually be undervalued relative to that of its peers.

- **P/S Ratio:** This is another indicator that XLX stock may actually be undervalued relative to that of its peers. However, this ratio alone does not account for cost structure, capital structure, or tax effects that should be evaluated before determining whether a stock is relatively overvalued or undervalued.

- **P/CF Ratio:** XLX and the industry have very similar P/CF ratios. This metric alone would indicate that the stock price for XLX is fairly valued.

- **P/B Ratio:** Relative to the value of its equity, XLS's stock price is higher than that of its peers. The stock may not necessarily be overvalued, as a higher P/B may indicate that the market thinks that XLX's net assets are undervalued.

Question 1
CPA-06137

Fernwell wants to buy shares of Gurst Company in two years. Fernwell uses a constant growth dividend discount model with a presumed dividend growth rate of 5 percent. If Fernwell's discount rate is 10 percent and Gurst's current year dividend is $20, what is the approximate price Fernwell will pay?

    a. $400
    b. $420
    c. $441
    d. $463

Question 2
CPA-06131

Coldwell is using a constant growth dividend discount model to forecast the value of a share of common stock. Inherent in Coldwell's assumptions is the idea that:

    a. Compounding growth is linear.
    b. Dividends will grow at a rate faster than the presumed discount rate.
    c. Stock price will grow at the same rate as the dividend.
    d. Stock price will grow at the same amount as the dividend.

Question 3
CPA-06133

Investors are likely to view a high price-earnings (P/E) ratio as an indication that:

    a. Earnings have growth potential.
    b. Earnings have peaked and will remain flat.
    c. Earnings have peaked and will likely fall.
    d. There is no logical conclusion to reach about the relationship between price and earnings.

1 Option Pricing Models

1.1 Definition of an Option

An option is a contract that entitles the owner (holder) to buy (call option) or sell (put option) a stock (or some other asset) at a given price within a stated period of time. American-style options can be exercised at any time prior to their expiration. European-style options can be exercised only at the expiration or maturity date of the option.

1.2 Valuing Options: The Black-Scholes Model

Different factors enter into the determination of the value of an option. A commonly used method for option valuation is the Black-Scholes model. The calculation is extremely complex and beyond the scope of the CPA Exam. However, you do need a high-level understanding of the concepts and assumptions that underlie Black-Scholes. Accountants may use this method in valuing stock options when accounting for share-based payments. Option price calculators are widely available, so you do not need to understand the complexity of the actual calculations to apply this method.

- Inputs into the Black-Scholes model (determinants of the call option value)
  - Current price of the underlying stock (higher price → higher option value)
  - Option exercise price
  - Risk-free interest rate (higher rate → higher option value)
  - Current time until expiration (longer time → higher call option value)
  - Some measure of risk for the underlying stock (higher risk → higher option value)
- Assumptions underlying the Black-Scholes model
  - Stock prices behave randomly.
  - The risk-free rate and volatility of the stock prices are constant over the option's life.
  - There are no taxes or transaction costs.
  - The stock pays no dividends, although the model can be adapted to dividend-paying stock.
  - The options are European-style (exercisable only at maturity).
- Limitations of the Black-Scholes model

  Despite its current use, the Black-Scholes model does have several limitations:
  - Due to the model's assumptions, results generated from the Black-Scholes model may differ from real prices.
  - It assumes instant, cost-less trading, which is unrealistic in today's markets.
  - The model tends to underestimate extreme price movements.
  - The model is not applicable to pricing American-style options.

1.3 Valuing Options: Binomial Model

Another option pricing model is the binomial or Cox-Ross-Rubinstein model. It is a variation of the original Black-Scholes model. The binomial model considers the underlying security over a period of time, as compared to the value at one point in time under the Black-Scholes model. This model is useful for valuing American-style options, which can be exercised over a period of time.

- The assumptions of the binomial model are:
  - a perfectly efficient stock market; and
  - the underlying security price will move up or down at certain points in time (called nodes) during the life of the option.

- The result of applying the model is a tree diagram showing the possible values of the options at different points in time or nodes. The math for this approach is also beyond the scope of the CPA Exam.

- The benefits of the binomial method are:
  - it can be used for American-style options; and
  - it can be used for stocks that pay dividends without modifying the model, as is necessary with Black-Scholes.

2 Valuing Debt Instruments

The value of a bond is equal to the present value of its future cash flows (which consist of interest payments and the principal payment at maturity). The cash flows may be discounted using a single interest rate or multiple interest rates aligned with the degree of risk for each cash flow.

Bonds paying a fixed coupon rate equal to the market rate for comparable bonds are issued at par (face) value. If a bond's coupon rate at issuance is less (more) than the market rate, the bond will be issued at a discount (premium). As market interest rates change, the market value of the bond will also change. For fixed-rate bonds, when market interest rates rise the market value of the bond falls, and vice versa.

Example 1	Debt Instruments

Facts: A $1,000 face value bond maturing in three years pays annual interest of 4 percent.

Required: Calculate the bond's price If the market rate at the time of issuance is 5 percent.

Solution: Because the bond pays a lower coupon rate than market rate, it will be issued at a discount to par. The calculation for the bond's price is as follows:

Year 1 payment: $40 / 1.05 = \$38.10$

Year 2 payment: $40 / (1.05)^2 = \$36.28$

Year 3 payment: $(40 + 1,000) / (1.05)^3 = \$898.39$

Total value: $\$38.10 + \$36.28 + \$898.39 = \$972.77$

---

3   Valuing Tangible Assets

Fixed assets represent the property (land), plant (buildings), and equipment (PP&E) held by a company to provide the infrastructure needed to support operations. GAAP and IFRS dictate how PP&E is reported on the balance sheet; the actual value of these assets can be determined using the following methods:

3.1   Cost Method

The value of the assets is based on the original cost paid to acquire the asset. Adjustments may be made for depreciation in order to reduce the value of the asset to reflect current utility.

3.2   Market Value Method

This method requires that similar assets be available in the marketplace in order to find a comparable value. Two iterations of the market value method are the replacement cost method (what it would cost to replace the valued asset) and the net realizable value method (the price at which the asset could be sold in the marketplace, reduced by any costs associated with selling the asset).

Illustration 1   Market Value Method

A company is assessing the value of the equipment at its headquarters. Using the market value method, the company determines that it would cost $6,200,000 today to replace all of its equipment. The company also determines that selling its equipment in the marketplace would generate $5,900,000 after accounting for selling/disposal costs. Either value may be used as a reasonable proxy for market value.

3.3   Appraisal Method

Under this method, a professional appraiser determines the value of the asset, assuming that the company can find an appraiser with knowledge and experience working with the specific asset(s) in question.

3.4   Liquidation Value

If the asset had to be sold today, the liquidation value represents the amount that the company would get upon sale assuming that there is an active market for the asset.

4   Valuing Intangible Assets

Intangible assets do not have a physical form, but like any asset, they provide probable future economic benefit to the entity that owns them. Intangible assets include patents, trademarks, intellectual property, copyrights, etc. The following methods may be used to value intangible assets.

4.1   Market Approach

This approach requires that actual arm's-length transactions (sales, transfers, licenses) in similar markets be used as a reference for the asset to be valued. Although this is a preferred approach to valuation, the unique nature of individual intangible assets and relative trading infrequency present challenges.

Illustration 2   Market Approach

A company has a patent in its intangibles portfolio that it is looking to monetize. In looking at recent transactions for comparable patent sales, the company discovers four within the last couple of years.

- Sale 1: $18.5 million
- Sale 2: $16.2 million
- Sale 3: $16.8 million
- Sale 4: $15.1 million

The company will look to assign a value within a range of $15.1 million to $18.5 million, perhaps using the median value of $16.5 million; or, the company may identify the transaction involving the asset that is closest to the nature of the patent the company is looking to sell and use that value.

4.2   Income Approach

Using this approach, future expected cash flows over the estimated useful life of the intangible asset are discounted to present value using discount rates reflecting the level of risk (including asset risk, industry risk, and market risk) associated with the income stream.

Illustration 3   Income Approach

Eagle Road Enterprises owns a patent that is expected to generate $4 million each year for the next 10 years. Using a discount rate of 5.5 percent and a discounting factor of 7.5376, the patent is worth $30.15 million today ($4 million × 7.5376 = $30.15 million).

4.3   Cost Approach

When there are no similar assets or transactions involving similar assets, and no reasonable estimates of future income, the cost approach can be used. Iterations of the cost approach include replacement cost (expenses required to create a similar asset) and reproduction cost (the expenses needed to reproduce the same asset). Costs incorporated will include materials, labor, overhead, legal and other fees, development costs, production costs, and opportunity costs.

Illustration 4   Cost Approach

Alpine Inc. looks to establish a value for the copyrights in its intangible asset portfolio. Using a valuation date of today, Alpine determines the following values for the costs associated with reproducing the same copyrights:

- Labor: $15,000
- Materials: $9,000
- Overhead: $11,000
- Legal and other fees: $22,000
- Development costs: $16,000
- Production costs: $13,000
- Opportunity costs: $26,000
- Total cost: $112,000

5   Valuation Using Accounting Estimates

Certain financial statement line items are valued using accounting estimates. For example:

- Accounts receivable is presented net of an allowance for uncollectible accounts.

- Inventory is reported at the lower of cost or market, or lower of cost and net realizable value, including write-downs of obsolete inventory.

- Fixed assets are offset by accumulated depreciation.

- Contingent liabilities are based on the best estimate of probable future losses.

5.1   Preparing Accounting Estimates

When preparing accounting estimates, management must consider the following data and factors:

- **Historical Information:** GAAP requires that the allowance for uncollectible accounts be estimated using historical information regarding the collectibility of a company's receivables from its customers. Historical patterns of fixed-asset usage may be used to justify the method used to depreciate fixed assets.

- **Market Information:** Information on the current value of inventory items should be used to determine the lower of cost or market and lower of cost and net realizable value, and should also be used to determine whether inventory should be written down or written off due to obsolescence.

- **Expected Usage:** Depreciation methods may be based on expected patterns of fixed-asset usage.

- **Estimates From Experts:** Attorneys are often used to provide estimates of probable future losses on pending or threatened litigation.

5.2   Review and Approval of Accounting Estimates

Accounting estimates should be supported by documentation that shows the assumptions and calculations upon which the estimates are based. Management should regularly review the support for material accounting estimates and should approve each estimate when reviewed.

Companies that use accounting estimates should expect their auditors to closely scrutinize the assumptions and support underlying the estimates. Auditors expect accounting estimates to be reasonable and look closely at any information that contradicts the assumptions made by management when preparing the estimates.

Financial Decision Models: Part 1

1 Cash Flows Related to Capital Budgeting

Capital budgeting is a process for evaluating and selecting the long-term investment projects of the firm. Proper capital budgeting is crucial to the success of an organization. The amount of cash the company takes in and pays out for an investment affects the amount of cash the company has available for operations and other activities of the company.

1.1 Cash Flow Effects

1.1.1 Direct Effect

When a company pays out cash, receives cash, or makes a cash commitment that is directly related to the capital investment, that effect is termed the direct effect. It has an immediate effect on the amount of cash available.

1.1.2 Indirect Effect

Transactions which are indirectly associated with a capital project or which represent noncash activity that produces cash benefits or obligations are termed indirect cash flow effects.

Illustration 1   Cash Flow Effects

Depreciation is a noncash expense taken as a tax deduction. Depreciation reduces the amount of taxable income and, consequently, the related taxes. The reduced tax bill resulting from increased depreciation expense associated with a new project decreases the cash paid out. This type of effect is termed an indirect effect (or tax effect) of capital budgeting.

1.1.3 Net Effect

The total of the direct and indirect effects of cash flows from a capital investment is called the net effect.

1.2 Stages of Cash Flows

Cash flows exist throughout the life cycle of a capital investment project. Cash flows are categorized in three general stages.

1.2.1 Inception of the Project (Time Period Zero)

Both direct cash flow effects (the acquisition cost of the asset) and indirect cash flow effects (working capital requirements or disposal of the replaced asset) occur at the time of the initial investment. The initial cash outlay for the project is often the largest amount of cash outflow of the investment's life.

- **Working Capital Requirements:** Working capital is defined as current assets minus current liabilities. When a capital project is implemented, the firm may need to increase or decrease working capital to ensure the success of the project.

  - **Additional Working Capital Requirements:** A proposed investment may be expected to increase payroll, expenses for supplies, or inventory requirements. This may result in an indirect cash outflow that is recognized at the inception of the project because part of the working capital of the organization will be allocated to the investment project and will be unavailable for other uses in the organization.

  - **Reduced Working Capital Requirements:** Implementing a just-in-time inventory system (in which the amount of inventory required to be on hand is reduced) represents a decrease in current assets and is recognized as an indirect cash inflow at the inception of the project.

- **Disposal of the Replaced Asset**

  - **Asset Abandonment:** If the replaced asset is abandoned, the net salvage value is treated as a reduction of the initial investment in the new asset. The abandoned asset's book value is considered a sunk cost, and therefore not relevant to the decision-making process. The remaining book value (for tax purposes) is deductible as a tax loss, which reduces the liability in the year of abandonment. This tax liability decrease is considered a reduction of the new asset's initial investment.

  - **Asset Sale:** If a new asset acquisition requires the sale of old assets, the cash received from the sale of the old asset reduces the new investment's value. If a gain or loss (for tax purposes) exists, there is also a corresponding increase or decrease in income taxes. The amount of income tax paid on a gain on a sale is treated as a reduction of the sales price (which increases the initial expenditure). Conversely, a reduction in tax resulting from a loss on a sale is treated as a reduction of the new investment.

1.2.2 Operations

The ongoing operations of the project will affect both direct and indirect cash flows of the company.

- The cash flows generated from the operations of the asset occur on a regular basis. These cash flows may be the same amount every year (an annuity) or may differ.

- Depreciation tax shields create ongoing indirect cash flow effects.

1.2.3 Disposal of the Project

Disposal of the investment at the end of the project produces direct or indirect cash flows.

- If the asset is sold, there is a direct effect for the cash inflow created on the sale and an indirect effect for the taxes due (in the case of a gain) or saved (in the case of a loss).

- Certain direct expenses may be incurred for the disposal (e.g., severance pay).

- If the asset is scrapped or donated, there may be a tax savings (an indirect effect) if the net tax basis is greater than zero (i.e., the asset has not been fully depreciated).

- There may be indirect effects associated with changes in the amount of working capital committed once the project is disposed of (e.g., employees who worked on the project may no longer be needed). A working capital commitment that was recognized as an indirect cash outflow at the inception of a project is recognized as an indirect cash inflow at the end of the project when the working capital commitment is released.

1.3   Calculation of Pretax and After-Tax Cash Flows

1.3.1   Pretax Cash Flows

The traditional computation of an asset's value is based on the cash flows it generates. Thus an investment's value is often based on the present value of the future cash flows that investors expect to receive from the investment. Larger cash outflows than inflows may indicate that a project is unprofitable.

1.3.2   After-Tax Cash Flows

After-tax cash flows are relevant to capital budgeting decisions and are computed using either of the following methods. Operating cash flow differs from net income because noncash expenses like depreciation must be added-back to net income to get to cash flow.

- **Method 1**
    1. Estimate net operating cash inflows (cash inflows minus cash outflows).
    2. Subtract noncash tax deductible expenses to arrive at taxable income.
    3. Compute income taxes related to a project's income (or loss) for each year of the project's useful life.
    4. Subtract tax expense from net cash inflows to arrive at after-tax cash flows.

- **Method 2**
    1. Multiply net operating cash inflows by (1 − Tax rate).
    2. Add the tax shield associated with noncash expenses such as depreciation (depreciation multiplied by the tax rate).
    3. The sum of these two amounts will equal the after-tax cash flows.

Illustration 2   Methods of Calculating After-Tax Cash Flows

Compute after-tax cash flows based on the following facts:

Annual cash inflows	$40,000
Depreciation	10,000
Tax rate	40%

Transaction Data	Method 1				Method 2
Cash inflows	$ 40,000	×	(1 − 40%)	=	$24,000
Depreciation	10,000	×	40%	=	+ 4,000
Pretax income	30,000				$28,000
Tax rate	(12,000)				
Net income	$ 18,000				
After-Tax Cash Flows					
Cash inflows	$ 40,000				
Taxes	(12,000)				
After-Tax Cash Flows	$ 28,000				

Example 1	Cash Flows for Capital Budgeting

Facts: The divisional management of Carlin Company has proposed the purchase of a new machine that will improve the efficiency of the operations in the company's manufacturing plant. The purchase price of the machine is $425,000. Costs associated with putting the machine into service include $10,000 for shipping, $15,000 for installation, and $6,000 for the initial training.

Carlin expects the machine to last six years and to have an estimated salvage value of $7,000. The machine is expected to produce 4,000 units a year with an expected selling price of $800 per unit and prime costs (direct materials and direct labor) of $750 per unit.

Tax depreciation will be computed under the accelerated straight-line rules (not MACRS) for five-year property with no consideration for salvage value (i.e., the entire asset amount capitalized will be depreciated). Carlin has a marginal tax rate of 40 percent.

Required: Calculate cash flows at the beginning of the first year (Year 0), for Years 1–5, and for Year 6, which is the final year.

Solution: Cash flow at the beginning of the first year for capital budgeting analysis

The net cash outflow at the beginning of the first year is calculated as follows:

Initial investment	$(425,000)	
Shipping	(10,000)	
Installation	(15,000)	
Training	(6,000)	
Total	$(456,000)	[Outflow]

Sample year: Net cash flow for Years 1–5 for capital budgeting analysis

Net cash flow from sales	$ 200,000	[4,000 × ($800 − $750)]
Less: taxes on net sales	(80,000)	[$200,000 × 0.40]
Add: net indirect effect of depreciation on machine	36,480	[($456,000 / 5) × 0.40]
Total	$ 156,480	[Inflow]

Net cash flow for the final year (Year 6) for capital budgeting analysis

Net cash flow from sales	$200,000	[per above]
Less: taxes on net sales	(80,000)	[per above]
Add: net indirect effect of depreciation on machine	-0-	No depreciation in Year 6
Salvage value	4,200	[$7,000 gain × 0.60, which is net of tax]
Total	$ 124,200	[Inflow]

2   Discounted Cash Flow (DCF)

DCF valuation methods (including the net present value and the internal rate of return methods) are techniques that use time value of money concepts to measure the present value of cash inflows and cash outflows expected from a project.

2.1   Objective and Components of Discounted Cash Flow as Used in Capital Budgeting

The objective of the discounted cash flow (DCF) method is to focus the attention of management on relevant cash flows appropriately discounted to present value. The factors used to evaluate capital investments under discounted cash flow include the dollar amount of the initial investment, the dollar amount of future cash inflows and outflows, and the rate of return desired for the project.

2.1.1   Rate of Return Desired for the Project

The rate used to discount future cash flows may be set by management using several different approaches. Management may use a weighted average cost of capital (WACC) method, a specific target rate assigned to new projects, or a rate that relates to the risk specific to the proposed project. If the proposed project is similar in risk to the ongoing projects of the company, WACC is appropriate because it reflects the market's assessment of the average risk of the company's projects.

2.1.2   Limitation of Discounted Cash Flow: Simple Constant Growth Assumption

Discounted cash flow methods are widely viewed as superior to methods that do not consider the time value of money. However, discounted cash flow methods do have an important limitation—they frequently use a single interest rate assumption. This assumption is often unrealistic because, over time, as management evaluates its alternatives, actual interest rates or risks may fluctuate.

3   Net Present Value Method (NPV)

3.1   Objective

The objective of the net present value method is to focus decision makers on the initial investment amount that is required to purchase (or invest in) a capital asset that will yield returns in an amount in excess of a management-designated hurdle rate.

NPV requires managers to evaluate the dollar amount of return rather than either percentages of return (as with the internal rate of return method) or years to recover principal (as with the payback methods) as a basis for screening investments.

3.2   Calculation of Net Present Value

Net present value is calculated as follows:

1. **Estimate the Cash Flows**

   Estimate all direct and indirect after-tax cash flows (both inflows and outflows) related to the investment.

   - **Ignore Depreciation (Unless a Tax Shield)**

     As with DCF methods, depreciation is ignored except to the extent that it reduces tax payments (i.e., a tax shield). Use of accelerated (instead of straight-line) depreciation methods increases the present value of the depreciation tax shield.

   - **Ignore Interest Expense**

     The discounting process itself deals with the cost of financing the project, and therefore finance costs are excluded from the cash flow forecast.

2. **Discount the Cash Flows**

   Discount all cash flows (both inflows and outflows) to present value using the appropriate discount factor based on the hurdle rate and the timing of the cash flow. The net present value method assumes that the cash flows are reinvested at the same rate used in the analysis.

3. **Compare**

   Compare the present values of inflows and outflows.

Pass Key

Discounted cash flow is the basis for net present value methods:

- **Step 1:** Calculate after-tax cash flows = Annual net cash flow × (1 − Tax rate)
- **Step 2:** Add depreciation benefit = Depreciation × Tax rate
- **Step 3:** Multiply result by appropriate present value of an annuity (assuming cash flows are an annuity)
- **Step 4:** Subtract initial cash outflow

Result: Net present value

3.3   Interpreting the NPV Method

The investment decision is based on whether the net present value is positive or negative. Note that if the net present value is equal to zero, management would be indifferent about accepting or rejecting the project. NPV is the theoretical dollar change in the market value of the firm's equity due to the project.

3.3.1 Positive Result = Make Investment

If the result is positive (greater than zero), the rate of return for the project is greater than the hurdle rate (the discount percentage rate used in the net present value calculation) and the investment should be made. If the company has unlimited funds, all projects with a net present value greater than zero should be accepted. Project ranking and acceptance techniques in circumstances involving limited capital are described below.

3.3.2 Negative Result = Do Not Make Investment

If the result is negative (less than zero), the rate of return for the project is less than the hurdle rate and the investment should not be made because it does not meet management's minimum rate of return. A negative NPV means that the internal rate of return on the investment is less than management's hurdle rate for the project.

3.4 Interest Rate Adjustments for Required Return

Net present value analysis may incorporate many types of hurdle rates, such as the cost of capital (the average rate of return demanded by investors), the interest rate of the opportunity cost, or some other minimum required rate of return. All rates are determined by management.

3.4.1 Adjustments to Rate

Rates may be modified (generally increased) to adjust for:

▪ **Risk:** Discount rates may be increased to further factor differences in risk into the analysis.

Illustration 3   Interest Rate Adjustment for Risk
Management would select a high hurdle rate for certain projects to factor risk into its consideration of acceptance of those projects. The higher hurdle rate discounts (reduces) future cash flows more, creating a smaller present value, which stands a larger chance of yielding an NPV below zero, with the project not being selected. By "devaluing" the cash flows for a project, the NPV model compensates for risk.

▪ **Inflation (Also Affects Cash Flows):** Rates may be raised to compensate for expected inflation.

Illustration 4   Interest Rate Adjustment for Inflation
Assume that management anticipates higher-than-normal inflation. To compensate for the falling value of the dollars it anticipates from its cash flows, the interest rate (discount factor) may be increased. In addition, the future cash flows also should be increased to the extent of predicted inflation. If management anticipates no change in tax rates, cash flows generated from the effects of depreciation would not be adjusted because they relate to the original investment.

3.4.2 Differing Rates

Different rates may be used for different time periods using the NPV method. For example, 12 percent might be the rate for the first three years, and 15 percent (which reflects a greater risk) might be the rate for subsequent years. If the NPV is greater than zero, the project will be acceptable.

Pass Key

The NPV method of capital investment valuation is considered to be superior to the internal rate of return (IRR) method because it is flexible enough to handle inconsistent rates of return for each year of the project.

3.4.3 Discount Rate Applied to Qualitatively Desirable or Non-optional Investments

A project that meets qualitative management criteria for investment (e.g., mandated technology investments) is subject to financing, rather than capital budgeting, considerations. In this case, the discount rate used for NPV evaluation should be the after-tax cost of borrowing, sometimes called the incremental borrowing rate.

Example 2	Net Present Value

Facts: McLean Inc. is considering the purchase of a new machine, which will cost $150,000. The machine has an estimated useful life of three years. Assume for simplicity that the equipment will be fully depreciated for tax purposes 30 percent, 40 percent, and 30 percent in each of the three years, respectively. The new machine will have a $10,000 resale value at the end of its estimated useful life. The machine is expected to save the company $85,000 per year in operating expenses. McLean uses a 40 percent estimated income tax rate and a 16 percent hurdle rate to evaluate capital projects.

Discount rates for a 16 percent rate are as follows:

	Present Value of $1	Present Value of an Ordinary Annuity of $1
Year 1	0.862	0.862
Year 2	0.743	1.605
Year 3	0.641	2.246

Required: Calculate the net present value of the proposed purchase of the new machine.

(continued)

(continued)

Solution:

1. **Annual Depreciation Shield**

    First, calculate the annual depreciation tax shield as follows (Depreciation × Tax rate):

	Years 1 and 3 (30%)	Year 2
Cost of asset	$150,000	$150,000
Depreciation %	× 30%	× 40%
Annual depreciation	$ 45,000	$ 60,000
Tax rate	× 40%	× 40%
Tax shield	$ 18,000	$ 24,000

2. **Annual Savings**

    Calculate the after-tax annual savings as follows [Savings × (1 − Tax rate)]:

    Annual savings = $85,000 [savings per year] × (1 − 0.40)

    Annual savings = $85,000 × 0.60

    Annual savings = **$51,000**

3. **Salvage Value Inflow**

    Calculate the salvage value inflow as follows:

Proceeds from salvage	$10,000	
Less: Basis of machine	—	[fully depreciated]
Gain on salvage	$10,000	
Less: Taxes	(4,000)	[$10,000 × 40%]
Cash inflow	$ 6,000	[$10,000 × (1 − 0.40)]

4. **Net Present Value Schedule and Calculation**

	Year 0	Year 1	Year 2	Year 3	
Equipment cost	$(150,000)				
Depreciation tax shield		$18,000	$24,000	$18,000	[from 1, above]
Annual savings		51,000	51,000	51,000	[from 2, above]
Salvage value inflow				6,000	[from 3, above]
After-tax cash flow	(150,000)	69,000	75,000	75,000	
Discount rate	× 1.00	× 0.862	× 0.743	× 0.641	
Present value	(150,000)	59,478	55,725	48,075	= **$13,278**

3.5   Advantages and Limitations of the Net Present Value Method

3.5.1   Advantages

The net present value method is flexible and can be used when there is no constant rate of return required for each year of the project.

3.5.2   Limitations

Even though NPV is considered the *best* single technique for capital budgeting, the net present value method of capital budgeting is limited by not providing the true rate of return on the investment. The NPV purely indicates whether an investment will earn the "hurdle rate" used in the NPV calculation.

3.6   Capital Rationing

The concept of capital rationing describes how limited investment resources are considered as part of investment ranking and selection decisions.

3.6.1   Unlimited Capital

Ideally, a company has virtually unlimited resources at its disposal, so the company may do everything (or nearly everything) that meets the company's screening criteria. Investments are undertaken in the order that they are ranked. If a company has unlimited capital, all investment alternatives with a positive NPV should be pursued.

3.6.2   Limited Capital

Realistically, a company has extremely limited resources that make its investment choices mutually exclusive (i.e., if one investment is chosen over another, the company does not have the option of "hedging its bet" with the second alternative because resources are entirely committed).

- **Importance:** Capital budgeting decisions involve a tremendous amount of money, time, and risk. If the company is down to two mutually exclusive choices, the importance of clearly defined calculations is just that much more critical.

- **Ranking and Acceptance:** If capital is limited and must be rationed, managers will allocate capital to the combination of projects with the maximum net present value. The ranking of projects from a group of qualifying investments (those that exceed the hurdle rate) is best accomplished using the profitability index (described below) and becomes especially important when projects are independent (i.e., mutually exclusive).

3.7   Profitability Index

The profitability index is the ratio of the present value of net future cash inflows to the present value of the net initial investment. The profitability index is also referred to as the excess present value index, or simply the present value index. Ranking and selection of investment alternatives anticipate positive net present values for all successfully screened investments. The profitability ratio likely will be over 1.0, which means that the present value of the inflows is greater than the present value of the outflows.

$$\text{Profitability index} \ = \ \frac{\text{Present value of cash flows}}{\text{Cost (present value) of initial investment}}$$

3.7.1 Application

The profitability index measures cash-flow return per dollar invested; the higher the profitability index, the more desirable the project. Projects that meet the screening criteria (e.g., positive NPV) are ranked in descending order by their profitability index. Limited capital resources are applied in the order of the index until resources are either exhausted or the investment required by the next project exceeds remaining resources.

Example 3	Capital Rationing

Facts: Beaman Enterprises has $50,000 of capital to invest in new projects for the coming fiscal year. The company must decide which projects to invest in given its budget constraints. The chart below shows the initial cost of the five investment options, along with the calculated present value of the future cash inflows.

Project	Initial Investment	PV Future Inflows
A	$16,000	$25,000
B	4,000	7,000
C	30,000	38,000
D	8,000	11,000
E	25,000	42,000

Required: Rank the investments using the profitability index and determine which project options Beaman should choose to pursue.

Solution: The first step is to calculate the profitability index for each project, which is done by dividing the present value of future inflows by the present value of the initial investment.

Project	PV Future Inflows	Initial Investment	Profitability Index
A	$25,000	$16,000	1.5625
B	7,000	4,000	1.75
C	38,000	30,000	1.267
D	11,000	8,000	1.375
E	42,000	25,000	1.68

The second step is to rank the projects from highest profitability index to lowest. The order would then be: Projects B, E, A, D, C.

The third and final step is to add the initial investments until the company's $50,000 threshold is reached.

$$B + E + A = \$4,000 + \$25,000 + \$16,000 = \$45,000$$

The next best project, which is D, would cost Beaman $8,000 and would push the company over the threshold of $50,000. Therefore, the projects Beaman will choose are projects B, E, and A.

Question 1 CPA-03283

In equipment-replacement decisions, which one of the following does *not* affect the decision-making process?

    a. Current disposal price of the old equipment.

    b. Original fair market value of the old equipment.

    c. Cost of the new equipment.

    d. Operating costs of the new equipment.

Question 2 CPA-03358

When the risks of the individual components of a project's cash flows are different, an acceptable procedure to evaluate these cash flows is to:

    a. Compute the net present value of each cash flow using the firm's cost of capital.

    b. Compare the internal rate of return from each cash flow to its risk.

    c. Utilize the accounting rate of return.

    d. Discount each cash flow using a discount rate that reflects the degree of risk.

Question 3 CPA-03337

If the net present value of a capital budgeting project is positive, it would indicate that the:

    a. Present value of cash outflows exceeds the present value of cash inflows.

    b. Internal rate of return is equal to the discount percentage rate used in the net present value computation.

    c. Present value index would be less than 100 percent.

    d. Rate of return for this project is greater than the discount percentage rate used in the net present value computation.

Question 4	CPA-06644

Salem Co. is considering a project that yields annual net cash inflows of $420,000 for Years 1 through 5, and a net cash inflow of $100,000 in Year 6. The project will require an initial investment of $1,800,000. Salem's cost of capital is 10 percent. Present value information is presented below:

Present value of $1 for five years at 10 percent is 0.62.

Present value of $1 for six years at 10 percent is 0.56.

Present value of an annuity of $1 for five years at 10 percent is 3.79.

What was Salem's expected net present value for this project?

a. $83,000
b. $(108,200)
c. $(152,200)
d. $(442,000)

NOTES

Financial Decision Models: Part 2

1 Application of NPV: Lease-vs.-Buy Decisions

1.1 The Issue

A company may acquire an asset by purchasing the asset or through a leasing arrangement. There are two main types of leases:

1. **Finance Lease:** Analogous to a lessee buying an asset and financing it with debt. Meets at least one of the **OWNES** criteria described earlier.

2. **Operating Lease:** Similar in concept to a finance lease. Does not meet any of the **OWNES** criteria described earlier.

The important issue for financial decision-making is the *cash flows* created by a lease, as compared with purchasing the asset.

1.2 Decision-Making

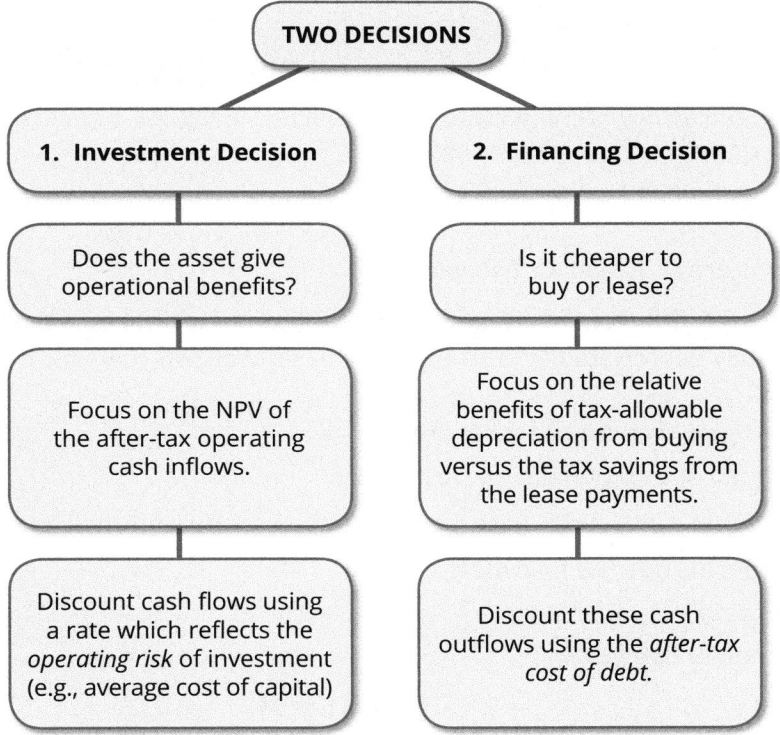

TWO DECISIONS

1. Investment Decision

Does the asset give operational benefits?

Focus on the NPV of the after-tax operating cash inflows.

Discount cash flows using a rate which reflects the *operating risk* of investment (e.g., average cost of capital)

2. Financing Decision

Is it cheaper to buy or lease?

Focus on the relative benefits of tax-allowable depreciation from buying versus the tax savings from the lease payments.

Discount these cash outflows using the *after-tax cost of debt.*

1.2.1 Investment Decision

- Discount the after-tax operating cash inflows at the firm's weighted average cost of capital (WACC).

1.2.2   Financing Decision

■   Discount the cash flows specific to each financing option at the after-tax cost of debt.

■   The preferred financing option is that with the lowest NPV of cost.

■   The relevant cash flows to consider include:

- Buy asset
    - —Purchase cost or present value of lease payments
    - —Tax savings from depreciation
    - —Scrap proceeds
- Lease asset
    - —Lease payments
    - —Tax savings on lease payments

Pass Key

If the PV of the cost of the best source of financing is less than the PV of the operating cash flows, then the project should be undertaken.

Example 1   Lease or Buy

Facts: Boulder Inc. is considering the acquisition of a new machine, either through an operating lease or by purchasing the asset.

The asset will cost $200,000 on January 1, Year 1, and will have a scrap value of $25,000 at the end of Year 2.

Operating inflows are $150,000 for two years.

The tax rate is 30 percent and the company's weighted average cost of capital is 9 percent.

The machine is fully depreciated on a straight-line basis over two years for both book and tax purposes.

Boulder's financing options for the asset are:

- using a bank loan at a 10 percent interest rate; or
- leasing for $92,500 a year, with lease payments due on January 1 of each year.

Relevant PV factors include the following:

PV of ordinary annuity at 9%	1.759
PV of annuity due at 7%	1.935

	PV of $1 at 7%
Year 1	0.935
Year 2	0.873

(continued)

(continued)

Required:

1. Determine the operational benefit of the project.

2. Determine how the project should be financed.

3. Determine the NPV of the investment.

Solution:

1. Operational Benefit

    PV of annual after-tax cash inflow = [$150,000 × (1 – 30%)] × 1.759

    PV of annual after-tax cash inflow = $105,000 × 1.759 = $184,695

2. Financing Decision

    After-tax cost of debt = 10% × (1 – 30%) = 7%

    a. Borrow and buy asset

    Annual depreciation tax shield = $100,000 × 30% = $30,000

    After-tax cash inflow from scrap = $25,000 × (1 – 30%) = $17,500

	Year 0	Year 1	Year 2
Cost of machine	$(200,000)		
Depreciation tax shield		$30,000	$30,000
Scrap	–	–	17,500
After-tax cash flow	(200,000)	30,000	47,500
Discount rate	1	0.935	0.873
Present value	$(200,000)	$28,050	$41,468 = $(130,483)

    b. Operating lease

    PV of annual after-tax cash outflow = [$92,500 × (1 – 30%)] × 1.935

    PV of annual after-tax cash outflow = $64,750 × 1.935 = $(125,291)

    Project should be financed using the operating lease because the NPV of the cost is lower.

3. Net Present Value

PV of operating inflows	$184,695
PV of lease financing	(125,291)
Net present value	$ 59,404

1.3   Effect on the Financial Statements

Financial accounting implications must be considered when making a lease-versus-buy decision.

This is certainly relevant for the managers of a public company as key ratios may be influenced—particularly financial risk indicators such as the firm's debt-to-equity ratio and interest coverage ratio.

The implications of each financing option can be summarized as follows:

- **Borrow to Buy**

    The bank loan will be recorded in non-current liabilities and will increase the firm's debt-to-equity ratio. Interest on the debt will reduce the firm's interest coverage ratio. However, the overall effect also depends on the profits generated by the asset as these will increase earnings and equity.

- **Finance Lease**

    A right-of-use (ROU) asset and lease liability will be recognized on the balance sheet of the lessee. Therefore, the debt-to-equity ratio would initially rise. Lease payments are split between interest expense and repayment of principal and therefore the liability is amortized over time and ultimately falls to zero. Interest expense in the early years is relatively high, decreasing the interest coverage ratio, but interest expense falls in later years as the liability decreases.

- **Operating Lease**

    Although the accounting treatment for operating leases is similar to finance leases (ROU asset and liability recognized) and the lease payments are recognized as lease expense on the income statement, an entity may elect to not recognize the asset and liability if the lease term is 12 months or less and there are no purchase options associated with the lease that the lessee is reasonably certain to exercise.

2   Internal Rate of Return (IRR)

The internal rate of return (IRR) is the expected rate of return of a project and is sometimes called the time-adjusted rate of return.

2.1   Objective

The IRR method determines the present value factor (and related interest rate) that yields an NPV equal to zero. (The present value of the after-tax net cash flows equals the initial investment on the project.)

The IRR method focuses the decision maker on the discount rate at which the present value of the cash inflows equals the present value of the cash outflows (usually the initial investment).

Pass Key

Although the NPV method highlights dollar amounts, the IRR method focuses decision makers on percentages.

2.2   Interpreting IRR for Investment Decisions

The targeted rate of return or hurdle rate is predetermined and is compared with the computed IRR. Note that management would be indifferent about accepting or rejecting the project if the IRR were equal to the hurdle rate.

- **Accept When IRR > Hurdle Rate:** Projects with an IRR greater than the hurdle rate will be accepted.

- **Reject When IRR < Hurdle Rate:** Projects with an IRR less than the hurdle rate will be rejected.

2.3   Limitations of IRR

2.3.1   Unreasonable Reinvestment Assumption

Cash flows generated by the investment are assumed in the IRR analysis to be reinvested at the internal rate of return. If internal rates of return are unrealistically high or unrealistically low, assumed returns on reinvested cash flows based on IRR rates could lead to inappropriate conclusions.

2.3.2   Inflexible Cash Flow Assumptions

The timing or the amount of cash flows used to determine IRR can be misleading when compared with the NPV method. The IRR method is less reliable than the NPV method when there are several alternating periods of net cash inflows and net cash outflows or the amounts of the cash flows differ significantly.

2.3.3   Evaluates Alternatives Based Entirely on Interest Rates

The IRR method evaluates investment alternatives based on the achieved IRR and does not consider the dollar impact of the project.

Illustration 1   Limitations of IRR

If an investment of $50 earns $100, then there is a 200 percent return [100 / 50 = 200%]. If an investment of $50,000 earns $25,000, then there is a 50 percent return [25 / 50 = 50%]. The IRR method would suggest that it would be best to invest $50 to earn $100 and receive a 200 percent return, while the NPV method would favor the larger $25,000 NPV on the $50,000 investment.

---

3   Payback Period Method

The payback period is the time required for the net after-tax operating cash inflows to recover the initial investment in a project.

3.1   Objective

The payback period method focuses decision makers on both liquidity and risk. The payback period method measures the time it will take to recover the initial investment in the project, thereby emphasizing the project's liquidity and the time during which return of principal is at risk. The payback method is often used for risky investments. The greater the risk of the investment, the shorter the payback period that is expected (tolerated) by the company.

3.2   Calculation

The formula for calculating the payback period is as follows, assuming equal annual cash flows:

$$\text{Payback period} = \frac{\text{Net initial investment}}{\text{Average incremental cash flow*}}$$

* Where cash flow per period is even.

3.3   Cash Flow Assumptions

3.3.1   Uniform Cash Inflows

The net cash inflows are generally assumed to be constant for each period during the life of the project. The payback period is computed at the point of initial investment using after-tax cash flows. Cash flows involve the following factors:

- **Project Evaluation:** In the case of a project, the net annual cash inflow would be the net cash receipts associated with the project.

- **Asset Evaluation:** In the case of the purchase of equipment, the net annual cash inflow will be the savings generated by use of the new equipment.

- **Depreciation Tax Shield:** Depreciation expense is not considered, except to the extent that it is a tax shield.

Example 2   Uniform Cash Flows

Facts: Helena Company is planning to acquire a $250,000 machine that will provide increased efficiencies, thereby reducing annual operating costs by $80,000. The machine will be depreciated by the straight-line method over a five-year life with no salvage value at the end of five years.

Required: Assuming a 40 percent income tax rate, calculate the machine's payback period.

Solution:

1. Calculate the annual net cash savings (also referred to as the average expected cash flows) as follows:

Expected cash flow savings		$ 80,000
Net income increase	$ 80,000	
Less: annual depreciation	(50,000)	
Net income before income taxes	$ 30,000	
Multiplied by 40% tax rate	× 40%	(12,000)
Net cash savings		$ 68,000

2. Calculate the payback period, as follows:

$$\frac{\text{Investment}}{\text{Net cash savings}} = \frac{\$250,000}{\$68,000} = 3.68 \text{ years}$$

3.3.2 Non-uniform Cash Flows (Use Cumulative Approach)

The standard payback formula shown above applies to uniform annual cash inflows. If cash flows are not uniform (i.e., they vary from period to period over the life of the project), a cumulative approach (rather than the standard payback formula) to determine the payback period is used. Net after-tax cash inflows are accumulated until the time they equal the initial net investment (at which point the end of the payback period is reached).

Example 3	Non-uniform Cash Flows

Facts: Radon Technologies is considering the purchase of a new machine costing $200,000 for its surfboard manufacturing plant in San Diego, CA. The management of Radon estimates that the new machine will last approximately four years and will be directly responsible for efficiencies that will increase the company's after-tax cash flows by the following amounts (non-uniform cash flow):

		Cumulative Amounts
Year 1	$90,000	$ 90,000
Year 2	80,000	170,000
Year 3	75,000	245,000
Year 4	60,000	305,000

Required: Calculate the payback period for this investment.

Solution: The cumulative cash flows reach the initial investment amount of $200,000 sometime in Year 3.

Therefore, the payback period would be more than two years and less than three years. Assume that the cash flow is earned evenly throughout the year. The payback period is then calculated as follows:

1. Amount of cash flow in Year 3 needed to attain $200,000 cumulative cash flows:

    $200,000 − $170,000 (Year 2's cumulative amount) = $30,000

2. Percentage of Year 3 until cumulative amount of $200,000 is attained:

    $$\frac{\$30,000}{\$75,000} = 40\%$$

3. 2 + 0.40 = 2.40 years payback

3.4 Advantages and Limitations of Payback

3.4.1 Advantages of the Payback Method

- **Easy to Use and Understand:** The simplicity of the objective and the absence of complex formulas or multiple steps make the payback method easy to use and understand.

- **Emphasis on Liquidity:** The computation focuses management on return of principal. The method's emphasis on liquidity is a very important consideration when making capital budgeting decisions (e.g., most companies will prefer shorter payback periods, all other factors being equal).

3.4.2 Limitations of the Payback Method

- The time value of money is ignored.

- Project cash flows occurring after the initial investment is recovered are not considered.

- Reinvestment of cash flows is not considered.

- Total project profitability is neglected.

4 Discounted Payback Method

Companies may use the discounted payback method as an alternative to the nondiscounted payback method. This variation computes the payback period using expected cash flows that are discounted by the project's cost of capital (the method considers the time value of money). Discounted payback is also referred to as the breakeven time method (BET).

4.1 Objective

The objective of the discounted payback method (or BET) is to evaluate how quickly new ideas are converted into profitable ideas.

- **Focus on Liquidity and Profit:** The measure focuses decision makers on the number of years needed to recover the investment from discounted net cash flows.

- **Evaluation Term:** The computation begins when the project team is formed and ends when the initial investment has been recovered (based on cumulative discounted cash flows).

- **Using Discounted Payback:** Discounted payback (or BET) is often used to evaluate new product development projects of companies that experience rapid technological changes. These companies want to recoup their investment quickly, before their products become obsolete.

4.2 Advantages and Limitations of Discounted Payback

The advantages and limitations of discounted payback are the same as the payback method (except that discounted payback incorporates the time value of money, a feature ignored by the payback method). Both focus on how quickly the investment is recouped rather than overall profitability of the entire project.

Example 4	Discounted Payback

Facts: Radon Technologies is considering the purchase of a new machine costing $200,000 for its surfboard manufacturing plant in San Diego, CA. The company's discount rate for projects of this type is 10 percent. The management of Radon estimates that the new machine will last approximately four years and will be directly responsible for efficiencies that will increase the company's after-tax cash flows by the following amounts (non-uniform cash flow):

Year 1	$90,000
Year 2	80,000
Year 3	75,000
Year 4	60,000

The present value interest factors for 10 percent are as follows:

Year 1	0.909
Year 2	0.826
Year 3	0.751
Year 4	0.683

Required: Calculate the discounted payback period for this investment.

Solution:

1. Calculate the present value of the future cash flows:

Year	Cash Flow Increase	Discount Factor	10% PV of Cash Flow	Cumulative PV
Year 1	$ 90,000	0.909	$ 81,810	$ 81,810
Year 2	80,000	0.826	66,080	147,890
Year 3	75,000	0.751	56,325	204,215
Year 4	60,000	0.683	40,980	245,195
	$305,000		$245,195	

2. Determine the discounted payback period:

The cumulative present value reaches the initial investment amount of $200,000 in Year 3. Therefore, the discounted payback period would be more than two years and less than three years. Assume that the cash flow is earned evenly throughout the year. The discounted payback period is then calculated as follows:

- Amount of cash flow in Year 3 needed to attain $200,000 cumulative cash flows:

  $200,000 − $147,890 (Year 2's cumulative amount) = $52,110

- Percentage of Year 3 until cumulative amount of $200,000 is attained:

  $$\frac{\$52,110}{\$56,325} = 92.5\%$$

- 2 + 0.925 = 2.925 years discounted payback

Pass Key

Calculating Time Value of Money Without Factors

Although the CPA Exam often will provide factors for use in time value of money calculations, it is very helpful for candidates to understand how to calculate these factors in the event that they are not given on the exam.

Present Value of $1

The formula to calculate present value is as follows:

$$PV = FV / (1 + r)^n$$

Where:

PV = Present value

FV = Future value

r = Interest rate

n = Number of years

Example: What is the factor for the present value of $1 to be received two years in the future at an interest rate of 6 percent?

$$PV = \dfrac{FV}{(1 + r)^n}$$

$$= \dfrac{1}{(1.06)^2}$$

$$= 0.890$$

Present Value of Annuity

The formula to calculate the present value of an annuity is as follows:

$$PV = PMT \times \dfrac{\left[1 - \dfrac{1}{(1 + r)^n}\right]}{r}$$

Where:

PMT = Annuity payment

Example: What is the factor for the present value of $1 to be received in each of the next three years at an interest rate of 6 percent?

$$PV = 1 \times \dfrac{\left[1 - \dfrac{1}{(1.06)^3}\right]}{0.06}$$

$$= 2.673$$

Question 1   **CPA-05785**

Which of the following statements about investment decision models is true?

- **a.** The discounted payback rate takes into account cash flows for all periods.
- **b.** The payback rule ignores all cash flows after the end of the payback period.
- **c.** The net present value model says to accept investment opportunities when their rates of return exceed the company's incremental borrowing rate.
- **d.** The internal rate of return rule is to accept the investment if the opportunity cost of capital is greater than the internal rate of return.

Question 2   **CPA-04836**

Which of the following statements is true regarding the payback method?

- **a.** It does not consider the time value of money.
- **b.** It is the time required to recover the investment and earn a profit.
- **c.** It is a measure of how profitable one investment project is compared to another.
- **d.** The salvage value of old equipment is ignored in the event of equipment replacement.

Question 3   **CPA-05309**

In considering the payback period for three projects, Fly Corp. gathered the following data about cash flows:

	Year 1	Year 2	Year 3	Year 4	Year 5
			Cash Flows by Year		
Project A	$(10,000)	$ 3,000	$ 3,000	$ 3,000	$ 3,000
Project B	(25,000)	15,000	15,000	(10,000)	15,000
Project C	(10,000)	5,000	5,000		

Which of the projects will achieve payback within three years?

- **a.** Projects A, B, and C.
- **b.** Projects B and C.
- **c.** Project B only.
- **d.** Projects A and C.

NOTES

Operations Management: Cost Accounting and Performance Management

Module

1 Cost Objects (or Objectives)

Cost objects (or cost objectives) are defined as resources or activities that serve as the basis for management decisions. Cost objects require separate cost measurement and may be products, product lines, departments, geographic territories, or any other classification that aids in decision making.

1.1 Focus of Cost Objectives

Integration of product costing with cost control measurement and assignment objectives maximizes the effectiveness of management accounting systems. Cost measurement and assignment may focus on valuation of product or inventory (i.e., product costing) or cost control (i.e., cost comparison to standards and budgets).

Pass Key

A single cost object can have more than one measurement. Inventory (product) costs for financial statements are usually different from costs reported for tax purposes. Both inventory (product) costs and costs reported for tax purposes are different from costs used by management to make decisions.

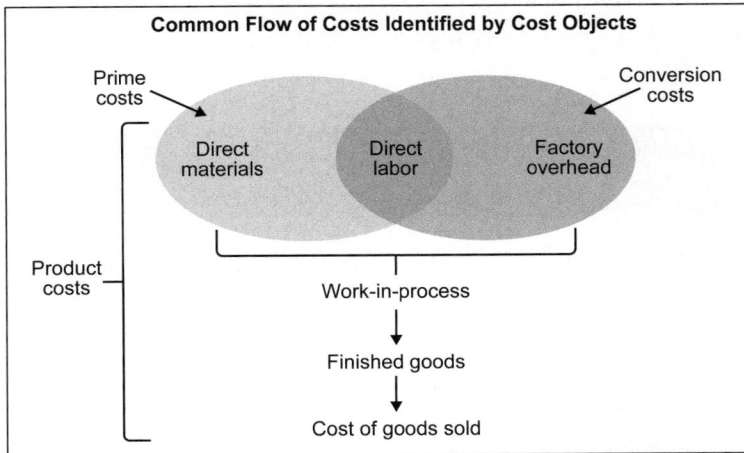

1.2 Common Cost Objects and Their Definitions

1.2.1 Product Costs

Product costs are all costs related to the manufacture of the product.

- **Inventory and Cost of Goods Manufactured and Sold:** Product costs are inventoriable (i.e., considered as assets before the product is sold). These costs attach to the units of output.

■ **Components:** Product costs consist of direct materials, direct labor, and manufacturing overhead applied.

1.2.2 Period Costs

Period costs are expensed in the period in which they are incurred and are not inventoriable.

■ **Expenses:** Period costs include selling, general, and administrative expenses as well as interest (financing) expense.

■ **Components:** Period costs are the costs of selling the product and administering and managing the operations of the firm.

1.2.3 Manufacturing Costs (Treated as Product Costs)

Manufacturing costs include all costs associated with the manufacture of a product.

■ **Inventory and Cost of Goods Manufactured and Sold:** Manufacturing costs are specifically capitalized to the cost of the manufactured product.

■ **Components:** Manufacturing costs consist of both direct and indirect costs (described later).

1.2.4 Nonmanufacturing Costs (Treated as Period Costs)

Nonmanufacturing costs are costs that do not relate to the manufacture of a product. These costs (e.g., selling, general, and administrative expenses) are expensed in the period incurred.

Pass Key

Cost accounting systems are designed to meet the goal of measuring cost objects or objectives. The most frequent objectives include:

- Product costing (inventory and cost of goods manufactured and sold)
- Income determination (profitability)
- Efficiency measurements (comparisons to standards)

Example 1   Product Costs and Period Costs

Facts: Thompson Manufacturing incurred the following costs during its recent fiscal year:

Wages for factory employees	$ 5,700,000
Wages for accounting department	840,000
Sales and promotion expense	325,000
Raw materials purchased	4,950,250
General and administrative costs	675,500
Manufacturing overhead	1,100,000
Interest expense	195,000

(continued)

(continued)

Required: Compute Thompson's product costs and period costs for the year.

Solution:

Product costs:

Wages for factory employees	$ 5,700,000
Raw materials purchased	4,950,250
Manufacturing overhead	1,100,000
Total product costs	**$11,750,250**

Period costs:

Wages for accounting department	$ 840,000
Sales and promotion expense	325,000
General and administrative costs	675,500
Interest expense	195,000
Total period costs	**$ 2,035,500**

2 Tracing Costs to Cost Objects

2.1 Direct Costs

A *direct cost* can be easily (i.e., without excessive cost and without significant effort) traced to a cost pool or object, as the cost directly relates to that item. Common direct costs include:

2.1.1 Direct Raw Materials

Direct raw materials are the costs of materials purchased to be used in production (including freight-in net of any applicable purchase discounts) plus a reasonable amount for normal scrap created by the process.

2.1.2 Direct Labor

Direct labor is the cost of the labor that is directly related to the production of a product or the performance of a service plus a reasonable amount of expected "downtime" for the labor (e.g., breaks, setup, training, etc.).

Illustration 1   **Direct Costs**

Spud Furnishings Inc. manufactures custom couches. Raw materials (fabric or leather) used in the production process of a custom order (a couch) are considered direct materials and are easily traced to the cost object, the custom order. The time spent by the upholsterer to make the couch is considered direct labor and is also easily traced to the cost object, the custom order.

2.2 Indirect Costs

An *indirect cost* is not easily traceable to a cost pool or cost object. Indirect costs are typically incurred to benefit two or more cost pools or objects. The specific benefit each cost gives to the cost pool or object cannot be determined without making some sort of reasonable estimate or using an allocation methodology. Indirect costs are known as *overhead*. In the manufacturing business, such costs are classified as *manufacturing overhead*.

2.2.1 Indirect Materials

The category *indirect materials* covers the cost of materials that were not used specifically or could not be traced to the completed product with ease.

Illustration 2	Indirect Materials

Spud Furnishings Inc. manufactures custom couches. In addition to the direct material for fabric, wood for framing, and springs it uses in the couches, the company purchases cleaning supplies used in the manufacturing area and small replacement parts for the manufacturing machines. These items are *indirect materials* that do not directly benefit any specific cost object. These costs are included in overhead.

2.2.2 Indirect Labor

Indirect labor is the cost of labor that is not easily traceable to a particular product, service, etc. Most often, this type of labor supports the manufacturing process but does not work directly on the specific job, etc.

Illustration 3	Indirect Labor

Spud Furnishings Inc. manufactures custom couches. In addition to upholsterers, Spud Furnishings employs forklift drivers, maintenance workers, shift supervisors, workers in the receiving department, janitorial staff, inspectors, engineers, training, and other human resources staff. These costs are *indirect labor* and are included in *manufacturing overhead*.

2.2.3 Other Indirect Costs

Other indirect costs are indirect costs other than those for materials or labor.

Illustration 4	Other Indirect Costs

Spud Furnishings Inc. incurs costs for depreciation of the facility and machinery, rent of the production warehouse, machine maintenance, property taxes on the building, insurance, rent, utilities, etc. These miscellaneous facility costs are *other indirect costs* and are included in *manufacturing overhead*.

2.3 Overhead Allocation Using Cost Drivers

Indirect costs are allocated (assigned) to benefiting cost pools or cost objects using cost drivers that are considered to have a strong relationship to the incurrence of these costs.

- **Allocation Bases**

  The cost drivers that are used to allocate indirect costs are referred to as allocation bases.

- **Accounting for Overhead**

  When traditional costing is used, all indirect costs are allocated to a single cost pool (or account) called "overhead" and allocated as a single pool. Overhead may also be allocated using activity-based costing.

3 Cost Behavior (Fixed vs. Variable)

Costs can be classified by their behavior, the degree to which the costs are either fixed or variable. Direct material and direct labor are generally variable costs, and indirect costs consist of both fixed and variable components.

Cost behaviors are graphically illustrated as follows:

Fixed vs. Variable

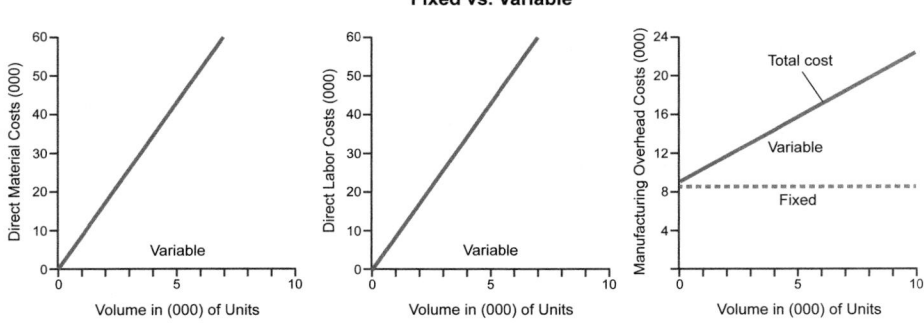

3.1   Variable Cost

- **Behavior:** A variable cost changes proportionally with the cost driver (e.g., typical cost drivers include sales volume and production volume).

- **Amount (Constant per Unit, Total Varies):** Variable costs change in total, but they remain constant per unit. As production volume increases (or decreases), the total variable cost will increase (or decrease), but the variable cost per unit will always remain the same.

- **Long-Run Characteristics:** The short-run and long-run effects of variable costs are the same within relevant ranges (the range of production over which cost behavior assumptions are valid).

3.2   Fixed Cost

- **Behavior:** In the short term and within a relevant range, a fixed cost does not change when the cost driver changes.

- **Amount (Varies per Unit, Total Remains Constant):** Fixed costs remain constant in total, but they vary per unit. As production volume increases (or decreases), fixed costs remain the same, but the cost per unit will decrease (or increase), respectively.

Pass Key

The distinction between variable costs and fixed costs allows managers to determine the effect of a given percentage change in production output on costs. *Be careful!* The examiners often attempt to trick candidates by providing a fixed cost per unit for a given volume of production. As fixed costs are "fixed," the candidate must convert this format to a dollar amount that will not change as production volume changes within a relevant range.

- **Long-Run Characteristics:** Given enough time (and a long enough relevant range), any cost can be considered variable.

Illustration 5   Long-Run Characteristics

Depreciation is typically a fixed cost in a relevant manufacturing range of units or up to production capacity but can be considered variable in the long run. A new building will have to be purchased if the production levels exceed plant capacity (thus possibly increasing depreciation expense, depending on the extent to which other facilities have been depreciated).

3.3   Semi-variable Costs (Mixed Costs)

Costs frequently contain both fixed and variable components. Costs that include components that remain constant over the relevant range and include components that fluctuate in direct relation to production are classified as *semi-variable*.

Example 2	Cost Behavior

Facts: Quality Ornaments Inc. (QOI) manufactures collector porcelain figurines and holiday ornaments in its single manufacturing facility. During the recently completed operating year, the company incurred manufacturing labor costs of $3,200,000 (including indirect labor of $200,000, which includes a base annual contractual amount and a variable rate amount for hours worked above a contractual threshold), raw material costs of $6,000,000, plant depreciation costs of $440,000 (straight-line method used), electricity costs of $250,000 (directly tied to hours of production), heating costs of $100,000 (annual rate), and delivery expenses of $25,000 (based on a formula per customer order). Additionally, QOI incurred $10,000 in building and equipment maintenance and repair expense that includes both a fixed contractual amount for weekday maintenance and a variable rate amount for maintenance performed on Saturdays and holidays.

Required: Based on the above scenario, calculate the company's variable costs, fixed costs, and semi-variable costs for the year.

Solution:

Cost Item	Variable Costs	Fixed Costs	Semi-variable Costs
Direct labor	$3,000,000		
Indirect labor			$200,000
Raw materials	6,000,000		
Depreciation		$440,000	
Electricity	250,000		
Heating		100,000	
Maintenance and Repair			10,000
Deliveries	25,000		
Total Costs	**$9,275,000**	**$540,000**	**$210,000**

3.4 Relevant Range

The *relevant range* is the range for which the assumptions of the cost driver (i.e., linear relationship with the costs incurred) are valid. When the cost driver activity is no longer within the relevant range, the variable and fixed cost assumptions for that cost driver cannot be used to allocate costs to cost objects. Relevant range is graphically illustrated as follows:

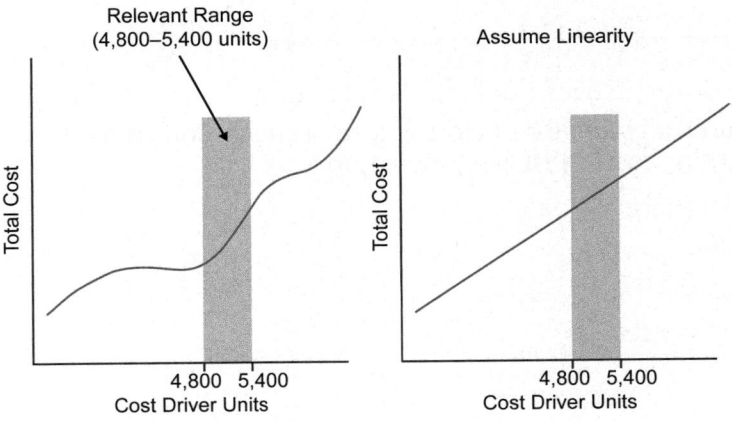

Illustration 6	Cost Behaviors

	Variable	Fixed	Semi-variable
Sales	✓		
Less: returns and allowances	✓		
Cost of sales			
Direct material	✓		
Direct labor	✓		
Indirect labor			✓
Fringe benefits (15% of labor)	✓		✓
Royalties (1% of product sales)	✓		
Maintenance and repairs of building			✓
Factory production supplies	✓		
Depreciation: straight-line		✓	
Electricity: used in the mfg. process	✓	✓	
Scrap and spoilage (normal)	✓		
Selling, general, and administrative expense			
Sales commissions	✓		
Officers' salaries		✓	
Fringe benefits (relate to labor)	✓	✓	
Delivery expenses	✓		
Advertising expenses (annual contract expenses)		✓	

Question 1	CPA-07083

If a product required a great deal of electricity to produce, and crude oil prices increased, which of the following costs most likely increased?

    a. Direct materials.

    b. Direct labor.

    c. Prime costs.

    d. Conversion costs.

1   Cost Accumulation Systems

Cost accumulation systems are used to assign costs to products. The system used is driven by the cost object involved. If the cost object is a custom order, job costing is used. If the cost object is a mass-produced, homogeneous product (e.g., steel), process costing is used.

Pass Key

Although the most commonly tested cost accumulation systems are job-order costing and process costing, there are many variations of cost accumulation systems that may appear on your examination:

- Operations costing uses components of both job-order costing and process costing.

- Backflush costing accounts for certain costs at the end of the process in circumstances in which there is little need for in-process inventory valuation.

Life-cycle costing seeks to monitor costs throughout the product's life cycle and expand on the traditional costing systems that focus only on the manufacturing phase of a product's life.

2   Cost of Goods Manufactured and Sold

Production costs may be summarized in a cost of goods manufactured statement and a cost of goods sold statement. These statements may be prepared separately or combined as a cost of goods manufactured and sold statement.

2.1   Cost of Goods Manufactured

The *cost of goods manufactured* statement accounts for the manufacturing costs of the products completed during the period. These costs consist of direct material, direct labor, and manufacturing overhead costs. The manufacturing costs incurred during the period are increased or decreased by the net change in work-in-process inventory (beginning WIP minus ending WIP) to equal cost of goods manufactured.

XYZ Company
Cost of Goods Manufactured
For the Month Ended November 30, Year 1

Work-in-process inventory, beginning		$ 40,000
Add: direct material used	$ 30,000	
Direct labor	50,000	
Manufacturing overhead applied	40,000	
Total manufacturing costs incurred		120,000
Total manufacturing costs available		160,000
Less: work-in-process inventory, ending		(10,000)
Cost of goods manufactured		$ 150,000

2.2 Cost of Goods Sold

A *cost of goods sold* statement for a manufacturer is very similar to one prepared for a retailer except that cost of goods manufactured is used in place of purchases made during the period.

XYZ Company
Cost of Goods Sold
For the Month Ended November 30, Year 1

Finished goods inventory, beginning	$ 20,000
Add: cost of goods manufactured	150,000
Cost of goods available for sale	170,000
Less: finished goods inventory, ending	(50,000)
Cost of goods sold	$120,000

3 Job-Order Costing

Job-order costing (or job costing) is the method of product costing that identifies the job (or individual units or batches) as the cost objective and is used when relatively few units are produced and when each unit is unique or easily identifiable.

3.1 Cost Objective Is the Job (or Unit)

Under job-order costing, cost is allocated to a specific job as it moves through the manufacturing process. Record keeping for job costing emphasizes the job as the cost objective.

3.2 Job-Cost Records

Job-cost records are maintained for each product, service, or batch of products, and they serve as the primary records used to accumulate all costs for the job. Job-cost records are also referred to as job-cost sheets or job orders. Job-cost records accumulate data from the following internal documents:

- **Materials Requisitions:** *Materials requisitions* are documents showing materials requested for use on the job.

- **Labor Time Tickets (Time Cards):** *Labor time tickets* (time cards) are documents that show the labor hours and labor rate associated with the time applied to the job.

- **Job-Order Costing:** *Job-costing systems* require a limited number of work-in-process accounts.

Pass Key

Job-costing systems are best suited for customized production environments such as construction, aircraft assembly, printing, etc. A new job-cost record would be started every time a new job (building project, airplane, or print job) is started.

Question 1	CPA-05321

Jonathon Manufacturing adopted a job-costing system. For the current year, budgeted cost driver activity levels for direct labor hours and direct labor costs were 20,000 and $100,000, respectively. In addition, budgeted variable and fixed factory overhead were $50,000 and $25,000, respectively.

Actual costs and hours for the year were as follows:

Direct labor hours	21,000
Direct labor costs	$110,000
Machine hours	35,000

For a particular job, 1,500 direct-labor hours were used. Using direct-labor hours as the cost driver, what amount of overhead should be applied to this job?

    a. $3,214

    b. $5,357

    c. $5,625

    d. $7,500

Overview: Job-Order Costing

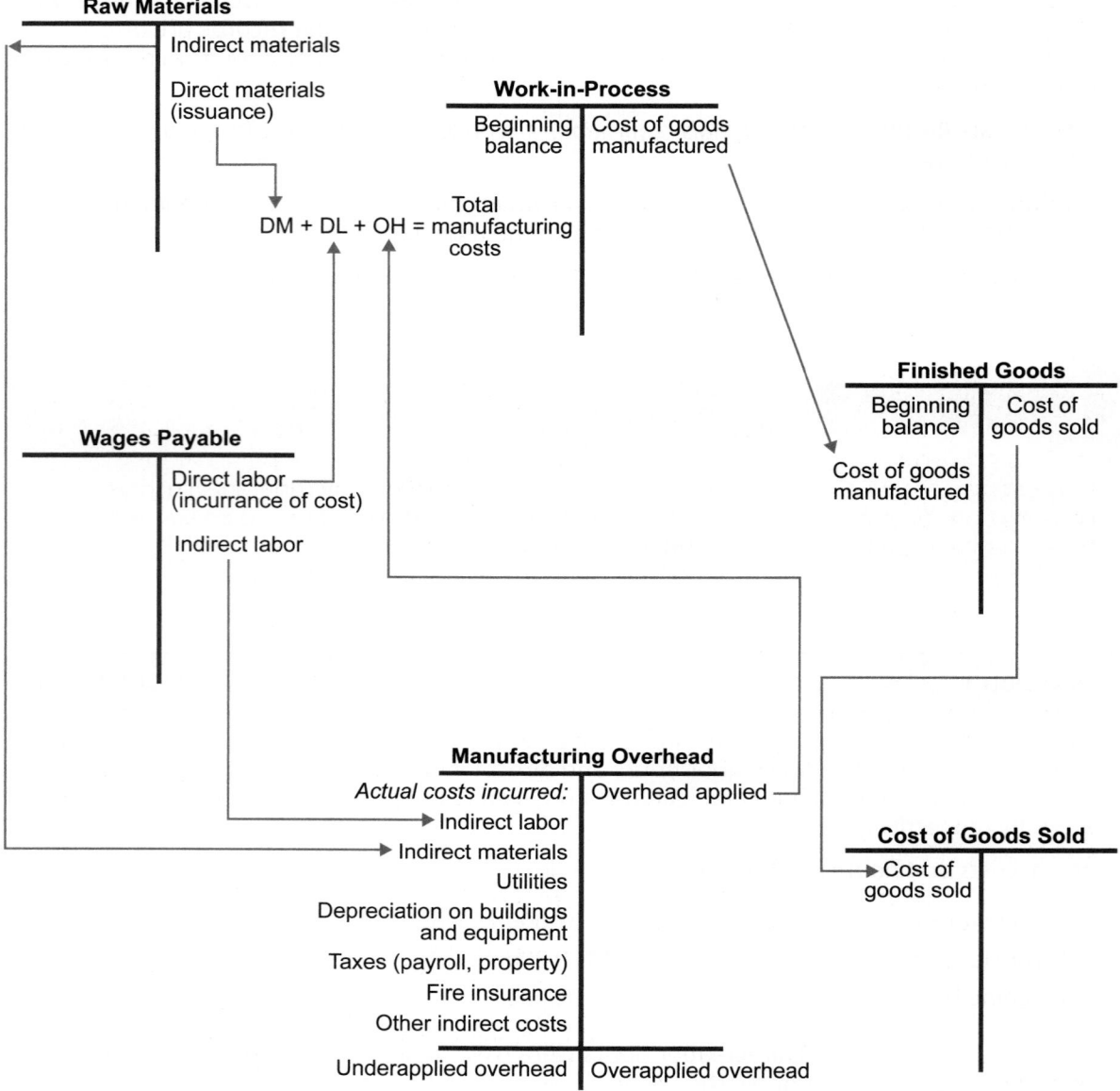

4   Process Costing

Process costing is a method of product costing that averages costs and applies them to a large number of homogeneous items using the following steps:

1. Summarize the flow of physical units (beginning with the production report).

2. Calculate "equivalent unit" output.

3. Accumulate the total costs to be accounted for (production report).

4. Calculate the average unit costs based on total costs and equivalent units.

5. Apply the average costs to the units completed and the units remaining in ending work-in-process inventory.

4.1   Units and Costs Collected on a Production Report

Costs incurred for a period as well as all units produced during that period are accumulated on a production report that accounts for the physical flow of units. The report includes the beginning inventory, the number of units started, the number of units completed, and the number of units remaining in inventory.

- **Unit (Quantity) Accounting**

    The number of units accounted for must equal the number of units charged to the department (or separate process).

- **Cost Accounting**

    The amount of costs accounted for must also equal the amount of costs charged to the department (or separate process).

Pass Key

The following shows the flow of inventory from beginning raw materials to ending finished goods inventory:

Inventory: Raw Materials	Inventory: Work-in-Process	Inventory: Finished Goods
Beginning inventory of raw materials	Beginning inventory of work-in-process	Beginning inventory of finished goods
Add: purchases of raw materials	Add: raw materials used plus direct labor and overhead used	Add: inventory transferred from work-in-process
Raw materials available for use	Work-in-process inventory available to be finished	Finished goods inventory available-for-sale
Subtract: raw materials used	Subtract: inventory transferred to finished goods	Subtract: cost of goods sold
Ending inventory of raw materials	Ending inventory of work-in-process	Ending inventory of finished goods

Illustration 1	Production Report	

Quantities

Charged to department:

In process, beginning	5,000
Transferred in	20,000
Total units charged to department	25,000

Units accounted for:

Transferred out	15,000
In process, end	10,000
Total units accounted for	25,000

Costs

Charged to department:

In process, beginning	$12,000
During the period	85,000
Total units charged to department	$97,000

Costs accounted for:

Transferred out	$60,000
In process, end	37,000
Total costs accounted for	$97,000

4.2   Equivalent Units

Costs must be attached to the completed units as well as to the units that are partially complete at the end of each period. This calculation is made by taking into account the partially completed units and by making use of equivalent units.

Pass Key

Accounting for the physical flow of units is an important step in process costing. Remember, however, that the pure physical flow of units will be different from the equivalent units of production.

4.2.1   Equivalent Unit Defined

An equivalent unit of direct material, direct labor, or conversion costs (direct labor plus factory overhead) is equal to the amount of direct material, direct labor, or conversion costs necessary to complete one unit of production.

Illustration 2   Equivalent Units

Company X would like to produce 10,000 units during the first quarter. The company obtains the raw material inputs prior to the production of each unit and has applied the necessary direct labor and manufacturing overhead to complete 75 percent of the production during the first two months (with the remaining production process to be performed during the third month).

When preparing its internal monthly production reports, Company X would indicate that it has 10,000 units 100 percent complete as to direct materials and 7,500 equivalent units of production as to direct labor and overhead at the February 28 month end.

4.2.2   Process Costing Assumptions

■ **Transfers In Are 100 Percent Complete**

Transfers in from other departments are always considered 100 percent complete. The transfer in costs of direct material from a previous department are treated as direct materials (DM), even though they are called "transfer in" costs or "previous department" costs.

■ **Timing of Addition of Direct Material**

•   **Addition at the Beginning or During a Process**

Direct material added at the beginning of or during a second or later process may either be 100 percent complete or "partially complete," depending on how much work has been done on that component of the process.

•   **Addition at the End of a Process**

Any material added at the (very) end of a process will not be in work-in-process inventory at the month end.

4.3   Calculations of Average Unit Costs

The calculation of average unit costs and the application of those costs to various segments of the process is complicated by a number of issues.

4.3.1   Averaging of Costs From Prior Month's WIP

Frequently, costs from the previous month's work-in-process inventory are different from costs of the current month. These costs must be averaged.

4.3.2   Cost Flow Assumptions

Cost averaging computations depend on FIFO and/or weighted (or moving) average cost flow assumptions. These computations require a well-labeled account analysis format for each unit of direct material, direct labor, or overhead.

4.4   Calculation Using First In, First Out (FIFO)

Under FIFO accounting, the ending inventory is priced at the cost of manufacturing during the period, assuming that the beginning inventory was completed during the period.

4.4.1 Equivalent Unit Components

The *equivalent units* are composed of three elements:

1. Completion of units on hand at the beginning of the period

2. Units started and completed during the period (Units completed − Beginning WIP)

3. Units partially complete at the end of the period

4.4.2 Cost Components

Current costs incurred during the period are allocated to the equivalent units produced during the period.

4.5 Calculation Using Weighted Average

The weighted average cost method averages the cost of production during the period with the costs in the beginning work-in-process inventory.

4.5.1 Equivalent Unit Components

The *equivalent units* are composed of two elements:

1. Units completed during the month (Beginning WIP + Units started and completed during the month)

2. Units partially complete at the end of the period

4.5.2 Cost Components

Total costs, including both the costs of beginning inventory and current costs, are allocated to equivalent units to arrive at a weighted average unit cost.

Example 1	Equivalent Units of Production

Facts: Assume the following information:

Work-in-process, beginning	100 units, 25% complete
Units completed and transferred out	600 units
Work-in-process, ending	200 units, 40% complete

Required: Compute the equivalent units of production using the FIFO method and the weighted average cost method.

Solution:

Weighted average equivalent units of production

Units completed and transferred out (always 100%)	600
Work-in-process, ending	
200 units × 40%	80
Equivalent units of production	680

(continued)

(continued)

FIFO equivalent units of production

Work-in-process, beginning		
100 units × 75% (to complete)		75
Units started and completed this period		
Units completed and transferred out	600	
Units in beginning inventory	(100)	500
Work-in-process, ending		
200 units × 40%		80
Equivalent units of production		655

4.6 Comparison of FIFO and Weighted Average

4.6.1 Equivalent Unit Calculation

Equivalent unit calculation under FIFO consists of three elements representing current period production, whereas the calculation under the weighted average method consists of only two elements, units completed and units available in beginning inventory.

4.6.2 Cost Components

FIFO represents only costs incurred in the current period. The weighted average approach includes both current period units plus prior period units.

Pass Key

Equivalent units of production may be computed using either the FIFO or weighted average methods. The FIFO method specifically accounts for work to be completed, and the weighted average method blends the units, as follows:

1. Weighted average (two steps)

Units completed		XXX
Ending WIP × % completed	+	XXX
Equivalent units		XXX

2. FIFO (three steps)

Beginning WIP × % to be completed		XXX
Units completed—Beginning WIP	+	XXX
Ending WIP × % completed	+	XXX
Equivalent units		XXX

Pass Key

Cost per equivalent unit is computed by dividing total costs by equivalent units. FIFO uses only current costs, and the weighted average method uses both beginning inventory and current costs.

1. Weighted average

$$\text{Weighted average} = \frac{\text{Beginning cost} + \text{Current cost}}{\text{Equivalent units}}$$

2. FIFO

$$\text{FIFO} = \frac{\text{Current cost only}}{\text{Equivalent units}}$$

Example 2   Process Costing

Facts:

Comprehensive Example
Process Costing Under FIFO and Weighted Average
May of Year 1

	Percent Complete	Materials	Conversion	Total
1. Units in process, May 1				
Materials	100%	4,000		
Conversion	40%		4,000	
2. Units started and completed in May				
Materials	100%	10,000		
Conversion	100%		10,000	
3. Units in process, May 31				
Materials	100%	2,000		
Conversion	80%		2,000	
4. Costs associated with May 1 WIP				
Materials		$ 1,000		$ 1,000
Conversion			$ 3,000	3,000
5. Costs associated with May production				
Materials		$24,000		$24,000
Conversion			$49,000	49,000
6. Total Costs				**$77,000**

(continued)

(continued)

Required:

1. Compute equivalent units of production using FIFO and weighted average.

2. Compute production costs using FIFO and weighted average.

3. Compute equivalent cost per unit using FIFO and weighted average.

Solution:

1. Equivalent units of production

	First In, First Out		Weighted Average	
	Materials (%)	Conversion (%)	Materials (%)	Conversion (%)
Units in process, May 1	– (0%)	2,400 (60%)	4,000 (100%)	4,000 (100%)
Units started and completed in May	10,000 (100%)	10,000 (100%)	10,000 (100%)	10,000 (100%)
Units in process, May 31	2,000 (100%)	1,600 (80%)	2,000 (100%)	1,600 (80%)
Total Units	**12,000**	**14,000**	**16,000**	**15,600**

2. Production costs

	First In, First Out		Weighted Average	
Costs in WIP, May 1	$ –	$ –	$ 1,000	$ 3,000
Costs during May	24,000	49,000	24,000	49,000
Total Costs	**$24,000**	**$49,000**	**$25,000**	**$52,000**

3. Equivalent cost per unit

	First In, First Out		Weighted Average	
Equivalent cost per unit	**$ 2.00**	**$ 3.50**	**$ 1.56**	**$ 3.33**

4.7 Spoilage (or Shrinkage)

Spoilage (or shrinkage) is generally taken care of automatically because the equivalent units added for the month are generally less than the actual units added during the month due to problems with the production process.

4.7.1 Normal Spoilage (Inventory Cost)

Normal spoilage occurs under regular operating conditions and is included in the standard cost of the manufactured product.

- **Computation**

  For normal spoilage (or shrinkage), per unit cost is automatically increased as a result of spoilage because actual costs are spread over fewer equivalent good units rather than actual units produced.

- **Accounting Treatment**

  Normal spoilage is capitalized as part of inventory cost. Normal spoilage costs, if accounted for separately, are allocated to good units produced.

4.7.2 Abnormal Spoilage (Period Expense)

Abnormal spoilage should not occur under normal operating conditions and is excluded from the standard cost of a manufactured product.

■ **Computation**

For abnormal spoilage (or shrinkage), the per unit cost is based on actual units. Equivalent units of production include spoiled units.

■ **Accounting Treatment**

The cost of abnormal spoilage is normally expensed separately on the income statement as a period expense.

Example 3	Spoilage Application

Facts: Fresh Baked Company produces ready-to-serve fruit pies for local restaurants and supermarkets. During the month of April, the company had the following costs related to the production of 20,000 pies:

Pie ingredients	$45,000
Baking labor	24,000
Plant production overhead	11,000
Sales and marketing expenses	500
General and administrative expenses	1,200
Normal spoilage	400
Abnormal spoilage	200

Required:

1. What is the per unit cost of the pies assigned to inventory for April?

2. What amount will the company assign as a period expense for April?

Solution:

1. Unit cost

Step 1: Determine inventory costs.

Pie ingredients	$45,000
Baking labor	24,000
Plant production overhead	11,000
Normal spoilage	400
Total inventory costs	**$80,400**

Step 2: Determine per unit cost.

Per unit cost (of pies) = $80,400 ÷ 20,000 pies

$4.02

2. Period expense

The period expenses assigned to April are as follows:

Sales and marketing expenses	$ 500
General and administrative expenses	1,200
Abnormal spoilage	200
Total period expenses	**$ 1,900**

Question 2   CPA-05798

Merry Co. has two major categories of factory overhead: material handling and quality control. The costs expected for these categories for the coming year are as follows:

Material handling	$120,000
Quality inspection	200,000

The plant currently applies overhead based on direct labor hours. The estimated direct labor hours are 80,000 per year. The plant manager is asked to submit a bid and assembles the following data on a proposed job:

Direct materials	$4,000
Direct labor (2,000 hours)	6,000

What amount is the estimated product cost on the proposed job?

    a. $8,000
    b. $10,000
    c. $14,000
    d. $18,000

Question 3   CPA-03601

Kerner Manufacturing uses a process costing system to manufacture laptop computers. The following information summarizes operations relating to laptop computer model No. KJK20 during the quarter ending March 31:

	Units	Direct Materials
Work-in-process inventory, January 1	100	$ 70,000
Started during the quarter	500	
Completed during the quarter	400	
Work-in-process inventory, March 31	200	
Costs added during the quarter		$750,000

Beginning work-in-process inventory was 50 percent complete for direct materials. Ending work-in-process inventory was 75 percent complete for direct materials. What were the equivalent units of production using the FIFO method, with regard to materials for the quarter ended March 31?

    a.   450
    b.   500
    c.   550
    d.   600

Question 4	**CPA-03644**

Kimbeth Manufacturing uses a process cost system to manufacture Dust Density Sensors for the mining industry. The following information pertains to operations for the month of May:

	Units
Beginning work-in-process inventory, May 1	16,000
Started in production during May	100,000
Completed production during May	92,000
Ending work-in-process inventory, May 31	24,000

The beginning inventory was 60 percent complete for materials and 20 percent complete for conversion costs. The ending inventory was 90 percent complete for materials and 40 percent complete for conversion costs.

Costs pertaining to the month of May are as follows:

- Beginning inventory costs are: materials, $54,560; direct labor, $20,320; and factory overhead, $15,240.

- Costs incurred during May are: materials used, $468,000; direct labor, $182,880; and factory overhead, $391,160.

Using the weighted average method, the equivalent unit cost of materials for May is:

    a. $4.50
    b. $4.60
    c. $5.03
    d. $5.46

1 Activity-Based Costing (ABC)

1.1 Types of Operational Cost Drivers

1.1.1 Volume-Based

Traditional costing systems assign overhead as a single cost pool with a single plant-wide overhead application rate using a single allocation base. These rates generally use volume-based cost drivers such as direct labor hours or machine hours. Assigning overhead costs based on volume can distort the amount of costs assigned to various product lines because all overhead costs do not fluctuate with volume.

1.1.2 Activity-Based

Activity-based costing (ABC) refines traditional costing methods and assumes that the resource-consuming activities (tasks, units of work, etc.) with specific purposes cause costs. ABC assumes that the best way to assign indirect costs to products (cost objects) is based on the product's demand for resource-consuming activities (i.e., costs are assigned based on the consumption of resources). Application of activity-based costing techniques attempts to improve cost allocation by emphasizing long-term product analysis.

1.2 Introduction to Activity-Based Costing

1.2.1 Terminology

- **Activity:** An *activity* is any work performed inside a firm. Activities are identified for ABC.
- **Resource:** A *resource* is an element that is used to perform (or applied to perform) an activity.
- **Cost Drivers:** *Cost drivers* used in ABC are activity bases that are closely correlated with the incurrence of manufacturing overhead costs in an activity center, and they are often used as allocation bases for applying overhead costs to cost objects.

Pass Key

A cost driver is a factor that has the ability to change total costs. Cost drivers (including nonfinancial, statistical measurements of activities such as sales or production volume) are identified by ABC and are related to one of multiple cost pools for cost allocation.

- **Resource Cost Driver:** A *resource cost driver* is the amount of resources that will be used by an activity.
- **Activity Cost Driver:** An *activity cost driver* is the amount of activity that a cost object will use, and it is used to assign the costs to the cost objects.
- **Activity Centers:** An operation necessary to produce a product is an *activity center*.

Illustration 1	ABC Terminology

Hope Hospital applies ABC to costing its services. The surgical unit is identified as an activity center that includes various professional service (surgeon and nurse) functions as well as facilities (operating room) functions. Resources used include hours of staff time for surgery and operating room preparation as well as for facilities maintenance. Resource drivers may include the complexity of surgical procedures (including setup time) and activity drivers may be purely admissions or scheduled surgeries.

- **Cost Pool:** A *cost pool* is a group of costs (e.g., raw material or direct labor) or a specially identified cost center (e.g., a department or a manager) in which costs are grouped, assigned, or collected.

1.2.2   Characteristics of ABC

ABC applies a more focused and detailed approach than using a department or plant as the level for gathering costs. ABC focuses on multiple causes (activities) and effects (costs) and then assigns costs to them. The cost of activities is used to "build up" the engineered cost of products using increased cost pools and allocations.

- ABC can be part of a job order system or a process cost system.

- ABC can be used for manufacturing or service businesses.

- ABC takes a long-term viewpoint and treats production costs as variable.

- The cost driver is often a nonfinancial variable.

- ABC may be used for internal but not for external purposes.

1.2.3   Transaction-Based Costing

Activity-based costing is also referred to as *transaction-based costing*. The cost driver is typically the number of transactions involved in a particular activity.

1.2.4   Focuses on Cost/Benefit of Activities

ABC focuses management on the cost/benefit of activities. Value-added activities increase the product value or service.

- **Value Chain (Value-Added Activities):** A *value chain* is a series of activities in which customer usefulness is added to the product. Support activities directly support value-added activities.

- **Non-Value-Added Activities:** *Non-value-added activities* do not increase product value or service and are targeted for elimination. Often, these types of activities (e.g., warehousing) should be eliminated.

1.3   Basic Operation of Activity-Based Costing

Activity-based costing is done using the following steps:

1. **Identify the Cost Drivers**
   Identify the activity centers and the activities that drive the costs in each activity center.

2. **Accumulate the Costs in Cost Pools**
   Many small cost pools are accumulated.

3. **Trace Indirect Costs to Activity Centers**
   Trace any indirect costs to the activity centers that can be assigned without allocation.

4. **Allocate Remaining Indirect Cost Pools**

   Costs of each activity are applied to cost objects based on the most appropriate cost drivers.

5. **Divide Assigned Costs by Level of Activity for the Cost Center**

   Divide the costs assigned to the activity center by the estimated level of activity for the center to derive an application rate for that center.

6. **Cost the Product**

   Cost the product by multiplying its demand for the resources of an activity center by the rate for that activity center.

1.4 Effects of Activity-Based Costing

An ABC system will apply high amounts of overhead to a product that places high demands on expensive resources. If a product places few demands on expensive resources, the system will assign little of that cost to the product. This will remove much of the cost distortion caused by traditional, volume-based overhead systems.

1.5 ABC and Standard Cost Systems

Standard cost systems are a natural extension of activity-based costing. Standards are set at activity levels based on cost drivers. Useful variances are calculated by comparing actual and standard costs that consider levels of activity. These variances can be due to price (rate for labor), usage (efficiency), or other factors. Further, flexible budgets are derived at the activity level.

- Normal and abnormal scrap or spoilage is estimated for activity levels.

- Standards may be difficult to set on a per unit basis.

  - Per unit costs are often inversely proportional to volume.

  - Assumption of a relevant range may be necessary to set a per unit standard.

Illustration 2   ABC Costing

Iowa Products makes two products at its Boone factory. The company has used a traditional cost accounting system for the application of overhead to the products. Currently it uses direct labor hours as an application base. One product, Can, incurred 150,000 direct labor hours and the other product, Bottle, incurred 45,000 direct labor hours. The company is considering converting to an activity-based costing system. The estimated data for its Year 1 operations is summarized below:

			Activity Level	
Activity Center	**Costs**	**Cost Driver**	**Cans**	**Bottles**
Units			500,000	150,000
Material handling	$ 480,000	Pounds	100,000	60,000
Production orders	90,000	Number of production orders	100	100
Product redesign	250,000	Number of changes	50	200
Plant utilities	2,300,000	Machine hours	150,000	80,000

(continued)

(continued)

1. Illustration of the overhead application rate under a *traditional system* using direct labor hours as an application base:

Material handling	$ 480,000
Production orders	90,000
Product redesign	250,000
Plant utilities	2,300,000
Total overhead costs	**$3,120,000**

$$\text{Overhead application rate} = \frac{\text{Total overhead costs}}{\text{Total direct labor hours}}$$

$$= \$3,120,000 / (150,000 + 45,000)$$

$$= \$16 \text{ per direct labor hour}$$

Cans: 150,000 direct labor hours × $16 = $2,400,000
$2,400,000 / 500,000 cans = $4.80 per can

Bottles: 45,000 direct labor hours × $16 = $720,000
$720,000 / 150,000 bottles = $4.80 per bottle

2. Illustration of the overhead application rate under an *activity-based costing system* using each activity as a cost pool:

Material handling: $480,000 / 160,000 pounds = $3 per pound
Production orders: $90,000 / 200 orders = $450 per order
Product redesign: $250,000 / 250 changes = $1,000 per change
Plant utilities: $2,300,000 / 230,000 machine hr. = $10 per machine hour

Cans:

Material handling, 100,000 lb. × $3	$ 300,000
Production orders, 100 orders × $450	45,000
Product redesign, 50 changes × $1,000	50,000
Plant utilities, 150,000 machine hr. × $10	1,500,000
Total overhead costs	**$1,895,000**

$1,895,000 / 500,000 cans = $3.79 per can

Bottles:

Material handling, 60,000 lb. × $3	$ 180,000
Production orders, 100 orders × $450	45,000
Product redesign, 200 changes × $1,000	200,000
Plant utilities, 80,000 machine hr. × $10	800,000
Total overhead costs	**$1,225,000**

$1,225,000 / 150,000 bottles = $8.167 per bottle

Bottle cost significantly increased with activity-based costing. This resulted because bottles required a large amount of the redesign resource. Redesign is a very costly resource and not related to volume. Because bottles required a large amount of this resource, a high amount of indirect cost was assigned to bottles. The cost of cans decreased significantly because that used comparatively little redesign resource.

1.6   Service Costs Allocation Using ABC

Companies in all sectors of the economy allocate service department costs to production or user departments and ultimately the final products produced.

Illustration 3   Service Cost Allocation

Hospitals use complex methods to allocate service-related costs such as patient admissions or housekeeping to the various hospital departments that ultimately affect patient billing. By allocating these service department costs to the individual production departments and the final product, the entity is recognizing that these service costs are an input into the production process.

1.6.1   Direct Method

- The *direct method* is the most widely used (and least complex) method to allocate service costs.

- Each service department's total costs are directly allocated to the production departments without recognizing that service departments themselves may use the services from other service departments.

1.6.2   Step-Down Method

- The *step-down method* or sequential method is a more sophisticated approach to allocate service costs in more complex situations.

- Service department costs are also allocated to other service departments as well as production departments.

- Step-down allocations assume that once a service department's costs have been allocated to another service department, there can be no subsequent costs allocated back to the other service department(s).

Example 1   Direct Method

Facts: Remington Company has two production departments, Division A and Division B. The company also has two service departments, which consist of Information Systems (IS) and Human Resources (HR). During the most recently completed operating year, the IS and HR departments had total service costs of $2,220,000 and $975,000, respectively.

Dept.	Activity Center	Cost Driver	Division A	Division B
IS	Planning and reporting	Computing hours	9,000	6,000
HR	Division administration	Performance appraisals	2,800	2,200

Required: Allocate the IS and HR departments' service costs to the two production divisions.

(continued)

(continued)

Solution:

Application rate using ABC system

Planning and reporting	$2,220,000 ÷ 15,000 hours = $148/hr.
Division administration	$975,000 ÷ 5,000 appraisals = $195/appraisal

Division A: Service cost allocation

IS—Planning and reporting: 9,000 hours × $148	$1,332,000
HR—Division administration: 2,800 appraisals × $195	546,000
Total service costs	**$1,878,000**

Division B: Service cost allocation

IS—Planning and reporting: 6,000 hours × $148	$ 888,000
HR—Division administration: 2,200 appraisals × $195	429,000
Total service costs	**$1,317,000**

Example 2   Step-Down Method

Facts: Assume the same facts as the Remington Company direct-method example, above, with the exception that the Information Systems (IS) department also uses the services of the Human Resources (HR) department. Specifically, performance appraisals administered by the HR department to the IS department accounted for an additional 200 appraisals during the recent operating year. Further, assume that because of data privacy issues, the HR department uses an outside contractor for its information technology needs instead of the IS department.

Note: The allocation of IT computing service hours to the other two production divisions remains the same as above, as there is no IT service allocation to HR.

Dept.	Activity Center	Cost Driver	Division A	Division B
HR	Division administration	Performance appraisals	2,800	2,200

Required: Allocate the service costs for performance appraisals from HR to IT and the two production divisions using ABC.

Solution:

HR application rate using ABC system

HR—Division administration	$975,000 ÷ 5,200 appraisals = $187.50/appraisal

IT service department: Service cost allocation (of HR)

HR—Division administration	200 appraisals × $187.50 = $37,500

(continued)

(continued)

IT application rate using ABC system

IT—Planning and reporting ($2,220,000 + $37,500) ÷ 15,000 hours = $150.50 per hour

Division A: Service cost allocation

IT—Planning and reporting: 9,000 hours × $150.50	$1,354,500
HR—Division administration: 2,800 appraisals × $187.50	525,000
Total service costs	**$1,879,500**

Division B: Service cost allocation

IT—Planning and reporting: 6,000 hours × $150.50	$ 903,000
HR—Division administration: 2,200 appraisals × $187.50	412,500
Total service costs	**$1,315,500**

It should be noted that under the step-down method, the HR (performance appraisal) allocation is lower to both Division A and Division B under ABC costing, given that HR costs are also allocated to the IS department.

2 Joint Product Costing and By-product Costing (Common Cost Allocation)

Accountants face the problem of allocating the cost of a single process (*joint costs*) among several final products (or by-products) if two or more final products are produced from the same raw material or input.

Illustration 4   Joint Costing

The meat-packing industry takes a single input, a steer, and produces many final products. Each product must be assigned a cost, including the different cuts of meat for human consumption, different food products for animal consumption (pet food), and basic ingredients for glue (by-product).

2.1 Terminology

- **Joint Products:** *Joint products* are two or more products that are generated from a common input.

- **By-products:** *By-products* are minor products of relatively small value that incidentally result from the manufacture of the main product.

- **Split-off Point:** The *split-off point* is the point in the production process at which the joint products can be recognized as individual products.

■ **Joint Product Costs (or Joint Costs):** *Joint product costs* are costs incurred in producing products up to the split-off point.

■ **Separable Costs:** *Separable costs* are costs incurred on a product after the split-off point.

■ **Joint Products:** *Joint products* represent outputs of significant value that are the object of a manufacturing process.

2.2 Allocation by Unit Volume Relationships

Example 3	Joint Cost Allocation by Unit Volume

Facts: Simple Manufacturing Company produces two products, Product A and Product B. Direct costs associated with manufacturing Product A and Product B were $25,000 and $50,000, respectively, with joint costs of production representing $10,000. In order to allocate joint costs, the company used the proportional gallons of production for its two products as follows:

	Volume
Product A	10,000 gal
Product B	20,000 gal
Total	**30,000** gal

Required: Determine the portion of *joint costs* that will be allocated to each product and the total cost of each product.

Solution:

Joint cost allocation

Product A:	(10,000/30,000) × $10,000	=	$ 3,333
Product B:	(20,000/30,000) × $10,000	=	6,667
			$10,000

Total cost

Product A:	$25,000 (direct) + $3,333 (joint)	=	$28,333
Product B:	$50,000 (direct) + $6,667 (joint)	=	$56,667

2.3   Relative Net Realizable Values at Split-off Point

Net realizable value equals sales value less cost of completion and disposal. Relative sales value at split-off point is used purely for inventory costing and is of little use for cost planning and control purposes.

2.3.1   Sales Price Quotations Available at Split-off

The relative sales value at split-off point can be used to allocate joint costs if sales price quotations are known or can be determined. The relative sales value approach assigns costs to the separate joint products in relation to their market values.

Example 4   **Joint Cost Allocation: Sales Values Known at Split-off**

Facts: Brown Company produces two products, A and B. Joint production costs incurred in the production of A and B totaled $1,000. At the split-off point, 100 units of A had a sales value of $20/unit and 400 units of B had a sales value of $15/unit.

Required: Compute the joint costs to be allocated to A and B using relative sales values at split-off.

Solution:

Allocation based on relative sales value:

Product A: 100 units @ $20	$2,000
Product B: 400 units @ $15	6,000
	$8,000

Joint cost allocated to A: $1,000 × ($2,000 ÷ $8,000)	=	$ 250
Joint cost allocated to B: $1,000 × ($6,000 ÷ $8,000)	=	750
Total allocated joint cost		**$1,000**

2.3.2   Sales Values Not Available at Split-off

If sales values at split-off are not available because there are no markets for the joint products at split-off, then sales values at split-off must be derived using the following formula:

Sales value at split-off ≈ Final selling price − Identifiable costs incurred after split-off

---

Example 5 — Joint Cost Allocation: No Sales Value at Split-off

Facts: Smith Company produces two joint products: F and G. Joint production costs for October were $30,000. During October, further processing costs beyond the split-off point (separable costs), needed to convert the products into saleable form, were $16,000 and $24,000 for 1,600 units of F and 800 units of G, respectively. F sells for $25 per unit and G sells for $50 per unit. Smith uses the net realizable value method for allocating joint product costs.

Required: Determine the joint costs to be allocated to F and G during October.

Solution:

Product F: Net realizable value		
Sales value, $25 per unit × 1,600 units	$40,000	
Further processing costs	(16,000)	
Net realizable value		$24,000
Product G: Net realizable value		
Sales value, $50 per unit × 800 units	$40,000	
Further processing costs	(24,000)	
Net realizable value		16,000
Total net realizable value		**$40,000**
Joint costs allocated to F: $30,000 × ($24,000 / $40,000)	$18,000	
Joint costs allocated to G: $30,000 × ($16,000 / $40,000)	12,000	
Total joint costs	**$30,000**	

2.4 Service Departments Cost Allocation to Joint Products

The allocation of service department costs to joint products can be accomplished by using the joint products unit-volume relationship.

Example 6 — Service Department Joint Cost Allocation

Facts: Simple Manufacturing Company manufactures two products (Product A and Product B) and allocates its joint costs using the proportional gallons of production for its two products as follows:

	Volume
Product A	10,000 gal
Product B	20,000 gal
Total	**30,000** gal

The company's lone service department is Janitorial Services. Costs incurred for this department were $6,000 for the operating year.

Required: Determine the portion of service department costs that will be allocated to each product based on the joint products unit-volume relationships.

Solution:

Product A:	(10,000/30,000) × $6,000 =	$2,000
Product B:	(20,000/30,000) × $6,000 =	4,000
		$6,000

2.5   By-products

By-products represent outputs of relatively minor value that are incidental to a manufacturing process. By-products have relatively low sale values that are not sufficient to cover their share of common costs (otherwise, they would be joint products). Revenue accounting can take one of two forms:

1. **Applied to Main Product**

   Any proceeds from the sale of by-products are a reduction to common costs for joint product costing. The revenue earned from their sale is credited to joint costs incurred either at the time of production or the time of sale.

2. **Miscellaneous Income**

   As an alternative, revenue from the sale of by-products may be credited to miscellaneous income.

2.6   By-product Costing vs. Joint Costing

Decisions regarding whether to use by-product costing or joint costing are practical ones, and they depend on relative demand.

Illustration 5   Joint vs. By-product Costing
Before the invention of the automobile, gasoline produced when oil was refined had no value and was scrap for disposal. After the invention of the automobile, gasoline was first priced as a by-product and then priced as a joint product (when demand for gasoline increased).

Question 1	CPA-08307
A manufacturing company has several product lines. Traditionally, it has allocated manufacturing overhead costs between product lines based on total machine hours for each product line. Under a new activity-based costing system, which of the following overhead costs would be most likely to have a new cost driver assigned to it?	

    a. Electricity expense

    b. Repair and maintenance expense

    c. Employee benefits expense

    d. Depreciation expense

Question 2   **CPA-03477**

A processing department produces joint products Ajac and Bjac, each of which incurs separable production costs after split-off. The following details pertain to a batch produced at a $60,000 joint cost before split-off:

Product	Separable costs	Sales value
Ajac	$ 8,000	$ 80,000
Bjac	22,000	40,000
	$30,000	$120,000

What is the joint cost assigned to Ajac if costs are assigned using the relative net realizable value?

    a. $16,000

    b. $40,000

    c. $48,000

    d. $52,000

1 Financial and Nonfinancial Performance Measures

Both *financial* and *nonfinancial measures* are ultimately designed to provide feedback that will motivate appropriate employee behaviors. Feedback tied to self-interest is most effective. The issue associated with any performance measurement system is the appropriate linkage of measures, incentives, and goals.

1.1 Financial Measures

Financial measures of performance include financial scorecards (including the balanced scorecard), costs of quality, return on investment, return on assets, return on equity, residual income, and economic value added.

1.2 Nonfinancial Measures

1.2.1 External Benchmarks: Productivity Measures

Productivity is defined as the measure of the ratio of the outputs achieved to the inputs of production. Productivity is a measure of efficiency and uses the relationships derived from actual performance in comparison to similar organizations over time. Two types of productivity ratios are generally recognized.

- **Total Factor Productivity Ratios (TFP)**

  Total factor productivity ratios (TFPs) reflect the quantity of all output produced relative to the costs of all inputs used. This ratio can be used to compare actual cost per unit production levels to budgeted (or a prior year's) production levels.

- **Partial Productivity Ratios (PPRs)**

  Partial productivity ratios (PPRs) reflect the quantity of output produced relative to the quantity of individual input(s) used. This ratio can be used to compare the actual levels of a production input needed to produce a given output, which may be used for a comparison with a budgeted (or a prior year's) input level. It is the most frequently used productivity measure.

Example 1	Productivity Ratios

Facts: Garden Furnishings Inc. produces outdoor garden sculptures for its high-end niche market. Each garden sculpture manufactured by the company includes two raw materials, with plastic being the largest product input. During the previous month, the company used 20,000 pounds of plastic and 5,000 pounds of cement to produce 1,000 garden sculptures. Material prices at time of production were $1.25/lb. and $1.75/lb. for plastic and cement, respectively.

Required: Calculate the partial productivity ratio for plastic and the total factor productivity ratio.

Solution:

Based on the above, the direct material (plastic) *partial productivity ratio* is calculated as follows:

$$
\begin{aligned}
\text{PPR} \;&=\; \text{Quantity of output produced / Quantity of input used} \\
&=\; 1,000 \text{ units of garden sculptures / } 20,000 \text{ lb. of plastic} \\
&=\; 0.05 \text{ sculpture units per lb. of plastic}
\end{aligned}
$$

Using the above, the *total factor productivity* ratio is calculated as follows:

$$
\begin{aligned}
\text{TFP} \;&=\; \text{Quantity of output produced / Costs of all inputs used} \\
&=\; 1,000 \text{ garden sculptures / } (20,000 \times \$1.25) + (5,000 \times \$1.75) \\
&=\; 1,000 \text{ garden sculptures / } \$33,750 \\
&=\; 0.02963 \text{ units of output per dollar of input cost}
\end{aligned}
$$

1.2.2 Internal Benchmarks: Techniques to Find and Analyze Problems

Internal benchmarks include a variety of techniques to find and analyze problems or measure performance. Among the most common quality-monitoring and investigative techniques are the procedures described below.

■ **Control Charts**

Control charts are an important tool used in statistical quality control (SQC). This graphical tool is used to plot a comparison of actual results by batch or other suitable constant interval to an acceptable range. Control charts show whether there is a trend toward improved quality conformance or deteriorating quality conformance.

Illustration 1   Control Chart

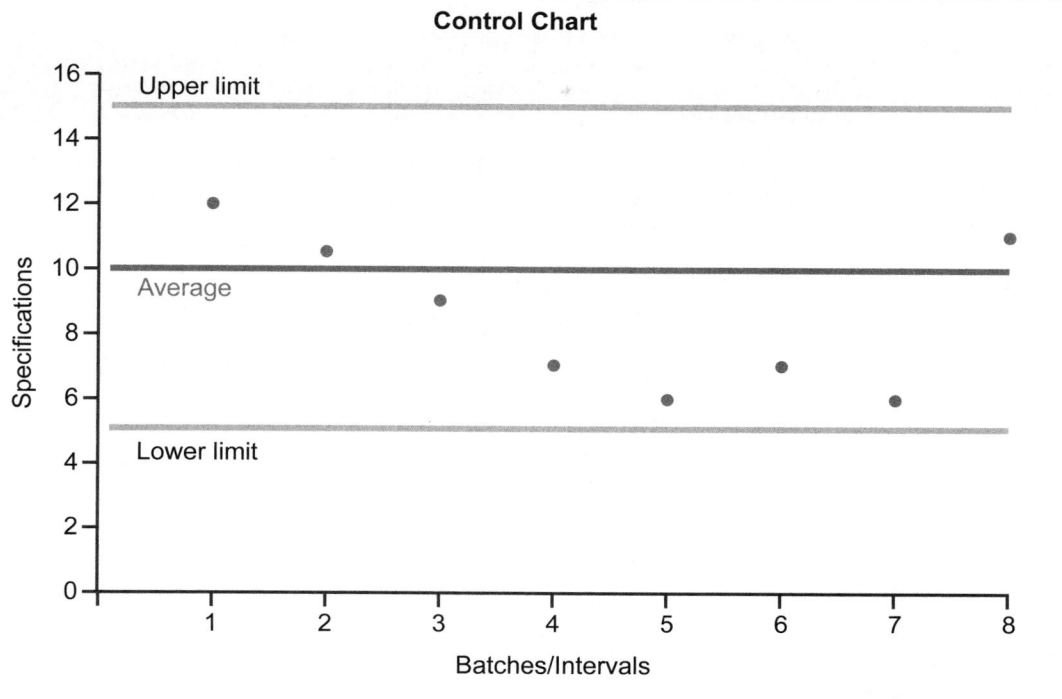

1. The control chart above demonstrates how individual batches/intervals of production fall within a range of quality specifications, from an acceptable upper limit of 15 occurrences to an acceptable lower limit of 5 occurrences, with production management establishing an average quality specification of 10 occurrences per batch/interval.

2. To further extrapolate the results of the control chart above, assume that the company's machine makes batches of rubber tires, with each batch consisting of 10,000 truck tires. Given management's historical experience with this production line, the company has set an upper-end defect rate of 15 tires per batch. The company has also established a lower-end defect rate of 5 tires per batch, as any amount set lower could result in production machine breakdown and repairs.

3. The results graphically displayed on the control chart above indicate that the individual tire production batches/intervals are all within the upper (15) and lower (5) limit tire defect specifications for production. Furthermore, the pattern of production shows a general decline in defects as more batches were produced for each subsequent monthly time interval; the very last batch (No. 8) is an outlier with more tire defects (11) than the average of 10.

Pareto Diagrams

Pareto diagrams are used to determine the quality-control issues that are most frequent and often demand the greatest attention. A Pareto diagram demonstrates the frequency of defects from highest to lowest frequency.

Illustration 2   Pareto Diagram

The Pareto diagram below shows the individual and cumulative frequency of six types of quality issues. Addressing half of the types of defects (Type 3, Type 2, and Type 1) would address three quarters (75 percent) of all defects.

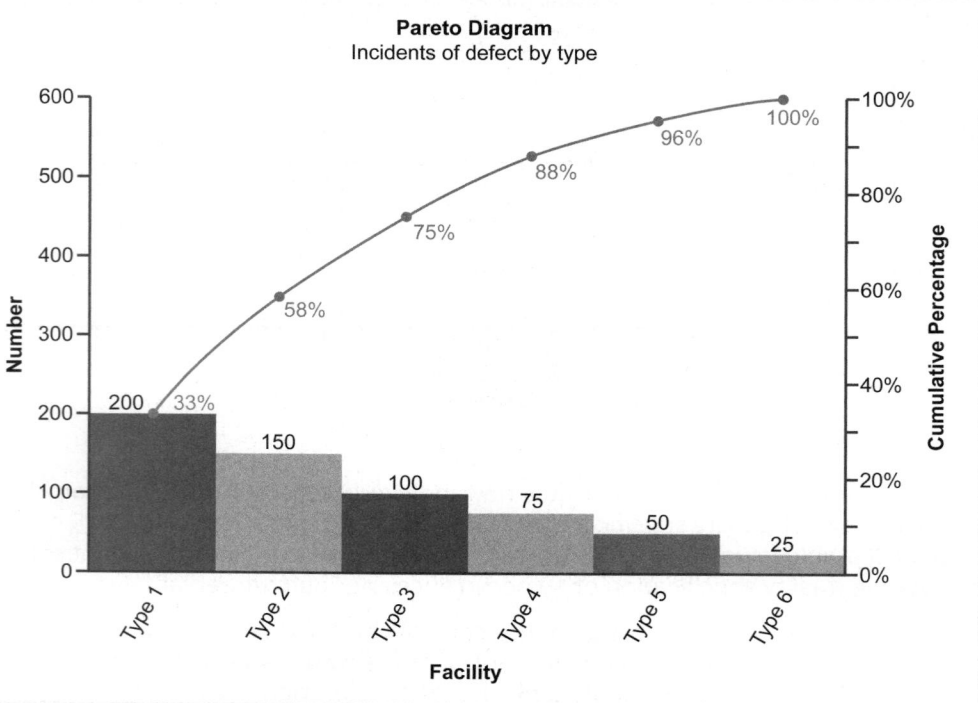

Cause-and-Effect (Fishbone) Diagram

Once the most frequently recurring and costly defects/problems are identified by the Pareto diagram, a cause-and-effect diagram may be used to further analyze the defect.

Cause-and-effect diagrams provide a framework for managers to analyze the problems that contribute to the occurrence of defects. Production processes that lead to the manufacture of an item are displayed along a production line in a manner that looks like a fishbone. Managers use the diagram to identify the sources of problems in the production process by resource and take corrective action.

Illustration 3   Fishbone Diagram

This fishbone diagram indicates that the main categories of potential causes of the defect (called "large bones") are machinery, method used, materials, and use of manpower. Individual factors under each primary factory can be added on ("bones") and provide more detailed reasons for the higher-level ("large bone") cause of the defect. For example, under "machinery," the diagram indicates that incorrect settings may be a specific cause for the defect. Although not shown here, additional "bones" may be added to the machinery "large bone," such as functional obsolescence and lack of sufficient machine downtime.

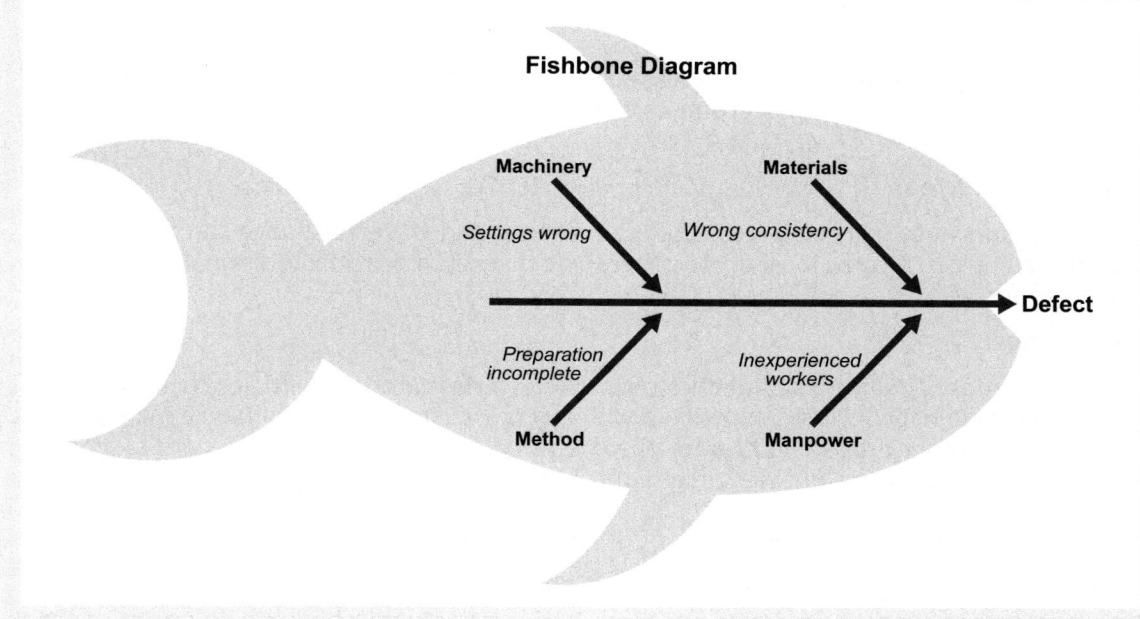

Fishbone Diagram

2   Financial Scorecards

Financial scorecards take many forms, including budget versus actual and other variance reports, as well as overall analysis of business performance. Financial performance is often a function of organizational decisions and the performance objectives given to each segment.

2.1   Types of Responsibility Segments

Responsibility segments, sometimes referred to as strategic business units (SBUs), are generally classified by four financial measures (performance objectives) for which managers may be held accountable. SBUs are highly effective in organizing performance requirements and in establishing accountability for financial responsibility.

1.   Cost SBU

Managers are held responsible for controlling costs.

2.   Revenue SBU

Managers are held responsible for generating revenues.

3.   Profit SBU

Managers are held responsible for producing a target profit (accountability for both revenues and costs).

4.   Investment SBU

Managers are held responsible for return on the assets invested to produce the earnings generated by the SBU.

2.2   Areas of Accountability in Financial Scorecards

The effectiveness of each strategic business unit is often subdivided into additional areas of accountability, including:

■   **Product Lines**

Some strategic business units involve multiple products. Costs, sales, profits, or returns associated with each of these products can be analyzed for further insight into the sources of profits or losses.

■   **Geographic Areas**

Strategic business units also cross geographic boundaries. Performance can generally be traced by geographic location or geographic market to provide additional insight into results.

■   **Customer**

Often the most significant segment classification is a classification by major customer. The relative profitability or losses associated with any one customer may influence management's decisions to either drop the customer or to reevaluate the relationship in regard to any marginal benefits to the business (e.g., contribution of the customer to fixed costs, etc.).

2.3   Contribution Reporting

Profit SBUs are normally responsible for generating a level of profit in relation to controllable costs. Contribution reporting formats are generally used to clearly show the degree to which the profit that strategic business units have generated has covered variable or controllable costs.

2.3.1   Contribution Margin

Contribution margin measures the excess of revenues over variable costs (or the contribution to fixed costs) for a company or division.

2.3.2   Controllable Margin

Contribution by SBU is a refinement of contribution margin reporting and represents the difference between contribution margin and controllable fixed costs. Controllable fixed costs are costs that managers can influence in less than one year (e.g., advertising and sales promotion).

2.3.3   Allocation of Common Costs

Managers have control over variable costs and over controllable fixed costs. Financial scorecards that use contribution reporting factor in these costs. Common costs are not controllable. Approaches to the rational allocation of central administrative costs must be understood by responsible managers and must be fair and logical. Employees are more motivated to achieve corporate goals if they believe that common costs do not represent an arbitrary burden.

Illustration 4 — Contribution Reporting

Delta Manufacturing has four regions that it has organized into profit strategic business units. Delta's management has designed a financial performance evaluation report that focuses on contribution margin and controllable margins. The report is designed as follows:

Delta Manufacturing Performance Evaluation

	Region 1	Region 2	Region 3	Region 4	Untraceable Costs	Total
Revenues	$ 200	$ 300	$ 150	$450	$ –	$1,100
Variable costs	(150)	(250)	(125)	(350)	–	(875)
Contribution margin	50	50	25	100	–	225
Controllable fixed costs	(25)	(25)	(10)	(50)	–	(110)
Controllable margin	25	25	15	50	–	115
Noncontrollable fixed costs	(15)	(15)	(6)	(44)	–	(80)
Contribution by SBU	10	10	9	6	–	35
Untraceable costs	–	–	–	–	(20)	(20)
Operating Income	$ 10	$ 10	$ 9	$ 6	$(20)	$ 15

2.4 Balanced Scorecard

The *balanced scorecard* gathers information on multiple dimensions of an organization's performance defined by critical success factors necessary to accomplish the firm's strategy. Critical success factors are classified as:

- Financial
- Internal business processes
- Customer satisfaction
- Advancement of innovation and human resource development (learning and growth)

Typically, the scorecard describes the classifications of critical success factors, the strategic goals, the tactics, and the related measures associated with strategic and tactical goals.

Illustration 5 Balanced Scorecard

Instafab Manufacturing is building its business using a cost leadership strategy. The management of Instafab has identified four strategic goals, one associated with each classification of critical success factors, to help its business grow. The strategic goals are:

1. Capturing additional market share
2. Maintaining low costs that are supported by low prices
3. Becoming a low-price leader
4. Linking strategy with reward and recognition

Help Instafab design tactics to achieve its strategic goals, define measures it might use, and organize them in the manner of a balanced scorecard.

Legend:

	Tactics	Measures
Financial Perspective		
Strategic goals	Capture increasing market share	Company vs. industry growth
Critical success factors	Maintain customer base	Volume trend line
Tactics and measures	Steadily expand services	Percentage of sales from new products
Internal Business Processes		
Strategic goals	Maintain low costs that are supported by low prices	Costs compared to competitor
Critical success factors	Maintain consistent production	First pass rates
Tactics and measures	Improve distribution efficiency	Percentage of perfect orders
Customer Perspective		
Strategic goals	Become a low-price leader	Our cost vs. competition
Critical success factors	Anticipate customer needs before competitors	Percentage of products in R&D being test-marketed
Tactics and measures	Increase customer satisfaction	Customer surveys
Advance Learning and Innovation (Human Resources)		
Strategic goals	Link strategy with reward and recognition	Net income per dollar of variable pay
Tactics and measures	Promote entrepreneurial culture	Annual reports

3   Costs of Quality

Quality is broadly defined by the marketplace as a product's ability to meet or exceed customer expectations.

The cost of quality includes costs associated with activities related to conformance with quality standards and opportunity costs or activities associated with correcting nonconformance with quality standards.

3.1   Conformance Costs

The costs of ensuring *conformance* with quality standards are classified as prevention and appraisal costs.

3.1.1   Prevention Costs

Prevention costs are incurred to prevent the production of defective units. This includes such cost elements as:

- Employee training
- Inspection expenses
- Preventive maintenance
- Redesign of product
- Redesign of processes
- Search for higher-quality suppliers

3.1.2   Appraisal Costs

Appraisal costs are incurred to discover and remove defective parts before they are shipped to the customer or the next department. These costs include:

- Statistical quality checks
- Testing
- Inspection
- Maintenance of the laboratory

3.2   Nonconformance Costs

The costs of nonconformance with quality standards are classified as internal and external costs. *Nonconformance costs* are often difficult to compute because most of these costs are in the form of opportunity costs (e.g., lost sales or reputation damage).

3.2.1   Internal Failure

Internal failure costs are the costs to cure a defect discovered before the product is sent to the customer. These costs include:

- Rework costs
- Scrap
- Tooling changes
- Costs to dispose
- Cost of the lost unit
- Downtime

3.2.2 External Failure

External failure costs are the costs to cure a defect discovered after the product is sent to the customer. These costs include:

- Warranty costs
- Cost of returning the good
- Liability claims
- Lost customers
- Reengineering an external failure

3.3 Quality Reporting

"Cost of quality" reports display the financial result of quality. An inverse relationship between conformance and nonconformance costs exists. Increased investment in conformance costs should result in decreases in nonconformance costs, while the consequence of reduced investment in conformance costs may result in increased nonconformance costs.

- **Appraisal** includes the costs incurred (e.g., statistical quality control, inspection, and testing) to identify defective products or services.
- **Prevention** includes the costs incurred (e.g., engineering or training) to prevent the production or delivery of defective products or services.
- **Internal** failure is the cost of defective parts or lost production time (e.g., scrap and rework).
- **External** failure is the cost of returns and lost customer loyalty due to defective products or services.

Illustration 6   Costs of Quality

Glass Products Inc. (GPI) experienced several internal failure costs in the past operating year, including significant production downtime and batch rework costs. Additionally, GPI had external failure costs after shipping glass products to its customers, including material costs pertaining to product returns and lost customers.

At the beginning of the current operating year, the company's production manager was replaced. The new manager, in his first week on the job, hired a statistical quality technician to test the products as they exited the production line. The new production manager then implemented quarterly employee training, preventive maintenance measures, and weekly inspections by line supervisors. Through the first half of the year, these appraisal and prevention measures have reduced production downtime by 90 percent and have reduced the company's scrap costs by 50 percent. As a result of these prevention measures, the company has also experienced fewer glass product returns and has lost no customers in the current operating year.

Question 1   **CPA-03883**

Listed below are selected line items from the Cost of Quality Report for Watson Products for last month.

Category	Amount
Rework	$ 725
Equipment maintenance	1,154
Product testing	786
Product repair	695

What is Watson's total prevention and appraisal cost for last month?

a. $786
b. $1,154
c. $1,849
d. $1,940

Question 2   **CPA-03890**

In a quality control program, which of the following is (are) categorized as internal failure costs?

I. Rework.
II. Responding to customer complaints.
III. Statistical quality control procedures.

a. I only.
b. II only.
c. III only.
d. I, II, and III.

NOTES

Performance Management: Part 2

1   Return on Investment

Return on investment (ROI) provides for the assessment of a company's percentage return relative to its capital investment risk. The ROI is an ideal performance measure for investment strategic business units (SBUs). In simplest terms, ROI is expressed as income divided by invested capital; however, ROI is also expressed as a product of profit margin and investment turnover.

> **ROI = Income / Investment capital**
>
> *Or:*
>
> **ROI = Profit margin × Investment turnover**

1.1   Components of ROI

Return on investment (ROI) can be disaggregated as indicated in the following flowchart, in which income is expressed as a percentage of sales (i.e., the profit margin calculation) and sales are expressed as a percentage of invested capital (i.e., the investment turnover calculation). The higher the percentage return, the better.

ROI Flowchart

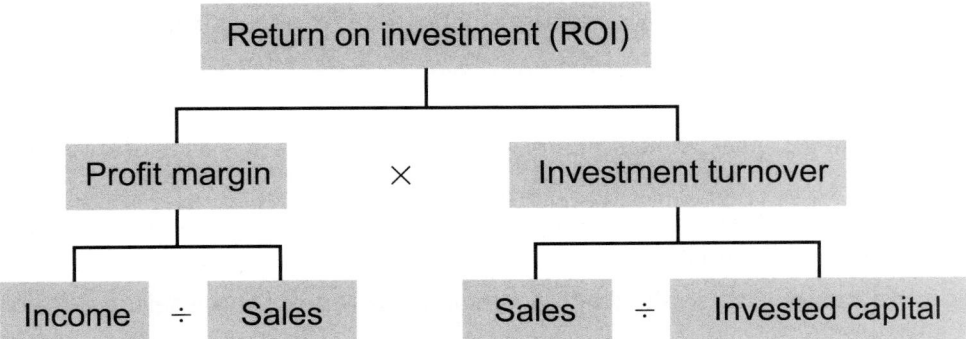

Example 1   **ROI**

Facts: Assume that sales are $1,000,000, net income is $40,000, and invested capital is $250,000. The organization's required rate of return (hurdle rate) is 12 percent.

Required: Determine whether the organization is meeting performance expectations using ROI.

Solution:

$$\frac{\$40,000}{\$1,000,000} \times \frac{\$1,000,000}{\$250,000} = \frac{\$40,000}{\$250,000} = 16\%$$

The organization is meeting its requirements based on ROI computations. The ROI of 16 percent exceeds the required rate of return of 12 percent.

1.2 Return on Assets

Return on assets (ROA) is similar to ROI, except that ROA uses average total assets in the denominator rather than invested capital.

$$\text{ROA} = \frac{\text{Net income}}{\text{Average total assets}}$$

1.3 ROI/ROA Issues

1.3.1 Variations on Asset Valuation

Asset valuations used in the ROI and ROA computations affect the results. The appropriate asset valuation depends on the strategic objectives of the company and the direction that leadership wants to give its managers. The following terms define different asset valuations.

- **Net Book Value:** Assets valued at net book value represent historical cost less accumulated depreciation.

- **Gross Book Value:** Assets valued at gross book value represent historical cost prior to the reduction for accumulated depreciation.

- **Replacement Cost:** Assets valued at replacement cost represent the cost to replace assets at their current level of utility.

- **Liquidation Value:** Assets valued at liquidation value represent the selling price of productive assets.

Pass Key

Adjustments to the ROI denominator raise the bar on asset, project, or company performance. The higher the denominator used in the ROI computation, the lower the return.

1.3.2 Limitations of ROI

ROI, like any performance measure, is designed to direct managers to achieve corporate objectives and provide a basis for incentives. ROI computations have the following limitations:

- **Short-Term Focus:** Use of ROI exclusively as a measure of the performance can inadvertently focus managers purely on maximizing short-term returns. The overemphasis of managers on investment return targets is referred to as investment myopia.

- **Disincentive to Invest:** Profitable units are reluctant to invest in additional productive resources because they could reduce ROI in the short term.

2 Return on Equity and the DuPont Model

2.1 Return on Equity

A critical measure for determining a company's effectiveness is its return on equity (ROE).

$$\text{ROE} = \frac{\text{Net income}}{\text{Equity}}$$

The advantage of this ROE formula is that it is simple to compute. However, additional breakouts of the components of ROE provide management with a much clearer picture of the efficiencies and leverage of a given company's operations.

2.2 DuPont Analysis

2.2.1 Components of DuPont ROE

The three-step DuPont model breaks ROE into three distinct components: Net profit margin, asset turnover, and financial leverage.

- **Net Profit Margin**

  Net profit margin is a measure of operating efficiency.

$$\text{Net profit margin} = \frac{\text{Net income}}{\text{Sales}}$$

▪ Asset Turnover

Asset turnover is a measure of the degree of efficiency with which a company is using its assets.

$$\text{Asset turnover} = \frac{\text{Sales}}{\text{Assets}}$$

▪ Financial Leverage

Financial leverage measures the extent to which a company uses debt in its capital structure.

$$\text{Financial Leverage} = \frac{\text{Assets}}{\text{Equity}}$$

2.2.2 Calculating DuPont ROE

The formula for DuPont ROE is:

$$\text{DuPont ROE} = \text{Net profit margin} \times \text{Asset turnover} \times \text{Financial leverage}$$

$$= \frac{\text{Net income}}{\text{Sales}} \times \frac{\text{Sales}}{\text{Assets}} \times \frac{\text{Assets}}{\text{Equity}}$$

Note that net profit margin and asset turnover can be multiplied to calculate return on assets (ROA). Therefore, DuPont ROE can also be calculated as:

$$\text{DuPont ROE} = \text{ROA} \times \text{Financial leverage}$$

2.2.3 Extended DuPont Model

The extended DuPont model further breaks out net profit margin into three distinct components: Tax burden, interest burden, and the operating income margin.

▪ Tax Burden

The *tax burden* is the extent to which a company retains profits after paying taxes.

$$\text{Tax burden} = \frac{\text{Net income}}{\text{Pretax income}}$$

- **Interest Burden**

    The *interest burden* reflects how much in pretax income a company retains after paying interest to debt holders.

    $$\text{Interest burden} = \frac{\text{Pretax income}}{\text{Earnings before interest and taxes (EBIT)}}$$

- **EBIT Margin**

    The *EBIT margin* is a measure of company profits earned on sales after paying operating and nonoperating costs (other than interest and taxes).

    $$\text{EBIT margin} = \frac{\text{EBIT}}{\text{Sales}}$$

- **Extended DuPont ROE Formula**

    The last two components of the ROE calculation remain the same, with the extended model shown below:

    $$
    \begin{aligned}
    \text{Extended DuPont ROE} &= \underset{\text{Tax burden}}{} \times \underset{\text{Interest burden}}{} \times \underset{\text{EBIT margin}}{} \times \underset{\text{Asset turnover}}{} \times \underset{\text{Financial leverage}}{} \\[4pt]
    &= \frac{\text{Net income}}{\text{Pretax income}} \times \frac{\text{Pretax income}}{\text{EBIT}} \times \frac{\text{EBIT}}{\text{Sales}} \times \frac{\text{Sales}}{\text{Assets}} \times \frac{\text{Assets}}{\text{Equity}}
    \end{aligned}
    $$

Pass Key

Average assets and average equity should be used when calculating ROE. However, if a CPA Exam question only gives ending assets and/or ending equity, these amounts may be used to calculate ROE.

Example 2	ROE

Facts: Blake Co. reports the following in its Year 5 financial statements:

Sales	$500,000	Assets	$900,000
COGS	275,000	Liabilities	300,000
Gross profit	225,000	Equity	600,000
SG&A	150,000		
EBIT	75,000		
Interest expense	15,000		
Pretax income (EBT)	60,000		
Tax (30% rate)	18,000		
Net income	$ 42,000		

Required: Calculate each of the individual component ratios for Blake, as well as the ROE for Blake using both the DuPont model and the extended DuPont model.

Solution:

Net profit margin = Net income / Sales
= $42,000 / $500,000
= **0.084**

Tax burden = Net income / Pretax income
= $42,000 / $60,000
= **0.70**

Interest burden = Pretax income / EBIT
= $60,000 / $75,000
= **0.80**

EBIT margin = EBIT / Sales
= $75,000 / $500,000
= **0.15**

Asset turnover = Sales / Assets
= $500,000 / $900,000
= **0.56**

Financial leverage = Assets / Equity
= $900,000 / $600,000
= **1.50**

DuPont ROE = Net profit margin × Asset turnover × Financial leverage
= 0.084 × 0.56 × 1.50
= **0.07 or 7%**

Extended DuPont ROE = Tax burden × Interest burden × EBIT margin × Asset turnover × Financial leverage
= 0.70 × 0.80 × 0.15 × 0.56 × 1.50
= **0.07 or 7%**

Pass Key

It is important to note that both methods of calculating ROE (DuPont and extended DuPont) produce the same number. By breaking out the calculation into different components, management can get a better understanding of what factors are driving ROE and how those factors compare relative to competing companies and to the industry overall.

3   Residual Income

The residual income method measures the excess of actual income earned by an investment over the return required by the company. The rate of return/hurdle rate for the company may be its WACC, cost of equity, or it may simply be the return established by management as a target rate. Although ROI provides a percentage measurement, residual income provides an amount. Like ROI, residual income is a performance measure for investment SBUs.

3.1   Formula

The formula for residual income is as follows:

> **Residual income = Net income (from the income statement) – Required return**
>
> **Where:**
>
> **Required return   =   Net book value (Equity) × Hurdle rate**

3.2   Interpretation

A positive residual income indicates that performance is meeting standards, and a negative residual income indicates that performance is not meeting standards.

Example 3   Residual Income

Facts: Instafab Manufacturing has an investment in its Southeast regional plant with a net book value of $200,000. Instafab's expected hurdle rate is 10 percent, and the division produces net income of $30,000.

Required: Calculate residual income.

Solution:

Net income		$30,000
Net book value	$200,000	
Hurdle rate	× 10%	
Required return		(20,000)
Residual income		**$10,000**

3.3   Benefits of Residual Income Performance Measures

Advantages of using residual income include the ease of measurement of actual dollars earned by an investment above its required amount.

3.3.1   Realistic Target Rates

Usually, the target rate in the residual income method will be less than the highest return rates actually earned by the best-performing investment centers in a company. Historical weighted average cost of capital is often used as the target or hurdle rate; however, the rate optimally used is the target return set by the company's management.

3.3.2   Focus on Target Return and Amount

Residual income controls and performance measures encourage managers to invest in projects that generate income in excess of the target or calculated rate, thereby improving company profits and promoting the congruence of individual and corporate goals. Divisions with high *rates* of return do not fear dilution of their rates and, therefore, do not avoid investments that demonstrate strong residual income performance.

3.4   Weaknesses of Residual Income Performance Measures

3.4.1   Reduced Comparability

Use of an absolute amount to compute performance distorts comparison of units with unequal size. Larger units of an organization may produce larger dollar volumes of residual income even though their performance is identical to a smaller unit on a percentage basis.

3.4.2   Target Rates Require Judgment

Reliance on computing a target rate of return may sometimes be difficult to establish.

4   Economic Value Added

The Economic Value Added™ (EVA™) method of performance evaluation is very similar to the residual income method. The residual income method computes required return based on a hurdle rate determined by management, and the EVA measures the excess of income after taxes (not counting interest expense) earned by an investment over the return rate defined by the company's overall cost of capital (WACC). The amount used to represent income after taxes is the firm's net operating profit after taxes (NOPAT), and it often incorporates several accounting adjustments prior to application into the model. Economic value added ensures that performance is measured in comparison to changes associated with all capital, debt, and equity. EVA is expressed as an amount and is considered a form of economic profit.

4.1   Formula

The formula for EVA is:

> **Economic value added = Net operating profit after taxes (NOPAT) − Required return**
>
> **Where:**
>
> **Required return   =   Investment × WACC**

4.2   Interpretation

■ **Positive EVA:** A *positive EVA* indicates that performance is meeting standards.

■ **Negative EVA:** A *negative EVA* indicates that performance is not meeting standards.

4.3   Economic Value Added Component Issues

Economic value added can be refined using investment or income adjustments to produce a more accurate analysis of economic profit (value added).

4.3.1   Investment Valuation Issues

■ **Capitalization of Research and Development:** The organization may *capitalize research and development* costs as part of its asset base along with other value-adding investments in advertising and training.

■ **Current Valuation of the Balance Sheet:** *Balance sheet* accounts are generally revalued to represent current cost.

4.3.2   Income Determination

NOPAT may be adjusted to eliminate the effect of certain transactions and thereby create a nearly cash basis income statement.

■ Adjustments to the balance sheet affect the income statement.

■ Deferred taxes are ignored.

Example 4	EVA

Facts: Instafab Manufacturing has an investment in its Southeast regional plant with an investment of $300,000 after adjustments for capitalization of research and development costs and revaluation of certain assets. The company's cost of capital is 12 percent, and its division produces a net operating profit after taxes of $50,000 after adjustments for current-year research and development, asset revaluations, and other accounting considerations.

Required: Calculate the economic value added.

Solution:

NOPAT		$50,000
Investment	$300,000	
Cost of capital	× 12%	
Required return		(36,000)
Economic value added		**$14,000**

Instafab's economic value added is positive. Instafab has added to shareholder value.

Question 1	CPA-06645

SkyBound Airlines provided the following information about its two operating divisions:

	Passenger	Cargo
Operating profit	$ 40,000	$ 50,000
Investment	250,000	500,000
External borrowing rate	6%	8%

Measuring performance using return on investment (ROI), which division performed better?

a. The Cargo division, with an ROI of 10 percent.

b. The Passenger division, with an ROI of 16 percent.

c. The Cargo division, with an ROI of 18 percent.

d. The Passenger division, with an ROI of 22 percent.

Question 2	CPA-04809

Minon Inc. purchased a long-term asset on the last day of the current year. What are the effects of this purchase on return on investment and residual income?

	Return on Investment	Residual Income
a.	Increase	Increase
b.	Decrease	Decrease
c.	Increase	Decrease
d.	Decrease	Increase

Question 3	CPA-08378

Spear Corp. had sales of $2,000,000, a profit margin of 11 percent, and assets of $2,500,000. Spear decided to reduce its debt ratio to 0.40 from 0.50 by selling new common stock and using the proceeds to repay principal on some outstanding long-term debt. After the refinancing, what is Spear's return on equity?

a. 3.5 percent

b. 5.3 percent

c. 14.7 percent

d. 22.9 percent

Question 4	**CPA-04818**

Zig Corp. provides the following information:

Pretax operating profit	$ 300,000,000
Tax rate	40%
Capital used to generate profits 50% debt, 50% equity	1,200,000,000
Cost of equity	15%
Cost of debt (after tax)	5%

Which of the following represents Zig's year-end economic value-added amount?

    a. $0

    b. $60,000,000

    c. $120,000,000

    d. $180,000,000

NOTES

BEC

4

Operations Management: Planning Techniques

Module

Projection and Forecasting Techniques: Part 1

1 Projection Techniques

Projections are prepared to show multiple, hypothetical ("what-if") scenarios and courses of action that a business might follow. Projections serve as the precursor to actual forecasts. Projections are typically prepared for internal use and can assist managers in making decisions regarding products, acquisitions, revenues, expenses, etc.

Sensitivity and scenario analyses are frequently used to project revenues, costs, and profitability.

1.1 Sensitivity Analysis

Sensitivity analysis is the process of experimenting with different parameters and assumptions regarding a model and cataloging the range of results to view the possible consequences of a decision. Sensitivity models often use probabilities to approximate reality.

Also called "what-if" analysis, sensitivity analysis is a risk management tool that is used to test the effect of specific variables on overall profitability. Managers incorporate sensitivity analysis into the budgeting process to determine which variables are the most sensitive to change and therefore will have the biggest effect on the bottom line.

The biggest drawback of sensitivity analysis is the implicit assumption that variables are independent. The reality is that variables do not typically operate in a vacuum, and a change in one will often result in changes in others that are difficult to predict with accuracy.

Example 1 | Sensitivity Analysis

Facts: July sales for Besser Company are projected to be $100,000, with cost of goods sold of $60,000 and general/administrative expenses of $25,000. The CFO has determined that variability in sales has the biggest impact on profitability and she wants to determine the effect on operating income if sales dollars are over-/underestimated by 25 percent.

In order to estimate the change in operating income, the CFO assumes that cost of goods sold will consistently be 60 percent of sales and general/administrative expenses will stay constant at $25,000.

Required: Project operating income using the assumptions that sales at $100,000 are overestimated by 25 percent, correct, or underestimated by 25 percent.

(continued)

(continued)

Solution:

	Sales Overestimated by 25%	Sales Correctly Estimated	Sales Underestimated by 25%
Sales	$75,000	$100,000	$125,000
Cost of goods sold	(45,000)	(60,000)	(75,000)
General/administrative	(25,000)	(25,000)	(25,000)
Operating Income	$ 5,000	$ 15,000	$ 25,000

Because cost of goods sold remains a fixed percentage of sales, and general/administrative expenses remain constant (and therefore independent of sales), the biggest impact on operating income will result from sales being different from estimates.

1.2 Scenario Analysis

In preparing models for future periods, managers may prepare multiple different scenarios which represent alternative possible outcomes. Budgets will be prepared under each scenario and then probabilities may be assigned in order to come up with weighted totals.

Example 2 Scenario Analysis

Facts: In preparing its budgets for the coming year, Ridge Company projects three scenarios for revenues:

- Optimistic scenario (30 percent likelihood): 5 percent sales growth
- Pessimistic scenario (20 percent likelihood): 5 percent sales decline
- Most likely scenario (50 percent likelihood): No sales growth/decline

Required: If sales in the previous fiscal year were $40 million, project sales for next year.

Solution:

- Expected sales growth/decline: (30% × 5%) + (20% × –5%) + (50% × 0%) = 0.5% growth.
- $40 million × (1.005) = $40.2 million in projected sales for next year.

2 Forecasting Techniques

Forecasting is driven by historical data and actual expectations rather than hypothetical scenarios. Projections are typically used internally, and forecasts are prepared for both internal and external audiences.

Forecasting techniques generally can be broken out into qualitative and quantitative methods. Qualitative forecasts are based on the opinions and judgment of management and other experts, and do not require historical data. Quantitative forecasts use historical data and are categorized as either time series methods or causal methods. Time series methods use past trends to predict future variables, and causal methods are based on cause-and-effect relationships between variables.

2.1 Forecasting Analysis

Forecasting (probability/risk) analysis is an extension of sensitivity analysis.

2.1.1 Purpose

Forecasting involves predicting future values of a dependent variable (the variable that one is trying to explain) using information from previous time periods. Historical relationships may be examined in order to use predictions about independent variables to forecast changes in dependent variables.

- **Forecasting Revenues:** On the revenue side, sales are a dependent variable that may be a by-product of independent variables such as expectations regarding the economy, personal income, product competition, growth of the industry, etc.

- **Forecasting Expenses:** On the expense side, total costs are a by-product of specific independent variables such as overall fixed costs and per-unit variable costs.

2.1.2 Application

Various quantitative methods (including regression analysis, explained below) are used in forecasting.

3 Regression Analysis

Linear regression is a method for studying the relationship between two or more variables. One use of linear regression is to predict the value of a dependent variable [e.g., total cost (y)] corresponding to given values of the independent variables [e.g., fixed costs (a), variable cost per unit (B), and production expressed in units (x)].

3.1 Simple Linear Regression Model

Regression analysis explains variation in a dependent variable as a linear function of one or more independent variables. Simple regression involves only one independent variable. Multiple regressions involve more than one independent variable.

- **Components of the Simple Linear Regression Model:** The simple linear regression model takes the following form:

> $$y = a + Bx$$
>
> **Where:**
>
> y = The dependent variable (the variable we are trying to explain). For example, y might be total costs measured in dollars for a cost function.
>
> x = The independent variable (the regressor). The variable that explains y. For example, in a cost function, x would be total activity (or output).
>
> a = The y-axis intercept of the regression line. For example, if y is total costs, a would measure total fixed costs.
>
> B = The slope of the regression line. For example, if y is total costs, and x is output, B measures the change in total costs due to a one-unit change in output (variable cost per unit).

- **Application:** If y is total costs and x is total activity or output, one goal of regression analysis would be to predict total costs (y, the dependent variable) based on observed total activity or output. Questions on the CPA Exam expect you to predict total cost.

3.2   Statistical Measures to Evaluate Regression Analysis

3.2.1   The Coefficient of Correlation (r)

- **Definition:** The coefficient of correlation measures the strength of the linear relationship between the independent variable (x) and the dependent variable (y). In standard notation, the coefficient of correlation is "r."

- **Interpretation:** The range of "r" is from −1.00 to +1.00, as follows:

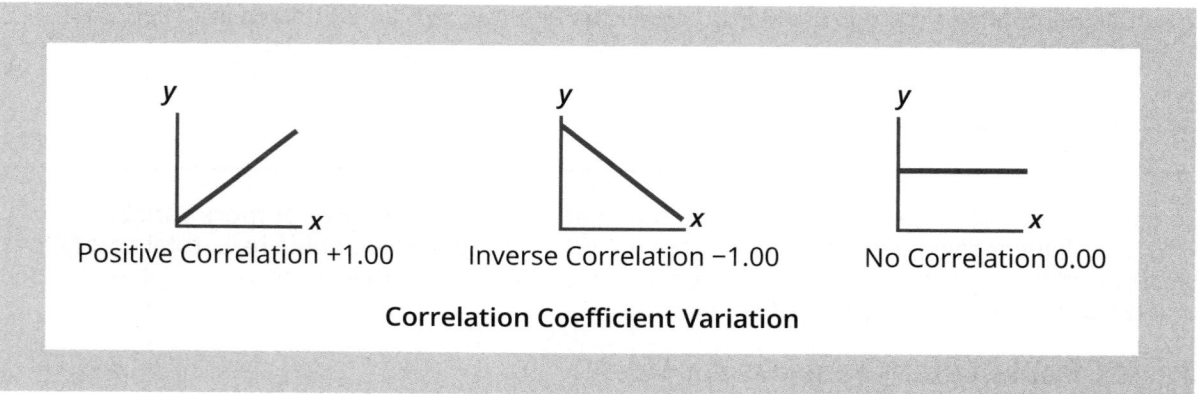

Positive Correlation +1.00   Inverse Correlation −1.00   No Correlation 0.00

Correlation Coefficient Variation

- **Perfect Positive Correlation (+1.00):** The dependent and independent variables move together in the same direction. An increase (decrease) in the independent variable produces an equivalent increase (decrease) in the dependent variable.

- **Perfect Inverse Correlation (−1.00):** The dependent and independent variables move in equivalent opposite directions. An increase (decrease) in the independent variable produces an equivalent decrease (increase) in the dependent variable.

- **No Correlation (0.00):** The dependent and independent variables are not related in a linear fashion. Movement in the independent variable cannot be used to predict the movement in the dependent variable.

■ **Projecting Total Cost:** When predicting total cost (the dependent variable) as a function of fixed costs, variable costs, and volume (the independent variable), management's expectation is that the correlation coefficient will be somewhere between 0.00 and 1.00. As more units of a given product are produced, a reasonable expectation is that total costs will increase.

3.2.2 The Coefficient of Determination (R^2)

■ **Definition:** The coefficient of determination (R^2) is the proportion of the total variation in the dependent variable (y) explained by the independent variable (x). Its value lies between zero and one.

■ **Interpretation:** The higher the R^2, the greater the proportion of the total variation in y that is explained by the variation in x. That is, the higher the R^2, the better the fit of the regression line.

Illustration 1	Coefficient of Determination

Based on looking at five years of data on fixed costs and variable costs per unit, Raxan Inc. determines that its fixed and variable costs in the next year will be $16,000 and $4.50 per unit, respectively. Raxan has determined that the correlation coefficient between the independent and dependent variable is equal to 0.90. The R^2 for the regression equation y (total costs) = $16,000 + 4.50x$, with x being volume, is equal to 0.81. An R^2 of 0.81 means that 81 percent of the change in total cost during a period can be attributed to changes in volume.

4   High-Low Method

The *high-low method* is a simple technique that is used to estimate the fixed and variable portions of cost, usually production costs.

4.1   Procedures

4.1.1   Gather Data

Compare the high and low volumes and costs (ignoring any obvious aberrations). Outliers, which are unusually high or low volumes, are eliminated.

4.1.2   Analyze Data

■ Divide the difference between the high and low dollar total costs by the difference in high and low volumes to obtain the variable cost per unit.

■ Use either the high volume or the low volume to calculate the variable costs by multiplying the volume times the variable cost per unit.

■ Subtract the total calculated variable cost from total costs to obtain fixed costs.

4.1.3   Formulate Results

The result enables preparation of a flexible/performance budget by identifying total fixed costs and variable costs per unit. This may be used to estimate total costs at any volume.

4.2   Flexible Budget Formula

The result of the high-low method is called a total cost formula and, sometimes, a flexible budget formula (or equation).

4.2.1   Flexible Budget

A *flexible budget* is a series of budgets that are prepared for a range of activity levels rather than a single activity (in which variable costs are adjusted to the level of activity and fixed costs are held constant).

4.2.2   Formula

This formula defines total costs as equal to the fixed costs plus the variable costs per unit times the units. The flexible budget formula is then used to estimate total cost at any volume.

$$\text{Total cost} = \text{Fixed cost} + \left[\frac{\text{Variable cost}}{\text{per unit}} \times \frac{\text{Number}}{\text{of units}} \right]$$

Illustration 2   High-Low Method

Period	Units/Volume	Cost
January	1,200	$9,000
February	1,000	8,450
March	1,050	8,600
April	1,130	8,750
May	1,400	9,550
June	1,200	9,000
High	1,400	9,550
Low	(1,000)	(8,450)
Difference between high and low	400	$1,100

Variable cost per unit = $1,100 / 400 units = $2.75 per unit

Using either the high or the low will produce the same total fixed-cost result:

	High	Or:	Low
Units	1,400		1,000
Total cost of units	$9,550		$8,450
Variable costs @ $2.75 per unit	(3,850)		(2,750)
Total fixed costs	$5,700	=	$5,700

Total costs = Fixed costs + [Variable costs per unit × Number of units]

Total costs = $5,700 + [$2.75 × Number of units]

---

5   Learning Curve

Learning curve analysis is based on the premise that as workers become more familiar with a specific task, the per-unit labor hours will decline as experience is gained and production becomes more efficient.

- This analysis is used to set standards and to project costs, as variable costs per unit should decline until a steady-state period is achieved. Once steady state occurs, labor hours per unit will remain constant.

- In order for learning curve analysis to be applied, the activity itself must be repetitive in nature, involve intense labor, and have little to no labor force turnover or breaks in production.

- The calculation begins with the first unit/batch. As cumulative production doubles (from one unit to two units, to four units, to eight units, etc.), cumulative average time per unit falls to a fixed percentage (the learning curve rate) of the previous average time.

Example 3	Learning Curve

Facts: It takes the Jones Production Company 50 hours to produce the first unit of its only product.

Required: Assuming a 70 percent learning curve, estimate the average time and total to produce 2 units, 4 units, and 8 units.

Solution:

2 Units

What is the average time it takes Jones to produce 2 units?

   Average time (2 units) = 50 hours × 0.70 = 35 hours

What is the total time it takes Jones to produce 2 units?

   Total time (2 units) = 35 hours × 2 units = 70 hours

4 Units

What is the average time it takes Jones to produce 4 units?

   Average time (4 units) = 35 hours × 0.70 = 24.5 hours

What is the total time it takes Jones to produce 4 units?

   Total time (4 units) = 24.5 hours × 4 units = 98 hours

8 Units

What is the average time it takes Jones to produce 8 units?

   Average time (8 units) = 24.5 hours × 0.70 = 17.15 hours

What is the total time it takes Jones to produce 8 units?

   Total time (8 units) = 17.15 hours × 8 units = 137.2 hours

| Example 4 | Learning Curve |

Facts: It takes the Jones Production Company 50 hours to produce the first unit, and 70 total hours to produce the first two units.

Required: Calculate the learning curve rate.

Solution: 70%. (70 total hours for 2 units)/(50 hours × 2 units) = 70/100 = 70%.

| Example 5 | Learning Curve |

Facts: It takes the Jones Production Company 50 hours to produce the first unit, and 35 hours, on average, to produce each of the first two units.

Required: Calculate the learning curve rate.

Solution: 70%. (35 hours on average for each unit) / (50 hours for the first unit).

| Question 1 | CPA-07088 |

The coefficient of determination, R^2, in a multiple regression equation is the:

a. Percentage of variation in the independent variables explained by the variation in the dependent variable.

b. Percentage of variation in the dependent variable explained by the variation in the independent variables.

c. Measure of the proximity of actual data points to the estimated data points.

d. Coefficient of the independent variable divided by the standard error of regression coefficient.

| Question 2 | CPA-04642 |

Trijonis Company estimated its material handling costs at two activity levels, as follows:

Kilos Handled	Cost
80,000	$160,000
60,000	$132,000

What is Trijonis' estimated cost for handling 75,000 kilos?

a. $150,000

b. $153,000

c. $157,500

d. $165,000

1 Cost-Volume-Profit (CVP) Analysis

Cost-volume-profit (CVP) analysis is used by managers to forecast profits at different levels of sales and production volume. The point at which revenues equal total costs is called the breakeven point. Cost-volume-profit analysis is synonymous with breakeven analysis.

1.1 Assumptions

1.1.1 General Assumptions

- All costs can be separated into either variable or fixed costs, depending on the behavior of the cost.

- Volume is the only relevant factor affecting cost.

- All costs behave in a linear fashion in relation to production volume.

- Cost behaviors are anticipated to remain constant over the relevant range of production volume because there is an assumption that the efficiency of production does not change.

- Costs show greater variability over time. The longer the time period, the greater the percentage of variable costs. The shorter the time period, the greater the percentage of fixed costs.

1.1.2 Use of Single Product

Although cost-volume-profit analysis can be performed for more than one product, in its simplest form, the model assumes that the product mix remains constant.

1.1.3 Contribution Approach (Direct Costing) Is Used Rather Than Absorption Approach

The contribution approach to the income statement is used for breakeven analysis. Identifying each element of cost as fixed or variable defines its relationship to volume and to the computation of breakeven.

1.1.4 Selling Prices Remain Unchanged

The volume of transactions produces a uniform contribution margin per unit and a predictable projected contribution margin based on volume.

2 Absorption Approach vs. Contribution Approach

2.1 Absorption Approach

The *absorption approach,* which is required for financial reporting under U.S. GAAP, does not segregate fixed and variable costs.

The equation for the absorption approach follows:

> **Revenue**
>
> **Less: cost of goods sold**
>
> **Gross margin**
>
> **Less: operating expenses**
>
> **Net income**

2.2   Contribution Approach

The *contribution approach* to the income statement uses *variable costing* (also called *direct costing*). Although it does not represent generally accepted accounting principles, the contribution approach is extremely useful for internal decision making.

The equation for the contribution approach follows:

> **Revenue**
>
> **Less: variable costs**
>
> **Contribution margin**
>
> **Less: fixed costs**
>
> **Net income**

Pass Key

Variable costs include direct labor, direct material, variable manufacturing overhead, shipping and packaging, and variable selling expenses.

Fixed costs include fixed overhead, fixed selling, and most general and administrative expenses.

- **Total or Per Unit:** Revenue, variable costs, and contribution margin may be expressed in total and on a per-unit basis.

- **Unit Contribution Margin:** *Unit contribution margin* is the unit sales price minus the unit variable cost.

- **Contribution Margin Ratio:** The *contribution margin ratio* is the contribution margin expressed as a percentage of revenue.

2.3   Absorption Approach vs. Contribution Approach

The difference between the *absorption approach* and the *contribution approach* is the treatment of fixed factory overhead. Selling, general, and administrative expenses are period costs under both methods.

2.3.1   Treatment of Fixed Factory Overhead

- **Absorption Approach—Product Cost:** Under the *absorption approach* (absorption costing), all fixed factory overhead is treated as a product cost and is included in inventory values. Cost of goods sold includes both fixed costs and variable costs.

- **Contribution Approach—Period Cost:** Under the *contribution approach* (variable costing), all fixed factory overhead is treated as a period cost and is expensed in the period incurred. Inventory values include only the *variable manufacturing costs*, so cost of goods sold includes only variable manufacturing costs.

2.3.2   Treatment of Selling, General, and Administrative Expenses

Selling, general, and administrative expenses are *period costs* used in the determination of net income under both methods.

- **Absorption Approach:** Under the *absorption approach*, both variable and fixed selling, general, and administrative expenses are part of operating expenses and are reported on the income statement separately from cost of goods sold.

- **Contribution Approach:** Under the *contribution approach*, the variable selling, general, and administrative expenses are part of the total variable costs for the contribution margin calculation.

2.3.3 Gross Margin vs. Contribution Margin

The general income statement formats of both methods are presented below:

Gross Margin *Absorption (Full Cost) Method*		Contribution Margin *Variable (Direct) Cost Method*	
Sales	$XX	Sales	$XX
Less: cost of goods sold	(X)	Less: variable cost of goods sold (excludes fixed overhead)	(X)
Gross margin*	XX	Less: variable selling and administrative expense	(X)
Less: variable selling and administrative expenses	(X)	Contribution margin	$XX
Fixed selling and administrative expenses	(X)	Less: fixed expenses	
Operating income	$XX	Fixed manufacturing overhead	(X)
		Fixed selling and administrative expenses	(X)
		Operating income	$XX

*Gross profit margin may also be stated as a percentage, which is calculated as gross margin (or profit) divided by net sales.

2.4 Effect on Income

If all production is sold every period, both methods produce the same operating income figures. However, if the number of units sold is more or less than the number of units produced, the operating income figures will be different.

2.4.1 Production Greater Than Sales

If units produced exceed units sold, then some units are added to ending inventory and income is higher under absorption costing than under variable costing.

■ Under absorption costing, a portion of the fixed manufacturing overhead is included with each unit in ending inventory.

■ Under variable (direct) costing, all fixed manufacturing overhead is considered a period cost and is expensed during the period.

2.4.2 Sales Greater Than Production

If units sold exceed units produced, then ending inventory is less than beginning inventory and income is lower under absorption costing than under variable costing.

■ Under absorption costing, the fixed manufacturing overhead carried over from a previous period as a part of beginning inventory is charged to cost of sales.

■ Under variable (direct) costing, those fixed costs were charged to income in a prior period (when they were incurred).

Pass Key

Examiners frequently ask about the difference between variable costing net income and absorption costing net income. Follow the simple steps below to compute the difference:

- **Step 1:** Compute fixed cost per unit (Fixed manufacturing overhead / Units produced)
- **Step 2:** Compute the change in income (Change in inventory units × Fixed cost per unit)
- **Step 3:** Determine the impact of the change in income:

No change in inventory: Absorption net income = Variable net income

Increase in inventory: Absorption net income > Variable net income

Decrease in inventory: Absorption net income < Variable net income

2.5 Benefits and Limitations of Each Method

2.5.1 Absorption (GAAP) Costing

■ **Benefits**

- *Absorption costing* is GAAP.
- The Internal Revenue Service requires the use of the absorption method for financial reporting.

■ **Limitations**

- The level of inventory affects net income because fixed costs are a component of product cost.
- The net income reported under the absorption method is less reliable (especially for use in performance evaluations) than under the variable method because the cost of the product includes fixed costs and, therefore, the level of inventory affects net income.

2.5.2 Variable (Direct) Costing

■ **Benefits**

- Variable and fixed costs are separated and can be easily traced to and controlled by management.
- The net income reported under the contribution income statement is more reliable (especially for use in performance evaluations) than under the absorption method because the cost of the product does not include fixed costs and, therefore, the level of inventory does not affect net income.
- Variable costing isolates the contribution margins in financial statements to aid in decision making (the contribution margin is defined as sales price less all variable costs, including variable sales and administrative costs, and breakeven analysis is often based on contribution margins).

■ **Limitations**

- Variable costing is not GAAP.
- The Internal Revenue Service does not allow the use of the variable cost method for financial reporting.

Illustration 1	Absorption vs. Variable Costing		
Costs	**Total Costs**	**Absorption Method Product Cost**	**Contribution Method Product Cost**
Direct materials	$1.00	$1.00	$1.00
Labor			
Direct	4.00	4.00	4.00
Indirect (fixed building maintenance)	0.50	0.50	–
Overhead			
Variable	1.50	1.50	1.50
Fixed	2.00	2.00	–
Commissions to salesman	1.00	–	–
Freight out	0.80	–	–
Total	$10.80	$9.00	$6.50

3   Breakeven Analysis

Breakeven analysis determines the sales required (in dollars or units) to achieve zero profit or loss from operations. In determining the amount in revenues required to break even, management must estimate both fixed costs overall and variable costs on a per-unit basis.

Example 1	Breakeven Analysis

Facts: The following information is applicable to Green Grass Industries and will be used for all of the examples in the next several sections:

- Sales price per unit of $125 and variable costs per unit of $50. The contribution margin per unit is $75 ($125 – $50) and the contribution margin ratio is 60% ($75/$125).

- Fixed costs of $150,000.

- Desired pretax profit of $60,000, a tax rate of 40%, and desired after-tax profit of $36,000.

- Potential unit sales of 2,500 at the current sales price, and a maximum of 3,000 in unit sales to reach market saturation.

3.1   Breakeven Point in Units

The contribution approach to the income statement makes it easy to calculate the breakeven point in either units or sales dollars.

The breakeven point in units can be determined by dividing the unit contribution margin into the total fixed costs:

$$\text{Breakeven point in units} = \frac{\text{Total fixed costs}}{\text{Contribution margin per unit}}$$

Example 1	Breakeven Analysis (continued)

Facts: The same as the first part of Example 1.

Required: Calculate Green Grass' breakeven point in units.

Solution: Breakeven point in units = $150,000 / $75 = 2,000 units

The company will need to sell 2,000 units in order to recover its variable costs of $75 per unit and its total fixed costs of $150,000.

3.2   Breakeven Point in Dollars

There are two approaches to computing breakeven in sales dollars.

1. **Contribution Margin per Unit:** Compute the breakeven point in units using the contribution margin per unit, and then multiply those breakeven units by the selling price per unit:

$$\text{Breakeven point in dollars} = \text{Unit price} \times \text{Breakeven point (in units)}$$

Example 1	Breakeven Analysis (continued)

Facts: The same as the first part of Example 1.

Required: Calculate Green Grass' breakeven point in dollars, using breakeven units.

Solution: Breakeven point in dollars = $125 × 2,000 units = $250,000

The company will need sales of $250,000 in order to cover total variable costs of $100,000 (2,000 units × $50 per unit) and total fixed costs of $150,000.

2. **Contribution Margin Ratio:** Divide total fixed costs by the contribution margin ratio (i.e., the contribution margin as a percentage of revenue per unit or unit price):

$$\text{Breakeven point in dollars} = \frac{\text{Total fixed costs}}{\text{Contribution margin ratio}}$$

Example 1   Breakeven Analysis (continued)

Facts: The same as the first part of Example 1.

Required: Calculate Green Grass' breakeven point in dollars, using the contribution margin ratio.

Solution: Breakeven point in dollars = $150,000 / 60% = $250,000

3.3   Required Sales Volume for Target Profit

Breakeven analysis can be extended to calculate the unit sales or sales dollars required to produce a targeted profit. Although profit figures are most relevant on an after-tax basis, the amount that must be added to the breakeven computation in order to calculate the required sales dollars/units must be a before-tax profit amount. This is done for the purposes of maintaining consistency with the pretax sales and pretax cost figures used in the calculation.

3.3.1   Sales Units Needed to Obtain a Desired Profit

The formula is modified to treat the desired net income before taxes as another fixed cost.

$$\text{Sales (units)} = (\text{Fixed cost} + \text{Pretax profit}) / \text{Contribution margin per unit}$$

Example 1   Breakeven Analysis (continued)

Facts: The same as the first part of Example 1.

Required: Calculate Green Grass' unit sales needed in order to achieve its desired pretax profit of $60,000.

Solution: Sales (units) = ($150,000 + $60,000) / $75 = 2,800 units

Green Grass must sell 2,800 units in order to cover its fixed and variable costs and to achieve its desired pretax profit of $60,000.

3.3.2 Sales Dollars Needed to Obtain a Desired Profit

There are two approaches to computing the sales dollars needed to achieve a desired profit.

1. Summation of Total Costs and Profits

> Sales dollars = Variable costs + Fixed costs + Pretax profit

---

Example 1   Breakeven Analysis (continued)

Facts: The same as the first part of Example 1.

Required: Calculate Green Grass' sales (in dollars) needed in order to achieve its desired pretax profit.

Solution: Total variable costs = 2,800 units × $50 per unit = $140,000

Sales (dollars) = $140,000 + $150,000 + $60,000 = $350,000

Green Grass must have sales of $350,000 in order to cover its variable and fixed costs and achieve its desired $60,000 pretax profit.

---

2. Contribution Margin Ratio

$$\text{Sales} = \frac{\text{Fixed cost + Pretax profit}}{\text{Contribution margin ratio}}$$

Example 1   Breakeven Analysis (continued)

Facts: The same as the first part of Example 1.

Required: Calculate Green Grass' sales (in dollars) needed in order to achieve its desired pretax profit.

Solution: Sales (dollars) = ($150,000 + $60,000)/60% = $350,000

3.4 Predicting Profits Based on Volume

After breakeven has been achieved, each additional unit sold will increase net income by the amount of the contribution margin per unit.

Example 1	Breakeven Analysis (continued)

Facts: The same as the first part of Example 1.

Required: Calculate Green Grass' profit if the company sells 2,500 units.

Solution: Profit = Units above the breakeven point × Contribution margin per unit
= 500 × $75 = $37,500.

The breakeven point calculated earlier was 2,000 units. For every unit sold above 2,000, the company will book a $75 profit. If it sells 2,500 units, that is 500 additional units above breakeven; those 500 units will provide a total profit of $37,500.

3.5 Setting Selling Prices Based on Assumed Volume

This analysis also may be used to derive a per-unit selling price necessary to cover all costs and the desired pretax profit given a specific volume limit.

> **Sale price per unit = (Fixed costs + Variable costs + Pretax profit) / Number of units sold**

Example 1	Breakeven Analysis (continued)

Facts: The same as the first part of Example 1.

Required: Calculate Green Grass' per-unit sales price needed to produce its desired pretax profit given the market saturation level of 3,000 units.

Solution: Per-unit sales price = [$150,000 + (3,000 units × $50 per unit) + $60,000]/3,000
= $120 per unit.

If the company can sell 3,000 units at $120 per unit, it will cover all fixed costs, variable costs, and the desired pretax profit.

3.6 Margin of Safety Concepts

The margin of safety is the excess of sales over breakeven sales, and generally is expressed as either dollars or a percentage.

3.6.1 Sales Dollars

The margin of safety expressed in dollars is calculated as follows:

> **Margin of safety (in dollars) = Total sales (in dollars) – Breakeven sales (in dollars)**

3.6.2 Percentage

The margin of safety also can be expressed as a percentage of sales, as indicated below:

$$\text{Margin of safety percentage} = \frac{\text{Margin of safety in dollars}}{\text{Total sales}}$$

3.7 Breakeven Charts

Breakeven charts graphically display the results of breakeven analysis.

Illustration 2   Breakeven Chart 1

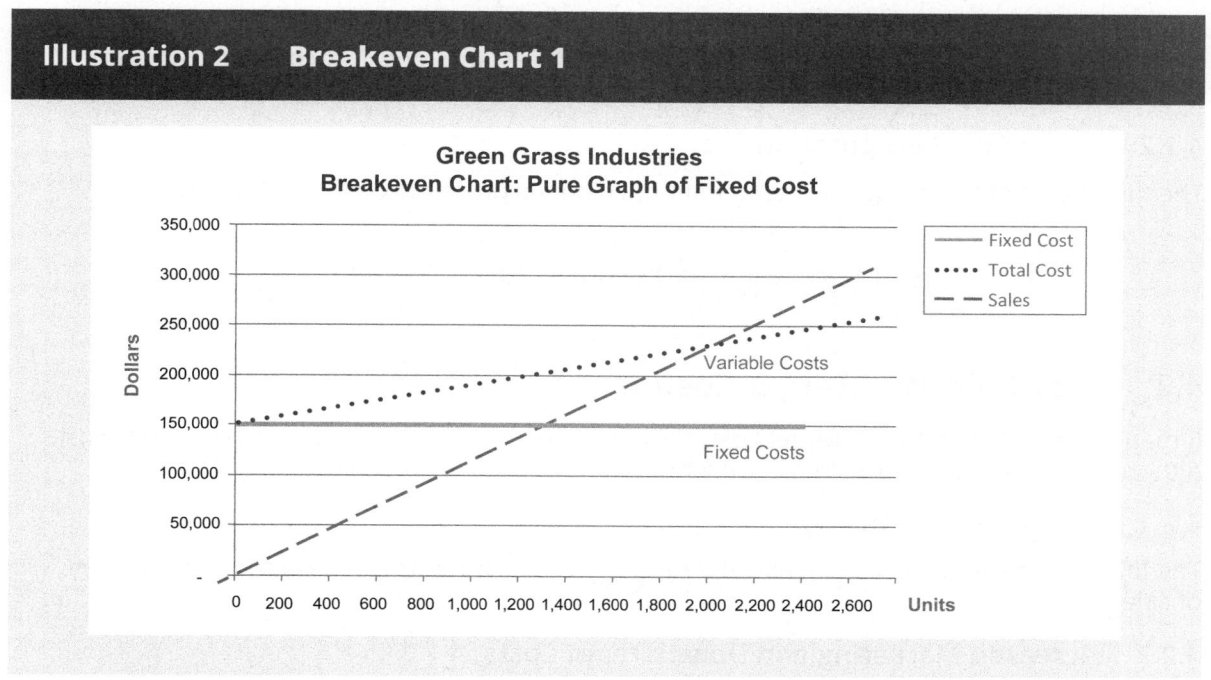

Illustration 3   Breakeven Chart 2

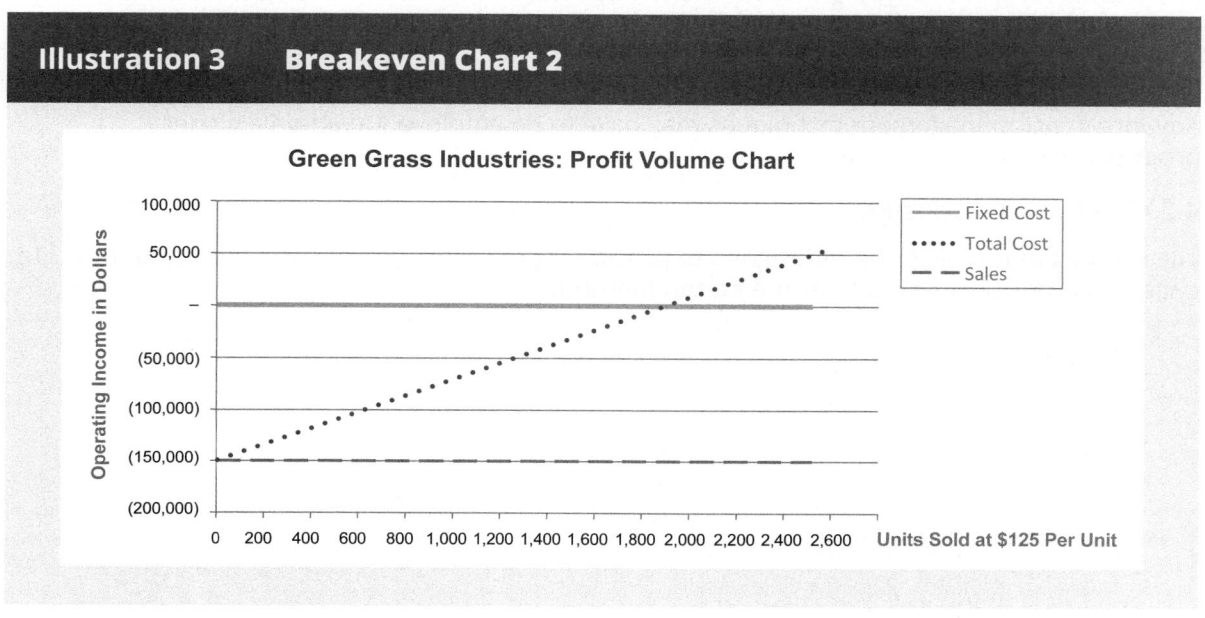

4 Target Costing (Used for Target Pricing)

Target costing is a technique used to establish the product cost allowed to ensure both profitability per unit and total sales volume.

4.1 Cost Determination

The concept of target costing uses the selling price of the product to determine the production costs to be allowed.

4.1.1 Market Circumstances Creating Target Costing

As competition (typically from a "cost leader") sets prices, any change in price could easily cause a customer defection. Target costing is the first step in establishing cost controls to ensure ongoing profitability.

4.1.2 Target Cost Computation

The target cost of the product is the market price minus profit calculated as follows:

Target cost = Market price – Required profit

4.2 Implications of Target Costing

If management commits to a target cost, serious measures must be employed to reduce costs. Although the mechanics are simple, the implications can be far-reaching.

4.2.1 Compromised Quality

The firm may have to sacrifice quality (by reducing costs), but this can have the effect of loss of sales.

4.2.2 Increased Marketing and Downstream Costs

Firms competing in this type of environment may incur increased downstream costs in an attempt to differentiate their products and create brand loyalty (and a competitive advantage).

4.2.3 Increased Complexity in Cost Measurement

Advanced cost management techniques may have to be employed to attain a higher productivity level.

4.2.4 Product Redesign

The product may have to be redesigned to provide for the reduction of costs throughout the life cycle of a product (referred to as the Kaizen method).

Question 1   CPA-03709

Breakeven analysis assumes that over the relevant range:

   a. Unit revenues are nonlinear.

   b. Unit variable costs are unchanged.

   c. Total costs are unchanged.

   d. Total fixed costs are nonlinear.

Question 2   CPA-04798

Waldo Company, which produces only one product, provides its most current month's data as follows:

Selling price per unit	$ 80
Variable costs per unit:	
Direct materials	21
Direct labor	10
Variable manufacturing overhead	3
Variable selling and administrative	6
Fixed costs:	
Manufacturing overhead	$76,000
Selling and administrative	58,000
Units:	
Beginning inventory	0
Month's production	5,000
Number sold	4,500
Ending inventory	500

Based on the above information, what is the total contribution margin for the month under the variable costing approach?

   a. $46,000

   b. $180,000

   c. $207,000

   d. $226,000

Question 3	CPA-04815

At the end of a company's first year of operation, 2,000 units of inventory are on hand. Variable costs are $100 per unit, and fixed manufacturing costs are $30 per unit. The use of absorption costing, rather than variable costing, would result in a higher net income of what amount?

    a. $60,000

    b. $140,000

    c. $200,000

    d. $260,000

Question 4	CPA-03676

At annual sales of $900,000, the Ebo product has the following unit sales price and costs:

Selling price per unit		$20
Prime cost	6	
Manufacturing overhead:		
Variable	1	
Fixed	7	
Selling and administrative costs:		
Variable	1	
Fixed	<u>3</u>	
		<u>18</u>
Profit		<u>$ 2</u>

What is Ebo's breakeven point in units?

    a. 25,000 units

    b. 31,500 units

    c. 37,500 units

    d. 45,000 units

1 Ratio Analysis: An Overview

Ratios are a quick and easy way to evaluate a company's past, current, and future performance and financial standing. The results of forecasts and projections can be analyzed using ratio analysis and by looking for correlations to and variations from key financial ratios.

Many of the ratios in this module are also presented elsewhere in the text. In this section, they are defined and interpreted in the context of projections and forecasts (with these terms used interchangeably for simplicity).

Pass Key

Ratio questions on the business exam may require a simple ratio calculation, an interpretation of what the ratio means, or an analysis of the effects of a change.

When asked to analyze whether a ratio is likely to increase or decrease, you can gain efficiency by knowing the following:

- The numerator has a direct relationship with the ratio. For example, an increase in the numerator results in an increase in the ratio.

$$\uparrow \frac{\text{Numerator}}{\text{Denominator}} = \text{Resulting ratio} \uparrow$$

- The denominator has an inverse relationship with the ratio. For example, an increase in the denominator results in a decrease in the ratio.

$$\frac{\text{Numerator}}{\uparrow \text{Denominator}} = \text{Resulting ratio} \downarrow$$

Sometimes, when both the numerator and denominator are affected by a given change, the final result (increase or decrease) is not easy to determine. The best way to answer questions such as these is to make up numbers and plug them into the ratio formula.

Illustration 1   Gi Company Forecast

Gi Company has used its Year 1 financial results and other information on the historical performance of the company to forecast its Year 2 financial results and has prepared the following forecasted financial statements for Year 2.

The company will use ratio analysis to determine the financial implications of the forecasted results.

Gi Company Balance Sheet

	12/31/Year 2	12/31/Year 1
Current assets		
Cash and cash equivalents	$ 50,000	$ 35,000
Trading securities (at fair value)	75,000	65,000
Accounts receivable	300,000	390,000
Inventory (at lower of cost or market)	290,000	275,000
Total current assets	715,000	765,000
Investments available for sale (at fair value)	350,000	300,000
Fixed assets:		
Property, plant, and equipment (at cost)	1,900,000	1,800,000
Less: accumulated depreciation	(180,000)	(150,000)
	1,720,000	1,650,000
Goodwill	30,000	35,000
Total assets	$2,815,000	$2,750,000

(continued)

(continued)

Current liabilities:

Accounts payable	$ 150,000	$ 125,000
Notes payable	325,000	375,000
Accrued and other liabilities	220,000	200,000
Total current liabilities	$ 695,000	$ 700,000

Long-term debt

Bonds and notes payable	650,000	700,000
Total liabilities	1,345,000	1,400,000

Stockholders' equity

Common stock (100,000 shares outstanding)	500,000	500,000
Additional paid-in capital	670,000	670,000
Retained earnings	300,000	180,000
Total equity	1,470,000	1,350,000
Total liabilities and equity	$2,815,000	$2,750,000

Gi Company Income Statement

	Year 2 (Forecasted)	Year 1 (Actual)
Sales	$1,800,000	$1,700,000
Cost of goods sold	(1,000,000)	(940,000)
Gross profit	800,000	760,000
Operating expenses	(486,970)	(476,970)
Interest expense	(10,000)	(10,300)
Net income before income taxes	303,030	272,730
Income taxes (34%)	(103,030)	(92,730)
Net income after income taxes	$ 200,000	$ 180,000
Earnings per share	$ 2.00	$ 1.80
Other financial information		
Operating cash flows	$275,000	$265,000
Dividends for the year	$0.80 per share	$0 for Year 1
Market price per share	$12	$11

Assumptions for forecast:

Sales: A forecasted increase of 100,000 in sales from 1,700,000 to 1,800,000.

COGS: A forecasted increase of 60,000 in COGS from 940,000 to 1,000,000 due to rising inventory costs.

Operating expenses: A forecasted increase of 10,000 tied to annual wage increases.

Interest expense: A forecasted decline of 300 due to pay down of a small amount of debt.

Operating cash flows: increase of $10,000.

2 Liquidity Ratios

The focus of liquidity ratios is on the current liabilities side of a company's balance sheet, and on whether a company will have enough in current assets and other funds to pay the liabilities when they are due. Key liquidity ratios include the current ratio, quick ratio, cash ratio, operating cash flow ratio, and working capital turnover ratio.

2.1 Working Capital

Working capital = Current assets – Current Liabilities

Year 2: $715,000 – $695,000 = $20,000

Year 1: $765,000 – $700,000 = $65,000

2.2 Current Ratio

$$\text{Current ratio} = \frac{\text{Current assets}}{\text{Current liabilities}}$$

$$\text{Year 2} = \frac{\$715,000}{\$695,000} = 1.03$$

$$\text{Year 1} = \frac{\$765,000}{\$700,000} = 1.09$$

(Industry average = 1.50)

The ratio, and therefore Gi Company's ability to meet its short-term obligations, is forecasted to decrease slightly and it is low compared with the industry average. The only components (current assets and current liabilities) needed to calculate this ratio come straight from totals on the balance sheet.

- **Projection Interpretations:** All else being equal, a higher current ratio is better because it implies that more current assets are available to pay short-term liabilities. If a company expects either decreases in current assets or increases in current liabilities, this will result in a lower forecasted current ratio, which can have a potential negative effect on future funding opportunities and business operations.

2.3　Quick Ratio

$$\text{Quick ratio} = \frac{\text{Cash and cash equivalents} + \text{Short-term marketable securities} + \text{Receivables (net)}}{\text{Current liabilities}}$$

$$\text{Year 2} = \frac{\$50{,}000 + \$75{,}000 + \$300{,}000}{\$695{,}000} = 0.61$$

$$\text{Year 1} = \frac{\$35{,}000 + \$65{,}000 + \$390{,}000}{\$700{,}000} = 0.70$$

(Industry average = 0.80)

This ratio is similar to the current ratio, except that it only includes the more liquid components of current assets such as cash, short-term marketable securities (investments), and receivables. Gi's ratio is forecasted to decrease from Year 1 to Year 2 and the industry average of 0.80 is higher than Gi's ratio, which together indicate that Gi may have trouble meeting short-term needs.

■ **Projection Interpretations:** Like the current ratio, a higher quick ratio is better because it implies that more current liquid assets are available to pay short-term liabilities. Projected shifts in dollars from liquid current assets to more illiquid assets or increases in current liabilities will result in a lower forecasted ratio.

Pass Key

When current assets are used to pay down current liabilities, the numerator and denominator of the current ratio and quick ratio decrease by the same amount. If the current ratio or quick ratio is already less than one, this will result in a lower ratio amount.

2.4   Operating Cash Flow Ratio

$$\text{Operating cash flow ratio} = \frac{\text{Cash flow from operations}}{\text{Ending current liabilities}}$$

$$\text{Year 2} = \frac{\$275,000}{\$695,000} = 0.40$$

$$\text{Year 1} = \frac{\$265,000}{\$700,000} = 0.38$$

(Industry average: 0.45)

This ratio measures how much cash a company has generated from operating activities to cover current liabilities. Gi forecasts an increase in this ratio from 0.38 to 0.40, which means that it expects to generate more from its core operations to cover its current liabilities. Although the output is still lower than the industry average, it is moving in the right direction and presumably strong for a relatively new company going into its second year.

- **Projection Interpretations:** A higher ratio is desired, as it implies that a company is generating more cash from its core activities to pay its current liabilities. Positive and sustainable cash flows from operations are crucial for the ongoing success of a company. If operating cash flows are projected to decline in the future, the company will have to look to investing and financing sources to cover the shortfall.

2.5   Working Capital Turnover

$$\text{Working capital turnover} = \frac{\text{Sales}}{\text{Average working capital}}$$

$$\text{Year 2} = \frac{\$1,800,000}{\left[(\$715,000 - \$695,000) + (\$765,000 - \$700,000)\right] / 2}$$

$$= 42.4 \text{ times}$$

(Industry average: 48.5 times)

The sales amount comes from the income statement, while working capital is calculated as the difference between current assets and current liabilities. This measure is used to evaluate the money used to fund the company's operations and the sales derived from the operations. Gi's forecasted working capital turnover ratio is slightly below industry average, indicating that the company is not doing as well as its peers at converting its working capital into sales. The expectation is that as the company matures, this ratio will improve.

- **Projection Interpretations:** All else being equal, a higher working capital turnover ratio is better. Higher projected net sales in future years will cause this ratio to increase. The ratio will also increase with projected declines in current assets or increases in current liabilities. A ratio that is too high could indicate a working capital amount that is too low.

3   Activity Ratios

Activity ratios are used to assess how efficient a company is at utilizing its resources to generate sales and profits. Key activity ratios include the days in inventory, days of payables outstanding, days sales in accounts receivable, operating cycle, and cash conversion cycle.

Pass Key

Turnover ratios generally use average balances [i.e., (beginning balance + ending balance) / 2] for balance sheet components. However, on some recent CPA Exam questions, candidates have been instructed to use year-end balances instead. Please be sure to read the question carefully to determine the appropriate method to use.

The ratios given in this module match the most recent ratios provided by the AICPA as an exhibit on task-based simulations requiring ratio calculations.

3.1   Days in Inventory

$$\text{Days in inventory} = \frac{\text{Ending inventory}}{\text{Cost of goods sold / 365}}$$

$$\text{Year 2} = \frac{290{,}000}{\$1{,}000{,}000 \text{ / } 365}$$

$$= 105.85 \text{ days}$$

(Industry average: 78 days)

This ratio indicates the average number of days required to sell inventory. Inventory will typically be averaged in this ratio in order to align the time period to cost of goods sold. Use ending inventory if data is not provided for multiple years. Gi is forecasting a Year 2 inventory conversion ratio that is significantly higher than the industry average, which means that it will take the company longer to convert its inventory into sales. This ratio will need to be reduced over the next several years, or the company will risk its inventory becoming obsolete (as well as potentially incurring higher carrying costs in order to sustain the inventory).

■   **Projection Interpretations:** This ratio reflects how long it takes on average to turn inventory into sales. The output will be in days, with a lower number of days indicating a company is more efficient in converting inventory into sales. Projected sales will affect projected inventory, which will influence the projected inventory conversion period.

3.2   Days Sales in Accounts Receivable

$$\text{Days sales in accounts receivable} = \frac{\text{Ending accounts receivable (net)}}{\text{Sales (net)} / 365}$$

$$\text{Year 2} = \frac{\$300,000}{\$1,800,000 / 365}$$

$$= 60.83 \text{ days}$$

(Industry average: 55 days)

This ratio indicates the receivables' quality and the success of the firm in collecting outstanding receivables. The net sales number from the income statement is equal to gross sales less sales returns and allowances. Receivables are often averaged in this ratio to align to the period covered by net sales on the income statement. Use ending receivables if data is not provided for multiple years. Although Gi is forecasting a 70-day receivables collection period (relative to the industry average of 55), it is forecasting an increase in sales along with a decrease in the receivables balance, implying that it expects to collect on much of its outstanding receivables while boosting revenue. Gi is still unfavorable relative to the industry, but it is moving in the right direction.

- **Projection Interpretations:** This measure provides an average number of days to convert sales into cash. A shorter number of days indicates that a company is doing a good job collecting on its outstanding receivables. Future expected growth in sales will likely tie to increases in receivables, unless a company projects a change in the percentage of credit sales relative to cash sales.

3.3   Days of Payables Outstanding

$$\text{Days of payables outstanding} = \frac{\text{Ending accounts payable}}{\text{Cost of goods sold} / 365}$$

$$\text{Year 2} = \frac{\$150,000}{\$1,000,000 / 365}$$

$$= 54.75 \text{ days}$$

(Industry average: 62 days)

Accounts payable will typically be averaged to align with the time period associated with cost of goods sold. Use ending accounts payable if data is not provided for multiple years. Here, Gi is forecasting a little over 50 days to pay its vendors, whereas the industry takes 62 days. As long as the company is meeting the payment terms of its vendors, it should look to extend this period in order to conserve cash.

- **Projection Interpretations:** This is a measure of how long it takes for a company to pay its vendors for goods purchased on credit. If a company wishes to conserve cash, it will project longer average time periods to pay its vendors.

3.4   Cash Conversion Cycle

Cash conversion cycle = Days in inventory + $\dfrac{\text{Days sales in}}{\text{accounts receivable}}$ − $\dfrac{\text{Days of payables}}{\text{outstanding}}$

Year 2 = 105.85 days + 60.83 days − 54.75 days

= 111.93 days

(Industry average: 71 days)

Gi is forecasting a cash conversion cycle that is significantly longer than that of its industry. Although it is expected that a relatively new company such as Gi will take some time to develop efficiencies and procedures designed to maximize its cash position, there is room for improvement in all three components that make up this cycle. Gi will have to address how fast it converts inventory into sales, how fast it collects outstanding receivables, and how long it takes Gi to pay its vendors. The biggest area for improvement is inventory conversion.

- **Projection Interpretations:** All else being equal, a lower cash conversion cycle is better because a company would want to minimize the number of days it takes to convert inventory into sales and sales into cash, while taking as long as possible to pay its vendors. Similar to the operating cycle, policy and forecasted cash flow decisions will influence this cycle time.

Example 1	Cash Conversion Cycle

Facts: A company expects to reduce its operating cycle by five full days as a result of new sales initiatives and more aggressive collection policies.

Required: If the cash conversion cycle is projected to be three days shorter than before, compute the change in the days of payables outstanding.

Solution: The operating cycle consists of the days in inventory and days sales in accounts receivable, which represents two thirds of the cash conversion cycle. If the overall cash conversion cycle is projected to be three days shorter and the operating cycle will be five days shorter, it must be a case that the days of payables outstanding is decreasing by two days.

4   Debt Ratios

Debt ratios measure the extent to which a company employs financial leverage in its capital structure. Although debt is cheaper than equity from a cost standpoint because of the tax benefits and lower interest rates, too much debt is risky for the borrowing company. Key debt ratios include the debt-to-equity ratio, debt-to-assets ratio, debt-to-total-capital ratio, interest coverage ratio, and debt service coverage ratio.

4.1   Debt-to-Equity

$$\text{Debt-to-equity ratio} = \frac{\text{Total liabilities}}{\text{Total equity}}$$

$$\text{Year 2} = \frac{\$1,345,000}{\$1,470,000} = 0.91$$

$$\text{Year 1} = \frac{\$1,400,000}{\$1,350,000} = 1.04$$

(Industry average = 0.75)

This ratio indicates the degree of protection to creditors in case of insolvency. A lower ratio is better. Gi is forecasting a reduction in this ratio, which is positive as both current and long-term liabilities are forecasted to decline and equity is forecasted to increase due to net income from Year 2. The goal for the company should be to get this ratio closer to the industry average, which can be accomplished by paying down debt. If new debt is added, there should be at least as much growth in equity to cover the debt increase.

- **Projection Interpretations:** A higher debt-to-equity ratio indicates that the company employs more risk. If a company anticipates issuing debt in the future or reducing the amount of outstanding stock, this ratio will increase. Ideally, a company will choose the mix of liabilities and equity that will minimize its overall cost of capital.

4.2   Total Debt Ratio

$$\text{Total debt ratio} = \frac{\text{Total liabilities}}{\text{Total assets}}$$

$$\text{Year 2} = \frac{\$1,345,000}{\$2,815,000} = 47.8\%$$

$$\text{Year 1} = \frac{\$1,400,000}{\$2,750,000} = 50.9\%$$

(Industry average: 40%)

Gi's total debt ratio is forecasted to improve due to an increase in assets and a decrease in liabilities. Because a higher ratio indicates higher risk, this forecast shows a positive trend and will get the company closer to the industry average.

- **Projection Interpretations:** Very similar to the debt-to-equity ratio, a company's risk level increases as this ratio increases. Forecasted future year asset and liability totals are compared to produce a projected total debt ratio. If a company wishes to lower its risk levels, it will have to reduce total liabilities or increase total assets without incurring more debt.

4.3   Times Interest Earned (Interest Coverage) Ratio

$$\text{Times interest earned ratio} = \frac{\text{Earnings before interest expense and taxes} (\text{EBIT})}{\text{Interest expense}}$$

$$\text{Year 2} = \frac{\$303,030 + \$10,000}{\$10,000} = 31.3 \text{ times}$$

$$\text{Year 1} = \frac{\$272,730 + \$10,300}{\$10,300} = 27.5 \text{ times}$$

(Industry average: 24.5 times)

Gi has a more favorable ratio than its peers. The ratio of 27.48 days for Year 1 is forecasted to increase to 31.30 days, which shows the company can cover its debt expenses.

- **Projection Interpretations:** A higher number implies that a company has more funding to cover its required interest expense associated with debt. By paying down old debt or replacing old debt with new debt carrying lower interest rates, interest expense can be lowered in the future, which will increase this ratio.

5   Profitability Ratios

The focus of profitability ratios is on determining how profitable a company is at various levels of its business. Although the bottom line is very important, cost controls earlier in the process can be extremely beneficial for a company. Common profitability ratios include the margins (gross, operating, and net), return on equity, and return on assets.

5.1   Gross Margin

$$\text{Gross margin} = \frac{\text{Sales (net)} - \text{Cost of goods sold}}{\text{Sales (net)}}$$

$$\text{Year 2} = \frac{\$1,800,000 - \$1,000,000}{\$1,800,000} = 44.4\%$$

$$\text{Year 1} = \frac{\$1,700,000 - \$940,000}{\$1,700,000} = 44.7\%$$

(Industry average: 48%)

This ratio is looking at profitability at the highest level. Gi is forecasting relatively flat gross margins in Year 2 relative to Year 1. As the company becomes more efficient in its operations and reduces costs relative to sales, this ratio should improve such that it meets or exceeds the industry average.

- **Projection Interpretations:** All profitability margins are interpreted the same way: All else being equal, higher is better. Sales are forecast to grow at a certain percentage each year based on a variety of factors described earlier in the text. For ease of calculation purposes, cost of goods sold is often forecast to remain a specific percentage of sales—keeping the gross margin constant.

5.2 Profit Margin

$$\text{Profit margin} = \frac{\text{Net income}}{\text{Sales (net)}}$$

$$\text{Year 2} = \frac{\$200,000}{\$1,800,000} = 11.1\%$$

$$\text{Year 1} = \frac{\$180,000}{\$1,700,000} = 10.6\%$$

(Industry average: 13%)

As with all margins, the goal is to increase the ratio. Gi is forecasting an increase in the net profit margin. Controlling growth in costs while continuing to increase sales will get the company closer to the industry average.

- **Projection Interpretations:** The higher the net profit margin the better, as this means a company is profitable after taking into account all costs associated with generating sales and operating its business. This is one of the key measures a company evaluates in making projections, as this will likely impact future capital structure decisions and stock growth.

5.3 Return on Equity (ROE)

$$\text{Return on equity (ROE)} = \frac{\text{Net income}}{\text{Average total equity}}$$

$$\text{Year 2} = \frac{\$200,000}{(\$1,470,000 + \$1,350,000) \, / \, 2}$$

$$= 14.2\%$$

(Industry average: 15%)

Gi's forecasted ROE for Year 2 is very close to the industry average. Continued growth in profitability while managing dividend outflows will boost this ratio. Because net income comes from the income statement and shareholders' equity comes from the balance sheet, it is common practice to use average shareholders' equity in the denominator.

- **Projection Interpretations:** A higher ROE is desirable, as higher net income for shareholders means greater profitability, higher earnings per share, and probable future stock growth. While equity is a by-product of future capital structure decisions, future net income (which also affects equity) will be a result of forecasted sales and costs.

5.4   Return on Assets (ROA)

$$\text{Return on assets}\,(\text{ROA}) = \frac{\text{Net income}}{\text{Average total assets}}$$

$$\text{Year 2} = \frac{\$200,000}{\$2,782,500}$$

$$= 7.2\%$$

(Industry average: 8%)

In line with other profitability and return measures, Gi's ROA is slightly below the industry average. As long as Gi can continue to increase its bottom-line profits at a rate faster than overall asset growth, this measure will improve. Similar to ROE, common practice is to take the average balance of assets at the beginning and end of the period in order to align with the period covered by net income.

- **Projection Interpretations:** A higher ROA implies that a company is generating more profits relative to its base of assets. Projected net income should be compared with projected assets to determine whether this ratio is increasing or decreasing in the future.

Question 1	CPA-03991

Which of the following transactions does not change the current ratio or total current assets?

    a.   A cash advance is made to a divisional office.

    b.   A cash dividend is declared.

    c.   Short-term notes payable are retired with cash.

    d.   Equipment is purchased with a three-year note and a 10 percent cash down payment.

Question 2	CPA-04009

An increase in sales collections resulting from an increased cash discount for prompt payment would be expected to cause a(n):

    a.   Increase in the operating cycle.

    b.   Increase in the average collection period.

    c.   Decrease in the cash conversion cycle.

    d.   Increase in bad debt losses.

NOTES

1 Terms Related to Marginal Analysis

The operational decision method, referred to as *marginal analysis*, is used when analyzing business decisions such as the introduction of a new product or changes in output levels of existing products, acceptance or rejection of special orders, making or buying a product or service, selling or processing further, and adding or dropping a segment. Marginal analysis focuses on the relevant revenues and costs that are associated with a decision.

1.1 Relevant Revenues and Costs

When making business decisions that will affect future periods, revenues and costs related to those decisions are deemed to be relevant only if they change as a result of selecting different alternatives. Although variable costs are more likely to be relevant because they change with production volume and output, relevant costs can be either fixed or variable.

Relevant costs often share similar characteristics, including their specific traceability to cost objects that may change as a result of selecting different alternatives. Ultimately, a cost's relevance pertains to its potential to affect the decision.

- **Direct Costs:** Costs that can be identified with or traced to a given cost object. Direct costs are usually relevant (variable costs are generally direct costs).

- **Prime Costs:** Direct material and direct labor costs, which are generally relevant.

- **Discretionary Costs:** Costs arising from periodic (usually annual) budgeting decisions by management to spend in areas not directly related to manufacturing. Discretionary costs are generally relevant.

Illustration 1   Discretionary Costs
Costs to maintain landscaping at a corporation's headquarters are generally viewed as discretionary.

- **Incremental Costs:** Also known as marginal costs, differential costs, or out-of-pocket costs, the additional costs incurred to produce an additional amount of the unit over the present output. Incremental costs are relevant costs and include all variable costs and any avoidable fixed costs associated with a decision.

- **Opportunity Costs:** The cost of foregoing the next best alternative when making a decision. Opportunity costs are relevant costs.

Illustration 2   Opportunity Costs

1. Costs related to a special device that is necessary if a special order is selected are relevant.

2. Costs associated with alternative uses of plant space are relevant.

- **Irrelevant Costs:** Costs that do not differ among alternatives are irrelevant and should be ignored in a marginal cost analysis.

- **Sunk Costs:** Costs that are unavoidable because they were incurred in the past and cannot be recovered as a result of a decision. Sunk costs are not relevant costs.

Illustration 3   Sunk Costs

Electramag Corporation is evaluating whether to replace a piece of equipment. The cost of the old equipment is a sunk cost and is not relevant to the replacement decision. Additionally, under either alternative (keep the old equipment or replace it), the anticipated cost of electricity remains the same. The cost of electricity is a variable cost. Even so, the cost of electricity is not relevant because it does not change regardless of the selected alternative.

- **Controllable Costs:** Costs that are authorized by the business unit manager or the decision maker. The ability to control cost is evaluated when analyzing business decisions. By classifying a cost as either controllable or uncontrollable, the specific level of management responsible for the cost is identified. Controllable costs are relevant if they will change as a result of selecting different alternatives.

- **Uncontrollable Costs:** Costs that were authorized at a different level in the organization. Uncontrollable costs are not relevant costs because they cannot be changed by the manager making the decision.

Illustration 4   Controllable vs. Uncontrollable Costs

A manufacturing department manager has control over the materials and supplies used in the manufacturing department (i.e., controllable costs), but that manager has no control over the fixed asset depreciation allocated to the department (i.e., uncontrollable costs).

- **Avoidable Costs and Revenues:** Costs and revenues that result from choosing one course of action instead of another. As a result, the firm avoids the cost and revenue associated with the course of action not selected. They are relevant to the decision.

- **Unavoidable Costs:** Costs that are the same regardless of the chosen course of action are unavoidable costs that are not relevant to future decisions. These costs will continue regardless of the course of action taken. They have no effect on the decision.

2 Special Order Decisions

Special order decisions are defined as opportunities that require a firm to decide whether a specially priced order should be accepted or rejected. Decisions of this character involve a comparison of the special order price to the relevant costs of the decision and an analysis of the strategic issues that relate to the acceptance or rejection of the order.

2.1 Determining Relevant Costs

2.1.1 Capacity Issues

Special orders are short-term decisions that often assume excess capacity. Fixed costs are generally not relevant to these decisions unless the special order will change total fixed costs.

- **Presumed Excess Capacity**

  If there is excess capacity, a comparison should be made of the incremental costs of the order to the incremental revenue generated by the order. The special order should be accepted if the selling price per unit is greater than the variable cost per unit.

- **Presumed Full Capacity**

  If the company is operating at full capacity, the opportunity cost of producing the special order should be included in the analysis.

  - The production that is forfeited to produce the special order is the next best alternative use of the facility.

  - The opportunity cost is the contribution margin that would have been produced if the special order were not accepted.

Example 1	Special Order With Excess Capacity

Facts: Kator Company is a manufacturer of industrial components. Product KB-96 is normally sold for $150 per unit and has the following costs per unit:

Direct materials	$20
Direct labor	15
Variable manufacturing overhead	12
Fixed manufacturing overhead	30
Shipping and handling costs	3
Fixed selling costs	10
Total cost	$90

Kator has received a special, one-time order for 1,000 units of KB-96.

Required: Assuming that Kator has excess capacity, calculate the minimum acceptable price for this one-time special order.

Solution: The fixed manufacturing overhead and the fixed selling costs are not relevant to the decision. The incremental per-unit production cost is the total variable cost per unit of $50. Kator should accept the special order only if the selling price per unit is greater than $50.

| Example 2 | Special Order With No Excess Capacity |

Facts: Assume the same costs as in the previous example. Kator has received a special, one-time order for 1,000 units of KB-96. Assume that Kator is operating at full capacity. Also assume that the next best alternative use of the capacity is the production of LB-64, which would produce a contribution margin of $10,000.

Required: Calculate the minimum acceptable price for this one-time special order.

Solution: Kator's next best alternative use of its capacity would produce a contribution margin of $10,000. If Kator produces 1,000 units of KB-96, this $10-per-unit ($10,000 / 1,000 units) opportunity cost would be added to the variable cost of $50 to determine the minimum justifiable price for the special order. Kator should accept the special order only if the selling price per unit is greater than $60.

2.2 Strategic Factors

The acceptance of a special order also requires consideration of a number of strategic factors, including:

- The effect on regular-priced sales and other long-term pricing issues.

- The possibility of future sales to this customer.

- The possibility of exceeding plant capacity or the complexities of the order itself.

- The pricing of the special order.

- The impact of income taxes.

- The effect on machinery and/or the scheduled machine maintenance program.

3 Make vs. Buy

The decision to make or buy a component (also referred to as insourcing versus outsourcing) is similar to the special order decision. Managers should select the lowest-cost alternative.

3.1 Determining Relevant Costs and Other Make-or-Buy Issues

3.1.1 Capacity Issues

- **Excess Capacity:** If there is excess capacity, the cost of making the product internally is the cost that will be avoided (or saved) if the product is not made. This will be the maximum outside purchase price.

- **No Excess Capacity:** If there is no excess capacity, the cost of making the product internally is the cost that will be avoided (saved) if the product is not made plus the opportunity cost associated with the decision.

Example 3	Make vs. Buy Decisions

Facts: Offset Manufacturing produces 20,000 units of part No. 125. The production costs are:

	Total Cost	Cost per Unit
Direct materials	$ 10,000	$ .50
Direct labor	40,000	2.00
Variable manufacturing overhead	20,000	1.00
Fixed factory overhead	40,000	2.00
Total cost	$110,000	$5.50

An outside manufacturer approaches Offset Manufacturing and offers to sell it the same part for $5 per unit. Offset has excess capacity. The $10,000 factory floor supervisor's salary is the only fixed cost that will be eliminated if Offset purchases the part.

Required: Determine whether Offset Manufacturing should make or buy the part.

Solution:

	Make Total	Make Per Unit	Buy Total	Buy Per Unit
Purchase cost			$100,000	$5.00
Direct materials	$10,000	$0.50		
Direct labor	40,000	2.00		
Variable factory overhead	20,000	1.00		
Fixed factory overhead (avoidable)	10,000	0.50		
Total relevant costs	$80,000	$4.00	$100,000	$5.00
Difference	$20,000	$1.00		

Offset will choose to make the part because it is the lowest-cost alternative when relevant costs are considered.

3.2 Strategic Factors

The following strategic factors should be considered when analyzing a make-or-buy decision:

- The quality of the product purchased compared with the quality of the product manufactured.
- The reliability of the purchased product.
- The value of service contracts or other warranties.
- The risks associated with outsourcing or buying outside the organization, including inflexibility, loss of control, and less confidentiality.
- The most efficient use of the entity's resources.

4 Sell or Process Further

The decision regarding *additional processing* is made based on profitability.

4.1 Joint Costs

Joint costs are the costs of a single process that yields multiple products (e.g., the processing of a pig to produce ham, bacon, and pork chops). Joint costs cannot be traced to an individual product. Joint costs are sunk costs that are not relevant to decisions of whether to sell or to process further.

4.2 Separable Costs

Separable costs are costs incurred after the split-off point that can be traced to individual products and are relevant to decisions of whether to sell or to process further.

4.3 Deciding Factors to Sell or Process Further

The decision on whether to sell at the split-off point is made by comparing the incremental cost and the incremental revenue generated after the split-off point.

If the incremental revenue exceeds the incremental cost, the organization should process further.

If the incremental cost exceeds the incremental revenue, the organization should sell at the split-off point.

Example 4 | Sell or Process Further

Facts: Jackson Inc. processes raw materials into beauty products. The Soap Division (Soap) processes fats and lye at a cost of $200 per batch, which yields 2,000 bars of soap. Soap can sell the soap for $0.50 per bar at this point. Alternatively, various fragrances and oils can be added to produce fine soaps for the high-end retail market from a given batch of raw materials. Soap could incur an additional cost of $1.20 per bar of soap for the perfumes and attractive packaging and create lavender-scented soap. Or, for an additional cost of $1.75 per bar, Soap could create rose-scented soap. The high-end soap would sell for $1.30 per bar for the lavender scent and $3 per bar for the rose scent.

Required: Determine whether the soap division will produce the lavender soap, rose-scented soap, or both.

Solution: The Soap Division will not produce the lavender soap because the costs after the split-off point are $1.20 per bar and the incremental revenue is only $0.80 ($1.30 for lavender soap minus the $0.50 revenue for basic soap). Incremental revenue is less than incremental costs.

If the company decides to produce rose-scented soap, incremental costs are $1.75 per bar and incremental revenue is $2.50 ($3 minus $0.50) per bar. Because the incremental revenue exceeds incremental costs, Soap would produce rose soap.

---

5   Keep or Drop a Segment

Relevant costs should be used to determine whether to *keep or drop a business* segment.

5.1   Classification of Costs

The fixed costs associated with the segment must be identified as either avoidable (relevant) or unavoidable, even if the segment is discontinued.

5.2   Decision Factors

A firm should compare the fixed costs that can be avoided if the segment is dropped (i.e., the cost of running the segment) to the contribution margin that will be lost if the segment is dropped.

- Keep the segment if the lost contribution margin exceeds avoided fixed costs.

- Drop the segment if the lost contribution margin is less than avoided fixed costs.

Example 5   Fixed Costs Are Unavoidable

Facts: The executives at Chowderhead Industries are evaluating each of their product lines. A variable costing analysis by product shows that the company's clam and corn chowder products are profitable but its conch chowder product is not.

Description	Clam	Conch	Corn	Total
Sales	$125,000	$75,000	$50,000	$250,000
Variable costs	90,000	60,000	25,000	175,000
Contribution margin	35,000	15,000	25,000	75,000
Fixed costs	20,000	20,000	20,000	60,000
Operating Income	$ 15,000	$ (5,000)	$ 5,000	$ 15,000

The conch chowder fixed costs are unavoidable.

Required: Determine whether Chowderhead should eliminate its conch chowder product line.

Solution: If the conch chowder fixed costs are unavoidable, they will be incurred even if conch chowder is eliminated.

Description	Clam	Conch	Corn	Total
Sales	$125,000	–	$50,000	$175,000
Variable costs	90,000	–	25,000	115,000
Contribution margin	35,000	–	25,000	60,000
Fixed costs	20,000	20,000	20,000	60,000
Net Income	$ 15,000	$(20,000)	$ 5,000	–

The conch chowder product line should not be eliminated. Elimination of the product would eliminate company-wide profits because the product makes a positive contribution to covering the entity's fixed costs.

Example 6	Some Fixed Costs Are Avoidable

Facts: Assume that $16,000 of the Conch Chowder fixed costs are avoidable advertising costs that will not be incurred if the product is eliminated.

Required: Given these new facts, determine whether Chowderhead Industries should eliminate its conch chowder product line.

Solution: If $16,000 of the fixed costs are avoidable, then only $4,000 are unavoidable and will be incurred even if conch chowder is eliminated.

Description	Clam	Conch	Corn	Total
Sales	$125,000	–	$50,000	$175,000
Variable costs	90,000	–	25,000	115,000
Contribution margin	35,000	–	25,000	60,000
Unavoidable fixed costs	15,000	4,000	16,000	35,000
Avoidable fixed costs	5,000	–	4,000	9,000
Operating Income	$ 15,000	$ (4,000)	$ 5,000	$ 16,000

The Chowderhead executives should eliminate the conch chowder product line because the avoidable fixed costs exceed the contribution margin that is lost when the product is eliminated. In this case, elimination of the conch chowder product line improves overall productivity from $15,000 to $16,000.

5.3 Strategic Factors

Important strategic factors to consider include:

- The complementary character of products and their relationship to the sales of other products. Manufacturers might produce and price certain products as loss leaders to promote sales of more profitable products.

- The impact of product addition or deletion on employee morale.

- The growth potential of each product regardless of individual profitability.

- Opportunity costs associated with available capacity.

Question 1   CPA-06169

The Danforth Corp. circuit production plant has a 12,000-unit capacity and currently produces 10,000 circuits per year. The company incurs $50,000 in variable costs for its current production and carries a $40,000 fixed cost burden.

If Danforth has an opportunity to fill a special order for 1,000 circuits, the price per unit for the order should exceed:

    a. $4.00

    b. $5.00

    c. $8.33

    d. $9.00

Question 2   CPA-06170

The Danforth Corp. circuit production plant has a 10,000-unit capacity and currently produces 10,000 circuits per year. The company incurs $50,000 in variable costs for its current production and carries a $40,000 fixed cost burden.

Danforth has explored other alternatives and knows that the next best alternative would produce a $2,000 contribution margin for a 1,000-unit run. If Danforth has an opportunity to fill a special order for 1,000 circuits, the price per unit of the order should exceed:

    a. $2.00

    b. $5.00

    c. $7.00

    d. $11.00

NOTES

1 Operational and Tactical Planning

Operational and tactical planning is the process of determining the specific objectives and means by which strategic plans will be achieved. Tactical plans are short term and cover periods up to 18 months.

1.1 Single-Use Plans

Tactical plans are also called *single-use plans* because they are developed to apply to specific circumstances during a specific time frame.

1.2 Annual Budget

An *annual budget* is a (type of) single-use tactical plan. Budgets translate the strategic plan and implementation into a period-specific operational guide. Placing responsibility for achievement of strategic goals in the hands of managers promotes routine accomplishment of strategy as part of the manager's job function.

2 Budget Policies

To effectively budget, an organization should implement formal *budget policies* that include the following key features.

2.1 Management Participation

Typically, a budget will extend for a period of one year and involve numerous individuals. The budget process normally involves a budget committee, which includes members of senior management. The budget committee is charged with resolving disputes and making final decisions regarding major budget changes.

2.2 Budget Guidelines

Top management should provide *guidelines* for budget preparation based on the entity's strategic goals and long-term plan. These guidelines should include:

2.2.1 Evaluation of Current Conditions

- Consideration of the changes to the environment since the adoption of the strategic plan.
- Organizational goals for the coming period.
- Operating results year-to-date.

2.2.2 Management Instructions

- Setting the tone for the budget (e.g., cost containment, innovation, etc.).
- Corporate policies (e.g., mandated downsizing).

3   Standards and Benchmarking

Budgets frequently revolve around the development of standards. Standards have been referred to as per-unit budgets and are integral to the development of flexible budgets.

3.1   Ideal and Currently Attainable Standards

Standards are often set below expectations to motivate productivity and efficiency, but those standard costs must be revised periodically (generally once a year) to reflect changes in previously determined standards. The best standard is the standard that leads to the accomplishment of strategic goals.

3.1.1   Ideal Standards

Ideal standards represent the costs that result from perfect efficiency and effectiveness in job performance. Ideal standards are generally not historical; they are forward-looking. No provision is made for normal spoilage or downtime.

- **Advantage:** An advantage of using ideal standards is the implied emphasis on continuous quality improvement (CQI) to meet the ideal.
- **Disadvantage:** A disadvantage is the demotivation of employees by the use of unattainable standards.

3.1.2   Currently Attainable Standards

Currently attainable standards represent costs that result from work performed by employees with appropriate training and experience but without extraordinary effort. Provisions are made for normal spoilage and downtime.

- **Advantage:** Fosters the perception that standards are reasonable.
- **Disadvantage:** Required use of judgment and potential manipulation.

3.2   Authoritative and Participative Standards

3.2.1   Authoritative Standards

Authoritative standards are set exclusively by management.

- **Advantage:** Authoritative standards can be implemented quickly and will likely include all costs.
- **Disadvantage:** Workers might not accept imposed standards.

3.2.2   Participative Standards

Participative standards are set by both managers and the individuals who are held accountable to those standards.

- **Advantage:** Workers are more likely to accept participative standards.
- **Disadvantage:** Participative standards are slower to implement.

4   Master Budgets

A *master budget* (or "annual business plan") documents specific short-term operating performance goals for a period, normally one year or less. The plan normally includes an operating (nonfinancial) budget as well as a financial budget that outlines the sources of funds and detailed plans for their expenditure.

4.1   Overview

4.1.1   Purpose

Annual business plans are prepared to provide comprehensive and coordinated budget guidance for an organization consistent with overall strategic objectives.

- **Control Objective:** The master budget serves to communicate the criteria for performance over the period covered by the budget.

- **Terminology:** Master budgets are alternatively referred to as static budgets, annual business plans, profit planning, or targeting budgets.

- **Use:** Annual business plans are appropriate for most industries but are particularly useful in manufacturing settings that require coordination of financial and operating budgets.

4.1.2   Components

A master budget generally comprises operating budgets and financial budgets prepared in anticipation of achieving a *single level of sales volume* for a specified period.

- **Pro Forma Financial Statements:** The ultimate output of the annual business plan is a series of pro forma financial statements, including a balance sheet, an income statement, and a statement of cash flows.

- **Assumptions:** Pro forma financial statements are supported by schedules that reflect the underlying operating assumptions that produce those statements.

4.1.3   Limitations of the Annual Plan

- **Master Budget Confined to One Year at a Single Level of Activity:** Budget amounts may be much different from actual results, even though the relationship between expenses and revenues is consistent. An annual static budget divided by 12 (to establish a monthly budget) may exaggerate variances due to seasonal or volume fluctuations.

- **Reporting Output:** The product of the process is a set of pro forma financial statements. Although familiar, pro forma financial statements may not provide the type of management information most useful to decision making.

4.2   Mechanics of Master Budgeting

The annual business-plan process produces the following budgets and reports:

4.2.1   Operating Budgets

Operating budgets are established to describe the resources needed and the manner in which those resources will be acquired. Operating budgets include:

- Sales budgets
- Production budgets
- Selling and administrative budgets
- Personnel budgets

4.2.2 Financial Budgets

Financial budgets define the detailed sources and uses of funds to be used in operations. Financial budgets include:

- Pro forma financial statements
- Cash budgets

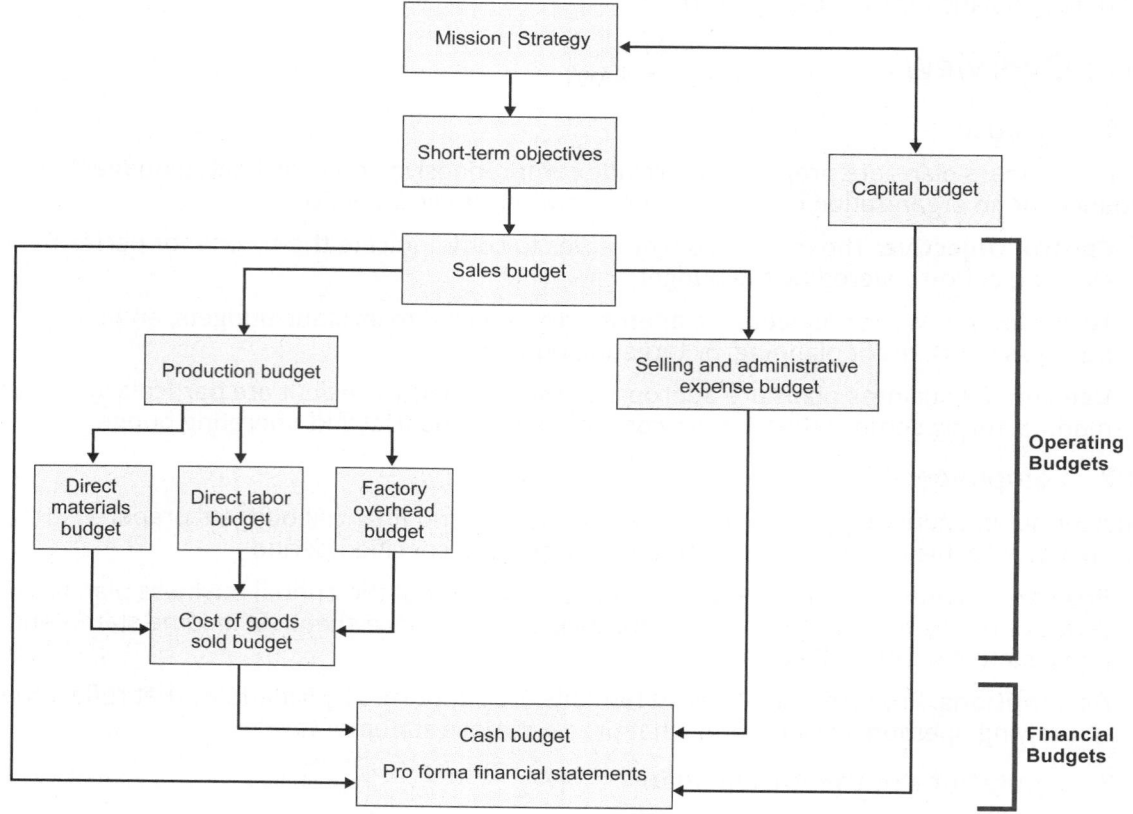

5   Operating Budgets: Sales Budget

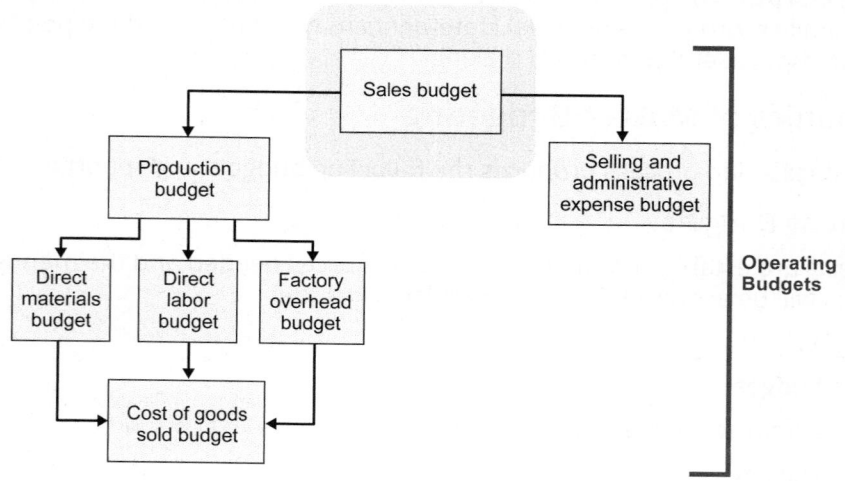

The sales budget is the foundation of the entire budget process. The sales budget represents the anticipated sales of the organization in units and dollars. The sales budget is the first budget prepared and it drives the development of most other components of the master budget. Sales budget units drive the number of units required by the production budget. Sales budget dollars drive the anticipated cash and revenue figures. Inventory levels, purchases, and operating expenses are coordinated with sales levels.

5.1   Sales Forecasting and Budgeting

The *sales budget* is based on the sales forecast. Sales forecasts are derived from input received from numerous organizational resources, including the opinions of sales staff, statistical analysis of correlation between sales and economic indicators, and opinions of line management. Sales forecasts are developed after consideration of the following factors:

- Past patterns of sales
- Sales force estimates
- General economic conditions
- Competitors' actions
- Changes in the firm's prices
- Changes in product mix
- Results of market research studies
- Advertising and sales promotion plans

Example 1   Sales Budget

Facts: Blanchforte Stereo is a retailer of audio equipment. Blanchforte's sales manager is working with the controller to develop the sales budget for the next year. Blanchforte's sales manager knows that sales volume is seasonal and that it can be influenced by price and by promotions. The sales manager has developed the following sales forecasts based on units to be sold and average selling price.

Assumptions for Forecasts

First-quarter sales are often weak. The sales manager projects the following sales volumes for aggregate units and average prices.

- 2,000 units at full retail of $75
- 2,500 units assuming discounts down to $60

Second-quarter sales strengthen somewhat for graduation and Father's Day promotions. A greater volume and ability to collect full retail can be anticipated based on promotions.

- 3,000 units at full retail of $75
- 4,000 units assuming discounts down to $60

Third-quarter sales historically decline despite summer vacation and back-to-school promotions.

- 1,500 units at full retail of $75
- 2,000 assuming discounts down to $50

(continued)

(continued)

Fourth-quarter sales spike in response to holiday spending.

- 7,000 units at full retail of $75
- 10,000 units at discounts down to $60

Required: Use the sales forecasts to develop the sales budget, assuming that the company has selected a cost-leadership strategy.

Solution:

	Q1	Q2	Q3	Q4	Total
Sales (units)	2,500	4,000	2,000	10,000	
Average price	× $60	× $60	× $50	× $60	
Total	$150,000 +	$240,000 +	$100,000 +	$600,000 =	$1,090,000

6   Operating Budgets: Production Budget

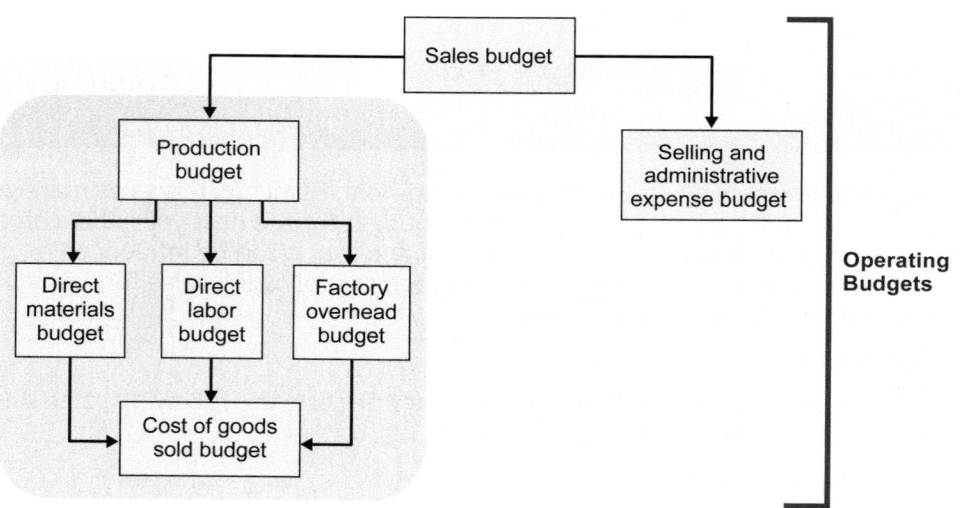

Production/inventory budgets are prepared for each product or each department based on the amount that will be produced, stated in units. The production budget is made up of the amounts spent for direct labor, direct materials, and factory overhead. The amount of the production budget is based on the amounts of inventory on hand and the inventory necessary to sustain sales.

6.1   Establishing Required Levels of Production

■   The relationship between production, sales, and inventory levels is displayed in the
following formula:

> **Budgeted sales**
> \+   **Desired ending inventory**
> –   **Beginning inventory**
> **Budgeted production**

■   Desired levels of inventory are normally a function of sales volume and seek to balance the
risk of stockouts with the cost of maintaining inventory.

Example 2	Production Budget

Facts: Carlisle Manufacturing is trying to estimate the level of production for the month
of June. Assume that Carlisle wants safety stock in beginning inventory of 30 percent of
estimated sales and that estimated sales for June and July are as follows:

June ⟶ 40,000
July ⟶ 30,000

Required: Compute the estimated inventory amounts and estimated production for June.

Solution:

Estimated inventory amounts:

	June	July
Sales	40,000	30,000
Safety stock percentage	× 30%	× 30%
Beginning inventory required	12,000	9,000

Estimated production for June:

Budgeted sales for June	40,000
Desired ending inventory	+ 9,000
Estimated beginning inventory	– 12,000
Budgeted production	37,000

■   **Other Factors Affecting the Production Budget**

- Company policies regarding stable production
- Condition of production equipment
- Availability of productive resources
- Experience with production yields and quality

6.2   Direct Materials Budgets

The direct materials required to support the production budget are defined by the direct materials purchases budget and the direct materials usage budget.

6.2.1   Direct Materials Purchases Budget

The *direct materials purchases budget* represents the dollar amount of purchases of direct materials required to sustain production requirements.

■   **Number of Units to Be Purchased:** The number of units of direct materials to purchase is calculated from the production budget. The formula is:

> Units of direct materials needed for a production period
>
> +   Desired ending inventory at the end of the period
>
> –   Beginning inventory at the start of the period
> _____
>
> Units of direct materials to be purchased for the period

■   **Cost of Direct Materials to Be Purchased:** The cost of direct materials purchased is calculated by applying the anticipated cost per unit of direct materials to the computed amount of direct materials to be purchased.

> Units of direct materials to be purchased for the period
>
> ×   Cost per unit
> _____
>
> Cost of direct materials to be purchased for the period (purchases at cost)

6.2.2   Direct Materials Usage Budget (Cost of Direct Materials Used)

The direct materials usage budget represents the number of units of direct materials required for production along with the related cost of those direct materials.

■   The extended costs associated with direct materials are derived as follows:

> Beginning inventory at cost
>
> +   Purchases at cost
>
> –   Ending inventory at cost
> _____
>
> Direct materials usage (cost of materials used)

6.2.3   Impact of Purchasing Policies

Purchases budgets are influenced by management's philosophy regarding required inventory levels, including safety stock and stockout decisions.

6.3 Direct Labor Budget

Direct labor budgets anticipate the hours and rates associated with workers directly involved in meeting production requirements. Direct labor hours are computed based on the hours necessary to produce each unit of finished goods.

	Budgeted production (in units)
×	Hours (or fractions of hours) required to produce each unit
	Total number of hours needed
×	Hourly wage rate
	Total wages

Example 3   Direct Materials and Labor Budgets

Facts: Carlisle Manufacturing computed its budgeted production at 37,000 units to sustain budgeted sales of 40,000 units in the month of June. Four pounds of direct material are needed to produce each unit of finished product. We assume that new direct materials cost $10 per pound and that they were previously acquired for $9 per pound. Carlisle has 48,000 pounds on hand at the beginning of June and has a desired direct materials ending inventory of 36,000.

Two hours of direct labor at $20 per hour are needed to convert the direct materials to finished goods.

Required: Prepare the direct materials and direct labor budgets for the month of June.

Solution:

Direct materials purchases

Units of direct materials needed for a production period		
Budgeted production	37,000	units
Pounds of direct material per unit	× 4	pounds
Total pounds needed	148,000	pounds
+ Desired ending inventory at the end of the period		
Pounds of direct material	36,000	pounds
− Beginning inventory at the start of the period		
Pounds of direct material	(48,000)	pounds
Direct material to be purchased	136,000	
Cost per pound	× $10	
Direct material purchases	$1,360,000	

(continued)

(continued)

Direct materials usage budget (cost of direct materials used)

Beginning inventory at cost (48,000 × $9)	$432,000
+ Purchases at cost	1,360,000
− Ending inventory at cost (36,000 × $10)	(360,000)
= Direct materials usage (cost of materials used)	$1,432,000

Direct labor budget

Budgeted production	37,000 units
Hours of direct labor per unit	× 2 hours
Total hours needed	74,000 hours
Rate per hour	× $20
Direct labor budget	$1,480,000

6.4 Factory Overhead Budget

Factory overhead includes the fixed and variable production costs that are not direct labor or direct materials. Factory overhead is applied to inventory (cost of goods manufactured and sold, below) based on a representative statistic (cost driver). Frequently, the rate is applied using direct labor hours.

Example 4 — Factory Overhead Budget

Facts: Carlisle Manufacturing uses direct labor hours to apply variable factory overhead and has determined that its variable overhead rate is $5 per hour. Assume that the company used 74,000 direct labor hours according to the direct labor budget.

Required: Compute the variable overhead to be applied to the cost of goods manufactured in the month of June.

Solution: Budgeted overhead = 74,000 direct labor hours × $5 per hour = $370,000

6.5 Cost of Goods Manufactured and Sold Budget

The *cost of goods manufactured and sold budget* accumulates the information from the direct labor, direct material, and factory overhead budgets.

6.5.1 Components of the Costs of Goods Manufactured and Sold Budget

The cost of goods manufactured represents the sum of the budgets for each element of manufacturing as follows:

- Direct labor
- Direct material
- Factory overhead

Cost of goods sold considers cost of goods manufactured in relation to beginning and ending inventories of finished goods as follows:

> Cost of goods manufactured
>
> \+ Beginning finished goods inventory
>
> – Ending finished goods inventory
> _____
> Cost of goods sold

Example 5   Cost of Goods Manufactured and Sold

Facts: Carlisle Manufacturing is preparing its budgeted cost of goods manufactured and budgeted cost of goods sold schedules for the month of June. It has developed the following information:

Direct materials used	$1,432,000
Direct labor	1,480,000
Factory overhead (variable)	370,000
Factory overhead (fixed)	300,000 (given)
Finished goods (beginning)	1,000,000 (given)
Finished goods (ending)	750,000 (given)

Required: Compute the cost of goods manufactured.

Solution:

Direct materials used	$1,432,000
Direct labor	1,480,000
Factory overhead (variable)	370,000
Factory overhead (fixed)	300,000
Total cost of goods manufactured	3,582,000
Plus finished goods, beginning	1,000,000
Goods available	4,582,000
Less finished goods, ending	(750,000)
Cost of goods sold	$3,832,000

6.5.2 Cost of Goods Sold and the Pro Forma Financial Statements

The budgeted cost of goods sold amount feeds directly into the pro forma income statement. Budgeted cost of goods sold is matched with budgeted sales as a basis for budgeted gross margin.

7 Operating Budgets: Selling and Administrative Expense Budget

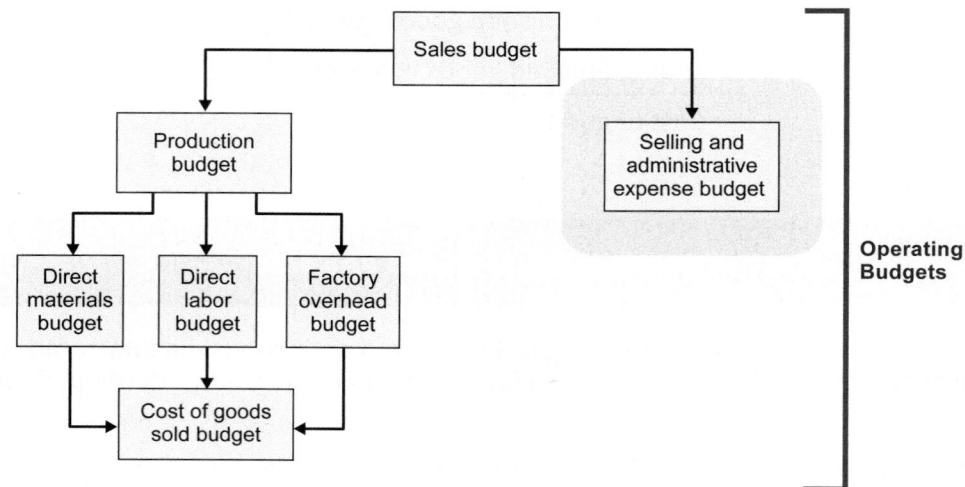

Selling and administrative expenses represent the fixed and variable nonmanufacturing expenses anticipated during the budget period.

7.1 Components of Selling and General Administration Expense

7.1.1 Variable Selling Expenses

■ Sales commissions

■ Delivery expenses

■ Bad-debt expenses

7.1.2 Fixed Selling Expenses

■ Sales salaries

■ Advertising

■ Depreciation

7.1.3 General Administrative Expenses (All Fixed)

■ Administrative salaries

■ Accounting and data processing

■ Depreciation

■ Other administrative expenses

7.2 Selling and Administrative Expenses and the Pro Forma Financial Statements

Selling and administrative expenses are not inventoried and are budgeted as period costs. Budgeted selling and administrative expenses are matched in their entirety against budgeted sales.

Question 1   CPA-05829

Which of the following listings correctly describes the order in which the four types of budgets must be prepared?

    a. Production, direct materials purchases, sales, cash disbursements.

    b. Sales, production, direct materials purchases, cash disbursements.

    c. Cash disbursements, direct materials purchases, production, sales.

    d. Sales, direct materials purchases, production, cash disbursements.

Question 2   CPA-04793

Johnson Co. is preparing its master budget for the first quarter of next year. Budgeted sales and production for one of the company's products are as follows:

Month	Sales	Production
January	10,000	12,000
February	12,000	11,000
March	15,000	16,000

Each unit of this product requires 4 pounds of raw materials. Johnson's policy is to have sufficient raw materials on hand at the end of each month for 40 percent of the following month's production requirements. The January 1 raw materials inventory is expected to conform with this policy.

How many pounds of raw materials should Johnson budget to purchase for January?

    a. 11,600

    b. 46,400

    c. 48,000

    d. 65,600

NOTES

1 Financial Budgets: Cash Budgets

Cash budgets represent detailed projections of cash receipts and disbursements. The cash budget is derived from other budgets based on cash collection and disbursement assumptions. Cash budgets provide management with information regarding the availability of funds for distribution to owners, for repayment of debt, and for investment. Cash budgets are generally divided into three major sections:

- Cash available
- Cash disbursements
- Financing

1.1 Cash Available

Cash available for use by the organization is normally associated with both balances available at the beginning of the period and cash collections.

1.1.1 Cash Balances

Cash balances are the amounts of cash on hand that can be used to liquidate expenses. Cash balances that are available for use are limited by management policies relative to minimum cash on hand and compensating balance agreements.

1.1.2 Cash Collections

Cash collection budgets specify the amounts of cash that will be received from sales, based on the sales budget and from anticipated loan proceeds.

- Cash collection budgets set standards for collections based on current-period sales (usually monthly) and prior-period sales (also usually monthly).

- Cash collection budgets make assumptions regarding the percentage of credit sales and the speed at which those collections will occur.

Example 1	Cash Collections

Facts: Beck-Con Inc. is a U.S. retailer creating its cash budget for September. Based on historical data, it assumes the following information regarding collections:

- 80 percent of credit sales collected in the next month after sale.
- 18 percent of credit sales collected in the second month after sale.
- The remaining 2 percent will not be collected.

Month	Type	Sales Dollars
July	Credit	$850,000
August	Credit	$925,000
September	Credit	$700,000
September	Cash	$170,000

Required: Calculate cash collections for September.

Solution:

July credit sales ($850,000 × 18%)	$ 153,000
+ August credit sales ($925,000 × 80%)	740,000
+ September cash sales	170,000
Total cash collections	$1,063,000

1.2 Cash Disbursements

Cash disbursements budgets represent the cash outlays associated with purchases and with operating expenses.

1.2.1 Purchases

Cash disbursements budgets (for purchases) indicate the amount that is expected to be paid for *purchases*.

- Cash disbursements budgets include:
  - Cash purchases for the current period (generally the current month).
  - Credit purchases (accounts payable) for the current period.
  - Cash disbursements required to pay accounts payable during the current period.
- Cash disbursements budgets are developed using the percentage of goods bought on credit, the age of payables liquidated, and the percentage of goods purchased for cash.

1.2.2 Operating Expenses

Cash disbursements budgets (for operating expenses) specify the amounts paid out to defray the costs of *operating expenses*.

▪ Cash disbursements budgets eliminate noncash operating expenses (such as depreciation).

▪ Cash disbursements budgets include:

- Percentage of prior month expenses to be paid in the current month.

- Current month expenses for which disbursement is deferred until the following month.

- Current month expenses paid in cash in the current month.

▪ Cash disbursements consider the effect of accounts payable (other operating expenses) and accrued payroll (wages).

Example 2   Cash Disbursements

Facts: To forecast its cash disbursements for September, Beck-Con divided its outflows into the following categories:

Cost Category	Applicable Dollar Amounts
Direct materials	$425,000 to be purchased in August, payable in September
Direct labor	$310,000 to be incurred and payable in September
Overhead	$150,000 in actual costs to be incurred and payable in September
Operating expenses	$145,000 in actual costs to be incurred and payable in September
Capital expenditures	$120,000 (from the capital expenditure budget)
Tax payments	None in September
Dividends	$35,000 payable in September, for the last quarter of the fiscal year

Required: Calculate Beck-Con's cash disbursements for September.

Solution: September cash disbursements are calculated as follows:

	Direct materials	$ 425,000
+	Direct labor	310,000
+	Overhead	150,000
+	Operating expenses	145,000
+	Capital expenditures	120,000
+	Dividends	35,000
	Total cash disbursements	$1,185,000

1.3   Financing

Financing budgets consider the manner in which operating (line of credit) financing will be used to maintain minimum cash balances or the manner in which excess or idle cash will be invested to ensure liquidity and adequate returns.

Illustration 1   Financing Budget

Beck-Con forecasts a beginning cash balance for September 1 of $80,000. The company would like to ensure that the ending cash balance is at least $50,000. In order to accomplish this, it plans to borrow $95,000 at the end of September from its established line of credit at an annual interest rate of 6 percent. The first interest payment would not be due until October 31.

1.4   Cash Budget Formats

Cash budgets represent statements of planned cash receipts and disbursements and are primarily affected by the amounts used in the budgeted income statement. Cash budgets consider:

- Beginning cash
- Cash collections from sales (add)
- Cash disbursements for purchases and operating expenses (subtract)
- Computed ending cash
- Cash requirements to sustain operations (subtract)
- Working capital loans to maintain cash requirements

Example 3   Combined Cash Budget

Facts: Beck-Con's cash budget includes a beginning balance of $80,000; cash collections of $1,063,000; cash payments of $1,185,000; and a letter of credit borrowing of $95,000.

Required: Prepare the cash budget that will allow the company to end September with a cash balance of $53,000.

Solution:

Beginning cash balance:	$ 80,000
+ Cash collections	1,063,000
Total cash available	1,143,000
Less cash payments:	(1,185,000)
Ending cash balance (before financing)	$ (42,000)
Financing:	
Borrowings	$ 95,000
Interest payments	0
Repayments	0
Ending cash balance	$ 53,000

---

2 Financial Budgets: Pro Forma Financial Statements

2.1 Pro Forma Income Statement

Key components of the budgeted income statement include the data described in the operating budgets:

- Sales budget
- Cost of goods sold budget (derived from the production budgets)
- Selling and administrative expense budget
- Interest expense budget (taken from the cash budget)

2.2 Pro Forma Balance Sheet

Budgeted balance sheets display the balances of each balance sheet account in a manner consistent with the income statement and cash budget plans developed above. Balance sheet accounts are adjusted for the cash collections and disbursements associated with the cash budget and the noncash transactions accounted for in the income statement.

2.3 Pro Forma Statement of Cash Flows

The budgeted statement of cash flows is derived from the budgeted income statement, the current and previous budgeted balance sheets, and then reconciled to the cash budget. Cash budgeting has the benefits of displaying the cash effects of the master budget on actual cash flows, assisting in the determination of whether additional sources of financing are required, and evaluating the optimal use of trade credit.

Example 4 — Pro Forma Income Statement

Facts: The CFO for Packer Company is creating a pro forma income statement for the upcoming fiscal year. The estimated current-year income statement shows:

Sales	$500,000
Cost of goods sold	(320,000)
SG&A	(60,000)
Interest expense	(20,000)
Pretax profit (EBT)	$100,000

For the next fiscal year, the CFO forecasts the following:

- Sales growth of 5 percent.
- An inventory increase of $25,000, along with projected cost of goods manufactured of $365,000.
- An increase in SG&A expenses of $10,000.
- A pay down of a substantial amount of debt, reducing interest expense by $15,000.

(continued)

(continued)

Required: Create a pro forma income statement for the upcoming fiscal year.

Solution:

Sales	$525,000	5 percent growth over prior year's $500,000.
Cost of goods sold	(340,000)	COGM of $365,000—Increase in inventory balance of $25,000.
SG&A	(70,000)	Increase of $10,000 over prior year's $60,000.
Interest expense	(5,000)	Decrease of $15,000 over prior year's $20,000.
Pretax profit (EBT)	$110,000	Overall $10,000 increase over prior year's $100,000.

3 Capital Budgets

Capital purchases budgets identify and allow management to evaluate the capital additions of the organization, often over a multiyear period. Financing is a significant component of the capital purchases budget. Capital budgets detail the planned expenditures for capital items (e.g., facilities, equipment, new products, and other long-term investments). Capital budgets are highly dependent on the availability of cash or credit, and they generally involve long-term commitments by the organization.

3.1 Pro Forma Balance Sheet

Planned additions of capital equipment and related debt from the capital budget are added to the balance sheet.

3.2 Pro Forma Income Statement

Planned additions of capital equipment are considered in developing budgeted depreciation expense; interest expense associated with planned financing is included as an expense.

3.3 Cash Budget

Planned financing expenses and principal repayments are included as disbursements on the cash budget.

4 Flexible Budgeting

A *flexible budget* is a financial plan prepared in a manner that allows for adjustments for changes in production or sales and accurately reflects expected costs for the adjusted output. Analysis focuses on substantive variances from standards rather than just simple changes in volume or activity. Flexible budgets represent adjustable economic models that are designed to predict outcomes and accommodate changes in actual activity. Revenues and expenses are adjusted to display anticipated levels for achieved outputs.

4.1 Assumptions and Uses

Flexible budgets include consideration of revenue per unit, variable costs per unit, and fixed costs over the relevant range within which the relationship between revenues and variable costs will remain unchanged and fixed costs will remain stable.

4.1.1 Yield

Flexible budgets consider the amount of cost per unit allowed for units of output.

4.1.2 Variance Analysis

Flexible budgets derive the expenses and revenues allowed from the output achieved for purposes of comparison to actual activity and performance evaluation.

4.2 Benefits and Limitations of the Flexible Budget

4.2.1 Benefits

Flexible budgets can display different volume levels within the relevant range to pinpoint areas in which efficiencies have been achieved or waste has occurred.

4.2.2 Limitations

Flexible budgets are highly dependent on the accurate identification of fixed and variable costs and the determination of the relevant range.

Example 5 — Flexible Budgeting

Facts: The Flex-o-matic Corp. produces the Flex-o-matic, a piece of exercise equipment. Corporate Controller Felix Flexmeister is developing a flexible budget. Felix has already developed a master budget but estimates that the relevant range extends 20 percent above and below the master budget.

Required: Calculate income over the relevant range in dollars assuming a selling price of $60 per unit, variable costs of $40 per unit, fixed costs of $100,000, and anticipated output according to the master budget of 5,000 units.

Solution:

	80% of Master	Master Budget	120% of Master
Sales	$240,000	$300,000	$360,000
Variable costs	(160,000)	(200,000)	(240,000)
Contribution margin	80,000	100,000	120,000
Fixed costs	(100,000)	(100,000)	(100,000)
Operating income	$ (20,000)	$ 0	$ 20,000

Question 1 CPA-03813

The basic difference between a master budget and a flexible budget is that a master budget is:

   a. Only used before and during the budget period and a flexible budget is only used after the budget period.

   b. For an entire production facility and a flexible budget is applicable to single departments only.

   c. Based on one specific level of production, and a flexible budget can be prepared for any production level within a relevant range.

   d. Based on a fixed standard and a flexible budget allows management latitude in meeting goals.

Question 2	**CPA-05867**

A company's controller is adjusting next year's budget to reflect the effect of an expected 5 percent inflation rate. Listed below are selected items from next year's budget before the adjustment:

Total salaries expense	$250,000
Health costs	100,000
Depreciation expense	65,000
Interest expense on 10-year fixed-rate notes	37,750

After adjusting for the 5 percent inflation rate, what is the company's total budget for the selected items before taxes for next year?

    a. $470,250

    b. $472,138

    c. $473,500

    d. $475,388

1 Actual vs. Plan

Variance analysis is a tool for comparing some measure of performance to a plan, budget, or standard for that measure. Variance analysis is used for planning and control purposes, and can be used to evaluate revenues and costs. Comparison of actual results to the annual business plan is the first and most basic level of control and evaluation of operations.

1.1 Performance Report

Actual results may be easily compared with budgeted results. However, usefulness is limited by the existence of budget variances that may be strictly related to volume.

Example 1   **Budget vs. Plan Performance Report**

Facts: Neostar Corporation has prepared its annual business plan for Year 1. The organization anticipated that it would sell 10,000 units of its product at $15 apiece, that its contribution margin percentage would be 20 percent, and that its fixed costs would be $25,000. Actual units sold numbered only 8,000 (totaling $112,000 in revenue); variable expenses materialized at $100,800 and fixed costs materialized at $24,000.

Required: Prepare a performance report comparing actual versus budgeted results.

Solution:

	Budget	Actual	Variance	
Revenue	$150,000	$112,000	$(38,000)	Unfavorable
Variable expenses	(120,000)	(100,800)	19,200	Favorable
Contribution margin	30,000	11,200	(18,800)	Unfavorable
Fixed costs	(25,000)	(24,000)	1,000	Favorable
Operating income	$ 5,000	$ (12,800)	$(17,800)	Unfavorable

Variances need significant analysis before they are useful. The favorable variance in variable expenses, for example, does not represent efficiencies. Budgeted contribution margin ratios are 20 percent; actual contribution margin ratios are 10 percent. Sales in units were off budget by 20 percent, yet revenue was down by 25 percent. Something is very wrong at Neostar, but what?

1.2 Use of Flexible Budgets to Analyze Performance

Budget variance analysis becomes progressively more sophisticated as managers review flexible budget comparisons. The flexible budget allows managers to identify how an individual change in a cost or revenue driver affects the overall cost of a process.

Example 2	Flexible Budget Performance Report

Facts: Management at Neostar has heard that flexible budgeting can provide more meaningful information.

Required: Prepare a flexible budget using the same information described in Example 1.

Solution:

Neostar Corporation
Flexible Budget Performance Report
For the year ended December 31, Year 1

	Actual Results @ Actual	Flexible Budget Variances	Flexible Budget @ Actual (Planned Cost)	Sales Activity (Volume) Variances	Master Budget
Units	8,000		8,000		10,000
Sales	$112,000	$ (8,000)	$120,000	$(30,000)	$150,000
Variable costs	(100,800)	(4,800)	(96,000)	24,000	(120,000)
Contribution margin	11,200	(12,800)	24,000*	(6,000)	30,000*
Fixed costs	(24,000)	1,000	(25,000)	–	(25,000)
Operating income	$ (12,800)	$(11,800)	$ (1,000)	$ (6,000)	$ 5,000
Flexible budget variances		(11,800)			
Sales activity (volume) variances				(6,000)	
Total master budget variances					(17,800)

*24,000 / 120,000 = 20%
  30,000 / 150,000 = 20%

Flexible budget variances show that revenue per unit was less than expected and variable costs per unit were greater than expected. The company has performed $11,800 worse than expected. Meanwhile, differences in volume produced a $6,000 unfavorable variance, yielding a total variance from the budget of $17,800.

Although we still do not know what is wrong with Neostar, we know where to look. Revenue is not materializing as expected despite efforts to discount our selling price (producing an unfavorable sales price variance of $8,000), and expenses are over budget (producing an unfavorable variable cost variance of $4,800 despite a favorable fixed-cost variance of $1,000).

---

2 Variance Analysis Using Standards

Variance analysis becomes increasingly sophisticated as the investigation of differences between budgeted and actual performance moves from the aggregate examinations associated with either performance reporting or flexible budget analysis to the computation of per-unit variances normally associated with the use of standard costing systems.

2.1 Standard Costing Systems

Standard costing systems are the most common cost-measurement systems. Standard costs, in the aggregate, measure the costs the firm expects that it *should* incur during production. In a standard costing system, standard costs are used for all manufacturing costs (i.e., raw materials, direct labor, and manufacturing overhead).

2.1.1 Calculations

▪ **Direct Costs**

> Standard direct costs = Standard price × Standard quantity

▪ **Indirect (Overhead) Costs**

> Standard indirect costs = Standard (predetermined) application rate × Standard quantity

2.1.2 Purposes of Standard Costing Systems

▪ Cost control

▪ Data for performance evaluations (variance analysis)

▪ Ability to learn from standards and improve various processes

2.2 Variance Calculations Using Standards

2.2.1 Standard Cost Objectives

The objective of using a standard costing system is to attain a realistic predetermined or budgeted cost for use in planning and decision making. It also greatly simplifies bookkeeping procedures.

2.2.2 Evaluating Variances From Standard

The differences between actual amounts and standard amounts are called variances.

▪ **Evaluating Results:** An actual cost lower than standard cost is called a *favorable* variance, and an actual cost higher than standard cost is called an *unfavorable* variance.

▪ **Evaluating Control:** If a variance from standard could have been prevented, it is called a controllable variance; if not, the variance is known as an *uncontrollable* variance.

2.2.3   Product Costs Subject to Variance Analysis

Product costs generally consist of direct materials, direct labor, and manufacturing overhead. A favorable or unfavorable variance in total is a composite of a number of variances. Variances are typically calculated for the following cost elements:

■   Direct materials (DM)

■   Direct labor (DL)

■   Variable manufacturing overhead (VOH)

■   Fixed manufacturing overhead (FOH)

2.3   Direct Materials and Direct Labor Variance

For direct materials and direct labor, two variances are typically calculated: a price (or rate) variance and a quantity (or efficiency) variance. The variance calculations may be approached in either an equation or a tabular format. Both are presented below:

2.3.1   Equation Format

> DM price variance = **Actual quantity purchased × (Actual price − Standard price)**
>
> DM quantity usage variance = **Standard price × (Actual quantity used − Standard quantity allowed)**
>
> DL rate variance = **Actual hours worked × (Actual rate − Standard rate)**
>
> DL efficiency variance = **Standard rate × (Actual hours worked − Standard hours allowed)**

Materials and labor variances are expense variances. When actual price/rate or actual quantity/hours exceed standards, variances are unfavorable. If standards exceed actuals, variances are favorable.

2.3.2   Tabular Format

The variance is computed by comparing two totals. If a figure on the left (actual) is larger than a figure on the right (standard), then the variance is unfavorable; if the figure on the left is smaller, the variance is favorable. The specific variances follow:

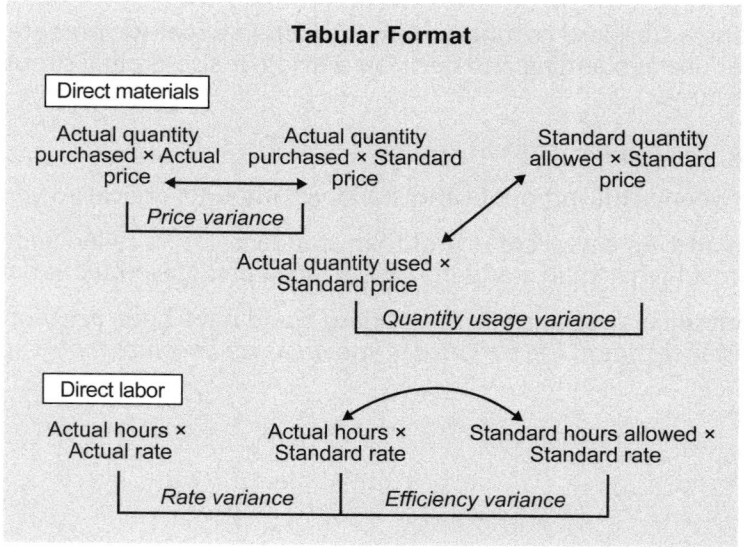

Illustration 1   Materials Variances Using Equation and Tabular Formats

Actual quantity purchased   200 units
Actual quantity used   110 units
Units standard quantity   100 units
Actual price paid $8 per unit
Standard price $10 per unit

$$
\begin{aligned}
\text{DM price variance} &= AQ_{purchased} \times (AP - SP) \\
&= 200 \text{ units} \times (\$8/\text{unit} - \$10/\text{unit}) \\
&= \$400 \text{ Favorable}
\end{aligned}
$$

$$
\begin{aligned}
\text{DM quantity variance} &= SP \times (AQ_{used} - SQ_{allowed}) \\
&= \$10/\text{unit} \times (110 \text{ units} - 100 \text{ units}) \\
&= \$100 \text{ Unfavorable}
\end{aligned}
$$

Actual quantity purchased × Actual price	Actual quantity purchased × Standard price	Standard quantity allowed × Standard price
200 × $8 = $1,600	200 × $10 = $2,000	100 × $10 = $1,000

Price variance = $400 F

Actual quantity used × Standard price

Quantity usage variance
110 × $10 = $1,100
= $100 U

Illustration 2   Labor Variances Using Equation and Tabular Formats

Actual hours worked   450 hours
Standard hours   500 hours
Actual paid rate $20 per hour
Standard rate $15 per hour

$$
\begin{aligned}
\text{DL rate variance} &= AH_{worked} \times (AR - SR) \\
&= 450 \text{ hours worked} \times (\$20/\text{hour} - \$15/\text{hour}) \\
&= \$2,250 \text{ Unfavorable}
\end{aligned}
$$

$$
\begin{aligned}
\text{DL efficiency variance} &= SR \times (AH_{worked} - SH_{allowed}) \\
&= \$15/\text{hour} \times (450 \text{ hours worked} - 500 \text{ hours allowed}) \\
&= \$750 \text{ Favorable}
\end{aligned}
$$

Actual hours × Actual rate	Actual hours × Standard rate	Standard hours allowed × Standard rate
450 × $20 = $9,000	450 × $15 = $6,750	500 × $15 = $7,500

Rate variance = $2,250 U   Efficiency variance = $750 F

2.4 Manufacturing Overhead Variance

At a high level, the analysis of manufacturing overhead compares the actual overhead incurred in a period to the applied overhead in that same period. Overhead is estimated and applied based on a predetermined overhead application rate.

2.4.1 Underapplied and Overapplied Overhead

If the actual amount of overhead incurred in the period exceeds the amount applied, overhead will be considered underapplied and the overhead account will have a net debit balance. This will result in an unfavorable variance because the actual amount of overhead incurred is higher than expected.

If the actual amount of overhead incurred is less than the amount applied, overhead will be considered overapplied and the overhead account will have a net credit balance. The variance will be favorable because the actual overhead incurred is less than expected.

2.4.2 Variable and Fixed Overhead Variances

The overall manufacturing overhead variance can be broken into variable and fixed overhead variances. The variable overhead (VOH) variance can be further broken into a rate (spending) variance and an efficiency variance. The fixed overhead (FOH) variance can be divided into a budget (spending) variance and a volume variance. Although the variable and fixed overhead spending variances can be combined for calculation purposes, they serve different functions from a strategic/analytical perspective.

Pass Key

The equations for the four overhead variances are as follows:

- VOH rate (spending) variance = Actual hours × (Actual rate – Standard rate)
- VOH efficiency variance = Standard rate × (Actual hours – Standard hours allowed for actual production volume)
- FOH budget (spending) variance = Actual fixed overhead – Budgeted fixed overhead
- FOH volume variance = Budgeted fixed overhead – Standard fixed overhead cost allocated to production*

*Based on Actual production × Standard rate

2.4.3 Establishing Overhead Application Rates

Overhead rates are applied using various cost drivers that most appropriately assign the components of overhead cost pools to production. Predetermined fixed and variable overhead rates are established by dividing planned fixed and variable overhead amounts by a suitable cost driver.

2.4.4 Application of Overhead

Overhead is applied to production based on the predetermined rate per cost driver times the standard cost driver allowed for the actual level of activity (hours worked, units produced, etc.).

Pass Key

When standard costing is used, the application of overhead is accomplished in two steps:

- **Step 1:** Calculated overhead rate = Budgeted overhead costs ÷ Estimated cost driver

- **Step 2:** Applied overhead = Standard cost driver for actual level of activity × Overhead rate (from Step 1)

2.4.5 Interpretation

Overhead variances represent the analysis of balance in the overhead account after overhead has been applied. Overapplied overhead (more credit) is favorable, as it will ultimately result in a credit to cost of goods sold at the end of the period and therefore a reduction in expenses (and increase in profits). Underapplied (more debit) is unfavorable, as the eventual debit to cost of goods sold will increase expenses and therefore decrease profits. Each component of the variance computation follows the same logic.

- If the number on the right is greater than the number on the left (more credit), then the variance is favorable.

- If the number on the left is greater than the number on the right (more debit), then the variance is unfavorable.

- The sum of all variances equals the net balance in the overhead account.

2.4.6 Variable Manufacturing Overhead Variances

- **Variable Overhead Rate (Spending) Variance**

$$\text{VOH rate (spending) variance} = \text{Actual hours} \times (\text{Actual rate} - \text{Standard rate})$$

This variance tells managers whether more or less was spent on variable overhead than expected. A favorable variance occurs when the standard rate exceeds the actual rate, which is beneficial to a company because it means that it paid less per labor hour than anticipated. An unfavorable variance occurs when the actual rate exceeds the standard rate, which means that the company paid more per labor hour than it expected to spend.

- **Variable Overhead Efficiency Variance**

$$\text{VOH efficiency variance} = \text{Standard rate} \times (\text{Actual hours} - \text{Standard hours allowed for actual production volume})$$

This variance is tied to the efficiency with which labor hours are utilized. The efficiency variance isolates the amount of total variable overhead variance that is due to using more or fewer direct labor hours than what was budgeted (assuming that direct labor hours is the cost driver). In other words, given what was produced in terms of output, did it require more or fewer labor hours than anticipated? A favorable variance results from using fewer labor hours than budgeted, and an unfavorable variance stems from using more labor hours than budgeted.

2.4.7 Fixed Manufacturing Overhead Variances

■ **Fixed Overhead Budget (Spending) Variance**

$$\text{FOH budget (spending) variance} = \text{Actual fixed overhead} - \text{Budgeted fixed overhead}$$

Companies budget an amount for fixed overhead costs every period, and this variance focuses at a high level on whether more or less was spent than budgeted. All of the actual fixed overhead costs are summed for the period and the total actual overhead is compared with the budgeted amount of fixed overhead. A favorable variance occurs when actual fixed overhead costs are less than budgeted, and an unfavorable variance results from actual fixed overhead costs exceeding the budgeted amount.

■ **Fixed Overhead Volume Variance**

$$\text{FOH volume variance} = \text{Budgeted fixed overhead} - \text{Standard fixed overhead cost allocated to production*}$$

*Based on actual production × Standard rate

Fixed overhead costs are typically applied using a rate derived from budgeted fixed overhead costs and expected volume (the cost driver). When the actual volume produced differs from the amount used to calculate the fixed overhead application rate, there will be a variance. A favorable variance occurs when volume is higher than anticipated, which implies that more units were produced using the same amount of fixed resources. An unfavorable variance occurs when volume is lower than anticipated, as fewer units were produced using a fixed amount of resources.

Example 3	Manufacturing Overhead Variance

Facts: Lucy Inc. produces widgets and applies overhead costs based on direct labor hours. The table below provides budgeted and actual information on the number of widgets, labor hours, variable overhead costs, and fixed overhead costs for January.

Required: Using this information, calculate the rate and efficiency variable overhead variances, the budget and volume fixed overhead variances, and the overall overhead variance.

(continued)

(continued)

Solution:

Number of Widgets		
Budgeted number of widgets	4,000 widgets	
Actual number of widgets	3,800 widgets	
Labor Hours		
Standard labor hours required per widget	1.00 labor hour	
Standard labor hours total (based on actual production)	3,800 hours	(3,800 widgets × 1.00 labor hour per widget)
Actual labor hours used	3,900 hours	
Variable Overhead		
Standard VOH Rate	$1.50 per hour	
Actual VOH Rate	$1.60 per hour	
Actual VOH Costs	$6,240	(3,900 hours × $1.60 per hour)
Fixed Overhead		
Standard FOH per widget	$3.00 per hour	
Budgeted FOH Costs	$12,000	(4,000 budgeted widgets × 1.00 labor hour per widget × $3.00 per hour)
Actual FOH Costs	$10,560	

VOH rate (spending): 3,900 hours × ($1.60 − $1.50) = $390 Unfavorable

VOH efficiency: $1.50 × [3,900 hours − (3,800 × 1.00 hour)] = $150 Unfavorable

FOH budget (spending): $10,560 − $12,000 = $1,440 Favorable

FOH volume: $12,000 − *$11,400 = $600 Unfavorable

*3,800 hours budgeted (for production of 3,800 widgets) × $3 per hour

Adding all of the variances produces a total overall favorable variance of $300: $390U + $150U − $1,440F + $600U = $300F

Overall variance: $16,800 actual − $17,100 applied = $300 Favorable

Actual overhead (FOH + VOH): $16,800

> *Actual FOH:* $10,560
> *Actual VOH:* $6,240

Applied overhead (FOH + VOH): $17,100

> *Applied FOH:* $11,400 [3,800 standard labor hours (to produce 3,800 widgets) × $3.00 per hour]
> *Applied VOH:* $5,700 [3,800 standard labor hours (to produce 3,800 widgets) × $1.50 per hour]

Interpretation	Driver
• Spending (VOH and FOH)	
—VOH rate: $390 Unfavorable	VOH rate was higher than anticipated
—FOH budget: $1,440 Favorable	Spent less than anticipated on FOH
• Efficiency (VOH only)	
—VOH efficiency: $150 Unfavorable	Took longer per unit than anticipated
• Volume (FOH only)	
—FOH volume: $600 Unfavorable	Produced fewer units than budgeted

2.5 Sales and Contribution Margin Variances

Sales and contribution margin variance analyses can be used to evaluate the effectiveness of an entity's identification of target markets and its strategies to capture those markets. The sales variance (the difference between actual sales revenue and budgeted sales revenue) has various components, as described below.

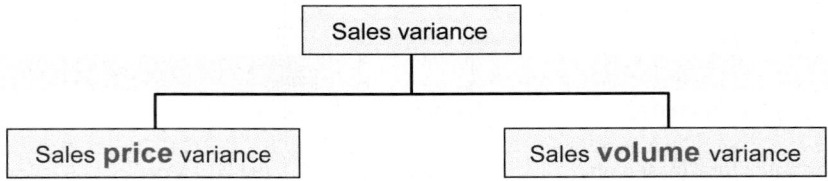

2.5.1 Sales Price Variance (or Sales Revenue Flexible Budget Variance)

The *sales price variance* measures the aggregate effect of a selling price different from the budget.

$$\text{Sales price variance} = \left[\frac{\text{Actual SP}}{\text{Unit}} - \frac{\text{Budgeted SP}}{\text{Unit}} \right] \times \text{Actual sold units}$$

- **Strategy and Mission:** Firms might reduce prices in an effort to move into a cost leadership strategy or increase prices in an effort to put a differentiation strategy into place. Variance results have specific implications in analyzing the effectiveness of a firm in reaching its target markets.

- **Interpretation:** A favorable variance in price (the actual sales price exceeds the budgeted sales price) can result in untapped profit potential for a firm. If a firm plans to increase its market share or sales volume simply by reducing sales prices, however, it can risk reducing the profitability of the firm if the expected volume increase is not enough to cover the reduction in price.

Example 4   **Sales Price Variance**

Facts: In Cascade Company's January budget, the company shows 3,000 budgeted units sold, a sale price of $16 per unit, and variable costs of $10 per unit. The company actually sells 4,000 units at a price of $14 per unit.

Required: Calculate Cascade's sales price variance for January.

Solution: Sales price variance = ($14 – $16) × 4,000 = $8,000 unfavorable. This variance is unfavorable because the per-unit selling price was less than anticipated.

2.5.2 Sales Volume Variance

The *sales volume variance* is a flexible budget variance that distills volume activity from other sales performance components. The basic sales volume variance is:

$$\text{Sales volume variance} = \left[\frac{\text{Actual}}{\text{sold units}} - \frac{\text{Budgeted}}{\text{sales units}} \right] \times \text{Standard contribution margin per unit}$$

A favorable variance exists when more units are sold than budgeted, and an unfavorable variance occurs when budgeted units exceed actual units.

Example 5   Sales Volume Variance

Facts: In Cascade Company's January budget, the company shows 3,000 budgeted units sold, a sale price of $16 per unit, and variable costs of $10 per unit. The company actually sells 4,000 units at a price of $14 per unit.

Required: Calculate Cascade's sales volume variance for January.

Solution: Sales volume variance = (4,000 − 3,000) × $6 = $6,000 Favorable. This variance is favorable because the company sold more units than it anticipated.

Question 1   CPA-03836

The standard direct material cost to produce a unit of Lem is 4 meters of material at $2.50 per meter. During May of the current year, 4,200 meters of material costing $10,080 were purchased and used to produce 1,000 units of Lem. What was the material price variance for May?

   a. $400 favorable
   b. $420 favorable
   c. $80 unfavorable
   d. $480 unfavorable

Question 2   CPA-05251

A company produces widgets with budgeted standard direct materials of 2 pounds per widget at $5 per pound. Standard direct labor was budgeted at 0.5 hour per widget at $15 per hour. The actual usage in the current year was 25,000 pounds and 3,000 hours to produce 10,000 widgets. What was the direct labor usage variance?

   a. $25,000 favorable
   b. $25,000 unfavorable
   c. $30,000 favorable
   d. $30,000 unfavorable

Question 3   CPA-05874

A company uses a standard costing system. At the end of the current year, the company provides the following overhead information:

Actual overhead incurred:

Variable	$90,000
Fixed	62,000
Budgeted fixed overhead	65,000
Variable overhead rate (per direct labor hour)	8
Standard hours allowed for actual production	12,000
Actual labor hours used	11,000

What amount is the variable overhead efficiency variance?

a. $8,000 favorable
b. $8,000 unfavorable
c. $6,000 favorable
d. $2,000 unfavorable

Question 4   CPA-03831

Baby Frames Inc. evaluates manufacturing overhead by using variance analysis. The following information applies to the month of May:

	Actual	Budgeted
Number of frames manufactured	19,000	20,000
Variable overhead costs	$ 4,100	$ 2 per direct labor hour
Fixed overhead costs	22,000	20,000 $1 per unit
Direct labor hours	2,100 hours	0.1 hour per frame

What is the production volume variance?

a. $1,000 favorable
b. $1,000 unfavorable
c. $2,000 favorable
d. $2,000 unfavorable

Question 5	CPA-06165

Anderson Corporation budgeted sales of 6,250 at $12 per unit but achieved sales of 5,000 at $15 per unit. Anderson would compute a selling price variance of:

    a. $0

    b. $3,750

    c. $15,000

    d. $18,750

NOTES

BEC
5

Economic Concepts and Analysis

Module

Economic and Business Cycles

1 Economics

Economics is defined as a science that studies human behavior as the relationship between ends and scarce means that have alternative uses. In essence, economics is about people (e.g., individuals, corporations, governments) and the choices they make. Because economics is a crucial component of the business environment which ultimately affects an individual's, company's, or government's performance (and financial reporting), it is considered an important area of study in the Business Environment and Concepts (BEC) curriculum.

2 Business Cycles

2.1 Introduction

Business cycles refer to the rise and fall of economic activity relative to long-term growth trends (i.e., the swings in total national output, income, and employment over time). Although the economy tends to grow over time, the growth in economic activity is not stable. Rather, economic activity is characterized by fluctuations, and these fluctuations are known as business cycles. Business cycles vary in duration and severity. The analysis of business cycles is part of the field of macroeconomics. Macroeconomics is the study of the economy as a whole. It examines the determinants of national income, unemployment, inflation, and how monetary and fiscal policies affect economic activity.

2.2 Measuring Economic Activity (Gross Domestic Product)

Because business cycles refer to the rise and fall of economic activity, it is important to first examine how economic activity is measured. The most common measure of the economic activity or output of an economy is gross domestic product (GDP). GDP is the total market value of all final goods and services produced within the borders of a nation in a particular period. The term "final goods and services" *excludes used* goods that have been resold; GDP is the nation's output of goods and services. Note that GDP includes all final goods and services produced by resources *within* a country regardless of who owns the resources. Thus, U.S. GDP includes the output of foreign-owned factories in the United States but excludes the output of U.S.-owned factories operating abroad.

2.3 Nominal vs. Real GDP

2.3.1 Nominal GDP

Nominal GDP (unadjusted) measures the value of all final goods and services in prices prevailing at the time of production. That is, nominal GDP measures the value of all final goods and services in current prices.

2.3.2 Real GDP

Real GDP (adjusted) measures the value of all final goods and services in constant prices. That is, real GDP is adjusted to account for changes in the price level (i.e., it removes the effects of inflation by using a price index). Real GDP is the most commonly used measure of economic activity and national output (i.e., the total output of an economy).

The price index used to calculate real GDP is called the GDP deflator. It is a price index for all goods and services included in GDP. Using the GDP deflator, real GDP is calculated as the ratio of nominal GDP to the GDP deflator times 100.

$$\text{Real GDP} = \frac{\text{Nominal GDP}}{\text{GDP deflator}} \times 100$$

Example 1 — Application of Price Index to Determine Real GDP

Facts: Assume that a local economist is attempting to measure an economy's real GDP and the change in real GDP from the prior year. Based on his research, the following economic data is gathered on the economy's production:

	Current Year	Prior Year
Nominal GDP ($ billions)	$3,450.3	$3,286.0
GDP deflator	107.0	105.0

Required: Using the table above, calculate the real GDP for the current year and prior year and the change in real GDP for the economy.

Solution: The following formula is used to measure real GDP:

$$\text{Real GDP} = \frac{\text{Nominal GDP}}{\text{GDP deflator}} \times 100$$

$$\text{Current year} = \frac{\$3,450.3}{107.0} \times 100$$

$$= \textbf{\$3,224.6 billion}$$

$$\text{Prior year} = \frac{\$3,286.0}{105.0} \times 100$$

$$= \textbf{\$3,129.5 billion}$$

The following formula is used to measure the change in real GDP:

$$\% \Delta \text{ Real GDP} = \frac{\text{Current year real GDP}}{\text{Past year real GDP}} - 1$$

$$= \frac{\$3,224.6}{\$3,129.5} - 1$$

$$= \textbf{+3.04\%}$$

2.3.3 Real GDP per Capita and Economic Growth

Real GDP per capita is real GDP divided by population. Real GDP per capita is typically used to compare standards of living across countries or across time. Real GDP per capita is also used to measure economic growth. Economic growth is the increase in real GDP per capita over time.

2.4 Summary Composition of Business Cycles

As noted previously, economic activity is characterized by fluctuations, and these fluctuations are known as business cycles. Business cycles typically comprise the following:

- **Expansionary Phase:** An expansionary phase is characterized by rising economic activity (real GDP) and growth. During an expansionary phase, economic activity is rising above its long-term growth trend. Firms' profits are likely to be rising during an expansionary phase as the demand for goods and services increases. Firms also are likely to increase their workforces during an expansion, and the prices of goods and services are likely to be rising.

- **Peak:** A peak is a high point of economic activity. It marks the end of an expansionary phase and the beginning of a contractionary phase in economic activity. At the peak of a business cycle, firms' profits are likely to be at their highest levels. Firms also are likely to face capacity constraints and input shortages (raw material and labor), leading to higher costs and higher overall price levels.

- **Contractionary Phase:** A contractionary phase is characterized by falling economic activity and growth, and follows a peak. During a contractionary phase, firms' profits are likely to be falling from their highest levels.

- **Trough:** A trough is a low point of economic activity. At this point of the business cycle, firms' profits are likely to be at their lowest levels. Firms also are likely to experience significant excess production capacity, leading them to reduce their workforces and cut costs.

- **Recovery Phase:** A recovery phase follows a trough. During a recovery phase, economic activity begins to increase and return to its long-term growth trend. Further, firms' profits typically begin to stabilize as the demand for goods and services begins to rise.

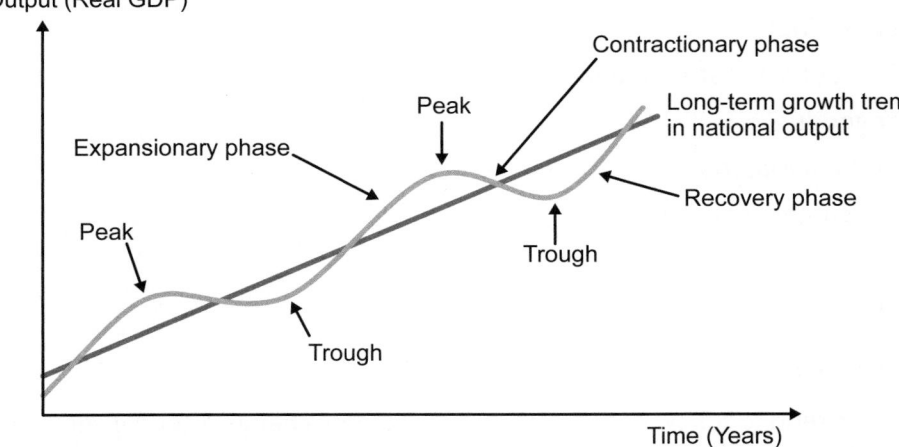

Business Cycles

2.5   Terminology Used in Describing Business Cycles

2.5.1   Recession

A recession occurs when the economy experiences negative real economic growth (declines in national output). Economists define a recession as two consecutive quarters of falling national output. During a recession, firms' profits tend to fall and many firms incur losses. Firms also are likely to have excess capacity. As a result, during a recession, resources (including labor) are likely to be underutilized and unemployment is likely to be high.

2.5.2   Depression

A depression is a very severe recession. It is characterized by a relatively long period of stagnation in business activity and high unemployment rates. As a result, firms experience significant excess capacity. Furthermore, due to the significant reduction in the demand for goods and services, it is likely that many firms will go out of business during a depression.

3   Economic Indicators

Although business cycles tend to be irregular and unpredictable, economists nevertheless attempt to predict business cycles and their severity and duration using economic indicators. Economic indicators (gathered by The Conference Board) are statistics that historically have been highly correlated with economic activity. They can be "leading indicators," "lagging indicators," or "coincident indicators."

3.1   Leading Indicators

Leading indicators tend to predict economic activity. They change before the economy starts to follow a certain trend. The government routinely revises the numbers as more data becomes available. Thus, leading indicators are subject to change.

Leading indicators include:

- Average new unemployment claims
- Building permits for residences
- Average length of the workweek
- Money supply (M2)
- Standard & Poor's 500 stock index
- Orders for goods
- Price changes of materials
- Index of consumer expectations
- Interest rate spread
- Index of supply deliveries

3.2   Lagging Indicators

Lagging indicators tend to follow economic activity; i.e., they change after a given economic trend has already started. They give signals after the fact. Economists measure lagging indicators to confirm or dispute previous forecasts and the effectiveness of policy directives.

Lagging indicators include:

- Prime rate charged by banks
- Average duration of unemployment
- Commercial and industrial loans outstanding
- Consumer price index for services
- Consumer debt-to-income ratio
- Changes in labor cost per unit of manufacturing output
- Inventories-to-sales ratio

3.3   Coincident Indicators

Coincident indicators change at approximately the same time as the whole economy, thereby providing information about the current state of the economy. A coincident indicator may be used to identify, after the fact, the timing of peaks and troughs in a business cycle.

Coincident indicators include:

- Industrial production
- Manufacturing and trade sales
- Industrial production (GDP)
- Personal income less transfer payments

4   Reasons for Fluctuations

Although there are a variety of theories regarding the cause of business cycles, economists generally agree that business cycles result from shifts in aggregate demand and/or aggregate supply. Aggregate demand and aggregate supply curves can be used to illustrate the relationship between a country's output (real GDP) and price level (the GDP deflator). They also are used to examine the causes of economic fluctuations.

4.1   Aggregate Demand (AD) Curve

The aggregate demand (AD) curve illustrates the maximum quantity of all goods and services that households, firms, and the government are willing and able to purchase at any given price level. The curve shows the relationship between total output (real GDP) of the economy and the price level. Note that this "aggregate" demand curve is the macroeconomic demand curve of the "total" demand in the economy as a whole. The x-axis is real GDP and the y-axis is the price level.

4.2   Aggregate Supply (AS) Curve

The aggregate supply (AS) curve illustrates the maximum quantity of all goods and services producers are willing and able to produce at any given price level. Note that this "aggregate" supply curve is the macroeconomic supply curve of the "total" supply in the economy as a whole.

4.2.1   Short-Run Aggregate Supply Curve

The short-run aggregate supply (SRAS) curve is upward sloping, illustrating that as the price level rises, firms are willing to produce more goods and services.

4.2.2   Long-Run Aggregate Supply Curve

The long-run aggregate supply (LRAS) curve is vertical, illustrating that in the long run, if all resources are fully utilized, output is determined solely by the factors of production. This curve corresponds to the potential level of output in the economy.

4.2.3   Potential Level of Output (Potential GDP)

Potential GDP refers to the level of real GDP (national output) that the economy would produce if its resources (capital and labor) were fully employed. When real GDP is below the potential level of output, the economy will typically be experiencing a recession. Similarly, when real GDP rises above the potential level of output, the economy typically will be experiencing an expansion.

Aggregate Demand and Aggregate Supply Curves

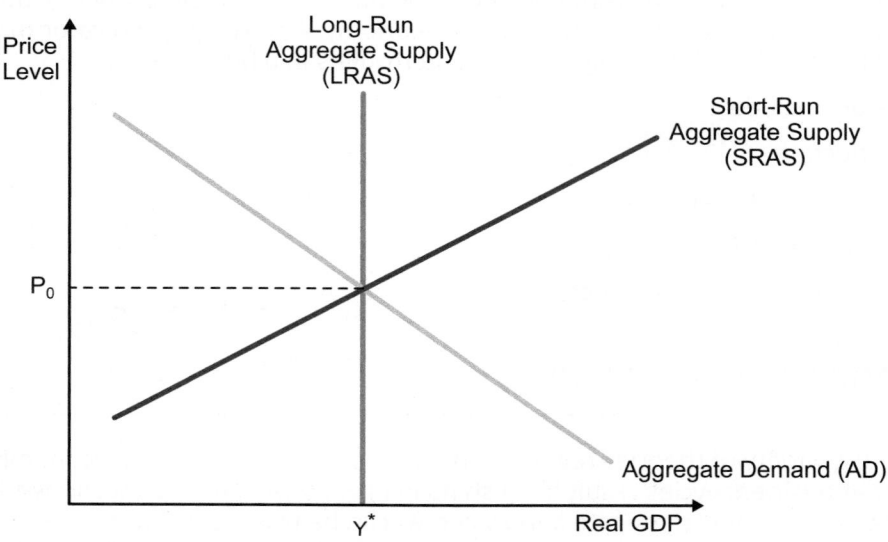

The intersection of the short-run aggregate supply (SRAS) curve and the aggregate demand (AD) curve determines the level of output (real GDP) and price level in the short run. The position of the long-run aggregate supply (LRAS) curve determines the level of output in the long run. The LRAS curve is vertical at the economy's potential level of output.

Y^* = GDP at the potential (equilibrium) level of output

4.3   Aggregate Demand, Aggregate Supply, and Economic Fluctuations

Business cycles, or economic fluctuations, result from shifts in aggregate demand and short-run aggregate supply (note that shifts in the long-run aggregate supply curve are associated with long-run growth in the economy and do not affect business cycles).

4.3.1   Reduction in Demand

If circumstances cause individuals, businesses, or governments to reduce their demand for goods and services, economic activity (real GDP) will decline, leading to a contraction in economic activity and possibly a recession. As a result, a reduction in demand tends to cause firms' profits to decline. Firms also are likely to experience an increase in excess capacity, leading them to reduce their workforces.

4.3.2   Increase in Demand

In contrast, if circumstances cause individuals, businesses, and governments to increase their demand for goods and services, economic activity will rise, leading to a recovery or an expansion in economic activity. As a result, an increase in demand tends to cause firms' profits to rise. Firms also are likely to experience a reduction in excess capacity, leading them to increase their workforces.

4.3.3   Reduction of Supply

If circumstances cause firms to reduce their supply of goods and services, economic activity will fall, leading to a contraction or possibly a recession. As firms reduce their supply, they also are likely to reduce their workforces, leading to higher unemployment.

4.3.4   Increase in Supply

If circumstances cause firms to increase their supply of goods and services, economic activity will rise, leading to an expansionary phase of economic activity. As firms increase their supply, they also are likely to increase their workforces, leading to lower unemployment.

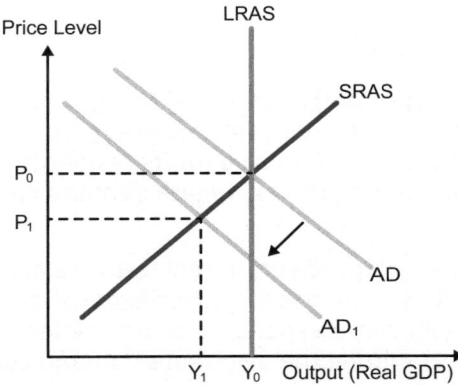

Shift in Aggregate Demand

A recession caused by a shift in the aggregate demand curve: A decrease in aggregate demand causes actual GDP to fall below potential GDP. This is illustrated as the leftward shift in aggregate demand. As a result, real GDP falls from Y_0 to Y_1.

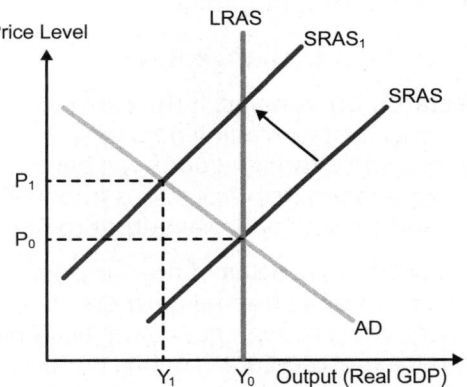

Shift in Short-Run Aggregate Supply

A recession caused by a shift in the short-run aggregate supply curve: A decrease in short-run aggregate supply causes actual GDP to fall below potential GDP. This is illustrated as the leftward shift in the short-run aggregate supply curve. As a result, real GDP falls from Y_0 to Y_1.

4.4   Factors That Shift Aggregate Demand

The primary factors that shift aggregate demand are:

4.4.1   Changes in Wealth

■   **Increase in Wealth:** An increase in real wealth causes the aggregate demand curve to shift to the right. Thus, an increase in wealth causes the economy to expand and leads to an increase in national output (real GDP).

■   **Decrease in Wealth:** A decrease in wealth causes the aggregate demand curve to shift to the left. A decrease in wealth does the opposite of an increase in wealth. For example, a large decline in stock prices would decrease consumer wealth and therefore shift the aggregate demand curve to the left. As a result, national output would fall, causing a contraction and possibly a recession.

4.4.2   Changes in Real Interest Rates

■   **Increase in Real Interest Rates:** An increase in interest rates increases the cost of capital and, therefore, tends to reduce consumer demand for durable goods, such as new cars and homes, and firms' demand for new plants and equipment. Therefore, an increase in real interest rates causes the cost of capital to rise and shifts the aggregate demand curve to the left, causing national output to fall.

■   **Decrease in Real Interest Rates:** A decrease in real interest rates reduces the cost of borrowing, thereby increasing the demand for investment goods and shifting the aggregate demand curve to the right, causing national output to rise.

4.4.3   Changes in Expectations About the Future Economic Outlook (Consumer Confidence)

■   **Confident Economic Outlook:** If households become confident about the economic outlook (consumer confidence increases), their willingness to acquire investments and consumer goods increases and the aggregate demand curve shifts right, causing national output to rise.

■   **Uncertain Economic Outlook:** When the economic outlook appears more uncertain, consumers tend to reduce current spending, shifting aggregate demand to the left and causing national output to fall.

4.4.4   Changes in Exchange Rates

■   **Appreciated Currencies:** If the currency of a country appreciates in real terms relative to the currencies of its trading partners, its goods will become relatively more expensive for foreigners, while foreign goods will become relatively less expensive for its residents. As a result, net exports (exports minus imports) will fall, shifting the aggregate demand curve to the left and causing national output to fall.

■   **Depreciated Currencies:** If the currency of a country depreciates in real terms relative to the currencies of its trading partners, its goods will become relatively less expensive for foreigners, while foreign goods will become relatively more expensive for its residents. As a result, net exports (exports minus imports) will rise, shifting the aggregate demand curve to the right and causing national output to rise.

4.4.5   Changes in Government Spending

■   **Increase in Government Spending:** An *increase* in government spending shifts the aggregate demand curve to the right, causing national output to rise.

■   **Decrease in Government Spending:** A *decrease* in government spending shifts the aggregate demand curve to the left, causing national output to fall.

4.4.6   Changes in Consumer Taxes

■   **Increase in Consumer Taxes:** An *increase* in consumer taxes (e.g., the personal income tax) reduces the disposable income (gross income minus taxes) of consumers and, therefore, shifts the aggregate demand curve to the left, causing national output to fall.

■   **Decrease in Consumer Taxes:** A *decrease* in consumer taxes increases the disposable income of consumers and therefore shifts the aggregate demand curve to the right, causing national output to rise.

Expansionary Fiscal Policy

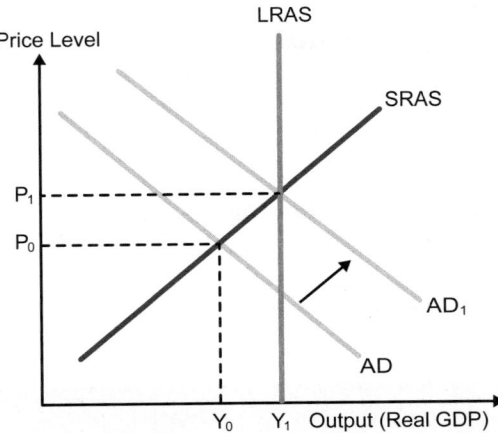

Contractionary Fiscal Policy

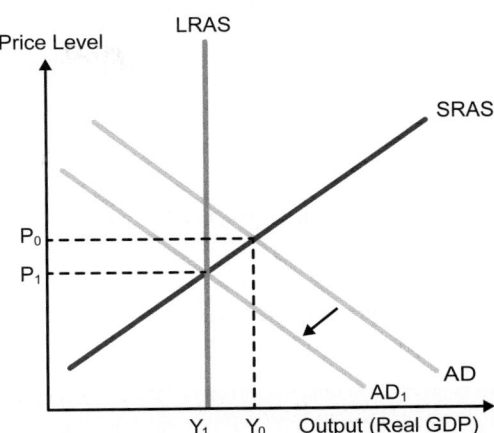

The economy is initially in a recession, illustrated as output level Y_0, which is below the potential level of output Y_1. The government can stimulate the economy by increasing government spending or decreasing taxes (or both), shifting the aggregate demand curve to the right and causing national output (real GDP) to rise.

The economy is initially in an expansionary phase, illustrated as output level Y_0, which is above the potential level of output Y_1. The government can contract the economy by decreasing government spending or increasing taxes (or both), shifting the aggregate demand curve to the left and causing national output (real GDP) to fall.

Pass Key

Remember the factors that shift aggregate demand as **TWICE G**overnment:

Taxes

Wealth

Interest rates

Consumer confidence

Exchange rates

Government spending

4.5   Multiplier Effect

The *multiplier effect* refers to the fact that an increase in consumer, company, or government spending produces a multiplied increase in the level of economic activity. For example, a $1 increase in government spending results in a greater than $1 increase in real GDP. The multiplier effect stems from the fact that increases in spending generate income for firms, which in turn spend that income. Their spending gives other households and firms income, and so on. Therefore, the effect of a $1 increase in spending is magnified by the multiplier effect. The multiplier effect results from the marginal propensity to consume (MPC). The MPC is the change in consumption due to a $1 increase in income. Because people tend to save part of their income, the MPC is typically less than one.

Using the MPC, the size of the multiplier effect can be calculated using the following formulas:

$$\text{Multiplier} = \frac{1}{(1 - \text{MPC})}$$

$$\text{Change in real GDP} = \text{Multiplier} \times \text{Change in spending}$$

Note: The examiners could refer to "1 – MPC" as the marginal propensity to save (MPS), so be aware of this terminology as well.

Example 2   Multiplier Effect

Facts: Suppose that the MPC is 0.8 (i.e., the change in consumption due to a $1 increase in income is 80 cents) and that spending increases by $100.

Required: Calculate the change in real GDP.

Solution:

$$\text{Change in real GDP} = \frac{1}{(1 - 0.8)} \times \$100 = \$500$$

Thus, a $100 increase in spending results in a $500 increase in real GDP.

4.6   Factors That Shift Short-Run Aggregate Supply

Recall that shifts in long-run aggregate supply are associated with economic growth, not business cycles. Therefore, when discussing business cycles, we focus on shifts in the short-run aggregate supply curve.

The primary factors that shift short-run aggregate supply are:

4.6.1   Changes in Input (Resource) Prices

- **Increase in Input Prices:** An *increase* in input prices (raw material prices, wages, etc.) causes the short-run aggregate supply curve to shift left. Thus, an increase in input prices causes the economy to contract and leads to a decrease in national output (real GDP).

Illustration 1   Increase in Input Prices

A large increase in oil prices (oil is a primary input in production) would shift the short-run aggregate supply curve to the left. As a result, national output would fall, causing a contraction and possibly a recession.

■ **Decrease in Input Prices:** A *decrease* in input prices causes the short-run aggregate supply curve to shift to the right. A decrease in input prices causes the economy to expand and leads to an increase in national output (real GDP).

4.6.2 Supply Shocks

■ **Supplies Are Plentiful:** If resource supplies become more plentiful, the short-run aggregate supply curve will shift to the right, causing national output to increase.

■ **Supplies Are Curtailed:** If resource supplies are curtailed (e.g., crop failures, damage to infrastructure caused by earthquakes, etc.), the short-run supply curve will shift to the left, causing national output (real GDP) to decline.

Question 1	CPA-03291

Which of the following is *not* likely to cause a rightward shift in the aggregate demand curve?

   a. An increase in wealth.

   b. An increase in the level of real interest rates.

   c. An increase in government spending.

   d. An increase in the general level of confidence about the economic outlook.

Question 2	CPA-05318

Which of the following statements is correct if there is an increase in the resources available within an economy?

   a. More goods and services will be produced in the economy.

   b. The economy will be capable of producing more goods and services.

   c. The standard of living in the economy will rise.

   d. The technological efficiency of the economy will improve.

NOTES

Economic Measures and Indicators

1 Overview

Economists and policy makers rely on a host of economic measures or indicators to determine the overall state of economic activity. Some of the most commonly cited economic measures are:

- Real gross domestic product (real GDP)
- Unemployment rate
- Inflation rate
- Interest rates

It is important to remember that these economic measures tend to move together. For example, when real GDP is rising, unemployment tends to be falling. Similarly, when the unemployment rate is rising, the inflation rate tends to be falling.

2 National Income Accounting System

The National Income and Product Accounting (NIPA) system was developed by the U.S. Department of Commerce to monitor the health and performance of the U.S. economy. The two methods for measuring GDP, expenditure approach and income approach, are calculated using NIPA. The combined economic output of the following four sectors is called gross domestic product (GDP), the total dollar value of all new final goods and services produced within the economy in a given period.

- Households (or consumers)
- Businesses
- Federal, state, and local governments
- Foreign sector

2.1 Two Methods of Measuring GDP

The two methods of measuring GDP are the *expenditure approach* and the *income approach*.

2.1.1 Expenditure Approach

Under the expenditure approach, GDP is the sum of the following four components:

- **Government** purchases of goods and services
- Gross private domestic **investment** (nonresidential fixed investment, residential fixed investment, and change in business inventories)
- Personal **consumption** expenditures (durable goods, nondurable goods, and services)
- Net **exports** (exports minus imports)

The first letters of the words in bold form the mnemonic **GICE**.

2.1.2 Income Approach

The income approach accounts for GDP as the value of resource costs and incomes generated during the measurement period. The income approach includes business profits, rent, wages, interest, depreciation, and business taxes. Under the income approach, GDP is the sum of the following eight components:

- **Income** of proprietors
- **Profits** of corporations
- **Interest** (net)
- **Rental** income
- **Adjustments** for net foreign income and miscellaneous items
- **Taxes** (indirect business taxes)
- **Employee** compensation (wages)
- **Depreciation** (also known as capital consumption allowance)

The first letters of the words in bold form the mnemonic **I PIRATED**.

2.2 Comparison of Approaches

The two different approaches are used to prepare an "income statement" for the domestic economy (the GDP), as shown in the following table.

- The aggregate expenditures approach on the left is a flow of product approach (at market prices).
- The income approach on the right is a flow of earnings and other resources that generate domestic income.

Comparison of Approaches (in Billions of Dollars)			
Expenditure Approach (Flow-of-Product)		**Income Approach (Earnings and Costs)**	
Government purchases	$1,314.70	**Income** of proprietors	$ 450.90
Investment	1,014.40	**Profits** of corporations	526.50
Consumption	4,698.70	**Interest** (net)	392.80
Exports (net)	(96.40)	**Rental** income	116.60
		Adjustments for net foreign income/ miscellaneous	45.00
		Taxes (indirect business)	572.50
		Employee compensation	4,008.30
		Depreciation (consumption of fixed capital)	818.80
Aggregate expenditure	$6,931.40	Domestic Income	$6,931.40

2.3   Other Measures of National Income

Although GDP is the most common measure of national income and an economy's output and performance, there are several other noteworthy measures.

- **Net Domestic Product (NDP):** *Net domestic product* is GDP minus depreciation (the capital consumption allowance).

- **Gross National Product (GNP):** *Gross national product* is defined as the market value of final goods and services produced by residents of a country in a given time period. GNP differs from GDP because GNP includes goods and services that are produced overseas by U.S. firms and excludes goods and services that are produced domestically by foreign firms.

- **Net National Product (NNP):** *Net national product* is defined as GNP minus economic depreciation (i.e., losses in the value of capital goods due to age and wear).

- **National Income (NI):** *National income* is NNP less indirect business taxes (e.g., sales tax).

- **Personal Income (PI):** *Personal income* is the income received by households and noncorporate businesses.

- **Disposable Income (DI):** *Disposable income* is personal income less personal taxes. It is the amount of income households have available either to spend or to save.

Illustration 1   GNP vs. GDP

If BMW produces cars in the United States, that production is counted as part of U.S. GDP, but it is not counted as part of U.S. GNP because BMW is a foreign-owned company.

---

3   Unemployment Rate

The *unemployment* rate measures the ratio of the number of people classified as unemployed to the total labor force. The total labor force includes all non-institutionalized individuals 16 years of age or older who either are working or are actively looking for work. (An unemployed person is defined as a person 16 years of age or older who is available for work and who has actively sought employment during the previous four weeks.) Note that to be counted as unemployed, a person must be actively looking for work. The unemployment rate can be expressed as:

$$\text{Unemployment rate} = \frac{\text{Number of unemployed}}{\text{Total labor force}} \times 100$$

3.1   Types of Unemployment

3.1.1   Frictional Unemployment

Frictional unemployment is normal unemployment resulting from workers routinely changing jobs or from workers being temporarily laid off. It is the unemployment that arises because of the time needed to match qualified job seekers with available jobs.

3.1.2 Structural Unemployment

Structural unemployment occurs when:

- jobs available in the market do not correspond to the skills of the workforce; and
- unemployed workers do not live where the jobs are located.

3.1.3 Seasonal Unemployment

Seasonal unemployment is the result of seasonal changes in the demand and supply of labor. For example, shortly before Christmas, the demand for labor in some industries increases and then decreases again after Christmas.

3.1.4 Cyclical Unemployment

Cyclical unemployment is the amount of unemployment resulting from declines in real GDP during periods of contraction or recession or in any period when the economy fails to operate at its potential. When real GDP is below the potential level of output, cyclical unemployment is positive. When real GDP is above the potential level of output, cyclical unemployment is negative. Thus, cyclical unemployment rises during a recession and falls during an expansion.

3.2 Natural Rate of Unemployment and Full Employment

3.2.1 Natural Rate of Unemployment

The *natural rate of unemployment* is the "normal" rate of unemployment around which the unemployment rate fluctuates due to cyclical unemployment. Thus, the natural rate of unemployment is the sum of frictional, structural, and seasonal unemployment or the employment rate that exists when the economy is at its potential output level.

3.2.2 Full Employment

Full employment is defined as the level of unemployment when there is no cyclical unemployment. Full employment does not mean zero unemployment. When the economy is operating at full employment, there is still frictional, structural, and seasonal unemployment.

4 Price Level and Inflation

4.1 Definitions

4.1.1 Inflation

Inflation is defined as a sustained increase in the general prices of goods and services. It occurs when prices on average are increasing over time.

4.1.2 Deflation

Deflation is defined as a sustained decrease in the general prices of goods and services. It occurs when prices on average are falling over time.

Most economists believe that deflation is a much bigger economic problem than inflation. During periods of deflation, firms are likely to experience significant excess production capacity. This occurs because consumers tend to hold off purchasing goods and services during a period of deflation because they realize that the price of goods and services is likely to continue to fall. Consequently, firm profits are likely to be falling during periods of deflation.

4.1.3   Inflation/Deflation Rate

The *inflation* or *deflation rate* is typically measured as the percentage change in the consumer price index (CPI) from one period to the next.

- **Consumer Price Index (CPI):** The *consumer price index* (CPI) is a measure of the overall cost of a fixed basket of goods and services purchased by an average household. The CPI is computed as follows:

$$CPI = \frac{\text{Current cost of market basket}}{\text{Base year cost of market basket}} \times 100$$

Example 1   Consumer Price Index

Facts: A doctoral student in economics is working on her dissertation. As part of her research, she selects four goods (products) that are consumed by college students on the local campus and then collects data to determine the average price changes for these products over the past 10 years. She gathers the following data for the four products.

	Time = 0 (Base year)	Time = Year 10 (Current year)
Product A	$ 3.00	$ 4.80
Product B	25.00	39.00
Product C	17.00	22.00
Product D	6.00	8.20
Total	$51.00	$74.00

Note: The prices for each product above are the average prices for T = 0 and T = 10.

Required: Compute the (consumer) price index for these four products.

Solution:

$$CPI = \frac{\$74.00 \times 100}{\$51.00}$$

$$= 145.1$$

- **Inflation Rate:** Using the CPI, the inflation rate is calculated as the percentage change in the CPI from one period to the next:

$$\text{Inflation rate} = \frac{CPI_{\text{this period}} - CPI_{\text{last period}}}{CPI_{\text{last period}}} \times 100$$

- **Producer Price Index (PPI):** The *producer price index* (PPI) measures the overall cost of a basket of goods and services typically purchased by firms.

4.2   Causes of Inflation and Deflation

Inflation and deflation are caused by shifts in the aggregate demand and short-run aggregate supply curves.

A rightward shift in the *aggregate demand* curve will cause the price level to rise, leading to inflation. Similarly, a leftward shift in the *short-run aggregate supply* curve will also cause the price level to rise, leading to inflation.

4.2.1   Demand-Pull Inflation

Demand-pull inflation is caused by increases in aggregate demand. Thus, demand-pull inflation could be caused by factors such as:

- increases in government spending;

- decreases in taxes;

- increases in wealth; or

- increases in the money supply.

4.2.2   Cost-Push Inflation

Cost-push inflation is caused by reductions in short-run aggregate supply. Thus, cost-push inflation could be caused by factors such as:

- an increase in oil prices; or

- an increase in nominal wages.

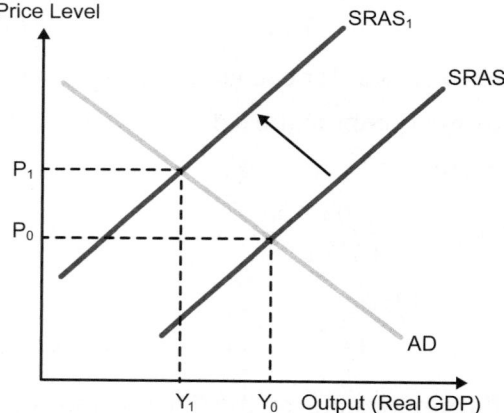

Demand-Pull Inflation

An increase in aggregate demand causes the short-run equilibrium price level to rise from P_0 to P_1.

Cost-Push Inflation

A decrease in short-run aggregate supply causes the short-run equilibrium price level to rise from P_0 to P_1.

4.2.3 Deflation

Deflation is also caused by shifts in aggregate demand or short-run aggregate supply. A shift left in aggregate demand (perhaps brought about by a stock market crash or a large increase in taxes) will cause the aggregate price level to fall. Similarly, a shift right in the short-run aggregate supply curve will also cause the aggregate price level to fall.

4.3 Inflation and the Value of Money

Inflation has an inverse relationship with purchasing power. As the price level rises, the value of money (purchasing power) declines.

4.3.1 Definitions

- **Monetary Assets and Liabilities:** *Monetary assets and liabilities* (e.g., cash, accounts receivable, notes payable, etc.) are fixed in dollar amounts regardless of changes in specific prices or the general price level.

- **Nonmonetary Assets and Liabilities:** The value of nonmonetary assets (e.g., a building, land, machinery, etc.) and nonmonetary liabilities (e.g., rent collected in advance) will fluctuate with inflation and deflation.

4.3.2 Holding Monetary Assets

During a period of inflation, those with a fixed amount of money or income (e.g., retired persons) will be hurt (i.e., their purchasing power will be eroded). Similarly, firms that loan money at fixed interest rates are likely to be hurt by inflation.

4.3.3 Holding Monetary Liabilities

During a period of inflation, those with a fixed amount of debt (e.g., those with home mortgages) will be aided (i.e., the debt will be repaid with inflated dollars). Thus, inflation also tends to benefit firms with large amounts of outstanding debt.

Illustration 2   OPEC and the Stagflation of the 1970s

From 1973 to 1974, OPEC (Organization of the Petroleum Exporting Countries) substantially curtailed its production of crude oil. As a result, the price of a barrel of crude oil rose from about $2 a barrel in late 1973 to $10 a barrel in late 1974.

This increase in the price of crude oil had a substantial effect on the U.S. economy. Specifically, rising crude oil prices represented an increase in input costs for U.S. firms. As a result, firms cut back production and the short-run aggregate supply curve shifted left.

As the short-run aggregate supply curve shifted left, national output (real GDP) began to decline, unemployment began to rise, and the aggregate price level began to rise (cost-push inflation).

The combination of falling national output and a rising price level is known as *stagflation*. The actions of OPEC in 1973–74 led to a recession in the U.S. that was particularly harsh because not only was the unemployment rate rising, but the newly unemployed were facing higher prices for goods and services due to inflation.

Illustration 3   The Great Depression and Deflation

The Great Depression began with the stock market crash of Oct. 29, 1929. By 1932, the Dow Jones Industrial Average had fallen 89 percent from its peak in 1929. In addition, shortly before the stock market crash, the Federal Reserve (the central bank of the U.S.) increased interest rates in an attempt to control inflation. It then increased interest rates again in early 1931.

Although the stock market crash was not the only cause of the Great Depression, it did mark the beginning of the Great Depression. The Great Depression was caused by a number of factors, including ill-timed interest rate hikes by the Federal Reserve and protectionist trade policies, as well as the stock market crash. The table below shows what happened to real GDP, the unemployment rate, and the price level (as measured by the CPI) from 1929 through 1933.

Year	Real GDP (Billions of 1987 Dollars)	Unemployment Rate	Price Level (CPI)
1929	821.8	3.15%	17.1
1930	748.9	8.71%	16.7
1931	691.3	15.91%	15.2
1932	599.7	23.65%	13.7
1933	587.1	24.87%	13.0

As the table illustrates, the Great Depression was characterized by falling output (falling real GDP), rising unemployment, and deflation. The deflation that occurred can be seen by noting that from 1929 through 1933, the price level fell continuously. Furthermore, at the height of the Great Depression, one out of every four workers was unemployed.

The data suggest that the Great Depression was caused by a shift left in aggregate demand. Specifically, the stock market crash reduced household wealth, which shifted the aggregate demand curve to the left. In addition, the interest rate hikes orchestrated by the Federal Reserve increased the cost of capital, thereby decreasing the demand for investment goods and shifting the aggregate demand curve even further to the left. As aggregate demand fell, the price level also fell and the nation experienced a period of deflation.

4.4   Inverse Relationship Between Inflation and Unemployment

The *Phillips curve* illustrates the inverse relationship between the rate of inflation and the unemployment rate. It illustrates the trade-off that exists in the short run between inflation and unemployment. Unemployment and inflation have historically moved in opposite directions, but during the oil shocks of the 1970s, the Phillips curve broke down. The oil crisis (a supply shock) caused a decrease in short-run aggregate supply that caused both unemployment and inflation.

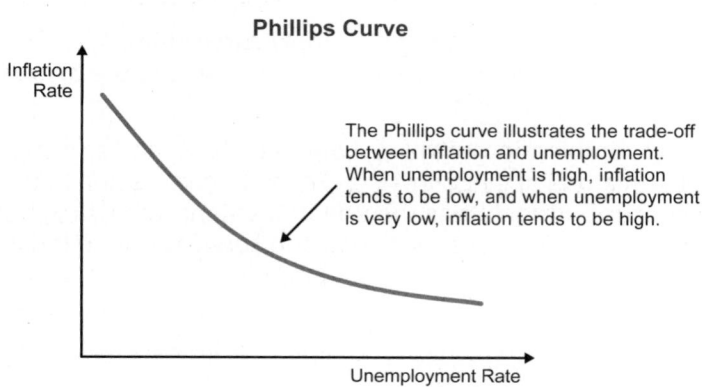

Phillips Curve

Inflation Rate

The Phillips curve illustrates the trade-off between inflation and unemployment. When unemployment is high, inflation tends to be low, and when unemployment is very low, inflation tends to be high.

Unemployment Rate

5   Budget Deficits and Surpluses

The budget is the federal government's plan for spending funds and raising revenues through taxation, fees, and other means (and for borrowing funds if necessary). The budget deficit and the budget surplus are important indicators of the current and future health of an economy.

5.1   Budget Deficits

A budget deficit occurs when a country spends more than it takes in (mostly in the form of taxes during the year).

5.1.1   Financing Budget Deficits

Budget deficits are usually financed by government borrowing, which affects interest rates. The government could also finance budget deficits by printing new money. Financing budget deficits by printing money, however, causes inflation.

5.1.2   Cyclical Budget Deficit

A *cyclical budget deficit* is caused by temporarily low economic activity. For example, a cyclical budget deficit might be caused by a recession and the resulting lower level of national output.

5.1.3   Structural Budget Deficit

A *structural budget deficit* is one that is caused by a structural imbalance between government spending and revenue. Structural deficits are not caused by temporarily low economic activity.

5.2   Budget Surpluses

A *budget surplus* occurs when government revenues exceed government spending during the year.

6   Interest Rates and the Money Supply

6.1   Nominal and Real Interest Rates

6.1.1   Nominal Interest Rate

The *nominal interest rate* is the amount of interest paid (or earned) measured in current dollars. When the economy experiences inflation, nominal interest rates are not a good measure of how much borrowers really pay or lenders really receive when they take out or make a loan. A more accurate measure of the interest borrowers pay or lenders receive is the *real interest rate*.

6.1.2   Real Interest Rate

The *real interest rate* is defined as the nominal interest rate minus the inflation rate. It is a measure of the purchasing power of interest earned or paid.

$$\text{Real interest rate} \ = \ \text{Nominal interest rate} \ - \ \text{Inflation rate}$$

Illustration 4	Real Interest Rate

If you take out a loan with a 10 percent nominal interest rate and the inflation rate is 3 percent, then your real interest rate is only 7 percent. That is, after adjusting for the fact that the dollars with which you will repay the loan in the future are worth less than current dollars due to inflation, you are really only paying 7 percent to borrow the money.

6.1.3   Relationship Between Nominal Interest Rates and Inflation

Nominal interest rates and inflation naturally move together. When the inflation rate increases, so does the nominal interest rate. The relationship between nominal interest rates and inflation may be shown by rearranging the above equation for real interest rates as follows:

$$\text{Nominal interest rate} \; = \; \text{Real interest rate} \; + \; \text{Inflation rate}$$

Thus, if *real interest rates* do not change, a one percent increase in the inflation rate will lead to a one percent increase in *nominal interest rates*.

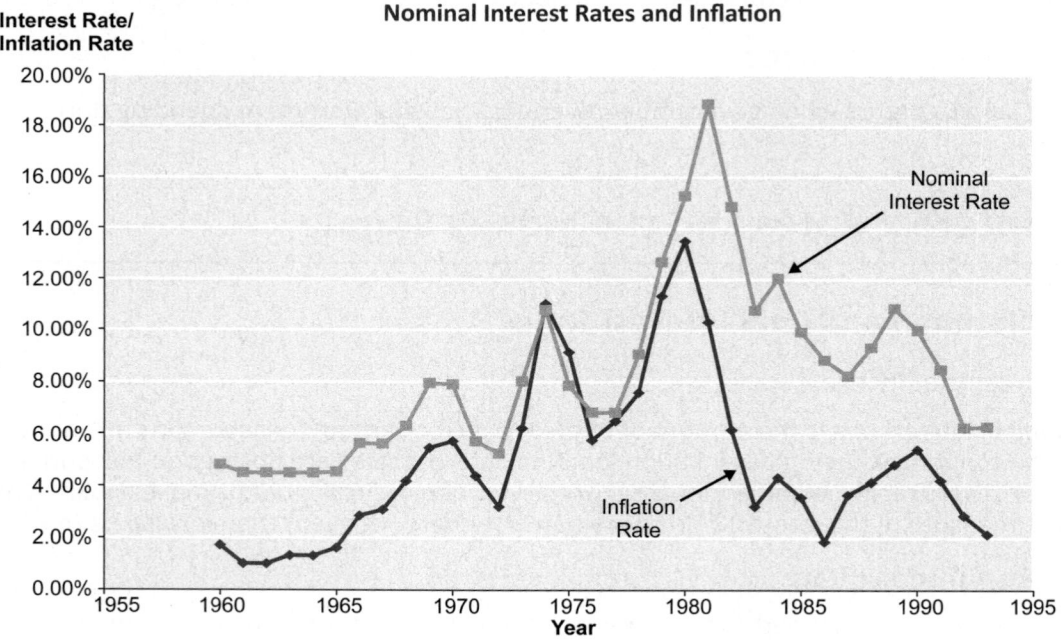

Note the close relationship between nominal interest rates and the inflation rate. As the inflation rate increases, the nominal interest rate also increases. Also note that about 1974–1975, the inflation rate was actually higher than the nominal interest rate, implying real interest rates were negative.

6.2   Definition of Money and the Money Supply

Money is the set of liquid assets generally accepted in exchange for goods and services. The money supply is defined as the stock of all liquid assets available for transactions in the economy at any given point in time. There are several definitions of money supply. M1 and M2 are the most common measures of money supply and are reported (periodically) in financial publications (for example, The Wall Street Journal).

6.2.1   M1

M1 is defined broadly as money that is used for purchases of goods and services. It typically includes coins, currency, checkable deposits (accounts that allow holders to write checks against interest-bearing funds within them), and traveler's checks. M1 does not include savings accounts or certificates of deposit (CDs).

6.2.2   M2

M2 is defined broadly as M1 plus liquid assets that cannot be used as a medium of exchange but that can be converted easily into checkable deposits or other components of M1. These include time certificates of deposit less than $100,000, money market deposit accounts at banks, mutual fund accounts, and savings accounts.

6.2.3   M3

M3 includes all items in M2 as well as time certificates of deposit of $100,000 or more.

Example 2 ▶ The Money Supply

Facts: Assume that at year-end, an economy had the following liquid assets (in billions of dollars):

Money market deposit accounts	$10,500
Checkable deposits	42,100
Certificates of deposits > $100,000	3,435
Traveler's checks	700
Mutual funds	24,650
Currency	85,284
Savings accounts	37,169

Required: Calculate the economy's M1, M2, and M3 money measures.

Solution:

M1 = Checkable deposits + Traveler's checks + Currency

$42,100 + $700 + $85,284 = **$128,084 billion**

M2 = M1 + Money market deposits + Mutual funds + Savings accounts

$128,084 + $10,500 + $24,650 + $37,169 = **$200,403 billion**

M3 = M2 + Certificates of deposits > $100,000

$200,403 + $3,435 = **$203,838 billion**

6.3   Interest Rates and the Demand for and Supply of Money

6.3.1   Demand for Money Is Inversely Related to Interest Rates

Changes in the money supply have a direct effect on interest rates because interest rates are determined by the supply of and demand for money. The demand for money is the relationship between how much money individuals want to hold and the interest rate. The demand for money is inversely related to the interest rate—as interest rates rise, it becomes more expensive to hold money (because holding money rather than saving or investing it means you do not earn interest), thus reducing the demand for money.

6.3.2   Supply of Money Is Fixed at a Given Point in Time

As noted above, the supply of money is determined by the Federal Reserve and is therefore fixed at any given point in time at the level set by the Federal Reserve.

6.3.3   The Money Market

The graph below illustrates the demand for and supply of money. The intersection of the money demand curve and the money supply line determines the interest rate.

- An increase in the money supply will cause interest rates to fall.

- Conversely, a decrease in the money supply will cause interest rates to rise.

The Money Market

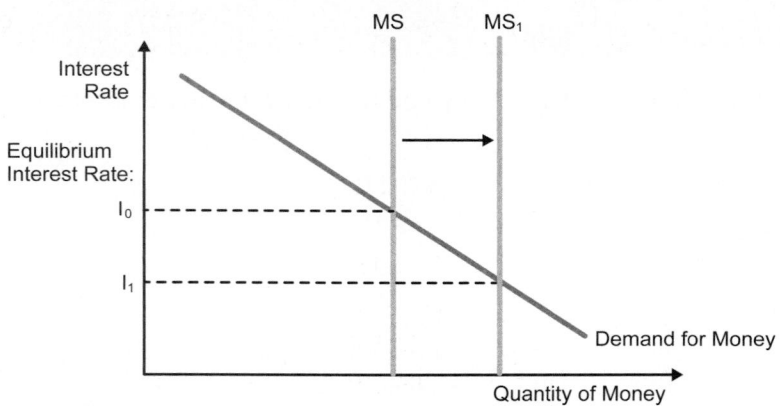

The equilibrium interest rate is found where the demand for money intersects the supply of money. The money supply curve is vertical since the Federal Reserve controls the supply of money (thus it is independent of the interest rate). If the Fed increases the money supply, interest rates will fall, as illustrated by the fall in interest rates from I_0 to I_1.

7   The Federal Reserve and Monetary Policy

Monetary policy is the use of the money supply to stabilize the economy. The Federal Reserve uses monetary policy to increase or decrease the money supply in an effort to promote price stability and full employment. Understanding the effects of changes in the money supply is important because changes in the money supply lead to changes in interest rates, changes in the price level, and changes in national output (real GDP).

7.1   Tools of the Federal Reserve

The Federal Reserve controls the money supply through the following mechanisms.

7.1.1   Open Market Operations (OMO)

Open market operations consist of the purchase and sale of government securities (Treasury bills and bonds) in the open market by the Federal Reserve as a means to expand or contract the existing money supply. Open market operations are the most common method used by the Federal Reserve to impact monetary policy.

- When the Federal Reserve purchases government securities, it increases the money supply (that is, puts money into circulation to pay for the securities). Specifically, the money supply is increased when the Federal Open Market Committee (FOMC) of the Federal Reserve decides to purchase government securities.

- When the Federal Reserve sells government securities, it decreases the money supply (that is, takes money out of circulation).

7.1.2   Changes in the Discount Rate

The *discount rate* is the interest rate the Federal Reserve charges member banks for short-term (normally overnight) loans. Member banks may borrow money from the Federal Reserve to cover liquidity needs, increase reserves, or make investments.

- Raising the discount rate discourages borrowing by member banks and decreases the money supply.

- Lowering the discount rate encourages borrowing by member banks and increases the money supply.

7.1.3   Changes in the Required Reserve Ratio (RRR)

The *required reserve ratio* is the fraction of total deposits banks must hold in reserve.

- Raising the reserve requirement decreases the money supply.

- Lowering the reserve requirement increases the money supply.

7.2   Expansionary Monetary Policy (Increase in the Money Supply)

Expansionary monetary policy results when the Fed increases the money supply, affecting the economy through the following chain of events:

1. An increase in the money supply causes interest rates to fall.

2. Falling interest rates reduce the cost of capital and hence stimulate the desired levels of firm investment and household consumption.

3. Increases in desired investment and consumption cause an increase in aggregate demand.

4. Aggregate demand shifts to the right, causing real GDP to rise, the unemployment rate to fall, and the price level to rise.

7.3 Contractionary Monetary Policy (Decrease in the Money Supply)

Contractionary monetary policy results when the Fed decreases the money supply. The effect is the exact opposite of expansionary monetary policy. Specifically:

1. A decrease in the money supply causes interest rates to rise.

2. Rising interest rates reduce the desired levels of firm investment and household consumption.

3. Decreases in desired investment and consumption cause a decrease in aggregate demand.

4. Aggregate demand shifts to the left, causing real GDP to fall, the unemployment rate to rise, and the price level to fall.

Question 1 CPA-03396

Assume the following data for the U.S. economy in a recent year:

Personal consumption expenditures	$5,015 billion
Exports	106 billion
Government purchases of goods/services	1,040 billion
M1	262 billion
Imports	183 billion
Gross private domestic investment	975 billion
Open market purchases by Federal Reserve	5 billion

Based on this information, which of the following was the U.S. GDP for the year in question?

a. $6,953 billion
b. $6,958 billion
c. $6,691 billion
d. $7,215 billion

Question 2 CPA-03404

What type of unemployment is shown when individuals do not have the qualifications or skills necessary to fill available jobs?

a. Frictional
b. Natural
c. Cyclical
d. Structural

Question 3	CPA-05857

Which of the following individuals would be most hurt by an unanticipated increase in inflation?

    a. A retiree living on a fixed income.

    b. A borrower whose debt has a fixed interest rate.

    c. A union worker whose contract includes a provision for regular cost-of-living adjustments.

    d. A saver whose savings was placed in a variable rate savings account.

Question 4	CPA-05869

Assume an economy is at the peak of the business cycle. Which of the following policy combinations is the most effective way to dampen the economy and prevent inflation?

    a. Increase government spending, reduce taxes, increase money supply, and reduce interest rates.

    b. Reduce government spending, increase taxes, increase money supply, and increase interest rates.

    c. Reduce government spending, increase taxes, reduce money supply, and increase interest rates.

    d. Reduce government spending, reduce taxes, reduce money supply, and reduce interest rates.

NOTES

1 The Laws of Demand and Supply

While macroeconomics focuses on how human behavior affects outcomes in highly aggregated markets (e.g., products, labor), microeconomics focuses on how human behavior affects the conduct of more narrowly defined units, including a single individual, household, or business firm. Basic principles of microeconomic theory are very important on the CPA Exam, but understanding the fundamentals is also important to the business manager. Managers are more likely to be successful if they understand how their actions and various governmental policies or collusive actions (for example, cartels) affect their market and firm. A market is simply a collection of buyers and sellers *meeting or communicating* in order to trade goods or services.

1.1 Demand

1.1.1 Definitions

- **Demand Curve**

    The *demand curve* illustrates the maximum quantity of a good that consumers are willing and able to purchase at each and every price (at any given price), all else being equal. Note that this demand curve is similar to the aggregate demand curve, except that the *x*-axis here is quantity and not real GDP. It does, however, illustrate the same kind of relationship. This demand curve is the microeconomics demand curve for a certain good or product and not the total demand in the economy as a whole.

- **Quantity Demanded**

    Quantity demanded is defined as the quantity of a good (or service) individuals are willing and able to purchase at each and every (given) price, all else being equal.

- **Change in Quantity Demanded (Movement Along the Demand Curve)**

    A *change in quantity demanded* is a change in the amount of a good demanded resulting solely from a change in price. Changes in quantity demanded are shown by *movements along the demand curve* (D). When assumptions regarding price or quantity change, the "demand point" will change along this demand curve. For example, if the price of a product increases, there will be a move up the demand curve.

- **Change in Demand (Movement of the Demand Curve)**

    A *change in demand* is a change in the amount of a good demanded resulting from a change in something other than the price of the good. A change in demand cannot be due to a change in price. A change in demand causes a shift in the demand curve.

1.1.2 Fundamental Law of Demand

The *fundamental law of demand* states that the price of a product (or service) and the quantity demanded of that product (or service) are inversely related. As the price of the product increases (decreases), the quantity demanded decreases (increases). Quantity demanded is inversely related to price for two reasons:

■ **Substitution Effect**

The *substitution effect* refers to the fact consumers tend to purchase more (less) of a good when its price falls (rises) in relation to the price of other goods. The substitution effect exists because people tend to substitute one similar good for another when the price of a good they usually purchase increases. For example, if the price of Pepsi decreases, it will be used as a substitute for Coca-Cola (a similar good).

■ **Income Effect**

The *income effect* means that as prices are lowered with income remaining constant (i.e., as purchasing power or real income increases), people will purchase more or all of the lower-priced products. For example, a decrease in the price of a good increases a consumer's real income even when nominal income remains constant. As a result, the consumer can purchase more of all goods.

1.1.3 Factors That Shift Demand Curves (Factors Other Than Price)

■ **Changes in Wealth**

A positive or negative change in wealth for people will result in a shift in the demand curve. For example, if people become wealthier it may increase (shift) their demand for luxury items (e.g., high-end sports cars).

■ **Changes in the Price of Related Goods (Substitutes and Complements)**

If the price of a similar good (a substitute good) increases, the demand curve will shift to the right (increase) for the original good, now perceived as a bargain. If the price of a good used in conjunction with the original good (referred to as a complementary good) decreases, the demand for the original good will increase (e.g., if personal computer prices fall, demand increases for peripherals, such as monitors and printers).

■ **Changes in Consumer Income**

An increase in consumers' incomes will shift the demand curve to the right (depicted as the shift from D_1 to D_2). Assume, for example, that employment in a local community is primarily retail-based. Because employees' commissions rise during the Christmas season, those employees will have additional consumer income and will demand more goods (demand curve shifts to right).

■ **Changes in Consumer Tastes or Preferences for a Product**

When consumers' preferences (tastes) for a given product increase or decrease, there is a shift in the demand curve. For example, if the clothing industry experiences a revival of the 1960s era, the demand for bell-bottom jeans (retro clothing) will increase. This is also depicted as the shift from D_1 to D_2.

■ **Changes in Consumer Expectations**

If consumers anticipate that there will be a future price increase, immediate demand will increase for that product (at the current, lower price). For example, if commuters expect that the price of a monthly or annual bus pass will increase 10 percent in the near term, there should be a spike in demand for bus passes.

■ **Changes in the Number of Buyers Served by the Market**

An increase in the number of buyers will shift the demand curve to the right. This is evident in a community in which there has been a steady rise in the population of people 65 and older. As the number of senior citizens grows, there will be more buyers of prescription drugs, resulting in a shift in the demand curve to the right.

Change in Quantity Demanded vs. Change in Demand

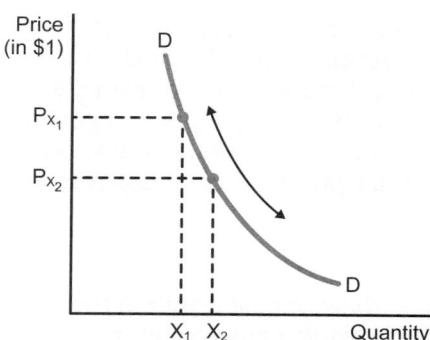

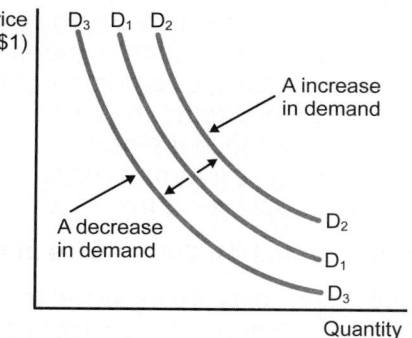

Change in quantity demanded:
Changes in price cause movements along the demand curve.

Change in demand:
Shift in demand curve caused by external influences (other than the price of the good).

1.2 Supply

1.2.1 Definitions

The fundamental law of supply states that price and quantity supplied are positively related (i.e., they have a positive correlation). The higher the price received for a good, the more sellers will produce (higher quantity).

- **Supply Curve**

  The *supply curve* illustrates the maximum quantity of a good that sellers are willing and able to produce at each and every price (at any given price), all else being equal. Note that this supply curve is similar to the aggregate supply curve, except that the *x*-axis here is quantity and not real GDP. It does, however, illustrate the same kind of relationship. This is the microeconomics supply curve for a certain good or product and not the total supply in the economy as a whole.

- **Quantity Supplied**

  Quantity supplied is the amount of a good that producers are willing and able to produce at each and every (given) price, all else being equal.

- **Change in Quantity Supplied (Movement Along the Supply Curve)**

  A *change in quantity* supplied is a change in the amount producers are willing and able to produce resulting solely from a change in price. A change in quantity supplied is represented by a *movement along the supply curve*. When price changes, there will be movement up or down the supply curve to find the new quantity that will be supplied.

- **Change in Supply (Movement of the Supply Curve)**

  A *change in supply* is a change in the amount of a good supplied resulting from a change in something other than the price of the good. A change in supply *cannot be due to a change in price*. A change in supply causes a shift in the supply curve.

1.2.2 Factors That Shift Supply Curves

■ **Changes in Price Expectations of the Supplying Firm**

If prices are expected to decrease, the firm will supply more now at each price level to take advantage of the currently higher prices. For example, Coffee Products Inc. produces gourmet coffee (in cans) sold primarily to the restaurant industry. Given expected favorable crop and market conditions, the company believes that the average price of gourmet coffee will decline by $1 a can in the next six months. Based on this forecast, the company will increase the supply of gourmet coffee now to maximize profitability. This is represented by the shift in the supply curve from S_1 to S_2.

■ **Changes in Production Costs (Price of Inputs)**

When production costs are expected to decline (rise) there will be a shift in the supply curve to the right (left). A decrease in wages paid to workers would cause a shift to the right in the supply curve because for a lower amount of production dollars, the firm is willing to supply more products. This is represented by the shift in the supply curve from S_1 to S_2.

■ **Changes in the Price or Demand for Other Goods**

A decrease (increase) in the demand for another good supplied by a firm would cause the firm to shift its resources and increase (decrease) the supply of its remaining goods. Assume that a firm produces two products, butter and margarine. If there is an industry-wide increase in the price of butter that also lowers butter demand, the firm will shift its production to make more margarine, causing a shift in the supply curve for margarine to the right.

■ **Changes in Subsidies or Taxes**

A decrease in taxes or an increase in subsidies would increase the amount supplied at each price level. In contrast, assume that a local company produces cigarettes and that a tax is levied on the sale of cigarettes in the state. If the company believes that this tax increase will negatively affect the demand for cigarettes, it will decrease the supply of cigarettes, which will shift the supply curve to the left.

■ **Changes in Production Technology**

An improvement in technology would cause a shift to the right of the supply curve. For example, a company has introduced a state-of-the art technology that would significantly increase the finished bottle output for a production day. Under this scenario, the company would increase supply, resulting in a shift in the supply curve to the right.

Change in Quantity Supplied vs. Change in Supply

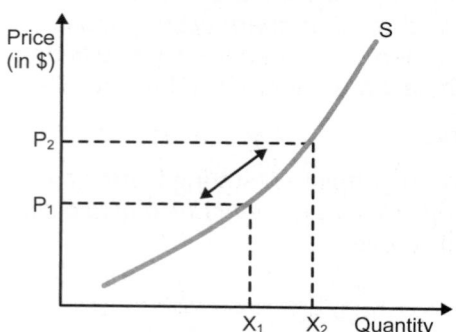

Change in quantity supplied:
Changes in price cause movements
along the supply curve.

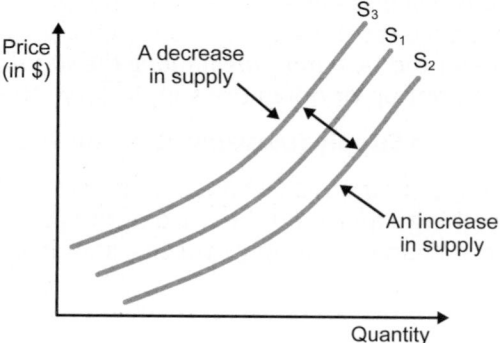

Change in supply:
Shift in supply curve caused by external factors
(other than price).

1.3   Market Equilibrium

A market is in equilibrium when there are no forces acting to change the current price/quantity combination. The market supplies just as much as is demanded, and there is no pressure to change prices.

■ The market's equilibrium price and output (quantity) is the point at which the supply and demand curves intersect. This is sometimes called the market clearing price.

■ The interaction of demand and supply determines equilibrium price.

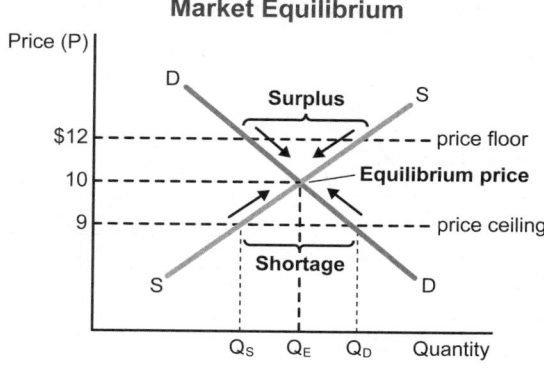

Market Equilibrium

- Price (P) is $10 at equilibrium, and the quantity supplied (Q) is Q_E.
- If the price is set below the equilibrium price, the quantity demanded will exceed the quantity supplied, and a shortage will result.
- If the price is set above the equilibrium price, the quantity demanded will be less than the quantity supplied, and a surplus will result.

1.3.1   Changes in Equilibrium

If supply and/or demand curves shift, the equilibrium price and quantity will change.

■ **Effects of a Change in Demand on Equilibrium**

A rightward shift (increase) in demand from curve D to curve D_1 (below, left) will result in an increase in price (from P to P_1) and an increase in market clearing quantity (from Q to Q_1). Conversely, a leftward shift (decrease) in demand from curve D to curve D_1 (below, right) will result in a decrease in price (from P to P_1) and a decrease in market clearing quantity (from Q to Q_1).

Effects of a Change in Demand on Equilibrium

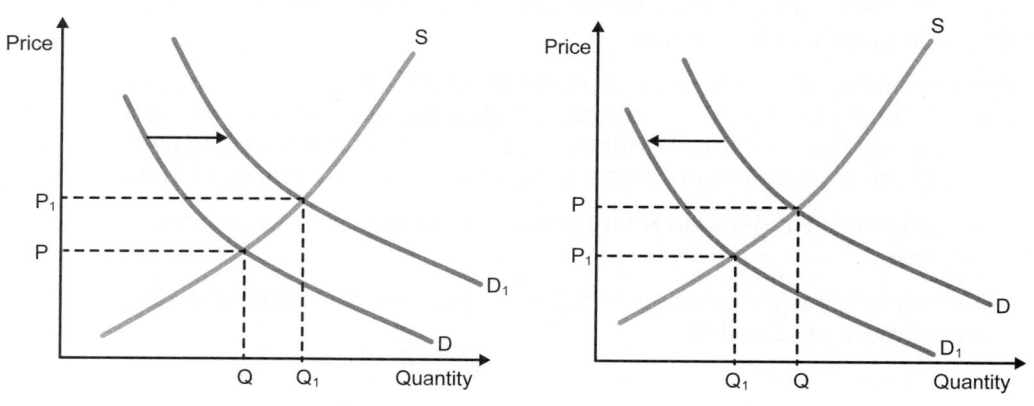

Module 3   B5–35

■ **Effects of a Change in Supply on Equilibrium**

A rightward shift (increase) in supply from curve S to curve S_1 (below, left) will result in a decrease in price (from P to P_1) and an increase in market clearing quantity (from Q to Q_1). Conversely, a leftward shift (decrease) in supply from curve S to curve S_1 (below, right) will result in an increase in price (from P to P_1) and a decrease in market clearing quantity (from Q to Q_1). Market clearing quantity is the equilibrium quantity. Market clearing is the idea that the market will "eventually" be cleared of all excess supply and demand (all surpluses and shortages), assuming that prices are free to change.

Effects of a Change in Supply on Equilibrium

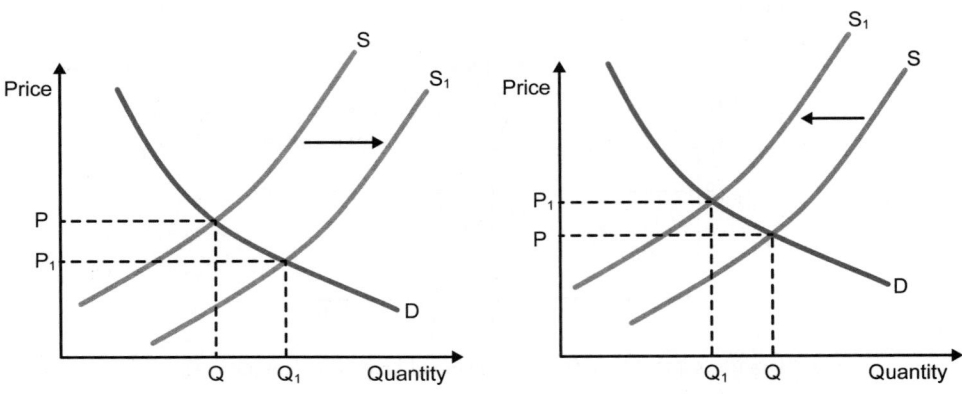

Illustration 1	Effects of Changes in Demand and Supply on Equilibrium

Consider the situation in the northeastern U.S. seaboard states during a recent hurricane. Prior to the hurricane, the market for generators was most likely in a state of equilibrium. However, as a result of the hurricane, residents began to demand more generators, causing a shortage. Suppliers of generators were motivated to increase the price of generators so fewer people wanted to purchase them. The price increase could potentially "clear" the market (both demand and supply), resulting in a state of equilibrium at the higher price.

■ **General Effects of Changes in Demand and Supply on Equilibrium**

• An increase in demand and supply results in an increase in equilibrium quantity, but the effect on price is indeterminate.

It is certain that the effect is an increase of equilibrium quantity (because both an increase in demand and an increase in supply cause quantity to increase); however, the effect on equilibrium price is indeterminate because an increase in demand and supply could cause an increase, decrease, or no change (if equal changes) in equilibrium price.

—If the increase in demand is larger than the increase in supply, the equilibrium price will rise.

—Conversely, if the increase in supply is larger than the increase in demand, the equilibrium price will fall.

- The effect of other complex scenarios such as 1) a decrease in demand and an increase in supply, 2) an increase in demand and a decrease in supply, or 3) a decrease in demand and a decrease in supply can be analyzed in a similar manner. The table below summarizes the effect of all four scenarios discussed above on equilibrium price and quantity. To understand them more fully, you should draw supply and demand diagrams for each case to verify the effects listed.

Change in Demand	Change in Supply	Effect on Equilibrium Quantity	Effect on Equilibrium Price
Increase	Increase	Increase	Indeterminate
Increase	Decrease	Indeterminate	Increase
Decrease	Decrease	Decrease	Indeterminate
Decrease	Increase	Indeterminate	Decrease

1.4 Government Intervention in Market Operations

Sometimes, the government will intervene in a market by mandating a price different from the "market price" (causing either a surplus or a shortage). This most often is accomplished by using *price ceilings* and *price floors*.

1.4.1 Price Ceilings

A *price ceiling* is a maximum price that is established *below* the equilibrium price which causes shortages to develop. Price ceilings cause prices to be artificially low, creating a greater demand than the supply available.

1.4.2 Price Floors

A *price floor* is a minimum price set *above* the equilibrium price which causes surpluses to develop. Price floors are minimum prices established by law, such as minimum wages and agricultural price supports.

Illustration 2   Government Intervention in Market Operations

Price Ceiling: Rent-controlled apartments exist in some places. The price is required by government mandate to remain at a certain level below the market price. The result is an artificially high demand for those apartments. (There may be policy reasons for having rent controls, but the economic result is that there is a shortage of apartments.)

Price Floors: You can always find supporters of increasing the minimum wage in the United States. However, businesses hiring minimum-wage workers counter that they will be able to hire fewer people at the higher rates, thus creating a higher unemployment rate among those workers. Again, there is competition between the social policy and the economic policy in this case.

2   Elasticity of Demand and Supply

Elasticity is a measure of how sensitive the demand for, or the supply of, a product is to a change in price.

2.1   Price Elasticity of Demand

The price elasticity of demand is the percentage change in quantity demanded divided by the percentage change in price.

$$E_p = \text{Price elasticity of demand} = \frac{\%\text{ change in quantity demanded}}{\%\text{ change in price}}$$

■ In a normal demand curve, the price elasticity of demand is usually negative. This negative price elasticity reflects the downward sloping demand curve; as price goes up (positive percentage change), the quantity demanded goes down (negative percentage change). A negative price elasticity coefficient results if the demand curve is normal.

■ Generally, the absolute value of the elasticity coefficient (positive value) is considered when elasticity problems are posed on the examination, because it is presumed that price elasticity is negative for a demand curve.

Example 1	Elasticity of Demand

Facts: Suppose that when the price of a product increases from $100 to $120, quantity demanded decreases from 1,000 units to 900 units.

Required: Using the point method, calculate the price elasticity of demand.

Solution:

$$\frac{\%\text{ change}}{\text{in quantity}} = \frac{900\ [\text{new demand}] - 1{,}000\ [\text{old demand}]}{1{,}000\ [\text{old demand}]} = \frac{-100\ \text{units}}{1{,}000\ \text{units}} = -10\%$$

Divided by:

$$\frac{\%\text{ change}}{\text{in price}} = \frac{\$120\ [\text{new price}] - \$100\ [\text{old price}]}{\$100\ [\text{old price}]} = \frac{\$20}{\$100} = 20\%$$

$$E_p = \text{Price elasticity of demand} = \frac{-10}{20}, \text{or} = -0.5\ [\text{absolute value} = 0.5]$$

2.1.1   Price Inelasticity (Absolute Price Elasticity of Demand < 1.0)

Demand for a good is *price inelastic* if the absolute price elasticity of demand is less than 1.0. The smaller the number the more inelastic the demand for the good.

- If price inelasticity is zero, demand is perfectly inelastic. Note also that perfectly inelastic demand curves are vertical, depicting that the quantity demanded stays the same no matter how the price changes (e.g., in the pharmaceutical industry, the demand for insulin by diabetics).

- The calculation above with a 0.5 value is an example of inelastic demand.

2.1.2 Price Elasticity (Absolute Price Elasticity of Demand > 1.0)

Demand is *price elastic* if the absolute price elasticity of demand is greater than 1.0. When the value is greater than 1.0 (defined as elastic), the greater the number, the more elastic the demand.

2.1.3 Unit Elasticity (Absolute Price Elasticity of Demand = 1.0)

Demand is *unit elastic* if the absolute price elasticity of demand is equal to exactly 1.0. Demand is unit elastic if the percentage change in the quantity demanded caused by a price change equals the percentage change in price.

2.1.4 Factors Affecting Price Elasticity of Demand

- Product demand is more elastic with more substitutes available but is inelastic if few substitutes are available. (Demand for soft drinks and fast-food restaurant meals are price elastic. Purveyors of those products must be careful in raising their prices.)

- The longer the time period, the more product demand becomes elastic because more choices are available.

2.1.5 Price Elasticity Effects on Total Revenue

If we know the price elasticity of demand for a good, we can determine how a change in price will affect a firm's total revenue. Total revenue is simply the price of a good multiplied by the quantity of the good sold.

- **Effects of Price Inelasticity on Total Revenue (Positive Relationship)**

  When demand is price inelastic, an increase in price results in a decrease in quantity demanded that is proportionally *smaller* than the increase in price. As a result, total revenue (equal to price times quantity) will increase.

- **Effects of Price Elasticity on Total Revenue (Negative Relationship)**

  When demand is price elastic, an increase in price results in a decrease in quantity demanded that is proportionally *larger* than the increase in price. As a result, total revenue (equal to price times quantity) will decrease.

- **Effects of Unit Elasticity on Revenue (No Effect)**

  If demand is unit elastic, a change in price will have no effect on total revenue.

- **Summary**

  The table below summarizes the relationship between the price elasticity of demand and total revenue.

Price Elasticity of Demand	Implied Elasticity	Impact of a Price Increase on Total Revenue	Impact of a Price Decrease on Total Revenue
Elastic	Greater than 1	Total revenue decreases	Total revenue increases
Inelastic	Less than 1	Total revenue increases	Total revenue decreases
Unit Elastic	Equal to 1	Total revenue is unchanged	Total revenue is unchanged

2.2   Price Elasticity of Supply

The *price elasticity of supply* is calculated the same way as the price elasticity of demand, except that we now measure the change in quantity supplied.

$$E_p = \text{Price elasticity of supply} = \frac{\%\text{ change in quantity supplied}}{\%\text{ change in price}}$$

Illustration 3   Elasticity of Supply

$$\frac{\%\text{ change}}{\text{in quantity}} = \frac{600\text{ (new supply)} - 500\text{ (old supply)}}{500\text{ (old supply)}} = \frac{100}{500} = 20\%$$

Divided by:

$$\frac{\%\text{ change}}{\text{in price}} = \frac{\$11\text{ (new price)} - \$10\text{ (old price)}}{\$10\text{ (old price)}} = \frac{1}{10} = 10\%$$

$$E_p = \text{Price elasticity of supply} = \frac{20\%}{10\%} = 2.0$$

2.2.1   Price Inelasticity (Supply < 1.0)

Supply is *price inelastic* if the absolute price elasticity of supply is less than 1.0. If supply is perfectly inelastic, the price elasticity of supply equals zero. Perfectly inelastic supply curves are vertical, which reflects that quantity supplied is insensitive to price changes.

2.2.2   Price Elasticity (Supply > 1.0)

Supply is *price elastic* if the absolute price elasticity of supply is greater than 1.0.

2.2.3   Unit Elasticity (Supply = 1.0)

Supply is *unit elastic* if the absolute price elasticity of supply is equal to 1.0.

2.2.4   Factors Affecting Price Elasticity of Supply

- The feasibility of producers storing the product will affect the price elasticity of supply. For example, a product that can be produced and stored until needed may have a high elasticity of supply. When the prices increase, the product is available to sell. Perishables, such as fresh flowers, cannot be stored very long and may have a low elasticity because it is more difficult to increase supply when prices rise.

- The time required to produce and supply the good will affect the price elasticity of supply. For example, longer production time leads to lower price elasticity.

2.3   Cross Elasticity

Cross elasticity of demand (or supply) is the percentage change in the quantity demanded (or supplied) of one good caused by the price change of another good. A producer of butter might want to know the cross elasticity of demand or supply for margarine.

$$C_e = \text{Cross elasticity of demand (supply)}$$

$$= \frac{\% \text{ change in number of units of X demanded (supplied)}}{\% \text{ change in price of Y}}$$

2.3.1 Substitute Goods (Positive Coefficient)

If the coefficient is positive (i.e., the price of Product Y goes up, causing the demand for Product X to go up), the two goods are substitutes (people stop buying the higher-priced goods and begin to buy the substitute). For example, some consumers would consider ground beef and ground turkey to be substitutes.

2.3.2 Complementary Goods (Negative Coefficient)

If the coefficient is negative (i.e., an increase in the price of Product A results in a decrease in quantity demanded for Product B), the commodities are complements. For example, peanut butter and jelly are complementary goods (assuming you like PB&J sandwiches). Printers and ink cartridges are complementary goods.

2.3.3 Unrelated Goods

If the coefficient is zero, the goods are unrelated.

Example 2	Cross Elasticity

Facts: The table below indicates how the price of sirloin steak will affect the quantity of steak sauce demanded (sold) at a local supermarket in a given week.

Required: Calculate the cross elasticity of demand for steak sauce if the price of sirloin steak (per pound) is increased from $6.50 to $7.00 this week (and the supermarket only carries sirloin steak and no hamburger).

Solution:

Price (lb.) Sirloin Steak	Quantity Steak Sauce Sold
$6.00	80
6.50	60
7.00	38
7.50	23

$$C_{\text{Steak Sauce}} = \text{Cross elasticity of demand/supply of steak sauce}$$

$$= \frac{\% \text{ change in quantity demanded of sauce}}{\% \text{ change in price of steak}}$$

% change in quantity demanded of sauce = (38 − 60)/60 = −0.3667

% change in the price of steak = ($7.00 − $6.50)/$6.50 = 0.0769

Cross elasticity of demand/supply of steak sauce = −0.3667/0.0769 = −4.77

Interpretation: The cross elasticity is negative; the goods are complementary.

2.4   Income Elasticity of Demand

The *income elasticity of demand* measures the percentage change in quantity demanded for a product for a given percentage change in income.

$$I_e = \text{Income elasticity of demand (supply)}$$

$$= \frac{\%\text{ change in number of units of X demanded (supplied)}}{\%\text{ change in income}}$$

2.4.1   Positive Income Elasticity (Normal Good)

If the income elasticity of demand is *positive* (e.g., demand increases as income increases), the good is a normal good. A *normal good* is a product whose demand is positively related to income. As income goes up, demand for normal goods increases (e.g., premium foods such as steak and lobster).

2.4.2   Negative Income Elasticity (Inferior Good)

If the income elasticity of demand is *negative* (e.g., demand decreases as income increases), the good is an *inferior good*. An inferior good is a product whose demand is inversely related to income (opposite of a normal good). As income goes up, demand for inferior goods decreases (e.g., generic-labeled vegetables or hamburger).

Example 3   Income Elasticity of Demand

Facts: Assume that the level of family annual income increases from $100,000 to $120,000, resulting in the following change in attendance at professional sports events:

Annual Family Income	Number of Sporting Events Attended
$ 80,000	3
100,000	5
120,000	9
140,000	11

Required: Using the data above, calculate the income elasticity of demand for sporting events attended in a year in which income increases from $100,000 to $120,000.

Solution:

$$I_e = \text{Income elasticity of demand for attendance at sporting events}$$

$$= \frac{\%\text{ change in quantity demanded of sporting events}}{\%\text{ change in income}}$$

% change in quantity demanded = (9 − 5) / 5 = 0.8

% change in income = ($120,000 − $100,000) / $100,000 = 0.2

Income elasticity of demand for sporting events = 0.8 / 0.2 = 4

Interpretation: Income elasticity of demand is positive; this is a normal good.

Question 1

CPA-03667

Which one of the following changes will cause the demand curve for gasoline to shift to the left?

  a.   The price of gasoline increases.
  b.   The supply of gasoline decreases.
  c.   The price of cars increases.
  d.   The price of cars decreases.

Question 2

CPA-05577

A city ordinance that freezes rent prices may cause:

  a.   The demand curve for rental space to fall.
  b.   The supply curve for rental space to rise.
  c.   The quantity demanded of rental space exceeds the quantity supplied.
  d.   The quantity supplied of rental space exceeds the quantity demanded.

Question 3

CPA-05770

Which of the following characteristics would indicate that an item sold would have a high price elasticity of demand?

  a.   The item has many similar substitutes.
  b.   The cost of the item is low compared to the total budget of the purchasers.
  c.   The item is considered a necessity.
  d.   Changes in the price of the item are regulated by governmental agency.

NOTES

1 Market Structures and Pricing

Operating environments influence a firm's strategic plan. Following is a brief discussion of the overall market structures in which firms may operate.

1.1 Perfect (Pure) Competition

In a perfectly competitive market, no individual firm can influence the market price of its product, nor shift the market supply sufficiently to make a good scarcer or more abundant.

1.1.1 Assumptions and Market Conditions

- A large number of suppliers and customers act independently. Firms are small relative to the industry.

- There are no barriers to entry because firms exert no influence over the market or price (thus, goods and services are produced at the lowest cost to the consumer in the long run).

- Very little product differentiation (homogeneous products).

- Firms are price takers. Price is set by the market.

- Firms control only the quantity produced. Each firm can sell as much or as little as it wants at the given market price.

- Demand is perfectly elastic.

- Because there are no barriers to entry, the entry and exit of new firms ensures that economic profits are zero in the long run; thus, firms earn a normal rate of return.

1.1.2 Strategies Under Perfect Competition

Under *perfect competition*, strategic plans may include maintaining the market share and responsiveness of the sales price to market conditions.

1.2 Monopolistic Competition

Monopolistic competition exists when many sellers compete to sell a differentiated product in a market into which the entry of new sellers is possible (e.g., brand-name cosmetic products).

1.2.1 Assumptions and Market Conditions

- There are numerous firms with differentiated products. Firms are small relative to the industry.

- Few barriers to entry exist.

- Firms exert some influence over the price and market through differentiation, but have more control over quantity produced than over price.

- Differentiation results in a highly elastic but downward-sloping demand curve.

- Because there are few barriers to entry under monopolistic competition, in the long run, monopolistically competitive firms will earn zero economic profits. If profits are positive in the short run, more firms will enter and drive down profits to zero. If firm profits are negative in the short run, firms will exit and drive up profits to zero.

1.2.2 Strategies Under Monopolistic Competition

Under *monopolistic competition*, strategic plans may include maintaining the market share (as with pure competition) but also will likely include a plan for enhanced product differentiation and extensive allocation of resources to advertising, marketing, product research, etc.

1.3 Oligopoly

An oligopoly is a market structure in which a few sellers (e.g., the "Big Three" U.S. automotive manufacturers) dominate the sales of a product and entry of new sellers is difficult or impossible.

1.3.1 Assumptions and Market Conditions

- Relatively few firms with differentiated products. Firms are large relative to the industry.

- There are fairly significant barriers to entry (e.g., high capital cost of designing a safety-tested car and building an auto plant).

- Products are differentiated and firms have control over both the quantity produced and the price charged.

- Firms are strongly interdependent.

- Oligopolists face a kinked demand curve because firms match price cuts of competitors but ignore price increases. This causes the demand curves to have different slopes above and below the prevailing price.

- Because of high barriers to entry, economic profits are positive in the long run.

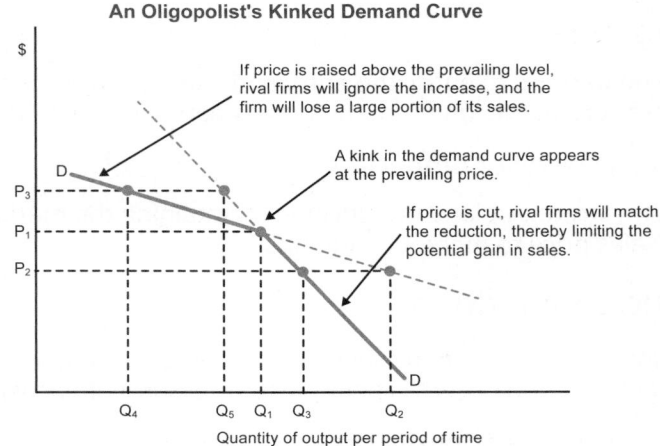

An Oligopolist's Kinked Demand Curve

The matching of price cuts and the ignoring of price increases by rival firms has the effect of making an oligopolist's demand curve highly elastic above the ruling (prevailing) price. This causes the demand curve to be kinked, illustrating that there is not a direct relationship between price and quantity at all points on the demand curve. Firms would be foolish to engage in price cutting because rivals merely match the price reduction (e.g., the airline industry).

1.3.2 Strategies Under Oligopoly

Under an oligopoly, strategic plans focus on market share and call for the proper amount of advertising (to ensure appropriate product differentiation) and ways to properly adapt to price changes or required changes in production volume.

1.4   Monopoly

Monopoly (e.g., the classic utility company, which was a "regulated" monopoly) represents concentration of supply in the hands of a single firm.

1.4.1   Assumptions and Market Characteristics of Monopoly

- There is a single firm with a unique product.

- Insurmountable barriers to market entry exist.

- Monopolies are "price setters," as opposed to firms in perfect competition (which are "price takers"). The firm sets both output and prices (e.g., through patents or regulatory restrictions against competition).

- There are no substitute products (the firm's demand curve is the same as the industry's demand curve). Demand is inelastic.

- Because of insurmountable barriers to entry, economic profits are positive in the long run.

1.4.2   Strategies Under Monopoly

Under a *monopoly*, strategic plans will likely ignore market share and focus on profitability from production levels that maximize profits.

Example 1   Market Structure

Facts: ABC Company ("ABC") and XYZ Company ("XYZ") operate in different industries. ABC is a relatively small firm in the men's clothing industry that focuses on the young men's niche by continuously producing and offering new fashion items to its retail customers. Although ABC has significant control over the quantity of fashion items produced, the pricing of these products to its retail customer base is more a function of the market.

XYZ manufactures hubcaps and wheel covers for the U.S. auto industry. XYZ is one of many competitors in this industry, in which the standard products offered are commodity-like and the prices offered to wholesalers for its products are driven entirely by market forces. XYZ's management continues to be concerned about the expansion of firms competing against XYZ in this industry.

Required:

1. Identify the most likely market structure for ABC and XYZ.

2. Identify one characteristic that is common to both ABC and XYZ.

3. Indicate a market strategy that should be used by ABC and XYZ.

Solution:

1. The market structures for ABC and XYZ are monopolistic competition and perfect competition, respectively.

2. Both ABC and XYZ would seek a zero economic profit over the long run.

3. ABC's market strategy would focus on maintaining its market share primarily through continued enhanced product differentiation. XYZ would also focus on maintaining its market share despite a continued saturation of new firms entering this market. To accomplish this, XYZ needs to ensure that its pricing of its products continuously responds to existing market conditions.

1.5 Market Assumptions and Conditions

- Regardless of the model that represents the industry, the firm will operate best when marginal revenue equals marginal cost (MR = MC).

- Microeconomic theory holds that firms make decisions based on marginal cost and marginal revenue (essentially ignoring fixed or sunk costs).

- The following table summarizes the market assumptions and conditions underlying perfect competition, monopolistic competition, oligopoly, and monopoly.

Summary Table: Market Structure				
Characteristic	Perfect Competition	Monopolistic Competition	Oligopoly	Monopoly
Number of firms in the industry	Many (Highly competitive)	Many (Highly competitive)	Few (Moderately competitive)	One (No competition)
Size of firms relative to industry	Small	Small	Large	100% of industry
Barriers to entry	None (Easy to enter industry)	Low (Easy to enter industry)	High (Difficult to enter industry because of economies of scale)	Insurmountable (No entry is possible)
Differentiation of product	None (All firms sell the same commodity product)	Some (Firms sell slightly different products that are close substitutes)	Various (Firms usually sell differentiated products)	None (One firm sells only one product)
Firm's control over price and quantity	Firm has control over quantity produced only; price is set by the market, firm must accept the market price	Firm has control mostly over quantity produced; price is primarily set by the market	Firm has control over both the quantity produced and the price charged	Firm has control over both price and quantity
Elasticity of demand	Perfectly elastic (Firm sells as much, or as little, as it wants at the given market price)	Highly elastic but downward sloping (Firm can adjust quantity of products sold without affecting the price very much)	Inelastic (Firms face a kinked downward-sloping demand curve)	Inelastic (Firm faces the entire demand curve for the product, which slopes downward)
Long-run profitability	Zero economic profit	Zero economic profit	Positive economic profit	Positive economic profit
Strategies	Maintaining market share and responsiveness of sales price to market conditions	Maintaining market share, enhanced product differentiation, and allocation of resources to advertising, marketing, and product research	Maintaining or enhancing market share, proper spending on advertising, and proper adaptation to price changes and changes in production volume	Ignore market share and focus on profitability from production levels that maximize profits

2   The Economy as a System of Markets

2.1   Production and Demand for Economic Resources

2.1.1   Factors of Production (Resources)

Businesses use resources to make final products. The primary resources from which final products are made consist of *land* (natural resources), *labor* (human capital), and *capital* (nonhuman physical capital accumulated through past investment). These resources are known as *factors of production*. Factors of production are bought and sold in markets just as final goods and services are bought and sold in markets.

▪ To maximize profits, firms need to decide on the optimal levels of inputs to employ.

▪ The price firms must pay for the factors of production is determined by the interaction of supply and demand in the input market.

2.1.2   Types of Inputs

▪ **Complementary Inputs:** Inputs are *complementary inputs* if an increase in the usage of one input results in an increase in the usage of the other input.

Illustration 1   Complementary Inputs

A firm opens two new factories (capital) and will need to hire more employees (human capital).

▪ **Substitute Inputs:** Inputs are *substitute inputs* if an increase in the usage of one input results in a decrease in the usage of the other input.

Illustration 2   Substitute Inputs

A firm that invests in production line automation (capital) may need fewer employees (human capital).

2.1.3   Derived Demand

Derived demand is the demand for factors of production. A firm's demand for inputs is derived from its decision to produce a good or service. Therefore, the demand for inputs is directly related to the demand for the goods and services those inputs produce.

▪ **Demand for Inputs Depends on Demand for Outputs**

The demand for any input depends on the demand for the product the input produces (i.e., the firm's output) and the marginal product of the input itself. (Recall that marginal product, or MP, is the change in total product resulting from a one-unit change in an input.)

• If the demand for a firm's output increases, the demand for the inputs used to produce that output will also increase.

• Similarly, if the marginal product of an input increases, the demand for that input will also increase.

- **Examples of Derived Demand**
  - The demand for labor is directly related to the demand for the goods and services that labor produces.
  - If the demand for medical services increases, the derived demand for doctors, nurses, and medical equipment will also increase.

2.2 The Labor Market

In modern economies, workers sell their services to employers in labor markets, where workers independently offer skills of a given quality to employers who compete for the workers' services. Just as in any other market, the supply of labor and demand for labor determines the price, or wage, of workers. Thus, in the labor market, wages are the price paid for labor. The laws of demand and supply prevail in labor markets as they do in product markets. The lower the wage, the greater the quantity of labor service demanded by employers.

The following graph illustrates equilibrium in the labor market. The equilibrium wage depends on the supply of and demand for labor. The equilibrium wage is found where the demand curve for labor intersects the supply curve for labor.

The Labor Market

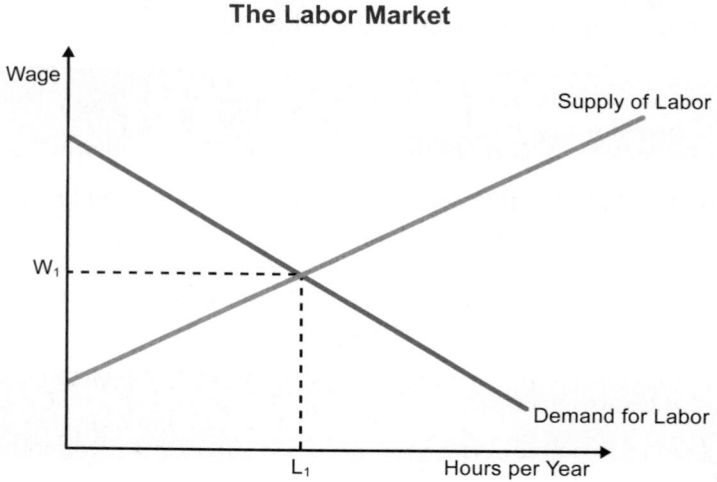

2.2.1 Labor Demand and Supply Under Monopsony

A *monopsony* occurs when there is only one employer in a market. For example, if a town contains a single firm, that firm is known as a monopsonist. Much like a monopolist has market power in the product market, a monopsonist has market power in the input (labor) market. Relative to a purely competitive labor market, a monopsony results in lower wages and lower levels of employment.

2.2.2 Unions and Wages

- **Effect on Unionized Workers**

  By forming a union and acting collectively, workers gain market power much in the same way that a monopoly or cartel has market power. The union may use its market power to bargain collectively for higher wages or restrict the supply of labor. As a result, wages of unionized workers increase.

Effect on Nonunionized Workers

Unions may also affect the wages of nonunionized workers. Suppose there are two worker sectors in an economy, one unionized and the other not. Because employment falls in the unionized sector, displaced workers may seek employment in the nonunion sector. As a result, wages in the nonunion sector may fall as the supply of labor in that sector increases. Thus, while wages rise in the unionized sector, they may fall in the sector that is not unionized.

2.2.3   Minimum Wage Laws

The use of minimum wage laws to increase the wages of low-skilled labor is controversial. If the minimum wage is set above the equilibrium wage, an excess supply of labor will result. In other words, if the minimum wage is above the equilibrium wage, the result is unemployment.

Furthermore, the imposition of a minimum wage increases the income of those workers who have a job, but it decreases the income of workers who find themselves unemployed as a result of the imposition of the minimum wage. The effect of a minimum wage is illustrated in the following graph.

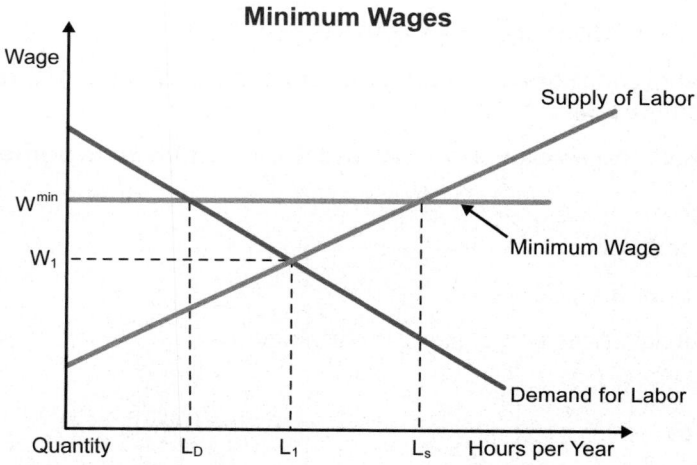

Minimum Wages

When the minimum wage is set at W^{min}, the quantity of labor demanded decreases from L_1 to L_D and the quantity of labor supplied increases from L_1 to L_s. As a result, the minimum wage causes unemployment, or an excess supply of labor, of $L_s - L_D$.

3   Factors That Influence Strategy

When determining the effects of the market on business strategy, a look at the overall macro-environment in which the firm operates is essential because it can significantly assist the company in developing and choosing the best strategy to meet its goals.

3.1   General Types of Factors That Influence Strategy

Firms use SWOT (Strengths, Weaknesses, Opportunities, and Threats) analysis to assist in developing their appropriate strategic plans. Any strategy must consider these factors in its development.

3.1.1   Internal Factors (Strengths and Weaknesses)

Factors internal to the organization that affect strategy are sources of strengths and weaknesses and include:

- Innovation of product lines
- Competence of management
- Core competencies (outstanding skills that are better than those of the competitors)
- Influence of high-level managers
- Capital improvements
- Leadership in research and development
- Cohesiveness of the values of the organization
- Marketing effectiveness
- Effectiveness of communication
- Clarity of the strategic mission

3.1.2   External Factors (Opportunities and Threats)

Factors external to the organization are sources of opportunities in the market and threats to the firm's ability to continue with its strategic plan.

- **Factors That Affect the Overall Industry and Competitive Environment of the Industry**
  - The economy
  - Regulations and laws
  - Demographics of the population
  - Technological advances and existing technology
  - Social values
  - Political issues
- **Factors That Affect the Competitive Environment of the Firm**
  - Barriers to market entry
  - Market competitiveness
  - Existence of substitute products
  - Bargaining power of the customers
  - Bargaining power of the suppliers

Illustration 3   SWOT Analysis

Diverse Company (DC) is an international firm that produces bottles and pumps for its three distinct business segments, including food, healthcare, and fragrance. The following SWOT analysis was prepared by an equity analyst to further understand the factors which affect the company's business strategy.

Strengths **(S):** Diverse Company has developed strong business relationships in many of its international markets, which has resulted in steadily increasing market shares for its product offerings. The company has been successful in implementing production efficiencies, which has led to improved operating margins.

Weaknesses **(W):** Despite its diversification, the company has significant exposure to the European market, which has been in a recession. The company's net earnings are also subject to foreign-exchange risk (exposure) as DC has operations in 12 countries.

Opportunities **(O):** There has been increased demand for personal healthcare products in emerging market countries. Although DC currently has limited product sales to emerging markets, management considers this a significant opportunity to expand its global market share.

Threats **(T):** While barriers to entry in the company's product markets are moderate, DC will have to increase its already significant investment in R&D to maintain its customer base. These additional operating costs, along with expected further compliance and regulatory costs, may erode the company's impressive operating margins.

Question 1   CPA-06642

Which of the following is an assumption in a perfectly competitive financial market?

    a. No single trader or traders can have a significant impact on market prices.

    b. Some traders can impact market prices more than others.

    c. Trading prices vary based on supply only.

    d. Information about borrowing/lending activities is only available to those willing to pay market prices.

Question 2   CPA-03493

Under an oligopoly structure, strategic plans focus on:

    a. Profitability from production levels that maximize profits.

    b. Maintaining the market share and being responsive to market conditions related to sales price.

    c. Maintaining the market share and planning for enhanced product differentiation.

    d. Maintaining the market share, ensuring product differentiation, and adapting to changes in price and/or production volume.

NOTES

1   Porter's Five Forces

The following five forces identified by Michael Porter of Harvard University have a significant effect on the competitive environment and profitability of the firm.

1.1   Barriers to Entry

The firm faces the threat of new firms entering the market in which it operates.

- **Types of Barriers to Entry**

  Often, rival firms face barriers to entry in the form of government regulation, supplier access, high up-front capital requirements, preexisting customer preferences and loyalties, economies of scale, learning-curve issues, and other up-front competitive cost disadvantages, including patents, trade barriers, and other restrictions.

- **When New Companies Will Attempt to Enter**

  New companies will attempt to enter the competition when barriers to entry are low, potential high profits exist in the market, and the risk of retaliation by other firms is low. If the industry as a whole is earning a profit, other firms will desire to enter the market. Unless barriers to entry exist, firms will enter until profits fall to a competitive level. It is also possible that the simple threat of new entrants will scare existing firms into keeping their prices at competitive levels.

1.2   Market Competitiveness (Intensity of Competition)

The existence of competition from rival firms is often the most significant of the five forces of competition.

- **Ability of Rival Firms to Respond to Change**

  If a firm is in competition with other firms that are all able to respond to changes in various components affecting business (e.g., regulation, input costs, labor issues, technology changes, consumer desires for improved quality and service, etc.), the firm faces a strong competitive force.

- **Advertising of Rival Firms**

  If rival firms are likely to spend large amounts of money on advertising aimed at changing customer preferences and creating loyalty, the impact of this competitive factor is increased.

- **Research and Development of Rival Firms**

  When rival firms spend large amounts of money on research and development to improve their products or create innovations in technology, the effect of this competitive factor is increased.

■ **Alliances of Rival Firms and Suppliers**

Often, rival firms focus on developing strong alliances with suppliers. This could affect the firm's ability to obtain its inputs to the production process at advantageous prices and, thus, reduce its competitive advantage. When alliances are created, the impact of this competitive factor is increased.

■ **Other Factors Increasing Competition**

Competition becomes an even stronger force affecting the firm when: the market is not growing fast (in contrast, in fast-growing markets, competitors are usually able to sustain profitability without having to take market share from their rivals); several equal-sized firms exist in the market; customers do not have strong brand preferences; the cost of exiting the market exceeds the cost of continuing to operate; some firms profit from making certain moves to increase market share; and the various firms employ different types of strategic plans.

1.3 Existence of Substitute Products

If the firm faces heavy competition from substitute products, the ability of a firm to sustain profits is significantly affected by the maximum amount that buyers are willing to pay for a product. This is especially true if the substitutes are readily available to consumers, have equal performance, and are priced at or below the price of the firm's product. The effect is further intensified when the costs of the buyer switching to the substitute product are low. If few substitutes exist, buyers have little choice of products and may be willing to pay a higher price for the products that are available. If close substitutes exist, buyers may have a limit on the maximum price that they are willing to pay, and this has a direct effect on the profits of the firm.

Illustration 1   Existence of Substitute Products

Both Chevrolet and Ford have strong market positions in the U.S. pickup truck market. If Ford is able to lower its model prices due to increased efficiencies in its production process, and consumers view their pickup truck models as comparable, there is a legitimate threat that Chevrolet could lose market share because switching costs are virtually nonexistent.

1.4 Bargaining Power of the Customers

If buyers are in the position to bargain with suppliers on the conditions of service, price, and quality, they are a strong force in the competitive market in which the firm operates. For example, Wal-Mart Stores Inc. is a retailer that is known to have a strong position when it comes to bargaining with its suppliers.

Buyers may be quite price sensitive and change products solely based on price, or they may have such brand loyalty and strong preferences that they will stay with a product regardless of price (oftentimes depending on the elasticity of demand).

■ **Large Volume of a Firm's Business (High Buyer Concentration)**

If one group of customers makes up a large volume of the firm's business, the bargaining power (negotiating power) of the customer will significantly affect the competitive environment of the firm, and the strategy of firms should focus on pleasing this group of customers.

■ **Availability of Information**

The more information that is available to the buyer, the more the buyer will be able to compare and contrast features of a product and choose one over the other.

■ **Buyer's Low Cost of Switching Products**

If the costs of switching from one product to another are low, the impact on the competitive environment from buyers is increased. This result is intensified if the firm cannot easily change production without incurring high costs to begin producing another product.

■ **High Number of Alternative Suppliers**

When many suppliers exist to serve the customers, the bargaining power of the buyer is increased.

1.5   Bargaining Power of the Suppliers

When the bargaining power of the suppliers of inputs to the production process is high, suppliers can take profits away from a firm simply by increasing the cost of the inputs to the firm's production process.

■ **Firm Is Unable to Change Suppliers**

If the firm is unable to use different suppliers or cannot change its inputs (i.e., no substitutes are available), changes in the operations of the supplier, and thus the price of the input, will affect the profitability of firms, especially when those input costs are a significant part of the overall product cost.

■ **Reputation of Supplier and Demand for Its Goods**

If the reputation of the supplier (e.g., the quality of its product) is excellent and crucial to the success of the firm's product, and the demand for its goods from other firms is high, the firm could be placed in a difficult situation, especially if the firm is not a large client of the supplier or if strategic alliances have been formed between the supplier and a competitor.

2   Types of Competitive Strategies

Building a successful competitive strategy requires being able to attain some sort of competitive advantage while still holding customer loyalty and having value for the customer.

2.1   Competitive Advantage in General

The overall competitive advantage of a firm is determined by the value the firm offers to its customers minus the cost of creating that value. Firms that seek to achieve competitive advantage with respect to products will choose from two basic forms of advantage.

2.1.1   Cost Leadership Advantage

The *cost leadership advantage* stems from the fact that the buyers of the product are better off because the firm has been able to produce and sell its product for less than its rivals. If the total costs of the firm are less than those of rival firms, the firm has a competitive market advantage. This advantage may be used by the firm in one of two ways:

■ **Build Market Share**

If the firm lowers the price of its product below the price of its competitors, it may be able to gain market share by securing a larger part of the market as its customer base while still maintaining the profits that are required.

■ **Match the Price of Rivals**

If a firm enjoys a low-cost competitive advantage, it will be able to match the price of its rivals and, because it has overall lower total costs, beat the profitability of its rivals.

2.1.2   Differentiation Advantage (Offering Advantage)

The *differentiation advantage* (product differentiation) stems from the fact that buyers are better off because the customer perceives the firm's product to be superior in some way to those of its rivals. Therefore, they are willing to pay a higher price for its uniqueness.

All parts of the buying decision are affected by the perceived value of the product (e.g., higher quality, timeliness of delivery, superior service, wide range of goods, fewer risks, performance measures, etc.). After the product has been differentiated, the firm must always be sure to remain profitable and recoup the cost of the "premium" included with the product. This advantage may be used by the firm in one of two ways:

- **Build Market Share**

   The firm may attempt to build market share by pricing its product below what it would charge to recoup the premium with a standard number of buyers and try to recover its costs because it captures more than an average share of the market.

- **Increase Price**

   The firm may increase the price of its product to the point at which it exactly offsets the value the customer perceives in the product.

2.2   Five Basic Types of Competitive Strategies

There are five types of competitive strategies that firms can employ:

1. Cost leadership focused on a broad range of buyers.
2. Cost leadership focused on a narrow range (niche) of buyers.
3. Differentiation focused on a broad range of buyers.
4. Differentiation focused on a narrow range (niche) of buyers.
5. Best cost provider.

2.3   Cost Leadership Strategies

Organizations may choose to achieve their organizational missions by selling their product or service for less than any other participant in the marketplace. Cost leaders undermine the profitability of their competitors as a means of achieving overwhelming market share.

Illustration 2   Cost Leadership Strategies

Toys-Only Company is an online toy retailer that sells toys to the mass consumer market. In order to increase its market share and to compete with the "brick and mortar" stores, the company's strategy has been focused on offering a complete line of toys at the lowest prices. This cost leadership strategy has been successful for Toys-Only given that it sells commodity-like products to the general U.S. toy retail market.

- **When Cost Leadership Strategies Work Well**

  Cost leadership strategies work well in markets in which buyers have large amounts of bargaining power and are able to switch between competitive products without incurring significant cost.

  Such strategies also are successful in markets with heavy price competition and where firms (especially new entry firms) can influence buyers to switch to their product and then increase their customer base simply by cutting the price of the product for a period.

- **When Cost Leadership Strategies Fail**

  If firms focus too much on cutting costs of the current process, they may overlook technological advances that could help lower costs (especially those that rivals have latched onto) or overlook the fact that consumers may want improvements to the product or may not care as much about the existence of a lower price in the desired product.

2.4 Differentiation Strategies (Product Differentiation)

Organizations may choose to achieve their organizational missions by creating the perception that their product is better or has a unique quality that differentiates it from competitors in the marketplace. Firms that successfully differentiate their products are able to command higher prices.

Illustration 3   Differentiation Strategies

Quality Bathroom Inc. sells high-end bathtubs and accessories to a regional market. Because the company offers unique features, designs, and materials, its bathtubs sell at premium prices. This strategy has been successful for the company given its ability to clearly offer value-added products (at higher prices) to its retail customer market.

- **When Differentiation Strategies Work Well**

  Differentiation strategies work well when customers are able to see value in a product, when the product appeals to different people for different reasons, and when the firms that are competing in the market choose different features to differentiate their products.

- **When Differentiation Strategies Fail**

  When a firm attempts to differentiate in an area without properly assessing the requirements of the consumer for desired features and preferences, or without creating value for the consumer, a differentiation strategy can fail.

  Further, firms that focus too much on one area (or the wrong area) may end up creating a product whose value does not exceed the higher price that must be charged for the feature.

  If a firm is in a market in which customers do not care about differentiation, will not pay extra for unique features, and are happy with paying a lower price for a more generic product, a differentiation strategy can fail.

2.5 Best Cost Strategies

The best cost strategy combines the cost leadership strategy with the differentiation strategy to give customers higher value for their purchase price (i.e., a high-quality product at a reasonable price). If a firm is able to achieve the lowest cost among its closest competitors while matching them on features desired by consumers, it will succeed.

Illustration 4	Best Cost Strategies

Wal-Mart Stores Inc. is a mass merchandiser that uses a best cost strategy to increase its market share. Because of sheer economies of scale (e.g., purchasing, distribution), the company is able to offer the lowest prices on its vast product lines, which include many name brands as well as its own generic brands. Wal-Mart's business strategy continues to be focused on offering customers superior products at the overall lowest prices.

- **When Best Cost Strategies Work Well**

  Best cost strategies work well when generic products are not acceptable to the varied needs and preferences of the buyers, but the buyers are still sensitive to the value that they are receiving for the money they are spending and the overall price they are paying.

- **When Best Cost Strategies Fail**

  Because the best cost strategist plays the "middle," it faces the risk of losing customers to other firms that are using cost leadership strategies or those that are specifically focused on differentiation.

2.6 Focus/Niche Strategies

Firms with cost leadership or differentiation strategies may choose to focus their chosen strategy on a select, small group of consumers, or a niche. Rather than having to address the needs and preferences of a broad range of consumers, these firms are able to focus on market niches where consumers have specialized needs and preferences.

Illustration 5	Focus/Niche Strategies

All-Star Baseball Gloves Inc. makes premium baseball gloves for the collegiate/professional niche market, which includes collegiate baseball, minor league baseball, and major league teams. The company has been successful because it uses the highest-quality leather materials and includes special features in each of the player position baseball gloves it manufactures and sells to the collegiate/professional niche market.

- **When Focus/Niche Strategies Work Well**

  The focus/niche strategy works well, provided the niche has a large enough demand to create a profit for the firm, the firm has the proper resources to adequately serve the needs of the niche group, and when few firms are focusing in an area where others cannot compete in price or are not addressing a particular feature.

- **When Focus/Niche Strategies Fail**

  When other firms see that the niche has been successful for those serving it, they will attempt to enter the market as competitors and take away some of the sales of the firm, likely reducing the firm's profits and its competitive advantage. The firm also faces a risk that those consumers in the current niche may find that they actually prefer the features of products that the overall market desires. If the firm is not easily responsive to change (flexible) for whatever reason, the focus/niche strategies can fail.

3   Value Chain Analysis

Value chain analysis is a *strategic tool* that assists a firm in determining how important its value is (as perceived by buyers) with respect to the market in which the firm operates. Managers must determine the flow of activities undertaken by the organization to produce a service or product and critique the value added to the customer by each link in the value chain. Once the firm is aware of how its product is perceived, value chain analysis is invaluable in assessing the ability of the firm to obtain a competitive advantage.

3.1   Approach of Value Chain Analysis

Firms must assess every part of the value chain to allow them to provide their customers with maximum value; they must determine the parts of the value chain that will provide them with the largest competitive advantage. Three major forms of analysis are performed.

3.1.1   Internal Costs Analysis

In order to determine the internal value-creating ability of a firm, the sources of profit and costs of the internal activities within the firm must be analyzed.

3.1.2   Internal Differentiation Analysis

The firm may analyze its ability to create value through differentiation (e.g., what are the sources of differentiation and what are the related costs?) when the customer perceives that the firm's product is superior to those of its rivals.

3.1.3   Vertical Linkage Analysis

Analyzing the vertical linkage of the firm means understanding the activities of the suppliers and buyers of the product (i.e., all links from the sources of the raw materials through the recycling and disposal of the product after use) and determining where value can be created external to the firm's operations.

3.2   Steps in Value Chain Analysis

There are four general steps in value chain analysis:

1. **Identify Value Activities**

    Organizations must *identify value activities* performed as part of their business. Value activities are generally those processes that are involved with *designing, preparing, manufacturing,* and *delivering* a good or service.

2. **Identify Cost Drivers Associated With Each Activity**

    Cost drivers represent factors that increase total cost. Identification of cost drivers assists the organization in determining those areas in which it has a competitive advantage. Organizations might also identify those areas in which outsourcing is valuable.

3. **Develop a Competitive Advantage by Reducing Cost or Adding Value**

    *   **Identify Competitive Advantage:** Firms with cost leadership strategies will look at cost-saving opportunities, and firms with differentiation strategies will look at opportunities for innovation.

    *   **Identify Opportunities for Added Value:** Product innovation for those organizations that depend on differentiation and reduced prices for those organizations that are focused on cost leadership will be the drivers of value chain analysis.

- **Identify Opportunities for Reduced Cost**: Analysis of the cost drivers should show where the organization is not competitive. Elimination or outsourcing of those items for which the organization is not cost competitive is generally proposed from this step in value chain analysis.

4. **Exploit Linkages Among Activities in the Value Chain**

   Analysis of the value chain may also show synergies or connections that can be used to create greater efficiencies or greater value. Each step of the value chain should produce some value.

   In some cases, that value not only benefits the specific activity in the chain, but also benefits other activities. For example, in-house customer service departments handle customer complaints in an efficient and courteous manner that establishes organizational responsiveness to the customer and creates loyalty. In-house customer service staff also can be alert for patterns of complaints that may influence product design.

Illustration 6   Value Chain Analysis

Boat Motors Inc. (BMI) is a low-cost manufacturer of motor boat engines for recreational fishing boats. Company management has prepared the following value chain analysis blueprint for the upcoming operating year.

BMI *Value Activities* include state-of-the-art design, production of low-cost efficient engines, and superior delivery and installation of boat engines.

BMI's primary *cost drivers* are focused on using high-quality raw materials, outsourcing certain production labor costs, lowering assembly and repair costs, and minimizing delivery costs.

BMI's *competitive advantage* will focus on further lowering product costs by expanding its outsourcing of direct and indirect labor, and designing a more efficient assembly production process. Given the company's extensive trucking network, BMI will attempt to maximize its economies of scale in trucking while reducing redundancies in delivery routes.

BMI will continue to strive to *improve the linkage* of its key production functions, including basic motor part production/purchases, motor design, motor assembly, and motor installation. In order to effectively reduce costs to the customer end-user, each production function will have a goal of lowering costs by a minimum of 5 percent in the upcoming year. The head of operations will accomplish this production goal by initiating monthly meetings between the production-function department heads and holding the managers more accountable for their goal achievement by restructuring their compensation packages.

3.3   Global Competitive Advantage and Value Chain Analysis

In addition to Michael Porter's look at the "five forces" that affect the profits and competitive environment of an industry, Porter focused on the competitive forces that exist globally by studying the ability of a nation to attain and sustain worldwide competitive advantage. When the various parts of the value chain exist in different parts of the world, this may pose problems of costs of transportation and lack of control and communication, which can negatively affect the overall customer value.

Porter identified four major factors that impact global competitive advantage:

1. **Conditions of the Factors of Production**

   If the nation has a strong set of factors of production (e.g., a skilled labor force) that are required in a given industry, it will fare better with regard to global competitive advantage.

2. **Conditions of Domestic Demand**

   If the nation's domestic demand for the product is high, the nation will fare better with regard to global competitive advantage.

3. **Related and Supporting Industries**

   If suppliers of material inputs exist within the nation, it may help the nation fare better with regard to global competitive advantage (unless the costs are prohibitively high). If other rival domestic firms that are competitive in the international environment exist, the nation's competitive advantage is increased.

4. **Firm Strategy, Structure, and Rivalry**

   The practices of a nation with respect to how companies are managed and organized, along with the laws of the nation that regulate the formation of companies and the intensity of rivalry among competing firms, all influence the ability of the nation to attain and sustain competitive advantage.

Question 1	CPA-04830

Under which of the following conditions is the supplier most able to influence or control buyers?

    a. When the supplier's products are not differentiated.

    b. When the supplier does not face the threat of substitute products.

    c. When the industry is controlled by a large number of companies.

    d. When the purchasing industry is an important customer to the supplying industry.

Question 2	CPA-03609

When do differentiation strategies fail?

    a. The firm's product appeals to different people for different reasons.

    b. The value of the firm's differentiation premium does not exceed its cost.

    c. Customers are able to see (or perceive) a value in the firm's product compared with products of other firms.

    d. The various rival firms have chosen different features on which to differentiate their products.

NOTES

1   Globalization

Globalization is defined as the distribution of industrial and service activities across an increasing number of nations. Globalization produces deeper integration of the world's individual national economies and makes them more interdependent. Reduced barriers to trade have created opportunities to conduct operations in multiple countries or conduct import/export operations within the context of a traditional domestic operation. Entities that conduct business outside the country in which they are organized are frequently referred to as *multinational corporations* (MNC).

Globalization is often measured by world trade as a percentage of GDP—the greater the percentage, the greater the degree of globalization.

1.1   Factors That Drive Globalization

- **Improvements in Transportation:** Increased efficiencies in transportation enhance the competitive status of importers in domestic markets.

- **Technological Advancements:** Knowledge-based products (such as technical support for software, etc.) eliminate the importance of location.

- **Deregulation of International Financial Markets:** Elimination of capital controls increases the options for direct foreign investment, although political and legal limitations are still an inherent risk of international commerce.

- **Organizational/Operational Options for International Business:** When conducting business internationally, an entity must decide whether to centralize or decentralize certain business operations or functions. The availability of human labor, raw materials, or transportation channels for a business region can affect the type of production, distribution, and marketing activities performed by a region.

2   Motivations for International Business Operations

Entities are encouraged to look beyond the political borders in which they were organized to maximize shareholder value. Several economic theories support international trade as a means of achieving improved shareholder value.

2.1   Comparative Advantage

Specialization in the production and trade of specific products produces a *comparative advantage* in relation to *trading* partners. Companies and countries use comparative advantage to maximize the value of their efforts and resources.

Illustration 1   Comparative Advantage

The island nation of Bermuda produces no gasoline or vehicles, yet its roadways are filled with vehicles of all types. The country specializes in tourism and uses the money it earns from its visitors to buy (import) vehicles and petroleum products. The country maximizes its resources by specializing in tourism and buying transportation resources elsewhere.

2.2 Imperfect Markets

Resource markets are often deemed to be *imperfect*. The ability to trade freely between markets is often limited by the physical immobility of the resource or regulatory barriers. In order to retrieve more resources, companies must trade outside their borders.

Illustration 2   Imperfect Markets

Hi-Tech Components Inc. requires special electronic components to build its state-of-the art antenna systems. Although the company purchases 50 percent of these components domestically, Hi-Tech has historically purchased 35 percent and 15 percent of the remaining specialized components from Asia and Europe, respectively.

Over the past six months, Hi-Tech has faced a significant increase in prices for these international components due to production shortages, higher shipping costs, and political tensions with several of the exporting countries. In order to remedy this risk, Hi-Tech is currently seeking other international trading partners for these specialized components.

2.3 Product Cycle

Product manufacture or delivery is subject to a definable cycle, starting with the initial development of the product to meet needs in the domestic markets. Product cycle theory predicts that domestic success will result in domestic competition, encouraging the export of products or services to meet foreign demand and to maintain efficient use of capacity. Foreign success will in turn promote foreign competition. The entity is then motivated to establish a business outside its boundaries to differentiate itself more effectively and to compete with foreign business rivals.

3   Methods of Conducting International Business Operations

Multinational operations are structured in any number of ways. The following terms help define different methods of organization:

- **International Trade:** Companies (and nations) conduct international trade by exporting/importing products or services.

- **Licensing:** Entities that provide the right to use processes or technologies in exchange for a fee are engaged in licensing activities.

Illustration 3   Licensing

Wireless Inc., a U.S. corporation, obligates itself to establishing and maintaining cellular telephone systems in Mexico in exchange for a licensing fee to use its technology.

- **Franchising:** Franchisors are entities whose marketing service or delivery strategy provides training and related service delivery resources in exchange for a fee.

Illustration 4   Franchising

Flip-a-Burger Inc., a U.S. corporation, obligates itself to providing training and the use of unique company logos to businesses that operate in Peru.

- **Joint Ventures:** *Joint ventures* take advantage of comparative advantage of one or both of the participants in marketing or delivering a product.

Illustration 5   Joint Ventures

Engulf & Devour Food Products, a U.S. corporation, teams with Chez Brule, a French concern, to distribute U.S. confections throughout France using Chez Brule's distribution network.

- **Direct Foreign Investment (DFI):** An entity may establish international operations by purchasing a foreign company as a subsidiary or by starting a subsidiary operation within the borders of a foreign country.
- **Global Sourcing:** *Global sourcing* is the synchronization of all levels of product manufacturing, including research and development, production, and marketing, on an international basis. Global sourcing is frequently implemented through a range of organizational and business arrangements (e.g., import/export operations, licensing, franchises, joint ventures).

4   Relevant Factors of Globalization

Factors relevant to assessing the effect of globalization on a company include:

- **Political and Legal Influences:** Conducting business internationally may involve certain political risks that could be potentially disruptive to an entity. The legal requirements for conducting business in a given foreign country should also be assessed.
- **Potential for Asset Expropriation:** Nations may expropriate (take) assets from the international companies that own the assets. Assessing the risk of political intervention is integral to business planning and financial reporting.
- **Taxes and Tariffs:** Governments may attempt to control economic activity through taxes and tariffs. Mitigation of this risk is typically handled through transfer pricing.

■ **Limitations on Asset Ownership or Joint Venture Participation:** Governments may limit the amount of ownership or entirely restrict any ownership of business ventures within their borders, thereby limiting joint ventures and direct investments.

■ **Content or Value Added Limits:** Sometimes referred to as sourcing requirements, governments may provide tariff reductions to companies whose imports include specified percentages of material and labor in their products.

■ **Foreign Trade Zones:** Governments may establish trade zones in which tariffs are waived until the goods leave the zone. The creation of foreign trade zones affects the government's control of imports and the location of import facilities.

■ **Economic Systems**

  ● **Centrally Planned Economies:** Some economies (such as China) are centrally planned. Factors of production (capital, land, etc.) are owned by the government and subject to restriction.

  ● **Market Economies:** Most industrialized economies (such as the United States and Japan) are market economies. The factors of production are owned by individuals.

  ● **Conglomerates:** Establishment of integrated conglomerates (e.g., the Japanese keiretsu or the Korean chaebol) creates self-sustaining entities that could not exist in the United States (fully integrated financing, manufacturing, and supplying organizations would likely violate antitrust laws).

■ **Culture:** Different *cultures* affect international business. *Culture* can be defined as the shared values and attitudes of a group. The cultures of nations or regions typically involve the following issues.

  ● **Individualism vs. Collectivism:** Some cultures (such as that of the United States) place a high value on individualism, and others (often Asian) are more likely to place a higher value on the collective.

  ● **Uncertainty Avoidance:** Certain cultures have difficulty dealing with *uncertainty*. The United States typically has a guarded ability to accept uncertainty, while Asian and South American cultures may be highly averse to dealing with uncertainty.

  ● **Short-Term vs. Long-Term Orientation:** Certain cultures are traditional, adapting more slowly to change, while others are more focused on immediate gratification. The United States tends to have a short-term orientation, and many Asian cultures have a longer-term focus.

  ● **Acceptance of Leadership Hierarchy:** Cultures have varying degrees of acceptance of vast differences between leadership and the rank and file. Some accept large differences in power and others anticipate greater levels of equality. The United States has a balanced view on this issue, although former European monarchies may be more accepting of wide differences in power. Less-developed former colonial counterparts in Asia and South America are often more distrustful of wide dispersions of power.

  ● **Technology and Infrastructure:** International business may require factoring in wide differences in:

    —Communications systems

    —Transportation systems

    —Power and water sources

    —Training of staff

    —Differences in accounting practices

5   Inherent Risks of International Business Operations

The risks associated with conducting international business operations are generally categorized by the following:

5.1   Exchange Rate Fluctuation

Exchange rate or currency risks (and mitigation techniques) are generally divided into three categories:

- Transaction risk
- Economic risk
- Translation risk

5.2   Foreign Economies

An operation within a *foreign economy* carries the risk of functioning within the general health or weakness of a particular economy. Domestic economies may be booming while international economies may be suffering and acting as a drag on a multinational company's overall performance. The state of the foreign economy in which the company operates is highly significant to risk evaluation.

5.2.1   Foreign Demand

A multinational corporation exporting to a foreign country is vitally concerned with demand within that country. Demand is directly affected by the health of the economy of the country in which it operates.

- Weakening demand may cause the foreign government to implement tariffs or other regulatory measures that reduce foreign penetration.

- Measures to reduce foreign penetration may require either curtailment of foreign operations or export of goods produced by the multinational inside the foreign country instead of selling within the foreign country.

5.2.2   Interest Rates

- Higher interest rates in the foreign country are indicators of slower economic growth and reduced demand.

- Lower interest rates in the foreign country may be indicative of increased growth and demand.

5.2.3   Inflation

- Higher local (economy) inflation reduces purchasing power, making imported goods more expensive and reducing local demand.

- Lower local (economy) inflation increases the purchasing power for imported goods, resulting in higher local demand.

5.2.4   Exchange Rates

- Weak local currency reduces demand for imported goods.
- Strong local currency increases demand for imported goods.

5.3 Political Risk

Political risks represent noneconomic events or environmental conditions that are potentially disruptive to financial operations. Ultimately, political climates or actions can disrupt cash flows. Although expropriation of productive resources represents the most extreme political risk, other features of political risk also must be considered, including:

- Bureaucracies and related inefficiencies or barriers to trade
- Corruption
- The host government's attitude toward foreign firms
- The attitude of consumers toward foreign firms
- Inconvertibility of foreign currency
- War

Question 1	CPA-08364

Each of the following is an effect from opening markets to foreign investment, *except*:

- **a.** An increase in the correlation of emerging stock markets with world markets.
- **b.** A change in the volatility of emerging stock market returns.
- **c.** A decrease in local firms' cost of capital.
- **d.** A decrease in investment growth rates.

Question 2	CPA-08365

Global companies that deal with the political and financial risks of conducting business in a particular foreign location face which of the following types of risk?

- **a.** Country risk
- **b.** Principal risk
- **c.** Interest rate risk
- **d.** Commodity price risk

1 Business Combinations

An entity can expand its operations by entering into a business combination. The four primary types of combinations include horizontal, vertical, circular, and diagonal combinations. Transactions include mergers, acquisitions, consolidations, tender offers, purchases of assets, and management acquisitions.

1.1 Types of Business Combinations

1.1.1 Horizontal Combination

A horizontal combination occurs when companies in the same industry that produce the same goods or provide the same services join together under single management/leadership. Both horizontal and vertical combinations (described next) offer benefits, such as reduced competition, economies of scale leading to reduced costs, expertise at various levels of production, minimized overproduction, and maximized profits.

Illustration 1	Horizontal Combination

Heinz and Kraft Foods, both in the business of selling processed food to consumers, merged into one company—the Kraft Heinz Company—in 2015. The expectation at the time of the merger was that the new company would become one of the largest food and beverage companies in both the United States and the world. The new company projected annual revenues of approximately $28 billion, along with an expected $1.5 billion in cost savings.

1.1.2 Vertical Combination

A vertical combination involves the combination of companies at different stages of the production process. The companies can be from the same industry or multiple industries. A vertical combination can assure the supply of raw materials (backward integration) or provide a stable market for products sold (forward integration).

Illustration 2	Vertical Combination

In 1996, Time Warner Inc. merged with Turner Broadcasting to create a massive, worldwide entertainment conglomerate. This merger provided Time Warner access to many of the basic cable television channels (and historical films) that were owned previously by Turner. Federal Trade Commission concerns about the merger's effect on competition in the cable industry kept the deal in limbo for months.

1.1.3 Circular Combination

A circular combination occurs when different business units with relatively remote connections come together under single management. The relationship could come from using similar distribution or advertising channels, or requiring similar production processes. Having one management group over the combined units reduces overall administrative and other operational costs.

Illustration 3   Circular Combination

Pharma Inc. is a leading company in the U.S. pharmaceuticals industry. In order to expand its business within its current consumer market and to take advantage of potential cost reductions, it acquires Letson Watson—a company specializing in building residential real estate for adult communities 55 and older.

1.1.4 Diagonal Combination

A diagonal combination occurs when a company that engages in an activity integrates with another company that provides ancillary support for that primary activity. The purpose is to ensure that the ancillary support is delivered in a timely and effective manner, which is crucial to the mission of the primary activity and business.

Illustration 4   Diagonal Combination

Landbright Farms breeds organic livestock and sells the meat to high-end grocery stores. Fresh Meats Inc. transports Landbright's products to market in refrigerated trucks. If Landbright were to merge with Fresh Meats, this would be an example of a diagonal combination.

1.2   Transactions

1.2.1   Merger

In a merger, two (or more) entities combine to form a single new corporation, with the stocks of all merging companies surrendered and replaced with new stock in the name of the new company. Mergers often involve the combination of like-sized companies.

Illustration 5   Merger

In 2016, Dell Inc. and EMC Corp. will merge to become Dell Technologies. The deal is expected to be worth close to $60 billion and will bring together two powerful technology franchises with strong capabilities in storage, servers, PCs, hybrid cloud, converged infrastructure, mobile, and security.

1.2.2 Acquisition

The acquisition of one company by another involves no new company. Only the acquirer remains after the acquisition. The acquired firm, which is generally smaller than the acquiring firm, may retain its legal structure and name, or it may be subsumed by the acquirer and cease to exist.

Illustration 6	Acquisition

In 1984, the U.S. Department of Justice instructed AT&T to divest its regional telephone companies. Twenty-two years later, AT&T reacquired Bell South in a deal worth more than $85 billion dollars. The company retained the name AT&T.

1.2.3 Tender Offer

In a tender offer, a company makes an offer directly to shareholders to buy the outstanding shares of another company at a specified price. The offer may be in the form of cash or securities of the acquiring corporation (stocks, warrants, debt issuances). Shareholders of the target company have the option of accepting or rejecting the offer.

Illustration 7	Tender Offer

Biltmore Inc. offers $13 per share to buy the stock directly from the shareholders of Alexander Co. (the target company). Alexander stock is currently selling at $11 per share, making the Biltmore offer very attractive to the target's shareholders. Assuming that the majority of shareholders agree to the terms, Biltmore will provide $13 per share. This is an example of a tender offer.

1.2.4 Purchase of Assets

A purchase of assets transaction occurs when a portion (or all) of the selling company's assets are purchased by the acquiring company, which may result in the dissolution of the selling company. As with a tender offer, shareholder approval must be obtained.

Illustration 8	Purchase of Assets

Lox Industries enters into an asset purchase agreement with Bright Star Inc. to purchase approximately 80 percent of the latter's buildings and equipment. As part of the agreement, Lox agrees to assume the liabilities associated with mortgages outstanding on the buildings and capital leases on the equipment purchased.

2 Divestiture

A divestiture involves the partial or full disposal of a component or business unit of a company. Divestiture transactions include sell-offs, spin-offs, and equity carve-outs.

2.1 Sell-off

A sell-off is an outright sale of a subsidiary because, for example, the subsidiary's core competencies do not align with the overall company's or because there is a lack of synergy between the company and its subsidiary. Legal action stemming from anticompetitive or antitrust practices may also require a sell-off.

Illustration 9   Sell-off

Management and shareholders of BeckCo Industries think that its ownership of Blended Ltd. is causing the overall entity to be undervalued from a market perspective. As a result, the company sells the assets and liabilities of Blended to another entity in the hopes that investors will react favorably to the sale, which will lead to an increase in the stock price.

2.2 Spin-off

A spin-off creates a new, independent company by separating a subsidiary business from a parent company. A spin-off can be completed by distributing stock in the new entity as a stock dividend to existing shareholders or by offering shareholders stock in the new company in exchange for their stock in the parent company. Spin-offs typically occur when a unit is less profitable and/or unrelated to the core parent business. The assumption is that the operations of the unit after a spin-off are expected to have more value than they did as part of the larger operation.

Illustration 10   Spin-off

In 1994, Eli Lilly and Company (a large, U.S.-based global pharmaceutical company) shifted its focus purely to pharmaceuticals and other similar businesses. As a result, Lilly spun off its medical devices division, which went public later that year under the name Guidant. Guidant focused on cardiovascular medical products, such as artificial pacemakers, stents, and cardioverter-defibrillators.

2.3 Equity Carve-out

An equity carve-out occurs when a subsidiary is made public through an initial public offering (IPO), thereby creating a new publicly listed company. Unlike a spin-off, in which no cash comes to the parent company, the sale of shares in the new company generates cash for the parent as well as providing the parent with a controlling interest in the subsidiary. The hope is this strategy will unlock the independent value of the subsidiary previously contained within the merged entity.

Illustration 11   Equity Carve-out

Teco Industries is a multinational company with several divisions specializing in unique product lines. Fearing that Teco is not focusing enough on its core business, management would like to divest one of the company's units. Management is interested in both a cash infusion from the divestiture and maintaining some degree of control. The equity carve-out is the most likely choice because it would provide cash while allowing management to retain a controlling interest.

Question 1   CPA-03934

Which of the following situations best illustrates a potential horizontal merger between Companies X and Y?

- **a.** Companies X and Y are competitors in the same industry.
- **b.** Company X supplies raw materials to the production processes for Company Y.
- **c.** Company X is a textile manufacturer, whereas Company Y operates as a wholesaler for Company X products.
- **d.** Company X operates in the financial services industry, whereas Company Y operates in the scientific research and development industry.

Question 2   CPA-03935

Gerard Incorporated is a leader in the home health services industry with operations primarily in the western United States. Gerard owns 100 percent of Brighton Greens, a company that operates nursing care facilities in the same region. Wanting to devote all of its corporate resources to home health care and hoping to generate cash, Gerard should look to divest its operation under which of the following mechanisms?

- **a.** Sell-off
- **b.** Spin-off
- **c.** Tender offer
- **d.** Equity carve-out

NOTES

Process Management and Information Technology

Module

NOTES

1 Introduction to Business Process Management

1.1 Approaches

Business process management (BPM) is a management approach that seeks to coordinate the functions of an organization toward an ultimate goal of continuous improvement in customer satisfaction. Customers may be internal or external to an organization. Process management seeks effectiveness and efficiency through promotion of innovation, flexibility, and integration with technology.

Business process management attempts to improve processes continuously. By focusing on processes, an organization becomes more nimble and responsive than hierarchical organizations that are managed by function.

1.2 Activities

Business process management activities can be grouped into five categories: design, modeling, execution, monitoring, and optimization.

- **Design:** The design phase involves the identification of existing processes and the conceptual design of how processes should function once they have been improved.

- **Modeling:** Modeling introduces variables to the conceptual design for what-if analysis.

- **Execution:** Design changes are implemented and key indicators of success are developed.

- **Monitoring:** Information is gathered and tracked and compared with expected performance.

- **Optimization:** Using the monitoring data and the original design, the process manager continues to refine the process.

1.3 Techniques

The general technique or approach to process management is as follows:

- **Define:** The original process is defined as a baseline for current process functioning or process improvement.

- **Measure:** The indicators that will show a change to the process (e.g., reduced time, increased customer contacts, etc.) are determined.

- **Analyze:** Various simulations or models are used to determine the targeted or optimal improvement.

- **Improve:** The improvement is selected and implemented.

- **Control:** Dashboards and other measurement reports are used to monitor the improvement in real time and apply the data to the model for improvement.

1.4   Plan, Do, Check, Act (PDCA)

Process management also has been commonly referred to as plan, do, check, act (PDCA).

- **Plan:** Design the planned process improvement.
- **Do:** Implement the process improvement.
- **Check:** Monitor the process improvement.
- **Act:** Continuously commit to the process and reassess the degree of improvement.

Illustration 1   PDCA

Brakes-Only Company (BOC) manufactures car brakes for each of the big three U.S. automakers. Over the past several years there has been an increase in the return of new brake systems by these automakers due primarily to the failure to meet all required design specifications.

In order to reverse this negative trend, the head of production at BOC has implemented the PDCA approach at the company. In the first quarter of the operating year, he designed a **plan** to ensure that all brake specifications are carefully reviewed prior to the production and shipment processes as well as to improve the communication among internal departments through enhanced internal reporting.

During the second quarter, the production manager implemented the process **(do)** at the company.

At the end of each the next two operating quarters, the production manager monitored **(check)** the effectiveness of the process by comparing year-to-date brake returns to the prior year.

This process continued the following operating year with BOC achieving a 10 percent reduction in brake system returns over an 18-month period. To further reduce the number of brake system returns, the production manager hired a full-time quality control manager. As part of his ongoing responsibilities, the quality control manager will continue to monitor **(act)** the effectiveness of the process and recommend any technological improvements to the production manager.

1.5   Measures

Measures or process metrics can be financial or nonfinancial and should correlate directly to the managed process. The measures are compared with expectations to monitor progress. Examples of measures include:

- **Gross Revenue:** *Gross revenue* is an appropriate measure for sales or other measures of revenue volume in sales-driven organizations.
- **Customer Contacts:** *Customer contacts* can be used in sales-driven organizations.
- **Customer Satisfaction:** Organizations using relationship marketing techniques may consider *customer satisfaction* measures.
- **Operational Statistics:** Manufacturing operations might use *operational statistics* such as throughput times, delivery times, or other logistical measures to determine the efficiency of a process.

1.6 Benefits

The benefits of a studied and systematic approach to process management allow the company to monitor the degree to which process improvements have been achieved. The benefits often mentioned for process management are:

- **Efficiency:** Fewer resources are used to accomplish organizational objectives.

- **Effectiveness:** Objectives are accomplished with greater predictability.

- **Agility:** Responses to change are faster and more reliable.

2 Shared Services, Outsourcing, and Offshore Operations

2.1 Shared Services

Shared services refers to seeking out redundant services, combining them, and then sharing those services within a group or organization. The distinguishing feature of shared services is that they are shared within an organization or group of affiliates.

Illustration 2   Shared Services

Financial Group Inc. is a financial services company with three distinct businesses including accounting, tax, and consulting. Currently, each division operates as a separate company with its own human resources, payroll, and legal departments. In order to more effectively manage the organization and reduce costs, the new CEO implements a shared services plan whereby all human resources, payroll, and legal department services will be consolidated into one centralized function. The CEO thinks that this shared services approach will eliminate redundant back-office functions and will reduce annual operating costs by $750,000.

Consolidation of redundant services creates efficiency but might also result in the following issues:

- **Service Flow Disruption:** The consolidation of work to a single location can create waste in the transition, rework, and duplication as well as increases in the time it takes to deliver a service.

- **Failure Demand:** The demand for a shared service caused by a failure to do something or to do something right for a customer is called failure demand. Failure demand results when a task must be performed for a second time because it was incorrectly performed the first time.

2.2 Outsourcing

Outsourcing is defined as the contracting of services to an external provider. Examples might include a payroll service or even a call center to provide support or back-office services for a fee. A contractual relationship exists between the business and its service provider.

Outsourcing can provide for efficiencies, but there are also risks. Those risks include:

- **Quality Risk:** An outsourced product or service might be defective. Suppliers might provide substandard products or services.

- **Quality of Service:** Poorly designed service agreements may impede the quality of service.

- **Productivity:** Real productivity may be reduced even though service provider employees are paid less.

- **Staff Turnover:** Experienced and valued staff whose functions have been outsourced may leave the organization.

- **Language Skills:** Outsourced services may go offshore. Language barriers may reduce the quality of service.

- **Security:** Security of information with a third party might be compromised.

- **Qualifications of Outsourcers:** Credentials of service providers may be flawed. Offshore degrees may not include the same level of training as domestic degrees.

- **Labor Insecurity:** Labor insecurity increases when jobs move to an external service provider or, as a result of globalization, out of the country.

2.3   Offshore Operations

Offshore operations relate to outsourcing of services or business functions to an external party in a different country. A computer manufacturer in the United States, for example, might have its call center in India. The most common types of offshore outsourcing are:

- Information technology

- Business process (call centers, accounting operations, tax compliance)

- Software research and development (software development)

- Knowledge process (processes requiring advanced knowledge and specialized skill sets, such as reading x-rays, etc.)

Business risks of offshore outsourcing are generally the same as outsourcing, but with greater emphasis on the lack of controls associated with proximity, as well as potential language issues.

3   Selecting and Implementing Improvement Initiatives

3.1   Selecting Improvement Initiatives

Rational and irrational methods may be used to select improvement initiatives.

3.1.1   Irrational

Irrational methods are intuitive and emotional. They lack structure and systematic evaluation. The irrational methods are based on fashion, fad, or trend. They may result from an immediate need for cost reduction, and stem from a very short-term viewpoint.

3.1.2   Rational

Rational assessments are structured and systematic and involve the following:

- **Strategic Gap Analysis:** External (environmental) assessments and internal (organizational) assessments performed to create a strategic gap analysis.

- **Review Competitive Priorities:** Review of price, quality, or other considerations.

- **Review Production Objectives:** Review of performance requirements.

- **Choose Improvement Program:** Decide how to proceed for improvement.

3.2   Implementing Improvement Initiatives

There are several crucial features of successful implementation activities.

- **Internal Leadership:** Senior management must provide direction and commit resources to the implementation.

- **Inspections:** Ongoing implementation must be monitored and measured.

- **Executive Support:** Executive management must be visibly supportive of the initiative.

- **Internal Process Ownership:** The individuals most deeply involved with process management must be committed to the need for process improvement and have the resources to carry it out.

4   Business Process Reengineering

Business process reengineering (BPR) refers to techniques to help organizations rethink how work is done to dramatically improve customer satisfaction and service, cut costs of operations, and enhance competitiveness. Development of sophisticated information technology systems and networks have driven many reengineering efforts.

Business process reengineering is not synonymous with business process management. Business process management seeks incremental change, and business process reengineering seeks radical changes.

4.1   Fresh Start

The basic premise of business process reengineering is the idea that management will "wipe the slate clean" and reassess how business is done from the ground up. Reengineering uses benchmarking and best practices to evaluate success.

4.2   Current Status

Reengineering is not as popular as it was when introduced in the mid-1990s. The technique has been criticized for what some believe was overaggressive downsizing. In addition, the programs have not produced the benefits that were originally anticipated.

Illustration 3   Business Process Reengineering

Decorations Inc. manufactures holiday ornaments and decorative lawn figurines. Over the past several years, rising manufacturing costs have significantly eroded the company's operating profit margins. Currently, the automated manufacturing process and manual labor process represent 30 percent and 70 percent of the total production costs, respectively.

In order to combat this negative operating trend, company management hired an outside consulting firm that will consider both business process management and business process reengineering.

(continued)

(continued)

After performing due diligence, the consultants recommended a business process management plan that involved cutting 10 percent of the production workforce over the next three years and replacing 15 percent of the manual production process with newly designed machines. After severance and machine upgrade costs, it is estimated that this business process management program will reduce annual operating costs by $1,000,000 in three years.

The consulting firm also completed a business process reengineering study (plan) that would eliminate 80 percent of the current production workforce over the next three years and fully automate the production process, with the exception of the quality control function and packaging supervision. Although the up-front costs to implement the business process reengineering program are more significant than the BPM, the BPR plan is expected to reduce annual operating costs by $2,500,000 in three years.

The consulting firm submits both plans to company management, who must decide whether incremental change or radical change is more appropriate given the up-front costs to execute the plans and the expected annual cost savings associated with each plan.

5   Management Philosophies and Techniques for Performance Improvement

Performance improvement philosophies and techniques seek to provide the highest-quality goods and services in the most efficient and effective manner possible.

5.1   Just-in-Time (JIT)

Just-in-time management anticipates achievement of efficiency by scheduling the deployment of resources just-in-time to meet customer or production requirements.

5.1.1   Inventory Does Not Add Value

The underlying concept of JIT is that *inventory does not add value*. The maintenance of inventory on-hand produces wasteful costs.

5.1.2   Benefits

The *benefits* of JIT implementation include:

- Synchronization of production scheduling with demand.
- Arrival of supplies at regular intervals throughout the production day.
- Improved coordination and team approach with suppliers.
- More efficient flow of goods between warehouses and production.
- Reduced setup time.
- Greater efficiency in the use of employees with multiple skills.

5.2   Total Quality Management

Total quality management (TQM) represents an organizational commitment to customer-focused performance that emphasizes both quality and continuous improvement. Total quality management identifies seven critical factors, outlined below.

5.2.1   Customer Focus

The TQM organization is characterized by the recognition that each function of the corporation exists to satisfy the customer. Customers are identified as both external customers and internal customers.

- **External Customers:** The external customer is the ultimate recipient or consumer of an organization's product or service.

- **Internal Customers:** Each link in the value chain (and within the value chain) represents an internal customer.

Illustration 4   TQM
Supplies inventory managers provide services to internal customers, such as production managers. A TQM organization will demand that the supplies inventory manager value the satisfaction of production managers in the timely delivery of supplies adequate to meet production requirements.

5.2.2   Continuous Improvement

Quality is not viewed as an achievement in a TQM organization. The organization constantly strives to improve its product and processes. Quality is not just the goal; it is embedded in the process.

5.2.3   Workforce Involvement

TQM organizations are characterized by team approaches and worker input to process development and improvement. Small groups of workers that use team approaches to process improvement are called *quality circles.*

5.2.4   Top Management Support

Top management must actively describe and demonstrate support for the quality mission of the organization. Management can communicate support by meaningful delegation of authority to quality circles and involvement of suppliers.

5.2.5   Objective Measures

Measures of quality must be unambiguous, clearly communicated, and consistently reported.

5.2.6   Timely Recognition

Acknowledgement of TQM achievements (in terms of compensation and general recognition) must occur to encourage the ongoing involvement of the workforce.

5.2.7   Ongoing Training

TQM training should occur on a recurring basis to ensure workforce understanding and involvement.

5.3   Quality Audits and Gap Analysis

5.3.1   Quality Audits

Quality audits are a technique used as part of the strategic positioning function in which management assesses the quality practices of the organization. Quality audits produce the following:

- Analysis that identifies strengths and weaknesses.

- A strategic quality improvement plan that identifies the improvement steps that will produce the greatest return to the organization in the short term and long term.

5.3.2   Gap Analysis

Gap analysis determines the gap, or difference, between industry best practices and the current practices of the organization. Gap analysis produces the following:

- Target areas for improvement.

- A common objective database from which to develop strategic quality improvement.

5.4   Lean Manufacturing

Lean manufacturing or lean production requires the use of only those resources required to meet the requirements of customers. It seeks to invest resources only in value-added activities.

5.4.1   Waste Reduction

The focus of *lean* is on waste reduction and efficiency. The concept of preserving value while expending only the effort necessary is not uncommon and has a long history in business and economics. Kaizen- and activity-based management initiatives are waste-reduction methodologies that use empirical data to measure and promote efficiencies.

5.4.2   Continuous Improvement (Kaizen)

"Kaizen" refers to *continuous improvement* efforts that improve the efficiency and effectiveness of organizations through greater operational control.

Kaizen occurs at the manufacturing stage, where the ongoing search for cost reductions takes the form of analysis of production processes to ensure that resource usage stays within target costs.

5.4.3   Process Improvements/Activity-Based Management

Activity-based costing (ABC) and activity-based management (ABM) are highly compatible with process improvements and total quality management (TQM).

- **Cost Identification**

  Activity-based costing and management systems highlight the costs of activities. The availability of cost data by activity makes the identification of costs of quality and value-added activities more obvious.

- **Implementation**

  Organizations with ABC and ABM programs are more likely to have the information they need to implement a TQM program. Process improvement results from a detailed process management program (sometimes referred to as an activity-based management system, or ABM).

5.5   Demand Flow

Demand flow manages resources using customer demand as the basis for resource allocation. Demand flow contrasts with resource allocations based on sales forecasts or master scheduling.

5.5.1   Relationship to Just-in-Time

Demand flow is akin to *just-in-time* processes that focus on the efficient coordination of demand for goods in production with the supply of goods in production. Kanban systems, which visually coordinate demand requirements on the manufacturing floor with suppliers, are used to coordinate demand flow.

5.5.2   Relationship to Lean

Demand flow is designed to maximize efficiencies and reduce waste. One-piece flow manufacturing environments, in which components move progressively from production function to production function, benefit from demand flow ideas.

5.6   Theory of Constraints (TOC)

Theory of constraints states that organizations are impeded from achieving objectives by the existence of one or more constraints. The organization or project must be consistently operated in a manner that either works around or leverages the constraint.

5.6.1   Constraints

A *constraint* is anything that impedes the accomplishment of an objective. Constraints for purposes of TOC are limited in total and, sometimes, organizations may face only one constraint.

- **Internal Constraints**

  Internal constraints are evident when the market demands more than the system can produce.

  - Equipment may be inefficient or used inefficiently.

  - People may lack the necessary skills or mind-set necessary to produce required efficiencies.

  - Policies may prevent the efficient use of resources.

- **External Constraints**

  External constraints exist when the system produces more than the market requires.

5.6.2   Five Steps

TOC generally involves five steps:

1. **Identification of the Constraint:** Use of process charts or interviews results in identification of the constraint that produces suboptimal performance.

2. **Exploitation of the Constraint:** Planning around the constraint uses capacity that is potentially wasted by making or selling the wrong products, improper procedures in scheduling, etc.

3. **Subordinate Everything Else to the Above Decisions:** Management directs its efforts to improving the performance of the constraint.

4. **Elevate the Constraint:** Add capacity to overcome the constraint.

5. **Return to the First Step:** Reexamine the process to optimize the results. Remain cognizant that inertia can be a constraint.

5.6.3   Buffer

The concept of *buffers* is used throughout TOC. Managers add buffers before and after each constraint to ensure that enough resources to accommodate the constraint exist. Buffers, therefore, eliminate the effect of the constraint on work flow.

Illustration 5   Internal Constraints

Advanced Printing Co. purchased several state-of-the art printing presses in the fourth quarter of last year. Despite this significant capital investment, the company's year-to-date production output and costs have not changed. Company management attributes this production trend to several internal constraints, including a lack of sufficient training for employees operating the new presses and the fact that the machines were used inefficiently during the production process.

In order to improve the new machines' productivity and generate a positive return on capital investment, management will begin scheduling periodic training sessions for operating them and will hire an outside consultant to determine the most effective way to maximize productivity. Once the study is completed, each machine line supervisor will meet with the outside consulting firm to go over the study's results, share ways to further improve productivity, and provide an effective way to monitor employees' ongoing production performance. Each Saturday after a weekly production run is completed, every machine line supervisor will be required to submit a weekly production report to the production manager, explaining any negative cost and production variances greater than 2 percent from the plan. Management believes that these buffers will eliminate the internal constraints identified from the current year's operating results.

5.7   Six Sigma

Six Sigma uses rigorous metrics in the evaluation of goal achievement. Six Sigma is a continuous quality-improvement program that requires specialized training. The program expands on the *Plan-Do-Check-Act* model of process management described earlier, and outlines methodologies to improve current processes and develop new processes.

5.7.1   Existing Product and Business Process Improvements (DMAIC)

- **Define the Problem:** Based on customer comments, failed project goals, or other issues, determine the existence of a problem.

- **Measure Key Aspects of the Current Process:** Collect relevant data.

- **Analyze Data:** Examine the relationships between data elements.

- **Improve or Optimize Current Processes:** Use models and data to determine how the process can be optimized.

- **Control:** Develop a statistical control process to monitor results.

5.7.2 New Product or Business Process Development (DMADV)

- **Define Design Goals:** Design goals that are consistent with customer demands.

- **Measure CTQ (Critical to Quality Issues):** Analyze the value chain to determine the features that provide value to the customer and the production capabilities that are available.

- **Analyze Design Alternatives:** Develop different methodologies to produce the new product.

- **Design Optimization:** Use modeling techniques to determine optimization of the proposed process.

- **Verify the Design:** Implement and test the plan.

Question 1	CPA-03895

The benefits of a just-in-time system for raw materials usually include:

    a. Elimination of non-value adding operations.

    b. Increase in the number of suppliers, thereby ensuring competitive bidding.

    c. Maximization of the standard delivery quantity, thereby lessening the paperwork for each delivery.

    d. Decrease in the number of deliveries required to maintain production.

NOTES

1 Overview

The role of information technology (IT) in an organization has evolved. The early focus was on automating transactions and reducing costs. Decision support systems (DSS) improved managers' decision making. Historically, IT was viewed as a support function for an organization. Today, IT is a strategic driver, making the IT governance function even more crucial and elevating it to the executive and board levels.

IT governance is a formal structure for how organizations align IT and business strategies, ensuring that companies stay on track to accomplish their strategies and goals, and implementing performance measures for IT.

An IT governance framework should answer key questions, such as how is the IT department functioning, what key metrics does management need, and what does IT return to the business.

2 Vision and Strategy

Technology and an entity's objectives are interconnected. The design of an information technology department's strategy has traditionally supported that of the overall organization. Technology decisions should be an input to the strategic process, defining innovations and helping to increase revenue.

Illustration 1   IT Strategy and Corporate Strategy

Bell, a computer manufacturer, wants to expand to global markets. IT strongly influences how management can accomplish this. Without the investment in technology for e-commerce, customer service, inventory management, market research, etc., this strategy would not be viable. IT should be viewed as a critical component of strategy development, and not simply a back-office support function.

Illustration 2   Technology-Driven Strategy

A brokerage firm was able to leverage faster computers and grid computing (large number of connected computers) to develop faster responses to customers who make inquiries online. Rather than have customers enter questions and data online and wait several hours to receive a response by e-mail, the response could be generated within seconds. This product innovation was extremely popular with customers.

3   Definition of IT Governance

IT governance is about how leadership accomplishes the delivery of mission-critical business capability using IT strategies, goals, and objectives. IT governance is concerned with the strategic alignment between the goals and objectives of the business and the utilization of its IT resources to effectively achieve the desired results. IT governance is the duty of executive management and the board of directors. IT governance is crucial to the governance of the entire organization. IT governance comprises leadership, organizational structures, policies and processes, IT strategy, and IT objectives. IT governance establishes chains of responsibility, authority, and communication. It also establishes measurement, policy, standards, and control mechanisms to enable people to carry out their roles and responsibilities.

3.1   Five Areas of Focus

According to the IT Governance Institute, there are five areas of focus, which follow.

3.1.1 Strategic Alignment

Linking business and IT so they work well together. Typically, the starting point is the planning process, and true alignment can occur only when the corporate side of the business communicates effectively with line-of-business leaders and IT leaders about costs, reporting, and effects.

3.1.2 Value Delivery

Making sure that the IT department does what is necessary to deliver the benefits promised at the beginning of a project or investment. The best way to get a handle on everything is by developing a process to ensure that certain functions are accelerated when the value proposition is growing, and eliminating functions when the value decreases.

3.1.3 Resource Management

One way to manage resources more effectively is to organize staff more efficiently—for example, by skills rather than by line of business. This allows organizations to deploy employees to various lines of business on a demand basis.

3.1.4 Risk Management

Instituting a formal risk framework that puts some rigor around how IT measures, accepts, and manages risk, as well as reporting on what IT is managing in terms of risk.

3.1.5 Performance Measures

Putting structure around measuring business performance. One popular method involves instituting an IT balanced scorecard, which examines where IT makes a contribution in terms of achieving business goals, being a responsible user of resources, and developing people. This method uses both qualitative and quantitative measures to find those answers.

4   IT Strategy

IT strategy should intersect with the overall strategies of the corporation.

4.1   Corporate-Level Strategy

Corporate-level strategy is developed by senior management. It encompasses new business opportunities, the closing of old business units, and the allocation of resources among departments.

4.2 Business-Level Strategy

Business-level strategy is found in organizations that have autonomous departments with the need to develop their own strategies. Business strategy should function within the broader aims of the corporate strategy. This level of strategy is typically not found in small businesses.

4.3 Functional-Level Strategy

Functional-level strategy involves establishing strategies for marketing, manufacturing, IT, and finance. An effective strategy at the functional level improves the entity's ability to execute its business-level and corporate-level strategies.

Illustration 3   Interaction of IT and Corporate Strategy

Development of e-commerce or a well-designed website as an IT strategy should improve the market share and performance of the overall entity.

---

5 Principles of Technology-Driven Strategy Development

1. Technology is a core input to the development of strategy, just as much as customers, markets, and competitors.

2. Because of the speed with which technology changes, strategy development must be a continual process, rather than something that is revisited every three to five years.

3. Innovative emerging business opportunities must be managed separately and differently from core businesses.

4. Technology has the power to change long-held business assumptions; managers and executives must be open to this.

5. Technology must be managed from two perspectives:

   - The ability of technology to create innovation in existing businesses; and

   - The ability of emerging technologies to create new markets/products.

6. The focus should be on customer priorities, internal efficiencies, and ways that IT can be maximized for the advantage of the entity.

6 Organization of IT Governance Structure

The IT governance structure within an organization must encompass the tone at the top; key stakeholders, including the steering committees; governance objectives and policies; and IT strategies and oversight.

6.1 The Tone at the Top

Technology plays a crucial role in enabling the *flow of information* in an organization. The selection of specific technologies to support an organization typically is a reflection of the:

1. entity's approach to risk management and its degree of sophistication;

2. types of events affecting the entity;

3. entity's overall information technology architecture; and

4. degree of centralization of supporting technology.

6.2   Stakeholders or Participants in Business Process Design

The participants in business process design form the project team, which typically includes the following parties:

6.2.1   Management

One of the most effective ways to generate systems development support is to send a clear signal from top management that user involvement is important. Top management's most important roles are providing support and encouragement for IT development projects and aligning information systems with corporate strategies. Because business process design often takes time away from other duties, management must ensure that team members are given adequate time and support to work on the project.

6.2.2   Accountants

Accountants may play three roles during systems design:

1.   As users of an *accounting information system* (AIS), the accountants should determine their information needs and system requirements, and communicate these to system developers.

2.   As members of the project development team or information systems steering committee, they can help manage system development.

3.   As accountants, they should take an active role in designing system controls, and periodically monitor and test the system to verify that the controls are implemented and functioning properly.

6.2.3   Information Systems Steering Committee

An executive-level *information systems steering committee*, also known as the project steering committee, should plan and oversee the information systems function and address the complexities created by functional and divisional boundaries.

1.   The committee often consists of high-level management, such as the controller and the systems and user-department management.

2.   Functions of the steering committee include:

-    setting governing policies for the various information systems within the company;

-    ensuring top-management participation, guidance, and control; and

-    facilitating the coordination and integration of information systems activities to increase goal congruence and reduce goal conflict.

6.2.4   Project Development Team

The team members planning each project are responsible for the successful design and implementation of the business system. The team should work to ensure both technical implementation and user acceptance. Their tasks include:

1.   Monitoring the project to ensure timely and cost-effective completion.

2.   Managing the human element (e.g., resistance to change).

3.   Frequently communicating with users and holding regular meetings to consider ideas and discuss progress so there are no surprises at project completion.

4.   Risk management and escalating issues that cannot be resolved within the team.

6.2.5   External Parties

Many people outside an organization play a role in systems development, including customers, vendors, auditors, and governmental entities. For example, a major retailer may require that its vendors implement and use *electronic data interchange* (EDI).

6.3 Governance Objectives

6.3.1 Strategic Alignment

The linkage between business and IT plans is referred to as *strategic alignment* and includes defining, maintaining, and validating the IT value proposition, with a focus on customer satisfaction.

6.3.2 Value Creation

Value creation is the key governance objective of any enterprise. It includes the provision by IT of promised benefits to the organization, while satisfying its customers and optimizing costs and risks.

6.3.3 Resource Management

Resource management focuses on the optimization of knowledge and infrastructure.

6.3.4 Risk Management

Risk management is defined as risk awareness by senior management, characterized by understanding risk appetite and risk management responsibilities (e.g., event identification, risk assessments, and responses).

Risk management begins with identification of risks faced followed by determining how the company will respond to the risk. The company can avoid the risk, mitigate the risk, share the risk, or ignore the risk.

Illustration 4   Dealing With Risk

A health care provider might *avoid* risk by not providing certain high-risk medical procedures, and instead focusing on low-risk basic care. An online retailer might *mitigate* risk by implementing strict controls over customer account information. Companies share risk by purchasing insurance. *Ignoring* risk would be an option only if the risk presents low impact and small probability.

6.3.5 Performance Measurement

Features of *performance measurement* include tracking and monitoring strategy implementation, project completion, resource usage, process performance, and service delivery. It is important to define milestones and/or deliverables throughout the project so that progress toward completion can be measured.

7 Risk Assessment Process

7.1 Prepare a Business Impact Analysis

The purpose of the *business impact analysis* (BIA) is to identify which business units, departments, and processes are essential to the survival of an entity. The BIA will identify how quickly essential business units and/or processes need to return to full operation following a disaster situation. The BIA will also identify the resources required to resume business operations.

For example, the department may utilize some special hardware/software, some special locations may be involved, or there may even be a dependence on someone else's information resources.

The objectives of the BIA are as follows:

- Estimate the financial impacts for each business unit, assuming a worst-case scenario.

- Estimate the intangible (operational) impacts for each business unit, assuming a worst-case scenario.

- Identify the organization's business unit processes and the estimated recovery time frame for each business unit.

7.2   Identify Information Resources

This includes any hardware, software, systems, services, people, databases, and related resources important to the department. These resources should be identified in a manner such that overlap is minimized. It might also be appropriate to have some clear point of accountability (that is, an individual who is responsible for specific hardware, a software package, or an office process).

7.3   Categorize Information Resources by Impact

This step helps to determine the criteria for categorizing the list of information resources as high, medium, or low related to the effect on day-to-day operations. Criteria include characteristics such as criticality, costs of a failure, publicity, legal and ethical issues, etc. It is important to agree upon and establish a common understanding of the criteria and their meaning. Resources can be categorized as follows:

7.3.1   High Impact (H)

Under a high-impact category, the department:

- cannot operate without this information resource for even a short period of time;

- may experience a high recovery cost;

- may realize harm or obstruction to achieving one's mission or to maintaining one's reputation.

7.3.2   Medium Impact (M)

Under a medium-impact category, the department:

- could work around the loss of this information resource for days or perhaps a week, but eventually restoration of the resource must occur;

- may experience some cost of recovery;

- may realize harm or obstruction to achieving one's mission or to maintaining one's reputation.

7.3.3   Low Impact (L)

Under a low-impact category, the department:

- could operate without this information resource for an extended (although perhaps finite) period of time, during which particular units or individuals may be inconvenienced and/or need to identify alternatives;

- may notice an effect on achieving one's mission or maintaining one's reputation.

7.4   Identify and Categorize Risks by Likelihood

"Risks," as used here, includes problems as well as threats. Risks must be tangible and specific with respect to one or more resources. When finalizing the list, eliminate duplicates, combine risks as appropriate, and include only the risks that team members agree are valid. Categorize the identified risks by likelihood of occurrence. The definitions for likelihood are as follows:

7.4.1   High Likelihood (H)

The risk (threat) source is highly motivated and sufficiently capable, and controls to prevent the vulnerability are ineffective.

7.4.2   Medium Likelihood (M)

The risk (threat) source is motivated and capable, but controls are in place that may impede successful exercise of the vulnerability.

7.4.3   Low Likelihood (L)

The risk (threat) source lacks motivation or capability, or controls are in place to prevent or significantly impede successful exercise of the vulnerability.

7.5   Information Resources, Associated Risks, and Corrective Actions

- List the high-impact information resources and document the risks associated with each information resource.
- Supply comments where needed to clarify a specific situation. Denote the risk likelihood.
- Finally, indicate the action decision by the team to mitigate each specified risk. Definitions for risk actions are as follows:
    1. High Action (H): Take corrective action as soon as possible.
    2. Medium Action (M): Implement corrective actions within a reasonable time frame.
    3. Low Action (L): Take no corrective action. Accept the level of risk.

7.6   Recommendations for Mitigating Risks

All high- and medium-risk actions associated with high-impact information resources need a documented recommendation or plan for mitigating each risk. If no high-impact information resources exist, the team should review identified high and medium risks and develop recommendations to mitigate those risks. The process for developing appropriate recommendations is as follows:

1. *Identify* each recommendation that might be implemented (this includes technical and manual solutions, as well as policies and procedures) and appropriately documented. It may be obvious at this early point only one recommendation is applicable. Document that fact and include documentation regarding the dismissal of other recommendations.

2. *Provide a justification* for each proposed recommendation: this may be the same for each or it could be different, in which case it will be useful in any evaluation. The obvious justification is that the recommendation will handle the problem, but a specific solution may not handle all risks.

3. *Develop a cost-benefit analysis* for each proposed recommendation (in some cases this may involve other departments or units). This should include (but not be limited to) capital and direct costs, staff costs, training and support, and any ongoing operating costs.

4. *Specify any known implementation plans or specific dates* for the recommendations. This could be an important consideration depending on the severity of the risk and the time frame involved for implementation.

Question 1	**CPA-06442**

Which of the following is the responsibility of an information technology steering committee?

    a. A steering committee plan shows how a project will be completed, including the modules or tasks to be performed and who will perform them, the dates they should be completed, and project costs.

    b. A steering committee must develop clear specifications. Before third parties bid on a project, clear specifications must be developed, including exact descriptions and definitions of the system, explicit deadlines, and precise acceptance criteria.

    c. A steering committee should be formed to guide and oversee systems development and acquisition.

    d. Steering committee must assess the operations of IT using system performance measurements. Common measurements include: throughput (output per unit of time), utilization (percentage of time the system is being productively used), and response time (how long it takes the system to respond).

Question 2	**CPA-07042**

The IT Governance Institute identifies five focus areas for IT governance, including which of the following:

    a. Systems analysis

    b. Programming

    c. Operations

    d. Value delivery

1 The Role of Big Data/Data Analytics and Statistics in Supporting Business Decisions

Most companies store digital versions of documents on servers and storage devices. These documents become instantly available within a company, regardless of an employee's geographical location. Companies are able to store and maintain a tremendous amount of historical data economically, and employees benefit from immediate access to the documents they need.

1.1 What Is Big Data?

"Big data" is a fast-evolving concept in data management and in information technology in general. There is no single, widely accepted definition of "big data," or even "big," in this context.

Rapid advances in software technology and data management systems allow companies to build more individual relationships with customers and even predict what customers want before they ask for it. Think about the times you receive recommendations for products as soon as you sign into a website, or even in a personal e-mail you receive. Big data analytics is focused on finding marketing and sales patterns, discovering previously unknown relationships, detecting new market trends, and being able to ferret out actual customer preferences.

For any business, there are boundless ways in which the processing of big data can improve the company's results. In order to benefit from "big data," companies must have the systems and people to mine it and refine it so that it is useful for making decisions. Increasingly, the individuals who work with "big data" are not just the typical accountant, but are data scientists, statisticians, programmers, data analysts, and database engineers, among other professionals.

1.2 Dimensions of Big Data

IBM Corp. describes four dimensions of big data:

1.2.1 Volume

The volume of data is too large for traditional database software to store. Storage is a huge challenge usually solved by a distributed system in which there is a network of interconnected databases, possibly even globally.

1.2.2 Velocity

The flow of data is continuous, so the real value is in being able to analyze data in real time.

1.2.3 Variety

The best "big data" comes from a variety of sources, including customer relationship management systems, social media feedback, point-of-sale records, and other sources.

1.2.4 Veracity

Biases or irrelevant data must be mined from big data in order to minimize the chance of making decisions based on the wrong data.

1.3   Data Analytics Processes

The three main data analytics processes are the following:

1.3.1   Descriptive Analytics

Descriptive analytics describes events that have already occurred, such as financial reports and historical operations reports, which enable learning from past behaviors.

1.3.2   Predictive Analytics

Predictive analytics use statistical techniques and forecasting models to predict what could happen.

1.3.3   Prescriptive Analytics

Prescriptive analytics use optimization and simulation algorithms to affect future decisions. This is the most complex of the three types of analytics to implement.

1.4   Uses of Data Analytics

Some of the top uses of data analytics in businesses currently are the following:

1.4.1   Customer Analytics

Customer analytics supports digital marketing, and allows the company to deliver timely, relevant, and anticipated offers to customers.

1.4.2   Operational Analytics

Operational analytics uses data mining and data collection tools to plan for more effective business operations; normally used to observe and analyze business operations in real time.

1.4.3   Risk and Compliance Analytics

Risk and compliance analytics are used in Enterprise Risk Management activities such as continuous monitoring, continuous auditing, and fraud detection.

1.4.4   New Products and Services Innovation Analytics

New products and services innovation analytics are used to determine where innovation is needed, and to isolate product qualities that are most important to customers.

2   Role of Information Systems in Key Business Processes Within an Entity

One of the most basic and vital information technology components of any business is the set of software referred to as the "business information system." Information technology is the enabler of business functions, processes, and outcomes. Below are some of the key components of information technology used in most businesses today.

2.1   Communication

For many companies, e-mail is the principal means of communication between employees, suppliers, and customers. Other communications tools have also evolved, such as live chat systems, online meeting tools, and videoconferencing systems. Voice over Internet Protocol (VoIP) telephones and smartphones offer additional ways to facilitate communication within the organization.

2.2   Management Information Systems

Management information systems (MIS) enable companies to use data as part of their strategic planning process as well as the tactical execution of that strategy. Management information systems often have subsystems called decision support systems (DSS) and executive information systems (EIS).

A management information system provides users predefined reports that support effective business decisions. MIS reports may provide feedback on daily operations, financial and nonfinancial information to support decision making across functions, and both internal and external information.

2.3   Decision Support Systems (DSS)

A *decision support system* is an extension of an MIS that provides interactive tools to support decision making. A DSS may provide information, facilitate the preparation of forecasts, or allow modeling of various aspects of a decision. It is sometimes called an expert system.

Illustration 1   DSS

Examples of decision support systems include production planning, inventory control, bid preparation, revenue optimization, traffic planning, and capital investment planning systems.

2.4   Executive Information Systems (EIS)

Executive information systems provide senior executives with immediate and easy access to internal and external information to assist in strategic decision making. An EIS consolidates information internal and external to the enterprise and reports it in a format and level of detail appropriate to senior executives.

Illustration 2   EIS

Examples of executive information systems include sales forecasting, profit planning, key performance indicators, macro-economic data, and financial reports.

2.5   Accounting Information Systems (AIS)

The business information system that is most important to an accountant is the *accounting information system* (AIS). An accounting information system is a type of management information system; it also may be partly a transaction processing system and partly a knowledge system.

There may be separate systems (often called modules) for each accounting function, such as accounts receivable, accounts payable, etc., or there may be one integrated system that performs all of the accounting functions, culminating in the general ledger and the various accounting reports.

A well-designed AIS creates an audit trail for accounting transactions. The audit trail allows a user to trace a transaction from source documents to the ledger and to trace from the ledger back to source documents. The ability to trace in both directions is important in auditing.

An example of a basic accounting audit trail follows. Source documents are often stored as electronic documents, thus alleviating the need to file paper documents. Sophisticated scanning systems can turn paper documents into electronic documents before they are processed.

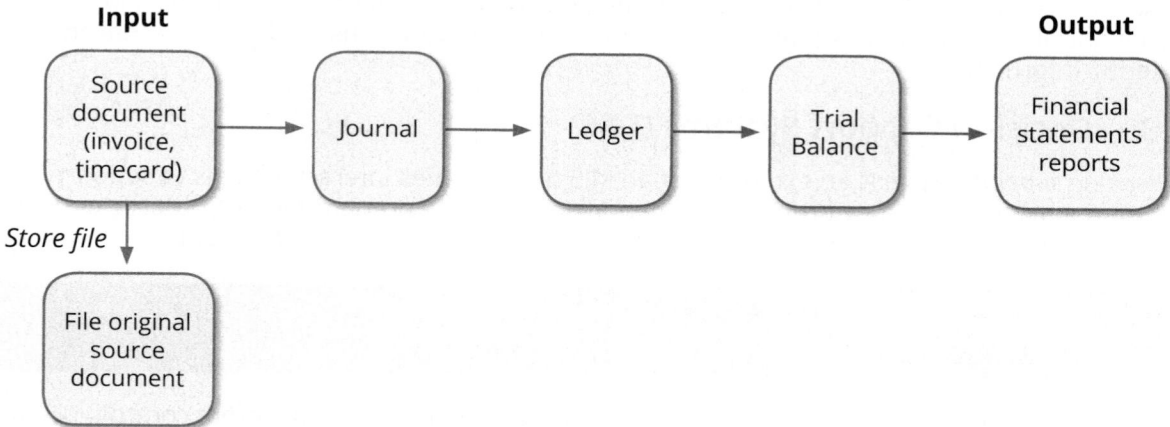

2.5.1 Objectives of an AIS

1. Record valid transactions;

2. Properly classify those transactions;

3. Record the transactions at their proper value;

4. Record the transactions in the proper accounting period; and

5. Properly present the transactions and related information in the financial statements of the organization.

2.5.2 Sequence of Events in an AIS

1. The transaction data from source documents is entered into the AIS by an end user. Alternatively, an order may be entered through the Internet by a customer.

2. The original source documents, if they exist, are filed.

3. The transactions are recorded in the appropriate journal.

4. The transactions are posted to the general and subsidiary ledgers.

5. Trial balances are prepared.

6. Adjustments, accruals, and corrections are entered. Financial reports are generated.

2.6 Inventory Management

Inventory management systems track the quantity of each item a company maintains, triggering an order when quantities fall below a predetermined level. These systems are best used when the inventory management system is connected to the point-of-sale (POS) system. The POS system ensures that each time an item is sold, one of that item is removed from the inventory count.

2.7   Customer Relationship Management System (CRM)

2.7.1   Purpose

Customer relationship management systems (CRM) provide sales force automation and customer services in an attempt to manage customer relationships. CRM systems capture every interaction a company has with a customer. CRM systems record and manage customer contacts; manage salespeople; forecast sales; manage sales leads; provide and manage online quotes, product specifications, and pricing; and analyze sales data.

If a customer contacts a call center with an issue, a customer support representative will be able to see what the customer purchased, view shipping information, call up the training manual for that item, and effectively respond to the issue. The entire interaction is stored in the CRM system, ready to be recalled if the customer calls again.

2.7.2   CRM Benefits

The objective of CRM (and of CRM systems) is to increase customer satisfaction and thus increase revenue and profitability. CRM attempts to do this by appearing to market to each customer individually. The assumptions are that 20 percent of customers generate 80 percent of sales and that it is 5 to 10 times more expensive to acquire a new customer than to obtain repeat business from an existing customer.

CRM also attempts to reduce sales costs and customer support costs. It attempts to identify the best customers and possibly provide those best customers with increased levels of service or simply drop the worst customers.

2.7.3   Categories of CRM

CRM is sometimes divided into two categories:

1. **Analytical CRM**

    Creates and exploits knowledge of a company's current and future customers to drive business decisions.

2. **Operational CRM**

    This is the automation of customer contacts or contact points.

2.8   Enterprise Resource Planning Systems (ERP)

An *enterprise resource planning system* (ERP) is a cross-functional enterprise system that integrates and automates the many business processes and systems that must work together in the manufacturing, logistics, distribution, accounting, project management, finance, and human resource functions of a business.

ERP software comprises a number of modules that can function independently or as an integrated system to allow data and information to be shared among all of the different departments and divisions of large businesses.

ERP software manages the various functions within a business (enterprise) related to manufacturing, from entering sales orders to coordinating shipping and after-sales customer service. In spite of the name, ERP normally does not offer anything in the way of planning. The enterprise part, however, is correct. ERP is often considered a back-office system, from the customer order to fulfillment of that order.

2.8.1   ERP Operations

1. ERP systems store information in a central repository so that data may be entered once and then accessed and used by the various departments.

2. ERP systems act as the framework for integrating and improving an organization's ability to monitor and track sales, expenses, customer service, distribution, and many other business functions.

3. ERP systems can provide vital cross-functional information quickly to managers across the organization in order to assist them in the decision-making process.

2.9   Supply Chain Management Systems (SCM)

2.9.1   Characteristics

Supply chain management (SCM) is concerned with the four important characteristics of every sale: what, when, where, and how much. For example, all customers, whether business or consumer, expect all of the following:

1. The goods received should match the goods ordered.

2. The goods should be delivered on or before the date promised.

3. The goods should be delivered to the location requested.

4. The cost of the goods should be as low as possible.

2.9.2   Integration

Supply chain management is the integration of business processes from the original supplier to the customer and includes purchasing, materials handling, production planning and control, logistics and warehousing, inventory control, and product distribution and delivery. SCM systems may perform some or all of these functions.

2.9.3   Objectives and Functions

The overall objectives of SCM are achieving flexibility and responsiveness in meeting the demands of customers and business partners. SCM might incorporate the following functions:

1. Planning (e.g., demand forecasting, product pricing, and inventory management)

2. Sourcing (e.g., procurement and credit and collections)

3. Making (e.g., product design, production scheduling, and facility management)

4. Delivery (e.g., order management and delivery scheduling)

3   E-Commerce Technologies

Electronic commerce, commonly written as e-commerce, is the trading or facilitation of trading in products or services using computer networks, such as the Internet.

3.1   Electronic Funds Transfer(s)

Electronic funds transfer systems (EFT) are a form of electronic payment for banking and retailing industries. EFT uses a variety of technologies to transact, process, and verify money transfers and credits between banks, businesses, and consumers. The Federal Reserve's financial services systems are used frequently in EFT to reduce the time and expense required to process checks and credit transactions.

EFT service is often provided by a *third-party vendor* who acts as the intermediary between the company and the banking system. That third party might accept transactions from a business and perform all of the translation services. EFT security is provided through various types of data encryption. EFT reduces the need for manual data entry, thus reducing the occurrence of data entry errors.

3.2   Application Service Providers (ASP)

Application service providers (ASP) provide access to application programs on a rental basis. They allow smaller companies to avoid the extremely high cost of owning and maintaining today's application systems by allowing them to pay only for what is used. The ASPs own and host the software and users access it via a Web browser. The ASP is responsible for software updates and usually will also provide backup services for the users' data. The provided software may be referred to as software as a service, apps on tap, or on-demand software.

3.2.1   Advantages of ASP

The benefits of utilizing an ASP are lower costs, from a hardware, software, and people standpoint, and greater flexibility. Small businesses especially benefit because they do not need to hire systems experts to provide the services performed by the ASP.

3.2.2   Disadvantages of ASP

The drawbacks of utilizing an ASP are the possible risks to the security and privacy of the organization's data, the financial viability or lack thereof of the ASP, and possible poor support by the ASP (a concern anytime anything is outsourced).

3.3   Web Stores

3.3.1   Stand-Alone Web Stores

Many small companies have stand-alone Web stores that are not integrated with larger accounting systems. Such stores are typically hosted by shopping cart software that manages a product catalog, user registrations, orders, e-mail confirmations, and so on.

Financial reports, such as order summaries, are generated as needed by the software. The reports are then imported into general accounting software.

3.3.2   Integrated Web Stores

Many larger companies and an increasing number of small companies have turned to ERP systems that integrate all the major accounting functions, as well as the Web store, into a single software system. Such systems process Web orders and then automatically update cash and revenue accounts, handle inventory reordering, and so on. In effect, such systems treat Web-store sales the same as sales made in retail stores.

3.4   Dynamic Content

Web 2.0 is associated with an increase in Web pages with dynamic content. Such content is often linked to databases, such as price lists and catalog product lists. Such data can be dynamically embedded in Web pages through XML, with the data stored in a database separate from the Web page.

Dynamic content is any content that changes frequently and can include video, audio, and animation. Dynamic content in the context of HTML and the World Wide Web refers to website content that constantly or regularly changes based on user interactions, timing, and other parameters that determine what content is delivered to the user. This means that the content of the site may differ for every user because of different parameters. Facebook is an example of a site that delivers dynamic content, as every user gets different content based on friends and social interactions, although the layout generally stays the same.

3.5　Mash-ups

Mash-ups are Web pages that are collages of other Web pages and other information. Google Maps (*maps.google.com*) is an example of a mash-up. Google Maps allows the user to view various sources of information (e.g., places of interest and street names) superimposed on a single map.

3.6　Cloud Computing

Cloud computing is defined as virtual servers available over the Internet. Cloud computing includes any subscription-based or pay-per-use service that extends an entity's existing information technology capabilities on a real-time basis over the Internet. A public cloud sells services to anyone on the Internet. A private cloud is a private network or data center that provides services to a limited number of customers.

Cloud computing can offer the advantage of professional management of hardware and software. Cloud providers generally will have sophisticated backup procedures as well as high level security for customer data.

3.6.1　Services

Cloud computing services can be divided into three categories:

1.　**Infrastructure-as-a-Service (IaaS):** Also known as Hardware-as-a-Service (HaaS), outsources storage, hardware, services, and networking components to customers, generally on a per-use basis. Amazon, Microsoft, Google, and Rackspace are providers in this market.

2.　**Platform-as-a-Service (PaaS):** Allows customers to rent virtual servers and related services that can be used to develop and test new software applications.

3.　**Software-as-a-Service (SaaS):** A method of software distribution in which applications are hosted by a vendor or service provider and made available to customers over the Internet. This is another name for the ASP (application service provider). An example is Salesforce.com.

Question 1	CPA-03682

Which of the following is usually a benefit of using electronic funds transfer for international cash transactions?

　　a.　Improvement of the audit trail for cash receipts and disbursements

　　b.　Creation of self-monitoring access controls

　　c.　Reduction of the frequency of data entry errors

　　d.　Off-site storage of source documents for cash transactions

Question 2	CPA-07012

An enterprise resource planning system is designed to:

　　a.　Allow nonexperts to make decisions about a particular problem.

　　b.　Help with the decision-making process.

　　c.　Integrate data from all aspects of an organization's activities.

　　d.　Present executives with the information needed to make strategic plans.

1 Protection of Information

Information security is a strategy including the processes, tools, and policies necessary to detect, prevent, document, and counter threats to both digital and physical information. Processes and policies often involve both digital and non-digital security measures to protect data from unauthorized access, use, replication, or destruction. Information security management can include various components such as mantraps, encryption, and malware detection.

Information security management programs are key for protecting the confidentiality, integrity and availability of IT systems and business data. Many large entities employ a dedicated security group to implement and maintain the organization's information security management program. The group is often led by a chief information security officer.

1.1 Security Policy Defined

An entity's information security policy is a document that states how an organization plans to protect its tangible and intangible information assets. Security policies include:

1. Management instructions indicating a course of action, a guiding principle, or an appropriate procedure.

2. High-level statements that provide guidance to workers who must make present and future decisions.

3. Generalized requirements that must be written and communicated to certain groups of people inside and, in some cases, outside the organization.

1.2 Security Policy Goal

The goal of a good information security policy is to require people to protect information, which in turn protects the organization, its employees, and its customers.

1.3 Types of Policies

Computer security policies start out at a high level and become more specific (granular) at the lower levels.

1.3.1 Program-Level Policy

Program-level policies are used for creating a management-sponsored computer security program. A program-level policy, at the highest level, might prescribe the need for information security and may delegate the creation and management of the program to a role within the IT department. This is the mission statement for the IT security program.

1.3.2 Program-Framework Policy

A program-framework policy establishes the overall approach to computer security (i.e., a computer security framework). A framework policy adds detail to the program by describing the elements and organization of the program and department that will carry out the security mission. This is the IT security strategy.

- **Issue-Specific Policy:** *Issue-specific policies* address specific issues of concern to the organization (e.g., cloud computing).

- **System-Specific Policy:** *System-specific policies* focus on policy issues that exist for a specific system (e.g., the payroll system).

2 Development and Management of Security Policies

A three-level model can be used to develop a comprehensive set of security policies:

2.1 Security Objectives

The first step is to define the *security objectives*. The objectives should consist of a series of statements to describe meaningful actions about specific resources. These objectives should be based on system functionality or mission requirements and also state the security actions to support the requirements. Security objectives might relate to confidentiality, data integrity, authorization, access, resource protection, and other issues.

2.2 Operational Security

Operational security should define the manner in which a specific data operation would remain secure (e.g., operational security for data integrity might consider a definition of authorized and unauthorized modification: the individuals authorized to make modifications, by job category, by organization placement, by name, etc.).

2.3 Policy Implementation

Security is normally enforced through a combination of technical and traditional management methods. Although technical means are likely to include the use of access control technology, other automated means of enforcing or supporting security policy exist. For example, technology can be used to block telephone system users from calling certain numbers. Intrusion detection software can alert system administrators to suspicious activity or take action to stop the activity. Personal computers can be configured to prevent booting from an external drive.

3 Policy Support Documents

Policies are defined as statements of management's intent. Documents that serve to support policies include:

3.1 Regulations

Laws, rules, and regulations generally represent governmentally imposed restrictions passed by regulators and lawmakers (i.e., the Sarbanes-Oxley Act of 2002, HIPPA, etc.).

3.2 Standards and Baselines

Topic-specific and system-specific documents that describe overall requirements for security are called, respectively, standards and baselines.

3.3   Guidelines

Guidelines provide hints, tips, and best practices in implementation.

3.4   Procedures

Procedures are step-by-step instructions on how to perform a specific security activity (configure a firewall, install an operating system, and others).

4   Logical and Physical Access Controls

Data and procedural controls are implemented to ensure that data is recorded, errors are corrected during processing, and output is properly distributed.

4.1   Logical Controls

Logical controls use software and data to monitor and control access to information and computing systems.

4.1.1   User Access

Because user accounts are the first target of a hacker, care must be used when designing procedures for creating accounts and granting access to information.

4.1.2   Initial Passwords and Authorization for System Access

The first point of contact for a new employee is generally the human resources (HR) department. HR should generate the request for a user account and system access rights. Depending on the level of access being granted, the information security officer also may need to approve the account.

4.1.3   Changes in Position

Changes in position require coordination of effort between HR and IT.

- It is important to have procedures to address changes in jobs/roles and to remove access that is no longer needed.

- There must be a mechanism to disable accounts when an employee leaves an organization. The ideal scenario is for HR to alert IT prior to termination, or otherwise, as soon as possible.

4.1.4   Managing Passwords

Passwords are designed to protect access to secure sites and information. The first rule in password policy is that every account must have a password. A strong password management policy must address the following password characteristics:

- **Password Length:** Longer passwords are generally more effective. Many organizations require a minimum of seven or eight characters.

- **Password Complexity:** Complex passwords are more effective and generally feature three of the following four characteristics:

    1. Uppercase characters
    2. Lowercase characters
    3. Numeric characters
    4. ASCII characters (e.g., !, @, #, $, %, ^, &, *, or ?)

Password Age

Although there is no true standard, passwords should be changed frequently in order to be effective; every 90 days is considered a good policy. Administrative passwords should be changed more frequently.

Password Reuse

Although there is no true standard, passwords should not be reused until a significant amount of time has passed. The goal is to prevent users from alternating between their favorite two or three passwords.

Two-Factor Authentication

This method allows for a second authentication key from a secondary device such as a smartphone or other key generator that is based on the time of log-in.

4.1.5 Network and Host-Based Firewalls

Default-Deny Policy

The firewall administrator lists the allowed network services, and everything else is denied.

Default-Allow Policy

The firewall administrator lists network services that are not allowed, and everything else is accepted.

A default-deny approach to firewall security is by far the more secure, but due to the difficulty in configuring and managing a network in that fashion, many networks instead use a default-allow approach.

4.1.6 Network Intrusion Detection Systems

These systems comprise devices or software programs that monitor network or system activities for malicious activities or policy violations and produce electronic reports for management.

4.1.7 Access Control Lists

These specify which users or system processes are granted access to objects, as well as what operations are allowed on given objects.

4.1.8 Data Encryption

Encryption is an essential foundation for electronic commerce. Encryption involves using a password or a digital key to scramble a readable (plaintext) message into an unreadable (ciphertext) message. The intended recipient of the message then uses another digital key to decrypt or decipher the ciphertext message back into plaintext.

With encryption keys, the longer the length of the key, the less likely is the message or transaction to be decrypted by the wrong party and the less likely the key is to be broken by a *brute-force attack*. In a brute-force attack, the attacker simply tries every possible key until the right one is found.

If encrypted content is communicated by an entity (a person or a machine) using cryptography, the sender is the entity that encrypts and the receiver is the entity that decrypts the content. Between the sender and the receiver lies the unsecured environment where the garbled message travels.

When encrypted content is stored, rather than transferred between a sender and a receiver, authorized users have the ability to encrypt and decrypt the content so they can use it for authorized purposes.

Illustration 1   Encryption

A local bank uses encryption methods and hashing in all of its online banking transfers. (Hashing is the process of changing a series of characters into a shorter, fixed length that represents the original string of characters. It is commonly used with encryption.)

The bank has previously used a digital certificate from a trusted certificate authority (CA), such as Symantec or Network Solutions. A bank customer wants to make an online transfer between accounts. The encrypted transaction will be processed as follows:

Step 1: When a bank customer visits the bank's website, the customer will notice the lock icon displayed at the bottom of the screen once he or she clicks on a "Money Transfer" button or its equivalent. The bank customer's browser software will then obtain the website's digital certificate, verify its validity, and open it to get the bank's public key. The bank's website software follows the same concept to acquire the user's public key.

Step 2: Once the bank customer clicks on the "money transfer" button to view his or her online banking transactions, the encryption software performs the following steps:

a. It creates a hash of the money transfer by using a hashing algorithm.

b. It creates a digital signature for the money transfer by encrypting the hash using the bank customer's private key.

c. It encrypts the money transfer using the advanced encryption standard (AES) symmetric key in order to protect the confidentiality of the bank customer because only those with the AES key can decrypt the transfer.

d. The AES key is encrypted by using the bank's public key in order to ensure that only the intended recipient (bank) will be able to decrypt the AES key needed for the money transfer.

Step 3: The encrypted money transfer (created in Step 2 c), the AES key needed to decrypt the money transfer (created in Step 2 d), and the user's digital signature (created in Step 2 b) are all sent over the Internet to the bank.

Step 4: Once the bank's computer system receives the package of information via the Internet, it performs the following steps:

a. The system uses the user's public key, obtained in Step 1, to decrypt the digital signature created in Step 2 b, in order to yield the hash of the money transfer that was created by the bank customer.

b. The system uses its own private key to decrypt the AES key sent by the customer in Step 2 d.

c. The system uses the AES key from Step 4 b to decrypt the encrypted money transfer created in Step 2 c in order to produce the plaintext version of the customer's transfer.

d. The system uses the same hashing algorithm used on the user's computer in Step 1 to hash the plaintext copy of the money transfer created in Step 4 c.

The system compares the hash created in Step 4 d with the one produced in Step 4 a. If there is a match, the bank's system knows that the money transfer has not been changed or corrupted during transmission.

Step 5: The bank sends the customer an acknowledgement that the money transfer has been received.

4.1.9   Digital Certificates

▪ *Digital certificates,* another form of data security, are electronic documents created and digitally signed by a trusted party that certify the identity of the owners of a particular public key. The digital certificate contains that party's public key.

▪ The term *public key infrastructure (PKI)* refers to the system and processes used to issue and manage asymmetric keys and digital certificates. The organization that issues public and private keys and records the public key in a digital certificate is called a certificate authority.

Digital certificates intended for e-business use are typically issued by commercial certificate authorities, such as Comodo and Verisign. The certificate authority hashes the information stored on a digital certificate and then encrypts that hash with its private key. That digital signature is then appended to the digital certificate, which provides the means for validating the authenticity of the certificate.

4.1.10 Digital Signatures vs. E-Signatures

Digital signatures use asymmetric encryption to create legally binding electronic documents. Web-based e-signatures are an alternative and are provided by vendors as a software product. The e-signature is a cursive-style imprint of a person's name that is applied to an electronic document. E-signatures are legally binding, just as if the user had really "signed" a paper copy of the document.

4.2   Physical Controls

Physical controls monitor and control the environment of the workplace and computing facilities. They also monitor and control access to and from such facilities.

4.2.1   Segregation of Duties

This ensures that an individual cannot complete a critical task by himself.

4.2.2   Monitoring and Control of Access to and From the Facilities

Can include the following examples: doors, locks with retina or fingerprint scanners, secure pass-throughs called mantraps, heating and air-conditioning, smoke and fire alarms, fire suppression systems, cameras, barricades, fencing, security guards, cable locks, etc. Separating the network and workplace into functional areas are also physical controls.

4.2.3   Backup Files

Data backups are necessary both for recovery in a disaster scenario and for recovery from processing problems. Copies of key master files and records should be stored in safe places located outside of the company. Copies of files kept on-site should be stored in fireproof containers or rooms.

▪ **Backup of Systems That Can Be Shut Down:** The backup process is relatively simple when a system can be shut down for backup and maintenance. When this is the case, files or databases that have changed since the last backup (or just all data) can be backed up, using the son-father-grandfather or similar concept.

▪ **Backups of Systems That Do Not Shut Down:** Effective backups are more difficult when an information system cannot be shut down. Recovery often includes applying a transaction log (a file of the transactions that had been applied to the databases) and reapplying those transactions to get back to the point immediately before the failure.

▪ **Mirroring:** Mirroring is the use of a backup computer to duplicate all of the processes and transactions on the primary computer. Mirroring, which can be expensive, is sometimes used by banks and other organizations for which downtime is unacceptable.

4.2.4   Uninterrupted Power Supply

An *uninterrupted power supply* (UPS) is a device that maintains a continuous supply of electrical power to connected equipment. A UPS is also called battery backup. A UPS is used to prevent a system from shutting down inappropriately during an outage. A UPS can prevent data loss and can protect the integrity of a backup while it is being performed. When a power failure occurs, the UPS switches to its own power source instantaneously so that there is no interruption in power to the system.

A UPS is not a backup standby generator; the battery will run out sooner or later. Because a backup generator will not provide protection from a momentary power interruption, it is critical that the UPS be able to provide power without any interruption so that data will not be corrupted.

4.2.5   Program Modification Controls

Program modification controls are controls over changes to programs being used in production applications. Program modification controls include both controls designed to prevent changes by unauthorized personnel and controls that track program changes so that there is a record of what versions of what programs are running in production at any specific point in time.

4.2.6   Malware Detection

Malware detection software on servers and clients detects the threat of viruses, worms, and file infectors, to protect information.

5   General Controls and Application Controls

5.1   General Controls

General controls are designed to ensure that an organization's control environment is stable and well-managed, and include:

1. Systems development standards
2. Security management controls
3. Change management procedures
4. Software acquisition, development, operations, and maintenance controls

5.2   Application Controls

Application controls prevent, detect, and correct transaction error and fraud and are application-specific, providing reasonable assurance as to system:

1. Accuracy
2. Completeness
3. Validity

6   Disaster Recovery/Business Continuity Plans

Disaster recovery consists of an entity's plans for restoring and continuing operations in the event of the destruction of program and data files, as well as processing capability. Short-term problems or outages do not normally constitute disasters. If processing can be quickly reestablished at the original processing location, then disaster recovery is not necessary. If processing cannot be quickly reestablished at the original processing site (possibly because the original processing site no longer exists), then disaster recovery is necessary.

6.1   Major Players in Disaster Recovery

Major players in a disaster recovery plan are the organization itself and the disaster recovery services provider (e.g., IBM or SunGard). If application software packages are utilized, the package vendors may be involved. For distributed processing, hardware vendors may be involved. Senior management support is absolutely necessary for an effective disaster recovery plan.

6.2   Steps in Disaster Recovery

The *steps in a disaster recovery* plan are to:

1. assess the risks;

2. identify mission-critical applications and data;

3. develop a plan for handling the mission-critical applications;

4. determine the responsibilities of the personnel involved in disaster recovery; and

5. test the disaster recovery plan.

Depending on the organization, the disaster recovery plan may be limited to the restoration of IT processing or may extend to restoration of functions in end-user areas (often called business continuity). One factor that must be considered in business continuity is the paper records that might normally be maintained in end-user areas and that might be lost in a disaster.

6.3   Advantages and Disadvantages of Disaster Recovery and Business Continuity

If an organization does not have a disaster recovery and business continuity plan and a disaster occurs, the organization may go out of business. The disadvantage is the cost and effort required to establish and maintain a disaster recovery plan.

6.4   Split-Mirror Backup

As the amount of data needed to support many large companies grows, so do the time and resources that it takes those companies to back up and recover their data. One often-used, effective backup method is known as a split-mirror backup, which is useful when the main systems must always be online. A split-mirror backup uses a remote server to back up large amounts of data offline that can be restored in the event of a disaster.

6.5   Data Backup and Recovery Procedures

6.5.1   Use of a Disaster Recovery Service

Some organizations contract with outside providers for disaster recovery services. Various levels and types of service can be provided, which could be one empty room or even complete facilities across the country where end users could be located. The major emphasis is on hardware and telecommunications services.

6.5.2   Internal Disaster Recovery

Some organizations with the requirement for instantaneous resumption of processing after a disaster (e.g., banks and houses) provide their own duplicate facilities in separate locations. Data might be mirrored (i.e., updated and stored in both locations), and processing can be switched almost instantaneously from one location to another. A duplicate data center and data mirroring are expensive, and most organizations adopt cheaper solutions.

6.5.3   Multiple Data Center Backups

▪ Using a data center to back up another or back up to a cloud provider, assuming that there is enough capacity to process the essential applications.

▪ Organizations also must decide what types of backups to perform in order to recover lost data.

    1. *Full backup* is an exact copy of the entire database. Full backups are time consuming, so most organizations only do full backups weekly and supplement them with daily partial backups.

    2. Two types of partial backups are possible:

      —An *incremental backup* involves copying only the data items that have changed since the last backup. This produces a set of incremental backup files, each containing the results of one day's transactions. Restoration involves first loading the last full backup and then installing each subsequent incremental backup in the proper sequence.

      —A *differential backup* copies all changes made since the last full backup. Thus, each new differential backup file contains the cumulative effects of all activity since the last full backup. Consequently, except for the first day following a full backup, daily differential backups take longer than incremental backups. Restoration is simpler, however, because the last full backup needs to be supplemented with only the most recent differential backup, instead of a set of daily incremental backup files. Many organizations make incremental and differential backups daily.

6.5.4   Alternative Processing Facilities

1. **Cold Site:** A *cold site* is an off-site location that has all the electrical connections and other physical requirements for data processing, but it does not have the actual equipment. Cold sites usually require one to three days to be made operational because equipment has to be acquired. Organizations that utilize a cold-site approach normally utilize generic hardware that can be readily (and quickly) obtained from hardware vendors. Cold sites are the cheapest form of off-site location.

2. **Hot Site:** A *hot site* is an off-site location that is equipped to take over the company's data processing. Backup copies of essential data files and programs may also be maintained at the location or a nearby data storage facility. In the event of a disaster, the organization's personnel need to be shipped to the disaster recovery facility to load the backup data onto the standby equipment.

    • **Telecommunications Network**

      The most difficult aspect of recovery is often the telecommunications network.

    • **Floor Space and Equipment Determination**

      Disaster recovery service providers normally have an extensive amount of floor space and an extensive amount of equipment, but they would have nowhere near enough if all customers (or even a significant number of similar customers) declare a disaster at the same time. How much is needed is determined on a probabilistic basis; to a disaster recovery services provider, geographic and industry diversification of customers is extremely important.

    • **Personnel Issues**

      Effective recovery, and especially rapid effective recovery, is often a function of having knowledgeable personnel involved.

3. **Warm Site:** A *warm backup site* is a facility that is already stocked with all the hardware that it takes to create a reasonable facsimile of the primary data center.

    In order to restore the organization's service, the latest backups must be retrieved and delivered to the backup site. Next, a bare-metal restoration of the underlying operating system and network must be completed before recovery work can be done. The advantage of the warm backup site is that a restoration can be accomplished in a reasonable amount of time. The disadvantage is that there is still a continued cost associated with the warm backup site because a contract must be maintained with the facility to keep it up-to-date. The warm backup site is the compromise between the hot backup site and the cold backup site.

Question 1	CPA-06630

When a client's accounts payable computer system was relocated, the administrator provided support through a virtual private network (VPN) connection to a server. Subsequently, the administrator left the company. No changes were made to the accounts payable system at that time. Which of the following situations represents the greatest security risk?

  a. User passwords are *not* required to be in alphanumeric format.

  b. Management procedures for user accounts are *not* documented.

  c. User accounts are *not* removed upon termination of employees.

  d. Security logs are *not* periodically reviewed for violations.

Question 2	CPA-04813

Which of the following procedures is most important to include in the disaster recovery plan for an information technology department?

  a. Replacement personal computers for user departments

  b. Identification of critical applications

  c. Physical security of warehouse facilities

  d. Cross-training of operating personnel

1 The Role of Input, Processing, and Output Controls

1.1 Input Controls

The following source data controls regulate the integrity of input, which is crucial to accurate and complete output:

1. Data validation at the field level (edit checks, meaningful error messages, input masks, etc.).

2. Prenumbering forms, making it possible to verify that all input is accounted for and that no duplicate entries exist.

3. Well-defined source data preparation procedures, which are used to collect and prepare source documents. (Sometimes, no source documents exist because the data is entered automatically by way of a Web-based application or document scanning.)

1.2 Processing Controls

Important processing controls include the following:

1.2.1 Data Matching

Matching two or more items of data before taking an action improves transaction processing (e.g., controls should include matching information on the vendor invoice to both the purchase order and the receiving report before paying a vendor).

1.2.2 File Labels

Use of *file labels* ensures that the correct and most current files are updated. External labels are readable by humans, while internal labels are written in machine-readable form on the data recording media. Both internal and external labels should be used. External labels are easily altered so that internal labels are more secure. Two important types of internal labels are header and trailer records.

- The header record is at the beginning of each file and contains the file name, expiration date, and other identification data.

- The trailer record is at the end of a file and contains the batch totals calculated during input.

1.2.3 Recalculation of Batch Totals

Comparison of amounts input to amounts output ensures that the volume of transactions processed is correct. Hash totals (such as a sum of invoice numbers) also can be used to confirm that the correct source documents are included. If someone substituted a different invoice with the same amount, the batch total would agree but the hash total would not.

1.2.4 Cross-Footing and Zero-Balance Tests

Testing the sum of a column of row totals to the sum of a row of column totals to verify identical results provides some assurances as to accuracy. A zero-balance test requires the use of control accounts.

For example, the payroll clearing account is debited for the total gross pay of all employees. It is then credited for the amount of all labor costs allocated to various expense categories. The payroll clearing account should have a zero balance after these entries have been made; a nonzero balance indicates a processing error.

1.2.5 Write-Protection Mechanisms

Common file protections guard against the accidental writing over or erasing of data files stored on magnetic media. However, it is important to remember that although these provide protection from accidental erasure, most write-protection mechanisms are easily removed.

1.2.6 Database Processing Integrity Procedures

Database systems use database administrators, data dictionaries, and concurrent update controls to ensure processing integrity.

1. The administrator establishes and enforces procedures for accessing and updating the database.

2. The data dictionary ensures that data items are defined and used consistently.

3. Concurrent update controls protect records from errors that occur when two or more users attempt to update the same record simultaneously. This is accomplished by locking out one user until the system has finished processing the update entered by the other.

1.3 Output Controls

Verification of system output provides additional control over processing integrity. *Output controls* include:

1.3.1 User Review of Output

Examination by users of system output for reasonableness, completeness, and verification that the output is provided to the intended recipient.

1.3.2 Reconciliation Procedures

Reconciliation of individual transactions and other system updates to control reports, file status, or update reports (e.g., reconcile input control totals to output control totals).

1.3.3 External Data Reconciliation

Reconciliation of database totals with data maintained outside the system (e.g., the number of employee records in the payroll file should be compared with the total from human resources to detect attempts to add fictitious employees to the payroll database).

1.3.4 Output Encryption

The authenticity and integrity of data outputs must be protected during transmission. Encryption techniques reduce the chance for data interception. Controls should be designed to minimize the risk of data transmission errors.

■ When a receiving unit detects a data transmission error, it requests the sending unit to retransmit that data. Generally, the system will do this automatically, and the user is unaware that it has occurred.

■ Parity checking and message acknowledgement techniques are two basic types of data transmission controls.

- Parity checking is the process of taking the sum of the bits in a byte and adding either a zero or one to make the byte even for even parity or odd for odd parity.

- If the message arrives and a bit has changed during transmission, then it is recognized and the message can be resent.

1.4   Correctly Functioning Controls

Completeness, accuracy, and continuous processing integrity are the goals of correctly functioning controls.

1. Completeness means to be whole and have nothing missing.

2. Accuracy means to be correct and precise.

3. Continuous processing integrity means to have data integrity that is consistent and accurate throughout the processing cycle.

2   Design and Operating Effectiveness of Application Controls

2.1   Information Technology Controls

It is important to establish controls related to the use of information technology resources. Budgets should be established for the acquisition of equipment and software, for operating costs, and for usage. Actual costs should be compared with budgeted amounts, and significant discrepancies should be investigated. Specific information technology control procedures include:

▤ A plan of organization that includes appropriate segregation of duties to reduce opportunities for anyone to be in a position to both perpetrate and conceal errors or irregularities in the normal course of his or her duties.

Illustration 1   Segregation of Duties

Programmers should not have access to source code and production data. They should only make changes in a test environment with test data. Otherwise, a programmer could alter the program to commit fraud and then change the program back so the fraud would be undetected.

▤ Procedures that include the design and use of adequate documents and records to help ensure the proper recording of transactions and events.

▤ Limits to asset access in accordance with management's authorization.

Illustration 2   Access to Assets

Only employees authorized to issue checks have access to the accounts payable module of the accounting system.

▤ Effective performance management, with clear definitions of performance goals and effective metrics to monitor achievement of goals.

▤ Information processing controls are applied to check for proper authorization, accuracy, and completeness of individual transactions.

- The proper design and use of electronic and paper documents and records help ensure the accurate and complete recording of all relevant transaction data.

- Implementation of security measures and contingency plans.

  - Security measures focus on preventing and detecting threats. Data security controls should be designed to ensure that authorization is required to access, change, or destroy storage media.

  - Contingency plans detail the procedures to be implemented when threats are encountered. One goal of the contingency plan would be to minimize disruption of processing while ensuring the integrity of data input and processing.

  - It is a well-accepted concept in information system security that some active threats cannot be prevented without making the system so secure that it is unusable.

2.2 Effectiveness of Control Policies

Evaluating the ongoing *effectiveness* of control policies and procedures provides added assurance that controls are operating as prescribed and achieving their intended purpose. A diagnostic control system compares actual performance with planned performance.

2.2.1 Diagnostic Controls

Diagnostic controls are designed to achieve efficiency in operations of the firm to get the most from resources used.

2.2.2 Control Effectiveness

The following principles of control should be applied to systems development and maintenance:

- **Strategic Master Plan:** To align an organization's information system with its business strategies, a multiyear *strategic master plan* should be developed and updated annually. The plan should show the projects that must be completed to achieve long-range company goals and address the company's hardware, software, personnel, and infrastructure requirements.

- **Data Processing Schedule:** All data processing tasks should be organized according to a *data processing* schedule.

- **Steering Committee:** A *steering committee* should be formed to guide and oversee systems development and acquisition.

- **System Performance Measurements:** For a system to be evaluated properly, it must be assessed using *system performance measurements*. Common measurements include throughput (output per unit of time), utilization (percentage of time the system is being productively used), and response time (how long it takes the system to respond).

3 Roles and Responsibilities of Information Technology Professionals

Information technology professionals include administrators (for the database, the network, and the Web), librarians, computer operators, and developers (for systems and applications). The roles and responsibilities of IT professionals are defined individually by each organization, and, as indicated previously, job titles and responsibilities can vary widely depending on the needs of the organization and, in some cases, the personal preferences of IT management.

3.1   System Analyst

3.1.1   Internally Developed System

- Works with end users to determine system requirements.

- Designs the overall application system.

- Determines the type of network needed.

3.1.2   Purchased System

- Integrates the application with existing internal and purchased applications.

- Provides training to end users.

3.2   Computer Programmer

Computer programmers include application programmers and system programmers.

3.2.1   Application Programmer/Software Developer (Software Engineers)

- An *application programmer* is the person responsible for writing and/or maintaining application programs. A considerable number of the new ideas for the IT industry have been devoted to techniques to minimize or facilitate program maintenance.

- For internal control purposes, application programmers should not be given write/update access to data in production systems or unrestricted and uncontrolled access to application program change management systems.

3.2.2   System Programmer

- A *system programmer* is responsible for installing, supporting (troubleshooting), monitoring, and maintaining the operating system. System programmers also may perform capacity planning functions. In complex computing environments, a considerable amount of time can be spent testing and applying operating system upgrades.

- For internal control purposes, system programmers should not be given write/update access to data in production systems or access to change management systems.

3.3   Computer Operator

Computer operators are responsible for scheduling and running processing jobs. Much of the job of scheduling and running jobs can be automated and, in large computing environments, must be automated due to the sheer volume of information processed.

3.4   IT Supervisor

IT supervisors manage the functions and responsibilities of the IT department.

3.5   File Librarian

File libraries store and protect programs from damage and unauthorized use, and file librarians control the file libraries. In large computing environments, much of this work is automated.

3.6   Data Librarian

In large companies, the data librarian has custody of and maintains the entity's data and ensures that production data is released only to authorized individuals when needed.

3.7   Security Administrator

Security administrators are responsible for the assignment of initial passwords and often the maintenance of those passwords (if the end users do not maintain their own passwords). Security administrators are responsible for the overall operation of the various security systems and the security software in general.

3.8   System Administrator

3.8.1   Database Administrator (DBA)

- *Database administrators* are responsible for maintaining and supporting the database software and performing certain security functions. Database administrators perform functions for database software that are similar to those system programmers perform for the operating system as a whole.

- Database administrators differ from data administrators; a database administrator is responsible for the actual database software, and a data administrator is responsible for the definition, planning, and control of the data within a database.

3.8.2   Network Administrator

Network administrators support computer networks through performance monitoring and troubleshooting. Sometimes, network administrators are called telecommunication analysts or network operators.

3.8.3   Web Administrator

Web administrators are responsible for information on a website.

3.9   End User

End users are any workers in an organization who enter data into a system or who use the information processed by the system. End users now routinely enter much of their own data or transactions.

4   Segregation of Duties Within Information Technology

In a well-structured IT department, the duties discussed below are segregated. Because many transactions in an IT environment are actually performed by the application software, segregation of duties normally revolves around granting and/or restricting access to production programs and to production data.

4.1   System Analysts vs. Computer Programmers

System analysts design an information system to meet user needs, whereas computer programmers use that design to create an information system by writing computer programs. Analysts often are in charge of hardware and programmers are in charge of application software. Theoretically, if the same person is in charge of hardware and software, that person could easily bypass security systems without anyone knowing and steal organizational information or assets (e.g., embezzling of funds).

4.2   Computer Operators vs. Computer Programmers

It is important that *computer operators* and *computer programmers* be segregated because a person performing both functions could make unauthorized and undetected program changes.

4.3   Security Administrators vs. Computer Operators and Computer Programmers

Security administrators are responsible for restricting access to systems, applications, or databases to the appropriate personnel. If the security administrator were also a programmer or an operator for that system, that person could give himself or another person access to areas they are not authorized to enter. This security bypass also would allow that person to steal organizational information or assets.

5   Design and Effectiveness of Information Technology Control Activities

5.1   Manual vs. Automated Controls

A *manual control* is a control performed by a person without making direct use of automated systems.

Illustration 3   Manual Control

When performing a quality assurance review, the reviewer evaluates the process and related requirements in order to confirm that the entire process was executed correctly.

An *automated control* is a control performed by an automated system, without interference of a person.

Illustration 4   Automated Control

In a point-of-sale credit limit check at a retail store:

Step 1: Customer swipes a credit card at the register.

Step 2: The retail point-of-sale (POS) terminal communicates with the credit card issuer to verify credit limit and amount of available credit.

Step 3: If the transaction is within the credit limit, the system approves the transaction. If the transaction is above the credit limit, the system declines the transaction.

■ **Value of Automated Controls**
- Accuracy
- Timeliness
- Efficiency
- Security

5.2 Controls Can Be Preventive, Detective, and Corrective

5.2.1 Preventive

Preventive controls refers to using administrative controls such as security awareness training, technical controls such as firewalls, and anti-virus software to stop attacks from penetrating the network. Most industry and government experts agree that security configuration management is probably the best way to ensure the best security configuration allowable, along with automated patch management and updating anti-virus software.

5.2.2 Detective

Employing a blend of technical controls such as anti-virus, intrusion detection systems, system monitoring, file integrity monitoring, change control, log management, and incident alerting can help to track how and when system intrusions are being attempted.

5.2.3 Corrective

Applying operating system upgrades, backup data restore and vulnerability mitigation, and other controls to make sure that systems are configured correctly and can prevent the irretrievable loss of data.

Question 1	CPA-06984

What is the primary objective of data security controls?

- **a.** To establish a framework for controlling the design, security, and use of computer programs throughout an organization.
- **b.** To ensure that storage media are subject to authorization prior to access, change, or destruction.
- **c.** To formalize standards, rules, and procedures to ensure the organization's controls are properly executed.
- **d.** To monitor the use of system software to prevent unauthorized access to system software and computer programs.

Question 2	CPA-08305

A company's new time clock process requires hourly employees to select an identification number and then choose the clock-in or clock-out button. A video camera captures an image of the employee using the system. Which of the following exposures can the new system be expected to change the *least*?

- **a.** Fraudulent reporting of employees' own hours
- **b.** Errors in employees' overtime computation
- **c.** Inaccurate accounting of employees' hours
- **d.** Recording of other employees' hours

1 Fundamental Risks Related to Systems Development and Maintenance

Organizations constantly improve or replace information systems for any of the following reasons:

1. Changes in needs of a business unit (because of growth, downsizing, mergers, new regulations, etc.).

2. Technological advances resulting in more effective but less costly systems.

3. Improvements in business processes leading to shorter processing times.

4. Competitive advantages as the result of improvements in quality, quantity, and speed of information gathering.

5. Productivity gains due to automation of clerical tasks.

6. System age and need for replacement.

1.1 Technology Risk

The need for technology risk management has intensified in recent years due to the speed of technological change, the degree to which technology is driving business, and the adoption of emerging and disruptive technologies that change the way business is done, such as cloud, connected devices, and mobile.

There are four general types of risks associated with information technology systems, whether the system is in development or in use.

1.1.1 Strategic Risk

Strategic risk includes the risk of choosing inappropriate technology. For example, an organization may choose a Web-based program to share data between remote offices in different parts of the world. If one of the offices is in a location that does have access to high-speed Internet connections, it will not be able to enter data at the same speed as the other offices. This problem may lead to the generation of reports thought to be up-to-date but actually missing data from the office that does not have high-speed access.

1.1.2 Operating Risk

Operating risk includes the risk of doing the right things in the wrong way. For example, assume that a payroll manager is supposed to run the biweekly payroll after the human resources manager enters newly hired employees into the system. If the payroll manager runs the payroll too early (i.e., before the newly hired employees are entered), the newly hired employees do not get paid, and the payroll report is inaccurate.

1.1.3 Financial Risk

Financial risk includes the risk of having financial resources lost, wasted, or stolen. For example, an inventory report lists several laptop computers, but some of the laptops were not returned when employees left the organization. This problem could lead to inaccurate financial reports that report assets that no longer exist.

1.1.4 Information Risk

Information risk includes the risk of loss of data integrity, incomplete transactions, or hackers. If a network system that is connected to the Internet does not have a secure firewall or another type of security measure, hackers may enter the system and corrupt or destroy data.

2   Managing IT Risk

2.1   Risk IT Framework

ISACA (formerly known as the Information Systems Audit and Control Association) developed the Risk IT Framework, which can be used with other frameworks (e.g., ERM), to achieve the following three objectives:

1. Integrate the management of IT risk into the overall risk management of the enterprise.

2. Make well-informed decisions about the nature and extent of the risk, the risk appetite, and the risk tolerance of the enterprise.

3. Develop a response to the risk.

2.2   IT Risk Defined

As defined in the Risk IT Framework, IT risk is the business risk associated with the use, ownership, operation, involvement, influence, and adoption of IT within an enterprise. It consists of IT-related events that could potentially affect the business. Examples are:

- Late project delivery

- Not achieving enough value from IT

- Compliance

- Obsolete or inflexible IT architecture

- IT service delivery problems

- Security issues

2.3   Categories of IT Risk

According to ISACA, there are three categories of IT risk, which are defined as separate from but interrelated to general business risks. These are:

1. **IT Benefit/Value Enablement Risk:** Related to missed opportunities to use technology to improve business processes.

2. **IT Program and Project Delivery Risk:** Related to the contribution of IT to new or improved business solutions.

3. **IT Operations and Service Delivery Risk:** Related to all aspects of the performance of IT systems and services.

3   Risk Assessment

Before risks can be managed, they must be assessed. The steps in risk assessment are to:

1.   identify threats;

2.   evaluate the probability that the threat will occur;

3.   evaluate the exposure in terms of potential loss from each threat;

4.   identify the controls that could guard against the threats;

5.   evaluate the costs and benefits of implementing controls; and

6.   implement controls that are determined to be cost effective.

The following chart lists some of the major risks that could affect systems development, operation, and maintenance. New threats constantly arise, so the list is not considered to be complete.

Sample of Potential Risks to IT				
Risks From Nature	*Risks From Current and Past Employees*	*Risks From Competitors*	*Risks From Hackers*	*Unintended Risks*
1. Earthquakes, volcanoes, fires, storms, and floods 2. Transportation accidents 3. Events related to hazardous materials	1. Human error 2. Sabotage 3. Fraud 4. Professional misconduct 5. Negligence 6. Passive-aggressive behavior 7. Workplace revenge 8. Insurance fraud 9. Lawsuits against employer	1. Intellectual property theft 2. Copyright infringement 3. Patent infringement 4. Price surveillance	1. Viruses 2. Eavesdropping 3. Spam 4. Phishing 5. Spyware 6. Malware 7. Password cracking 8. Website defacement 9. Transmission control protocol and Internet protocol (TCP/IP) hijacking 10. System tampering	1. Software defects 2. Loss of data due to hardware failure or employee error 3. Unavailability of key personnel due to disaster or illness 4. Failure to keep computers up-to-date with operating system, antivirus, or firewall software 5. Having insufficient personnel or personnel who are not adequately trained 6. Inadequate physical security 7. Employees sharing passwords or other access 8. Loss of outsourced services 9. Inadequate budgets to maintain appropriate software and hardware

4   Risks Related to New Technology

Developing high-quality, error-free software is difficult, expensive, and time-consuming. An established fact in business is that most software projects deliver less, cost more, and take longer than expected. This does not address the projects that get canceled before completion.

The AICPA has published lessons learned by a major corporation in a recent system implementation that stressed the importance of the following points, adapted from the AICPA:

- **Defining the integration points to the governance processes.** Successfully moving a strategic plan from concept to reality depends on clear, well-defined integration points with the budgeting, governance, and decision-making processes within IT. Decision makers must understand the strategic directions and make decisions consistent with their intent. If localized, sub-optimal decisions will be made and the plan will not succeed.

- **Defining and managing planning data.** A wealth of data flows throughout the strategic planning process. To lend focus to the process and avoid wasted efforts, deliverables for each step of the process must be clearly defined from the start. This helps ensure that the correct data is developed for effective decision making and also builds support for the process by informing stakeholders of the expected output of each step.

- **Defining and publicizing the planning calendar.** When multiple levels of planning occur simultaneously, publicizing a planning calendar lets everyone know what's happening—and when—so that everyone involved is on the same page.

- **Realizing that timing is essential.** Each step in the planning process must support the next stage. Direct influence is lost if there are timing missteps along the way.

- **Clearly defining roles and responsibilities.** Core team members include a business process manager who defines, communicates, facilitates, and improves the process through each cycle. Subject matter experts develop the data, analysis, and ideas that are used throughout the process. It is best to have a broad, virtual team from across the organization participating in the process to make sure the output is challenged and supported from a number of different perspectives. Decision makers should review, discuss, and debate the strategic planning data and set the direction for the organization. Clearly defining the decision makers early on helps avoid organizational conflict later.

- **Communicating data and messages well.** Effectively communicating the strategic planning messages and associated data to middle and first-line managers helps them educate their personnel. Well-informed employees are most likely to commit to and support the plan.

5   Risks Related to Legacy Systems

The incentives to stick with legacy software do not negate the risks. One of the most powerful disincentives is the unguarded security vulnerabilities of legacy products. The cost of a breach that leaks Social Security or credit card information now averages more than $7 million.

5.1   Reasons for Persistence of Legacy Systems

Many entities choose to continue to use legacy systems due to:

- **Investment in Deployment:** The company already paid for the product, so there is an incentive to use it for as long as possible.

- **Investment in Training:** The employees have already invested time in learning the product, so again there is a built-in incentive to leverage that.

- **Dependencies on Supportive Technology:** The legacy software might only run on a legacy system, which would be burdensome to upgrade.

- **Dependencies Built on the Legacy Product:** The organization may have built custom products using the legacy software, creating a huge disincentive to abandon it and risk having to rebuild in-house software.

- **Risk Over Reward:** Saving time and money by continuing to use legacy software might seem like a reward, but it is often illusory. A security breach easily can result in a disaster, which is far more time-consuming and potentially costly than maintaining up-to-date software.

5.2   Risks of Legacy Systems

Using legacy systems exposes an entity to the following risks:

- **Lack of Vendor Support:** It costs money for a vendor to continue updating a product. Eventually, support may end and new vulnerabilities may not be caught. Vendors concentrate more of their resources on developing, updating, and promoting new products rather than maintaining old ones.

- **Old "Threatscape":** Older products possess less sophisticated security mechanisms. Legacy software was, by definition, developed at a time when the understanding of the security threatscape was less advanced than the present. Many of the techniques developed by hackers to compromise systems, as well as strategies created by security professionals to protect them, were less mature in the past.

- **Code Reutilization:** Often, software products incorporate some amount of code from a predecessor or other products. This can incorporate security vulnerabilities that predate even the legacy product.

- **Educated Hackers:** When security flaws are discovered in software, they are published so they can be known and acted on. This also educates the hackers, and for a legacy product the known vulnerabilities have been exposed for years, providing ample time for hackers to learn, understand, and develop tools to exploit them.

- **Patch Lag:** Many organizations are slow to install patches, allowing legacy products to remain exposed for a long period, during which the knowledge about those flaws is increasingly available.

- **Evolving Hacker Tools:** When a new security flaw is discovered in a contemporary product, many times it can be exploited only by the most sophisticated hackers with a high degree of technical savvy. Over time, the hacker toolkit evolves, and compromises which once required the most advanced knowledge can be executed by more rudimentary hackers using simple tools, often guided by online tutorials.

- **Dependency on Insecure Platform:** In some cases, a legacy product may only run in a legacy environment. Even if the legacy product in question does not itself pose a security risk, the fact that it forces you to continue using a highly exploited platform can put an organization in a vulnerable position.

5.3   Mitigating Risk in Legacy Systems

An entity can mitigate the risks related to its legacy systems by:

- **Isolating the System:** One of the many great uses of virtualization is to sandbox a risky platform to keep it isolated from your important systems. It is possible to run legacy apps within a self-contained window on a modern, secure system. In addition, the virtual system can be cut off from network access to the outside world.

- **Virtual Patches:** Sometimes, no security patch is available to directly modify and harden a legacy product. But a so-called virtual patch can address a known vulnerability upstream of the insecure application. A virtual patch could consist of rules in a firewall packet inspector or Web server that look for and detect SQL injection syntax and block the request before it ever reaches the vulnerable legacy product.

6 Information System Testing Strategies

6.1 Purpose of Testing

Software testing is intended to accomplish the following:

1. Find defects created during the development of the software.

2. Determine the level of quality of the software.

3. Ensure that the end product meets the business and user requirements.

6.2 Guidelines for Successful Testing

- Specify testing objectives explicitly. For example, load testing is a process of testing the behavior of software by applying maximum load in terms of accessing and manipulating large input data. This type of testing identifies the maximum capacity of software and its behavior at peak time.

- Identify categories of users for the software and develop a profile for each. Develop a test plan that emphasizes rapid cycle testing. The goal of rapid testing is to identify major bugs early in the development process, requiring integration of test planning, execution, and reporting throughout the life cycle.

- Build robust software that is designed to test itself.

- Use effective formal reviews as a filter prior to testing.

- Conduct formal technical reviews to assess the test strategy and test cases.

- Develop a continuous improvement approach for the testing process.

6.3 Types of Tests

An effective testing strategy includes automated, manual, and exploratory tests to efficiently reduce risk and tighten release cycles. A discussion of some popular approaches to testing follows.

6.3.1 Unit Tests

Used to validate the smallest components of the system, ensuring that they handle known input and output correctly. This type of testing is performed by developers before the setup is handed over to the testing team to formally execute the test cases. The goal of unit testing is to isolate each part of the program and show that individual parts are correct in terms of requirements and functionality.

6.3.2 Integration Tests

Exercise an entire subsystem and ensure that a set of components operates smoothly together. Integration testing can be done in two ways:

1. **Bottom-Up Integration Testing:** This testing begins with unit testing, followed by tests of progressively higher-level combinations of units called modules or builds.

2. **Top-Down Integration Testing:** The highest-level modules are tested first and progressively lower-level modules are tested thereafter.

6.3.3   Validation Tests

Focus on visible user actions and user-recognizable outputs from the system. These tests answer the question, "Did we build the right thing?"

- Validation tests are based on the use-case scenarios, the behavior model, and the event flow diagram created in the analysis phase of the development.
    - Tests must ensure that each function or performance characteristic conforms to its specification.
    - Deviations (deficiencies) must be negotiated with the customer to establish a means for resolving the errors.
- Configuration review or audit is used to ensure that all elements of the software configuration have been properly developed, cataloged, and documented to allow its support during its maintenance phase.

6.3.4   Acceptance Tests

Make sure the software works correctly for the intended user in his or her normal work environment. This is arguably the most important type of testing, as it is conducted by a quality assurance (QA) team that gauges whether the application meets the intended specifications and satisfies the client's requirement. The QA team will have a set of prewritten scenarios and test cases that will be used to test the application.

- **Alpha Test:** Version of the complete software is tested by the customer under the supervision of the developer at the developer's site.
- **Beta Test:** Version of the complete software is tested by the customer at his or her own site without the developer being present.

6.3.5   System Testing

System testing tests the system as a whole. Once all the components are integrated, the application as a whole is tested rigorously to determine whether it meets the specified quality standards. This type of testing is performed by a specialized testing team.

1. **Steps in System Testing**
    - **Recovery Testing:** Checks the system's ability to recover from failures.
    - **Security Testing:** Verifies that system protection mechanisms prevent improper penetration or data alteration.
    - **Stress Testing:** Program is checked to see how well it deals with abnormal resource demands (i.e., quantity, frequency, or volume).
    - **Performance Testing:** Designed to test the run-time performance of software, especially real-time software.
    - **Deployment (or Configuration) Testing:** Exercises the software in each of the environments in which it is to operate.

2. **Importance of System Testing**
    - System testing is the first step in the software development life cycle, where the application is tested as a whole.
    - The application is tested thoroughly to verify that it meets the functional and technical specifications.
    - The application is tested in an environment that is very close to the production environment in which the application will be deployed.
    - System testing enables QA to test, verify, and validate both the business requirements as well as the application architecture.

Question 1   CPA-03483

All of the following are different types of reporting risk that an accountant must recognize as threats to accuracy of reports, *except*:

- **a.** Strategic risk.
- **b.** Financial risk.
- **c.** Information risk.
- **d.** Data integrity risk.

Question 2   CPA-04827

Which of the following risks can be minimized by requiring all employees accessing the information system to use passwords?

- **a.** Collusion
- **b.** Data entry errors
- **c.** Failure of server duplicating function
- **d.** Firewall vulnerability

NOTES

1. CPA-06748

Choice "d" is correct. The principle of external communications asserts that matters affecting the achievement of financial reporting should be communicated with outside parties.

Choice "a" is incorrect. The principle of financial reporting information conveys the idea that information should be identified, captured, used at all levels of the company, and distributed in a manner that supports achievement of financial reporting objectives.

Choice "b" is incorrect. Internal control information is needed to facilitate the function of control components and is identified, captured, used, and distributed in a timely manner that enables personnel to fulfill their responsibilities.

Choice "c" is incorrect. The principle of internal communications asserts that communications should enable and support understanding and execution of internal control objectives, processes, and individual responsibilities.

2. CPA-06483

Choice "d" is correct. The financial reporting competencies principle of the control environment component of internal control integrated framework suggests stronger controls and encourages the company to retain qualified personnel to handle financial reporting.

Choice "a" is incorrect. The integrity and ethical values principle of the control environment component of internal control integrated framework suggests stronger controls with high standards of ethical conduct for top management, but does *not* address retention of qualified personnel to handle financial reporting.

Choice "b" is incorrect. The management philosophy and operating style principle of the control environment component of internal control integrated framework suggests strong controls and encourages management's attitudes to be congruent with strong financial controls, but does *not* address retention of qualified personnel to handle financial reporting.

Choice "c" is incorrect. The accountability principle of the control environment component of internal control integrated framework suggests strong controls and encourages management to hold individuals accountable for their internal control responsibilities, but does *not* address retention of qualified personnel to handle financial reporting.

1. CPA-06480

Choice "a" is correct. The governance and culture component of the enterprise risk management (ERM) framework includes foundational elements such as defining desired culture, establishing and operating structure, the organization's commitment to core values, and similar issues that influence the tone of the organization.

Choice "b" is incorrect. The strategy and objective-setting component of the ERM framework includes principles that relate to the definition of risk appetite and development of strategy and objectives, not core values.

Choice "c" is incorrect. The performance component of the ERM framework includes principles that relate to the evaluation of risk and development of appropriate responses, not to commitment to core values.

Choice "d" is incorrect. The review and revision component of the enterprise risk management framework includes principles that relate to the pursuit of improvements to enterprise risk management and reviews of risk and performance, not commitment to core values.

2. CPA-06754

Choice "c" is correct. Insuring against losses or entering into joint ventures to address risk is known as risk sharing.

Choice "a" is incorrect. A response to risk that involves the disposal of a business unit, product line, or geographical segment is called risk avoidance. Obtaining appropriate insurance is not avoidance.

Choice "b" is incorrect. A response to risk that involves the diversification of product offerings rather than elimination of product offerings is called reduction. Obtaining appropriate insurance is not reduction, it is sharing (the risk has not changed; it has been shifted to another party).

Choice "d" is incorrect. Self-insuring or simply tolerating the full exposure to risk is known as acceptance. Obtaining appropriate insurance is not acceptance of risk.

Business 1, Module 3

1. CPA-07014

Choice "c" is correct. The financial expert serving on the audit committee of an issuer must have experience with internal controls. The financial expert qualifies through education or past experience as an auditor or finance officer for an issuer of similar complexity.

Choice "a" is incorrect. The financial expert qualifies through education or past experience as an auditor or finance officer for an issuer of similar complexity. The expert should have an understanding of GAAP, application of GAAP, an understanding of internal controls, and an understanding of audit committee functions. There is no requirement to have a limited understanding of GAAS.

Choice "b" is incorrect. The financial expert qualifies through education or past experience as an auditor or finance officer for an issuer of similar complexity. The expert should have an understanding of GAAP, application of GAAP, an understanding of internal controls, and an understanding of audit committee functions. There is no requirement to have education and experience as a certified financial planner.

Choice "d" is incorrect. The financial expert qualifies through education or past experience as an auditor or finance officer for an issuer of similar complexity. The expert should have an understanding of GAAP, application of GAAP, an understanding of internal controls, and an understanding of audit committee functions. There is no requirement to have experience in tax return preparation.

2. CPA-06491

Choice "c" is correct. Issuers are generally prohibited from making personal loans to directors or executive officers under the Sarbanes-Oxley Act of 2002. Exceptions exist for loans made in the ordinary course of business.

Choice "a" is incorrect. Although there is no 10 percent cap on ownership, disclosures are required for persons who generally directly or indirectly own more than 10 percent of any class of most any equity security.

Choice "b" is incorrect. Although there is no 10 percent cap on ownership, disclosures are required for persons who generally directly or indirectly own more than 10 percent of any class of most any equity security.

Choice "d" is incorrect. There are no prohibitions on perquisite compensation but disclosures may be required.

1. CPA-05788

Choice "b" is correct. The effective rate of interest rate is 10 percent. The effective interest rate represents the actual finance charges associated with a borrowing after reducing loan proceeds for charges and fees.

The above scenario indicates that finance charges are $40,000 ($500,000 × 8%), and the net proceeds or amount available under the loan is $400,000 (the face value of $500,000 net of the 20 percent compensating balance of $100,000 [$500,000 × 20%]).

The effective rate of interest is the finance charge of $40,000 divided by the net proceeds of $400,000:

$40,000 ÷ $400,000 = 10%

Choice "a" is incorrect. The stated rate of the loan (8 percent) is not the effective rate of interest.

Choice "c" is incorrect. The compensating balance (20 percent) percentage is not the effective rate of interest.

Choice "d" is incorrect. The sum of the stated rate and the compensating balance (28 percent) is not the effective rate of interest.

1. CPA-05860

Choice "a" is correct. Foreign currencies are like anything else: their value can go up or down. If the dollar price of the euro rises, then the euro is getting more expensive. That means that the dollar is getting less expensive. Another way to say the same thing is that the dollar is depreciating against the euro.

Choice "b" is incorrect. This choice is backward.

Choice "c" is incorrect. The euro is the currency of Europe (or at least a large portion of Europe). If the price of the euro increases relative to the U.S. dollar, it will not buy fewer European goods. When the price of the euro rises, the price of European goods will also increase, and the euro will buy the same amount of European goods, but more U.S. goods.

Choice "d" is incorrect. When the price of the euro rises, the euro will buy more, not fewer, U.S. goods.

2. CPA-05590

Choice "a" is correct. As a foreign competitor's currency becomes weaker compared with the U.S. dollar, the product becomes less expensive in U.S. dollars. The less expensive product will increase demand and result in an advantage in the U.S. market.

Choice "b" is incorrect. The opposite effect occurs, as described in choice "a" above.

Choice "c" is incorrect. Foreign currency exchange rates affect both sales and possibly cost of goods sold of a competing domestic company. Sales within U.S. markets will deteriorate as the currency of foreign competitors deteriorates and makes the domestic company's goods more expensive. As a foreign competitor's currency appreciates, sales within U.S. markets by a domestic company should also increase as goods manufactured in the U.S. become less expensive. Cost of goods sold may fluctuate if foreign suppliers are used.

Choice "d" is incorrect. It is better for a U.S. company when the value of the U.S. dollar weakens, not strengthens. A weak U.S. dollar makes domestic goods relatively less expensive than imported goods.

3. CPA-05767

Choice "c" is correct. Because Platinum is going to receive euros in 30 days, it will want to lock in the price of euros now. The way to do that is to enter into a forward contract (referred to in the text as a forward hedge) to sell euros in 30 days. The price will be fixed now, but the transaction will not occur until the end of the 30-day period. A futures contract also might be able to be used. Note that, with the fixed price, Platinum will not be hurt if the price of euros in terms of dollars falls, but it will also not benefit if the price of euros in terms of dollars rises. In this question, the treasurer was concerned about the price of euros dropping.

Choice "a" is incorrect. Buying 30,000 euros now will not reduce the risk of a drop in the value of the euro. In fact, the risk will double because the company will have 60,000 euros in 30 days.

Choice "b" is incorrect. Buying an interest rate swap will do nothing to reduce the risk of a drop in the value of the euro. Interest rate swaps might reduce the risk of changes in interest rates.

Choice "d" is incorrect. Platinum can reduce the risk of a drop in the value of the euro by using the appropriate hedge. Hedges are often used to reduce currency risk.

NOTES

1. CPA-03385

	Debt		Equity		Total
Investment dollars	$15 mil	+	$35 mil	=	$ 50 mil
Investment structure	30%		70%		100%
Cost of investment	× 7%		× 12%		
Weighted avg. cost of capital	2.1%	+	8.4%	=	10.5%

Choice "a" is correct. 10.50 percent weighted average cost of capital.

Choices "b", "c", and "d" are incorrect, per the above calculation.

2. CPA-03420

Choice "d" is correct. The CAPM holds that:

Cost of retained earnings = Risk-free rate + [Beta × (Market return − Risk-free rate)]

Substituting

Cost of retained earnings = 6% + 1.25 (14% − 6%)

= 6% + 10%

= 16% (Choice "d")

Choices "a", "b", and "c" are incorrect, per the above calculation.

1. CPA-03431

Choice "c" is correct. Financial leverage increases when the debt-to-equity ratio increases. Using a higher percentage of debt (bonds) for future investments would increase financial leverage.

Choice "a" is incorrect. This results in no change in total equity and, consequently, no change in financial leverage.

Choice "b" is incorrect. This would result in increased equity and decreased debt, which would decrease financial leverage.

Choice "d" is incorrect. This would increase equity, decrease the debt-to-equity ratio and decrease financial leverage.

Business 2, Module 3

1. CPA-03528

Choice "b" is correct. Working capital (WC) increases only if current assets are increased or current liabilities are decreased. Exchanging accounts payable (current liability) for a two-year note payable (long-term liability) would decrease current liabilities and increase working capital.

Choice "a" is incorrect. This would not impact WC.

Choice "c" is incorrect. This would not have an impact on WC (decrease of both CA and CL).

Choice "d" is incorrect. This would decrease WC.

2. CPA-03456

Choice "d" is correct. The current ratio is current assets divided by current liabilities. The sale of land would increase cash and therefore current assets without increasing current liabilities. This would increase the current ratio. Furthermore, the sale of land at a loss would decrease net profit.

Choice "a" is incorrect. The payment of a tax payment would not decrease net profit because the expense was accrued last year.

Choice "b" is incorrect. The use of cash to retire a long-term bond would reduce current assets without reducing current liabilities. This would reduce the current ratio.

Choice "c" is incorrect. As above, this would reduce cash without reducing current liabilities.

Business 2, Module 4

1. CPA-03458

Choice "d" is correct. 36.7% annual cost of credit if cash discount is not taken.

$$\frac{360}{(30 - 10)} \times \frac{2\%}{(100\% - 2\%)} = 36.7\%$$

Choices "a", "b", and "c" are incorrect, per the above calculation.

2. CPA-06627

Choice "b" is correct. An increase in the cost of carrying inventory would lead to a reduction in average inventory. Suppose item A is required to be refrigerated so that it will not spoil. If electricity prices are rising, management would prefer to have a lower inventory of item A on hand because of the electricity (i.e., carrying) cost of that item.

Choice "a" is incorrect. An increase in the cost of placing an order would lead to an increase in average inventory. Management would increase the amount of inventory per order to reduce the number of orders, thereby causing the company to on average hold more inventory.

Choice "c" is incorrect. Increased demand would likely increase average inventory to avoid stockout costs.

Choice "d" is incorrect. An increase in lead time would likely lead to an increase in average inventory. A higher safety stock likely would be needed to accommodate the lead time to ensure that requirements are met.

1. CPA-05315

Choice "d" is correct. The primary reason for a company to agree to a debt covenant limiting the percentage of its long-term debt is to reduce the coupon rate on NEW bonds being sold. A debt covenant is a provision in a bond indenture (contract between the bond issuer and the bond holders) that the bond issuer will either do (affirmative covenants) or not do (negative covenants) certain things. In this question, the issuer would agree not to issue bonds in the future over a certain percentage of its long-term debt. Such a provision would be good for the potential bondholders and would probably reduce the coupon rate on the bonds being sold.

Choice "a" is incorrect. The primary reason for a company to agree to a debt covenant limiting the percentage of its long-term debt is not to cause the price of the company's stock to rise. Bond covenants affect bonds, not equity (at least not directly).

Choice "b" is incorrect. The primary reason for a company to agree to a debt covenant limiting the percentage of its long-term debt is not to lower the company's bond rating. Such a covenant might raise, not lower, a company's bond rating because there would be less risk.

Choice "c" is incorrect. The primary reason for a company to agree to a debt covenant limiting the percentage of its long-term debt is not to reduce the risk of existing bondholders, although a reduction in the risk of the existing bondholders certainly might result from such a covenant. As a general rule, more debt means more risk, and less debt means less risk. So less debt would reduce the risk of all bondholders.

1. CPA-06137

Choice "d" is correct. Fernwell will pay approximately $463, computed as follows:

Step 1, Compute dividend in subsequent year:

$$P_t = D_{(t+1)} / (R - G)$$
$$D_{(t+1)} = \$20 \times 1.05^2$$
$$D_{(t+1)} = \$20 \times 1.1025$$
$$D_{(t+1)} = \$22.05$$

Step 2, Apply growth rate to computed dividend:

$$P_t = D_{(t+1)} / (R - G)$$
$$P_t = \$22.05 \times 1.05 / (0.10 - 0.05)$$
$$P_t = \$23.15 \times 0.05$$
$$P_t = \$463$$

Terms are defined as:

P_t = Current price (price at period "t")

$D_{(t+1)}$ = Dividend one year after period "t"

R = Required return

G = Growth rate

Choice "a" is incorrect. $400 presumes a zero growth model.

Choice "b" is incorrect. $420 presumes only one year of growth, not two.

Choice "c" is incorrect. $441 does not properly account for growth. Specifically, it does not properly include the compounding in the year following the first two years of compounding.

2. CPA-06131

Choice "c" is correct. An underlying assumption of the constant growth model is the idea that the stock price will grow at the same rate as the dividend, thereby producing a constant growth rate.

Choice "a" is incorrect. Compounding growth is exponential, not linear.

Choice "b" is incorrect. The constant growth model assumes that the growth rate is less than the discount rate.

Choice "d" is incorrect. An underlying assumption of the constant growth model is the idea that the stock price will grow at the same rate (not amount) as the dividend as a means of producing a constant growth rate.

3. CPA-06133

Choice "a" is correct. The P/E ratio measures the amount that investors are willing to pay for each dollar of earnings per share. Higher P/E ratios generally indicate that investors are anticipating more growth and are bidding up the price of the shares in advance of performance.

Choice "b" is incorrect. High P/E ratios generally indicate investor confidence in earnings growth, not performance that has peaked.

Choice "c" is incorrect. High P/E ratios generally indicate investor confidence in earnings growth, not that performance will fall.

Choice "d" is incorrect. High P/E ratios give some insight into investor confidence of earnings growth.

Business 2, Module 8

1. CPA-03283

Choice "b" is correct. The original FMV of the old equipment is a sunk cost that does not affect equipment-replacement decisions.

All of the following items affect the decision process:

- Current disposal price of the old equipment
- Cost of the new equipment
- Operating costs of the new equipment

2. CPA-03358

Choice "d" is correct. Discount rates may be adjusted to factor differences in risk into cash flow analysis. For example, a 12 percent discount rate may be used for the first three years of a project and a 15 percent discount rate for subsequent years to reflect the greater risk associated with the cash flows in the later time periods. Discount rates may also be adapted to compensate for expected inflation.

Choices "a", "b", and "c" are incorrect, per above.

3. CPA-03337

Choice "d" is correct. If the net present value of a project is positive, it would indicate that the rate of return for the project is greater than the discount percentage rate (hurdle rate) used in the net present value computation.

Choice "a" is incorrect. If the present value of cash outflows exceeds the present value of cash inflows, then the net present value is negative and the rate of return for the project is less than the discount percentage rate (hurdle rate).

Choice "b" is incorrect. If the internal rate of return is equal to the discount percentage rate (hurdle rate) used in the net present value computation, the net present value will be zero.

Choice "c" is incorrect. The present value index will be greater (not less) than 100 percent if the net present value of a project is positive.

4. CPA-06644

Choice "c" is correct. Net present value is computed as the difference between project inflows and outflows, discounted to present value as follows:

Inflows

Years 1 through 5: $420,000 × 3.79 =	$1,591,800
Year 6: $100,000 × 0.56 =	56,000
Present value of all inflows	1,647,800
Outflow (today, discount factor of 1.0)	1,800,000
Net present value	$ 152,200

Choices "a", "b", and "d" are incorrect, based on the above explanation.

Business 2, Module 9

1. CPA-05785

Choice "b" is correct. The payback period computation ignores cash flows after the initial investment has been recovered. The payback method focuses on liquidity and the time it takes to recover the initial investment.

Choice "a" is incorrect. The discounted payback period considers the time value of money but, like any other payback method, it ignores cash flows after the initial investment has been recovered.

Choice "c" is incorrect. The net present value method measures the amount of absolute return and not a rate. Although a positive net present value would confirm that the entity's investment exceeds the hurdle rate established by management, it neither measures the rate specifically nor assumes a hurdle rate equal to the incremental borrowing rate.

Choice "d" is incorrect. When using the internal rate of return, the analyst recommends acceptance of the investment in the event that the IRR is greater than the hurdle rate established by management.

2. CPA-04836

Choice "a" is correct. The payback method determines the number of years that it will take for a company to recoup or be paid back for its investment. The payback method does not consider the time value of money.

Choice "b" is incorrect. The payback method determines the number of years that it will take for a company to recoup or be paid back for its investment. Although the payback method focuses on liquidity, project cash flows after the initial investment are not considered; thus, profitability is ignored.

Choice "c" is incorrect. The payback method determines the number of years that it will take for a company to recoup or be paid back for its investment. Although the payback method focuses on liquidity, project cash flows after the initial investment are not considered; thus, profitability is ignored.

Choice "d" is incorrect. Salvage value is specifically considered as part of payback computations because it contributes to the incoming cash flow when the asset is sold.

3. CPA-05309

Choice "b" is correct. Projects B and C achieve payback by the end of Year 3. The payback period for Project A is somewhere between the end of Year 4 and Year 5. For all three projects, Year 1 appears to be a combination of cash outflows (initial cost) and cash inflows (return of investment), but it really does not make any difference. When the cumulative cash flow (both inflow and outflow) is zero, the project has paid back.

Choice "a" is incorrect. Project A does not pay back within three years even though Projects B and C do.

Choice "c" is incorrect. Projects B and C, *not* just Project B, pay back within three years.

Choice "d" is incorrect. Project A does *not* pay back within three years even though Project C does.

1. CPA-07083

Choice "d" is correct. Conversion costs include both direct labor and overhead. Increases in crude oil prices are likely to impact the cost of generating electricity (and, by extension, the rate for electricity). Electricity is significant in manufacture of the product in the fact pattern and would likely increase the overhead costs of the manufacturer.

Choice "a" is incorrect. Electricity is not included in direct materials. Direct material costs would likely not increase.

Choice "b" is incorrect. Electricity is not included in direct labor. Direct labor costs would likely not increase.

Choice "c" is incorrect. Prime costs are the sum of direct materials and direct labor. Electricity is not included in prime costs. Prime costs would likely not increase.

1. CPA-05321

Choice "c" is correct. Using direct labor hours, the overhead applied consists of both variable overhead and fixed overhead. The calculation is as follows:

Variable overhead rate = $50,000 / 20,000 hours = $2.50 per direct labor hour

Fixed overhead rate = $25,000 / 20,000 hours = $1.25 per direct labor hour

Total overhead rate = $2.50 + $1.25 = $3.75

Overhead applied to the job = $3.75 × 1,500 = <u>$5,625</u>

Choices "a" and "b" are incorrect, per the above calculation.

Choice "d" is incorrect. This answer incorrectly used a $5.00 overhead application rate, with the variable overhead rate applied twice instead of applying both a fixed and variable overhead rate.

2. CPA-05798

Choice "d" is correct. The estimated product cost is equal to the sum of prime costs and applied overhead or $18,000.

Prime costs are the sum of direct labor and direct material:

Direct labor	$ 6,000	
Direct material	4,000	
Subtotal, prime costs		$10,000

Applied overhead is equal to the overhead rate times the estimated hours:

Computations of rate—total overhead:		
Material handling	$120,000	
Quality inspection	200,000	
Total overhead	$320,000	
Total cost driver	80,000	
Rate	$ 4.00	
Applied overhead:		
Estimated hours	2,000	
Rate	× 4.00	
Applied overhead		$ 8,000
Estimated costs		$18,000

Choice "a" is incorrect. The proposed solution incorrectly anticipates that the product cost is equal to only applied overhead, exclusive of prime costs.

Choice "b" is incorrect. The proposed solution incorrectly anticipates that the product cost is equal to only prime costs, exclusive of applied overhead.

Choice "c" is incorrect. The proposed solution incorrectly anticipates that the product cost is equal to the sum of only direct labor and applied overhead, exclusive of direct material.

3. CPA-03601

Choice "b" is correct. Under the FIFO method, the equivalent units of production is composed of three parts: (i) the completion of units on hand at the beginning of the period; (ii) the units started and completed during the period; and (iii) the units partially completed at the end of the period. Applying these principles to the given fact pattern, the total equivalent units of production for the quarter is determined as follows:

Equivalent units for the first quarter:		
Work in process, beginning (100 units × 50% to complete)		$50
Units started and completed:		
Units completed and transferred out	400	
Units in beginning inventory	(100)	300
Work in process, ending (200 units × 75% complete)		150
Equivalent units of production		$500

Choices "a", "c", and "d" are incorrect, per the above.

4. CPA-03644

Choice "b" is correct. $4.60 equivalent unit cost of materials using the weighted-average method, calculated as follows:

Units completed	92,000
Ending WIP x % completed	21,600 [= 24,000 x 90%]
Equivalent units	113,600

Total costs:

Beginning cost + Current cost = $54,560 + $468,000 = $522,560

Cost per equivalent unit = $522,560/113,600 = $4.60

Choices "a", "c", and "d" are incorrect, per the above explanation.

Business 3, Module 3

1. CPA-08307

Choice "c" is correct. Activity-based costing seeks to assign overhead costs in a manner that identifies consumption of resources. Employee salaries or even head count are more appropriate cost drivers than machine hours for employee benefits expense. Machine hours would be more likely identified as cost drivers for electric, repairs and maintenance, and depreciation expense.

Choice "a" is incorrect. Machine hours are likely an appropriate cost driver for electricity expense.

Choice "b" is incorrect. Machine hours are likely an appropriate cost driver for repairs and maintenance expense.

Choice "d" is incorrect. Machine hours are likely an appropriate cost driver for depreciation expense.

2. CPA-03477

Choice "c" is correct. Using the relative net realizable value method of allocating the joint costs, the net realizable value of both products is calculated as follows:

	Ajac	Bjac
Sales	$80,000	$40,000
Separable costs	(8,000)	(22,000)
Net realizable value	$72,000	$18,000

The joint costs are allocated based on relative net realizable values. The two products together have a net realizable value of $90,000 ($72,000 + $18,000). Ajac contributes 80% of this total (72,000 / $90,000 = 80%). 80% of the joint costs are thus allocated to Ajac: 80% x $60,000 = $48,000.

Choice "a" is incorrect. This answer uses only the separable costs, not the net realizable value. The sales value must also be taken into consideration.

Choice "b" is incorrect. This answer uses only the sales value, not the net realizable value. The separable costs must also be taken into consideration.

Choice "d" is incorrect. The net realizable value (sales value less separable costs) must be computed in order to allocate the joint costs using the net realizable value method.

Business 3, Module 4

1. CPA-03883

Choice "d" is correct. $1,940 total prevention and appraisal cost.

Equipment maintenance (prevention)	$1,154
Product testing (appraisal)	786
	$1,940

Rework is an internal failure cost.

Product repair (warranty) is an external failure cost.

Choices "a", "b", and "c" are incorrect, based on the above explanation.

2. CPA-03890

Choice "a" is correct. In a quality control program, internal failure costs are incurred because nonconforming products and services are detected prior to being shipped to customers. Examples are rework, scrap, reinspection, and retesting.

Choice "b" is incorrect. Responding to customer complaints is an external failure cost incurred because products or services failed to conform to requirements after being delivered to customers.

Choice "c" is incorrect. Statistical quality control procedures are appraisal costs incurred to detect defects.

Choice "d" is incorrect. Only rework represents an internal failure cost as described above.

1. CPA-06645

Choice "b" is correct. The passenger division has an ROI of 16% ($40,000 operating profit divided by $250,000 investment). The cargo division has ROI of 10% ($50,000 operating profit divided by $500,000 investment). The passenger division performed better than the cargo division based on ROI.

Notice that a performance measure based on ROI considers the amount invested to yield return rather than the absolute amount of operating profit. Also note that the rate associated with financing is not relevant.

Choice "a" is incorrect. The cargo division ROI is 10%. However, the cargo division's ROI is lower than the passenger division's ROI of 16%. The passenger division performed better than the cargo division as measured by ROI.

Choices "c" and "d" are incorrect. Both answers incorrectly add the external borrowing rate.

2. CPA-04809

Choice "b" is correct. The addition of an asset at year-end serves to reduce both return on investment and residual income. The addition of an asset increases the denominator in the ROI computation and increases the threshold earnings required using the residual income approach. Both measures would suffer as a result of addition of assets. See illustration below:

Assumptions

Income	$ 100,000
Assets	$1,000,000
Required return	10%
Additional asset	$ 200,000

	Return on Investment				*Residual Income*		
	Before	*Purchase*	*After*		*Before*	*Purchase*	*After*
Income	$ 100,000		$ 100,000	Assets	$1,000,000	$200,000	$1,200,000
Assets	$1,000,000	$200,000	$1,200,000	Required Return		10%	10%
Return	10%		8%	Required Income	$ 100,000		$120,000
				Income	$ 100,000		$100,000
				Difference	$ -		$(20,000)

The purchase of the additional asset reduces ROI from 10% to 8% and produces negative residual income.

Choices "a", "c", and "d" are incorrect, per the above illustration.

3. CPA-08378

Choice "c" is correct. Return on equity (ROE) is calculated as follows:

$$ROE = \frac{\text{Net income}}{\text{Sales}} \times \frac{\text{Sales}}{\text{Assets}} \times \frac{\text{Assets}}{\text{Equity}}$$

The three terms in the calculation (in order) are known as the net profit margin, asset turnover, and financial leverage, respectively. For Spear, these amounts given in the question are reflected in the formula below:

$$ROE = 0.11 \times \frac{2,000,000}{2,500,000} \times \frac{2,500,000}{2,500,000\,(1 - 0.40)} = 0.1467, \text{ or } 14.7\%$$

Note that equity is derived using the new debt ratio of 0.40. If debt represents 40 percent of total assets, equity must represent 60 percent.

Choices "a", "b", and "d" are incorrect, based on the above calculation.

4. CPA-04818

Choice "b" is correct. Economic value added (EVA) is computed as after-tax income in excess of required return. EVA is applied to the fact pattern as follows:

Pretax operating profit				$300,000,000
Less: taxes (40%)				(120,000,000)
After tax income				$180,000,000
Less: required return				

	Weight	Capital	Return	
Cost of equity	50%	× $1,200,000,000 ×	15%	= $90,000,000
Cost of debt	50%	× $1,200,000,000 ×	5%	= 30,000,000
Total required return				120,000,000
Economic value added (EVA)				$ 60,000,000

Earnings after taxes of $180,000,000 net of the required return of 15% on half of the investment funded by equity and 5% on the other half of the investment funded by debt ($120,000,000) yields an EVA of $60,000,000.

Choice "a" is incorrect, per the above computation.

Choice "c" is incorrect. The amount of the required return is not the EVA.

Choice "d" is incorrect. The amount of the after-tax income is not the EVA.

1. CPA-07088

Choice "b" is correct. The coefficient of determination (R^2) is the proportion of the total variation in the dependent variable (y) explained by the independent variable (x).

Choice "a" is incorrect. The independent variable is not explained by the dependent variable. Changes in the independent variable drive the variation in the dependent variable. The coefficient of determination (R^2) is the proportion of the total variation in the dependent variable (y) explained by the independent variable (x).

Choice "c" is incorrect. The measure of proximity of actual data points to estimated data points is not the coefficient of determination. The coefficient of determination (R^2) is the proportion of the total variation in the dependent variable (y) explained by the independent variable (x).

Choice "d" is incorrect. The coefficient of determination (R^2) is the proportion of the total variation in the dependent variable (y) explained by the independent variable (x), not the coefficient of the independent variable divided by the standard error of regression coefficient.

2. CPA-04642

Choice "b" is correct. Using the high-low method, the variable cost per kilo can be determined by dividing the change in cost ($160,000 − $132,000) by the change in volume (80,000 − 60,000):

$$\frac{\$160,000 - \$132,000}{80,000 - 60,000} = \$1.40 \text{ per kilo}$$

The fixed portion of the cost can be determined by substituting the volume and variable in the equation $Y = a + bx$, or

$$Y = a + bx$$
$$\$160,000 = a + \$1.40(80,000)$$
$$a = \$48,000$$

At 75,000 kilos, the total cost would be:

$$Y = \$48,000 + \$1.40x$$
$$Y = \$48,000 + \$1.40(75,000)$$
$$\mathbf{Y = \$153,000}$$

Choices "a", "c", and "d" are incorrect. Using the high-low method, the variable cost per kilo can be determined by dividing the change in cost by the change in volume. The fixed portion of the cost can be determined by substituting the volume and the variable in the equation $Y = a + bx$.

1. CPA-03709

Choice "b" is correct. Breakeven analysis assumes that all variable costs and revenues are constant on a per-unit basis and are linear over a relevant range. Fixed costs in total are constant.

Choice "a" is incorrect. Breakeven analysis assumes that all variable costs and revenues are constant on a per-unit basis and linear over a relevant range.

Choice "c" is incorrect. Total costs do change over a relevant range. Breakeven analysis assumes that all variable costs and revenues are constant per unit and linear within a relevant range.

Choice "d" is incorrect. Total fixed costs are assumed to be constant (representing a linear relationship) over a relevant range.

2. CPA-04798

Choice "b" is correct. Under variable costing, all fixed factory overhead is treated as a period cost and is expensed in the period incurred. The cost of inventory includes only variable manufacturing costs, so the cost of goods sold includes only variable costs. Also, the variable selling, general, and administrative expenses are part of total variable costs.

	Unit Price	Units		Total
Sales	$80.00	4,500		$360,000
Direct materials	$21.00	4,500	$94,500	
Direct labor	$10.00	4,500	45,000	
Variable mfg. O/H	$3.00	4,500	13,500	
Variable S&A	$6.00	4,500	27,000	
Total variable costs				180,000
Contribution margin				180,000
Fixed mfg. O/H			76,000	
Fixed S&A			58,000	
Total fixed costs				134,000
Net income				$ 46,000

Choice "a" is incorrect. The net income is not the contribution margin.

Choice "c" is incorrect per the above computation.

Choice "d" is incorrect. The contribution margin is not the difference between sales and fixed costs ($360,000 − $134,000 = $226,000).

3. CPA-04815

Choice "a" is correct. The difference between variable and absorption costing is the manner in which fixed manufacturing costs are treated. Under variable costing, only variable costs are included in inventory. Consequently, the difference in net income under variable costing rather than absorption costing is the amount of fixed manufacturing costs (accounted for in inventory under absorption costing) multiplied by the change in inventory. An increase in inventory indicates that a portion of the fixed costs associated with inventory under absorption costing are expensed under variable costing. Absorption costing, therefore, produces greater income than variable costing as inventory levels increase, as follows:

Change in inventory (increase)	2,000 units
Fixed manufacturing cost per unit (absorbed into inventory, excluded from cost of goods sold)	$ 30
Higher net income under absorption costing	$60,000

Choice "b" is incorrect. The difference between the fixed costs in inventory and the variable costs in inventory is not the difference in net income when comparing the two methods.

Choice "c" is incorrect. The change in inventory times the variable cost per unit does not define the difference in net income per above. Variable costs are included in inventory and, therefore, reduce cost of goods sold under both methods.

Choice "d" is incorrect. The change in inventory times total cost does not define the difference in net income. Inventory does receive a value under variable costing; however, it is limited to variable costs.

4. CPA-03676

Choice "c" is correct.

Step 1: Determine how many units were sold to generate the $900,000 in sales shown in the fact pattern: $900,000/$20 per unit = 45,000 units sold

Step 2: Determine the total fixed costs:

Unit costs:

Fixed manufacturing costs	$ 7
Fixed selling and administrative costs	3
Total fixed cost per unit	$10

Total fixed costs = $10 per unit × 45,000 units = $450,000

Step 3: Determine the contribution margin per unit:

Selling price per unit	$20
Prime costs	(6)
Variable overhead costs	(1)
Variable selling and administrative costs	(1)
Contribution margin per unit	$12

Step 4: Determine the breakeven in units:

$$\text{Breakeven in units} = \frac{\text{Fixed costs}}{\text{C.M. per unit}}$$

$$\frac{450,000}{12} = 37,500 \text{ units}$$

Choices "a", "b", and "d" are incorrect, per the explanation above.

1. CPA-03991

Choice "a" is correct. This does not change the current assets or the current ratio because the reduction of cash is offset by an increase in accounts receivable.

Choice "b" is incorrect. A cash dividend increases current liabilities without increasing current assets. Although current assets remain unchanged (until the payment happens), the current ratio will change.

Choice "c" is incorrect. Cash is reduced and current liabilities are reduced. Total current assets will change (they will be reduced).

Choice "d" is incorrect. The payment of cash reduces current assets. Long-term assets are increased, as well as long-term and short-term liabilities. The current ratio is reduced.

2. CPA-04009

Choice "c" is correct. An increase in sales collections would decrease the cash conversion cycle.

Choice "a" is incorrect because the operating cycle (as well as the cash conversion cycle) would decrease.

Choice "b" is incorrect, as the average collection period would decrease.

Choice "d" is incorrect. Bad debt losses would decrease from an increase in sales collections.

1. CPA-06169

Choice "b" is correct. Assuming available capacity, the minimum cost per unit of a special order is equal to the variable cost per unit. Fixed costs are irrelevant.

Choice "a" is incorrect. The fixed cost per unit is not the minimum charge.

Choice "c" is incorrect. The variable cost per unit plus the fixed costs spread over available capacity is not the minimum charge. Fixed costs are irrelevant.

Choice "d" is incorrect. The variable cost per unit plus the fixed costs spread over current utilization is not the minimum charge. Fixed costs are irrelevant.

2. CPA-06170

Choice "c" is correct. At capacity, the minimum price for a special order is the sum of the variable costs of current utilization plus the contribution margin from the next best alternative.

Variable costs ($50,000 ÷ 10,000)	$5
Contribution margin, next best ($2,000 ÷ 1,000)	2
Total	$7

Choice "a" is incorrect. The minimum price is not purely the contribution margin on the next best alternative.

Choice "b" is incorrect. The minimum price is not purely the variable costs associated with existing capacity.

Choice "d" is incorrect. The minimum price is not the sum of the total cost plus the contribution from the next best alternative.

1. CPA-05829

Choice "b" is correct. The order of budget preparation begins with the sales budget, which logically drives the production budget (to support sales), which in turn drives the direct materials purchases (to support production), from which the cash disbursements budget is derived.

Choice "a" is incorrect. Budgets are driven by sales forecasts. To begin with, the production budget is illogical and presumes that the budget preparer can mandate sales levels based on production or is not constrained by inventory levels.

Choice "c" is incorrect. Budgets are driven by sales forecasts that ultimately determine cash flows. Beginning with cash disbursements is incorrect.

Choice "d" is incorrect. Although the order presented in this selection properly begins with sales, it does not logically support anticipated sales with production. The placement of direct materials before production appears to indicate that direct material purchases are determined independently of production as determined by sales. That relationship is generally not logical.

2. CPA-04793

Choice "b" is correct.

		Final Units	Safety Stock Percentage	WIP Conversion	WIP Units	
Beginning	Inventory	12,000	40%	4	19,200	↓
Additions	Purchases	N/A	N/A	N/A	**46,400**	Squeeze
Subtractions	(Production)	12,000	N/A	4	48,000	
Ending	Inventory	11,000	40%	4	17,600	↑

The computation derives purchases using the BASE mnemonic where B is the beginning inventory computed at 40 percent of January's production requirements and E is the ending inventory at 40 percent of February's production requirements. Both are multiplied by the 4 pounds of raw material needed. Amounts subtracted from inventory, the "S," are the items produced in January, multiplied by the 4 pounds of raw materials needed. We then squeeze the purchases from the formula: Ending inventory of 17,600 + 48,000 units produced − Beginning inventory of 19,200, which equals 46,400.

Choice "a" is incorrect. It does not consider the raw material conversion of 4 pounds per unit.

Choice "c" is incorrect. This response simply considers the amount of units sold converted to raw materials.

Choice "d" is incorrect. This response is the sum of the units sold in February and the ending inventory requirements.

Business 4, Module 6

1. CPA-03813

Choice "c" is correct. A master budget is an overall budget, consisting of many smaller budgets, that is based on one specific level of production. A flexible budget is a series of budgets based on different activity levels within the relevant range.

Choice "a" is incorrect. The usefulness of master budgets and flexible budgets is not limited to specific periods.

Choice "b" is incorrect. The master budget includes the entire company, not just the production facility. The flexible budget can cover many levels of activity, not just one department.

Choice "d" is incorrect. Flexible budgets do not allow management latitude in meeting goals, but they do give management the opportunity to compare actual results to the budget for the activity level achieved.

2. CPA-05867

Choice "a" is correct. A 5 percent inflation rate would affect salary and health care costs but would not affect depreciation expense (based on historical cost), and would not affect interest expense (fixed based on amortization schedule). The budget would be computed as follows:

Salaries expense	$250,000 × 1.05 =	$262,500
Health costs	100,000 × 1.05 =	105,000
Depreciation expense	65,000 × 1.00 =	65,000
Interest expense on 10-year fixed-rate notes	37,750 × 1.00 =	37,750
Total budget		**$470,250**

Choice "b" is incorrect. The proposed solution improperly inflates interest expense.

Choice "c" is incorrect. The proposed solution improperly inflates depreciation expense.

Choice "d" is incorrect. The proposed solution improperly inflates all presented expenses.

Business 4, Module 7

1. CPA-03836

Choice "b" is correct. Material price variance is the difference between actual price and standard price times actual quantity.

$$\text{Material price variance} = (AP - SP) \times AQ$$
$$= [(\$10,080 \div 4,200) - \$2.50] \times 4,200$$
$$= (\$2.40 - \$2.50) \times 4,200$$
$$= \underline{420}$$

The variance is favorable because the actual cost ($2.40) was less than the standard cost ($2.50).

Choice "a" is incorrect. The material price variance equals the difference in prices times the quantity purchased.

Choice "c" is incorrect. The total material variance is $80 unfavorable ($10,000 − $10,080). This total variance needs to be separated into price and quantity variances.

Choice "d" is incorrect. The material price variance equals the difference in prices times the quantity purchased.

2. CPA-05251

Choice "c" is correct. The direct labor usage (efficiency) variance is computed as follows:

Direct labor usage variance = Difference in standard and actual hours × Standard rate
Direct labor usage variance = [(10,000 units × 0.5 hour) − 3,000 hours] × $15 per hour
Direct labor usage variance = $30,000 favorable

The usage variance is favorable because the actual hours were less than the standard hours.

Choice "a" is incorrect. It is unclear how the $25,000 variance can be calculated in this question, but $25,000 favorable or unfavorable is certainly not correct.

Choice "b" is incorrect. It is unclear how the $25,000 variance can be calculated in this question, but $25,000 favorable or unfavorable is certainly not correct.

Choice "d" is incorrect. The variance was favorable, *not* unfavorable, because the actual hours were less than the standard hours.

3. CPA-05874

Choice "a" is correct. The efficiency variance compares the amount of the variable overhead applied (at standard) with the amount of variable overhead that would have been applied at actual. If more was applied than would have been incurred, the results are favorable.

Standard hours allowed	12,000
Application rate	$ 8
Total	96,000
Actual hours	11,000
Application rate	$ 8
Total	(88,000)
Variable efficiency variance	$ 8,000

Choice "b" is incorrect. Results are favorable, not unfavorable.

Choice "c" is incorrect. The proposed amount is the budget variance, the amount applied compared with the amount spent.

Choice "d" is incorrect. The proposed answer is the variable spending variance (the actual amount spent compared with the amount applied at actual).

4. CPA-03831

Rule: The formula for the production volume variance component for overhead variances is computed as applied overhead minus budgeted overhead based on standard hours. The sole difference between these two calculated amounts is the application of fixed factory overhead.

Choice "b" is correct. Volume variances are computed as follows:

Applied overhead:

(Standard variable overhead rate × Standard direct labor hours allowed) + (Standard fixed overhead rate × Actual production)	$22,800

Budgeted overhead based on standard hours:

(Standard variable overhead rate × Standard direct labor hours allowed) + (Standard fixed overhead rate × Standard production) = ($2.00 × .1 × 19,000) + ($1.00 × 20,000) =	<u>$23,800</u>

Difference:

Unfavorable variance	<u>$ (1,000)</u>

Choices "a", "c", and "d" are incorrect, per the computation above.

5. CPA-06165

Choice "c" is correct. The selling price variance is computed as follows:

$$\text{Selling price variance} = \left[\frac{\text{Actual SP}}{\text{Unit}} - \frac{\text{Budgeted SP}}{\text{Unit}} \right] \times \text{Actual sold units}$$

Choice "a" is incorrect. Even though the budgeted and actual sales both compute to equal $75,000 ($15 × 5,000 for actual and $12 × 6,250 for budget), the selling price variance is not zero.

Choice "b" is incorrect. The selling price variance is not equal to the difference in price times the difference in volume.

Choice "d" is incorrect. The selling price variance is not equal to the difference in price multiplied by standard units.

1. CPA-03291

Choice "b" is correct. An increase in real interest rates increases the cost of capital, which shifts the aggregate demand curve to the left.

Choice "a" is incorrect. An increase in wealth shifts the aggregate demand curve to the right.

Choice "c" is incorrect. An increase in government spending shifts the aggregate demand curve to the right.

Choice "d" is incorrect. An increase in consumer confidence shifts the aggregate demand curve to the right.

2. CPA-05318

Choice "b" is correct. If there is an increase in the resources available in an economy, the economy will be capable of producing more goods and services. This increase is really an increase in the long-run aggregate supply (potential GDP). On the aggregate supply and demand chart, the long-run aggregate supply line (LRAS) is the vertical line that represents the potential or equilibrium level of output. If that line shifts to the right, then the economy is capable of expanding, but it will not automatically expand just because the line shifts to the right.

Choice "a" is incorrect. Just because there is an increase in the resources available in an economy, it does not mean that more goods and services will automatically be produced. There would have to be increased demand (a shift upward in the aggregate demand line) for more goods and services to actually be produced by suppliers.

Choice "c" is incorrect. If there is an increase in the resources available in an economy, the standard of living in the economy will not necessarily rise. It could rise, but it will not necessarily do that.

Choice "d" is incorrect. If there is an increase in the resources available in an economy, the technological efficiency of the economy will not automatically improve. This statement is backwards. An increase in technological efficiency of an economy will normally increase the resources available in the economy and potentially result in increased productivity.

1. CPA-03396

Choice "a" is correct. GDP = G + I + C + E (Exports − Imports)

	$1,040 billion
+	975 billion
+	5,015 billion
+	106 billion
−	183 billion
	$6,953 billion

2. CPA-03404

Choice "d" is correct. Structural unemployment occurs when the jobs available do not match the skills of the unemployed individuals or when the individuals do not live where jobs are available with their skills.

Choice "a" is incorrect. Frictional unemployment exists when workers are in the process of changing jobs or are temporarily laid off from their jobs.

Choice "b" is incorrect. The natural unemployment rate is the sum of frictional, structural, and seasonal unemployment or the unemployment rate that exists when the economy reaches its potential output level.

Choice "c" is incorrect. Cyclical unemployment is due to a downturn (recession) in the economy, which leads to a decline in real GDP and higher unemployment.

3. CPA-05857

Choice "a" is correct. Inflation is the sustained increase in the general price of goods and services. A retiree living on a fixed income would be most hurt by an unanticipated increase in inflation because the retiree's income would not increase to offset the negative effects of the inflation.

Choice "b" is incorrect. A borrower whose debt has a fixed interest rate would benefit from inflation because the borrower would be paying back the debt in cheaper dollars.

Choice "c" is incorrect. A union worker whose contract includes a provision for regular cost-of-living adjustments theoretically would have cost of living increases to offset the effects of the inflation. There would be a lag because the cost-of-living adjustments would be after-the-fact, but at least there would be some protection.

Choice "d" is incorrect. A saver whose savings were placed in a variable rate savings account would have the same kind of protection as the union worker (in choice "c"). The interest rate on the savings accounts would theoretically increase with the inflation. Again, there would probably be a lag, but at least there would be some protection.

4. CPA-05869

Choice "c" is correct. The economy can be dampened by reducing government spending and by increasing taxes (thus giving consumers less money to spend), both of which are fiscal policy. The economy can also be dampened by reducing the money supply (thus effectively decreasing prices) and increasing interest rates (thus giving consumers less money to spend because they are spending more money on interest), both of which are monetary policy.

Choice "a" is incorrect. All of these policies would stimulate the economy further.

Choice "b" is incorrect. Increasing money supply will stimulate the economy, not dampen it.

Choice "d" is incorrect. Reducing both taxes and interest rates will stimulate the economy, not dampen it.

1. CPA-03667

Choice "c" is correct. A shift left in any demand curve represents a decrease in demand (at all price levels) for that product. Because gasoline and cars are considered complementary goods, the demand for gasoline is directly impacted by the demand for cars. If the price for cars increases, the demand for cars will decrease, causing the demand for gasoline to decrease, and the gasoline demand curve to shift left.

Choice "a" is incorrect. An increase in the price for gasoline will decrease the quantity demanded but will not affect overall demand across all price levels and quantities (as represented by a left shift in the demand curve).

Choice "b" is incorrect. A change in the supply curve will not cause a shift in the demand curve.

Choice "d" is incorrect. A decrease in the price of cars would have the opposite effect and cause a right shift in the demand curve.

2. CPA-05577

Choice "c" is correct. A city ordinance that freezes rent prices (such as rent control and rent stabilization in New York City) may cause the quantity demanded for rental space to exceed the quantity supplied. This occurs if the rent controlled price is set below the market clearing price. At the controlled price, the quantity supplied will be constrained due to the low rent prices for the rent-controlled and rent-stabilized properties; builders will not want to build and rent properties for less than they are worth on the open market. The quantity demanded for the rental space will still be artificially high due to the city ordinance, which sets the controlled price below the market price. Thus, the quantity demanded will exceed the quantity supplied. New York City rent control is a perfect example of the effect of a price ceiling and the problems that it can cause.

Choice "a" is incorrect. A city ordinance that freezes rent prices will not cause the demand curve for rental space to fall. Price changes cause movements along the demand curve, not shifts in the demand curve.

Choice "b" is incorrect. A city ordinance that freezes rent prices will not cause the supply curve for rental space to rise. Price changes cause movements along the supply curve, not shifts in the supply curve.

Choice "d" is incorrect. A city ordinance that freezes rent prices will not cause the quantity supplied to exceed the quantity demanded; it would cause the reverse effect.

3. CPA-05770

Choice "a" is correct. If an item has many similar substitutes, its price elasticity of demand will be high. Customers can always switch to a substitute, so a change in price may affect demand substantially.

Choice "b" is incorrect. If the cost of an item is low compared to the total budget of the purchasers, it will make little difference how much it costs. For example, in a business the cost of paper clips will probably not be a significant factor.

Choice "c" is incorrect. If an item is considered a necessity (e.g., insulin to diabetics), the price elasticity of demand will be relatively low (i.e., inelastic). Purchasers will buy it regardless of the cost, and demand will not change all that much.

Choice "d" is incorrect. If the price of an item is regulated by a government agency, the demand may not be highly price elastic because any price changes (if made) will be controlled and implemented gradually over time.

1. CPA-06642

Choice "a" is correct. The inability of market participants (a single trader in this instance) to influence market prices is an attribute of perfect (pure) competition. Attributes of perfect competition also include a large number of suppliers, customers acting independently, very little product differentiation (homogeneous products), and no barriers to entry exist.

Choice "b" is incorrect. Market participants cannot influence prices in perfectly competitive markets.

Choice "c" is incorrect. Trading prices are based on both supply and demand in perfectly competitive markets.

Choice "d" is incorrect. Pricing information is available to all market participants in perfectly competitive markets.

2. CPA-03493

Choice "d" is correct. Under oligopoly, strategic plans focus on maintaining market share and call for the proper amount of advertising (to ensure product differentiation) and ways to properly adapt to price changes or required changes in production volume.

Choices "a", "b", and "c" are incorrect because they are characteristics of other types of market structures.

1. CPA-04830

Choice "b" is correct. When there are few good substitutes for a supplier's product, the supplier has market power (think of a monopoly). As a result, the supplier is better able to control buyers and act as a price setter rather than a price taker.

Choice "a" is incorrect. When supplier's products are not differentiated, buyers will be indifferent about which supplier they purchase from. In other words, if firms sell identical products (think of perfect competition) the product of one firm is a perfect substitute for the product of another firm. In this case, firms are price takers, not price setters.

Choice "c" is incorrect. When there are a large number of firms, no one firm has much market power. This is the case of either perfect competition (if all firms sell identical products) or monopolistic competition (if all firms sell slightly differentiated products).

Choice "d" is incorrect. If the purchasing industry is an important customer of the supplier, the *purchasing industry* (i.e., the buyer) will have some market power. This will diminish the ability of the supplier to influence or control the buyer.

2. CPA-03609

Choice "b" is correct. If a firm must pay a higher cost for the premium related to the differentiation than it is able to recoup in the market for that feature, then its profits will decrease, the firm will lose competitive advantage, and the differentiation strategy will fail.

Choices "a", "c", and "d" are incorrect, as these are all situations in which differentiation strategies work well.

1. CPA-08364

Choice "d" is correct. Opening markets to foreign investment is encompassed within globalization, which is the distribution of industrial and service activities across many nations. Investment growth rates will likely increase (rather than decrease) through globalization, as there are more opportunities for investment and growth.

Choice "a" is incorrect. Emerging markets will become more correlated (integrated) with world markets as globalization increases.

Choice "b" is incorrect. Emerging markets on their own tend to be highly volatile, but integration with world markets will help to reduce that volatility.

Choice "c" is incorrect. Local firms will likely see a decrease in their cost of capital because of an increase in growth and demand.

2. CPA-08365

Choice "a" is correct. Country risk encompasses the political risk, economic risk, transfer risk, sovereign risk, and exchange rate risk associated with engaging in business with foreign countries.

Choice "b" is incorrect. Principal risk relates to the risk of losing an investment (money).

Choice "c" is incorrect. Interest rate risk relates to the fluctuation in value of an investment as a result of changes in interest rates.

Choice "d" is incorrect. Commodity price risk relates to market values and future cash inflows that are affected by fluctuations in commodity prices.

1. CPA-03934

Choice "a" is correct. When two companies operating in the same industry merge, it represents a horizontal merger.

Choice "b" is incorrect. If a company merges with one of its suppliers, this represents a vertical merger.

Choice "c" is incorrect. This is likely to represent either a vertical or diagonal combination, depending on the extent of the relationship between the two companies.

Choice "d" is incorrect. This situation represents a circular combination, as the two companies appear to be in relatively unrelated industries.

2. CPA-03935

Choice "a" is correct. A sell-off would allow Gerard to raise cash while separating itself from Brighton Greens so that it can focus on its core business.

Choice "b" is incorrect. A spin-off would not result in cash for Gerard.

Choice "c" is incorrect. A tender offer is a form of business combination, not a divestiture.

Choice "d" is incorrect. An equity carve-out would allow Gerard to generate cash for the company through the sale of Brighton stock. However, equity carve-outs are typically used when the parent wants to retain control of the new entity, which is not the case in this question.

NOTES

1. CPA-03895

Choice "a" is correct. The just-in-time system focuses on expediting the production process by having materials available as needed without having to store them prior to usage. Thus, the non-value adding operation of storing materials is eliminated.

Choice "b" is incorrect. A just-in-time system is designed to facilitate the flow of materials whether the materials come from one or more suppliers. Competitive bidding is not a major benefit of the just-in-time system.

Choice "c" is incorrect. Maximizing the delivery quantity of materials may increase the need to store the materials prior to using them. The just-in-time system focuses on minimizing storage time and storage costs. Lessening paperwork is not a focus of the just-in-time system.

Choice "d" is incorrect. With a just-in-time system, deliveries are made as materials are needed. A decrease in deliveries may increase the delivery quantity, thus increasing the need to store the materials prior to using them. The just-in-time system focuses on minimizing storage time and storage costs.

1. CPA-06442

Choice "c" is correct. A steering committee has broad objectives that include the oversight of systems development and acquisition after an assessment of data processing needs.

Choice "a" is incorrect. IT project planning and monitoring is the responsibility of the committee or group charged with project controls.

Choice "b" is incorrect. Development of specifications and acceptance criteria is the responsibility of the committee or group charged with post implementation review.

Choice "d" is incorrect. Evaluating IT performance using system performance measurements is the responsibility of managers involved in IT operations, not the direct responsibility of the information technology steering committee.

2. CPA-07042

Choice "d" is correct. Value delivery is one of the five focus areas identified by the IT Governance Institute for IT governance. Value delivery anticipates execution of the IT value proposition throughout the delivery cycle such that IT services consistently satisfy customer requirements. Other areas of IT governance include:

- Strategic alignment
- Resource management
- Risk management
- Performance measurement

Choice "a" is incorrect. Systems analysis is an important IT activity, but it is not a focus area of IT governance.

Choice "b" is incorrect. Programming is an important IT activity, but it is not a focus area of IT governance.

Choice "c" is incorrect. Operations are an important IT activity, but are not a focus area of IT governance.

Business 6, Module 3

1. CPA-03682

Choice "c" is correct. Use of electronic funds transfer for any funds transfer reduces the need for manual data entry, thus reducing the occurrence of data entry errors.

Choice "a" is incorrect. Use of electronic funds transfer is likely to result in a reduction of the paper audit trail surrounding cash receipts and disbursements.

Choice "b" is incorrect. Use of electronic funds transfer creates a need for more stringent access controls.

Choice "d" is incorrect. Use of electronic funds transfer does not affect company policy regarding storage of source documents (e.g., an accounts payable invoice) for cash transactions.

2. CPA-07012

Choice "c" is correct. Enterprise resource planning (ERP) is designed to integrate data from all aspects of an organization's activity. ERP is defined as a cross-functional system that integrates and automates the many business processes that must work together in manufacturing, logistics, distribution, accounting, etc.

Choice "a" is incorrect. Although ERP systems can provide cross-functional information across the organization to assist managers in decision making, the system assumes a high level of sophistication among users and does not automate decision making. The focus of ERP is cross-functional information integration.

Choice "b" is incorrect. ERP provides integrated information that can assist with decision making; however, it is designed to automate the accumulation of cross-functional information.

Choice "d" is incorrect. ERP is primarily meant to provide integrated information for operational managers, not strategic information to executives.

1. CPA-06630

Choice "c" is correct. User accounts should immediately be disabled or removed upon termination of any employee. Enabled accounts for terminated employees present a great security risk since they allow unauthorized access to the system.

Choice "a" is incorrect. Passwords are usually required to be a combination of characters, but in comparison to failing to disable accounts for former employees, weak passwords do not present the greatest risk. Passwords, however weak they may be, provide at least some security.

Choice "b" is incorrect. Although management procedures should always be documented, lack of documentation does not present a high security risk as long as there are procedures in place that are being used.

Choice "d" is incorrect. Security logs should be reviewed periodically by the administrator regardless of whether employees have left the company. Although reviewing logs might detect unauthorized system access, allowing former employees to maintain active passwords has a high security risk of allowing the unauthorized access.

2. CPA-04813

Choice "b" is correct. The identification of critical applications will be found in almost all disaster recovery plans and thus is the best answer.

Choice "a" is incorrect. Replacement of PCs could be in some disaster recovery plans, but even when it is, the plan is more likely to be called a business continuity plan. PCs can be readily purchased, and many firms will decide to purchase replacements only when they need to.

Choice "c" is incorrect. Although the physical security of warehouses may be in another function's disaster recovery plan, it is not likely to be a part of the IT function's disaster recovery plan. It will most likely be included in a supply chain business continuity plan.

Choice "d" is incorrect. Cross-training could be included in some disaster recovery plans, assuming that the "operating personnel" means computer operations personnel (if it means something else, it will not be).

1. CPA-06984

Choice "b" is correct. The objective of data security controls is to ensure that storage media are only accessed, changed, or deleted after appropriate authorization. The objective is to protect information.

Choice "a" is incorrect. Policies establish an overall approach to computer security and are sometimes referred to as the IT security strategy. Data security controls are designed to protect information, not to establish strategy or policy.

Choice "c" is incorrect. Policy support documents, such as procedures, formalized standards, rules, and procedures to ensure the organization's controls are properly executed. Data security controls may be included in procedures, but development of procedures is not their objective.

Choice "d" is incorrect. Change management and related control activities anticipate monitoring the use of system software to prevent unauthorized access to system software and computer programs.

2. CPA-08305

Choice "b" is correct. Controls over time and attendance will not be effective in preventing or detecting errors in the computation of employee overtime. Miscalculation of the wage or overtime premium amount could occur even if hours worked are accurately controlled and captured by the time and attendance system.

Choice "a" is incorrect. Controls over time and attendance systems would be designed to be effective in preventing fraudulent reporting of an employee's own hours. The video image would be very helpful in this regard.

Choice "c" is incorrect. Controls over time and attendance systems would be designed to be effective in preventing inaccurate accounting for employees' hours. The video image would be very helpful in this regard.

Choice "d" is incorrect. Controls over time and attendance systems would be designed to be effective in preventing recording of other employees' hours. The video image would be very helpful in this regard.

Business 6, Module 6

1. CPA-03483

Choice "d" is correct. There is no separate data integrity risk category.

Choice "a" is incorrect. Strategic risk includes risks such as choosing inappropriate technology.

Choice "b" is incorrect. Financial risk includes risks such as having financial resources lost, wasted, or stolen.

Choice "c" is incorrect. Information risk includes risks such as loss of data integrity, incomplete transactions, or hackers.

2. CPA-04827

Choice "d" is correct. Because the primary purpose of a firewall is to prevent unauthorized access to a network, requiring all users to have a password helps to minimize vulnerability.

Choice "a" is incorrect. Collusion would not be minimized at all by requiring employees to have passwords; the employees conspiring to do bad things could merely share their passwords.

Choice "b" is incorrect. Passwords would not do anything about data entry errors.

Choice "c" is incorrect. The usage of passwords or the lack of passwords would have no effect on failure of the server duplicating function.

Blueprint

BEC

Summary blueprint

Content area allocation	Weight
I. Corporate Governance	17–27%
II. Economic Concepts and Analysis	17–27%
III. Financial Management	11–21%
IV. Information Technology	15–25%
V. Operations Management	15–25%

Skill allocation	Weight
Evaluation	–
Analysis	20–30%
Application	50–60%
Remembering and Understanding	15–25%

Business Environment and Concepts

Area I – Corporate Governance (17–27%)

A. Internal control frameworks

Content group/topic	Skill				Representative task
	Remembering and Understanding	Application	Analysis	Evaluation	
1. Purpose and objectives	✓				Define internal control within the context of the COSO internal control framework, including the purpose, objectives and limitations of the framework.
2. Components and principles	✓				Identify and define the components, principles and underlying structure of the COSO internal control framework.
		✓			Apply the COSO internal control framework to identify entity and transaction level risks (inherent and residual) related to an organization's compliance, operations and reporting (internal and external, financial and non-financial) objectives.
		✓			Apply the COSO internal control framework to identify risks related to fraudulent financial and non-financial reporting, misappropriation of assets and illegal acts, including the risk of management override of controls.
		✓			Apply the COSO internal control framework to identify controls to meet an entity's compliance, operations and reporting (internal and external, financial and non-financial) objectives, throughout an entity's structure, from entity-wide through sub-units, down to the transactional level.
		✓			Apply the COSO internal control framework to identify an appropriate mix of automated and manual application controls, (e.g., authorization and approval, verifications, physical controls, controls over standing data, reconciliations and supervisory controls) to prevent and detect errors in transactions.
		✓			Describe the corporate governance structure within an organization (tone at the top, policies, steering committees, oversight, ethics, etc.).

Area I – Corporate Governance
(17–27%) (continued)

Content group/topic	Skill				Representative task
	Remembering and Understanding	Application	Analysis	Evaluation	
B. Enterprise risk management (ERM) frameworks					
1. Purpose and objectives	✓				Define ERM within the context of the COSO ERM framework, including the purpose and objectives of the framework.
2. Components and principles	✓				Identify and define the components, principles and underlying structure of the COSO ERM framework.
	✓				Understand the relationship among risk, business strategy and performance within the context of the COSO ERM framework.
		✓			Apply the COSO ERM framework to identify risk/opportunity scenarios in an entity.
C. Other regulatory frameworks and provisions					
	✓				Identify and define key corporate governance provisions of the Sarbanes-Oxley Act of 2002 and other regulatory pronouncements.
		✓			Identify regulatory deficiencies within an entity by using the requirements associated with the Sarbanes-Oxley Act of 2002.

BEC8

Business Environment and Concepts

Area II — Economic Concepts and Analysis (17–27%)

Content group/topic	Skill				Representative task
	Remembering and Understanding	Application	Analysis	Evaluation	
A. Economic and business cycles - measures and indicators					
	✓				Identify and define business cycles (trough, expansion, peak, recession) and conditions and government policies that impact an entity's industry or operations.
		✓			Use appropriate inputs to calculate economic measures and indicators (e.g., Nominal and Real GDP, Consumer Price Index, Aggregate Demand Curve, Money Supply, etc.) and apply leading, coincident and lagging indicators (e.g., bond yields, new housing starts, personal income, unemployment, etc.).
		✓			Use economic measures and indicators to explain the impact on an entity's industry and operations due to changes in government fiscal policy, monetary policy, regulations, trade controls and other actions.
		✓			Use economic measures and indicators to explain the impact on an entity's industry and operations due to changes in business cycles and economic conditions, caused by factors such as exchange rates, inflation, productivity, state of the global economy, unemployment levels, etc.
B. Market influences on business					
		✓			Identify and define the key factors related to the economic marketplace (e.g., competition, currencies, globalization, supply and demand, trade, etc.) and how they generally apply to a business entity.
		✓			Identify and define market influences (e.g., economic, environmental, governmental, political, legal, social and technological, etc.).
			✓		Determine the impact of market influences on the overall economy (e.g., consumer demand, labor supply, market prices, production costs, volatility, etc.).
			✓		Determine the impact of market influences on an entity's business strategy, operations and risk (e.g., increasing investment and financial leverage, innovating to develop new product offerings, seeking new foreign and domestic markets, undertaking productivity or cost-cutting initiatives, etc.).
			✓		Determine the business reasons for, and explain the underlying economic substance of, significant transactions (e.g., business combinations and divestitures, product line diversification, production sourcing, public and private offerings of securities, etc.).

Uniform CPA Examination Blueprints: Business Environment and Concepts (BEC)   BEC9

Business Environment and Concepts

Area II – Economic Concepts and Analysis
(17–27%) (continued)

Content group/topic	Skill				Representative task
	Remembering and Understanding	Application	Analysis	Evaluation	
C. Financial risk management					
1. Market, interest rate, currency, liquidity, credit, price and other risks		✓			Calculate and use ratios and measures to quantify risks associated with interest rates, currency exchange, liquidity, prices, etc. in a business entity.
2. Means for mitigating/controlling financial risks		✓			Identify strategies to mitigate financial risks (market, interest rate, currency, liquidity, etc.) and quantify their impact on a business entity.

Uniform CPA Examination Blueprints: Business Environment and Concepts (BEC)

BEC10

Business Environment and Concepts

Area III – Financial Management (11–21%)

Content group/topic	Skill				Representative task
	Remembering and Understanding	Application	Analysis	Evaluation	
A. Capital structure					
	✓				Describe an organization's capital structure and related concepts, such as cost of capital, asset structure, loan covenants, growth rate, profitability, leverage and risk.
		✓			Calculate the cost of capital for a given financial scenario.
			✓		Compare and contrast the strategies for financing new business initiatives and operations within the context of an optimal capital structure, using statistical analysis where appropriate.
B. Working capital					
1. Fundamentals and key metrics of working capital management		✓			Calculate the metrics associated with the working capital components, such as current ratio, quick ratio, cash conversion cycle, inventory turnover and receivables turnover.
			✓		Detect significant fluctuations or variances in the working capital cycle using working capital ratio analyses.
2. Strategies for managing working capital			✓		Compare inventory management processes, including pricing and valuation methods, to determine the effects on the working capital of a given entity.
			✓		Compare accounts payable management techniques, including usage of discounts, factors affecting discount policy, uses of electronic funds transfer as a payment method and determination of an optimal vendor payment schedule in order to determine the effects on the working capital of a given entity.
			✓		Distinguish between corporate banking arrangements, including establishment of lines of credit, borrowing capacity and monitoring of compliance with debt covenants in order to determine the effects on the working capital of a given entity.
			✓		Interpret the differences between the business risks and the opportunities in an entity's credit management policies to determine the effects on the working capital of a given entity.
			✓		Analyze the effects on working capital caused by financing using long-term debt and/or short-term debt.

Uniform CPA Examination Blueprints: Business Environment and Concepts (BEC)

BEC11

Business Environment and Concepts

Area III – Financial Management
(11–21%) (continued)

Content group/topic	Skill				Representative task
	Remembering and Understanding	Application	Analysis	Evaluation	
C. Financial valuation methods and decision models					
	✓				Identify and define the different financial valuation methods and their assumptions, including but not limited to fair value, Black-Scholes, Capital Asset Pricing Model and Dividend Discount Model.
	✓				Identify and define the different financial decision models and assumptions involved in making decisions relating to asset and investment management, debt, equity and leasing.
	✓				Identify the sources of data and factors that management considers in forming the assumptions used to prepare an accounting estimate.
	✓				Describe the process and framework within which management exercises its responsibilities over the review and approval of accounting estimates.
		✓			Calculate the value of an asset using commonly accepted financial valuation methods.
			✓		Compare investment alternatives using calculations of financial metrics (payback period, net-present value, economic value added, cash flow analysis, internal rate of return etc.), financial modeling, forecasting, projection and analysis techniques.
			✓		Compare options in a lease vs. buy decision scenario.

BEC12

Uniform CPA Examination Blueprints: Business Environment and Concepts (BEC)

Business Environment and Concepts

Area IV – Information Technology (15–25%)

Content group/topic	Remembering and Understanding	Application	Analysis	Evaluation	Representative task
A. Information technology (IT) governance					
1. Vision and strategy	✓				Identify the role that the IT function plays in determining/supporting an organization's vision and strategy.
2. Organization		✓			Describe the IT governance structure within an organization (tone at the top, policies, steering committees, IT strategies, oversight, etc.).
3. Risk assessments		✓			Conduct an IT risk assessment, identify risks and suggest mitigation strategies.
B. Role of information technology in business					
	✓				Recognize the role of big data/data analytics and statistics in supporting business decisions.
		✓			Identify the role of information systems in key business processes within an entity.
		✓			Identify the role of e-commerce in key business processes within an entity.
C. Information security/availability					
1. Protection of information		✓			Recognize the risks and controls associated with protecting sensitive and critical information within an organization's IT environment (the use of mobile technology, data storage devices, data transmission, cybersecurity, etc.).
2. Logical and physical access controls		✓			Identify weaknesses and mitigation strategies within an entity's IT environment in relation to logical and physical access controls.
		✓			Identify weaknesses and mitigation strategies within an entity's IT environment in relation to IT general and application controls.
3. System disruption/ resolution		✓			Describe an entity's disaster recovery/business continuity plans, including threat identification and mitigation strategies, data backup and recovery procedures, alternate processing facilities, etc.

Uniform CPA Examination Blueprints: Business Environment and Concepts (BEC)

BEC13

Business Environment and Concepts

Area IV – Information Technology
(15–25%) (continued)

Content group/topic	Skill				Representative task
	Remembering and Understanding	Application	Analysis	Evaluation	
D. Processing integrity (input/processing/output controls)					
		✓			Describe the role of input, processing and output controls within an entity to support completeness, accuracy and continued processing integrity.
		✓			Determine the appropriateness of the design and operating effectiveness of application controls (authorizations, approvals, tolerance levels, input edits, etc.).
		✓			Identify issues related to the design and effectiveness of IT control activities, including manual vs. automated controls, as well as preventive, detective and corrective controls.
E. Systems development and maintenance					
	✓				Identify different information system testing strategies.
		✓			Recognize the fundamental issues and risks associated with implementing new information systems or maintaining existing information systems within an entity.

Business Environment and Concepts

Area V – Operations Management (15–25%)

Content group/topic	Skill				Representative task
	Remembering and Understanding	Application	Analysis	Evaluation	
A. Financial and non-financial measures of performance management					
		✓			Calculate financial and non-financial measures appropriate to analyze specific aspects of an entity's performance (e.g., Economic Value Added, Costs of Quality-Prevention vs. Appraisal vs. Failure, etc.).
			✓		Determine which financial and non-financial measures are appropriate to analyze specific aspects of an entity's performance and risk profile (e.g., Return on Equity, Return on Assets, Contribution Margin, etc.).
B. Cost accounting					
1. Cost measurement concepts, methods and techniques		✓			Apply cost accounting concepts, terminology, methods and measurement techniques within an entity.
		✓			Differentiate the characteristics of fixed, variable and mixed costs within an entity.
		✓			Compare and contrast the different costing methods such as absorption vs. variable and process vs. job order costing.
2. Variance analysis			✓		Determine the appropriate variance analysis method to measure the key cost drivers by analyzing business scenarios.

Uniform CPA Examination Blueprints: Business Environment and Concepts (BEC)

BEC15

Business Environment and Concepts

Area V – Operations Management (15–25%) (continued)

Content group/topic	Skill				Representative task
	Remembering and Understanding	Application	Analysis	Evaluation	
C. Process management					
1. Approaches, techniques, measures, benefits to process-management driven businesses	✓				Identify commonly used operational management approaches, techniques and measures within the context of business process management.
2. Management philosophies and techniques for performance improvement	✓				Identify commonly used management philosophies and techniques for performance and quality improvement within the context of business process management.
D. Planning techniques					
1. Budgeting and analysis		✓			Prepare a budget to guide business decisions.
			✓		Reconcile results against a budget or prior periods and perform analysis of variances as needed.
2. Forecasting and projection		✓			Use forecasting and projection techniques to model revenue growth, cost and expense characteristics, profitability, etc.
		✓			Prepare and calculate metrics to be utilized in the planning process, such as cost benefit analysis, sensitivity analysis, breakeven analysis, economic order quantity, etc.
			✓		Analyze results of forecasts and projections using ratio analysis and explanations of correlations to, or variations from, key financial indices.
			✓		Compare and contrast alternative approaches (such as system replacement, make vs. buy and cost/benefit) proposed to address business challenges or opportunities for a given entity.

BEC16

Uniform CPA Examination Blueprints: Business Environment and Concepts (BEC)

NOTES

Absorption Costing: Absorption costing is a method of product costing that includes fixed manufacturing overhead costs, along with direct material, direct labor, and variable manufacturing costs, in the cost of the product. This method is also referred to as "full costing." Absorption costing is GAAP for financial statement purposes. Absorption costing is frequently contrasted with variable costing. The difference between absorption costing and variable costing methods is the treatment of fixed manufacturing overhead. Absorption costing includes fixed overhead as product costs, while variable costing treats all fixed costs as period costs. Fixed selling, general, and administrative costs are treated the same (as period costs) under both methods. *See also* variable costing *and* activity-based costing.

Access Control List (ACL): An access control list, in a computer security context, is a list of permissions attached to a piece of data. The access control list specifies who (which users or groups of users or roles) can access the data and what they can do to/with it (read, write, delete, and/or execute).

Access Controls: Access controls are controls that limit access to program documentation, data files, programs, and computer hardware to those who require it in the performance of their job responsibilities. These controls include physical access controls and electronic access controls. *See also* physical access controls *and* electronic access controls.

Access Point: An access point is a device that connects wireless communication devices to form a wireless network. An access point is often called a wireless access point (WAP, but different from the other WAP, wireless application protocol). The access point normally connects to a wired network. Several WAPs can link together to form a larger network that allows a larger roaming area. Wireless access points have IP addresses for configuration and management of the network.

Accounting Costs: Accounting costs are the explicit costs of operating a business (e.g., purchases of input services). *See also* explicit costs *and* accounting profit.

Accounting Information System (AIS): An accounting information system is a type of management information system; it may also be partly a transaction processing system and partly a knowledge system. There may be separate systems for each accounting function such as accounts receivable, accounts payable, etc., or there may be one integrated system that performs all of the accounting functions, culminating in the general ledger and the various accounting reports. *See also* decision support system *and* executive information system *and* management information system.

Accounting Profit: Accounting profit is the difference between total revenue and total explicit costs. No allowance is made for the opportunity cost of the equity capital of the firm's owners or other implicit costs. *See also* explicit costs *and* implicit costs *and* opportunity costs.

Accounts Receivable Turnover: Accounts receivable turnover is sales (net) divided by average accounts receivable (net).

Activity-Based Costing: Activity-based costing is a costing system that divides production into activities where costs are accumulated into multiple cost pools and allocated to the product based on the level of activities (defined by cost drivers) demanded by the product. Activity-based costing is normally used as a supplement to, rather than a replacement for, a firm's absorption costing system. Activity-based costing normally allocates costs in addition to normal manufacturing costs, and the cost drivers are often nonfinancial activities. Absorption costing is frequently contrasted with traditional cost allocation, a method that assumes a single cost pool and a single cost driver. *See also* variable costing *and* absorption costing *and* cost pool.

Ad Hoc Reports: An ad hoc (done for a particular purpose) report is a report that does not currently exist but that can be created on demand, without involving a software developer or programmer. This capability is often called a user report writer.

Aggregate Demand (AD): Aggregate demand is the maximum quantity of all goods and services that households, firms, and governments are willing and able to purchase at any given price. The aggregate demand curve has the general price level on the y-axis and real GDP on the x-axis. The aggregate demand curve normally slopes down and to the right, indicating that the quantity of goods and services demanded increases as prices decline. Factors that shift the aggregate demand are changes in wealth, changes in real interest rates, changes in consumer confidence, changes in foreign currency exchange rates, changes in government spending, and changes in consumer taxes. *See also* aggregate supply *and* long-run aggregate supply.

Aggregate Supply (AS): Aggregate supply is the maximum quantity of all goods and services that providers are willing and able to produce at any given price. The aggregate supply curve has the general price level on the y-axis and the real GDP on the x-axis. The aggregate supply curve normally slopes upward and to the right, meaning that firms are willing to produce more goods and services at higher prices. The supply in this case is the short-run aggregate supply. Factors that shift aggregate supply are changes in resource prices and supply shocks. *See also* aggregate demand *and* long-run aggregate supply.

Annual Percentage Rate (APR): The annual percentage rate is the interest rate calculated by considering all of the added costs (points, application fee, closing costs, etc.) for a given loan. The calculation spreads these costs over the life of the loan, along with the interest rate, to arrive at a more accurate annualized percentage rate than the stated interest rate alone. The annual percentage rate for a given loan is equal to the stated interest rate if there are no added costs. The APR must be disclosed. *See also* stated interest rate.

Application Controls: Application controls are controls that apply to the processing of individual transactions and are built into the application itself. *See also* access controls *and* electronic access controls *and* physical access controls.

Application Firewall: An application firewall supplements the standard network firewall. A standard network firewall (which is what is meant when the word "firewall" is used by itself) inspects data in packet headers of packets that are coming from or going to certain ports (packet filtering) based on the set firewall access rules. An application firewall (also known as a proxy or an application layer gateway, if implemented hardware) examines data in the packets themselves. Note that the word "application" in this context does not refer to application software such as an accounts receivable application, but to the application layer in a network protocol.

Application Service Provider (ASP): Application service providers provide access to application programs on a rental basis. They allow smaller companies to avoid the extremely high cost of owning and maintaining more sophisticated application systems by allowing them to pay only for what is used. The ASPs own and host the software. *See also* on-demand computing.

Application Software: Application software includes the diverse group of systems and programs that an organization uses to accomplish its objectives. Application software can be generic (e.g., word processors, spreadsheets, or databases) or custom-developed for a specific application or a specific organization. Application software is made up of application programs. Application software can be purchased from an outside vendor or developed internally. *See also* system software.

Appraisal Costs: In quality control, appraisal costs are the costs to discover and remove defective parts before they are shipped to the customer. These costs include statistical quality checks, testing, and inspection. *See also* prevention costs.

Artificial Intelligence: Artificial intelligence is a field of study in which researchers attempt to develop software that can reason and think like humans.

Asset Turnover: Asset turnover is sales (net) divided by average total assets. *See also* return on assets.

Attribute Standards: Attribute standards published by the Institute of Internal Auditors (IIA) address many of the same issues as the general standards under generally accepted auditing standards. Issues related to auditor independence, technical proficiency, and professional care are addressed here.

Audit Trail: The path of a transaction through a data processing system from beginning to end. An audit trail provides a way to check the accuracy and validity of ledger postings and trace all changes in general ledger accounts from their initial balance to their final balance.

Avoidable Costs: Avoidable costs are costs that can be eliminated in whole or in part by choosing one alternative over another. *See also* incremental costs.

B2B: When a business sells its products or services to other businesses, it is called a Business-to-Business (B2B) transaction. *See also* B2C.

B2C: When a business sells its products or services to the public, it is called a Business-to-Consumer (B2C) transaction. *See also* B2B.

Backdoor: A backdoor is a means of access to a program or system that bypasses normal security mechanisms. A programmer will sometimes install a backdoor so that the program or system can be easily accessed for troubleshooting or other purposes. Backdoors should be eliminated. *See also* software vulnerability.

Backflush Costing: Backflush costing (or delayed costing) is a cost system that works backward from the final product to apply manufacturing costs. Backflush costing is used to simplify cost accounting when tracking work-in-process is not important. Backflush costing is often used with just-in-time systems to reduce inventory to very low levels. *See also* just-in-time.

Backup: Backup (or file backup) is the copying of data so that copies of the data will be available if the original data are damaged or destroyed. Backups are necessary in normal operations (where individual files or groups of files might be damaged by an incorrect application program, for example) or for disaster recovery. Backups may be full backups (where "all" of the data are backed up) or incremental backups (where only changed data after the last full backup or the last incremental backup are backed up). A hot backup is a backup of a database that is in use.

Balanced Budget: A balanced budget occurs when taxes and other governmental revenues equal governmental spending. *See also* budget surplus *and* budget deficit.

Balanced Scorecard: A balanced scorecard reports information on multiple dimensions of a firm's performance defined by the critical success factors necessary to accomplish the firm's business objective. A balanced scorecard normally includes both financial and nonfinancial data.

Bandwidth: Bandwidth is a measure of a communication medium's information-carrying capacity.

Banker's Acceptance: A banker's acceptance is a short-term credit investment created by a nonfinancial firm and guaranteed by a bank. Banker's acceptances are traded at a discount from face value in the secondary market. For corporations, a banker's acceptance acts as a negotiable time draft for financing imports, exports, or other transactions in goods. They are especially useful when the creditworthiness of a foreign trade partner is unknown. One advantage is that they do not need to be held until maturity. Instead they can be sold off in the secondary markets, where investors and institutions constantly trade them. *See also* trade acceptance *and* commercial paper *and* draft.

Batch Processing: With batch processing, input documents/transactions are collected and grouped by type of transaction. These groups (called batches) are processed periodically (e.g., daily, weekly, monthly, etc.). Batch processing systems may use either sequential storage devices (e.g., magnetic tape) or random access storage devices (i.e., disks).

Batch Total: A batch total is a total of a field in a transaction that might normally be added, such as dollar amounts. *See also* hash total.

Benchmarking: Benchmarking is the process of identifying standards for the critical success factors of the firm used in comparison to actual performance, determination of gaps in performance, and implementing improvements to meet or exceed the benchmark. Best practices represent world-class performance standards.

Best Cost Strategy: A best cost strategy is a competitive strategy that combines cost leadership strategies with differentiation strategies to give customers higher value for their money. *See also* cost leadership strategy *and* differentiation strategy *and* niche strategy.

Beta Coefficient: Beta coefficient is a statistical measure of an individual company's stock price variability in relation to the market as a whole. The beta coefficient is a key component of the capital asset pricing model (CAPM).

Biases: Biases, in the context of behavioral finance, anticipate human tendencies that distort financial analysis, including excessive optimism, overconfidence, and the illusion of control.

Bill of Materials: A bill of materials is a list that shows the quantity of each type of material in a unit of finished product. *See also* materials requirements planning.

Biometric Authentication: Biometric authentication (sometimes just biometrics) is the use of such things as fingerprints or eye-prints or voice-prints (physical characteristics of the user) in addition to or in place of access cards for physical or electronic access to a location or to a network. *See also* electronic access controls.

Bit: A bit is a binary digit (0 or 1) with which all computer data is stored. *See also* byte *and* field.

Bond Indenture: A bond indenture is the contract between a bond issuer/borrower and the bondholders that sets forth the obligations of the issuer and the rights of the bondholders. *See also* loan covenant.

Bond Yield Plus Risk Premium Method: The bond yield plus risk premium method is a method for determining the cost of equity capital (common stock or retained earnings) as the firm's cost of debt capital plus an equity risk premium (the compensation for taking the additional risk of equity ownership versus the holding of debt). *See also* capital asset pricing model *and* dividend yield plus growth rate method.

Boycott: A boycott is an organized group refusal to conduct market transactions with a target group or individual (using only social pressure, not legal obligation).

Breakeven Point: The breakeven point is the level of sales or the level of volume at which revenue equals expenses. It is also calculated as the ratio of fixed costs to the contribution margin. Profit is zero at the breakeven point because the total of fixed and variable expenses exactly equals sales revenue. *See also* cost-volume-profit analysis *and* contribution margin *and* margin of safety.

BRIC: The acronym BRIC refers to the four leading emerging economies of the world: Brazil, Russia, India and China.

Budget (Controllable) Variance: In a two-way overhead variance, the budget variance is the difference between the actual overhead and the budget based on the standard hours worked for the actual output. This budget variance is equal to the total of the spending variance and the efficiency variance in a three-way overhead variance. *See also* spending variance *and* efficiency variance *and* volume variance.

Budget Deficit: A budget deficit occurs when taxes and other governmental revenues are less than governmental spending. *See also* budget surplus *and* balanced budget.

Budget Surplus: A budget surplus occurs when taxes and other governmental revenues are greater than government spending. *See also* budget deficit *and* balanced budget.

Bundling: Bundling is the selling of a combination of products at a lower price than if the products were sold separately (e.g., a telecommunication company bundling a phone line, cable Internet, and cable TV).

Business Continuity: Business continuity planning deals with the safeguards for ensuring the continuity of a business as a whole.

Business Cycle: The business cycle is the rise and fall of economic activity (GDP) relative to the long-term growth trend of the economy. Business cycles typically comprise an expansionary phase, a peak, a contractionary phase, a trough, and a recovery phase. *See also* recession *and* depression.

Business Information Systems: A business information system is a set of interrelated components (hardware, software, networks, people, and data) that collect, process, store, transform, and distribute data and information to support decision making in an organization.

Business Model: A business model describes how a business produces, delivers, and sells its products or services so as to bring value to its customers.

Business Process: A business process is a unique set of tasks and actions that organizations develop and utilize to produce specific business results. A particular business process may or may not utilize information technology, but IT is becoming increasingly involved in most business processes.

Business Process Reengineering (BPR): Business process reengineering generally involves a comprehensive rethinking of how work is performed to emphasize customer service and reduce costs (improve effectiveness and efficiency). Implementation of new technologies is often a strong motivation for process reengineering.

Business Strategy: A business strategy is adopted by a company to both sustain and grow as a value-adding organization.

Byte: A byte is a group of normally 8 bits that can represent a number or a letter, with the specific form dependent on what internal representation format is being used. Sometimes, bytes are called characters. *See also* bit *and* field.

Call Provision: A call provision in a bond is a provision that allows the bond issuer to pay off part or all of a bond's principal before the maturity date. A call provision is beneficial to the bond issuer because it allows the issuer to pay off the bonds if interest rates decline (and to issue new debt at the lower interest rate). A call provision is thus detrimental to the bondholders since the bondholders will have to reinvest their proceeds at the lower interest rates. If callable, bonds are normally called at a (call) premium.

Capacity Management: Capacity management is the process of planning, sizing, and controlling computer processing or IT infrastructure capacity to satisfy user demand at a reasonable cost. The goal of capacity management is to optimize the capability of the IT infrastructure and supporting organization in order to deliver a cost-effective and sustained level of availability that enables a company to satisfy its business objectives.

Capital Asset Pricing Model (CAPM): The capital asset pricing model is a model for determining the cost of equity capital (common stock or retained earnings) or pricing risk. The CAPM assumes that investors must be compensated for the time value of money plus systematic risk, as measured by the stock's beta. The primary conclusion of the CAPM is that the risk of an individual stock is its contribution to the risk of a well-diversified portfolio. The CAPM can be used to determine the cost of common stock and retained earnings in determining the weighted average cost of capital. CAPM is computed as the risk-free rate plus (beta times the difference between the market rate and the risk-free rate). *See also* beta coefficient *and* nondiversifiable risk *and* bond yield plus risk premium method *and* dividend yield plus growth-rate method.

Capital Budgeting: Capital budgeting decisions are decisions that involve an outlay or outlays now (or soon) in order to obtain some return in the future. Capital budgeting decisions are often made for individual projects to determine if those projects will be undertaken. Capital investments that are independent should be made if they add value to a firm; otherwise, they should be rejected. Four common approaches to capital budgeting decisions are the payback method, the discounted payback method, the net present value method, and the internal rate of return method. Sometimes, the accounting rate of return method is also used. *See also* payback method *and* discounted payback method *and* net present value method *and* internal rate of return method.

Capital Rationing: Capital rationing is used when investment funding is limited. Capital is rationed among competing projects either by using a higher cost of capital or by setting a maximum for the entire capital budget. If capital is rationed, and there are no other constraints, capital is normally allocated to the projects with the highest net present value. A profitability index may be used to rank the projects. *See also* profitability index.

Carrying Costs: Carrying costs are the costs incurred to carry an asset (e.g., the costs incurred to carry inventory). Examples of carrying costs include the opportunity cost of the funds that are being used to carry the asset (i.e., the next best investment alternative), storage of the asset, insurance for loss of the asset, costs of obsolescence, various types of shrinkage, etc.

Cartel: A cartel is a group of firms acting together to coordinate output decisions and control prices so that the joint profit of the members of the cartel will be maximized. The cartel will attempt to create a monopoly. *See also* monopoly.

Cash Conversion Cycle: The cash conversion cycle is the length of time between the date of the cash expenditures for production and the date of cash collection from customers (cash to cash). The cash conversion cycle is the days in inventory plus days sales in accounts receivable less days of payables outstanding. *See also* days in inventory, days sales in accounts receivable, *and* days of payables outstanding.

Cause-and-Effect Diagram: In quality control, a cause-and-effect diagram identifies potential causes of failures or defects. *See also* Pareto diagram *and* statistical quality control.

Centralized Processing: Centralized processing environments maintain all data and perform all data processing at a central location. If end-user PCs are used merely to connect to a LAN to allow data entry from remote locations, and all editing and other such processing is accomplished by programs running on the central processors, the processing would be considered centralized. *See also* distributed processing.

Change Control: Change control (sometimes called program change control or change management if used in a more general context) is a formal process to ensure that a computer program is modified only with approved changes. Some system of change control (normally at least partly automated these days) is necessary to know exactly what versions of what programs are running in production at a particular point in time. In addition to normal planned changes, there are usually emergency changes (that bypass the normal change control procedure) to keep a system up and running.

Check Digit: Check digits exist when some kind of technique is used to compute a digit or digits to add to an existing number and other programs use the same computation when that number is used. *See also* field check *and* validity check.

Cloud: The cloud is the representation in network diagrams of the public switched data network (PSDN). Cloud computing involves information technology as a service rather than as a collection of products. Most carriers offer service-level agreements for transmission within the cloud.

Coefficient of Correlation: In regression analysis, the coefficient of correlation is the square root of the coefficient of determination. It measures the interdependence of the dependent variable and the independent variable. Its value lies between -1 and $+1$. The absence of correlation would be 0; perfect positive correlation would be $+1$; and perfect negative correlation would be -1. The algebraic sign of the correlation coefficient is the same as that of the regression coefficient b in the regression line equation. *See also* regression analysis *and* coefficient of determination *and* standard error of the estimate.

Coefficient of Determination: In regression analysis, the coefficient of determination ($R2$) is the proportion of the total variation in the dependent variable explained by the independent variable. Its value lies between zero and 1. The greater the coefficient of determination, the better the fit of the regression line. *See also* regression analysis *and* coefficient of correlation *and* standard error of the estimate.

Cold Site: For disaster recovery, a cold site is an off-site location that has all the electrical connections and other physical requirements for data processing, but it does not have the actual equipment. Cold sites usually require one to three days to be made operational because equipment has to be acquired. Cold sites are the cheapest form of off-site location. *See also* hot site.

Commercial Paper: Commercial paper is short-term, unsecured promissory notes that are generally sold by large, creditworthy corporations on a discount basis to institutional investors and other corporations. Maturities of commercial paper are usually no longer than nine months, with maturities of one to two months common. Commercial paper is usually issued in denominations of $100,000 or more. *See also* banker's acceptance *and* trade acceptance.

Committed Costs: Committed costs are those costs that cannot be altered in the short run. Committed costs establish the present level of operating capacity. Committed costs are normally fixed costs. Committed costs can be contrasted to discretionary costs. *See also* discretionary costs.

Committee of Sponsoring Organizations (COSO): The COSO is an independent private sector initiative which was initially established to study the factors that can lead to fraudulent financial reporting. The private "sponsoring organizations" included the five major financial professional associations in the United States: the American Accounting Association, the American Institute of Certified Public Accountants, the Financial Executives Institute, the Institute of Internal Auditors, and the Institute of Management Accountants. The COSO has issued Internal Control–Integrated Framework, as well as Enterprise Risk Management–Integrated Framework, to assist organizations in developing comprehensive assessments of internal control effectiveness. The COSO is sometimes referred to as the Treadway Commission after its original chairman, James C. Treadway, Jr.

Common Cost: A common cost is a cost that is incurred to support a number of cost objects but that cannot be traced to them individually. Common costs are allocated to the cost objects on some basis. A common cost is a particular type of indirect cost. *See also* cost object *and* indirect costs *and* joint costs.

Common Gateway Interface (CGI): CGI is a standard protocol to interface external application software with a server such as a Web server, which allows the server to pass requests from a browser to the external application and for the external application to return output to the browser.

Common Stock: Common stock is a class of stock that will carry with it all rights of stock ownership and entitle the owner to rights of governance.

Comparative Advantage: When production possibility curves are drawn with the same products on the same axes, the country whose production possibility curve has the steepest slope has the comparative advantage in the product on the vertical axis and the other country has the comparative advantage in the product on the horizontal axis. Countries should concentrate on producing those products in which they have the comparative advantage. *See also* production possibility curve.

Compensating Balance: A compensating balance is a required minimum amount of funds (10 to 20 percent) that a firm receiving a loan or a line of credit must keep in a non-interest bearing checking account at the bank.

Competitive Strategies: Competitive strategies are (1) cost leadership focused on a broad range of buyers; (2) cost leadership focused on a narrow range of buyers; (3) product differentiation focused on a broad range of buyers; (4) product differentiation focused on a narrow range of buyers; and (5) best cost.

Compilation: The translation of a program from source code to object code so that the program can be executed. The source code is not necessarily translated line-by-line and is often optimized for execution speed. *See also* interpretation *and* source code *and* object code.

Complements: Complements or complementary products are products that are usually consumed jointly. Complements are related such that a decrease in the price of one product will cause an increase in demand of the other product. *See also* substitutes.

Compound Interest: Compound interest is interest computed with compounding (i.e., interest on principal and interest both). *See also* simple interest.

Computer Operator: In mainframe computing environments, computer operators are responsible for scheduling processing jobs, running or monitoring scheduled production jobs, hanging tapes, and possibly printing and distributing reports. Much of the job-scheduling and job-running work can be automated and, in large computing environments, must be automated due to the sheer volume of the processing that occurs. A computer operator is not a person entering data into a system. In most situations, computer operators have nothing to do with data. *See also* computer programmer *and* system programmer *and* end user.

Computer Programmer: A computer/application programmer is the person responsible for writing and/or maintaining application programs. The application programmer also normally handles the testing of application programs and the preparation of computer operator instructions, if there are any computer operators in the organization. Applications programmers are also sometimes called software engineers. *See also* system programmer *and* computer operator.

Concentration Banking: Concentration banking is a payment collection procedure in which payments are made to regionally dispersed collection centers. Checks are collected at these centers several times a day and deposited in local banks for quick clearing. *See also* zero balance account.

Conceptual Design: During the conceptual design phase, a company decides how to meet user needs.

Constant Returns to Scale: Constant returns to scale is the state in which the long-run average total cost stays the same as the quantity of output produced increases or decreases (i.e., the unit cost stays the same regardless of the number of units produced).

Consumer Price Index (CPI): The consumer price index is an index that is used to adjust for inflation. It is designed to measure the effect of price changes on the cost of a typical basket of goods purchased by urban consumer households. The current base (100) year for the consumer price index is 1982–1984. Inflation is the CPI of the current period less the CPI of the previous period, divided by the CPI of the previous period times 100. *See also* GDP deflator.

Contractionary Monetary Policy: Contractionary monetary policy is the reduction of the money supply by the Federal Reserve. *See also* monetary policy *and* expansionary monetary policy.

Contribution Margin: The contribution margin (also called marginal income) is sales minus variable costs or selling price per unit minus variable cost per unit. For this purpose, variable costs include variable manufacturing costs (direct material, direct labor, and variable manufacturing overhead) and variable selling costs. *See also* breakeven point *and* cost-volume-profit analysis and contribution margin ratio.

Contribution Margin Ratio: The contribution margin ratio is the contribution margin divided by sales. *See also* contribution margin.

Control Activities: As a component of the Internal Control–Integrated Framework (the Framework), control activities include the policies and procedures that will mitigate the risk of material misstatement of financial statements. As a component of Enterprise Risk Management–Integrated Framework (ERM), the concept is broadened to include the implementation of risk response strategies into operations through policies and procedures that consider not only a risk assessment but also a separate risk response component.

Control Chart: In quality control, a control chart is a graphical display of a quality characteristic that has been measured or computed from a sample versus the sample number or time. The chart contains a center line that represents the average value of the quality characteristic corresponding to the in-control state. Two other horizontal lines, called the upper control limit (UCL) and the lower control limit (LCL), are also drawn. These control limits are chosen so that if the process is in control, nearly all of the sample points will fall between them. As long as the sample points plot within the control limits, the process is assumed to be in control, and no action is necessary. *See also* statistical quality control *and* Pareto diagram *and* cause-and-effect diagram.

Control Clerk: In the old days of complete batch processing, control clerks logged or scheduled input and output and maintained error and correction logs. The control clerks also controlled the flow of batches through data entry and editing, monitored processing, and controlled distribution of reports and other output. In many large computing environments, this function is obsolete because the responsibilities have either been automated (and are now done by software and/or hardware) or have been distributed to the end users.

Control Environment: A component of the Internal Control–Integrated Framework (the Framework) that defines the "tone at the top" including integrity and ethical values, management operating styles, financial reporting competencies, etc.

Conversion: Conversion is the process of changing from an old application system to a new application system. There may be a direct cutover or some kind of parallel processing where both the old application system and the new application system are run and the results are compared (often a quite difficult comparison to make if the new and old systems do not perform the same functions in the same way).

Conversion Costs (and Conversion Cost Pricing): Conversion costs are direct labor and manufacturing overhead costs needed to convert raw materials into a finished product (i.e., they do not include raw materials). Pricing can be determined using conversion costs (i.e., "conversion cost pricing") when customers furnish the material to be used in the manufacturing process. *See also* prime costs.

Core Competency: A core competency is fundamental knowledge, ability, or expertise in a specific subject area or skill set.

Corrective Control: Corrective controls are controls that correct errors after they have occurred and have been detected. *See also* preventive control *and* detective control.

Cost Assignment: Cost assignment is the assignment of costs to either a cost pool or a cost object. Distinguishing between the direct and indirect components of a cost is required for proper cost assignment.

Cost Driver: A cost driver is a factor that has the ability to change total cost. Typically, cost drivers are activity bases that are closely correlated with the incurrence of manufacturing overhead costs in an activity center, and they are often used as allocation bases for applying overhead costs to cost objects. Cost drivers may be based on volume (output), activity, value added, or any other operational characteristics. *See also* cost object *and* cost pool.

Cost Leadership Strategy: A cost leadership strategy is a competitive strategy that emphasizes lowest overall cost. *See also* differentiation strategy *and* best cost strategy *and* niche strategy.

Cost Object: A cost object is the object of the assignment of a cost. Although a product is the object that many people think of first, a cost object can be customers, strategic business units (SBUs), services, etc. *See also* cost driver *and* strategic business unit.

Cost of Goods Manufactured: The cost of goods manufactured is beginning work-in-process inventory plus total manufacturing costs less ending work-in-process inventory. Manufacturing costs are the direct material used, the direct labor used, and the manufacturing overhead applied. *See also* direct material *and* direct labor *and* overhead.

Cost of Goods Sold: The cost of goods sold is beginning finished goods inventory plus cost of goods manufactured less ending finished goods inventory.

Cost of Long-Term Debt: The cost of long-term debt is the current yield prevailing in the market on newly issued par value bonds of equal risk to that already outstanding. The cost of long-term debt is computed on an after-tax basis as the product of the yield times (1 – the company's marginal tax rate). The after-tax cost of debt is used to compute the weighted average cost of capital. *See also* weighted average cost of capital *and* cost of preferred stock *and* cost of retained earnings.

Cost of Preferred Stock: The cost of preferred stock is the current yield prevailing in the market on newly issued preferred stock of equal risk to that already outstanding. The cost of preferred stock is computed as the preferred dividends divided by the net (of flotation cost) issuing price of the preferred stock. There is no pretax or after-tax cost of preferred stock since preferred dividends are not deductible for income tax purposes. The cost of preferred stock is used to compute the weighted average cost of capital. *See also* weighted average cost of capital *and* cost of long-term debt *and* cost of retained earnings.

Cost of Retained Earnings: The cost of retained earnings is the return prevailing in the market for common stock of equal risk to that already outstanding. The cost of retained earnings is also called the cost of internal capital or the cost of internal equity. The cost of retained earnings is computed using one of three methods: the capital asset pricing model, the dividend yield plus growth rate method (also called the discounted cash flow method), or the bond yield plus risk premium method. Since these various methods will normally provide different results, an average of the three results is often used for the weighted average cost of capital. *See also* weighted average cost of capital *and* cost of long-term debt *and* cost of preferred stock.

Cost Pool: A cost pool is a group of costs (e.g., raw material or direct labor) or a specially identified cost center (e.g., a department or a manager) in which costs are grouped, assigned, or collected. *See also* cost driver *and* cost assignment.

Cost Push Inflation: Cost push inflation is inflation caused by reductions in short-run aggregate supply (i.e., by a leftward shift in the short-run aggregate supply curve). *See also* demand pull inflation *and* aggregate supply.

Cost-Volume-Profit Analysis: Cost-volume-profit-analysis (sometimes called breakeven analysis) determines the effects of selling and production volume on revenues, costs, and net income. Assumptions of cost-volume-profit analysis are that the selling price is constant, costs are linear, the sales mix is constant, and inventories do not change. *See also* breakeven point *and* contribution margin.

Country Risk: Country risk is the risk of political and economic uncertainty in a foreign country that affects the value of loans or investments in that country.

Coupon Interest Rate: The coupon interest rate is the interest rate that will actually be paid on a bond. The coupon rate of interest is normally fixed and the interest is normally paid semiannually in the U.S. If the coupon rate is not fixed, then the bond is called a floating rate bond. *See also* effective interest rate *and* floating rate securities.

Covered Interest Arbitrage: In an interest arbitrage transaction, the foreign exchange risk can be covered (covered interest arbitrage) if, at the same time the investor exchanges the domestic currency for the foreign currency to make the foreign investment, the investor also engages in a forward sale of an equal amount of the foreign currency to coincide with the maturity of the investment. *See also* interest arbitrage *and* forward hedge.

Credit Risk: Credit risk is the risk of loss due to the "other" party, called a counterparty, defaulting on a contract or, more generally, the risk of loss due to some "credit event." Traditionally, credit risk is applied to bonds where the debt holders were concerned that the counterparty might default on a payment (coupon or principal). Credit risk is sometimes called default risk. *See also* interest rate risk *and* reinvestment risk.

Cross Elasticity of Demand: The cross elasticity of demand is the percentage change in the quantity demanded of one good divided by the percentage change in the price of a related good.

Cross Elasticity of Supply: The cross elasticity of supply is the percentage change in the quantity supplied of one good divided by the percentage change in the price of a related good.

Cross Hedging: Cross hedging is hedging the exposure in one currency by the use of futures, forwards, or other contracts in a second currency that is correlated with the first currency. *See also* currency variability.

Currency Appreciation: Currency appreciation is the strengthening of a currency in relation to another currency. Appreciation occurs when, because of a change in currency exchange rates, a unit of one currency buys more units of another currency.

Currency Depreciation: Currency depreciation is the weakening of a currency in relation to another currency. Depreciation occurs when, because of a change in currency exchange rates, a unit of one currency buys fewer units of another currency.

Currency Variability: Overall currency exposure can be assessed by considering each currency position together with that currency's variability and the correlations among the currencies (how much two currencies tend to increase and decrease together). The standard deviation of historical data serves as one measure of currency variability. Currency variability levels may change over time.

Current Ratio: The current ratio is current assets divided by current liabilities. *See also* working capital *and* quick ratio.

Currently Attainable Standards: Currently attainable standards represent standard costs that result from work performed by employees with appropriate training and experience but without extraordinary effort. Provision is made for normal spoilage and down time. *See also* ideal standards *and* standard costs.

Customer Relationship Management (CRM): Customer relationship management systems provide sales force automation and customer services in an attempt to manage customer relationships. CRM systems record and manage customer contacts, manage salespeople, forecast sales and sales targets and goals, manage sales leads and potential sales leads, provide and manage online quotes and product specifications and pricing, and analyze sales data. *See also* enterprise resource planning (ERP).

Customization: Customization is the changing of a purchased application software package to meet a customer's specific requirements. The software must be recustomized each time there is a new release of the software.

Cyclical Unemployment: Cyclical unemployment is unemployment resulting from business cycles, especially recessions or depressions. *See also* recession *and* depression *and* unemployment rate *and* structural unemployment *and* seasonal unemployment.

Dashboard Reporting: Reports provided to management with critical data presented in a summary format to quickly show the extent to which the entity's activities are operating within prescribed limits.

Data: Data are raw facts (e.g., a quantity, a name, or a dollar amount). Data are stored in computer systems in various ways. *See also* information.

Data Administrator: A data administrator is responsible for the definition, planning, and control of the data within a database or databases. *See also* database administrator *and* database.

Data Encryption: Data encryption offers a form of security, and it is based on the idea of keys. Each party has a public and private key for their data (public key encryption is one type of encryption). The public key is distributed to others in a separate transmission. The sender of a message uses the private key (which never goes anywhere) to encrypt the message, and the receiver uses the public key to decrypt the message. An encrypted message must properly process through the encryption algorithm after the keys are applied. As long as the private key is secure, the encryption scheme should provide a secure transmission. All encryption keys can be cracked, but the longer the key is, the harder it is. *See also* digital signature *and* digital certificate.

Data Flow Diagram: A data flow diagram is a graphic representation of information flow in a system.

Data Matching: Data matching is the combination of two or more data items that are combined to improve processing controls.

Data Mining: Data mining is the use of analytical techniques to identify trends, patterns, and relationships in data.

Data Processing Cycle: The data processing cycle is defined by four functional areas that affect the handling of data, including data input, data storage, data processing, and information output.

Data Redundancy: Data redundancy is the storage of the same data in more than one place in an organization. This can cause problems, because if data are stored in more than one place, reported values are likely to differ.

Database: A database is an integrated collection of data records and data files. It comprises nothing more than stored data. A database most often centralizes data and minimizes redundant data (think of the data as all being in one place, although it may or may not be physically stored that way). The structure of the data in the database often provides the data relationships that start to change the data into information. *See also* database management system *and* database administrator *and* schema *and* data administrator *and* structured query language (SQL).

Database Administrator (DBA): Within a database environment, database administrators are responsible for maintaining and supporting the database software. The database administrator may also perform some or all of the security functions for the database. Database administrators perform somewhat the same functions for database software as system programmers perform for the operating system as a whole. *See also* system programmer *and* data administrator *and* database.

Database Management System (DBMS): In organizations that employ mainframe and midrange computer systems, a database management system is a very important software package because it controls the development, use, and maintenance of the databases used by the organization. Quite often, the terms "database" and "DBMS" are used interchangeably. This usage is inaccurate. *See also* database *and* database administrator *and* data administrator.

Database Structure: Database structure is the structure of a database such as a hierarchical structure, relational structure, or object-oriented structure. *See also* database.

Database Tuning: Database tuning is the testing of a database to ensure that the database is operating effectively and efficiently. *See also* database.

Days in Inventory: Days in inventory is ending inventory divided by (cost of goods sold/365).

Days of Payables Outstanding: The days of payables outstanding is ending accounts payable divided by (cost of goods sold/365). *See also* cash conversion cycle *and* days in inventory *and* days sales in accounts receivable.

Days Sales in Accounts Receivable: Days sales in accounts receivable is ending accounts receivable (net) divided by (sales [net]/365).

Debenture: A debenture is an unsecured bond. *See also* subordinated debenture.

Debt Securities: Debt securities are bonds. A debt security represents a creditor-debtor relationship with the corporation whereby the corporation has borrowed funds from "outside investors" and promises to repay them.

Debt-to-Equity Ratio: The debt-to-equity ratio is total liabilities divided by total equity. The debt-to-equity ratio indicates what percentage of permanent capital is financed with debt and thus a firm's long-term debt-paying ability.

Debugging: Debugging is the process of removing as many bugs (programming errors) as possible. *See also* desk checking.

Decision Support System (DSS): A decision support system is a computer-based information system that provides interactive support for managers during the decision-making process. A DSS is an extension of an MIS and is useful for developing information directed toward making particular decisions. DSS do not automate decisions, but rather provide managers with interactive, computer-aided tools that combine their subjective judgments and insights with objective analytical data to guide the decision. DSS address problems where the procedure for arriving at a solution may not be fully predefined in advance. DSS may automate decision procedures, may provide information about certain aspects of the decision, may facilitate the preparation of forecasts based on the decision, or may allow the simulation of various aspects of the decision. DSS are often divided into data-driven and model-driven systems. DSS are sometimes called expert systems. *See also* accounting information system *and* executive information system *and* management information system *and* expert system *and* artificial intelligence.

Default Risk: Default risk is another word for credit risk. *See also* credit risk *and* liquidity risk *and* maturity risk premium.

Defective Units: Spoiled goods (goods that do not meet quality specifications or standards) that may be salvaged through rework or resale (at a reduced price) are termed defective units.

Deflation: Deflation is a sustained decrease in the general prices of goods and services. *See also* inflation.

Demand Curve: A demand curve is a curve that illustrates the relationship between the price of a good or service and the quantity demanded of that good or service. Price is plotted on the y-axis and quantity is plotted on the x-axis. *See also* supply curve.

Demand Flow: Demand flow is a management philosophy or business strategy that develops business processes in response to customer demand. (Demand pull is a similar concept.) At its most sophisticated level, demand flow uses quantitative techniques that connect processes in a flow and links them to daily changes in demand. Demand flow is the opposite of a schedule-push philosophy that would use sales forecasts to determine a production schedule.

Demand Pull Inflation: Demand pull inflation is inflation caused by increases in aggregate demand (i.e., by a rightward shift in the aggregate demand curve). *See also* cost push inflation.

Demand Reporting: Reports giving a user access to a report at any time. These reports are also referred to as response reports because an end user can log on to a workstation and obtain a response in the form of a report without waiting for the scheduled reporting time.

Depreciation Tax Shield: A depreciation tax shield is the tax reduction associated with depreciation. Depreciation is not considered in determining cash flows in capital budgeting models, except to the extent that it is a tax shield, since it is deductible for income tax purposes. The depreciation tax shield is the depreciation times the marginal tax rate. *See also* capital budgeting.

Depression: A depression is a very severe recession. *See also* recession *and* business cycle.

Derived Demand: Derived demand is the demand for the factors of production of a good caused by the demand for a final good.

Desk Checking: Traditionally, desk checking (reviewing printed listings of the program) was used to discover and eliminate bugs. *See also* debugging.

Detective Control: Detective controls are controls that discover errors after they have occurred. *See also* preventive control *and* corrective control.

Differential Costs: Differential costs are the difference in costs between two or more alternatives. Differential costs are also called incremental costs. The words differential and incremental can also be used for revenues to quantify the different revenues associated with two or more alternatives.

Differentiation Strategy: A (product) differentiation strategy is a competitive strategy that emphasizes the perception that a company's products are better or have a unique quality that differentiates them from competing products. *See also* cost leadership strategy *and* best cost strategy.

Digital Cash: Digital cash (also electronic cash or E-cash) is currency in an electronic form that moves outside the normal channels of money. Digital cash can be used to make purchases over the Internet without having to use credit cards. An example of digital cash is PayPal.

Digital Certificate: Digital certificates are a form of data security. An individual wishing to send an encrypted message applies for a digital certificate from a certificate authority. The certificate authority issues an encrypted digital certificate containing the applicant's public key and a variety of other identification information. The certificate authority makes its own public key readily available through print publicity or perhaps over the Internet. The recipient of an encrypted message uses the certificate authority's public key to decode the digital certificate attached to the message, verifies it as issued by the certificate authority, and then obtains the sender's public key and identification information contained in the certificate. With this information, the recipient can send an encrypted reply. *See also* data encryption *and* digital signature.

Digital Checking: Digital checking is an electronic check with a secure digital signature.

Digital Signature: Digital signatures, which authenticate a document by using a form of data encryption, are a form of data security. A mathematically condensed version of the message is produced and encrypted by the sender's private key. It is attached to the original message. The message and the digital signature can be unlocked by an authorized receiver (anybody with the public key). The original message can be compared with the condensed version to ensure that the original message has not been changed. *See also* data encryption *and* digital certificate.

Direct Costs: Direct costs are costs that can be identified with or traced to a given cost object in an economical manner. Direct costs are usually relevant to a costing decision. Variable costs are generally direct costs. *See also* indirect costs *and* cost object *and* variable costs *and* fixed costs.

Direct Labor: Direct labor is labor that can be identified with or traced to a given cost object in an economic manner. *See also* direct material *and* overhead *and* cost of goods manufactured.

Direct Labor Efficiency Variance: The direct labor efficiency variance is the standard rate times the difference between the actual hours worked and the standard hours allowed for the actual production. *See also* direct labor rate variance *and* direct material quantity variance.

Direct Labor Rate Variance: The direct labor rate variance is the actual hours worked times the difference between the actual rate and the standard rate. *See also* direct labor efficiency variance *and* direct material price variance.

Direct Material: Direct material is material that can be identified with or traced to a given cost object in an economical manner. *See also* direct labor *and* overhead *and* cost of goods manufactured.

Direct Material Price Variance: The direct material price variance is the actual quantity purchased times the difference between the actual price and the standard price, assuming that the price variances are isolated at the time of purchase. *See also* direct labor rate variance *and* direct material usage variance.

Direct Material Usage Variance: The direct material usage variance is the standard price times the difference between the actual quantity used and the standard quantity allowed for the actual production. *See also* direct material price variance *and* direct labor efficiency variance.

Disaster Recovery: Disaster recovery is the plan for or the actual resumption of computer processing after a disaster (which is more serious than just a temporary system outage).

Discount Rate: The discount rate is the interest rate that the Federal Reserve charges banks for short-term loans.

Discounted Cash Flow Methods: Discounted cash flow methods are capital budgeting methods that measure cash inflows and cash outflows at a single point in time, normally the current time, by incorporating the time value of money. Discounted cash flow methods, which include the net present value method and the internal rate of return method, are considered superior to methods that do not consider the time value of money. *See also* net present value method *and* internal rate of return method.

Discounted Payback Method: The discounted payback method is a capital budgeting method that calculates the amount of time to recover the initial investment for a project. The discounted payback method uses after-tax cash flows discounted at the project's cost of capital as the discount rate. *See also* payback method.

Discretionary Costs: Discretionary costs are costs that might or might not be incurred. They normally are fixed costs, have no causal relationship to the outputs of the costs, and are typically incurred because of an annual (or other periodic) decision regarding the amount of the cost to be incurred.

Examples of discretionary costs include human resource costs, advertising, training of executives, and other costs that are not generally crucial to the production process or other significant activity of the organization. Discretionary costs can be contrasted to committed costs. *See also* committed costs.

Diseconomies of Scale: Diseconomies of scale is the state in which the long-run average total cost increases as the quantity of output produced increases. *See also* economies of scale.

Disintermediation: Disintermediation is the removal of organizational or business process layers responsible for intermediate steps in a value chain. The process of shifting or moving intermediate steps in a value chain is called re-intermediation.

Disposable Income: Disposable income is personal income less personal taxes. *See also* personal income.

Distributed Processing: Distributed or decentralized processing occurs when computing power, applications, and work is spread out (or distributed) over many locations (i.e., via a LAN or WAN). Decentralized processing environments often use distributed processing techniques, where each remote computer performs a portion of the processing (e.g., a portion of the data validation), thus reducing the processing burden on the central computer or computers. *See also* centralized processing.

Diversifiable Risk: Diversifiable risk (also called unsystematic risk) is the risk of an individual stock (in a portfolio) that can be eliminated by diversification. Diversifiable risk is caused by such random events as lawsuits, strikes, successful and unsuccessful marketing programs, and other events that are unique to a particular firm. *See also* nondiversifiable risk.

Dividend Yield Plus Growth Rate Method: The dividend yield plus growth rate method is a method to determine the cost of common stock or retained earnings as the expected (at the end of the year) yield on the common stock plus the expected growth rate in the dividends per share after that. Unfortunately, this method is sometimes called the discounted cash flow method. *See also* capital asset pricing model *and* bond yield plus risk premium method.

Dividends: A dividend is a distribution of corporate profits as ordered by the directors and paid to the shareholders.

Domain Name System (DNS): The domain name system is the system of domain names that is employed by the Internet. The Internet is based on IP addresses, not domain names, and each Web server requires a domain name server to translate domain names into IP addresses.

Draft: A draft is an unconditional order in writing—signed by a person, usually an exporter in international trade financing—ordering the importer to pay, on demand or at a fixed future date (time draft), the amount specified on its face. *See also* banker's acceptance.

Drill Down: Drill down is moving from a piece of summary data to lower and lower levels of detail. The ability to drill down in this manner is a necessary function of an executive information system. *See also* executive information system.

DSL: DSL is an acronym for digital subscriber line, which is a mechanism to use high-speed access to the Internet through a regular telephone line.

E-Business: E-business refers to any use of information technology, particularly networking and communications technology, to perform business processes in an electronic form. The exchange of this electronic information may or may not relate to the purchase and sale of goods or services. E-commerce (by contrast) relates to buying and selling transactions. *See also* e-commerce.

E-Commerce: E-commerce is the electronic consummation of exchange (buying and selling) transactions. E-commerce uses a private network or the Internet as the communications provider. Certain types of e-commerce involve communication between previously known parties or between parties that have had no prior contracts or agreements with each other. *See also* e-business.

Economic Costs: Economic costs are accounting (explicit) costs plus implicit costs. *See also* explicit costs and implicit costs *and* opportunity costs.

Economic Exposure: Economic exposure is the risk that the present value of a firm's cash flows could increase or decrease as a result of changes in exchange rates. *See also* transaction exposure *and* translation exposure.

Economic Order Quantity (EOQ): The economic order quantity is the order quantity that minimizes the combination of the ordering and carrying costs of inventory.

Economic Profit: Economic profit is the difference between total revenue and total explicit costs and implicit costs. *See also* explicit costs *and* implicit costs *and* opportunity costs.

Economic Value Added (EVA): Economic value added is a firm's net operating profit after taxes less its after-tax cost of capital. After-tax cost of capital is the weighted average cost of capital times (total assets less current liabilities). EVA is similar to residual income, which is the excess of a firm's net income over its required rate of return. *See also* residual income.

Economies of Scale: Economies of scale is the state in which long-run average total cost declines as the quantity of output produced increases. *See also* diseconomies of scale.

Effective Interest Rate: The effective interest rate is the market interest rate at the date bonds are issued. If the market interest rate is equal to the coupon rate, the bonds will sell at par; if the market interest rate is greater than the coupon rate, the bonds will sell at a discount; and if the market interest rate is less than the coupon rate, the bonds will sell at a premium. *See also* coupon interest rate *and* floating rate securities.

Efficiency Variance: The efficiency variance is the budget based on the actual hours worked less the budget based on standard hours allowed for the actual output. If variable overhead only is being analyzed, the formula can be expressed as the standard rate times the difference between the actual hours and the standard hours, and the formula corresponds to the direct material usage variance and the direct labor efficiency variance. *See also* direct material usage variance *and* direct labor efficiency variance *and* spending variance *and* budget variance *and* volume variance.

Electronic Access Controls: Electronic access controls are nonphysical controls over access to data and application programs such as user identification codes, assignment and maintenance of security levels, file attributes, firewalls, etc. *See also* access controls *and* physical access controls.

Electronic Data Interchange (EDI): EDI is computer-to-computer exchange of business transaction documents (e.g., purchase orders, confirmations, invoices, etc.) in structured formats that allow the direct processing of the data by the receiving system. Any standard business document (including an information request) that one organization can exchange with another can be exchanged via EDI, provided both organizations have made the proper preparations. *See also* value added network (VAN).

Electronic Funds Transfer (EFT): Electronic funds transfer systems are a form of electronic payment for the banking and retailing industries. EFT uses a variety of technologies to transact, process, and verify money transfers and credits between banks, businesses, and consumers. The Federal Reserve's financial services system is used frequently in EFT to reduce the time and expense required to process checks and credit transactions.

E-mail Archiving: E-mail archiving is a form of backup for the secure preservation of e-mail for regulatory compliance and other purposes. An e-mail archiving system normally extracts message contents and attachments, indexes them, and stores them in a read-only format so that they cannot be altered.

Emerging Nations: Emerging nations represent those economies outside the world's largest industrial nations that are experiencing rapid growth.

Encryption: Encryption is the use of a password or digital key to scramble a readable (plaintext) message into an unreadable (ciphertext) message. The intended recipient of the message then uses the same (or different, depending on encryption method) digital key to convert the ciphertext message back into plaintext.

End User: An end user is a person who actually uses a system or application.

End User Computing (EUC): EUC is the hands-on use of computers by end users.

Engineered Costs: Engineered costs (including direct and indirect costs and variable and fixed costs) typically have a causal relationship between the incurrence of the cost and the output associated with the cost.

Enterprise Resource Planning (ERP): An enterprise resource planning system is a cross-functional enterprise system that integrates and automates the many business processes that must work together in the manufacturing, logistics, distribution, accounting, finance, and human resource functions of a business. ERP software is composed of a number of modules that can function independently or as an integrated system to allow data and information to be shared among all of the different departments and divisions of large businesses. ERP is often considered a back office system, from the customer order to fulfillment of that order. *See also* customer relationship management (CRM).

Enterprise Risk Management Integrated Framework: The COSO publication Enterprise Risk Management–Integrated Framework (ERM) builds upon the COSO publication Internal Control–Integrated Framework (Framework) to provide a more extensive evaluation of the broader concept of enterprise risk management. ERM identifies four categories of business objectives including strategic operational, reporting and compliance and expands the five components in the internal control framework to include three additional components (objective setting, event identification and risk response) to support the risk assessment components of the framework and expand on the framework to embrace operations.

Equity Securities: Equity securities are stocks. An equity security is an instrument representing an investment in the corporation whereby its holder becomes a part owner of the business.

Equivalent Unit (EQU): An equivalent unit is the amount of work expressed in completed units of a product. For example, if 1,000 units are 80 percent complete as to direct material, direct labor, and manufacturing overhead, there are 800 equivalent units of production. Normally, however, there will be a different number of equivalent units for direct material, direct labor, and manufacturing overhead. For equivalent unit calculations, transfers in from previous departments are assumed to be 100 percent complete. Materials may be added either at the beginning or the end of the process in a particular department as is stated in the question. *See also* process costing.

Escrow: Escrow (of source code) is the holding of the source code of an application system by an independent third party (escrow agent) so that it can be made available to the purchaser if something happens to the vendor (e.g., filing for bankruptcy) or if the vendor fails to maintain the software as promised in the licensing agreement.

Eurobonds: A Eurobond is a bond issued in one country but denominated in the currency of some other country.

Eurodollars: Eurodollars are U.S. dollar-denominated time deposits at banks outside the U.S. The Eurodollar market evolved in Europe (specifically London), but Eurodollars can be held anywhere outside the U.S. Interest rates on Eurodollar deposits (and loans) are tied to LIBOR. *See also* LIBOR.

Event Identification: A component of the Enterprise Risk Management–Integrated Framework (ERM) that defines the process for identifying events that may positively or negatively impact the organization. Positive events are opportunities and negative events are risks.

Exception Reporting: Exception reports are produced when a specific condition or exception occurs. In other words, specific criteria are established, and any transaction or entity that meets the criteria is reported on the exception report.

Exchange Rate: An exchange rate is the price of one unit of foreign currency in terms of the domestic currency. These days most exchange rates are floating, which means that they are established in the foreign exchange market.

Exchange Rate Risk: Exchange rate risk (also called currency risk) is the risk that the exchange rate between the currency in which a cash flow is denominated (a bond denominated in Euros, for example) and the currency of the investor (the U.S. dollar, for example) might change.

Executive Information System (EIS): Executive information systems, or executive support systems, provide senior executives with immediate and easy access to internal and external information to assist the executives in monitoring business conditions in general. EIS assist in strategic, not daily, decision-making. EIS are collectors and synthesizers of business and economic information. A premium is normally placed on ease of use so that the systems can be used by executives who might lack full computer literacy. Extensive graphics are often used in presentation. A drill-down capability is often provided so that detail can be obtained in areas of interest. *See also* accounting information system *and* decision support system *and* management information system *and* drill down.

Expansionary Monetary Policy: Expansionary monetary policy is the expansion of the money supply by the Fed. *See also* monetary policy *and* contractionary monetary policy.

Expected Value: Expected value is the weighted average of the probable outcomes of a variable where the weights are the probabilities of each outcome occurring. Expected value is found by multiplying the probability of each outcome by its payoff and summing the results. *See also* probability *and* subjective probability *and* objective probability.

Expenditure Approach: One way to measure GDP is to measure expenditures for products bought by consumers, products bought by businesses, products bought by governments, and net exports, or exports minus imports (i.e., a flow of products approach). *See also* gross domestic product *and* gross domestic income *and* income approach.

Expenditure Cycle: The expenditure cycle is a transaction cycle characterized by the purchase of goods or services that use cash or produce debt or other obligations. *See also* transaction cycles.

Experience Curve: The experience curve is an extension of learning curve theory applied to groups of people undertaking a range of tasks. The experience curve anticipates that the amount of time required for a group of tasks will decrease as experience increases.

Expert System: An expert system is a class of computer programs. The programs are made up of a set of rules that analyze information about a specific class of problem and then provide an analysis of the problem or recommend a course of action. The problems solved by an expert system are the kind of problems that would be solved by a human "expert." *See also* decision support system *and* artificial intelligence.

Expired Costs: Expired costs are costs that cannot be justifiably carried forward because they have no benefit to future periods. *See also* sunk costs *and* unexpired costs.

Explicit Costs: Explicit costs are documented out-of-pocket expenses (e.g., wages, cost of raw materials, etc.). *See also* implicit costs *and* opportunity costs.

External Factors: In value chain analysis, external factors are sources of opportunities in the market and threats to the firm's ability to continue with its strategic plan. *See also* internal factors *and* value chain *and* value chain analysis.

External Failure Costs: External failure costs are costs to cure a defect discovered after a product is sent to the customer. These costs include warranty costs, costs of returning the goods, liability claims, and the cost of lost customers. *See also* internal failure costs.

Extranet: Extranets permit company suppliers, customers, and business partners (a general term for customers, suppliers, etc.) to have direct access to the company's network. *See also* intranet.

Factoring: Factoring is the selling of a firm's accounts receivable at a discount. Factoring may be on a recourse basis, where any uncollectible receivables can be returned, or nonrecourse, where the factor takes the risk of collectibility.

Factors of Production: Factors of production are the inputs or resources used to produce final goods and services. Factors of production are bought and sold in markets.

Federal Reserve (Fed): The Federal Reserve is the central bank of the United States.

Field: A field is a group of bytes in which a specific data element such as an employee number or name is stored. *See also* bit and byte *and* file and record.

Field Check: A field check is a data validation step performed on a data element to ensure that it is of the appropriate type (alphabetic, numeric, etc.). *See also* check digit *and* validity check.

FIFO Method of Process Costing: The FIFO method of process costing calculates equivalent units and production costs differently from the weighted average method of process costing. In the FIFO method, the equivalent units are the equivalent units in the beginning inventory plus the units started and completed during the period (100 percent) plus the equivalent units in the ending inventory. Production costs to be accounted for are the costs added during the month. Cost per equivalent unit is the production cost divided by the equivalent units. Normally, a separate cost per equivalent unit is calculated for direct materials and conversion costs (labor and overhead). *See also* weighted average method of process costing.

File: A file is a collection of related records often arranged in some kind of sequence, such as a customer file made up of customer records and organized by customer number. Traditionally, files were often classified as master files, which were stored permanently, and transaction files, which were used to update the master files and were normally not retained permanently. *See also* bit and byte *and* field and record.

File Attribute: File attributes are read/write indicators on files that restrict reading and writing/updating of the files. For example, if a file is marked read only, it cannot be updated.

File Librarian: File libraries store and protect programs and tapes from damage and unauthorized use. File librarians control the file libraries.

Final Products: In the computation of GDP, final products are products that do not undergo any further processing during the measurement period. Final products are either sold to end-users or remain as inventories. Intermediate products are products that are not final products. Total production is final products plus intermediate products. *See also* gross domestic product.

Financial Leverage: Financial leverage is defined as the degree to which a firm uses fixed financial costs to magnify the effects of a given percentage change in earnings before interest and taxes on the percentage change in its earnings per share. Financial leverage is an extension of operating leverage that purely focuses on one type of fixed cost, debt financing. A low financial fixed cost eliminates financial leverage as a consideration in operations. *See also* operating leverage.

Financial Risk: Financial risk includes the risk of having financial resources lost, wasted, or stolen. For example, an inventory report lists several laptop computers, but some of the laptops were not returned when employees left the organization. This problem could lead to inaccurate financial reports that are reporting assets that no longer exist. *See also* information risk *and* operating risk.

Financing Cycle: The financing cycle is a transaction cycle associated with equity and debt financing, including issuance of stock or debt, payment of dividends or debt service payments, etc. *See also* transaction cycles.

Firewall: A firewall is a system, often both hardware and software, of user identification and authentication that prevents unauthorized users from gaining access to network resources; acting as a gatekeeper, it isolates a private network from a public network. The term firewall may also be applied to a network node used to improve network traffic and to set up a boundary that prevents traffic from one network segment from crossing over to another. *See also* application firewall.

Fiscal Policy: Fiscal policy is the use of government spending and taxation policies to promote price stability, full employment, and economic growth. *See also* monetary policy.

Fixed Costs: Fixed costs are costs that remain constant in total over a relevant range of production activity (they may change from one relevant range to another). Fixed costs are fixed in total but variable on a per unit basis. *See also* variable costs *and* mixed costs *and* relevant range.

Flexible Budget: A flexible budget is a budget that is adjusted for changes in sales or production volumes. *See also* master budget.

Float: Float is the difference between a firm's cash account in its accounting records and the same account at the bank. Float, sometimes called net float, is the difference between collection float and disbursements float.

Floating Rate Securities: Floating rate securities are securities that pay coupon interest rates that are not fixed but that are set by a coupon formula based on some reference rate, such as LIBOR. *See also* Eurodollars *and* LIBOR.

Flowchart: A flowchart is a chart that depicts some aspect of a system. A flowchart may be a system flowchart or a program flowchart.

Foreign Trade Zones: Trade zones established by government in which tariffs are waived until the goods leave the zone. The creation of foreign trade zones has obvious implications on the government's control of imports and the location of import facilities.

Forward Exchange Rate: A forward exchange rate is the price at which foreign exchange can be bought or sold with payment/delivery set for some day in the future. Spot rates and forward exchange rates for the same currency are normally different. The term forward rate by itself, without the word exchange, is an interest rate that is expected to exist at some point in the future (and has nothing to do with currency or forward exchange). *See also* spot rate.

Forward Hedge: A forward hedge is a hedge transacted in the forward market for foreign currencies. A forward contract is a private agreement between two parties to enter into a transaction at some future date and at a price agreed to at the time the agreement is made. In terms of foreign currencies, a forward hedge entitles a firm to either purchase or sell units of an individual foreign currency for a negotiated price at a future time. Outside the foreign currencies market, the instrument is normally called a forward, without the word hedge. *See also* futures hedge *and* options hedge *and* money market hedge.

Frictional Unemployment: Frictional unemployment is unemployment resulting from workers routinely changing jobs or from workers being temporarily laid off. *See also* unemployment rate *and* structural unemployment *and* cyclical unemployment *and* seasonal unemployment.

Full Employment: Full employment is the level of unemployment when there is no cyclical unemployment. Full employment does not mean zero unemployment. *See also* cyclical unemployment *and* unemployment rate.

Full Product Costing: Full product costing is a product costing technique that considers all inputs in arriving at product costs, not just traditional inventoriable costs. Full product costs include such costs as research and development, product design, marketing, distribution, and customer service in product cost. Full product costs do not include finance or administrative costs. *See also* inventoriable costs.

Functional Currency: The functional currency is the currency of the primary economic environment in which a firm operates; normally that is the currency of the environment in which the firm primarily generates and expends cash. *See also* translation exposure.

Functional Interdependence: Functional interdependence (of nations and their economies) contemplates the participation of nations in world-wide institutions such as the United Nations (U.N.), World Trade Organization (WTO), and International Monetary Fund (IMF).

Futures Hedge: A futures hedge is a hedge transacted in the futures market for foreign currencies. A futures contract is an agreement between two parties to enter into a transaction at some future date and at a price agreed to at the time the agreement is made. For this purpose, the main difference between a forward hedge and a futures hedge is that futures are exchange traded and are much more standard than forward contracts. In terms of foreign currencies, a futures hedge entitles a firm to either purchase or sell units of an individual currency for a negotiated price at a future time. Outside the foreign currencies market, the instrument is normally called a future, without the word hedge. *See also* forward hedge *and* options hedge *and* money market hedge.

G6: The G6 is the group of the six largest industrial economies, including the United States, Japan, the United Kingdom, Germany, France, and Italy. The largest industrial nations are sometimes referred to as the G7, which comprises the G6 nations and Canada.

Gateway: A gateway is a combination of hardware and software that connect different types of networks by translating from one set of network protocols to another.

GDP Deflator: The GDP deflator is an index similar to the consumer price index. It is designed to measure the impact of price changes on the cost of a typical basket of goods purchased by consumers, businesses, governments, and foreigners (i.e., those goods that make up the GDP). *See also* consumer price index *and* real GDP *and* nominal GDP.

General Controls: General controls are controls over data center operations, system software acquisition and maintenance, access security, and application system development and maintenance. *See also* application controls.

Gigabyte (GB): A gigabyte is approximately 1 billion bytes (actually 1,073,741,824 bytes).

Globalization: Globalization represents the distribution of industrial and service activities across an increasing number of nations. Globalization makes the world's economies increasingly integrated and interrelated.

Global Sourcing: Synchronization of all levels of a product manufacture, from research and development to production, to marketing on an international basis.

Gross Domestic Income (GDI): Gross domestic income is the amounts that were paid for the resources that were used to make the products produced during the measurement cycle. The amounts that were paid are the same as the incomes of the owners of those resources. Gross domestic income is also wages plus interest plus rent plus indirect business taxes plus net income to foreigners plus depreciation plus the profits of producers. *See also* gross domestic product.

Gross Domestic Product (GDP): Gross domestic product is the total market value of all final goods and services produced within the borders of a nation within a particular time period. It is also the value added by work done by people and machines. *See also* final products *and* gross national product *and* gross domestic income.

Gross National Product (GNP): Gross national product is the total market value of all final goods and services produced by "residents" of a country within a particular time period. It includes goods and services that are produced overseas by U.S. firms (the residents) and excludes goods and services that are produced domestically by overseas firms (the nonresidents). *See also* gross domestic product *and* final products.

Hacker: Hacker is used to denote a person who gains unauthorized access to software or computer system, most often for nefarious purposes.

Hardware: Hardware is the actual physical computer or computer peripheral device. For example, a PC or some other kind of workstation, a mainframe, a disk drive, a tape drive, a monitor, a mouse, a printer, a scanner, and a keyboard are all considered hardware. *See also* software.

Hash Total: A hash total is a total of a field in a transaction that would not normally be added, such as a total of employee numbers. *See also* batch total.

Hedge Transaction: A hedge transaction is a transaction designed to protect against a price change that would negatively affect profits. There are two kinds of hedges: long hedges in which futures (or other) contracts are bought in anticipation of (or to protect against) price increases, and short hedges in which futures (or other) contracts are sold to guard against price declines. *See also* forward hedge *and* futures hedge *and* options hedge *and* money market hedge.

Heuristic: Heuristic means "rule of thumb" in common language. In finance, heuristics are generally agreed-upon benchmarks that can lead, dangerously, to poor decisions. In IT, heuristic has a technical meaning and can sometimes be used as an adjective and other times as a noun. Heuristic algorithms (heuristic used as an adjective) are algorithms that produce "good enough" answers. Algorithms are sets of detailed instructions that produce a predictable end from a known beginning (a computer program is an algorithm). In computer science, a heuristic (heuristic used as a noun) is a technique designed to solve a problem ignoring whether the solution can be proven to be correct but producing that "good enough" answer. An expert system might be called a heuristic system. *See also* expert system *and* decision support system.

Heuristic (Behavioral Finance): Heuristic means "rule of thumb" in common language. In behavioral finance it relates to assumptions that can distort the objective evaluation of financial evidence. Use of heuristics (e.g., a price earnings ratio should be at a certain level) promotes stereotyping, use of intuition instead of analysis, and exclusive use of easily available data.

High-Low Method: The high-low method is a technique to determine a regression line by using the high and low values of a set of data. It is one step up from using a ruler to determine the line. The method of least squares can be used to determine a more exact line. *See also* regression analysis *and* coefficient of correlation *and* coefficient of determination *and* standard error of the estimate *and* t-value.

Hot Site: For disaster recovery, a hot site is an off-site location that is equipped to take over the company's data processing. Backup copies of essential data files and programs may also be maintained at the location or a nearby data storage facility. *See also* cold site.

Human Resources Cycle: The human resources cycle is a transaction cycle associated with all phases of employee administration (hiring, determining compensation, paying employees, benefits administration and termination). *See also* transaction cycles.

Hurdle Rate of Return: The hurdle rate of return is the desired (or minimum) rate of return that is set to evaluate investments or projects. The hurdle rate of return is used to discount the various cash flows in the net present value method. The hurdle rate of return may be adjusted (increased) to reflect risk or to compensate for expected inflation. Different rates may be used for different time periods. *See also* net present value method *and* internal rate of return method.

Hypertext Markup Language (HTML): HTML is a tag-based formatting language used for Web pages. It provides a way to describe the structure of text-based information in a document and to replicate that information in a Web page by using tags in the text. An extension of HTML is XHTML (extensible HTML), which conforms to the extensible markup language (XML) format. The ability to read and work with HTML documents is built into browsers, and the ability to read XHTML is built into all new browsers. XML, on the other hand, needs a "parser" to translate it before it can be used in standard browsers.

Ideal Standards: Ideal standards are standard costs that result from perfect efficiency and effectiveness. *See also* currently attainable standards *and* standard costs.

Implementation standards: Implementation standards published by the Institute of Internal Auditors (IIA) are imbedded within the attribute and reporting standards to address the requirements of implementing both assurance and consulting activities.

Implicit Costs: Implicit costs are opportunity costs supplied by owners. *See also* explicit costs *and* opportunity costs.

Importing Data: Data files can be imported into a different program that can interpret the same data file (an inventory program "dumps" data concerning the latest inventory count into a data file that can be imported by the accounting program). In importing and exporting data, a standard format (e.g., a text file format) is used. Importing and exporting of data is not the same as data transfers from one application or system to another by data interface. With data interfaces, the transferor program and the transferee program both use a specialized format to transfer the data.

Income Approach: One way to measure GDP is to determine the gross domestic income (i.e., an earnings and cost approach). *See also* gross domestic product *and* gross domestic income *and* expenditure approach.

Income Bonds: Income bonds are bonds that pay interest only upon the achievement of target income levels (i.e., only if the interest is earned). *See also* debenture *and* subordinated debenture *and* junk bonds.

Income Elasticity of Demand: Income elasticity of demand is the percentage change in the quantity demanded of a good or service divided by the percentage change in consumer income.

Incremental Costs: Incremental costs are the difference in costs between two alternatives. In other words, they are also the additional costs incurred to produce an additional unit of product in excess of the current output. Incremental costs are also called differential costs. The words differential and incremental can also be used for revenues. *See also* differential costs.

Indirect Costs: An indirect cost is a cost that cannot be identified with or traced to a given cost object in an economic manner. Indirect material and indirect labor fit into this category. Indirect costs are accumulated in a cost pool and are then allocated to the various cost objects on some reasonable basis. Indirect costs are part of overhead and normally include both fixed and variable components. *See also* direct material *and* direct labor *and* overhead and common costs *and* cost pool.

Inferior Good: An inferior good is a good whose demand is negatively related to income (negative income elasticity of demand). *See also* normal good *and* income elasticity of demand.

Inflation: Inflation is a sustained increase in the general prices of goods and services. *See also* deflation.

Information: Information is organized and processed data that is meaningful to somebody. *See also* data.

Information and Communication: As a component of the Internal Control–Integrated Framework (the Framework), information and communication contemplates financial and internal control information as well as internal and external communication, while as a component of Enterprise Risk Management–Integrated Framework (ERM), the concept is broadened to include information and communication for general business operations.

Information Risk: Information risk includes the risk of loss of data integrity, incomplete transactions, or hackers. *See also* financial risk *and* operating risk.

Information Technology Policy: An information technology policy is management's formal notification to employees regarding the entity's technology objectives.

Infrastructure: Infrastructure (specifically IT infrastructure) is a collection of the shared hardware, software, storage technology, and network resources of an organization.

Infrastructure Costs: Infrastructure costs are those costs that exist because a firm has an infrastructure (e.g., a building, various machinery, etc.). Examples include depreciation and long-term leases. As these costs typically benefit a firm for a longer period of time than most other costs, capital budgeting is often necessary, and management pays particular attention to the outlay for these types of expenditures. Infrastructure costs can be contrasted to engineered costs and discretionary costs. *See also* engineered costs *and* discretionary costs.

Input Controls: Input controls are programmed controls that verify that transaction data is valid, complete, and accurate. *See also* processing controls.

Intellectual Property: Intellectual property is a term used to describe intangible products of the human intellect that have economic value (e.g., software and artistic works). Intellectual property can be protected as trade secrets or by copyrights or by patents.

Interest Arbitrage: Interest arbitrage is the transfer of funds from one currency to another to take advantage of higher rates of return. In order to make the foreign investment, the domestic (sometimes called home) currency must be converted into the foreign currency. Then, when the investment matures or is liquidated, the foreign currency must be reconverted back into the domestic currency. A foreign exchange risk arises because during the period of the

investment, the spot exchange rate of the foreign currency may fall so that the investor gets back fewer domestic currency units than were originally paid. This fall may wipe out some or all of the extra interest earned on the foreign over the domestic investment and may even lead to an actual loss. *See also* covered interest arbitrage.

Interest Rate Risk: Interest rate risk is the risk that bond prices will decline when interest rates increase. When the coupon rate on a bond is equal to the market rate, the bond will sell at par. When the coupon rate on a bond is greater than the market rate (because the market rate has declined), the bond will sell at a premium. When the coupon rate is less than the market rate (because the market rate has increased), the bond will sell at a discount. The market rate adjusts the price of the bond to produce a market yield based on the coupon amount. Interest rate risk is a function of the bond's maturity (longer-term bonds are more volatile than short-term bonds), the bond's coupon rate (if a bond's coupon rate is lower, it will experience greater volatility), and the bond's yield (the higher the yield, the lower the volatility). Interest rate risk is measured by a calculated factor called duration. *See also* credit risk *and* default risk *and* reinvestment risk.

Internal Control–Integrated Framework: The COSO publication Internal Control–Integrated Framework (the Framework) describes internal control as a process that is designed to provide reasonable assurance in regard to the efficiency and effectiveness of operations, financial reporting, and compliance. The Framework identifies five major components, including control environment, risk assessment, control activities, information and communication, and monitoring.

Internal Controls: It is the process of directing, measuring and monitoring an organization's resources to provide reasonable assurance that the control objectives are achieved.

Internal Environment: A component of the Enterprise Risk Management–Integrated Framework (ERM) that defines the "tone at the top" including integrity and ethical values, risk appetite and risk management philosophy, and organizational structure.

Internal Factors: In value chain analysis, internal factors are the strengths and weaknesses of the firm. *See also* external factors *and* value chain *and* value chain analysis.

Internal Failure Costs: Internal failure costs are the costs to cure a defect before the product is sent to a customer. Internal failure costs include rework costs, scrap, tooling changes, and downtime. *See also* external failure costs.

Internal Rate of Return Method: The internal rate of return method is a capital budgeting method that determines the rate of return of an investment's or project's cash flows. The internal rate of return method is the inverse of the net present value method because it determines the rate at which the net present value of the investment is zero. *See also* net present value method *and* hurdle rate of return.

International Monetary Fund (IMF): The IMF is a global financial institution established to help stabilize exchange rates among the world's currencies and make loans as appropriate to improve the economies of member nations. Nearly 200 nations belong to the IMF, including the United States.

Internet: The Internet is a global network of computers. *See also* extranet *and* intranet.

Internet-Based Networks: Internet-based networks use Internet protocols and public communications channels to establish network communications.

Interpretation: The line-by-line translation of program source code to object code. Programs that are interpreted normally execute much more slowly than programs that are compiled because there is no optimization for execution speed. *See also* compilation.

Intranet: Intranets connect geographically separate LANs within a company. *See also* extranet *and* Internet.

Inventoriable Costs: Inventoriable costs are manufacturing costs (direct and indirect costs). *See also* full product costing.

Inventory Turnover: Inventory turnover is the cost of goods sold divided by the average inventory.

IP Address: An IP address is an address assigned to users of a network or the Internet (assigned by the network information center [NIC]). IP addresses are written in dotted decimal notation (e.g., 123.11.1.123).

Issue-Specific Policy: An issue-specific policy addresses a specific issue of concern to the organization.

Job Order Costing: Job order costing, sometimes called job costing, is a cost accounting technique that involves the simple accumulation of all costs associated with a job, order, project, or activity. Job order costing is most effective for customized activities with easily traceable costs. Direct material and direct labor are traced to the individual jobs. Manufacturing overhead is applied to the individual jobs based on an overhead rate normally calculated at the beginning of the year based on the budgeted overhead costs divided by the estimated costs driver (such as the estimated number of units to be produced). *See also* process costing *and* cost driver.

Joint Costs: Joint costs are costs incurred in the production of two or more inseparable products from the same raw material or input. Joint costs stop at the split-off point where the products become separable; after that, the costs are called separable costs. The accounting treatment of joint costs depends on the character and value of the resulting products.

1. Joint products have relatively high values, and common costs must be allocated by some arbitrary means.

2. By-products have relatively low values, and any proceeds from their sale are a reduction of common costs or treated as miscellaneous income.

3. Scrap has little or no value, and any disposal cost adds to joint costs. Joint costs are often allocated using net realizable values at the split-off point.

Junk Bonds: Junk bonds are extremely risky bonds that are characterized by a high return to compensate for the risk. *See also* debenture *and* subordinated debenture *and* income bonds.

Just-in-Time (JIT): Just-in-time inventory systems, also called lean production systems, are inventory systems that minimize inventories by arranging for materials and sub-components to arrive just as they are needed and for goods to be made just in time to be shipped to customers. It is based on a "pull" approach, in which an item is produced only when it is requested further downstream in the production cycle. Raw materials are purchased in small quantities, enough only to meet immediate production demands.

Kaizen: Kaizen is continuous improvement. In practice, Kaizen can be implemented by improving every aspect of a business process in a step-by-step approach, while gradually developing employee skills through training, education, and increased involvement. The principles in Kaizen implementation are: (1) human resources are the most important firm asset; (2) processes must evolve by gradual improvement rather than by radical changes; and (3) improvement must be based on statistical/quantitative evaluation of process performance. *See also* statistical quality control.

Kanban: The Japanese refer to kanban as a simple parts-movement system that depends on cards and boxes/containers to take parts from one station to another on a production line. The essence of the kanban concept is that a supplier or the warehouse should deliver components to a production line only as they are needed so that there is no storage in the production area. Within a kanban system, stations located along production lines produce/deliver desired components only when they receive a card and an empty container indicating that more parts will be needed in production. *See also* just-in-time.

Kilobyte (KB): A kilobyte is approximately 1,000 bytes (actually 1,024 bytes).

Kinked Demand Curve: A kinked demand curve is the demand curve of an oligopolist. The kinked demand curve has different slopes above and below the prevailing price. *See also* oligopoly.

Knowledge Management: Knowledge management is gathering, management, and use of knowledge by an organization. It is also the process of improving an organization's management of its knowledge.

Lagging Indicator: A lagging indicator is an indicator (economic measure) that tends to follow economic activity. *See also* leading indicator.

Law of Demand: The law of demand is an economic proposition that states that the price of a product (or service) and the quantity demanded of that product (or service) are inversely related. *See also* law of supply.

Law of Diminishing Returns: The law of diminishing returns is the property by which output increases at a decreasing rate, as more and more units of an input are combined with a fixed amount of other inputs.

Law of Supply: The law of supply is an economic proposition that states that the price of a product or service and the quantity supplied of that product are positively related. *See also* law of demand.

Leading Indicator: A leading indicator is an indicator (economic measure) that tends to predict economic activity. *See also* lagging indicator.

Lean: Lean is shorthand for lean manufacturing or lean production. Lean anticipates that a production process can be made more efficient by identifying those efforts that add value to the customer and to limit efforts to those processes.

Learning Curve: Learning curve analysis is a step-by-step method of projecting costs for repetitive tasks where learning is a variable. The theory of learning recognizes that repetition of the same operation results in less time or effort expended on that operation. The direct labor hours necessary to complete a unit of production will decrease by a constant percentage each time the production quantity is doubled. While the learning curve emphasizes time, it can be easily extended to cost as well. The learning curve itself is a graphical representation of increased productivity per unit of time (e.g., per hour) as workers gain more experience with repetitive tasks.

LIBOR: LIBOR is a standard benchmark or reference rate for short-term interest rates. LIBOR stands for the London Interbank Offer Rate and is the rate of interest at which banks borrow funds from other banks in the London interbank market. *See also* Eurodollars.

Line of Credit: A line of credit is an informal agreement between a borrower and a bank indicating the maximum credit the bank will extend to the borrower. A revolving credit agreement is a formal line of credit.

Liquidity Risk: Liquidity risk is the risk that a security will not be able to be sold quickly without giving up a large price concession. *See also* default risk *and* maturity risk premium *and* interest rate risk.

Loan Covenant: Loan covenants are provisions in a bond indenture. The covenants can be either affirmative covenants or negative covenants. Affirmative covenants contain the activities that the issuer promises to do, such as a promise to pay interest and principal on a timely basis, a promise to keep certain assets (the collateral) in good condition and in working order, or a promise to submit periodic reports to the trustee. Negative covenants contain limitations and restrictions on the issuer's activities, such as restrictions on the issuer's ability to issue additional debt. *See also* bond indenture.

Local Area Network (LAN): LANs permit shared resources (software, hardware, and data) among computers within a limited area. LANs are normally privately owned, which means that they do not use telephone lines or that they use private lines leased from telecommunications providers. *See also* network *and* server *and* wide area network (WAN).

Lockbox: A lockbox system is a payment collection procedure in which payers send their payments to a nearby post office box that is emptied by the firm's bank several times a day. *See also* concentration banking *and* zero balance account.

Long Run: The long run is the period of time during which all of the costs of production are variable (i.e., a time frame that is long enough for fixed production facilities, technology, or institutional arrangements to be changed). *See also* short run.

Long-Run Aggregate Supply (LRAS): Long-run aggregate supply (potential GDP) is the economy's maximum rate of sustainable output given its current resource base, level of technology, and institutional arrangements. It is the optimal productive capacity of the economy that is dictated by the fixed plant and equipment assets currently in place. The long-run aggregate supply curve is vertical. Factors that shift the long-run aggregate supply curve are investment in new physical capital, improved technologies, additions to the raw materials resources, increases in the labor force, changes in institutional arrangements, and improvements in efficiency. The long-run aggregate supply is increased when people work harder and smarter. *See also* aggregate demand *and* aggregate supply.

M1: M1 is a measure of the money supply that includes cash, demand deposits, and traveler's checks. *See also* M2 *and* M3.

M2: M2 is a measure of the money supply that includes M1 plus savings deposits, time deposits less than $100,000, and money market mutual fund shares. *See also* M2 *and* M3.

M3: M3 is a measure of the money supply that includes M2 plus time deposits of more than $100,000. *See also* M1 *and* M2.

Macro: A macro is a series of prerecorded commands that will be executed on the occurrence of certain events.

Magnetic Ink Character Reader (MICR): A MICR reader is equipment that reads the magnetic ink characters on checks and similar documents.

Maintenance: Maintenance refers to both hardware maintenance (fixing the hardware) and software or application maintenance (fixing the software).

Major Deficiency: A material internal control deficiency or combination of deficiencies that significantly reduces the likelihood that an organization can achieve its objectives.

Management by Objective: Management by objective is a performance evaluation method that begins with the mutual development of goals for the upcoming performance evaluation period.

Management Information System (MIS): Management information systems, sometimes called management reporting systems, are a type of business information system. A management information system provides managerial and other end users with reports. *See also* accounting information system *and* decision support system *and* executive information system.

Manufacturing Overhead: Manufacturing overhead includes all costs associated with the manufacturing process that cannot easily be identified as part of the cost of the finished product. It can also be defined as all direct manufacturing costs other than direct materials and direct labor. Manufacturing overhead includes indirect material and indirect labor; factory rent; factory heat, light, and power; factory insurance; and factory depreciation. *See also* direct materials *and* direct labor.

Margin of Safety: The margin of safety is the excess of sales over sales at the breakeven point. *See also* breakeven point.

Marginal Cost (MC): Marginal cost is the change in total cost due to a one unit increase in output. *See also* marginal revenue *and* perfect competition.

Marginal Product (MP): Marginal product is the change in total product due to a one unit increase in the quantity of a variable input employed. *See also* marginal revenue product *and* total product.

Marginal Propensity to Consume (MPC): The marginal propensity to consume is the change in consumption due to a $1 increase in income. *See also* multiplier effect.

Marginal Revenue (MR): Marginal revenue is the change in total revenue due to a one unit increase in sales of the product. *See also* marginal cost *and* perfect competition.

Marginal Revenue Product (MRP): Marginal revenue product is the change in total revenue that results from employing an additional unit of input. It is computed as the marginal product of an input times the price of a firm's output. *See also* marginal product.

Market Equilibrium: Market equilibrium is the state in which there are no forces acting to change the current price/quantity combination of a good or service. It is the state of balance in a market.

Market Risk: Market risk is the risk of an individual stock or risk in a portfolio that cannot be eliminated by diversification. Market risk stems from factors that systematically affect most or all firms. Market risk is also called nondiversifiable risk. *See also* diversifiable risk *and* beta coefficient.

Market Share Variance: In target market analysis, market share variance is the budgeted contribution margin per unit times the actual units sold, times the difference between the actual market share and the budgeted market share. *See also* market size variance.

Market Size Variance: In target market analysis, market size variance is the budgeted contribution margin per unit times the budgeted market share, times the difference between the actual market size in units and the expected market size in units. *See also* market share variance.

Master Budget: A master budget is a budget for all of the planned activities of a firm. It normally is developed for a year at a time and normally includes an operating budget as well as a financial budget. The operating budget would include a sales budget; a production budget; and a selling, general, and administrative expenses budget. The financial budget would include a cash budget and pro forma (as if) financial statements. *See also* flexible budget.

Materials Requirements Planning (MRP): Materials resource planning systems extend the idea of computerized inventory control to manufacturing. Sales personnel estimate how many products will be sold in the future. The MRP system backtracks using estimated times to assemble each product. The system then explodes the product into lists of parts needed, using bills of materials for each product. The needed parts are ordered at times backdated from the assembly dates. *See also* bill of materials.

Maturity Risk Premium: A maturity risk premium is an interest premium to compensate investors for a longer maturity of bonds. *See also* credit risk *and* default risk *and* liquidity risk.

Mbps: Megabits per second (Mbps) is a measurement of data transmission speed. A megabit is 1 million bits. A T1 communications line is rated at 1.544 Mbps. Other common measures are kilobits per second (kbps), gigabits per second (Gbps), and terabits per second (Tbps).

Megabyte: A megabyte is approximately 1 million bytes (actually 1,048,576 bytes).

Merger: A merger involves one or more corporations merging into another corporation. One corporation survives the merger and continues in existence and the other merging corporations cease to exist following the merger.

Mirroring: Mirroring is the use of a backup computer to duplicate all of the processes and transactions on the primary computer. If the primary computer fails, the backup computer immediately takes its place without any interruption in service. Mirroring is often used by banks and other such organizations where any downtime is not acceptable.

Mixed Costs: Mixed costs are semi-variable costs and include both a fixed and a variable component. *See also* fixed costs *and* variable costs *and* relevant range.

Monetary Assets and Liabilities: Monetary assets and liabilities are assets and liabilities that are fixed in dollar amounts regardless of changes in specific prices or the general price level. *See also* nonmonetary assets and liabilities.

Monetary Policy: Monetary policy is the setting of the money supply by the Fed through the use of monetary policy tools to promote full employment and price stability. *See also* fiscal policy *and* contractionary monetary policy *and* expansionary monetary policy.

Money Market Hedge: A money market hedge is the simultaneous borrowing and lending transactions in two different currencies to lock in the domestic currency value of a foreign currency transaction. *See also* forward hedge *and* futures hedge *and* options hedge.

Money Supply: The money supply is the stock of all liquid assets (currency, checking account funds, and traveler's checks) available for transactions in the economy at any given point in time. *See also* M1 *and* M2 *and* M3.

Monitoring: As a component of the Internal Control–Integrated Framework (the Framework), monitoring contemplates ongoing and separate evaluations of the effectiveness of controls over financial reporting as well as reports of deficiencies, while as a component of Enterprise Risk Management–Integrated Framework (ERM) the concept is broadened to include general business operations.

Monopolistic Competition: Monopolistic competition is a market structure that consists of many firms each selling a slightly differentiated product. Under monopolistic competition, there are few barriers to entry but significant non-price competition in the market. *See also* perfect competition *and* monopoly.

Monopoly: A monopoly is a market structure that consists of one firm that is the only seller of a product. Under monopoly there are significant barriers to entry and no close substitutes for the good sold by the monopolist. Monopolists are price setters. *See also* price setter *and* oligopoly *and* natural monopoly.

Monopsony: A monopsony is a market in which there is only one buyer. In a labor market, there is only one employer. A monopsony, where there is only one buyer, is similar to a monopoly, where there is only one seller. *See also* monopoly.

Mortgage Bond: Mortgage bonds are bonds that are secured by liens on real assets of the issuer. *See also* debentures *and* subordinated debentures *and* junk bonds *and* income bonds.

Multiplier Effect: The multiplier effect is the magnified effect that an increase in household, firm, or government spending has on real GDP (i.e., a $1 increase in spending by households, firms, or the government results in a greater than $1 increase in real GDP). *See also* GDP *and* real GDP *and* nominal GDP *and* marginal propensity to consume.

Multipolar: The term multipolar is used to describe a world economy in which several nations have significant and potentially competing power. The growth of the world's emerging economies creates a multipolar environment.

Multipolarity: Multipolarity anticipates distributed power among nations and their economies.

Multiprocessing: Multiprocessing is the coordinated processing of programs by more than one processor. Multiprocessing is a general term that is divided into symmetric multiprocessing (in which one operating system controls the processing) and parallel processing (in which each processor has its own operating system). When multiple processors or computers process the same program, there is an efficiency loss to provide the control of the overall processing. *See also* multiprogramming *and* parallel processing.

Multiprogramming: Multiprogramming is several parts of a program running at the same time on a single processor. *See also* multiprocessing *and* parallel processing.

National Income: National income is net national product less indirect business taxes (sales taxes). *See also* net national product.

National Income Accounting: The national income accounting system is the process by which economic activity is measured on a national scale. *See also* national income.

Natural Monopoly: A natural monopoly is a monopoly that arises because economic and/or technical conditions permit only one efficient supplier. *See also* monopoly.

Natural Rate of Unemployment: The natural rate of unemployment is the normal rate of unemployment around which unemployment fluctuates due to cyclical unemployment. *See also* unemployment rate *and* cyclical unemployment.

Net Book Value: Net book value is the historical cost of an asset less its accumulated depreciation.

Net Domestic Product: Net domestic product is gross domestic product less depreciation. *See also* gross domestic product.

Net National Product: Net national product is gross national product less depreciation. *See also* gross national product *and* national income.

Net Present Value Method (NPV): The net present value method is a capital budgeting method that measures cash inflows and cash outflows of an investment at a single point in time by incorporating the time value of money and discounting each of the cash flows to that single point in time. One discount rate or different discount rates to reflect risk or inflation may be used. If the net present value is greater than zero (which means that the investment will at least earn the hurdle rate of return), the investment should be accepted; if the net present value is less than zero (which means that the investment will not earn the hurdle rate of return), the investment should not be accepted. *See also* internal rate of return method *and* hurdle rate of return.

Network: A network is an interconnected group of interconnected computers and terminals. The components of a network are computers, terminals, communications channels, communications processors, and communications software.

Network Administrator: Network administrators support computer networks. A network administrator sets up and configures a computer network so that multiple computers can share the same data and information. After a network is established, the work is mostly monitoring and troubleshooting. Sometimes, network administrators are called telecommunication analysts or network operators. *See also* security administrator.

Network Monitoring: Network monitoring is the monitoring of networks and the systems attached to them for slow or failing systems. Normally networks are monitored by a network management/monitoring system, with a network administrator checking for notifications and addressing problems. Intrusion detection software monitors the network for outside intrusions.

Network Operating System (NOS): A network operating system manages communication over a network. It may be either a peer-to-peer system (in which all nodes share in communications management) or a client/server system (in which a central machine serves as the mediator of communication on the network). *See also* operating system.

Network Protocol: Various pieces of hardware and software perform the various functions, all of which communicate by adhering to a common set of rules that allow them to communicate. The set of rules is called a communication or network protocol.

Niche Strategy: A niche strategy is a competitive strategy that focuses on a select group of consumers. *See also* cost leadership strategy *and* differentiation strategy *and* best cost strategy.

Nominal GDP: Nominal GDP is GDP measured in current (nominal) dollars (i.e., with current prices). *See also* GDP *and* real GDP *and* GDP deflator.

Nominal Interest Rate: The nominal interest rate is the amount of interest paid (or earned) measured in current dollars. Interest rates that are quoted in the financial press are nominal interest rates. *See also* real interest rate *and* inflation.

Noncumulative Preferred Shares: Shares with a preference usually are entitled to a fixed amount of money before distributions can be made with respect to nonpreferred shares. Unless the dividend is cumulative, the right to a dividend preference is extinguished if it is not declared for that year.

Nondiversifiable Risk: Nondiversifiable risk is another word for market or systematic risk. *See also* diversifiable risk.

Nonmonetary Assets and Liabilities: Nonmonetary assets and liabilities are assets and liabilities whose values fluctuate due to changes in specific prices or the general price level. *See also* monetary assets and liabilities.

Normal Good: A normal good is a good whose demand is positively related to income (positive income elasticity of demand). *See also* income elasticity of demand *and* inferior good.

Normalization: Normalization is the process of separating data into logical tables. Often, a process of data modeling is used. Before a relational database can be designed, a process of normalization has to occur. *See also* database *and* database administrator.

Objective Probability: An objective probability is a probability based on past outcomes/historical data. The objective probability of an event is equal to the number of times that the event will occur divided by the total number of possible outcomes. Objective probabilities are also called empirical probabilities. Most people would assign approximately the same values to them. *See also* probability *and* subjective probability *and* expected value.

Objective Setting: A component of the Enterprise Risk Management–Integrated Framework (ERM) that defines the process for setting objectives, including strategic objectives, related objectives, and selected objectives, within the context of the risk appetite and tolerance of organization leadership.

Oligopoly: An oligopoly is a market structure that consists of a small number of firms selling similar products. Under an oligopoly, there are significant barriers to entry and strong interdependence among the firms within the market. *See also* monopoly *and* monopolistic competition.

On-Demand Computing: On-demand computing (also called utility computing) is the off-loading of peak demand processing to other data processing centers. Organizations can purchase and pay for computing power from central computing centers as that computing power is needed.

Open Market Operations: Open market operations are the buying and selling of government securities (Treasury bills and bonds) by the Fed.

Operating Agreement: An operating agreement is the internal document signifying the agreement between members of a limited liability company.

Operating Leverage: Operating leverage is the degree to which a firm uses fixed operating costs (as opposed to variable operating costs) to magnify the effects of a given percentage change in sales on the percentage change in earnings before interest and taxes. It is calculated by the ratio of fixed operating costs to variable operating costs. *See also* financial leverage.

Operating Risk: Operating risk includes the risk of doing the right things in the wrong way. For example, assume that a payroll manager is supposed to run the biweekly payroll after the human resources manager enters newly hired employees into the system. If the payroll manager runs the payroll too early (i.e., before the newly hired employees are entered), the newly hired employees do not get paid, and the payroll report generated is inaccurate. *See also* financial risk *and* information risk.

Operating System: An operating system provides the interface between the user and the hardware. It defines what commands can be issued and how they are issued (e.g., typing in a command, pointing at an icon and clicking, issuing a verbal command, etc.). The operating system also controls all input and output to main memory, and it may include certain utility programs that might be used stand-alone or in application software. *See also* system programmer *and* network operating system *and* Unix.

Operational Audit: An operational audit provides a three-dimensional look at a company. Financial statements can illustrate problems, but normally cannot pinpoint the causes of the problems. During an operational audit, an objective third party probes deep inside the company, reviewing its operational and financial objectives, processes, tools, and controls, and focusing on the efficient or inefficient use of resources.

Operational Costing: Operational costing is a technique that blends concepts from job order costing and process costing and is applied to a batch production of homogeneous units processed through a sequence of activities. Work is organized by batch, similar to job order costing. Each activity (or each unit within a batch) is treated exactly the same, similar to process costing. Work orders initiate production for each job in operational costing. Materials are specific to the work order. Conversion costs (direct labor and manufacturing overhead) are applied on an average cost per unit basis, similar to process costing. *See also* job order costing *and* process costing.

Opportunity Costs: Opportunity costs are costs that would have been saved or the profit that would have been earned if another decision alternative had been selected. Accounting records do not record opportunity costs.

Optimal Capital Structure: The optimal or target capital structure is the capital structure that produces the lowest weighted average cost of capital and maximizes the price of a firm or at least of the firm's stock.

Options Hedge: An options hedge is a hedge transacted in the options market for foreign currencies. An option contract is an agreement between two parties where the purchaser of the option has the right, but not the obligation, to enter into a transaction at some future date and at a price agreed to at the time the agreement is made. In terms of foreign currencies, an options hedge entitles the option purchaser the right to either purchase or sell units of an individual currency for a negotiated price on a certain date. Outside the foreign currencies market, the instrument is normally called an option, without the word hedge. *See also* futures hedge *and* forward hedge *and* money market hedge.

Output Controls: Controls where system outputs are verified to enhance processing integrity.

Outstanding Shares: Outstanding shares are shares in shareholder's hands.

Overapplied Overhead: Overapplied overhead is manufacturing overhead applied to products that is greater than the actual overhead cost incurred. Depending on materiality, overapplied overhead is either allocated between ending inventory and cost of goods sold or just written off to cost of goods sold. *See also* underapplied overhead *and* overhead.

Overhead: Overhead is any manufacturing cost that is not material or labor. Overhead includes both fixed and variable components and is "applied" to the products. *See also* direct material *and* direct labor *and* overapplied overhead *and* underapplied overhead.

Packet: Packets are small pieces of data that travel over a network; they are normally small parts of the complete message. Each packet has a packet header to identify the packet and to indicate its sending and receiving locations. The whole thing is called the packet. *See also* packet filtering *and* firewall *and* application firewall.

Packet Filtering: Packet filtering examines packets of data as they pass through the firewall according to the rules that have been established for the source of the data, the destination of the data, and the network ports the data was sent from. Packet filtering is the simplest type of firewall configuration, but it can be circumvented by an intruder who forges an acceptable address (called IP spoofing). *See also* packet *and* firewall *and* application firewall.

Par Value: Par value is a specific face value placed on stock.

Parallel Processing: Parallel processing is the simultaneous use of more than one computer to execute a program, which first has to be divided into parts that can be executed separately. *See also* multiprocessing *and* multiprogramming.

Pareto Diagram: A Pareto diagram plots data in a hierarchical order, which allows the most significant or most frequent problems to be corrected first; it is a combination of a histogram with a line graph that displays the cumulative occurrence of the problems. The Pareto analysis technique is used primarily to identify and evaluate nonconformities, although it can summarize all types of data. Most quality problems result from a small number of problems, the so-called 80–20 rule (80 percent of the quality problems can be traced to 20 percent of the output). *See also* control chart *and* statistical quality control *and* cause-and-effect diagram.

Payback Method: The payback method is a capital budgeting method that calculates the amount of time to recover the initial investment for an investment or project (i.e., the payback period). The shorter the payback period, the better. The normal payback method uses nondiscounted after-tax cash flows. *See also* discounted payback method.

Perfect Competition: Perfect competition is a market structure that consists of a very large number of sellers, each of which sells a nearly identical product. Under perfect competition, there are few barriers to entry and firms are price takers. Under perfect competition, short-run profits are maximized when prices are set so that marginal revenue equals marginal cost (Price = MR = MC). *See also* marginal revenue *and* marginal cost.

Performance Standards: Performance standards published by the Institute of Internal Auditors (IIA) address many of the same issues as fieldwork standards and reporting standards under GAAS. Issues related to planning and supervision of the engagement and documentation of evidence or basis for conclusions are addressed here along with generic reporting requirements.

Period Costs: Period costs are costs that are not the costs of producing the product manufactured and are thus not inventoriable. Period costs are charged to the period in which they are incurred. Selling and general and administrative costs are almost always period costs. *See also* product costs.

Permanent File: Master files represent data at a certain point in time. There are many different iterations of a master file; one for each point in time the master file is updated. Master files are permanent files and may be retained permanently or semi-permanently. Older iterations of a master file are often needed if significant processing problems are discovered and data has to be reconstructed. Master files that are kept permanently are called permanent files. *See also* temporary file.

Personal Income: Personal income is the income received by households and noncorporate businesses.

Phillips Curve: The Phillips curve is a curve that illustrates the typical inverse relationship between the rate of inflation and the unemployment rate. In the Phillips curve, the inflation rate is plotted on the y-axis and the unemployment rate is plotted on the x-axis. The curve normally slopes down to the right. *See also* inflation *and* unemployment rate.

Phishing: Phishing is the sending of phony e-mails to try to lure people to phony websites asking for financial information.

Physical Access Controls: Physical access controls encompass the physical security of IT assets, including access to facilities and access to programs and data. *See also* access controls *and* electronic access controls *and* application controls.

Physical Design: During the physical design phase, a company uses the conceptual design to develop detailed specifications to code and test the computer programs.

Portal: A portal (also corporate portal or enterprise portal) is a browser-based application that allows knowledge workers and other workers in an organization to gain access to, collaborate with, make decisions on, and take other actions on a wide variety of business-related information over a network. Web portals (e.g., Yahoo) are another type of portal that collect Web information and provide it to individual users.

Practical Capacity: Practical capacity is the maximum production that can be reached during normal operations with an allowance for normal downtime.

Preventive Control: Preventive controls are controls that reduce the occurrence of errors in the first place, i.e., they prevent errors from happening. *See also* corrective control *and* detective control.

Prevention Costs: In quality control, prevention costs are costs to prevent the production of defective units. These costs include inspection costs, preventive maintenance, redesign of products, redesign of processes, and the search for higher-quality suppliers. *See also* appraisal costs.

Price Ceiling: A price ceiling is a maximum price for a good or service established by law (e.g., rent control). If the price ceiling is set below the equilibrium price in a market, a shortage will develop. *See also* price floor.

Price Elastic Demand: Price elastic demand is when a 1 percent increase in price results in a greater than 1 percent decrease in the quantity demanded (i.e., when the absolute value of the price elasticity of demand is greater than 1). *See also* price inelastic demand.

Price Elasticity of Demand: Price elasticity of demand is the percentage change in quantity demanded divided by the percentage change in the price of a good or service.

Price Elasticity of Supply: Price elasticity of supply is the percentage change in quantity supplied divided by the percentage change in the price of a good or service.

Price Floor: A price floor is a minimum price for a good or service established by law (e.g., minimum wage). If the price floor is set above the equilibrium price in a market, a surplus will develop. *See also* price ceiling.

Price Inelastic Demand: Price inelastic demand is when a 1 percent increase in price results in a less than 1 percent decrease in quantity demanded (i.e., when the absolute value of the price elasticity of demand is less than 1). *See also* price elastic demand.

Price Inelastic Supply: Price inelastic supply is when a 1 percent increase in price results in a less than 1 percent increase in quantity supplied (i.e., when the price elasticity of supply is less than 1). *See also* price elasticity of supply.

Price Searcher: A price searcher is a firm that faces a downward sloping demand curve for its products. The amount that the firm will be able to sell is inversely related to the price that it charges. *See also* price taker *and* perfect competition.

Price Setter: The opposite of a price taker, a price setter has the power to set prices. For instance, a firm that faces a downward sloping demand curve can choose its price. *See also* price taker *and* monopoly.

Price Taker: A price taker is a firm that must take the market price in order to sell its products. Because each price taker's output is small in relation to the total market, price takers can sell all of their output at the market price, but they are unable to sell any of their output at a price higher than the market price. *See also* price searcher *and* perfect competition.

Primary Market: The primary market is where securities are created/initially issued. For stocks, this market is also called the initial public offering (IPO market). *See also* secondary market.

Prime Costs: Prime costs include direct material and direct labor. Prime costs are generally relevant to a costing decision. *See also* direct costs *and* indirect costs *and* cost object *and* variable costs *and* fixed costs.

Probability: A probability is the chance that an event will occur. Probabilities are assigned values between zero (0) and one (1). A zero probability indicates that there is no chance the event will ever occur (i.e., an impossibility). A probability of one indicates that the event will always occur (i.e., a certainty). *See also* objective probability *and* subjective probability *and* expected value.

Process Costing: Process costing is a cost accounting technique that is used when products are produced in a more-or-less continuous basis and when the products are indistinguishable from each other. Costs are accumulated by department, rather than by order as in job order costing, and are applied uniformly to all units that pass through the process during a period. Process costing is normally FIFO or weighted average. *See also* job order costing *and* cost driver *and* FIFO method of process costing *and* weighted average method of process costing.

Process Management: Process management represents a collection of different contemporary business concepts that include planning and monitoring the performance of a process to continuously improve the process and the resulting product to achieve objectives. Project management and business process reengineering are related to the concept of process management.

Processing Controls: Processing controls are programmed controls that verify that all transactions are processed correctly (completely and accurately) during file maintenance. *See also* input controls.

Product Costs: Product costs are the costs of producing the product manufactured and are thus inventoriable. Direct material, direct labor, and manufacturing overhead are product costs. Product costs normally become part of the cost of goods manufactured when the products are completed and the cost of goods sold when the products are sold. *See also* period costs.

Production Cycle: The production cycle is a transaction cycle characterized by the conversion of resources (e.g., raw material or time) into products or services. *See also* transaction cycles.

Production Function: The production function is the relationship between the firm's input of productive resources and its output of goods and services.

Production Possibilities Curve: A production possibilities curve identifies the amount of two different goods or services that can be produced with a given amount of resources when those resources are fully employed. Production possibilities curves are often used in the analysis of international trade. *See also* comparative advantage.

Profit: Profit is total revenue less total cost.

Profitability Index: The profitability index is used to rank qualifying investments. The index is the present value of the future cash flows divided by a project's or an investment's initial cost (or the present value of the cash outflows if the investment is not all at time 0). Mathematically, for independent investments, if the net present value of a project or an investment is greater than zero, its internal rate of return will be greater than the hurdle rate of return and the profitability index will be greater than 1.0.

Program-Framework Policy: A program-framework policy establishes an organization's approach to computer security (i.e., a computer security framework).

Program-Level Policy: A program-level policy is used to create a management-sponsored computer security program.

Programming Language: Programming languages allow programmers to write programs in source code. The programs are then translated into object code for execution. There are many different programming languages, each with strengths and weaknesses.

Project: A project is a temporary undertaking intended to produce a unique service, product, or result. Unlike continuing operations, a project has a definite beginning and an end.

Push Reporting: Under push reporting, information can actually be "pushed" and sent to a computer screen or computer desktop. Push reporting requires determination of the data that is to be selected for an end user, selection of the specified data by the push reporting software, and delivery of the specified data to the end user, but it can be more automated, even from the Internet. Delivery of the information can be to a PC, a PDA, or a cellular phone, depending on volume of the response. Push reports can be specific internal reports of a particular organization, or they can be general industry reports or information downloaded and possibly aggregated from the Internet.

Quality: Quality embraces a wide variety of concepts, including the perceived quality of products to consumers that result from enhanced features (a luxury vs. an economy car) or the engineering or manufacturing definitions of quality that pertain to conformance of goods to manufacturing specifications within tolerable limits.

Quantity Demanded: The quantity demanded is the maximum quantity of a good or service that consumers are willing and able to purchase at each and every price.

Quantity Supplied: The quantity supplied is the maximum amount of a good or service that a firm is willing and able to produce at each and every price.

Quick Ratio: The quick ratio is (cash and cash equivalents plus short-term marketable securities plus receivables [net]) divided by current liabilities. *See also* current ratio *and* working capital.

Real GDP: Real GDP is GDP measured in dollars adjusted for inflation (i.e., in dollars of constant purchasing power). Inflation is measured by the GDP deflator, which is a measure of inflation somewhat like the more widely known consumer price index. *See also* GDP deflator *and* consumer price index.

Real Interest Rate: The real interest rate is the amount of interest paid (or earned) adjusted for inflation. The real interest rate is the nominal interest rate minus the inflation rate. *See also* nominal interest rate *and* inflation.

Recession: A recession occurs when the economy experiences negative real economic growth for two consecutive quarters. *See also* depression *and* business cycle.

Record: A record is a group of fields that represents the data that is being stored for a particular entity, such as a customer or an account receivable. *See also* bit and byte *and* file and field.

Referential Integrity: In a relational database, referential integrity prevents the deletion of key values in related records (tables). For instance, if there is a relational database with customer records (tables) and invoice records (tables), the invoice records normally contain a customer number that references back to the customer record. If a customer is deleted, the invoice records with that customer's numbers should be updated or deleted. Referential integrity is enforced by the database management system.

Regression Analysis: Regression analysis is a method for determining the relationship between two or more variables. Simple regression analysis involves one dependent variable and one independent variable. Multiple regression analysis involves more than one independent variable. Often, the determination of whether there is a relationship, and the strength of that relationship if there is one, is called correlation analysis. Regression analysis is purely the determination of the actual regression equation (the intercept and slope coefficients of the regression line). *See also* coefficient of correlation *and* coefficient of determination *and* standard error of the estimate *and* high-low method.

Reinvestment Risk: Reinvestment risk is the risk that intermediate cash flows from a bond (interest payments or proceeds from a bond refunding) will have to be invested at a lower interest rate than the original bond (if interest rates have decreased in the meantime). *See also* interest rate risk *and* credit risk.

Relevant Costs: Relevant costs are future costs that will change as a result of selecting different alternatives. Costs that will not change as a result of selecting different alternatives are not relevant because they will not impact the total costs that will result from the decision. *See also* sunk costs.

Relevant Range: The relevant range is a range of activity levels in which cost behavior characteristics (fixed or variable) are valid. Within a relevant range, fixed costs are assumed to remain the same (i.e., they do not change). *See also* fixed costs *and* variable costs *and* mixed costs.

Replication: Replication (file or database replication) is the duplication of files or databases in their entirety, normally in different physical locations.

Reporting Currency: The reporting currency is the currency in which an entity prepares its financial statements, normally the U.S. dollar. *See also* functional currency.

Required Reserves Ratio (RRR): The required reserves ratio is the fraction of total deposits the Fed requires banks to hold in reserve (not be loaned). The required reserves ratio is the inverse of the multiplier.

Residual Income: Residual income is the excess of a firm's net income over its required rate of return. *See also* economic value added.

Responsibility Accounting: Responsibility accounting is an accounting system that provides information to management about the performance of other parts of the organization by the type of responsibility assigned to each part of the organization (e.g., responsibility for cost containment in cost centers and responsibility for revenue production in revenue centers). *See also* strategic business unit.

Return on Assets (ROA): Return on assets is a firm's net income divided by average total assets. *See also* asset turnover.

Return on Equity (ROE): Return on equity is a firm's net income divided by average total equity.

Return on Investment (ROI): Return on investment is a firm's net income divided by average invested capital.

Return on Sales (ROS): Return on sales is a firm's income before interest income, interest expense, and taxes divided by sales (net).

Revenue Cycle: The revenue cycle is a transaction cycle characterized by the sales of goods or services that produce cash or other assets (e.g., receivables). *See also* transaction cycles.

Rework: The process and related cost of converting defective units into goods meeting production specifications is termed rework. Some imperfections are anticipated as part of the manufacturing process. Normal rework is included in standards and is included in manufacturing overhead.

Risk Assessment: As a component of the Internal Control–Integrated Framework (the Framework), risk assessment includes the risk of material misstatement of financial statements. As a component of Enterprise Risk Management–Integrated Framework (ERM), the concept is broadened to embrace the evaluation of risk as part of overall operational management and the criteria and techniques that might be used to fully assess risk.

Risk Averse: Risk averse means that the investor does not seek out risk and thus will demand a higher return for accepting risk in an investment.

Risk-Free Rate: The risk-free rate is the interest rate that would be paid on a riskless security. It is approximated by the interest rate on short-term U.S. Treasury securities. The real risk-free rate assumes no inflation; the nominal risk-free rate assumes inflation so that the nominal risk-free rate is the real risk-free rate plus an inflation risk premium.

Risk Response: A component of the Enterprise Risk Management–Integrated Framework (ERM) that defines the process for identifying the range of responses to enterprise risk.

Safety Stock: A safety stock is the level of inventory that is maintained to ensure that supply requirements are met.

Sales Mix Variance: In target market analysis, sales mix variance is the budgeted contribution margin per unit times the actual units sold times the difference between the actual sales mix and the budgeted sales mix. The sales mix variance is also the sales volume variance less the sales quantity variance.

Sales Quantity Variance: In target market analysis, sales quantity variance is the budgeted contribution margin per unit times the budgeted sales mix times the difference between the actual units sold and the budgeted sales volume. The sales quantity variance is also the sales volume variance less the sales mix variance.

Sales Volume Variance: In target market analysis, sales volume variance is the standard contribution margin per unit times the difference between the actual units sold and the budgeted sales volume.

Sarbanes-Oxley Act of 2002: Legislation that amended federal securities laws after a series of corporate financial scandals exposed serious weaknesses in the self-regulating system that had been intended to provide reliable company financial statements. Provisions of the act expand the responsibility of both auditors and corporate financial managers to annually assess the adequacy of internal controls.

Scalability: Scalability is the ability of a computer, computer product, or system to expand to serve a greater amount of users.

Schema: A description of the types of data elements that are in a database, the relationships among the data elements, and the structure used to organize the data. *See also* database.

Scorched Earth Policy: When a corporation is faced with the prospect of being taken over and the board of directors wants to resist the takeover attempt, it will sell off assets or take out loans that would make the company less financially attractive.

Scrap: Materials remaining after the manufacturing process that have a minor value in relation to primary products. Scrap is generally either sold or reused.

Seasonal Unemployment: Seasonal unemployment is the unemployment that arises from seasonal changes in the demand and supply of labor. *See also* structural unemployment *and* unemployment rate.

Secondary Market: Secondary markets are markets other than the primary market, where securities are traded among investors. *See also* primary market.

Secondary Storage: Secondary storage devices (e.g., hard drives or magnetic disks, flash drives, CD-ROM disks, optical disks, and magnetic tape) are a means to permanently store programs and data. With sequential storage devices (such as tapes), data is accessed sequentially. With random storage devices, data is normally accessed randomly.

Security Administrator: Security administrators are responsible for the assignment of initial passwords and often the maintenance of those passwords (if the end users do not maintain their own passwords). Security administrators are responsible for the overall operation of the various security systems and the security software in general. *See also* database administrator *and* system programmer *and* network administrator.

Segregation of Duties: Segregation of duties is defined as dividing responsibilities for different portions of a transaction (authorization, recording, and custody) among several different people or departments. The objective is to prevent any one person from having total control over all aspects of the transaction. Because many transactions in an IT environment are actually performed by the application software, segregation of duties in an IT environment normally revolves around granting and/or restricting access to production programs and to production data.

Selling Price Variance: In target market analysis, selling price variance is the actual units sold times (the actual selling price per unit less the budgeted selling price per unit). *See also* sales mix variance *and* sales volume variance.

Sensitivity Analysis: Sensitivity analysis is the process of experimenting with different parameters and assumptions regarding a model and recording the results.

Server: A server is a node dedicated to providing services or resources to the rest of the network (e.g., a file server maintains centralized application and data files, a print server provides access to high-quality printers, a database server provides access to a specific database, etc.). A server is generally not directly accessible by individual users but only through the network software. *See also* local area network (LAN).

Service-Level Agreement: From a telecommunications standpoint, a service-level agreement (SLA) is an agreement by a PSDN provider (carrier) to provide a certain level of service within the cloud. Service-level agreements can also be used wherever levels of service can be quantified and measured.

Shareholder: A shareholder is a party owning an interest in a corporation (also called a stockholder). A shareholder has a limited right to manage.

Shareware: Terminology for some types of application software includes groupware/shareware (which is short for group working software), software that lets different people work on the same documents and coordinate their work activities.

Shifts in the Economic Balance of Power: The ability of the world's emerging nations to contend with the economies of the industrialized world for power, resources, influence, etc., is a change or shift in the economic balance of power from previous decades. Balance of power theory holds that the states that are members of the global economy can either engage in balancing or bandwagoning behavior. An emerging nation might side with the United States or other industrialized nations in adopting standards that reduce greenhouse emissions that contribute to global warming (bandwagoning) or could join with other emerging nations in ignoring the leadership of the United States (balancing). The significance of an emerging nation's possible decision to change the impact of the effectiveness of environmental controls represents an important shift in the balance of economic power.

Short Run: The short run is a period of time during which some of the costs of production are fixed (i.e., a time frame that is not long enough for fixed production facilities, technology, or institutional arrangements to be changed). *See also* long run.

Simple Interest: Simple interest is interest computed without any compounding. *See also* compound interest.

Six Sigma: Six Sigma is a process improvement strategy initially adopted in manufacturing. The name Six Sigma is based on a statistical quality measurement that indicates near zero defects. The foundational premise of Six Sigma is the idea that product defects can be removed by improving business processes and eliminating variability of the manufacturing process. Quality management methods that utilize statistical techniques characterize Six Sigma. Methods are so technical that they often require specially trained individuals to fully implement the ideas. Degrees of expertise in Six Sigma are identified by titles borrowed from the martial arts (e.g., Black Belts, Green Belts, etc.). Six Sigma projects follow a defined sequence of steps and have quantified targets.

Software: Software is the systems and programs that process data and turn that data into information. Software can be very general and be used by any organization (e.g., a word processing program such as WordPerfect® or Microsoft Word®). Software also can be very specific (e.g., an internal auditing program). Software can be developed internally by the organization or can be purchased as an application package from an outside vendor. Software can be divided into the categories of system software, programming languages, and application software. *See also* system programmer.

Software Distribution: Software distribution refers to the process of distributing software updates and also to the various parts of an organization that use the software (e.g., an organization with multiple branch offices using the same software at each branch will want to have the same version of the software running at each office).

Software Piracy: Software piracy is the illicit copying of software and selling it. Software piracy is a subset of copyright infringement of software.

Software Vulnerability: A software vulnerability is a weakness in a system that allows attacks on the system.

Source Code: Source code is the program instructions written by a programmer. Source code is compiled (to produce object code) or interpreted.

Spam: Spam is unsolicited commercial e-mail, sent in bulk to many users in substantially the same form at the same time.

Spending Variance: The spending variance is the actual overhead less the budget based on the actual hours worked. If variable overhead only is being analyzed, the formula can be expressed as the actual hours times (the difference between the actual rate and the standard rate), and the formula corresponds to the direct material price variance and the direct labor rate variance. *See also* direct material price variance *and* direct labor rate variance *and* efficiency variance *and* budget variance *and* volume variance.

Spoilage: Spoilage is generally defined as waste. Accounting treatment for spoilage depends on the character of the spoilage. Normal spoilage is waste that cannot be avoided; it occurs under normal efficient operations. Normal spoilage is a product cost. Equivalent units of production include spoiled units (normal spoilage). Abnormal spoilage is waste that is not expected to occur during normal operations. Abnormal spoilage is a period cost as a separate component of cost of goods sold.

Spoiled Goods: Spoiled goods are products that fail to meet quality specifications or standards.

Spot Rate: The spot rate, sometimes called the spot exchange rate, is the price at which foreign exchange can be bought or sold with payment set for the same day. The term spot rate also means the current interest rate for a bond of a specific maturity (and has nothing to do with currency or forward exchange). *See also* forward exchange rate.

Spyware: Spyware is a broad category of malicious software designed to take control or partial control of a computer's operation without the informed consent of the computer's owner and gather information with the user's consent (e.g., keystroke loggers and screen capture programs).

Standard Costs: Standard costs are a firm's target costs, or the costs it hopes to attain or expects to incur in a production process, based on the information used to determine the standards. In a standard costing system, standard costs are used for all manufacturing costs. *See also* ideal standards *and* currently attainable standards.

Standard Error of the Estimate: In regression analysis, the standard error of the estimate is a measure of how good the estimate is. The standard error indicates the closeness of the estimate to the actual results (i.e., how perfect the regression line is in predicting the dependent variable). *See also* regression analysis *and* coefficient of correlation *and* coefficient of determination.

Stated Interest Rate: The stated interest rate is the coupon rate on the bond. *See also* effective interest rate *and* annual percentage rate.

Statistical Quality Control: Statistical quality control, or statistical process control, is a formal means of distinguishing between random variations and nonrandom variations in an operating or production process. *See also* control chart *and* Pareto diagram *and* Kaizen.

Steering Committee: A steering committee is a committee formed by organizations to guide and oversee systems development and acquisition.

Step-Variable Costs: The term step-variable costs is a synonym for semi-variable or semi-fixed costs and contemplates an increase in costs with an increase in capacity. Step-variable costs behave like fixed costs over a portion of the relevant range and then increase incrementally in a stairstep manner as capacity increases. For example, insurance expense may be fixed over a particular range of production within the overall relevant range but may increase incrementally as the number of locations or number of hours worked increases.

Stockout Cost: The cost of a stockout, which includes loss of income from product unavailability, the cost of restoring customer goodwill, and additional expenses to expedite shipping.

Strategic Business Unit (SBU): A strategic business unit, sometimes called a responsibility center, is any part of an organization whose manager has control over cost, revenue, or investment funds. SBUs are divided into cost SBUs (managers are responsible for controlling costs), revenue SBUs (managers are responsible for generating revenues), profit SBUs (managers are responsible for producing a target profit), and investment SBUs (managers are responsible for producing a target return on investment). *See also* responsibility accounting.

Strategic Risk: Strategic risk includes the risk of choosing inappropriate technology. For example, an organization may choose a Web-based program to share data between remote offices in different cities. If one of the offices does not have a high-speed Internet connection and cannot enter data at the same speed as the other offices, this problem could lead to the generation of reports thought to be up-to-date but in reality missing data from the office with the slow Internet connection. *See also* financial risk *and* information risk *and* operating risk.

Structural Unemployment: Structural unemployment is the unemployment that arises when the skills of workers do not match the skills demanded by employers and when qualified workers do not live where jobs they are qualified for are located. *See also* seasonal unemployment *and* cyclical unemployment *and* frictional unemployment *and* unemployment rate.

Structured Query Language (SQL): Database query is most often provided in a relational database by a language called SQL. SQL provides the ability to "select" data from individual tables in a database based on the data satisfying certain conditions (customers who had ordered more than a certain amount in a certain period) and to "join" certain tables such as suppliers and part numbers, etc. SQL consists of a data definition language (DDL), which is used to define the database; a data manipulation language (DML), which is used to query the database; and a data control language (DCL). *See also* database.

Subjective Probability: A subjective probability is the probability based on an individual's belief about the likelihood that a given event will occur. It is estimated based on judgment and past experience of the likelihood of future events. *See also* probability *and* objective probability *and* expected value.

Subordinated Debenture: A subordinated debenture is a debenture that is subordinated to (lower than) other debt in terms of payment in the event of bankruptcy. Subordinated debentures may be subordinated to certain types of debt or to all other debt. *See also* debenture.

Substitutes: Substitutes or substitute products are products that serve similar purposes. They are related such that an increase in the price of one will cause an increase in demand for the other. *See also* complements.

Sunk Costs: Sunk costs are previously incurred costs that have already been incurred and that cannot be avoided regardless of what a decision maker might decide. Sunk costs are irrelevant to a particular decision. For example, depreciation on existing equipment is a sunk cost as long as the equipment is retained. Ignoring a change in accounting principle, sunk costs can be changed only if the equipment is disposed of. *See also* expired costs *and* unexpired costs *and* committed costs.

Supply Chain Management (SCM): Supply chain management is the integration of business processes from the customer to the original supplier and includes purchasing, materials handling, production planning and control, logistics and warehousing, inventory control, and product distribution and delivery. SCM systems may perform some or all of these functions. *See also* ERP *and* CRM.

Supply Curve: A supply curve is a curve that illustrates the relationship between the price of a good or service and the quantity supplied of that good or service. Price is plotted on the y-axis and quantity is plotted on the x-axis. *See also* demand curve.

Supply Shock: A supply shock is a surprise occurrence that temporarily increases or decreases current output. Supply shocks will thus decrease short-run aggregate supply without directly affecting long-run aggregate supply. *See also* short-run aggregate supply *and* long-run aggregate supply.

System Access Log: System access logs are electronic lists of who has accessed or attempted to access systems or parts of systems or data or subsets of data. *See also* electronic access controls *and* system access log.

System Analysis: System analysis is the phase of the system development life cycle where management gathers information needed to purchase or develop a new system.

System Analyst: The information technology professional charged with design of an internally developed application system and, depending on the application system, the type of computer network needed, and changes to the overall network. The system analyst's responsibility is to work with the end users to determine the requirements for a system, and then design the specifics of the system to satisfy those requirements. The roles of system analysts are sometimes combined with that of programmers to create programmer/analysts. If an application package is purchased from an outside vendor and installed, system analysts may be called system integrators. In that case, his/her responsibilities may be to learn the purchased application (so that the system can be maintained after it is installed), to integrate that application with existing internal and package applications by designing interfaces with the existing applications, to determine how to convert the initial data for the application from other applications or manually, and to provide training to end users.

System Design: System design is the phase of the system development life cycle that includes specifying the input, processing, output, user interface, and file or database design. It is also when controls and security should be developed.

System Development Life Cycle (SDLC): SDLC is a framework for planning and controlling the detailed activities associated with system development.

System Programmer: A system programmer is responsible for installing, supporting (troubleshooting), monitoring, and maintaining the operating system (and often the related hardware if that function is not performed by a separate hardware technician). System programmers may also forecast hardware capacity and perform other capacity planning functions. In complex computing environments, a considerable amount of time can be spent testing and applying operating system upgrades. *See also* application software *and* application service provider.

System Software: System software consists of the programs that run the computer and support system management operations. *See also* application software *and* system programmer.

Systematic Interdependence: Systematic interdependence (of nations and their economies) acknowledges that all members of the global community share planet Earth. Actions of governments that adversely affect the climate or reduce our safety (nuclear proliferation) affect all nations.

System-Specific Policy: A system-specific policy is a policy that management has decided to implement for a specific system (e.g., the payroll system).

Target Costs: Target costs are standard costs developed in connection with a known selling price. Target costing backs into the level of costs that can be allowed for a given product in order to meet profitability objectives.

TCP: Transport control protocol (TCP) is the transmission protocol of the Internet protocol suite.

TCP/IP: TCP/IP is the network protocol used on the Internet. TCP/IP creates a packet-switching network, where a message is split into pieces by the sending end and put back together by the receiving end. The sending end attaches a header to each piece of each message, and the header information (which includes the destination address) is used to put the message back together again.

Temporary File: Temporary files are files that are not permanent files. *See also* permanent file.

Terabyte (TB): A terabyte is approximately 1 trillion bytes (actually 1,099,511,627,776 bytes).

Theory of Constraints (TOC): The theory of constraints is a management philosophy that contends that manageable systems and processes are limited from achieving their goals by one or more identifiable constraints. The TOC process seeks to identify the constraint(s) and restructure the business operations around the constraint(s). Business process improvement using theory of constraints anticipates the use of five focusing steps to work around the constraint, including identifying the constraint; taking organization-wide measures to exploit, leverage, or eliminate the constraint; and then verify that the process is working.

Threat: A threat is any eventuality that represents a danger to an asset or a capability linked to hostile intent. *See also* vulnerability.

Throughput Costing (Super-Variable Costing): Throughput costing is a relatively recent development in costing methods. This method assumes that the only truly variable costs are the costs for direct materials, so these are the only costs assigned to the product. All other costs (including direct labor) are expensed on the throughput contribution margin statement in the period in which they occur. *See also* absorption costing *and* variable costing.

Token: A token is a physical device similar to an identification card that identifies a particular user.

Total Cost (TC): Total cost is the amount a firm must pay for the resources used to produce its products. Total cost is the sum of the total fixed cost plus the total variable cost. *See also* total fixed cost *and* total variable cost.

Total Cost of Ownership (TCO): Total cost of ownership (TCO) is the total cost of hardware or software, including the original purchase price, ongoing maintenance, and support costs.

Total Debt Ratio: The total debt ratio is total liabilities divided by total assets.

Total Fixed Cost (TFC): Total fixed cost is the total of the fixed costs of a firm. *See also* total variable cost.

Total Leverage: Total leverage is operating leverage plus financial leverage. *See also* operating leverage *and* financial leverage.

Total Output (Q): Total output is another name for total product.

Total Product: Total product is the total amount of output produced by a firm.

Total Quality Management (TQM): Total quality management represents an organizational commitment to customer performance that emphasizes both quality and continuous improvement. The factors of TQM are customer focus, continuous improvement, workforce involvement, top management support, objective measures of quality, timely recognition of achievements, and ongoing training.

Total Revenue (TR): Total revenue is the price of a product times the number of units sold.

Total Variable Cost (TVC): Total variable cost is the total of the variable costs of a firm. *See also* total fixed cost.

Trade Acceptance: A trade acceptance is a draft drawn by the seller of goods on the buyer and accepted by a commercial enterprise at a specified future date. The trade acceptance may be marketable at a discount depending on the buyer's creditworthiness. *See also* banker's acceptance.

Trade Credit: Trade credit is the use of credit from suppliers to finance current operations. It includes accounts payable, accrued expenses (expenses that have not become accounts payable yet), notes payable (accounts payable that have been formalized in notes), and trade acceptances.

Transaction Cycles: Similar economic events are typically grouped for repetitive processing into five transaction cycles. Transaction cycles are most frequently revenue, expenditure, production, human resources, and financing. Individual industries might have additional or customized transaction cycles.

Transaction Exposure: Transaction exposure is the risk that a firm could suffer economic loss or experience economic gain upon settlement of individual transactions as a result of change in foreign exchange rates. *See also* translation exposure *and* economic exposure.

Transaction Processing System: Transaction processing systems are the systems that process and record the routine daily transactions necessary to conduct the business. The functions of such a system are normally predefined and highly structured. *See also* decision support system *and* executive information system *and* management information system.

Transfer Price: A transfer price is the price charged for a good or service by one division (or segment) of a business to another division (or segment) of a business. Transfer prices may be based on market price, cost, or a negotiated amount.

Translation Exposure: Translation exposure is the risk that a company's equity, assets, or income will change in value as a result of foreign exchange rate changes. Translation exposure is also known as accounting exposure. *See also* transaction exposure *and* economic exposure.

Treasury Bills: Treasury bills, or T-Bills, are short-term securities that can be purchased either directly from the U.S. Treasury or through a bank or broker. Treasury bills are sold at a discount and are issued at maturities of one year or less.

Treasury Bonds: Treasury bonds are coupon securities (they pay interest) issued by the U.S. Treasury and whose original maturities are more than 10 years.

Treasury Notes: Treasury notes are coupon securities (they pay interest) issued by the U.S. Treasury and whose original maturities are more than one year and up to 10 years.

Treasury Shares: Treasury shares are issued shares that are sometimes repurchased by the corporation (called "issued but not outstanding").

Trojan Horse: A Trojan horse is a seemingly innocuous program in which malicious or harmful program code is hidden.

T-Value: In sampling with a normal distribution, a factor called the z-value is used for determining confidence intervals around a sample mean. The z-value is used when the data in the population are normally distributed with a known standard deviation. When the data in the population are not normally distributed or the standard deviation of the population is not known, the appropriate factor to use for the same purpose is called a t-value. It is based on the t-distribution, which approximates the normal distribution, especially as the sample size increases. *See also* regression analysis *and* coefficient of correlation *and* coefficient of determination *and* standard error of the estimate.

Underapplied Overhead: Underapplied overhead is manufacturing overhead applied to products that is less than the actual overhead cost incurred. Depending on materiality, underapplied overhead is either allocated between ending inventory and cost of goods sold or just written off to cost of goods sold. *See also* overapplied overhead.

Unemployment Rate: The unemployment rate is the ratio of the number of people classified as unemployed to the total labor force. The total labor force includes all noninstitutionalized individuals 16 years of age or older who are either working or actively looking for work. An unemployed person is defined as a person 16 years of age or older who is available for work and who has actively sought employment during the previous four weeks.

Unexpired Costs: Unexpired costs are costs that are reasonably expected to benefit future periods and should be carried forward as an asset. *See also* expired costs *and* sunk costs.

Uniform Resource Locator (URL): A uniform resource locator (URL) is a string of characters that refers to specific resources on a computer. URLs consist of three parts: (1) the protocol that will be used (e.g., the http in http://); (2) the computer on which the requested resource is located (e.g., www.beckerreview.com/); and (3) the resource (file) requested (e.g., students).

Uninterruptible Power Supply (UPS): A UPS is a device that maintains a continuous supply of electrical power to connected equipment. UPS is also called battery backup.

Unipolar: The term unipolar is used to describe a system (such as the world economy) with one dominant power. Currently the United States is the lone super power in the world. U.S. dominance is an illustration of unipolarity.

Unipolarity: Unipolarity anticipates concentration of economic power in one nation and its economy.

Unit Elastic Demand: Unit elastic demand is when a 1 percent increase in price results in a 1 percent decrease in quantity demanded (i.e., when the absolute value of the price elasticity of demand is equal to 1). *See also* price elasticity of demand.

United Nations (U.N.): The United Nations consists of nearly 200 countries. The goals of the U.N. include facilitating cooperation in international law and security, economic development, and the achievement of world peace.

UNIX: UNIX is an operating system designed for minicomputers.

Unshielded Twisted Pair (UTP): UTP is the standard telephone wiring (two strands of wire twisted together).

Validity Check: A validity check is a validation step performed on a data element to ensure that it is in a valid code table, such as product numbers, or that the data is within an appropriate range or that the data is otherwise valid in combination with other data elements. *See also* check digit *and* field check.

Value Added Activities: Value added activities in a value chain are those activities that increase product value. Non-value added activities are activities that do not add value. *See also* value chain.

Value Added Network (VAN): Value added networks are privately owned and managed communications networks that provide additional services beyond standard data transmission. VANs are often used for electronic data interchange. *See also* electronic data interchange (EDI).

Value at Risk: Value at risk is a calculation that allows a firm to estimate the maximum amount that it might expect to lose in an asset portfolio in a given time period with a given probability. It is a measure used to estimate how the value of the portfolio might decrease over a certain time period under usual conditions. It has two parameters: the time period and the confidence level at which the estimate is made. The time period is usually one day or 10 days. Confidence levels are usually 99 or 95 percent.

Value Chain: The value chain defines each major activity that adds value to the products or services produced by a firm. Comprehensive value chains typically begin with product development and end with product delivery. *See also* value added activities.

Value Chain Analysis: The value chain defines each of the major activities that add value to the products or services produced by an organization. Comprehensive value chains are typically represented as beginning with product development and ending with product delivery. Value chain analysis is the determination of what constitutes the value chain. Steps in value chain analysis are (1) identifying the value chain activities; (2) identifying the cost drivers associated with each activity; and (3) developing a competitive advantage by reducing cost or adding value.

Value Engineering: Value engineering is the identification of the functions of a product or service with the objective of providing those functions at the lowest total cost. Value engineering incorporates the systematic application of recognized techniques to identify product and service functions.

Variable (Direct) Costing: Variable costing is a method of product costing that includes only variable manufacturing costs (i.e., direct materials, direct labor, and variable manufacturing overhead) as part of product costs. All other costs, including fixed manufacturing overhead, are treated as period costs. Variable costing is not GAAP for financial statement purposes.

Variable Cost Ratio: The variable cost ratio is defined as variable costs divided by total sales.

Variable Costs: Variable costs are costs that change proportionately in total relative to changes in production within the relevant range. Variable costs per unit remain constant, but vary directly in total with changes in units. Almost any cost is variable in the long term (because the relevant range will change over time). *See also* fixed costs *and* mixed costs *and* relevant range.

Variance Analysis: Variance analysis is an analysis of the variances between standard costs and actual costs for direct material, direct labor, and overhead. *See also* standard costs.

Vertical Integration: Vertical integration is the improvement of a value chain through the supply end and the demand end in the same industry (i.e., when a firm expands its business into areas that are at different points of the same production path).

Virtual Memory: Virtual memory or virtual storage is not real memory. Portions of a program that are not being executed are stored on a disk as virtual memory pages and are retrieved and brought into actual physical memory when they are needed. Virtual memory provides the capability to run programs that require more memory than is physically available.

Virtual Private Network (VPN): A virtual private network is a private network configured within a public network to take advantage of the economies of scale of the public network. A VPN hides data in the private network in a wrapper to hide its contents. VPNs can be either encrypted (secure) or unencrypted (trusted).

Virus: A virus is a self-replicating computer program or piece of program code that spreads by inserting copies of itself into other programs or data. A virus can enter a system as an e-mail attachment, a file downloaded from the Internet, or other infected media. Not all malicious software programs are viruses; worms and Trojan horses are also considered malicious software.

VOIP: VOIP means voice over Internet protocol. VOIP is used for making phone calls using a high-speed connection to the Internet.

Volume Variance: In a two-way or three-way analysis of overhead variance, the volume variance is the budget based on standard hours allowed for the actual units and the applied overhead. There will be a volume variance only when fixed and variable overhead are both being analyzed because, for variable overhead, the budget based on standard hours allowed will be the same as the applied overhead (which is based on the standard rate times the actual units). *See also* spending variance *and* efficiency variance *and* budget variance.

Vulnerability: For business information systems, a vulnerability is a characteristic of a design, implementation, or operation that renders the system susceptible to a threat.

Warm Site: A warm backup site is a facility that is stocked with all the hardware necessary to create a reasonable facsimile of a primary data center. It is the compromise between the hot backup site and the cold backup site.

Waste: Waste includes scrap with no value or productive materials lost in the production process. A certain amount of shrinkage is anticipated and considered a normal part of production.

Web 2.0: Web 2.0 refers to change and innovation in the ways that software developers and users utilize the Internet.

Web Administrator: Web administrators, often called webmasters, are responsible for information on a website. *See also* network administrator.

Web Hosting Service: A Web hosting service is an organization that maintains a number of Web servers and provides space to users to maintain their websites.

Web Server: A Web server is a computer that delivers Web pages upon request. Any computer can be turned into a Web server by installing Web server software and connecting it to the Internet.

Weighted Average Cost of Capital (WACC): The weighted average cost of capital is the weighted average of the costs of the various components of capital (debt, preferred stock, and common stock or retained earnings). The weights are the market values of the different securities.

Weighted Average Method of Process Costing: The weighted average method of process costing calculates equivalent units and production costs differently from the FIFO method of process costing. In the weighted average method, the equivalent units are the units transferred out plus the equivalent units of the ending work in process. Production costs to be accounted for are the cost of beginning work in process plus costs added during the month. Cost per equivalent units is the production cost divided by the equivalent units. Normally, a separate cost per equivalent units is calculated for direct materials and conversion costs (labor and overhead). *See also* FIFO method of process costing.

Wide Area Network (WAN): WANs allow national and international communications. They usually employ non-dedicated public communications channels (e.g., fiber optic, terrestrial microwave, or satellite) as their communications media. WAN communication services may be provided by value added networks, Internet-based networks, or point-to-point networks (direct private/proprietary network links normally using leased lines). *See also* local area network (LAN).

Wi-Fi: Wi-Fi is the set of standards for wireless LANs, also called the 802.11 standards.

Working Capital: Working capital is current assets minus current liabilities. *See also* current ratio *and* quick ratio.

Workstation: A workstation is a node (usually a PC) that is used by end users.

World Trade Organization (WTO): The World Trade Organization is an international institution that deals with regulation of trade between nations including formalizing trade agreements and assisting in the resolution of trade disputes. The WTO has more than 150 member nations.

Worm: A worm is a self-replicating computer program, similar to a virus. Worms are self-contained and do not need to be part of other programs to propagate. Worms are generally designed to travel over networks such as the Internet.

XBRL (Extensible Business Reporting Language): XBRL is a license-free means of communicating business and financial data between businesses and via the Internet through the use of, for example, identifying tags that are assigned to data. Advantages of this language include cost savings and improved efficiency, accuracy, and reliability. XBRL is a very flexible program, able to handle various languages and accounting standards.

XML (Extensible Markup Language): XML is a technology that is being developed to transmit data in flexible formats, instead of the standard formats of EDI. XML tells systems the format of data and also what kind of information the data is. XML utilizes user-defined tags similar to the data formatting tags that are used in HTML for the display of Web pages in browsers. *See also* hypertext markup language (HTML).

Zero Balance Accounts: A zero balance account is a bank account that allows for automatic same-day transfers to or from a concentration account. A zero balance account allows a firm to move excess cash balances into a single account or to control the disbursement of funds from a central pool of money. The balance in the account is maintained at zero by transferring money to a concentration account. *See also* concentration banking.

Zero-Based Budget: A zero-based budget is a budget that requires justification of all expenditures every year.

Zero-Coupon Bonds: Zero-coupon bonds are discount bonds that do not pay interest. They are purchased at a discount and mature at par.

NOTES

Index

BEC

A

H

I

J

K

L